WEBSTER'S
STUDENT
DICTIONARY
&THESAURUS

WEBSTER'S
STUDENT
DICTIONARY
&THESAURUS

Reader's
Digest

NEW YORK

A READER'S DIGEST BOOK

This edition published by The Reader's Digest Association, Inc.,
by arrangement with Geddes & Grosset.

FOR GEDDES & GROSSET
Section Editors: Pronunciation Guide:
Alice Grandison   Dr. Scott Montgomery
Joanne Shepherd   Dr. Bettina Montgomery
Sheila Ferguson   Consultant: Dr. Helen Fraser
Edwinna von Baeyer
Roz Paterson

Project Director: Ron Grosset
Production Manager: Craig Brown
Production Editor: Eleanor Cowan
Designer: Mark Mechan

FOR READER'S DIGEST
Copy Editor: Marilyn Knowlton
Canadian Project Editor: Pamela Johnson
Associate Art Director: George McKeon
Executive Editor, Trade Publishing: Dolores York
Associate Publisher: Rosanne McManus
President and Publisher, Trade Publishing: Harold Clarke

World maps created by Lovell Johns Limited, Oxfordshire
England

Atlas of World History
Co-authors: Liz Wyse and Caroline Lucas
Design and illustration: Ralph Orme, with additional
illustrations (of Canada) supplied by Domex, India
Maps: Malcolm Porter, assisted by Andrea Fairbrass and
A Bereznay
Additional maps by Lovell Johns Limited

Library of Congress Cataloging-in-Publication Data:
Webster's Student Dictionary and Thesaurus
     p. cm.
ISBN 13: 978-0-7621-0858-9
ISBN 10: 0-7621-0858-4
   1. English language--Dictionaries. 2. English language--
Synonyms and antonyms.
   I. Reader's Digest Association. II. Title: Student
dictionary and thesaurus.

PE1628.W56396 2007
423—dc22   2006050427

We are committed to both the quality of our products and the service we provide to our customers.
We value your comments, so please feel free to contact us.

The Reader's Digest Association, Inc.
Adult Trade Publishing
Reader's Digest Road
Pleasantville, NY 10570-7000

For more Reader's Digest products and information, visit our website:
www.rd.com (in the United States)
www.readersdigest.ca (in Canada)

Printed and bound in Poland

POLSKABOOK

Geddes & Grosset, David Dale House, New Lanark, ML11 9DJ, Scotland

Typeset by Geddes & Grosset using Bitstream Dutch and Linotype Frutiger fonts

This book is not published by the original publishers of
Webster's Dictionary or *Webster's Thesaurus* or by their successors.

1 3 5 7 9 10 8 6 4 2

Contents

Elements in the Dictionary

guide words

● indicates a variation, a common phrase or idiom related to the head-word

at-a-glance, spelled-out pronunciation guide

stresses shown by bolds

syllable division shown by hyphens

different parts of speech indicated by ●

parts of speech in italic

examples of the word in use

numbered senses within a definition

abrasive /a-**bray**-ziv/ *adj* 1 causing abrasion (*abrasive movements*). 2 harsh or irritating (*abrasive personality*). ● *n* something that causes abrasion (*use abrasive to remove the paint*).

abreast /a-**brest**/ *adv* side by side (*competitors running abreast*). ● **abreast of the times** up-to-date.

abridge /a-**bridge**/ *vb* to make shorter (*abridge the story*). ● *n* **abridg(e)ment** /a-**bridge**-ment/.

abroad /a-**brawd**/ *adv* 1 out of your own country (*holidays abroad*). 2 far and wide (*spread the news abroad*).

abrupt /a-**brupt**/ *adj* 1 sudden, hasty (*an abrupt departure*). 2 discourteous (*an abrupt reply*). ● *adv* **abruptly** /a-**brupt**-ly/. ● *n* **abruptness** /a-**brupt**-ness/.

abscess /**ab**-sess/ *n* a boil, a gathering of pus in some part of the body.

absence *see* **absent**¹.

absent /**ab**-sent/ *adj* not present (*absent from school/absent friends*). ● *n* **absence** /**ab**-sence/.

absentee /ab-sen-**tee**/ *n* someone who is not present.

absentminded /ab-sent-**mind**-ded/ *adj* not thinking of what you are doing.

absolute /**ab**-so-lute, ab-so-**lute**/ *adj* 1 complete (*absolute perfection*). 2 free from controls or conditions (*absolute power*). ● *adv* **absolutely** /**ab**-so-lute-ly, ab-so-**lute**-ly/.

absolution *see* **absolve**.

absolve /ab-**solve**/ *vb* to set free, as from guilt or punishment (*absolve from blame*). ● *n* **absolution** /ab-so-**loo**-shen/.

absorb /ab-**sorb**/ *vb* 1 to soak up (*a material that absorbs liquid*). 2 to take up all the attention of.

absorbed /ab-**sorbd**/ *adj* giving the whole mind to (*people absorbed in their work*).

absorbent /ab-**sor**-bent/ *adj* drinking in.

absorption /ab-**sorp**-shen/ *n* 1 act of absorbing. 2 full attention.

abstain /ab-**stain**/ *vb* 1 to keep yourself from, to hold back from (*abstain from smoking*). 2 not to vote (*three voted against and two abstained*). ● *n* **abstainer** /ab-**stainer**/. ● *n* **abstention** /ab-**sten**-shen/.

abstract /**ab**-stract/ *n* a summary (*an abstract of the lecture*). ● *adj* /**ab**-stract, ab-**stract**/ 1 existing in the mind only. 2 portraying ideas rather than realistic images (*an abstract painting*).

absurd /ab-**surd**/ *adj* foolish. ● *n* **absurdity** /ab-**sur**-di-tee/.

abundance /a-**bun**-dance/ *n* more than enough, plenty (*an abundance of apples this year*). ● *adj*

abundant /a-**bun**-dant/. ● *adv* **abundantly** /a-**bun**-dant-lee/.

abuse /a-**byooz**/ *vb* 1 to make wrong use of (*abuse power*). 2 to ill-treat, to maltreat, especially physically or sexually (*abuse their children*). 3 to use insulting language (*a drunk abusing the barman*). ● *ns* **abuse** /a-**byoos**/, **abuser** /a-**byoo-zer**/.

abusive /a-**byoo**-sive/ *adj* 1 ill-treating, cruel (*abusive treatment*). 2 insulting (*abusive language*). ● *adv* **abusively** /a-**byoo**-siv-lee/.

abysmal /a-**biz**-mal/ *adj* very bad (*an abysmal performance*).

abyss /a-**biss**/ *n* a very deep pit or ravine.

academic /a-ca-**de**-mic/ *adj* 1 of or concerning education, especially in a college or university (*an academic career*). 2 not practical or useful, theoretical (*of academic interest*). ● *n* teacher in a college or university

academy /a-ca-de-**mee**/ *n* 1 a high school. 2 a school for special studies (*a military academy*). 3 a society for advancing arts and sciences (*the Royal Academy*).

accelerate /ac-**sel**-le-rant / *vb* to increase speed. ● *n* **acceleration** /ac-sel-le-**ray**-shen/.

accelerator /ac-**sel**-le-ray-tor/ *n* a device that controls the speed of an automobile.

accent /**ac**-sent/ *n* 1 a special emphasis given to part of a word (*the accent is on the first syllable*). 2 the mark that indicates such emphasis. 3 a way of speaking peculiar to certain persons or groups (*a New York accent*). ● *vb* **accent** /ac-**sent**/ to emphasize a certain part of a word.

accentuate /ac-**sen**-shoo-ate/ *vb* to emphasize (*a dress accentuating the blue of her eyes*).

accept / ak-**sept**/ *vb* 1 to receive something offered (*accept the gift with thanks/accept his apology*). 2 to regard as true, reasonable, satisfactory, etc. (*accept his excuse/accept their criticism*). ● *n* **acceptance** /ak-**sep**-tance/.

acceptable /ak-**sep**-ta-bl/ *adj* 1 pleasant to receive (*a very acceptable gift*). 2 satisfactory, good enough (*acceptable work*). 3 allowable, tolerable (*acceptable levels of radiation*).

access /**ak**-sess/ *n* a way or means of approach. ● *vb* to find on a computer file (*access secret data illegally*).

accessible /ak-**sess**-i-bl/ *adj* 1 easily approached (*an accessible manager*). 2 easily reached (*villages that are scarcely accessible*). 3 easily obtained or understood (*accessible information*). ● *n* **accessibility**.

homographs, in separate numbered definitions

Elements in the Thesaurus

guide words

tells the reader to look for further information: usage details, word history, or a common phrase or idiom related to the headword shown by shaded boxes

Source or origins of phrases shown between pointed brackets <>

English idioms explained

chart 523 **choke**

lead a charmed life regularly to have good fortune and to avoid misfortune, harm or danger (*The racing driver seems to lead a charmed life. He has been in many serious accidents but has never been badly injured*) <It is as though someone has cast a spell on him or her to ensure protection>.
work like a charm to be very effective, to work very well (*His efforts to get the old woman to like him worked like a charm*) <It is as though a sorcerer has cast a spell>.

chart *n* (*record the information in the form of charts*) table, graph, diagram.
chase *vb* **1** (*the hounds were chasing the fox*) run after, pursue, follow. **2** (*they chased away the burglar*) put to flight, drive away. ⬦

chase (after) rainbows to spend time and effort in thinking about, or in trying to obtain, things that it is quite impossible for one to achieve (*He is always applying for jobs that are away beyond his qualifications. He should concentrate on finding a job which he can do and stop chasing rainbows*).

cheap *adj* **1** (*fruit is very cheap in the summer there*) inexpensive, low-cost, low-priced, reasonable, economical. **2** (*she wears cheap and gaudy jewelry*) inferior, shoddy, tawdry, trashy, tatty, cheap-jack, (*inf*) tacky.
cheat *vb* **1** (*he cheated the old lady into giving him her savings*) deceive, trick, swindle, dupe, hoodwink. **2** (*his brother cheated him out of his inheritance*) deprive of, deny, thwart, prevent from.
check *vb* **1** (*the police checked the car's tires*) examine, inspect, look at, scrutinize, test. **2** (*you must check that the door is locked*) confirm, make sure, verify. **3** (*they had to find some way to check the vehicle's progress*) stop, halt, slow down, delay, obstruct, impede.
cheeky *adj* (*he was scolded for being cheeky to the teacher*) impertinent, impudent, insolent, disrespectful, forward .
cheer *vb* **1** (*the crowds began to cheer*) applaud, shout hurrah, hurrah. **2** (*the arrival of her friends cheered her*) brighten up, buoy up, perk up, enliven, hearten, exhilarate, gladden, elate.
cheerful *adj* **1** (*they were in a cheerful mood when the sun shone*) happy, merry, bright, glad, light-hearted, carefree, joyful. **2** (*she was wearing a dress in cheerful colors*) bright.

cherish *vb* **1** (*she cherishes memories of her father*) treasure, prize, hold dear, revere. **2** (*the children cherish their pets*) look after, care for, tend, protect. **3** (*they cherish hopes of success*) have, entertain, cling to, harbor.
chest *n* **1** (*he was wounded in the chest*) breast, sternum. **2** (*the miser kept his treasure in a chest*) box, trunk, casket, coffer, container, receptacle. ⬦

get (something) off one's chest to tell (someone) about (something) that is upsetting, worrying, or annoying one (*If you know something about the accident you must get it off your chest and tell the police*).

chew *vb* (*children told to chew their food thoroughly*) munch, crunch, champ, masticate. ⬦

chew the cud to think deeply about something (*You will have to chew the cud before coming to a decision on such an important issue*) <A reference to cows literally chewing the cud>.

chief *adj* **1** (*the chief man of the tribe*) head, leading, foremost, principal. **2** (*we must discuss the chief points in the report*) main, principal, most important, essential, prime, key, central.
child *n* **1** (*when he was a child*) young one, little one, youngster, young person, (*inf*) kid. **2** (*parents and their child*) offspring, progeny, son/daughter. ⬦

child's play something that is very easy to do (*With your experience you will find the work child's play*).

choice *n* **1** (*you have some choice in the matter—the meeting is not compulsory*) option, selection, preference. **2** (*there is a wide choice of fruit and vegetables in the supermarket*) selection, range, variety. **3** (*we have little choice but to go*) option, alternative, possibility. ⬦

Hobson's choice no choice at all; a choice between accepting what is offered or having nothing at all (*The hotel has only one room available for tonight. It's Hobson's choice, I'm afraid*).

choke *vb* **1** (*the murderer choked her to death*) strangle, throttle. **2** (*he choked to death on the smoke from the fire*) suffocate, smother, stifle, asphyxiate. **3** (*the drains are choked and had to be cleared*) block, clog, obstruct.

examples of words in use

numbered senses within a definition

parts of speech in italic

English idioms shown in use

homographs, in separate numbered definitions

Preface

Introduction

This books aims to be an accessible and comprehensive modern dictionary with a difference. As well as providing over 35,000 concise, up-to-date dictionary definitions, with specially commissioned, crystal-clear pronunciation guides, it also includes many sections invaluable for students of all disciplines, from fifth grade upwards, and is a fascinating reference volume for all the family.

It includes a thesaurus of 25,000 synonyms with a unique phrasefinder to help find and explain common English idiomatic phrases; a full-color atlas; a full-color atlas of world history; US state maps; Canadian territories and provinces; world flags; the United States Constitution; the Declaration of Independence; Presidents of the USA; and Prime Ministers of Canada.

How to use the dictionary

Alphabetical order

Strict alphabetical order is followed. All compound words and hyphenated words are alphabetized as if they are one word.

Headwords that contain contractions, such as St, are alphabetized as would the whole word; thus St is alphabetized just as Saint would be.

Abbreviations and acronyms are alphabetized as if the abbreviation is a whole word. Capitalized headwords come before lower case headwords. Numerals take precedence over letters.

Variations

Variant spellings appear in bold type and in brackets next to the headword.

Other terms, of a different part of speech, that are related to the headword are given at the end of an entry in bold preceded by ●.

Inflected forms of verbs and plural forms of nouns appear in bold and in brackets following the headword.

Parts of speech

Parts of speech are indicated in italic by the abbreviations shown on page xii, and the bold headword. Other parts of speech after the main headword are indicated by a full point (.) and ●.

Senses and definitions

Within entries synonyms are separated by commas (,). Different senses within parts of speech are numbered. Parts of speech are separated by full points (.) and ●.

Homographs

Words of different origins but with the same spelling are given separate, numbered entries.

Abbreviations and acronyms

Headwords which are abbreviations or acronyms appear with the label *abbr* and are followed by an equals sign (=).

Register

Level of registers are indicated by the following labels: formal, informal, slang, derogatory, dialect, offensive.

Pronunciation in the dictionary

The aim of the pronunciation guide

Unlike some languages, English spelling does not always correspond to pronunciation. There are many very obvious examples of this, for example, *yacht* is not pronounced as it is spelled. Because of this difficulty, it is important to have a pronunciation guide in an English dictionary.

The pronunciation system in this book is a readable one. There are no phonetic symbols, and there is even no need for a key as there is in some other dictionaries with "spelled-out" pronunciation.

To achieve this, each entry in the dictionary includes a syllable-based "spelling pronunciation." This means that the pronunciation of the word stays as close to the original spelling of the word as is usefully possible and uses the conventions of English spelling to provide an easy-to-understand guide to pronunciation. This system is used in this book whether the word is easy to pronounce from the spelling, e.g., *bit* /bit/, or where the spelling is not a good guide to the word's pronunciation, *e.g., yacht* /yot/.

Reasons for using "spelling pronunciation"

Many readers, especially younger ones, may find pronunciation guides using the International Phonetic Alphabet (IPA) hard to follow and the symbols rather offputting. Research has shown that pronunciation guides that stay as close as possible to the actual spelling of a word provide the most accessible guide for the reader[1]. Also, when encountering a new word, there is a tendency for a reader, in the absence of a pronunciation guide, to produce what is known as a spelling pronunciation[2]. Put simply, given a word with which they are not familiar, readers will try to work out how it is pronounced by drawing from what they already know of the rules of English spelling and pronunciation.

Consider how people might say the name *Sean* if they were unaware of the correct pronunciation. The reader will assume it is pronounced /seen/ if they do not know it should be /shawn/ because they know *sea* is pronounced /see/.

Obviously, if a word's spelling is a direct reflection of its pronunciation, then the word is easier to pronounce without aid than a word that is not. Our pronunciation guide in this book taps into this natural tendency and provides a spelling pronunciation for every word.

Of course, many English words are not simple spelling pronunciations. We cannot use the spelling of such a word on its own as a guide to the word's pronunciation. So despite the obvious benefits of using conventional spelling as a pronunciation guide, all words do not lend themselves to this.

Our solution

To help our readers pronounce the words in our dictionary, we have used the norms of the English sound/spelling system broken into manageable syllables. Syllables break down words into smaller units. Our words often have more than one syllable, with one syllable in each word more prominent than others. This is known as the stressed syllable.

It is the tendency of readers to naturally want to produce the most simple pronunciation of any given string of letters (a spelling pronunciation). In basic terms, we have broken down words which do not have an obvious pronunciation into syllables which have pronunciations that are obvious from the spelling. For example: *earache* /**ee**-rake/, *eccentricity* /ek-sen-**tri**-si-tee/.

We have produced, for each word, a series of syllable blocks—divided by hyphens—which when read, reveal the pronunciation of the word. The main stress is marked in bold. The result is a clear and intuitive spelling pronunciation which is based on the sound and spelling norms of the English Language at a syllabic level. Look at the following:

Thi re-**zult** is a clear and in-**choo**-wi-tiv **spe**-ling pro-nun-see-**ay**-shun which is baist on thi sound and **spe**-ling normz ov thi **ing**-glish **lang**-gwidge at a si-**la**-bic **le**-vel and which iz i-**mee**-dee-it-lee in-**choo**-wi-tiv.

As you will notice in this passage, some words are changed, and some are not. Where the word's pronunciation cannot be made clearer, its own spelling is used as the pronunciation guide—with hyphens inserted to indicate syllables. However, many words require the syllables to be rewritten in a simpler way to provide a clear pronunciation. The system is elegant in its simplicity, with the benefit that pronunciations are generated without the need for reference tables or the necessity of dealing with phonemes or symbols.

Variation

Each word has to be individually transcribed into the syllable-based spelling pronunciation—there cannot be a systematic approach because we are not using a key or a system of symbols to describe the pronunciation. The result of this is accuracy of pronunciation achieved without the need for any new skills from the reader because the rules of English spelling/pronunciation automatically lead the reader to the pronunciation.

Conclusion

Ultimately, English spelling is inconsistent. English pronunciations from the spellings are even more varied. When we cannot assume the reader is familiar with a system such as the IPA, a system that employs syllable-based spelling pronunciations is the most intuitive and clear method of generating pronunciations. It is simple; it draws on the reader's own knowledge and it ensures pronunciations are accessible even to those unfamiliar with any kind of pronunciation system ... all without the need for a key.

Dr Scott Montgomery

Footnotes/References

1. Fraser, H. (1996) "Guy-dance with pro-nun-see-yay-shun." English Today 47, Vol.12, No.3 (July 1996).
2. Montgomery, S. (2005) "Lax Vowels, Orthography and /´/: the need for orthographic primacy." *Linguistische Berichte*, 201: 41-64.

Abbreviations

abbr	abbreviation	*naut*	nautical
adj	adjective	*neut*	neuter
adv	adverb	*nf*	noun feminine
anat	anatomy	*npl*	noun plural
approx	approximately	*n sing*	noun singular
arch	archaic	*NT*	New Testament
archit	architecture	*obs*	obsolete
astrol	astrology	*off*	offensive
astron	astronomy	*orig*	original, originally, origin
Austral	Australia, Australasia	*OT*	Old Testament
aux	auxiliary	*p*	participle
biol	biology	*pers*	person, personal
bot	botany	*philos*	philosophy
Br	Britain, British	*photog*	photography
c	circa, about	*pl*	plural
cap	capital	*poet*	poetical
Cdn	Canadian	*poss*	possessive
cent	century	*pp*	past participle
chem	chemical, chemistry	*prep*	preposition
compar	comparative	*pres t*	present tense
comput	computing	*print*	printing
conj	conjunction	*pron*	pronoun
derog	derogatory, derogatorily	*pr p*	present participle
e.g.	exempli gratis, for example	*psychol*	psychology
etc.	etcetera, and so on	*pt*	past tense
fig	figuratively	*RC*	Roman Catholic
form	formal	*reflex*	reflexive
geog	geography	*Scot*	Scotland
geol	geology	*sing*	singular
geom	geometry	*sl*	slang
gram	grammar	*superl*	superlative
her	heraldry	*theat*	theatre
hist	history	*TV*	television
i.e.	id est, that is	*TM*	trademark
imper	imperative	*UK*	United Kingdom
incl	including	*US*	United States
inf	informal	*USA*	United States of America
interj	interjection	*var*	variant
math	mathematics	*vb*	verb
mech	mechanics	*vb aux*	auxiliary verb
med	medicine	*vi*	intransitive verb
mil	military	*vt*	transitive verb
mus	music	*vti*	transitive or intransitive verb
myth	mythology	*vulg*	vulgar, vulgarly
n	noun	*zool*	zoology

DICTIONARY

A

A, a /a/ *n* **1** the first letter of the English alphabet. **2** in music, the sixth note of the scale of C. **3** a human blood type (*blood type A*). **4** the best grade in a school paper (*he got an A for algebra*).

a /a/ *indefinite article* (**an** before a vowel) **1** any, some, one (*have a cookie*). **2** one single thing (*there's not a store for miles*). **3** per, for each (*take this twice a day*).

aardvark /**ard**-vark/ *n* an African mammal with a long snout that feeds on ants.

abacus /a-ba-kus, a-**ba**-kus/ *n* a child's counting frame with beads.

abalone /a-ba-**lo**-nee, a-ba-lo-nee/ *n* an edible sea snail with a shell that is shaped like an ear.

abandon /a-**ban**-don/ *vb* **1** to give up (*abandon the attempt*). **2** to depart from forever, desert (*abandon his wife and children*). ● *n* freedom from care (*dance with abandon*).

abandoned /a-**ban**-dond/ *adj* **1** deserted (*an abandoned house*). **2** immoral, shameless (*abandoned young women*).

abate /a-**bate**/ *vb* to lessen (*the storms are abating*). ● *n* **abatement** /a-**bate**-ment/.

abbess /a-bess/ *n* the chief nun in a convent.

abbey /a-bee/ *n* **1** a monastery or convent. **2** a church, once part of a monastery or convent.

abbot /a-bot/ *n* the chief monk in a monastery.

abbreviate /a-**bree**-vee-ate/ *vb* to shorten (*abbreviate a word*). ● *n* **abbreviation** /a-**bree**-vee-**ay**-shon/.

abdicate /**ab**-di-kate/ *vb* to give up high office, especially a throne. ● *n* **abdication** /ab-di-**kay**-shon/.

abdomen /**ab**-do-men/ *n* the part of the body between your chest and your thighs. ● *adj* **abdominal** /ab-**dom**-in-al/.

abduct /ab-**duct**/ *vb* to kidnap. ● *ns* **abduction, abductor.**

abhor /ab-**hor**/ *vb* to loathe. ● *n* **abhorrence** /ab-**hor**-rence/.

abhorrent /ab-**hor**-rent/ *adj* loathsome.

abide /a-**bide**/ *vb* to put up with (*she cannot abide untidiness*). ● **abide by** to obey, to remain true to (*abide by the rules*).

abiding /a-**bide**-ing/ *adj* lasting (*an abiding love*).

ability /a-**bil**-it-ee/ *n* **1** skill or power to do a thing (*the ability to do the job*). **2** cleverness (*children of ability do well in school*).

ablaze /a-**blaze**/ *adj and adv* on fire, in flames.

able /**ay**-bl/ *adj* **1** having skill or power to do a thing. **2** clever. ● *adv* **ably.**

able-bodied /**ay**-bl-**bod**-eed/ *adj* someone who is able to walk and is physically healthy.

abnormal /ab-**nor**-mal/ *adj* different from the usual (*abnormal levels of lead*). ● *adv* **abnormally** /ab-**nor**-mal-lee/.

abnormality /ab-nor-**mal**-it-ee/ *n* an unusual quality.

aboard /a-**board**/ *adv and prep* onboard, on a ship, train, airplane, etc.

abode /a-**bode**/ *n* (*fml or hum*) house, home (*our humble abode*).

abolish /a-**bol**-ish/ *vb* to put an end to, to do away with (*abolish slavery*). ● *ns* **abolition** /a-bol-**ish**-en/, **abolitionist** /a-bo-**lish**-en-ist/.

abominable /a-**bom**-na-bl/ *adj* hateful.

aboriginal /a-bor-**ridge**-nal, a-bor-**ri**-ji-nal/ *adj* describing a feature that is native to a country.

Aboriginal /a-bor-**ridge**-nal, a-bor-**ri**-ji-nal/ *adj* describing the native peoples of Australia. ● *n* (also called native Australian) a descendant of the people who inhabited Australia before the arrival of the Europeans. ● *Usage*: **Aboriginal**, rather than **Aborigine**, is now the preferred term.

aborigine /a-bor-**ridge**-nee, a-bor-**ri**-ji-nee/ *n* **1** one of the original inhabitants of a country, who has been there since the earliest times. **2** (*with cap*) **Aborigine** another name for an Australian **Aboriginal**. ● *adj* **aboriginal, Aboriginal.**

abort /a-**bort**/ *v* to stop something, especially in the early stages (*abort the space shuttle take off*).

abortive /a-**bor**-tive/ *adj* unsuccessful because done too soon (*an abortive attempt*).

abound /a-**bound**/ *vb* to be plentiful (*large houses abound there*).

about /a-**bout**/ *adv and prep* **1** concerning (*a letter about money*). **2** around (*dash about the house*). **3** near to (*somewhere about here*). **4** nearly (*costing about $5*). **5** on the point of (*just about to go*).

above /a-**buv**/ *adv and prep* **1** over (*pictures above the fireplace/an apartment above the store*). **2** higher [than] (*above average*).

aboveboard /a-**buv**-board/ *adj* honest, fair (*the deal was honest and aboveboard*).

abrasion /a-**bray**-zhen/ *n* **1** the act of rubbing away at something (*abrasion can cause scratches*). **2** an area of skin that has been scraped (*cuts and abrasions*).

abrasive /a-**bray**-ziv/ *adj* **1** causing abrasion (*abrasive movements*). **2** harsh or irritating (*abrasive personality*). ● *n* something that causes abrasion (*use abrasive to remove the paint*).

abreast /a-**brest**/ *adv* side by side (*competitors running abreast*). ● **abreast of the times** up-to-date.

abridge /a-**bridge**/ *vb* to make shorter (*abridge the story*). ● *n* **abridg(e)ment** /a-**bridge**-ment/.

abroad /a-**brawd**/ *adv* **1** out of your own country (*holidays abroad*). **2** far and wide (*spread the news abroad*).

abrupt /a-**brupt**/ *adj* **1** sudden, hasty (*an abrupt departure*). **2** discourteous (*an abrupt reply*). ● *adv* **abruptly** /a-**brupt**-ly/. ● *n* **abruptness** /a-**brupt**-ness/.

abscess /**ab**-sess/ *n* a boil, a gathering of pus in some part of the body.

absence *see* **absent**[1].

absent /**ab**-sent/ *adj* not present (*absent from school/absent friends*). ● *n* **absence** /**ab**-sence/.

absentee /ab-sen-**tee**/ *n* someone who is not present.

absentminded /ab-sent-**mind**-ded/ *adj* not thinking of what you are doing.

absolute /**ab**-so-lute, ab-so-**lute**/ *adj* **1** complete (*absolute perfection*). **2** free from controls or conditions (*absolute power*). ● *adv* **absolutely** /**ab**-so-lute-ly, ab-so-**lute**-ly/.

absolution *see* **absolve**.

absolve /ab-**solve**/ *vb* to set free, as from guilt or punishment (*absolve from blame*). ● *n* **absolution** /ab-so-**loo**-shen/.

absorb /ab-**sorb**/ *vb* **1** to soak up (*a material that absorbs liquid*). **2** to take up all the attention of.

absorbed /ab-**sorbd**/ *adj* giving the whole mind to (*people absorbed in their work*).

absorbent /ab-**sor**-bent/ *adj* drinking in.

absorption /ab-**sorp**-shen/ *n* **1** act of absorbing. **2** full attention.

abstain /ab-**stain**/ *vb* **1** to keep yourself from, to hold back from (*abstain from smoking*). **2** not to vote (*three voted against and two abstained*). ● *n* **abstainer** /ab-**stainer**/. ● *n* **abstention** /ab-**sten**-shen/.

abstract /**ab**-stract/ *n* a summary (*an abstract of the lecture*). ● *adj* /**ab**-stract, ab-**stract**/ **1** existing in the mind only. **2** portraying ideas rather than realistic images (*an abstract painting*).

absurd /ab-**surd**/ *adj* foolish. ● *n* **absurdity** /ab-**sur**-di-tee/.

abundance /a-**bun**-dance/ *n* more than enough, plenty (*an abundance of apples this year*). ● *adj*

abundant /a-**bun**-dant/. ● *adv* **abundantly** /a-**bun**-dant-lee/.

abuse /a-**byooz**/ *vb* **1** to make wrong use of (*abuse power*). **2** to ill-treat, to maltreat, especially physically or sexually (*abuse their children*). **3** to use insulting language (*a drunk abusing the barman*). ● *ns* **abuse** /a-**byoos**/, **abuser** /a-**byoo**-zer/.

abusive /a-**byoo**-sive/ *adj* **1** ill-treating, cruel (*abusive treatment*). **2** insulting (*abusive language*). ● *adv* **abusively** /a-**byoo**-siv-lee/.

abysmal /a-**biz**-mal/ *adj* very bad (*an abysmal performance*).

abyss /a-**biss**/ *n* a very deep pit or ravine.

academic /a-ca-**de**-mic/ *adj* **1** of or concerning education, especially in a college or university (*an academic career*). **2** not practical or useful, theoretical (*of academic interest*). ● *n* teacher in a college or university

academy /a-**ca**-de-mee/ *n* **1** a high school. **2** a school for special studies (*a military academy*). **3** a society for advancing arts and sciences (*the Royal Academy*).

accelerate /ac-**sel**-le-rant / *vb* to increase speed. ● *n* **acceleration** /ac-sel-le-**ray**-shen/.

accelerator /ac-**sel**-le-ray-tor/ *n* a device that controls the speed of an automobile.

accent /**ac**-sent/ *n* **1** a special emphasis given to part of a word (*the accent is on the first syllable*). **2** the mark that indicates such emphasis. **3** a way of speaking peculiar to certain persons or groups (*a New York accent*). ● *vb* **accent** /ac-**sent**/ to emphasize a certain part of a word.

accentuate /ac-**sen**-shoo-ate/ *vb* to emphasize (*a dress accentuating the blue of her eyes*).

accept / ak-**sept**/ *vb* **1** to receive something offered (*accept the gift with thanks/accept his apology*). **2** to regard as true, reasonable, satisfactory, etc. (*accept his excuse/accept their criticism*). ● *n* **acceptance** /ak-**sep**-tance/.

acceptable /ak-**sep**-ta-bl/ *adj* **1** pleasant to receive (*a very acceptable gift*). **2** satisfactory, good enough (*acceptable work*). **3** allowable, tolerable (*acceptable levels of radiation*).

access /**ak**-sess/ *n* a way or means of approach. ● *vb* to find on a computer file (*access secret data illegally*).

accessible /ak-**sess**-i-bl/ *adj* **1** easily approached (*an accessible manager*). **2** easily reached (*villages that are scarcely accessible*). **3** easily obtained or understood (*accessible information*). ● *n* **accessibility**.

accessory /ak-**sess**-or-ee/ *n* **1** an assistant, especially in crime. **2** an additional part or tool (*car accessories*). **3** an additional item worn with a woman's clothing (*accessories such as purses*).

accident /ak-sid-ent/ *n* **1** an unexpected happening (*we met by accident*). **2** an unexpected event that causes damage or injury (*a road accident*). ● *adj* **accidental**.

acclaim /a-**claim**/ *vb* to greet with applause.

acclamation /ak-la-**may**-shun/ *n* a shout of joy or approval.

acclimatize /a-**clime**-a-tize/ *vb*, also **acclimatise** (*Br*) to accustom to a new climate or situation. ● *n* **acclimatization, acclimatisation** (*Br*).

accolade /a-ko-lade/ *n* **1** the touching on the shoulder with a sword in the ceremony of making someone a knight. **2** praise or approval (*receive accolades for his bravery*).

accommodate /a-**com**-o-date/ *vb* **1** to provide lodgings for (*accommodate the travelers in the hotel*). **2** to have space for (*a garage accommodating three cars*). **3** to supply with (*accommodate them with a loan*). **4** to make suitable, to adapt (*accommodate his way of life to his salary*).

accommodating /a-**com**-o-date-ing/ *adj* obliging (*an accommodating friend*).

accommodation /a-com-o-**day**-shuns/ *n* lodgings (*cheap accommodation for student travelers*).

accompaniment /a-**com**-pan-ee-ment/ *n* the music played with a singer or player (*musical accompaniment for the voice*).

accompanist /a-**com**-pan-ist/ *n* someone who plays the accompaniment for a singer or player (*the accompanist played piano*).

accompany /a-**com**-pan-ee/ *vb* **1** to go with (*accompany her to the concert*). **2** to join a singer or player by playing a musical instrument.

accomplice /a-**com**-pliss/ *n* a helper, especially in crime (*the burglar's accomplice*).

accomplish /a-**com**-plish/ *vb* to perform successfully, to finish (*accomplish the task*).

accomplished /a-**com**-plisht/ *adj* **1** finished (*the accomplished task*). **2** skilled (*an accomplished pianist*).

accomplishment /a-**com**-plish-ment/ *n* **1** something done successfully. **2** completion.

accord /a-**cord**/ *vb* **1** to agree (*his account of the accident accords with hers*). **2** to give (*accord them a warm welcome*). ● *n* agreement. ● **of your own accord** by your own wish.

accordance /a-**cor**-dans/ *n* agreement.

accordingly /a-**cor**-ding-lee/ *adv* therefore.

according to /a-**cor**-ding to/ *prep* **1** in keeping with (*act according to the rules*). **2** as stated by (*according to the teacher*).

accordion /a-**cor**-dee-on/ *n* a portable musical instrument played by keys and worked by bellows. ● *n* **accordionist** /a-**cor**-dee-on-ist/.

accost /a-**cost**/ *vb* to speak to first, to address.

account /a-**count**/ *vb* (*fml*) to consider, to reckon (*account him an honest man*). ● *n* **1** a statement of money received and paid, a bill. **2** a report, description (*an account of the accident*). ● **account for** give an explanation of (*account for his absence*). ● **of no account** of no importance. ● **on account of** because of.

accountable *adj* /a-**count**-a-bl/ responsible (*not accountable for his brother's crime*).

accountancy /a-**count**-an-see/ *n* the work of an accountant (*he studied accountancy*).

accountant /a-**count**-ant/ *n* someone who keeps or examines money accounts.

accumulate /a-**kyoom**-yoo-late/ *vb* **1** to increase, to heap up (*garbage accumulated*). **2** to collect (*accumulate wealth*).

accumulation /a-**kyoom**-yoo-lay-shun/ *n* growth, a large collection.

accuracy /ak-yoo-rass-ee/ *n* exactness, precision (*to aim with accuracy*).

accurate /ak-yoo-rit/ *adj* **1** correct, exact (*an accurate answer*). **2** correct, careful (*an accurate worker*). ● *adv* **accurately**.

accursed /a-**curst**/ *adj* lying under a curse, doomed (*he seemed to be an accursed man*).

accusation /a-kyoo-**zay**-shun/ *n* a charge brought against anyone (*accusation of theft*).

accuse /a-**kyooz**/ *vb* to charge with wrongdoing (*accuse them of stealing cars*). ● *n* **accuser** /a-**kyooz**-er/.

accused /a-**kyoozd**/ *n* someone charged with wrongdoing (*the accused was found guilty*).

accustom /a-**cuss**-tom/ *vb* to make well known by use (*accustom yourself to a different climate*).

accustomed /a-**cuss**-tomd/ *adj* **1** usual (*his accustomed evening walk*). **2** used (to), familiar with (*not accustomed to being treated rudely*).

ace /ace/ *n* **1** one at cards, dice, or dominoes (*the ace of hearts*). **2** someone good at sports (*an ace on the running track*). ● **within an ace of** on the very point of.

acetic /a-**set**-ic/ *adj* sour, of vinegar.

acetylene /a-**set**-ill-een/ *n* a gas used for giving light and heat, and commonly used with oxygen for welding or cutting metal.

ache /ake/ *vb* to be in or to give prolonged pain. ● *n* a prolonged or throbbing pain.

achieve /a-**cheev**/ *vb* 1 to succeed in doing (*achieve what we set out to do*). 2 to gain (*achieve success*).

achievement /a-**cheev**-ment/ *n* 1 something done successfully (*the achievement of his aims*). 2 a feat (*a remarkable achievement*).

acid /a-sid/ *n* a sour substance (*a solution of dilute sulfuric acid*). ● *adj* sour; sharp to the taste; bitter (*an acid personality*).

acid rain /a-sid **rane**/ *n* rain that has been polluted by acid from factory waste, car exhausts, etc. and is harmful to the environment

acid test /a-sid **test**/ *n* a test that indicates the worth or value of something (*the acid test of his invention will be if it works*).

acidity /a-**sid**-it-ee/ *n* sourness.

acknowledge /ak-**naw**-ledge/ *vb* 1 to admit as true (*acknowledge that he was wrong/acknowledge defeat*). 2 to admit the receipt of (*acknowledge the letter*). ● *n* **acknowledg(e)ment** /ak-**naw**-ledge-ment/.

acne /ak-nay/ *n* a skin condition that causes pimples.

acorn /ay-corn/ *n* the fruit or seed of the oak tree.

acoustic /a-**coos**-tik/ *adj* 1 having to do with hearing and sound (*the acoustic problems of the old hall*). 2 (*of a musical instrument*) making its natural sound, not electric (*an acoustic guitar*).

acoustics /a-**coos**-tiks/ *npl* the science of sound.

acquaint /a-**kwaint**/ *vb* 1 to make familiar with (*acquaint yourself with the new system*). 2 to inform (*acquaint them with the facts*).

acquaintance /a-**kwain**-tanse/ *n* 1 a person you know (*friends and acquaintances*). 2 knowledge (*a slight acquaintance with the plays of Tennessee Williams*).

acquire /a-**kwire**/ *vb* to gain, to obtain.

acquit /a-**kwit**/ *vb* 1 to declare innocent. 2 to conduct yourself (*acquit yourself well*).

acquittal /a-**kwi**-tal/ *n* a setting free.

acre /ay-kr/ *n* a measure of land (=4840 square yards or 4046.9 square meters).

acrobat /a-cro-bat/ *n* a high-wire or trapeze artiste. ● *adj* **acrobatic**. ● *npl* **acrobatics**.

acronym /a-cro-nym/ *n* an abbreviation, made from the initial letters, or from combinations of letters from a word, which itself can be pronounced as a word (*NATO is an acronym of North Atlantic Treaty Organization*).

act /act/ *vb* 1 to do (*act quickly*). 2 to conduct yourself (*act wisely*). 3 to perform on the stage, in movies, or on television. 4 to produce an effect (*drugs acting quickly*). ● *n* 1 a deed (*a kind act*). 2 a law. 3 a part of a play.

action /ac-shon/ *n* 1 something done (*take swift action*). 2 a movement (*good wrist action*). 3 the producing of an effect. 4 the events in a narrative or drama. 5 a battle. 6 a lawsuit.

active /ac-tiv/ *adj* 1 energetic (*active children*). 2 taking part, involved (*an active member of the club*). 3 being in action, working, operative (*an active volcano*).

activity *n* /ac-**ti**-vi-tee/ 1 energy. 2 occupation or pastime (*spare-time activities*).

actor /ac-tor/ *n* a man who performs in a play.

actress /ac-tress/ *n* a woman who performs in a play or movie or on television.

actual /ac-chul/ *adj* 1 real, not imaginary (*actual children, not characters in a television play*). 2 true (*the actual cost of the repairs*).

actuality /ac-chu-**wa**-li-tee/ *n* reality.

actually /ac-cha-lee/ *adv* really, as a matter of fact.

acupuncture /a-kyoo-punk-cher/ *n* a treatment used in alternative medicine in which fine needles are inserted into the skin at certain points along energy paths known as meridians.

acute /a-**kyoot**/ *adj* 1 coming to a sharp point. 2 sharp-witted. 3 (*of emotions or diseases*) intense but short-lasting. ● *adv* **acutely**.

acute angle /a-**kyoot ang**-gl/ *n* an angle less than 90°.

ad /ay dee/ *abbr* = **Anno Domini**: a Latin phrase meaning "in the year of our Lord," used to describe the years following the birth of Jesus.

ad /ad/ *n* short for **advertisement**.

adage /a-didge/ *n* a proverb, an old wise saying.

adamant /a-da-mant/ *adj* determined, firm (*adamant that they were right*).

adapt /a-**dapt**/ *vb* 1 to make suitable, to fit to a different use (*adapt the evening dress for day wear*). 2 to change, adjust (*adapt to new surroundings*).

adaptable /a-**dap**-ta-bl/ *adj* easily fitted to new uses or conditions. ● *n* **adaptability** /a-dap-ta-**bi**-li-tee/.

adaptation /a-dap-**tay**-shun/ *n* the action or result of adapting.

adapter /a-**dap**-ter/ *n* a device for connecting electrical plugs with a socket.

add /add/ *vb* 1 to join one thing to another. 2 to

increase (*add to their misery*). **3** to say more (*add a word of thanks*).

adder /a-der/ *n* a small poisonous snake, a viper.

addict /a-dict/ *n* a person who is dependent on and so unable to give up a habit, especially a harmful one such as drug-taking (*a drug addict*).

addicted /a-dic-ted/ *adj* dependent on, unable to give up (*addicted to alcohol/an addicted drug-user*). ● *n* **addiction** /a-dic-shen/.

addition /a-di-shen/ *n* **1** act of adding. **2** something added (*an addition to the family*). ● *adj* **additional** /a-di-she-nel/.

additive /a-di-tiv/ *n* a substance added to another, especially to add flavor or color (*food additives*).

address /a-dress/ *vb* **1** to speak to (*address the crowds*). **2** to direct a letter. **3** to direct your attention or energy to (*address the task*). ● *n* **address, address** /a-dress, a-dress/ **1** the place where a person lives or works. **2** the directions on a letter or envelope. **3** a formal talk (*the head teacher's address on speech day*).

adenoids /a-de-noid/ *npl* soft, natural growth at the back of the nose that hinders breathing.

adept /a-dept/ *adj* very skillful (*adept at tennis*). ● *n* someone who is skilled.

adequate /a-de-kwit/ *adj* **1** enough (*adequate supplies*). **2** satisfactory (*adequate for the job*). ● *adv* **adequately.** ● *n* **adequacy.**

adhere /ad-heer/ *vb* **1** to stick (to). **2** to remain loyal to (*adhere to your principles*). ● *n* **adherence** /ad-hee-rents/.

adhesive /ad-hee-ziv/ *adj* sticky. ● *n* a sticky substance, glue.

adieu /a-dyoo/ *interj* the French word for farewell, goodbye. ● *n* (*pl* **adieus** *or* **adieux** /a-dyooz/) a farewell.

adios /a-dee-oss/ *interj* the Spanish word for good-bye.

adjacent /a-jay-sent/ *adj* lying near (to) (*the fire spread to adjacent buildings*).

adjective /a-jec-tiv/ *n* a word that describes a noun. ● *adj* **adjectival** /a-jec-tie-val/. ● *adv* **adjectivally.**

adjourn /a-jurn/ *vb* **1** to put off to another time (*adjourn the meeting*). **2** to go to another place (*adjourn to the next room*). ● *n* **adjournment** /a-jurn-ment/.

adjust /a-just/ *vb* **1** to set right. **2** to put in order. ● *adj* **adjustable** /a-jus-ta-bl/. ● *ns* **adjuster** /a-jus-ter/, **adjustment** /a-just-ment/.

administer /ad-mi-ni-ster/ *vb* **1** to manage, to govern (*administer the firm's finances*). **2** to carry out (*administer the law*). **3** (*fml*) to give (*administer medicine*).

administration /ad-mi-ni-stray-shun/ *n* **1** the management of a business or a government. **2** people involved in this. ● *adj* **administrative** /ad-mi-ni-stra-tiv/.

administrator /ad-mi-ni-stray-tor/ *n* a person who works in administration (*hospital administrators*).

admirable /ad-mi-ra-bl/ *adj* deserving admiration or praise (*admirable work*). ● *adv* **admirably** /ad-mi-ra-blee/.

admiral /ad-mi-ral/ *n* the highest rank of naval officer.

admiration /ad-mi-ray-shun/ *n* a feeling of pleasure and respect (*look at the painting with admiration*).

admire /ad-mire/ *vb* to think very highly of (*admire her work*). ● *n* **admirer** /ad-mire-rer/.

admission /ad-mi-shen/ *n* **1** permission to enter (*women being refused admission*). **2** the amount payable for entry (*admission $4*). **3** a confession (*an admission of guilt*).

admit /ad-mit/ *vb* **1** to allow to enter (*the ticket admits two people*). **2** to accept as true or just (*admit that they are right*). **3** to confess (*admit his crime*).

admittance /ad-mi-tanse/ *n* (*fml*) right or permission to enter (*fail to gain admittance*).

admittedly /ad-mi-ted-lee/ *adv* it cannot be denied.

admonish /ad-mo-nish/ *vb* to give a warning or scolding to. ● *n* **admonition** /ad-mo-ni-shun/. ● *adj* **admonitory** /ad-mon-ni-to-ree/.

ado /a-doo/ *n* fuss, trouble (*let us get on our way without further ado*).

adobe /a-doe-bee/ *n* **1** a building material made of sun-dried earth and straw. **2** a building made of this material.

adolescent /a-doe-less-sent/ *adj* growing up from youth to adulthood. ● *n* a person of either sex when adolescent. ● *n* **adolescence** /a-doe-less-sens/.

adopt /a-dopt/ *vb* **1** to take as your own (*adopt a child*). **2** to take over and use (*adopt foreign customs*). **3** to choose formally (*adopt a candidate*). ● *n* **adoption** /a-dop-shun/.

adorable /a-doe-ra-bl/ *adj* lovable.

adore /a-dore/ *vb* **1** to worship (*adore God*). **2** to love or like very much (*adore their mother/adore spicy food*). ● *n* **adoration** /a-do-ray-shun/.

adorn *vb* /a-dorn/ to decorate, to make beautiful (*adorn the tree with Christmas lights*). ● *adj* **adorned.**

adornment /a-**dorn**-ment/ *n* an ornament.

adrift /a-**drift**/ *adj* and *adv* floating without control.

adrenaline /a-**dre**-na-lin/ *n* a chemical produced by your body when you are scared or excited.

adulation /a-je-**lay**-shun/ *n* extreme praise, flattery.

adult, adult /a-**dult**, a-dult/ *adj* grown-up (*an adult animal*). ● *n* adult a grown-up person.

adulterate /a-**dul**-te-rayt/ *vb* to lower in value by mixing with something of less worth (e.g., to mix wine with water, gold with tin, etc.). ● *n* adulteration /a-dul-te-ray-shun/.

advance /ad-**vanse**/ *vb* 1 to put forward (*advance a theory*). 2 to go forward (*armies advancing*). 3 to help promote (*advance the cause of freedom*). 4 to lend (*the bank advanced him $5000*). ● *n* 1 a forward movement (*the advance of the army*). 2 progress (*little advance in the discussions*). 3 a loan (of money), especially a payment made before the normal time (*an advance on his paycheck*). 4 increase (*any advance on $500 for this picture?*). ● **in advance** in front; before.

advanced /ad-**vanst**/ *adj* 1 far on (in life, time, etc.) (*of advanced years/an illness at an advanced stage*). 2 at a high level, not elementary (*advanced studies*). 3 modern and new and sometimes not yet generally accepted (*advanced ideas*).

advantage /ad-**van**-tidge/ *n* 1 a better position or something that puts someone in a better position (*he has the advantage of being older*). 2 gain, profit, benefit (*little advantage in having a car if you can't afford to run it*).

advantageous /ad-van-**tey**-jess/ *adj* profitable; helpful. ● *adv* advantageously /ad-van-**tey**-jess-lee/.

advent /ad-vent/ *n* a coming, an arrival (*the advent of train travel*).

Advent /ad-vent/ *n* in the Christian church, the period from the fourth Sunday before Christmas to Christmas Day.

adventure /ad-**ven**-cher/ *n* an exciting or dangerous deed or undertaking.

adventurer /ad-**ven**-cher-rer/ (*m/f*), adventuress /ad-**ven**-che-ress/ (*f*) *n* 1 someone who seeks adventures. 2 someone who lives by his or her wits.

adventurous /ad-**ven**-che-russ/ *adj* 1 daring, eager for adventure (*adventurous children*). 2 dangerous, involving risk (*an adventurous journey*).

adverb /ad-verb/ *n* a word that modifies the meaning of a verb, an adjective, or another adverb. ● *adj* adverbial /ad-**ver**-bee-al/.

adversary /ad-ver-se-ree/ *n* an enemy.

adverse /ad-**verse**, ad-verse/ *adj* acting against, unfavorable (*adverse weather conditions/adverse criticism*). ● *adv* adversely /ad-**verse**-lee/.

adversity /ad-**ver**-si-tee/ *n* misfortune.

advertise /ad-ver-tize/ *vb* to make known to the public. ● *n* advertiser /ad-ver-tie-zer/.

advertisement /ad-ver-**tize**-ment/ *n* an announcement to the public.

advice /ad-**vice**/ *n* 1 a helpful opinion offered to another (*seek expert financial advice*). 2 a formal letter, etc., giving information (*a sales advice*).

advisable /ad-**vie**-za-bl/ *adj* wise; correct in the circumstances. ● *n* advisability /ad-vie-za-**bi**-li-tee/.

advise /ad-vize/ *vb* 1 to give advice (*advise them to leave*). 2 to inform (*advise us of the cost*).

adviser /ad-**vie**-zer/ *n* someone who gives advice.

advisory /ad-**vie**-zo-ree/ *adj* for the purpose of giving advice.

advocate /ad-vo-cat/ *n* 1 someone who speaks for another. 2 a lawyer who pleads a cause in court. ● *vb* to recommend, to speak in favor of (*advocate a change of climate for his health*).

aerial /ae-ree-al/ *adj* of or from the air (*aerial photography*). ● *n* (*Br*) a radio or television antenna.

aerobatics /ae-ro-**ba**-tics/ *npl* difficult exercises performed by an aircraft.

aerobics /ae-**ro**-bics/ *n* a type of physical exercise that strengthens the heart and lungs by temporarily increasing the heart rate. ● *adj* aerobic /ae-ro-bic/.

aerodynamic /ae-ro-die-**na**-mic/ *adj* streamlined for smooth movement through the air.

aeronautics /ae-ro-**naw**-tics/ *n* the science of the operation and flight of aircraft.

aerosol /ae-ro-sol/ *n* 1 a liquid under pressure in a container, which is released in a fine spray (*deodorants in the form of aerosols*). 2 the container for this (*aerosols of perfume*).

affable /a-fa-bl/ *adj* pleasant, polite, easy to talk with. ● *n* affability /a-fa-**bi**-li-tee/. ● *adv* affably.

affair /a-**fair**/ *n* 1 business (*affairs of state*). 2 a matter, a concern (*no affair of yours*). 3 happenings or events connected with a particular person or thing (*the Watergate affair*). 4 a love affair.

affect /a-**fect**/ *vb* 1 to act upon (*a disease affecting his eyes*). 2 to move the feelings (*deeply affected by his death*). 3 to pretend (*affect grief*).

affected /a-**fec**-ted/ *adj* full of affectation (*an affected young woman*).

affectation /a-fec-**tay**-shun/ *n* manner or behavior that is not natural, pretense (*her helplessness is just an affectation*).

affection /a-**fec**-shun/ *n* fondness, love.

affectionate /a-**fec**-shi-nit/ *adj* loving. ● *adv* **affectionately** /a-**fec**-shi-nit-lee/.

affiliate /a-**fi**-lee-ay-ted/ *v* to be joined or be connected with something (*affiliate yourself with that club*). ● *n* **affiliation** /a-fi-lee-**ay**-shun/.

affinity /a-**fi**-ni-tee/ *n* **1** relationship (*languages having an affinity with one another*). **2** attraction (*an affinity between them*).

affirm /a-**firm**/ *vb* to state with certainty.

affirmation /a-fir-**may**-shun/ *n* **1** a statement. **2** a solemn statement of the truth.

affirmative /a-**fir**-ma-tiv/ *adj* answering "yes". ● *n* an answer meaning "yes". ● **answer in the affirmative** to say "yes"

afflict /a-**flict**/ *vb* to cause pain, distress, etc., to (*she is afflicted with poor health/the economic problems afflicting the country*). ● *n* **affliction** /a-**flic**-shun/.

affluence /a-**floo**-ents/ *n* wealth.

affluent /a-**floo**-ent/ *adj* wealthy.

afford /a-**ford**/ *vb* **1** to be able to pay for (*unable to afford a vacation*). **2** to be able to do, spend, etc., something without trouble, loss, etc. (*unable to afford the time*). **3** (*fml*) to give (*the occasion afforded him much pleasure*).

afloat /a-**float**/ *adj* and *adv* floating.

aforesaid /a-**fore**-said/ *adj* already mentioned.

afraid /a-**frade**/ *adj* frightened.

afresh /a-**fresh**/ *adv* again (*begin afresh*).

African American /a-fri-can a-**me**-ri-can/ *n* a United States citizen who has African ancestors. ● *adj* describing African Americans, or their culture, history, etc.

African Canadian /a-fri-can ca-**nay**-dee-an/ *n* a Canadian citizen who has African ancestors. ● *adj* describing Black Canadians, or their culture, history, etc.

aft /**aft**/ *adj* and *adv* at or near the stern of a ship.

after /**af**-ter/ *adv* and *prep* **1** later in time (than) (*after the meal*). **2** behind (*come after them*).

aftermath /**af**-ter-math/ *n* the period of time, or consequences, following an unpleasant or unfortunate event (*the aftermath of the war*).

afternoon /af-ter-**noon**/ *n* the time from noon to evening.

afterthought /**af**-ter-thot/ *n* **1** a fresh thought after an act or speech. **2** something added or done later, not part of an original plan (*added on as an afterthought*).

afterward /**af**-ter-ward/ *adv* later.

again /a-**gen**/ *adv* once more.

against /a-**genst**/ *prep* **1** in opposition to (*people against the new law*). **2** supported by (*lean against the wall*).

agate /a-**get**/ *n* a very hard precious stone.

age /**ayj**/ *n* **1** the length of time a person or thing has lived or existed. **2** (*inf*) a long time (*wait ages for a bus*). **3** the state of being old (*improve with age*). **4** a particular period in history (*the Stone Age*). ● *vb* **1** to become old. **2** to make old (*worry has aged her*).

aged /**ay**-jed/ *adj* **1** at the age of (*boys aged ten*). **2** old (*my aged grandfather*).

ageless /**ayj**-less/ *adj* never becoming old.

agency /**ay**-jen-see/ *n* the office or business of an agent.

agenda /a-**jen**-da/ *n* a list of matters to be discussed at a meeting.

agent /**ay**-jent/ *n* **1** someone or something that acts (*cleaning agents that harm the skin*). **2** a person who acts on behalf of someone else.

aggravate /a-gra-vate/ *vb* **1** to make worse (*aggravate the situation by losing his temper*). **2** (*inf*) to make angry (*children aggravating their mother*). ● *adj* **aggravating**. ● *n* **aggravation**.

aggression /a-**gre**-shun/ *n* **1** an attack. **2** hostile feelings.

aggressive /a-**gre**-siv/ *adj* **1** always ready to attack, quarrelsome. **2** forceful, determined (*an aggressive sales campaign*). ● *adv* **aggressively** /a-**gre**-siv-lee/.

aggressor /a-**gre**-sor/ *n* the first to attack.

agile /a-jile/ *adj* quick of movement, nimble. ● *n* **agility** /a-ji-li-tee/.

agitate /a-ji-tate/ *vb* **1** to excite, to make anxious (*delay agitates her*). **2** to try to stir up public feeling (*agitate for prison reform*). **3** (*fml*) to shake (*agitate the bottle*). ● *n* **agitation** /a-ji-**tay**-shun/.

agitator /a-ji-tay-tor/ *n* someone who tries to cause public discontent or revolt.

agnostic /ag-**naw**-stic/ *n* someone who believes that the existence of God cannot be proved.

ago /a-**go**/ *adv* in the past (*a long time ago*).

agonizing /a-gon-eye-zing/ *adj, also* **agonising** (*Br*) **1** causing great pain. **2** causing great distress.

agony /a-gon-ee/ *n* **1** great pain (*in agony from a gunshot wound*). **2** great distress (*the agony of divorce*).

agree /a-**gree**/ *vb* **1** to be of the same opinion (*agree that everyone should go*). **2** to be alike (*statements* *that agree*). **3** to suit (*a climate that agrees with her*).

agreeable /a-**gree**-a-bl/ *adj* **1** pleasant (*an agreeable climate*). **2** ready to agree (*we were not all agreeable to vote that way*). ● *adv* **agreeably** /a-**gree**-a-blee/.

agreement /a-**gree**-ment/ *n* **1** sameness of opinion (*in agreement about the new plans*). **2** likeness (*little agreement in their statements*). **3** a contract (*sign an agreement*).

agriculture /a-gri-**cul**-cher/ *n* the science of cultivating the land, farming. ● *adj* **agricultural** /a-gri-**cul**-chu-rel/.

aground /a-**ground**/ *adv* on or on to the sea bed.

ahead /a-**hed**/ *adv* **1** in front (*go on ahead to clear the way*). **2** forward, for the future (*plan ahead*).

AI /ay eye/ *abbr* = **artificial intelligence**: the study of the capacity of computers to simulate human intelligence.

aid /aid/ *vb* to help. ● *n* help.

aide /aid/ *n* (*pl* **aides-de-camp**) an officer in attendance on a king, general or other high official (*a White House aide*).

AIDS, Aids /aidz/ *n* a serious disease that affects the body's immune system, greatly reducing resistance to infection (*AIDS is an acronym of Acquired Immune Deficiency Syndrome*).

ailing /**ay**-ling/ *adj* **1** unwell (*his ailing wife*). **2** weak (*the country's ailing economy*).

ailment /**ayl**-ment/ *n* a minor health problem.

aim /aim/ *vb* **1** to point a weapon (at). **2** to intend, to try (*aim to win*). ● *n* **1** the act of aiming a weapon. **2** intention, goal, purpose (*our aim is to win*).

aimless /**aim**-less/ *adj* without purpose (*aimless discussions*).

air /air/ *n* **1** the mixture of gases composing the earth's atmosphere (*the air we breathe*). **2** a light breeze (*the sea air*). **3** a tune (*play a familiar air*). **4** manner (*an air of confidence*). **5** *pl* a manner that is not genuine (*put on airs*). ● *vb* **1** to expose to fresh air (*air the room by opening the windows*). **2** to expose to warm air, to dry (*air the laundry*). **3** to speak openly about (*air your views*).

air bag /**air**-bag/ *n* an inflatable safety device in automobiles that blows up on impact to cushion the driver.

air-conditioning /air-con-**dish**-un-ing/ *n* a system for controlling the temperature and quality of the air in a building. ● *adj* **air-conditioned** /air-con-**dish**-end/. ● *n* **air-conditioner** /air-con-**dish**-ner/.

aircraft /**air**-craft/ *n* (*pl* **aircraft**) a flying machine.

airfield /**air**-feeld/ *n* a starting and landing place for aircraft.

airily /**air**-ill-ee/ *adv* in an airy manner.

airing /**air**-ing/ *n* **1** act of exposing to fresh or warm air. **2** an outing in the open air.

airless /**air**-less/ *adj* stuffy.

airline /**air**-line/ *n* a company providing regular aircraft services.

airliner /**air**-line-er/ *n* a large passenger aircraft.

airmail *n* a postal service where mail is carried by airplane.

airplane /**air**-plane/ *n* a heavier-than-air flying machine with wings.

air pocket /**air** pock-it/ *n* a stream of air that carries an aircraft suddenly up or down.

airport /**air**-port/ *n* a station for passenger aircraft.

air raid /**air**-rade/ *n* an attack by aircraft.

airship /**air** ship/ *n* an aircraft kept aloft by a gas-filled balloon and driven by a motor.

airtight /**air**-tite/ *adj* so sealed that air can pass neither in nor out (*preserve fruit in an airtight bottle*).

airy /**ay**-ree/ *adj* **1** with plenty of fresh air (*an airy room*). **2** lacking seriousness (*an airy disregard for authority*).

aisle /ile/ *n* **1** the side part of a church, often separated from the central part by a row of pillars. **2** a passage in a church. **3** a passage in a theater or store.

ajar /a-**jar**/ *adv* partly open (*doors left ajar*).

akimbo /a-**kim**-bo/ *adv* with the hand on the hip and the elbow outward (*arms akimbo*).

akin /a-**kin**/ *adj* similar (*problems akin to ours*).

alabaster /a-la-**bas**-ter/ *n* a soft marble-like stone.

alarm /a-**larm**/ *n* **1** a warning of danger (*hear a burglar alarm*). **2** sudden fear (*news causing alarm*). ● *vb* to frighten.

alarm clock *n* a clock that can be set to ring or buzz to wake you.

alarming /a-**larm**-ing/ *adj* frightening. ● *adv* **alarmingly**.

alarmist /a-**larm**-ist/ *n* someone who needlessly spreads frightening news or rumors. ● *adj* causing needless fear.

alas /a-**las**/ *interj* a cry of grief or pity.

albatross /**al**-ba-tross/ *n* a large white seabird.

albino /al-**bee**-no/ *n* a person or animal with white skin and hair and pink eyes because he or she has no natural coloring.

album /**al**-bum/ *n* **1** a blank book into which may be put autographs, photographs, stamps, etc. **2** a collection of songs on a CD or other recording (*the band's latest album*).

alcohol /al-co-hol/ *n* **1** pure spirit. **2** strong liquor containing such spirit (*addicted to alcohol*).

alcoholic /al-co-**hol**-ic/ *n* someone who is addicted to alcohol. ● *adj* having to do with alcohol (*alcoholic drinks*).

alcove /al-cove/ *n* a recess, a section of a room, etc., that is set back from the main part.

ale /ale/ *n* a light-colored, bitter beer.

alert /a-**lert**/ *adj* **1** attentive (*sentries must be alert on duty*). **2** quick (*mentally alert*). ● *n* a warning of danger. ● *n* **alertness**.

alfalfa /al-**fal**-fa/ *n* a green plant used as cattle food.

algebra /**al**-ji-bra/ *n* a method of calculation in which letters and symbols are used to represent numbers. ● *adj* **algebraic** /al-ji-**bray**-ic/.

alias /**ay**-lee-ass/ *adv* otherwise (*Fred Jones, alias Martin Smith*). ● *n* a false name (*the alias adopted by the spy*).

alibi /a-li-buy/ *n* the plea that you were elsewhere when a crime was committed (*establish an alibi*).

alien /**ay**-lee-an/ *adj* **1** foreign (*find ourselves in an alien land*). **2** different, strange (*attitudes that are alien to ours*). ● *n* **1** a foreigner, a person who is not a naturalized citizen of the country where he or she is living. **2** a being from another world.

alienate /**ay**-lee-an-ate/ *vb* to make unfriendly (*alienate his family with his violence*).

alight[1] /a-**lite**/ *vb* **1** to get down (from) (*alight from the bus*). **2** to settle upon (*butterflies alighting on the leaves*).

alight[2] /a-**lite**/ *adv* on fire.

align /a-**line**/ *vb* **1** to put in line, to straighten. **2** to join, ally yourself with (*align himself with the enemy*). ● *n* **alignment** /a-**line**-ment/.

alike /a-**like**/ *adj* like, similar. ● *adv* in the same way.

alimentary canal /a-li-**men**-tree ca-**nal**/ *n* the passage through the body by which food is received and digested.

alimony /**a**-li-mone-ee/ *n* the money payable regularly by a man or woman to his or her former wife or husband after legal separation or divorce.

alive /a-**laiv**/ *adj* **1** living (*wounded soldiers still alive*). **2** lively (*eyes alive with excitement*). **3** aware of (*alive to danger*).

alkali /**al**-ka-lie/ *n* a substance such as potash or soda that neutralizes acids and unites with oil or fat to form soap.

all /ol/ *adj* **1** every one of (*all the girls*). **2** the whole of (*all the cake*). ● *n* **1** everyone (*all left*). **2** everything (*eat it all*). ● *adv* wholly, entirely.

Allah *n* the Islamic name for God.

allay /a-**lay**/ *vb* to calm (*allay their fears*).

all-dressed /ol-**drest**/ *adj* (*Cdn*) describing an item of food, such as a pizza or a hot dog, that is topped with all available garnishes.

allege /a-**ledge**/ *vb* to state without proof (*allege that he had been attacked*). ● *n* **allegation** /a-le-**gay**-shun/ (*can you provide proof of that allegation?*). ● *adj* **alleged** /a-**ledge**-ed/ (*the alleged thief sat in the courtroom*).

allegiance /a-**lee**-jance/ *n* loyalty.

allegory /**a**-li-go-ree/ *n* a story with a hidden meaning different from the obvious one. ● *adj* **allegorical** /a-li-**go**-ri-cal/.

allegro /a-le-**gro**/ *adv* (*mus*) briskly.

allergy /**a**-ler-jee/ *n* a reaction of the body to some substance (*break out in a rash because of an allergy to cats*). ● *adj* **allergic** /a-**ler**-jic/.

alleviate /a-**lee**-vee-ate/ *vb* to lessen (*alleviating pain*). ● *n* **alleviation** /a-lee-vee-**ay**-shun/.

alley /**a**-lee/ *n* **1** a narrow walk or passage. **2** a lane for bowling. **3** a building containing lanes for bowling.

alliance /a-**lie**-anse/ *n* a union between families, governments, etc.

allied *see* **ally**.

alligator /**a**-li-gay-tor/ *n* a reptile related to the crocodile found in North America, South America and China.

alliteration /a-lit-er-**ay**-shon/ *n* the repetition of a sound at the beginning of words especially in poetry, for example, "Peter Piper picked a peck of pickled pepper." ● *Compare* **assonance**.

allocate /**a**-lo-cate/ *vb* to share out, to distribute (*allocating tasks to each of the children*). ● *n* **allocation** /a-lo-**cay**-shon/.

allot /a-**lot**/ *vb* (**allotted**, **allotting**) to give a share, to distribute (*allot the money collected to various charities*).

allotment /a-**lot**-ment/ *n* **1** act of allotting. **2** a small piece of land for growing vegetables, etc.

allow /al-**ow**/ *vb* **1** to permit (*allow them to go*). **2** to provide, to set aside (*allow three hours for the journey*).

allowable /al-**ow**-a-bl/ *adj* permissible.

allowance /al-**ow**-anse/ *n* a sum of money granted for a special purpose (*a dress allowance*). ● **make allowance for** take into consideration.

alloy /a-loy/ *n* a mixture of metals.

all right /ol **rite**/ *adj* **1** acceptable or satisfactory (*the show was all right*). **2** safe or well (*I am feeling all right now*). ● *adv* an expression of agreement (*all right, I will*).

allude /a-**lood**/ *vb* to refer to, to mention (*allude to several new developments in his speech*). ● *n* **allusion** /a-**loo**-zhen/. ● *adj* **allusive** /a-**loo**-siv/.

allure /a-**loor**/ *vb* to attract (*allure them to new jobs with promises of high salaries*). ● *n* attraction, charm (*the allure of the stage*). ● *n* **allurement** /a-**loor**-ment/. ● *adj* **alluring** /a-**loor**-ing/.

allusion *see* **allude**.

ally /a-**lie**/ *vb* to join with another for a special purpose (e.g., by marriage or by treaty) (*ally ourselves with the blue team*). ● *adj* **allied** /a-**lied**/. ● *n* **1** a helper (*one of the President's closest allies*). **2** a nation bound to another by treaty of friendship (*a victory for the allies against the enemy*).

almanac /**ol**-man-ac/ *n* a book containing a calendar and information about anniversaries, tides, stars, and planets, etc.

almighty /ol-**mite**-ee/ *adj* **1** (*often cap*) all-powerful (*Almighty God*). **2** (*inf*) very great, strong, loud, etc. (*an almighty crash*). ● *n* **The Almighty** God.

almond /a-**mond**/ *n* a brown oval nut.

almost /**ol**-most/ *adv* nearly (*almost midnight/almost at my mother's house/she almost fell*).

aloe /a-**loe**/ *n* a plant with a bitter juice used in medicines, especially for the skin.

aloft /a-**loft**/ *adv* high up in the air (*hold the flag aloft*).

aloha /a-**loe**-ha/ *interj* a Hawaiian word, meaning love, used to say hello or goodbye.

alone /a-**lone**/ *adj and adv* **1** without company (*live alone/go on vacation alone*). **2** taken by itself (*money alone is not enough*).

alongside /a-**long**-side/ *adv and prep* by the side of (*draw up alongside their car*).

aloof /a-**loof**/ *adv* apart, distant (*stand aloof from his friends' quarreling*). ● *adj* distant, cool (*aloof people who do not make friends*). ● *n* **aloofness**.

aloud /a-**loud**/ *adv* so as can be heard (*read aloud*).

alp /alp/ *n* a high mountain.

alphabet /**al**-fa-bet/ *n* the set of letters used in writing a language. ● *adj* **alphabetical** /al-fa-**bet**-i-cal/ (*in alphabetical order*).

alpine /**al**-pine/ *adj* having to do with high mountains, especially the Swiss Alps (*alpine plants*).

already /ol-**red**-ee/ *adv* **1** before this time, previously (*I have already seen the movie*). **2** now or

before the expected time (*are you leaving already?*).

altar /**ol**-ter/ *n* **1** a raised place or table on which sacrifices are offered. **2** a communion table.

alter /**ol**-ter/ *vb* to change (*alter your lifestyle/alter a dress/neighborhoods that have altered*). ● *n* **alteration** /ol-te-**ray**-shun/.

alternate /**ol**-ter-nit/ *adj* **1** first one coming, then the other (*a pattern with alternate squares and circles*). **2** every second (*visit on alternate Tuesdays*). **3** alternative (*offer an alternate appointment*). ● *n* an alternative. ● *vb* /**ol**-ter-nate / **1** to do, use, cause, arrange, etc., by turns (*alternating reading with watching television*). **2** to happen by turns (*rainy days alternated with dry ones*). ● *adv* **alternately** /**ol**-ter-nate-lee/. ● *n* **alternation** /ol-ter-**nay**-shun/.

alternative /ol-**ter**-na-tiv/ *n* **1** a choice between two things (*the alternatives are to go or stay*). **2** (*inf*) a choice of two or more possibilities. ● *adj* offering such a choice. ● *adv* **alternatively** /ol-**ter**-na-tiv-lee/.

although /ol-**tho**/ *conj* though.

altitude /**al**-te-tood/ *n* height.

alto /**al**-toe/ *n* **1** the highest male voice. **2** a low female voice, properly called **contralto** /con-**tral**-toe/. ● *also adj*.

altogether /ol-te-**ge**-ther/ *adv* **1** wholly (*not altogether satisfied*). **2** including everything (*$20 altogether*). **3** on the whole (*altogether the vacation was a success*).

altruism /**al**-troo-izm/ *n* acting to please others rather than yourself. ● *n* **altruist** /**al**-troo-ist/. ● *adj* **altruistic** /al-tru-is-tic/.

aluminum /a-**loo**-me-nem/ *n* a soft, white, light metal.

always /**ol**-waze/ *adv* at all times.

am /am/ *vb* the form of the verb *to be* used with *I*.

a.m. /ay em/ *abbr* = **ante meridiem** /an-tee mer-id-ee-um/: a Latin phrase meaning before midday.

amalgam /a-**mal**-gam/ *n* a mixture, especially of mercury with another metal.

amalgamate /a-**mal**-ga-mate/ *vb* to unite, to join together (*amalgamate the clubs/the clubs amalgamated*). ● *n* **amalgamation** /a-mal-ga-**may**-shun/.

amass /a-**mass**/ *vb* to collect a large amount of.

amateur /a-ma-ter, a-ma-cher/ *n* **1** someone who takes part in any activity for the love of it, rather than for money (*a tennis tournament open only to*

amateurs). **2** a person without skill or expertise in something (*repairs carried out by an amateur*). ● *n* **amateurism** /a-ma-te-rizm, a-ma-che-rizm.
amateurish /a-ma-te-rish, a-ma-che-rish/ *adj* inexpert, unskillful (*his amateurish repair of the fence*).
amaze /a-**maze**/ *vb* to astonish (*her rudeness amazed me/amazed by his skill*). ● *n* **amazement** /a-**maze**-ment/.
ambassador /am-**bass**-sa-dor/ *n* a high-ranking official appointed to represent his or her government in a foreign country. ● *adj* **ambassadorial** / am-bass-sa-**do**-ree-al/.
amber /am-ber/ *n* a clear yellowish substance used for ornaments. ● *adj* **1** made of amber (*amber beads*). **2** brownish yellow (*amber eyes*).
ambidextrous /am-bi-**dek**-strus/ *adj* able to do things equally well with either hand.
ambiguous /am-**bi**-gyoo-uss/ *adj* having more than one meaning (*the ambiguous statement left him in doubt*). ● *n* **ambiguity** /am-bi-**gyoo**-e-tee/.
ambition /am-bi-shen/ *n* **1** desire for power, determination to succeed (*people of ambition struggling for promotion*). **2** a goal, aim (*his ambition is to play football for his country*). ● *adj* **ambitious** / am-**bi**-shess/.
amble /am-bl/ *vb* to walk at an easy pace (*ambling along although late for school*). ● *n* **1** an easy pace. **2** a slow walk. ● *n* **ambler** /am-bler/.
ambulance /am-byoo-lanss/ *n* a vehicle for carrying the sick or injured.
ambush /am-boosh/ *n* **1** a body of people so hidden as to be able to make a surprise attack on an approaching enemy. **2** the place where such people hide. **3** a surprise attack made by people in hiding (*killed in a terrorist ambush*). ● *vb* to lie in wait, to attack from an ambush.
ameba, amoeba /a-**mee**-ba/ *n* (*pl* amebae, amoebae*) a tiny living creature found in water. ● *adj* **amebic, amoebic** /a-**mee**-bic/.
ameliorate /a-**meel**-ye-rayt/ *vb* **1** to make better (*medicines ameliorating her condition*). **2** to grow better (*conditions have ameliorated slightly*). ● *n* **amelioration** /a-meel-ye-**ray**-shun/.
amen /ay-**men**/ *interj* may it be so!; so be it!
amenable /a-**mee**-na-bl/ *adj* ready to be guided or influenced (*amenable to your suggestions/amenable people*).
amend /a-**mend**/ *vb* **1** (*fml*) to change for the better (*amend your ways*). **2** to correct (*amend the author's manuscript*). **3** to alter slightly (*amend

the law). ● **to make amends** to make up for a wrong done.
amendment /a-**mend**-ment/ *n* **1** improvement. **2** an alteration (e.g. in a law).
amenities /a-**mee**-ne-tees, a-**mee**-ne-tees / *npl* things that make life easier or more pleasant (*the amenities of the town, such as the library, theater, bowling alley, etc.*).
American /a-**me**-ri-can/ *adj* **1** describing the United States of America (*the American flag*). **2** describing North America, Central America, or South America. ● *n* **1** a person from the United States of America. **2** a person from North America, Central America, or South America.
American Indian /a-**me**-ri-can **in**-dee-an/ *n* a native person of the United States or Canada. ● *adj* describing the native people of the United States and Canada and their languages, customs, etc.
amethyst /a-**me**-thest/ *n* a precious stone of a bluish-violet or purple color.
amiable /ay-mee-abl/ *adj* friendly, pleasant (*an amiable young man/in an amiable mood*). ● *n* **amiability** /ay-mee-a-**bi**-li-tee/.
amicable /a-**mi**-ca-bl/ *adj* friendly (*settle the dispute in an amicable way*).
amid, amidst /a-**mid**, a-**midst**/ *preps* in the middle of, among.
amigo *n* /a-**mee**-go/ the Spanish word for "male friend," used informally in English. ● *n* **amiga** female friend.
amiss /a-**miss**/ *adv* wrong (*something amiss*). ● **take amiss** to take offense at.
ammonia /a-**mo**-nee-a/ *n* **1** a strong-smelling, colorless gas. **2** a solution of ammonia gas and water (*ammonia may be used for cleaning*).
ammunition /am-ye-**ni**-shen/ *n* **1** powder, bullets, shells, etc. **2** facts, etc., used against someone in an argument, etc.
amnesia /am-**nee**-zha/ *n* loss of memory (*a blow to the head caused his amnesia*).
amnesty /am-ne-stee/ *n* a general pardon (*an amnesty for all political prisoners*).
amoeba (*Br*) see **ameba**.
among, amongst /a-**mong**/ *preps* **1** in the middle of (*a house among the trees/roses amongst the weeds*). **2** in shares or parts to each person (*share the candy among you*). **3** in the group of (*the best among his novels*).
amorous /a-mo-rus, am-rus/ *adj* feeling or expressing love or sexual desire (*amorous glances*).
amount /a-**mount**/ *vb* **1** to add up to (*bills amounting

to $3000). **2** to be equal to (*a reply amounting to a refusal*). ● *n* the sum total.

amp *see* **ampere**.

ampere /am-pir/ *n* the unit used in measuring electric current, usually shortened to **amp**.

ampersand /am-per-sand/ *n* a character (&) that stands for "and" (*Jones & Son*).

amphibian /am-fi-bee-an/ *n* **1** a creature that can live both on land and in water (*frogs are amphibians*). **2** a vehicle designed to move over land or water. **3** an aircraft that can take off from or land on either land or water. ● *adj* **amphibious** /am-fi-bee-uss/.

amphitheater /am-fe-thee-e-ter/ *n, also* **amphitheatre** (*Br, Cdn*) an oval or circular theater or building in which the seats rise in tiers around and above a central stage or arena.

ample /am-pl/ *adj* **1** large (*a lady with an ample bosom*). **2** enough, sufficient, more than enough (*ample time to get there/ample opportunity*).

amplification *see* **amplify**.

amplifier /am-ple-fie-er/ *n* an instrument for making sounds louder.

amplify /am-ple-fy/ *vb* **1** to enlarge (*amplify his statement with further details*). **2** to make louder (*amplify the music from the guitar*). ● *n* **amplification** /am-pli-fee-**kay**-shun/.

amplitude /am-pli-tood/ *n* size, extent, abundance.

amply /am-plee/ *adv* fully, sufficiently (*amply paid*).

amputate /am-pye-tate/ *vb* to cut off (a limb). ● *n* **amputation** /am-pye-**tay**-shon/.

amulet /am-ye-let/ *n* an ornament worn as a charm against evils.

amuse /a-**myooz**/ *vb* **1** to entertain, to give pleasure (*amuse the children by reading to them*). **2** to make laugh or smile (*amused by the comedian's jokes*). ● *adj* **amusing** /a-**myoo**-zing/.

amusement /a-**myooz**-ment/ *n* **1** pleasure, entertainment (*play the piano purely for her own amusement*). **2** entertainment, pastime (*a wide variety of amusements, such as pool, badminton, table tennis*).

anaconda /a-na-**con**-da/ *n* a large snake of South America.

anaemia (*Br, Cdn*) *see* **anemia**.

anaemic (*Br, Cdn*) *see* **anemic**.

anaesthesia (*Br, Cdn*) *see* **anesthesia**.

anaesthetic (*Br, Cdn*) *see* **anesthetic**.

anaesthetist (*Br, Cdn*) *see* **anesthetist**.

anagram /a-na-gram/ *n* a word or words formed by arranging the letters of a word or phrase in a new order (e.g. *mite* from *time*).

analog /a-na-log/ *n* an object, e.g., such as a pointer on a dial, used to measure something else.

analogous /a-na-lo-gus/ *adj* similar (*in a situation analogous to our own*).

analogy /a-na-lo-jee/ *n* **1** likeness (*the analogy between the human heart and a pump*). **2** the process of reasoning based on such similarity (*explain the movement of light as an analogy with that of water*).

analysis /a-na-li-siss/ *n* (*pl* **analyses** /a-na-li-seez/) **1** the process of analyzing (*subject the food to analysis*). **2** a statement of the results of this. **3** short for **psychoanalysis** /sa-ee-co a-na-li-siss/. ● *adj* **analytical** /a-na-li-ti-cal/.

analyst /a-na-list/ *n* someone who analyzes, especially in chemistry.

analytical *see* **analysis**.

analyze /a-na-lize/ *vb, also* **analyse** (*Br*) to break a thing up into its parts or elements (*analyze the food for signs of poison/ analyze the facts and figures*).

anarchist /a-nar-kist/ *n* who wishes to do away with all government.

anarchy /a-nar-kee/ *n* **1** lawlessness. **2** absence of government.

anathema /a-**na**-the-ma/ *n* **1** a solemn curse. **2** a thing that is accursed or hateful. **3** something or someone that one detests or strongly disapproves of (*bullying is an anathema to him*).

anatomy /a-**na**-ta-mee/ *n* **1** the study of the way the body is put together (*study anatomy*). **2** the cutting up of a body to study its parts and their relation to one another. **3** the body (*leaving some parts of his anatomy uncovered*). ● *adj* **anatomical** /a-na-**to**-mi-cal/. ● *n* **anatomist** /a-**na**-to-mist/.

ancestor /an-sess-tor/ *n* forefather, a person from whom you are descended. ● *adj* **ancestral**.

ancestry /an-sess-tree/ *n* line of forefathers.

anchor /ang-kor/ *n* **1** a heavy iron hook that grips the sea bed and holds a ship at rest in the water. **2** a person or thing that provides support, stability or security (*his wife was his anchor*). ● *vb* **1** to hold fast by an anchor. **2** to drop an anchor. ● **to weigh anchor** to take up an anchor before sailing.

anchorage /ang-ko-ridge/ *n* a place where a ship can anchor.

anchovy /an-tcho-vee/ *n* a small strong-tasting fish of the herring family.

ancient /**ayn**-shent/ *adj* **1** old, existing since early times (*ancient customs*). **2** belonging to old times (*ancient civilizations*). **3** (*inf*) very old (*still wearing that ancient coat*). ● **the ancients** those who lived long ago, especially the Greeks and Romans.

ancillary /**ant**-si-le-ree/ *adj* supporting, helping, subsidiary (*doctors and ancillary medical staff*).

andante /an-**dan**-tay/ *adj* (*mus*) with slow and graceful movement.

anecdote /**a**-nec-dote/ *n* a short, interesting or amusing story about a person or event.

anemia /a-**nee**-mee-a/ *n, also* **anaemia** (*Br, Cdn*) a condition caused by lack of red corpuscles in the blood, which causes pallor and fatigue.

anemic /a-**nee**-mic/ *adj, also or* **anaemic** (*Br, Cdn*) **1** suffering from anemia. **2** pale, colorless (*wearing an anemic shade of pink*). **3** lifeless, lacking spirit (*an anemic performance*).

anemone /a-**ne**-me-nee/ *n* the wind-flower, a kind of garden plant with red, purple, or white flowers.

anesthesia /a-ness-**thee**-zha/ *n, also* **anaesthesia** (*Br, Cdn*) loss of feeling.

anesthesiologist /a-ness-thee-zee-**o**-lo-gist/ *n, also* **anaesthesiologist** (*Br, Cdn*) a doctor who gives anesthetics.

anesthetic /a-ness-**thet**-ic/ *n, also* **anaesthetic** (*Br, Cdn*) a substance that causes loss of feeling for a time, either in the whole body (**general anesthetic**) or in a limited area of the body, such as a leg (**local anesthetic**) (*given an anesthetic before the operation*). ● *also adj.* ● *vb* **anesthetize** /a-**nees**-the-tize/, *also* **anaesthetise** (*Br*) .

anesthetist /a-**nes**-the-tist/ *n, also* **anaesthetist** (*Br, Cdn*) **1** a nurse who gives anesthetics. **2** (*Br, Cdn*) a medical doctor specializing in anesthetics.

anew /a-**nyoo**/ *adv* (*fml or old*) again, in a new or different way (*begin the attempt anew*).

angel /**ayn**-jel/ *n* **1** in Christianity, a spirit created to serve God (*angels are usually shown in pictures with wings and wearing white*). **2** a very good and helpful person (*she was an angel to lend me the money*). ● *adj* **angelic** /an-**je**-lic/.

angel food cake /**ayn**-jel **food** cake/ *n* a very light, pale-colored cake.

anger /**ang**-ger/ *n* a feeling of rage or fury. ● *vb* to enrage (*angered by his rudeness*).

angina /an-**jie**-na/ *n* a disease of the heart, causing sudden, sharp pains.

angle[1] /**ang**-gl/ *n* **1** the space between two meeting lines (*an angle of 90˚*). **2** a corner (*a room full of*

angles). **3** point of view (*looking at things from the parents' angle*).

angle[2] /**ang**-gl/ *vb* **1** to fish with hook and bait. **2** to try to get by indirect means (*angle for an invitation*).

angling /**ang**-gling/ *n* the art of fishing with a rod. ● *n* **angler** /**ang**-gler/.

angora /ang-**go**-ra/ *n* a long-haired wool from a goat.

angry /**ang**-gree/ *adj* feeling or showing anger (*an angry man/angry words*). ● *adv* **angrily** /**ang**-gri-lee/.

anguish /**ang**-guish/ *n* very great pain, of body or mind (*suffer anguish until the lost child was found*). ● *adj* **anguished** /**ang**-guishd/.

angular /**ang**-gyoo-lar/ *adj* **1** sharp-cornered (*an angular building*). **2** thin and bony (*clothes hanging loosely on her angular body*).

animal /**a**-ni-mal/ *n* **1** a living being with the power to feel and to move at will. **2** such a living being other than human beings (*care about animals as well as people*). **3** a four-footed creature, as distinct from a bird, fish, or insect. **4** a wild or uncivilized person.

animate /**a**-ni-mate/ *vb* **1** to give life to. **2** to enliven, to make lively and interesting (*need to animate our weekly discussions*). ● *adj* living.

animation /a-ni-**may**-shun/ *n* liveliness, excitement.

animosity /a-ni-**mo**-si-tee/ *n* strong dislike, hatred (*cause animosity between neighbors*).

ankle /**ang**-kl/ *n* the joint that connects the foot with the leg.

annex, annexe (*Br*) /a-**neks**, a-neks/ *vb* **1** to add to the end (*annex a personal note to her report*). **2** to take possession of (*small countries annexed by the emperor*). ● *n* a part added to or situated near a building (*the school annex*). ● *n* **annexation** /a-neks-**say**-shun/.

annihilate /a-**nie**-e-late/ *vb* to destroy completely (*annihilate the entire army/annihilate their argument*). ● *n* **annihilation** /a-ni-hi-**lay**-shun/.

anniversary /an-ni-**ver**-sa-ree/ *n* the yearly return of the date on which some event occurred and is remembered (*their wedding anniversary/the anniversary of the end of the war*).

annotate /**an**-no-tate/ *vb* to write notes upon. ● *n* **annotation**.

announce /a-**nounse**/ *vb* to make known (*announce their engagement*). ● *n* **announcement** /a-**nounse**-ment/.

announcer /a-**noun**-ser/ *n* in broadcasting, someone who makes known the programs or reads news items.

annoy /an-**noy**/ *vb* to vex; to tease; to be troubled by something you dislike. ● *n* **annoyance** /an-**noy**-ans/.

annual /an-ye-wel/ *adj* **1** yearly (*her annual salary*). **2** happening every year or only once a year (*an annual festival*). ● *n* **1** a plant lasting only for one year. **2** a book of which a new edition is published yearly (*children's annuals published for Christmas*). ● *adv* **annually** /an-ye-wel-lee/.

anoint /a-**noint**/ *vb* to put oil on, especially with the intention of making holy.

anomaly /a-**nom**-a-lee/ *n* something unusual, irregular or not normal (*a bird with no wings is an anomaly/anomalies in the tax system*). ● *adj* **anomalous** /a-**nom**-a-less/.

anon[1] /a-**non**/ *adv* (*old or hum*) soon (*see you anon!*).

anon[2] /a-**non**/ *abbr* = **anonymous** (*the author of the poem is anon*).

anonymous /a-**non**-ni-muss/ *adj* nameless, of unknown name (*an anonymous donor*). ● *n* **anonymity** /a-no-**nim**-mi-tee/.

anorexia /a-ne-**rek**-see-a/ *n* an eating disorder in which someone refuses to eat in order to lose weight, although already very thin. ● *adj* **anorexic** /a-ne-**rek**-sic/.

answer /an-ser/ *vb* **1** to reply to (*answer a letter/answer her questions*). **2** to be suitable, to fit (*answer the firm's needs/answer the description*). **3** to accept blame for or punishment (*have to answer for your crimes*). **4** to be responsible to (*answer to a new boss*). ● *n* **1** a reply. **2** a solution (to a problem).

answerable /an-se-re-bl/ *adj* open to blame for (*answerable for the damage*).

answering machine /an-se-ring ma-**sheen**/ *n* a machine that records telephone messages while someone is out.

ant /ant/ *n* a small, social insect, that lives in a colony made up of winged males, wingless sterile females, and fertile females known as queens.

antagonism /an-**ta**-ge-nizm/ *n* opposition, ill feeling (*cause antagonism between the partners*).

antagonist /an-**ta**-ge-nist/ *n* an opponent.

antagonistic /an-ta-ge-**nis**-tic/ *adj* opposed to, hostile.

antagonize /an-**ta**-ge-nize/ *vb*, also **antagonise** (*Br*) to make an enemy of (*antagonize neighbors with noisy behavior*).

antacid /an-**tass**-id/ *n* a medicine that makes the stomach less acidic and relieves pain caused by this (*take an antacid for indigestion*).

Antarctic /ant-**arc**-tic/ *adj* of south polar regions. ● *n* **the ~** Antarctica, the continent around the South Pole.

anteater /an-tee-ter/ *n* a mammal with a long snout that feeds on ants and termites.

antecedent /an-te-**see**-dent/ *adj* (*fml*) going before (*antecedent events*). ● *npl* **antecedents** the previous family, history, etc., of a person.

antelope /an-te-lope/ *n* a graceful, delicate animal like the deer.

antenatal /an-ti-**nay**-tal/ *adj* before birth (*antenatal exercises*).

antenna /an-**ten**-na/ *n* **1** (*pl* **antennae** /an-**ten**-nee/) the feeler of an insect. **2** (*pl* **antennas**) a wire or rod, etc., for receiving radio waves or television signals.

anthem /**an**-thum/ *n* a hymn or song of praise to God.

anthology /an-**tho**-le-jee/ *n* a collection of pieces of poetry or prose by different authors.

anthracite /ant-thre-site/ *n* a type of coal that burns almost without flame or smoke.

anthrax /an-thraks/ *n* a disease attacking sheep or cattle and sometimes infecting humans.

anthropology /an-thre-**po**-le-jee/ *n* the study of human beings in relation to their surroundings.

anti- /an-tie/ *prefix* against.

antibiotic /an-ti-bie-**o**-tic/ *n* a substance used in medicine to destroy bacteria that cause disease (*given an antibiotic, such as penicillin, to cure a sore throat*). ● *also adj*.

antibody /an-ti-bo-dee/ *n* a protein your body produces to fight infections and illnesses (*antibodies in the blood*).

anticipate /an-**ti**-si-pate/ *vb* **1** to expect (*anticipate trouble at the rally*). **2** to take action in advance of (*we anticipated their arrival at the camp by getting there first*). **3** to foresee (*anticipate how they would act*). ● *n* **anticipation** /an-ti-se-**pay**-shun/.

anticlimax /an-ti-**clie**-maks/ *n* an unexpectedly dull ending to a striking series of events (*after the weeks of preparation, the actual festival seemed an anticlimax*).

antics /an-tiks/ *npl* absurd or exaggerated behavior (*the antics of the clowns*).

antidote /an-ti-dote/ *n* a medicine that counteracts the effects of poison or disease (*given an antidote when bitten by a snake*).

antipathy /an-**ti**-pa-thee/ *n* dislike, opposition to (*feel antipathy toward the man who caused the accident*).

antiquated /an-te-**kway**-ted/ *adj* old-fashioned, out of date (*antiquated ideas*).

antique /an-**teek**/ *adj* **1** made in an earlier period and usually valuable (*antique furniture*). **2** (*fml*) connected with ancient times. ● *n* a piece of furniture, jewelry, etc., made in an earlier period and considered valuable.

antiquity /an-**ti**-kwe-tee/ *n* **1** ancient times, especially those of the Greeks and Romans. **2** great age.

antiseptic /an-ti-**sep**-tic/ *adj* having the power to kill germs. ● *n* an antiseptic substance (*clean the wound with an antiseptic*).

antithesis /an-**ti**-thi-sis/ *n* (*pl* **antitheses**) **1** contrast of ideas, emphasized by similarity in expressing them. **2** the exact opposite. ● *adj* **antithetical** /an-ti-**thet**-i-cal/.

antler /**ant**-ler/ *n* a branch of a stag's horn. ● *adj* **antlered**.

antonym /**an**-ti-nim/ *n* a word meaning the opposite of (*ugly is the antonym of beautiful*).

anxious /**ang**-shus/ *adj* worried about what will happen or has happened (*anxious parents waiting for their lost children/anxious about flying*). ● *n* **anxiety** /ang-**zie**-e-tee/.

any /**en**-ee/ *adj* **1** one out of many (*any of those hats will do*). **2** some (*do you have any sugar?*). **3** every (*any mother would be proud of you*). ● *adv* at all (*is it any warmer in there?*).

anybody /**en**-ee-baw-dee/ *pron* any person (*is anybody there?*).

anyhow /**en**-ee-how/ *adv* **1** in any way, whatever (*just paint the wall anyhow*). **2** in any case (*I never liked him anyhow*).

anymore /en-ee-**more**/ *adv* now, from now on (*I don't like it anymore*).

anyone /**en**-ee-won/ *pron* any person, anybody (*is anyone there?*).

anyplace /**en**-ee-place/ *adv* in, at, or to anywhere (*have you been anyplace special?*)

anything /**en**-ee-thing/ *pron* any object, event, fact etc. (*he'll believe anything*). ● *n* a thing, no matter what kind (*have you got anything to polish silver?*). ● *adv* at all (*he doesn't look anything like his brother*).

anytime /**en**-ee-time/ *adv* at any hour, day, week, etc. (*come visit anytime you are passing*).

anyway /**en**-ee-way/ *adv* in any case (*I didn't want to go anyway*). ● *adv* **any way** in any manner (*go any way you like*).

anywhere /**en**-ee-ware/ in, at, or to any place (*I can go anywhere*).

aorta /ae-**or**-ta/ *n* the great artery leading from the heart, carrying blood to all parts of the body.

Apache /a-**patch**-ee/ *n* one of a group of American Indians of the United States who made their home in the southwest part of the country.

apart /a-**part**/ *adv* separately (*married but now living apart*).

apartheid /a-**part**-hide/ *n* a policy where different races are kept apart (*South Africa used to have a racial political policy called apartheid*).

apartment /a-**part**-ment/ *n* **1** a room (*the private apartments that cannot be visited in the palace*). **2** a set of rooms rented as a dwelling (*share an apartment*).

apartment house /a-**part**-ment **house**/ *n* a building divided up into apartments.

apathy /a-**path**-ee/ *n* lack of feeling or interest (*people failing to vote in the election because of apathy*). ● *adj* **apathetic** /a-pa-**thet**-ic/.

ape /ape/ *n* a mammal resembling a tailless monkey (e.g., gorilla, chimpanzee, orangutan, gibbon). ● *vb* to imitate exactly.

aperture /a-per-**choor**/ *n* an opening, a hole (*peek through an aperture in the fence*).

apex /**ay**-peks/ *n* (*pl* **apexes** *or* **apices**) the top or highest point (*the apex of the triangle/the apex of his career*).

aphid /**ay**-fid/ *n* an insect that lives on the sap of green plants.

aphorism /a-**for**-iz-um/ *n* a short, wise saying.

apiary /**ay**-pee-ar-ee/ *n* a place where bees are kept.

apiece /a-**peess**/ *adv* to or for each one (*plants costing 40 cents apiece*).

apocalyptic /a-poc-a-**lip**-tic/ *adj* **1** telling of great misfortune in the future (*apocalyptic warning about the environment*). **2** relating to an event of great importance, particularly an event of disastrous or catastrophic importance.

apocryphal /a-**poc**-ra-fal/ *adj* not likely to be genuine, doubtful or untrue (*the stories about his adventures are thought to be apocryphal*).

apologetic /a-pol-o-**je**-tic/ *adj* making excuses, expressing regret (*an apologetic refusal to the invitation*).

apologize /a-**pol**-o-jize/ *vb, also* **apologise** (*Br*) to express regret for a fault or error, to say you are sorry (*apologize for being late*).

apology /a-**pol**-o-jee/ *n* an admission that wrong has been done, an expression of regret.

apostle /a-**pos**-l/ *n* **1** someone sent to preach the gospel. **2** one of the twelve disciples of Christ.

apostrophe /a-**pos**-tro-fee/ *n* a mark (') indicating the possessive case or omission of certain letters.

appall /a-**pawl**/ *vb also* appal (*Br*) to shock, to horrify (*appalled at the state of the starving children*). ● (*US, Cdn*) appalls, appalled, appalling; *also* (*Br*) appals, appalled, appalling.

appalling /a-**paw**-ling/ *adj* shocking, terrible, horrific.

apparatus /a-pa-**ra**-tus/ *n* tools or equipment for doing work (*gymnastic apparatus/laboratory apparatus*).

apparel /a-**par**-el/ *n* clothing. ● *vb* (*old*) to dress.

apparent /a-**pa**-rent/ *adj* **1** easily seen, evident (*it was apparent that he was very ill/worries that were apparent to everyone*). **2** seeming but not necessarily real (*her apparent concern for her friend*).

apparently /a-**pa**-rent-lee/ *adv* evidently, seemingly.

appeal /a-**peel**/ *vb* **1** to make an earnest and strong request for (*appeal for money to feed her children*). **2** to carry (a law case) to a higher court. **3** to interest, to please (*films that appeal to me*). ● *also n.*

appear /a-**peer**/ *vb* **1** to come into sight (*figures appearing out of the mist*). **2** to seem (*she appears sad*). ● *n* appearance.

appease /a-**peez**/ *vb* **1** to calm, to make peaceful (*appease the angry father by apologizing*). **2** to satisfy by giving what is wanted (*appease their curiosity*). ● *n* appeasement.

append /a-**pend**/ *vb* to add, to attach (*append their signatures to the document*).

appendage /a-**pen**-dige/ *n* **1** something added or attached (*signatures as appendages to the document*). **2** something forming a part or attached to something larger or more important (*appendages, like elephants' trunks*).

appendicitis /a-pend-ih-**sie**-tis/ *n* a painful disease of the appendix, requiring surgical removal.

appendix /a-**pen**-diks/ *n* (*pl* appendixes *or* appendices /a-**pen**-dis-ees/) **1** information added at the end of a book. **2** in your digestive system, a short, closed tube leading off the bowels.

appetite /a-**pe**-tite/ *n* desire to have something, especially food or pleasure (*invalids with little appetite for hospital food/no appetite for love*).

appetizer /a-**pe**-tize-er/ *n* something eaten or drunk to stimulate the appetite (*savories served as an appetizer*).

appetizing /a-**pe**-tize-ing/ *adj* increasing the desire for food (*appetizing smells from the kitchen*).

applaud /a-**plod**/ *vb* to praise by clapping or shouting (*applauded warmly by the audience*). ● *n* applause /a-**ploz**/.

apple /a-pl/ *n* **1** a tree with many varieties, and pink or white blossom. **2** the sweet fruit of this tree.

appliance /a-**plie**-anse/ *n* an instrument intended for some particular use (*modern kitchen appliances*).

applicable /a-pli-ca-bl/ *adj* that may be applied, suitable under the circumstances (*rules not applicable to the situation*). ● *n* applicability /a-pli-ca-**bi**-li-tee/.

applicant /a-plic-ant/ *n* someone who asks for, a person who applies for or makes a formal request for (*several applicants for the post*).

application /a-pli-**cay**-shon/ *n* **1** the act of applying. **2** a formal request (*make an application for a council grant*). **3** perseverance, hard work (*application is required to pass the exams*).

apply /a-**ply**/ *vb* **1** to put or spread on (*apply the ointment to the wound*). **2** to use (*apply force*). **3** to pay attention (to), to concentrate (*apply yourself to your work*). **4** to ask for, to put in a formal request for (*apply for the post of manager*). **5** to concern or be relevant to (*the usual rules apply*).

appoint /a-**point**/ *vb* **1** to choose for a job or position (*appoint her to the post of manager*). **2** (*fml*) to fix or decide on (*appoint a date for the meeting*).

appointment /a-**point**-ment/ *n* **1** a post or position (*a teaching appointment*). **2** a meeting arranged for a certain time (*have several appointments today/a doctor's appointment*).

appraisal /a-**prase**-al/ *n* the assessment of the value or quality of (*give an appraisal of his assistant's work*).

appraise /a-**prase**/ *vb* to judge the value, quality, ability, etc., of (*appraise her suitability for the job*).

appreciable /a-**pree**-sha-bl/ *adj* enough to be noticed (*no appreciable difference*). ● *adv* appreciably.

appreciate /a-**pree**-shee-ate/ *vb* **1** to recognize the value or good qualities of, to enjoy (*appreciate good food*). **2** to understand fully, to recognize (*I appreciate your concern*). **3** to be grateful for (*appreciate your kindness*). **4** to rise in value (*houses appreciating in value*).

appreciation /a-pree-shee-**ay**-shon/ *n* **1** a good or just opinion of (*audiences showing their appreciation by applauding*). **2** gratitude (*in appreciation of his good work*). **3** understanding (*some* *appreciation of your problem*). **4** increase in value (*appreciation of property values*).

appreciative /a-**pree**-sha-tive/ *adj* **1** willing to understand and praise justly (*appreciative of good music/an appreciative audience*). **2** grateful (*appreciative of his kindness*). ● *adv* **appreciatively** / a-**pree**-sha-tive-lee/.

apprehend /a-pre-**hend**/ *vb* (*fml*) to arrest, to seize (*apprehended by the police*).

apprehension /a-pre-**hen**-shon/ *n* **1** (*fml*) fear, dread (*view the arrival of the new manager with some apprehension*). **2** (*fml*) arrest, seizure (*the apprehension of the bank robbers*). **3** (*fml*) understanding (*no apprehension of the difficulties involved*).

apprehensive /a-pre-**hen**-sive/ *adj* afraid of what may happen (*apprehensive about the exams*).

apprentice /a-**pren**-tiss/ *n* someone who is learning a trade or skill while working at it. ● *vb* to bind by agreement to serve as an apprentice.

apprenticeship /a-**pren**-tiss-ship/ *n* the time served as an apprentice.

approach /a-**proch**/ *vb* **1** to move nearer (to) (*approaching the village/Christmas is approaching*). **2** to seek an opportunity to speak to someone (*approach him for a donation to the charity*). ● *n* **1** act of approaching. **2** the way leading to a place.

approachable /a-**pro**-cha-bl/ *adj* **1** able to be approached (*villages not approachable by the road in winter*). **2** easy to speak to (*he's unfriendly and not at all approachable*).

approbation /a-pro-**bay**-shon/ *n* praise, approval.

appropriate /a-**pro**-pree-ate/ *vb* **1** to take and use as your own (*appropriate the firm's money*). **2** to set apart for a particular purpose or use (*money appropriated by the government for training*). ● *adj* suitable. ● *adv* **appropriately** /a-**pro**-pree-ate-lee/. ● *ns* **appropriation** /a-pro-pree-**ay**-shun/, **appropriateness** /a-**pro**-pree-ate-ness/.

approve /a-**proov**/ *vb* **1** to think well of, to accept as good (*approve of your choice*). **2** to agree to, to accept (*approve the application*). ● *n* **approval** / a-**proov**-al/. ● **on approval** for a period of trial before purchase.

approximate /a-**prok**-si-mat/ *vb* to come near to (*a story approximating to the truth*). ● *adj* nearly correct (*an approximate price*).

approximately /a-**prok**-si-mat-lee/ *adv* nearly (*approximately 9 o'clock/approximately four miles*).

approximation /a-prok-si-**may**-shon/ *n* a nearly correct result (*the figure is an approximation*).

apricot /**ay**-pri-cot, **a**-pri-cot / *n* an orange-yellow fruit of the peach family.

April /**ay**-pril/ *n* the fourth month of the year.

apron /**ay**-pron/ *n* a garment or cloth worn in front to protect the clothes.

apt /apt/ *adj* **1** suitable, appropriate (*an apt reply*). **2** ready to learn (*an apt pupil*). **3** having a tendency to (*a car that is apt to break down*).

aptly /**apt**-lee/ *adv* appropriately.

aptitude /**ap**-ti-tood/ *n* skill, cleverness (*an aptitude for foreign languages*).

aptness /**apt**-ness/ *n* suitability (*the aptness of the remark*).

aquarium /a-**kwa**-ree-um/ *n* (*pl* **aquariums** or **aquaria**) a tank for (live) fish and water animals and water plants.

aquatic /a-**kwa**-tic/ *adj* **1** living or growing in water (*aquatic plants*). **2** taking place in water (*aquatic sports*).

aqueduct /a-**kwi**-duct/ *n* **1** a man-made channel for carrying water. **2** a bridge built to carry water.

aqueous /a-**kwee**-us/ *adj* of or like water, watery (*an aqueous solution*).

aquiline /a-**kwi**-leen/ *adj* hooked like the beak of an eagle (*an aquiline nose*).

Arab /**a**-rab/ *n* a native of Arabia. ● *adj* describing Arabia or the Arabs.

Arabic /a-ra-bic/ *n* a language spoken by people in North Africa and Middle Eastern countries. ● *adj* describing the Arab language and the countries in which it is spoken.

Arabic numerals /a-ra-bic **noo**-mer-als/ *n* the numbers 0, 1, 2, 3, 4, 5, 6, 7, 8, and 9.

arable /**a**-ra-bl/ *adj* suitable for plowing.

arbiter /**ar**-bi-ter/ *n* someone chosen by the parties concerned to settle a dispute, an umpire (*appoint an arbiter in the dispute between unions and management*).

arbitrary /**ar**-bi-tre-ree/ *adj* **1** not decided by rules, laws, etc., but by a person's own opinion (*a decision that was completely arbitrary/an arbitrary choice*). **2** uncontrolled, unrestrained (*arbitrary power/an arbitrary ruler*). ● *adv* **arbitrarily** /ar-bi-**tre**-ri-lee/.

arbitrate /**ar**-bi-trate/ *vb* to act as an umpire or referee, especially in a dispute (*asked to arbitrate in the dispute between neighbors*). ● *n* **arbitrator** / **ar**-bi-trate-or/. ● *n* **arbitration** /ar-bi-**tray**-shon/.

arbor /**ar**-bor/ *n, also* **arbour** (*Br, Cdn*) a shady recess in a garden.

arc /ark/ *n* **1** a curve. **2** a part of the circumference of a circle.

arcade /ar-**cade**/ *n* **1** a covered walk. **2** a covered street containing shops.

arch- /arch-/ *prefix* chief.

arch¹ /arch/ *n* a curved structure, usually supporting a bridge or roof.

arch² /arch/ *adj* cunning, roguish (*an arch smile*). ● *adv* **archly** /arch-lee/. ● *n* **archness** /arch-ness/.

archaeology /ar-kee-aw-lo-jee/ *n see* **archeology**.

archaic /ar-**kay**-ic/ *adj* **1** old-fashioned (*archaic medical methods*). **2** (*of words*) no longer in current use ("*methinks" is an archaic expression for" I think*").

archaism /ar-kay-ism/ *n* a word or expression not in present-day use.

archbishop /arch-**bish**-op/ *n* a chief bishop, with other bishops under his rule.

archeology /ar-kee-aw-lo-jee/ *n, also* **archaeology** (*Br, Cdn*) the study of the remains and monuments of ancient times. ● *adj* **archeological**, *also* **archaeological** (*Br, Cdn*) /ar-kee-o-**law**-ji-cal/. ● *n* **archeologist**, *also* **archaeologist** (*Br, Cdn*) /ar-kee-aw-lo-jist/.

archer /ar-cher/ *n* someone who uses a bow and arrow.

archery /ar-cher-ee/ *n* the art of shooting with bow and arrow.

archipelago /ar-ki-**pe**-la-go/ *n* (*pl* **archipelagos** *or* **archipelagoes**) **1** a sea dotted with many islands. **2** a group of islands.

architect /ar-ki-tect/ *n* **1** someone who plans buildings. **2** someone who plans, designs or creates something (*the architect of our modern political system*).

architecture /ar-ki-tect-choor/ *n* **1** the art or science of planning or designing buildings (*study architecture*). **2** a special fashion in building (*Gothic architecture*). ● *adj* **architectural** /ar-ki-tect-choor-al/.

archives /ar-kives/ *npl* **1** historical records (*the firm's archives go back to the early 19th century*). **2** the place where they are kept. ● *n* **archivist** /ar-ki-vist/.

arctic /arc-tic/ *adj* very cold (*arctic conditions*).

ardent /ar-dent/ *adj* eager, enthusiastic, passionate (*ardent fans/ardent lover*). ● *adv* **ardently**.

arduous /ar-joo-us/ *adj* difficult, requiring a lot of effort (*an arduous task/an arduous climb*).

are *see* **be**.

area /ay-ree-a/ *n* **1** any open space, place, region (*a residential area/dry areas of the world*). **2** a subject, topic or activity (*in the area of politics*). **3** the extent of a surface (*a room 144 square feet in area*).

area code /ay-ree-a **code**/ *n* a three-digit number dialed to identify a particular area when telephoning.

arena /a-**ree**-na/ *n* **1** an open space of ground for contests or games. **2** area of activity or conflict (*the arena of party politics*).

argue /ar-gyoo/ *vb* **1** to give reasons for believing something to be true (*argue against uniting the two firms*). **2** to discuss in an unfriendly or quarrelsome way (*argue about whose toy it is*). **3** to quarrel (*brother and sister are always arguing*). ● *adj* **arguable** /ar-gyoo-a-bl/.

argument /ar-gyoo-ment/ *n* **1** reasons for holding a belief (*the argument for going to college*). **2** a dispute, an unfriendly discussion (*an argument about money*). **3** a quarrel. **4** a summary of a book.

argumentative /ar-gyoo-**men**-ta-tive/ *adj* given to discussing or disputing (*in an argumentative mood*).

arid /a-rid/ *adj* **1** very dry (*arid soil/arid areas of the world*). **2** unproductive, uninteresting (*arid discussions*). ● *n* **aridity** /a-ri-di-tee/.

arise /a-rise/ *vb* (*pt* **arose** /a-rose/, *pp* **arisen** /a-ri-zen/) **1** to come into being, to appear (*difficulties that may arise/when the need arises*). **2** to result from (*matters arising from our discussion*). **3** (*old*) to get up (*arise and go*).

aristocracy /a-ri-**stock**-ra-see/ *n* **1** government by the nobility of birth. **2** the nobility.

aristocrat /a-**ri**-sto-crat/ *n* a person of noble birth. ● *adj* **aristocratic** /a-ri-sto-**crat**-ic/.

arithmetic /a-**rith**-me-tic/ *n* the science of numbers; the art of working with numbers. ● *adj* **arithmetical** /a-rith-**met**-ic-al/.

ark /ark/ *n* **1** a wooden chest (e.g., *Ark of the Covenant*). **2 the Ark** in the Old Testament of the Bible, the vessel in which Noah was saved from the Flood.

arm /arm/ *n* **1** one of the upper limbs, the part of the body from the shoulder to the hand. **2** anything resembling this (*the arm of the chair*). **3** the part of a garment that covers the arm. **4** power (*the arm of the law*). **5** *pl* **arms** weapons or armor used in fighting. **6** *pl* the badge of a noble family, town, etc. (*coat of arms*). ● *vb* **1** to take up weapons. **2** to provide with weapons.

armada /ar-ma-da/ *n* a fleet of armed ships (*the Spanish Armada*).

armadillo /ar-ma-**dil**-ow/ *n* a South American animal with a bony protective shell.

armament /**ar**-ma-ment/ *n* **1** the guns on a ship, tank, etc. **2** *npl* all the weapons used in war.

armistice /**ar**-mi-stis/ *n* in war, an agreement to stop fighting for a time.

armlet /**arm**-let/ *n* a band worn round the arm (*mourners with black armlets*).

armor /**ar**-mor/ *n, also* **armour** (*Br, Cdn*) **1** protective covering. **2** (*old*) a metal covering worn by soldiers to protect their bodies. **3** the tank force of an army.

armory /**arm**-ree/ *n, also* **armoury** (*Br, Cdn*) a place for keeping arms.

armpit /**arm**-pit/ *n* the hollow under the shoulder, between the arm and the body.

army /**ar**-mee/ *n* **1** a large number of soldiers organized for war. **2** a large number of persons engaged on a common task (*an army of voluntary workers*).

aroma /a-**rome**-a/ *n* a pleasant smell (*the aroma of newly baked bread*).

aromatic /a-rome-**at**-ic/ *adj* sweet-smelling (*aromatic cooking herbs*).

around /a-**round**/ *prep* **1** on all sides of or in a circle, about (*flowers grew around the tree/children dancing around the maypole*). **2** here and there, at several places in (*books lying around the room*). **3** approximately (*around 4 o'clock/around four miles away*). **4** near to (*restaurants around here*). ● *adv* **1** on every side, here and there (*pick up the books lying around*). **2** in the surrounding area (*he's somewhere around*). **3** available (*no money around*). **4** in the opposite direction (*turn around*).

arouse /a-**rouz**/ *vb* **1** to stir up (*arouse their anger*). **2** to make awake or active (*arouse them from sleep*).

arrange /a-**range**/ *vb* **1** to put into order (*arrange the books on the shelves*). **2** to make plans, to make preparations for (*arrange a meeting*). ● *n* **arrangement** /a-**range**-ment/.

arrant /**a**-rant/ *adj* thoroughly (bad), out-and-out (*an arrant coward*).

arras /**a**-ras/ *n* a hanging of ornamental cloth on a wall.

array /a-**ray**/ *vb* **1** to set in order (*soldiers arrayed for battle*). **2** to dress up (*dancers arrayed in beautiful ballgowns*). ● *n* **1** order. **2** dress.

arrears /a-**rirz**/ *npl* that which remains unpaid or undone (*her rent is in arrears*).

arrest /a-**rest**/ *vb* **1** to take as prisoner, especially in the name of the law. **2** (*fml*) to catch or attract (*arrest the attention of the crowd*). **3** to stop (*arrest the economic growth of the country*). ● *n* **1** the act of stopping. **2** the act of arresting in the name of the law.

arrival /a-**rive**-al/ *n* **1** the act of arriving (*the late arrival of the visitors*). **2** someone who arrives (*recent arrivals in the village*).

arrive /a-**rive**/ *vb* **1** to come (*the day of the wedding arrived*). **2** to reach (*arrive home*).

arrogant /**a**-ro-gant/ *adj* proud, haughty (*too arrogant to listen to others' advice*). ● *n* **arrogance** /**a**-ro-ganss/.

arrow /**a**-ro/ *n* a pointed stick or similar missile for shooting from a bow.

arrowroot /**a**-ro-root/ *n* a West Indian plant from which an edible starch is obtained.

arsenal /**ar**-snal/ *n* a place where weapons of war are made or stored, usually on behalf of a government.

arsenic /**ar**-snic/ *n* a toxic chemical poison.

arson /**ar**-son/ *n* the crime of setting fire to property on purpose.

art /art/ *n* **1** a particular ability or skill (*the art of conversation/the art of cooking*). **2** (*fml*) cunning, trickery (*get her own way by art*). **3** the practice of painting, sculpture, and architecture, etc. (*studying art at college*). **4** examples of painting, sculpture, etc. (*a gallery showing modern art*). ● **the Arts** subjects of study that are intended to broaden the mind rather than (or as well as) to teach practical skill.

artery /**ar**-te-ree/ *n* a tube carrying blood from the heart.

artful /**art**-ful/ *adj* deceitful, cunning (*an artful child/an artful dodge*). ● *adv* **artfully** /**art**-ful-ee/.

artichoke /**ar**-ti-choke/ *n* **1** (**globe artichoke**) a tall plant, somewhat like a thistle, part of the leaves of which can be eaten. **2** (**Jerusalem artichoke**) a type of sunflower with edible underground stems.

article /**ar**-tic-l/ *n* **1** a thing (*articles of clothing*). **2** an essay on a single topic in a newspaper, periodical, or encyclopedia. **3** a single item in a list or statement (e.g., a treaty). **4** *pl* a written agreement (*articles of apprenticeship*).

articulate /ar-**tic**-yoo-late/ *adj* **1** distinct, clear (*articulate speech*). **2** able to express yourself clearly. ● *vb* **1** to join together (*bones articulated with others*). **2** to speak distinctly (*articulate your words so that you can be heard at the back*).

articulation /ar-**tic**-yoo-lay-shon/ *n* **1** a joint. **2** the act of joining. **3** forming of sounds in speech.

artifice /**ar**-ti-fis/ *n* **1** a trick (*use artifice to gain entrance*). **2** trickery (*gain entrance by artifice*).

artificial /ar-ti-**fish**-al/ *adj* **1** man-made and so not natural (*artificial flowers/artificial light*). **2** not genuine, unnatural (*an artificial smile*). ● *n* **artificiality** /ar-ti-fish-ee-**ah**-li-tee/.

artillery /ar-**til**-ree/ *n* **1** big guns. **2** the part of an army that cares for and fires such guns.

artisan /**ar**-ti-zan/ *n* a skilled manual workman.

artist /**ar**-tist/ *n* **1** a professional painter (*Constable and other British artists*). **2** one skilled in some art (*a culinary artist*). **3** an artiste.

artiste /ar-**teest**/ *n* a public entertainer, such as a professional singer or dancer.

artistic /ar-**tis**-tic/ *adj* **1** having to do with art or artists (*artistic works*). **2** having or showing love for what is beautiful (*an artistic child/an artistic flower arrangement*).

artistry /**ar**-tis-tree/ *n* artistic skill.

artless /**art**-less/ *adj* simple, sincere. ● *adv* **artlessly** /**art**-less-lee/.

asbestos /as-**bes**-tos/ *n* a soft white mineral that cannot burn.

ascend /a-**send**/ *vb* (*fml*) **1** to go upward (*the elevator ascended*). **2** to climb (*ascend the mountain*).

ascent /a-**sent**/ *n* (*fml*) **1** act of going up (*the ascent of the hill*). **2** an upward slope (*a rocky ascent*).

ascribe /a-**scribe**/ *vb* to explain as the result of something else (*ascribe his behavior to his violent upbringing*).

ash[1] /**ash**/ *n* a tree.

ash[2] /**ash**/ *n or* **ashes** /**ash**-eez/ *npl* the dust left after anything has been burned.

ashamed /a-**shaymd**/ *adj* feeling shame (*ashamed of his actions*).

ashore /a-**shore**/ *adv* on or to land (*go ashore*).

ashtray /**ash**-tray/ *n* a small dish for cigarette ash.

aside /a-**side**/ *adv* **1** on one side (*put some money aside every week for a holiday*). **2** to one side, apart (*take her aside to tell her the secret*).

ask /**ask**/ *vb* **1** to request (*ask for directions*). **2** to inquire (*ask how old they are*).

askew /a-**skyoo**/ *adv* to one side, crookedly (*wear his cap askew*).

asleep /a-**sleep**/ *adj and adv* sleeping (*remain asleep despite the noise*).

asp /**asp**/ *n* a small poisonous snake.

asparagus /a-**spa**-ra-gus/ *n* a plant, the tops of which can be eaten as a vegetable.

aspect /a-**spect**/ *n* **1** (*fml*) appearance (*of frightening aspect*). **2** the direction in which a building, etc., faces (*a house with a southern aspect*). **3** a particular part or feature of something (*consider the financial aspects of the situation*).

aspen /a-**spen**/ *n* a type of poplar tree.

asphalt /**ass**-folt/ *n* a type of pitch used in road-making.

asphyxiate /ass-**fik**-see-ate/ *vb* to choke, to suffocate. ● *n* **asphyxiation** /ass-fik-see-**ay**-shon/.

aspiration /ass-pi-**ray**-shon/ *n* eager desire, ambition (*aspirations to greatness*).

aspire /a-**spire**/ *vb* to try very hard to reach (something ambitious, difficult, etc.) (*aspire to high office in the government*).

aspirin /a-**sprin**/ *n* a drug that relieves pain.

ass /**ass**/ *n* **1** a donkey. **2** a foolish person.

assail /a-**sale**/ *vb* (*fml*) to attack (*assail him with violent blows/assail them with questions*).

assailant /a-**sale**-ant/ *n* an attacker.

assassin /a-**sass**-in/ *n* someone who kills by surprise or secretly.

assassinate /a-**sass**-in-ate/ *vb* to murder by surprise or treachery, often for political reasons (*try to assassinate the president*). ● *n* **assassination** /a-sass-in-**ay**-shon/.

assault /a-**solt**/ *n* a sudden violent attack. ● *vb* to attack.

assay /a-**say**/ *n* a test of the quality of a metal, to find out whether it is pure or an alloy. ● *vb* to test the quality, especially of metals.

assemble /a-**sem**-bl/ *vb* **1** to bring or put together (*assemble the family together/assemble all the parts*). **2** to come together (*people assembling on the wharf*). ● *n* **assemblage** /a-**sem**-blage/.

assembly /a-**sem**-blee/ *n* a gathering of people to discuss and take decisions (*school assembly*).

assent /a-**sent**/ *vb* to agree (*assent to the proposal*). ● *n* consent; permission.

assert /a-**sert**/ *vb* to state firmly (*assert that he is innocent*). ● **assert yourself** to stand up for your rights.

assertion /a-**ser**-shon/ *n* a firm statement.

assertive /a-**ser**-tive/ *adj* confident, tending to assert yourself.

assess /a-**sess**/ *vb* **1** to fix an amount payable (*assess your tax contribution*). **2** to estimate the value, worth, quality, etc., of (*assess his worth to the firm*). ● *n* **assessor** /a-**sess**-or/.

assessment /a-**sess**-ment/ *n* the amount or value fixed.

asset /a-set/ *n* a help, an advantage (*he is an asset to the team*).

assets /a-sets/ *npl* the entire property of a person or company.

assign /a-**sine**/ *vb* 1 to give as a share, duty, task, etc. (*assign household tasks to each of the children*). 2 to appoint (*assign three men to the job*). 3 to fix, to name (*assign Wednesdays for our meetings*).

assignment /a-**sine**-ment/ *n* 1 the share or amount (of work, etc.) given to a person or group. 2 a piece of homework.

assimilate /a-**sim**-i-late/ *vb* to take in and absorb (*plants assimilating food from the soil/assimilate people from different countries into America/try to assimilate the facts*). ● *n* **assimilation** /a-si-mi-lay-shun/.

assist /a-**sist**/ *vb* to help (*assist with teaching duties/assist her in cooking the meal*).

assistance /a-**sis**-tanse/ *n* help, aid.

assistant /a-**sis**-tant/ *n* a helper (*a teacher and two nursery assistants*).

associate /a-**so**-she-ate/ *vb* 1 to keep company with, to join with (*associate with criminals*). 2 to join or connect in the mind (*associate childhood with happiness*). ● *n* a companion, a partner, a colleague.

association /a-so-she-**ay**-shon/ *n* 1 act of associating. 2 a group of persons meeting for a common purpose (*an athletics association*). 3 the bringing together of connected ideas (*the association of home with security*).

assorted /a-**sor**-ted/ *adj* mixed (*a bag of assorted sweets*). ● **ill-assorted** badly matched (*an ill-assorted pair*).

assortment /a-**sort**-ment/ *n* a mixed collection (*an assortment of books sold as one lot*).

assume /a-**soom**/ *vb* 1 to take for granted (*assume that he is honest*). 2 to take over (*assume responsibility for the running of the school*). 3 (*fml*) to put on, to pretend (*assume an air of innocence although guilty*). 4 (*fml*) to take on, to begin to have (*the situation gradually assumed the quality of a nightmare*).

assumption /a-**sum**-shon/ *n* 1 act of assuming (*his assumption of the leadership*). 2 something supposed, but not proved, to be true (*making an assumption that he is guilty before his trial/proceed on the assumption that he is innocent*).

assurance /a-**shoo**-ranse/ *n* 1 confidence (*a post requiring a great deal of assurance*). 2 a promise (*you have my assurance that I shall be there*).

assure /a-**shoor**/ *vb* 1 to make certain (*his success in his career is now assured*). 2 to tell as a sure fact, to state positively (*I assure you that everything possible has been done*).

assuredly /a-**shoo**-rid-lee/ *adv* certainly.

aster /as-ter/ *n* a flower with the shape of a star.

asterisk /a-ster-isk/ *n* a star-shaped mark (*) used in printing.

asthma /az-ma/ *n* a disease marked by difficulty in breathing. ● *adj* **asthmatic** /az-ma-tic/.

astonish /a-**ston**-ish/ *vb* to surprise greatly, to amaze (*we were astonished at the news*). ● *n* **astonishment** /a-**ston**-ish-ment/.

astound /a-**stound**/ *vb* to shock with surprise, to surprise greatly.

astral /a-stral/ *adj* belonging to the stars.

astray /a-**stray**/ *adv* out of the right way (*parcels that have gone astray*).

astride /a-**stride**/ *adv* with the legs apart or on each side of a thing.

astringent /a-**strin**-jent/ *adj* 1 helping to close open wounds, cuts, or pores (*astringent lotions*). 2 stern, severe (*astringent comments*). ● *n* **astringency** /a-**strin**-jen-see/.

astrology /a-**strol**-o-jee/ *n* the study of the stars in order to learn about future events. ● *n* **astrologer** /a-**strol**-o-jer/.

astronaut /a-stre-nawt/ *n* a member of the crew of a spaceship.

astronomical /a-stre-**no**-mi-cal/ *adj* 1 connected with astronomy. 2 extraordinarily large (*an astronomical sum of money*).

astronomy /a-**straw**-ne-mee/ *n* the scientific study of the stars. ● *n* **astronomer** /a-**straw**-ne-mer/.

astute /a-**styoot**/ *adj* clever, shrewd (*an astute businessman*). ● *n* **astuteness** /a-**styoot**-ness/.

asylum /a-**sie**-lem/ *n* 1 a place of refuge or safety (*seek political asylum in another country*). 2 (*old*) a home for the care of helpless or mentally ill people.

ate *pt of* **eat**.

Athapaskan /a-tha-**pas**-kan/ *n* a group of First Nations languages in northwest Canada; a member of a First Nations people who speaks one of these languages. ● *adj* describing these peoples or their languages. — *also* **Athabaskan** /a-tha-**bas**-kan/.

atheism /ay-thee-izm/ *n* the belief that there is no God.

atheist /ay-thee-ist/ *n* someone who believes that there is no God. ● *adj* **atheistic** /ay-thee-**is**-tic/.

athlete /ath-leet/ *n* someone good at sports, especially outdoor sports.

athletic /ath-**let**-ic/ *adj* **1** having to do with sport or athletics (*athletic events*). **2** physically strong and active (*athletic young people*).

athletics /ath-**let**-ics/ *npl* **1** sporting activities. **2** (*Br*) see **track-and-field**.

atigi /a-ti-gee, a-**ti**-gee/ *n* a type of Inuit parka.

atlas /**at**-lass/ *n* a book of maps.

ATM /**ay-tee-em**/ *abbr* = **automated/automatic teller machine**: a machine that allows you to take money from your bank account using a card and a PIN (personal identification number).

atmosphere /**at**-mes-fear/ *n* **1** the air surrounding planet Earth. **2** the gas surrounding any star. **3** the air in a particular place (*a stuffy atmosphere in the hall*). **4** the feelings given rise to by an incident, place, story, etc., mood (*a friendly atmosphere*).

atmospheric /at-mes-**fer**-ic/ *adj* **1** connected with the air (*atmospheric conditions*). **2** creating a certain atmosphere or mood (*atmospheric music*).

atoll /**a**-tawl/ *n* a ring-shaped coral island.

atom /**a**-tom/ *n* **1** the smallest possible particle of an element that can be shown to have the properties of that element. **2** anything very small (*not an atom of truth*).

atomic /a-**tom**-ic/ *adj* connected with atoms.

atomic energy /a-**tom**-ic e-ner-jee/ *n* the power obtained by separating the electrical units in an atom.

atone /a-**tone**/ *vb* to make up for, to pay for a wrong (*atone for his crime by paying compensation to his victim*). ● *n* **atonement** /a-**tone**-ment/.

atrocious /a-**tro**-shess/ *adj* **1** very cruel or wicked (*atrocious crimes*). **2** very bad (*atrocious weather*).

atrocity /a-**traw**-se-tee/ *n* a very cruel act.

attach /a-**tach**/ *vb* to join (by tying, sticking, etc.) (*attach the rope to the boat*).

attaché /a-ta-**shay**/ *n* an official at an embassy.

attaché case /a-ta-**shay** case/ *n* a small case for papers, etc.

attached /a-**tachd**/ *adj* **1** joined onto (*read the attached document*). **2** fond of (*she is very attached to her sister*).

attachment /a-**tach**-ment/ *n* **1** something joined on (*a food mixer with various attachments*). **2** fondness (*feels a strong attachment to his old school*).

attack /a-**tack**/ *vb* **1** to use force against, to begin to fight against (*armies attacking each other*). **2** to speak or act strongly against (*attack the politician in a newspaper article*). **3** to begin to deal with vigorously, to tackle (*attack the pile of correspondence*). ● *also n.* ● *n* **attacker** /a-**tack**-er/.

attain /a-**tane**/ *vb* to reach (*attain a position of power/attain your goal*).

attainable /a-**tay**-na-bl/ *adj* able to be reached.

attainment /a-**tane**-ment/ *n* **1** act of attaining (*the attainment of early ambitions*). **2** something, such as a skill or ability, learned successfully (*attainments in the field of music*).

attempt /a-**tempt**/ *vb* to try to do (*attempt to cheat*). ● *n* an effort (*an attempt at cheating*).

attend /a-**tend**/ *vb* **1** to be present at (*attend the meeting of the committee*). **2** to take care of (*doctors attending to their patients/attend to the needs of the patient*). **3** (*fml*) to fix the mind on (*attend to what the teacher is saying*). **4** to wait on (*the queen—attended by her ladies-in-waiting*).

attendance /a-**ten**-dense/ *n* **1** presence. **2** the persons present.

attendant /a-**ten**-dent/ *n* **1** someone who waits on another. **2** a servant.

attendee /a-ten-**dee**/ *n* someone who is present.

attention /a-**ten**-shen/ *n* **1** care (*a wound in need of urgent attention*). **2** heed, notice (*pay attention to what is said/attract her attention*). **3** concentration (*her attention tends to wander*).

attentive /a-**ten**-tiv/ *adj* giving attention, paying heed (*attentive students*).

attest /a-**test**/ *vb* to bear witness to, to vouch for (*attest to the truth of her statement*). ● *n* **attestation** /a-tes-**tay**-shun/.

attic /**a**-tic/ *n* a room just under the roof of a house.

attire /a-**tire**/ *vb* to dress (*attired in silk*). ● *n* dress.

attitude /a-ti-**tood**/ *n* **1** position of the body (*artists painting models in various attitudes*). **2** way of thinking or behaving (*a hostile attitude*).

attorney /a-**tor**-ney/ *n* **1** a lawyer. **2** someone appointed to act for another. ● **power of attorney** the right to act on another's behalf.

attract /a-**tract**/ *vb* **1** to cause to come nearer (*magnets attracting steel*). **2** to cause to like or desire (*always attracted to amusing people*). **3** to arouse (*attract their attention*).

attraction /a-**tract**-shen/ *n* **1** act of attracting (*the attraction of moths to the light/the attraction of television for children*). **2** the power to attract (*her attraction lies in her personality*). **3** something that attracts (*the attractions of the resort*).

attractive /a-**trac**-tiv/ *adj* **1** having the power to attract, interesting, pleasing, etc. (*an attractive offer*). **2** good-looking, pretty, handsome (*an attractive young woman*).

attributable /a-**tri**-byoo-ta-bl/ *adj* able to be attributed (*crimes easily attributable to him*).

attribute /a-**tri**-byoot *vb* **1** to think of as being caused by (*attribute his silence to guilt*). **2** to regard as being made, written, etc., by (*attribute a play to Shakespeare*). ● *n* **attribute** /a-tri-byoot/ a quality, a characteristic (*the right attributes for the job*).

attune /a-**toon**/ *vb* to make to agree, bring into harmony (*unable to attune our ideas to theirs*).

ATV *abbr* = **all-terrain vehicle**: a vehicle like a motorcycle but with three wheels or more that can be driven over rough ground.

aubergine (*Br*) *see* **eggplant**.

auburn /**aw**-bern/ *adj* reddish brown.

auction /**awk**-shen/ *n* a public sale at which an object is sold to the person offering the highest price or bid.

auctioneer /awk-she-**neer**/*n* the person who conducts the sale at an auction.

audacious /aw-**day**-shess/ *adj* **1** bold, daring (*an audacious scheme*). **2** bold, shameless (*an audacious young woman*). ● *n* **audacity** /aw-**da**-si-tee/.

audible /**aw**-de-bl/ *adj* able to be heard (*a voice scarcely audible*). ● *n* **audibility** /aw-de-**bi**-le-tee/.

audience /**aw**-dee-ense/ *n* **1** the people who listen (e.g. to a speech, concert, etc.). **2** an interview granted by a ruler or person of high authority (*an audience with the pope*).

audition /aw-**di**-shen/ *n* a test given to an actor or singer to see how good he or she is (*hold auditions for the part of Hamlet*).

auditorium /aw-di-**to**-ree-um/ *n* the part of a hall open to the audience.

auditory /**aw**-di-to-ree/ *adj* having to do with the sense of hearing (*auditory organs*).

augment /awg-**ment**/ *vb* to increase (*augment income*). ● *n* **augmentation** /awg-men-**tay**-shun/.

august /aw-**gust**/ *adj* (*fml*) noble, worthy of reverence (*an august personage*).

August /**aw**-gust/ *n* the eighth month of the year.

auk /**awk**/ *n* a northern sea bird expert at swimming and diving.

aunt /**ant** or **ont**/ *n* the sister of someone's mother or father.

au pair /aw **pair**/ *n* a young person from abroad who helps with childcare and domestic work in exchange for board and a small salary.

aural /**aw**-ral/ *adj* having to do with the ear or hearing (*aural comprehension tests*).

aurora /aw-**ro**-ra/ *n* **1** the dawn. **2** the brightness seen in the sky in the extreme north or south (*the Aurora Borealis*, or Northern Lights, can be seen near the Arctic Circle*).

auspicious /aw-**spi**-shess/ *adj* promising future good (*an auspicious beginning*).

austere /aw-**steer**/ *adj* **1** simple and severe (*an austere way of life*). **2** stern (*her austere manner*). **3** plain, without decoration (*an austere room*). ● *n* **austerity** /aw-**ster**-i-tee/.

authentic /aw-**then**-tic/ *adj* true, genuine (*an authentic signature/authentic documents*). ● *n* **authenticity** /aw-then-**ti**-si-tee/.

authenticate /a-**then**-ti-cate/ *vb* to show the authenticity of, to prove genuine.

author /**aw**-ther/ *n* **1** a writer of books, etc. **2** (*fml*) a person who creates or begins something (*the author of this particular scheme*). ● *n* **authorship** /**aw**-ther-ship/.

authoritative /a-**tho**-re-tay-tiv/ *adj* **1** having or showing power (*an authoritative tone of voice*). **2** reliable, providing trustworthy information (*an authoritative book on a subject*).

authority /a-**tho**-re-tee/ *n* **1** the power or right to rule or give orders (*the authority to sack people*). **2** a person or group of persons having this power or right.

authorize /**aw**-the-rize/ *vb, also* **authorise** (*Br*) to give to another the right or power to do something (*authorizing him to sign the firm's checks*).

autism /**aw**-ti-zum/ *n* a condition in which someone has unusual difficulty in communicating or in relating to other people or the world around him or her. ● *adj* **autistic** /aw-**tis**-tic/.

auto- /**aw**-toe/ *prefix* self.

auto /**aw**-toe/ *n* an automobile.

autobiography /aw-to-bie-**aw**-gre-fee/ *n* the story of a person's life written by himself or herself.

autograph /**aw**-to-graf/ *n* a person's own handwriting or signature.

automated/automatic teller machine *see* **ATM**.

automatic /aw-to-**ma**-tic/ *adj* **1** working by itself (*an automatic washing machine*). **2** done without thought (*the automatic process of breathing/an automatic response*). ● *adv* **automatically** /aw-to-**ma**-ti-clee/.

automation /aw-to-**may**-shun/ *n* the act of replacing human labor by machines.

automobile /**aw**-te-mo-beel/ *n* a four-wheeled motor vehicle that can hold a small number of people.

autopsy /**aw**-top-see/ *n* an examination of a dead body to discover the cause of death.

autumn /**aw**-tum/ *n* the season between summer and winter also know as **fall**.

autumnal /aw-**tum**-nal/ *adj* having to do with the fall (*autumnal colors*).

auxiliary /og-**zil**-ye-ree/ *n* a person or thing that helps (*the Coast Guard Auxiliary*). ● *also adj*.

avail /a-**vail**/ *vb* to make use of (*avail yourself of any help offered*). ● *n* use, help.

available /a-**vail**-e-bl/ *adj* at hand if wanted (*all the available money/not so far available*).

avalanche /a-ve-lansh/ *n* **1** a great mass of snow, earth, and ice sliding down a mountain. **2** a great amount (*an avalanche of offers*).

avarice /a-va-riss/ *n* greed for gain and riches. ● *adj* **avaricious**.

avenge /a-**vendge**/ *vb* to take revenge for a wrong (*to avenge her brother's death by killing his murderer/to avenge herself on her attacker by damaging his car*). ● *n* **avenger** /a-**ven**-jer/.

avenue /a-ven-yoo/ *n* **1** a way of approach. **2** a broad street. **3** a double row of trees, with or without a road between them.

average /a-ve-ridge/ *n* the figure found by dividing the total of a set of numbers by the number of numbers in the set. ● *adj* **1** calculated by finding the average of various amounts, etc. (*average expenditure per person*). **2** ordinary (*the average person/his work is average*). ● *vb* to find the average.

averse /a-**verse**/ *adj* not in favor of.

aversion /a-**ver**-shen/ *n* **1** dislike (*have an aversion to people smoking*). **2** something disliked (*housework is one of her pet aversions*).

avert /a-**vert**/ *vb* to turn away (*avert your eyes*).

aviary /**ay**-vee-a-ree/ *n* a place for keeping birds.

aviation /ay-vee-**ay**-shun/ *n* the science of flying aircraft.

aviator /**ay**-vee-ay-tor/ *n* an airman.

avid /a-vid/ *adj* eager, keen (*an avid reader/avid for news*). ● *n* **avidity** /a-**vi**-di-tee/.

avocado /a-ve-ka-do/ *n* a pear-shaped fruit with a hard, dark green skin, soft, pale green flesh, and a large stone, used in salads, etc.

avoid /a-**voyd**/ *vb* to keep away from (*avoid trouble/avoid walking in the streets at night/avoid inquisitive neighbors*). ● *adj* **avoidable** /a-**voy**-de-bl/. ● *n* **avoidance** /a-**voy**-dents/.

await /a-**wate**/ *vb* (*fml*) to wait for (*await further instructions*).

awake /a-**wake**/ *vb* (*pt* **awoke**, *pp* **awoken**) **1** (*fml*) to rouse from sleep (*the noise awoke me*). **2** (*fml*) to stop sleeping (*we awoke early*). **3** to stir up, to rouse (*awake old memories*). ● *adj* **1** not sleeping (*people not yet fully awake*). **2** aware of, conscious of (*awake to the dangers*).

awaken /a-**way**-ken/ *vb* **1** to awake. **2** to rouse (*awaken old fears*).

award /a-**ward**/ *vb* to give after judgment or examination (*award compensation for his injuries/award him first prize*). ● *n* what is awarded, a prize.

aware /a-**ware**/ *adj* **1** having knowledge of, interested, concerned (*young people who are politically aware*). **2** conscious of (*aware of the difficulties*).

awe /aw/ *n* fear mixed with respect or wonder (*look at the huge cathedral with awe/hold his grandfather in awe*).

awesome /**aw**-sum/ *adj* **1** causing awe (*the awesome sight of the huge waterfall*). **2** (*inf*) excellent, marvelous (*an awesome achievement/an awesome performance*).

awful /**aw**-ful/ *adj* **1** very bad or unpleasant, terrible (*an awful accident*). **2** (*inf*) very great (*I am in an awful hurry*). **3** (*old or lit*) causing awe (*the awful sight of the towering mountain*).

awfully /**aw**-ful-lee/ *adv* (*inf*) very (*awfully kind*).

awkward /**aw**-kward/ *adj* **1** clumsy, unskilled (*awkward with his hands*). **2** difficult to use or deal with (*furniture of an awkward shape/awkward customers*). **3** inconvenient (*an awkward time*). ● *adv* **awkwardly** /**aw**-kward-lee/.

ax or **axe** /aks/ *n* a tool for hewing or chopping. ● *n* **1** to dismiss someone suddenly (*ax workers*). **2** to end or cancel something suddenly (*ax a TV show*)

axiom /**ak**-see-em/ *n* a statement accepted as true without need for proof.

axis /**ak**-sis/ *n* (*pl* **axes**) the straight line, real or imaginary, on which a body turns (*the axis of the earth*).

axle /**aks**-l/ *or* **axle-tree** *n* the pole on which a wheel turns.

Aztec *n* an ancient Mexican Indian people who created a great civilization.

azure /a-zher/ *adj* sky-blue. ● *n* **1** a bright blue color. **2** the sky.

B

B, b /**bee**/ 1 the second letter of the alphabet. 2 the seventh note of the scale of C major.

BA / bee **ay**/ *abbr* = **Bachelor of Arts**: a degree award.

babble /**ba**-bl/ *vb* 1 to make indistinct sounds (*babies babbling in their baby carriages*). 2 to chatter continuously and without making a lot of sense (*what's he babbling about?*). 3 to make a sound, as of running water (*brooks babbling*). ● *n* 1 indistinct sounds, 2 foolish chatter. 3 murmur, as of a stream.

babe /babe/ *n* 1 a baby. 2 (*slang*) a pretty young woman (*she blushed when they called her a babe*).

baboon /ba-**boon**/ *n* a type of large African monkey.

baby /**bay**-bee/ *n* the young of a person or animal.

babysitter /**bay**-bee-sit-er/ *n* a person who is paid to look after someone else's children for a short time. ● *vb* **babysit**.

bachelor /**bach**-lor/ *n* 1 an unmarried man. 2 someone who has passed certain university examinations (*a bachelor of science*). ·

back /**back**/ *n* a part of the body, describing from the bottom of your neck to the base of your spine, also **backbone**; something that is behind. ● *also adj* and *adv*. ● *vb* 1 to go or move backward (*back out of the garage*). 2 to support (*back plans for expansion*).

backboard /**back**-bored/ *n* the area, made of wood or plastic, at the back of a basketball hoop.

backbone /**back**-bone/ *n* 1 the spine. 2 firmness, determination. 3 the chief support (*workers who are the backbone of the industry*).

backer /**back**-er/ *n* a supporter or helper (*financial backers of the scheme*).

backfire /**bak**-fire/ *n* an explosive noise made by a motor vehicle. ● *vb* **backfire** 1 to explode. 2 (*of a plan*) to go wrong in such a way that it harms its maker.

backgammon /**back**-ga-mon/ *n* a board game played with checker pieces and dice.

background /**back**-ground/ *n* 1 the area behind the principal persons in a picture, scene, or conversation. 2 a series of events leading up to something (*the background to the quarrel between the families*). 3 a person's origins, upbringing, education, etc. (*come from a wealthy background*).

backhand /**back**-hand/ *n* 1 writing in which the letters slope backward. 2 in tennis, a stroke played with the hand turned outward.

backhanded /**back**-hand-ded/ *adj* 1 made with the back of the hand. 2 indirect and sometimes with a double meaning (*backhanded compliments*).

backpack /**back**-pack/ *n* a large bag with straps carried on the back by hikers, etc. to hold their luggage. ● *vb* to travel from place to place with your belongings in a backpack. ● **backpacker** *n*.

backstroke /**back**-stroke/ *n* in swimming, a stroke where the swimmer floats on his or her back.

backward /**back**-ward/ *adj* 1 toward the back (*a backward glance*). 3 behind others in progress (*backward countries*). 4 shy, reserved (*too backward to be noticed in a crowd*). ● *n* **backwardness**.

backwater /**back**-wat-er/ *n* 1 a piece of water supplied by a river, but not out of its current. 2 a remote place, unaffected by modern progress.

backwoods /**back**-woods/ *npl* land not cleared of forest.

backyard /**back**-**yard**/ *n* an area behind someone's house (*play in your own backyard*).

bacon /**bay**-con/ *n* meat taken from the back and sides of a pig, often salted or smoked.

bacteria /**back**-**tee**-ree-a/ *npl* (*sing* **bacterium** /bac-**tee**-ree-um/) very tiny living things that are often the cause of disease.

bacteriology /bac-tee-ree-**ol**-o-jee/ *n* the study of bacteria. ● *n* **bacteriologist** /bac-tee-ree-**ol**-o-jist/.

bad /**bad**/ *adj* 1 not good (*I'm worried; your flu seems bad*). 2 naughty, mischievous (*he was sent to his room for being bad*). 3 serious (*the mistake was a bad one*). 4 rotten or spoiled (*the meat had to be thrown away because it had gone bad*). 5 sorry, apologetic (*she feels bad about her mistake*). ● *adj* **worse, worst**.

badge /**badge**/ *n* something worn as a sign of membership, office, rank, etc. (*a school badge on a blazer*).

badger /**ba**-jer/ *n* a night animal that lives in a burrow. ● *vb* to worry, to pester (*badger their mother for more pocket money*).

badminton /**bad**-min-ton/ *n* a game like tennis played with shuttlecocks batted with rackets across a net.

bad tempered /bad **tem**-perd/ *adj* grouchy or cross.

baffle /**ba**-fl/ *vb* 1 to puzzle, to bewilder (*baffled by the exam question/police baffled by the crime*). 2 to make someone's efforts useless (*baffle the enemy's attempt to gain entrance*). ● *n* **bafflement**.

bag /**bag**/ *n* 1 a container for carrying things. ● *vb*

(bagged, bagging) 1 to put into a bag (*bag all this stuff for taking to the refuse dump*). **2** (*inf*) to take possession of (*bag that empty table*). **3** to catch or kill (*bag a few rabbits*). **4** to hang loosely, to bulge (*trousers bagging at the knee*).

bagel /**bay**-gl/ *n* a ring-shaped bread roll that has a shiny surface (*a bagel and cream cheese*).

baggage /**ba**-gidge/ *n* **1** luggage. **2** stores of a moving army.

baggy /**ba**-gee/ *adj* **1** loose (*wear fashionable baggy trousers*). **2** out of shape (*trousers baggy at the knees*).

bagpipes /**bag**-pipes/ *npl* a musical wind instrument in which a bag serves as bellows (*it takes a great control of the breath to play the bagpipes*).

baguette /ba-**get**/ *n* a long crusty loaf of bread.

bail[1] /**bale**/ *n* **1** someone ready to pay a sum of money to obtain freedom for a person charged with a crime until the day of his or her trial. **2** money paid to release someone from jail, which is lost if the person does not appear for trial. ● *vb* **bail out** to help someone out, usually by giving them money.

bail[2] /**bale**/ *n* a small bar placed on the top of the stumps in cricket (*the ball hit the bail*).

bail[3] /**bale**/ *vb* to throw water out of a boat, a little at a time (*to bail out the canoe*).

bailiff /**bay**-lif/ *n* an official who takes charge of prisoners when they appear in court.

bait /**bate**/ *n* **1** food to trap or attract animals or fish. **2** a temptation (*shops offering free goods as a bait to customers*). ● *vb* **1** to put bait on a hook or in a trap. **2** to torment (*pupils baiting the new boy because he was so small*).

bake /**bake**/ *vb* **1** to dry, to harden by fire. **2** to cook in an oven.

baker /**bay**-ker/ *n* one who makes or sells bread.

bakery /**bay**-ker-ee/ *n* a place where bread is made.

baking powder /**bay**-king **pow**-der/ *n* a powder containing baking soda, used instead of yeast in baking to make dough rise.

balalaika /ba-la-**ly**-ka/ *n* a type of guitar used in Russia.

balance /**ba**-lanse/ *n* **1** a pair of weighing scales. **2** equality of weight, power, etc. (*the major countries of the world trying to achieve a balance of power*). **3** a state of physical steadiness (*lose one's balance*). **4** a state of mental or emotional steadiness (*while the balance of her mind was disturbed*). **5** the difference between the amount of money possessed and the amount owed. ● *vb* **1** to make equal. **2** to keep steady or upright (*acrobats balancing themselves on a tightrope*). **3** to add

up two sides of an account to show the difference between them. ● **in the balance** doubtful; about to be decided.

balcony /**bal**-co-nee/ *n* **1** a railed platform outside a window or along the wall of a building. **2** an upper floor in a hall or theater.

bald /**bawld**/ *adj* **1** without hair (*a bald old man*). **2** bare, without the usual or required covering (*bald tires*). **3** plain (*the bald truth*). ● *n* **baldness**.

bald eagle /**bawld ee**-gl/ *n* an eagle with a brown body and white feathers on its head that makes it appear bald.

balderdash /**bawld**-er-dash/ *n* senseless talk, nonsense.

bale /**bale**/ *n* a large bundle or package (*a bale of hay*).

balk /**bawlk**/ *n* a large beam of timber. ● *vb* to stop short of, to be reluctant or unwilling to be involved in (*balk at actually committing a crime*).

ball[1] /**bawl**/ *n* **1** anything round in shape (*a ball of wool*). **2** a round or roundish object used in games (*a tennis ball/a golf ball/a football*). **3** a rounded part of something (*the ball of the foot*).

ball[2] /**bawl**/ *n* a party held for the purpose of dancing. ● *n* **ballroom**.

ballad /**ba**-lad/ *n* **1** a simple poem relating a popular incident. **2** a short, romantic song.

ballast /**ba**-last/ *n* heavy material carried in a ship or other vehicle to keep it steady.

ball-bearings /bawl-**bay**-rings/ *npl* small metal balls that help a machine to work more smoothly.

ballerina /ba-le-**ree**-na/ *n* a female ballet dancer.

ballet /ba-**lay**/ *n* a performance in which dancing, actions, and music are combined to tell a story.

ball game /**bawl** game/ *n* **1** any game played with a ball. **2** baseball. **3** (*inf*) any situation (*"We want to get married in June, not February." "Oh—well, that's a whole different ball game."*).

ball park /**bawl** park/ *n* **1** a field where baseball is played. **2 ball park figure** a number that is close, but not exactly, the same as the correct amount (*give me a ballpark figure as to how much the kitchen will cost*). ● **in the right ball park** a figure that is close to the right amount (*$100 for the table is in the right ball park*).

balloon /ba-**loon**/ *n* **1** a small brightly colored rubber bag that can be blown up and used as a toy or as a decoration at parties, etc. **2** originally, a large bag of light material that floats in the air when filled with air or light gas, with a large basket hanging below for carrying passengers. ● *n* **balloonist** /ba-**loon**-ist/.

ballot /ba-lot/ *n* a way of voting secretly by putting marked cards into a box. ● *also vb*. ● *n* **ballot box** /**ba**-lot **boks**/.

ballpoint /**bawl**-point/ *n* a pen that writes by means of a small rotating ball fed by a tube of ink.

balm /bom/ *n* **1** a sweet-smelling oil. **2** a pain-relieving ointment. **3** something that heals or soothes (*a balm to his wounded pride*).

balmy /bom-ee/ *adj* gentle, soft (*balmy breezes*).

balsa /**bawl**-sa/ *n* a tree with light, corky wood.

balsam /**bawl**-sam/ *n* **1** a flowering plant. **2** a sweet-smelling, healing oil.

bamboo /bam-**boo**/ *n* a giant tropical reed from which canes, etc., are made.

ban /ban/ *n* an order forbidding something (*impose a ban on smoking in public places*). ● *vb* (**banned** /band/, **banning**/**ban**-ing/) to forbid (*banned from driving*).

banal /ban-**al**/ *adj* unoriginal, commonplace; uninteresting (*a few banal remarks*). ● *n* **banality** / ba-**nal**-i-tee/.

banana /ba-**na**-na/ *n* a tropical fruit that is yellow in color, long and curved.

banana split /ba-**na**-na **split**/ *n* a desert that includes a banana, halved lengthwise, with ice cream, whipped cream, nuts and syrup.

band¹ /band/ *n* **1** anything used to bind or tie together (*a band to tie her hair back*). **2** a strip of cloth round anything (*skirt waistbands*).

band² /band/ *n* a group of persons united for a purpose, especially to play music together. ● *vb* to join (together) (*local people banding together to fight crime*).

bandage /**ban**-dage/ *n* a strip of cloth used in dressing a wound or injury. ● *also vb*.

bandanna, bandana /ban-**da**-na/ *n* a brightly colored handkerchief often worn over the head or around the neck.

bandit /**ban**-dit/ *n* an outlaw, a robber.

bandy¹ /**ban**-dee/ *vb* **1 to bandy words** to quarrel. **2 to bandy about/around** to mention something (repeatedly) and hint at its importance in connection with something (*his name was bandied about after the money went missing*).

bandy² /**ban**-dee/, **bandy-legged** /**ban**-dee **leg**-(e)d/ *adjs* (*inf, Brit*) having legs curving outward.

bane /bane/ *n* **1** ruin. **2** a cause of ruin or annoyance (*that child is the bane of our existence*).

baneful /**bane**-ful/ *adj* causing harm, hurtful.

bang /bang/ *n* **1** a sudden loud noise (*the door shut with a bang*). **2** a blow or knock (*get a bang on the head*). ● *vb* **1** to close with a bang (*the door banged shut*). **2** to hit or strike violently, often making a loud noise (*children banging drums/banged on the leg by a baby buggy*). **3** to make a sudden loud noise (*guns banging away*). ● See also **big bang**. ● *npl see* **bang**².

bang² /bang/ *n* often **bangs** *pl* a fringe of hair across the forehead (*cut your hair in bangs*).

bangle /**bang**-gl/ *n* a ring worn around the wrist or ankle.

bangs /bangz/ *npl* a fringe of hair that hangs over the forehead.

banish /**ban**-ish/ *vb* **1** to order to leave the country (*banished from his native land*). **2** to drive away (*banish all their doubts*). ● *n* **banishment**.

banister /**ban**-iss-ter/ *n* a post or row of posts supporting a rail at the side of a staircase.

banjo /**ban**-jo/ *n* a stringed musical instrument played with the fingers.

bank /bangk/ *n* **1** a ridge or mound of earth, etc. (*banks of snow at the edge of the road/stand on a grassy bank full of wild flowers*). **2** the ground at the side of a river, lake, etc. **3** a place where money is put for safekeeping. ● *vb* **1** to heap up (*snow banked up at the sides of the road*). **2** to cover a fire with small coal to make it burn slowly. **3** to put money in a bank. **4** to make an airplane slope one wing tip down when turning.

banker /**bang**-ker/ *n* **1** one who runs or manages a bank. **2** one who holds the money staked in gambling games.

banking /**bang**-king/ *n* the business of a banker.

bankrupt /**bang**-krupt/ *n* one who is unable to pay his or her debts (*declared bankrupt*). ● *also adj*. ● *n* **bankruptcy** /**bang**-krup-see/.

banner /**ban**-ner/ *n* a flag.

banquet /**bang**-kwet/ *n* a feast.

banter /**ban**-ter/ *vb* to poke fun at; to tease. ● *also n*.

baptism /**bap**-tiz-um/ *n* **1** the ceremony by which one is received into the Christian church. **2** a first experience of something, an initiation. ● *adj* **baptismal**.

baptize /**bap**-tize/ *vb, also* **baptise** (*Br*) **1** to dip in or sprinkle with water during a **baptism** (*baptize the baby*). **2** to christen or give a name to (*she was baptized Mary Elizabeth*).

bar /bar/ *n* **1** a solid piece of wood, metal, etc., that is longer than it is wide (*a gold bar/a bar of chocolate*). **2** a length of wood or metal across a door or window to keep it shut or prevent entrance through it (*iron bars on the prison windows*). **3** an obstacle (*a bar to progress*). **4** the bank of sand, etc., at the mouth of a river which hinders entrance. **5** a counter at which food or drink may be bought and consumed (*a sandwich bar*). **6** a counter at which alcoholic drinks are served (*place two beers on the bar*). **7** a place where alcoholic drinks are sold, a public house (*the Station Bar*). **8** the rail behind which a prisoner stands in a courtroom. **9** a division in music. ● *vb* (**barred, barring**) **1** to fasten with a bar or belt (*bar the door*). **2** to hinder or prevent (*bar their advance*). **3** to forbid, to ban (*bar women from joining the club*). ● *prep* except.

barb /barb/ *n* **1** sharp points facing in more than one direction. **2** a backward-curving spike on a fish-hook or arrow.

barbarian /bar-**bay**-ree-an/ *n* **1** an uncivilized person. **2** one who does not respect the arts or learning.

barbaric /bar-**ba**-ric/ *adj* connected with barbarism.

barbarism /**bar**-bar-izm/ *n* the state of being uncivilized.

barbarity /bar-**ba**-ri-tee/ *n* savage cruelty.

barbarous /**bar**-ba-russ/ *adj* **1** savage, uncivilized (*a barbarous tribe*). **2** cruel (*his barbarous treatment of prisoners of war*).

barbecue /**bar**-bi-kyoo/ *n* **1** a framework on which meat, etc., may be cooked over a charcoal fire, usually outside. **2** a large outdoor party where food is cooked on a barbecue. ● *vb* to cook on a barbecue (*barbecuing steaks*).

barbed /barbd/ *adj* **1** having a **barb** or barbs (*barbed wire*). **2** intended to hurt someone's feelings (*barbed comments*).

barber /**bar**-ber/ *n* a man's hairdresser.

bar code /**bar**-code/ *n* a pattern of vertical lines of differing widths that represent numbers. It is printed on something, such an item for sale, and contains information, such as the price, which can be scanned by a computer.

bard /bard/ *n* **1** a Celtic minstrel. **2** a poet.

bare /bare/ *adj* **1** uncovered (*bare hillsides/bare floors*). **2** empty (*bare cupboards*). **3** naked (*children stripped bare*). ● *vb* to uncover, to expose (*bare his chest/dogs baring their teeth*).

barefaced /bare-**fayst**/ *adj* shameless.

barely /**bare**-lee/ *adv* **1** only just. **2** scarcely.

bargain /**bar**-gin/ *n* **1** an agreement about buying and selling. **2** an agreement. **3** something bought cheaply. ● *vb* **1** to argue about the price before paying. **2** to make an agreement. ● **to bargain for** to expect. ● **into the bargain** in addition.

barge /barge/ *n* a flat-bottomed boat for carrying cargoes on inland waters. ● *vb* to move clumsily and often rudely (*barge on to the bus in front of us*).

baritone /**ba**-ri-tone/ *n* a male singing voice that can go neither very high nor very low.

bark[1] /bark/ *n* the outer covering of a tree. ● *vb* to scrape the skin off (*bark one's shin*).

bark[2] /bark/ *n* the noise made by a dog, wolf, etc. ● *also vb*.

barley /**bar**-lee/ *n* a grain used for making malt.

bar mitzvah /bar-**mits**-va/ *n* a ceremony held on the thirteenth birthday of a Jewish boy whereby he becomes an adult.

barn /barn/ *n* a farm building for the storage of grain, hay, etc.

barnacle /**bar**-ni-cl/ *n* a type of shellfish.

barn dance /**barn**-dance/ *n* a country dance.

barometer /ba-**rom**-i-ter/ *n* **1** an instrument for measuring air pressure, thus showing what the weather may be. **2** something that indicates change (*opinion polls are a barometer of the popularity of the government*).

baron /**bar**-on/ *n* (*Br*) a nobleman of the lowest rank. ● *f* **baroness** /ba-**ron**-ess/.

baronet /**bar**-on-et/ *n* (*Br*) a titled rank just below that of a nobleman. ● *n* **baronetcy** /**bar**-on-et-see/.

barracks /**bar**-aks/ *n pl* a building for housing soldiers.

barracuda /ba-ra-**coo**-da/ *n* a fish with a long body and many sharp teeth.

barrage /**bar**-azh/ *n* **1** a bar across a river to make the water deeper. **2** a concentration of heavy gunfire on a certain area. **3** a large number (of questions, etc.) made rapidly one after the other (*a barrage of comments from the audience*).

barrel /**bar**-el/ *n* **1** a round wooden cask or container with flat ends and curved sides (*a barrel of beer*). **2** the tube of a gun.

barren /**bar**-en/ *adj* **1** producing no fruit or seed (*barren apple trees*). **2** (*old*) unable to produce young, infertile (*barren women*). **3** unable to produce crops (*barren soil*). **4** useless, not productive (*barren discussions*). ● *n* **barrenness**.

barricade /ba-ri-**cade**/ *n* a barrier, often temporary and quickly constructed, to prevent people from passing or entering. ● *also vb*.

barrier /**bar**-ee-er/ *n* **1** a kind of fence put up to control or restrain (*barriers along the sides of the street to keep the crowds back*). **2** an obstacle (*a barrier to progress*). **3** something that separates or keeps people apart (*a language barrier*).

barrow /**bar**-oe/ *n* **1** a small handcart (*wheel grass* *cuttings away in a barrow*). **2** (*old*) a mound over a grave.

bartender /**bar**-ten-der/ *n* someone who serves drinks at a public bar.

barter /**bar**-ter/ *n* trade by exchange of goods instead of money payments. ● *vb* to trade by barter, to exchange.

basalt /bi-**solt**, **bay**-solt/ *n* a dark volcanic rock.

base[1] /**base**/ *n* **1** that on which a thing stands or is built up (*the base of the column*). **2** the place in which a fleet or army keeps its main stores and offices. **3** a fixed point in certain games. ● *vb* **1** to use as a foundation or grounds (*base one's decision on the evidence*). **2** to establish, to place (*a company based in Boston*).

base[2] /**base**/ *adj* low, worthless, vile (*a base villain/a base act*). ● *adv* **basely** /**base**-lee/.

baseball /**base**-bawl/ *n* **1** a game played with bat and ball and two teams of nine players. **2** the ball used in this game.

baseless /**base**-less/ *adj* without foundation, groundless (*baseless suspicions*).

basement /**base**-ment/ *n* the ground floor, below ground level.

bash /**bash**/ *vb* to beat, to hit with great force.

bashful /**bash**-ful/ *adj* modest, shy (*too bashful to speak in public*).

basic /**base**-ic/ *adj* **1** providing a foundation or beginning (*the basic rules of science/basic steps in mathematics*). **2** without more than is necessary, simple, plain (*a room with basic furniture*).

basin /**base**-in/ *n* **1** a deep broad dish (*a pudding basin*). **2** a hollow place containing water. **3** a dock. **4** the land drained by a river.

basis /**base**-iss/ *n* (*pl* **bases** /**base**-eez/) that on which a thing is built up, the foundation or beginning (*arguments that have a firm basis*).

bask /**bask**/ *vb* **1** to lie in the sun. **2** (*fml*) to enjoy (*bask in his employer's approval*).

basket /**bas**-ket/ *n* a container made of thin sticks or coarse grass plaited together (*a basket of groceries*).

bas mitzvah *see* **bat mitzvah**.

bass[1] /**bass**/ *n* **1** the lowest part in music. **2** the lowest male voice.

bass[2] /**bass**/ *n* a type of fish.

bassoon /ba-**soon**/ *n* a musical wind instrument, with low notes only.

baste /**baste**/ *vb* **1** to drip or pour fat on meat while roasting. **2** to sew with long, loose stitches.

bastion /**bas**-chen/ *n* **1** a tower jutting out from the wall of a fort to allow the defenders to aim arrows, bullets, etc., at the flanks of the attackers. **2** a person or thing that provides strong support or defense (*the last bastions of the traditional village way of life*).

bat[1] /**bat**/ *n* a piece of wood prepared for striking a ball in certain games. ● *vb* to use the bat for striking the ball

bat[2] /**bat**/ *n* a flying creature with a body like a mouse and large wings.

batch /**batch**/ *n* **1** a quantity of bread, etc., baked at one time. **2** a set or group (*a new batch of army recruits*).

bath /**bath**/ *n* **1** act of washing the body. **2** a large vessel in which the body is washed. **3** a large tank in which one can swim. ● *vb* (*Br*) to wash the body in a bath.

bathe /**bathe**/ *vb* **1** to wash the body in a bath. **2** to go for a swim (*bathe in the sea*) **3** to apply water to in order to clean (*bathe the wound*). ● *n* (*Br*) act of swimming or playing in water.

bat mitzvah /**bat**-mits-va/ *n* a ceremony for a Jewish girl similar to a **bar mitzvah**. *Also called* a **bas mitzvah** /**bas**-mits-va/.

baton /ba-**ton**/ *n* **1** a short stick used by the director of a band or choir. **2** a short club carried by policemen as a weapon. **3** a stick passed by one member of a team of runners to the next runner in a relay race.

battalion /ba-**tal**-yen/ *n* a body of infantry, about 1000 strong.

batten[1] /ba-**ten**/ *n* **1** a long board or strip of wood. **2** a strip of wood used to fasten down the hatches of ships. ● *vb* to close firmly with battens (*batten down the hatches, there's a storm coming*).

batten[2] /ba-**ten**/ *vb*. ● **to batten on** to live well or thrive by taking advantage of someone else (*landlords battening on their poor tenants*).

batter /ba-**ter**/ *vb* to beat with violence. ● *n* a mixture of flour and liquid combined for cooking.

battering ram /ba-te-ring **ram**/ *n* a heavy piece of wood with an iron head formerly used for battering down castle walls or doors.

battery /ba-te-ree/ *n* **1** a group of guns and the people who serve them. **2** a number of connected cells for providing or storing electric current. **3** a violent attack.

battle /ba-tl/ *n* **1** a fight between armies, fleets, etc. **2** a struggle (*a battle for promotion*). ● *vb* to fight or struggle (*battling for top place in the league*).

battlement /ba-tl-ment/ *n* the top wall of a castle, with openings through which weapons can be aimed.

bauble /baw-bl/ n a small, worthless ornament or piece of jewelry (*baubles on the Christmas tree*).

baulk see **balk**.

bawl /bawl/ vb to shout or cry loudly. ● *also* n.

bay¹ /bay/ adj reddish-brown. ● n a bay horse.

bay² /bay/ n 1 an inlet of the sea. 2 a recess in a wall.

bay³ /bay/ n the laurel tree.

bay⁴ /bay/ n the bark of a dog, the low cry of a hunting dog. ● **to stand at bay** to stop running away and turn to defend oneself. ● **to keep at bay** to keep at a safe distance. ● vb to give the bark or cry of a dog (*hounds baying*).

bayonet /bay-o-net/ n a weapon, like a dagger, for fixing on to a rifle. ● vb to stab with a bayonet.

bay window /bay win-doe/ n a window built into a section of the wall that juts out.

bazaar /be-zar/ n 1 in the East, a marketplace or group of shops. 2 a sale of articles held to raise money for a special purpose (*a church bazaar to raise money for roof repairs*).

bc /bee see/ abbr = **before Christ**: referring to a date occurring before the birth of Jesus Christ.

beach /beech/ n the shore of a sea or lake. ● vb to run or pull (a vessel) onto a beach (*beach the canoe*).

beachcomber /beech comb-er/ n 1 in the Pacific, one who lives by what he or she finds on the beach (e.g., pearls, wreckage). 2 a vagrant who lives around harbors or beaches.

beacon /bee-con/ n 1 a signal fire. 2 a high hill on which a beacon could be lighted. 3 a signal of danger.

bead /beed/ n 1 a small object, usually round, of glass or other material, with a hole through it for a string (*a necklace of colored beads*). 2 a drop or bubble (*beads of sweat*). 3 pl a rosary.

beady /bee-dee/ adj small and bright (*with beady eyes*).

beagle /bee-gl/ n a small hunting dog.

beak /beek/ n the bill of a bird.

beaker /bee-ker/ n 1 a glass vessel used in scientific experiments. 2 a large cup usually with a lip from which to pour liquid.

beam /beem/ n 1 a thick piece of wood. 2 a main timber in a building. 3 the greatest breadth of a ship. 4 a ray of light. 5 radio waves sent out in one particular direction, as a ray. ● vb to smile brightly (*beam with pleasure*).

bean /bean/ n a plant whose seed or seed pod is eaten as a vegetable (*broad beans/lima beans*).

bear¹ /bare/ vb (pt **bore**, pp **borne**) 1 (fml) to carry (*bearing gifts*). 2 to put up with (*bear the pain*). 3 to support (*bear his weight*). 4 to have or show (*still bearing a scar*). 5 to move (*bear left*). 6 (pp **born**) to bring into existence. 7 (pp **borne**) to produce (*bear fruit*).

bear² /bare/ n a wild animal with thick fur and claws.

bearable /bare-a-bl/ adj able to be put up with (*pain scarcely bearable*).

beard /beerd/ n the hair on the chin and lower jaw. ● vb to defy openly (*beard the lion in its den*).

bearer /bare-rer/ n a carrier (*the bearer of bad news*).

bearing /bare-ring/ n 1 the way a person holds himself or herself or behaves (*of noble bearing*). 2 (usually pl) direction (*lose one's bearings*). 3 connection, influence (*their statement had no bearing on our decision*).

beast /beest/ n 1 a four-footed animal. 2 a person who behaves in an animal-like way, a hateful person. ● adj **beastly**. ● n **beastliness**.

beat /beet/ vb (pt **beat**, pp **beaten**) 1 to strike several times. 2 to defeat or win against (*beat the home team*). 3 to throb (*with heart beating*. 4 to mix with a fork or a spoon (*beat two eggs*). ● n 1 a repeated stroke. 2 a policeman's round. 3 a regular rhythm (e.g., the pulse, a drum).

beau /bo/ n (pl **beaux**) 1 (old) a man who is taken up with matters of dress and manners, a dandy. 2 (old or fml) a male sweetheart (*her latest beau*).

beautify /byoo-ti-fie/ vb to make beautiful (*girls beautifying themselves at the mirror*).

beauty /byoo-tee/ n 1 that which is pleasing to the senses. 2 a beautiful woman (*she was a beauty in her youth*). 3 (inf) a very fine specimen (*his new car is a real beauty*). 4 (inf) advantage (*the beauty of the job is the short hours*). ● adj **beautiful**.

beaver /bee-ver/ n an animal with a wide, flat tail that can live both on land and in water.

because /be-coz/ con a word meaning "for the reason that" (*I cried because you hurt me*).

beckon /be-kon/ vb to make a sign inviting a person to approach (*beckon to them to move forward*).

become /be-come/ vb (pt **became**, pp **become**) 1 to come to be (*become a fine young woman/become a doctor*). 2 to suit (*green becomes her*).

becoming /be-come-ing/ adj 1 (fml) fitting, suitable, appropriate (*behavior that was far from becoming in the circumstances*). 2 suiting the wearer (*a becoming dress*).

bed /bed/ *n* **1** a thing to sleep or rest on. **2** the channel of a river. **3** a piece of ground prepared for growing flowers, plants, etc.

bedclothes /**bed**-cloe(th)z/ *npl* the coverings on a bed.

bedding /**bed**-ing/ *n* bedclothes.

bedraggled /bi-**drag**-geld/ *adj* wet and dirty, muddy (*bedraggled from her walk through the storm*).

bedridden /**bed**-rid-n/ *adj* having to stay permanently in bed (*bedridden invalids*).

bedrock /**bed**-rock/ *n* **1** the solid rock underlying the broken rock formations near the earth's surface. **2** basic facts or principles (*the bedrock of his beliefs*).

bedroom /**bed**-room/ *n* a room in which to sleep.

bedspread /**bed**-spred/ *n* a quilt used as a bed covering.

bedstead /**bed**-sted/ *n* a frame for supporting a bed.

bee /bee/ *n* a flying, honey-making insect.

beech /beech/ *n* a type of tree. ● *n* **beechnut** /**beech**-nut/.

beef /beef/ *n* the flesh of an ox or cow.

beehive /**bee**-hive/ *n* a place, often dome-shaped, where bees are kept.

beeline /**bee**-line/ *n* the shortest way. ● **make a beeline for** to go directly and quickly toward (*make a beeline for the prettiest girl at the party*).

beer /beer/ *n* a drink made from barley and hops.

beeswax /**beez**-waks/ *n* the wax made by bees for their honeycombs. ● *vb* to polish with beeswax.

beet /beet/ *n* a plant with a root eaten as a vegetable (*also* **sugar beet**).

beetle[1] /**bee**-tl/ *n* a common insect. ● *vb* (*inf*) to hurry, to scurry (*beetle off home*).

beetle[2] /**bee**-tl/ *n* a heavy wooden tool, like a mallet, used to beat such things as paving stones into place.

beetle[3] /**bee**-tl/ *vb* to jut, to hang over (*cliffs beetling over the sea*).

beetroot /**beet**-root/ *n* the root of the beet.

befall /bi-**fol**/ *vb* (*pt* **befell**, *pp* **befallen**) (*fml*) to happen (*troubles that befell her*).

befit /bi-**fit**/ *vb* (**befitted**, **befitting**) (*fml*) to suit, to be appropriate for (*his behavior does not befit a man of his position*).

befitting /bi-**fit**-ing/ *adj* suitable (*behave with a befitting degree of modesty*). ● *adv* **befittingly**.

beforehand /bi-**fore**-hand/ *adv* earlier (*pay for the tickets beforehand*).

befriend /bi-**frend**/ *vb* to act as a friend to, to be kind to (*befriend the orphan girl*).

beg /beg/ *vb* (**begged**, **begging**) **1** to ask for money (*beg on the streets*). **2** to ask earnestly (*beg for forgiveness/beg a favor*). ● **to beg the question** to take a fact for granted without proving its truth.

beggar /**beg**-er/ *n* one who asks for money or food.

begin /bi-**gin**/ *vb* (*pt* **began**, *pp* **begun**, *prp* **beginning**) **1** to start (*begin to play/the trouble began in June*). **2** to be the first to do or take the first step in doing (*begin the discussion*).

beginner /bi-**gi**-ner/ *n* one starting to learn (*a beginner's class*).

begonia /bi-**goan**-ya/ *n* a plant with brightly colored flowers.

behalf /bi-**half**/ *n*. ● **on behalf of** in the name of (*speak on behalf of his mother*).

behave /bi-**hayv**/ *vb* **1** to conduct oneself. **2** to conduct oneself well. **3** to act.

behavior /bi-**hay**-vyer/ *n*, *also* **behaviour** (*Br, Cdn*) conduct.

behead /bi-**hed**/ *vb* to cut off the head.

behold /bi-**hold**/ *vb* (*pt, pp* **beheld**) to see; to watch. ● *n* **beholder**.

belated /bi-**lay**-ted/ *adj* too late (*a belated apology*).

belch /belch/ *vb* to send out forcefully, especially gas through the mouth.

belfry /**bell**-free/ *n* a bell tower.

belief /be-**leef**/ *n* **1** faith (*belief in God*). **2** trust (*shake her belief in his ability*). **3** opinion (*it is my belief that she is guilty*).

believe /be-**leeve**/ *vb* **1** to accept as true or real (*believe in ghosts*). **2** to trust (*believe in her husband*). **3** to have faith, especially in God. **4** to think. ● *adj* **believable**. ● *n* **make-believe** pretense.

believer /be-**lee**-ver/ *n* one who has faith, especially in God.

belittle /bi-**li**-tl/ *vb* to make to seem small or unimportant (*belittle his achievements*).

bell /bell/ *n* a hollow metal vessel that gives a ringing sound when struck.

belle /bell/ *n* a lady of great beauty.

bellow /**bell**-o/ *vb* **1** to shout loudly (*bellow to his children to make less noise*). **2** to roar (*bulls bellowing*). ● *also n*.

bellows /**bell**-oez/ *npl* an instrument that makes a draft of air by forcing wind out of an airtight compartment.

belly /**bell**-ee/ *n* **1** the part of the human body between the breast and thighs. **2** the under part of an animal's body. ● *vb* to bulge out (*sails bellying in the wind*).

belly button /bel-lee-bu-ton/ (*inf*) the informal name for the naval.

belong /bi-**long**/ *vb* **1** to be the property (of). **2** to be a member. **3** to be connected with.

belongings /bi-**long**-ing-z/ *npl* the things that are one's own property.

beloved /bi-**luvd**/ *adj* greatly loved. ● *n* one who is greatly loved (*having lost his beloved*).

belt /belt/ *n* **1** a strap or band for putting round the waist. **2** a leather band used to carry the motion of one wheel onto another in a piece of machinery. **3** a space that is much longer than it is broad (*a belt of trees dividing two fields*). **4** an area that has a particular quality or characteristic (*the industrial belt of the country*). **5** (*inf*) an act of hitting, a blow. ● *vb* **1** to put on a belt. **2** to hit with a strap. **3** to hit, to attack with blows (*belt his brother*). ● **below the belt 1** below the waistline. **2** unfair.

bemused /bi-**myoozd**/ *adj* confused, bewildered (*motorists bemused by the traffic system/wearing a bemused expression*).

bench /bench/ *n* **1** a long seat (*children sitting on benches in the school hall*). **2** a worktable (*benches in the science lab*). **3** the seat of a judge in court. **4** all the judges, as a body.

benchmark /bench mark/ *n* **1** a mark on a fixed object indicating height. **2** a standard for judging or measuring (*his work was regarded as a benchmark for that of his classmates*).

bend /bend/ *vb* (*pt, pp* **bent**) **1** to curve (*a road bending sharply*). **2** to make to curve (*bend the branch*). **3** to incline the body, to stoop (*bend to pick up a coin*). ● *n* **1** a curving turn on a road. **2** an angle.

benediction /be-ne-**dic**-shen/ *n* blessing. ● *adj* **benedictory**.

benefactor /be-ne-**fac**-tor/ *n* one who gives help to another. ● *f* **benefactress**.

beneficial /be-ne-**fi**-shal/ *adj* helpful, having a good effect (*a diet beneficial to health*).

beneficiary /be-ne-**fi**-shee-ree/ *n* **1** one who receives money or property by will. **2** one who benefits from another's kindness.

benefit /be-ne-fit/ *n* **1** advantage, gain (*the benefits of a healthy lifestyle/advice that is of benefit to us*). **2** (*Br*) the money to which an insured person has the right when unemployed, ill, etc. ● *vb* **1** to do good to (*the holiday clearly benefited her*). **2** to be of advantage to (*he benefited from having educated parents*).

benevolence /be-**ne**-vol-ense/ *n* kindness, generosity.

benevolent /be-**ne**-vol-ent/ *adj* kindly, generous.

benign /bi-**nine**/ *adj* **1** kindly, gentle (*a benign smile*). **2** not malignant, not cancerous (*a benign tumor*). ● *adv* **benignly**.

bent[1] /bent/ *pt, pp of* **bend**.

bent[2] /bent/ *adj* (*inf*) dishonest (*a bent lawyer*).

bent[3] /bent/ *n* a natural skill in (*a musical bent*).

bequeath /bi-**kweeth**/ *vb* to leave by will (*bequeath her jewelry to her granddaughter*).

bequest /bi-**kwest**/ *n* the money or property left by will; a legacy.

berate /bi-**rate**/ *vb* to scold.

bereave /bi-**reev**/ *vb* (*pt, pp* **bereaved** *or* **bereft**) to take away (*war bereft her of her sons*). ● *n* **bereavement** /bi-**reev**-ment/.

bereaved /bi-**reev**-d/ *adj* having lost, by death, a near relative (*the bereaved mother*). ● *n* one who has lost a relative by death (*comfort the bereaved*).

bereft /bi-**reft**/ *adj* having been deprived of something (*so amazed that she was bereft of words*).

beret /be-**ray**/ *n* a round flat cap with no peak or brim.

berry /be-**ree**/ *n* a small fruit containing seeds.

berserk /ber-**serk**/ *adj* uncontrollably angry (*he went berserk when he saw the damage*).

berth /berth/ *n* **1** the place where a ship lies when at anchor or in dock. **2** a place for sleeping in a ship or train. ● *vb* to moor a ship. ● **to give a wide berth to** to keep well clear of (*give a wide berth to troublemakers*).

beseech /bi-**seech**/ *vb* (*pt, pp* **besought** *or* **beseeched**) (*fml*) to ask earnestly, to beg for (*beseech her employer not to dismiss her*). ● *adv* **beseechingly**.

beset /bi-**set**/ *vb* (**beset, besetting**) to attack from all sides, to surround (*trouble beset them from all sides*).

besiege /bi-**seedge**/ *vb* **1** to surround a fortress with soldiers in order to bring about its capture. **2** to surround, to crowd round (*reporters besieging the princess on her tour*). **3** to overwhelm (*reporters besieging the police with questions*). ● *n* **besieger**.

besom /bee-zom/ *n* a broom.

besotted /bi-**sot**-ted/ *adj* silly, muddled (*besotted with love*).

bespatter /bi-**spat**-ter/ *vb* to sprinkle (with dirt, etc.) (*traffic bespattering pedestrians with mud*).

best /best/ *adj* (*superl of* **good**) good in the utmost degree (*his best attempt*). ● *vb* to do better than, to win against (*best them in their attempt at victory*).

bestial /bes-chal/ *adj* like an animal, beastly, disgusting (*a bestial crime*).

bestiality /bes-chee-a-li-tee/ *n* animal-like behavior.

bestow /bi-sto/ *vb* (*fml*) to give (to) (*bestow a gift of money*).

bestride /bi-stride/ *vb* to sit or stand across something, with a leg on either side of it.

bet /bet/ *n* money put down in support of an opinion, to be either lost or returned with interest, a wager. ● *vb* (**betting, bet**) to stake money in a bet.

betake /bi-take/ *vb*. ● **betake oneself to** (*old or fml*) to go (*betake oneself to the hospital*).

betide /bi-tide/ *vb* (*fml or lit*) to happen (*whatever may betide*).

betoken /bi-to-ken/ *vb* to be a sign of, to indicate (*houses betokening great wealth*).

betray /bi-tray/ *vb* **1** to give up to an enemy. **2** to be false to, to be a traitor to (*betray one's country*). **3** to reveal, to show (*nervousness betraying guilt*). ● *n* **betrayer**.

betrayal /bi-tray-al/ *n* act of betraying.

betroth /bi-troth/ *vb* to promise in marriage. ● *n* **betrothal** /bi-troth-al/.

between /bi-tween/ *prep* **1** the space, time, etc., separating (two things) (*between meetings*). **2** connecting from one or the other (*the bond between them*).

betwixt /bi-twikst/ *prep* between.

bevel /be-vel/ *vb* (**beveled, beveling**) to cut to a slope. ● *n* a sloping edge.

beverage /bev-ridge/ *n* a drink.

bevy /be-vee/ *n* **1** a group (*a bevy of beautiful girls*). **2** a flock of birds.

bewail /bi-wale/ *vb* (*fml*) to lament aloud, to regret (*bewail the loss of his fortune*).

beware /bi-ware/ *vb* to be cautious or careful of (*warned to beware of thieves*).

bewilder /bi-will-der/ *vb* to puzzle, to confuse. ● *adj* **bewildering**. ● *n* **bewilderment**.

bewitch /bi-wich/ *vb* **1** to put under a spell. **2** to charm, to fascinate (*he was bewitched by her beauty*). ● *n* **bewitchment**.

bewitching /bi-wich-ing/ *adj* charming, fascinating (*a bewitching smile*).

beyond /bi-yond/ *prep* on the farther side of. ● *adv* at a distance.

bias /bie-ess/ *n* **1** the greater weight on one side of a bowl that causes it to roll off the straight. **2** an unreasonable dislike (*a bias against foreigners*). **3** a preference (*a bias toward blonde women*). **4** in dress-making, a line across the weave of a fabric. ● *vb* to incline to one side, to prejudice (*his early childhood had biased him against foreigners*).

bias(s)ed /bie-esst/ *adj* prejudiced.

bib /bib/ *n* a cloth tied under a child's chin to keep him or her clean while eating.

Bible /bie-bel/ *n* the Holy Scriptures of the Christian religion. ● *adj* **biblical** /bi-bli-cal/.

bibliography /bi-blee-og-ra-fee/ *n* a list of books dealing with a particular subject. ● *n* **bibliographer** /bi-blee-og-ra-fer/. ● *adj* **bibliographical** /bi-blee-og-gra-fi-cal/.

bibliophile /bi-blee-o-file/ *n* (*fml*) a lover of books.

bicentennial /bie-sen-te-nee-al/ *n* the two hundredth year (after a certain event).

biceps /bie-seps/ *n* a muscle in the upper part of the arm.

bicker /bik-er/ *vb* to quarrel frequently over unimportant things.

bicycle /bie-si-cl/ *n* a machine with two wheels that can be ridden on. ● *also vb*.

bid /bid/ *vb* (*pt* **bid** *or* **bade**, *pp* **bidden** *or* **bid**, *prp* **bidding**) **1** to offer (*bid $600 for the vase at the auction*). **2** to ask, to order (*bid them come in*). ● *n* **1** an offer of money, especially at a sale. **2** a strong effort (*make a bid to take over the company*).

bidder /bid-der/ *n* one offering a price.

bide /bide/ *vb* (*pt, pp* **bided** *or* **bode**). ● **bide one's time** to wait for a good opportunity (*biding his time until he tries to get her job*).

biennial /bie-en-ee-al/ *adj* **1** lasting for two years (*biennial plants*). **2** happening every second year (*a biennial event*). ● *n* a plant that flowers only in its second year, then dies. ● *adv* **biennially** /bie-en-ee-al-ee/.

bier /bir/ *n* a stretcher for carrying a dead body or coffin to the grave.

big bang /big bang/ *n* (*inf*) the name of the theory that the whole universe was created by the explosion of one tiny superdense mass, and that universe is still expanding. ● **big-bang theory**.

bigamy /bi-ga-mee/ *n* the state of having two wives or two husbands at the same time. ● *n* **bigamist** /bi-ga-mist/. ● *adj* **bigamous** /bi-ga-mus/.

bigot /bi-get/ *n* one who accepts without question certain beliefs and condemns the different beliefs held by others (*a religious bigot*). ● *adj* **bigoted.** ● *n* **bigotry.**

bikini /bi-**kee**-nee/ *n* a two-piece swimsuit for women.

bilateral /bie-**la**-te-ral/ *adj* **1** two-sided. **2** concerning two parties (*a bilateral agreement*).

bilberry /**bil**-bi-ree/ *n* a small blue berry.

bile /**bile**/ *n* **1** a fluid, coming from the liver, that aids digestion. **2** (*fml*) anger (*arouse his bile*).

bilingual /bie-**ling**-gwel/ *adj* able to speak two languages.

bilious /**bil**-i-yes/ *adj* **1** relating to bile. **2** sick (*feeling bilious*). ● *n* **biliousness.**

bilk /**bilk**/ *vb* to cheat, to defraud.

bill[1] /**bill**/ *n* the beak of a bird.

bill[2] /**bill**/ *n* **1** the form of a proposed law, as put before congress for discussion. **2** a piece of paper money. **3** a printed notice (*a bill on the noticeboard announcing the meeting*) **4** (*Br*) *see* **check.** ● *vb* to advertise by bills.

billboard /**bill**-board/ *n* a large sign that is pasted with advertisements.

billet /**bill**-let/ *n* a lodging, especially for soldiers. ● *vb* to lodge (e.g. soldiers) in people's houses.

billfold /**bill**-fold/ *n* a pocket-sized flat case, often leather, for holding paper money and credit cards.

billiards /**bill**-yardz/ *n* a game, played on a cloth-covered table, with cues and balls.

billion /**bill**-yon/ *n* **1** in America, and often now in Britain, one thousand millions. **2** in Britain, one million millions.

billow /**bill**-low/ *n* a great wave of the sea. ● *vb* to swell out. ● *adj* **billowy.**

billy goat /**bill**-lee goat/ *n* a male goat.

bin /**bin**/ *n* **1** a large box for corn, meal, etc. (*a bread bin*). **2** a container for garbage.

bind /**biynd**/ *vb* (*pt, pp* **bound**) **1** to tie (*bind the wound with bandages*). **2** to fasten together (*bind his hands together*). **3** to cover (a book) (*a book bound in leather*). **4** to put an edging on (*bind the seams of the dress*). **5** (*fml*) to put under an obligation (*the contract binds you to pay me $1500 per month*). ● **bind oneself** to promise.

binding /**biynd**-ing/ *n* the cover and sewing of a book.

binoculars /bi-**nok**-ye-lers/ *npl* a pair of field glasses.

biochemistry /bie-o-**ke**-me-stree/ *n* the chemistry of living things. ● *adj* **biochemical** /bie-o-**ke**-mi-kel/. ● *n* **biochemist** /bie-o-**ke**-mist/.

biodegradable /bie-o-di-**gray**-da-bl/ *adj* decaying naturally as the result of the action of bacteria and so not causing pollution to the environment (*plastic is not biodegradable*).

biographer /bie-**og**-re-fer/ *n* a writer of biography (*the biographer of Samuel Johnson*).

biography /bie-**og**-re-fee/ *n* the written life story of a person. ● *adj* **biographical** /bie-e-**gra**-fi-kl/.

biology /bie-**ol**-e-jee/ *n* the study of life and living creatures. ● *adj* **biological** /bie-e-**lo**-ji-kl/. ● *n* **biologist** /bie-**ol**-e-jist/.

biped /**bie**-ped/ *n* an animal with two feet.

biplane /**bie**-plane/ *n* an airplane with two wings, one above the other.

birch /**berch**/ *n* **1** a tree. **2** a bundle of sticks tied together at one end and used for flogging.

bird /**berd**/ *n* a creature with feathers and wings that usually flies.

birth /**berth**/ *n* **1** the act of being born (*happy at the birth of her son*). **2** the beginning (*the birth of civilization*).

birthday /**berth**-day/ *n* the day on which one is born, or its anniversary.

birthmark /**berth**-mark/ *n* a mark on the body from birth (*a purple birthmark on her face*).

birthright /**berth**-rite/ *n* any right one possesses by birth.

biscuit /**bis**-ket/ *n* **1** a small round bread made with flour and with baking soda as a raising agent. **2** (*Br*) *see* **cookie.**

bisect /bie-**sect**/ *vb* (*fml*) to cut into two equal parts (*bisect the circle*).

bishop /**bi**-shep/ *n* in the RC Church, Anglican Church, or Eastern Orthodox Church, the chief clergyman of a district.

bison /**bie**-sen/ *n* a type of wild ox.

bit /**bit**/ *n* **1** a small piece (*tear the paper to bits*). **2** a piece of (*a bit of cake/a bit of advice*). **3** part (*the bit in the film where the hero dies*). **4** a tool for boring holes. **5** the metal bar attached to the bridle and put in the mouth of a horse. **4** a unit of value equivalent to an eighth of a dollar.

bite /**bite**/ *vb* (*pt* **bit**, *pp* **bitten**) **1** to cut, pierce, etc., with the teeth (*the dog that bit the postman/bite the apple*). **2** to take the bait (*fish biting today*). ● *n* **1** the amount bitten off. **2** the wound made by biting. **3** a taking of the bait by fish.

biting /**bite**-ing/ *adj* **1** sharp (*biting wind*). **2** hurtful (*a biting remark*). ● *adv* **bitingly.**

bitter /**bit**-ter/ *adj* **1** sharp to the taste (*bitter oranges*). **2** severe, piercing (*the bitter cold*). **3** painful (*from bitter experience*). **4** feeling or showing hatred, hostility, envy, disappointment, etc. (*feeling bitter about her divorce/a bitter quarrel*). ● *adv* **bitterly**. ● *n* **bitterness**.

bivalve /**bie**-valve/ *n* an animal or fish whose shell is in two parts joined by hingelike cartilage. ● *adj* **bivalvular** /bie-**val**-vyoo-lar/.

biweekly /bie-**week**-lee/ *adj* **1** happening once every two weeks (*a biweekly magazine*). **2** twice in one week (*biweekly meetings*).

bizarre /be-**zar**/ *adj* strange, peculiar, weird (*his bizarre appearance/a bizarre crime*).

black /black/ *n* **1** a dark color like coal. **2** (*sometimes with cap*) a member of one of the dark-skinned races of people. ● *also adj.* ● *n* **1** to make black (*black his eye in a fight*). **2** to clean with black polish (*black his shoes*). ● *n* **blackness**.

blackbird /**black**-berd/ *n* a type of thrush.

blackboard /**black**-board/ *n* a dark-colored board used for writing on with a light-colored chalk.

blacken /**black**-en/ *vb* **1** to make black (*smoke blackening the walls*). **2** to become black or dark (*skies blackening*).

blacklist /**black**-list/ *n* a list of persons suspected of doing wrong.

blackmail /**black**-male/ *vb* to obtain money by threatening to reveal a secret. ● *also n.* ● *n* **blackmailer**.

blackout /**black**-out/ *n* **1** a sudden putting out of all lights (*a blackout caused by an electrical power failure*). **2** a period when all lights must be put out or covered (*blackouts ordered by the government to guard against enemy air attacks*). **3** a sudden, short loss of consciousness (*have a blackout after hitting her head on a beam*).

blacksmith /**black**-smith/ *n* a metal-worker who works with iron.

bladder /**bla**-der/ *n* **1** a part of the body in which urine collects. **2** a bag of thin leather, rubber, etc., containing air (*the bladder of a football*).

blade /blade/ *n* **1** a leaf (of grass, corn, etc.). **2** the cutting part of a sword or knife. **3** the flat part of an oar.

blame /blame/ *vb* **1** to find fault with (*I don't blame you for being angry*). **2** to regard as guilty or responsible (*blame him for his brother's death/blame the rise in prices on the government*). ● *n* **1** fault. **2** guilt. ● *adjs* **blameless, blameworthy**.

blancmange /ble-**mandge**/ *n* a jelly-like milk dessert.

bland /bland/ *adj* **1** so mild as to be almost tasteless (*bland food*). **2** so mild or gentle as to be without personality or emotion (*bland smiles/bland articles about the government's problems*).

blank /blank/ *adj* **1** not written on or marked (*blank sheets of paper*). **2** empty, without expression (*blank faces*). ● *n* an empty space (*leave blanks for unanswered questions in the exam paper*).

blanket /**blang**-ket/ *n* **1** a woolen, etc., bed covering. **2** a covering (*a blanket of snow*).

blare /blare/ *vb* to make a loud sound (*trumpets blaring*). ● *also n.*

blaspheme /blass-**feem**/ *vb* **1** to speak mockingly or disrespectfully of God. **2** to swear or curse (*drunks blaspheming when thrown out of the pub*). ● *n* **blasphemer** /blas-**fee**-mer/. ● *adj* **blasphemous** /**blass**-fe-mess/. ● *n* **blasphemy** /**blass**-fe-mee/.

blast /blast/ *n* **1** a sudden, strong gust of wind. **2** a loud sound (*the blast of a trumpet*). **3** an explosion (*killed in the bomb blast*). ● *vb* **1** to blow up or break up by explosion (*blast rock*). **2** to make a loud noise (*music blasting from the radio*). **3** (*old or lit*) to cause to wither (*frost blasted the oak trees*). **4** to ruin (*blast their hopes*). **5** (*inf*) to criticize severely (*the critics blasted their performance*).

blatant /**blay**-tant/ *adj* very obvious, shameless (*a blatant disregard for the law*).

blaze[1] /blaze/ *n* **1** a bright fire or flame (*dry wood makes a good blaze*). **2** a bright glow of light or color (*the garden was a blaze of color in the summer*). **3** a large, often dangerous, fire (*several people killed in the blaze*). **4** an outburst (*leave in a blaze of anger*). ● *vb* **1** to burn brightly. **2** to shine like a flame.

blaze[2] /blaze/ *n* a mark, especially as made on a tree by cutting off a piece of bark. ● *vb* to show a trail by such marks.

blazer /**blay**-zer/ *n* a kind of jacket (*school blazers*).

bleach /bleech/ *vb* **1** to make white or whiter (*curtains bleached by the sun*). **2** to become white. ● *n* a substance that bleaches (*soak sheets in diluted bleach*).

bleak /bleek/ *adj* **1** dreary, cold (*a bleak winter's day*). **2** not hopeful or encouraging (*a bleak future*). ● *n* **bleakness**.

bleat /bleet/ *vb* to cry, as a sheep. ● *also n.*

bleed /bleed/ *vb* (*pt, pp* **bled**) **1** to lose blood. **2** to take blood from (*doctors used to bleed people to treat disease*). **3** (*inf*) to take money from illegally or dishonestly (*moneylenders bleeding their clients*).

blemish /**blem**-ish/ n a stain, a fault. ● vb to stain; to spoil.

blend /**blend**/ vb to mix together (*blend the cake ingredients/blend colors*). ● n a mixture.

bless /**bless**/ vb 1 to pronounce holy (*bless the new church*). 2 to ask God's favor for (*priests blessing newborn children*).

blessed /**blest**/ adj 1 holy (*blessed saints*). 2 happy, fortunate.

blessing /**bless**-ing/ n 1 a thing that brings happiness (*the blessing of children*). 2 a prayer (*say a blessing at the christening*).

blight /**blite**/ n 1 a disease in plants that causes them to wither. 2 a cause of ruin (*the blight of all their hopes*). ● vb 1 to cause to wither. 2 to ruin.

blimp n an airship.

blind /**blinde**/ adj 1 having no sight. 2 unable or unwilling to understand (*blind to the truth*). 3 closed at one end (*a blind alley*). ● n 1 a window screen. 2 (*inf*) a pretense (*his business was a blind for drug-smuggling*). ● vb 1 to make blind. 2 to dazzle (*blinded by the light*). ● adv **blindly**. ● n **blindness**.

blindfold /**blinde**-folde/ vb to cover the eyes with a bandage. ● also adj.

blink /**blink**/ vb 1 to wink. 2 to twinkle (*lights blinking*). ● n 1 a glimpse. 2 a quick gleam of light.

blinker /**bling**-ker/ n a piece of leather put over a horse's eyes to prevent it from seeing sideways.

bliss /**bliss**/ n 1 great happiness. 2 the happiness of heaven.

blissful /**bliss**-ful/ adj very happy.

blister /**bliss**-ter/ n a bag of skin containing watery matter (*blisters on their feet after the long walk*). ● vb to raise a blister.

blizzard /**bli**-zard/ n a violent storm of wind and snow.

bloated /**blo**-ted/ adj blown out, swollen (*I feel bloated after the large meal*).

blob /**blob**/ n a drop, a small round mass (*a blob of paint*).

block /**block**/ n 1 a solid piece of wood, stone, etc. (*a block of stone/a block of ice*). 2 the piece of wood on which people were beheaded. 3 a group of connected buildings (*a block of flats*). 4 a piece of wood in which a pulley is placed. 5 an obstacle (*a block to further progress*). ● vb to stop the way.

blockade /**block**-ade/ n the surrounding of a place with soldiers and/or ships to prevent people and food from going in or leaving. ● also vb.

blockhead /**block**-hed/ n a stupid fellow.

blond /**blond**/ adj having fair hair and skin. ● f **blonde**. ● also ns.

blood /**blud**/ n 1 the red liquid in the bodies of people and animals. 2 family or race (*of noble blood*).

bloodhound /**blud**-hound/ n a large dog often used in tracking.

bloodless /**blud**-less/ adj 1 without blood or killing (*a bloodless victory*). 2 pale, anemic. 3 without spirit or energy.

bloodshed /**blud**-shed/ n the spilling of blood, slaughter.

bloodshot /**blud**-shot/ adj (*of the eye*) red and inflamed with blood.

bloodthirsty /**blud**-thur-stee/ adj eager to shed blood, taking pleasure in killing.

blood vessel /**blud**-vess-l/ n a vein or artery.

bloody /**blud**-ee/ adj 1 bleeding, covered with blood (*a bloody nose*). 2 stained with blood (*a bloody handkerchief*). 3 with a lot of death or killing (*a bloody battle*).

bloom /**bloom**/ n 1 a blossom, a flower (*the first blooms of spring*). 2 the state of flowering (*flowers in bloom*). 3 freshness, perfection (*in the bloom of youth*). ● vb to blossom.

blot /**blot**/ n 1 a spot or stain, often of ink. 2 disgrace (*a blot on the family's honor*). 3 something that spoils something beautiful or good (*that industrial plant is a blot on the beautiful landscape*). ● vb (**blotted, blotting**) 1 to spot, to stain, especially with ink. 2 to dry ink with blotting paper.

blotch /**blotsh**/ n a large spot or mark (*a blotch of ink/red blotches on her skin*).

blouse /**blouse**/ n a loose upper garment.

blow[1] /**blo**/ vb (*pt* **blew**, *pp* **blown**) 1 to cause air to move. 2 to breathe hard (at or into) (*blow into one's hands to warm them*). 3 to pant (*blowing hard after a climb*). ● vb **blow up** to destroy by explosives.

blow[2] /**blo**/ n 1 a stroke. 2 a misfortune.

blow[3] /**blo**/ vb (*pt* **blew** /**bloo**/, *pp* **blown**) to bloom.

blowlamp /**blo** lamp/ n a lamp producing heat by a rush of air.

blowy /**blo**-ee/ adj (*inf*) windy (*a blowy day*).

blubber /**blub**-er/ n the fat of whales, etc. ● vb (**blubbered, blubbering**) to weep noisily.

bludgeon /**blud**-zhen/ n a short club. ● vb to strike repeatedly with something heavy (*bludgeoned to death*).

blue /**bloo**/ n a primary color, as that of the sky on a clear day. ● also adj.

bluebell /bloo-bel/ n 1 the harebell. 2 in Scotland, the wild hyacinth.

blueberry /bloo-ber-ee/n a round, sweet blue berry grown on a bush.

bluebottle /bloo-botl/ n a large bluish fly.

blue fish /bloo-fish/ n a silvery-blue, ocean-living fish.

blue jay /bloo-jay/ n a North American crested bird with blue and white feathers.

blue jeans /bloo-jeenz/ n pants made of blue denim material.

blueprint /bloo-print/ n 1 a photographic print of a plan for a structure (the blueprints for the new office block). 2 a detailed plan or scheme (a blueprint for success).

bluff /bluf/ n 1 a cliff, a steep headland. 2 a pretense (their threat to kill the hostage was just a bluff). ● adj frank and abrupt but good-natured. ● vb to try to deceive by a show of boldness (they said they had guns but we knew they were bluffing).

blunder /blun-der/ vb 1 to make a foolish mistake (you blundered when you mistook her for her mother). 2 to stumble about or into something (blundering about in the dark looking for candles). ● also n.

blunt /blunt/ adj 1 not sharp (blunt knives). 2 short and plain in speech (a blunt young man). 3 outspoken (a few blunt remarks). ● vb 1 to make less sharp. 2 to weaken.

blur /blur/ n 1 an indistinct mass (people only a blur in the distance). 2 a stain, a blot, a smear. ● vb (blurred, blurring) to make unclear (blur his vision/blur memories).

blurb /blurb/ n a short description of something written to make people interested in it (the blurb on a paperback).

blurt /blurt/ vb to speak suddenly or thoughtlessly (blurt out the truth to the teacher).

blush /blush/ vb to become red in the face from shame, modesty, etc. ● n the reddening of the face so caused. ● adv blushingly.

bluster /blust-er/ vb 1 (of wind) to blow violently. 2 to talk boastfully, noisily or threateningly. ● n boastful, noisy or threatening talk.

boa /boe-a/ n 1 a snake that kills by crushing its victim. 2 a scarf of fur or feathers.

boa constrictor /boe-a con-stric-ter/ n a type of boa snake.

boar /bore/ n 1 a male pig. 2 a wild pig.

board /bored/ n 1 a long, broad strip of timber (nail boards together to make a raft). 2 food (ask for board as well as lodging). 3 a group of people who meet, for example, for business reasons (board of directors). 4 the deck of a ship. 5 pl the stage. 6 a flat surface, often marked with a pattern on which certain games are played (a Scrabble board). ● vb 1 to cover with boards (board the broken windows up). 2 to supply with food and accommodation (board the pupils during term time). 3 to take meals, and usually have accommodation, in (workers boarding at my mother's house). 4 to enter a ship. 5 to get onto (board a bus).

boarder /bore-der/ n one who receives food and lodging at an agreed price.

boarding house /bore-ding-house/ n a house where food and lodging may be obtained.

boarding school /bore-ding-skool/ n a school in which pupils live as boarders.

boast /boste/ vb 1 to speak with too much pride about oneself or one's belongings, etc. (boast about his victory/boast about her big house). 2 to possess (something to be proud of) (a town boasting three theaters). ● n proud speech; a proud claim.

boastful /boste-ful/ adj fond of or given to boasting.

boat /bote/ n 1 a ship, especially a small one. 2 a dish shaped like a boat (a gravy boat). ● vb to go in a boat. ● n boatman /bote-man/.

boatswain /boe-sun/ n a petty officer on board ship.

bob /bob/ vb (bobbed, bobbing) 1 to move quickly up and down (boats bobbing up and down on the water). 2 to cut short (bob her hair). ● also n.

bobbin /bob-in/ n a pin or cylinder around which thread is wound, a reel.

bode /bode/ vb. ● bode ill or well to be a bad or good sign of future events (the team's victory bodes well for the championship).

bodice /bod-iss/ n 1 a woman's tight-fitting, sleeveless garment worn on the upper body. 2 the upper part of a woman's dress (a dress with a low-cut bodice).

bodily /bod-il-ee/ adj having to do with the body (convicted of doing bodily harm to her). ● adv by taking hold of the body (remove him bodily from the building).

bodkin /bod-kin/ n 1 an instrument, like a needle, for piercing holes. 2 a blunt needle with a large eye for threading tape through a hem.

body /bod-ee/ n 1 the physical structure of a human being or animal. 2 the main part of anything (the body of the text of the book/the body of the hall). **3** a group of persons (*a body of spectators*). **4** a dead body, a corpse (*police looking for a body*).

bodyguard /**bod**-ee-gard/ *n* a guard to protect a person from attack.

bog /**bog**/ *n* soft, wet ground, a marsh.

bogey, bogy /**boe**-gee/ *n* **1** (*also* **bogeyman**) a goblin, an imaginary evil spirit. **2** an object of fear (*the bogey of unemployment*). **3** in golf, one stroke over par on a hole.

bogie /**boe**-gee/ *n* **1** a four-wheeled truck supporting the front of a railway engine. **2** (*Br*) a low truck.

bogus /**boe**-gus/ *adj* not genuine, sham (*a bogus workman/a bogus passport*).

bogy *see* **bogey**.

bohemian /boe-**hee**-mee-an/ *n* anyone who pays little heed to the customs or conventions of the time.

boil[1] /**boil**/ *vb* **1** to bubble from the action of heat (*water boiling*). **2** to cook in boiling water (*boil the potatoes*). ● *n* **boiler** /**boy**-ler/.

boil[2] /**boil**/ *n* a painful swelling containing poisonous matter.

boisterous /**boy**-struss/ *adj* **1** stormy. **2** noisy and cheerful (*a boisterous party*).

bold /**bolde**/ *adj* **1** daring, brave. **2** large and clear (*bold type*).

boldness /**bolde**-ness/ *n* courage.

bole /**bole**/ *n* the trunk of a tree.

boll /**bole**/ *n* a seed-container, as of the cotton or flax plant.

boll weevil /**bole**-wee-vil/ *n* an insect that destroys cotton bolls.

bolster /**bole**-ster/ *n* a long pillow. ● *vb* to hold up, to support (*get a loan to bolster up the firm's financial state*).

bolt /**bolte**/ *n* **1** an arrow. **2** a thunderbolt. **3** a bar of a door. ● *vb* **1** to fasten with a bolt. **2** to run away (*horses bolting in fright*). **3** to eat too quickly (*bolt one's food*).

bomb /**bom**/ *n* a hollow metal missile containing high explosive, gas, etc. (*buildings blown up by a bomb*). ● *vb* to attack with bombs (*the enemy air force bombing the city*).

bombard /bom-**bard**/ *vb* **1** to fire many guns at. **2** to direct many questions, statements of criticism, etc., at (*reporters bombarding the police with questions about the murder*). ● *n* **bombardment** /bom-**bard**-ment/.

bombshell /**bom**-shell/ *n* a very surprising piece of news, often bad news (*the closing of the factory was a real bombshell to the town*).

bonbon /**bon**-bon/ *n* (*fml*) a candy.

bond /**bond**/ *n* **1** that which binds (*the bond of friendship/the bond between twins*). **2** a written agreement, especially to pay money. **3** (*fml*) *pl* chains, fetters (*prisoners in bonds*).

bondage /**bon**-dage/ *n* slavery.

bone /**bone**/ *n* **1** the hard substance forming the skeleton of human beings and animals (*flesh and bone*). **2** any one of the pieces of this (*break a bone in the leg*). ● *vb* to take out the bones from (*bone fish*).

bonfire /**bon**-fire/ *n* a large, open-air fire.

bonnet /**bon**-et/ *n* **1** a headdress. **2** (*Br*) *see* **hood**.

bonny /**bon**-ee/ *adj* **1** pretty. **2** healthy-looking.

bonus /**boe**-nus/ *n* an extra payment, made for a special effort or services (*a productivity bonus/a Christmas bonus*).

bony /**boe**-nee/ *adj* **1** having many bones (*bony fish*). **2** having protruding bones (*his bony back*).

booby /**boo**-bee/ *n* a stupid person.

booby prize /**boo**-bee prize/ *n* a prize given to the worst performer.

booby trap /**boo**-bee trap/ *n* a trap hidden in a place so obvious that no one suspects it.

book[1] /**book**/ *n* printed matter, bound between covers.

book[2] /**book**/ *vb* to reserve in advance (*booked a hotel room/book theater tickets*)

bookish /**boo**-kish/ *adj* fond of reading or study.

bookkeeper /**book**-kee-per/ *n* one who keeps accounts. ● *n* **bookkeeping** /**book**-kee-ping/.

bookmaker /**book**-may-ker/ *n* (*also inf*) **bookie** / **boo**-kee/) one who makes his or her living by accepting and paying out on bets.

bookworm /**book**-wurm/ *n* one who reads a great deal.

boom[1] /**boom**/ *n* **1** a long pole to stretch the bottom of a sail. **2** a barrier set up across a harbor entrance or river.

boom[2] /**boom**/ *n* a long deep sound. ● *also vb*.

boom[3] /**boom**/ *n* a time of rapid increase or growth (*a tourist boom/a baby boom*). ● *vb* to increase or grow quickly (*business is booming*).

boomerang /**boo**-me-rang/ *n* a curved throwing stick that returns to the thrower, used by Australian Aboriginals. ● *vb* (*of an action, plan, etc.*) to go wrong in such a way that harm or damage is caused to the person responsible.

boon /**boon**/ *n* **1** (*old*) a favor, a special request. **2** an advantage, a blessing.

boor /**boor**/ *n* a rough, ill-mannered person. ● *adj* **boorish**.

boot /**boot**/ *n* **1** a covering for the foot and lower leg. 2 (*Br*) *see* **trunk.** ● *vb* to kick (*boot the ball into play*).

bootleg /boot-leg/ *vb* to smuggle (alcoholic liquor). ● *n* **bootlegger.** ● *adj* a cut of pants where the hems flare out slightly.

booth /booth/ *n* 1 a tent at a fair. 2 a covered stall at a market. 3 a small, enclosed structure (*a phone booth*).

booty /boo-tee/ *n* 1 goods seized and divided by the victors after a battle. 2 goods taken by thieves. 3 (*slang*) the human bottom.

border /bor-der/ *n* 1 the outer edge of anything (*a handkerchief with a lace border/a white border round the picture*). 2 the boundary between two countries (*show one's passport at the border*). 3 a flowerbed round a lawn, etc. (*borders of pansies*). ● *vb* to be next to (*the farm bordering ours*). ● **border (up)on** to come close to, to be almost (*a crime bordering on treason*).

bore[1] /bore/ *vb* to make a hole in. ● *n* 1 the hole made by boring. 2 the greatest breadth of a tube, especially of a gun.

bore[2] /bore/ *vb* to weary by uninteresting talk, etc. (*an audience bored by a long speech*). ● *n* a person whose talk is wearisome. ● *adj* **boring.**

bore[3] /bore/ *n* a large tidal wave.

bored /board/ *adj* weary and dissatisfied with one's circumstances (*bored children with nothing to do*).

boredom /bore-dom/ *n* the state of being bored.

born /born/ *pp of* **bear**, sense 6.

borne /born/ *pp of* **bear**, senses 1–5, 7.

borrow /bor-o/ *vb* to ask or receive as a loan (*borrow money from the bank/borrow a library book*). ● *n* **borrower** /bor-o-wer/.

bosom /boo-zum/ *n* 1 the breast (*an ample bosom*). 2 (*lit or fml*) the heart, considered as the seat of desires and feelings (*hope stirred in his bosom*). ● *adj* close, well-loved (*bosom friends*).

boss[1] /boss/ *n* a knob.

boss[2] /boss/ *n* (*inf*) a master, a manager(ess). ● *vb* 1 to be in charge. 2 to order about (*older boys bossing younger ones*).

bossy /boss-ee/ *adj* (*inf*) fond of ordering others about (*bossy people/in a bossy manner*).

botany /bot-(a)-nee/ *n* the science or study of plants. ● *adjs* **botanic** /bo-ta-nic/, **botanical** /bo-ta-nic-al/. ● *n* **botanist** /bot-a-nist/.

bother /baw-ther/ *vb* 1 to annoy (*stop bothering your mother for candy*). 2 to trouble oneself (*don't bother to get up*). ● *n* a trouble.

bottle /baw-tl/ *n* 1 a container, usually of glass, with a narrow neck. 2 (*inf*) courage, boldness (*lose one's bottle*). ● *vb* to put into bottles (*bottle wine*).

bottleneck /baw-tl-neck/ *n* 1 a narrow or busy part of a road where traffic has to slow down or stop 2 something that slows down progress (*production held up by a bottleneck in the system*).

bottom /bot-um/ *n* 1 the lowest part (*at the bottom of the well/the bottom of the cupboard*). 2 the buttocks. ● *adj* lowest (*the bottom drawer/the bottom flat*). ● *adj* **bottomless.**

boudoir /boo-dwar/ *n* (*fml*) a lady's private room.

bough /ba-oo/ *n* (*fml*) the branch of a tree.

bought /bot/ *pt of* **buy.**

bouillon /bool-yon/ *n* a strong broth.

boulder /bole-der/ *n* a large smooth stone.

boulevard /boo-le-vard/ *n* a wide street, with trees planted along either side.

bounce /bounse/ *vb* to jump or rebound suddenly (*balls that bounce easily/children bouncing with joy*). ● *also n.*

bouncing /boun-sing/ *adj* big, strong (*a bouncing baby*).

bound[1] /bound/ *n* a limit or boundary beyond which one must not go. ● *vb* to form a limit or boundary.

bound[2] /bound/ *vb* to jump, to leap. ● *also n.*

bound[3] /bound/ *adj* 1 on the way to (*homeward bound*). 2 (*pt of* **bind**). 3 obliged (*feel bound to report him*). 4 sure (to do something) (*bound to fail*). 5 tied (*with bound hands*). 6 covered (*bound books*).

boundary /boun-dar-ee/ *n* 1 an outer limit. 2 a border.

boundless /bound-less/ *adj* without limit, endless (*with boundless energy*).

bountiful /boun-tee-ful/ *adj* (*fml*) giving generously.

bounty /boun-tee/ *n* (*fml*) 1 generosity, kindness. 2 a gift of money above what is earned.

bouquet /boo-kay/ *n* 1 a bunch of flowers. 2 perfume of wine.

bout /bout/ *n* 1 a period of action (*bouts of activity*). 2 an attack (of illness) (*a bout of flu*). 3 a contest (*a boxing bout*).

boutique /boo-teek/ *n* a small shop selling fashionable clothes (*a boutique selling only designer clothes*).

bovine /boe-veen/ *adj* 1 like an ox. 2 slow and stupid.

bow[1] /bo/ *vb* 1 to bend, especially in respect or greeting (*bow to the queen*). 2 to lower (*bow his* *head*). ● *n* a bending of the head or body in respect or greeting.

bow[2] /bo/ *n* **1** a weapon for shooting arrows. **2** a looped knot. **3** a stick for playing a stringed instrument (e.g. the violin).

bow[3] /bo/ *n* the curved front part of a ship.

bowed /bode/ *adj* bent, stooping (*with head bowed in prayer*).

bowels /ba-wels/ *npl* **1** the inside of the body, the intestines. **2** the organ by means of which waste matter is expelled from the body.

bowie knife /ba-wee nife/ *n* a long curved hunting knife.

bowl[1] /bole/ *n* a roundish dish or basin (*a pudding bowl*).

bowl[2] /bole/ *n* **1** a heavy wooden ball. **2** *pl* the game played with such balls. ● *vb* **1** to play bowls. **2** to deliver the ball at cricket.

bowlegged /boe-le-ged/ *adj* having legs wide apart at the knees.

bowler[1] /boe-ler/ *n* one who bowls.

bowler[2] /boe-ler/, **bowler hat** (*Br*) *see* **derby**.

bowline /boe-lin, boe-leen/ *n* **1** a rope on a sailing ship. **2** a knot that does not slip.

bowling /boe-ling/ *n* a game where you attempt to knock down 10 pins by rolling a large, heavy ball down an alley.

bow tie *n* /boe-tie/ a tie, tied in the shape of a bow, usually for formal occasions.

bow window /bow win-doe/ *n* a window built into a section of wall that curves out and back.

box[1] /boks/ *n* a type of hardwood tree.

box[2] /boks/ *n* **1** a case or container (*a box of chocolates/boxes of books*). **2** in a theater, a separate compartment with seats, overlooking the stage. ● *vb* to put in a box (*a job boxing apples*).

box[3] /boks/ *vb* **1** to strike (*box the boy's ears*). **2** to fight in sport, wearing padded gloves. ● *n* **boxer** /bok-ser/.

boxing /bok-sing/ *n* the sport of fighting with padded gloves on.

Boxing Day /bok-sing day/ *n* (*Br*) the day after Christmas Day.

box room /boks room/ *n* a storage room in a house.

boy /boy/ *n* **1** a male child (*have two boys and a girl*). **2** a young male person. ● *n* **boyhood** /boy-hood/.

boycott /boy-cot/ *vb* to refuse to have any dealings with (*workers boycotting firms whose employees are not union members*). ● *also n*.

Boy Scout /boy scout/ *n* formerly the name given

to a member of an international youth organization for boys, now **Scout**.

bra /bra/ *n abbr* = **brassiere** /bra-zeer/: underwear worn by women to support the breasts.

brace /brase/ *n* **1** a support. **2** a pair or a couple (*a brace of pheasants*). **3** a boring tool. **4** (*Br*) *see* **suspenders**. ● *vb* to steady or prepare oneself (*brace yourself for some bad news*).

bracelet /brase-let/ *n* an ornament for the wrist.

bracing /bray-sing/ *adj* giving strength (*a bracing climate*).

bracket /bra-ket/ *n* **1** a support for something fixed to a wall (*lights supported by brackets*). **2** *pl* marks in printing to enclose a word, as {}, //, (), or < >. ● *vb* **1** to enclose in brackets (*bracket the information*). **2** to link or connect (*bracket the two cases together*).

brag /brag/ *n* a boast. ● *vb* (**bragged, bragging**) to boast (*brag about the cost of her jewels*).

braid /brade/ *vb* to twist together into one (*braid her hair*). ● *n* **1** a plait of cords or of hair so twisted together. **2** a narrow edging of decorated tape.

braided /bray-did/ *adj* edged with braid.

Braille /bray-el/ *n* a system of printing for blind people in which the letters of the alphabet and numbers are printed as raised dots that can be read by touching them.

brain /brane/ *n* **1** the soft matter within the skull, the center of the nervous system (*an operation on the brain*). **2** *pl* cleverness, intelligence (*the job requires someone with a brain*). **3** (*inf*) someone very clever or intelligent. ● *vb* to dash the brains out.

brainless /brane-les/ *adj* stupid.

brainy /bray-nee/ *adj* (*inf*) clever.

brake[1] /brake/ *n* **1** a fern. **2** a clump of bushes or undergrowth.

brake[2] /brake/ *n* **1** a large wagon. **2** an apparatus for slowing or stopping a vehicle. ● *vb* to apply the brake (*brake sharply*).

bramble /bram-bl/ *n* **1** a prickly bush, especially the blackberry bush. **2** the berry from this bush.

bran /bran/ *n* the husks of corn when separated from the grain.

branch /branch/ *n* **1** a shoot growing out of the trunk or one of the boughs of a tree. **2** any connected part of a larger body (e.g., office, store, bank, etc.) (*branches responsible to head office*). ● *vb* to divide into branches (*the road branches here*). ●

branch out 1 to begin something new (*after working for the family firm, he's branching out on his* *own*). **2** to expand (*the firm is branching out into computers*).

brand /brand/ *n* **1** (*fml*) a burning piece of wood. **2** a mark made with a hot iron to identify cattle, etc. **3** a trademark, a special make of article (*several brands of tinned soup*). **4** variety (*his own brand of humor*). ● *vb* **1** to mark with a hot iron (*brand cattle*). **2** to mark down (as being bad).

brandish /bran-dish/ *vb* to wave, to shake (*brandish a sword in the air*).

brandy /bran-dee/ *n* a strong drink made from wine.

brass /brass/ *n* **1** an alloy of copper and zinc. **2** (*inf*) impudence (*have the brass to call me a liar*). ● *adj* **brassy**.

brassiere *see* **bra**.

brat /brat/ *n* an ill-mannered child.

bravado /bre-va-do/ *n* pretended courage, boastful talk.

brave /brave/ *adj* courageous, daring (*a brave man/a brave action*). ● *vb* **1** to defy (*brave the opposition*). **2** to face with courage (*brave the dangerous journey*). ● *n* a North American Indian warrior.

bravery /bray-ve-ree/ *n* courage, daring.

brawl /brawl/ *vb* to quarrel noisily (*drunks brawling in the pub*). ● *n* a noisy row. ● *n* **brawler**.

brawn /brawn/ *n* muscle, strength.

brawny /braw-nee/ *adj* muscular, strong.

bray /bray/ *vb* to make a loud, harsh sound, as an ass. ● *also n*.

brazen /bray-zen/ *adj* **1** made of brass. **2** impudent, bold (*a brazen young woman*). ● *vb* to face boldly and impudently.

breach /breech/ *n* **1** act of breaking (*a breach of the law*). **2** (*fml*) a gap (*breach in the wall*). **3** a fault (*breach in security*). **4** a quarrel, separation (*breach between two sections of the club*). ● *vb* to make a gap or opening in.

bread /bred/ *n* a food made from flour or meal and baked.

breadth /bredth/ *n* the distance from side to side, width.

breadwinner /bred-win-er/ *n* the person whose earnings supply the needs of the family.

break /brake/ *vb* (*pt* **broke**, *pp* **broken**) **1** to separate into two or more parts, usually by force (*break a vase*). **2** to become unusable or in need of repair (*the machine is broken*). **3** to tame (*break in the new horses*). **4** to fail to keep (*break a promise/break the law*). **5** to tell gently (*break the news*). **6** to go with force (*break out from the prison*). **7** to do better than (*break a record*). ● *n*

1 an opening. **2** a separation. **3** a pause. ● *adj* **breakable**.

breakage /brake-idge/ *n* **1** a breaking. **2** the thing broken.

breaker /bray-ker/ *n* a wave broken by rocks.

breakfast /brek-fast/ *n* the first meal in the day. ● *vb* to eat breakfast.

breakthrough /brake-throo/ *n* an important new development (*a breakthrough in the treatment of cancer*).

breakwater /brake-wa-ter/ *n* a wall to break the force of the waves.

breast /brest/ *n* **1** (*fml*) the front part of the body from the neck to the stomach, the chest (*a soldier stabbed in the breast*). **2** each of the milk-producing glands in a female. ● *vb* **1** to face (*breast the waves*). **2** to touch (*breast the tape*). **3** to come to the top of (*breast the hill*).

breastplate /brest-plate/ *n* armor for the breast.

breath /breth/ *n* **1** the air taken into and put out from the lungs. **2** a gentle breeze.

breathe /breethe/ *vb* **1** to take air into one's lungs and put it out again. **2** (*fml*) to live (*while he breathes he will be loyal*). **3** (*fml*) to whisper (*breathe a reply in her ear*).

breathless /breth-less/ *adj* **1** out of breath, panting (*breathless after climbing the hill*). **2** excited, eager (*in breathless expectation*). ● *adv* **breathlessly**.

breech /breech/ *n* **1** the back part of a gun barrel. **2** *pl* **breeches** pants that fasten just below the knee.

breed /breed/ *vb* (*pt, pp* **bred**) **1** to produce young (*rabbits breeding rapidly*). **2** to keep (animals) for the purpose of breeding young (*he breeds Alsatians*). **3** to be the cause of (*breed disaster*). ● *n* a type, variety, species (*a breed of cattle/a new breed of men*).

breeding /bree-ding/ *n* **1** the bearing of offspring. **2** good manners.

breeze /breez/ *n* a light wind.

breezy /bree-zee/ *adj* **1** windy. **2** lively (*in a breezy manner*). ● *adv* **breezily**.

brethren /breth-ren/ *npl* (*old or relig*) brothers.

brevity /bre-vi-tee/ *n* (*fml*) shortness (*the brevity of the statement*).

brew /broo/ *vb* **1** to make (beer). **2** to make (tea). **3** to be about to start (*a storm brewing/trouble brewing*). ● *n* the mixture made by brewing. ● *n* **brewer**.

brewery /broo-e-ree/ *n* a factory where beer is made.

briar *see* **brier**.

bribe /bribe/ n a reward offered to win unfairly favor or preference (*get into the country by bribing the border guard*). ● vb to win over by bribes. ● n **bribery** /bribe-ree/.

bric-a-brac /bri-ke-brak/ n small ornaments (*a shelf covered by bric-a-brac*).

brick /brick/ n **1** a block of baked clay. **2** (*inf*) a good or helpful person.

brickbat /brick-bat/ n a piece of criticism (*a play receiving only brickbats*).

bricklayer /brick-lay-er/ n one who builds with bricks.

bridal /bride-al/ adj concerning a bride or a wedding (*the bridal party*).

bride /bride/ n a woman about to be married, or newly married.

bridegroom /bride-groom/ n a man about to be married, or newly married.

bridesmaid /briedz-made/ n a girl who attends the bride at a wedding.

bridge[1] /bridge/ n **1** a roadway built across a river, etc. **2** the small deck for a ship's captain. **3** the piece of wood that supports the strings of a violin, etc. ● vb **1** to build a bridge over. **2** to close a gap or pause to make a connection (*bridging the awkward silence with a few remarks*).

bridge[2] /bridge/ n a card game.

bridle /bride-l/ n **1** the head straps and metal bit by which a horse is guided. **2** a check (*act as a bridle on her extravagance*). ● vb **1** to put a bridle on (*bridle a horse*). **2** to check (*bridle his anger*). **3** to toss the head in anger, etc. (*bridle at his criticism*). **4** to show anger or indignation.

brief /breef/ n a summary of an argument especially a law case for use in court. ● adj short (*a brief statement*). ● vb to provide with a summary of the facts.

briefcase /breef-case/ n a case for carrying papers.

brier, briar /brie-er/ n a thorn bush, the wild rose.

brigade /bri-gade/ n an army unit consisting usually of three battalions.

brigadier /bri-gad-ir/ n an officer commanding a brigade.

brigand /bri-gand/ n (*old*) a member of a band of robbers.

bright /brite/ adj **1** shining (*a bright light*). **2** strong, vivid (*a bright red color*). **3** lively, cheerful (*the invalid is a bit brighter*). **4** clever (*a bright pupil*). ● n **brightness**.

brighten /brie-ten/ vb to make or become bright (*candles brightening the room/something to brighten her mood*).

brill /bril/ n a type of flatfish.

brilliant /bril-yant/ adj **1** sparkling. **2** very bright. **3** very clever. ● n a diamond. ● ns **brilliance** /bril-yanse/, **brilliancy** /bril-yan-see/.

brim /brim/ n **1** the rim (*the brim of the cup*). **2** the edge (*the brim of the hat*).

brimful /brim-ful/, **brimming** /brim-ing/ adj full to the brim (*glasses brimful with wine*).

brimstone /brim-stone/ n sulfur.

brindled /brin-duld/ adj marked with streaks (*a brindled terrier*).

brine /brine/ n salt water. ● **the briny** /brine-ee/ the sea.

bring /bring/ vb (*pt, pp* **brought** /brawt/) **1** to fetch, to carry (*bring food with you/bring a friend to the party*). **2** to cause (*death bringing sadness and grief*). ● **bring about** to cause to happen. ● **bring off** to succeed (*bring off a victory*). ● **bring up 1** to rear, to educate (*bring up three children*). **2** to raise (a subject for discussion).

brink /bringk/ n **1** the edge of a steep place (*at the brink of the waterfall*). **2** the edge, the point (*on the brink of disaster*).

brisk /brisk/ adj keen; lively. ● adv **briskly**. ● n **briskness**.

brisket /briss-ket/ n a cut of meat from the breast of an animal.

bristle /briss-el/ n a short, stiff hair. ● vb to stand on end.

bristly /briss-(u)-lee/ adj having bristles, rough (*a bristly chin*).

brittle /bri-tl/ adj hard but easily broken (*brittle wood/brittle bones*).

broach /broach/ vb **1** (*fml*) to open up (*broach a new bottle of wine*). **2** to begin to speak of (*broach the question of money*).

broad /brawd/ adj **1** wide (*a broad piece of ribbon*). **2** not detailed, general (*a broad description*). **3** (*of speech*) with a strong local accent. ● n **broadness**.

broadcast /brawd-cast/ vb (*pt, pp* **broadcast**) **1** to make widely known (*broadcast his views to the whole office*). **2** to send out by radio or television (*broadcast the game*). **3** to scatter widely (*broadcast seed*). ● also n.

broaden /braw-den/ vb to make or become broad or broader (*broaden the road/the road broadens here*).

broad-minded /brawd-mine-ded/ adj ready to listen to and consider opinions different from one's own, liberal.

brocade /bro-**kade**/ *n* a silk cloth with a raised pattern.

broccoli /**broc**-o-lee/ *n* a green vegetable.

brochure /bro-**shoor**/ *n* a small book, a pamphlet (*a brochure advertising the hotel*).

broil /**broyl**/ *vb* to cook over a fire, to grill.

broiler /**broy**-ler/ *n* the part of a stove that cooks using direct heat, usually above, the food.

broker /**bro**-ker/ *n* **1** one who buys and sells for others for a commission. **2** a stockbroker.

bronchial /**brong**-kee-al/ *adj* having to do with the **bronchi**, the branches of the windpipe to the lungs.

bronchitis /**bronk**-eye-tis/ *n* an illness affecting the windpipe to the lungs.

bronco, broncho /**brong**-co/ *n* a half-tamed horse.

brontosaurus /bron-to-**saw**-rus/*n* a very large plant-eating dinosaur.

bronze /**bronz**/*n* **1** an alloy of copper and tin. **2** a reddish brown color. ● *vb* to give or become a reddish brown color.

brooch /**broach**/*n* an ornamental pin.

brood /**brood**/ *vb* **1** to sit on eggs. **2** to think deeply or anxiously about (*brood about her money problems*). ● *n* **1** children. **2** a family of young birds.

broody /**brood**-ee/*adj* **1** hatching eggs. **2** badly wanting to have children (*feels broody when she looks at a newborn baby*).

brook[1] /**brook**/ *n* a small stream.

brook[2] /**brook**/ *vb* (*fml*) to bear, to tolerate (*brook no interference*).

broom /**broom**/ *n* **1** a plant with yellow flowers. **2** a brush, especially one of twigs.

broomstick /**broom**-stick/ *n* the handle of a broom.

broth /**brawth**/ *n* a meat soup with vegetables.

brother /**bru**-ther/ *n* (*pl* **brothers** *or* (*old or relig*) **brethren** /**breth**-ren/) **1** a son of the same parents. **2** a member of the same group.

brotherhood /**bru**-ther-hood/ *n* **1** the relation of a brother. **2** a group with one common purpose.

brotherly /**bru**-ther-lee/ *adj* of or like a brother.

brought /**braw**-t/ *pt of* **bring.**

brow /**braoo**/ *n* **1** the forehead. **2** the jutting-out edge of a cliff or hill (*the brow of the hill*).

browbeat /**braoo**-beet/ *vb* to bully (*browbeat the younger boy into doing his work*).

brown /**braoon**/ *adj* of a dark color. ● *also n.* ● *vb* to make or become brown.

brownie /**braoo**-nee/ *n* **1** a small, rich, chocolate cake, usually square, with nuts. **2** a kindly fairy. **3** a junior member of the **Girl Scouts.**

browse /**braooz**/ *vb* **1** to feed upon (*cows browsing in the fields*). **2** to glance through a book (*browse through the catalog*).

bruise /**brooz**/ *n* a dark spot on the skin, caused by a knock. ● *vb* to cause a bruise on (*bruise her face in the accident/apples bruised by falling from the tree*).

brunette /broo-**net**/ *n* a woman with dark brown hair.

brunt /**brunt**/ *n* the main force or shock of something, the worst effects (*the mother bore the brunt of the father's violence*).

brush /**brush**/ *n* **1** an instrument for cleaning, sweeping, or smoothing. **2** an instrument for putting paint on to something. **3** the tail of a fox. **4** small trees and bushes. **5** a short battle. **5** (*inf*) a slight disagreement or hostile encounter (*a brush with the police*). ● *vb* **1** to clean with a brush. **2** to touch lightly (*brush her cheek with his lips*).

brushwood /**brush**-wood/ *n* **1** small trees and bushes. **2** a thicket.

brusque /**brusk**/ *adj* blunt, rude and abrupt in speech or manner. ● *adv* **brusquely.** ● *n* **brusqueness.**

Brussels sprout /**brus**-sel-sprout/ *n* a small, round, green vegetable like a very small cabbage.

brutal /**broo**-tal/ *adj* cruel, savage (*a brutal murder*).

brutality /broo-**ta**-li-tee/ *n* cruelty, savagery.

brute /**broot**/ *n* **1** an animal. **2** (*inf*) a cruel person (*he was a brute to leave her like that*).

bubble /**bu**-bul/ *n* a film of water or other liquid, containing air (*bubbles in the glasses of champagne*). ● *vb* to form bubbles. ● *adj* **bubbly** /**bu**-blee/.

buccaneer /bu-ca-**neer**/ *n* a pirate.

buck /**buck**/ *n* **1** a male deer, goat, rabbit, etc. **2** (*old*) a dandy, a lively young man. **3** (*inf*) a dollar. ● *vb* to jump straight up with the back arched.

bucket /**bu**-ket/ *n* a vessel for carrying water, a pail.

buckle /**bu**-kl/ *n* a fastener for joining the ends of a belt or band. ● *vb* **1** to fasten (*buckle on his belt*). **2** to bend out of shape (*metal buckling in the intense heat*).

buckskin /**buck**-skin/ *n* a soft leather.

bud /**bud**/ *n* a leaf or flower before it opens. ● *vb* (**budded, budding**) to put out buds.

Buddhist /**boo**-dist/ *n* a person who believes in the religious teaching of Buddha. ● *n* **Buddhism** /**boo**-di-zum/.

budding /**bu**-ding/ *adj* promising (*a budding young artist*).

budge /budge/ *vb* (*inf*) to move, to stir (*I can't budge this heavy wardrobe/she won't budge from that seat*).

budgerigar /bu-je-ree-gar/ *n* a type of small parrot that can be trained to talk.

budget /bu-jet/ *n* **1** a statement of government taxation and intended spending for the coming year. **2** a plan to ensure that household expenses or those of a firm or organization will not be greater than income (*keep within our monthly budget*). ● *vb* **1** to make such a plan (*I try to budget, but I always seem to spend too much*). **2** to allow for something in a budget (*they hadn't budgeted for such a large phone bill*).

buff /buf/ *n* **1** a type of leather. **2** a pale dull yellow color. ● *adj* light yellow.

buffalo /buf-a-lo/ *n* (*pl* **buffalos** *or* **buffaloes**) a type of ox.

buffer /buf-er/ *n* an apparatus to lessen the force of a collision or shock.

buffet[1] /bu-fay/ *n* **1** a sideboard. **2** a counter or bar at which refreshments may be obtained (*the station buffet*). **3** a meal, often cold, set out on tables so that people can help themselves (*have a buffet supper*).

buffet[2] /buf-ay/ *n* (*fml*) a blow, a slap (*give his son a buffet on the side of the head*). ● *vb* **1** to strike. **2** to knock about (*boats buffeted by strong winds*).

buffoon /bu-foon/ *n* **1** a clown. **2** a person who plays the fool.

bug /bug/ *n* **1** a blood-sucking insect (*bedbugs*). **2** any insect (*bugs crawling over our picnic*). **3** (*inf*) an infection (*a stomach bug*). **4** (*inf*) a hidden microphone used to record other people's conversations secretly (*a bug in his hotel room*). **5** a defect or error in a computer program or system. ● *vb* (**bugged**, **bugging**) (*inf*) **1** to install or use a hidden microphone (*bug his room*). **2** (*inf*) to annoy (*what's bugging you?*).

bugle /byoo-gul/ *n* a small brass instrument like a trumpet. ● *n* **bugler**.

build /bild/ *vb* (*pt*, *pp* **built** /bilt/) to put together materials in order to make something, to construct. ● *n* **builder**.

building /bild-ing/ *n* the thing built.

bulb /bulb/ *n* **1** the round root of certain flowers. **2** a pear-shaped glass globe surrounding the element of an electric light.

bulbous /bul-bus/ *adj* bulb-shaped, swollen.

bulge /bulge/ *n* a swelling. ● *vb* to swell out (*his muscles are bulging after weight-training*). ● *adj* **bulgy** /bul-jee/.

bulimia /boo-lee-mee-ya/ *n* an eating disorder in which bouts of over-eating are followed by bouts of vomiting in order to lose weight. ● **bulimic** *adj*.

bulk /bulk/ *n* **1** the size, especially of large things (*the package is not heavy but its sheer bulk makes it difficult to move*). **2** the main part (*the bulk of their money goes on housing*). ● **in bulk** in a large quantity. ● *vb* to make fuller, to increase in size (*use weights to bulk up your muscles*). ● **bulk large** (*fml*) to be important or prominent (*education does not bulk large in his plans*).

bulkhead /bulk-hed/ *n* an inside wall between one part of a ship and another.

bulky /bul-kee/ *adj* very large and awkward to move or carry.

bull[1] /bool/ *n* **1** the male of cattle. **2** the male ox, elephant, whale, etc.

bull[2] /bool/ *n* a ruling by the pope.

bulldog /bool-dog/ *n* a type of dog.

bulldozer /bool-doe-zer/ *n* a heavy tractor for clearing away obstacles and making land level.

bullet /boo-let/ *n* a small piece of metal shot from a rifle or pistol.

bulletin /boo-le-tin/ *n* **1** a short, official report of news. **2** a printed information sheet or newspaper (*the company bulletin*).

bulletproof /boo-let-proof/ *adj* not able to be pierced by bullets (*a bulletproof vest*).

bullfrog /bool-frog/ *n* a large frog.

bullion /bool-yon/ *n* uncoined gold and silver in lumps.

bulls-eye /boolz-eye/ *n* **1** the center of a target. **2** a shot that hits it. **3** a type of candy.

bully /boo-lee/ *n* a person who uses his or her strength to hurt or to terrify those who are weaker. ● *vb* to intimidate, oppress, or hurt (*bullying younger boys/bullied people into doing what he wants*).

bulrush /bool-rush/ *n* a tall weed.

bumblebee /bum-bel-bee/ *n* a large type of bee.

bump /bump/ *n* **1** a heavy blow, or the dull noise made by it (*receive a bump on the head in the accident*). **2** a lump caused by a blow. ● *vb* to knock against. ● *adj* **bumpy**

bumper /bum-per/ *n* **1** (*old*) a full glass or cup. **2** a protective bar at the front and the back of an automobile. ● *adj* unusually large or full (*a bumper harvest*).

bumptious /bum(p)-shes/ *adj* conceited, too full of oneself.

bun /bun/ *n* **1** a small cake. **2** hair styled in a rounded mass.

bunch /bunch/ *n* **1** a group or collection of things of the same kind (*a bunch of flowers/a bunch of bananas/a bunch of keys*). **2** (*inf*) a group of people (*her friends are a nice bunch*). ● *vb* to come or put together in groups or bunches (*traffic bunching on motorways/players bunched up on the field*).

bundle /bun-del/ *n* a collection of things tied together. ● *vb* **1** to tie in a bundle (*bundle up the old clothes for the rummage sale*). **2** to force to go in a hurry (*bundle the children off to school*).

bungalow /bung-ga-loe/ *n* a low house usually of one story.

bungee jumping /bun-jee jum-ping/ *n* the act of jumping from a high place while the ankles are secured by an elastic cord.

bungle /bung-gul/ *vb* to do badly or clumsily (*bungle a deal and lose the firm money*). ● *also n.*

bunion /bun-yon/ *n* a swelling on the foot, especially on the big toe.

bunk /bungk/ *n* **1** a narrow bed, especially in a ship. **2** one of a pair of beds placed one above the other (*bunk beds*).

bunker /bung-ker/ *n* **1** a ship's coal store. **2** a large chest for storing coal. **3** (*Br*) *see* **sand trap**.

bunny /bu-nee/ *n* the informal name for a rabbit.

Bunsen burner /bun-sin bur-ner/ *n* a pipe mounted on a stand through which gas flows and which is lit to make a flame. It is used in science classes and laboratories.

bunt /bunt/ *v* to hit a baseball very lightly.

bunting /bun-ting/ *n* **1** a material used for making flags. **2** flags.

buoy /boy/ *n* an object floating in a fixed position to show ships the safe course. ● *vb* **1** to keep afloat. **2** to support, to keep high (*profits buoyed up by the export market/buoy up his hopes*). **3** to raise the spirits of (*thoughts of going home buoyed him up*).

buoyant /boy-ant/ *adj* **1** floating, able to float easily (*cork is a buoyant material*). **2** cheerful, optimistic (*in buoyant mood*). ● *n* **buoyancy** /boy-an-see/.

bur, burr /bur/ *n* the prickly seed container of certain plants.

burden /bur-den/ *n* **1** a load. **2** the chorus of a song. **3** the leading idea (of). ● *vb* to load heavily. ● *adj* **burdensome** /bur-den-sum/ (*a burdensome task*).

bureau /byoo-ro/ *n* (*pl* **bureaux** *or* **bureaus**) **1** (*Br*) a writing desk with drawers (*an antique bureau*). **2** an office (*an accommodation bureau/an exchange bureau*).

bureaucracy /byoo-rok-ra-see/ *n* **1** a system of government by paid officials working for a government (*civil service bureaucracy*). **2** these officials taken as a group. **3** a system of doing things officially, often unnecessarily complicated and time-consuming (*complain about the bureaucracy involved in getting a license*).

burger /bur-ger/ *n see* **hamburger**.

burglar /bur-glar/ *n* a thief who breaks into a house.

burglary /bur-gla-ree/ *n* the crime of breaking into a house.

burgle /bur-gul/ *vb* to commit burglary.

burial /ber-ee-al/ *n* the act of putting into a grave.

burlap /bur-lap/ *a* course material used in making sacks.

burlesque /bur-lesk/ *n* a comic or mocking imitation, a parody, a caricature. ● *also adj and vb.*

burly /bur-lee/ *adj* stout, big and strong (*troublemakers thrown out by burly doormen*).

burn /burn/ *vb* (*pt, pp* **burned** /burnd/ *or* **burnt** /burnt/) **1** to be alight, to give out heat (*wood that burns easily*). **2** to be on fire (*the house is burning*). **3** to destroy or damage by fire (*all their possessions were burned in the blaze*). **4** to hurt or injure by fire (*he was badly burned in the fire*). **5** to be very hot (*burn with fever*). **6** to feel great anger, passion, etc. ● *n* a hurt caused by fire (*receive severe burns in the fire*).

burner /bur-ner/ *n* the part of a stove, etc., from which the flame comes.

burnish /bur-nish/ *vb* to polish. ● *also n.*

burr /bur/ *n* a bur.

burrito /bu-ree-toe/ *n* a Mexican dish of a **tortilla** wrapped around spicy beans or meat.

burrow /bu-ro/ *n* a hole in the earth made by certain animals, e.g., rabbits, foxes, etc. ● *vb* **1** to make by digging (*burrow a hole*). **2** to search for something (*burrow in her pocket for keys*).

burst /burst/ *vb* (*pt, pp* **burst**) **1** to break in pieces (*the balloon burst*). **2** to rush, to go suddenly or violently (*burst into the room*). ● *n* a sudden outbreak (*a burst of applause*).

bury /ber-ee/ *vb* **1** to put into a grave. **2** to put under ground.

bus /bus/ *n* a large road vehicle for carrying

passengers (short for **omnibus**). ● *vb* (**bussed, bussing** *or* **bused, busing**) to transport by bus (*bus the children to school*).

bush /**boosh**/ *n* **1** a small low tree. **2** wild, uncleared country; forest country.

bushel /**boo**-shel/ *n* a dry measure (35.3 liters) for grain, etc.

bushy /**boo**-shee/ *adj* **1** full of bushes. **2** thick-growing (*bushy hair*).

business /**biz**-nis/ *n* **1** one's work or job (*selling furniture is his business*). **2** trade and commerce (*a career in business*). **3** a matter that concerns a particular person (*none of your business*). ● **businesslike** *adj*.

bust /**bust**/ *n* **1** a statue showing only the head, shoulders, and breast of a person (*a bust of Shakespeare*). **2** the shoulders and breast.

bustle[1] /**bu**-sel/ *vb* to move about busily and often fussily (*bustling about preparing a meal*). ● *n* noisy movement, hurry.

bustle[2] /**bu**-sel/ *n* a frame or pad once worn to hold out the back of a woman's skirt.

busy /**bi**-zee/ *adj* **1** always doing something (*too busy to visit her family*). **2** at work, engaged in a job, etc. (*he's busy and will call you back*). **3** full of people, traffic, etc. (*busy shops/busy streets*). ● *vb* to occupy (*busy oneself with Christmas preparations*). ● *adv* **busily** /**bi**-zi-lee/.

busybody /**bi**-zee-bod-ee/*n* one who shows too a lot of interest in the affairs of others, a meddler.

butcher /**boo**-cher/ *n* **1** one who kills and sells animals for food. **2** a cruel killer (*the leader of the enemy army was a butcher*). ● *vb* **1** to kill for food. **2** to kill cruelly.

butchery /**boo**-che-ree/ *n* cruel slaughter.

butler /**but**-ler/ *n* the chief manservant in a household, formerly in charge of the wine cellar.

butt[1] /**but**/ *n* **1** a large barrel. **2** the thicker end of a thing (*the butt of a rifle*). ● *vb* to strike with the head or horns (*butted by a ram*).

butt[2] /**but**/ *n* **1** a mark to be shot at. **2** the mound behind the targets for rifle practice. **3** a person who is always being made fun of (*the butt of his jokes*).

butter /**but**-er/ *n* an oily food made from milk.

buttercup /**but**-er-cup/ *n* a common yellow wild flower.

butterfly /**but**-er-flaee/ *n* **1** an insect with large colorful wings. **2** a frivolous unreliable person.

buttermilk /**but**-er-milk /*n* the milk that remains after the butter has been made.

butterscotch /**but**-er-scotch/ *n* a hard toffee.

button /**but**-on/ *n* **1** a knob or disc to fasten one part of a garment to another. **2** something shaped like a button, especially a knob or switch on an electrical appliance (*press the red button to switch on*). ● *vb* to fasten with buttons (*button up your coat*).

buttonhole /**but**-on-hole/ *n* **1** a hole for a button. **2** a flower worn in a buttonhole. ● *vb* to stop and hold in conversation (*he buttonholed me and bored me with his holiday plans*).

buy /**bye**/ *vb* (*pt, pp* **bought**) to obtain by paying for.

buyer /**bye**-yer/ *n* **1** one who buys. **2** one whose job is to buy goods (*the buyer in the dress department*).

buzz /**buz**/ *n* a humming noise. ● *also vb*.

buzzard /**bu**-zard/ *n* a type of hawk.

by /**bye**/ *prep* **1**. next to (*sit by me*). **2** by the means of (*it was built by hand/ we traveled by train*). **3** through the work of (*built by the Egyptians*) ● *adv* **1** near (*it's by the door*). **2** past (*in times gone by*).

by and by /bye-an-**bye**/ *adv* soon (*I'll see you by and by*). ● *n* **by-and-by** a future occasion or time.

bye /**bye**/ *n* **1** in cricket, a run made from a ball that is not hit. **2** in a competition, a pass without contest into the next round.

bye-law *see* **bylaw**.

by-election /**bye**-e-lec-shun/ *n* an election held when the person elected at a general election has resigned or has died.

bygone /**bye**-gon/ *adj* (*fml*) past (*in bygone days*). ● *npl* **bygones** past events.

bylaw, bye-law /**by**-law/ *n* a law made by a local body and applying to the area in which the body has authority.

by-product /**by**-prod-uct/ *n* something made in the course of making a more important article.

byroad *n see* **byway**.

bystander /**bye**-stan-der/ *n* an onlooker, a spectator (*bystanders at the accident scene giving statements to the police*).

byte /**bite**/ *n* the unit of storage in a computer memory.

byway /**bye**-way/ *n* a side road.

C

C, c /see/ **1** the third letter of the alphabet. **2** (*mus*) the first note of the scale of C major.

cab /cab/ *n* **1** (*inf*) a taxi. **2** (*old*) a horse carriage for public hire. **3** the driver's part of a railway engine or truck.

cabaret /ca-ba-**ray**/ *n* a form of light entertainment consisting of songs and dancing, usually performed in a nightclub or restaurant (*diners watching the cabaret*).

cabbage /ca-bidge/ *n* a common vegetable with edible leaves formed into a bud.

cabin /ca-bin/ *n* **1** a small, simple house, a hut (*a log cabin*). **2** a room on a ship for passengers to stay in. **3** the space available for passengers or crew on an aircraft. **4** the covered part of a yacht.

cabinet /cab-net/ *n* **1** a display case. **2** a piece of furniture with drawers (*a filing cabinet*). **3** a case or container for a radio, television, etc. **4** (*often cap*) the body of official advisers to a president, governor, etc.: in the US, composed of the heads of various governmental departments.

cable /cay-bl/ *n* **1** a strong rope, often of wire. **2** a chain attached to a ship's anchor. **3** an undersea or underground telegraph or telephone line. **4** a bundle of electric wires enclosed in a pipe. **5** a message sent by cable. **6** cable television. ● *vb* to send a message by cable.

cablegram /cay-bl-gram/ *n* a more formal name for cable, sense **5**.

cable television /cay-bl te-le-vi-zhon/ *n* a television service that is supplied by using underground cables.

cacao /ca-kaow/ *n* a tropical tree that bears seeds from which chocolate and cocoa are made.

cackle /ca-kl/ *n* **1** the shrill, broken sound of a hen or goose. **2** noisy chatter (*the cackle of people gossiping*). **3** loud unpleasant laughter (*try to ignore the cackle coming from the other room*). ● *also vb.*

cacophony /ca-cof-u-nee/ *n* (*fml*) loud, unpleasant mixture of different sounds. ● *adj* **cacophonous** /ca-cof-u-nuss/.

cactus /cac-tus/ *n* (*pl* cacti /cac-tie/) a desert plant with fleshy stems, reduced or prickly leaves, and often bright, colorful flowers.

CAD /see-ay-dee/ *abbr* = **1 computer-aided design**: design (of products) using a computer. **2 Canadian dollars**: CAD is the symbol used by currency exchanges.

cadet /ca-det/ *n* **1** someone training in the armed forces. **2** a boy at a military school. **3** (*fml*) a younger son.

café /ca-fay/ *n* a coffeehouse, a small restaurant serving light meals.

cafeteria /ca-fe-tir-ee-ya/ *n* a restaurant in which a person serves him or herself from a variety of meals that are displayed on or behind a counter.

caffeine /ca-feen/ *n* a chemical that is a stimulant and is in tea, coffee and some soft drinks.

cage /cage/ *n* **1** a box with one or more walls consisting of bars or wire netting in which animals or birds can be kept. ● *vb.* to shut in a cage or prison (*cage the rabbits/cage the prisoners*).

cake /cake/ *n* **1** a dessert, made from flour, eggs, milk, sugar, etc., that is baked and usually covered with icing. **2** a small, usually flat amount of dough, or some other food, that is baked or fried. **3** a small, flat lump (*a cake of soap*).

calamity /ca-la-mi-tee/ *n* **1** a tragedy (*the earthquake was a calamity for the whole area*). **2** a serious misfortune (*losing his job was a calamity for the family*). ● *adj* **calamitous**.

calcium /cal-see-um/ *n* a soft, silver-white metal that is found in chalk, marble, etc., and is the basic part of bones, teeth, and shells.

calculate /cal-kyu-late/ *vb* **1** to work with numbers and mathematics. **2** to estimate (*calculate the cost of the repair work*). **3** to plan for a purpose (*a question calculated to trick us*). ● *adj* **calculable** / cal-kyu-la-bl/.

calculating /cal-kyu-late-ing/ *adj* **1** scheming, clever, or sly, especially in a selfish way.

calculation /cal-kyu-lay-shun/ *n* **1** the act or process of calculating (*the calculation of the cost*). **2** a sum (*made a mistake in the calculation*).

calculator *n* a small electronic machine used to make arithmetical and mathematical calculations.

calendar /ca-len-dar/ *n* a table showing the relation of the days of the week to the dates of a particular year.

calf[1] /caf/ *n* (*pl* calves /cavz/) the young of the cow, elephant, whale, etc.

calf[2] /caf/ (*pl* calves /cavz/) the fleshy back part of the leg below the knee.

calfskin /caf-skin/ *n* a type of leather made from a calf's skin.

calico /ca-li-co/ *n* **1** a kind of cotton cloth from India.

2 a cat with a coat that is a mix of black, brown, yellow, or orange.

calk *see* **caulk.**

call /cawl/ *vb* **1** to say or read in a loud voice; to shout or announce. **2** to give a name (*call her daughter Amy*) **3** to ask to come (*call the next witness*). **4** to make a short visit (*call on her mother on her way home*). ● *n* **1** a cry (*a call for help*). **2** a short visit. **3** a telephone call. **4** need, demand (*there is no call for that brand of coffee in this store*). ● **a close call** a narrow escape.

calligraphy /ca-lig-ro-fee/ *n* **1** handwriting as an art. **2** the art of writing well.

calling /caw-ling/ *n* (*fml*) **1** profession or employment. **2** an inner urging toward some profession.

callous /ca-lus/ *adj* hardened, unfeeling, insensitive (*a callous treatment of animals*). ● *n* **callousness** /ca-lus-ness/.

calm /cahm/ *adj* **1** quiet, still (*a calm day*). **2** unexcited, not agitated (*remained calm when the building went on fire*). ● *n* **1** stillness. **2** freedom from excitement (*admire her calm during the bomb scare*). ● *vb* to make calm. ● *n* **calmness** /cahm-nes/.

calorie /ca-lo-ree/ *n* **1** a measure of heat. **2** a unit for measuring the energy value of food (*diet by reducing the number of calories eaten*).

calve /cav/ *vb* to give birth to a calf.

calypso /ca-lip-so/ *n* songs sung as originally by the native people of Trinidad, with stresses and short, emphasized rhythms.

cam /cam/ *n* a wheel-like part of a machine that creates a straight movement from a rotating one.

camcorder /cam-cor-der/ *n* a portable video camera that records pictures and sound.

camel /ca-mel/ *n* an animal, found in Asian and African deserts, that has a long neck, cushioned feet, and one or two humps on its back (*Arabian camels have one hump, and Bactrian camels have two humps*).

cameo /ca-me-o/ *n* **1** a raised carving (usually of the side view of a person's head) on a gem or shell, with a different-colored background. **2** a precious stone with a raised design carved on it, often of a different color. **3** a small but important role in a film or play performed by a celebrity.

camera /ca-me-ra/ *n* a device for taking photographs, consisting of a closed box containing film on which an image is formed when light enters through a lens.

camisole /ca-mi-sole/ *n* a woman's light undergarment, usually sleeveless and trimmed in lace,

worn on the upper part of the body (*wear a camisole under a sheer blouse*).

camp /camp/ *n* **1** a place where people live in tents, caravans, huts, etc. (*a holiday camp/a military camp*). **2** a group of tents, caravans, huts, or other kinds of temporary shelter. ● *vb* to stay in or set up a camp.

campaign /cam-pane/ *n* **1** a battle or series of battles in a war. **2** any series of actions, meetings, etc. directed to one purpose (*a campaign to save the school*). ● *vb* to take part in or conduct a campaign (*campaigning against the new highway*).

camphor /cam-for/ *n* a strong-smelling chemical mixture used in protecting fabrics from moths, in making plastics, and in medicine.

campus /cam-pus/ *n* the grounds of a school or college.

can[1] /can/ *vb* am, are, or is able to.

can[2] /can/ *n* a small metal container. ● *vb* (**canned, canning**) to put into tins to preserve (*employed to can vegetables*).

canal /ca-nal/ *n* a humanmade waterway.

canary /ca-nay-ree/ *n* a small, yellow bird often kept as a pet. ● *adj* bright yellow.

cancel /can-sel/ *vb* (**canceled, canceling**) **1** to cross out. **2** to do away with. ● *n* **cancellation** /can-se-lay-shum/.

cancer /can-ser/ *n* **1** a harmful, sometimes fatal growth in the body (*he needs surgery for cancer of the lung*). **2** a growing evil (*meaningless violence is a cancer in modern society*).

Cancer /can-ser/ *n* **1** a northern constellation shaped like a crab. **2** a sign of the zodiac, used in astrology. **3** a person who was born under this astrological sign.

candid /can-did/ *adj* very honest or frank in what you say (*my candid opinion/a candid person*). ● *adv* **candidly.**

candidate /can-di-date/ *n* **1** someone who seeks a post or position (*interview candidates for the job of manager*). **2** someone who takes an exam.

candle /can-dl/ *n* a mass of formed, shaped wax or tallow containing a wick for lighting.

candlestick /can-del-stick/ *n* a holder for a candle.

candour /can-dor/ *n* frankness.

candy /can-dee/ *n* **1** sugar hardened by boiling. **2** any sweet or sweets (*a box of candy*). ● *vb* to preserve by boiling with sugar.

cane /cane/ *n* **1** a usually bendable, slender, jointed, hollow stem, such as bamboo, sugar cane, etc. **2** a walking stick (*an old man leaning on his cane*). ● *vb* to beat with a cane.

cane sugar /**cane**-shu-gar/ n sugar obtained from the sugar cane.

canine /**cay**-nine/ adj having to do with dogs or other animals in the dog family. ● n one of the pointed teeth in the front of the mouth (*also* **canine tooth**).

canister /**ca**-nis-ter/ n a small box or tin (*a canister of tea*).

cannibal /**ca**-ni-bal/ n **1** a person who eats human flesh. **2** an animal that eats flesh of its own species. ● n **cannibalism** /**ca**-ni-ba-li-zum/.

cannon /**ca**-non/ n a large, mounted weapon.

cannonball /**ca**-nun-bol/ n an iron ball fired from a cannon.

cannot *often shortened to* **can't** v to be unable to do something (*he cannot swim*).

canoe /ca-**noo**/ n a narrow, light boat moved by paddles.

canola /ca-**no**-la/ n the seeds of a variety of the rape plant, used to make cooking oil.

canon /**ca**-non/ n **1** the law or laws of a church. **2** a member of clergy who lives according to the laws in a church.

canopy /**ca**-no-pee/ n a hanging cover forming a shelter above a throne, bed, etc. (*a canopy over the porch to keep out the sunlight*).

cant¹ /**cant**/ n **1** a special way of speaking used by a particular group of people (*thieves' cant*). **2** meaningless or insincere talk (*just political cant*).

cant² /**cant**/ vb to tilt up (*the ship began to cant*). ● n a tilt (*a table with a definite cant*).

can't *contraction* a shortened form of **cannot**.

cantaloupe /**can**-ta-lope/ n a type of melon with sweet orange flesh.

canteen /can-**teen**/ n **1** a place where food and drink can be obtained in a camp, factory, office, etc. **2** a small metal or plastic container used to carry water.

canter /**can**-ter/ vb to gallop at a smooth, easy pace (*horses cantering over the meadow*). ● *also* n.

cantor /**can**-ter/ n someone who leads the singing and prayer in a synagogue.

canvas /**can**-vas/ n **1** a coarse cloth of cotton, hemp, or linen, often unbleached, and used for sails, tents, etc. **2** the sails of a ship. **3** an oil painting (*sell a canvas by Picasso*).

canvass /**can**-vas/ vb **1** to ask for votes or orders (*politicians knocking on people's doors to canvass for votes*). ● n **canvasser**. **2** to look at or discuss in detail.

canyon /**can**-yin/ n a long, narrow valley between cliffs, often with a river or stream flowing through it.

cap /**cap**/ n **1** a covering for the head with no brim or only part of one (*boys wearing school caps*). **2** a cover or top piece (*the cap of a bottle*). ● vb (**capped, capping**) **1** to put a cap on (*cap the bottle*). **2** to improve on (*cap his opponent's performance*). **3** to impose an upper limit on (*cap local government spending*).

capable /**cay**-pa-bl/ adj **1** able to (*capable of doing better*). **2** likely to (*capable of committing violent acts*). **3** able to do things well, efficient (*a capable manager*). ● n **capability** /cay-pa-**bi**-li-teel/.

capacity /ca-**pa**-si-tee/ n **1** ability to hold or contain (*a capacity of 10 gallons/a seating capacity of 2000*). **2** ability to produce or perform, experience, etc. (*a great capacity for hard work*). **3** (*fml*) position (*in his capacity as chairman*).

cape¹ /**cape**/ n a short cloak for covering the shoulders, a sleeveless cloak.

cape² /**cape**/ n a piece of land jetting out into the water (*Cape Cod is a popular vacation spot*).

caper¹ /**cay**-per/ vb to jump about playfully (*children capering about in excitement*). ● n **1** a jump or leap. **2** a prank, a mischievous act. **3** a robbery.

caper² /**cay**-per/ n a kind of tree or shrub that has tiny, green flower buds that are picked and used to flavor food (*fish with a caper sauce*).

capillary /ca-**pil**-a-ree/ adj very small and thin, hairlike. ● npl **capillaries** small blood vessels.

capital /**ca**-pi-tal/ adj **1** chief (*the capital city*). **2** punishable by death (*a capital offence*). **3** (*inf*) excellent (*capital entertainment*). ● n **1** the top of a column or pillar. **2** the chief city. **3** money, especially when used for business (*borrow capital from the bank*). **4** a large letter, as used first in proper names.

capital punishment /**ca**-pi-tal **pun**-ish-ment/ n punishment by death (*in some states, murderers are subjected to capital punishment*).

capitalist /**ca**-pi-tal-ist/ n a wealthy businessman, a person who owns capital.

capitalism /**ca**-pi-ta-li-zum/ n an economic system where production is privately owned and run to make a profit.

caprice /ca-**preess**/ n a sudden desire or fancy, a whim (*a caprice made her change her plans*).

capricious /ca-**pri**-shus/ adj changeable, unreasonable (*too capricious to be relied on*).

capsize /cap-**size**/ vb to overturn or upset (*in the storm, the ship capsized*).

capsule /**cap**-sul/ n **1** a hollow pill containing medicine. **2** the part of a spacecraft containing the instruments and crew.

captain /**cap**-tin/ n **1** a commander. **2** an officer. **3** a leader (*the captain of the football team*). ● also vb.

caption /**cap**-shon/ n the heading over (or under) a newspaper report or picture.

captivate /**cap**-ti-vate/ vb to charm, to fascinate (*captivated by her beauty*).

captive /**cap**-tiv/ n a prisoner.

captivity /cap-**ti**-vi-tee/ n the state of being a prisoner.

captor /**cap**-tor/ n someone who takes a prisoner or holds something or someone captive.

capture /**cap**-shur/ vb **1** to take prisoner, to catch (*capture convicts trying to escape*). **2** to take control of (*capture the castle/capture the imagination*). ● n **1** act of taking prisoner. **2** the thing so taken.

car /**car**/ n **1** a wheeled vehicle (*a tramcar*). **2** a motorcar. **3** a carriage (*the dining car in the train*).

carafe /ca-**raf**/ n a glass bottle (*a carafe of wine*).

caramel /**ca**-ra-mel/ n **1** burnt sugar used as coloring in cooking (*ice cream flavored with caramel*). **2** a type of candy made with sugar, milk, etc. (*chew a caramel*).

carat /**ca**-rat/ n a unit of weight used for jewelry, equal to 200 milligrams

caravan /**ca**-ra-van/ n **1** a large, covered vehicle for passengers, circus animals, etc. **2** a group of people traveling together for safety.

caraway /**ca**-ra-way/ n a plant whose seeds are used to flavor cakes, breads, cheese, etc.

carbohydrate /car-bo-**hie**-drate/ n the substance in foods that gives you energy.

carbon /**cahr**-bun/ n a natural element, found in coal, charcoal, soot, etc.

carbon dioxide /**car**-bun die-**oc**-side/ n a gas without color or smell that is breathed out by people and animals and absorbed by plants.

carbon monoxide /**car**-bun mon-**oc**-side/ n a poisonous gas, without color or smell, produced by the exhaust systems of cars, etc.

carbon paper /**car**-bun **pay**-per/ n thin, prepared paper used to make copies of letters as they are written.

carburetor /**car**-bu-ray-tor/ n the part of a motor engine in which air is mixed with gasoline, etc., to make a vapor that will burn.

carcass /**car**-cas/ n the dead body of an animal (*carcasses in a butcher's shop*).

card[1] /**card**/ n a small piece of thick paper for various purposes (*playing cards/business cards/membership card/credit card*).

card[2] /**card**/ vb to comb wool or flax before making it into thread. ● n an instrument for combing wool or flax. ● n **carder** /**cor**-der/.

cardboard /**card**-bored/ n stiff, thick paper.

cardiac /**car**-dee-ac/ adj having to do with the heart (*cardiac disease*).

cardigan /**car**-di-gan/ n a sweater that buttons down the front.

cardinal /**car**-di-nal/ adj **1** very important, principal (*a cardinal virtue*). ● n in the Roman Catholic Church, a high-ranking official with the right to take part in the election of the pope. **2** a bright red, crested bird.

care /**care**/ n **1** worry (*a life full of care*). **2** attention (*read the article with care*). **3** being looked after (*in the care of a social worker*). ● vb **1** to be concerned or interested (*I don't care what you say*). **2** to look after (*cares for her neighbor's children*). **3** to have a liking or love (for) (*still cares for his wife*).

career /ca-**reer**/ n someone's work or profession in life (*a career in law*). ● vb to move at full speed (*the car careered downhill out of control*).

careful /**care**-ful/ adj **1** taking trouble. **2** cautious. ● adv **carefully**.

careless /**care**-less/ adj taking little or no trouble. ● adv **carelessly**. ● n **carelessness**.

caress /ca-**ress**/ vb to touch or stroke lovingly (*caressed her cheek*). ● also n.

caretaker /**care**-tay-ker/ n someone who looks after a building or place.

cargo /**car**-go/ n the goods carried by a ship, plane, etc. (*a cargo of tropical fruit*).

caribou /**ca**-ri-boo/ n the North American reindeer.

caricature /**ca**-ri-ca-choor/ n a cartoon picture that of a person or thing that shows a particular feature as being elaborated to make others laugh. ● vb to draw a caricature. ● n **caricaturist** /ca-ri-ca-choo-rist/.

carnage /**car**-nidge/ n widespread killing, slaughter (*the carnage of World War I*).

carnal /**car**-nal/ adj having to do with the body rather than the spirit.

carnation /car-**nay**-shun/ n a plant with usually double flowers of white, pink, or red that smell of cloves.

carnival /**car**-ni-val/ n **1** a time of feasting and merriment just before Lent, a Christian time of fasting. **2** a circus or fair (*the carnival is in town*).

carnivore /**car**-ni-vore/ *n* a flesh-eating animal (*lions are carnivores*). ● *adj* **carnivorous** /car-**ni**-vo-russ/.

carol /**ca**-rol/ *n* a song of joy, especially one sung at Christmas. ● *vb* (**caroled, caroling**) to sing joyfully.

carotid /ca-**rot**-id/ *n* having to do with the two large arteries in the neck.

carousal /ca-**row**-zul/ *n* (*fml*) a noisy drinking party.

carouse /ca-**rowz**/ *vb* (*fml*) to drink freely.

carousel, carrousel /ca-ro-**sel**/ *n* a merry-go-round; a rotating conveyor belt.

carp[1] /**carp**/ *vb* to find fault or complain, often unreasonably (*carping about petty details*).

carp /**carp**/ *n* a freshwater fish.

carpenter /**car**-pen-ter/ *n* someone who builds and repairs wooden things, especially for houses, ships, etc. ● *n* **carpentry** /**car**-pen-tree/.

carpet /**car**-pet/ *n* **1** a thick covering of wool or other material for a floor. **2** a covering (*a carpet of leaves*). ● *vb* **1** to cover with a carpet (*carpeted the stairs*). **2** to cover (*snow carpeting the fields*). **3** (*inf*) to scold, to reprimand (*carpet him for being late*).

carpetbag /**car**-pet-bag/ *n* an old-fashioned traveling bag made of carpeting.

carriage /**ca**-ridge/ *n* **1** act of carrying. **2** the price of carrying (*carriage extra*). **3** the way someone stands or moves (*she has a noble carriage*). **4** a cart with wheels or other passenger vehicle (*a royal carriage/a railway carriage*).

carrier /**ca**-ree-yer/ *n* **1** someone who carries or transports goods. **2** anyone or anything that carries (*a carrier of disease*).

carrier pigeon /**ca**-ree-yer **pi**-jin/ *n* a pigeon used for carrying letters.

carrion /**ca**-ree-yon/ *n* rotten flesh (*vultures feeding on carrion*).

carrot /**ca**-rot/ *n* an orange-red root vegetable.

carry /**ca**-ree/ *vb* **1** to take from one place to another (*carry chairs from the van to the hall*). **2** to go from one place to another (*the sound of his voice carried tothe next room*). **3** to have or hold (*carry great responsibility/carry a whole range of goods*). ● **carry on 1** to continue to do (*carry on speaking*). **2** to behave badly or in an uncontrolled manner. ● **carry out** to perform (*carry out the operation*).

cart /**cart**/ *n* a two-wheeled vehicle or wagon for carrying goods. ● *vb* to carry by cart (*cart the rubbish to the dump*). ● *n* **carter** /**car**-ter/.

cartilage /**car**-ti-lige/ *n* an elastic substance surrounding the joints of bones.

cartography /car-**tog**-ra-fee/ *n* the art of mapmaking. ● *n* **cartographer** /cor-**tog**-ra-fer/.

carton /**car**-ton/ *n* a cardboard box (*a carton of milk*).

cartoon /car-**toon**/ *n* **1** a comic drawing. **2** an animated drawing. ● *n* **cartoonist** /car-**too**-nist/.

cartridge /**car**-tridge/ *n* **1** the container for the explosive that fires the bullet or shell from a gun. **2** any small container that carries a substance for a larger device (*the ink cartridge for our printer is empty*).

carve /**carve**/ *vb* **1** to cut into a special shape (*carve a piece of wood into the shape of an animal*). **2** to make by cutting wood or stone (*carve animals out of stone*). **3** to cut into slices (*carve the meat*).

carver /**car**-ver/ *n* **1** someone who carves. **2** a carving knife.

cascade /ca-**scade**/ *n* **1** a waterfall. **2** something like a waterfall (*a cascade of hair down her back*). ● *vb* to fall or drop in a cascade.

case[1] /**case**/ *n* **1** a box or container (*a watch in a case/a case of wine*). **2** a covering (*seed cases of plants*). **3** a suitcase. **4** a piece of furniture for displaying or containing things (*a glass case in the jewelry shop/a bookcase*).

case[2] /**case**/ **1** an event, instance, or example (*in that case you must go now/it's a case of having to spend less/a case of measles/a case of blackmail*). **2** a person having medical, etc., treatment (*a psychiatric case*). **3** a statement of facts and arguments or reasons (*there's a good case for believing him*). **4** a question to be decided in a court of law, a lawsuit.

cash /**cash**/ *n* **1** coins or paper money, not checks or credit cards, etc. **2** immediate payment rather than by credit (*a discount for paying cash*). **3** (*inf*) money generally (*make a lot of cash*). ● *vb* to turn into money (*cash traveler's checks*).

cashier /ca-**sheer**/ *n* someone who has charge of money in a store or a bank. ● *vb* to dismiss (an officer from the army, navy, etc.) in disgrace.

cash machine *see* automatic teller machine.

cashmere /**cazh**-meer/ *n* a fine, soft, woolen material.

casino /ca-**see**-no/ *n* a hall for dancing or gambling.

cask /**cask**/ *n* a barrel.

casket /**cas**-ket/ *n* **1** a jewel case. **2** a coffin, or box in which a dead body is buried.

casserole /**ca**-se-role/ *n* **1** a glass or earthenware dish in which food can be cooked in an oven and then served at table. **2** the food so prepared (*a beef casserole*).

cassette /ca-**set**/ *n* a flat plastic case containing tape for recording or playing back sounds or pictures.

cassock /**ca**-sok/ *n* a long, close-fitting robe worn by clergymen and those taking part in services.

cast /cast/ *vb* (*pt, pp* **cast**) **1** to throw (*cast a pebble in the pool*). **2** to throw off (*snakes casting their skins*). **3** to shape (melted metal) in a mold. **4** to give parts to actors in (*cast his new play*). ● *n* **1** a throw. **2** a squint (in the eye). **3** a model made in a mold. **4** the actors in a play.

castaway /**cas**-ta-way/ *n* a shipwrecked person.

caste /cast/ *n* in India, the social class or rank into which someone is born.

caster /**ca**-ster/ **1** a small jar or bottle with holes in the top for sprinkling salt, sugar, etc. **2** a small wheel on a piece of furniture, making it easy to move (*a wardrobe on casters*).

castigate /**ca**-sti-gate/ *vb* (*fml*) to scold or criticize severely (*employees castigated for arriving late*). ● *n* **castigation** /ca-sti-**gay**-shon/.

cast iron /**ca**-sting eye-urn/ *n* iron that has been melted and shaped in a mould. ● *adj* very strong.

castle /**ca**-sel/ *n* **1** a large building, usually one strengthened against attack (*Windsor Castle*). **2** a piece in chess. ● **castles in the air** a daydream.

casual /**cazh**-yoo-ul/ *adj* **1** happening by chance (*find out from a casual remark*). **2** not regular (*casual work in the summer*). **3** uninterested (*casual attitude to his work*). **4** not careful, not thorough (*take a casual glance at the page*). **5** informal (*casual clothes*). ● *adv* **casually**.

casualty /**ca**-zhul-tee/ *n* **1** an accident, especially a fatal one (*there's been a casualty at the mine*). **2** an injured or wounded person (*no casualties in the train accident*). **3** something that is damaged or destroyed as a result of an event (*the library has closed—a casualty of spending cuts*).

cat /cat/ *n* **1** an animal with soft fur and sharp claws, commonly kept as a pet. **2** a family of meat-eating animals (*lions are members of the cat family*).

catacomb /**ca**-ta-com/ *n* an underground tomb.

catalog /**ca**-ta-lawg/ *n* a complete list arranged in a special order so that the items can be found easily (*a catalog of the books in the library*). ● *vb* to make a list (*cataloging the books according to the alphabetical order of the authors' last names*).

catalyst /**ca**-ta-list/ *n* **1** a substance that aids a chemical reaction but is not itself changed. **2** something or someone that causes a change in a

situation or has a marked effect on the course of events (*World War I was a catalyst for social change*).

catamaran /ca-ta-me-**ran**/ *n* a sailing boat made in long, narrow parts joined by a bridge.

catapult /**ca**-ta-pult/ *n* a machine used for hurling heavy stones in war.

cataract /**ca**-ta-ract/ *n* **1** a large waterfall. **2** a disease of the eye, causing gradual loss of sight.

catastrophe /ca-**ta**-stro-fee/ *n* a sudden, great disaster (*the flood was a catastrophe for the whole area*). ● *adj* **catastrophic** /ca-ta-**strof**-ic/.

catch /catch/ *vb* (*pt, pp* **caught** /cot/) **1** to take and hold (*catch the ball*). **2** to capture (*catch the remaining prisoners*). **3** to become accidentally attached or held (*her skirt caught on the door handle*). **4** to surprise in the act of (*catch him stealing*). **5** to succeed in hearing (*catch what he said*). **6** to get by infection (*catch measles from his sister*). **7** to be in time for, to get on (*catch the first bus in the morning*). ● *n* **1** the act of catching. **2** the number of fish caught at one time. **3** a fastener (*a gate catch*). **4** a snag (*a catch in the plan*). **5** a song in which the same words and tune are repeated by several singers starting at different times.

catchy /**ca**-chee/ *adj* memorable (*a catchy tune*).

categorical /ca-te-**gawr**-ic-al/ *adj* definite (*give a categorical denial*). ● *adv* **categorically**.

category /**ca**-te-go-ree/ *n* a class or group of things in a system of grouping (*various categories in the dog-judging competition/books in categories of fiction, nonfiction, and reference*).

cater /**cay**-ter/ *vb* **1** to supply with food and drinks, especially at social occasions (*the restaurant catering for the wedding reception*). **2** to provide what is needed or desired by (*cater for a wide range of tastes*). ● *n* **caterer**.

caterpillar /**ca**-ter-pi-lar/ *n* **1** the wormlike larvae of insects such as the butterfly or moth.

cathedral /ca-**thee**-dral/ *n* the main church in a district in which a bishop has his throne.

catholic /**cath**-lic/ *adj* wide-ranging, broad, including many different things (*a catholic taste in books meant she read everything from comic books to Shakespeare*). ● *n* **catholicity** /ca-the-li-se-tee/.

Catholic /**cath**-lic/ *n* a member of the Roman Catholic Church. ● *also adj*.

catkin /**cat**-kin/ *n* the furry blossom of the willow, hazel, etc.

CAT scan /**cat**-scan/ *n* (CAT is short for **computerized axial tomography**) a series of X-rays that create a three-dimensional image of the body (*a CAT scan of the chest area*).

cattle /**cat**-tl/ *n pl* cows, bulls, and oxen.

caucus /**caw**-kes/ *n* a private meeting of leaders of a political party to decide policy, choose candidates, etc. (*the presidential candidate was decided at the caucus*).

caught *pt of* **catch**.

cauldron /**col**-drun/ *n* a large boiling pot (*the witch's cauldron*).

cauliflower /**caw**-li-fla-wer/ *n* a type of cabbage, of which the white, fleshy flower is eaten as a vegetable.

cause /**cawz**/ *n* **1** something or someone that produces an effect or result (*an electrical fault was the cause of the fire/he was the cause of his father's unhappiness*). **2** the reason for an action, a motive (*no cause to treat her so badly/little cause for complaint*). **3** a purpose, aim (*in the cause of peace*). ● *vb* to make happen.

causeway /**cawz**-way/ *n* **1** a road or path raised on a mound above the surrounding country, as over wet ground or water. **2** a paved road.

caustic /**caw**-stic/ *adj* **1** burning (*a caustic chemical substance*). **2** bitter, severe (*caustic remarks*). ● *adv* **caustically**.

caution /**caw**-shen/ *n* **1** carefulness, especially to avoid risk or danger (*cross the busy road with caution*). **2** warning (*receive a caution from the police to stop speeding*). ● *vb* **1** to warn against possible danger (*caution children against talking to strangers*). **2** to give a warning to, often with the threat of future punishment (*this time the police just cautioned him for careless driving*).

cautious /**caw**-shess/ *adj* careful, showing caution (*a cautious driver/cautious about spending a lot of money*).

cavalcade /ca-val-**cade**/ *n* a procession (*the president travels with a cavalcade of cars*) (originally, of people on horseback).

cavalier /ca-va-**leer**/ *n* an armed horseman. ● *adj* offhand, casual, and disrespectful (*a cavalier disregard for other people's feelings*). ● *adv* **cavalierly**.

cavalry /**ca**-val-ree/ *n* originally soldiers on horses, but now often riding in armored trucks or tanks.

cave /**cave**/ *n* a hollow place in the earth, as in a hillside extending back. ● **cave in** to fall in over a hollow.

cave man /**cave** man/ *n* **1** (*old*) a human who, in the earliest times, lived in a cave. **2** a man with very rough manners, especially toward women.

cavern /**ca**-vern/ *n* a large cave. ● *vb* to hollow out.

cavernous /**ca**-ver-nus/ *adj* large and hollow, like a cavern (*the lion opened its cavernous mouth*).

caviar(e) /**ca**-vee-ar/ *n* the eggs of sturgeon, salmon, and similar fish eaten as a delicacy.

cavity /**ca**-vi-tee/ *n* **1** a hollow place. **2** a hole (*a cavity in his tooth*).

cayenne /kie-**yen**/ *n* a very hot red pepper.

CCTV /**see**-**see**-**tee**-**vee**/ *abbr* = **closed-circuit television**: a type of surveillance camera system (*The thieves were seen on CCTV robbing the jeweler's shop*).

CD /**see dee**/ *abbr* = **compact disk** or **compact disc** (*Br*): a small, mirrored, plastic disk that stores music, images, or files that are read optically by a laser beam.

CD-ROM /**see**-dee-**rom**/ *abbr* = **compact disk read-only memory**: a disk that holds files that can be read by a computer, but the files cannot be altered.

cease /**sees**/ *vb* **1** to stop (*soldiers were ordered to cease firing/the factory has ceased making weapons*). **2** to come to an end (*the noise finally ceased*).

ceaseless /**sees**-less/ *adj* endless, continuous (*ceaseless chatter*).

cedar /**see**-dar/ *n* **1** a large, cone-bearing tree or its wood.

ceiling /**see**-ling/ *n* **1** the inside roof of a room. **2** the greatest height to which a particular aircraft can climb. **3** an upper limit (*a wages ceiling of 3%*).

celebrate /**se**-le-brate/ *vb* **1** to perform a religious ceremony. **2** to honor an event by feasting and rejoicing (*celebrate her birthday*). ● *n* **celebration** /se-le-**bray**-shon/.

celebrated /**se**-le-bray-ted/ *adj* famous (*the celebrated artist*).

celebrity /se-**le**-bri-tee/ *n* a famous person (*the new hall was opened by a local celebrity*).

celery /**se**-le-ree/ *n* a kind of vegetable, of which the green stem is eaten either cooked or raw.

celestial /se-**les**-chal/ *adj* **1** heavenly (*celestial beings such as angels*). **2** having to do with the sky (*celestial bodies such as planets*).

celibacy /**se**-li-ba-see/ *n* the state of being unmarried, not having sexual relationships.

celibate /**se**-li-bet/ *adj* unmarried, not having sexual relationships (*Catholic priests must remain celibate*).

cell /**sell**/ *n* **1** a small, bare room, especially in a prison or monastery. **2** a space in a honeycomb.

3 a single unit of living matter (*red blood cells*). **4** a unit of an electric battery. **5** a small group of people working toward the same end (*a terrorist cell*).

cellar /se-lar/ *n* an area underneath a house, often used for storage.

cello /che-lo/ (*short for* **violoncello**) a musical instrument of the violin family, between the viola and bass in size and pitch.

cellophane /se-lo-fane/ *n* a thin, transparent wrapping material (*wrap the flowers in cellophane*).

cell phone /sell fone/ *n* a cellular telephone.

cellular /sell-ye-lar/ *adj* having cells, made up of cells (*cellular tissue*).

cellular telephone /sell-ye-lar te-le-fone/ *n* a portable phone that transmits signals by radio waves.

cellulose /sell-ye-loze/ *n* a substance obtained from wood or plants and used in making paper, imitation silk, film, etc.

Celsius /sell-see-es/ *adj* a way of measuring temperature so that 0 degrees is the freezing point and 100 degrees is the boiling point.

cement /si-ment/ *n* a powdered substance that, mixed with liquid, forms a solid material used to make things stick together (*bricks stuck together with cement*). ● *vb* **1** to join with cement. **2** to unite closely (*cement their relationship by marrying*).

cemetery /se-me-te-ree/ *n* a burial ground, a graveyard.

censer /sen-ser/ *n* a decorated container in which incense is burned.

censor /sen-ser/ *n* someone who examines letters, books, films, etc., to see if they contain anything inappropriate, offensive, or harmful to society (*censors remove anything offensive in the film*). ● *also vb*. ● *n* **censorship** /sen-ser-ship/. ● *adj* **censorious** /sen-saw-ree-es/.

census /sen-ses/ *n* **1** an official counting of a country's population. **2** an official counting of other things (*take a traffic census on the new highway*).

cent /sent/ *n* a coin that is worth one-hundredth of a dollar, a penny.

centaur /sen-tawr/ *n* in Greek stories, an imaginary creature that is half man and half horse.

centenarian /sen-te-ne-ree-an/ *n* a person at least one hundred years old.

centenary /sen-tee-ne-ree/ *n* the one hundredth year after a certain event (*the centenary of the opening of the school*).

centennial /sen-ten-ee-al/ *adj* happening once every one hundred years.

center /sen-ter/ *n* **1** the middle point or part of anything (*the center of the circle/the center of the town*). **2** a place where certain activities or facilities are concentrated (*a shopping center*). **3** a political position that is not extreme (*people in the center of the party*). ● *vb* **1** to put into the middle (*centered the picture on the wall*). **2** to collect or concentrate at or around (*interests centering on sport*).

centimeter /sen-ti-mee-ter/ *n* one-hundredth of a meter.

centipede /sen-ti-peed/ *n* a small, insect-eating, caterpillar-like animal with a segmented body and many feet.

central /sen-tral/ *adj* **1** in the middle (*the central barrier in a highway*). **2** chief (*the central character in the novel*).

centralize /sen-tra-lize/ *vb, also* **centralise** (*Br*) to bring together to one place (*regions object to government being centralized*). ● *n* **centralization** /sen-tra-lie-zay-shon/ *also* **centralisation** (*Br*).

centrifugal /sen-trif-yew-gul/ *adj* describing a physical force that causes an object, that is rotating around a central point, to move away from that point.

centripetal /sen-trip-it-ul/ *adj* describing a physical force that pulls something toward the center point it is rotating around.

centurion /sen-choo-ree-en/ *n* (*old*) the captain of a hundred men, especially in an ancient Roman army.

century /sen-choo-ree/ *n* one hundred years.

ceramic /se-ra-mic/ *adj* having to do with pottery, earthenware, tile, etc.

ceramics /se-ra-mics/ *n* the art or work of making pottery, earthenware, tile, etc.

cereal /si-ree-al/ *adj n* **1** any grain that can be eaten (*wheat and barley are cereals*). **2** food made from such grain, often eaten at breakfast.

cerebral /se-ree-bral/ *adj* **1** having to do with the brain (*a cerebral tumor*). **2** intellectual rather than emotional (*cerebral poetry*).

ceremonial /se-re-mo-nee-al/ *n* the actions connected with a ceremony. ● *adj* having to do with a ceremony.

ceremonious /se-re-mo-nee-es/ *adj* (*fml*) full of ceremony, very formal (*ceremonious events*).

ceremony /se-re-mo-nee/ *n* **1** the performing of certain actions in a fixed order for a religious or other serious purpose (*a wedding ceremony*). **2** formal behavior, formality (*an occasion of great ceremony*).

certain /ser-ten/ *adj* 1 sure (*a certain victory*). 2 particular (*certain people*).

certainly /ser-ten-lee/ *adv* 1 undoubtedly. 2 willingly.

certainty /ser-ten-tee/ *n* 1 the state of being certain or sure (*I can say with certainty that he will succeed*). 2 that which is certain (*it's a certainty that they will win*).

certificate /ser-ti-fi-cate/ *n* a written statement of fact (*birth certificate/a certificate of insurance*).

certify /ser-ti-fie/ *vb* 1 to confirm formally the truth of a statement (*certify that he is the owner of the car*). 2 officially to declare a person crazy (*the patient was certified and sent to a mental hospital*).

chafe /chafe/ *vb* 1 to warm by rubbing. 2 to make sore or wear away by rubbing. 3 to be angry.

chain /chain/ *n* 1 a number of metal rings joined to form a rope (*the dog was fastened to the fence by a chain/prisoners in chains/a silver chain around her neck*). 2 a number of connected facts or events, a series (*a chain of events*). 3 a measure of length. 4 a range (of mountains). ● *vb* to bind or fasten with a chain (*chain the dog to the fence*).

chair /chair/ *n* 1 a movable seat with a back. 2 chairperson. 3 the seat or place of an official (e.g., of a professor in a university or a person controling a meeting). ● *vb* to be in charge of a meeting (*chairing the annual general meeting*).

chairman, chairperson, chairwoman /chair-man, chair-per-son, chair-wu-man/ *n* someone who controls a meeting.

chalet /sha-lay/ *n* a wooden house or hut with a steeply sloping roof, common in Switzerland.

chalice /cha-lis/ *n* 1 (*old*) a drinking cup. 2 a cup with a stem, especially used in church services.

chalk /chawk/ *n* 1 a soft, white limestone. 2 a piece of chalk used for writing on a blackboard. ● *vb* to mark with chalk. ● *adj* **chalky**.

chalk board /chawk bored/ *n* a smooth black or slate surface, usually in a classroom, which can be written on with chalk.

challenge /cha-lenj/ *vb* 1 to call on another to fight or play a match to see who is the better (*challenge him to a duel/challenge him to a game of darts*). 2 to doubt the truth of (*challenge his statement that the substance was safe/challenge his right to be present*). ● *n* 1 the daring of another to a contest. 2 a statement or action that questions something (*a challenge to the leader's authority*). 3 a difficult or exciting task (*his new job is a challenge*). ● *n* **challenger**.

chamber /chame-ber/ *n* 1 (*old*) a room. 2 a room in which a meeting takes place (*the judge asked the lawyers to meet in his chamber*). 3 an administrative group (*the Chamber of Commerce*). 4 the part of a gun in which the cartridge is held.

chamber music /chame-ber myoo-zik/ *n* music written to be played by only a few people (such as a quartet) for a small group, as in a room rather than a hall.

chameleon /ca-meel-yen/ *n* a type of lizard that can change the color of its skin.

champ /champ/ *vb* to chew noisily with the teeth (*horses champing hay*). ● *n* short for champion.

champagne /sham-pain/ *n* a type of sparkling white wine.

champion /cham-pee-en/ *n* 1 someone who has beaten all his or her rivals or opponents (*the club tennis champion*). 2 someone who fights for a certain cause, or for another person (*a champion of animal rights*). ● *vb* to defend or support (*champion the cause of freedom*).

championship /cham-pee-en-ship/ *n* 1 a series of contests or matches to discover the champion. 2 the state of being a champion.

chance /chans/ *n* 1 accident (*we met by chance*). 2 opportunity (*the chance to get a better job*). 3 risk (*take a chance and try to escape*). ● *vb* 1 (*fml*) to happen (*I chanced to see him yesterday*). 2 to risk (*it may rain on our picnic, but we'll just have to chance it*). ● *adj* accidental (*a chance meeting*).

chancel /chan-sel/ *n* the altar end of a church.

chancellor /chan-se-ler/ *n* 1 a country's leader or high government official (*Angela Merkel is the first female Chancellor of Germany*). 2 the chief judge of England. 3 the head of a university. ● **Chancellor of the Exchequer** in Britain, the chief minister of finance in the government.

chandelier /shan-de-lir/ *n* a hanging lamp frame with branches to hold lights (formerly candles).

change /change/ *vb* 1 to become different (*her lifestyle has changed/the wind changed*). 2 to make different (*change someone's attitude/change your clothes*). 3 to put or take one thing in place of another, to exchange (*change your library books*). ● *n* 1 a difference or alteration (*see a change in her/a change in the direction of the wind*). 2 money given in return for money received (*given the wrong change by the shop assistant*). 3 small coin (*I have only a $10 bill—I have no change*). ● *adj* **changeable**. ● *adj* **changeless**.

changeling /change-ling/ *n* (*myth*) a child put by fairies in the place of another, as told in folk tales.

channel /**cha**-nel/ *n* **1** the course of a river. **2** the deep part of a river where ships can sail safely. **3** a narrow sea.

chant /**chant**/ *vb* **1** to sing. **2** to recite slowly in a singing voice. ● *n* **1** a song. **2** a way of singing sacred music.

chaos /**kay**-as/ *n* a state of utter confusion, disorder (*the chaos in the room during the children's party*).

chaotic /kay-a-tic/ *adj* completely without order or arrangement (*chaotic traffic conditions in the snow*).

chap[1] /**chap**/ *vb* (**chapped, chapping**) to crack (*hands chapped by the cold*). ● *n* a crack in the skin, caused by cold and wet.

chap[2] /**chap**/ *n* (*inf*) a man, a fellow (*a friendly chap*).

chapel /**cha**-pel/ *n* a small church.

chaperon /**sha**-pe-rone/ *n* **1** especially formerly, an older person, usually a woman, who accompanies young unmarried people when they go out. **2** a person who supervises young people on an outing (*the chaperon of the Sunday school group*). ● *vb* to act as chaperon to.

chaplain /**cha**-plen/ *n* **1** the clergyman serving a private chapel. **2** a clergyman with the army, navy, or air force.

chaps /**chaps**/ *npl* protective leather leggings worn by people riding on horseback.

chapter /**chap**-ter/ *n* **1** a division of a book. **2** a meeting of the canons of a cathedral.

char /**char**/ *vb* (**charred, charring**) **1** to burn in part (*furniture charred in the fire*). **2** to burn the outside (*char the steak*).

character /**ca**-ric-ter/ *n* **1** a letter or figure or, as in Chinese, a symbol standing for a whole word. **2** a person's nature as known by words, deeds, etc. **3** a reputation (*not of very good character*). **4** a person in a story or play (*the chief characters in the novel*). **5** (*inf*) an odd, humorous, or interesting person (*he's quite a character*). **6** (*inf*) a person (*a nasty character*).

characteristic /**ca**-ric-te-**ris**-tic/ *n* a single point in a person's character, a special and recognizable quality in someone or something (*generosity is not one of his characteristics/a characteristic of the disease*). ● *adj* typical (*signs characteristic of the disease*).

characterize /**ca**-ric-te-rize/ *vb, also* **characterise** (*Br*) **1** to be characteristic or typical of. **2** (*fml*) to describe as (*characterize the terrorist attack as a bid for freedom*).

charade /sha-**rayd**/ *n* **1** a word game in which players guess the word clue without saying anything, just using motions. **2** something that is easily seen to be false (*the trial was just a charade as they had decided he was guilty*).

charcoal /**char**-cole/ *n* partly burned wood used as fuel (*steak grilled over charcoal*).

charge /**charge**/ *vb* **1** to ask a price (*charge $6 a ticket*). **2** to accuse (*charge him with murdering his brother*). **3** to rush (*children charging into the room*). **4** to attack at speed (*charge the enemy*). **5** to fill with electricity or energy (*charge the battery*). **6** to tell a person to do something as a duty (*charge them with getting the groom to the church*). ● *n* **1** a load of electricity or energy. **2** a price (*the hotel's expensive charge*). **3** a duty, especially that of a clergyman. **4** a violent attack. **5** an accusation (*bring a charge of murder*). ● *adj* **chargeable**. ● **take charge** to take command, take control.

chariot /**cha**-ree-et/ *n* (*old*) a horse-drawn, two-wheeled cart used in ancient times for war, racing, parades, etc.

charioteer /**cha**-ree-e-**teer**/ *n* (*old*) the driver of a chariot.

charity /**cha**-ri-tee/ *n* **1** a love of other human beings. **2** kindness to others. **3** generosity in giving to the poor. ● *adj* **charitable**. **4** an organization that raises money to help people in need or other good causes (*collecting money in aid of a children's charity*).

charlatan /**shar**-la-tan/ *n* someone who deceives by pretending to have special knowledge or skill (*the supposed doctor was a charlatan*).

charm /**charm**/ *n* **1** a magic spell (*the witch reciting a charm*). **2** an object or words possessing magical power (*wear a charm*). **3** any small ornament worn as decoration on a necklace, bracelet, or other jewelry (*one of the charms on her bracelet was of a flower*). **4** attractiveness of character, a pleasant quality (*succeeded in deceiving people because of her great charm*). **5** *pl* (*fml*) beauty (*use her charms to get her way*). ● *vb* **1** to put under a spell (*charmed by the wizard*). **2** to delight (*charmed by her personality*).

chart /**chart**/ *n* **1** a map, especially one for sailors. **2** a paper showing information in a graph or table (*a chart showing production progress*).

charter /**char**-ter/ *n* a written document granting certain rights. ● *vb* to hire (*charter a boat*).

chase[1] /**chase**/ *vb* **1** to run after (*chase the man who stole the old lady's bag*). **2** to drive away (*chase* *away the boys who were stealing the apples*). ● *n* a pursuit, a hunt.

chase^2 /**chase**/ *vb* **1** to engrave or cut figures on metal. **2** *n* a groove cut into a wall to provide space for a pipe.

chasm /**ka**-zm/ *n* **1** a wide, deep crack in the surface of the earth, a gorge, a canyon. **2** a wide gap or difference of opinion, attitudes, feelings, etc. (*the chasm between the two families*).

chaste /**chaste**/ *adj* pure, decent, or modest in nature.

chasten /**chay**-sen/ *vb* to teach by suffering or punishment (*chastened by the thought that he had caused his brother's death*).

chastise /chas-**tize**/ *vb* to punish severely, especially by beating. ● *n* **chastisement** /chas-**tize**-ment/.

chastity /**chas**-ti-tee/ *n* purity, the state of being chaste.

chat /**chat**/ *vb* (**chatted, chatting**) to talk about unimportant matters (*chat on the phone to her friend*). ● *n* a friendly talk.

chat room, chatroom /**chat** room/ *n* an Internet Web site that allows several members to send each other typed instant messages.

château /sha-**toe**/ *n* (*pl* **châteaux**) a French castle or country house.

chattel /**cha**-tel/ *n* **1** movable belongings, someone's possessions. **2** a slave or slaves.

chatter /**cha**-ter/ *vb* **1** to talk quickly and continuously, usually about something unimportant (*children chattering when the teacher was out of the room*). **2** to make meaningless sounds (*monkeys chattering*). ● *also n.* ● *n* **chatterer**.

chatterbox /**cha**-ter boks/ *n* one who chatters a great deal.

chauffeur /sho-**fer**/ *n* a person employed to drive someone's car. ● *also vb*.

chauvinism /**sho**-vi-ni-zm/ *n* too great a pride in one's country, race, sex, etc., leading to a dislike or mistreatment of others. ● *n* **chauvinist** /**sho**-vi-nist/.

cheap /**cheep**/ *adj* **1** of a low price. **2** of little value.

cheapen /**chee**-pen/ *vb* to lessen the price or value of.

cheat /**cheet**/ *vb* to deceive, to use unfair means. ● *n* **1** a trick. **2** a swindler.

check /**check**/ *vb* **1** to stop. **2** to slow down. **3** to scold. **4** to look at something to see if it is correct or in order. ● *n* **1** a sudden halt or obstacle. **2** a control. **3** a bill at a restaurant or bar. **4** (*Br* **cheque**) a slip of paper with a person's bank details on it used as payment, an order to the bank to pay out a sum of money from an account. ● *adj* divided into or marked by squares.

checkers /**che**-kers/ *npl* a game that is played between two people using 12 round, flat pieces on a board divided into checks, the objective being to capture the other player's pieces.

checkmate /**check**-mate/ *n* the winning move in chess. ● *vb* to defeat another's plans.

cheddar /**che**-der/ *n* a variety of cheese.

cheek /**cheek**/ *n* the side of the face (*kiss her on the cheek*).

cheep /**cheep**/ *n* a faint squeak, a chirp (*the cheep of a young bird*). ● *also vb*.

cheer /**cheer**/ *n* **1** (*old*) mood, disposition (*be of good cheer*). **2** a shout of joy or encouragement (*the cheers of the football supporters*). ● *vb* **1** to brighten up (*cheered him up by taking him to the movies/cheer the room up with some new curtains*). **2** to encourage, especially by shouts (*cheering on their football team*).

cheerful /**cheer**-ful/ *adj* **1** happy and lively (*a cheerful person/a cheerful mood*). **2** bright and attractive (*cheerful colors*).

cheerless /**cheer**-less/ *adj* sad, gloomy (*a cheerless room*).

cheese /**cheez**/ *n* a solid food made from milk.

cheetah /**chee**-ta/ *n* a large, wild animal of the cat family that is lean, fast and has a coat with black spots on it.

chef /**shef**/ *n* a cook in charge of a kitchen.

chemical /**ke**-mi-cal/ *adj* having to do with chemistry. ● *n* a substance studied in chemistry.

chemist /**ke**-mist/ *n* **1** someone who studies or works in chemistry.

chemistry /**ke**-mis-tree/ *n* the science that separates and studies the substance(s) of which all things are made.

cherish /**cher**-ish/ *vb* **1** to treat lovingly, to hold dear (*cherish his only daughter*). **2** to keep in the mind or heart (*cherish hopes of becoming wealthy/cherish her memory*).

Cherokee *n* the name of an American Indian nation, and its members, who live in Oklahoma and North Carolina.

cherry /**cher**-ee/ *n* **1** a small, pitted fruit. **2** a tree bearing cherries.

cherub /**cher**-ub/ *n* (*pl* **cherubs** *or* **cherubim**) **1** an angel. **2** in art, an angel pictured as a winged child. **3** a beautiful, innocent-looking child.

cherubic /che-**roo**-bic/ *adj* angelic.

chess /chess/ *n* a game of skill played on a checkered board by two people with 16 chessmen that are limited in their movements according to kind, the object being to capture the king.

chessmen /chess-men/ *n* game pieces used in chess, including a king, a queen, two rooks (or castles), two knights, two bishops, and eight pawns.

chest /chest/ *n* **1** a large, strong box. **2** the front, upper part of the body, from the shoulders to the lowest ribs.

chestnut /chest-nut/ *n* **1** a nut. **2** a tree bearing chestnuts. **3** a reddish brown horse. ● *adj* reddish brown.

chevron /shev-ron/ *n* a V-shaped strip of cloth worn on the sleeve as a sign of rank in the military.

chew /choo/ *vb* to crush with the teeth.

Cheyenne /sheye-en/ *n* the name of an American Indian nation, and its members, who live in Oklahoma and Montana.

chic /sheek/ *adj* smart, fashionable (*chic dress shop*).

chicanery /shi-cane-ree/ *n* trickery (*persuaded the old lady to leave him her money by chicanery*).

Chicana /ch-kah-na/ *n* a Mexican American woman.

Chicano /chi-kah-no/ *n* a Mexican American man.

chick /chick/ *n* a young bird.

chicken /chi-ken/ *n* **1** a farm bird raised for its eggs and meat. **2** a person who is afraid, not brave, timid.

chickenpox /chi-ken poks/ *n* a disease involving fever and red itchy spots, usually affecting children.

chickpea *n* a large kind of pea.

chicory /chi-ko-ree/ *n* a plant used in salads or in cooking, also sometimes mixed with coffee.

chide /chide/ *vb* to scold (*chiding the children for talking in class*).

chief /cheef/ *adj* **1** highest in rank (*the chief clerk*). **2** most important, main (*the chief crops of the country*). ● *n* a head, a leader. ● *adv* **chiefly**.

chieftain /cheef-tin/ *n* a chief, the head of a clan or tribe.

chiffon /shi-fon/ *n* a thin, silky cloth.

chigger /chig-er/ *n* a tiny parasitic insect that can cause a rash on the skin.

child /childe/ *n* (*pl* **children** /chil-dren/) **1** a young boy or girl, an adolescent (*I have lived here since I was a child*). **2** a son or daughter (*they have two children*). ● *n* **childhood**.

child-care /childe-care/ *n* the care of children, especially by people other than the parents, when they are at work (*most of her salary goes to pay for childcare*).

childish /chile-dish/ *adj* **1** like a child (*childish voices*). **2** silly, immature (*their childish behavior in not speaking to their neighbors*).

children *see* **child**.

chili /chi-lee/ *n* (*pl* **chilies**) the small red or green seed pod of a type of hot pepper, used in cooking spicy food.

chill /chil/ *n* **1** coldness (*a chill in the air*). **2** coldness of manner, unfriendliness. ● *vb* **1** to make cold (*children were chilled after their walk in the snow*). **2** to make cold without freezing (*chill the wine*). **3** to discourage (*chill their hopes*). ● *adj* cold (*a chill wind*).

chilly /chi-lee/ *adj* **1** cold (*a chilly day*). **2** unfriendly (*a chilly welcome*).

chime /chime/ *n* **1** the sound of a bell. **2** the music of bells. **3** *pl* a set of bells. ● *vb* to ring musically. ● **chime in** to agree.

chimney /chim-nee/ *n* a passage by which smoke may escape from a fireplace.

chimney pot /chim-nee pot/ *n* a pipe at the top of a chimney.

chimney sweep /chim-nee sweep/ *n* someone who cleans chimneys.

chimpanzee /chim-pan-zee/ *n* a type of ape in Africa with black fur and large ears.

china /chine-a/ *n* **1** a fine, thin porcelain or ceramic ware. **2** cups, plates, ornaments, etc., made of this (*put out the best china for her guests*).

chinchilla /chin-chi-la/ *n* **1** a small rodent valued for its fur. **2** the fur from this animal.

chink /chingk/ *n* **1** a very narrow opening (*peer through a chink in the door*). **2** ringing or jingling sound (*the chink of money in his pockets*). ● *vb* to jingle.

chintz /chints/ *n* a gaily patterned cotton material that is usually glazed.

chip /chip/ *n* a small piece (*wood chips*). **2** a counter or token used in games. ● *vb* (**chipped, chipping**) **1** to cut into small pieces (*chip a small hole in the woods*). **2** to break off a small piece, often accidentally (*paint chipped off the wall*).

chipmunk /chip-munk/ *n* a type of small squirrel with black stripes down its head and back, living mainly in the ground and found in North America.

chirp /chirp/ *vb* to make a short, sharp whistling sound (*birds chirping*). ● *also n*.

chisel /chi-zel/ *n* a tool used for cutting or chipping wood, stone, etc. ● *also vb* (**chiseled, chiseling**).

chivalry /shi-val-ree/ *n* **1** (*old*) the rules of good behavior laid down for knights in the Middle Ages, gentlemanly behavior. **2** good manners, especially toward women. ● *adjs* **chivalric** /shi-**val**-ric/, **chivalrous** /shi-val-rus/.

chloride /**clo**-ride/ *n* a mixture of chlorine with another substance.

chlorine /**clo**-reen/ *n* a poisonous chemical gas used as a bleaching agent.

chlorophyll /**claw**-ro-fil/ *n* the green coloring of plants.

chocolate /**choc**-lat/ *n* a paste, powder, syrup, or bar made from cacao seeds that have been roasted and ground, a kind of candy bar. ● *adj* chocolate-colored, i.e., reddish brown.

choice /**choiss**/ *n* **1** act of choosing (*he left his job by choice*). **2** that which is chosen (*like their choice of song/Italy was her first choice*). ● *adj* very good, excellent (*choice fruit*).

choir /**kwire**/ *n* **1** a group of singers. **2** the part of the church where the choir sits.

choke /**choke**/ *vb* **1** to be unable to breathe (*people choking in the fumes from the fire*). **2** to prevent breathing by pressing the windpipe. **3** to block up (*the man in the restaurant was choking on a piece of food*). ● *n* **1** a fit of choking or its sound. **2** a part that controls the flow of air in a carburetor.

cholera /**co**-le-ra/ *n* a serious stomach illness.

choose /**chooz**/ *vb* (*pt* **chose**, *pp* **chosen**) to take what you prefer (*choose a dish from the menu/choosing the members of his team/he has chosen between the two jobs*).

chop /**chop**/ *vb* (**chopped, chopping**) **1** to cut with a quick strong blow. **2** to cut into pieces (*chop the vegetables*). ● *n* a piece of pork or mutton on a rib bone (*a pork chop*).

choppy /**chop**-ee/ *adj* rough (*a choppy sea*).

chops /**chops**/ *npl* the jaws (*dogs licking their chops*).

chopsticks /**chop**-stiks/ *npl* two long, thin sticks held in one hand, used in some Asian countries instead of a knife and fork.

choral /**core**-al/ *adj* having to do with a chorus or choir (*choral music*).

chord /**cawrd**/ *n* **1** the playing of several musical notes at once in harmony.

chore /**chore**/ *n* a regular job about the house (*chores such as washing the dishes*).

chorus /**co**-rus/ *n* **1** a group of singers and dancers. **2** a song or part of a song in which all may join (*ask the audience to sing the chorus*). ● *vb* to sing or speak together (*"Goodbye," chorused the children to their teacher*).

christen /**cris**-en/ *vb* **1** to baptize, or make part of the Christian church (*have their son christened in church*). **2** to name (*she calls herself Kate, although she was christened Catherine*) **3** to make use of for the first time. ● *n* **christening**.

Christian /**cris**-chin/ *adj* having to do with Christ and his teaching. ● *n* a believer in Christ.

Christmas /**cris**-mas/ *n* December 25, the day each year on which the birth of Christ is celebrated.

chronic /**cron**-ik/ *adj* lasting for a long time (*a chronic illness*).

chronicle /**cron**-ik-al/ *adj* a record of events, set down in the order in which they happened (*a chronicle of the events leading up to the war*). ● also *vb*. ● *n* **chronicler**.

chronological /cron-o-**lodge**-ik-al/ *adj* arranged in order of time (*announce the dates of the meetings in chronological order*).

chrysalis /**cris**-sa-lis/ *n* an early stage in the life of a flying insect, when it is shut up in a cocoon until its wings grow.

chrysanthemum /cri-**zanth**-e-mum/ *n* a garden plant with a large, bushy flower.

chubby /**chu**-bee/ *adj* plump (*chubby babies*).

chuck wagon /**chuk wag**-on/ *n* a portable kitchen on a covered wagon.

chuckle /**chu**-kl/ *vb* to laugh quietly (*chuckling over his comic*). ● also *n*.

chum /**chum**/ *n* (*inf*) a close friend (*old school chums*). ● *adj* **chummy**.

chunk /**chungk**/ *n* a thick piece (*a chunk of cheese*).

church /**church**/ *n* **1** a building set aside for worship. **2** a group of people having the same beliefs and religious organization. **3** those in charge of a religious organization

churn /**churn**/ *n* a vessel or machine for making butter. ● *vb* to shake or stir (cream) so as to make butter.

chute /**shoot**/ *n* **1** a waterfall. **2** a sloping passage or slide (*children sliding down the chute in the playground*).

chutney *n* a savory preserve or relish made, usually, from fruit, vegetables and spices.

cider /**sie**-der/ *n* a drink made from pressed apple juice.

cigar /si-**gar**/ *n* a roll of tobacco for smoking, consisting of cut tobacco rolled in a whole tobacco leaf.

cigarette /si-ga-**ret**/ *n* tobacco finely cut and rolled in thin paper for smoking.

cinder /**sin**-der/ *n* partly burned coal or wood.

cinema /**si**-ne-ma/ *n* **1** a building in which movies

are shown. **2** the industry of making movies. ●
adj **cinematic.**

cinnamon /si-na-mon/ *n* a yellowish brown spice
made from the dried inner bark of several kinds
of trees and shrubs of the laurel family, used in
cooking.

circle /sir-kl/ *n* **1** a perfectly round figure. **2** a group
of people (*a small circle of close friends*). ● *vb* **1**
to move round (*dancers circling the room*). **2** to
draw a circle around (*circled the correct word*).

circlet /sir-klet/ *n* an ring or circular band worn as
an ornament.

circuit /sir-kit/ *n* **1** a path round (*Earth's circuit
around the sun*). **2** the act of moving around (*do
a circuit of the city streets*). **3** the journey of a judge
round a district to hold courts of law in several
places. **4** the path of an electric current.

circular /sir-kyi-lar/ *adj* round (*a circular shape*). ●
n a letter, copies of which are sent to many people (*sent a circular to the parents about school
sports day*).

circularize /sir-kyi-la-rize/ *vb, also* **circularise** (*Br*)
to send circulars to (*circularize the members to
get their views*).

circulate /sir-kyi-late/ *vb* **1** to move in a circle or a
fixed path (*water circulating in the pipes of the
heating system*). **2** to pass around, to spread (*circulate information*). **3** to move from one person
to another (*a hostess circulating among the
guests*).

circulation /sir-kyi-lay-shun/ *n* **1** the act of circulating. **2** the movement of the blood through the
body. **3** the number of readers (of a newspaper,
etc.).

circumference /sir-cum-frense/ *n* the line marking
the limits of a circle.

circumnavigate /sir-cum-na-vi-gate/ *vb* (*fml*) to sail
around (*circumnavigate the world*).

circumstance /sir-cum-stanse/ *n* **1** (*usually pl*) a
condition relating to or connected with an act or
event (*the circumstances surrounding the robbery/
given the circumstances the police let him go*). **2** *pl*
state of affairs, position (often financial) (*in very
bad circumstances*).

circus /sir-cus/ *n* **1** a traveling show given largely by
skilled acrobats and trained animals.

cistern /sis-tern/ *n* a tank for storing water.

citadel /si-ta-del/ *n* a fortress above a city for its
defense.

cite /site/ *vb* **1** to call to appear in court. **2** to quote.
3 to give as an example.

citizen /si-ti-zen/ *n* **1** an inhabitant of a city. **2** a
member of a state.

citizenship /si-ti-zen-ship/ *n* being, or having the
rights of, a citizen.

citrus /si-trus/ *adj* of a group of related fruits, including the lemon, orange, lime, and grapefruit.

city /si-tee/ *n* a center of population larger than a
town or village.

civic /si-vic/ *adj* **1** having to do with a city (*a civic
function*). **2** having to do with citizens or citizenship (*your civic duty*). ● *npl* **civics** the study of
the rights and duties of citizens.

civil /si-vil/ *adj* **1** having to do with citizens (*civil
disorder*). **2** having to do with those citizens who
are members of neither the armed forces nor the
clergy (*civil, not military, government*). **3** polite
(*shop assistants who are scarcely civil*). ● *adv* **civ-
illy.** ● *n* **civility** /si-vil-i-tee/.

civilian /si-vil-yen/ *n* someone not in the armed
forces.

civilization /si-vi-li-zay-shun/ *n, also* **civilisation**
(*Br*) **1** a well-organized and polished society (*the
ancient civilizations of Greece and Egypt*). **2** the
state of being civilized (*living with a savage tribe
far from civilization*).

civilize /si-vi-lize/ *vb, also* **civilise** (*Br*) **1** to bring or
come out of a primitive condition. **2** to make more
polite and well-mannered). ● *adj* **civilized,** *also*
civilised (*Br*).

civil war /si-vil wor/ *n* a war between citizens of the
same country.

clad /clad/ *pp of* **clothe** (*he was clad in ceremonial
dress*).

claim /clame/ *vb* to demand as a right (*claimed the
throne/claiming his share of the goods*). ● *also n.*

clam /clam/ *n* a type of shellfish.

clamber /clam-ber/ *vb* to climb with difficulty, to
scramble (*children clambering over the rocks*). ●
also n.

clammy /cla-mee/ *adj* damp, cold, and sticky
(*clammy hands/the weather was clammy before
the storm*).

clamor /cla-mur/ *n, also* **clamour** (*Br, Cdn*) loud
shouting, a general outcry, especially demanding
something (*a clamor from the audience to get their
money back*). ● *vb* to shout (for something).

clamorous /cla-mo-rus/ *adj* noisy (*clamorous protesters*).

clamp /clamp/ *n* a device used for holding things
firmly together. ● *vb* to fasten with a clamp.

clan /clan/ *n* an early social group of families with

the same name thought to be related who were ruled by a chief. ● *n* **clansman** /**clanz**-man/, **clanswoman** /**clanz**-woo-man/.

clang /clang/ *n* a loud ringing sound, as of metal against metal. ● *vb* to make this noise (*the iron gates clanged shut*).

clank /clangk/ *n* a short, sharp ringing sound (*the clank of chains*). ● *also vb*.

clap /clap/ *vb* (**clapped** /clapt/, **clapping**) **1** to smack the hands together noisily (*the audience clapped when the singer appeared*). **2** to slap or tap, usually in a friendly way (*clap him on the back in congratulation*). **3** to put suddenly and quickly (*clap the wrongdoers in jail*). ● *n* **1** the noise made by clapping the hands. **2** a sudden sound (e.g. of thunder).

clarify /**cla**-ri-fy/ *vb* to make clear or clearer (*clarified the instructions/clarifying the situation*). ● *n* **clarification** /cla-ri-fi-**cay**-shun/.

clarinet /cla-ri-**net**/ *n* a musical wind instrument with a wooden reed in the mouthpiece. ● *n* **clarinetist** /cla-ri-**net**-ist/, *also* (*Br*) **clarinettist**.

clarity /**cla**-ri-tee/ *n* clearness (*the clarity of his speech/the clarity of the instructions*).

clash /clash/ *vb* **1** to strike together noisily (*clash the cymbals*). **2** to disagree strongly about (*the two sides clashed over money*). **3** to happen at the same time, as in events (*the concert clashed with my birthday party*). ● *n* **1** the loud noise of two objects coming violently together. **2** a quarrel.

clasp /clasp/ *n* **1** a metal fastener (*the clasp of a brooch*). **2** a firm hold (*hold her hand in a firm clasp*). ● *vb* **1** to fasten. **2** to hold firmly (*clasp her mother's hand*).

class /class/ *n* **1** a group of persons or things of the same kind (*plants divided into classes*). **2** a group of pupils or students. **3** a rank, a standard of excellence (*of the first class*). **4** the system according to which people are divided into social groups. **5** one of these social groups (*the upper class*). ● *vb* to put in a class, to regard as being of a certain type (*class him as being unfit for work*).

classic /**cla**-sic/ *adj* of the best kind or standard. ● *n* **1** a great writer or book. **2** *pl* **the classics** Greek and Roman literature.

classical /**cla**-si-cal/ *adj* **1** classic. **2** having to do with Greek and Roman literature, art, or customs.

classify /**cla**-si-fy/ *vb* to arrange in classes (*classified the books as fiction or nonfiction*). ● *n* **classification** /cla-si-fi-**cay**-shun/.

clatter /**cla**-ter/ *vb* to make rattling noises (*clattered up the wooden stairs*). ● *n* a rattling noise.

clause /clawz/ *n* **1** a group of words forming a part of a sentence. **2** a section of an agreement (*a clause in the contract allowing either side to withdraw*).

claustraphobia /claw-stri-**foe**-bee-a/ *n* the fear of being confined in any small enclosed space.

claw /claw/ *n* **1** the hooked nail of a bird or other animal. **2** a foot with such nails. ● *vb* to scratch or tear with claws or nails (*clawed at his face with her nails*).

clay /clay/ *n* a moist, formable earth that hardens when dried, used to make sculptures and pottery. ● *adj* **clayey** /**clay**-ee/.

clean /cleen/ *adj* **1** free from dirt (*clean hands/a clean shirt*). **2** pure, free from guilt, evil, crime, sickness, etc. (*a clean bill of health/a clean record*). **3** complete (*a clean break*). ● *adv* completely (*the handle came away clean in my hand*). ● *vb* to remove dirt, dust, etc., from (*cleaned the dress/cleaning the kitchen*). ● *n* **cleaner**. ● *n* **cleanness** /**cleen**-ness/.

cleanly /**clen**-lee/ *adj* having clean habits (*a cleanly animal*). ● *adv* in a clean manner, neatly. ● *n* **cleanliness** /**clen**-lee-ness/.

cleanse /clenz/ *vb* to make clean or pure (*the soap cleansed her skin/cleansing his soul*). ● *n* **cleanser**.

clear /cleer/ *adj* **1** easy to hear, see, or understand (*a clear description*). **2** bright (*clear skies*). **3** free from difficulties or obstacles (*the way is now clear to go on with our plans*). **4** obvious (*a clear case of guilt*). ● *vb* **1** to make or become clear (*the skies cleared*). **2** to prove innocent (*clearing his name*). **3** to remove difficulties or obstacles from (*clear the way*). **4** to pass through or over (*clear the fence*). ● *adv* **clearly**.

clearance /**clee**-ranse/ *n* **1** act of clearing (*the clearance of trees/the clearance of goods from the shelves*). **2** permission for something to be done (*receive clearance from the boss*).

clearing /**clee**-ring/ *n* a wide open part of a forest with no trees.

clef /clef/ *n* a mark to show the pitch in music.

cleft /cleft/ *n* a crack, a split.

clench /clench/ *vb* to press tightly together (*clench your fist/clench your teeth*).

clergy /**cler**-jee/ *n* persons who are in charge of and who lead religious services, ministers, priests, rabbis, etc.

cleric /**cle**-ric/ *n* a a member of clergy.

clerical /**cle**-ri-cal/ *adj* **1** having to do with the clergy. **2** having to do with a clerk (*clerical work*).

clerk /clark/ *n* an office employee doing written work.

clever /cle-ver/ *adj* 1 able to learn quickly. 2 able to think quickly. 3 able to do things well with the hands, skilful. ● *adv* **cleverly.** ● *n* **cleverness.**

cliché /clee-**shay**/ *n* a stock phrase in common use.

click /click/ *n* a light, sharp sound (*the click of her heels*). ● *also vb.*

client /clie-ent/ *n* 1 a customer (*a hairdresser's clients*). 2 someone who employs a member of some profession (*a lawyer's clients*).

clientele /clee-on-**tel**/ *n* all the clients of a professional or customers of a shopkeeper.

cliff /cliff/ *n* a high, steep rock face.

climate /clie-mit/ *n* the usual weather conditions of a place. ● *adj* **climatic** /clie-**ma**-tic/.

climax /clie-max/ *n* the highest or most exciting point, the most dramatic moment (*the climax of his career/the climax of the play*). ● *adj* **climactic** / clie-**mac**-tic/.

climb /clime/ *vb* 1 to rise or ascend (*the plane climb to its cruising height/the stock prices climbed over the weekend*). 2 to go up, by using the feet and often the hands. ● *n* **climber.**

clinch /clinch/ *vb* 1 to settle (*clinched the deal*). 2 in boxing, to stand so close that no strong punches may be given. ● *also n.*

cling /cling/ *vb* (*pt, pp* **clung**) 1 to stick to (*mud clinging to her shoes*). 2 to hold firmly to (*clung to her mother's skirt*).

clinic /cli-nic/ *n* a building or a part of a hospital for people needing special medical treatment or advice (*a skin clinic*). ● *adj* **clinical.**

clink /clingk/ *n* a sharp, thin ringing sound. ● *also vb.*

clip[1] /clip/ *vb* (**clipped** /clipt/, **clipping** /cli-ping/) 1 to cut (*clip the hedge*). ● *n* something that has been clipped. 2 a sharp blow.

clip[2] *n* a fastener (*she put her hair up in a clip*). ● *vb* (**clipped, clipping**) to fasten.

clipper /cli-per/ *n* 1 an instrument for clipping (*nail clippers*). 2 a fast sailing ship.

clique /cleek/ *n* a small group of people who keep together, not mixing with others.

cloak /cloke/ *n* 1 a loose outer garment. 2 something that hides or covers. ● *vb* 1 to cover as with a cloak. 2 to conceal.

cloakroom /cloke-room/ *n* 1 a room where you can leave outer garments, packages, etc., in a public place.

clock /clock/ *n* an instrument for telling the time. ●

vb to measure time (*he clocked me running a mile in 8.27 minutes*).

clockwise /clock-wise/ *adj* going around in the direction of the hands of a clock.

clockwork /clock-wurk/ *n* machinery like that inside a clock. ● **like clockwork** regularly and smoothly.

clod /clod/ *n* 1 a lump of earth. 2 a clumsy or stupid person.

clog /clog/ *n* 1 a shoe with a wooden sole. 2 something that blocks or gets in the way of. ● *vb* (**clogged** /clogd/, **clogging** /clog-ing/) to block, to choke (*clog the drains*).

cloister /cloy-ster/ *n* 1 a monastery or other place where religious people choose to be by themselves. 2 a covered walkway in a monastery, church, etc., that leads to a garden or courtyard.

clone /clone/ *n* 1 an animal or plant that has been produced or manufactured from the cells of another and is, therefore, an exact copy. 2 a person or thing that is very like someone or something else (*the teenagers all wear the same clothes and look like clones of one another*). ● *vb* to produce an exact copy of an animal or plant from its own cells.

close[1] /cloze/ *vb* 1 to shut (*close the gates*). 2 to finish (*close the meeting*). 3 to bring or come near (*his arms closed around her*). ● *n* the end.

close[2] /cloze/ *adj* 1 shut in. 2 stuffy (*the air was close in the crowded hall*). 3 near, not far (*the station is quite close*).

closed-circuit television *see* **CCTV.**

closet /cloz-it/ *n* a large cupboard or small room in which clothes are kept. ● *vb* to shut up (*closeted themselves in a private room*).

closure /clo-zhur/ *n* (*fml*) closing, end (*the closure of the factory*).

clot /clot/ *n* a soft lump formed on or in liquid (*a clot of blood*). ● *vb* (**clotted** /clot-id/, **clotting** /clot-ing/) 1 to form into clots. 2 to thicken.

cloth /cloth/ *n* a material made by weaving threads of wool, cotton, etc.

clothe /clothe/ *vb* (*pt, pp* **clothed** *or* **clad**) to put clothes on (*clothe herself in silk*).

clothes /cloze/ *npl* garments.

clothes pin /cloze-pin/ *n* a wooden or plastic clip that holds washed clothes on a line to dry (*in Britain a clothes pin is called a peg*).

clothing /clothe-ing/ *n* garments (*warm clothing*).

cloud /cloud/ *n* 1 a mass of water vapor floating high in the sky. 2 a great many (*a cloud of insects*). 3 cause of gloom or trouble (*a cloud on their* *happiness*). ● *vb* to darken. ● *adjs* **cloudy** /clou-dee/, **cloudless** /cloud-less/.

cloudburst /cloud-burst/ *n* a sudden, very heavy rainstorm.

clove /clove/ *n* **1** a plant bud from a tree used as a spice. **2** a part of a bulb, such as garlic.

clover /clo-ver/ *n* a three-leaved plant grown as food for cattle.

clown /cloun/ *n* **1** a fool. **2** one who plays the fool to amuse others. ● *vb* to play the fool (*boys clowning around*).

club /club/ *n* **1** a heavy stick. **2** a golf stick. **3** a group of people who meet for a common purpose. **4** their meeting place (*a golf club*). **5** a place, usually one selling drinks, where people go to listen to music and dance. **6** *pl* a suit of playing cards. ● *vb* (**clubbed** /clubd/, **clubbing** /clu-bing/) **1** to beat with a club.

cluck /cluck/ *n* a low, sharp, clicking sound, like the sound made by a hen.

clue /cloo/ *n* a fact that, when understood, helps one to find the answer to a problem, a hint (*police looking for clues/find a clue to her whereabouts*).

clump /clump/ *n* a closely packed group, a cluster (*a clump of trees*). ● *vb* to walk heavily (*clump angrily upstairs*).

clumsy /clum-zee/ *adj* **1** awkward in movement, shape, etc. (*the clumsy person always dropped things*). **2** badly done (*a clumsy apology*). ● *n* **clumsiness** /clum-zee-ness/.

cluster /cluss-ter/ *n* a number of things growing very close together, a closely packed group (*a cluster of grapes*). ● *vb* to grow or stand close together.

clutch /cluch/ *vb* **1** to seize (*clutched the rope that was thrown*). **2** to hold tightly (*clutches her bag*). ● *n* **1** a firm hold. **2** *pl* power, control (*in the clutches of criminals*). **3** eggs being hatched at one sitting. **4** in a car, a lever that puts an engine in or out of action. **5** a woman's small handbag or purse.

clutter /clu-ter/ *vb* to fill or cover untidily (*papers cluttering the desk*). ● *n* an untidy mass.

co- /co-/ *prefix* together.

coach /coach/ *n* **1** (*old*) a closed four-wheeled horse carriage. **2** a railway carriage. **3** a private teacher (*employ a coach to improve their son's French*). **4** one who trains athletes (*an football coach*). ● *vb* **1** to give private lessons (*coach him in French*). **2** to prepare (a person or a team) for a contest (*coach the football players*).

coal /cole/ *n* a black rock dug from a mine, used as fuel for fires.

coalition /co-wa-li-shun/ *n* **1** a joining together. **2** the joining together of different political parties for a special purpose (*a country ruled by a coalition*).

coarse /coarse/ *adj* **1** rough (*coarse material*). **2** rude, vulgar, unrefined (*a coarse sense of humor*). ● *adv* **coarsely**. ● *n* **coarseness**.

coarsen /coar-sen/ *vb* to make coarse (*hands coarsened by washing floors*).

coast /coast/ *n* the side of the land next the sea. ● *vb* **1** to sail alongside the coast. **2** to move without the use of power (*cars coasting downhill*). **3** to go on without much effort (*coast along without doing much studying*). ● *adj* **coastal** /co-stal/.

coast guard /coast-gard/ *n* the coast police (*an empty boat spotted by the coast guard*).

coastline /coast-line/ *n* the line of the coast or shore.

coat /coat/ *n* **1** an outer garment with sleeves. **2** the natural cover of an animal (e.g., hair, wool, fur). **3** anything that covers (*a coat of paint*). ● *vb* to cover (*cookies that were coated with chocolate*).

coating /co-ting/ *n* a covering.

coat of arms /coat-of-arms/ *n* the design on a shield or badge representing a person, family, country, or organization.

coax /coaks/ *vb* to get someone to do something by speaking kindly or petting.

cob /cob/ *n* **1** a corncob. **2** a male swan. **3** a short-legged, thickset riding horse.

cobble /cob-ul/ *vb* **1** (*old*) to mend (shoes) (*he cobbled boots*). **2** to mend or put together roughly (*cobble together a makeshift table*). ● *n* a cobblestone.

cobbler /cob-ler/ *n* a mender of shoes.

cobblestone /cob-ul-stone/ *n* a rounded stone used to pave roads (*Macondray Lane has cobblestones*).

cobra /co-bra/ *n* a poisonous snake that has loose skin behind its head that stiffens into a hood when the snake is excited, scared, or angry, found in Africa and Asia.

cobweb /cob-web/ *n* the spider's web, usually one found in a house and that has collected dust.

cocaine /co-cane/ *n* a drug that deadens pain, but is very addictive and can be fatal.

cock /cock/ *n* **1** a male bird. **2** a tap or faucet. **3** the hammer of a gun. ● *vb* **1** to turn upward, to tilt (*cock his hat*). **2** to raise, to cause to stand up (*the dog cocked its ears*). **3** (*of a gun*) to draw back the hammer before firing.

cockatoo /cock-a-too/ *n* a type of parrot.

cockerel /**cock**-rel/ *n* a young cock.

cocker spaniel /**cock**-er span-**yel**/ *n* a small, long-haired, long-eared dog.

cockle /**cock**-ul/ *n* a type of shellfish.

cockleshell /**cock**-ul-shell/ *n* **1** the shell of the cockle. **2** a small, light boat.

cockpit /**cock**-pit/ *n* **1** (*old*) a pit in which cocks were made to fight each other. **2** the pilot's place in an aircraft.

cockroach /**cock**-roach/ *n* a kind of black beetle with long antennae and flat bodies.

cocktail /**cock**-tale/ *n* a strong drink made by mixing alcohol with juice, soda, or other drinks.

cocky /**cock**-ee/ *adj* absolutely sure, overconfident.

cocoa /**co**-co/ *n* **1** a powder made from cacao seeds. **2** a drink made from this powder, hot chocolate.

coconut /**co**-co-nut/ *n* the fruit of the coconut palm tree, with a white inside flesh covered in a brown husk surrounded by a hard shell.

coconut palm /**co**-co-nut pom/ *n* a tropical palm tree.

cocoon /co-**coon**/ *n* a silky case spun by many insects as they grow and transform, as from a caterpillar to a butterfly.

COD /see-oh-**dee**/ *abbr* = **1 collect on delivery**. **2 cash on delivery**: a person receiving a package must pay for it when he or she receives it.

cod /cod/ *n* a large sea fish.

coddle /**cod**-ul/ *vb* **1** to pet, to treat with too much care (*coddles her youngest child*). **2** to cook gently (*coddle eggs*).

code /code/ *n* **1** a collection of laws, rules, or signals. **2** a method of sending secret messages by using signs, sounds, or words (*try to decipher the message in code/the Morse code*).

coerce /co-**erse**/ *vb* to make to do, to force (*enemy soldiers coercing the villagers into providing them with food and shelter*). ● *n* **coercion** /co-**er**-shun/. ● *adj* **coercive** /co-**er**-siv/.

coexist /co-eg-**zist**/ *vb* to live at the same time or in the same place with another, especially peacefully (*the warring neighbors finally succeeded in coexisting happily*). ● *n* **coexistence** /co-eg-**zis**-tanse/.

coffee /**co**-fee/ *n* a dark brown drink brewed from the roasted, ground seeds of the coffee tree or shrub.

coffin /**co**-fin/ *n* a box in which a dead body is put for burial.

cog /cog/ *n* the tooth of a wheel for receiving motion by fitting between the teeth of another wheel, as on the gears for a bicycle.

coherent /co-**hee**-rent/ *adj* clear and logical (*a coherent argument*). ● *n* **coherence** /co-**hee**-rense/.

cohesion /co-**hee**-zhen/ *n* **1** the force that makes the parts of a a substance is held together. **2** coherence. ● *adj* **cohesive** /co-**hee**-siv/.

coil /coil/ *vb* to wind in a series of rings (*a snake coiling itself around a tree*). ● *n* a ring or rings into which a rope, etc., is wound.

coin /coin/ *n* a metal piece of money. ● *vb* **1** to make money out of metal. **2** to invent (*coin a word*).

coinage /**coy**-nage/ *n* **1** the act of coining. **2** all coined money. **3** the coined money in use in a particular country. **4** a newly invented word.

coincide /co-in-**side**/ *vb* **1** to happen at the same time (*their arrival coincided with our departure*). **2** to be in agreement (*their opinions coincide*).

coincidence /co-**win**(t)-si-dense/ *n* the accidental happening of one event at the same time as another (*it was a coincidence that we both arrived together*). ● *adjs* **coincident** /co-**win**(t)-si-dent/, **coincidental** /co-win(t)-si-**den**-tal/.

coke /coke/ *n* coal from which most of the gas has been extracted by heating, used as industrial fuel.

colander /**col**-an-der/ *n* a strainer.

cold /coald/ *adj* **1** not hot or warm (*a cold day/cold food*). **2** without emotion or excitement, unenthusiastic (*his performance left me cold*). **3** unfriendly (*a cold welcome*). ● *n* **1** absence of heat (*cannot stand the cold*). **2** an illness, usually consisting of a runny or stuffy nose, sneezing, coughing, aches, and pains. (*catch a cold*).

cold-blooded /coald blu-ded/ *adj* **1** having blood colder than the air or water, as fish, snakes, etc. **2** completely unfeeling, cruel (*cold-blooded murder*).

collaborate /co-**la**-bo-rate/ *vb* **1** to work together, especially in writing, study, art, or science (*collaborating on a book*). **2** to work with another to betray secrets, etc. (*collaborating with the enemy*). ● *ns* **collaboration** /co-la-bo-**ray**-shun/, **collaborator** /co-la-bo-rate-or/.

collapse /co-**lapse**/ *n* **1** a fall (*the collapse of the bridge*). **2** a sudden loss of consciousness. **3** a failure (*the collapse of the firm/the collapse of the talks*). ● *vb* **1** to fall down (*the bridge collapsed*). **2** to fall down unaware of one's surroundings (*collapsing in the extreme heat*). **3** to fail completely (*the company collapsed*).

collar /**col**-ar/ *n* **1** the part of the clothing that covers or surrounds the neck. **2** a strap or band put round the neck of an animal. ● *vb* (*inf*) to take hold of, to seize (*police collaring criminals*).

colleague /col-eeg/ *n* a fellow worker.

collect /co-lect/ *vb* **1** to bring together (*collect the glasses*). **2** to come together (*a crowd collected*). **3** to gather and keep things of the same kind (*collect stamps*). **4** to obtain money by contributions (*collecting for charity*).

collected /co-lek-ted/ *adj* **1** gathered together. **2** calm, cool, in control.

collection /co-lek-shun/ *n* **1** act of collecting. **2** the things collected. **3** the gathering of money for a special purpose. ● *n* **collector** /co-lek-tor/.

collective /co-lek-tive/ *adj* taken as a whole, joint (*our collective strength*). ● *n* a collective enterprise, as a farm. ● *adv* **collectively** /co-lek-tive-lee/.

college /col-edge/ *n* **1** a society of learned or professional people that have certain duties (*the electoral college*). **2** a place of further education after high school, where one might obtain a bachelor's or associate's degree.

collide /co-lide/ *vb* to run into, to strike against (*collide with another car*/*two cars colliding*). ● *n* **collision** /co-li-zhon/.

collie /col-ee/ *n* a long-haired dog with a long, narrow head, originally bred for herding sheep.

collision *see* **collide**.

colloquial /co-lo-kwee-al/ *adj* conversational, having to do with the spoken language of ordinary people (*colloquial language*).

colloquialism /co-lo-kwee-a-li-zum/ *n* a popular expression.

collusion /co-loo-zhun/ *n* a secret agreement to do something wrong (*witnesses acting in collusion to deceive the courts*).

colon /co-lon/ *n* **1** a mark of punctuation (:). **2** a part of the bowel, or lower intestine.

colonel /cur-n(e)l/ *n* a military officer.

colonial /co-lo-nee-al/ *adj* **1** having to do with a colony. **2** (*often cap*) having to do with the 13 British colonies that became the United States.

colonist /col-un-ist/ *n* a settler in a colony.

colonize /col-un-ise/ *vb, also* **colonise** (*Br*) to form or set up a colony in (*the British colonized parts of America*).

colonnade /col-un-ade/ *n* a row of columns or pillars.

colony /col-un-ee/ *n* **1** a community of settlers in a new land. **2** the place in which they settle.

color /cul-ur/ *n, also* **colour** (*Br, Cdn*) **1** a quality that objects have and that can be seen only when light falls on them (*what color is her new dress?*/

bright colors such as red and yellow). **2** paint (*watercolors*). **3** redness (of the face) (*brings color to her cheeks*). **4** a skin color varying with race (*was unliked because of the color of her skin*). **5** brightness (*a description full of color*). **6** *pl* a flag. ● *vb* **1** to paint, to put color on or into (*color the walls yellow*). **2** to give interesting qualities to, to elaborate (*an account colored by her imagination*). **3** to affect (*a view of life colored by childhood experiences*). **4** to blush (*coloring with embarrassment*).

colorblind /cul-ur blinde/ *n, also* **colourblind** (*Br, Cdn*) *adj* unable to see the difference between colors or certain colors.

colorful /cul-ur-ful/ *adj, also* **colourful** (*Br, Cdn*) **1** full of color, bright. **2** bright and interesting (*a colorful account*).

colorless /cul-ur-less/ *adj, also* **colourless** (*Br, Cdn*) **1** without color. **2** uninteresting (*a colorless description*/*a colorless young woman*).

colossal /cu-law-sal/ *n adj* very big, gigantic.

colt /colt/ *n* a young, male horse or donkey.

columbine /col-um-bine/ *n* a kind of wild flower of the buttercup family.

column /col-um/ *n* **1** a pillar used to support or ornament a building. **2** something similar in shape (*a column of smoke*). **3** a body of troops standing one behind the other in one or more lines. **4** a row of numbers, one below the other. **5** a narrow division of a page. ● *adj* **columnar** /col-um-nar/ *n* **1** a quality that objects have and that can be seen only when light falls on them (*what color is her new dress?*/*bright colors such as red and yellow*). **2** paint (*watercolors*).

columnist /col-um-nist/ *n* the writer of a regular series of articles for a newspaper or magazine.

coma /co-ma/ *n* a long-continuing state of being unconscious or not awake or aware of one's surroundings (*in a coma after the head injury*).

comatose /co-ma-toze/ *adj* **1** of, like, or in a coma. **2** (*inf*) very sleepy, drowsy (*comatose after a large meal*).

comb /coam/ *n* **1** a toothed instrument for passing through and arranging hair, wool, etc. **2** the crest of a cock. ● *vb* to pass through or arrange with a comb.

combat /com-bat/ *vb* (**combated** /com-ba-ted/, **combating** /com-ba-ting/) to fight against, to try to defeat, destroy, etc. (*combat disease*). ● *n* a fight.

combatant /com-ba-tant/ *n* one taking part in a fight. ● *also adj*.

combative /com-**ba**-tive/ *adj* liking to fight (*in a combative mood*).

combination /com-bi-**nay**-shun/*n* **1** a joining, a union (*a combination of the new and the old/work in combination with overseas firms*). **2** *pl* a one-piece undergarment covering the upper and lower body.

combine /com-**bine**/ *vb* to join (*he combines wit and skill/the two firms have combined*).

combust /com-**bust**/ *vb* to burn.

combustible /com-**bus**-ti-bul/ *adj* able to take light and burn easily.

combustion /com-**bus**-chin/ *n* the process of burning.

come /cum/ *vb* (*pt* **came**, *pp* **come**) to move toward (*opposite of* **go**). ● *n* **coming**. ● **come across** to discover (something) by accident (*come across some valuable books in an old shop*). ● **come to pass** (*old or fml*) to happen (*it came to pass that they married*).

comedian /cu-**mee**-dee-an/ *n* **1** a performer who tells jokes, a comic. **2** one who is always trying to make others laugh. ●*f* **comedienne** /cu-mee-dee-**yen**/.

comedy /**com**-ed-ee/ *n* **1** a light or amusing play with a happy ending. **2** an amusing happening, the amusing side of something (*the comedy of the situation*).

comely /**cum**-lee/ *adj* (*old or fml*) pleasant-looking, graceful (*a comely young woman*). ● *n* **comeliness** /**cum**-lee-ness/.

comet /**com**-et/ *n* a bright heavenly body made up of frozen dust and gas that orbits the sun, seen only rarely, with a tail of light.

comfort /**cum**-furt/ *vb* to give comfort to, to cheer (someone) up (*comfort the widow at the funeral*). ● *n* **1** the state of being free from anxiety, worry, pain, etc., and having all one's physical needs satisfied, ease (*a life of comfort*). **2** something that satisfies one's physical needs (*all modern comforts*). **3** strength, hope, sympathy, etc. (*offer comfort to the widow*). **4** the cause of comfort to others (*a comfort to her mother*).

comfortable /**cumf**-te-bl/ *adj* **1** at ease, free from anxiety, worry, etc. (*not feel comfortable in her presence*). **2** providing comfort, soft and restful, relaxing (*a comfortable bed*).

comforter /**cum**-fe-te(r)/ *n* **1** someone who comforts. **2** (*old*) a quilted bed covering.

comic /**com**-ic/ *adj* **1** having to do with comedy (*a comic act/comic opera*). **2** amusing, laughable (*a comic situation*). ● *also n*.

comical /**com**-ic-al/ *adj* funny, amusing (*look comical in that funny hat*).

comma /**com**-a/ *n* a mark of punctuation (,).

command /co-**man**/ *vb* **1** to order (*command them to come at once*). **2** to be in charge (of). **3** to control. **4** to overlook (a place) (*command a view of the sea*). ● *n* **1** an order. **2** mastery.

commander /cu-**man**-der/ *n* **1** an officer in charge of troops. **2** an officer in the navy.

commanding /cu-**man**-ding/ *adj* arousing respect.

commandment /cu-**mand**-ment/ *n* an order, a law.

commemorate /cu-**mem**-o-rate/ *vb* to make people remember something by holding a service or doing something special (*commemorating those who died in the war*). ● *n* **commemoration** /cu-mem-o-**ray**-shun/.

commence /cu-**mense**/ *vb* (*fml*) to begin. ● *n* **commencement** /cu-**mense**-ment/.

commend /cu-**mend**/ *vb* **1** to praise (*her teaching was highly commended*). **2** (*fml*) to recommend (*I commend you to try the new restaurant*).

commendable /cu-**men**-da-bl/ *adj* deserving praise.

commendation /com-en-**day**-shun/ *n* praise.

comment /**com**-ent/ *vb* **1** to say something about, to remark on (*friends commenting on her unhappiness*). **2** to write notes in explanation of. ● *n* **1** a remark. **2** an explanation.

commentary /**com**-en-te-ree/ *n* **1** a series of remarks or notes. **2** a spoken description of an event as it happens. ● **running commentary** a description of an event as it happens, given by an onlooker.

commentator /**com**-en-tay-tor/ *n* **1** one who comments. **2** the writer or speaker of a commentary.

commerce /**com**-erse/ *n* the buying and selling of goods, trade.

commercial /co-**mer**-shal/ *adj* **1** having to do with trade or commerce (*commercial law*). **2** profit-making (*a commercial business*). ● *n* a paid advertisement for radio or television.

commiserate /co-**miz**-u-rate/ *vb* to pity, to sympathize with (*commiserate with her on her misfortune*). ● *n* **commiseration** /co-miz-u-**ray**-shun/ pity, sympathy.

commission /co-**mi**-shun/ *n* **1** act of committing. **2** an order for a work of art (*receive a commission to paint the president's portrait*). **3** a group of people appointed to study and report on a particular matter (*a commission to look into government spending*). **4** money paid to someone who has helped to arrange a business deal (*his commission for selling the painting/the commission paid* by the writer to his agent). ● *vb* to give an order or request to, to appoint (*commission him to paint a portrait*).

commit /co-**mit**/ *vb* (**committed, committing**) **1** to perform or do, especially something illegal (*commit a crime*). **2** to make a definite agreement (that one will do something) (*commit oneself to raising $1000 for the charity*). **3** to give (someone) into care (*he committed his brother to a mental hospital*). **4** (*fml*) to put in or on (*commit the facts to paper*).

commitment /co-**mit**-ment/ *n* **1** the act of committing (*the commitment of facts to paper*). **2** a promise, a duty, a responsibility (*family commitments*). **3** state of being devoted (*looking for someone with commitment to his work*).

committee /co-**mi**-tee/ *n* a group of people appointed from a larger body to manage its affairs or perform a particular duty (*the prom committee*).

commodity /co-**mod**-i-tee/ *n* (*often pl*) anything bought and sold, a useful thing (*household commodities*).

common /**com**-on/ *adj* **1** belonging to everyone, of no special rank or quality (*their common desire to be free*). **2** found everywhere (*a common wild flower*). **3** ordinary (*a common member of the public*). **4** frequent (*a common occurrence*). **5** rough, regarded as being low class (*regarded as common because of her dress and speech*). ● *n* **1** land belonging to or open to the community (*common ground*)

common denominator /**com**-on di-**nom**-in-ay-tor/ *n* a denominator shared by two or more fractions.

commonplace /**com**-on-place/ *n* a well-known remark, an ordinary or unoriginal remark. ● *adj* ordinary, not regarded as special (*a commonplace speech*).

common sense /**com**-on **sense**/ *n* practical, good sense, knowledge of how to act in everyday matters (*brilliant but with little common sense*).

commonwealth /**com**-on-welth/ *n* **1** a state in which everyone has a say in the type of government. **2** a group of states united by certain common interests.

commotion /co-**mo**-shun/ *n* confused movement, disorder (*awakened by a commotion in the street*).

communal /cu-**myoo**-nal/ *adj* shared by all (*a communal changing room*).

commune /cu-**myoon**/ *vb* (*fml*) to talk together (with), to exchange thoughts or feelings with (*claims he can commune with plants*).

communicable /cu-**myoo**-ni-ca-bl/ *adj* **1** able to be passed to others (*a communicable disease*). **2** able to be communicated or explained to others (*ideas only communicable to experts*).

communicant /cu-**myoo**-ni-cant/ *n* one who receives Holy Communion, a religious ceremony practiced in some Christian churches.

communicate /cu-**myoo**-ni-cate/ *vb* **1** to make known to, to tell (*communicate the facts to her*). **2** to get in touch with (*communicate with each other by phone*). **3** to make known information, ideas, feelings, etc., clearly to others (*necessary to be able to communicate in this job*). **4** to pass (something) to another (*communicate a disease*).

communication /cu-myoo-ni-**cay**-shun/ *n* **1** a message (*receive a secret communication*). **2** a means of communicating (*telephone communications*).

communicative /cu-**myoo**-ni-ca-tiv/ *adj* talkative, ready to give information (*find the witnesses not very communicative*).

communion /cu-**myoon**-yun/ *n* the act of sharing. ● **Holy Communion** a religious ceremony practiced in some Christian churches.

communism /**com**-yoo-ni-zum/ *n* the belief in an economic system that based on all property being owned by the whole community and not by the individual.

communist /**com**-yoo-nist/ *n* a believer in communism. ● *adj* to do with communism. ● *adj* **communistic** /com-yoo-**nis**-tic/.

community /cu-**myoo**-ni-tee/ *n* the whole body of the people living in a town, district, country, etc. (*the mining disaster affected the whole community*).

commute /cu-**myoot**/ *vb* **1** to daily travel from the place where one lives to the place where one works (*commute by rail*). **2** to change into something less unpleasant (*commute the death sentence to one of life imprisonment*). ● *adj* **commutable** /cu-myoo-ta-bl/. ● *n* **commutation** /com-ye-**tay**-shun/.

commuter /cu-**myoo**-ter/ *n* one who commutes (*commuters affected by the rail strike*).

compact /com-**pact**/ *adj* **1** tightly packed, firm (*a compact mass of sand*). **2** fitted neatly together in a small space (*a compact kitchen*). **3** short, concise (*a compact account of the events/a compact style*). ● *n* **compact** a flat case for face powder. ● *n* **compactness** /cum-**pact**-ness/.

compact disc /**com**-pact **disc**/ *n* a small, hard, plastic disc on which sound or information is recorded in a form readable by a laser, often called **CD**.

companion /com-**pan**-yon/ *n* **1** a friend, a person, etc., who regularly accompanies another (*his dog* *was his constant companion/miss his companions at the club*). **2** one who goes with or accompanies (*her companion on her walk*). **3** a person employed to live with someone and keep him or her company (*the old lady's companion*). **4** one of a matching pair or set of things (*the companion to this volume*). ● *n* **companionship**.

companionable /com-**pan**-yu-na-bl/ *adj* liking company (*companionable people enjoy a social life*).

companionway /com-**pan**-yun-way/ *n* stairs on a ship from deck to cabin.

company *n* **1** a number of people gathered together by chance or invitation (*tell the company to help themselves*). **2** being together with another or others (*enjoy his company*). **3** a group of persons who have put together money to run a business. **4** a group of people working together (*a theatrical company*). **5** a body of soldiers commanded by a captain. **6** the crew of a ship.

comparable /com-**pa**-ra-bl/ *adj* **1** able to be compared (*a comparable job*). **2** nearly or just as good as (*a book that is comparable with the greatest novels*).

comparative /com-**pa**-ra-tive/ *adj* judged alongside something else, relative (*comparative luxury*).

compare /com-**pare**/ *vb* **1** to consider things together to see how they are alike and different (*compare the two accounts of the accident*). **2** to point out the likeness between (*compare his novels to those of Dickens*).

comparison /com-**pa**-ris-son/ *n* **1** act of comparing (*a small city in comparison with New York*). **2** likeness, similarity (*no comparison between fresh food and frozen*).

compartment /com-**part**-ment/ *n* **1** a part (e.g., of a drawer) divided off from the rest. **2** one of the small rooms in a railway carriage.

compass /**com**-pass/ *n* **1** a direction-finding instrument containing a magnetic needle that always points north. **2** (*fml*) full extent or range (*not within the compass of his power*). **4** *pl* **compasses** /**com**-pa-siz/ an instrument for drawing circles, consisting of two pointed legs connected at one end.

compassion /com-**pa**-shun/ *n* pity, deep sympathy (*show compassion for the refugees*).

compassionate /com-**pa**-shu-nate/ *adj* feeling or showing pity or deep sympathy.

compatible /com-**pa**-ti-bl/ *adj* **1** able to exist together peacefully (*husbands and wives should be compatible*). **2** in agreement with (*their accounts of the accident are not compatible*).

compatriot /com-**pay**-tree-ut/ *n* a person from the same country.

compel /com-**pel**/ *vb* (**compelled, compelling**) to make to do, to force (*compel him to pay his share*). ● *adj* **compelling** very interesting, attractive.

compendium /com-**pen**-dee-um/ *n* a summary containing the important aspects of a subject (*a compendium of sport*).

compensate /**com**-pen-sate/ *vb* **1** to give something to make up for harm or injury done (*compensate him for his injury at work*). **2** to undo or counteract the effect of a disadvantage, loss, etc. (*her aunt's love compensated for her parents' neglect*).

compensation /com-pen-**say**-shun/ *n* something given to make up for harm or injury.

compete /com-**peet**/ *vb* **1** to try to do better than one's fellows in work, games, etc. (*two teams competing for a place in the finals/two firms competing for a government grant*). **2** to take part in the hope of winning a prize (*a record number of teams competing*).

competence /**com**-pe-tense/, **compotency** /**com**-pe-ten-see/ *ns* **1** ability, skill (*no one doubts his competence as a statesman*). **2** (*old*) a sufficient amount of money to live on.

competent /**com**-pe-tent/ *adj* **1** good at one's job (*a competent teacher*). **2** well-done (*a competent job*). **3** (*fml*) having the necessary powers (*a court not competent to deal with the matter*). ● *adv* **competently** /**com**-pe-tent-lee/.

competition /com-pe-**ti**-shun/ *n* **1** the act of competing, rivalry (*a lot of competition for the post of manager*). **2** a contest for which a prize is offered (*enter the golf competition*). **3** people competing for a prize, etc. (*the competition is very strong*).

competitive /com-**pe**-ta-tive/ *adj* encouraging competition or rivalry (*a competitive industry*).

competitor /com-**pe**-ti-tor/ *n* **1** one who competes (*line up the competitors in the race*). **2** a rival (*a shop charging less than its competitors*).

compile /com-**pile**/ *vb* to collect (facts and figures, etc.) and put together in an orderly form. ● *n* **compiler** /com-**pile**-er/. ● *n* **compilation** /com-pi-**lay**-shun/.

complacence /com-**play**-sense/, **complacency** /com-**play**-sen-see/ *ns* satisfaction, especially self-satisfaction, smugness.

complacent /com-**play**-sent/ *adj* smug, satisfied with oneself and one's actions, etc. (*he's complacent about his position as champion but there are many new young players in the competition*).

complain /com-**plane**/ vb **1** to grumble (*complaining about the cold weather*). **2** to say that one is not satisfied (*complain to the manager about the faulty goods*).

complainant /com-**play**-nant/ n one who accuses another of an offence against the law.

complaint /com-**playnt**/ n **1** a grumble (*complaints about the weather*). **2** an expression of dissatisfaction (*write a letter of complaint to the manager*). **3** an illness (*childhood complaints*). **4** an accusation (*lodge a complaint against his noisy neighbor*).

complaisant /com-**play**-sant/ adj agreeable, ready to please (*a complaisant husband*). ● n **complaisance** /com-**play**-sanse/.

complement /com-pli-ment/ n **1** that which completes (*a good dessert is a complement to a good dinner*). **2** the number or quantity needed to make something complete (*have their full complement of office staff*).

complementary /com-pli-**men**-ta-ree/ adj adding what is necessary to make complete (*a dessert that is complementary to a dinner/a complementary amount*).

complete /com-**pleet**/ adj **1** finished (*a task that will soon be complete*). **2** whole (*a complete set of Shakespeare's plays*). **3** perfect (*a complete gentleman*). ● vb **1** to finish (*complete the task*). **2** to make whole (*complete their happiness*). ● n **completion** /com-**plee**-shun/.

complex /com-**plex**/ adj **1** having many parts (*complex machinery*). **2** not simple (*a complex plan*). ● n **1** a group of connected or similar things (*a shopping complex/a leisure complex*). **2** an abnormal mental state, often caused by past experiences or suppressed desires or fears, that influences a person's behavior (*an inferiority complex/have a complex about being short*).

complexion /com-**plek**-shun/ n the color, texture, and general appearance of the skin, especially the face.

complexity /com-**plek**-si-tee/ n **1** the state of being complex. **2** difficulty (*deal with the complexities of the situation*).

compliant /com-**plie**-ant/ adj giving in easily to others (*so compliant that everyone takes advantage of him*). ● n **compliance** /com-**plie**-anse/.

complicate /**com**-pli-cate/ vb to make difficult (*it will complicate matters if we travel separately*).

complicated /**com**-pli-cay-ted/ adj **1** difficult to understand (*a complicated problem*). **2** confusing because of having many parts (*a complicated machine*).

complication /com-pli-**cay**-shun/ n **1** a confused state of affairs. **2** an event or fact that makes things difficult.

complicity /com-**pli**-si-tee/ n helping to do something wrong (*accused of complicity in the robbery*).

compliment /**com**-pli-ment/ n **1** praise, a flattering remark (*pay her a compliment on her appearance*). **2** pl (fml) good wishes (*compliments of the season/free dessert with the compliments of the owner*). ● vb to praise, to express admiration.

complimentary /com-pli-**men**-ta-ree/ adj **1** flattering, showing admiration (*complimentary remarks*). **2** free (*complimentary tickets*).

comply /com-**ply**/ vb **1** to agree to (*complying with their request*). **2** to obey (*complied with the rules*).

component /com-**po**-nent/ n a part necessary to the whole object (*car components*). ● also adj.

comport /com-**poart**/ vb (fml) to behave (*comport oneself with dignity*).

compose /com-**poze**/ vb **1** to make up by putting together. **2** to write (*compose a poem/compose a piece of music*). **3** to calm (*take time to compose oneself*).

composed /com-**pozed**/ adj calm.

composer /com-**po**-zer/ n one who writes music.

composite /com-**poz**-it/ adj made up of several parts (*a composite picture painted by all the children in the class*).

composition /com-po-**zi**-shun/ n **1** act of putting together. **2** the arrangement of parts to form a pleasing whole (*studying the composition of the chemical*). **3** the thing composed or written (*children writing a composition/a composition for violins*). **4** a mixture (*a chemical composition*).

compost /**com**-post/ n rotting vegetable matter, etc., used as a fertilizer (*a compost heap*).

composure /com-**po**-zhur/ n calmness.

compote /**com**-pote/ n preserved or stewed fruit (*compote and cream for dessert*).

compound[1] /com-**pound**/ vb **1** to put together, to mix (*a painkiller compounded of two chemicals*). **2** to increase greatly (*the usual difficulties compounded by bad weather conditions*). ● adj **compound** /**com**-pound/, made up of two or more parts (*a compound substance*). ● n a mixture of two or more substances.

compound[2] /**com**-pound/ n an enclosed space with a building or buildings in it.

comprehend /com-pre-**hend**/ vb **1** to understand (*unable to comprehend his attitude*). **2** (fml) to include (*his estate comprehends all the land from the sea to the castle*).

comprehensible /com-pre-**hen**-si-bl/ *adj* able to be understood (*his speech was scarcely comprehensible*).

comprehension /com-pre-**hen**-shun/ *n* the power of understanding (*beyond our comprehension*).

comprehensive /com-pre-**hen**-sive/ *adj* taking in as much as possible (*a comprehensive survey*).

compress /com-**press**/ *vb* to press together into a smaller space (*compress all his belongings into a small case/compress all his material into a ten-minute speech*). ● *n* **compression** /com-pre-shun/. ● *n* **compress** /**com**-press/ a soft pad (*a cold compress to reduce the swelling*).

comprise /com-**prize**/ *vb* to be made up of (*a committee comprising only women/a house comprising three bedrooms, three public rooms, a bathroom, and a kitchen*).

compromise /**com**-pro-mize/ *vb* 1 to reach agreement by giving way on certain points (*we couldn't agree on a vacation destination, so we both had to compromise and choose somewhere acceptable to both of us*). 2 to leave open to suspicion or criticism (*politicians compromising themselves by accepting hospitality from business firms*). ● *n* an agreement reached when each party gives way on certain points.

compulsion /com-**pul**-shun/ *n* 1 force (*they left only under compulsion*). 2 an irresistible urge (*a sudden compulsion to run away*).

compulsory /com-**pulse**-ree/ *adj* forced, compelled (*the wearing of a school uniform is compulsory/compulsory safety helmets*).

compunction /com-**punc**-shun/ *n* regret, feeling of guilt (*feel no compunction about leaving work early*).

compute /com-**pyoot**/ *vb* (*fml*) to calculate or estimate (*compute the likely cost*). ● *n* **computation** /com-pyoo-**tay**-shun/.

computer /com-**pyoo**-ter/ *n* an electronic machine capable of storing and processing large amounts of information and of doing calculations. ● **computerize** /com-**pyoo**-te-rize/ *vb, also* **computerise** (*Br*) 1 to store (information) on a computer (*begin to computerize hospital records*) 2 to use computers to do the work connected with something (*production at the factory has now been fully computerized*). ● **computerization**, *also* **computerisation** (*Br*) /com-pyoo-te-ri-**zay**-shun/.

computer-aided design *n* the use of a computer to create plans and drawings.

computer graphics *npl* artwork or design that is created on a computer.

comrade /**com**-rade/ *n* a friend, a companion.

comradeship /**com**-rade-ship/ *n* good fellowship.

con[1] /con/ *vb* (**conned** /cond/, **conning** /**con**-ing/) to deceive, to trick (*con him into lending her money*).

con[2] /con/ *n* a reason, vote, or position in opposition (*make a list of the pros and cons*).

concave /**con**-cave/ *adj* hollow, curved inward (like a bowl).

conceal /con-**seel**/ *vb* to hide, to keep from others (*conceal the money/conceal his feelings*).

concealment /con-**seel**-ment/ *n* act of concealing.

concede /con-**seed**/ *vb* 1 to admit as true (*conceding that we may be wrong*). 2 to give up (*conceded his right to a part of his father's estate*).

conceit /con-**seet**/ *n* 1 too high an opinion of oneself. 2 (*fml*) a fanciful or imaginative idea (*a poem full of conceits*).

conceited /con-**see**-ted/ *adj* too proud of oneself, vain (*so conceited that she couldn't imagine losing the contest*).

conceivable /con-**see**-va-bl/ *adj* able to be thought of or imagined (*it was hardly conceivable that they were still alive*).

conceive /con-**seev**/ *vb* 1 to grasp clearly with the mind. 2 to imagine. 3 to become pregnant.

concentrate /**con**-sen-trate/ *vb* 1 to bring together to one point. 2 to bring all the powers of the mind to bear on. 3 to make a substance stronger by reducing its volume. 4 to pack tightly. ● *n* a concentrated substance. ● *n* **concentration** /con-sen-**tray**-shun/.

concentric /con-**sen**-tric/ *adj* having the same center (*concentric circles*).

concept /**con**-sept/ *n* a general idea (*scientific concepts*). ● *adj* **conceptual** /con-**sep**-chu-wal/.

conception /con-**sep**-shun/ *n* 1 act of conceiving. 2 an idea.

concern /con-**sern**/ *vb* 1 to have to do with (*the problem concerns all of us*). 2 to take interest (*concern themselves in other people's business*). 3 (*fml*) to be anxious about (*his absence concerned us*). ● *n* 1 an affair (*his financial concerns*). 2 interest (*of little concern to other people*). 3 anxiety (*the invalid's condition giving cause for concern*). 4 a business (*a profitable concern*).

concerning /con-**ser**-ning/ *prep* having to do with, about (*problems concerning work*).

concert /**con**-sert/ *n* a musical entertainment.

concerted /con-**ser**-ted/ *adj* planned together, worked out together (*a concerted effort*).

concertina /con-ser-**tee**-na/ *n* a musical wind instrument similar to an accordian but with buttons instead of a keyboard.

concerto /con-**cher**-toe/ *n* a musical composition for a solo player accompanied by an orchestra.

concession /con-**se**-shun/ *n* **1** the action of giving up (*the concession of his claim to his father's estate*). **2** a thing conceded, a favor (*he always wore jeans, but as a concession to his mother, he agreed to wear a suit to the dinner party*).

conch /**conch**/ *n* the large, spiral seashell of certain shellfish.

conciliate /con-**si**-lee-ate/ *vb* **1** (*fml*) to make less angry or more friendly (*try to conciliate her by bringing her some flowers*). **2** to create peace between (*conciliate the two parties in the argument*).

conciliation /con-si-lee-**ay**-shun/ *n* the bringing together in peace or friendship of those who have quarreled (*attempts at conciliation between the two sides*).

conciliatory /con-**sil**-ya-toe-ree/ *adj* calming, peacemaking (*some conciliatory words*).

concise /con-**saeess**/ *adj* short and to the point, brief (*a concise account of the events*). ● *n* **conciseness** /con-**saeess**-ness/.

conclave /con-clave/ *n* **1** in Catholicism, the meeting of cardinals to choose a new pope. **2** a meeting held in private (*a meeting in conclave*).

conclude /con-**clood**/ *n* **1** (*fml*) to end, to bring to an end (*conclude the meeting*). **2** to arrange, to settle on (*concluding an agreement*). **3** to come to believe after consideration of the facts (*after hearing the evidence, we conclude that he is guilty*).

conclusion /con-**cloo**-zhun/ *n* **1** (*fml*) end (*at the conclusion of the meeting*). **2** the idea finally reached after thinking something out (*come to the conclusion that he was innocent*).

conclusive /con-**cloo**-siv/ *adj* convincing, putting an end to doubt (*conclusive evidence*).

concoct /con-**coct**/ *vb* **1** to make by mixing (*concocting something for dinner*). **2** to make up, invent (*concocted an excuse for being late*).

concoction /con-**coc**-shun/ *n* food or drink made by mixing several things.

concomitant /con-**com**-i-tant/ *adj* (*fml*) accompanying, going together (*an important job and its concomitant responsibilities*). ● *also n.*

concord /con-cord/ *n* (*fml*) **1** agreement (*little concord among the committee members*). **2** peace and friendship (*neighboring countries living in concord*).

concordance /con-**cor**-danse/ *n* **1** agreement. **2** an alphabetical list of the most important words used in a book or by a writer and exactly where they can be found.

concordat /con-**cor**-dat/ *n* a treaty, a formal agreement.

concourse /con-coarse/ *n* **1** a large, open space for people (*the railway station concourse*). **2** (*fml*) a gathering, a crowd.

concrete /con-**creet**/ *adj* **1** solid, having a real bodily existence (unlike an idea) (*concrete evidence*). **2** definite (*no concrete plans*). ● *n* a mixture of cement, sand, and gravel with water.

concur /con-**cur**/ *vb* (**concurred** /con-**curd**/, **concurring** /con-**cur**-ing/) **1** to happen at the same time. **2** to agree (*we concurred with their plans*).

concurrence /con-**cur**-ense/ *n* **1** happening together at the same place. **2** (*fml*) agreement (*the concurrence of their opinions*).

concurrent /con-**cur**-ent/ *adj* **1** in agreement. **2** happening at the same time (*concurrent events/concurrent prison sentences*). ● *adv* **concurrently** /con-**cur**-ent-lee/.

concussion /con-**cu**-shun/ *n* **1** a violent shaking. **2** an injury that affects the function of an organ, especially the brain, as a result of a violent blow or impact (*had a concussion when he fell on the concrete floor*).

condemn /con-**dem**/ *vb* **1** to blame. **2** to find guilty. **3** to name a punishment for a guilty person. ● *n* **condemnation** /con-dem-**nay**-shun/.

condemnatory /con-**dem**-na-toe-ree/ *adj* laying the blame on.

condense /con-**dense**/ *vb* **1** to make shorter or smaller (*condense his original speech into a few sentences*). **2** to make a substance more solid (e.g., to change vapor into liquids). ● *n* **condensation** /con-den-**say**-shun/.

condescend /con-di-**send**/ *vb* to descend to the level, regarded as lower, of the person or people with whom one is dealing, usually in an ungracious, proud manner (*she condescended to speak to the workers*). ● *adj* **condescending** /con-di-**sen**-ding/. ● *n* **condescension** /con-di-**sen**-shun/.

condiment /con-di-ment/ *n* a seasoning, sauce, or relish eaten with food to bring out its flavor or enhance its taste (*salt and pepper and other condiments*).

condition /con-**di**-shun/ *n* **1** state (*furniture in poor condition/patients in no condition to be sent home*). **2** something that must be or happen before something else can take place (*a condition of the agreement/he can go on condition that he reports to the police*).

conditional /con-**dish**-nal/ *adj* depending on something else happening (*a conditional acceptance to university/an acceptance to the university conditional on his passing his exams*).

condolence /con-**doa**-lense/ *n* (*often pl*) expression of sympathy (*express our condolences to the widow*).

condone /con-**doan**/ *vb* to forgive, to pardon, to overlook a wrong (*condone his bad behavior because of his unhappy home life*).

condor /con-dor/ *n* a large vulture with black feathers, a bald head and neck, and soft, white feathers at the base of the neck.

conducive /con-**dyoo**-sive/ *adj* helping to produce, leading (*conducive to good health*).

conduct /con-**duct**/ *vb* 1 to lead, to guide (*conduct us to our seats*). 2 to carry (*pipes conducting water*). 3 to direct (*conducted the orchestra*). 4 (*fml*) to behave (*conduct oneself well*). ● *n* **conduct** / con-duct/ behavior.

conductor /con-**duc**-tor/ *n* 1 the director of an orchestra. 2 the person who takes the fares on a bus. 3 a substance that passes on heat or electricity to something else. ● *f* **conductress** /con-**duc**-tress/.

conduit /**con**-dwit/ *n* 1 a pipe or channel made to carry fluids. 2 tubing or piping that protects electric wires.

cone /**cone**/ *n* 1 a figure with a circular base and a pointed top. 2 the fruit of pines and firs. 3 any object shaped like a cone (*an ice-cream cone*).

confection /con-**fec**-shun/ *n* 1 the act of process of making something by mixing. 2 any kind of candy or other sweet treat.

confectionary /con-**fec**-shu-na-ree/ *adj* of or like a confection, of confectioners or their work.

confectioner /con-**fec**-shu-ner/ *n* a person whose work is making or selling candy and sweets.

confectionery /con-**fec**-shu-na-ree/ *n* 1 candy or other sweet treats. 2 the buisiness or work of a confectioner. 3 a candy store.

confederate /con-**fe**-de-rit/ *adj* joined together by agreement or common purpose (*confederate nations*). ● *n* 1 a supporter, a helper, often in wrongdoing (*the bully and his confederates*). 2 (*cap*) a southern supporter of the Confederate States of America during the Civil War (1860 to 1865).

confederation /con-fe-de-**ray**-shun/ *n* a group of states or nations that have agreed to act together.

confer /con-**fer**/ *vb* (**conferred, conferring**) 1 to talk together (*conferring over the plans*). 2 to give (*confer an honor on him*).

conference /**con**-frense/ *n* a meeting held to discuss matters (*an international conference on the environment*).

confess /con-**fess**/ *vb* to own up, to admit fault or guilt (*confess to the crime/confess one's sins*).

confession /con-**fe**-shun/ *n* the act of confessing, an account of the wrong one has done (*make a confession to the police*).

confessional /con-**fesh**-nal/ *n* in the Catholic church, the small room in which a priest hears confessions.

confessor /con-**fe**-sor/ *n* 1 a person who confesses. 2 in the Catholic church, a priest who hears confessions.

confetti /con-**fe**-tee/ *n* small pieces of colored paper thrown during celebrations.

confidant /**con**-fi-dawnt/ *n* a person trusted with a secret. ● *f* **confidante**.

confide /con-**fide**/ *vb* to give or tell something to a person one trusts (*confide her personal problems to a friend/confide in a friend*).

confiding /con-**fie**-ding/ *adj* trusting (*a confiding nature*).

confidence /**con**-fi-dense/ *n* 1 trust (*gain his confidence*). 2 belief in one's own abilities (*lose one's confidence*).

confident /**con**-fi-dent/ *adj* having no fear of failure (*confident competitors/confident of success*). ● *adv* **confidently** /**con**-fi-dent-lee/.

confidential /con-fi-**den**-shal/ *adj* 1 trusted (*a confidential secretary*). 2 secret (*confidential information*). ● *adv* **confidentially** /con-fi-den-shee-a-li-tee/.

configuration /con-fig-yu-**ray**-shun/ *n* (*fml*) shape that is determined by the arrangement of various parts.

configure /con-**fi**-gyer/ *vb* to arrange in a certain way.

confine /con-**fine**/ *vb* 1 to shut up (*confine prisoners in a cell*). 2 to keep within limits (*confine yourself to subjects that you know about*). ● *n* a limit, a boundary.

confinement /con-**fine**-ment/ *n* 1 imprisonment (*sentenced to a confinement of five years*). 2 childbirth.

confirm /con-**firm**/ *vb* 1 to say that something is undoubtedly certain or true (*confirm her alibi*). 2 to give final approval to (*confirmed his appointment as governor*).

confirmation /con-fir-**may**-shun/ *n* 1 proof (*receive confirmation of his innocence*). 2 the ceremony by which one becomes a full member of certain churches.

confirmed /con-**firmd**/ *adj* settled, habitual (*a confirmed bachelor*).

confiscate /**con**-fi-skate/ *vb* to seize a person's private property, especially as a punishment (*officials confiscating illegal drugs/the teacher confiscated the sweets*). ● *n* **confiscation** /con-fi-**skay**-shun/.

conflagrant /con-**flay**-grant/ *adj* burning.

conflagration /con-fla-**gray**-shun/ *n* (*fml*) a big, destructive fire.

conflict /**con**-flict/ *n* 1 a state of disagreement (*unions in conflict with management*). 2 a fight (*armed conflict*). ● *vb* **conflict** /con-**flict**/ to disagree, to clash (*modern ideas that conflict with traditional ones*).

conflicting /con-**flic**-ting/ *adj* 1 going against each other, fighting, or quarreling (*on conflicting sides*). 2 clashing, disagreeing (*conflicting opinions*).

confluence /**con**-floo-ense/ *n* 1 a flowing together. 2 the meeting of streams. ● *adj* **confluent** /con-floo-ent/.

conform /con-**fawrm**/ *vb* 1 to act or think like most other people, to accept the laws and practices of the time or place (*people who want to rebel don't conform to society*). 2 to obey, to be in accordance with (*conform to school rules/conform to safety standards*).

conformation /con-for-**may**-shun/ *n* the way in which a thing is put together, shape (*the conformation of the crystal*).

conformity /con-**fawr**-mi-tee/ *n* 1 behavior, attitudes, etc., that are the same as most people's. 2 agreement, obedience (*in conformity with the law/ not in conformity with safety standards*).

confound /con-**found**/ *vb* 1 to defeat completely. 2 to confuse, to mix up.

confront /con-**frunt**/ *vb* to meet face to face (*confront the enemy/confront the problems*). ● *n* **confrontation** /con-fron-**tay**-shun/.

confuse /con-**fyooz**/ *vb* 1 to put into disorder, to muddle (*confuse the arrangements/confuse the argument*). 2 to puzzle, to bewilder (*confused by the questions on the form*). 3 to mistake one person or thing for another (*confuse the two sisters*).

confusion /con-**fyoo**-zhun/ *n* 1 disorder (*a room in total confusion*). 2 puzzlement, bewilderment (*confusion over the meaning of the word*).

confute /con-**fyoot**/ *vb* to prove (someone) wrong, to prove untrue (*confute their argument/confute their accusation*). ● *n* **confutation** /con-fyu-**tay**-shun/.

congeal /con-**jeel**/ *vb* 1 to become thick by cooling or freezing. 2 to become solid and stiff (*blood congeals*).

congenial /con-**jee**-nee-al/ *adj* 1 having the same likes and dislikes (*a congenial companion*). 2 pleasing (*a congenial climate*).

congenital /con-**jen**-i-tal/ *adj* dating from birth (*a congenital brain defect*).

conger /**cong**-ger/ *n* a saltwater eel with a long fin on its back, sharp teeth, and powerful jaws.

congested /con-**jess**-tid/ *adj* 1 overcrowded (*congested roads*). 2 too full of blood or mucus (*congested arteries/nose is congested*). ● *n* **congestion** /con-**jess**-chun/.

conglomerate /con-**glom**-rit/ *adj* stuck together in a lump. ● *n* 1 a cluster. 2 a rock of different kinds of pebbles sticking together. 3 a large corporation formed by merging several different firms (*an international conglomerate*).

conglomeration /con-glom-e-**ray**-shun/ *n* a mixed collection (*a conglomeration of old toys*).

congratulate /con-**gra**-chu-late/ *vb* to express pleasure at another's success, a happy event, etc. (*congratulate him on getting onto the football team/ congratulate him on his engagement*. ● *n* **congratulation** /con-gra-chu-**lay**-shun/. ● *adj* **congratulatory** /con-**gra**-chu-la-tore-ree/.

congregate /**cong**-gri-gate/ *vb* to meet, to form a crowd (*the people congregated in the town hall*).

congregation /cong-gri-**gay**-shun/ *n* a gathering of people, especially at a church service.

congress /**cong**-gress/ *n* 1 a formal meeting of statesmen, etc., to settle certain questions. 2 **Congress** the part of the US government that makes laws, consisting of two parts: the Senate and the House of Representatives. ● *adj* **congressional** /cong-**gresh**-nal/.

congruent /**cong**-groo-ent/ *adj* suitable, agreeing (*behavior congruent with his position*). ● *n* **congruity** /cong-**groo**-i-tee/.

congruous /**cong**-groo-us/ *adj* suitable, agreeing (*punishment congruous with the crime*).

conic /**con**-ic/, **conical** /**con**-i-cal/ *adjs* cone-shaped.

conifer /**con**-i-fer/ *n* a cone-bearing tree. ● *adj* **coniferous** /con-i-**fe**-rus/.

conjectural /con-**jec**-che-ral/ *adj* due to guesswork, not certain (*opinions that are purely conjectural*).

conjecture /con-**jec**-cher/ *vb* to guess, to suppose. ● *n* guess.

conjoin /con-**join**/ *vb* (*fml*) to join, unite (*conjoin in marriage*).

conjoint /con-**joint**/ *adj* (*fml*) joined, united. ● *adv* **conjointly** /con-**joint**-lee/.

conjugal /**con**-ji-gal/ *adj* having to do with marriage or the relationship between husband and wife (*conjugal bonds*).

conjugate /**con**-ji-gate/ **1** *adj* joined, especially in a pair, coupled. **2** *vb* to give the forms (i.e. mood, tense, person, etc.) of a verb. ● *n* **conjugation** / con-ji-**gay**-shun/.

conjunction /con-**jung**-shun/ *n* **1** a connection. **2** in grammar, a joining word, such as and, but, or. ● *adj* **conjunctive** /con-**jung**-tiv/.

conjuncture /con-**jungk**-cher/ *n* (*fml*) a combination of events or situations, especially one causing difficulties (*a depressing conjuncture in their lives*).

conjure /**con**-jer/ *vb* **1** to do magic, to do tricks so quickly and skillfully that the onlooker cannot see how they are done. **2** to summon, to cause to appear as if by magic.

conjurer or **conjuror** /**con**-ju-rer/ *n* one who entertains by doing tricks, one who performs magic.

connect /co-**nect**/ *vb* **1** to join (*connect the two pipes*). **2** to see that a thing or idea is related to another, to associate in the mind (*he didn't connect the middle-aged woman with the girl he used to know/the police are connecting the two murders*). ● **well-connected** related to important or powerful people.

connection /co-**nec**-shun/ *n* **1** something that joins (*a loose connection between the two pipes*). **2** a relation by blood or marriage. **3** something that makes one think of a certain person, place, event, etc., when one sees another (*police making a connection between the crimes*).

connive /co-**nive**/ *vb* **1** to pretend not to see wrongdoing (*her parents connived at the girl's truancy*) **2** to cooperate secretly with someone, especially in wrongdoing. ● *n* **connivance** /co-**nie**-vanse/.

connoisseur /con-i-**sur**/ *n* one with expert knowledge of something and the ability to tell what is bad from what is good (*a connoisseur of opera*).

connotation /con-i-**tay**-shun/ *n* what is suggested by a word in addition to its actual meaning (*"armchair" has connotations of comfort*).

connote /co-**note**/ *vb* to suggest in addition to the actual meaning (*the word "plump" usually connotes cheerfulness*).

connubial /co-**noo**-bee-al/ *adj* (*fml*) having to do with marriage or married life (*connubial bliss*).

conquer /**cong**-ker/ *vb* **1** to win by war (*conquer the neighboring state*). **2** to defeat (*conquer the enemy/conquer his opponent*). **3** to overcome (*conquer her fears*). ● *n* **conqueror** /**cong**-ke-ror/.

conquest /**con**-kwest/ *n* **1** act of conquering. **2** the thing gained by force.

conscience /**con**-shense/ *n* one's sense of right and wrong (*have a bad conscience about her treatment of her friend*).

conscientious /con-she-**en**-shus/ *adj* careful to do one's duty at work (*conscientious pupils*). ● *n* **conscientiousness** /con-she-**en**-shus-ness/.

conscientious objector /con-she-**en**-shus ob-**jec**-tor/ *n* one who, in war, refuses to fight because he or she believes it is wrong to do so.

conscious /**con**-shus/ *adj* **1** knowing what is going on around one (*badly hurt but still conscious*). **2** aware (*conscious that he was being watched*). ● *n* **consciousness** /**con**-shus-ness/.

conscript /**con**-script/ *n* one made by law to serve in the armed services.

conscription /con-**scrip**-shun/ *n* the act of making people serve in the armed services by law.

consecrate /**con**-si-crate/ *vb* **1** to make holy (*consecrate a new church*). **2** to devote, to set apart (*consecrate his life to helping others*). ● *n* **consecration** /con-si-**cray**-shun/.

consecutive /con-**sec**-yu-tiv/ *adj* following one after the other, in order (*consecutive numbers/on consecutive days*).

consensus /con-**sen**-sis/ *n* general agreement (*fail to reach a consensus on the issue*).

consent /con-**sent**/ *vb* to agree, to give one's permission (*to consent to the operation*). ● *n* agreement, permission.

consequence /**con**-se-kwense/ *n* **1** a result, an effect (*have to face the consequences of their actions*). **2** importance (*matters of no consequence*).

consequent /**con**-se-kwent/ *adj* (*fml*) following, resulting (*his illness and consequent death*).

consequential /con-se-**kwen**-shal/ *adj* **1** following upon. **2** self-important.

conservatism /con-**ser**-va-ti-zum/ *n* dislike of changes, especially in the way of governing.

conservative /con-**ser**-va-tiv/ *adj* **1** disliking change. **2** moderate, cautious, safe.

conservatory /con-**ser**-va-toe-ree/ *n* **1** a room enclosed in glass for showing or growing plants, a greenhouse. **2** a school of fine arts, specifically music.

conserve /con-**serv**/ vb **1** to keep something as it is (*conserving the environment*). **2** to keep from being wasted (*conserved our supplies*). ● n two or more fruits preserved in sugar, a kind of jam. ● n **conservation** /con-ser-**vay**-shun/.

consider /con-**si**-der/ vb **1** to think about (*consider what's best to do*). **2** to think seriously (*take time to consider before acting*). **3** to take into account (*consider the effect on others*). **4** to regard as (*considered him a hero*).

considerable /con-**si**-der-a-bl/ adj fairly large, great (*a considerable amount of money/considerable influence*).

considerate /con-**sid**-rit/ adj thoughtful of others.

consideration /con-si-de-**ray**-shun/ n **1** serious thought (*give consideration to her future*). **2** thought for others and their feelings (*show consideration to elderly people*). **3** a payment or reward (*do the work for a consideration*).

considering /con-**si**-de-ring/ prep allowing for.

consign /con-**sine**/ vb (*fml*) **1** to deliver to, to put in the care of another (*consign the body to the grave*). **2** to send (*goods consigned to you by rail*).

consignment /con-**sine**-ment/ n the goods sent (*a consignment of drugs found by police*).

consist /con-**sist**/ vb to be made up of (*a stew that consists of beef and vegetables*).

consistency /con-**sis**-ten-see/ n **1** degree of thickness (*the consistency of the jam*). **2** the quality of being consistent.

consistent /con-**sis**-tent/ adj **1** fixed, having a regular pattern (*show consistent improvement*). **2** agreeing with (*action consistent with the company's policy/a statement not consistent with the previous one*). **3** always thinking or acting on the same principles (*the judge's punishments are harsh, but he is always consistent*).

consolation /con-so-**lay**-shun/ n **1** comfort (*bring consolation to those that have suffered*). **2** a person or thing that brings comfort in sorrow or sadness (*the new baby was a consolation to the unhappy family*).

console[1] /con-**sole**/ vb to comfort (*consoling the unhappy little girl with some sweets*). ● adj **consolatory** /con-so-**la**-toe-ree/.

console[2] /con-**sole**/ n the raised portion between the two front seats in a car, containing storage compartments, switces, and/or controls.

consolidate /con-**sol**-i-date/ vb **1** to make solid or firm, to strengthen (*consolidating your present position*). **2** to unite or combine into a single whole, to merge (*consolidated four small firms into one large one*). ● n **consolidation** /con-sol-i-**day**-shun/.

consonance /con-si-nanse/ n (*fml*) agreement.

consonant /con-si-nant/ n a speech sound or letter other than a vowel. ● adj in agreement with.

consort /con-sort/ n a partner, a husband or wife (*the gentleman's consort*). ● vb **consort** /con-**sort**/ (*fml*) to go out together, to associate with (*object to his daughter consorting with criminals*).

conspicuous /con-**spic**-yoo-us/ adj easily seen, very noticeable (*she was conspicuous in her red coat*).

conspiracy /con-**spi**-ra-see/ n **1** a coming together to plan wrongdoing (*arrested on charges of conspiracy*). **2** a plot (*discover the conspiracy to kill the king*).

conspire /con-**spire**/ vb **1** to plan secretly together to do something unlawful (*terrorists conspiring to bring down the government*). **2** to unite (*events that conspired to bring about his ruin*). ● n **conspirator** /con-**spi**-ra-tor/.

constant /con-stant/ adj **1** never stopping (*constant noise/constant rain*). **2** unchanging (*temperatures at a constant level*). **3** (*fml*) faithful, loyal (*friends forever constant*). ● n **constancy** /con-stan-see/.

constantly /con-stant-lee/ adv **1** again and again, nearly always, regularly (*children constantly nagging*). **2** without stopping (*lights burning constantly*).

constellation /con-ste-**lay**-shun/ n a group of stars, usually named for an object or animal that is resembles.

consternation /con-ster-**nay**-shun/ n great surprise, dismay (*to our great consternation our team lost*).

constipated /con-sti-pay-ted/ adj having difficulty in clearing the bowels. ● n **constipation** /con-sti-**pay**-shun/.

constipation /con-sti-**pay**-shun/ n a condition in which clearing the bowels is difficult.

constituency /con-**stich**-wan-see/ n the people of a district who vote for a governmental representative.

constituent /con-**stich**-wint/ adj being part of, forming (*the constituent parts of the machine*). ● n **1** a necessary part (*a constituent of the chemical compound*). **2** a member of a constituency (*a meeting of the politician's constituents*).

constitute /con-sti-toot/ vb **1** (*fml*) to be (*his dismissal constitutes a breach of the rules*). **2** to make up, to form (*twelve months constitute one year/five people constitute the committee*).

constitution /con-sti-**too**-shun/ n **1** the way something is made up (*the constitution of the* committee). **2** the general health of the body (*have a strong constitution*). **3** the body of law with which a country is governed. **4** (*cap*) the document containing the fundamental laws and rights of the citizens of the United States.

constitutional /con-sti-**toosh**-nal/ *adj* having to do with the laws of a country. ● *n* (*old*) a short walk taken to improve the health.

constrain /con-**strane**/ *vb* to force, to compel (*you must not feel constrained to go/I feel constrained to write and complain*).

constraint /con-**straint**/ *n* **1** force, compulsion (*leave only under constraint*). **2** a limit (*no constraints on your freedom*). **3** strained manner, lack of friendliness (*aware of a certain constraint between the two people*).

constrict /con-**strict**/ *vb* **1** to make smaller or narrower, to make tight (*a drug constricting blood vessels*). **2** to prevent free movement (*constricted by lack of money*). ● *n* **constriction** /con-**stric**-shun/.

constrictor /con-**stric**-tor/ *n* a large snake that crushes its prey.

construct /con-**struct**/ *vb* **1** to build (*construct a new building*). **2** to make by putting the parts together (*construct an idea*).

construction /con-**struc**-shun/ *n* **1** act of constructing. **2** the thing constructed (*a large construction*). **3** the way of arranging words to give a certain meaning. **4** (*fml*) meaning (*what construction do you put on his statement?*).

constructive /con-**struc**-tiv/ *adj* useful and helpful (*constructive criticism*).

construe /con-**stroo**/ *vb* **1** to translate into another language. **2** to explain, to interpret (*construing his remark as an insult*).

consul /**con**-sul/ *n* a person appointed to look after the interests of his or her country in a foreign country.

consular /**con**-si-lar/ *adj* having to do with a consul.

consulate /**con**-si-lit/ *n* the office of a consul.

consult /con-**sult**/ *vb* **1** to ask advice, information, or help from (*consult a doctor*). **2** to discuss matters with (*consult his partners*). **3** to look up (*consult a dictionary*). ● *n* **consultation** /con-sul-**tay**-shun/.

consultant /con-**sul**-tant/ *n* one able to advise, especially a doctor who is an expert in a particular branch of medicine (*a chest consultant*).

consume /con-**soom**/ *vb* **1** to eat (*consume quantities of chocolate*). **2** to use up (*consume our supply of firewood*). **3** to destroy, to waste (*a building consumed by fire*).

consumer /con-**soo**-mer/ *n* one who buys or uses (*consumers' rights*).

consummate /**con**-su-mate/ *vb* to finish, to make complete or perfect (*the award consummated his life's work*). ● *adj* complete, perfect (*a consummate performance*). ● *n* **consummation** /con-su-**may**-shun/.

consumption /con-**sum**-shun/ *n* **1** the act of using. **2** the amount used (*low electricity consumption*). **3** (*old*) a disease of the lungs (tuberculosis).

consumptive /con-**sum**-tiv/ *adj* suffering from the disease of consumption (tuberculosis). ● *also n*.

contact /**con**-tact/ *n* **1** touch (*come into contact with dangerous chemicals/in contact with someone with measles*). **2** communication (*keep in contact with old friends*). ● *vb* to get in touch with, to communicate with (*contact her by phone*).

contact lens /**con**-tact **lenz**/ *n* a small round piece of thin plastic or glass placed on the front of the eye to help the wearer see better.

contagious /con-**tay**-jus/ *adj* (*of disease*) able to be passed on by touch, quickly spreading to others. ● *n* **contagion** /con-**tay**-jun/.

contain /con-**tane**/ *vb* **1** to have in it (*a bucket containing a gallon of water*). **2** to keep control of (*contain the fire*).

container /con-**tay**-ner/ *n* anything made to hold something else in it (*a plant container*).

contaminate /con-**ta**-mi-nate/ *vb* to make dirty, infected, or impure, to pollute (*chemical waste contaminating the water*). ● *n* **contamination** /con-ta-mi-**nay**-shun/.

contemn /con-**tem**/ *vb* (*old or lit*) to look down on, to despise.

contemplate /**con**-tem-plate/ *vb* **1** to look at thoughtfully (*contemplating the bottom of his glass*). **2** to think deeply about (*contemplated her future*). **3** to think of doing (*contemplate moving*). ● *n* **contemplation** /con-tem-**play**-shun/.

contemplative /con-**tem**-pla-tiv/ *adj* **1** thoughtful (*in a contemplative mood*). **2** spending a lot of time in prayer.

contemporary /con-**tem**-po-ra-ree/ *adj* **1** belonging to the same time (*contemporary musicians/a contemporary record of the war*). **2** modern (*contemporary styles*). ● *n* one who lives at the same time as another (*a contemporary of Bach*).

contempt /con-**temt**/ *n* the feeling that another person or thing is worthless and to be looked down on, scorn (*the wealthy businessman's contempt for unsuccessful people*).

contemptible /con-**tem**-ti-bl/ *adj* deserving to be looked down on (*contemptible behavior*).

contemptuous /con-**tem**-choo-us/ *adj* showing contempt or scorn (*a contemptuous smile*).

contend /con-**tend**/ *vb* **1** to struggle against (*contend against financial difficulties*). **2** to compete (*contending for the trophy*). **3** to maintain, to state (*contended that he was innocent*). ● *n* **contender** / con-**tend**-er/.

content[1] /**con**-tent/ *n* that which is in something else (*the content of his speech*).

content[2] /con-**tent**/ *adj* satisfied, pleased, not wanting more than one has (*content with their humble way of life/content with his exam results*). ● *also vb and n.* ● *n* **contentment** /con-**tent**-ment/.

contention /con-**ten**-shun/ *n* **1** disagreement, argument (*much contention in the town about the new road*). **2** competition (*in contention for the trophy*). **3** an opinion (*his contention is that he is innocent*).

contentious /con-**ten**-shus/ *adj* quarrelsome (*contentious neighbors*).

contest /con-**test**/ *vb* **1** to try to prove wrong (*contest the will*). **2** to try hard to gain (*contest the boxing title*). ● *n* **contest** /**con**-test/ **1** a struggle (*a contest for promotion*). **2** a competition (*an athletics contest*).

contestant /con-**tes**-tant/ *n* one who contests (*the contestants in the quiz show*).

context /**con**-tecst/ *n* **1** the parts of a sentence, book, paragraph, etc., surrounding a word or meaning (*took the quotation out of context*). **2** circumstances, the whole situation, background, or environment to a particular event (*in the context of his unhappy childhood*).

contiguous /con-**ti**-joo-us/ *adj* (*fml*) touching, next to, neighboring (*his farm and contiguous fields*). ● *n* **contiguity** /con-ti-**joo**-wi-tee/.

continence /**con**-ti-nense/ *n* self-control.

continent[1] /**con**-ti-nent/ *adj* able to control oneself.

continent[2] /**con**-ti-nent/ *n* one of the large land masses in the world (e.g., Africa).

continental /con-ti-**nen**-tal/ *adj* having to do with a continent.

contingency /con-**tin**-jen-see/ *n* something that may happen but is not certain to do so (*prepared for all possible contingencies*).

contingent /con-**tin**-jent/ *adj* **1** happening only if something else happens first (*success contingent upon hard work*). **2** accidental (*contingent advantages*). ● *n* a body of soldiers, scouts, etc.

continual /con-**tin**-yoo-wal/ *adj* **1** going on all the time (*live in continual fear*). **2** happening again and again, repeated (*continual interruptions*).

continuance /con-**tin**-yoo-wanse/ *n* the going on or lasting of.

continuation /con-tin-yoo-**way**-shun/ *n* **1** act of going on or carrying on. **2** something that continues from something else (*this is a continuation of the street where they live*).

continue /con-**tin**-yoo/ *vb* **1** to go on doing (*continue working although in pain*). **2** to carry on with later (*continue with his work after dinner*). **3** to go or move further (*the forest continuing as far as one can see*). **4** to remain (*continued in the same job*).

continuity /con-ti-**nyoo**-wi-tee/ *n* uninterrupted connection, a series, the fact or quality of being continuous (*ensure continuity of supplies*).

continuous /con-**tin**-yoo-wus/ *adj* **1** never stopping (*continuous noise*). **2** unbroken (*a continuous line*).

contort /con-**tort**/ *vb* to twist out of shape (*his face contorted in rage*).

contortion /con-**tor**-shun/ *n* **1** act of twisting. **2** a twisting of the body.

contortionist /con-**tor**-shu-nist/ *n* one who entertains people by twisting his or her body into strange shapes, an acrobat.

contour /**con**-toor/ *n* **1** an outline, a shape (*the smooth contours of the sculpture*). **2** a line drawn on a map through all places of the same height.

contraband /**con**-tra-band/ *n* **1** goods that it is forbidden by law to bring into the country. **2** goods brought into the country against the law. ● *adj* (*of goods*) forbidden by law.

contract /**con**-tract/ *vb* **1** to arrange by agreement (*contract to build the house*). **2** to make or become smaller or shorter (*metals contract as they cool*). **3** to begin to have (*contract a fatal illness*). ● *n* **contract** /**con**-tract/ a legal written agreement (*sign a contract*).

contraction /con-**trac**-shun/ *n* **1** something becoming smaller or shorter. **2** a shortened form (*"I'm" is a contraction of "I am"/muscles contract when they are being used*).

contractor /**con**-trac-tor/ *n* one who undertakes to do certain jobs (*a building contractor*).

contradict /con-tra-**dict**/ *vb* **1** to say the opposite (*his story contradicts hers*). **2** to say that something is not true (*she contradicted what he said about the accident*). ● *n* **contradiction** /con-tra-**dic**-shun/.

contradictory /con-tra-**dic**-tree/ *adj* saying the opposite (*contradictory statements*).

contralto /con-**tral**-toe/ *n* **1** a very low singing voice for a woman. **2** a singer with a voice in this range.

contraption /con-**trap**-shun/ *n* an unusual machine or instrument (*an inventor always building strange contraptions*).

contrariety /con-tra-**rie**-i-tee/, **contrariness** /con-tra-ree-ness/ *ns* opposition.

contrary /**con**-tra-ree/ *adj* **1** opposite (*hold contrary opinions/opinions contrary to ours*). **2** always choosing to act differently from others, difficult to deal with. ● *n* **contrary** the opposite (*on the contrary*).

contrast /con-**trast**/ *vb* **1** to put things together to show clearly the differences between them (*contrast their neat garden with our sloppy one*). **2** to appear very different from (*a black dress contrasting with her blonde hair*). ● *n* **contrast** /**con**-trast/ a clear difference.

contravene /con-tra-**veen**/ *vb* to go against, to disagree with in an argument. ● *n* **contravention** /con-tra-**ven**-shun/.

contribute /con-**tri**-byut/ *vb* **1** to give part of what is needed (*contributing to her going-away present/contributed $20 to the charity*). **2** to write something for (*contribute several articles to the magazine*). ● *n* **contribution** /con-tri-**byoo**-shun/. ● *n* **contributor** /con-**tri**-byu-ter/.

contributory /con-**tri**-byu-toe-ree/ *adj* giving a share, helping.

contrite /con-**trite**/ *adj* showing or feeling guilt or sorrow for something one has done (*a contrite apology*). ● *n* **contrition** /con-**tri**-shun/.

contrive /con-**trive**/ *vb* **1** to succeed in, usually with difficulty (*contriving to hold a surprise party for her*). **2** to succeed in bringing about, usually with difficulty (*contrived a meeting between the two rivals*).

control /con-**trole**/ *n* **1** power over the movements and actions of another person or thing (*a country under the control of a tyrant*). **2** power over one's own thoughts and feelings (especially self-control) (*keep her temper under control*). **3** *pl* those parts of a machine that start, stop, or change the movement of all other parts (*the controls of the plane*). ● *vb* (**controlled** /con-**trold**/, **controlling** /con-**trole**-ing/) **1** to have power or authority over (*controlled the whole department*). **2** to direct the movements of (*control the car*). **3** to hold back, to restrain (*control yourself*). **4** to regulate, to cause to keep to a fixed standard (*control prices*). ● *n* **controller** /con-**troe**-ler/.

control tower /con-**trole** tow-er/ *n* an airport building from which messages are sent by radio to aircraft, telling them when, where, and how it is safe to land or take off.

controversial /con-tro-**ver**-shal/ *adj* causing disagreement, discussion, argument (*a controversial decision*).

controversy /**con**-tro-ver-see/ *n* disagreement, discussion, argument (*a lot of controversy over the decision to close the local school*).

controvert /**con**-tro-vert/ *vb* to argue or reason against (*a statement that cannot be controverted*).

conundrum /co-**nun**-drum/ *n* a riddle whose the answer is a play on words.

convalesce /con-va-**less**/ *vb* to recover gradually after an illness (*home from hospital to convalesce*). ● *n* **convalescence** /con-va-**le**-sense/. ● *adj and n* **convalescent** /con-va-**le**-sent/.

convection /con-**vec**-shun/ *n* warming by the spreading of heat from a portion of water or air to that surrounding it until a current of warmth is set up.

convector /con-**vec**-tor/ *n* a heater that works by convection.

convene /con-**veen**/ *vb* **1** to call together (*convened a meeting*). **2** to meet (*the committee is convening for an emergency meeting*).

convener /con-**vee**-ner/ *n* **1** one who calls members to a meeting. **2** the chairman of a committee.

convenience /con-**veen**-yense/ *n* **1** quality of being convenient or suitable (*come at your convenience/the convenience of the house to the station/the convenience of her kitchen*). **2** comfort (*a house full of modern conveniences*).

convenient /con-**veen**-yent/ *adj* **1** suitable, not causing trouble or difficulty (*find a convenient date/when it is convenient for you*). **2** easy to reach, accessible (*a house convenient for the train station*). **3** easy to use or manage (*a convenient size of house*).

convent /**con**-vent/ *n* a community of nuns or sometimes monks living under strict religious vows. ● *adj* **conventual** /con-**ven**-chal/.

convention /con-**ven**-shin/ *n* **1** a large meeting called for a special purpose (*a convention on mental health*). **2** an agreement (*a convention to ban nuclear weapons*). **3** a way of behaving that has been in use for so long that it is regarded as necessary, a custom (*a common convention when meeting someone new is to shake hands/a matter of convention*).

conventional /con-**vench**-nal/ *adj* **1** following convention (*a conventional way of behaving*). **2** accepting the manners and ideas of others, not original (*a very conventional person*).

converge /con-**verge**/ *vb* to move from different directions toward one point (*converging on the* *town from all directions).* ● *n* **convergence** /con-ver-jense/. ● *adj* **convergent** /con-**ver**-jent/.

conversant /con-**ver**-sant/ *adj* having knowledge of (*not conversant with modern methods*).

conversation /con-ver-**say**-shun/ *n* talk, speech with others.

conversational /con-ver-**say**-shnal/ *adj* having to do with talk or speech with others (*in conversational tones*).

conversationalist /con-ver-**say**-shna-list/ *n* one who is good at talking easily with others.

converse[1] /con-**verse**/ *vb* (*fml*) to talk.

converse[2] /**con**-verse/ *n* the exact opposite (*the converse of what he says is true*). ● *also adj.*

conversely /con-**verse**-lee/ *adv* looked at in the opposite way.

conversion /con-**ver**-zhun/ *n* a change, especially in belief or way of life (*his conversion to Christianity*).

convert /con-**vert**/ *vb* **1** to change from one state or form to another (*coal converted to gas/a sofa that converts to a bed/convert dollars to pounds*). **2** to get another to change his or her ideas, especially on religion. ● *n* **convert** /**con**-vert/ one who has changed his or her beliefs or way of life.

convertible /con-**ver**-ti-bl/ *adj* able to be changed into something else (*a sofa convertible to a bed/a convertible sofa*). ● *n* a car whose roof rolls or folds back so that the driver and passengers are riding in open air.

convex /con-**veks**/ *adj* curved outward (like a bowl when upside down). ● *n* **convexity** /con-**vek**-si-tee/.

convey /con-**vay**/ *vb* **1** to carry, to take from one place to another (*pipes conveying oil/buses conveying children/trucks conveying food*). **2** to pass (e.g., property) from one person to another. **3** to make known (*convey our apologies to our hostess*).

conveyance /con-**vay**-anse/ *n* **1** any kind of automobile that carries people or things (*go by public conveyance rather than private car*). **2** the document by which property is passed from one person to another.

conveyancing /con-**vay**-an-sing/ *n* the preparing of the papers to make a change in ownership lawful.

convict /con-**vict**/ *vb* to prove guilty, especially in a court of law (*convict him of robbery*). ● *n* **convict** /**con**-vict/ a person imprisoned for a crime.

conviction /con-**vic**-shun/ *n* **1** a proving of guilt (*the conviction of the accused*). **2** a strong belief (*a woman of strong convictions*).

convince /con-**vince**/ *vb* to persuade a person that

something is true (*convincing the teacher of his innocence/I am convinced he is lying*).

convincing /con-**vin**-sing/ *adj* **1** able to convince (*a convincing argument*). **2** clear (*a convincing victory*).

convivial /con-**viv**-yal/ *adj* **1** having to do with a feast or festive activity. **2** fond of eating, drinking, and good company. ● *n* **conviviality** /con-vi-vee-al-i-tee/.

convocation /con-vo-**cay**-shun/ *n* a meeting, especially for religious or academic purposes.

convoke /con-**voke**/ *vb* to call together.

convolution /con-vo-**loo**-shun/ *n* **1** a twisting or winding together (*a carving with curves and convolutions*). **2** complication (*the convolutions of the plot*). ● *adj* **convolute** /con-vo-**loot**/. ● *vb* **convolve** /con-**volv**/.

convoy /**con**-voy/ *vb* to go with to protect (*a warship convoying ships across the Atlantic/parents convoying children to and from school*). ● *n* **convoy 1** warships accompanying other ships to protect them. **2** the ships so protected. **3** a number of army wagons traveling together for protection.

convulse /con-**vulse**/ *vb* **1** to shake violently (*convulsing with laughter*). **2** to agitate, to disturb (*a country convulsed with revolution*).

convulsion /con-**vul**-shun/ *n* a fit, shaking (*go into convulsions/suffer from convulsions*).

convulsive /con-**vul**-sive/ *adj* sudden and jerky (*convulsive movements*).

cony *see* **coney**.

coo /coo/ *vb* to make a soft, murmuring sound as a dove would, to speak gently and lovingly. ● *also n.*

cook /cook/ *vb* to prepare food by heating it. ● *n* one who prepares food for eating.

cookery /**coo**-ke-ree/ *n* the art, practice, or work of preparing food.

cookie /**coo**-kee/ *n* **1** a small, sweet cake, usually either crispy or chewy. **2** a small file placed on a computer by a Web site or online service, to store information about the user.

cool /cool/ *adj* **1** slightly cold, pleasantly cold (*a cool drink on a hot day*). **2** calm, not easily excited (*keep cool in difficult situations*). ● *vb* **1** to make or become colder (*drinks cooling in the fridge*). **2** to become calmer or less interested (*she was very angry, but she's cooled down/he was in love with her, but he's cooled off*). ● *n* **coolness**.

coolly /**cool**-lee/ *adv* calmly, without excitement

coop /coop/ *n* a cage for hens or other small animals (*a chicken coop*). ● *vb* to shut up in a small space (*cooped up in a small office*).

cooper /**coo**-per/ *n* one who makes or repairs barrels.

cooperate, co-operate /co-op-er-ate/ *vb* to work or act together (*pupils cooperating on a project/the public cooperating with the police*). ● *n* **cooperation, co-operation** /co-op-er-ay-shun/.

cooperative, co-operative /co-op-er-a-tive/ *adj* **1** willing to work with others, helpful (*the cooperative attitude of the staff*). **2** made, done, etc., by people working together (*a cooperative effort/a cooperative farm*).

co-opt /co-**opt**/ *vb* to elect into a society or committee by the votes of the members.

coordinate, co-ordinate /co-or-di-nate/ *vb* to make things work or happen together for the same purpose (*coordinate her movements/coordinate the various parts of the campaign/coordinate our efforts*). ● *npl* **coordinates** /co-**ord**-nats/ figures that indicate a position on a map or squared paper. ● *n* **coordination, co-ordination** /co-or-di-**nay**-shun/.

coot /coot/ *n* a ducklike freshwater bird.

cope[1] /cope/ *n* a capelike garment worn by a clergyman on certain occasions.

cope[2] /cope/ *vb* to deal with, especially successfully (*coping with tired children/single mothers finding it difficult to cope/unable to cope with his work*).

coping /co-ping/ *n* the top row of stones, bricks, or concrete on a wall, usually sloped to carry off water.

copious /co-pee-us/ *adj* plentiful (*copious supplies of food*).

copper /cop-er/ *n* **1** a reddish brown metal, used to make pennies. **2** a large metal container.

copperplate /cop-er **plate**/ *n* **1** a plate of copper on which something has been engraved. **2** a print made from this.

copse, *or* **coppice** /cops/ *ns* a group of small trees or bushes growing close together.

copy /cop-ee/ *n* **1** a thing done or made in exactly the same way as another (*keep a copy of the letter/this picture is not by Picasso—it is a copy*). **2** a single example of a newspaper, magazine, book, etc. (*order several copies of the book*). **3** written material given to the printer for printing. ● *vb* to imitate, to make a copy of.

copyright /cop-ee-rite/ *n* the right, given to one person or publisher only, to print and sell books, music, or pictures for a certain number of years.

coquette /co-ket/ *n* a woman who flirts. ● *adj* **coquettish** /co-ke-tish/.

coracle /cawr-a-cl/ *n* a boat made of basketwork or wicker and covered with animal skins.

coral /cawr-al/ *n* a rocklike material built under the sea from the skeletons of tiny creatures (polyps).

cord /cawrd/ *n* **1** a thin rope, a thick string (*tie the box up with cord*). **2** a length of electrical cable attached to an electrical device. **3** a part of the body resembling this (*the spinal cord/vocal cords*).

cordial /cawr-jal/ *adj* **1** very friendly (*a cordial welcome*). **2** heartfelt (*cordial thanks*). ● *n* a refreshing drink.

cordiality /cawr-jee-a-li-tee/ *n* friendliness (*greet his guests with great cordiality*).

cordon /cawr-don/ *n* a line of soldiers, police, etc., to prevent people from entering an area (*crowds kept back from the accident by a police cordon*). ● *vb* to surround with a cordon (*police cordoned off the area and the house held by the gunman*).

corduroy /cawr-du-roy/ *n* a strong cotton cloth with raised, cordlike lines running from one end to the other (*pants made of brown corduroy*).

core /core/ *n* **1** the central part of a fruit in which the seeds are stored (*apple core*). **2** the innermost part, the most important part (*the core of the problem*).

cork /cawrk/ *n* **1** the cork tree or its bark. **2** a stopper made from cork (*the cork from a wine bottle*). ● *vb* to stop a bottle with a cork.

corkscrew /cawrk-scroo/ *n* an instrument for taking the cork out of a bottle.

corn[1] /cawrn/ *n* **1** a small, hard seed or seedlike fruit, kernel (*peppercorn*). **2** a cereal plant, with the grain growing on cobs enclosed in husks. ● *vb* to put salt on or soak in salt water to preserve (*corned beef*).

corn[2] /cawrn/ *n* a hard, painful growth of skin on the toe or foot.

corncob /cawrn-cob/ *n* the woody core of an ear of corn where the kernels grow.

cornea /cawr-nee-ya/ *n* the clear covering of the eyeball.

corner /cawr-ner/ *n* **1** the meeting place of two walls (*a table standing in the corner*). **2** a bend in a road (*the car took the corner too quickly*). **3** a difficult position (*he is in a tight corner financially*). ● *vb* **1** to drive into a position from which there is no escape (*cornered the wild animal/police succeeded in cornering the escaped prisoner*). **2** to put into a difficult situation (*corner the politician by asking awkward questions*). **3** to gain total control of (*corner the market in pine furniture*).

cornerstone /cawr-ner **stone**/ *n* **1** a stone put at the corner of the foundation of a new building. **2** something very important, something on which everything is based (*the cornerstone of the firm's success*).

cornet /**cawr**-net/ *n* a musical instrument similar to a trumpet.

cornflour /**cawrn**-flaoo-wer/ *n* (*Br*) cornstarch.

cornflower /**cawrn**-flaoo-wer/ *n* a plant with white, pink, or blue flowers that form a round head at the top of the stem.

cornice /**cawr**-nis/ *n* **1** a plaster decoration running along the top of a wall of a room (*a cornice of flowers*). **2** an ornamental line of stone sticking out at the top of a wall of a building.

cornstarch /**cawrn** starch/ *n* flour made from corn (*Chinese cooking often uses cornstarch*).

corollary /**cor**-ol-la-ree/ *n* something that must be true if another thing is proved true.

coronation /caw-ro-**nay**-shun/ *n* the crowning of a king or queen.

coroner /**caw**-ro-ner/ *n* an officer of the law who determines the cause of death when not obviously due to natural causes (*a case sent to the coroner*).

corporal[1] /**cawr**-pral/ *adj* (*fml*) having to do with the body (*corporal punishment*).

corporal[2] /**cawr**-pral/ *n* an officer in the military.

corporal punishment /**cawr**-pral **pun**-ish-ment/ *n* punishing by beating the body.

corporate /**cawr**-pe-rit/ *adj* **1** forming one group (*several individuals forming a corporate body*). **2** of or shared by all the members of a group (*corporate responsibility*). ● *adv* **corporately** /**cawr**-pe-rit-lee/.

corporation /cawr-pe-**ray**-shun/ *n* a group of people allowed by the law to act as one person in certain cases (e.g., in business matters).

corps /core/ *n* **1** a large body of soldiers, a division of an army. **2** a group of people working together for one purpose (*the Peace Corps*).

corpse /cawrps/ *n* the dead body of a person.

corpulent /**cawr**-pyu-lent/ *adj* (*fml*) fat, stout (*Santa Claus is corpulent and jolly*). ● *n* **corpulence** /**cawr**-pyu-lense/.

corral /co-**ral**/ *n* **1** an enclosure for horses or cattle. **2** a defensive area made by drawing up covered wagons to form a circle in which to take cover.

correct /co-**rect**/ *adj* right, having no mistakes (*the correct spelling*). ● *vb* **1** to set right, to remove mistakes from (*correct her spelling*). **2** to point out or mark mistakes (*corrected the student's homework*). ● *n* **correctness** /co-**rect**-ness/.

correction /co-**rect**-shun/ *n* **1** act of correcting. **2** the right thing put in place of a mistake (*write corrections in red*). **3** (*old or fml*) punishment (*a house of correction*).

corrective /co-**rec**-tive/ *adj* putting right or improv-

ing what is wrong (*corrective treatment/corrective punishment*). ● *also n.*

correspond /caw-re-**spond**/ *vb* **1** to write letters to (*correspond with a friend overseas*). **2** to fit in with, to agree with (*your written statement does not correspond with your spoken one*). **3** to be like, to be the equal of (*the elephant's trunk corresponding to the human nose*).

correspondence /caw-re-**spon**-dense/ *n* **1** all the letters a person or office sends or receives. **2** likeness.

correspondent /caw-re-**spon**-dent/ *n* **1** one who writes letters to another (*the two old friends have been correspondents for many years*). **2** one who sends special reports to a newspaper (*a foreign correspondent*).

corresponding /caw-re-**spon**-ding/ *adj* like or similar.

corridor /**cawr**-i-dore/ *n* an indoor passage or hallway (*several doors leading off the hotel corridor*).

corroborate /co-**rob**-e-rate/ *vb* to support or confirm the story or idea of another (*a statement corroborating other evidence*). ● *n* **corroboration** /co-rob-e-**ray**-shun/. ● *adj* **corroborative** /co-**rob**-e-ray-tive/.

corrode /co-**rode**/ *vb* to eat or wear away slowly (*rust corroding the metal*). ● *n* **corrosion** /co-**roe**-zhun/.

corrosive /co-**roe**-siv/ *adj* able to eat away (*acids are corrosive substances*). ● *also n.*

corrugate /**caw**-ru-gate/ *vb* to shape into an uneven, wavy, grooved surface. ● *adj* **corrugated** /**caw**-ru-gay-ted/.

corrupt /co-**rupt**/ *vb* to make or become evil or morally bad (*young people corrupted by drug-dealers*). ● *adj* **1** evil (*corrupt drug-dealers*). **2** ready to act dishonestly for money (*corrupt officials accepting bribes*). ● *n* **corruption** /co-**rup**-shun/. ● *adv* **corruptly** /co-**rupt**-lee/.

corset /**cawr**-set/ *n* a stiff, tight-fitting undergarment (*corsets worn by women to make them look slimmer/corsets worn by people with back problems*).

cosmetic /coz-**met**-ic/ *n* something used to make the face and/or hair more beautiful (*cosmetics such as lipstick*). ● *adj* **1** intended to improve the appearance (*cosmetic preparations/cosmetic surgery following a car accident*). **2** dealing only with outside appearances (*cosmetic changes to the law*).

cosmic /**coz**-mic/ *adj* **1** having to do with the universe. **2** (*inf*) very great (*changes of cosmic proportions*).

cosmology /coz-**mol**-o-jee/ *n* the study of the universe as a whole.

cosmopolitan /coz-mo-**pol**-i-tan/ *adj* **1** consisting of people from many different parts of the world (*a cosmopolitan city*). **2** having or showing wide experience of different people and places (*a cosmopolitan attitude*).

cosmos /**coz**-mus/ *n* the whole universe as an orderly system (*all the planets in the cosmos*).

cosset /**cos**-et/ *vb* to treat with great or too much kindness, to pamper (*cosseting her by giving her breakfast in bed*).

cost /**cost**/ *vb* (*pt, pp* **cost**) **1** to be on sale at a certain price (*apples costing 20 cents each*). **2** to cause loss or suffering (*the battle cost many lives*). ● *n* **1** the price (*the cost of the house*). **2** loss (*at the cost of many lives*). **3** *pl* the money needed to pay for a lawsuit (*lose the case and have to pay costs*).

costly /**cost**-lee/ *adj* having a high price (*costly silk clothes*).

costume /**cos**-toom/ *n* the clothes worn in a special place or at a special time (*bathing costume/a Halloween costume*).

costumer /**cos**-too-mer/ *n* a person who makes, sells, or rents costumes.

cot /**cot**/ *n* a bed that can be folded and stored away, generally used for overnight guests.

cottage /**cot**-idge/ *n* a small house. ● *n* **cottager** /**cot**-a-jer/ a person who lives in a cottage.

cotton /**cot**-on/ *n* **1** a soft white substance from the cotton plant. **2** thread or cloth made of cotton. ● *also adj*.

cotton wool /cot-on-**wool**/ *n* raw cotton before it is made into thread or cloth (*wipe the wound with cotton wool*).

couch /**couch**/ *n* a sofa, something on which one lies. ● *vb* (*fml*) to put into words (*couch his statement in simple words*). **couchant** /**caoo**-shint/ *adj* (*of an animal*) lying down but on all four paws with the head up (*a statue of a lion couchant*).

cougar /**coo**-ger/ *n* a puma or mountain lion, a large, wild animal of the cat family.

cough /**cof**/ *vb* to force air noisily from the throat, often to clear it of some matter, such as dust or phlegm. ● *n* **1** a noisy forcing of the air from the throat. **2** an illness marked by frequent coughing (*have a bad cough*).

council /**coun**-sil/ *n* a group of people chosen to make decisions, to advise, or to discuss issues affecting a larger number (*city council*).

councilor /**coun**-si-lor/ *n* a member of a council.

counsel /**coun**-sil/ *n* **1** (*fml*) advice (*refuse to listen to his father's counsel*). **2** professional advice given by a counselor (*debt counsel*). **3** the lawyer who presents a case in a court of law. ● *vb* (**counsel**) to advise.

counseling /**coun**-sel-ing/ *n* the act of listening to people's difficulties or problems and giving professional advice as to how to cope with them or solve them (*counseling for survivors of the tragedy*).

counselor /**coun**-se-lor/ *n* an adviser, one who gives (professional) advice on a variety of personal problems (*a marriage counselor*).

count[1] /**count**/ *vb* **1** to number (*count the people as they enter*). **2** to consider (*count him among her friends*). **3** to matter (*money doesn't count with her*). ● *n* a numbering (*a count of the votes*).

count[2] /**count**/ *n* a European nobleman.

countenance /**coun**-te-nanse/ *n* (*fml*) **1** the face (*a beautiful countenance*). **2** the expression of the face (*a fierce countenance*). ● *vb* (*fml*) to tolerate, to allow (*refuse to countenance such behavior*).

counter /**coun**-ter/ *n* **1** a person or thing that counts (*the counters of votes at elections*). **2** a small flat object used in some games to keep score. **3** the table in a shop across which goods are sold. ● *vb* to act in order to oppose or defend oneself against (*counter the enemy attack by bringing in more soldiers*).

counter- /**coun**-ter/ *prefix* against, opposite to.

counteract /coun-te-**ract**/ *vb* to undo or prevent the effect of by opposite action (*a drug that counteracts the effect of the poison*).

counterattack /**coun**-ter-a-tac/ *n* an attack made in reply to an enemy attack. ● *also vb*.

counterbalance /**coun**-ter-**ba**-lanse/ *vb* to put something of equal weight or importance on the other side (*the expense of the project is counterbalanced by its usefulness*).

counterclockwise /**coun**-ter **clock**-wise/ (*Br* **anti-clockwise**) *adv* revolving in the direction opposite to the way the hands of a clock would turn.

counterfeit /**coun**-ter-fit/ *vb* **1** to copy or imitate to deceive (*accused of counterfeiting 20-dollar bills*). **2** (*fml*) to pretend (*counterfeit cheerfulness*). ● *adj* **1** not real. **2** made alike deceive. **3** pretended. ● *n* something copied, not real or true. ● *n* **counterfeiter**.

counterpart /**coun**-ter-part/ *n* a person or thing almost exactly the same as another (*his counterpart in the opposing team*).

counterpoint /**coun**-ter-point/ *n* (*mus*) the art of arranging two different tunes so that they can be played together.

countess /**coun**-tess/ *n* the wife of a count or of an earl.

countless /**count**-less/ *adj* too many to be counted (*countless visitors*).

country /**cun**-tree/ *n* **1** the land of one nation or people. **2** the land outside and away from towns (*a quiet weekend in the country*). **3** an area or stretch of land (*hilly country*). ● *adj* having to do with the country rather than the town (*country districts*).

countryside /**cun**-tree-side/ *n* country or rural areas (*admire the beauty of the countryside*).

county /**coun**-tee/ *n* a district of a country or state.

coup /**coo**/ *n* a sudden successful action (*pull off a coup by taking business away from the competition*).

coupé /coo-**pay**/ *n* a two-door car.

couple /**cu**-pl/ *n* **1** (*inf*) two. **2** husband and wife. **3** two people who are in a committed relationship. ● *vb* **1** to join (*couple the carriage to the train/bad weather coupled with illness kept many people away*). **2** to link or associate with (*their names have been coupled*).

couplet /**cu**-plet/ *n* two lines of poetry, one after the other, that rhyme.

coupling /**cu**-pling/ *n* a joining link, as that between two railway carriages.

coupon /**coo**-pon/ *n* a ticket that can be exchanged for money or goods.

courage /**cur**-age/ *n* bravery.

courageous /cur-**ay**-jus/ *adj* brave, fearless.

courier /**coo**-ree-yer/ *n* **1** a messenger (*packages delivered by courier*). **2** a guide in charge of a party of travelers.

course /**coarse**/ *n* **1** the way along which a thing moves or runs (*the course of the river/the usual course of events*). **2** the ground on which a race is run or golf is played. **3** a number of lectures or lessons given for the same purpose (*take a course in English literature*). **4** a row or layer, as of bricks in a wall or shingles on a roof **5** part of a meal served at one time (*a meal consisting of three courses*). ● *vb* **1** to chase. **2** (*fml*) to move quickly (*tears coursing down her cheeks*).

court /**coart**/ *n* **1** an open area surrounded or partly surrounded by buildings, houses, or walls, a courtyard. **2** a place marked out for tennis, racketball, etc. **3** a king and queen and all their advisers and attendants. **4** the building in which judges hear cases and give decisions. **5** all the judges and officials in a court of law. **6** attentions paid to someone to gain favor (*pay court to her in the hope that she would marry him/pay court to wealthy people*). ● *vb* **1** to pay attention to someone to try and gain the love of.

2 (*fml*) to try to gain (*court the audience's approval*). **3** to act in a way that is likely to bring about (something unpleasant) (*court disaster*).

courteous /**core**-tee-us/ *adj* polite, considerate, and respectful (*a courteous young man/a courteous reply*).

courtesy /**core**-ti-see/ *n* politeness, good manners (*treat people with courtesy/have the courtesy to apologize*).

courtier /**core**-tee-yer/ *n* someone who attends the court of a king or queen.

court-martial /**court**-mar-shal/ *n* (*pl* **courts-martial**) a military court, with officers acting as judges. ● *vb* **court-martial** /**coart**-mar-shal/ (**court-martialed, court-martialing**) to try by court-martial (*court-martialed for taking leave without permission*).

courtship /**coart**-ship/ *n* courting or wooing in hopes of obtaining love.

courtyard /**coart**-yard/ *n* an open space surrounded or partly surrounded by buildings, walls, or houses.

cousin /**cu**-zin/ *n* the child of an uncle or aunt, the child of a parent's brother or sister.

cove /**coav**/ *n* a small bay or inlet (*build sandcastles in a sandy cove*).

covenant /**cuv**-nant/ *n* a written agreement (*sign a covenant to give money regularly to a charity*). ● *vb* to enter into written agreement, to promise

cover /**cu**-ver/ *vb* **1** to spread over (*cover the table with a cloth/the ground covered in snow*). **2** to protect (*cover her eyes in the sunlight*). **3** to wrap (up) (*covering her head from the cold*). **4** to include (*the cost covers the hotel stay and meals*). ● *also n.*

covering /**cuv**-ring/ *n* anything that covers (*a covering of snow*).

covert /**coe**-vert/ *adj* secret, hidden (*exchange covert glances/the covert activities of the spy*). ● *n* **1** a shelter. **2** a group of bushes or trees in which hunted birds or animals can hide.

covet /**cu**-vet/ *vb* to want to have something belonging to another (*she coveted her friend's diamond ring*). ● *adj* **covetous** /**cu**-ve-tus/. ● *n* **covetousness** /**cu**-ve-tus-ness/.

cow /**cow**/ *n* the female of certain animals (e.g., of cattle, oxen, elephants, whales).

coward /**ca**-ward/ *n* one easily frightened in the face of danger.

cowardice /**ca**-war-diss/ *n* fear of danger (*showed his cowardice by running away*).

cowardly /**ca**-ward-lee/ *adj* having no bravery, showing fear (*too cowardly to admit his mistakes*).

cowboy /**cow**-boy/ *n* a man who looks after cattle on a ranch on horseback. ● *fem* **cowgirl**.

cower /**cow**-er/ *vb* to crouch or shrink back out of fear (*cowered in a corner as the bully threatened him*).

cowherd /**cow**-herd/ *n* one who looks after cows.

coy /**coy**/ *adj* **1** shy, bashful, especially excessively so. **2** hesitant to give information (*coy about her age*). ● *adv* **coyly** /**coy**-lee/.

coyote /kie-**yo**-te/ *n* an animal of the dog family resembling a small wolf, found in North America.

cozy /**co**-zee/ *adj* pleasantly comfortable or warm (*a cozy room/cozy pajamas*). ● *n* a teapot or egg cover. ● *adv* **cozily** /**co**-zi-lee/.

crab[1] /**crab**/ *n* **1** a sea creature with eight legs and two pincers, a flat shell, and a short, wide belly. **2** the sideways motion of an aircraft. ● *vb* to fish for crab.

crab[2] /**crab**/ *adj* bad-tempered, cross, alwayss complaining (*don't be such a crab/he can be crabby at times*).

crab apple /**crab**-a-pl/ *n* **1** very small apples growing wild or grown for making jellies or preserves. **2** a tree bearing crab apples.

crack /**crak**/ *n* **1** a sudden, sharp noise (*the crack of thunder*). **2** a break in which the parts remain together (*a crack in the vase*). **3** a sharp blow (*a crack on the head*). **4** (*sl*) a form of the drug cocaine. ● *also vb*.

cracked /**krakt**/ *adj* **1** broken, but not in pieces. **2** (*inf*) crazy (*don't listen to him—he's completely cracked*).

cracker /**cra**-ker/ *n* a crisp, thin wafer or biscuit (*crackers with cheese*).

crackle /**cra**-kl/ *vb* to go on making short, sharp, popping noises, to rustle (*dry leaves crackling as they walked*). ● *n* the act or sound of crackling.

crackling /**cra**-kling/ *n* the producing of short, popping noises, rustling.

cradle /**cray**-dl/ *n* **1** a baby's bed that can be rocked or swung. **2** the frame in which something is cradled, such as the frame under a ship when it is being built or the base of a telephone where the receiver is placed. **3** the place of a thing's early development (*the cradle of civilization*). ● *vb* to lay or rock as in a cradle (*cradle the head of the dying man in her arms*).

craft /**craft**/ *n* **1** a special skill, especially with the hands (*a craft such as woodworking*). **2** cleverness, especially in deceiving (*gain entry to the house by craft*). **3** a ship (*a seaworthy craft*).

craftsperson /**crafts**-per-sun/ *n* a skilled worker, especially with the hands. ● *ns* **craft(s)manship** / **craft(s)**-man-ship/.

crafty /**craf**-tee/ *adj* good at deceiving, clever, tricky (*criminals too crafty to get caught by the police*). ● *adv* **craftily** /**craf**-ti-lee/.

crag /**crag**/ *n* a steep, rough rock that rises above others or projects from a rock mass. ● *adj* **craggy** /**cra**-gee/.

cram /**cram**/ *vb* (**crammed** /**cramd**/, **cramming** /**cra**-ming/) **1** to fill very full by pressing or squeezing (*cram the suitcase full of clothes*). **2** to learn many facts right away for a test.

crammer /**cra**-mer/ *n* a teacher who prepares someone for a test by making him or her learn many facts in a short time.

cramp /**cramp**/ *n* a sudden, sharp pain in a muscle (*suffer from stomach cramps*). ● *vb* to prevent free movement, to hinder (*lack of money cramps his style*).

cranberry /**cran**-be-ree/ *n* a sour, red berry used in making juice, in cooking, and in baking.

crane /**crane**/ *n* **1** a long-legged, long-necked water bird. **2** a machine for lifting or moving heavy weights by using a moving beam or arm anchored to its base by an overhead support. ● *vb* to stretch out one's neck (*craning his neck to see over the crowd*).

cranium /**cray**-nee-um/ *n* (*fml*) the skull (*suffer injury to the cranium*). ● *adj* **cranial**.

crank /**crank**/ *n* **1** in machines, a part that changes an up-and-down or side-to-side movement into a round-and-round movement (or the other way round). **2** a person who complains a lot. **3** a person with fixed, obsessive ideas, a person with strange ideas (*a health-food crank*). ● *vb* to turn or wind.

cranny /**cra**-nee/ *n* a small narrow opening, a crack (*insects in the crannies of the walls*).

crash /**crash**/ *vb* **1** to fall with a loud noise (*the vase crashed to the floor*). **2** to dash violently against something (*crashing his fist into the wall*). ● *n* **1** the loud noise of a breakage or wreckage. **2** the sudden failure of a business (*the crash of his firm*).

crass /**crass**/ *adj* very stupid, insensitive.

crate /**crate**/ *n* a large box, basket, or packing case, made with wooden boards or out of wicker.

crater /**cray**-ter/ *n* **1** the bowl-shaped mouth of a volcano. **2** a deep wide hole in the earth.

cravat /**cra**-vat/ *n* a piece of cloth worn round the neck (*a silk cravat tucked into the neck of his shirt*).

crave /**crave**/ vb **1** (fml) to beg for (crave forgiveness). **2** to desire very much (craving a chocolate bar/craved admiration).

craving /**cray**-ving/ n a strong desire.

crawfish see **crayfish**.

crawl /**crawl**/ vb **1** to move with the body on or near the ground, to move on the hands and knees (crawl along the tunnel/babies learning to crawl). **2** to move slowly (time crawled by). ● n **1** act of crawling. **2** a style in swimming.

crayfish /**cray**-fish/, also **crawfish** n small, usually freshwater shellfish that look like little lobsters.

crayon /**cray**-on/ n a stick of colored chalk, wax, or charcoal used for drawing, coloring, or writing. ● vb to draw with crayons.

craze /**craze**/ vb to drive insane. ● n a popular fashion, a temporary excitement for (a 1970s craze for flared pants).

crazy /**cray**-zee/ adj **1** (inf) insane (he must be crazy to think that). **2** very excited, liking very much (crazy about horror films/crazy about the girl next door).

creak /**creek**/ vb to make a harsh grating or squeaking sound (stairs creaking as he crept upstairs). ● also n. ● adj **creaky** /**cree**-kee/.

cream /**creem**/ n **1** the oily, yellowish part of the milk that rises to the top, and from which butter is made. **2** any sweet, smooth substance that is made from cream (cream-filled cupcake) **3** the best of anything (the cream of the crop). **4** a creamlike substance for rubbing into the skin (hand cream). **5** the color of cream.

creamery /**creem**-ree/ n a place where milk is made into butter and cheese.

creamy /**cree**-mee/ adj like cream (a creamy dessert).

crease /**creess**/ n a mark made by folding, crushing, or pressing. ● vb to make creases in (her skirt creased from sitting too long).

create /**cree**-ate/ vb **1** to bring into existence (from a lump of clay, he created a scupture). **2** to make (create a bad impression/create a fuss/fashion designers creating a new line).

creation /**cree-ay**-shun/ n **1** act of creating. **2** anything made or invented (designers showing their latest creations).

creative /**cree-ay**-tiv/ adj **1** involving creation (the creative process). **2** able to create or invent, producing original ideas and works (a creative writer).

creator /**cree-ay**-tor/ n one who creates or invents (he was the creator of the masterpiece). ● **the Creator** God, the Supreme Being.

creature /**cree**-chur/ n anything created, especially humans, animals, and other living things.

credence /**cree**-dense/ n belief, trust (give no credence to what he says).

credentials /cri-**den**-shals/ npl papers saying that the owner of them may be trusted (ask candidates for the job for their credentials).

credible /**cre**-di-bl/ adj able to be believed (a scarcely credible story). ● n **credibility** /cre-di-**bi**-li-tee/.

credit /**cre**-dit/ n **1** belief, trust in (place no credit in their policies). **2** approval or praise (give him credit for capturing the thief). **3** a cause of honor (a credit to his school). **4** a system of buying goods or services and paying for them later (buy the video on credit). **5** the quality of being able to pay debts (her credit is good). **6** the money a person has in a bank (an account in credit). ● vb **1** to believe. **2** to sell or lend in trust. **3** to write in on the credit side of an account. **4** to consider as having (a good quality).

creditable /**cre**-di-ta-bl/ adj deserving praise (a creditable achievement).

credit card /**cre**-dit card/ n a plastic card with which goods can be purchased and paid for later.

creditor /**cre**-di-tor/ n one to whom money is owed.

credulous /**cre**-ju-lus/ adj too ready to believe, too trusting (credulous people who would believe anything). ● n **credulity** /cre-**joo**-li-tee/.

creed /**creed**/ n **1** that which one believes, especially in religion (people of every creed). **2** a statement of one's faith or beliefs.

creek /**creek**/ n a small stream, somewhat larger than a brook.

creel /**creel**/ n a basketlike cage for catching fish.

creep /**creep**/ vb (pt, pp **crept** /**crept**/) **1** to move with the body on or near the ground. **2** to move slowly and silently (creep upstairs). **3** to shiver with horror (her flesh crept at the ghostly sight). ● n a person regarded as annoying or disgusting.

creeper /**cree**-per/ n **1** a person, animal, or thing that creeps. **2** a plant that grows along the ground or up walls, trees, etc.

creepy /**cree**-pee/ adj (inf) eerie, strange, causing fear or disgust (a creepy story/a creepy old house).

cremate /**cree**-mate/ vb to burn a dead body to ashes.

cremation /cree-**may**-shun/ n act of cremating.

crematory /cre-ma-**toe**-ree/ n a place where dead bodies are cremated. ● also **crematorium** /cre-ma-**toe**-ree-um/.

Creole /**cree**-ole/ n **1** a person born in the West Indies, Central America, tropical South America, or Gulf States but with European parents. **2** a descendant of such persons, specifically a person descended from the French settlers of Louisiana (New Orleans area). **3** French, as spoken by Creoles. **4** *adj* (*lowercase*) prepared with sautéed tomatoes, green peppers, onions, and spices.

creosote /**cree**-u-zote/ *n* an oily liquid taken from tar and used to disinfect or preserve wood from decay.

crepe /**crep**/ *n* **1** a thin, soft, crinkly cloth (*a dress of blue crepe*). **2** any crinkly material (*crepe paper*). **3** a thin pancake, generally served rolled or folded with a filling.

crescendo /cri-**shen**-doe/ *n* **1** a sign used in writing music. **2** a gradual increase in loudness.

crescent /**cre**-sent/ *n* **1** the shape of the moon in its first and last quarter. **2** a narrow, tapering curve. **3** a curving street. ● *adj* shaped like a crescent.

cress /**cress**/ *n* an edible water plant.

crest /**crest**/ *n* **1** a tuft or comb on the heads of certain birds (*a cock's crest*). **2** a bunch of feathers on the top of a helmet. **3** a sign or badge of a family, seen on a coats-of-arms, writing paper, etc. **4** the top of a slope, wave, etc. (*surfing on the crest of a wave*). ● *vb* to get to the top of.

crestfallen /**crest**-faw-len/ *adj* sad, disappointed (*feel crestfallen at missing the party*).

cretin /**cree**-tin/ *n* **1** a person who is suffering from cretinism. **2** (*inf*) a foolish or stupid person.

crevasse /cri-**vas**/ *n* **1** a deep crack in a glacier. **2** a break in the outside walls of a river.

crevice /**cre**-vis/ *n* a narrow opening caused by a crack or split (*crevices in the stone wall*).

crew /**croo**/ *n* **1** the sailors of a ship. **2** a group of people working or classed together, a gang. **3** the rowers on a rowing team.

crib /**crib**/ *n* **1** a baby's bed. **2** something copied dishonestly from someone else. **3** a translation of a text. **4** the house, apartment, ect where a person lives. ● *vb* (**cribbed** /**cribd**/, **cribbing** /**crib**-ing/) to copy unfairly the work of another.

cribbage /**crib**-idge/ *n* a card game for up to four players in which the object is to form various combinations for points.

crick /**crick**/ *n* a painful stiffness, especially of the neck. ● *vb* to cause this (*cricked her neck looking over her shoulder*).

cricket[1] /**cri**-ket/ *n* a small, black, jumping insect that makes chirping noises with its legs.

cricket[2] /**cri**-ket/ *n* an outdoor game played with a flat bat and red leather ball with a team of eleven. ● *n* **cricketer**.

crime /**crime**/ *n* a breaking of the law (*the crime of murder*).

criminal /**cri**-mi-nal/ *adj* **1** against the law (*convicted of a criminal act*). **2** wrong, wicked (*it was criminal to cut down such a beautiful tree*). ● *n* one who breaks the law.

crimp /**crimp**/ *vb* **1** to compress into small folds or ridges (*crimp the cloth*). **2** to curl (*crimp her hair*).

crimson /**crim**-zon/ *n* a deep red color. ● *also adj*. ● *vb* to make or become red.

cringe /**cringe**/ *vb* **1** to shrink back in fear (*cringe from the bully/cats cringing at the sight of the dogs*). **2** to behave too humbly toward (*cringe in the presence of the boss*).

crinkle /**cring**-kl/ *vb* to twist or bend into many folds, to wrinkle. ● *n* a fold or wrinkle.

cripple /**cri**-pl/ *n* an offensive, informal word for a person who is unable to use some or all of his or her limbs. ● *vb* **1** to make unable to move freely, to make lame (*the accident crippled her foot*). **2** to make less strong, to not work as well, etc. (*debts cripple the country's economy*). ● *Usage*: see **disabled**.

crisis /**crie**-sis/ *n* (*pl* **crises** /**crie**-seez/) **1** a turning point at which things must become either better or worse (*the crisis of the illness*). **2** a very serious state of affairs (*the firm recovered from a financial crisis*).

crisp /**crisp**/ *adj* **1** hard but easily broken (*crisp crackers*). **2** tight (*crisp curls*). **3** fresh and firm (*crisp apples*). **4** firm and clear (*give crisp orders*). **5** dry and clear (*a crisp day*). ● *vb* to curl or twist. ● *adv* **crisply** /**cri**-splee/.

criterion /cri-**tee**-ree-on/ *n* (*pl* **criteria** /cri-**tee**-ree-ya/) a rule or standard with which things may be compared to judge their value, a test (*criteria used in judging a novel*).

critic /**cri**-tic/ *n* **1** one who judges something by pointing out its good and bad points (*a theater critic*). **2** one who finds fault, a person who expresses dislike and disapproval of (*one of the government's critics*).

critical /**cri**-ti-cal/ *adj* **1** pointing out both good and bad (*a critical analysis of the play*). **2** hard to please, ready to find fault (*a very critical person/ in a critical mood*). **3** having to do with a crisis (*a critical point in his career*). **4** most important (*at the critical moment*).

criticism /**cri**-ti-si-zum/ *n* **1** judgment (*literary criticism*). **2** fault-finding (*a plan open to criticism/ tired of her constant criticism*).

criticize /**cri**-ti-size/ *vb*, *also* **criticise** (*Br*) **1** to point out the good and bad in (*the journalist appointed* *to criticize the play*). **2** to find fault with (*always criticizing his clothes*).

critique /cri-**teek**/ *n* an essay in which a criticism is made.

croak /croak/ *vb* to make a low, hoarse noise in the throat (*frogs croaking/croaking because of a sore throat*). ● *also n.* ● *adj* **croaky** /**croa**-kee/.

crochet /croa-**shay**/ *n* a type of knitting done with one hooked needle. ● *vb* to knit in this way(*crocheting a blanket*).

crock[1] /crok/ *n* a pot or jar (*a crock of salt*).

crock[2] /crok/ *n* an old, broken-down animal, anything useless. ● *vb* to injure.

crockery /**crok**-e-ree/ *n* earthenware or china cups, plates, and other dishes.

crocodile /**crok**-o-dile/ *n* a large, lizardlike reptile with a long snout, long tail, large teeth, and a scaly body that lives in or around water.

crocodile tears /crok-o-dile **teerz**/ *npl* pretended sorrow or grief (*she seemed upset when we left, but I think it was a case of crocodile tears*).

crocus /**cro**-cus/ *n* a spring plant grown from a bulb with yellow, purple, or white flowers that bloom in early spring.

croissant *n* /craw-**sont**/ a light, crescent-shaped roll made of flaky pastry eaten at breakfast.

crone /crone/ *n* (*old*) an old woman.

crony /**cro**-nee/ *n* (*inf*) a close friend (*get together with his cronies*).

crook /crook/ *n* **1** a bend, curve (*in the crook of one's arm*). **2** a stick, hook-shaped at one end, as carried by a shepherd or bishop. **3** (*inf*) a dishonest person, a criminal (*a crook who eventually went to jail*). ● *vb* to bend, to shape like a hook.

crooked /**croo**-ked/ *adj* **1** not straight, twisted (*a crooked stick/a crooked smile*). **2** dishonest, illegal (*a crooked business deal*). **3** dishonest, not to be trusted (*a crooked businessman*). ● *n* **crookedness** /**croo**-ked-ness/.

croon /croon/ *vb* to sing softly (*crooning a lullaby to the child*).

crop /crop/ *n* **1** a pocket in the throat of birds in which the food is partly digested before passing to the stomach. **2** a riding whip. **3** the whole amount of grain, fruit, etc. that is grown or gathered at one place or time (*the wheat crop/a fine crop of green beans/a disappointing crop of apples*). **4** a short haircut. ● *vb* (**cropped** /cropt/, **cropping** /**crop**-ing/) **1** to cut short (*crop his hair*). **2** to bite off (*sheep cropping the grass*). **3** to sow or gather (a crop). ●
crop up to turn up unexpectedly (*difficulties that*

cropped up/one of the subjects that crop up). ● **come a cropper 1** to fall heavily (*come a cropper on the icy surface*). **2** to fail completely (*he came a cropper when he tried to expand his business*).

croquet /cro-**kay**/ *n* a game in which wooden balls are hit through hoops with long hammer-shaped wooden clubs.

cross /crawss/ *n* **1** a mark made by drawing one straight line across another, e.g., +, x. **2** one piece of wood fastened across another in the shape of a cross. **3** anything made in the shape of a cross (*wear a cross around her neck*). **4** the sign of the Christian religion. **5** (*old*) a cross-shaped wooden frame to which criminals were fixed as a punishment. **6** a place where roads meet. **7** a monument in the shape of a cross (*a cross in the middle of the town*). **8** a source of suffering or sorrow (*a cross to bear*). **9** an animal or plant that is the offspring of different breeds or varieties (*a mule is a cross between a horse and a donkey*). ● *vb* **1** to draw a line through or across (*cross out the mistakes*). **2** to go from one side to the other side (*cross the road*). **3** to pass across each other (*the roads cross before the town*). **4** to put or place something across or over something of the same type (*crossing her fingers*). **5** to hinder, to obstruct (*he doesn't like to be crossed*). ● *adj* angry, bad-tempered (*feeling cross about ripping her tights*). ● **crosser** /**craw**-ser/ *n* **crossly** /**crawss**-lee/ *adv* **crossness** /**crawss**-ness/ *n*.

crossbow /**crawss**-boe/ *n* a bow fixed across a support or stand onto which the string was looped when drawn back, then fired by a trigger.

crossbreed /**crawss**-breed/ *n* a mixture of two breeds. ● *also vb.*

cross-country /**crawss**-**cun**-tree/ *adj* going across fields, etc., instead of along roads (*people taking part in a cross-country race*).

cross-examine /**crawss**-ig-**za**-min/ *vb* to ask a person questions about a statement he or she has made to test its truth, especially in a court of law (*cross-examine the witness for the defense*). ● *n* **cross-examination** /**crawss**-ig-za-mi-**nay**-shun/.

cross-eyed /**crawss**-eyed/ *adj* an abnormal condition in which the eyes are turned toward each other, facing inward.

crossing /**craw**-sing/ *n* a place at which one may cross a street, river, etc. (*cross the road at the pedestrian crossing by the school*).

cross-purpose /**crawss**-**pur**-pus/ *n*. ● **to be at crosspurposes** to disagree with another through a misunderstanding (*they were at cross-purposes—*

they were talking about different people without realizing it).

cross-question /**crawss**-**kwess**-chin/ *vb* to cross-examine.

cross-reference /**crawss**-re-frense/ *n* the mention in a book of another passage or book in which the same subject is discussed.

crossroads /**crawss**-roadz/ *n* the place where two roads cross.

crossword /**crawss**-wurd/ *n* a word puzzle with squares and clues, in which each answer is part of another answer.

crotchet /**croch**-et/ *n* **1** a strange desire or idea, a whim. **2** a hook.

crotchety /**cro**-che-tee/ *adj* **1** (*old*) having strange desires or ideas. **2** cross, bad-tempered (*a crotchety old man*).

crouch /**crouch**/ *vb* to bend low (*crouch down to look at the plant*).

croup /**croop**/ *n* a disease of the throat in children consisting of a swollen throat, a hoarse cough, and trouble breathing.

croupier /**croo**-pee-er/ *n* the person who takes in and gives out the money at a gambling table.

crow /**croe**/ *n* **1** a large black bird. **2** the cry of a rooster (*sleepers disturbed by the crow of the rooster*). **3** a baby's cry of pleasure (*crows of delight*). ● *vb* **1** to cry like a rooster. **2** (*of a baby*) to make sounds expressing pleasure. **3** (*inf*) to boast (*crowing about his new car*). ● **as the crow flies** following the straightest and shortest way from one place to another.

crowbar /**croe**-bar/ *n* a bar of iron used to raise heavy objects or open things that are stuck (*prise the load up with a crowbar*).

crowd /**croud**/ *n* a large number of people gathered together, especially into a small space (*a crowd packed the hall*). ● *vb* **1** to come together in large numbers (*the people crowded together in the square*). **2** to fill too full by coming together in (*crowd the streets*).

crowded /**crou**-ded/ *adj* full of people or objects.

crown /**croun**/ *n* **1** an ornamental head-covering worn by a king or queen as a sign of office. **2** a wreath worn on the head (*a crown of flowers*). **3** the top of certain things (*the crown of the hill/the crown of the head/the crown of the hat*). ● *vb* **1** to put a crown on (*crown the king*). **2** to finish with a success (*the award crowned a fine career*). **3** (*inf*) to hit on the head (*crowned him with an iron bar*).

crows-feet /**croze**-feet/ *npl* the little lines on the face at the outside corners of the eye.

crozier *see* **crosier**.

crucial /**croo**-shal/ *adj* of the greatest importance, needing a clear decision (*take the crucial step of resigning/the next game is a crucial one for the championship*).

crucible /**croo**-si-bl/ *n* a melting pot.

crucifix /**croo**-si-fiks/ *n* a figure of Jesus Christ on a cross.

crucifixion /croo-si-**fik**-shun/ *n* act of crucifying. ● **the Crucifixion** the crucifixion and death of Jesus Christ.

crucify /**croo**-si-fy/ *vb* **1** to put to death by fastening on a cross and being left. **2** to treat cruelly, to deal with severely (*a politician crucified by the press about his private life*).

crude /**crood**/ *adj* **1** rough (*crude garden furniture*). **2** in the natural state (*crude oil/crude sugar*). **3** coarse, vulgar, not civilized (*crude manners/crude voices*). ● *n* **crudity** /**croo**-di-tee/.

cruel /**crool**/ *adj* **1** taking pleasure in making others suffer, hard-hearted (*a cruel tyrant*). **2** causing pain (*a cruel blow/cruel punishment*). ● *n* **cruelty** /**crool**-tee/.

cruet /**croo**-et/ *n* a small, glass bottle for vinegar, salt, oil, etc.

cruise /**crooz**/ *vb* **1** to sail from place to place, often now for pleasure. **2** to travel at the speed that uses the least amount of fuel. ● *also n*.

cruiser /**croo**-zer/ *n* **1** a fast warship. **2** anything that cruises.

crumb /**crum**/ *n* **1** a very small bit, especially of some form of bread (*biscuit crumbs/toast crumbs*). **2** a small piece (*a crumb of comfort*).

crumble /**crum**-bl/ *vb* **1** to break into small bits or dust (*crumble the bread*). **2** to fall to pieces or into dust (*ancient walls gradually crumbling*). **3** gradually to get into a poor state and come to an end (*empires crumble/hopes crumble*).

crumple /**crum**-pl/ *vb* **1** to press into many folds, to crush out of shape (*crumpling her dress*). **2** to fall down suddenly (*she crumpled down in a faint*). **3** to collapse, to fail (*all resistance to the enemy suddenly crumpled*). ● *also n*.

crunch /**crunch**/ *vb* to crush noisily with the teeth (*the dog crunching a bone*). ● *also n*.

crusade /croo-**sade**/ *n* **1** an attempt by Christian armies from the eleventh to thirteenth centuries to win back control of the Holy Land from Muslims. **2** any attempt by a number of people to do what is considered to be good or work against what is considered to be evil (*a crusade against dishonest officials*). ● *n* **crusader** /croo-**say**-der/.

crush /crush/ *vb* **1** to squeeze or press together with force. **2** to press out of shape. **3** to defeat completely. ● *n* the crowding together of things or persons. ● *adj* **crushing** /**cru**-shing/.

crust /crust/ *n* the hard, crispy, or crunchy outside of anything (e.g. bread). ● *vb* to cover with a crust.

crusty /**cru**-stee/ *adj* **1** having a distinctive crust (*a crusty pizza base*). **2** short-tempered (*a crusty old man*). ● *adv* **crustily** /**cru**-sti-lee/.

crutch /cruch/ *n* **1** a stick, with a top made to fit under the armpits, to support people whose legs have been injured. **2** a person or thing that provides help and/or support (*her teddy bear is a crutch*).

crux /cruks/ *n* the most important or difficult part of a matter, issue, etc. (*lack of money is the crux of the problem*).

cry /craee/ *vb* **1** to make shrill, loud sounds of weeping, joy, etc. (*cried for help*). **2** to weep. **3** to shout. ● *also n.*

crying /**craee**-ying/ *adj* needing to be put right (*a crying need for more books*).

crypt /cript/ *n* an underground chamber or vault, found in some churches, often used as a burial place.

cryptic /**crip**-tik/ *adj* difficult to understand, sometimes on purpose (*a cryptic remark/a cryptic message*).

crystal /**cri**-stal/ *n* **1** a clear, bright glass. **2** a hard, glassy-looking stone. **3** one of the regular shapes in which the atoms of certain bodies are arranged. ● *also adj.*

crystalline /**cri**-sta-line/ *adj* **1** clear (*crystalline water*). **2** made of or like crystal.

crystallize /**cri**-sta-lize/ *vb, also* **crystallise** (*Br*) **1** to form into crystals. **2** to make or become clear or definite (*plans beginning to crystallize*). ● *n* **crystallization** /cri-sta-li-**zay**-shun/, *also* **crystallisation** (*Br*).

cub /cub/ *n* **1** the young of certain animals (e.g. the bear, fox, etc.).

cube /cyoob/ *n* **1** a solid body with six equal square sides. **2** the answer got by multiplying a number twice by itself (e.g. 2 x 2 x 2 = 8, therefore 8 is the *cube* of 2, 2 is the **cube root** of 8).

cubic /**cyoo**-bic/ *adj* **1** cube-shaped. **2** having to do with cubes.

cubicle /**cyoo**-bi-cal/ *n* **1** a small sleeping area in a dormitory. **2** any small compartment in a larger room (*changing cubicles at the swimming pool*).

cuckoo /**coo**-coo/ *n* a grayish brown bird with white on the bottom, whose call sounds similar to its name.

cucumber /**cyoo**-cum-ber/ *n* a creeping plant with a long green fruit a lot of used in salads.

cud /cud/ *n* the food that certain animals bring up from their stomachs to chew again.

cuddle /**cu**-dl/ *vb* **1** to hug lovingly (*cuddled the baby*). **2** to lie close and comfortably (*children cuddling to keep warm*).

cue /cyoo/ *n* **1** a word or sign that reminds a person of what to say or do next (*the last words of an actor's speech act as a cue to the next speaker*). **2** the long stick used for striking the balls in billiards and pool.

cuff[1] /cuf/ *n* the part of a sleeve near the wrist.

cuff[2] /cuf/ *n* a blow (*a cuff on the ear*). ● *also vb.*

cuisine /cwi-**zeen**/ *n* a style of cooking (*French cuisine/Italian cuisine*).

cul-de-sac /**cul**-di-sac/ *n* a street closed at one end, a dead-end street.

culinary /**cu**-li-ne-ree/ *adj* having to do with cooking (*culinary skills*).

cull /cul/ *vb* **1** to gather, choose, or select (*information culled from many sources*). **2** to select and destroy (*the librarian culled some needless books*).

culminate /**cul**-mi-nate/ *vb* to reach the highest point (*small battles culminating in a full-scale war*). ● *n* **culmination** /cul-mi-**nay**-shun/.

culprit /**cul**-prit/ *n* a wrongdoer, one accused of a crime (*catch the culprit committing the crime*).

cult /cult/ *n* a particular, often temporarily, fashionable system of beliefs, especially religious.

cultivate /**cul**-ti-vate/ *vb* **1** to prepare (land) for the growing of crops. **2** to make to grow (*cultivating several types of vegetable*). **3** to improve (the mind) (*reading books and listening to music to cultivate her mind*). ● *n* **cultivation** /cul-ti-**vay**-shun/. ● *n* **cultivator** /cul-ti-**vay**-tor/.

culture /**cul**-chur/ *n* **1** the character of an age and people as seen in customs, arts, etc. (*learn about Roman culture*). **2** learning and good taste (*people of culture*). **3** the rearing of creatures or growing of plants in conditions not natural to them. ● *adj* **cultural**.

cultured /**cul**-churd/ *adj* having learning and good taste (*cultured people interested in the arts*).

cumbersome /**cum**-ber-sum/ *adj* **1** heavy and difficult to move (*cumbersome parcels/cumbersome furniture*). **2** slow and not working to the best ability (*a cumbersome method of government*).

cumulative /**cyoom**-yu-la-tive/ *adj* (*fml*) growing gradually larger by being added to (*cumulative damage to the to the atmosphere/frequent small doses of a drug with a cumulative effect*). ● *vb* **cumulate** /**cyoom**-yu-late/.

cumulus /**cyoom**-yu-lus/ *n* a mass of white rounded clouds. ● *adj* **cumulous**.

cunning /**cun**-ing/ *adj* **1** clever, skillful, crafty (*a cunning trick*). **2** good at deceiving (*a cunning cheat*). **3** clever (*a cunning device*). ● *n* skill, deceit.

cup /**cup**/ *n* a small drinking vessel. ● *vb* (**cupped** /cupt/, **cupping** /**cup**-ing/) to put into the shape of a cup (*cup her hands around the flower/cup his hands to catch the ball*).

cupboard /**cu**-board/ *n* a shelved place for storing food, dishes, etc.

cupcake /**cup**-cake/ *n* a small sponge cake, cooked in a paper case, usually with frosting on top.

cupful /**cup**-ful/ *n* the amount a cup holds.

curator /**cyoo**-ray-tor/ *n* one in charge of a museum, art gallery, etc.

curb /**curb**/ *vb* to control, to keep in check (*curb his anger/curb their spending*). ● *n* **1** anything that controls or holds in check (*a curb on their expenditure*). **2** a chain or strap fastened to the bit in a horse's mouth. **3** the concrete edging along a street that separates it from the sidewalk or guttering.

curd /**curd**/ *n* a solid substance that forms in sour milk, and from which cheese is made.

curdle /**cur**-dl/ *vb* to thicken, to become solid (*a creamy sauce curdling when boiled*).

cure /**cyoor**/ *n* **1** act of healing. **2** that which heals or gives back health (*a cure for cancer*). **3** (*fml*) the care of souls. ● *vb* **1** to heal. **2** to preserve meat, fish, etc.

curfew /**cur**-fyoo/ *n* **1** (*old*) a bell rung in the evening as a signal to put out all lights. **2** a military order for people to be indoors and keep the streets empty after a certain hour (*impose a curfew after the riots*). **3** the time at which people have to be indoors or in their homes.

curiosity /cyoo-ree-**oss**-i-tee/ *n* **1** the desire to learn, or to find out about (*a child showing curiosity about how the car works/full of curiosity about her neighbors' lives*). **2** a rare or strange object (*an shop full of curiosities*).

curious /**cyoo**-ree-us/ *adj* **1** wanting to learn (*curious about the origin of mankind*). **2** wanting to know the private affairs of others (*neighbors curious about where she goes in the evenings*). **3** strange (*rather a curious figure/it's curious that he has disappeared*).

curl /**curl**/ *vb* **1** to form into ringlets. **2** to twist around (*smoke curling from the chimney*). **3** to play at the game of curling. ● *n* a ringlet.

curling /**cur**-ling/ *n* a winter game played on ice, involving sliding heavy smooth stones toward a target.

curly /**cur**-lee/ *adj* having curls (*curly hair*).

currant /**cur**-ant/ *n* **1** a small dried grape (*buns made with currants*). **2** a type of sour, red, black, or white berry growing on certain shrubs and used in jellies or jams.

currency /**cur**-en-see/ *n* **1** the money in present use in a country. **2** the state of being widely known (*the currency of the rumors*).

current /**cur**-ent/ *adj* **1** in general use (*words no longer current*). **2** belonging to the present time (*current fashions*). ● *n* **1** a stream of water or air moving in a certain direction. **2** a flow of electricity.

curriculum /cu-ri-cyu-lum/ *n* a course of study at a school, university, etc. (*several foreign languages on the curriculum*).

curry[1] /**cu**-ree/ *n* a dish of meat, vegetables, etc., cooked with a spicey sauce.

curry[2] /**cu**-ree/ *vb* to rub down a horse with a comb. ● **curry favor** to try to win the favor of another by pleasing (*curries favor with the teacher by giving her presents*).

curse /**curse**/ *vb* **1** to use bad language (*not allowed to curse at home*). **2** to call down harm and evil upon (*she cursed the man who killed her son*). ● *n* **1** the wish that another may suffer harm and evil (*put a curse on his enemy*). **2** a great evil or cause of suffering (*the curse of drug-dealing*). **3** a swear word.

cursor /**cur**-sor/ *n* a movable pointer on a computer screen that shows, for example, where the next piece of text would be typed.

cursory /**cur**-so-ree/ *adj* quick, careless (*give the instructions a cursory glance*).

curt /**curt**/ *adj* **1** abrupt, rude (*a curt answer/he was very curt with us*). **2** brief, abrupt (*a curt reply*). ● *n* **curtness** /**curt**-ness/.

curtail /cur-**tale**/ *vb* (*fml*) to cut short (*have to curtail our vacation/curtailing our spending*). ● *n* **curtailment** /cur-**tale**-ment/.

curtain /**cur**-tin/ *n* a cloth hung up to darken, or to hide things behind it. ● *also vb*.

curtsy /**curt**-see/ *n* a bow made by women in a respectful greeting by bending the knees with a slight lowering of the upper body (*a curtsy to the queen*). ● *also vb*.

curve /**curv**/ *n* **1** a line that is not straight and that changes direction without angles (*a curve on the graph*). **2** something shaped like this (*curves in the road/her attractive curves*). ● *vb* to bend into a curve.

cushion /**coo**-shin/ *n* **1** a cloth bag filled with soft material, for sitting, leaning, or kneeling on. **2** anything that takes the force of a blow or shock (*his savings acted as a cushion when he lost his job*). ● *vb* to lessen a blow or shock.

custard /**cu**-stard/ *n* a dish of milk, eggs, and sugar, baked or boiled.

custodian /cu-**sto**-dee-an/ *n* a keeper, one who takes care, especially of a museum or other public building.

custody /**cu**-sto-dee/ *n* **1** care (*a mother given custody of her children*). **2** safekeeping (*leave her jewelry in the custody of the bank*). **3** imprisonment (*taken into custody while awaiting trial*).

custom /**cu**-stom/ *n* **1** the usual way of doing something (*traditional country customs*). **2** something done often as a habit (*it was her custom to have an afternoon nap*). **3** the buying of certain things at one particular shop, etc. (*threaten to take her custom elsewhere when the assistant was rude*). **4** *pl* the taxes payable on goods brought into a country. **5** *pl* the office where such taxes are paid, or the officials collecting them.

customary /**cu**-sto-me-ree/ *adj* usual (*the customary route for his walk*).

customer /**cu**-sto-mer/ *n* one who usually buys things (in a particular shop) (*the local shop with a few regular customers*).

cut /**cut**/ *vb* (**cut**, **cutting** /**cu**-ting/) **1** to make an opening with a sharp instrument (*cut her hand*). **2** to divide into pieces with a sharp instrument (*cut up the meat*). **3** to shorten or shape by cutting (*cut his hair*). **4** to divide a pack of cards. **5** to lessen (*cut costs*). **6** to refuse to look at or speak to (*cut out his old friend*). ● *n* **1** an opening made by cutting (*a cut in the cloth*). **2** a wound (*a deep cut in her leg*). **3** the way a thing is shaped (*the cut of her coat/a haircut*). **4** a lessening (*a cut in their spending*). **5** a piece of meat (*an expensive cut of meat*).

cutback /**cut**-back/ *n* a reduction in the amount of something (*cutbacks in public spending*).

cute /**cyoot**/ *adj* **1** (*inf*) cunningly clever (*he was too cute to be caught/a cute trick*). **2** pretty, attractive, especially in a lively way.

cuticle /**cyoo**-ti-cl/ *n* **1** the outer skin of a plant or of the body. **2** the hardened skin that gathers at the base of the fingernails and toenails.

cutlass /**cut**-lass/ *n* a short, curving sword.

cutlery /**cut**-le-ree/ *n* knives, forks, spoons, etc.

cutlet /**cut**-let/ *n* a thin slice of meat, usually from a rib or leg, a chop (*lamb cutlets*).

cutter /**cu**-ter/ *n* **1** a light sailing boat. **2** the tailor who cuts out the cloth.

cutting /**cu**-ting/ *adj* hurting the feelings (*a cutting remark*). ● *n* **1** a piece of a plant cut off for replanting (*take cuttings from the geranium*). **2** a piece cut out of a newspaper (*save cuttings about the pop star*). **3** a passage cut through rock for a road or railway.

cuttlefish /**cu**-tul-fish/ *n* a sea creature with eight legs that gives out a black liquid when attacked.

cycle /**sie**-cul/ *n* **1** a series of events that are regularly repeated in the same order (*the cycle of the seasons*). **2** a number of stories, songs, etc., about the same person or event (*a Schubert song cycle*). **3** (*inf*) a bicycle. ● *vb* to ride a bicycle (*cycling to school*).

cyclic /**sie**-clic/ *adj* happening in cycles.

cyclist /**sie**-clist/ *n* one who rides a bicycle.

cyclone /**sie**-clone/ *n* a violent storm of wind that moves in a circular motion, such as a hurricane or tornado.

cygnet /**sig**-net/ *n* a young swan.

cylinder /**si**-lin-der/ *n* **1** a solid or hollow shape with circular ends and straight sides. **2** an object or container shaped like this (*a cylinder of oxygen*). ● *adj* **cylindrical**.

cymbal /**sim**-bal/ *n* one of two brass plates used as a musical instrument and struck together to make a clanging noise.

cynic /**si**-nic/ *adj* one who believes that people do not do things for good or kindly reasons but for their own advantage (*cynics who believe that politicians are interested only in keeping their seats*). ● *also adj*. ● *adj* **cynical** /**si**-ni-cal/. ● *n* **cynicism** /**si**-ni-si-zum/.

cyst /**sist**/ *n* a small bag full of liquid that forms on or in the body (*have a cyst removed*).

czar /**zar**/ *n* the title of former emperors of Russia, or any person having great or unlimited power. ● *f* **czarina** /za-**ree**-na/. *See also* **tsar**, **tzar**.

D

D, d /dee/ **1** the fourth letter of the alphabet. **2** (*mus*) the second note of the scale of C major.

DA /dee-ay/ *abbr* = **District Attorney**: the prosecuting officer of a district.

dab[1] /dab/ *vb* (**dabbed** /dabd/, **dabbing** /da-bing/) to touch or hit gently with something soft or damp (*dab the wound with absorbent cotton*). ● *n* **1** a gentle touch (*give the wet ink a dab with some blotting paper*). **2** a small lump of anything soft or damp (*a dab of butter*).

dab[2] /dab/ *n* a flatfish.

dabble /da-bul/ *vb* **1** to splash, to wet (*dabble her fingers in the water*). **2** to take up in a small way (*dabble in witchcraft*). ● *n* **dabbler** /da-bler/.

dachshund /daks-hoont/ *n* a small dog with a long body and short legs.

dad /dad/, **daddy** /da-dee/ *n* (*inf*) father.

daddy long legs /da-dee long-legs/ *n* the informal name for the crane fly, a fly with a long thin body and long spindly legs.

daffodil /da-fo-dil/ *n* a yellow bell-shaped spring flower.

daft /daft/ *adj* (*inf*) foolish, silly (*a daft idea/daft behavior*).

dagger /da-ger/ *n* a short sharp-pointed sword.

daily /day-lee/ *adj* happening every day (*a daily walk to the park*). ● *also adv.* ● *n* a daily newspaper (*the San Francisco Examiner is a daily*).

dainty /dane-tee/ *adj* small, delicate, and pretty (*a dainty little girl/dainty porcelain*).

daintily /dane-ti-lee/ *adv* **1** in a dainty way (*dress daintily*). **2** with very great care (*eat daintily*). ● *n* **daintiness** /dane-tee-ness/.

dairy /day-ree/ *n* a place where milk is sold, or made into butter or cheese.

dais /day-us/ *n* a low platform (*a speaker addressing the school from a dais*).

daisy /day-zee/ *n* a usually white, common wild flower with many petals and yellow center.

dalmatian /dal-may-shun/ *n* a large black-and-white-spotted dog.

dam[1] /dam/ *n* a wall to stop or control the flow of water (*the dam in the river*). ● *vb* (**dammed** /damd/, **damming** /da-ming/) to keep back by a dam.

dam[2] /dam/ *n* (*of animals*) a mother.

damage /da-midge/ *n* **1** injury, harm (*storms causing a lot of damage/rumors doing damage to his reputation*). **2 damages** /da-mi-jeez/ money paid to make up for loss or harm (*sue the driver of the car that hit her for damages*). ● *vb* to harm.

dame /dame/ *n* **1** the status of a lady of the same rank as a knight. **2** (*inf*) a woman.

damn /dam/ *vb* **1** in religion, to send to everlasting punishment (*damn his soul*). **2** to condemn, to declare to be bad (*a play damned by the critics*). **3** to curse (*damn you!*). ● *n* a curse.

damp /damp/ *adj* slightly wet (*damp hair/damp clothing*). ● *n* slight wetness. ● *vb* to make slightly wet (*damp her hair*). ● *n* **dampness** /damp-ness/.

dampen /dam-pen/ *vb* **1** to make or become damp (*dampen the shirt before ironing*). **2** to make less strong, etc. (*dampen his enthusiasm*).

dance /dance/ *vb* **1** to move in time to music. **2** to move in a lively way (*children dancing about in excitement*). ● *n* **1** act of dancing. **2** a social gathering for the purpose of dancing (*invite her to a formal dance*). ● *n* **dancer** /dan-ser/.

dandelion /dan-dee-lie-on/ *n* a wild plant with a yellow flower.

dandruff /dan-druff/ *n* small pieces of dead skin on the scalp.

dandy[1] /dan-dee/ *n* a man who pays what is considered to be too much attention to his appearance and clothes. ● *adj* **dandified** /dan-di-fied/.

dandy[2] /dan-dee/ *adj* great or fine (*that's just dandy!*).

danger /dane-jer/ *n* **1** the risk of hurt or harm (*with her life in danger*). **2** something that may cause harm, injury, death, etc. (*wild animals that are a danger to the villagers/the dangers of modern living*).

dangerous /dane-je-russ/ *adj* full of risks (*a dangerous journey*).

dangle /dang-gul/ *vb* to hang loosely (*with her purse dangling from her wrist*).

dank /dangk/ *adj* cold and damp (*a dank cellar*).

dapple /da-pel/, **dappled** /da-puld/ *adjs* marked with spots of a different shade (*dappled ponies*).

dare /dare/ *vb* **1** to be brave enough (to), to undertake to do (*he dared to ask the boss for more money/who would dare to climb Mount Everest?*). **2** to challenge (*dare the boy to climb to the roof*). ● *n* a challenge.

daredevil /dare-de-vil/ *n* a person who is ready to face any danger.

daring /dare-ing/ *adj* brave, fearless (*a daring young man/a daring attempt*). ● *n* courage.

dark /dark/ *adj* **1** without light (*dark nights/dark rooms*). **2** having black or brown hair (*a tall dark stranger*). **3** evil (*dark deeds*). ● *n* **darkness** /dark-ness/.

darken /dar-ken/ *vb* to make or become darker (*a complexion darkened by the sun*).

darkroom /dark-room/ *n* a room that is kept dark in which photographs are developed and printed.

darling /dar-ling/ *n* a person who is dearly loved (*you are a darling/come here, darling*). ● *also adj* (*his darling wife/a darling little cottage*).

darn /darn/ *vb* to mend holes in clothes. ● *also n.*

dart /dart/ *n* **1** a pointed weapon thrown by hand. **2** a sudden quick movement (*in one dart the child escaped*). **3** in needlework, a small pleat. ● *npl* **darts** a game in which darts are thrown at a target. ● *vb* to move quickly (*the child darted out the door*).

dash /dash/ *vb* **1** to run quickly. **2** to smash against (*waves dashing against the rocks*). **3** to discourage (*dash all their hopes*). ● *n* **1** a quick movement. **2** a small amount (*a dash of milk*). **3** a mark of punctuation (—).

dasher /da-sher/ *n* **1** someone who dashes. **2** a part of a cream churn. **3** one of the boards surrounding a hockey rink.

dashboard /dash-board/ *n* the instrument board in a car.

data /day-ta/ *npl* (*now often regarded as a singular noun, see also* **datum** /day-tum/) a known fact or piece of information (*consider all the data relating to population/process computer data*).

database /day-ta-base/ *n* a collection of data that is stored in a computer.

date[1] /date/ *n* **1** the day and month and/or year in which something happened or is going to happen (*the date of the next meeting*). **2** (*inf*) an arrangement to meet at a certain time, especially a social meeting with a member of the opposite sex. ● *vb* **1** to write the date on (*dated the letter*). **2** (*inf*) to make a date, often to see a romantic partner (*dating the boy next door*). ● **date from** to have a beginning at a certain time (*houses dating from the 18th century*). ● **out of date** no longer in use (*machinery that is out of date*).

date[2] /date/ *n* the edible fruit of the date palm.

dateline /date-line/ *n* the line in the Pacific where one day is regarded as beginning and another as ending.

datum *sing of* **data**.

daub /dawb/ *vb* **1** to put on in lumps or smears (*clothing daubed with mud/daub paint on*). **2** to paint roughly (*daub the walls red with paint*). ● *n* a smear (*a daub of mud*).

daughter /daw-ter/ *n* a female child.

daughter-in-law /daw-ter-in-law/ *n* (*pl* **daughters-in-law**) the wife of a son.

daunt /dawnt/ *vb* to make less brave, to discourage (*she refused to be daunted by the remarks of her critics/not be daunted by the difficulty of the journey*). ● *adj* **dauntless** /dawnt-less/.

dawdle /daw-dul/ *vb* to move slowly, often stopping, to waste time (*dawdling along, late for school*).

dawn /dawn/ *n* **1** the beginning of day. **2** a beginning (*at the dawn of civilization*). ● *vb* to grow light. ● **dawn on** to become clear eventually (*it suddenly dawned on me that I was on the wrong train*).

day /day/ *n* **1** during daylight. **2** 24 hours.

daybreak /day-brake/ *n* the beginning of day, dawn (*set out on our journey at daybreak*).

day care /day-care/ *n* **1** the taking care of children, during daytime, usually while their parents are at work. **2** the place where children go to be taken care of.

daydream /day-dreem/ *vb* to dream while awake (*daydream of being rich one day*). ● *also n.*

daylight /day-lite/ *n* the light of day.

daytime /day-time/ *n* the hours of day.

daze /daze/ *vb* to confuse, to bewilder (*dazed by the bang on the head/dazed by the bad news*). ● *n* confusion.

dazzle /da-zul/ *vb* **1** to prevent from seeing clearly with strong light (*car headlights dazzling rabbits*). **2** to confuse or impress (*dazzled by her beauty*).

dead /ded/ *adj* **1** without life (*dead bodies*). **2** dull, lifeless (*a dead expression*). **3** absolute, complete (*come to a dead stop*). **4** not working (*the phone is dead*). ● *adv* **1** completely (*dead tired*). **2** straight (*dead ahead*). ● *n* the quietest time (*dead of night*). ● *npl* dead people (*prayers for the dead*).

deaden /de-den/ *vb* to dull, to lessen (*deaden the pain/deaden the sounds*).

dead end /de-dend/ *n* a road that is closed at one end.

deadline /ded-line/ *n* a time by which something must be done (*tomorrow is the deadline for applications for the job*).

deadlock /ded-lock/ *n* a complete disagreement (*talks between the two sides have reached deadlock*).

deadly /**ded**-lee/ adj 1 causing death (a deadly disease/a deadly blow). 2 (inf) very boring (what a deadly talk!). ● n **deadliness** /**ded**-lee-ness/.

deaf /def/ adj 1 unable to hear (are you deaf?) 2 (with cap) relating to the Deaf and to their culture (the Deaf community communicates using American Sign Language [ASL]). 3 unwilling to listen (deaf to our request for mercy). ● n 1 (used with **the**) Deaf people considered as a group. 2 the community of deaf people who use American Sign Language. ● **Usage**: There is a distinction between deaf and Deaf. The capitalized form is used to refer to deaf people who use American Sign Language as their preferred means of communication. ● n **deafness** /**def**-ness/.

deafen /**def**-en/ vb to make deaf (noise that would deafen you). ● adj **deafening** /**def**-e-ning/.

deal /deel/ n 1 an amount (a great deal of money/a good deal of rain). 2 the giving out of playing cards. 3 a business agreement (sign an important export deal). ● vb (pt, pp **dealt** /delt/) 1 to give out (cards). 2 to cope with, to handle (deal with the problem). 3 to do business with (will deal only with the owner of the firm).

dealer /**dee**-ler/ n 1 a person who buys and sells (a dealer in antiques). 2 a person who gives out playing cards in a game.

dealings /**dee**-lingz/ npl acts of business, relations (wish to have no further dealings with them).

dean /deen/ n 1 a leader of the church in charge of a cathedral. 2 the head of a university faculty.

dear /deer/ adj 1 well-loved (my dear mother). 2 expensive, high in price (dear food/zucchini are dear today). ● n a loved person. ● adv dearly. ● n **dearness** /**deer**-ness/. ● adv **dearly** /**deer**-lee/.

death /deth/ n state of being dead.

deathly /**deth**-lee/ adj and adv like death (deathly pale).

deathtrap /**deth**-trap/ n (inf) a place that is very dangerous (the floor of that old cottage is a real deathtrap).

debate /de-**bate**/ n 1 an argument (a lot of debate over where to go on vacation). 2 the formal discussion of a question in public (a debate in the Senate). ● vb 1 to argue. 2 to discuss. ● adj **debatable** /de-**bay**-ta-bul/.

debilitate /de-**bi**-li-tate/ vb to weaken (debilitated by a long illness).

debility /de-**bi**-li-tee/ n weakness (the debility of the invalid).

debit /**de**-bit/ n (Br, Cdn) the written note in an account book of a sum owed. ● vb to note the sum owed.

debris /**de**-bree/ n 1 the remains of something broken, destroyed, etc., wreckage (the debris of the crashed plane). 2 garbage, etc. (clear up the debris after the party).

debt /det/ n anything owed.

debtor /**de**-tor/ n a person who owes.

debug /dee-**bug**/ n to correct the errors in a computer program.

debut /**day**-byoo, day-**byoo**/ n a first appearance in public (a young actress making her debut).

decade /**de**-cade/ n 1 a period of 10 years. 2 (inf, exaggeration) a long time (I haven't seen her in decades).

decaffeinated /dee-ca-fi-nay-ted/ adj of a drink such as coffee, having had most of the caffeine removed, often abbreviated to **decaf** /**dee**-caf/.

decagon /**de**-ca-gon/ n a figure with 10 sides. ● adj **decagonal** /de-**ca**-go-nal/.

decamp /di-**camp**/ vb to go away secretly (decamp without paying their bills).

decant /di-**cant**/ vb to pour carefully from one vessel to another (decant wine from a bottle into a carafe).

decanter /di-**can**-ter/ n a stoppered bottle in which wine or spirits is served.

decapitate /di-**ca**-pi-tate/ vb to cut off the head of. ● n **decapitation** /di-ca-pi-**tay**-shun/.

decathlon /di-**cath**-lon/ n a track-and-field event in which people compete in 10 different sports.

decay /di-**cay**/ vb 1 to go rotten (teeth decaying). 2 to fall into ruin (buildings decaying from lack of maintenance). ● also n.

deceased /di-**seesst**/ adj dead. ● n a dead person (bury the deceased).

deceit /di-**seet**/ n anything said or done to deceive, trickery (capable of great deceit/use deceit to get the old lady's money). ● adj **deceitful** /di-**seet**-ful/.

deceive /di-**seev**/ vb to make someone believe what is not true, to trick (deceive them into believing he was a real doctor). ● n **deceiver** /di-**see**-ver/.

December /di-**sem**-ber/ n the 12th month of the year.

decency see **decent**.

decent /**dee**-sent/ adj 1 proper, not shocking (the school rules say wear a skirt of a decent length). 2 reasonable, satisfactory (get a decent meal). ● n **decency** /**dee**-sen-see/.

deception /di-**sep**-shun/ n 1 act of deceiving. 2 a trick, pretense (gain entrance by a deception). ● adj **deceptive** /di-**sep**-tiv/.

decibel /**de**-si-bel/ *n* a unit for measuring how loud something is.

decide /di-**side**/ *vb* **1** to make up your mind (*decided to go on vacation*). **2** to settle a question, etc. (*a goal deciding the match*).

decided /di-**sie**-ded/ *adj* **1** firm. **2** definite.

decidedly /di-**sie**-ded-lee/ *adv* undoubtedly (*feel decidedly sick*).

deciduous /di-**si**-joo-wus/ *adj* having leaves that drop off in the fall.

decimal /**de**-si-mal/ *adj* counted by tens, hundreds, etc.. ● *n* a fraction worked out to the nearest tenth, hundredth, etc.. (*0.25 is the decimal way of expressing one quarter*).

decimal point *n* a period, or full stop, in a number that is used to show fractions. The numbers appearing to the right of the period are less than 1. (*The number 1.75 is the numeral 1 and the fraction three quarters. The fraction appears after the decimal point.*)

decimal system /**de**-si-mal **si**-stem/ *n* a system of weights, measures, and money based on multiplying and dividing by 10.

decipher /di-**sie**-fer/ *vb* to work out the meaning of (*decipher her bad handwriting/decipher the enemy's code*).

decision /di-**si**-zhun/ *n* **1** act of deciding. **2** a judgment (*the judge's decision is final/come to a decision*). **3** (*fml*) firmness (*act with decision*).

decisive /di-**sie**-siv/ *adj* **1** firm (*stop changing your mind and be decisive*). **2** settling a matter finally (*a decisive battle*).

decisively /di-**si**-siv-lee/ *adv* firmly, clearly.

deck /deck/ *vb* (*fml*) to cover, to decorate (*deck the room with holly/deck yourself out in your best*). ● *n* the covering or floor on a ship.

declare /di-**clare**/ *vb* **1** to make known, to announce (*declared war/declaring their intention to marry*). **2** to state firmly (*"I am going home early," she declared*). ● *n* **declaration** /de-cla-**ray**-shun/.

decline /di-**cline**/ *vb* **1** to refuse (*decline the invitation*). **2** to slope downward. **3** to become worse or weaker (*her state of health is declining*). **4** to give the cases of a noun or adjective. ● *n* a gradual worsening or weakening (*a noticeable decline in standards*).

decode /dee-**code**/ *vb* to work out the meaning of a message in code.

decompose /dee-com-**poze**/ *vb* to decay, to rot (*vegetables decomposing on the compost heap/bodies decomposing in the heat*). ● *n* **decomposition** /dee-com-po-**zi**-shun/.

decontaminate /dee-con-**ta**-mi-nate/ *vb* to free from what is infectious or harmful (*decontaminating the radioactive area*). ● *n* **decontamination** /dee-con-ta-mi-**nay**-shun/.

décor, decor /day-**cawr**/ *n* the style of decoration in a room or house.

decorate /**de**-cu-rate/ *vb* **1** to make beautiful or ornamental (*decorating the Christmas tree*). **2** to put wallpaper, paint, etc., on the walls of (*decorate the kitchen*). **3** to give a badge or medal of honor to (*decorate the soldiers for bravery*). ● *n* **decoration** /de-cu-**ray**-shun/.

decorative /**de**-cra-tiv/ *adj* ornamental (*a fireplace that was purely decorative*).

decorator /**de**-cu-rate-or/ *n* a person who paints and wallpapers houses.

decoy /**dee**-coy/ *n* anything intended to lead people, animals, etc., into a trap (*use her child as a decoy to get her into the car*). ● *vb* to lead into a trap, to trick into a place of danger by using a decoy (*decoyed him into the cellar by saying his son was there*).

decrease /di-**creess**/ *vb* to become or make less (*the number of students is decreasing/decrease the amount of money allowed*). ● *n* **decrease** /**dee**-creess/ a lessening (*a decrease in the number of patients*).

decree /di-**cree**/ *n* **1** an order or law (*a decree forbidding hunting*). **2** a judgment at law. ● *vb* to make a decree.

decrepit /di-**crep**-it/ *adj* broken down with age (*decrepit old man/decrepit furniture*). ● *n* **decrepitude** /di-**cre**-pi-tood/.

dedicate /**de**-di-cate/ *vb* **1** to set apart for a special purpose (*dedicating her life to medicine*). **2** to offer to God. **3** to write another's name at the beginning of a book to show that you think highly of him or her. ● *n* **dedication** /de-di-**cay**-shun/. ● *adj* **dedicatory** /de-di-**cay**-toe-ree/.

deduce /di-**dooss**/ *vb* to work out a truth from things already known (*from the evidence the police deduced that he was guilty*). ● *adj* **deductive** /di-**duc**-tiv/.

deduct /di-**duct**/ *vb* to subtract, to take away (*deduct the price of the broken vase from her pay check*).

deduction /di-**duc**-shun/ *n* **1** an amount taken away (*tax deductions from his pay check*). **2** a conclusion worked out from things already known (*the deduction made by the police*).

deed /deed/ *n* **1** that which is done, an act (*a brave* *deed/a foolish deed*). **2** a written agreement (*sign a deed transferring her house to her daughter*).

deem /**deem**/ *vb* (*fml*) to judge, to consider (*deem her unworthy to marry her son*).

deep /**deep**/ *adj* **1** going far down (*a deep hole/a deep lake*). **2** difficult to understand (*thoughts too deep for me/a very deep person*). **3** strongly felt (*deep feelings*). **4** cunning (*a deep plot*). **5** (*of sounds*) low in pitch. **6** (*of color*) strong, dark, intense (*a deep purple*). ● *n* **the deep** the sea.

deepen /**dee**-pen/ *vb* to become or make deep (*his voice deepened/deepen the hole*).

deer /**deer**/ *n* (*pl* **deer**) a swift-moving animal with hooves and horns (e.g., the reindeer).

deface /di-**face**/ *vb* to damage, to spoil the appearance of (*deface the walls with graffiti*). ● *n* **defacement** /di-**face**-ment/.

default /di-**fawlt**/ *n* **1** failure to do what is necessary. **2** failure to pay a debt. **3** the action that a computer takes unless you give it a different command. ● *also vb.* ● *n* **defaulter** /di-**fawl**-ter/.

defeat /di-**feet**/ *vb* **1** to beat in a fight or contest. **2** to make to fail. ● *n* a lost fight or contest.

defeatist /di-**fee**-tist/ *adj* expecting or being ready to accept defeat or failure (*don't be so defeatist— if you start work now, you could still pass your exams*). ● *n* a defeatist person. ● *n* **defeatism** /di-**fee**-ti-zum/.

defect[1] /**dee**-fect/ *n* a fault or flaw (*a defect in the fabric/a defect in his character*).

defect[2] /di-**fect**/ *vb* to desert a country, army, group, or political party to join an opposing one (*soldiers defecting to the enemy/voters defecting to another party*). ● *n* **defection** /di-**fec**-shun/.

defective /di-**fec**-tiv/ *adj* **1** below average or normal (*mentally defective*). **2** faulty, flawed (*defective goods*).

defend /di-**fend**/ *vb* **1** to protect or guard against attack (*defend the city against the invaders*). **2** to give reasons in support of your ideas (*defend their economic policy*). **3** to present the case for an accused person (*the barrister defending the accused*).

defendant /di-**fen**-dant/ *n* in law, the person accused.

defense /di-**fense**/ *n, also* **defence** (*Br, Cdn*) **1** the act of holding off an attack (*join in the defense of the city against the invader*). **2** that which protects (*thick castle walls acting as a defense*). **3** the arguments in favor of an accused person, especially in a court of law.

defenseless /di-**fense**-less/ *adj, also* **defenceless** (*Br, Cdn*) without protection (*defenseless children*).

defensible /di-**fen**-si-bul/ *adj* able to be defended (*behavior that is scarcely defensible*).

defensive /di-**fen**-siv/ *adj* **1** suitable for defense, protecting (*defensive weapons*). **2** ready to defend against attack (*she always adopts a defensive attitude against criticism*). ● *n* state of defending.

defer[1] /di-**fer**/ *vb* (**deferred** /di-**ferd**/, **deferring** /di-**fe**-ring/) to put off until later (*defer the meeting planned for today*). ● *n* **deferment** /di-**fer**-ment/.

defer[2] /di-**fer**/ *vb* (**deferred** /di-**ferd**/, **deferring** /di-**fe**-ring/) to give in to another's wishes from respect (*defer to more experienced people*).

defiance /di-**fie**-anse/ *n* defiant behavior (*in defiance of her teachers/in defiance of the law*).

defiant /di-**fie**-ant/ *adj* fearlessly and boldly refusing to obey (*a defiant child/a defiant attitude*).

deficiency /di-**fi**-shen-see/ *n* lack, want (*a deficiency of vitamin C*).

deficient /di-**fi**-shent/ *adj* lacking something, not having something that you should have (*a diet deficient in fresh fruit/deficient in common sense*).

deficit /**de**-fi-sit/ *n* the amount by which a sum of money falls short of what is needed, a shortage (*annual accounts showing a deficit of thousands of dollars*).

define /di-**fine**/ *vb* **1** to mark out the limits of (*define the boundary of their land*). **2** to explain exactly (*defining a difficult word/define your terms*).

definite /**de**-fi-nit/ *adj* fixed, certain (*definite plans*). ● *adv* **definitely** /**de**-fi-nit-lee/.

definition /de-fi-**ni**-shun/ *n* an exact meaning or explanation.

definitive /de-**fi**-ni-tiv/ *adj* **1** clear and certain. **2** final.

deflate /di-**flate**/ *vb* **1** to let the air out of (*deflating tires*). **2** to reduce, especially someone's pride, importance, etc. ● *n* **deflation** /di-**flay**-shun/.

deflect /di-**flect**/ *vb* to make to change direction, to turn aside (*deflect the blow with his arm/deflect her from her chosen career*). ● *n* **deflection** /di-**flec**-shun/.

deforest /dee-**faw**-rest/ *vb* to clear a forest by cutting down or burning trees in an area. ● *n* **deforestation** /dee-faw-res-**tay**-shun/.

deform /di-**form**/ *vb* to spoil the shape or appearance of (*her beauty was deformed by a birthmark/ deform the landscape with buildings*).

deformed /di-**formd**/ *adj* badly or unnaturally shaped. ● *n* **deformity** /di-**for**-mi-tee/.

defraud /di-**frawd**/ vb to cheat (*defraud the old man of his savings*).

defrost /di-**frawst**/ vb to thaw out frozen food.

deft /**deft**/ adj skillful (*deft fingers/deft at pottery/a deft handling of the situation*). ● n **deftness** /**deft**-ness/.

defunct /di-**funct**/ adj dead, out of existence (*customs now defunct*).

defuse /dee-**fyooz**/ vb 1 to remove the fuse from (*defuse the bomb*). 2 to calm down (*defuse the situation*).

defy /di-**fie**/ vb 1 to challenge. 2 to refuse to obey or to respect. 3 to care nothing for.

degenerate /di-**jen**-er-rate/ vb to become worse, to lose good qualities (*the meeting started off well but degenerated into a loud argument*). ● also adj. ● /di-**jen**-rit/ n a person whose character has become worse (*a moral degenerate*). ● ns **degeneracy** /di-**jen**-ra-see/, **degeneration** /di-je-ne-**ray**-shun/.

degrade /di-**grade**/ vb 1 to lower in rank or importance. 2 to disgrace (*the family were degraded by their son's brutal behavior*). ● n **degradation** /de-gra-**day**-shun/.

degree /di-**gree**/ n 1 a step or stage (*be promoted by degrees/make progress by degrees*). 2 a unit of measurement for heat, angles, etc. 3 the title given by a university to those who reach a certain standard of learning.

dehydrate /dee-**hie**-drate/ vb 1 to take the water out of (*dehydrated vegetables*). 1 to lose water from the body (*dehydrated from walking in the severe heat*).

de-ice /dee-**ice**/ vb to remove ice or frost from a vehicle's windshield, etc. ● n **de-icer** /dee-**ie**-ser/.

deity /**day**-i-tee/ n a god or goddess. ● **the Deity** God.

déjà vu /day-zha-**voo**/ n the feeling that you have experienced something before.

dejected /di-**jec**-tid/ adj sad, discouraged (*felt dejected when he failed to win*). ● n **dejection** /di-**jec**-shun/.

delay /di-**lay**/ vb 1 to put off till later (*delaying the start of the meeting*). 2 to make late (*a plane delayed by fog*). 3 to wait before going on (*we delayed a bit before starting out*). ● also n.

delectable /di-**lec**-ta-bul/ adj (*fml*) delightful, very pleasing (*the creamy dessert was a delectable sight*).

delegate /de-**le**-git/ vb 1 to send a person to act or speak for others. 2 to give certain powers to an-

other. ● n a person who acts or speaks for others (*our union delegate at the conference*).

delegation /de-le-**gay**-shun/ n a body of delegates.

delete /de-**leet**/ vb to rub out, to cross out (*deleting the second paragraph of the report*). ● n **deletion** /de-**lee**-shun/.

deli see **delicatessen**

deliberate /de-li-be-rate/ vb 1 (*fml*) to think over carefully, to consider (*take time to deliberate whether to go or not/deliberating on his financial problems*). 2 to talk over (*deliberated with her co-workers about the correct course of action*). ● adj /de-li-be-rit/ 1 done on purpose (*a deliberate attempt to hurt her*). 2 slow (*with a deliberate tread*).

deliberation /de-li-be-**ray**-shun/ n (*fml*) 1 careful thought. 2 discussion.

delicate /de-li-cate/ adj 1 fine, easily hurt, or damaged (*delicate skin/delicate porcelain*). 2 fine, dainty (*delicate features*). 3 not very healthy, easily made ill (*his wife is delicate/of a delicate constitution*). 4 light, subtle (*delicate shades of pink/delicate flavors*). ● n **delicacy** /de-li-ca-see/.

delicatessen /de-li-ca-**te**-sen/ n a store, or part of one, that sells cold meats and cheese and specialty foods from other countries. Often shortened to **deli**.

delicious /di-li-shus/ adj very pleasing, especially to the taste (*delicious food/delicious smells*).

delight /di-**lite**/ n great joy or pleasure (*take delight in reading/one of the delights of living in the country*). ● vb to gladden, to give great joy (*delighted by the news*).

delightful /di-**lite**-ful/ adj causing delight, pleasant (*a delightful day/a delightful personality*). ● adv **delightfully** /di-**lite**-fu-lee/.

delinquency /di-**ling**-kwen-see/ n 1 (*fml*) failure to do duty (*the soldier's delinquency in being asleep on duty*). 2 wrongdoing, minor crime (*juvenile delinquency*).

delinquent /di-**ling**-kwent/ adj 1 (*fml*) not doing your duty. 2 doing wrong, committing minor crimes (*delinquent young people*). ● n 1 a person who does not do his or her duty. 2 a wrongdoer, especially a young one.

delirious /di-li-**ree**-us/ adj 1 wandering in the mind (*delirious after the blow to his head*). 2 highly excited (*children delirious with excitement at the idea of going to the theme park*). ● n **delirium** /di-li-**ree**-um/.

deliver /di-li-ver/ vb 1 (*fml*) to set free, to rescue (*deliver them from slavery*). 2 to hand over (*deliver the parcel*). **3** to make (a speech). **4** to aim (*deliver a blow*).

delivery /di-**li**-ve-ree/ *n* **1** childbirth (*present at the delivery of his son*). **2** a giving out of letters (*postal delivery*). **3** manner of speaking in public (*a clear delivery*).

dell /dell/ *n* a small valley.

delta /**del**-ta/ *n* the land between the branches of a river with two or more mouths.

delude /di-**lood**/ *vb* to deceive, to trick (*deluding his parents into thinking she was doing well at school*).

deluge /**del**-yoodge/ *n* a great flood.

delusion /di-**loo**-zhun/ *n* a mistaken belief (*parents under the delusion that their children were studying*).

delusive /di-**loo**-siv/ *adj* deceiving, misleading (*the results were delusive*),

delusory /di-**loo**-su-ree/ same as **delusive**.

de luxe /di-**luks**/ *adj* luxurious, top-quality.

delve /delv/ *vb* (*old*) to dig, to search deeply (*delving in her purse for change/delved into old records for details of her family history*).

demand /di-**mand**/ *vb* **1** to ask for firmly or sharply (*demand to see the manager/demand her rights*). **2** require or need (a situation demanding tact). ● *n* **1** a claim. **2** a pressing request.

demean /di-**meen**/ *vb* to lower (yourself) (*refuse to demean yourself to associate with a thief*).

demeanor /di-**mee**-nor/ *n* (*fml*), also **demeanour** (*Br, Cdn*) behavior, manner (*a cheerful demeanor*).

demi- /**de**-mee/ *prefix* half.

demigod /**de**-mee god/ *n* in fable, a being that is half-human, half-divine.

demise /de-**mize**/ *n* **1** (*fml*) death (*after the demise of his father*). **2** end, often due to failure (*the demise of his business*).

democracy /de-**mok**-ra-see/ *n* **1** government by the people. **2** a state that is governed by the people or by persons elected by the people.

democrat /**de**-mo-crat/ *n* a person who believes in democracy. ● *adj* **democratic** /de-mo-**cra**-tik/.

Democrat /**de**-mo-crat/ *n* a member or supporter of the Democratic Party. ● *adj* **Democratic** /de-mo-**cra**-tik/.

Democratic Party /de-mo-**cra**-tik **par**-tee/ *n* one of the main political parties of the United States of America (*the symbol of the Democratic Party is the donkey*).

demolish /de-**mol**-ish/ *vb* **1** to pull down (*demolish the dangerous old buildings*). **2** to destroy (*demolish their argument*). ● *n* **demolition** /de-mo-li-shun/.

demon /**dee**-mon/ *n* an evil spirit, a devil.

demonstrate /**de**-mon-strate/ *vb* **1** to show (*demonstrated his affection by bringing her flowers*). **2** to show how something works (*demonstrate the new washing machine*). **3** to take part in a public show of strong feeling or opinion, often with marching, large signs, etc. (*students demonstrating against cuts in grants*).

demonstration /de-mon-**stray**-shun/ *n* **1** a proof (*flowers in demonstration of his affection*). **2** actions taken by a crowd to show their feelings (*a demonstration against racism*). **3** a display to show how something works (*a demonstration of the new vacuum cleaner*).

demonstrative /de-**mon**-stra-tiv/ *adj* **1** indicating the person or thing referred to (*a demonstrative pronoun*). **2** quick to show feelings, showing feelings openly (*a demonstrative person/so demonstrative that she gave him a hug*).

demonstrator /**de**-mon-stray-tor/ *n* a person who shows how something works.

demoralize /di-**maw**-ra-lize/ *vb*, also **demoralise** (*Br*) to weaken the courage or self-confidence of (*a defeat that demoralized the troops*). ● *n* **demoralization** /di-maw-ra-li-**zay**-shun/, also **demoralization** (*Br*).

demure /di-**myoor**/ *adj* serious and modest in manner (*a demure young girl*). ● *n* **demureness** /di-**myoor**-ness/.

den /den/ *n* **1** the home (cave, hole, etc) of a wild beast (*the lion's den*). **2** a secret meeting place (*a den of thieves*). **3** (*inf*) a small room for studying in.

Dene /de-**nay**/ *n* (*Cdn*) a member of a First Nations people in the Canadian north. ● *adj* describing this people.

denim /**de**-nim/ *n* a cotton material used for overalls, etc. (*jeans made of blue denim*).

denomination /di-nom-in-**ay**-shun/ *n* **1** a class or unit of measurement or money (*coins of low denomination*). **2** all those sharing the same religious beliefs.

denominational /di-nom-in-**aysh**-nal/ *adj* having to do with a religious group or sect (*the school was non-denominational*).

denominator /di-**nom**-in-ay-tor/ *n* the number below the line in a vulgar fraction (*in $^3/_4$ the denominator is 4*).

denote /di-**note**/ *vb* **1** to be a sign of, to mean (*a silence that probably denoted guilt/a sign denoting a missing word*).

denounce /di-**nounse**/ *vb* to speak openly against, to accuse publicly (*the principal denounced the culprits at assembly*). ● *n* **denunciation** /di-nun-see-**ay**-shun/.

dense /**dense**/ *adj* **1** thick (*dense fog*). **2** closely packed (*a dense crowd*). **3** stupid (*dense students*).

density /**den**-si-tee/ *n* the thickness of anything.

dent /**dent**/ *n* a hollow made by a blow or by pressure on the surface (*a dent in his car after the collision/the dent in the pillow made by her head*). ● *also vb*

dental /**den**-tal/ *adj* having to do with the teeth (*dental treatment*).

dental floss /**den**-tal floss/ *n* a fine string used to clean between the teeth. ● *also* **floss**.

dentist /**den**-tist/ *n* a person who takes out or repairs bad teeth, makes false teeth, and in general cares for the teeth of others. ● *n* **dentistry** /**den**-tis-tree/.

denture /**den**-chur/ *n* a set of artificial teeth.

denunciation *see* **denounce**.

deny /di-**nie**/ *vb* **1** to say that something is not true (*deny that he is guilty/deny the accusations*). **2** to refuse (*deny them the opportunity to go to the concert*). ● *n* **denial** /di-**nie**-al/.

deodorant /dee-oe-de-rant/ *n* a liquid or powder that takes away or hides bad smells (*an underarm deodorant*).

deodorize /dee-oe-de-rize/ *vb* (*fml*), *also* **deodorise** (*Br*) to take away the smell from.

dépanneur /day-pa-**noor**/ *n* (*Cdn*) in Quebec, a small store with extended hours that sells food and other items.

depart /di-**part**/ *vb* **1** (*fml*) to go away, to set out (*the train departs from platform six/we depart at dawn*). **2** to cease to follow (*depart from our usual routines*). **3** (*fml*) to die (*depart this life*). ● *n* **departure** /di-**par**-chur/.

department /di-**part**-ment/ *n* a separate part (*the sales department/the toy department*).

department store /di-**part**-ment store/ *n* a large store that has many different sections, each selling a different type of goods.

departure *see* **depart**.

depend /di-**pend**/ *vb* **1** to be likely to happen only under certain conditions (*our vacation depends on our having enough money*). **2** to trust, to rely on (*depend on his assistant*). **3** to need for your

support (*charities depend on the public for donations*).

dependable /di-**pen**-da-bul/ *adj* trustworthy (*dependable employees*).

dependant /di-**pen**-dant/ *n* a person who looks to another for support or livelihood (*have a wife and three children as dependants*).

dependence /di-**pen**-dense/ *n* the state of depending.

dependency /di-**pen**-den-see/ *n* a country governed by another country.

dependent /di-**pen**-dent/ *adj* **1** relying on another for support (*countries dependent on foreign aid*). **2** to be decided by (*whether we have a picnic is dependent on the weather*).

depict /di-**pict**/ *vb* **1** to describe (*the book depicts Victorian London*). **2** to draw, paint, etc. (*a painting depicting a cornfield*).

deplete /di-**pleet**/ *vb* to lessen in amount, size, or numbers (*the number of spectators was depleted by the weather*). ● *n* **depletion** /di-**plee**-shun/.

deplorable /di-**plo**-ra-bul/ *adj* very bad, regrettable (*deplorable behavior*).

deplore /di-**ploar**/ *vb* to regret, to express disapproval of (*deploring their behavior*).

deploy /di-**ploy**/ *vb* to spread out over a wide front (*deployed troops*). ● *n* **deployment** /di-**ploy**-ment/.

deport /di-**poart**/ *vb* **1** to send a person out of the country in punishment (*formerly criminals were deported from Britain to Australia*). **2** (*fml*) to behave (yourself) (*deport yourself well*).

deportation /dee-pore-**tay**-shun/ *n* act of sending out of the country.

deportment /di-**poart**-ment/ *n* (*fml*) the manner in which you stand, move, etc. (*improve your deportment*).

depose /di-**poze**/ *vb* to remove from high office or the throne (*deposing the king*). ● *n* **deposition** /de-po-**zi**-shun/

deposit /di-**poz**-it/ *vb* **1** (*fml*) to lay down (*deposit the books on the table*). **2** to put in a safe place (*depositing her jewelry in the bank*). ● *n* **1** an amount paid into a bank (*make several large deposits*). **2** a first payment toward a larger amount (*put down a deposit on a TV set*). **3** solid matter in liquid, collecting at the bottom (*the deposit at the bottom of a bottle of wine*).

depository /di-**poz**-i-toe-ree/ *n* a storehouse.

depot /dee-po/ *n* **1** a storehouse. **2** a military station or headquarters. **3** a garage for buses.

depreciate /di-**pree**-shee-ate/ *vb* **1** to lower the value of (*houses depreciating in value/cars depreciating rapidly*). **2** (*fml*) to represent as being of little value (*try to depreciate his contribution*). ● *n* **depreciation** /di-pree-shee-**ay**-shun/.

depress /di-**press**/ *vb* **1** to press down, to lower (*depress the lever to start the machine*). **2** to make sad (*winter depresses him*).

depression /di-**pre**-shun/ *n* **1** gloom, sadness (*suffer from depression*). **2** a hollow (*a depression in the soil where the box had stood*). **3** low atmospheric pressure, causing unsettled or stormy weather.

deprivation /de-pri-**vay**-shun/ *n* **1** loss (*the deprivation of their rights*). **2** want, hardship (*live in deprivation*).

deprive /di-**prive**/ *vb* to take away from (*war depriving them of their father/people deprived of their rights*).

depth /depth/ *n* **1** deepness (*the depth of the water*). **2** strength (of feeling) (*the depth of her love/ the depth of public feeling*). ● *npl* **depths** the deepest or most central part (*in the depths of the ocean/ the depths of winter*).

depute /di-**pyoot**/ *vb* **1** to send someone to act or speak for others. **2** to hand over to someone else to do (*deputing the task of collecting the money to him*). ● *adj* acting for another. ● *vb* **deputize** /de-pyoo-tize/ *also* **deputise** (*Br*).

deputy /de-pyoo-tee/ *n* a person who acts for another (*the principal's deputy*).

derail /dee-**rail**/ *vb* to cause to leave the rails (*trains derailed in a collision*). ● *n* **derailment** /dee-rail-ment/.

deranged /di-**rainjd**/ *adj* mad, insane (*so deranged that he is a danger to himself and others*).

derelict /de-re-lict/ *adj* left as useless (*derelict old houses*).

derivation /de-ri-**vay**-shun/ *n* the history of a word back to its earliest known form.

derivative /di-**ri**-va-tiv/ *n* a word made from another word. ● *adj* not original, copying others (*a derivative style of painting*).

derive /di-**rive**/ *vb* **1** to obtain from (*deriving comfort from their presence/derive cheese from milk*). **2** to come from (*a word derived from Latin/her popularity derives from her pleasantness*).

dermatology /der-ma-**tol**-o-jee/ *n* the study of the skin and its diseases. ● *n* **dermatologist** /der-ma-tol-o-jist/.

derrick /der-ick/ *n* a type of crane (used in drilling oil wells).

descend /di-**send**/ *vb* **1** to climb down (*descending the mountain*). **2** to attack (*thieves descended on the travelers*). **3** to have as an ancestor (*descended from Abraham Lincoln*).

descendant /di-**sen**-dant/ *n* someone who has a certain person as an ancestor (*a descendant of Abraham Lincoln*).

descent /di-**sent**/ *n* **1** (*fml*) act of climbing down (*the descent of the mountain*). **2** a slope (*a slippery descent*). **3** a sudden attack (*the terrorists' descent on the tourists*). **4** a line of ancestors (*proud of his royal descent*).

describe /di-**scribe**/ *vb* **1** to tell what happened (*describing the visit of the president/described how the accident happened*). **2** to tell what a thing or person is like (*asked to describe her attacker*). ● *n* **description** /di-scrip-shun/. ● *adj* **descriptive** / di-**scrip**-tiv/.

desert[1] /**de**-zert/ *adj* without inhabitants (*a desert island*). ● *n* a large area of barren, often sandy, land (*camels in the desert*).

desert[2] /di-**zert**/ *vb* **1** to leave, to run away from (*desert his wife and children*). **2** to go away from (your duty) (*soldiers deserting their posts*). ● *n* **desertion** /di-**zer**-shun/.

deserter /di-**zer**-ter/ *n* a person who leaves the army, navy, etc., without permission.

deserts /di-**zerts**/ *npl* that which is deserved (good or bad) (*get your just deserts*).

deserve /di-**zerv**/ *vb* to be worthy of (*deserve a medal for bravery*). ● *adj* **deserving**.

deservedly /di-**zer**-ved-lee/ *adv* justly (*punished deservedly*).

design /di-**zine**/ *vb* **1** to make a plan of (*design a swimming pool/design clothing*). **2** to plan, to intend (*a scheme designed to save money*). ● *n* **1** a plan or drawing of something to be made (*the design for the new building*). **2** a plan, a purpose (*they met by design*). **3** a pattern (*a checkered design*).

designate /de-**zig**-nate/ *vb* **1** to name (*an area designated a bird sanctuary*). **2** to point out (*crosses on the map designating churches*). **3** to appoint to a particular post or position (*designated sportswoman of the year*). ● *adj* appointed to a post, but not yet in it (*vice-president designate*).

designation /de-zig-**nay**-shun/ *n* (*fml*) name, title (*a firm trading under a new designation*).

designer /di-**zie**-ner/ *adj* made by a famous designer and bearing a label with that name on it (*unable to afford designer clothing*).

designing /di-**zie**-ning/ *adj* always planning cunningly or to gain advantage (*a designing woman who craves fame at any cost*).

desirable /di-**zie**-ra-bul/ *adj* **1** much wanted (*a desirable job*). **2** arousing longing for (*a desirable woman*). ● *n* **desirability** /di-zie-ra-**bi**-li-tee/.

desire /di-**zire**/ *vb* **1** (*fml*) to wish for, to long for (*desiring happiness*). **2** to be physically attracted to. ● *n* **1** a longing, a wish (*their desire for peace/express a desire to emigrate*). **2** a strong physical attraction to someone. **3** something or someone that is desired (*his heart's desire*). ● *adj* (*fml*) **desirous** /di-**zie**-rus/

desk /**desk**/ *n* a table for reading or writing at.

desktop /**desk**-top/ *n* **1** the surface of a desk. **2** (*comput*) the backdrop on a computer screen on which icons and windows appear. ● *adj* suitable for use on a desk (*a desktop computer*).

desktop publishing /**desk**-top **pu**-bli-shing/ *n* the act or business of printing and publishing material by means of a desktop computer.

desolate /**de**-so-lit/ *adj* **1** deserted and miserable (*a desolate part of the world*). **2** miserable, lonely (*desolate at the death of his wife*). ● *vb* to lay waste.

desolation /de-so-**lay**-shun/ *n* **1** loneliness, grief (*the desolation of the widow*). **2** a wilderness (*areas of desolation*).

despair /di-**spare**/ *vb* to be without hope, to give up hope (*despair of ever getting a job*). ● *n* hopelessness.

despatch *see* **dispatch**.

desperate /**de**-sprit/ *adj* **1** hopeless, and therefore ready to take risks (*a desperate criminal/prisoners desperate to escape*). **2** without hope (*a desperate cause*). **3** urgent and despairing (*a desperate appeal for help*). ● *n* **desperation** /de-spe-**ray**-shun/.

despicable /di-**spi**-ca-bul/ *adj* mean, deserving to be despised (*a despicable trick*).

despise /di-**spize**/ *vb* to look down upon, to consider worthless (*despised him for hitting a child*).

despite /di-**spite**/ *prep* in spite of.

despondent /di-**spon**-dent/ *adj* without hope, downcast (*despondent after her failure in the exam*). ● *n* **despondency** /di-**spon**-den-see/.

dessert /di-**zert**/ *n* the sweet course at the end of a meal (*have fresh fruit for dessert*).

destination /des-ti-**nay**-shun/ *n* the place to which a person or thing is going (*arrive at our destination*).

destined /**des**-tinned/ *adj* marked out for a special purpose (*a young woman destined for greatness*).

destiny /**des**-ti-nee/ *n* a power that seems to arrange people's lives in advance, fate.

destitute /**des**-ti-toot/ *adj* in great want, very poor (*homeless and destitute*). ● *n* **destitution** /des-ti-**too**-shun/.

destroy /di-**stroy**/ *vb* **1** to break to pieces (*a house destroyed by fire*). **2** to ruin (*destroying all our hopes*). **3** to kill (*a poison that destroys rats*).

destroyer /di-**stroy**-er/ *n* **1** a person who destroys. **2** a fast-moving warship.

destructible /di-**struc**-ti-bul/ *adj* able to be destroyed.

destruction /di-**struc**-shun/ *n* **1** the act of destroying (*the destruction of the house by fire*). **2** ruin (*the destruction of our hopes/the destruction of the Roman Empire*). **3** death (*the destruction of the rats by poison*).

destructive /di-**struc**-tiv/ *adj* **1** causing ruin (*destructive fire*). **2** unhelpful (*destructive criticism*).

detach /di-**tach**/ *vb* **1** to unfasten (*detach the lead from the dog's collar*). **2** to take away from the rest (*a group of soldiers detached to guard the castle*).

detachable /di-**ta**-cha-bul/ *adj* able to be detached (*a coat with a detachable hood*).

detached /di-**tacht**/ *adj* **1** separate, not joined to others (*a detached house*). **2** not influenced by others, impartial (*take a detached view/a detached judgment*).

detachment /di-**tach**-ment/ *n* **1** a group of soldiers taken away from a larger group. **2** freedom from prejudice, impartiality (*judges require detachment*).

detail /di-**tale**, **dee**-tale/ *vb* **1** (*fml*) to give a very full account or description (*detailing the tasks to be carried out*). **2** to set apart for a particular job (*detailed soldiers to guard the castle*). ● *n* **detail**, **detail** /di-**tale**, **dee**-tale/ a small part or item (*the plan has been drawn up but not the details*).

detailed /di-**taild**, **dee**-taild/ *adj* very full and exact (*a detailed report*).

detain /di-**tane**/ *vb* **1** to prevent from leaving or doing something, to delay (*detained by several telephone calls/the doctor has been detained*). **2** to arrest, to keep in custody (*detained by the police*). ● *n* **detainee** /di-tay-**nee**/. ● *n* **detention** /di-**ten**-shun/.

detect /di-**tect**/ *vb* **1** to find out, to notice, to discover (*detect smoke/detect a note of sadness*). **2** to investigate and solve (*police detecting a murder*). ● *n* **detection** /di-**tec**-shun/.

detective /di-**tec**-tiv/ *n* a person whose job it is to find those guilty of crimes (*detectives seeking clues*).

detention *see* **detain**.

deter /di-ter/ *vb* (**deterred** /di-terd/, **deterring** /di-te-ring/) to keep from, to discourage (*deterred from leaving by fear*).

detergent /di-**ter**-jent/ *n* a chemical material used instead of soap for washing and cleansing (*wash clothing in detergent*).

deteriorate /di-**ti**-ree-o-rate/ *vb* to become worse (*the patient's condition is deteriorating*).

determination /di-ter-mi-**nay**-shun/ *n* strength of will, firmness (*have the determination to succeed*).

determine /di-**ter**-min/ *vb* **1** to fix, to decide on (*determine the date for the meeting*). **2** to find how exactly (*determining the cause of the accident*).

determined /di-**ter**-mind/ *adj* strong-willed (*a determined young woman/a determined attitude*).

deterrent /di-**te**-rent/ *n* something that keeps people from acting in a certain way (*prison acting as a deterrent to those who might break the law*). ● *also adj*.

detest /di-**test**/ *vb* to hate, to loathe (*detest violence*). ● *adj* **detestable** /di-**te**-sti-bul/. ● *n* **detestation** /dee-te-**stay**-shun/.

detonate /de-tu-nate/ *vb* to explode (*a bomb detonated by remote control*). ● *n* **detonation** /de-tu-**nay**-shun/.

detonator /de-tu-nay-tor/ *n* a mechanism that sets off an explosion.

detour /**dee**-toor/ *n* a roundabout way (*forced to make a detour to avoid the Center City*).

detract /di-**tract**/ *vb* to take away from (*a crack detracting from the value of the antique vase/detract from our enjoyment*). ● *n* **detraction** /di-**trac**-shun/.

detriment /**de**-tri-ment/ *n* (*fml*) harm, damage, disadvantage (*to the detriment of her health/with inevitable detriment to his reputation*).

detrimental /de-tri-**men**-tal/ *adj* harmful, disadvantageous (*conditions detrimental to health/detrimental effects*).

devalue /dee-**val**-yoo/ *vb* to reduce the value of. ● *n* **devaluation** /dee-val-yu-**ay**-shun/.

devastate /**de**-va-state/ *vb* **1** to lay waste (*war devastating the country*). **2** to overwhelm with grief or disappointment (*devastated at the news of her death/devastated by his defeat in the championship*). ● *n* **devastation** /de-va-**stay**-shun/.

develop /di-**ve**-lop/ *vb* **1** to grow bigger or better (*he is developing into a fine young man/the plan is slowly developing*). **2** to make to grow bigger or

better (*exercises to develop muscles/develop the scheme further*). **3** in photography, to treat a film with chemicals to make the picture appear.

developing country /di-**ve**-lop-ing **cun**-tree/ *n* a relatively poor country that is working toward improving its industrial production and living conditions.

development /di-**ve**-lop-ment/ *n* **1** growth (*watch the child's development/the development of the business*). **2** a stage of growth (*the latest development*). **3** a new product or invention (*exciting developments in the car industry*).

deviate /**dee**-vee-ate/ *vb* to turn aside (*deviating from the usual procedure*).

deviation /dee-vee-**ay**-shun/ *n* a turning aside from the normal or expected course (*little deviation from her routine*).

device /di-**vice**/ *n* **1** a plan, scheme, trick (*a supposed illness that was just a device to get off work*). **2** an invention, a tool, or mechanism (*a labor-saving device for the kitchen/an explosive device*). **3** an emblem or sign (*the heraldic device on the family crest*).

devil /**de**-vil/ *n* **1** an evil spirit. **2** Satan. **3** a very wicked person. **4** a person who does detailed or routine work for a professional person (e.g., a lawyer, printer, etc.).

devilish /**de**-vul-ish/ *adj* very evil (*a devilish plan*).

devilment /**de**-vil-ment/, **deviltry** /**de**-vil-tree/ *ns* mischief, naughtiness (*children full of devilment*).

devious /**dee**-vee-us/ *adj* **1** roundabout, indirect (*a devious route*). **2** not direct, not straightforward and honest (*use devious means to get his own way/a very devious person*).

devise /de-**vise**/ *vb* to plan, to invent, to work out, especially cleverly (*devising a scheme*).

devoid /de-**void**/ *adj* lacking in, free from (*devoid of humor/devoid of trouble*).

devote /di-**vote**/ *vb* to give up wholly to (*devoting his life to helping the poor*).

devoted /di-**vo**-ted/ *adj* loving (*her devoted parents*).

devotee /de-vu-**tee**/ *n* a very keen follower.

devotion /di-**vo**-shun/ *n* **1** great love, dedication (*her devotion to her children*). **2** (*fml*) prayer (*at his devotions*).

devour /di-**vour**/ *vb* **1** to eat greedily (*devour the chocolate*). **2** to destroy (*a forest devoured by fire*). **3** to possess completely (*devoured by hate/devoured by jealousy*). **4** to read eagerly (*devour the story hungrily*).

devout /di-**vout**/ *adj* **1** given to prayer and worship, religious (*a devout Christian*). **2** sincere, deeply felt (*it is our devout hope that we will be able to help*).

dew /**doo**/ *n* tiny drops of water that fall on the ground when air cools during the night. ● *adj* **dewy** /**doo**-wee/.

dexterity /dek-**ste**-ri-tee/ *n* cleverness with the hands, skill (*admire the dexterity of the juggler*). ● *adj* **dext(e)rous** /**dek**-st(e-)rus/.

diabetes /die-a-**bee**-teez/ *n* a disease causing too much sugar in the body (*suffer from diabetes and have to take insulin*). ● *adj and n* **diabetic** /die-a-**bet**-ic/.

diabolic /die-a-**bol**-ic/, **diabolical** /die-a-**bol**-ic-al/ *adjs* **1** devilish. **2** very wicked, very cruel (*a diabolical plan to murder his wife*). **3** (*inf*) very bad (*her cooking is diabolical*).

diagnose /**die**-ag-noaz/ *vb* to decide by examining a sick person the kind of illness that he or she has (*diagnosing chickenpox/diagnose the patient as having chickenpox*). ● *n* **diagnosis** /die-ag-**no**-sis/.

diagonal /die-**ag**-u-nal/ *adj* going from corner to corner. ● *n* a line joining opposite corners. ● *adv* **diagonally** /die-**ag**-na-lee/ at a slant (*a path going diagonally across a field*).

diagram /**die**-a-gram/ *n* a plan or sketch, a drawing made to help to explain something (*a diagram of the parts of the body*).

dial /**die**-al/ *n* **1** the face of a watch or clock (*a watch with a digital dial*). **2** the numbered disc or pad by means of which you ring a telephone number. ● *vb* (**dialed** /**die**-ald/, **dialing** /**die**-a-ling/) to ring a telephone number (*dial 911*).

dialect /**die**-a-lect/ *n* the way of speaking in a particular part of a country (*the Southern dialect*).

dialog /**die**-a-lawg/ *n* a conversation between two or more people (*the play is a dialog between two old men about the past*).

diameter /die-**a**-me-ter/ *n* a straight line passing from one side of a circle to the other through its center.

diametrically /die-a-**met**-ri-ca-lee/ *adv*: **diametrically opposed** exactly opposite (*hold diametrically opposed views*).

diamond /**die**-mond/ *n* **1** a hard, very valuable precious stone. **2 diamonds** /**die**-mondz/ a suit of playing cards.

diamond wedding /**die**-mond **wed**-ing/ *n* the 60th anniversary of marriage.

diaper /**die**-per/ *n* a piece of absorbent material fastened around a baby's bottom.

diaphragm /**die**-a-fram/ *n* a muscle separating the chest from the abdomen.

diarrhea /die-a-**ree**-a/ *n*, *also* **diarrhoea** (*Br*, *Cdn*) looseness of the bowels (*suffering from diarrhea*).

diary /**die**-a-ree/ *n* a book in which you write something every day (*writes his appointments in his diary/writes an account of her day in her diary*).

dice /**dice**/ *pl of* **die²** /**die**/. ● *vb* to cut into pieces shaped like cubes (*dicing vegetables for soup*).

dictate /dic-**tate**, **dic**-tate/ *vb* **1** to speak aloud something to be written down by another (*dictating letters for his secretary to type*). **2** to give orders, to order about (*workers trying to dictate how the factory should be run*). **3** to fix, to determine (*the amount of work done by the charity is dictated by money*). ● *n* **dictate** /**dic**-tate/ *n* an order. ● *n* **dictation** /dic-**tay**-shun/.

dictator /dic-**tay**-tor/ *n* one person with complete power of government (*a people terrified of the dictator*). ● *n* **dictatorship** /dic-**tay**-tor-ship/.

dictatorial /dic-ta-**toe**-ree-al/ *adj* **1** like a dictator (*a dictatorial manner*). **2** liking to order others about (*so dictatorial that people will not work for her*).

diction /**dic**-shun/ *n* **1** choice of words (*poetic diction*). **2** way of speaking (*clear diction/try to improve her diction*).

dictionary /**dic**-shu-**ne**-ree/ *n* a book in which words are arranged in alphabetical order and their meanings and other information about them given.

die¹ /**die**/ *vb* **1** to stop living. **2** to fade away (*hope died*).

die² /**die**/ *n* **1** (*pl* **dice**) a small cube, its sides marked with numbers from 1 to 6, used in games of chance. **2** (*pl* **dies**) a stamp for marking designs on paper, coins, etc.

diesel /**dee**-zel/ *n* **1** a petroleum oil, heavier than gasoline, used as fuel. **2** a vehicle driven by diesel.

diesel engine /**dee**-zel **en**-jin/ *n* an engine that works by burning diesel oil using heat produced by compressing air.

diet /**die**-it/ *n* **1** food, the type of food on which you live (*a healthy diet/a vegetarian diet*). **2** a course of limited foods designed to lose weight, treat a medical condition, etc. (*go on a strict diet/a low-cholesterol diet*). ● *vb* to eat certain foods only, especially in order to lose weight.

dietary /**die**-i-ter-ee/ *adj* concerning diet (*religious dietary restrictions*).

differ /**di**-fer/ *vb* 1 to be unlike (*people differing from each other in their attitude to money/differ in size*). 2 to disagree (*two sides differing over the site of the new building/agree to differ*).

difference /**di**-frense/ *n* 1 unlikeness (*a marked difference in the state of her health/the difference between the two cars*). 2 a disagreement, a quarrel (*settle their differences*).

different /**di**-frent/ *adj* 1 unlike, not the same (*sisters quite different from each other/a different hairstyle*). 2 (*inf*) unusual, special (*well, her new hairstyle is certainly different*).

differentiate /di-fe-**ren**-shee-ate/ *vb* 1 to see or point out the difference between (*able to differentiate a robin from a sparrow*). 2 to make different (*what differentiates the two models of car?*). 3 to treat differently (*differentiating between men and women in terms of pay*).

difficult /**di**-fi-cult/ *adj* 1 hard to do (*a difficult task*). 2 hard to please (*a difficult old woman*). 3 troublesome (*a difficult period*). ● *n* **difficulty** /**di**-fi-cul-tee/.

diffident /**di**-fi-dent/ *adj* bashful, not sure of yourself (*a diffident young woman/diffident of expressing opinions in public*). ● *n* **diffidence** /**di**-fi-dense/.

diffuse /di-**fyooz**/ *vb* (*fml*) to spread widely (*diffusing light/diffused happiness*). ● *adj* **diffuse** /di-**fyoos**/ 1 widely spread (*diffuse light*). 2 longwinded, wordy (*a diffuse style of writing*). ● *n* **diffusion** /di-**fyoo**-zhun/.

dig /dig/ *vb* (**dug** /dug/, **digging** /**di**-ging/) 1 to turn up earth or soil. 2 to prod, to poke (*dig her in the ribs*). 3 (*inf*) to search (*dig in her purse for her keys*). ● *n* a prod, a sharp push. ● *n* **digger** /**di**-ger/.

digest /die-**jest**/ *vb* 1 to dissolve in the stomach (*digest a heavy lunch*). 2 to think over and understand fully (*take time to digest what he said*).

digestible /die-**jes**-ti-bul/ *adj* able to be digested (*able to eat foods that are easily digestible*).

digestion /die-**jes**-chun/ *n* the process of digesting food.

digestive /die-**jes**-tiv/ *adj* concerning digestion (*the human digestive system*).

digit /**di**-jit/ *n* 1 any figure from 0 to 9. 2 (*fml*) a finger or toe.

digital /**di**-ji-tal/ *adj* 1 showing information in the form of numbers (*a digital watch*). 2 recording or transmitting information as numbers in the form of very small signals. 3 to do with the fingers or toes. ● *adv* **digitally** /**di**-ji-ta-lee/.

digital television /**di**-ji-tal **te**-le-vi-zhun/ *n* a system of television in which the picture is transmitted as a digital signal and decoded by a device attached to the viewer's television set.

digital video disk *see* **DVD**.

dignified /**dig**-ni-fied/ *adj* noble in manner, stately (*dignified behavior/a dignified exit/a dignified old lady*).

dignify /**dig**-ni-fie/ *vb* 1 to give grace or nobility to (*a procession dignified by the presence of the mayor*). 2 to give an important-sounding name to something (*dignifying his patch of grass with the title of lawn*).

dignitary /**dig**-ni-ter-ee/ *n* a person of high rank (*a formal dinner attended by local dignitaries*).

dignity /**dig**-ni-tee/ *n* 1 goodness and nobleness of character, worthiness (*human dignity*). 2 seriousness, calmness, formality (*the dignity of the situation/keep her dignity while being booed by the crowd*).

digress /die-**gress**/ *vb* to speak or write on a subject other than the one being considered (*keep digressing from the main issue/unable to follow the speaker as he often digresses*). ● *n* **digression** /die-**gre**-shun/.

dike, dyke /dike/ *n* 1 a ditch or wall. 2 a bank built up to hold back the sea or floods.

dilapidated /di-**la**-pi-day-ted/ *adj* completely worn out, falling to bits (*dilapidated property/in a dilapidated condition*). ● *n* **dilapidation** /di-la-pi-**day**-shun/.

dilate /**die**-late/ *vb* 1 to become larger or wider (*eyes dilating in fear*). 2 to cause to become larger or wider (*a substance that had dilated her pupils*). ● *ns* **dilatation** /die-lay-**tay**-shun/, **dilation** /die-**lay**-shun/.

dilemma /di-**le**-ma/ *n* a choice between two things or actions, usually equally unpleasant.

diligent /**di**-li-jent/ *adj* very careful, painstaking, hardworking (*diligent students/diligent workers*). ● *n* **diligence** /**di**-li-jense/.

dilly-dally /**di**-lee-da-lee/ *vb* (*inf*) to waste time, to wait about (*dilly-dallying instead of getting down to work*).

dilute /die-**loot**/ *vb* 1 to water down, to reduce in strength by adding water or another liquid (*diluting lime juice with water*). 2 to weaken in force, effect, etc. (*the president's power has been diluted/tried to dilute the force of her critical speech with a smile*). ● *n* **dilution** /di-**loo**-shun/.

dim /dim/ *adj* **1** faint, not bright (*a dim light*). **2** indistinct (*a dim figure in the distance*). **3** (*inf*) not intelligent, not understanding clearly (*he's a bit dim*). ● *vb* (**dimmed** /dimd/, **dimming** /di-ming/) to make or become dim (*dim the lights/the lights dimmed in the theater*).

dime /dime/ *n* a silver coin that is a 10th part of a dollar, 10 cents.

dimension /di-**men**-shun/ *n* **1** the measure of length, breadth, and depth (*a beast of huge dimension*). **2** (*often pl*) size, extent (*take the dimensions of the room*).

diminish /di-**mi**-nish/ *vb* to make or become less (*enthusiasm has gradually diminished/strength diminished by a poor diet*)

diminutive /di-**mi**-nyu-tiv/ *adj* very small, tiny (*diminutive little girls/look diminutive beside the tall man*). ● *n* a word or part of a word suggesting smallness (e.g., -*kin* in *lambkin*).

dimple /dim-pul/ *n* a small hollow, especially on the cheek or chin. ● *vb* to show dimples (*dimpling prettily as she smiled*).

din /din/ *n* a loud noise that lasts a long time (*complain about the din from the neighbor's television*). ● *vb* (**dinned** /dind/, **dinning** /di-ning/) **1** to go on saying the same thing again and again (*try to din the information into her*). **2** to make a continuing loud noise (*music from his car radio dinning in our ears*).

dine /dine/ *vb* to eat dinner (*dining at eight o'clock/dined on oysters*). ● *n* **diner** /di-ner/.

dinghy /ding-ee/ *n* a small boat, a ship's boat.

dingy /din-jee/ *adj* dull, dirty-looking, faded (*dingy wallpaper/a dingy room/dingy colors*). ● *n* **dinginess** /din-jee-ness/.

dinner /di-ner/ *n* the principal meal of the day (*eat dinner in the evening*).

dinosaur /**die**-no-sawr/ *n* a very large lizard-like animal of prehistoric times.

dip /dip/ *vb* (**dipped** /dipt/, **dipping** /di-ping/) **1** to put into liquid for a moment (*dip the strawberry in chocolate sauce/dip his bread in the soup*). **2** to lower sheep into a liquid that disinfects them or kills insects. **3** to lower for a short time (*dip his headlights*). **4** to take a sudden downward slope (*the road suddenly dipped*). ● *n* **1** (*inf*) a quick wetting, a bathe (*go for a dip in the river*). **2** a liquid or semi-liquid substance into which something is dipped (*a cheese dip*). **3** a cleansing liquid for dipping sheep. **4** a downward slope (*a dip in the road*).

diploma /di-plo-ma/ *n* a printed paper showing that a person has passed certain examinations.

diplomacy /di-**plo**-ma-see/ *n* **1** the discussing of affairs and making of agreements with foreign countries (*solving the differences between the two countries by diplomacy rather than war*). **2** the ability to get people to do things without annoying them (*use diplomacy to get his friends to stop quarreling*).

diplomat /**di**-plo-mat/ *n* **1** a person who represents his or her country in discussions with foreign governments. **2** a person who is good at managing people (*you have to be a bit of a diplomat to be a good human-resources manager*).

diplomatic /di-plo-**ma**-tic/ *adj* **1** having to do with or good at diplomacy. **2** tactful (*a diplomatic reply*).

dipper /**di**-per/ *n* **1** a cup with a long handle used top scoop up liquid. **2** (*Cdn*) a small lidless saucepan.

dire /dire/ *adj* very great, extreme, terrible (*in dire poverty/in dire need of food/in dire trouble*).

direct /di-**rect**, die-rect/ *adj* **1** straight (*the most direct route*). **2** without any other reason or circumstances coming between (*his sickness is a direct result of damp housing*). **3** saying openly what you think (*a very direct person/a direct way of speaking*). ● *vb* **1** to point or aim at (*directed a gun at him*). **2** to show or tell the way to (*directed her to the station*). **3** to control (*directed the whole operation*). **4** (*fml*) to order (*direct her to go immediately*). **5** to address (*directed his remarks to us*).

direction /di-**rec**-shun/ *n* **1** the way in which you are looking, pointing, going, etc. (*in a northerly direction/have no sense of direction*). **2** control (*the direction of the military operation*). **3** an order (*obey directions*). **4** an address. **5** **directions** /di-**rec**-shunz/ information as to how to do something (*get directions to the station/read the directions for putting the machine together*).

directly /di-**rect**-lee/ *adv* **1** in a direct manner (*tell her directly what he thinks of her behavior*). **2** at once, very soon (*I'll be with you directly*).

director /di-**rec**-tor/ *n* **1** one of a group of people who manage a business, etc. (*on the board of directors*). **2** a person in charge of putting on a play or making a movie.

directory /di-**rec**-tree/ *n* **1** a book containing people's names, addresses, telephone numbers, etc. (*a telephone directory*). **2** in a computer, a folder that contains files.

dirge /dirge/ *n* a song of mourning, a lament (*play a dirge at the funeral*).

dirt /durt/ *n* **1** anything not clean (*remove the dirt from the wound/brush the dirt from the clothing*). **2** (*inf*) gossip, scandal (*spread dirt about her*). **3** (*inf*) something obscene.

dirty /dur-tee/ *adj* **1** unclean (*dirty hands/dirty clothes*). **2** mean or unfair (*a dirty trick*). **3** (*inf*) obscene (*dirty books*). **4** (*of weather*) rough. ● *also vb*.

dis /dis/ *vb* (**dissed** /dist/, **dissing** /di-sing/) (*slang*) to treat with disrespect (*don't dis me*).

disable /di-**say**-bul/ *vb* **1** (*fml*) to take away the power from (*disabled from voting*). **2** to deprive of some physical or mental ability (*disabled by the accident*). ● *ns* **disability** /di-sa-**bi**-li-tee/, **disablement** /di-**say**-bul-ment/.

disabled /di-**say**-buld/ *adj* describing someone who is physically or mentally restricted in some way.

disadvantage /di-sad-**van**-tidge/ *n* something unfavorable or harmful to your interests, a drawback (*a disadvantage to be small in a basketball team*). ● *adj* **disadvantageous** /di-sad-van-**tay**-jus/.

disadvantaged /di-sad-**van**-tijd/ *adj* suffering from a disadvantage, especially with regard to your economic situation, family background, etc.

disagree /di-sa-**gree**/ *vb* **1** to differ (*the two accounts of the event disagree*). **2** to have different opinions, etc. (*two sides disagreeing*). **3** to quarrel (*children disagreeing*). **4** to have a bad effect on (*food that disagrees with her*). ● *n* **disagreement** /di-sa-**gree**-ment/.

disagreeable /di-sa-**gree**-a-bul/ *adj* unpleasant (*a disagreeable woman/a disagreeable situation*).

disallow /di-sa-**laoo**/ *vb* (*fml*) to refuse to allow (*disallowed by a local law to play football there*).

disappear /di-sa-**peer**/ *vb* **1** to go out of sight (*the sun disappearing behind a cloud*). **2** to leave or become lost, especially suddenly or without explanation (*two children have disappeared*). **3** to cease to exist (*a species of bird that has disappeared*). ● *n* **disappearance** /di-sa-**pee**-ranse/.

disappoint /di-sa-**point**/ *vb* **1** to fail to do what is hoped or expected. **2** (*fml*) to fail to fulfill (*disappoint their hopes*). **3** to cause sorrow by failure (*she was disappointed at losing the race/disappoint the children by not coming*). ● *n* **disappointment** /di-sa-**point**-ment/.

disapprove /di-sa-**proov**/ *vb* to believe that something is wrong or bad (*disapproving of the new*

changes in education). ● *n* **disapproval** /di-sa-**proo**-val/.

disarm /di-**sarm**/ *vb* **1** to take away weapons from (*police disarming the gunman*). **2** to do away with weapons of war (*countries beginning to disarm*). **3** to make less angry, to charm (*disarmed by her frankness/a disarming smile*).

disarrange /di-sa-**range**/ *vb* (*fml*) to set in the wrong order, to untidy (*the wind had disarranged her hair*). ● *n* **disarrangement** /di-sa-**range**-ment/.

disarray /di-sa-**ray**/ *n* disorder or untidiness.

disaster /di-**za**-ster/ *n* **1** a great misfortune (*a firm affected by financial disaster*). **2** an accident affecting many people or causing a lot of damage (*natural disasters such as floods and earthquakes*). **3** a complete failure (*an attempt at dressmaking that was a complete disaster*). ● *adj* **disastrous** /di-**za**-struss/.

disband /dis-**band**/ *vb* to break up and separate (*disband his private army/the club has disbanded*). ● *n* **disbandment** /dis-**band**-ment/.

disbelieve /dis-bi-**leev**/ *vb* to refuse to believe (*see no reason to disbelieve his statement*). ● *n* **disbelief** /dis-bi-**leef**/.

disc /disc/ *n* (*Br*) see **disk**.

discard /dis-**card**/ *vb* to throw away (*discard old furniture*).

discharge /dis-**charge**/ *vb* **1** to unload (*a plane discharging its passengers*). **2** to set free (*discharge the prisoner*). **3** to fire (*discharged the gun*). **4** to send away (*discharge the members of the jury*). **5** to give or send out (*a wound discharging pus*). **6** to do, to carry out (*discharge your duty*). **7** to pay (*discharge your account*). ● *n* **discharge** /dis-charge/ **1** act of discharging. **2** the matter coming from a sore or wound (*a bloody discharge*).

disciple /di-**sie**-pul/ *n* a person who believes in the teaching, etc., of another, a follower (*Christ's disciples/disciples of Martin Luther King*).

disciplinarian /di-si-pli-**nay**-ree-an/ *n* a person who controls others firmly or severely. ● *adj* **disciplinary** /di-si-**pli**-na-ree/.

discipline /di-si-plin/ *n* **1** training of mind or character (*the discipline of the monks' way of life*). **2** ordered behavior (*the discipline shown by the soldiers*). **3** punishment (*students claiming unfair discipline*). **4** a branch of knowledge (*study other disciplines as well as science*). ● *vb* **1** to train to be obedient (*a well-disciplined team*). **2** to punish (*disciplining his son by not allowing him to go to the movies*).

disk jockey /**disc**-jock-ee/ *n* a person who introduces and plays recorded pop music on a radio or television show or at a club.

disclose /dis-**cloaz**/ *vb* **1** to make known (*disclosing family secrets/disclosed his whereabouts*). **2** to uncover (*disclose the contents of the box*).

disclosure /dis-**clo**-zher/ *n* the telling or showing of something previously hidden (*disclosures made in the newspapers about a member Congress*).

disco /**dis**-co/ *n* a club to which people go to dance to recorded pop music.

discolor /dis-**cu**-lur/ *vb, also* **discolour** (*Br, Cdn*) to spoil the color of, to stain (*the painting is discolored by direct sunlight*). ● *n* **discoloration** / dis-cu-lu-**ray**-shun/, *also* **discolouration** (*Br, Cdn*).

discomfort /dis-**cum**-furt/ *n* the fact or state of being uncomfortable. ● *vb* to make uncomfortable.

disconcert /dis-con-**sert**/ *vb* to make uneasy (*disconcerted by the fact that he ignored her*).

disconnect /dis-cu-**nect**/ *vb* **1** to unfasten (*disconnect the carriages from the train*). **2** to break the connection (*disconnect a gas supply*).

disconnected /dis-cu-**nec**-ted/ *adj* showing little connection between (*a disconnected stream of words*).

disconsolate /dis-**con**-so-lit/ *adj* sad, disappointed (*disconsolate because of her canceled vacation*).

discontent /dis-con-**tent**/ *n* the state of not being satisfied, displeasure (*a sign of discontent in the workforce*). ● *adj* **discontented** /dis-con-**ten**-tid/. ● *n* **discontentment** /dis-con-**tent**-ment/.

discontinue /dis-con-**ti**-nyoo/ *vb* to stop or put an end to (*discontinue the bus service/discontinuing that range of goods*).

discord /**dis**-cawrd/ *n* **1** two or more notes of music that sound unpleasing when played together. **2** (*fml*) disagreement, quarreling (*marital discord/some discord between the families*). ● *adj* **discordant** /dis-**cawr**-dant/.

discount /**dis**-count/ *n* a reduction in the cost or price of (*receive a discount on the car for paying cash/a discount on goods sold to staff*). ● *vb* **discount** /dis-**count**/ **1** to give a discount. **2** to regard as unimportant or untrue (*discount anything they say since they have no knowledge of the situation*).

discourage /dis-**cu**-ridge/ *vb* **1** to dishearten (*his early failure discouraged him*). **2** to persuade not to do (*smoking is discouraged here*). ● *n* **discouragement** /dis-**cu**-ridge-ment/.

discourse /**dis**-coarse/ *n* a speech, a lecture (*a long discourse on manners delivered by the principal*). ● *vb* **discourse** /dis-**coarse**/ to talk.

discourteous /dis-**cur**-tee-us/ *adj* rude, impolite. ● *n* **discourtesy** /dis-**cur**-ti-see/.

discover /dis-**cu**-ver/ *vb* **1** to find (*discover America/discover a great new restaurant*). **2** to find out (*discover the truth about him/discover how to work the machine*).

discoverer /dis-**cu**-ve-rer/ *n* an explorer.

discovery /dis-**cu**-ve-ree/ *n* **1** act of finding (*a voyage of discovery*). **2** the thing found (out) (*a number of important discoveries*).

discredit /dis-**cre**-dit/ *vb* **1** to refuse to believe (*discrediting all she says*). **2** to cause to be disbelieved (*theories discredited by experts*). **3** to damage the good reputation of (*try to discredit the president*). ● *n* shame, dishonor (*bring discredit on his family*).

discreditable /dis-**cre**-di-ta-bul/ *adj* shameful (*discreditable behavior*).

discreet /dis-**creet**/ *adj* thinking carefully before acting or speaking, cautious, not saying anything that is likely to cause trouble (*discreet behavior/is discreet about her boss's affairs*).

discrepancy /dis-**cre**-pan-see/ *n* the difference between what a thing is and what it ought to be or is said to be (*a discrepancy between the two accounts of the accident/a discrepancy between the amount of money taken in and the amount in the cash register*).

discretion /dis-**cre**-shun/ *n* **1** discreetness (*you can rely on her discretion—she won't tell anyone*). **2** judgment, caution (*use your discretion on how much to charge*).

discriminate /dis-**cri**-mi-nate/ *vb* **1** to see differences, however small. **2** to show judgment. ● *n* **discrimination** /dis-cri-mi-**nay**-shun/.

discriminating /dis-**cri**-mi-nay-ting/ *adj* having good judgment.

discus /**di**-scus/ *n* in track-and-field, a heavy disk-shaped object that is thrown in a field event.

discuss /di-**scus**/ *vb* to talk about, to consider. ● *n* **discussion** /di-**scu**-shun/.

disdain /dis-**dane**/ *vb* to look down upon, to be too proud to, to refuse because of pride (*disdain our company/disdain our offers of help*). ● *n* scorn. ● *adj* **disdainful**.

disease /di-**zeez**/ *n* an illness or unhealthy condition (*kidney disease/disease of oak trees/violence is a disease of today*).

diseased /di-**zeezd**/ *adj* suffering from a disease (*diseased fruit trees*).

disenchant /di-sen-**chant**/ *vb* to free from mistaken beliefs (*many former admirers have been disenchanted by her behavior*). ● *adj* **disenchanted** /di-sen-**chant**-ed/.

disentangle /di-sen-**tang**-gul/ *vb* 1 to take the knots out of (*disentangling the string*). 2 to free from a position that is difficult to escape from (*disentangled herself from an unhappy marriage*). 3 to separate from a confused condition (*disentangle the truth from a mass of lies*).

disfigure /dis-**fi**-gyur/ *vb* to spoil the appearance of (*a face disfigured by a huge scar*). ● *n* **disfigurement** /dis-**fi**-gyur-ment/.

disgrace /dis-**grace**/ *n* 1 shame, loss of favor or respect (*bring disgrace on his family*). 2 a person or thing that should cause shame (*work that is a disgrace*). ● *vb* to bring shame or dishonor upon (*disgracing his family by going to prison*).

disgraceful /dis-**grace**-ful/ *adj* shameful). ● *adv* **disgracefully** /dis-**grace**-fu-lee/.

disguise /dis-**gize**/ *vb* to change the appearance of, to change so as not to be recognized. ● *n* changed dress or appearance so as not to be recognized.

disgust /dis-**gust**/ *n* strong dislike, loathing (*look with disgust at the rotting meat/feel disgust for his evil behavior*). ● *vb* to cause to loathe or hate (*disgusted by the smell of rotting meat/disgusted by his cruel treatment of his wife*).

disgusting /dis-**gu**-sting/ *adj* sickening (*a disgusting mess*).

dish /dish/ *n* 1 a broad open vessel for serving food (*a casserole dish*). 2 a particular kind of food (*a French dish*). 3 food mixed and prepared for the table (*a dish of meat and potatoes*). ● *vb* to put into a dish (*dish the potatoes*). ● **dish out** 1 to distribute and give out (*dish out leaflets to people*). 2 (*inf*) to give out generously (*dish out compliments*).

dishearten /dis-**har**-ten/ *vb* to discourage (*disheartened by his failure*).

dishevel /di-**shev**-el/ *vb* (**disheveled** /di-**shev**-eld/, **disheveling** /di-**shev**-e-ling/) to untidy (*hair disheveled by the wind*).

dishonest /di-**son**-est/ *adj* not honest (*dishonest salesman/dishonest means*). ● *n* **dishonesty** /di-**son**-es-tee/.

dishonor /di-**son**-ur/ *n, also* **dishonour** (*Br, Cdn*) shame, disgrace (*bring dishonor on her family by stealing*). ● *vb* 1 to bring shame on (*dishonor his regiment*). 2 (*fml*) to treat in a shameful way (*dishonor his wife*).

dishonorable /di-**son**-e-ra-bul/ *adj, also* **dishonourable** (*Br, Cdn*) not honorable, shameful (*dishonorable conduct*).

dishwasher /dish-**waw**-sher/ *n* a machine for washing dishes and flatware.

disillusion /di-si-**loo**-zhun/ *vb* to free from a wrong idea or belief (*disillusion her that he was not interested only in her money/disillusioned with the legal system*). ● *n* **disillusionment** /di-si-**loo**-zhun-ment/.

disinfect /di-sin-**fect**/ *vb* to free from infection (*disinfect the wound/disinfect the toilet*). ● *n* **disinfection** /di-sin-**fec**-shun/.

disinfectant /di-sin-**fec**-tant/ *adj* destroying germs, killing infection. ● *n* a disinfectant substance (*clean the bathroom with a disinfectant*).

disinherit /di-sin-**her**-it/ *vb* to take from a son or daughter the right to receive anything by the will of a dead parent.

disintegrate /di-**sin**-ti-grate/ *vb* 1 to break up into parts (*a damp cardboard box that just disintegrated*). 2 to fall to pieces (*plans disintegrating/families disintegrating*). ● *n* **disintegration** /di-sin-ti-**gray**-shun/.

disinterested /di-**sin**-tre-stid/ *adj* favoring no side (*referees must be disinterested*).

disjointed /dis-**join**-tid/ *adj* having no clear connection between ideas, rambling (*a disjointed piece of prose/a few disjointed ideas*).

disk *or* **disc** (*Br*) /**disk**/ *n* 1 a round flat object (*wear an identity disk*). 2 an audio recording, especially a compact disk (*recorded on disk*). 3 a circular plate, coated with magnetic material, on which data can be recorded in a form that can be used by a computer. 4 a layer of cartilage between the bones of the spine.

dislike /dis-**like**/ *vb* not to like (*dislikes her very much/disliking his habit of asking questions/dislike tasteless food*). ● *also n.*

dislocate /**dis**-lo-cate/ *vb* 1 to put out of joint (*dislocated a bone in his foot*). 2 (*fml*) to throw into disorder (*dislocating the computer system*). ● *n* **dislocation** /dis-lo-**cay**-shun/.

dislodge /dis-**lodge**/ *vb* to move from its place (*dislodging the fish bone from his throat/dislodge the stone from the horse's hoof*).

disloyal /dis-**loy**-al/ *adj* 1 unfaithful (*disloyal to her husband*). 2 not true to (*disloyal to their leader*). ● *n* **disloyalty** /dis-**loy**-al-tee/.

dismal /**diz**-mal/ *adj* dark, gloomy (*a dismal place/a dismal mood*).

dismantle /dis-**man**-tul/ *vb* to take to pieces (*dismantling the machine*).

dismay /dis-**may**/ *vb* to make afraid, anxious, discouraged, etc. (*they were dismayed to find the door locked/dismayed at the news of his disappearance*). ● *also n.*

dismiss /dis-**mis**/ *vb* **1** to send away (*dismiss the visitor with a wave of her hand/dismiss ideas of promotion*). **2** to send away from your job (*dismiss him for dishonesty*). ● *n* **dismissal** /dis-**mis**-al/.

dismount /dis-**mount**/ *vb* to get down from a horse, etc. (*dismounting from his bicycle*).

disobey /dis-o-**bay**/ *vb* to refuse to do what you are told (*disobeying orders/disobey his boss*). ● *n* **disobedience** /dis-o-**beed**-yense/. ● *adj* **disobedient** / dis-o-**beed**-yent/.

disorder /dis-**awr**-der/ *vb* to put things out of their places, to untidy. ● *n* **1** untidiness (*criticize the disorder of the room*). **2** disturbance, riot (*the meeting broke up in disorder*). **3** a sickness, disease (*a disorder of the stomach*).

disorderly /dis-**awr**-der-lee/ *adj* **1** untidy (*a disorderly office*). **2** out of control (*a disorderly crowd*).

disorganize /dis-**awr**-ga-nize/ *vb, also* **disorganise** (*Br*) to put out of order, to throw into confusion (*wedding plans totally disorganized when the bride changed her mind*). ● *n* **disorganization** /dis-awr-ga-ni-**zay**-shun/, *also* **disorganisation** (*Br*).

disown /dis-**oan**/ *vb* to refuse to have anything to do with, to refuse to acknowledge as belonging to yourself (*disowned his son because of his dishonest behavior*).

disparage /dis-**pa**-ridge/ *vb* to suggest, especially unfairly, that something or someone is of little value or importance (*disparaging his achievements*). ● *n* **disparagement** /dis-**pa**-ridge-ment/.

disparate /**dis**-pa-rit/ *adj* unlike, completely different (*totally disparate personalities*).

disparity /dis-**pa**-ri-tee/ *n* difference, inequality (*the disparity in age between husband and wife*).

dispassionate /dis-**pash**-nit/ *adj* not influenced by emotion, taking no side, impartial (*a dispassionate account of the accident*).

dispatch, despatch /dis-**patch**/ *vb* **1** to send off (*dispatch a letter/dispatch a messenger*). **2** (*old*) to kill. **3** (*fml*) to do quickly (*dispatch several pieces of work*). ● *n* **1** the act of sending off (*the dispatch of a letter*). **2** a written official report (*a dispatch from the military line/mentioned in dispatches*). **3** (*fml*) quickness in doing (*act with dispatch*).

dispel /dis-**pel**/ *vb* (**dispelled** /dis-**peld**/, **dispelling** / dis-**pe**-ling/) to drive away, to make disappear (*dispel all doubts*).

dispensable /dis-**pen**-si-bul/ *adj* able to be done without (*workers regarded as being dispensable*).

dispensary /dis-**pen**-sa-ree/ *n* a place where medicines are prepared and given out.

dispensation /dis-**pen**-say-shun/ *n* a permission, often from the church, not to do something (*by dispensation of the bishop*).

dispense /dis-**pense**/ *vb* **1** (*fml*) to give out (*dispensing money to the poor/dispense justice*). **2** to prepare and give out (medicines). ● **dispense with** to do without (*dispense with the need for regular checking*).

dispenser /dis-**pen**-ser/ *n* **1** a person who prepares medicines. **2** a machine from which something can be obtained by the insertion of money (*a soap dispenser/a drinks dispenser*).

disperse /dis-**perse**/ *vb* to scatter (*crowds dispersing/clouds dispersed by the wind*). ● *ns* **dispersal** / dis-**per**-sal/, **dispersion** /dis-**per**-shun/.

dispirited /dis-**pi**-ri-ted/ *adj* discouraged, in low spirits (*feel dispirited after his defeat*).

displace /dis-**place**/ *vb* **1** (*fml*) to put out of place (*papers displaced by the burglar*). **2** to take the place of (*displacing his wife in his affections*).

displacement /dis-**place**-ment/ *n* **1** act of displacing. **2** the amount of liquid put out of place when an object is placed in it.

display /dis-**play**/ *vb* **1** to show, to make obvious (*displaying your lack of knowledge*). **2** to put where it can be easily seen (*display ornaments in a glass-fronted cabinet/display the paintings in a gallery*). ● *n* **1** show (*goods on display*). **2** a parade. **3** an exhibition (*a display of the work of local artists*).

displease /dis-**please**/ *vb* to anger, to annoy (*displeased by their failure*).

displeasure /dis-**ple**-zhur/ *n* annoyance (*show his displeasure by frowning*).

disport /dis-**port**/ *vb* (*fml*) to play about, to amuse yourself actively (*children disporting themselves on the beach*).

disposable /dis-**po**-za-bul/ *adj* designed to be used once and then thrown awaay (*disposable diapers*).

disposal /dis-**po**-zal/ *n* **1** act of getting rid of (*the disposal of garbage*). **2** the way that people or things are arranged (*the disposal of the troops*). **3** use (*a firm's car at his disposal*).

dispose /dis-**poze**/ *vb* **1** (*fml*) to arrange (*troops* *disposed in battle formation*). **2** (*fml*) to make willing (*I am not disposed to be of assistance to them*). **3** to get rid (of) (*disposing of the evidence*).

disposition /dis-po-**zi**-shun/ *n* **1** arrangement (*the general's disposition of the troops*). **2** a person's character as revealed by his or her normal behavior (*of a bad-tempered disposition*).

dispossess /dis-po-**zess**/ *vb* to take away from (*dispossess them of their houses*).

disproportion /dis-pro-**poar**-shun/ *n* lack of proper or usual relation between things (*a disproportion between his height and weight*).

disproportionate /dis-pro-**poar**-shu-nit/ *adj* too great (or too small) in the circumstances (*a head disproportionate to her body*).

disprove /dis-**proov**/ *vb* to prove to be false (*difficult to disprove his allegations*).

disputation /dis-pyu-**tay**-shun/ *n* an argument, a debate.

dispute /dis-**pyoot**/ *vb* **1** to argue, to quarrel (*farmers disputing whose land it is*). **2** to refuse to agree with, to question the truth or rightness of (*dispute the truth of what he said/dispute his right to the throne*). ● *also n.*

disqualify /dis-**kwaw**-li-fy/ *vb* **1** to make unable (*his ill-health disqualified him from joining the army*). **2** to put out of a competition, etc., usually for breaking a rule (*a relay team disqualified for dropping the baton*). ● *n* **disqualification** /dis-kwaw-li-fi-cay-shun/.

disquiet /dis-**kwie**-it/ *n* anxiety (*felt disquiet when the children were late*). ● *vb* to make anxious. ● *n* **disquietude** /dis-**kwie**-i-t(y)ood/.

disregard /dis-ri-**gard**/ *vb* to take no notice of (*disregard the rules/disregard safety instructions*). ● *n* neglect.

disrepair /dis-ri-**pair**/ *n* a bad state due to lack of repairs (*property in disrepair*).

disreputable /dis-**rep**-yu-ta-bul/ *adj* **1** having a bad character. **2** in a bad condition, shabby.

disrepute /dis-ri-**pyoot**/ *n* disgrace, bad reputation (*brought his team into disrepute by using drugs*).

disrespect /dis-ri-**spect**/ *n* rudeness, failure to behave in a proper way (*show disrespect to his elders by being very late*). ● *adj* **disrespectful** /dis-ri-**spect**-ful/.

disrobe /dis-**robe**/ *vb* (*fml*) to take off clothing, especially ceremonious or official clothing (*judges disrobing*).

disrupt /dis-**rupt**/ *vb* to put into a state of disorder (*disrupt the traffic/a strike disrupting holiday*

flights). ● *n* **disruption** /dis-**rup**-shun/.

disruptive /dis-**rup**-tiv/ *adj* causing disorder (*disruptive students/disruptive behavior*).

dissatisfied /di-**sa**-tis-fied/ *adj* not satisfied, discontented (*a dissatisfied customer/dissatisfied with the result*).

dissatisfy /di-**sa**-tis-fie/ *vb* to fail to satisfy, to displease (*a standard of work that dissatisfied the teacher*). ● *n* **dissatisfaction** /di-sa-tis-**fac**-shun/.

dissect /di-**sect**/ *vb* **1** to cut into separate parts in order to examine (*dissecting a rat in the biology class*). **2** to study carefully (*dissect the election result*). ● *n* **dissection** /di-**sec**-shun/.

dissemble /di-**sem**-bul/ *vb* to pretend not to be what you are, to hide your feelings, intent, etc. (*he said he loved her but he was dissembling*). ● *n* **dissembler** /di-**sem**-bler/.

disseminate /di-**se**-mi-nate/ *vb* (*fml*) to spread far and wide (*disseminating information*). ● *n* **dissemination** /di-se-mi-**nay**-shun/.

dissension /di-**sen**-shun/ *n* disagreement, quarreling (*the proposal caused some dissension among committee members*).

dissent /di-**sent**/ *vb* to disagree, to think differently from (*the vote was almost unanimous but one committee member dissented*). ● *also n.*

dissertation /di-ser-**tay**-shun/ *n* a lecture or essay (*students required to write a dissertation*).

disservice /di-**ser**-vis/ *n* a bad turn (*do him a disservice by letting him copy your homework*).

dissident /**di**-si-dent/ *adj* disagreeing. ● *n* a person who disagrees with a government's policies, especially one who is punished (*political dissidents*).

dissimilar /di-**si**-mi-lar/ *adj* unlike (*have totally dissimilar tastes*).

dissipate /**di**-si-pate/ *vb* **1** to scatter (*a crowd that dissipated when the police arrived*). **2** to spend or use wastefully (*dissipating a fortune on gambling*). **3** to waste (*dissipate the natural resources of the country*). ● *n* **dissipation** /di-si-**pay**-shun/.

dissipated /**di**-si-pay-ted/ *adj* given to living wildly, indulging in drinking and foolish or dangerous pleasures (*dissipated young men/lead a dissipated life*).

dissociate /di-**so**-shee-ate/ *vb* **1** to separate from (*try to dissociate his private life from his public one*). **2** to refuse to be connected with (*dissociating yourself from the behavior of your co-workers*). ● *n* **dissociation** /di-so-shee-**ay**-shun/.

dissolute /**di**-so-loot/ *adj* living wickedly, immoral (*dissolute drunks/a dissolute life*).

dissolution /di-so-**loo**-shun/ *n* act of dissolving (*the dissolution of Parliament/the dissolution of the Roman Empire*).

dissolve /di-**zolv**/ *vb* **1** to make or become liquid by placing in liquid (*dissolving pills in water*). **2** to break up, to put an end to (*dissolve Parliament/dissolve a marriage*).

dissuade /di-**swade**/ *vb* to advise not to do (*try to dissuade them from resigning*). ● *n* **dissuasion** / di-**sway**-zhun/. ● *adj* **dissuasive** /di-**sway**-siv/.

distance /**dis**-tanse/ *n* **1** being far off (*live at a distance from her mother*). **2** the space between two points or places (*a distance of three miles between the villages*). **3** (*fml*) unfriendliness (*notice a certain distance in his manner*).

distant /**dis**-tant/ *adj* **1** far off (*travel to distant lands*). **2** not close (*a distant relative*). **3** cold or unfriendly in manner (*he seemed rather distant to his old friends*).

distaste /dis-**taste**/ *n* dislike or disgust (*look at her dirty fingernails with distaste*).

distasteful /dis-**taste**-ful/ *adj* unpleasant (*a distasteful duty to have to declare people redundant/ a subject that is distasteful to her*).

distemper /dis-**tem**-per/ *n* **1** a disease of dogs. **2** (*old*) an oil-less paint for walls.

distend /dis-**tend**/ *vb* to stretc h, to swell (*children's stomachs distended from lack of food in the famine area*). ● *n* **distension**/dis-**ten**-shun/.

distill /dis-**til**/ *vb* **1** to fall in drops. **2** to purify a substance by heating it until it turns into vapor, and then cooling the vapor until it becomes liquid.

distillation /dis-ti-**lay**-shun/ *n* act of distilling.

distiller /dis-**ti**-ler/ *n* a maker of whiskey or other alcoholic liquor.

distillery /dis-**ti**-le-ree/ *n* a factory where whiskey, etc., is made.

distinct/dis-**tingkt**/ *adj* **1** separate (*two distinct types of bird*). **2** easily heard, seen, etc. (*a distinct improvement*).

distinction /dis-**ting**-shun/ *n* **1** difference (*make a distinction between high school and college students*). **2** excellence (*a writer of distinction*). **3** a special mark of honor (*win a distinction for bravery*).

distinctive /dis-**ting**-tiv/ *adj* different in a special way (*a distinctive style of dress/wear a distinctive perfume*).

distinguish /dis-**ting**-gwish/ *vb* **1** to see or point out the differences (between) (*unable to distinguish one twin from the other/distinguish right from*

wrong). **2** to make different (*the ability to speak distinguishes humans from animals*). **3** to make (yourself) outstanding (*distinguished himself in battle*). **4** to see, to make out (*be just able to distinguish a figure in the distance*).

distinguished /dis-**ting**-gwishd/ *adj* famous (*a distinguished writer*).

distort /dis-**tawrt**/ *vb* **1** to twist out of shape (*a face distorted in agony*). **2** to give a false meaning to (*the facts distorted by some newspapers*). ● *n* **distortion** /dis-**tawr**-shun/.

distract /dis-**tract**/ *vb* to draw the attention away (*distract him from his work*).

distracted /dis-**trac**-ted/ *adj* almost mad with grief or anxiety (*parents distracted by the loss of their children*).

distraction /dis-**trac**-shun/ *n* **1** anything that draws the attention away (*too many distractions for her to be able to study properly*). **2** confusion of mind (*driven to distraction by the constant noise*).

distraught /dis-**trawt**/ *adj* almost mad with grief or anxiety (*a distraught mother looking for her missing child*).

distress /dis-**tress**/ *n* **1** great pain or anxiety (*an accident victim in great distress*). **2** suffering caused by lack of money (*in financial distress*). **3** danger (*a ship in distress*). ● *vb* to cause anxiety, sorrow, or pain.

distribute /dis-**tri**-byoot/ *vb* **1** to give out, to give each his or her share (*distributing food to the poor*). **2** to spread out widely (*hamburger restaurants distributed throughout the country*). ● *n* **distribution** /dis-tri-**byoo**-shun/.

distributor /dis-**tri**-byoo-ter/ *n* **1** a person who gives away or shares something. **2** part of a motor engine.

district /**dis**-trict/ *n* **1** part of a country. **2** an area marked off for some special purpose.

distrust /dis-**trust**/ *vb* to have no confidence or belief in (*distrust that old car/have a distrust of strangers*). ● *n* doubt, suspicion. ● *adj* **distrustful** /dis-**trust**-ful/.

disturb /dis-**turb**/ *vb* **1** to throw into disorder (*disturb the papers on the desk*). **2** to trouble (*disturbed by the lack of news*). **3** to interrupt (*disturbed his sleep*).

disturbance /dis-**tur**-banse/ *n* **1** disorder, riot (*police called to a disturbance in the local tavern*). **2** disarrangement (*notice the disturbance of the papers on his desk*). **3** an interruption (*unable to work with all the disturbance*). **4** mental illness (*suffer an emotional disturbance*).

disuse /dis-**yoos**/ n a state of not being used, neglect (old laws fallen into disuse). ● adj **disused** /dis-**yoozd**/.

ditch /**ditch**/ n a long narrow trench for carrying away water. ● vb to make a ditch.

ditto /**di**-toe/ n the same as before, indicated by the sign " (used to show that the same word, phrase, figure, etc., is to be repeated, in writing, often shortened to **do**).

ditty /**di**-tee/ n a short simple song.

divan /di-**van**/ n **1** a long low sofa without back or arms. **2** a kind of bed like this.

dive /**dive**/ vb (**dove** /**dove**/, **diving** /**die**-ving/) **1** to plunge into water head first. **2** to move quickly downward (rabbits diving into holes). ● n **1** a plunge. **2** a sudden downward move.

diver /**die**-ver/ n **1** one who, with special equipment, is able to work under water (deep-sea divers). **2** a diving bird.

diverge /die-**verge**/ vb to go off in a different direction, to branch in different directions (the road and railway line diverge near the village/with the subject of politics, that is where our opinions diverge). ● n **divergence** /die-**ver**-jense/. ● adj **divergent** /die-**ver**-jent/.

diverse /die-**verse**/ adj different, unlike (have many diverse reasons to go/people of diverse backgrounds).

diversify /die-**ver**-si-fy/ vb to make or become different (diversifying their range of goods/engineering firms diversifying into computers). ● n **diversification** /die-ver-si-fi-**cay**-shun/.

diversion /die-**ver**-shun/ n **1** (fml) amusement (swimming and other diversions for the children). **2** something that distracts the attention (his friend created a diversion while he stole sweets from the store). **3** a turning aside from the main route (e.g., to avoid an obstacle) (a diversion ahead because of roadworks).

diversity /die-**ver**-si-tee/ n difference, variety.

divert /die-**vert**/ vb **1** to turn in another direction (divert the traffic on to a side road). **2** to draw away (diverting their attention from their personal problems). **3** to amuse (diverted by the clown's antics).

diverting /die-**ver**-ting/ adj amusing.

divest /die-**vest**/ vb **1** to take away, to strip (divest the tyrant of his power). **2** to take off, especially ceremonial clothes (bishop divesting himself of his robes).

divide /di-**vide**/ vb **1** to break up into parts (divid-

ing the class into three groups). **2** to share out (divide the chocolate among them). **3** to separate (a wall divided the gardens). **4** in mathematics, to see how many times one number is contained in another.

divided highway /di-**vie**-ded **hie**-way/ n a wide road which has a strip of grass or barrier in the middle to separate two lines of traffic moving in opposite directions.

dividend /**di**-vi-dend/ n **1** in mathematics, a number to be divided. **2** a share of profit. **3** the rate at which the profits of a company are divided among shareholders.

dividers /di-**vie**-derz/ npl an instrument for measuring distances on paper, etc.

divine /di-**vine**/ adj **1** of or belonging to God. **2** (inf) extremely good (a divine dancer). ● vb **1** to foretell, to guess (divining the future). **2** to learn or discover by intuition, insight (divine a sudden change in her manner). ● n **divination** /di-vi-**nay**-shun/.

divining rod /di-**vie**-ning-rod/ n a Y-shaped rod, usually of hazel, used to find underground water.

divinity /di-**vi**-ni-tee/ n **1** a god. **2** the study of religion.

divisible /di-**vi**-zi-bul/ adj able to be divided.

division /di-**vi**-zhun/ n **1** the act of dividing (the division of responsibility). **2** one of the parts into which something is divided (the sales division of the firm). **3** disagreement (some division in the family). **4** a large army group.

divisional /di-**vizh**-nal/ adj having to do with a division (the divisional head).

divisor /di-**vie**-zor/ n in mathematics, the number by which another number (the **dividend** /**di**-vi-dend/) is divided in a sum.

divorce /di-**voarss**/ n **1** legal permission to separate from your married partner and to marry someone else if so desired. **2** separation. ● vb **1** officially to end a marriage (parents who divorce). **2** to separate (try to divorce his private life from his public life/she seems divorced from reality).

divulge /di-**vulge**/ vb to make known, to reveal (divulging secrets to the press/divulge information about the robbery to the police).

Diwali /di-**wa**-lee/ n a Hindu festival held in the fall, particularly associated with Lakshmi, the goddess of prosperity.

DNA /**dee**-en-ay/ n a substance in your body that stores genetic information, an abbreviation of deoxyribonucleic acid.

DIY /dee-eye-why/ n the act of making, repairing, or decorating things yourself, as opposed to employing a tradesman, an abbreviation of do-it-yourself.

dizzy /di-zee/ adj giddy, having the feeling that everything is spinning around (children whirling around until they are dizzy/feel dizzy at the top of a ladder). ● n **dizziness** /di-zee-ness/.

do[1] /doo/ vb (pt **did** /did/, pp **done** /dun/) **1** to perform, to carry out (do his duty). **2** to attend to (do the dishes). **3** to act or behave (do as you are told). **4** to be enough or suitable (will this hat do for the wedding?).

do[2] see **ditto**.

docile /do-sul/ adj easily managed, controlled, or influenced, quiet (a docile pony/docile children). ● n **docility** /do-si-li-tee/.

dock[1] /dock/ n **1** an enclosure in a harbor where enough water can be kept to float a ship when it is being loaded or unloaded, repaired, etc. **2** the box in which prisoners stand in a court of law. ● vb to sail into dock (when the ship was docking/dock the ship).

dock[2] /dock/ vb to cut short, to remove part of (dock the dog's tail).

dock[3] /dock/ n a common weed.

docket /dock-et/ n a label tied to goods (a docket listing the contents).

dockyard /dock-yard/ n a place where ships are built and repaired.

doctor /doc-tor/ n **1** a person who is qualified by medical training to attend the sick and injured. **2** a person who receives a degree granted by universities to those learned in a certain field (a doctor of philosophy). ● vb **1** to give medical treatment to (doctoring her cold with Tylenol and hot drinks). **2** to make different in order to deceive, to tamper with (doctor the evidence).

doctorate /doc-trit/ n the degree of doctor.

doctrinal /doc-tri-nal/ adj having to do with a doctrine or set of beliefs held by a religious society (doctrinal differences between the two faiths).

doctrinaire /doc-tri-nare/ adj believing in or trying to put into action a system of ideas without considering the practical difficulties of doing so.

doctrine /doc-trin/ n a set of beliefs held by a person or group (the Protestant doctrine/socialist doctrine).

document /doc-yu-ment/ n a written or printed paper that can be used as proof (secret government documents/documents of sale). ● vb to bring forward written evidence (local history that is well documented).

documentary /doc-yu-men-tu-ree/ adj **1** having to do with documents (documentary evidence). **2** giving facts and explanations (a documentary film). ● also n.

dodder /dod-er/ vb to move unsteadily or shakily (an elderly man doddering along).

dodge /dodge/ vb **1** to make a quick movement to avoid someone or something (succeed in dodging the blow/dodge the police). **2** to avoid by cleverness or trickery (politicians dodging reporters' questions). ● n **1** a quick movement aside (a footballer making a sudden dodge to the right). **2** a trick (up to his old dodges).

dodger /dodge-er/ n a trickster, a person who is not to be trusted.

dodo /doe-doe/ n (pl **dodoes** or **dodos** /doe-doaz/) a type of flightless bird no longer in existence (dead as the dodo).

doe /doe/ n the female of many animals (e.g., deer, rabbit, etc.).

doff /doff/ vb (fml) to take off (doffed his cap).

dog /dawg/ n **1** a common domestic animal. **2** (hum or contemp) a fellow. ● vb (**dogged** /dawgd/, **dogging** /daw-ging/) to follow closely, to pursue (dog his footsteps/a family dogged by bad luck).

dogcart /dawg-cart/ n a two-wheeled cart or carriage.

dog collar /dawg-caw-ler/ n **1** a collar for a dog. **2** the collar worn by a member of the clergy.

dog-eared /daw-gird/ adj with the corners of the pages turned down (a dog-eared paperback).

dogfish /dawg-fish/ n a type of small shark.

dogged /daw-ged/ adj determined, unwilling to give in (a dogged attempt to get to the top). ● n **doggedness** /daw-ged-ness/.

doggerel /daw-ge-rel/ n bad poetry.

dogma /dawg-ma/ n a belief or set of beliefs put forward by an authority to be accepted as a matter of faith (Christian dogma/tired of his political dogma).

dogmatic /dawg-ma-tic/ adj **1** relating to dogma (dogmatic theology). **2** holding your beliefs very strongly and expecting other people to accept them without question (so dogmatic about the best way to educate children). ● n **dogmatism** /dawg-ma-ti-zum/.

dog rose /dawg-roaz/ n the wild rose.

Dog Star /dawg-star/ n Sirius, the brightest of the fixed stars.

dogwatch /**dawg**-watch/ *n* on a ship, a short watch of two hours.

doily, doyley /**doi**-lee/ *n* a small fancy napkin or mat (*the doily under the cake*).

doldrums /**doal**-drumz/ *npl* seas near the equator where there is little or no wind. ● **in the doldrums** in a sad mood.

dole /**dole**/ *vb* to give out shares of, often in small amounts (*dole out daily rations to the refugees*/ *dole out spending money*).

doleful /**dole**-ful/ *adj* gloomy, sad (*looking doleful*/ *doleful news*). ● *adv* **dolefully** /**dole**-fu-lee/.

doll /**dol**/ *n* a toy in the shape of a person (*a baby doll*).

dollar /**dol**-ar/ *n* an American, Australian, or Canadian currency (=100 cents).

Dolly Varden /dol-ee **var**-den/ *n* **1** a brightly spotted trout of western North America. **2** a large lopsided hat worn by women. **3** a sponge cake made with spices and dried fruit.

dolorous /**dol**-o-rus/ *adj* (*fml*) sad, sorrowful. ● *n* **dolor** /**dol**-or/, *also* **dolour** (*Br, Cdn*).

dolphin /**dol**-fin/ *n* a sea animal like the porpoise, belonging to the whale family.

dolt /**doalt**/ *n* a stupid person.

domain /doe-**mane**/ *n* **1** the land that you own. **2** the country that a monarch rules. **3** an area of interest, knowledge, influence, etc. (*lie within the domain of science fiction*).

dome /**dome**/ *n* **1** a rounded top on a building. **2** something of this shape (*the dome of his bald head*). ● *adj* **domed** /**doamd**/.

dome fastener /**doam** fas-ner/ *n* a small fastener for articles of clothing or other items that has a rounded portion that snaps into a socket.

domestic /du-**mes**-tic/ *adj* **1** belonging to or having to do with the house (*appliances for domestic use*). **2** concerning your personal or home life (*domestic happiness*). **3** tame and living with or used to people (*domestic animals*). **4** having to do with your own country (*goods sold on the domestic market*). **5** (*inf*) interested in and good at cooking, housework, etc. (*she's very domestic*). ● *n* a house servant.

domesticated /du-**mes**-ti-cay-ted/ *adj* **1** accustomed to living near and being used by people (*domesticated animals*). **2** fond of and/or good at doing jobs associated with running a house (*a domesticated person*).

domesticity /du-mes-**ti**-si-tee/ *n* **1** home life. **2** the state of being fond of and good at running a home.

domicile /**dom**-i-sile/ *n* (*fml*) a house, a home, the place where a person is living.

dominant /**dom**-i-nant/ *adj* **1** controlling others (*a dominant personality*). **2** most important (*the dominant issue at the meeting*). ● *n* **dominance** / **dom**-i-nanse/.

dominate /**dom**-i-nate/ *vb* **1** to have complete control over (*dominate the meeting*/*dominate the rest of the class*). **2** to be the most important (*financial problems that dominated his thoughts*). **3** to rise high above (*mountains dominating the village*). ● *n* **domination** /dom-i-**nay**-shun/.

domineer /dom-i-**neer**/ *vb* to bully (*tired of being domineered by his elder brother*). ● *adj* **domineering** /dom-i-**nee**-ring/.

dominion /du-**min**-yun/ *n* **1** (*fml*) rule, government (*an emperor holding dominion over millions of people*). **2** the territory governed (*the vast dominions of the empire*).

Dominion Day /du-**min**-yun day/ *n* former name for Canada Day.

dominoes /**dom**-i-noaz/ *n* a game played with small flat pieces of wood, ivory, etc., marked with dots.

don[1] /**don**/ *vb* (**donned** /**dond**/, **donning** /**don**-ing/) (*fml*) to put on (*donned his coat*).

don[2] /**don**/ *n* a teacher in a university or college.

donate /**doa**-nate/ *vb* to give, especially to a charity, etc., to contribute (*donating hundreds of dollars to a children's charity*). ● *n* **donation** /doa-**nay**-shun/.

done /**dun**/ *pp* of **do** /**doo**/ 1. ● *adj* (*inf*) utterly exhausted (*completely done after the long walk*).

donkey /**dong**-kee/ *n* an ass.

donor /**doa**-nur/ *n* **1** a person who gives or contributes (*money given to the charity by anonymous donors*). **2** a person who provides blood for transfusion, organs for transplantation, etc. (*a blood donor*/*a kidney donor*).

doodle /**doo**-dul/ *vb* to draw or scribble casually or absent-mindedly. ● *also n.*

doom /**doom**/ *n* death, ruin, destruction, terrible and inevitable fate (*meet your doom*). ● *vb* to cause to suffer something unavoidable and terrible, such as death, ruin, or destruction (*doomed to a life of unemployment*).

doomsday /**doomz**-day/ *n* the day of judgment at the end of the world.

door /**dore**/ *n* a moving barrier in an entrance to a building or room.

doorway /**dore**-way/ *n* an entrance to a building or room,

dope /dope/ *n* (*inf*) a fool, a stupid person.

doré /doa-**ray**/ *n* (*Cdn*) a walleye (fish).

dormant /**dawr**-mant/ *adj* not at present active (*a dormant volcano*).

dormer /**dawr**-mer/ *n* a small window in a sloping roof.

dormitory /**dawr**-mi-toe-ree/ *n* a sleeping room with many beds (*the dormitories in the boarding school*).

dormouse /**dawr**-mouse/ *n* (*pl* **dormice** /**dawr**-mice/) a small mouse like animal that sleeps in winter.

dorsal /**dawr**-sal/ *adj* having to do with the back (*the dorsal fin of the shark*).

dory /**doe**-ree/ *n* a sea fish (often **John Dory**).

dosage /**doe**-sidge/ *n* the amount to be given in a dose (*exceed the recommended dosage*).

dose /doas/ *n* the amount of medicine given at one time (*a dose of cough mixture*). ● *vb* to give medicine to (*dosing herself with cough mixture*).

dossier /daws-**yay**/ *n* a collection of papers dealing with one particular subject or person (*firms keeping dossiers on members of staff*).

dot /dot/ *n* a small point or mark (*a pattern of black and white dots*). ● *vb* (**dotted** /**dot**-ed/, **dotting** /**dot**-ing/) to mark with dots. ● **dotted with** having (things) placed here and there (*a sky dotted with stars*).

dotage /**doe**-tidge/ *n* the weak-mindedness of old age (*an old man in his dotage*).

dote /doat/ *vb* **1** to show great fondness of, especially in a foolish way (*doting on his daughter and thinking she can do no wrong*). **2** (*old*) to become weaker in mind when old.

double /**du**-bul/ *adj* **1** twice as much as usual or normal (*a double helping of dessert/his income is double that of his brother*). **2** for two people (*a double bed/a double ticket*). **3** forming a pair (*a double window/double yellow lines*). **4** combining two things or qualities (*a double meaning/a double life*). ● *n* **1** twice the amount (*double the price*). **2** a person or thing looking the same as another (*the double of her mother at that age*). **3** a glass of alcoholic liquor holding twice the standard amount. **4** a running pace (*leave at the double*). ● *vb* **1** to multiply by two, to cause to become twice as large or numerous. **2** to fold in two (*doubling the blanket over for extra warmth*). **3** to have two uses, jobs, etc. (*the sofa doubles as a bed*). ● *adv* **doubly**. ● **double back** to turn back in the opposite direction, especially unexpectedly.

double-bass /du-bul-**base**/ *n* a large, low-toned stringed instrument.

double-cross /du-bul-**crawss**/ *vb* to deceive someone who trusts you and believes that you are their friend.

double-dealing /du-bul-**dee**-ling/ *n* deceit, dishonesty. ● *adj* devious, not to be trusted (*a double-dealing business partner*).

doublet /**du**-blet/ *n* **1** a close-fitting body garment worn by men in the 14th to 17th centuries. **2** one of a pair of words having the same meaning.

doubt /dout/ *vb* to be uncertain about, to be unwilling to believe or trust (*doubt his word/I doubt whether they'll come*). ● *n* **1** a feeling of uncertainty. **2** distrust. ● *adj* **doubtful** /**dout**-ful/. ● *adv* **doubtless** /**dout**-less/.

douche /doosh/ *n* a stream of water directed on to the body to clean it. ● *also vb.*

dough /doe/ *n* **1** flour moistened with water and pressed into a paste ready for baking (*dough for making bread*). **2** (*inf*) money.

doughnut /**doe**-nut/ *n* a type of sweet cake in the shape of a ring.

douse, dowse /douz/ *vb* **1** to drench in water (*dousing the fire/douse him with a bucket of water*). **2** to put out (*douse the candles*).

dove /duv/ *n* a bird of the pigeon family.

dove-cote, dove-cot /**duv**-cot(e)/ *ns* a pigeon house.

dovetail /**duv**-tail/ *n* a sticking-out end of wood shaped like a dove's tail to fit into a hole in another piece of wood to lock the two together. ● *vb* to fit neatly or exactly together (*plans neatly dovetailing with theirs*).

dowager /**dow**-i-jer/ *n* the title given to the widow of a nobleman.

dowdy /**dow**-dee/ *adj* badly or shabbily dressed, unfashionable, drab (*a dowdy woman/dowdy clothes*). ● *n* **dowdiness** /**dow**-dee-ness/. ● *adv* **dowdily** /**dow**-di-lee/.

down[1] /down/ *prep* in a descending direction in, on, along, or through (*water flows down/go down the hill*). ● *adv* **1** from a higher to a lower position, to a lying or sitting position (*she fell down*). **2** toward or to the ground, floor, or bottom (*climb down*). **3** to or in a lower status or in a worse condition (*prices are going down*). **4** in cash. **5** to or in a state of less activity (*the children quietened down*). ● *adj* **1** occupying a low position, especially lying on the ground. **2** (*inf*) depressed (*she is feeling down*). ● *n* **1** a low period. **2** (*inf*) a dislike. **3** in Canadian and US football, one of a series of attempts by the team on offence to advance the ball ten yards. ● *vb* **1** to go or cause to go or come down. **2** to defeat. **3** to swallow.

down² /down/ *n* the fine soft feathers of a bird (*the down of a swan/pillows filled with down*). ● *adj* **downy** /dow-nee/.

down-and-out /dow-nan-**dout**/ *adj* having no job and no home, and no money (*down-and-out people sleeping rough under the bridge*). ● *n* a down-and-out person.

downcast /**down**-cast/ *adj* **1** directed downward (*with eyes downcast*). **2** sad, in low spirits (*feeling downcast at the news of his failure*).

downfall /**down**-fawl/ *n* **1** ruin, fall from power, prosperity, etc. (*overconfidence led to his downfall*). **2** a heavy fall of rain.

down-hearted /**down**-har-tid/ *adj* discouraged, in low spirits (*down-hearted after the failure of his business*).

download /**down**-load/ *vb* to copy or transfer data or a program from one computer to another.

downpour /**down**-poar/ *n* a heavy fall of rain (*get soaked in the downpour*).

downright /**down**-rite/ *adj* **1** thorough, complete (*a downright lie*). **2** frank, straightforward, saying exactly what you think (*a downright kind of man*).

downsize /**down**-size/ *vb* to reduce the number of people who work in a company, usually in order to reduce costs (*downsize the workforce*).

dowry /**dow**-ree/ *n* the property a woman brings to her husband at marriage.

dowse *see* **douse**.

doyley *see* **doily**.

doze /doaz/ *vb* to be half asleep (*dozing in his chair after lunch*). ● *n* light sleep.

dozen /**du**-zen/ *n* twelve.

drab /drab/ *adj* **1** of a dull grayish brown color (*wearing drab clothes*). **2** dull, uninteresting (*lead a drab existence*).

draft¹ /draft/ *n* **1** the amount taken in one drink (*a long draft of cold beer*). **2** a stream of air through a room (*drafts coming in the window*). **3** the depth a ship sinks in water.

draft² /draft/ *n* **1** a number of soldiers picked to go somewhere on duty. **2** a written order to pay money to someone. **3** a rough copy or plan of work to be done (*a draft of his essay*). ● *vb* **1** to prepare a plan or rough copy (*draft the contract*). **2** to pick and send off (*draft police to control the football crowds*).

draftsman /**draft**-sman/ *n* **1** a man whose job it is to draw plans for buildings, etc. **2** a piece in a game of checkers.

drafty /**draf**-tee/ *adj* cold because of a stream of air (*large drafty rooms*).

drag /drag/ *vb* (**dragged** /dragd/, **dragging** /dra-ging/) **1** to pull along with force (*drag the fallen tree*). **2** to trail on the ground (*with her long skirt dragging in the mud*). **3** (*inf*) to go very slowly (*the evening seemed to drag*). **4** to search underwater with hooks or a net (*drag the canal for the dead body*). ● *n* anything that causes to go slowly.

dragon /**dra**-gon/ *n* **1** in fables, a winged monster. **2** a fierce, stern person (*his grandmother's a real old dragon*).

dragonfly /**dra**-gon-fly/ *n* a winged insect.

dragoon /dra-**goon**/ *n* a horse soldier. ● *vb* to force to obey, to bully into (*dragoon them into helping him paint the house*).

drain /drane/ *vb* **1** to draw off liquid by pipes, ditches, etc. (*drain the water tank*). **2** to empty completely (*drain his glass*). **3** to cause to become dry as liquid flows away (*drain the plates*). ● *n* a pipe or channel to carry away liquid (*a blocked drain*).

drainage /**dray**-nidge/ *n* all the means used to draw water away from a certain area.

drake /drake/ *n* a male duck.

dram /dram/ *n* **1** a small measure of weight (1/16 ounce). **2** a small drink of whisky, etc.

drama /**dra**-ma/ *n* **1** a play (*a television drama*). **2** plays as a branch of literature and as a performing art (*study drama*). **3** an exciting event, a series of exciting events (*a real-life hospital drama*). **4** excitement (*a life that seems full of drama*).

dramatic /dra-**ma**-tic/ *adj* **1** having to do with drama (*a dramatic society/a dramatic representation of the novelist's life*). **2** sudden or exciting (*a dramatic improvement*). **3** showing too much feeling or emotion (*she's so dramatic about the least thing*). ● *adv* **dramatically** /dra-**ma**-ti-ca-lee/.

dramatist /**dra**-ma-tist/ *n* a writer of plays.

dramatize /**dra**-ma-tize/ *n, also* **dramatise** (*Br*) **1** to turn into a stage play (*dramatizing a novel*). **2** to exaggerate the importance or significance of (*she dramatized what was a minor injury/a situation that was dramatized by the press*). ● *n* **dramatization** /dra-ma-ti-**zay**-shun/, *also* **dramatisation** (*Br*).

drape /drape/ *vb* **1** to cover or decorate with cloth, etc., in folds (*drape the sofa with a large length of brown velvet*). **2** to cause to hang or rest loosely (*draping his legs over the end of the sofa*).

draper /**dray**-per/ *n* a person who sells clothes.

drapery /**dray**-pe-ree/ *n* **1** cloth, linen. **2** a draper's shop.

drapes /**draips**/ *npl* pieces of fabric hung at a window.

drastic /**dra**-stic/ *adj* acting with strength or violence, thorough (*take drastic measures to reduce expenditure*). ● *adv* **drastically** /**dra**-sti-clee/.

draught /**draft**/ *see* (*Br*) **draft**.

draughts /**drafts**/ *n* (*Br*) *see* **checkers**.

draw /**draw**/ *vb* (*pt* **drew** /**droo**/, *pp* **drawn** /**drawn**/) **1** to pull along or toward (*a tractor drawing a trailer/draw a gun out/drew a file from the cabinet*). **2** to move toward or away from (*the crowd drew nearer/the car drew away from the curb*). **3** to attract (*try to draw his attention to the lack of money*). **4** to receive money (as wages, for a check, etc.) (*draw $1500 per month*). **5** to make a picture or pictures of, usually with a pencil, crayons, etc. (*ask the child to draw a picture of the house/draw his mother*). **6** (*of a game or contest*) to end with nobody winning (*the two football teams drew*). **7** (*of a ship*) to sink to a certain depth in the water. ● *n* **1** an attraction (*the new singer is a real draw at the club*). **2** a game or contest won by nobody (*the football match ended in a draw*). **3** the selecting of winning tickets in a raffle, lottery, etc. ● **draw the line at** to refuse to have do (*draw the line at lying*). ● **draw up 1** to stop (*cars drawing up at the curb*). **2** to prepare, especially in writing (*draw up a contract*).

drawback /**draw**-**back**/ *n* a disadvantage (*he found his poor eyesight a drawback*).

drawbridge /**draw**-**bridge**/ *n* a bridge that can be lifted at one end to prevent crossing.

drawer /**drawr**/ *n* **1** a sliding box or container in a table, closet, etc. **2** (*pl*) *see* **drawers** /**drawrz**/.

drawers /**drawrz**/ *npl* (*old*) an undergarment with legs for the bottom part of the body.

drawing /**draw**-ing/ *n* **1** a picture made with a pencil, crayons, etc. (*a pen-and-ink drawing of the house*). **2** the art of making such pictures (*study drawing*).

drawing room /**draw**-ing room/ *n* a sitting room, especially a large one in which guests are received.

drawl /**drawl**/ *vb* to speak slowly or lazily (*drawl his words in an irritating way*). ● *also n.*

dread /**dred**/ *n* fear, terror (*live in dread of being attacked*). ● *adj* (*fml*) causing great fear, terrible. ● *vb* to fear greatly (*dread losing his job*).

dreadful /**dred**-ful/ *adj* **1** terrible (*a dreadful accident/a dreadful storm/in dreadful pain*). **2** very unpleasant, bad (*a dreadful noise/a dreadful dress*). ● *adv* **dreadfully** /**dred**-ful-ee/.

dreadlocks /**dred**-loks/ *npl* hair that is twisted into long thick braids hanging down from the scalp.

dream /**dreem**/ *n* **1** the ideas or fancies passing through the mind of a person sleeping. **2** memories of the past or thoughts of what may happen (*dreams of becoming a millionaire*). **3** state of being occupied by your thoughts, daydream. **4** (*inf*) a beautiful or wonderful person or thing (*a dream of a dress*). ● *vb* (*pt, pp* **dreamed** /**dreemd**/ or **dreamt** /**dremt**/) **1** to have dreams. **2** to imagine.

dreamer /**dree**-mer/ *n* a person who is more interested in thoughts or fancies than facts.

dreamy /**dree**-me/ *adj* **1** given to or relating to daydreaming (*a dreamy kind of person/in a dreamy mood*). **2** extremely attractive (*he is so dreamy*).

dreary /**dree**-ree/ *adj* cheerless, gloomy (*a dreary November day/a dreary style of decoration*).

dredge[1] /**dredge**/ *n* a machine for bringing up mud, fish, etc., from the bottom of a river or the sea. ● *vb* **1** to bring up with a dredge (*dredge up the body from the riverbed*). **2** to clear with a dredge (*dredging the canal*). **3** to mention something from the past (*dredge up the old scandal about her*).

dredge[2] /**dredge**/ *vb* to sprinkle with (*dredging doughnuts with sugar*).

dredger /**dre**-jer/ *n* a ship fitted to clear mud from the channel in a river or harbor.

dregs /**dregz**/ *npl* tiny pieces of matter that sink to the foot of a standing liquid (*wine dregs/coffee dregs*).

drench /**drench**/ *vb* **1** to make very wet (*get drenched in the storm*). **2** to force (an animal) to drink.

dress /**dress**/ *vb* **1** to put on clothes (*dress yourself/dress the child warmly*). **2** to wear evening or formal dress (*do we have to dress for dinner?*). **3** to straighten, to set in order (*dress the shop window*). **4** to bandage (*dress a wound*). **5** to prepare for use (*dress a turkey for the oven*). ● *n* **1** clothing (*casual dress*). **2** a woman's outer garment (*a summer dress*). ● **dress up 1** to put on the clothing of another person, nation, etc. (*dress up for the fancy-dress party*). **2** to put on your best clothing (*dress up for the formal ball*).

dress circle /**dress**-**sir**-cul/ *n* the second-floor gallery in a theater.

dresser /**dre**-ser/ *n* **1** a kitchen sideboard (*plates displayed on the dresser*). **2** a person who helps an actor to dress.

dressing /**dre**-sing/ *n* **1** the ointments, bandages, etc., put on a wound. **2** something put on as a covering (*give the plants a dressing of fertilizer*). **3** sauce for food, especially a mixture of oil and vinegar, etc., for putting on salads.

dress rehearsal /dres-ri-**her**-sal/ *n* a practice before a performance, in the appropriate costume.

dressy /**dre**-see/ *adj* **1** (*inf*) fond of nice clothes (*a dressy young man*). **2** elegant or elaborate, suitable for special occasions (*dressy clothes*).

dribble /**dri**-bul/ *vb* **1** to fall or let fall in small drops (*water dribbling from the faucet*). **2** to allow saliva to run from the mouth (*babies dribbling*). **3** to keep a moving ball under control by little kicks or taps (*a footballer dribbling toward the goal*).

driblet /**dri**-blet/ *n* a small amount (*water coming out in driblets*).

drift /**drift**/ *n* **1** that which is driven by wind (e.g., snow, sand) or water (e.g., seaweed). **2** meaning (*I didn't get the drift of his speech*). ● *vb* **1** to be driven by wind or water current (*boats drifting*). **2** to do something aimlessly (*just drifting without any ambition*).

drifter /**drif**-ter/ *n* a fishing boat using **drift nets** (i.e., nets kept near the surface of the water by cork).

drill[1] /**drill**/ *n* **1** a tool for boring holes (*an electric drill*). **2** training practice (*military drill*). **3** procedures to be followed in a certain situation, such as an emergency (*fire drill*). ● *vb* **1** to make holes with a drill (*drill holes for screws/drill for oil*). **2** to teach something by making learners do it again and again (*drill the class in spelling rules*). **3** to practice military exercises (*soldiers drilling*).

drill[2] /**drill**/ *n* **1** a machine for sowing seeds. **2** a row of seeds. ● *vb* to sow in rows.

drily *see* **dry**.

drink /**dringk**/ *vb* (*pt* **drank** /**drangk**/, *pp* **drunk** / **drungk**/) **1** to swallow (a liquid) (*drink milk*). **2** to take alcoholic liquor, especially in too great amounts (*her husband drinks*). ● *n* **1** an act of drinking (*have a drink of water*). **2** a liquid suitable for drinking (*soft drinks*). **3** alcoholic liquor (*take to drink*). **4** a glass of alcoholic liquor (*buy the drinks*).

drip /**drip**/ *vb* (**dripped** /**dript**/, **dripping** /**dri**-ping/) to fall or let fall in drops (*water dripping from the ceiling/his umbrella dripping water*). ● *n* a drop (*drips from the ceiling*).

dripping /**dri**-ping/ *n* the fat that drops from roasting meat.

drive /**drive**/ *vb* (*pt* **drove** /**drove**/, *pp* **driven** /**dri**-ven/) **1** to control or guide (a car, etc.) (*drive a sports car*). **2** to ride in a car or other vehicle (*driving with his friends to the coast*). **3** to force or urge along (*drive cows to market*). **4** to hit hard (*drive the nail through the wood*). ● *n* **1** a ride in a car or carriage. **2** a private road up to a house. **3** a hard hit (at a ball). **4** energy.

drive-by /**drive-by**/ *adj* carried out from a moving car (*a drive-by shooting*).

drive-in /**drie**-vin/ *n* a cinema, restaurant, etc. which you can use while staying in your car.

drivel /**dri**-vel/ *n* (*inf*) foolish talk, nonsense (*talk a lot of drivel*). ● *vb* (**driveled** /**dri**-veld/, **driveling** / **dri**-ve-ling/) to talk nonsense (*drivel on about unimportant problems*).

driver /**drie**-ver/ *n* **1** a person who drives (*truck drivers*). **2** a golf club with a wooden head.

drive shed /**drive**-shed/ *n* (*Cdn*) a large shed for storing vehicles or farm machinery.

drizzle /**dri**-zel/ *vb* to rain in small drops. ● *n* a fine rain (*get caught in the drizzle*).

droke /**droak**/ *n* (*Cdn*) in the Atlantic Provinces, a grove of trees; a steep-sided valley.

droll /**drole**/ *adj* amusing, odd (*a droll child/a droll story*).

dromedary /**drom**-e-de-ree/ *n* a camel with one hump on its back.

drone /**drone**/ *n* **1** the male or nonworking bee. **2** a lazy person (*the drones in the office*). **3** a humming sound (*the drone of traffic*). ● *vb* **1** to make a humming sound (*an airplane droning overhead*). **2** to speak boringly (*the speaker droned on as most of the audience left*).

drool /**drool**/ *vb* **1** to dribble saliva from the mouth. **2** (*inf*) to admire very enthusiastically (*drooling over her favorite actor*).

droop /**droop**/ *vb* **1** to hang down (*with the hem of her dress drooping*). **2** to become weak (*drooping visibly after a hard day at the office*). ● *also n*.

drop /**drop**/ *n* **1** a very small amount of liquid (*not a drop spilled*). **2** the act of falling (*a drop in temperature*). **3** the distance that a person may fall (*a drop of 300 feet from the castle wall*). ● *vb* (**dropped** /**dropt**/, **dropping** /**drop**-ing/) **1** to fall or let fall in drops. **2** to fall or let fall (*drop a plate on the floor/the dish dropped to the floor*). **3** to fall or cause to fall to a lower level or amount (*the price dropped sharply/forced to drop his speed*). **4** to stop seeing, talking about, doing, etc. (*we've discussed this too long—let's drop the subject*).

drought /drout/ *n* a long spell of dry weather, lack of rain, dryness (*crops dying in the drought*).

drove /drove/ *n* a herd or flock on the move (*a drove of cattle*).

drover /dro-ver/ *n* a person who drives cattle.

drown /droun/ *vb* 1 to die under water by water filling the lungs (*drown while trying to rescue his friend from the river*). 2 to kill by keeping under water (*drown the kittens in the river*). 3 to flood, to submerge (*farmland drowned by the floods*). 4 to put too much liquid in or on (*meat drowned in a sickly sauce*). 5 to prevent from being heard by making a noise (*her speech was drowned out by the noise of the traffic*).

drowsy /drou-zee/ *adj* sleepy (*feeling drowsy after a large lunch*). ● *n* **drowsiness** /drou-zee-ness/.

drub /drub/ *vb* (**drubbed** /drubd/, **drubbing** /dru-bing/) to beat, to thrash (*drub the other team*). ● *n* **drubbing** /dru-bing/.

drudge /drudge/ *vb* to work hard, to slave (*drudging away in the factory*). ● *n* a person who does hard or boring work (*drudges washing dishes in the hotel kitchen*).

drudgery /dru-je-ree/ *n* dull or hard work.

drug /drug/ *n* 1 any substance used as or in a medicine (*pain-killing drugs*). 2 a substance that causes sleep or loss of feeling, especially a habit-forming one (*drugs such as cocaine and heroin*). ● *vb* (**drugged** /drugd/, **drugging** /dru-ging/) to give drugs to in order to make insensible (*drug him before kidnaping him*).

druggist /dru-gist/ *n* a person who dispenses and sells medicines.

drugstore /drug-store/ *n* a store selling medicines and other assorted goods.

druid /droo-id/ *n* a priest of the Celts in ancient Britain before the Christian era.

drum /drum/ *n* 1 a musical instrument in which skin is stretched tightly over the ends of a box and then beaten to produce a booming sound. 2 the tight skin across the inside of the ear. 3 something shaped like a drum (*an oil drum*). ● *vb* (**drummed** /drumd/, **drumming** /dru-ming/) 1 to beat a drum. 2 to make a noise by beating or tapping (*drumming impatiently on the table/drumming her fingers impatiently on the table*). ● *n* **drummer** /dru-mer/.

drumstick /drum-stick/ *n* a stick for beating a drum.

drunk /drungk/ *adj* overcome or overexcited by too much alcoholic liquor (*too drunk to drive*). ● *also adj* **drunken** /drung-ken/. ● *n* **drunkenness** /drung-ken-ness/.

drunkard /drung-kard/ *n* a person who is often drunk.

dry /drie/ *adj* 1 not wet or damp (*paint not yet dry/is the washing dry?*). 2 with little rainfall (*a dry spell/dry parts of the world*). 3 not legally allowed to sell alcohol (*a dry area*). 4 not sweet (*a dry wine*). 5 (*inf*) thirsty (*dry after their long walk*). 6 uninteresting (*a very dry book*). 7 (*of humor*) quiet, not easily noticed. ● *vb* to make or become dry (*dried the washing on the radiators/paint taking a long time to dry*). ● *adv* **drily, dryly** /drie-lee/. ● *n* **dryness** /drie-ness/.

dryad /drie-ad/ *n* a mythical spirit of the woods.

dry-clean /drie-cleen/ *vb* to clean with chemicals instead of water. ● *n* **dry-cleaner** /drie-clee-ner/.

dry dock /drie-dock/ *n* a dock out of which water can be drained so that a ship may be repaired.

dry rot /drie-rot/ *n* a disease of wood that makes it crumble away (*houses affected by dry rot*).

dual /dool/ *adj* consisting of two, double (*have dual nationality/play a dual role in the movie*). ● *n* **duality** /doo-a-li-tee/.

dual carriageway /jool-ca-ridge-way/ (*Br*) *see* **divided highway**.

dub /dub/ *vb* (**dubbed** /dubd/, **dubbing** /du-bing/) 1 to make someone a knight by touching him with a sword. 2 to give a nickname or title to (*dubbed "Ginger" by his friends*).

dubbin, dubbing /du-bin(g)/ *ns* a grease for softening leather.

dubious /doo-bee-us/ *adj* 1 feeling doubt (*I am rather dubious about his suitability for the job*). 2 causing doubt, of uncertain worth, etc., possibly dishonest (*of dubious character*). ● *n* **dubiety** / doo-bie-i-tee/.

duchess /du-chess/ *n* the wife or widow of a duke.

duchy /du-chee/ *n* 1 the lands of a duke. 2 a country ruled by a duke.

duck[1] /duck/ *n* a type of common waterfowl, both domestic and wild, whose flesh is used as a food (*ducks swimming on the pond/duck served in orange sauce*).

duck[2] /duck/ *vb* 1 to plunge or dip under water (*duck her in the river*). 2 to bend to avoid something or to avoid being seen (*duck to avoid hitting his head on the branch/duck down behind the window to avoid being seen by the police*). 3 to avoid or dodge (*duck his responsibilities*).

duckish /du-kish/ *n* (*Cdn*) in Newfoundland, twilight or the time between sunset and darkness.

duckling /duck-ling/ *n* a young duck.

duct /duct/ *n* **1** a pipe or tube for carrying liquid, gas, electric wires, etc. (*air-conditioning ducts*). **2** a tube in the body or in plants through which fluid, etc., passes (*tear ducts*).

dud /dud/ *adj* (*inf*) of no use (*dud fireworks/a dud manager*). ● *also n.*

dude /dood/ *n* (*inf*) a man, a guy.

dudgeon /du-jun/ *n* annoyance, anger (*left the meeting in high dudgeon*).

due /doo/ *adj* **1** owed. **2** proper. **3** expected. ● *adv* directly (*due north*). ● *n* **1** an amount owed. **2** a right. **3** dues /dooz/ a sum payable. ● **due to** caused by.

duel /doo-ul/ *n* **1** an arranged fight between two armed people (*challenged him to a duel when he insulted his honor*). **2** a contest or struggle between two people (*a duel of wits*). ● *also vb* (**dueled** /doo-uld/, **dueling** /doo-ul-ing/).

duet /doo-wet/ *n* a piece of music for two singers or players (*pianists playing a duet*).

duffel, **duffle** /du-ful/ *n* a rough woolen cloth (*a duffel coat*).

dugout /du-gout/ *n* **1** an underground shelter (*a military dugout*). **2** a boat made from a hollowed-out tree.

duke /dook/ *n* **1** the highest rank of nobleman. **2** in some parts of Europe, especially formerly, a ruling prince.

dulcet /dul-set/ *adj* (*often hum*) sweet, tuneful (*good to hear your dulcet tones*).

dulcimer /dul-si-mer/ *n* a musical instrument played by small hammers striking strings, the forerunner of the piano.

dull /dull/ *adj* **1** slow, stupid (*a dull student*). **2** uninteresting (*a dull TV show/rather a dull young woman*). **3** cloudy, sunless, gloomy (*a dull, wet day*). **4** not bright (*dull colors*). **5** not sharp (*a dull pain/a dull noise*). ● *vb* to make dull, to blunt. ● *n* **dullness** /dull-ness/. ● *adv* **dully** /doo-lee/.

dullard /du-lard/ *n* a dull or stupid person.

duly /doo-lee/ *adv* **1** properly (*duly elected MP for the area*). **2** at the due and proper time (*the taxi they ordered duly arrived*).

dumb /dum/ *adj* **1** unable to speak (*people who have been dumb since birth*). **2** silent (*remain dumb throughout the police officer's questioning/struck dumb with amazement*). **3** (*inf*) stupid, unintelligent (*she's obviously a bit dumb*). ● *n* **dumbness** /dum-ness/.

dumbbells /dum-belz/ *npl* weights used when exercising the arm muscles (*dumbbells used in weight training*).

dumbfound /dum-**found**/ *vb* to astonish greatly (*she was dumbfounded by his rude behavior*).

dummy /du-mee/ *n* **1** a model of the human figure, used for displaying or fitting clothing (*a tailor's dummy*). **2** an imitation article (*dummies in the window, not real boxes of candy*). ● *adj* pretended, not real.

dump /dump/ *vb* **1** to throw away, to get rid of (*dump garbage*). **2** (*inf*) to let fall or set down heavily (*dump his suitcase on the doorstep*). **3** to sell goods in another country at a low price. ● *n* **1** a garbage heap (*take the garbage to the dump*). **2** a military store (*an ammunition dump*). **3** (*inf*) a dirty, untidy, or uninteresting place (*the apartment's a real dump*). **4** (*pl*) *see* **dumps**.

dumper truck, **dump truck** *n* a heavy truck the back of which can be tilted back and up to unload cargo such as earth, gravel, rocks, etc.

dumpling /dum-pling/ *n* a food consisting of a thick paste, sometimes rolled into balls, or sometimes filled with fruit or meat.

dumps /dumps/ *npl* low spirits.

dun /dun/ *adj* of a pale yellowish or grayish brown color (*a horse of a dun color*).

dunce /dunse/ *n* a slow learner, a stupid student (*the class dunce*).

dune /doon/ *n* a low sandhill, especially on the seashore (*children playing on the dunes*).

dung /dung/ *n* the waste matter passed from the bodies of animals (*dung used as a fertilizer by farmers*). ● *vb* to mix dung with earth to fertilize it.

dungarees, **dungarees** /dung-ga-**reez**/ *npl* outer garments worn to protect the clothing (*workmen in dungarees*).

dungeon /dun-jin/ *n* a dark prison, an underground prison cell (*the dungeons beneath the castle*).

dunk /dungk/ *vb* to dip into liquid for a moment (*dunked his doughnut in his coffee*).

duo /doo-oe/ *n* a group of two people, especially two musicians.

duodenum /doo-oe-**dee**-num/ *n* part of the bowel. ● *adj* **duodenal** /doo-oe-**dee**-nal/.

dupe /doop/ *vb* to cheat (*duping the old lady by pretending to be a telephone engineer*). ● *n* a person who is cheated or deceived.

duplicate /doo-pli-cate/ *adj* exactly the same, exactly like another (*duplicate keys*). ● *n* an exact copy (*keep a duplicate of the letter in the office files*). ● *vb* to make a copy or copies of (*duplicating the documents for the meeting*). ● *n* **duplication** /doo-pli-**cay**-shun/.

duplicity /doo-**pli**-si-tee/ *n* deceit, trickery.

durable /doo-ra-bul/ *adj* **1** lasting, hard-wearing (*pants of a durable material*). **2** lasting or able to last (*hopes of a durable peace are fading*). ● *n* **durability** /doo-ra-bi-li-tee-cate/.

duration /doo-**ray**-shun/ *n* the time for which a thing lasts (*for the duration of the storm/a disease of short duration*).

duress /doo-**ress**/ *n* use of force, threats, etc. (*agree to go only under duress*).

during /doo-ring/ *prep* **1** in the course of (*he died during the night*). **2** throughout the time of (*a shortage of food during the war*).

dusk /**dusk**/ *n* partial darkness, twilight (*dusk sets in early in the winter*). ● *adj* **dusky** /**dus**-kee/.

dusky /**dus**-kee/ *adj* dark.

dust /**dust**/ *n* tiny dry particles of earth or matter (*dust settling on the furniture*). ● *vb* **1** to remove dust (*dust the piano*). **2** to sprinkle with powder (*dust the cake with confectioners' sugar*). ● *adj* **dusty** /**dus**-tee/.

dustbin /**dust**-bin/ (*Br*) *see* **garbage can**.

duster /**dust**-cloth/ *n* a cloth for removing dust, etc. (*polishing the silver with a duster*).

dustman /**dust**-man/ *n* (*Br*) *see* **garbage man**.

dutiable /doo-tee-a-bul/ *adj* able to be taxed (*dutiable goods such as wine and other alcoholic liquor*).

dutiful /doo-tee-ful/ *adj* obedient, careful to do your duty (*a dutiful son*).

duty /**doo**-tee/ *n* **1** that which you ought to do (*do your duty as a responsible citizen*). **2** an action or task requiring to be done, especially one attached to a job (*perform his duties as a junior doctor/on night duty*). **3** a tax on goods (*duty paid on cigarettes*).

duvet /doo-vay/ (*Br*) *see* **comforter**.

DVD /dee-vee-**dee**/ a kind of compact disk on which particularly large amounts of information, especially photographs and video material, can be stored.

dwarf /**dwawrf**/ *n* (*pl* **dwarfs** /**dwawrfs**/ *or* **dwarves** /**dwawrvz**/) **1** a person, animal, or plant that is much smaller than average. **2** in fairy tales, a creature like a very small man who has magical powers (*dwarfs and fairies*). ● *adj* undersized, very small (*dwarf fruit trees*). ● *vb* to make seem small (*he was so tall that he dwarfed the rest of the team*). ● *adj* **dwarfish** /**dwawr**-fish/.

dwell /**dwell**/ *vb* (*pt*, *pp* **dwelt** /**dwelt**/ *or* **dwelled** / **dweld**/) **1** (*old or lit*) to live in (*dwell in a house by the sea*). **2** to talk or think a lot about (*try not to dwell on your health problems*).

dwelling /**dwe**-ling/ *n* (*fml or old*) a house.

dwindle /**dwin**-dul/ *vb* to grow gradually less or smaller (*his hopes of success dwindled/the population of the village is dwindling*).

dye /**die**/ *vb* to give a new color to, to stain (*dye a white skirt red*). ● *n* a coloring substance. ● *n* **dyer** /**die**-er/.

dyke /**dike**/ *see* **dike**.

dynamic /die-**na**-mic/ *adj* active, energetic (*a dynamic new salesman*).

dynamics /die-**na**-mics/ *n* the science of matter and movement.

dynamite /**die**-na-mite/ *n* a powerful explosive (*bridges blown up with dynamite*).

dynamo /**die**-na-mo/ *n* a machine for making electric current.

dynasty /**die**-na-stee/ *n* a line of rulers of the same family (*the Tudor dynasty in England*). ● *adj* **dynastic** /die-**na**-stic/.

dysentery /**di**-sen-te-ree/ *n* a disease of the bowels.

dysfunctional /**dis**-fung-shnal/ *adj* not functioning in what is considered the normal fashion (*a dysfunctional family*).

dyslexia /dis-**lek**-see-a/ *n* difficulty with reading and spelling caused by a slight disorder in the brain.

E

E, e /ee/ **1** the fifth letter of the alphabet. **2** (*mus*) the third note of the scale of C major.

each /eech/ *pron, adj* every one taken singly or separately (*each pupil is to bring money for the school trip/give a cake to each of the children*).

eager /ee-ger/ *adj* full of desire, keen (*eager to learn/eager pupils/eager for news*). ● *n* **eagerness**.

eagle /ee-gl/ *n* a large bird of prey.

eagle-eyed /ee-gl-eyed/ *adj* having very keen sight (*the eagle-eyed teacher saw the children exchange notes*).

eaglet /ee-glet/ *n* a young eagle.

ear[1] /eer/ *n* **1** the organ of hearing. **2** the ability to hear the difference between sounds (*a musical ear*). **3** attention (*have the president's ear*).

ear[2] /eer/ *n* a head or spike of corn.

earache /ee-rake/ *n* a pain in the ear.

eardrum /eer-drum/ *n* the tight skin across the inside of the ear that enables a person to hear sounds.

early /ur-lee/ *adj* **1** before the time arranged (*the baby's early arrival*). **2** near the beginning (*in the early part of the century*). **3** belonging to the first stages of development, etc. (*early musical instruments*). **4** (*fml*) soon (*we look forward to an early reply*). ● *adv* **1** near the beginning (of a period of time, etc.) (*early in the afternoon*). **2** sooner than usual, sooner than expected, sooner than often, etc. (*arrive early for work*).

earmark /eer-mark/ *vb* to set aside for a special purpose (*earmark some money for their children's education*).

earmuffs /eer-mufs/ *npl* pads that fit over the ears to keep them from getting cold (*earmuffs made from fake fur*).

earn /urn/ *vb* **1** to get money in return for work (*earn $30,000 per year*). **2** to deserve (*earn their respect*).

earnest /ur-nest/ *adj* **1** serious. **2** determined. ● *n* **earnestness** /ur-nest-ness/. ● **in earnest** meaning what one says (*they thought he was joking about leaving, but he was in earnest*).

earnings /ur-nings/ *npl* wages, money paid for work done (*pay tax on earnings*).

earring /ee-ring/ *n* an ornament worn on the ear.

earshot /eer-shot/ *n* the distance within which one can hear something (*be quiet—he's within earshot*).

earth /urth/ *n* **1** the planet on which we live (*people used to think that the earth was flat*). **2** the world as opposed to heaven (*heaven and earth*). **3** dry land, the ground or soil (*the earth, sea and sky/fill a plant pot with earth*). **4** the hole of a fox, badger, etc. **5** (*Br*) see **ground**. ● **earthen** /urth-en/ *adj*.

earthly /urth-tlee/ *adj* having to do with the world, of worldly rather than heavenly things (*earthly pleasures*).

earthquake /urth-kwake/ *n* a shaking movement of the surface of the earth.

earthwork /urth-wurk/ *n* a defensive wall of earth.

earthworm /urth-wurm/ *n* a worm (of the family *Lumbricidae*) that lives in the soil.

earthy /urth-ee/ *adj* **1** like, or of, earth (*an earthy smell*). **2** coarse, not refined (*earthy humor*).

ease /eez/ *n* **1** freedom from anxiety or pain (*a mind at ease*). **2** lack of difficulty (*do the job with ease*). **3** freedom from work, rest, comfort (*a life of ease*). **4** naturalness (*ease of manner*). ● *vb* **1** to lessen (*easing the pain/the pain has eased*). **2** to move gently or gradually (*ease the piano through the door*).

easel /ee-zel/ *n* a stand to hold a picture, blackboard, etc., upright (*an artist's easel*).

east /eest/ *n adj* and *adv* one of the four chief points of the compass, the direction in which the sun rises. ● *adjs* **eastern** /ee-stern/, **eastward** /eest-ward/. ● **the East** the countries of Asia.

Easter /ee-ster/ *n* a Christian festival that commemorates the rising of Christ from the dead.

easterly /ee-ster-lee/ *adj* from or toward the east (*easterly winds*).

easy /ee-zee/ *adj* **1** not difficult (*easy tasks/easy exams*). **2** free from anxiety or pain (*an easy mind*). **3** comfortable (*an easy life*). **4** relaxed, leisurely (*walk with an easy stride*).

easy-going /ee-zee-go-wing/ *adj* not easily worried or angered (*an easy-going mother who is not upset by her children's noise*).

eat /eet/ *vb* (*pt* **ate** /ate/, *pp* **eaten** /ee-ten/) **1** to chew and swallow, as food (*eat a lot of chocolate/eat only vegetarian food*). **2** to wear away (*acids eating metal*).

eating disorder /ee-ting-di-**sawr**-der/ *n* an emotional disorder in which the sufferer has an irrational attitude toward food.

eaves /eevz/ *npl* that part of the roof that comes out beyond the walls.

eavesdrop /eevz-drop/ *vb* (**eavesdropped** /eevz-dropt/, **eavesdropping** /eevz-drop-ing/) to try to hear what others are saying to each other privately (*find out their secrets by eavesdropping on their conversation/open the door suddenly and find her eavesdropping*). ● *n* **eavesdropper** /eevz-drop-er/.

ebb /eb/ *n* **1** the flowing back of the tide. **2** a falling away or weakening (*the ebb of the emperor's power*). ● *vb* **1** to flow back (*the tide ebbing*). **2** to grow less, weak, faint, etc. (*enthusiasm began to ebb*).

ebony /e-bu-nee/ *n* a hard black wood. ● *adj* **1** made of ebony (*the ebony keys on the piano*). **2** black (*an ebony skin*).

eccentric /ek-sen-tric/ *adj* **1** odd, strange (*an eccentric old woman/eccentric behavior*). **2** (*of circles*) not drawn round the same center. ● *n* a person who behaves in an odd or unusual manner (*one of the village's eccentrics*). ● *n* **eccentricity** /ek-sen-tri-si-tee/.

echo /e-co/ *n* (*pl* **echoes** /e-coaz/) **1** the repeating of a sound by the reflection of sound waves from a surface (*hear the echo in the cave*). **2** an imitation (*work that is an echo of Shakespeare*). ● *vb* **1** to repeat, to throw back a sound (*the cave echoed back his shout*). **2** to imitate (*echoing their leader's behavior*).

eclipse /e-clips/ *n* **1** the cutting off of the light from the sun by the moon coming between it and the earth. **2** the darkening of the face of the moon by the earth coming between it and the sun. **3** a failure caused by the unexpected success of another (*a writer who suffered an eclipse when younger writers gained popularity*). ● *vb* **1** to cut off the light from, to darken. **2** to make another seem inferior by outdoing (*eclipsing her husband as a painter/eclipsed by her beautiful talented sister*).

ecology /e-col-o-jee/ *n* **1** the science of the life of things in their physical surroundings (*study ecology*). **2** the relation of plants and living creatures to each other and to their surroundings (*pollution affecting the ecology of the area*). ● **ecological** *adj*.

e-commerce /ee-com-erse/ *n* electronic commerce, business conducted online.

economic /e-co-nom-ic/ *adj* **1** having to do with economics (*the government's economic policy*). **2** designed to give a profit (*charge an economic rent/not economic for the shop to open in the evening*).

economical /e-co-nom-i-cal/ *adj* careful of money, not wasteful (*an economical meal/be economical with cream in cooking*).

economics /e-co-nom-ics/ *n* the study of the means of increasing the wealth of a community or nation.

economist /e-con-o-mist/ *n* a person who studies economics.

economize, economise (*Br*) /e-con-o-mize/ *vb* to spend or use carefully, to save, to be economical (*economizing on gas by walking to work*).

economy /e-con-o-mee/ *n* **1** careful management of the wealth, money, goods, etc., of a home, business or country. **2** sparing use of money (*have to practice economy*).

ecosystem /e-co-sis-tem/ *n* all the plants and living creatures that live in an area and depend on one another together with their habitat (*The ecosystem of the lakeshore is being threatened by factory waste*).

ecstasy /ec-sta-see/ *n* great delight or joy (*religious ecstasy/be in ecstasies after her victory*).

ecstatic /ec-sta-tic/ *adj* delighted, carried away by joy (*ecstatic at the birth of their child/ecstatic players celebrated their win*).

eczema /ig-zee-ma/ *n* a skin disease.

eddy /ed-ee/ *n* a whirling current of water or air, a whirlpool or whirlwind (*eddies of mist on the mountain tops*). ● *vb* to move in eddies (*mist eddied round the mountaintops*).

Eden /ee-den/ *n* (in the Old Testament) the garden of Adam and Eve, paradise.

edge /edge/ *n* **1** the sharp side of a blade (*put an edge on the knife*). **2** a border or boundary (*the edge of the lake*). **3** keenness, sharpness (*a wit with an edge/add an edge to her appetite*). ● *vb* **1** to move gradually, especially with small sideways movements (*edged his way toward the front of the line/edging away from their angry mother*). **2** to put a border on (*edge a lawn with flowers/edge a handkerchief with lace*).

edgewise /edge-wize/ *adj* sideways (*get the wardrobe through the door edgewise*). ● *also* (*Br*) **edgeways**.

edging /e-jing/ *n* a border or fringe (*the edging on the woolen shawl*).

edible /ed-i-bl/ *adj* able or fit to be eaten (*food that is scarcely edible/edible berries*).

edit /e-dit/ *vb* to prepare for printing or publication (*edited a manuscript*).

edition /e-di-shun/ *n* the number of copies of a book

or newspaper published at one time (*the late edition of the newspaper*).

editor /e-di-tor/ *n* **1** a person who edits (*the editor of a manuscript*). **2** a person who collects the material for a newspaper or magazine and selects what is to be published or who is in charge of a newspaper or part of a newspaper (*a fashion editor*).

editorial /e-di-**toe**-ree-al/ *adj* of an editor. ● *n* an article by the editor or someone chosen by him or her on a matter of immediate interest (*an editorial on the country's economic situation*).

educate /e-ju-cate/ *vb* to teach or train (*educating children to the age of sixteen*). ● *n* **education** /e-ju-**cay**-shun/.

educational /e-ju-**cay**-shu-nal/ *adj* having to do with education (*educational opportunities*).

eel /eel/ *n* a snakelike fish.

eerie, eery /**ee**-ree/ *adj* strange and frightening (*eerie sounds in the night/the eerie feeling of a graveyard at night*).

effect /i-**fect**/ *n* **1** result, power to bring about a change (*a medicine that had little effect/angry words that had no effect on the child's behavior*). **2** impression (*flower arrangements creating a colorful effect*). **3** *pl* goods, property (*personal effects*). **4** *pl* lighting and sounds used in a play, film, etc. (*special effects in the horror film*). ● *vb* to bring about, to succeed in doing, to produce (*effecting a market change*).

effective /i-**fec**-tive/ *adj* **1** doing what is intended or desired, successful (*an effective cure*). **2** striking (*an effective use of color*). **3** actual, real (*in effective control of the film*). **4** in operation, working (*a new system of taxation effective from next week*).

effeminate /i-**fe**-mi-nit/ *adj* womanish, unmanly (*a man walking in an effeminate way*). ● *n* **effeminacy** /i-**fe**-mi-ni-see/.

effervesce /e-fer-**vess**/ *vb* to bubble or sparkle (*champagne effervescing in the glasses*). ● *n* **effervescence** /e-fer-**ve**-sense/.

effervescent /e-fer-**ve**-sent/ *adj* **1** bubbling, sparkling (*effervescent wine*). **2** lively and enthusiastic (*young people in an effervescent mood*).

efficient /e-fi-shent/ *adj* **1** able to do what is necessary or intended without wasting time, energy, etc. (*an efficient filing system*). **2** good at one's job, capable (*an efficient administrator*). ● *n* **efficiency** /e-fi-shen-see/.

effigy /e-fi-jee/ *n* **1** a likeness in the form of a picture, statue or carving (*stone effigies of Buddha*). **2** the head on a coin. **3** an imitation figure of a person (*burn an effigy of the dictator*).

effluent /e-floo-ent/ *adj* flowing out from. ● *n* **1** the discharge of liquid waste matter, sewage, etc. (*the effluent from the factory*). **2** a stream flowing from a larger stream. ● *n* **effluence** /e-floo-ense/.

effort /e-fort/ *n* **1** an energetic attempt (*make a real effort to arrive on time*). **2** the making use of strength or ability (*take a lot of effort to move the rock*).

effortless /e-fort-less/ *adj* with ease, without trying hard (*playing with effortless skill/what seemed an effortless victory*).

effusive /i-**fyoo**-siv/ *adj* expressing one's feelings too freely, pretending to feel more than one really feels (*an effusive welcome by the hostess*). ● *n* **effusiveness** /i-**fyoo**-siv-ness/.

egg /eg/ *n* **1** object, usually covered with a hard brittle shell, laid by a bird, reptile, etc., from which a young one is hatched. **2** such an object laid by the domestic hen used as food (*have a boiled egg for breakfast*). **3** in the female mammal, the cell from which the young is formed, the ovum.

egg on /eg-on/ *vb* to try to get somebody (to do something), to urge, to encourage (*egg his friend on to steal the apples*).

eggplant /eg-plant/ *n* a vegetable with a shiny, dark purple skin, often egg-shaped or long and pear-shaped, used in cooking.

ego /ee-go/ *n* **1** the image a person has of himself or herself. **2** self confidence to the point of being conceited, **egotism**.

egoism /ee-gu-i-zum/ *n* **1** selfishness, self-centeredness. **2** egotism. **3** a theory that states that self-interest is the foundation for morality.

egoist /ee-gu-wist/ *n* a selfish person, someone who believes in and practices egoism (*such an egoist that she sees things only from her point of view*). ● *adj* **egoistic** /ee-gu-**wiss**-tic/.

egotism /ee-go-tizm/ *n* **1** excessive talking about yourself. **2** and exaggerated opinion of yourself. **3** extreme selfishness.

egotist /ee-gu-tist/ *n* a person always talking of himself or herself (*he's such an egotist that he bores everyone with tales of his personal life*). ● *n* **egotism** /ee-gu-ti-zum/. ● *adjs* **egotistic** /ee-gu-ti-stic/, **egotistical** /ee-gu-**ti**-sti-cal/.

egress /ee-gress/ *n* **1** (*fml*) a way out (*two means of egress from the building*). **2** the right or power of going out (*no egress through his property*).

eider /ie-der/ *n* the Arctic duck.

eiderdown /ie-der-down/ *n* a warm bedcovering stuffed with the soft feathers of the eider.

either /ee-ther/ *pron* and *adj* one or other of two (*either book will do/either of the restaurants is suitable*).

eject /i-ject/ *vb* to throw out (*people employed to eject troublemakers from the club*).

ejection /i-jec-shun/ *n* **1** act of throwing out. **2** putting somebody out of a house rented by him or her (*the ejection of tenants for nonpayment of rent*).

elaborate /i-la-bo-rate/ *adj* **1** worked out with great care (*elaborate preparations*). **2** having many parts (*elaborate machines*). **3** very decorative (*an elaborate carving*). ● *vb* **1** to work out very carefully, to add to and improve upon (*elaborating their plans*). **2** to explain fully (*elaborate on what you said*). ● *n* **elaboration** /i-la-bo-ray-shun/.

elapse /ee-lapse/ *vb* (*fml*) (of time) to pass (*a few years had elapsed*).

elastic /ee-la-stic/ *adj* able to stretch or be stretched easily, but returning immediately to its former shape (*a skirt with an elastic waistband*). ● *n* **1** a rubber band. **2** a strip of material lined with rubber to make it elastic.

elasticity /ee-la-sti-si-tee/ *n* springiness.

elate /ee-late/ *vb* to make very glad or proud (*they were elated by the news of his victory*). ● *n* **elation** /ee-lay-shun/.

elated /ee-lay-ted/ *adj* to be filled with happiness or pride (*the elated parents watched their son graduate*).

elbow /el-bo/ *n* **1** the joint between the forearm and upper arm. **2** a sharp bend or corner (*an elbow in the pipe*). ● *vb* to push with the elbow.

elder[1] /el-der/ *adj* older (*a younger sister and an elder brother*). ● *n* **1** an older member of a community (*the elders of the tribe*). **2** an official in certain Christian churches (e.g., the Presbyterian).

elder[2] /el-der/ *n* a small tree with purple berries.

elderly /el-der-lee/ *adj* old, getting old (*seats reserved for elderly people*).

eldest /el-dest/ *adj* oldest (*her eldest daughter*).

elect /i-lect/ *vb* **1** (*fml*) to choose (*elect to go by train*). **2** to choose by voting (*elect a new president*). ● *adj* chosen. ● *n* **1** those chosen. **2** those chosen by God.

election /i-lec-shun/ *n* act of choosing, especially by vote (*a presidential election*).

elector /i-lec-tor/ *n* a person with the right to vote (*politicians trying to convince the electors*).

electoral /i-lec-tu-ral/ *adj* having to do with electors (*the electoral roll*).

electorate /i-lec-tu-rit/ *n* all those having the right to vote on a certain occasion (*a high proportion of the electorate do not bother to vote*).

electric /i-lec-tric/ *adj* **1** having to do with electricity. **2** exciting, thrilling (*an electric performance*). ● *npl* **electrics** electric fittings.

electrical /i-lec-tri-cal/ *adj* having to do with electricity, worked by electricity.

electrician /i-lec-tri-shun/ *n* a person who works with electricity or electrical apparatus.

electricity /i-lec-tri-si-tee/ *n* an energy produced by chemical or other action, a natural force that can be harnessed to give heat, light and power.

electrify /i-lec-tri-faee/ *vb* **1** to put electricity into (*electrify the railway line*). **2** to thrill (*electrified by the orchestra's performance*).

electrocute /i-lec-tri-cyoot/ *vb* to kill by electricity (*in some states convicted murderers are electrocuted*). ● *n* **electrocution** /i-lec-tri-cyoo-shun/.

electrode /i-lec-trode/ *n* either of the two conductors through which electricity enters or leaves something, such as a battery.

electron /i-lec-tron/ *n* the negative electrical unit in an atom.

electronic /i-lec-tron-ic/ *adj* of a device, having many small parts, such as microchips and transistors, which control and direct an electric current (*an electronic calculator*).

electronics /i-lec-tron-ics/ *n* the branch of technology that is concerned with electronic devices such as computers and televisions.

elegant /e-le-gant/ *adj* **1** graceful, smart, stylish (*an elegant woman/an elegant suit*). **2** stylish, polished (*an elegant style of writing*). ● *n* **elegance** /e-le-ganse/.

elegy /e-le-jee/ *n* a mourning or sorrowful poem.

element /e-le-ment/ *n* **1** a necessary part (*have all the elements of a good crime novel/a sensible economic policy is a vital element of government*). **2** a substance that cannot be broken down into any other substances and from which all other things are made up (*elements such as hydrogen*). **3** *pl* knowledge without which a subject cannot be properly understood (*fail to grasp the elements of mathematics*). **4** *pl* **elements** nature, the weather (*exposed to the elements without shelter*).

elemental /e-le-men-tal/ *adj* **1** having to do with

elements, like the powers of nature (*the elemental forces of nature*). **2** basic (*elemental truths*).

elementary /e-le-**men**-tu-ree/ *adj* **1** having to do with the beginning (*elementary steps in mathematics*). **2** simple, easy (*elementary questions*).

elephant /e-le-fant/ *n* a large very thick-skinned animal with a trunk and ivory tusks. ● **white elephant** a gift or purchase that turns out to be of no use, a useless possession that is troublesome to keep up or retain (*that dresser we bought is a real white elephant—we've no space to keep it*).

elevate /e-le-vate/ *vb* **1** (*fml*) to make finer, better, more educated, etc. (*elevating the minds of his pupils*). **2** to raise to a higher place or rank (*elevated him to the rank of captain*).

elevation /e-le-**vay**-shun/ *n* **1** the act of raising. **2** (*fml*) a hill (*from an elevation above the city*). **3** height (*at an elevation of 1500 meters*). **4** a plan showing a building as seen from one side. **5** the angle measuring height.

elevator /e-le-vay-tor/ *n* a platform or cage for carrying people and goods to different levels (*take the elevator to the top floor*).

eleven /i-le-ven/ *n* the number that is one more than ten. ● *adj* **eleventh** /i-le-venth/.

elf /elf/ *n* (*pl* **elves** /elvz/) in fairy tales, a mischievous fairy. ● *adjs* **elfin** /el-fin/, **elfish** /el-fish/, **elvish** /el-vish/.

eligible /e-li-ji-bl/ *adj* able to be chosen, suitable (*eligible for the post/an eligible bachelor*). ● *n* **eligibility** /e-li-ji-**bi**-le-tee/.

eliminate /i-li-mi-nate/ *vb* to get rid of (*eliminating him from our list of suspects/eliminate errors from the manuscript*). ● *n* **elimination** /i-li-mi-**nay**-shun/.

elite /i-**leet**/ *n* a group that is at a higher level or rank, professionally, socially or in ability, etc. (*the elite of the tennis club/the elite of Boston society*).

elixir /i-**lik**-sir/ *n* (*old*) a magic liquid that, alchemists believed, could change any metal into gold, or enable people to live forever.

elk /elk/ *n* a type of large deer.

ellipse /i-**lips**/ *n* an oval figure.

elm /elm/ *n* a type of tree.

elongate /i-**long**-gate/ *vb* **1** to make longer (*figures in the painting that are too elongated*). **2** to stretch out (*feel that the speaker had unnecessarily elongated his speech*). ● *n* **elongation** /ee-long-**gay**-shun/.

elope /i-**lope**/ *vb* to leave home secretly with one's lover (*decided to elope when their parents forbade them to marry*). ● *n* **elopement** /i-**lope**-ment/.

eloquent /e-lo-kwent/ *adj* **1** able to speak well, especially in public and express one's ideas and opinions effectively (*an eloquent speaker*). **2** showing or using such an ability (*an eloquent appeal to possible blood donors*). ● *n* **eloquence** /e-lo-kwense/.

else /elss/ *adj* **1** besides, also (*what else did he say?/who else spoke?*). **2** other than that already mentioned (*someone else/decide to live somewhere else*).

elsewhere /elss-where/ *adv* in another place (*unhappy in his job and applying for jobs elsewhere*).

elude /i-**lood**/ *vb* **1** to escape or avoid by quickness, cleverness or trickery (*a criminal who has eluded the police for many years*). **2** to be difficult, etc., to understand or remember (*a name that eludes me/a cure for cancer that has eluded the researchers*).

elusive /i-**loo**-siv/ *adj* **1** hard to remember, express, identify, etc. (*an elusive perfume*). **2** hard to catch or track down (*elusive criminals*).

elves, **elvish** *see* **elf**.

email, **e-mail** /ee-male/ *n* **1** electronic mail, a system for sending communications from one computer to another, using a telephone connection and a modem. **2** a message sent by email. ● *vb* to send (a message) by email (*email the list of club members*).

emanate /e-ma-nate/ *vb* (*fml*) to come from (*interesting smells emanating from the kitchen/information emanating from an unknown source*). ● *n* **emanation** /e-ma-**nay**-shun/.

emancipate /i-**man**-si-pate/ *vb* to free from control (*emancipate from slavery*). ● *n* **emancipation** /i-man-si-**pay**-shun/.

embalm /im-**balm**/ *vb* to preserve a dead body with spices.

embankment /im-**bank**-ment/ *n* a mound of stones and earth built to shut in a river or to carry a road, railway, etc., over low ground.

embargo /im-**bar**-go/ *n* (*pl* **embargoes** /im-**bar**-goaz/) an official order forbidding something, especially trade with another country (*put an embargo on trade with countries practicing racism*).

embark /im-**bark**/ *vb* **1** to put or go on board ship. **2** to start (upon) (*embarking on a new career*). ● *n* **embarkation** /im-bar-**kay**-shun/.

embarrass /im-**ba**-ras/ *vb* **1** to cause to feel shy or uncomfortable (*embarrass her by paying her compliments*). **2** to involve in difficulties (*find himself financially embarrassed*). ● *n* **embarrassment** /im-**ba**-ras-ment/.

embassy /em-ba-see/ *n* **1** the duties of an ambassador. **2** the house of an ambassador. **3** a group of people sent by a country to act for it in another country.

embed /im-**bed**/ *vb* to fix firmly and deeply into something (*the stone was embedded in his foot/the instructions were embedded in her brain*).

embers /**em**-berz/ *npl* **1** live cinders of a dying fire (*stare into the embers of the fire*). **2** the fading remains (*trying to rekindle the embers of their love*).

embezzle /im-**be**-zul/ *vb* to steal money that one has been trusted with by other people. ● *n* **embezzlement** /im-**be**-zul-ment/.

embitter /im-**bi**-ter/ *vb* to make someone feel bitter, to increase anger or hatred (*embittered by the disloyalty of his followers*).

emblem /**em**-blem/ *n* an object that is regarded as a sign of something (*the dove is the emblem of peace*). ● *adjs* **emblematic** /em-ble-ma-tic/, **emblematical** /em-ble-ma-ti-cal/.

embodiment /em-**bod**-ee-ment/ *n* a living example (*he is the embodiment of the old-fashioned gentleman/the embodiment of politeness*).

embody /em-**bod**-ee/ *vb* **1** to give a solid form to, to express in a real or physical form (*a country's constitution that embodies the principles of freedom*). **2** to include (*a computer system embodying many new features*).

embolden /em-**bole**-den/ *vb* to give courage, to make bold (*emboldened by the silence they moved forward*).

emboss /im-**boss**/ *vb* to make a raised pattern on (*embossing leather with a pattern/with the firm's name and address embossed on the writing paper*).

embrace /im-**brase**/ *vb* **1** to hold in the arms, to hug (*embracing his wife fondly*). **2** to include (*a speech that embraced many topics*). ● *n* a holding in the arms, a hug (*a farewell embrace*).

embroider /im-**broy**-der/ *vb* **1** to decorate with needlework (*embroidering a handkerchief with a border of roses*). **2** to add interesting or exaggerated details to a story (*embroidered the account of his unhappy childhood*).

embroidery /im-**broy**-de-ree/ *n* **1** the art of decorating with needlework. **2** the act of adding interesting or exaggerated detail to. **3** decorative needlework.

embryo /**em**-bree-oe/ *n* **1** the form of any creature before it is born or grows (*an egg containing the embryo of a chicken*). **2** the beginning stage of anything (*plans that are yet in embryo*).

emerald /**em**-rald/ *n* a bright green precious stone. ● *adj* bright green (*an emerald dress*).

emerge /i-**merge**/ *vb* **1** to come out (*swimmers emerging from the water*). **2** to become known (*facts beginning to emerge/it emerged that she had been in prison*). ● *n* **emergence** /i-**mer**-jense/. ● *adj* **emergent** /i-**mer**-jent/.

emergency /i-**mer**-jen-see/ *n* a state of affairs requiring immediate action (*call 911 in an emergency/use one's savings only in an emergency*).

emery /**em**-ree/ *n* a very hard mineral, made into powder and used for polishing or sharpening metals.

emigrant /**e**-mi-grant/ *n* a person who emigrates. ● *also adj*.

emigrate /**e**-mi-grate/ *vb* to leave one's country and go to live in another (*emigrating to find work overseas*). ● *n* **emigration** /e-mi-**gray**-shun/.

eminence /**e**-mi-nense/ *n* **1** (*fml*) a high place, a hill (*the view from the eminence above the town*). **2** fame (*achieve eminence as an artist*). **3** the title given to a cardinal in the Roman Catholic Church.

eminent /**e**-mi-nent/ *adj* distinguished, very well-known (*one of our most eminent writers*).

emit /e-**mit**/ *vb* (**emitted** /e-mi-ted/, **emitting** /e-mi-ting/) to send or give out (*chimneys emitting smoke/emit a cry of pain*). ● *n* **emission** /e-mi-shun/.

emotion /i-**mo**-shun/ *n* **1** strong or deep feeling (*an emotion such as love or hate*). **2** the moving or upsetting of the mind or feelings (*overcome by emotion*).

emotional /i-**mo**-she-nal/ *adj* **1** of the emotions (*emotional problems*). **2** causing or showing deep feelings (*an emotional farewell*). **3** easily moved by emotion (*a very emotional person*).

empathy /**em**-path-ee/ *n* the ability to imagine oneself in another's situation (*I felt empathy for what he was going through*). ● *vb* **empathize** /**em**-path-ize/, *also* **empathise** (*Br*).

emperor /**em**-pe-ror/ *n* the ruler of an empire. ● *f* **empress** /**em**-press/.

emphasis /**em**-fa-sis/ *n* (*pl* **emphases** /**em**-fa-seez/) **1** the added force with which certain words or parts of words are spoken (*place the emphasis on the first syllable*). **2** special meaning, value, importance, etc. (*the emphasis in the firm is on efficiency*).

emphasize /**em**-fa-size/ *vb, also* **emphasise** (*Br*) **1** to say with emphasis (*emphasizing the first syllable of the word*). **2** to call attention to specially, to stress (*emphasized the trustworthiness of his friends*).

emphatic /im-**fa**-tic/ *adj* forceful, firm and definite (*an emphatic denial*).

empire /**em**-pire/ *n* **1** a group of countries under the rule of one of their number. **2** a large industrial organization controlling many firms (*a fast-food empire*).

employ /im-**ploy**/ *vb* **1** to give work to (*a firm employing hundreds of factory workers*). **2** to use (*employed tact*).

employee, employee /im-**ploy**-ee/ *n* a person paid to work for another person or for a firm (*sack several employees*).

employer /im-**ploy**-er/ *n* a person who gives work to another.

employment /im-**ploy**-ment/ *n* job, occupation (*seek employment in industry*).

emporium /im-**po**-ree-um/ *n* (*pl* **emporia** /im-**po**-ree-ya/ *or* **emporiums** /im-**po**-ree-umz/) **1** a market. **2** a large store in which many different kinds of things are sold.

empower /im-**pou**-wer/ *vb* to give the right or power to (*police empowered to stop and search cars*).

empress *see* **emperor**.

empty /**em**-tee/ *adj* having nothing inside (*empty barrels/empty shops*). ● *vb* **1** to take everything out of (*empty the bottle/empty the cupboard*). **2** to become empty (*shops emptying at closing time*). ● *n* **emptiness** /**em**-tee-ness/.

emu /**ee**-myoo/ *n* a large Australian flightless bird.

emulate /**em**-yoo-late/ *vb* (*fml*) to try to be as good as or better than (*try to emulate his elder brother on the football field*).

emulation /em-yoo-**lay**-shun/ *n* act of emulating, rivalry.

emulsion /i-**mul**-shun/ *n* a mixture of two liquids that remain separate until shaken up (e.g., oil and vinegar).

enable /i-**nay**-bl/ *vb* to give the power or means to do something (*more money enabling the firm to expand*).

enact /i-**nact**/ *vb* **1** to lay down by law, to pass a law (*laws enacted in Congress*). **2** to act, perform (*enact scenes from Shakespeare*).

enamel /i-**na**-mel/ *n* **1** a smooth, glossy coating put on metals or wood to preserve or decorate them. **2** the outer covering of the teeth. ● *vb* (**enamelled** /i-**na**-meld/, **enamelling** /i-**na**-mel-ing/) to cover with enamel.

encase /in-**case**/ *vb* to put in a case or covering (*encasing the broken leg in plaster*).

enchant /in-**chant**/ *vb* **1** (*old*) to put a magic spell on (*the enchanted wood*). **2** to delight (*children enchanted by the ballet*). ● *n* **enchanter** /in-**chan**-ter/. ● *f* **enchantress** /in-**chan**-tress/. ● *n* **enchantment** /in-**chant**-ment/.

encircle /in-**sir**-cl/ *vb* to surround (*a field encircled by trees/troops encircling the enemy*). ● *n* **encirclement** /in-**sir**-cl-ment/.

enclose /in-**cloaz**/ *vb* **1** to shut in, to fence in (*enclosing the garden within a wall*). **2** to send with a letter (*enclose an application form*).

enclosure /in-**cloa**-zher/ *n* **1** a space shut or fenced in (*an enclosure for ponies*). **2** something sent with a letter (*a check sent as an enclosure*).

encompass /in-**cum**-pass/ *vb* **1** to surround. **2** to include or comprise (*a course encompassing a wide range of subjects*).

encore /**on**-core *or* **ong**-core/ *adv* again, once more. ● *n* **1** a call to a performer to repeat something or perform something else. **2** the repetition of part of a performance or a further performance by the same person or people given after the main performance. ● *also vb*.

encounter /in-**coun**-ter/ *n* **1** a meeting, especially an unexpected one (*a brief encounter with an old friend*). **2** a fight or quarrel (*an encounter between the opposing armies*). ● *vb* to meet (*encountered her ex-husband in the street/encountering several problems*).

encourage /in-**cu**-rage/ *vb* **1** to make bold (*their victory encouraged the troops*). **2** to urge on (*encouraging the pupils to stay on at school*). ● *n* **encouragement** /in-**cu**-rage-ment/.

encyclopedia /in-sie-clo-**pee**-dee-a/ *n* , **encyclopaedia** (*Br, Cdn*) a book or set of books containing information about every subject or about every branch of one subject.

encyclopedic /in-sie-clo-**pe**-dic/ *adj* very detailed or complete (*encyclopedic knowledge*).

end /end/ *n* **1** the last part of anything (*the end of the book/the end of the journey*). **2** death (*meet a violent end*). **3** purpose or aim (*with this end in view/strive toward such an end*). ● *vb* to bring or come to an end (*ending his life/the book ends happily*).

endanger /in-**dane**-jer/ *vb* to put someone or something in a dangerous or harmful situation (*endanger their health by smoking*). ● **endangered** /in-**dane**-jerd/ *adj* in danger or at risk, especially of ceasing to exist (*trying to conserve an endangered species*).

endear /in-**deer**/ *n* to make dear (*she endeared herself to him by being kind to his mother*).

endeavor /in-**dev**-ur/ *vb, also* **endeavour** (*Br, Cdn*) to try, to try hard (*endeavoring to win*). ● *n* attempt, effort (*make every endeavor to succeed*).

endemic /in-**dem**-ic/ *adj* found specially among one people or in one place (*endemic diseases*).

endless /**end**-less/ *adj* **1** having no end (*an endless conveyor belt*). **2** seemingly having no end (*the endless noise*).

endorse /in-**dorss**/ *vb* **1** to sign one's name on the back of a check or document. **2** to express approval or support (*his proposals endorsed by the committee/endorsing the new product*). ● *n* **endorsement** /in-**dorss**-ment/.

endow /in-**dow**/ *vb* **1** to provide with a permanent income. **2** to give, to grant (*endowed with great charm*). ● *n* **endowment** /in-**dow**-ment/.

endurance /in-**joo**-ranse/ *n* the ability to endure or bear patiently (*the marathon race is a test of endurance/bear pain with endurance*).

endure /in-**joor**/ *vb* **1** (*fml*) to last (*houses built to endure*). **2** to bear patiently (*enduring a lot of pain*). **3** to put up with (*hard to endure noisy neighbors*).

enemy /**e**-ne-mee/ *n* **1** a person who is unfriendly, someone who acts against another (*make a lot of enemies in business*). **2** those with whom one is at war (*form an alliance against the enemy*). ● *also adj*.

energetic /e-ner-**je**-tic/ *adj* active, powerful, vigorous.

energize /**e**-ner-jize/ *vb, also* **energise** (*Br*) to give energy to (*healthy food energizing him*).

energy /**e**-ner-jee / *n* active power, force, vigor (*set about the work with energy/lack energy since her illness*).

enforce /in-**foarss**/ *n* to cause to be obeyed or carried out (*police enforcing traffic laws*). ● *n* **enforcement** /in-**foarss**-ment/.

engage /in-**gage**/ *vb* **1** (*fml*) to bind oneself by a promise, to promise (*engage to pay the money back in installments*). **2** to begin to employ (*engaging a gardener*). **3** to begin fighting (*the armies engaged at dawn*). **4** to busy (oneself) with (*engage oneself in household activities*). **5** to attract and keep (*engaging the child's attention*).

engaging /in-**gay**-jing/ *adj* pleasing, attractive (*an engaging smile*).

engagement /in-**gage**-ment/ *n* **1** (*fml*) a written agreement (*unable to meet all his financial engagements*). **2** a promise to marry (*announce their engagement*). **3** an arrangement to meet someone, an appointment (*a previous engagement*). **4** a battle (*an engagement that ended the war*).

engine /**in**-jin/ *n* **1** a machine that produces power (*a car engine*). **2** a railway locomotive.

engineer /in-ji-**neer**/ *n* **1** a person who looks after engines. **2** a person who makes or designs machinery, roads, bridges, etc. **3** a person who drives a railway locomotive. ● *vb* to arrange for or cause something to happen, usually by clever, cunning or secret means (*engineered a surprise party for her birthday/engineering his son's promotion*).

engineering /in-ji-**nee**-ring/ *n* the science of making and using machines.

engrave /in-**grave**/ *vb* **1** to cut or carve on metal, stone, wood, etc. (*engraving his name on the trophy that he won/engrave flowers on the table top*). **2** to cut a picture on a metal plate in order to print copies of it.

engraving /in-**gray**-ving/ *n* a print from an engraved plate.

engross /in-**grose**/ *vb* to take up one's whole time or attention (*children engrossed by the film*). ● *n* **engrossment** /in-**grose**-ment/.

engulf /in-**gulf**/ *vb* to swallow up (*a flood that threatened to engulf the town/people engulfed with grief*).

enhance /in-**hanse**/ *vb* to increase in amount, value, importance, etc., to increase, to improve (*qualifications enhancing her job prospects/a color that enhanced her beauty*). ● *n* **enhancement** /in-**hanse**-ment/.

enigma /in-**nig**-ma/ *n* a person or thing that is difficult to understand, a mystery (*we've known her for years, but she is still a bit of an enigma to us/his background is an enigma to us*).

enigmatic /in-nig-ma-tic/, **enigmatical** /in-nig-ma-ti-cal/ *adjs* having to do with an enigma, mysterious (*an enigmatic smile*).

enjoy /in-**joy**/ *vb* **1** to take pleasure in (*enjoy reading/enjoying a walk in the hills*). **2** to possess (*enjoy good health/enjoy a comfortable income*). ● *adj* **enjoyable** /in-**joy**-a-bl/. ● *n* **enjoyment** /in-**joy**-ment/.

enlarge /in-**large**/ *vb* **1** (*fml*) to make larger (*enlarging the lawn*). **2** to reproduce (a photograph) on a larger scale. **3** to talk at length about (*enlarge on his previous comments*).

enlargement /in-**large**-ment/ *n* **1** act of making larger. **2** a larger copy of a photograph.

enlighten /in-**lite**-en/ *vb* (*fml*) to give more and correct information or knowledge about (*enlighten me as to the cause of the fire*). ● *n* **enlightenment** /in-**lite**-en-ment/.

enlist /in-**list**/ *vb* **1** to join the armed forces. **2** to obtain support (*enlist friends to help paint the house*). **3** to obtain from (*enlist help from the neighbors*). ● *n* **enlistment** /in-**list**-ment/.

enliven /in-**lie**-ven/ *vb* to brighten, to cheer (*enliven a dull party*).

enormity /i-**nawr**-mi-tee/ *n* **1** immensity (*the enormity of the task*). **2** a great wickedness (*the enormity of the crime*). **3** a crime, an act of great wickedness (*enormities committed during the war*).

enormous /i-**nawr**-mus/ *adj* huge, very large (*an enormous creature/enormous sums of money*).

enough /i-**nuf**/ *adj* as many or as much as is required (*enough food for the four of them*). ● *n* a sufficient amount (*I have eaten enough*).

enquire *see* **inquire**.

enrage /in-**rage**/ *vb* to make very angry (*enraged by the child's impertinence*).

enrapture /in-**rap**-chur/ *n* (*fml*) to fill with delight (*enraptured by the dancer's performance*).

enrich /in-**rich**/ *vb* **1** to make rich (*a country enriched by its oil resources*). **2** to improve greatly in quality (*enriching the soil/enrich the mind*). ● *n* **enrichment** /in-**rich**-ment/.

enroll /in-**role**/ *vb* (**enrolled** /in-**roald**/, **enrolling** /in-**role**-ing/) **1** to write (a name) in a list (*enroll her daughter in the ballet class*). **2** to join or become a member (*decide to enroll in the aerobics class*). ● *n* **enrolment** /in-**role**-ment/.

ensemble /on-**som**-bul/ *n* **1** a group of musicians regularly performing together (*a woodwind ensemble*). **2** clothing made up of several items, an outfit (*wear a green ensemble to the wedding*). **3** all the parts of a thing taken as a whole (*the furniture of the room forms a pleasing ensemble*).

enslave /in-**slave**/ *vb* (*fml*) to make a slave of (*enslaved by her beauty*).

ensue /in-**soo**/ *vb* to follow upon, to result from (*the fire and the panic that ensued*).

ensure /in-**shoor**/ *vb* to make sure (*he ensured that the family was well provided for/ensuring their success*).

entail /in-**tale**/ *vb* **1** to leave land or property to be passed down through a succession of heirs. **2** to

make necessary, to involve (*a post that entails a lot of hard work*). ● *n* land or property so left.

entangle /in-**tang**-gul/ *vb* **1** to cause to become twisted, tangled or caught (*a bird entangled in wire netting/a long scarf entangled in the rose bushes*). **2** to get into difficulties or complications (*become entangled in an unhappy love affair*).

entanglement /in-**tang**-gul-ment/ *n* a difficult situation, involvement (*his entanglement with the police*).

enter /**en**-ter/ *vb* **1** to go or come into (*entered the building by the back door*). **2** to become a member of (*enter politics*). **3** to put down in writing (*entering the money spent*).

enterprise /**en**-ter-prize/ *n* **1** an undertaking or project, especially one that is difficult or daring (*a new business enterprise*). **2** willingness to take risks or to try out new ideas (*show enterprise by starting their own business*).

enterprising /**en**-ter-prie-zing/ *adj* having or showing enterprise (*an enterprising young man/an enterprising scheme*).

entertain /**en**-ter-tane/ *vb* **1** to receive as a guest (*entertain them in your own home*). **2** to please, to amuse (*a magician to entertain the children at the birthday party*). **3** (*fml*) to consider (*refuse to entertain the idea*).

entertainment /**en**-ter-tane-ment/ *n* **1** the act of entertaining (*the entertainment of dinner guests/ the entertainment of children at the party*). **2** amusement (*children seeking entertainment*). **3** something that entertains, such as a public performance (*a musical entertainment*).

enthrall /in-**thrawl**/ *vb* (**enthralled** /in-**thrawld**/, **enthralling** /in-**thraw**-ling/) to delight, to enchant (*enthralled by her performance*).

enthrone /in-**throne**/ *vb* (*fml*) to place on a throne (*enthroning the new king*). ● *n* **enthronement** / en-**throne**-ment/.

enthuse /in-**thooz**/ *vb* to be, become or cause to be enthusiastic, to show enthusiasm (*enthusing over the new fashions*).

enthusiasm /in-**thoo**-zee-a-zum/ *n* great eagerness, keenness (*show no enthusiasm for the new scheme/play the game with great enthusiasm*).

enthusiast /in-**thoo**-zee-ast/ *n* a person who is very keen (*a baseball enthusiast*).

enthusiastic /in-thoo-zee-a-stic/ *adj* full of enthusiasm (*enthusiastic about the new house/enthusiastic theatergoers*).

entice /in-**tice**/ *vb* to tempt, to attract by offering something (*enticing the child into his car by giving her sweets*). ● *n* **enticement** /in-**tice**-ment/. ● *adj* **enticing** /in-**tice**-ing/.

entire /in-**tire**/ *adj* whole, complete (*paint the entire house/spend her entire fortune*). ● *adv* **entirely** /in-**tire**-lee/.

entirety /in-**tie**-ri-tee/ *n* completeness.

entitle /in-**tite**-ul/ *vb* **1** to give a right to (*a ticket entitling us to attend the exhibition*). **2** to give a name to (*a book entitled "Green Dragons"*).

entity /**en**-ti-tee/ *n* **1** existence. **2** anything that exists (*separate political entities*).

entrails /**en**-traylz/ *npl* the bowels, the internal organs of the body (*a sheep's entrails*).

entrance[1] /in-**transe**/ *vb* to delight, to fill with wonder (*children entranced by the lights on the Christmas tree*).

entrance[2] /**en**-transe/ *n* **1** coming or going in (*applaud the entrance of the actor*). **2** a place by which one enters (e.g., a door or gate) (*the side entrance of the building*).

entrant /**en**-trant/ *n* a person who puts his or her name in for or joins (*entrants in the race/the youngest entrant won the competition*).

entrap /in-**trap**/ *vb* (**entrapped** /in-**trapt**/, **entrapping** /in-**tra**-ping/) to catch in a trap or by a trick.

entreat /in-**treet**/ *vb* (*fml*) to ask earnestly (*entreat her to help him*).

entreaty /in-**tree**-tee/ *n* an earnest request (*the tyrant refused to listen to her entreaties for mercy*).

entrée /on-**tray**/ *n* a main course at dinner.

entrench /in-**trench**/ *vb* **1** to dig ditches around, thus putting oneself in a strong position (*with the enemy army entrenched across the river*). **2** to establish firmly or in a strong position (*entrenched in that job for years/entrenched in old-fashioned ideas and attitudes*).

entrust /in-**trust**/ *vb* to give into the care of (*entrust her children to him*).

entry /**en**-tree/ *n* **1** act of entering (*try to gain entry to the locked building/their country's entry into the war*). **2** a way in (*the entry to the apartment block*). **3** something written in a diary, cash book, etc. (*read out the entry for yesterday*).

enunciate /i-**nun**-see-ate/ *vb* to speak or state, to pronounce in a distinct way (*enunciating his words clearly*). ● *n* **enunciation** /i-nun-see-**ay**-shun/.

envelop /in-**ve**-lop/ *vb* to cover or surround completely (*mountains enveloped in mist/a long coat enveloping a small figure*).

envelope /**en**-ve-lope/ *n* **1** a wrapper or cover, especially one made of paper for a letter (*address the envelope*).

enviable /**en**-vee-a-bl/ *adj* causing envy, very desirable (*an enviable lifestyle*).

envious /**en**-vee-us/ *adj* full of envy, jealous (*friends envious of her achievement/envious neighbors looking at her new car*).

environment /in-**vie**-ron-ment/ *n* **1** surroundings. **2** all the conditions and surroundings that influence human character. **3** the natural world in which people, animals and plants live (*pollution affecting the environment*). ● **environmental** /in-vie-ron-**men**-tal/ *adj*.

envisage /in-**vi**-zage/ *vb* (*fml*) to picture to oneself (*I could not envisage myself agreeing to such a plan/impossible to envisage him as a young man*).

envoy /**en**-voy/ *n* a messenger, especially one sent to speak for his or her government in another country (*envoys sent to discuss a peace treaty with France*).

envy /**en**-vee/ *n* **1** a feeling of discontent caused by someone else's good fortune or success, especially when one would like these for oneself (*try to hide their envy at his winning the medal/his success arousing envy/look with envy at her new car*). **2** something that causes envy (*a dress that was the envy of her friends*). ● *vb* to feel envy toward or at (*envy him his good luck/envy her lifestyle*).

eon see **aeon**.

epaulette /e-pu-**let**/ *n* a flap of material, sometimes of another color, worn on the shoulder of a uniform jacket (*a soldier's epaulettes*).

ephemeral /i-**fem**-ral/ *adj* lasting for only a short time (*ephemeral pleasures/ephemeral fashions in dress*).

epic /**e**-pic/ *n* **1** a long poem telling of heroic deeds (*Homer's Iliad is a famous epic*). **2** a story, movie, etc., dealing with heroic deeds and exciting adventures (*watch an epic about the Roman empire*). ● *adj* of or like an epic, heroic, in the grand style (*an epic journey*).

epidemic /e-pi-**dem**-ic/ *n* a disease or condition that attacks many people at the same time (*an epidemic of influenza/a measles epidemic*).

epilepsy /**e**-pi-lep-see/ *n* a disease causing fits of unconsciousness and sudden attacks of uncontrolled movements of the body. ● *adj* and *n* **epileptic**.

epilog /**e**-pi-log/ *n, also* **epilogue** (*Br Cdn*) **1** a speech addressed to the audience at the end of a play (*the epilogue in Hamlet*). **2** a part or section added at the end of a book, program, etc. *See also* **prolog.**

Epiphany /e-pi-fa-nee/ *n* the Christian festival that commemorates the revealing of Jesus Christ to the Magi, or three wise men from the East.

episode /e-pi-soad/ *n* **1** a particular event or a series of events that is separate from but forms part of a larger whole (*enjoy the episode in the novel where the hero meets an elephant/episodes in her youth that she wants to forget*). **2** a part of a radio or television serial that is broadcast at one time (*miss last week's episode*).

episodic /e-pi-**sod**-ic/ *adj* consisting of events not clearly connected with one another.

epitaph /e-pi-taf/ *n* words referring to a dead person, inscribed on his or her tombstone.

epitome /i-**pi**-to-mee/ *n* **1** a person or thing that is a perfect example of a quality, type, etc. (*she is the epitome of kindness/he is the epitome of the perfect gentleman*). **2** something that in a small way perfectly represents a larger or wider idea, issue, etc. (*the family's hardship was the epitome of the poverty affecting the whole country*). **3** (*fml*) a summary, an abstract (*an epitome of the talks given at the conference*).

epitomize /i-**pi**-to-mize/ *vb, also* **epitomise** (*Br*) **1** to be an epitome of (*he epitomizes the computer nerd/the downturn epitomizes the country's economic problems*). **2** (*fml*) to summarize, to describe briefly (*epitomizing the lecture in a few paragraphs*).

epoch /e-pok/ *n* **1** a period of time in history, life, etc., especially one in which important events occurred (*an epoch characterized by wars*). **2** the start of such a period.

equal /ee-kwal/ *adj* **1** the same in size, number, value, etc. (*earn an equal amount of money*). **2** able (to do something) (*not equal to the task*). ● *n* a person the same as another in rank or ability (*her intellectual equal*). ● *vb* (**equalled** /ee-kwald/, **equalling** /ee-kwa-ling/) to be equal to (*sales figures that equal last year's*).

equality /i-**kwol**-i-tee/ *n* the state of being equal (*fighting for equality of women in salary scales/seeking racial equality*).

equalize /ee-kwol-ize/ *vb, also* **equalise** (*Br*) to make or become equal (*the home team equalized*).

equate /i-kwate/ *vb* **1** to state that certain things are equal. **2** to think of as equal or the same (*equating financial success with happiness*).

equation /i-**kway**-zhun/ *n* a statement that two things are equal (*a mathematical equation*).

equator /i-**kway**-tor/ *n* an imaginary line round the earth, halfway between the poles.

equatorial /i-kwa-**toe**-ree-al/ *adj* **1** having to do with the equator (*an equatorial climate*). **2** on or near the equator (*the equatorial rain forest*).

equi- /e-kwee/ *prefix* equal.

equilateral /ee-kwi-**la**-te-ral/ *adj* having all sides equal (*equilateral triangle*).

equilibrium /ee-kwi-**li**-bree-um/ *n* **1** a balance between equal weights (*scale in equilibrium*). **2** steadiness (*a disease of the ear affecting his equilibrium*). **3** balanced state of the mind, emotions, etc. (*try to maintain his equilibrium in a difficult situation*).

equinox /ee-kwi-noks/ *n* either of the two times in the year at which the sun crosses the equator and day and night are equal. ● *adj* **equinoctial** /ee-kwi-**nok**-shal/.

equip /i-**kwip**/ *vb* (**equipped** /i-**kwipt**/, **equipping** /i-**kwi**-ping/) to provide the things necessary for doing a job, to fit out (*equip a new operating theater/equip themselves with climbing gear*).

equipment /i-**kwip**-ment/ *n* outfit, the set of things needed for a particular activity (*mountaineering equipment/video equipment*).

equity /e-kwi-tee/ *n* fairness, justice (*try to establish equity in sentencing criminals*).

equivalent /i-**kwi**-va-lent/ *adj* **1** equal in value, amount, meaning, etc. (*a sum of money equivalent to $15,000*). ● *n* an equivalent thing (*the equivalent of 500 grams*).

era /i-ra/ *n* **1** a long period of time, starting from some important or particular event (*the Cold War era*). **2** a period of time marked by an important event or events (*the era of the steam engine*).

eradicate /i-ra-di-cate/ *vb* to root out, to destroy completely (*eradicating weeds from the garden/eradicate corruption/try to eradicate violence*). ● *n* **eradication** /i-ra-di-**cay**-shun/.

erase /i-**raze**/ *vb* to rub out, to remove (*erasing pencil marks from the manuscript/erased all memories of him from her mind/erase data from a CD*).

erasure /i-**ray**-zher/ *n* a rubbing out.

ere /eer/ *adv, conj and prep* (*old or lit*) before (*ere break of day*).

erect /i-**rect**/ *adj* standing up straight (*soldiers standing erect*). ● *vb* **1** to build (*erect apartment blocks*). **2** to set upright (*erect a tent*). ● *n* **erection** /i-**rec**-shun/.

ermine /er-min/ n **1** a type of weasel. **2** its white winter fur (robes trimmed with ermine).

erode /i-rode/ vb to destroy or wear away gradually (rocks eroded by the sea/a need for low prices eroding standards of quality). ● n **erosion** /i-ro-zhun/.

erotic /i-rot-ic/ adj having to do with love or sexual desire (erotic literature).

err /er/ vb (fml) to make a mistake, to do wrong (admit that he erred in leaving his wife).

errand /e-rand/ n **1** a short journey made to give a message, deliver goods, etc., to someone (send the child on an errand). **2** the purpose of such a journey (accomplish her errand).

errant /e-rant/ adj **1** (old) wandering (knight errant). **2** (fml) wrongdoing (errant husbands).

erratic /e-ra-tic/ adj not steady, irregular, uneven, unpredictable (people of erratic behavior/an erratic sales pattern).

error /e-ror/ n **1** a mistake (a spelling error). **2** the state of being mistaken (a letter sent to your address in error).

erupt /i-rupt/ vb to break or burst out (volcanoes erupting/father erupting in anger).

eruption /i-rup-shun/ n act of breaking or bursting out (e.g., of a volcano).

escalate /e-sca-late/ vb **1** to rise or increase (house prices escalating). **2** to increase in intensity (a war escalating rapidly).

escalator /e-sca-lay-tor/ n a moving staircase (take the escalator to the second floor).

escapade /e-sca-pade/ n a foolish or risky adventure (a childhood escapade such as stealing apples from an orchard/the romantic escapades of the heroine).

escape /i-scape/ vb **1** to get out of the way of, to avoid (escape punishment). **2** to free oneself from (escape from prison). **3** to leak (gas escaping). **4** to avoid being noticed, remembered, etc. (a name that escapes me). ● n **1** act of escaping. **2** a leakage.

eschew /e-shoo/ vb (fml) to keep away from, to avoid (try to eschew crowded places/aim to eschew trouble).

escort /is-coart/ vb to go with as a guard, as a partner, to show the way or as an honor (supply ships escorted by a warship/escort the members of the audience to their seats/escort his cousin to the ball). ● n **escort** /ess-coart/ **1** a guard, a bodyguard (ships acting as an escort to the royal yacht). **2** a partner, a companion (he was her escort to the ball).

Eskimo /ess-ki-mo/ n a member of a group of people who live in Northern Canada, parts of Alaska, Greenland and parts of Siberia, many of whom, especially in North America and Greenland, prefer to be called **Inuit** and regard Eskimo as offensive.

esophagus /i-sof-a-gus/ n the tube that goes from your throat to your stomach.

especial /i-spe-shal/ adj (fml) more than ordinary, particular (an especial favorite of hers/with especial care).

especially /i-spesh-lee/ adv specially, particularly, markedly (especially pleased to see her today).

espionage /es-pee-o-nazh/ n spying (involved in espionage during the war).

essay /e-say/ vb (fml or old) to try (foolish to essay that task). ● n **1** (fml or old) an attempt (an unsuccessful essay at climbing the mountain). **2** essay a written composition (pupils asked to write an essay on holidays).

essence /e-sense/ n **1** the nature or necessary part of anything (confidence could be said to be the essence of success). **2** a substance obtained from a plant, etc., in concentrated form (vanilla essence).

essential /e-sen-shal/ adj **1** necessary, very important, that cannot be done without (essential equipment for diving/it is essential to take warm clothing). **2** of the basic or inner nature of something, fundamental (the essential difference between the two methods). ● n something that cannot be done without (air conditioning is an essential).

establish /i-sta-blish/ vb **1** to set up (establish a local branch of the society/take time to establish a new business). **2** to place or fix in a position, etc., usually permanently (establish herself as the local bridge expert). **3** to prove, to show to be true (establish an alibi).

establishment /i-sta-blish-ment/ n **1** act of setting up (the establishment of a new business). **2** a group of people employed in an organization, the staff of a household (in charge of a large establishment). **3** a place of business, the premises of a business organization or large institution (an educational establishment). ● **the Establishment** the people holding important positions in a country, community, etc., and usually supporting traditional ways, etc.

estate /i-state/ n **1** all one's property and money (on her death her estate is to be divided between her children). **2** area of land, especially in the country, with one owner (*owns a large estate in Connecticut*). **3** (*old*) political or social group or class (*the nobility, the clergy, and the commons comprise the Three Estates*). **4** (*fml or old*) condition (*the holy estate of matrimony*).

estate agent /i-**state** ay-jent/ *n* (*Br*) *see* **real estate agent.**

esteem /i-**steem**/ *vb* to think highly of (*the artist's work is highly esteemed*). ● *n* respect, regard (*hold him in high esteem as a teacher*).

estimate /e-sti-mate/ *vb* **1** to judge size, amount, etc., roughly, to guess (*estimating the distance at 10 miles*). **2** to calculate the probable cost of (*estimate the repairs to the house at $2000*). ● *n* **1** an opinion. **2** a judgment as to the value or cost of a thing.

estimation /e-sti-**may**-shun/ *n* **1** judgment (*give his estimation as to the value of the vase*). **2** opinion (of someone) (*she was not a good artist in his estimation/go down in their estimation*).

estuary /e-styoo-a-ree/ *n* the mouth of a river as far as the tide flows up it.

etc. /et-se-te-re/ *abbr* = **et cetera.**

et cetera, etcetera /et-**se**-te-re/ *adv* and all the rest (*clear up all the plates, et cetera*).

etch /ech/ *vb* to cut a picture on a metal plate by use of acids in order to print copies of it.

etching /e-ching/ *n* a picture printed by etching (*etchings of the harbor hanging on the wall*).

eternal /i-**ter**-nal/ *adj* **1** everlasting, without beginning or end (*believe in eternal life*). **2** seeming never to stop (*tired of their eternal arguments*).

eternity /i-**ter**-ni-tee/ *n* **1** everlasting existence, with no beginning and no end, unending life after death. **2** (*inf*) a very long time (*wait an eternity for a bus*).

ether /**ee**-ther/ *n* **1** the clear upper air. **2** formerly, an invisible substance supposed to fill all space and to pass on electric waves. **3** a colorless liquid, often formerly used as an anesthetic.

ethical /e-thi-cal/ *adj* **1** having to do with right and wrong (*the doctor's behavior was not considered ethical*). **2** relating to ethics (*ethical problems*).

ethics /e-thics/ *n* **1** the study of right and wrong. **2** rules or principles of behavior (*the ethics of protecting a member of the family from the police*).

ethnic /**eth**-nic/ *adj* having to do with human races or their customs, food, dress, etc. (*ethnic restaurants*).

etiquette /e-ti-ket/ *n* the rules of polite behavior, good manners (*a book on wedding etiquette*).

etymology /e-ti-**mol**-o-jee/ *n* **1** the study of the history of words. **2** derivation, an explanation of the history of a particular word (*dictionaries giving etymologies*). ● *adj* **etymological** /e-ti-mo-**lodge**-i-cal/. ● *n* **etymologist** /e-ti-**mol**-o-jist/.

EU /**ee-yoo**/ *abbr* = **European Union:** a group of European countries that have joined together for economic and political purposes (*the United Kingdom is a member of the EU*).

eucalyptus /yoo-ca-**lip**-tus/ *n* **1** an Australian gum tree. **2** the oil from its leaves, used in the treatment of colds.

euphemism /**yoo**-fe-mi-zum/ *n* the use of mild words or phrases to say something unpleasant (e.g., *fairy tale* for *lie*). ● *adj* **euphemistic** /yoo-fe-**mi**-stic/.

euro /**yoo**-ro/ *n* the common unit of currency in the following European countries: Austria, Belgium, Finland, France, Germany, Greece, Ireland, Italy, Luxembourg, the Netherlands, and Portugal.

European Union /**yoo**-ro-pee-an **yoon**-yun / *see* **EU.**

evacuate /i-va-cyoo-ate/ *vb* **1** to go away from (a place) (*evacuating the area as the enemy army approached*). **2** (*fml*) to make empty (*evacuate the bowels*). **2** to send to a place of safety in wartime (*children evacuated from areas likely to be bombed in World War II*). ● *n* **evacuation** /i-va-cyoo-**ay**-shun/.

evade /i-**vade**/ *vb* **1** to keep oneself away from (*evading the police/evade an attack*). **2** to dodge, to find a way of not doing something, especially by using trickery, deception, etc. (*evaded military service by pretending to suffer from asthma*). **3** to refuse to answer directly (*evade the question*). ● *n* **evasion** /i-**vay**-zhun/.

evaluate /i-**val**-yoo-ate/ *vb* to work out the value of (*difficult to evaluate his success as a writer on such little evidence*). ● *n* **evaluation** /i-val-yoo-**ay**-shun/.

evangelic /ee-van-je-lic/, **evangelical** /ee-van-je-li-cal/ *adjs* **1** having to do with the Christian Gospels. **2** accepting the Bible as the only guide to faith.

evangelist /ee-**van**-je-list/ *n* **1** one of the four Gospel writers. **2** a preacher of the Gospel.

evaporate /i-**va**-po-rate/ *vb* **1** to turn into vapor and disappear (*the water in the puddles soon evaporated in the heat*). **2** to disappear (*all hope gradually evaporating*). ● *n* **evaporation** /i-va-po-**ray**-shun/.

evasion *see* **evade**.

evasive /i-vay-siv/ *adj* **1** having the purpose of evading (*take evasive action*). **2** not straightforward, not frank (*give evasive answers*).

eve /eev/ *n* **1** (*old*) evening. **2** the day before (*Christmas Eve*). **3** the time before an important event (*on the eve of the battle*).

even /ee-vin/ *adj* **1** level (*an even temperature*). **2** smooth (*even ground*). **3** equal (*scores now even*). **4** divisible by 2 (*even numbers*). **5** calm (*of even temper*). ● *adv* just (*even as we speak*). ● *vb* **1** to make smooth or level (*even the ground*). **2** to make equal (*even the score*). ● *n* **evenness** /ee-vin-ness/.

evening /eev-ning/ *n* the close of day.

event /i-vent/ *n* **1** anything that happens, an incident (*the events leading up to the war*). **2** a single race or contest at sports or races (*athletic events*).

eventful /i-vent-ful/ *adj* full of interesting or exciting happenings (*an eventful life/an eventful day*).

eventual /i-ven-sha-wul/ *adj* happening as a result, final (*his criminal behavior and eventual imprisonment*).

eventuality /i-ven-cha-**wa**-li-tee/ *n* a possible happening (*try to allow for any eventuality in planning the celebration*).

eventually /i-**ven**-cha-wa-lee/ *adv* finally, at length (*after many attempts, he eventually passed the exam*).

ever /e-ver/ *adv* always, at all times.

evergreen /e-ver-green/ *n* a tree or plant that has green leaves all the year round. ● *adj* always green (*evergreen trees*).

everlasting /e-ver-**la**-sting/ *adj* **1** never ending (*everlasting life*). **2** seemingly without end, frequent (*their everlasting complaints*).

evermore /e-ver-**more**/ *adv* forever (*promise to love her evermore*).

every /**ev**-ree/ *adj* each one (*every child was present*).

everybody /**ev**-ree-bu-dee/ *pron* every person (*everybody should take regular exercise*).

everyday /**ev**-ree-day/ *adj* **1** happening every day (*everyday duties*). **2** usual, ordinary (*everyday clothes*).

everyone /**ev**-ree-wun/ *pron* every person (*everyone suddenly burst out singing*).

everything /**ev**-ree-thing/ *pron* all things being considered as a group (*everything in this room is filthy*).

evict /i-vict/ *vb* to put out of a house or off land by order of a court (*evict tenants for not paying rent*). ● *n* **eviction** /i-**vic**-shun/.

evidence /e-vi-dense/ *n* **1** information given to show a fact is true (*produce evidence of his innocence*). **2** the statement made by a witness in a court of law (*give evidence at the murder trial*).

evident /e-vi-dent/ *adj* clear, easily understood, obvious (*it was evident that she was ill/her evident unhappiness*).

evil /ee-vil/ *adj* **1** wicked, bad, sinful (*an evil man/evil deeds*). **2** unpleasant, nasty (*an evil smell*). ● *n* **1** wickedness (*feel surrounded by evil in that house*). **2** anything bad or harmful (*the evils of the world*).

evoke /i-**voke**/ *vb* **1** to call up (*evoking memories of childhood*). **2** to give rise to, to cause (*her tears evoked sympathy from the crowd*). ● *n* **evocation** /ee-vo-**cay**-shun/.

evolution /e-vu-**loo**-shun/ *n* **1** the belief that life began in lower forms of creature and that these gradually changed over millions of years into the highest forms, such as humans (*Darwin's theory of evolution*). **2** development (*the evolution of a modern political system*).

evolve /i-**volve**/ *vb* **1** to work out (*evolving an efficient filing system in the office*). **2** to develop gradually (*a system of efficient government evolved*).

ewe /yoo/ *n* a female sheep (*ewes and rams*).

exact /ig-**zact**/ *adj* **1** absolutely correct, accurate in every detail (*the exact measurements/an exact copy of the antique vase*). **2** showing or taking great care (*require to be very exact in that kind of work*). ● *vb* **1** to force to make payment. **2** to demand and obtain.

exacting /ig-**zac**-ting/ *adj* needing a lot of work or attention (*an exacting job*).

exaggerate /ig-**za**-je-rate/ *vb* **1** to speak or think of something as being better or more (or worse or less) than it really is (*exaggerating her unhappiness to gain people's sympathy*). **2** to go beyond the truth in describing something (*you can't believe what she says—she always exaggerates*). ● *n* **exaggeration** /ig-za-je-**ray**-shun/.

exalt /ig-**zolt**/ *vb* **1** (*fml*) to raise in power or rank (*he has been exalted to general*). **2** to praise highly (*exalt God*). ● *n* **exaltation** /ig-zol-**tay**-shun/.

examine /ig-**za**-min/ *vb* **1** to look at closely and carefully in order to find out something (*the doctor examined the child/customs officials examining baggage*). **2** to question (*witnesses examined by the counsel*). **3** to test a learner's knowledge by questions (*examine the pupils in French*). ● *n* **examination** /ig-za-mi-**nay**-shun/. ● *n* **examiner** / ig-**za**-mi-ner/.

examinee /ig-za-mi-**nee**/ *n* a person who is being examined.

example /ig-**zam**-pl/ *n* **1** one thing chosen to show what others of the same kind are like, a model (*an example of the artist's work/an example of his bad behavior*). **2** a person or thing deserving to be imitated (*the saint's patience was an example to us all*).

exasperate /ig-**za**-spe-rate/ *vb* to make angry (*exasperating their mother with their endless questions*). ● *n* **exasperation** /ig-za-spe-**ray**-shun/.

excavate /**ek**-sca-vate/ *vb* **1** to uncover by digging (*excavating Roman remains*). **2** to dig up, to hollow out (*excavate a building site*). ● *n* **excavator** / **ek**-sca-vay-tor/.

excavation /ek-sca-**vay**-shun/ *n* **1** act of excavating. **2** a hole or trench made by digging.

exceed /ik-**seed**/ *vb* **1** to go beyond (*exceed the speed limit*). **2** to be greater or more numerous than (*a price not exceeding $7000*).

exceedingly /ik-**see**-ding-lee/ *adv* very, extremely (*exceedingly difficult tasks*).

excel /ik-**sel**/ *vb* (**excelled** /ik-**seld**/, **excelling** /ik-**se**-ling/) to do very well at, to get exceptionally good at (*excel at tennis/excel at playing the piano*).

excellence /**ek**-se-lense/ *n* perfection, great merit (*recognize her excellence as a musician/the excellence of his work*).

excellent /**ek**-se-lent/ *adj* very good, of a very high standard (*excellent work/an excellent performance*).

except[1] /ik-**sept**/ *vb* (*fml*) to leave out (*only children are excepted from the admission charge*).

except[2] /ik-**sept**/, **excepting** /ik-**sep**-ting/ *preps* leaving out (*everyone except my brother*).

exception /ik-**sep**-shun/ *n* a person or thing that does not follow the rule (*everyone will pay an admission fee with the exception of children*). ● **take exception** to object (*took exception to his remarks*).

exceptional /ik-**sep**-shu-nal/ *adj* different from others, unusual, remarkable (*show exceptional understanding/have an exceptional musical talent*). ● *adv* **exceptionally**.

excerpt /**ek**-serpt/ *n* a short passage taken out of a longer piece of writing or music.

excess /ik-**sess**/ *n* **1** too much (*an excess of alcohol*). **2** the amount by which a thing is too much

(*the check was wrong, and we paid an excess of $10*). **3** bad and uncontrolled behavior (*his drunken excesses*).

excessive /ik-**se**-siv/ *adj* more than is right or correct (*an excessive amount of salt in the soup/excessive alcohol in his blood/find the price excessive*).

excessively /ik-**se**-siv-lee/ *adv* very.

exchange /iks-**change**/ *vb* to give one thing and receive another in its place (*exchanging his dollars for euros*). ● *n* **1** the act of exchanging (*an exchange of views/give food in exchange for gardening work*). **2** a place where merchants meet to do business. **3** the changing of the money of one country into that of another. **4** a telephone center where lines are connected to each other.

excise[1] /**ek**-size/ *n* a tax on certain goods made within the country.

excise[2] /ik-**size**/ *vb* to cut out, to cut away (*surgeons excising the diseased tissue*). ● *n* **excision**.

excitable /ik-**site**-a-bl/ *adj* easily excited.

excite /ik-**site**/ *vb* **1** to stir up feelings of happiness, expectation, etc. (*children excited by thoughts of Christmas*). **2** to rouse (*exciting feelings of envy in her friends*). ● *n* **excitement** /ik-**site**-ment/. ● *adj* **exciting** /ik-**site**-ing/.

exclaim /ik-**sclame**/ *vb* to cry out suddenly (*"Oh my goodness!" she exclaimed in surprise*). ● *adj* **exclamatory** /ik-**sclam**-a-toe-ree/.

exclamation /ek-scla-**may**-shun/ *n* a word or words said suddenly or with feeling (*utter an exclamation of amazement*).

exclamation mark /ek-scla-**may**-shun **mark**/ *n* a mark of punctuation (!).

exclude /ek-**sclood**/ *vb* **1** to shut out (*exclude air from the bottle*). **2** to leave out (*excluding her from membership of the club*). **3** to leave out, not to include (*the price excludes drinks*). ● *n* **exclusion** / ek-**scloo**-zhen/.

exclusive /ek-**scloo**-siv/ *adj* **1** open to certain people only (*an exclusive club*). **2** sole (*your exclusive role*). **3** not shared (*exclusive rights*). ● *adv* **exclusively** /ek-**scloo**-siv-lee/.

excrement /**eks**-cre-ment/ *n* waste matter put out from the body (*stepped in dog's excrement*).

excrete /ik-**screet**/ *vb* to put out what is useless from the body (*excreting abnormal quantities of urine*). ● *adj* **excretory** /**ek**-scre-to-ree/.

excruciating /ik-**scroo**-she-ate-ing/ *adj* **1** very great, intense (*an excruciating pain in his back*). **2** terrible, very bad (*an excruciating performance on the violin*).

excursion /ik-**scur**-zhon/ *n* a trip made for pleasure, an outing (*a bus excursion to the beach*).

excuse /ek-**scyooz**/ *vb* **1** to let off (*excused from playing baseball because of illness*). **2** to forgive, to overlook (*excuse her late arrival/excusing him for being late*). **3** to give reasons showing or intended to show that someone or something cannot be blamed (*nothing could excuse such behavior*). ● *n* /ek-**scyoos**/ a reason given for failure or wrongdoing. ● *adj* **excusable** /ek-**scyoo**-za-bl/.

execute /ek-si-cyoot/ *vb* **1** to perform (*executing a dance step*). **2** to carry out (*execute orders*). **3** to put to death by law (*execute murderers*).

execution /ek-si-**cyoo**-shun/ *n* **1** the carrying out, performance, etc., of something (*execution of orders/execution of difficult dance steps*). **2** skill in performing music. **3** the act of putting to death by order of the law.

executioner /ek-si-**cyoo**-shu-ner/ *n* an officer who puts condemned criminals to death.

executive /ig-**zec**-yoo-tiv/ *adj* **1** concerned with making and carrying out decisions, especially in business (*an executive director/executive powers*). **2** having the power to carry out government's decisions and laws. ● *n* **1** a person involved in the management of a firm. **2** the part of government that puts laws, etc., into effect.

executor /ig-**zec**-yoo-tor/ *n* a person who sees that a dead person's written will is carried out (*appoint two executors*).

exemplify /ig-**zem**-pli-fy/ *vb* **1** to be an example (*this machine exemplifies the firm's high standard of work*). **2** to illustrate by example (*exemplify the problems*).

exempt /ig-**zempt**/ *vb* to free from, to let off (*exempt certain goods from tax/exempt him from military service*). ● *adj* free. ● *n* **exemption** /ig-**zem**-shun/.

exercise /ek-ser-size/ *n* **1** an action performed to strengthen the body or part of the body. **2** a piece of work done for practice. **3** training (*military exercises*). **4** use (*the exercise of patience*). ● *vb* **1** to use, to employ (*exercising patience*). **2** to perform some kind of physical exercises. **3** to give exercise to, to train (*exercise the horses*).

exert /ig-**zert**/ *vb* to apply (*exert influence to get his son a job/have to exert force*). ● **exert oneself** to try hard.

exertion /ig-**zer**-shun/ *n* effort (*tired after the exertion of climbing the hill*).

exhale /eks-**hale**/ *vb* to breathe out. ● *n* **exhalation** /eks-ha-**lay**-shun/.

exhaust /ig-**zawst**/ *vb* **1** to use up completely (*exhaust our food supplies*). **2** to tire out (*the journey exhausted her*). **3** to say everything possible about (*exhaust the subject*). ● *n* **1** a passage by which used steam or gases are carried away from an engine (*a car's exhaust*). **2** these gases.

exhausting /ig-**zaw**-sting/ *adj* very tiring (*an exhausting journey/an exhausting day*).

exhaustion /ig-**zaw**-chun/ *n* **1** the state of being tired out. **2** lack of any strength.

exhaustive /ig-**zaw**-stiv/ *adj* **1** very thorough, complete (*an exhaustive search*). **2** dealing with every possible aspect of a subject.

exhibit /ig-**zi**-bit/ *vb* **1** to show in public (*exhibit Picasso's early works/exhibit roses at the flower show*). **2** (*fml*) to display, to show (*exhibiting no sign of emotion*). ● *n* a thing shown in public.

exhibition /ek-si-**bi**-shun/ *n* **1** act of exhibiting. **2** a collection of many things brought together to be shown to the public (*an art exhibition*).

exhibitionist /ek-si-**bi**-shu-nist/ *n* a person who behaves in such a way as to draw attention to himself or herself.

exhibitor /ig-**zi**-bi-tor/ *n* a person who exhibits at a show (*exhibitors in the art gallery*).

exhilarate /ig-**zi**-li-rate/ *vb* to make lively or happy (*a swim in cold water exhilarates him*). ● *n* **exhilaration** /ig-zi-li-**ray**-shun/.

exile /**eg**-zile/ *n* **1** long or unwilling absence from one's home or country (*an ex-general forced to live in exile*). **2** a person living in a country other than his or her own (*exiles talking about the old country*). ● *vb* to send someone out of his or her own country as a punishment (*they were exiled for taking part in a conspiracy against the government*).

exist /ig-**zist**/ *vb* **1** to be. **2** to live. ● *n* **existence** /ig-zi-stense/. ● *adj* **existent** /ig-**zi**-stent/.

exit /**eg**-zit/ *n* **1** a way out (*several exits in the hall*). **2** a going out (*an exit by the crowd*). ● *also vb.*

exodus /**ek**-so-dus/ *n* a going out or away by many people (e.g., the departure of the Jews from Egypt) (*an exodus of people to the beach in the summer*).

exorcise, exorcize /**ek**-sawr-size/ *vb* to drive out evil spirits (*exorcising the haunted house*).

exorcism /**ek**-sawr-si-zum/ *n* act of exorcising. ● *n* **exorcist** /**ek**-sawr-sist/.

exotic /ig-**zot**-ic/ *adj* **1** foreign, introduced from another country (*exotic fruits*). **2** striking and unusual (*exotic clothes*).

expand /ik-**spand**/ *vb* **1** to make or become larger (*metals expand when heated*). **2** to spread out (*his face expanded in a smile/his waistline has expanded*). **3** to become more friendly or talkative (*her guests were beginning to expand after a few drinks*).

expanse /ik-**spanse**/ *n* a wide area (*an expanse of green*).

expansion /ik-**span**-shun/ *n* act of expanding.

expansive /ik-**span**-siv/ *adj* **1** wide (*an expansive gesture with his arms*). **2** ready to talk freely (*become expansive when drunk*).

expatriate /ek-**spa**-tree-ate/ *vb* to send someone out of his own country. ● *n* a person living or working in a country other than his or her own (*expatriates living abroad*).

expect /ik-**spect**/ *vb* **1** to wait for (*expect a letter from her daughter*). **2** to think it likely that something will happen (*she expects to arrive today*). **3** to require as a right or duty (*teachers expecting obedience from the pupils*).

expectancy /ik-**spec**-tan-see/ *n* state of being expectant.

expectant /ik-**spec**-tant/ *adj* hopeful, waiting for something to happen (*children with expectant faces on Christmas morning*). ● **expectant mother** a woman who is pregnant.

expectation /ek-spec-**tay**-shun/ *n* **1** hope that something will happen (*enter the competition full of expectation*). **2** that which is expected (*have high expectations on entering the competition*).

expedience /ik-**spee**-dee-ence/, **expediency** /ik-**spee**-dee-en-see/ *ns* doing things not because they are right or moral but because they are likely to be successful or to one's advantage (*the government was not interested in people's feelings—it was a question of expedience*).

expedition /ek-spe-**di**-shun/ *n* **1** a journey made for a particular purpose (*on a shopping expedition*). **2** (*fml*) speed (*carry out the tasks with expedition*).

expel /ik-**spel**/ *vb* (**expelled** /ik-**speld**/, **expelling** /ik-**spe**-ling/) **1** to drive out (*air expelled from the lungs*). **2** to force to go away (*foreign journalists expelled from the war zone*). **3** to dismiss officially from a school, club, etc. (*expel pupils for drug-taking*). ● *n* **expulsion** /ik-**spul**-shun/.

expend /ik-**spend**/ *vb* to spend, to use up (*expend all his energy*).

expenditure /ik-**spen**-di-cher/ *n* **1** the amount spent (*try to reduce your annual expenditure*). **2** the act of spending (*the expenditure of money*).

expense /ik-**spense**/ *n* **1** cost (*purchase the car at his own expense*). **2** spending of money, etc.

expensive /ik-**spen**-siv/ *adj* dear, costing a lot (*expensive clothes/an expensive house*).

experience /ik-**spi**-ree-ense/ *n* **1** a happening in one's own life. **2** knowledge gained from one's own life or work. ● *vb* **1** to meet with. **2** to feel. **3** to undergo.

experiment /ik-**spe**-ri-ment/ *n* something done so that the results may be studied, a test (*scientific experiments*). ● *vb* to do an experiment (*object to scientists experimenting on animals*). ● *adj* **experimental** /ik-spe-ri-**men**-tal/.

expert /**ek**-spert/ *adj* very skillful (*an expert tennis player*). ● *n* **expert** a person having special skill or knowledge (*an expert in antiques*).

expiration /ek-spi-**ray**-shun/ *n* (*fml*) **1** act of breathing out. **2** end (*the expiration of the contract*).

expire /ik-**spire**/ *vb* **1** (*fml*) to die (*soldiers expiring on the battlefield*). **2** (*fml*) to breathe out. **3** to come to an end (*a bus pass that has expired*).

expiry /ik-**spie**-ree/ *n* end (*expiry of the lease on the apartment*).

explain /ik-**splane**/ *vb* **1** to make clear (*explain the instructions*). **2** to give reasons for (*explain his absence*).

explanation /ek-spla-**nay**-shun/ *n* a statement of the meaning of or the reasons for.

explanatory /ek-**spla**-na-toe-ree/ *adj* helping to make clear (*explanatory notes*).

expletive /ek-**splee**-tiv/ *n* a swear word.

explicable /ek-**spli**-ca-bl/ *adj* able to be explained (*behavior that seems scarcely explicable*).

explicit /ek-**spli**-sit/ *adj* **1** stating exactly what is meant (*explicit instructions*). **2** with full details, with nothing hidden (*explicit sex scenes*).

explode /ik-**spload**/ *vb* **1** to burst or blow up with a loud noise (*a bomb exploding/a gas boiler exploding*). **2** to show to be untrue, to destroy (*explode a myth*).

exploit /ik-**sploit**/ *n* **1** a brave or outstanding deed (*a film about the exploits of pilots during World War II*). ● *vb* to make use of, especially for selfish reasons (*rich employers exploiting illegal immigrants by paying low wages*). ● *n* **exploitation** /ik-sploy-**tay**-shun/.

explore /ik-**sploar**/ *vb* **1** to examine closely (*explore all possibilities*). **2** to travel through a country to find out all about it. ● *n* **exploration** /ek-splo-**ray**-shun/. ● *n* **explorer** /ik-**splo**-rer/.

explosion /ik-**splo**-zhun/ *n* **1** going off or bursting with a loud noise. **2** an outburst (*an explosion of anger*).

explosive /ik-**splo**-siv/ *adj* able to cause an explosion. ● *n* any substance that will explode (*the police found explosives in a barn*).

exponent /ik-**spo**-nent/ *n* **1** a person who explains and supports a theory, belief, etc. (*an exponent of Marxism*). **2** a person who is good at (*an exponent of mime*).

export /ek-**spoart**/ *vb* to send goods to another country. ● *n* **export** /ek-spoart/ an article that is exported. ● *n* **exportation** /ek-spoar-**tay**-shun/.

expose /ek-**spoaz**/ *vb* **1** to uncover (*dig and expose the roots of the tree/exposing white teeth/expose her legs to the sun*). **2** to make known the truth about (*newspapers exposing scandals about politicians*). **3** to allow light to fall on (*a photographic film*).

exposition /ek-spo-**zi**-shun/ *n* **1** (*fml*) a collection of things brought together to be shown to the public (*an exposition of modern art*). **2** a full explanation (*an exposition of the company's sales policy*).

exposure /ek-**spo**-zher/ *n* **1** act of exposing (*exposure to the sun/the newspaper's exposure of fraud*). **2** the effect on the body of being out in cold weather for a long time (*climbers dying of exposure*).

expound /ik-**spound**/ *vb* (*fml*) to explain fully (*expound his theory*).

express /ik-**spress**/ *vb* **1** to put into words, to state (*expresses his ideas*). **2** to make known by words or actions (*express her anger by stamping her feet*). ● *adj* **1** swift (*by express post*). **2** clearly stated (*express instructions*). ● *n* a fast train.

expressly /ik-**spress**-lee/ *adv* **1** clearly (*I expressly forbade you to do that*). **2** specially, with a certain definite purpose.

expression /ik-**spre**-shun/ *n* **1** a word or phrase (*foreign expressions*). **2** the look on one's face (*a surprised expression*). **3** ability to read, play music, etc., with meaning or feeling.

expressive /ik-**spre**-siv/ *adj* with feeling or meaning (*expressive eyes*).

expulsion /ik-**spul**-shun/ *see* **expel**.

expunge /ik-**spunge**/ *vb* to rub out, to wipe out (*expunging some passages from the book/expunge the tragedy from your memory*).

expurgate /ek-**spur**-gate/ *vb* to cut out of a book unsuitable or objectionable passages. ● *n* **expurgation** /ek-spur-**gay**-shun/.

exquisite, exquisite /ek-**skwi**-zit/ *adj* **1** beautiful and delicate, very fine (*exquisite china/exquisite*

workmanship/exquisite beauty*). **2** (*fml*) strongly felt, acute (*exquisite pain*).

extant /ek-**stant**/ *adj* still existing (*customs still extant*).

extemporaneous /ek-stem-po-**ray**-nee-uss/ *adj* (*fml*) unprepared (*an extemporaneous speech*).

extempore /ik-**stem**-po-ree/ *adv and adj* without preparation (*speak extempore at the meeting*).

extemporize /Ik-**stem**-po-rize/ *vb, also* **extemporise** (*Br*) **1** to speak without preparation. **2** to make up music as one is playing.

extend /ik-**stend**/ *vb* **1** to stretc h out (*extend his arms*). **2** to reach or stretc.h (*a forest extending for miles*). **3** to offer (*extend an invitation*). **4** to make longer or bigger (*extend the garden*).

extension /ik-**sten**-shun/ *n* **1** an addition (*build an extension to the house*). **2** an additional period of time (*get an extension to write his essay*).

extensive /ik-**sten**-siv/ *adj* **1** large (*extensive grounds*). **2** wide, wide-ranging (*extensive interests*).

extent /ik-**stent**/ *n* **1** the area or length to which something extends (*the extent of his estate*). **2** amount, degree (*the extent of the damage*).

extenuate /ik-**sten**-yoo-ate/ *vb* (*fml*) to make excuses for in order to make seem less bad (*nothing could extenuate such behavior*). ● *n* **extenuation** /ik-sten-yoo-**ay**-shun/.

extenuating /ik-**sten**-yoo-ay-ting/ *adj* making a crime, etc., seem less serious by showing there is some excuse for it (*extenuating circumstances*).

exterior /ek-**sti**-ree-or/ *adj* outer (*exterior walls*). ● *n* the outside.

exterminate /ik-**ster**-min-ate/ *vb* to kill to the last one, to destroy completely (*exterminating rats on the farm*). ● *n* **extermination** /ik-ster-mi-**nay**-shun/.

external /ek-**ster**-nal/ *adj* on the outside (*external walls*).

extinct /ik-**stingt**/ *adj* **1** no longer found in existence (*an extinct species*). **2** no longer burning (*extinct volcanoes*).

extinction /ik-**sting**-shun/ *n* **1** act of destroying. **2** the state of being no longer living (*species threatened with extinction*). **3** the putting out of (*the extinction of lights/the extinction of fires*).

extinguish /ik-**sting**-wish/ *vb* **1** to put out (*extinguish the fire*). **2** to put an end to (*extinguish all hope*).

extirpate /ek-**stir**-pate/ *vb* (*fml*) to destroy completely, to root out (*a tyrant extirpating all opposition to him/attempt to extirpate poverty from our society*). ● *n* **extirpation** /ek-stir-**pay**-shun/.

extol, extoll /ik-**stoal**/ *vb* (**extolled** /ik-**stoald**/,

extolling /ik-**stoe**-ling/) (*fml*) to praise highly (*extol the merits of the new product/extol her daughter's virtues*).

extort /ik-**stawrt**/ *vb* to take from by force or threats (*bullies extorting money from younger boys*). ● *n* **extortion** /ik-**stawr**-shun/.

extortionate /ik-**stawr**-shu-nate/ *adj* **1** far too expensive (*extortionate prices*). **2** asking too much (*extortionate demands*).

extra /**ek**-stra/ *adj* additional, more than is usual, expected or necessary (*workers asking for extra money/require extra workers*). ● *adv* more than usually. ● *n* something additional (*school fees and extras such as dancing*).

extract /ek-**stract**/ *vb* **1** to draw, take or pull out (*extract teeth/try to extract information*). **2** to select a passage from a book. ● *n* **extract** /**ek**-stract/ **1** a passage taken from a book (*a book of extracts from Shakespeare's plays*). **2** a substance drawn from a material and containing all its qualities (*yeast extract*).

extraction /ek-**strac**-shun/ *n* **1** act of drawing out (*the extraction of teeth*). **2** connection with a certain family or race (*Spanish by extraction*).

extradite /**ek**-stra-dite/ *vb* to hand over a foreign criminal to the police of his own country. ● *n* **extradition** /ek-stra-**di**-shun/.

extramural /ek-stra-**myoo**-ral/ *adj* **1** organized for those who are not members (e.g., of a university) (*extramural studies*). **2** separate from or outside the area of one's studies (*extramural activities*).

extraneous /ek-**stray**-nee-uss/ *adj* having nothing to do with the subject.

extraordinary /ek-**strawr**-di-na-ree/ *adj* **1** very unusual, remarkable (*what extraordinary behavior*). **2** (*fml*) additional to what is usual or ordinary (*an extraordinary meeting of the committee*).

extraterrestrial /ek-stra-te-**re**-stree-al/ *adj* existing or happening beyond the earth's atmosphere (*the possibility of extraterrestrial life*).

extravagance /ek-**stra**-vi-gense/ *n* **1** wasteful spending. **2** wastefulness.

extravagant /ek-**stra**-vi-gent/ *adj* **1** spending or using a great deal, wasteful (*extravagant use of materials/live in an extravagant way*). **2** spending foolishly (*an extravagant young woman*). **3** foolish and improbable (*extravagant schemes*).

extreme /ek-**streem**/ *adj* **1** farthest away (*the extreme ends of the continent/at the extreme edge of the forest*). **2** greatest possible (*in extreme pain*). **3** far from moderate, going beyond the limits, not sharing the views of the majority (*extreme views/extreme members of the party*). **4** intense, strong, not ordinary or usual (*calling for extreme measures of punishment*). ● *n* **1** the end, the farthest point (*the extremes of the earth*). **2** something as far or as different as possible from something else (*the extremes of wealth and poverty*). **3** the greatest or highest degree (*the extremes of heat in the desert*). ● *adv* **extremely** /ek-**streem**-lee/.

extremist /ek-**stree**-mist/ *n* a person who holds extreme ideas (*a political extremist*). ● *also adj*.

extremity /ek-**stre**-mi-tee/ *n* **1** the farthest point (*the extremities of the earth*). **2** (*fml*) a situation of great misfortune, distress or danger (*in an extremity of poverty*). **3** (*fml*) the farther parts of the body, i.e. the hands and feet (*poor circulation in her extremities*).

extricate /**ek**-stri-cate/ *vb* to set free from a difficult position (*extricating the dog from the hole in which he was stuck/extricate the firm from its financial difficulties*).

extrovert /**ek**-stro-vert/ *n* a person who is extremely outgoing and self-assured). ● *also adj*.

exuberant /ig-**zoo**-ber-ant/ *adj* **1** vigorous, strong (*exuberant growth of plants*). **2** in high spirits (*in exuberant mood*). ● *n* **exuberance** /ig-**zoo**-ber-anse/.

exude /ig-**zood**/ *vb* to ooze out, to give off (*exuding perspiration/exude confidence*).

exult /ig-**zult**/ *vb* to rejoice very much, to express joy (*exulting over their victory*). ● *adj* **exultant** / ig-**zul**-tant/. ● *n* **exultation** /ig-zul-**tay**-shun/.

eye /ie/ *n* **1** the organ by means of which we see. **2** a small hole in a needle. **3** the seed bud of a potato. ● *vb* **1** to look at, to watch closely (*eying his friend's cake with envy/eyed the policeman warily*).

eyebrow /**ie**-brow/ *n* an arc of hair on the brow bone above the eye.

eye-opener /**ie**-oa-pe-ner/ *n* something very surprising.

eyelash /**ie**-lash/ *n* each of the short hairs extending from the edge of the eyelid.

eyelid /**ie**-lid/ *n* the fold of skin that can be lowered to close the eye.

eyesight /**ie**-sight/ *n* a person's ability to see.

eyesore /**ie**-sore/ *n* something very ugly (*apartment blocks that are an eyesore on the landscape*).

eyewitness /**ie**-wit-ness/ *n* a person who sees an event happen (*eyewitnesses of the accident*).

eyrie *n see* **aerie**.

F

F, f /eff/ **1** the sixth letter of the alphabet. **2** (*mus*) the fourth note of the scale of C major.

fable /fay-bl/ *n* a short story, usually about animals, etc., who talk and behave like humans, meant to teach people to do what is right (*Aesop's fable about the fox and the grapes*).

fabric /fa-bric/ *n* **1** the framework of a building (*the fabric of the building is crumbling*). **2** manufactured cloth (*a woolen fabric*).

fabricate /fa-bri-cate/ *vb* **1** to make or build, to manufacture. **2** to make up or invent (*fabricating an excuse*). ● *n* **fabrication** /fa-bri-cay-shun/.

fabulous /fa-byoo-lus/ *adj* **1** (*fml*) existing only in fable or legend (*the dragon is a fabulous animal*). **2** (*inf*) wonderful, marvelous, very good (*a fabulous dress/a fabulous performance*).

facade /fa-sad/ *n* **1** the front of a building. **2** outer appearance (*frightened in spite of his brave facade*).

face /fayss/ *n* **1** the front part of the head, from forehead to chin (*a beautiful face*). **2** the front part of anything (*break the face of his watch*). ● *vb* **1** to stand looking toward, to turn toward (*a house facing south*). **2** to meet or encounter boldly (*face the enemy/face his problems*). **3** to cover with a surface of different material (*face the wall with plaster*).

facet /fa-set/ *n* **1** one of many small sides, as of a diamond. **2** an aspect (*a humorous facet to the situation*).

facial /fay-shal/ *adj* having to do with the face (*facial hair*). ● *n* a treatment to improve the appearance of the skin on the face.

facile /fa-sul/ *adj* **1** done with ease, often done too easily (*a facile victory*). **2** without depth, not sincere (*a facile remark*).

facilitate /fa-si-li-tate/ *vb* to make easy (*facilitating the bill's progress through Congress*). ● *n* **facilitation** /fa-si-li-tay-shun/.

facility /fa-si-li-tee/ *n* **1** (*fml*) ease, skill (*perform the tasks with facility*). **2** *pl* the means or conditions for doing something easily.

facsimile /fac-si-mi-lee/ *n* **1** an exact copy (*a facsimile of the legal document*). **2** an image produced by facsimile transmission (*also* **fax**). ● **facsimile transmission** a system of sending written, printed, or pictorial documents over a telephone line by scanning it and then reproducing the image in a different location.

fact /fact/ *n* **1** something known to be true or to have happened (*geographical facts about the country*). **2** truth (*it is a fact that Earth is round*). **3** a deed, an event (*after the fact*).

factor /fac-tor/ *n* **1** a person who does business for another, someone who manages another's land (*the estate's factor*). **2** a cause, element (*one of the factors in his lack of success*). **3** a number that divides exactly into another number.

factory /fac-to-ree/ *n* a building where large quantities of goods are made (*a car factory*).

factual /fac-chu-wul/ *adj* having to do with facts (*a factual, rather than fictional, account of the war*).

faculty /fa-cul-tee/ *n* **1** a special ability (*a faculty for putting people at their ease*). **2** the power to do something (*the faculty of speech*). **3** all the teachers of a school, college, or university or of a school's departments (*the science faculty*).

fad /fad/ *n* a craze, a short-lived fashion (*bell-bottom jeans were a fad in the 1960s*).

fade /fade/ *vb* **1** to wither. **2** to lose color. **3** to disappear gradually (*hopes fading*).

Fahrenheit /fa-ren-hite/ *adj* of a scale of temperature in which the freezing point of water is 32° and the boiling point is 212°, named for a German physicist.

fail /fale/ *vb* **1** not to succeed (*fail his driving test/fail in his attempt at the record*). **2** to break down (*a car engine that failed*). **3** to disappoint (*feel that she failed her mother*). **4** to owe so much money that debts cannot be paid (*a company that is bound to fail*).

failing /fay-ling/ *n* a fault, a weakness (*laziness is his major failing*).

failure /fale-yer/ *n* **1** lack of success (*disappointed at their failure in the tournament*). **2** a person who has not succeeded (*regard himself as a failure*). **3** a breakdown (*engine failure*).

fain /fane/ *adj* (*old or lit*) glad. ● *adv* gladly.

faint /faint/ *vb* to become weak, to fall down unconscious (*faint from lack of food*). ● *n* act of falling down unconscious. ● *adj* **1** weak, dizzy. **2** lacking clearness or brightness (*writing grown faint over the years*). **3** slight (*chances of winning are now faint*).

fair[1] /fare/ *adj* **1** light in color, having light-colored hair or skin (*one daughter is fair and the other dark*). **3** quite good (*a fair piece of work*). **3** just (*a fair sentence given by the judge*). **4** (*of weather*) not rainy (*hope the weather will be fair for the picnic*). **5** (*old or lit*) attractive (*a fair young maiden*).

fair² /**fare**/ *n* **1** a market or sale, often with shows and amusements. **2** a trade exhibition (*a book fair*).

fairly /**fare**-lee/ *adv* somewhat (*fairly sure that he is at work this morning/do fairly well*).

fairway /**fare**-way/ *n* **1** the deep part of a river where ships usually sail. **2** the part of a golf course where the grass is cut short.

fairy /**fay**-ree/ *n* an imaginary small being, supposed to have magic powers.

fairy tale /**fay**-ree tale/ *n* a story about fairies, giants, magic deeds, etc.

faith /**faith**/ *n* **1** belief, especially in God. **2** trust, being sure of something (*have faith in her ability*). **3** religion (*Christianity and other faiths*). **4** a person's word of honor, loyalty (*keep faith with his friends*).

faithful /**faith**-ful/ *adj* **1** true to one's friends or one's promises (*the king's faithful followers*). **2** loyal to one's marriage vows (*a faithful wife*). **3** true to the facts or an original (*a faithful account of the situation/a faithful copy*).

faithless /**faith**-less/ *adj* (*fml*) **1** disloyal, dishonest (*faithless friends*). **2** unreliable.

fajita /fa-**hee**-ta/ *n* grilled chicken or beef wrapped in a soft tortilla with vegetables and sauce.

fake /**fake**/ *n* someone or something that deceives by looking other than he, she, or it is (*that painting is not an original Picasso—it's a fake*). ● *vb* **1** to change something so that it falsely appears better, more valuable, etc. (*faking the test results*). **2** to copy something so as to deceive (*faked the man's signature*). **3** (*inf*) to pretend (*fake illness to stay home from school*).

falafel /fa-**lof**-el/ *n* a small patty of ground chickpeas, other vegetables, and spices that is deep-fried.

falcon /**fal**-con/ *n* a bird of prey trained to hunt smaller birds.

falconry /**fal**-con-ree/ *n* **1** the art of training falcons to hunt game. **2** the sport of hunting with falcons.

fall /**fawl**/ *vb* (*pt* **fell** /**fel**/, *pp* **fallen** /**faw**-len/) **1** to drop down (*trip over a stone and fall*). **2** to become less or lower (*prices falling*). **3** to hang down (*hair falling to her waist*). **4** to happen or occur (*the holiday falls on a Sunday*). **5** to enter into a

certain state or condition (*fall asleep/fall silent*). **6** to be taken by an enemy (*Rome fell to the enemy*). **7** to be killed in battle (*soldiers who fell in the war*). ● *n* **1** a drop or descent (*injured in a fall from the cliff*). **2** a lessening or lowering (*a fall in the birth rate*). **3** loss of power (*the government's fall*). **4** a waterfall. **5** autumn. ● **fall back** to go back. ● **fall on** *or* **upon** to attack. ● **fall out** (*inf*) to quarrel. ● **fall through** to fail (*plans falling through*).

fallacy /**fa**-la-see/ *n* a wrong idea or belief, usually one that is generally believed to be true, false reasoning (*it is a fallacy that more expensive things are always of better quality*). ● *adj* **fallacious** /fa-**lay**-shus/.

fallible /**fa**-la-bl/ *adj* (*fml*) able to make mistakes (*all humans are fallible*). ● *n* **fallibility** /fa-la-**bi**-li-tee/.

fallout /**faw**-lout/ *n* particles of radioactive dust that are in the air and fall to the ground after an atomic explosion.

fallow /**fa**-lo/ *adj* ploughed but left unplanted for a season or more to kill weeds, make soil richer, etc. (*fields lying fallow*). ● *also n.*

false /**fawlse**/ *adj* **1** not true (*a false account of what happened*). **2** disloyal (*false friends*). **3** not real, fake (*a false beard*). ● *ns* **falseness** /**fawlse**-ness/, **falsity** /**fawl**-si-tee/.

falsehood /**fawlse**-hood/ *n* (*fml*) a lie (*tell falsehoods*).

falter /**fawl**-ter/ *vb* **1** to speak or say in an uncertain or hesitant way (*"I didn't know what to say," she faltered/falter out a few words of apology*). **2** to stumble (*he faltered as he went down the slippery steps*).

fame /**fame**/ *n* the state of being well-known (*prefers personal happiness to fame*).

famed /**faymd**/ *adj* (*fml*) well-known (*famed for her cooking*).

familiar /fa-**mil**-yar/ *adj* **1** well-known because often seen (*a familiar figure in the town*). **2** having good knowledge of (*familiar with the layout of the town*). **3** too friendly, disrespectful (*object to his talking to her in such a familiar way*). ● *n* **1** a close friend. **2** in folklore, an evil spirit constantly with someone and usually dwelling within an animal. ● *n* **familiarity** /fa-mi-lee-**ya**-ri-tee/.

familiarize /fa-**mil**-ya-rize/ *vb*, *also* **familiarise** (*Br*) to make used to (*familiarizing himself with the rules of the game*).

family /**fam**-lee/ *n* **1** a household, parents and

children. **2** one's children (*a couple with no family*). **3** people descended from the same ancestors. **4** a group of things in some way related to one another (e.g., races, animals, etc.).

family tree /**fam**-lee **tree**/ *n* a chart that shows the members of a family, their ancestors, and their relationship to one another.

famine /**fa**-min/ *n* a shortage of food (*people starving during the famine*).

famish /**fa**-mish/ *vb*. ● **to be famished** (*inf*) to be very hungry.

famous /**fay**-mus/ *adj* well-known to all (*famous actor/a famous building/a famous painting*).

fan[1] /**fan**/ *n* an instrument or machine that causes a current of air (*use an electric fan in hot weather*). ● *vb* (**fanned** /**fand**/, **fanning** /**fa**-ning/) to move the air with a fan. ● **fan out** to spread out over a wider front (*police fanning out over the fields to look for evidence*).

fan[2] /**fan**/ *n* a follower or supporter (*football fans*).

fanatic /fa-**na**-tic/ *n* someone who holds a belief, especially a religious or political belief, so strongly that he or she can neither discuss it reasonably nor think well of those who disagree with it (*a health food fanatic*). ● *n* **fanaticism** /fa-**na**-ti-si-zum/.

fanatical /fa-**na**-ti-cal/ *adj* having the views of a fanatic (*fanatical about cleanliness*).

fan belt /**fan**-belt/ *n* a tough, thin belt on most car engines.

fanciful /**fan**-si-ful/ *adj* **1** imaginative, inclined to have strange, unreal ideas (*a fanciful child*). **2** imaginary, unreal (*fanciful ideas*).

fancy /**fan**-see/ *n* **1** (*fml*) the imagination (*poets relying on fancy*). **2** a false idea or belief, something imagined (*just an old person's fancy*). **3** a sudden desire (*a pregnant woman with a fancy for oranges*). **4** a liking for, often a romantic one (*a fancy for the girl next door*). ● *adj* not plain, ornamented. ● *vb* **1** (*fml*) to imagine (*he fancied that he saw a ghost*). **2** (*inf*) to like (*fancying a drink*). **3** to be romantically or sexually attracted to (*Robert fancies Susan*).

fanfare /**fan**-fare/ *n* the sounding of many trumpets in greeting (*a fanfare introducing the queen*).

fang /**fang**/ *n* **1** a long, pointed tooth (*the fangs of the wolf*). **2** the tooth of a snake that is used to inject venom, or poison, into its prey.

fantail /**fan**-tale/ *n* **1** a part, tail, or end that is spread out like a fan. **2** any of several kinds of birds with a very broad tail.

fantasia /fan-**tay**-zha/ *n* a light or fanciful piece of music.

fantastic /fan-**ta**-stic/ *adj* **1** strange or weird (*amazed by her fantastic design*). **2** created in the mind, fanciful, unrealistic (*fantastic hopes of wealth*). **3** (*inf*) very large (*a fantastic sum of money*). **4** (*inf*) very good, excellent (*a fantastic performance*).

fantasy /**fan**-ta-see/ *n* **1** an unusual or far-fetched idea, a dream (*have fantasies about lying on a sun-drenched beach*). **2** a story with highly imaginative characters or settings that are not part of the real world (*he read a fantasy that had unicorns and dragons in it*).

far /**far**/ *adj* distant (*far places*). ● *adv* at a distance in time, space, or degree (*to travel far*).

faraway /**far**-a-way/ *adj* **1** distant in time, space, or degree. **2** dreamy, distracted (*a faraway look*).

farce /**farse**/ *n* **1** a stage play intended only to arouse laughter. **2** a laughable or senseless, unreasonable situation (*the trial was a farce—they had already decided he was guilty*).

farcical /**far**-si-cal/ *adj* laughable, senseless, unreasonable.

fare /**fare**/ *vb* (*fml or old*) to be or do (ill or well) (*he fared well on his travels*). ● *n* **1** food. **2** the cost of a travel ticket (*unable to afford the train fare*). **3** a passenger on a bus or in a taxi (*taxi drivers picking up fares*).

farewell /**far**-**well**/ *interj* goodbye.

farfel /**for**-fel/ *n* noodle dough formed into small grains.

far-fetched /**far**-fecht/ *adj* so unlikely as to be almost impossible (*far-fetched stories of his adventures*).

farina /fa-**ree**-na/ *n* a hot cereal made from wheat, potatoes, nuts, etc.

farm /**farm**/ *n* an area of land prepared for crops and/or herds by the owner. ● *vb* to use land as a farm (*farm the land next to ours*). ● *n* **farmer** /**for**-mer/. ● **farm out** to give out to be done by others (*farm out work*).

farmstead /**farm**-sted/ *n* a land and buildings of a farm.

farrow /**fa**-ro/ *n* a litter of baby pigs.

farseeing /**far**-see-ing/ *adj* wise, having shown good judgment.

farsighted /**far**-sie-tid/ *adj* **1** having better vision for distant objects than for near ones. **2** *see* farseeing.

farther /**far**-ther/ *adj* **1** at or to a greater distance. **2** additional.

fascinate /fa-si-nate/ *vb* to attract or interest very strongly, to charm (*she was fascinated by his travel stories/her beauty fascinated him*). ● *n* **fascination** /fa-si-**nay**-shun/.

fascism /fa-shi-zum/ *n* a strict political movement based on one person/group being in charge of the country in a militaristic way, incorporating racist views. ● *n* and *adj* **fascist** /fa-shist/.

fashion /fa-shin/ *n* **1** the way in which a thing is done or made (*paint after the fashion of van Gogh*). **2** the kinds of clothes popular at a certain time (*1920s fashion*). ● *vb* to shape, to make (*fashion a figure out of clay*).

fashionable /fash-na-bl/ *adj* **1** following a style that is currently popular (*fashionable clothes/fashionable furniture*). **2** used or visited by people following a current fashion (*a fashionable hotel*).

fast¹ /fast/ *vb* to do without food, especially for religious reasons (*Muslims fasting during Ramadan/patients fasting before being operated on*). ● *n* act or time of fasting.

fast² /fast/ *adj* **1** firm, fixed (*make fast the rope*). **2** quick, swift (*at a fast pace*). ● *adv* **1** firmly (*made fast*). **2** quickly (*run fast*). **3** (*old*) near.

fasten /fa-sen/ *vb* **1** to fix firmly (*fasten the gate*). **2** to fix to (*fasten a brooch to her dress*).

fastener /fa-sner/ *ns* **1** a device that joins together or fixes one thing to another (*a zip fastener*). **2** someone who fastens.

fastening /fa-se-ning/ *see* **fasten 1**.

fast-food /fast-food/ *n* hot food that is prepared and served very quickly, often taken away to be eaten (*fast-food such as hamburgers and French fries*).

fastidious /fa-**sti**-dee-us/ *adj* hard to please (*fastidious about what she eats*). ● *n* **fastidiousness** /fa-**sti**-dee-us-ness/.

fast lane /fast lane/ *n* a lane on a highway for moving at a higher speed or for passing other automobiles.

fastness /fast-ness/ *n* **1** the quality of being fast or quick. **2** a fort, a stronghold.

fast track /fast track/ *n* a career path offering rapid advancement.

fat /fat/ *adj* well fed, fleshy. ● *n* **1** an oily substance in animal bodies (*cut the fat off the meat*). **2** this substance or the oily substance found in some plants when in solid or almost solid form, used as a food or in cooking (*fry the chicken in vegetable fat*).

fatal /fay-tal/ *adj* **1** causing death (*a fatal accident*). **2** bringing danger or ruin, or having unpleasant results.

fatality /fay-**ta**-li-tee/ *n* **1** death caused by accident, war, etc. (*a bomb attack resulting in several fatalities*). **2** (*fml*) deadliness (*the fatality of certain diseases*).

fate /fate/ *n* **1** a power that is supposed to decide future events before they happen (*decide to take no action and leave it up to fate*). **2** what will happen to someone in the future (*a judge deciding the accused person's fate*).

fateful /fate-ful/ *adj* important for one's future (*a fateful decision*).

father /fa-ther/ *n* **1** a male parent. **2** a person who begins, invents, or first makes something (*the founding fathers of the United States*). **3** a priest. ● *vb* **1** to be the father of (*father several children*). **2** to start an idea or movement (*fathered the Scout movement*).

fatherhood /fa-ther-hood/ *n* the state of being a father.

father-in-law /fa-ther-in-law/ *n* the father of someone's spouse.

fathom /fa-thom/ *n* a measurement of 6 feet or 1.8 meters, especially of the depth of water. ● *vb* to understand fully.

fatigue /fa-**teeg**/ *n* **1** weariness, great tiredness (*suffering from fatigue after climbing the mountain*). **2** an unpleasant or tiring job. ● *vb* to tire out.

fatten /fa-ten/ *vb* to make fat (*fattening turkeys for Thanksgiving*).

fatty /fa-tee/ *adj* containing fat.

faucet /faw-set/ *n* a device for regulating the flow of a liquid from a pipe (*turn off the faucet while brushing your teeth*).

fault /fawlt/ *n* **1** a mistake (*the accident was his fault*). **2** a weakness in character (*his main fault is laziness*). **3** an imperfection, something wrong with something (*a fault in the machine*). ● *adj* **faulty**. **4** a break in the rock of Earth's crust that moves against, above, or below the other side.

faun /fawn/ *n* in Roman legend, a minor god, half man and half goat.

fauna /faw-na/ *n* all the animals found in a country or region.

favor /fay-vur/ *n*, *also* **favour** (*Br, Cdn*) **1** a feeling of kindness or approval toward (*look with favor on the suggestion*). **2** an act done out of kindness (*do him a favor and give him a ride to work*). **3** something (e.g., a flower, rosette, etc.) worn as a sign of good will or support (*favors worn by the politician's supporters*). ● *vb* **1** (*fml*) to show more kindness to one person than to another (*favor* *his son over his daughter*). **2** to prefer (*she favors the yellow dress*). **3** to give an advantage (*the weather favored the other team*).

favorable /**fay**-vu-ra-bl/ *adj, also* **favourable** (*Br, Cdn*) kindly, helpful (*favorable weather conditions*).

favorite /**fay**-vu-rit/ *n, also* **favourite** (*Br, Cdn*) a person or thing preferred to others (*accused of being the teacher's favorite*). ● *also adj.*

favoritism /**fay**-vu-ra-ti-zum/ *n, also* **favouritism** (*Br, Cdn*) showing more liking for one person than for others (*show favoritism to the youngest of her children*).

fawn[1] /fawn/ *n* **1** a young deer. **2** a yellowish brown color. ● *adj* yellowish brown.

fawn[2] /fawn/ *vb* to flatter or behave like a servant to gain another's favor (*fawning on his rich uncle*). ● *adj* **fawning** /**faw**-ning/.

fax /faks/ *n* **1** a machine that sends and receives documents electronically along a telephone line and then prints them out, see **facsimile**, also called **fax machine**. **2** a document sent in this way. ● *vb* to send by fax machine (*fax the exam results*).

FBI /ef-bee-eye/ *abbr* = **Federal Bureau of Investigation**: an governmental organization that solves crimes.

fear /feer/ *n* dread, terror, anxiety (*have a fear of spiders/the noises in the night filled her with fear*). ● *also vb.*

fearful /**feer**-ful/ *adj* **1** afraid (*fearful of being attacked*). **2** terrible (*a fearful storm/a fearful sight*). **3** (*inf*) very bad, very great (*a fearful liar*).

fearless /**feer**-less/ *adj* unafraid (*fearless explorers*).

fearsome /**feer**-sum/ *adj* (*fml*) causing fear (*a fearsome sight*).

feasible /**fee**-zi-bl/ *adj* possible, able to be done (*a feasible plan/it is not feasible to use that method*). ● *n* **feasibility** /fee-zi-**bi**-li-tee/.

feast /feest/ *n* **1** a meal with plenty of good things to eat and drink. **2** something extremely pleasing (*the view was a feast for the eyes*). **3** a day or period of time kept in memory, especially in religion, such as in honor of God or a saint. ● *vb* **1** to eat well. **2** to provide a good meal for others.

feat /feet/ *n* a deed notable for courage, skill, etc.

feather /**fe**-ther/ *n* one of the growths that cover a bird's body. ● *vb* to line or cover with feathers. ● **feather one's nest** to make a profit for oneself by taking advantage of a situation.

feature /**fee**-chur/ *n* **1** an outstanding part of anything (*his eyes are his most striking feature*). **2** a special long article in a newspaper (*a feature on children's rights*). **3** *pl* the face (*have small features*). ● *vb* to give or have a position, especially an important one (*money features largely in his life*).

February /**feb**-ye-wa-ree/ *n* the second month of the year.

feckless /**fec**-less/ *adj* **1** helpless (*so feckless she can't boil an egg*). **2** careless.

federal /**fe**-de-ral/ *adj* united under one central government, but keeping local control of certain matters.

federation /fe-de-**ray**-shun/ *n* **1** a group of states that give up certain powers to a common central government. **2** a joining of certain groups of people.

fee /fee/ *n* **1** a payment made for special professional services, a charge or payment (*a lawyer's fee*). **2** money paid for entering or being taught in a school, college, etc.

feeble /**fee**-bl/ *adj* very weak (*the old lady has grown very feeble/hear a feeble cry*). ● *n* **feebleness** /**fee**-bl-ness/.

feed /feed/ *vb* (*pt, pp* **fed** /fed/) **1** to give food to (*feed the children early*). **2** to eat (*cats feeding on mice*). **3** to provide what is necessary for (*feed the furnace/feed the imagination*). **4** to put into (*feed data into the computer*). ● *n* food.

feedback /**feed**-back/ *n* information about how good or bad something or someone has been (*feedback about the athlete's performance*).

feel /feel/ *vb* (*pt, pp* **felt** /felt/) **1** to touch (*feel the bump on his head*). **2** to find out by touching (*feel the quality of the cloth*). **3** to experience or be aware of (*feel a sudden anger/feel the cold*). **4** to believe or consider (*feel that she is too old*). **5** to be moved by, to have pity (*feel for the orphaned children*). ● *n* the sense of touch, a quality as revealed by touch (*the smooth feel of silk*).

feeler /**fee**-ler/ *n* **1** the threadlike organ of touch on an insect. **2** something said to try to get others to give their opinions (*put out feelers to test the market*).

feeling /**fee**-ling/ *n* **1** the sense of touch (*lose the feeling in the fingers of her right hand*). **2** emotion (*a feeling of sadness*). **3** kindness for others (*have no feeling for the orphaned children*). **4** an impression or belief (*I have a feeling that he is lying*). ● *adj* able to understand the emotions of others.

feet *see* **foot**.

feign /fane/ *vb* to pretend (*feign sleep*).

feint /**faynt**/ n a pretended movement (*the hockey player made a feint on one side of the goal before landing it in the other side*). ● *also vb*.

feisty /**fie**-stee/ *adj* energetic, full of spirit.

feline /**fee**-line/ *adj* **1** catlike. **2** of the cat family.

fell[1] /**fel**/ *pt of* **fall**

fell[2] /**fel**/ *vb* to cut down, to knock down (*felled trees for firewood*).

fell[3] /**fel**/ *adj* (*old*) cruel, savage, deadly (*a fell blow*).

fell[4] /**fel**/ *n* an animal's hide or skin.

fell[5] /**fel**/ *n* (*Br*) a rocky, bare hill, a moor.

fellow /**fe**-lo/ *n* **1** one of a pair (*the fellow to the glove*). **2** a companion and an equal (*school fellows*). **3** a member of a learned society or a college. **4** (*inf*) a man (*quite a nice fellow*).

fellowship /**fe**-lo-ship/ *n* **1** company (*seek the fellowship of his co-workers*). **2** friendship (*feelings of fellowship among the staff*). **3** an association (*a youth fellowship*). **4** a grant of money given to someone to enable him or her to do advanced studies.

felon /**fe**-lon/ *n* (*fml*) a criminal (*convicted of being a felon*).

felony /**fe**-lo-nee/ *n* (*fml*) a serious crime (*commit a felony*).

felt[1] /**felt**/ *pt and pp of* **feel**.

felt[2] /**felt**/ *n* a cloth made of wool and hair or fur being worked together by pressure, heat, etc. instead of by weaving (*a felt hat*).

female /**fee**-male/ *adj* **1** consisting of girls or women (*the female changing area*). **2** of or relating to the sex that produces offspring (*our female dog is having puppies soon*). ● *also n*.

feminine /**fe**-mi-nin/ *adj* **1** having the qualities considered suitable for a woman (*wear feminine clothes*). **2** of a woman (*a feminine voice*).

feminism /**fe**-mi-nis-zum/ *n* the principle that men and women should have equal rights. ● *n* **feminist** /**fe**-mi-nist/.

femininity /fe-mi-**ni**-ni-tee/ *n* the state of being female or womanly (*the femininity of her style of decoration*).

femur /**fee**-mur/ *n* (*fml*) the thighbone (*break his femur*). ● *adj* **femoral** /**fe**-mo-ral/.

fence /**fense**/ *n* **1** a wall made of wood or of wooden posts and wire to enclose a field (*a fence made of wire netting*). **2** the art of self defense with a sword. **3** (*inf*) a receiver of stolen goods (*the burglars handed on the stolen jewelry to a fence*). ● *vb* **1** to put a fence around (*fence in the garden*). **2** to take part in swordplay. **3** to avoid giving direct answers

to questions, especially by quibbling over minor points. ● **sit on the fence** to give no decision either way, to be neutral (*sit on the fence and not give one's support to either side*).

fencing /**fen**-sing/ *n* **1** the materials for making a fence. **2** swordplay as a sport.

fend /**fend**/ *vb* **1** to keep off, to turn aside (*fend off blows/fend off attackers*). **2** to look after (*fend for oneself*).

fender /**fen**-der/ *n* **1** a guard around the fireplace. **2** a pad made of rope, canvas, or wood to protect the side of a ship when at a pier. **3** a metal or plastic enclosure over the wheels of an automobile.

fennel /**fe**-nel/ *n* a sweet-smelling plant used as a herb and vegetable.

ferment /**fer**-ment/ *n* **1** that which causes fermentation. **2** excitement (*children in a state of ferment before Christmas*). ● *vb* **ferment** /fer-**ment**/ **1** to cause or undergo fermentation (*ferment alcohol*). **2** to excite (*ferment trouble among the workers*).

fermentation /fer-men-**tay**-shun/ *n* a chemical change that causes solids to break up and mix and liquids to froth and bubble.

fern /**fern**/ *n* a plant with no flowers and feathery leaves that reproduces by spores.

ferocious /fe-ro-shus/ *adj* fierce, cruel, savage (*a ferocious dog/a ferocious attack*). ● *n* **ferocity** /fe-**ros**-i-tee/.

ferret /**fe**-ret/ *n* **1** a small weasel-like animal used in hunting rabbits. **2** a rare, black-footed weasel. ● *vb* **1** to search busily and persistently (*ferreting about in the cupboard*). **2** to find something carefully hidden (*ferret out her secret diary/ferret out details of her past*).

Ferris wheel /**fe**-ris wheel/ *n* a large, upright wheel that rotates and that has seats on it; used as an amusement-park ride.

ferry /**fe**-ree/ *vb* **1** to carry over water in a boat or airplane (*ferrying passengers to the island*). **2** to transport (*ferried the children to and from school*). ● *n* **1** a boat that ferries (*the ferry that sank*). **2** the place where a ferry crosses.

fertile /**fer**-tile/ *adj* **1** able to produce a lot of, fruitful (*fertile land*). **2** inventive (*a fertile imagination*). ● *n* **fertility** /fer-**ti**-li-tee/.

fertilize /**fer**-ti-lize/ *vb, also* **fertilise** (*Br*) to make fertile or fruitful, to enrich (*fertilizing the soil with manure*).

fertilizer /**fer**-ti-lie-zer/ *n, also* **fertiliser** (*Br*) a material mixed into soil to make it more fertile.

fervent /**fer**-vent/ *adj* 1 eager, devoted, sincere (*a fervent supporter of the local team*). 2 hot, burning, glowing.

fervid /**fer**-vid/ *adj* (*fml*) hot, glowing (*a fervid desire*).

fervor /**fer**-vor/ *n, also* **fervour** (*Br, Cdn*) strength of feeling (*speak with great fervor*).

fester /**fess**-ter/ *vb* 1 (*of a wound*) to become full of poisonous matter, to become infected. 2 to give rise to bitter feelings, to become bitter (*memories of the insult festering in his mind/resentment festered over the years*).

festival /**fe**-sti-val/ *n* 1 a day or number of days spent in joy, celebrating, etc. (*a religious festival*). 2 a season of plays, films, concerts, etc. (*a musical festival*).

festive /**fe**-stiv/ *adj* suited to a feast, merry, joyous (*a festive occasion*).

festivity /fe-**sti**-vi-tee/ *n* joyful celebration, merrymaking (*join in the festivities*).

festoon /fe-**stoon**/ *n* a drooping chain of flowers, ribbons, etc., put up as a decoration, a hanging wreath. ● *n* to decorate with festoons, etc. (*a room festooned with balloons*).

feta /**fe**-ta/ *n* a soft, white cheese first made in Greece.

fetal /**fee**-tal/ *adj* of or like a baby that has not yet been born.

fetch /**fech**/ *vb* 1 to go and bring (*fetch water from the well*). 2 to be sold for (*an old vase fetching $2000*).

fetching /**fe**-ching/ *adj* attractive (*a fetching red hat*).

fetish /**fe**-tish/ *n* 1 an object that is worshipped and believed to have magic power. 2 something regarded with too much attention or respect (*make a fetish of cleanliness*).

fetus /**fee**-tus/ *n* an unborn baby.

feud /**fyood**/ *n* a lasting quarrel or strife between persons, families, etc. (*a feud between the families for 200 years*).

feudal /**fyoo**-dal/ *adj* having to do with feudalism.

feudalism /**fyoo**-da-li-zum/ *n* a system in medieval Europe under which people worked and lived on land in exchange for military or other services.

fever /**fee**-ver/ *n* 1 a disease causing great heat in the body (*scarlet fever*). 2 an abnormally high body temperature (*symptoms of flu such as fever and aching limbs*). 3 excitement (*in a fever of impatience*).

fevered /**fee**-verd/, **feverish** /**fee**-ve-rish/ *adjs* 1 hot with fever (*the child is feverish/a fevered brow*). 2 excited (*with feverish haste*).

few /**fyoo**/ *adj* not many, a small number of.

fez /**fez**/ *n* a brimless red cap with a black tassel.

fiancé /fee-on-**say**/ *n* a man engaged to be married. ● *f* **fiancée** /fee-on-**say**/ a woman engaged to be married.

fiasco /fee-a-**sco**/ *n* (*pl* **fiascoes** *or* **fiascos**) a complete failure, a laughable failure (*the show was a complete fiasco*).

fib /**fib**/ *n* a not very serious lie or untruth (*children scolded for telling fibs*). ● *vb* (**fibbed, fibbing** /**fi**-bing/) to tell untruths. ● *n* **fibber** /**fi**-ber/.

fiber /**fie**-ber/ *n* 1 a threadlike part of an animal or plant (*cotton fibers/nerve fibers*). 2 a material made of fibers (*woolen fiber for spinning*).

fiberglass /**fie**-ber **glass**/ *n* finely spun, cottonlike glass.

fibrous /**fie**-bruss/ *adj* like or made of fibers (*a fibrous substance*).

fibula /**fi**-byu-la/ *n* (*fml*) the outer of the two bones between the knee and the ankle (*fracture her fibula*).

fickle /**fi**-cul/ *adj* quickly changing, not faithful (*a fickle friend*). ● *n* **fickleness** /**fi**-cul-ness/.

fiction /**fic**-shun/ *n* 1 a made-up story (*the account of the event was a complete fiction*). 2 the art of writing stories (*works of fiction*). 3 novels (*publish fiction*).

fictitious /fic-**ti**-shus/ *adj* imaginary, invented (*fictitious characters/a fictitious town*).

fiddle /**fi**-dl/ *n* a violin. ● *vb* 1 to play the violin. 2 to play about with (*a girl fiddling with her hair*). 3 to prepare or alter dishonestly to one's own advantage (*an accountant fiddling the books*). ● *n* **fiddler** /**fid**-ler/.

fiddlehead /**fi**-dl-hed/ *n* 1 a carved decoration on a ship's bow, curved like a violin head. 2 the coiled tip of a young fern often cooked and eaten as a vegetable.

fiddler crab /**fid**-ler crab/ *n* a small, burrowing crab, the male of which has one claw much bigger than the other.

fiddlesticks /**fi**-dl-sticks/ *interj* (*old*) nonsense.

fidelity /fi-**de**-li-tee/ *n* 1 faithfulness, loyalty (*rely on his followers' fidelity*). 2 exactness (*the fidelity of the translation*).

fidget /**fi**-jet/ *vb* to move about restlessly (*children fidgeting with impatience*). ● *also n*.

field /**feeld**/ *n* 1 open country. 2 an enclosed area of ground. 3 a battlefield. 4 a sports ground. ● *vb* 1 to catch and return a ball. **2** to put a team or player in the field for a game. **3** to deal with, or handle (*to field phone calls*).

fielder /**feel**-dur/ n a baseball player whose position is in the outfield.

field goal /**feeld**/ n **1** in football, a goal in which a ball is kicked from the field and scores three points. **2** in basketball, a basket which is scored while the ball is in play, which score two or three points.

field hockey /**feeld**-hok-ee/ n a team game played on a field in which players use long sticks with a curved, flat bottom to hit a small, hard ball into the other team's goal.

field trip /**feeld**-trip/ n a trip away from the classroom to learn something new first hand.

fiend /**feend**/ n **1** a devil. **2** a very cruel person (*the guard in the prison was a real fiend*). • adj **fiendish** /**feen**-dish/.

fierce /**feerse**/ adj wild, angry (*a fierce tiger/a fierce wind/a fierce look*). • n **fierceness** /**feerse**-ness/.

fiery /**fie**-ree/ adj **1** having to do with fire. **2** easily angered or excited.

fiesta /fee-**ess**-ta/ n a festival or celebration, especially a religious one.

fife /**fife**/ n a small flute with six to eight finger holes.

fig /**fig**/ n the fig tree or its fruit.

fight /**fite**/ vb (pt, pp **fought** /**fot**/) **1** to use force against another (*boys fighting*). **2** to take part in war or battle (*armies fighting*). **3** to quarrel, to argue (*brother and sister always fighting*). **4** to try hard to succeed (*fighting for his life*). • n **1** a struggle in which force is used, a battle. **2** a hard effort (*a fight for poor people to survive*).

figure /**fi**-gyur/ n **1** the shape of the body (*have a slim figure*). **2** a person or a shape of a thing (*see three figures in the distance*). **3** lines drawn to show a shape (*a six-sided figure*). **4** a number. **5** a price (*the house will fetch a high figure*). **6** a diagram or illustration (*number the figures in the book*). • vb **1** to work out the answer to a sum or problem. **2** to appear (*she figures in his account of the event*). **3** (inf) to think or consider (*I figure he will arrive soon*).

figurehead /**fi**-gyur-hed/ n **1** a carved figure fixed on the front of a ship (*a figurehead in the shape of a woman*). **2** a person who has a high position but no real power (*the owner is now just a figurehead in the company*).

figure of speech /**fi**-gyur ov-**speech**/ n the use of words in an unusual meaning or order to express ideas with greater understanding or feeling.

figure skating /**fi**-gyur **skay**-ting/ n ice skating in which the skater makes elaborate figures on the ice and shows his or her ability by balancing and leaping in dancelike ways.

figurine /fi-gyu-**reen**/ n a small, molded sculpture.

filament /**fi**-la-ment/ n **1** a very thin thread. **2** the thin wire in a light bulb.

file[1] /**file**/ n **1** a number of papers arranged in order (*a file relating to the house sale*). **2** any device that keeps these papers in order (*a cardboard file*). **3** in a computer, a collection of related information stored under a particular name. **4** a row of persons, one behind the other (*a file of schoolgirls*). • vb **1** to put in place in a file (*file the correspondence*). **2** to walk in file (*people filing out of church*).

file[2] /**file**/ n a tool with a rough face for smoothing or cutting. • vb to smooth or cut away with a file (*filing her nails/filed through the metal bars*).

filings /**fi**-lingz/ npl the small pieces rubbed off by a file (*iron filings*).

fill /**fil**/ vb **1** to make full (*fill the bathtub with hot water/the news filled him with sadness*). **2** to become full (*the hall filled quickly*). **3** to stop up (*fill the holes in the wall*). **4** to occupy (*fill a teaching post*). • n as much as fills or satisfies, often to a great extent (*have one's fill of the excellent food/have one's fill of his advice*).

fillet /**fi**-let/ n **1** a thin strip or band worn around the head to keep the hair in place. **2** a flat, boneless meat or fish (*fillet of chicken*). • vb to take the bones out of and slice.

filling /**fi**-ling/ n **1** the act of one that fills. **2** a thing used to fill something else. **3** the metal, plastic, etc. that a dentist puts into a prepared cavity.

filly /**fi**-lee/ n a young female horse.

film /**film**/ n **1** a thin skin or covering (*a film of dust over the furniture*). **2** the thin roll of material on which pictures are taken by a camera. **3** a movie (*a horror film*). • vb to take a moving picture.

filter /**fil**-ter/ n a strainer, a device through which liquid is passed to clean it. • vb to clean or separate by passing through a filter (*filter the coffee*).

filth /**filth**/ n **1** dirt (*clean the filth from his clothes*). **2** anything considered foul, indecent, or offensive.

filthy /**filth**-ee/ adj **1** very dirty (*filthy clothes after walking through the mud*). **2** disgusting, foul.

fin /**fin**/ n a small winglike organ by means of which a fish swims.

final /fie-nal/ *adj* **1** last (*the final chapter of the book*). **2** putting an end to (*my final offer/the judge's decision is final*). ● *n* finality /fi-na-li-tee/. ● *adv* **finally** /fi-na-lee/.

finale /fi-na-lee/ *n* the last part of a piece of music, a play, etc. (*the whole cast took part in the finale*).

finalist /fie-na-list/ *n* a person who takes part in the final round of a contest.

finance /fi-**nanse**/ *n* **1** having to do with money (*seek a career in finance*). **2** *pl* money resources (*keep his finances in order*). ● *vb* **finance** /fi-**nanse**/ to find or provide the money for (*financing his son's business*). ● *adj* **financial** /fi-nan-shal/. ● *n* **financier** /fi-nan-**seer**/.

finch /finch/ *n* one of many kinds of small singing birds.

find /finde/ *vb* (*pt, pp* **found** /found/) **1** to come upon what a person is looking for (*find the lost ring*). **2** to discover (*he was too late to find oil*). **3** to decide (*found the accused guilty*). ● *n* a valuable discovery.

finding /fine-ding/ *n* a decision or opinion reached (*the jury's findings*).

fine[1] /fine/ *adj* **1** very thin or small (*fine bones*). **2** excellent (*a fine performance*). **3** delicate, beautiful (*fine china*). **4** bright, sunny (*a fine day/fine weather*). **5** healthy (*ill yesterday but feeling fine today*). **6** slight (*a fine difference*).

fine[2] /fine/ *n* money paid as a punishment. ● *vb* to punish by fine (*fined for a driving offence*).

finesse /fi-ness/ *n* great skill and cleverness (*handle the situation with great finesse*).

finger /fing-ger/ *n* one of the five points that extend from the hand or glove. ● *vb* to touch with the fingers (*finger the piano keys/fingered the material*).

fingering /fing-ge-ring/ *n* the use of the fingers in playing a musical instrument.

fingernail /fing-ger-nale/ *n* the horny substance growing from the end of the finger.

fingerpicking /fing-ger-pi-king/ *n* a style of guitar playing in which the thumb plays the bass notes and the index and middle fingers play the rest, often heard in country music and done with fingerpicks, special metal or plastic picks that fit on each finger. ● *n* **fingerpick** the picks defined above.

fingerprint /fing-ger-print/ *n* **1** the mark made by the tips of the fingers (*burglars who left no fingerprints anywhere*). **2** an ink print of the lines on the fingertips for identification purposes (*a police file of fingerprints*).

fingertips /fing-ger-tips/ *npl* the tips of the fingers. ● **have at one's fingertips** to have ready knowledge of (*have the facts of the situation at their fingertips*).

finicky /fi-ni-kee/ *adj* **1** fussy, too particular (*finicky tastes in food/a finicky eater*). **2** needing a lot of attention to detail (*a finicky job*).

finish /fi-nish/ *vb* **1** to bring to an end (*unable to finish the job*). **2** to come to an end (*the show finished early*). ● *n* **1** the end (*the finish of the race*). **2** extra touches to make perfect (*furniture with a fine finish/manners lacking finish*).

finite /fie-nite/ *adj* having an end, limited (*human knowledge is finite*).

fiord *see* **fjord.**

fir /fur/ *n* a cone-bearing (coniferous) tree.

fire /fire/ *n* **1** the activity of burning, which gives out heat and light (*a forest fire*). **2** (*fml*) strong feeling, excitement (*patriotic fire*). ● *vb* **1** to start a fire. **2** to bake (*fire pottery*). **3** to cause to explode (*firing a gun*). **4** to arouse interest and/or excitement (*fired them up with enthusiasm*). **5** (*inf*) to dismiss (from a job) (*fired his assistant for being late*).

firearm /fire-arm/ *n* a gun, rifle, or pistol (*the police issued with firearms*).

firecracker /fire-cra-ker/ *n* a usually small paper covered cylinder with an explosive inside and a fuse that makes a sharp noise when set off.

fire engine /fire-en-jin/ *n* a truck that carries equipment for putting out fires and the firefighters.

fire escape /fire-i-scape/ *n* a long ladder or steps by which people can escape from a burning building.

fire extinguisher /fire ex-**ting**-gwish-er/ *n* a portable container used to put out fires.

firefighter /fire-fie-ter/ *n* a person who is trained to put out fires.

firefly /fire-flie/ *n* any of the beetles that glow in the dark.

fire house /fire-howss/ *n* the building where fire engines are kept and firefighters stay when on duty.

fireplace /fire-plase/ *n* a framed opening in the wall of a house to hold a fire (*a marble fireplace*).

fireproof /fire-proof/ *adj* that cannot be set on fire (*fireproof material for children's clothes*).

fire side /fire-side/ *n* the area next to the fireplace in a home.

fire station /fire-stay-shun/ *n* another term for **fire house.**

firewood /fire-wood/ *n* wood, such as sticks or logs, which will be burned as fuel to heat a home.

fireworks /fire-wurks/ *npl* explosives of different colors and styles set off in the dark for a showy celebration (*let off fireworks on the Fourth of July*).

firm[1] /firm/ *adj* **1** steady, not easily moved (*a table that is not quite firm/a firm grip*). **2** determined (*a firm refusal/she was quite firm about not going*). ● *n* **firmness** /firm-ness/.

firm[2] /firm/ *n* a business company organized to manufacture or trade in goods (*a publishing firm*).

first /furst/ *adj* before all others (*the first person to arrive/his first visit*). ● *adv* **1** before all others (*speak first*). **2** before doing anything else (*speak first and then act*).

first aid /fur-stade/ *n* treatment given to an injured person before the doctor arrives, simple medical attention (*received first aid when he got hurt playing football*).

first base /furst-base/ *n* the base to the left of the pitcher in baseball, the first of four the runner must run around to score.

firstborn /furst-bawrn/ *n* (*fml*) eldest child.

first class /furst-class/ adj of the highest class, rank, excellence, etc.

first family /furst-fa-mi-lee/ *n* the family of the US president.

first lady /furst-lay-dee/ *n* the wife of the US president.

first mate /furst-mate/ *n* a ship's officer next in rank below the captain.

first name /furst-name/ *n* a personal name that comes before the family name or surname and is given at birth, also called **forename** and sometimes **Christian name** (*his first name is Joe*).

fish /fish/ *n* a coldwater animal with gills and fins that lives in water. ● *vb* **1** to try to catch fish. **2** (*inf*) to search for (*fishing in her bag for her keys*). **3** (*inf*) to try to get by indirect means (*fish for compliments*).

fisher /fi-sher/ *n* a person who fishes.

fishhook /fish-hook/ *n* a hook, usually barbed, for catching fish.

fishing pole /fi-shing-pole/ *n* a simple device with a line extending out from it used to catch fish.

fishing rod /fi-shing-rod/ *n* a slender pole with an attached line, hook, and reel used in fishing.

fishmonger /fish-mong-ger/ *n* someone who buys and sells fish.

fishtail /fish-tale/ *vb* to move forward with a side-to-side swinging motion of the rear (*the car fishtailed on the ice*).

fishy /fi-shee/ *adj* **1** of or like fish (*a fishy smell*). **2** doubtful, arousing suspicion (*rather a fishy story/fishy situation*).

fission /fi-shun/ *n* the splitting into parts.

fist /fist/ *n* the hand tightly shut (*fight with their fists*).

fit[1] /fit/ *adj* **1** suitable, proper, right (*a fit person for the job/not fit behavior/food not fit to be eaten*). **2** in good health. ● *n* the particular way in which something fits (*a good fit/a tight fit*). ● *vb* (**fitted**, **fitting**) **1** to be of the right size (*a coat that fits beautifully*). **2** to suit (*a punishment that fits the crime*). **3** to make suitable (*fit the punishment to the crime*).

fit[2] /fit/ *n* **1** a sudden attack of illness, fainting, etc. (*coughing fits*). **2** a sudden feeling (*a fit of anger*).

fitful /fit-ful/ *adj* occurring in short periods, not regularly or steadily (*in fitful bursts of energy/fitful sleep*).

fitness /fit-ness/ *n* suitability (*question his fitness for the job*).

fitter /fi-ter/ *n* someone who puts the parts of machinery together.

fitting /fi-ting/ *adj* suitable, proper (*fitting behavior/a fitting end to his career*). ● *n* **1** a thing fixed in position (*kitchen fittings*). **2** the trying on of clothes to see if they fit (*a fitting for a wedding dress*).

five-and-ten-cent store /fie-van-ten-sent-store/ *n* a store that sells inexpensive items, originally mostly marked for five or ten cents each.

Five Civilized Tribes /five si-vi-liezd triebz/ *n* the Native American groups the Cherokees, Chickasaws, Choctaws, Creeks, and Seminoles as a group.

Five Nations /five nay-shunz/ *n* the Native American groups the Mohawks, Oneidas, Onodagas, Cayugas, and Senecas.

fix /fiks/ *vb* **1** to make firm (*fix the loose tiles*). **2** to arrange (*fixing a meeting*). **3** to fasten (*fixed a brooch to her dress*). **4** to repair (*fix the broken radio*). **5** (*inf*) to arrange the result of dishonestly (*fix the result of the election*). ● *n* (*inf*) a difficulty.

fixate /fik-sate/ *vb* to focus on. ● *n* **fixation** /fik-say-shun/.

fixative /fik-sa-tiv/ *n* a substance used to make something permanent, prevents fading, etc.

fixed /fikst/ *adj* firm, not moving or changing (*a fixed stare/a fixed price*). ● *adv* **fixedly** /fik-sed-lee/.

fixture /**fiks**-chur/ *n* **1** anything fastened in place (*bathroom fixtures*). **2** any person or thing that has remained in a situation so long as to seem fixed there.

fizz /**fiz**/ *vb* to release or give off many bubbles (*soda pop fizzing in the glass*). ● *n* **1** bubbles of gas in a liquid (*soda pop that has lost its fizz*). **2** the sound of fizzing. **1** (*inf*) enthusiasm, liveliness, excitement (*the fizz went out of the party*). ● *adj* fizzy.

fizzle /**fi**-zl/ *vb* to fail, to come to nothing (*after an enthusiastic start our plans fizzled out*).

fjord /fee-**awrd**/ *n* a long, narrow bay running inland between steep rocky hills.

flab /**flab**/ *n* sagging flesh.

flabbergast /**fla**-ber-gast/ *vb* to astonish (*flabbergasted by the expense of the vacation*). ● *adj* **flabbergasted**.

flabby /**fla**-bee/ *adj* **1** soft, hanging loosely (*flabby muscles*). **2** having soft loose flesh (*get flabby after giving up exercise*). ● *n* **flabbiness** /**fla**-bee-ness/.

flaccid /**fla**-sid/ *adj* soft and weak, flabby, hanging in loose folds (*flaccid muscles*).

flag[1] /**flag**/ *n* **1** a square or oblong piece of material with a pattern on it representing a country, party, association, etc. (*the French flag*). **2** a colored cloth or paper used as a sign or signal (*red flags at dangerous beaches*). ● *vb* (**flagged, flagging**) **1** to signal with flags (*flag dangerous beaches*). **2** to cause a vehicle to stop by signaling to the driver (*police flagging down speeding motorists*).

flag[2] /**flag**/ *n* any of the wild irises with flat fans of sword-shaped leaves and white, blue, or yellow flowers.

flag[3] /**flag**/ *n* a flat paving stone.

flag[4] /**flag**/ *vb* (**flagged** /**flagd**/, **flagging** /**fla**-ging/) (*fml*) to become tired (*flagging after a hard day's work*).

Flag Day /**flag** day/ *n* June 14, the day in 1777 when the US flag was adopted.

flagpole /**flag**-pole/ *n* a pole on which a flag is raised and flown.

flair /**flare**/ *n* **1** a natural ability (*a flair for languages/a flair for organizing*). **2** style, stylishness, an original and attractive quality (*dress with flair*).

flake /**flake**/ *n* **1** a small thin piece of anything, especially a small loose piece that has broken off something (*flakes of paint/flakes of chocolate*). **2** a very light piece (e.g., of snow). ● *vb* to come off in flakes (*paint flaking off*). ● *adj* flaky.

flamboyant /flam-**boy**-ant/ *adj* **1** very brightly colored or decorated (*flamboyant clothes*). **2** showy and confident (*a flamboyant person/with flamboyant gestures*).

flame /**flame**/ *n* a tongue of fire, a blaze (*a candle flame*). ● *vb* **1** to burn brightly (*the fire flamed suddenly*). **2** (*inf*) to become suddenly angry (*she was flaming*).

flaming /**flay**-ming/ *adj* **1** burning with flames. **2** excited, violent (*in a flaming temper*). **3** very bright (*flaming red hair*).

flamenco /fla-**meng**-co/ *n* a Spanish gypsy style of dance or music featuring stamping, clapping, etc.

flamingo /fla-**ming**-go/ *n* (*pl* **flamingoes** /fla-**ming**-goaz/) a brightly colored water bird with long legs and neck.

flammable /**fla**-ma-bl/ *adj* likely to catch fire and burn easily (*gasoline is very flammable*).

flan /**flan**/ *n* **1** a piece of shaped metal ready to be made into a coin by a stamp. **2** a dessert tart filled with custard, fruit, etc. **3** a Spanish dessert of custard covered with a burnt-sugar syrup.

flange /**flange**/ *n* a rim that sticks out, as on a wheel that runs on rails.

flank /**flangk**/ *n* **1** the fleshy part of an animal's side between the ribs and the hip (*stroke the horse's flank*). **2** the side of anything (e.g., an army, a mountain, etc.). ● *vb* to be at the side of, to move to the side of (*the prisoner flanked by the policemen*).

flannel /**fla**-nel/ *n* **1** a soft, loosely woven woolen cloth (*blankets made of flannel*). **2** a shirt or other piece of clothing made from this material.

flap /**flap**/ *n* **1** anything fixed at one end and hanging loose at the other (*the flap of the tent*). **2** the sound made by such a thing when it moves (*the flap of the clothes hanging on the line*). **3** (*inf*) panic, agitation (*don't get in a flap*). ● *vb* (**flapped** /**flapt**/, **flapping** /**fla**-ping/) **1** to flutter, to move up and down, to make a sound as of fluttering (*clothes flapping on the line*). **2** (*inf*) to get into a panic, to become confused or excited (*people flapping in an emergency*).

flapjack /**flap**-jack/ *n* a pancake.

flare /**flare**/ *vb* **1** to blaze up, to burn brightly but unsteadily (*a match flared in the darkness*). **2** to spread out (*jeans flaring at the bottom*). ● *n* **1** a bright, unsteady light. **2** a light used as a signal (*ships firing off emergency flares*). **3** a gradual widening, especially of a skirt.

flare-up /**flare**-up/ *n* a sudden outburst of flame, anger, trouble, etc. (*a flare-up of his illness*).

flash /flash/ *n* **1** a quick or sudden gleam (*a flash of light*). **2** (*inf*) a moment (*all over in a flash*). **3** anything lasting for a very short time (*a flash of humor*). **4** a device for producing a short burst of electric light used to take photographs in the dark. ● *vb* **1** to shine out suddenly (*lights flashing*). **2** to move very quickly (*days seeming to flash past*).

flashback /flash-back/ *n* **1** an section of a story, play, film, etc. by the telling of something that happened in the past. **2** a sudden, clear, detailed memory of something in the past.

flashcard /flash-card/ *n* one of a set of cards with words, numbers, etc. on them flashed one by one for a quick answer, used in the classroom or as a study aid.

flash flood /flash-flud/ *n* a sudden, violent flood, as after a heavy rain.

flashlight /flash-lite/ *n* **1** an electric torch (*find his way in the dark by flashlight*). **2** a short burst of electric light used to take photographs in the dark.

flashy /flash-shee/ *adj* gaudy, showy (*flashy clothes/a flashy car*).

flask /flask/ *n* **1** a kind of bottle with a narrow neck, used in laboratories. **2** a pocket bottle (*a hip flask of water*).

flat /flat/ *adj* **1** level (*flat land*). **2** uninteresting, dull, and lifeless (*things a bit flat after Christmas*). **3** (*of music*) below the right note. **4** lying full length (*people flat on the ground after the explosion*). **5** deflated, without enough air in it (*a flat tire*). **6** clear, strong, firm (*a flat denial*). **7** no longer fizzy (*soda pop gone flat*). ● *n* **1** a level area (*cycle on the flat*). **2** the flat part or side (*with the flat of my hand*). **3** a musical sign (b) showing that a note is to be played a semitone lower. **4** a flat tire (*went to fix the flat*). ● *n* **flatness**.

flatbed /flat-bed/ *adj* of a truck, trailer, etc., having a bed or platform without sides or stakes.

flatbread /flat-bred/ *n* bread made into thing, circular pieces or sheets, such as pita or matzo.

flatfish /flat-fish/ *n* a kind of fish, such as a flounder or sole, that is very flat to the bottom of the water with, as an adult, both eyes and mouth on one side of its body.

flatten /fla-ten/ *vb* to make flat (*flatten the uneven ground*).

flatter /fla-ter/ *vb* **1** to praise a lot or insincerely (*flatter his mother by complimenting her on her dress because he wanted to borrow the car*). **2** to make appear better than is true (*candlelight flatters the room*). ● *n* **flatterer** /fla-te-rer/.

flattery /fla-te-ree/ *n* insincere or a lot of praise.

flatulence /fla-chu-lense/ *n* gas in the stomach or bowels. ● *adj* **flatulent** /fla-chu-rent/.

flatware /flat-ware/ *n* flat tableware, such as knives, forks, spoons, etc.

flaunt /flawnt/ *vb* to show off, to try to draw attention to (*flaunt his wealth by buying expensive clothes*).

flauta /flaw-ta/ *n* a Mexican dish consisting of a tortilla rolled tightly around a filling, such as shredded chicken or beef, and deep fried.

flavor /flay-vor/ *n*, *also* **flavour** (*Br, Cdn*) **1** a taste (*have the flavor of strawberries*). **2** the taste special to a thing. ● *vb* to add something to a dish to improve its taste (*flavor the sauce with herbs/flavor the ice cream with vanilla*).

flavoring /flay-vor-ing/ *n*, *also* **flavouring** (*Br, Cdn*) something added to improve the taste (*artificial flavoring*).

flaw /flaw/ *n* **1** a crack, a defect, an imperfection (*the flaw reduces the price of the old vase*). **2** any weakness that makes a person or thing less than perfect, less effective, etc. (*flaws in her character/spot the flaws in his argument*). ● *adj* **flawed** /flawd/.

flawless /flaw-less/ *adj* without any imperfections or defects.

flax /flaks/ *n* a plant with narrow leaves and blue flowers, the fibers of which are made into linen and the seeds of which are made into linseed oil.

flaxen /flak-sen/ *adj* **1** like or of flax. **2** light yellow in color (*flaxen hair*).

flea /flee/ *n* a small, jumping, bloodsucking insect (*dogs with fleas*).

flea market /flee-mar-ket/ *n* a bazaar, usually outdoors, dealing mainly in cheap, secondhand goods.

fleck /flek/ *n* a spot (*flecks of dirt on the white towels/flecks of white on the cat's black fur*). ● *vb* to mark with spots (*black fur flecked with white*).

fledgling /fledge-ling/ *n* a young bird learning to fly.

flee /flee/ *vb* (*pt, pp* **fled** /fled/) to run away, to run away from (*people fleeing from the invading army*).

fleece /fleese/ *n* the woolly coat of a sheep or similar animal. ● *vb* **1** to cut the wool off (*shepherds fleecing sheep*). **2** (*inf*) to overcharge (*fleece the customers*).

fleet[1] /fleet/ *n* **1** a large number of ships, motorcars, airplanes, etc., together. **2** a large group of warships commanded by an admiral.

fleet[2] /fleet/ *adj* (*fml*) quick-moving (*fleet of foot*). ● *vb* (*fml*) to pass quickly (*time fleeting past*).

fleeting /flee-ting/ *adj* (*fml*) passing quickly (*fleeting moments*).

flesh /flesh/ *n* 1 the soft substance that covers the bones of an animal to form its body (*the trap cut into the rabbit's flesh*). 2 this as food (*animals that eat flesh rather than plants*). 3 the edible part of fruit (*the flesh of a melon*). 4 the body. 5 the desires of the body.

fleshly /flesh-lee/ *adj* having to do with the body and its desires.

fleshy /flesh-ee/ *adj* fat (*fleshy arms*).

flew /floo/ *pt of* **fly**.

flex /fleks/ *vb* to bend (*flexing his muscles/flex one's toes*). ● *n* a cord of rubber-covered wires used to carry electric currents.

flexible /flek-si-bl/ *adj* 1 easily bent (*flexible tubing*). 2 easily changed, adaptable (*flexible plans*). 3 willing and able to change according to the situation, adaptable (*flexible people*). ● *n* **flexibility** / flek-si-**bi**-li-tee/.

flick /flik/ *vb* to strike lightly and quickly (*flick a piece of dirt from his sweater/flick the light switch on*). ● *also n*.

flicker /fli-ker/ *vb* 1 to shine or burn unsteadily (*a candle flickering*). 2 to flutter, to move quickly and lightly (*with eyes flickering*). ● *also n*.

flier /flie-er/ *see* **fly**.

flight /flite/ *n* 1 the act of flying (*the airplane was in flight*). 2 the act of running away (*the flight of the refugees*). 3 the movement or path of a thing through the air (*the flight of an arrow*). 4 a journey made by air (*a long-distance flight*). 5 a number of birds flying together (*a flight of geese*). 5 a set of stairs or steps (*a flight of wooden stairs*).

flight attendant /flite a-**ten**-dant/ *n* a person whose job it is to look after passengers in an aircraft.

flight control /flite con-**trole**/ *n* 1 the control from the ground by radio of aircraft in flight. 2 a station using such control.

flight deck /flite deck/ *n* the upper deck of an aircraft carrier, which is used as a runway.

flight plan /flite plan/ *n* a pilot's oral or written report that states the speed, altitude, and destination of a flight.

flighty /flie-tee/ *adj* 1 changeable, unreliable (*flighty young girls*).

flimsy /flim-zee/ *adj* 1 thin (*a dress of flimsy material*). 2 not strong, easily broken or destroyed (*a flimsy box*). 3 weak (*a flimsy excuse*).

flinch /flinch/ *vb* to draw back in fear or pain (*flinched as the bully raised his hand*).

fling /fling/ *vb* (*pt*, *pp* **flung** /flung/) 1 to throw (*fling papers on the floor*). 2 to move suddenly and forcefully (*fling from the room in a temper*). ● *n* 1 a throw. 2 a brief love affair. 3 a trial effort.

flint /flint/ *n* 1 a hard stone (*rock containing a lot of flint*). 2 a piece of hard mineral from which sparks can be made when struck (*a flint for his lighter*). ● *also adj*.

flip /flip/ *vb* (**flipped** /flipt/, **flipping** /fli-ping/) 1 to turn over lightly but sharply (*flip over the pages of the book*). 2 to toss (*flip a coin in the air*). ● *also n*. ● *adj* disrespectful, not serious (*don't be flip with me*).

flippant /fli-pant/ *adj* not serious, disrespectful (*a flippant remark*). ● *n* **flippancy** /fli-pan-see/.

flipper /fli-per/ *n* a broad, flat part or limb used by certain sea creatures (e.g., seal, turtle, penguin) when swimming.

flirt /flurt/ *vb* 1 to show interest in for a time only (*flirt with the idea of moving*). 2 to behave toward another as if attracted by or to attract (*she was flirting with all the men at the party*). ● *n* someone who plays at making love. ● *n* **flirtation** /flur-**tay**-shun/.

flirtatious /flur-**tay**-shus/ *adj* fond of flirting.

float /float/ *vb* 1 to remain on the surface of a liquid (*rafts floated on the water/swimmers floating on their backs*). 2 to start (a new business or company) by selling shares to the public. 3 to suggest, to put forward (*float a few ideas at the meeting*). ● *n* 1 anything that floats (e.g., a raft, a buoy, etc.) or helps to make something else float (e.g., the floats of a seaplane). 2 a low, flat, decorated automobile for carrying things in a parade. 3 a cold beverage with ice cream floating in it (*a root beer float*).

flock[1] /flok/ *n* 1 a company of birds or animals (*a flock of sheep*). 2 a number of people together (*people arriving in flocks*). 3 a congregation (*a priest and his flock*). ● *vb* to come together in a crowd (*people flocking to the sales*).

flock[2] /flok/ *n* 1 a tuft or flake of wool. 2 waste wool used for stuffing cushions, etc. (*a mattress made of flock*).

floe /flo/ *n* a large sheet of floating ice.

flog /flog/ *vb* (**flogged** /flogd/, **flogging** /flog-ing/) to beat, to thrash (*flog wrongdoers*). ● *n* **flogging** /flog-ing/.

flood /flud/ *n* 1 an overflowing of water onto dry

land. **2** a rush (of water, people, etc.) (*a flood of correspondence*). **3** the flowing in of the tide. ● *vb* **1** to overflow, to cover with water (*water flooding the town*). **2** to arrive in great quantities (*letters flooded in*).

floodlight /flud-lite/ *n* a very bright lamp directed on to the outside of a building at night to light it up. ● *also vb*. ● *n* **floodlighting** /flud-lite-ing/.

flood plain /flud-plane/ *n* a plain that borders a river, made up of the soil deposited by the river after it floods.

floor /flore/ *n* **1** the bottom surface of a room on which a person walks (*an uncarpeted floor*). **2** any bottom surface (*the floor of the ocean*). **3** all the rooms, etc., on the same level in a building (*rent the first and second floors*). ● *vb* **1** to make a floor (*floor the room with pine*). **2** to knock down (*the boxer floored his opponent with one blow*). **3** (*inf*) to astound (*completely floored by his announcement to get married*).

floorboard /flore-board/ *n* the wooden boards that make up the floor to a house or building.

flooring /flore-ing/ *n* a floor, or material for making a floor.

floor plan /flore-plan/ *n* a scaled drawing of the layout of the rooms of a house or building.

flop /flop/ *vb* (**flopped** /flopt/, **flopping** /flop-ing/) **1** to sit or fall down heavily or loosely (*flop down exhausted in a chair*). **2** to hang or swing heavily or loosely (*long hair flopping*). **3** to fail completely, to be unsuccessful (*the play flopped*). ● *n* a complete failure.

floppy /flop-ee/ *adj* hanging loosely, not stiff (*a floppy hat*).

floppy disk /flop-ee-disk/ *n* a small disk made of magnetic material on which computer data is stored. *See* **hard disk**.

flora /flo-ra/ *n* all the plants in a country or region.

floral /flo-ral/ *adj* having to do with flowers (*a floral arrangement/a floral pattern*).

florist /flo-rist/ *n* someone who grows or sells flowers (*ask the florist to make up a bouquet*).

floss /floss/ *n* **1** rough silk. **2** any fluffy substance. **3** waxed thread for cleaning between the teeth. ● *vb* to clean teeth with floss.

flotsam /flot-sam/ *n* floating wreckage (*the flotsam from the wrecked ship*).

flounce[1] /flounse/ *vb* to move sharply or quickly (*flounced out in a temper*). ● *also n*.

flounce[2] /flounse/ *n* a gathered strip of cloth sewn by its upper edge round a skirt or dress and left hanging (*a skirt with lace flounces*). ● *n* **flouncing** /floun-sing/.

flounder[1] /floun-der/ *n* a type of flatfish, the fluke.

flounder[2] /floun-der/ *vb* **1** to struggle helplessly or awkwardly (*walkers floundering in the mud*). **2** to be in doubt as to what to say next, to hesitate, to struggle when speaking (*he lost his notes and floundered helplessly when giving the lecture*).

flour /flour/ *n* grain, especially wheat or corn, ground into powder (*whole wheat flour*).

flourish /flur-ish/ *vb* **1** to get on well, to be very successful, to prosper (*a company that is flourishing*). **2** to grow well, to bloom (*flowers flourished*). **3** to wave about in a showy manner (*flourish his letter of acceptance*). ● *n* **1** spoken words or handwriting that attract attention by being unusual. **2** a sudden short burst of music (*a flourish of trumpets*). **3** a bold, sweeping movement or gesture (*open the door to his guests with a flourish*).

floury /flou-ree/ *adj* **1** covered with flour (*floury hands*). **2** like flour (*floury potatoes*).

flout /flout/ *vb* to pay no attention to, to disobey openly and scornfully (*flouting the school rules*).

flow /flo/ *vb* **1** to move steadily and easily, as water (*tears flowing/keep the traffic flowing*). **2** to proceed evenly and continuously (*conversation flowing*). **3** to fall or hang down loosely and freely (*hair that flowed to her waist*). **4** to be plentiful (*the drinks were flowing at the party*). ● *n* **1** a flowing movement, a stream. **2** the rise of the tide. **3** a continuous stream or supply (*the flow of conversation/a flow of information*).

flowchart /flo-chart/ *n* a diagram showing the order of stages in a process or system (*a flowchart of the production process*).

flower /flour/ *n* **1** a blossom, consisting of petals and bearing pollen. **2** the best part of (*the flower of the nation's young men*). ● *vb* to blossom or bloom.

flowerpot /flour-pot/ *n* a container in which plants can be grown.

flowery /flou-ree/ *adj* **1** full of flowers (*flowery meadows*). **2** patterned with flowers (*a flowery wallpaper*). **3** ornate, overelaborate (*flowery language*).

flu /floo/ *n* short for influenza, a sickness caused by a virus.

fluctuate /fluc-che-wate/ *vb* **1** to rise and fall, as a wave (*prices fluctuating*). **2** to vary, to change continually and irregularly (*opinions that fluctuate*). ● *n* **fluctuation** /fluc-che-way-shun/.

flue /floo/ *n* a passage in a chimney for carrying away air or smoke.

fluent /**floo**-ent/ *adj* able to speak or write quickly and easily (*fluent in French/a fluent French speaker*). ● *n* **fluency** /**floo**-en-see/.

fluff /fluf/ *n* any soft or feathery material (*fluff from blankets on his dark suit/the fluff on baby chickens*).

fluffy /**fluf**-ee/ *adj* like fluff, soft and downy (*fluffy little ducklings*).

fluid /**floo**-id/ *adj* 1 able to flow, flowing. 2 able to change quickly (*fluid arrangements*). 3 smooth and graceful (*dance with fluid movements*). ● *n* any substance that flows, as liquid or gas.

fluke[1] /flook/ *n* a type of flatfish, a flounder.

fluke[2] /flook/ *n* 1 the part of an anchor that hooks into the seabed. 2 one of the pointed parts on a whale's tail.

fluke[3] /flook/ *n* (*inf*) a lucky chance (*win by a fluke*).

flume /floom/ *n* a human-made channel or chute for carrying water, usually down a mountainside.

fluorescence /floo-**re**-sense/ *n* a quality in certain substances that enables them to give off very bright light.

fluorescent /floo-**re**-sent/ *adj* having or showing fluorescence (*fluorescent paint*).

fluoride /**flaw**-ride/ *n* a chemical compound that is sometimes added to toothpaste and water supplies to prevent tooth decay.

flurry /**flu**-ree/ *n* 1 confused movement (*in a flurry of excitement when the visitors were coming*). 2 a sudden rush of air, rain, etc. (*a flurry of snow*). ● *vb* to make anxious or confused (*unexpected visitors always flurried her*).

flush /flush/ *vb* 1 to become suddenly red in the face (*flush with embarrassment/flushed with the heat*). 2 to cleanse by a flow of water (*flush the toilet*). ● *n* 1 a sudden redness in the face (*heat bringing a flush to her face*). 2 a rush of water. 3 freshness, vigor (*in the first flush of youth*). ● *adj* 1 (*inf*) having plenty of money (*he is flush because he has just been paid*). 2 level (*flush with the wall*).

fluster /**flu**-ster/ *vb* to make confused, to overexcite (*get flustered in an emergency*). ● *also n*.

flute /floot/ *n* 1 a wooden musical wind instrument. 2 a shallow hollow carved in a pillar. ● *vb* 1 to play the flute. 2 to carve hollows or grooves.

flutter /**flut**-er/ *vb* 1 to move the wings up and down quickly without flying (*moths fluttering*). 2 to move about quickly (*flags fluttering in the breeze/fluttered her eyelashes*). ● *n* 1 quick movement (*with a flutter of her eyelashes*). 2 (*inf*) excitement (*the new arrival caused a flutter in the office*). 3 (*inf*) a bet, a gamble (*have a flutter on the horses*).

fly /flie/ *vb* (*pt* **flew** /floo/, *pp* **flown** /flone/) 1 to move through the air on wings (*birds flying*). 2 to travel by airplane (*prefer to fly than to go by train*). 3 to move quickly (*I must fly—I'll be late*). 4 to run away (*fly from the invading army*). ● *n* 1 a common flying insect (*the house fly*). 2 a fishing hook covered with feathers to make it look like a fly. 3 a flap, especially one that closes the entrance to a tent. ● *n* **flier, flyer** /**flie**-er/.

FM /ef-em/ *abbr* = **frequency modulation**: a system that uses waves to send and receive sound (*we listen to 88.1 FM on the radio for news*).

foal /foal/ *n* a young horse, mule, donkey, etc. ● *vb* to give birth to a foal.

foam /foam/ *n* bubbles on the top of liquid, froth (*the foam on a glass of root beer*). ● *vb* to gather or produce foam (*a mad dog foaming at the mouth*).

focaccia /fo-**coch**-ee-a/ *n* a round, flat Italian yeast bread that has a crispy crust and contains olive oil, herbs, etc.

focal /**fo**-cal/ *adj* 1 of a focus. 2 central, main (*the room's focal point is a marble fireplace*).

focus /**fo**-cus/ *n* (*pl* **foci** /**fo**-kie/ *or* **focuses** /**fo**-cu-seez/) 1 a point at which rays of light meet. 2 a center of interest or attention (*the beautiful woman was the focus of everyone's attention*). ● *vb* 1 to bring to bear on one point (*focus his attention on the firm's financial problems*). 2 to get a clear image in the lens of a camera before taking a photograph.

fodder /**fod**-er/ *n* dried food for cattle, horses, sheep, etc.

foe /fo/ *n* (*fml*) an enemy (*the country's foe/regard his rival as a foe*).

fog /fog/ *n* a thick mist.

fogey, fogy /**fo**-gee/ *n* a person whose ideas are out of date (*teenagers think he is an old fogey for not liking loud rock music*).

foggy /**fog**-ee/ *adj* 1 misty (*a foggy day*). 2 confused, vague (*have just a foggy impression of what she looked like*).

foil[1] /foyl/ *vb* to cause to fail, to defeat (*foil their attempt at the prize*).

foil[2] /foyl/ *n* 1 a very thin sheet of metal (*wrap the leftovers in aluminum foil*). 2 the metal coating on the back of a mirror.

foil[3] /foyl/ *n* a long, thin sword with a cap or button on the tip to prevent injury, used in fencing.

fold¹ /foald/ *vb* **1** to bend one part of a thing all the way over to cover another part (*fold the blanket in half*). **2** to enclose (*fold her in his arms*). ● *n* **1** a line or crease made by folding (*iron out the folds in the sheets*). **2** the part doubled over.

fold² /foald/ *n* a place where sheep are kept.

folder /foal-der/ *n* a stiff cover for holding papers, letters, etc. (*keep his important documents in a folder*).

foliage /fo-lee-idge/ *n* (*fml*) the leaves of trees or other plants (*a plant with silvery green foliage*).

folio /fo-lee-yo/ *n* **1** a sheet of paper folded so that it opens to two equal, opposing pages. **2** the number of pages in a book.

folk /foak/ *n* **1** (*inf*) people (*the friendly folk next door*). **2** the people of a country or a particular part of a country (*townsfolk*). **1** (*inf*) *pl* relatives, parents (*take him home to meet her folks*).

folklore /foak-loar/ *n* all the stories, songs, beliefs, etc., that have been passed on from one generation of people to another (e.g., **folk dance, folk song, folktale**).

follow /fol-oa/ *vb* **1** to go or come after (*follow her mother down the path*). **2** to be next in order to (*autumn follows summer*). **3** to go along (*follow the mountain path*). **4** to accept as a leader or a teacher (*some people are taught to follow God*). **5** to result from (*disease that followed the drought*). **6** to understand (*I don't follow what you mean*).

follower /fol-oa-er/ *n* a supporter (*followers of the football team*).

following /fol-oa-ing/ *n* all one's supporters (*a football team with a huge following*). ● *adj* next in order (*the following day*).

folly /fol-ee/ *n* **1** foolishness (*their folly is lending him money*). **2** a foolish act (*regret their follies*).

fond /fond/ *adj* **1** having a love or liking for (*fond of music/fond of her parents*). **2** loving (*fond glances*). **3** foolishly loving, indulging, doting (*spoilt by fond parents*). **4** hoped for but not likely to be realized (*fond hopes*). ● *n* **fondness** /fond-ness/.

fondle /fon-dl/ *vb* to stroke, to touch lovingly (*fondling the dog's ear*).

font /font/ *n* **1** the basin holding the water for baptism. **2** a set of type of the same size and style.

food /food/ *n* that which can be eaten (*a shortage of food*).

food chain /food-chane/ *n* a series of living things, each of which feeds on the one below it in the series (*cats are above mice in the food chain/humans are at the top of the food chain*).

fool /fool/ *n* **1** a silly or stupid person (*he was a fool to leave his job*). **2** (*old*) a jester (*the fool in Shakespeare's plays*). ● *vb* **1** to deceive (*succeed in fooling his friends*). **2** to behave as if someone were a fool (*fool around with the children*).

foolish /foo-lish/ *adj* silly, stupid (*a foolish thing to do/a foolish young man*). ● *n* **foolishness** /foo-lish-ness/.

foolproof /fool-proof/ *adj* unable to go wrong even when foolishly used (*the filing system is meant to be foolproof*).

foot /foot/ *n* (*pl* **feet** /feet/) **1** the part of the leg below the ankle. **2** the lowest part of anything (*the foot of the stairs/the foot of the page*). **3** a measure of length equal to 12 inches. **4** foot-soldiers. ● *vb* (*inf*) to pay (*foot the bill*).

football /foot-bol/ *n* **1** a team game with eleven players on each side, the object of which is to score points by kicking field goals through the goal posts or running the ball in for a touchdown. **2** the ball used to play this game.

foothills /foot-hilz/ *npl* low hills at the bottom of mountains (*the foothills of the Rocky Mountains*).

footing /foo-ting/ *n* **1** a safe place for the feet (*a climber seeking a footing*). **2** balance (*miss his footing and fall*). **3** foundation, basis (*a business on a firm footing*). **4** relationship (*on a friendly footing with the boss*).

footlights /foot-lites/ *npl* lights on the floor at the front of the stage in a theater.

footnote /foot-note/ *n* a note at the bottom of a page (*footnotes explaining part of the text*).

footpath /foot-path/ *n* a narrow path used by walkers only.

footprint /foot-print/ *n* the mark left by a foot (*police examining footprints at the murder scene*).

footstep /foot-step/ *n* the sound or mark made by the foot of someone walking (*hear footsteps behind me*).

footstool /foot-stool/ *n* a low stool to support the feet of a person seated.

for /for/ *prep* **1** in place of (*to use coats for blankets*). **2** in the interest of (*to speak for another*). **3** for the purpose of going (*she left for the day*). **4** in search of (*look for the lost glove*). **5** as being (*he knew for a fact*). **6** the length of (*for an hour*).

forage /faw-ridge/ *n* food for cattle or horses. ● *vb* **1** to gather food for cattle or horses. **2** to go out and look for food. **3** to search, to hunt, to rummage (*foraging around in the cupboard*).

forbid /fawr-bid/ *vb* (*pt* **forbade** /fawr-bade/, *pp*

forbidden /fawr-**bi**-den/) to order not to do (*forbid his son to drive his car*).

forbidding /fawr-**bi**-ding/ *adj* frightening (*rather a forbidding expression*).

force /**foarse**/ *n* **1** strength, power (*the force of the wind*). **2** violence (*have to use force to get him into the car*). **3** an organized body of people (*the police force*). **4** *pl* the army, navy, and air force (*the military forces*). **5** a person or thing that has great power (*a force in the local council*). ● *vb* **1** to make (somebody do something) (*force him to clean his room*). **2** to get something by strength, violence, or effort (*forcing his way through the crowd*). **3** to grow plants out of season under artificial conditions.

forced /**foarst**/ *adj* brought about by force, unnatural, strained (*a forced smile*).

forceful /**foarse**-ful/ *adj* strong, energetic (*a forceful speech/a forceful personality*). ● *adv* **forcefully** /**foarse**-fu-lee/.

forceps /**fawr**-seps/ *n* an instrument like tongs or pincers used by doctors and dentists to hold, lift, or grip things.

forcible /**foar**-si-bl/ *adj* done by force (*forcible entry to the house*).

ford /**foard**/ *n* a place where a river is shallow enough to be crossed. ● *vb* to wade across.

fore /**foar**/ *adj* and *adv* in front. ● *interj* (*in golf*) look out!

forearm[1] /fo-**rarm**/ *n* the arm from the elbow to the wrist (*tennis players have strong forearms*).

forearm[2] /fore-**arm**/ *vb* to arm or prepare in advance (*forearmed by a list of the questions the audience were likely to ask*).

foreboding /fore-**bo**-ding/ *n* a feeling that evil is going to happen (*a foreboding that he was going to die in the battle/look upon the future with foreboding*).

forecast /**fore**-cast/ *vb* (*pt, pp* **forecast**) to say what will happen in the future (*impossible to forecast the result of the match/try to forecast the weather*). ● *also n.*

forefather /**fore**-fa-ther/ *n* an ancestor (*his forefathers went from Ireland to America*).

forefinger /**fore**-fing-ger/ *n* the finger next to the thumb, index finger (*point with his forefinger*).

forefront /**fore**-frunt/ *n* the front part (*in the forefront of the campaign against nuclear weapons*).

forego[1] /**fore**-go/ *vb* (*pt* **forewent** /**fore**-went/, *pp* **foregone** /**fore**-gon/) to go before.

forego[2] /**fore**-go/ *see* **forgo**.

foregoing /**fore**-go-ing/ *adj* earlier, previous (*the foregoing passage in the book*).

foregone /**fore**-gon/ *adj* previously determined, predicted (*it was a foregone conclusion that he would win*).

foreground /**fore**-ground/ *n* **1** the nearest objects shown in a picture (*a house in the background and two figures in the foreground*). **2** the nearest part of a view.

forehead /**fore**-hed/ *n* the part of the face above the eyebrows and below the hairline (*frown lines in her forehead*).

foreign /**fawr**-un/ *adj* **1** belonging to or concerning another country (*foreign customers/a foreign vacation*). **2** strange (*meanness was foreign to her nature*). **3** out of place (*a foreign object in her body*).

foreigner /**fawr**-u-ner/ *n* a person from a different country from where they are (*considered foreigners when visiting Brazil*).

foreleg /**fore**-leg/ *n* one of the front legs of an animal (*the racehorse broke its left foreleg*).

foremost /**fore**-most/ *adj* **1** most famous, best (*the foremost writer of his generation*). **2** most important (*the foremost issue before the committee*).

foremother /**fore**-mu-ther/ *n* a woman ancestor.

forename /**fore**-name/ *see* **first name**.

forensic /fo-**ren**-zic/ *n* **1** having to do with the law or courts of law (*forensic medicine*). **2** having to do with applying scientific, especially medical, knowledge to legal matters, as in crime investigation.

foreperson /**fore**-per-sun/ *n* **1** the person in charge of a group of workers (*the foreperson on the building site*). **2** the chief person in a jury (*the foreperson of the jury delivered the verdict*).

forerunner /**fore**-ru-ner/ *n* **1** (*old*) someone who goes before with a message or announcement. **2** a person or thing that comes before another (*a forerunner of the jet plane*). ● *vb* **forerun** /**fore**-run/.

foresee /**fore**-see/ *vb* (*pt* **foresaw** /**fore**-saw/, *pp* **foreseen** /**fore**-seen/) to see what is going to happen (*no one could have foreseen the accident*).

foreshadow /**fore**-sha-doe/ *vb* to be a sign of future events (*his personal defeat in his own event foreshadowed the defeat of the whole team*).

foresight /**fore**-sight/ *n* the ability to guess and prepare for future events (*have the foresight to save for his old age*).

foreskin /**fore**-skin/ *n* the fold of skin that covers the tip of the penis, this is sometimes removed by circumcision for religious or medical reasons.

forest /faw-rest/ *n* a large area covered by trees and undergrowth.

forestall /fore-stawl/ *vb* to guess what another is going to do and act before him or her.

forestation /fore-stay-shun/ *n* the planting and caring for forests.

forested /faw-re-sted/ *adj* covered with trees and undergrowth.

forester /faw-re-ster/ *n* a person in charge of a forest.

forestry /faw-re-stree/ *n* the study of planting and looking after forests.

foretell /fore-tell/ *vb* (*pt, pp* **foretold** /fore-toald/) to say what will happen in the future (*claim to be able to foretell the future from the stars/she foretold that he would go to prison*).

forethought /fore-thot/ *n* care that the results of actions will be good (*have the forethought to book tickets in advance*).

forever /fu-rev-er/ *adv* for always, endlessly, at all times.

forewarn /fore-wawrn/ *vb* to warn in advance (*try to forewarn his brother that their father was angry*).

foreword /fore-word/ *n* a piece of writing at the beginning of a book as an introduction.

forfeit /fawr-fit/ *vb* to lose or give up (*forfeit his right to the throne/the team had to forfeit because not enough players could come*). ● *n* that which is so lost or given up, a fine.

forge /foarge/ *n* **1** a blacksmith's workshop. **2** a furnace for heating metal. ● *vb* **1** to beat hot metal into shape. **2** to make by hard effort (*forging a new career*). **3** to imitate something to deceive (*forged the old man's signature on the will*).

forger /fore-jer/ *n* a person who forges.

forgery /fore-je-ree/ *n* **1** act of imitating something dishonestly, especially another's writing. **2** the imitation so made (*this is not his handwriting on the will—it's a forgery*).

forget /fore-get/ *vb* (*pt* **forgot** /fore-got/, *pp* **forgotten** /fore-got-en/) to fail to remember (*she forgot his name/forget to bring her notes*).

forgetful /fore-get-ful/ *adj* bad at remembering (*getting forgetful as she grows older*). ● *n* **forgetfulness** /fore-get-ful-ness/.

forget-me-not /fore-get-me-not/ *n* a small blue flower.

forgive /fore-giv/ *vb* (*pt* **forgave** /fore-gave/) **1** to pardon (*forgive her disloyalty*). **2** to stop being

angry or bitter toward, to stop blaming or wanting to punish (*forgive his son for crashing the car*). ● *n* **forgiveness** /fore-giv-ness/. ● *adj* **forgivable** / fore-gi-va-bul/.

forgiving /fore-gi-ving/ *adj* quick to forgive (*a forgiving nature*).

forgo, forego /for-go/ *vb* to give up, to do without (*make up her mind to forgo meat for life*).

fork /fork/ *n* **1** an instrument with two or more pointed prongs used for digging, eating, etc. **2** a place where two roads meet. **3** a place where a tree or branch divides. ● *vb* **1** to raise or dig with a fork (*fork the hay/fork the soil*). **2** to divide into branches (*the road forks outside the town*).

forked /forkt/ *adj* divided into branches or sections (*the snake had a forked tongue*).

forklift /fork-lift/ *n* a device on the front of a truck for lifting heavy objects.

forlorn /fur-lawrn/ *adj* left alone, miserable (*standing forlorn on the platform after the train pulled away*).

form /fawrm/ *n* **1** shape (*forms such as triangles/a cake in the form of a train*). **2** a paper so printed that a message or information can be written in prepared spaces (*fill in an application form for the job*). **3** kind (*training in several different forms*). **4** arrangement (*poetic form*). **5** a fixed way of doing things (*the correct form of the ceremony*). ● *vb* **1** to make, to cause to take shape (*how do you form the past tense of the verb?/form the matches into a triangle/children forming an orderly line*). **2** to come into existence, to take shape (*icicles forming on the edge of the garage roof/ideas forming in her mind*).

formal /fawr-mal/ *adj* **1** following the accepted rules or customs (*a formal invitation*). **2** stiff in manner (*rather a formal old woman*). ● *n* a dance (*invited to the spring formal*). ● *adv* **formally** /fawr-ma-lee/.

formality /fawr-ma-li-tee/ *n* **1** stiffness of manner. **2** something done only to carry out a rule (*sending you a letter of acceptance was a formality*). **3** care to follow rules and customs (*observe the formalities of the wedding ceremony*).

format /fawr-mat/ *n* the general shape and size of anything (*the format of the book*). ● *vb* to prepare a computer disk so that data can be recorded and stored on it.

formation /fawr-may-shun/ *n* **1** act of forming. **2** an orderly arrangement (*planes flying in formation*).

formative /**fawr**-ma-tiv/ *adj* helping to shape or develop (*in her formative childhood years*).

former /**fawr**-mer/ *adj* earlier, past (*in former times*). ● *pron* the person or thing previously mentioned.

formerly /**fawr**-mer-lee/ *adv* in earlier times (*he formerly worked in a bank*).

formidable /fawr-**mi**-da-bl/ *adj* **1** to be feared (*her mother seems rather formidable*). **2** difficult (*a formidable task*).

formless /**fawrm**-less/ *adj* having no definite shape or regular plan.

formula /**fawrm**-yu-la/ *n* (*pl* **formulae** /**fawrm**-yu-lay/ *or* **formulas** /**fawrm**-yu-laz/) **1** a fixed arrangement of words or numbers. **2** a rule in arithmetic set down with signs or letters so that it can be used for any sum. **3** in chemistry, the use of signs or letters to show how substances are made up.

formulate /**fawrm**-yu-late/ *vb* (*fml*) to express or set down clearly (*find it difficult to formulate her objections*).

forsake /fawr-**sake**/ *vb* (*pt* **forsook** /fawr-**sook**/, *pp* **forsaken** /fawr-**say**-ken/) to give up, to abandon (*forsake his family/forsake her religion*).

fort /**foart**/ *n* **1** a place prepared for defense against an enemy. **2** a permanent military post.

forte[1] /**foart**/ *n* one's strong point, the thing at which a person is best (*tact is not her forte*).

forte[2] /**fawr**-tay/ *adv* (*mus*) loud.

forth *adv* **1** /**foarth**/ onward in time, place, or order (*from that time forth*). **2** out (*go forth*).

forthcoming /foarth-**cu**-ming/ *adj* **1** about to happen, coming soon (*the forthcoming election*). **2** open, responsive (*a forthcoming personality*).

forthright /**foarth**-rite/ *adj* saying what one thinks (*a forthright person/a forthright reply*).

fortify /**fawr**-ti-fie/ *vb* **1** to strengthen or enrich (*cereal fortified with vitamins*). **2** to build defenses around (*fortify the city against attack*).

fortitude /**fawr**-ti-tood/ *n* ability to suffer without complaint, courage, patience (*the dying woman bore her pain with fortitude*).

fortress /**fawr**-tress/ *n* a place prepared with strong defenses against attackers (*a fortress built on the hill*).

fortunate /**fawr**-chi-net/ *adj* lucky (*a fortunate young lady/come at a fortunate time*).

fortune /**fawr**-chin/ *n* **1** luck, chance (*she had the good fortune to win the lottery*). **2** wealth, a large amount of money (*make a fortune on the stock exchange*). **3** the supposed power that affects one's life (*fortune is on his side*).

forum /**fo**-rum/ *n* (*pl* **forums** /**fo**-rumz/ *or* **fora** /**fo**-ra/) **1** (*old*) the market place in a Roman town. **2** any place of public discussion (*the town hall is a forum for all local issues*). **3** a meeting involving a public discussion (*a forum on the subject of the local traffic policy*).

forward /**fawr**-wurd/ *adv* toward the front (*step forward*). ● *adj* **1** advancing (*a forward movement*). **2** near the front (*the forward part of the bus*). **3** in advance (*forward planning*). **4** developing more quickly than usual (*forward plans*). **5** bold, not shy (*a forward person*). ● *vb* **1** to help move along (*forwarding our plans*). **2** to send on (*forward mail*).

fossil /**fos**-il/ *n* **1** the remains of a plant or animal that have hardened into stone and so been preserved in rock or earth. **2** a person whose ideas are out of date (*children regarding their parents as fossils*).

fossil fuel /**fos**-il fyool/ *n* a natural substance, such as coal or oil, found underground and formed in an earlier time, used as a source of energy.

fossilize /**fos**-il-ize/ *vb, also* **fossilise** (*Br*) to change into a fossil.

foster /**faws**-ter/ *vb* **1** to look after for a time, to bring up a child that is not one's own (*fostering the boy while his mother was unable to look after him*). **2** to encourage (*foster hopes/foster her daughter's talent*).

foster child /**faws**-ter childe/ *n* (*pl* **foster children** /**faws**-ter **chil**-dren/) a child nursed and brought up by someone who is not his or her parent. ● *also ns* **foster brother**, **foster sister**.

foster father /**faws**-ter fa-ther/, **foster mother** /**faws**-ter mu-ther/ *ns*, **foster parents** /**faws**-ter pay-rints/ *npl* those who bring up the child(ren) of other parents.

foster home /**faws**-ter hoam/ *n* a home in which foster children are cared for by people other than their families.

fought *see* **fight**.

foul /**foul**/ *adj* **1** dirty, disgusting (*a foul smell/a foul mess*). **2** stormy (*foul weather*). **3** against the rules (*foul play*). **4** nasty (*he was foul to his wife*). **5** bad (*use foul language*). ● *vb* **1** to make or become dirty (*fouling the streets*). **2** to become entangled (*ropes getting fouled*). **3** to break the rules of a game (*foul his opponent*). ● *n* an act against the rules of a game (*the referee said she committed a foul*).

foul line /**foul**-line/ *n* the line that surrounds the area of play in a game.

foul play /foul-play/ *n* **1** unfair play. **2** violence or murder (*police suspected foul play when they saw the body*).

found[1] /found/ *pt of* **find**.

found[2] /found/ *vb* **1** to start from the beginning, to set up (*found a new club*). **2** to give money to start a school, hospital, etc. ● *n* **founder** /foun-der/.

foundation /foun-**day**-shun/ *n* **1** the lowest part of a building on which the walls stand (*lay the foundations of the new theater*). **2** the amount of money given to start a school, hospital, etc. **3** the place started with such money.

founder[1] /foun-der/ *vb* **1** to fill with water and sink (*ships foundering*). **2** to come to nothing, to fail (*our plans foundered*).

founder[2] /foun-der/ a person who founds or establishes something.

Founding Father /foun-ding fa-ther/ *n* a person who took part in the Constitutional Convention in 1787, especially one who signed the Constitution.

foundry /foun-dree/ *n* a workshop where metals are melted and shaped.

fount /fount/ *n* **1** (*old*) a spring of water. **2** (*fml*) a cause or beginning (*the fount of knowledge*).

fountain /foun-tin/ *n* **1** a spring of water. **2** a jet of water thrown into the air from a pipe (*take a drink from the drinking fountain in the park*). **3** (*fml*) a beginning or source (*the fountain of knowledge*).

fountain pen /foun-tin pen/ *n* a pen containing a supply of liquid ink.

four-poster /fore-**po**-ster/ *n* a bed with four tall corner posts that sometimes hold up a decorative drape.

Fourth of July /foarth-ov-ju-**lie**/ *n* a holiday celebrating the signing of the Declaration of Independence.

four-way /**foar**-way/ *adj* giving passage in four different directions.

fowl /foul/ *n* a bird, especially the farmyard chicken or rooster (*a boiling fowl*).

fox /foks/ *n* **1** a doglike animal with reddish brown or gray fur and a bushy tail. **2** a cunning or deceitful person. ● *f* **vixen** /**vik**-sen/.

foxhole /foks-hole/ *n* a hole dug in the ground as a temporary protection for soldiers.

foxhound /foks-hound/ *n* a kind of dog with black, tan, and white fur and trained for hunting.

foxy /fok-see/ *adj* **1** cunning (*with foxy cleverness*). **2** like a fox (*a foxy smell*). **3** reddish brown (*hair of a foxy color*). **4** attractive (*a foxy lady*).

foyer /foy-er/ *n* an entrance hall (*hotel foyer*).

fraction /frac-shun/ *n* **1** a part of a whole. **2** a small part (*a fraction of the cost*). **3** in arithmetic, part of a whole number, e.g., $\frac{1}{2}$, $\frac{1}{4}$, etc.

fractional /frac-shnal/ *adj* very small (*a fractional improvement*).

fracture /frac-cher/ *n* **1** a break (*a fracture in the pipe*). **2** the breaking of a bone. ● *vb* to break, to suffer a fracture (*fracturing a bone in his leg*).

fragile /fra-jul/ *adj* **1** easily broken (*fragile goods*). **2** not strong (*fragile after her illness*).

fragment /frag-ment/ *n* **1** a part broken off (*fragments of china*). **2** a small part (*not a fragment of common sense*). ● *vb* **fragment** /frag-**ment**/ to break into fragments.

fragrance /fray-granse/ *n* **1** scent, sweet smell (*the fragrance of flowers*). **2** perfume (*market a new fragrance*).

fragrant /fray-grant/ *adj* sweet-smelling (*fragrant flowers*).

frail /frale/ *adj* **1** weak, feeble, delicate (*frail old ladies*). **2** (*old*) easily tempted to do wrong.

frame /frame/ *vb* **1** to make, to construct (*framing a sentence/framed a reply/frame a plan*). **2** to put in a frame (*frame the painting*). **3** (*inf*) to cause someone to seem guilty of a crime (*they framed him by putting the stolen goods in his shed*). ● *n* **1** the supports around which the rest of a thing is built (*the frame of the ship*). **2** the border of metal, wood, etc., placed around a picture (*a photograph frame*). **3** the body (*a slender frame*).

framer /fray-mer/ *n* a person or thing that frames.

framework /frame-wurk/ *n* the supports around which the rest of a thing is built (*the framework of the ship/the framework of their plans*).

franc /frangk/ *n* a money that was formerly used in France, Belgium, and Luxembourg (now the euro).

franchise /fran-chize/ *n* **1** the right to vote (*when women got the franchise*). **2** a special right given or sold by a company to one person or group of people to sell the company's goods or services in a particular place (*a hamburger franchise*).

frank[1] /frangk/ *adj* **1** saying what one really thinks, honest (*a frank person/a frank reply*). **2** open, honest-looking (*a frank face*). ● *n* **frankness** /frangk-ness/.

frank[2] /frangk/ *vb* to put an official mark on a letter.

frankfurter /frangk-fur-ter/ *n* a long, thin smoked sausage, a hot dog.

frankincense /frang-kin-sense/ *n* a gum giving a sweet-smelling smoke when burned.

frantic /fran-tic/ *adj* 1 very anxious or worried (*frantic about her missing children/frantic mothers*). 2 wildly excited, hurried (*frantic pace of modern life*).

fraternal /fra-ter-nal/ *adj* brotherly (*fraternal love*).

fraternity /fra-ter-ni-tee/ *n also* **frat** /frat/ 1 a group of men meeting for a common purpose. 2 (*fml*) the state of being brothers or like brothers.

fraternize /fra-ter-nize/ *vb, also* **fraternise** (*Br*) to mix with in a friendly or brotherly way (*accused of fraternizing with the enemy*).

fraud /frawd/ *n* 1 dishonesty (*found guilty of fraud*). 2 a deceiving trick (*carry out a frauds on a trusting person*). 3 a person who deceives (*the doctor turned out to be a fraud*).

fraudulent /fraw-ju-lent/ *adj* dishonest (*fraudulent behavior*).

fray[1] /fray/ *n* 1 a fight. 2 a noisy quarrel.

fray[2] /fray/ *vb* 1 to wear away by rubbing (*rubbing against the wall had frayed the rope*). 2 to become worn at the edges (*material fraying easily*). 3 to upset (*with nerves frayed*).

freak /freek/ *n* 1 a living creature of unnatural form. 2 a strange, unexpected happening (*by some freak, snow fell in July*). ● *adj* strange, unusual (*a freak accident*).

freakish /free-kish/ *adj also* **freaky** /free-kee/ very unusual, strange (*a freakish result*).

freckle /fre-kul/ *n* a brownish yellow spot on the skin. ● *adj* **freckled**.

free /free/ *adj* 1 at liberty, able to do what a person wants (*former prisoners now free/animals free to wander*). 2 not forced or persuaded to act, think, speak, etc., in a particular way (*the right to free speech*). 3 not occupied (*no rooms free in the hotel*). 4 generous (*free with his money*). 5 costing nothing (*free goods/goods given free*). 6 open, frank (*a free manner*). ● *n* 1 to set at liberty (*freeing the prisoner*). 2 to set free from (*freed him from his responsibility*).

freedom /free-dum/ *n* 1 the state of being at liberty (*ex-prisoners enjoying their freedom*). 2 the right to act, think, speak, etc., as a person pleases (*freedom of speech*). 3 the state of being without (*freedom from pain*). 4 the unlimited use of something (*have the freedom of the house*).

freelance /free-lanse/ *n* someone who works for himself or herself and not any particular company. ● *vb* to work in such a way (*freelancing for various newspapers*).

free-range /free-range/ *adj* of eggs, laid by hens that are allowed to move around freely.

freestyle /free-stile/ *adj* (*sports*) not limited to one specific style.

freethinker /free-thing-ker/ *n* someone who tries to work out his or her own ideas about God, religion, politics, morals, etc.

free throw /free-thro/ *n* in basketball, a clear shot at the basket from a certain line allowed to a player because the other team had done something wrong.

free trade /free-trade/ *n* the exchanging of goods without making a customs charge on imports.

free verse /free-verse/ *n* poetry without rhyme or a standard, regular pattern.

freeze /freez/ *vb* (*pt* froze /froze/, *pp* frozen /frozen/) 1 to harden because of cold (*a dessert left to freeze*). 2 to become or make into ice (*the pond sometimes freezes*). 3 to be very cold (*it's freezing today*). 4 to make (food) very cold so as to preserve it (*freeze raspberries*). 5 to become suddenly still (*he froze when he saw the gunman*).

freezer /free-zer/ *n* a piece of electrical equipment or the part of a refrigerator that freezes and preserves food or other things at very low temperatures.

freight /frate/ *n* 1 the cargo of a ship. 2 the load on a train carrying goods. 3 the cost of transporting goods (*freight included in the price of the goods*).

freight car /frate car/ *n* a railroad car used to transport goods.

freighter /fray-ter/ *n* a cargo ship.

French /french/ *adj* of or relating to France. ● *n* the language spoken in France.

French bread /french-bred/ *n* a long, slender loaf of white bread with a hard, crisp crust.

French cuff /french-cuff/ *n* a double cuff, on the sleeves of a shirt, that is turned back on itself and fastened with cuff links.

French doors /french-doarz/ *npl* two glass doors that are right next to each other and are hinged at the opposite sides of a doorway so that they open together in the middle.

French dressing /french-dre-sing/ *n* a salad dressing made from oil, vinegar and seasoning; also known as vinaigrette.

French fries /french-frize/ *n* strips of potato that have been deep fried.

French horn /french-hawrn/ *n* a brass musical instrument consisting of a long, spiral tube ending in a flared bell.

French toast /french-toast/ *n* sliced bread dipped in an egg batter and then fried in a pan.

French twist /french-**twist**/ *n* a woman's hairstyle in which the hair is gathered at the back and twisted into a vertical coil running down the back of her head.

frenzied /**fren**-zeed/ *adj* wild, uncontrolled (*a frenzied dance*).

frenzy /**fren**-zee/ *n* 1 a sudden attack of madness (*yelled at his friend in a frenzy*). 2 uncontrollable excitement or feeling (*the fans at the rock concert worked themselves into a frenzy*).

frequency /**free**-kwen-see/ *n* 1 the number of times something happens (*increase the frequency of his visits to his father*). 2 the number of waves, vibrations, etc., per second.

frequent /**free**-kwent/ *adj* happening often, common (*a frequent visitor*). ● *vb* /free-**kwent**/ to visit often (*frequent the store at the corner*).

fresh /fresh/ *adj* 1 new (*no fresh news*). 2 not tired (*feeling fresh after a night's sleep*). 3 cool (*fresh air*). 4 not stale (*fresh bread*). 5 not frozen or canned (*fresh vegetables*). 6 not salted (*fresh butter*).

freshen /**fre**-shen/ *vb* 1 to make or become fresh (*the air has freshened*). 2 to cause to become less untidy, etc. (*freshen up for dinner*). ● *n* **freshener** /**fre**-she-ner/.

freshman /**fresh**-man/ *n* a student in the first year of high school or college.

freshwater /**fresh**-waw-ter/ *n* not saltwater. ● *adj* of or relating to those things that live in freshwater.

fret /fret/ *vb* (**fretted** /**fre**-tid/, **fretting** /**fre**-ting/) 1 to wear away by rubbing (*rope becoming fretted*). 2 to worry, to be anxious (*children fretting while their mother is away*).

fretful /**fret**-ful/*adj* troubled, irritable (*overtired children getting fretful*).

friar /**frie**-er/ *n* a member of a Roman Catholic religious order.

friary /**frie**-e-ree/ *n* a house of friars.

friction /**fric**-shun/ *n* 1 rubbing, a rubbing together (*a rope worn by friction*). 2 the resistance felt when one object is moved against another (*friction between the wheels of a car and the road*). 3 disagreement (*some friction between the two departments*).

Friday /**frie**-dee/ *n* one of the seven days of the week, between Thursday and Saturday.

fridge /fridge/ *n* a refrigerator.

friend /frend/ *n* a close companion. ● **Society of Friends** the religious group also known as the Quakers.

friendly /**frend**-lee/ *adj* 1 kind (*friendly people*). 2 fond of or liking one another (*they have been friendly since their schooldays*). ● *n* **friendliness** /**frend**-lee-ness/.

friendship /**frend**-ship/ *n* the state of being friends (*form a friendship/value her friendship*).

frieze /freez/ *n* a decorative border around the top of the wall of a room.

frigate /**fri**-git/ *n* a small fast warship.

fright /frite/ *n* a sudden feeling of fear, a shock (*get a fright when she saw the strange man*).

frighten /**frie**-ten/ *vb* to make afraid (*the strange noise frightened the children*).

frightful /**frie**-ful/ *adj* 1 dreadful, causing fear (*a frightful experience when the car crashed*). 2 (*inf*) very bad, dreadful (*wearing a frightful dress/the film was frightful*).

frigid /**fri**-jid/ *adj* 1 (*fml*) cold, frozen (*the frigid areas of the world*). 2 cold and unemotional, unfriendly (*give a frigid stare/a frigid welcome*). ● *n* **frigidity** /fri-ji-di-tee/.

frill /fril/ *n* 1 a loose ornamental edging of cloth gathered or pleated at one end and sewn on to a garment. 2 an unnecessary ornament (*a plain room with no frills*). ● *adj* **frilly** /**fri**-lee/.

fringe /fringe/ *n* 1 an ornamental edging of hanging threads (*a skirt with a fringe round the hem*). 2 the edge (*the fringe of the lake*). ● *vb* to border.

frisbee /**friz**-bee/ *n* 1 a simple game in which a flat, plastic disk is flung between players. 2 the disk used to play this game.

frisk /frisk/ *vb* 1 to jump and dance about, to play about joyfully (*lambs frisking about*). 2 to search quickly.

frisky /**fri**-skee/ *adj* playful, active (*frisky kittens*).

frittata /fri-**tot**-a/ *n* an omelet with vegetables, meat, etc. in the egg mixture and cooked slowly until fluffy and served without folding.

fritter /**fri**-ter/ *n* any sweet or tasty food cut small, fried in batter, and served hot (*banana fritters*). ● *vb* to waste (*frittering away money on sweets/fritter away her time*).

frivolity /fri-**vol**-i-tee/ *n* fun, lack of seriousness.

frivolous /**fri**-vu-lus/ *adj* 1 interested only in amusement (*frivolous nature/a frivolous man*). 2 not taking important matters seriously, silly (*make frivolous comments*). 3 not serious, playful, light-hearted (*frivolous pleasures*).

frizz /friz/ *vb* to form into small, tight curls. ● *adj* **frizzy** /**fri**-zee/.

frizzle /**fri**-zul/ *vb* 1 to form into small, tight curls.

2 to fry with a sputtering, hissing noise (*bacon frizzling in the pan*).

fro /fro/ *adv.* ● **to and fro** forward and back again (*wander to and fro along the sea front*).

frog /frawg/ *n* a cold-blooded, four-footed land and water creature that can leap long distances (*tadpoles growing into frogs*).

frogman /frawg-man/ *n* a person trained and equipped for underwater work.

frolic /frol-ic/ *vb* (**frolicked** /frol-ict/, **frolicking** /frol-i-cing/) to play about, to dance or jump about happily (*children frolicking around the garden/lambs frolicking*). ● *n* a trick played for fun, lively amusement.

from /from/ *prep* **1** beginning at (*leave from the airport*). **2** starting with (*from two until three*). **3** out of (*money from his wallet*). **4** with (*a shed made from wood*). **5** out of the whole of (*take four from three*). **6** as not being like (*tell one brother from the other*). **7** because of (*to scream from fright*).

frond /frond/ *n* a leaf, especially of a palm or fern.

front /frunt/ *n* **1** the forward part of anything. **2** in war, the place where the fighting is going on (*news from the front*). ● *also adj.* ● *vb* to face, to stand before.

frontier /frun-teer/ *n* **1** the boundary between one country and another (*show passports at the frontier*). **2** that part of a settled, civilized country that is still underdeveloped and somewhat wild.

frost /frawst/ *n* frozen dew or moisture freezing (*young plants killed by a late frost*). ● *vb* **1** to cover with frost (*fields frosted over in winter*). **2** to cover with icing (*frost the birthday cake*). **3** to treat glass so that it cannot be seen through (*frosted glass on the bathroom window*).

frostbite /frawst-bite/ *n* injury caused to the body by very severe cold. ● *adj* **frostbitten** /frawst-bi-ten/.

frosting /fraw-sting/ *n* icing for cakes (*pink frosting on the birthday cake*).

frosty /fraw-stee/ *adj* **1** covered with frost (*frosty roofs*). **2** cold because of frost (*a frosty day*). **3** unfriendly (*a frosty manner*).

froth /frawth/ *n* a mass of tiny bubbles on the surface of liquid, foam (*the froth on a glass of root beer*). ● *vb* to throw up froth (*root beer frothing in the glass*). ● *adj* **frothy** /fraw-thee/.

frown /froun/ *vb* to wrinkle the forehead, to scowl, to look angry (*frown at the children's bad behavior/frown in disapproval*). ● *also n*. ● **frown on** to discourage, to disapprove of (*frown on staff leaving early*).

fructose /fruke-toze/ *n* a sugar found in fruit and honey.

frugal /fru-gal/ *adj* **1** careful, not wasteful, thrifty (*he's frugal with money*). **2** very small, not much (*a frugal meal*). ● *n* **frugality** /fru-ga-li-tee/.

fruit /froot/ *n* **1** the part of a plant that produces the seed, many times eaten as a food (*apples, pears, and other fruits*). **3** result (*the fruits of his research*).

fruit bat /froot-bat/ *n* any fruit-eating bat, such as the flying fox.

fruitcake /froot-cake/ *n* **1** a rich cake containing nuts, fruit, spices, etc. **2** (slang) a foolish person.

fruit cup /froot-cup/ *n* mixed diced fruits served in a small bowl as a dessert or appetizer (*also* **fruit cocktail**).

fruit fly /froot-flie/ *n* a small fly that feeds on fruit.

fruitful /froot-ful/ *adj* **1** (*old*) fertile. **2** having good results (*fruitful discussions*).

fruition /froo-wi-shun/ *n* fulfillment, a successful ending (*plans finally coming to fruition*).

fruitless /froot-less/ *adj* unsuccessful (*a fruitless search*).

fruity /froo-tee/ *adj* like fruit in taste or smell.

frump /frump/ *n* a badly or unfashionably dressed woman (*she's such a frump, although she is very wealthy*). ● *adj* **frumpy** /frum-pee/.

frustrate /fru-strate/ *vb* **1** to make to fail (*frustrating their attempt*). **2** to cause to have feelings of disappointment or dissatisfaction (*frustrated by the dullness of her job/delays that frustrated her*). ● *n* **frustration** /fru-stray-shun/.

fry[1] /frie/ *vb* to cook in fat (*fry bacon*). ● *n* anything fried.

fry[2] /frie/ *n* (*pl* **fry**) young fish.

fry bread /frie-bred/ *n* a kind of bread that is deep fried until light brown and puffy, made by Native Americans in the southwestern United States.

fryer /frie-er/ *n* a person or thing that fried.

frying pan /frie-ing-pan/ *n* a shallow pan with a handle for frying food.

fuchsia /fyoo-sha/ *n* **1** a shrub with long, hanging, bell-shaped flowers of a pink, red, or purple color. **2** purplish red.

fudge /fudge/ *n* a soft sweet. ● *vb* to refuse to commit or give a direct answer.

fuel /fyool/ *n* **1** material to keep a fire going (*coal and logs as fuel*). **2** material used for producing heat or power by burning (*high fuel bills because of the central heating system*).

fugitive /fyoo-ji-tiv/ *n* someone who is running away. ● *adj* **1** (*fml*) passing quickly (*fugitive hours*). **2** escaping (*fugitive prisoners*). ● *n* a person who flees from danger, pursuit, or duty.

fugue /fyoog/ *n* a piece of music for a definite number of parts or voices.

fulfill /ful-**fil**/ *vb* (**fulfilled** /ful-**fild**/, **fulfilling** /ful-fi-ling/), also **fulfil** (Br, Cdn) **1** to carry out successfully, to complete (*fulfill tasks/fulfill promises*). **2** to satisfy, to meet (*fulfill the entrance requirements*). ● *n* **fulfillment** /ful-**fil**-ment/, also **fulfilment** (Br, Cdn).

full[1] /ful/ *adj* **1** holding as much as possible (*a full bucket of water*). **2** complete (*a full report*). ● *n* **fullness** /**ful**-ness/.

full[2] /ful/ *vb* to clean and thicken cloth. ● *n* **fuller** / **foo**-ler/.

fullback /**ful**-back/ *n* in football, one of the players used for blocking the other team members.

full-blown /ful-**bloan**/ *adj* in full bloom, fully opened (*full-blown roses*).

full-bodied /ful-**bod**-eed/ *adj* having a rich, strong flavor.

full dress /ful-**dress**/ *n* formal clothes worn on special occasions. ● *adj* **full-dress**.

full-fledged /ful-**flejd**/ *adj* having a complete set of feathers, completely developed.

full-grown /ful-**groan**/ *adj* having reached full size.

full-length /ful-**lenth**/ *adj* showing or covering the full length of an object or all of a person's figure, said of pictures, mirrors, etc.

full moon /ful-**moon**/ *n* the phase of the Moon when its entire face can be seen from Earth.

full sail /ful-**sale**/ *adj* with every sail set up and in use.

full-service /ful-**ser**-vis/ *adj* offering all the services for a business of its kind (*a full-service bank/a full-service gas station*).

full-time /ful-**time**/ *adj* engaged in work, study, etc. for the full extent of the working hours of the day.

fulmar /**fool**-mar/ *n* a type of sea bird.

fulminate /**ful**-mi-nate/ *vb* **1** (*fml*) to thunder. **2** to speak loudly and threateningly (*father fulminating about her coming in late*). ● *n* **fulmination** /ful-mi-**nay**-shun/.

fulsome /**ful**-sum/ *adj* overmuch (*fulsome praise/fulsome apologies*).

fumble /**fum**-bul/ *vb* **1** to feel for something not seen (*fumbling in the dark for the light switch*). **2** to handle clumsily (*fumble the catch and drop the ball*).

fume /**fyoom**/ *n* smoke, vapor (*paint fumes/gas fumes*). ● *vb* **1** to give off fumes. **2** (*inf*) to show anger (*fuming about his insulting remarks*).

fumigant /**fyoo**-mi-gant/ *n* the substance used in fumigation.

fumigate /**fyoo**-mi-gate/ *vb* to disinfect by means

of fumes (*fumigating the room after the patient died of scarlet fever*). ● *n* **fumigation** /fyoo-mi-**gay**-shun/.

fun /fun/ *n* merriment, amusement, enjoyment (*children having fun in the park*). ● *adj* amusing, enjoyable (*have a fun time*).

function /**fung**-shun/ *n* **1** the work that a thing is made or planned to perform, use (*the function of the car's engine/the function of the liver*). **2** duties (*his function is to supervise the workers*). **3** (*fml*) a public ceremony or party (*the firm's holiday function*). ● *vb* **1** to work as intended. **2** to act.

functional /**fung**-shu-nal/ *adj* designed with a view to its use (*functional rather than decorative furniture*).

functionary /**fung**-shu-ne-ree/ *n* (*fml*) an official (*council functionaries*).

fund /fund/ *n* **1** an amount laid aside till needed (*a vacation fund*). **2** money collected or kept for a purpose (*the church repair fund*).

fundamental /fun-da-**men**-tal/ *adj* having to do with the beginning or most necessary parts of something, of great importance (*the fundamental principles of mathematics/a fundamental difference*). ● *also n*.

fundamentalism /fun-da-**men**-ta-li-zum/ *n* the belief that the whole of the Bible is to be believed and lived by exactly as written.

fundraiser /**fund**-ray-zer/ *n* an event put together to raise money for an organization, cause, etc.

funeral /**fyoon**-ral/ *n* **1** burial of the dead. **2** the ceremonies performed at burial.

funeral director /**fyoon**-ral di-**rec**-tor/ *n* a person who manages funerals.

funeral home /**fyoon**-ral hoam/ *n* a place of business where the dead are prepared for burial and where services can be held.

funerary /**fyoo**-ne-re-ree/ *adj* of or having to do with a funeral.

funereal /fyoo-**ni**-ree-al/ *adj* gloomy, sad, dark (*funereal music/a funereal atmosphere*).

fungal /**fung**-gal/ *adj* having to do with or caused by a fungus (*a fungal infection*).

fungus /**fung**-gus/ *n* (*pl* **fungi** /**fung**-gie/ *or* **funguses** /**fung**-gu-seez/) **1** a mushroom, toadstool, or similar plant. **2** an unhealthy growth on an animal or plant (*roses affected by a fungus*).

funk[1] /fungk/ *vb* (*inf*) to fear to do, to be frightened (*funk telling his mother about the broken window*). ● *n* a state of fear (*in a funk about telling his parents about failing his exams*).

funk² /fungk/ n **1** a musty, unpleasant odor. ● adj funky.

funk³ /fungk/ n a style of music with a jerky baseline, popular since the 1970s.

funnel /fu-nel/ n **1** a hollow cone used for pouring liquids into bottles etc. (use a plastic funnel to pour cooking oil into a bottle). **2** a passage by which smoke etc., escapes (the funnel of a steamship).

funnies /fu-neez/ npl comic strips.

funny /fu-nee/ adj **1** amusing, humorous (a funny joke). **2** strange, odd (he's a funny man—he doesn't like chocolate).

funny bone /fu-nee-bone/ n a place on the elbow that gives a strange, tingling sensation when it is hit.

funny car /fu-nee-car/ n a type of racing car with large rear tires and a one-piece body.

fur /fur/ n **1** the short soft hair of certain animals (a cat's fur). **2** the skin of an animal with the hair still attached, used as a garment (wear a stole made of silver fox fur). **3** a coating (e.g., on the tongue).

furbish /fur-bish/ vb (fml) to polish, to make bright by rubbing (furbish the family silver).

furious /fyoo-ree-us/ see fury.

furl /furl/ vb to roll up (a sail, flag, etc.).

furlong /fur-lawng/ n one eighth of a mile (220 yards).

furlough /fur-lo/ n (fml) permission to be absent from work for a certain time (obtain furlough from the army).

furnace /fur-nis/ n an enclosed place in which great heat can be produced by fire (a furnace for melting iron ore/a furnace that provides the office's central heating).

furnish /fur-nish/ vb **1** to provide what is necessary (furnish them with all the necessary information). **2** to put tables, chairs, beds, and other necessary articles in a house (furnish the house gradually).

furnishings /fur-ni-shingz/ npl the fittings in a house.

furniture /fur-ni-cher/ n the articles (tables, chairs, etc.) needed in a house or office.

furor /fyoo-ror/ n, also **furore** (Br) great excitement, craze, frenzy (the furor of the fire drill).

furrier /fu-ree-er/ n someone who deals in furs.

furrow /fu-ro/ n **1** the trench cut in the earth by a plough. **2** a wrinkle (furrows in her brow). ● vb **1** to plough. **2** to wrinkle (furrowed her brow).

furry /fu-ree/ adj covered with fur (furry toy animals).

further /fur-ther/ adv **1** besides (he is hardworking—further, he is honest). **2** farther (unable to go any further without a rest). ● adj **1** more

distant. **2** more (no further use). ● vb to help forward (furthering the cause of freedom).

furthermore /fur-ther-more/ adv besides, in addition (he is poor—furthermore he is homeless).

furthermost /fur-ther-most/ adj most distant (the furthermost point in the British Isles) (also **furthest** /fur-thest/).

furtive /fur-tiv/ adj careful, done secretly (cast a furtive look around before letting herself into the house).

fury /fyoo-ree/ n rage, great anger (fly into a fury on discovering the damage to his property). ● adj **furious** /fyoo-ree-us/.

fuse¹ /fyooz/ vb **1** to melt by heat (lead fuses at a low temperature). **2** to melt together as a result of great heat (copper and tin fuse to form bronze). **3** (of an electrical appliance or circuit) to stop working or cause to stop working because of the melting of a fuse (fusing all the lights). **4** to join together (ideas that fused). ● n easily melted wire used to complete an electric current.

fuse² /fyooz/ n a tube of slow-burning substance used to explode shells, bombs, dynamite, etc. (light the fuse).

fuselage /fyoo-su-lazh/ n the body of an airplane.

fusible /fyoo-zi-bul/ adj that can be fused or easily melted.

fusion /fyoo-zhun/ n **1** act of melting (a metal formed by the fusion of two other metals). **2** a joining to make one (a literary work that is a fusion of several different styles).

fuss /fuss/ n anxiety or excitement over unimportant things.

fussy /fu-see/ adj worrying over details, hard to please.

futile /fyoo-til/ adj having no useful result (a futile search/futile attempts). ● n **futility** /fyoo-ti-li-tee/.

futon /foo-ton/ n a thin cushion placed on a frame that can be used as a bed or folded into a chair or couch.

future /fyoo-cher/ adj about to happen, coming (present and future projects). ● n the time to come (in the future we will take more care/the future of the factory is uncertain).

futuristic /fyoo-che-ri-stic/ adj of or having to do with the future, so advanced in design, etc. as to seem from the future.

fuzz /fuzz/ n **1** a mass of fine, light hair or similar substance (apricots covered in fuzz). **2** (inf) the police.

fuzzy /fu-zee/ adj **1** covered in fuzz (toy fuzzy animals). **2** not clear, blurred (a fuzzy television picture).

FX /ef-eks/ abbr = **1 foreign exchange. 2** (cinema) **special effects.**

G

G, g /jee/ **1 t**he seventh letter of the alphabet. **2** (*mus*) the fifth note of the scale of C major.

gab /gab/ *vb* (**gabbed** /gabd/, **gabbing** /ga-bing/) (*sl*) to chatter or talk idly. ● *n* idle chat. ● **gift of gab** the ability to speak well or at length (*it is important for salespeople to have the gift of the gab*).

gable /**gay**-bl/ *n* the pointed top to the end wall of a building with a sloping roof.

gadget /ga-jet/ *n* a small useful tool or machine (*labor-saving kitchen gadgets*).

gag /gag/ *vb* (**gagged** /gagd/, **gagging** /ga-ging/) to stop someone speaking by forcibly stopping the mouth (*burglars gagging the bank workers*). ● *n* **1** something put in the mouth to prevent speech (*use a scarf as a gag*). **2** a joke (*comedians telling the same old gags*).

gaggle /ga-gl/ *n* **1** a flock of geese. **2** a disorderly group of people (*a gaggle of neighbors gossiping about the accident*).

gaily /**gay**-lee/ *see* gay.

gain /**gane**/ *vb* **1** to obtain (*gain an advantage/gain support for the scheme*). **2** to have an increase in (*gain weight/gain speech*). **3** to reduce between oneself and someone or something (*gain on the car in front*). **4** (*fml*) to reach (*gain the safety of her home*). ● *n* profit, advantage.

gainful /**gane**-ful/ *adj* (*fml*) paid, profitable (*gainful employment*).

gait /gate/ *n* manner of walking (*walk with a rolling gait*).

gala /ga-la/ *n* a day or time of feasting and rejoicing (*a miners' gala*).

galaxy /ga-lak-see/ *n* **1** a belt of stars stretching across the sky (e.g., the Milky Way). **2** a company of well-known, impressive, etc., people (*a galaxy of stars at the movie premiere*).

gale /gale/ *n* a strong wind (*ships wrecked in the gale*).

gallant /ga-lant, ga-**lant** / *adj* (*fml*) brave, noble (*a gallant soldier*). ● *adj* **gallant** (*especially old*) polite and attentive to women (*be gallant and open the door for the lady*).

galleon /gal-yun/ *n* (*old*) a large sailing ship with several decks, as used by the Spaniards in the 15th and 16th centuries.

gallery /ga-le-ree/ *n* **1** a raised floor over part of a church, theater (*a good view of the stage from the front row of the gallery*). **2** a narrow passage in a mine. **3** a room in which pictures, etc. are dis-

played (*an exhibition of modern art at the local gallery*).

galley /ga-lee/ *n* **1** (*old*) a long low ship with sails and oars. **2** a ship's kitchen.

gallon /ga-lon/ *n* a measure for liquids or grain (=4 quarts, 3.785 liters, or 231 cubic inches).

gallop /ga-lop/ *n* a horse's fastest speed. ● *vb* **1** to go at a gallop (*racehorses galloping to the finish*). **2** (*inf*) to move or do very quickly (*children galloping through their homework so that they can watch TV*).

gallows /ga-loze/ *n or npl* a wooden frame for hanging criminals.

galore /ga-**lore**/ *adj* in plenty (*bargains galore at the sales*).

galoshes /ga-**losh**-ez/ *npl* overshoes, usually of rubber, which protect the shoes in wet weather.

galvanize /gal-va-nize/ *vb, also* **galvanise** (*Br*) **1** to give an electric shock. **2** to put on a coat of metal by electricity, to electroplate. **3** to rouse to activity (*galvanized into action under threat of losing his job*).

gamble /gam-bl/ *vb* **1** to play for money, to bet. **2** to take risks (*the burglars gambled on there being no one in the house*). ● *n* a risk. ● *n* **gambler** / gam-bler/. ● *n* **gambling** /gam-bling/.

gambol /gam-bl/ *vb* to jump about playfully. ● *also n*.

game[1] /**game**/ *n* **1** a sporting contest (*interested in games such as football and hockey*). **2** a single part of a set into which a game is divided (*lose a game at tennis*). **3** an amusement or diversion, a pastime (*it was just a game—not to be taken seriously*). **4** (*inf*) a scheme, a trick (*wonder what his little game is*). **5** birds or animals hunted for sport (*shoot game such as pheasants*). ● *adj* **1** brave, plucky (*game enough to go on playing after being injured*). **2** willing, ready (*if you want to go to the movies, I'm game*). ● *vb* to gamble (*to make money gaming*). ● **make game of** (*fml*) to make fun of, mock (*make game of him for being small*).

game[2] /**game**/ *adj* lame, injured (*his game leg*).

gaming /gay-ming/ *n* **1** gambling (*lose a fortune on gaming*). **2** the playing of computer games.

gander /gan-der/ *n* a male goose.

gang /gang/ *n* **1** a group of people, especially friends. **2** a group of people working on the same job (*the gang working on the new road*). **3** a group of criminals working together (*the gang that held up the bank*).

gangrene /**gang**-green/ *n* the rotting away of a part of the body (*had his foot amputated because of gangrene*). ● *adj* **gangrenous** /**gang**-gri-nus/.

gangster /**gang**-ster/ *n* a member of an organized gang of criminals (*local store-owners terrorized by gangsters threatening to rob them*).

gangway /**gang**-way/ *n* **1** a movable footbridge from a ship to the shore. **2** a passage between rows of seats (*the gangway in a theater*).

gap /**gap**/ *n* **1** an opening (*a gap in the fence*). **2** a space between (*bridge the gap between the banks*). **3** something missing (*the gap in his knowledge*).

gape /**gape**/ *vb* **1** to stare open-mouthed (*stand gaping at the piles of gold*). **2** to be wide open (*the entrance to the cellar gaped open*).

garage /ga-**rozh**/ *n* **1** a building in which an automobile can be kept (*a garage attached to the house*). **2** a shop where automobiles are repaired.

garb /**garb**/ (*old*) *n* dress, clothes. ● *vb* to clothe (*garbed in silk*).

garbage /**gar**-bage/ *n* **1** waste food (*household garbage*). **2** (*inf*) nonsense, anything of little value (*newspaper reporting that was nothing but garbage*).

garbled /**gar**-buld/ *adj* mixed up and muddled (*a garbled account of the accident*).

garden /**gar**-den/ *n* a piece of land on which flowers or vegetables are grown. ● *vb* to look after a garden, often as a hobby (*try to find time to garden*). ● *n* **gardener** /**gar**-de-ner/. ● *n* **gardening** /**gard**-ning/.

gargle /**gar**-gl/ *vb* to wash the throat with a mouthful of liquid by blowing it up and down in the back of the mouth. ● *n* a liquid prepared for gargling.

gargoyle /**gar**-goyl/ *n* a grotesquely carved spout in the form of a person's or animal's head, for carrying away water from a roof gutter (*a cathedral with gargoyles*).

garish /**gay**-rish/ *adj* flashy, unpleasantly bright (*garish colors*).

garland /**gar**-land/ *n* a wreath of flowers (*wear a garland round her neck*). ● *vb* to decorate with a garland.

garlic /**gar**-lic/ *n* a plant with a strong-smelling bulb used in cookery (*chop up cloves of garlic*).

garment /**gar**-ment/ *n* (*fml*) any article of clothing (*a store selling only ladies' garments*).

garnet /**gar**-net/ *n* a red mineral, sometimes a precious stone.

garnish /**gar**-nish/ *vb* to decorate (*garnish the dish with parsley*).

garrison /**ga**-ri-son/ *n* the soldiers sent to a place to defend it.

garter /**gar**-ter/ *n* **1** a band of elastic to hold up a stocking. **2** a strap hanging from a kind of belt or corset to hold up a stocking.

gas /**gas**/ *n* **1** matter in the form of an airlike vapor. **2** any of various gases or mixtures of gases used as fuel (*natural gas/coal gas*). **3** the vapor given off by a substance at a certain heat. **4** a feeling of discomfort caused by swallowing too much air when eating or drinking. **5** gasoline. ● *adj* **gaseous** /**ga**-shus/.

gash /**gash**/ *n* a wide deep wound or cut. ● *vb* to cut deep (*gash his thumb with a carving knife*).

gas mask /**gas**-mask/ *n* a mask that enables one to breathe when surrounded by poisonous gas (*gas masks issued in World War II*).

gasoline /**ga**-so-leen/ *n* a liquid obtained from a mixture of gas and petroleum, used as a fuel for motor vehicles.

gasp /**gasp**/ *vb* **1** to breathe with difficulty, to pant (*gasping for breath*). **2** to draw in the breath suddenly through the mouth (*gasp in horror at the sight*). ● *n* the act or sound of gasping (*his dying gasp/a gasp of horror*).

gassy /**ga**-see/ *adj* full of gas, fizzy (*gassy drinks*).

gastric /**ga**-stric/ *adj* having to do with the stomach (*a gastric complaint*).

gastronomic /ga-stri-**nom**-ic/, **gastronomical** /ga-stri-**nom**-i-cal/ *adjs* having to do with gastronomy (*the gastronomic delights of France*).

gastronomy /ga-**stron**-o-mee/ *n* the art of good eating.

gate /**gate**/ *n* **1** a movable frame of wood, iron, etc., to close an opening in a wall or fence (*the garden gate*). **2** an entrance or way out, especially in an airport (*the boarding gate*). **3** the number of people who pay to see a game (*expecting a large gate for the basketball game*). **4** the total sum of money paid for entrance to a sports ground.

gateux, **gâteau** /ga-**toe**/ *n* (*pl* **gateaux** *or* **gateaus**) a large cake, often filled and decorated with cream (*a chocolate gateau for dessert*).

gatecrash /**gate**-crash/ *vb* to attend a party, etc., without an invitation. ● *n* **gatecrasher** /**gate**-cra-sher/.

gateway /**gate**-way/ *n* **1** the opening closed by a gate (*the gateway to the orchard*). **2** the way or path to (*the gateway to a successful career*).

gather /**ga**-ther/ *vb* **1** to bring or come together (*a crowd gathered*). **2** to collect, to pick (*gather flowers*). **3** to draw cloth together in small folds (*gathered at the waist*). **4** to come to the conclusion (*we gather he is sick*). ● *n* a fold in cloth held in position by thread.

gathering /**ga**-ther-ing/ *n* a meeting (*a gathering of protesters against the new freeway*).

gaudy /**gaw**-dee/ *adj* showy, flashy, too bright (*gaudy colors*). ● *adv* **gaudily** /**gaw**-di-lee/. ● *n* **gaudiness** /**gaw**-dee-ness/.

gauge /**gage**/ *vb* **1** to measure (*instruments that gauge the diameter of the wire*). **2** to make an estimate of (*gauging the strength of the wind from the movement of trees*). **3** to make a judgment about, to judge (*try to gauge his likely reaction*). ● *n* **1** a measuring rod. **2** a measuring instrument. **3** the distance between the two rails of a railroad. **4** a help to guessing accurately (*a reliable gauge of his character*).

gaunt /**gawnt**/ *adj* very thin, haggard (*the gaunt faces of starving people*).

gauntlet /**gawnt**-let/ *n* **1** (*old*) an iron glove worn as part of a suit of armor. **2** a type of glove covering the wrist (*driving gauntlets*). ● **run the gauntlet** to be criticized or attacked from all sides (*have to run the gauntlet of a lot of newspaper articles on his private life*). ● **throw down the gauntlet** to challenge (*throw down the gauntlet and challenge him to a tennis match*).

gauze /**gawz**/ *n* a light cloth that one can see through (*bandages of gauze*). ● *adj* **gauzy** /**gaw**-zee/.

gave /**gave**/ *pt of* **give**.

gawky /**gaw**-kee/, **gawkish** /**gaw**-kish/ *adjs* clumsy, awkward (*gawky teenagers*).

gay /**gay**/ *adj* lively, fond of enjoyment, cheerful (*in a gay mood/gay music/streets gay with Christmas lights*). ● *adv* **gaily** /**gay**-lee/.

gaze /**gaze**/ *vb* to look hard at without looking away (*gaze at him in disbelief/gazing into space*). ● *n* a fixed look.

gazelle /ga-**zel**/ *n* a small antelope.

gazette /ga-**zet**/ *n* a government news sheet containing official notices, appointments, etc.

gazetteer /ga-ze-**teer**/ *n* a book listing places in alphabetical order and telling where they can be found on a map (*a world gazetteer*).

gear /**geer**/ *n* **1** the set of tools, equipment, etc., used for a particular job, sport, expedition, etc. (*camping gear*). **2** any arrangement of levers, toothed wheels, etc., that passes motion from one part of a machine to another (*put the car into reverse gear*).

geese /**geese**/ *see* **goose**.

gel /**jel**/ *n* a smooth, soft substance resembling jelly, often used in products for the skin or hair (*shower gel*).

gelatin, **gelatine** /**je**-la-tin/ *n* a jellylike substance made from boiled-down bones, etc., used as a thickening agent in jellies, etc.

gelignite /**je**-lig-nite/ *n* a powerful explosive (*blow up the bridge with gelignite*).

gem /**jem**/ *n* **1** a precious stone. **2** anything or anyone that is thought to be especially good (*the gem of his stamp collection/her mother is a gem*).

gender /**jen**-der/ *n* (*gram*) **1** a grouping of nouns roughly according to the sex (masculine, feminine, or neuter) of the things they name. **2** of a person or animal: the state of being male or female (*discriminated against on the grounds of gender*).

gene /**jeen**/ *n* any of the basic elements of heredity passed from parents to their offspring, that cause the offspring to have certain features that the parents have.

genealogist /jee-nee-**ol**-o-jist/ *n* one who studies genealogy.

genealogy /jee-nee-**ol**-o-jee/ *n* **1** the tracing of the history of a family to discover all its ancestors and branches. **2** a diagram showing this. ● *adj* **genealogical** /jee-nee-o-**lo**-ji-cal/.

genera /**je**-ne-ra/ *see* **genus**.

general /**je**-ne-ral/ *adj* **1** including every one of a class or group (*a general lowering of prices throughout the industry/wet weather that is general throughout the state*). **2** not specialized (*general knowledge*). **3** common, usual, normal (*the general procedure*). **4** taken as a whole, overall (*the invalid still has a weak arm but her general condition is good*). **5** widespread, public (*information that has become general*). **6** without details (*a general report*). ● *n* **1** a high-ranking army officer. **2** the commander of an army.

generalize /**je**-ne-ra-lize/ *vb*, *also* **generalise** (*Br*) **1** to work out from a few facts an idea that covers a great number of cases (*you must not generalize from just two examples*). **2** to talk in general terms without details (*generalizing about educational problems*). ● *n* **generalization** /je-ne-ra-li-**zay**-shun/.

generally /**je**-ne-ra-lee/ *adv* in most cases (*generally it is hot in summer*).

generate /**je**-ne-rate/ *vb* to bring into life, to produce, to be the cause of (*a meeting generating ideas/a misunderstanding that generated ill-feeling in the office*).

generation /je-ne-**ray**-shun/ *n* **1** the act of bringing into existence or producing (*the generation of new ideas*). **2** a single step in family descent (*three generations at the old man's birthday party*). **3** people living at the same time (*most of the people of her generation are dead*).

generator /**je**-ne-ray-tor/ *n* a machine for producing electricity, steam, etc.

generic /je-**ne**-ric/ *adj* applies to a member of a group or class (*see* **genus**). ● *n* (*of a drug, etc.*) a product not patented or sold with a brand name.

generous /je-ne-rus/ *adj* **1** giving or given freely and gladly (*generous hosts/a generous donation*). **2** ready to see the good in others. ● *n* **generosity** / je-ne-**ros**-i-tee/. ● *adv* **generously** /je-ne-rus-lee/.

genesis /je-ne-sis/ *n* (*fml*) beginning, origin. ● *n* **Genesis** the first book of the Christian Bible.

genetic /je-**ne**-tic/ *adj* of genes, of genetics (*a genetic defect*).

genetics /je-**ne**-tics/ *n* the science of breeding and family characteristics.

genial /jee-nee-al/ *adj* friendly in manner, cheerful (*genial hosts/new neighbors who seem genial*). ● *n* **geniality** /jee-nee-a-li-tee/. ● *adv* **genially** /jee-nee-a-lee/.

genie /jee-nee/ *n* (*pl* **genii** /jee-nee-ie/) a good or evil spirit in Eastern tales (*the genie of the lamp in the tale of Aladdin*).

genital /je-ni-tal/ *adj* having to do with reproduction (*genital organs*). ● *npl* **genitals** the genital organs. ● *n* **genitalia**.

genius /jeen-yus/ *n* **1** extraordinary skill or ability (*amazed at the genius of Emily Dickinson*). **2** a person of extraordinary intelligence (*Einstein was a genius*). **3** (*inf*) a natural ability (*a genius for offending people*).

genome *n* a full set of chromosomes.

genteel /jen-teel/ *adj* over-refined in manners, affected (*use a genteel voice on the telephone*).

gentile /jen-tile/ *adj* non-Jewish. ● *also n*.

gentility /jen-**ti**-li-tee/ *n* the state of having good manners or being of good birth.

gentle /jen-tul/ *adj* **1** (*old*) well-born (*people of gentle birth*). **2** not rough or violent in manner, unwilling to hurt anyone (*her gentle handling of the situation/gentle with the injured animal*). ● *n* **gentleness** /jen-tul-ness/. ● *adv* **gently** /jent-lee/.

gentleman /jen-tul-man/ *n* **1** (*old*) a man of good birth. **2** a well-mannered and kindly man (*he was a gentleman and rose to give the old lady his seat in the bus*).

gentlemanly /jen-tul-man-lee/ *adj* well-mannered.

gentry /jen-tree/ *n* the people of good but not noble birth (*landed gentry*).

genuflect /jen-yu-flect/ *vb* (*fml*) to bend the knee in respect (*courtiers genuflecting before the king*). ● *n* **genuflection** /jen-yu-**flec**-shun/.

genuine /jen-yoo-in/ *adj* **1** true, real (*a genuine Van Gogh painting*). **2** sincere, without pretense or dishonesty (*feel genuine concern for her situation*). ● *adv* **genuinely** /jen-yoo-in-lee/. ● *n* **genuineness** /jen-yoo-in-ness/.

genus /jee-nus/ *n* (*pl* **genera** /je-ne-ra/) a kind or class of animals, plants, etc., with certain characteristics in common. ● *adj* **generic** /je-ne-ric/.

geography /jee-**og**-ra-fee/ *n* the study of the surface of the earth and its climate, peoples, cities, etc. ● *n* **geographer** /jee-**og**-ra-fer/. ● *adjs* **geographic** /jee-o-**gra**-fic/, **geographical** /jee-o-**gra**-fi-cal/.

geology /jee-o-lo-jee/ *n* the study of the rocks, etc., forming the earth's crust. ● *n* **geologist** /jee-o-lo-jist/. ● *adj* **geological** /jee-o-**loj**-i-cal/.

geometry /jee-**om**-e-tree/ *n* a branch of mathematics dealing with the measurement of lines, figures, and solids. ● *adjs* **geometric** /jee-o-**met**-ric/, **geometrical** /jee-o-**met**-ri-cal/.

geranium /je-**ray**-nee-um/ *n* a strongly scented plant, with red, pink, or white flowers.

gerbil /jer-bil/ *n* a small ratlike rodent, often kept as a pet.

germ /jerm/ *n* **1** a tiny living cell that has the power to grow into a plant or animal. **2** the beginning of anything (*the germ of an idea*). **3** a disease-carrying microbe (*a disinfectant claiming to kill all germs*).

germicide /jer-mi-side/ *n* a substance that kills germs.

germinate /jer-mi-nate/ *vb* to begin to grow (*seeds germinating*).

gesticulate /je-**sti**-cyu-late/ *vb* to make meaningful signs with the hands especially while speaking, usually for emphasis (*gesticulating wildly/gesticulate to her to go away*). ● *n* **gesticulation** / je-sti-cyu-**lay**-shun/.

gesture /jes-chur/ *n* **1** a movement of the hands, head, etc., to express feeling (*with a gesture of despair*). **2** an action showing one's attitude or intentions (*a gesture of friendship*). ● *vb* to make a gesture.

get /get/ *vb* (**got** /got/, **getting** /ge-ting/, *pp* **gotten** /go-ten/) **1** to obtain (*get money*). **2** to reach (*get there*). **3** to become (*get older*).

geyser /gie-zer/ *n* a hot water spring that shoots up into the air (*geysers in Iceland*).

ghastly /gast-lee/ *adj* **1** (*fml or lit*) deathly pale (*his face ghastly with fear*). **2** horrible, terrible (*a ghastly murder/a ghastly experience*). **3** (*inf*) very bad, ugly, etc. (*a ghastly mistake/a ghastly dress*). **4** (*inf*) unwell, upset (*feel ghastly after a drinking bout*). ● *n* **ghastliness** /gast-lee-ness/.

gherkin /ger-kin/ *n* a small cucumber used for pickling.

ghetto /ge-toe/ n (pl **ghettos** or **ghettoes** /ge-toaz/) **1** the Jewish quarter of a town. **2** a part of a city, often poor, in which a certain group of people, often immigrants, lives.

ghost /goast/ n the spirit of a dead person appearing to one living. ● adjs **ghostlike** /goast-like/, **ghostly** /goast-lee/. ● n **ghostliness** /goast-lee-ness/.

ghoul /gool/ n **1** a spirit said to prey on corpses. **2** a person who takes an unusually great interest in death, disaster, and other horrible things (ghouls at the scene of the fatal accident). ● adj **ghoulish** /goo-lish/.

giant /jie-ant/ n **1** in fairy stories, a huge man (the giant in "Jack and the Beanstalk"). **2** a person of unusually great height and size (the giants in the basketball team). **3** a person of very great ability or importance (one of the political giants of the 19th century). ● f **giantess** /jie-an-tess/.

gibberish /ji-be-rish/ n nonsense, meaningless words (talk gibberish).

gibbon /gi-bon/ n a type of ape.

gibe /jibe/ vb to mock, to jeer at (gibe at their ragged clothes/gibing at his attempts to climb the tree). ● also n.

giddy /gi-dee/ adj **1** dizzy (feel giddy at the top of the ladder). **2** changeable, not serious in character, fond of amusement (giddy young girls). ● n **giddiness** /gi-dee-ness/.

gift /gift/ n **1** a present (Christmas gifts). **2** a natural ability to do something (a gift for public speaking). ● vb to give as a present (money gifted by alumni).

gifted /gif-ted/ adj having exceptional natural ability (gifted children).

gig /gig/ n **1** (inf) a single booking for a jazz or pop band, etc., a single night's performance. **2** (old) a light two-wheeled carriage.

gigantic /jie-gan-tic/ adj huge, giantlike (a gigantic machine).

giggle /gi-gl/ vb to laugh quietly, but in a silly way (children giggling at the practical joke).

gild /gild/ vb to cover with gold (a gilded statue).

gill[1] /gil/ n a quarter of a pint.

gill[2] /gil/ n the organ through which a fish breathes.

gilt /gilt/ adj covered with gold or gold paint (a gilt brooch). ● n the gold or imitation of gold used in gilding.

gimmick /gi-mic/ n an ingenious gadget or device to attract attention (a sales gimmick).

gin[1] /gin/ n a strong drink flavored with juniper berries (gin and tonic).

gin[2] /gin/ n **1** a trap or snare (a rabbit caught in a gin). **2** a machine for separating cotton from its seeds.

ginger /jin-jer/ n **1** a hot-tasting root used as a spice (crystallized ginger/chop ginger for an Indian dish). ● adj of a reddish yellow color (ginger hair).

gingerbread /jin-jer-bred/ n treacle cake flavored with ginger.

gingerly /jin-jer-lee/ adv carefully, cautiously (walk gingerly on the icy road).

gingham /ging-am/ n a striped or checked cotton cloth (gingham tablecloths).

gipsy /jip-see/ (Br) see **gypsy**.

giraffe /ji-raf/ n an African animal with a very long neck and long legs.

girder /gir-der/ n a heavy beam of iron or steel used to bridge an open space when building.

girdle /gir-dl/ n **1** a kind of belt. **2** (fml or lit) anything that surrounds (a girdle of green around the village). ● vb to surround as with a belt.

girl /girl/ n **1** a female child (a baby girl). **2** a young woman. **3** a daughter (they have two boys and a girl). ● n **girlhood** /girl-hood/.

girlfriend /girl-frend/ n **1** a female friend (she is having lunch with her girlfriends). **2** a female romantic partner (he is out on a date with his girlfriend).

girlish /gir-lish/ adj like or of a girl (a girlish figure/girlish laughter).

Girl Scout /girl-scout/ n a member of an international youth organization for girls.

girth /girth/ n **1** the measurement around the waist (a man of enormous girth). **2** the distance around something cylindrical in shape (the girth of the tree). **3** a strap that holds the saddle in place on a horse's back.

gist /jist/ n the meaning, the most important part (follow the gist of what he was saying).

give /giv/ vb (pt **gave** /gave/, pp **given** /gi-ven/) **1** to make a present of (give him a book for his birthday). **2** to hand over to (give the money to the bank). **3** to allow (given a chance). **4** to utter (give a shout). **5** to produce (cows giving milk). **6** to organize, to hold (give a party). **7** to yield, bend, break, etc. (the heavy door gave under pressure). ● n **giver** /gi-ver/. ● **give away 1** to give as a gift. **2** to tell something secret (give away their hiding place). ● **give ground** to go backward (the army had to give ground). ● **give in** to admit defeat (after a long argument he gave in and admitted he was wrong). ● **give out** to report (give out the news of her death). ● **give up 1** to leave to be taken by others (*give up a seat to a pregnant woman*). **2** to stop (*give up eating meat*). **3** to lose hope (*so long unemployed that he has given up*). ● **give way 1** to stop in order to allow someone or something to pass (*give way to traffic coming from the left*). **2** to be replaced by (*anger that gave way to fear*). **3** to break and fall (*a bridge that gave way*). ● **give and take** allowing some of another's views to be correct.

glacial /**glay**-shal/ *adj* **1** of ice. **2** icy, very cold (*glacial winds*). **3** (*fml*) very cold in manner (*a glacial stare*).

glacier /**glay**-sher/ *n* a large slow-moving river of ice.

glad /**glad**/ *adj* pleased, cheerful (*glad for her success*). ● *adv* **gladly** /**glad**-lee/. ● *n* **gladness** /**glad**-ness/.

gladden /**gla**-den/ *vb* to make glad (*news that gladdened his heart*).

glade /**glade**/ *n* (*fml*) a clear space in a wood.

gladiator /**gla**-dee-ay-tor/ *n* in Ancient Rome, a man trained to fight with other men or wild animals for public entertainment. ● *adj* **gladiatorial** /gla-dee-a-**toe**-ree-al/.

glamour /**gla**-mur/ *n* apparent charm and attractiveness that depends entirely on the outer appearance, dress, etc. (*the glamor of the movie star/the glamor of the stage*). ● *adj* **glamorous** /**gla**-mu-rus/. ● *vb* **glamorize**, *also* **glamourize** (*Cdn*) *also* **glamourise** (*Br*).

glance /**glanse**/ *n* a quick look (*give a glance over her shoulder*). ● *vb* **1** to look at for a moment (*glance at the newspaper*). **2** to hit the side of something and fly off in another direction (*the bullet glanced off the wall*).

gland /**gland**/ *n* an organ in the body that produces certain fluids necessary to the health of the body (*the thyroid gland*). ● *adj* **glandular** /**glan**-ju-lar/.

glare /**glare**/ *n* **1** a dazzling light (*the glare of the car's headlights*). **2** an angry or fierce look (*give her a glare for going before him in the queue*). ● *also vb*.

glaring /**glay**-ring/ *adj* **1** having a fierce look. **2** very obvious (*a glaring error*). ● *adv* **glaring** *adj* **1** having a fierce look. **2** very obvious (*a glaring error*). ● *adv* **glaringly** /**glay**-ring-lee/.

glass /**glass**/ *n* **1** hard, easily broken transparent material (*a door made of glass*). **2** a mirror (*look in the glass/a looking glass*). **3** a glass drinking vessel (*a glass of milk*). ● *adj* made of glass.

glasses /**gla**-siz/ *see* **eyeglasses**.

glaze /**glaze**/ *vb* **1** to fit with glass (*glaze the new windows*). **2** to cover with a smooth shiny surface (*glaze a cake with frosting/glazed fruit*). **3** to become fixed or glassy-looking (*eyes glazing over*). ● *n* a smooth shiny surface (*a glaze on the tiles*).

glazier /**glay**-zher/ *n* one who fixes glass in windows.

gleam /**gleem**/ *n* **1** a small ray of light, especially one that disappears quickly (*the gleam of a match in the darkness*). **2** a temporary appearance of some quality (*a faint gleam of humor/a gleam of hope*). ● *vb* **1** to shine softly (*lights gleaming/polished tables gleaming*). **2** to be expressed with a sudden light, to be bright (*eyes gleaming with excitement/excitement gleamed in her eyes*).

glee /**glee**/ *n* pleasure, joy (*full of glee at their victory*).

gleeful /**glee**-ful/ *adj* joyful (*gleeful at his enemy's defeat*). ● *adv* **gleefully** /**glee**-fu-lee/.

glen /**glen**/ *n* (*Scot*) a narrow valley.

glib /**glib**/ *adj* **1** quick to answer, able to find words easily, fluent (*a glib salesperson*). **2** spoken fluently and without hesitation (*a glib reply*). ● *n* **glibness** /**glib**-ness/.

glide /**glide**/ *vb* to move smoothly or without effort (*skiers gliding down the mountain*).

glider /**glie**-der/ *n* an aircraft with no engine.

glimmer /**gli**-mer/ *vb* to burn low and unsteadily, to shine faintly (*a candle glimmering at the end of the dark passage*). ● *n* **1** a low and unsteady light (*the glimmer from the candle*) **2** a slight sign or amount (*a glimmer of hope*).

glimpse /**glimss**/ *n* a quick or passing view of (*catch a glimpse of her in the crowd*). ● *vb* to see for a moment only (*glimpsing her red hat in the crowd*).

glint /**glint**/ *vb* to flash, to sparkle (*eyes glinting with anger*). ● *n* **1** a brief flash of light. **2** a brief indication (*glint of anger in her eyes*).

glisten /**gli**-sen/ *vb* (*especially of wet or polished surfaces*) to shine, to give a bright, steady light, to sparkle (*dew drops glistening on the grass/bodies glistening with sweat*). ● *also n*.

glitch /**glich**/ *n* something that goes unexpectedly wrong, especially with computers (*a computer glitch meant I could not save the file*).

glitter /**gli**-ter/ *vb* to sparkle, to give a bright flickering light (*stars glittering in the clear sky/diamonds glittering at her throat*). ● *also n*. ● *adj* **glittery** /**gli**-te-ree/.

gloat /**gloat**/ *vb* to look at with greedy or evil enjoyment (*gloat over her neighbor's misfortune/a miser gloating over his gold*).

global /**glo**-bal/ *adj* **1** affecting the whole world (*a global issue like poverty*). **2** relating to or including the whole of something (*the industry is seeking a* *global pay settlement*). ● *adv* **globally** /glo-ba-lee/.

globalization /glo-ba-li-**zay**-shun/ *n, also* **globalisation** (*Br*) the process by which a business firm or organization begins to operate on an international basis (*the globalization of the insurance industry*).

global warming /glo-bal **wawr**-ming/ *n* a gradual increase in the world's temperatures believed to be caused, in part at least, by the **greenhouse effect** (*see below*).

globe /globe/ *n* **1** a ball, a sphere. **2** anything ball-shaped (*a new globe for the light*). **3** the earth (*from all parts of the globe*). **4** a map of the earth printed on to a ball.

globular /glob-yu-lar/ *adj* ball-shaped.

globule /glob-yul/ *n* a drop, a very small ball (*globules of wax from a candle*).

gloom /gloom/ *n* **1** darkness. **2** sadness.

gloomy /gloo-mee/ *adj* **1** dark, dim (*gloomy corridors*). **2** sad-looking, depressed (*gloomy about the future/in a gloomy mood*).

glorify /glo-ri-fie/ *vb* **1** to praise or worship (*glorifying God*). **2** to make seem better, more beautiful, more important, etc. (*a book that glorified war*). ● *n* **glorification** /glo-ri-fi-**cay**-shun/.

glorious /glo-ree-us/ *adj* **1** splendid, magnificent (*a glorious summer's day/a glorious sunset*). **2** famous (*a glorious victory/glorious deeds*).

glory /glo-ree/ *n* **1** honor, fame (*win glory on the battlefield*). **2** brightness, beauty, splendor (*the glory of the sunset*). **3** worship, adoration (*glory to God*). **4** a special cause for pride, respect, honor, etc. (*one of the glories of American justice*). ● *vb* to take pride in, to rejoice (*glorying in one's freedom/gloried in her success*).

gloss[1] /gloss/ *n* a bright or shiny surface. ● *vb* to give a shine to. ● **gloss over** to try to make appear pleasing or satisfactory.

gloss[2] /gloss/ *n* **1** a note written in the margin or between lines (*a gloss explaining the word*). **2** an explanation, interpretation (*politicians putting different glosses on the situation*). ● *vb* to provide with glosses, to annotate (*expressions that need to be glossed*).

glossary /glos-a-ree/ *n* a list of words with their meanings (*a glossary of cooking terms in the recipe book*).

glossy /gloss-ee/ *adj* smooth and shining (*glossy hair*).

glove /gluv/ *n* a covering of cloth or leather for the hand, each finger being separately covered (*gloves wet from throwing snowballs*).

glow /glo/ *vb* **1** to give out light and heat but no flame (*coal glowing in the grate/a cigarette glowing in the dark*). **2** to look or feel warm or red (*cheeks glowing after exercise*). ● *n* **1** a bright steady light (*the glow of the furnace*). **2** a warm look or feeling (*a healthy glow after their walk*). **3** a good feeling (*feel a glow of satisfaction*).

glower /glaoo-er/ *vb* to give an angry look (*glower at the person who bumped his car*).

glowing /glo-ing/ *adj* **1** full of praise (*a glowing account of her work*). **2** giving out heat (*glowing coal*).

glow-worm /glo-wurm/ *n* an insect that sends out a light in the dark.

glucose /gloo-cose/ *n* grape sugar, a natural sugar found in fruits and plants.

glue /gloo/ *n* a sticky substance used for sticking things together. ● *vb* to stick with glue (*gluing the pieces of the vase together/glued the newspaper cuttings in a scrapbook*).

gluey /gloo-ee/ *adj* sticky.

glum /glum/ *adj* **1** sad, gloomy (*glum expressions*). **2** downcast (*feel glum about the future*).

glut /glut/ *vb* (**glutted** /glu-ted/, **glutting** /glu-ting/) **1** to fill too full, to supply with more than is needed (*glut the market with cheap foreign goods*). **2** to stuff, to gorge oneself (*glutted with food*). ● *n* too great an amount (*a glut of soft fruit on the market*).

gluten /gloo-ten/ *n* (*fml*) a sticky protein found in wheat and some other cereal grains.

glutinous /gloot-nus/ *adj* (*fml*) sticky (*a glutinous substance*).

glutton /glu-ten/ *n* **1** a person who eats too much. **2** (*inf*) a person who is always ready for more (*a glutton for work*).

gluttonous /glut-nus/ *adj* greedy, too fond of food.

gluttony /glut-nee/ *n* a fondness for eating a good deal, love of food (*disgusted by his gluttony*).

glycerin /glis-rin/ *n* a colorless sweet liquid obtained from fats.

GM /jee-em/ *abbr* = **genetically modified**: food, such as a plant, whose genetic material or structure has been altered by technological means to improve growth or treat disease.

gnarled /narld/ *adj* twisted and having a rough surface (*gnarled tree trunks/hands gnarled with age*).

gnash /nash/ *vb* to strike the teeth together, to grind the teeth, often as a sign of emotion (*gnash his teeth in rage*).

gnat /nat/ *n* a small biting insect.

gnaw /naw/ *vb* **1** to keep on biting at in order to

wear away gradually (*dogs gnawing bones*). **2** to cause continued distress to (*guilt gnawing away at her*).

gnome /nome/ *n* in fairytales, a mischievous fairy supposed to live underground.

gnu /noo/ *n* a large African antelope.

go /go/ *vb* (*pt* **went** /went/, *pp* **gone** /gon/) **1** to move (*go backward*). **2** to become (*go mad/go white-haired with age*). ● *n* **going**. ● **go for** to attack (*the dog went for the postman*). ● **go hard with** (*fml*) to turn out badly for (*it went hard with our army in the battle*). ● **go in for** to take interest in (*she works hard and doesn't go in for hobbies*). ● **go under** to fail (*hope that the firm does not go under*).

go-ahead /go-a-hed/ *adj* ready to try out new ideas (*a go-ahead firm*). ● *n* permission to proceed (*get the go-ahead for the new road*).

goal /goal/ *n* **1** an aim, target, object of one's efforts (*his main goal in life*). **2** in some games, the wooden frame through which players try to pass the ball (*the goalkeeper guarding the goal in the hockey match*). **3** a score at football, hockey, etc. (*the team that scored a goal*).

goalkeeper /goal-kee-per/ *n* the player who defends a goal.

goat /goat/ *n* an animal with horns, related to the sheep.

goatee /go-tee/ *n* a neat pointed beard on a man's chin.

gobble /gob-ul/ *vb* **1** to eat quickly (*children gobbling down their food before going out to play*). **2** to make a noise like a turkey.

go-between /go-bee-tween/ *n* one who arranges an agreement between two other parties (*act as a go-between in the talks between the firms*).

goblet /gob-let/ *n* a drinking cup without a handle (*silver wine goblets*).

goblin /gob-lin/ *n* in fairytales, a mischievous fairy.

god /god/ *n* any being worshiped for having more than natural powers (*the Roman god of war*).

God /god/ *n* **1** in various religions, the creator of the world, the Supreme Being. **2** a man of superior charms or excellence.

goddess /god-ess/ *n* **1** a female god (*the Greek goddess of beauty*). **2** a woman of superior charms or excellence.

godfather /god-fa-ther/ *n* a man who makes the promises for a child at a Christian baptism. ● *f* **godmother** /god-mu-ther/. ● *also* **godchild, god-daughter, god-parent, godson**.

God-fearing /god-fee-ring/ *adj* deeply religious (*a god-fearing old man/a god-fearing people*).

godless /god-less/ *adj* (*fml*) not believing in God, wicked (*a godless people*).

godlike /god-like/ *adj* **1** like God. **2** like a god (*a godlike beauty*).

godly /god-lee/ *adj* religious, following God's laws (*a godly man/a godly life*). ● *n* **godliness** /god-lee-ness/.

goggles /gog-ulz/ *npl* a type of eyeglasses, especially those worn to protect the eyes (*machine operators wearing protective goggles*).

go-kart /go-kart/ *n* a small racing vehicle made of an open frame on four wheels with an engine (*go-kart racing*).

gold /goald/ *n* **1** a precious metal (*rings made of gold*). **2** wealth, money (*a miser counting his gold*). **3** the color of gold (*hair of gold*).

golden /goal-den/ *adj* **1** made of gold. **2** of the color of gold (*golden sands/golden hair*). **3** valuable (*a golden opportunity*).

goldfinch /goald-finch/ *n* a beautiful singing bird.

goldfish /goald-fish/ *n* a small red Chinese carp, often kept in an aquarium or pond.

goldsmith /goald-smith/ *n* a worker in gold.

golf /golf/ *n* an outdoor game played with clubs and a hard ball (*play a few rounds of golf*). ● *also vb*. ● *n* **golfer** /gol-fer/.

gondola /gon-du-la/ *n* **1** a long narrow boat used on the canals of Venice. **2** the car of an airship.

gondolier /gon-du-leer/ *n* a man who rows a gondola.

gone /gon/ *pp of* **go**.

gong /gong/ *n* a flat metal plate that makes a ringing sound when struck (*sound the gong for dinner*).

good /good/ *adj* **1** right, morally acceptable, virtuous (*a good deed/a good life*). **2** of a high quality (*a good performance/good eyesight*). **3** pleasant, agreeable, welcome (*good news/good to see some sunshine*). **4** fit, competent (*a good teacher*). **5** well-behaved (*tell the children to be good*). **6** kindly (*the good fairy in the story*). **7** clever (*good at math*). **8** fit to be eaten (*good fruit affected by the bad*). **9** beneficial (*food that is good for one*).

goodbye, good-bye /good-bie/ *n and interj* a farewell greeting.

Good Friday /good frie-day/ *n* the Friday before Easter on which Christians cemmemorate the crucifixion and death of Christ.

good-looking /good-loo-king/ *adj* handsome.

good-natured /good-nay-churd/ *adj* kindly (*good-natured neighbors*).

goodness /good-ness/ *n* the quality of being good.

goods /goodz/ *npl* **1** movable property (*stolen goods*). **2** things for buying or selling (*a range of electrical goods*).

goodwill /good-will/ *n* **1** kindly feeling (*full of goodwill even toward people who treat him badly*). **2** the good name and popularity of a store or business (*the price she was charging for her store took into consideration the goodwill of the business*).

goose /gooss/ *n* (*pl* **geese** /geess/) **1** a web-footed farmyard fowl. **2** (*fml or old*) a foolish person (*she was a goose to believe them*).

gooseberry /gooss-be-ree/ *n* **1** a thorny shrub. **2** its edible berry. **3** an unwanted third person when two people, especially lovers, want to be alone.

goose bumps /gooss-bumps/ *npl* a roughness or bumpiness of the skin due to cold or fear.

gore[1] /gore/ *vb* to wound with a tusk or horn (*a farmhand gored by a bull*).

gore[2] /gore/ *n* (*fml or lit*) blood from a dead or wounded person, especially when formed into solid lumps (*a battlefield covered in gore/a movie with too much gore*). ● *adj* **gory** /goa-ree/.

gorge /gorge/ *n* **1** (*old*) the throat (*a bone stuck in his gorge*). **2** (*found in place names*) a deep narrow pass between hills (*the Cheddar Gorge*). ● **make one's gorge rise** to sicken, to fill with disgust. ● *vb* to overeat, to eat greedily.

gorgeous /gawr-jus/ *adj* **1** (*inf*) very beautiful and glamorous (*gorgeous models*). **2** splendid, magnificent, richly decorated or colored (*walls covered with gorgeous tapestries/gorgeous silks and satins*). **3** (*inf*) giving a lot of pleasure, marvelous (*a gorgeous meal/a gorgeous day*).

gorilla /gaw-ri-la/ *n* a large African ape.

gory *see* **gore**.

gosling /goz-ling/ *n* a young goose.

gospel /gos-pel/ *n* **1** (*usually cap*) the teaching of Jesus Christ. **2** in the Christian New Testament, the story of the life of Christ as written by Matthew, Mark, Luke, or John. **3** any complete system of beliefs (*spread the gospel of a healthy diet*). **4** (*inf*) the truth (*I thought his story was untrue but he swore that it was gospel*). **5** religious music in a popular or folk style and African-American in origin.

gossamer /gos-a-mer/ *n* **1** cobweblike threads floating in the air or resting on bushes. **2** any very light material (*a wedding veil of gossamer*). ● *adj* very light.

gossip /gos-ip/ *n* **1** one who likes to hear and spread news about the private affairs of others (*the village gossips starting whispering in the post office*). **2** idle talk (*spread gossip about her*). ● *vb* **1** to spread stories about others. **2** to talk idly or chatter, often about other people (*neighbors gossiping over the fence*).

got *pt of* **get**.

Gothic /goth-ic/ *adj* in the pointed-arch style of architecture common in the Middle Ages.

gotten *pp of* **get**.

Gouda /gou-da/ *n* a mild, round Dutch cheese.

gouge /goudge/ *n* a chisel with a curving blade for cutting grooves. ● *vb* **1** to make a groove or hole in (*gouging holes in the paintwork*). **2** to scoop out, to force out (*gouge her eyes out as a torture*).

gourd /goard/ *n* **1** a large fleshy fruit (e.g., cucumber, melon). **2** the hollow skin of a gourd used as a bottle or a cup.

gourmand /goor-mawnd/ *n* **1** (*fml*) a greedy eater, a glutton. **2** a person who likes good food, often to excess.

gourmet /goor-may/ *n* a person who is a good judge of wines and food (*a restaurant guide written by a gourmet*).

gout /gout/ *n* a disease causing painful swelling of the joints.

govern /gu-vern/ *vb* **1** to control and direct the affairs of (*a country governed by a dictator*). **2** to control, to guide, to influence (*price of goods governed to some extent by demand/a business policy governed by several factors*). **3** to exercise restraint over, to control, to regulate (*try to govern her temper*).

governess /gu-ver-ness/ *n* a woman who looks after and teaches children in their home.

government /gu-ver-ment/ *n* **1** the act or way of ruling (*a democratic system of government*). **2** the group of people who direct the affairs of a country (*ministers resigning from the government*). ● *adj* **governmental** /gu-ver-men-tal/.

governor /gu-ve-nor/ *n* **1** in the United States, a person who is elected as head of a state (*the Governor of Texas*). **2** a member of the committee of people who govern a school, hospital, etc. (*on the school's board of governors*). **3** (*old*) a person governing a province or colony (*the former governor of Australia*).

gown /goun/ *n* **1** a woman's dress, usually formal (*an evening gown*). **2** a long robe worn by members of clergy, teachers, lawyers, etc. (*students required to wear academic gowns to graduate*).

grab /grab/ *vb* (**grabbed** /grabd/, **grabbing** /gra-bing/) **1** to take hold of with a sudden quick movement (*grab the child to prevent her being run over/a robber grabbing the money from the bank clerk*). **2** to get or take something quickly and sometimes unfairly (*grab a sandwich/grab her seat*). **3** (*inf*) to affect, to influence, to find favor with (*how does a trip to the movies grab you?*). ● *also n.*

grace /grase/ *n* **1** the mercy or kindness associated with God. **2** a sense of what is right or decent (*he finally had the grace to apologize*). **3** a delay allowed as a favor (*a few days' grace to repay the loan*). **4** beauty and effortlessness of movement (*dance with grace*). **5** a short prayer said at meal times. **6** a title of respect used to dukes, archbishops, etc. (*Your Grace*). ● *n* **1** to honor (*grace the dinner with her presence*). **2** to adorn (*flowers gracing the table*).

graceful /grase-fool/ *adj* beautiful in appearance or movement (*graceful dancers*). ● *adv* **gracefully** / grase-foo-lee/.

gracious /gray-shus/ *adj* kind, pleasant, polite (*our gracious hostess*). ● *adv* **graciously** /gray-shus-lee/.

grade /grade/ *n* **1** a placing in an order according to one's merit, rank, performance, etc. (*grades achieved in exams*). **2** rank (*various grades in the army*). ● *vb* **1** to arrange in grades (*grade the wool according to quality/grading eggs according to size*). **2** to assign a grade to (*the teacher is grading papers*). **3** to pass or change from one thing to another gradually (*blues and reds grading into purple*).

gradient /gray-dee-ent/ *n* **1** a slope (*the child tumbled down the steep gradient*). **2** the steepness of a slope (*the gradient of the hill/a gradient of 1 in 7*).

gradual /gra-ju-wul/ *adj* slow and steady, little by little (*a gradual improvement/a gradual rise in temperature*). ● *adv* **gradually** /gra-ju-wa-lee/.

graduate /gra-ju-wit/ *vb* **1** to receive an academic degree or diploma. **2** (*fml*) to divide into stages or equal spaces (*a thermometer graduated in degrees/a graduated tax system*). ● *n* a person who holds an academic degree or diploma (*a graduate of the University of Pennsylvania*). ● *adj* relating to people who already hold one academic degree or diploma (*a graduate student*).

graduation /gra-ju-**way**-shun/ *n* the receiving of an academic degree or dilpoma.

graffiti /gra-**fee**-tee/ *npl* (*sing* **graffito** /gra-**fee**-toe/ (*rare*) writing or drawings, often humorous or rude, scribbled or sprayed unofficially or illegally on walls or other surfaces in public places (*the subway walls are covered in graffiti*).

graft[1] /graft/ *vb* **1** to fix a piece cut from one plant onto another so that it grows into it. **2** to put skin cut from one part of the body on to another part (*graft skin from his thigh to his arm after he was scalded*). **3** to replace an organ of the body by one belonging to someone else, to transplant (*graft a kidney from his brother in the patient*). ● *n* the cutting or skin so grafted.

graft[2] /graft/ *n* (*inf*) **1** bribery and corruption (*accused of graft by his political opponents*). **2** wealth made by illegal use of office. **3** hard work (*make money by sheer hard graft*).

graham cracker /**gram** cra-ker/ *n* a cracker made with graham flour.

graham flour /**gram** flour/ *n* wholewheat flour.

Grail /grale/ *see* **Holy Grail**.

grain /grane/ *n* **1** a seed of wheat, corn, etc. **2** corn in general (*grain ground into flour*). **3** a very small hard particle (*a grain of salt*). **4** a very small amount (*not a grain of truth in it*). **5** the smallest measure of weight (1 pound=7000 grains). **6** the pattern of markings in wood, leather, etc. ● *vb* to imitate the grain of wood when painting doors, etc.

gram /gram/ *n* the basic unit of weight in the metric system.

grammar /gra-mer/ *n* the science of the correct use of language. ● **grammarian** /gra-**may**-ree-an/.

grammatical /gra-**ma**-ti-cal/ *adj* correct in grammar (*a grammatical sentence*).

granary /gra-na-ree/ *n* a storehouse for grain.

grand /grand/ *adj* **1** noble, magnificent, splendid (*a very grand procession/generals looking very grand in their uniforms*). **2** important, proud, too proud (*grand ladies looking down on poor people/too grand to go out for a drink with his old colleagues*). **3** (*inf or dial*) pleasant (*a grand day*). **4** wonderful, highly respected (*a grand old man*). **5** dignified (*write in a grand style*).

grandeur /gran-jur/ *n* nobility, magnificence, splendidness.

grandfather /gran-fa-ther/ *n* the father of one's father or mother. ● *f* **grandmother** /gran-mu-ther/. ● *also* **grandchild**, **grand-daughter**, **grand-parent**, **grandson**.

grandiose /gran-dee-oas/ *adj* meant to be splendid, intended to be impressive (*he has grandiose ideas, but no money to carry them out*).

grand piano /grand-**pee**-a-no/ *n* a large piano in which the strings are horizontal.

grandstand /grand-stand/ *n* rows of seats built on a rising slope to allow people a good view of a sports contest. ● *vb* to show off to the audience or onlookers.

granite /gra-nit/ *n* a hard rock (*houses built of granite*).

granny /gra-nee/ *n* (*inf*) a grandmother (*a little girl asking for her granny*).

grant /grant/ *vb* 1 to give, to agree to, to allow (*grant him permission to go/grant him a favor*). 2 (*fml*) to admit as true (*I grant that he is hardworking*). ● *n* something allowed or given, especially money given for a certain purpose (*a grant to build a new wing for the university library*).

granular /gran-yu-lar/ *adj* 1 of or like grains (*granular substances like salt*). 2 rough to the touch, rough in appearance (*rather granular skin*).

granulate /gran-yu-late/ *vb* to break into grains or small pieces (*granulated sugar*).

granule /gran-yool/ *n* a small grain (*granules of sugar*).

grape /grape/ *n* the fruit of the vine (*wine made from grapes*).

grapefruit /grape-froot/ *n* a large yellowish sharp-tasting fruit (*have half a grapefruit for breakfast*).

graph /graf/ *n* a diagram in which different numbers, quantities, etc., are shown by dots on a piece of squared paper, and then joined up by lines so that they can be easily compared (*a graph showing the annual variations in sales*).

graphic /gra-fic/ *adj* 1 so well told that the events, etc., can be seen in the mind's eye (*a graphic description of what was going on in the war zone*). 2 drawn, concerned with drawing, painting, etc. (*the graphic arts*). ● **graphics** *npl* information in the form of illustrations or diagrams (*the graphics in the book make the text easier to understand*).

graphite /gra-fite/ *n* a soft black form of carbon used in pencils.

grapple /gra-pl/ *vb* 1 to fight hand to hand, to take hold of and struggle with (*grapple with the burglar who had entered his house*). 2 to struggle with (*grappling with math for the exam*).

grasp /grasp/ *vb* 1 to take firm hold of (*grasp his hand in farewell*). 2 to understand (*unable to grasp the urgency of the situation*). ● *n* 1 firm hold (*shake his hand in a grasp*). 2 reach (*the job was within his grasp*). 3 understanding (*a good grasp of the subject*).

grasping /gra-sping/ *adj* mean, always wanting more money (*grasping moneylenders/grasping merchants overcharging customers*).

grass /grasp/ *n* the common plant covering of the ground, usually green. ● *adj* **grassy**.

grasshopper /grass-hop-er/ *n* a small jumping insect.

grate¹ /grate/ *n* a metal frame in a fireplace for holding the fire (*a fire burning steadily in the grate*).

grate² /grate/ *vb* 1 to break down by rubbing on something rough (*grate cheese*). 2 to make a harsh sound, as of metal rubbing on metal (*chalk grating on a blackboard*). 3 to annoy, to irritate (*a voice that really grates on people*).

grateful /grate-ful/ *adj* thankful (*grateful for your help/with grateful thanks*)). ● *adv* **gratefully** /grate-fu-lee/.

grater /gray-ter/ *n* an instrument with a rough surface for breaking down to crumbs or powder (*a cheese grater*).

gratification /gra-ti-fi-**cay**-shun/ *n* pleasure, satisfaction (*a sense of gratification at finishing the job on time*).

gratify /gra-ti-fy/ *vb* 1 to please, to delight (*we were gratified to hear that they liked our present*). 2 to satisfy (*able to gratify her desire to go to the opera*).

grating /gray-ting/ *n* a framework of metal bars.

gratitude /gra-ti-tood/ *n* thankfulness (*express his gratitude for their help/be filled with gratitude for her kindness*).

gratuitous /gra-**too**-wi-tus/ *adj* 1 unasked-for, unwanted (*gratuitous advice*). 2 unnecessary, unjustified (*scenes of gratuitous violence in the movie*).

grave¹ /grave/ *n* the hole dug in the earth for a dead body.

grave² /grave/ *adj* serious, important (*a matter of grave importance/wear a grave expression*).

gravel /gra-vel/ *n* 1 small stones or pebbles (*throw gravel at the bedroom window to wake her*). 2 a mixture of small stones and sand used to make the surface of roads and paths (*the child fell on the gravel*).

gravestone /grave-stone/ *n* a memorial stone placed over a grave.

graveyard /grave-yard/ *n* a piece of land set aside for graves.

gravitate /gra-vi-tate/ *vb* 1 to move toward the center. 2 to move in a certain direction as if drawn there by some force (*children gravitating toward the toy store*). ● *n* **gravitation** /gra-vi-**tay**-shun/.

gravity /gra-vi-tee/ *n* 1 seriousness, importance (*understand the gravity of the situation*). 2 (*fml*) weight. 3 the force drawing bodies toward the center of the earth (*the force of gravity*).

gravy /gray-vee/ *n* the juice got from meat when it is being cooked, often thickened and served as a sauce with the meat.

gray /**gray**/ *adj* **1** black mixed with white in color (*a gray dress*). **2** of the color of hair whitened by age (*gray hair*). ● *also n.*

graze[1] /**graze**/ *vb* **1** to touch or rub against lightly in passing (*the car grazed the garage door*). **2** to scrape along the surface. ● *n* **1** a passing touch. **2** a scraping of the skin (*bandage the graze on the child's knee*).

graze[2] /**graze**/ *vb* to eat growing grass, to feed on grass (*cows grazing in the field*).

grazing /**gray**-zing/ *n* land with grass suitable for feeding cattle (*hire out the grazing to a neighboring farmer*).

grease /**greese**/ *n* **1** fat in a soft state (*the grease from cooking bacon*). **2** fatty or oily matter (*use grease on his hair/lubricate the hinges with grease*). ● *vb* to smear with grease. ● *adj* **greasy**.

great /**grate**/ *adj* **1** large in amount, number, or size (*a great crowd*). **2** important (*a great painting/a great discovery*). **3** famous (*a great leader*). **4** long in time (*a great age*). **5** more than is usual (*great kindness*). **6** noble. **7** having possessed and made full use of extraordinary ability. ● *adv* **greatly** /**grate**-lee/. ● *n* **greatness** /**grate**-ness/.

great-grandfather /**grate**-gran-fa-ther/ *n* the father of one of one's grandparents. ● *f* **great-grandmother** /**grate**-gran-mu-ther/. ● *also* **great-grandchild**, **great-grandparent**, etc.

greed /**greed**/ *n* **1** the desire to have more and more for oneself (*the greed of the miser as he got more and more money*). **2** love of eating (*eat not from hunger but from greed*).

greedy /**gree**-dee/ *adj* always wanting more than one has (*greedy miser/greedy eaters*). ● *adv* **greedily** /**gree**-di-lee/. ● *n* **greediness** /**gree**-dee-ness/.

green /**green**/ *adj* **1** the color of grass (*a green dress*). **2** fresh, not ripe (*green bananas*). **3** inexperienced (*young workers so green that they believed his jokes*). **3** concerned with the protection and conservation of the environment (*discussing green issues*). ● *n* **1** green color (*she always wears green*). **2** a piece of ground covered with grass (*the village green*). **3** a person who is concerned with the protection and conservation of the environment (*the greens*). ● *n* **greenness** /**green**-ness/. ● *npl* **greens** /**greenz**/ green vegetables (e.g., cabbage) (*children told to eat their greens*).

greenery /**green**-ree/ *n* green plants, foliage (*arrange the flowers with some greenery*).

greenhouse /**green**-house/ *n* a glasshouse for growing plants (*grow tomatoes in a greenhouse*).

greenhouse effect /**green**-house ee-**fect**/ *n* an increase in the earth's atmosphere of the amount of carbon dioxide and other gases that trap the heat of the sun and prevent it from escaping into space, thought to be a major cause of **global warming** (*see above*).

greet /**greet**/ *vb* **1** to welcome (*greet the guests at the front door*). **2** to speak or send good wishes to someone (*greeted his neighbors in the street*). **3** to receive (*greet the news with relief/the statement was greeted with disbelief*).

greeting /**gree**-ting/ *n* **1** welcome (*a few words of greeting to the guests*). **2** (*often pl*) good wishes (*send greetings to her parents*).

gregarious /gre-**ga**-ree-us/ *adj* **1** fond of company (*too gregarious to live alone*). **2** (*fml*) living in flocks or herds (*gregarious animals*).

grenade /gre-**nade**/ *n* a small bomb thrown by hand.

grew /**groo**/ *pt of* **grow**.

grey /**gray**/ (*Br, Cdn*) *see* **gray**.

greyhound /**gray**-hound/ *n* a lean fast-running dog, used in dog-racing.

grid /**grid**/ *n* **1** a framework of metal bars (*a grid to keep cattle from leaving the field*). **2** a gridiron. **3** a large number of electric wires, rail lines, etc., crossing and going in different directions. **4** the division of a map into squares to make map-reading easier.

griddle /**gri**-dul/ *n* a flat iron plate for baking cakes, etc., on a fire or the top of a stove.

gridiron /**grid**-ie-urn/ *n* **1** a framework of iron bars used for cooking meat over a fire (*broil steaks over a gridiron*). **2** a field for American football.

grief /**greef**/ *n* great sorrow (*their grief at their friend's death*). ● **come to grief** to fail, to suffer a misfortune (*they'll come to grief if they oppose his scheme*).

grievance /**gree**-vanse/ *n* a cause of complaint (*workers giving management a list of grievances*).

grieve /**greeve**/ *vb* **1** to sorrow, to mourn (*widows grieving for their dead husbands*). **2** (*fml*) to cause sorrow (*it grieved him to leave her*).

grievous /**gree**-vus/ *adj* (*fml*) **1** causing pain or sorrow (*grievous loss*). **2** severe, serious (*grievous bodily harm*).

grill /**grill**/ *n* **1** a framework of metal bars used in cooking that directs heat downward for cooking meat, etc. (*cook the hamburgers on the grill*). **2** food cooked on a grill (*a mixed grill*). **3** an informal restaurant or diner. **4** a grille. ● *vb* **1** to cook on a grill (*grill the steak*). **2** (*inf*) to question intensively (*grilled by the police*).

grille /grill/ *n* a framework of metal bars fitted into a counter or door, or outside a window (*bank clerks protected by a grille*).

grim /grim/ *adj* **1** angry-looking, unsmiling (*looked grim when he heard the news*). **2** unpleasant, depressing (*the grim prospect of unemployment*). **3** severe, harsh (*a grim struggle for survival*). **4** stubborn, determined (*with grim determination*). ● *n* **grimness** /**grim**-ness/.

grimace /**gri**-mas/ *vb* to twist the face to show one's feelings (*grimacing with disgust at the sight*). ● *also n.*

grime /grime/ *n* dirt, filth (*the grime on the city buildings*). ● *adj* **grimy** /**grie**-mee/.

grin /grin/ *vb* (**grinned** /grind/, **grinning** /**gri**-ning/) to smile widely in pleasure. ● *also n.*

grind /grinde/ *vb* (*pt, pp* **ground** /ground/) **1** to rub or crush to powder or small pieces (*grind the coffee/ground beef*). **2** to sharpen by rubbing (*grind the knives*). **3** to press together noisily (*grind his teeth*). **4** (*inf*) to work hard (*grind away at her studies*). ● *n* hard and uninteresting work.

grinder /**grin**-der/ *n* a person or thing that grinds (*a coffee grinder*).

grip /grip/ *vb* (**gripped** /gript/, **gripping** /**gri**-ping/) **1** to take a firm hold of, to hold very tightly (*a child gripping his mother's hand*). **2** to seize the attention of (*an audience gripped by the play*). ● *n* a firm or tight hold (*keeping a tight grip on his wallet*).

gripe /gripe/ *vb* **1** (*fml*) to cause a sharp pain in the stomach. **2** (*inf*) to complain (*always griping about something*). ● *n* **1** a pain in the stomach. **2** (*inf*) a complaint.

grisly /**griz**-lee/ *adj* dreadful, frightening (*the grisly sight of the headless corpse*).

the mill).

gristle /**gri**-sul/ *n* a tough elastic substance surrounding the joints of the bones (*unable to eat the meat that was full of gristle*). ● *adj* **gristly** /**gri**-slee/.

grit /grit/ *n* **1** grains of sand or dust (*spread grit on icy roads*). **2** courage, determination (*it took grit to face up to the bullies*). ● *vb* (**gritted** /**gri**-ted/, **gritting** /**gri**-ting/) **1** to press (the teeth) tightly together. **2** to spread grit on (roads). ● *adj* **gritty** /**gri**-tee/.

grits /grits/ *npl* boiled grain eaten as a side dish.

grizzly /**griz**-lee/ *n* a large fierce North American bear.

groan /groan/ *vb* to utter a low, deep sound expressing pain or anxiety (*victims groaning with pain after the accident/groaned in despair*). ● *also n.*

grocer /**gro**-ser/ *n* a person who sells dry and tinned foods, tea, sugar, household supplies, etc. (*prefer the grocer's store to the supermarket*).

grog /grog/ *n* (*old*) a mixture of strong drink and cold water.

groggy /**grog**-ee/ *adj* not steady on the feet, weak (*feeling groggy after the surgical procedure*).

groin /groin/ *n* the hollow part of the body where the legs join the trunk (*strain a muscle in the groin*).

groom /groom/ *n* **1** a person who cares for horses (*the grooms at the racing stables*). **2** a man who is being married (*the bride and groom*).

groomsman /**groomz**-man/ *n* a male friend or relative who accompanies the bridegroom at a wedding.

groove /groov/ *n* a long, narrow hollow, such as that made by a tool in wood (*the groove in a record/the groove for a sliding door*). ● *vb* to make a groove in.

grope /grope/ *vb* to feel for something unseen by feeling with one's hands (*groping for the light switch*).

gross /grawss/ *adj* **1** fat and overfed (*feel gross beside the slender models*). **2** coarse, vulgar, impolite (*gross behavior/gross language*). **3** (*inf*) disgusting, repulsive (*that movie is so gross*). **4** very noticeable, glaringly obvious (*gross negligence*). **5** whole, complete, total (*gross weight/gross profit*). ● *n* **1** twelve dozen, 144. **2** the whole. ● *adv* **grossly** /**grawss**-lee/.

grossness /**grawss**-ness/ *n* rudeness, vulgarity (*the grossness of his behavior*).

grotesque /gro-**tesk**/ *adj* **1** strangely shaped, distorted, fantastic (*grotesque masks*). **2** ridiculously exaggerated, unreasonable, absurd, foolish (*a grotesque distortion of the truth/look grotesque in clothes too young for them*).

grotto /**graw**-toe/ *n* (*pl* **grottoes** /**graw**-toaz/) a cave, often an artificial one in a park or store (*Santa's grotto*).

ground[1] /ground/ *n* **1** the surface of the earth, land (*dead birds falling to the ground/plant seeds in the ground*). **2** a piece of land used for a particular purpose (*sports ground*). **3** (*often pl*) a reason (*grounds for complaint*). ● *vb* **1** (*of a ship*) to run ashore (*ships grounded in the storm*). **2** (*of an airplane*) to come to or keep on the ground (*ground airplanes in bad weather conditions*). **3** to base (*an argument that is grounded on lies*). **4** to teach the basic facts to (*ground the pupils in* mathematics. **4** to teach the basic facts to (*ground the pupils in mathematics.* **5** to punish (a child) by not allowing him or her to go out for a specified period (*she is grounded for a week*). ● *npl* **grounds** /groundz/ **1** the tiny pieces of matter that sink to the bottom of a liquid (*coffee grounds*). **2** the land surrounding a large house, castle, etc. (*extensive grounds*).

ground² /ground/ *pt and pp of* **grind**.

ground floor /ground-flore/ (*Br*) *see* **first floor**.

grounding /groun-ding/ *n* knowledge of the elementary part of a subject (*receive a good grounding in English grammar*).

groundless /ground-less/ *adj* without a reason (*fears that proved groundless*).

groundskeeper /groundz-kee-per/ *n* the man in charge of a sports field.

groundwork /ground-wurk/ *n* work that must be done well in the beginning if later work on the subject or task is to succeed (*a book that required a great deal of groundwork in the form of research/lay the groundwork for talks between the heads of state*).

group /groop/ *n* **1** a number of persons or things taken together (*a group of horses/a group of languages/a drama group*). **2** a set of people who play or sing together (*a pop group*). ● *vb* to put or go into a group (*group the books according to subject*).

grouse¹ /grouse/ *n* (*pl* **grouse**) a small fowl hunted on the moors as game.

grouse² /grouse/ *vb* (*inf*) to grumble, to complain (*grousing about the high prices*). ● *also n.*

grove /grove/ *n* (*fml*) a small wood.

grovel /grov-el/ *vb* **1** to lie face downward in humility or fear (*grovel before the emperor*). **2** to humble oneself, to behave with humility (*grovel to her parents for a loan*).

grow /gro/ *vb* (*pt* **grew** /groo/, *pp* **grown** /groan/) **1** to become bigger (*children growing*). **2** (*of plants*) to have life (*plants that can grow in any soil*). **3** to become (*grow old*). **4** to plant and rear (*grow potatoes in the back garden*). ● *n* **growth** /groath/.

growl /groul/ *vb* to utter a low harsh sound, as a dog when angry (*growling at the children who were disturbing him*). ● *also n.*

grown-up /gro-nup/ *n* a fully grown person (*children wishing to have dinner with the grown-ups*).

growth *see* **grow**.

grub /grub/ *vb* (**grubbed** /grubd/, **grubbing** /gru-bing/) **1** to dig, to root out (*grub out all the weeds*). **2** to search for by digging (*pigs grubbing around for food*). **3** (*inf*) to search around for (*reporters grubbing around for information*). ● *n* **1** the form of an insect when it comes out of the egg. **2** (*inf*) food.

grubby /gru-bee/ *adj* dirty (*children grubby after a day's play/wash his grubby clothes*).

grudge /grudge/ *vb* **1** to be unwilling to give (*grudging the money spent on traveling to work*). **2** to be displeased by another's success, to envy (*grudge the actor his part in the play*). ● *n* a deep feeling of ill-will, dislike, resentment, etc. (*bore a grudge against his brother for marrying his girlfriend*).

gruel /grool/ *n* (*old*) a light food made by boiling meal in water.

grueling /groo-ling/ *adj* very difficult and tiring (*a grueling climb up the mountain*).

gruesome /groo-sum/ *adj* horrible, very unpleasant (*a gruesome murder/the gruesome sight of rotting meat*).

gruff /gruff/ *adj* **1** deep and rough (*a gruff voice*). **2** rough, angry-sounding (*a gruff reply*).

grumble /grum-bul/ *vb* to complain, to express discontent (*grumbling about being overworked*). ● *also n.* ● *n* **grumbler** /grum-bler/.

grumpy /grum-pee/ *adj* (*inf*) cross, ill-tempered (*feeling grumpy first thing in the morning*).

grunt /grunt/ *vb* to make a noise like a pig (*he grunted that he was too busy to talk*). ● *also n.*

guarantee /ga-ran-tee/ *n* **1** a promise to pay money on behalf of another person if that person fails to pay money he or she has promised to pay. **2** a person who undertakes to see that another keeps his or her promise, especially to repay money, a guarantor. **3** a promise, usually in the form of a written statement, that if an article bought is unsatisfactory, it will be repaired or replaced (*a manufacturer's guarantee*). **4** a thing that makes something likely or certain (*there's no guarantee that we will have enough money*). ● *vb* **1** to promise (*guaranteed that he'd be there*). **2** to undertake to see that a promise is kept (*guaranteeing that the money will be repaid*).

guarantor /ga-ran-tawr/ *n* one who hands over something as a guarantee and loses it if the promise is not kept.

guard /gard/ *vb* **1** to watch over, to protect (*guard the children*). **2** to defend against attack (*guard the city from enemy attack*). ● *n* **1** something that protects (*a fire guard/guards to protect players' shins*). **2** a person, such as a soldier or prison officer, who watches over a person or place to prevent escape, attack, etc. **3** a group of persons whose duty it is to watch over and defend something or someone (*the changing of the guard at Buckingham Palace*). **4** the official in charge of a train. **5** a position in which one can defend or protect oneself, a state of watchfulness (*be on his guard walking through the unlit streets*).

guarded /**gar**-did/ *adj* careful, cautious (*give a guarded reply*).

guardian /**gar**-dee-an/ *n* **1** a person who has the legal duty to take care of a child (*when her parents were killed her uncle was appointed her guardian*). **2** (*fml*) a keeper (*the guardian of the castle*).

guava /**gwa**-va/ *n* a tropical tree or its fruit.

guerrilla, guerilla /gu-**ri**-la/ *n* a member of an unofficial small military group that makes sudden, unexpected attacks (*the president and his staff were ambushed by guerrillas in the mountains/ guerrilla warfare*).

guess /**ges**/ *vb* **1** to put forward an opinion or solution without knowing the facts (*I would guess that it is a distance of 20 miles/try to guess the weight of the cake*). **2** (*inf*) to suppose, to consider likely (*I guess you might know him*). ● *n* an opinion or judgment that may be wrong as it is formed on insufficient knowledge (*I think he's about 60, but it's just a guess*).

guesswork /**ges**-wurk/ *n* a number of connected guesses (*reach the right answer by guesswork*).

guest /**gest**/ *n* **1** a visitor to a house (*be rude to her mother's guests/have guests for Thanksgiving*). **2** a person staying in a hotel (*have room for 20 guests*).

guffaw /gu-**faw**/ *vb* to laugh loudly or rudely (*guffawed at his vulgar jokes*). ● *also n.*

guidance /**gie**-danse/ *n* help and advice (*career guidance*).

guide /**gide**/ *vb* **1** to lead to the place desired (*guiding guests to their seats*). **2** to show the way (*guide them up the mountain*). **3** to direct, to influence (*be guided by one's common sense*). ● *n* **1** a person who shows the way (*a mountain guide*). **2** an adviser, a person who directs or influences one's behavior (*his father was also his guide and friend*). **3** a guidebook (*a guide to New York*). **4** a person who leads people around a place, pointing out things of interest (*a guide taking tourists around the castle*). **5** a thing that helps one to form an opinion or make a calculation (*sales as a guide to the firm's financial situation*).

guidebook /**gide**-book/ *n* a book describing a place and giving information about it.

guide dog /**gide**-dog/ *n* a dog trained to lead a blind person.

guild /**gild**/ *n* a group of people who meet for a particular purpose (formerly, the members of one trade) (*the American Newspaper Guild*).

guilder /**gil**-der/ *n* formerly the currency unit of the Netherlands, until the introduction of the euro in 2002.

guile /**gile**/ *n* (*fml*) deceit, trickery, cunning skill (*used guile to gain access to the old lady's house*). ● *adjs* **guileful** /**gile**-fool/, **guileless** /**gile**-less/.

guillotine /**gi**-le-teen/ *n* **1** a machine formerly used in France for beheading people. **2** a machine for cutting paper.

guilt /**gilt**/ *n* **1** the fact of having done wrong, the fact of having committed a crime (*the police established his guilt*). **2** blame or responsibility for wrongdoing (*where the guilt lies*). **3** a sense of shame, uneasiness, etc., caused by the knowledge of having done wrong (*unable to sleep because of feelings of guilt/racked with guilt*). ● *adj* **guiltless** /**gilt**-less/.

guilty /**gilt**-lee/ *adj* **1** having done wrong, having broken a law (*found guilty of the crime*). **2** responsible for behavior that is morally wrong or socially unacceptable (*a local authority guilty of spending too much money on hospitality*). **3** feeling or showing a sense of guilt or shame (*feel guilty about keeping them waiting*).

guinea fowl /**gi**-nee-foul/ *n* a large spotted edible bird.

guinea pig /**gi**-nee-pig/ *n* **1** a small tailless rodent, often kept as a pet. **2** a person made use of for the purpose of an experiment (*guinea pigs for their mother's cookery experiments*).

guise /**gize**/ *n* **1** dress. **2** appearance (*under the guise of friendship*).

guitar /gi-**tar**/ *n* a six-stringed musical instrument.

gulch /**gulch**/ *n* a rocky valley.

gulf /**gulf**/ *n* **1** an inlet of the sea, a long bay. **2** a deep hollow. **3** an area of serious difference or separation (*a gulf between brother and sister*).

gull[1] /**gul**/ *n* a long-winged sea bird.

gull[2] /**gul**/ *vb* (*old*) to cheat, to deceive (*gulled into lending her money*). ● *n* one who has been cheated, one easily deceived.

gullet /**gu**-let/ *n* the food passage from the mouth to the stomach, the throat (*get a piece of food stuck in her gullet*).

gullible /**gu**-li-bul/ *adj* easily deceived (*so gullible that she believed him when he pretended to be Italian*).

gully /**gu**-lee/ *n* a deep channel worn by running water.

gulp /gulp/ *vb* **1** to eat quickly, to swallow in large mouthfuls (*gulped his food down and rushed out*). **2** to make a swallowing movement (*gulped with fear as he saw the policeman*). ● *also n.*

gum[1] /gum/ *n* the flesh in which the teeth are set.

gum[2] /gum/ *n* **1** the sticky juice of trees. **2** a liquid used for sticking things together (*children using gum to stick pieces of colored paper on cardboard*). ● *vb* (**gummed, gumming**) to stick with gum (*gum the cuttings into a scrapbook*).

gumboil /gum-boil/ *n* a painful swelling on the gum.

gumboot /gum-boot/ *n* a rubber boot (*children wearing gumboots to walk in the muddy fields*).

gummy /gu-mee/ *adj* sticky.

gumption /gum-shun/ *n* common sense, good sense (*not have the gumption to think for himself*).

gum tree /gum-tree/ *n* a tree from which gum is obtained.

gun /gun/ *n* any weapon that fires bullets or shells by means of explosive. ● *vb* (**gunned** /gund/, **gunning** /gu-ning/) to shoot or hunt with a gun.

gunboat /gun-boat/ *n* a small warship.

gundog /gun-dog/ *n* a dog trained to accompany hunters and to fetch game shot down.

gunfire /gun-fire/ *n* the sound of guns being fired.

gunmetal /gun-met-al/ *n* **1** a mixture of copper and tin. **2** a dull-gray color (*shoes of gunmetal*).

gunnel /gu-nel/ *see* **gunwale**.

gunner /gu-ner/ *n* a man trained to fire large guns.

gunpowder /gun-pou-der/ *n* a type of explosive.

gunrunning /gun-ru-ning/ *n* taking guns into a country against its laws (*terrorists involved in gunrunning*).

gunshot /gun-shot/ *n* **1** the firing of a gun (*heard gunshot the night his neighbor was murdered*). **2** the distance a gun can fire (*within gunshot*).

gunsmith /gun-smith/ *n* a person who makes or repairs guns.

gurgle /gur-gul/ *vb* **1** to flow with a bubbling sound (*water gurgling from the taps*). **2** to make a noise resembling this (*babies gurgling in their prams*). ● *also n.*

guru /goo-roo/ *n* a spiritual leader or guide.

gush /gush/ *n* a sudden or strong flow (*a gush of water from the faucet/a gush of blood from the wound/a gush of enthusiasm*). ● *vb* **1** to flow out strongly (*water gushing from the faucets/blood gushing from the wound*). **2** to talk as if one felt something very deeply, to speak insincerely (*gushing about how grateful she was*).

gusset /gu-set/ *n* a triangular piece of cloth put into a garment to strengthen part of it.

gust /gust/ *n* a sudden violent rush of wind (*papers blown away by a gust of wind*).

gusto /gu-sto/ *n* keen enjoyment, eagerness (*eat the meal with gusto/play the piano with gusto*).

gusty /gu-stee/ *adj* **1** windy (*a gusty day*). **2** in short violent bursts (*a gusty wind*).

gut /gut/ *n* **1** a tube in the body that takes the waste matter from the stomach. **2** a strong cord used for violin strings, fishing lines, etc. ● *vb* (**gutted** /gu-ted/, **gutting** /gu-ting/) **1** to take out the inner parts (*gut the fish*). **2** to remove or destroy all except the walls of a building (*fire gutted the house*). ● *npl* **guts** /guts/ (*inf*) **1** the bowels, intestines (*a bad pain in the guts*). **2** bravery, courage (*not have the guts to admit the truth*).

gutter /gu-ter/ *n* **1** a passage at the edge of a roof or at the side of the road to carry away water (*blocked gutters*). **2** the lowest poorest level of society (*she was born in the gutter but became famous*). ● *vb* to run down in drops, as wax on a candle.

guttural /gu-te-ral/ *adj* **1** having to do with the throat. **2** made or seeming to be made in the throat, harsh (*a guttural accent*).

guy[1] /gie/ *n* a rope to steady anything (e.g., a tent).

guy[2] /gie/ *n* **1** a man or boy (*guys and girls*). **2** (*inf*) a person (*come on, you guys!*).

guzzle /gu-zul/ *vb* (*inf*) to eat or drink greedily (*guzzling all the ice cream*).

gym /jim/ *n* a gymnasium.

gymkhana /jim-ka-na/ *n* a sports meeting for races, horse racing, horse jumping, etc. (*children riding ponies at the local gymkhana*).

gymnasium /jim-nay-zee-um/ *n* (*pl* **gymnasia** /jim-nay-zee-a/ *or* **gymnasiums** /jim-nay-zee-umz/) a room or hall with equipment for physical exercise (*the school gymnasium*).

gymnast /jim-nast/ *n* a person who is skilled in gymnastics. ● *adj* **gymnastic** /jim-nast-ic/.

gymnastics /jim-nast-ics/ *npl* exercises to develop the muscles of the body.

gypsy /jip-see/ *n* a member of a traveling people (*a gypsy woman telling fortunes*).

gyrate /jie-rate/ *vb* **1** to move in circles (*dancers gyrating to the music*). **2** to spin round (*a spinning top gyrating*). ● *n* **gyration** /jie-ray-shun/.

gyroscope /jie-ro-scope/ *n* an instrument that is sometimes used to keep steady ships, aircraft, etc.

H

H, h /**aitch**/ the eighth letter of the alphabet.

ha /ha/ *interj* **1** a sound used to express surprise, wonder, triumph. **2** the sound of a laugh.

habit /**ha**-bit/ *n* **1** a fixed way of doing something without having to think about it, someone's ordinary way of doing things, something that a person does regularly (*he has a bad habit of biting his nails/it is her habit to go for a walk before going to bed*). **2** dress, especially of a monk or rider.

habitable /**ha**-bi-ta-bul/ *adj* that may be lived in (*houses that are scarcely habitable*).

habitat /**ha**-bi-tat/ *n* the place or surroundings in which a plant or animal is usually found (*the usual habitat of the bear*).

habitation /ha-bi-**tay**-shun/ *n* **1** the act of living in a place (*houses unfit for human habitation*). **2** the place where a person lives.

habitual /ha-**bich**-wul/ *adj* **1** usual. **2** having formed a certain habit (*habitual runner*).

habituate /ha-**bi**-chu-wate/ *vb* (*fml*) to make used to (*become habituated to a hot climate*).

hacienda /ha-see-**en**-da/ *n* a large estate, ranch, or plantation, the main dwelling on any of these.

hack¹ /**hack**/ *vb* **1** to cut roughly or unevenly (*hack meat into chunks/hack a path through the jungle*). **2** to foul by striking an arm in basketball. ● *n* **1** a tool for cutting or hacking. **2** a dry, harsh cough.

hack² /**hack**/ *n* **1** a hired horse. **2** a person hired to do uninteresting written work (*employed as a hack in the company*).

hack³ /**hack**/ *n* a rack for drying cheese or fish, or for holding food for cattle, etc.

hacker /**ha**-ker/ *n* **1** a person who hacks. **2** a highly skilled computer user who tries to access unauthorized files.

hacksaw /**hak**-saw/ *n* a saw for cutting metal.

had /had/ *vb* past tense of have.

haddock /**ha**-dock/ *n* a sea fish of the cod family, used as food.

haft /**haft**/ *n* (*fml or lit*) a handle (*the haft of a sword*).

hag /**hag**/ *n* **1** a female demon or evil spirit. **2** an ugly old woman who is often mean.

haggard /**ha**-gard/ *adj* pale, thin-faced, and tired looking (*looking haggard after being up all night*).

haggis /**ha**-gis/ *n* a Scottish dish in which the heart, liver and lungs of a sheep are minced, mixed with oatmeal and seasoning and boiled in a sheep's stomach.

haggle /**ha**-gul/ *vb* to try to get a seller to lower his or her price (*in some countries customers are expected to haggle with merchants*).

haiku /**hie**-koo/ *n* a kind of Japanese poem of three unrhymed lines of five, seven, and five syllables, often about nature.

hail¹ /**hail**/ *n* **1** frozen rain. **2** a shower of anything (*a hail of arrows*). ● *vb* **1** to rain hail (*it was hailing when we left*). **2** to pour down.

hail² /**hail**/ *vb* **1** to call to, to greet (*she hailed her neighbor cheerfully*). **2** to shout to a person to try to catch his or her attention (*hail a taxi*). ● *interj* a call of greeting. ● **hail from** to come from (*he hails from the country*).

hailstone /**hail**-stone/ *n* a pellet of hail.

hailstorm /**hail**-storm/ *n* a storm in which hail falls.

hair /**hair**/ *n* any or all of the threadlike growths covering the skin of humans and animals (*she had pretty long, dark hair*). ● *adjs* **hairless** /**hair**-less/, **hairy** /**hay**-ree/. ● **to split hairs** to point out differences so slight that they could be overlooked.

hairbrush /**hair**-brush/ *n* a brush for grooming the hair.

haircut /**hair**-cut/ *n* a cutting of the hair of the head or the style in which this is done.

hairdo /**hair**-do/ *n* the style in which hair is arranged.

hairdresser /**hair**-dre-ser/ *n* a person who cuts, styles, etc., hair as a job (*an appointment with my hairdresser*).

hairnet /**hair**-net/ *n* a net cap for keeping the hair in place (*kitchen workers wear hairnets so their hairs do not get in the food*).

hairpiece /**hair**-peess/ *n* a wig.

hairpin /**hair**-pin/ *n* a small, usually *u*-shaped, piece of wire for keeping the hair in place or a headdress on. ● *adj* shaped like a hairpin (*a hairpin turn*).

hair-raising /**hair**-ray-zing/ *adj* terrifying, thought of as causing the hair to stand on end (*driving with him is hair-raising because he drives so fast*).

hair spray /**hair**-spray/ *n* a liquid sprayed on the hair to hold it in place.

hairstyle /**hair**-stile/ *n* a style of hairdressing, often one that is fashionable.

hairy /**hay**-ree/ *adj* covered with hair.

hajj /**hadge**/ *n* the religious trip to Mecca that every Muslim is expected to make at least once.

hajji or **haji** /**ha**-jee/ *n* the title given to a Muslim who has made a religious trip to Mecca.

hake /hake/ *n* a fish like the cod, used as food.

halal /ha-**lal**/ *n* meat from an animal that has been killed according to Muslim law.

halcyon /**hal**-see-yon/ *n* the kingfisher. ● *adj* calm, peaceful. ● **halcyon days** a time of happiness and peace (*recall the halcyon days of her youth*).

half /haf/ *n* (*pl* **halves** /havz/) one of two equal parts (*she cut the apple and gave her sister half*). ● *also adj*.

half brother /**haf**-bru-ther/ *n* a brother by one parent only.

halfhearted /haf-**har**-ted/ *adj* lacking interest and energy, not eager (*make a halfhearted attempt*).

half-hour /haf-**our**/ *n* 30 minutes.

half-moon /haf-**moon**/ *n* 1 the moon in its first or last quarter phase. 2 anything shaped like a half-moon or crescent.

half note /**haf**-note/ *n* in music, a note having one half the duration of a whole note.

half pint /**haf**-pint/ *n* 1 a unit of measure equaling 8 ounces. 2 (*inf*) a small person.

half sister /**haf**-si-ster/ *n* a sister by one parent only.

halftime /haf-**time**/ *n* the rest period between the halves of a football game, basketball game, etc.

halfway /haf-**way**/ *adj* equally distant between two places.

halibut /**ha**-li-but/ *n* a large flatfish, used as food.

hall /hol/ *n* 1 a large public room (*a concert hall/the town hall*). 2 the room or passage at the entrance to a house (*stand in the hall waiting for her hostess*).

hallel /**ha**-lale/ *n* a part of Jewish religious services during which certain things are recited or sung on festivals.

hallelujah /ha-le-**loo**-ya/ *n* an exclamation or song of praise to God. ● *interj*.

hallmark /**hawl**-mark/ *n* any mark or symbol that shows the quality of a person, thing, etc. (*politeness is the hallmark of a gentleman*).

hallow /**ha**-lo/ *vb* 1 to make holy (*the priest was asked to hallow the ground*). 2 to treat as being holy.

hallowed /**ha**-lode/ *adj* sacred or holy.

Halloween /ha-lo-**ween**/ *n* the eve of All Saints' Day (i.e., October 31), now generally celebrated by dressing in costume for fun (*ghosts are supposed to be seen on Halloween/trick-or-treating on Halloween*).

hallucinate /ha-**loo**-si-nate/ *vb* to see something that is not there.

hallucination /ha-loo-si-**nay**-shun/ *n* 1 the seeing of something that is not there (*hallucination can be the result of mental illness*). 2 something imagined as though it is really there (*he thought he saw a ghost but it was a hallucination*). ● *adj* **hallucinatory** /ha-**loo**-si-na-toe-ree/.

hallway /**hawl**-way/ *n* a passageway between the entrance and interior of the house.

halo /**hay**-loe/ *n* 1 a circle of light around the Sun or Moon. 2 a colored ring or ring of light around the head of a holy person in a painting (*the saint painted with a halo*).

halt[1] /holt/ *vb* to stop (*the guard halted the train/halt progress/the car halted*). ● *n* a stop (*trains coming to a halt*).

halt[2] /holt/ *vb* 1 (*old*) to limp (*halting badly after the accident to his leg*). 2 to hesitate (*a reader halting over some difficult words*). ● *adj* lame, limping.

halter /**hawl**-ter/ *n* 1 a rope or strap fitted on to the head of a horse for leading it. 2 a rope for hanging a person. 3 a dress or top formed by a strap that goes round the wearer's neck leaving the shoulders bare.

halve /hav/ *vb* to cut or break into halves (*halve the apple/halving the cost*).

halves *see* **half**.

ham /ham/ *n* 1 the back of the thigh (*strain a ham muscle*). 2 the thigh of a pig salted and dried and used as food (*slices of baked ham*). 3 (*inf*) an actor who exaggerates his or her actions and speech (*Hamlet performed by a real ham*).

hambone /**ham**-bone/ *n* the bone of a ham.

hamburger /**ham**-bur-ger/ a flat round patty made of ground beef, fried or grilled, and usually eaten in a bun, also known as **burger** /**bur**-ger/.

hamlet /**ham**-let/ *n* a very small village.

hammer /**ham**-er/ *n* 1 a tool for pounding nails, beating metal, etc. 2 part of a machine or device that strikes (*the hammers in a piano*). ● *vb* 1 to drive or beat with a hammer (*hammer the nail into the wall*). 2 to strike hard (*police hammering at the door*).

hammered /**ham**-erd/ *adj* shaped or marked by hammer blows.

hammerhead /**ham**-er-hed/ *n* 1 the part of the hammer that strikes its object. 2 any of a family of large sharks with large, mallet-shaped heads.

hammertoe /**ham**-er-toe/ *n* a condition in which the first joint of a toe is bent downward permanently.

hammock /**ham**-ock/ *n* a bed made of a strip of canvas or network hung up at the ends (*lying on a hammock in the outside*).

hamper[1] /**ham**-per/ *n* a large basket (*a picnic hamper*).

hamper[2] /**ham**-per/ *vb* to prevent from moving freely (*the broken tools hampered progress*).

hamster /**ham**-ster/ *n* a small rodent with large cheek pouches, often kept as a pet.

hamstring /**ham**-string/ *n* the tendon behind the knee (*strain a hamstring playing football*). ● *vb* (*pt, pp* **hamstrung** /**ham**-strung/) **1** to make lame by cutting the hamstring. **2** to prevent from acting freely (*they were hamstrung by lack of money*).

hand /hand/ *n* **1** the end of the arm below the wrist. **2** a worker (*a factory hand*). **3** a sailor on a ship (*all hands on deck!*). **4** the cards given to one player in a card game (*deal someone a good hand*). **5** a person's style of writing (*write in a neat hand*). **6** the pointer of a clock or watch (*the minute hand*). **7** a measure of 0.1 meters, used in measuring a horse's height at the shoulder. ● *vb* to give with the hand (*hand him the book*). **8** a share, a part, an influence (*suspect he had a hand in the robbery*). ● **hand in glove with** in league with (*suspect that the house owner was hand in glove with the burglar to get insurance money*). ● **hand-to-hand** at close quarters (*hand-to-hand combat*). ● **hand-to-mouth** with only just enough money to live on with nothing for the future (*earns so little that the family lives hand-to-mouth*). ● **out of hand** out of control (*the party got out of hand and the police came*). ● **upper hand** control (*he had the upper hand in the tennis match*). ● **to wash one's hands of** to refuse to have anything more to do with (*if you won't take any notice of my advice, I am washing my hands of you*).

handbag /**hand**-bag/ *n* a small bag that contains the owner's possessions, usually carried by women.

handball /**hand**-bol/ *n* **1** a game in which a small ball is batted against a wall by hand by opposing players. **2** the ball used in this game.

handbarrow /**hand**-ba-ro/ *n* a large tray with handles at either end, for carrying loads.

handbill /**hand**-bill/ *n* a small printed notice (*handbills advertising the jumble sale*).

handbook /**hand**-book/ *n* a small useful book giving information or instructions (*a handbook explaining the parts of the car*).

handcart /**hand**-cart/ *n* a small cart, often with two wheels, pulled or pushed by hand.

handcraft /**hand**-craft/ *vb* to make by hand with craftsmanship.

handcuff /**hand**-cuff/ *vb* to put handcuffs on (*the police handcuffed the criminal*). ● *npl* **handcuffs** /**hand**-cuffs/ metal rings joined by a chain, locked on the wrists of prisoners.

hand-feed /**hand**-feed/ *vb* to feed by hand.

handful /**hand**-fool/ *n* **1** as much as can be held in one hand (*children given a handful of nuts each*). **2** a small number or amount (*only a handful of people turned up*).

hand glass /**hand**-glass/ *n* **1** a magnifying glass. **2** a small mirror with a handle.

hand grenade /**hand**-gri-nade/ *n* a small, round, handheld bomb that is thrown at its target after pulling out a fuse.

handgun /**hand**-gun/ *n* any firearm that is held and fired while being held in only one hand.

handheld /**hand**-held/ *adj* small enough to be held in the hand while being used.

handhold /**hand**-hoald/ *n* a secure grip or hold with the hand.

handicap /**han**-di-cap/ *vb* (**handicapped** /**han**-di-capt/, **handicapping** /**han**-di-ca-ping/) **1** in sports or races, to give a certain advantage to weaker competitors so that they have an equal chance of winning. **2** to obstruct, to put at a disadvantage (*in the race she was handicapped by a knee injury/a firm handicapped by having too little capital*). ● *n* **1** in sports or games, an arrangement that allows all competitors to start with an equal chance of winning. **2** an obstruction, a disadvantage (*her lack of height is a handicap in basketball*). **3** a physical or mental disability.

handicraft /**han**-di-craft/ *n* skilled work done by hand. ● *n* **handicraftsperson** /**han**-di-craft-sper-sun/.

handily /**han**-di-lee/ *adv* with no trouble, easily.

handiwork /**han**-di-wurk/ *n* **1** work done with a person's hands (*examples of the students' handiwork on show in the classroom*). **2** something done or caused by someone (*they think the fire in the school was the handiwork of a former student*).

handkerchief /**hang**-ker-chif/ *n* a cloth for wiping the nose.

handknit /**hand**-nit/ *adj* knit by hand instead of by machine.

handle /**han**-dul/ *vb* **1** to feel, use, or hold with the hand (*wash your hands before handling food*). **2** to deal with (*handle the situation well*). ● *n* that part of a thing made to be held in the hand (*the handle of the cup*).

handlebar /**han**-dul-bar/ *n* the bent rod with which a person steers a bicycle.

handler /**hand**-ler/ *n* a person or thing that handles, trains, or manages (*the handler led the dog in front of the judges*).

handmade /**hand**-**made**/ *adj* made by hand, not by machine.

hand-me-down /**hand**-mee-down/ *n* something that has been used and then passed along to someone else (*she was tired of her sister's hand-me-downs and wanted new clothes of her own*).

handoff /**han**-dof/ *n* in football, when the quarterback hands the ball directly to another player.

handout /**han**-dout/ *n* **1** a gift of food, clothing, etc., as to a poor person. **2** a leaflet or printed notice handed out for information.

handpick /hand-**pick**/ *vb* to pick by hand, to choose with care for a special purpose.

handprint /**hand**-print/ *n* a mark made by a hand.

hand puppet /**hand**-pu-pet/ *n* a puppet that fits over the hand and is moved by the fingers.

handrail /**hand**-rail/ *n* a rail used as a guard or support, as along a staircase.

handsaw /**hand**-saw/ *n* a hand-held saw.

handsel /**hand**-sel/ *n* a present for good luck.

handset /**hand**-set/ *n* a telephone mouthpiece, receiver, and dial buttons in a single unit.

handshake /**hand**-shake/ *n* a gripping and shaking of each other's hand in greeting.

handsome /**hand**-sum/ *adj* **1** good-looking (*a handsome young man*). **2** generous (*a handsome gift*).

handspring /**hand**-spring/ *n* a tumble in which a person turns over in midair with one or both hands touching the ground.

handstamp /**hand**-stamp/ *n* a rubber stamp used by the post office.

handstand /**hand**-stand/ *n* the act of standing upside down on the hands.

handwriting /**hand**-rie-ting/ *n* the way a person writes.

handwritten /**hand**-ri-ten/ *adj* written by hand, with pen, pencil, etc.

handy /**han**-dee/ *adj* **1** clever in using the hands, skillful (*handy around the house*). **2** useful and simple (*a handy little gadget*). **3** ready, available (*keep a flashlight handy*). **4** near (*a house handy for the station*). ● *n* **handiness** /**han**-dee-ness/.

hang /hang/ *vb* **1** (*pt, pp* **hung** /hung/) to fix one part to something above and allow the rest to drop (*hang the picture from a hook/hang the curtains from a rail*). **2** to remain steady in the air, as certain birds (*hawks hanging*). **3** to let fall (*hang her head in shame/with hair hanging down her back*). **4** (*pt, pp* **hanged**) to kill a criminal by putting a rope round the neck and then letting him or her drop suddenly so that the neck is broken.

hangar /**hang**-ar/ *n* a large shelter in which airplanes are kept.

hanger /**hang**-er/ *n* a thing from which a garment is hung (*clothes on metal hangers/coat-hangers*).

hanger-on /**hang**-er-on/ *n* (*pl* **hangers-on**) a person who supports another in the hope of gaining some advantage (*since she won the lottery, she has been surrounded by hangers-on*).

hang gliding /**hang** glie-ding/ *n* the sport of gliding through the air while hanging from a large kite-like device.

hangman /**hang**-man/ *n* a person whose job it is to hang criminals.

hangnail /**hang**-nale/ *n* a bit of torn skin hanging at the side or base of a fingernail.

hangout /**hang**-out/ *n* a place where a group of people go frequently.

hangover /**hang**-oa-ver/ *n* the sick feeling a person gets from drinking too much alcohol.

hang time /**hang**-time/ *n* **1** the length of time a kicked football remains in the air. **2** the length of time a jumping person stays in the air, as in basketball.

hang-up /**hang**-up/ *n* a problem or difficulty.

hank /hangk/ *n* a coil of thread or wool.

hanker /**hang**-ker/ *vb* to want greatly, to long for (*hankering for a chocolate bar*).

hankie /**hang**-kee/ *n* a handkerchief.

hansom /**han**-sum/ *n* (*old*) a two-wheeled carriage pulled by one horse.

Hanukkah /**hon**-i-ca/ *n* an 8-day Jewish festival taking place in November or December.

haphazard /hap-**ha**-zard/ *adj* chance, unplanned (*the town had developed in a haphazard way/vacation plans that are rather haphazard*). ● *adv* **haphazardly** /hap-**ha**-zard-lee/.

hapless /**hap**-less/ *adj* (*fml*) unfortunate, unlucky (*the hapless victim*).

happen /**ha**-pen/ *vb* **1** to take place (*a terrible thing happened*). **2** to come about by chance (*it happened that they arrived at the same time*).

happening /**ha**-pe-ning/ *n* an event (*an unfortunate happening*).

happy /**ha**-pee/ *adj* **1** lucky (*by a happy chance*). **2** pleased, joyous (*she was happy to see him*). **3** pleasant, joyful (*a happy occasion*). **4** suitable (*a happy turn of phrase*). ● *n* **happines** /**ha**-pee-ness/.

happy-go-lucky /**ha**-pee-go-**lu**-kee/ *adj* not easily worried, carefree (*too happy-go-lucky to worry about the future*).

happy hour /**ha**-pee-our/ *n* a time when a bar sells its drinks at reduced prices.

harangue /ha-**rang**/ *n* a loud speech. ● *vb* to speak loudly and forcefully (*the manager haranguing the work force about the importance of being on time*).

harass /ha-**rass**/ *vb* **1** to attack again and again (*troops harassing the enemy army*). **2** to worry or disturb constantly or frequently (*children harassing their mother for more pocket money*).

harbor /**har**-bur/ *n, also* **harbour** (*Br, Cdn*) **1** a place of safety for ships. **2** a place of shelter (*they regarded his house as a harbor for criminals*). ● *vb* **1** to give shelter (*it is an offense to harbor criminals who are wanted by the police*). **2** to keep in the mind (*harbor anger*).

hard /hard/ *adj* **1** firm, solid (*a hard shell*). **2** unfeeling, unkind, cruel (*a hard master/a hard look*). **3** difficult (*a hard task*). **4** harsh, severe (*a hard punishment/a hard life*). ● *adv* **1** with force (*hit him hard/raining hard*). **2** with great effort (*work very hard*). **3** close (*follow hard on his heels*). **4** with great attention (*stare hard*). ● **hard of hearing** fairly deaf. ● **hard up** (*inf*) having little money.

hardball /**hard**-bol/ *n* **1** a kind of baseball in which the ball is pitched overhanded. **2** the ball used in baseball. **3** any forceful, competitive form of politics, business, etc.

hardboard /**hard**-board/ *n* a building material made by pressing and heating wood chips.

hard-boiled /hard-**boild**/ *adj* cooked in boiling water until it is solid throughout, as in eggs.

hard copy /**hard**-caw-pee/ *n* a computer printout.

hard disk /**hard**-**disk**/ *n* a computer disk on which data and programs are stored.

hard drive /hard-**drive**/ *n* a computer drive for hard disks.

harden /**har**-den/ *n* to make hard or harder (*leave the toffee to harden/harden a person's heart*).

hardily /**har**-di-lee/ *adv* in a hardy manner.

hardiness /**har**-dee-ness/ *n* toughness, strength.

hardly /**hard**-lee/ *adv* **1** almost not (*we hardly ever see her*). **2** only just, not really (*I hardly know him*). **3** with difficulty (*she could hardly hear him*).

hardness /**hard**-ness/ *n* the state of being hard (*the hardness of the plastic*).

hardship /**hard**-ship/ *n* poor or difficult conditions (*poor people enduring hardship*).

hardtop /**hard**-top/ *n* a car, truck, etc., with a permanent roof made of hard material.

hardware /**hard**-ware/ *n* **1** household articles and tools made of metal (*a shop selling hardware*). **2** the mechanical and electronic parts of a computer system.

hard-wired /**hard**-wirde/ *adj* directly connected to a computer.

hardwood /**hard**-wood/ *n* any tough, heavy timber with a compact grain.

hardy /**har**-dee/ *adj* **1** strong, tough (*have to be hardy to work such long hours out in the winter cold*). **2** (*old*) bold (*hardy warriors*).

hare /hare/ *n* a fast-running animal with rabbit-like ears and long hind legs. ● **hare and hounds** a game in which some people (the *hounds*) chase others (the *hares*) across country by following a trail of paper scattered by them.

harebell /**hare**-bell/ *n* a bluebell-shaped flower.

harebrained /**hare**-braned/ *adj* thoughtless, careless, hasty (*a harebrained scheme/it was harebrained of her to leave her job*).

harelip /**hare**-lip/ *n* an upper lip divided in the center, like that of the hare.

haricot /**ha**-ri-co/ *n* **1** a type of stew made with lamb and vegetables. **2** a type of French bean.

harm /harm/ *n* hurt, damage, wrong (*do his reputation harm/try to cause harm to his rival*). ● *also vb*. ● *adjs* **harmful** /**harm**-fool/, **harmless** /**harm**-less/.

harmonic /har-**mon**-ic/ *adj* having to do with harmony.

harmonica /har-**mon**-i-ca/ *n* a mouth organ played to make music.

harmonics /har-**mon**-ics/ *n* the study of harmony in music.

harmonious /har-mo-nee-us/ *adj* **1** pleasant-sounding (*harmonious sounds*). **2** friendly (*a harmonious atmosphere/relations between them are not harmonious*). **3** pleasant to the eye (*a harmonious group of colors*).

harmonium /har-**mo**-nee-um/ *n* a musical wind instrument, like a small organ.

harmonize /har-mo-nize/ *vb, also* **harmonise** (*Br*) **1** to cause to be in harmony or agreement, to be in harmony or agreement (*colors that do not really harmonize*). **2** to play or sing notes that sound pleasantly with the others.

harmony /**har**-mo-nee/ *n* **1** agreement, friendship (*they used to be enemies but they now live in harmony*). **2** the pleasant effect made by parts combining into a whole (*the harmony of colors in the flower garden*). **3** the playing at one time of musical notes that are pleasant when sounded together. **3** pleasant sound.

harness /**har**-ness/ *n* the straps, etc., by which a horse is fastened to its load. ● *vb* to put a harness on. ● **to die in harness** to die while still doing a job (*he did not retire—he died in harness*).

harp /harp/ *n* a stringed musical instrument played

by the fingers. ● *also vb.* ● *n* **harpist.** ● **harp on** to keep on talking about one subject (*I wish he would stop harping on about his unhappy childhood*).

harpoon /har-**poon**/ *n* a long spear used in hunting whales. ● *vb* to strike with a harpoon.

harpsichord /**harp**-see-cawrd/ *n* a string instrument played by striking keys (as a piano).

harpy /**har**-pee/ *n* **1** in Greek legend, a monster with the head and upper body of a woman and the lower body of a bird. **2** a cruel or nasty woman.

harrowing /**ha**-ro-wing/ *adj* very distressing (*seeing her father die in the accident was a harrowing experience for her*).

harsh /harsh/ *adj* **1** rough and unpleasant to hear, see, etc. (*a harsh voice/harsh colors*). **2** unkind, severe, cruel (*a harsh sentence/a harsh attitude*).

hart /hart/ *n* a stag or male deer.

harvest /**har**-vest/ *n* **1** the time when the ripe crops are cut and gathered (*take on extra staff for the harvest*). **2** the crops so gathered. ● *vb* to cut and gather (*harvesting grapes*). ● *n* **harvester** /**har**-ve-ster/.

has /haz/ *vb* to hold, to possess.

has-been /**haz**-bin/ *n* a person or thing that was popular but is no longer so.

hash /hash/ *n* **1** a dish of finely chopped or shredded meat. **2** (*inf*) something done badly, a mess (*make a hash of the job*). ● *vb* to finely chop or shred.

hash browns /hash-**brounz**/ *n* potatoes that have been mashed and then fried in a pan.

hassle /**ha**-sul/ (*inf*) *vb* to annoy someone, especially by repeatedly asking them to do something. ● *n* a difficult or troublesome situation (*finding enough volunteers is a real hassle*).

haste /haste/ *n* speed, hurry (*change the subject with haste/make haste*).

hasten /**hay**-sen/ *vb* (*fml*) to hurry (*worry hastened his death/hasten home*).

hasty *adj* **1** done in a hurry (*eat a hasty meal*). **2** done too quickly, rash (*a hasty decision*). **3** quick to lose one's temper.

hat /hat/ *n* a head covering.

hatch[1] /hach/ *vb* **1** to produce (young) from eggs (*hens hatching chicks*). **2** to break out of the egg (*chickens hatching*). **3** to work out in secret (*hatch a cunning plan*). ● *n* the young hatched from eggs.

hatch[2] /hach/ *n* **1** an open space in a wall or roof or the deck of a ship. **2** the lower half door of a door.

hatch[3] /hach/ *vb* to decorate (in drawing, stonecarving) with thin lines that cross one another.

hatchback /**hach**-back/ *n* a car with a rear door or section that swings up to provide storage area.

hatcheck /**hat**-check/ *adj* of, for, or working in a room where a person can leave their hats, coats, etc.

hatchet /**ha**-chet/ *n* a small ax. ● **bury the hatchet** to end a quarrel (*they did not speak for years, but they've now buried the hatchet*).

hatchling /**hach**-ling/ *n* a recently hatched bird, fish, turtle, etc.

hatchway /**hach**-way/ *n* **1** an opening in the ship's deck through which cargo is loaded. **2** a similar opening in the floor or roof of a building

hate /hate/ *vb* to dislike greatly (*hating his job/hate her sister*). ● *n* great dislike (*full of hate for his rival*).

hate crime /**hate**-crime/ *n* a crime against a person that has been committed because of race, religion, gender, etc.

hateful /**hate**-fool/ *adj* deserving or causing hate (*a hateful job/a hateful person*).

hatred /**hate**-red/ *n* great dislike (*look at his rival with hatred*).

hatter /**ha**-ter/ *n* one who makes, sells, or cleans hats.

hat trick /**hat**-trick/ *n* **1** the scoring of three goals in a game, such as soccer, ice hockey, etc. (*the soccer player scored a hat trick*). **2** the act of achieving something three times.

haughty /**haw**-tee/ *adj* proud, behaving as if better than others (*a haughty young woman/a haughty expression*). ● *n* **haughtiness** /**haw**-tee-ness/.

haul /hawl/ *vb* to pull by force, to drag (*haul the fishing nets up/hauling the felled trees from the forest*). ● *n* **1** a pull (*give the rope a haul*). **2** an amount taken or caught (e.g., of fish).

haunch /hawnch/ *n* the thick part of the body around the hips (*squat on his haunches*).

haunt /hawnt/ *vb* **1** to visit again and again, to go often to (*haunt the local movie theater*). **2** to visit as a ghost (*supposedly haunted by a gray lady*). **3** to be always in the thoughts of someone (*she was haunted by thoughts of his wretched appearance*). ● *n* a place often visited. ● *n, adj* **haunting** /**hawn**-ting/.

haunted /**hawn**-tid/ *adj* visited by ghosts (*a haunted house*).

haunting /**hawn**-ting/ *adj* often recurring in the mind, not easily forgotten (*a haunting song*).

have /hav/ *vb* (*pt, pp* **had** /had/; *indicative* **I have, he has; we, they have**) **1** to possess, to own, to hold (*he has a fast car/I have a book*). **2** to be forced (to do) (*he has to leave tomorrow*). ● **to**

have to do with to be concerned in (*he has nothing to do with the school*).

haven /**hay**-ven/ *n* **1** (*old*) a harbor. **2** (*fml*) a place of safety, a shelter (*the shelter is a haven for the homeless*).

haversack /**ha**-ver-sack/ *n* a bag carried on the back, used for carrying food, etc., on a journey.

havoc /**ha**-voc/ *n* destruction, ruin (*the storm created havoc in town/create havoc with our plans*).

haw /**haw**/ *n* the berry of the hawthorn.

hawk[1] /**hawk**/ *n* a bird of prey. ● *vb* to hunt with a hawk.

hawk[2] /**hawk**/ *vb* to sell (*peddlers hawking things to townspeople*). ● *n* **hawker** /**haw**-ker/.

hawthorn /**haw**-thawrn/ *n* a thorny tree with white, pink, or red flowers and small berries.

hay /**hay**/ *n* grass cut and dried (*give hay to the horses*).

hay fever /**hay**-fee-ver/ *n* an illness caused by an allergy to dust or pollen (*sufferers from hay fever sneezing uncontrollably*).

hayfield /**hay**-feeld/ *n* a field of grass to be made into hay.

hayloft /**hay**-loft/ *n* a loft or upper story of a barn for storing hay.

hayride /**hay**-ride/ *n* a ride in a wagon partly filled with hay taken by a group for fun.

haystack /**hay**-stack/ *n* a large pile of hay.

haywire /**hay**-wire/ *adj* (*inf*) tangled up, mixed up, in a state of disorder (*the computer system went haywire*).

hazard /**ha**-zard/ *n* **1** risk (*allow for driving hazards such as icy roads*). **2** (*fml*) chance (*a game of hazard*). **3** a piece of rough ground or a sand trap on a golf course. ● *vb* **1** to risk (*hazard his earnings on a bet*). **2** to put in danger (*hazarding their lives to save others*). **3** to put forward (*hazard a guess*).

hazardous /**ha**-zar-dus/ *adj* risky, dangerous (*a hazardous journey*).

haze /**haze**/ *n* **1** a thin mist (*an early morning haze over the fields*). **2** vagueness of mind (*in a haze about the future*).

hazel /**hay**-zel/ *n* **1** a tree with edible nuts. **2** a greenish brown color (*eyes of hazel*).

hazelnut /**hay**-zel-nut/ *n* the nut of a hazel tree.

hazy /**hay**-zee/ *adj* **1** misty (*hazy weather*). **2** not clear (*only a hazy idea of what is involved*). **3** doubtful (*she's a bit hazy about what happened*). ● *n* **haziness** /**hay**-zee-ness/.

H-bomb /**aich**-bom/ *n* hydrogen bomb, a very powerful weapon of mass destruction.

he /**hee**/ *pron* the man, boy, or male animal previously mentioned.

head /**hed**/ *n* **1** the top part of the body. **2** a person's mind (*have a good head*). **3** a chief person (*the head of the department/the head teacher*). **4** the top or front part (*the head of the line*). **5** a division in an essay or speech (*a chapter divided into various heads*). **6** the beginning of a stream. **7** a piece of high land jutting out into the sea. ● *vb* **1** to lead. **2** to be first (*heading the field*). **3** to direct (*headed the firm*). **4** to strike (a ball) with the head. ● *adj* **1** belonging to the head. **2** chief, principal (*the head teacher*). **3** coming from the front (*head winds*).

headache /**hed**-ake/ *n* pain in the head (*suffer from headaches*).

headband /**hed**-band/ *n* a band worn around the head for decoration.

head cold /**hed**-coald/ *n* a common cold resulting in a clogged or blocked nose and head.

head count /**hed**-count/ *n* the act of counting people in a certain group.

headdress /**hed**-dress/ *n* a covering for the head (*the Native American's headdress*).

header /**hed**-er/ *n* (*inf*) **1** a fall or dive forward (*slip and take a header into the water*). **2** the act of hitting a ball with the head.

headfirst /hed-**furst**/ *adv* with the head in front, headlong.

headhunter /**hed**-hun-ter/ *n* **1** a member of certain primitive peoples that remove the heads of enemies and keep them as trophies. **2** an agent whose job it is to find highly skilled people for employment.

heading /**hed**-ing/ *n* the words written at the top of a page or above a piece of writing (*a chapter divided into various headings*).

headland /**hed**-land/ *n* a piece of high land jutting out into the sea.

headlight /**hed**-lite/ *n* a light at the front, especially of a car, truck, etc. (*see the headlights of an approaching car*).

headline /**hed**-line/ *n* **1** the line in large print above a piece of news in a newspaper (*have a look at the headlines*). **2** the line of print at the top of a page of a book. ● *v* **1** to give something a headline. **2** to be the leading performer (*Tom Cruise headlined*).

headliner /**hed**-lie-ner/ *n* the leading performer (*Tom Cruise was the headliner*).

head linesman /hed-**lienz**-man/ *n* in football, the person who judges each play and measures the yardage afterward.

headlock /hed-loc/ *n* in wrestling, a hold in which one person's head is held between the arm and the body of another.

headlong /hed-long/ *adv* **1** hastily and rashly (*rush headlong into one impossible job after another*). **2** with the head first (*fall headlong into the mud*). ● *adj* **1** rash. **2** headfirst (*a headlong fall*).

headmaster /hed-ma-ster/ *n* the man who is head of a school. ● *f* **headmistress** /hed-mi-stress/.

headmost /hed-moast/ *adj* in the lead.

head-on /hed-on/ *adj, adv* with the head or front being first (head-on collision).

headphone /hed-foan/ *n* a listening device made of small speakers held to the ears by a band.

headpiece /hed-peess/ *n* a covering for the head.

headquarters /hed-kwawr-terz/ *n* the office of those who are in control or command (*the firm's headquarters are in New York*).

headrest /hed-rest/ *n* a support for the head, as on a chair.

headroom /hed-room/ *n* the space available above a person's head.

headsail /hed-sale/ *n* any said forward of the mast.

headset /hed-set/ *n* a headphone with a small microphone for two-way communication.

headship /hed-ship/ *n* the position of a leader or person of authority.

headshrinker /hed-shring-ker/ *n* a headhunter who shrinks the heads of his victims.

headsman /hedz-man/ *n* (*old*) a person who cuts off the head of a guilty criminal.

headspring /hed-spring/ *n* a fountain, or source.

headstand /hed-stand/ *n* the act of standing upside down on the head, usually helped by the hands.

headstone /hed-stone/ *n* the stone placed over a dead person's grave in his or her memory.

headstream /hed-stream/ n a stream forming the source of another, larger stream or river.

headstrong /hed-strong/ *adj* determined to have one's own way (*so headstrong that he refused to listen to anyone's advice*).

heads-up /hed-zup/ *adj* alert and resourceful.

head-to-head /hed-to-hed/ *adj, adv* in direct confrontation.

headwaters /hed-waw-terz/ *n* the beginnings of a large stream or river.

headway /hed-way/ *n* advance, improvement (*boats making little headway against the storm/he is not making much headway with his plans*).

head wind /hed-wind/ *n* a wind blowing directly opposite the direction a person is trying to go.

heady /hed-ee/ *adj* **1** excited (*the heady feeling of success/heady with triumph*). **2** strong, having a quick effect on the senses (*a heady wine*).

heal /heel/ *vb* to make or become well or healthy, to cure (*a wound that would not heal/given ointment to heal the wound*).

healer /hee-ler/ *n* one who heals or cures (*a faith healer*).

health /helth/ *n* **1** the state of being well. **2** the state of being free from illness (*in sickness and in health*).

healthcare /helth-care/ *n* the treatment of illness.

health club /helth-club/ *n* a private club for exercise.

healthful /helth-ful/ *adj* (*fml*) causing good health.

health spa /helth-spa/ *n* a place people go to exercise.

healthy /helth-ee/ *adj* **1** having good health (*a healthy young woman/in a healthy state*). **2** causing good health (*a healthy climate/a healthy diet*).

heap /heep/ *n* a number of things lying one on top of another (*a heap of leaves/a heap of old newspapers*). ● *vb* to put one on top of another, to pile (*leaves heaped up against the door/heap the old newspapers together*).

hear /heer/ *vb* (*pt, pp* **heard** /herd/) **1** to perceive sounds by the ear. **2** to listen (*wait and hear what they say*).

hearer /hee-rer/ *n* a person or animal who listens.

hearing /hee-ring/ *n* **1** the power to hear sounds (*have sharp hearing*). **2** the distance at which a person's can be heard (*they made remarks about him within his daughter's hearing*). **3** the examining of evidence by a judge.

hearing aid /hee-ring-ade/ *n* a small, battery-powered device that helps a person to hear better.

hearing-impaired /hee-ring im-paird/ *adj* deaf.

hearsay /heer-say/ *n* what people say though not perhaps the truth, gossip (*no one knows why she left—it's all hearsay*).

hearse /hurss/ *n* a car or carriage for a coffin at a funeral.

heart /hart/ *n* **1** the organ that keeps the blood flowing through the body (*suffer from heart disease*). **2** the central or most important part of anything (*the heart of the forest/the heart of the town*). **3** the center of a person's thoughts and emotions (*know in his heart that he was dying*). **4** the cause of life in anything. **5** enthusiasm, determination (*the heart went out of them when their leader died*). **6** kindly feelings, especially love (*he had given her his heart*).

7 *npl* a suit of playing cards. **8** a thing shaped like a heart (*a valentine with hearts in it*). ● **learn by heart** to memorize. ● **take to heart** to feel deeply about (*take her criticism to heart*).

heartache /**har**-take/ *n* sorrow (*the heartache of losing a child*).

heart attack /**har**-ta-tack/ *n* a sudden, painful, sometimes fatal medical condition in which the heart stops working normally (*he died of a heart attack*).

heartbeat /**hart**-beet/ *n* the pulse of the heart pumping blood through the body.

heartbreak /**hart**-brake/ *n* sorrow, grief. ● *adj* **heartbreaking** /**hart**-bray-king/.

heartbreaker /**hart**-bray-ker/ *n* someone or something that causes heartbreak.

heartbroken /**hart**-bro-ken/ *adj* overcome by sorrow or grief (*heartbroken by his wife's death*).

heartburn /**hart**-burn/ *n* a burning feeling in the stomach, caused by indigestion.

hearten /**har**-ten/ *vb* to encourage, to cheer up (*heartened by winning the first game*).

heart failure /**hart**-fale-yur/ *n* the failure of the heart to beat or to pump blood through the body.

heartfelt /**hart**-felt/ *adj* sincere (*their heartfelt thanks*).

hearth /**harth**/ *n* **1** the floor of a fireplace. **2** the fireside (*sit by the hearth*). **3** the center of family life.

heartily /**har**-ti-lee/ *adv* sincerely, friendly, with zest (*thank him heartily for his help*).

heartland /**hart**-land/ *n* a geographically central area having importance in politics, strategy, etc.

heartless /**hart**-less/ *adj* having no kind feelings (*heartless people/heartless remarks*).

heart-rending /**hart**-ren-ding/ *adj* causing great sorrow or grief (*the heart-rending sobs of the child*).

heartsease /**harts**-eez/ *n* **1** peace of mind. **2** the pansy.

heartsick /**hart**-sick/ *adj* (*old*) very sad or sorrowful.

heartstrings /**hart**-stringz/ *n* deepest feelings.

heart-to-heart /**hart**-to-**hart**/ *adj* intimate.

heartwarming /**hart**-wawr-ming/ *adj* such as to cause a warm glow of good feelings.

heartwood /**hart**-wood/ *n* the hard, nonliving, older wood at the center of a tree trunk.

hearty /**har**-tee/ *adj* **1** cheerful, sometimes too cheerful (*he annoys people by being so hearty first thing in the morning*). **2** sincere (*hearty thanks*). **3** healthy. **4** large (*a hearty breakfast*).

heat /**heet**/ *n* **1** hotness, warmth (*the heat of the sun/the effect of heat on metal*). **2** anger, excitement (*in the heat of the moment*). **3** a division of a race from which the winners go on to the final. ● *vb* to make or become warm or hot (*a small fire to heat a large room/heat the soup*).

heated /**hee**-ted/ *adj* **1** hot. **2** angry (*a heated argument*).

heater /**hee**-ter/ *n* a device for heating a room, car, water, etc.

heat exhaustion /**heet**-ig-zawss-chun/ *n* a sickness consisting of dizziness, nausea, clammy skin, and low body temperature caused by loss of salt and water in the body, usually resulting from working too hard in a hot environment.

heath /**heeth**/ *n* **1** a stretch of wasteland, especially in Britain, that is covered in low shrubs **2** a low-growing evergreen shrub.

heathen /**hee**-then/ *n* **1** a person who is not a Jew, Christian, or Muslim, someone who believes in more than one God. **2** a person who is not religious. ● *also adj*.

heather /**he**-ther/ *n* a low-growing shrub with purple or white flowers.

heat shield /**heet**-sheeld/ *n* any heat protecting device, especially those fastened to a spacecraft.

heatstroke /**heet**-stroke/ *n* a serious failure of the body's ability to regulate its heat, resulting in high fever, dry skin, collapse, and sometimes coma.

heat wave /**heet**-wave/ *n* a long spell of hot weather (*forbidden to use garden hoses during the heat wave*).

heave /**heev**/ *vb* **1** to lift, to raise with effort (*heave the luggage into the car*). **2** to move up and down regularly (*shoulders heaving with laughter*). **3** to pull hard (*sailors heaving ropes*). **4** to utter with effort (*heave a sigh of relief*). ● *n* **1** an upward throw. **2** a pull. ● **heave to** (*of a ship*) to stop moving.

heaven /**he**-ven/ *n* **1** the sky. **2** the everlasting presence of God. **3** the dwelling place of the gods. **4** the happiness enjoyed by good people after death (*Christians believe that people go to heaven after death*).

heavenly /**he**-ven-lee/ *adj* **1** having to do with heaven or the sky. **2** (*inf*) delightful (*a heavenly dress/a heavenly performance*).

heavy /**he**-vee/ *adj* **1** having weight, of great weight (*lead is a heavy metal/how heavy is the package?*). **2** of more than the usual size, amount, force, etc. (*heavy traffic/heavy losses in the battle*). **3** dull, dark, and cloudy (*a heavy sky*). **4** sleepy (*children* *with heavy eyes/heavy with tiredness*). **5** sad (*with heavy heart*). **6** difficult to digest (*a heavy meal/ a heavy book*). **7** busy, full of activity (*a heavy day/a heavy program*). ● *n* **heaviness** /he-vee-ness/. ● *adv* **heavily** /he-vi-lee/.

heavy-duty /he-vee-doo-tee/ *adj* strong and not easily damaged or worn out (*heavy-duty boots*).

heavy-handed /he-vee-han-did/ *adj* **1** without a light touch. **2** cruel.

heavy metal /he-vee-me-tal/ *n* **1** any metal that has a gravity greater than 5. **2** a form of rock that features loud rhythms, guitar, and lyrics that are sometimes shouted.

heavyweight /he-vee-wate/ *n* **1** a person or animal weighing much more than average. **2** an athlete who is in the heaviest weight division.

Hebrew /hee-broo/ *n* **1** the language of the Jewish people. **2** a Jew. ● *also adj.* ● *adj* **Hebraic** /hi-bray-ic/.

heckle /he-cul/ *vb* to put difficult questions to a public speaker (*a politician heckled by his opponent's supporters*). ● *n* **heckler** /he-cler/.

hectare /hec-tare/ *n* a unit of measurement equal to 10,000 square meters or 2.471 acres.

hectic /hec-tic/ *adj* **1** feverish. **2** confusion, excitement.

hedge /hedge/ *n* **1** a fence of bushes, shrubs, etc. (*plant a hedge along the front of the garden*). **2** means of defense or protection (*as a hedge against inflation*). ● *vb* **1** to surround with a hedge (*hedge the yard*). **2** to avoid giving a clear, direct answer (*politicians hedging when asked questions*).

hedgehog /hedge-hog/ *n* a small animal, covered with prickles, that can roll itself into a ball.

hedgerow /hedge-ro/ *n* a line of bushes, shrubs, etc., forming a hedge.

heed /heed/ *vb* to pay attention to, to notice (*you should heed your parents' advice*). ● *n* care, attention (*pay little heed to his work*). ● *adjs* **heedful** /heed-ful/, **heedless** /heed-less/.

heel[1] /heel/ *n* **1** the back part of the foot (*have blisters on her heel*). **2** the part of a shoe, etc., under the heel of the foot (*shoes with high heels*). ● *vb* **1** to strike with the heel (*heeling the ball away*). **2** to put a heel on (*have the boots heeled*). ● **bring to heel** to get control over (*bring the rebels to heel*). ● **down at heel** poorly or untidily dressed. ● **take to one's heels** to run away (*he took to his heels when he saw the police*).

heel[2] /heel/ *vb* to lean over to one side (*boats heeling over in the storm*).

hefty /hef-tee/ *adj* **1** rather heavy, big and strong (*a hefty young woman*). **2** large and heavy (*a hefty load*). **3** powerful (*a hefty blow*). **4** (*inf*) large, substantial (*a hefty salary*). ● *n* **heft** /heft/ weight, heaviness, bulk.

heifer /he-fer/ *n* a young cow.

height /hite/ *n* **1** the distance from top to bottom (*the height of the fence*). **2** the state of being high (*his height is an advantage in some games*). **3** a high place (*be afraid of heights*). **4** a hill (*scale the heights above the town*). **5** the highest degree of something (*the height of summer/the height of her acting career*).

heighten /hie-ten/ *vb* **1** to make higher (*heighten the fence*). **2** to increase.

Heimlich maneuver /hime-lick ma-noo-ver/ *n* a way of stopping a person from choking by which the user puts sudden, sharp pressure to the stomach area to force wind up through the windpipe clearing the blockage.

heinie /hie-nee/ *n* the buttocks.

heinous /hey-nous/ *adj* very bad, wicked (*a heinous crime*).

heir /air/ *n* a person who receives property or a title after the death of the previous owner (*the duke's heir is his son*). ● *f* **heiress** /ae-ress/.

heirloom /air-loom/ *n* a valuable object that has been the property of a family for many generations (*her diamond pin is a family heirloom*).

heist /hiest/ *n* a robbery.

held *v* see **hold**.

helicopter /he-li-cop-ter/ *n* a type of aircraft with propellers that enable it to go straight up or down (*survivors rescued from the sea by helicopter*).

helium /hee-lee-um/ *n* a very light gas.

hell /hell/ *n* **1** in some religions, the place where the wicked are punished after death. **2** everlasting banishment from God. **3** a place of great evil or suffering.

hellish /he-lish/ *adj* **1** having to do with or like hell. **2** (*inf*) very bad, extremely unpleasant (*a hellish crime*).

hello /he-lo/ *interj* used as a greeting or to attract attention.

helm /helm/ *n* a steering wheel or handle on a ship. ● **at the helm** in control or command (*the firm's owner has retired and there is a new man at the helm*).

helmet /hel-met/ *ns* **1** (*old*) head armor. **2** a protective covering for the head (*motorcyclists wearing helmets*).

help /help/ *vb* **1** to aid, to assist (*help the old lady* *across the road/help them to find the book*). **2** to give what is needed (*help him to vegetables*). **3** to serve someone in a shop (*can I help you?*). **4** to make it easier for something to happen (*it would help if he left*). **5** to avoid (doing) (*she could not help laughing*). ● *n* aid, assistance. ● *n* **helper** /**hel**-per/.

helpful /**help**-ful/ *adj* **1** willing to help (*helpful neighbors*). **2** useful (*a helpful suggestion*).

helping /**help**-ing/ *n* a person's share of a dish of food (*a second helping of dessert*).

helpless /**help**-less/ *adj* unable to help oneself (*helpless children*).

helter-skelter /**hel**-ter-**skel**-ter/ *adv* **1** in a hurry and confusion (*the children ran helter-skelter from the bus to the beach*).

hem /**hem**/ *n* the border of a garment folded back and sewn (*put a hem on the skirt to shorten it*). ● *vb* (**hemmed** /**hemd**/, **hemming** /**he**-ming/) to sew a hem. ● **hem in** to surround closely (*a house hemmed in by blocks of flats*).

he-man /**hee**-man/ *n* a strong man.

hematology /**hee**-ma-**tol**-u-jee/ *n, also* **haematology** (*Br, Cdn*) the study of the blood.

hemisphere /**he**-mi-sfeer/ *n* **1** half of the world. **2** a map showing half of the world.

hemline /**hem**-line/ *n* the bottom edge of a skirt, coat, etc., which is usually hemmed.

hemlock /**hem**-lock/ *n* a poisonous plant.

hemoglobin /**hee**-mo-glo-bin/ *n, also* **haemoglobin** (*Br, Cdn*) the red matter that gives blood its color.

hemophilia /**hee**-mo-**fil**-ee-a/ *n, also* **haemophilia** (*Br, Cdn*) a condition where the blood does not clot properly when a person bleeds.

hemorrhage /**hem**-ridge/ *n, also* **haemmorhage** (*Br, Cdn*) heavy bleeding.

hemorrhoid /**hem**-a-roid/ *n, also* **haemmorrhoid** (*Br, Cdn*) a painful swelling of a vein near the anus, usually with bleeding.

hemp /**hemp**/ *n* **1** a grasslike plant from whose fibers ropes are made. **2** a drug from the plant.

hen /**hen**/ *n* a female bird, especially a farmyard fowl (*keep hens for their eggs*).

henchman /**hench**-man/ *n* a follower, a trusty supporter (*a people controlled by the dictator and his henchmen*).

henna /**he**-na/ *n* **1** a plant with white or red flowers. **2** a dye taken from the leaves of this plant. **3** reddish brown.

hepatitis /**he**-pa-**tie**-tis/ *n* irritation and swelling of the liver.

heptagon /**hep**-ta-gon/ *n* a seven-sided figure.

heptathlon /**hep**-**tath**-lon/ *n* a contest for women in which there are seven events, 100-meter hurdles, shot put, high jump, 200-meter dash, long jump, javelin throw, and 800-meter run.

her /**hur**/ *pron* the woman or female animal being referred to.

herald /**he**-rald/ *n* **1** (*old*) a person who makes important announcements to the public. **2** a sign of something to come (*flowers that are a herald of spring*). ● *vb* **1** to announce the approach of someone or something (*heavy footsteps heralded his approach*). **2** to be a sign of (*flowers heralding the arrival of spring*).

herb /**herb**/ *n* **1** any plant whose stem dies away during the winter. **2** a plant used for medicine or for flavoring food (*add herbs to the spaghetti sauce*).

herbaceous /**her**-**bay**-shus/ *adj* having to do with or full of herbs. ● **herbaceous border** a flowerbed with plants that flower year after year.

herbal /**her**-bal/ *adj* of herbs (*herbal remedies*).

herbalist /**her**-ba-list/ *n* a person who studies or sells herbs (*go to a herbalist for a cure for his allergy*).

herbivore /**her**-bi-vore/ *n* an animal that eats plants and grasses (*sheep are herbivores*). ● **herbivorous** /**her**-**bi**-vo-rus/ *adj* eating grass or herbs (*herbivorous animals such as cows*).

herd /**herd**/ *n* **1** a flock of animals (*a herd of cows/a herd of deer*). **2** a large crowd of people (*herds of people doing Christmas shopping*). ● *vb* **1** (*inf*) to crowd or collect together (*people herded into the hall to hear the speaker*). **2** to look after a herd (*herd the cows in the field*). **3** to drive (*herd the cows to market*).

herdsman /**herdz**-man/ *n* a person who looks after a herd.

here /**heer**/ *adv* at or in this place.

hereafter /**hi**-raf-ter/ *adv* after this time. ● *n* the life after death.

hereby /**heer**-bie/ *adv* by or through this, by this means.

hereditary /**hi**-re-di-ta-ree/ *adj* passed on from parents to children (*a hereditary disease*).

heredity /**hi**-re-di-tee/ *n* the passing on of qualities of character, etc., from parents to children (*health factors associated with heredity*).

heretic /**he**-re-tic/ *n* a person who teaches a heresy. ● *adj* **heretical** /**he**-re-ti-cal/.

heritable /**he**-ri-ta-bul/ *adj* able to be passed on from parents to children (*heritable property*).

heritage /**he**-ri-tage/ *n* **1** that which is passed on to a person by his or her parents (*the farm was part of his heritage*). **2** things that have been passed on from earlier generations (*the art collection is part of our national heritage*).

hermit /**her**-mit/ *n* a person who lives alone or away from other people, often originally for religious reasons.

hernia /**her**-nee-a/ *n* a break in the wall of muscle in the front of the stomach (*have an operation to repair a hernia*).

hero /**hee**-ro/ *n* (*pl* **heroes** /**hee**-roaz/) **1** a brave person, someone admired for his brave deeds (*treated as a hero for saving the cat from the fire*). **2** the chief character in a play or novel (*the hero of the novel is a young boy*). ● *f* **heroine** /**he**-ro-in/.

heroic /he-**ro**-ic/ *adj* **1** brave (*heroic deeds*). **2** having to do with heroes (*heroic legends*).

heroin /**he**-ro-in/ *n* a habit-forming drug obtained from opium.

heroine *see* **hero**.

heroism /**he**-ro-i-zum/ *n* bravery (*receive a medal for his heroism in battle*).

heron /**he**-ron/ *n* a water bird with long legs and neck (*a heron catching fish*).

herpes /**her**-peez/ *n* a disease that causes small blisters on the skin.

herpetology /her-pe-**tol**-o-jee/ *n* the study of reptiles.

herring /**he**-ring/ *n* a small sea fish used as food.

herringbone /**he**-ring-bone/ *adj* with a pattern like the backbone of a herring (*a herringbone tweed*).

herring gull /**he**-ring-gull/ *n* the common sea gull of the Northern Hemisphere with gray and white feathers and black wing tips.

hers /herz/ *pron* belonging to her.

herself /her-**self**/ *pron* her real, true, or actual self.

hertz /herts/ *n* a unit of measurement for the number of waves, vibrations, etc. per unit of time.

hesitance /**he**-zi-tanse/, **hesitancy** /**he**-zi-tan-see/, **hesitation** /he-zi-**tay**-shun/ *ns* doubt, act of hesitating, indecision (*her hesitance about accepting the invitation*).

hesitant /**he**-zi-tant/ *adj* doubtful, undecided (*a hesitant person/a hesitant step/a hesitant remark*).

hesitate /**he**-zi-tate/ *vb* **1** to stop for a moment before doing something or speaking (*she hesitated before answering the question*). **2** to be undecided (*they are hesitating about whether to go*).

hessian /**he**-shan/ a coarse cloth used for bags. *See* **burlap**.

heterosexual /he-te-ro-**sek**-shal/ *adj* of different sexes, being attracted to the opposite sex.

hew /hyoo/ *n* (*fml*) to cut by a number of strong blows, to chop as with an ax (*hew down a tree*). ● *adj* **hewn** /hyoon/.

hex /heks/ *n* a spell believed to bring bad luck, a jinx.

hexagon /**hek**-sa-gon/ *n* a six-sided figure. ● *adj* **hexagonal** /hek-**sa**-gu-nal/.

hexagram /**hek**-sa-gram/ *n* a six-sided star.

hey /hay/ *interj* used to attract attention or express surprise, delight, sometimes used as a greeting.

heyday /**hay**-day/ *n* full strength, the time of life when a person's abilities, etc., reach their full power (*when silent films were in their heyday*).

hi /hie/ *interj* hello.

hiatus /hie-**ay**-tus/ *n* **1** a break in a piece of writing or a speech (*notice a hiatus in the play*). **2** a gap (*the talks resumed after a week's hiatus*).

hibernate /**hie**-ber-nate/ *vb* to pass the winter in sleep, as certain animals do (*bears hibernating*). ● *n* **hibernation** /hie-ber-**nay**-shun/.

hibiscus /hi-**bi**-scuss/ *n* a kind of plant or shrub with large, colorful flowers.

hiccup /**hi**-cup/ *n* **1** a sudden, short stoppage of the breath. **2** the sound caused by this. **3** a small delay or interruption (*a hiccup in our timetable because of the absence of one of the speakers*). ● *vb* (**hiccupped** /**hi**-cupt/, **hiccupping** /**hi**-cu-ping/) to have hiccups.

hickory /**hic**-ree/ *n* an North American tree with very hard wood.

Hidatsa /hi-**dat**-sa/ *n* a Native American people now living in North Dakota, the language of these people.

hide[1] /hide/ *vb* (**hid** /hid/, *pp* **hidden** /**hi**-den/) **1** to put or keep out of sight (*hide the presents from the children until Christmas*). **2** to keep secret (*hide her disappointment*). ● *n* a camouflaged place used by bird-watchers, hunters, etc.

hide[2] /hide/ *n* the skin of an animal (*an elephant's hide*).

hide-and-seek /hide-and-**seek**/ *n* a game in which one player tries to find the other players, who have all hidden.

hideaway /**hie**-da-way/ *n* a place where a person can hide.

hideous /hi-**dee**-us/ *adj* **1** frightful (*a hideous scream*). **2** very ugly (*a hideous dress*).

hide-out /**hie**-dout/ *n* a place to hide (*a hideout in the forest where they were safe from enemies*).

hiding[1] /hie-ding/ *n* the condition of being hidden (*he went into hiding after he gave evidence at the trial*).

hiding[2] /hie-ding/ *n* a thrashing, a beating (*their father threatened them with a hiding if they got into trouble again*).

hierarchy /hie-rar-kee/ *n* **1** an arrangement in order, putting the most important first (*his place in the firm's hierarchy*). **2** the group of people in an organization who have power or control. ● *adj* **hierarchal** /hie-rar-kal/.

hieroglyph /hie-ro-glif/, **hieroglyphic** /hie-ro-gli-fic/ *ns* a picture or sign standing for a letter, as in ancient Egyptian writing.

hieroglyphics /hie-ro-gli-fics/ *n* **1** a system of writing that uses hieroglyphs. **2** (*inf*) writing that is difficult to read.

high /hie/ *adj* **1** being a certain distance up (*a wall six feet high*). **2** being above normal level (*high blood pressure/a high temperature*). **3** raised above (*a high window*). **4** of important rank (*high officials*). **5** morally good (*of high ideals*). **6** expensive (*high costs*). ● *also adv*. ● **on a high horse** wanting to be treated with great respect, haughty (*when anyone criticizes her, she gets on her high horse and won't speak to anyone*).

higher education /hie-er e-joo-cay-shun/ *n* college or university education.

high-five /hie-five/ *n* the slapping of another persons upraised, open hand in celebration.

high jump /hie-jump/ *n* a contest to see who can jump the highest over a bar set up between two posts.

highland /hie-land/ *n* land well above sea level, land containing many hills or mountains.

highlander /hie-lan-der/ *n* a person who lives in the mountains.

highlight /hie-lite/ *n* a part on which light is brightest (*she has blond highlights in her hair*). ● *v* to mark with something to make lighter or brighter (*highlighted the sections to study*).

highlighter /hie-lie-ter/ *n* a pen that is used to highlight parts of text.

highly /hie-lee/ *adv* greatly, very (*highly amused/highly spiced/highly unlikely*)

highness /hie-ness/ *n* **1** the quality or state of being high. **2** a title of honor given to royalty.

high-rise /hie-rize/ *adj* of a tall apartment house, office building, etc. ● *n*.

high school /hie-skool/ *n* a secondary school that includes grades 10, 11, and 12, and sometimes 9.

high seas /hie-seez/ *npl* the open seas (*pirates sailing the high seas*).

high-strung /hie-strung/ *adjs* very nervous, easily excited (*she's very high strung and easily gets upset*).

high-tech /hie-tek/ *adj* using very advanced modern machinery and methods, especially electronic ones, also **hi-tech**.

high tide /hie-tide/ *n* the time of day when the water level is highest.

high-top /hie-top/ *n* a sneaker or athletic shoe that extends over the ankle.

high water /hie-waw-ter/ *n* high tide.

highway /hie-way/ *n* a public road, a main road.

high wire /hie-wire/ *n* a wire stretched high between two supports across which people will walk and perform tricks, as in a circus, fair, etc.

hijack /hie-jack/ *vb* to steel or take control of a car, truck, train, etc. illegally during a journey (*terrorists hijacking a plane*). ● **hijacker** /hie-ja-ker/ *n*.

hike /hike/ *vb* to go on a long walk in the country, especially over rough ground (*hiking over the mountain on Saturday morning*). ● *n* **hiker** /hie-ker/.

hilarious /hi-lay-ree-us/ *adj* **1** extremely amusing or funny (*a hilarious account of the party/hilarious jokes*). **2** noisily merry (*a hilarious party*). ● *n* **hi-larity** /hi-la-ri-tee/.

hill /hill/ *n* a low mountain, a raised part of the earth's surface.

hillside /hill-side/ *n* the side of a hill.

hilltop /hill-top/ *n* the top of a hill.

hilly /hi-lee/ *adj* having many hills (*hilly ground*).

hilt /hilt/ *n* the handle of a sword, dagger, or knife.

him /him/ *pron* the man or male animal being referred to.

himself /him-self/ *pron* his real, true, or normal self.

hind[1] /hinde/ *n* a female red deer.

hind[2] /hinde/ *adj* at the back (*the dog's hind legs*).

hinder[1] /hin-der/ *adj* at the back.

hinder[2] /hin-der/ *vb* to stop or delay the advance or development of, to put difficulties in the way of (*hinder progress/hinder them in their escape plan*).

Hindi /hin-dee/ *n* the main language in India.

hindrance /hin-dranse/ *n* something or someone that makes action or progress difficult (*the new assistant was more of a hindrance than a help/her injured arm was a hindrance in her work*).

hindsight /hinde-site/ *n* **1** the rear sight of a firearm. **2** the ability to see, after the event, what should have been done.

Hindu /hin-doo/ *n* a believer in Hinduism.

Hinduism /hin-doo-i-zum/ *n* a religion held by many

in India focused on three things: Dharma, the universal law; Karma, the effects of personal actions; and Samsara, the cycle of rebirth.

hinge /hindge/ *n* a folding joint to which a door or lid is fixed so that it can turn on it (*gate hinges in need of being oiled*). ● *vb* **1** to fix hinges to (*the cupboard door is hinged on the right*). **2** to depend (*his promotion hinges on passing the exam*).

hint /hint/ *vb* to suggest indirectly (*she hinted that he was not completely honest*). ● *n* **1** an indirect suggestion (*he received a hint that the firm would be sold*). **2** a helpful suggestion (*mother's cookery hints*). **3** a small amount (*a hint of parsley*).

hip[1] /hip/ *n* the upper part of the thigh (*stand with her hands on her hips*).

hip[2] /hip/ *n* the fruit of the wild rose.

hip[3] /hip/ *adj* aware, fashionable, stylish, associated with hippies or hipsters.

hip boots /hip-boots/ *n* high, usually waterproof boots that reach the top of the legs.

hip-hop /hip-hop/ *n* a form of music that combines rap, funk, street sounds, and melody.

hippies /hi-peez/ *npl* young people of the 1960s and 1970s who believed in peace, lived together in separate communities, and dressed in a similar, casual way.

hippo /hi-po/ *n* informal word for hippopotamus.

hippopotamus /hi-po-**paw**-ta-mus/ *n* (*pl* **hippopotamuses** /hi-po-**paw**-ta-mu-seez/ *or* **hippopotami** /hi-po-**paw**-ta-mie/) a large, plant-eating river animal with thick skin, an almost hairless body, and short legs found in Africa.

hire /hire/ *n* **1** the renting of something (*a boat for hire*). **2** the money paid for the use of a thing or for the work of another (*pay the hire of the hall in advance*). ● *vb* **1** to get the use of a thing by paying for it (*hire a boat for a week*). **2** to lend to another for payment (*hiring out his boat to tourists*).

his /hiz/ *pron* belonging to him.

Hispanic /hi-**spa**-nic/ *adj* of or relating to Hispanics. ● *n* a usually Spanish-speaking person of Latin American birth or descent.

hiss /hiss/ *vb* to make a sound like that of the letter s, often as a sign of disapproval (*the audience hissed at the comedian's bad jokes*). ● *n* the act or sound of hissing (*the hiss of a snake*).

historian /hi-**sto**-ree-an/ *n* a person who writes about and studies history (*a historian specializing in the nineteenth century*).

historic /hi-**staw**-ric/ *adj* of lasting importance (*a historic battle*).

historical /hi-**staw**-ri-cal/ *adj* having to do with history (*historical studies*).

history /hi-sto-ree/ *n* **1** the study of past events (*study American history in school*). **2** an account of past events, conditions, ideas, etc. (*the history of the English language/told him her life history*).

hit /hit/ *vb* (**hit, hitting** /hi-ting/) **1** to strike (*hit the ball with the racket/hit his attacker in the face*). **2** to reach, to arrive at (*hit a bad patch*). ● *n* **1** a blow. **2** a success (*the show was a hit*).

hit-and-miss /hi-tan-**miss**/ *adj* resulting in both successes and failures.

hit-and-run /hi-tan-**run**/ *adj* of an accident in which the driver involved flees from the scene.

hitch /hich/ *vb* **1** to hook or fasten (on to) (*hitch the carriage on to the train*). **2** to try to get a ride in someone else's car (*try to hitch to Philadelphia*). ● *n* **1** a jerk, a pull (*give his trousers a hitch*). **2** a type of knot. **3** a difficulty, a snag (*a slight hitch in the proceedings*).

hitchhike /hich-hike/ *vb* to travel by asking for rides from others along the way.

hi-tech *see* **high tech.**

hither /hi-ther/ *adv* (*fml or old*) to this place (*come hither*).

hitherto /hi-ther-too/ *adv* (*fml*) until now (*hitherto he has been on time but he was late today*).

hit man /hit-man/ *n* a man paid to kill someone.

hit-or-miss /hi-tor-**miss**/ *adj* random.

HIV /aych-ie-vee/ *abbr* = **Human Immunodeficiency Virus**: a virus that affects the body's immune system, or its ability to protect itself from infection, can lead to **AIDS**.

hive /hive/ *n* **1** a home made for bees. **2** a place of great activity (*the small office was a real hive of industry*).

hives /hievz/ *n* an allergic reaction that causes itching, burning, stinging, and red patches on the skin.

ho /ho/ *interj* used to attract attention.

hoard /hoard/ *n* a hidden supply (*the miser's hoard of gold*). ● *vb* **1** to store secretly (*a miser hoarding gold coins*). **2** to collect (*hoard food in case there is a shortage*).

hoarse /hoarse/ *adj* having a rough or husky voice (*children hoarse from shouting*).

hoarsen /hoar-sen/ *vb* to make or become hoarse.

hoax /hoaks/ *n* a trick or joke intended to deceive (*the phone call about the fire was a hoax*). ● *vb* to deceive, to trick.

hob /hob/ *n* an shelf at the side or rear of a fireplace for pots, etc.

hobble /hob-ul/ vb 1 to limp (hobbling in shoes that were too tight). 2 to tie the legs of an animal to one another to stop it running away.

hobby /hob-ee/ n a favorite subject or interest for a person's spare time, an interesting pastime (work so hard that they had no time for hobbies/play golf as a hobby).

hobo /ho-bo/ n a person who travels from place to place doing various jobs, a homeless person.

hock /hock/ n the joint in the middle of an animal's back leg.

hockey /hock-ee/ n 1 a game in which the players are skating on ice and trying to score by hitting a puck into a goal with a long stick (there are eleven players in a hockey team). 2 (Br) a team game played with a ball or puck and sticks curved at the end played indoors, in a field, or on pavement.

hod /hod/ n a V-shaped wooden container on a pole used for carrying bricks, etc.

hodgepodge /hodge-podge/ n a kind of stew, any jumbled mixture or mess.

hoe /ho/ n a garden tool with a thin, flat blade at the end of a long handle for loosening the earth around plants. ● vb to dig with a hoe (hoeing the weeds).

hoedown /ho-down/ n a lively dance, often a square dance.

hog /hog/ n 1 a pig. 2 a greedy or filthy person (he's such a hog that he ate all the food before the others arrived).

hogan /ho-gan/ n the dwelling of the Navajo, built of earthen walls supported by timber.

hogwash /hog-wash/ n 1 garbage fed to hogs. 2 useless talk, writing, etc.

ho-hum /ho-hum/ interj used to suggest boredom.

hoist /hoist/ vb to lift, to raise, especially by some device (hoist the load with a crane). ● n a lift for goods.

hold /hoald/ vb (pt, pp **held** /held/) 1 to have or take in the hand(s) or arms (hold a newborn baby/holding a knife in one hand). 2 to bear the weight of, to support (the bridge wouldn't hold them). 3 to be able to contain (a jug holding two liters). 4 to have (an opinion) (he holds the view that all people are equal). 5 to cause to take place (hold a meeting). ● n 1 grasp (have a firm hold of the wheel). 2 the lowest part of a ship, where the cargo is stored. ● **hold forth** (fml) to speak in public or at length (held forth about his political opinions). ● **hold your own** to keep advantages without gaining any more (held his own in a fight). ● **hold up 1** to attack and rob. 2 to delay, to hinder. 3 to last. 4

to raise. 5 to support. ● **hold with** to agree with (he does not hold with new educational ideas).

holder /hole-der/ n one who holds or possesses (the holder of the lease).

hole /hole/ n 1 a hollow or empty space in something solid (a hole in the road). 2 an opening (a hole in the fence). 3 an animal's den (the fox's hole). 4 (inf) a difficulty (in a bit of a hole financially). ● vb to make a hole in (a ship holed by a rock).

holiday /hol-i-day/ n a day of freedom from work, a day set aside for rest or amusement (the Christmas holiday). ● n **holiday-maker** /hol-i-day may-ker/.

holiness /ho-lee-ness/ n the state of being holy. ● **Holiness** a title given to the pope.

holler /hol-er/ vb to shout or yell.

hollow /hol-o/ adj 1 not solid. 2 empty inside (hollow trees). 3 worthless (a hollow victory). 4 not sincere (hollow promises). 5 sounding as if coming from a hollow place, echoing (hollow sounds). ● n 1 a sunken place, something hollow (hollows in the cheeks). 2 a low place between folds, ridges, etc. 3 a valley. ● vb 1 to make hollow. 2 to take out the inside leaving the outside untouched (hollow out the melon).

holly /hol-ee/ n an evergreen bush with dark green spiky leaves and red berries.

holocaust /ho-lo-cawst/ n 1 (old) the burning of an animal as a sacrifice. 2 killing or destruction on a huge scale, often by fire (fear a nuclear holocaust).

hologram /ho-lo-gram/ n a 3-dimensional photographic image created by using a laser beam.

holograph /ho-lo-graf/ n a document in the person's own handwriting whom it is about (a will in the form of a holograph).

holster /hole-ster/ n a pistol case that can be fixed to a belt (remove his gun from his holster).

holy /ho-lee/ adj 1 good and trying to be perfect in the service of God (holy men). 2 set aside for the service of God (holy places).

Holy Communion /ho-lee cu-myoon-yun/ n in the Christian faith, the receiving of bread and wine to remember Jesus's last meal with his followers before his death.

holy day /ho-lee-day/ n any day set aside for a religious purpose.

homage /om-idge/ n 1 (old) the promise to do certain duties for an overlord. 2 respect, things said or done to show great respect (come to do homage at the great man's funeral/pay homage to the famous writer).

home /home/ n 1 a person's house, the place where a

person lives (*the doctor visited her in her home*). **2** where a person was born, the place where a person or thing originally comes from (*the home of jazz*). **3** a place where children without parents, old people, people who are ill, etc., are looked after (*an old people's home*). ● *adj* **1** having to do with a person's home (*home comforts*). **2** made or done at home (*home cooking*). ● *adv* to or at home (*go home*).

homeboy /home-boy/ *n* a boy or man from the same town, neighborhood, etc.

homegirl /home-girl/ *n* a girl or woman from the same town, neighborhood, etc.

homeless /home-less/ *adj* having no home.

homely /home-lee/ *adj* **1** plain, simple (*homely tastes*). **2** like home, comfortable (*a homely place*).

homemade /home-made/ *adj* made at home or at the place where it is being offered, sold, etc.

homemaker /home-may-ker/ *n* a person who manages a home.

homeopathy /ho-me-aw-pa-thee/ *n, also* **homoe-opathy** (*Br, Cdn*) a system of medical treatment based on the belief that certain illnesses can be cured by giving the patient small doses of a drug that would cause a mild form of the illness in a healthy person. ● *adj* **homeopathic** /ho-me-o-pa-thic/.

homeowner /ho-moa-ner/ *n* a person who owns the house that he or she lives in.

home page /home-page/ *n* the first Web page found on an Internet site.

homeplate /home-plate/ *n* in baseball, the base from where the batter hits and to where the runners run to score.

homeroom /home-room/ *n* the room where a class in school meets every day to make sure the students are all there and to give any announcements.

home run /home-run/ *n* in baseball, a hit that allows the batter to run around all the bases to score.

home schooling /home skoo-ling/ *n* the process of teaching his or her own children in the home rather than sending them to a school.

homesick /home-sick/ *adj* having a longing for home (*homesick at boarding school*). ● *n* **home-sickness** /home-sick-ness/.

homespun /home-spun/ *n* cloth made in the home. ● *adj* **1** made of cloth spun at home. **2** plain and simple (*homespun remedies*).

homestead /home-sted/ *n* **1** a house with grounds and outbuildings around it, especially a farm. **2** a piece of public land granted to a person by the US government to be developed as a farm (per the Homestead Act of 1862).

hometown /home-town/ *n* the town where a person lives or grew up.

homeward /home-ward/ *adv* (*fml*) toward home (*travel homeward*).

homework /home-wurk/ *n* work to be done or lessons to be studied at home.

homicide /hom-i-side/ *n* **1** the act of killing another human being (*guilty of homicide*). **2** a person who kills another human being (*homicides in jail*). ● *adj* **homicidal** /hom-i-sie-dal/.

homogenize /ho-modge-i-nize/ *vb, also* **homog-enise** (*Br*) to make the same in texture, mixture, quality by breaking down and blending the different parts (*we drink homogenized milk so the cream doesn't separate*).

homonym /hom-o-nim/ *n* a word sounding the same as another but having a different meaning (e.g., here, hear).

homophobia /ho-mo-fo-bee-a/ *n* irrational fear or hatred of homosexuals or homosexuality.

Homo sapiens /ho-mo-say-pee-enz/ *n* the scientific name for human beings.

homosexual /ho-mo-sek-shwal/ *adj* of or having to do with sexual desire for those of the same sex. ● *n* **homosexuality** /ho-mo-sek-shoo-wa-li-tee/.

honest /on-est/ *adj* **1** free from deceit, upright, truthful, not cheating, stealing, etc. (*honest workers*). **2** open and frank (*to be honest with you*). **3** typical of an honest person, open (*an honest face*). **4** true (*an honest report*). ● *n* **honesty** /on-est-ee/.

honey /hu-nee/ *n* a sweet fluid made by bees from flowers.

honeybee /hu-nee-bee/ *n* a bee that makes honey.

honeycomb /hu-nee-coam/ *n* the waxy cells in which bees store their honey.

honeymoon /hu-nee-moon/ *n* the vacation taken by a newly married couple immediately after marriage.

honeysuckle /hu-nee-su-cul/ *n* a sweet-smelling climbing plant (*honeysuckle surrounding the door*).

honk /hongk/ *n* the call of a wild goose or any similar sound, like that of a car horn.

honor /on-ur/ *n, also* **honour** (*Br, Cdn*) **1** good name, reputation (*fight for his country's honor*). **2** high principles and standards of behavior (*a man of honor*). **3** glory (*bring honor to the school*). **4** a person or thing that brings pride or glory (*he is an honor to the school*). **5** a title of respect used when talking to or about certain important people such as judges, mayors, etc. **6** respect (*in honor of the dead*). ● *vb* **1** to respect. **2** to raise in rank or dignity. **3** to pay (a bill) when due.

honorable /on-ur-a-bul/ *adj, also* **honourable** (*Br, Cdn*) **1** worthy of respect or honor (*honorable deeds*). **2** honest, of high principles (*an honorable man*). **3** just.

honorary /on-ur-ra-ree/ *adj* **1** unpaid (*honorary secretary of the organization*). **2** given to a person as a mark of respect for his or her ability (*an honorary degree*).

honor society /on-ur so-**sie**-i-tee/ *n, also* **honour society** (*Cdn*) a college or high school organization for students who get high marks.

honor system /on-ur **sis**-tem/ *n, also* **honour system** (*Cdn*) a system whereby people are trusted to obey rules, do their work, etc. without direct supervision.

hood /hood/ *n* **1** a covering for the head and neck (*the monk's hood*). **2** anything that looks like a hood or can be used as such (*the hood of a baby carriage/the hood of a car*).

hoodlum /hod-lum/ *n* a wild, lawless person, often a member of a gang of criminals.

hoodwink /hood-wingk/ *vb* to deceive (*hoodwink her into lending him money*).

hoof /hoof/ *n* (*pl* **hooves** /hoovz/ *or* **hoofs** /hoofs/) the horny part of the foot in certain animals (*a horse's hoof*). ● *adj* **hoofed** /hooft/ having hoofs.

hook /hook/ *n* **1** a piece of metal or plastic bent for catching hold or for hanging things on (*a hook on the bathroom door for robes*). **2** a short, curved cutting instrument. ● *vb* to catch, hold, or fasten with a hook (*hook a large salmon*). ● *adjs* **hooked, hook-shaped.** ● **by hook or by crook** by any means, fair or unfair (*he will get the money by hook or by crook*).

hook shot /hook-shot/ *n* in basketball, a one handed shot in which the arm is brought up sideways over the head to toss the ball into the hoop.

hooligan /hoo-li-gan/ *n* a wild, lawless person, often a member of a gang of criminals (*young hooligans fighting in the street and damaging property*). ● *n* **hooliganism** /hoo-li-ga-ni-zum/.

hoop /hoop/ *n* **1** a band of metal around a cask. **2** a large ring of wood, metal, etc. (*dogs jumping through hoops*).

hoot /hoot/ *vb* **1** to cry as an owl. **2** to make a loud noise of laughter or disapproval (*hooting with laughter*). ● *n* **1** the cry of an owl. **2** a shout of laughter or disapproval.

hooves *see* **hoof**.

hop[1] /hop/ *vb* (**hopped** /hopt/, **hopping** /hop-ing/) **1** to jump on one leg (*hurt his foot and have to hop to the car*). **2** to jump (*he hopped over the wall*). ● *n* a jump, especially on one leg.

hop[2] /hop/ *n* a plant with bitter-tasting cones used in making beer, ale, etc.

hope /hope/ *vb* to wish and expect for things good in the future (*he hopes for better things/she hopes to get a job soon*). ● *n* a wish or expectation for the future (*her hopes of getting to university/live in hope*).

hope chest /hope-chest/ *n* a chest in which a young woman collects linen, clothing, etc. in hopes of getting married one day.

hopeful /hope-ful/ *adj* **1** full of hope (*in a hopeful mood*). **2** giving cause for hope (*hopeful signs*).

hopeless /hope-less/ *adj* **1** without hope. **2** giving no cause for hope (*a hopeless cause*). **3** (*inf*) poor, not good (*a hopeless cook*).

Hopi /ho-pee/ *n* a member of a Native American people living in northeastern Arizona, the language spoken by these people.

hopping /hop-ing/ *adj* very busy or active (*the nightclub was hopping*).

hopscotch /hop-scotch/ *n* a game in which a player tosses a stone or other object into a section of a figure drawn on the ground and hops from section to section to pick to the stone up after the toss.

horde /hoard/ *n* **1** a wandering camp or tribe. **2** a huge crowd (*hordes of people at the January sales*). ● *v* to collect into a large group.

horizon /ho-rie-zun/ *n* **1** the line along which the earth and sky seem to meet. **2** the breadth of a person's understanding and experience (*extend his horizons by studying*).

horizontal /ho-ri-**zon**-tal/ *adj* parallel to the horizon, flat, level (*in a horizontal line*).

hormone /hawr-moan/ *n* a substance made in the body that has a specific job or effect.

horn /horn/ *n* **1** a hard, pointed growth on the heads of some animals (*a bull's horns*). **2** anything shaped like a horn (e.g., snail's feelers). **3** a musical wind instrument (*play the French horn*). **4** on a car, truck, etc., an instrument that makes warning noises (*beep his horn as a warning for the other car*). ● *adj* made of horn.

horned /hornd/ *adj* having horns (*horned cattle*).

hornet /hor-net/ *n* a large, stinging insect of the wasp family colored yellow and black.

hornist /**hor**-nist/ *n* a person who plays the French horn.

hornpipe /**horn**-pipe/ *n* **1** a lively dance, a sailor's dance. **2** music for such a dance. **3** a musical instrument no longer widely used with a bell and mouthpiece made of horn.

horoscope /**haw**-ro-scope/ *n* **1** a plan showing the positions of the stars in the sky at a particular time, especially the hour of a person's birth, made in the belief that from it features and future events can be foretold (*cast a horoscope*). **2** a forecast of a person's future based on such a plan (*a horoscope printed in the newspaper*).

horrendous /haw-**ren**-dus/ *adj* horrible, frightful.

horrent /**haw**-rent/ *adj* bristly, horrified.

horrible /**haw**-ri-bul/ *adj* **1** causing horror, dreadful, terrible (*a horrible accident*). **2** (*inf*) unpleasant, nasty (*a horrible person/horrible weather*). ● *adv* **horribly** /**haw**-ri-blee/.

horrid /**haw**-rid/ *adj* **1** (*fml*) horrible, dreadful (*horrid crimes*). **2** (*inf*) horrible, unpleasant, nasty (*a horrid girl*).

horrify /**haw**-ri-fie/ *vb* to shock with unpleasant news, etc. (*we were horrified to hear the news of his accident*). ● *adj* **horrific** /haw-**ri**-fic/.

horror /**haw**-ror/ *n* **1** terror, great fear or dislike (*have a horror of snakes*). **2** (*inf*) a horrible or disagreeable person or thing (*the child is a real horror*). ● *adj* (*like to watch horror movies*).

horrorstruck /**haw**-ror-struck/ *adj* horrified.

hors d'oeuvre /awr-**durv**/ *n* an appetizer, a small portion of food served before a meal or at a cocktail party.

horse /horss/ *n* **1** an animal that can be used for riding on or pulling loads. **2** a device or frame with legs to support something. **3** a padded block on four legs used by gymnasts in vaulting.

horseback /**hawrss**-back/ *adv* on the back of a horse.

horsefly /**hawrss**-flie/ *n* a large fly that typically feeds on the blood of horses and cattle.

horseplay /**hawrss**-play/ *n* rough play (*children breaking things while indulging in horseplay*).

horsepower /**hawrss**-pou-er/ *n* the pulling power of a horse, taken as a measure of power equal to the power needed to raise 33,000 pounds 1 foot in 1 minute (*the horsepower of a car*).

horseradish /**hawrss**-ra-dish/ *n* a plant with a sharp-tasting edible root used for sauce or relish (*roast beef with horseradish*).

horseshoe /**hawrss**-shoo/ *n* **1** a curved iron shoe for horses. **2** anything of this shape.

horticultural /hawr-ti-**cul**-chu-ral/ *adj* having to do with gardening or growing plants, vegetables, etc.

horticulture /**hawr**-ti-cul-chur/ *n* the art or science of gardening or growing flowers, vegetables, etc.

horticulturist /**hawr**-ti-cul-chu-rist/ *n* a person skilled in gardening.

hosanna /ho-**za**-na/ *n* a cry of praise to God.

hose /hoaz/ *n* **1** (*fml*) stockings, socks, etc. (*a shop selling hose*). **2** a movable pipe of rubber, plastic, etc., used for carrying water (*a garden hose*). ● *vb* to spray with a hose.

hosiery /**ho**-zhe-ree/ *n* the articles sold by a hosier.

hospice /**hos**-pis/ *n* **1** (*old*) a place of rest or shelter for travelers. **2** a hospital for sufferers of incurable diseases (*cancer patients in hospices*).

hospitable /hos-**pi**-ta-bul/ *adj* kind to guests and visitors (*she was very hospitable to the visitors and welcomed them into her home*).

hospital /**hos**-pi-tal/ *n* a building for the care of the sick.

hospitality /hos-pi-**ta**-li-tee/ *n* kindness to guests and visitors.

hospitalization /hos-pi-ta-lie-**zay**-shun/ *n, also* **hospitalisation** (*Br*) the condition of being put into the hospital for a time.

host[1] /hoast/ *n* **1** one who receives guests (*their host at the dinner party*). **2** (*old*) an innkeeper or hotelkeeper. ● *f* **hostess** /ho-**stess**/. ● *vb* to act as a host (to a party, television show, etc.).

host[2] /hoast/ *n* **1** (*old*) an army. **2** a very large number (*a whole host of people came to the meeting*).

host[3] /hoast/ *n* in some Christian services, the bread taken during Holy Communion.

hostage /**hos**-tidge/ *n* a person held prisoner until certain conditions have been carried out (*the hijackers of the plane took the passengers as hostages*).

hostel /**hos**-tel/ *n* a building in which persons away from home (students, travelers, etc.) can pay to stay if they agree to keep its rules.

hostelry /**hos**-tel-ree/ *n* (*old*) an inn.

hostess *see* **host**.

hostile /**hos**-til/ *adj* **1** unfriendly (*hostile toward anyone who disagrees with her*). **2** having to do with an enemy (*hostile troops*).

hostility /hos-**ti**-li-tee/ *n* **1** unfriendliness. **2** *pl* warfare.

hot /hot/ *adj* **1** very warm (*a hot day*). **2** easily excited (*a hot temper*). **3** having a sharp, burning taste (*hot food*).

hot air /**hot**-air/ *n* writing or speech that claims to be important but really is not.

hotbed /**hot**-bed/ *n* **1** in a garden, a piece of earth kept warm so that plants will grow in it more quickly. **2** a place where things develop quickly (*a hotbed of rebellion*).

hotch-potch *see* **hodgepodge**.

hot dog /**hot**-dog/ *n* a frankfurter, usually served on a long, soft roll.

hotel /ho-**tel**/ *n* a building where people sleep and eat when away from home, an inn (*stay at a hotel when away on business*).

hotheaded /hot-**he**-ded/ *adj* easily excited, rash (*he's so hotheaded that he rushes into things without thinking*). ● *n* **hothead** /**hot**-hed/.

hot plate /**hot**-plate/ *n* a small, portable device for cooking food or for keeping it warm.

hot seat /**hot**-seet/ *n* any stressful, difficult position to be in.

hotshot /**hot**-shot/ *n* a person who is regarded an expert at an activity or very important, aggressive, or skillful at something.

hot spring /**hot**-spring/ *n* a spring with water that is hotter than the temperature of the human body.

hot-tempered /**hot-tem**-perd/ *adj* easily angered (*so hot-tempered that children are afraid of him*).

hot tub /**hot**-tub/ *n* a large tub in which several people soak in hot water together.

hot water bottle /hot-**water**-botl/ *n* a rubber container holding hot water which is used to warm a person in bed.

hound /hound/ *n* **1** a hunting dog (*foxhounds*). **2** (*inf*) a rascal (*that thieving hound*). ● *vb* to hunt. ● **hound out** to drive out (*hounded out of the town*).

hour /our/ *n* **1** 60 minutes. **2** the time fixed for doing something, the time at which something is usually done (*business hours*).

hourglass /**our**-glass/ *n* a sand-filled glass for measuring time.

houri /**hoo**-ree/ *n* in the Muslim faith, any of the beautiful young women in paradise.

hourly /**our**-lee/ *adj* happening every hour (*hourly reports*).

house /house/ *n* **1** a building in which people, often a family, live. **2** a place or building used for a particular purpose (*a house of worship*). **3** a theater audience (*a full house at the evening performance*). ● *vb* /**houze**/ **1** to provide a house for. **2** to shelter.

houseboat /**house**-boat/ *n* a large, flat-bottomed boat used as a home (*a houseboat on the Mississippi*).

housebroken /**house**-bro-ken/ *adj* trained to go outside to urinate, etc., said of dogs.

housefly /**house**-fly/ *n* a kind of fly that feeds on garbage, food, etc. and found around houses.

houseguest /**house**-gest/ *n* a person who stays at least one night in a person's home.

household /**house**-hoald/ *n* all who live in a house (*the whole household helped with the cooking*). ● *adj* having to do with a house or those who live in it (*household pets/household insurance*).

househusband /**house**-huz-band/ *n* a married man whose primary job it is to manage the home.

housekeeper /**house**-kee-per/ *n* a person in charge of a house (*the man employed a housekeeper*).

housekeeping /**house**-kee-ping/ *n* the work of a housekeeper.

house music /**house**-myoo-zic/ *n* a kind of dance music developed in Chicago with a low base and rap sound.

House of Representatives /**house**-of-re-pri-**zen**-ta-tivz/ *n* a part of the US government responsible for creating laws.

house party /**house**-par-tee/ *n* a party of guests that stay overnight or for a few days.

house physician /**house** fi-**zi**-shun/ *n* a resident doctor at a hospital, hotel, etc.

houseplant /**house**-plant/ *n* a plant that is grown indoors for decoration.

house-raising /**house**-ray-zing/ *n* a gathering of the members of a community to help build a neighbor's house or its framework.

housesit /**house**-sit/ *vb* to stay in and care for a house while its owners are absent.

housewife /**house**-wife/ *n* a woman whose primary job it is to manage the home and family.

housework /**house**-wurk/ *n* the work involved in housekeeping such as cleaning, cooking, etc.

housing /**hou**-zing/ *n* shelter or lodging, the act of providing shelter.

hovel /**hu**-vel/ *n* a small, dirty house (*disease spreads rapidly in a hovel*).

hover /**hu**-ver/ *vb* **1** to stay in the air without moving (*hawks hovering*). **2** to stay near (*hover around to try and talk to the celebrity*).

hovercraft /**hu**-ver-craft/ *n* a type of car or boat that can skim over the surface of smooth land or water on a cushion of air.

how /**how**/ *adv* **1** in what manner or way (*how will you do this?*). **2** in what state or condition (*how do you feel?*). **3** for what reason or purpose (*how do you know that?*). **4** at what price (*how could you?*).

however /how-e-ver/ adv **1** in whatever way (get there however we can). **2** no matter how (however bad the conditions). **3** yet (he is very old—however, he is healthy).

howl /howl/ vb to give a long, loud cry, as a dog or wolf (the wind howling/people howling with laughter). **2** to wail, to cry (children howling with pain). ● also n.

hub /hub/ n **1** the central part of a wheel. **2** a center of interest or activity (the area is the hub of the business community).

hubcap /hub-cap/ n a cap over the center of a wheel on a car, truck, etc.

huckleberry /hu-cul-be-ree/ n a plant with dark blue berries, the berries from this plant.

huckster /huck-ster/ n a person who sells things from door to door or in the street (hucksters selling fruit and vegetables off their carts).

huddle /hu-dul/ vb to crowd together (people huddling together for warmth). ● n a close crowd (in a huddle to discuss the plan).

hue[1] /hyoo/ n (fml or lit) **1** color (materials of every hue). **2** shade of a color.

hue[2] /hyoo/ n. ● **hue and cry** **1** pursuit after a criminal. **2** a noisy expression of anger, a noisy protest (a hue and cry after the new road was canceled).

huevos rancheros /hway-voos-ran-che-ros/ n fried eggs with a creole sauce.

huff /huff/ n a fit of temper (he goes into a huff when he does not get his own way).

huffy /hu-fee/ adj easily angered.

hug /hug/ vb (**hugged** /hugd/, **hugging** /hu-ging/) **1** to hold tightly in the arms, to take lovingly in the arms. **2** to keep close to (cars hugging the side of the road in the fog). ● n a close grip, an embrace (an affectionate hug).

huge /hyoodge/ adj very big, enormous (a huge monster/a huge sum of money). ● n **hugeness** /hyoodge-ness/.

huh /hu/ interj used to express surprise, used to ask a question.

huipil /wee-peel/ n a loose-fitting, often colorful garment worn by women from Mexico and Guatemala.

hula /hoo-la/ n a native Hawaiian dance marked by flowing movements.

Hula-Hoop /hoo-la-hoop/ n a light hoop made of plastic that is twirled around the body.

hulk /hulk/ n **1** the body of an old ship. **2** anything difficult to move (a hulk of an old wardrobe). **3** a big, clumsy person or thing.

hulking /hul-king/ adj big and awkward (a hulking old dresser).

hull /hull/ n **1** the outer covering of a grain or seed. **2** the frame or body of a ship. ● vb to strip off the husk (hull raspberries).

hullabaloo /hu-la-ba-loo/ n noise and confusion.

hum /hum/ vb (**hummed** /humd/, **humming** /hu-ming/) **1** to make a buzzing sound (bees humming/machines humming). **2** to sing without words or with the mouth closed (hums a tune as she works). ● n **1** a buzzing noise (the hum of machinery). **2** the noise made by a bee when flying.

human /hyoo-man/ adj having to do with people (human diseases/human remains). ● n person.

humane /hyoo-mane/ adj kindly, merciful (it is humane to put to sleep very ill animals).

humanism /hyoo-ma-ni-zum/ n **1** love of literature and learning. **2** the belief that humans are the most important subject of study (she believes in humanism, not Christianity). ● n **humanist** /hyoo-ma-nist/.

humanitarian /hyoo-ma-ni-tay-ree-an/ n a person who works to lessen human suffering (humanitarians who go to poor areas to help the local people). ● also adj.

humanity /hyoo-ma-ni-tee/ n **1** all humankind. **2** kindness, feeling for others (he is cruel and totally lacking in humanity).

humanize /hyoo-ma-nize/ vb, also **humanise** (Br) **1** to civilize. **2** to make gentler, to make kind (marriage seemed to humanize him).

humankind /hyoo-man-kind/ n all people as a race.

humble /hum-bul/ adj thinking oneself unimportant, not proud, seeking no praise (too humble to see that she was being taken advantage of/show a humble attitude to his seniors). ● vb **1** to make humble (humbling herself by begging for her job back). **2** to lessen the importance or power of (humble the proud king). ● adv **humbly** /hum-blee/.

humdrum /hum-drum/ adj dull, ordinary, boring (lead a humdrum existence).

humerus /hyoo-me-rus/ n the bone that extends from the shoulder to the elbow.

humid /hyoo-mid/ adj moist, damp (a humid heat/humid weather).

humidify /hyoo-mi-di-fy/ vb to make damp, to moisten.

humidity /hyoo-mi-di-tee/ n dampness, the amount of moisture in the air.

humiliate /hyoo-mi-lee-ate/ vb to embarrass, to lessen the importance or power of, to lower the dignity or pride of (*humiliating her in front of the rest of the class by making her stand in the corner*). ● *n* **humiliation** /hyoo-mi-lee-**ay**-shun/.

humility /hyoo-**mi**-li-tee/ *n* the state of being humble (*people in lower positions in the firm were expected to behave with humility*).

hummingbird /**hu**-ming-burd/ *n* a small, brightly colored bird whose wings make a humming sound when it is flying.

hummus /**hu**-mus/ *n* a Middle Eastern dish made of mashed chickpeas and eaten as an appetizer.

humor /**hyoo**-mur/ *n, also* **humour** (*Br, Cdn*) **1** any fluid or juice of an animal or plant. **2** a comical or amusing quality (*a sense of humor/see the humor in the situation*). **3** a state of mind, mood (*in a good humor*).

humorist /**hyoo**-mu-rist/ *n* a person who writes or talks amusingly (*a humorist who has had several books published*).

humorous /**hyoo**-mu-rus/ *adj* **1** funny, amusing (*tell a humorous story*). **2** having or displaying a sense of humor (*a humorous person*).

hump /**hump**/ *n* a rounded lump, especially on the back (*camels have humps*). ● *adj* **humped** /**humpt**/, **humpy** /**hum**-pee/.

humpback /**hump**-back/ *n* a person with a lump on his or her back.

humph /**humf**/ *interj* used to express doubt, disgust.

humus /**hyoo**-mus/ *n* rotted leaves, etc., mixed into the earth (*humus fertilizing the soil*).

hunch /**hunch**/ *n* **1** a rounded hump, especially on the back. **2** (*inf*) an intuitive feeling, a hint (*I have a hunch that she is hiding something*).

hunchback /**hunch**-back/ *n* a person with a hunch on his or her back. ● *adj* **hunchbacked** /**hunch**-backt/.

hundred /**hun**-dred/ *n* 10 times 10, number after 99. ● *adj* **hundredth** /**hun**-dredth/.

hung *see* **hang**.

hunger /**hung**-ger/ *n* **1** a strong desire for food (*try to suppress his hunger until lunchtime*). **2** lack of food (*die of hunger*). **3** any strong desire (*a hunger for fame*). ● *vb* **1** (*old*) to feel hunger. **2** to desire greatly (*hunger for love*).

hungry /**hung**-gree/ *adj* **1** needing food, feeling or showing hunger (*hungry children asking for food*). **2** having a strong need or desire for (*hungry for love*).

hunk /**hungk**/ *n* (*inf*) a large piece, a chunk (*a hunk of cheese*).

hunker /**hung**-ker/ *vb* to creep or settle down.

hunt /**hunt**/ *vb* **1** to chase wild animals to kill or capture them (*hunting stags*). **2** to look for

(*hunting for his other sock*). **3** to follow so as to catch (*police hunting the escaped prisoner*). ● *n* **1** the act of hunting. **2** a group of people who meet to hunt wild animals.

hunter /**hun**-ter/ *n* a person who hunts (*f* **huntress** /**hun**-tress/).

huntsman /**hunts**-man/ *n* a person who hunts.

Hupa /**hoo**-pa/ *n* a member of a North American people from northwestern California, the language of this people.

hurdle /**hur**-dl/ *n* **1** a gatelike movable frame of wood or metal. **2** a wooden frame over which people or horses must jump in certain races (*the horse refused to jump the last hurdle*). **3** obstruction, obstacle (*their major hurdle is lack of money*).

hurl /**hurl**/ *vb* to throw with force (*hurling a brick through the window/hurl abuse*).

Huron /**hyoo**-ron/ *n* a member of a group of Native American peoples that lived between Georgian Bay and Lake Ontario, that now live in Oklahoma and Quebec, the language of this people.

hurrah /hu-**ra**/, **hurray** /hu-**ray**/ *interj* a cry of joy.

hurricane /**hu**-ri-cane/ *n* a violent storm, a very strong wind (*parts of America flattened by a hurricane*).

hurried /**hu**-reed/ *adj* **1** done quickly, often too quickly, hasty (*a hurried exit/a hurried reply*).

hurry /**hu**-ree/ *vb* **1** to do or go quickly (*hurrying to catch a train*). **2** to make to go quickly (*hurried the children along*). ● *n* haste, speed (*in a hurry*).

hurt /**hurt**/ *vb* (*pt, pp* **hurt** /**hurt**/) **1** to cause pain to, to wound, to injure (*hurt his hand on broken glass*). **2** to upset (*hurt by his remarks*). ● *n* (*fml*) **1** a wound, an injury. **2** harm.

hurtful /**hurt**-ful/ *adj* harmful (*hurtful remarks*).

husband /**huz**-band/ *n* a married man (*husband and wife*). ● *vb* to use or spend carefully (*husband their resources*).

husbandry /**huz**-ban-dree/ *n* **1** (*old*) farming. **2** (*fml*) careful spending.

hush /**hush**/ *n* silence, stillness (*in the hush of the evening/a hush descended on the room*). ● *vb* **1** to make silent (*try to hush the children*). **2** to become silent (*ask the children to hush*). ● **hush up** to prevent something becoming generally known (*try to hush up the family scandal*). ● *interj* quiet! silence!

husk /**husk**/ *n* the dry outer covering of a grain or seed, or of certain fruits.

husky[1] /**huss**-kee/ *adj* **1** hoarse, dry, and rough (*a husky voice*). **2** hefty, strong.

husky[2] /**huss**-kee/ *n* an Arctic sled dog.

hut /hut/ *n* a small, roughly built house, a wooden shed (*a garden hut*).

hutch /hutch/ *n* a boxlike cage for rabbits.

hyacinth /**hie**-a-sinth/ *n* a bulbous plant with bell-like flowers and a strong scent.

hybrid /**hie**-brid/ *n* a plant or animal resulting from the mixing of two different kinds or species (*a mule is a hybrid of a horse and a donkey*). ● *adj* bred from two different kinds. ● *vb* **hybridize** /**hie**-bri-dize/, *also* **hybridise** (*Br*).

hydrant /**hie**-drant/ *n* a pipe from the main water pipe of a street from which water may be drawn direct (*firemen attaching their hose to a hydrant*).

hydraulic /hie-**draw**-lic/ *adj* worked by the pressure of water or other liquid (*hydraulic brakes*).

hydro- /**hie**-dro/ *prefix* having to do with water.

hydroelectric /hie-dro-we-**lec**-tric/ *adj* having to do with electricity obtained by water power.

hydrogen /**hie**-dro-jen/ *n* an invisible gas with no color or smell that with oxygen forms water.

hydrogen bomb /**hie**-dro-jen **bom**/ *n* an extremely destructive nuclear bomb.

hydroplane /**hie**-dro-plane/ *n* **1** an attachment of an airplane that enables it to glide along the water. **2** a speedboat that skims the surface of the water. ● *also vb.*

hyena /hie-**ee**-na/ *n* a doglike animal that eats dead flesh (*hyenas make a sound like a human laughing*).

hygiene /**hie**-jeen/ *n* **1** the study of clean and healthy living. **2** clean and healthy living (*careful about personal hygiene*).

hygienic /hie-**jee**-nic/ *adj* having to do with hygiene, clean (*a kitchen that was not hygienic*).

hymn /him/ *n* a song of praise, especially to God.

hymnal, hymnary /**him**-nal/ *n* a book of hymns.

hype /hipe/ *vb* to promote in an extravagant way. ● *n* such promotion.

hyperactive /hie-per-**ac**-tiv/ *adj* too active and unable to sit still for very long (*a hyperactive child*).

hyperbole /hie-**per**-bo-lee/ *n* a figure of speech by which a statement is exaggerated in a striking way, i.e. he is as strong as an ox. ● *adj* **hyperbolic** /hie-per-**bol**-ic/.

hypertension /**hie**-per-ten-shun/ *n* very high blood pressure.

hyphen /**hie**-fen/ *n* a short dash (-) between syllables or between words joined to express a single idea.

hypnosis /hip-**no**-sis/ *n* a sleeplike state in which the person who induced the hypnosis has a certain amount of control over the sleeper's actions

(*she wondered if hypnosis could cure her addiction to smoking*).

hypnotic /hip-**not**-ic/ *adj* producing sleep (*a hypnotic state*).

hypnotism /**hip**-no-ti-zum/ *n* the art of producing hypnosis.

hypnotist /**hip**-no-tist/ *n* a person who has the power to hypnotize others.

hypnotize /**hip**-no-tize/ *vb, also* **hypnotise** (*Br*) to will a person into a sleeplike state and to then control the sleeper's actions.

hypochondria /hie-po-**con**-dree-a/ *n* a condition in which someone is overanxious about his or her health, constantly believing that he or she is ill when he or she is not (*she is physically healthy but she is a hypochondriac*). ● **hypochondriac** /hie-po-**con**-dree-ac/ *n* a person who suffers from hypochondria.

hypocrisy /hi-**poc**-ri-see/ *n* the pretence of being good or of having beliefs or feelings that one does not have (*it was hypocrisy for him to tell me to clean my room because his is messier than mine*).

hypocrite /**hi**-po-crit/ *n* a person who pretends to be good but is not so, a person who says one thing and does another.

hypocritical /hi-po-**cri**-ti-cal/ *adj* not sincere, false.

hypotenuse /hie-paw-**te**-nooz/ *n* the side opposite the right angle of a triangle, the longest side of a right triangle.

hypothermia /hie-po-**ther**-mee-a/ *n* a serious medical condition in which the body temperature is much lower than normal because of prolonged exposure to cold.

hypothesis /hie-**poth**-e-sis/ *n* an idea accepted as true for the basis of an argument, something supposed true but not proved so. ● *adj* **hypothetical** /hie-po-**thet**-ic-al/.

hysterectomy /hi-ste-**rec**-to-me/ *n* the surgical removal of all or part of the uterus.

hysteria *n* **1** a disorder of the nerves, causing a person to laugh or cry violently, have imaginary illnesses, etc. (*she suffers from bouts of hysteria*). **2** lack of control, uncontrolled excitement (*the mass hysteria of the crowd when the president was killed*).

hysterics /hi-**ste**-rics/ *n* **1** a fit of hysteria (*she went into hysterics when she heard of his death*). **2** (*inf*) an uncontrollable fit of laughter (*the audience was in hysterics at the comic's jokes*).

hysterical /hi-**ste**-ri-cal/ *adj* **1** suffering from hysteria. **2** caused by hysteria (*a hysterical illness*). **3** (*inf*) very funny (*a hysterical sight*).

I

I, i /eye/ the ninth letter of the alphabet.

I /eye/ pron meaning the person speaking or writing.

ice /eyess/ n 1 frozen water (take some ice from the freezer for the drinks). ● vb 1 to cool in ice. 2 to cover with icing.

Ice Age /eye-sage/ n a time when large amounts of ice and glaciers cover many areas of the earth.

iceboat /eyess-boat/ n a light boatlike frame set on runners and designed to be ridden on ice by wind going through a sail.

icebox /eyess-boks/ n a cabinet, box, or room with ice in it for keeping things cold.

icebreaker /eyess-bray-ker/ n a ship designed for cutting its way through ice.

ice cap /eyess-cap/ n a dome-shaped mass of ice that spreads slowly outward from the center.

ice cream /eyess-creem/ n 1 cream or a mixture of creamy substances flavored, sweetened, and frozen (a store selling ice cream). 2 a portion of ice cream (buy two ice creams).

ice fishing /eyess-fi-shing/ fishing on a frozen lake or stream through a hole in the ice.

ice floe /eyess-flo/ n a large sheet of floating ice.

ice hockey /eyess-hock-ee/ see hockey.

ice pack /eyess-pack/ n ice collected and put into a bag or container of some kind, used to cool things down (put the ice pack in the cooler for the picnic/ put an ice pack on her knee to reduce the swelling).

ice pick /eyess-pick/ n a sharp, pointed metal tool used to chip ice pieces away from a larger block of ice.

ice skate /eyess-skate/ n footwear with a blade on the bottom, used for skating on the ice.

ichthyosaur /ic-thee-o-sawr/ n a huge fishlike prehistoric reptile.

icicle /eye-si-cul/ n a long, hanging, pointed piece of ice formed by the freezing of falling water (icicles hanging from the roof).

icily /eye-si-lee/ adv in an icy manner, very coldly.

icing /eye-sing/ n a mixture of fine powdery sugar with liquid used to cover cakes (cover the cake with chocolate icing). ● also frosting.

icon /eye-con/ n 1 a religious picture or statue, an image. 2 a famous person or thing that many people admire and regard as a symbol of a way of life, set of beliefs. 3 a small symbol on a computer screen that represents a program or file (click on that icon using the mouse). ● adj iconic /eye-con-ic/.

icy /eye-see/ adj 1 very cold (icy weather). 2 covered with ice (icy roads). 3 unfriendly (an icy stare).

ID /eye-dee/ abbr = identification.

idea /eye-dee-ya/ n 1 a plan, thought, or suggestion (I have an idea for a book). 2 a picture in the mind (an idea of the house that they are looking for). 3 an opinion or belief (political ideas).

ideal /eye-deel/ n 1 a perfect example (her ideal of what a husband should be). 2 high principles or perfect standards, a person's standard of behavior, etc. (a person of high ideals). ● adj 1 perfect (an ideal wife/an ideal job). 2 extremely suitable (a tool that is ideal for the job). 3 expressing possible perfection that is unlikely to exist (ideal happiness). ● adv ideally /eye-dee-lee/.

idealism /eye-dee-li-zum/ n the desire to achieve perfection, the state of having high principles or perfect standards (he is full of idealism about marriage). ● n idealist /eye-dee-list/. ● adj idealistic /eye-dee-li-stic/.

idealize, idealise /eye-dee-lize/ vb to think of as perfect or better than reality (he gives an idealized account of life at the beginning of the century).

identical /eye-den-ti-cul/ adj 1 the very same (this is the identical car that was here yesterday). 2 the same, exactly alike (they were wearing identical dresses).

identification /eye-den-ti-fi-cay-shun/ n 1 act of recognizing (identification of the mysterious gentleman was difficult). 2 something that is proof of or a sign of identity (you require identification to get into the club). 3 the feeling that one shares ideas, feelings, etc., with another person (her identification with the unhappy woman whom she was reading about).

identify /eye-den-ti-fie/ vb 1 to think of as being the same (she identifies wealth with happiness). 2 to recognize as being a certain person or thing (she had to identify her attacker in a lineup). 3 to discover or recognize (identified the cause of the problem).

identity /eye-den-ti-tee/ n 1 (fml) the state of being the same. 2 who a person is (have to prove her identity).

ideology /eye-dee-**ol**-o-jee/ *n* **1** the study of the nature and origin of ideas. **2** a system of ideas (*political ideologies*).

idiocy /i-dee-u-see/ *n* **1** the state of being an idiot. **2** a foolish action (*the idiocies committed by fast drivers in the fog*).

idiom /i-dee-um/ *n* **1** the language or dialect of a certain group of people (*the idiom of American English*). **2** a group of words that together have an unexpected meaning different from the exact sense (*the expression "white elephant" is an idiom for an object that is of value to someone other than the owner*).

idiosyncrasy /i-dee-yo-**sing**-cra-see/ *n* an odd way of behaving (*it is one of her idiosyncrasies to talk to herself*). ● *adj* **idiosyncratic** /i-dee-yo-sing-**cra**-tic/ (*an idiosyncratic habit of putting salt on pudding*).

idiot /i-dee-yot/ *n* **1** (*old or fml*) a person with very low intelligence. **2** a foolish or stupid person (*he was an idiot to drive without a license*). ● *adj* **idiotic** /i-dee-**yaw**-tic/. ● *adv* **idiotically** /i-dee-**yaw**-tic-lee/. ● *see* **idiocy**.

idle /**eye**-dul/ *adj* **1** doing nothing, not working, not in use (*workers forced to be idle for lack of work/ machines lying idle*). **2** lazy (*idle people who don't want to work*). **3** having no effect or results (*idle threats*). ● *vb* **1** (*fml*) to be idle, to do nothing (*enjoy idling on holiday*). **2** (*of a machine*) to run without doing work (*the car engine was idling*). ● *n* **idleness** /**eye**-dul-ness/. ● *n* **idler** /**eyed**-ler/. ● *adv* **idly** /**eyed**-lee/.

idol /**eye**-dul/ *n* **1** a statue or other object that is worshipped. **2** a person regarded with too great love and respect (*he made an idol out of his father*).

idolize, idolise (*Br*) /**eye**-dol-ize/ *vb* to love or admire very greatly (*he idolizes his wife, although she is not very pleasant*).

idyll /**eye**-dil/ *n* a poem about simple country life (*an idyll about a shepherd and his sweetheart*).

idyllic /eye-**di**-lic/ *adj* **1** perfectly happy, pleasant (*an idyllic marriage*). **2** charming, picturesque (*a cottage in an idyllic setting*).

if /**if**/ *conj* on condition that, in case, supposing (*if I were you*).

igloo /i-**gloo**/ *n* an Eskimo house or hut, usually dome shaped and made of blocks of frozen snow.

igneous /**ig**-nee-us/ *adj* (*of rocks*) formed from lava from a volcano.

ignite /ig-**nite**/ *vb* **1** to set fire to (*drop a match and ignite the gasoline*). **2** to catch fire (*the gasoline leaking from the car ignited*).

ignition /ig-**ni**-shun/ *n* **1** act of setting fire to. **2** the part of a motor engine that sets fire to the fuel that drives the engine (*turn the key in the ignition*).

ignoble /ig-**no**-bul/ *adj* **1** (*fml*) mean, dishonorable (*an ignoble action*). **2** (*old*) of low birth.

ignoramus /ig-ni-**ray**-mus/ *n* a person with little or no knowledge (*she's an ignoramus when it comes to cooking*).

ignorance /**ig**-ni-ranse/ *n* **1** want of knowledge (*his ignorance of mathematics*). **2** lack of awareness or knowledge (*his ignorance of what they were really doing*).

ignorant /**ig**-ni-rant/ *adj* **1** having little or no knowledge (*ignorant about financial matters*). **2** unaware of (*he was ignorant of the true facts*).

ignore /ig-**nore**/ *vb* to take no notice of, to refuse to pay attention to (*she completely ignored her old friend/try to ignore her problems/ignoring his advice*).

iguana /ig-**wa**-na/ *n* any of a large family of lizards with spines along its back and that eats vegetation or insects.

ihram /i-ram/ *n* **1** a costume worn by Muslims when traveling to Mecca consisting of one piece of white cotton around the waist and hips and another over the shoulder. **2** the rules that have to be followed when dressed in this way.

ill /**ill**/ *adj* **1** sick (*ill patients*). **2** bad (*ill health*). **3** evil, harmful (*ill luck*). ● *n* **1** evil, harm (*wish him ill*). **2** trouble (*all the ills of the world*). ● *adv* badly (*treat him ill*).

I'll /**eyel**/ *contraction* I will.

illegal /i-**lee**-gal/ *adj* against the law. ● *n* **illegality** /i-le-**ga**-li-tee/.

illegible /i-**le**-ji-bul/ *adj* that cannot be read, badly written (*illegible handwriting*).

illegitimate /i-le-**ji**-ti-mit/ *adj* born of unmarried parents (*his illegitimate daughter*). ● *n* **illegitimacy** /i-le-**ji**-ti-mi-see/.

illicit /i-**li**-sit/ *adj* unlawful, against the law (*the illicit trade in drugs*).

Illinois /i-li-**noy**/ *n* a member of a group of native American people who lived in northern Illinois, southern Wisconsin and parts of Iowa and Missouri, the language spoken by these people.

illiterate /i-**li**-trit/ *adj* **1** unable to read or write (*illiterate people seeking help with reading lessons*). **2** uneducated (*an illiterate note*). ● *n* **illiteracy** /i-**li**-tra-see/.

illness /**ill**-ness/ *n* sickness, the state of being unwell (*off work because of illness/childhood illnesses*).

illogical /i-**lodge**-ic-al/ *adj* **1** not using reasoning, not reasonable (*illogical people*). **2** against the rules of reasoning (*his action was completely illogical*). ● *n* illogic the state of being illogical.

illuminate /i-**loo**-mi-nate/ *vb* **1** (*old*) to light up (*strings of little lights illuminating the garden*). **2** (*of books, etc.*) to decorate with bright colors (*early illuminated manuscripts prepared by monks*). **3** to explain, to make clear (*could you illuminate a few points in the legal agreement*).

illumination /i-loo-mi-**nay**-shun/ *n* (*fml*) **1** a lighting up. **2** decorative lights (*the town's Christmas illuminations*). **3** a picture or decoration painted on a page of a book (*illuminations on early manuscripts*). **4** explanation, clarification (*a few points in need of illumination*).

illusion /i-**loo**-zhun/ *n* **1** a deception, an unreal image or appearance (*an optical illusion*). **2** a wrong belief, a false idea (*she had illusions that she was very beautiful*). ● *adj* illusory /i-**loo**-su-ree/.

illusionist /i-**loo**-zhu-nist/ *n* a person who performs tricks that deceive the eye, a magician.

illusive /i-**loo**-siv/ *adj* unreal.

illustrate /i-lu-strate/ *vb* **1** to make clear by examples (*illustrating the movement of traffic by a diagram*). **2** to provide pictures for a book or magazine (*she illustrates children's books*).

illustration /i-lu-**stray**-shun/ *n* **1** an example that makes something easier to understand or demonstrates something (*an illustration of his meanness*). **2** a picture in a book or magazine (*color illustrations*).

illustrative /i-lu-stra-tiv/ *adj* helping to explain (*illustrative examples*).

illustrious /i-**lu**-stree-us/ *adj* (*fml*) famous (*illustrious former pupils*).

ill will /ill-**will**/ unfriendly feeling, hate, dislike.

image /i-midge/ *n* **1** a likeness, form (*an image in the mirror*). **2** a likeness or copy of a person, etc., made of stone, wood, etc. (*images of famous people*). **3** a statue or picture that is worshipped. **4** a picture formed of an object in front of a mirror or lens. **5** a picture in the mind (*have an image of what life would be like in 10 years*). **6** the impression that a person or organization gives to the public (*we must improve the firm's image*).

imagery /i-**midge**-ree/ *n* figures of speech, words chosen because they call up striking pictures in the mind (*the poet's use of imagery*).

imaginable /i-**ma**-ji-na-bul/ *adj* that can be imagined.

imaginary /i-**ma**-ji-na-ree/ *adj* existing in the mind only, not real (*a child with an imaginary friend*).

imagination /i-ma-ji-**nay**-shun/ *n* **1** the power of inventing stories, persons, etc., creative ability (*it requires a lot of imagination to write for children/ a play showing a great deal of imagination*). **2** the power of forming pictures in the mind (*able to see it all in her imagination*). **3** the seeing or hearing of things that do not exist (*she said that she heard noises in the night, but it was just her imagination*).

imaginative /i-**ma**-ji-na-tiv/ *adj* **1** having a good imagination (*an imaginative person*). **2** demonstrating imagination (*an imaginative production of the play/imaginative designs*).

imagine /i-**ma**-jin/ *vb* **1** to form a picture in the mind (*I can imagine her reaction*). **2** to form ideas of things that do not exist or of events that have not happened (*she imagined that she met an alien*). **3** to suppose (*I imagine that he will arrive on time*).

imam /i-**mam**/ *n* the leader of prayer in a Muslim mosque, any of various Muslim leaders.

imbalance /im-**ba**-lanse/ *n* lack of balance.

imbecile /**im**-bu-sil/ *n* **1** (*fml*) a weak-minded person. **2** a fool, an idiot. ● *n* imbecility /im-bu-**si**-li-tee/.

imitate /i-mi-tate/ *vb* to copy, to try to be, behave, or look the same as (*imitating his voice/imitate her style of writing*). ● *n* imitator /i-mi-**tay**-tor/.

imitation /i-mi-**tay**-shun/ *n* **1** act of imitating. **2** a copy (*not the original painting but an imitation*).

imitative /i-**mi**-ta-tiv/ *adj* **1** done as a copy (*an imitative piece of work*). **2** fond of copying (*an imitative poet*).

immaculate /i-**ma**-cyu-lit/ *adj* **1** (*old*) pure. **2** spotless, perfectly clean (*immaculate white shorts*). **3** perfect (*an immaculate performance*).

immaterial /i-ma-**tee**-ree-al/ *adj* **1** not consisting of matter, spiritual. **2** unimportant (*it is immaterial how you get here as long as you do*).

immature /i-ma-**toor**/ *adj* **1** unripe. **2** not fully grown. **3** lacking experience and wisdom. ● *n* immaturity /i-ma-**too**-ri-tee/.

immeasurable /i-**mezh**-ra-bul/ *adj* huge, that cannot be measured, vast (*immeasurable damage*).

immediate /i-**mee**-dee-it/ *adj* **1** happening at once (*an immediate improvement*). **2** direct, without anyone or anything coming between (*her* *immediate successor*). **3** near, close (*her immediate surroundings*). ● *n* **immediacy** /i-**mee**-dee-a-see/ the quality or condition of being immediate.

immediately /i-**mee**-dee-it-lee/ *adv* **1** at once (*you must reply immediately*). **2** closely (*houses immediately next to the station*).

immense /i-**mense**/ *adj* huge (*an immense improvement/an immense stretch of grassland*). ● *n* **immensity** /i-**men**-si-tee/.

immerse /i-**merse**/ *vb* **1** to put into water (*immersing the vegetables in boiling water*). **2** to give a person's whole attention to (*immersed in his work*). ● *n* **immersion** /i-**mer**-shun/.

immigrant /i-mi-grant/ *n* a person who immigrates, or moves to another country (*immigrants came to America to start a new life*). ● *adj* of or relating to immigrants.

immigrate /i-mi-grate/ *vb* (*fml*) to enter and settle in a new country. ● *n* **immigration** /i-mi-**gray**-shun/.

imminent /i-mi-nent/ *adj* just about to happen, near in time (*in imminent danger*). ● *n* **imminence** /i-mi-nense/.

immobile /i-**mo**-bul/ *adj* not moving, unable to move (*lying there immobile as if dead/he is immobile since breaking both legs*). ● *n* **immobility** /i-mo-bi-li-tee/. ● vb **immobilize** /i-**mo**-bi-lize/, *also* **immobilise** (*Br*).

immoderate /i-**mod**-rit/ *adj* more than is proper, uncontrolled (*immoderate spending*).

immodest /i-**mod**-est/ *adj* (*fml*) **1** shameless, indecent (*the immodest behavior of the young people/an immodest outfit*). **2** not modest (*an immodest pride in his own achievements*). ● *n* **immodesty** /i-**mod**-es-tee/.

immoral /i-**maw**-ral/ *adj* wrong, evil, wicked (*immoral actions/an immoral person*). ● *n* **immorality** /i-maw-ra-li-tee/.

immoralist /i-**maw**-ra-list/ *n* an immoral person.

immortal /i-**mawr**-tul/ *adj* **1** living or lasting forever. **2** famous for all time (*Shakespeare is immortal*).

immortality /i-**mawr**-ta-li-tee/ *n* **1** everlasting life. **2** undying fame (*the undoubted immortality of Shakespeare*).

immortalize /i-**mawr**-tu-lize/ *vb, also* **immortalise** (*Br*) **1** to make immortal. **2** to make famous for all time (*she was immortalized in a poem by her lover*).

immovable /i-**moo**-va-bul/ *adj* **1** not able to be moved (*immovable objects*). **2** not changing easily (*immovable opinions*).

immune /i-**myoon**/ *adj* **1** free from, specially protected from (*immune from taxation*). **2** not to be infected by (*immune from chicken pox because she has had it already*). ● *n* **immunity** /i-**myoo**-ni-tee/.

immune system /i-**myoon sis**-tem/ *n* the system that protects the body from disease.

immunize /i-**myoo**-nize/ *vb, also* **immunise** (*Br*) to inject disease germs into the blood stream to cause a mild attack of an illness and so make the person immune to it (*immunizing the children so they won't get measles*).

immunology /i-myu-**nol**-o-jee/ *n* the study of the immune system.

imp /imp/ *n* **1** in fairy tales, an evil spirit, a devil's child. **2** a mischievous child (*the little imp stole an apple*).

impact /im-**pact**/ *n* **1** the force with which one thing strikes another (*thrown out of the car by the impact of it hitting the wall*). **2** a collision (*the car was wrecked on impact with the wall*). **3** a strong effect or impression (*the impact on the audience of the politician's speech*).

impair /im-**pair**/ *vb* to make worse, to weaken (*his vision is impaired*).

impale /im-**pale**/ *vb* to fix upon something sharp, to pierce (*he fell out of the window and was impaled on the railings below*).

impart /im-**part**/ *vb* (*fml*) **1** to tell (*impart new information*). **2** to give or share (*impart courage to his troops*).

impartial /im-**par**-shal/ *adj* fair, just, not taking sides (*an impartial judgment*).

impartiality /im-par-shee-a-li-tee/ *n* fairness, treating all parties or persons in the same way.

impassive /im-**pa**-siv/ *adj* **1** not showing strong feeling, not feeling pain (*a totally impassive expression*). **2** calm, unexcited (*he remained impassive as the judge passed sentence*).

impatient /im-**pay**-shent/ *adj* not willing to wait, easily angered by delay (*a very impatient person/in an impatient mood*). ● *n* **impatience** /im-**pay**-shense/.

impeach /im-**peech**/ *vb* **1** to charge with a crime. **2** to charge an important person with a crime (*politicians impeached for accepting bribes*). **3** (*fml*) to raise doubts about (*impeach the character of the manager*). ● *n* **impeachment** /im-**peech**-ment/.

impeccable /im-**pe**-ca-bul/ *adj* faultless (*his behavior was impeccable*).

imperative /im-**pe**-ra-tiv/ *adj* **1** commanding. **2**

necessary, urgent (*it is imperative that we get more supplies*).

imperfect /im-**per**-fect/ *adj* having faults, not perfect (*goods that are slightly imperfect*). ● *n* **imperfection** /im-per-**fec**-shun/.

imperial /im-**pee**-ree-al/ *adj* **1** having to do with an empire or emperor (*Great Britain's former imperial power*). **2** of a country that has control over other countries or colonies.

impersonal /im-**per**-snal/ *adj* **1** not influenced by personal feelings (*an impersonal account of the situation/impersonal places such as hospitals*). **2** (*of verbs*) occurring only in the third person singular, usually with "it" as the subject (*it is snowing*). ● *vb* **impersonalize** /im-**per**-sna-lize/, *also* **impersonalise** (*Br*).

impersonate /im-**per**-su-nate/ *vb* to pretend to be someone else (*she impersonated her older sister to get into the club*).

impertinent /im-**pert**-nent/ *adj* not showing proper manners, purposely disrespectful (*punish the impertinent children*). ● *n* **impertinence** /im-**pert**-nense/.

impetuous /im-**pech**-wus/ *adj* acting without thinking first, rash, hasty (*an impetuous young woman/regret his impetuous decision*). ● *n* **impetuosity** /im-pe-che-**wos**-i-tee/.

impish /im-pish/ *adj* mischievous (*an impish sense of humor*).

implant /im-plant/ *vb* **1** to plant firmly. **2** to place in. **3** to teach.

implement /im-ple-ment/ *n* a tool, an instrument (*garden implements*). ● *vb* **implement** /im-ple-ment/ to put into practice (*implement an agreement*).

implicate /im-pli-cate/ *vb* to show that a person is involved or connected with (an affair), to mix up in (*when he was arrested, his statement implicated two of his friends*).

implication /im-pli-**cay**-shun/ *n* something hinted at but not said openly (*by implication, he was accusing her of lying*).

implicit /im-**pli**-sit/ *adj* **1** understood but not said (*his implicit criticism*). **2** unquestioning, without doubts (*implicit faith*).

implode /im-**plode**/ *vb* to burst or collapse inward. ● *n* **implosion** /im-**plo**-zhun/.

implore /im-**plore**/ *vb* to ask earnestly, to beg (*imploring him to forgive her*).

imply /im-**ply**/ *vb* to suggest something without saying it openly, to hint (*he implied that she was lying*).

impolite /im-pu-**lite**/ *adj* (*fml*) rude, ill-mannered (*impolite table manners*).

import /im-**poart**/ *vb* to bring in goods from abroad (*import silk from China*). ● *n* **import** /im-**poart**/ something brought in from abroad. ● *n* **importer** /im-poar-ter/.

important /im-**poar**-tant/ *adj* **1** deserving great attention (*an important book*). **2** having results that affect many people (*important decisions*). **3** having a high position (*important people in the land*). ● *n* **importance** /im-**poar**-tanse/. ● *adv* **importantly** /im-**poar**-tant-lee/.

importation /im-poar-**tay**-shun/ *n* an importing or being imported.

impose /im-**poaz**/ *vb* **1** to lay on or place (as a duty, tax, etc.). **2** to force to accept (*imposing his authority on others*). ● **impose on** to take advantage of, to exploit, to make unfair demands on (*they imposed on her by getting her to baby-sit free of charge*).

imposing /im-**poa**-zing/ *adj* important-looking, stately (*an imposing building*).

imposition /im-pu-**zi**-shun/ *n* **1** the act of laying on or placing (*the imposition of taxes*). **2** a tax. **3** an unfair demand (*it was an imposition to get him to give her a lift to work every day*).

impossible /im-**poss**-i-bul/ *adj* not able to be done or achieved (*an impossible dream*). ● *n* **impossibility** /im-poss-i-**bi**-li-tee/.

impostor or **imposter** /im-**poss**-tor/ *n* a person who pretends to be someone else, a deceiver (*they realized he was an impostor when the real policeman turned up*).

imposture /im-**poss**-chur/ *n* the act or practice of an impostor, fraud, deception.

impotent /im-pu-tent/ *adj* lacking power, helpless, weak (*impotent against the force of the storm/full of impotent rage*).

impractical /im-**prac**-ti-cal/ *adj* not practical, not workable or useful.

imprecise /im-pri-**sise**/ *adj* not precise, exact, or definite.

impregnate /im-**preg**-nate/ *vb* **1** to fill with (*water impregnated with salt*). **2** to fertilize or make pregnant.

impress /im-**press**/ *vb* **1** to mark by pressing into, to stamp (*impress a pattern on the clay pots before baking them*). **2** to fix in the mind (*try to impress the details in her memory*). **3** to stress, to emphasize the importance of (*impress the need for them to hurry*). ● *adj* **impressible** /im-**pre**-si-bul/.

impression /im-**pre**-shun/ n **1** the mark left by pressing or stamping (*the impression of his heel in the mud*). **2** the number of copies of a book printed at one time. **3** an effect on the mind or feelings (*his appearance creates a bad impression*). **4** a not very clear idea or memory (*I have a vague impression that she left early*). **5** an attempt to copy, in a humorous way, someone else's voice, behavior, appearance, etc. (*he does impressions*).

impressionable /im-**presh**-na-bul/ adj easily influenced (*impressionable people were fooled by him*).

impressionism /im-**pre**-shu-ni-zum/ n an way of painting created by artists who attempted to represent scenes just as they appeared at a certain moment by using color and brush strokes in a specific way; also used to describe similar attempts in writing and music.

impressionist /im-**pre**-shu-nist/ n **1** an artist who practices impressionism. **2** a person who does impressions of people, especially as a form of entertainment. ● *also adj.*

impressive /im-**pre**-siv/ adj **1** important-looking (*an impressive building*). **2** causing deep feeling, such as admiration (*an impressive performance*).

imprint /im-**print**/ vb **1** to make a mark by pressing or printing. **2** to fix in the memory (*her sad expression is imprinted on my memory*). ● n **imprint** /**im**-print/ **1** that which is imprinted. **2** a publisher's name, address, etc., on a book.

imprison /im-**pri**-zon/ vb to put into prison, to shut in.

imprisonment /im-**pri**-zon-ment/ n the act of imprisoning or the state of being imprisoned (*the accused is facing imprisonment*).

improbable /im-**prob**-a-bul/ adj not likely to happen or to be true (*an improbable ending to the story*). ● n **improbability** /im-prob-a-bi-li-tee/.

impromptu /im-**prom**-too/ adj not prepared (*an impromptu speech*). ● adv without preparation.

improper /im-**prop**-er/ adj **1** wrong (*accused of improper use of the company's funds*). **2** not suitable, not polite (*improper behavior on such a formal occasion*). **3** indecent (*make improper suggestions to a colleague*).

improper fraction /im-**prop**-er **frac**-shun/ n a fraction greater than 1, in which the denominator is less than the numerator (e.g., $^5/_2$).

impropriety /im-pru-**prie**-i-tee/ n (*fml*) incorrect or impolite behavior, the quality of being improper (*accused of impropriety in conducting the legal case*).

improve /im-**proov**/ vb to make or become better (*do something to improve the situation/a patient beginning to improve*). ● n **improvement** /im-**proov**-ment/.

improvise /im-pru-**vize**/ vb **1** to make something from material that is available (*improvising a shelter*). **2** to make something up at the moment required without preparation (*the pianist had no music and so had to improvise*). ● n **improvisation** /im-pru-vi-**zay**-shun/.

imprudent /im-**proo**-dent/ adj rash, acting without forethought, unwise (*it was imprudent of her to give up her job before she found another one*). ● n **imprudence** /im-**proo**-dense/.

impudent /im-**pyu**-dent/ adj disrespectful, shameless, saucy (*the impudent child stuck her tongue out at the teacher*). ● n **impudence** /**im**-pyu-dense/.

impulse /**im**-pulse/ n **1** a force causing movement (*an electrical impulse*). **2** a sudden desire or decision to act at once (*she bought the new dress on impulse*).

impulsive /im-**pul**-siv/ adj **1** done without forethought (*an impulsive decision to buy an expensive dress*). **2** acting without thinking first (*an impulsive young man*). ● n **impulsiveness** /im-**pul**-siv-ness/.

impure /im-**pyoor**/ adj **1** dirty, polluted (*impure water*). **2** mixed with something else (*impure drugs*). **3** sinful (*impure thoughts*). ● n **impurity** /im-**pyoo**-ri-tee/.

in /in/ prep **1** contained or enclosed by (*in the room*). **2** wearing, clothed by (*dress in her best*). **3** during the course of (*done in a day*). **4** at or before the end of (*return in an hour*). **5** being a member of or worker at (*in the navy*).

inability /i-na-**bi**-li-tee/ n lack of power, state of being unable (*his inability to control his dog*).

inaccessible /i-nac-**se**-si-bul/ adj not able to be reached or approached (*towns made inaccessible by the storm*).

inaccurate /i-**na**-cyu-rit/ adj **1** not correct (*an inaccurate answer to the mathematical problem*). **2** not exact (*an inaccurate description*). ● n **inaccuracy** /i-**na**-cyu-ri-see/.

inaction /i-**nac**-shun/ n idleness, lack of action (*local councilors accused of inaction following the floods*).

inactive /i-**nac**-tiv/ adj **1** not taking much exercise (*inactive office workers*). **2** no longer working or operating (*an inactive volcano*). **3** not taking an active part (*inactive members of the political party*).

inadequate /i-**na**-de-kwit/ *adj* **1** not good enough (*inadequate attempts*). **2** not sufficient (*inadequate supplies*). ● *n* **inadequacy** /i-na-de-kwi-see/.

inadmissible /i-nad-**mi**-sa-bul/ *adj* not able to be allowed (*evidence that is inadmissible in court*).

inadvertent /i-nad-**ver**-tent/ *adj* **1** without care or attention (*inadvertent damage*). **2** not on purpose (*an inadvertent insult*). ● *n* **inadvertence** /i-nad-ver-tense/.

inadvertently /i-nad-**ver**-tent-lee/ *adv* not purposely (*he inadvertently damaged his neighbor's gate with his car*).

inadvisable /i-nad-**vie**-za-bul/ *adj* not wise, not advisable.

inane /i-**nane**/ *adj* foolish, silly, lacking sense (*make inane remarks*). ● *n* **inanity** /i-**na**-ni-tee/.

inanimate /i-**na**-ni-mit/ *adj* without life (*rocks are inanimate objects*).

inappropriate /i-na-**pro**-pree-it/ *adj* not suitable, fitting, or proper (*an inappropriate remark/wear inappropriate clothes*).

inapt /i-**napt**/ *adj* not suitable, not appropriate, not proper (*inapt humorous remarks at a serious meeting*).

inarticulate /i-nar-**ti**-cyu-lit/ *adj* **1** not clear (*an inarticulate account*). **2** unable to express oneself clearly (*too inarticulate to give a clear account of the accident*).

inattentive /i-na-**ten**-tiv/ *adj* not attentive, neglectful, absentminded (*inattentive pupils*).

inaudible /i-**naw**-di-bul/ *adj* that cannot be heard (*inaudible remarks/the speaker was inaudible at the*

inauspicious /i-naw-**spi**-shus/ *adj* unlucky, being a sign of bad luck to come (*an inauspicious beginning*).

inborn /in-**bawrn**/ *adj* existing in a person since birth, natural (*an inborn ability to play musical instruments*).

inbound /in-**bound**/ *adj* traveling or going inward.

inbounds /in-**boundz**/ *adj* of or relating to putting the ball in play from out of bounds in a game of basketball (*throw an inbounds pass*).

inbred /in-**bred**/ *adj* **1** having become part of a person's nature as a result of early training (*her inbred politeness*). **2** bred from closely related parents, resulting from inbreeding.

inbreed /in-**breed**/ *vb* to breed by mating closely related parents.

Inca /**ing**-ka/ *n* a member of a group of peoples in ancient Peru who had a highly developed civilization.

incalculable /in-**cal**-cyu-la-bul/ *adj* very great, too many or too much to be counted (*incalculable damage*).

incandescent /in-can-**de**-sent/ *adj* white-hot or glowing with heat. ● *n* **incandescence** /in-can-de-sense/. ● *vb* **incandesce** /in-can-**des**-sense/.

incantation /in-can-**tay**-shun/ *n* words sung or spoken as a spell or charm (*witches reciting an incantation*).

incapable /in-**cay**-pa-bul/ *adj* **1** not good at a job. **2** not able, helpless. ● *n* **incapability** /in-cay-pa-**bi**-li-tee/.

incapacitate /in-ca-**pa**-si-tate/ *vb* to make unfit or unable (*incapacitated by his injured leg*).

incapacity /in-ca-**pa**-si-tee/ *n* **1** unfitness. **2** lack of ability.

incarcerate /in-**car**-se-rate/ *vb* (*fml or hum*) to imprison (*incarcerated in jail*). ● *n* **incarceration** /in-car-se-**ray**-shun/.

incense[1] /in-sense/ *n* a mixture of spices burned to give a sweet-smelling smoke.

incense[2] /in-**sense**/ *vb* to make angry (*he was incensed when the boy broke his window*).

incentive /in-**sen**-tiv/ *n* something for which someone is prepared to work hard, a reason for action (*award a prize as an incentive to the pupils*).

incessant /in-**se**-sant/ *adj* not stopping, going on all the time (*incessant rain/her incessant complaining*).

incest /in-sest/ *n* **1** sex between people who are too closely related to marry legally. **2** sexual abuse of a child by a close relative. ● *adj* **incestuous** /in-ses-chu-wus/.

inch /inch/ *n* one-twelfth of a foot in length. ● *vb* to move a little at a time (*try to inch nearer the front of the crowd*).

incidence /in-si-dense/ *n* **1** the extent or rate of frequency of something (*the incidence of burglaries in the area*). **2** the act, fact, or manner of falling on or influencing.

incident /in-si-dent/ *n* **1** a happening, an event (*it was a sad incident in his life*). **2** an event involving violence or law-breaking (*police called to an incident in the house*).

incidental /in-si-**den**-tal/ *adj* **1** happening as a result of something, though not the most important result (*an incidental effect of the meeting*). **2** accompanying (*incidental music to the play*).

incidentally /in-si-**den**-ta-lee/ *adv* by the way (*incidentally, it has started to rain*).

incinerate /in-**si**-ne-rate/ *vb* to burn to ashes (*incinerating the garbage*).

incinerator /in-**si**-ne-ray-tor/ *n* a furnace for burning anything to ashes.

incise /in-**size**/ *vb* to cut into with a sharp tool. ● *adj* **incised** /in-**siexd**/.

incision /in-**si**-zhun/ *n* **1** act of cutting. **2** a cut, a deep cut (*the incision made by the surgeon*).

incisive /in-**sie**-siv/ *adj* clear and sharp, to the point (*incisive criticism/incisive comments*).

incisor /in-**sie**-zor/ *n* a cutting tooth in the front of the mouth.

incite /in-**site**/ *vb* to stir up, to urge on (*a speech that incited the crowd to take action*). ● *n* **incitement** /in-**site**-ment/.

inclement /in-**cle**-ment/ *adj* (*fml*) **1** stormy, unpleasant (*inclement weather*). **2** merciless (*an inclement judge*). ● *n* **inclemency** /in-**cle**-men-see/.

inclination /in-cli-**nay**-shun/ *n* **1** a slope (*a slight inclination in the road*). **2** a bow (*with an inclination of his head*). **3** a liking, preference (*have an inclination to travel*). **4** a tendency (*an inclination to think negatively*).

incline /in-**cline**/ *vb* **1** to slope. **2** to bend (*incline the head*). **3** to move gradually off the straight away. ● **be inclined to 1** to feel a desire or preference (*I am inclined to accept their story*). **2** to have a tendency to (*he is inclined to be lazy*). ● *n* **incline** /in-cline/ a slope.

include /in-**clude**/ *vb* to count as a part or member (*including them on the invitation list*). ● *n* **inclusion** /in-**cloo**-zhun/.

inclusive /in-**cloo**-siv/ *adj* including everything mentioned or understood (*Monday to Friday inclusive/a price inclusive of postage*).

incognito /in-cog-**nee**-toe/ *adj* in disguise, under a false name (*the prince was traveling incognito so as not to be recognized*). ● *f* **incognita** /in-cog-**nee**-ta/.

incoherent /in-co-**hir**-ent/ *adj* **1** having no clear connection between the parts, muddled (*an incoherent account of what had happened*). **2** not speaking or writing clearly, difficult to follow or understand (*she was so upset that she was incoherent*). ● *n* **incoherence** /in-co-**hir**-ense/.

income /**ing**-cum/ *n* the money earned or gained (*his annual income*).

income tax /**ing**-cum-taks/ *n* the tax charged on income.

incomparable /in-com-**pa**-ra-bul/ *adj* **1** that cannot be equaled (*an incomparable performance*). **2** having no equal (*an incomparable pianist*).

incompatible /in-com-**ba**-ti-bul/ *adj* **1** unable to get along (*they loved each other but they were totally incompatible*). **2** not in agreement (*the statements from the witnesses were incompatible*). ● *n* **incompatibility** /in-com-ba-ti-**bi**-li-tee/.

incompetent /in-**com**-pe-tent/ *adj* **1** unable to do a job well, unskillful (*an incompetent manager*). **2** not good enough (*an incompetent piece of work*). ● *ns* **incompetence** /in-**com**-pe-tense/, **incompetency** /in-**com**-pe-ten-see/.

incomplete /in-com-**pleet**/ *adj* unfinished (*the poet's final work is incomplete*).

incomprehensible /in-com-pre-**hen**-si-bul/ *adj* that cannot be understood (*incomprehensible behavior*). ● *n* **incomprehension** /in-com-pre-**hen**-shun/.

inconceivable /in-con-**see**-va-bul/ *adj* unable to be imagined (*it seemed inconceivable that she could treat her own child so cruelly*).

inconclusive /in-con-**cloo**-siv/ *adj* not final, not leading to a definite result.

inconsiderable /in-con-**si**-der-(a)-bul/ *adj* very small, of no importance (*an inconsiderable difference*).

inconsiderate /in-con-**sid**-(e)-rit/ *adj* having no thought for the feeling of others, thoughtless (*it is inconsiderate to play loud music late at night*).

inconsistent /in-con-**sis**-tant/ *adj* **1** not agreeing with what was said or done before or elsewhere (*the judge's decision is inconsistent with the one he made last week*). **2** changeable, erratic (*her work is extremely inconsistent*). **3** contradictory (*sending his children to private school is inconsistent with his political views*). ● *n* **inconsistency** /in-con-**sis**-tan-see/.

inconsolable /in-con-**soe**-la-bul/ *adj* not to be comforted, broken-hearted (*the inconsolable widow*).

inconspicuous /in-con-**spic**-yu-wus/ *adj* not easily seen (*try to make herself inconspicuous in the crowd by wearing dark clothes*).

inconstant /in-**con**-stant/ *adj* **1** often changing. **2** not always behaving in the same way. ● *n* **inconstancy** /in-**con**-stan-see/.

incontinent /in-**con**-ti-nent/ *adj* unable to control the bladder and/or bowels (*incontinent elderly people*). ● *n* **incontinence** /in-**con**-ti-nense/.

inconvenience /in-con-**veen**-yense/ *n* trouble, annoyance (*apologize for any inconvenience caused by his absence*). ● *vb* (*fml*) to cause trouble or difficulty (*visitors who inconvenienced them by staying too late*).

inconvenient /in-con-**veen**-yent/ *adj* causing trouble, unsuitable (*come at an inconvenient time*).

incorporate /in-**cawr**-po-rit/ *vb* **1** to bring together in one (*incorporating the smaller firm in the international company*). **2** to make to form a part of, to include (*incorporate their suggestions in his report*). ● *n* **incorporation** /in-cawr-po-**ray**-shun/.

incorrect /in-caw-**rect**/ *adj* **1** wrong (*incorrect answers*). **2** not according to accepted standards (*incorrect behavior*).

increase /in-**creess**/ *vb* to make or become greater in size or number (*the number of club members has increased/the temperature has increased*). ● *n* **increase** /in-creess/ a rise in amount, numbers, or degree (*an increase in membership/an increase in temperature*).

incredible /in-**cre**-di-bul/ *adj* **1** unbelievable, hard to believe (*I find his story completely incredible*). **2** amazing, wonderful (*it was an incredible performance*). ● *n* **incredibility** /in-cre-di-**bi**-li-tee/.

incredulous /in-**cre**-ju-lus/ *adj* not willing to believe, unbelieving (*she gave him an incredulous look*). ● *n* **incredulity** /in-cre-**doo**-li-tee/.

increment /**in**-cre-ment/ *n* an increase in money or value, often in salary (*receive an annual increment*).

incriminate /in-**cri**-mi-nate/ *vb* to show that a person has taken part in a crime (*the accused tried to incriminate several other people in the bank robbery*).

incubate /**ing**-cyu-bate/ *vb* **1** to sit on eggs, to keep eggs warm until the young come out of them. **2** (*of eggs*) to be kept warm until the young birds come out. **3** (*of a disease or infection*) to develop until signs of disease appear. **4** to be holding in the body an infection that is going to develop into a disease (*she must have been incubating chickenpox*).

incubation /ing-cyu-**bay**-shun/ *n* **1** act of incubating. **2** the time between the catching of a disease and the showing of symptoms (*the incubation period of measles*).

incubator /**ing**-cyu-bay-tor/ *n* **1** an apparatus for hatching eggs. **2** an apparatus for keeping alive premature babies.

incurable /in-**cyoo**-ra-bul/ *adj* that cannot be cured (*incurable diseases*).

indebted /in-**det**-id/ *adj* owing thanks, owing something to someone or something (*indebted to them for their help*). ● *n* **indebtedness** /in-**det**-id-ness/.

indecent /in-**dee**-sent/ *adj* **1** not decent, morally offensive, improper (*indecent remarks*). **2** not

suitable, not in good taste (*marry in indecent haste after her husband's death*). ● *n* **indecency** /in-**dee**-sen-see/.

indecision /in-di-**si**-zhun/ *n* doubt, hesitation, inability to make up the mind (*full of indecision about whether to change jobs*).

indecisive /in-di-**sie**-siv/ *adj* **1** uncertain, having difficulty in making decisions (*too indecisive to make up her mind and stick to the decision*). **2** settling nothing (*an indecisive verdict*).

indeed /in-**deed**/ *adv* truly (*yes indeed he will be there*).

indefensible /in-de-**fen**-si-bul/ *adj* that cannot or should not be defended (*his attitude toward her is indefensible*).

indefinable /in-de-**fine**-a-bul/ *adj* that cannot be clearly described or explained (*an indefinable difference*).

indefinite /in-**def**-nit/ *adj* **1** not fixed or exact, without clearly marked outlines or limits (*guests staying for an indefinite time*). **2** not clear, not precise, vague (*give indefinite replies*).

indelicate /in-**de**-li-cit/ *adj* **1** slightly indecent, improper (*indelicate language for a lady*). **2** lacking in tact (*an indelicate question*). ● *n* **indelicacy** /in-**de**-li-ca-see/.

indent /in-**dent**/ *vb* **1** to make a notch or zigzag in (*a coastline indented by the sea*). **2** to begin a line in from the margin. **3** to order goods in writing (*the soldier indented for a new uniform*). ● *n* **indent** /**in**-dent/ an order for goods.

indentation /in-den-**tay**-shun/ *n* **1** a notch or piece cut out of a straight edge (*the indentations in the coastline*). **2** the starting of a line in from the margin.

independence /in-di-**pen**-dense/ *n* freedom to act or think as one likes, freedom (*a colony that gained independence several hundred years ago*).

independent /in-di-**pen**-dent/ *adj* **1** thinking and acting for oneself (*too independent to let others tell her what to do*). **2** free from control by others (*independent countries*). **3** having enough money to live without working or being helped by others (*financially independent/a woman of independent means*).

in-depth /in-**depth**/ *adj* carefully worked out, thorough.

indescribable /in-di-**scrie**-ba-bul/ *adj* that cannot be described (*indescribable cruelty*).

indestructible /in-di-**struc**-ta-bul/ *adj* that cannot be destroyed (*indestructible courage*).

indeterminable /in-di-**ter**-mi-na-bul/, **indetermi-nate** /in-di-**ter**-mi-nit/ *adj* not fixed, uncertain (*indeterminate plans*).

index /**in**-deks/ *n* (*pl* **indexes** /**in**-dek-siz/ or **indices** /**in**-di-seez/) **1** the pointer on the dial or scale of an instrument. **2** something that indicates or points to (*the results of the opinion poll are an index to public opinion*). **3** an alphabetical list of names, subjects, etc., at the end of a book (*consult the index to see on what page the battle is mentioned*).

Indian /**in**-dee-an/ *adj* **1** of India. **2** having to do with Native Americans.

indicate /**in**-di-cate/ *vb* **1** to point out, to show (*arrows indicating the way to the X-ray department*). **2** to be a sign of (*her attitude indicates an unwillingness to go*). **3** to show to be necessary or desirable (*drastic action is indicated*).

indication /in-di-**cay**-shun/ *n* a sign (*she gave no indication that she intended to leave*).

indicative /in-**di**-ca-tiv/ *adj* showing, being a sign of (*a rash indicative of measles*).

indicator /**in**-di-cay-tor/ *n* **1** a needle or pointer on a machine that indicates something or gives information about something (*the indicator on the gasoline gauge*). **2** one of the lights on a car, truck, etc. that flashes to show which way the car is turning.

indifference /in-**di**-frense/ *n* lack of interest.

indifferent /in-**di**-frent/ *adj* **1** taking no interest, not caring (*indifferent to the suffering of others/indifferent to whether he goes or stays*). **2** neither good nor bad (*rather an indifferent musical performance*).

indigenous /in-**di**-je-nus/ *adj* born or growing naturally in a country (*plants indigenous to America/ the indigenous people of the country*). ● *n* **indigene** /**in**-di-jeen/.

indigestible /in-di-**je**-sti-bul/ *adj* not easily digested (*food that he finds indigestible*).

indigestion /in-di-**jes**-chun/ *n* illness or pain caused by failure to dissolve food properly in the stomach (*certain foods give her indigestion*). ● *adj* **indigestive** /in-di-**jes**-tiv/.

indignant /in-**dig**-nant/ *adj* angry, annoyed by what is unjust (*she was indignant at the way she had been treated by the sales assistant/an indignant customer*). ● *n* **indignation** /in-dig-**nay**-shun/.

indignity /in-**dig**-ni-tee/ *n* treatment that makes a person feel shame or loss of respect (*suffer the indignity of being taken to the police station for questioning*).

indigo /**in**-di-go/ *n* a blue dye obtained from certain plants. ● *adj* deep blue.

indirect /in-di-**rect**/ *adj* **1** not leading straight to the destination, roundabout (*take an indirect route home*). **2** not direct, not straightforward, not frank (*give indirect answers to the questions*). **3** not intended, not directly aimed at (*an indirect result of the meeting*). ● *n* **indirection** /in-di-**rec**-shun/.

indiscreet /in-di-**screet**/ *adj* **1** unwise, thoughtless. **2** done or said without thought of results.

indiscretion /in-di-**scre**-shun/ *n* **1** thoughtless behavior. **2** an act done without thought of its results. **3** lack of good judgment.

indiscriminate /in-di-**scrim**-nit/ *adj* taking no notice of differences, choosing without care (*indiscriminate in their choice of books/indiscriminate killing of hostages*). ● *n* **indiscrimination** /in-di-scri-mi-**nay**-shun/.

indispensable /in-di-**spen**-si-bul/ *adj* that cannot be done without, absolutely necessary (*no one is really indispensable*).

indisputable /in-di-**spyoo**-ti-bul/ *adj* that cannot be denied or contradicted (*his indisputable right to vote as he pleases*).

indistinct /in-di-**stingt**/ *adj* not seen or heard clearly, faint (*her voice on the telephone was indistinct*).

indistinguishable /in-di-**sting**-gwi-sha-bul/ *adj* that cannot be made out as being different or separate (*the twins were indistinguishable from each other*).

individual /in-di-**vij**-u-wal/ *adj* **1** single (*label each individual item*). **2** intended for, used by, etc., one person only (*individual attention*). **3** special to one person (*a very individual style of painting*). ● *n* **1** a single person (*the rights of the individual*). **2** (*inf*) a person (*a strange individual*).

individualism /in-di-**vij**-wa-li-zum/ *n* **1** the belief that the rights of the single person are more important than those of society. **2** the belief that the state exists for the individual and not the individual for the state. **3** a person's individual character.

individualist /in-di-**vij**-wa-list/ *n* a person who believes in doing things in his or her own way (*an individualist who disregards fashion*).

individuality /in-di-vi-je-**wa**-li-tee/ *n* a person's own character and qualities (*express her individuality in her style of dress*).

individualize /in-di-**vij**-wa-lize/ *vb, also* **individualise** (*Br*) to mark as different from other persons or things, to suit the taste, requirements, etc., of a particular individual.

individually /in-di-**vij**-wa-lee/ *adv* separately, one by one (*they went individually to see the principal*).

indivisible /in-di-**vi**-zi-bul/ *adj* that cannot be divided (*an indivisible number*).

indoctrinate /in-**doc**-tri-nate/ *vb* **1** to instruct in a belief (*indoctrinating children with the idea that qualifications are important*). **2** to bring to accept a system of belief unquestioningly (*indoctrinating children with his own political ideas*).

indoor /in-**dore**/ *adj* done in a house or building (*an indoor sport*).

indoors /in-**doarz**/ *adv* within doors, inside a house (*hold the party indoors*).

inducement /in-**doos**-ment/ *n* something that leads a person to try to do something, an attractive reason for doing something (*offer her the inducement of a company car to get her to stay*).

indulge /in-**duldge**/ *vb* **1** to take pleasure in something, without trying to control oneself (*indulging in too much rich food*). **2** to give in to the wishes of (*indulge her child too much/indulge herself by going on a shopping trip*).

indulgence /in-**dul**-jense/ *n* **1** act of indulging. **2** in the Roman Catholic Church, a setting free from the punishment due to sinners.

indulgent /in-**dul**-jent/ *adj* kindly, easygoing, ready to give in to the wishes of others (*parents who are too indulgent*).

industrial /in-**du**-stree-al/ *adj* having to do with the manufacturing of goods (*an industrial, rather than an agricultural, country*).

industrialism /in-**du**-stree-a-li-zum/ *n* social and economic organization featuring large industries, machine production, concentration of workers in cities, etc.

Industrial Revolution /in-**du**-stree-al re-vu-**loo**-shun/ *n* the change in social and economic organization resulting from replacing hand tools with machine and power tools and the development of mass production, beginning in England about 1760 and spreading to other countries.

industrious /in-**du**-stree-us/ *adj* hardworking, busy, skillful, clever (*industrious children studying for their exams*).

industry /in-du-stree/ *n* **1** (*fml*) the ability to work hard (*he owes his success to industry as well as ability*). **2** in trade or commerce, the work that is done to make goods ready for selling, the manufacturing and selling of goods (*workers involved in industry rather than agriculture*).

inedible /i-**ne**-di-bul/ *adj* that should not or cannot be eaten (*salty food that was totally inedible*).

ineffective /i-ne-**fec**-tiv/ *adj* useless, having no effect (*ineffective methods/ineffective people*). ● *n* **ineffectiveness** /i-ne-**fec**-tiv-ness/.

ineffectual /i-ne-**fec**-chal/ *adj* **1** not having the desired effect (*ineffectual remedies*). **2** powerless, not able to get things done (*ineffectual people*).

inefficient /i-ni-**fi**-shent/ *adj* **1** not good at a job, unable to do the job required (*sack the inefficient workers*). **2** not producing results in the best, quickest, and/or cheapest way (*inefficient methods of production*). ● *n* **inefficiency** /i-ni-**fi**-shen-see/.

inept /i-**nept**/ *adj* **1** clumsy, awkward (*an inept attempt at making a dress*). **2** foolishly unsuitable (*embarrass them by her inept remarks*).

ineptitude /i-**nep**-ti-tood/ *n* **1** clumsiness, awkwardness. **2** foolish unsuitability.

inequality /i-ne-**kwol**-i-tee/ *n* lack of equality, unevenness (*inequalities in the law*).

inert /i-**nert**/ *adj* **1** without the power to move (*lying inert on the bed as if dead*). **2** not wanting to take action, not taking action (*she remained inert as though she could not think of what to do*). **3** not acting chemically when combined with other substances (*inert gases*).

inertia /i-**ner**-sha/ *n* **1** unwillingness or inability to move (*feelings of inertia caused by the heat*). **2** the inability of matter to set itself in motion or to stop moving.

inescapable /i-ne-**scay**-pa-bul/ *adj* that cannot be avoided.

inevitable /i-**ne**-vi-ta-bul/ *adj* certain to happen (*defeat seemed inevitable*). ● *n* **inevitability** /i-ne-vi-ta-**bi**-li-tee/.

inexact /i-**nig**-zact/ *adj* not quite correct (*an inexact science/inexact figures*). ● *n* **inexactitude** /i-nig-**zac**-ti-chood/.

inexcusable /i-nik-**scyoo**-za-bul/ *adj* that cannot be forgiven or pardoned (*inexcusable behavior*).

inexpensive /i-nik-**spen**-siv/ *adj* cheap, not expensive (*inexpensive presents for Christmas stockings*).

inexperience /i-nik-**spee**-ree-ense/ *n* lack of skill or practice (*the accident was caused by the driver's inexperience*). ● *adj* **inexperienced** /i-nik-**spee**-ree-enst/.

inexplicable /i-nik-**spli**-ca-bul/ *adj* that cannot be explained, understood, or accounted for (*inexplicable delays*).

infallible /in-**fa**-la-bul/ *adj* **1** unable to make a mistake (*supposedly infallible judges*). **2** that cannot fail (*supposedly infallible methods*). ● *n* **infallibility** /in-fa-la-**bi**-li-tee/.

infamous /**in**-fa-mus/ *adj* having a bad reputation, famous for something bad or wicked (*infamous criminals*). ● *n* **infamy** /**in**-fa-mee/ the quality of being infamous, an infamous act.

infancy /**in**-fan-see/ *n* **1** babyhood (*she died in infancy*). **2** the early stages of anything (*the computer industry was in its infancy then*).

infant /**in**-fant/ *n* a very young child, a baby.

infantile /**in**-fan-tile/ *adj* **1** childish (*the infantile behavior of the two men*). **2** having to do with infants (*infantile diseases*).

infantry /**in**-fan-tree/ *n* foot soldiers.

infatuate /in-**fa**-chu-wate/ *vb* **1** to make foolish. **2** to inspire with foolish love or affection.

infatuated /in-**fa**-chu-way-tid/ *adj* loving foolishly or unreasonably (*the young girl is infatuated with a much older man*). ● *n* **infatuation** /in-fa-chu-**way**-shun/.

infect /in-**fect**/ *vb* **1** to pass on a disease to another (*the hotel worker infected others with the illness*). **2** to make impure by spreading disease into it (*food that is infected*). **3** to pass on or spread (*infect others with his love of life*).

infection /in-**fec**-shun/ *n* the passing on or spreading of disease, or anything harmful.

infectious /in-**fec**-shus/ *adj* that can be passed on to others (*infectious diseases/infectious laughter*).

infer /in-**fer**/ *vb* (**inferred** /in-**ferd**/, **inferring** /in-**fe**-ring/) **1** to work out an idea from the facts known (*what can we infer from the evidence given*). **2** (*inf*) to suggest by hints.

inference /**in**-frense/ *n* an idea or conclusion worked out from the known facts.

inferior /in-**fee**-ree-ur/ *adj* **1** of lesser value or importance (*people of inferior qualifications were promoted before her*). **2** of bad quality (*inferior goods*). ● *n* a person lower in rank (*he is her inferior in the company's staff structure*).

infertile /in-**fer**-tile/ *adj* not fertile, barren.

infest /in-**fest**/ *vb* to be present in very large numbers in (*a building infested with mice*).

infiltrate /**in**-fil-trate/ *vb* **1** to pass through, a few at a time (*soldiers infiltrating enemy lines*). **2** to enter and secretly, gradually become part of, usually with an unfriendly purpose (*enemy spies infiltrated the government department*). ● *n* **infiltration** /in-fil-**tray**-shun/.

infinite /**in**-fi-nit/ *adj* **1** having neither beginning nor end, limitless (*infinite space*). **2** (*inf*) very great (*with infinite patience*).

infinitive /in-**fi**-ni-tiv/ *n* the form of a verb that expresses action without referring to a person, number, or tense (e.g., to go, to live, to see).

infinity /in-**fi**-ni-tee/ *n* **1** space, time, or quantity that is without limit or is immeasurably great or small (*the grassy plains seemed to stretch into infinity*). **2** an indefinitely large number, quantity, or distance.

infirm /in-**firm**/ *adj* weak, sickly (*infirm old people unable to live alone*).

infirmary /in-**firm**-ree/ *n* a hospital.

infirmity /in-**fir**-mi-tee/ *n* illness, weakness (*old people suffering from a range of infirmities*).

inflammable /in-**fla**-ma-bul/ *adj* **1** easily set on fire (*children's pajamas should not be made of inflammable material*). **2** excitable.

inflammation /in-fla-**may**-shun/ *n* a swelling on part of the body, accompanied by heat and pain (*his sore throat was the result of inflammation of the tonsils*).

inflammatory /in-**fla**-ma-toe-ree/ *adj* causing excitement or anger (*an inflammatory speech*).

inflate /in-**flate**/ *vb* **1** to puff up (*her success inflated her sense of her own importance*). **2** to make to swell by filling with air or gas (*inflate the tire/inflating the balloon*). **3** to increase in price or value (*inflate house prices*). ● *adj* **inflatable** /in-**flat**-ta-bul/.

inflation /in-**flay**-shun/ *n* **1** act of inflation. **2** a situation in a country's economy where prices and wages keep forcing each other to increase. ● *adj* **inflationary** /in-**flay**-shu-na-ree/.

inflexible /in-**flek**-si-bul/ *adj* **1** that cannot be bent, stiff and firm (*inflexible materials*). **2** not easily changed (*inflexible attitudes*). **3** not giving in (*we tried to persuade her to change her mind but she was inflexible*). ● *n* **inflexibility** /in-flek-si-**bi**-li-tee/.

inflict /in-**flict**/ *vb* to force something unpleasant or unwanted on someone (*inflict pain on his parents/inflict a heavy burden on them*).

infliction /in-**flic**-shun/ *n* **1** the act of inflicting. **2** punishment.

in-flight /**in**-flite/ *adj* done, occurring, shown, etc. while an aircraft is in flight (*the in-flight movie was very boring*).

influence /**in**-floo-ense/ *n* **1** the ability to affect other people or the course of events (*his childhood* *unhappiness had an influence on his way of thinking*). **2** the power to make requests to those in authority (*he has some influence with the local authorities*). ● *vb* to have an effect on (*she tried not to influence the decision*).

influential /in-floo-**en**-shal/ *adj* having power, important (*influential people in the community*).

influenza /in-floo-**en**-za/ *n* a type of infectious illness, usually causing headache, fever, cold symptoms, etc.

infomercial /in-fo-mer-shal/ *n* a long television commercial to introduce a product and tell, show, etc. what it is capable of.

inform /in-**fawrm**/ *vb* **1** to tell, to give information (*inform her of the changes/inform him that she was leaving*). **2** to teach, to give knowledge to. **3** to tell facts to the police or authorities about a criminal, etc. (*he informed against his fellow thieves*).

informal /in-**fawr**-mal/ *adj* **1** without ceremony (*an informal dance*). **2** not bound by rules or accepted ways of behaving (*an informal agreement*). **3** suitable for ordinary everyday situations (*informal clothes*). ● *n* **informality** /in-**fawr**-ma-li-tee/.

information /in-fur-**may**-shun/ *n* facts told, knowledge in the form of facts, news, etc. (*receive information about new products/gather information about foreign customs*).

information technology /in-fur-**may**-shun tek-**nol**-o-jee/ *n* the use of computers and other electronic equipment to produce, store, and communicate information.

informative /in-**fawr**-ma-tiv/ *adj* giving news or facts (*an informative television documentary*).

informer /in-**fawr**-mer/ *n* someone who gives away the plans of others (*a police informer*).

infrequent /in-**free**-kwent/ *adj* not happening often. ● *n* **infrequency** /in-**free**-kwen-see/.

infuriate /in-**fyoo**-ree-ate/ *vb* to madden, to make very angry (*she was infuriated by his superior attitude toward women*).

infuse /in-**fyooz**/ *vb* **1** to put into (*infuse some enthusiasm into the class*). **2** to steep in hot liquid (as in making tea) (*infusing chamomile to make an herbal tea*).

infusion /in-**fyoo**-zhun/ *n* **1** act of infusing. **2** a liquid given taste or color by something steeped in it (*an infusion of chamomile*).

ingenious /in-**jeen**-yus/ *adj* **1** having good or new ideas, inventive (*ingenious at thinking of ways to keep the children entertained*). **2** cleverly thought out (*an ingenious plan*).

ingenuity /in-je-**noo**-i-tee/ *n* **1** cleverness, inventiveness (*the ingenuity of the plan*). **2** the ability to invent, cleverness (*use her ingenuity to make a meal from very few ingredients*).

ingot /**ing**-gut/ *n* a bar or block of metal, especially gold or silver, got from a mold.

ingrained /in-**graind**/ *adj* fixed firmly in (*an ingrained sense of duty/ingrained dirt*). ● *vb* **ingrain** /in-**grain**/.

ingredient /in-**gree**-dee-ent/ *n* one of the things in a mixture (*the ingredients for a cake/the ingredients for a happy life*).

ingrown /**in**-groan/ *adj* grown within, inward, or into, especially grown into the flesh (*an ingrown hair*). ● *n* **ingrowth** /**in**-groath/.

inhabit /in-**ha**-bit/ *vb* to live in (*an area mainly inhabited by retired people*).

inhabitable /in-**ha**-bi-ta-bul/ *adj* that can be lived in (*houses that are inhabitable*).

inhabitant /in-**ha**-bi-tant/ *n* a person who lives in a certain place (*the older inhabitants of the town*).

inhabited /in-**ha**-bi-tid/ *adj* having inhabitants, lived in, occupied.

inhalation /in-ha-**lay**-shun/ *n* **1** act of breathing in (*the inhalation of car exhaust fumes*). **2** something that is breathed in (*prepare an inhalation to try to cure her cold*).

inhale /in-**hale**/ *vb* to breathe in (*inhaling the smoke from other people's cigarettes*).

inhaler /in-**hay**-ler/ *n* a device for giving medicine in the form of a vapor by inhalation.

inherit /in-**he**-rit/ *vb* **1** to receive something from another at his or her death (*inherited his father's estate*). **2** to receive certain qualities through the parents (*inherit his mother's good looks*). ● *n* **inheritor** /in-**he**-ri-tor/.

inheritance /in-**he**-ri-tanse/ *n* that which is inherited (*he has spent most of his inheritance already*).

inhibit /in-**hi**-bit/ *vb* **1** to prevent or hinder, to hold back from doing (*a tight skirt that inhibited walking/a financial situation that inhibited expansion of the company*). **2** to make someone inhibited (*his presence seems to inhibit her*). ● *n* **inhibitor** /in-**hi**-bi-tor/.

inhibited /in-**hi**-bi-tid/ *adj* unable to relax and express feelings in an open and natural way (*too inhibited to speak in public*).

inhibition /in-hi-**bi**-shun/ *n* a belief or fear of which a person is not aware but which may prevent him or her from performing certain actions (*have inhibitions about being seen in a swimsuit*).

inhospitable /in-hos-**pi**-ta-bul/ *adj* not welcoming visitors, not kind to strangers (*it was inhospitable not to offer the visitors anything to eat or drink*). ● *n* **inhospitality** /in-hos-pi-ta-**bi**-li-tee/.

inhuman /in-**hyoo**-man/ *adj* not having the qualities considered normal to or for humans, cruel, brutal, unkind.

inhumane /in-hyoo-**mane**/ *adj* unmoved by the suffering of others, cruel, merciless, brutal, unkind.

inhumanity /in-hyoo-**ma**-ni-tee/ *n* the quality or condition of being inhuman or inhumane.

inimitable /i-**ni**-mi-ta-bul/ *adj* that cannot be copied, too good to be equalled (*an inimitable performance*).

initial /i-**ni**-shal/ *adj* first, happening at the beginning (*the initial reaction was favorable*). ● *adv* **initially** /i-**ni**-sha-lee/. ● *vb* (**initialed** /i-**ni**-shald/, **initialing** /i-**ni**-sha-ling/) to mark or write initials (*initial the order form to authorize it*). ● *npl* **initials** /i-**ni**-shalz/ the first letters of each of a person's names.

initiate /i-**ni**-she-ate/ *vb* **1** to begin (*initiating a new system of accounting*). **2** to teach the ways of a society to a new member (*the boys initiated their friend into their club*). ● *n* **initiation** /i-ni-she-**aye**-shun/.

initiative /i-**ni**-sha-tiv/ *n* **1** the ability to make decisions and take action without asking for help and advice (*he had to use his initiative when he was stranded on the island*). **2** the first movement or action that starts something happening (*take the initiative in organizing the garage sale*).

inject /in-**ject**/ *vb* **1** to put into the bloodstream through a hollow needle (*injected with a drug to fight the infection*). **2** to put in (*her arrival injected some life into the party*). ● *n* **injection** /in-**jec**-shun/.

injure /**in**-joor/ *vb* **1** to hurt (*she was badly injured in the car accident*). **2** to harm, to damage (*the incident injured his reputation*).

injury /**in**-ju-ree/ *n* **1** damage, harm, hurt (*an accident that caused injury to his spine/injury to his reputation*). **2** a physical hurt or wound (*he died later from his injuries*).

injustice /in-**ju**-stiss/ *n* **1** unfairness (*felt there was injustice in the way he was treated*). **2** an unfair act (*complain about the injustices of the system*).

ink /ingk/ *n* a colored liquid used for writing or printing. ● *vb* to mark with ink.

inkblot /**ingk**-blot/ *n* any of a group of irregular patterns made by blots of ink and used in certain kinds of tests, as for the way a person thinks.

inkjet /**ingk**-jet/ *adj* of a high-speed printing process in which ink droplets are formed into printed characters on paper.

inky /**ing**-kee/ *adj* **1** stained with ink (*inky hands*). **2** like ink in color, dark (*an inky sky*).

inlaid *see* **inlay**.

inland /**in**-land/ *n* the part of a country away from the sea coast or border. ● *adj* **1** having to do with a country's own affairs (*inland trade*). **2** away from the coast or border (*inland waterways*). ● *also adv*.

in-law /**in**-law/ *n* a relative by marriage.

inlay /in-**lay**/ *vb* (*pt, pp* **inlaid** /in-**laid**/) to decorate by filling carved designs with gold, silver, ivory, etc. (*the box is inlaid with precious stones*). ● *adj* **inlaid** /in-**laid**/. ● *n* **inlay** /**in**-lay/.

inlet /**in**-let/ *n* **1** a way in (*a fuel inlet*). **2** a small bay (*boats sheltering in an inlet*).

in-line skate /**in**-line-skate/ *n* a kind of roller skate having wheels arrange in a straight line like a blade from toe to heel.

inmate /**in**-mate/ *n* a person living with others in the same house, hospital, prison, etc.

inmost /**in**-most/ *adj* farthest in (*the inmost depths of the cave*).

inn /in/ *n* an establishment where travelers may pay to eat, drink, and/or stay for the night.

innards /**i**-nerdz/ *n* the inner parts of anything.

innate /i-**nate**/ *adj* existing naturally rather than being acquired, that seems to have been in a person since birth.

inner /**i**-ner/ *adj* farther in (*the inner room*).

innkeeper /**in**-kee-per/ *n* the person who is in charge of an inn.

innocence /**i**-no-sense/ *n* freedom from blame or wickedness (*the innocence of the young children/try to prove his innocence*).

innocent /**i**-no-sent/ *adj* **1** not guilty (*innocent of the crime/innocent people accused*). **2** having no knowledge or experience of evil (*innocent young children*).

innocuous /i-**noc**-yu-wus/ *adj* harmless (*drugs thought to be innocuous/a perfectly innocuous remark*).

innovation /i-no-**vay**-shun/ *n* **1** a new way of doing something, a new thing or idea (*innovations in marketing methods*). **2** the introduction of new things or ideas (*he is set in his ways and dislikes innovation*). ● *vb* **innovate** /**i**-no-vate/ to renew, to introduce new ways of doing things.

innuendo /i-nyoo-**wen**-doe/ *n* (*pl* **innuendoes** *or*

innuendos /i-nyoo-**wen**-doaz/) **1** a way of speaking that makes one understand what is meant without actually saying it (*a newspaper that goes in for innuendo*). **2** an indirect hint (*he made innuendoes about where she got all the money*).

innumerate /i-**nyoo**-me-ret/ *adj* unable to do math and arithmetical problems.

inoculate /i-**noc**-yu-late/ *vb* to infect slightly with the germs of a disease to prevent more serious infection (*inoculating the children against measles*). ● *n* **inoculation** /i-**noc**-yu-lay-shun/.

inoffensive /i-no-**fen**-siv/ *adj* not causing harm or trouble (*a quiet inoffensive man/be insulted at a perfectly inoffensive remark*).

inpatient /**in**-pay-shent/ *n* a patient who is lodged and kept in a hospital for more than a day.

input /**in**-poot/ *n* **1** the act of putting in. **2** what is put in, as in the amount of money, material, effort, opinion, etc.

inquire, enquire /in-**kwire**/ *vb* **1** to ask (*inquire the way to the station*). **2** to ask for information about (*inquire about times of trains to New York*). **3** to try to discover the facts of (*the police are inquiring into the accident*).

inquiring /in-**kwie**-ring/ *adj* seeking information, curious (*an inquiring mind*).

inquiry, enquiry /in-**kwie**-ree/ *n* **1** a question (*reply to his inquiry about times of trains*). **2** a careful search for information, an investigation (*an official inquiry into the train accident*).

inquisition /in-kwi-**zi**-shun/ *n* **1** (*fml*) an official inquiry (*subjected to an inquisition about his movements on the previous evening*). **2** (*old*) an examination consisting of a series of questions. ● *n* **inquisitor** /in-**kwi**-zi-tor/.

inquisitive /in-**kwi**-zi-tiv/ *adj* seeking information, especially about other people (*inquisitive neighbors*).

inroad /**in**-road/ *n* a raid, a sudden attack.

insane /in-**sane**/ *adj* **1** mentally ill (*a murderer declared insane*). **2** (*inf*) very unwise, very foolish (*it was insane to give up his job*).

insanity /in-**sa**-ni-tee/ *n* the state of being insane, mental illness.

inscribe /in-**scribe**/ *vb* to write in a book or engrave on stone, etc. (*the words inscribed on the tombstone*).

inscription /in-**scrip**-shun/ *n* words written on something, often as a tribute (*the inscription on the tombstone*).

insect /**in**-sect/ *n* any of a large group of small creatures that have a body divided into three sections, six legs, and usually wings.

insecure /in-si-**cyoor**/ *adj* **1** anxious and unsure of oneself, lacking confidence (*children feeling insecure when their parents separated*). **2** (*fml*) not safe, likely to be lost (*an insecure job*). **3** (*fml*) not safe or firmly fixed (*the insecure leg of the table*). ● *n* **insecurity** /in-si-**cyoo**-ri-tee/.

insensible /in-**sen**-si-bul/ *adj* **1** too small to be noticed (*an insensible change*). **2** without feeling, indifferent (*insensible to their distress*). **3** unconscious (*knocked insensible by the blow*).

insensitive /in-**sen**-si-tiv/ *adj* **1** not noticing the feelings of others. **2** not quick to feel or notice.

inseparable /in-**se**-pra-bul/ *adj* that cannot be put apart (*the two issues are inseparable/childhood friends who were inseparable*).

insert /in-**sert**/ *vb* to put in or among (*insert the key in the lock*).

insertion /in-**ser**-shun/ *n* **1** something inserted (*an advertising insertion in the newspaper*). **2** the act of inserting (*the insertion of the key in the lock*).

inset /**in**-set/ *n* an extra piece set in (e.g., a small picture in a larger one). ● *vb* **inset** /**in**-set/ (**inset, insetting** /**in**-se-ting/).

inside /in-**side**/ *n* **1** the inner side or part (*the inside of the house*). **2** *pl* (*inf*) the internal organs, stomach, bowels. ● *adj* **1** internal (*inside furniture*). **2** known only to insiders, secret (*inside information*). ● *adv* **1** on or in the inside, within, indoors. **2** (*inf*) in prison. ● *prep* in or within.

insider /in-**sie**-der/ *n* **1** a person inside a given place or group. **2** a person having or likely to have secret information.

insidious /in-**si**-dee-us/ *adj* developing gradually without being noticed and causing harm (*cancer is an insidious disease*).

insight /**in**-site/ *n* ability to see the real meaning or importance of something, thorough knowledge (*his poverty-stricken childhood gave him an insight into the lives of the homeless*). ● *adj* **insightful** /in-**site**-ful/.

insignia /in-**sig**-nee-ya/ *npl* badges of rank, membership, or honor (*the insignia of his regiment*).

insignificant /in-sig-**ni**-fi-cant/ *adj* of little importance (*an insignificant sum of money/rather an insignificant person*). ● *n* **insignificance** /in-sig-**ni**-fi-canse/.

insincere /in-sin-**sir**/ *adj* not meaning what is said, false, not truly meant (*his sympathy was insincere/insincere compliments*). ● *n* **insincerity** /in-sin-**se**-ri-tee/.

insinuate /in-**sin**-yu-wate/ *vb* **1** to make way gradually and cunningly (*insinuating herself into her aunt's favor to receive money*). **2** to hint in an unpleasant way (*she insinuated that he was not honest*). ● *n* **insinuation** /in-sin-yu-**way**-shun/.

insipid /in-**si**-pid/ *adj* **1** having no taste or flavor (*insipid food*). **2** uninteresting, dull (*an insipid story*).

insist /in-**sist**/ *vb* **1** to state firmly, to demand or urge strongly (*he insisted on paying the bill*). **2** to keep on saying (*she insisted that she was innocent*).

insistent /in-**sis**-tent/ *adj* **1** firm (*he was insistent that we all go home*). **2** wanting immediate attention (*her insistent demands*). ● *n* **insistence** /in-**sis**-tense/.

insolate /in-so-late/ *vb* to expose to the sunlight so as to dry, bleach, etc.

insolation /in-so-**lay**-shun/ *n* **1** the act of insolating. **2** the treatment of sickness by exposure to sunlight.

insole /in-sole/ *n* the inside sole of a shoe.

insolent /in-so-lent/ *adj* rude, boldly insulting or disrespectful (*an insolent stare*). ● *n* **insolence** /in-so-lense/.

insoluble /in-**sol**-yu-bul/ *adj* **1** impossible to dissolve (*a chemical insoluble in water*). **2** that cannot be solved (*an insoluble problem*).

insomnia /in-**som**-nee-ya/ *n* sleeplessness (*suffering from insomnia*).

inspect /in-**spect**/ *vb* to look at closely, to examine (*inspect the work/officials from the insurance company inspecting the damage*).

inspection /in-**spec**-shun/ *n* an examination (*a troop inspection*).

inspector /in-**spec**-tor/ *n* **1** someone who inspects. **2** someone who examines the work of others to see that it is done properly. **3** a rank of police officer.

inspectorate /in-**spec**-trit/ *n* a body or group of inspectors (*the school inspectorate*).

inspiration /in-spi-**ray**-shun/ *n* **1** (*fml*) the breathing in of air. **2** a person or thing that encourages a person to use his or her powers, gifts, talent, etc. (*the poet's work was an inspiration to young writers*). **3** the encouragement so given (*she provided the inspiration for his latest novel*). ● *adj* **inspirational** /in-spi-**ray**-shnal/.

inspire /in-**spire**/ *vb* **1** (*fml*) to breathe in (*he was asked by the doctor to inspire*). **2** to encourage someone with the desire and ability to take action by filling with eagerness, confidence, etc. (*she was inspired to work hard by her mother's example*). **3** to be the force that produces something, to be the origin of (*she inspired his love of poetry*). **4** to arouse in someone (*inspiring confidence in others*).

instability /in-sta-**bi**-li-tee/ *n* unsteadiness (*the instability of his character*).

install /in-**stawl**/ *vb* **1** to place in office, especially with ceremony (*install the new bishop*). **2** to put in place (*have central heating installed*). ● *n* **installation** /in-stu-**lay**-shun/.

installment /in-**stawl**-ment/ *n* **1** payment of part of a sum of money owed (*the first installment on the television set*). **2** part of a serial story published or broadcast at one time.

instance /in-stanse/ *n* an example (*several instances of car theft in the area*). ● **for instance** for example. ● *vb* to give or quote as an example (*instancing violence as one of the features of modern life*).

instancy /in-stan-see/ *n* urgency.

instant /in-stant/ *adj* **1** immediate (*demand instant attention*). **2** pressing or urgent (*an instant need*). **3** concentrated or precooked for quick preparation (*instant soup*). ● *n* **1** a moment (*he did not believe her for an instant*). **2** the exact moment (*he loved her the instant he saw her*). ● **instantly** /in-stant-lee/ *adv* at once (*she died instantly*).

instantaneous /in-stan-**tay**-nee-us/ *adj* happening or done very quickly (*an instantaneous reaction*).

instate /in-**state**/ *vb* to put in a particular status, position, or rank.

instead /in-**sted**/ *adv* in place of (*he attended the meeting instead of his father*).

instep /in-step/ *n* the upper part of the foot between the ankle and the toes.

instill /in-**still**/ *vb* (**instilled** /in-**stilld**/, **instilling** /in-**sti**-ling/) to put in little by little into the mind of (*instill the need for honesty into him from an early age*).

instinct /in-stingt/ *n* a natural tendency to behave or react in a particular way without having been taught (*in winter birds fly south by instinct/instinct made them run from danger*).

instinctive /in-**sting**-tiv/ *adj* done at once without thinking, natural (*an instinctive urge to run away*).

institute /in-sti-toot/ *vb* to set up for the first time (*instituting a new computer system*). ● *n* **1** a society working to achieve a certain purpose (*the Women's Institute*). **2** the building in which such a society meets or works.

institution /in-sti-**too**-shun/ *n* **1** an organization, usually a long-established or well-respected one (*schools, hospitals, and other institutions*). **2** the building used by such an organization. **3** an accepted custom or tradition (*the institution of marriage*). ● *adj* **institutional** /in-sti-**too**-shnal/.

institutionalize /in-sti-**too**-shna-lize/ *vb, also* **institutionalise** (*Br*) **1** to make into an institution. **2** to place in an institution.

instruct /in-**struct**/ *vb* **1** to teach (*instruct the children in French*). **2** to order (*she instructed her children to arrive home early*).

instruction /in-**struc**-shun/ *n* **1** teaching (*receive instruction in French*). **2** an order (*his instructions were to leave immediately*). **3** *pl* information on how to use something correctly (*a leaflet giving instructions on how to put the furniture together*).

instructive /in-**struc**-tiv/ *adj* giving knowledge or information (*an instructive television show*).

instructor /in-**struc**-tor/ *n* a teacher, a coach, someone who instructs (*a sports instructor*).

instrument /**in**-stru-ment/ *n* **1** a tool, especially one used for delicate work (*surgical instruments*). **2** a device producing musical sound (*stringed instruments*). **3** a device for measuring, recording, controlling, etc., especially in an aircraft.

instrumental /in-stru-**men**-tal/ *adj* **1** being the cause of (*she was instrumental in getting him hired*). **2** played on musical instruments (*instrumental music*). ● *n* **instrumentality** /in-stru-men-ta-li-tee/ the state of being instrumental.

instrumentation /in-stru-men-**tay**-shun/ *n* **1** the arrangement of music for instruments. **2** the act of using instruments, especially scientific instruments. **3** the instruments used.

insubstantial /in-sub-**stan**-shal/ *adj* **1** weak or flimsy. **2** not real, imaginary.

insufferable /in-**suf**-ra-bul/ *adj* unbearable (*an insufferable bore*).

insufficient /in-su-**fi**-shent/ *adj* not enough (*insufficient evidence*). ● *n* **insufficiency** /in-su-fi-shen-see/.

insular /**in**-soo-lar/ *adj* **1** (*fml*) having to do with an island. **2** narrow-minded (*an insular outlook on life*).

insularity /in-su-**la**-ri-tee/ *n* narrow-mindedness.

insulate /**in**-su-late/ *vb* **1** to keep apart (*a wealthy family insulated from the financial problems of ordinary people*). **2** to cover with a special material to prevent the loss of electricity or heat. ● *n* **insulation** /in-su-**lay**-shun/.

insulator /**in**-su-lay-tor/ *n* a material that does not allow electricity or heat to pass through it.

insulin /**in**-s(u)-lin/ *n* a substance that if given as a medicine helps to use up the sugar in the body when there is too much of it (*people suffering from diabetes sometimes have to take insulin*).

insult /in-**sult**/ *vb* to speak rude or hurtful words to or of (*she was insulted when he called her an old lady*). ● *n* **insult** /**in**-sult/.

insupportable /in-su-**pore**-ta-bul/ *adj* unbearable, not capable of being upheld or supported (*insupportable burdens*).

insure /in-**shoor**/ *vb* to pay regular sums to a society on condition that the payer receives an agreed amount of money in case of loss, accident, death, etc. (*insuring his life/insure his house against fire and theft*). ● *n* **insurance** /in-**shoo**-ranse/.

insured /in-**shoord**/ *n* a person whose life, property, etc. is insured against loss or damage.

insurer /in-**shoo**-rer/ *n* a person or company that insures others against loss or damage.

insurmountable /in-sur-**moun**-ta-bul/ *adj* that cannot be passed over or overcome (*insurmountable difficulties*).

intact /in-**tact**/ *adj* untouched, unharmed, with no part missing (*the police recovered the box of jewels intact/her self-confidence remained intact*).

intake /**in**-take/ *n* the act or process of taking in (*intake of breath*).

intangible /in-**tan**-ji-bul/ *adj* **1** that cannot be touched (*air is intangible*). **2** not able to be clearly defined or understood (*an intangible air of hopelessness*).

integer /**in**-ti-jer/ *n* a whole number.

integral /**in**-ti-gral/ *adj* necessary to make something complete (*an integral part of the case against him*). ● *also n*.

integrate /**in**-ti-grate/ *vb* **1** to join in society as a whole, to mix freely with other groups (*newcomers trying to integrate into American life*). **2** to fit parts together to form a whole (*integrating everyone's comments into the report on the conference*). ● *n* **integration** /in-ti-**gray**-shun/.

integrator /**in**-ti-gray-tor/ *n* a person or thing that integrates.

integrity /in-**te**-gri-tee/ *n* **1** the state of being whole and undivided, completeness (*integrity as a nation*). **2** honesty, sincerity (*a man of absolute integrity*).

intellect /**in**-ti-lect/ *n* **1** the mind, the power to think and understand. **2** someone with great intellect (*one of the world's greatest intellects*).

intellectual /in-ti-**lec**-chu-wal/ *adj* **1** having a high intellect (*her intellectual friends*). **2** having to do with the intellect (*intellectual interests*). ● *also n*.

intelligence /in-**te**-li-jense/ *n* **1** cleverness, quickness of mind or understanding (*the intelligence of the pupils*). **2** (*fml*) news (*receive intelligence of his death*).

intelligent /in-te-li-jent/ *adj* having a quick mind, clever (*intelligent pupils*).

intelligible /in-te-li-ji-bul/ *adj* clear, that can be understood (*instructions that are scarcely intelligible*).

intemperate /in-tem-prit/ *adj* **1** lacking self-control, given to taking too much, especially strong drink (*intemperate habits*). **2** more than is desirable (*an intemperate amount of alcohol*). **3** excessive, unrestrained (*intemperate language*). **4** extreme (*an intemperate climate*). ● *n* **intemperance** /in-tem-pranse/.

intend /in-tend/ *vb* **1** to have as a purpose (*she intends to leave tomorrow*). **2** to mean (*the bullet was intended for the president*). ● *adj* **intended** /in-ten-did/ meant, planned for the future (*his intended wife*).

intense /in-tense/ *adj* **1** very great (*intense heat*). **2** very serious (*intense young women*).

intensify /in-ten-si-fie/ *vb* to make greater or more severe (*intensified their interest in the subject*). ● *n* **intensifier** /in-ten-si-fie-er/ a person or thing that makes greater or more severe.

intension /in-ten-shun/ *n* **1** determination. **2** the quality of being intense, degree of intensity.

intensity /in-ten-si-tee/ *n* **1** strength (*the intensity of the heat*). **2** seriousness, earnestness (*the intensity of the young poet*). **3** great energy, emotion, thought.

intensive /in-ten-siv/ *adj* increasing or degree or amount (*intensive care at the hospital*).

intent /in-tent/ *adj* **1** attending carefully (*intent on his work/with an intent expression*). **2** eager, planning or wanting to do something (*intent on going abroad*). ● *n* (*fml*) purpose (*it was his intent to move out of the area*).

intention /in-ten-shun/ *n* purpose, aim in doing something (*it was his intention to leave early*).

intentional /in-tench-nal/ *adj* done on purpose (*intentional damage to his car*).

inter /in-ter/ *vb* (**interred** /in-terd/, **interring** /in-te-ring/) (*fml*) to bury (*inter him in the churchyard*).

inter- /in-ter/ *prefix* between, among.

interact /in-te-ract/ *vb* to act on each other (*chemicals that interact*). ● *n* **interaction** /in-te-rac-shun/.

intercede /in-ter-seed/ *vb* **1** to try to settle a dispute or quarrel between others (*interceding in the wage dispute between management and the union*). **2** to speak in defense of another (*he interceded with the king to save his friend's life*).

intercept /in-ter-sept/ *vb* to stop or catch on the way from one place to another (*intercept the enemy message*). ● *n* **interception** /in-ter-sep-shun/.

interchange /in-ter-change/ *vb* **1** to change places with each other. **2** to give and receive in return (*interchange ideas*). ● *n* an exchange.

interchangeable /in-ter-chane-ja-bul/ *adj* that which can be exchanged for each other (*the two words are interchangeable*).

interest /in-trest/ *n* **1** something in which a person takes part eagerly (*his main interests are tennis and football*). **2** advantage (*it was in his interest to agree*). **3** eager attention (*give the matter all his interest*). **4** concern (*of interest to all of us*). **5** the money paid for the use of a loan of money (*the rate of interest on his bank loan*). ● *vb* to gain the attention of.

interesting /in-tres-ting/ *adj* arousing interest (*interesting information*).

interface /in-ter-face/ *n* the point at which two subjects affect each other or are connected (*the interface between production and sales*).

interfere /in-ter-fere/ *vb* **1** to get in the way of, to prevent from working or happening (*outside interests that interfere with his work*). **2** to force oneself into the affairs of others (*interfering in other people's private business*). **3** to touch or move something that is not supposed to be touched or moved (*interfere with his private papers*).

interference /in-ter-fee-rense/ *n* **1** act of interfering (*object to his interference in their affairs*). **2** the interruption of radio broadcasts by atmospherics or other broadcasts.

intergalactic /in-ter-ga-lac-tic/ *adj* existing or occurring between or among galaxies.

interim /in-te-rim/ *n* the meantime, the time between two events (*the new head arrives next week—in the interim the deputy head is in charge*). ● *adj* acting for a time only (*take interim measures*).

interior /in-tee-ree-ur/ *adj* **1** inner. **2** inland. ● *n* **1** the inner part (*the interior of the house*). **2** the inland part (*the interior of the country*).

interject /in-ter-ject/ *vb* **1** to say something short and sudden. **2** to put in a remark when another is speaking.

interjection /in-ter-jec-shun/ *n* **1** a short word expressing surprise, interest, disapproval, etc. ("*oh*" *is an interjection*). **2** a remark made when another is speaking (*the speaker objected to his rude interjections*).

interlude /in-ter-lood/ *n* **1** an interval between the acts of a play, etc. **2** the music or other entertainment provided during such an interval. **3** a period of time that comes between two events or activities (*a brief interlude of peace between the two wars*).

intermediate /in-ter-**mee**-dee-it/ *adj* coming between two other things, in the middle (*at an intermediate stage of the language course*).

interminable /in-**ter**-mi-na-bul/ *adj* without, or apparently without, end, seeming to last forever.

intermission /in-ter-mi-shun/ *n* an interval, a time between two parts (*have a drink at the theater bar in the intermission*).

intermittent /in-ter-**mi**-tent/ *adj* stopping for a time, then going on again, happening at intervals (*intermittent showers*).

intern /in-tern/ *n* a person, especially a student, working in a professional field to gain experience in the work place. ● *vb* to detain or confine people, ships, etc. as during a war. ● *n* **internment** /in-**tern**-ment/.

internal /in-**ter**-nal/ *adj* **1** having to do with the inside, especially of the body (*internal organs*). **2** of a person's own country (*internal trade*).

international /in-ter-**nash**-nal/ *adj* having to do with several or many countries (*an international trading treaty*). ● *n* a person associated with two different countries.

Internet /**in**-ter-net/ *n* the worldwide system of linked computer networks.

interplay /**in**-ter-play/ *n* the action of one thing on another (*the interplay of light and shade in his painting*).

interpret /in-**ter**-pret/ *vb* **1** to explain the meaning of (*how do you interpret these lines of poetry?*). **2** to understand the meaning to be (*he interpreted her silence as a refusal*). **3** to translate from one language into another (*he spoke in French, and his English assistant interpreted his speech for the audience*). ● *adj* **interpretive** /in-**ter**-pre-tiv/.

interpretation /in-ter-pre-**tay**-shun/ *n* **1** act of interpreting. **2** the meaning given to a work of art by a critic or performer.

interpreter /in-**ter**-pre-ter/ *n* someone who translates from one speaker's language into another's.

interracial /in-ter-**ray**-shal/ *adj* between, among, or involving members of different races.

interrogate /in-**te**-ro-gate/ *vb* to put questions to (*police interrogated the accused for several hours*).

interrogation /in-te-ro-**gay**-shun/ *n* **1** the act of interrogating (*the interrogation of the accused by the police*).

interrogative /in-te-**rog**-a-tiv/ *adj* asking a question, having to do with questions (*an interrogative remark*). ● *n* a word used in asking questions (e.g., why).

interrupt /in-te-**rupt**/ *vb* **1** to break flow of speech or action (*interrupt the broadcast to announce the death of the president/interrupt his lunch break to ask him to move his car*). **2** to stop a person while he or she is saying or doing something (*he interrupted the speaker to ask a question*). **3** (*fml*) to cut off (*build a block of flats that interrupted our view of the lake*). ● *n* **interrupter** /in-te-**rup**-ter/ a person who interrupts.

interruption /in-te-**rup**-shun/ *n* a remark or action that causes a stoppage (*the noisy interruptions by the audience during the politician's speech*).

intersect /in-ter-**sect**/ *vb* to cut across each other (*the roads intersect outside the town*).

intersection /in-ter-**sec**-shun/ *n* the point at which lines or roads cross each other (*an intersection without traffic lights*).

intersperse /in-ter-**sperse**/ *vb* to scatter over, to put here and there (*intersperse seeds amongst the soil*).

interstate /**in**-ter-state/ *adj* between or among states. ● *n* one of a network of US highways connecting 48 of the United States.

interstellar /in-ter-**ste**-lar/ *adj* among or between the stars.

intertwine /in-ter-**twine**/ *vb* to twist together (*roses intertwine around the door*).

interval /**in**-ter-val/ *n* **1** the time or distance between (*the interval between snow showers*). **2** a break, a spell of free time (*pupils having a snack in their interval*). **3** a short break in a play, concert, etc. (*have a drink at the theater bar during the interval*). **4** the difference of pitch between two musical sounds.

intervene /in-ter-**veen**/ *vb* **1** to interrupt, to interfere (*intervening to try to stop them quarrelling*). **2** to be or to happen between (in time) (*a few years intervened before they met again*). **3** to happen so as to prevent something (*he was going to go to college but the war intervened and he became a soldier*). ● *n* **intervention** /in-ter-**ven**-shun/.

interview /**in**-ter-vyoo/ *n* **1** a meeting at which a person applying for a job is questioned (*several candidates had an interview*). **2** a meeting with a person to get information or to do business (*the journalist asked for an interview with the president*). ● *also vb.*

intestinal /in-**tes**-ti-nal/ *adj* having to do with the intestines (*intestinal problems*).

intestines /**in**-te-stinz/ *npl* the inner parts of the body, especially the bowels (*the intestines consist of the large intestine and the small intestine*).

intifada /in-ti-**fa**-da/ *n* an uprising, specifically the uprising of Palestinian Arabs against Israeli military forces in occupied territories of the Gaza Strip and the west bank of the Jordon River, begun in 1987.

intimacy /in-ti-ma-see/ *n* closeness, close relationship (*enjoy the intimacy that exists between old school friends*).

intimate /in-ti-mit/ *adj* **1** having a close relationship. **2** having a close knowledge of (*an intimate knowledge of the area*). ● *n* a close friend. ● *vb* [in'-tim-āt] (*fml*) to make known (*intimating his intention to leave*).

intimation /in-ti-**may**-shun/ *n* **1** (*fml*) a hint (*he gave no intimation of his intention to leave*). **2** an announcement (*intimations of births, marriages, and deaths in the newspaper*).

intimidate /in-ti-mi-date/ *vb* to make afraid, e.g., by making threats (*she was intimidated by the sight of the huge man/the boy intimidating younger boys into giving him money*). ● *n* **intimidation** /in-ti-mi-**day**-shun/.

into /in-too/ *prep* **1** from the outside to the inside (*jumped into the pool*). **2** continuing to the midst of (*danced into the night*). **3** to the form, substance, or condition of (*turned into a butterfly*). **4** so as to strike, against (*bumped into the wall*). **5** to the work or activity of (*go into teaching*).

intolerable /in-**tol**-ra-bul/ *adj* that cannot or should not be put up with (*intolerable pain/intolerable behavior*).

intolerant /in-**tol**-rant/ *adj* not willing to put up with actions or opinions that are different from a person's own, narrow-minded (*intolerant people who dislike those who hold views that are different from theirs*). ● *n* **intolerance** /in-**tol**-ranse/.

intonation /in-tu-**nay**-shun/ *n* the rise and fall of the voice while speaking (*a boring voice with very little intonation*).

intoxicate /in-**tok**-si-cate/ *vb* **1** to make drunk or stupefied (*he had drunk enough beer to intoxicate him*). **2** to excite greatly (*he was intoxicated by his success*). ● *n* **intoxication** /in-tok-si-**cay**-shun/.

intra- /in-tra/ *prefix* within, inside.

intragalactic /in-tra-ga-**lac**-tic/ *adj* occurring within a galaxy.

intranet /**in**-tra-net/ *n* a private computer network using Internet technology but keeping access limited to members of a particular organization.

intransitive /in-**tran**-zi-tiv/ *adj* (*of verbs*) not taking an object.

intravenous /in-tra-**vee**-nus/ *adj* in or directly into a vein or veins.

intrepid /in-**tre**-pid/ *adj* fearless, brave (*the intrepid explorer*).

intricate /in-tri-cit/ *adj* having many small parts, complicated (*an intricate pattern/an intricate story*). ● *n* **intricacy** /**in**-tri-ca-see/.

intrigue /in-**treeg**/ *n* **1** a secret plot. **2** a secret love affair. ● *vb* **1** to plot secretly. **2** to interest greatly. ● *adj* **intriguing** /in-**tree**-ging/.

intrinsic /in-**trin**-zic/ *adj* being part of the nature or character of, belonging to a thing as part of its nature (*his intrinsic generosity/furniture of no intrinsic worth*).

introduce /in-tro-**doos**/ *vb* **1** to bring in or put forward, especially something new (*introducing a new system of accounting*). **2** to make one person known to another (*introduce her two friends to each other*).

introduction /in-tru-**duc**-shun/ *n* **1** act of introducing (*the introduction of new methods/ask for an introduction to her friend*). **2** a short section at the beginning of a book to make known its purpose (*an introduction explaining how to use the encyclopedia*).

introductory /in-tru-**duc**-tree/ *adj* coming at the beginning, giving an introduction (*an introductory course/a few introductory remarks*).

introspective /in-tro-**spec**-tiv/ *adj* thinking a lot about one's own actions and ideas (*poetry of an introspective nature/so introspective that she is frequently rather depressed*). ● *n* **introspection** /in-tro-**spec**-shun/. ● *vb* **introspect** /**in**-tro-spect/ to look into one's own mind.

introvert /**in**-tro-vert/ *n* someone who is always thinking about his or her own ideas and aims (*he is an introvert, but his sister is a real extrovert*).

intrude /in-**trood**/ *vb* to come or go where not wanted (*he was intruding, since they obviously wanted to be alone/she intruded on their private grief*). ● *n* **intrusion** /in-**troo**-zhun/.

intruder /in-**troo**-der/ *n* **1** someone who intrudes. **2** a person who breaks into a house to steal, a burglar (*he heard an intruder downstairs*).

intrusive /in-**troo**-siv/ *adj* tending to intrude (*intrusive neighbors/intrusive questions*).

intuition /in-too-**wi**-shun/ *n* **1** immediate knowledge of the truth gained without having to think (*she had an intuition that he was a wrongdoer, and she was right*). **2** the ability to know things in this way (*she knew by intuition that something was wrong with her sister*). ● *adj* **intuitive** /in-**too**-wi-tiv/. ● *vb* **intuit** /in-**too**-wit/ to know or learn by intuition.

Inuit /i-noo-wit/ *n* an Eskimo of northern North America or Greenland, the language of this people.

Inuktitut /i-**nook**-ti-toot/ *n* a group of Eskimo languages spoken in the eastern and central parts of arctic Canada.

inundate /i-nun-date/ *vb* **1** to flow over (*fields inundated with flood water*). **2** to flood, to come in very large amounts (*they were inundated with correspondence*).

Inupiaq /i-**noo**-pee-yak/ *n* the language of the Inupiat, spoken in northern Alaska, Canada, and Greenland.

Inupiat /i-**noo**-pee-yat/ *n* a member of the Eskimo people of northern Alaska, Canada, and Greenland.

invade /in-**vade**/ *vb* **1** to enter as an enemy, to attack (*the king ordered his army to invade the neighboring country*). **2** to interfere with (*invading his neighbor's privacy*).

invalid[1] /in-va-lid/ *adj* **1** not valid (*an invalid ticket*). **2** useless, unreliable (*an invalid argument*).

invalid[2] /in-va-lid/ *adj* weak, sickly (*her invalid aunt*). ● *n* a sick person. ● *vb* to send away because of illness (*he was invalided by the disease*).

invalidate /in-**va**-li-date/ *vb* to make to have no value or effect (*his claims to be an expert on local history were completely invalidated*).

invalidism /in-**va**-li-di-zum/ *n* the state of being an invalid, long-term ill health or disability.

invaluable /in-**val**-yu-bul/ *adj* of very great value, more valuable than can be paid for (*her invaluable help/the information was invaluable*).

invariable /in-**vay**-ree-ya-bul/ *adj* unchanging, constant. ● *n*.

invariant /in-**vay**-ree-ant/ *adj* constant, unchanging.

invasion /in-**vay**-zhun/ *n* **1** entry into a country by enemy forces (*their invasion of a neighboring country*). **2** interference (*the invasion of his privacy*). ● *adj* **invasive** /in-**vay**-siv/.

invent /in-**vent**/ *vb* **1** to think of and plan something new (*invent the motor car*). **2** to make up (*she invented a story about her car breaking down to account for her lateness*). ● *n* **inventor** /in-**ven**-tor/.

invention /in-**ven**-shun/ *n* **1** a thing thought of and made for the first time (*the telephone was one of his inventions*). **2** the ability to think of new ideas (*her powers of invention*).

inventive /in-**ven**-tiv/ *adj* good at thinking of new or unusual ideas (*an inventive writer*).

inventory /in-ven-toe-ree/ *n* a list of goods or articles (*take an inventory of the contents of the house before she rented it out*).

inverse /in-verse/ *adj* opposite or reverse (*their enthusiasm for their work seemed to be in inverse proportion to their salaries*).

inversion /in-**ver**-shun/ *n* **1** act of turning upside down. **2** a change in the usual order of words in a sentence.

invert /in-**vert**/ *vb* to turn upside down, to turn the other way round (*he inverted his glass to trap the wasp/invert the clauses in the sentence*).

invertebrate /in-**ver**-te-brate/ *adj* having no backbone (*invertebrate creatures such as worms*). ● *n* an animal without a backbone.

invest /in-**vest**/ *vb* **1** to mark someone's entry to rank or office by clothing him or her with the robes belonging to it (*invest the new bishop*). **2** to surround a fort with an army. **3** to lend money so as to increase it by interest or a share in profits (*he invested his savings in her new restaurant*).

investigate /in-**ve**-sti-gate/ *vb* to examine, to find out everything about (*police investigating the murder*). ● *n* **investigator** /in-**ve**-sti-gay-tor/.

investigation /in-ve-sti-**gay**-shun/ *n* a careful examination, an inquiry (*the police have mounted a murder investigation*).

investigative /in-**ve**-sti-ga-tiv/ *adj* inclined to investigate.

investment /in-**vest**-ment/ *n* **1** the act of investing. **2** a sum of money invested (*she has an investment of $14,000 in her husband's business*). **3** the thing money has been invested in (*she had to sell all her investments, including her house*).

investor /in-**ve**-stor/ *n* someone who invests money (*all the investors in her business lost their money*).

inveterate /in-**ve**-trit/ *adj* **1** firmly fixed in a habit (*an inveterate liar*). **2** firmly established (*an inveterate dislike of flying*).

invincible /in-**vin**-si-bul/ *adj* that cannot be defeated (*they thought their army was invincible*). ● *n* **invincibility** /in-vin-si-**bi**-li-tee/.

invisible /in-**vi**-zi-bul/ *adj* that cannot be seen (*germs are invisible*). ● *n* **invisibility** /in-vi-si-**bi**-li-tee/.

invite /in-**vite**/ *vb* **1** to ask politely, to ask to come, especially as a guest (*inviting them to dinner/invited them to join their club*). **2** to attract (*the talks invited press attention*). ● *n* **invitation** /in-vi-**tay**-shun/.

inviting /in-**vie**-ting/ *adj* attractive (*an inviting prospect*).

invoice /in-voiss/ *n* **1** a list of goods sent to a buyer, with prices. **2** a list of work done and payment due. ● *vb* to send an invoice.

invoke /in-**voke**/ *vb* **1** to bring into use or operation (*invoking a little-known law to justify their actions*). **2** to call on God or a god in prayer. **3** to request or beg for (*invoke their assistance*). **4** to make an urgent request to (*invoke the law for their protection*).

involuntary /in-**vol**-un-te-ree/ *adj* unintentional, done without conscious effort or intention (*involuntary movements of the muscles/he gave an involuntary cry*).

involve /in-**volve**/ *vb* **1** to include (*the accident involved a car and a truck*). **2** to mix up in (*he became involved in drug-smuggling*). **3** to cause as a result (*a job involving a lot of overtime*).

involved /in-**volvd**/ *adj* complicated (*an involved explanation*).

invulnerable /in-**vuln**-ra-bul/ *adj* that cannot be wounded.

inward /in-ward/ *adj* **1** inner. **2** having to do with the mind (*a feeling of inward satisfaction*). ● *adv* toward the inside.

inwardly /in-ward-lee/ *adv* on the inside, in the mind (*inwardly disapproving*).

iodine /**eye**-o-deen/ *n* a chemical used in medicine to clean wounds, instruments, etc. (*a solution of iodine used as an antiseptic*).

iodize /**eye**-o-dize/ *vb, also* **iodise** (*Br*) to treat with iodine.

ion /**eye**-on/ *n* an electrically charged atom. ● *adj* **ionic** /eye-**on**-ic/.

ionosphere /eye-**on**-oe-sfeer/ *n* the outer part of the earth's atmosphere.

iota /**eye**-oe-ta/ *n* **1** a Greek letter. **2** a tiny amount (*not care an iota about his family*).

Iowa /**eye**-oe-wa/ *n* a member of a Native American people previously living in Iowa and Missouri, now living in Nebraska, Kansas, and Oklahoma, the language of these people.

IQ /eye-**kyoo**/ *abbr* = **Intelligence Quotient**: a person's level of intelligence as measured by a special test.

irate /eye-**rate**/ *adj* very angry, furious (*the irate farmer chased the boys who had let his cows out*).

ire /ire/ *n* (*fml or lit*) anger.

iridescent /i-ri-**des**-ant/ *adj* colored like the rainbow, brightly colored, having or showing shifting colors (*iridescent patches of oil on the street*). ● *n* **iridescence** /i-ri-**des**-anse/.

iris /**eye**-ris/ *n* **1** the colored circle of the eye. **2** a flowering plant. **3** the rainbow.

irk /urk/ *vb* to annoy, to bother (*it irks her that he earns more than she does*).

irksome /**irk**-sum/ *adj* troublesome, tedious, annoying (*irksome household tasks*).

iron /**eye**-urn/ *n* **1** the most common of metals. **2** a tool or instrument made of iron, especially for smoothing clothes. **3** *pl* chains (*prisoners in irons*). ● *adj* **1** made of iron. **2** strong, hard (*an iron will*). ● *vb* to smooth (clothes) with an iron (*iron shirts*). ● **to have too many irons in the fire** to be trying to do too many things at once.

ironic /eye-**ron**-ic/, **ironical** /eye-**ron**-ic-al/ *adjs* expressing irony (*an ironic remark/it was ironic that he stole money that he was going to get as a gift*).

irony /**eye**-ro-nee/ *n* **1** a remark made in such a way that the meaning is understood to be the opposite of what is said ("*a fine fellow you are,*" *she said with irony*). **2** the result of an action that has the opposite effect to that intended (*the irony of his action was that he stole money that she was going to give him*).

Iroquoian /i-ro-**kwaw**-yan/ *n* a family of Native American languages including Oneida, Mohawk, Huron, Tuscarora, and Cherokee, a member of the peoples speaking these languages.

Iroquois /i-ro-**kwoy**/ *n* a member of a group of Native American peoples that lived in upstate New York and included the Senecas, Cayugas, Onondagas, Oneidas, Mohawks, and the Tuscaroras, any of the languages spoken by the Iroquois.

irradiate /i-**ray**-dee-ate/ *vb* **1** (*fml or lit*) to make bright by throwing light on (*a garden irradiated with light from the lanterns*). **2** to treat with radiation (*irradiating the cancer*). ● *n* **irradiation** /i-ray-dee-**aye**-shun/ exposure to radiation, an irradiating of.

irrational /i-**ra**-shnal/ *adj* **1** not rational, not reasonable, not sensible (*an irrational decision*). **2** not able to reason, not using reason. ● *n* **irrationalism** /i-**ra**-shna-li-zum/ irrational thought.

irregular /i-**reg**-yu-lar/ *adj* **1** not in agreement with the rules, not according to accepted standards (*his behavior was most irregular*). **2** not straight or even (*irregular features/irregular road surfaces/ an irregular coastline*). **3** not happening, etc., regularly (*irregular school attendance*). ● *n* **irregularity** /i-reg-yu-**la**-ri-tee/.

irrelevant /i-**re**-le-vant/ *adj* having nothing to do with the subject, not to the point (*please do not raise irrelevant issues at the meeting*). ● *ns* **irrelevance** /i-**re**-le-vanse/, **irrelevancy** /i-**re**-le-van-see/.

irreplaceable /i-re-**play**-sa-bul/ *adj* not replaceable, that cannot be replaced.

irrepressible /i-re-**pre**-si-bul/ *adj* that cannot be kept down or held back (*irrepressible cheerfulness*).

irresistible /i-re-**zi**-sta-bul/ *adj* **1** that cannot be resisted (*an irresistible force*). **2** very strong (*find his argument irresistible*). **3** very attractive, charming (*find newborn babies irresistible*).

irrespective /i-re-**spec**-tiv/ *adj* showing disregard for persons, not troubling about.

irresponsible /i-re-**spon**-si-bul/ *adj* not caring about the consequences of actions (*irresponsible of him to leave the children on their own*).

irrigate /i-ri-gate/ *vb* to supply water to dry land by canals, etc. ● *n* **irrigation** /i-ri-**gay**-shun/. ● *adj* **irrigable** /i-ri-ga-bul/.

irritable /i-ri-ta-bul/ *adj* easily angered or annoyed (*he is always irritable first thing in the morning*). ● *n* **irritability** /i-ri-ta-**bi**-li-tee/.

irritant /i-ri-tant/ *n* something that irritates, annoys, angers, inflames, makes sore, etc. (*the irritant that caused her sore eye/regard all children as irritants*).

irritate /i-ri-tate/ *vb* **1** to annoy, to anger (*irritated by their lack of interest*). **2** to cause to itch, become inflamed, red, swollen, etc. (*the washing-up liquid irritating her skin*). ● *n* **irritation** /i-ri-**tay**-shun/.

is /iz/ *vb* third-person usage of the verb "to be" (*she is going away*).

Islam /iz-lam/ *n* **1** the Muslim religion founded by Mohammed in which the god is called Allah. **2** all Muslims. **3** all the lands in which Islam is the main religion. ● *adj* **Islamic** /i-**sla**-mic/.

island /**eye**-land/ *n* a piece of land surrounded by water (*a desert island*).

islander /**eye**-lan-der/ *n* a native of an island.

isle /ile/ *n* (*lit*) an island, especially a small island.

islet /**eye**-let/ *n* a very small island.

isolate /**eye**-so-late/ *vb* **1** to place apart or alone (*isolate the patient with the unknown fever*). **2** to cut off (*towns isolated in snowy weather*). **3** to separate (*isolating and examining the chemical substance*). ● *n* **isolation** /eye-so-**lay**-shun/.

isosceles /eye-**sos**-leez/ *adj* (*of a triangle*) having two sides equal.

issue /i-shoo/ *vb* **1** to go or come out (*people issuing from the building/noises issuing from the room*). **2** to send out (*issue reminders about unpaid bills*). **3** to flow out (*blood issued from the wound*). **4** to give out (*issue new uniforms to all soldiers*). **5** to

publish. ● *n* **1** a flowing out (*the issue of blood from the wound*). **2** (*fml*) children (*married couples with no issue*). **3** (*fml*) a result (*await the issue of their debate*). **4** a question under discussion (*this issue is an international one*). **5** the number of books, papers, etc., published at one time (*the Christmas issue of the magazine*).

it /it/ *pron* the person, animal, or thing previously mentioned, also used as the subject to an impersonal verb (e.g., it is snowing).

IT /eye-**tee**/ *abbr* = **information technology**: the study or use of computers and telecommunication sytems.

italicize, italicise (*Br*) /i-**ta**-li-size/ *vb* to print in italics (*italicizing the names of books and plays in essays*).

italic(s) /i-ta-lics/ *n* in printing, letters in sloping type (e.g., *italics*). ● *adj*.

itch /itch/ *n* **1** an irritation of the skin that causes a desire to scratch (*she has an itch where the flea bit her*). **2** a longing (*an itch to travel*). ● *vb* **1** to feel an itch. **2** to feel a strong desire (to do something). ● *adj* **itchy** /**it**-chee/.

item /**eye**-tem/ *n* **1** a single one out of a list or number of things (*the items on her shopping list/items of clothing*). **2** a piece of news (*an interesting item in the newspaper*). ● *adv* also, in the same way.

itemize /**eye**-tem-ize/ *vb, also* **itemise** (*Br*) to specify the items of (*an itemized bill shows each thing purchased*).

itinerant /eye-**ti**-ne-rant/ *adj* not settling in any one place, moving from place to place (*an itinerant salesman*). ● *n* one who is always on the move from place to place.

itinerary /eye-**ti**-ne-ra-ree/ *n* a note of the places visited or to be visited on a journey (*receive an itinerary from the travel agent*).

its /its/ *pron* that or those belonging to it, the possessive form of "it."

it's /its/ *contraction* shortened form of **it is** or **it has**.

itty-bitty /i-tee-**bi**-tee/ *adj* (*inf*) very small, tiny.

ivory /**eye**-vree/ *n* the hard white substance forming the tusks of elephants, etc. (*decorations made of ivory*). ● *adj* of or like ivory, creamy white (*an ivory blouse*).

ivy /**eye**-vee/ *n* a climbing vine with a woody stem and evergreen leaves (*trees covered in ivy*).

J

J, j /jay/ the tenth letter of the alphabet.

jab /jab/ *vb* (**jabbed** /jabd/, **jabbing** /ja-bing/) to prod or poke suddenly (*she jabbed him in the arm as she spoke*). ● *n* **1** a sudden prod or poke. **2** (*Br inf*) an injection (*get a jab against measles*).

jabber /ja-ber/ *vb* to chatter, to speak quickly and indistinctly (*unable to understand what the excited children were jabbering about*).

jack /jack/ *n* **1** a tool for lifting heavy weights (*a car jack*). **2** the small white ball aimed at in the game of bowls. **3** the knave in cards. **4** a flag. ● *vb* to raise with a jack (*jack the car up*). ● **every man jack** (*inf*) every single one (*every man jack of us will have to help*).

jackal /ja-cal/ *n* a doglike wild animal.

jackass /ja-cass/ *n* **1** a male donkey. **2** (*inf*) a fool.

jacket /ja-cet/ *n* **1** a short coat (*a man's woolen jacket*). **2** a loose paper cover for a book (*the book has a striking design on its jacket*).

jack-of-all-trades /jack-of-awl-**traydz**/ *n* someone who is able to do any kind of job (*he is not only a joiner—he is a jack-of-all-trades*).

Jacuzzi /ja-**coo**-zee/ (*trademark*) a kind of whirlpool bath with a system of underwater jets which massage the body.

jade /jade/ *n* a green precious stone.

jaded /jay-did/ *adj* tired, bored, uninterested (*after all the Christmas parties he feels a bit jaded and can't be bothered going out*).

jagged /ja-ged/ *adj* having rough edges or having sharp points (*jagged rocks*).

jaguar /ja-gwar/ *n* an animal like the leopard, found in South America.

jail /jale/ *n* a prison (*sentenced and sent to jail*).

jailer /jay-ler/ *n* a prison guard (*locked up at night by jailers*).

jam¹ /jam/ *n* fruit boiled with sugar to preserve it; jelly; preserve (*spread raspberry jam on the bread*).

jam² /jam/ *vb* (**jammed** /jamd/, **jamming** /ja-ming/) **1** to squeeze in, to fix so tightly that movement is impossible, to wedge in (*he jammed his foot in the doorway*). **2** to crowd full (*the hall was jammed with protesters*). **3** to prevent the receiving of radio messages by broadcasting sounds on the same wavelength. **4** to take part in an unplanned music making session (*I jammed with the saxophonists/we were jamming*). ● *n* **1** a pile-up of traffic (*bad traffic jams in the town during rush hour*). **2** an unplanned music-making session (the jazz musicians in the club had a jam). ● *also* **jam/jamming session**.

jangle /jang-gl/ *n* a harsh ringing noise (*hear the jangle of the shop doorbell*). ● *vb* **1** to make or cause to make a jangle. **2** (*inf*) to irritate (*jangling one's nerves*).

janitor /ja-ni-tor/ *n* **1** a doorkeeper. **2** one who takes care of a building.

January /jan-yoo-a-ree/ *n* the first month of the year.

jar /jar/ *n* a glass or earthenware vessel with a wide mouth (*a jar of jam*).

jargon /jar-gon/ *n* words special to a group or profession (*the jargon of the advertising business*).

Jasmine /jaz-min/, **jessamine** /jess-min/ *ns* a climbing bush with sweet-smelling flowers.

jasper /ja-sper/ *n* a precious stone, yellow, red or brown in color.

jaundice /jon-diss/ *n* an illness marked by yellowness of the eyes and skin.

jaundiced /jon-dist/ *adj* **1** suffering from jaundice. **2** full of envy, disappointment, etc., thinking of everything as bad or unlucky (*have a jaundiced view of life*).

jaunt /jont/ *n* a short pleasure trip (*go on a jaunt to the seaside*). ● *vb* to go from place to place.

jaunty /jon-tee/ *adj* **1** cheerful-looking, confident (*wear his hat at a jaunty angle*). **2** pleased with oneself (*in a jaunty mood*).

javelin /ja-ve-lin/ *n* a light throwing spear.

jaw /jaw/ *n* one of the bones in the mouth that hold the teeth (*get a broken jaw in a fight*).

jay /jay/ *n* a bird of the crow family with brightly colored feathers.

jaywalk /jay-wawk/ *vb* to walk across the street carelessly or without obeying the rules of the road. ● *n* **jaywalker** /jay-waw-ker/.

jazz /jazz/ *n* syncopated music and dancing of African-American origin.

jealous /je-luss/ *adj* **1** disliking rivals in love, having feelings of dislike for any possible rivals (*a jealous husband/he is jealous of any man she speaks to*). **2** disliking another because he or she is better off than you in some way; envious (*jealous of her friend's beauty*). **3** (*fml*) very careful of (*jealous of her reputation*). ● *n* **jealousy** /je-lu-see/.

jean /jeen/ *n* a cotton cloth. ● *npl* **jeans** /jeenz/ close-fitting trousers often made of denim.

Jeep /jeep/ (*trademark*) a light truck, military or otherwise, for going over rough ground.

jeer /jeer/ *vb* to laugh or shout at disrespectfully, to mock, (*jeering at the football player who was playing badly*). ● *n* insulting words.

jehad /ji-**had**/ *see* jihad.

Jehovah /ji-**ho**-va/ *n* from the Old Testament of the bible, a name for God.

Jell-O /**je**-lo/ *n* (*trademark*) a sweet food made by boiling the juice of fruit with sugar and mixing with gelatin to make it set (*serve orange Jell-O to the children*).

jelly /**je**-lee/ *n* **1** a type of preserved fruit; jam (*spread grape jelly and peanut butter on bread*). **2** a food made from fruit juice boiled with sugar, from meat juices, or from gelatin (*the juice from the roast chicken turned to jelly*). **3** a material that is in a state between solid and liquid. **4** (*Br*) Jell-O.

jellyfish /**je**-lee-fish/ *n* a jellylike sea creature often with stinging tentacles.

jeopardize /**je**-par-dize/ *vb, also* **jeopardise** (*Br*) to put in danger, to risk (*jeopardizing the rescue operation by his careless action*).

jeopardy /**je**-par-dee/ *n* danger.

jerk /jerk/ *vb* **1** to give a sudden pull or push (*jerk the cord that operates the light*). **2** to move suddenly and quickly (*she jerked back as the car came toward her*). ● *n* a sudden, quick movement (*after a series of jerks the car came to a halt*).

jerkin /**jer**-kin/ *n* a close-fitting jacket or short coat.

jerky[1] /**jer**-kee/ *adj* moving by jerks (*a jerky way of walking*).

jerky[2] /**jer**-kee/ *n* dried, preserved meat that can be kept for a long time even when not in a refrigerator (*eat some beef jerky*).

jersey /**jer**-zee/ *n* **1** a fine wool (*a dress of jersey*). **2** (*Br*) **sweater**.

jest /jest/ *n* a joke, something done or said in fun (*make a jest about their being newly married/he said it in jest*). ● *vb* to joke.

jester /**je**-ster/ *n* (*old*) one paid to make jokes, as in a king's or nobleman's household.

Jesuit /**je**-zoo-it/ *n* a priest or brother in the Society of Jesus, a Roman Catholic religious order.

jet[1] /jet/ *n* a hard black substance, often used for ornamental purposes (*a necklace made of jet*).

jet[2] /jet/ *n* **1** a stream of liquid or gas forced through a narrow opening. **2** a spout through which a

narrow stream of liquid or gas can be forced (*the water jet is blocked*). **3** a jet plane.

jet lag *n* tiredness which results from traveling across several time zones.

jet plane /jet-plane/ *n* an airplane that is jet-propelled, i.e., driven forward by the force of jets of gas forced out to the rear.

jetsam /**jet**-sum/ *n* goods thrown overboard to make a ship lighter.

jettison /**je**-ti-son/ *vb* **1** to throw (goods, etc.) overboard. **2** to get rid of (*decide to jettison the idea*).

jetty /**je**-tee/ *n* **1** a pier. **2** a wall built to protect a harbor from high seas.

jewel /**joo**-ul/ *n* **1** a precious stone (*diamonds, emeralds and other jewels*). **2** something valued highly (*the jewel of his art collection*).

jeweler /**joo**-u-ler/, **jeweller** (*Br, Cdn*) *n* someone who buys and sells jewels.

jewelry /**joo**-ul-ree/ *n, also* **jewellery** (*Cdn, Brit*), jewels, personal ornaments, as rings, necklaces, etc.

jib /jib/ *n* **1** a triangular sail raised in front of a ship's foremast. **2** the arm of a crane. ● *vb* to pull a sail round to the other side. ● **to like the cut of someone's jib** to like someone.

jibe *same as* **gibe**.

jiffy /**ji**-fee/ *n* (*inf*) a moment, an instant (*she said that she would be down in a jiffy*).

jig /jig/ *n* a lively dance tune. ● *vb* (**jigged** /jigd/, **jigging** /**ji**-ging/) **1** to dance a jig. **2** to move up and down quickly in a jerky way (*children jigging with excitement*).

jigsaw /**jig**-saw/ *n* a picture that has been cut into different shapes and the puzzle is to try to fit them together again (*the jigsaw was of a battle scene*).

jihad /ji-**had**/ *n* a holy war waged by Muslims against nonbelievers; a crusade for or against a cause. ● *also* **jehad**.

jilt /jilt/ *vb* to leave someone after promising to love or marry him or her (*jilted her at the altar*).

jingle /**jing**-gul/ *n* a light ringing noise made by metal against metal, as by small bells or coins (*the jingle of coins in his pocket*). ● *vb* to ring lightly, to clink.

jitters /**ji**-terz/ *npl* (*inf*) great nervousness.

jittery /**ji**-te-ree/ *adj* (*inf*) nervous (*in a jittery mood/get jittery at the sight of a policeman*).

jive /jive/ *n* **1** a type of jazz music. **2** the way of dancing to it. ● *also vb*.

job /job/ *n* **1** a piece of work (*make a good job of mending the table*). **2** someone's employment (*a job in an office). **3** (*inf*) a crime (*serving three years in jail for the job he did*).

jockey /**jaw**-key/ *n* a rider in horse races. ● *vb* to persuade or manipulate a person gradually and skillfully into doing something he or she is unwilling to do (*succeeded in jockeying him into joining them*).

jocular /**joc**-yu-lar/ *adj* **1** intended to be humorous (*a few jocular remarks*). **2** fond of joking (*a jocular fellow*).

jodhpurs /**jod**-purz/ *npl* riding breeches reaching to the ankle.

jog /jawg/ *vb* (**jogged** /jawgd/, **jogging** /**jaw**-ging/) **1** to nudge, to prod (*he jogged me and I spilled the coffee*/*jog someone's memory*). **2** to walk or run at a slow, steady pace (*jog round the park for exercise*). ● *n* **1** a nudge, a slight shake. **2** a slow walk or trot.

join /join/ *vb* **1** to put or fasten together (*join the two pieces of string*). **2** to take part in with others (*join the search for the missing child*). **3** to become a member of (*join the golf club*). ● *n* a place where things join (*unable to see the join in the wallpaper*). ● **join battle** to begin fighting (*the enemies joined battle at dawn*).

joiner /**joy**-ner/ *n* a carpenter, a worker in wood, who makes furniture, etc.

joint /joint/ *n* **1** a place at which two things meet or are fastened together (*seal the joints in the pipe*). **2** a place where two things are joined, but left the power of moving (as at, e.g., the elbow, a hinge) (*old people suffering from stiff joints*). **3** a large piece of meat containing a bone (*roast a joint of beef*). ● *adj* **1** shared between two or among all (*a joint bank account*). **2** done by several together (*a joint achievement*). ● *also vb*.

jointed /**join**-ted/ *adj* having joints.

jointly /**joint**-lee/ *adv* together (*write the book jointly*).

joist /joist/ *n* one of the beams of wood supporting the floor or ceiling.

jojoba /ho-**ho**-ba/ *n* an evergreen shrub from which oil is extracted for use in creams and shampoos.

joke /joke/ *n* something said or done to cause laughter (*a speech full of jokes that were not funny*). ● *also vb*.

jollification /jol-i-fi-**cay**-shun/ *n* merrymaking and feasting (*much jollification when they won the football competition*).

jollity /**jol**-i-tee/ *n* gaiety, cheerfulness.

jolly /**jol**-ee/ *adj* merry, cheerful (*in a jolly mood*/*jolly, amusing people*).

Jolly Roger /jol-ee **raw**-jer/ *n* the black pirate flag with the skull and crossbones.

jolt /joalt/ *vb* **1** to give a sudden jerk to (*he jolted my arm as he passed*). **2** to move along jerkily (*a bus jolting along country lanes*). ● *n* **1** a sudden jerk (*the car gave a jolt and stopped suddenly*). **2** a shock (*get a jolt when he failed the exam*).

jonquil /jon-kwil/ *n* a small daffodil.

jostle /**joss**-ul/ *vb* to knock or push against (*people jostling to get into the cinema*).

jot /jot/ *n* a small amount (*have not a jot of sympathy*). ● *vb* (**jotted, jotting**) to write down in short form (*jot down his address*).

jotting /**jot**-ing/ *n* a short note.

journal /**jur**-nal/ *n* **1** (*usually in titles*) a daily newspaper. **2** a weekly or monthly magazine (*The Canadian Journal of Surgery*). **3** a record of the events of every day (*keep a journal of her travels*).

journalism /**jur**-na-li-zum/ *n* the work of preparing or writing for newspapers and magazines (*a career in journalism*).

journalist /**jur**-na-list/ *n* someone whose job is journalism.

journalistic /jur-na-li-**stic**/ *adj* having to do with journalism (*a journalistic career*).

journey /**jur**-nee/ *n* a distance traveled, especially over land (*long journeys by train and bus*). ● *vb* (*fml or old*) to travel (*journeyed for three days*).

journeyman /**jur**-nee-man/ *n* a person who has served an apprenticeship to learn a craft or a trade and is now employed by another.

joust /joust/ *n* (*old*) a contest between two armed knights on horseback at a tournament. ● *also vb*.

jovial /jo-**vee**-al/ *adj* merry, joyful, cheerful (*a jovial old man*/*in a jovial mood*). ● *n* **joviality** /jo-vee-a-li-tee/.

jowl /jowl/ *n* the jaw, the lower part of the cheek (*a face with heavy jowls*). ● **cheek by jowl** very close together (*a meeting to promote peace where terrorists stood cheek by jowl with churchmen*).

joy /joy/ *n* **1** delight, gladness (*bring joy to their lives*). **2** a cause of great happiness (*their child was a great joy to them*).

joyful /**joy**-ful/, **joyous** /**joy**-us/ *adjs* full of joy (*a joyful occasion*).

joy ride /**joy**-ride/ *n* (*inf*) a drive for pleasure in a car (often one that does not belong to the driver) (*teenagers stealing cars for joy rides*). ● *vb* **joy-ride**.

joystick /**joy**-stick/ *n* **1** the pilot's lever to control an airplane. **2** a control lever on a computer.

jubilant /joo-bi-lant/ *adj* rejoicing greatly, triumphant, very glad (*jubilant after winning the match*).

jubilation /joo-bi-**lay**-shun/ *n* triumphant joy.

jubilee /joo-bi-**lee**/ *n* **1** a special anniversary of an event (*the firm celebrated its golden jubilee*). **2** a celebration of this. ● **golden jubilee** a 50th anniversary. ● **silver jubilee** a 25th anniversary. ● **diamond jubilee** a sixtieth anniversary.

Judaism /joo-day-iz-um/ *n* the religion of the Jews.

judge /**judge**/ *n* **1** someone who presides in a court of law giving advice on matters of law and deciding on the punishment for guilty persons (*the judge sentenced him to two years in prison*). **2** someone asked to settle a disagreement (*appointed judge in their dispute*). **3** someone able to distinguish what is good from what is bad (*a good judge of wine*). ● *vb* **1** to act as judge in a court of law. **2** to decide, to give an opinion on (*judging a school by its exam results*). **3** to decide which is the best in a competition (*judge a singing competition*). **4** (*fml*) to criticize or blame someone (*quick to judge others*).

judgment, judgement (*Br*) /**judge**-ment/ *n* **1** act or power of judging (*his judgment is not to be trusted*). **2** the decision given at the end of a law case. **3** good sense (*a business decision showing poor judgment*). **4** an opinion (*in my judgment he is a good player*). ● **Judgment** the Last Judgment of the Old Testament.

judicature /joo-di-ca-chur/ *n* all the judges or law courts of a country.

judicial /joo-**di**-shal/ *adj* having to do with a judge or court of law (*our judicial system*).

judiciary /joo-**di**-sha-ree/ *adj* having to do with a court of law. ● *n* judges as a body.

judicious /joo-**di**-shus/ *adj* wise, showing good sense (*a judicious decision/an action that was far from being judicious*).

judo /**joo**-do/ *n* a Japanese system of unarmed combat adapted as a competitive sport from jujitsu.

jug /**jug**/ *n* a deep vessel for holding liquids, with a handle (*a jug of milk*). ● *vb* (**jugged** /jugd/, **jugging** /**ju**-ging/) (*old*) to cook in a jar or jug.

juggernaut /**ju**-ger-not/ *n* **1** a large destructive force (*the juggernaut of bureaucracy*). **2** a very large lorry (*juggernauts roaring through country villages from the ports*).

juggle /**ju**-gul/ *vb* **1** to keep on throwing things up, catching them and throwing them up again with great quickness of hand (*an entertainer juggling plates*). **2** to change the arrangement of something in order to get a satisfactory result or to deceive (*the accountant juggled the company's end-of-year figures*). ● *n* **juggler** /**ju**-gler/.

jugular /**ju**-gyu-lar/ *adj* having to do with the neck or throat.

jugular vein /**ju**-gyu-lar **vane**/ *n* the large vein at the side of the neck.

juice /**joos**/ *n* the liquid of a fruit or plant (*orange juice*). ● *adj* **juicy** /**joo**-see/.

ju-jitsu /ju-**jit**-soo/ *n* a form of self-defense first used in Japan.

jujube /**joo**-joob/ *n* a small Chinese tree or the fruit of this tree (also know as Chinese date).

jukebox /**jook**-boks/ *n* a machine in a café, pub, etc. that automatically plays a selected record or compact disc when a coin is inserted.

julep /**joo**-lep/ *n* a tall glass of bourbon or brandy and sugar over crushed ice, garnished with mint.

July /joo-**lie**/ *n* the seventh month of the year.

jumble /**jum**-bul/ *vb* to mix in an untidy heap (*a cupboard with shoes and clothes all jumbled up*). ● *n* a muddle (*a jumble of books and papers*).

jumbo /**jum**-bo/ *n* something very large of its kind. ● *adj* very large (*a jumbo jet*).

jump /**jump**/ *vb* **1** to push off the ground with the feet so that the whole body moves through the air (*the dog jumped over the wall*). **2** to make a sudden quick movement or start, as when surprised (*he jumped when the door banged*). ● *n* **1** a leap (*a parachute jump*). **2** a sudden, quick movement (*give a jump in his sleep*). **3** an obstacle to be jumped over (*the jumps in a horse race*). ● *n* **jumper** /**jum**-per/. ● **jump at** to accept willingly (*jump at the chance of working abroad*). ● **jump to conclusions** to take things as true without waiting for them to be proved so.

jumper /**jum**-per/ *n* (*Brit*) a sweater.

jumpy /**jum**-pee/ *adj* (*inf*) nervous, anxious (*feel jumpy when she was alone in the house*). ● *n* **jumpiness** /**jum**-pee-ness/.

junction /**jungk**-shun/ *n* **1** (*fml*) a joining point. **2** a station where several railway lines meet.

juncture /**jungk**-chur/ *n* moment, point, stage (*at this juncture he decided to leave*).

June /**joon**/ *n* the sixth month of the year.

jungle /**jung**-gul/ *n* land especially in the tropics, covered with trees and matted undergrowth.

junior /**joon**-yer/ *adj* **1** younger (*the junior children*). **2** lower in rank (*junior members of staff*). ● *also n*.

juniper /**joo**-ni-per/ *n* an evergreen shrub.

junk[1] /jungk/ n odds and ends, old or unwanted things, rubbish (*the shop is supposed to sell antiques but it's full of junk*).

junk[2] /jungk/ n a Chinese sailing vessel.

junket /jung-ket/ n 1 the thickened part of sour milk sweetened with sugar. 2 a feast. ● vb to feast.

junk food /jungk-food/ n food which is low in nutritional value, often eaten as snacks (*eating junk food instead of well-balanced meals*).

junk mail /jungk-mail/ n mail that you receive without having asked for it, usually containing advertisements.

junkyard /jungk-yard/ n a place used to store and eventually dispose of discarded objects such as old cars.

Jupiter /joo-pi-ter/ n the fifth planet from the sun.

juror /joo-ror / n a member of a jury (*the jurors in a murder trial*).

jury /joo-ree/ n a number of persons who have sworn to give a fair and honest opinion of the facts related in a law case (*the jury reached a verdict of not guilty*).

just /just/ adj 1 right and fair (*a just decision/it's only just that she pays*). 2 honest, fair, moral (*a just man*). 3 reasonable, based on one's rights (*a just claim*). 4 deserved (*his just reward*). ● adv 1 exactly (*just what he needs*). 2 on the point of (*just coming in the door*). 3 quite (*a house that is just as nice as theirs*). 4 merely, only (*he's just a child*).

5 barely (*just enough milk for two*). 6 very lately or recently (*she has just left*).

justice /ju-stiss/ n 1 fairness or rightness in the treatment of other people (*laws based on justice/there was no justice in her treatment of him*). 2 a judge.

justice of the peace /ju-stiss-ov-thi-peess/ n a person appointed to help administer the law in a certain district.

justifiable /ju-sti-fie-a-bul/ adj that may be shown right, excusable (*try to make us believe that his behavior was justifiable*).

justification /ju-sti-fi-cay-shun/ n a reason for doing something, a defense (*no justification for his bad behavior*).

justify /ju-sti-fie/ vb to show that something is right, just, reasonable or excusable (*unable to justify spending all that money/try to justify his behavior*).

jut /jut/ vb (**jutted** /ju-tid/, **jutting** /ju-ting/) to stick out (*balconies jutting out over the sea*).

jute /joot/ n a fiber from the bark of certain plants, from which rope, canvas, etc., are made.

juvenile /joo-vi-nul/ adj 1 having to do with young people (*juvenile courts*). 2 typical of young people, childish (*middle-aged people behaving in a juvenile way*). ● n a young person.

juxtapose /juk-sta-poaz/ vb to place side by side or close together, especially to show a contrast (*juxtaposing two phrases for effect*).

juxtaposition /jux-sta-po-zi-shun/ n a placing near, or side by side.

K

K, k /kay/ the eleventh letter of the alphabet.

kabob *or* **kebob** /ka-**bab**/ *n* small pieces of meat and vegetables cooked on a metal or wooden skewer under a broiler or over flames.

kail *see* **kale**.

kale /kale/ *n* a type of cabbage with dark, crinkled leaves.

kaleidoscope /ka-**lie**-do-scope/ *n* **1** a toy consisting of a tube in which quickly changing colors and shapes are seen through an eyehole. **2** a constantly and quickly changing pattern (*the kaleidoscope of history*).

kaleidoscopic /ka-lie-do-**scop**-ic/ *adj* **1** with many changing colors. **2** quickly changing.

kamik /ka-**mik**/ *n* an Inuit boot made from caribou hide.

kangaroo /kang-ga-**roo**/ *n* an Australian mammal with a pouch for its young and long strong hind legs by means of which it jumps along.

kapok /ka-pok/ *n* a light cottonlike fiber used for stuffing cushions, etc.

karaoke /ka-ree-o-kay/ *n* a type of entertainment in which a machine plays a tape of popular music while people take it in turns to sing the words of the songs.

karate /ka-ra-tay/ *n* a Japanese form of unarmed combat using the feet, hands and elbows.

katydid /**kay**-tee-did/ *n* a large green insect related to the grasshopper.

kayak /ka-yak/ *n* an Inuit canoe, made from seal-skin.

kebab *see* **kabob**.

kedgeree /**kedge**-e-ree/ *n* a dish made of rice, fish and eggs (*the English serve kedgeree for breakfast*).

keel /keel/ *n* the long beam or girder along the bottom of a ship from which the whole frame is built up. ● *vb* **keel over 1** to turn over to one side, to capsize (*the boat keeled over in the storm*). **2** (*inf*) to fall down, to collapse (*people keeling over in the heat*).

keen /keen/ *adj* **1** sharp (*a keen mind/keen eyesight*). **2** eager, very interested (*keen pupils/keen to go/keen on cooking*). ● *n* **keenness** /**keen**-ness/.

keep /keep/ *vb* (*pt, pp* **kept** /kept/) **1** to have something without being required to give it back (*told to keep the change*). **2** not to give or throw away, to preserve (*keep old family photographs/keep a secret*). **3** to remain in a certain state (*keep calm*).

4 to have charge of, to look after (*keep his watch for him/keep hens*). **5** to pay for and look after (*keep his family*). **6** to hold back. **7** to carry out (*keep an engagement*). **8** to go on doing (*keep walking*). **9** (*inf*) to remain in good condition (*food that won't keep*). ● *n* **1** (*fml*) care (*leave the children in his keep*). **2** a strong tower in the centre of a castle. **3** (*inf*) maintenance, food and lodging (*pay for his keep*). ● **keep at** to go on trying to do. ● **keep body and soul together** to help to keep alive (*she does two jobs to try to keep body and soul together*). ● **keep one's hand in** to practice enough to remain good at (*she no longer plays in an orchestra but she plays the piano enough to keep her hand in*).

keeper /**kee**-per/ *n* someone who keeps or looks after (*the lock-keeper/the gate-keeper*).

keeping /**kee**-ping/ *n* care, charge (*money given into the bank's keeping*).

keepsake /**keep**-sake/ *n* a gift valued because of the giver (*she gave him a lock of her hair as a keepsake*).

keg /keg/ *n* a small barrel (*a keg of beer*).

kelp /kelp/ *n* **1** a type of seaweed. **2** ashes of seaweed, used in making glass, iodine, etc.

ken /ken/ *n*. ● **beyond one's ken** outside the extent of your understanding (*how he made his money was beyond our ken*).

kennel /**ke**-nel/ *n* **1** a house for dogs (*a kennel in the garden for the dog*). **2** a pack of hounds.

kerb *see* **curb**.

kerchief /**ker**-chuf/ *n* a cloth for covering the head (*wearing a red kerchief to protect her head from the sun*).

kernel /**ker**-nel/ *n* **1** the edible part in the centre of a nut or fruit stone. **2** the most important part (*the kernel of the problem*).

kerosene /**ke**-ro-seen/ *n* an oil made from petroleum, paraffin.

kestrel /**ke**-strel/ *n* a small falcon.

ketchup /**ke**-chup/ *n* a sauce, usually made of tomatoes, onions, salt and sugar (*tomato ketchup*).

kettle /**ke**-tul/ *n* a metal vessel, with a spout and handle, used for boiling water (*boil water for the tea in an electric kettle*). ● **a kettle of fish** a great difficulty.

kettledrum /**ke**-tul-drum/ *n* a drum made of skin or parchment stretched across the mouth of a rounded metal frame.

key /kee/ *n* **1** an instrument for opening locks, winding clocks, etc. (*turn the key in the lock*). **2** one of the levers struck by the fingers on a piano, typewriter, etc. **3** the relationship of the notes in which a tune is written. **4** something that when known enables you to work out a code, problem, etc. (*the key to the puzzle*). **5** a translation. **6** a general mood, tone or style (*in a low key*).

keyboard /kee-board/ *n* the set of levers struck by the fingers on a piano, typewriter, etc. (*the keyboard of the computer*). ● *vb* to use a keyboard.

keyhole /kee-hole/ *n* the hole through which a key is put in a lock (*looking through the keyhole to see what they were doing*).

kg /kay-jee/ *abbr* = **kilogram.**

khaki /ka-kee/ *adj* dust-colored. ● *n* yellowish brown cloth originally used in making army uniforms.

kibbutz /ki-boots/ *n* in Israel, a small community in which the members all live and work together.

kibbutznik /ki-boots-nik/ *n* a member of a kibbutz.

kick /kick/ *vb* **1** to strike with the foot (*kick the ball*). **2** (*of a gun*) to jerk back when fired. ● *n* **1** a blow given with the foot (*his leg injured by a kick from a horse*). **2** the recoil of a gun. **3** (*inf*) a thrill, a feeling of pleasure (*get a kick from fast cars*). **4** strength, effectiveness (*a drink with a kick in it*).

kick-off /ki-cawff/ *n* the beginning of a game of football or soccer.

kid /kid/ *n* **1** (*inf*) a child (*work hard to give his kids everything*). **2** a young goat. **3** goatskin leather. ● *vb* (**kidded** /ki-did/, **kidding** /ki-ding/) (*inf*) to deceive in fun (*she was offended, but then she realized that he was only kidding*).

kidnap /kid-nap/ *vb* (**kidnapped** /kid-napt/, **kidnapping** /kid-na-ping/) to carry off a person by force (*kidnap the child of the millionaire to get money*). ● *n* **kidnapper** /kid-na-per/.

kidney /kid-nee/ *n* **1** one of two glands that cleanse the blood and pass the waste liquid out of the body. **2** the kidneys of certain animals used as food.

kill /kill/ *vb* **1** to put to death. **2** to put an end to (*kill all their hopes*). ● *n* the animal(s) killed in a hunt. ● **kill time** to make time seem to pass more quickly by occupying or amusing yourself in some way (*kill time by looking round the shops*).

kiln /kiln/ *n* a furnace or oven for heating or hardening anything, especially bricks and pottery.

kilo- /kee-lo/ *prefix* one thousand.

kilogram /kee-lo-gram/ *n* a measure of weight = 1000 grams (about 2.2 lbs).

kilometer /ki-lom-i-ter/ *n, also* **kilometre** (*Cdn, Br*) a measure of length = 1000 meters (about $^5/_8$ mile).

kilowatt /ki-lo-wat/ *n* a measure of electric power = 1000 watts.

kilt /kilt/ *n* a short pleated skirt worn by Scotsmen as part of Highland dress.

kimono /ki-mo-no/ *n* a Japanese long loose robe, tied with a sash, worn by women.

kin /kin/ *n* (*fml*) relatives, by blood or marriage (*all his kin are dead*).

kind /kined/ *n* **1** sort, type, variety (*fruit of various kinds/people of that kind*). **2** nature, character (*differ in size but not in kind*). ● *adj* thoughtful and friendly, generous (*kind neighbors/kind acts*). ● *n* **kindness** /kinde-ness/. ● **pay in kind** to pay by goods, etc., not money (*they gave us apples and we paid them in kind by giving them eggs*).

kindergarten /kin-der-gar-ten/ *n* a school for children ages four to six.

kindle /kin-dul/ *vb* **1** to set on fire, to light (*kindling the fire in the hearth*). **2** to stir up (*kindle love*).

kindling /kin-dling/ *n* small pieces of wood used for lighting a fire (*chop kindling for the fire*).

kindly /kine-dlee/ *adj* kind, friendly (*a kindly old woman/a kindly smile*). ● *also adv.* ● *n* **kindliness** /kine-dlee-ness/.

kindred /kin-dred/ *n* **1** (*fml*) relatives, especially by blood (*all his kindred were killed in the battle*). **2** relationship (*claim kindred with him*). ● *adj* **1** related (*kindred languages*). **2** congenial (*kindred spirits*).

kinetics /ki-ne-tics/ *n* the study of the connection between force and motion. ● *adj* **kinetic** /ki-ne-tic/.

king /king/ *n* **1** the male ruler of a state. **2** a playing card with a king's picture. **3** a piece in chess (*kings and castles and bishops*).

kingdom /king-dom/ *n* a state ruled by a king.

kingfisher /king-fi-sher/ *n* a small brightly colored bird that dives for fish.

kink /kingk/ *n* **1** a backward twist in a rope, chain, etc. (*a kink in the garden hose*). **2** an unusual or strange way of thinking about things (*a curious kink in his character*).

kinship /kin-ship/ *n* **1** a family connection. **2** any close connection.

kinsman /kinz-man/ *n* a male relative. ● *f* **kinswoman** /kinz-woo-man/.

kiosk /kee-osk/ *n* **1** a small hut or stall for the sale of newspapers, sweets, etc. (*buy sandwiches at the station kiosk*). **2** a public telephone booth.

kipper /ki-per/ *vb* to preserve by splitting open, salting and drying. ● *n* a fish so preserved, especially a herring, and used as food (*have grilled kippers for breakfast*).

kirk /kirk/ *n* (*Scot*) a church.

kiss /kiss/ *vb* to touch with the lips as a sign of love or respect (*kiss their parents goodnight/kiss each other when they met/he kissed her hand*). ● *also n.*

kit /kit/ *n* all the tools, etc., needed to do a job (*his athletics kit*).

kitbag /kit-bag/ *n* a bag for necessary tools, clothes, etc., as carried by soldiers, sailors, etc.

kitchen /kit-chen/ *n* the room in which cooking is done (*a kitchen fitted with labor-saving machines*).

kite /kite/ *n* **1** a type of hawk. **2** a toy made of paper or cloth stretched on a tight framework, flown in the air at the end of a string (*the child was flying a kite in the shape of a dragon*).

kitten /ki-ten/ *n* a young cat.

kiwi /kee-wee/ *n* **1** a wingless tailless bird of New Zealand. **2** the fruit of an Asian vine.

Kleenex /klee-neks/ *n* (*trademark*) tissue paper used as a handkerchief.

kleptomania /klep-toe-**may**-nee-a/ *n* an uncontrollable desire to steal things (*she was accused of shoplifting, but she was suffering from kleptomania*). ● *n* **kleptomaniac** /klep-toe-**may**-nee-ac/.

knack /nak/ *n* knowledge of the right way to do a thing, skill gained by practice (*there is a knack to tossing pancakes/he has the knack of making people feel welcome*).

knapsack /nap-sack/ *n* (*old*) a bag strapped to the back, worn by soldiers or travelers.

knave /nave/ *n* **1** a rascal, a dishonest rogue (*the knaves who stole his horse*). **2** the third picture in a pack of cards, the jack.

knead /need/ *vb* to press into a dough or paste (*knead the dough to make bread*).

knee /nee/ *n* the joint between the upper and lower parts of the leg (*pray on his knees*).

kneel /neel/ *vb* (*pt, pp* **knelt** /nelt/ *or* **kneeled** /neeld/) to go down or rest on the knees.

knell /nell/ *n* (*fml or lit*) the sound of a bell, especially at a funeral. ● *vb* **1** (*of a bell*) to ring a knell (*church bells knelling*). **2** to summon by, or as by, a knell.

knickerbockers /ni-ker-bok-erz/ *npl* (*old*) loose breeches ending at the knee.

knickers /ni-kerz/ *npl* (*inf*) a woman's undergarment with elastic round the waist, panties.

knick-knack /nik-nak/ *n* a small or dainty ornament (*a row of knick-knacks on her mantelpiece*).

knife /nife/ *n* (*pl* **knives** /nivez/) a tool with a sharp edge for cutting (*stab him with a knife/carve the meat with a knife/eat his food with a knife and fork*). ● *vb* to stab with a knife (*he planned to knife her to death*).

knight /nite/ *n* **1** in olden days, someone of honorable military rank (*knights fighting in a tournament*). **2** a rank awarded for service to society, entitling the holder to be called Sir (*the Queen made him a knight*). **3** a piece in chess. ● *vb* to make (someone) a knight (*a famous footballer knighted by the Queen*).

knight errant /nite-**er**-ant/ *n* (*old*) a knight who traveled in search of adventure.

knighthood /nite-hood/ *n* the rank of a knight (*receive a knighthood for services to charity*).

knightly /nite-lee/ *adj* having to do with a knight (*knightly behavior*).

knit /nit/ *vb* (**knitted** /ni-teed/, **knitting** /ni-ting/) **1** to make woolen thread into garments by means of needles (*knit a cardigan*). **2** to join closely (*broken bones that failed to knit*).

knitting /ni-ting/ *n* the thing knitted (*leave her knitting on the bus*).

knitting needle /ni-ting **nee**-dul/ *n* a long needle used for knitting.

knives *see* **knife**.

knob /nob/ *n* **1** a rounded part sticking out from a surface (*the knobs on the trunk of a tree*). **2** the round handle of something (*wooden door knobs*). **3** a round control switch (*the knobs on the television set*). **4** a small lump of something (*a knob of butter*).

knobbly /**nob**-lee/ *adj* covered with lumps, bumpy (*knobbly knees*).

knock /nok/ *vb* **1** to strike (*he knocked his head on the low ceiling*). **2** to rap on a door (*knock at the door*). **3** (*inf*) to criticize (*stop knocking him—he's doing his best*). ● *n* **1** a blow (*a knock on the head*). **2** a rap on the door.

knocker /nok-er/ *n* a hammer attached to a door for knocking (*brass door-knockers*).

knock-kneed /nok-need/ *adj* having knees that touch in walking.

knoll /nole/ *n* (*fml or lit*) a little rounded hill (*a grassy knoll*).

knot /not/ *n* **1** the twisting of two parts or pieces of string, etc., together so that they will not part until untied (*put a knot in the string to tie the parcel*). **2** a hard piece of the wood of a tree, from which a branch grew out. **3** a small group of people (*a knot of people gossiping at the street corner*). **4** a measure of speed at sea (about 1.15 miles per hour). ● *vb* to tie in a knot.

knotty /**not**-ee/ *adj* difficult (*a knotty problem*).

know /no/ *vb* (*pt* **knew** /noo/, *pp* **known** /noan/) **1** to be aware that (*she knew that he was present*). **2** to have information or knowledge about (*she knows the office system thoroughly*/*know all the facts*). **3** to have learned and remember (*know a poem by Keats*). **4** to be aware of the identity of, to be acquainted with (*I know Mary Jones*). **5** to recognize or identify (*I would never have known her after all these years*).

knowing /**no**-wing/ *adj* showing secret understanding (*a knowing smile*).

knowledge /**nol**-idge/ *n* **1** that which is known, information (*he had considerable knowledge about America*). **2** the whole of what can be learned or found out (*branches of knowledge, such as astronomy*).

knuckle /**nu**-cul/ *n* a finger joint (*graze his knuckles*). ● *vb* **knuckle down** to start working hard. ●

knuckle under to be forced to accept the authority of someone, to give in to (*he was disobedient, but the new teacher made him knuckle under*).

knuckle-duster /**nu**-cul du-ster/ *n* a blunt metal instrument fixed on to the hand as a weapon.

koala /ko-**a**-la/ *n* a small bearlike animal found in Australia.

kook /kook/ *n* someone who behaves in a crazy or silly way. ● *adj* **kooky** /**koo**-kee/.

kookaburra /**koo**-ka-bu-ra/ *n* an Australian bird (the laughing jackass).

Koran *or* **Qu'ran** /ku-**ran**/ *n* the holy book of Islam, the book of the Muslim religion.

kosher /**ko**-sher/ *adj* **1** of food that has been prepared according to the rules of Jewish law. **2** (*inf*) genuine, honest, legal (*I don't think his qualifications are kosher*).

kudos /**koo**-dos/ *n* glory, fame, credit (*gain a lot of kudos in the village from being interviewed on television*).

kung fu /kung-**foo**/ *n* a Chinese form of unarmed combat using the hands and feet, similar to karate.

Kwanza *or* **Kwanzaa** /**kwan**-za/ *n* an African-American holiday celebrated for seven days between December 26 and January 1.

L

L, l /el/ the twelfth letter of the alphabet.

lab /lab/ *n* short for laboratory.

label /**lay**-bel/ *n* a piece of paper or card fixed to something to give information about it (*read the ingredients on the label/a label with washing instructions*). ● *vb* (**labeled, labeling,** (*Br*) **labeled** /**lay**-beld/, (*Br*) **labelling** /**lay**-bu-ling/) to fix a label to (*make sure all the parcels are labeled*).

labor /**lay**-bur/ *n, also* **labour** (*Br, Cdn*) **1** hard work (*manual labor/the labor involved in tidying up the garden*). **2** childbirth. **3** all workers as a body (*have difficulty in getting local labor*). ● *also adj*. ● *vb* **1** to work hard (*laboring away at their homework*). **2** to be employed to do hard and unskilled work (*laboring at the building site*). **3** to do something slowly or with difficulty (*laboring up the hill*).

laboratory /la-**bra**-toe-ree/ *n* a workshop used for scientific experiments (*the firm's research laboratory*).

Labor Day /**lay**-bur-day/ *n, also* **Labour Day** (*Cdn*) a legal holiday celebrated in the US on the first Monday in September.

labored /**lay**-burd/ *adj, also* **laboured** (*Br, Cdn*) showing a lot of effort or hard work (*a labored styled of writing*).

laborer /**lay**-bu-rer/ *n, also* **labourer** (*Br, Cdn*) a person who does unskilled work (*laborers on the building site*).

lace /lace/ *n* **1** a cord used for tying opposite edges together (*a shoe lace*). **2** an ornamental network of thread (*handkerchiefs edged with lace*). ● *vb* to fasten with a lace (*lacing up her shoes*).

lacerate /**la**-se-rate/ *vb* **1** to tear, to wound (*her leg lacerated by a barbed wire fence*). **2** to hurt badly (*he lacerated her with his cruel words*). ● *n* **laceration** /la-se-**ray**-shun/.

lack /lak/ *vb* to want, to need, to be without (*she lacks confidence/the organization lacks funds*). ● *n* want, need (*a lack of money*).

lackey /**la**-kee/ *n* **1** (*old*) a servant. **2** someone who behaves like a servant (*she is always surrounded by lackeys*).

lackluster /**lack**-lu-ster/ *adj, also* **lacklustre** (*Br, Cdn*) dull, lacking brightness (*a lackluster piano recital*).

laconic /la-**con**-ic/ *adj* using few words to express a meaning (*a laconic way of speaking*).

lacquer /**la**-ker/ *n* **1** a varnish. **2** a substance used to keep hair in place (*spray her hair with lacquer*). ● *vb* to paint with lacquer.

lacrosse /la-**cross**/ *n* a team ball game played with long-handled rackets.

lactic /**lac**-tic/ *adj* having to do with milk.

lacuna /la-**coo**-na/ *n* (*pl* **lacunae** /la-**coo**-nay/) (*fml*) a gap, a blank (*a lacuna in the manuscript/a lacuna in her knowledge of the subject*).

lad /lad/ *n* a boy, a young man (*employ a lad to deliver papers/just a lad*).

ladder /**la**-der/ *n* **1** a frame of two poles or planks, joined by short crossbars, used as steps for going up or down (*climb the ladder to get to the roof*). **2** a tear that runs up or down a stocking or tights (*bang her leg and get a ladder in her tights*).

laden /**lay**-den/ *adj* loaded (*trees laden with apples/women laden with shopping/laden with worries*).

ladle /**lay**-del/ *n* a large long-handled spoon for lifting liquids (*a soup ladle*). ● *vb* to lift with a ladle (*ladling soup into the plates*).

lady /**lay**-dee/ *n* **1** a woman of rank or with good manners (*behave like a lady*). **2** (*Brit, with cap*) the title of the wife of a knight or of a man of higher rank. ● *n* **your Ladyship** the title used in speaking to or of a lady of high rank.

ladybug /**lay**-dee-bug/ *or* **ladybird** /**lay**-dee-burd/ (*Brit*) *n* a small beetle, usually red with black spots.

lag /lag/ *vb* (**lagged** /lagd/, **lagging** /**la**-ging/) **1** to go too slowly, not to keep pace with, to fall behind (*lagging behind the rest of the walkers*). **2** not to keep up with (*wage increases lagging behind those in other industries*). ● *n* (*inf*) an old convict.

lager /**la**-ger/ *n* a light, clear beer of German origin (*a pint of lager*).

lagoon /la-**goon**/ *n* a shallow saltwater lake cut off from the sea by sandbanks or rocks.

laid /laid/ *pt of* **lay**.

laid-back /laid-**back**/ *adj* relaxed, easygoing.

lair /lair/ *n* a wild beast's den (*the fox's lair*).

lake[1] /lake/ *n* a large stretch of water surrounded by land (*Lake Michigan*).

lake[2] /lake/ *n* a deep red color (*artists using lake*).

lamb /lam/ *n* a young sheep (*newborn lambs frolicking*).

lame /lame/ *adj* **1** unable to walk well because of an injured or badly formed leg (*horses gone lame*). **2**

not good, inadequate (*a lame excuse*). ● *vb* to make lame. ● *n* **lameness.**

lament /la-**ment**/ *vb* **1** to show grief or sorrow for, to mourn for (*lament the death of the king*). **2** to express regret for (*lament the passing of old traditions*). ● *n* **1** the expressing of great grief. **2** a mournful song or tune. ● *n* **lamentation** /la-men-**tay**-shun/.

lamentable /la-**men**-ta-bul/ *adj* much to be regretted, extremely unsatisfactory (*show a lamentable lack of knowledge/the council's lamentable record*).

laminate /la-mi-nate/ *vb* to put a thin layer (e.g., of plastic) over something (*laminating table tops*). ● *also n.*

lamp /**lamp**/ *n* a vessel for giving light (*electric lamps*).

lampoon /lam-**poon**/ *n* something written specially to make another seem foolish or wicked (*journalists lampooning the members of the cabinet*).

lance /**lanse**/ *n* a long spear used by horse soldiers. ● *vb* **1** to wound or hit with a lance. **2** to cut open with a lancet (*lancing a boil*).

lance-corporal /**lanse**-cawr-pral/ *n* the lowest appointed rank in the British Army, just below that of a corporal.

land /**land**/ *n* **1** the solid part of the earth's surface (*prefer land to sea*). **2** country (*visit lands overseas*). **3** ground, soil (*the farmer's land is very fertile*). ● *vb* to bring, put, or go ashore; to touch down.

landed /**lan**-did/ *adj* possessing land (*landed gentry*).

landfall /**land**-fawl/ *n* **1** a ship's approach to land at the end of a voyage. **2** the land approached.

landfill site /**land**-fill site/ *n* a place where waste material is buried under layers of earth, often excavated for this purpose.

landing /**lan**-ding/ *n* **1** the act of going ashore. **2** a place for going on shore (*tie the boat up at the landing*). **3** the corridor opening on to the rooms at the top of a flight of stairs (*children standing on the landing looking through the banisters*).

landlady /**land**-lay-dee/ *n* **1** a woman who keeps an inn or boarding house (*seaside landladies*). **2** a woman who rents out rooms, flats or houses (*their landlady calls to collect the rent*).

landlord /**land**-lawrd/ *n* **1** a man who rents out rooms, flats or houses (*the landlord put up the rent*). **2** a man who keeps an inn or boarding house.

landmark /**land**-markt/ *n* **1** an easily recognized object from which travelers can tell where they are. **2** a very important event (*a landmark in British history*).

landscape /**land**-scape/ *n* **1** a view of the country seen from one position. **2** a picture of the countryside (*he paints watercolor landscapes*).

landslide /**land**-slide/ *n* the falling of a mass of earth, etc., down the side of a mountain (*the car was buried in the rocks from a landslide*).

landslip /**land**-slip/ *n* a landslide.

landward /**land**-ward/ *adj and adv* toward land.

lane /**lane**/ *n* **1** a narrow road (*country lanes*). **2** a narrow passage or alley between buildings, often found in place names (*Macondray Lane is cobbled*). **3** any of the parallel parts into which roads are divided for a single line of traffic (*the fast lane on the freeway*). **4** the route intended for or regularly used by ships or aircraft (*shipping lanes*). **5** a marked strip of track, water, etc., for a competitor in a race (*swimming lanes*).

language /**lang**-gwidge/ *n* **1** meaningful speech (*humans, unlike animals, use language*). **2** the speech of one people (*the French language*). **3** words (*obscene language*).

languid /**lang**-gwid/ *adj* lacking energy, weak, slow-moving (*languid movements*).

languish /**lang**-gwish/ *vb* to lose strength, to become weak (*she languishes when her lover is away*). **2** to experience long suffering (*languish in prison*).

lank /**langk**/ *adj* **1** tall and thin, lanky. **2** straight and limp (*lank hair*).

lanky /**lang**-kee/ *adj* ungracefully tall and thin (*lanky male teenagers*).

lanolin(e) /**la**-no-lin/ *n* a soothing ointment made from fat obtained from sheep's wool.

lantern /**lan**-tern/ *n* a case, usually of glass, that encloses and protects a light (*the farmer carried a lantern to go out to the barn*).

lap[1] /**lap**/ *n* **1** the seat formed by the knees and thighs of a person sitting (*a child sitting on her mother's lap*). **2** one round of a course in a race (*a race of ten laps*).

lap[2] /**lap**/ *vb* (**lapped** /**lapt**/, **lapping** /**la**-ping/) **1** to lick up (*cats lapping milk*). **2** to wash against in little waves (*the sea lapping the rocks*). ● *n* the sound made by small waves.

lapdog /**lap**-dog/ *n* a small pet dog.

lapel /la-**pel**/ *n* the folded back part of the breast of a coat or jacket (*wearing a rose in his lapel*).

lapis lazuli /la-pis-**la**-zu-lee/ *n* a blue precious stone.

lapse /**lapse**/ *n* **1** a mistake, a small error or fault (*apart from occasional lapses, her work is first class/brief memory lapses*). **2** the passing (of time) (*with a lapse of several years*). ● *vb* **1** to fall out of use (*local customs that have lapsed*). **2** to come to an end (*their contract has lapsed*). **3** to pass gradually into a less active or less desirable state (*standards have lapsed*).

laptop /**lap**-top/ *n* a small, light computer that can be operated by battery and can be used on someone's lap.

larch /**larch**/ *n* a type of deciduous, cone-bearing tree.

lard /**lard**/ *n* the fat of pigs, prepared for use in cooking (*they fry the potatoes in lard, not oil*).

larder /**lar**-der/ *n* a room or cupboard for storing food.

large /**large**/ *adj* more than usual in size, number or amount, big (*large sums of money/a large lake/a large house*). ● **at large** free, at

lariat /**la**-ree-at/ *n* **1** a rope. **2** a rope with a running knot for catching animals, like a lasso.

lark /**lark**/ *n* **1** a songbird. **2** something done for fun. ● *vb* to play tricks.

larva /**lar**-va/ *n* (*pl* **larvae** /**lar**-vay/) the form of an insect on coming out of the egg, a grub.

larynx /**la**-rinks/ *n* the upper part of the windpipe, containing the vocal chords which produce the voice.

lasagne /la-**zan**-ya/ *n* an Italian dish made from layers of flat, wide pasta, a meat or vegetable sauce and a cheese sauce.

laser /**lay**-zer/ *n* a device that produces a narrow beam of concentrated light (*a laser beam*).

lash /**lash**/ *n* **1** the cord of a whip. **2** a blow given with a whip. ● *vb* **1** to whip, to strike hard or often. **2** to fasten by tying tightly.

lass /**lass**/ *n* a girl.

lasso /la-**soo**/ *n* (*pl* **lassos** *or* **lassoes** /la-**sooz**/) a rope with a running knot for catching animals. ● *vb* to catch with a lasso.

last[1] /**last**/ *adj* **1** coming after all others. **2** latest. **3** final. ● *adv* at the last time or place. ● **at last** in the end.

last[2] /**last**/ *n* a foot-shaped block on which shoes are made or repaired.

last[3] /**last**/ *vb* **1** to go on. **2** to continue.

lasting /**la**-sting/ *adj* **1** going on for a long time. **2** remaining in good condition.

latch /**lach**/ *n* a small piece of wood or metal for keeping a door shut. ● *vb* to fasten with a latch.

latchkey /**lach**-kee/ *n* the key for the main door of a house (*children given latchkeys to let themselves into their homes*).

late /**late**/ *adj* **1** arriving after the time fixed (*late for the meeting*). **2** far on in time (*late afternoon*). **3** now dead (*her late husband*). **4** recent (*her latest novel/the latest news*). ● *adv* after the time fixed. ● *n* **lateness** /**late**-ness/. ● **of late** (*fml*) recently (*she seems tired of late*).

lately /**late**-lee/ *adv* in recent times, recently (*I have not seen him lately*).

latent /**lay**-tent/ *adj* present but not yet noticeable, not fully developed (*latent talent*).

lateral /**la**-te-ral/ *adj* on, at or from the side (*lateral movements*).

lathe /**lathe**/ *n* a machine for turning around wood, metal, pottery, etc., while it is being shaped (*turn the piece of wood on a lathe*).

lather /**la**-ther/ *n* **1** froth of soap and water (*the lather on his face while he is shaving*). **2** froth from sweat (*the lather on a horse after a race*). ● *vb* **1** to cover with lather (*lather his face before shaving*). **2** to become frothy (*soap that lathers easily*).

Latin /**la**-tin/ *n* the language of ancient Rome. ● *adj* **1** having to do with the ancient Romans (*the Latin language*). **2** having to do with the peoples of France, Italy, Portugal and Spain (*Latin peoples*).

latitude /**la**-ti-tood/ *n* **1** distance north or south of the equator. **2** freedom from controls (*they give their children a good deal of latitude*).

latrine /la-**treen**/ *n* a lavatory, especially in a camp or institution.

latter /**la**-ter/ *adj* **1** near the end of a period of time (*in the latter part of his life*). **2** second of two just spoken of (*she prefers the former suggestion, but I prefer the latter*).

latterly /**la**-ter-lee/ *adv* recently, lately, in the last part of a period of time.

lattice /**la**-tis/ *n* a network of crossed bars or strips as of wood (*a lattice of pastry on the tart*). ● *adj* **latticed** /**la**-tist/.

laugh /**laf**/ *vb* to make a sound expressing amusement or pleasure (*laugh at his jokes*). ● *n* the sound of laughing.

laughable /**la**-fa-bul/ *adj* causing people to laugh, ridiculous (*his laughable attempts to jump the wall*).

laughter /**laf**-ter/ *n* the act or sound of laughing (*listen to the children's laughter*).

launch /lawnch/ *vb* **1** to put into motion, to send on its course (*launch a missile*). **2** to cause (a ship) to move into the water (*launch a new liner*). **3** to put into action, to set going (*launch an attack*). ● *n* **1** the act of launching. **2** a large motorboat.

launder /lawn-der/ *vb* to wash and iron (*launder his shirts*).

laundry /lawn-dree/ *n* a place where clothes, etc., are washed and ironed (*take the sheets to the laundry*).

laurel /law-rel/ *n* **1** a bay tree whose leaves are used for making wreaths of honor. **2** a special honor (*win academic laurels*).

lava /la-va/ *n* the melted rock emitted by a volcano.

lavatory /la-va-toe-ree/ *n* a toilet.

lavender /la-ven-der/ *n* **1** a plant with sweet-smelling flowers (*lavender bushes/branches of dried lavender*). **2** a light purple color.

lavish /la-vish/ *adj* **1** giving freely, generous (*a lavish spender*). **2** given or spent in great quantities (*lavish praise*). ● *vb* to give or spend lavishly (*lavish money on unsound business schemes/lavish attention on his wife*).

law /law/ *n* **1** a rule or set of rules laid down for a people or a group of people by a person or persons with recognized authority (*the laws of the land*). **2** in science, a statement of the way in which objects regularly behave.

law-abiding /law-a-bide-ing/ *adj* obeying the law (*law-abiding people living next door to vandals*).

lawful /law-ful/ *adj* allowed by law (*his lawful wife*).

lawless /law-less/ *adj* not keeping the laws, wild (*a lawless mob destroying property*).

lawn[1] /lawn/ *n* a stretch of carefully kept grass in a garden (*mow the lawn*).

lawn[2] /lawn/ *n* a type of fine linen (*a dress of white lawn*).

lawnmower /lawn-mo-wer/ *n* a machine for cutting grass.

lawsuit /law-soot/ *n* claiming before a judge that another has broken the law (*start a lawsuit against the person who slandered her*).

lawn tennis /lawn-te-nis/ *n* tennis played on a grass court (*the lawn tennis finals at Wimbledon*).

lawyer /law-yer/ *n* someone skilled in the law (*the lawyer who arranged the divorce*).

lax /laks/ *adj* not sufficiently strict or severe (*lax lax/lax security/teachers too lax with the pupils*).

laxative /lak-sa-tiv/ *n* a medicine that causes or helps the bowels to empty. ● *also adj*.

lay[1] /lay/ *pt of* **lie**.

lay[2] /lay/ *vb* (*pt, pp* **laid** /lade/) **1** to cause to lie (*lay the injured woman on the ground*). **2** to place (*lay the books on the table*). **3** to make ready (*lay the table*). **4** to produce eggs. **5** to bet. ● **lay by, lay up** to store for the future (*lay by supplies for the winter*). ● **lay oneself open to** to put yourself into the position of receiving (*lay yourself open to accusations of theft*).

lay[3] /lay/ *n* (*old*) a poem or song.

lay[4] /lay/ *adj* **1** having to do with people who are not members of the clergy. **2** not expert (*lay people who do not understand technical language*).

layer /lay-er/ *n* an even spread of one substance over the surface of another (*a cake made of layers of chocolate sponge*).

layman /lay-man/ *n* **1** someone who is not a clergyman. **2** someone who is not an expert or specialist (*the doctor tried to explain the situation in layman's terms*).

laze /laze/ *vb* to be lazy, to do nothing (*holiday-makers lazing on the beach*). ● *n* **laziness**.

lazy /lay-zee/ *adj* unwilling to work, liking to do nothing (*too lazy to do any work/feel lazy in the heat*).

lead[1] /leed/ *n* **1** a soft heavy metal (*roof covering made of lead*). **2** the stick of black lead or graphite in a pencil. **3** a piece of lead attached to a cord for finding the depth of water. **4** *pl* **leads** /leeds/ the sheets of lead used for covering roofs.

lead[2] /leed/ *vb* (*pt, pp* **led** /led/) **1** to go in front to show the way, to guide (*lead the mountaineers up the cliff face*). **2** to act as a chief or commander (*he was leading the attacking troops*). **3** to influence (*she is easily led*). **4** to spend (life) in a certain way (*lead a quiet life*). ● *n* **1** a guiding suggestion or example (*follow their lead/police looking for a lead*). **2** a chief part (*she has the lead in a local production of "Saint Joan."*) **3** the position ahead of all others (*she is in the lead in the race*). **4** a cord, etc., for leading a dog (*put the dog's lead on to take him for a walk*).

leader /lee-der/ *n* **1** someone who shows the way (*act as leader up the mountain track*). **2** someone who gives orders or takes charge (*the leader of the attacking force*). **3** a person or thing that is ahead of others (*the leader in the competition*) **4** a newspaper article giving an opinion on a news item of interest (*also* **leading article**). ● *n* **leadership** /lee-der-ship/.

leading /lee-ding/ *adj* chief, most important (*leading politicians*).

leading question /lee-ding kwes-chun/ n a question asked in such a way as to suggest the answer desired.

leaf /leef/ n (pl **leaves** /leevz/) **1** one of the thin, flat usually green blades growing out of the stem of a plant or the branch of a tree (*leaves changing color in autumn*). **2** a single sheet of paper in a book with pages printed on both sides (*turn over the leaves of the book*). **3** the movable part of a table-top or double door (*put in the extra leaf in the table*). ● **turn over a new leaf** to begin to live or act in a better way (*he has been in prison but he has decided to turn over a new leaf*).

leaflet /leef-let/ n **1** a printed sheet of paper, usually folded and free of charge, containing information (*an advertising leaflet/a leaflet on dental care*).

leafy /lee-fee/ adj full of leaves (*leafy lanes*).

league[1] /leeg/ n a measure of distance (about three miles).

league[2] /leeg/ n **1** a group of people or nations bound by agreement to help one another (*the League of Nations*). **2** a group of sports clubs or players that play matches among themselves (*the National Football League/a darts league*). ● vb (*fml*) to join together, to unite (*leaguing together to plot against the king*).

leak /leek/ n **1** a hole by which water escapes (e.g., from a pipe) or enters a dry place. **2** a small accidental hole or crack through which something flows in or out. **3** the accidental or intentional making public of secret information (*a leak to the press about confidential government matters*). ● vb **1** to let water in or out (*the roof is leaking*). **2** to get out through a hole or crack (*gas leaking*). **3** to make public that which is secret (*leak confidential information to the press*).

leakage /lee-kage/ n act of leaking.

leaky /lee-kee/ adj (*inf*) having leaks (*leaky roof*).

lean[1] /leen/ vb (pt, pp **leaned** /leend/ or **leant** /lent/) **1** to slope to one side (*the building leans to the right*). **2** to bend (*she leaned down to pat the dog*). **3** to rest against (*the ladder was leaning against the wall*). **4** to have a preference for (*he leans toward the right of the political party*).

lean[2] /leen/ adj **1** not having much fat (*lean meat*). **2** thin, healthily thin (*fit, lean athletes*). ● n meat without fat. ● n **leanness** /leen-ness/.

leaning /lee-ning/ n preference, liking (*what are his political leanings*).

leap /leep/ vb (pt, pp **leaped** /leept/ or **leapt** /lept/) to jump (*leap out of bed/the deer leapt the fence*). ● n **1** a jump (*clear the wall in one leap*). **2** the height or distance jumped.

leapfrog /leep-frawg/ n a game in which one player leaps over the others while they are bent over.

leap year /leep-year/ n a year in which there are 366 days, occurring once every 4 years.

learn /lern/ vb (pt, pp **learned** /lernd/ or **learnt** /lernt/) **1** to gain knowledge or skill, to find out how to do something (*learn French/learn how to swim*). **2** to come to understand, to realize (*she must learn that she has to consider others*). **3** to memorize, to fix in the memory (*learn a poem by Keats*).

learned /ler-ned/ adj having much knowledge, gained by study.

learner /ler-ner/ n someone who is learning (*a learner driver/learners of English as a foreign language*).

learning /ler-ning/ n knowledge gained by study (*a man of learning*).

learning disability /ler-ning dis-a-bil-i-tee/ n often shortened to LD, a problem that someone has in learning basic skills such as reading, which is caused by a physical condition.

lease /leese/ n an agreement by which the use of house or land is given to another in return for a fixed annual amount or rent. ● vb to give or take on lease (*leasing a house*).

leash /leesh/ n a cord or strap for leading animals (*asked to keep her dog on a leash in the park*). ● vb to hold on a leash.

least /leest/ adj smallest (*the least inconvenience*). ● also n. ● adv in the smallest degree (*I don't mind in the least*).

leather /le-ther/ n material made by preparing animal skins in a certain way (*coats made of leather*). ● also adj. ● vb (*inf*) to beat, to thrash (*leathered by his father for lying*). ● adj **leathery** /le-ther-ee/.

leave /leev/ n **1** permission (*she received leave to go home early*). **2** permitted absence (*on sick leave*). **3** holiday (*on annual leave*). **4** farewell (*he took his leave from them*). ● vb (pt, pp **left** /left/) **1** to give to another at your death (*he left all his money to his son*). **2** to cause to be or remain in a particular state or condition (*leave the door open/leave the country without a leader*). **3** to go without taking (*leave her gloves on the counter*). **4** to depart (*leave home at an early age*). **5** to desert (*he has left his wife*). **6** to entrust to another (*leave getting the food to him*). **7** to allow to remain unused, untaken, uneaten, etc. (*she left most of the meal*).

leaves *see* **leaf**.

lectern /**lec**-tern/ *n* a reading desk for standing at (*the lectern on the stage of the hall*).

lecture /**lec**-cher/ *n* **1** a talk on a certain subject (*go to a lecture on local history*). **2** a scolding (*get a lecture from their mother on good manners*). ● *vb* **1** to give a lecture. **2** to scold.

lecturer /**lec**-che-rer/ *n* **1** someone giving a talk (*introduce the lecturer on local history*). **2** someone who teaches in a college or university.

led /led/ *pt of* **lead**.

ledge /**ledge**/ *n* **1** a narrow shelf (*a window ledge*). **2** a ridge (*climbers sheltering on a ledge*).

ledger /**le**-jer/ *n* the chief account book of a business.

leech /**leech**/ *n* **1** a blood-sucking worm (*leeches used to be used in medicine*). **2** (*old*) a doctor.

leek /**leek**/ *n* a vegetable with broad flat leaves (*a soup made with leeks*).

leer /**leer**/ *vb* to look at sideways in a sly or unpleasant way (*he leered at the girl*). ● *also n.*

left[1] /**left**/ *pp of* **leave**.

left[2] /**left**/ *n* **1** the side opposite to the right (*drive on the left of the road*). **2** in politics, the Socialist party. ● *also adj.* ● **the extreme left** the Communist party.

left-handed /**left-han**-did/ *adj* better able to use the left hand than the right (*left-handed people*).

leg /**leg**/ *n* **1** one of the limbs on which an animal stands or moves. **2** a support for a table, chair, etc. (*a table with uneven legs*). ● **on one's last legs** near the end of your power, life, etc. (*the firm is on its last legs*). ● **pull a person's leg** to play a joke on someone (*he was pulling her leg when he said there was a bear standing behind her*).

legacy /**le**-ga-see/ *n* that which is left to someone by will (*receive a legacy from his uncle*).

legal /**lee**-gal/ *adj* **1** having to do with the law (*legal proceedings*). **2** allowed by law (*legal activities*).

legality /li-**ga**-li-tee/ *n* lawfulness (*question the legality of his actions*).

legalize /**lee**-ga-lize/ *vb, also* **legalise** (*Br*) to make lawful (*a suggestion that some drugs should be legalized*).

legend /**le**-jend/ *n* **1** an ancient story passed on by word of mouth (*legends about giants*). **2** the words written under a picture, etc. (*the legend below the illustration is wrong*).

legendary /**le**-jen-da-ree/ *adj* **1** having to do with

ancient legends, famous in story, existing only in story (*legendary beasts/legendary kings*). **2** very famous (*legendary folk singer/her legendary beauty*).

leggings /**le**-gingz/ *npl* a thick covering for the lower leg (*girls wearing leggings and short skirts*).

leggy /**le**-gee/ *adj* (*inf*) having very long legs (*leggy young women*).

leghorn /**leg**-horn/ *n* a type of hen.

legible /**le**-ji-bul/ *adj* possible to read (*handwriting that is scarcely legible*). ● *n* **legibility** /le-ji-**bi**-li-tee/.

legion /**lee**-jun/ *n* **1** a Roman regiment or division (3000–6000 soldiers). **2** a great number (*people came to hear him in their legions*).

legionary /**lee**-ju-ne-ree/ *n* a soldier belonging to a legion.

legislate /**le**-ji-slate/ *vb* to make laws (*legislating against smoking in public buildings*).

legislation /le-ji-**slay**-shun/ *n* **1** the act of making laws. **2** the laws made (*new legislation brought in against the import of certain goods*).

legislative /**le**-ji-slay-tiv/ *adj* having the power or right to make laws (*a legislative assembly*).

legislator /**le**-ji-slay-tor/ *n* someone who makes laws.

legislature /**le**-ji-slay-chur/ *n* the part of a government that makes laws.

legitimate /li-**ji**-ti-mat/ *adj* **1** allowed by law, lawful (*a legitimate claim/a legitimate business*). **2** born of married parents (*they married just before their daughter was born so that she would be legitimate*).

legume /**lay**-goom/ *n* a plant that bears seeds in pods (e.g., peas, beans, etc.).

leisure /**lee**-zhur/ *n* spare time, time free from work (*little time for leisure/leisure activities*).

leisurely /**lee**-zhur-lee/ *adj* slow, unhurried (*work at a leisurely pace*). ● *also adv.*

lemming /**le**-ming/ *n* a small ratlike animal of far northern regions.

lemon /**le**-mon/ *n* **1** a pale, yellow, sharp-tasting fruit (*buy lemons to flavor the drinks*). **2** the tree bearing this fruit. **3** a pale yellow color (*paint the walls lemon*).

lemonade /le-mo-**nade**/, **lemon squash** /**le**-mon skwash/ *ns* a drink made from or tasting of lemon juice.

lemur /**lee**-mur/ *n* a monkeylike animal.

lend /**lend**/ *vb* (*pt, pp* **lent** /**lent**/) to give something to another on condition that it is returned after use (*lend her a book/lend my car to my brother*). ● *n* **lender** /len-der/.

length /lenth/ *n* measurement from end to end of space or time (*measure the length of the room/estimate the length of a journey*). ● **at length 1** at last (*at length we understood what he was trying to say*). **2** taking a long time, in detail (*she explained it at length*).

lengthen /lenth-en/ *vb* to make or become longer (*curtains requiring to be lengthened*).

lengthwise /lenth-wize/ *adv, also* **lengthways** (*Br*) /lenth-waze/ in the direction of the length (*measure the room lengthways*).

lengthy /lenth-ee/ *adj* very long (*a lengthy sermon/a lengthy delay*).

lenient /leen-yent/ *adj* **1** merciful (*a lenient judge*). **2** not severe (*a lenient sentence*). ● *ns* **lenience** /leen-yense/, **leniency** /leen-yen-see/.

lens /lenz/ *n* a transparent substance, usually glass, with a surface curved in such a way that objects seen through it appear bigger or smaller.

Lent /lent/ *n* the period between Ash Wednesday and Easter during which Christ's fast in the desert is commemorated.

lentil /len-til/ *n* the edible seed of a pealike plant (*a soup made of lentils*).

leopard /le-pard/ *n* a large, spotted animal of the cat family.

leper /le-per/ *n* a person with leprosy.

leprechaun /le-pre-con/ *n* in fairy tales, an elf, especially in Ireland.

leprosy /le-pru-see/ *n* an infectious disease that eats away the skin and parts of the body. ● *adj* **leprous** /le-prus/.

lesion /lee-zhun/ *n* (*fml*) an injury, a wound (*lesions on his back caused by his accident*).

less /less/ *adj* smaller, not so much (*earn less money*). ● *n* a smaller amount (*she gave him less*). ● *adv* not so greatly, not so much (*she likes him less now*).

lessen /le-sun/ *vb* to make or become less (*try to lessen the pain*).

lesser /le-ser/ *adj* less, smaller (*a lesser problem*).

lesson /le-sun/ *n* **1** something that is learned or taught (*give French lessons/take piano lessons*). **2** a period of teaching (*feel ill during the science lesson*). **3** a passage read from the Bible (*read the lesson in church*). **4** an example (*her courage is a lesson to us all*).

let /let/ *vb* (**let** /let/, **letting** /le-ting/) **1** to allow (*let the children go to the cinema*). **2** to allow the use

of for rent or payment (*let a room in their house to a student*). ● *n* the act of letting for rent (*a short-term let*).

lethal /lee-thal/ *adj* causing death (*a lethal dose of poison*).

lethargic /le-thar-jic/ *adj* sleepy, slow-moving, lacking interest (*feel lethargic after her illness*).

lethargy /le-thar-jee/ *n* lack of energy and interest (*the lethargy brought on by extreme heat*).

letter /le-ter/ *n* **1** a sign standing for a sound (*the letter "h"*). **2** a written message (*write a letter of apology*). **3** (*fml*) *pl* literature, learning (*men of letters*). ● **letter of credit** a letter allowing the holder to draw money when away from home. ● **to the letter** exactly (*carry out her instructions to the letter*).

lettered /le-terd/ *adj* (*fml*) well read.

lettering /le-te-ring/ *n* letters that have been drawn, painted, etc. (*lettering on shop windows*).

lettuce /le-tus/ *n* a plant whose leaves are used in salads (*a salad of lettuce and tomatoes*).

leukaemia /loo-kee-mee-a/ *n* a serious disease in which too many white blood cells are produced.

levee /le-vee/ *n* **1** (*old*) a morning party at which guests were introduced to the king or queen. **2** a raised bank at the side of a river.

level /le-vel/ *n* **1** a flat, even surface (*he can walk on the level but not uphill*). **2** a sealed tube filled with alcohol and containing an air bubble that is stationary in the middle of the tube when it is level. **3** a general standard of quality or quantity (*a high level of achievement/wages falling below last year's level*). **4** a horizontal division or floor in a house, etc. (*a garden on two levels*). ● *adj* **1** flat. **2** even. **3** on the same line or height. ● *vb* (**leveled** /le-veld/, **leveling** /le-ve-ling/) **1** to make flat (*level the ground*). **2** to make equal (*level the score*). **3** to destroy, to demolish (*the bulldozer leveled the block of flats*). **4** to aim (*level his gun at the enemy soldier*).

level crossing /le-vel craw-sing/ *n* a place where a railway line crosses the surface of a road (*the car had to stop at the level crossing until the train passed*).

level-headed /le-vel he-ded/ *adj* sensible (*he is very level-headed and dealt with the emergency calmly and efficiently*).

lever /lee-ver/ *n* a bar for raising heavy objects (*use a lever to remove the tire from the wheel*).

leverage /lee-ve-rige/ *n* power gained by the use of a lever (*not enough leverage to raise the huge metal block*).

leveret /**le**-ve-ret/ *n* a young hare.

leviathan /li-**vie**-a-thin/ *n* **1** a sea monster. **2** anything very large.

levity /**le**-vi-tee/ *n* (*fml*) lack of seriousness (*treating the matter of her exams with too much levity*).

levy /**le**-vee/ *vb* **1** to bring together men to form an army. **2** to collect money for a tax (*levied taxes on alcohol*). ● *n* **1** the soldiers thus assembled. **2** the money thus collected.

lewd /**lood**/ *adj* indecent, obscene (*singing lewd songs*). ● *n* **lewdness** /**lood**-ness/.

lexicographer /lek-si-**cog**-ra-fer/ *n* someone who prepares a dictionary.

lexicon /**lek**-si-con/ *n* a dictionary.

liability /lie-a-**bi**-li-tee/ *n* **1** debt (*liabilities that exceed his assets*). **2** the state of being liable (*his liability to colds/exempt from any liability in the matter*). **3** something for which someone is responsible (*the dog is his liability*).

liable /**lie**-a-bul/ *adj* **1** likely to have to do or suffer from (*liable to lose her temper/liable to catch cold/liable to flood*). **2** legally responsible for (*liable for his wife's debts*). **3** likely to get, be punished with, etc. (*trespassers are liable to a large fine*).

liaison /lee-**ay**-zon/ *n* **1** a close connection or working association (*important that the two departments maintain a liaison*). **2** (*fml*) an unlawful sexual relationship (*he had a liaison with a married women*).

liar /**lie**-ar/ *n* someone who tells lies.

libel /**lie**-bel/ *n* something written that damages a person's reputation (*being sued for libel*). ● *also vb* (**libeled** /**lie**-beld/, **libeling** /**lie**-bel-ing/).

libelous /**lie**-bel-us/ *adj* hurtful to someone's reputation (*a libelous statement in the newspapers*).

liberal /**lib**-ral/ *adj* **1** generous (*a liberal supply of food*). **2** ready to accept new ideas (*liberal attitudes*). **3** (*of education*) intended solely to develop the powers of the mind. ● *n* someone who believes in greater political freedom.

liberality /li-ber-a-li-tee/ *n* (*fml*) readiness to give to others (*the liberality of their host*).

liberate /**li**-ber-rate/ *vb* to set free (*liberating the city held by the enemy*). ● *n* **liberation** /li-be-**ray**-shun/.

libertine /**lib**-er-teen/ *n* (*fml*) someone who openly leads a wicked, immoral life.

liberty /**lib**-er-tee/ *n* **1** freedom (*ex-prisoners enjoying newfound liberty*). **2** the right to do as you like (*you are at liberty to leave if you wish*). **3** too great freedom of speech or action (*it was taking a liberty to borrow my car without permission*).

librarian /lie-**bray**-ree-an/ *n* someone in charge of a library.

library /**lie**-bre-ree/ *n* **1** a collection of books (*a fiction library and a reference library*). **2** a room or building in which books are kept (*build a new library*).

libretto /li-**bre**-toe/ *n* (*pl* **libretti** /li-**bre**-tee/) the book of words of an opera or musical work (*he wrote the music and his wife the libretto*).

lice /**lice**/ *see* **louse**.

licence /**lie**-sense/ *n* **1** a written permission to do or keep something (*a license to drive a car*). **2** (*fml*) too great freedom of action (*allow his children too much license*).

license /**lie**-sense/ *vb* to give a license to (*he is licensed to sell alcohol*).

licensee /lie-sen-**see**/ *n* someone to whom a license is given (*the owner of the pub is the licensee*).

licentious /lie-**sen**-shus/ *adj* (*fml*) behaving in an immoral or improper way, indecent (*he was licentious as a young man but regrets it now*). ● *n* **licentiousness** /lie-**sen**-shus-ness/.

lichen /**lie**-ken/ *n* a moss that grows on rocks, tree trunks, etc.

licit /**li**-sit/ *adj* (*fml*) lawful (*licit pleasures*).

lick /**lick**/ *vb* **1** to pass the tongue over (*the dog licked her hand*). **2** to take (food or drink) into the mouth with the tongue (*lick the ice cream*). **3** (*inf*) to defeat (*we licked the other team*). **4** (*inf*) to thrash (*he will get licked for breaking the window*). ● *n* **1** act of passing the tongue over. **2** a blow.

licking /**li**-king/ *n* (*inf*) a thrashing (*get a good licking for breaking the window*).

licorice /**li**-crish/ *n* **1** a black sweet-tasting root used in making medicines and sweets. **2** a kind of sweet made from this.

lid /**lid**/ *n* the movable cover of a pot, box, etc. (*the lid of the jar is stiff*).

lie[1] /**lie**/ *n* a statement that the maker knows to be untrue (*tell a lie to try to avoid being punished*). ● *vb* (**lied** /**lied**/, **lying** /**lie**-ing/) to tell a lie (*it was obvious that he was lying*).

lie[2] /**lie**/ *vb* (**lay** /**lay**/, **lying** /**lie**-ing/, *pp* **lain** /**lane**/) **1** to put the body full length upon (*she wants to lie on the beach all day*). **2** to be or remain in a certain place (*the book was lying on the table*). ● *n* the way in which something lies.

liege /**leedge**/ *n* (*old*) **1** someone owing certain duties to a lord. **2** a lord.

lieu /**loo**/ *n*. ● **in lieu of** instead of (*extra holiday in lieu of wages for working overtime*).

lieutenant /loo-**ten**-ant/ *n* **1** (*fml*) someone who does the work of another, deputy (*sent one of her lieutenants to deal with the complaint*). **2** a naval or army officer.

life /life/ *n* (*pl* **lives** /lievz/) **1** the state of being alive (*there is no life left in the injured man*). **2** the force existing in animals and plants that gives them the ability to change with the passing of time. **3** liveliness, activity (*a house without life after the children left*). **4** the time someone has been alive (*he worked hard all his life*). **5** the story of someone's life (*publish a life of the poet*).

lifebelt /life-belt/ *n* a belt of a material that floats easily and so helps to prevent the wearer sinking when in water.

lifeboat /life-boat/ *n* a boat that goes to the help of those in danger at sea.

lifebuoy /life-boy/ *n* an object that floats easily and to which shipwrecked people can hold until help arrives.

life cycle /life-sie-cul/ *n* the series of forms into which a living thing changes during its development (*the life cycle of the frog*).

lifeless /life-less/ *adj* **1** dead (*pull the lifeless bodies from the sea*). **2** dull (*lifeless hair*). **3** not lively (*a lifeless performance*).

lifelike /life-like/ *adj* seeming to have life (*a lifelike portrait*).

lifelong /life-long/ *adj* lasting through life (*a lifelong friendship*).

life-size /life-size/, **life-sized** /life-siezd/ *adj* of the same size as the person or thing represented (*a life-size statue of the king*).

life span /life-span/ *n* the length of time that someone is likely to live or something is likely to function (*the life span of the average person was much shorter in those days*).

lifestyle /life-stile/ *n* the way in which someone lives (*an affluent lifestyle*).

lifetime /life-time/ *n* the length of time a person lives (*he experienced several wars in his lifetime*).

lift /lift/ *vb* **1** to raise up higher (*lift the flag above his head*). **2** to take up (*lift the baby from the pram*). ● *n* **1** a machine by which people or goods are carried from floor to floor of a building. **2** a free ride in a private vehicle (*get a lift to work from his neighbor*).

ligament /li-ga-ment/ *n* a band of tough substance joining bones together at joints (*strain a ligament*).

ligature /li-ga-chur/ *n* **1** (*fml*) a bandage. **2** a cord for tying up the end of a blood vessel during an operation. **3** two letters joined together in type (e.g., æ).

light¹ /lite/ *n* **1** that which makes it possible for the eye to see things. **2** anything that gives light, as the sun, a lamp, etc. (*a bedside light*). **3** knowledge, understanding (*unable to throw any light on the problem*). **4** brightness in the eyes or face (*a light in his eye*). ● *adj* **1** clear, not dark (*it's getting light*). **1** not deep or dark in color (*light green/light hair*). ● *vb* (*pt, pp* **lit** /lit/) to give light to, to set fire to (*light the fire*).

light² /lite/ *adj* **1** not heavy (*light loads*). **2** not difficult (*light tasks*). **3** not severe (*a light punishment*). **4** small in amount (*a light rainfall*). **5** not serious, for entertainment (*light reading*). **6** graceful (*light on her feet*). **7** happy, merry (*light of heart*).

light³ /lite/ *vb* to come upon by chance (*light upon the solution*).

light bulb *or* **lightbulb** /lite-bulb/ a glass bulb containing a wire (filament) or a gas that glows when it is supplied with electricity.

lighten¹ /lie-ten/ *vb* **1** to make bright (*lighten the mood*). **2** to flash.

lighten² /lie-ten/ *vb* to make less heavy (*try to lighten the load*).

lighter¹ /lie-ter/ *n* a device for setting something (e.g., a cigarette) alight.

lighter² /lie-ter/ *n* a large boat, usually flat-bottomed, for carrying goods from ship to shore.

light-fingered /lite-fing-gerd/ *adj* (*inf*) thieving (*detectives watching for light-fingered people in shops*).

light-footed /lite-foo-ted/ *adj* nimble, quick on your feet (*light-footed dancers*).

light-headed /lite-he-ded/ *adj* giddy, dizzy (*feel light-headed after drinking the wine*).

light-hearted /lite-har-ted/ *adj* **1** merry, cheerful (*people on holiday in light-hearted mood*). **2** not serious (*a light-hearted account of the event*).

lighthouse /lite-house/ *n* a tower with a light to guide ships.

lightning /lite-ning/ *adj* the electric flash seen before thunder is heard (*a tree struck by lightning*).

lightning conductor /lite-ning con-**duc**-tor/, **lightning rod** /lite-ning rod/ *ns* a metal rod that protects a building from lightning by conducting the flash to the earth.

lights /lites/ *npl* the lungs of an animal, such as sheep, used as food.

lightship /lite-ship/ *n* an anchored ship with a light to guide other ships.

light year /lite-year/ *n* the distance light travels in a year.

lignite /lig-nite/ *n* a type of brown coal.

like[1] /like/ *adj* nearly the same, resembling (*have like attitudes/of like mind/they are as like as two peas*). ● *prep* in the same way as (*she walks like her mother*). ● *n* a person or thing nearly the same as or equal to another (*you will not see his like again*).

like[2] /like/ *vb* 1 to be pleased by (*she liked the play*). 2 to be fond of (*she likes children/she does not like her next-door neighbor*).

likeable, likable /like-a-bul/ *adj* attractive, pleasant.

likelihood /like-li-hood/ *n* probability (*have little likelihood of success*).

likely /like-lee/ *adj* 1 probable (*the likely result*). 2 suitable (*the more likely of the candidates*). ● *adv* probably (*they'll very likely arrive late*).

liken /like-en/ *vb* to compare (*she likened her relationship with him to a battle*).

likeness /like-ness/ *n* 1 resemblance (*I saw little likeness between mother and daughter*). 2 a picture of a person (*the artist's likeness of his wife*).

likes /likes/ *npl* things that are pleasing to someone (*we all have our likes and dislikes*).

likewise /like-wize/ *adv* 1 in the same way (*he left early and she did likewise*). 2 also (*Mr Jones was sacked and likewise Mr Smith*).

liking /like-ing/ *n* a fondness or preference for (*a liking for classical music/a liking for fast food*).

lilac /lie-lac/ *n* 1 a type of small tree with light purple or white flowers (*the sweet smell of lilac*). 2 a light purple color. ● *adj* light purple (*lilac wool*).

lilt /lilt/ *vb* to sing cheerfully. ● *n* 1 a regular pattern of rising and falling sound (*Scots people speaking with a lilt*). 2 a cheerful song. 3 a tune with a strongly marked rhythm.

lilting /lil-ting/ *adj* having a strongly marked lilt (*a lilting voice*).

lily /li-lee/ *n* a flower grown from a bulb, often white in color.

lily of the valley /li-lee-ov-the-va-lee/ *n* a flower with small white bells and a distinctive sweet smell.

limb /lim/ *n* 1 an arm, leg or wing (*fracture a limb*). 2 a branch of a tree (*a cat stuck on a limb of the oak tree*).

limber[1] /lim-ber/ *n* (*old*) a small two-wheeled ammunition carriage that travels with a gun.

limber[2] /lim-ber/ *adj* moving and bending easily, supple (*he is elderly but still very limber*). ● *vb*

limber up to exercise in order to make more supple (*dancers limbering up for a performance*).

limbo /lim-bo/ *n* 1 a place where, it is supposed, the souls of those who die in complete ignorance of God spend eternity. 2 a place where someone is forgotten or neglected, a state of uncertainty (*she is in limbo waiting to get the results of three job interviews*).

lime[1] /lime/ *n* a white substance got by heating certain kinds of rock.

lime[2] /lime/ *n* 1 a small lemon like, yellowish-green fruit (*flavor the dessert with the juice of a lime*). 2 the tree bearing this fruit. 3 the linden tree.

lime juice /lime-joose/ *n* a drink made from the juice of the lime.

limelight /lime-lite/ *n*. ● **in the limelight** in a position in which someone's actions are followed with interest by many people (*senior members of the government always in the limelight*).

limerick /lim-e-rick/ *n* a nonsense poem written in a special five-line stanza.

limestone /lime-stone/ *n* rock containing a lot of lime.

limit /li-mit/ *n* 1 a boundary (*the limits of his estate*). 2 that which you may not go past (*the limit of his patience*). 3 the greatest or smallest amount or number that is fixed as being correct, legal, necessary, desirable, etc. (*the government imposed a 4% limit on pay increases*). ● *vb* to keep within bounds (*try to limit your expenditure on entertainment to $50 per week/we must limit the audience to 200*).

limitation /li-mi-tay-shun/ *n* 1 that which limits (*the limitations imposed by time*). 2 inability to do something, weakness (*all of us have our limitations*).

limited /li-mi-ted/ *adj* 1 small in amount (*a limited supply of food*). 2 not very great, large, wide-ranging, etc. (*of limited experience*).

limn /lim/ *vb* (*old*) to draw or paint.

limp[1] /limp/ *vb* to walk lamely (*he limps after the accident to his leg*). ● *also n*.

limp[2] /limp/ *adj* 1 not stiff, drooping (*limp lettuce leaves*). 1 without energy or strength (*feel limp after her illness/a limp handshake*).

limpet /lim-pet/ *n* a shellfish that clings tightly to rocks.

limpid /lim-pid/ *adj* clear, transparent (*look into the limpid stream*).

linchpin /linch-pin/ *n* 1 the pin passed through the end of an axle to keep the wheel on it. 2 a person who is very important to the running of a form or organization (*the senior secretary is the linchpin of the whole firm*).

linden /**lin**-den/ *n* a kind of tree with yellow sweet-smelling flowers, the lime tree.

line /**line**/ *n* **1** a small rope or cord (*washing hanging on the line to dry*). **2** a thin mark made with a pen, pencil, etc. (*put a line under the important words*). **3** a row of persons or things (*a line of people waiting to get tickets from the box office*). **4** a row of words on a page (*there were fifty lines on one page of the book*). **5** a short letter (*drop him a line to say hello*). **6** a railway track (*the main London line*). **7** ancestors and descendants (*of the royal line*). **8** a fleet of steamers, airplanes, etc., providing regular services (*a passenger line*). **9** (*inf*) the equator. **10** a telephone wire. **11** (*inf*) way of behaving or of earning your living (*what line is he in?*). **12** *pl* the positions of an army ready to attack or defend (*behind the enemy lines*). ● *vb* **1** to mark with lines (*age had lined her face*). **2** to arrange in a row or rows (*lining the children up*). **3** to cover on the inside (*line the dress with silk*).

lineage /**li**-nee-age/ *n* someone's ancestors (*of royal lineage*).

lineal /**li**-nee-al/ *adj* passed down from father to son.

lineament /**li**-nee-a-ment/ *n* (*fml*) a noticeable feature of the face (*admire her noble lineaments*).

linear /**li**-nee-ar/ *adj* having to do with lines (*a linear diagram*).

linen /**li**-nen/ *n* cloth made of flax (*dresses made of white linen*).

liner /**lie**-ner/ *n* **1** a large ocean-going passenger ship. **2** something that lines.

linesman /**line**-zman/ *n* someone who assists an umpire or referee by signaling when a ball is out of play (*linesmen on the football pitch*).

ling /**ling**/ *n* **1** a fish of the cod family. **2** heather.

linger /**ling**-ger/ *vb* **1** to delay before going (*let's not linger—it's getting dark*). **2** to stay about, to last or continue for a long time (*the smell lingered/doubts that lingered*).

lingerie /**lon**-je-ree/ *n* women's underclothing (*the shop's lingerie department*).

lingo /**ling**-go/ *n* (*inf*) a language (*he didn't learn the language of the country and complained about not understanding the lingo*).

lingua franca /**ling**-gwa-**frang**-ka/ *n* a mixed language in which people of different languages may speak to one another.

lingual /**ling**-gwal/ *adj* (*fml*) **1** having to do with the tongue. **2** having to do with language.

linguist /**ling**-gwist/ *n* someone skilled in foreign languages (*a linguist looking for work as a translator*).

linguistic /ling-**gwi**-stic/ *adj* having to do with the study of languages (*note some linguistic changes*). ● *n* **linguistics** /ling-**gwi**-stics/.

liniment /**li**-na-ment/ *n* an ointment or oil rubbed into the body to prevent stiffness (*athletes rubbing liniment into their legs*).

lining /**lie**-ning/ *n* the covering of the inside of something, such as a garment or box (*a coat with a fake fur lining*).

link /**lingk**/ *n* **1** one ring of a chain (*break one of the links of the silver chain round her neck*). **2** that which connects one thing with another (*a link between poverty and crime*). **3** $^1/_{100}$ part of a chain (= 7.92 inches). ● *vb* to connect, to join (*the police are linking the three robberies*).

links /**lingks**/ *npl* **1** flat sandy, grassy ground by the seashore. **2** a seaside golf course.

linoleum /li-**no**-lee-um/ *n* a floor covering made of cloth coated with linseed oil.

linotype /**li**-no-tipe/ *n* a machine that prepares whole lines of printing type at a time.

linseed /**lin**-seed/ *n* the seed of flax.

lint /**lint**/ *n* linen specially prepared for dressing open wounds (*cover the grazed knee with lint and a bandage*).

lintel /**lin**-tel/ *n* the wood or stone across the top of a window or door (*the tall man hit his head on the lintel of the door*).

lion /**lion**/ *n* **1** a large flesh-eating animal of the cat family (*the large tawny mane of the lion*). **2** a famous and important person (*the after-dinner speaker will be one of our literary lions*). ● *f* **lioness** /**lion**-ess/. ● **lion's share** the largest share (*her greedy big brother always took the lion's share of the food*).

lion-hearted /**lion**-har-ted/ *adj* very brave.

lionize /**lion**-ize/ *vb, also* **lionise** (*Br*) to treat a person as if he or she were famous (*he is only a minor poet but he is lionized by the people in the village where he lives*).

lip /**lip**/ *n* **1** either of the edges of the opening of the mouth (*she bit her lip to try to stop crying*). **2** the edge or brim of anything (*the lip of the cup*).

lip-read /**lip**-reed/ *vb* to understand what a person is saying from the movements of his or her lips (*she is deaf and she lip-reads well*).

lipstick /**lip**-stick/ n a kind of pencil or crayon used to color the lips (*wear bright red lipstick*).

liquefy /**li**-kwi-fie/ vb to make or become liquid (*butter that liquefied in the heat of the kitchen*). ● n **liquefaction** /li-kwi-fi-**cay**-shun/.

liqueur /li-**cur**/ n a sweetly flavored alcoholic drink (*drink liqueurs after dinner/a liqueur flavored with coffee*).

liquid /**li**-kwid/ adj **1** in the form of a liquid (*liquid soap*). **2** clear (*liquid eyes*). **3** (*of sounds*) smooth and clear, as the letter r or l. ● n a substance that flows and has no fixed shape, a substance that is not a solid or gas.

liquidate /**li**-kwi-date/ vb **1** to pay debts. **2** to close down a business when it has too many debts. **3** to put an end to, to get rid of, to destroy (*liquidating the terrorist leader*). ● n **liquidation** /li-kwi-**day**-shun/.

liquor /**li**-cur/ n **1** strong drink, such as spirits (*drink beer but not liquor*). **2** the liquid produced from cooked food (*the liquor from the baked ham*).

liquorice see **licorice**.

lisp /lisp/ vb **1** to say the sound th for s when speaking. **2** to speak as a small child does (*a little girl lisping a poem*). ● also n.

list[1] /list/ n a series of names, numbers, etc., written down in order one after the other (*making a shopping list/have a long list of people waiting for houses*). ● vb to write down in order (*list the people present*).

list[2] /list/ vb to lean over to one side (*boats listing in the storm*). ● also n.

listen /**li**-sen/ vb **1** to try to hear (*listen to music as she worked*). **2** to pay attention to (*listen to his mother's advice*). ● n **listener** /**li**-sner/.

listless /**list**-less/ adj lacking energy, uninterested (*feel listless after the long winter*).

lit pt of **light**.

litany /**li**-ta-nee/ n a form of public prayer with responses given by the worshippers.

liter /**li**-ter/ n in the metric system, a measure of liquid (about 1 ³/₄ pints).

literacy /**li**-tra-see/ n the ability to read and write (*teachers are worried about the lack of literacy in the country*).

literal /**li**-tral/ adj **1** with each word given its ordinary meaning, word for word (*a literal translation*). **2** following the exact meaning without any exaggeration or anything added from the imagination (*a literal account of what happened*). ● adv **literally** /**li**-tra-lee/.

literary /**li**-te-ra-ree/ adj having to do with literature or with writing as a career (*have literary tastes*).

literate /**li**-te-rat/ adj **1** able to read and write (*a disturbing number of people who are scarcely literate*). **2** having read a great deal (*literate people who enjoy discussing books*).

literature /**li**-te-ra-chur/ n **1** the books, etc., written on a particular subject (*all the literature relating to drug abuse*). **2** written works of lasting interest and of fine quality and artistic value (*study English literature*).

lithe /lithe/ adj able to bend or twist easily and gracefully (*the lithe bodies of the young gymnasts*).

litmus /**lit**-mus/ n a blue dye turned red by acids.

litter /**li**-ter/ n **1** (*old*) a light bed that can be carried about, a stretcher. **2** bedding of straw, etc., for animals. **3** the young of an animal born at one time (*a litter of five pups*). **4** (*Br*) trash; scraps of paper and rubbish lying about (*pick up the litter and put it in a bin*). ● vb **1** to throw away untidily (*litter the streets with the packaging from fast food*). **2** (*of animals*) to give birth to.

little /**li**-tul/ adj **1** small (*little black birds*). **2** short (*he was only a little fellow*). **3** young (*little children*). ● n **1** a small amount (*pay a little at a time*). **2** a short time (*I'll be there in a little*). ● adv not much (*think little of her work*).

live[1] /liv/ vb **1** to have life, to exist, to be alive (*everything that lives/the right to live*). **2** to continue to be alive (*he is very ill but he will live*). **3** to dwell, to have your home (*she lives in the country*). **4** to behave in a certain way (*live dangerously*). **5** to keep oneself alive, obtain the food or goods necessary for life (*earn barely enough to live/live by hunting*). **6** to pass or spend one's life (*living a life of luxury*). ● **live down** to live in a way that makes others overlook one's past faults (*he will never live it down if his neighbors discover he has been in prison*).

live[2] /live/ adj **1** having life, alive (*a cat with a live mouse*). **2** full of energy, capable of becoming active (*live electrical wires*). **3** heard or seen as the event takes place, not recorded (*a live broadcast*). **4** burning (*live coals*).

livelihood /**live**-lee-hood/ n the work by which one earns one's living (*earn his livelihood by driving taxis*).

livelong /**liv**-long/ adj **1** seeming long (*he snored the livelong night*). **2** (*fml*) whole (*children playing in the sun the livelong day*).

lively /**live**-lee/ adj active, energetic, cheerful (*a *lively child/a lively discussion).* ● *n* **liveliness** /live-lee-ness/.

liven /lie-ven/ *vb* to make more cheerful (*try to liven up the party*).

liver /li-ver/ *n* **1** an organ inside the body that helps to cleanse the blood (*get a liver transplant*). **2** this organ from certain animals used as food (*liver and onions*).

livery /li-ve-ree/ *n* a special uniform worn by servants in one household (*footmen wearing the queen's livery*).

livestock /live-stock/ *n* animals kept on a farm.

live wire /live-**wire**/ *n* **1** a wire through which an electric current is passing. **2** a person with a lot of energy (*she's a real live wire who's fun to have around*).

livid /li-vid/ *adj* **1** discolored, black and blue (*livid bruises*). **2** (*old*) pale (*a livid face*). **3** (*inf*) very angry (*she was livid with her son for being late*).

living /li-ving/ *n* **1** a means of providing oneself with what is necessary for life (*what does he do for a living?*). **2** employment as a member of clergy in the Church of England.

lizard /li-zard/ *n* a four-footed reptile with a long tail.

llama /la-ma/ *n* a South American animal of the camel family.

llano /la-no/ *n* one of the vast grassy plains of South America.

lo /lo/ *interj* (*old or lit*) look! (*lo! a light has suddenly appeared*).

load /load/ *vb* **1** to put a burden on the back of an animal (*load the donkey*). **2** to put goods into a vehicle (*load the van*). **3** to put a heavy weight on (*load him with responsibility*). **4** to put ammunition into a gun (*load his revolver*). **5** to put film into a camera. ● *n* **1** that which is carried (*the lorry's load*). **2** a weight (*a load on her mind*). **3** a cargo (*the ship's load*).

loadstar *same as* **lodestar**.

loadstone *same as* **lodestone**.

loaf[1] /loaf/ *n* (*pl* **loaves** /loavz/) bread made into a shape convenient for selling (*a loaf of brown bread*).

loaf[2] /loaf/ *vb* to pass time without doing anything, to laze around (*loafing around street corners instead of going to work*). ● *n* **loafer** /lo-fer/.

loam /loam/ *n* a sand and clay soil. ● *adj* **loamy** /lo-mee/.

loan /loan/ *n* that which is lent (*get a loan from the bank*).

loath, loth /loath/ *adj* unwilling (*she was loath to leave home*).

loathe /loathe/ *vb* to hate (*she loathed the nasty old man/loathes living there*).

loathing /loathe-ing/ *n* hate, disgust (*look at him with sheer loathing*).

loathsome /loathe-sum/ *adj* hateful, disgusting (*a loathsome creature*).

loaves *see* **loaf**.

lob /lob/ *vb* (**lobbed** /lobd/, **lobbing** /lob-ing/) to hit, kick or throw a ball gently into the air (*lob the tennis ball over the net*). ● *also n*.

lobby /lob-ee/ *n* **1** an entrance hall (*hotel lobbies*). **2** a group of people trying to influence the decisions of the government (*the anti-motorway lobby*). ● *vb* to try to influence decisions of the government.

lobe /loab/ *n* the fleshy hanging part of the ear (*earrings are worn on the lobes of the ears*).

lobelia /lo-beel-ya/ *n* a kind of garden flower, often blue, white or red in color.

lobster /lob-ster/ *n* a long-tailed jointed shellfish.

lobster pot /lob-ster pot/ *n* a baited basket for trapping lobsters.

local /lo-cal/ *adj* having to do with a particular place (*local history/local people*).

local color /lo-cal cul-ur/ *n* in a picture or story, accuracy over details of place to make it more realistic (*his descriptions of the village inhabitants added local color to his novel*).

locality /lo-cal-i-tee/ *n* a district, area, neighborhood (*she has lived in the same locality for years*).

localize /lo-ca-lize/ *vb, also* **localise** (*Br*) to keep to one place or district (*the disease seems to be localized*).

locate /lo-cate/ *vb* **1** to find the place of (*try to locate the source of the infection*). **2** to fix or set in a certain place (*the houses are located by the village green*).

location /lo-cay-shun/ *n* **1** place (*live in a pleasant location*). **2** the place where a story is filmed (*the filming was carried out on location in Scotland*).

loch /lok/ *n* **1** a lake, especially in Scotland. **2** an arm of the sea.

lock /lok/ *n* **1** a fastening bolt moved by a key (*turn the key in the lock*). **2** the part of a gun by which it is fired. **3** a section of a canal, enclosed by gates, in which the amount of water can be increased to raise a ship to a higher level, or vice versa. **4** a firm grasp (*the wrestler held his opponent in a lock*). **5** a curl of hair. ● *vb* **1** to fasten with lock and key (*lock the door/lock the safe*). **2** to hold firmly (*lovers locked in a passionate embrace*). **3** to jam, to become fixed or blocked (*the car's wheels have locked*). ● **lock, stock and barrel** altogether, completely (*he moved out of the flat, lock, stock and barrel*).

locker /**lok**-er/ *n* a small cupboard with a lock (*his locker in the changing rooms*).

locket /**lok**-et/ *n* a small metal case, often containing a picture, worn on a chain round the neck as an ornament (*a silver locket containing a lock of her husband's hair*).

lockjaw /**lok**-jaw/ *n* **1** (*fam*) tetanus. **2** a condition in which the muscles of the jaw become so stiff that the mouth cannot be opened, usually a sign of tetanus.

locksmith /**lok**-smith/ *n* one who makes or repairs locks.

lock-up /**lok**-up/ *n* **1** a cell in a prison (*he's in a lock-up in the local police station*). **2** a garage in which a car can be locked away (*his lock-up is some way from his house*).

locomotion /lo-co-**mo**-shun/ *n* (*fml*) movement from place to place (*the sideways locomotion of a crab*).

locomotive /lo-co-**mo**-tiv/ *n* a railway engine.

locust /**lo**-cust/ *n* a large grasshopper that feeds on and destroys crops.

lode /**lode**/ *n* a vein of metal in a crack in a rock.

lodestar /**lode**-star/ *n* **1** the star by which one sets a course, the Pole star. **2** a guide or example to follow (*he was so successful that he acted as a lodestar to his fellow workers*).

lodestone /**lode**-stone/ *n* a stone containing magnetic iron, formerly used as a compass.

lodge /**lodge**/ *n* **1** a small house originally for a gatekeeper at the entrance to a park, church, etc. (*he lives in the manor house and his mother in the lodge*). **2** the meeting place of a society (e.g., Freemasons) or the members meeting there (*a Masonic lodge*). **3** a house for a hunting party (*live at the shooting lodge for the stag-hunting season*). **4** a house or cabin used occasionally for some seasonal activity (*a ski lodge*). ● *vb* **1** to put in a certain place (*lodge documents with his solicitor*). **2** to stay in another's house on payment (*students lodging with locals*). **3** to fix in (*a bullet lodged in her shoulder*). ● **lodge a complaint** to make a complaint before an official.

lodger /**lod**-jer/ *n* one who stays in hired rooms in another's house (*take in lodgers to make money to live*).

lodging /**lod**-jing/ *n* a place where one pays to stay (*look for cheap lodging in town*).

loft /**loft**/ *n* **1** the space or room under the roof of a building (*keep old toys and furniture in the loft*). **2** a room over a stable. **3** a gallery in a hall or church. ● *vb* to strike upward (*loft the ball*).

lofty /**lof**-tee/ *adj* **1** (*lit*) very high (*the lofty walls of the city*). **2** of high moral quality (*lofty aims*). **3** proud, haughty (*with a lofty disregard for other people's feelings*). ● *n* **loftiness**.

log /**log**/ *n* **1** a piece sawn from the trunk or one of the large branches of a tree (*cut logs for the fire*). **2** an instrument for measuring the speed of ships. **3** an official written record of a journey (*a ship's log*).

loganberry /**lo**-gan-be-ree/ *n* a fruit like a raspberry.

logarithms /**law**-ga-ri-thumz/ *n* numbers arranged in a table by referring to which calculations can be done quickly.

logbook /**lawg**-book/ *n* **1** a book in which the rate of progress of a ship is written daily. **2** an official record of a journey (*details of the flight found in the logbook*). **3** the registration document of a car.

loggerheads /**law**-ger-hedz/ *npl.* ● **at loggerheads** quarreling (*she's been at loggerheads with her neighbors for years*).

logic /**law**-jic/ *n* **1** the art or science of reasoning (*study logic*). **2** a particular way of thinking or reasoning (*we were unable to follow her logic*). **3** (*inf*) reasonable thinking, good sense (*there's no logic in her decision*).

logical /**law**-ji-cal/ *adj* **1** having to do with logic. **2** well-reasoned (*a logical argument*). **3** able to reason correctly (*logical people*).

logician /**law**-ji-shun/ *n* one skilled in logic.

logo /**lo**-go/ *n* a special symbol or design that an organization uses on its products, notepaper, etc. (*the firm's logo resembled a thistle*).

loin /**loin**/ *n* **1** a piece of meat cut from the back of an animal (*a loin chop*). **2** *pl* the part of the human back below the ribs. ● **gird up one's loins** to prepare for action.

loin-cloth /**loin**-cloth/ *n* a piece of cloth worn round the loins (*loin-clothes are worn in hot countries, usually by poor people*).

loiter /**loi**-ter/ *vb* **1** to stand about idly (*they were loitering near the bank, looking suspicious*). **2** to go slowly, often stopping (*don't loiter—you'll be late for school*).

loll /**lol**/ *vb* **1** to sit back or lie lazily (*they lolled in their armchairs while she washed the dishes*). **2**

(*of the tongue*) to hang out (*thirsty dogs with their tongues lolling*).

lollipop /**law**-lee-pop/ *n* a candy on a stick (*children sucking red lollipops*).

lone /**lone**/ *adj* alone, single, without others (*a lone piper/a lone figure on the deserted beach*).

lonely /**lone**-lee/ *adj* sad because alone (*lonely old people/lonely since her husband died*).

lonesome /**lone**-sum/ *adj* (*inf*) lonely (*feel lonesome when the others are away*).

long /**long**/ *adj* **1** not short, in time or space (*a long meeting/a long journey*). **2** having length, covering a certain distance from one end to the other or a certain time (*a garden 30 meters long/a film two hours long*). **3** (*of drinks*) containing little or no alcohol and served in a long glass. ● *adv* for a long time. ● *vb* to want very much (*she longs to see her friend again*).

longboat /**long**-boat/ *n* the largest and strongest boat carried on board a ship.

longbow /**long**-bo/ *n* a bow, drawn by hand, for firing arrows. ● **draw the longbow** to tell untrue and improbable stories.

longevity /lan-**je**-vi-tee/ *n* very long life (*a family noted for its longevity*).

longheaded /**lawng**-hed-ed/ *adj* wise, farseeing, shrewd.

longing /**lawng**-ing/ *n* an eager desire (*a longing to be free/a longing for freedom*).

longish /**lawng**-ish/ *adj* (*inf*) quite long (*a longish journey*).

longitude /**lon**-ji-tud/ *n* **1** length. **2** distance in degrees east or west of an imaginary line from pole to pole, running through Greenwich (London).

longitudinal /lon-ji-**tood**-nal/ *adj* having to do with length or longitude.

longshoreman /**lawng**-shore-man/ *n* one who lives or works on the coast or shore.

long-sighted /lawng-**sie**-ted/ *adj* able to see distant objects more clearly than near ones (*he is long-sighted and wears glasses for reading*).

long-suffering /lawng-su-fring/ *adj* patient, ready to put up with troubles without complaint (*their long-suffering mother tried to sort out all their problems*).

long-winded /lawng-**win**-ded/ *adj* speaking or writing in an unnecessarily roundabout way (*a long-winded lecturer who bored the whole audience/a piece of long-winded prose*).

loofa(h) /**loo**-fa/ *n* **1** a marrowlike plant. **2** the fibrous framework of the plant stripped of the fleshy part and used in washing as a sponge (*a loofah at the side of the bath*).

look /**look**/ *vb* **1** to turn the eyes toward so as to see (*look at the picture/look at her with dislike*). **2** to have a certain appearance (*she looks ill/it looks as if it will rain*). **3** to face in a certain direction (*a house looking south*). ● *n* **1** act of looking (*do have a look to see if they are coming*). **2** a glance (*have a look at the essay*). **3** the appearance, especially of the face (*the look of one who has seen a ghost*). ● **look after** to take care of (*look after the children while their mother is away*). ● **look down on** to despise (*look down on people less well-off than she is herself*). ● **look for 1** to try to find (*look for the lost book*). **2** to hope for (*look for mercy from the king*). ● **look on** to watch (*the other boys looked on while the bully hit the younger boy*). ● **look out 1** to be careful (*look out in case you slip*). **2** to watch out for (*look out for my sister at the concert*). ● **look over** to examine. ● **look a gift-horse in the mouth** to say that one is not pleased with a present or to criticize it.

looker-on /**loo**-ker-on/ *n* one who watches or spectates (*the lookers-on should have stopped the boys fighting*).

looking glass /**loo**-king-glass/ *n* a mirror (*the fairy tale told of an enchanted looking glass*).

lookout /**loo**-kout/ *n* **1** watchman. **2** a post from which one watches. **3** a careful watch (*be on the lookout for thieves*).

loom[1] /**loom**/ *n* a machine for weaving cloth.

loom[2] /**loom**/ *vb* **1** to appear gradually and dimly, as in the dark, to seem larger than natural (*shapes looming out of the mist*). **2** to seem threateningly close (*with exams looming*).

loon /**loon**/ *n* a northern diving bird.

loop /**loop**/ *n* **1** a line that curves back and crosses itself (*the road makes a loop*). **2** a rope, cord, etc., that so curves (*loops of ribbon*). ● *vb* **1** to make a loop (*loop the ribbon*). **2** to fasten in a loop.

loophole /**loop**-hole/ *n* a way of escaping or avoiding something (*a loophole in the contract that meant he could withdraw*).

loose /**looss**/ *adj* **1** untied, not packed together in a box, etc. (*buy loose tomatoes/the string had come loose*). **2** free, at liberty (*the dog had broken loose from the rope*). **3** not definite (*a loose arrangement*). **4** careless. **5** not tight (*wear loose clothes*). **6** indecent, immoral (*loose behavior*). ● *vb* **1** to untie (*loose the string*). **2** to set free (*loose the cows from the barn/loose the prisoners*).

loose-leaf /**looss**-leef/ adj describing a notebook that can hold pages with perforations which can be added or removed.

loosen /**loo**-sen/ vb to make or become loose or less tight (loosen his belt after a heavy meal).

loot /loot/ n that which is stolen or carried off by force (the police caught the burglar but failed to find his loot).

lop[1] /lop/ vb (**lopped** /lopt/, **lopping** /**lop**-ing/) to cut off (lop branches off the tree/lop a bit off the price).

lop[2] /lop/ vb (**lopped** /lopt/, **lopping** /**lop**-ing/) to hang loosely.

lop-sided /**lop**-sie-ded/ adj leaning to one side (she looked lop-sided because she carried a heavy bag in one hand/a lop-sided account of the events).

lord /lawrd/ n 1 a master. 2 a ruler. 3 a nobleman. 4 a title of honor given to noblemen and certain high officials (e g., judges). 5 an owner. ● n **Lord** God. ● vb to rule strictly or harshly.

lordly /**lawrd**-lee/ adj 1 proud, grand. 2 commanding.

lordship /**lawrd**-ship/ n 1 the state of being a lord. 2 the power of a lord. 3 the title by which one addresses noblemen, judges, etc.

lore /lore/ n 1 (old) learning. 2 all that is known about a subject, usually that which is handed down by word of mouth (sea lore).

lorry /**law**-ree/ n (Br) a truck.

lose /looz/ vb (pt, pp **lost** /lost/) 1 to cease to have (lose his eye in an accident). 2 to fail to keep in one's possession (lose her gloves). 3 to be defeated in (lose the battle/lose the match). 4 to fail to use, to waste (lose no time in asking for a loan). 5 to miss (lose an opportunity). 6 (of a watch or clock) to work too slowly (my watch loses about five minutes a day). 7 to have less of (lose weight). ● **lose one's head** to become too excited to act sensibly.

loser /**loo**-zer/ n one who loses (the loser of the tennis match congratulated the winner).

loss /loss/ n 1 act of losing (the loss of his wife/the loss of her home). 2 that which is lost (she is a loss to the firm). 3 harm, damage (forced to pay for the losses). ● **at a loss** not knowing what to do (at a loss to know what to do).

lost pt of **lose**.

lot /lot/ n 1 one of a set of objects, a separate part (one lot of clothes). 2 a set of objects sold together at an auction (bid for lot number 3). 3 the way of life that one has to follow (it was his lot in life to work hard and earn little). 4 a large number (a lot of people/a lot of books). 5 a piece of land (a building lot/a parking lot).

loth see **loath**.

lotion /**lo**-shun/ n a liquid for healing wounds, cleansing the skin, etc. (apply a lotion to her sunburn).

lottery /**lot**-e-ree/ n a game of chance in which prizes are shared out among those whose tickets are picked out in a public draw (she had the winning numbers in the lottery).

lotus /**lo**-tus/ n a type of water-lily whose flower was once said to make those who ate it forget everything.

loud /loud/ adj 1 easily heard (a loud voice). 2 noisy (a loud party). 3 unpleasantly bright, showy (loud colors).

loudspeaker /**loud**-spee-ker/ n a radio apparatus by which sound is transmitted and made louder when necessary (use a loudspeaker to get the competitors to leave the field).

lough /laak/ n a lake, especially in Ireland.

lounge /**loundge**/ vb 1 to stand about lazily, to move lazily, to spend time in an idle way (some workers lounging around while others were working hard). 3 to sit or lie back in a comfortable position (lounge in an armchair). ● n 1 a comfortably furnished sitting room (take her guests into the lounge). 2 a public room in a hotel (the residents' lounge). ● n **lounger** /**loun**-jer/.

lounge suit /**loundge**-soot/ n a man's suit of clothes for everyday wear (it's not an occasion for evening wear—a lounge suit will do).

lour same as **lower**.

louse /louss/ n (pl **lice** /lice/) a wingless insect that lives on the bodies of animals (tramps offered baths to get rid of lice).

lousy /**lou**-zee/ adj 1 full of or covered with lice. 2 (inf) very bad, poor (lousy food/lousy weather).

lout /**loute**/ n a rude and clumsy fellow (the lout who bumped into the old woman).

lovable /**lu**-va-bul/ adj worthy of love (a lovable puppy).

love /luv/ n 1 a strong liking for (a love of good food). 2 a feeling of desire for (full of love for his wife). 3 the person or thing loved (his first love). 4 (in some games) no score (the score was forty love). ● vb 1 to be fond of, to like (I love Mexican food). 2 to be strongly attracted to, to be in love with (he loved her and was heartbroken when she left). ● n **lover** /**lu**-ver/.

loveless /**luv**-less/ adj 1 with no love (a loveless

marriage). **2** unloved (*when her mother died, the child felt completely loveless*).

lovelorn /**luv**-lawrn/ *adj* (*old*) sad because left by one's lover.

lovely /**luv**-lee/ *adj* **1** beautiful (*a lovely girl*). **2** (*inf*) very pleasing (*a lovely day/a lovely meal*). ● *n* **loveliness** /**luv**-lee-ness/.

loving /**lu**-ving/ *adj* full of love, fond (*a loving smile/ a loving mother*).

low[1] /**lo**/ *vb* **1** to bellow, as an ox. **2** to moo like a cow (*cattle lowing in the field*). ● *n* **lowing** /**lo**-wing/.

low[2] /**lo**/ *adj* **1** not far above the ground (*the picture is too low*). **2** not tall, not high (*low buildings*). **3** small in degree, amount, etc. (*low temperatures*). **4** not high in rank or position (*low positions in the firm*). **5** cheap (*low prices*). **6** vulgar, coarse (*low humor*). **7** dishonorable (*a low thing to do*). **8** soft, not loud (*a low voice*). **9** sad, unhappy. ● **low spirits** a sad mood.

lower[1] /**laoo**-er/ *vb* **1** to make less high (*lower the height of the ceiling*). **2** to let or bring down (*lower the flag*). **3** to make of less value or worth (*the building of the motorway lowered the value of their property*).

lower[2], **lour** /**laoo**-er/ *vb* **1** to frown (*lower angrily at the news that he had lost*). **2** to become dark (*skies lowering*).

lowland /**lo**-land/ *n* low-lying or level country.

lowlander /**lo**-lan-der/ *n* one born or living in low-lands.

lowly /**lo**-lee/ *adj* **1** (*fml or hum*) humble, not high in rank (*workers too lowly for the owner of the firm to speak to/a lowly clerk*). **2** (*old or lit*) gentle in manner.

loyal /**loy**-al/ *adj* **1** faithful to one's friends, duty, etc. (*loyal followers*). **2** true (*loyal to the cause*). ● *n* **loyalty** /**loy**-al-tee/.

loyalist /**loy**-a-list/ *n* one who supports the lawful government of the country.

lozenge /**loz**-endge/ *n* **1** a diamond-shaped figure (*a sweater with a lozenge design*). **2** a small candy, or medicine in the form of a sweet (*cough loz-enges*).

lubricant /**loo**-bri-cant/ *n* oil or grease used to make machinery run smoothly (*engine lubricant*).

lubricate /**loo**-bri-cate/ *vb* to oil something to make it run smoothly (*lubricating the parts of the ma-chine*). ● *ns* **lubrication** /loo-bri-**cay**-shun/, **lubri-cator** /loo-bri-**cay**-tor/.

lucid /**loo**-sidt/ *adj* clear, easily understood (*a lu-cid explanation*). ● *n* **lucidity** /loo-**si**-di-tee/.

lucifer /**loo**-si-fer/ *n* (*old*) a match. ● **Lucifer 1** the morning star. **2** Satan.

luck /**luck**/ *n* **1** the good or bad things that happen by chance, fate, fortune (*only luck is involved, not skill/she had bad luck/a bit of good luck*). **2** something good that happens by chance, good luck (*luck was with her*).

luckless /**luck**-less/ *adj* (*fml*) unfortunate (*the luck-less loser*).

lucky /**lu**-kee/ *adj* fortunate, having good luck (*she is very lucky and is always winning things*).

lucrative /**loo**-cra-tiv/ *adj* bringing in much money or profit (*a lucrative occupation*).

ludicrous /**loo**-di-crus/ *adj* funny, silly and laugh-able (*she looks ludicrous in that hat/it was ludi-crous to think he could win*).

lug /**lug**/ *vb* (**lugged** /**lugd**/, **lugging** /**lu**-ging/) to pull, draw or carry with difficulty (*lug the trunk down from the attic/lug her bags to the station*).

luge /**loozh**/ *n* a sled used for high-speed racing.

luggage /**lu**-gidge/ *n* a traveler's baggage (*check her luggage in at the airport*).

lukewarm /luke-**wawrm**/ *adj* **1** quite warm, neither hot nor cold (*lukewarm water*). **2** not eager (*rather lukewarm about the idea*).

lull /**lull**/ *vb* **1** to calm (*lull her fears*). **2** to send to sleep (*the rocking of the cradle lulled the child to sleep*). ● *n* an interval of calm.

lullaby /**lu**-la-by/ *n* a song sung to a baby to make it sleep.

lumbago /lum-**bay**-go/ *n* muscular pain in the lower part of the back (*have difficulty in bending be-cause of lumbago*).

lumbar /**lum**-bar/ *adj* having to do with the lower part of the back (*pain in the lumbar region*).

lumber /**lum**-ber/ *n* **1** unused or useless articles (*clear the lumber out of the attic*). **2** wood of trees cut into timber. ● *vb* **1** to move heavily and clum-sily (*a bear was lumbering toward them*). **2** to give someone an unpleasant or unwanted responsi-bility or task (*she got lumbered with taking notes at the meeting*).

lumberjack /**lum**-ber-jack/ *n* someone whose job it is to cut down trees.

luminary /**loo**-mi-na-ree/ *n* **1** (*lit*) a body that gives light (e.g., the sun). **2** (*fml*) a person well-known for his or her knowledge, expertise or talent (*sev-eral luminaries from the world of the theater were there*).

luminous /**loo**-mi-nuss/ *adj* shining, giving light (*luminous paint/a luminous watch face*).

lump /lump/ *n* **1** a shapeless mass (*a lump of dough*). **2** a hard swelling (*a lump on his head after being hit with an iron bar*). ● *vb* **1** to put together as one, to consider together (*he lumps all women together as inefficient*).

lump sum /lump-sum/ *n* a single large amount of money instead of several smaller payments (*get a lump sum when he retired instead of monthly amounts*).

lumpy /lum-pee/ *adj* full of lumps (*lumpy custard*).

lunacy /loo-na-see/ *n* madness (*it was lunacy to walk alone in that district at night*).

lunar /loo-nar/ *adj* having to do with the moon.

lunatic /loo-na-tic/ *n* a mad person. ● *adj* mad, insane, very foolish (*what a lunatic thing to do*).

lunch /lunch/ *n* a midday meal (*have sandwiches for lunch/have a working lunch*). ● *vb* to take lunch (*lunch on fresh salmon*).

lung /lung/ *n* one of the two bodily organs by means of which we breathe (*have a collapsed lung*).

lunge /lundge/ *n* a sudden move or thrust forward (*make a lunge at her with a knife*). ● *vb* to make a sudden onward movement (*she lunged at him with a knife*).

lupin /loo-pine/ *n* a kind of garden plant with a tall stem covered in many flowers.

lurch /lurch/ *vb* to roll or sway to one side (*drunks lurching down the road*). ● *n* a sudden roll (*the bus gave a sudden lurch*). ● **leave in the lurch** to leave (someone) in difficulty (*he left her in the lurch on her own with a baby*).

lure /loor/ *n* something that attracts or leads on (*a lure to customers of free offers*). ● *vb* to attract, to lead on, as by promise or gifts (*try to lure him to join the firm by promises of a high salary*).

lurid /loo-rid/ *n* **1** too brightly colored, too vivid (*lurid sweaters*). **2** horrifying, shocking (*the lurid details of the accident/a lurid sight*).

lurk /lurk/ *vb* **1** to remain out of sight (*photographers lurking behind trees to try to take shots of the filmstar*). **2** to lie hidden, to exist unseen (*danger might be lurking*).

luscious /lu-shus/ *adj* very sweet in taste (*luscious peaches*).

lush /lush/ *adj* **1** growing very plentifully, thick (*lush vegetation*). **2** (*inf*) affluent, luxurious (*lush surroundings*).

lust /lust/ *n* a strong or uncontrollable desire, especially for sexual pleasure. ● *vb* to desire eagerly (*older men lusting after young girls*). ● *adj* **lustful**.

luster /lu-ster/ *n* **1** brightness (*the luster of the polished surface*). **2** glory (*his brave actions brought luster to the family*). **3** dress material with a shiny surface.

lusterless /lu-ster-less/ *adj* dull (*lusterless hair*).

lustrous /lu-struss/ *adj* bright, shining (*lustrous eyes*).

lusty /lu-stee/ *adj* **1** strong and healthy, full of energy (*lusty young men*). **2** strong or loud (*lusty singing*).

lute /loot/ *n* (*old*) a stringed musical instrument, rather like the guitar.

luxuriant /lug-zhoo-ree-ant/ *adj* growing in great plenty (*luxuriant vegetation/luxuriant hair*).

luxuriate /lug-zhoo-ree-ate/ *vb* to live in or enjoy great comfort (*luxuriate in a hot, scented bath/luxuriating in the comfort of a high-class hotel*).

luxurious /lug-zhoo-ree-uss/ *adj* **1** fond of luxury. **2** splendid and affluent (*a luxurious hotel/a luxurious lifestyle*).

luxury /luk-shu-ree/ *n* **1** great ease and comfort (*wealthy people living in luxury*). **2** a desirable or pleasing thing that is not a necessity of life (*afford luxuries such as perfume*).

Lycra /lie-cra/ *n* (*trademark*) a stretchy, shiny artificial fabric used for swimsuits, sportswear, etc.

lying /lie-ing/ *pres p of* **lie**. ● *also adj*.

lymph /limf/ *n* a colorless liquid in the body (*the lymph glands*).

lynch /linch/ *vb* to seize someone, judge him or her on the spot and put to death without a proper trial (*the mob lynched the child's murderer before he could be tried*).

lynx /links/ *n* an animal of the cat family noted for keen sight.

lyre /lire/ *n* (*old*) a U-shaped stringed musical instrument similar to a harp, played by the ancient Greeks.

lyre-bird /lire-burd/ *n* a bird with a tail shaped like a lyre.

lyric /li-ric/ *n* **1** a short poem expressing the writer's feelings. **2** *pl* the words of a song (*the song has rather sad lyrics*).

lyrical /li-ri-cal/ *adj* **1** expressing feeling (*lyrical verse*). **2** enthusiastic, effusive (*lyrical about the beauty of her new baby*).

M

M, m /em/ the thirteenth letter of the alphabet.

ma'am /mam/ *n* madam.

macabre /ma-**cab**/ *adj* horrible, causing a shudder of horror (*a macabre murder*).

macaroni /ma-ca-**roe**-nee/ *n* flour paste rolled into long tubes (*a dish of macaroni and cheese*).

macaroon /ma-ca-**roon**/ *n* a small cake containing powdered almonds or coconut.

macaw /ma-**caw**/ *n* a large type of parrot.

mace /mase/ *n* **1** (*old*) a spiked club used as a weapon of war. **2** a heavy ornamental stick carried before certain officials as a sign of their office (*the mayor's mace*).

machete /ma-**shet**-ee/ *n* a large heavy knife sometimes used as a weapon.

machine /ma-**sheen**/ *n* **1** any apparatus for producing power or doing work (*a washing machine*). **2** a system under which the work of different groups is directed to one end (*the political party's machine*).

machine gun *n* a gun that fires many bullets in a short time before it has to be reloaded.

machinery /ma-**shee**-ne-ree/ *n* **1** machines (*buy new machinery for the factory*). **2** parts of a machine (*something wrong with the machinery of the tumble dryer*). **3** organization (*the machinery of government*).

machinist /ma-**shee**-nist/ *n* a person who makes, looks after or operates machinery (*she was a machinist in a clothing factory*).

mackerel /ma-krel/ *n* an edible sea fish (*smoked mackerel*).

mad /mad/ *adj* **1** insane (*the murderer pretended to be mad*). **2** out of your mind with anger, pain, etc. (*mad with grief*). **3** (*inf*) very angry (*she was mad at the naughty children*). **4** (*inf*) very unwise, crazy (*a mad plan*).

madam /ma-dam/ *n* the title used in addressing a woman politely.

Madame /ma-**dam**/ *n* the French form of **Mrs**.

madcap /mad-cap/ *n* a wild or reckless person. ● *adj* reckless, very thoughtless (*a madcap plan to make money quickly*).

madden /ma-din/ *vb* to make mad (*an animal maddened with pain*). ● *adj* **maddening** /mad-ning/.

madly /mad-lee/ *adv* very much (*madly in love*).

madman /mad-man/ *n* a person who is mad (*the killer must have been a madman*).

madness /mad-ness/ *n* **1** insanity. **2** folly.

Madonna /ma-**don**-a/ *n* **1** the Virgin Mary. **2** a picture or statue of the Virgin Mary.

magazine /ma-ga-zeen/ *n* **1** a store for firearms and explosives (*the military magazine*). **2** a weekly or monthly paper containing articles, stories, etc. (*women's magazines*).

magenta /ma-**jen**-ta/ *n* a crimson dye. ● *adj* crimson.

maggot /**ma**-got/ *n* the grub of certain insects, especially the fly or bluebottle (*find maggots on the rotting meat*).

Magi /**may**-jie/ *npl* **1** (*old*) priests of ancient Persia. **2** in Christianity, the wise men from the East who visited the infant Jesus.

magic /**ma**-jic/ *n* **1** the art of controlling spirits, and so gaining knowledge of the future or commanding certain things to happen, witchcraft (*black magic*). **2** the art of producing illusions by tricks or sleight of hand (*the magic practiced by the stage magician*). **3** fascination (*the magic of the theater*). ● *adj also* **magical** /**ma**-ji-cal/ **1** having to do with magic (*a magic spell/a magic act*). **2** (*inf*) marvelous, very good (*the match was magic*). ● *adv* **magically** /**ma**-ji-ca-lee/.

magician /ma-**ji**-shun/ *n* **1** a person who has magic powers (*the magician in the fairy tale*). **2** a person who practices the art of producing illusions by tricks or sleight of hand (*a magician with his own television show*).

magisterial /ma-ji-**sti**-ree-al/ *adj* **1** having the manner of a person who is used to giving commands. **2** having to do with magistrates.

magistracy /**ma**-ji-stra-see/ *n* the office of magistrate.

magistrate /**ma**-ji-strate/ *n* a person who has the authority to try and sentence those who break the law, a judge (*appear before the magistrate*).

magnanimous /mag-**na**-ni-mus/ *adj* generous, especially to enemies or dependants, unselfish (*he was magnanimous to forgive those who had attacked him*). ● *n* **magnanimity** /mag-na-**ni**-mi-tee/.

magnate /**mag**-nate/ *n* a person of great wealth or importance (*industrial magnates*).

magnesia /mag-**nee**-sha/ *n* a white powder made from magnesium, used as a medicine (*take milk of magnesia for indigestion*).

magnesium /mag-**nee**-zee-um/ *n* a white metal that burns with a bright white light.

magnet /**mag**-net/ *n* **1** a piece of iron that attracts to it other pieces of iron and that when hung up points to the north. **2** a person or thing that attracts (*he told such interesting stories that he was a magnet for all the children*).

magnetic /mag-**net**-ic/ *adj* **1** acting like a magnet (*magnetic forces*). **2** attractive (*a magnetic personality*).

magnetism /**mag**-ne-ti-zum/ *n* **1** the power of the magnet. **2** the science that deals with the power of the magnet. **3** personal charm or attraction (*by his sheer magnetism he always took charge of situations*).

magnification /mag-ni-fi-**cay**-shun/ *n* **1** the act or power of magnifying. **2** an exaggeration (*the magnification of her troubles*).

magnificent /mag-**ni**-fi-sent/ *adj* splendid, grand (*a magnificent royal parade/magnificent clothes*). ● *n* **magnificence** /mag-**ni**-fi-sense/.

magnify /**mag**-ni-fie/ *vb* **1** to make appear larger, to exaggerate (*her parents seemed to magnify the crime that she had committed*). **2** to praise (*magnify God*).

magnifying glass /**mag**-ni-fie-ing-glass/ *n* a glass with a curved surface that makes things appear larger.

magnitude /**mag**-ni-tood/ *n* **1** greatness of size or extent (*a star of great magnitude*). **2** importance (*the magnitude of the crime*).

magnolia /mag-**nole**-ya/ *n* a tree with beautiful foliage and large pale-colored flowers.

magnum /**mag**-num/ *n* a two-quart bottle or container (*a magnum of wine*).

magpie /**mag**-pie/ *n* a black-and-white bird of the crow family (*magpies are known for their habit of collecting bright things*).

maharaja(h) /ma-ha-**ra**-ja/ *n* an Indian prince.

maharanee /ma-ha-**ra**-nee/ *n* an Indian princess.

mahatma /ma-**hat**-ma/ *n* an Indian title of respect for a very holy person.

mahogany /ma-**hog**-a-nee/ *n* a reddish-brown wood often used for furniture (*old-fashioned wardrobes made of mahogany*).

maid /made/ *n* **1** (*old*) a young girl. **2** a female servant (*only very wealthy families have maids nowadays*). **3** a woman who is employed to clean other people's houses. **4** (*old*) a virgin.

maiden /**may**-den/ *n* (*old*) a young unmarried woman.

maidenly /**may**-den-lee/ *adj* modest, gentle.

maiden name /**may**-den-name/ *n* the surname of a married woman before marriage (*Mrs Franklin's maiden name is Jones*).

maiden voyage /**may**-den **voy**-idge/ *n* the first voyage of a new ship (*the ship sank on its maiden voyage*).

mail[1] /male/ *n* **1** the postal service (*the check is in the mail*). **2** letters, parcels, etc., sent by mail (*some mail has gone astray*). ● *vb* to send by mail (*mailed the parcel*).

mail[2] /male/ *n* (*old*) armor (*knights clad in mail*).

mail order /**male**-awr-der/ *n* a system of buying goods from a catalog and having them delivered to your home.

maim /mame/ *vb* to disable (*maimed for life in the accident*).

main /mane/ *adj* chief, principal (*his main source of income/the main branch of the store*). ● *n* **1** the greater part. **2** (*old*) the ocean. **3** a pipe under the street for water, gas, etc. **4** strength (*might and main*).

mainframe /**mane**-frame/ *n* a large fast computer that serves a lot of terminals.

mainland /**mane**-land/ *n* land, as distinct from nearby islands (*the children on the island go to school on the mainland*).

mainly /**mane**-lee/ *adv* chiefly (*they sell mainly magazines and candy*).

mainstay /**mane**-stay/ *n* **1** the rope holding up the mast of a ship. **2** the chief support (*the office manager is the mainstay of the firm*).

mainstream /**mane**-streem/ *n* the prevailing way of thinking or of doing something (*in the mainstream of contemporary music*).

maintain /mane-**tain**/ *vb* **1** to feed and clothe (*difficulty in maintaining his family*). **2** to keep up (*maintain a good standard of living*). **3** to keep in good repair (*houses that are expensive to maintain*). **4** to defend a point of view (*maintain his innocence*).

maintenance /**maint**-nanse/ *n* upkeep, support (*pay for the maintenance of his children*).

maize /maze/ (*Br*) *n* corn.

majestic /ma-**je**-stic/ *adj* dignified, stately.

majesty /**ma**-je-stee/ *n* **1** grandeur, dignity (*the majesty of the occasion*). **2** the title given to a king or queen.

major /**may**-jor/ *adj* **1** the greater in number, size, or quantity (*the major part of the audience*). **2** the more important (*the major medical discoveries*). ● *n* an army officer just above a captain in rank.

majority /ma-**jaw**-ri-tee/ *n* **1** the greater number (*she is liked by the majority of the class*). **2** in voting, the amount by which the number of votes cast for one candidate exceeds that cast for another (*the government won by a majority of 20*). **3** (*fml*) the age at which you have full civil rights (*she has not yet achieved her majority*).

make /make/ *vb* (*pt, pp* **made** /made/) **1** to create (*stories of how God made the earth*). **2** to construct by putting parts or substances together (*make a model airplane out of a kit*). **3** to cause to be (*the win made him famous*). **4** to force (*they made her go*). **5** to add up to (*two plus two makes four*). **6** to earn (*he makes $50,000 a year*). ● *n* **1** the way something is made. **2** shape. ● **make for** to go toward (*they made for the nearest town*). ● **make good** to succeed, to do well (*people from poor backgrounds who make good*). ● **make off** to run away. ● **make out 1** to decipher (*unable to make out the faint writing*). **2** (*inf*) to succeed. ● **make up 1** to invent (a story) (*she made up an excuse for not going to the party*). **2** to put paint, powder, etc. (on the face) (*she made up her face in the cloakroom*). **3** to bring (a quarrel) to an end, to try to become friendly with (*she wanted to make up but he was still angry*).

make-believe /make-bi-leev/ *n* pretense (*it was just make-believe that she was a princess*). ● *also vb*.

make-over /make-oe-ver/ *n* the process of trying to improve the appearance of a person or place.

maker /make-er/ *n* a person who makes (*a maker of model airplanes/a tool-maker*). ● **your Maker** God.

makeshift /make-shift/ *adj* used or done because nothing better can be found or thought of (*they made a makeshift shelter on the desert island*). ● *also n*.

make-up /make-up/ *n* **1** mascara, lipstick, and other substances used to enhance the appearance of the face (*a range of make-up in her bag*). **2** your character (*it was not in his make-up to be mean*).

malaria /ma-**ler**-ee-ya/ *n* a fever caused by a mosquito bite.

male /male/ *adj* of the sex that can become a father (*a male elephant*). ● *also n*.

malevolent /ma-**le**-vo-lent/ *adj* wishing harm to others, spiteful (*give his rival a malevolent glance*). ● *n* **malevolence** /ma-**le**-vo-lense/.

malformed /mal-**fawrmd**/ *adj* out of shape, wrongly shaped (*a malformed foot*). ● *n* **malformation** /mal-fawr-**may**-shun/.

malfunction /mal-**fung**-shun/ *vb* to fail to work correctly (*the machine is malfunctioning*).

malice /ma-**liss**/ *n* pleasure in the misfortunes of others, spite, a desire to harm others (*full of malice toward the person who beat him in the match*).

malicious /ma-**li**-shus/ *adj* spiteful, full of malice.

malign /ma-**line**/ *vb* to speak ill of (*he maligned the person who had helped him*). ● *adj* evil, harmful (*a malign influence*).

malignancy /ma-**lig**-nan-see/ *n* **1** great hatred. **2** a desire to do harm.

malignant /ma-**lig**-nant/ *adj* **1** able to cause death (*a malignant cancer*). **2** very harmful (*a malignant influence*). **3** feeling great hatred (*malignant feelings toward his rival*).

mall /mawl/ *n* a large indoor shopping center.

mallard /ma-lard/ *n* a wild duck.

mallet /ma-let/ *n* **1** a wooden hammer (*fix the fence posts in place with a mallet*). **2** the stick used in croquet.

malnutrition /mal-noo-**tri**-shun/ *n* a state caused by eating too little food or food that does not supply the needs of the body (*children suffering from malnutrition*).

malt /mawlt/ *n* barley or other grain prepared for making beer or whiskey. ● *vb* to make into or become malt. ● *adj* **malty** /mawl-tee/.

malted milk /mawlted milk/ *n* milk, flavored with malt, and sometimes mixed with ice cream.

maltreat /mal-**treet**/ *vb* to treat badly, to ill-use (*accused of maltreating his dog*). ● *n* **maltreatment** /mal-**treet**-ment/.

mam(m)a /ma-ma/ *n* (*inf*) mother.

mammal /ma-mal/ *n* an animal that suckles its young.

mammoth /ma-moth/ *n* a type of large elephant, no longer existing. ● *adj* huge (*a mammoth shopping mall*).

man /man/ *n* (*pl* **men** /men/) **1** the human race (*man has destroyed much of the environment*). **2** a human being (*all men must die*). **3** a male human being (*men, women, and children*). **4** (*inf*) a husband. **5** a male servant (*his man packed his suitcase*). ● *vb* (**manned** /mand/, **manning** /ma-ning/) to provide with people to go to or to be in the place where a duty is to be performed (*man the lifeboats*).

manage /ma-nidge/ *vb* **1** to control, to be in charge of (*managing the firm*). **2** to succeed (in doing something) (*she managed to get there on time*).

manageable /ma-ni-ja-bul/ *adj* easily controlled (*manageable children/manageable hair*).

management /ma-nidge-ment/ *n* **1** control, direction (*under the management of an experienced businessman*). **2** the group of persons who control or run a business (*management in dispute with the labor unions*).

manager /ma-na-jer/ *n* a person who controls a

business or part of it (*the manager of the accounts department*).

managerial /ma-ni-**ji**-ree-al/ *adj* having to do with the management of a business (*a managerial post*).

mandarin /**man**-d(a-)rin/ *n* **1** a Chinese official. **2** a variety of small orange.

Mandarin /**man**-d(a-)rin/ *n* the chief dialect of the Chinese language.

mandate /**man**-date/ *n* **1** a command (*by mandate of the queen*). **2** power given to one person, group, or nation to act on behalf of another (e.g., by voters to the governing party) (*claim they had a mandate to increase taxes*).

mandatory /**man**-da-toe-ree/ *adj* compulsory (*attendance is mandatory*).

mandible /**man**-di-bul/ *n* the lower jawbone.

mandolin(e) /man-do-**lin**/ *n* a musical stringed instrument, like the guitar but with a rounded back.

mane /mane/ *n* the long hair on the neck of certain animals (*the lion's mane*).

maneuver /ma-**noo**-ver/ *n, also* **manoeuvre** (*Br, Cdn*) **1** a planned movement of armies or ships. **2** a skillful or cunning plan intended to make another behave as you want him or her to (*a maneuver to get rid of his boss, and get the job*). **3** **maneuvers** /ma-**noo**-verz/ *npl, also* **manoeuvres** (*Br, Cdn*) practice movements of armies or ships (*troops on maneuvers*). ● *vb* **1** to move armies or ships. **2** to move or act cunningly to gain your ends (*she maneuvered him out of his job to get promotion*).

manful /**man**-ful/ *adj* brave (*a manful attempt*). ● *adv* **manfully** /**man**-fu-lee/.

manganese /**mang**-ga-neez/ *n* a hard, easily broken gray metal.

mange /mange/ *n* a skin disease of dogs, etc.

manger /**main**-jer/ *n* a raised box or trough out of which horses or cattle feed (*the Bible tells us that the baby Jesus lay in a manger*).

mangle /**mang**-gul/ *vb* to cut or tear so as to be unrecognizable (*bodies badly mangled in the accident*).

mango *n* (*pl* **mangoes**) **1** an Indian fruit with a large stone (*have fresh mango for dessert*). **2** the tree on which it grows.

mangrove /**man**-grove/ *n* a tropical tree growing in wet or muddy ground.

mangy /**main**-jee/ *adj* **1** affected with mange. **2** shabby or dirty.

manhandle /**man**-han-dul/ *vb* **1** to move by hand (*manhandling the huge wardrobe up the stairs*). **2** to treat roughly (*he complained that the police manhandled him*).

manhole /**man**-hole/ *n* a hole in the ground or floor through which a person may enter an underground shaft or tunnel (*get down to the sewer through a manhole*).

manhood /**man**-hood/ *n* the state of being a man or of having the qualities of a man (*till he reaches manhood*).

mania /**may**-nee-ya/ *n* **1** madness (*suffering from mania*). **2** a very great interest (in), an obsession (*he has a mania for fast cars*).

maniac /**may**-nee-yac/ *n* a madman (*killed by a maniac*).

maniacal /ma-**nie**-a-cul/ *adj* completely mad (*a maniacal attack*).

manicure /**ma**-ni-cyoor/ *n* the care of the hands and fingernails (*have a manicure*). ● *also vb.*

manicurist /**ma**-ni-cyoo-rist/ *n* a person whose job it is to care for hands and nails (*train as a manicurist*).

manifest /**ma**-ni-fest/ *adj* (*fml*) easily seen or understood, obvious (*her lack of interest was manifest*). ● *vb* to show clearly (*she manifested very little enthusiasm*).

manifestation /ma-ni-fe-**stay**-shun/ *n* an open showing, a display (*a manifestation of his love for her*).

manifestly /**ma**-ni-fest-lee/ *adv* clearly, obviously (*she was manifestly sick*).

manifesto /ma-ni-**fe**-sto/ *n* a public announcement of future plans (*the political party published its manifesto*).

manil(l)a /ma-**ni**-la/ *n* **1** a material used for making ropes. **2** a type of thick strong brown paper (*manila envelopes*).

manipulate /ma-**ni**-pyu-late/ *vb* **1** to handle skillfully (*manipulating the bones back into position*). **2** to manage skillfully (often in a dishonest way) (*a barrister accused of trying to manipulate the jury*). ● *n* **manipulation** /ma-ni-pyu-**lay**-shun/.

mankind /man-**kinde**/ *n* the human race.

manly /**man**-lee/ *adj* having the qualities of a man (*manly behavior*).

mannequin /**ma**-ni-kin/ *n* **1** a dummy used to display clothes in a clothes shop (*a mannequin in the shop window*). **2** another word for a fashion model (*mannequins at the fashion show*).

manner /**ma**-ner/ *n* **1** the way in which anything is done or happens (*the manner of his dying*). **2** the way a person speaks or behaves to others (*he has an open, frank manner*). **3** **manners** /**ma**-nerz/ courteous behavior.

mannerism /ma-ne-ri-zum/ *n* a way of behaving, writing, etc., that has become a habit (*constantly flicking back his hair is one of his mannerisms*).

mannish /ma-nish/ *adj* like a man.

manoeuvre /ma-noo-ver/ (*Br, Cdn*) *see* **maneuver**

manor /ma-ner/ *n* the land or house belonging to a lord. ● *adj* **manorial** /ma-noe-ree-al/.

mansion /man-shun/ *n* a large dwelling house.

manslaughter /man-slaw-ter/ *n* the unlawful but unintentional killing of a person (*found guilty of manslaughter rather than murder*).

mantelpiece /man-tel-peess/, **mantel** /man-tel/ *ns* **1** an ornamental surround built on either side of and above a fireplace. **2** the shelf above a fireplace (*ornaments on the mantelpiece*).

mantilla /man-tee-ya/ *n* a lace veil used as a head covering (*a Spanish lady wearing a mantilla*).

mantle /man-tel/ *n* **1** (*old*) a loose sleeveless cloak (*a velvet mantle over her evening dress*). **2** a coating or covering (*a mantle of snow*).

manual /man-yoo-wul/ *adj* done by hand (*manual tasks*). ● *n* **1** a small book containing all the important facts on a certain subject (*have lost the manual for the washing machine*). **2** the keyboard of an organ). ● *adv* **manually** /man-yoo-wu-lee/.

manufacture /man-yoo-fac-chur/ *n* **1** the making of goods or materials (*the manufacture of computers*). **2** an article so made (*importing many foreign manufactures*). ● *vb* to make, especially by machinery, in large quantities (*manufacturing cars*). ● *n* **manufacturer** /man-yoo-fac-chu-rer/.

manure /ma-noor/ *n* dung or some other substance used to make soil more fertile (*farmers spreading manure on their fields*). ● *vb* to treat with manure.

manuscript /man-yoo-script/ *n* **1** a paper or book written by hand (*look at many manuscripts in his research on local history*). **2** the written material sent by an author for publishing.

many /men-ee/ *adj* great in number (*many people*). ● *n* a large number (*many of my friends*).

Maori /maoo-ree/ *n* one of the original inhabitants of New Zealand. ● *also adj.*

map /map/ *n* a plan of any part of the earth's surface (*a map of France*). ● *vb* (**mapped** /mapt/, **mapping** /ma-ping/) to make a map of. ● **map out** to plan (*map out their campaign*).

maple /may-pul/ *n* a tree from whose sap sugar is made (*pancakes with maple syrup*).

mar /mar/ *vb* (**marred** /mard/, **marring** /ma-ring/) to spoil, to damage (*something marred the performance/mars her beauty*).

marathon /ma-ra-thon/ *n* **1** a long race of about 26 miles along roads. **2** something that takes a long time and requires a great deal of effort (*digging the weed-filled garden was a real marathon*).

marauder /ma-raw-der/ *n* (*fml*) a robber (*marauders raiding the border area*). ● *adj* **marauding** / ma-raw-ding/.

marble /mar-bul/ *n* **1** a type of hard stone used for buildings, statues, etc. (*a mantelpiece made of marble*). **2** a small ball of stone or glass used in children's games.

march /march/ *vb* to walk with a regular step (*soldiers marching*). ● *n* **1** movement of a body of soldiers on foot. **2** the distance walked (*a march of 15 miles*). **3** music suitable for marching to (*the band played a stirring march*). ● *n* **marcher** /mar-cher/.

March /march/ *n* the third month of the year (*the cold winds of March*).

mare /mare/ *n* the female of the horse.

margarine /mar-je-reen/ *n* a substance made from vegetable or animal fat, often used instead of butter (*spread margarine on bread*).

margin /mar-jin/ *n* **1** (*fml*) edge, border (*the margin of the lake*). **2** the part of a page that is not usually printed or written on (*comments in the margin*). **3** an amount more than is necessary, something extra (*leave a margin for error in the estimated calculations*).

marginal /mar-ji-nal/ *adj* **1** on or near the edge, border, or limit. **2** very small or unimportant (*a marginal improvement*). ● *adv* **marginally** /mar-ji-na-lee/.

marigold /ma-ri-goald/ *n* a bright yellow or orange flower.

marina /ma-ree-na/ *n* a harbor for the use of yachts and small boats.

marine /ma-reen/ *adj* **1** having to do with the sea (*marine animals*). **2** having to do with shipping (*marine insurance*). ● *n* **1** shipping. **2** a soldier serving on board ship.

mariner /ma-ri-ner/ *n* (*fml*) a seaman.

marionette /ma-ree-u-net/ *n* a doll that can be moved by strings, a puppet.

marital /ma-ri-tal/ *adj* (*fml*) having to do with marriage (*marital problems*).

maritime /ma-ri-time/ *adj* of or near the sea (*maritime areas*).

marjoram /mar-ju-ram/ *n* a sweet-smelling herb used in cooking (*add marjoram to the sauce*).

mark[1] /mark/ *n* **1** a sign, spot, or stamp that can be seen (*a cat with a white mark on its chest*). **2** a thing aimed at (*the arrow was wide of the mark*). **3** a number or letter indicating the standard reached (*her essay got a mark of 60%*). **4** an acceptable level of quality (*work that is not up to the mark*). **5** a stain or dent (*sooty marks on his white shirt*). **6** an indication, a sign (*give flowers as a mark of respect*). ● *vb* **1** to make a mark on (*a tablecloth marked with fruit stains*). **2** to indicate by a mark the standard reached (*mark the essays*). **3** (*old*) to watch closely, to pay attention to (*mark my words*). **4** to show the position of (*a cross marks the spot where he died*). **5** to be a sign of (*mark the beginning of change*). ● **beside the mark** (*fml*) off the subject (*a guess that was beside the mark*). ● **mark time 1** to move the legs up and down as if walking, but without going backward or forward. **2** to fill in time (*mark time while he's waiting to go to college*).

mark² /mark/ *n* a former German currency (*Germany now uses the euro instead of the mark*).

marked /markt/ *adj* noticeable, important (*a marked change*).

markedly /mar-kid-lee/ *adv* noticeably (*he is markedly healthier*).

marker /mar-ker/ *n* **1** a person who keeps the score. **2** a person or thing used to mark a place (*buoys as markers for the yacht race*).

market /mar-ket/ *n* **1** a public place for buying and selling, a coming together of people to buy and sell (*buy fruit at a street market*). **2** a demand or need (*a market for lightweight cotton clothing*). ● *vb* to sell in a market (*they market their books all over the world*).

marketable /mar-ke-ta-bul/ *adj* that can be sold (*products that are no longer easily marketable*).

marketing /mar-ke-ting/ *n* the promoting and selling of a product.

marketplace /mar-ket-place/ *n* the open space where a market is held (*a wide range of stalls in the marketplace*).

market research /mar-ket-**ree**-serch/ *n* the collection and study of data on which products or services people want.

marksman /marks-man/ *n* a person who shoots well (*a police marksman*).

marmalade /mar-ma-lade/ *n* a jam made from oranges or lemons (*marmalade on toast*).

marmoset /mar-mo-set/ *n* a type of small monkey.

marmot /mar-mot/ *n* a small squirrel-like animal.

maroon¹ /ma-**roon**/ *n* a brownish-crimson color. ● *adj* of this color (*a book with a maroon cover*).

maroon² /ma-**roon**/ *vb* to abandon (*marooned on a desert island*).

marquee /mar-**kee**/ *n* a large tent (*a marquee on the large lawn for a wedding*).

marquetry /mar-ke-tree/ *n* work in which a design is made by setting differently colored pieces of wood into another piece of wood.

marriage /ma-ridge/ *n* **1** the ceremony of marrying or being married (*there were 60 guests at their marriage*). **2** life together as husband and wife (*their marriage is over*).

marrow /ma-roe/ *n* a soft fatty substance filling the hollow parts of bones.

marry /ma-ree/ *vb* **1** to join together as husband and wife (*married by the local minister*). **2** to take as husband or wife (*he is marrying his sister's friend*).

Mars /marz/ *n* **1** a planet. **2** the Roman god of war.

marsh /marsh/ *n* low watery ground, a swamp (*have difficulty walking over the marsh*). ● *adj* **marshy** /mar-shee/.

marshal /mar-shal/ *n* **1** an officer of high rank in the army or air force. **2** a law-enforcement officer. **3** an official who makes arrangements for public processions, etc. ● *vb* to arrange in order (*marshal the troops/marshal your facts*).

marshmallow /marsh-me-loe/ *n* a type of soft sweet confection (*toasted marshmallows*).

marsupial /mar-**soo**-pee-al/ *n* an animal that carries its young in a pouch (*kangaroos are marsupials*).

marten /mar-ten/ *n* a type of weasel valued for its fur.

martial /mar-shal/ *adj* **1** (*fml*) warlike (*a martial nation*). **2** having to do with war (*martial arts/martial music*).

martin /mar-tin/ *n* a bird of the swallow family.

martyr /mar-tir/ *n* **1** a person who suffers death for his or her beliefs (*Christian martyrs*). **2** a person who suffers continuously from a certain illness (*a martyr to asthma*). ● *vb* to put to death for refusing to give up his or her faith (*she was martyred for her faith*). ● *n* **martyrdom** /mar-tir-dom/.

marvel /mar-vel/ *n* a wonder. ● *vb* to wonder (at), to feel astonishment (*marvel at the parachutists' jumping*).

marvelous/mar-ve-lus/ *adj, also* **marvellous** (*Br, Cdn*) **1** wonderful, astonishing, extraordinary (*a marvelous new discovery*). **2** (*inf*) very good, excellent (*a marvelous vacation*).

marzipan /mart-si-pan/ *n* a sweet made from

ground almonds, sugar, etc. (*put marzipan on the cake before the frosting*).

mascara /ma-**sca**-ra/ *n* a substance used for darkening eyelashes (*brush mascara on her lashes*).

mascot /ma-scot/ *n* a person, animal, or thing supposed to bring good luck (*a silver horseshoe as a mascot*).

masculine /ma-skyu-lin/ *adj* **1** of the male sex (*masculine characteristics*). **2** manly (*women who like masculine men*). **3** like a man (*a woman with a masculine walk*).

mash /mash/ *vb* to crush food until it is soft (*mash potatoes/mash bananas*). ● *n* a mixture of crushed grain, etc., given to animals as food (*prepare a mash for the pigs*).

mask /mask/ *n* **1** a cover for the face or part of the face (*surgeons wearing masks to prevent the spread of infection*). **2** an animal or human face painted on paper, etc., and worn at parties or processions (*wear a cat's mask to the Halloween party*). **3** any means of concealing what is really going on (*her smile was a mask for her grief*). **4** (*usually called* **masque**) a poetical play. ● *vb* **1** to cover with a mask. **2** to hide (*try to mask her amusement*).

mason /may-son/ *n* **1** a person who is skilled in shaping stone or building (*a mason making large gravestones*). **2** a Freemason. ● *adj* **masonic** /ma-**son**-ic/.

masonry /may-sun-ree/ *n* **1** stonework (*the masonry of the statue is crumbling*). **2** the skill or work of a mason. **3** freemasonry.

masquerade /ma-ske-**rade**/ *n* a ball at which masks are worn. ● *vb* **1** to go in disguise. **2** to pretend to be another (*a criminal masquerading as a social worker*).

mass /mass/ *n* **1** a lump or quantity of matter (*a land mass*). **2** (*fml*) the quantity of matter in a body (*the mass of the rock*). **3** (*often pl*) a crowd (*there were masses at the protest*). **4** the larger part (*the mass of the people are in favor*). ● *vb* **1** to gather into a mass. **2** to form a crowd.

Mass /mass/ *n* in the Roman Catholic Church, the celebration of the Lord's Supper.

massacre /ma-sa-cur/ *n* the killing of large numbers of men, women, and children. ● *vb* to kill in large numbers (*the invading army massacred the townspeople*).

massage /ma-**sazh**/ *n* rubbing and pressing the muscles to strengthen them or make them less stiff (*athletes having a massage after the race*). ● *also vb*.

masseur /ma-**soor**/ *n* a man who gives massages.

masseuse /ma-**sooz**/ *n* a woman who gives massages.

massive /ma-siv/ *adj* huge, big and heavy (*a massive rock/a massive rise in unemployment*).

mast /mast/ *n* on a ship, an upright pole on which sails may be set (*attach a flag to the mast*).

master /ma-ster/ *n* **1** a person who is in charge or gives orders (*the dog's master*). **2** a male teacher (*the French master*). **3** an expert (*a master of the art of conversation*). ● *vb* **1** to gain complete knowledge of (*master the art of public speaking*). **2** to overcome (*master her shyness*).

masterful /ma-ster-ful/ *adj* commanding, used to giving orders (*a masterful personality*).

masterly /ma-ster-lee/ *adj* showing great skill (*a masterly performance*).

mastermind /ma-ster-minde/ *n* **1** a very intelligent person. **2** a person who plans and organizes a complex scheme, especially a crime. ● *vb* to plan and organize a complex scheme.

masterpiece /ma-ster-peess/ *n* the best piece of work done by an artist (*regarded as Vincent van Gogh's masterpiece*).

mastery /ma-ste-ree/ *n* **1** control, command (*gain mastery over the enemy*). **2** thorough knowledge (*his mastery of foreign languages*).

masticate /ma-sti-cate/ *vb* (*fml*) to chew (*masticating food before swallowing*). ● *n* **mastication** /ma-sti-**cay**-shun/.

mastiff /ma-stif/ *n* a large powerful dog.

mat /mat/ *n* **1** a small piece of coarse cloth or plaited fiber used as a floor covering or foot-wiper (*a mat at the front door*). **2** a piece of cloth or other material placed under a plate or dish (*table mats*). ● *adj* matt. ● *vb* (**matted** /ma-tid/, **matting** /ma-ting/) to twist together, to entangle (*matted hair*).

matador /ma-ta-dor/ *n* in Spain, the man who fights the bull in a bullfight.

match[1] /match/ *n* a small stick tipped with a substance that catches fire when rubbed on certain prepared surfaces (*light the fire with a match*).

match[2] /match/ *n* **1** a person or thing the same or nearly the same as another (*find a match for the wool*). **2** an equal (*she was his match in any argument*). **3** a sporting contest or game (*a football match*). **4** a marriage (*a love match*). ● *vb* **1** to be equal to (*the restaurant does not match our local one for home cooking*). **2** to be like or to go well with something else (*the dress matches her eyes*).

matchbox /match-boks/ *n* a box for holding matches.

matchmaker /match-may-ker/ *n* a person who tries to arrange a marriage between others (*try to act* *as matchmakers by asking her female friend and his male friend to dinner*).

mate /**mate**/ n **1** a companion, a colleague (*schoolmates*). **2** (*inf*) a husband or wife (*she is looking for a mate*). **3** a ship's officer below the captain in rank. **4** a workman's assistant (*a plumber's mate*). **5** an animal with which another is paired for producing offspring (*looking for a suitable mate for her pedigree dog*). ● *vb* to come together for breeding (*animals mating*).

material /ma-**tir**-ee-al/ *adj* **1** made of matter. **2** worldly, not spiritual (*a material person/material interests*). **3** (*fml*) important (*it is not material how he feels about it*). ● *n* **1** the substance out of which a thing is made (*use only good-quality materials in his buildings*). **2** cloth (*coats of a warm material*).

materialism /ma-**tir**-ee-al-iz-um/ *n* **1** the belief that nothing exists but matter. **2** the state of being interested only in worldly things such as wealth (*her materialism led her to marry for money not love*).

materialist /ma-**tir**-ee-al-ist/ *n* **1** a person who believes in materialism. **2** a person who is concerned more with wealth and comfort than with ideas (*a materialist who has no interest in music or poetry*). ● *adj* **materialistic** /ma-tir-ee-al-**i**-stic/.

materialize, **materialise** /ma-**tir**-ee-al-ize/ *vb* **1** to become real, to happen (*her dreams of happiness never materialized*). **2** to appear (*a figure of a man materialized out of the mist*).

materially /ma-**tir**-ee-al-ee/ *adv* to a large extent, considerably (*circumstances have changed materially*).

maternal /ma-**ter**-nal/ *adj* of or like a mother (*no maternal feelings*).

maternity /ma-**ter**-ni-tee/ *n* motherhood.

math /**math**/ *n* (*inf*) mathematics.

mathematical /ma-thi-**ma**-ti-cal/ *adj* having to do with mathematics (*a mathematical problem*).

mathematics /ma-thi-**ma**-tics/ *n* the science of space and number. ● *n* **mathematician** /ma-thi-ma-**ti**-shun/.

matinee /mat-**nay**/ *n* an afternoon performance in a theater (*the children went to the Saturday matinee*).

matriculate /ma-**tri**-cyu-late/ *vb* to enroll or be accepted as a student in a university or college. ● *n* **matriculation** /ma-tri-cyu-**lay**-shun/.

matrimony /ma-tri-**moe**-nee/ *n* (*fml*) the state of marriage (*joined in holy matrimony*). ● *adj* **matrimonial** /ma-tri-**moe**-nee-al/.

matrix /**may**-triks/ *n* (*pl* **matrices** /**may**-tri-seez/) **1** in mathematics, the arrangement of a set of

quantities in rows and columns. **2** a mold in which hot molten metal is shaped.

matron /**may**-tron/ *n* **1** (*old*) an older married woman. **2** a woman in a school in charge of medical care, etc. (*matron bandaged the child's grazed knee*).

matronly /**may**-tron-lee/ *adj* **1** middle-aged and rather plump (*a matronly figure*). **2** dignified, serious.

matt(e) /**mat**/ *adj* dull, without gloss or shine (*matt paint*).

matter /**ma**-ter/ *n* **1** that out of which all things are made (*the different kinds of matter of the universe*). **2** a subject of conversation or writings. **3** affair (*a family matter/a matter of great importance*). **4** the infected liquid contained in a wound or sore (*matter oozing from a boil*). ● *vb* to be of importance (*it doesn't matter if you can't be there*).

matter-of-fact /ma-ter-ov-**fact**/ *adj* without imagination or exaggeration, containing facts only (*a matter-of-fact description*).

matting /**ma**-ting/ *n* material used as mats (*coconut matting*).

mattress /**ma**-tress/ *n* a flat bag filled with soft material or light springs, placed under a sleeper for comfort (*prefer a firm mattress*).

mature /ma-**toor**/ *adj* **1** ripe (*mature fruit*). **2** fully grown (*mature turkeys*). **3** fully developed in body or mind (*employers looking for mature people*). ● *vb* **1** to ripen (*fruit maturing early*). **2** to become mature (*young people beginning to mature*). **3** to be due in full (*an insurance policy that matures next year*).

maturity /ma-**too**-ri-tee/ *n* **1** ripeness. **2** full growth or development.

maul /**mawl**/ *vb* **1** to injure badly (*mauled by a lion*). **2** to handle roughly (*accuse her boss of mauling her*).

mausoleum /maw-zu-**lee**-um/ *n* a magnificent tomb (*mausoleums of ancient kings*).

mauve /**mawv**/ *n* a purple dye or color. ● *adj* light purple (*mauve eye shadow*).

maxim /**mak**-sim/ *n* a wise saying, a rule for behavior ("*do as you would be done by*" *is a maxim*).

maximize /**mak**-si-mize/ *vb*, *also* **maximise** (*Br*) to make as large or as important as possible (*maximize the window to fill the screen*).

maximum /**mak**-si-mum/ *n* the greatest possible number or amount (*the maximum that we can afford*). ● *also adj*.

may[1] /**may**/ *vb* (*pt* **might** /**mite**/) used to express possibility or permission (*I may go to the mall later*).

may /**may**/ *n* hawthorn blossom.

May /**may**/ *n* the fifth month of the year (*the flowers of May*).

maybe /**may**-be/ *adv* perhaps (*maybe he'll come and maybe he won't*).

Mayday /**may**-day/ *n* the first day of May.

mayonnaise /**may**-u-naze/ *n* a salad dressing of eggs, oil, etc.

mayor /**may**-ur/ *n* the chief magistrate of a city or borough.

maze /**maze**/ *n* **1** a confusing system of paths or passages through which it is difficult to find your way (*get lost in the maze at the stately home*). **2** a confusing network of streets, etc. (*lost in a maze of side streets*).

me /**mee**/ *pron* the form of "I" used when the object of a sentence (*you don't know me*).

meadow /**me**-doe/ *n* rich grassland (*cows grazing in the meadows*).

meager /**mee**-ger/ *adj, also* **meagre** (*Br, Cdn*) scanty, not enough (*a meager amount of food/a meager diet*).

meal[1] /**meel**/ *n* food taken at one time (*evening meal*).

meal[2] /**meel**/ *n* grain ground to powder.

mean[1] /**meen**/ *adj* **1** nasty, unkind over small things (*mean to her younger sister*). **2** unwilling to spend or give away (*too mean to give presents*). **3** (*old or lit*) poor (*a mean dwelling*). **4** (*old or lit*) of low birth or behavior (*of mean birth*). ● *n* **meanness** /**meen**-ness/.

mean[2] /**meen**/ *vb* (*pt, pp* **meant** /**ment**/) **1** to intend (*we did not mean to hurt her*). **2** to have a certain purpose (*this carpet was meant for the sitting room*). **3** to express a certain idea (*she did not know what the word meant*).

mean[3] /**meen**/ *adj* **1** middle (*the mean point*). **2** halfway between numbers, amounts, extremes, etc., average (*the mean annual rainfall*). ● *n* **1** the average (*the mean of the quantities*). **2** a middle state (*finding the mean between being too harsh and being too kind*). **3** (*pl*) *see* **means** /**meenz**/.

meander /mee-**an**-der/ *vb* to follow a winding course, as a river over very flat land (*paths that meander over the hills*).

meaning /**mee**-ning/ *n* **1** the idea expressed by a word or words (*a word with several meanings*). **2** the sense in which something is intended to be understood (*the meaning of his action/a look full of meaning*). ● *adjs* **meaningful** /**mee**-ning-ful/, **meaningless** /**mee**-ning-less/.

means /**meenz**/ *npl* **1** that by which something is done or carried out (*means of transport*). **2** money or property (*a man of means*).

meantime /**meen**-time/ *n* the time between two events (*in the meantime*). ● *adv* meanwhile.

meanwhile /**meen**-while/ *n* the time between two events, meantime. ● *adv* **1** in or during the intervening time. **2** at the same time (*he will be late— meanwhile you will have to wait*).

measles /**mee**-zulz/ *n* an infectious disease with a red rash (*catch measles from a friend*).

measly /**mee**-zlee/ *adj* worthless, mean (*a measly sum of money*).

measure /**me**-zhur/ *n* **1** a unit by which you express size, weight, etc. (*a liter is a measure of capacity*). **2** size, weight, etc., so expressed (*a room of small measure*). **3** an instrument used in finding size, weight, etc. (*a tape measure*). **4** a course of action (*emergency measures*). **5** a law proposed but not passed (*new taxation measure*). ● *vb* **1** to find out size quantity, etc., with an instrument (*measuring the window for new drapes*). **2** to judge (*measure his skill as a pianist*). **3** to weigh out (*measure out a pound of sugar*). ● *n* **measurement** /**me**-zhur-ment/.

measured /**me**-zhurd/ *adj* (*fml*) steady, regular (*a measured pace*).

meat /**meet**/ *n* the flesh of animals used as food (*vegetarians eat no meat*).

meaty /**mee**-tee/ *adj* **1** full of meat (*meaty pies*). **2** full of information (*a meaty lecture*).

mechanic /me-**ca**-nic/ *n* a person who looks after a machine (*a car mechanic*).

mechanical /me-**ca**-ni-cal/ *adj* **1** done or worked by machine (*mechanical toy cars*). **2** having to do with machinery (*mechanical engineering*). **3** done by habit, done without awareness (*a mechanical task*). ● *adv* **mechanically** /me-**ca**-ni-ca-lee/.

mechanics /me-**ca**-nics/ *n* the science of motion and force.

mechanism /**me**-ca-ni-zum/ *n* the machinery that makes something work (*something wrong with the mechanism of the washing machine*).

medal /**me**-dal/ *n* a flat piece of metal with a picture or writing stamped on it, made in memory of some person or event or as a reward of merit (*soldiers given medals for bravery*).

medalist /**me**-da-list/ *n* the winner of a medal (*medalists in the singing competition*).

medallion /me-**dal**-yun/ *n* a large medal.

meddle /**me**-dul/ *vb* to interfere (*object to her meddling in our private affairs*). ● *n* **meddler** /**med**-dler/.

meddlesome /**me**-dul-sum/ *adj* given to interfering (*meddlesome neighbors*).

media *see* **medium**.

medial /**mee**-dee-al/, **median** /**mee**-dee-an/ *adjs* (*fml*) in the middle (*the medial point*).

mediate /mee-dee-ate/ *vb* to try to settle a dispute between others (*mediating between workers and employers*). ● *n* **mediator** /mee-dee-ay-tor/.

mediation /mee-dee-ay-shun/ *n* an attempt to settle a dispute between others.

medical /me-di-cal/ *adj* **1** having to do with medicine (*medical, rather than surgical, treatment*). **2** having to do with the work of a doctor, medicine, or healing (*medical care/medical insurance*). ● *adv* **medically** /me-di-ca-lee/.

medicate /me-di-cate/ *vb* (*fml*) **1** to give medicine to. **2** to soak in medicine (*medicated shampoo*).

medication /me-di-**cay**-shun/ *n* (*fml*) medicine, treatment by medicine (*on medication for a heart condition*).

medicine /me-di-sin/ *n* **1** the science of bringing the sick back to health (*study medicine*). **2** any substance that cures or heals (*cough medicine*). **3** the science of curing or treating by means other than surgery. ● *adj* **medicinal** /me-**di**-si-nal/. ● *adv* **medicinally** /me-**di**-si-na-lee/.

medieval /me-**dee**-val/ *adj, also* **mediaeval** (*Br, Cdn*) having to do with the Middle Ages (*medieval knights*).

mediocre /mee-dee-**oe**-car/ *adj* not very good, ordinary (*a mediocre performance*). ● *n* **mediocrity** /mee-dee-**oc**-ri-tee/.

meditate /me-di-tate/ *vb* **1** to think deeply about (*meditating on possible solutions to his problems*). **2** to spend short regular periods in deep, especially religious, thought (*he meditates every day*).

meditation /me-di-**tay**-shun/ *n* deep thought.

meditative /me-di-ta-tiv/ *adj* (*fml*) thoughtful (*in a meditative mood*).

medium /mee-dee-um/ *n* **1** (*pl* **media** /mee-dee-ya/) the means by which something is done (*expressing his feelings through the medium of paint*). **2** (*especially in pl*) a means by which news is made known (*the medium of newspapers/the medium of television/a story put out by the media*). **3** (*pl* **mediums** /mee-dee-umz/) a person who is able to receive messages from spirits at a meeting held for that purpose. ● *adj* middle or average in size, quality, etc. (*a medium jar of coffee*).

medley /med-lee/ *n* **1** a mixture (*a medley of colors*). **2** a selection of tunes played as one item (*the band played a medley from the 1960s*).

meek /meek/ *adj* gentle, kind, unresisting (*too meek to insist on her rights*). ● *adv* **meekly** /meek-lee/.

meet /meet/ *vb* (*pt, pp* **met** /met/) **1** to come face to face with, often by chance (*I met my neighbor in the mall*). **2** to come together by arrangement (*we meet for lunch once a week*). **3** to pay (*unable to meet his debts*). **4** to satisfy (*meet their requirements/meet their demands*). **5** to answer (*meet force with force*). ● *n* a coming together of huntsmen on horseback with hounds for a hunt.

meeting /mee-ting/ *n* a coming together for a special purpose (*a committee meeting/a meeting of parents and teachers*).

megabyte /me-ga-bite/ *n* in computing, a unit of storage capacity equal to approximately 1,000,000 bytes.

megaphone /me-ga-foan/ *n* a large device for making the voice louder (*the policeman used a megaphone to ask the crowd to move back*).

melancholy /me-lan-col-ee/ *n* sadness, depression (*a tendency to melancholy on dark winter days*). ● *also adj*.

mellow /me-loe/ *adj* **1** soft with ripeness. **2** made kindly by age. ● *vb* to make or become mellow. ● *n* **mellowness** /me-loe-ness/.

melodic /me-**lod**-ic/ *adj* relating to melody (*simple melodic style*).

melodious /me-**loe**-dee-us/ *adj* sweet-sounding (*melodious pieces of music*).

melodrama /me-lo-dra-ma/ *n* a thrilling or sensational play, usually with an improbable plot (*Victorian melodramas*).

melodramatic /me-lo-dra-**ma**-tic/ *adj* more like a play than real life, theatrical, exaggerated (*her melodramatic reaction to the news*).

melody /me-lo-dee/ *n* **1** a tune (*old-fashioned melodies*). **2** the principal part in a piece of harmonized music.

melon /me-lon/ *n* a large juicy fruit that grows on the ground (*have a slice of melon as the first course of the meal*).

melt /melt/ *vb* **1** to make or become liquid by heat, to soften, to dissolve (*melt the butter*). **2** to disappear (*the crowd melted away*). **3** to make or become gentler (*his heart melted at the sight of the children*).

member /mem-ber/ *n* **1** one of a society or group (*become a member of the chess club*). **2** (*fml or old*) a limb of the body.

membership /mem-ber-ship/ *n* **1** the state of being a member (*renew his membership of the chess club*). **2** all the members of a society (*the membership voted against the idea*).

membrane /mem-brane/ *n* a thin layer of skin covering or connecting parts inside the body (*the eyeballs are covered by a thin membrane*).

memento /mu-**men**-toe/ *n* an object kept or given to remind you of a person or event (*gave him a painting of the house as a memento of his holiday*).

memo *see* **memorandum**.

memoir /**mem**-war/ *n* **1** a written account of past events. **2 memoirs** /**mem**-warz/ the story of a person's life (*the memoirs of a famous political leader*).

memorable /**mem**-ra-bul/ *adj* worth remembering (*a memorable occasion/a memorable victory*). ● *adv* **memorably** /**mem**-ra-blee/.

memorandum /me-mu-**ran**-dum/ *n* (*pl* **memoranda** /me-mu-**ran**-da/) (*often abbreviated to* **memo**) a written note of something you want to remember (*a memorandum about staffing levels sent to all heads of department*).

memorial /me-**moe**-ree-al/ *n* an object, often a monument, that helps people to remember a person or event (*a memorial to the soldiers who died in the war*).

memorize /**me**-mu-rize/ *vb, also* **memorise** (*Br*) to learn by heart (*memorizing the telephone number/memorize the poem*).

memory /**me**-mu-ree/ *n* **1** the power of the mind to recall past events or to learn things by heart (*have a poor memory*). **2** the mind's store of remembered things (*a memory full of useful facts*). **3** something remembered (*childhood memories*). **4** the part of a computer that stores information.

menace /**me**-nis/ *n* **1** a threat, a person or thing likely to cause harm or danger (*regard him as a menace to their security*). **2** a threat, a show of hostility (*demand money with menaces/ a look full of menace*). ● *vb* (*fml*) to threaten (*a country menaced by talk of war*).

menacing /**me**-ni-sing/ *adj* **1** threatening to harm (*menacing letters/a menacing look*). **2** threatening-looking (*a menacing sky*).

menagerie /me-**nadge**-ree/ *n* a collection of wild animals for public show.

mend /**mend**/ *vb* **1** to repair (*mend the broken chair*). **2** to improve (*told to mend his ways*). **3** (*inf*) to become well or healthy again (*his broken leg has mended nicely*). ● *n* the hole or crack that has been mended (*see the mend in the shirt*).

menial /**mee**-nee-al/ *adj* humble, unskilled (*have to do all the menial tasks in the hotel*).

meningitis /**me**-nin-**jie**-tis/ *n* a serious disease affecting the membrane around the brain.

menstrual cycle /men-stroo-al/ *n* a series of changes that take place in a woman's body, roughly over a 28-day period, which prepare her body for possible pregnancy.

menstruation /men-stroo-**way**-shun/ *n* also called a **period**; a monthly discharge of blood from a woman's womb at the end of the normal menstrual cycle if pregnancy does not take place. ● *vb* **menstruate** /**men**-stroo-wate/.

mental /**men**-tal/ *adj* **1** having to do with the mind (*mental illness*). **2** done in the mind without anything being written (*mental arithmetic*). ● *adv* **mentally** /**men**-ta-lee/.

mentality /men-**ta**-li-tee/ *n* **1** mental power (*a person of low mentality*). **2** the way of thinking typical of a person, the character of a person's mind (*I cannot understand the mentality of someone who would attack an old woman*).

menthol /**men**-thol/ *n* a substance made from mint and used as a medicine (*cough drops containing menthol*).

mention /**men**-shun/ *vb* **1** to speak of, to refer to, to say the name of (*mentioned various people who had helped him*). **2** to say briefly or indirectly (*she mentioned that she was thinking of leaving*). ● *n* a remark about or reference to.

mentor /**men**-tawr/ *n* (*fml*) a wise adviser (*his university lecturer was the young writer's mentor*).

menu /**men**-yoo/ *n* **1** a list of foods that can be ordered for a meal in a restaurant (*the menu was written in French*). **2** a list of options on a computer display.

meow /mee-**ow**/ *see* **mew**.

mercenary /**merse**-(u)-ne-ree/ *adj* **1** working for money (*foreign mercenary soldiers*). **2** doing things only to obtain money, greedy for money (*he's too mercenary to help anyone free of charge*). ● *n* a soldier hired to fight for a country not his or her own.

merchandise /**mer**-chan-dize/ *n* goods bought and sold (*poor-quality merchandise*).

merchant /**mer**-chant/ *n* a person who buys and sells goods in large quantities (*a wine merchant*).

merciful /**mer**-si-ful/ *adj* showing mercy, forgiving (*a merciful judge/be merciful to the criminal because of her youth*). ● *adv* **mercifully** /**mer**-si-fu-lee/.

merciless /**mer**-si-less/ *adj* pitiless (*a merciless tyrant*). ● *adv* **mercilessly** /**mer**-si-less-lee/.

mercurial /mer-**cyoo**-ree-al/ *adj* quickly changing mood (*a mercurial personality*).

mercury /**mer**-cyu-ree/ *n* a liquid silvery-white metal used in thermometers.

mercy /**mer**-see/ *n* kindness and pity, forgiveness, willingness not to punish (*show mercy to his captured enemy/treat the wrongdoers with mercy because of their youth*).

mere /**meer**/ *adj* no more or less than (*a mere child/ win by a mere 10 votes/earns a mere $5 per hour*).

merely /**meer**-lee/ *adv* only (*she's merely a child*).

merge /**merge**/ *vb* **1** to join together to make one (*they merged the two branches of the bank*). **2** to become part of a larger whole (*firms that have merged*).

merger /**mer**-jer/ *n* the joining together of two or more businesses (*a merger of two banks*).

meridian /me-**ri**-dee-an/ *n* an imaginary line encircling the earth from pole to pole.

meringue /mu-**rang**/ *n* a light sweet or cake made from sugar and white of egg (*a pie with a topping of meringue*).

merit /**me**-rit/ *n* **1** the quality of deserving praise or reward, worth or excellence (*recognize the merit of the performance*). **2** good point (*a merit of the system*). **3 merits** good qualities. ● *vb* to deserve.

mermaid /**mer**-maid/ *n* an imaginary sea creature, half woman and half fish. ● *also* **merman** /**mer**-man/.

merry /**me**-ree/ *adj* joyous, happy, full of fun (*a merry mood/a merry evening*). ● *adv* **merrily** /**mer**-ri-lee/. ● *n* **merriment** /**me**-ri-ment/.

merry-go-round /**me**-ree-go-round/ *n* a large revolving circular platform with seats in the shape of animals, etc., on which people may ride for amusement at an amusement park.

mesh /**mesh**/ *n* the space between the threads of a net.

mesmerize /**mez**-me-rize/ *vb, also* **mesmerise** (*Br*) **1** to hold the complete attention of and make seemingly unable to move or speak (*they seemed mesmerized by her beauty*). **2** (*old*) to hypnotize.

mess[1] /**mess**/ *n* **1** a muddle (*the files are in a mess*). **2** a dirty or untidy state (*the house is in a mess*). ● *vb* **1** to make dirty or untidy (*mess up the house*). **2** to do badly or inefficiently (*mess up the job*).

mess[2] /**mess**/ *n* **1** a company of people who take their meals together as in the armed services. **2** the place where they eat (*the officers' mess*).

message /**me**-sidge/ *n* **1** information or news sent to another by word of mouth or in writing (*send a message of congratulation/receive a telephone message canceling the meeting*). **2** a piece of instruction, an important idea (*a story with a message*).

messenger /**me**-sin-jer/ *n* a person who bears a message (*the king's messenger*).

Messiah /me-**sie**-ya/ *n* **1** the deliverer promised by God to the Jews. **2** Jesus Christ, believed by Christians to be the Messiah.

Messrs /**me**-surz/ *npl* plural of **Mr**, short for **Messieurs** /mus-**yur**/, usually found in addresses on envelopes (*Messrs Lopez and Smith*).

messy /**me**-see/ *adj* dirty or untidy.

met /**met**/ *pt of* **meet**.

metabolism /me-**ta**-bo-li-zum/ *n* the system of chemical changes in the cells of the body that provide energy (*the rate of metabolism has slowed down*). ● *adj* **metabolic** /me-ta-**bol**-ic/.

metal /**me**-tal/ *n* a class of substances, such as gold, copper, iron, tin, etc. (*boxes made of metal*).

metallic /me-**tal**-ic/ *adj* of or like metal (*metallic paint*).

metallurgy /me-**tal**-ur-jee/ *n* the art of working with metals. ● *n* **metallurgist** /me-**tal**-ur-jist/.

metamorphosis /me-ta-**mawr**-fu-sis/ *n* (*pl* **metamorphoses** /me-ta-**mawr**-fu-seez/) **1** a change in form or kind (*a caterpillar's metamorphosis into a butterfly*). **2** a complete change (*he's undergone a metamorphosis since he married*).

metaphor /**me**-ta-fawr/ *n* a way of comparing two things by identifying them and speaking about one as if it were the other (*"The camel is the ship of the desert" is a metaphor*). ● *adjs* **metaphoric** /me-ta-**faw**-ric/, **metaphorical** /me-ta-**faw**-ri-cal/. ● *adv* **metaphorically** /me-ta-**faw**-ri-ca-lee/.

metaphysics /me-ta-**fi**-zics/ *n* the study of the nature of existence and of the mind. ● *adj* **metaphysical** /me-ta-**fi**-zi-cal/.

mete /**meet**/ *vb* (*old*) to measure (*mete out punishment*).

meteor /**mee**-tee-or/ *n* a shining body that can be seen moving across the sky, a shooting star.

meteoric /me-tee-**awr**-ic/ *adj* rapid but often short-lasting (*his meteoric rise to fame*).

meteorite /**mee**-tee-u-rite/ *n* a meteor that falls to earth as a piece of rock.

meteorological /mee-tee-u-rol-**odge**-i-cal/ *adj* having to do with meteorology (*meteorological charts/ meteorological changes*).

meteorology /mee-tee-u-**rol**-o-jee/ *n* the study or science of the earth's weather. ● *n* **meteorologist** /mee-tee-u-**rol**-o-jist/.

meter[1] /**mee**-ter/ *n* an instrument for measuring things (*a gas meter*).

meter[2] /**mee**-ter/ *n, also* **metre** (*Br, Cdn*) a measure of length (39.37 inches) in the metric system (*measure the cloth in meters*).

meter[3] /**mee**-ter/ *n, also* **metre** (*Br, Cdn*) the systematic arrangement of stressed and unstressed syllables that give poetic rhythm.

methane /**me**-thane/ *n* a flammable gas produced by decaying matter and used as a fuel.

methinks /mee-**thingks**/ *vb* (*old or hum*) it seems to me (*methinks he is not telling the truth*).

method /me-thod/ *n* **1** a way of doing something (*their method of doing business*). **2** an orderly way of arranging or doing things (*a system lacking method*).

methodical /me-thod-ic-al/ *adj* orderly in following a plan or system (*a methodical person/a methodical approach*). ● *adv* **methodically** /me-thod-ic-al-ee/.

Methodist /me-thod-ist/ *n* a member of a Christian sect founded by John Wesley.

methyl /me-thil/ *n* a substance from which wood-alcohol can be made.

methylated spirits /me-thi-lay-tid spi-rits/ *n* a type of alcohol unfit for drinking but used for burning, cleaning, etc. (*use methylated spirits to clean the glass*).

meticulous /me-ti-cyu-lus/ *adj* extremely careful about details or small matters (*prepare the accounts with meticulous attention*).

metre (*Br*) *see* **meter**.

metrical /me-tri-cal/ *adj* (*of poetry*) having a regular rhythm or meter.

metric system /me-tric sis-tem/ *n* a system of weights and measures in which each unit is divisible into 10 parts.

metronome /me-tro-nome/ *n* an instrument with a pendulum that can be set to mark time correctly for a musician (*a metronome on the piano*).

metropolis /me-trop-lis/ *n* (*fml or hum*) a large city, especially the capital (*the metropolis of New York*).

metropolitan /me-tro-pol-i-tan/ *adj* belonging to a metropolis (*the metropolitan area*).

mettle /me-tul/ *n* spirit, courage (*admire their mettle in trying again*).

mew /myoo/, **miaow**, **meow** /mee-aoo/ *n* the cry of a cat. ● *vb* to make a high-pitched cry like a cat (*hear a cat mewing*).

mezzo-soprano /met-so su-pra-noe/ *n* a female voice between soprano and contralto (*a musical role for a mezzo-soprano*).

miaow *see* **mew**.

mice *see* **mouse**.

Michaelmas /mi-cal-mus/ *n* the feast of St Michael, September 29.

microbe /mie-crobe/ *n* a tiny living creature, especially one causing disease (*scientists examining microbes under microscopes*).

microchip /mie-cro-chip/ *n* a very small piece of a material, usually silicon, which acts as a semi-conductor and forms the base on which an electronic circuit is printed.

microcosm /mie-cru-caw-zum/ *n* a little world, a small copy (*a fish tank that is a microcosm of life on the sea bed*).

microphone /mie-cru-fone/ *n* in a telephone or radio, the instrument by which the sound of the voice is changed into electric waves, used to make sounds louder (*the news reporter spoke into a microphone/the singer used a microphone so that everyone in the theater could hear*).

microscope /mie-cru-scope/ *n* an instrument containing an arrangement of curved glasses by means of which very tiny objects can be seen larger and studied.

microscopic /mie-cru-scop-ic/ *adj* **1** very small, tiny, seen only with the help of a microscope (*microscopic bacteria*). **2** (*inf*) tiny (*a microscopic improvement*).

microwave /mie-cro-wave/ *n* a microwave oven, an oven that cooks or heats up food very quickly using electromagnetic radiation. ● *vb* to cook or heat in a microwave.

mid /mid/ *adj* having to do with the middle, in the middle of (*in mid-air, in mid-career*).

midday /mid-day/ *n* noon or the time about noon (*lunch at midday*).

middle /mi-dul/ *adj* equally distant from the ends or limits (*the middle seat in the row*). ● *n* the center, the middle part or point (*stand in the middle of the circle*).

middle-aged /mi-dul-ayjd/ *adj* neither old nor young, between youth and old age (*a middle-aged man and woman*).

Middle Ages /mi-dul ay-jez/ *npl* the period between AD 500 and AD 1500 in European history.

middle class /mi-dul-class/ *n* those who are well enough off to live in comfort, but are neither wealthy nor of noble birth. ● *adj* **middle-class** having to do with the middle class (*political policies appealing more to middle-class voters than to the working class*).

Middle East /mi-dul-eest/ *n* Asian countries west of India and China.

middleman /mi-dul-man/ *n* a trader who buys goods in large quantities from the maker or producer and sells them again at a profit to store owners.

middleweight /mi-dul-wate/ *n* a boxer who fights in the class with a maximum weight of 160 lb.

middling /mi-dul-ing/ *adj* (*inf*) neither very good nor very bad, average (*of middling ability*).

midget /mid-jet/ *n* a very small person or thing.

midland /mid-land/ *adj* far from the coasts or borders of a country.

midnight /mid-nite/ *n* 12 o'clock at night (*go to bed at midnight*).

midriff /mid-rif/ *n* the part of the body containing the muscles separating the stomach from the lungs (*a sweater that left her midriff bare*).

midshipman /mid-ship-man/ *n* a naval rank between cadet and sublieutenant.

midst /midst/ *n* the middle (*in the midst of the battle*).

midsummer /mid-su-mer/ *n* the middle of summer.

midtown /mid-town/ *n* the part of a city between uptown and downtown.

midway /mid-way/ *n* **1** halfway (*their house is midway between the two towns*). ● *also adv*. **2** an area with sideshows at a fair.

midwife /mid-wife/ *n* (*pl* **midwives** /mid-wievz/) a person who assists a mother at the birth of a baby (*the midwife delivered the baby*).

midwifery /mid-wi-free/ *n* the knowledge or study of the work of a midwife.

midwinter /mid-win-ter/ *n* the middle of winter (*the severe cold of midwinter*).

might[1] /mite/ *pt of* **may**[1].

might[2] /mite/ *n* power, strength (*crushed by the might of the enemy army*).

mighty /mie-tee/ *adj* **1** powerful, strong (*a mighty blow/a mighty nation*). **2** huge (*a mighty oak tree*). ● *adv* very (*mighty fine*).

migraine /mie-grane/ *n* a severe headache, often accompanied by a feeling of sickness and visual disturbances.

migrant /mie-grant/ *n* a person or a bird that migrates. ● *also adj*.

migrate /mie-grate/ *vb* **1** to move your home from one land to another, to go from one place to another (*tribes that migrated to find food*). **2** (*of birds*) to move to another place at the season when its climate is suitable. ● *n* **migration** /mie-gray-shun/.

migratory /mie-gra-toe-ree/ *adj* used to migrating (*migratory birds, such as swallows*).

mike /mike/ *n* (*inf*) a microphone.

mild /milde/ *adj* **1** gentle, merciful, not severe (*a mild punishment/a mild sentence*). **2** calm (*a mild sea*). **3** (*of weather*) not cold (*mild days in late spring*). ● *adv* **mildly** /milde-lee/. ● *n* **mildness** /milde-ness/.

mildew /mil-doo/ *n* a tiny but destructive growth that appears and spreads on leaves or on damp paper, leather, etc. (*mildew on old books*).

mileage, milage /mile-idge/ *n* distance in miles (*what mileage does your car have?*).

mile /mile/ *n* a measure of length (= 1760 yards) (*distances measured in miles*).

milestone /mile-stone/ *n* **1** a stone by the roadside telling the distance in miles to places in the neighborhood. **2** a time at which you can consider the progress made (*reach a milestone in her career*).

militant /mi-li-tant/ *adj* **1** fighting, warlike (*a militant nation*). **2** active in a campaign (*militant members of the feminist movement*). ● *n* **militancy** /mi-li-tan-see/.

militarism /mi-li-ta-ri-zum/ *n* belief in the use of armies or war in politics (*the militarism of the country in invading others*). ● *n* **militarist** /mi-li-ta-rist/.

military /mi-li-ta-ree/ *adj* having to do with soldiers or battles (*a military force*). ● *n* the army, soldiers (*join the military*).

militate /mi-li-tate/ *vb* **1** to act or stand (against) (*militating against injustice*). **2** to act as a reason against (*his criminal record militated against him/the recession militated against house sales*).

militia /mi-li-sha/ *n* a reserve army, consisting of people trained in the use of arms, and called out in an emergency. ● *n* **militiaman** /mi-li-sha-man/.

milk /milk/ *n* **1** the liquid produced by female mammals to feed their babies (*a baby getting milk from its mother*). **2** such milk produced by cows or goats and drunk by humans or made into butter and cheese (*have bottles of milk delivered*). ● *vb* to draw milk from (e.g., a cow).

milkmaid /milk-maid/ *n* a woman who milks cows.

milkman /milk-man/ *n* a man who sells or delivers milk.

milk shake /milk-shake/ *n* a cold frothy drink made from milk shaken up with flavoring and ice cream.

milk tooth /milk tooth/ *n* one of a child's first set of teeth (*baby's first milk tooth came through*).

milky /mil-kee/ *adj* **1** like milk (*a milky liquid*). **2** containing a lot of milk (*a milky drink*).

Milky Way /mil-kee-way/ *n* a bright band across the night sky, made up of countless stars.

mill /mill/ *n* **1** a machine for grinding corn, coffee, etc. **2** the building in which corn is ground into flour. **3** a factory (*steel mills/paper mills/cotton mills*). ● *vb* **1** to grind (*mill corn*). **2** to stamp a coin and cut grooves around its edge.

millennium /mi-len-ee-um/ *n* (*pl* **millennia** /mi-len-ee-ya/ *or* **milleniums** /mi-len-ee-umz/) **1** a period of 1000 years. **2** according to the Bible, the 1000 years for which Christ will reign on the Earth.

miller /mi-ler/ *n* a person who keeps a corn mill.

millet /mi-let/ *n* a grass bearing edible grain.

mill hand /mil-hand/ *n* a factory worker (*mill hands no longer able to find work*).

milligram /mi-li-gram/ *n* the thousandth part of a gram (*measure the drug in milligrams*).

millimeter /mi-li-mee-ter/ *n, also* **millimetre** (*Br, Cdn*) the thousandth part of a meter.

milliner /mi-li-ner/ *n* a person who makes or sells ladies' hats (*the number of milliners has decreased with the decline in hat wearing*).

millinery /mi-li-ne-ree/ *n* hats made or sold by a milliner.

million /mil-yun/ *n* **1** a thousand thousand (1,000,000). **2** (*inf*) a very great many (*excuses by the million*).

millionaire /mil-yu-**nare**/ *n* a person who possesses a million or more dollars (*lottery winners who are now millionaires*).

millipede /mi-li-peed/ *n* an insect with many feet.

millstone /mil-stone/ *n* **1** a heavy round stone used for grinding corn into flour. **2** a very heavy load or handicap (*she has the millstone of a lazy husband*).

millwheel /mil-wheel/ *n* the large wheel, turned by water power, that drives the machinery inside a mill.

mime /mime/ *n* **1** a play without words carried on by facial expressions, gestures, and actions. **2** using actions without language (*we showed her by mime that we wanted to find a restaurant because we did not speak the language*). ● *vb* **1** to mouth the words to a recorded song. **2** to act without speaking (*he mimed that he wanted a drink*).

mimic /mi-mic/ *vb* (**mimicked** /mi-mict/, **mimicking** /mi-mi-king/) to imitate, especially in order to make fun of (*she mimics his way of walking to amuse her classmates*). ● *n* a person who imitates.

mimicry /mi-mi-cree/ *n* imitation (*impressed by the performer's mimicry of the prime minister*).

mimosa /mi-**mo**-sa/ *n* a tree with sweet-smelling flowers.

minaret /mi-na-**ret**/ *n* the tower of a Muslim mosque.

mince /minse/ *vb* to cut into very small pieces (*mince up the beef*). ● **not to mince matters** to speak the plain truth (*not to mince matters, he's a liar*).

mincemeat /minse-meet/ *n* **1** minced meat. **2** currants, etc., chopped up small and mixed with spices (*pies made with mincemeat for Christmas*).

mind /minde/ *n* **1** the power by which human beings understand, think, feel, will, etc. (*have a sharp mind/an adult with the mind of a child*). **2** a person of great mental ability (*one of the great minds of the century*). **3** memory (*unable to call his name to mind*). ● *vb* **1** to take care of (*mind the baby*). **2** to take heed, to be careful (*mind you don't fall on the ice*). **3** to object to (*I do not mind if you leave early*). ● **mind your p's and q's** to be careful what you say or do (*mind your p's and q's*

when you visit his parents*). ● **mind your own business** not to interfere in another's affairs (*he told his neighbor to mind her own business when she asked him if he was still working*).

minded /**mine**-did/ *adj* desirous, inclined (*serious-minded*).

mindful /**minde**-ful/ *adj* not forgetful, paying attention to (*always mindful of possible dangers*).

mindless /**minde**-less/ *adj* unthinking, stupid (*a mindless act of violence*).

mine[1] /mine/ *poss pron* belonging to me (*the pen is mine*).

mine[2] /mine/ *n* **1** a deep hole made in the earth so that minerals can be taken from beneath its surface (*a coal mine/a gold mine*). **2** a container filled with an explosive charge to blow something up (*military tanks blown up by enemy mines*). **3** a person or place from which much may be obtained (*a mine of information*). ● *vb* **1** to make tunnels into and under the earth (*the area is extensively mined*). **2** to dig for in a mine (*mining coal*). **3** to place explosive mines in position (*the enemy mined the beaches*). **4** to blow up with mines (*ships mined in the war*).

minefield /**mine**-feeld/ *n* **1** an area in which there are many mineral mines. **2** an area in which many explosive mines are placed. **3** something full of hidden dangers (*her situation at work is a minefield*).

minelayer /**mine**-lay-er/ *n* a ship that places mines in a minefield.

miner /**mine**-er/ *n* a person who works in a mine (*a coal miner*).

mineral /**min**-ral/ *n* an inorganic substance found naturally in the earth and mined (*coal and salt are minerals*). ● *adj* having to do with minerals (*the country's mineral wealth*).

mineralogy /mi-ne-**rol**-o-jee/ *n* the study of minerals. ● *n* **mineralogist** /mi-ne-**rol**-o-jist/.

mineral water /**min**-ral **waw**-ter/ *n* water that comes from a natural spring and contains minerals, sometimes sold still and sometimes carbonated (*a bottle of gassy mineral water*).

mine-sweeper /**mine**-swee-per/ *n* a ship that clears an area of mines.

mingle /**ming**-gul/ *vb* **1** to mix together (*comments that mingled praise with blame*). **2** to mix with (*police mingling with the crowds*).

miniature /mi-nee-a-chur/ *n* a very small painting (*a miniature of the artist's mother*). ● *adj* very small, tiny (*a miniature bottle of whiskey/a miniature model railroad*).

minim /mi-nim/ (*Br*) *a* **half note.**

minimize, minimise /mi-ni-mize/ *vb* to make seem less important (*minimizing the problems*).

minimum /mi-ni-mum/ *n* the smallest amount possible (*we want the minimum of fuss*). ● *also adj.* ● *adj* **minimal** /mi-ni-mal/.

minion /min-yun/ *n* **1** a slavelike follower or employee, a person who always does as his or her employer orders (*the manager and his minions treated the rest of us badly*).

minister /mi-ni-ster/ *n* **1** a member of the clergy (*the minister's sermon*). **2** (*Br*) a person in charge of a government department (*Minister of Transport*). **3** the principal representative of a government in another country. ● *vb* to give help, to serve (*she ministers to his every need*).

ministerial /mi-ni-**stee**-ree-al/ *adj* having to do with a minister (*ministerial duties*).

ministry /mi-ni-stree/ *n* **1** the clergy (*join the ministry*). **2** (*Br*) a department of government in charge of a minister.

mink /mingk/ *n* (*pl* **mink**) a small stoatlike animal valued for its fur (*breed mink in captivity/a mink coat*).

minnow /mi-no/ *n* a very small freshwater fish.

minor /mie-nor/ *adj* **1** smaller, of less importance (*minor issues*). **2** (*mus*) lower than the corresponding major by a half step (*a minor key*). ● *n* **1** a person below the age when you have full civil rights (*he committed murder while still a minor*). **2** (*mus*) a minor key, interval, or scale (*played in A minor*).

minority /mi-**naw**-ri-tee/ *n* **1** the state of being below the age when you have full civil rights. **2** the smaller number in a group or assembly, less than half (*a minority of people voted against the suggestion/the objectors were in the minority*).

minstrel /min-strel/ *n* **1** in olden times, a wandering singer and poet. **2** (*old*) a singer.

mint[1] /mint/ *n* **1** a place where coins are made, especially by the government. **2** (*inf*) a large amount (*he earns a mint*). ● *vb* to make coins.

mint[2] /mint/ *n* a sweet-smelling herb whose leaves are used as flavoring in cooking (*lamb flavored with mint*).

minuet /min-yu-et/ *n* (*old*) **1** a slow, graceful dance. **2** music for this dance.

minus /mie-nus/ *prep* **1** less (*10 minus 3 is 7*). **2** (*inf*) not having (*we are minus two members of staff*). ● *adj* less than zero (*a minus quantity*). ● *n* the sign of subtraction (−).

minuscule /mi-ni-scyool/ *adj* extremely small.

minute[1] /mi-nit/ *n* **1** the 60th part of an hour. **2** the 60th part of a degree. **3** a short time (*I'll be with you in a minute*). **4** a written note or comment. **5** **minutes** a short account of what was discussed and decided at a meeting. ● *vb* to make a written note of.

minute[2] /mie-**nyoot**/ *adj* **1** very small (*minute quantities of the drug*). **2** exact (*minute attention to detail*).

minutiae /mie-**noo**-shee-a/ *npl* small details (*get to the main point and ignore the minutiae*).

minx /mingks/ *n* a forward or impertinent girl (*the minx told her grandmother to keep quiet*).

miracle /mi-ra-cul/ *n* **1** an extraordinary event believed by some to be brought about by the interference of God with the natural course of events. **2** any extraordinary event for which there is no known explanation (*it is a miracle that the family can survive on that income*).

miraculous /mi-ra-cyu-lus/ *adj* **1** caused by a miracle, marvelous (*the miraculous cures of Christ*). **2** amazing, extraordinary (*his miraculous recovery*). ● *adv* **miraculously** /mi-ra-cyu-lus-lee/.

mirage /mi-**razh**/ *n* imaginary objects (eg water, trees) that appear real to a traveler because of certain atmospheric conditions, such as shimmer caused by heat (*they thought they saw an oasis in the desert, but it was a mirage*).

mire /mire/ *n* (*fml or lit*) wet, muddy ground, mud (*vehicles stuck in the mire*).

mirror /mi-rur/ *n* a looking glass. ● *vb* to reflect as in a mirror.

mirth /mirth/ *n* laughter, merriment (*collapse with mirth at the antics of the clown*). ● *adjs* **mirthful** /mirth-ful/, **mirthless** /mirth-less/.

misadventure /mi-sad-**ven**-chur/ *n* (*fml or old*) an unlucky happening (*death by misadventure*).

misanthrope /mi-san-thrope/, **misanthropist** /mi-san-thru-pist/ *ns* (*fml*) a person who hates humankind (*a misanthrope who stays away from other people as much as possible*). ● *adj* **misanthropic** /mi-san-**throp**-ic/. ● *n* **misanthropy** /mi-san-thru-pee/.

misapprehend /mi-sa-pri-**hend**/ *vb* (*fml*) to misunderstand (*misapprehend their intentions*). ● *n* **misapprehension** /mi-sa-pri-**hen**-shun/.

misappropriate /mi-sa-**pro**-pree-at/ *vb* (*fml*) to put to a wrong use, to use dishonestly for yourself (*misappropriating the firm's money and running off with it*).

misbehave /mis-bee-**have**/ *vb* to behave badly. ● *n* **misbehavior** /mis-bee-**have**-yur/, *also* **misbehaviour** (*Br, Cdn*).

miscalculate /mis-**cal**-cyu-late/ *vb* to work out an answer or likely result wrongly (*miscalculating the cost of the journey*). ● *n* **miscalculation** /mis-cal-cyu-**lay**-shun/.

miscarriage /mis-**ca**-ridge/ *n* the loss of a baby from the womb before it is able to survive. ● **miscarriage of justice** a mistaken finding by a court that an innocent person is guilty of a crime.

miscarry /mis-**ca**-ree/ *vb* to have a miscarriage (*the expectant mother miscarried*).

miscellaneous /mi-se-**lay**-nee-us/ *adj* mixed, of different kinds (*a miscellaneous collection of old books*).

miscellany /mi-**se**-la-nee/ *n* (*fml*) a mixture, a collection of things of different kinds (*a miscellany of old books*).

mischance /mis-**chanse**/ *n* (*fml*) an unlucky happening (*killed by mischance*).

mischief /**mis**-chif/ *n* 1 (*fml*) harm done on purpose (*the mischief done to their property by vandals*). 2 children's naughtiness (*children punished for their mischief*).

mischievous /**mis**-chi-vus/ *adj* 1 harmful, intended to cause trouble (*mischievous gossip*). 2 naughty (*mischievous children*). ● *adv* **mischievously** /**mis**-chi-vus-lee/.

misconception /mis-con-**sep**-shun/ *n* a mistaken idea, misunderstanding (*she was under the misconception that he was not married*).

misconduct /mis-**con**-duct/ *n* bad or wrong behavior (*workers sacked for misconduct on duty*).

misconstrue /mis-con-**stroo**/ *vb* (*fml*) to give a wrong meaning or significance to (*misconstruing his instructions*). ● *n* **misconstruction** /mis-con-**struc**-shun/.

miscreant /**mis**-cree-ant/ *n* (*fml*) a wicked person (*miscreants sent to prison by the judge*).

misdeed /mis-**deed**/ *n* (*fml*) a wrongful action, a crime (*punished for their misdeeds*).

misdemeanor /mis-di-**mee**-nor/ *n* 1 an act that breaks the law, a petty crime (*fined for the misdemeanor*). 2 an act of misbehavior (*the child's misdemeanor*).

misdirect /mis-di-**rect**/ *vb* to give wrong instructions to (*accused of misdirecting the jury*). ● *n* **misdirection** /mis-di-**rec**-shun/.

miser /**mie**-ser/ *n* a person who dislikes spending money (*too much of a miser even to eat properly*).

miserable /**mi**-zer-bul/ *adj* 1 very unhappy (*a miserable child/feel miserable*). 2 causing unhappiness or discomfort (*a miserable day/a miserable place to live*). 3 low in quality or quantity (*a*

miserable performance/a miserable amount of money*). ● *adv* **miserably /**mi**-zer-blee/.

miserly /**mie**-zer-lee/ *adj* very mean (*a miserly employer*).

misery /**mi**-ze-ree/ *n* great unhappiness or suffering (*the misery of their existence*).

misfire /mis-**fire**/ *vb* 1 (*of guns*) to fail to go off. 2 to fail (*plans that misfired*). ● *also n*.

misfit /**mis**-fit/ *n* a person unsuited to his or her circumstances (*as a shy person, he is a misfit in the sales industry*).

misfortune /mis-**fawr**-chun/ *n* 1 bad luck (*have the misfortune to have her car break down*). 2 a piece of bad luck (*suffer one misfortune after another*).

misgiving /mis-**gi**-ving/ *n* a feeling of fear, doubt, or mistrust (*last-minute misgivings about marrying someone whom he did not know well*).

misguided /mis-**gie**-did/ *adj* showing bad judgment (*a misguided attempt to help*).

mishandle /mis-**han**-dul/ *vb* (*fml*) to manage badly (*mishandling the situation*).

mishap /**mis**-hap/ *n* an unlucky event, usually not serious (*he had a mishap while parking the car*).

misinform /mi-sin-**fawrm**/ *vb* (*fml*) to give wrong information (*we were misinformed about the time of the meeting*).

misinterpret /mi-sin-**ter**-pret/ *vb* to give a wrong meaning to (*misinterpreted what they were asked to do*). ● *n* **misinterpretation** /mi-sin-ter-pre-**tay**-shun/.

misjudge /mis-**judge**/ *vb* to judge wrongly, to form a wrong opinion (*you are misjudging him—he is a very pleasant person*).

mislay /mis-**lay**/ *vb* (*pt, pp* **mislaid** /mis-**laid**/) to put (something) down and forget where you have put it (*mislaid the book that she was reading*).

mislead /mis-**leed**/ *vb* (*pt, pp* **misled** /mis-**led**/) to deceive, to give the wrong idea to (*he tried to mislead the police by giving wrong evidence*).

mismanage /mis-**ma**-nidge/ *vb* to manage badly (*mismanaging his finances*). ● *n* **mismanagement** /mis-**ma**-nidge-ment/.

misnomer /mis-**no**-mer/ *n* a wrong or unsuitable name ("*assistant*" *was a misnomer—she never did a thing to help me do the job*).

misogynist /mi-**sodge**-in-ist/ *n* a man who hates women (*he never married—he's a misogynist who even hates his sister*).

misplace /mis-**place**/ *vb* to put in a wrong place (*misplace a book*).

misprint /**mis**-print/ *n* a mistake in printing (*correct* *the misprint before the book is published*). ● *vb* **misprint** /mis-**print**/.

mispronounce /mis-pro-**nounse**/ *vb* to pronounce wrongly (*don't mispronounce his name*). ● *n* **mispronunciation** /mis-pro-nun-see-**ay**-shun/.

misquote /mis-**kwoat**/ *vb* to quote wrongly, to make mistakes in trying to repeat another's words. ● *n* **misquotation** /mis-kwo-**tay**-shun/.

misread /mis-**reed**/ *vb* (*pt, pp* **misread** /mis-**red**/) to read wrongly (*misread the instructions*).

misrepresent /mis-re-pri-**zent**/ *vb* to give an untrue account of another's ideas or opinions (*in court he misrepresented what I had said*). ● *n* **misrepresentation** /mis-re-pri-zen-**tay**-shun/.

misrule /mis-**rule**/ *vb* to rule or govern badly. ● *also n.*

miss[1] /**miss**/ *vb* **1** to fail to hit, find, meet, catch, or notice (*the batter missed the ball/we were meant to meet, but we missed each other/he missed the bus*). **2** to leave out (*he missed a bit when he was painting*). **3** to regret the loss or absence of (*she missed her friend when he went abroad*). ● *n* a failure to hit or catch.

miss[2] /**miss**/ *n* (*pl* **misses** /**mi**-seez/) (*old*) an unmarried woman, a girl.

missal /**mi**-sal/ *n* a Roman Catholic prayer book containing prayers, etc., for Mass.

misshapen /mis-**shay**-pen/ *adj* badly formed, deformed, ugly (*misshapen oak trees*).

missile /**mi**-sile/ *n* **1** any object thrown or fired from a gun to do harm. **2** an explosive flying weapon with its own engine, which can be aimed at distant objects (*nuclear missiles*).

missing /**mi**-sing/ *adj* lost (*the missing letter/his son has gone missing*).

mission /**mi**-shun/ *n* **1** persons sent to carry out a certain task (*an American trade mission sent to the UK*). **2** the task itself (*the group's mission was to blow up the enemy bridge*). **3** your chief aim in life (*her mission is to help people*). **4** a group of persons sent to a foreign land to teach their religion. **5** the building(s) in which they live (*the mission also provides medical services*).

missionary /**mi**-shu-ner-ee/ *n* a person who is sent to a foreign land to teach his or her religion. ● *also adj.*

misspell /mis-**spel**/ *vb* to spell wrongly (*she misspelled his name*). ● *n* **misspelling** /mis-**spe**-ling/.

misspend /mis-**spend**/ *vb* (*pt, pp* **misspent** /mis-**spent**/) to spend wastefully or unprofitably (*she misspent her dead mother's savings*).

mist /**mist**/ *n* **1** rain in fine, tiny drops. **2** a cloud

resting on the ground (*cars having to drive slowly in the mist*).

mistake /mi-**stake**/ *vb* **1** to understand wrongly (*she mistook what he said*). **2** to confuse one person or thing with another (*she mistook him for his brother*). ● *n* an error.

mistaken /mi-**stay**-ken/ *adj* in error, wrong (*a mistaken interpretation of the situation*).

mister /**mi**-ster/ *n* the title put before a man's name (usually written **Mr**).

mistime /mis-**time**/ *vb* to time badly, to do something at a wrong time (*they mistimed their arrival*).

mistletoe /**mi**-sul-toe/ *n* an evergreen plant with white berries (*hang bunches of mistletoe at Christmas*).

mistreat /mi-**street**/ *vb* to treat badly.

mistress /**mi**-stress/ *n* **1** (*usually written* **Mrs**) the title put before the name of a married woman. **2** a woman having charge or control (of) (*she is the mistress of the house*). **3** a woman teacher. **4** a woman who is the lover of a man and sometimes maintained by him but not married to him (*his wife does not know he has a mistress*).

mistrust /mi-**strust**/ *vb* to suspect, to doubt. ● *also n.*

misty /**mi**-stee/ *adj* **1** darkened or clouded by mist (*misty hills*). **2** not clear (*her eyes were misty with tears*).

misunderstand /mi-sun-der-**stand**/ *vb* to take a wrong meaning from (*they misunderstood his directions and got lost*).

misunderstanding /mi-sun-der-**stan**-ding/ *n* a disagreement, especially one due to failure to see another's meaning or intention (*they have not spoken to each other for years, and it was all because of a misunderstanding*).

misuse /mis-**yooz**/ *vb* to use in the wrong way, to use badly (*the machine broke because they misused it*). ● *n* improper or wrong use (*his misuse of the firm's money*).

mite /**mite**/ *n* **1** a type of very small insect. **2** a small child (*a poor little mite dressed in rags*). **3** a very small amount.

miter /**mie**-ter/ *n* **1** the tall pointed headgear worn by bishops. **2** a way of joining two boards meeting at right angles.

mitigate /**mi**-ti-gate/ *vb* **1** to make less serious, to excuse to some extent (*the lawyer hoped that the fact that the accused murdered in self-defense would mitigate the offense*). **2** to make less severe (*a drug for mitigating the pain*). ● *n* **mitigation** /mi-ti-**gay**-shun/.

mitt /**mit**/, **mitten** /**mi**-ten/ *ns* **1** a type of glove that covers the hand but not the fingers and thumb. **2**

a glove without separate places for the fingers (*the little girl wore mittens and a matching hat*).

mix /miks/ *vb* **1** to put together to form one (*mix the butter and sugar*). **2** to go together or blend successfully (*oil and water do not mix*). **3** to join in (with others) (*she did not mix at the party*).

mixed /mikst/ *adj* **1** made up of different things or kinds (*mixed feelings*). **2** relating to people of different sexes (*a mixed school/mixed doubles at tennis*).

mixture /miks-cher/ *n* the result of mixing things or people together (*a mixture of eggs, flour, and milk/a mixture of nationalities*).

mnemonic /ne-**mon**-ic/ *adj* helping the memory. ● *n* something easily remembered that helps you to remember something else (*mnemonics to remind him how to spell certain words*).

moan /moan/ *vb* **1** to make a low sound expressing sorrow or pain (*moaning in agony*). **2** (*inf*) to complain (*she's always moaning about the weather*). ● *also n.*

moat /moat/ *n* a trench, often filled with water, around a castle or fort.

mob /mob/ *n* a disorderly crowd (*football mobs*). ● *vb* (**mobbed** /mobd/, **mobbing** /mob-ing/) to crowd around in a disorderly way (*the movie star was mobbed by photographers*).

mobile /mo-bul/ *adj* **1** that can be moved (*a mobile library*). **2** easily moved (*mobile office units*). **3** able to move easily, active (*old people no longer mobile*). ● *n* **1** a decoration that hangs from the ceiling by threads or wire and that has attached to it several small objects that move when the surrounding air moves (*a mobile made of plastic fish*). **2** see **mobile phone**.

mobile phone /mo-bul-**foan**/ *n* a handheld, portable phone that works by means of radio networks. Also **cell phone**.

mobility /mo-**bi**-li-tee/ *n* ability to move about (*old people annoyed at their lack of mobility*).

mobilize, mobilise /mo-bi-lize/ *vb* **1** to call upon to serve as soldiers (*officers told to mobilize their men*). **2** to organize for a particular reason (*mobilizing supporters for the party rally*). ● *n* **mobilization** /mo-bu-li-**zay**-shun/, *also* **mobilisation** (*Br*).

moccasin /mok-a-sin/ *n* a shoe or slipper made of deerskin or sheepskin.

mock /mock/ *vb* **1** to make fun of (*they mocked his attempts to improve himself*). **2** to imitate in order to make appear foolish (*the boys mocked the way the lame old man walked*). ● *adj* false, not real (*mock leather*).

mockery /**mock**-ree/ *n* **1** the act of mocking. **2** a person or thing mocked (*make a mockery of his attempts*).

mock heroic /mock-he-**ro**-ic/ *adj* imitating the grand style of writing when dealing with an unimportant subject.

mockingbird /**mok**-ing-burd/ *n* a type of thrush that imitates the song of other birds, etc.

mode /mode/ *n* **1** (*fml*) the way of doing something (*his mode of expressing himself*). **2** (*old*) a fashion in clothing (*Paris modes*).

model /mo-del/ *n* **1** a person or thing to be copied (*use the essay as a model*). **2** a copy, usually smaller, of a person or thing (*models of aircraft*). **3** a small copy of (e.g., a building or ship made from a plan to show what the finished object will look like) (*show would-be buyers a model of the condo*). **4** a living person who sits or stands still to let an artist draw him or her (*act as a model for the art class*). **5** a person who is employed to display clothes by wearing them (*the models at the Paris fashion show*). **6** an artificial figure used in display (*store-window models*). ● *adj* worth copying, perfect (*model behavior*). ● *vb* **1** to give shape to (*model the clay into a bowl*). **2** to make a model of (*model the head of the president in clay*). **3** to wear clothes to show to possible buyers (*model the new season's fashions*).

modem /mo-dem/ *n* a piece of equipment that links a computer to the telephone system so that information can be sent to other computers.

moderate /mod-rit/ *adj* **1** not going to extremes (*of moderate views*). **2** within sensible limits (*moderate prices*). **3** average (*someone of only moderate ability*). ● *vb* **1** to prevent from going to extremes (*moderate your demands*). **2** to lessen (*the storm is moderating*). ● *adv* **moderately** /mod-rit-lee/.

moderation /mod-e-**ray**-shun/ *n* avoidance of extremes, self-control (*drink liquor in moderation*).

modern /mod-ern/ *adj* **1** belonging to the present day (*modern language changes*). **2** belonging to recent centuries (*modern history*). **3** up-to-date (*parents who have modern ideas on education*). ● *n* **modernity** /mo-**der**-ni-tee/.

modernize /**mod**-er-nize/ *vb*, *also* **modernise** (*Br*) to bring up-to-date (*modernizing machinery to keep ahead of the competition*).

modest /mod-est/ *adj* **1** not having too high an opinion of yourself (*a very modest young woman*). **2** not boastful (*modest about her success*). **3** decent (*always modest in her dress*). **4** not very large (*a modest increase in salary*). ● *adv* **modestly** /mod-est-lee/. ● *n* **modesty** /mod-e-stee/.

modicum /mod-i-cum/ *n* (*fml*) a small amount (*not a modicum of truth in what he says*).

modification /mod-i-fi-**cay**-shun/ *n* an alteration, a small change (*minor modifications to the house plans*).

modify /mod-i-fie/ *vb* **1** to alter in part (*modified the design*). **2** to make less severe (*modify his extreme views*).

modish /mod-ish/ *adj* (*fml*) fashionable (*a modish style of dress*).

modulate /maw-ju-late/ *vb* **1** to raise or lower the tone or pitch of the voice when speaking or singing (*actors learning to modulate their voices*). **2** in music, to change from one key to another. ● *n* **modulation** /mo-ju-lay-shun/.

module /maw-jul/ *n* **1** one of several parts that together form a larger structure. **2** a unit of a course of study.

mohair /mo-hair/ *n* **1** the silky hair of an Angora goat. **2** the wool or cloth made from it (*a mohair sweater*).

moist /moist/ *adj* slightly wet, damp (*clean it with a moist cloth/his moist brow*).

moisten /moi-sten/ *vb* to make damp (*moistened a cloth to wipe the child's face*).

moisture /mois-chur/ *n* dampness, wetness caused by tiny drops of water in the atmosphere (*soil in need of moisture*).

moisturizer /mois-chu-rie-zer/ *n* cream or lotion applied to treat dry skin.

molar /mo-lar/ *n* one of the back teeth that grind food.

molasses /mo-la-siz/ *n* a thick sticky dark liquid left over when sugar is made from sugarcane.

mold[1]/moald/ *n, also* **mould** (*Br, Cdn*) **1** a shaped vessel into which hot molten metal is poured so that when it cools, it has the same shape as the vessel. **2** a vessel used to food. ● *vb* **1** to form in a mold (*the metal is molded into bars*). **2** to work into a shape (*mold the clay into a ball*). **3** to shape or influence (*mold a child's character*).

mold[2]/moald/ *n, also* **mould** (*Br, Cdn*) a fluffy growth consisting of tiny plants on stale food or damp surfaces.

molder /moal-der/ *vb, also* **moulder** (*Br Cdn*) to rot away, to crumble (*walls of the old house moldering away/talent left to molder away*).

molding/moal-ding/ *n, also* **moulding** (*Br Cdn*) **1** anything given shape in a mold. **2** an ornamental

pattern on a wall or ceiling or on a picture frame (*a molding on the ceiling in the form of leaves*).

moldy /moal-dee/ *adj, also* **mouldy** (*Br Cdn*) **1** covered with mold. **2** (*inf*) of little value, unpleasant, dull (*the child complained about getting a moldy old $10 bill for Christmas*).

mole[1] /mole/ *n* **1** a dark spot on the human skin (*he had a mole on his shoulder*). **2** a spy who works from within an organization, passing information to another organization.

mole[2] /mole/ *n* a small furry burrowing animal (*piles of earth on his lawn caused by moles*).

molecular /mol-e-cyu-lar/ *adj* having to do with molecules (*the molecular structure of the substance*).

molecule /mol-i-cyool/ *n* the smallest particle of a substance that can exist while still retaining the chemical qualities of that substance.

molehill /mole-hill/ *n* the heap of earth thrown up by a burrowing mole (*molehills on the lawn*).

moleskin /mole-skin/ *n* a strong ribbed cotton cloth.

molest /mo-lest/ *vb* **1** to disturb or annoy (*molested by members of the press*). **2** to make a bodily, often sexual, attack upon. ● *n* **molestation** /mol-es-**tay**-shun/.

mollify /mol-i-fie/ *vb* to make less angry, to calm down (*mollified their mother by giving her flowers*).

mollusk /mol-usk/ *n*, **mollusc** (*Br, Cdn*) a soft-bodied animal with a hard shell, as a snail, oyster, etc. (*edible mollusks*).

mollycoddle /mol-ee-cod-ul/ *vb* to take too great care of (*she mollycoddles her children*).

molt /moalt/ *vb, also* **moult** (*Br, Cdn*) to lose the hair or feathers, to fall off (*dogs molting*).

molten /moal-ten/ *adj* **1** melted (*molten metal*). **2** made by having been melted (*molten casts*).

mom /mom/ *n* mother (*short for* **mommy** /mom-ee/).

moment /mo-ment/ *n* a very short time (*it took only a moment*).

momentarily /mo-men-**ter**-i-lee/ *adv* **1** for a moment (*momentarily blinded by the bright light*). **2** shortly (*I'll be with you momentarily*).

momentary /mo-men-ter-ee/ *adj* lasting only a moment (*a momentary pause*).

momentous /mo-**men**-tus/ *adj* very important (*a momentous discovery*).

momentum /mo-**men**-tum/ *n* the force of a moving body (*the rock gathered momentum as it rolled downhill*).

mommy /mo-mee/ *n* (*inf*) mother.

monarch /mon-ark/ *n* a single supreme ruler, a sovereign, a king or queen (*the ruling monarch*).

monarchist /**mon**-ar-kist/ *n* a person who believes in monarchy (*some people would prefer a republic, but he is a monarchist*).

monarchy /**mon**-ar-kee/ *n* a state or system of government in which power is, in appearance or reality, in the hands of a single ruler (*Britain is a monarchy*).

monastery /**mon**-a-stree/ *n* a house for monks.

monastic /mu-**na**-stic/ *adj* having to do with monks or monasteries (*a monastic way of life*).

Monday /**mun**-day/ *n* the second day of the week.

monetary /**mon**-i-te-ree/ *adj* having to do with money (*monetary considerations*).

money /**mu**-nee/ *n* metal coins and printed banknotes used in making payments, buying, and selling.

moneyed /**mu**-need/ *adj* rich (*the moneyed classes*).

moneylender /**mu**-nee-**len**-der/ *n* a person who lives by lending money on condition that interest is paid to him or her for the time of the loan.

mongoose /**mong**-goos/ *n* (*pl* **mongooses** /**mong**-goo-siz/) a small weasel-like animal that kills snakes.

mongrel /**mong**-grel/ *adj* of mixed breed or race (*a mongrel dog*). ● *n* a dog of mixed breed.

monitor /**mon**-i-tor/ *n* **1** in school, a student who helps a teacher to keep order. **2** a device for checking electrical transmission without interfering with it. **3** an instrument that receives and shows continuous information about the working of something. **4** a screen for use with a computer. **5** a small screen in a television studio showing the picture that is being broadcast at any given time. ● *vb* to observe and check something regularly (*monitor the patient's condition*).

monk /mungk/ *n* a man who, with the intention of devoting his life to prayer, joins a religious society and spends his life in a monastery.

monkey /**mung**-kee/ *n* **1** a long-tailed animal resembling a human being in shape. **2** (*inf*) a mischievous child (*the little monkey tricked me*). ● *vb* to play about (with) (*somebody had monkeyed about with the computer*).

monkey puzzle /**mung**-kee **pu**-zul/ *n* an evergreen tree whose branches are covered with short prickly leaves.

mono- /**mon**-oe/ *prefix* one.

monochrome /**mon**-oe-crome/ *adj* in one color, or in black and white (*a monochrome monitor*).

monocle /**mon**-i-cul/ *n* a single eyeglass (*the old colonel always wore a monocle*).

monogamy /mo-**nog**-a-mee/ *n* marriage to one husband or wife only. ● *n* **monogamist** /mo-**nog**-a-mist/. ● *adj* **monogamous** /mo-**nog**-a-mus/.

monogram /**mon**-o-gram/ *n* letters, especially initials, written one on top of another to make a single design (*has his monogram on his T-shirt*).

monolith /**mon**-o-lith/ *n* a single standing stone like a pillar or ornament. ● *adj* **monolithic** /mon-o-**li**-thic/.

monolog /**mon**-o-log/ *n*, *also* **monologue** (*Br, Cdn*) a scene or play in which only one person speaks (*the play closed with a monolog*).

monoplane /**mon**-o-plane/ *n* an airplane with only one pair of wings.

monopolize /mu-**nop**-o-lize/ *vb*, *also* **monopolise** (*Br*) **1** to have or obtain complete possession or control of (*they used to monopolize the ice-cream market there*). **2** to take up the whole of (*monopolizing the teacher's attention*).

monopoly /mu-**nop**-lee/ *n* **1** complete control of the trade in a certain article by a single person or company (*they had a monopoly of the car market once*). **2** possession of or control over something that is not shared by others (*she thinks that she has a monopoly on beauty*).

monosyllable /**mon**-o-si-la-bul/ *n* a word of one syllable (*she was scarcely polite and spoke in monosyllables*). ● *adj* **monosyllabic** /mon-o-si-la-bic/.

monotone /**mon**-o-tone/ *n* a single unvarying tone of voice when speaking (*an audience almost sent to sleep by the speaker's monotone*).

monotonous /mu-**not**-nus/ *adj* **1** dull from lack of variety (*a monotonous job*). **2** in a monotone (*a monotonous voice*).

monotony /mu-**not**-nee/ *n* dullness, lack of variety, sameness (*the monotony of his existence*).

monsoon /mon-**soon**/ *n* a south Asian wind, blowing from the southwest in summer and the northeast in winter, usually bringing heavy rain.

monster /**mon**-ster/ *n* **1** a huge frightening creature (*a fairy tale about sea monsters*). **2** anything huge (*the turnip was a monster/a monster turnip*). **3** an unnaturally cruel or wicked person (*a monster to treat his wife so badly*).

monstrosity /mon-**stros**-i-tee/ *n* something, usually large, that is very ugly (*my aunt left us a monstrosity of a wardrobe*).

monstrous /**mon**-struss/ *adj* **1** huge (*monstrous trucks rushing down the freeway*). **2** unnaturally cruel or wicked (*a monstrous crime*).

montage /**mon**-tazh/ *n* a picture made by putting together many separate images.

month /munth/ n one of the 12 periods of time into which the year is divided.

monthly /munth-lee/ adj happening once a month or every month (a monthly magazine). ● also adv.

monument /mon-yu-ment/ n a statue, stone, etc., set up in memory of a person or event (a monument to the soldiers killed in the war).

monumental /mon-yu-men-tal/ adj 1 huge (a monumental painting covering the whole wall). 2 outstanding (a monumental achievement).

mood /mood/ n 1 a state of the mind and feelings, a person's temper at a certain moment (he is in a bad mood). 2 a state of bad temper (she is in a mood). 3 in grammar, a verb form that tells whether the verb is used to express a command, desire, statement of fact, etc.

moody /moo-dee/ adj tending to change mood suddenly or often, often bad-tempered (moody people). ● adv **moodily** /moo-di-lee/. ● n **moodiness** /moo-dee-ness/.

moon /moon/ n 1 the heavenly body that moves around the earth and reflects the light of the sun. 2 any smaller heavenly body that moves around a larger one. ● vb (inf) to walk about in a dreamy way (mooning about waiting for her boyfriend to ring).

moonbeam /moon-beem/ n a ray of light from the moon.

moonlight /moon-lite/ n the light from the moon (a walk in the moonlight). ● adj **moonlit** /moon-lit/.

moonstone /moon-stone/ n a precious stone, bluish white in color.

moor[1] /moor/ n a large extent of poor land on which only coarse grass, heather, etc., will grow, a heath (the Yorkshire moors).

moor[2] /moor/ vb to fasten a ship by ropes, cables, etc. (moors his yacht at the local harbor).

Moor /moor/ n an Arab inhabitant of Morocco, or any part of northwest Africa. ● adj **Moorish** /moo-rish/.

moorage /moo-ridge/ n a place for mooring a ship (pay for a moorage near his house).

moorcock /moor-cock/, **moorfowl** /moor-foul/ ns the red grouse.

moorhen /moor-hen/ n the water-hen.

mooring /moo-ring/ n, **moorings** /moo-ringz/ npl 1 the ropes, cables, etc., by which a ship is fastened (the moorings came loose). 2 the place where a ship is so fastened.

moorland /moor-land/ n a moor, moors (an area of moorland).

moose /mooss/ n the elk, a type of deer found in North America.

moot /moot/ vb (fml) to put forward for discussion.

moot point /moot-point/ n a matter on which two or more opinions may be upheld, an undecided matter (it's a moot point whose land it is).

mop /mop/ n strips of coarse cloth, yarn, etc., fixed together to a handle and used for washing floors, etc. ● vb (mopped /mopt/, mopping /mop-ing/) to clean with a mop, to wipe (mop the floor).

mope /moap/ vb to be gloomy or sad (a dog moping for its owner).

moral /maw-ral/ adj 1 having to do with what is right or wrong in action (a moral problem). 2 living according to the rules of right conduct (a very moral person). ● n 1 the lesson to be learned from a story (Aesop's fables had morals). 2 **morals** /maw-ralz/ your beliefs as to what is right or wrong in action (he seems to have no morals). 3 **morals** /maw-ralz/ standards of behavior (complain about the morals of the teenagers). ● adv **morally** /maw-ra-lee/.

morale /mu-ral/ n belief in your ability to do what is asked of you, courage (he tried to boost the team's morale by telling them how well they were playing).

moralist /maw-ra-list/ n a person who studies questions of right and wrong.

morality /maw-ra-li-tee/ n 1 moral principles. 2 a particular system of moral principles (Christian morality). 3 the quality of an action, as estimated by a standard of right and wrong.

moralize /maw-ra-lize/ vb, **moralise** (Br) to discuss questions of morals (the minister used his sermon to moralize to his congregation).

morbid /mawr-bid/ adj 1 unhealthy, diseased (a morbid condition of the foot). 2 thinking too much about what is gloomy or disgusting (morbid curiosity/have a morbid view of the future). ● n **morbidity** /mawr-bi-di-tee/. ● adv **morbidly** /mawr-bid-lee/.

more /more/ adj greater in amount, number, etc. (ask for more money). ● also n. ● adv 1 to a greater extent or degree (he has traveled more). 2 again (once more).

morgue /mawrg/ n a mortuary.

Mormon /mawr-mon/ n a member of the Church of Jesus Christ of the Latter-day Saints founded by Joseph Smith in 1830. ● also adj.

morn /mawrn/ n (lit) morning.

morning /mawr-ning/ n the early part of the day (go to work in the morning).

morning star /mawr-ning-star/ n the planet Venus when seen before sunrise.

morocco /mo-**roc**-o/ *n* a fine goatskin leather originally prepared in Morocco.

moron /mo-ron/ *n* **1** a feeble-minded person. **2** (*inf*) a very stupid person (*you were a moron to drive without a license*). ● *adj* **moronic** /mo-**ron**-ic/.

morose /mo-**rose**/ *adj* gloomy and ill-natured (*in a morose mood after he lost the chess match*).

morphia /mawr-fee-a/, **morphine** /mawr-feen/ *ns* a drug made from opium that causes sleep and lessens pain (*addicted to morphia*).

morse /mawrss/ *n* a signaling code in which dots and dashes (or short and long sounds or flashes) represent the letters of the alphabet (*morse code*).

morsel /mawr-sel/ *n* a small piece, a bite (*not able to eat another morsel*).

mortal /mawr-tal/ *adj* **1** having to die (*all humans are mortal*). **2** causing death (*a mortal blow*). ● *n* a human being (*mortals must die*). ● *adv* **mortally** /mawr-ta-lee/.

mortality /mawr-**ta**-li-tee/ *n* **1** the state of being mortal (*mortality is one of the few certain things in life*). **2** the number who die from a certain cause (*infant mortality is still high there*).

mortar /mawr-tar/ *n* **1** a bowl in which substances are crushed into powder (by a pestle) (*she ground the spices in a mortar and pestle*). **2** a gun with a short barrel. **3** a cement made of lime and sand and used in building.

mortar-board /mawr-tar-board/ *n* a square-topped cap worn with an academic gown (*wear a mortar-board for her graduation ceremony*).

mortgage /mawr-gidge/ *n* giving to a person who has lent money the control of certain property that he or she may sell if the loan is not repaid but must return when the loan is repaid in full (*take out a mortgage on their new house*). ● *vb* to give control over property to another to obtain a loan (*mortgaging the house to the buildings and loan*).

mortify /mawr-ti-fie/ *vb* to make ashamed (*she was mortified when she discovered that she was wearing non-matching shoes*). ● *n* **mortification** /mawr-ti-fi-**cay**-shun/.

mortise /mawr-tis/ *n* a hole cut in a piece of wood, etc., so that part of another piece (the tenon) may fit into it (*a mortise lock*).

mortuary /mawr-chu-we-ree/ *n* a building in which dead bodies are kept until burial (*the murdered corpse was removed to the mortuary*).

mosaic /mo-**zay**-ic/ *n* design made by placing together differently colored pieces of glass, stone, etc.

mosque /mosk/ *n* a Muslim place of worship.

mosquito /mo-**skee**-toe/ *n* (*pl* **mosquitoes** /mo-**skee**-toaz/) a stinging insect that sometimes carries the germs of malaria (*her leg swelled up when the mosquito bit her*).

moss /mawss/ *n* a tiny flowerless plant growing on walls and tree trunks and in damp places (*stones covered in moss*).

mossy /maw-see/ *adj* overgrown with moss (*mossy rocks*).

most /moast/ *adj* greatest in number, amount, etc. (*she got most votes/most people believed him*). ● *also n.* ● *adv* **1** in or to the greatest degree or extent (*most importantly*). **2** very (*most accomplished*).

mostly /moast-lee/ *adv* mainly.

motel /mo-tel/ *n* a hotel with special facilities for motorists (*the motel had space for the cars next to the rooms*).

moth /mawth/ *n* **1** a winged insect that flies by night (*moths are like butterflies but not so brightly colored*). **2** the clothes moth (*moths had made holes in the clothing stored in the attic*).

mother /mu-ther/ *n* **1** a female parent. **2** the female head of a convent of nuns. ● *vb* to care for, as would a mother (*mothered the orphans*).

motherhood /mu-ther-hood/ *n* the state of being a mother.

mother-in-law /mu-ther-in-law/ *n* (*pl* **mothers-in-law** /mu-ther-zin-law/) the mother of the person to whom you are married.

motherly /mu-ther-lee/ *adj* like a mother (*a motherly kind of person*).

mother-of-pearl /mu-ther-ov-perl/ *n* the hard pearl-like lining of certain shells (*a jewel box lined with mother-of-pearl*).

mother tongue /mu-ther-tung/ *n* your native language (*English is his mother tongue*).

motif /mo-teef/ *n* a repeated theme in an artistic or a literary work.

motion /mo-shun/ *n* **1** act of moving (*the motion of the boat made her feel sick*). **2** a movement (*with a motion of his hand*). **3** an idea put to a meeting so that it can be voted on (*he proposed the motion that fees be raised*). ● *vb* to make a movement as a sign.

motionless /mo-shun-less/ *adj* unmoving (*the bird lay unmoving on the ground*).

motion picture /mo-shun-pic-shur/ *n* a series of still pictures captured on film which, when run through a projector are displayed as moving pictures; a movie (*the motion picture industry*).

motivate /mo-ti-vate/ *vb* to give a reason or urge to act. ● *n* **motivation** /mo-ti-**vay**-shun/.

motive /mo-tiv/ *n* a reason for doing something. ● *adj* causing movement.

motor /mo-tor/ *n* an engine that by changing power into motion drives a machine (*the car needs a new motor*). ● *adj* causing movement or motion (*the accident affected his motor muscles/a motor nerve*). ● *vb* to travel by motor car (*he motors to work every day*).

motorbike /mo-tor bike/ *n* a bicycle driven by a motor. ● *similarly* **motor-boat** /mo-tor boat/, **motor car** /mo-tor car/.

motorist /mo-tu-rist/ *n* a person who drives a motor car (*a motorist driving without a license*).

motorway /mo-tur-way/ (*Br*) *see* **freeway**.

mottle /mot-ul/ *vb* to mark with spots or blotches (*have a mottled complexion*).

motto /mot-oe/ *n* (*pl* **mottoes** /mot-oaz/) **1** a wise saying that can be used as a rule of life (*"Early to bed, early to rise" is his motto*). **2** the word or words on a coat of arms. **3** a printed saying (*mottoes in fortune cookies*).

mound /mound/ *n* **1** a low hill. **2** a heap of earth or stones.

mount /mount/ *n* **1** (*usually in names*) a hill, a mountain (*Mount Everest*). **2** an animal, especially a horse, for riding (*he chose a mount*). **3** a card or paper surrounding a painting or photograph. ● *vb* **1** to go up, to climb (*mount the ladder*). **2** to get on to (*mount the bus*). **3** to place in position (*mount the photograph*). **4** to get on horseback (*mount the chestnut horse*).

mountain /moun-tin/ *n* **1** a high hill (*the highest mountain in the United States*). **2** a large heap (*a mountain of garbage*).

mountain ash /moun-ti-nash/ *n* a type of tree, the rowan.

mountaineer /moun-ti-neer/ *n* a person who climbs mountains (*mountaineers climbing Everest*). ● *n* **mountaineering** /moun-ti-nee-ring/.

mountainous /moun-ti-nus/ *adj* **1** having many mountains (*a mountainous region*). **2** huge (*a mountainous man*).

mounted /moun-tid/ *adj* on horseback (*mounted police*).

mourn /moarn/ *vb* to show sorrow, to feel grief, especially after a loss or death (*mourning her dead sister/she mourns his death*). ● *n* **mourner** /moar-ner/.

mournful /moarn-ful/ *adj* sad, sorrowful (*a mournful expression*). ● *adv* **mournfully** /moarn-ful-ee/.

mourning /moar-ning/ *n* **1** sorrow, grief (*her mourning for her dead sister*) **2** black clothing worn as a sign of grief for another's death (*the widow was wearing mourning*).

mouse /mouse/ *n* (*pl* **mice** /mice/) **1** a small rodent animal found in houses or in the fields. **2** (*computing*) (*pl* **mouses** /mouses/, **mice** /mice/) a handheld device which allows the user to control some computer functions without the keyboard.

moustache *see* **mustache.**

mouth /mouth/ *n* **1** the opening in the face for eating and uttering sounds (*she opened her mouth to scream*). **2** the opening into anything hollow (*the mouth of the jar*). **3** the part of a river where it flows into the sea. ● *vb* to twist the mouth into different shapes (*mouth the answer silently to him*).

mouthful /mouth-ful/ *n* the amount placed in the mouth at one time (*eat the cake in two mouthfuls*).

mouthpiece /mouth-peess/ *n* **1** the part of a musical instrument or pipe placed in the mouth. **2** a person who speaks for others.

movable, moveable /moo-va-bul/ *adj* able to be moved (*movable property*). ● *npl* **movables** /moo-va-bulz/ property that can be moved, especially furniture.

move /moov/ *vb* **1** to cause to change place or position (*move the chairs to the next room*). **2** to go from one place to another (*she moved from the chair to the sofa*). **3** to change houses (*they are moving to Philadelphia*). **4** to set in motion. **5** to stir up the feelings (*her performance moved them deeply*). **6** to rouse to action (*she moved them to protest*). **7** at a meeting, to put forward an idea to be voted on (*he moved that they sell the building*). ● *n* **1** a change of position or place. **2** a change of house (*their second move in one year*). **3** an action (*wonder what his next move will be*). **4** in chess, etc., the act of moving a piece.

movement /moov-ment/ *n* **1** act of moving (*police are watching his movements*). **2** change of position (*the sudden movement made the dog bark*). **3** a number of people working for the same purpose (*the women's movement*). **4** a complete part of a long musical work (*the slow movement*).

movie /moo-vee/ *n* a cinema picture, a motion picture. ● *npl:* **the movies** a showing of a motion picture (*let's go to the movies*).

moving /moo-ving/ *adj* stirring up the feelings (*a moving story/the moving sight of the little girl in tears*).

moving picture /moo-ving pic-chur/ *n* a cinema picture, a movie.

mow /moe/ *vb* (*pp* **mown** /moan/) **1** to cut (grass) (*mowing the lawn*). **2** to knock down, to kill in large numbers (*a group of children mown down by a huge truck*).

mower /moe-er/ *n* a person or machine that mows (*a lawn mower*).

much /much/ *adj* great in amount or quantity (*not much money*). ● *n* a great amount (*he does not earn much*). ● *adv* greatly.

muck /muck/ *n* (*inf*) wet filth, dirt. ● *vb* (*inf*) **1** to dirty. **2** to make a mess of (*muck up the clean kitchen*). **3** to spoil (*muck up our plans*). **4** to bungle (*muck up the interview*).

mucky /mu-kee/ *adj* (*inf*) filthy (*children with mucky hands*).

mucous /myoo-cus/ *adj* producing mucus, slimy.

mucous membrane /myoo-cus mem-brane/ *n* the inner skin lining the nose, mouth, etc.

mucus /myoo-cus/ *n* the shiny liquid coming from the mucous membrane of the nose (*the mucus that comes from your nose when you have a cold*).

mud /mud/ *n* soft, wet earth (*cars stuck in the mud*).

muddle /mu-dul/ *vb* **1** to confuse (*she felt a bit muddled about the directions*). **2** to mix up (*she muddled the dates*). **3** to act without plan (*muddling through the meeting*). ● *n* confusion, disorder.

muddy /mu-dee/ *adj* covered with mud (*muddy clothing*). ● *vb* **1** to make dirty or muddy (*dirt muddying water*). **2** to make unclear.

muesli /myoo-zlee/ *n* a kind of breakfast cereal consisting of grains, nuts, and dried fruit.

muff[1] /muff/ *n* a cover of warm material (often fur) for both hands (*gloves are usually worn now instead of muffs*).

muff[2] /muff/ *vb* (*inf*) **1** to fail to hold (*muff a catch at baseball*). **2** to do badly (*given an opportunity to succeed but muffed it*).

muffin /mu-fin/ *n* an individual sweet quick bread, usually eaten warm.

muffle /mu-ful/ *vb* **1** to wrap up to keep warm (*children muffled up in scarves and hats*). **2** to deaden sound (*a gag muffling his cries*). **3** to make a sound less loud (*muffle the sound of the car's exhaust*).

muffler /mu-fler/ *n* **1** a warm scarf. **2** a device that makes a sound less loud, especially in a car's exhaust system.

mug[1] /mug/ *n* a drinking vessel with a handle and more or less straight sides (*a mug of coffee*).

mug[2] /mug/ *n* (*inf*) a gangster or thug. ● *vb* (**mugged**

/mugd/, **mugging** /mu-ging/) to attack and rob (*I was mugged at knifepoint*). ● *n* **mugger** /mu-ger/.

muggy /mu-gee/ *adj* unpleasantly warm and damp (*muggy weather*).

mulberry /mul-ber-ee/ *n* **1** a tree bearing dark red edible berries. **2** a dark reddish purple color.

mule /myool/ *n* the offspring of an ass and a horse, supposedly famous for its stubbornness (*used a mule to carry their load/stubborn as a mule*).

mulish /myoo-lish/ *adj* stubborn (*too mulish to admit that she is in the wrong*). ● *n* **mulishness** / myoo-lish-ness/.

mull[1] /mull/ *vb*. ● **mull over** to think carefully about (*mull over your proposal*).

mull[2] /mull/ *vb* to heat, sweeten, and spice (wine, ale, etc.) (*have mulled wine at Christmas*).

mullet /mu-let/ *n* an edible sea fish.

mullion /mul-yin/ *n* an upright bar between the divisions of a window.

multi- /mul-tee/ *prefix* many.

multicolored /mul-tee-cu-lurd/ *adj* of many colors (*multicolored summer shirts*).

multilateral /mul-tee-lat-ral/ *adj* **1** having many sides. **2** (*fml*) concerning more than two groups (*a multilateral agreement*).

multimedia /mul-tee-mee-dee-ya/ *adj* **1** using several different methods and media (*a multimedia approach to advertising*). **2** in computing, using sound and video images as well as data.

multiple /mul-ti-pul/ *adj* **1** having or affecting many parts (*accident victims receive multiple injuries*). **2** involving many things of the same kind (*a multiple crash on the freeway*). ● *n* a number that contains another an exact number of times (*12 is a multiple of 4*).

multiplex /mul-ti-pleks/ *n* a building that contains several movie theaters.

multiplier /mul-ti-plie-er/ *n* the number by which another is multiplied.

multiply /mul-ti-plie/ *vb* **1** to find the number obtained by adding a number to itself a certain number of times (*if you multiply 4 by 3 you get 12*). **2** to increase (*their misfortunes seem to multiply/multiplied their chances of success*).

multitude /mul-ti-tood/ *n* **1** (*old*) a crowd (*the leader spoke to the multitude*). **2** a great number (*a multitude of objections*).

multitudinous /mul-ti-tood-nus/ *adj* (*fml or hum*) very many (*his multitudinous relatives*).

mum /mum/ *adj* silent (*keep mum*). ● *n* (*Br*) *see* **mom.**

mumble /mum-bul/ *vb* to speak in a low, indistinct

voice (*mumbling the answer so that the teacher could not hear her*).

mumbo-jumbo /mum-bo-**jum**-bo/ *n* meaningless talk.

mummy[1] /**mu**-mee/ *n* a human body kept from decay by being treated with certain drugs and wrapped tightly in cloth (*Egyptian mummies*). ● *vb* **mummify** /**mu**-mi-fie/.

mummy[2] /**mu**-mee/ (*Br*) *see* **mommy**.

mumps /**mumps**/ *n* an infectious disease that causes swelling of the neck and face (*in bed with mumps*).

munch /**munch**/ *vb* to chew noisily, to crush with teeth (*munch cookies/munch on an apple*).

mundane /mun-**dane**/ *adj* **1** (*fml*) having to do with this world (*mundane, not spiritual, pleasure*). **2** ordinary, with nothing exciting or unusual (*a mundane job*).

municipal /myoo-**ni**-si-pal/ *adj* having to do with a city or town (*municipal buildings*).

municipality /myoo-ni-si-**pa**-li-tee/ *n* a city or town with certain powers of self-government.

munificent /myoo-**ni**-fi-sent/ *adj* (*fml*) generous (*a munificent gift of diamonds*). ● *n* **munificence** /myoo-**ni**-fi-sense/.

munitions /myoo-**ni**-shunz/ *npl* the guns, shells, etc., used in making war (*a munitions factory*).

mural /**myoo**-ral/ *n* a painting that is painted directly on to the walls of a building (*a mural in the hospital corridor showing people being healed*).

murder /**mur**-der/ *n* act of unlawfully and intentionally killing another (*commit murder*). ● *also vb.* ● *ns* **murderer** /**mur**-de-rer/, **murderess** /**mur**-de-ress/.

murderous /**mur**-de-rus/ *adj* **1** used to commit murder (*murderous thugs*). **2** cruel, savage (*a murderous attack*).

murky /**mur**-kee/ *adj* **1** dark, gloomy (*a murky night*). **2** vague or obscure (*he has a murky past*).

murmur /**mur**-mur/ *n* **1** a low, indistinct sound, as of running water (*the murmur of the stream*). **2** a soft, low continuous sound (*a murmur of voices in the next room*). **3** a grumble (*murmurs against his handling of the situation*). ● *vb* **1** to make a low indistinct sound. **2** to talk in a low voice (*he murmured something in his sleep*). **3** to grumble (*murmur about their lack of money*).

muscle /**mu**-sul/ *n* the elastic fibers in the body that enable it to make movements (*strain a muscle by lifting a heavy weight*).

muscular /**mu**-skyu-lar/ *adj* **1** having well-developed muscles, strong (*a muscular young man*). **2** having to do with muscles (*muscular strain*).

muse[1] /**myooz**/ *n* **1** in legend, one of the nine goddesses of the arts and learning. **2** (*fml*) inspiration to write (e.g., poetry) (*the muse deserted him*).

muse[2] /**myooz**/ *vb* to think deeply about, to ponder (*musing on the events of the day*).

museum /myoo-**zee**-um/ *n* a building in which objects of scientific, artistic, or literary interest are kept (*the ancient tools in the museum*).

mushroom /**mush**-room/ *n* an edible plant with a soft whitish pulpy top (*steak in mushroom sauce*). ● *vb* to grow in size very rapidly (*new supermarkets mushrooming*).

music /**myoo**-zic/ *n* **1** the art of arranging sounds to give melody or harmony (*studying music*). **2** the sounds so arranged when played, sung, or written down (*orchestral music*).

musical /**myoo**-zi-cal/ *adj* **1** having to do with music. **2** pleasant-sounding (*a musical voice*). ● *n* a play or a movie that includes a lot of songs. ● *adv* **musically** /**myoo**-zi-ca-lee/.

musician /myoo-zi-shun/ *n* a person who is skilled in music (*the musicians in the orchestra*).

musk /**musk**/ *n* a sweet-smelling substance obtained from the musk deer and used in making perfume.

musket /**mus**-ket/ *n* (*old*) a handgun formerly carried by soldiers.

musketeer /**mus**-ke-teer/ *n* (*old*) a soldier armed with a musket.

muskrat /**musk**-rat/ *n* a large water rat found in North America.

musky /**mus**-kee/ *adj* smelling of musk (*a perfume with a musky smell*).

Muslim /**muz**-lim/ *n* a person who follows the religion known as Islam. ● *also adj.*

muslin /**muz**-lin/ *n* a fine, thin cotton cloth.

musquash /**muz**-kwawsh/ *n* the fur of the muskrat.

mussel *n* an edible shellfish enclosed in a double shell (*have mussels as a first course*).

must /**must**/ *vb* to have to (*I must go home now*).

mustache, moustache /**mus**-tash/ *n* the hair growing on the upper lip (*he had a black mustache*).

mustang /**mus**-tang/ *n* a wild horse native to the United States, descended from horses brought by the Spanish.

mustard /**mus**-tard/ *n* **1** a plant with hot-tasting seeds. **2** a type of seasoning made from these for flavoring food, especially meat (*spread mustard on the beef sandwiches*).

musty /**mu**-stee/ *adj* stale (*a musty smell in the old house/the musty smell of old books*).

mutable /**myoo**-ta-bul/ *adj* (*fml*) changeable (*mutable attitudes*).

mutation /myoo-**tay**-shun/ *n* change, alteration (*new kinds of plants can sometimes be caused by mutation of the genes*). ● *n* **mutant** /**myoo**-tant/.

mute /**myoot**/ *adj* 1 silent (*a mute appeal for mercy*). 2 unable to speak (*mute since birth*). 3 not pronounced (*a mute "l" has no sound*). ● *n* 1 a dumb person. 2 an attachment that lessens or modifies the sound of a musical instrument.

muted /**myoo**-tid/ *adj* 1 having the sound altered by a mute. 2 subdued (*muted enthusiasm*). 3 soft in hue, shade, etc. (*muted colors*).

mutilate /**myoo**-ti-late/ *vb* to damage seriously by removing a part, especially a limb (*the murderer mutilated the corpse*). ● *n* **mutilation** /myoo-ti-**lay**-shun/.

mutineer /myoo-ti-**neer**/ *n* a person who takes part in a mutiny.

mutinous /**myoo**-ti-nus/ *adj* 1 taking part in a mutiny (*the mutinous sailors*). 2 obstinate and sulky, as if going to disobey (*mutinous children objecting to the cancellation of the party*).

mutiny /**myoo**-ti-nee/ *n* refusal to obey those in charge, especially a rising of people in the armed services against their officers (*a mutiny of sailors protesting about poor food*). ● *also vb*.

mutter /**mu**-ter/ *vb* to speak in a low voice, without sounding the vowels clearly, especially when grumbling or insulting (*mutter a complaint*). ● *also n*.

mutton /**mu**-tun/ *n* the flesh of sheep as meat (*roast mutton*).

mutual /**myoo**-chu-wal/ *adj* 1 given and received in the same degree by those concerned (*mutual help/their dislike was mutual*). 2 common to, or shared by, two or more persons or parties (*a mutual back garden for the apartment block*). ● *adv* **mutually** /**myoo**-chu-wa-lee/.

muzzle /**mu**-zul/ *n* 1 the mouth and nose of an animal (*a black dog with a gray muzzle*). 2 a cage or set of straps fastened on an animal's mouth to prevent it biting (*the dog was apt to attack people and so it was made to wear a muzzle*). 3 the open end of a gun. ● *vb* 1 to put a muzzle on an animal's mouth. 2 to prevent from speaking freely.

my /**mie**/ *adj* belonging to me (*I cut my finger*).

myopia /mie-**oe**-pee-a/ *n* short-sightedness (*her myopia makes distant objects look blurry*).

myopic /mie-**op**-ic/ *adj* short-sighted (*too myopic to recognize people across the street*).

myriad /**mi**-ree-ad/ *n* a very large number (*a myriad of reasons*). ● *also adj*.

myrrh /**mur**/ *n* 1 a tree from which is obtained a sweet-smelling gum. 2 the gum so obtained.

myrtle /**mur**-tul/ *n* an evergreen shrub with sweet-smelling white flowers.

myself /mie-**self**/ *pron* (*used reflexively or for emphasis*) me (*I hurt myself*).

mysterious /mi-**stee**-ree-us/ *adj* difficult to understand or explain (*the mysterious stranger/his mysterious behavior*). ● *adv* **mysteriously** /mi-**stee**-ree-us-lee/.

mystery /**mi**-ste-ree/ *n* 1 a religious truth that cannot be fully understood by the human mind. 2 anything difficult to understand or explain (*his background was a mystery*). 3 a secret way of doing something, known only to a few (*the mysteries of making whiskey*).

mystic /**mi**-stic/ *adj* having to do with religious mysteries or secrets (*mystic rites*). ● *n* a person who believes that through prayer or sympathy he or she has understood in part the mysteries of life and the existence of God.

mystical /**mi**-sti-cal/ *adj* mystic (*mystical beliefs*).

mysticism /**mi**-sti-si-zum/ *n* the beliefs or practices of a mystic.

mystify /**mi**-sti-fie/ *vb* to puzzle, to bewilder (*mystified by his odd behavior*). ● *n* **mystification** /mi-sti-fi-**cay**-shun/.

mystique /mi-**steek**/ *n* a mysterious quality.

myth /**mith**/ *n* 1 a story about the gods or goddesses of ancient peoples, especially one containing their beliefs about the facts of nature. 2 something that is popularly thought to be true but is not (*the myth that elephants have good memories*).

mythical /**mi**-thi-cal/ *adj* existing in myths or legends, imaginary (*mythical creatures such as dragons*).

mythologist /mi-**thol**-o-jist/ *n* a person who studies myths.

mythology /mi-**thol**-o-jee/ *n* 1 a collection of myths (*in Scandinavian mythology*). 2 the study of myths. ● *adj* **mythological** /mi-tho-**lodge**-ic-al/.

N

N, n /**en**/ the fourteenth letter of the alphabet.

nab /**nab**/ *vb* (*inf*) (**nabbed** /**nabd**/, **nabbing** /**na**-bing/) **1** to catch or capture. **2** to arrest (*police nabbed the criminal*).

nachos /**na**-choaz/ *n* tortilla chips spread with a mixture, such as beans, beef, peppers, onions, etc., covered with cheese, and then broiled.

nag[1] /**nag**/ *n* a horse, especially a small, weak, or old one (*he rents out horses but they are just nags*).

nag[2] /**nag**/ *vb* (**nagged** /**nagd**/, **nagging** /**na**-ging/) to keep on annoying or finding fault with (*nag the boy into getting a haircut*).

nail /**nail**/ *n* **1** the horny growth on the tips of the fingers or toes. **2** the claw of a bird or animal. **3** a thin piece of metal with a pointed end and a flattened head, used for joining together pieces of wood (*hammer a nail into the wall to hang the picture from*). ● *vb* to fasten with a nail (*nail a sign to the post*).

nail-biter /**nail**-bie-ter/ *n* a situation or activity, such as a movie or sports game, that has such an uncertain outcome that it creates a lot of anxiety and nervousness. ● *adj* **nail-biting** /**nail**-bie-ting/.

nailbrush /**nail**-brush/ *n* a small, stiff brush for cleaning fingernails and toenails.

nail file /**nail**-file/ *n* a small, flat file for smoothing and shaping fingernails and toenails.

nail head /**nail**-hed/ *n* the flattened end of a nail.

nail set /**nail**-set/ *n* a tool used to drive the head of a nail even with or below the wood surface.

naïve /**na**-eev/ *adj* **1** simple and natural, innocent (*naïve young girls*). **2** ignorantly simple, too trustful (*naïve enough to believe he really was a prince*). ● *n* **naïveté** /**na**-ee-vi-tee/. ● *n* **naïf** /**na**-eef/ a naïve person.

naked /**nay**-ked/ *adj* **1** wearing no clothes (*naked when taking a bath*). **2** uncovered (*a naked flame*). **3** plain, unconcealed (*the naked truth*). ● *n* **nakedness** /**nay**-ked-ness/.

name /**name**/ *n* **1** the word by which a person or thing is known. **2** reputation (*make a name for himself in the art world*). ● *vb* **1** to give a name to (*naming the baby Alice*). **2** to speak about by name (*name all the presidents of the United States*). ● *adj* **1** having a good reputation (*a name brand*). **2** carrying a name (*a name tag*).

nameless /**name**-less/ *adj* **1** unknown (*a nameless poet of the twelfth century*). **2** having no name

(*nameless graves*). **3** wanting his/her name to be concealed (*the giver of the money wishes to remain nameless*). **4** too bad to be mentioned by name (*nameless acts of cruelty*).

namely /**name**-lee/ *adv* that is to say (*only one student was absent, namely Peter*).

nameplate /**name**-plate/ *n* a metal or wooden plate on which the name of a person, firm, etc., is engraved (*polish the nameplate on the door*).

namesake /**name**-sake/ *n* a person with the same name as another (*her niece is her namesake*).

nan /**nan**/ *n* a kind of flat bread of India made with white flour.

nana /**na**-na/ *n* a child's term for grandmother.

nanny /**na**-nee/ *n* a person employed to take care of children, a children's nurse (*their mother works and they have a full-time nanny*).

nanny goat /**na**-nee-goat/ *n* a female goat.

nanogram /**na**-no-gram/ *n* one-billionth of a gram.

nanosecond /**na**-no-se-cond/ *n* one-billionth of a second.

nap[1] /**nap**/ *n* a short sleep, a doze (*have a nap after lunch*). ● *vb* (**napped** /**napt**/, **napping** /**na**-ping/) to take a short sleep. ● **caught napping** taken by surprise (*the police were caught napping and the bank robbers escaped*).

nap[2] /**nap**/ *n* the woolly or hairy surface of cloth.

nape /**nape**/ *n* the back part of the neck (*hair cut close at the nape of the neck*).

napkin /**nap**-kin/ *n* a small cloth or paper used at the table to keep the clothes clean (*a tablecloth with matching napkins*).

narcissism /**nar**-si-si-zum/ *n* too much interest in a person's own appearance, comfort, importance, etc. ● *adj* **narcissistic** /nar-si-si-stic/. ● *n* **narcissist** /**nar**-si-sist/ a person who is like this.

narcissus /**nar**-si-sus/ *n* (*pl* **narcissi** /nar-si-sie/) a flower of the daffodil family, but with white petals.

narcotic /**nar**-cot-ic/ *n* a drug that causes sleep and eases pain (*addicted to narcotics such as opium*). ● *adj* causing sleep.

narrate /**nar-rate**/ *vb* to tell (a story) (*narrating his adventures in Africa*).

narration /**nar-ray**-shun/ *n* a story, the act of telling a story.

narrative /**na**-ra-tiv/ *adj* **1** telling a story (*a narrative poem*). **2** having to do with storytelling (*her narrative technique*). ● *n* a story.

narrator /na-**ray**-tor/ *n* the teller of a story (*the narrator in the book was the main character*).

narrow /na-ro/ *adj* **1** not broad, measuring little from side to side (*a very narrow bridge/narrow ribbon*). **2** (*also* **narrow-minded**) unwilling to accept new ideas or ways of doing things (*narrow views on education*). **3** not extensive, not wide-ranging (*narrow interests*). **4** only just avoiding the opposite result (*a narrow escape*). ● *n* (*usually pl*) a narrow part of a river or sea. ● *vb* to make or become narrow (*the road suddenly narrows/narrow the street*).

narrowly /na-ro-lee/ *adv* barely, only just (*narrowly escape death*).

narwhal /nar-wal/ *n* a type of whale with one large tusk.

NASA /na-sa/ *abbr* = **National Aeronautics and Space Administration**: the organization in the United States that deals with space travel and exploration.

nasal /**nay**-zal/ *adj* **1** having to do with the nose (*nasal infections*). **2** sounded through the nose (*a nasal accent*). ● *n* a vowel or consonant so sounded.

nasty /na-stee/ *adj* **1** unpleasant. **2** dirty. **3** disagreeable. **4** unkind. ● *n* **nastiness**.

natal /**nay**-tal/ *adj* (*fml*) having to do with birth.

nation /**nay**-shun/ *n* all the people belonging to one country and living under the same government (*nations getting together to prevent war*).

national /na-shnal/ *adj* **1** having to do with a nation (*the maple leaf is the national emblem of Canada*). **2** of concern to all the people in a country (*national rather than local issues*).

nationalism /**na**-shna-li-zum/ *n* devotion to a person's own country, excessive patriotism, the belief that national interests are more important than international interests.

nationalist /**na**-shna-list/ *n* a person who has great pride in and love of his or her country and considers it superior to others.

nationality /na-shu-**na**-li-tee/ *n* membership of a particular nation (*her nationality is French*).

nationalize /**na**-shna-lize/ *vb, also* **nationalise** (*Br*) to transfer ownership and control of land, resources, industry, etc. to the national government.

national monument /**na**-shnal **mon**-yu-ment/ *n* a natural feature or historic site such as a mountain, canyon, old fort, etc., that is preserved by the government for the public to visit.

national park /**na**-shnal-**park**/ *n* an area of scenic beauty or historical interest that is preserved by the government for the public to visit.

national seashore /**na**-shnal **see**-shore/ *n* any of the coastal areas with beaches, fishing, etc. reserved by the government for public use.

nationwide /**nay**-shun-**wide**/ *adj* by or throughout the whole nation.

native /**nay**-tiv/ *adj* **1** of the place where one was born (*his native language*). **2** belonging to a country (*a native plant*). ● *n* (*now often considered offensive*) an original inhabitant of a place.

Native American /**nay**-tiv ah-**mer**-i-cans/ *n* one of the people, and their descendants, that originally occupied North and South America before Europeans began to settle there. ● *also adj*.

nativity /na-**ti**-vi-tee/ *n* birth, especially with reference to place, time, or conditions. ● **the Nativity** the birth of Jesus.

natural /**na**-chu-ral/ *adj* **1** not caused or altered by humans, occurring in nature. **2** born in a person (*natural musical talents*). **3** normal (*natural in a boy of that age*). **4** real, genuine (*a natural blonde*). **5** (*mus*) neither sharp nor flat. ● *n* **1** (*old*) an idiot. **2** (*inf*) a person who is naturally good at something (*as a singer, he's a natural*). **3** (*mus*) a natural note and the mark by which it is shown.

natural gas /**na**-chu-ral **gas**/ *n* a gas that occurs naturally and is often used for fuel.

natural history /**na**-chu-ral **hi**-stree/ *n* the study of the earth and all that grows on it.

naturalism /**na**-chu-ra-li-zum/ *n* **1** action or thought based on natural desires. **3** the belief that the natural world is all that exists and that there is no spiritual world dealing with creation or control. **3** the belief that all religious truth can be gotten from the natural world.

naturalist /**na**-chu-ra-list/ *n* one who studies plant and animal life (*naturalists collecting wild flowers*).

naturalize /**na**-chu-ra-lize/ *vb, also* **naturalise** (*Br*) to accept someone as a member of a nation to which he or she does not belong by birth (*he was not born in the United States, but he is a naturalized US citizen*). ● *n* **naturalization** /na-chu-ra-li-**zay**-shun/, *also* **naturalisation** (*Br*).

naturally /**na**-chu-ra-lee/ *adv* **1** in a natural way (*she's naturally beautiful and does not need makeup*). **2** of course (*naturally, he will be paid for the work he has done*).

natural resource /**na**-chu-ral ri-**zoarse**/ *n* a form of wealth supplied by nature, such as coal, oil, water power, etc.

natural science /**na**-chu-ral **sie**-enss/ *n* any of the branches of knowledge and study of nature, which includes zoology, chemistry, geology, etc.

natural selection /na-chu-ral si-**lec**-shun/ *n* the process by which a kind of animal or plant will take on certain features and not others to help it adapt to its surroundings.

nature /**nay**-chur/ *n* **1** all existing and happening in the universe that is not the work of humans, such as plants, animals, mountains, lakes, etc. **2** the sum of those qualities that make any creature or thing different from others (*the nature of the new drug*). **3** the character of a person (*a sweet nature*). **4** kind, sort (*the nature of his injuries*).

naught /nawt/ *n* (*old or lit*) nothing (*his plans came to naught*).

naughty /**naw**-tee/ *adj* mischievous, badly behaved (*naughty children/children punished for being naughty*). ● *n* **naughtiness** /**naw**-tee-ness/.

nausea /**naw**-zee-ya/ *n* **1** a feeling of sickness, as if needing to vomit (*feel nausea as the boat rocked*). **2** great disgust (*vegetarians filled with nausea at the thought of eating meat*).

nauseate /**naw**-zee-ate/ *vb* **1** to sicken (*nauseated by the smell of the rotting meat*). **2** to disgust (*nauseated by the terrible murder*).

nauseous /**naw**-shess/ *adj* disgusting, sickening.

nautical /**naw**-ti-cal/ *adj* having to do with the sea, sailors, or ships (*a nautical way of life*).

nautical mile /**naw**-ti-cal **mile**/ *n* a unit for measuring distance at sea; about 1.2 miles, or about 6076 feet (1.8 kilometers).

nautilus /**naw**-ti-lus/ *n* a sea creature living in a shell that twists round in a spiral.

Navajo /**na**-va-ho/ *n* a member of a Native American people living in Arizona, New Mexico, and Utah, the language of this people.

naval /**nay**-vul/ *adj* having to do with a navy or warships (*a naval career/a naval officer*).

nave¹ /nave/ *n* the main part of a church where people worship (*the nave in the church is between two aisles*).

nave² /nave/ *n* the central part of a wheel.

navel /**nay**-vul/ *n* **1** a little scar, sometimes shaped like a hollow, in the center of the belly where, before birth, a baby is attached to its mother (*some people wear a jewel in the navel for decoration*). **2** any centrally located part of place.

navigable /**na**-vi-ga-bul/ *adj* that can be steered, that ships can sail through (*navigable waters*).

navigate /**na**-vi-gate/ *vb* **1** to steer, to sail (a ship) (*navigating the ship between the dangerous rocks*). **2** to work out the correct course for a ship, aircraft, etc., and direct it on that course (*looking for someone to navigate in the yacht race*).

navigation /**na**-vi-**gay**-shun/ *n* **1** the science of working out the course or position of a ship, aircraft, etc. **2** act of sailing a ship.

navigator /**na**-vi-gay-tor/ *n* a person who navigates (*employed as a ship's navigator*).

navy /**nay**-vee/ *n* the warships of a nation, their crews, and their equipment.

navy blue /**nay**-vee **blue**/ *adj* very dark blue (*a navy blue uniform*).

Nazi /**nat**-see/ *n* a political party, or one of its followers, in Germany between 1919 and 1945. It took control of the country in 1933 under Adolph Hitler and promoted nationalism, racism, and political aggression. The party was dissolved after World War II in 1945. ● *adj* referring to this time, party, belief system, etc. (*in Nazi Germany there was much hardship*).

Neanderthal /nee-**an**-der-tawl/ *adj* of a form of early human being. ● *n* **1** a Neanderthal human being. **2** a crude, primitive person.

Neapolitan /nee-ya-**pol**-i-tan/ *adj* **1** of Naples. **2** of various flavors and colors (*Neapolitan ice cream*). ● *n* **1** a person from Naples. **2** ice creams of various flavors served together, usually vanilla, chocolate, and strawberry.

near /neer/ *adj* **1** close, not distant in time or place (*the station is near/her birthday is near*). **2** only just missed or avoided (*a near miss/a near accident*). ● *prep* close to. ● *adv* almost. ● *vb* to approach.

nearby /**neer**-bie/ *adj, adv* near, close by.

nearer /**nee**-rer/ *adv, adj, prep* less distant from (*a planet nearer the sun than the Earth*).

nearest /**nee**-rest/ *adv, adj, prep* least distant from (*Mercury is nearest to the sun*).

nearly /**neer**-lee/ *adv* almost (*he nearly died/it's nearly time to go*).

nearsighted /neer-**sie**-ted/ *adj* short-sighted, having better vision for near objects than for distant ones (*he is nearsighted and unable to see numbers on buses as they approach*).

neat /neet/ *adj* **1** tidily arranged (*a neat room/neat appearance*). **2** skillfully done or made (*a neat job*). **3** not mixed with anything, said of alcoholic drinks. ● *n* **neatness** /**neet**-ness/. ● *vb* **neaten** /**nee**-ten/.

nebula /**ne**-byu-la/ *n* (*pl* **nebulae** /**ne**-byu-lay/) a cloudy patch in the night sky, sometimes caused by a number of very distant stars.

nebulous /**ne**-byu-lus/ *adj* not clear, cloudy (*plans that are rather nebulous/only a nebulous idea of the work involved*).

necessary /**ne**-si-se-ree/ *adj* needed, unavoidable, that cannot be done without (*take the necessary classes/it will be necessary for all of us to go*). ● *adv* **necessarily** /ne-si-se-ri-lee/.

necessitate /ni-**se**-si-tate/ *vb* to make necessary (*lack of money necessitated a reduction in staff*).

necessity /ni-**se**-si-tee/ *n* **1** that which a person needs (*have money only for the necessities of life*). **2** the condition of being necessary or unavoidable (*is there any necessity to employ more staff*). **3** events forcing a person to act or behave in a certain way (*necessity made him take a low-paying job*).

neck /neck/ *n* **1** the part of the body joining the head to the shoulders (*broke his neck in the accident*). **2** the narrow part near the mouth of a bottle. **3** a narrow strip of land joining two larger masses of land. ● **neck and neck** exactly level (*the two horses are neck and neck approaching the finish*).

neckband /**neck**-band/ *n* a band worn around the neck.

neckerchief /**ne**-ker-chif/ *n* a large handkerchief or scarf worn around the neck.

necklace /**ne**-cliss/ *n* a chain of gold, silver, etc. or a string of beads or jewels worn around the neck (*diamond necklaces*).

neckline /**ne**-cline/ *n* the line formed by the edge of a piece of clothing around or nearest the neck.

neckpiece /**neck**-peess/ *n* a decorative scarf, especially of fur.

necktie /**neck**-tie/ *n* (*usually* **tie**) a band of cloth worn around the neck, under the shirt collar, and tied in the front (*wear a black necktie at the funeral*).

nectar /**nec**-tar/ *n* **1** in Greek legend, the drink of the gods. **2** a sweet liquid found in flowers (*bees collecting nectar*). **3** a delicious drink (*a cup of tea seemed like nectar to the tired woman*).

nectarine /**nec**-ta-reen/ *n* a type of peach with a smooth skin.

need /need/ *n* **1** a want (*in need of food*). **2** that which one requires (*people with few needs*). **3** poverty (*families living in need*). ● *vb* **1** to be in want of, to require (*they need food and warm clothing/need help*). **2** to have to (*they will need to work harder*).

needful /**need**-ful/ *adj* necessary (*take the needful steps to avoid infection*).

needle /**nee**-dul/ *n* **1** a small, sharply pointed piece of steel used for drawing thread through cloth in sewing. **2** a short, pointed stick used for knitting wool. **3** a small metal pointer on a dial, compass, etc. **4** the long pointed leaf of a pine tree, fir, etc. (*needles falling off the Christmas tree*).

needlepoint /**nee**-dul-point/ *n* decorative sewing done with thread on canvas used for pillow covers, decorative hangings, etc.

needless /**need**-less/ *adj* not needed, unnecessary (*inflict needless suffering on animals*).

needlework /**nee**-dul-wurk/ *n* sewing done by hand with a needle such as crocheting, embroidering, knitting, etc. (*take needlework at school*).

needy /**nee**-dee/ *adj* poor, living in want (*give food to needy families*).

negate /ni-**gate**/ *vb* (*fml*) **1** to deny (*negate his accuser's statement*). **2** to cause to have no effect (*negating all their attempts to improve the situation*).

negation /ni-**gay**-shun/ *n* **1** a denial. **2** a word or phrase saying no.

negative /**ne**-ga-tiv/ *adj* **1** saying no (*a negative reply*). **2** criticizing, but putting forward no alternative plan or idea (*a negative report*). ● *n* **1** a word like no, not, etc., expressing refusal or denial (*answer in the negative*). **2** the image on a photographic film or plate in which light seems dark and shade light.

neglect /ni-**glect**/ *vb* **1** to fail to take care of (*neglect their children*). **2** to leave undone (*neglected to mail the letter*). **3** to pay no or little attention to, to give too little care to (*neglect his work*). ● *n* want of care or attention.

neglectful /ni-**glect**-ful/ *adj* heedless, careless (*neglectful parents*).

negligee /ne-gli-**zhay**/ *n* a woman's light, thin robe or dressing gown.

negligence /**ne**-gli-jense/ *n* carelessness, lack of proper care (*a driver accused of negligence*).

negligent /**ne**-gli-jent/ *adj* careless (*negligent drivers*).

negligible /**ne**-gli-ji-bul/ *adj* too little to bother about, unimportant (*the damage to the car was negligible*).

negotiable /ni-**go**-sha-bul/ *adj* **1** able to be settled or changed through discussion (*a negotiable salary*). **2** that can be exchanged for money (*a negotiable check*). **3** able to be passed (*icy roads scarcely negotiable*).

negotiate /ni-**go**-she-ate/ *vb* **1** to try to reach agreement, to bargain (*management and workers negotiating over pay*). **2** to arrange, usually after a long discussion (*negotiate a peace treaty*). **3** to obtain or give money for (*negotiate a check*). **4** to pass (over, through, etc.) successfully (*negotiate the sharp bend*). ● *n* **negotiation** /ni-**go**-she-ay-shun/. ● *n* **negotiator** /ni-**go**-shee-ay-tor/.

Negro /**nee**-gro/ *n* (*pl* **Negroes** /**nee**-groaz/) (*sometimes considered offensive*) a person belonging to a dark-skinned race, especially from the area of Africa south of the Sahara. *See* **African American**.

neigh /**nay**/ *n* the cry of a horse, a whinny. ● *also vb*.

neighbor/**nay**-bur/ *n*, *also* **neighbour** (*Br, Cdn*) **1** a person living near (*all the neighbors collected money to help her*). **2** a person living next door (*she talks to her neighbor over the fence*).

neighborhood/**nay**-bur-hood/ *n*, *also* **neighbourhood** (*Br, Cdn*) **1** the surrounding area or district (*in the neighborhood of the lake*). **2** a group of people and their homes forming a small area within a larger one (*live in a quiet neighborhood of the city*).

neighboring/**nay**-bu-ring/ *adj*, *also* **neighbouring** (*Br, Cdn*) close at hand, near (*the neighboring town*).

neighborly/**nay**-bur-lee/ *adj*, *also* **neighbourly** (*Br, Cdn*) friendly, helpful (*people in the town are very neighborly*).

neither /**nee**-ther, **neye**-ther/ *adj, pron, conj and adv* not either.

Neolithic /nee-yo-**li**-thic/ *adj* having to do with the later Stone Age, during which people used polished stone tools, made pottery, reared stock, etc.

neon /**nee**-on/ *n* a gas that glows brightly when electricity passes through it (*neon lighting*).

nephew /**ne**-fyoo/ *n* the son of a person's brother or sister.

nepotism /**ne**-pu-ti-zum/ *n* unjust use of a person's power by giving good positions to relatives (*he was accused of nepotism when his daughter got a job in the department that he managed*).

Neptune /**nep**-toon/ *n* in Roman mythology, the god of the sea.

nerd /**nurd**/ *n* a person thought of as dull, awkward, etc., especially if they are overly interested in computers or schoolwork.

nerve /**nerv**/ *n* **1** one of the threadlike fibers along which messages pass to and from the brain (*damage a nerve in his back*). **2** courage (*he was going to walk along a tightrope but he lost his nerve*). **3** (*inf*) self-confidence, cheek (*she had the nerve to come to the party uninvited*). **4** *pl* excitement, nervousness (*she suffered from nerves before the exam*). ● *vb* to give strength.

nerveless /**nerv**-less/ *adj* without strength or power.

nervous /**ner**-vus/ *adj* easily excited or upset, timid (*too nervous to stay in the house overnight by herself*/*nervous about her exam results*). ● *n* **nervousness** /**ner**-vus-ness/.

nervous breakdown /**ner**-vus-**brake**-down/ *n* a dis-order that keeps a person's body from functioning normally.

nervous system /**ner**-vus-sis-tem/ *n* all the nerve cells and tissues in a body that control responses and behavior.

nest /**nest**/ *n* **1** a place built by a bird in which it lays its eggs and brings up its young. **2** the home built by certain small animals and insects (*a wasp's nest*/*the nest of some mice*). **3** a comfortable shelter. **4** a set of things that fit one inside another (*a nest of tables*). ● *vb* to build a nest and live in it (*birds nesting*).

nest egg /**ne**-steg/ *n* **1** a sum of money put aside for future use (*try to get a nest egg together for her retirement*). **2** a real or fake egg put into a nest to get a hen to lay more eggs there.

nestle /**ne**-sul/ *vb* **1** to lie close to (*the children nestled together for warmth*). **2** to settle comfortably (*nestling down in the sofa to read a book*).

nestling /**ne**-sling/ *n* a bird too young to leave the nest.

net[1] /**net**/ *n* **1** crisscrossing strings knotted together at the crossing places. **2** an extent of this used for catching fish, animals, etc., and for many other purposes (*a butterfly net*/*put the ball in the net*). **3** a fabric made like this (*net curtains*). ● *vb* (**netted, netting**) **1** to catch in a net (*net several fish*). **2** to cover with a net (*net the fruit trees to keep off the birds*). **3** to hit or kick into a net (*net the ball*).

net[2] /**net**/ *adj* left after one has subtracted the amount due for taxes, expenses, etc. (*earn $500 net per month*). ● *vb* (**netted** /**ne**-tid/, **netting** /**ne**-ting/) to bring in as profit (*net a record annual profit*).

nether /**ne**-ther/ *adj* (*fml or hum*) lower (*the nether regions*).

nethermost /**ne**-ther-moast/ *adj* farthest down.

netherworld /**ne**-ther-wurld/ *n* the world of the dead or of punishment after death, hell.

netting /**ne**-ting/ *n* **1** material made in the form of a net (*wire netting to keep the chickens in*). **2** the act or process of making nets.

nettle /**ne**-tul/ *n* a weed covered with stinging hairs (*stung by a nettle*). ● *vb* to anger, to annoy (*his remarks nettled her*).

network /**net**-wurk/ *n* **1** anything in which lines, roads, railways, etc., cross and recross one another. **2** a widespread organization (*a radio network*).

neural /**noo**-ral/ *adj* of a nerve, nerves, or the nervous system.

neurological /noo-ro-**lodge**-i-cal/ *adj* having to do with the nerves (*a neurological disorder*).

neurology /noo-**rol**-o-jee/ *n* the study of the nerves. ● *n* **neurologist** /noo-**rol**-o-jist/.

neurosis /noo-**ro**-sis/ *n* a type of mental illness in which a person suffers from great anxiety, depression and/or fear.

neurotic /noo-**rot**-ic/ *adj* 1 in a nervous state, unreasonably anxious or sensitive (*a neurotic man/ a neurotic dog*). 2 suffering from a neurosis.

neuter /**noo**-ter/ *adj* having no sexual organ. ● *n* an animal that has been spayed or castrated, an animal that has been fixed. ● *vb* to spay, castrate, or fix an animal.

neutral /**noo**-tral/ *adj* 1 not taking sides, neither for nor against, impartial (*a country that was neutral in the war/require someone neutral to referee the match*). 2 not strong or definite (*neutral colors*). ● *n* a neutral person or party.

neutrality /noo-**tra**-li-tee/ *n* the state of being neutral.

neutralize, neutralise /**noo**-tra-lize/ *vb* to cause to have no effect, to make useless, to balance by an opposite action or effect (*neutralize the acid*).

never /**ne**-ver/ *adv* at no time, not ever.

nevermore /ne-ver-**more**/ *adv* never again.

never-never land /ne-ver **ne**-ver land/ *n* an unreal place or situation.

nevertheless /ne-ver-the-**less**/ *adv* for all that, despite everything (*he is young—nevertheless he is highly qualified*).

new /**noo**/ *adj* 1 never known before (*the discovery of a new star/new ideas*). 2 just bought or made, fresh (*new clothes/new cars*). 3 changed from an earlier state, different (*a new job*). ● *n* **newness** /**noo**-ness/.

newborn /**noo**-bawrn/ *n* a recently born infant.

newcomer /**noo**-cu-mer/ *n* a person who has recently arrived (*newcomers to the town welcomed by the older residents*).

newfound /noo-**found**/ *adj* newly gained.

newly /**noo**-lee/ *adv* recently (*newly laid eggs*).

newlywed /**noo**-lee-wed/ *n* a recently married person.

new moon /noo-**moon**/ *n* the first phase of the moon when it is between the Earth and the sun with its dark side facing the Earth.

news /**nooz**/ *n* 1 information about what is going on (*we have no news of the missing child*). 2 an account of recent events (*listen to the news on the radio*).

newsletter /**nooz**-le-ter/ *n* a printed sheet of news sent to members of a group, organization, etc. (*a newsletter sent to all members of staff*).

newspaper /**nooz**-pay-per/ *n* a number of printed sheets (usually issued daily) containing the latest news, articles, advertisements, etc.

newsprint /**nooz**-print/ *n* a cheap, low-grade paper used for printing newspapers.

newsreel /**nooz**-reel/ *n* a film showing recent events.

newsstand /**nooz**-stand/ *n* a stand at which newspapers, magazines, etc. are sold.

newsy /**noo**-zee/ (*pl* **newsies** /**noo**-zeez/) *n* (*inf*) a person, especially a child or teenager, who sells newspapers.

newt /**noot**/ *n* a small lizardlike creature that can live both on land and in water.

New Testament /**noo**-te-sta-ment/ *n* the part of the Christian Bible that deals with the life and teachings of Jesus.

next /**nekst**/ *adj* nearest, just before or just after in time, place, degree, or rank (*live in the next street/ the next day*). ● *also adv, prep, n.*

next-door /**neks(t)**-door/ *adj* in or at the next house or building.

next of kin /nek-stov-**kin**/ *n* someone's closest relative (*contact the dead man's next of kin*).

nib /**nib**/ *n* 1 the bill or beak of a bird. 2 the point of a pen (*the nib of a fountain pen*).

nibble /**ni**-bul/ *vb* to take small bites at (*mice nibbling the cheese*). ● *also n.*

nice /**nice**/ *adj* 1 pleasing (*a nice day/a nice meal*). 2 (*old*) particular when choosing, hard to please. 3 (*fml*) fine, delicate, precise (*a nice distinction/a nice sense of timing*).

nicety /**nie**-si-tee/ *n* 1 the quality or the state of being nice. 2 exactness, precise detail (*consider the niceties of the two firms joining together*). 3 a very small difference (*the nicety of the distinction*).

niche /**nich**/ *n* 1 a hollow place in a wall for a statue, etc. (*a niche by the staircase for the statue*). 2 the work, place, or position for which a person or thing is best suited (*find her niche in teaching/a niche in the market for luxury apartments*).

nick /**nick**/ *n* 1 the small hollow left when a piece is cut or chipped out of something, a notch (*a nick in the door/a nick in his skin from shaving*). ● *vb* 1 to cut notches in. ● **in the nick of time** just in time (*we arrived in the nick of time to catch the train*).

nickel /**ni**-cel/ *n* 1 a hard silver-white metal used for plating utensils and mixed with other metals because it doesn't rust (*steel plated with nickel*). 2 a five-cent piece.

nickel-and-dime /ni-cel-and-**dime**/ *vb* 1 to spend very little money. 2 to weaken, destroy, etc. by the constant spending of small sums or repeated small actions against.

nickelodeon /ni-ce-**lo**-dee-an/ *n* an early-twentieth-century theater to which the admission was five cents.

nickname /**nic**-name/ *n* a name used instead of one's real name in friendship or mockery (*William's nickname is Bill*). ● *vb* to give a nickname to.

nicotine /**ni**-co-teen/ *n* the toxic oily liquid from tobacco that is addictive (*fingers stained with nicotine*).

niece /**neess**/ *n* the daughter of a person's brother or sister.

night /**nite**/ *n* the time between sunset and sunrise, darkness (*animals that come out at night*) (*also* **nighttime** /**nite**-time/).

nightcap /**nite**-cap/ *n* **1** a cap worn in bed. **2** a drink taken last thing at night (*take a glass of hot milk as a nightcap*).

nightclothes /**nite**-cloathz/ *n* clothes worn in bed, pajamas.

nightclub /**nite**-club/ *n* a place of entertainment open at night for eating, drinking, dancing, etc.

nightfall /**nite**-fawl/ *n* evening, the approach of darkness (*insist that the children are home by nightfall*).

nightgown /**nite**-goun/ *n* a loose gown worn to bed by women or girls (*also* **nightie** /**nie**-tee/).

nightingale /**nie**-ting-gale/ *n* a type of small bird that sometimes sings at night.

night light /**nite**-lite/ *n* a small, faint light burning all night, as in a hallway or child's room.

nightly /**nite**-lee/ *adj* happening every night (*listen to the nightly news program*). ● *adv* every night.

nightmare /**nite**-mare/ *n* a frightening dream (*a nightmare about being attacked by sharks*).

night owl /**nite**-owl/ *n* **1** an owl active mostly at night. **2** a person who works at night or who generally stays up late.

nightshirt /**nite**-shirt/ *n* a long, loose-fitting, shirt worn to bed.

night watch /**nite**-watch/ *n* a watching or guarding during the night.

night watchman /**nite**-watch-man/ *n* a man who looks after buildings, etc., by night (*the night watchman disturbed the burglars*).

nightwear /**nite**-ware/ *n* nightclothes.

nil /**nil**/ *n* nothing, zero (*the score at the end of the soccer match was three-nil*).

nimble /**nim**-bul/ *adj* active, quick-moving (*elderly people who are still nimble/nimble young gymnasts*). ● *n* **nimbleness** /**nim**-bul-ness/.

nimbus /**nim**-bus/ *n* (*pl* **nimbi** /**nim**-bie/ *or* **nimbuses** /**nim**-bu-seez/) **1** a rain cloud. **2** the halo around the head of an angel in paintings.

nine /**nine**/ *adj* the number between eight and ten.

nine ball /**nine**-bawl/ *n* a kind of pool game in which the winner is the one who pockets the nine ball.

nineteen /**nine**-teen/ *adj* ten more than nine.

nineteenth /**nine**-teenth/ *adj* preceded by 18 others in a series.

ninetieth /**nine**-tee-eth/ *adj* preceded by 89 others.

nine-to-five /**nine**-to-five/ *adj* of or referring to the time between 9am and 5am, the period of business hours on a weekday.

ninety /**nine**-tee/ *n* the number before 89 and 91.

ninja /**nin**-ja/ *n* a Japanese warrior that is highly trained a spy and killer.

ninth /**nine**-th/ *adj* any of the nine equal parts of something.

nip /**nip**/ *vb* (**nipped** /**nipt**/, **nipping** /**ni**-ping/) **1** to pinch (*nip the child's arm*). **2** to bite (*the dog nipped him on the ankle*). **3** to stop the growth (*fruit trees nipped by frost*). ● *n* **1** a pinch (*he gave the other child a nip*). **2** biting cold (*a nip in the air*). **3** a small drink. ● **nip in the bud** to destroy at an early stage (*nip the conspiracy in the bud*).

nipple /**ni**-pul/ *n* **1** the point of the breast (*babies sucking at their mothers' nipples*). **2** anything so shaped. **3** a rubber stopper with a small hole in it through which liquid may pass, a teat.

nippy /**ni**-pee/ *adj* cold in a stinging way.

nirvana /nir-**va**-na/ *n* **1** in Buddhism, the state of being perfectly blessed after death and taken into the supreme spirit. **2** complete peace and happiness. 3 in Hinduism, a blowing out of the flame of life through reunion with Brahma, the god of creation.

nisei /nee-**say**/ *n* a native US or Canadian citizen born of immigrant Japanese parents and educated in America.

nit /**nit**/ *n* a young louse or the egg of a louse or other small insect (*find nits in her child's hair*).

nitpick /**nit**-pick/ *vb* to find fault with someone or something in a manner that is finicky or minor.

nitrogen /**nie**-tro-jen/ *n* a colorless, odorless, and tasteless gas that makes up about four-fifths of the air. ● *adj* **nitrogenous** /nie-**trodge**-en-us/.

nitroglycerin /nie-tro-**glis**-ren/ *n* an explosive.

nitty gritty /ni-tee-**gri**-tee/ *n* the basic or most important details of something (*we must get down to the nitty gritty of the traffic problem*).

nitwit /**nit**-wit/ *n* a foolish, stupid, or silly person (*he was a nitwit to buy a second-hand car without testing it*).

no *adv* not ever, the opposite of yes, it cannot be so.

nobility /no-**bi**-li-tee/ *n* **1** goodness of character. **2** the class of nobles of a country (*a member of the nobility*).

noble /**no**-bul/ *adj* **1** fine in character, honorable (*of noble character*). **2** of high rank (*people of noble birth*). **3** stately (*of noble carriage*). ● *n* a person of high rank. ● *adv* **nobly** /**no**-blee/.

nobleman /**no**-bul-man/ *n* a man in the noble class.

noblewoman /**no**-bul-woo-man/ *n* a woman in the noble class.

nobody /**no**-bu-dee/ *n* **1** no one (*she was warned to tell nobody the secret*). **2** (*inf*) a person of no importance (*she's just a nobody in the firm, but she tries to order everyone around*).

no-brainer /no-**bray**-ner/ *n* (*inf*) something so obvious or simple as to require little thought.

nocturnal /noc-**tur**-nal/ *adj* **1** (*fml*) happening at night (*a nocturnal visitor*). **2** active by night (*nocturnal animals, such as bats*).

nocturne /noc-**turn**/ *n* **1** a dreamy piece of music. **2** a painting of a night scene.

nocuous /**noc**-yu-wus/ *adj* harmful, poisonous.

nod /nod/ *vb* (**nodded** /**nod**-id/, **nodding** /**nod**-ing/) **1** to bow the head slightly (*she nodded in agreement/nod to her neighbor as he passed*). **2** to let the head drop forward in tiredness (*old ladies nodding by the fire*). ● *n* a slight bow of the head.

nodal /**no**-dal/ *adj* of or like a node.

node /node/ *n* **1** the place where a leaf joins the stem. **2** the point at which a curve crosses itself. **3** a swelling or a roundish lump, as on a tree trunk or a person's body (*lymph nodes*).

nodule /**nod**-jul/ *n* a small rounded lump. ● *adj* **nodular** /**nod**-yu-lar/.

Noël /no-**wel**/ *n* Christmas.

no-hitter /no-**hi**-ter/ *n* a baseball game in which the pitcher allows the other team no base hits.

noise /noyz/ *n* **1** a sound (*the noise made by a fire truck*). **2** loud or unpleasant sounds, din (*complain about the noise from the party*). ● *vb* (*fml or old*) to make public (*noising the news of his dismissal*). ● *adj* **noisy** /**noy**-zee/.

noiseless /**noyz**-less/ *adj* not making any sound.

noisemaker /**noyz**-may-ker/ *n* a person or thing that makes noise, especially for a celebration.

nomad /**no**-mad/ *n* **1** a wanderer. **2** a member of a group of people that has no permanent home but moves around constantly in search of food, pastures, etc.

nomadic /no-**ma**-dic/ *adj* wandering (*nomadic peoples*).

no man's land /**no**-manz-land/ *n* **1** land that belongs to no one (*a piece of no man's land between the two farms*). **2** land lying between two opposing armies (*the soldier was shot crossing no man's land*).

nominal /**nom**-in-al/ *adj* **1** existing in name but not in reality (*her father is the nominal head of the firm, but she runs it*). **2** having to do with a noun or nouns. **3** very small compared to others (*charge his son a nominal amount of money for the car*).

nominate /**nom**-in-ate/ *vb* **1** to put forward another's name for a certain office (*nominating him for captain*). **2** to appoint (*nominated her brother as her representative*). ● *n* **nomination** /nom-in-**ay**-shun/.

nominative /**nom**-in-a-tiv/ *adj* **1** having the name of a person on it. **2** in grammar, of or in the case of the subject of a verb.

nominee /nom-i-**nee**/ *n* a person who is nominated (*several nominees for the office of president*).

non- /non/ *pref* not, the opposite of, used to give a negative meaning to a word.

nonagenarian /non-i-ji-**nay**-ree-an/ *n* a person who is 90 years old or between 90 and 100.

nonchalant /**non**-sha-lont/ *adj* calm, unexcited, showing little interest, cool, without warmth or concern (*nonchalant about the idea of going into battle*). ● *n* **nonchalance** /**non**-sha-lonse/.

nondescript /non-di-**script**/ *adj* not easily described, not very interesting (*wear nondescript clothes*).

none /nun/ *pron* not one, not anyone, no persons or things.

nonentity /non-**en**-ti-tee/ *n* a person of no importance, a person of little ability or character (*she considered the party to be full of nonentities and left early*).

nonesuch /**nun**-such/ *n* a person or thing unequaled.

nonetheless /nun-thi-**less**/ *adv* in spite of that, nevertheless.

nonexistence /non-ig-**zi**-stanse/ *n* the condition of not existing.

nonflammable /non-**fla**-ma-bul/ *adj* not likely to catch fire or burn easily (*nonflammable nightwear for children*).

no-no /**no**-no/ *n* (*inf*) something that is forbidden or unwise to do.

no-nonsense /no-**non**-sense/ *adj* practical and serious.

nonplus /non-**plus**/ *vb* (**nonplussed** /non-**plust**/, **nonplussing** /non-**plu**-sing/) to puzzle completely, to leave speechless (*we were nonplussed by her strange behavior*).

nonsense /**non**-sense/ *n* foolish or meaningless words, ideas, etc. (*talk nonsense/it was nonsense to accuse him of lying*).

nonsensical /non-**sen**-si-cal/ *adj* meaningless, absurd (*a nonsensical thing to do*).

nonstop /non-**stop**/ *adj and adv* without any stop or pause (*nonstop pop music*).

noodle /**noo**-dul/ *n* a long thin strip of pasta used especially in Chinese or Italian cooking, often eaten with sauce or soup (*chicken soup with noodles*).

nook /**nook**/ *n* **1** a corner (*a nook by the fire*). **2** an out-of-the-way place (*shady nooks*).

noon /**noon**/ *n* Midday, 12pm (*lunch at noon*).

noose /**nooss**/ *n* a cord or rope with a loop at one end fastened by a running knot (*throw a noose round the ball to catch it/hang him with a noose*). ● *vb* to catch in a noose.

Nootka /**noot**-ka/ *n* the Native American people living on Vancouver Island, the language of these people.

nope /**noap**/ *adv, interj* no, a negative reply.

nor /**nor**/ *conj, prep* **1** (preceded by *neither*) and not (*neither rich nor poor*). **2** or not; not either (*they weren't clever—nor were they funny*).

norm /**norm**/ *n* the usual rule, an example or standard with which others may be compared (*his height is below the norm for his age/wage increases above the national norm*).

normal /**nor**-mal/ *adj* usual, according to what is expected, average (*normal body temperature/normal behavior/his normal routine*). ● *n* **normality** /nor-**ma**-li-tee/.

normalize /**nor**-ma-lize/ *vb, also* **normalise** (*Br*) to make normal.

north /**north**/ *n* **1** one of the chief points of the compass. **2** (*often cap*) the northern part of the country. **3** the northern regions of the world.

north /**north**/, **northern** /**nor**-then/, **northerly** /**nor**-ther-lee/ *adjs* **1** having to do with the north. **2** of or from the north (*a northern accent/a north wind*).

northbound /**north**-bound/ *adj* traveling north (*the north°bound train*).

northeast /north-**east**/ *n* the point of the compass halfway between north and east. ● *also adj* **northeastern** /north-**ee**-stern/.

northeastward /north-**eest**-ward/ *adj, adv* toward the northeast.

northern /**nor**-thern/ *adj* in, of, to, toward, or facing the north.

northerner /**nor**-ther-ner/ *n* (*often cap*) a person living in or coming from the north (*northerners moving to the south to find work*).

northern lights /nor-thern-**lites**/ *npl* bright rays of colored light sometimes seen in the region of the North Pole; its proper name is the *aurora borealis*.

northernmost /**nor**-thern-moast/ *adj* farthest to the north (*the northernmost part of America*).

North Pole /north-**pole**/ *n* the northernmost part of the Earth, in the middle of the Arctic regions.

northward /**north**-ward/ *adv* toward the north (*trains traveling northward*).

northwest /**north**-west/ *n* the point of the compass halfway between north and west. ● *also adj*.

northwestern /north-**we**-stern/ *adj* in, of, to, toward, or facing the northwest.

northwestward /north-**west**-ward/ *adv, adj* toward the northwest.

nose /**noze**/ *n* **1** the part of the face between the eyes and mouth that allows people and animals to breathe and smell (*a boxer with a broken nose*). **2** a sense of smell (*dogs with good noses*). **3** the part that juts out in the front of anything (*the nose of an airplane*). ● *vb* **1** to smell. **2** to find by smell (*the dog nosed out the drugs*). **3** to look or search around in (*nosing about in her neighbor's shed*). **4** to discover by searching (*reporters nosing out the details of the scandal*). **5** to move slowly (*the car nosed out into the traffic*).

nosebleed /**noze**-bleed/ *n* a bleeding from the nose.

nose dive /**noze**-dive/ *n* **1** a nose-first dive earthward by an airplane. **2** a sudden and great fall or drop (*house prices took a nose dive*). ● *vb* to take a nose dive.

nosepiece /**noze**-peess/ *n* that part of a helmet that covers and protects the nose.

nose ring /**noze**-ring/ *n* **1** a metal ring passed through the nose of an animal for leading it about. **2** a ring worn in the nose as a piece of jewelry.

nostalgia /nos-**tal**-ja/ *n* a longing or feeling of fondness for things past (*music that fills him with nostalgia for his native land*). ● *adj* **nostalgic** /nos-**tal**-jic/.

nostril /**nos**-tril/ *n* one of the two openings of the nose.

nosy /**no**-zee/ *adj* (*inf*) curious about the affairs of others (*nosey neighbors*).

not /**not**/ *adv* in no manner, to no degree.

notable /**no**-ta-bul/ *adj* worthy of notice, deserving to be remembered (*notable events of the year/notable achievements*). ● *n* **notability** /no-ta-**bi**-li-tee/.

notation /no-**tay**-shun/ *n* a set of signs or symbols that stand for letters, numbers, notes in music, etc.

notch /notch/ *n* a small V-shaped cut (*cut a notch on the stick to mark the child's height*). ● *vb* to make a notch in.

note /note/ *n* **1** a short letter (*write them a note to thank them*). **2** a short written account of what is said or done (*taking notes at the committee meeting*). **3** a written explanation (*a note at the foot of the page*). **4** a single musical sound or the sign standing for it. **5** fame, good reputation (*politicians of note*). ● *vb* **1** to put down in writing (*the policeman noted the details of the accident*). **2** to take notice of (*they noted a change in his behavior*).

notebook /note-book/ *n* a book into which notes may be written.

noted /no-tid/ *adj* famous, well known (*noted actors*).

notepad /note-pad/ *n* a small pad of paper.

notepaper /note-pay-per/ *n* paper for writing notes or letters on (*notepaper with matching envelopes*).

noteworthy /note-wur-thee/ *adj* deserving to be noticed or remembered (*nothing noteworthy occurred*).

nothing /nu-thing/ *n* **1** no thing, not anything (*absolutely nothing in the cupboard*). **2** a thing of no importance (*her friendship's nothing to him*).

notice /no-tiss/ *n* **1** a written or printed announcement (*a notice on the wall forbidding smoking*). **2** warning (*change the rules without notice*). **3** attention (*he took no notice of the warning*). **4** advance information (*receive notice about a meeting*). ● *vb* **1** to pay attention to. **2** to see. ● *adj* noticeable.

notify /no-ti-fie/ *vb* to inform, to make known (*notified the police about the accident*). ● *n* **notification** /no-ti-fi-cay-shun/.

notion /no-shun/ *n* **1** idea, opinion, view (*old-fashioned notions about what is women's work*). **2** a sudden desire (*he had a notion to go to the seaside for the day*).

notoriety /no-tu-rie-i-tee/ *n* bad reputation.

notorious /no-toe-ree-us/ *adj* well known for something bad (*a notorious criminal/a notorious accident spot*).

notoriously /no-toe-ree-us-lee/ *adv* as is well known for something bad (*a notoriously inefficient firm*).

nougat /noo-gat/ *n* a white toffeelike sweet containing nuts.

noun /noun/ *n* in grammar, a word that names a person, place, quality, or thing.

nourish /nu-rish/ *vb* **1** to feed, to give what is needed to grow or stay healthy (*foods that will nourish the children/well-nourished babies*). **2** to keep in the mind (*nourish resentment against his rival*).

nourishment /nu-rish-ment/ *n* food, especially food of value to health (*little nourishment in fast foods*).

nova /no-va/ *n* a type of star that suddenly increases in brightness and then decreases in brightness over time.

novel /nov-el/ *adj* new and often of an unusual kind (*a novel suggestion/a novel way of dealing with the problem*). ● *n* a long story of which all or some of the events are imaginary.

novelist /nov-list/ *n* a person who writes novels.

novelty /nov-el-tee/ *n* **1** newness, the quality of being novel (*the novelty of the idea*). **2** a new or unusual thing (*it was a novelty for him to take a holiday*). **3** an unusual, small, cheap object (*Christmas novelties*).

November /no-vem-ber/ *n* the eleventh month of the year (*Thanksgiving is in November*).

novice /nov-iss/ *n* **1** a beginner (*just a novice at skiing*). **2** a person who has newly joined a religious order but has not yet taken vows (*the novices in the convent*).

novitiate /no-vi-shate/ *n* **1** the time spent as a novice (*the novitiate of the nun*). **2** a novice.

now /now/ *n* **1** at the present time (*she is living in London now*). **2** at once (*Go now!*).

nowadays /now-a-daze/ *adv* in modern times (*nowadays the rate of unemployment is high*).

nowhere /no-whare/ *adv* in no place (*he was nowhere to be seen*).

noxious /nok-shus/ *adj* (*fml*) harmful, hurtful (*noxious fumes*).

nozzle /noz-ul/ *n* a spout or pipe fitted on to the end of a hose, etc., to direct the liquid (*the nozzle of the garden hose*).

nuance /noo-onse/ *n* a slight difference in meaning, color, etc. (*fail to appreciate the nuances in the arguments*).

nub /nub/ *n* the most important point (*the nub of the problem*).

nuclear /noo-clee-ar/ *adj* having to do with the atomic nucleus (*nuclear power stations*).

nuclear bomb /noo-clee-ar bom/ *n* an atomic bomb or a hydrogen bomb, capable of destroying a large area.

nuclear energy /noo-clee-ar en-er-jee/ *n* the energy in an atomic nucleus.

nuclear family /noo-clee-ar fa-mi-lee/ *n* a basic family unit consisting of parents and their children living in one household.

nuclear physics /noo-clee-ar fi-zics/ *n* the science of the forces within the nucleus of the atom.

nuclear reactor /noo-clee-ar ree-**ac**-tor/ *n* a machine for producing atomic energy.

nucleus /noo-clee-us/ *n* (*pl* **nuclei**) **1** the central part of an atom, seed, etc. **2** the central part of anything around which the rest grows up (*the nucleus of the library*).

nude /nood/ *adj* naked, wearing no clothes (*a nude model for the artist*). ● *n* a naked person (*a painting of a nude*).

nudge /nudge/ *vb* to push with the elbow (*nudging the child to warn him to keep quiet*). ● also *n*.

nudist /noo-dist/ *n* a person who believes that it is healthy to wear no clothes (*a nudist colony*).

nudity /noo-di-tee/ *n* nakedness (*object to the nudity of the characters in the play*).

nugget /nu-get/ *n* a lump, as of gold, silver, etc.

nuisance /noo-sanse/ *n* a person, action, or thing that annoys.

null /nul/ *adj*. ● **null and void** having no legal force (*a contract declared null and void by the court*).

numb /num/ *adj* unable to feel (*fingers numb with cold/numb with grief*). ● *vb* to take away the power of feeling sensations (*hands numbed with cold/numbed by the break-up of her marriage*). ● *adj* **numbing** /nu-ming/.

number /num-ber/ *n* **1** a word or sign that tells how many (*a phone number*). **2** a collection of several (persons, things, etc.) (*a small number of viewers*). **3** a single copy of a magazine, etc., printed at a particular time, an issue (*the current number of the magazine*). **4** a piece of popular music or a popular song usually forming part of a longer performance (*one of the numbers on her latest album*). ● *vb* **1** (*fml*) to reach as a total (*the spectators numbered a thousand*). **2** to give a number to (*number the pages*). **3** to include (*he is numbered among our greatest scientists*).

numerable /noom-ra-bul/ *adj* that can be numbered or counted.

numeral /noom-ral/ *n* a word or figure standing for a number (*Roman numerals*).

numerate /noo-me-rate/ *vb* (*fml*) to count. ● *adj* able to do arithmetic and mathematics (*people who are scarcely numerate*). ● *n* **numeration** /noo-me-**ray**-shun/.

numerator /noo-mer-ay-tor/ *n* in fractions, the number above the line, which tells how many parts there are.

numerical /noo-**mer**-ic-al/ *adj* having to do with numbers (*numerical information/in numerical order*).

numerous /noo-mer-uss/ *adj* many (*numerous reasons for leaving*).

nun /nun/ *n* a woman who joins a convent and vows to devote her life to the service of God.

nunnery /nun-ree/ *n* a convent, a house for nuns.

nuptial /nup-shal/ *adj* (*fml*) having to do with marriage (*a nuptial ceremony*). ● *npl* **nuptials** a marriage.

nurse /nurss/ *n* a person trained to look after the young, sick, or aged (*a hospital nurse*). ● *vb* **1** to look after as a nurse (*nurse the patient*). **2** to give milk from the breast, to suckle (*mothers nursing babies*). **3** to look after with great care (*nurse his tomato plants*). **4** to keep in existence (*nurse hopes of success*).

nursemaid /nur-smade/ *n* a woman hired to take care of a child or children.

nursery /nur-sree/ *n* **1** a room in a house for children to sleep or play in. **2** a place where young children are looked after (*newborns stay in a nursery*). **3** a place where young plants are grown for sale (*buy tomato plants from the local nursery*).

nursery rhyme /nur-sree-rime/ *n* a short, rhymed poem for children.

nursery school /nur-sree-skool/ *n* a school for young children of preschool age.

nursing /nur-sing/ *n* the duties of or care given by a nurse.

nursing home /nur-sing-home/ *n* a small private hospital for invalids, sick people, or old people who are unable to take care of themselves.

nurture /nur-chur/ *n* care and training (*nurture of children by their parents*). ● *vb* **1** to care for (*parents nurturing children*). **2** to help to grow or develop (*nurture ideas of independence*).

nut /nut/ *n* **1** a fruit with a hard outer shell and an edible kernel inside it (*crack the nut*). **2** the edible kernel (*put nuts in the cake*). **3** a screw that is turned on to one end of a bolt to fasten it. ● **in a nutshell** in a few words.

nutcracker /nut-cra-ker/ *n* an instrument for cracking nuts.

nutmeg /nut-meg/ *n* the hard seed of a certain kind of tree, used as a spice in cooking (*add grated nutmeg to the sauce*).

nutrient /noo-tree-ent/ *n* a substance in food that is good for the body.

nutriment /**noo**-tri-ment/ *n* food needed for life and growth (*soil low in nutriments for the plants*).

nutrition /noo-**tri**-shun/ *n* **1** food, nourishment (*poor standards of nutrition*). **2** the process of giving or getting food (*in charge of the children's nutrition*).

nutritious /noo-**tri**-shus/ *adj* good for the health of the body (*nutritious food/a nutritious diet*).

nuzzle /**nu**-zul/ *vb* **1** to push or rub with the nose (*a horse nuzzling its owner*). **2** to press close up to (*she nuzzled her head against his shoulder*).

nylon /**nie**-lon/ *n* **1** a human-made fiber for thread or cloth (*shirts made of nylon*). **2** a stocking made from this (*a pair of nylons*).

nymph /**nimf**/ *n* in legend, a goddess of forests, rivers, trees, etc.

O

O, o /oh/ the fifteenth letter of the alphabet.

oaf /oaf/ n a stupid or clumsy person (*the oaf painted the wrong door*).

oak /oak/ n a hardwood tree that bears acorns.

oar /oar/ n a pole with a flat broad end, used for rowing a boat (*he lost one of the oars*).

oarlock /oar-lock/ n a U-shaped device on the side of a boat for keeping an oar in place.

oarsman /oarz-man/ n a rower (*the oarsmen in the boat race*). ● n oarsmanship /oarz-man-ship/.

oasis /oa-ay-sis/ n (*pl* oases /oa-ay-seez/) a place in the desert where there is water and trees and plants grow.

oat /oat/ n, oats /oats/ npl a grain often used for food.

oatcake /oat-cake/ n a thin cake made of oatmeal.

oath /oath/ n 1 a solemn promise, especially one made in God's name (*take the oath in court*). 2 a swear word (*object to his oaths in front of children*).

oatmeal /oat-meel/ n oats ground to powder (*take some oatmeal to make porridge*).

obedient /oa-bee-dee-ent/ adj willing to do what you are told (*obedient children/followers obedient to their leader*). ● n obedience.

obelisk /ob-el-isk/ n a tall four-sided stone monument, narrowing to a point at its top.

obese /oa-beess/ adj (*fml*) very fat. ● n obesity /oa-bee-si-tee/.

obey /oa-bay/ vb 1 to do what you are told (*when her mother tells her to do something, she obeys*). 2 to carry out (*obey instructions*).

obituary /oa-bi-chu-we-ree/ n 1 a list of deaths. 2 a newspaper account of the life of a person who has recently died (*an obituary of the famous poet*).

object /ob-ject/ n 1 anything that can be perceived by the senses. 2 aim, purpose (*his object is to make money quickly*). 3 in grammar, a word governed by a verb or preposition. ● vb object /ob-ject/ 1 to express dislike. 2 to speak against.

objection /ob-jec-shun/ n a reason against (*raise objections against the proposed new road*).

objectionable /ob-jec-shu-na-bul/ adj deserving to be disliked, unpleasant (*a really objectionable young man*).

objective /ob-jec-tiv/ adj not depending on, or influenced by, personal opinions (*judges have to be objective*). ● n aim, purpose (*his objective is a job that he will enjoy*). ● adv objectively /ob-jec-tiv-lee/.

objector /ob-jec-tor/ n a person who objects (*objectors to the new road scheme*).

obligation /ob-li-gay-shun/ n 1 a duty, a promise that must be kept (*he is under an obligation to support his children*). 2 gratitude due to another for kindness or help.

obligatory /o-bli-ga-toe-ree/ adj that which has to be done (e.g., as a duty), compulsory (*attendance at the meeting is obligatory*).

oblige /o-blije/ vb 1 (*fml*) to force or make it necessary to do (*she was obliged to stop working because of ill health*). 2 to do a kindness to or service for (*could you oblige us by lending us your lawnmower*).

obliging /o-blie-jing/ adj ready to help, kind (*obliging neighbors*).

oblique /o-bleek/ adj 1 slanting (*an oblique line*). 2 indirect, roundabout (*an oblique reference to his dishonesty*).

obliterate /o-bli-te-rate/ vb 1 to destroy utterly (*a town obliterated by enemy bombs*). 2 to blot out (*snow obliterating the footprints in the mud*). ● n obliteration /o-bli-te-ray-shun/.

oblivion /o-bli-vee-on/ n 1 the state of being unaware, forgetfulness (*in total oblivion of what had happened*). 2 the state of being forgotten (*he used to be famous, but after his death his name sank into oblivion*).

oblivious /o-bli-vee-us/ adj unaware of, not paying attention to (*completely oblivious to what was happening around him*).

oblong /ob-long/ n 1 a four-sided figure with all angles right angles and one pair of sides longer than the other pair. 2 a figure or object so shaped. ● adj having this shape.

obnoxious /ob-nok-shus/ adj very unpleasant, hateful (*obnoxious people/obnoxious smells*).

oboe /o-bo/ n a wooden wind instrument. ● n oboist /o-bo-ist/.

obscene /ob-seen/ adj disgusting, indecent (*obscene passages in the film had to be removed*). ● adv obscenely /ob-seen-lee/. ● n obscenity /ob-sen-i-tee/.

obscure /ob-scyoor/ adj 1 (*fml*) dark (*an obscure corner of the room*). 2 not clear in meaning (*an obscure reference to an earlier work*). 3 not well-known, not famous (*an obscure poet*). ● *vb* **1** to darken. **2** to hide from view. **3** to make more difficult.

obscurity /ob-**scyoo**-ri-tee/ *n* the state of being obscure (*a once famous poet now in obscurity*).

observance /ob-**zer**-vanse/ *n* **1** the act of observing (*the observance of religious holidays*). **2** the act of obeying (*the observance of the law*).

observant /ob-**zer**-vant/ *adj* quick to notice things (*not observant enough to take the license number of the car*).

observation /ob-zer-**vay**-shun/ *n* **1** the act, power, or habit of observing (*the police officer's observation of the criminal's activities*). **2** a remark (*he made the observation that things were going badly for the president*).

observatory /ob-**zer**-va-toe-ree/ *n* a place from which scientists study the stars, the planets, and the heavens.

observe /ob-**zerv**/ *vb* **1** (*fml*) to see, to notice (*observe a change in the weather*). **2** to watch carefully (*police told to observe the movements of the accused*). **3** to carry out (*observing local customs*). **4** to say, to make a remark (*he observed that the weather was mild for the time of year*).

observer /ob-**zer**-ver/ *n* **1** a person who observes. **2** a person whose job it is to take careful notice of what is going on.

obsess /ob-**sess**/ *vb* to take up all your thoughts and interest (*obsessed by her rival's activities*). ● *adj* **obsessive** /ob-**se**-siv/.

obsession /ob-**se**-shun/ *n* an idea or interest that takes up all your attention so that you never think about other things.

obsolete /ob-so-**leet**/ *adj* no longer in use, out-of-date (*obsolete computer*).

obstacle /**ob**-sta-cul/ *n* that which is in the way and prevents progress (*lack of money was the obstacle to the firm's plans for expansion*).

obstacle race /**ob**-sta-cul race/ *n* a race in which the runners have to find their way under, over, or through certain objects placed on the course to hinder them.

obstinate /**ob**-sti-nit/ *adj* **1** determined to hold to your own opinions, etc., stubborn. **2** not easy to cure or remove (*an obstinate stain*). ● *n* **obstinacy** /**ob**-sti-na-see/.

obstruct /ob-**struct**/ *vb* **1** to stop up. **2** to prevent from moving or acting freely.

obstruction /ob-**struc**-shun/ *n* **1** a cause of delay. **2** an obstacle.

obstructive /ob-**struc**-tiv/ *adj* causing delay (*obstructive tactics*).

obtain /ob-**tane**/ *vb* to get (*interested in obtaining a share of the business*).

obtainable /ob-**tay**-na-bul/ *adj* that can be gotten (*goods that are no longer obtainable*).

obtuse /ob-**toos**/ *adj* **1** stupid, slow to understand (*they accused him of being deliberately obtuse in not understanding the instructions*). **2** (*of an angle*) greater than a right angle.

obvious /**ob**-vee-us/ *adj* easily seen or understood (*an obvious solution to the problem*). ● *adv* **obviously** /**ob**-vee-us-lee/.

occasion /o-**cay**-zhun/ *n* **1** a particular time (*decide not to complain on this occasion*). **2** a special event (*the wedding was the occasion of the year for the family*). **3** (*fml*) a reason (*no occasion to be angry*). **4** (*fml*) opportunity (*if the occasion arises*). ● *vb* to cause.

occasional /o-**cay**-zhnal/ *adj* **1** happening now and then (*pay the occasional visit*). **2** having to do with a particular event or occasion (*occasional poems*). ● *adv* **occasionally** /o-**cay**-zhna-lee/.

occult /o-**cult**/ *adj* secret, mysterious, having to do with magic (*occult powers/occult ceremonies*).

occupancy /**ok**-yu-pan-see/ *n* **1** act of going to live in a house (*their occupancy of the new house*). **2** the time during which you live there (*an occupancy of five years*).

occupant /**oc**-yu-pant/, **occupier** /**oc**-yu-pie-er/ *ns* the person living in a house (*owner-occupiers*).

occupation /oc-yu-**pay**-shun/ *n* **1** act of occupying (*their occupation of the house/the enemy army's occupation of the city*). **2** the time during which a place is occupied (*during the occupation, many people tried to leave the country*). **3** your job (*looking for a new occupation*). **4** that which you are doing at a certain time (*various leisure occupations*). ● *adj* **occupational** /oc-yu-**pay**-shnal/.

occupy /**oc**-yu-pie/ *vb* **1** to take possession of (*a town occupied by the enemy*). **2** to live in (*he occupies the whole house*). **3** to fill (*occupying an important post*). **4** to keep busy (*she keeps herself occupied by doing voluntary work*). **5** to take up (space, time, etc.) (*his collection of model trains occupies a whole room*).

occur /u-**cur**/ *vb* (**occurred** /u-**curd**/, **occurring** /u-**cu**-ring/) **1** to happen (*accidents occurring*). **2** to come to the mind (*it suddenly occurred to me where he was*). **3** to be found here and there.

occurrence /u-**cu**-rense/ *n* a happening, an event (*a daily occurrence*).

ocean /o-shin/ *n* **1** the vast body of salt water surrounding the land on the earth (*on land or in the ocean*). **2** a large sea (*the Pacific Ocean*). ● *adj* **oceanic** /o-she-a-nic/.

ocelot /oss-uh-lot/ n a spotted wildcat from southwestern United States, Central America and parts of South America.

o'clock /u-clock/ *adv* according to the clock (*the movie starts at eight o'clock*).

octagon /oc-ta-gon/ *n* a figure or shape with eight angles and sides.

octagonal /oc-**tag**-nal/ *adj* eight-sided.

octave /oc-tave/ *n* **1** (*mus*) a scale of eight notes beginning and ending with a note of the same tone but a different pitch. **2** a stanza of eight lines.

octet /oc-**tet**/ *n* a piece of music for eight singers or instruments.

October /oc-**toe**-ber/ *n* the tenth month of the year (*Hallowe'en is October 31*).

octogenarian /oc-ta-je-**nay**-ree-an/ *n* a person who is 80 years old or between 80 and 90.

octopus /oc-to-pus/ *n* a sea creature with eight arms.

odd /odd/ *adj* **1** (*of a number*) not even, that cannot be divided by two without leaving a remainder of one (*nine is an odd number*). **2** strange, unusual (*an odd character/an odd thing to say*). **3** unmatched (*six pairs of gloves and one odd one*). ● *adv* **oddly** /od-lee/.

oddity /od-i-tee/ *n* something strange or unusual, a strange person (*he's a bit of an oddity*).

oddment /od-ment/ *n* a piece left over (*oddments of material*).

odds /odz/ *npl* the chances in favor of a certain happening or result (*the odds are that he will win*). ● **at odds with** on bad terms with (*two branches of the firm at odds with each other*). ● **by all odds** in every way, without question (*by all odds—the best movie ever*). ● **odds and ends** extra pieces or things of various kinds (*go shopping for some odds and ends*).

ode /ode/ *n* a poem in which the writer expresses his or her ideas or feelings on a certain subject at some length (*Keats's "Ode to Autumn"*).

odious /oe-dee-us/ *adj* hateful, disgusting (*an odious smell/an odious man*).

odium /oe-dee-um/ *n* (*fml*) hatred, widespread dislike or blame (*bring odium on his family*).

odor /oe-dur/ *n*, also **odour** (*Br, Cdn*) any smell, pleasant or unpleasant (*the odor of a fish in the boat*).

odorless /oe-dur-less/ *adj*, also **odourless** (*Br, Cdn*) having no smell (*odorless face creams*).

odorous /oe-du-rus/ *adj* having a smell, especially a characteristic one (*the odorous smell of lilies*).

odyssey /od-i-see/ *n* (*lit*) a long adventurous journey.

o'er /oar/ *prep* and *adv* (*lit*) over.

oesophagus /i-sof-a-gus/ (*Br, Cdn*) see **esophagus**.

of /ov/ *prep* **1** belonging to (*the shore of the lake*). **2** relating to (*a tale of the Wild West*). **3** made of (*a band of gold*). **4** from (*south of the border*).

off /off/ *adv* **1** away (*they drove off*). **2** distant (*a few miles off*). ● *adj* **1** not happening (*the match is off*). **2** (*inf*) not fit to eat, bad, rotten (*this meat is off*). ● *prep* away from, not on (*keep off the grass/ take your foot off the table*).

offal /of-al/ *n* the inner organs of an animal sold as food or regarded as waste matter (*offal such as heart and liver*).

offence see **offense**.

offend /o-**fend**/ *vb* **1** to displease, to hurt someone's feelings (*she was offended at not being asked to their party*). **2** (*fml*) to do wrong (*offend against society*). **3** to be unpleasant or disagreeable (*his bad language offended her*).

offender /o-**fen**-der/ *n* **1** a person who does wrong (*a first offender who was not sent to prison*). **2** a person who causes offense.

offense, offence /o-**fense**/ *n* **1** a wrongful act (*it's an offense to drive in the dark without lights*). **2** hurt done to the feelings, a feeling that you have been insulted (*a remark that gave offense to his family*). **3** those players in a sports team whose job is to score goals.

offensive /o-**fen**-siv/ *adj* **1** unpleasant (*an offensive smell/an offensive person*). **2** insulting (*an offensive remark*). **3** having to do with attack (*offensive weapons*). ● *n* an attack (*the army took the offensive*).

offer /of-er/ *vb* **1** to give someone the chance of taking (*offer him a job*). **2** to say that you are willing (to do something) (*to offer to help*). **3** to give as a sacrifice (*offer a lamb to God*). ● *n* **1** act of offering. **2** the thing or amount offered (*an offer of $250,000 for their house*).

offering /of-er-ing/ *n* **1** (*fml or hum*) a gift (*a humble offering*). **2** (*old*) that which is sacrificed to God. **3** a sum of money given at a religious service, used for the work of the church.

offhand /of-**hand**/ *adj* careless, thoughtless (*his offhand treatment of others*).

office /of-is/ *n* **1** a special duty. **2** a job, especially one in the service of the public (*the office of mayor/the political party in office*). **3** a room or building in which business is carried on (*the head office of the company*). **4** (*fml*) an act of kindness (*thanks to his good offices*).

officer /of-i-ser/ *n* a person who holds a post with certain powers or duties, especially in the armed forces (*an army officer*).

official /o-fi-shal/ *adj* **1** having to do with an office or the duties attached to it (*his official tasks*). **2** given out or announced by those with the right to do so (*receive official permission*). ● *n* a person who holds a post with certain powers or duties. ● *adv* **officially** /o-fish-lee/.

officialdom /o-fi-shal-dom/ *n* **1** all those holding public office. **2** an unbending attitude of holding to regulations and routine (*thanks to officialdom, her visa took weeks to come through*).

off-peak /off-peek/ *adj* happening when, for example, the city is less busy (*buy an off-peak travel ticket*).

off-putting /of-poo-ting/ *adj* discouraging.

offset /awf-set/ *vb* (**offset**, **offsetting**) to make up for (*her enthusiasm offsets her lack of training*).

offshoot /awf-shoot/ *n* **1** a branch or shoot growing out from the main stem of a plant. **2** something growing out of something else (*the firm is an offshoot of a large business*).

offshore /awf-shore/ *adj* toward the sea. ● *adv* **offshore**.

offside /awf-side/ *adv* and *adj* in soccer or hockey, in a position disallowed by the rules when the ball was last kicked or struck.

offspring /awf-spring/ *n* a child or children (*the couple have badly behaved offspring*).

often /aw-fen/ *adv* frequently (*we often see them*).

ogle /o-gul/ *vb* to look sidewise at, to look or stare at because of admiration or physical attraction.

ogre /o-gur/ *n* in fairy tales, a man-eating giant. ● *f* **ogress** /o-gress/.

ohm /oam/ *n* the unit of measurement of electrical resistance.

oil /oil/ *n* a greasy liquid obtained from vegetable, animal, or mineral sources, and used as a fuel, lubricant, etc. (*put more oil in the car engine/fry the food in sunflower oil*). ● *npl* **oils** /oilz/ oil paints or painting (*a portrait in oils*). ● *vb* to put or drop oil on, as on the parts of a machine to make them work smoothly (*oil the hinges of the gate*).

oil painting /oil-pane-ting/ *n* a picture done in oils (*an oil painting of their house*).

oilskin /oil-skin/ *n* a cloth made waterproof with oil.

oily /oi-lee/ *adj* **1** covered with oil (*oily hands*). **2** greasy (*oily food*).

ointment /oint-ment/ *n* an oily paste rubbed on the skin to heal cuts or sores.

OK /o-kay/ *adv and adj* (*fml*) all right.

old /oald/ *adj* **1** not new (*old clothing*). **2** aged (*old people*). **3** belonging to the past (*old customs*). **4** not fresh (*old bread*).

old-fashioned /oald-fa-shund/ *adj* out-of-date (*old-fashioned clothing*).

olive /ol-iv/ *n* **1** an evergreen tree bearing a small, sharp-tasting fruit, from which oil can be obtained. **2** its fruit, used as food (*olives stuffed with peppers*). ● *adj* yellowish green. ● *n* **olive oil**.

olive branch /ol-iv branch/ *n* a sign of peace (*we hadn't spoken to our neighbors for years but we decided to hold out an olive branch to them*).

olive-skinned /ol-iv-skind/ *adj* having a yellowish-brown skin (*olive-skinned people*).

Olympic /o-lim-pic/ *adj* having to do with Olympia in Greece, and the games held there every four years in ancient times.

Olympic Games /o-lim-pic-gaymz/ *n* an international athletic contest held every four years, each time in a different country.

omelet, **omelette** /om-let/ *n* eggs beaten and fried in a pan, usually served folded in half.

omen /o-men/ *n* a sign of a future event, good or bad (*clouds are an omen of bad weather*).

ominous /om-in-us/ *adj* signifying future trouble or disaster (*ominous black clouds*).

omit /o-mit/ *vb* (**omitted** /o-mi-tid/, **omitting** /o-mi-ting/) **1** to fail to do (*omit to post the letters*). **2** to leave out (*omit a few passages from the report*). ● *n* **omission** /o-mi-shun/.

omnibus /om-ni-bus/ *n* **1** (*fml*) a bus. **2** a book containing several works by the same author or on the same subject (*an omnibus edition of the crime writer's works*).

omnivorous /om-niv-rus/ *adj* (*fml or hum*) eating all kinds of food (*omnivorous animals*).

on /on/ *adv* **1** being worn (*put your shoes on*). **2** forward (*they walked on*). ● *adj* in operation (*the TV is on*). ● *prep* on top of (*on the table*).

once /wunse/ *adv* **1** on one occasion only (*I met him only once*). **2** formerly (*they were friends once*). ● **once and for all** once and never again (*they told her once and for all to go*). ● **at once** immediately (*I shall come at once*).

oncoming /**on**-cu-ming/ *adj* approaching (*oncoming traffic*).

one /wun/ *adj* single. ● *pron* a person.

one-sided /wun-**sie**-did/ *adj* favoring one party or point of view only (*giving a one-sided version of events*).

one-way /wun-**way**/ *adj* of a street, allowing movement of traffic in one direction only.

ongoing /**on**-go-wing/ *adj* continuing, continuing to develop (*an ongoing process*).

onion /**un**-yun/ *n* a strong-smelling edible bulb, often used in cooking.

online /on-**line**/ *adj* controlled by or connected to a central computer or connected to the Internet.

onlooker /**awn**-loo-ker/ *n* a spectator, a person who looks at what is happening but takes no part in it (*police asked the onlookers to move from the scene of the accident*).

only /**oan**-lee/ *adv* no more than (*only two days*). ● *conj* except that (*I would love to take a vacation, only I can't afford it*).

only child /**oan**-lee-childe/ *n* a person who has no brothers or sisters.

onomatopoeia /on-o-ma-to-**pay**-a/ *n* forming words by imitating sounds (e.g., hiss, bang). ● *adj* onomatopoeic /on-o-ma-to-**pay**-ic/.

onrush /**awn**-rush/ *n* a rapid advance (*the onrush of the protesting demonstrators*).

onset /**awn**-set/ *n* the first attack of or the beginning of (*the onset of the illness*).

onshore /**awn**-shore/ *adj* toward the shore. ● *adv* onshore /**awn**-shore/.

onslaught /**awn**-slot/ *n* a fierce attack (*try to withstand the enemy onslaught/a politician making an onslaught on the government*).

onward /**awn**-ward/ *adj* forward. ● *adv* onward /**awn**-ward/.

onyx /**aw**-niks/ *n* a precious stone containing layers of different colors.

ooze /ooz/ *n* soft mud, slime. ● *vb* 1 to flow very slowly (*blood oozing from the wound*). 2 to have flowing from (*a wound oozing pus*).

opacity *see* opaque.

opal /**o**-pal/ *n* a white precious stone that changes color when turned in the light.

opaque /o-**pake**/ *adj* that cannot be seen through, letting no light through (*opaque glass*). ● *n* opacity /o-**pa**-si-tee/.

open /**o**-pen/ *adj* 1 not shut, uncovered (*an open gate*). 2 ready for business (*the stores are open*). 3 not hidden (*an open show of affection*). 4 free from obstructions (*the road is open now*). 5 public (*an open meeting*). 6 sincere (*an open manner*). 7 clear. ● *vb* 1 to make or become open (*open the door*). 2 to unlock (*open the safe*). 3 to begin (*open the meeting*). ● in the open air outside. ● keep open house to welcome all visitors. ● open up to build roads, etc., in a country to make progress possible.

open-handed /o-pen-**han**-did/ *adj* (*fml*) generous (*an open-handed host*).

opening /**ope**-ning/ *n* 1 beginning (*the opening of the fête*). 2 a gap, a way in or out (*an opening in the fence*). 3 an opportunity (*job openings*).

openly /**o**-pen-lee/ *adv* publicly, not secretly (*discuss the matter openly*).

open-minded /o-pen-**mine**-did/ *adj* ready to consider new ideas, unprejudiced.

opera¹ /**aw**-pra/ *n* a musical drama in which all or some of the words are sung (*operas by Wagner*).

opera² *see* opus.

opera glasses /**aw**-pra **gla**-siz/ *npl* glasses used in the theater to magnify the stage and players.

operate /**aw**-pe-rate/ *vb* 1 (*of a machine*) to work or to cause to work (*machines operated by hand*). 2 (*of a surgeon*) to cut the body in order to cure or treat a diseased part (*the doctor will operate to remove her appendix*).

operatic /aw-pe-**ra**-tic/ *adj* having to do with opera (*operatic tenors*).

operating system /**aw**-pe-ray-ting-si-stem/ *n* the software that controls the operation of a computer.

operation /aw-pe-**ray**-shun/ *n* 1 action (*a rescue operation/a plan now in operation*). 2 the way a thing works (*the operation of the machine*). 3 the cutting of the body by a doctor or surgeon to cure or treat a diseased part (*an operation to remove tonsils*).

operative /**aw**-pra-tiv/ *adj* 1 in action. 2 having effect. ● *n* a worker in a factory.

operator /**aw**-pe-ray-tor/ *n* a person who looks after a machine (*the elevator operator*).

operetta /aw-pe-**re**-ta/ *n* a short, not too serious, musical play (*an operetta by Gilbert and Sullivan*).

ophthalmic /of-**thal**-mic/ *adj* having to do with the eye(s).

opinion /o-**pin**-yun/ *n* 1 that which you think or believe about something (*listen to the opinions of others*). 2 judgment (*too ill to work, in the doctor's opinion*).

opinionated /o-**pin**-yu-nay-tid/, **opinionative** /o-**pin**-yu-na-tiv/ *adjs* sure that your opinions are correct (*an opinionated young woman who refuses to listen to the advice of others*).

opium /**o**-pee-yum/ *n* a sleep-producing drug made from poppy seeds.

opossum /o-**poss**-um/ *n* a small animal that carries its young in a pouch.

opponent /o-**po**-nent/ *n* an enemy, a person whom you try to overcome in a game, argument, etc. (*his opponent in the tennis match*).

opportune /op-or-**toon**/ *adj* happening at the right time (*arrive at the opportune moment*).

opportunist /op-or-**too**-nist/ *n* a person who takes advantage of opportunities that occur. ● *adj.*

opportunity /op-or-**too**-ni-tee/ *n* happening at the right time (*arrive at the opportune moment*).

oppose /o-**poaz**/ *vb* **1** to act or speak against (*opposing the bill in Parliament*). **2** to resist (*oppose change*).

opposite /**op**-u-zit/ *adj* **1** facing (*the house opposite*). **2** in the same position on the other side. **3** different in every way (*have opposite tastes in music/go in opposite directions*). ● *n* something in every way different (*"good" is the opposite of "bad"*). ● *adv* and *prep* across from.

opposition /op-u-**zi**-shun/ *n* **1** the act of going or speaking against, resistance (*their opposition to the new road*). **2** (*often cap*) in politics, the party that criticizes or resists the governing party (*leader of the Opposition*).

oppress /o-**press**/ *vb* **1** to govern harshly or unjustly, to treat cruelly (*a tyrant who oppressed the people*). **2** to make gloomy or anxious (*oppressed by news of the war*). ● *n* **oppression** /o-**pre**-shun/.

oppressive /o-**pre**-siv/ *adj* **1** harsh and unjust (*an oppressive form of government*). **2** (*of the weather*) hot and tiring.

opt /**opt**/ *vb* to choose (*I opted for the rack of lamb*). ● **opt out** to choose not to do something.

optic /**op**-tic/, **optical** /**op**-ti-cal/ *adjs* having to do with sight or the eye(s).

optician /op-**ti**-shan/ *n* a person who makes or sells glasses for the eyes (*an appointment at the optician's for an eye test*).

optics /**op**-tics/ *n* the science of light or sight.

optimal /**op**-ti-mal/ *adj* best (*the optimal time*).

optimism /**op**-ti-mi-zum/ *n* the belief that all that happens is for the best, cheerful hope that all will go well (*they were full of optimism, although we thought they had little chance of success*).

optimist /**op**-ti-mist/ *n* a cheerfully hopeful person.

optimistic /op-ti-**mi**-stic/ *adj* having to do with or characterized by optimism (*optimistic people/an optimistic view of life*). ● *adv* **optimistically** /op-ti-**mi**-sti-clee/.

optimum /**op**-ti-mum/ *adj* and *n* best.

option /**op**-shun/ *n* choice (*no option but to go*).

optional /**op**-shnal/ *adj* that may or may not be done by choice (*some school subjects are optional*).

opulence /**op**-yu-lense/ *n* (*fml*) riches, wealth (*the opulence of the king*).

opulent /**op**-yu-lent/ *adj* (*fml*) rich, wealthy.

opus /**o**-pus/ *n* (*pl* **opuses** /**o**-pu-seez/ or **opera** **aw**-pra/) **1** (*fml*) a work of art (*the latest opus of the author*). **2** a musical work numbered in order of composition (*Beethoven's opus 106*).

or /**awr**/ *conj* used to link alternatives (*would you like milk or orange juice?*)

oracle /**aw**-ra-cul/ *n* **1** in legend, the answer given to a question by or on behalf of a god. **2** the place where such answers were given. **3** a person who answers on behalf of a god. **4** (*often hum*) a wise or knowledgeable person (*she is the oracle on company law in the office*).

oral /**aw**-ral/ *adj* spoken, not written (*an oral exam*). ● *adv* **orally** /**aw**-ra-lee/.

orange /**aw**-ranj/ *n* **1** a juicy fruit with a reddish yellow skin (*peel the rind from an orange*). **2** the tree bearing it. **3** its color, reddish-yellow. ● *adj* of orange color.

orangutan /**aw**-**rang**-u-tan/ *n* a large man-like ape with long arms.

oration /**aw**-**ray**-shun/ *n* (*fml*) a formal public speech (*a funeral oration*).

orator /**aw**-ra-tor/ *n* a skilled public speaker (*an eloquent orator*).

orb /**awrb**/ *n* (*lit*) a sphere, a round object.

orbit /**awr**-bit/ *n* the curved path of a planet, comet, rocket, etc., around a larger heavenly body (*a satellite in orbit around the earth*). ● *adj* **orbital** **awr**-bi-tal/.

orchard /**awr**-chard/ *n* a field in which fruit trees are grown (*an apple orchard*).

orchestra /**awr**-ke-stra/ *n* **1** a group of musicians skilled in different instruments who play together (*she plays the flute in the orchestra*). **2** the place where they sit in a hall or theater.

orchestral /awr-ke-stral/ *adj* suitable for performance by an orchestra (*orchestral music*).

orchestrate /**awr**-ke-strate/ *vb* **1** to arrange for an orchestra (*orchestrating the music*). **2** to organiz or arrange (*orchestrate the campaign*). ● *n* **orchestration** /awr-ke-**stray**-shun/.

orchid /**awr**-kid/ *n* a showy flower with unusually shaped petals.

ordain /awr-**dane**/ *vb* **1** (*fml*) to order (*prisoners freed as the king ordained*). **2** to admit to office as a priest or minister of religion.

ordeal /awr-**deel**/ *n* a difficult, painful experience (*being taken hostage was a terrible ordeal*).

order /**awr**-der/ *n* **1** a methodical arrangement (*put the books in order*). **2** a command (*obey the officer's order*). **3** rank, class (*the various orders of plants*). **4** obedience to law (*law and order*). **5** tidiness (*lack of order in the room*). **6** an instruction to make or supply something (*an order for books*). **7** a body or brotherhood of people of the same rank profession, etc., a religious brotherhood obeying a certain rule (*an order of monks*). ● *vb* **1** to arrange (*order the book alphabetically*). **2** to command (*order them to leave*). **3** to give an instruction to make or supply (*orders books from them*).

orderly /**awr**-der-lee/ *adj* **1** tidy, well-arranged (*an orderly room*). **2** well-behaved (*an orderly group of children*). ● *n* **1** a soldier who carries the orders and messages of an officer. **2** a hospital attendant.

ordinal /**awr**-di-nal/ *adj* showing the place in an order (*first, second, third, etc., are ordinal numbers*).

ordinance /**awr**-di-nanse/ *n* (*fml*) a law, a command (*obey the king's ordinance*).

ordinary /**awr**-di-ne-ree/ *adj* usual, common, not exceptional (*an ordinary working day*). ● *adv* **ordinarily** /awr-di-**na**-ri-lee/.

ordination /awr-di-**nay**-shun/ *n* the act or ceremony of admitting to office as a priest or minister of religion.

ore /ore/ *n* rock from which metal is obtained (*iron ore*).

oregano /aw-re-**ga**-no/ *n* the dried leaves of the herb marjoram, used in cooking.

organ /**awr**-gan/ *n* **1** part of an animal or plant that serves some special purpose (*the respiratory organs*). **2** a large musical instrument supplied with wind through pipes and played by a keyboard (*play the church organ*). **3** a means of conveying views or information to the public (e.g., a newspaper) (*the organ of the political party*).

organic /awr-**ga**-nic/ *adj* **1** having to do with an organ (*an organic disorder*). **2** produced by living organs (*organic compounds*). **3** grown without the use of artificial fertilizers (*organic vegetables*). ● *adv* **organically** /awr-**ga**-ni-clee/.

organism /**awr**-ga-ni-zum/ *n* **1** any living thing (*all the organisms in a pond*). **2** anything in which the parts all work together to serve one purpose.

organist /**awr**-ga-nist/ *n* a person who plays the organ.

organization /awr-ga-ni-**zay**-shun/ *n* also **organisation** (*Br*) **1** orderly arrangement (*try to establish some organization in the office system*). **2** a group of people working systematically to carry out a common purpose (*a business organization*). ● *adj* **organizational** /awr-ga-ni-**zay**-shnal/, also **organisational** (*Br*).

organize /**awr**-ga-nize/ *vb*, also **organise** (*Br*) **1** to put together in an orderly way, to make to work systematically (*organizing the office filing system*). **2** to arrange (*organize a party*). ● *n* **organizer** /**awr**-ga-ni-zer/, also **organiser** (*Br*).

orgy /**awr**-jee/ *n* a wild or drunken feast (*have an orgy while his parents are away*).

Orient /**oa**-ree-ent/ *n* the East.

orient /**oa**-ree-ent/ *vb* to orientate.

oriental /oa-ree-**en**-tal/ *adj* Eastern, Asian. ● *n* a native of an Eastern or Asian country.

Orientalist /oa-ree-**en**-ta-list/ *n* a person who studies Eastern languages.

orientate /**oa**-ree-en-tate/ *vb* **1** to find out north, south, east, and west from the point where you are standing (*the climbers were lost in the mist and tried to orientate themselves*). **2** to arrange or direct toward (*a course orientated to adult learners*). ● *n* **orientation** /oa-ree-en-**tay**-shun/.

orienteering /oa-ree-en-**tee**-ring/ *n* the sport of following a route on foot as quickly as possible, using a map and compass.

orifice /**aw**-ri-fiss/ *n* (*fml*) an opening (*bodily orifices*).

origami /aw-ri-**ga**-mee/ *n* the Japanese art of paper-folding.

origin /**aw**-ri-jin/ *n* **1** the place or point at which a thing begins, beginning (*the origin of the river/the origin of the word*). **2** cause (*the origin of his problem*).

original /aw-**ri**-ji-nal/ *adj* **1** new, not thought of before (*an original idea*). **2** first in order (*the original inhabitants of the country*). **3** ready to think or act in a new way (*an original thinker*). **4** not copied (*an original painting*). ● *n* **1** an original work of art, etc. **2** a creative or eccentric person. ● *adv* **originally** /aw-**ri**-ji-na-lee/.

originality /aw-ri-ji-**na**-li-tee/ *n* the ability to think or act in a new way.

originate /aw-**ri**-ji-nate/ *vb* **1** to bring into being (*originating a new club*). **2** to come into being (*a sport that originated in China*).

oriole /**oa**-ree-ole/ *n* a bird with golden-yellow feathers.

ornament /**awr**-na-ment/ *n* that which decorates or makes more attractive. ● *vb* **ornament** /**awr**-na-ment/ to decorate. ● *n* **ornamentation** /awr-na-men-**tay**-shun/.

ornamental /awr-na-**men**-tal/ *adj* decorative (*fireplaces that are purely ornamental*).

ornate /awr-**nate**/ *adj* with a great deal of ornament, richly decorated (*ornate furniture*).

ornithology /awr-na-**thol**-o-jee/ *n* the study of birds. ● *n* **ornithologist** /awr-na-**thol**-o-jist/ *n* a person who studies birds (*ornithologists going on a bird-watching trip*).

orphan /**awr**-fan/ *n* a child whose parents are dead (*made an orphan by the plane crash*). ● *vb* to cause to become an orphan. ● *also adj.*

orphanage /**awr**-fa-nidge/ *n* a home for orphans.

orthodontist /**awr**-tha-dawn-tist/ *n* a dentist who straightens teeth.

orthodox /**awr**-tho-doks/ *adj* **1** having the same beliefs or opinions as most other people (*orthodox people*). **2** agreeing with accepted belief (*orthodox views*). ● *n* **orthodoxy** /**awr**-tho-dok-see/.

orthopedic /awr-tho-**pee**-dic/ *adj* having to do with injury or diseases of the bones or joints (*an orthopedic surgeon*).

osprey /**aw**-spray/ *n* a hawk that feeds on fish.

ostensible /aw-**sten**-si-bul/ *adj* as far as can be seen, apparent (*his ostensible reason for leaving*). ● *adv* **ostensibly** /aw-**sten**-si-blee/.

ostentatious /aw-sten-**tay**-shus/ *adj* showy, fond of display (*an ostentatious wedding despite their lack of money*).

osteopath /**aw**-stee-o-path/ *n* a person who practices osteopathy (*he attended an osteopath for his backache*).

osteopathy /aw-stee-**op**-a-thee/ *n* cure of disease by massage or otherwise handling the bones.

ostracize /**aw**-stra-size/ *vb*, *also* **ostracise** (*Br, Cdn*) to drive out of society, to refuse to have anything to do with (*workers ostracizing people who worked during the strike*). ● *n* **ostracism** /**aw**-stra-si-zum/.

ostrich /**aw**-strich/ *n* a large swift-running bird valued for its feathers.

other /**u**-ther/ *adj* **1** one of two things (*the other hand*). **2** addition (*we have other problems*). those not mentioned, present, etc. (*other people*)

otherwise /**u**-ther-wize/ *adv* **1** in a different wa (*they think otherwise*). **2** if this were not so (*yo must pay—otherwise they will sue you*).

otter /**aw**-ter/ *n* a fish-eating animal of the weas family.

Ottoman /**aw**-to-man/ *adj* (*old*) Turkish. ● *n* **1** (*old* a Turk. **2** (*without cap*) a sofa without back o arms.

ought /awt/ *vb* should (*she ought to see a doctor*)

ounce /ounse/ *n* **1** a unit of weight ($^1/_{16}$ lb). **2** a sma amount (*not an ounce of common sense*).

our /our/ *adj* belonging to us. ● *prons* **ours** /ourz **ourselves** /our-**selvz**/.

oust /oust/ *vb* to put out, to drive out (*oust hir from his post*).

out /out/ *adv* **1** not inside (*the children are out i the garden*). **2** away (*he was told to get out*). ● *pre* out of, out through, outside. ● *adj* **1** external. asleep or unconscious (*out to the world*).

out-and-out /ou-tan-(**d**)**out**/ *adj* thorough (*an out and-out villain*).

outback /**out**-back/ *n* a remote area of Australia wit very few inhabitants.

outbid /out-**bid**/ *vb* (**outbid, outbidding** /out-**bi** ding/) to offer a higher price than another (*sh outbid him for the antique furniture*).

outboard /**out**-board/ *adj* attached to the outsid of a boat (*an outboard motor*).

outbreak /**out**-brake/ *n* a sudden beginning, breaking out (*the outbreak of war*).

outburst /**out**-burst/ *n* a bursting out, an explosio (*an outburst of applause/an outburst of anger*).

outcast /**out**-cast/ *adj* driven away from your hom and friends. ● *n* a person who is so driven awa (*an outcast from society*).

outcome /**out**-come/ *n* the result (*the outcome c the discussion*).

outcrop /**out**-crop/ *n* a layer of rock that shows abov the surface of the earth.

outcry /**out**-cry/ *n* widespread complaint (*there wa an outcry at the closure of the bridge*).

outdated /out-**day**-tid/ *adj* old-fashioned, out-of date (*outdated ideas about child care*).

outdo /out-**doo**/ *vb* to do better than (*try to outd him in giving her expensive presents*).

outdoor /out-**dore**/ *adj* done in the open air (*a outdoor display*).

outdoors /out-**doarz**/ *adv* in the open air (*hav lunch outdoors*).

outer /ou-ter/ *adj* 1 farther out (*outer space*). 2 outside (*the outer layer of clothing*).

outermost /ou-ter-moast/ *adj* farthest out (*the outermost ring of a target*).

outer space /ou-ter-**space**/ *n* space beyond the earth's atmosphere.

outfield /out-feeld/ *n* the part of a baseball field that extends outward from the diamond. ● *n* **outfielder** /out-feel-der/.

outfit /out-fit/ *n* 1 all the articles necessary for a certain job (*a bicycle repair outfit*). 2 a set of articles of clothing (*buy a new outfit for the wedding*).

outgoings /out-go-ingz/ *npl* the money spent (*their outgoings came to more than their income*).

outgrow /out-**gro**/ *vb* 1 to grow taller than (*he has outgrown his elder brother*). 2 to grow too big or too old for (*children outgrowing their clothing*).

outing /ou-ting/ *n* a short trip made for pleasure (*take the children on an outing to the shore*).

outlast /out-**last**/ *vb* to last longer than.

outlaw /out-law/ *n* (*old*) someone whose person and property are no longer protected by the law (*Billy the Kid was an outlaw*). ● *vb* 1 to declare an outlaw. 2 to declare not legal (*outlaw drinking and driving*).

outlet /out-let/ *n* 1 an opening outward (*an outlet from the main water tank*). 2 an activity that allows you to make use of your powers or of a particular ability (*an outlet for his musical talent*).

outline /out-line/ *n* 1 a line showing the shape of a thing (*children asked to draw the outline of a face*). 2 an account of the most important points, etc. (*an outline of the proposals for improvement*). ● *vb* 1 to draw in outline. 2 to describe without giving details (*outlining the plans for expansion*).

outlive /out-**liv**/ *vb* to live longer than (*he outlived his son*).

outlook /out-look/ *n* 1 a view (*a house with a beautiful outlook*). 2 what seems likely to happen in future (*the financial outlook for the firm is not good*). 3 a point of view (*a gloomy outlook on life*).

outmoded /out-**mo**-did/ *adj* out of fashion (*outmoded ideas*).

outnumber /out-**num**-ber/ *vb* to be greater in number than (*the children outnumbered the adults*).

out-of-date /out-ov-**date**/ *adj* old-fashioned (*out-of-date clothing*).

outpatient /out-pay-shent/ *n* a person who visits a hospital for treatment but does not stay there (*attend as an outpatient to have his broken arm attended to*).

outpost /out-poast/ *n* 1 a defended place close to enemy territory and in front of the main positions. 2 a settlement far from towns and main roads (*the last outpost of civilization*).

output /out-poot/ *n* the total amount produced by a machine, factory, worker, etc. (*increase output by 10%*).

outrage /out-rage/ *n* 1 a violent and wicked deed (*outrages committed by enemy soldiers*). 2 a deed that shocks or causes widespread anger (*regard the decision to cut workers' wages as an outrage*). ● *vb* 1 to injure. 2 to insult.

outrageous /out-**ray**-jus/ person who rides on horseback or on a motorcycle beside or in front of a vehicle (*police outriders with a very large truck*).

outright /out-**rite**/ *adv* 1 completely and at once (*they paid for the furniture outright/kill him outright*). 2 openly, frankly (*tell me outright what you feel*). ● *adj* complete (*an outright refusal*).

outrun /out-**run**/ *vb* to run faster than (*outrun the other horses in the race*).

outset /out-set/ *n* beginning (*realized the plan was a failure from the outset*).

outside /out-side/ *n* 1 the outer part or parts (*the outside of the orange*). 2 the part farthest from the center (*standing on the outside of the group*). ● *adj* 1 being on the outside, external (*outside help*). 2 outdoor (*an outside hot tub*). 3 slight (*an outside chance*). ● *adv* on or to the outside. ● *prep* on or to the exterior of, beyond.

outsider /out-**sie**-der/ *n* 1 a person who is not accepted as a member of a certain group (*still regarded as an outsider by the family, although she is married to one of the sons*). 2 a person who is believed to have little chance of winning (*a horse regarded as an outsider won the race*).

outskirts /out-skirts/ *npl* the parts of a town or city farthest from the center (*live on the outskirts of the city*).

outsmart /out-**smart**/ *v* to outwit someone (*the fox outsmarted the hunters*).

outspoken /out-**spo**-ken/ *adj* saying just what you think, frank (*outspoken people stating their objections*).

outstanding /out-**stan**-ding/ *adj* 1 exceptionally good (*an outstanding student/an outstanding performance*). 2 (*fml*) still in existence (*outstanding debts*).

outward /**out**-ward/ *adj* **1** on the outside or surface (*her outward cheerfulness*). **2** away from a place (*the outward journey*). ● *advs* **outward, outwardly** /**out**-ward-lee/.

outwit /out-**wit**/ *vb* to outdo or overcome by greater cleverness, to deceive (*succeed in outwitting the police*).

ova *see* **ovum.**

oval /**oa**-val/ *adj* egg-shaped (*an oval face*). ● *n* an oval shape or figure.

ovary /**oa**-va-ree/ *n* **1** a bodily organ in which eggs are formed (*a woman's ovaries*). **2** the seed case of a plant.

ovation /oa-**vay**-shun/ *n* enthusiastic applause (*a standing ovation*).

oven /**u**-ven/ *n* a small chamber heated by a fire or stove and used for cooking (*an electric oven*).

over /**oa**-ver/ *prep* **1** above (*a picture over the mantel*). **2** across (*jump over the wall*). **3** more than (*over three miles*). ● *adv* **1** above (*planes flying over*). **2** across (*water boiling over*). **3** from one side to the other or another (*roll over*). **4** more than the quantity assigned (*food left over*). **5** completed (*it's all over*). **6** from beginning to end (*think it over*).

overalls /**oa**-ver-awlz/ *npl* a garment worn over your usual clothing to keep it clean (*workers wearing overalls*).

overawe /oa-ver-**aw**/ *vb* to frighten into obeying or being silent, to fill with silent respect (*children overawed by the great man*).

overbalance /oa-ver-**ba**-lanse/ *vb* **1** to lean too much in one direction and fall (*the tightrope walker overbalanced*). **2** to cause to fall in this way.

overbearing /oa-ver-**bay**-ring/ *adj* proud and commanding (*overbearing people who try to bully others*).

overboard /**oa**-ver-board/ *adv* over the side of a ship (*fall overboard*).

overcast /**oa**-ver-cast/ *adj* clouded over (*an overcast sky*).

overcharge /oa-ver-**charge**/ *vb* to ask for too great a price (*he was overcharging customers*).

overcoat /**oa**-ver-coat/ *n* a warm outer garment (*wear an overcoat over his suit*).

overcome /oa-ver-**cum**/ *vb* **1** to defeat (*overcome the enemy*). **2** to get the better of (*overcome difficulties*).

overdo /oa-ver-**doo**/ *vb* **1** to do too much (*the invalid was told not to overdo it*). **2** to cook for too long (*overdo the steak*).

overdose /**oa**-ver-doass/ *n* too large a dose (*take an overdose of the drug, intending to commit suicide*) ● *also vb.*

overdraft /**oa**-ver-draft/ *n* the amount of money drawn from a bank in excess of what is available in an account (*try to pay off their overdraft*).

overdraw /oa-ver-**draw**/ *vb* to take more from a bank than you have in your account (*overdraw his account*).

overdress /oa-ver-**dress**/ *vb* to dress too well for the occasion (*she felt overdressed because everyone else was wearing jeans and sweaters*).

overdue /oa-ver-**doo**/ *adj* after the time fixed or due.

overestimate /oa-ver-e-sti-mate/ *vb* to set too high a value on (*overestimating their ability*).

overexpose /oa-ver-ek-**spoaz**/ *vb* to expose a photographic film to too much light.

overflow /**oa**-ver-flo/ *vb* to flood, to flow over the edge or limits of (*the river overflowed its banks*) ● *n* **1** what flows over the sides (*a pipe for the overflow*). **2** the amount by which something is too much (*another hall for the overflow of the audience*).

overgrown /oa-ver-**groan**/ *adj* grown beyond the normal size.

overhand /**oa**-ver-hand/ *adj* something done with your arm raised above your shoulder (*an overhand pitch*).

overhaul /oa-ver-**haul**/ *vb* **1** to examine thoroughly and carry out necessary repairs (*overhauling the car engine*). **2** to catch up (*overhaul the other runners*). ● *n* **overhaul** /**oa**-ver-haul/.

overhead[1] /oa-ver-**head**/ *adj* and *adv* in the sky above (*overhead cables*).

overhead[2] /oa-ver-**head**/ *n* the cost of running a business (*the overhead is too expensive*).

overhear /oa-ver-**heer**/ *vb* to hear what you are not intended to hear (*overhear his parents' conversation*).

overjoyed /oa-ver-**joyd**/ *adj* **1** extremely happy.

overland /**oa**-ver-land/ *adv* across land (not sea) (*journey overland*). ● *adj* **overland** /**oa**-ver-land/ passing by land.

overlap /oa-ver-**lap**/ *vb* to cover partly and go beyond (*tiles overlapping*).

overleaf /oa-ver-**leef**/ *adv* on the reverse side of a page (*turn overleaf*).

overload /oa-ver-**load**/ *vb* to put too heavy a load on.

overlook /oa-ver-**look**/ *vb* **1** to look down on from above (*balconies overlooking the sea*). **2** to for give, to let off without punishment (*overlook the children's naughtiness*). **3** not to notice, to miss (*defects that are easily overlooked*).

overnight /oa-ver-**nite**/ *adv* during the night (*have to stay overnight after the party*). ● *adj* done in or lasting the night (*an overnight journey*).

overpower /oa-ver-**pow**-er/ *vb* to defeat by greater strength (*succeed in overpowering the burglar*).

overpowering /oa-ver-**pow**-er-ing/ *adj* too great to bear (*an overpowering urge to scream*).

overrate /oa-ver-**rate**/ *vb* to think a person or thing better than he, she, or it really is (*he thinks the artist is overrated*).

override /oa-ver-**ride**/ *vb* to decide to pay no attention to (*override their objections*).

overrule /oa-ver-**rool**/ *vb* to use your power to change the decision or judgment of another (*the appeal court judge overruled the previous judgment*).

overrun /oa-ver-**run**/ *vb* **1** to spread over in large numbers (*a building overrun with rats*). **2** to continue beyond the expected time (*the show overran*).

oversea(s) /oa-ver-**seez**/ *adj* and *adv* across the sea (*go overseas to work*).

oversee /oa-ver-**see**/ *vb* to direct the work of others (*oversee production*). ● *n* **overseer** /oa-ver-**see**-er/.

overshadow /oa-ver-**sha**-doe/ *vb* **1** to make less happy (*a wedding overshadowed by the threat of war*). **2** to make seem less important (*her achievements were overshadowed by those of her sister*).

overshoot /oa-ver-**shoot**/ *vb* to go beyond before stopping (*planes overshooting the runway*).

oversight /**oa**-ver-site/ *n* a mistake, a failure to do something (*fail to invite her because of an oversight*).

oversleep /oa-ver-**sleep**/ *vb* to sleep later than intended (*oversleep and be late for work*).

overstep /oa-ver-**step**/ *vb* to go beyond the limits of (*overstep her authority*).

overt /oa-**vert**/ *adj* done or said openly, not hidden (*their overt dislike of him*). ● *adv* **overtly** /oa-**vert**-lee/.

overtake /oa-ver-**take**/ *vb* to catch up with (*the car went fast to overtake the truck*).

overthrow /oa-ver-**throe**/ *vb* to defeat, to remove from power (*overthrow the government*). ● *also n.*

overtime /**oa**-ver-time/ *n* time worked beyond the regular hours (*be paid extra for overtime*). ● *also adj and adv.*

overture /**oa**-ver-choor/ *n* **1** a proposal, an offer (*overtures of peace*). **2** the music played by the orchestra before an opera, etc.

overturn /oa-ver-**turn**/ *vb* **1** to turn upside down

(*overturn the bucket*). **2** to make fall, to defeat, to ruin (*overturn the government*).

overweight /oa-ver-**wate**/ *adj* weighing more than the proper amount. ● *n* excess weight.

overwhelm /oa-ver-**whelm**/ *vb* **1** to defeat utterly (*overwhelm the enemy*). **2** to overcome all your powers, to make feel helpless (*overwhelmed by the volume of work*). ● *adj* **overwhelming** /oa-ver-**whel**-ming/. ● *adv* **overwhelmingly** /oa-ver-**whel**-ming-lee/.

overwork /oa-ver-**wurk**/ *vb* to work too hard (*students overworking for their exams*). ● *n* too much work.

ovoid /**oa**-void/ *adj* egg-shaped.

ovum /**oa**-vum/ *n* (*pl* **ova** /**oa**-va/) an egg.

owe /oa/ *vb* **1** to be in debt to (*owe his brother $100*). **2** to be obliged to (someone), to feel grateful to (*owe his parents a lot*). ● **owing to** because of (*the flight was canceled owing to bad weather*).

owl /owl/ *n* a night bird of prey.

owlet /**ow**-let/ *n* a young owl.

own /oan/ *adj* belonging to yourself. ● *vb* to possess (*they own a car*). ● **own up** to admit (*she owned up that she was guilty*). ● *n* **owner** /**oa**-ner/. ● *n* **ownership** /**oa**-ner-ship/.

ox /oks/ *n* (*pl* **oxen** /**ok**-sen/) a bull or cow. ● *npl* **oxen** cattle.

oxidation /ok-si-**day**-shun/ *n* compounding with oxygen.

oxide /**ok**-side/ *n* a compound of oxygen with another element.

oxidize, oxidise /**ok**-si-dize/ *vb* to unite with oxygen.

oxygen /**ok**-si-jen/ *n* a gas without color, taste, or smell that is present in air and water, and is necessary for all life.

oxygenate /**ok**-si-je-nate/, **oxygenize** /**ok**-si-je-nize/, *also* **oxygenise** (*Br*) *vbs* to mix with oxygen.

oxymoron /ok-si-**mo**-ron/ *n* a figure of speech in which an adjective seems to contradict the noun it accompanies (e.g., *busy idler*).

oyster /**oy**-ster/ *n* an edible shellfish with a double shell in which pearls are sometimes found (*oysters and champagne*).

oyster-catcher /**oy**-ster-ca-cher/ *n* a bird of the seashore.

ozone /**oa**-zone/ *n* **1** a kind of colorless gas with a chlorinelike smell. **2** (*inf*) clean bracing air as found at the shore.

ozone layer /**oa**-zone-lair/ *n* a layer of ozone in the stratosphere that absorbs ultraviolet rays from the sun.

P

P, p /**pee**/ the sixteenth letter of the alphabet.

pace /**payss**/ n **1** a step with the foot. **2** the distance so covered. **3** speed. ● vb **1** to walk slowly. **2** to measure by steps.

pacific /pa-**si**-fic/ adj (fml) peace-loving (a pacific nation).

pacification /pa-si-fi-**cay**-shun/ n act of bringing peace.

pacifier /pa-si-fie-er/ n a rubber teat given to babies to suck on.

pacifism /pa-si-fi-zum/ n the belief that war is never right.

pacifist /pa-si-**fist**/ n someone who works for the end of all war (pacifists who refused to join the armed services).

pacify /pa-si-fie/ vb **1** to restore peace, to end a war in. **2** to calm, to soothe (pacified the crying baby).

pack /**pack**/ n **1** a bundle of things fastened or strapped together (the pack on the hiker's back). **2** a set of playing cards. **3** individual items grouped together into one package (a pack of cigarettes). **4** a number of animals acting or hunting together (a pack of hounds). **5** a gang (a pack of thieves). **6** a mass of floating pieces of ice. ● vb **1** to make into a bundle, to put things into a case, etc. (pack for their vacation/pack their clothes). **2** to fill. **3** to fill to overflowing (pack the hall). **4** to fill with a person's own supporters (pack the jury).

package /pa-kidge/ n **1** a wrapped and sealed container, along with its contents (a package of cookies). **2** a parcel, a bundle (packages delivered by mail).

packaging /pa-ka-jing/ n the materials in which objects are wrapped before they are put on sale.

pack animal /pack-a-ni-mal/ n an animal used for carrying loads (a pack horse).

packet /pa-kit/ n **1** a small parcel (a packet containing a watch). **2** a mail boat.

pack-ice /**pack**-ice/ n a mass of floating pieces of ice.

packing /pa-king/ n the paper, cardboard, etc., used to protect goods being delivered (unwrap the china and throw away the packing).

pact /**pact**/ n an agreement (sign a peace pact).

pad[1] /**pad**/ n **1** a small cushion (kneel on a pad to scrub the floor). **2** soft material used to protect or to alter shape (shoulder pads). **3** sheets of paper fixed together (tear a sheet from the pad). **4** the soft flesh on the foot of certain animals (a dog's pad). ● vb (padded, padding) **1** to fill out with soft material (pad the shoulders of the coat). **2** to make longer with unnecessary words (having little to say, she padded out the essay as much as possible).

pad[2] /**pad**/ vb to walk steadily and usually softly (children padded down the hall in their slippers).

padding /pa-ding/ n **1** soft material used for stuffing or filling out. **2** words, sentences, etc., put in merely to make something longer.

paddle /pa-dul/ n a short oar with a broad blade, sometimes at each end. ● vb **1** to row with a paddle (paddle the boat downstream). **2** to walk in water with bare feet (children paddling at the seaside). **3** to punish by spanking.

paddle steamer /pa-dul-stee-mer/ n a steamer driven by two large wheels turning in the water to make it move.

paddle wheel /pa-dul-wheel/ n the wheel of a paddle steamer.

paddock /pa-dick/ n **1** a small enclosed field (the paddock for the pony near the house). **2** an enclosure in which horses are assembled before a race.

paddy field /pa-dee-feeld/ n a field in which rice is grown.

padlock /pad-lock/ n a metal locking device that closes over two rings and thus fastens something (the padlock on the gate). ● vb to close with a padlock (padlock the trunk).

pagan /pay-gan/ n **1** someone who is not Christian, Jewish or Muslim. **2** someone who worships many gods. **3** someone who has no religion; heathen (modern paganism is sometimes described as nature religion). ● n paganism /pay-ga-ni-zum/.

page[1] /paidge/ n **1** a boy servant, usually uniformed, in a hotel, club, etc. (tell the page to take a message). **2** a boy attendant on a bride at a wedding. **3** (old) a boy attendant of a knight or nobleman.

page[2] /paidge/ n one side of a sheet of paper in a book, etc. (turn over the pages of the magazine).

pageant /pa-jint/ n **1** a performance or procession often presenting scenes from history (a pageant to celebrate the centenary of the village). **2** a fine display or show (a colorful pageant).

pageantry /pa-jin-tree/ n splendid display.

pagoda /pa-goe-da/ n a pyramid-shaped temple in Eastern countries.

pail /pail/ *n* an open vessel with a handle for carrying liquids (*carry a pail of water*).

pain /pain/ *n* **1** suffering of body or mind (*the pain in his back/the pain of her grief*). **2** *pl* **pains** /painz/ trouble, care (*be at pains to explain why he refused*). ● *vb* (*fml*) to cause suffering to (*it pained him to leave his family*). ● *adjs* **painful** /pain-ful/, **painless** /pain-less/. ● **on pain of death** with death as a punishment.

painstaking /pain-stay-king/ *adj* **1** very careful (*a painstaking report*). **2** taking great trouble (*a painstaking student*).

paint /paint/ *n* a coloring substance spread over the surface of an object with a brush (*buy cans of blue paint to decorate the bedroom/the artist's clothes were covered in paint*). ● *vb* **1** to put on paint (*paint the bedroom/paint a picture*). **2** to paint a picture (*he paints as a hobby*). ● *n* **painter**

paintbrush /paint-brush/ *n* **1** a brush used for decorating a house with paint. **2** a brush used for painting pictures.

painting /pain-ting/ *n* a painted picture (*a painting of their house*).

pair /pair/ *n* **1** two things of the same kind, a set of two (*a pair of gloves/two socks that are not a pair*). **3** a couple, two people, animals, etc., often one of either sex, who are thought of as being together (*a pair of rabbits/our neighbors are an inquisitive pair*). ● *vb* **1** to arrange in twos. **2** to join one to another.

pal /pal/ *n* (*inf*) a friend, comrade (*his best pal*).

pajamas, pyjamas /pa-ja-maz/ *npl* a loose, lightweight pants and shirt set, worn in bed.

palace /pa-liss/ *n* a large and splendid house, especially the house of a king or queen (*Buckingham Palace*). ● *adj* **palatial** /pa-lay-shal/.

palate /pa-lit/ *n* **1** the roof of the mouth. **2** the sense of taste, the ability to tell good food or wine from bad (*get him to choose the wine because he has a good palate*). **3** a taste or liking (*novels that are not to his palate*).

pale¹ /pale/ *adj* **1** lacking color, whitish (*ill people looking pale*). **2** not dark in color (*pale colors*). ● *vb* to make or become pale (*she paled with fear*).

pale² /pale/ *n* **1** a pointed stake of wood driven into the ground as part of a fence. **2** (*old*) a boundary. ● **beyond the pale** beyond the limit of proper behavior (*his drunken behavior was beyond the pale*).

paleolithic /pay-lee-o-li-thic/ *adj*, *also* **palaeolithic** (*Br, Cdn*) having to do with the early Stone Age (*paleolithic remains*).

paleontology /pay-lee-on-tol-uh-jee/ *n*, *also* **palaeontology** (*Br, Cdn*) the study of fossils and ancient life forms.

paleontologist /pay-lee-on-tol-uh-jee/ *n*, *also* **palaeontology** (*Br, Cdn*) someone who studies paleontology.

palette /pa-lit/ *n* a thin board on which an artist mixes paints.

palindrome /pa-lin-droam/ *n* a word whose letters when read from end to beginning spell the same word (e.g., noon).

palisade /pa-li-sade/ *n* **1** (*old*) a defensive fence of stakes. **2** *npl* **palisades** /pa-li-saydz/ a line of high cliffs.

pallet /pa-let/ *n* **1** a wooden platform on which goods can be carried by a fork-lift truck. **2** (*old*) a bed of straw.

pallor /pa-lur/ *n* paleness (*the invalid's pallor*).

palm¹ /pam/ *n* the inner part of the hand between the wrist and fingers. ● *vb* **palm off** to get to accept something worthless (*palm off the painting as genuine, although it was a copy*).

palm² /pam/ *n* a tall tropical tree with a crown of long broad leaves at the top of the trunk (*coconut palms*).

palmist /pa-mist/ *n* a person who claims to tell someone's future from the lines on their hand (*have her future told by a palmist*). ● *n* **palmistry** /pa-mis-tree/.

Palm Sunday /pam-sun-day/ *n* the Sunday before Easter.

palsy /pawl-zee/ *n* a disease causing trembling of the limbs. ● *adj* **palsied** /pawl-zeed/.

paltry /pawl-tree/ *adj* **1** contemptibly small, worthless (*a paltry sum of money*). **2** mean (*a paltry trick*).

pampas /pam-paz/ *npl* the vast grassy treeless plains of South America.

pamper /pam-per/ *vb* to spoil by trying to please too much (*pamper the child*).

pamphlet /pam-flit/ *n* a small paper-covered book (*a pamphlet giving the aims of the campaign*).

pan /pan/ *n* **1** a metal pot used for cooking (*a frying pan/pans sitting on the stove*). **2** the tray of a balance or set of scales. ● *vb* **1** to criticize severely. **2 pan out** to turn out, to result.

Pan /pan/ *n* in legend, the Greek god of nature and shepherds.

pan- /pan/ *prefix* all.

panacea /pa-na-see-ya/ *n* a cure for all diseases or evils (*look for a panacea for the world's ills*).

panache /pa-nash/ *n* style, a dramatic show of skill, etc. (*introduce the guest with great panache*).

pancake /**pan**-cake/ *n* a thin cake of batter cooked in a pan or on a griddle (*toss the pancakes*).

pancreas /**pan**-cree-as/ *n* a gland in the body that produces a fluid that helps digestion and produces insulin that helps the body to use glucose (*a malfunctioning pancreas caused the boy to develop diabetes*).

panda /**pan**-da/ *n* a large black-and-white animal found in China.

pandemonium /pan-di-**moe**-nee-um/ *n* a scene of noisy disorder, uproar (*there was pandemonium when the crowds were refused entrance to the rally*).

pander /**pan**-der/ *vb* to give in to the desires of a person or group (*pander to the children by letting them stay up late*).

pane /**pane**/ *n* a single piece of glass in a window.

panel /**pa**-nul/ *n* **1** a thin board fitted into the framework of a door or on a wall or ceiling (*an old house with indoor walls made of wooden panels*). **2** a group of people who discuss or answer questions put to them by others (*a panel of experts answering questions asked by television viewers*).

pang /**pang**/ *n* **1** a sudden sharp pain (*pangs of hunger*). **2** a sudden sharp feeling (*pangs of regret*).

panic /**pa**-nic/ *n* **1** a sudden uncontrollable fear (*she felt the panic rising*). **2** sudden fear spreading through a crowd and causing wild disorder (*there was panic in the theater when the fire broke out*). ● *also adj.*

panic-stricken /**pa**-nic-**stri**-kin/ *adj* filled with panic (*the panic-stricken crowd*).

panorama /pa-nu-ra-ma/ *n* **1** a wide view (*a breathtaking panorama from the top of the mountain*). **2** a scene painted on a strip of material and gradually unrolled before an audience. **3** a general representation in words or pictures (*a book giving a panorama of life in the Prohibition Era*).

pansy /**pan**-zee/ *n* a large type of violet.

pant /**pant**/ *vb* **1** to take short quick breaths (*runners panting at the end of the race*). **2** to long for (*pant for the chance to sing*). ● *n* a gasp.

panther /**panth**-er/ *n* a leopard, especially the black variety.

panties /**pan**-tees/ *npl* women or children's underwear.

pantomime /**pan**-tu-mime/ *n* **1** a story told through mime. **2** (*Br*) an amusing Christmas play, popular with children, with music and songs, based on a well-known story or fairy tale.

pantry /**pan**-tree/ *n* **1** a small room for keeping food (*keep the food cool in the pantry*). **2** a room in which food, dishes, cutlery, etc., are stored.

pants /**pants**/ *npl* **1** a piece of clothing that has two legs and fastens at the waist. **2** (*Br*) underpants.

pantyhose /**pan**-tee-hose/ *n* a woman's undergarment covering the legs and bottom, similar to tights, made from nylon or silk.

paparazzi /pa-pa-**rat**-see/ *npl* (*sing* **paparazzo** /pa-pa-**rat**-so/) photographers who follow famous people (often intrusively) in order to take their photographs to sell to newspapers and magazines.

papaw, pawpaw /**paw**-paw/ *n* a North American tree with edible fruit.

papaya /pa-**pie**-ya/ *n* a yellow or orange, melonlike sweet-tasting tropical fruit.

paper /**pay**-per/ *n* **1** a material made from wood pulp, rags, etc., and used for writing, printing, wrapping and many other purposes (*waste paper*). **2** a newspaper (*a daily paper*). **3** an essay (*write a paper on the poetry of John Keats*). **4** a set of examination questions on a subject or part of a subject (*the maths paper*). ● *vb* to cover with paper (*paper the walls*).

paperback /**pay**-per-back/ *n* a soft book with a cover of thin card (*wait for the novel to come out in paperback*).

paper chase /**pay**-per-chase/ *n* a cross-country run in which certain runners throw down a trail of paper for the others to follow.

paper money /pay-per-**mu**-nee/ *n* banknotes.

paperweight /**pay**-per-wate/ *n* a heavy object placed on top of loose papers to keep them in place.

papier mâché /pay-per **ma**-shay, pa-pee-ay ma-shay/ *n* a substance consisting of paper pulp and used for making boxes, ornaments, etc (*children making models out of papier mâché*).

papoose /pa-**pooss**/ *n* an American Indian baby.

paprika /pa-**pree**-ka/ *n* red pepper (*sprinkle paprika on the savories*).

papyrus /pa-**pie**-rusk/ *n* (*pl* **papyri** /pa-**pie**-ree/) **1** reed from which paper was made in ancient times. **2** the paper thus made (*manuscripts written on rolls of papyrus*).

par /**par**/ *n* **1** the state of being equal (*cities on a par in terms of tourist popularity*). **2** the normal value, amount or degree of something (*work not up to par*). **3** in golf, the number of strokes that should be taken on a round by a good player (*a score of two over par*).

parable /**pa**-ra-bul/ *n* a simple story made up to illustrate the difference between right and wrong.

parabola /pa-ra-bu-la/ *n* **1** a curved line so drawn that it is throughout its length the same distance from both a fixed point and a line. **2** a section obtained by cutting a cone by a plane parallel to its side.

parachute /pa-ra-shoot/ *n* an apparatus that opens like an umbrella and enables people to jump from an airplane and drop to the ground safely (*he did a parachute jump for charity*).

parade /pa-rade/ *n* **1** a public procession (*a parade of decorated floats*). **2** display, show (*a parade of his knowledge*). **3** soldiers, etc., standing in lines under the command of their officers. ● *vb* **1** to show off (*parade his knowledge*). **2** to take up places in an orderly body (e.g., of soldiers). **3** to march in procession (*children parading in fancy dress*). **4** to walk up and down (*she paraded up and down impatiently waiting for him*).

paradise /pa-ra-dice/ *n* **1** heaven. **2** the garden of Eden. **3** (*inf*) a place or state of great happiness (*regard a day without work as paradise*).

paradox /pa-ra-doks/ *n* a statement that seems to contradict itself (*"more haste, less speed" is a paradox*). ● *adj* **paradoxical** /pa-ra-dok-si-cal/.

paraffin /pa-ra-fin/ *n* a waxy substance obtained from shale or coal and used for making candles or made into oil for lamps, etc.

paragon /pa-ra-gon/ *n* a perfect example of some good quality (*a paragon of good manners*).

paragraph /pa-ra-graf/ *n* a distinct division of a piece of writing beginning on a new line, often with its first word slightly in from the left-hand margin.

parakeet /pa-ra-keet/ *n* a small parrot.

parallel /pa-ra-lel/ *adj* **1** (*of lines*) at the same distance from each other at all points. **2** similar (*a parallel case/parallel circumstances*). ● *n* **1** a like or similar example, a comparison (*see a parallel in the two cases*). **2** one of the lines drawn on maps through all places at the same distance from the equator.

parallelogram /pa-ra-lel-lo-gram/ *n* a four-sided figure whose opposite sides are parallel.

paralyze, paralyse /pa-ra-lize/ *vb* **1** to make helpless or powerless (*a country paralyzed by a transport strike*). **2** to strike with paralysis (*he has been paralyzed since the accident that injured his spine*).

paralysis /pa-ra-li-sis/ *n* a condition causing loss of feeling and the power to move in part of the body (*suffering from paralysis below the waist*).

paralytic /pa-ra-li-tic/ *adj* suffering from paralysis. ● *also n*.

paramedic /pa-ra-med-ic/ *n* a person who is trained to give someone a certain amount of medical treatment until the patient can be treated by a doctor.

parameter /pa-ra-mi-ter/ *n* a factor that determines the limits (*working within the parameters of the resources available to them*).

paramount /pa-ra-mount/ *adj* highest, greatest (*of paramount importance*).

paranoia /pa-ra-noy-a/ *n* a form of mental illness that can result in delusions or feelings of persecution.

parapet /pa-ra-pit/ *n* a safety wall at the side of a bridge, at the edge of a roof, etc.

paraphernalia /pa-ra-fer-nale-ya/ *npl* a large collection of objects, often personal belongings, or all the tools necessary for a job or hobby (*the paraphernalia necessary to take a baby on a journey*).

paraphrase /pa-ra-fraze/ *vb* to express the sense of a passage by using other words (*the teacher paraphrased the difficult poem*). ● *also n*.

parasite /pa-ra-site/ *n* **1** someone who lives at another's expense (*a parasite who moves from one friend's house to another*). **2** a plant or animal that lives on or in another (*fleas are parasites*). ● *adj* **parasitic** /pa-ra-si-tic/.

parasol /pa-ra-sawl/ *n* a sunshade in the form of an umbrella (*carry a parasol in the midday sun*).

paratroop(er) /pa-ra-troo-per/ *n* a soldier trained to drop from an airplane by parachute.

parboil /par-boil/ *vb* to boil slightly (*parboil the potatoes before roasting*).

parcel /par-sul/ *n* **1** a small bundle or package (*send the present in a parcel*). **2** a small piece of land, especially part of a large piece (*the large estate has been divided into parcels of land*). ● *vb* (**parceled** / par-suld/, **parceling** /par-su-ling/) **1** to divide into shares (*parcel out the food to the homeless*). **2** to wrap up in paper, etc. (*parcel up the presents*).

parch /parch/ *vb* to dry up (*grass parched by the sun*).

parched /parcht/ *adj* **1** dried out (*parched land*). **2** (*inf*) very thirsty (*parched after the long walk*).

parchment /parch-ment/ *n* **1** a skin prepared for writing on. **2** what is written on it.

pardon /par-dun/ *vb* to forgive, to let off without punishment (*the priest pardoned his wrongdoing*). ● *n* forgiveness.

pardonable /par-du-na-bul/ *adj* that can be forgiven (*crimes that are not pardonable*).

pare /pare/ *vb* to cut off the skin or edge of (*paring the rind from the cheese*).

parent /**pay**-rint/ n a father or mother.

parentage /**pay**-rin-tidge/ n parents and ancestors, birth (*of noble parentage*).

parental /pa-**ren**-tal/ adj of a parent (*parental responsibilities*).

parenthesis /pa-**ren**-thi-sis/ n 1 a group of words put into the middle of a sentence interrupting its sense, often enclosed in brackets. 2 either of a pair of brackets. ● adj parenthetical /pa-ren-**thet**-i-cal/.

parish /**pa**-rish/ n 1 a district with its own church and priest or minister. 2 local government division in Louisiana, equivalent to a county in the other states. 3 (*Br*) a division of a county for administrative purposes. ● adj having to do with a parish (*a parish church/a parish council*).

paring /**pay**-ring/ n a piece of skin cut off (*feed vegetable parings to the pigs*).

parity /**pa**-ri-tee/ n equality, the state of being equal (*women seeking salary parity with men*).

park /**park**/ n 1 an enclosed piece of ground for the use of the public (*children playing in the park*). 2 a large enclosed space of open ground around a country house (*a mansion with an extensive park*). 3 see **parking lot**. ● vb to leave (a motor car, etc.) standing (*park his car illegally on a double yellow line*).

parka /**par**-kah/ n a heavy jacket with a hood.

parking lot /**par**-king-lot/ n a place where motor cars, etc., may be left.

parkway /**park**-way/ n a wide road that has trees, shrunbs, grass or flowers planted down the middle or along the sides.

parliament /**par**-li-ment/ n 1 an assembly that discusses and makes laws. 2 (*Br*) (*usually with cap*) in the United Kingdom, the House of Commons and the House of Lords. ● adj parliamentary / par-li-**men**-ta-ree/.

parlor /**par**-lur/ n 1 (*old*) a sitting room. 2 a shop providing some kind of personal service (*a beauty parlor/a funeral parlor*).

parody /**pa**-ru-dee/ n 1 a humorous imitation of a serious work of literature. 2 a weak and unsuccessful copy or absurd imitation (*his statement was a parody of the truth*). ● vb 1 to make a parody of. 2 to imitate in order to make fun of (*he parodied the judge's closing speech*).

parole /pa-**role**/ n the release of a prisoner before the end of his or her sentence on condition that he or she does not break the law (*prisoners released on parole*).

parrot /**pa**-rut/ n a brightly colored tropical bird able to imitate human speech (*keep a parrot in a cage as a pet*).

parse /**parss**/ vb to tell what part of speech a word is and its relation to other words in the sentence. ● n parsing /**par**-sing/.

parsley /**par**-slee/ n a garden herb used in cooking (*use parsley to flavor the soup*).

parsnip /**par**-snip/ n a vegetable with a yellow edible root.

parson /**par**-sun/ n a member of clergy (*married by the local parson*).

part /**part**/ n 1 one of the pieces into which a thing can be divided. 2 some but not all. 3 the character played by an actor. 4 the division made when the hair is brushed in two directions (*a center part*) 5 pl ability, talents. ● adj and adv in part. ● vb 1 to divide. 2 to separate. ● adv partly /**part**-lee/. ● in good part without being angry (*take the news of the defeat in good part*). ● part and parcel a necessary part.

partake /par-**take**/ vb (*fml*) 1 to take a share in, to take part in (*partaking in the decision*). 2 to eat (*partake of a large meal*).

partial /**par**-shul/ adj 1 in part only (*a partial improvement*). 2 favoring one side or person (*a partial decision/a partial umpire*). 2 fond (of) (*partial to sweet things*).

partiality /par-shee-a-**li**-tee/ n 1 (*fml*) the favoring of one more than others, unfairness (*an umpire accused of partiality*). 2 liking (for) (*a partiality for chocolate*).

participant /par-**ti**-si-pant/, participator /par-**ti**-si-pay-tor/ ns someone who takes part in (*participants in the quiz*).

participate /par-**ti**-si-pate/ vb to take part in, to have a share in (*participating in the discussions*). ● n participation /par-ti-si-**pay**-shun/.

participle /**par**-ti-si-pul/ n a part of the verb that does the work of an adjective.

particle /**par**-ti-cul/ n a very small part (*particles of dust/not a particle of truth*).

particular /par-**ti**-cyu-lar/ adj 1 different from others, special. 2 careful, exact. 3 difficult to please ● n a single fact, a detail.

particularize, particularise /par-**ti**-cyu-la-rize/ vb to describe in detail.

parting /**par**-ting/ n 1 separation (*the parting of the ways*). 2 act of going away or leaving (*a sad parting at the station*). 3 (*Br*) see **part** sense 4. ● adj done when going away, final (*her parting words*).

partition /par-**ti**-shun/ n 1 a dividing wall or screen

(*a partition dividing the bedroom into two*). **2** division (*the partition of India*). **3** a part divided off from the rest (*a partition for changing*). ● *vb* **1** to divide up (*partition the country into states*). **2** to set up a dividing wall, etc.

partner /**part**-ner/ *n* **1** someone who works or plays with another in a certain undertaking, game, etc. (*business partners/tennis partners*). **2** a husband or wife, someone with whom one lives or is in a long-term relationship (*he and his partner were invited to the party*). ● *vb* to go with or give to as a partner (*she partnered him to the dance*).

partnership /**part**-ner-ship/ *n* **1** the state of being partners (*go into partnership*). **2** a group of people working together for the same purpose (*a business partnership*). **3** people playing on the same side in a game (*a successful tennis partnership*).

partridge /**par**-tridge/ *n* a game bird with gray, brown and white feathers, hunted in sport.

part-time /**part**-**time**/ *adj* for some of the time only (*part-time work*).

party /**par**-tee/ *n* **1** a group of people who have the same or similar beliefs and opinions (*political parties*). **2** a number of people meeting for enjoyment (*a birthday party*). **3** a person or organization taking part (*one of the parties involved in the scheme*).

pass /**pass**/ *vb* **1** to go past (*pass the church on the way to the station*). **2** to go on one's way (*watch the soldiers pass on their way to war*). **3** to move (something) from one place or person to another (*could you pass the salt?*). **4** to die (*the invalid passed away*). **5** (*of time*) to go by (*as the hours passed*). **6** to spend (time) (*pass the summer reading*). **7** to overtake (*a car passing the truck*). **8** to succeed at examination. **9** to recognize as good enough, to approve (*pass his application for a license*). **10** to utter (*pass a remark*). **11** to set up as by vote (*congress passing a new bill*). **12** (*fml*) to be too great for (*pass their understanding*). ● *n* **1** a narrow valley between mountains. **2** a written permission to visit certain places. **3** success in an examination (*get a pass in maths*). ● **a pretty pass** a bad state of affairs (*things have come to a pretty pass when people are begging in the streets*).

passable /**pa**-sa-bul/ *adj* **1** fairly good (*a passable pianist*). **2** that can be crossed or traveled on (*roads scarcely passable in the winter*).

passage /**pa**-sidge/ *n* **1** a way through (*force a passage through the crowds*). **2** act of passing (*the passage of time*). **3** a journey, especially by sea (*pay for his passage to Australia by cooking for the*

crew). **4** a corridor (*a large house with long dark passages*). **6** part of a book, poem, etc. (*learn a passage from the poem by heart*).

passbook /**pass**-book/ *n* a book showing the amounts paid into and drawn from a bank account.

passenger /**pa**-sin-jer/ *n* someone traveling in a ship, car, train, etc. (*a car with room for passengers*).

passe-partout /pa-spar-**too**/ *n* (*fml*) a sticky tape used in framing pictures, photographs, etc.

passer-by /pa-sur-**bie**/ *n* (*pl* **passers-by** /pa-surz-**bie**/) someone who is walking past (*a beggar ignored by the passers-by*).

passing /**pa**-sing/ *adj* **1** moving or going by (*a passing stranger*). **2** lasting for a short time only (*a passing thought*).

passion /**pa**-shin/ *n* **1** a strong feeling, such as love (*their passion for each other*). **2** anger (*a fit of passion*). **3** great enthusiasm (*his passion for football*). **4** (*fml*) great suffering. ● **the Passion** the last sufferings of Christ.

passionate /**pash**-nit/ *adj* **1** having or showing strong feelings (*a passionate love of freedom*). **2** very enthusiastic (*a passionate interest in sport*).

passion flower /**pa**-shin-flour/ *n* a tropical flower, so-called because of an imagined resemblance to Christ's crown of thorns.

passion fruit /**pa**-shin-froot/ *n* an edible purple fruit of the passion flower.

passive /**pa**-siv/ *adj* **1** acted on (*passive verbs*). **2** showing no emotion, interest, etc. (*she remained passive on hearing the bad news*). **3** unresisting (*accept the situation with passive resignation*). ● *n* **passivity** /pa-**si**-vi-tee/.

passive smoking /**pa**-siv-smo-king/ *n* the breathing in of other people's cigarette smoke (*passive smoking can damage health*).

Passover /**pa**-so-ver/ *n* a Jewish feast in memory of their escape from Egypt.

passport /**pass**-poart/ *n* a document giving a person permission to travel in foreign countries (*showing their passports at the border*).

password /**pass**-wurd/ *n* a secret word, knowledge of which shows that a person is friendly.

past /**past**/ *adj* **1** gone by (*in past times*). **2** belonging to an earlier time (*past presidents*). ● *n* **1** time gone by (*in the past he was very poor*). **2** one's earlier life (*his past is unknown to his present employers*). ● *prep* **1** beyond (*the building past the church*). **2** after (*past 3 o'clock*). ● *adv* by (*watch the soldiers march past*).

pasta /**pa**-sta/ *n* an Italian food made from flour,

eggs and water and formed into different shapes, such as spaghetti, often dried before use (*pasta and tomato sauce*).

paste /paist/ *n* **1** flour mixed with water, etc., to make dough for cooking. **2** a sticky mixture of this used as an adhesive (*wallpaper paste*). **3** food crushed so that it can be spread like butter (*fish paste*). **4** the material of which imitation gems are made (*a necklace of paste*). ● *vb* to stick with paste (*pasting the pictures to a piece of card*).

pasteboard /paist-board/ *n* cardboard.

pastel /pa-stul/ *n* **1** a colored chalk or crayon. **2** a drawing done with pastel. ● *adj* soft, quiet, not bright (*pastel colors*).

pasteurize, pasteurise /pa-styu-rize/ *vb* to heat in order to kill all harmful germs (*pasteurized milk*).

pastille /pa-stul/ *n* **1** a small sweet-smelling lozenge. **2** a lozenge containing medicine (*cough pastilles*).

pastime /pa-stime/ *n* a hobby, a game, an interest for one's spare time (*his pastimes are chess and golf*).

past master /past-ma-ster/ *n* an expert, someone with great skill (*a past master at the art of conversation*).

pastor /pa-stur/ *n* the minister of a church.

pastoral /pa-stu-ral/ *adj* **1** (*fml*) having to do with the country or country life (*pastoral scenes*). **2** having to do with a member of the clergy or his or her duties (*pastoral duties*). ● *n* a poem describing country life.

past participle /past par-ti-si-pul/ *n* a form of verb, that often ends in -ed or –en, that shows that an action happened in the past (*sang is the past participle of sing*).

past perfect /past-per-fect/, **pluperfect** /plu-per-fect/ *ns* a tense indicating that an action took place before a past action (e.g., *I had written*).

pastry /pay-stree/ *n* **1** paste of flour, water etc., made crisp by baking (*puff pastry*). **2** a pie or tart (*a store selling pastries*).

pasture /pa-schur/ *n* grassland where farm animals graze. ● *vb* **1** to put cattle to graze. **2** to eat grass on.

pasty /pay-stee/ *adj* white and unhealthy, pale (*a pasty complexion*).

pat /pat/ *n* **1** a tap, a light touch (*a pat on the back*). **2** a small lump (*a pat of butter*). ● *vb* (**patted** /pa-tid/, **patting** /pa-ting/) to tap, to hit lightly (*pat the dog*). ● *adj* ready, coming too easily (*an explanation that was too pat to be convincing*).

patch /patch/ *n* **1** a piece of material sewed or put on to cover a hole (*a patch on the knee of her*

jeans). **2** a small piece of ground (*a vegetable patch in the garden*). ● *vb* to mend by covering over (*patch the elbows of his jacket*).

patchwork /patch-wurk/ *n* many small pieces of material sewn together (*a quilt made of patchwork*).

patchy /pa-chee/ *adj* **1** full of small areas of differing quality (*patchy paintwork*). **2** (*inf*) sometimes good, sometimes bad (*his schoolwork is patchy*).

pâté /pa-tay/ *n* finely minced meat, such as liver, that is spreadable.

patent /pa-tint/ *n* **1** a written document giving someone the sole right to make or sell a new invention. **2** the granting of land titles by the government. ● *adj* **1** protected by patent (*a patent cough cure*). **2** (*fml*) obvious, clear (*his patent dishonesty*). ● *vb* **1** to obtain a patent for (*patenting his new machine*). **2** to grant land titles by a patent.

patent leather /pa-tint-le-ther/ *n* leather with a very high gloss (*dancing shoes of patent leather*).

paternal /pa-ter-nal/ *adj* **1** fatherly, like a father (*paternal love*). **2** related by blood to one's father (*his paternal grandmother*).

paternity /pa-ter-ni-tee/ *n* the state of being a father (*question his paternity of the child*).

path /path/ *n* **1** a narrow way made by the treading of feet, a track (*mountain paths*). **2** the course followed by a person or thing (*a new career path*).

pathetic /pa-thet-ic/ *adj* sad, causing pity (*a pathetic sight/a pathetic person*).

pathless /path-less/ *adj* (*fml*) without a path, unexplored (*pathless tracts of the jungle*).

pathological /pa-thu-lodge-ic-al/ *adj* **1** having to do with the study of disease (*pathological research*). **2** (*inf*) unreasonable, unnatural (*a pathological hatred of his brother*).

pathology /pa-thol-u-jee/ *n* the study of diseases. ● *n* **pathologist** /pa-thol-u-jist/.

pathos /pay-thos/ *n* the quality that excites pity or sadness (*the pathos of the sight of the orphan child*).

pathway /path-way/ *n* a path (*the mountain pathways/the pathway to fortune*).

patience /pay-shince/ *n* **1** the ability to suffer or wait long without complaining, calmness despite delay or difficulty (*bear her long illness with patience/her lack of patience in lines*). **2** (*Br*) see **solitaire**.

patient /pay-shint/ *adj* suffering delay, pain, irritation, etc. quietly and without complaining (*a patient acceptance of her long illness/be patient and wait your turn in the line*). ● *n* a person receiving treatment from a doctor (*the general practitioner's patients*).

patio /pa-tee-o/ *n* a paved area outside a house where people can sit, plants can be grown in containers, etc.

patriarch /pay-tree-ark/ *n* (*fml*) **1** the head of a tribe or family. **2** a senior bishop. **3** a head of the Greek church. **4** a very old man (*the patriarchs of the village sitting in the square*). ● *adj* **patriarchal** / pay-tree-**ar**-cal/.

patriot /pay-tree-ut/ *n* someone who loves his or her country (*a patriot who died for his country*). ● *n* **patriotism** /pay-tree-u-ti-zum/.

patriotic /pay-tree-ot-ic/ *adj* loving one's country (*sing the national anthem with patriotic enthusiasm*).

patrol /pa-**trole**/ *n* **1** a group of men, ships, etc., sent out as a moving guard (*enemy aircraft spotted by the patrol*). **2** the act of patrolling (*soldiers on patrol*). **3** a small group of Scouts or Guides. ● *vb* (**patrolled** /pa-**troald**/, **patrolling** /pa-**tro**-ling/) to move about on guard or to keep watch (*security guards patrolling the factory grounds*).

patrolman /pa-**trole**-man/ *n* a police officer responsible for a particular beat.

patron /pay-trun/ *n* **1** someone who encourages, helps or protects (*a patron of the arts*). **2** a regular customer (*a patron of the local hairdresser*).

patronage /pay-tru-nidge/ *n* **1** the help or protection given by a patron (*his patronage of the arts*). **2** the right of appointing to certain offices (*the chairman's patronage secured his son's appointment*). **3** a manner that shows that one thinks oneself superior (*her patronage of the younger members of staff*).

patronize, patronise /pay-tru-nize/ *vb* **1** to behave to another as if superior to him or her (*the manager's secretary who patronizes the younger secretaries*) **2** (*fml*) to encourage or help, as a patron (*patronizing young artists*). **3** to go somewhere regularly as a patron (*I patronize Burke's Bistro*).

patron saint /pay-trun-**saint**/ *n* a saint believed to give special protection (*Andrew is the patron saint of Scotland*).

patter[1] /pa-ter/ *vb* **1** to make a light tapping sound (*rain pattering on the roof*). **2** to run with quick light steps (*mice pattering around the attic*). ● *n* the sound of pattering (*the patter of rain on the roof*).

patter[2] /pa-ter/ *n* fast talk, especially persuasive talk (*the patter of a salesman*).

pattern /pa-tern/ *n* **1** a model that can be copied (*a dress pattern*). **2** an example (*the pattern of good behavior*). **3** a design as on cloth, a carpet, etc. (*a flower pattern on the curtains*). **4** the way in which

something happens or develops (*the pattern of the illness*).

patty /pa-tee/ *n* a little pie (*meat patties*).

patsy /pat-see/ *n* someone who can be used or manipulated.

paunch /pawnch/ *n* the belly, especially a large protruding one (*develop a paunch from drinking too much beer*).

pauper /paw-per/ *n* a person too poor to support himself or herself (*he was wealthy once, but he died a pauper*).

pause /pawz/ *vb* to stop for a time (*pause for a moment before answering*). ● *n* a short stop (*a pause for breath/a pause for a cup of tea*).

pave /pave/ *vb* to make a road or pathway by laying down flat stones (*paving the road leading to the new houses*). ● **pave the way for** to prepare for (*the opening of the new shopping mall paved the way for further property developments*).

pavement /pave-mint/ *n* (*Br*) see **sidewalk**.

pavilion /pa-vil-yun/ *n* **1** a building put up quickly for a special purpose (*the exhibition pavilions*). **2** a large tent. **3** a small, decorative building in a park or garden.

paw /paw/ *n* the foot of an animal that has claws (*a dog's paws*). ● *vb* **1** to scrape with the forefoot (*horses pawing the ground*). **2** to handle clumsily and often in too familiar a way (*he was pawing the woman he was dancing with*).

pawn[1] /pawn/ *n* **1** in chess, the piece of least value. **2** a person made use of by another to do his or her will (*the child was used as a pawn in the quarrel between his divorced parents*).

pawn[2] /pawn/ *vb* to hand over in return for money lent (*pawning his watch*). ● *n* a thing handed over in return for a loan of money and returned when the loan is repaid. ● **pawnbroker** /pawn-bro-ker/ *n* someone who lends money to those who pawn goods with him or her until the loan is repaid (*take his watch to the pawnbroker to get money for Christmas*).

pay /pay/ *vb* (*pt, pp* **paid** /paid/) **1** to give money for goods, service, etc. (*pay for their groceries/paying the gardener for his work*). **2** to suffer for faults, crimes, etc. (*murderers who must be made to pay for their crimes*). **3** to give (*pay attention/pay heed*). **4** to produce a profit (*find a product that pays*). **5** to let run out (*pay out the rope to let the boat into the water*). ● *n* wages, salary. ● **pay through the nose** (*inf*) to pay too much for something (*he paid through the nose for that old car*).

payment /**pay**-mint/ *n* **1** the act of paying (*the payment of their debts*). **2** the amount paid (*payment received in full*).

payroll /**pay**-role/ *n* a list of persons to be paid (*people on the factory payroll*).

PC /pee-**see**/ *abbr* = **1 personal computer**: a computer designed to be used by one person. **2 politically correct**: nonoffensive terminology. **3** (*Br*) **police constable**.

pea /pee/ *n* **1** a climbing plant with pods containing round edible seeds. **2** one of the seeds (*soup made from peas*).

peace /peess/ *n* **1** quiet, calm (*peace reigned after the children went to bed*). **2** freedom from war or disorder (*people in a country at war longing for peace*). **3** the agreement to end a war (*talks on peace*).

peaceful /**peess**-ful/ *adj* **1** quiet, calm, untroubled (*a peaceful village in the country*). **2** without war (*peaceful countries*).

peach /peech/ *n* a juicy fruit with a rough stone and soft velvety skin (*ripe golden peaches*).

peacock /**pee**-cock/ *n* a bird, the male of which has a large brightly colored spreading tail. ● *f* **peahen** /**pee**-hen/.

peak /peek/ *n* **1** the highest point (*the peak of his political career*). **2** the pointed top of a mountain (*snow-covered peaks*). **3** the jutting-out brim at the front of a cap (*a blue cap with a red peak*). ● *adj* connected with the time of greatest use or demand (*peak TV viewing times*). ● *vb* to reach the highest point (*his career peaked in his early 40s*).

peaked /peekt/ *adj* having a jutting-out brim in front (*a peaked cap*).

peal /peel/ *n* **1** a sudden noise (*a peal of thunder*). **2** the loud ringing of bells (*the peal of the church bells*). **3** a set of bells for ringing together. ● *vb* to sound or ring loudly.

peanut /**pee**-nut/ *n* a type of edible nut (*peanut butter*).

pear /pare/ *n* a juicy fruit narrower at one end than at the other (*pears grow in the orchard*).

pearl /perl/ *n* **1** a shining white jewel found in shellfish, especially oysters (*a necklace of pearls*). **2** (*inf*) something highly valued (*the pearl of his collection of antiques*). **3** mother-of-pearl (*pearl handles*).

peasant /**pe**-zant/ *n* a person who works on the land, especially in a poor, primitive or underdeveloped area (*local peasants plowing with oxen*).

peasantry /**pe**-zan-tree/ *n* peasants, country people.

peat /peet/ *n* turf containing decayed vegetable matter dried and used as fuel (*peat fires in the Scottish Highlands*).

pebble /**pe**-bul/ *n* a small stone made round by the action of water (*a beach of pebbles*). ● *adj* **pebbly** /**pe**-blee/ (*a pebbly beach*).

peck[1] /peck/ *n* a measure for grain, etc. (= 2 gallons).

peck[2] /peck/ *vb* **1** to strike with the beak (*have his fingers pecked by his pet bird*). **2** to pick up with the beak (*birds pecking at seed*). **3** to eat slowly in small mouthfuls, to nibble (*a child who only pecks at her food*).

peculiar /pi-**cyool**-yar/ *adj* **1** strange, odd (*meat that tastes peculiar*). **2** belonging to one person, place or thing in particular and to no other (*his peculiar style of walking/the peculiar charm of the village*).

peculiarity /pi-cyool-**ya**-ri-tee/ *n* **1** a quality, custom, etc., that belongs to a particular person, thing, etc. **2** an odd way of behaving.

pedal /**pe**-dal/ *n* a lever worked by foot to control the working of a machine (*the bicycle pedal/the piano pedal*). ● *vb* (**pedaled** /**pe**-dald/, **pedaling** /**pe**-da-ling/) to work a pedal by foot (*pedal the bicycle uphill*).

pedant /**pe**-dant/ *n* **1** someone who shows off his or her learning. **2** someone who attaches too much importance to small details and unimportant rules (*a pedant who kept finding problems with the wording of the contract*). ● *adj* **pedantic** /pe-**dan**-tic/.

pedantry /**pe**-dan-tree/ *n* **1** showing off one's learning. **2** over-insistence on rules, etc.

peddle /**pe**-dal/ *vb* to sell from door to door (*salesmen peddling cleaning products*).

peddler, *also* **pedlar**, **pedler** /**ped**-ler/ *n* someone who travels about selling small objects (*peddlers selling things from door to door*).

pedestal /**pe**-di-stal/ *n* the block of stone at the base of a column or under a statue (*a bust of Shakespeare on a pedestal*). ● **put on a pedestal** to treat with very great, often too much, respect (*he put his wife on a pedestal, but she did not deserve his respect*).

pedestrian /pi-de-**stree**-an/ *n* someone who goes on foot, a walker (*pedestrians looking for a place to cross the street/a pedestrian crossing*). ● *adj* **1** going on foot (*pedestrian passengers on the ferry*). **2** dull, uninteresting (*a pedestrian style of writing*). ● *adj* of streets in which traffic is not allowed so that pedestrians can walk safely (*a pedestrian mall*).

pedigree /**pe**-di-gree/ *n* **1** a written table showing one's ancestors (*get a copy of the dog's pedigree*).

2 one's ancestors (*a young woman of aristocratic pedigree*). ● *adj* of good birth (*a pedigree spaniel*).

pediment /pe-di-ment/ *n* the triangular topmost part at the front of a building.

pedlar, pedler *see* **peddler**

pedometer /pi-**dom**-i-ter/ *n* an instrument that measures distance walked (*walkers wearing pedometers*).

peel /peel/ *vb* **1** to strip off. **2** to cut the skin off a fruit or vegetable. **3** to come off, as does skin or like the bark of a tree (*oranges that peel easily*). ● *n* skin, rind, bark.

peeling /pee-ling/ *n* a piece peeled off.

peep[1] /peep/ *vb* to chirp, to squeak. ● *n* **1** a chirp or squeak. **2** any of various small sandpipers.

peep[2] /peep/ *vb* **1** to look at through a narrow opening. **2** to look at for a moment only. **3** to begin to appear (*the sun peeped through the clouds*). ● *n* **1** a quick or secret look. **2** a look through a narrow opening. **3** a first appearance.

peephole /peep-hole/ *n* a small hole for looking through (*a peephole in the front door*).

peer[1] /peer/ *vb* **1** to strain one's eyes to see. **2** to look closely.

peer[2] /peer/ *n* **1** an equal, one's equal in age, ability, rank (*a child ahead of his peers at school*). **2** a British nobleman (*a peer in the House of Lords*). ● *f* **peeress** /pee-**ress**/.

peerage /pee-ridge/ *n* **1** all the noblemen of a country. **2** the rank or title of a British nobleman.

peerless /peer-less/ *adj* (*fml*) unequaled (*her peerless beauty*).

peevish /pee-vish/ *adj* irritable, full of complaints (*a peevish old man who is difficult to please*).

peg /peg/ *n* a nail, pin or fastener (*tent pegs*). ● *vb* (**pegged** /pegd/, **pegging** /pe-ging/) to fasten with a peg (*peg the tent to the ground*). ● **take down a peg** to humble, to humiliate (*she was so conceited that they felt they had to take her down a peg or two*).

pelican /pe-li-can/ *n* a water bird with a large beak containing a pouch for storing fish.

pellet /pe-lit/ *n* **1** a small ball of anything (*give the birds pellets of bread*). **2** a pill. **3** one of a number of small lead balls packed in a cartridge and fired from a gun.

pell-mell /pel-mel/ *adv* in great disorder (*the children ran pell-mell into the yard*).

pelt[1] /pelt/ *n* the raw skin of an animal (*sell mink pelts for profit*).

pelt[2] /pelt/ *vb* **1** to attack by throwing things at (*the*

audience pelting the comedian with rotten fruit). **2** (*of rain*) to fall heavily (*it was pelting down*).

pelvis /pel-vis/ *n* the bony frame and the lower end of the trunk, into which the hip bones fit.

pen[1] /pen/ *n* an instrument for writing in ink (*a fountain pen*). ● *vb* to write.

pen[2] /pen/ *n* a female swan.

pen[3] /pen/ *n* a small enclosure, especially for animals (*a sheep pen*). ● *vb* (**penned** /pend/, **penning** /pen-ing/) to shut up in a small space (*pen the stray dogs up*).

penal /pee-nal/ *adj* having to do with punishment (*the penal system*).

penalize /pee-na-lize/ *vb*, *also* **penalise** (*Br*) to punish (*penalizing the baseball player/penalize his attempt at cheating*).

penalty /pe-nal-tee/ *n* **1** due punishment (*the death penalty*). **2** a disadvantage of some kind that must be suffered for breaking the rules (*a football penalty*).

penance /pe-nanse/ *n* punishment willingly accepted as a sign of sorrow for sin (*do penance for his sins*).

pence /pense/ (*Br*) *see* **penny**.

penchant /pon-**shont**/ *n* (*fml*) a liking for, a preference for (*a penchant for spicy food*).

pencil /pen-sil/ *n* a writing or drawing instrument. ● *vb* (**penciling** /pen-si-ling/, **penciled** /pen-sild/) to write or draw with pencil (*pencil in a few corrections*).

pendant /pen-dant/ *n* **1** an ornament hanging from a necklace or bracelet (*a diamond pendant*). **2** an earring. **3** anything hanging (e.g., a lamp from a roof).

pending /pen-ding/ *adj* not yet decided (*the matter is still pending*). ● *prep* waiting for (*pending a decision*).

pendulous /pen-ju-luss/ *adj* (*fml*) hanging (*branches pendulous with fruit*).

pendulum /pen-ju-lum/ *n* a swinging weight, as in a large clock.

penetrable /pe-ni-tra-bul/ *adj* that can be penetrated (*roads scarcely penetrable in winter*).

penetrate /pe-ni-trate/ *vb* **1** to pass through (*light penetrating the thin curtains*). **2** to make a hole in or through (*a bullet penetrated his shoulder*). **3** to reach the mind of (*it didn't seem to penetrate that her husband was dead*).

penetrating /pe-ni-tray-ting/ *adj* **1** sharp (*a penetrating stare*). **2** loud and clear (*a penetrating voice*).

penetration /pe-ni-**tray**-shun/ *n* **1** act of passing through or making a hole in. **2** clear understanding, intelligence.

pen friend /**pen**-frend/ *n* a person one gets to know only through exchanging letters. ● *also* **pen pal**.

penguin /**pen**-gwin/ *n* a web-footed bird with very short wings that it uses for swimming, not flying (*penguins are found in the Antarctic regions*).

penicillin /pe-ni-**si**-lin/ *n* a kind of germ-killing drug obtained from mould (*take penicillin to cure her sore throat*).

peninsula /pe-**nin**-su-la/ *n* a piece of land almost surrounded by water.

penitent /**pe**-ni-tent/ *adj* sorrowful for having done wrong (*children penitent for having broken the window*). ● *n* someone who is penitent. ● *n* **penitence** /**pe**-ni-tense/.

penitential /pe-ni-**ten**-shal/ *adj* (*fml*) having to do with penitence (*a penitential attitude*).

penitentiary /pe-ni-**ten**-shree/ *n* a prison.

penknife /**pen**-nife/ *n* a folding pocket knife.

penmanship /**pen**-man-ship/ *n* (*fml*) the art of writing (*admire his penmanship*).

pen name /**pen**-name/ *n* a pretended name under which an author writes (*the author's pen name*).

pennant /**pe**-nant/, **pennon** /**pe**-nun/ *ns* **1** a long narrow triangular flag. **2** a flag symbolizing a particular sports championship.

penniless /**pe**-nee-less/ *adj* having no money (*penniless people begging*).

penny /**pe**-nee/ *n* (*pl* **pennies** /**pe**-neez/, **pence** /penss/) a British bronze coin worth one-hundredth of a pound. 100 pence = £1.

pen pal *see* **pen friend**.

pension /**pen**-shun/ *n* money paid regularly to someone for the rest of his or her lifetime after he or she has stopped working or after some misfortune (*receive a company pension*). ● *vb* to give a pension to (*pension the older workers off*).

pensioner /**pen**-shu-ner/ *n* someone who receives a pension.

pensive /**pen**-siv/ *adj* (*fml*) thoughtful (*in pensive mood*).

pentagon /**pen**-ta-gon/ *n* a five-sided figure.

Pentagon /**pen**-ta-gon/ *n* the headquarters of the Department of Defense.

Pentecost /**pen**-ta-cawst/ *n* a Christian and Jewish festival.

penthouse /**pent**-house/ *n* **1** an apartment, usually luxurious, at the top of a building (*a fine view from the penthouse*). **2** a shed with down-sloping roof built against a wall.

penultimate /pe-**nul**-ti-mit/ *adj* (*fml*) the last but one (*it was the TV series' penultimate episode*).

peony /**pee**-u-nee/ *n* a garden plant with large white or red flowers.

people /**pee**-pul/ *n* **1** persons in general (*people who care about others*). **2** (*pl* **peoples**) all those belonging to one nation or country (*the people of America*). **3** the ordinary persons of a country and not their rulers, etc. (*the people rebelled against their rulers*). ● *vb* **1** to fill with people (*a building peopled with office workers*). **2** to inhabit (*tribes who people the plains*).

pep /pep/ *n* vitality, high spirits.

pepper /**pe**-per/ *n* **1** a plant whose seeds are ground into a hot-tasting powder and used for flavoring food. **2** the powder so used (*season the dish with salt and pepper*).

peppercorn /**pe**-per-cawrn/ *n* the seed of the pepper plant.

peppermint /**pe**-per-mint/ *n* **1** a plant with sharp-tasting oil. **2** a sharp-tasting candy (*suck a peppermint*).

peppery /**pe**-per-ee/ *adj* **1** like pepper, hot (*a peppery sauce*). **2** easily angered (*a peppery old man*).

per /per/ *prep* **1** for each (*apples $2 per pound*). **2** during each (*work 40 hours per week*). **3** (*inf*) according to (*as per instructions*).

perceive /per-**seev**/ *vb* to know through one of the senses, to see, to understand (*perceive a reason for their distress*).

percent, per cent /per-**sent**/ in each hundred (%).

percentage /per-**sen**-tidge/ *n* the number of cases in every hundred (*a percentage of the injured animals die*).

perceptible /per-**sep**-ti-bul/ *adj* able to be perceived (*no perceptible difference*).

perception /per-**sep**-shun/ *n* **1** the ability to perceive. **2** intelligence.

perceptive /per-**sep**-tiv/ *adj* **1** quick to notice or understand (*perceptive people who reported him to the police*). **2** showing the ability to notice or understand (*perceptive comments*).

perch[1] /perch/ *n* a freshwater fish.

perch[2] /perch/ *n* **1** the bar on which a bird stands when resting. **2** a high place. ● *vb* **1** to rest on a bar or high place (*parrots perching on bars in their cages*). **2** to put or be in a high position.

perchance /per-**chanse**/ *adv* (*old*) perhaps.

percussion /per-**cu**-shun/ *n* **1** the striking of one thing against another. **2** the sound thus made. **3** the drums and cymbals section of an orchestra.

perdition /per-**di**-shun/ *n* **1** entire ruin (*an army* led to perdition by an incompetent general). **2** condemnation to hell (sinners facing perdition).

peremptory /pe-**remp**-tree/ adj short and commanding (a peremptory manner).

perennial /pe-**ren**-ee-yal/ adj **1** lasting forever, continual (their perennial complaints). **2** (of a plant) growing again year after year. ● n a perennial plant.

perfect /**per**-fect/ adj **1** without fault, excellent (a perfect piece of work). **2** exact (a perfect copy). **3** complete, utter (a perfect fool). ● vb **perfect** /per-**fect**/ to finish, to make perfect. ● n **perfection** / per-**fec**-shun/.

perforate /**per**-fu-rate/ vb to make a hole or row of holes through (perforating paper/a perforated ulcer).

perforation /per-fu-**ray**-shun/ n a row of small holes, often to make tearing easy, as in sheets of stamps, etc.

perform /per-**fawrm**/ vb **1** to do, to carry out (perform her duties satisfactorily). **2** to show in a theater (perform a production of "Hamlet"). **3** to act in a play (they performed in a musical production).

performance /per-**fawr**-manss/ n **1** act of doing or carrying out (the performance of their duties). **2** that which is done (admire their musical performance). **3** the acting of a play or part (see a performance of "Othello").

performer /per-**fawr**-mer/ n an actor, musician, etc.

performing /per-**fawr**-ming/ adj trained to act, do tricks, etc. (performing animals).

perfume /**per**-fyoom/ n **1** a sweet smell (the perfume of roses). **2** a sweet-smelling liquid, scent (buy a bottle of perfume). ● vb **perfume** /per-**fyoom**/ **1** to apply perfume to. **2** to give a pleasant smell to (roses perfuming the garden).

perfumer /per-**fyoo**-mer/ n someone who makes perfume.

perfumery /per-**fyoo**-mer-ee/ n **1** a place where perfumes are made or sold. **2** the art of making perfumes (a training in perfumery).

perfunctory /per-**fung**(k)-tree/ adj done carelessly or without interest, badly done (a perfunctory cleaning of the room).

perhaps /per-**haps**/ adv it may be, possibly.

peril /**pe**-ril/ n risk, danger (the perils of travel in those parts).

perilous /**pe**-ri-lus/ adj dangerous (a perilous journey).

perimeter /pe-**ri**-mi-ter/ n **1** the total length of the line(s) enclosing a certain space or figure. **2** the boundaries of a camp or piece of land (the perimeter of the city).

period /**pee**-ree-ud/ n **1** a certain length of time (a period of three months). **2** an age in history (the period of the Depression). **3** the dot or full stop marking the end of a sentence. **4** a time of menstruation.

periodic /pee-ree-**od**-ic/ adj happening at regular intervals (periodic breakdowns in the system).

periodical /pee-ree-**od**-ic-al/ n a newspaper or magazine that appears at regular intervals (e.g. of a week, month, etc.) (a scientific periodical). ● adj periodic.

periodic table /pee-ree-od-ic-**tay**-bul/ n a chart showing the arrangement of chemical elements and their connections to one another.

periphery /pee-**ri**-free/ n a boundary line (on the periphery of the city/on the periphery of the subject that she is studying).

periscope /**pe**-ri-scope/ n an instrument in which mirrors are so arranged that one can see things on the surface of the land or sea when in a trench or submarine.

perish /**pe**-rish/ vb **1** to die (soldiers who perished in the battle). **2** to pass away completely (a way of life that perished). **3** to rot away (rubber that perished).

perishable /**pe**-ri-sha-bul/ adj that will rot away under ordinary conditions (perishable food).

perjury /**per**-ju-ree/ n the act of saying under oath that a statement is true when one knows it to be false (a witness who committed perjury).

perk[1] /perk/ vb ● **perk up** (inf) to cheer up (she perked up when she heard the news).

perk[2] n see **perquisite**.

perky /**per**-kee/ adj lively, cheerful (in a perky mood). ● n **perkiness** /**per**-kee-ness/.

perm /perm/ n an artificial wave in the hair.

permanent /**per**-ma-nent/ adj lasting (a permanent dye/a permanent job). ● n **permanence** /**per**-ma-nense/.

permanent wave /**per**-ma-nent-wave/ n see **perm**.

permeable /**per**-mee-a-bul/ adj allowing liquid, gases, etc., to pass through.

permeate /**per**-mee-ate/ vb **1** to pass through, to spread through every part of (damp permeating the whole house/an organization permeated with politics).

permissible /per-**mi**-su-bul/ adj (fml) that can be allowed (it is not permissible to leave school early).

permission /per-**mi**-shun/ n leave, consent (get permission to leave early).

permissive /per-**mi**-siv/ adj (fml) allowing freedom (a permissive regime).

permit /per-**mit**/ vb (**permitted** /per-**mi**-tid/,

permitting /per-**mi**-ting/) to allow (*the children are not permitted to leave the school premises*). ● *n* **permit** /**per**-mit/ a paper giving the holder the right to do certain things (*a permit to sell things in the market*).

permutation /per-myoo-**tay**-shun/ *n* **1** all the ways in which a series of things, numbers, etc., can be arranged. **2** one of these ways.

peroration /pe-ru-**ray**-shun/ *n* **1** (*fml*) the closing part of a speech. **2** a grand long speech, often meaningless.

peroxide /per-**ok**-side/ *n* **1** a mixture of oxygen with another element to contain the greatest possible amount of oxygen. **2** a substance used for bleaching, e.g., the hair.

perpendicular /per-pen-**di**-cyu-lar/ *adj* **1** at right angles. **2** upright. ● *n* a line at right angles to another.

perpetrate /**per**-pi-trate/ *vb* to commit, to do (*perpetrating a crime*). ● *ns* **perpetration** /per-pi-**tray**-shun/, **perpetrator** /**per**-pi-tray-tur/.

perpetual /per-**pe**-chu-wal/ *adj* **1** lasting forever (*perpetual life*). **2** continuing endlessly, uninterrupted (*perpetual noise*).

perpetuate /per-**pe**-chu-wate/ *vb* to make lasting (*a system that perpetuates the old faults*). ● *n* **perpetuation** /per-pe-chu-**way**-shun/.

perpetuity /per-pe-**choo**-wi-tee/ *n* (*fml*) everlasting time. ● **in perpetuity** forever.

perplex /per-**pleks**/ *vb* to puzzle, to bewilder (*perplexed by the flashing traffic signals*).

perplexity /per-**plek**-si-tee/ *n* puzzlement, bewilderment.

perquisite /**per**-kwi-zit/ *n* (*usually shortened to* **perk** /**perk**/) money, goods, etc., gained from a job in addition to wages or salary.

persecute /**per**-si-cyoot/ *vb* to ill-treat, especially because of one's beliefs, to treat cruelly (*persecuted for their religious faith*). ● *n* **persecution** /per-si-**cyoo**-shun/. ● *n* **persecutor** /**per**-si-cyoo-tur/.

perseverance /per-si-**vee**-ranse/ *n* the quality of continuing to try until one succeeds.

persevere /per-si-**veer**/ *vb* to keep on trying (*if you don't succeed at first, persevere/persevering with singing lessons*).

persist /per-**sist**/ *vb* **1** to keep on doing (*persist in telling lies*). **2** to last (*an infection that persisted*). **3** not to give in despite difficulty.

persistence /per-**si**-stense/ *n* the quality of persisting, obstinacy.

persistent /per-**si**-stent/ *adj* **1** keeping on trying, not giving in easily. **2** long, continuing (*a persistent infection*).

persnickety /per-**sni**-ki-tee/ *adj* overly fussy.

person /**per**-sun/ *n* **1** a human being, a man, woman or child. **2** (*fml*) one's body (*drugs about one's person*).

personal /**per**-snal/ *adj* **1** concerning a person's own private life (*personal belongings*). **2** (*of remarks*) unkind.

personal identification number *see* **PIN**.

personality /per-su-**na**-li-tee/ *n* **1** the union of qualities that makes someone's character different from those of other people (*a cheerful personality*). **2** a strong, distinct character (*a woman of personality*). **3** a well-known person (*television personalities*).

personally /**pers**-na-lee/ *adv* as far as one is concerned oneself (*personally, I think she is honest*).

personate /**per**-su-nate/ *vb* (*fml*) to act the part of, to pretend to be (someone else).

personify /per-**son**-i-fie/ *vb* **1** to speak or write of a thing, quality, etc., as if it were a human being (*innocence personified as a baby*). **2** to be a perfect example of (*he personifies optimism*). ● *n* **personification** /per-son-i-fi-**cay**-shun/.

personnel /per-su-**nel**/ *n* the persons employed in an organization (*highly qualified personnel*).

perspective /per-**spec**-tiv/ *n* **1** the art of drawing objects on a flat surface so that they appear farther or nearer as they do to the eye. **2** (*fml*) a view. ● **see in perspective** to see the real value or importance of things when compared with others (*so upset that she was unable to see things in perspective*).

Perspex /**per**-speks/ *n* a trademark for a tough transparent glasslike plastic.

perspicacious /per-spi-**cay**-shus/ *adj* (*fml*) quick to notice or understand (*perspicacious enough to spot the errors*).

perspicacity /per-spi-**ca**-si-tee/ *n* quickness or clearness of understanding.

perspire /per-**spire**/ *vb* to sweat (*runners perspiring in the heat*). ● *n* **perspiration** /per-spi-**ray**-shun/.

persuade /per-**swade**/ *vb* to convince a person or get him or her to do as one wants by argument (*persuading them to take part*).

persuasion /per-**sway**-zhun/ *n* **1** act of persuading. **2** (*fml*) a belief or set of beliefs (*of the Christian persuasion*). **3** a group holding certain beliefs.

persuasive /per-**sway**-siv/ *adj* good at gaining the agreement of others, able to influence others (*a persuasive young man/a persuasive argument*).

pert /pert/ *adj* forward, cheeky (*a pert young woman*). ● *n* **pertness** /**pert**-ness/.

pertain /per-**tain**/ *vb* to belong, to have to do with (*remarks not pertaining to the situation*).

pertinent /**per**-ti-nent/ *adj* to the point, having to do with the subject. ● *ns* **pertinence** /**per**-ti-nense/, **pertinency** /**per**-ti-nen-see/.

perturb /per-**turb**/ *vb* to make worried or anxious, to disturb (*perturbed by rumors of war*). ● *n* **perturbation** /per-tur-**bay**-shun/.

perusal /pe-**roo**-zal/ *n* reading, study.

peruse /pe-**rooz**/ *vb* (*fml*) to read through, to examine carefully (*perusing the contract*).

pervade /per-**vade**/ *vb* to spread through (*an area pervaded by disease*).

pervasive /per-**vay**-siv/ *adj* spreading through all parts.

perverse /per-**verse**/ *adj* 1 holding firmly to a wrong opinion. 2 continuing to do things that one knows to be wrong, unacceptable or forbidden (*it was perverse of her to disobey her father*).

perversion /per-**ver**-zhun/ *n* putting to a wrong or evil use (*an unnatural perversion*).

perversity /per-**ver**-si-tee/ *n* the quality of being perverse.

pervert /per-**vert**/ *vb* 1 to put to a wrong use (*perverting the course of justice*). 2 to teach wrong ways to. ● *n* **pervert** /**per**-vert/ someone who has formed unnatural habits (*a pervert who preys on the young*).

pervious /**per**-vee-us/ *adj* (*fml*) that can be passed through.

peseta /pi-**say**-ta/ *n* a former Spanish coin.

pessimism /**pe**-si-mi-zum/ *n* the belief that things generally turn out for the worst. ● *n* **pessimist** /**pe**-si-mist/.

pessimistic /pe-si-mi-**stic**/ *adj* having to do with pessimism, gloomy (*a pessimistic outlook on life*).

pest /pest/ *n* 1 something harmful. 2 a nuisance (*that child is just a pest*). 3 a destructive animal, insect, etc. (*farmers spraying crops to kill pests*).

pester /**pe**-ster/ *vb* to keep on annoying (*children pestering their mother to buy ice cream*).

pesticide /**pe**-sti-side/ *n* a chemical substance used to kill pests, especially insects that are harmful to crops and other plants (*spray the roses with pesticide*).

pestilence /**pe**-sti-lense/ *n* any deadly disease that spreads quickly, plague. ● *adj* **pestilential** /pe-sti-len-shal/.

pestilent /**pe**-sti-lent/ *adj* causing pestilence or disease.

pestle /**pe**-sul/ *n* an instrument for pounding substances to powder (*a mortar and pestle*).

pet /pet/ *n* 1 a favorite child (*a teacher's pet*). 2 a tame animal kept in the house as a companion (*keep a dog as a pet*). ● *adj* best-loved, favorite. ● *vb* (**petted** /**pe**-tid/, **petting** /**pe**-ting/) 1 to treat lovingly. 2 to fondle.

petal /**pe**-tal/ *n* the leaf-shaped part of a flower.

peter /**pee**-ter/ *vb*. ● **peter out** to stop or disappear gradually (*a mild protest that petered out*).

petite /pi-**teet**/ *adj* tiny, dainty (*a petite blonde*).

petition /pi-**ti**-shun/ *n* 1 a request. 2 a written request signed by a number of people (*sign a petition against the new superhighway being built*). 3 a prayer. ● *vb* 1 to make a request to someone able to grant it. 2 to put forward a written request. ● *n* **petitioner** /pi-**ti**-shner/.

petrel /**pe**-trul/ *n* a sea bird.

petrifaction /pe-tri-**fac**-shun/ *n* 1 turning into stone. 2 terror, amazement.

petrify /**pe**-tri-fie/ *vb* 1 to turn into stone. 2 to terrify, to astound (*children petrified by the eerie music*).

petrol /**pe**-trul/ *n* (*Br*) *see* **gasoline**.

petroleum /pi-**tro**-lee-um/ *n* a heavy oil obtained from under the surface of the earth.

petrology /pi-**trol**-u-jee/ *n* the study of the formation, composition and erosion of rocks.

petticoat /**pe**-tee-coat/ *n* a woman's undergarment.

pettish /**pe**-tish/ *adj* sulky (*in a pettish mood*).

petty /**pe**-tee/ *adj* 1 small, unimportant, trivial (*petty crime*). 2 mean-spirited (*petty, spiteful people*).

petty cash /pe-tee-**cash**/ *n* money held in readiness to meet small expenses (*take the money for stationery from petty cash*).

petty officer /pe-tee-**aw**-fi-ser/ *n* in the navy, a noncommissioned officer.

petulant /**pe**-chu-lant/ *adj* easily angered or annoyed, peevish (*get tired of his petulant behavior*). ● *n* **petulance** /**pe**-chu-lanse/.

petunia /pe-**toon**-ya/ *n* 1 a flowering garden plant of various colors but often purple. 2 the purplish color of this flower.

pew /pyoo/ *n* a seat in a church.

pewter /**pyoo**-ter/ *n* a mixture of tin and lead (*goblets made of pewter*).

pH /pee-**aich**/ *n* the measurement of the acid or alkaline content of a solution.

phaeton /**fay**-u-tun/ *n* (*old*) an open four-wheeled carriage drawn by a pair of horses.

phalanx /**fa**-langks/ *n* 1 (*fml or old*) a body of foot soldiers standing close to each other in battle. **2** a body of persons or animals standing close to one another (*a phalanx of police officers holding back the crowds*).

phantom /**fan**-tum/ *n* a ghost.

pharaoh /**fay**-ro/ *n* a king of ancient Egypt.

pharisee /**fa**-ri-see/ *n* (*inf*) a hypocrite.

pharmaceutical /far-ma-**soo**-ti-cal/ *adj* having to do with the making up of drugs or medicines.

pharmacy /**far**-ma-see/ *n* **1** the making up of drugs or medicines (*study pharmacy*). **2** a shop in which medicines are made up and sold (*take the prescription to the pharmacy*). ● *n* **pharmacist** /**far**-ma-sist/.

pharyngitis /fa-rin-**jie**-tis/ *n* inflammation of the pharynx.

pharynx /**fa**-rinks/ *n* the back part of the mouth.

phase /faze/ *n* **1** a distinct stage in growth or development (*the first phase of the building project*). **2** apparent shape (e.g., of the moon).

pheasant /**fe**-zant/ *n* a large bird hunted for sport (*have roast pheasant for dinner*).

phenix /**fee**-niks/ *n* in ancient fables, a bird said to burn itself and rise again from its own ashes.

phenomenon /fi-**nom**-i-nun/ *n* (*pl* **phenomena** /fi-**nom**-i-na/) **1** any natural happening that can be perceived by the senses. **2** anything unusual or extraordinary (*snow in that part of the world is a phenomenon*).

phenomenal /fi-**nom**-i-nal/ *adj* unusual, extraordinary (*a phenomenal talent*).

phial /**fie**-al/ *n* a small glass bottle (*a phial of poison*).

philander /fi-**lan**-der/ *vb* to flirt (*he is always philandering with married women*). ● *n* **philanderer** /fi-**lan**-der-er/.

philanthropy /fi-**lan**-thru-pee/ *n* love of humankind, shown by giving money, etc., to help those in need or to benefit the public. ● *adj* **philanthropic** /fi-lan-**throp**-ic/. ● *n* **philanthropist** /fi-**lan**-thru-pist/.

philately /fi-**la**-tu-lee/ *n* stamp collecting. ● *n* **philatelist** /fi-**la**-tu-list/.

philharmonic /fil-er-**mon**-ic/ *adj* musical.

philistine /**fi**-li-stine/ *n* an uncultured person (*a philistine with no interest in books or the arts*).

philology /fi-**lol**-u-jee/ *n* the study of languages, their history and development. ● *n* **philologist** /fi-**lol**-u-jist/.

philosopher /fi-**los**-u-fer/ *n* **1** someone who tries to find by reasoning the causes and laws of all things. **2** someone who treats life calmly.

philosophic(al) /fi-lu-**sof**-ic-al/ *adjs* **1** having to do with philosophy. **2** calm, not easily annoyed (*of a philosophical turn of mind*).

philosophy /fi-**los**-u-fee/ *n* **1** the study of the causes and laws of all things (*study philosophy at university*). **2** a particular way of thinking (*his philosophy of life is to enjoy himself*).

philter /**fil**-ter/ *n* (*fml*) a magic drink supposed to make the drinker fall in love.

phlebitis /fli-**bie**-tus/ *n* inflammation of a vein of the body.

phlegm /flem/ *n* the thick, slimy liquid coughed up from the throat.

phlegmatic /fleg-ma-tic/ *adj* cool, not easily excited.

phlox /floks/ *n* a garden plant with brightly colored flowers.

phobia /**foe**-bee-ya/ *n.* an unreasoning fear or dread (*have a phobia about heights*).

phone /foan/ *n* the common short form of **telephone** /te-le-foan/.

phonetic /fu-**ne**-tic/ *adj* having to do with the sounds of speech or pronunciation (*the phonetic alphabet*). ● *npl* **phonetics** /fu-**ne**-tics/ the study of the sounds of speech.

phonic /**fon**-ic/ *adj* having to do with sound.

phonograph /**fon**-u-graph/ *n* (*old*) an instrument for recording sounds and playing them back.

phony /**foe**-nee/ *adj* (*inf*) not genuine, not sincere, unreal (*a phony workman/a phony interest in the arts*).

phosphate /**fos**-fate/ *n* a type of salt mixed into soil to make it more fertile.

phosphorescence /fos-fu-**re**-sense/ *n* a faint shining visible only in the dark.

phosphorescent /fos-fu-**re**-sent/ *adj* giving out a faint light in the dark (*phosphorescent paint*).

phosphorous /**fos**-fu-rus/ *n* a yellowish substance, easily set alight, giving out a faint light.

photo /**fo**-toe/ *n* the common short form of **photograph** /**fo**-toe-graph/.

photocopy /**fo**-toe-cop-ee/ *n* a photographed copy (*take a photocopy of the document*). ● *vb* to make a photographed copy.

photogenic /fo-toe-**jen**-ic/ *adj* suitable for photographing (*photogenic enough to be a professional model*).

photograph /**fo**-toe-graph/ *n* (*abbr* = **photo** /**fo**-toe/) a picture taken with a camera by means of the action of light on specially prepared glass or celluloid. ● *vb* to take a photograph. ● *n* **photographer** /fu-**tog**-ra-fer/. ● *adj* **photographic** /fo-toe-**graf**-ic/.

photography /fo-**tog**-ra-fee/ *n* the art of taking photographs.

photometer /fo-**tom**-i-ter/ *n* an instrument for measuring intensity of light.

phrase /**fraze**/ *n* **1** a small group of connected words expressing a single idea. **2** (*mus*) a group of connected notes. ● *vb* to express in words (*phrase his statement in simple language*).

phraseology /fray-zee-**ol**-u-jee/ *n* a manner or style of expressing in words (*expressed in simple phraseology*).

phrenology /fri-**nol**-u-jee/ *n* **1** the belief that a person's intelligence and abilities may be judged from the shape of his or her skull. **2** study of the shape of the skull based on this belief. ● *n* **phrenologist** /fri-**nol**-u-jist/.

physical /**fi**-zi-cal/ *adj* **1** having to do with the body (*a physical abnormality*). **2** having to do with the natural world (*the physical sciences*).

physical therapy /fi-zi-cal-**ther**-a-pee/ *n* the use of exercise or massage to improve mobility after illness or injury.

physician /fi-**zi**-shun/ *n* a doctor, especially as opposed to a surgeon.

physicist /**fi**-zi-sist/ *n* a student of physics.

physics /**fi**-zics/ *n* the study of matter, its properties, and the forces affecting it (e.g., heat, electricity, etc.).

physiology /fi-zee-**ol**-u-jee/ *n* the study of living bodies, their organs and the way they work. ● *adj* **physiological** /fi-zee-u-**lodge**-ic-al/. ● *n* **physiologist** /fi-zee-**ol**-u-jist/.

physique /fi-**zeek**/ *n* **1** the structure of a person's body. **2** strength of body (*athletes trying to improve their physique*).

pianissimo /pee-a-**ni**-si-mo/ *adv* (*mus*) very softly.

pianist /pee-a-nist/ *n* someone who plays on a piano.

piano[1] /pee-a-no/, **pianoforte** /pee-a-no-**for**-tay/ *ns* a musical instrument played by pressing down keys that cause little hammers to strike tuned strings.

piano[2] /pee-a-no/ *adv* (*mus*) softly.

piazza /pee-**at**-za/ *n* **1** an open square surrounded by buildings (*cafés around the piazza*). **2** (*Br*) a path under a roof supported by pillars.

piccolo /**pi**-ca-lo/ *n* a small high-pitched flute.

pick[1] /**pick**/ *vb* **1** to choose (*pick a cookie from the plateful*). **2** to pull or gather (*pick flowers/pick raspberries*). **3** to eat by small mouthfuls (*pick at one's food*). **4** to open (a lock) with a tool. **5** to steal from (a pocket). ● *n* choice, the best. ● **pick holes in** to point out the faults in (*pick holes in*

the argument). ● **pick up 1** to take up (*pick up his tools*). **2** to learn as if by chance (*pick up a foreign language*). **3** to come upon by chance (*pick up some interesting jewelry*).

pick[2] /**pick**/, **pickax** /**pi**-caks/ *ns* a tool with a long pointed head, used for breaking up hard ground. etc. (*laborers breaking up the road surfaces with picks*).

picket /**pi**-cit/ *n* **1** a pointed wooden post. **2** a small group of soldiers acting as a guard. **3** a number of people on strike who try to prevent others from going to work (*pickets stopping trucks on the way into the factory*). ● *vb* **1** to send out soldiers, strikers, etc., on picket. **2** to tie to a post.

pickle /**pi**-cul/ *n* **1** salt water or vinegar in which food is preserved (*serve pickles with cold roast beef*). **2** (*inf*) a difficult or unpleasant situation (*in a fine old pickle*). **3** *pl* vegetables, especially cucumber, preserved in vinegar. ● *vb* to preserve by putting in salt water, vinegar, etc.

pickpocket /**pic**-poc-it/ *n* someone who steals from pockets.

picnic /**pic**-nic/ *n* an outing taken for pleasure, during which meals are eaten out of doors. ● *also vb*.

pictorial /pic-**toe**-ree-al/ *adj* told or illustrated by pictures (*a pictorial description*).

picture /**pic**-chur/ *n* a painting, drawing or other likeness, a portrait. ● *vb* **1** to imagine clearly (*try to picture their distress*). **2** (*fml*) to represent in a painting (*the artist has pictured him as an old man*).

picturesque /pic-chu-**resk**/ *adj* that would make a good picture, striking in appearance, beautiful (*a picturesque village*).

pie /**pie**/ *n* meat or fruit in or under a crust of pastry (*a steak pie*).

piece /**peess**/ *n* **1** a bit (*a piece of chewing gum*). **2** a distinct part (*put it together piece by piece*). **3** a literary or musical composition. **4** a gun. **5** a short distance (*down the road a piece*). **6** a coin (*a ten-cents piece*). ● *vb* **1** to put (together). **2** to patch.

piecemeal /**peess**-meel/ *adv* **1** in or by pieces. **2** little by little.

piecework /**peess**-wurk/ *n* work paid by the amount done, not by time.

pied /**pied**/ *adj* (*fml*) of different colors, spotted.

pier /**peer**/ *n* **1** a stone pillar supporting an arch, etc. **2** (*Br*) boardwalk; a wooden platform built out into the sea, often used as a landing place by boats.

pierce /**peerss**/ *vb* **1** to make a hole through. **2** to go through (*a dagger pierced her heart*).

piercing /**peer**-sing/ *adj* **1** high-sounding (*a piercing scream*). **2** bright and intelligent-looking, staring (*a piercing stare*).

pig /pig/ *n* **1** a common farm animal (*we get pork and bacon from pigs*). **2** a rough block or bar of smelted metal. ● *vb* (**pigged** /pigd/, **pigging** /**pi**-ging/) (*inf*) to live in dirty or untidy surroundings (*pig it in a student apartment*). ● **buy a pig in a poke** to buy something without examining it first (*buying goods at an auction can be like buying a pig in a poke*).

pigeon /**pi**-jin/ *n* **1** a bird like a dove, but slightly larger. **2** (*slang*) someone who is easily fooled. **2** (*slang*) a young woman.

pigeon-hole /**pi**-jin-hole/ *n* one of several compartments in a desk for storing papers, letters, etc.

piggy bank /**pi**-gee bank/ *n* a small savings bank shaped like a pig.

pig-headed /pig-**he**-did/ *adj* foolishly stubborn (*too pig-headed to listen to advice*).

pigment /**pig**-mint/ *n* any substance used for coloring (*a red pigment*).

pigmy *n* same as **pygmy**.

pigpen /**pig**-pen/ *n* an enclosure for pigs.

pig-sticking /**pig**-sti-king/ *n* hunting wild boar with spears.

pigtail, /**pig**-tale/ *n* a plait of hair hanging down the back or from each side of the head (*a girl with pigtails*).

pike[1] /pike/ *n* a large freshwater fish.

pike[2] /pike/ *n* (*old*) a long spear.

pilchard /**pil**-churd/ *n* a small edible sea fish.

pile[1] /pile/ *n* **1** a heap (*a pile of rubbish*). **2** (*inf*) a large and grand building (*a stately pile*) **3** a large amount of money (*he made a pile from that contract*). ● *vb* to heap up (*rubbish piling up*).

pile[2] /pile/ *n* one of a number of wooden posts driven into the ground as the foundation for a building.

pile[3] /pile/ *n* the soft wooly hair on cloth, carpets, etc.

pilfer /**pil**-fur/ *vb* to steal small amounts or articles of small value (*pilfer money from the cash register*). ● *n* **pilferer** /**pil**-fu-rer/.

pilgrim /**pil**-grim/ *n* **1** someone who travels, often very far, to a holy place to worship. **2** *npl* **the Pilgrims** a group of people who left England because they were being persecuted for their religion, and came to America, founding Plymouth Colony in 1620.

pilgrimage /**pil**-gri-midge/ *n* a journey made by a pilgrim (*a pilgrimage to Bethlehem*).

pill /pill/ *n* a tiny ball of medicine (*vitamin pill*).

pillar /**pi**-lar/ *n* **1** an upright of stone, wood, etc., for supporting an arch, roof, etc. **2** any person or thing that gives support (*a pillar of the local tennis club*).

pillow /**pi**-lo/ *n* a soft cushion for the head.

pillowcase /**pi**-lo-case/ *n* the cover put over a pillow.

pilot /**pie**-lut/ *n* **1** someone who steers an airplane **2** someone who guides a ship in and out of harbor. ● *vb* **1** to steer an airplane (*he pilots military aircraft*). **2** to guide, to show the way (*piloting the ship into harbor*).

pimple /**pim**-pul/ *n* a small swelling on the skin.

pimply /**pim**-plee/ *adj* (*inf*) covered with pimples (*a pimply youth*).

pin /pin/ *n* **1** a short pointed bar of wire with a flattened head, used for fastening cloth, paper etc. (*put up the hem of the dress with pins*). **2** a wooden, metal, or plastic peg (*have a pin put in his injured arm*). **3** a bolt. **4** a narrow brooch (*a silver pin*). ● *vb* (**pinned** /pind/, **pinning** /**pi**-ning/) **1** to fasten with pins. **2** to hold firmly (to) (*she pinned him against the wall*). ● **pins and needles** a tingling feeling in a limb as the blood starts to flow freely through it again.

PIN /pin/ *abbr* = **personal identification number**: a number, consisting of several digits, used to identify a person (*enter your PIN to get money from the automated teller machine*).

piñata /pi-**nya**-ta/ *n* a container, often shaped like a horse and covered in colored tissue paper, full of candy and gifts and used at parties. It is hung from the ceiling and hit with sticks until its contents spill out.

pincers /**pin**-surz/ *npl* **1** a tool for gripping things firmly, used especially for pulling out nails. **2** claws (e.g., as of a crab).

pinch /pinch/ *vb* **1** to take or nip between the finger and thumb (*pinch his arm*). **2** to squeeze the flesh until it hurts (*pinch him to get him to wake up*). **3** (*inf*) to steal (*pinch money from her mother's pocketbook*). ● *n* **1** the amount that can be taken between the finger and thumb. **2** a small amount (*a pinch of salt*). **3** need, distress (*feeling the pinch having no job*).

pine[1] /pine/ *n* a cone-bearing evergreen tree.

pine[2] /pine/ *vb* **1** to waste away with sorrow, pain, etc. **2** to long for.

pineapple /**pine**-a-pul/ *n* a cone-shaped tropical fruit.

pine cone /**pine**-cone/ *n* the scaly fruit of the pine (*burn pine cones on the fire*).

ping /ping/ n a sharp sound, as of a bullet in flight.

pink[1] /pingk/ n **1** a garden flower. **2** a light red color. **3** the best of condition (*in the pink*). ● also adj.

pink[2] /pingk/ vb to cut a zig-zag edge on cloth (*pink the edges of the seams*).

pinnacle /pi-na-cul/ n **1** a pointed tower or spire on a building. **2** a pointed mountain. **3** the highest point (*the pinnacle of her success*).

pinstripe /pin-stripe/ n a very thin stripe running through a material.

pint /pinte/ n the eighth part of a gallon, 0.57 liter.

pioneer /pie-u-neer/ n **1** someone who goes before the main body to prepare the way, someone who is the first to try out new ideas etc. (*a pioneer of medical research in cancer*). **2** an explorer. ● vb **1** to begin (*pioneer the research*). **2** to explore.

pious /pie-us/ adj loving and worshipping God, religious (*the congregation's pious members*). ● n **piety**.

pip /pip/ n **1** seed of fruit (*orange pips*). **2** the spot on a card, dice, domino, etc. **3** one of the badges worn on an army officer's shoulder to show his rank.

pipe /pipe/ n **1** a musical wind instrument (*the pipes of Pan*). **2** a long tube (*water pipes*). **3** a tube with a bowl at one end for smoking tobacco (*smoke a pipe*). **4** a shrill voice. **5** a bird's note. **6** (*fml*) a measure of wine. ● vb **1** to play upon a pipe. **2** to make (water, gas, etc.) pass through pipes (*piping oil to the refinery*). **3** to speak in a shrill voice. **4** to whistle. ● **piping hot** very hot.

pipeline /pipe-line/ n a long line of pipes to carry water, oil, etc. ● **in the pipeline** in preparation (*plans in the pipeline*).

piper /pie-per/ n someone who plays a pipe or bagpipes. ● **pay the piper** to pay the bill.

piquant /pee-kant/ adj **1** sharp-tasting, appetizing (*a piquant sauce*). **2** witty, arousing interest. ● n **piquancy** /pee-kan-see/.

pique /peek/ n irritation, anger caused by wounded pride. ● vb to wound the pride of, to offend (*piqued at her lack of interest*).

pirate /pie-rit/ n **1** someone who attacks and robs ships at sea. **2** a person who does something without legal right (*pirates who publish books without permission*). ● also vb. ● n **piracy**.

pirouette /pi-ro-wet/ vb to turn round on the points of the toes like a ballet dancer would. ● also n.

pistachio /pi-sta-shee-o/ n a nut with a green kernel.

pistil /pi-stul/ n the seed-bearing part of a flower.

pistol /pi-stul/ n a small firearm fired with one hand.

piston /pi-stun/ n a plug that fits closely into a hollow cylinder inside which it moves up and down (*the pistons in the engine*).

pit[1] /pit/ n **1** a deep hole in the earth. **2** the passageway leading down to a mine. **3** a mine (for coal, etc.). **4** the area in front of the stage in a theater where the orchestra sits. **5** a trading area in a commodities exchange. ● vb (**pitted** /pi-tid/, **pitting** /pi-ting/) **1** to lay in a pit. **2** to set against in order to outdo (*pit his wits against theirs*).

pit[2] /pit/ n the stone of fruits such as the peach, plum, or cherry.

pitch[1] /pitch/ vb **1** to set up (*pitch a tent*). **2** to throw (*pitch a ball*). **3** to fall heavily (*he suddenly pitched forward*). **4** to set the keynote of (a tune). **5** (*of a ship*) to dip down headfirst after rising on a wave. ● n **1** a throw. **2** the highness or lowness of a note in music. **3** the ground marked out for a game (*a baseball pitch*). ● **pitched battle** a set battle between two prepared armies.

pitch[2] /pitch/ n a thick dark substance obtained from tar (*as black as pitch*).

pitcher[1] /pi-cher/ n a container for liquids (*a pitcher of water*).

pitcher[2] /pi-cher/ n the person who throws the ball to the batter in baseball.

pitchfork /pitch-fawrk/ n a long-handled tool with prongs for moving hay. ● vb **1** to move with a pitchfork. **2** to put suddenly into a new situation.

pitfall /pit-fawl/ n a trap (*the pitfalls of business*).

pith /pith/ n **1** material just under the skin of an orange, etc. **2** the soft center of the stem of a plant. **3** the most important part (*the pith of his speech*).

pithy /pith-ee/ adj short and to the point, forceful.

pitiable /pi-tee-ya-bul/ adj deserving pity (*a pitiable sight*).

pitta (bread) /pi-ta-bred/ n an oval-shaped type of flat bread that which can be opened to insert a filling.

pittance /pi-tanse/ n a small allowance or wage (*earn a pittance*).

pitted /pi-tid/ adj marked with little hollows, like the skin after smallpox.

pity /pi-tee/ n sympathy for the pain or sorrow of others (*feel pity for the homeless*). ● vb to feel sorry for. ● adjs **pitiful** /pi-ti-ful/, **pitiless** /pi-tee-less/.

pivot /pi-vut/ n **1** the pin on which anything (e.g., a wheel) turns. **2** the central point of anything (*the pivot of the organization*).

pivotal /pi-vu-tal/ adj holding a central or important position (*a pivotal role in the firm*).

pixel /piks-ul/ *n* in computing or photography, a tiny dot that makes up a larger picture (*the picture is made up of 350 pixels per square inch*).

pixie, pixy /pik-see/ *n* a fairy.

pizza /peet-sa/ *n* a baked circle of dough covered with cheese, tomatoes, etc.

pizzeria /peet-se-ree-a/ *n* a restaurant where pizzas are baked and sold.

placard /pla-card/ *n* a notice put up in a public place to announce or advertise something (*carry a placard protesting against the new bill*).

placate /pla-**cate**/ *vb* to make calm or peaceful (*placating their angry mother*).

place /place/ *n* **1** an open space in a town. **2** a particular part of space. **3** a village, town, etc. **3** the post or position held by someone. **4** rank in society. **5** a passage in a book. ● *vb* **1** to put or set. **2** to decide from where a thing comes or where it ought to be. **3** to recognize. **4** to find a job for.

placebo /pla-**see**-bo/ *n* **1** an ineffective medication given to a control group in an experiment. **2** an action or assurance designed to humor someone.

placid /pla-sid/ *adj* calm, not easily angered or upset, gentle (*a placid baby*). ● *n* **placidity** /pla-si-di-tee/.

plagiarism /**play**-ja-ri-zum/ *n* the act of stealing from another author's works. ● *n* **plagiarist** /play-ja-rist/.

plagiarize /**play**-ja-rize/ *vb, also* **plagiarise** (*Br*) to use the words or ideas of another and pretend they are one's own (*plagiarizing his friend's essay*).

plague /plaig/ *n* **1** a very infectious and dangerous disease (*the Black Death was a dangerous plague in the Middle Ages*). **2** (*inf*) a nuisance. ● *vb* (*inf*) to keep on annoying, to pester (*plaguing us with questions*).

plaice /place/ *n* an edible flat fish (*plaice and chips*).

plaid /plad/ *n* **1** a type of checked cloth. **2** a large woolen shawl-like wrap, often of tartan, worn as part of Scottish Highland dress.

plain /plain/ *adj* **1** clear, easily understood (*plain English*). **2** simple, bare, undecorated (*plain living*). **3** obvious (*it was plain that she was guilty*). ● *n* a stretc.h of level country.

plain sailing /plain-**say**-ling/ *n* something easy (*getting into the building was plain sailing*).

plain-spoken /plain-**spo**-kin/ *adj* saying what one thinks, frank.

plaintiff /**plain**-tif/ *n* the person who brings a suit before a court of law.

plaintive /**plain**-tiv/ *adj* sad, expressing sorrow (*a plaintive sound*).

plait /plat/, **pleat** /pleet/ *ns* **1** a pigtail of intertwined hair. **2** a fold (e.g. in material). ● *vb* to twist together into a plait.

plan /plan/ *n* **1** a drawing of the outlines made by an object on the ground, a map (*a plan of the building*). **2** a scheme of what is to happen on a future occasion (*make plans for defeating the enemy*). ● *vb* (**planned** /pland/, **planning** /pla-ning/) **1** to draw a plan of. **2** to arrange beforehand what should happen (*plan their future actions*). ● *n* **planner**.

plane[1] /plane/ *n* **1** a smooth or level surface. **2** a carpenter's tool for giving wood a smooth surface. **3** a common short form of **airplane** /air-plane/. ● *adj* level, smooth. ● *vb* to make smooth (*planing the rough wood*).

plane[2], **plane tree** /plane-tree/ *n* a tall broad-leaved tree.

planet /pla-nit/ *n* one of the heavenly bodies moving in orbit round the sun.

planetarium /pla-ni-**tay**-ree-um/ *n* a model of the planetary system.

planetary /pla-ni-te-ree/ *adj* having to do with the planets (*planetary influences*).

plank /plangk/ *n* a long, flat piece of timber (*a floor made of planks*).

plankton /plangk-tun/ *n* small living organisms found in the sea.

plant /plant/ *n* **1** anything growing from the earth and feeding on it through its roots (*garden plants*). **2** the machinery and equipment used in a factory (*industrial plant*). ● *vb* **1** to put in the ground to grow (*plant potatoes*). **2** to set firmly (*plant his feet on the ground*).

plantain[1] /plan-tin/ *n* a type of herb with broad leaves.

plantain[2], **plantain tree** /plan-tin tree/ *n* a tropical tree with fruit like a banana.

plantation /plan-**tay**-shun/ *n* **1** a wood planted by man. **2** a colony. **3** an estate on which a large amount of sugar, tea, cotton, etc., is cultivated.

planter /plan-ter/ *n* the owner or manager of a plantation (*a rubber planter*).

plaque /plak/ *n* **1** an ornamental plate of metal, etc. (*a plaque on the wall in memory of the dead soldier*). **2** a deposit of saliva and bacteria that forms on the teeth.

plasma /plaz-ma/ *n* the liquid part of blood.

plaster /pla-ster/ *n* **1** a mixture of lime, water and sand spread over the walls of buildings to make them smooth. **2** an adhesive bandage used for dressing wounds, etc. (*put a plaster on his grazed knee*). ● *vb* **1** to cover with plaster. **2** to spread over the surface of.

plaster cast /**pla**-ster-cast/ *n* a rigid casing put around a broken limb for support while it is healing.

plasterer /**pla**-stu-rer/ *n* someone who plasters walls.

plastic /**pla**-stic/ *adj* easily shaped or molded. ● *n* one of a group of man-made substances that can be molded into any shape (*chairs made of plastic*).

plastic surgery /**pla**-stic-**sur**-ju-ree/ *n* the reshaping of the human body by surgery (*have plastic surgery to reshape his nose*).

plate /**plate**/ *n* **1** a shallow dish for food (*serve the meat on the plates*). **2** a flat piece of metal, glass, etc. (*the name of the company engraved on a plate on the wall*). **3** gold and silver household articles (*burglars stole the family plate*). **4** a picture printed from an engraved piece of metal, etc. ● *vb* to cover with a thin coat of metal.

plateau /**pla**-toe/ *n* (*pl* **plateaux** /**pla**-toe/ *or* **plateaus** /**pla**-toaz/) an extent of high level land, a tableland.

platform /**plat**-fawrm/ *n* **1** a raised part of the floor (for speakers, etc.). **2** a bank built above ground level for those entering trains, etc. **3** statement of the aims of a group (*the animal rights platform*).

plating /**play**-ting/ *n* the art of covering articles with a thin coat of metal (*silver plating*).

platinum /**plat**-num/ *n* a valuable heavy grayish white metal.

platonic love /pla-**ton**-ic-**luv**/ *n* purely spiritual love between two human beings (*a platonic relationship*).

platoon /pla-**toon**/ *n* a small division of a company of infantry.

platter /**pla**-ter/ *n* a large flat plate or dish (*a platter of cold meat*).

platypus /**pla**-ti-pus/ *n* an Australian mammal with jaws like a duck's bill.

plausible /**plau**-zi-bul/ *adj* that which sounds convincing, seemingly true or truthful (*a plausible excuse*). ● *n* **plausibility** /plau-zi-**bi**-li-tee/.

play /**play**/ *vb* **1** to amuse oneself (*children playing*). **2** to take part in a game (*play darts*). **3** to gamble. **4** to act a part in a drama (*play Hamlet*). **5** to perform on a musical instrument (*to play the piano*). **6** to trifle with (*she played with his affections*). ● *n* **1** a drama (*go to see a play in the local theater*). **2** trifling amusement or sport (*children engaged in play*). **3** gambling. **4** free movement (*the play of the rope*).

player /**play**-er/ *n* **1** someone who takes part in a sport or drama. **2** a musical performer (*piano-player*).

playful /**play**-ful/ *adj* fond of sport or amusement.

playground /**play**-ground/ *n* a piece of ground set aside for children to play in.

playhouse /**play**-house/ *n* **1** (*especially in titles*) a theater. **2** a toy house large enough for children to play inside.

playmate /**play**-mate/ *n* a childhood companion (*his playmates at nursery school*).

plaything /**play**-thing/ *n* a toy.

playwright /**play**-rite/ *n* someone who writes plays.

plea /**plee**/ *n* **1** an excuse. **2** an earnest request. **3** the prisoner's answer to the charge in a law court (*a plea of not guilty*).

plead /**pleed**/ *vb* (*pt, pp* **pled** /**pled**/ *or* **pleaded** /**plee**-did/) **1** to request earnestly (*plead for his friend's release*). **2** to put forward in excuse (*plead that he was somewhere else*). **3** to present one's case or one's client's case in a court of law.

pleasant /**ple**-zant/ *adj* agreeable, enjoyable (*a pleasant companion/a pleasant day*).

please /**pleez**/ *vb* **1** to make happy or content (*do anything to please her*). **2** to seem good to (*music is pleasing to her*). **3** to be so kind as to (*close the window, please*).

pleasurable /**plezh**-ra-bul/ *adj* giving pleasure (*a pleasurable occasion*).

pleasure /**ple**-zhur/ *n* **1** delight, joy (*get pleasure in her son's happiness*). **2** will or choice (*at their pleasure*).

pleat *see* **plait**.

plectrum /**plec**-trum/ *n* a small instrument for plucking the strings of stringed instruments.

pledge /**pledge**/ *n* **1** a solemn promise (*a pledge that he would look after her*). **2** an object handed over to another to keep until a debt has been paid back to him or her. **3** a toast. ● *vb* **1** to promise solemnly (*pledge that he would be present*). **2** (*fml*) to give to keep until a debt has been repaid (*pledging his watch at the pawnbroker's*). **3** to drink to the health of.

plenitude /**ple**-ni-tood/ *n* an abundance, completeness.

plentiful /**plen**-ti-ful/ *adj* enough, more than enough (*a plentiful supply*).

plenty /**plen**-tee/ *n* all that is necessary, more than is necessary (*there is plenty of food*).

plethora /**ple**-tho-ra/ *n* more than enough of anything (*a plethora of secondhand clothes*).

pliable /**plie**-a-bul/ *adj* **1** easily bent. **2** easily influenced (*pliable people doing what she says*). ● *n* **pliability** /plie-a-**bi**-li-tee/.

pliant /**plie**-ant/ *adj* **1** easily bent. **2** easily influenced. ● *n* **pliancy** /**plie**-an-see/.

pliers /**plie**-urs/ *npl* a small tool for gripping things firmly and for cutting wire (*use pliers to pull out the nail*).

plight[1] /**plite**/ *n* a difficult condition, situation (*in an awkward financial plight*).

plight[2] /**plite**/ *vb* (*old*) to promise (*plight their troth*).

plinth /**plinth**/ *n* the square slab at the foot of a pillar or under a statue.

plod /**plod**/ *vb* (**plodded** /**plod**-id/, **plodding** /**plod**-ing/) to walk or work slowly and steadily (*plodding home at the end of the day*).

plodder /**plod**-er/ *n* someone who, though not clever, makes progress by hard work.

plot /**plot**/ *n* **1** a small piece of ground (*a plot in the cemetery*). **2** the planned arrangement of the events of a story, play, etc. **3** a secret plan against one or more persons (*conspirators in a plot against the government*). ● *vb* (**plotted** /**plot**-id/, **plotting** /**plot**-ing/) **1** to plan. **2** to form a plan against (*plot against the government*). **3** to mark out or set down on paper (*plot a graph*). ● *n* **plotter** /**plot**-er/.

plow /**plow**/ *n*, *also* **plough** (*Br, Cdn*) an instrument for turning up soil before seeds are sown. ● *vb* to turn up with a plow.

plowman /**plow**-man/ *n* someone who plows, a farm laborer.

plowshare /**plow**-share/ *n* the cutter or blade of a plow.

ploy /**ploy**/ *n* a devious tactic (*his ploy to get rid of them worked*).

pluck /**pluck**/ *vb* **1** to pick or gather (*pluck roses*). **2** to snatch (*pluck the log from the fire*). **3** to pull the feathers (*pluck the pheasant for dinner*). ● *n* courage (*have the pluck to face danger*).

plucky /**plu**-kee/ *adj* brave (*plucky fighters*).

plug /**plug**/ *n* an object that fits into a hole and stops it, a stopper. ● *vb* (**plugged** /**plugd**/, **plugging** /**plug**-ing/) **1** to stop with a plug. **2** (*inf*) to publicize (*plugging his new book on radio*).

plum /**plum**/ *n* a smooth-skinned, purple-colored fruit with a pit. ● *adj* **1** a dark, purple-red color. **2** desirable (*a plum job*).

plumage /**ploo**-midge/ *n* the feathers of a bird.

plumb /**plum**/ *n* a piece of lead on a string, lowered from the top of a wall to see that it is at right angles to the ground. ● *adj* straight up and down. ● *adv* **1** exactly (*plumb between the eyes*). **2** straight up and down. **3** really, incredibly (*plumb crazy*). ● *vb* **1** to measure depth. **2** to study thoroughly (*plumb the human mind*).

plumber /**plu**-mer/ *n* a workman skilled in mending or fitting pipes, faucets, etc.

plumbing /**plu**-ming/ *n* **1** the work of a plumber. **2** all the pipes, faucets, etc., in a house (*faulty plumbing*).

plumbline /**plum**-line/ *n* the string by which the plumb is lowered.

plume /**ploom**/ *n* **1** a feather. **2** an ornament of feathers in a hat, etc. ● *vb* (*fml*) **1** to decorate with feathers. **2** to pride (oneself) (*pluming himself on his building expertise*).

plummet /**plu**-mit/ *vb* to drop down, to plunge.

plump[1] /**plump**/ *adj* fat and rounded. ● *vb* to grow fat, to fatten (*plump the turkeys for Christmas*). ● *n* **plumpness** /**plump**-ness/.

plump[2] /**plump**/ *vb* **1** to sit or fall suddenly (*plump down on the sofa*). **2** to choose (*plump for the older candidate*). ● *adv* suddenly or directly.

plum pudding /plum-**poo**-ding/ *n* a pudding containing currants, raisins, etc., flavored with spices.

plunder /**plun**-der/ *vb* to steal by force, to rob. ● *n* that which is taken away by force (*plunder taken by the enemy from the city*).

plunge /**plunj**/ *vb* **1** to thrust into water (*plunging the vegetables into boiling water*). **2** to jump or dive into water (*plunge into the lake*). **3** to rush (into) (*plunge into marriage*). ● *n* **1** a dive. **2** act of rushing.

pluperfect /**ploo**-per-fect/ *n* see **past perfect**.

plural /**plu**-ral/ *adj* more than one in number. ● *n* the form(s) of a word indicating more than one.

pluralist /**plu**-ra-list/ *n* (*fml*) someone who holds more than one office.

plurality /plu-**ra**-li-tee/ *n* (*fml*) **1** a number consisting of more than one. **2** the majority.

plus /**plus**/ *prep* with the addition of (*brains plus beauty*). ● *adj* **1** more than (*children who are twelve plus*). **2** to be added, extra (*a plus factor*). ● *n* the sign (+) of addition.

plush /**plush**/ *n* (*inf*) a velvety kind of cloth. ● *adj* luxurious.

ply[1] /**plie**/ *vb* **1** to work at (*plying his trade*). **2** to go regularly between two places (*a ferry plied between the island and the mainland*). **3** to use skillfully.

ply[2] /**plie**/ *n* a layer (*four-ply wood*).

plywood /**plie**-wood/ *n* strong board made up of several thin layers of wood stuck together.

p.m. /pee em/ *abbr* = **post meridiem**: from the Latin, meaning after noon.

pneumatic /noo-**ma**-tic/ *adj* filled with air, moved by air.

pneumonia /noo-**moe**-nee-a/ *n* an inflammation of the lungs.

poach[1] /**poach**/ *vb* to cook (fish, eggs, etc.) lightly in liquid.

poach[2] /**poach**/ *vb* to hunt unlawfully on another's land (*poach pheasants*). ● *n* **poacher** /**poa**-cher/.

pocket /**pock**-it/ *n* **1** a small bag attached to a garment, billiard table, suitcase, etc. (*a handkerchief in his top pocket*). **2** a hollow in earth or rock filled with metal ore. **3** the hollow in a baseball mitt for catching the ball. ● *vb* **1** to put into a pocket (*pocketing his winnings*). **2** to steal. **3** to conceal (*pocketed his pride*).

pocketbook /**pock**-it-book/ *n* a small case for holding paper money, letters, etc., in one's pocket.

pocket money /**pock**-it-mu-nee/ *n* money carried about for immediate personal use.

pockmarked /**pock**-markt/ *adj* marked with small hollows on the skin as a result of smallpox.

pod /**pod**/ *n* the covering of the seed of plants, such as peas, beans, etc.

podcast /**pod**-cast/ n an audio or video file, downloadable (usually for free) from a Web site and playable on computers or mp3 players.

podgy /**pod**-jee/ *adj* (*inf*) short and fat.

poem /**poa**-em/ *n* a piece of writing set down in memorable language and in lines with a recognizable rhythm.

poet /**poa**-et/ *n* someone who writes poetry. ● *f* **poetess** /**poa**-e-tess/.

poetic /**poa**-e-tic/, **poetical** /**poa**-e-ti-cal/ *adjs* **1** having to do with poetry. **2** suitable for poetry (*poetic language*).

poetry /**poa**-e-tree/ *n* ideas, feelings, etc., expressed in memorable words and rhythmical language.

poignant /**poi**-nant/ *adj* painful and deeply felt (*poignant memories*).

point /**point**/ *n* **1** the sharp end of anything (*the point of the knife*). **2** a headland. **3** a dot. **4** the exact place or time. **5** the purpose for which something is said or written (*fail to see the point of his speech*). **6** a single stage in an argument or list. **7** the unit of scoring in certain games (*a team three points ahead*). **8** *pl* (*Br*) *see* **switch**. ● *vb* **1** to show the direction of with a finger, stick, etc. (*point out the house to them*). **2** to sharpen. **3** to aim (*point the gun at them*). **4** (*of dogs*) to show the direction of game with the nose. ● **make a point of** to attach special importance to. ● **on the point of** about to (*on the point of leaving*).

pointed /**poin**-tid/ *adj* **1** sharp (*with a pointed edge*). **2** meant to be understood in a certain way (*a pointed remark*).

pointer /**poin**-ter/ *n* **1** a rod for pointing with (*indicate the place on the map with a pointer*). **2** a dog trained to point out game.

pointless /**point**-less/ *adj* having no meaning, having no sensible purpose (*a pointless exercise*).

poise /**poiz**/ *n* **1** balance. **2** calmness and good sense (*enough poise to cope with the situation*). ● *vb* **1** to balance. **2** to hover (*poised ready to intervene*).

poison /**poi**-zun/ *n* **1** any substance that when taken into a living creature (animal or vegetable), harms or kills it. **2** any idea, etc., that when spread through society causes standards of judgment to become lower. ● *vb* **1** to give poison to. **2** to kill by poison.

poisonous /**poi**-zu-nuss/ *adj* **1** being or containing poison (*poisonous berries*). **2** having a very harmful influence (*poisonous influences on society*).

poke /**poke**/ *vb* to push with something pointed (e.g., a finger, stick, etc.), to prod. ● *n* a prod given with something pointed (*a poke in the ribs*). ● **poke fun at** to make fun of. ● **poke one's nose into** to interfere in what does not concern one.

poker /**po**-ker/ *n* **1** a metal rod for stirring the coal, etc., in a fire. **2** a card game, usually played for money.

poky /**po**-kee/ *adj* (*inf*) small and cramped (*a family living in a poky apartment*).

polar /**po**-lar/ *adj* of or near one of the poles of the earth (*the polar regions*).

polar bear /**po**-lar-bare/ *n* the white bear of Arctic regions.

polarize /**po**-la-rize/ *vb, also* **polarise** (*Br*) **1** to make to work in the same direction. **2** to divide into groups based on two completely opposite opinions, attitudes, etc.

pole[1] /**pole**/ *n* **1** a long rod. **2** a long rounded post. **3** a measure of length (= 5.03 meters).

pole[2] /**pole**/ *n* **1** one of the ends of the axis of the earth. **2** one of the points in the sky opposite the poles of the earth (*celestial poles*). **3** the end of either of the two arms of a magnet.

polecat /**pole**-cat/ *n* a weasel-like animal that throws out a foul-smelling liquid when attacked.

polestar, Pole Star /**pole**-star/ *n* a particular star at or near the celestial North Pole, used for finding directions.

police /pu-**leess**/ *n* a body of persons whose job is to keep public order and see that the law is kept. ● *vb* to see that law and order are kept (*policing the area*). ● *ns* **policeman** /pu-**leess**-man/, **police officer** /pu-**leess**-aw-fi-ser/, **policewoman** /pu-**leess**-woo-man/.

policy /**pol**-i-see/ *n* 1 the methods or plans of a government or party. 2 a course of action (*a marketing policy*). 3 a written agreement with an insurance company (*a household policy*).

polish /**pol**-ish/ *vb* 1 to make smooth and shining by rubbing (*polish the table*). 2 to improve, to refine (*manners requiring polishing*). ● *n* 1 a smooth, shiny surface. 2 any substance rubbed on to make smooth and shiny. 3 good manners, refinement (*sent to finishing school to acquire polish*).

polite /pu-**lite**/ *adj* well-mannered, refined (*polite children*). ● *n* **politeness** /pu-**lite**-ness/.

political /pu-**li**-ti-cal/ *adj* having to do with politics (*political motives*).

politically correct /pu-li-**tic**-lee-cu-**rect**/ *adj* of language that is designed to avoid giving offence to particular groups of people, usually people who are often discriminated against, often abbreviated to **PC**. ● **political correctness** /pu-li-ti-cal-cu-**rect**-ness/ *n*.

politician /pol-i-**ti**-shun/ *n* 1 a statesman whose work is concerned with the public affairs or government of a country. 2 someone who seeks political office for selfish motives.

politics /**pol**-i-tics/ *n* the art or study of government, political matters (*go in for politics*).

polka /**pol**-ka/ *n* a quick lively dance.

poll /pole/ *n* 1 an election (*a poll to elect a president*). 2 the number of votes (*a small poll*). ● *vb* 1 to vote. 2 to receive a vote or votes (*he polled over 20,000 votes*).

pollen /**pol**-in/ *n* the yellow dust on a flower that when, united to seeds, makes them grow.

pollinate /**pol**-in-ate/ *vb* to make pollen unite with the seed. ● *n* **pollination** /pol-in-**ay**-shun/.

pollutant /pu-**loo**-tant/ *n* something that pollutes.

pollute /pu-**loot**/ *vb* to make filthy or unfit for use (*water polluted by industrial waste*). ● *n* **pollution** /pu-**loo**-shun/.

polo /**po**-lo/ *n* a game like hockey played on horseback.

poltergeist /**pole**-ter-giest/ *n* a mischievous spirit or ghost (*believe that a poltergeist was throwing things around the room*).

poly- /**pol**-ee/ *prefix* many.

polyester /po-le-**es**-ter/ *n* a synthetic fiber used to make fabric.

polythene /**pol**-i-theen/ *n* a man-made plastic material resistant to chemicals and moisture (*bags made of polythene*).

pomegranate /**pom**-e-gra-nit/ *n* a large thick-skinned fruit containing many red, juicy, edible seeds.

pomp /pomp/ *n* splendid show or display, grandeur (*a procession full of pomp*).

pomposity /pom-**pos**-i-tee/ *n* act of being pompous.

pompous /**pom**-pus/ *adj* trying to appear dignified or important (*a pompous old fool*).

poncho /**pon**-sho/ *n* a circular or rectangular cloak with a hole in the middle to put the head through.

pond /pond/ *n* a large pool of standing water.

ponder /**pon**-der/ *vb* (*fml*) to think deeply, to consider carefully (*ponder the problems of the situation*).

ponderous /**pon**-drus/ *adj* 1 (*fml*) very heavy (*a ponderous load*). 2 slow, dull (*with ponderous steps*).

pontiff /**pon**-tif/ *n* 1 a bishop. 2 the pope. ● **Supreme Pontiff** the pope.

pontifical /pon-**ti**-fi-cal/ *adj* 1 having to do with a bishop or the pope. 2 pompous.

pontificate /pon-**ti**-fi-cate/ *vb* 1 (*fml*) to state one's opinions pompously, as if stating undoubted facts (*pontificating on the state of the country*). 2 to act as a pontiff. ● *n* the office or reign of a pontiff.

pontoon¹ /pon-**toon**/ *n* a card game, usually played for money.

pontoon² /pon-**toon**/ *n* a flat-bottomed boat used as a support for a bridge. ● *n* **pontoon bridge**.

pony /**poe**-nee/ *n* a small horse.

poodle /**poo**-dul/ *n* a small pet dog with curly hair, often clipped to leave part of its body bare.

pooh /poo/ *interj* an exclamation of contempt.

pooh-pooh /poo-**poo**/ *vb* (*inf*) to sneer at, to speak of (an idea) as foolish (*pooh-poohed their efforts to help*).

pool¹ /pool/ *n* 1 a puddle. 2 a deep place in a stream or river. 3 an area of still water (*a swimming pool*).

pool² /pool/ *n* 1 all the money bet on a certain game or event. 2 a collection of resources, money, etc., for sharing, communal use etc. (*a typing pool*). ● *vb* to put together the goods, etc., of individuals for use by the whole group (*pooling their resources*).

poop¹ /poop/ *n* the back part of a ship, the stern.

poop² /poop/ *vb* to make exhausted (*he was pooped after all his exertions*).

poor /poor/ *adj* 1 having little money. 2 unfortunate (*sorry for the poor soul*). 3 bad (*poor weather*).

poorly /poor-lee/ *adj* unwell (*too poorly to go to work*).

pop /pop/ *n* a sharp, low sound (*the pop of a cork being pulled from a bottle*). ● *vb* (**popped** /popt/, **popping** /pop-ing/) **1** to make a sharp low sound. **2** to move quickly or suddenly (*the child popped out from behind the door*).

pope /pope/ *n* the head of the Roman Catholic Church.

poplar /pop-lar/ *n* a tall slender tree.

pop music /pop-myoo-zic/ *n* popular tunes of the day.

poppy /pop-ee/ *n* a plant with brightly colored flowers (*red poppies*).

populace /pop-yu-lis/ *n* (*fml*) the common people (*ideas disliked by the populace*).

popular /pop-yu-lar/ *adj* **1** having to do with the people (*popular issues*). **2** well-liked by most people (*a popular young woman*).

popularity /pop-yu-la-ri-tee/ *n* the state of being liked by most people.

popularize /pop-yu-la-rize/ *vb, also* **popularise** (*Br*) to make popular (*popularizing the fashion for short skirts*).

populate /pop-yu-late/ *vb* to provide with inhabitants (*an island mainly populated by old people*).

population /pop-yu-lay-shun/ *n* all the people living in a place.

populous /pop-yu-lus/ *adj* having many inhabitants (*the more populous areas of the world*).

porcelain /pore-slin/ *n* fine pottery.

porch /poarch/ *n* a roofed approach to a door.

porcupine /pawr-cyu-pine/ *n* an animal like the rat, covered with prickly quills.

pore[1] /pore/ *n* a tiny opening, especially in the skin (*blocked pores*).

pore[2] /pore/ *vb*. ● **pore over** to study closely (*poring over the map*).

pork /poark/ *n* the meat obtained from a pig (*roast pork*).

porous /po-rus/ *adj* having small holes through which liquid may pass (*porous substances*).

porpoise /pawr-poiz/ *n* a sea animal about 1.5 meters long.

porridge /paw-ridge/ *n* a food made from oatmeal boiled in water or milk to make a thick broth (*have porridge for breakfast*).

port[1] /poart/ *n* **1** a harbor. **2** a place with a harbor (*a small port in the south of the country*).

port[2] /poart/ *n* an opening in the side of a ship.

port[3] /poart/ *n* the left side of a ship (looking forward), larboard.

port[4] /poart/ *n* a dark sweet red wine (*serve port after dinner*).

portable /poar-ta-bul/ *adj* able to be carried about (*a portable television*).

portal /poar-tal/ *n* (*fml*) a doorway, a gateway.

portcullis /poart-cu-lis/ *n* a grating of crisscrossed iron bars that could be lowered suddenly to close the gateway of a castle against attackers.

porter[1] /poar-tur/ *n* (*Br*) a doorkeeper.

porter[2] /poar-tur/ *n* **1** someone who carries loads, baggage, etc., for others (*a station porter*). **2** a dark brown beer.

portfolio /poart-foe-lee-o/ *n* **1** a case for carrying loose papers, drawings, etc. **2** the office of a minister of state (*the trade and industry portfolio*).

porthole /poart-hole/ *n* a small window in the side of a ship.

portico /poar-ti-co/ *n* (*pl* **porticoes** *or* **porticos** /poar-ti-coaz/) **1** a roof supported by a row of pillars, jutting out at the front of a building. **2** a roofed approach to a door. **3** a path covered by a roof supported by pillars.

portion /poar-shun/ *n* **1** a share (*take a portion of the blame*). **2** a helping (*a large portion of cake*). **3** the money and property given to a woman at the time of her marriage. **4** (*fml or old*) one's fate (*poverty has been her portion*). **5** a part (*the front portion of the train*). ● *vb* **1** to divide up. **2** to give a share to.

portly /poart-lee/ *adj* stout (*a portly old gentleman*).

portrait /poar-trait/ *n* **1** a picture of a person (*paint her portrait in oils*). **2** a good description (*a pen portrait of her grandmother*).

portraiture /poar-tri-chur/ *n* **1** the drawing of portraits. **2** describing in words.

portray /poar-tray/ *vb* **1** to draw or paint (*a painting portraying children playing*). **2** to describe (*in her account of the accident the driver of the car is portrayed as a very stupid man*).

portrayal /poar-tray-al/ *n* the act of portraying.

pose /poze/ *vb* **1** to put (*posing a question*). **2** to put on or take up a certain attitude (*pose for an artist*). **3** to pretend to be what one is not (*burglars posing as laborers*). ● *n* **1** position, attitude. **2** a pretense of being what one is not. **3** a false manner or attitude.

position /pu-zi-shun/ *n* **1** place (*the house's position by the lake*). **2** rank, grade (*finish in second position in the race*). **3** job (*a junior position in the firm*). **4** state of affairs (*their financial position*). **5** a place occupied by troops during battle. ● *vb* to place.

positive /pos-i-tiv/ *adj* **1** sure (*positive that she saw* *him*). **2** certain, definite (*positive proof*). **3** confident (*a positive manner*). **4** greater than 0 (*a positive number*). **5** really existing. **6** active, leading to practical action (*positive action*).

positively /**pos**-i-tiv-lee/ *adv* completely, really (*positively the last time*).

posse /**pos**-ee/ *n* **1** a small body of people, especially police. **2** (*inf*) a group of people with a shared interest.

possess /pu-**zess**/ *vb* **1** to have as one's own (*possess great wealth*). **2** (*fml*) to control the mind of (*possessed by a great rage*). ● *adj* **possessed** /pu-**zest**/.

possession /pu-**ze**-shun/ *n* **1** the act of possessing. **2** ownership. **3** control by evil spirits.

possessive /pu-**ze**-siv/ *adj* **1** showing possession (*a possessive pronoun*). **2** liking to possess or own, unwilling to share (*a possessive lover*).

possessor /pu-**ze**-sur/ *n* someone who possesses (*the possessor of a new car*).

possibility /paw-si-**bi**-li-tee/ *n* something possible (*no possibility of improvement*).

possible /**paw**-si-bul/ *adj* **1** that may be true (*it is possible that she is dead*). **2** that may exist (*possible proof*). **3** that can be done (*possible courses of action*).

possibly /**paw**-si-blee/ *adv* perhaps, maybe.

post[1] /**poast**/ *n* a strong pole or length of wood stuck upright in the ground (*posts to make a fence*). ● *vb* to put up on a post, noticeboard, etc. (*post notices about the show*).

post[2] /**poast**/ *n* **1** one's place of duty (*soldiers at their posts*). **2** one's job (*seek a new post*). **3** a military camp. **4** a settlement. **5** (*Br*) see **mail**. ● *vb* **1** to send to a certain place of duty (*post soldiers overseas*). **2** (*old*) to hurry. **3** (*old*) to travel on horseback changing horses at regular intervals. **4** to supply with the latest news (*keep them posted*). **5** (*Br*) see **mail**.

post- /**poast**/ *prefix* after.

postage /**poa**-stidge/ *n* the charge for sending something by mail (*postage has gone up*).

postal service /**poast**-ul ser-viss/ *n* the agency that sells stamps, and collects and delivers the mail in the United States.

postcard /**poast**-card/ *n* a card on which a message may be written and which can be mailed without an envelope (*postcards sent on vacation*).

postdate /**poast**-date/ *vb* to put on a date later than the actual one (*postdating a check*).

poster /**poas**-ter/ *n* a large printed notice for public display (*a poster advertising the concert*).

posterior /pu-**sti**-ree-ur/ *adj* (*fml*) **1** later. **2** placed behind.

posterity /pos-**te**-ri-tee/ *n* one's descendants, later generations (*paintings preserved for posterity*).

posthumous /**pos**-chu-mus/ *adj* **1** happening after someone's death (*he was awarded a posthumous medal for bravery*). **2** born after the father's death (*a posthumous son*). **3** published after the author's death (*a posthumous novel*).

postmortem /**poast**-mawr-tum/ *adj* after death. ● *n* an examination of a body after death to find out the cause of death (*a postmortem after sudden death*).

postnatal /**poast**-**nay**-tal/ *adj* after birth.

post office /**poast**-**awf**-iss/ *n* **1** an office where stamps may be bought, letters posted, etc. **2** a government department in charge of postal services.

postpone /**poast**-**pone**/ *vb* to put off until a later time (*postponing the meeting until next week*). ● *n* **postponement** /**poast**-**pone**-mint/.

postscript /**poast**-script/ *n* something extra written at the end of a letter after the signature.

posture /**pos**-chur/ *n* **1** a way of holding oneself (*a slouched posture*). **2** an attitude. ● *vb* **1** to hold oneself in a certain way. **2** (*fml*) to behave in a way not natural to oneself (*posturing in front of an audience*).

posy /**poe**-zee/ *n* a small bunch of flowers (*bridesmaids carrying posies*).

pot /**pot**/ *n* **1** a vessel for cooking in (*a pot of soup*). **2** a vessel for holding plants, liquids, etc. (*a plant pot*). ● *vb* (**potted** /**pot**-id/, **potting** /**pot**-ing/) **1** to put in a pot (*pot plants*). **2** to shoot at and kill (*pot rabbits*).

potash /**pot**-ash/ *n* a substance obtained from the ashes of certain plants.

potassium /pu-**ta**-see-um/ *n* the metallic base of potash.

potato /pu-**tay**-toe/ *n* (*pl* **potatoes** /pu-**tay**-toaz/) a plant the swellings (tubers) on whose roots are eaten as vegetables (*mash potatoes*).

potency /**poe**-ten-see/ *n* power.

potent /**poe**-tent/ *adj* strong, powerful (*a potent influence*).

potential /pu-**ten**-shal/ *adj* existing but not made use of, possible (*potential trouble*). ● *n* the unrealized ability to do something.

potentiality /pu-ten-shee-a-**li**-tee/ *n* unused or undeveloped power(s) (*the potentiality of the pupils*).

pothole /**pot**-hole/ *n* **1** a hole in the surface of a road (*potholes made driving difficult*). **2** a deep hole in limestone.

potholing /pot-hole-ing/ *n* the exploring of limestone potholes.

potion /po-shun/ *n* (*lit*) a dose, a liquid medicine (*a love potion*).

pot luck /pot luck/ *n* **1** whatever food is available (*come for a meal and take pot luck*). **2** whatever is available (*go to the movies and take pot luck*).

potluck /pot-**luck**/ *n* a dinner party where guests bring dishes to share (*come to the church potluck*).

potpourri /po-poo-**ree**/ *n* **1** (*old*) a dish of several foods cooked together. **2** a mixture of dried pieces of sweet-smelling flowers and leaves. **3** (*fml*) a selection of writings or pieces of music, a miscellany.

pottage /pot-idge/ *n* (*old*) a thick soup or porridge.

potter[1] /pot-er/ *n* someone who makes earthenware vessels.

potter[2] /pot-er/ *vb* (*Br*) *see* **putter**.

pottery /pot-er-ee/ *n* **1** cups, plates, etc., made of earthenware (*a shop selling pottery*). **2** a potter's workshop.

pouch /pouch/ *n* a small bag (*a tobacco pouch*).

poulterer /pole-tu-rer/ *n* someone who buys and sells poultry.

poultice /pole-tiss/ *n* a dressing containing some soft material often heated and placed on or over a sore part of the body (*put a poultice on the boil*). ● *vb* to put a poultice on.

poultry /pole-tree/ *n* farmyard fowls (*a shop selling poultry*).

pounce /pounse/ *n* **1** a sudden jump on (*with one pounce she was on him*). **2** the claw of a bird. ● *vb* **1** to jump on suddenly (*the cat pouncing on the mouse*). **2** to attack suddenly (*the mugger pounced on the old man*).

pound[1] /pound/ *n* **1** a measure of weight (= 16 ounces or 0.454 kilogram). **2** a British unit of money (100 pence) (*a pound coin*).

pound[2] /pound/ *vb* **1** to beat hard (*with heart pounding*). **2** to crush into powder or small pieces (*pound the nuts into a paste*). **3** to walk or run heavily (*patrolmen pounding the beat*).

pound[3] /pound/ *n* **1** an enclosure for lost cattle. **2** a place for stray cats and dogs.

pour /pore/ *vb* **1** to cause to flow (*pour milk from the jug*). **2** to flow strongly (*blood poured from the wound*). **3** to rain heavily (*it was pouring*). **4** to move in great quantity or in large numbers (*children pouring out of school*).

pout /pout/ *vb* to thrust out the lips in displeasure, to look sulky (*the child pouted when she did not get what she wanted*). ● *n* a sulky look.

poverty /po-vur-tee/ *n* lack of money or goods, want, the state of being poor (*live in poverty*).

poverty-stricken /po-vur-tee-stri-kin/ *adj* very poor.

powder /pow-der/ *n* **1** any substance in the form of tiny dry particles (*talcum powder*). **2** gunpowder. ● *vb* **1** to make into a powder. **2** to put powder on (*powder her face*).

powdery /pow-dree/ *adj* **1** dustlike (*powdery snow*). **2** covered with powder.

power /pow-er/ *n* **1** the ability to act or do (*the power of speech*). **2** strength, force (*hit the rock with great power*). **3** influence (*use her power on the committee*). **4** control (*people in his power*). **5** a strong nation (*the great powers of the world*). **6** mechanical energy (*the car's power*). ● *adjs* **powerful** /pow-er-ful/, **powerless** /pow-er-less/.

powerhouse /pow-er-house/ *n* **1** a power station. **2** (*inf*) a strong or energetic person, team, etc.

power station /pow-er-stay-shun/ *n* a place where electrical power is generated.

powwow /pow-wow/ *n* **1** (*inf*) a friendly discussion. **2** (*old*) a conference among American Indians.

practicable /prac-ti-ca-bul/ *adj* that can be done, possible (*a plan that is simply not practicable*).

practical /prac-ti-cal/ *adj* **1** skillful in work, able to deal with things efficiently (*a practical person dealing with household emergencies*). **2** that can be carried out, useful (*practical suggestions*). **3** concerned with action rather than with ideas. ● *adv* **practically** /prac-ti-ca-lee/.

practicality /prac-ti-ca-li-tee/ *n* usefulness.

practice /prac-tiss/ *n* **1** (*fml*) habit, frequent use (*it was his practice to walk to work*). **2** the doing of an action often to improve one's skill (*piano practice*). **3** a doctor or lawyer's business. ● *vb* **1** to do frequently (*practicing self-control*). **2** to do often in order to improve one's skill (*practice playing the piano*). **3** to carry on a profession (*practice medicine*).

practitioner /prac-**tish**-ner/ *n* someone who practices a profession (*a medical practitioner*).

pragmatic /prag-ma-tic/ *adj* concerned with practicalities rather than theories (*a pragmatic solution to the problem*).

pragmatism /prag-ma-ti-zum/ *n* the judging of actions or events by their practical outcome.

prairie /pray-ree/ *n* an extent of level treeless grassland.

praise /praise/ *vb* **1** to speak well of, to speak in honor of (*praising the boy for rescuing his friend/praising his brave action*). **2** to worship, as by singing hymns, etc. (*praise God*). ● *n* **1** an expression of credit or honor. **2** glory, worship expressed through song.

praiseworthy /praise-wur-thee/ *adj* deserving to be spoken well of (*a praiseworthy act*).

prance /pranss/ *vb* **1** to jump about (*children prancing about with delight/horses prancing*). **2** to walk in a showy manner (*prance about, showing off her new shoes*).

prank /prangk/ *n* a trick played in fun (*children playing pranks on their parents*).

prattle /pra-tul/ *vb* to talk a lot and foolishly, to chatter like a young child (*prattling about her vacation*). ● *n* foolish or childish talk.

prawn /prawn/ *n* an edible shellfish like a large shrimp.

pray /pray/ *vb* **1** to beg for, to ask earnestly (*pray for forgiveness*). **2** to speak to God in worship, thanksgiving, etc.

prayer /prare/ *n* **1** an earnest request. **2** words addressed to God in worship, thanksgiving, etc.

prayer book /prare book/ *n* a book containing prayers, order of services, etc.

pre- /pree/ *prefix* before.

preach /preech/ *vb* **1** to speak in public on a religious or sacred subject (*ministers preaching to their congregations on Sunday*). **2** to give advice on how to behave correctly (*parents preaching the importance of studying hard*). ● *n* **preacher** /pree-cher/.

preamble /pree-am-bul/ *n* (*fml*) the introductory part of a statute or constitution, speech, piece of writing, etc. (*bored by the long preamble to the novel*).

prearrange /pre-a-range/ *vb* to arrange beforehand.

precarious /pri-cay-ree-us/ *adj* uncertain, dangerous (*a precarious existence*).

precaution /pri-caw-shun/ *n* something done to prevent future trouble. ● *adj* **precautionary** /pri-caw-shun-ree/.

precede /pree-seed/ *vb* to come or go before in time, place or importance (*the tenants preceding him*).

precedence /pre-si-dense/ *n* **1** being earlier in time. **2** greater importance (*give precedence to the subject at the meeting*). **3** order according to rank (*admirals take precedence over vice-admirals*).

precedent /pre-si-dent/ *n* an earlier case that helps one to decide what to do in like circumstances (*the judge basing his sentence on precedents*).

preceding /pri-see-ding/ *adj* previous (*during the preceding month*).

precinct /pree-singkt/ *n* **1** a division within a city for administrative or policing purposes. **2** an electoral district. **3** the land around and belonging to a building. **4** *pl* the grounds. **5** a part laid out for a particular use (*a shopping precinct/a pedestrian precinct*).

precious /pre-shus/ *adj* **1** of great worth or value. **2** too deliberate, too concerned with perfection or unimportant detail (*a precious prose style/precious manners*).

precipice /pre-si-piss/ *n* a very steep cliff.

precipitate /pri-si-pi-tate/ *vb* **1** to rain, hail, sleet or snow. **2** (*fml*) to throw down headfirst (*the horse precipitated him into the ditch*). **3** to make happen at once (*his speech precipitated war*). **4** to hasten (*his mother's illness precipitated his departure*). **4** to cause the solid matter in a liquid to sink to the foot. ● *adj* thoughtless, overhasty (*a precipitate action*). ● *n* the solid matter that settles at the bottom of a liquid.

precipitation /pri-si-pi-tay-shun/ *n* the fall of water from the sky in the form of rain, hail sleet or snow.

precise /pri-siess/ *adj* **1** exact, clearly expressed (*precise instructions*). **2** careful (a precise speaker). **3** exact, particular, very (*at that precise moment*). ● *n* **precision** /pri-si-zhun/.

precocious /pri-co-shus/ *adj* (*of a child*) too clever for one's age, forward. ● *n* **precocity** /pri-cos-i-tee/.

predator /preh-da-tor/ *n* an animal that hunts other animals for food (*a lion is a predator*).

predatory /preh-da-toe-ree/ *adj* living by killing or robbing others (*predatory animals such as foxes*).

predecessor /pree-di-se-sur/ *n* someone who held a certain post before another (*younger than his predecessors*).

predestination /pree-de-sti-nay-shun/ *n* the belief that God has settled beforehand everything that is to happen, including the fate of people in the afterlife.

predestine /pree-de-stin/ *vb* to settle or decide beforehand (*the plan seemed predestined to fail*).

predetermine /pree-di-ter-min/ *vb* (*fml*) to decide beforehand (*predetermine the problem areas*).

predicament /pri-di-ca-ment/ *n* a difficulty, an unpleasant situation (*an embarrassing predicament*).

predicate /**pre**-di-cit/ *n* the part of sentence, containing a verb, which tells you what the subject or object does, or what it has done to it.

predict /pri-**dict**/ *vb* to say what will happen in the future, to foretell (*predict a change in the weather*). ● *n* **prediction** /pri-**dic**-shun/.

predilection /pre-di-**lec**-shun/ *n* (*fml*) a preference (*a predilection for expensive perfume*).

predispose /pree-di-**spoaz**/ *vb* to influence, to make more likely to be affected by.

predisposition /pree-dis-pu-**zi**-shun/ *n* a tendency to be influenced or affected by (*children with a predisposition to asthma*).

predominance /pri-**dom**-in-anse/ *n* 1 control (*predominance over other political parties*). 2 superiority in numbers, etc. (*the predominance of objectors*).

predominant /pri-**dom**-in-ant/ *adj* 1 outstanding (*the predominant color*). 2 largest (*a predominant number of protesters*).

predominate /pri-**dom**-in-ate/ *vb* 1 to have control over (*the left wing of the party is said to predominate*). 2 to be most or greatest (*the "no" votes predominating over the "yes" votes*).

preempt /pree-**empt**/ *vb* to take action to stop something from happening (*he preempted his tenant's complaint by fixing the roof*).

preen /**preen**/ *vb* 1 (*of birds*) to trim the feathers with the beak. 2 to tidy one's hair, clothes, etc. (*preening herself in front of the mirror*).

prefabricate /pree-**fa**-bri-cate/ *vb* to make ready the parts (especially of a building) for putting together on site (*prefabricated houses*).

preface /**pre**-fiss/ *n* an explanatory passage at the beginning of a speech or book. ● *vb* to begin with some explanation or other remarks.

prefect /**pree**-fect/ *n* 1 someone placed over others. 2 a senior pupil who helps to keep order in a school.

prefer /pri-**fer**/ *vb* (**preferred** /pri-**ferd**/, **preferring** /pri-**fer**-ing/) to like better, to choose before others (*prefer lamb to beef/prefer his brother to him*).

preferable /**pref**-ra-bul/ *adj* more likable, chosen before others (*leaving seemed preferable to staying*).

preference /**pref**-rense/ *n* a liking for one more than another (*a preference for smaller cars*).

preferential /pre-fe-**ren**-shal/ *adj* giving, receiving or showing preference (*accused of giving members of his family preferential treatment in the firm*).

prefix /pree-**fiks**/ *vb* to put at the beginning. ● *n*
prefix /**pree**-fiks/ a meaningful syllable or word put at the beginning of a word to alter its meaning.

pregnant /**preg**-nant/ *adj* 1 carrying unborn young within the body. 2 full of (*pregnant with meaning*). 3 full of meaning (*a pregnant look*). ● *n* **pregnancy** /**preg**-nan-see/.

prehensile /pree-**hen**-sul/ *adj* (*fml*) able to grasp or hold (*the prehensile tail of the monkey*).

prehistoric /pre-hi-**stor**-ic/ *adj* before the time of written records.

prejudge /pre-**judge**/ *vb* to decide or form an opinion before hearing all the facts (*prejudging the issue*).

prejudice /**pre**-ju-diss/ *n* 1 an unreasonable feeling for or against (*prejudice on the grounds of race*). 2 an opinion formed without full knowledge of the facts (*a prejudice against the accused*). 3 (*fml*) harm, injury (*to the prejudice of his health*). ● *vb* 1 to influence unreasonably for or against (*accused of prejudicing the jury*). 2 (*fml*) to harm, to spoil (*being late will prejudice her chances of getting the job*).

prejudicial /pre-ju-**di**-shal/ *adj* (*fml*) harmful (*actions prejudicial to her career*).

preliminary /pri-**li**-mi-na-ree/ *adj* coming before what is really important, introductory (*preliminary talks*). ● *also n.*

prelude /**prel**-yood/ *n* 1 a piece of music played before and introducing the main musical work. 2 something done or happening before an event, helping to prepare one for it (*a prelude to peace negotiations*).

premature /pree-ma-**choor**/ *adj* 1 happening or done too soon (*their rejoicing was premature*). 2 before the natural or proper time (*premature birth*).

premeditate /pree-**med**-i-tate/ *vb* (*fml*) to plan beforehand (*premeditated murder*).

premeditation /pree-med-i-**tay**-shun/ *n* (*fml*) thought about something before doing it.

premier /pri-**meer**/ *adj* first, chief. ● *n* the prime minister.

premiere /pri-**myur**/ *n* the first public performance of a play, film, etc. ● *also vb.*

premise /**pre**-miss/ *n* 1 (*fml*) a statement accepted as true for the purpose of an argument based on it (*take it as a premise that the world is round*). 2 *pl* a building, its outhouses and grounds (*the builder's premises went on fire*).

premium /**pree**-mee-um/ *n* 1 the amount paid for an insurance policy (*the premium for his house insurance*). 2 a reward, especially an inducement to buy. 3 something given free or at a reduced price with a purchase. ● **at a premium** of greater value than usual, difficult to obtain (*tickets for the concert are at a premium*).

premonition /pre-mu-**ni**-shun/ *n* a feeling that something particular is about to happen (*have a premonition that her son would die in battle*).

prenatal /pree-**nay**-tal/ *adj* before birth.

preoccupation /pree-oc-yu-**pay**-shun/ *n* a concern that prevents one thinking of other things (*his preoccupation with money*).

preoccupied /pree-**oc**-yu-pide/ *adj* thinking of other things (*preoccupied with personal problems*).

prepaid /**pree**-paid/ *adj* paid in advance.

preparation /pre-pe-**ray**-shun/ *n* **1** the act of preparing (*the preparation of food*). **2** something done to make ready (*party preparations*). **3** that which is made ready (*a medicinal preparation*).

preparatory /pri-**pa**-ri-toe-ree/ *adj* helping to prepare, making ready for something that is to follow (*preparatory steps*).

prepare /pri-**pare**/ *vb* **1** to make ready (*preparing the meal*). **2** to get oneself ready (*prepare for war*).

preposition /pre-pu-**zi**-shun/ *n* a word showing the relation between a noun or pronoun and another word.

preposterous /pri-**pos**-truss/ *adj* completely absurd, foolish (*a preposterous suggestion*).

prerogative /pri-**rog**-a-tiv/ *n* a special power or right attached to a certain office (*the king's prerogative*).

prescribe /pri-**scribe**/ *vb* **1** (*fml*) to lay down what is to be done (*prescribing how others should behave*). **2** to order a certain medicine (*prescribe antibiotics for his sore throat*).

prescription /pri-**scrip**-shun/ *n* a written order by a doctor for a certain medicine (*get antibiotics on prescription*).

prescriptive /pri-**scrip**-tiv/ *adj* indicating how something must be done.

presence /**pre**-zinss/ *n* **1** the state of being in the place required. **2** someone's appearance and bearing. ● **presence of mind** ability to behave calmly in the face of difficulty or danger (*her presence of mind prevented an accident*).

present[1] /**pre**-zent/ *adj* **1** in the place required or mentioned (*they were present at the meeting*). **2** now existing or happening (*the present situation*). ● *n* the time in which we live (*think about the present—forget the past*).

present[2] /**pre**-zent/ *n* a gift. ● *vb* **present** /pre-**zent**/ **1** to give, to offer (*present the celebrity with flowers*). **2** to introduce (one person to another)

(*present his wife to his employer*). **3** to show (*present a frightening appearance*). **4** to put forward (*present the case for the defense*). **5** to point (a rifle).

presentable /pri-**zen**-ta-bul/ *adj* fit to be seen or shown (*made himself presentable for the interview*).

presentation /pre-zen-**tay**-shun/ *n* **1** the act of handing over a present, especially in public (*the presentation of a gold watch on his retirement*). **2** something given by a group of people to mark a special occasion (*a presentation by his colleagues on his retirement*). **3** the way in which things are shown or arguments put forward (*a presentation to advertise their new product*).

presently /**pre**-zent-lee/ *adv* soon (*he will be here presently*).

preservation /pre-zer-**vay**-shun/ *n* **1** the act of preserving. **2** safeguarding.

preservative /pre-**zer**-va-tiv/ *n* an ingredient or application that prevents something from going bad (*put a preservative on the wood*). ● *also adj*.

preserve /pri-**zerv**/ *vb* **1** (*fml*) to keep from harm (*preserving the children from danger*). **2** to keep from rotting or decaying (*try to preserve the wood/preserve soft fruit*). **3** to keep safe or in good condition (*preserve old customs*). ● *n* **1** fruit, etc., treated so as to prevent it from going bad, jam. **2** a place where animals, birds, etc., are protected.

preside /pri-**zide**/ *vb* to control a meeting, to act as chairman (*presiding at the board meeting*).

presidency /**pre**-zi-den-see/ *n* the job or office of president.

president /**pre**-zi-dent/ *n* **1** the elected head of state of a republic. **2** the head of a company, etc., a chairman.

presidential /pre-zi-**den**-shal/ *adj* having to do with a president (*the presidential elections*).

press[1] /press/ *vb* **1** to push on or against with force (*press the doorbell*). **2** to squeeze (*press grapes*). **3** to smooth and flatten (*press trousers*). **4** to try to persuade (*press her into joining them*). ● *n* **1** a crowd. **2** a printing machine. **3** a machine for crushing or squeezing. **4** the newspapers. **5** a cupboard. ● *adj*.

press[2] /press/ *vb* (*old*) to force to serve in the armed forces.

press gang /**press**-gang/ *n* (*old*) a body of seamen sent out to seize men and force them to serve in the navy. ● *vb* **press-gang** /**press**-gang/ **1** (*old*) to seize someone and force him or her to serve in the navy. **2** to make someone do something by forceful persuasion (*she was press-ganged into organizing the event*).

pressing /**press**-ing/ *adj* requiring immediate action, urgent (*pressing matters*).

pressure /**pre**-shur/ *n* **1** the act of pressing force. **2** forceful influence (*agree to go under pressure from his parents*). **3** stress (*workers under pressure*).

prestige /pre-**steezh**/ *n* good name, high reputation (*his writing brought him prestige*).

presumably /pri-**zoo**-ma-blee/ *adv* apparently.

presume /pri-**zoom**/ *vb* **1** to take for granted, to accept as true without proof (*we presumed that they would be present/he is missing, presumed dead*). **2** (*fml*) to act in a bold or forward way (*he presumed to borrow her car without permission*).

presumption /pri-**zum**-shun/ *n* **1** something supposed to be true. **2** (*fml*) forwardness, boldness of manner.

presumptive /pri-**zum**-tiv/ *adj* (*fml*) probable.

presumptuous /pri-**zum**-chu-wus/ *adj* (*fml*) over-confident, bold in manner (*it was presumptuous of him to attend without an invitation*).

presuppose /pree-su-**poaz**/ *vb* to take for granted.

pretense /pri-**tense**/ *n* **1** the act of pretending. **2** a deception. **3** a false claim.

pretend /pri-**tend**/ *vb* **1** to make believe by words or actions that one is other than one really is (*he pretended to be a doctor*). **2** to behave as if one were in other circumstances (*she pretends absent-mindedness*). **3** to claim (*he does not pretend to understand*).

pretender /pri-**ten**-der/ *n* (*fml*) someone making a certain claim (*a pretender to the throne*).

pretension /pri-**ten**-shun/ *n* **1** a claim, true or false (*he has no pretensions to musical skill*). **2** pretentiousness.

pretentious /pri-**ten**-shus/ *adj* claiming much for oneself, too proud (*he is just an ordinary person, but he is so pretentious*).

preterit /**pre**-tu-rit/ *n* the past tense of a verb.

pretext /**pree**-tekst/ *n* a pretended reason, an excuse (*he left under the pretext of feeling ill*).

pretty /**pri**-tee/ *adj* pleasing to the eye, attractive (*a pretty girl/a pretty dress*). ● *adv* quite (*pretty good*). ● *n* prettiness /**pri**-tee-ness/.

prevail /pri-**vail**/ *vb* **1** to overcome, to prove better or stronger than (*common sense prevailed*). **2** to be in general use (*customs still prevailing*). **3** to persuade (*prevail on him to stay*).

prevailing /pri-**vay**-ling/ *adj* **1** common, most widely accepted, etc. (*the prevailing fashion*). **2**

that usually blows over an area (*the prevailing wind*).

prevalent /**pre**-va-lent/ *adj* common, widespread (*tuberculosis was prevalent then/prevalent rumors*). ● *n* prevalence /**pre**-va-lense/.

prevent /pri-**vent**/ *vb* to stop from happening (*prevent an accident/prevent progress*). ● *n* prevention /pri-**ven**-shun/.

preventive /pri-**ven**-ta-tiv/ *adj* helping to prevent (*preventive medical care*). ● *also n*.

preview, prevue /**pree**-vyoo/ *n* an advance showing of a film, performance, etc. before its official opening

previous /**pree**-vee-us/ *adj* earlier, happening before (*his previous crimes*).

prey /**pray**/ *n* **1** an animal or bird hunted and killed by another animal or bird (*the lion's prey*). **2** someone who suffers (from) (*a prey to headaches*). ● *vb* **1** to hunt and kill for food (*foxes preying on chicken*). **2** to keep on attacking and robbing (*frauds preying on old ladies*). **3** to trouble greatly (*worries preying on his mind*).

price /**price**/ *n* **1** the money asked or paid for something on sale (*the price of a loaf of bread*). **2** what is required to obtain something (*the price of freedom*).

priceless /**price**-less/ *adj* of great value (*priceless jewels*).

prick /**prick**/ *vb* **1** to stab lightly with the point of a needle, dagger, etc. **2** to make a tiny hole in. **3** to make to stand up straight. ● *n* **1** a sharp point. **2** a tiny hole. **3** a sting. **4** a thorn.

prickle /**pri**-cul/ *n* a small sharp point growing out from a plant or an animal (*the prickles on a rose bush*).

prickly /**pri**-clee/ *adj* covered with small sharp points.

prickly heat /**pri**-clee-heet/ *n* a skin disease causing severe itching.

pride /**pride**/ *n* **1** a feeling of pleasure at one's own abilities, deeds, etc. (*take a pride in her work*). **2** too great an opinion of oneself, one's deeds, etc. (*people disliked her because of her pride*). **3** the most valuable person or thing (*the pride of the town*). ● pride oneself on to take pleasure in.

priest /**preest**/ *n* a clergyman, a minister of religion. ● *f* priestess /**pree**-stess/.

priesthood /**preest**-hood/ *n* **1** the office of priest. **2** priests in general.

prim /**prim**/ *adj* **1** stiff in manner, formal and correct (*prim old ladies*). **2** neat, restrained (*prim clothes*).

primacy /**prie**-ma-see/ *n* **1** the office of archbishop.

2 the state of being first in time, order, rank, etc.

prima donna /pri-ma-**don**-a/ *n* **1** the chief female singer in an opera. **2** someone who is prone to tantrums if his or her wishes are not met.

primal /**prie**-mal/ *adj* (*fml*) original, having to do with early times (*mankind's primal innocence*).

primary /**prie**-mer-ee/ *adj* **1** first (*the primary stages of the disease*). **2** chief (*the primary reason for his absence*). ● *n* a preliminary election in which the candidates are chosen. ● *adv* **primarily** /prie-**mer**-il-ee/.

primary colors /prie-mer-ee-**cu**-lurz/ *npl* the colors red, yellow and blue, from which other colors may be made.

primary school /prie-mer-ee-**skool**/ *n* a school for children that includes the grades one to four, and kindergarten.

primate /**prie**-mate/ *n* **1** an archbishop. **2** one of the highest kinds of animals, including men and monkeys.

prime /**prime**/ *adj* **1** most important (*her prime reason*). **2** excellent in quality (*prime steak*). **3** that cannot be divided by any smaller number (*prime numbers*). ● *n* the best time (*people in their prime*). ● *vb* **1** to provide with information (*priming the witness about the kind of questions that she would be asked*). **2** to prepare (a gun) for firing. **3** to prepare for painting (*prime the wood*).

prime minister /prime-**mi**-ni-ster/ *n* the chief minister in a parliamentary government (*the Prime Minister of Canada*).

prime number /prime-**num**-ber/ *n* a number that can be divided only by itself and the number 1.

primer /**prie**-mer/ *n* **1** the mechanism that sets off the explosive in a shell, etc. **2** (*old*) a child's first reading book. **3** (*old*) a simple book on any subject. **4** an undercoat of paint (*put a primer on the new wood*).

primeval /prie-**mee**-val/ *adj* having to do with the first ages of the world (*primeval swamps*).

priming /**prie**-ming/ *n* the powder in a gun.

primitive /**pri**-mi-tiv/ *adj* **1** of the earliest times (*primitive tribes*). **2** simple or rough (*a primitive boat/camp in primitive conditions*).

primordial /prie-**mawr**-dee-al/ *adj* (*fml*) existing from the beginning (*primordial forests*).

primrose /**prim**-roze/ *n* **1** a pale yellow early spring flower. **2** a pale yellow color. ● *adj* pale yellow (*primose walls*).

primula /**prim**-yu-la/ *n* a flowering plant of the primrose family.

prince /**prinss**/ *n* **1** a ruler. **2** the son of a king or emperor.

princely /**prinss**-lee/ *adj* **1** of or like a prince. **2** (*fml*) magnificent, splendid (*a princely gift/a princely salary*).

princess /**prin**-sess/ *n* **1** the wife of a prince. **2** the daughter of a king or emperor.

principal /**prin**-si-pal/ *adj* chief, most important (*the principal cause of the dispute*). ● *n* **1** the head of a school, college, etc. **2** a amount of money lent at interest.

principality /prin-si-**pa**-li-tee/ *n* a country ruled by a prince.

principally /**prin**-si-pa-lee/ *adv* chiefly (*he is principally engaged in research*).

principle /**prin**-si-pul/ *n* **1** a general truth from which other truths follow (*the principle of gravity*). **2** a rule by which one lives (*moral principles*).

print /**print**/ *vb* **1** to make a mark by pressure. **2** to reproduce letters, words, etc., on paper by use of type (*get invitations printed*). **3** to publish in printed form (*his new novel is being printed*). **4** to write without joining the letters (*print your name*). **5** to stamp. **6** to stamp a design on cloth. **7** to produce a picture from a photographic negative. **8** to write in large clear lettering. ● *n* **1** a mark made by pressure (*footprints*). **2** letters, words, etc., reproduced on paper by use of type (*italic print*). **3** a copy of a picture taken from a photographic negative or engraving. **4** cloth with a design stamped on it (*a flower print*).

printer /**prin**-ter/ *n* someone who prints books, newspapers, etc.

printing machine /prin-ting-ma-**sheen**/, **printing press** /prin-ting-**press**/ *ns* a machine for printing with type.

prior[1] /**prie**-ur/ *adj* earlier, previous (*a prior engagement*).

prior[2] /**prie**-ur/ *n* **1** the head of a house of monks. **2** a monk next in rank to an abbot.

prioress /**prie**-ur-ess/ *n* the head of a house of nuns

priority /prie-**aw**-ri-tee/ *n* **1** the state or right of coming before others in position or time (*homeless people will get priority for aid*). **2** something or someone that must be considered or dealt with first (*our first priority is to save the children*).

priory /**prie**-ur-ee/ *n* a house of monks or nuns ruled by a prior(ess).

prise /**prize**/ *vb* (*Br*) see **prize**[2]

prism /**pri**-zum/ *n* **1** a solid body with ends the same in shape and size and parallel to one another, and sides that are parallelograms. **2** a triangular glass solid used for breaking up light into colors.

prismatic /priz-**ma**-tic/ *adj* **1** of or like a prism. **2** (*of colors*) very bright.

prison /**pri**-zun/ *n* a building in which criminals convicted of serious crimes are held.

prisoner /**priz**-ner/ *n* **1** someone kept in prison. **2** a person captured by the enemy in war (*prisoner of war*).

pristine /**pri**-steen/ *adj* **1** former, of earlier times (*restore the old palace to its pristine splendor*). **2** pure, undamaged clean (*a book in pristine condition*).

privacy /**pri**-va-see/ *n* **1** undisturbed quiet (*little privacy at a table in a small noisy restaurant*). **2** secrecy (*the privacy of the government documents*).

private /**prie**-vit/ *adj* **1** belonging to oneself only, not open to other people (*private possessions*). **2** not public (*private houses*). **3** secret (*private government documents*). ● *n* a common soldier who has not been promoted.

privateer /prie-vi-**teer**/ *n* a privately owned ship licensed to carry arms and attack enemy vessels.

privation /prie-**vay**-shun/ *n* lack of food and comforts, hardships (*suffer privation in the war*).

privatize /**prie**-vu-tize/ *vb, also* **privatise** (*Br*) to transfer something from public to private ownership (*privatize the steel industry*). ● *n* **privatization** /prie-vi-tie-**zay**-shun/, *also* **privatisation** (*Br*).

privilege /**priv**-lidge/ *n* **1** a right or advantage allowed to a certain person or group only (*old people are given certain privileges*). **2** advantage possessed because of social position, wealth, etc. (*people of privilege*). ● *vb* to allow a privilege to.

prize¹ /**prize**/ *n* **1** something given as a reward for merit or good work (*awarded a prize for French at school*). **2** that which is won by competition (*win a prize in a travel competition*). **3** anything seized from an enemy. ● *vb* to value highly (*prizing the vase/prize their freedom*).

prize² /**prize**/ *vb* to force open (*prizing open the lid of the paint tin*).

prizefight /**prize**-fite/ *n* a boxing match for a prize.

pro- /**pro**/ *prefix* **1** before. **2** in favor of. ● **pros and cons** reasons for and against.

probability /prob-a-**bi**-li-tee/ *n* likelihood.

probable /**prob**-a-bul/ *adj* **1** likely to happen, likely to be true (*the probable result/it is probable that he is guilty*). **2** easy to believe (*a probable story*).

probably /**prob**-u-blee/ *adv* very likely.

probate /**pro**-bate/ *n* proving before a court that a will has been properly and lawfully made. ● *also vb*.

probation /pro-**bay**-shun/ *n* **1** the testing of a person's conduct, work or character. **2** a time of trial or testing, especially for a young person found guilty of a crime, but not sentenced on condition that his or her conduct improves (*the young car thieves are on probation*).

probation officer /pro-bay-shun-**aw**-fi-ser/ *n* someone whose duty it is to watch over young persons on probation.

probationary /pro-**bay**-shu-ne-ree/ *adj* being tested, on approval (*have the job for a probationary period*).

probationer /pro-**bay**-shu-ner/ *n* **1** someone whose fitness for certain work is being tested. **2** someone who is on trial for a certain time.

probe /**probe**/ *n* a blunt metal instrument used by doctors when examining a wound closely. ● *vb* **1** to examine with a probe. **2** to examine carefully, to inquire into thoroughly (*police probing the homicide case*).

probity /**pro**-bi-tee/ *n* (*fml*) honesty, uprightness.

problem /**prob**-lem/ *n* a question or difficulty to which the answer is hard to find (*their problem is lack of staff/financial problems*).

problematic(al) /prob-lem-a-**ti**-cal/ *adj* doubtful.

proboscis /pru-**boss**-iss/ *n* (*fml*) **1** the trunk of an elephant. **2** the tube through which certain animals or insects suck food to their mouths.

procedure /pro-**see**-jur/ *n* way of conducting business (*usual legal procedure*).

proceed /pru-**seed**/ *vb* **1** to move forward (*passengers should proceed to gate 5/work is proceeding*). **2** to go on doing, to continue (*give permission to proceed with the scheme*). **4** (*fml*) to go to law (against). ● *npl* **proceeds** money made on a particular occasion (*the proceeds from the show are going to charity*).

proceeding /pru-**see**-ding/ *n* **1** something happening. **2** a course of action.

process /**pro**-sess/ *n* **1** the way in which a thing is done or made (*use a new process to waterproof cloth*). **2** a number of actions, each of which brings one nearer to the desired end (*the production process/the process of growing up*). **3** (*fml*) a legal case.

procession /pro-**se**-shun/ *n* a body of people moving forward in an orderly column (*the carnival procession*).

processional /pro-**se**-shnal/ *adj* having to do with a procession. ● *n* a hymn sung during a religious procession.

proclaim /pro-**claim**/ *vb* to announce publicly, to tell openly (*proclaim the birth of a prince*).

proclamation /pro-cla-**may**-shun/ *n* a public announcement.

procrastinate /pro-**cra**-sti-nate/ *vb* to put off until later (*procrastinating when there is work to be done*).

procrastination /pro-cra-sti-**nay**-shun/ *n* delay, a habit of putting things off until later.

prod /**prod**/ *vb* (**prodded** /**prod**-id/, **prodding** /**prod**-ing/) **1** to push with something pointed (*prod the cows with a stick to get them to move*). **2** to nudge (*he prodded her to wake her*). **3** to urge into action (*you will have to prod him to get him to work*). ● *also n.*

prodigal /**prod**-i-gal/ *adj* (*fml*) wasteful, spending too freely (*a prodigal young woman*). ● *n* a waster, a spendthrift.

prodigious /pru-**di**-jus/ *adj* (*fml*) **1** wonderful, extraordinary (*a prodigious sight*). **2** huge (*a prodigious sum of money*).

prodigy /**prod**-i-jee/ *n* **1** (*fml*) a wonder (*one of nature's prodigies*). **2** a person of extraordinary abilities (*a child prodigy won the music prize*).

produce /pro-**doos**/ *vb* **1** to bring forward, to bring into view (*produce a handkerchief from his pocket*). **2** to bear, to yield (*trees producing rubber*). **3** to cause or bring about (*a remark that produced laughter*). **4** to make or manufacture (*a factory producing furniture*). **5** to give birth to (*the cow produced twin calves*). **6** (*in geometry*) to cause, to make (a line) longer. ● *n* **produce** /**pro**-doos/ things grown, crops.

producer /pru-**doo**-ser/ *n* **1** a person or country that grows or makes certain things. **2** someone who gets a play or program ready for performance (*a television producer*).

product /**prod**-uct/ *n* **1** that which grows or is made (*a factory producing wooden products*). **2** result (*the product of much research*). **3** the number given by multiplying other numbers together.

production /pru-**duc**-shun/ *n* **1** the act of making or growing (*the production of furniture*). **2** the amount produced (*increase production*). **3** a performance or series of performances of a program, play, opera, etc.

productive /pru-**duc**-tiv/ *adj* **1** fertile (*productive soil*). **2** having results (*a productive meeting*).

productivity /pru-duc-**ti**-vi-tee/ *n* the rate of producing something (*increase productivity in the factory*).

profane /pro-**fane**/ *adj* not showing respect for what is holy. **2** coarse or vulgar (*profane language*). ● *vb* to treat irreverently.

profanity /pru-**fa**-ni-tee/ *n* **1** bad language. **2** lack of respect for what is holy.

profess /pru-**fess**/ *vb* **1** to say openly (*profess his love for her*). **2** to claim skill or ability (*he professed to be an expert*). **3** to declare one's beliefs (*profess his religious faith*). **4** to pretend (*he professed that he had been absent because of illness*).

professed /pru-**fest**/ *adj* openly admitted or declared.

profession /pru-**fe**-shun/ *n* **1** an employment requiring special learning (*professions such as teaching*). **2** the people involved in such employment (*the teaching profession*). **3** a public declaration (*a profession of faith*).

professional /pru-**fesh**-nal/ *adj* **1** having to do with a profession (*professional skills*). **2** paid for one's skill (*a professional pianist*). **3** done for a living (*professional singing*). **4** of a very high standard (*a professional performance*). ● *n* someone who makes his or her living by arts, sports, etc. (*opposite of* **amateur**).

professor /pru-**fe**-sur/ *n* a teacher in a university or college (*the professor of French*).

professorial /pro-fi-**soe**-ree-al/ *adj* having to do with a professor (*a professorial post*).

proficient /pru-**fi**-shent/ *adj* highly skilled, expert (*a proficient pianist*). ● *n* **proficiency** /pru-**fi**-shun-see/.

profile /**pro**-file/ *n* **1** an outline, a short description (*a profile of the winner of the literary prize*). **2** a head or an outline of it in side view (*a photograph of her profile*).

profit /**prof**-it/ *n* **1** an advantage (*little profit to be had from delaying*). **2** a gain, especially of money (*the profit from the sale*). ● *vb* **1** to gain an advantage (*profit from the deal*). **2** to be of use to (*the experience profited her*).

profitable /**prof**-i-ta-bul/ *adj* **1** bringing profit or gain (*a profitable deal*). **2** useful (*a profitable experience*).

profiteer /prof-i-**teer**/ *n* someone who makes money by selling scarce goods at very high prices. ● *vb* to make money thus.

profound /pru-**found**/ *adj* **1** deep (*a profound sleep*). **2** showing much knowledge or intelligence (*a profound thinker*). **3** intense (*a profound love*).

profundity /pro-**fun**-di-tee/ *n* **1** depth. **2** the state of being profound.

profuse /pro-**fyoos**/ *adj* very plentiful (*profuse thanks*).

profusion /pro-**fyoo**-zhun/ *n* great plenty (*a profusion of flowers*).

prognosis /prog-**no**-sis/ *n* a forecast, especially of the progress of a disease (*the prognosis is not good*).

program[1] /**pro**-gram/ *n* a sequence of instructions fed into a computer. ● *vb* (**programmed** /**pro**-gramd/, **programming** /**pro**-gra-ming/) **1** to feed a program into a computer. **2** to write a computer program.

program[2] /**pro**-gram/ *n* **1** a plan or scheme (*a program of social reforms*). **2** a list of the items in a concert, etc. (*the conference program*). **3** a scheduled radio or television broadcast. ● *also vb* (**programed** /**pro**-gramd/, **programing** /**pro**-gra-ming/).

progress /**pro**-gress/ *n* **1** movement forward, advance (*the progress of civilization*). **2** improvement (*technological progress*). ● *vb* **progress** /pro-**gress**/ **1** to advance (*the line of cars progressed slowly*). **2** to improve (*her condition is progressing*).

progression /pru-**gre**-shun/ *n* **1** onward movement. **2** a steady and regular advance.

progressive /pru-**gre**-siv/ *adj* **1** moving forward, advancing (*the progressive decline in trade*). **2** believing in trying new ideas and methods (*progressive educational methods*).

prohibit /pro-**hi**-bit/ *vb* **1** to forbid (*prohibit smoking in restaurants*). **2** to prevent (*the high cost of organic food prohibits wide sale*).

prohibition /pro-hi-**bi**-shun/ *n* **1** an order not to do something. **2** the forbidding by law of the making or selling of all strong drink in a country.

prohibitive /pro-**hi**-bi-tiv/ *adj* so high (in price) that people are unable to buy (*prohibitive house prices*).

project /pro-**ject**/ *vb* **1** to throw (*project a missile into space*). **2** to plan (*project a visit to France*). **3** to stick out (*a sign projecting from the wall*). **4** to make pictures appear on screen by using a projector. ● *n* **project** /**prodge**-ect/ a plan.

projectile /pro-**jec**-tile/ *n* **1** something thrown. **2** something fired from a gun, a shell.

projection /pro-**jec**-shun/ *n* a part that sticks out.

projector /pro-**jec**-tur/ *n* **1** someone who forms plans. **2** an apparatus for showing pictures on a screen.

proletariat /pro-li-**tay**-ree-at/ *n* the lowest class in society, the working people (*the proletariat threatening to rebel against the aristocracy*). ● *adj* **proletarian** /pro-li-**tay**-ree-an/.

prolific /pru-**li**-fic/ *adj* producing much (*a prolific writer*).

prolog /**pro**-log/ *n* , *also* **prologue** (*fml*) **1** (*fml*) an introduction (*the prologue to the poem*). **2** some lines spoken to the audience before a play begins. **3** an event that leads to another (*serve as a prologue to the signing of the treaty*).

prolong /pro-**long**/ *vb* to make longer (*no point in prolonging the discussion*). ● *n* **prolongation** /pro-long-**gay**-shun/.

prolonged /pro-**longd**/ *adj* very long (*a prolonged stay*).

promenade /prom-i-**nad**/ *n* **1** (*fml*) a short walk for pleasure (*take a promenade in the evening sunshine*). **2** (*abbr* = **prom** /prom/) a formal dance in a high school or college. **3** (*Br*) (*abbr* = **prom**) a wide road or sidewalk, especially along a seafront. ● *vb* (*fml*) **1** to take a short walk. **2** to walk up and down.

prominence /**prom**-i-nense/ *n* **1** the state or act of being prominent (*the prominence of his chin/the prominence of the news item*). **2** something that sticks out or is prominent (*prominences on the landscape*).

prominent /**prom**-i-nent/ *adj* **1** easily seen. **2** well-known (*prominent local people*). **3** sticking out (*a prominent nose*).

promiscuous /pru-**mi**-skyu-wus/ *adj* **1** (*fml*) mixed. **2** having many sexual relationships. ● *n* **promiscuity** /prom-i-**skyoo**-i-tee/.

promise /**prom**-iss/ *vb* **1** to say that one will do or not do something, to give one's word (*she promised that she would be there/promising to go*). **2** to give hope of a good result (*his work promises well*). ● *n* **1** act of giving one's word. **2** a sign of future success (*a promise of victory*).

promising /**prom**-iss-ing/ *adj* likely to do well in the future (*a promising young actor*).

promontory /**prom**-un-toe-ree/ *n* a headland.

promote /pru-**mote**/ *vb* **1** to raise to a higher position or rank. **2** to help on (*promoting the cause of freedom*). **3** to help to start (*promote a business*). ● *n* **promoter** /pru-**mo**-ter/. ● *n* **promotion** /pru-**mo**-shun/.

prompt /prompt/ *adj* **1** ready, quick to take action (*prompt to criticize other people*). **2** done without delay, quick (*a prompt reply*). ● *vb* **1** to cause another to take action (*his behavior prompted us to call the police*). **2** to help someone (especially an actor) who cannot remember what he or she ought to say.

prompter /**prom**(p)-ter/ *n* someone whose job it is to whisper words to an actor who cannot remember them.

prone /prone/ *adj* **1** lying face downward (*his prone* *body/lying prone*). **2** inclined (to) (*people who are prone to lose their temper*).

prong /**prong**/ *n* the spike of a fork, etc. ● *adj* **pronged** /**prongd**/.

pronoun /**pro**-noun/ *n* a word used instead of a noun ("*he*" *is a pronoun*).

pronounce /pru-**nounse**/ *vb* **1** to make the sound of (*pronounce the h*). **2** to declare publicly (*pronouncing him dead*). **3** to speak.

pronounced /pru-**nounst**/ *adj* very noticeable (*a pronounced foreign accent*).

pronouncement /pru-**nounse**-ment/ *n* **1** a statement to an assembly. **2** a firm statement.

pronunciation /pru-nun-see-**ay**-shun/ *n* the way of making the sounds of a language.

proof /**proof**/ *n* **1** an argument, fact, etc., that shows clearly that something is true or untrue (*police seeking proof that he was the murderer*). **2** (*fml*) a test or trial (*courage put to the proof*). **3** (*in printing*) a first printing made solely for correction. **4** the statement of strength of some spirits, e.g., whiskey. ● *adj* not affected by, able to resist.

proofreader /**proof**-ree-der/ *n* someone whose job it is to read first printings and mark errors.

prop /**prop**/ *n* **1** a support (*a roof supported by wooden props/she acted as a prop to the whole family*). **2** a piece of stage equipment. ● *vb* (**propped** /**propt**/, **propping** /**prop**-ing/) to support, to hold up.

propaganda /prop-a-**gan**-da/ *n* the organized spreading of certain ideas, beliefs etc., to large numbers of people (*political propaganda*).

propagandist /prop-a-**gan**-dist/ *n* someone who spreads ideas, etc., by propaganda.

propagate /**prop**-u-gate/ *vb* (*fml*) **1** to spread widely (*propagating their political ideas*). **2** to increase in numbers by sowing seeds or producing young (*propagate plants/propagate their species*). ● *n* **propagation** /prop-u-**gay**-shun/.

propel /pru-**pel**/ *vb* (**propelled** /pru-**peld**/, **propelling** /pru-**pe**-ling/) to drive or push forward (*a boat propelled by a diesel engine*).

propeller /pru-**pe**-lur/ *n* a revolving screw with sloping blades attached for moving forward ships, airplanes, etc.

propensity /pru-**pen**-si-tee/ *n* a natural leaning or tendency to behave in a certain way (*a propensity to drop things*).

proper /**prop**-er/ *adj* **1** correct, suitable, decent, polite (*proper behavior/the proper method*). **2** (*inf*) thorough, complete (*a proper mess*).

properly /**prop**-er-lee/ *adv* **1** correctly, suitably (*prop-*

erly dressed). **2** strictly (speaking) (*properly speaking, she's not qualified*).

property /**prop**-er-tee/ *n* **1** anything owned, that which belongs to one (*the car is his property*). **2** someone's land (*trespassing on her property*). **3** a quality or characteristic (*properties of the chemical substance*). **4** (*abbr* = **prop**) an object needed on the stage during a play.

prophecy /**prof**-i-see/ *n* **1** the foretelling of future events. **2** something foretold.

prophesy /**prof**-i-sye/ *vb* to tell what will happen in the future, to foretell (*the old man prophesied that there would be a cold winter*).

prophet /**prof**-it/ *n* **1** someone who foretells the future. **2** someone who tells men a message or command from God (*Old Testament prophets*). ● *f* **prophetess** /prof-i-**tess**/. ● *adj* **prophetic**(**al**) /pru-**fe**-ti-cal/.

proponent /pru-**po**-nent/ *n* someone who argues in favor of something (*a great proponent of organic foods*).

proportion /pru-**pore**-shun/ *n* **1** the size of a part when compared with the whole (*the proportion of his salary that goes in tax*). **2** the size of one object, number, etc., when compared with that of another (*the proportion of men to women in the firm*). **3** a share. **4** *pl* size (*a house of huge proportions*).

proportional /pru-**pore**-shnal/, **proportionate** /pru-**pore**-shu-nate/ *adjs* in correct or proper proportion.

proposal /pru-**poe**-zal/ *n* **1** a suggestion or plan put forward (*proposals for expansion*). **2** an offer to marry.

propose /pru-**poze**/ *vb* **1** to put forward for consideration. **2** to intend. **3** to offer to marry.

proposition /prop-u-**zi**-shun/ *n* **1** a plan or suggestion put forward. **2** an offer. **3** a statement, a statement that is to be proved true. **4** (*in geometry*) a problem to be solved.

proprietary /pru-**pri**-u-tree/ *adj* **1** owned by a person or group of persons (*proprietary brands of cookies*). **2** possessive (*a proprietary manner toward her boyfriend*).

proprietor /pru-**prie**-u-tur/ *n* an owner. ● *f* **proprietress** /pru-**prie**-u-tress/, **proprietrix** /pru-**prie**-u-triks/.

propriety /pru-**prie**-u-tee/ *n* (*fml*) correctness of behavior, fitness (*behave with propriety*).

propulsion /pru-**pul**-shun/ *n* a driving or pushing forward (*jet propulsion*).

prosaic /pro-**zay**-ic/ *adj* dull, commonplace, unpoetic (*a prosaic piece of writing*).

proscribe /pro-**scribe**/ *vb* (*fml*) **1** to declare an outlaw. **2** to forbid the use of (*proscribing the sale of alcohol*). ● *n* **proscription** /pru-**scrip**-shun/.

prose /proze/ *n* **1** the language of ordinary speech and writing. **2** all writing not in verse.

prosecute /**pros**-i-cyoot/ *vb* **1** to accuse in a court of law (*prosecute him for trespassing*). **2** (*fml*) to carry on (*police prosecuting a line of inquiry*). ● *n* **prosecution** /pros-i-**cyoo**-shun/.

prosecuting attorney, prosecutor /**pros**-i-cyoo-ting-a-**tur**-nee/ *n* a lawyer who acts on behalf of the government in court.

prosecutor /**pros**-si-cyoo-tur/ *n* **1** the person who makes the accusation in a court of law. **2** *see* **prosecuting attorney** /**pros**-i-cyoo-ting-a-**tur**-nee/.

prosody /**proz**-u-dee/ *n* (*fml*) rules for the writing of poetry.

prospect /**pros**-pect/ *n* **1** (*fml*) a view (*the prospect from the mountain top*). **2** an idea of what the future may hold (*not much prospect of arriving on time/the prospect of being homeless*). **3** chance of future success (*a young man with prospects*). ● *vb* **prospect** to explore, to search for places where mines may be sunk for oil, metals, etc.

prospective /pru-**spec**-tive/ *adj* expected, probable (*their prospective son-in-law*).

prospector /pru-**spec**-tor/ *n* someone who searches for gold or other minerals.

prospectus /pru-**spec**-tus/ *n* a written description of some undertaking or of the training offered by a school (*a college prospectus*).

prosper /**pros**-per/ *vb* to do well, to succeed (*the business is prospering*).

prosperity /pru-**spe**-ri-tee/ *n* success, good fortune.

prosperous /**pros**-prus/ *adj* successful, well-off (*a prosperous businesswoman*).

prostate /**pros**-tate/ *n* (*also* **prostate gland** /**pros**-tate-gland/) a gland in males in front of the bladder.

prostrate /**pros**-trate/ *adj* **1** lying flat with the face to the ground (*the prostrate body of the injured man*). **2** exhausted (*prostrate after climbing the mountain*). ● *vb* **1** to throw flat on the ground. **2** to bow in reverence (*prostrating themselves before the emperor*). **3** to tire out. ● *n* **prostration** /pros-**tray**-shun/.

protagonist /pru-**ta**-gu-nist/ *n* **1** someone playing a leading part in a drama or in an exciting situation in real life. **2** a leader (*one of the protagonists of socialism*). **3** someone taking part in a contest.

protect /pru-**tect**/ *vb* to keep safe from danger, loss, etc., to defend (*protect their property/protect rare birds*).

protection /pru-**tec**-shun/ *n* **1** defense, watchful care. **2** the taxing of goods brought in from other countries so that goods made at home will be cheaper than them.

protectionist /pru-**tec**-shu-nist/ *n* someone who believes in taxing goods from abroad to protect home goods.

protective /pru-**tec**-tiv/ *adj* giving defense, care or safety (*a mother protective of her children*).

protector /pru-**tec**-tur/ *n* a person or thing that protects.

protectorate /pru-**tec**-trit/ *n* a country that is defended and governed by another until it can look after itself.

protégé /pro-ti-zhay/ *n* (*fml*) someone under the care of another (*a protégé of the famous ballerina*).

protein /**proe**-teen/ *n* a substance contained in certain foods (e.g., meat, eggs) that helps the body to grow and become stronger.

protest /pro-**test**/ *vb* **1** to object (*protest about the building of the new road/protest against the umpire's decision*). **2** to strongly disapprove. **3** to declare (*protest their innocence*). ● *n* **protest** /**pro**-test/ a statement of disagreement or disapproval (*listen to their protests against his decision*).

Protestant /**prot**-i-stant/ *n* a member of one of the Christian groups separated from the Roman Catholic Church at the Reformation. ● *also adj*.

Protestantism /**prot**-i-stan-ti-zum/ *n* the Protestant religion.

protestation /prot-u-**stay**-shun/ *n* **1** an objection (*their protestation against the injustice of the decision*). **2** a declaration (*their protestations of innocence*).

proto- /**pro**-to/ *prefix* first.

protocol /**pro**-to-col/ *n* **1** correct procedure or behavior (*diplomatic protocol*). **2** a treaty.

proton /**pro**-ton/ *n* part of the nucleus of an atom that contains positive electricity.

protoplasm /**pro**-to-pla-zum/ *n* the living substance from which plants and animals grow.

prototype /**pro**-to-tipe/ *n* the first model from which others are copied, a pattern (*the prototype of the plan*).

protozoan /pro-to-**zo**-a/ *n* a tiny living creature, the lowest form of animal life. ● *npl* **protozoans, protozoa**.

protract /pru-**tract**/ *vb* to make long, to make last longer (*protract the talks unnecessarily*).

protractor /pru-**trac**-tur/ *n* an instrument for measuring angles.

protrude /pru-**trood**/ vb (fml) to stick out, to stand out from (his ears protrude too much/a gun protruding from his pocket). ● n **protrusion** /pru-**troo**-zhun/. ● adj **protrusive** /pru-**troo**-siv/.

protuberance /pru-**troo**-branse/ n (fml) a swelling, a part that bulges out (protruberances on tree trunks).

protuberant /pru-**troo**-brant/ adj (fml) bulging out (a protruberant stomach).

proud /**proud**/ adj 1 having too high an opinion of oneself, one's deeds or possessions. 2 rightly satisfied with oneself and what one has done.

prove /**proov**/ vb 1 to show the truth of (proving his guilt/they proved that he was guilty). 2 to turn out to be (she proved to be a natural teacher). 3 to test (require to prove oneself).

proverb /**prov**-erb/ n a popular truth or belief expressed in a short memorable sentence.

proverbial /pru-**ver**-bee-al/ adj 1 well-known to all (his proverbial bad temper). 2 expressed in a proverb.

provide /pru-**vide**/ vb 1 to supply what is needed (providing food for all). 2 to make ready beforehand, to prepare for (provide for their future).

provided (**that**) /pru-**vie**-did-that/ conj on condition (that) (he can stay provided that he keeps quiet).

providence /**prov**-i-dense/ n 1 care for the future, foresight. 2 Christians' belief in God's care of His creatures.

provident /**prov**-i-dent/ adj (fml) 1 taking care of the future. 2 not spending too much (provident housekeepers).

province /**prov**-inss/ n 1 a division of a country (a province of Canada). 2 the limits of one's powers, knowledge, etc. (the administration lies within her province). 3 pl all the parts of a country outside the capital (live in the provinces).

provincial /pru-**vin**-shal/ adj 1 like or in a province (provincial government). 2 having limited or local interests, unsophisticated (city people regarding other people as provincial).

provision /pru-**vi**-zhun/ n 1 something provided for the future (the provision of education). 2 pl food (buy provisions for the weekend). ● vb to supply with stores of food.

provisional /pru-**vizh**-nal/ adj for a time only, that may be changed (a provisional arrangement/a provisional government).

provocation /prov-u-**cay**-shun/ n a cause of anger or annoyance.

provocative /pru-**voc**-a-tiv/ adj intended to anger or annoy, arousing the emotions or passions (provocative remarks).

provoke /pru-**voke**/ vb 1 to make angry (provoked by his insulting remark). 2 to give rise to (events that provoked a war).

prow /**prow**/ n the front part of a ship or boat.

prowess /**prow**-ess/ n skill or ability (admire his prowess as a pianist).

prowl /**prowl**/ vb to keep moving about as if searching for something, to move quietly about looking for the chance to do mischief (hear someone prowling in the garden).

prowler /**prow**-ler/ n someone who moves stealthily especially a thief (hear a prowler in the garden).

proximate /**prok**-si-mit/ adj (fml) nearest.

proximity /prok-**si**-mi-tee/ n nearness, neighborhood (the proximity of the house to the station).

proxy /**prok**-see/ n 1 the right to act or vote for another. 2 someone with the right to act or vote for another (act as a proxy for her mother at the shareholders' meeting).

prude /**prood**/ n a person who makes a show of being very modest and correct in behavior (too much of a prude to change in a communal changing room). ● n **prudery** /**prood**-ree/.

prudence /**proo**-dense/ n foresight, caution (have the prudence to save for their old age).

prudent /**proo**-dent/ adj thinking carefully before acting, wise, cautious (it would be prudent to check the times of the train).

prudential /proo-**den**-shal/ adj (fml) careful about the future, prudent.

prudery see **prude**.

prudish /**proo**-dish/ adj over correct in behavior.

prune[1] /**proon**/ n a dried plum (have prunes for breakfast).

prune[2] /**proon**/ vb 1 to cut off the dead or overgrown parts of a tree (pruning the rose bushes). 2 to shorten by cutting out what is unnecessary (prune the report).

pry[1] /**prie**/ vb to inquire closely, especially into the secrets of others, to examine closely (pried into her private affairs/neighbors prying into the details of their relationship).

pry[2] /**prie**/ vb to force open (prying open the lid of the paint tin).

psalm /**sam**/ n a sacred song or hymn.

psalmist /**sam**-ist/ n a writer of sacred songs.

pseudo /**soo**-doe/ adj false, not real (a pseudo interest in the subject).

pseudonym /**soo**-du-nim/ n a name used instead

of one's real name (e.g., a pen-name) (*write under a pseudonym*).

psychiatry /sie-**kie**-u-tree/ *n* the treatment of diseases of the mind. ● *n* **psychiatrist** /sie-**kie**-u-trist/.

psychic /**sie**-kik/, **psychical** /**sie**-ki-kal/ *adjs* **1** having to do with the mind (*psychic disorders*). **2** (*of influences and forces*) that act on the mind and senses but have no physical cause (*psychic research*). **3** (*of a person*) sensitive to these influences. **4** able to communicate with spirits.

psychoanalysis /sie-ko-a-**na**-li-sis/ *n* treatment of mental disease by trying to find out by questioning problems, fears, etc., that exist in the patient's mind without his or her being aware of them. ● *n* **psychoanalyst** /sie-ko-a-ni-list/. ● *vb* **psychoanalyze** /sie-ko-**a**-na-lize/.

psychology /sie-**kol**-u-jee/ *n* **1** the study of the human mind. **2** the mental process of a person (*fail to understand his psychology*). ● *adj* **psychological** / sie-ku-**lodge**-ic-al/. ● *n* **psychologist** /sie-**kol**-u-jist/.

psychopath /**sie**-ko-path/ *n* someone with a personality disorder which can lead him or her to commit often violent acts without guilt.

pterodactyl /ter-u-**dac**-tul/ *n* a prehistoric winged reptile known of from fossils.

pub /pub/ *n* (*Br*) a public house.

puberty /**pyoo**-bur-tee/ *n* the age by which a young person has fully developed all the characteristics of his or her sex (*reach puberty*).

public /**pu**-blic/ *adj* **1** open to all (*public gardens/the public library*). **2** having to do with people in general (*a public campaign*). **3** well-known (*a public figure*). ● *n* the people in general.

publication /pu-bli-**cay**-shun/ *n* **1** the act of publishing (*the publication of his novel*). **2** a published book, magazine or paper (*weekly publications*).

public school /pub-**lick**/ *n* a school that provides free education.

publicity /pu-**bli**-si-tee/ *n* **1** making something widely known, advertising (*the publicity for her new novel*). **2** the state of being well-known (*filmstars who like publicity*). ● *vb* **publicize** /**pu**-bli-size/, *also* **publicise** (*Br*).

publish /**pu**-blish/ *vb* **1** (*fml*) to make widely known (*publish the news of the president's death*). **2** to print for selling to the public (*publish novels*).

publisher /**pu**-bli-sher/ *n* someone who publishes books, etc.

puck /puck/ *n* a small hard rubber disk used instead of a ball in ice hockey.

pucker /**pu**-ker/ *vb* to gather into small folds or wrin-

kles (*a material that puckers easily/her face puckered and she began to cry*). ● *n* a fold or wrinkle.

pudding /**poo**-ding/ *n* a sweet soft dessert served at the end of a meal (*Christmas pudding/a fruit pudding*).

puddle /**pu**-dul/ *n* a small pool of dirty water. ● *vb* to make watertight with clay.

pudgy /**pu**-jee/ *adj* (*inf*) short and fat (*a pudgy child*).

puff /puff/ *n* **1** a short sharp breath or gust of wind (*a puff of wind blew the letter away*). **2** a small cloud of smoke, steam, etc., blown by a puff (*puffs of smoke from his pipe*). **3** a soft pad for powdering the skin. **4** a kind of light pastry (*puff paste*). ● *vb* **1** to breathe quickly or heavily, as when short of breath (*puffing after climbing the hill*). **2** to blow in small blasts (*puff cigarette smoke in their faces*). **3** to blow up, to swell (*her eyes were puffed up*). **4** to praise too highly (*puff up his role in the rescue*).

puffin /**pu**-fin/ *n* a diving bird with a brightly colored beak.

puffy /**pu**-fee/ *adj* blown out, swollen (*a puffy face*).

pug, pug dog /**pug**-dawg/ *ns* a type of small dog with an upturned nose.

pugnacious /pug-**nay**-shus/ *adj* (*fml*) quarrelsome, fond of fighting (*he becomes pugnacious when he has taken too much alcohol*). ● *n* **pugnacity** /pug-**na**-si-tee/.

pug nose /**pug**-noze/ *n* a short upturned nose. ● *adj* **pug-nosed** /**pug**-noazd/.

puke /pyook/ *vb* (*inf*) to bring up the contents of the stomach, to vomit.

pule /pyool/ *vb* (*fml*) to whine, to cry peevishly (*infants puling*).

pull /pool/ *vb* **1** to draw toward one, to draw in the same direction as oneself (*pull the door open*). **2** to bring along behind one while moving (*a horse pulling a cart*). **3** to remove (flowers etc.) from the ground (*pull roses*). **4** to gather (*pull raspberries*). **5** to row with oars (*pull toward the shore*). ● *n* **1** act of pulling (*give the door a pull/with a pull of the rope*). **2** (*inf*) advantage, special influence (*have some pull with the committee*).

pulley /**poo**-lee/ *n* a grooved wheel with a cord running over it used for raising weights.

pulmonary /**pul**-mu-ne-ree/ *adj* (*fml*) having to do with the lungs.

pulp /pulp/ *n* **1** the soft juicy part of a fruit (*peach pulp*). **2** soft substance obtained by crushing rags, wood, etc., and made into paper. ● *vb* to make into pulp, to become pulpy (*pulp the fruit/pulp the rags*).

pulpit /**pool**-pit/ *n* a raised platform enclosed by a half wall for preaching in a church.

pulsate /pul-**sate**/ *vb* to beat or throb (*the music pulsated through the building*). ● *n* **pulsation** /pul-**say**-shun/.

pulse[1] /**pulss**/ *n* 1 the throb of the heart or of the blood passing through the arteries (*his pulse is too fast*). 2 a place on the body where the throb of the blood can be felt (*find the patient's pulse*). ● *vb* to beat or throb (*blood pulsing through his veins*).

pulse[2] /**pulss**/ *n* any of the edible seeds of peas, beans, lentils, etc. (*make a dish with pulses instead of meat*).

pulverize /**pul**-vu-rize/ *vb*, *also* **pulverise** (*Br*) 1 to make into dust or powder (*pulverizing the rock*). 2 (*inf*) to defeat thoroughly (*pulverize his opponent*).

puma /**poo**-ma *or* **pyoo**-ma/ *n* a large wild cat, the cougar.

pumice /**puhm**-iss/ *n* a light stone with a rough surface, used for cleansing or polishing.

pummel /**pu**-mul/ *vb* [**pummeled** /**pu**-muld/ **pummeling** /**pu**-mu-ling/; *also* **pummelled, pummelling** (*Br, Cdn*)] to keep on striking with the fist(s) (*pummeling the pillow with his fists*).

pump[1] /**pump**/ *n* 1 a machine for raising water from a well. 2 a machine for raising any liquid to a higher level (*central-heating pump*). 3 a machine for taking air out of or putting air into things (*a bicycle pump*). ● *vb* 1 to work a pump. 2 to raise with a pump. 3 (*inf*) to get information from someone by asking them constant questions (*pump the children about the details of their parents' income*).

pump[2] /**pump**/ *n* a light shoe for dancing.

pumpkin /**pum**(p)-kin/ *n* a large fleshy fruit with a thick yellow skin (*make a pumpkin into a lantern at Halloween*).

pun /**pun**/ *n* the witty or amusing use of a word like another in sound but different in meaning. ● *vb* (**punned** /**pund**/, **punning** /**pu**-ning/) to make a pun.

punch /**punch**/ *vb* 1 to strike with the fist (*he punched the other boy on the nose*). 2 to herd or drive cattle. 3 to make a hole with a special tool or machine (*punch holes in the papers for filing*). ● *n* 1 a blow with the fist. 2 a tool or machine for making holes.

punch /**punch**/ *n* a drink made from wine or spirit mixed with sugar, hot water, fruit, etc. (*serve punch at their Christmas party*).

punctual /**pungk**-chu-wal/ *adj* 1 up to time, not late (*be sure to be punctual*). 2 good at arriving at the correct time (*she is always punctual/punctual*

workers). ● *n* **punctuality** /pungk-chu-**wa**-li-tee/.

punctuate /**pungk**-chu-wate/ *vb* 1 to divide up written work with full stops, commas, etc. 2 to interrupt repeatedly. ● *n* **punctuation** /pungk-chu-**way**-shun/.

puncture /**pungk**-chur/ *n* a hole made by a sharp point (*a puncture in her bicycle tire*). ● *vb* to make a hole in, to pierce.

pundit /**pun**-dit/ *n* (*fml*) an expert (*pundits discussing the political situation on television*).

pungent /**pun**-jent/ *adj* 1 sharp to taste or smell (*the pungent smell of frying onions*). 2 sharp (*pungent criticism*). ● *n* **pungency** /**pun**-jen-see/.

punish /**pu**-nish/ *vb* 1 to cause someone to suffer for doing wrong (*punish naughty children/punish criminals*). 2 to deal roughly with (*punish the engine by driving at that speed/a punishing exercise schedule*).

punishment /**pu**-nish-ment/ *n* pain, loss, etc., inflicted on a wrongdoer (*capital punishment*).

punitive /**pyoo**-ni-tiv/ *adj* (*fml*) done by way of punishment, inflicting punishment (*punitive measures such as imprisonment*).

punster /**pun**-ster/ *n* someone who makes puns.

punt[1] /**punt**/ *n* a flat-bottomed boat moved by means of a pole. ● *vb* to move a punt with a pole (*students punting up the river*).

punt[2] /**punt**/ *vb* to kick a ball dropped from the hands before it touches the ground. ● *also n.*

puny /**pyoo**-nee/ *adj* small and weak (*his puny arms*).

pup /**pup**/ *n* a puppy, a young dog.

pupa /**pyoo**-pa/ *n* (*pl* **pupae** /**pyoo**-paez/ *or* **pupas** /**pyoo**-paz/) 1 a stage in the growth of an insect just before it develops wings. 2 an insect in this stage.

pupil /**pyoo**-pil/ *n* 1 someone being taught, a learner (*pupils at the high school*). 2 the round opening in the center of the eye through which light passes.

puppet /**pu**-pit/ *n* 1 a doll whose movements are controlled by strings, etc. 2 someone who obeys without question all the orders given him or her by another (*the king was a mere puppet—the nobles ruled the country*).

puppet show /**pu**-pit-sho/ *n* a performance by puppets (dolls).

puppy /**pu**-pee/ *n* a young dog.

purchase /**pur**-chis/ *vb* to buy. ● *n* 1 the thing bought (*carry home his purchases*). 2 a position that allows one to apply all one's strength (*the purchase required to lift the iron chest*).

purchaser /**pur**-chi-ser/ *n* a buyer.

pure /**pyoor**/ adj **1** clear (*pure sounds*). **2** unmixed (*a sweater of pure wool*). **3** clean, free from dirt or harmful matter (*pure drinking water*). **4** free from guilt or evil (*pure young children/pure thoughts*). **5** complete, absolute (*a pure accident*).

purée /**pyoo-ray**/ n food crushed to pulp and passed through a sieve (*tomato purée/fruit purée*).

purely /**pyoor**-lee/ adv **1** wholly (*he passed the exam purely because of hard work*). **2** only, merely (*he did it purely for a joke*). **3** in a pure manner.

purge /**purge**/ vb **1** to make pure and clean (*purge your mind of wicked thoughts*). **2** to get rid of unwanted persons (*purging the party of troublemakers*). **3** to clear the body of waste matter, to empty the bowels.

purification /pyoo-ri-fi-**cay**-shun/ n **1** act of purifying. **2** a ceremonial cleansing.

purify /**pyoo**-ri-fie/ vb **1** to cleanse (*purified the air/purifying the water*). **2** to make pure.

puritan /**pyoo**-ri-tan/ n someone who is very strict in matters of morals or religion. ● adj **puritanic(al)** /pyoo-ri-**ta**-ni-cal/. ● n **puritanism** /**pyoo**-ri-ta-ni-zum/.

purity /**pyoo**-ri-tee/ n the state of being pure.

purl[1] /**purl**/ n the rippling sound made by a stream. ● vb to ripple.

purl[2] /**purl**/ n a type of knitting stitch. ● also vb.

purple /**pur**-pul/ n **1** a color of red and blue mixed (*dressed in purple*). **2** (*fml*) the purple robe of a king or cardinal. **3** (*fml*) the rank of king or cardinal. ● adj of purple color (*a purple dress*).

purpose /**pur**-puss/ n **1** the reason for an action, an intention or plan (*a journey for business purposes/his purpose in going*). **2** use or function (*the purpose of the tool*). **3** determination (*a man of purpose*). ● vb to intend.

purposeful /**pur**-pus-ful/ adj **1** having a clear intention in mind (*a purposeful young woman*). **2** determined (*with a purposeful air*).

purposely /**pur**-pus-lee/ adv intentionally, on purpose.

purr /**pur**/ n the low sound made by a cat when pleased. ● also vb.

purse /**purss**/ n **1** a woman's handbag. **2** a sum of money offered as a prize. **3** (*Br*) see **pocketbook**. ● vb to pull in (*pursing her lips in disapproval*).

pursue /pur-**soo**/ vb **1** to follow in order to catch (*police pursuing the escaped prisoner*). **2** to carry on (an activity) (*pursue studies in French*).

pursuer /pur-**soo**-er/ n someone who chases (*the pursuers of the escaped criminal*).

pursuit /pur-**soot**/ n the act of pursuing (*the police in pursuit of a criminal/her pursuit of an interesting career*).

pursy /**pur**-see/ adj (*fml*) fat and short-winded.

purvey /pur-**vay**/ vb (*fml*) to provide food or meals. ● n **purveyor** /pur-**vay**-or/.

pus /**puss**/ n yellow matter from an infected sore or wound (*pus exuding from the boil*).

push /**poosh**/ vb **1** to press against with force (*push the door shut*). **2** to move by force, to shove (*push the cart uphill*). **3** to try to make someone do something (*push him into applying*). **4** (*inf*) to promote, to advertise (*push his new product*). ● n **1** a shove. **2** strong effort. **3** (*inf*) energy (*people with some push*). **4** an attack by a large army.

pushing /**poo**-shing/ adj **1** energetic. **2** eager to get on.

pusillanimous /poo-si-**la**-ni-muss/ adj (*fml*) timid, cowardly. ● n **pusillanimity** /poo-si-la-mi-tee/.

puss /**pooss**/, **pussy** /**poo**-see/ ns (*inf*) a cat.

pustule /**pus**-tchul/ n (*fml*) a small pimple containing poisonous matter (*the pustules on his face caused by the disease*).

put /**poot**/ vb (**put, putting** /**poo**-ting/) **1** to set down in or move into a certain place (*put the cups on the table/put the car in the garage*). **2** to ask (*put a question*). **3** to express in words (*put his refusal politely*). **4** to throw from the shoulder with a bent arm (*put the shot*). ● n act of throwing a weight in sport (*the shot put*). ● **put by** to keep for future use. ● **put up** to give accommodation to (*put up his friend for the night*). ● **put up with** to bear without complaining (*put up with noisy neighbors*).

putative /**pyoo**-tay-tiv/ adj supposed, commonly believed to be (*the putative father of the child*).

putrefy /**pyoo**-tri-fie/ vb (*fml*) to become rotten, to decay (*meat putrefied by the heat*). ● n **putrefaction** /pyoo-tri-**fac**-shun/.

putrid /**pyoo**-trid/ adj (*fml*) rotten, decayed (*putrid meat*). **2** (*inf*) very bad, poor (*a putrid performance*).

putt /**putt**/ vb (**putted** /**pu**-tid/, **putting** /**poo**-ting/) (*in golf*) to hit the ball into the hole on the green. ● n (*in golf*) a hit intended to send the ball into the hole.

putter[1] /**pu**-ter/ n a golf club for putting.

putter[2] /**pu**-ter/ vb to work slowly and without much attention (*spend Saturdays puttering about*).

putting green /**pu**-ting-green/ n (*in golf*) the smooth green near a hole.

putty /**pu**-tee/ *n* a paste made from chalk and linseed oil, used for fitting glass in windows, etc. ● *vb* to cement with putty.

puzzle /**pu**-zul/ *vb* 1 to present with a difficult problem or situation, to baffle, to perplex (*they were puzzled by the last question in the exam/ puzzled by her behavior*). 2 to think long and carefully about (*puzzling over the instructions*). ● *n* 1 a difficult question or problem (*how they got there was a puzzle*). 2 a game or toy intended to test one's skill or cleverness (*a crossword puzzle/a jigsaw puzzle*). ● *n* **puzzlement** /**pu**-zul-ment/.

PVC /pee-vee-**see**/ *abbr* = **polyvinyl chloride**: a tough kind of plastic (*a waterproof coat made of PVC*).

pygmy, pigmy /**pig**-mee/ *n* 1 a member of a race of very small people in Africa. 2 (*inf*) a very small person or animal. ● *also adj*.

pyjamas /pi-**ja**-maz/ *npl* (*Br*) *see* **pajamas**.

pylon /**pie**-lon/ *n* 1 a hollow skeleton pillar for carrying overhead cables. 2 a tower or pillar built aᵗ an airdrome as a guiding mark.

pyramid /pi-ra-mid/ *n* 1 a solid body with triangular sides meeting in a point at the top. 2 a monument of this shape.

pyre /**pire**/ *n* a pile of wood, etc., on which a deac body is placed for burning.

pyrotechnic /pie-ro-**tec**-nic/ *adj* having to witɦ fireworks.

pyrotechnics /pie-ro-**tec**-nics/ *n* the art of makinɡ or using fireworks.

Pyrrhic /**pi**-ric/ *adj.* ● **Pyrrhic victory** a victory iɪ which the victors suffer very heavy losses.

Pythagorean /pie-thag-u-**ree**-an/ *adj* having to dc with Pythagoras or his philosophy, which taughᵗ that after death the soul went into another body

python /**pie**-thon/ *n* a large nonpoisonous snake that crushes its prey in its coils.

Q

Q, q /kyoo/ the seventeenth letter of the alphabet.

quack[1] /kwak/ *n* the harsh cry of a duck. ● *vb* to make the cry of a duck (*ducks quacking by the pond*).

quack[2] /kwak/ *n* **1** a person who pretends to have knowledge or skill that he or she does not have, especially in medicine (*illnesses made worse by quacks*). **2** (*inf*) a doctor (*the quack told him to give up smoking*). ● *n* **quackery** /kwa-kree/ the claims or methods of a quack.

quad /kwad/ *n short for* **quadrangle** /kwad-rang-gul/ (of a school or college) (*I'll meet you in the quad*).

quadr- /kwad-r/ *prefix* four.

quadrangle /kwad-rang-gul/ *n* **1** a figure with four sides and four angles. **2** a square or rectangular courtyard enclosed by a building or buildings, especially at a school or college (*students walking in the quadrangle*).

quadrant /kwad-rant/ *n* **1** the fourth part of a circle. **2** an instrument for measuring angles.

quadrate /kwad-rate/ *adj* square or almost square. ● *n.*

quadratic /kwad-**ra**-tic/ *adj* in algebra, having to do with the square of an unknown quantity, but with no higher power.

quadrennial /kwad-**re**-nee-al/ *adj* **1** happening every four years (*a quadrennial festival*). **2** lasting for four years.

quadrennium /kwad-**re**-nee-um/ *n* a period of four years.

quadriceps /kwad-ri-seps/ *n* the large muscles at the front of the thighs.

quadrilateral /kwad-ri-lat-rul/ *n* a four-sided figure.

quadrille /kwad-ril/ *n* **1** a dance for four couples, each forming the side of a square. **2** a kind of card game played by four people.

quadruped /kwad-ru-ped/ *n* (*fml*) an animal with four feet (*quadrupeds such as dogs and lions*).

quadruple /kwad-**roo**-pul/ *adj* four times as great. ● *vb* to make or become four times greater (*the rent has quadrupled in five years*).

quadruplet /kwad-**roo**-plet/ *n* (*often abbreviated to* **quad**) one of four children born at one birth (*give birth to quadruplets*).

quaff /kwaf/ *vb* (*fml*) to drink a lot at one swallow (*quaffing a glass of water after his long run*).

quaggy /kwa-gee/ *adj* soft and flabby.

quagmire /kwag-mire/ *n* soft, very wet ground, bog, marsh (*cars stuck in the quagmire*).

quahog /k(w)o-hawg/ *n* an edible clam from the East Coast of North America.

quail[1] /kwail/ *vb* to bend or draw back in fear (*children quailing at the sound of angry voices*).

quail[2] /kwail/ *n* a small bird of the partridge family.

quaint /kwaint/ *adj* unusual or old-fashioned in a pleasing way (*quaint customs/quaint town*).

quake /kwake/ *vb* to shake, to tremble (*quaking with fear*).

Quaker /kway-ker/ *n* a member of the religious group the Society of Friends.

qualification /kwal-i-fi-**cay**-shun/ *n* an ability, skill, etc., that fits a person for a certain position or job (*after this class I will have the right qualification for the job*).

qualify /kwal-i-fie/ *vb* **1** to achieve the standards required before entering a business, filling a certain position, getting a job, etc. (*qualified as a doctor*). **2** to make fit (*his low salary qualifies him for financial aid*). **3** to change but not alter completely (*qualifying a person's statement*).

qualitative /kwal-i-tay-tiv/ *adj* (*fml*) having to do with quality.

quality /kwal-i-tee/ *n* **1** a feature of a person or thing (*qualities of leadership/the exciting quality of his writing*). **2** the degree to which something is good or excellent, a standard of excellence (*high-quality cloth/low-quality paper*). **3** excellence (*goods of quality*). ● *adj* **qualitative** /kwal-i-tay-tiv/.

qualm /kwam/ *n* doubt, a fear that a person is about to do something that is wrong (*have qualms about giving up his job to write a book/no qualms about getting married*).

quandary /kwan-dree/ *n* a state of uncertainty, doubt as to what a person ought to do (*in a quandary about whether to go or to stay*).

quantify /kwan-ti-fie/ *vb* to express the amount of, to measure.

quantitative /kwan-ti-tay-tiv/ *adj* (*fml*) able to be measured, having to do with quantity.

quantity /kwan-ti-tee/ *n* **1** size, amount (*the quantity of paper needed*). **2** a large amount (*buy food in quantity*). **3** the length of a vowel sound.

quantum /kwan-tum/ *n* an amount.

quarantine /kwaw-ren-teen/ *n* a period of time during which a person, animal, or ship that may carry infection is kept apart (*dogs going into Great Britain have to go into quarantine in case they have rabies*).

quarrel /kwaw-rel/ *n* an angry argument or disa-greement. ● *vb* [**quarreled** /kwaw-reld/, **quarreling** /kwaw-re-ling/; *also* **quarreled, quar-relling**] (*Br, Cdn*) **1** to exchange angry words with, to fall out (with) (*quarrel with his business part-ner over money*). **2** (*fml*) to disagree (*find no rea-son to quarrel with her account of the event*).

quarrelsome /kwaw-rel-sum/ *adj* fond of quarreling (*quarrelsome children*).

quarry[1] /kwaw-ree/ *n* an intended prey (*the mouse was the cat's quarry*).

quarry[2] /kwaw-ree/ *n* a place from which stone, slate, etc., may be cut. ● *vb* to dig or cut from a quarry (*quarried slate*).

quart /kwawrt/ *n* a measurement of liquid (1136 liters, 2 pints, or $^1/_4$ gallon).

quarter /kwawr-ter/ *n* **1** the fourth part of anything (*leave a quarter of his fortune to each of his four sons*). **2** a measure of weight, a quarter of a hun-dredweight (25 pounds). **3** one fourth of an hour (*it's quarter to eight at night*). **4** a district in a town (*the business quarter*). **5** *pl* lodgings. ● *vb* **1** to divide into four equal parts (*quarter the orange*). **2** (*fml*) to provide with lodgings (*soldiers quar-tered in the town*).

quarterback /kwawr-ter-back/ *n* a football player that takes the ball from the center and passes or hands it off at an attempt to score.

quartered /kwawr-terd/ *adj* divided into four parts.

quarterfinal /kwawr-ter-fie-nal/ *adj* having to do with the matches or games right before the semi-finals in a contest.

quarter horse /kwawr-ter-hawrse/ *n* any of a breed of light, strong horses that are solid, usually dark in color, and used in rodeos and in range work.

quarter-hour /kwawr-ter-hour/ *n* 15 minutes.

quartering /kwawr-ter-ing/ *adj* **1** moving toward a ship so as to strike either quarter (*a quartering wind*). **2** lying at right angles. ● *n* **1** the act of dividing into quarters. **2** the act of passing back and forth over an area, as in hunting. **3** the providing of lodging for sol-diers. **4** the division of a shield into quarters.

quarterly /kwawr-ter-lee/ *adj* happening every three months (*a quarterly magazine*). ● *also n.* ● *adv* once every three months.

quartet /kwawr-tet/ *n* **1** a piece of music written for four performers (*a Mozart quartet*). **2** a group of four singers or players (*she plays in a quartet*). **3** a set or group of four.

quartz /kwawrts/ *n* a type of mineral found in rocks, usually in the form of crystals.

quasar /kway-zar/ *n* a distant starlike heavenly body that emits light and radio waves.

quash /kwawsh/ *vb* **1** to set aside (an order or judg-ment), to cancel (*quash the criminal sentence*). **2** to put down, to put an end to (*quash the mutiny*).

quasi- /kway-zie/ *prefix* almost, to some extent but not really (*quasi-religious faith*).

quassia /kwa-sha/ *n* a South American tree with a bitter-tasting bark used in medicines.

quatrain /kwaw-train/ *n* a poem or section of a poem of four lines, usually rhyming alternately.

quaver /kway-ver/ *vb* **1** to shake, to tremble (*her voice quavered*). **2** to speak in a trembling, un-certain voice (*quaver a reply*). ● *n* **1** a trembling of the voice. **2** a trill in music.

quay /kee/ *n* a landing place for the loading and unloading of ships (*ships moored at the quay*).

queasy /kwee-zee/ *adj* **1** feeling sick, easily made sick (*feel queasy on the sea voyage*). **2** (*fml*) hav-ing fears or doubts, unwilling (*feel rather queasy about accepting his invitation*).

queen /kween/ *n* **1** the wife of a king (*the king and his queen*). **2** a woman royal ruler of a country (*she be-came queen when her father died*). **3** the female bee, ant, etc. **4** a picture playing card. **5** a piece in chess.

queenly /kween-lee/ *adj* like a queen (*a queenly manner*).

queen mother /kween-mu-ther/ *n* a former queen who is mother of the reigning king or queen.

queer /kweer/ *adj* strange, unusual (*a queer feel-ing/a queer person*).

quell /kwell/ *vb* **1** to put down completely, to crush (*quell the rebellion*). **2** to put an end to (*quell the children's fears*).

quench /kwench/ *vb* **1** to put out (*quench the fire*). **2** to satisfy (*quench thirst*). **3** (*fml*) to keep down (*quench a revolt*).

querulous /kwe-ru-lus/ *adj* complaining (*in queru-lous tones*).

query /kwee-ree/ *n* **1** a question (*answer their queries*). **2** a question mark (?). ● *vb* **1** (*fml*) to ask a question. **2** to doubt (*queried the truth of his statement*).

quesadilla /ke-sa-dee-ya/ *n* a Mexican dish made of a flour tortilla filled with cheese or a spicy mix-ture, folded, and deep fried.

quest /kwest/ (*fml or lit*) *n* a search (*a quest for happiness*). ● *vb* to go in search of.

question /kwes-chun/ *n* **1** a request for news, infor-mation, knowledge, etc. (*reply to questions about the president's health*). **2** words spoken or arranged in such a way that an answer is called for (*questions* *rather than statements*). **3** a problem (*exam questions*). **4** the matter under consideration (*questions of international importance*). ● *vb* **1** to ask questions. **2** to doubt. ● *n* **questioner** /**kwes**-chu-ner/.

questionable /**kwes**-chu-na-bul/ *adj* **1** doubtful (*it is questionable whether he will arrive on time*). **2** open to suspicion (*of questionable character*).

questionnaire /kwes-chu-**nare**/ *n* a set of written questions chosen for a particular purpose (*answer a questionnaire about house-buying*).

quibble /**kwi**-bul/ *n* an objection or argument, especially an unimportant objection or argument (*quibbles over the contract*). ● *vb* to argue about small, unimportant details (*quibbling about the price of some of the items on the restaurant's menu*).

quiche /keesh/ *n* an unsweetened egg custard baked in a tart with onions, cheese, bacon, etc.

quick /kwick/ *adj* **1** fast-moving (*a quick pace*). **2** clever (*a quick pupil/a quick brain*). **3** done in a short time (*a quick drink*). **4** (*old*) living. ● *n* the very tender flesh under the nails or just below the skin. ● *adv* quickly.

quicken /**kwi**-ken/ *vb* **1** to give life to (*quicken his interest*). **2** to become alive or lively. **3** to make or become faster (*quicken the pace/his pace quickened*).

quickly /**kwik**-lee/ *adv* at once, rapidly (*read the document quickly*).

quicksand /**kwik**-sand/ *n* loose, wet sand into which anything of weight (e.g., ships, people) may sink.

quicksilver /**kwik**-sil-ver/ *n* mercury.

quiet /**kwie**-et/ *adj* **1** at rest. **2** noiseless, not noisy. **3** calm, peaceful, gentle. **4** (*of colors*) not bright. ● *n* **1** rest, peace. **2** silence. ● *vb* **1** to calm. **2** to make silent.

quill /kwill/ *n* **1** a large feather from a goose or other bird, used as a pen. **2** the hollow stem of a feather. **3** one of the prickles on the back of a porcupine.

quilt /kwilt/ *n* a bedcover padded with feathers, wool, etc. (*huddle under the quilt to get warm*). ● *vb* to make (a cover, etc.) filled with padding separated into small compartments by cross-stitching (*a quilted waistcoat*).

quince /kwinss/ *n* **1** a sour pear-shaped fruit often used in jams. **2** a kind of fruit-bearing tree.

quintet /kwin-**tet**/ *n* **1** a piece of music written for five performers. **2** a group of five singers or players (*play in a quintet with her four sisters*). **3** a set or group of five.

quintuple /kwin-**too**-pul/ *adj* five times as great. ● *vb* to make or become five times greater (*quintupling the firm's profit in three years*).

quintuplet /kwin-**tu**-plet/ *n* (*often abbreviated to* **quin**) one of five children born at one birth (*give birth to quintuplets*).

quip /kwip/ *n* a joking or witty remark (*good at making quips*). ● *vb* (**quipped** /kwipt/, **quipping** /**kwi**-ping/) to make such remarks.

quirk /kwirk/ *n* **1** a way of behaving or doing something peculiar to oneself (*one of his quirks is to keep stroking his beard*). **2** a strange or unexpected happening (*by a sudden quirk of fate*).

quit /kwit/ *vb* (**quitted** /**kwi**-tid/ *or* **quit**, **quitting** /**kwi**-ting/) **1** to leave (*given notice to quit/tired of his job and decided to quit*). **2** to give up (*try to quit smoking*).

quite /kwite/ *adv* **1** completely, wholly (*quite recovered*). **2** fairly, rather (*quite clever*).

quits /kwits/ *adj* on even terms, owing nothing to each other (*call it quits*).

quittance /**kwi**-tanse/ *n* (*fml*) a setting free from debt, guilt, etc.

quiver[1] /**kwi**-ver/ *n* a case for carrying arrows.

quiver[2] /**kwi**-ver/ *vb* to tremble (*a voice quivering with rage/children quivering with fear*). ● *n* a shudder, a slight trembling (*a quiver of fear*).

quixotic /kwik-**sot**-ic/ *adj* trying to achieve impossible or unrealistic aims, especially when these are to help others and bring danger to oneself (*quixotic gestures*).

quiz /kwiz/ *vb* (**quizzed** /kwizd/, **quizzing** /**kwi**-zing/) to examine by questioning (*quiz them about their parents*). ● *n* a number of questions set to test a person's knowledge (*a television quiz*).

quizzical /**kwi**-zi-cal/ *adj* as if asking a question, especially mockingly or humorously (*a quizzical look*).

quota /**kwo**-ta/ *n* the share of the whole to which each member of a group has a right (*the quota of fish allowed to be caught by the local fishermen*).

quotation /kwo-**tay**-shun/ *n* **1** the words or passage quoted (*a quotation from Shakespeare*). **2** a price stated (*a quotation for painting the house*).

quotation marks /kwo-**tay**-shun-marks/ *npl* punctuation marks (" " *or* ' ') placed at the beginning and end of a written quotation.

quote /kwoat/ *vb* **1** to repeat or write down the exact words of another person, making it known that they are not anyone else's (*quoting her mother/quoted Shakespeare*). **2** to say the price of (*quote $500 for decorating the room*). ● *n* (*inf*) **1** a quotation. **2** a quotation mark.

quotidian /kwo-ti-**dee**-an/ *adj* (*fml*) daily.

quotient /**kwo**-shent/ *n* the answer to a division problem.

R

R, r /ar/ the eighteenth letter of the alphabet.

rabbi /ra-bie/ *n* a person who is learned in the law and doctrine of the Jews, a Jewish leader and teacher.

rabbit /ra-bit/ *n* a small long-eared burrowing animal.

rabble /ra-bul/ *n* a noisy or disorderly crowd (*there was a rabble in the square demanding the president's resignation*).

rabid /ra-bid/ *adj* **1** fanatical (*a rabid nationalist*). **2** (*of dogs*) suffering from rabies.

rabies /ray-beez/ *n* a disease, usually caught from a bite from another infected animal, that causes madness, and often death, in dogs and other animals (*the bat carried the rabies virus*).

raccoon, racoon /ra-coon/ *n* an American animal of the bear family.

race¹ /race/ *n* **1** a contest to see who can reach a given mark in the shortest time (*a horse race*). **2** a strong quick-moving current of water. ● *vb* **1** to take part in a race. **2** to run or move very quickly (*race to catch the bus*).

race² /race/ *n* **1** any of the main groups into which human beings can be divided according to their physical characteristics (*the white races*). **2** the fact of belonging to one of these groups (*discrimination on the grounds of race*). **3** a group of people who share the same culture, language, etc. (*the Nordic races*). **4** ancestors, family (*a man of noble race*).

race car /race-car/ *n* a car designed to race and to travel at high speed.

racehorse /race-hawrss/ *n* a horse bred for racing.

racetrack /race-track/, **race course** /race-coarss/ *n* the ground on which races are run.

racial /ray-shul/ *adj* having to do with a race or nation (*racial characteristics/racial hatred*).

racism /ray-si-zum/ *n* prejudice or discrimination against people on the grounds of race, sometimes accompanied by violent behavior. ● *adj* **racist** (*a racist remark*). ● *n* **racist**.

rack /rack/ *n* **1** a frame for holding articles (*a wine rack*). **2** (*old*) instrument for torturing people by stretching their joints. ● *vb* to cause great pain or trouble to (*racked by guilt*). ● **rack your brains** to think as hard as possible.

racket¹ /ra-kit/ *n* a bat (usually a frame strung with crisscrossing cords) for playing tennis, badminton, etc.

racket² /ra-kit/ *n* **1** an uproar, a din (*kept awake by a racket from the party next door*). **2** a dishonest method of making a lot of money (*in the drug racket*).

racketeer /ra-ki-teer/ *n* a person who makes money by dishonest or violent methods. ● *n* **racketeering** /ra-ki-tee-ring/.

racoon *see* **raccoon**.

radar /ray-dar/ *n* the sending out of radio signals to determine the position of ships, airplanes, etc.

radial /ray-dee-al/ *adj* **1** of or in rays. **2** arranged like spokes.

radiance /ray-dee-anse/ *n* brightness, brilliance (*the radiance of the sun/the radiance of her smile*).

radiant /ray-dee-ant/ *adj* **1** showing great joy or happiness. **2** sending out rays of light or heat (*radiant sun/radiant heat*). **3** glowing. **4** shining.

radiate /ray-dee-ate/ *vb* **1** to send out rays of light or heat (*heaters radiated warmth*). **2** to shine with (*a face radiating happiness*) **3** to send out or spread from a central point (*roads radiating from center city*). ● *n* **radiation** /ray-dee-ay-shun/.

radiator /ray-dee-ay-tur/ *n* **1** an apparatus (an electric or gas fire, hot-water pipes, etc.) for warming a room by radiating heat. **2** an apparatus for cooling the engine of an automobile.

radical /ra-di-cal/ *adj* **1** having to do with the root or basic nature (*radical faults in the system*). **2** seeking great political, social, or economic change (*a radical party*). **3** very thorough (*radical changes*). ● *n* a person who desires to make far-reaching changes in society or in methods of government. ● *adv* **radically** /ra-di-ca-lee/.

radii *see* **radius**.

radio /ray-dee-o/ *n* **1** the sending or receiving of sounds through the air by electric waves. **2** an apparatus for receiving sound broadcast through the air by electric waves. **3** the radio broadcasting industry.

radioactive /ray-dee-o-ac-tiv/ *adj* giving off rays of force or energy which can be dangerous but that can be used in medicine, etc. ● *n* **radioactivity** /ray-dee-o-ac-ti-vi-tee/.

radiographer /ray-dee-og-ra-fer/ *n* a person who is trained to take X-ray photographs.

radiography /ray-dee-og-ra-fee/ *n* the obtaining of photographs by X-rays.

radiology /ray-dee-ol-u-jee/ *n* the study of

radioactivity as a means of treating disease. ● *n* **radiologist** /ray-dee-**ol**-u-jist/.

radiotherapy /ray-dee-o-**ther**-a-pee/ *n* the treatment of disease by rays (e.g., X-rays). ● *n* **radiotherapist** / ray-dee-o-**ther**-a-pist/.

radish /**ra**-dish/ *n* a plant with an edible hot-tasting red root.

radium /**ray**-dee-um/ *n* a rare metallic substance that gives off rays of heat and light used in the treatment of disease.

radius /**ray**-dee-us/ *n* (*pl* **radii** /**ray**-dee-eye/) **1** a straight line from the center of a circle to any point on the circumference. **2** a bone in the forearm.

radon /**ray**-don/ *n* a radioactive gas that can be produced from the earth and rock.

raffle /**ra**-ful/ *n* a sale in which people buy tickets for an article that is given to the person whose name or number is drawn by lottery. ● *vb* to sell by raffle.

raft /raft/ *n* logs fastened together to make a floating platform or a flat boat without sides.

rag /rag/ *n* a torn or tattered piece of cloth, a left-over piece of material (*use a rag to dust the furniture*). ● *npl* **rags** /ragz/ old tattered clothes (*orphan children clad in rags*).

rage /rage/ *n* **1** violent anger, fury. **2** inspiration. **3** something very popular or fashionable at a certain time. ● *vb* **1** to be furious with anger. **2** to behave or talk violently.

ragged /**ra**-gid/ *adj* **1** torn or tattered. **2** wearing old tattered clothing. **3** rough-edged.

ragtime /**rag**-time/ *n* a highly syncopated form of music of African-American origin, an early form of jazz.

raid /raid/ *n* a sudden quick attack made by a group intending to return to their starting point (*a raid behind enemy lines*). ● *also vb.* ● *n* **raider** /**ray**-der/.

rail /rail/ *n* **1** a level or sloping bar of wood or metal linking up a line of posts, banisters, etc. (*hold on to the ship's rail*). **2** a strip of metal molded to a certain shape and laid down as part of a railroad track or streetcar line (*the rail to Washington is blocked by snow*). ● *vb* **1** to enclose with railings. **2** to send by railroad.

railing /**ray**-ling/ *n* a fence made of posts some distance apart linked together by crossbars or a rail.

railroad /**rail**-road/ *n* a track laid with parallel metal strips so molded that a train can run on them.

railway /**rail**-way/ (*Br*) *see* **railroad**.

rain /rain/ *n* moisture falling from the clouds in drops. ● *vb* **1** to fall in drops (*it was raining heavily*). **2** to fall or throw down in large numbers (*arrows raining down*). ● *ns* **raindrop** /**rain**-drop/, **rainwater** /**rain**-waw-ter/.

rainbow /**rain**-bo/ *n* a semicircular colored band that often appears in the sky when the sun shines through raindrops.

rainfall /**rain**-fawl/ *n* the amount of rain that falls in a certain place during a certain length of time (*exceed the average rainfall*).

rainforest /**rain**-faw-rest/ *n* a dense tropical forest where there is a high rainfall.

rainy /**rain**-ee/ *adj* wet, raining (*a rainy day/rainy weather*).

raise /raiz/ *vb* **1** to lift upward, to move to a higher position (*raise the flag high*). **2** to breed (*raise pigs*). **3** to make higher (*raise the wall a few meters*). **4** to cause to grow, to cultivate (*raise wheat*). **5** to increase in amount, size, etc. (*raise prices*). **6** to begin to talk about (*raise a new point*). **7** to collect (*raise money for charity*). **8** to make louder (*raise her voice in anger*). **9** to give up (*raise a siege*). ● *n* **1** an increase (*a raise in pay*). **2** an upward slope. **3** a small hill.

raisin /**ray**-zin/ *n* a dried grape (*cakes with raisins*).

rake /rake/ *n* a metal or wooden toothed crossbar fixed to a pole and used for scraping the ground, pulling together cut grass or hay, smoothing the soil, etc. ● *vb* **1** to scrape, pull together, smooth, etc., with a rake (*rake up dead leaves*). **2** to search very carefully (*rake through his papers for evidence of guilt*).

rally /**ra**-lee/ *vb* **1** to bring or come together again in one body (*rally the troops/troops rallying around the general*). **2** to regain some of your strength, health, etc., after weakness or illness (*a patient who suddenly rallied after the procedure*). ● *n* **1** a coming together in large numbers. **2** recovery of strength, health, good spirits, etc.

ram /ram/ *n* **1** a male sheep. **2** any heavy instrument used for breaking down walls, doors, etc. (*a battering ram*). ● *vb* (**rammed** /ramd/, **ramming** /**ra**-ming/) **1** to run into with great force. **2** to push down, into, or onto with great force (*ram the post into the ground*). **3** (*of a ship*) to strike another ship head-on in order to make a hole in its side. **4** to strike violently.

RAM /ram/ *n* an acronym standing for Random Access Memory, meaning memory that is lost when a computer is switched off.

Ramadan /**ra**-ma-dan/ *n* the ninth month of the Muslim year during which Muslims fast between the hours of sunrise and sunset.

ramble /**ram**-bul/ *vb* **1** to change from one subject to another in a foolish, purposeless way (*ramble on about his youth/rambling after the knock on his head*). **2** to walk as and where you like for pleasure (*rambling through the woods*). **3** to grow in all directions (*rambling roses*). ● *n* a walk taken for pleasure.

rambler /ram-bler/ *n* **1** a wanderer. **2** a climbing plant, especially a type of rose.

ramification /ra-mi-fi-**cay**-shun/ *n* a consequence, especially one of many and an indirect one (*unable to foresee the ramifications of his actions*).

ramp /ramp/ *n* a slope (*a ramp to allow cars to drive on to the ship*).

rampage /ram-page/ *vb* to rush about, to rage (*children rampaging about/elephants rampaging through the jungle*). ● *n* great anger or excitement.

rampant /ram-pant/ *adj* **1** uncontrolled (*rampant violence*). **2** growing uncontrollably (*rampant weeds*). **3** in heraldry, standing on the hind legs (*a lion rampant*).

rampart /ram-part/ *n* a defensive wall or mound of earth.

ramshackle /ram-sha-kul/ *adj* broken-down, nearly falling down (*ramshackle property*).

ranch /ranch/ *n* a large cattle farm.

rancher /ran-cher/ *n* a person who owns or works on a ranch.

rancid /ran-sid/ *adj* bad, unpleasant to taste or smell (*rancid butter*).

random /ran-dum/ *adj* without plan or purpose (*ask a random sample of people*). ● **at random** without plan or purpose (*choose people at random*).

range /range/ *vb* **1** to extend (*an area ranging from the city boundaries to the next town*). **2** to vary between certain limits (*ages ranging from 10 to 70*). **3** to set in a line, to place in order (*range the books on the shelf*). **4** (*fml*) to wander (*country children ranging over the hills*). ● *n* **1** a variety (*a range of exotic plants*). **2** extent (*voice range*). **3** a line or row, e.g., of mountains. **4** the distance between a gun and the fall of the shot, the distance over which an object can be sent or thrown, sound carried, heard, etc. (*out of hearing range*). **5** an area of land where animals roam and graze. **6** a piece of ground for firing practice. **7** an enclosed kitchen fireplace for cooking and baking (*a stew simmering on the range*).

ranger /rane-jer/ *n* a person in charge of a national park or forest.

rank[1] /rangk/ *n* **1** a position of authority, a level of importance (*promoted to the rank of colonel*). **2** a social class (*the upper ranks of society*). **3** a row or line (*ranks of police officers keeping back the crowds*). **4** a row of soldiers standing side by side. ● *vb* **1** to put or be in a certain class or in an order of merit. **2** to arrange in a row or line. ● **rank and file** the common people.

rank[2] /rangk/ *adj* **1** very bad (*the rank smell of rotting meat/rank stupidity*). **2** overgrown (*a garden rank with weeds*). **3** growing thickly and untidily (*rank weeds*).

rankle /rang-kul/ *vb* to go on causing anger or dislike (*his defeat still rankles with him*).

ransack /ran-sack/ *vb* **1** to search thoroughly (*burglars ransacking houses looking for money*). **2** to plunder (*enemy soldiers ransacking the town*).

ransom /ran-sum/ *n* a sum of money paid to free someone from captivity (*asked for a ransom in exchange for their kidnapped children*). ● *vb* to pay to obtain freedom, to redeem.

rant /rant/ *vb* to talk in a loud, uncontrolled manner, often using words for fine sound rather than meaning (*ranting on about how badly he was treated*). ● *also n*. ● *n* **ranter**.

rap /rap/ *n* **1** a quick light blow, a knock (*a rap on the door*). **2** a style of popular music in which (usually rhyming) words are spoken in a rhythmic chant over an instrumental backing. **3** (*inf*) talk, conversation. **4** (*inf*) a reputation (*a bum rap*). ● *vb* (**rapped** /rapt/, **rapping** /ra-ping/) **1** to give a rap to (*rap the door*). **2** (*inf*) to chat, converse. **3** to perform a rap. ● **not worth a rap** worthless (*a promise not worth a rap*). ● *n* **rapper**.

rapid /ra-pid/ *adj* very quick-moving (*rapid changes at a rapid pace*). ● *n* (*usually pl*) a quick-flowing stretch of river running downhill. ● *n* **rapidity** /ra-pi-di-tee/. ● *adv* **rapidly** /ra-pid-lee/.

rapier /ray-pee-er/ *n* a long, thin sword.

rappel /ra-pel/ *vb* to go down a very steep slope, such as a cliff face or a very tall building, using a rope secured at the top and passed around the body in a kind of harness.

rapport /ra-poar/ *n* a friendly relationship between people who understand one another.

rapt /rapt/ *adj* giving your whole mind (*with rapt attention*).

rapture /rap-chur/ *n* (*fml*) delight, great joy (*in raptures at the news of their success*).

rapturous /rap-chu-rus/ *adj* full of delight, very happy.

rare /rare/ *adj* **1** uncommon, unusual. **2** valuable. **3** very good. **4** very lightly cooked. **5** not thick. ● *n* **rareness** /rare-ness/.

rarefied /ray-ri-fied/ *adj* thin, with less oxygen than usual (*the rarefied air of high altitudes*).

rarely /rare-lee/ *adv* seldom, not often (*we rarely see them*).

rarity /ray-ri-tee/ *n* **1** a thing seldom met with (*such birds are rarities in this area*). **2** rareness (*stamps valuable because of their rarity*).

rascal /ra-scal/ *n* **1** a rogue, a scoundrel (*a rascal who deserved to be sent to prison*). **2** a naughty boy (*a rascal who tries to avoid going to school*). ● *adj* **rascally** /ra-sca-lee/.

rash[1] /rash/ *n* a redness of the skin caused by illness (*a measles rash*).

rash[2] /rash/ *adj* **1** acting without forethought (*she tends to be rash*). **2** hasty (*a rash decision*). **3** foolishly daring (*a rash action*). ● *adv* **rashly** /rash-lee/. ● *n* **rashness** /rash-ness/.

rasher /ra-sher/ *n* a thin slice of bacon.

rasp /rasp/ *n* **1** a file with a very rough face. **2** a harsh, grating sound. ● *vb* **1** to rub with a rasp. **2** to make a harsh, grating sound (*a rasping voice/metal rasping on metal*). **3** to say in a harsh, angry voice.

raspberry /rasp-be-ree/ *n* **1** a common shrub. **2** its edible red berry (*raspberry jam*).

Rastafarian /ra-sta-**fay**-ree-an/ *n* a member of a religious group that originated in Jamaica and worships the late Ethiopian emperor Haile Selassie.

rat /rat/ *n* a gnawing animal like, but larger than, the mouse. ● *vb* (**ratted** /ra-tid/, **ratting** /ra-ting/) to inform on someone.

ratchet /rat-chit/ *n* a toothed wheel with which a catch automatically engages as it is turned, preventing it from being turned in the reverse direction.

rate /rate/ *n* **1** the amount of one thing measured by its relation to another (*the death rate is the number of people who die yearly to every thousand of the population/a failure rate of 10%*). **2** speed (*the rate of increase*). **3** price (*charged at the rate of $50 per day*). ● *vb* **1** (*fml*) to consider (*he is rated by his neighbors as a kind man*). **2** to value (*we rate his abilities highly*). **3** to assign to a position on a scale (*rated number 15 in the world's tennis players*). ● *adj* **ratable** /ray-ta-bul/.

rather /ra-ther/ *adv* **1** preferably, more willingly (*she would rather die than marry him*). **2** fairly, quite (*she is rather talented*). **3** more exactly, more truly (*she is thoughtless rather than cruel*).

rating /ray-ting/ *n* **1** value or rank according to some kind of classification (*his rating as an international tennis player*). **2** in the navy, a sailor who is not an officer.

ratio /ray-sho/ *n* one number or amount considered in relation or proportion to another (*the ratio of students to teachers*).

ration /ra-shun/ *n* **1** a fixed amount of something allowed every so often (*the child's weekly candy ration*). ● *npl* **rations** /ra-shunz/ (*old*) food. ● *vb* to limit to fixed amounts (*rationed gasoline to 30 liters per person*).

rational /ra-shnul/ *adj* **1** having the power to think things out (*human beings are rational animals*). **2** reasonable, sensible (*a rational decision*). ● *adv* **rationally** /ra-shna-lee/.

rationalist /ra-shna-list/ *n* a person who tries to find natural causes for all things, including miracles. ● *n* **rationalism** /ra-shna-li-zum/.

rationalize /ra-shna-lize/ *vb*, *also* **rationalise** (*Br*) **1** to try to find reasons for all actions. **2** to explain as due to natural causes. **3** to reorganize a business firm in order to improve efficiency.

rat race /rat-race/ *n* the competitive, aggressive struggle to survive and be successful in the modern world (*she has opted out of the rat race*).

rattle /ra-tul/ *vb* **1** to make a number of short quick noises one after the other (*windows rattling in the storm*). **2** to shake something to cause such noises (*collectors rattling their cans*). **3** to speak or say quickly (*rattle off the instructions so that no one understood*). ● *n* **1** an instrument or toy for rattling (*a baby's rattle*). **2** a rattling sound (*the rattle of milk bottles*).

rattlesnake /ra-tul-snake/ *n* an American snake able to make a rattling sound with horny rings on its tail.

raucous /raw-cus/ *adj* hoarse, harsh-sounding (*the man shouted his instructions in a raucous voice*).

ravage /ra-vidge/ *vb* to lay waste, to plunder, to destroy far and wide (*crops ravaged by storms*). ● *n* damage, destruction.

rave /rare/ *vb* **1** to talk wildly or madly (*he was very ill and was raving in his sleep*). **2** (*inf*) to praise very highly (*critics raving about his new play*).

raven /ray-vin/ *n* a bird of prey of the crow family. ● *adj* black (*her raven hair*).

ravenous /ra-vi-nus/ *adj* very hungry (*ravenous after their long walk*). ● *adv* **ravenously** /ra-vi-nus-lee/.

ravine /ra-**veen**/ *n* a narrow valley with steep sides.

ravioli /ra-vee-o-lee/ *n* an Italian dish consisting of small squares of pasta with a meat or vegetable filling.

ravish /ra-vish/ *vb* **1** to take or carry off by force. **2** to delight (*ravished by her beauty*).

ravishing /ra-vi-shing/ *adj* delightful, wonderful (*her ravishing beauty*). ● *adv* **ravishingly** /ra-vi-shing-lee/.

raw /raw/ *adj* **1** uncooked (*raw meat*). **2** in its natural state (*raw cotton/a raw recruit*). **3** sore. **4** (*of part of the body*) uncovered by skin, scraped (*raw wounds*). **5** cold and damp (*a raw day*).

ray[1] /ray/ *n* **1** a line of light, heat, etc., getting broader as it goes further from its origin (*the sun's rays*). **2** a little, a very small amount (*a ray of hope*).

ray[2] /ray/ *n* a species of flatfish.

rayon /ray-on/ *n* artificial silk.

raze /raze/ *vb* to destroy completely, to wipe out (*cities razed to the ground by enemy armies*).

razor /ray-zor/ *n* an implement for shaving hair (*he shaves every day with an electric razor*).

razorblade /ray-zor-blade/ *n* a very sharp blade for use in certain kinds of razor.

reach /reech/ *vb* **1** to stretch out (*reach out a hand*). **2** to stretch out a hand or arm for some purpose (*reach for a book*). **3** to obtain by stretching out for (*unable to reach the book on the highest shelf*). **4** to arrive at, to get as far as (*reach the summit of the mountain*). **5** to pass with the hand (*reach him the salt*). ● *n* **1** the distance you can extend the hand from the body (*the telephone was within reach*). **2** a distance that can be easily traveled (*an airport within easy reach*). **3** a straight stretch of river (*the upper reaches of the stream*).

react /ree-act/ *vb* **1** to act, behave, or change in a certain way as a result of something said or done (*react badly to criticism*). **2** to do or think the opposite (*react against their strict upbringing*).

reaction /ree-ac-shun/ *n* **1** action or behavior given rise to by something said or done (*his reaction to the defeat*). **2** opposition to progress (*reaction against computerization*). **3** in chemistry, the change in a substance when certain tests are made on it.

reactionary /ree-ac-shun-ree/ *adj* wanting to return to things as they were before, opposed to progress (*reactionary older writers*). ● *also n.*

read /reed/ *vb* (*pt, pp* **read** /red/) **1** to look at and understand (*read the instructions*). **2** to speak aloud what is written or printed (*read out the message in the letter*). **3** in computing, to extract (data) from a storage system. **4** to study (*reading English at university*). **5** to be written or worded (*his letter reads as follows*).

readable /ree-da-bul/ *adj* easy to read, interesting (*readable books*).

reader /ree-der/ *n* **1** a person who enjoys reading (*children who are not readers*). **2** a person whose job it is to report on manuscripts sent in to publishers or to read and correct proofs. **3** a reading book for

schools (*a basic reader*). ● *n* **readership** /ree-der-ship/.

readily /re-di-lee/ *adv* willingly, cheerfully (*she readily agreed*).

reading /ree-ding/ *n* **1** the study of books (*reading is her main hobby*). **2** words read out from a book or written paper (*readings from the Talmud*). **3** an explanation of what is written (*there is more than one possible reading of the passage*). **4** the figure recorded on an instrument.

readjust /ree-a-just/ *vb* **1** to put right or in the proper place again (*readjust the driving mirror*). **2** to make changes needed for altered circumstances (*try to readjust to life at home after life overseas*). ● *n* **readjustment** /ree-a-just-ment/.

ready /re-dee/ *adj* **1** prepared and fit for use (*the food is ready*). **2** quick (*people of ready will*). **3** willing (*always ready to help people*). ● *n* **readiness** /ree-dee-ness/.

real /reel/ *adj* **1** actually existing (*real life*). **2** true, genuine, not false or fake (*real gold/his real reason*). **3** utter, complete (*a real idiot*). ● *adv* very (*a real nice guy*).

real estate /ree-li-state/ *n* property consisting of lands and houses.

realism /ree-li-zum/ *n* **1** the belief that only objects perceptible by the senses actually exist. **2** trying to make works of art as true to life as possible (*the school of realism*). **3** the habit of taking a sensible, practical view of life (*forced to think of the future with realism*).

realist /ree-list/ *n* a person who believes in realism.

realistic /ree-li-stic/ *adj* **1** lifelike (*a realistic painting*). **2** taking a sensible, practical view of life (*a realistic idea of what job he is qualified for*). ● *adv* **realistically** /ree-li-sti-clee/.

reality /ree-a-li-tee/ *n* **1** that which actually exists (*prefer dreams to reality*). **2** truth. **3** things as they actually are (*the realities of life*).

realize /ree-a-lize/ *vb, also* **realise** (*Br*) **1** to understand fully (*they realize that he is telling the truth*). **2** to make real (*realize ambitions*). **3** to sell for money (*realize their assets*). ● *n* **realization** /ree-a-lie-zay-shun/, *also* **realisation** (*Br*).

really /ree-lee/ *adv* **1** actually, in fact (*describes things as they really are*). **2** very (*a really pleasant day*).

realm /relm/ *n* **1** (*fml*) a kingdom. **2** one particular aspect or sphere of life (*the realm of sport*).

realty /reel-tee/ *n* real estate.

reap /reep/ *vb* **1** to cut down (crops), to gather in. **2** to receive as a reward (*reap the benefits of hard work*).

reaper /**ree**-per/ *n* **1** a person who reaps. **2** a machine for reaping.

reappear /ree-a-**peer**/ *vb* to appear again. ● *n* **reappearance** /ree-a-**pee**-ranse/.

rear[1] /reer/ *n* **1** the part behind (*the rear of the building*). **2** the back part of an army or fleet.

rear[2] /reer/ *vb* **1** to bring up (*rear children*). **2** to breed (*rearing pigs*). **3** to stand on the hind legs (*the horse reared up*). **4** to raise (*the horse reared its head*).

reason /**ree**-zun/ *n* **1** cause for acting or believing (*the reason for her sadness/the reason for his actions/the reason why she left*). **2** the power to think things out (*lose his reason*). **3** good sense (*he would listen to reason*). ● *vb* **1** to think out step by step (*we reasoned that they would attack at dawn*). **2** to try to convince by arguing (*reason them into being less hasty*).

reasonable /**reez**-na-bul/ *adj* **1** sensible (*a reasonable suggestion*). **2** willing to listen to another's arguments (*a reasonable person*). **3** not excessive (*a reasonable amount to drink*). ● *adv* **reasonably** /**reez**-na-blee/.

reasoning /**ree**-zu-ning/ *n* **1** use of the power of reason. **2** arguments used to convince (*find his reasoning unconvincing*).

reassure /ree-a-**shoor**/ *vb* to take away the doubts or fears of (*reassuring the child that his mother would soon return*). ● *n* **reassurance** /ree-a-**shoo**-ranse/.

rebate /**ree**-bate/ *n* part of a payment given back to the payer (*a tax rebate*).

rebel /**re**-bel/ *n* a person who revolts against authority. ● *vb* **rebel** /ri-**bel**/ (**rebelled** /ri-**beld**/, **rebelling** /ri-**be**-ling/) **1** to take up arms (against) (*rebel against the army leaders*). **2** to refuse to obey those in authority (*children rebelling against strict teachers*).

rebellion /ri-**bel**-yun/ *n* open resistance to or fighting against authority.

rebellious /ri-**bel**-yuss/ *adj* **1** ready to rebel, disobedient (*at a rebellious age*). **2** fighting against authority (*the rebellious troops*).

rebirth /ri-**bel**-yun/ *n* a revival of something.

reboot /ree-**boot**/ *vb* to start a computer again (*you have to reboot after installing the software*).

rebound /ree-**bound**/ *vb* to bounce back off, to spring back (*the ball rebounded off the wall*). ● *also n.*

rebuke /ri-**byook**/ *vb* to scold, to find fault with (*rebuked the child for being naughty*). ● *n* a scolding.

rebut /ri-**but**/ *vb* (**rebutted** /ri-**but**-id/, **rebutting** /ri-**bu**-ting/) to refuse to accept as true (*rebut their accusation*). ● *n* **rebuttal** /ri-**bu**-tal/.

recall /ri-**cawl**/ *vb* **1** to remember (*unable to recall his name*). **2** to call back (*recall certain cars because of a mechanical defect*). ● *n* an order to return (*the recall of the ambassador*).

recede /ri-**seed**/ *vb* **1** to move back (*his hair is receding at the front*). **2** to slope back (*her chin recedes*).

receipt /ri-**seet**/ *n* **1** a written statement that a sum of money or an article has been received (*ask for a receipt when you pay the check*). **2** the act of receiving (*her receipt of the goods*).

receive /ri-**seev**/ *vb* **1** to come into possession of, to get (*receive a letter/receive good news*). **2** to welcome (*receive guests*).

receiver /ri-**see**-ver/ *n* **1** a person who accepts stolen goods from a thief. **2** the earpiece of a telephone. **3** a radio set.

recent /**ree**-sint/ *adj* not long past (*recent events/recent developments*). ● *adv* **recently** /**ree**-sint-lee/.

receptacle /ri-**sep**-ti-cal/ *n* a place or vessel for holding things (*a large receptacle such as a bucket*).

reception /ri-**sep**-shun/ *n* **1** the act of receiving or being received, the welcoming of guests (*a room in the building for the reception of visitors/his reception of the news*). **2** a formal party (*invited to a reception for the ambassador*). **3** welcome (*received a warm reception*). **4** the quality of radio or television signals.

receptionist /ri-**sep**-shu-nist/ *n* a person who is employed by a hotel, doctor, business, etc., to receive guests, clients, callers, etc.

receptive /ri-**sep**-tiv/ *adj* quick to learn (*a receptive mind*). ● *n* **receptivity** /ree-sep-**ti**-vi-tee/.

recess /**ree**-sess/ *n* **1** a break from work or study (*school recess/parliament in recess*). **2** part of a room set back into the wall (*an old-fashioned room with a recess for a bookcase*).

recession /ri-**se**-shun/ *n* a period of reduced trade and business activity (*people losing their jobs in the recession*).

recipe /**re**-si-pee/ *n* instructions on how to make or prepare a certain dish (*a recipe for chocolate cake*).

recipient /ri-**si**-pee-ent/ *n* a person who receives (*the recipient of good news*).

recital /ri-**sie**-tal/ *n* **1** a detailed account (*a recital of the events at the party*). **2** a public musical performance, especially by one performer (*a piano recital*).

recitation /re-si-**tay**-shun/ *n* that which is recited (e.g., a poem).

recite /ri-**site**/ *vb* to repeat aloud from memory (*children asked to recite a poem*).

reckless /**reck**-less/ *adj* rash, heedless of danger (*a reckless young man/reckless driving*). ● *adv* **recklessly** /**rek**-less-lee/.

reckon /**re**-kun/ *vb* **1** to think or consider (*I reckon she is the best worker in the company*). **2** to guess, to estimate (*we reckon they owe us $100*). **3** (*fml*) to count (*reckon the cost*).

reckoning /**re**-ku-ning/ *n* **1** a calculation, estimate (*by our reckoning, we should be there by midnight*). **2** (*old*) a settlement of accounts, a bill.

reclaim /ri-**claim**/ *vb* **1** to demand the return of (*to reclaim their baggage*). **2** to bring under cultivation waste land, land covered by the sea, etc. ● *n* **reclamation** /re-cla-**may**-shun/.

recline /ri-**cline**/ *n* to sit or lie back at your ease, to rest (*recline on a couch*).

recluse /ri-**clooss**/ *n* a person who prefers to live away from human society (*he has become a recluse since his wife's death*). ● *adj* **reclusive** /ri-**cloo**-siv/.

recognition /re-cug-**ni**-shun/ *n* **1** act of recognizing (*he was so sick that he showed no recognition when his family arrived*). **2** acknowledgment (*a medal given in recognition of his courage*).

recognizable /re-kug-**nie**-za-bul/ *adj*, *also* **recognisable** (*Br*) that may be recognized (*she was scarcely recognizable after going to the beauty salon*).

recognize /**re**-kug-nize/ *vb*, *also* **recognise** (*Br*) **1** to know again (*recognize an old friend*). **2** to greet or salute (*she refused to recognize her ex-husband*). **3** to admit (*recognize his mistakes*). **4** to accept (*qualification not recognized overseas*). **5** to reward (*recognize the man's courage by giving him a medal*).

recoil /ree-**coil**/ *vb* **1** to go suddenly backward in horror, fear, etc. (*recoil in horror at the sight of the corpse*). **2** (*of a gun*) to move sharply backward on firing. ● *n* **1** a shrinking backward. **2** the backward kick of a gun on firing.

recollect /re-cu-**lect**/ *vb* to remember (*recollect a previous incident*).

recollection /re-cu-**lec**-shun/ *n* **1** memory. **2** something remembered.

recommend /re-cu-**mend**/ *vb* **1** to speak in praise

of, to suggest that something or someone is good, suitable, etc. (*recommend her for promotion/recommend the medicine as a cure for sore throats*). **2** to advise (*his teacher recommended him to apply for university*).

recommendation /re-cu-men-**day**-shun/ *n* **1** act of praising or speaking in favor of (*his recommendation of him as a reliable employee*). **2** a letter praising a person's good points.

reconcile /**re**-con-sile/ *vb* **1** to make or become friendly again (*they did not become reconciled until several years after the quarrel*). **2** to make (yourself) accept something new or strange (*try to reconcile yourself to the changes*).

reconciliation /re-cun-si-lee-**ay**-shun/ *n* a renewal of friendship.

reconsider /ree-kun-**si**-der/ *vb* to think about again with a view to changing your mind (*reconsider his resignation*). ● *n* **reconsideration** /ree-con-si-de-**ray**-shun/.

reconstruct /ree-con-**struct**/ *vb* **1** to rebuild (*reconstruct damaged buildings*). **2** to try to build up a description or picture of, to work out exactly what happened when all the facts are not known (*police reconstructing the crime*). ● *n* **reconstruction** /re-con-**struc**-shun/.

record /ri-**cawrd**/ *vb* **1** to put down in writing (*record the score in a notebook*). **2** to preserve sounds or images by mechanical means, on a CD, tape, etc. (*record the radio concert/record the TV show*). **3** to sing songs, play music, etc., which is recorded on a CD or tape (*record her latest hit*). ● *n* **1** a recorded account. **2** a book containing written records, a register (*parish records*). **3** the best performance yet known in any type of contest. **4** a disk for playing on a CD player or phonograph. **5** what is known about a person's past (*a good work record*). **6** a criminal record (*his record was well known to the police*).

recorder /ri-**cawr**-der/ *n* **1** a person who keeps registers or records. **2** a judge in certain cities. **3** simple form of flute (*play the recorder*).

recount /ri-**count**/ *vb* **1** to tell in detail (*recount their adventures*). **2** to count again. ● *n* **recount** /ree-count/ another counting, e.g., of votes after an election.

recoup /ri-**coop**/ *vb* to get back all or part of a loss (*recoup the cost of the car repairs*).

recover /ri-**cu**-ver/ *vb* **1** to cover again (*recover the couch*). **2** to get back, to regain (*recover their strength*). **3** to make or become better after sickness or weakness (*the accident victim is unlikely to recover*).

recovery /ri-**cu**-vu-ree/ *n* **1** a return to health after sickness (*a speedy recovery from flu*). **2** the regaining of anything after losing some or all of it.

recreation /rec-ree-**ay**-shun/ *n* **1** rest and amusement after work (*find some form of recreation*). **2** a sport, a pastime (*recreations such as gardening*).

recriminate /ri-**cri**-mi-nate/ *vb* to accuse in return, to accuse your accuser

recrimination /ri-cri-mi-**nay**-shun/ *n* the act of recriminating, a counteraccusation (*his accusation of his classmates led to recrimination*).

recruit /ri-**croot**/ *n* **1** a soldier who has just joined the army. **2** a new member (*the latest recruits to the advertizing campaign*). ● *vb* to enlist new soldiers, members (*try to recruit new members*). ● *n* **recruitment** /ri-**croot**-ment/.

rectangle /**rec**-tang-gul/ *n* a four-sided figure with all its angles right angles and one pair of sides longer than the other. ● *adj* **rectangular** /rec-**tang**-gyu-lar/.

rectify /**rec**-ti-fie/ *vb* **1** to put right, to correct (*rectify the mistake*). **2** (*chemistry*) to purify. ● *n* **rectification** /rec-ti-fi-**cay**-shun/.

rectum /**rec**-tum/ *n* the part of the large intestine that leads to the anus.

recuperate /ri-**coo**-pe-rate/ *vb* to regain health or strength after illness (*take a vacation to recuperate*). ● *n* **recuperation** /ri-coo-pe-**ray**-shun/.

recur /ri-**cur**/ *vb* (**recurred** /ri-**curd**/, **recurring** /ri-**cu**-ring/) to happen again and again (*a mistake that kept recurring*). ● *n* **recurrence** /ri-**cu**-rense/.

recurrent /ri-**cu**-rent/ *adj* happening or appearing again and again (*a recurrent dream*).

recycle /ri-**sie**-cul/ *vb* to put something through some kind of process so that it can be used again (*recycle your newspapers by placing them in the blue container*).

red /red/ *adj* **1** of a color like blood (*a red coat/hands red with cold*). **2** of a color that varies between a golden brown and a reddish brown (*red hair*). **3** (*inf*) communist. ● *n* **1** the color red. **2** a communist. ● **see red** to become suddenly very angry (*she saw red when the child disobeyed*).

Red Cross /red-**crawss**/, **Red Crescent** /red **cress**-ent/ *n* an international organization that looks after sick and wounded people in time of war, and protects the rights of prisoners of war.

redden /**re**-den/ *vb* **1** to make or become red (*redden her lips*). **2** to blush (*reddening in embarrassment*).

reddish /**re**-dish/ *adj* slightly red (*a reddish sky*).

redeem /ri-**deem**/ *vb* **1** to buy back (*redeeming the goods that he had pawned*). **2** to buy freedom for (*redeem the hostages by paying the ransom*). **3** to carry out (a promise) (*the government is being asked to redeem its election promises*). **4** to make up for (*the lead actor's performance redeemed a bad production*). **5** to save from the punishment due to sin.

redeeming /ri-**dee**-ming/ *adj* canceling out bad by good (*his one redeeming feature*).

redemption /ri-**dem**-shun/ *n* the act of redeeming.

red-handed /red-**han**-did/ *adj* in the very act of doing wrong (*caught red-handed stealing the money*).

redhead /**red**-hed/ *n* a person who has reddish brown hair.

red herring /red-**herr**-ing/ *n* something mentioned that takes attention away from the subject being discussed (*he said something to the police that made them follow a red herring*).

redoubtable /ri-**dow**-ta-bul/ *adj* to be feared, deserving respect (*a redoubtable opponent*).

red tape /red-**tape**/ *n* excessive attention to rules and regulations so that business is delayed.

reduce /ri-**dooss**/ *vb* **1** to make less, smaller, or less heavy (*reducing prices/reduce the load*). **2** to change into another, and usually worse state, form, etc. (*reduce the city to a ruined heap*). **3** to bring or force to do something less pleasant, etc., than usual (*be reduced to begging on the streets*). ● *n* **reduction** /ri-**duc**-shun/.

redundant /ri-**dun**-dant/ *adj* more than necessary (*redundant words*). ● *n* **redundancy** /ri-**dun**-dan-see/.

reed /reed/ *n* **1** a tall grasslike water plant with a hollow stem. **2** that part of certain wind instruments that vibrates and so causes the sound when the instrument is blown.

reedy /**ree**-dee/ *adj* **1** covered with reeds. **2** high-pitched and thin (*a reedy voice*).

reef[1] /reef/ *n* **1** a ridge of rock or sand just above or just below the surface of the water (*a ship stuck on a reef*). **2** a crack in a rock containing gold.

reef[2] /reef/ *n* one of the parts of a sail that can be rolled or folded up. ● *vb* to roll or fold up the reefs of a sail.

reef knot /**reef**-not/ *n* a symmetrically tied double knot.

reek /reek/ *n* a strong unpleasant smell (*the reek of burnt grass*). ● *vb* **1** to give off a smell, especially an unpleasant one (*breath reeking of garlic*). **2** to show or suggest strongly something bad or unpleasant (*a situation reeking of bribery*).

reel /reel/ *n* **1** a frame or roller around which string, thread, photographic film, etc., may be wound. **2** a lively Scottish dance. ● *vb* **1** to wind on to a reel. **2** to stagger (*people reeling down the street*). ● **reel off** to tell without stopping or hesitating (*able to reel off the names of every person at the meeting*).

refer /ri-fer/ *vb* (**referred** /ri-ferd/, **referring** /ri-fe-ring/) **1** to make mention of (*refer to the help of his parents in his speech*). **2** to advise to consult elsewhere (*the doctor referred her to a specialist*). **3** to look up a certain item in a book (*refer to a dictionary*). **4** to pass (a matter) on to another for decision (*refer the complaint to his manager*).

referee /re-fe-ree/ *n* **1** a person who is chosen to give a clear decision in case of doubt (*take the dispute to a referee*). **2** in games, a person who sees that the rules are kept (*the football referee*).

reference /ref-rense/ *n* **1** mention (*there was a reference in his speech to his parents' help*). **2** directions as to where to find certain items, passages, etc., in a book (*a map reference*). **3** a person who is ready to supply information about the character, behavior, etc., of another (*his former schoolteacher acted as a referee for his job application*). **4** a letter giving information about the character, behavior, etc., of a person who applies for a job (*they refused to give her a reference because her work was so bad*).

reference book /ref-rense-book/ *n* a book (e.g., a dictionary like this one) that supplies information.

refill /ree-fill/ *vb* to fill again (*refill your cup*). ● *n* **refill** /ree-fill/ the act of refilling something (*free refills of coffee*).

refine /ri-fine/ *vb* **1** to purify (*refined oil*). **2** to make more polite and civilized (*a school supposed to produce refined young ladies*). ● *adj* **refined** /ri-finde/.

refinery /ri-fie-ne-ree/ *n* a place for purifying sugar, oil, etc.

reflect /ri-flect/ *vb* **1** (*of a mirror*) to show the image of. **2** to throw back, especially rays of light or heat. **3** to think about carefully (*reflect on the best course of action*). **4** to be a cause (of praise or blame) for (*his behavior reflects badly on his parents*).

reflection /ri-flec-shun/ *n* **1** the image seen in a mirror, etc. (*her reflection in the store window*). **2** the act of reflecting (light, an image, etc.). **3** a deep or careful thought (*on reflection I think we*

will go). **4** blame (*his bad conduct is a reflection on his parents*).

reflective /ri-flec-tiv/ *adj* thoughtful (*in a reflective mood*).

reflector /ri-flec-tor/ *n* a polished surface for reflecting light or heat.

reflex /ree-fleks/ *adj* automatic (*jerking your leg when the kneecap is tapped is a reflex action*). ● *n* an unintentional movement of the body caused by something outside it.

reflex angle /ree-fleks ang-gel/ *n* an angle between 180 degrees and 360 degrees.

reform /ri-fawrm/ *vb* **1** to make or become better (*reform the system*). **2** to give up bad habits (*a criminal who promised to reform*). ● *n* a change for the better. ● *n* **reformer** /ri-fawr-mer/.

reformation /re-fur-**may**-shun/ *n* a thorough change for the better. ●

refract /ri-fract/ *vb* to change the direction of (a ray of light, sound, etc.). ● *n* **refraction** /ri-frac-shun/.

refrain[1] /ri-frain/ *vb* to hold (yourself) back from doing something (*refrained from saying what they thought*).

refrain[2] /ri-frain/ *n* a line or phrase that is repeated several times in a song or poem, a chorus.

refresh /ri-fresh/ *vb* to give new strength, energy, power, etc. (*felt refreshed after a night's sleep*). ● *adj* **refreshing** /ri-fre-shing/. ● *adv* **refreshingly** /ri-fresh-ing-lee/.

refreshment /ri-fresh-ment/ *n* (*often pl*) a light meal, a snack, a drink (*provide refreshments for the party guests*).

refrigerate /ri-fri-je-rate/ *vb* to make cold, to freeze (*refrigerate the meat to keep it fresh*). ● *n* **refrigeration** /ri-fri-je-ray-shun/.

refrigerator /ri-fri-je-ray-tur/ *n* an apparatus for preserving food, etc., by keeping it cold.

refuel /ree-fyool/ *vb* (of an aircraft or a ship) to take on more fuel.

refuge /ref-yoodge/ *n* a place of shelter from danger or distress (*a national wildlife refuge*).

refugee /re-fyoo-jee/ *n* a person who is fleeing from danger, a person who leaves his or her country to seek shelter in another (*refugees from the famine area*).

refund /ri-fund/ *vb* to repay. ● *n* **refund** /ree-fund/ **1** the act of refunding. **2** the amount refunded (*get a refund for the faulty goods*).

refurbish /ri-fur-bish/ *vb* to redecorate or restore (*the restaurant was completely refurbished*).

refusal /ri-**fyoo**-zal/ *n* act of refusing (*their refusal of the invitation/his refusal to go*).

refuse[1] /ri-**fyooz**/ *vb* **1** not to accept (*refuse the invitation*). **2** to say that you will not do or give something (*refuse to plead guilty*).

refuse[2] /**ref**-yooss/ n (*Br*) *see* **garbage**.

refute /ri-**fyoot**/ *vb* to prove (an argument) wrong (*refuting the suggestion that he was wrong*). ● *n* **refutation** /ri-**fyoo**-tay-shun/.

regain /ri-**gain**/ *vb* **1** to get possession of again (*regain the throne*). **2** to reach again (*regain the shore*).

regal /**ree**-gal/ *adj* of or like a king, royal, magnificent (*a regal procession*).

regale /ri-**gale**/ *vb* **1** to supply with plenty of food and drink. **2** to entertain (*regaling them with stories of his adventures*).

regalia /ri-**gay**-lee-a/ *npl* objects worn or carried as signs of royalty (e.g., a crown, etc.) or high office.

regard /ri-**gard**/ *vb* **1** to consider (*regarded as a nuisance by his teachers*). **2** (*fml*) to look at (*he regarded her questioningly*). ● *n* **1** respect (*she is held in high regard*). **2** (*fml*) attention (*have regard to the icy roads*). ● *npl* **regards** good wishes (*send your mother my regards*).

regarding /ri-**gar**-ding/ *prep* concerning (*suggestions regarding the new plans*).

regardless /ri-**gard**-less/ *adv* paying no attention, not caring about (*regardless of cost*).

regatta /ri-**ga**-ta/ *n* a race meeting for boats and yachts.

regency /**ree**-jen-see/ *n* **1** rule by a regent. **2** the office of regent. **3** the period during which a regent rules.

regenerate /ri-**je**-ne-rate/ *vb* to improve after a period of worsening, to give fresh faith or energy to (*try to regenerate the club by bringing in young members*). ● *n* **regeneration** /ri-je-ne-**ray**-shun/.

regent[1] /**ree**-jent/ *n* a person who governs during the youth, absence, or illness of a monarch.

reggae /**re**-gay/ *n* a type of popular music of West Indian origin.

regime /ray-**zheem**/ *n* a method or system of government (*a military regime*).

regiment /**re**-ji-ment/ *n* a body of soldiers commanded by a colonel, an army unit consisting of several battalions.

regimental /re-ji-**men**-tal/ *adj* having to do with a regiment (*a regimental mascot*).

regimentation /re-ji-men-**tay**-shun/ *n* strict organization and control.

region /**ree**-jun/ *n* **1** a part of a country, often a large area of land (*the coastal region*). **2** neighborhood (*a pain in the region of his kidney/a price in the region of $5000*). ● *adj* **regional** /**reej**-nal/.

register /**re**-ji-ster/ *n* **1** an official list (*a register of qualified doctors*). **2** a book in which records (e.g., of births, deaths, school attendance, etc.) are kept. **3** the distance from the highest to the lowest note of a singing voice or musical instrument. ● *vb* **1** to write down in a register (*register a complaint*). **2** to give details to an official for writing in a register (*register the baby's birth*). **3** to pay extra postage to ensure that a letter or parcel reaches its destination safely (*register the parcel containing the medicine*). **4** to show (what one is feeling) (*her face registered dismay*).

registrar /**re**-ji-strar/ *n* an official who keeps a register.

registration /re-ji-**stray**-shun/ *n* act of registering.

registry /**re**-ji-stree/ *n* an office where official records of births, deaths, marriages, etc., are kept.

regress /ri-**gress**/ *vb* to move backward (*the patient's condition is regressing*). ● *adj* **regressive** /ri-**gre**-siv/.

regression /ri-**gre**-shun/ *n* backward movement, a falling away.

regret /ri-**gret**/ *vb* (**regretted** /ri-**gre**-tid/, **regretting** /ri-**gre**-ting/) **1** to be sorry for what one has said or done (*he regrets his foolish action*). **2** to remember with sorrow (*regrets his criminal days*). ● *n* sorrow, grief (*feel regret for his foolish actions/feel regret at her absence*). ● *adj* **regretful** /ri-**gret**-ful/. ● *adv* **regretfully** /ri-**gret**-fu-lee/.

regrettable /ri-**gre**-ta-bul/ *adj* unfortunate, unwelcome (*it is regrettable that such behavior is allowed*). ● *adv* **regrettably** /ri-**gre**-ta-blee/.

regular /**re**-gyu-lar/ *adj* **1** normal, usual (*his regular route*). **2** done always in the same way or at the same time (*regular habits*). **3** occurring acting, etc. with equal amounts of space, time, etc. between (*a regular pulse/guards placed at regular intervals*). **4** belonging to the regular army. **5** the same on both or all sides (*a girl with regular features*). **6** ordinary, normal (*just a regular guy*). ● *n* **1** a habitual customer (*one of the local pub's regulars*). **2** a soldier of the regular army. ● *n* **regularity** /re-gyu-**la**-ri-tee/. ● *adv* **regularly** /**re**-gyu-lar-lee/.

regular army /**re**-gyu-lar-**ar**-mee/ *n* that part of the army in which people who wish to make soldiering their career are kept in training.

regulate /**re**-gyu-late/ *vb* **1** to control (*regulate expenditure*). **2** to alter (a machine) until it is working properly (*regulate a watch*).

regulation /re-gyu-**lay**-shun/ *n* a rule, an order, an instruction (*obey the club's regulations*). ● *adj* as laid down in the rules (*regulation sportswear*).

regulator /**re**-gyu-lay-tur/ *n* **1** a lever by which you can control a machine. **2** a person who controls.

regurgitate /ri-**gur**-ji-tate/ *vb* (*fml*) **1** to throw up again from the stomach (*the sick dog regurgitated its food*). **2** to repeat without change (*simply regurgitating what his teacher told him*).

rehabilitate /ree-ha-**bi**-li-tate/ *vb* to bring back to a normal life or normal standards of behavior by treatment or instruction (*rehabilitate criminals/ rehabilitate soldiers wounded in battle*). ● *n* **rehabilitation** /ree-ha-bi-li-**tay**-shun/.

rehearsal /ri-**her**-sal/ *n* a practice before a performance (*the last rehearsal before the opening night*).

rehearse /ri-**herss**/ *vb* **1** to practice, especially in preparation for public performance (*rehearse for the performance*). **2** (*fml*) to repeat aloud, to give a list of (*rehearse the various rules*).

reign /**rane**/ *n* **1** rule. **2** the time during which a king or queen has ruled. ● *vb* **1** to rule as a sovereign. **2** to exist (*silence reigned*).

reimburse /ree-im-**burse**/ *vb* to repay what someone has lost or spent (*have his travel expenses reimbursed by the company*). ● *n* **reimbursement** /ree-im-**burse**-ment/.

rein /**rane**/ *n* **1** the strap by which a driver or rider directs a horse. **2** control (*keep a tight rein on expenses*). ● *vb* to check or control with the rein (*rein in the horse*).

reindeer /**rane**-deer/ *n* a deer found in northern parts of America and Europe.

reinforce /ree-in-**force**/ *vb* **1** to make stronger (*reinforce the elbows of the coat with leather patches*). **2** to supply with more soldiers, helpers, etc. (*reinforce the aid workers with new recruits*).

reinforcement /ree-in-**foarss**-ment/ *n* the act of reinforcing. ● *npl* **reinforcements** /ree-in-**foarss**-ments/ more or fresh troops, etc. (*the aid workers require reinforcements*).

reinstate /ree-in-**state**/ *vb* to put back in a former position (*he was fired from his post but has been reinstated*). ● *n* **reinstatement** /ree-in-**state**-ment/.

reiterate /ree-**i**-te-rate/ *vb* to repeat again and again (*reiterate the instructions*). ● *n* **reiteration** /ree-i-te-**ray**-shun/.

reject /ri-**ject**/ *vb* **1** to refuse to accept (*reject the criticism*). **2** to throw back or away (*reject goods that were not up to standard*). ● *n* **reject** someone or something that has been rejected. ● *n* **rejection** /ri-**jec**-shun/.

rejoice /ri-**joiss**/ *vb* to be glad or joyful, to make glad, to express your joy (*the team rejoicing at their victory*).

rejoicing /ri-**joy**-sing/ *n* a feeling or expression of joy. ● *npl* **rejoicings** celebrations.

rejuvenate /ri-**joo**-vi-nate/ *vb* to make feel young again. ● *n* **rejuvenation** /ri-joo-vi-**nay**-shun/.

relapse /ri-**lapss**/ *vb* to fall back into evil or sickness after improving (*she was getting better after surgery, but she has suffered a relapse*). ● *n* **relapse** /ri-lapss/.

relate /ri-**late**/ *vb* **1** to show or see the connection between (*the rise in crime may be related to poverty*). **2** (*fml*) to tell (*related the story of his escape*). ● *adj* **related** /ri-**lay**-tid/.

relation /ri-**lay**-shun/ *n* **1** a person who belongs to the same family by birth or marriage (*invite all their relations to the wedding*). **2** a connection (*a possible relation between crime and unemployment*). **3** (*fml*) a story, an account. ● *n* **relationship** /ri-**lay**-shun-ship/.

relative /**re**-la-tiv/ *adj* **1** considered in comparison with others (*the relative methods of the two systems*). **2** having to do with (*facts relating to the present situation*). **3** (*fml*) (*in grammar*) referring to an earlier word in the sentence. ● *n* a person who belongs to the same family, by birth or marriage (*relatives on the mother's side*).

relatively /**re**-la-tiv-lee/ *adv* **1** quite (*she is still relatively young*). **2** when compared with others (*compared with flying, rail travel is relatively cheap*).

relax /ri-**laks**/ *vb* **1** to take a complete rest, to become less tense or worried (*relax by listening to music*). **2** to loosen (*relaxed his grip on the rope*). **3** to become or make less strict or severe (*relaxed the rules toward the end of the semester*).

relaxation /ree-lak-**say**-shun/ *n* **1** rest, amusement after work (*go to the movies for relaxation*). **2** loosening (*relaxation of his grip*). **3** making less severe (*relaxation of the rules*).

relaxing /ri-**lak**-sing/ *adj* **1** restful. **2** causing a feeling of tiredness.

relay /**ree**-lay/ *n* **1** a supply of fresh men or horses to take over from tired ones (*a relay of firefighters*). **2** a relay race. **3** the sending out of a radio or television signal or show that has been received from somewhere else. ● *vb* to rebroadcast a radio message or show received from elsewhere.

relay race /**ree**-lay-race/ *n* a team race in which each member of a team covers part of the whole distance.

release /ri-**leess**/ *vb* **1** to set free (*release the prisoner*). **2** to let go (*released his hold of the rope*). **3** to unfasten (*release the safety catch on the gun*). **4** to make public (*released the details of the president's death*). ● *also n*.

relegate /**re**-li-gate/ *vb* to put down to a lower position (*the story was relegated to page 16*).

relent /ri-**lent**/ *vb* to become less severe, to give way (*their mother relented and let the children go to the party*).

relentless /ri-**lent**-less/ *adj* without pity, unmerciful, continuous (*relentless criticism*). ● *adv* **relentlessly** /ri-**lent**-less-lee/.

relevant /**re**-li-vant/ *adj* having to do with the matter under consideration (*discuss matters relevant to the situation*). ● *ns* **relevance** /**re**-li-vanse/, **relevancy** /**re**-li-van-see/.

reliability /ri-lie-a-**bi**-li-tee/ *n* trustworthiness.

reliable /ri-**lie**-a-bul/ *adj* able to be trusted (*reliable witness*). ● *adv* **reliably** /ri-**lie**-a-blee/.

reliance /ri-**lie**-anse/ *n* trust, confidence (*put their reliance in his judgment*).

reliant /ri-**lie**-ant/ *adj* relying on, depending on (*reliant on the financial help of her parents*).

relic /**re**-lic/ *n* something old-fashioned that still exists (*a village custom that is a relic of colonial times*). ● *npl* **relics** /**re**-lics/ (*fml*) a dead body.

relief /ri-**leef**/ *n* **1** complete or partial freeing from pain or worry (*treatment that gave her some relief*). **2** money, etc., given to the poor or those who have lost everything in a disaster (*charitable organizations sent relief to the refugees*). **3** a person who takes another's place on duty (*the bus driver waited for his relief*). **4** forcing an enemy to end the siege of a town (*the relief of Mafeking*). **5** a piece of sculpture in which the design stands out just beyond a flat surface. **6** a clear outline.

relieve /ri-**leev**/ *vb* **1** to set free from or lessen (pain or worry) (*a medicine to relieve her back pain*). **2** to give help to. **3** to take another's place on duty (*relieve the soldier on duty*). **4** to force an enemy to end the siege of a town (*the army marched to relieve the city*).

religion /ri-**li**-jun/ *n* **1** belief in and worship of a god or gods. **2** belief, faith. **3** love of God.

religious /ri-**li**-jus/ *adj* **1** loving God. **2** holy. ● *adv* **religiously** /ri-**li**-jus-lee/.

relinquish /ri-**ling**-kwish/ *vb* to give up (*relinquish his post as manager*).

relish /**rel**-ish/ *vb* **1** to enjoy the taste of (*relish a glass of good wine*). **2** to like or enjoy (*relish a competitive game of tennis*). ● *n* **1** a taste, flavor. **2** enjoyment. **3** a sharp-tasting sauce (*put relish on your hamburger*).

relive /ree-**liv**/ *vb* to remember (an experience) in detail as if living through it again.

reluctant /ri-**luc**-tant/ *adj* unwilling (*reluctant to speak in public*). ● *n* **reluctance**. ● *adv* **reluctantly** /ri-**luc**-tant-lee/.

rely /ri-**lie**/ *vb* **1** to trust in (*relying on his judgment*). **2** to depend on (*relied on her parents for financial help*).

remain /ri-**main**/ *vb* **1** to stay on in a place (*asked to remain in the house*). **2** to be left over (*a little money remained after the bills had been paid*). **3** to continue to be (*they remained friends*).

remainder /ri-**main**-der/ *n* that which is left over or behind (*for the remainder of the evening*).

remains /ri-**mainz**/ *npl* **1** that which is left (*the remains of the meal*). **2** (*fml*) a dead body (*bury his remains this afternoon*).

remand /ri-**mand**/ *vb* to send back to prison while further inquiries are being made (*the accused has been remanded*). ● *n* **1** act of remanding. **2** the state of being remanded.

remark /ri-**mark**/ *vb* **1** to say (*she remarked that it was a pleasant day*). **2** to comment (on) (*he remarked on her beautiful ring*). ● *n* **1** something said (*he made a remark about her appearance*). **2** (*fml*) notice, attention (*clothing that could not escape remark*).

remarkable /ri-**mar**-ka-bul/ *adj* worthy of notice, extraordinary (*of remarkable intelligence/a remarkable performance*). ● *adv* **remarkably** /ri-**mar**-ka-blee/.

remedial /ri-**mee**-dee-al/ *adj* intended or helping to cure.

remedy /**re**-mi-dee/ *n* **1** a cure (*a remedy for headaches*). **2** a medicine (*herbal remedies*). **3** any way of putting right what is wrong (*seek a remedy for truancy*). ● *vb* **1** to cure. **2** to put right (*remedy the injustice*).

remember /ri-**mem**-ber/ *vb* **1** to keep in mind (*remember her youth with pleasure*). **2** to recall to the mind (*try to remember his name*). **3** to give greetings from another (*remember me to your father*).

remembrance /ri-**mem**-branss/ *n* **1** memory. **2** a souvenir.

remind /ri-**minde**/ *vb* to cause to remember (*you will have to remind him to come to the meeting*).

reminder /ri-**mine**-der/ *n* something that helps you to remember (*sent him a reminder about the unpaid bill*).

reminisce /re-mi-**niss**/ *vb* to tell stories of your past (*old people reminiscing about their youth*).

reminiscence /re-mi-**ni**-sense/ *n* **1** a memory of your past (*a childhood reminiscence*). **2** the remembering of the past. ● *npl* **reminiscences** /re-mi-**ni**-sen-seez/ stories about your past.

reminiscent /re-mi-**ni**-sent/ *adj* **1** remembering the past (*in a reminiscent mood*). **2** reminding of the past (*a style reminiscent of Renoir*).

remiss /ri-**miss**/ *adj* (*fml*) careless, not doing your duty properly (*it was remiss of them to forget their father's birthday*).

remission /re-mi-**shun**/ *n* **1** the reduction of a prison sentence (*you will be given six months' remission for good behavior*). **2** a period when an illness is less severe (*the cancer patient is in remission at the moment*).

remnant /**rem**-nant/ *n* a small piece or part left over, especially of fabric (*make an apron with the remnant*).

remorse /re-**mawrss**/ *n* great sorrow for having done wrong (*he showed remorse for his crimes*). ● *adj* **remorseful** /re-**mawrss**-ful/. ● *adv* **remorsefully** / re-**mawrss**-fu-lee/.

remorseless /re-**mawrss**-less/ *adj* feeling no remorse, pitiless (*a remorseless tyrant*). ● *adv* **remorselessly** /re-**mawrss**-less-lee/.

remote /ri-**mote**/ *adj* **1** distant, far away, out of the way (*a remote village*). **2** not closely related (*a remote cousin/a remote connection*). **3** not friendly, withdrawn (*a remote manner*). **4** slight (*a remote chance of success*). ● *adv* **remotely** /ri-**mote**-lee/.

remote control /ri-mote-cun-**trole**/ *n* **1** a system that allows a device or machine to be controlled from a distance, using electrical, electronic, or radio signals (*a model boat operated by remote control*). **2** *also* (*inf*) **remote** a handheld device that enables the user to operate a television set, etc. from a distance.

removal /ri-**moo**-val/ *n* **1** act of removing (*the removal of the stain from the fabric*). **2** a change of dwelling place (*the removal will be completed by the weekend*).

remove /ri-**moov**/ *vb* **1** to take from its place (*re-move a book from the shelf*). **2** to take off (*remove his socks*). **3** to dismiss (*remove him from the post of manager*). ● *adj* **removable** /ri-**moo**-va-bul/.

Renaissance /ri-nay-**sanss**/ *n* a revival, especially of interest in arts and learning, as in the 15th century.

render /**ren**-der/ *vb* **1** to give (*for services rendered*). **2** to perform in a certain way (*a piano solo beautifully rendered*). **3** to translate (*render the Latin passage into English*). **4** to cause to be (*her reply rendered him speechless*).

rendering /**ren**-dring/ *n* **1** a translation. **2** a particular performance.

rendezvous /**ron**-day-voo/ *n* **1** (*fml*) an agreed meeting place (*the summer house was the lovers' usual rendezvous*). **2** a meeting (*a midnight rendezvous*).

rendition /ren-**di**-shun/ *n* a particular performance (*his rendition of "Danny Boy"*).

renew /ri-**noo**/ *vb* **1** to make new again (*renew his club membership*). **2** to begin again (*renew their assault on the town*). ● *adj* **renewable** /ri-**noo**-a-bul/. ● *n* **renewal** /ri-**noo**-al/.

renounce /ri-**nounss**/ *vb* **1** to give up (*renounce his claim to the throne*). **2** to state that you will have nothing more to do with (*renounce his religion*). ● *n* **renunciation** /ri-nun-see-**ay**-shun/.

renovate /**re**-nu-vate/ *vb* to make like new, to repair and clean (*renovate the old building/renovate the couch*). ● *n* **renovation** /re-nu-**vay**-shun/.

renown /ri-**noun**/ *n* fame, glory (*he won renown as a writer*).

renowned /ri-**nound**/ *adj* famous (*a renowned scientist*).

rent[1] /**rent**/ *n* a payment made for the use of land, a house, etc. ● *vb* **1** to get the use of by paying rent (*students rent a house from him*). **2** to let or hire out for rent (*rent his apartment to students*).

rent[2] /**rent**/ *n* (*fml*) a tear, a split (*a rent in the drapes*).

rental /**ren**-tal/ *n* rent, the sum paid in rent (*TV rental*).

repair /ri-**pair**/ *vb* **1** to mend (*repair the broken fence*). **2** to put right, make up for (*repair the wrong done to them*). **3** to go. ● *n* **1** returning to good condition, mending. **2** a mended place (*the obvious repair to the dress*). **3** condition for using (*in poor repair*).

repay /ri-**pay**/ *vb* **1** to pay back (*repay the money borrowed*). **2** to treat in a like way (*repay her kindness with abuse*).

repayment /ri-**pay**-ment/ *n* **1** the act of repaying. **2** the sum repaid.

repeal /ri-**peel**/ *vb* to withdraw, to set aside, to abolish (*to repeal the law*). ● *also n.*

repeat /ri-**peet**/ *vb* **1** to do or say again (*repeat the order/repeat the task*). **2** to speak aloud something learned by heart (*repeat a poem*). ● *n* (*Br*) *see* **rerun** /**ree**-run/.

repeatedly /ri-**pee**-tid-lee/ *adv* again and again (*he hit the target repeatedly*).

repel /ri-**pel**/ *vb* (**repelled** /ri-**peld**/, **repelling** /ri-**pe**-ling/) **1** to cause dislike (*he is so dirty he repels me*). **2** to drive back (*repel the enemy army*).

repellent /ri-**pe**-lent/ *adj* causing dislike or disgust (*a repellent sight*). ● *n* that which is able to repel or drive away something (*an insect repellent*).

repent /ri-**pent**/ *vb* to feel sorry for having said or done something (*repent his wickedness*). ● *n* **repentance** /ri-**pen**-tanse/. ● *adj* **repentant** /ri-**pen**-tant/.

repertoire /**re**-per-twar/ *n* **1** a performer's stock of musical pieces, poems, etc. (*the comedian's repertoire of jokes*). **2** a company's stock of plays that are ready for acting.

repetition /re-pi-**ti**-shun/ *n* **1** act of repeating (*his repetition of the instructions*). **2** saying from memory (*the child's repetition of the poem*). ● *adj* **repetitious** /re-pi-**ti**-shus/.

replace /ri-**place**/ *vb* **1** to put back in place (*replacing the book on the shelf*). **2** to take the place of (*she replaced him as school principal*).

replacement /ri-**place**-ment/ *n* **1** act of replacing. **2** a person or thing that takes the place of another.

replenish /ri-**ple**-nish/ *vb* to fill up again (*replenish the guests' glasses*). ● *n* **replenishment** /ri-**ple**-nish-ment/.

replica /**re**-pli-ca/ *n* **1** an exact copy of a work of art (*a replica of the original piece*). **2** a reproduction, especially of a smaller size (*a replica of the Statue of Liberty*).

replicate /**re**-pli-cate/ *vb* to make an exact copy of.

reply /ri-**plie**/ *vb* to answer (*replied to their questions/replying to their initiative*). ● *n* an answer.

report /ri-**poart**/ *vb* **1** to give as news or information, to tell (*report a new medical development*). **2** to write an account of, especially for a newspaper (*she reported on foreign affairs for a national newspaper*). **3** to make a complaint about for having done wrong (*report the boys who played hooky to the teacher*). **4** to tell someone in authority (*report the theft to the police*). ● *n* **1** a spoken or writ-ten account of work performed (e.g., by a committee, a student). **2** an account of something that has been said or done, especially when written for a newspaper. **3** a rumor (*there were reports that he had married*). **4** a loud noise (*a report from a gun*).

reporter /ri-**poar**-ter/ *n* a person who reports for a newspaper or television/radio broadcast.

repose /ri-**poaz**/ *vb* **1** (*fml*) to lay at rest, to lie at rest. **2** to place (*repose her trust in someone not worthy of it*). ● *n* **1** rest, sleep (*seek repose*). **2** calmness (*her face in repose*).

represent /re-pri-**zent**/ *vb* **1** to stand for, or make to stand for, as a sign or likeness (*the white dove representing peace*). **2** to be a picture or statue of. **3** to have the right to speak or act for (*the lawyer representing her*). **4** to describe or declare, perhaps falsely (*he represented himself as someone whom they could trust*). **5** (*fml*) to be, to constitute (*it represented a considerable improvement on previous attendance figures*). **6** to be the representative of (a firm).

representation /re-pri-zen-**tay**-shun/ *n* **1** the act of representing or being represented. **2** an image or likeness (*a representation of the king in oils*). **3** (*fml*) a protest or objection (*make representations about the rise in fees*).

representative /re-pri-**zen**-ta-tiv/ *adj* typical, standing for others of the same class (*a representative sample*). ● *n* **1** a person who acts for another (*the lawyer acted as her representative*). **2** a person who sells goods for a business firm (*a representative for a publisher*). **3** an elected member of the house of representatives.

repress /ri-**press**/ *vb* to keep under control, to keep down, to restrain (*repress a desire to laugh*).

repression /ri-**pre**-shun/ *n* strict control, restraint.

repressive /ri-**pre**-siv/ *adj* (*fml*) intended to keep down or restrain (*a repressive form of government*).

reprieve /ri-**preev**/ *vb* to let off punishment, to pardon (*he faced the death sentence but was reprieved*). ● *also n.*

reprimand /**re**-pri-mand/ *n* a severe scolding. ● *vb* to scold severely (*reprimand the children for their manners*).

reprint /ree-**print**/ *vb* to print again. ● *n* **reprint** /**ree**-print/ a new printing or edition.

reprisal /ri-**prie**-zal/ *n* something done by way of punishment or revenge (*their raid was a reprisal for our earlier attacks*).

reproach /ri-**proach**/ *vb* to accuse and blame, to scold, usually with a suggestion of sadness or disappointment (*she reproached him for letting everyone down*). ● *n* **1** scolding, blame (*a look of reproach/words of reproach*). **2** something that brings shame (*his bad conduct brought reproach on his family*).

reproachful /ri-**proach**-ful/ *adj* accusing, shameful.

reproduce /ree-pru-**dooss**/ *vb* **1** to cause to be heard, seen, or done again (*unable to reproduce the results/try to reproduce the atmosphere of the last party/reproduce sound*). **2** to increase by having offspring (*rabbits reproduce rapidly*). ● *n* **reproduction** /ree-pru-**duc**-shun/. ● *adj* **reproductive** /ree-pru-**duc**-tiv/.

reptile /**rep**-tile/ *n* a class of cold-blooded animals that crawl or creep (e.g., snake, lizard).

republic /ri-**pub**-lic/ *n* a state entirely governed by elected persons, there being no sovereign.

republican /ri-**pu**-bli-can/ *adj* having to do with a republic. ● *n* a person who prefers republican government.

Republican /ri-**pu**-bli-can/ *n* a member or supporter of the Republican Party (*the elephant is the emblem of the Republican Party*). ● *adj* **Republican** / ri-**pu**-bli-can/.

repugnance /ri-**pug**-nanse/ *n* disgust.

repugnant /ri-**pug**-nant/ *adj* (*fml*) very unpleasant, disgusting (*a repugnant smell*).

repulse /ri-**pulss**/ *vb* (*fml*) **1** to drive back, to defeat (*repulse the enemy attacks*). **2** to refuse sharply (*to repulse his offer*). ● *n* **1** a defeat. **2** a refusal.

repulsion /ri-**pul**-shun/ *n* dislike, disgust.

repulsive /ri-**pul**-siv/ *adj* hateful, disgusting (*a repulsive sight/a repulsive, dirty old man*).

reputable /**re**-pyu-ta-bul/ *adj* having a good name, respectable (*a reputable real-estate agent*).

reputation /re-pyu-**tay**-shun/ *n* **1** your good name, your character as seen by other people (*it would damage her reputation to be seen with such a crook*). **2** fame (*establish a reputation as an artist*).

repute /ri-**pyoot**/ *n* reputation. ● *vb* to consider to be.

reputed /ri-**pyoo**-tid/ *adj* supposed (to be) (*she is reputed to be very wealthy*).

reputedly /ri-**pyoo**-tid-lee/ *adv* as is commonly supposed.

request /ri-**kwest**/ *vb* to ask for (*request them to order a book/request a piece of music to be played*). ● *n* **1** the act of asking for something (*go there at his request*). **2** a favor asked for (*grant his request*).

requiem /**re**-kwee-em/ *n* **1** a church service in which prayers are said for a dead person. **2** a musical composition for the dead.

require /ri-**kwire**/ *vb* **1** to need (*we have all we require to make the meal*). **2** to demand by right, to order (*the children are required to attend school*).

requirement /ri-**kwire**-ment/ *n* **1** a need, something needed (*a store that is able to supply all our requirements*). **2** a necessary condition (*a requirement for entry to university*).

rerun /**ree**-run/ *n* a television show that is broadcast again.

rescue /**re**-scyoo/ *vb* to save from danger or evil (*rescue the dog from drowning*). ● *n* act of rescuing. ● *n* **rescuer** /**re**-scyoo-er/.

research /ree-**search**/ *n* careful study to discover new facts (*engaged in medical research*). ● *also v.*

resemble /ri-**zem**-bul/ *vb* to be like (*she resembled her mother*). ● *n* **resemblance** /ri-**zem**-blanss/.

resent /ri-**zent**/ *vb* to be angered by, to take as an insult (*resent their interference in her life*).

resentful /ri-**zent**-ful/ *adj* showing anger, full of annoyance (*resentful of their interference/a resentful look*). ● *adv* **resentfully** /ri-**zent**-fu-lee/.

resentment /ri-**zent**-ment/ *n* anger, indignation (*feel resentment at their treatment*).

reservation /re-zer-**vay**-shun/ *n* **1** something kept back. **2** a condition. **3** land set aside for some special purpose (e.g., as a place for Native Americans to live). **4** a booked place or seat.

reserve /ri-**zerv**/ *vb* **1** (*fml*) to keep back for future use (*reserve some food for later*). **2** to order or book for future use (*reserve seats at the movies*). ● *n* **1** something kept back for future use (*a reserve of money for emergencies*). **2** land set aside for some special purpose (*a nature reserve*). **3** shyness, unwillingness to show your feelings (*her reserve made her appear unfriendly*). ● *npl* **reserves** /ri-**zervz**/ troops kept out of battle for use where and when needed.

reserved /ri-**zervd**/ *adj* shy, not showing what you are thinking or feeling (*a very reserved young woman*).

reservoir /**re**-zerv-war/ *n* **1** a place where the water supply of a city is stored. **2** a store (*a reservoir of oil/a reservoir of information*).

reside /ri-**zide**/ *vb* to dwell, to live (in).

residence /**re**-si-denss/ *n* dwelling, house.

residency /**re**-si-den-sees/ *n* the house of an official, e.g., a governor.

resident /**re**-si-dent/ *n* a person who lives somewhere (*a resident of Boston*). ● *also adj.*

residential /re-si-**den**-shal/ *adj* **1** suitable for living in. **2** (*of a district*) having many dwelling houses.

residual /ri-**zi**-ju-wal/ *adj* (*fml*) left after the rest has been taken (*his residual income after the bills were paid*).

residue /**re**-zi-doo/ *n* the remainder, what is left over (*he left most of his estate to his children, and the residue was divided among his nephews*).

resign /ri-**zine**/ *vb* **1** to give up (*resigned his post as manager*). **2** to give up an office or a post (*he threatened to resign*). **3** to accept with complaint (*he resigned himself to defeat*). ● *n* **resignation** /ri-zig-**nay**-shun/.

resigned /ri-**ziend**/ *adj* accepting trouble with complaint, patient (*a resigned attitude to trouble/she was resigned to a life of poverty*).

resilient /ri-**zil**-yint/ *adj* **1** able to spring back to a former position after being bent (*rubber is a resilient material*). **2** having good powers of recovery (*she has had much misfortune but has been very resilient*). ● *n* **resilience** /ri-**zil**-yinss/.

resin /**re**-zin/ *n* a sticky substance that oozes from certain plants, e.g., firs, pines, etc. ● *adj* **resinous** /**rez**-nuss/.

resist /ri-**zist**/ *vb* **1** to stand against, to fight against, to oppose (*resist the enemy advances*). **2** to face or allow yourself not to accept (*she cannot resist chocolate cake*).

resistance /ri-**zis**-tanse/ *n* the act or power of resisting, opposition (*to put up no resistance to the invading army*).

resistant /ri-**zis**-tant/ *adj* offering resistance.

resolute /**re**-zu-loot/ *adj* determined, bold, having the mind made up (*resolute in their efforts to succeed*). ● *adv* **resolutely** /**re**-zu-**loot**-lee/.

resolution /re-zu-**loo**-shun/ *n* **1** determination (*proceed with resolution*). **2** a firm intention (*a New Year's resolution to take more exercise*). **3** a proposal for a meeting to vote on (*those in favor of the resolution raised their hands*). **4** the decision of a meeting on a certain matter (*pass a resolution to change the rules*). **5** (*fml*) the act of solving (*the resolution of the problem*).

resolve /ri-**zolv**/ *vb* **1** to determine (*resolve to try again*). **2** to break up into parts or elements (*resolve a chemical substance*). **3** to solve (*resolve the problem*). ● *n* **1** a fixed purpose (*his resolve was to make a lot of money*). **2** determination (*proceed with resolve*).

resonant /**re**-zu-nant/ *adj* **1** echoing. **2** deep-sounding (*a resonant voice*). ● *n* **resonance** /**re**-zu-nanse/.

resort /ri-**zawrt**/ *vb* to make use of, to turn to (*resort to crime to pay his debts*). ● *n* **1** a place to which you go frequently. **2** a place where many people go on vacation. ● **as a last resort** as a last possibility (*as a last resort he can borrow from his father*).

resound /ri-**zound**/ *vb* to echo, to give back the sound of (*the cave resounded to the children's shouts*).

resounding /ri-**zoun-ding**/ *adj* **1** echoing. **2** very great (*a resounding success*).

resource /ri-**zoarss**/ *n* **1** a means of obtaining help, something turned to in time of need (*the local library was a useful learning resource*). **2** (*often pl*) a source of economic wealth, especially of a country (*oil is one of this nation's most valuable resources*).

resourceful /ri-**zoarss**-ful/ *adj* full of clever plans (*his resourceful use of materials saved money*).

respect /ri-**spect**/ *vb* **1** to think highly of (*respect him as a writer*). **2** to pay attention to (*respect their wishes*). ● *n* **1** honor (*treat older people with respect*). **2** care or attention (*treat their wishes with respect*). ● *npl* **respects** /ri-**spects**/ good wishes (*send his respects to the old man*).

respectability /ri-spec-ta-**bi**-li-tee/ *n* **1** state of deserving respect. **2** decency.

respectable /ri-**spec**-ta-bul/ *adj* **1** deserving respect, decent (*not thought respectable by the neighbors*) **2** socially acceptable (*respectable clothing*). **3** large enough, good enough, etc. (*a respectable score*). ● *adv* **respectably** /ri-**spec**-ta-blee/.

respectful /ri-**spect**-ful/ *adj* showing respect or honor to (*children told to be respectful to their elders/a respectful silence at the funeral*). ● *adv* **respectfully** /ri-**spect**-ful-ee/.

respecting /ri-**spec**-ting/ *prep* (*fml*) having to do with (*respecting his position in the firm*).

respective /ri-**spec**-tiv/ *adj* each to his/her own, proper to each (*they all went to their respective homes*).

respectively /ri-**spec**-tiv-lee/ *adv* belonging to each in the order already mentioned (*James and John got grades of A and B plus, respectively*).

respiration /re-spi-**ray**-shun/ *n* (*fml*) breathing.

respirator /**re**-spi-ray-tor/ *n* a mask with a filter worn over the nose and mouth to purify the air breathed in.

respiratory /**resp**-ra-toe-ree/ *adj* (*fml*) having to do with breathing (*a respiratory infection*).

respond /ri-**spond**/ *vb* **1** to answer (*failed to respond to the question*). **2** to do as a reaction to something that has been done (*he smiled, but she did not respond*).

respondent /ri-**spon**-dent/ *n* (*fml*) the defendant in a lawsuit, especially in divorce.

response /ri-**sponss**/ *n* **1** an answer, a reply (*in response to the question*). **2** a reaction (*a magnificent response to the charity's appeal*).

responsible /ri-**spon**-si-bul/ *adj* **1** able to be trusted (*responsible members of staff*). **2** having to say or explain what you have done (*he is responsible for his actions*). **3** being the cause of something (*responsible for the confusion*). ● *n* **responsibility** /ri-spon-si-**bi**-li-tee/. ● *adv* **responsibly** /ri-**spon**-si-blee/.

responsive /ri-**spon**-siv/ *adj* quick to react (*responsive to the suggestions*).

rest[1] /**rest**/ *n* **1** a pause in work. **2** inactivity. **3** sleep (*a good night's rest*). **4** a support or prop (*he aimed the rifle using the wall as a rest*). ● *vb* **1** to cease from action. **2** to stop work for a time (*rest for a few minutes*). **3** to be still or quiet (*the young children are resting*). **4** to sleep or repose. **5** to be supported (by) (*his feet resting on the table*).

rest[2] /**rest**/ *n* that which is left, the remainder.

restaurant /**re**-strawnt/ *n* a place where one may buy and eat meals.

restaurateur /re-stu-ra-**tur**/ *n* a person who keeps a restaurant.

restful /**rest**-ful/ *adj* peaceful, quiet (*have a restful vacation*).

restive /**re**-stiv/ *adj* unable to keep still, impatient (*children getting restive at their desks*).

restless /**rest**-liss/ *adj* **1** always on the move (*too restless to stay in one job for long*). **2** not restful, giving no rest (*spent a restless night*).

restore /ri-**store**/ *vb* **1** to bring back (*restore law and order*). **2** to put back (*they restored him to his former post*). **3** to make strong again (*restored by his vacation*). **4** to bring back to an earlier state or condition (*restore old furniture*). ● *n* **restoration** /re-sto-**ray**-shun/.

restrain /ri-**strain**/ *vb* to hold back, to check (*restrain the dog from biting people*).

restraint /ri-**straint**/ *n* **1** self-control. **2** lack of freedom.

restrict /ri-**strict**/ *vb* to set limits to, to keep down (the number or amount of) (*restrict the amount of money spent/restrict their freedom*).

restriction /ri-**stric**-shun/ *n* a rule or condition that lessens freedom.

restrictive /ri-**stric**-tiv/ *adj* (*fml*) lessening freedom, keeping under control (*restrictive clothing*).

result /ri-**zult**/ *n* **1** that which happens as the effect of something else, the outcome (*the result of the election/as a result of the accident*). **2** the final score in a sports contest. ● *vb* **1** to follow as the effect of a cause (*blindness resulting from the accident*). **2** to end (in) (*the research resulted in a new drug on the market*).

resume /ri-**zoom**/ *vb* **1** (*fml*) to begin again (*he will resume his studies*). **2** to take back (*resume his seat after speaking*).

résumé /**re**-zu-may/ *n* **1** a summary (*the résumé of what happened at the meeting*). **2** a brief list of a person's qualifications, work experience and accomplishments.

resumption /ri-**zum**-shun/ *n* the act of resuming.

resurgence /ri-**sur**-jinse/ *n* (*fml*) a rising again (*a resurgence of terrorist activity*).

resurrect /re-zu-**rect**/ *vb* **1** to raise or bring back again (*resurrect an old law*). **2** to raise to life again after death (*Christians believe Christ was resurrected*).

resurrection /re-zu-**rec**-shun/ *n* a rising again from the dead.

resuscitate /ri-**su**-si-tate/ *vb* to bring back to life or consciousness (*try to resuscitate the man who had a heart attack*). ● *n* **resuscitation** /ri-su-si-**tay**-shun/.

retail /**ree**-tail/ *vb* **1** to sell direct to the public in small amounts (*he retails tobacco goods*). **2** to sell (*these sweaters retail at $50 each*). ● *n* the sale of goods in small quantities (*the retail trade*). ● *n* **retailer** /**ree**-tay-ler/.

retain /ri-**tain**/ *vb* **1** to continue to use, have, remember, etc. (*retain control of the firm/a town that has retained its churches*). **2** to hold back (*a wall built to retain the water*). **3** to engage someone's services by paying a fee in advance (*retain a lawyer*).

retainer /ri-**tay**-ner/ *n* **1** (*old*) a follower (*the king's retainers*). **2** an advance fee for someone's services (*the lawyer is paid a retainer*).

retaliate /ri-**ta**-lee-ate/ *vb* to return like for like, to get your own back (*she retaliated by punching him*). ● *n* **retaliation** /ri-ta-lee-**ay**-shun/.

retard /ri-**tard**/ *vb* to make slow or late, to make go more slowly, to delay (*the bad weather retarded the growth of the crops*). ● *n* **retardation** /ree-tar-**day**-shun/.

retch /**retch**/ *vb* to try to vomit. ● *also n*.

retention /ri-**ten**-shun/ *n* (*fml*) act of retaining.

reticent /**re**-ti-sent/ *adj* unwilling to speak to others, silent (*a reticent person/reticent about the cause of the quarrel*). ● *n* **reticence** /**re**-ti-senss/.

retina /re-ti-na/ *n* the inner layer of the eye to which are connected the ends of the nerves that enable us to see.

retire /ri-tire/ *vb* **1** to leave your work forever because of old age, illness, etc. (*he retired at the age of 60*). **2** to go to bed (*retire shortly after midnight*). **3** (*fml*) to go back or away (*the jury retired to consider their verdict*).

retired /ri-tierd/ *adj* **1** having given up your business or profession (*a retired businessman*). **2** out-of-the-way, quiet (*a retired country village*).

retirement /ri-tire-ment/ *n* **1** the act of retiring (*his early retirement was due to poor health*). **2** the time after you have finished your working life (*he spent his retirement enjoying his hobbies*).

retiring /ri-tie-ring/ *adj* shy, not fond of company (*he was a retiring young man who did not enjoy parties*).

retort /ri-tawrt/ *vb* to reply quickly or sharply. ● *n* **1** a quick or sharp reply. **2** a thin glass bottle with a long bent-back neck, used for heating chemicals.

retrace /re-trace/ *vb* to go back over again (*retrace your steps to look for the lost ring*).

retract /ri-tract/ *vb* to say that a previous opinion was wrong, to take back what you have said (*retract your accusation*). ● *n* **retraction** /ri-trac-shun/.

retreat /ri-treet/ *vb* **1** to go back (*they had to retreat from the fire*). **2** (of an army) to move back away from the enemy. ● *n* **1** act of retreating (*the retreat of the enemy*). **2** a quiet, out-of-the-way place, a place of peace and safety (*a popular country retreat*). **3** a period of rest, meditation, prayer, etc. (*spend a week in retreat*).

retribution /re-tri-byoo-shun/ *n* just punishment for wrong done (*take retribution on the terrorists*).

retrieve /ri-treev/ *vb* **1** to find again (*retrieve the glove she left behind*). **2** to find and bring back (*gun dogs retrieve birds killed by hunters*). **3** to undo harm or loss undergone (*apologize to try to retrieve the situation*).

retriever /ri-tree-ver/ *n* a dog trained to fetch birds shot by hunters.

retro- /re-troe/ *prefix* backward.

retrospect /re-troe-spect/ *n* looking back to the past (*in retrospect, he wasn't so bad really*).

retrospection /re-troe-spec-shun/ *n* a looking-back to the past.

retrospective /re-troe-spec-tiv/ *adj* looking back to the past (*a retrospective mood*).

return /ri-turn/ *vb* **1** to come or go back (*they returned to the house*). **2** to give or send back (*return*

his present unopened). ● *n* **1** a coming or going back (*their return from vacation*). **2** what is given or sent back (*the return of the library books*). **3** profit (*a good return from their investment*). **4** a written statement of certain facts, expenses, figures, etc. (*their annual tax return*).

reunion /ri-yoon-yun/ *n* a meeting again of old friends or comrades (*a school reunion*).

reunite /ri-yoo-nite/ *vb* to join together again (*reunited with her sister whom she had not seen for 20 years*).

re-use /ree-yooz/ *vb* to use again (*reuse wrapping paper*). ● *also n*. ● *adj* **reusable**.

rev /rev/ *vb*. ● **rev up** to increase the speed of a motor.

Rev, Rev. /rev/ *short for* **Reverend**.

reveal /ri-veel/ *vb* **1** to show what was hidden (*open the box to reveal a diamond*). **2** to make known (*reveal what should have been confidential information*).

reveille /re-va-lee/ *n* a morning call on the bugle, etc., to waken soldiers.

revel /re-vul/ *n* merrymaking, a noisy feast (*student revels*). ● *vb* **1** (*old*) to make merry. **2** to take great delight (in) (*she revels in the misfortune of others*). ● *n* **reveler** /re-vler/.

revelation /re-ve-lay-shun/ *n* **1** act of making known (*the revelation of her secrets*). **2** a surprising discovery or piece of information (*the revelation caused great dismay*).

revelry /re-vel-ree/ *n* noisy feasting or merrymaking.

revenge /ri-venj/ *n* making someone suffer for a wrong done to another, repaying evil with evil (*he wanted revenge for his brother's death*). ● *also vb*. ● *adj* **revengeful** /ri-venj-ful/.

revenue /re-vi-noo/ *n* money made by a person, business, or state (*increase in annual revenue*).

reverberate /ri-ver-bi-rate/ *vb* to echo (*the caves reverberated with the child's laughter*). ● *n* **reverberation** /ri-ver-bi-ray-shun/.

revere /ri-veer/ *vb* (*fml*) to feel great respect for (*young writers revering the great author*).

reverence /rev-rense/ *n* respect and admiration (*treat the great artist with reverence*).

Reverend /rev-rend/ *n* (*abbr = Rev, Rev.*) a title given to a member of clergy.

reverent /rev-rent/ *adj* showing or feeling great respect (*a reverent attitude toward writers*).

reverential /re-ve-ren-shal/ *adj* full of reverence (*his reverential attitude toward other artists*).

reverse /ri-**verse**/ *vb* **1** to turn back to front or upside down (*reverse the tablecloth*). **2** to go or move backward (*he reversed the car into the garage*). **3** to change to the opposite (*reverse her opinion*). ● *n* **1** a defeat (*armies retreating after a major reverse*). **2** a failure (*firms facing a reverse during the recession*). **3** the opposite (*she thinks the reverse of what he does*). **4** the back of a coin, medal, etc. ● *adj* **1** opposite. **2** back.

reversible /ri-**ver**-si-bul/ *adj* **1** able to be reversed (*a reversible opinion*). **2** that which can be turned inside out (*a reversible coat*).

revert /ri-**vert**/ *vb* **1** to go back to a former condition, custom, or subject (*revert to the old bad habits*). **2** to return or be returned to the previous owner or member of his/her family (*when she dies, the land reverts to her brother's family*).

review /ri-**vyoo**/ *vb* **1** to look over again, to consider with a view to changing (*review the situation*). **2** to inspect (*the general reviewing the troops*). **3** to write your opinion of (books, plays, etc.). ● *n* **1** a looking back on the past (*a review of the year's news*). **2** reconsideration or revision (*a review of company policy*). **3** an article in a newspaper, magazine, etc., giving an opinion on a book, play, etc. (*a review of the latest movie*). **4** a magazine that reviews books, plays, etc. (*a literary review*).

reviewer /ri-**vyoo**-er/ *n* a person who writes reviews, a critic (*the play was praised by the reviewer*).

revile /ri-**vile**/ *vb* to speak insultingly about or to (*revile the government*).

revise /ri-**vize**/ *vb* to go over again and correct or improve (*revise the manuscript*). ● *n* **reviser** /ri-**vie**-zer/.

revision /ri-**vi**-zhun/ *n* the act of revising.

revitalize /ree-**vie**-ta-lize/ *vb, also* **revalitalise** (*Br*) to put new life or strength into (*this movie revitalized her career*).

revival /ri-**vie**-val/ *n* **1** the act of reviving. **2** the arousing of fresh enthusiasm for religion.

revivalist /ri-**vie**-va-list/ *n* a person who tries to arouse fresh enthusiasm for religion.

revive /ri-**vive**/ *vb* **1** to bring back to life, health, or consciousness (*able to revive the man who nearly drowned*). **2** to bring back to use or an active state (*revive an old custom*). **3** to give new vigor or energy to (*revive their interest in sport*). **4** to produce an old play in the theater (*revive an early musical*).

revoke /ri-**voke**/ *vb* to do away with, to withdraw (*revoke an existing rule*). ● *n* **revocation** /ree-vo-**cay**-shun/.

revolt /ri-**voalt**/ *vb* **1** to rebel (*the townspeople revolting against the government*). **2** to shock or disgust (*the sight of blood revolts him*). ● *n* a rebellion, a rising against the government.

revolting /ri-**vole**-ting/ *adj* disgusting, shocking (*a revolting sight*).

revolution /re-vu-**loo**-shun/ *n* **1** one complete turn of a wheel, etc. **2** a complete change (*the technological revolution*). **3** a movement or rebellion as a result of which a new method of government is introduced (*the French Revolution*).

revolutionary /re-vu-**loo**-shun-ree/ *adj* desiring to bring about a complete change (*revolutionary developments in technology*). ● *n* a person who works for a complete change of government.

Revolutionary War /re-vu-**loo**-shun-ree war/ *n* the war, lasting from 1775 to 1783, in which 12 American colonies won independence from Britain. It is also know as the American Revolution.

revolutionize /re-vu-**loo**-shu-nize/ *vb, also* **revolutionise** (*Br*) to bring about a complete change in (*revolutionize the whole industry*).

revolve /ri-**volv**/ *vb* **1** to turn around and around. **2** to move around a center or axis.

revolver /ri-**vol**-ver/ *n* a pistol able to fire several shots without reloading.

revue /ri-**vyoo**/ *n* a light theatrical entertainment with music, songs, dances, etc.

revulsion /ri-**vul**-shun/ *n* a sudden complete change of feeling, disgust (*feel revulsion at the sight of blood*).

reward /ri-**wawrd**/ *n* **1** something given in return for work done, good behavior, bravery, etc. (*a reward for saving the drowning man*). **2** a sum of money offered for finding or helping to find a criminal, lost or stolen property, etc. (*a reward is offered for the return of his car*). ● *vb* to give as a reward. ● *adj* **rewarding** /ri-**war**-ding/.

rhapsodize /**rap**-su-dize/ *vb, also* **rhapsodise** (*Br*) (*fml*) to talk in an excited, disconnected manner (*rhapsodizing over their vacation in Mexico*).

rhapsody /**rap**-su-dee/ *n* **1** a piece of writing or music or a speech full of excited feeling and therefore not following the usual rules of composition ("*Gershwin's Rhapsody in Blue*") **2** (*usually pl*) an expression of excited approval (*go into rhapsodies over the new baby*).

rhetoric /**re**-tu-ric/ *n* **1** the art of speaking and writing well. **2** words that sound well but say little of importance (*they thought the politician's speech was just rhetoric*). ● *n* **rhetorician** /re-tu-**ri**-shun/.

rhetorical /ri-**tawr**-ic-al/ *adj* high-sounding.

rhetorical question /ri-**tawr**-ic-al-**kwes**-chun/ *n* a question asked for effect where no answer is expected.

rheumatism /**roo**-ma-ti-zum/, **rheumatics** /roo-**ma**-tics/ *ns* a disease causing painful swelling in the joints (*he has difficulty moving around because of his rheumatism*). ● *adj* **rheumatic** /roo-**ma**-tic/.

rhinoceros /rie-**nos**-rus/ *n* a large thick-skinned animal with a horn (or two horns) on its nose.

rhododendron /ro-du-**den**-drun/ *n* an evergreen shrub with large brightly colored flowers (*pink rhododendrons growing along the driveway*).

rhombus /**rom**-bus/ *n* (*pl* **rhombuses** /**rom**-bu-seez/ *or* **rhombi** /**rom**-bie/) a parallelogram with equal sides but angles that are not right angles.

rhubarb /**roo**-bard/ *n* a garden plant with juicy stalks edible when cooked, and roots sometimes used in medicines (*rhubarb jam*).

rhyme, rime /**rime**/ *n* **1** sameness of sound at the ends of words or lines of poetry. **2** a word that rhymes with another. **3** a poem with rhymes. ● *vb* **1** to find words ending in the same sound(s). **2** to end in the same sound(s) as. **3** to write poetry. ● **without rhyme or reason** foolish, unreasonable.

rhythm *n* **1** the regular beat of words (especially in poetry, music, or dancing) (*tapped her feet to the rhythm of the music*). **2** a regular repeated pattern of movements, graceful motion (*the rhythm of the dancers*).

rhythmic /**rith**-mic/, **rhythmical** /**rith**-mi-cal/ *adjs* having a regular beat, regular. ● *adv* **rhythmically** /**rith**-mi-ca-lee/.

rib /**rib**/ *n* **1** one of the curved bones of the breast (*cracked a rib in the accident/a rib of beef*). **2** a low, narrow ridge or raised part of a material. **3** a curved piece of wood attached to the keel of a ship and going up to the deck.

ribald /**ri**-bald/ *adj* coarse, indecent, vulgar (*ribald jokes/ribald laughter*).

ribaldry /**ri**-bald-ree/ *n* coarse talk.

ribbon /**ri**-bun/ *n* a narrow decorative band of silk or other material (*tie a ribbon in her hair*).

rice /**rice**/ *n* a white edible grain often grown in hot countries, especially in river valleys (*served with fried rice*).

rice paper /**rice**-pay-per/ *n* **1** a kind of fine paper. **2** a special form of this that can be eaten and is used in cookery.

rich /**rich**/ *adj* **1** having much money, wealthy (*a rich man*). **2** fertile (*rich soil*). **3** valuable (*a rich silk*). **4** plentiful (*a rich source of gold*). **5** containing much fat or sugar (*rich sauces*). **6** deep, strong (*a rich voice/rich colors*). ● *n* **richness** /**rich**-ness/.

riches /**ri**-chiz/ *npl* wealth.

richly /**rich**-lee/ *adv* **1** in a rich manner (*richly dressed*). **2** with riches (*richly rewarded*).

rick /**rick**/ *n* a heap or stack of hay, etc.

rickety /**ri**-ki-tee/ *adj* shaky, unsteady (*a rickety table*).

rickshaw /**rik**-shaw/ *n* a light two-wheeled carriage pulled by a man.

ricochet /**ri**-cu-shay/ *n* the skimming of a bullet off a flat surface. ● *vb* to hit something and bounce away at an angle (*the bullet ricocheted off the wall*).

rid /**rid**/ *vb* (**rid** *or* **ridded** /**ri**-did/, **ridding** /**ri**-ding/) to make free from, to clear (*try to rid themselves of their boring guests*).

riddle[1] /**ri**-dul/ *n* a puzzling question.

riddle[2] /**ri**-dul/ *n* a large sieve (*use a riddle to separate stones from the soil*). ● *vb* **1** to sift. **2** to fill with holes.

ride /**ride**/ *vb* (*pt* **rode** /**rode**/, *pp* **ridden** /**ri**-din/) **1** to be carried on the back of an animal or on a vehicle (*ride a donkey*). **2** to be able to ride on and control a horse, bicycle, etc. (*she is learning to ride*). ● *n* a trip on an animal's back or in a vehicle.

rider /**rie**-der/ *n* **1** a person who rides (*a horseback rider*). **2** something added to what has already been said or written (*the teacher added the rider that he expected everyone to be on time*).

ridge /**ridge**/ *n* **1** a long, narrow hill. **2** the raised part between two lower parts (*the ridge of the roof*). **3** a mountain range.

ridicule /**ri**-di-cyool/ *n* mockery. ● *vb* to mock, to make fun of (*she was ridiculed by her classmates*).

ridiculous /ri-**di**-cyu-lus/ *adj* deserving to be laughed at, absurd (*the large hat made her look ridiculous*). ● *adv* **ridiculously** /ri-**di**-cyu-lus-lee/.

riding habit /**rie**-ding-ha-bit/ *n* the clothes worn for riding.

rife /**rife**/ *adj* found everywhere or in large numbers or quantities, extremely common (*disease and poverty were rife*).

rifle[1] /**rie**-ful/ *n* a handgun with a grooved barrel that makes the bullet spin in flight. ● *vb* to make grooves in a gun barrel.

rifle[2] /**rie**-ful/ *vb* to search through and steal anything valuable (*the burglar rifled through her papers*).

rift /**rift**/ *n* **1** a disagreement between two friends (*a rift between neighbors*). **2** a split or crack in the ground.

rig /rig/ *vb* (**rigged** /rigd/, **rigging** /ri-ging/) **1** to provide clothing (*rig the child out for the party*). **2** to provide tools or equipment. **3** to provide (a ship) with ropes, sails, etc. **4** to set up (*rig up a shelter*). **5** to arrange wrongfully to produce a desired result, often an unfair or unlawful one (*rig the election*). ● *n* the particular way in which a ship's masts, sails, etc., are arranged.

rigging /ri-ging/ *n* a ship's spars, ropes, etc.

right /rite/ *adj* **1** correct (*the right answer*). **2** true (*is it right to say he left early?*). **3** just, morally correct (*it is not right to let him go unpunished*). **4** straight (*go right ahead*). **5** on the side of the right hand (*stand at her right side*). **6** in good condition (*call a plumber to put the washing machine right*). **7** suitable, appropriate (*the right man for the job*). ● *vb* **1** to put back in position, to set in order. **2** to mend, to correct. ● *n* **1** that which is correct, good, or true (*they are in the right*). **2** something to which you have a just claim (*freedom of speech is a right*). **3** the right-hand side (*stand on her right*). **4** in politics, the party or group holding the more traditional, conservative beliefs (*a politician of the right*). ● *adv* **1** straight. **2** exactly. **3** to the right-hand side.

right angle /rite-ang-gul/ *n* an angle of 90 degrees.

righteous /rie-chus/ *adj* **1** having just cause (*righteous indignation*). **2** good-living, virtuous (*a righteous life/a righteous man*). ● *adv* **righteously** /rie-chus-lee/. ● *n* **righteousness** /rie-chus-ness/.

rightful /rite-ful/ *adj* lawful, just (*the rightful owner*). ● *adv* **rightfully** /rite-fu-lee/.

right-handed /rite-han-ded/ *adj* using the right hand more easily than the left.

rightly /rite-lee/ *adv* **1** justly (*rightly or wrongly he was blamed*). **2** correctly (*we rightly assumed he would refuse*).

rigid /ri-jid/ *adj* **1** that cannot be bent (*a rigid frame*). **2** stern, strict, not willing to change (*rigid in his views*). **3** not to be changed (*rigid rules*). ● *n* **rigidity** /ri-ji-di-tee/. ● *adv* **rigidly** /ri-jid-lee/.

rigmarole /rig-ma-role/ *n* long and confused or meaningless talk (*give clear instructions, not a rigmarole*).

rigor /ri-gur/ *n, also* **rigour** (*Br, Cdn*) (*fml*) strictness, severity, harshness (*the rigors of life in the orphanage*). ● *adj* **rigorous** /rig-russ/. ● *adv* **rigorously** /rig-rus-lee/.

rile /rile/ *vb* to make angry (*his rudeness riled me*).

rim /rim/ *n* **1** the outer hoop of a wheel. **2** the outer edge, brim (*the rim of the glass*).

rime[1] /rime/ *n* white or hoarfrost.

rime[2] /rime/ *another spelling of* **rhyme**.

rind /rinde/ *n* **1** the skin of some fruits (*lemon rind*) **2** the skin of bacon, cheese, etc.

ring[1] /ring/ *n* **1** a hoop of gold or other metal for the finger (*a wedding ring*). **2** anything in the form of a circle (*the children gathered in a ring*). **3** a space enclosed by ropes for a boxing match. ● *vb* (*pt, pp* **ringed** /ringd/) to surround, to encircle.

ring[2] /ring/ *vb* (*pt* **rang** /rang/, *pp* **rung** /rung/) **1** to make a clear sound as a bell. **2** to cause a bell to sound (*ring the doorbell*). **3** to echo (*his voice ringing in her ears*). ● *n* the sound of a bell.

ringleader /ring-lee-der/ *n* the leader of a gang (*police failed to catch the ringleader*).

ringlet /ring-let/ *n* a curl of hair (*a little girl with ringlets falling to her shoulders*).

rink /ringk/ *n* **1** a level stretch of ice for skating or curling. **2** a floor for roller-skating.

rinse /rinss/ *vb* **1** to wash by pouring water over (*rinse the cup under the faucet*). **2** to dip in water and wash lightly. **3** to put in clean water to remove soap (*wash the clothes by hand and rinse them*).

riot /rie-ut/ *n* **1** a noisy or violent disorder caused by a crowd (*there was a riot when the police arrested the protester*). **2** (*inf*) something or someone that is very funny (*the comedian is a riot*). **3** a bright and splendid show (*a riot of color*). ● **read the riot act** to give clear warning that unruly behavior must stop. ● **run riot** to go wild, to go out of control (*with the teacher gone the children would run riot*).

riotous /rie-u-tuss/ *adj* noisy, disorderly (*a riotous party*).

rip /rip/ *vb* (**ripped** /ript/, **ripping** /ri-ping/) to tear or cut open, to strip off (*she ripped her skirt on the fence*). ● *n* a tear, a rent.

ripe /ripe/ *adj* **1** ready to be gathered or picked, ready for eating (*ripe apples*). **2** suitable or ready for (*a company ripe for takeover*). ● *n* **ripeness** /ripe-ness/.

ripen /rie-pin/ *vb* **1** to become ripe (*the apples would slowly ripen*). **2** to cause to become ripe (*ripen fruit in a greenhouse*).

ripple /ri-pul/ *n* **1** a little wave (*a ripple on the water*). **2** the sound of shallow water running over stones. **3** a sound resembling this (*a ripple of laughter*). ● *vb* **1** to flow in ripples. **2** to cause tiny waves to appear on. **3** to flow with a murmuring sound.

rise /rize/ *vb* (*pt* **rose**, *pp* **risen** /ri-zin/) **1** to get up from bed (*rise early*). **2** to stand up (*she rose to go*). **3** to go upward (*smoke rising from the chimney*). **4** to increase (*prices rising*). **5** to rebel (*th* *people rose up against the king*). **6** to move to a higher position (*he has risen to become manager*). **7** (*of a river*) to have its source or beginning. ● **give rise to** to cause or bring about (*their relationship would give rise to scandal*). ● **rise to the occasion** to do all that is necessary at a difficult time (*he was nervous about speaking in public but we knew he could rise to the occasion*). ● **take a rise out of** (*inf*) to play a joke or trick on.

rising /**rie**-zing/ *n* **1** the act of rising. **2** a rebellion (*a rising against the tyrant*).

risk /**risk**/ *n* **1** danger. **2** possible harm or loss. ● *vb* **1** to put in danger, to lay open to the possibility of loss (*risk his health/risk his life*). **2** to take the chance of something bad or unpleasant happening (*risk defeat/risk losing his business*).

risky /**ri**-skee/ *adj* dangerous (*a risky journey*).

risotto /ri-**zot**-o/ *n* an Italian rice dish cooked with meat, vegetables, etc. (*mushroom risotto*).

rite /**rite**/ *n* an order or arrangement of proceedings fixed by rule or custom (*marriage rites*).

ritual /ri-chu-wal/ *adj* having to do with or done as a rite (*a ritual sacrifice*). ● *n* **1** a set of rites. **2** ceremonies performed to worship God. ● *adv* **ritually** /ri-chu-wa-lee/.

rival /**rie**-val/ *n* **1** a person who is trying to do better than another (*rivals for the same girl*). **2** a competitor for the same prize (*rivals in the tennis competition*). ● *vb* to be as good or nearly as good as (*her beauty rivals her sister's*). ● *n* **rivalry** /ri-val-ree/.

river /**ri**-ver/ *n* a large running stream of water.

rivet /**ri**-vit/ *n* a bolt driven through metal plates, etc., to fasten them together and then hammered flat at both ends. ● *vb* to fix (the eyes or mind) firmly upon (*they were riveted by the magician's tricks*).

rivulet /**ri**-vyu-lit/ *n* a small stream.

road /**road**/ *n* **1** a prepared public way for traveling on (*the road was icy*). **2** a street (*he lives in the next road*). **3** a way (*the road to Key West*).

roadhog /**road**-hog/ *n* (*inf*) a dangerously reckless motorist.

roadhouse /**road**-houss/ *n* a tavern or restaurant on or near a highway.

roadrunner /**road**-run-er/ *n* a small, brown bird with a long tail, found in the southwestern United States (*roadrunners run instead of flying*).

roam /**roam**/ *vb* to wander about (*wild animals roam the plain*).

roar /**roar**/ *vb* to give a roar (*roar in pain/roar with laughter*). ● *n* **1** a loud shout or cry (*he gave a roar*

of pain). **2** the full loud cry of a large animal (*the lion's roar*).

roast /**roast**/ *vb* to cook before a fire or in an oven (*roast the meat slowly*). ● *n* roasted meat (*have a roast for Sunday lunch*).

rob /**rob**/ *vb* (**robbed** /robd/, **robbing** /rob-ing/) **1** to steal from (*rob the rich/rob a bank*). **2** (*fml*) to cause someone not to get what he or she ought to get (*war robbed her of her sons*). ● *n* **robber** /rob-er/.

robbery /**rob**-er-ee/ *n* the act of robbing.

robe /**robe**/ *n* a long, loose-fitting garment. ● *npl* **robes** clothes worn as a sign of rank or position. ● *vb* to put on robes, to put robes on someone else.

robin /**rob**-in/ *n* a red-breasted songbird, about the size of a pigeon (*the American robin is a much larger bird than the little European robin*).

robot /**ro**-bot/ *n* **1** a machine made to carry out certain tasks usually done by people. **2** a person who does his or her work mechanically without thinking or asking questions. ● *adj* **robotic** /ro-bot-ic/.

robust /ro-**bust**/ *adj* **1** healthy and strong (*robust children*). **2** vigorous, rough (*a robust sense of humor*). ● *adv* **robustly** /ro-bust-lee/. ● *n* **robustness** /ro-bust-ness/.

rock¹ /**rock**/ *vb* **1** to move from side to side, or backward and forward in turn (*rock the cradle/rock the baby*). **2** to sway from side to side (*boats rocking on the waves*). ● *n* a type of loud popular music with a strong beat.

rock² /**rock**/ *n* **1** the hard, solid part of the earth's crust. **2** a large mass or piece of stone (*a rock fell from the cliff*).

rock and roll, rock 'n' roll /rock-un-**roll**/ *n* a type of popular dance music that originated in the 1950s.

rock climbing /**rock** clime-ing/ *n* a sport that involves the climbing of steep cliffs and rock faces, usually with ropes.

rocker /**rock**-er/ *n* a curved piece of wood fastened to the foot of a chair, cradle, etc., to enable it to rock (*fix rockers to the chair*).

rockery /**rock**-er-ee/ *n* part of a garden consisting of a heap of earth and large stones or small rocks with plants growing between them (*flowers growing in the rockery*).

rocket /**rock**-it/ *n* **1** a cylinder that is propelled through the air by a backward jet of gas. **2** a spacecraft launched in this way (*send a rocket into orbit*). **3** a firework that flies up into the air as it is burning out, often used as a signal (*rockets went off on the 4th of July*).

rocking chair /**rock**-ing-chair/ *n* a chair on rockers.

rocking horse /**rock**-ing-hawrss/ *n* a toy horse on rockers.

rock salt /**rock**-sawlt/ *n* common salt found in solid lumps in the earth.

rocky /**rock**-ee/ *adj* **1** shaky (*a rocky table*). **2** full of rocks (*a rocky shore*). **3** hard as rock.

rod /rod/ *n* a straight slender stick or bar (*a fishing rod*).

rodent /**roe**-dint/ *n* any animal that gnaws, e.g., a mouse or rat.

rodeo /**roe**-dee-o/ *n* **1** a gathering together of cattle for marking. **2** a display of riding skill by cowboys.

roe[1] /roe/ *n* **1** a female deer (*stags and roes*). **2** a small type of deer.

roe[2] /roe/ *n* all the eggs in a female fish (*cod roe*).

roebuck /**roe**-buck/ *n* a male roe deer.

rogue /roag/ *n* **1** a dishonest person (*the rogue stole money from the old lady*). **2** a naughty mischievous child.

roguish /**roe**-gish/ *adj* **1** dishonest. **2** mischievous, teasing (*a roguish smile*).

role /role/ *n* **1** the part played by an actor (*he played the role of Hamlet*). **2** your actions or duties (*his role in the company*).

role model /**role**-mod-el/ *n* a person whom some other people admire and try to copy (*the footballer was a role model for many teenage boys*).

roll /role/ *vb* **1** to move by going around and around, like a wheel or ball (*roll the stone down the hill*). **2** to rock or sway from side to side (*ships rolling at anchor*). **3** to flatten with a roller (*roll the pastry*). **4** to make a loud long noise (*the drums rolled*). ● *n* **1** paper, cloth, etc., rolled into the form of a cylinder. **2** a list of names (*the school roll*). **3** a turning or rocking movement (*rolled his eyes*). **4** a long-drawn-out noise (*a roll of thunder*).

roll call /**role**-cawl/ *n* the calling over of a list of names (*the school roll call*).

roller /**roe**-ler/ *n* **1** anything made in the form of a cylinder so that it can turn around and around easily (for flattening something) (*garden rollers*). **2** a long swelling wave.

Rollerblade™ /**roe**-ler-blade/ *n* a type of roller skate that has the wheels set in one straight line. ● *n* **rollerblading** /**roe**-ler-blay-ding/.

roller coaster /**roe**-ler-coe-ster/ *n* a fairground ride like an elevated railroad with steep sharp curves.

roller skate /**roe**-ler-skate/ *n* a skate mounted on small wheels. ● *vb* **roller-skate** /**roe**-ler-skate/.

rollicking /**ro**-li-king/ *adj* noisy and merry (*a rollicking party*).

rolling pin /**roe**-ling-pin/ *n* a roller for kneading dough.

Roman /**roe**-man/ *adj* having to do with Rome.

Roman Catholic /roe-man-**cath**-lic/ *n* a member of that part of the Christian Church that is governed by the Pope, the Bishop of Rome.

romance /roe-**manse**/ *n* **1** a love affair (*she had several romances before she married*). **2** a love story (*a writer of romances*). **3** a story of wonderful or fanciful events (*a romance about a prince and a princess*). ● *adj* (*of a language*) derived from Latin.

Roman numerals /roe-man-**noom**-ralz/ *npl* numbers represented by letters (e.g., IV, V, VI for 4, 5, 6, etc.).

romantic /roe-**man**-tic/ *adj* **1** showing feelings of love (*a romantic gesture*). **2** dealing with love (*a romantic novel*). **3** imaginative, fanciful (*she has romantic notions of becoming a movie star*). ● *adv* **romantically** /roe-**man**-tic-lee/.

roman type /**roe**-man tipe/ *n* ordinary upright type (not italics).

romp /romp/ *vb* **1** to play roughly or noisily (*children romping around the garden*). **2** to do swiftly and easily (*romp through the examinations*). ● *n* rough or noisy play.

romper /**rom**-per/ *n* a one-piece garment for a small child.

roof /roof/ *n* **1** the outside upper covering of a house, building, vehicle, etc. (*mend the roof of the castle*). **2** the upper part of the mouth. ● *vb* to cover with a roof (*roofed the new house*).

rook /rook/ *n* **1** a piece in chess. **2** (*Br*) a black bird of the crow family. ● vb to cheat someone.

room /room/ *n* **1** an apartment in a house (*three rooms upstairs*). **2** space (*room for three in the back*). **3** space for free movement (*no room to dance*). **4** scope (*room for improvement*). ● *npl* **rooms** /roomz/ lodgings.

roomy /**roo**-mee/ *adj* having plenty of space (*a roomy car*).

roost /roost/ *n* the pole on which birds rest at night ● *vb* to rest or sleep on a roost.

rooster /**roo**-ster/ *n* a cock.

root /root/ *n* **1** the part of a plant that is fixed in the earth and draws nourishment from the soil. **2** the beginning or origin, a first cause from which other things develop (*the root of the problem*). **3** a word from which other words are formed (*from the Latin root*). **4** a factor of a number that when multiplied by itself gives the original number. ● *vb* **1** to fix firmly (*he felt rooted to the spot*). **2** to search about for (*rooting around for misplaced keys*).

rope /rope/ *n* a strong thick cord, made by twisting together strands of hemp, wire, etc. ● *vb* **1** to fasten with a rope (*rope the donkeys together*). **2** to mark off with a rope (*rope off an area of the hall for the choir*).

rosary /roe-za-ree/ *n* in the Roman Catholic Church, a series of prayers, or a string of beads each of which represents a prayer in the series.

rose /roze/ *n* **1** a beautiful, sweet-smelling flower growing on a thorny shrub (*a bunch of roses*). **2** a shrub bearing roses (*plant roses*). **3** a light red or pink color (*a dress of pale rose*). **4** a nozzle full of holes at the end of the spout of a watering can.

rosemary /roze-me-ree/ *n* an evergreen sweet-smelling shrub used as a herb in cooking (*lamb flavored with rosemary*).

rosette /roe-zet/ *n* **1** a badge, like a rose in shape, made of ribbon (*the politicians all wore their rosettes*). **2** a rose-shaped ornament carved in stone, etc.

rosewood /roze-wood/ *n* a hard dark-colored wood smelling of roses when fresh cut (*a table made of rosewood*).

Rosh Hashana /rosh-ho-za-na/ (or **Hashanah** /ho-za-nah/) *n* the Jewish New Year festival, held in September or October.

rosy /roe-zee/ *adj* **1** red. **2** giving cause for hope.

rot /rot/ *vb* (**rotted** /rot-id/, **rotting** /rot-ing/) **1** to go bad from age or lack of use, to decay (*fruit rotting on the trees*). **2** to cause to decay (*damp had rotted the woodwork*). ● *n* decay (*rot in the wood paneling*).

rotary /roe-ta-ree/ *adj* turning around on an axle. ● *n* a meeting place of roads with a central circle around which vehicles must go until they turn off (*give way at the rotary*).

rotate /roe-tate/ *vb* **1** to turn around a center or axis (*wheels rotating*). **2** to move like a wheel (*trainees are rotating from department to department*).

rotation /roe-tay-shun/ *n* **1** movement around a center or axis. **2** a regular order repeated again and again (*rotation of crops*).

rotten /rot-in/ *adj* **1** decaying, having gone bad (*rotten fruit*). **2** (*inf*) mean (*a rotten thing to do*).

Rottweiler /rot-wie-ler/ *n* a breed of very large, strong dog with a black and brown coat.

rotund /roe-tund/ *adj* round, fattish (*a rotund little man*). ● *n* **rotundity** /ro-tun-di-tee/.

rouble *see* **ruble**.

rouge /roozh/ *n* red coloring for the cheeks (*she wears too much rouge*).

rough /ruf/ *adj* **1** not smooth, uneven (*a rough road surface*). **2** wild, stormy (*rough weather*). **3** not polite (*rough manners*). **4** not gentle (*a rough voice*). **5** coarse, violent (*a rough hooligan*). **6** badly finished (*a rough building job*). **7** not exact (*a rough estimate*). ● *n* a violent, badly behaved person. ● *adv* **roughly** /ruf-lee/. ● *n* **roughness** /ruf-ness/.

roughage /ru-fidge/ *n* food that conatins a lot of fiber, which aids digestion.

roughen /ru-fin/ *vb* to make or become rough (*hands roughened by scrubbing floors*).

roulette /roo-let/ *n* a gambling game played on a revolving board with a ball that falls into one of a number of holes when the board ceases spinning (*play roulette at the casino*).

round /round/ *adj* like a ball or circle in shape. ● *n* **1** a round object. **2** a duty visit to all the places under your care (*the doctor's rounds*). **3** a part song in which singers join at different times and begin again when they have finished. **4** a shell or bullet for firing. **5** a division of a boxing match (*a knockout in the second round*). **6** a complete part of a knock-out competition (e.g., in soccer). **7** a game of golf. **8** a spell or outburst (*a round of applause*). ● *adv* **1** in the opposite direction (*he turned round*). **2** in a circle (*stand all round*). **3** from one person to another (*pass the wine round*). **4** from place to place (*drive round*). ● *prep* **1** on every side of (*sit round the table*). **2** with a circular movement about (*sail round the world*). ● *vb* **1** to give a round shape to (*he rounded the corners with sandpaper*). **2** to go around (*ships rounding the bay*).

roundabout /roun-da-bout/ *n* (*Br*) *see* **rotary**. ● *adj* **1** indirect. **2** using too many words.

roundly /round-lee/ *adv* plainly (*told her roundly what he thought*).

round trip /round-trip/ *n* a journey to a place and back again.

roundup /round-up/ *n* **1** the gathering of cattle or other farm animals for market. **2** a gathering of something (*a roundup of this week's news*).

rouse /rouz/ *vb* **1** to awaken (*rouse from sleep*). **2** to stir up to action (*his words roused the crowd to rebellion*).

rousing /rou-zing/ *adj* stirring, exciting.

rout /rout/ *vb* to defeat and put to disordered flight (*rout the enemy army*). ● *n* **1** a disorderly and hasty retreat after a defeat. **2** a complete defeat (*a rout of the enemy*).

route /root/ *n* a way from one place to another (*take the scenic coastal route*).

routine /roo-**teen**/ *n* a regular way or order of doing things (*tired of her working routine*). ● *adv* **routinely** /roo-**teen**-lee/.

rove /rove/ *vb* **1** to wander about. **2** to wander.

rover /**roe**-ver/ *n* **1** a wanderer (*too much of a rover to settle down*). **2** (*old*) a pirate.

row[1] /roe/ *n* a line of people or things (*a row of trees*).

row[2] /roe/ *vb* to move a boat by means of oars. ● *n* **1** a spell of rowing. **2** a trip in a boat moved by oars (*a row up the river*).

row[3] /row/ *n* **1** noise, disturbance (*the row from the party next door*). **2** a quarrel (*a family row*). **3** a public argument (*a row over the federal immigration laws*). ● *vb* (*inf*) to quarrel (*husband and wife rowing*).

rowdy /**row**-dee/ *adj* noisy and quarrelsome (*a rowdy crowd*). ● *n* **rowdiness** /**row**-dee-ness/. ● *n* **rowdyism** /**row**-dee-i-zum/.

royal /**roy**-al/ *adj* **1** having to do with a king or queen (*the royal family*). **2** splendid, kingly (*a royal feast*). ● *adv* **royally** /**roy**-a-lee/.

royalist /**roy**-a-list/ *n* a supporter of a king or queen.

royalty /**roy**-al-tee/ *n* **1** a royal person or persons (*royalty was present at the dinner*). **2** a share of the profits paid to authors, inventors, etc., for the use of their work (*receive royalties for her work*).

rub /rub/ *vb* (**rubbed** /rubd/, **rubbing** /**ru**-bing/) to move one thing to and fro against another (*I rub my eyes*). ● *n* act of rubbing (*rub with a cloth*).

rubber /**ru**-ber/ *n* **1** a tough elastic substance made from the juice of certain tropical trees (*tires made of rubber*). **2** a piece of rubber used to remove marks by rubbing (*a rubber to remove her mistake*). ● *adj* **rubbery** /**ru**-bree/.

rubbish /**ru**-bish/ *n* **1** things of no value that you would throw away. **2** nonsense (*she talked a lot of rubbish*).

rubble /**ru**-bul/ *n* broken pieces of bricks or stones (*search the rubble for earthquake survivors*).

ruble /**roo**-bul/ *n* the main Russian unit of currency.

ruby /**roo**-bee/ *n* a red precious stone (*a ring with a valuable ruby*). ● *adj* **1** containing rubies. **2** red.

ruck /ruck/ *n* the mass of ordinary people (*dreams of getting out of the ruck and becoming famous*).

rudder /**ru**-der/ *n* a flat hinged plate at the stern of a ship or the tail of an aircraft for steering.

rude /rood/ *adj* **1** impolite (*the child was rude to the teacher*). **2** sudden and unpleasant (*a rude shock*) **3** (*old*) roughly made (*a rude hut*). **4** (*old*) uncivilized, untaught, vulgar. ● *adv* **rudely** /**rood**-lee/. ● *n* **rudeness** /**rood**-ness/.

ruff /ruff/ *n* a stiff frilled collar worn in olden times (*ruffs were worn in Tudor times*).

ruffian /**ru**-fee-an/ *n* a rough brutal fellow, a violent lawbreaker (*mugged by a gang of ruffians*).

ruffle /**ru**-ful/ *vb* **1** to disturb the smoothness of, to disarrange (*the wind ruffling her hair*). **2** to anger or annoy (*he was ruffled by her comments*). ● *n* a frill (*a party dress with ruffles*).

rug /rug/ *n* **1** a mat for the floor (*a rug on the floor*). **2** a thick woolen coverlet or blanket (*put a rug over the lady's legs*).

rugby /**rug**-bee/ *n* a form of football in which the ball, oval in shape, may be carried in the hands.

rugged /**ru**-gid/ *adj* **1** rough, uneven (*rugged coastline*). **2** strongly built (*rugged young men*).

ruin /**roo**-in/ *n* **1** destruction (*ancient buildings fallen into ruin*). **2** downfall, overthrow, state of having lost everything of value (*the company faced ruin during the recession*). **3** (*often pl*) remains of old buildings (*visit the castle ruins*). ● *vb* **1** to destroy (*all chances of success were ruined/the floods ruined her carpets*). **2** to cause to lose everything of value (*he was ruined when he lost the lawsuit*).

rule /rool/ *n* **1** government (*under foreign rule*). **2** a regulation or order (*school rules*). **3** an official or accepted standard (*as a rule he is home by midnight*). **4** the usual way that something happens (*spelling rules*). ● *vb* **1** to govern, to manage (*a king ruling the country*). **2** to give an official decision (*the judge ruled that he had to go to prison*). **3** to draw a straight line with the help of a ruler.

ruler /**roo**-ler/ *n* **1** a person who governs or reigns (*rebel against their ruler*). **2** a flat rod for measuring length (*draw a straight line with a ruler/measure with a ruler*).

ruling /**roo**-ling/ *adj* greatest, controlling (*the ruling party*). ● *n* a decision (*the ruling of the judge*).

rum /rum/ *n* spirit made from sugar cane.

rumba /**rum**-ba/ *n* a dance of Cuban origin.

rumble /**rum**-bul/ *vb* to make a low, rolling noise (*thunder rumbling*). ● *also n*.

ruminant /**roo**-mi-nant/ *adj* chewing the cud (*ruminant animals such as cows*). ● *n* an animal that chews the cud.

ruminate /**roo**-mi-nate/ *vb* **1** to chew the cud (*cow ruminating*). **2** (*fml*) to think deeply (*ruminating about his chances of success*).

rummage /**ru**-midge/ *vb* to search thoroughly but untidily (*rummage through her purse for a comb*). ● *also n*.

rumor /roo-mur/ *n, also* **rumour** (*Br, Cdn*) **1** a widely known story that may not be true (*he is not in prison—that was just a rumor*). **2** common talk, gossip (*a story based on rumor*).

rump /rump/ *n* **1** the end of an animal's backbone. **2** the buttocks (*smack the horse's rump*).

rumple /rum-pul/ *vb* to crease, to spoil the smoothness of (*clotheing rumpled after the long journey*).

rumpus /rum-pus/ *n* a noisy disturbance or quarrel, an uproar (*there was a rumpus when the concert was canceled*).

run /run/ *vb* (**ran** /ran/, **running** /ru-ning/, *pp* **run** /run/) **1** to move quickly (*run to catch the bus*). **2** to move from one place to another (*a train running from Philadelphia to New York*). **3** to take part in a race (*he runs in local race meetings*). **4** to flow (*blood running from the wound*). **5** to organize or manage (*she runs the local branch of the company*). **6** to smuggle (*run drugs across the border*). **7** to last or continue (*a play running for a year*). **8** to compete in a competition or an election (*run for governor*). ● *n* **1** act of running (*go for a run*). **2** the length of time for which something runs (*a run of six months*). **3** a widespread demand for (*a sudden run on bathing costumes*). **4** an enclosed place for animals or fowls (*a chicken run*). ● **run down 1** to say bad things about (*she is supposed to be his friend, but she is always running him down*). **2** to stop working because of lack of power (e.g., because a spring is unwound) (*a clock running down*). ● **run over 1** to read or repeat quickly (*run over the words of the poem*). **2** to knock over in a vehicle (*she ran over the dog*).

runaway /ru-na-way/ *n* **1** a deserter, a person who runs away (*police looking for a runaway*). **2** an animal or vehicle that is out of control.

rung /rung/ *n* a step of a ladder (*climb the ladder rung by rung*).

runner /ru-ner/ *n* **1** a person who runs (*the runners in the race*). **2** a messenger (*a runner for the advertizing agency*). **3** a long spreading stem of a plant. **4** a long narrow cloth for a table or carpet for a stair. **5** any device on which something slips or slides along (*the runners on the sledge*).

runner-up /ru-ner-up/ *n* (*pl* **runners-up** /ru-nerz-up/) the person or team second to the winner.

running /ru-ning/ *adj* **1** going on all the time (*a running commentary*). **2** in succession (*two years running*). ● *n* **1** the act of moving quickly. **2** that which runs or flows. ● **in the running** with a chance of success.

running mate /ru-ning-mate/ *n* a candidate for the lesser of two political posts, such as vice-president.

runny /ru-nee/ *adj* liquid, flowing (*runny soup*).

runway /run-way/ *n* a flat road along which an aircraft runs before taking off or after landing.

rupee /roo-pee/ *n* the main unit of currency in India and Pakistan.

rupture /rup-chur/ *n* **1** a clean break. **2** a quarrel or disagreement. **3** the thrusting of part of the intestine through the muscles of the abdomen. ● *vb* **1** to break. **2** to thrust. **3** to quarrel.

rural /roo-ral/ *adj* having to do with the country or its way of life (*the rural way of life*).

ruse /rooz/ *n* a trick (*a ruse to get into the party*).

rush[1] /rush/ *vb* **1** to move quickly and with force (*he rushed to help her*). **2** to do hastily (*rush the job*). **3** to make someone hurry (*rush him to make a decision*). **4** to capture by a sudden quick attack (*rush the enemy fortress*). ● *n* **1** hurry (*always in a rush*). **2** a fast and forceful move (*a rush toward the exit*). **3** a sudden demand (*a rush on toys at Christmas*). **4** a sudden advance (*a rush by the enemy army*).

rush[2] /rush/ *n* a tall grasslike plant growing in damp or marshy ground.

rust /rust/ *n* the red coating formed on iron and steel left in a damp place. ● *vb* to decay by gathering rust (*water pipes rusting through*).

rustic /ru-stic/ *adj* (*fml*) having to do with the country or country people (*a rustic way of life*).

rustle[1] /ru-sul/ *vb* to make a low whispering sound (*leaves rustling in the wind*). ● *also n.*

rustle[2] /ru-sul/ *vb* to steal (cattle). ● *n* **rustler** /ru-slur/.

rusty /ru-stee/ *adj* **1** covered with rust. **2** out of practice (*her piano playing is a bit rusty*).

rut /rut/ *n* a deep track made by a wheel (*ruts in the road made by trucks*). ● **in a rut** so tied by habits and customs that you are no longer interested in new or better methods (*in a rut and looking for another job*).

rutabaga /roo-ta-bay-ga/ *n* a swede; a Swedish turnip; a thick bulbous edible root

ruthless /rooth-less/ *adj* cruel, merciless, showing no pity (*a ruthless judge who imposes harsh sentences*). ● *adv* **ruthlessly** /rooth-less-lee/. ● *n* **ruthlessness** /rooth-less-ness/.

rye /rie/ *n* **1** a grain used for making bread. **2** rye bread.

rye bread /rie-bred/ *n* bread made with rye flour.

rye grass /rie-grass/ *n* a type of grass used as fodder for animals.

S

S, s /ess/ the nineteenth letter of the alphabet.

Sabbath /sa-buth/ *n* **1** the seventh day of the week, Saturday, set aside for rest and worship, observed by Jews and some Christian groups. **2** Sunday, the usual day of Christian rest and worship.

saber /say-ber/ *n* a heavy sword with a slightly curved blade.

sable /say-bul/ *n* **1** a type of weasel with dark-colored fur. **2** its fur. ● *adj* black, dark.

sabotage /sa-bu-tazh/ *n* the destroying, wasting, or ruining of something on purpose. ● *also vb.* ● *n* **saboteur** /sa-bu-**toor**/ a person who destroys, wastes, or ruins something on purpose.

sac /sac/ *n* a small bag of liquid inside an animal or plant.

saccharine /sa-ca-rin/ *n* a very sweet substance used instead of sugar. ● *adj* **saccharine** too sweet or syrupy.

sachem /sa-chem/ *n* the chief of certain Native American groups.

sachet /sa-shay/ *n* a small, sealed envelope or bag that contains perfumed powder or dried herbs and/ or flowers and is kept in dresser drawers, closets, etc. to scent clothing.

sack¹ /sack/ *n* **1** a bag made of coarse cloth for holding flour, wool, etc. ● *vb* (*inf*) to dismiss someone from his or her job.

sack² /sack/ *vb* to rob and destroy a town after capturing it. ● *also n.*

sacred /say-crid/ *adj* holy, set apart for the service of God (*sacred music*).

sacrifice /sa-cri-fice/ *n* **1** an offering to a god or God. **2** the act of giving up something desirable. **3** something given up in this way (*parents making sacrifices for their children*). ● *vb* **1** to make an offering to God or a god. **2** to give up something that is important to that person. ● *adj* **sacrificial** /sa-cri-fi-shal/.

sacrilege /sa-cri-lidge/ *n* disrespectful or insulting treatment of something holy. ● *adj* **sacrilegious** /sa-cri-li-jus/.

sacrosanct /sa-cro-sangt/ *adj* **1** very holy. **2** to be treated only with great respect (*private papers regarded as sacrosanct*).

sad /sad/ *adj* sorrowful, unhappy.

sadden /sa-den/ *vb* to make sad.

saddle /sa-dul/ *n* **1** a seat for a rider on a horse or bicycle. **2** meat taken from an animal's back (*saddle of beef*). ● *vb* **1** to put a saddle on. **2** to give (to another) something troublesome (*saddle others with his responsibilities*). ● **in the saddle** in control.

sadist /say-dist/ *n* a person who takes pleasure in giving pain to another. ● *n* **sadism** /say-di-zum/. ● *adj* **sadistic** /sa-**dis**-tic/.

safari /sa-fa-ree/ *n* a hunting trip, especially one in Africa.

safe /safe/ *adj* **1** out of harm or danger (*children safe in bed*). **2** not likely to cause harm, danger, or risk (*a safe job*). ● *n* a strong box or room for valuables. ● *adv* **safely**.

safeguard /safe-gard/ *n* any person or thing that protects. ● *also vb.*

safekeeping /safe-**kee**-ping/ *n* a keeping or being kept in safety.

safety /safe-tee/ *n* freedom from danger, harm, or loss.

safety belt /safe-tee-belt/ *n* **1** a belt that attaches a person to another object to keep him/her safe (*the window washer used a safety belt*). **2** a belt that attaches a driver or passenger to the seat in a car, plane, etc.

safety pin /safe-tee-pin/ a pin bent back on itself so as to cover the point when fastened.

saffron /saf-ron/ *n* a type of flower, purple in color with yellow orange in the middle, used to color or flavor food. ● *adj* deep yellow.

sag /sag/ *vb* (**sagged** /sagd/, **sagging** /sa-ging/) **1** to sink in the middle. **2** to droop, to hang down. ● *adj* **saggy** /sa-gee/.

saga /sa-ga/ *n* **1** a Scandinavian story of heroes, customs, battles, etc. **2** a very long adventure story.

sagamore /sa-ga-more/ *n* the second in command of certain Native American groups.

sage¹ /saydge/ *adj* wise. ● *n* a wise person.

sage² /saydge/ *n* **1** a sweet-smelling plant, used as a herb in cooking. **2** a grayish green color.

sagebrush /saydge-brush/ *n* a kind of plant with small leaves and small flowers that grows in the western United States.

sage grouse /saydge-grouse/ *n* a large bird that lives among the sagebrush in the western United States.

sago /sa-go/ *n* a type of flour, used in certain puddings.

saguaro /sa-**wa**-ro/ *n* a giant cactus with a thick spiny stem and white flowers native to the southwestern United States and northern Mexico.

aid /sed/ *pt of* **say**.

ail /sale/ *n* **1** a canvas spread to catch the wind. **2** a trip in a boat moved by sails. **3** the arm of a windmill. ● *vb* **1** to travel on water by way of a sail. **2** to move along without effort.

ailboard /sale-board/ *n* a board, used in windsurfing, similar to a surfboard with a sail attached to it.

ailboat /sale-boat/ *n* a boat or ship that has sails, by which it moves through the water.

ailer /say-ler/ *n* a ship or boat that has sails, used with reference to the way it sails (*a swift sailer*).

ailing /say-ling/ *n* **1** the act of a thing or person that sails. **2** the sport of managing a sailboat, as for racing.

ailor /say-lor/ *n* a person who makes a living by sailing.

ailplane /sale-plane/ *n* a light glider especially designed for soaring.

aint /saint/ *n* **1** a person who is very good, patient, helpful, etc. **2** a title given to an especially holy person by certain Christian churches. ● *adj* **saintly** /saint-lee/. ● *adj* **sainted** /sane-tid/.

ainthood /saint-hood/ *n* the status or rank of a saint.

ake¹ /sake/ *n*. ● **for the sake of** to get (*for the sake of peace and quiet*). ● **for my sake** to please me.

ake² /sake/ *n* a Japanese alcoholic drink made from rice.

alaam /sa-lom/ *n* **1** a greeting, meaning peace, used among Muslims. **2** in India, a greeting made by bowling low with the palm of the right hand on the forehead.

alable /say-la-bul/ *adj* that can be sold.

alacious /sa-lay-shus/ *adj* indecent, obscene.

alad /sa-lad/ *n* a dish of lettuce and other vegetables, mostly raw but sometimes cooked and sometimes including meat, fish, cheese, or fruit, usually served with a dressing.

alamander /sa-la-man-der/ *n* a lizardlike animal that can live both on land and in water.

alami /sa-la-mee/ *n* a highly spiced, salted sausage of pork and beef.

alary /sal-ree/ *n* the fixed sum of money paid to someone for work over an agreed length of time, usually a month or a year.

le /sale/ *n* **1** the act of selling. **2** the exchange of anything for money. **3** a selling of goods more cheaply than usual (*January sales*).

lesman /saylz-man/, **saleswoman** /saylz-woo-man/, **salesperson** /saylz-per-sun/ *ns* a person engaged in selling products.

salesmanship /saylz-man-ship/ *n* skill in selling things.

sales tax /saylz-taks/ a tax on things that are sold, usually a percentage (*some states have a high sales tax*).

salient /sale-yent/ *adj* **1** sticking outward. **2** most important (*the salient points of his plan*). ● *n* in war, a narrow strip of land jutting into enemy territory.

salina /sa-lee-na/ *n* a salt marsh, lake, or pond.

saline /say-leen/ *adj* containing salt. ● *n* a salt lake or spring.

salinize /sa-lin-nize/ *vb, also* **salinise** (*Br*) to put salt into.

saliva /sa-lie-va/ *n* the liquid that keeps the mouth moist, spittle. ● *adj* **salivary** /sa-lie-va-ree/.

salivate /sa-li-vate/ *vb* to produce excess saliva (*salivating in front of the chocolate cake*).

sallow¹ /sa-lo/ *n* a type of willow tree.

sallow² /sa-lo/ *adj* having a slightly yellow skin.

salmi /sal-mee/ *n* a highly seasoned dish of meat partly roasted then stewed in wine.

salmon /sa-mun/ *n* a large fish with pinkish flesh and silver scales, greatly valued for food and sport.

salmonella /sal-mu-ne-la/ *n* a kind of bacteria that can cause sickness in people or animals.

salon /sa-lon/ *n* **1** a public room in a home, hotel, etc., where people gather. **2** a building or room used for a particular business, such as hairdressing, the selling of fashionable clothes, etc.

saloon /sa-loon/ *n* **1** a large public room in a passenger ship. **2** a bar, a place where alcoholic drinks are sold and drunk.

salsa /sal-sa/ *n* **1** a type of Latin American dance music. **2** a spicy tomato sauce eaten with Mexican food.

salt /sawlt/ *n* **1** a white mineral element, obtained from sea water or by mining, used to give flavor to or to preserve food. ● *vb* to flavor or preserve with salt. ● *adj* containing or tasting of salt. ● *adj* **salty** /sawl-tee/.

salt-and-pepper /sawl-tand-pe-per/ *adj* dotted or specked with black and white.

saltcellar /sawlt-se-ler/ *n* a small dish for holding salt for use at table.

salter /sawl-ter/ *n* a person who makes or sells salt.

saltine /sawl-teen/ *n* a flat, crisp cracker with salt grains baked onto its top.

saltire /sawl-tire/ *n* a Saint Andrew's cross (X).

saltshaker /sawlt-shay-ker/ *n* a container for salt with a top that has holes in it for shaking over food.

saltwater /**sawlt**-waw-ter/ *adj* having to do with salt water or the sea (*saltwater fish tank*).

salutation /sal-yu-**tay**-shun/ *n* a greeting.

salute /sa-**loot**/ *vb* **1** to greet. **2** to make a gesture of respect by raising the right hand to the forehead or cap, firing guns, etc. ● *n* **1** the gesture of respect made by saluting. **2** the firing of guns as a welcome or mark of respect.

salvage /**sal**-vidge/ *n* **1** the saving of a ship or its cargo from loss. **2** the saving of property from any sort of destruction. **3** property saved in this way. ● *vb* to save from destruction, shipwreck, fire, etc.

salvation /sal-**vay**-shun/ *n* **1** the saving or being saved from danger, evil, difficulty, destruction, etc.

salve /salv/ *n* a medicine applied to wounds, burns, etc., to sooth or heal.

samba /**sam**-ba/ *n* **1** a South American dance of African origin. **2** music for this dance.

same /**same**/ *adj* in no way different (*the same person/the same mistake*). ● *n* the same person or thing (*I'll have the same*). ● *adv* in a like manner.

sameness /**same**-ness/ *n* lack of change or variety.

same-sex /**same**-seks/ *adj* of or relating to people of the same sex.

samosa /sa-**mo**-sa/ *n* a small pastry turnover, originally from India, filled with a spicy meat or vegetable mixture.

sampan /**sam**-pan/ *n* a small flat-bottomed boat used in China.

sample /**sam**-pul/ *n* a part or piece given to show what the whole is like (*a sample of the artist's work*). ● *vb* to try something to see what it is like (*sample the cake*).

sampler /**sam**-pler/ *n* a cloth sewn with designs, words, etc., in different types of stitches to show a beginner's skill.

samsara /sam-**sar**-a/ *n* in Hinduism, the cycle in which the same soul is reborn again and again.

samurai /sa-mu-rie/ *n* a member of the Japanese military class of people.

sanctify /**sang**-ti-fie/ *vb* to make holy or sacred. ● *n* **sanctification** /sang-ti-fi-**cay**-shun/.

sanctimonious /sang-ti-**mo**-nee-us/ *adj* pretending to be holy or religious. ● *n* **sanctimony** /**sang**-ti-mo-nee/.

sanction /**sang**-shun/ *n* **1** permission (*with the sanction of the police*). **2** a punishment imposed to make people obey a law (*trade sanctions imposed on countries that invade other countries*). ● *vb* to permit.

sanctity /**sang**(k)-ti-tee/ *n* holiness.

sanctuary /**sang**(k)-che-wer-ee/ *n* **1** a place where a person is safe from pursuit or attack. **2** a place providing protection, such as a reserve for wildlife. a holy place such as a church or temple.

sanctum /**sang**(k)-tum/ *n* **1** a person's private room where he or she is not to be bothered. **2** a sacred place.

sand /sand/ *n* **1** loose, gritty pieces of tiny particles of rock, shell, etc. **2** *pl* stretches of sand on the seashore. ● *vb* to rub with sandpaper to make smooth.

sandal /**san**-dal/ *n* a type of shoe to protect the sole leaving the upper part of the foot largely uncovered except by straps, etc.

sandalwood /**san**-dal-wood/ *n* any of several kinds of sweet-smelling wood.

sandbag /**sand**-bag/ *n* a bag filled with sand and used for protection against enemy attack or to protect against floods.

sandbar /**sand**-bar/ *n* a ridge of sand formed in a river or along a shore by the currents or tides.

sandbox /**sand**-boks/ *n* a box or pit filled with sand in which children can play.

sand dollar /**sand**-dol-ar/ *n* a kind of flat, round, spiny-skinned sea creature that lives on ocean beds.

sander /**san**-der/ *n* a person or tool that sands.

sand hopper /**sand**-hop-er/ *n* any of the various tiny animals that jump like fleas on beaches.

sandiness /**san**-dee-ness/ *n* a sandy state or quality.

sandlot /**sand**-lot/ *adj* having to do with games, especially baseball, played by people who were not professionals.

sandman /**sand**-man/ *n* a fairy-tale person who is thought to make children sleepy by dusting sand in their eyes.

sand painting /**sand**-pane-ting/ *n* in Navajo healing ceremonies, the sprinkling of colored sands into designs.

sandpaper /**sand**-pay-per/ *n* paper made rough by a coating of sand, used for smoothing and polishing.

sandpiper /**sand**-pie-per/ *n* a wading bird of the snipe family.

sandstone /**sand**-stone/ *n* a stone made up of sand pressed together.

sandstorm /**sand**-stawrm/ *n* a windstorm in which large amounts of sand are blown about in the air near the ground.

sandwich /**san**(d)-wich/ *n* two slices of bread with meat, cheese, salad, etc., in between them. ● *vb* to fit between two other things.

sandy /**san**-dee/ *adj* **1** covered with sand, full of sand. **2** the color of sand, a reddish yellow.

sane /sane/ *adj* **1** having a normal, healthy mind. **2** sensible.

sangria /sang-**gree**-ya/ *n* a punch made with wine, fruit juice, pieces of fruit, and soda water.

sanitarium /sa-ni-**ter**-ee-um/ *n* a quiet resort where people go to rest and regain their health, usually taking advantage of natural resources such as mineral springs.

sanitary /sa-ni-tree/ *adj* having to do with health or cleanliness.

sanitary napkin /sa-ni-tree **nap**-kin/ *n* a cotton-filled pad worn by women during menstruation.

sanitation /sa-ni-**tay**-shun/ *n* **1** the process or methods of keeping places clean and healthy. **2** a drainage or sewage system.

sanitize /sa-ni-tize/ *vb, also* **sanitise** (*Br*) to make sanitary.

sanity /sa-ni-tee/ *n* **1** the condition of being sane. **2** good sense.

sannup /sa-nup/ *n* a married Native American man.

sans /sanz/ *prep* without, lacking.

sansei /san-**say**/ *n* a native US or Canadian citizen whose grandparents were Japanese immigrants.

Sanskrit /san-skrit/ *n* an ancient language of India. ● *also adj*.

sap /sap/ *n* the juice that flows in plants, trees, etc., and feeds the various parts. ● *vb* (**sapped** /sapt/, **sapping** /sa-ping/) to weaken gradually (*sap a person's strength*).

sapling /sap-ling/ *n* a young tree.

sapphire /sa-fire/ *n* **1** a precious stone of a rich blue color. **2** its color. ● *also adj*.

sappy /sa-pee/ *adj* foolish, silly.

sarcasm /sar-ca-zum/ *n* a mocking remark intended to hurt another's feelings.

sarcastic /sar-ca-stic/ *adj* **1** given to sarcasm. **2** mocking, scornful.

sarcophagus /sar-**caw**-fa-gus/ *n* (*pl* **sarcophagi** /sar-**caw**-fa-gie/) a stone coffin.

sardine /sar-**deen**/ *n* a small fish of the herring family.

sardonic /sar-**don**-ic/ *adj* bitterly sneering, mocking.

sari /sa-ree/ *n* the dress of women in India, Pakistan, etc., consisting of a long piece of cloth wrapped around the body to form an ankle length skirt with the other end draped across the chest, over the shoulder, and sometimes over the head.

sarong /sa-**rong**/ *n* an item of clothing consisting of a length of often brightly colored cloth worn wrapped around the waste like a skirt by both men and women.

sarsaparilla /sar-spa-**ri**-la/ *n* **1** any of a number of tropical, woody vines of the lily family with fragrant roots and heart-shaped leaves. **2** the dried roots of these plants, formerly used in medicine. **3** a sweetened, carbonated drink flavored with sarsaparilla.

sash[1] /sash/ *n* an scarf worn around the waist or across the body over one shoulder.

sash[2] /sash/ *n* a window frame.

sashay /sa-**shay**/ *vb* to move, walk, etc. in such a way as to attract attention or show off.

sashimi /sa-**shu**-mee/ *n* a Japanese dish of thin slices of fresh raw fish served with soy sauce.

sasquatch /sa-skwatch/ *n* a large, hairy, humanlike creature with long arms said to live in the mountains of northwestern North America.

sass /sass/ *n* rash talk. ● *vb* to talk rashly, to talk without thinking of the consequences. ● *adj* **sassy** /sa-see/.

sassafras /sa-sa-fras/ *n* **1** a small eastern North American tree having a pleasant smelling bark. **2** the dried root bark of this tree used as a flavoring.

Satan /say-tin/ *n* **1** in Judaism, any of various beings that accuse or criticize humanity. **2** in Christian belief, the enemy of humankind and of goodness, the devil.

satanic /sa-**tan**-ic/ *adj* of, like, or having to do with the devil.

Satanism /say-ta-ni-zum/ *n* worship of Satan.

satay /sa-**tay**/ *n* a dish consisting of chunks of flavored meat broiled on sticks and dipped in a spicy peanut sauce.

satchel /sa-chel/ *n* a small bag worn on the shoulder or back for carrying books, clothes, etc.

sate /sate/ *vb* to satisfy a want fully.

satellite /sa-tu-lite/ *n* **1** a body that moves through the heavens in around a larger body, including those launched by man and those that are there naturally. **2** a person who depends completely on another. **3** a country that is totally in the power of another.

satellite dish /sa-tu-lite-dish/ *n* bowl-shaped device on the outside of a building for receiving television signals sent by a satellite.

satiate /say-shee-ate/ *vb* **1** to satisfy fully. **2** to give more than enough.

satiety /su-**tie**-i-tee/, **satiation** /say-shee-**ay**-shun/ *ns* **1** the state of having more than enough. **2** over-fullness.

satin /**sa**-tin/ *n* a silk and nylon cloth that is shiny on one side.

satire /**sa**-tire/ *n* a piece of writing in which persons, customs, actions, etc., are mocked and made to appear foolish. ● *adj* **satirical** /sa-**ti**-ri-cal/.

satirist /**sa**-ti-rist/, *n* a person who writes satires.

satirize /**sa**-ti-rize/ *vb, also* **satirise** (*Br*) to make seem foolish in satire.

satisfaction /sa-tis-**fac**-shun/ *n* **1** contentment. **2** the feeling of having enough.

satisfactory /sa-tis-**fac**-tree/ *adj* **1** good enough (*a satisfactory answer*). **2** quite good (*satisfactory work*).

satisfy /**sa**-tis-fie/ *vb* **1** to give all that is requested or expected (*satisfy her demand*). **2** to be enough (*satisfy their appetites*). **3** to convince (*satisfy them that he was innocent*).

satori /sa-**toe**-ree/ *n* the understanding of truth spiritually, used in Zen Buddhism.

satsuma /sat-**soo**-ma/ *n* a small, loose-skinned kind of orange.

saturate /**sa**-chu-rate/ *vb* to soak something so thoroughly that it cannot take in any more liquid. ● *n* **saturation** /sa-chu-**ray**-shun/.

Saturday /**sa**-tur-day/ *n* the seventh day of the week.

satyr /**say**-tur/ *adj* a mythical creature, half man, half goat.

sauce /saws/ *n* **1** a liquid poured on foods to improve or bring out the flavor. **2** (*inf*) rash talk, sass.

saucepan /**saws**-pan/ *n* a small pot with a lid and handle.

saucer /**saw**-ser/ *n* a small plate placed under a cup.

saucy /**saw**-see/ *adj* **1** rude. **2** stylish or smart.

sauerkraut /**sa**-wer-krout/ *n* chopped cabbage soaked in its own juice and salt.

sauna /**saw**-na/ *n* a bath of dry, hot air produced by dropping small amounts of water onto very hot stones, usually followed by a plunge into icy cold water.

saunter /**sawn**-ter/ *vb* to walk slowly, to stroll. ● *also n*.

sausage /**saw**-sidge/ *n* a roll of minced meat and seasonings in a thin skin.

sauté /saw-**tay**/ *adj* to fry quickly in a pan with a small amount of oil.

savage /**sa**-vidge/ *adj* **1** wild, untamed, or uncivilized (*savage animals*). **2** fierce, cruel (*savage blows*). ● *n* a very cruel person.

savagery /**sa**-vidge-ree/ *n* **1** cruelty. **2** the state of being wild or uncivilized.

savanna(h) /sa-**van**-a/ *n* a grassy, treeless plain.

save /save/ *vb* **1** to rescue from danger or harm. **2** to keep for future use (*save gift bows*). **3** to keep money instead of spending it (*save for your old age*). ● *prep* except.

savings /**say**-vingz/ *npl* money put aside for future use.

savior /**save**-yur/ *n, also* **saviour** (*Br, Cdn*) a person who saves from danger or harm.

savor /**say**-vur/ *n, also* **savour** (*Br, Cdn*) taste, flavor. ● *vb* **1** to taste. **2** to have a taste of, to suggest the idea of (*savor of disloyalty*).

savory /**say**-vu-ree/ *adj, also* **savoury** (*Br, Cdn*) tasty, arousing appetite (*savory smells*). **2** salty, meaty, or sharp, rather than sweet (*savory pastries*). ● *n* an appetizing dish served at the beginning or end of dinner.

savoy /sa-**voy**/ *n* a type of cabbage with crinkled leaves.

savvy /**sa**-vee/ (*inf*) *n* shrewdness, understanding, know-how.

saw[1] /saw/ *n* a tool with a toothed edge used for cutting wood, etc. ● *vb* to cut with a saw.

saw[2] /saw/ *n* a wise old saying.

saw[3] /saw/ *pt of* **see**.

sawdust /**saw**-dust/ *n* small fragments of wood made by sawing.

sawfish /**saw**-fish/ *n* a large, tropical, shark-like ray, its head prolonged into a flat, saw-like snout edged with large teeth on either side.

sawmill /**saw**-mill/ *n* a mill with a mechanical saw for cutting wood.

sax /saks/ *n* short for saxophone.

saxophone /**sak**-su-fone/ *n* a brass wind instrument with a single reed and keys.

say /say/ *vb* (*pt* **said** /sed/) **1** to utter in words, to speak. **2** to state (*say what you mean*). ● *n* the right to give an opinion.

saying /**say**-ing/ *n* a proverb, something commonly said.

scab /scab/ *n* a crust that forms over a healing sore. ● *adj* **scabby** /**sca**-bee/.

scabbard /**sca**-bard/ *n* the case of a sword.

scabies /**scay**-beez/ *n* an itchy skin disease.

scaffold /**sca**-foald/ *n* the platform on which people stand during the erecting, repairing, or painting of a building, etc.

scalawag /**sca**-li-wag/ *n* **1** a rascal. **2** a Southern white person who supported the Republicans during the post-Civil War Reconstruction.

scald /scawld/ *vb* to burn with hot liquid. ● *n* a burn caused by hot liquid.

scale[1] /scale/ *n* one of the thin flakes or flat plates on the skin of fish, reptiles, etc. ● *vb* to remove the scales from (*scale fish*). ● *adj* **scaly** /scay-lee/ covered with scales, like a fish.

scale[2] /scale/ *n* a balance or weighing machine.

scale[3] /scale/ *n* **1** a series of successive musical notes between one note and its octave. **2** the size of a map compared with the amount of area it represents (*a scale of ten miles to the inch*). **3** a measure (*the scale on a thermometer*). **4** a system of units for measuring (*the decimal scale*). **5** a system of grading (*the social scale*). **6** size, extent (*entertain on a large scale*). ● *vb* to climb (*scale the wall*).

scalene /scay-leen/ *adj* (*of a triangle*) having unequal sides and angles.

scallion /scal-yun/ *n* any of various onions or onion-like plants, such as the shallot, green onion, or leek.

scallop /sca-lup/ *n* **1** an edible shellfish, the shell of which has an uneven and toothed edge. **2** a series of even curves. ● *vb* to cut in scallops. ● *adj* **scalloped** with an edge shaped like that of the scallop shell.

scalp /scalp/ *n* the skin and hairs on top of the head. ● *vb* to cut off the scalp.

scalpel /scal-pul/ *n* a light, very sharp knife used by a surgeon.

scam /scam/ *n* a swindle, cheat, or fraud. ● *also vb.*

scamp /scamp/ *n* a rascal.

scamper /scam-per/ *vb* to run quickly or hurriedly, as if afraid. ● *n* a quick or hurried run.

scampi /scam-pee/ *n* a large shrimp broiled or fried with its tail on and served hot.

scan /scan/ *vb* (**scanned** /scand/, **scanning** /sca-ning/) **1** to look at closely or carefully (*scan the area for survivors*). **2** to obtain an image of an internal part (of the body) by using X-rays, ultrasonic waves, etc. ● *n* a medical examination in which part of the body is scanned (*a brain scan*).

scandal /scan-dal/ *n* **1** widespread talk about someone's wrongdoings, real or supposed (*listen to scandal*). **2** a disgrace (*their failure to act is a scandal*). **3** disgraceful behavior that gives rise to widespread talk (*a series of political scandals*).

scandalize /scan-da-lize/ *vb*, also **scandalise** (*Br*) to shock.

scandalous /scan-da-luss/ *adj* disgraceful.

scanner /sca-ner/ *n* a person or thing that scans.

scant /scant/ *adj* barely enough, very little (*pay scant attention*).

scanty /scan-tee/ *adj* barely enough, very little (*a scanty meal*).

scapegoat /scape-goat/ *n* a person who takes the blame for wrong done by others.

scar[1] /scar/ *n* the mark left by a healed wound. ● *vb* (**scarred** /scard/, **scarring** /sca-ring/) to leave or cause a scar.

scar[2] /scar/ *n* a cliff.

scarab /sca-rab/ *n* a beetle considered sacred in ancient Egypt.

scarce /scayrss/ *adj* **1** few and hard to find (*such birds are scarce now*). **2** not enough (*food is scarce*).

scarcely /scare-slee/ *adv* hardly, surely not.

scarcity /scare-si-tee/ *n* shortage, lack of what is necessary.

scare /scare/ *vb* to frighten. ● *n* a fright, panic.

scarecrow /scare-croe/ *n* **1** anything (e.g., a dummy man) set up to frighten away birds. **2** someone dressed in rags.

scaremonger /scare-mung-ger/ *n* a person who purposely scares people.

scarf /scarf/ *n* (*pl* **scarfs** /scarfs/ *or* **scarves** /scarvz/) a strip of material worn around the neck and over the shoulders.

scarify /scay-ri-fie/ *vb* to make many scratches or small cuts in the skin, as for surgery.

scarlet /scar-let/ *n* a bright red color. ● *also adj.*

scarlet fever /scar-let-fee-ver/ *n* a very infectious disease causing a red rash on the skin, sore throat, and fever.

scarp /scarp/ *n* a steep slope.

scary /skay-ree/ *adj* causing alarm, frightening.

scathe /skathe/ *vb* to injure.

scathing /skay-thing/ *adj* hurtful, bitter, harsh.

scatter /sca-ter/ *vb* **1** to throw about on all sides (*scatter confetti*). **2** to go away or drive in different directions (*crowds scattering*).

scatterbrain /sca-ter-brane/ *n* a foolish person, a person not capable of serious thinking. ● *adj* **scatterbrained** /sca-ter-braind/.

scattershot /sca-ter-shot/ *adj* having to do with a shotgun shell that spreads the shot in a broad pattern to cover more area.

scavenger /sca-vin-jer/ *n* an animal or person that searches for or lives on discarded or decaying material. ● *vb* **scavenge** /sca-vinge/.

scavenger hunt /sca-vin-jer-hunt/ *n* a party game in which people are sent out to find miscellaneous items without buying them.

scenario /si-nar-ee-yo/ *n* **1** an outline of the main incidents in a play or film. **2** an outline for any planned series of events.

scene /seen/ *n* **1** the place where something happens (*the scene of the crime*). **2** what a person can see from a certain viewpoint. **3** a distinct part of a play. **4** a painted background set up on the stage to represent the place of the action. **5** a quarrel or open show of strong feeling in a public place. ● **behind the scenes** in private.

scenery /seen-ree/ *n* **1** the painted backgrounds set up during a play to represent the places of the action. **2** the general appearance of a countryside (*an area of beautiful scenery*).

scenic /see-nic/ *adj* **1** having to do with scenery. **2** picturesque.

scent /sent/ *n* **1** a smell, especially a pleasant one. **2** the smell of an animal left on its tracks. **3** the sense of smell. ● *vb* **1** to smell. **2** to find by smelling. **3** to make something smell pleasant.

scepter /sep-ter/ *n* the staff held by a ruler as a sign of authority.

schedule /ske-jul/ *n* a list of details, a timetable (*production schedules*). ● *vb* to plan.

scheme /skeem/ *n* **1** a plan of what is to be done (*a work scheme*). **2** a plot (*a scheme to kill the president*). ● *vb* **1** to plan. **2** to plot. ● *n* **schemer** /skee-mer/. ● *adj* **scheming** /skee-ming/ given to planning schemes.

scholar /skoll-ar/ *n* **1** a learned person. **2** a school pupil.

scholarly /skoll-ar-lee/ *adj* learned.

scholarship /skoll-ar-ship/ *n* **1** learning. **2** wide knowledge. **3** a grant of money given to students to help pay for their education.

scholastic /sku-lass-tic/ *adj* having to do with schools or scholars.

school¹ /skool/ *n* **1** a place where instruction is given, where people learn. **2** a group of writers, thinkers, painters, etc., having the same or similar methods, principles, aims, etc. ● *vb* to train (*to school horses*).

school² /skool/ *n* a large number of fish of the same kind swimming together.

schoolbook /skool-book/ *n* a book used for study in schools.

schooling /skoo-ling/ *n* training or education.

schoolroom /skool-room/ *n* a room in which students are taught.

schoolteacher /skool-tee-cher/ *n* a person whose job it is to teach in a school.

schoolwork /skool-wurk/ *n* lessons worked on in classes for school or done as homework.

schooner /skoo-ner/ *n* **1** a large sailing ship with two masts. **2** a kind of large glass (*a schooner of water*).

sciatic /see-ya-tic/ *adj* having to do with the hip.

sciatica /see-ya-ti-ca/ *n* pain in the hip or thigh.

science /sie-ense/ *n* **1** all that is known about a subject, arranged in a systematic manner (*the science of geography*). **2** the study of the laws and principles of nature (*biology, physics and other branches of science*). **3** trained skill (*games requiring science rather than speed*).

science fiction /sie-ense-fic-shun/ *n* a form of fiction that deals with imaginary scientific developments or imaginary life on other planets, often abbreviated to **sci-fi**.

scientific /sie-en-ti-fic/ *adj* **1** having to do with science. **2** done in a systematic manner.

scientist /sie-en-tist/ *n* a person learned in one of the sciences.

sci-fi /sie-fie/ *see* **science fiction**.

scissor /si-zur/ *vb* to cut with scissors.

scissors /si-zurz/ *n* a cutting tool consisting of two blades moving on a central pin.

scoff /scoff/ *vb* to mock (at). ● *n* mocking words, a jeer.

scold /scoald/ *vb* to find fault with angrily.

scone /scone/ *n* a round, sweet biscuit served with butter.

scoop /scoop/ *vb* **1** to gather and lift up, as with the hands (*scoop up sand in your hands*). **2** to hollow with a knife, etc. (*to scoop a hollow in the melon half*). ● *n* **1** a deep shovel for lifting grain, earth from a hole, etc. **2** a piece of important news known only to one newspaper.

scoot /scoot/ *vb* to go or move quickly.

scooter /scoo-ter/ *n* a child's toy for riding on with a footboard, wheels at either end, and a raised handlebar for steering, moved by pushing off the ground with one foot.

scope /scope/ *n* **1** the range of matters being dealt with (*the scope of the book*). **2** opportunity (*scope for improvement*).

scorch /scawrch/ *vb* **1** to burn the outside of (*scorch the meat*). **2** to singe or blacken by burning (*scorched the shirt with the iron*).

scorcher /scawr-cher/ *n* **1** anything that scorches. **2** a very hot day.

score /score/ *n* **1** a set of 20. **2** a mark or line cut on the surface of. **3** a note of what is to be paid. **4** in games, the runs, goals, points, etc., made by those taking part. **5** a piece of music written down to show the parts played by different instruments. ● *vb* **1** to make marks or scratches on the surface of. **2** to gain an advantage. **3** to keep the score of a game. **4**

to arrange music in a score. ● **score off** to strike out. ● **score off** to get the better off. ● *n* **scorer** /sco-rer/.

scoreboard /score-board/ *n* a large board for posting the score and other details of a game.

scorekeeper /score-kee-per/ *n* a person who keeps score at a game or contest.

scorn /scawrn/ *vb* 1 to feel dislike for. 2 to refuse to have anything to do with (*scorn her friendly advances*). ● *n* dislike, complete lack of respect for.

scornful /scawrn-ful/ *adj* mocking, full of dislike.

scorpion /scawr-pee-on/ *n* a small creature related to the spider with eight legs and a lobsterlike tail containing a poisonous sting, found in warm regions.

scoundrel /scoun-drel/ *n* a thoroughly wicked person, a rascal.

scour[1] /scour/ *vb* to clean or brighten by rubbing.

scour[2] /scour/ *vb* to go back and forward over, searching carefully (*scour the fields for clues*).

scourge /scurdge/ *n* 1 a whip. 2 a cause of great trouble or suffering. ● *vb* 1 to whip. 2 to make suffer greatly.

scourings /scou-ringz/ *n* dirt or remains removed by scouring.

scout /scout/ *n* 1 a person sent in front to see what lies ahead and bring back news. 2 a person employed to find new talent. ● *vb* 1 to go out as a scout. 2 to search or explore (*to scout around for an open shop*).

Scout /scout/ *n* a member of the Boy Scouts or Girl Scouts, youth organizations that stress ability and skill in a wide range of activities.

scowl /scowl/ *vb* to lower the brows and wrinkle the forehead in anger or disapproval. ● *also n.*

scrabble /scra-bul/ *vb* 1 to scratch, scrape, or paw as though looking for something. 2 to struggle. 3 to scribble, to make meaningless marks.

scrabbly /scra-blee/ *adj* 1 having a scratching sound. 2 scrubby, poor, etc.

scrag /scrag/ *n* 1 a lean, scrawny person or animal. 2 a thin, stunted tree or plant. 3 the neck or back of the neck of certain kinds of meat.

scraggly /scrag-lee/ *adj* sparse, irregular, uneven, ragged, etc., in growth and form.

scraggy /scrag-ee/ *adj* thin and bony.

scram /scram/ *vb* to leave or get out, especially in a hurry.

scramble /scram-bul/ *vb* 1 to climb using both hands and feet. 2 to move awkwardly or with difficulty. 3 to struggle to obtain (*scramble for a seat in the*

bus) 4 to throw together randomly, to collect without any method. ● *n* a pushing and struggling for something.

scrap /scrap/ *n* 1 a small piece (*scraps of cloth*). 2 a picture, often cut to shape, for pasting in a book. 3 *pl* what is left over (*dogs feeding on scraps*). ● *vb* (**scrapped** /scrapt/, **scrapping** /scra-ping/) to throw away as no longer useful (*scrap the plans*).

scrapbook /scrap-book/ *n* a book for keeping scraps, cuttings from newspapers, pictures, etc.

scrape /scrape/ *vb* 1 to clean by rubbing with an edged instrument. 2 to make a harsh, unpleasant sound by rubbing along. 3 to save or gather with difficulty (*scrape together the food*). 4 to scratch by rubbing, as if by a fall (*she fell down the steps and scraped her knees*). ● *n* 1 a scratch. 2 something caused by scraping or its sound. 3 (*inf*) a small fight. 4 (*inf*) a difficult situation.

scrap heap /scrap-heep/ *n* a place for waste material, a garpage heap.

scraping /scray-ping/ *n* the act of a person or thing that scrapes, the sound of this.

scrappy /scra-pee/ *adj* 1 made up of bits and pieces. 2 fond of fighting.

scratch /scratch/ *vb* 1 to mark or wound the surface with something pointed. 2 to rub with the fingernails to stop itching. 3 to tear with the fingernails or claws. 4 to rub out or cross off (*scratch his name from the list*). 5 to withdraw from a competition or contest. ● *n* a slight mark or wound, especially one made by scratching. ● *adj* 1 without a plus or minus handicap (*scratch golfer*). 2 put together hastily (*scratch meal*). ● **up to scratch** as good as usual.

scratchy /scratch-ee/ *adj* that scratches, scrapes, itches, etc. (*scratchy throat with a cold/scratchy sweater*).

scrawl /scrawl/ *vb* to write untidily or carelessly. ● *n* untidy or careless handwriting.

scrawny /scraw-nee/ *adj* very thin, skinny, bony, small, etc.

scream /screem/ *vb* to shout in a loud, high-pitched voice, to shriek. ● *also n.*

screamer /scree-mer/ *n* a person who screams.

scree /scree/ *n* loose stones, etc., on a slope or at the foot of a cliff.

screech /screech/ *vb* to utter a loud, high-pitched cry. ● *also n.*

screed /screed/ *n* a long and uninteresting written statement.

screen /screen/ *n* 1 a movable piece of furniture, similar to a section of fence, that can be used to block a draft, to conceal part of a room, etc. **2** a surface on which movies are shown. **3** a frame covered with mesh of wire or plastic and fixed into windows or doors so that when they are open no insects can get in. **4** the front glass surface of a television, computer, etc., on which pictures or items of information are shown. **5** a sieve for separating smaller pieces of coal, stones, etc., from larger. ● *vb* **1** to protect (*trees screening the garden from the public view*). **2** to hide (*screen his son from the police*). **3** to put through a test (*screen all applicants for jobs in the office*). **4** to carry out medical tests on a large number of people to check whether they have a particular disease or not (*screen women over 50 for breast cancer*). **5** to show on film or television.

screenplay /screen-play/ *n* the script from which a film is produced.

screen saver /screen-say-ver/ *n* a program that prolongs the life of a computer monitor.

screenwriter /screen-rie-ter/ *n* the writer of a script for a film.

screw /scroo/ *n* **1** a type of nail with a spiral thread so that it can be twisted into wood, etc., instead of hammered. **2** a twist or turn. ● *vb* **1** to fasten by means of a screw. **2** to twist.

screwdriver /scroo-drie-ver/ *n* a tool that can fit into the slot on the head of a screw and turn it into wood, plaster, etc.

scribble /scri-bul/ *vb* to write carelessly or hurriedly. ● *n* something written quickly or carelessly. ● *n* **scribbler** /scri-bler/ a person who writes carelessly.

scribe /scribe/ *n* **1** a person whose job it was to copy books, pamphlets, poems, etc., by hand before the invention of the printing machine. **2** a writer or author.

scrim /scrim/ *n* a light, sheer, loosely woven cloth used for curtains, linings, etc.

scrimmage /scri-midge/ *n* **1** a confused fight or struggle. **2** a practice session or game between two different teams or two units of the same team.

scrimp /scrimp/ *vb* to give or use too little (*scrimp on food*).

script /script/ *n* **1** handwriting. **2** a printing type like handwriting. **3** a written outline of the actions, speaking, etc., in a film. **4** the text of a show, film, or play.

scripture(s) /scrip-chur(z)/ *n* **1** anything written. **2** a holy book or set of writings, such as the Bible, the Koran, etc. ● *adj* **scriptural** /scrip(t)-shral/.

scrounge /scrounj/ *vb* to try to get something for free (*the dog was scrounging around for food*).

scrub[1] /scrub/ *vb* (**scrubbed** /scrubd/, **scrubbing** /scrubbing/) **1** to clean by rubbing hard, especially with a stiff brush. **2** (*inf*) to cancel, to remove. ● *n* **scrubber** /scru-ber/ any person or thing that scrubs.

scrub[2] /scrub/ *n* small stunted bushes or trees, brushwood. ● *adj* **scrubby** /scru-bee/.

scrubland /scrub-land/ *n* land or a region that has much scrub plant life.

scrubs /scrubz/ *n* specially cleaned clothing worn by doctors, nurses, etc. when they perform surgery, etc

scruff /scruff/ *n* the back of the neck.

scruffy /scru-fee/ *adj* shabby, untidy.

scrumptious /scrum-chus/ *adj* very pleasing, attractive, etc., especially to the taste, delicious.

scrutinize /scroo-ti-nize/ *vb, also* **scrutinise** (*Br*) to look at closely or carefully. ● *n* **scrutinizer** /scroo-ti-nie-zer/, *also* **scrutiniser** (*Br*).

scrutiny /scroo-ti-nee/ *n* a close or careful look.

scuba /soo-ba/ *n* an acronym that stands for self-contained underwater breathing apparatus, what is worn by divers for breathing underwater, usually consisting of air tanks strapped to the back and connected by a hose to a mouthpiece.

scud /scud/ *vb* (**scudded** /scu-did/, **scudding** /scu-ding/) **1** to run quickly. **2** (*of a ship*) to sail quickly before a following wind. ● *n* spray, rain, or snow driven along by the wind.

scuff /scuff/ *vb* **1** to scrape with the feet. **2** to wear a rough place or places on the surface of.

scuffle /scu-ful/ *n* a confused or disorderly struggle.

scull /scull/ *n* one of a pair of short oars. ● *vb* **1** to row with sculls. **2** to move a boat by rowing with one oar at the front.

sculpt /sculpt/ *vb* to carve or model a figure, design, image, etc.

sculptor /sculp-tur/ *n* a person skilled in sculpture.

sculpture /sculp-chur/ *n* **1** the art of carving or modeling in wood, stone, clay, etc. **2** a work of sculpture.

scum /scum/ *n* **1** dirt and froth that gathers on the surface of liquid. **2** wicked or worthless people (*the scum who mugged the old man*). ● *adj* **scummy** /scu-mee/.

scurf /scurf/ *n* small dry flakes of skin.

scurrilous /scu-ri-lus/ *adj* **1** using bad or indecent language. **2** very insulting.

scurry /scur-vee/ *vb* to run hurriedly. ● *also n*.

scurvy /scur-vee/ *n* a disease caused by lack of fresh fruit or vegetables. ● *adj* mean, nasty.

scuttle[1] /scu-tul/ *n* a box or pail for keeping coal at the fireside.

scuttle² /**scu**-tul/ n a hole with a lid in the deck or side of a ship. ● vb to sink (a ship) by making a hole in it.

scuttle³ /**scu**-tul/ vb to run away hurriedly.

scythe /**sythe**/ n a tool consisting of a long, curving, very sharp blade set at an angle to a long handle, used for cutting grass, etc. ● vb to cut with a scythe.

sea /**see**/ n **1** the salt water that covers much of Earth's surface. **2** a large extent of this. **3** the ocean or part of it. **4** the swell of the sea. **5** a large amount or extent of anything (a sea of papers on her desk). ● **at sea** on the sea.

seabed /**see**-bed/ n the ocean floor, especially the areas with rich mineral or oil deposits.

seabird /**see**-bird/ n a bird living on or near the sea.

seaboard /**see**-board/ n land or coastal region near the sea.

seafood /**see**-food/ n food prepared from or consisting of saltwater fish or shellfish.

sea gull /**see**-gull/ n a kind of bird that lives along the seacoast.

sea horse /**see**-hawrse/ n a kind of small, tropical, bony fish with the head and nose looking somewhat like those of a horse.

seal¹ /**seel**/ n **1** wax with a design, etc., stamped on it, used to fasten shut envelopes, boxes, etc. **2** a stamp with a design, initials, etc., engraved on it. **3** a substance or thing that closes, fixes, or prevents leakage (a bottle seal). ● vb **1** to fasten with a seal. **2** to close firmly. **3** to make airtight (seal jars of preserved fruit). **4** to confirm (seal the agreement).

seal² /**seel**/ n a sea animal valued for its oil and fur.

sealant /**see**-lant/ n any substance used for sealing, such as wax, plastic, etc.

sea level /**see**-le-vel/ n the level of the sea's surface at half-tide.

sea lion /**see**-lie-un/ n a large seal.

sealskin /**seel**-skin/ n **1** the skin or pelt of the fur seal, especially with the outer fur removed exposing the soft underfur. **2** an article of clothing made from this.

seam /**seem**/ n the line made by two pieces of something joined together, such as the stitching joining two pieces of cloth.

seamless /**seem**-less/ adj made without a seam.

seamstress /**seem**-stress/ n a woman who makes her living by sewing.

séance /**say**-onss/ n a meeting, especially of people who believe they can call up the spirits of the dead.

seaplane /**see**-plane/ n an airplane with floats that enable it to take off from or land on water.

seaport /**see**-poart/ n a town with a harbor.

sear /**seer**/ vb **1** to burn with sudden powerful heat. **2** to wither (grass seared by the sun). ● adj dry, withered.

search /**serch**/ vb to look for, to explore, to try to find. ● n act of looking for. ● n **searcher** /**ser**-cher/.

search engine /**serch**-en-jin/ n computer software designed to locate items on a given topic.

searching /**ser**-ching/ adj thorough, testing thoroughly.

searchlight /**serch**-lite/ n a powerful electric lamp able to throw a beam of light on distant objects.

seasick /**see**-sick/ adj sick because of the rocking of a ship at sea.

seaside /**see**-side/ n the land near or beside the sea.

season¹ /**see**-zun/ n **1** one of the four divisions of the year (e.g., winter, summer). **2** a time of the year noted for a particular activity (the football season).

season² /**see**-zun/ vb **1** to make (wood) hard and fit for use by drying gradually. **2** to add something to food to give it a good taste.

seasonable /**seez**-na-bul/ adj **1** happening at the right time (seasonable advice). **2** suitable to the season of the year (seasonable weather).

seasonal /**seez**-nal/ adj having to do with one or all of the seasons (seasonal variations in the weather).

seasoning /**seez**-ning/ n anything added to food to bring out or improve its taste.

season ticket /**see**-zun-ti-ket/ a ticket that can be used many times over a stated period.

seat /**seet**/ n **1** anything on which a person sits. **2** a piece of furniture for sitting on. **3** the right to site as a member. ● vb **1** to place on a seat. **2** to have or provide seats for (a hall seating 500).

seat belt /**seet**-belt/ n a belt worn across the lap and sometimes chest to keep a person in place while driving, flying, riding, etc.

sea urchin /**see**-ur-chin/ n a sea creature living in a round prickly shell.

seaweed /**see**-weed/ ns sea plants.

secede /si-**seed**/ vb to break away from (during the Civil War, US states were seceding from the union).

secession /si-**se**-shun/ n act of seceding. ● n **secessionist** /si-**se**-shu-nist/ a person who favors or takes part in a secession.

seclude /si-**clood**/ vb to keep away from others, to make private or hidden.

secluded /si-**cloo**-did/ adj **1** out of the way (a secluded part of the garden). **2** private, quiet (a secluded life).

seclusion /si-**cloo**-zhun/ n quietness and privacy.

seclusive /si-**cloo**-siv/ *adj* fond of or seeking seclusion.

second[1] /**se**-cund/ *adj* coming immediately after the first. ● *n* 1 a person who comes after the first. 2 a person who supports and assists another in a fight or duel. 3 *npl* goods that because of some flaw are sold more cheaply. ● *vb* 1 to support (*second a proposal*). 2 to assist (*second him in the duel*). ● *vb* **second** /si-**cond**/ to transfer from normal duties to other duties (*second him to the advertising department for a month*).

second[2] /**se**-cund/ *n* the 60th part of a minute.

secondary /**se**-cun-de-ree/ *adj* 1 of less importance (*secondary considerations*). 2 coming after that which is first in a series of events, states, etc.

second-guess /se-cund-**gess**/ *vb* remaking a decision.

secondhand /se-cund-**hand**/ *adj* not new, having been used by another.

second hand /se-cund-**hand**/ *n* the hand on a clock or watch that times the seconds.

second nature /se-cund-**nay**-chur/ *n* habits fixed so deeply that they seem a part of a person's nature.

second-rate /se-cund-**rate**/ *adj* not of high quality.

second sight /se-cund-**site**/ *n* the ability to see things happening elsewhere or to foresee the future.

second wind /se-cund-**wind**/ *n* the ability to breathe smoothly again after having been out of breath.

secrecy /**see**-cre-see/ *n* 1 the habit of keeping information to oneself. 2 concealment (*the secrecy surrounding the meeting*).

secret /**see**-cret/ *adj* 1 hidden from others. 2 known or told to few (*a secret drawer/a secret meeting*). 3 private (*secret thoughts*). ● *n* 1 a piece of information kept from others. 2 privacy (*a meeting in secret*). 3 a hidden reason or cause (*the secret of their success*).

secretarial /sec-re-**ter**-ee-al/ *adj* having to do with the work of a secretary.

secretary /**sec**-re-ter-ee/ *n* 1 a person whose job it is to deal with letters and help to carry out the day-to-day business of his or her employer. 2 a high government official or minister (*the foreign secretary*).

secrete /si-**creet**/ *vb* 1 to hide away (*secreting the documents in a locked box*). 2 to produce a substance or fluid within the body by means of glands or other organs.

secretion /si-**cree**-shun/ *n* 1 the act of secreting. 2 the substance or fluid secreted (e.g., saliva).

secretive /**see**-cri-tiv/ *adj* 1 keeping information to oneself. 2 fond of concealing things.

sect /sect/ *n* a body of persons holding the same beliefs, especially in religion.

sectarian /sec-**ter**-ee-an/ *adj* 1 having to do with a sect or sects. 2 concerned with or relating to the interests of a person's own group, etc.

section /**sec**-shun/ *n* 1 a distinct part. 2 a part cut off (*a section of apple*). ● *adj* **sectional** /**sec**-shnal/.

sector /**sec**-tor/ *n* 1 a section of a circle. 2 one of the parts into which an area is divided (*the Italian sector of the city*). 3 part of a field of activity (*the private sector of industry*). ● *adj* **sectorial**.

secular /**se**-cyu-lar/ *adj* 1 having to do with this world, not with a faith or religion; not sacred. 2 having to do with lay, not church, affairs. ● *n* **secularity** /se-cyu-**la**-ri-tee/ the state or quality of being secular. ● *vb* **secularize** /**se**-cyu-la-rize/, *also* **secularise** (*Br*) to change from religious to civil ownership or use. ● *n* **secularism** /**se**-cyu-la-ri-zum/.

secure /si-**cyoor**/ *adj* 1 free from care or danger (*a secure home life*). 2 safe (*a secure place for the jewels*). ● *vb* 1 to make safe. 2 to fasten securely. 3 to seize and hold firmly.

security /si-**cyoo**-ri-tee/ *n* 1 safety. 2 precautions taken to protect someone or something from attack, crime, danger, etc. (*increased security measures at airports*). 3 something given as proof of a person's willingness or ability to repay a loan. 4 *pl* documents stating that a person has lent a sum of money to a business, etc., and is entitled to receive interest on it.

sedan /si-**dan**/ *n* a car with either two or four doors, a full-sized rear seat, and a hard top.

sedate /si-**date**/ *adj* calm, quiet, and relaxed (*a sedate conversation*). ● *vb* to make calm or sleepy.

sedation /si-**day**-shun/ *n* the act or process of reducing excitement or nervousness.

sedative /**se**-da-tiv/ *adj* having a calming effect. ● *n* a sedative drug.

sedentary /**se**-den-ter-ee/ *adj* inactive, requiring much sitting.

sediment /**se**-di-ment/ *n* the particles of matter that sink to the bottom of liquid. ● *adj* **sedimentary** /se-di-**men**-tu-ree/ of, having the nature of, or containing sediment.

sedition /se-**di**-shun/ *n* words or actions intended to stir up rebellion against the government. ● *adj* **seditious** /se-**di**-shus/.

seduce /si-**dooss**/ *vb* 1 to persuade someone to do what is wrong or immoral. 2 to persuade to have sexual intercourse. ● *n* **seducer** /si-**doo**-ser/.

seduction /si-**duc**-shun/ *n* the act of seducing.

seductive /si-**duc**-tiv/ *adj* **1** tempting, attracting to do wrong. **2** sexually attractive.

see[1] /**see**/ *vb* (*pt* **saw** /**saw**/, *pp* **seen** /**seen**/) **1** to look at with the eye. **2** to notice. **3** to understand. **4** to visit or interview. ● **see about** to attend to. ● **see off 1** to go so far with a person who is leaving. **2** (*inf*) to get rid of. ● **see through 1** to keep on with to the end. **2** to understand thoroughly (someone's character, etc.). ● **seeing that** since, because.

see[2] /**see**/ *n* the district over which a bishop has control.

seed /**seed**/ *n* **1** the grain or germ from which, when placed in the ground, a new plant grows. **2** children, descendants. ● *vb* to produce seed, to plant seeds. ● **go to seed, run to seed 1** (*of a plant*) to shoot up too quickly. **2** to grow careless and lazy. **3** to become weak.

seedbed /**seed**-bed/ *n* a bed of soil, usually covered with glass, in which seedlings are grown.

seedling /**seed**-ling/ *n* a young plant grown from a seed.

seedy /**see**-dee/ *adj* **1** shabby (*a seedy part of the town*). **2** unwell. **3** containing many seeds.

seeing /**see**-ing/ *n* the sense or power of sight, the act of using the eyes to see.

Seeing Eye dog /**see**-ing-**eye**-dawg/ *n* a dog trained to guide a blind person, a guide dog.

seek /**seek**/ *vb* (*pt*, *pp* **sought** /**sawt**/) **1** to look for. **2** to try to get, to ask.

seem /**seem**/ *vb* to appear to be, look as if.

seeming /**see**-ming/ *adj* having the appearance of, apparent.

seemly /**seem**-lee/ *adj* proper, fitting, decent (*seemly behavior*).

seep /**seep**/ *vb* to leak, drip, or flow slowly out through small openings. ● *n* **seepage** the act or process of seeping, the liquid that seeps.

seer /**seer**/ *n* a person who foresees the future, a prophet.

seersucker /**seer**-su-ker/ *n* a crinkled fabric of linen, cotton, etc., usually with a striped pattern.

seesaw /**see**-saw/ *n* **1** a plank that is balanced in the middle and on which children sit at either end so that when one end goes up the other end goes down. **2** the act of moving up and down or back and forth. ● *adj* moving up and down like a seesaw. ● *vb* **1** to play on a seesaw. **2** to move up and down or back and forth (*prices continually seesawing*).

seethe /**seethe**/ *vb* **1** to boil. **2** to be full of anger, excitement, etc.

see-through /**see**-throo/ *adj* that ccan be seen through, more or less transparent.

segment /**seg**-ment/ *n* **1** a piece cut off. **2** part of a circle cut off by a straight line. ● *vb* to cut into segments. ● *adj* **segmental** /seg-**men**-tal/.

segmentation /seg-men-**tay**-shun/ *n* a dividing or being divided into segments.

segregate /**seg**-ri-gate/ *vb* to set apart or separate from others (*segregate the girls and boys*). ● *n* **segregation** /seg-ri-**gay**-shun/.

seismic /**size**-mik/ *adj* having to do with earthquakes.

seismograph /**size**-mo-graf/ *n* an instrument showing the force of an earthquake and the direction in which it has occurred.

seismology /size-**mol**-u-jee/ *n* the science of earthquakes.

seize /**seez**/ *vb* **1** to take by force (*seize a hostage*). **2** to take firm hold of (*seize a branch or an opportunity*).

seizure /**see**-zhur/ *n* **1** act of taking by force. **2** a sudden attack of illness.

seldom /**sel**-dum/ *adv* rarely.

select /se-**lect**/ *vb* to choose, to pick out. ● *adj* specially chosen. ● *n* **selector** /se-**lec**-tur/ the person or thing that selects.

selection /se-**lec**-shun/ *n* **1** act of choosing. **2** what is chosen.

selective /se-**lec**-tiv/ *adj* choosing carefully, rejecting what is not wanted.

self /**self**/ *n* (*pl* **selves** /**selvz**/) a person's own person or interest.

self- /**self**/ *prefix* of oneself or itself.

self-awareness /self-a-**ware**-ness/ *n* awareness of oneself as an individual.

self-centered /self-**sen**-turd/ *adj* selfish, thinking chiefly of oneself and one's interests.

self-confident /self-**con**-fi-dent/ *adj* sure of oneself and one's powers.

self-conscious /self-**con**-shus/ *adj* thinking about oneself too much, shy because one thinks others are watching.

self-contained /self-cun-**taind**/ *adj* **1** keeping to oneself, not showing one's feelings. **2** (*of a house*) complete in itself and separate from other houses.

self-control /self-cun-**trole**/ *n* the ability to control one's temper, excitement, etc.

self-destruct /self-di-**struct**/ *vb* to destroy itself automatically. ● *n* **self-destruction** /self-di-**struc**-shun/. ● *adj* **self-destructive** /self-di-**struc**-tiv/.

self-employed /self-im-**ployd**/ *adj* working for oneself, with direct control over work, services, etc.

self-esteem /self-i-**steem**/ *n* one's opinion of oneself, self-respect.

self-help /self-**help**/ *n* care of or betterment of oneself by one's own efforts.

self-important /self-im-**pore**-tant/ *adj* full of one's own importance, pompous. ● *n* **self-importance** / self-im-**pore**-tanse/.

selfish /**sel**-fish/ *adj* thinking only of oneself and one's own advantage. ● *n* **selfishness** /**sel**-fish-ness/.

selfless /**self**-less/ *adj* concerned about other's welfare or interests and not one's own.

self-respect /self-re-**spect**/ *n* proper care of one's own character and reputation.

self-righteous /self-**rie**-chus/ *adj* too aware of what one supposes to be one's own goodness.

self-sacrificing /self-**sa**-cri-fie-sing/ *adj* ready to give up one's own desires for the good of others.

self-service /self-**ser**-viss/ *adj* (*of a shop, restaurant, etc.*) helping oneself. ● *also n.*

self-sufficient /self-su-**fi**-shent/ *adj* needing no help from others (*a country self-sufficient in food*).

sell /sell/ *vb* (*pt, pp* **sold** /soald/) to give in exchange for money.

seller /**se**-ler/ *n* a person who sells.

sellout /**se**-lout/ *n* the act of betraying someone or something, a person who betrays someone or something.

seltzer /**selt**-ser/ *n* carbonated mineral water.

selves /selvz/ *see* **self**.

semantic /se-**man**-tic/ *adj* of or regarding meaning, especially meaning in language.

semaphore /**sem**-ah-fore/ *n* a system of conveying messages using flags.

semblance /**sem**-blanse/ *n* outward appearance (*the semblance of order*).

semester /si-**mes**-ter/ *n* a school term of about 18 weeks.

semen /**see**-men/ *n* the white fluid produced by the reproductive organs of male mammals, also called sperm.

semi- /**se**-mee/ *prefix* half.

semicircle /**se**-mee-sir-cul/ *n* a half circle. ● *adj* **semicircular** /se-mee-**sir**-cyu-lar/.

semicolon /se-mee-**co**-lon/ *n* a mark of punctuation (;).

semifinal /se-mee-**fie**-nal/ *adj* coming just before the final match, as in a tournament.

seminar /**se**-mi-nar/ *n* a group of students working together under the guidance of a teacher.

seminary /**se**-mi-ne-ree/ *n* a school or college, especially one training people to be priests, ministers, rabbis, etc.

Seminole /**se**-mi-nole/ *n* **1** a member of a Native American group now living in Florida and Okahoma. **2** the variety of languages spoken by this group of people.

Semite /**se**-mite/ *n* **1** a member of any of the peoples who speak a Semitic language, including the Hebrews, Arabs, Assyrians, etc. **2** used loosely, a Jewish person.

Semitic /se-**mi**-tic/ *adj* **1** having to do with Semites.

senate /**se**-nit/ *n* **1** a group of officials elected to make laws. **2** (*with cap*) one of the two houses of the United States Congress. **3** the governing body of certain universities.

senator /**se**-ni-tor/ *n* a member of a senate. ● *adj* **senatorial** /se-ni-**toe**-ree-al/.

send /send/ *vb* (*pt, pp* **sent** /sent/) **1** to have taken from one place to another (*send a package*). **2** to order to go (*send them away*). ● *n* **sender** /**sen**-der/.

Seneca /**se**-ne-ca/ *n* **1** a member of a Native American group now living in New York and Ontario. **2** the language spoken by this group.

senile /**see**-nile/ *adj* weak in the mind from old age. ● *n* **senility** /si-**ni**-li-tee/.

senior /**seen**-yur/ *adj* **1** older. **2** higher in rank or importance. ● *n* **1** one older (*she is her brother's senior/the seniors in the school*). **2** a person having longer service or higher rank (*the senior partners in the law firm*). ● *n* **seniority** /seen-**yawr**-i-tee/.

sensation /sen-**say**-shun/ *n* **1** the ability to perceive through the senses, feeling (*lose sensation in her legs*). **2** a feeling that cannot be described (*a sensation of being watched*). **3** great excitement (*murder trials causing a sensation*). **4** an event that causes great excitement (*the news article was a sensation*).

sensational /sen-**say**-shnal/ *adj* causing great excitement. ● *vb* **sensationalize** /sen-**say**-shna-lize/, *also* **sensationalise** (*Br*).

sensationalism /sen-**say**-shna-li-zum/ *n* a liking for exciting news and events.

sense /senss/ *n* **1** one of the five powers (sight, hearing, taste, smell, touch) by which people and animals gain knowledge of things outside themselves. **2** wisdom in everyday things (*have the sense to keep warm*). **3** understanding (*no sense of direction*). **4** meaning (*words with several senses*).

senseless /**senss**-less/ *adj* **1** foolish, pointless (*a senseless act*). **2** unconscious (*senseless after a blow to the head*).

sensibility /sen-si-**bi**-li-tee/ *n* **1** the ability to feel emotions strongly. **2** delicacy of feeling.

sensible /**sen**-si-bul/ *adj* **1** having or showing good judgment, wise (*a sensible decision*). **2** aware (*sensible of the feelings of others*). **3** practical (*sensible shoes*).

sensitive /**sen**-si-tiv/ *adj* **1** quick to feel things (*too sensitive for the rough language of others*). **2** easily hurt or damaged (*sensitive skin*). **3** able to feel emotions strongly (*a sensitive reading of the poem*). ● *n* **sensitivity** /sen-si-**ti**-vi-tee/.

sensor /**sen**-sawr/ *n* a tool designed to detect, measure, or record things such as heat, temperature, pressure, etc.

sensory /**sen**-sree/ *adj* having to do with the senses.

sensual /**sen**-shwal/ *adj* **1** having to do with the pleasures of the body (*the sensual pleasure of soaking in a scented bath*). **2** fond of the pleasures of the body. ● *n* **sensuality** /sen-shu-**wa**-li-tee/.

sensuous /**sen**-shwus/ *adj* **1** having to do with the senses. **2** pleasing to the senses (*the sensuous pleasure of music*).

sentence /**sen**-tense/ *n* **1** a group of words, containing at least a subject and a verb, that are grammatically correct and make complete sense. **2** a judgment given in a court of law (*pass sentence*). **3** the punishment given to a wrongdoer by a judge (*a sentence of five years*). ● *vb* to state the punishment given to a wrongdoer.

sentient /**sen**-shent/ *adj* having the power of feeling. ● *n* **sentience** /**sen**-shense/ ability to feel.

sentiment /**sen**-ti-ment/ *n* **1** what a person feels or thinks about something (*I share your sentiments*). **2** an expression of feeling (*a song full of patriotic sentiment*). **3** tender or kindly feeling (*sentiments printed on birthday cards*).

sentimental /sen-ti-**men**-tal/ *adj* **1** showing, causing, etc., excessive tender feeling or emotion (*a sentimental love song*). **2** concerning the emotions rather than reason (*a watch with sentimental value*). ● *n* **sentimentality** /sen-ti-men-**ta**-li-tee/.

sentinel /**sen**-ti-nel/ *n* a person or animal that guards a group.

sentry /**sen**-tree/ *n* a soldier on guard.

sentry box /**sen**-tree-boks/ *n* a shelter for a sentry.

separate /**sep**-rate/ *vb* **1** to put apart. **2** to go away from. **3** to stop living together (*their parents have separated*). **4** to go different ways (*they separated at the crossroads*). **5** to divide into parts. ● *adj* unconnected, distinct, apart. ● *adj* **separable** /**se**-pra-bul/.

separation /se-pe-**ray**-shun/ *n* **1** act of separating. **2** an agreement by a married couple to live apart from each other.

separatism /**se**-pra-ti-zum/ *n* the condition of political, religious, or racial separation. ● *n* **separatist** /**se**-pra-tist/ a person who believes in separatism.

sepia /**see**-pee-ya/ *n* a dark, reddish brown dye or color made from fluid obtained from the cuttlefish.

September /sep-**tem**-ber/ *n* the ninth month of the year.

septic /**sep**-tic/ *adj* infected and poisoned by germs.

septic tank /**sep**-tic-tangk/ *n* an underground tank for waste matter to be stored and broken down.

septuagenarian /sep-ti-wa-je-**ner**-ee-an/ *n* one who is seventy years old or between seventy and eighty.

septuplet /**sep**-tu-plet/ *n* one of seven babies born at a single birth.

sepulchral /se-**pul**-cral/ *adj* **1** having to do with a tomb. **2** (*of a voice*) deep and gloomy.

sepulture /**se**-pul-chur/ *n* burial.

sequel /**see**-kwel/ *n* **1** that which follows, a result or consequence (*a sequel to the official inquiry was that standards improved*). **2** a novel, film, etc., that continues the story of an earlier one.

sequence /**see**-kwense/ *n* a number of things, events, etc., following each other in a natural or correct order.

sequential /si-**kwen**-shal/ *adj* of, relating to, or forming a sequence.

sequin /**see**-kwin/ *n* a tiny disc of bright metal sewn onto a dress for ornament, usually one of many. ● *adj* **sequined** /**see**-kwind/ decorated with sequins.

sequoia /**see**-kwee-ya/ *n* a large redwood tree.

seraph /**se**-raf/ *n* (*pl* **seraphs** /**se**-rafs/ *or* **seraphim** /**se**-ra-fim/) an angel of the highest rank.

seraphic /se-**ra**-fic/ *adj* angelic, pure.

serenade /se-ra-**nade**/ *n* a musical work played outside at night, especially by a lover under the window of his sweetheart. ● *vb* to sing or play a serenade.

serendipidy /se-ren-**di**-pi-tee/ *n* a seeming gift for finding something good accidentally.

serene /se-**reen**/ *adj* calm, undisturbed.

serenity /se-**re**-ni-tee/ *n* calmness, peace.

serf /**serf**/ *n* a slave, a person bound to his or her master's land and transferred with it to any new owner.

serge /**serge**/ *n* a strong woolen cloth.

sergeant /**sar**-jint/ *n* **1** in the US Army and US Marine Corps, a noncommissioned officer a rank above corporal. **2** in the US Air Force, a noncommissioned officer a rank above airman first class.

3 in the police, an officer just below a captain or lieutenant.

serial /**see**-ree-al/ *n* a story published or broadcast in parts or installments. ● *adj* **1** happening in a series (*serial murders*). **2** in successive parts (*a serial story*).

series /**see**-reez/ *n* (*pl* **series** /**se**-reez/) a number of things arranged in a definite order.

serious /**see**-ree-us/ *adj* **1** thoughtful (*in a serious mood*). **2** important (*more serious issues*). **3** likely to cause danger (*a serious wound*).

sermon /**ser**-mun/ *n* **1** a talk given by a priest, minister, or rabbi on a religious subject. **2** a talk containing advice or warning. ● *vb* **sermonize** /**ser**-mu-nize/, *also* **sermonise** (*Br*).

serpent /**ser**-pent/ *n* a snake.

serrate /se-**rate**/, *or* **serrated** /se-**ray**-tid/ *adj* having notches like the edge of a saw.

serration /se-**ray**-shun/ *n* the condition of being serrate.

serum /**see**-rum/ *n* **1** the watery part of the blood. **2** liquid taken from the blood of an animal and injected into a person's blood to protect against a disease. **3** the thin, watery part of plant fluid.

servant /**ser**-vant/ *n* **1** a person who works for and obeys another (*politicians regarded as servants of the people*). **2** a person employed to do tasks about the house (*houses looked after by a team of servants in colonial times*).

serve /serv/ *vb* **1** to work for and obey. **2** to hand food to at the table. **3** to supply with (food, etc.). **4** to be helpful. **5** (*in tennis, volleyball, etc.*) to hit the ball into play. ● **serves you right** that is just what you deserve.

server /**ser**-ver/ *n* **1** a person who serves. **2** the central computer in a network to which other computers are connected so that software and files can be shared.

service /**ser**-viss/ *n* **1** the work of a servant or employee (*five years' service with the company*). **2** time spent in the forces, police, etc. **3** use, help (*people who can be of service to us*). **4** a religious ceremony. **5** a set of dishes for use at table (*a dinner service*). **6** in tennis, the hit intended to put the ball into play. **7** *pl* the armed forces.

serviceable /**ser**-vi-sa-bul/ *adj* useful.

service station /**ser**-vis-stay-shun/ *n* a place that sells gasoline, oils, some other car requirements and often drinks and snacks, and usually provides toilet facilities.

servile /**ser**-vul/ *adj* behaving like a slave, too ready to obey. ● *n* **servility** /ser-**vi**-li-tee/.

servitude /**ser**-vi-tood/ *n* slavery, the condition of being a slave, serf, etc.

sesame /**se**-sa-mee/ *n* a plant whose seeds are used in cooking and from which an oil, used in cooking and salads, is obtained. ● **open sesame** a sure means of gaining admission (*his wealth was an open sesame to all clubs*).

session /**se**-shun/ *n* a meeting of a group or sitting of a court or assembly.

set /set/ *vb* (**set**, **setting** /**se**-ting/) **1** to put. **2** to fix in position (*set a broken bone*). **3** to put to music. **4** to become hard or solid (*leave jellies to set*). **5** (*of the sun, etc.*) to sink below the horizon (*the sun setting*). ● *n* **1** a number of things of the same kind. **2** a group of people with similar interests. **3** a group of games in a tennis match. ● *adj* fixed, regular. ● **set off, set out** to begin a journey. ● **set upon** to attack.

setback /**set**-back/ *n* something that keeps a person from doing something, from carrying out a plan.

set point /**set**-point/ *n* in a game such as tennis, when the next point scored by a player decides the winner of the set.

settee /se-**tee**/ *n* a small sofa.

setting /**se**-ting/ *n* **1** surroundings (*a house in a woodland setting*). **2** background (*a story with its setting in colonial times*). **3** music written to go with certain words.

settle /**se**-tul/ *n* a bench with arms and a high back. ● *vb* **1** to set up home in a certain place (*decide to settle in the country*). **2** to come to rest on (*a butterfly settling on a flower*). **3** to put an end to by giving a decision or judgment (*settle the argument*). **4** to make or become quiet or calm (*the baby was slow to settle*). **5** to pay (a bill, etc.). **6** to sink to the bottom of (*coffee grinds settling at the bottom of the cup*).

settlement /**se**-tul-ment/ *n* **1** a decision or judgment that ends an argument. **2** money or property given to someone under certain conditions. **3** payment of a bill. **4** a colony.

settler /**set**-ler/ *n* someone who makes his or her home in a new colony or land that has not previously been occupied.

set-to /**set**-too/ *n* a fight.

setup /**se**-tup/ *n* **1** the way in which something is set up. **2** a contest or plan that is arranged to go a certain way.

seven /**se**-ven/ *n* the number between six and eight.

sevenfold /**se**-ven-foald/ *adj* **1** having seven parts. **2** having seven times as much or as many.

seventeen /se-ven-teen/ *n* seven more than 10.

seventeenth /se-ven-teenth/ *adj* coming after 16 others.

seventh /se-venth/ *adj* coming after six others.

seventieth /se-ven-tee-eth/ *adj* coming after 69 others.

seventy /se-ven-tee/ *n* the number between 69 and 71.

sever /se-ver/ *vb* 1 to cut or tear apart or off (*sever his arm from his shoulder*). 2 to break (*the rope severed in two/sever relations with other countries*). ● *n* **severance** /se-ve-ranse/.

severable /sev-ra-bul/ *adj* that can be severed.

several /sev-ral/ *adj* 1 more than two, but not very many. 2 separate, various (*go their several ways*).

severe /se-veer/ *adj* 1 strict, harsh (*a severe punishment*). 2 plain and undecorated (*a severe dress*). 3 very cold (*a severe winter*). ● *n* **severity** /se-ve-ri-tee/.

sew /so/ *vb* (*pt* **sewed** /soad/, *pp* **sewn** /soan/) to join by means of needle and thread. ● *n* **sewer** /so-er/ a person or thing that sews.

sewage /soo-widge/ *n* waste matter of a house or town

sewan /se-wan/ *n* shells used as money by the Algonquian Native Americans.

sewer /soor/ *n* an underground drain to carry away water, waste matter, etc.

sewerage /soo-ridge/ *n* a system of underground drains or sewers.

sex /seks/ *n* 1 the state of being male or female. 2 the qualities by which an animal or plant is seen to be male or female. 3 sexual intercourse.

sexagenarian /sek-se-je-ner-ee-an/ *n* someone who is 60 years old or between 60 and 70.

sexism /sek-si-zum/ *n* the treatment of someone in a different, often unfair way on the grounds of that person's sex, especially against women. ● *adj, n* **sexist** /sek-sist/.

sextet /sek-stet/ *n* a song written for six voices.

sextuplet /sek-stoo-plet/ *n* one of six babies born at a single birth.

sexual /sek-shwal/ *adj* having to do with sex.

sexuality /sek-shu-wa-li-tee/ *n* the state or quality of being sexual.

sexy /sek-see/ *adj* exciting or intended to excite sexual desire. ● *n* **sexiness** /sek-see-ness/ *n* a sexy state or quality.

sh /sh/ *interj* used to urge or request silence.

shabby /sha-bee/ *adj* 1 untidy through much wear, threadbare, dressed in threadbare or untidy clothes. 2 mean, ungenerous (*a shabby trick*). ● *n* **shabbiness** /sha-bee-ness/.

shack /shack/ *n* a hut, small house, cabin.

shackle /sha-cul/ *vb* 1 to fasten with a chain (*prisoners with hands shackled together*). 2 to limit freedom of action or speech (*shackled by old-fashioned rules*). ● *npl* **shackles** /sha-culz/ chains for fastening the limbs.

shade /shade/ *vb* 1 to protect from light or sun (*shade your eyes*). 2 to darken. 3 to color (*shade wooded parts on the map*). ● *n* 1 any device that protects from light or sun. 2 a place in a shadow cast by the sun, half-darkness (*tables in the shade*). 3 a slight difference (*many shades of opinion*). 4 a little (*a shade warmer*).

shadiness /shay-dee-ness/ *n* a shady state or quality.

shading /shay-ding/ *n* the effects used to suggest darkness in a picture.

shadow /sha-doe/ *n* 1 a dark patch on the ground caused by the breaking of rays of light by a body (*in the shadow of the large building*). 2 shade. 3 someone who follows another around. 4 a ghost. ● *vb* to follow someone closely without his or her knowing it.

shadowy /sha-doe-wee/ *adj* 1 in shadow, shaded, dark (*shadowy parts of the garden*). 2 dark and unclear (*shadowy figures in the mist*).

shady /shay-dee/ *adj* 1 protected from light or sun. 2 dishonest, untrustworthy. ● *adv* **shadily** /shay-di-lee/ in a shady manner.

shaft /shaft/ *n* 1 the long handle of any tool or weapon. 2 an arrow. 3 a connecting rod in a machine, one of the poles of a carriage to which a horse is tied. 4 the main part of a pillar. 5 a deep tunnel leading down to a mine. 6 a ray of light.

shag /shag/ *n* 1 a kind of haircut that is shorter in front and longer in back with many layers. 2 heavy, rough woolen cloth.

shaggy /sha-gee/ *adj* 1 having rough, long hair (*shaggy dogs*). 2 rough (*a shaggy coat*).

shake /shake/ *vb* (*pt* **shook** /shook/, *pp* **shaken** /shay-ken/) 1 to move quickly up and down or to and fro (*shake the bottle*). 2 to tremble (*her hands shook*). 3 to make weaker or less firm (*shake the foundations/shake a person's faith*). ● *n* 1 trembling. 2 a sudden jerk. 3 a shock. 4 short for milk shake.

shaker /shay-ker/ *n* 1 a person or thing that shakes. 2 (*with cap*) a member of the United Society of Believers, an American religious community which believes in living with simplicity.

shaky /**shay**-kee/ *adj* **1** not steady (*a chair with a shaky leg*). **2** weak after illness.

shale /**shale**/ *n* a soft rock that was formed by the hardening of clay and that breaks apart easily. ● *adj* **shaly** /**shay**-lee/.

shall /**shall**/ *vb* will, especially used in formal writing (*I shall pay the lawyer*).

shallot /**sha**-lot/ *n* a small onion.

shallow /**sha**-lo/ *adj* **1** not deep (*shallow water*). **2** not thinking deeply (*a shallow writer*). ● *n* a place where water is not deep.

shalom /**sha**-lom/ *n* a Jewish way of saying either hello or goodbye.

sham /**sham**/ *n* **1** a person pretending to be what he or she is not (*the doctor turned out to be a sham*). **2** a thing made to look like something else (*trials in that country are a sham*). **3** a trick or fraud (*their marriage was a sham*). ● *adj* not real, pretended. ● *vb* (**shammed** /**shamd**/, **shamming** /**sha**-ming/) to pretend.

shaman /**shay**-man/ *n* a priest or medicine man, especially among some Asian people, who is believed to be able to heal and to tell the future by contacting good and evil spirits.

shamanism /**shay**-ma-ni-zum/ *n* the religion of certain peoples in good and evil spirits that can be contacted by a shaman.

shamble /**sham**-bul/ *vb* to walk clumsily. ● *also n.*

shambles /**sham**-bulz/ *npl* a scene of great disorder and confusion (*the house was a shambles after the robbery*).

shame /**shame**/ *n* a feeling of sorrow for wrongdoing or for the inability to do something, disgrace, a painful feeling of having lost the respect of others. ● *vb* to make ashamed, to disgrace.

shamefaced /**shame**-faist/ *adj* showing shame or embarrassment.

shameful /**shame**-ful/ *adj* disgraceful, shocking, bringing or causing shame.

shameless /**shame**-less/ *adj* not easily made ashamed, bold.

shampoo /**sham**-poo/ *vb* to wash and rub the head and hair. ● *n* **1** act of shampooing. **2** a preparation used for shampooing (*sachets of shampoo*).

shamrock /**sham**-rock/ *n* a small plant with three leaves on each stem, the national symbol of Ireland.

shank /**shangk**/ *n* **1** the leg from the knee to the ankle. **2** the long handle or shaft of certain tools.

shanty[1] /**shan**-tee/ *n* a poorly built hut, a shack.

shantytown /**shan**-tee-town/ *n* the section of a city where there a many shanties or small, rundown shacks.

shape /**shape**/ *n* **1** the form or outline of anything (*clouds of different shapes*). **2** (*inf*) condition, state (*players in good shape*). ● *vb* **1** to form (*shape the sand into a castle*). **2** to give a certain shape to (*shape his career*). ● **in good shape** in good condition.

shapeless /**shape**-less/ *adj* ugly or irregular in shape.

shapely /**shape**-lee/ *adj* well-formed (*shapely legs*).

shard /**shard**/ *n* a piece of broken pottery or glass.

share /**share**/ *n* **1** part of a thing belonging to a particular person. **2** one of the equal parts of the money of a company or business, lent by persons who may then receive a part of the profits. **3** the cutting part of a plough. ● *vb* **1** to divide among others. **2** to receive a part of.

sharecrop /**share**-crop/ *vb* to work for a share of the crop, especially as a tenant farmer.

shareholder /**shape**-hole-der/ *n* a person who owns shares in a company or business.

shareware /**share**-ware/ computer software that is provided for free for a limited time, with an option to buy.

sharia, shariah /**sha**-ree-ah/ *n* the religious law of Islam.

shark /**shark**/ *n* **1** a large meat-eating fish. **2** (*inf*) one ready to use unfair means to get as much money as possible (*a loan shark*).

sharp /**sharp**/ *adj* **1** having a thin edge for cutting with, having a fine point (*a sharp knife*). **2** quick and intelligent (*a sharp child*). **3** hurtful, unkind (*a sharp tongue*). **4** stinging, keen (*a sharp pain*). **5** in singing, higher than the correct note. **6** rather sour (*a sharp taste*). ● *n* a musical sign to show that a note is to be raised half a tone (#). ● *adv* (*of time*) exactly. ● *n* a needle.

sharpen /**shar**-pen/ *vb* to make sharp (*sharpen knives*).

sharper /**shar**-per/ *n* a person who cheats, especially at cards.

sharpie /**shar**-pee/ *n* a long, narrow, flat-bottomed New England fishing boat with a centerboard and one or two masts, each with a triangular sail.

sharp-tongued /**sharp**-tungd/ *adj* using severe or harshly critical language.

sharp-witted /**sharp**-wi-tid/ *adj* quick and clever.

shatter /**sha**-ter/ *vb* **1** to break into pieces, to smash (*the cups shattered when they were dropped*). **2** to put an end to (*shatter their hopes*).

shatterproof /sha-ter-proof/ *adj* that will resist shattering.

shave /shave/ *vb* **1** to cut off hair with a razor (*he shaves every morning*). **2** to cut strips off the surface (*shaving a thin strip from the edge of the door*). **3** to pass very close to without touching (*the car shaved the wall*). ● *n* **1** act of shaving, especially the face. **2** a close hair cut. **3** a narrow escape.

shaven /shay-ven/ *adj* closely trimmed, shaved.

shaver /shay-ver/ *n* a person or instrument that shaves.

shaving /shay-ving/ *n* a thin strip cut off the surface (*wood shavings*).

shawl /shawl/ *n* a cloth folded and worn loosely over the shoulders, especially by women.

Shawnee /shaw-nee/ *n* a member of a Native American group, at different times living in the East and Midwest, now primarily in Oklahoma, the language of these people.

she /she/ *pron* the woman, girl, female animal, or sometimes the thing referred to as female (as a boat) referred to.

sheaf /sheef/ *n* (*pl* **sheaves** /sheevz/) a number of things in a bundle (*a sheaf of paper/sheaves of wheat*).

shear /sheer/ *vb* (*pp* **shorn** /shawrn/) **1** to cut with shears (*shear his curls off*). **2** to clip the wool from (*shearing sheep*). **3** to cut or cause to break (*the tree fell and sheared through the telephone line*). ● *npl* **shears** /sheerz/ a pair of large scissors (e.g., for cutting off the wool of a sheep).

shearer /shee-rer/ *n* a person who shears (*sheep shearer*).

shearing /shee-ring/ *n* the action of cutting with or as with shears.

shearling /sheer-ling/ *n* a sheep whose wool has been cut off only once.

sheath /sheeth/ *n* a close-fitting case or container (*pull the sword from the sheath*).

sheathe /sheethe/ *vb* to put into a sheath (*sheathing the sword*).

sheaves *see* **sheaf**.

shebang /shi-bang/ *n* **1** a shack or hut. **2** an affair, business, thing, etc. (*the whole shebang*).

shed[1] /shed/ *vb* (**shed**, **shedding** /shed-ing/) **1** to let fall down or off (*trees shedding leaves*). **2** to spread about (*lamps shed a soft light*).

shed[2] /shed/ *n* a hut, a small building used for storage (*a garden shed*).

sheen /sheen/ *n* brightness, shininess (*the sheen on the polished table*).

sheep /sheep/ *n* **1** a farm animal valued for its wool and its meat. **2** a person who follows the lead of others without question.

sheepdog /sheep-dawg/ *n* a dog trained to look after and herd sheep.

sheepish /sheep-ish/ *adj* awkward or embarrassed because of having done something wrong (*looked sheepish when they discovered that he was lying*).

sheepskin /sheep-skin/ *n* the skin of a sheep, especially one dressed with the fleece on it, as for a coat.

sheer[1] /sheer/ *adj* **1** very steep (*sheer cliffs*). **2** (*of material*) very fine or transparent (*sheer silk*). **3** thorough, complete (*a sheer accident*).

sheer[2] /sheer/ *vb* to swerve, to move suddenly in another direction (*the car sheered to the right to avoid the truck*).

sheet /sheet/ *n* **1** a broad thin piece of anything. **2** a bedcovering of linen, cotton, etc. **3** a broad stretch of water, flame, ice, etc. **4** a rope tied to the lower corner of a sail.

sheik(h) /sheek/ *n* an Arab chief of a family, tribe, or village.

shekel /shek-el/ *n* **1** an ancient Jewish weight or coin. **2** *pl* (*inf*) money (*have run out of shekels*). **3** the unit of currency in Israel.

shelf /shelf/ *n* (*pl* **shelves** /shelvz/) **1** a board fixed to a wall or fastened in a cupboard, used for placing things on. **2** a ledge, a long flat rock or sandbank.

shell /shell/ *n* **1** a hard outer covering (*a nutshell/the shell of the tortoise/a seashell*). **2** a thick metal case filled with explosive and fired from a gun. ● *vb* **1** to take the shell off. **2** to fire shells at (*the city shelled by the enemy*).

she'll /sheel/ *contraction* shortened form of *she will* or *she shall*.

shellac /she-lac/ *n* a type of resin used for making varnish. ● *vb* to apply this to something.

shellfish /shell-fish/ *n* a fish with a shell covering (*shellfish such as mussels*).

shelter /shel-ter/ *n* **1** a place that gives protection from the weather or safety from danger. **2** protection. ● *vb* to protect, to go for protection.

shelve /shelv/ *vb* **1** to place on a shelf. **2** to put aside for a time. **3** to slope.

shelves *see* **shelf**.

shelving /shel-ving/ *n* **1** material for shelves. **2** a set of shelves.

shepherd /shep-urd/ *n* a person who looks after or herds sheep. ● *f* **shepherdess** /shep-ur-dess/. ● *vb* to guide a flock or group.

shepherd's pie /**shep**-urdz-pie/ *n* a meat pie with a layer of mashed potatoes serving as a top crust.

sherbet /**sher**-bet/ *n* a frozen, fruit-flavored dessert.

sherif /**sher**-if/ *n* a descendant of Mohammed through his daughter Fatima.

sheriff /**sher**-if/ *n* the chief law officer or judge of a county.

sherry /**sher**-ee/ *n* a Spanish wine (*have a glass of dry sherry before dinner*).

Shevat /**shev**-at/ *n* the fifth month of the Jewish year.

shield /**sheeld**/ *n* 1 a piece of metal or strong leather held in front of the body to defend it against sword strokes, etc. (*the knight's shield*). 2 a protector or protection (*an eye shield*). ● *vb* to defend, to protect (*put his arm up to shield his eyes from the sun*).

shift /**shift**/ *vb* 1 to change (*shift position*). 2 to move (*shift the blame*). 3 to remove, get rid of (*stains that are difficult to shift*). ● *n* 1 a change (*a shift of emphasis*). 2 a group of workers who carry on a job for a certain time and then hand over to another group. 3 the period during which such a group works. 4 a simple dress or nightgown (*a cotton shift*).

shifty /**shif**-tee/ *adj* untrustworthy, deceitful (*have a shifty appearance*).

shiitake /shee-**tak**-ee/ *n* an edible Japanese mushroom.

shimmer /**shi**-mer/ *vb* to shine with a flickering light (*pavements shimmering in the rain*). ● *also n.*

shimmy /**shi**-mee/ *n* a dance popular in the 1920s. ● *vb* to shake or wobble, to dance the shimmy.

shin /**shin**/ *n* the front part of the leg below the knee. ● *vb* (**shinned** /**shind**/, **shinning** /**shi**-ning/) to climb, gripping with the legs.

shine /**shine**/ *vb* (*pt, pp* **shone** /**shawn**/) 1 to give off light (*street lights shining*). 2 to direct a light or lamp (*shine the light in their eyes*). 3 to polish (*shine his shoes*). 4 (*inf*) to be very good at (*the student shines at math*). ● *n* brightness, polish.

shingle /**shing**-gul/ *n* 1 a thin, wedge-shaped piece of wood, slate, etc. laid with others in a series of overlapping rows as a covering for roofs and the sides of houses. 2 a woman's short haircut in which the hair at the back of the head is shaped close to the head.

Shinto /**shin**-toe/ *n* the native religion of Japan.

shiny /**shie**-nee/ *adj* bright, glossy, as if polished (*a shiny material*). ● *n* shininess /**shie**-nee-ness/.

ship /**ship**/ *n* a large seagoing boat. ● *vb* (**shipped** /**shipt**/, **shipping** /**shi**-ping/) 1 to put or take, as on board ship (*ship the goods to their new home*). 2 to go on board a ship.

shipbuilding /**ship**-bil-ding/ *n* the act of making ships.

shipmate /**ship**-mate/ *n* a fellow sailor on the same ship.

shipment /**ship**-ment/ *n* 1 the sending of goods by ship. 2 the goods put on board a ship (*a shipment of fruit*).

shipping /**shi**-ping/ *n* 1 all the ships of a port, country, etc. 2 ships in general. 3 the act or business of sending goods.

shipshape /**ship**-shape/ *adj* in good order, neat and tidy (*have the house shipshape for his mother's return*).

shipwreck /**ship**-reck/ *n* the loss or destruction of a ship at sea. ● *also vb.*

shipyard /**ship**-yard/ *n* a place where ships are built or repaired.

shire /**shire**/ *n* a county.

shirk /**shirk**/ *vb* to avoid (*shirk duty*). ● *n* shirker /**shir**-ker/.

shirt /**shurt**/ *n* a kind of upper garment (*button up his shirt*).

shish kabob *or* **shish kebob** /**shish**-ki-bob/ *n* a dish consisting of small chunks of meat placed on sticks with vegetables, such as tomatoes, peppers, onions, that is broiled or grilled.

shiva /**shi**-va/ *n* in Judaism, the mourning period of seven days after someone has died.

shiver /**shi**-ver/ *vb* 1 to tremble (*shivering with cold*). 2 to break into small pieces. ● *n* 1 a shaking or trembling. 2 a small piece (*a shiver of glass*).

shivery /**shi**-ve-ree/ *adj* trembling, as with cold or fear.

shoal[1] /**shoal**/ *n* a shallow place in the sea, a sandbank. ● *vb* to become shallow.

shoal[2] /**shoal**/ *n* 1 a large number of fish swimming together. 2 (*inf*) a crowd (*shoals of visitors*).

shock[1] /**shock**/ *n* a mass of long untidy hair (*a shock of black hair*).

shock[2] /**shock**/ *n* 1 the sudden violent striking of one thing against another (e.g., in a collision). 2 weakness of body or confusion of mind caused by a violent blow or collision (*suffer from shock after an accident*). 3 sorrow or a state of upset caused by sudden bad news, etc. (*the shock at hearing that he had died*). 4 an involuntary movement of the body, caused by passing electricity through it. ● *vb* 1 to cause sudden pain or sorrow. 2 to horrify to disgust (*shocked by the treatment of his wife*).

shocker /**shock**-er/ *n* a person or thing that shocks.

shocking /**shock**-ing/ *adj* very bad, disgusting, indecent.

shockproof /**shock**-proof/ *adj* able to absorb shock without being damaged (*shockproof watch*).

shoddy /**shod**-ee/ *adj* cheap, of poor quality (*shoddy clothes*). ● *n* cheap cloth made up from the clippings of other material.

shoe /shoo/ *n* 1 a covering for the foot (*high-heeled shoes*). 2 a U-shaped metal plate nailed to the hoof of a horse. ● *vb* to fit a horse with shoes.

shoehorn /**shoo**-hawrn/ *n* a curved piece of horn, metal, etc., to help the foot to slip easily into a shoe.

shoelace /**shoo**-lace/ *n* a length of cord, leather, etc., used for tying a shoe.

shoo /shoo/ *interj* go away, get out.

shoo-in /**shoo**-in/ *n* a person who is expected to win easily an election, contest, etc.

shoot /shoot/ *vb* (*pt, pp* **shot** /shot/) 1 to fire a bullet from a gun (*start shooting*). 2 to let fly (*shoot an arrow from a bow*). 3 to move suddenly or quickly (*the child shot across the road*). 4 to hit or kill with a bullet from a gun (*shoot rabbits*). 5 (*in games*) to kick or hit at goal. 6 to begin to grow (*plants shooting up*). 7 to make a moving film (*a film shot in Los Angeles*). ● *n* 1 a young branch or bud. 2 a sloping way down which water may flow or objects slide. 3 an outing for shooting and hunting.

shooter /**shoo**-ter/ *n* a person or thing that shoots.

shooting /**shoo**-ting/ *n* the act of shooting a gun.

shooting gallery /**shoo**-ting-ga-lu-ree/ *n* a place where people can safely practice shooting guns at targets.

shooting star /shoo-ting-**star**/ *n* what looks like a moving star but is really a glowing fragment of a heavenly body flying through space.

shootout /**shoo**-tout/ *n* a battle with handguns.

shop /shop/ *n* 1 a place where goods are sold (*a flower shop/the corner shop*). 2 a place where work is done with tools or machines. ● *vb* (**shopped** /shopt/, **shopping** /**shop**-ing/) to visit shops to buy things (*shop for groceries*). ● **talk shop** to talk about work (*she bores everyone by constantly talking shop*).

shopkeeper /**shop**-kee-per/ *n* a person who owns or runs a shop where goods are sold.

shoplifter /**shop**-lif-ter/ *n* a person who steals from the shops he or she is visiting (*threaten to prosecute all shoplifters*). ● *vb* **shoplift** /**shop**-lift/.

shopper /**shop**-er/ *n* a person who shops.

shore[1] /shore/ *n* the land beside the sea, a river, lake, etc.

shore[2] /shore/ *n* a wooden prop or support. ● *vb* to prop up or support (*shoring up the damaged wall*).

shoreline /**shore**-line/ *n* the edge of a body of water.

shorn /shawrn/ *pp of* **shear**.

short /shawrt/ *adj* 1 not long or tall (*a short distance/short people*). 2 not enough (*short measures*). 3 without enough of (*short of money*). 4 not lasting long (*a short vacation*). 5 quick and almost impolite (*she was very short on the phone*). 6 (*of pastry, etc.*) crumbling easily. ● *adv* **shortly** /**shawrt**-lee/ briefly, soon. ● *npl* **shorts** /**shawrt**-lee/ trousers reaching not lower than the knees. ● **in short** in a few words.

shortage /**shawr**-tidge/ *n* a lack of, not enough of (*a staff shortage/shortage of supplies*).

shortbread /**shawrt**-bred/ *n* a cookielike cake made of flour, butter, and sugar.

shortcake /**shawrt**-cake/ *n* a crisp, light cake or biscuit served with fruit and whipped cream as a dessert.

short circuit /shawrt-**sir**-kit/ *n* the touching of two electric wires so that current passes from one to the other instead of straight on, usually accidental and causing damage.

shortcoming /**shawrt**-cu-ming/ *n* a falling short of what is needed.

shortcut /**shawrt**-cut/ *n* a quicker way (*drivers trying to find a shortcut to avoid the heavy traffic*).

shorten /**shawr**-ten/ *vb* to make less in length or time (*shorten the dress/shorten the working day*).

shortening /**shawrt**-ning/ *n* fat for making pastry, etc., crumbles easily when cooked.

shorthand /**shawrt**-hand/ *n* a type of writing, featuring symbols, in which a person can write as fast as a speaker speaks.

short-handed /shawrt-**han**-did/ *adj* not having the number of helpers or workers required (*short-handed at the factory*).

shorthorn /**shawrt**-hawrn/ *n* a breed of cattle with short horns.

short-lived /shawrt-**livd**/ *adj* living or lasting for a short time only (*her pleasure was short-lived*).

short-run /**shawrt**-run/ *adj* lasting for a short period of time.

shorts *see* **short**.

short-sighted /shawrt-**sie**-tid/ *adj* 1 unable to see clearly things that are distant. 2 lacking foresight (*it was short-sighted of them not to save for their old age*).

shortstop /**shawrt**-stop/ *n* in baseball, the infielder who plays near second base and often covers second base.

short-tempered /shawrt-**tem**-perd/ *adj* easily

angered (*keep the child away from the short-tempered man*).

Shoshone /shu-shone/ *n* a member of a group of Native Americans scattered over Idaho, Nevada, Utah, Wyoming, and California, the language of these people.

shot[1] /shot/ *pt of* **shoot** /shoot/. ● *n* **1** the firing of a gun, etc. (*kill the animal with one shot*). **2** small lead bullets. **3** a solid metal ball fired from a gun. **4** a person able to shoot (*a good shot*). **5** (*inf*) a single attempt at doing something (*have another shot at learning to drive*). **6** a series of pictures of a scene taken at one time by a camera. **7** (*inf*) an injection (*a flu shot*).

shot[2] /shot/ *adj* having threads of a different color interwoven.

shotgun /shot-gun/ *n* a kind of gun usually used in hunting small animals.

shot put /shot-put/ *n* a contest in which a heavy metal ball is thrown as far as possible from the shoulder.

should /shood/ *vb* used to express duty, what a person is supposed to do (*he should be at work today*).

shoulder /shole-der/ *n* **1** the joint connecting an arm, wing, or foreleg to the body. **2** anything jutting out like a shoulder (*the shoulder of the highway*). ● *vb* **1** to push with the shoulder. **2** to put on to the shoulder (*shoulder the planks of wood*). **3** to bear, to accept, to take on (*shoulder responsibilities*).

shoulder blade /shole-der-blade/ *n* the broad flat bone of the shoulder.

shout /shout/ *vb* to utter a loud cry (*shout for help*). ● *n* a loud cry, a call.

shove /shuv/ *vb* (*inf*) to push (*shoving him out of the way*). ● *also n.*

shovel /shu-vel/ *n* a spade with a broad blade for lifting earth, gravel, etc. ● *vb* [**shoveled** /shu-veld/, **shoveling** /shuv-ling/; *also* **shovelled, shovelling** (*Br, Cdn*)] to move with a shovel (*shovel coal*).

show /shoa/ *vb* **1** to let be seen, to display (*she showed them the new dress*). **2** to point out (*show them the way*). **3** to be in sight (*a light showing*). **4** to prove (*it showed how the system worked*). ● *n* **1** a display. **2** a performance or entertainment (*get tickets for the show*). **3** a gathering at which flowers, animals, etc., are displayed to the public (*the agricultural show*).

show business /shoa-biz-ness/ *n* the world of entertainment, e.g., theater, films, television.

shower /shou-er/ *n* **1** a short fall of rain. **2** a great number of things falling or arriving at one time (*a shower of arrows*). **3** a piece of bathroom equipment that produces a spray of water so that people standing underneath it can wash themselves. ● *vb* **1** to give to or let fall on in large numbers. **2** to take a shower.

showerproof /shou-er-proof/ *adj* waterproof against light rain only.

showery /shou-ree/ *adj* rainy, marked by many showers (*showery weather*).

showroom /shoa-room/ *n* a room or shop in which things are on display to the public (*a furniture showroom*).

shrapnel /shrap-nel/ *n* **1** a shell packed with bullets or pieces of metal that are scattered when it explodes. **2** a fragment of the case of a bomb or shell.

shred /shred/ *vb* (**shredded** /shred-id/, **shredding** /shred-ing/) to tear or cut into small pieces (*shred paper/shred lettuce*). ● *n* a scrap, a rag, a piece cut or torn off. ● *n* **shredder** a person or thing that shreds (*use a shredder at the office for destroying certain documents*).

shrew /shroo/ *n* **1** a small mouse-like animal. **2** a bad-tempered or sharp-tongued woman (*a shrew of a wife*).

shrewd /shrood/ *adj* clever in practical matters, cunning, good at judging (*too shrewd to be deceived by them*).

shriek /shreek/ *vb* to scream (*shrieking with fright*). ● *also n.*

shrift /shrift/ *n* the confession of sins to a priest. ● **short shrift** little mercy.

shrill /shrill/ *adj* high and piercing in sound (*shrill children's voices*).

shrimp /shrimp/ *n* **1** a small edible shellfish. **2** (*inf*) a very small person (*her shrimp of a son*). ● *vb* to fish for shrimps.

shrine /shrine/ *n* **1** a box or tomb containing something connected with a holy person or thing. **2** a place revered because of a connection with a holy person or event.

shrink /shringk/ *vb* **1** to make or become smaller (*clothes that shrink in the wash*). **2** to go back in fear, horror, etc. (*shrink at the sight of the burglar*).

shrinkage /shring-kidge/ *n* the amount by which something becomes smaller.

shrink-wrap /shringk-rap/ *vb* to wrap in a tough, clear plastic material that shrinks to size when heated.

shrive /shrive/ *vb* (*pt* **shrove** /shroav/ *or* **shrived** /shrievd/, *pp* **shriven** /shri-ven/) (*fml or old*) to hear the confession and forgive the sins of (*priests shriving sinners*).

shrivel /shri-vel/ *vb* [**shriveled** /shri-veld/, **shriveling** /shri-vel-ing/; *also* **shrivelled**, **shrivelling** (*Br, Cdn*)] **1** to dry up and become smaller (*plants shriveling in the heat*). **2** to become wrinkled (*skin shriveled with age*).

shroud /shroud/ *n* **1** a garment or covering for a dead body. **2** *pl* the set of ropes supporting a mast of a ship. ● *vb* **1** to put in a shroud. **2** to cover, to hide (*clouds shrouding the sun*).

shrub /shrove-chooz-day/ *n* a short treelike bush with a short trunk.

shrubbery /shru-bree/ *n* a place where many shrubs are growing close together (*children hiding in the shrubbery*).

shrug /shrug/ *vb* (**shrugged** /shrugd/, **shrugging** /shru-ging/) to raise the shoulders in surprise, doubt, etc. (*she shrugged in disbelief*).

shrunken /shrung-kin/ *adj* grown smaller, shriveled.

shudder /shu-der/ *vb* to tremble from fear, etc., to shiver with cold (*shudder from the winter chill in the air*). ● *also n.*

shuffle /shu-ful/ *vb* **1** to make a noise by moving the feet on the ground (*people shuffling around in their slippers*). **2** to mix cards before giving them out. ● *also n.*

shuffleboard /shu-ful-board/ *n* a game in which disks are pushed along a smooth lane toward numbered areas to get points.

shun /shun/ *vb* (**shunned** /shund/, **shunning** /shu-ning/) to avoid, to keep away from (*she shuns crowds*).

shunpike /shun-pike/ *n* a secondary road used to avoid a turnpike or highway.

shunt /shunt/ *vb* **1** (*of a railway engine or train*) to move on to a different track or side line. **2** to move or turn to the side, to turn the other way.

shush /shush/ *interj* used to tell another to be quiet.

shut /shut/ *vb* (**shut**, **shutting** /shu-ting/) to close (*shut the door/shut the suitcase*).

shut-eye /shu-tie/ *n* sleep.

shutout /shu-tout/ *n* a game in which one team has not been able to score.

shutter /shu-ter/ *n* a covering that can be placed or closed over a window or other opening to keep out light (*close the wooden shutters*).

shuttle /shu-tul/ *n* **1** the part of a weaving or sewing machine that carries the thread to and fro. **2** a traveling back and forth over an often short route, as by train, bus, airplane, etc. **3** space shuttle, an aircraft that can go into space and return to Earth.

shuttlecock /shu-tul-cock/ *n* a cork rounded at one end and stuck with feathers, used for a ball in badminton.

shy[1] /shie/ *adj* timid, easily frightened, keeping to oneself in front of others (*she was too shy to speak to her parents' friends*). ● *vb* to jerk or jump to the side in fear, etc. (*horses shying*). ● *n* **shyness** /shie-ness/.

shy[2] /shie/ *vb* to throw. ● *n* a throw.

sibling /sib-ling/ *n* a brother or sister.

sibyl /si-bul/ *n* in ancient times, a prophetess or fortune teller.

sick /sick/ *adj* **1** ill (*too sick to go to work*). **2** bringing up food from the stomach by vomiting, about to vomit (*always get sick on board a ship*). **3** tired of through having too much (*sick of gardening/sick of meatloaf*).

sickbed /sick-bed/ *n* the bed in which a sick person stays.

sicken /si-ken/ *vb* **1** to make or become sick (*she sickened and died*). **2** to disgust (*the sight of the dead rabbit sickened her*). ● *adj* **sickening** /sick-ning/ causing sickness or nausea, disgusting or revolting.

sickle /si-cul/ *n* a knife with a curved blade for cutting corn, etc.

sickly /si-clee/ *adj* **1** often ill (*a sickly child*). **2** pale (*a sickly complexion*). **3** oversentimental (*sickly love songs*).

sickness /sick-ness/ *n* **1** illness. **2** vomiting.

siddur /si-dur/ *n* the Jewish prayer book.

side /side/ *n* **1** one of the surfaces of a body, the part of the body between either shoulder and thigh (*a pain in her side*). **2** edge, border (*the side of the lake*). **3** slope (*the side of the mountain*). **4** one of two opposing parties or teams (*the home side*). ● *adj* on, at, or toward the side. ● *vb* to support one party against another.

sideboard /side-board/ *n* a piece of furniture for storing dishes, cutlery, linen, etc.

sideburns /side-burnz/ *n* the hair on a man's face just in front of the ears, especially when the rest of the beard is shaved.

side effect /side-ef-ect/ *n* a negative effect of taking medication.

sidekick /side-kick/ *n* a close friend, a partner.

sideline /side-line/ *n* an activity carried on in addition to a person's real job (*he serves in a bar as a sideline*).

sidelong /side-lawng/ *adj* to the side, slanting (*a sidelong glance*). ● *also adv.*

sideshow /**side**-shoa/ *n* a less important show at a fair, circus, exhibition, etc.

sidetrack /**side**-track/ *vb* to turn someone away from what he or she was about to do (*he was going to study, but he got sidetracked*).

sidewalk /**side**-wawk/ *n* a footpath at the side of a road.

sideways /**side**-wayz/ *adv* on or toward one side (*move sideways*).

sidewinder /**side**-wine-der/ *n* a snake that slithers across the sand sideways.

siding /**sie**-ding/ *n* **1** a covering for an outside wall of a building or house. **2** a short railway track off the main line, used for shunting, etc.

siege /**seej**/ *n* surrounding a fort, town, etc., with an army to take it or make its garrison surrender.

sienna /see-**ye**-na/ *n* an earthy coloring matter, yellowish brown in the natural state and reddish brown when burned.

sierra /see-**ye**-ra/ *n* a range of mountains with pointed peaks.

siesta /see-**ye**-sta/ *n* a nap or rest taken after the noon meal, especially in Spain and some Latin American countries.

sieve /**siv**/ *n* a container with a net bottom or a bottom full of holes, used for separating small particles of anything from larger pieces. ● *vb* to pass through a sieve (*sieving flour*).

sift /**sift**/ *vb* **1** to pass through a sieve. **2** to examine closely (*sifting the evidence*). ● *n* **sifter** /**sif**-ter/. ● **sift out** to separate good from bad.

sigh /**sie**/ *vb* a long, deep, easily heard breath expressing pain, sadness, unreturned love, etc. ● *vb* **1** to draw such a breath (*sighing with boredom*). **2** (*lit*) to long (for) (*sigh for her lost love*).

sight /**site**/ *n* **1** the power of seeing (*lose her sight*). **2** that which is seen (*the sight of her in that hat was hilarious*). **3** something worth seeing (*the sights of the town*). **4** the area within which things can be seen by someone (*the children were out of sight*). **5** (*often pl*) a device attached to a gun to make it easier to aim straight. ● *vb* to see, to notice. ● **out of sight** too far away to be seen.

sighting /**sie**-ting/ *n* an observation of something rare or unusual (*a UFO sighting*).

sightseeing /**site**-see-ing/ *n* going around the places of interest in a town, district, etc. ● *n* **sightseer** /**site**-see-urr/.

sign /**sine**/ *n* **1** a mark, movement, gesture, etc., representing an accepted meaning (*a sign that she agrees*). **2** a mark by which a person or thing can be recognized. **3** a notice to give directions or advertise (*shop signs*). ● *vb* **1** to write a person's name on (*sign an autograph book*). **2** to convey meaning by a movement of the head, hands, etc.

signage /**sie**-nidge/ *n* the signs displayed in a particular area.

signal /**sig**-nal/ *n* **1** a sign to give information, orders, etc., from a distance (*give them a signal to keep quiet*). **2** a tool used to give such signs to drivers of railway engines. **3** a message conveyed by such signs. ● *adj* notable, important. ● *vb* [**signaled** /**sig**-nald/, **signaling** /**sig**-na-ling/; *also* **signalled**, **signalling** (*Br, Cdn*)] to make signals to (*signal them to stop*). ● *n* **signaler** /**sig**-na-ler/, *also* **signaller** (*Br, Cdn*).

signatory /**sig**-na-toe-ree/ *n* a person who has signed an agreement (*signatories of the contract*).

signature /**sig**-ni-chur/ *n* a person's name written by oneself.

significance /sig-**ni**-fi-canse/ *n* meaning, importance (*fail to understand the significance of her words*).

significant /sig-**ni**-fi-cant/ *adj* full of meaning, important (*no significant change in the patient's condition/significant events*).

signify /**sig**-ni-fie/ *vb* **1** to show by a sign (*she signified her agreement by a nod*). **2** to mean (*what her remark signified*). **3** to be important.

sign language /**sine**-lang-gwidge/ *n* a method of communication using the hands, used especially to communicate with deaf people.

signpost /**sine**-poast/ *n* a post indicating the direction and sometimes also the distance to a place (*see a signpost to the city*).

Sikh /**seek**/ *n* a member of an Indian religion called **Sikhism** /**see**-ki-zum/, originally connected with Hinduism, but now based on a belief that there is only one God.

silage /**sie**-lidge/ *n* green food for farm animals kept in a silo.

silence /**sie**-linss/ *n* lack of sound, quietness. ● *vb* to cause to be quiet (*silencing the children with a look*).

silencer /**sie**-lin-ser/ *n* a device for reducing the noise of an engine, gun, etc. (*the car's silencer*).

silent /**sie**-lint/ *adj* **1** making no sound (*machines that are virtually silent*). **2** not talking, speaking little (*they were silent on the journey*). **3** with no noise or sound (*a silent house*).

silhouette /si-lu-**wet**/ *n* the dark outline and flat shape of an object, especially of a face from the side, as seen with a light behind it.

silica /si-li-ca/ *n* the dioxide form of silicon (SiO$_2$) a glassy, hard, colorless mineral found as quartz or in agate, etc.

silicon /si-li-con/ *n* a chemical element found in rocks and minerals, with symbol Si.

silk /silk/ *n* **1** the fine thread produced by the silkworm. **2** a soft material woven from this.

silken /sil-ken/ *adj* (*lit*) made of silk.

silkworm /silk-wurm/ *n* a caterpillar that spins silk thread to enclose its cocoon.

silky /sil-kee/ *adj* **1** made of silk. **2** soft, smooth (*silky hair*).

sill /sill/ *n* the ledge of stone or wood at the foot of a window.

silly /si-lee/ *adj* foolish, unwise (*a silly thing to do*).

silo /si-lo/ *n* a tower or pit in which green fodder (grass, etc.) is stored until needed as food for animals.

silt /silt/ *n* the earth, sand, etc., deposited by a moving river. ● *vb* to block or become blocked with silt. ● *adj* **silty** /sil-tee/.

silvan *see* **sylvan**.

silver /sil-ver/ *n* **1** a precious metal of shining white color (*jewelery made of silver*). **2** coins, dishes, etc., made of silver (*the burglar stole the family silver*). **3** (*old*) money. ● *adj* made of silver. ● *vb* to coat with silver. ● *adj* **silvery** /sil-ver-ee/ **1** like silver (*silvery hair*). **2** clear in tone (*her silvery voice*).

silverware /sil-ver-ware/ *n* dishes and utensils made of silver.

simian /si-mee-an/ *adj* like a monkey or ape.

similar /si-mi-lar/ *adj* like, resembling (*have similar attitudes*).

similarity /si-mi-la-ri-tee/ *n* likeness, resemblance (*the similarity of their attitude*).

simile /si-mi-lee/ *n* a striking comparison of one thing with another.

simmer /si-mer/ *vb* to keep on boiling slowly without boiling over (*a sauce simmering in the pan on the stove*).

simper /sim-per/ *vb* to smile in a silly or insincere way (*girls simpering at the boys*). ● *also n.*

simple /sim-pul/ *adj* **1** unmixed, without anything added, pure (*the simple truth*). **2** not complicated (*a simple explanation*). **3** plain (*a simple dress*). **4** trusting, innocent, and inexperienced (*simple country girls*). **5** foolish, easily tricked (*simple enough to believe him*). ● *n* (*old*) an herb used as medicine.

simplicity /sim-pli-si-tee/ *n* **1** easiness. **2** sincerity. **3** plainness. **4** innocence.

simplification /sim-pli-fi-cay-shun/ *n* the act of making easier to do or understand.

simplify /sim-pli-fie/ *vb* to make easier to do or understand (*simplified the process*).

simply /sim-plee/ *adv* **1** in a clear way (*explained simply*). **2** absolutely (*simply wonderful*). **3** plain (*live simply*). **4** just, merely (*do it simply for the money*).

simulate /sim-yu-late/ *vb* (*fml*) to pretend (*simulating interest*). ● *n* **simulation** /sim-yu-lay-shun/.

simultaneous /si-mul-tay-nee-us/ *adj* taking place at the same time (*a simultaneous ringing of the two phone lines*).

sin /sin/ *n* **1** a thought, word, or action that breaks the law of God. **2** a wicked act. ● *vb* (**sinned** /sind/, **sinning** /si-ning/) **1** to do wrong. **2** to commit sin. ● *n* **sinner** /si-ner/.

since /sinse/ *prep* from (a certain time till now). ● *adv* ago. ● *conj* **1** from the time that. **2** because.

sincere /sin-seer/ *adj* real, genuine, meaning what is said, frank (*sincere friends/a sincere promise/sincere words of thanks*).

sincerity /sin-se-ri-tee/ *n* honesty of mind, genuineness.

sinew /sin-yoo/ *n* a tendon, a tough cordlike substance that joins muscle to bone, muscular power.

sinewy /sin-yoo-wee/ *adj* strong, tough (*sinewy workmen*).

sinful /sin-ful/ *adj* full of sin, wicked (*sinful thoughts*).

sing /sing/ *vb* (*pt* **sang** /sang/, *pp* **sung** /sung/) to make music with the voice, with or without words (*singing love songs/be taught to sing*). ● *n* **singer** /sing-er/.

singe /sinj/ *vb* to burn slightly, to burn the surface or ends of. ● *also n.*

single /sing-gul/ *adj* **1** one only, alone (*a single sheet of paper/the single cause*). **2** unmarried (*single people*). ● *vb* to pick out one (for special attention, etc.).

single-handed /sing-gul-han-did/ *adj* **1** having only one hand. **2** using or needing the use of only one hand. **3** without help, done or working alone.

single-minded /sing-gul-mine-did/ *adj* concentrating on one main purpose (*single-minded attempts to get a job*).

singly /sing-glee/ *adv* one by one, one at a time (*leave the meeting singly*).

singular /sing-gyu-lar/ *adj* **1** (*fml*) remarkable, unusual, odd, strange (*a singular happening*). **2** (*in grammar*) referring to one only (*a singular noun*).

singularity /sing-gyu-**la**-ri-tee/ *n* **1** peculiarity, strangeness. **2** an unusual feature.

singularly /sing-gyu-lar-lee/ *adv* (*fml*) strangely, remarkably (*she was singularly beautiful*).

sinister /**si**-ni-ster/ *adj* **1** evil looking (*a sinister stranger*). **2** threatening harm or evil (*a sinister warning*).

sink /singk/ *vb* (*pt* **sank** /sangk/, *pp* **sunk** /sungk/) **1** to go slowly down (*the sun was sinking*). **2** to go below the surface of water (*the boat sank*). **3** to become worse or weaker (*the invalid is sinking fast*). **4** (*of an idea*) to be understood gradually (*his death has not sunk in yet*). **5** to dig (*sink a well*). **6** to cause to go underwater. ● *n* a basin with a drainpipe leading from it, used when washing.

sinker /**sing**-ker/ *n* a weight attached to a fishing line.

sinner /**si**-ner/ *n* a person who commits a sin.

sinus /**sie**-nus/ *n* a small hollow in a bone, especially that connecting the nose with the skull (*have an infection of the sinuses*).

Sioux /**soo**us/ *n* an ethnic name given to different Algonquian Native American languages and several non-Algonquian Native American groups.

sip /sip/ *vb* (**sipped** /sipt/, **sipping** /**si**-ping/) to drink in small mouthfuls (*sip a cold drink*). ● *also n.*

siphon /**sie**-fun/ *n* **1** a bent tube for drawing liquids out of one vessel into another. **2** a bottle of aerated water in which the liquid is forced out up a tube by the pressure of the gas.

sir /sur/ *n* **1** a word of respect used to men. **2** the title given to a knight or baronet.

sire /sire/ *n* **1** father. **2** male parent of a horse or other animal (*the pony's sire*). **3** a title of respect used when addressing a king. ● *vb* (*of animals*) to procreate.

siren /**sie**-run/ *n* **1** a mythical creature, half-woman, half-bird, who by the beauty of her song lured sailors to destruction. **2** an attractive but dangerous woman. **3** a loud horn sounded as a time signal or as a warning of danger (*a siren warning of a bombing raid*).

sirloin /**sir**-loin/ *n* the upper part of a loin of beef.

sister /**si**-ster/ *n* **1** a girl or woman born of the same parents as another person. **2** nun. **3** a woman fellow member of the same race, church, profession, etc.

sisterhood /**si**-ster-hood/ *n* **1** the state of being sisters. **2** a society of women, usually carrying out religious or charitable works.

sister-in-law /**si**-ster-in-law/ *n* **1** the sister of a husband or wife. **2** the wife of a person's brother.

sisterly /**si**-ster-lee/ *adj* like a sister.

sit /sit/ *vb* (**sat** /sat/, **sitting** /**si**-ting/) **1** to take a rest on a seat. **2** to rest upon eggs to hatch them. **3** (*of government, courts, etc.*) to meet to do business. **4** to rest upon (*books sitting on the table*). ● **sit up 1** to sit straight. **2** to stay out of bed when it is time to sleep (*parents sitting up until their children come in*).

sitar /**si**-tar/ *n* an Indian stringed instrument with a long neck and gourdlike bottom.

sit-down /**sit**-down/ *n* a strike in which the strikers stay inside a factory, etc., refusing to leave or to work.

site /site/ *n* the ground on which a building or number of buildings stands or is to stand (*the site of the new building*). ● *vb* to choose a place for.

sit-in /**si**-tin/ *n* a method of protesting against the government, a business, etc. in which people sit in a public place and refuse to leave.

sitter /**si**-ter/ *n* **1** a person who visits an artist to have his or her portrait done. **2** short for babysitter, a person who watches children while parents or guardians are away.

sitting /**si**-ting/ *n* **1** a single uninterrupted meeting. **2** a single visit to an artist doing one's portrait. **3** the act or position of one that sits.

sitting room /**si**-ting-room/ *n* the room in which a family sits when not working, a living room.

situate /**si**-chu-wate/ *vb* to put in a certain place. ● *adj* **situated** /**si**-chu-way-tid/ placed.

situation /si-chu-**way**-shun/ *n* **1** a place or position (*a house in a lovely situation*). **2** (*fml*) a job (*seek a new situation*). **3** circumstances (*their financial situation*).

sit-up /**si**-tup/ *n* a stomach exercise in which a person lies flat on the back and rises to a sitting position without using the hands.

six /siks/ *adj* one more than five.

sixfold /**siks**-foald/ *adj* having six parts, having six times as much or as many.

sixteen /sik-**steen**/ *adj* six more than 10.

sixteenth /sik-**steenth**/ *adj* coming after 15 others.

sixth /siksth/ *adj* coming after five others.

sixtieth /**sik**-stee-ith/ *adj* coming after 59 others.

sixty /**sik**-stee/ *adj* the number between 59 and 61.

sizable /**sie**-za-bul/ *adj* quite large or bulky.

size[1] /size/ *n* bigness, bulk. ● *vb* to arrange in order according to size (*sizing the eggs*). ● **size up** to form an opinion about (*size up the opposition*).

size[2] /size/ *n* a thin glue used as a varnish on paper, cloth, etc.

izzle /si-zul/ *vb* to make a hissing or spluttering sound, as when frying (*sausages sizzling on the grill*).

ka /ska/ *n* a form of dance music originally from Jamaica.

kate[1] /skate/ *n* a steel blade fastened to a boot to allow a gliding movement on ice. ● *vb* to move on skates or roller skates.

kate[2] /skate/ *n* a large edible flatfish.

kateboard /skate-board/ *n* a short narrow board on small wheels on which a person stands and moves rapidly or performs jumps and stunts. ● *n* **skateboarding** /skate-boar-ding/.

kating rink /skay-ting-ringk/ *n* an area of ice prepared for skating.

kedaddle /ski-da-dul/ *vb* (*inf*) to run off or run away, to leave in a hurry.

keleton /ske-le-tun/ *n* **1** the bony framework of a body. **2** an outline of a plot or plan (*give a skeleton of the plan to the committee*). ● **skeleton in the closet** something in a person's past life that he/she keeps secret for fear of disgrace (*newspaper reporters anxious to find a skeleton in the film star's closet*).

keleton key /ske-le-tun-kee/ *n* a key that will open a number of different locks of a similar pattern (*the skeleton key held by the hotel manager*).

keleton staff /ske-le-tun-staff/ *n* the least number of people needed to keep a factory, etc., working.

keptic /skep-tik/ *adj*, *also* **sceptic** (*Br, Cdn*) a person who doubts things that others believe are true (*a skeptic might question whether God exists*). ● *adj* **skeptical** /skep-ti-cal/, *also* **sceptical** (*Br, Cdn*).

ketch /sketch/ *n* **1** a rough drawing or painting, sometimes to be finished later. **2** an outline or short account (*a sketch of their future plans*). **3** a short amusing play. ● *vb* **1** to make a quick or rough drawing. **2** to give a short account or outline of, to draw (*sketching out their plans*).

ketchbook /sketch-book/ *n* a book of drawing paper for making sketches.

ketchy /sket-chee/ *adj* incomplete, leaving out details (*a sketchy description of their plans*).

kew /skoo/ *adj* slanting, not straight.

kewer /skyoo-ur/ *n* a wooden or metal pin for fastening meat in shape while cooking (*meat cooked on skewers*).

ki /skee/ *n* a long strip of wood, metal, etc., fixed to the feet to allow gliding movement over snow. ● *ns* **skier** /skee-er/, **skiing** /skee-ing/. ● *also vb* to glide over snow on skis.

kid /skid/ *n* **1** a wooden or metal block put under a wheel to stop it turning. **2** a sort of runner fixed to the under part of an airplane. **3** a sideways movement of a wheel on the ground. ● *vb* (**skidded** /skid-id/, **skidding** /skid-ing/) **1** to move sideways on wheels that fail to turn (*cars skidding on the ice*). **2** to stop turning by placing a block under (a wheel).

skill /skill/ *n* ability gained by practice, natural cleverness at doing something (*her skill as a pianist/improve her typing skills*).

skilled /skild/ *adj* expert.

skillet /ski-let/ *n* **1** a frying pan. **2** (*Br*) small pot with a long handle and legs.

skillful /skil-ful/ *adj*, *also* **skilful** (*Br, Cdn*) expert, clever (at doing something) (*she was a skillful pianist*). ● *adv* **skillfully** /skil-ful-ee/, *also* **skilfully** (*Br, Cdn*).

skim /skim/ *vb* (**skimmed** /skimd/, **skimming** /ski-ming/) **1** to remove anything floating on the surface of a liquid (*skim the grease off the stew*). **2** to pass quickly over the surface of. **3** to read quickly and without attention (*skim the headlines*).

skim milk /skim-milk/ *n*, *also* **skimmed milk** (*Br*) /skimd-milk/ milk from which the cream has been removed.

skimp /skimp/ *vb* to give less than is needed, to give or use sparingly (*skimp on the curtain material*).

skimpy /skim-pee/ *adj* barely or not quite enough (*a skimpy dress/skimpy helpings of food*).

skin /skin/ *n* **1** the natural outer covering of animals or vegetables (*apple skins*). **2** a thin layer or covering (*the skin on rice pudding*). **3** a container made of skin. ● *vb* (**skinned** /skind/, **skinning** /skin-ing/) to take the skin off.

skinny /skin-ee/ *adj* (*inf*) very thin (*children who are too skinny*).

skintight /skin-tite/ *adj* clinging closely to the body.

skip[1] /skip/ *vb* (**skipped** /skipt/, **skipping** /skip-ing/) **1** to jump about lightly. **2** to keep on jumping over a rope swung over the head and then under the feet alternately. **3** to miss out something, e.g., to leave out parts of a book when reading it (*skip the descriptive parts in the novel*). ● *n* a light jump.

skip[2] /skip/ *n* the captain of a curling or bowling team.

ski plane /skee-plane/ *n* an airplane fitted with skis instead of wheels for landing and taking off in the snow.

skipper /skip-er/ *n* the captain of a ship or team.

skirmish /skir-mish/ *n* **1** a fight in which the main armies are not engaged. **2** a fight broken off before serious harm is done to either side. ● *vb* to fight in small parties.

skirt /skirt/ *n* **1** the part of a garment below the waist (*the skirt of the ball dress*). **2** a woman's garment stretching from the waist down. **3** the border or outer edge. ● *vb* to pass along the edge or border.

skit /skit/ *n* a piece of writing in which persons, events, etc., are imitated in a way that makes fun of them.

skittish /skit-ish/ *adj* easily excitable (*in a skittish mood*).

skulk /skulk/ *vb* to try to keep out of sight for fear or with evil intentions (*burglars skulking in the garden watching the empty house*).

skull /skull/ *n* the bony case that contains the brain.

skullcap /skull-cap/ *n* a light, close-fitting, brimless cap usually worn indoors.

skunk /skungk/ *n* **1** a black-and-white animal that sprays a bad-smelling fluid when attacked. **2** (*inf*) a mean or contemptible person (*he was a skunk to betray his friend*).

sky /skie/ *n* the space around Earth as visible to our eyes.

sky blue /skie-bloo/ *adj* light blue, azure.

sky box /skie-box/ *n* an elevated room at a sport stadium where the event can be viewed in luxurious surroundings.

sky dive /skie-dive/ *vb* to jump from a plane and fall for as long as possible without opening a parachute.

skylark /skie-lark/ *n* a small bird that sings as it flies upward. ● *vb* to play about noisily, to play tricks.

skylight /skie-lite/ *n* a window in the roof of a building (*the skylight in the attic*).

skyline /skie-line/ *n* the horizon.

skyscraper /skie-scray-per/ *n* a very tall building.

skyward /skie-wurdz/ *adv* upward from the earth.

slab /slab/ *n* a large flat piece of anything (*a slab of cheese*).

slack[1] /slack/ *adj* **1** loose, not tight (*a slack waistband*). **2** careless, lazy (*workers becoming slack under poor management*). **3** not busy (*their slack time of year*). ● *n* the loose part of a rope, etc. ● *vb* **1** to work lazily or carelessly. **2** to lose speed.

slack[2] /slack/ *n* coal dust and tiny pieces of coal.

slacken /sla-ken/ *vb* **1** to loosen. **2** to lose force or speed (*trains slackening speed*). **3** to become less (*demand slackening*).

slacker /sla-ker/ *n* (*inf*) a person who does not work hard.

slackness /slack-ness/ *n* **1** looseness (*the slackness of the waistband*). **2** carelessness.

slacks /slacks/ *npl* loose-fitting pants.

slake /slake/ *vb* **1** to satisfy (thirst). **2** to mix lime with water (when making cement).

slalom /sla-lum/ *n* a skiing race downhill over a zigzag course marked by poles.

slam /slam/ *vb* (**slammed** /slamd/, **slamming** /slamming/) to shut or put down noisily (*slam the door angrily*). ● *n* a bang.

slam-dunk /slam-dungk/ *n* in basketball, a dunk shot in which the ball is slammed through the basket

slander /slan-der/ *n* an untrue story written or said to injure a person's character (*take them to court on a charge of slander*). ● *vb* to spread such a story

slanderous /slan-druss/ *adj* harmful to the reputation.

slang /slang/ *n* words and phrases in common use but not accepted as good English.

slant /slant/ *n* slope (*draw a line at a slant*). ● *vb* **1** to slope or cause to slope. **2** to express or describe something in such a way as to emphasize a certain point or show favor toward a particular point of view.

slap /slap/ *n* a blow with the open hand. ● *vb* (**slapped** /slapt/, **slapping** /sla-ping/) to strike with the flat of the hand or anything flat.

slapdash /slap-dash/ *adj* careless, done in a hurry (*slapdash in their attitude to their work*). ● *adv* carelessly.

slapstick /slap-stick/ *adj* causing laughter by silly actions, such as falling down or bumping into things. ● *also n*.

slash /slash/ *vb* **1** to make a sweeping cut at with a knife, etc., to make long cuts in. **2** to reduce sharply (*slash prices*). ● *n* a long cut.

slat /slat/ *n* a thin strip of wood, etc.

slate[1] /slate/ *n* **1** a type of rock that splits easily into thin layers. **2** a shaped piece of slate for covering a roof or for writing on. ● *vb* to cover with slate (*slating the roof*).

slate[2] /slate/ *vb* **1** to scold angrily. **2** to criticize severely (*a play slated by the critics*).

slaughter /slaw-ter/ *n* **1** killing in great numbers. **2** the act of killing. ● *vb* **1** to kill in great numbers (*slaughter every soldier*). **2** to kill for food (*slaughter cattle*).

slaughterhouse /slaw-ter-house/ *n* a place where animals are killed for food.

slave /slave/ *n* **1** a person who is the property of another person and has to work for him or her. **2** a person who has to do the dirty or unpleasant work ● *vb* to work very hard (*slaving away to try to pass the exam*).

lavery /**slave**-vu-ree/ *n* **1** the state of being a slave, the owning or keeping of slaves as a practice. **2** hard, unpleasant, and badly paid work (*it was sheer slavery working in the hotel kitchen*). **3** lack of all freedom.

lave ship /**slave**-ship/ *n* a ship for moving slaves, as from taking them from Africa to the Americas.

lave state /**slave**-state/ *n* any of the states in which slavery was legal before the Civil War.

lave trade /**slave**-trade/ *n* the buying and selling of people as slaves.

lay /slay/ *vb* (*pt* **slew** /sloo/, *pp* **slain** /slane/) to kill.

leazy /**slee**-zee/ *adj* shoddy, shabby, morally low. ● *n* **sleaze** /sleez/.

led /sled/, **sledge** (*Br*) /sledge/ *n* a vehicle on runners for use in the snow. ● *vb* to ride on a sled, to carry on a sled. ● *n* **sledding** /**sled**-ing/ the riding or carrying on a sled (*went sledding on the snow day*).

ledgehammer /**sledge**-ha-mer/ *n* a long-handled, heavy hammer usually held with two hands.

leek /sleek/ *adj* **1** smooth and shiny (*sleek hair*). **2** well-fed and cared for (*sleek cats*).

leep /sleep/ *vb* to rest the body, with the eyes shut, unaware of the surroundings. ● *n* a complete rest for the body, as at night. ● *adv* **sleepily** /**slee**-pi-lee/ in a drowsy, sleepy manner.

leeper /**slee**-per/ *n* **1** a person or animal who is asleep. **2** a long rectangular block that supports railway lines. **3** a coach on a train with bunks for sleeping passengers.

leeping bag /**slee**-ping-bag/ *n* a large, warmly lined, zippered bag in which a person can sleep, especially outdoors.

leeping pill /**slee**-ping-pill/ *n* a drug that makes a person sleepy and drowsy, so as to help him/her to sleep.

leepless /**sleep**-less/ *adj* **1** unable to sleep (*lie sleepless all night*). **2** without sleep (*a sleepless night*).

leepover /**sleep**-oa-ver/ *n* (*inf*) a party where (usually) children spend the night at a place other than home. Also called a **slumber party** or a **pajama party**. The participants will be allowed to stay up late and play games.

leepwalker /**sleep**-waw-ker/ *n* a person who walks about in his or her sleep. ● *vb* **sleepwalking** /**sleep**-waw-king/.

leepy /**slee**-pee/ *adj* wanting to sleep, drowsy (*feel sleepy after a large meal*).

leet /sleet/ *n* falling snow mixed with rain or hail. ● *adj* **sleety** /**slee**-tee/.

leeve /sleev/ *n* **1** the part of a garment that covers the arm. **2** a tube or tubelike part fitting over or around another part. **3** a thin paper or plastic cover for protecting a record.

sleigh /slay/ *n* a vehicle on runners for use in snow; a sled.

sleight /slite/ *n* cunning or craft used to trick.

sleight of hand /slite-ov-**hand**/ *n* quickness with the hands, jugglery (*admire the magician's sleight of hand*).

slender /**slen**-der/ *adj* **1** slim (*a slender figure*). **2** thin, scanty, only just enough (*of slender means*).

sleuth /slooth/ *n* a detective (*the sleuth in the crime story*).

slew /sloo/ *n* a large number, a group.

slice /slice/ *vb* **1** to cut into thin pieces (*slicing bread*). **2** to strike a ball in a glancing blow that makes it spin. ● *n* **1** a thin, broad piece cut off (*a slice of bread*). **2** a flat utensil for serving food (*a fish slice*).

slick /slick/ *adj* **1** quick and clever (*flip the pancake with a slick movement*). **2** smart but not trustworthy (*a slick salesman*).

slide /slide/ *vb* (*pt, pp* **slid** /slid/) to move smoothly over a surface, as of ice, to slip. ● *n* **1** a slope or track for sliding on (*the children's slide in the park*). **2** a small glass plate with an object to be examined through a microscope or a picture to be shown on a screen (*scientists examining bacteria on a slide*).

slider /**slie**-der/ *n* **1** a person or thing that slides. **2** in baseball, a pitch with the speed of a fastball and the movement of a curve.

slight /slite/ *adj* **1** small, lightly built (*too slight to push the heavy car*). **2** small, not great, not serious (*matters of slight importance/a slight problem*). ● *n* an insult. ● *vb* to treat as unimportant, to treat insultingly. ● *adj* **slighting** /**slie**-ting/.

slim /slim/ *adj* thin, lightly built, small (*slim young women*). ● *vb* (**slimmed** /slimd/, **slimming** /**sli**-ming/) to reduce weight by exercises, not eating certain foods, etc. (*go on a diet to try to slim*).

slime /slime/ *n* any soft, moist, slippery, sometimes sticky matter.

slimy /**slie**-mee/ *adj* **1** covered with slime, slippery. **2** untrustworthy (*a slimy character*).

sling /sling/ *vb* (*pt, pp* **slung** /slung/) **1** to throw with the outstretched arm (*sling a stone in the river*). **2** to cause to hang from (*a gun slung from his shoulder*). ● *n* **1** a strap or band used for hurling stones. **2** a bandage hanging from the neck to support an injured arm. **3** a band passed around something to help to lift or support it (*a baby sling*).

slingshot /**sling**-shot/ *n* a Y-shaped piece of wood, metal, etc. with an elastic band attached to the upper tips for shooting stones, etc.

slink /slingk/ *vb* (*pt, pp* **slunk** /slungk/) to go away quietly as if ashamed (*the dog slunk away after being punished*).

slinky /sling-kee/ *adj* **1** sneaking. **2** graceful in movement.

slip /slip/ *vb* (**slipped** /slipt/, **slipping** /sli-ping/) **1** to move smoothly along. **2** to go quietly or unseen. **3** to lose footing. **4** to escape (the memory). ● *n* **1** the act of slipping. **2** a careless mistake. **3** a narrow piece of paper. **4** a twig. **5** a loose cover (e.g. a pillowcase). **6** a woman's undergarment or petticoat. **7** a prepared downward slope along which newly built, repaired, or laid-up ships can slide into the sea. ● **give the slip to** to go away from without being noticed.

slipcase /slip-case/ *n* a boxlike container for a book or set of books, open at one end to show the spine(s) of the book(s).

slipcover /slip-cu-ver/ *n* a removable, fitted cloth cover for a chair, sofa, etc.

slipknot *n* a knot that can be moved.

slippage /sli-pidge/ *n* the act of slipping, the amount of slipping.

slipper /sli-per/ *n* a loose shoe for wearing in the house.

slippery /sli-pree/ *adj* **1** hard to stand on without sliding or falling (*slippery ground*). **2** hard to hold without the grip sliding (*slippery fish*). **3** (*inf*) untrustworthy (*a slippery character*).

slipshod /slip-shod/ *adj* careless, untidy (*the interior decoration was slipshod*).

slit /slit/ *vb* (**slitted** /sli-tid/, **slitting** /sli-ting/) to make a long cut in (*slit the envelope open*). ● *n* a long narrow cut or opening.

slither /sli-ther/ *vb* to slide clumsily or without control, to slip or slide on (*people slithering on icy pavements/a snake slithering along the ground*).

sliver /sli-ver/ *n* a thin piece cut off, a splinter (*a sliver of cheese*).

slob /slob/ *n* a sloppy or gross person.

slobber /slob-er/ *vb* to let saliva run or fall from the mouth.

slog /slog/ *vb* (**slogged** /slogd/, **slogging** /slog-ing/) (*inf*) **1** to hit hard. **2** to work hard (*slogging away at his homework*). ● *n* **slogger**.

slogan /slo-gan/ *n* **1** a war cry. **2** a party cry or catchword. **3** an easily memorized saying used to advertise a product or campaign.

sloop /sloop/ *n* a small sailing boat with one mast.

slop /slop/ *vb* (**slopped** /slopt/, **slopping** /slop-ing/) to spill through, carelessness, to overflow a little at a time. ● *n* **1** a puddle of spilled liquid. **2** (*usually pl*) dirty or waste water. **3** (*usually pl*) liquid food.

slope /slope/ *n* **1** a rise or fall from the level. **2** a slant. ● *vb* **1** to rise or fall from the level (*fields sloping down to the sea*). **2** to slant.

sloppy /slop-ee/ *adj* (*inf*) **1** wet, muddy. **2** careless and untidy (*sloppy work*). **2** foolishly sentimental (*sloppy love stories*).

sloppy joe /slop-ee-joe/ *n* a sandwich made of ground beef mixed with tomato sauce and spices served on a bun.

slosh /slosh/ *vb* to shake a liquid, to apply a liquid, to splash through water.

slot /slot/ *n* a narrow opening or hole, especially one made to receive coins (*the slot in a parking meter*).

sloth /slawth/ *n* **1** laziness. **2** a slow-moving South American animal that lives in trees.

slothful /slawth-ful/ *adj* very lazy.

slouch /slouch/ *vb* to stand, walk, or sit with bent back and head and shoulders sloping inward (*slouching in his chair*). ● *n* a lazy, unhealthy, and improper way of standing and walking. ● *adj* **slouchy** /slou-chee/.

slough /sluf/ *n* the cast-off skin of a snake. ● *vb* **1** to cast off (*snakes sloughing their skin*). **2** to throw off (*slough off a feeling of depression*).

slovenly /slu-ven-lee/ *adj* dirty and untidy, very careless (*slovenly habits/a slovenly housekeeper*).

slow /sloa/ *adj* **1** not quick or fast. **2** taking a long time to do things. **3** not clever (*slow pupils*). **4** behind the correct time (*the clock is slow*). ● *vb* to go or cause to go less quickly.

sludge /sludge/ *n* soft, thick mud.

slug[1] /slug/ *n* a shell-less snail that is harmful to plants.

slug[2] /slug/ *vb* (**slugged** /slugd/, **slugging** /slu-ging/) **1** to shoot. **2** to hit hard. ● *n* a small solid metal bullet.

sluggish /slu-gish/ *adj* slow-moving (*feel sluggish in the morning/trade is sluggish*).

slum /slum/ *n* part of a town in which poor people live in overcrowded, dirty, and unhealthy houses.

slumber /slum-ber/ *vb* to sleep. ● *n* sleep.

slump /slump/ *n* a sudden fall in prices, wages, etc (*a slump in house prices*). ● *vb* **1** to go suddenly down in price, etc. **2** to fall suddenly or heavily (*she slumped into a chair*).

slur /slur/ *vb* (**slurred** /slurd/, **slurring** /slu-ring/) **1** to pass over quickly or without attention. **2** to make (sounds) unclear by running them together (*a tired man slurring his words*). ● *n* **1** a bad point in a person's character or reputation. **2** (*mus*) a curved mark over two notes to be played smoothly one after the other.

slurp /slurp/ *vb* to drink or eat noisily.

slush /slush/ *n* **1** half-melted snow. **2** (*inf*) foolishly sentimental writing or talk (*the slush on some greetings cards*). ● *adj* **slushy** /slu-shee/.

sly /slie/ *adj* cunning, tricky, doing things in a secret and untrustworthy way. ● **on the sly** secretly.

smack[1] /smack/ *vb* **1** to hit with the flat of the hand (*mothers smacking children*). **2** to part the lips so as to make a sharp noise. ● *n* a **1** slap. **2** a loud kiss.

smack[2] /smack/ *n* a taste, a flavor or suggestion of. ● *vb* **1** to taste (of). **2** to remind of, to suggest (*the situation smacks of bribery*).

smack[3] /smack/ *n* a small fishing boat with sails.

small /smawl/ *adj* **1** little (*small people*). **2** not much (*small reason to rejoice*). ● *n* the lower part of the back.

small intestine /small in-tess-tin/ *n* the part of the digestive system where nutrients are absorbed from food and passed into the bloodstream.

smallpox /smawl-poks/ *n* a dangerous infectious disease that leaves little pocks on the skin.

small talk /smawl-tok/ *n* conversation about unimportant matters (*trying to make small talk with his neighbor*).

smart /smart/ *adj* **1** quick, clever (*smart pupils/smart thinking*). **2** well-dressed (*smart wedding guests*). ● *vb* to feel or cause a quick keen pain (*a burn that was smarting*).

smarten /smar-ten/ *vb* to make smart or smarter (*told to smarten up his appearance*).

smash /smash/ *vb* to break into pieces (*smash crockery*). ● *n* **1** act of breaking into pieces. **2** the noise caused by breakage. **3** an accident involving one or more vehicles (*a motorway smash*). **4** a disaster, downfall. ● **smash and grab** a theft carried out by smashing a shop window and taking articles behind it.

smear /smeer/ *vb* **1** to spread (something sticky or dirty) over the surface (*smear jam over his bread*). **2** to smudge, to make or become blurred (*smear the lettering*). ● *n* **1** a dirty mark, a blot. **2** a story intended to harm a person's good name (*a smear campaign*). ● *adj* **smeary** /smee-ree/.

smell /smell/ *n* **1** the sense that enables animals to become aware of by breathing in through the nose (*dogs finding the criminal by smell*). **2** scent, odor. ● *vb* (*pt, pp* **smelled** /smeld/) **1** to perceive by smell. **2** to give off an odor. ● **smell a rat** to be suspicious.

smelly /smel-ee/ *adj* (*inf*) having an unpleasant odor (*smelly socks*).

smelt[1] /smelt/ *vb* to melt metal out of rock. ● *n* **smelter** /smel-ter/.

smelt[2] /smelt/ *n* a small edible fish of the salmon family.

smile /smile/ *vb* **1** to show joy, amusement, etc., by an upward movement of the lips. **2** to be favorable (*the future smiling on them*). ● *n* a look of pleasure or amusement. ● *adj* **smiley** /smie-lee/.

smirk /smurk/ *vb* to smile in a silly or unnatural manner (*stand smirking while being photographed*). ● *n* a smug or scornful smile (*a self-satisfied smirk*).

smite /smite/ *vb* (**smote** /smote/, **smiting** /smie-ting/, *pp* **smitten** /smi-ten/) (*old or fml*) **1** to strike hard. **2** to cause to suffer from (*smitten with flu*).

smith /smith/ *n* a craftsperson who works in metals.

smock /smock/ *n* **1** a loose overall worn to protect a person's clothes. **2** a woman's loose dress.

smog /smog/ *n* a smoky fog, pollution.

smoke /smoke/ *n* the sooty vapor rising from a burning substance (*smoke rising from the chimney*). ● *vb* **1** to give off smoke (*fires smoking*). **2** to draw in the tobacco smoke from a cigarette, pipe, etc. **3** to preserve in smoke (*smoked fish*). **4** to drive out by smoke. ● *adj* **smoky** /smo-kee/.

smokehouse /smoke-house/ *n* a building where meats are smoked to preserve them.

smoker /smo-ker/ *n* **1** a person who smokes tobacco. **2** a compartment in a train in which smoking is allowed.

smoke screen /smoke-screen/ *n* **1** thick clouds of smoke sent out to conceal movements. **2** something intended to conceal activities (*his store was a smoke screen for his drug-smuggling*).

smokestack /smoke-stack/ *n* the chimney of a steamer or factory.

smolder /smole-der/ *vb*, *also* **smoulder** (*Br, Cdn*) to burn and smoke without flame.

smooth /smooth/ *adj* **1** having an even surface, not rough. **2** free from difficulties (*the smooth running of the club*). **3** having good yet not pleasing manners. ● *vb* to make smooth or level (*smooth the rough wooden surface*).

smooth-tongued /smooth-tungd/ *adj* able to speak in a very polite or flattering manner.

smorgasbord /smawr-gas-board/ *n* a wide variety of tasty foods laid out in a buffet.

smother /smu-ther/ *vb* to kill by keeping air from.

smudge /smudge/ *n* a dirty mark, a stain. ● *vb* **1** to make a dirty mark on. **2** to make or become blurred or smeared (*smudging the painting*). ● *adj* **smudgy** /smu-jee/.

smug /smug/ *n* self-satisfied, too pleased with oneself.

smuggle /smu-gul/ *vb* **1** to bring goods into the country secretly, without paying customs duties on them. **2** to bring in or pass secretly (*smuggling food into the movies*).

smuggler /smu-gler/ *n* a person who smuggles goods.

smut /smut/ *n* **1** a flake of soot. **2** a dirty mark or stain. **3** dirty or indecent talk (*object to the smut of the comedian*). ● *adj* **smutty** /smu-tee/.

snack /snack/ *n* a light, quick meal (*a midmorning snack*) **2** something, such as a piece of fruit, eaten between meals. ● *vb* to eat between meals.

snag *n* **1** an unexpected difficulty (*their plans hit a snag*). **2** a log just below the water surface, dangerous to boats. ● *adj* **snaggy** /sna-gee/.

snail /snail/ *n* a slow-moving soft-bodied creature with a shell on its back.

snake /snake/ *n* **1** a long creature that slithers along the ground with no legs and a scaly skin, a serpent. **2** an untrustworthy or deceitful person (*the snake betrayed his friend*).

snap /snap/ *vb* (**snapped** /snapt/, **snapping** /sna-ping/) **1** to bite or seize suddenly. **2** to break with a sharp sound (*twigs snapping as they walked*). **3** to speak in a quick, angry manner (*mothers snapping at their children*). **4** to take a photograph of with a hand camera. ● *n* **1** a sudden bite. **2** a short, sharp sound. **3** a lock that springs shut when released. **4** a spell of weather (*a cold snap*). **5** a card game. **6** a snapshot.

snapdragon /snap-dra-gun/ *n* a plant with a showy white, yellow, red, or purple flower.

snappish /sna-pish/ *adj* irritable, short-tempered.

snappy /sna-pee/ *adj* **1** snappish (*a snappy remark*). **2** (*inf*) quick (*ask for a snappy response*).

snapshot /snap-shot/ *n* **1** a quick shot. **2** a photograph taken with a hand camera.

snare /snare/ *n* **1** a kind of musical drum. **2** a trap for catching birds or animals, especially one made with a running noose. **3** a temptation (*her beauty was a snare*). ● *vb* to catch by a snare (*snaring rabbits*).

snarl /snarl/ *vb* **1** to growl angrily and show the teeth (*dogs snarling*). **2** to speak rudely or angrily (*an old man snarling at the children*). ● *also n*.

snatch /snatch/ *vb* to seize quickly or suddenly. ● *n* **1**

a sudden seizing. **2** a small part.

sneak /sneek/ *vb* **1** to go quietly, as a thief (*sneak up the stairs at midnight*). **2** to tell of another's wrongdoing to a person in authority (*children sneaking on their friends*). **3** to behave meanly. ● *n* **1** a tattletale. **2** a mean person.

sneaker /snee-ker/ *n* an athletic shoe.

sneaking /snee-king/ *adj* underhand, secret.

sneaky /snee-kee/ *adj* mean.

sneer /sneer/ *vb* to show scorn by a look or remark (*sneer at his attempts to row the boat*). ● *n* a mocking smile or remark.

sneeze /sneez/ *vb* to expel air noisily through the nose and mouth in a sudden, explosive action (*people with colds often sneeze*). ● *n* the act or sound of sneezing.

snicker /sni-ker/ *vb* to laugh under the breath or secretly, to giggle nervously or unpleasantly. ● *also n*.

snide /snide/ *adj* cutting, slyly mean, nasty.

sniff /sniff/ *vb* **1** to breathe noisily inward. **2** to smell (*sniff the smell of the sea*). ● *n* **1** the act or sound of sniffing. **2** a slight smell. ● **sniff at** to show scorn for.

sniffle /sni-ful/ *vb* to sniff repeatedly, as when a person has a cold or the flu. ● *n* **the sniffles** a cold.

snigger /sni-ger/ same as **snicker**.

snip /snip/ *vb* (**snipped** /snipt/, **snipping** /sni-ping/) to cut as with scissors, to cut off with one sharp movement (*snip off a lock of her hair*). ● *n* **1** the act or sound of scissors closing to cut. **2** a small piece cut off (*a snip of the material*).

snipe[1] /snipe/ *n* a game bird with a long bill, found in marshy places.

snipe[2] /snipe/ *vb* to shoot at from a hiding place. ● *n* **sniper** /snie-per/.

snippet /sni-pit/ *n* **1** a small piece cut off. **2** a short item of news (*snippets of gossip*).

snivel /sni-vul/ *vb* (**sniveled** /sni-vuld/, **sniveling** /sni-vu-ling/) **1** to run at the nose. **2** to go on crying or complaining, to whimper (*snivel about being cold*).

snob /snob/ *n* a person who looks down on others because they are less wealthy or of lower rank in society (*his former friends accuse him of being a snob*). ● *n* **snobbery** /snob-ree/. ● *adj* **snobby** /snob-ee/.

snobbish /snob-ish/ *adj* behaving like a snob.

snooker /snoo-ker/ *n* a billiards game in which players have to knock, with a white cue ball, 15 red and then in order six colored balls into pockets on a table.

snoop /snoop/ vb to go about secretly or stealthily to find out something (*snooping among her friend's papers*). ● n **snooper** /snoo-per/.

snooty /snoo-tee/ adj (*inf*) haughty, proud, distant in manner (*snooty neighbors who won't speak to other people*).

snooze /snooz/ n (*inf*) a short, light sleep. ● vb to take a short nap (*snoozing on the plane*).

snore /snore/ vb to breathe noisily while asleep, as if grunting. ● n the noise so made.

snorkel /snawr-kul/ n a tube that extends above the water through which a person can breathe while swimming just below the surface of the water.

snort /snawrt/ vb to blow air out noisily through the nose (*snort with disbelief*). ● also n.

snot /snot/ n the mucus of the nose.

snout /snout/ n **1** the long nose and mouth of an animal (*the pig's snout*). **2** the nozzle of a pipe.

snow /sno/ n vapor frozen in the air and falling in flakes. ● vb to fall as snow, to cover as with snow. ● adj snowy /sno-wee/.

snowball /sno-bawl/ n snow pressed into a hard ball.

snowboard /sno-board/ n a long, wide board with bindings for the feet on which people slide down slopes. ● n **snowboarding** /sno-bore-ding/.

snowbound /sno-bound/ adj shut in or blocked off by snow.

snowcap /sno-cap/ n a cap of snow, as on a mountain.

snowdrift /sno-drift/ n snow heaped up by the wind to form a bank.

snowdrop /sno-drop/ n a small white flower that grows in early spring.

snowfall /sno-fawl/ n a falling of snow.

snowflake /sno-flake/ n a single piece of snow.

snow line /sno-line/ n the level above which snow never melts.

snowmobile /sno-mu-beel/ n a motor vehicle for traveling over snow, usually with steerable runners and tractor treads.

snowplow /sno-plow/ n, also **snowplough** (*Br, Cdn*) an implement for clearing snow from roads or railways.

snowshoe /sno-shoo/ n a light, broad frame worn on the feet for walking on snow.

snub /snub/ vb (**snubbed** /snubd/, **snubbing** /snu-bing/) to show dislike or disapproval of a person by taking no notice of or speaking rudely to him or her (*she was snubbed when she tried to be friendly to them*). ● n rude lack of notice, an unfriendly act or speech. ● adj (*of a nose*) short and turned up.

snuff[1] /snuff/ vb to sniff powdered tobacco, etc., up the nose. ● n tobacco powdered for sniffing up the nose.

snuff[2] /snuff/ vb **1** to cut off the burnt part of the wick of a candle. **2** to put out a candle. ● n **snuffer** /snu-fer/ a tool used to put out a candle.

snuffbox /snuff-boks/ n a box for carrying snuff in the pocket.

snuffle /snu-ful/ vb **1** to make sniffing noises. **2** to speak through the nose (*children with colds snuffling*).

snug /snug/ adj warm and comfortable, cosy (*children snug in their beds/a snug room*).

snuggle /snu-gul/ vb to lie close for warmth, to settle comfortably (*children snuggling under the blankets*).

so /so/ adv **1** in this or that manner (*do it so*). **2** to that extent (*so wet that we stayed in*). **3** thus (*she was tired and so left the party*). **4** very (*so happy*). ● conj therefore (*be quiet so I can think*).

soak /soak/ vb **1** to wet thoroughly. **2** to steep (*soak the stained clothing*). **3** to suck up (*blotting paper soaking up ink*).

soap /soap/ n **1** a substance made of oil or fat and certain chemicals, used in washing **2** a soap opera. ● vb to rub with soap. ● adj soapy /soa-pee/ having to do with or containing soap (*soapy water*).

soapbox /soap-boks/ n **1** a box or crate for soap. **2** a platform used by a person making an informal speech to people on the street.

soap opera /soap-op-ra/ n a radio or television drama serial that deals with the day-to-day lives and problems of the same group of characters [originates from the soap-powder-selling sponsors of such shows in the 1950s in the United States].

soar /soar/ vb **1** to fly upward. **2** to tower up (*mountains soaring above the town*).

sob /sob/ vb (**sobbed** /sobd/, **sobbing** /sob-ing/) to draw in the breath noisily when weeping or short of breath. ● also n.

sober /so-ber/ adj **1** not drunk. **2** serious, quiet (*a sober person*). **3** dark in color (*wear sober clothes to the funeral*).

sobriety /so-brie-i-tee/ n the state of being sober.

so-called /so-cawld/ adj given a name or title to which a person has no right (*a so-called lady*).

soccer /soc-er/ n a game played with a round ball by two teams of 11 players on a field with a goal at either end; the ball is moved by kicking or by striking with any part of the body accept the hands and arms.

sociable /**so**-sha-bul/ *adj* fond of company.

social /**so**-shal/ *adj* 1 having to do with society (*social problems*). 2 living in an organized group (*social creatures*).

socialism /**so**-sha-li-zum/ *n* the belief that all means of producing national wealth (e.g., mines, etc.) are the property of the community and should be used for the benefit of all.

socialist /**soash**-list/ *n* a person who believes in socialism.

social science /**so**-shal-**sie**-inss/ *n* the study of people living together in groups, families, etc.

social security /**so**-shul si-**cure**-i-tee/ *n* a government program that pays money to people who are not working or who are unable to work.

social work /**so**-shal-wurk/ *n* (*sometimes with caps*) any service designed to advance the welfare of the community and the individual through counseling services, health clinics, playgrounds, etc.

society /su-**sie**-u-tee/ *n* 1 a group of people living together in a single organized community. 2 a group of people who meet regularly for a special purpose, mixing with other people (*a debating society*). 3 the wealthy or high-ranking members of a community (*mix in society*).

sociology /so-she-**ol**-u-jee/ *n* the study of the nature, growth, and problems of human society. ● *n* sociologist /so-she-**ol**-u-jist/. ● *adj* sociological /so-she-ul-**odge**-ic-al/.

sock /sock/ *n* a short stocking, a cloth covering of the foot.

socket /**sock**-it/ *n* a hole or hollow for something to fit into or turn in (*an electric socket/an eye socket*).

sod /sod/ *n* a piece of earth held together by the roots of the grass growing in it.

soda /**so**-da/ *n* 1 a powder used in washing, baking, etc. 2 soda pop, a sweet, fizzy beverage.

soda water /**so**-da-wa-ter/ *n* water containing soda powder and made fizzy by gas.

sodden /**sod**-en/ *adj* wet through, soaking (*their sodden clothes*).

sodium /**so**-dee-um/ *n* an element found in salt, with the chemical symbol Na.

sofa /**so**-fa/ *n* a couch with a cushioned seat, back, and arms.

sofa bed /**so**-fa-bed/ *n* a sofa that can be opened into a bed.

soft /soft/ *adj* 1 not hard (*soft cheese*). 2 easily reshaped by pressing (*a soft substance*). 3 not loud (*soft music*). 4 (*of color*) not bright. 5 gentle (*a soft breeze*). 6 not strict (*teachers who are too soft*). 7 not alcoholic (*soft drinks*). 8 foolishly kind (*Don't be soft!*). ● *adv* quietly, gently.

softball /**soft**-bawl/ *n* a kind of baseball played with underhand pitching, the ball used in this game similar to a baseball but larger.

soft drink /**soft**-dringk/ a nonalcoholic drink, such as lemonade or cola.

soften /**sawf**-en/ *vb* 1 to make or become soft. 2 to become less harsh or angry (*her attitude softened*). ● *n* softener /**sawf**-ner/ something that softens.

software /**soft**-ware/ *n* the programs used in computers.

soggy /**sog**-ee/ *adj* soft and wet (*soggy toast/soggy ground*).

soil /soil/ *n* the ground, earth, especially that in which plants are grown. ● *vb* to dirty, to spoil (*the children were told not to soil their clothes in the sand*).

solace /**sol**-iss/ *vb* to cheer, to comfort. ● *n* that which gives cheer or comfort (*the widow found her child a solace*).

solar /**so**-lar/ *adj* having to do with the sun (*solar power*).

solarium /su-**lay**-ree-um/ *n* a glassed-in porch, roof, etc., where people sun themselves, as in treating illness.

solar system /**so**-lar-sis-tem/ n the sun and the planets that move around it.

sold /soald/ *pt of* sell.

solder /**sole**-dur/ *n* a metal alloy that when melted can be used for cementing together pieces of metal. ● *vb* to join with solder.

soldier /**sole**-jur/ *n* a person serving in an army. ● *n* soldiery /**sole**-ju-ree/ a group of soldiers, the profession of being a soldier.

sole[1] /sole/ *n* the underside of the foot, stocking, or shoe (*boots with leather soles*). ● *vb* to put a sole on (a shoe).

sole[2] /sole/ *n* a small flatfish.

sole[3] /sole/ *adj* only, single (*his sole objection*). ● *adv* solely /**sole**-lee/.

solemn /**sol**-um/ *adj* 1 serious in manner or appearance (*a solemn child*). 2 slow, stately (*a solemn meeting*).

solemnity /su-**lem**-ni-tee/ *n* seriousness.

sol-fa /**sole**-fa/ *n* the use of the sounds *doh*, *ray*, *me*, *fah*, *soh*, *lah*, *te* in singing the scale. ● *also adj*.

solicit /su-**li**-sit/ *vb* to ask earnestly or repeatedly (*soliciting a loan*). ● *n* solicitation /su-li-si-**tay**-shun/.

solid /**sol**-id/ *adj* 1 not hollow, consisting of hard matter throughout (*solid pieces of metal*). 2 not liquid or gaseous (*solid substances*). 3 firm (*solid* flesh). **4** reliable (*a solid citizen*). ● *n* a body consisting of hard matter throughout.

solidarity /sol-i-**da**-ri-tee/ *n* sameness of interests, complete unity (*workers joined by solidarity*).

solidify /su-li-di-fie/ *vb* to make or become solid (*water solidified in the pipes*).

soliloquy /su-li-lu-kwee/ *n* (*fml*) a speaking to oneself (*the actor's soliloquy*).

solitaire /sol-i-tair/ *n* **1** a single diamond or other gem set by itself in a ring. **2** a game for one player.

solitary /sol-i-tree/ *adj* **1** alone, without companions (*solitary travelers/a solitary tree*). **2** living or being alone by habit or preference (*solitary people*). **3** single (*a solitary reason*). ● *n* a person who lives alone and away from others.

solitude /sol-i-tood/ *n* loneliness, being alone, a lonely place.

solo /so-lo/ *n* **1** a piece of music for a single performer. **2** a performance by one person (*a piano solo*). **3** a single person's unaccompanied flight in an aiplane.

soloist /so-lo-ist/ *n* a solo singer or performer.

solstice /sol-stiss/ *n* the time when the sun is farthest north (June 21) or south (December 21), giving in the Northern Hemisphere the longest and shortest days, respectively.

soluble /sol-yu-bul/ *adj* **1** able to be melted or dissolved in liquid. **2** (*fml*) to which an answer or solution can be found (*soluble problems*). ● *n* **solubility** /sol-yu-**bi**-li-tee/.

solution /su-**loo**-shun/ *n* **1** a liquid containing another substance dissolved in it (*a salty solution*). **2** the answer to or explanation of a problem, etc. (*the solution to a crossword puzzle*).

solvable /sol-va-bul/ *adj* that can be solved.

solve /solv/ *vb* to find the right answer to or explanation of (*solving the problem/solved the puzzle*).

solvent /sol-vent/ *adj* **1** able to pay your debts (*firms that are scarcely solvent*). **2** able to dissolve. ● *n* a liquid able to dissolve another substance (*get some solvent to remove the grease from his shirt*).

somber /som-bur/ *adj, also* **sombre** (*Br, Cdn*) dark, gloomy, cheerless (*somber colors/in a somber mood*).

sombrero /sum-**bre**-ro/ *n* a broad-brimmed felt or straw hat.

some /sum/ *adj* a certain number or amount (of). ● *pron* **1** certain people (*some would not agree*). **2** a little (*have some*). ● *ns and prons* **someone** /sum-wun/, **something** /sum-thing/, **something**.

somebody /sum-bod-ee/ *n and pron* **1** some person. **2** a person of importance.

somehow /sum-how/ *adv* in some way or other (*we'll get there somehow*).

somersault /su-mer-sawlt/ *n* a leap or roll in which the heels turn completely over the head.

sometime /sum-time/ *adj* (*fml*) former (*his sometime teacher*).

sometimes /sum-tiemz/ *adv* now and then.

somewhat /sum-what/ *adv* in some degree, a little (*somewhat annoyed*).

somewhere /sum-whare/ *adv* in some place (*they have to live somewhere*).

son /sun/ *n* a male child.

sonar /so-nar/ *n* a machine that finds objects underwater by reflecting sound waves.

sonata /su-**na**-ta/ *n* a piece of music in several movements, usually for a solo instrument.

song /song/ *n* **1** words set to music for the voice. **2** the sounds uttered by a bird. **3** a short poem, poetry.

songbird /song-burd/ *n* a bird that sings or a woman who sings.

songbook /song-book/ *n* a book containing a collection of songs, both the words and the notes.

sonic /son-ic/ *adj* of or having to do with sound.

son-in-law /sun-in-law/ *n* the man married to a person's daughter.

sonnet /son-et/ *n* a poem of 14 lines, usually following fixed rhyming patterns. ● *n* **sonneteer** /son-i-tir/ a person who writes sonnets.

soon /soon/ *adv* **1** in a short time (*they'll be here soon*). **2** early (*it's too soon to know*). **3** willingly (*I would just as soon go*).

soot /soot/ *n* black particles that rise with the smoke from burning matter.

sooth /sooth/ *adj* true or real, fact.

soothe /soothe/ *vb* to calm, to comfort (*soothing the baby/soothe the pain*).

sooty /soo-tee/ *adj* **1** like soot. **2** black (*a sooty cat*).

sophisticated /su-fi-sti-cay-tid/ *adj* **1** (*fml*) not natural. **2** having a great deal of experience and wordly wisdom, knowledge of how to dress elegantly, etc. ● *n* **sophistication** /su-fi-sti-**cay**-shun/. ● *vb* **sophisticate** /su-**fi**-sti-cit/.

sophomore /sof-u-more/ *n* a student in the second year of college or the tenth grade in high school.

soporific /sop-u-**rif**-ic/ *adj* (*fml*) causing sleep. ● *n* a drug that causes sleep.

soppy /sop-ee/ *adj* **1** wet through. **2** foolishly sentimental (*soppy love songs*).

soprano /su-**pran**-o/ *n* **1** the highest female or boy's singing voice. **2** a singer with such a voice.

sorbet /**sawr**-bay/ *n* a tart ice, as of fruit juice, served as a dessert or sometimes between meals.

sorcerer /**sore**-su-rer/ *n* a person who works magic. ● *f* **sorceress** /**sore**-su-ress/.

sorcery /**sore**-su-ree/ *n* magic, witchcraft.

sordid /**sawr**-did/ *adj* mean, dirty, disgusting (*a sordid neighborhood/a sordid crime*).

sore /**sore**/ *adj* painful, hurtful (*sore legs*). ● *n* a painful cut or growth on the body (*people who are confined to bed may suffer from bed sores*).

sorely /**sore**-lee/ *adv* **1** very much. **2** painfully.

sorority /su-**raw**-ri-tee/ *n* a group of women or girls joined together by common interests, for fellowship, etc.

sorrel /**saw**-rel/ *n* **1** a plant with sour-tasting leaves. **2** a reddish brown color. **3** a horse of that color.

sorrow /**sor**-o/ *n* sadness caused by loss or suffering, grief (*her sorrow at the death of her friend*). ● *vb* to mourn, to grieve. ● *adj* **sorrowful** /**sor**-o-ful/.

sorry /**sor**-ee/ *adj* **1** feeling pity or regret, sad because of wrongdoing (*sorry for what he had done*). **2** wretched (*a sorry sight*).

sort /**sawrt**/ *n* a kind, class, or set. ● *vb* to arrange in classes or sets (*sorting the library books*). ● **out of sorts** not well.

soufflé /**soo**-**flay**/ *n* a light dish made from beaten egg whites (*a cheese soufflé*).

sought /**sawt**/ *pt of* **seek**.

soul /**sole**/ *n* **1** the spiritual part of a person. **2** (*inf*) a person (*poor souls*). **3** a kind of rhythm-and-blues music.

soulful /**sole**-ful/ *adj* full of feeling (*soulful music*).

soulless /**sole**-less/ *adj* **1** without soul; without spirit (*I thought the actor's performance was soulless*). **2** mean-spirited.

soul mate /**sole**-mate/ *n* a person with whom a person has a deeply personal relationship.

sound[1] /**sound**/ *adj* **1** healthy (*sound in mind and body*). **2** strong (*sound reasons for going*). **3** without serious error or weakness (*his work is quite sound*). ● *adv* completely.

sound[2] /**sound**/ *n* **1** a noise. **2** that which is heard. ● *vb* **1** to make a noise (*alarms sounding*). **2** to touch or strike so as to cause a noise (*sound the dinner bell*).

sound[3] /**sound**/ *n* a long narrow piece of water between two land masses, a strait. ● *vb* **1** to find depth by lowering a lead weight on a cord. **2** to try to discover someone's opinion by questioning (*sound out his views on the new project*).

soundproof /**sound**-proof/ *adj* that keeps sound from coming through.

soundtrack /**sound**-track/ *n* the part of a film on which sounds are recorded.

sound wave /**sound**-wave/ *n* a vibration that carries a sound through a substance, for example, the air.

soup /**soop**/ *n* a liquid food made by boiling meat, vegetables, etc. together (*chicken noodle soup*). ● *adj* **soupy** /**soo**-pee/.

sour /**sour**/ *adj* **1** sharp or bitter in taste (*the sour taste of lemons*). **2** ill-tempered and hard to please (*a sour old man complaining about the child's crying*). ● *vb* to make sour.

source /**soarss**/ *n* **1** that from which anything begins. **2** the spring from which a river flows. **3** origin or cause.

sousaphone /**soo**-za-foan/ *n* a brass instrument of the tuba family.

south /**south**/ *n* **1** one of the four points of the compass, opposite north. ● *adj* being in the south, facing south. ● *also adv*. ● *adj and adv* **southward** /**south**-ward/, **southbound** /**south**-bound/.

southeast /**sou**-theest/ *n* the point midway between south and east. ● *also adj*. ● *adjs* **southeasterly** /sou-**thees**-ter-lee/, **southeastern** /sou-**thees**-tern/, **southeastward** /sou-**thees**-tward/.

southerly /**su**-ther-lee/ *adj* lying toward or coming from the south (*southerly winds*).

southern /**su**-thern/ *adj* in or of the south (*the southern part of the country*). ● *n* **Southerner** /**su**-the(r)-ner/ a person living in or coming from the South.

Southern Hemisphere /**su**-thern **hem**-iss-feer/ *n* the half of the earth south of the equator.

southernmost /**su**-thern-moast/ *adj* farthest south.

South Pole /**south**-pole/ *n* the place on Earth that is the absolutely farthest south.

south-southeast /**south**-south-eest/ *n* the direction halfway between south and southeast.

south-southwest /**south**-south-west/ *n* the direction halfway between south and southwest.

southwest /**south**-west/ *n* the point midway between south and west. ● *also adj*. ● *adjs* **southwesterly** /south-**wes**-ter-lee/, **southwestern** /south-**wes**-tern/, **southwestward** /south-**wes**-tward/.

souvenir /**soo**-vin-ir/ *n* an object kept to remind a person of another person or past event (*a souvenir of their vacation*).

sovereign /**sov**-rin/ *adj* above all others, chief. ● *n* ruler, a king or queen.

sovereignty /**sov**-rin-tee/ *n* supreme power.

sow[1] /**sou**/ *n* a female pig (*sows with their piglets*).

sow[2] /**soe**/ *vb* (*pp* **sown** /**soan**/) **1** to scatter (*sow seeds*). **2** to plant with seeds (*sow a new lawn*).

soybean /**soy**-been/ *n* a type of bean used for making flour or oil, as fodder for cattle, and in food that is free of meat or dairy products, such as **soy milk** /**soy**-milk/.

soy sauce /**soy**-sawss/ *n* a dark, salty sauce made from soybeans and generally used in Chinese and/or Japanese dishes.

spa /**spa**/ *n* a place at which natural mineral waters may be drunk for better health, a health resort at a mineral spring.

space /**space**/ *n* **1** the whole extent of the universe not occupied by solid bodies. **2** the distance between one body or object and another. **3** the place occupied by a person or thing. **4** a length of time (*in the space of a year*). ● *vb* to arrange with intervals between (*spacing the new trees out across the field*).

spacecraft /**space**-craft/ *n* a vehicle used for space travel.

spaceship /**space**-ship/ *n* a spacecraft when people travel in it.

spacing /**spay**-sing/ *n* the arrangement of spaces.

spacious /**spay**-shus/ *adj* roomy, having or giving more than enough room (*spacious cars*).

spade /**spade**/ *n* **1** a tool with a broad blade, used for digging. **2** *pl* a suit of playing cards. ● **call a spade a spade** to say exactly what a person thinks.

spadework /**spade**-wurk/ *n* the hard work needed to start an enterprise (*do all the spadework when they opened the office*).

spaetzle /**shpet**-slu/ *n* egg noodles or dumplings.

spaghetti /spa-**ge**-tee/ *n* long thin strings of pasta made from flour (*spaghetti with tomato sauce*).

span /**span**/ *n* **1** the distance between the tip of the thumb and the little finger fully extended (about 9 inches [23 cm] in an adult). **2** the spread of an arch. **3** the distance from end to end of a bridge. **4** a space of time (*a span of five years*). **5** a number of horses or oxen yoked together to draw a cart, etc. ● *vb* (**spanned** /spand/, **spanning** /**spa**-ning/) **1** to extend from one point in space or time to another (*his employment with the company spans 10 years*). **2** to measure with outstretched fingers.

spangle /**spang**-gul/ *n* a small, glittering metal ornament.

spaniel /**span**-yul/ *n* a sporting or pet dog with long silky hair and drooping ears.

spank /**spangk**/ *vb* **1** to slap with the hand (*the child was spanked by her mother*). **2** to move along quickly.

spar[1] /**spar**/ *n* **1** a long piece of wood. **2** a pole attached to the mast, used for holding sails in position.

spar[2] /**spar**/ *vb* (**sparred** /spard/, **sparring** /**spa**-ring/) to box, to fight with the fists, to argue.

spare /**spare**/ *adj* **1** scarce. **2** thin. **3** more than is needed, kept in reserve. ● *vb* **1** to let off punishment or suffering, to show mercy to. **2** to do without. **3** to use up slowly and carefully.

spare ribs /**spare**-ribz/ *n* a cut of meat, especially pork, consisting of the thin end of the ribs with most of the meat cut away.

spark /**spark**/ *n* **1** a tiny piece of burning matter. **2** a tiny flash made by electricity passing from one wire to another. **3** a bright or clever young person. ● *vb* to give off sparks. ● *adj* **sparky** /**spar**-kee/.

sparkle /**spar**-kul/ *vb* **1** to throw off sparks, to gleam or shine in flashes, to glitter or glisten. **2** to be lively and intelligent (*she was sparkling at the party*). ● also *n*. ● *n* **sparkler** /**spar**-kler/ someone or something that sparkles.

spark plug /**spark**-plug/ a device for causing an electric spark to ignite the gas that drives an engine.

sparrow /**spa**-ro/ *n* a common small bird.

sparse /**sparse**/ *adj* **1** thinly scattered (*sparse vegetation*). **2** scanty, scarcely enough (*our information is rather sparse*). ● *n* **sparsity** /**spar**-si-tee/.

spasm /**spa**-zum/ *n* **1** a sudden movement of the body not done on purpose, caused by a tightening of muscles, as in cramp, a fit (*an muscle spasm*). **2** a feeling or activity that does not last long (*a spasm of coughing*).

spasmodic /spaz-**mod**-ic/ *adj* done occasionally for short periods (*spasmodic coughing*).

spat /**spat**/ *n* a brief, petty quarrel.

spatial /**spay**-shal/ *adj* (*fml*) having to do with space (*spatial problems*).

spatter /**spa**-ter/ *vb* to throw or scatter (liquid, mud, etc.) in drops, to splash (*cars spattering people with mud*).

spatula /**spa**-chu-la/ *n* a broad thin blade used in spreading or scraping plaster, paint, ointment, food, etc. (*a spatula for turning eggs in the pan*).

spawn /**spawn**/ *n* the eggs of fish, frogs, etc. ● *vb* **1** to produce spawn. **2** to produce, usually in large numbers (*a lot of new committees have been spawned*).

speak /**speek**/ *vb* (*pt* **spoke** /spoke/, *pp* **spoken** /**spo**-ken/) **1** to utter words, to talk (*children learning to speak*). **2** to make a speech (*speak after dinner*). **3** to pronounce.

speaker /**spee**-ker/ *n* **1** a person who speaks. **2** the chief officer of the House of Representatives.

spear /**speer**/ n a weapon with a long straight handle and a pointed metal head. ● vb to pierce with a spear.

spearhead /**speer**-hed/ n 1 the pointed head of a spear. 2 the leading person in a military attack.

special /**spe**-shal/ adj 1 having to do with one particular thing, person, or occasion (a special tool for the job). 2 not common or usual, distinctive (a special occasion). ● n **specialty** /**spe**-shal-tee/. ● adv **specially** /**spesh**-lee/ in a special manner.

specialist /**spe**-shlist/ n a person who makes a particular study of one subject or of one branch of a subject (a cookery specialist/a specialist in internal medicine).

specialty /**spesh**-ul-tee/, **speciality** /spe-shee-a-li-tee/ (Br) n 1 a special field of work or study (cosmetic surgery is his specialty). 2 something made or sold only by a certain trader (the specialty of the house).

specialize /**spe**-sha-lize/ vb, also **specialise** (Br) to make a particular study of (one subject) (a doctor specializing in skin disorders).

species /**spee**-sheez/ n kind, sort, a group of things (e.g. plants, animals) with certain features in common.

specific /spe-**si**-fic/ adj 1 definite (something specific he wants to ask). 2 exact (specific instructions). 3 particular (a specific tool for the job). ● n a remedy for a particular disease.

specification /spe-si-fi-**cay**-shun/ n an exact statement of the details of a piece of work to be done (measurements, materials to be used, etc.) (the specifications for the new factory).

specify /**spe**-si-fie/ vb to state exactly or in detail (specified his reasons for leaving).

specimen /**spe**-si-men/ n a sample, a part taken as an example of the whole (take a blood specimen).

speck /**speck**/ n a tiny particle, spot, or stain (a speck of soot).

speckle /**spe**-cul/ n a small spot on a differently colored background.

speckled /**spe**-culd/ adj marked with speckles (the speckled breast of the bird).

spectacle /**spec**-ta-cul/ n 1 something worth looking at, a wonderful or magnificent sight (crowds gathering to see the spectacle of the military parade). 2 pl glasses worn in front of the eyes to assist the eyesight.

spectacular /spec-**ta**-cyu-lar/ adj 1 magnificent, wonderful, or splendid to look at (a spectacular parade). 2 impressive, dramatic (a spectacular change in his appearance).

spectator /**spec**-tay-tur/ n a person who looks on. ● vb **spectate** /**spec**-tate/ to be a spectator at an event.

specter /**spec**-ter/ n, also **spectre** (Br, Cdn) a ghost.

spectral /**spec**-tral/ adj ghostly (spectral figures).

spectrum /**spec**-trum/ n a band of colors, as in a rainbow, produced by passing light through a prism.

speculate /**spe**-cyu-late/ vb 1 to think about, to guess without having the necessary facts (speculating on his reasons for leaving). 2 to buy shares in the hope of selling them later at a profit.

speculation /spec-cyu-**lay**-shun/ n 1 act of speculating. 2 a guess or theory (some speculation that they were getting married).

speculative /**spec**-yu-la-tiv/ adj 1 risky (a speculative venture). 2 hesitant, uncertain. 3 given to trying to think out the reasons for things (some speculative thinking).

speculator /**spec**-yu-lay-tur/ n a person who buys things (especially of uncertain value) in the hope of making a large profit on them.

speech /**speech**/ n 1 the ability to speak (children learning speech). 2 a talk given in public (an after-dinner speech).

speechless /**speech**-less/ adj unable to speak for love, surprise, fear, etc. (speechless with rage).

speed /**speed**/ n 1 quickness of movement (the speed of the car). 2 haste (move with speed). ● vb (pt **sped** /**sped**/) 1 to go fast. 2 to drive a car, truck, etc. very fast, often illegally fast (fined for speeding). 3 to succeed or make succeed.

speedboat /**speed**-boat/ n a motorboat built for speed.

speedometer /spi-**dom**-i-ter/ n an tool to show how fast a car, motorcycle, etc., is traveling.

speedup /**spee**-dup/ n an increase in speed.

speedwell /**speed**-well/ n a plant with small blue flowers.

speedy /**spee**-dee/ adj fast, quick-moving (seek a speedy end to the strike).

spell[1] /**spell**/ vb (pt, pp **spelt** /**spelt**/ or **spelled** /**speld**/) to say or write the letters of a word in order. ● n **speller** a person who spells words (a poor speller). ● n **spelling** /**spe**-ling/ the act of a person who spells.

spell[2] /**spell**/ n certain words uttered in order to make something happen by magic, a charm, a strange or magical power.

spell[3] /**spell**/ n 1 a length of time (spells of bad weather). 2 a turn at doing work (a spell at digging the garden).

spellbound /**spell**-bound/ adj fascinated, made still by wonder or magic. ● vb **spellbind** /**spell**-binde/.

spell-checker /**spell**-che-cker/ *n* a computer program that checks a document for misspelled words.

spelling bee /**spe**-ling-bee/ *n* a spelling contest.

spelunker /spi-**lung**-ker/ *n* a person who explores caves as a hobby. ● *n* **spelunking** /spi-**lung**-king/.

spend /**spend**/ *vb* (*pt, pp* **spent** /**spent**/) **1** to pay out (money). **2** to use or use up. **3** to pass (time).

spender /**spen**-der/ *n* a person who spends, especially someone who spends too much.

spendthrift /**spend**-thrift/ *n* a person who spends money wastefully and carelessly.

spent /**spent**/ *adj* **1** tired out (*spent after the day's work*). **2** used up (*spent energy*).

sperm /**sperm**/ *n* **1** a male reproductive cell. **2** semen.

spew /**spyoo**/ *vb* **1** (*inf*) to vomit. **2** to come out in a flood (*lava spewed out of the volcano*).

sphere /**sfeer**/ *n* **1** a ball. **2** a sun, star, or planet. **3** the extent of a person's work, knowledge, influence, etc. (*in the sphere of television*).

spherical /**sfe**-ri-cal/ *adj* round like a sphere.

sphinx /**sfinks**/ *n* a winged mythical monster, half-woman, half-lion.

spice /**spice**/ *n* **1** a sharp-tasting substance used to flavor food (*add spices to the sauce*). **2** something exciting or interesting (*add a bit of spice to life*). ● *vb* to flavor with spice, etc.

spicy /**spie**-see/ *adj* **1** sharp-tasting (*spicy food*). **2** lively and witty (*spicy stories*).

spider /**spie**-der/ *n* an eight-legged creature that spins a web to catch insects for food.

spidery /**spie**-de-ree/ *adj* like a spider, long and thin like a spider's legs.

spike /**spike**/ *n* **1** a short piece of pointed metal, a large nail (*spikes along the top of the wall to keep people out*). **2** an ear of corn. **3** many small flowers forming a single head along a stalk. ● *vb* **1** to fasten with spikes. **2** to pierce with a spike. **3** to put a gun out of action by driving a spike into it.

spiky /**spie**-kee/ *adj* having spikes, shaped like a spike (*the porcupine is spiky*).

spill[1] /**spill**/ *vb* (*pt, pp* **spilled** /**spild**/ *or* **spilt** /**spilt**/) to let run out or overflow (*spill the tea as she pours it*). ● *n* **1** a fall. **2** something spilled.

spill[2] /**spill**/ *n* a thin strip of wood or twisted paper for lighting cigarettes, candles, etc.

spillage /**spi**-lidge/ *n* the thing that is spilled.

spillover /**spi**-lo-ver/ *n* the act of spilling over.

spin /**spin**/ *vb* (**spun** /**spun**/, **spinning** /**spi**-ning/) **1** to draw out (wool, cotton, etc.) and twist into threads. **2** to turn quickly around one point (*she spun*

around to face him). **3** (*inf*) to make up (*spin a yarn about being attacked*). ● *n* **1** a short or rapid trip. **2** a dive made by an aiplane turning around at the same time.

spinach /**spi**-nich/ *n* a vegetable whose leaves are eaten as food.

spinal /**spie**-nal/ *adj* having to do with the spine (*spinal injuries*).

spinal cord /**spie**-nal-cawrd/ *n* the thick cord of nerves that runs down the spine.

spindle /**spin**-dul/ *n* on a spinning machine, the bar onto which the newly made thread is wound.

spindly /**spin**-dlee/ *adj* very long and thin (*spindly legs*).

spine /**spine**/ *n* **1** the backbone. **2** a pointed spike on an animal or fish. **3** a thorn.

spineless /**spine**-less/ *adj* **1** having no spine. **2** weak, lacking courage or willpower (*too spineless to stand up for himself*).

spine-tingling /**spine**-ting-gling/ *adj* very moving, thrilling, or terrifying.

spinning /**spi**-ning/ *n* **1** the act of amking thread or yarn. **2** the act fo fishing with a certain kind of rod. ● *adj* that spins or used in spinning.

spinning wheel /**spi**-ning-wheel/ *n* a home spinning machine operated by a wheel driven by a pedal.

spinster /**spin**-ster/ *n* **1** a woman who spins thread or yarn. **2** a woman who has never been married.

spiny /**spie**-nee/ *adj* full of prickles or thorns (*spiny bushes*).

spiral /**spie**-ral/ *adj* winding around like the thread of a screw (*a spiral staircase*). ● *also n*.

spire /**spire**/ *n* a tall tower, tapering to a pointed top.

spirit /**spi**-rit/ *n* **1** the soul. **2** a ghost. **3** courage, liveliness (*sing with spirit*). **4** mood (*the spirit of the times*). **5** the intention (*the spirit, not the letter, of the law*). **6** *pl* strong alcoholic liquor. ● *vb* to remove in a mysterious way.

spirited /**spi**-ri-tid/ *adj* **1** lively (*a spirited musical performance*). **2** showing courage (*a spirited defense of her tennis title*).

spiritless /**spi**-rit-less/ *adj* without courage or liveliness.

spirit level /**spi**-rit-le-vul/ *n* another term for **level**, see **level** *n* sense **2**.

spiritual /**spi**-ri-chu-wal/ *adj* **1** having to do with the soul or spirit (*the children's spiritual welfare*). **2** religious, holy. ● *n* an American religious song, originating among Southern blacks in the 18th and 19th centuries combining African and European styles of music.

spiritualism /spi-ri-chu-wa-li-zum/ *n* the belief that only the soul or spirit has real existence, the belief that it is possible to communicate with the souls of the dead. ● *n* **spiritualist** /spi-ri-chu-wa-list/.

spirituality /spi-ri-chu-**wa**-li-tee/ *n* concern with religion and matters of the soul.

spiritualize /spi-ri-chu-wa-lize/ *vb, also* **spiritualise** (*Br*) to make spiritual, to give a spiritual meaning or sense to.

spit[1] /spit/ *n* **1** a long, thick pin on which meat is roasted over a fire (*a pig turning on a spit*). **2** a long piece of lowland running out into the sea. ● *vb* (**spitted** /spi-tid/, **spitting** /spi-ting/) to put on a spit, to pierce.

spit[2] /spit/ *vb* (**spat** /spat/, **spitting** /spi-ting/) **1** to blow from the mouth (*spit out chewing gum*). **2** to put saliva, etc., out of the mouth (*he spat on the pavement*). ● *n* a quantity of saliva put out of the mouth.

spite /spite/ *n* ill-feeling against another, a desire to hurt or harm another. ● *vb* to do something to hurt or harm another. ● **in spite of** without paying attention to (*she got the job in spite of her lack of qualifications*).

spiteful /spite-ful/ *adj* desiring or intended to hurt or harm another (*a spiteful person/a spiteful action*).

spitfire /spit-fire/ *n* a quick-tempered person.

splash /splash/ *vb* to throw or scatter drops of mud or liquid onto (*splash bath oil into the water/rain splashing in the puddles*). ● *n* **1** act of splashing. **2** the sound made by a body striking water. **3** a spot of mud or liquid (*splashes on her white dress*).

splashboard /splash-board/ *n* any screen or board used to protect a person or thing from water splashing.

splashdown /splash-down/ *n* a spacecraft's soft landing in the sea.

splat /splat/ *n* a wet, slapping sound.

splatter /spla-ter/ *n* spatter or splash. ● *also vb*.

splay /splay/ *vb* to slope or turn outward. ● *adj* (*of feet*) turned outwards and flat.

spleen /spleen/ *n* **1** an organ near the stomach that helps purify the blood. **2** ill-temper, gloom (*vent his spleen on his colleagues*).

splendid /splen-did/ *adj* **1** bright, shining, brilliant (*a splendid palace*). **2** excellent (*a splendid performance*).

splendor /splen-dur/ *n, also* **splendour** (*Br, Cdn*) brightness, magnificence.

splice /splice/ *vb* **1** to join the ends of two ropes together by interweaving their strands. **2** to fit one piece of wood into another so as to join them. ● *n* a joint so made.

splint /splint/ *n* a piece of wood to keep a broken bone in position (*the ambulance driver put a splint on the injured man's leg*).

splinter /splin-ter/ *n* a sharp-edged or pointed piece of glass, wood, metal, etc., broken off a larger piece. ● *vb* to break into small pieces (*the store window splintered*).

split /split/ *vb* (**split, splitting** /spli-ting/) **1** to cut or break from end to end. **2** to separate into parts or smaller groups (*split the class into teams*). ● *n* **1** a long break or crack (*a split in the wood*). **2** a division (*a split in the committee*). **3** *pl* the trick of going down upright on the ground with the legs spread out at each side at right angles to the body.

splurge /splurge/ *vb* an excessive spending, spending by way of treating oneself.

splutter /splu-ter/ *vb* **1** to utter confused, indistinct sounds (*spluttering in rage*). **2** to make a spitting noise (*the candle spluttered*). ● *also n*.

spoil /spoil/ *vb* (*pt, pp* **spoiled** /spoild/ *or* **spoilt** /spoilt/) **1** to make or become useless or unpleasant (*food spoiling in the heat/spoil his chances of getting the job*). **2** to rob, to plunder. **3** to harm someone's character by always allowing him or her his or her own way (*spoil the children*). ● *n* things stolen or taken by force.

spoiler /spoi-ler/ *n* a person or thing that spoils.

spoilsport /spoil-spoart/ *n* a person who spoils the pleasure of others.

spoke[1] /spoke/ *pt of* **speak** /speak/. ● *pp* **spoken** /spo-ken/.

spoke[2] /spoke/ *n* one of the bars running from the hub to the rim of a wheel.

spokesman /spoaks-man/, **spokeswoman** /spoaks-woo-man/, **spokesperson** /spoaks-per-sun/ *n* a person who speaks for others (*the workers elected a spokesperson to talk to management*).

sponge /spunge/ *n* **1** a type of sea animal. **2** a kind of light absorbent washcloth made from or to be like the soft frame of a sponge (*a child's sponge in the shape of a bear*). **3** one who lives on the money or favors of another. ● *vb* **1** to wipe with a sponge. **2** to live on the money or favors of another (*sponging on his friends*).

spongecake *n* (*Br*) see **angel food cake**.

spongy /spun-jee/ *adj* soft and absorbent, soft, squishy.

sponsor /spon-sur/ *n* **1** a person who introduces someone or something and takes responsibility for it (*the sponsor of a new law*). **2** a business that pays for an event, show, etc., in return for advertising. **3** a person who agrees to pay someone money for charity if he or she completes a specified activity. **4** a godfather or godmother. ● *vb* **1** to put forward and support (*sponsor the new bill*). **2** act as a sponsor (*a soft-drinks firm sponsors the football match/ sponsor the child in a charity swim*).

spontaneous /spon-**tay**-nee-us/ *adj* **1** done willingly. **2** not caused by an outside agency. **3** done without previous thought. ● *n* **spontaneity** /spon-ti-**nee**-i-tee/.

spoof /spoof/ *n* a joke.

spook /spook/ *n* (*inf*) a ghost.

spooky /spoo-kee/ *adj* of, like, or suggesting a spook, eerie, easily fearful.

spool /spool/ *n* a reel on which thread, film, etc., may be wound.

spoon /spoon/ *n* **1** a domestic tool consisting of a shallow bowl and a handle, used in cooking, eating, or feeding. **2** a wooden golf club. ● *vb* to lift or scoop with a spoon.

spoonful /**spoon**-ful/ *n* the amount that a spoon contains.

spore /spore/ *n* the seed of a flowerless plant.

sport /spoart/ *n* **1** outdoor or athletic indoor games in which certain rules are obeyed (*children interested in sport*). **2** one of these games (*sports such as football and swimming*). **3** (*fml*) something done for fun or amusement (*hunt the deer for sport*). **4** (*fml*) a person fond of fun or amusement. ● *vb* to play, to have fun.

sporting /**spore**-ting/ *adj* **1** fond of sports. **2** used in sport (*sporting equipment*). **3** fair-minded and generous, especially in sports (*it was sporting of him to admit the ball was out*).

sportsman /**spoarts**-man/, **sportswoman** /**spoarts**-woo-man/, **sportsperson** /**spoarts**-per-sun/ *n* **1** a person who takes part in a sport. **2** a person who likes to see every person or group given an equal chance of success. ● *adj* **sportsmanlike** /**spoarts**-man-like/.

sportsmanship /**spoarts**-man-ship/ *n* the spirit of fair play.

sportswear /**spoarts**-ware/ *n* the clothing made for and worn while playing sports.

spot /spot/ *n* **1** a small mark, stain, or blot (*a black spot on her new dress*). **2** a tiny piece. **3** the exact place where something happened (*X marks the spot*). ● *vb* (**spotted** /spot-id/, **spotting** /spot-ing/) **1** to stain. **2** to see or catch sight of.

spotless /**spot**-less/ *adj* unmarked, very clean (*a spotless floor*).

spotlight /**spot**-lite/ *n* a strong beam of light shone on a particular person or place.

spotty /**spot**-ee/ *adj* **1** covered with spots. **2** irregular, uneven.

spouse /spouss/ *n* a husband or wife.

spout /spout/ *n* **1** a long tube sticking out from a pot, jug, pipe, etc., through which liquid can flow (*the spout of the teapot*). **2** a jet or gush of liquid. ● *vb* **1** to gush or make to gush in a jet. **2** (*inf*) to talk at length (*spouting on about his vacation*).

sprain /sprain/ *n* the painful twisting of a joint in the body, causing damage to muscles or ligaments. ● *vb* to twist a joint in such a way (*sprain her ankle*).

sprawl /sprawl/ *vb* **1** to sit or lie with the limbs spread out awkwardly. **2** to be spread out untidily (*towns sprawled along the seashore*).

spray[1] /spray/ *n* **1** a twig or stem with several leaves or flowers growing out from it (*a spray of cherry blossom*). **2** an arrangement of flowers (*a bridal spray*).

spray[2] /spray/ *n* **1** a cloud of small drops of liquid moving through the air. **2** liquid to be sprayed under pressure. **3** a can or container holding this. ● *vb* to sprinkle with fine drops of liquid (*sprayed the roses with insecticide*).

spread /spred/ *vb* (*pt, pp* **spread**) **1** to lay out over an area (*spread butter on bread*). **2** to grow bigger, so covering more space (*towns spreading rapidly*). **3** to make or become more widely known or believed (*spread the information*). **4** to affect more people (*the disease is spreading*). ● *n* **1** an area covered, extent. **2** a good meal, a feast.

spreader /**spre**-der/ *n* a person or thing that spreads.

spreadsheet /**spred**-sheet/ *n* a computer program that organizes information.

spree /spree/ *n* **1** a lively activity (*a shopping spree*). **2** a period of drinking.

sprig /sprig/ *n* **1** a small shoot or twig (*a sprig of cherry blossom*). **2** a small nail without a head.

sprightly /**sprite**-lee/ *adj* lively (*people sprightly for their age*). ● *n* **sprightliness** /**sprite**-lee-ness/.

spring /spring/ *vb* (*pt* **sprang** /sprang/, *pp* **sprung** /sprung/) **1** to jump. **2** to flow up from under the ground. **3** to be caused by (*his lack of confidence sprang from his unhappy childhood*). **4** to bud. **5** to cause (a mine) to explode. ● *n* **1** a jump. **2** a piece or coil of metal that after being compressed returns to its earlier shape or position. **3** water flowing up from under the ground (*hot springs*). **4** the season following winter when plants begin to grow again. ● **spring a leak** to have a hole through which water can come in. ● **spring a surprise** to give a surprise.

springboard /**spring**-board/ n a springy board for jumping or diving from (*the springboard at the swimming pool*).

spring-cleaning /spring-**clee**-ning/ n a thorough cleaning of the entire house, as is sometimes done in the spring.

springtime /**spring**-time/ n the season of spring.

spring tide /**spring**-tide/ the high tide at new and full moon.

springy /**spring**-ee/ adj 1 having elasticity, having a light bounciness. 2 light on the feet.

sprinkle /**spring**-kul/ vb to scatter in small drops or tiny pieces (*sprinkling water on flowers*).

sprinkler /**spring**-kler/ n a person or thing that sprinkles (*the sprinkler waters the lawn*).

sprinkling /**spring**-kling/ n a very small number or quantity (*a sprinkling of snow*).

sprint /**sprint**/ vb to run as fast as possible for a short distance. ● n 1 a short foot race. 2 a short fast run (*a sprint for the bus*).

sprite /**sprite**/ n an elf or fairy.

spritzer /**sprit**-ser/ n a drink made of wine and soda water.

sprout /**sprout**/ vb to begin to grow, to bud (*bulbs sprouting*). ● n a young plant, a shoot of a plant.

spruce[1] /**sprooss**/ adj neat, smart and tidy (*look spruce for his job interview*).

spruce[2] /**sprooss**/ n a type of fir tree, valued for its white timber.

spume /**spyoom**/ n froth, foam.

spunk /**spungk**/ n (*inf*) courage, spirit, liveliness. ● adj **spunky** /**spung**-kee/.

spur /**spur**/ n 1 a pointed instrument or spiked wheel attached to a horserider's heel and dug into the horse's side to make it move more quickly. 2 anything that urges on to greater effort (*the promise of a good job acted as a spur to his studying*). 3 the sharp point on the back of the legs of certain birds. 4 a ridge or line of hills running out at an angle from a larger hill or hills. ● vb (**spurred** /**spurd**/, **spurring** /**spu**-ring/) 1 to prick with a spur. 2 to urge to greater effort. ● **on the spur of the moment** without previous thought.

spurious /**spyoo**-ree-us/ adj false (*a spurious interest in her opinions*).

spurn /**spurn**/ vb 1 to push away, as with the foot. 2 to refuse with scorn (*spurn their offers of help*).

spurt /**spurt**/ vb to burst out in a jet. ● n 1 a gush of liquid. 2 a special effort. 3 a sudden short burst of extra speed (*put on a spurt at the end of a race*).

sputter /**spu**-tter/ vb 1 to spit when speaking. 2 to throw out small drops of liquid. 3 to make spitting and hissing noises (*sausages sputtering in the pan*).

spy /**spie**/ n 1 a person who tries to obtain secret information about a country on behalf of an enemy country. 2 a person who tries to find out another's secrets (*an industrial spy*). ● vb 1 to catch sight of (*she spied her friend in the distance*). 2 to act as a spy.

spyglass /**spie**-glass/ n a small telescope.

squabble /**skwob**-ul/ vb to quarrel noisily over unimportant matters (*children squabbling over their toys*). ● also n.

squad /**skwod**/ n a small party of soldiers or workers.

squadron /**skwod**-run/ n 1 a group of warships under the one commander. 2 a group of 12 airplanes commanded by a squadron leader. 3 a unit of cavalry.

squalid /**skwol**-id/ adj dirty and unpleasant, wretched (*squalid living conditions*).

squall /**skwol**/ vb to scream loudly (*kept awake by a cat squalling*). ● n 1 a loud scream. 2 a sudden violent gust of wind, a brief, violent windstorm.

squally /**skwol**-ee/ adj gusty, stormy and windy (*squally weather*).

squalor /**skwol**-ur/ n, also **squalour** (*Br, Cdn*) excessive dirt, filth, the condition of being squalid.

squander /**skwon**-der/ vb to spend wastefully, to use up needlessly (*squander her savings*).

square /**skware**/ adj 1 having four equal sides and four right angles. 2 forming a right angle. 3 just, fair (*a square deal*). 4 even, equal (*the two teams are now square*). ● n 1 a square figure. 2 an open space in a town with buildings on its four sides (*a war monument in the town square*). 3 the number obtained when a number is multiplied by itself. 4 an L- or T-shaped instrument for drawing right angles. ● vb 1 to make square. 2 to pay money due. 3 to bribe. 4 to multiply (a number) by itself. 5 to agree with.

square dance /**skware**-danse/ n a lively dance with various steps, figures, etc. in which the couples are grouped in a particular form.

square root /skware-**root**/ n the number that must be multiplied by itself to obtain a given number (2 is the square root of 4).

squash[1] /**skwosh**/ vb 1 to crush, to press or squeeze into pulp (*squash fruit*). 2 to speak sharply or rudely to someone to silence him or her (*the speaker squashed the people who were shouting criticisms*). ● *n* **1** a crowd, a crush. **2** a indoor game similar to tennis played with a rubber ball.

squash² /skwosh/ *n* a fruit of the gourd family eaten as a vegetale (*butternut squash*).

squat /skwot/ *vb* (**squatted** /skwot-id/, **squatting** /skwot-ing/) **1** to sit down on the heels. **2** to make a home on a piece of land or in a building to which that person has no legal right. ● *adj* short and broad.

squatter /skwot-er/ *n* a person who settles on land or in a building without legal right to do so.

squawk /skwawk/ *vb* to utter a harsh cry (*parrots squawking*). ● *also n*.

squeak /skweek/ *vb* to utter a short, high-pitched sound (*mice squeaking*). ● *also n*.

squeal /skweel/ *vb* to cry with a sharp shrill voice. ● *also n*.

squeamish /skwee-mish/ *adj* **1** easily made sick, feeling sick (*squeamish at the sight of blood*). **2** easily shocked or upset.

squeeze /skweez/ *vb* **1** to press from more than one side (*squeezing oranges*). **2** to hug. **3** to push through a narrow space (*squeeze into the crowded hall*). ● *n* **1** the act of squeezing. **2** a hug. **3** a tight fit.

squeezebox /skweez-boks/ *n* an accordion or concertina.

squelch /skwelch/ *vb* to make a sucking noise, as when walking over sodden ground (*squelch up the muddy road in boots*). ● *also n*.

squib /skwib/ *n* a small firework.

squid /skwid/ *n* a cuttlefish, a long slender sea creatures with eights arms and two tentacles.

squint /skwint/ *vb* **1** to look or peer with the eyes partly closed, as when the light is too strong. **2** to look sideways without turning the head. 3 to be cross-eyed. ● *n* **1** the act of looking with eyes partly closed. **2** eyes looking in different directions. **3** (*inf*) a quick look (*take a squint at the papers on the boss's desk*).

squire /skwire/ *n* (*old*) a person who accompanied and helped a knight.

squirm /skwirm/ *vb* to wriggle about, to move by wriggling (*fish squirming in the nets/squirm with embarrassment*).

squirrel /skwurl/ *n* a small bushy-tailed animal living in trees.

squirt /skwurt/ *vb* to force or be forced out in a thin, fast stream (*squirt water on the dry clothes*).

● *n* **1** a jet. **2** an instrument for throwing out a jet of liquid.

squish /skwish/ *vb* to squash. ● *n* the sound of something being squashed.

squishy /skwi-shee/ *adj* making a squishing sound.

stab /stab/ *vb* (**stabbed** /stabd/, **stabbing** /sta-bing/) to wound with a pointed weapon. ● *n* **1** a wound made with a pointed weapon. **2** a thrust with a dagger or pointed knife (*kill him with one stab*). **3** a sharp feeling (*a stab of pain/a stab of fear*).

stability /sta-bi-li-tee/ *n* steadiness, security.

stabilize /stay-bu-lize/ *vb, also* **stabilise** (*Br*) to make firm or steady. ● *n* **stabilizer** /sta-bi-li-tee/ *also* **stabiliser** (*Br*) a thing that makes something firm or steady.

stable¹ /stay-bul/ *n* a building or shelter for horses, cattle, etc. ● *vb* to keep in a stable.

stable² /stay-bul/ *adj* **1** firm, secure, not easily moved, upset, or changed (*stable shelves/stable marriages/stable institutions*). **2** likely to behave reasonably (*he's not very stable*).

stablemate /stay-bul-mate/ *n* any of the horses sharing a stable.

stabling /stay-bling/ *n* buildings available as stables.

staccato /stu-ca-toe/ *adj* in music, having each note sounded clearly and distinctly. ● *also n*.

stack /stack/ *n* **1** a large orderly pile of hay, wood, papers, etc. **2** a group of chimneys built in together. **3** a very tall chimney. ● *vb* to pile together.

stadium /stay-dee-um/ *n* (*pl* **stadia** /stay-dee-a/ *or* **stadiums** /stay-dee-umz/) a large ground for sports and athletics.

staff /staff/ *n* **1** a stick or rod used as a support. **2** a stick as a sign of office. **3** the set of five parallel lines on and between which musical notes are written. **4** a group of officers chosen to assist a general. **5** any body of employees (*the office staff*). ● *vb* to provide with workers or employees (*an office staffed mainly by women*).

staff officer /staff-of-i-ser/ *n* a member of a general's staff.

stag /stag/ *n* a male red deer.

stage /stage/ *n* **1** a raised platform for actors, performers, speakers, etc. **2** the theater (*she went on the stage*). **3** a halting place. **4** the distance that may be traveled after paying a certain fare. **5** a certain point in development or progress (*stages in the production process*). ● *vb* to produce (a play) on a stage (*staging Hamlet*).

stagecoach /stage-coach/ *n* formerly, a horse-drawn coach providing a regular service for passengers.

stage fright /**stage**-frite/ *n* the nervousness felt on appearing on the stage in public.

stagger /**sta**-ger/ *vb* **1** to walk unsteadily, to lurch to the side, to reel. **2** to amaze. **3** to arrange breaks, vacations, etc., so that they do not begin and end at the same times as those of others (*stagger the staff's lunch hours so that there are always people in the office*). ● *adj* **staggering** /**sta**-gring/.

stagnant /**stag**-nant/ *adj* **1** not flowing and often dirty (*stagnant water*). **2** not developing or growing, inactive (*a production process that remained stagnant*).

stagnate /stag-**nate**/ *vb* **1** to cease to flow. **2** to cease to develop or make progress. **3** to become dull. ● *n* **stagnation** /stag-**nay**-shun/.

staid /staid/ *adj* serious, steady, unwilling to move with the times.

stain /stain/ *vb* **1** to make dirty (*stain their hands*). **2** to change the color of (*stain the table dark brown*). **3** to make marks of a different color on. **4** to spoil, to disgrace (*stain her reputation*). ● *n* **1** a dirty mark or discoloration that cannot be removed. **2** a paint or dye. **3** disgrace.

stained glass /**staind**-glass/ *n* colored glass, held together by lead strips, used for church windows, decorations, lamp shades, etc.

stainless /**stain**-less/ *adj* **1** not easily stained or rusted. **2** without fault or disgrace (*a stainless reputation*).

stair /stare/, **staircase** /**stare**-case/, **stairway** /**stare**-way/ *n* a series of connected steps, usually with a railing, leading from one place to another on a different level (*a dramatic spiral staircase led to the ballroom*).

stairwell /**stare**-well/ *n* a vertical shaft in a building that contains a staircase.

stake[1] /stake/ *n* **1** a stout piece of wood pointed at one end for driving into the ground. **2** formerly, the post to which was tied a person condemned to death by burning. ● *vb* to mark with stakes.

stake[2] /stake/ *n* the amount of money, or anything else of value, bet or risked. ● *vb* to bet (money), to risk. ● **at stake** able to be lost.

stalactite /sta-**lac**-tite/ *n* a mass of mineral matter hanging like an icicle from the roof of a cave (caused by dripping water that gradually deposits the mineral).

stalagmite /sta-**lag**-mite/ *n* a mass of mineral matter rising like a spike from the floor of a cave (caused by the drips of water coming off of the cave roof or of a stalactite).

stale /stale/ *adj* **1** not fresh (*stale bread*). **2** not new (*stale news*). **3** uninteresting (*a stale piece of writing*).

stalemate /**stale**-mate/ *n* **1** in chess, a position from which neither player can win. **2** a situation or argument in which neither side can gain an advantage over the other (*management and workers reached a stalemate on the subject of wages*).

stalk[1] /stock/ *n* **1** the stem of a plant. **2** a tall chimney. ● *adj* **stalky** /**stock**-ee/.

stalk[2] /stock/ *vb* **1** to walk holding oneself stiffly upright (*stalk out of the room in anger*). **2** to approach an animal quietly and without being seen when hunting it (*stalking stags*) **3** to follow someone around, often someone famous, regularly and annoy or frighten him/her with unwanted attention (*accused of stalking the filmstar*). ● *n* **stalking** /**stock**-ing/, **stalker** /**stock**-er/.

stall /stawl/ *n* **1** a division of a stable in which one animal is kept. **2** a counter on which goods are laid out for sale. **3** a small, sometimes temporary, shop set up in an open place. **4** a ground-floor seat in a theater. **5** a seat in the choir of a church. ● *vb* **1** (*of an airplane*) to lose speed and get out of control. **2** (*of a motor car engine*) to stop working (*the car stalled at the traffic lights*). **3** to avoid giving a direct answer (*the politician stalled when he was asked about unemployment*).

stallion /**stal**-yun/ *n* a male horse, especially one kept for breeding.

stamen /**stay**-men/ *n* one of the little pollen-bearing stalks in the middle of a flower.

stamina /**sta**-mi-na/ *n* staying power, ability to endure (*he does not have the stamina to have a full-time job*).

stammer /**sta**-mer/ *vb* to have difficulty in uttering the sounds at the beginning of words, sometimes attempting them several times before succeeding. ● *n* such difficulty in speaking.

stamp /stamp/ *vb* **1** to strike the foot forcefully or noisily downward. **2** to print a mark on (*have his passport stamped*). **3** to put a postage stamp on. ● *n* **1** a forceful or noisy downward movement of the foot. **2** a mark or paper affixed to a letter or package to show that postage has been paid. **3** a mark consisting of letters, numbers, a pattern, etc., printed on paper, cloth, coins, etc. **4** a machine for making such a mark.

stampede /stam-**peed**/ *n* a sudden panic-stricken rush of many people or animals. ● *vb* to take sudden flight (*the buffaloes stampeded/people stampeding to get free tickets*).

stance /stanse/ *n* the way a person or animal stands.

stand /stand/ *vb* (*pt* **stood** /stood/) **1** to be upright on the feet, legs, or end (*boys standing in the* *corner*). **2** to rise up (*she stood and left*). **3** to set upright (*stand the tables up*). **4** to stop moving. **5** to stay motionless. **6** to be in a certain place (*a house standing on the riverbank*). **7** to bear, to put up with (*unable to stand the loud noise*). **8** to become a candidate for election. ● *n* **1** a halt. **2** a small table, rack, etc., on which things may be placed or hung. **3** a structure with seats arranged in tiers for spectators (*the stands at the football game*). **4** a base or support on which an object may be placed upright (*a stand for the statue*). **5** resistance to an attack (*take a stand against the enemy/take a stand against racism*). ● **stand by** to support, to be ready to help (*stood by their friend*). ● **stand down** to withdraw. ● **stand fast** to remain firm. ● **stand out 1** to be prominent or noticable (*the new building stands out in the old square*). **2** to refuse to give in (*stand out against the enemy*). ● **stand up** to get to the feet. ● **stand up for** to defend. ● **stand up to** to resist.

standard /stan-dard/ *n* **1** a fixed measure. **2** an average level of accomplishment with which other work is compared (*work below standard*). **3** an upright post, etc. used for support. ● *adj* **1** fixed. **2** fixed by rule. **3** usual. **4** standing upright.

standardize /stan-dar-dize/ *vb, also* **standardise** (*Br*) to see that all things are made or done in the same way (*standardizing the testing system in schools*).

standby /stand-bie/ *n* a person or thing that can always be depended on and ready to be put into service when needed.

standing /stan-ding/ *n* rank, position, reputation (*her standing in the community*). ● *adj* **1** upright (*standing stones*). **2** not flowing (*standing water*). **3** permanent, fixed (*a standing joke*).

standpoint /stand-point/ *n* a point of view (*from the average person's standpoint*).

standstill /stand-still/ *n* a stoppage (*work at the factory is at a standstill*).

stanza /stan-za/ *n* in poetry, a number of lines arranged in a certain pattern that is repeated throughout the poem.

staple /stay-pul/ *n* **1** a U-shaped nail or pin. **2** a principal product or article of trade. **3** a main item (*the staples of her diet*). ● *adj* chief, principal.

stapler /stay-pler/ *n* a tool used to drive staples into papers, wood, etc. to bind them or attach them.

star /star/ *n* **1** a heavenly body seen as a twinkling point of light in the night sky. **2** any object like a twinkling star in shape. **3** an asterisk (*). **4** a leading actor or actress. ● *vb* (**starred** /stard/, **starring** /

sta-ring/) to have the leading part in a play, etc. (*star in the new film*). ● *adj* **starry** /sta-ree/ full of stars, like stars (*a starry sky*).

starboard /star-board/ *n* the right-hand side of a ship as one faces the bows. ● *also adj*.

starch /starch/ *n* **1** a vegetable substance found in potatoes, cereals, etc. **2** a white powder mixed with water and used to make cloth stiff.

starchy /star-chee/ *adj* **1** containing starch. **2** stiff with starch (*starchy collars*). **3** stiff or unfriendly in manner (*her grandmother is rather starchy*).

stardom /star-dum/ *n* fame as an entertainer, sportsman, etc.

stardust /star-dust/ *n* a cluster of stars too far away to be seen separately with the naked eye.

stare /stare/ *vb* to look at fixedly, to look at with wide-open eyes (*staring at him in amazement*). ● *also n*.

starfish /star-fish/ *n* a star-shaped sea creature.

stark /stark/ *adj* **1** bare or simple, often in a severe way (*the stark landscape/the stark truth*). **2** utter, complete (*stark idiocy*). ● *adv* completely.

starless /star-less/ *adj* with no stars visible (*a starless night*).

starlet /star-let/ *n* **1** a small star. **2** a young actress being promoted as a future star.

starlight /star-lite/ *n* the light given off by stars.

starling /star-ling/ *n* a bird, with black-brown feathers, of the crow family.

start /start/ *vb* **1** to begin (*start working/start to work*). **2** to set in motion (*start a new business*). **3** to jump or make a sudden movement (*start in alarm at the eerie sound*). ● *n* **1** a beginning (*at the start of the working day*). **2** a sudden sharp movement (*give a start at the noise*). **3** the distance certain runners are allowed to start a race in front of the others.

starter /star-ter/ *n* **1** a device for starting a motor engine. **2** a person who gives the signal to begin. **3** a person who takes part in a race.

startle /star-tul/ *vb* to frighten, to give a sudden surprise to (*animals startled by the sudden noise*).

starve /starv/ *vb* **1** to die of hunger, to suffer greatly from hunger. **2** to keep without food. **3** to suffer for want of something necessary (*children starved of affection*). ● *n* **starvation** /star-vay-shun/.

state /state/ *n* **1** condition, circumstances, situation (*the state of the house/the state of the housing market*). **2** the people of a country organized under a form of government. **3** the governmental institutions of a country. **4** (*fml*) pomp or ceremonious display. ● *adj* **1** having to do with the government. **2** public. ● *vb* **1** to say as a fact. **2** to put clearly into words, spoken or written.

stately /**state**-lee/ *adj* dignified, grand in manner or behavior.

statement /**state**-ment/ *n* **1** a clear spoken or written account of facts (*an official statement about the president's illness*). **2** an account of money due or held (*a bank statement*).

state-of-the-art /**state**-ov-thi-art/ *adj* using the most modern, advanced methods (*using state-of-the-art computing equipment*)

statesman /**staytss**-man/, **stateswoman** /**staytss**-woo-man/ *n* **1** a person skilled in the art of government. **2** a person who has held high political office.

static /**sta**-tic/ *adj* motionless, at rest (*static electricity*).

station /**stay**-shun/ *n* **1** (*old*) position, rank (*his station in life*). **2** a regular stopping place for trains, buses, etc. **3** a headquarters from which a public service is operated (*fire station, police station*). ● *vb* to put in or send to a certain place.

stationary /**stay**-shu-ne-ree/ *adj* fixed, not moving (*stationary traffic*).

stationer /**stay**-shu-ner/ *n* a person who sells stationery.

stationery /**stay**-shu-ne-ree/ *n* paper, pens, and all other writing materials (*a shop selling stationery*).

station wagon /**stay**-shun wag-on/ *n* an automobile with a large storage area where the trunk would usually be.

statistician /sta-ti-**sti**-shun/ *n* a person who makes up or studies statistics.

statistics /sta-**tis**-tics/ *n* **1** the science of turning facts into figures and then classifying them. **2** the study of figures to deduce facts. **3** figures giving information about something (*unemployment statistics*).

statue /**sta**-choo/ *n* the carved or molded figure of a person or animal in stone, etc. (*a statue of the famous writer in the town square*).

statuesque /sta-choo-**esk**/ *adj* **1** like a statue. **2** motionless, not showing changes in expression.

statuette /sta-choo-**et**/ *n* a small statue.

stature /**sta**-chur/ *n* **1** height of the body. **2** importance, reputation (*a writer gaining in stature*).

status /**stay**-tus/ *n* rank, social position.

status quo /**stay**-tus-kwoe/ *n* an unchanged state of affairs (*wish to return to the status quo after the changes*).

status symbol /**stay**-tus-sim-bul/ *n* a possession that seems to mark a higher social position.

statute /**sta**-choo/ *n* a law.

statutory /**sta**-chu-toe-ree/ *adj* required by law or statute (*the statutory conditions of employment*).

staunch[1] /stawnch/ *adj* loyal, firm, reliable (*staunch followers of the president*). ● *vb* see **staunch**[2].

staunch[2] /stawnch/, **stanch** /stanch/ *vb* to stop blood flowing from a cut, etc. (*apply a tourniquet to staunch the blood*).

stave /stave/ *n* **1** one of the strips of wood forming the sides of a barrel. **2** the set of five parallel lines on and between which musical notes are written. **3** a verse of a song, a stanza. ● *vb* to break inward. ● **stave off** to keep away, to put off.

stay /stay/ *vb* **1** to remain (*stay calm*). **2** to live in a place for a time (*stayed in New York for a few years*). **3** (*fml*) to delay, to stop (*stay the execution*). ● *n* **1** time spent in a place. **2** a delay. **3** one of the ropes supporting the mast in its upright position.

steadfast /**sted**-fast/ *adj* loyal, firm, unmoving.

steady /**ste**-dee/ *adj* **1** firm (*hold the ladder steady*). **2** not easily changing (*steady temperatures*). **3** regular (*steady work*). **4** reliable, sensible (*steady workers*). ● *n* **steadiness** /**ste**-dee-ness/.

steak /stake/ *n* a slice of meat or fish for cooking (*tuna steak*).

steakhouse /**stake**-house/ *n* a restaurant that specializes in beef steaks.

steal /steel/ *vb* (*pt* **stole** /stole/, *pp* **stolen** /**sto**-len/) **1** to take what belongs to another. **2** to move slowly and quietly (*steal upstairs late at night*).

stealth /stelth/ *n* **1** secrecy. **2** acting quietly or slyly so as not to be seen or heard.

stealthy /**stel**-thee/ *adj* quiet, sly, secretive (*stealthy footsteps*).

steam /steem/ *n* the vapor of hot liquid, especially water. ● *vb* **1** to give off steam. **2** to cook in steam (*steam vegetables*). **3** to move driven by steam power (*a ship steamed into harbor*). ● *adj* **steamy** /**stee**-mee/ of or like stam, covered or filled with steam.

steamboat /**steem**-boat/, **steamer** /**stee**-mer/, **steamship** /**steem**-ship/ *ns* a ship driven by steam power.

steam engine /**steem**-in-jin/ *n* an engine driven by steam power.

steamroller /**steem**-ro-ler/ *n* a steam-driven vehicle with wide, heavy wheels, used for flattening road surfaces.

steed /steed/ *n* (*old*) a horse.

steel /steel/ *n* **1** an alloy consisting of iron hardened by carbon. **2** a steel bar on which knives may be sharpened. ● *adj* made of steel. ● *vb* to harden, to strengthen (*steeling herself to sack the boy*).

teely /stee-lee/ *adj* hard, unsympathetic (*a steely gaze*).

teep¹ /steep/ *adj* having a rapid slope up or down (*steep cliffs*). ● *n* a cliff or precipice. ● *vb* **steepen** / stee-pen/ to become more steep.

teep² /steep/ *vb* to soak, to leave in water for a time (*steep stained clothes*).

teeple /stee-pul/ *n* a tall church tower, sometimes tapering to a point.

teeplechase /stee-pul-chase/ *n* a cross-country race over obstacles for horses or runners.

teeplejack /stee-pul-jack/ *n* a person who climbs steeples, tall chimneys, etc., to repair them.

teer¹ /steer/ *n* a young ox.

teer² /steer/ *vb* to keep a moving object pointed in the right direction, to guide or control (*steer the car/steer the conversation*).

tegosaurus /ste-gu-saw-rus/ *n* a kind of dinosaur that has a small head and bony plates and sharp spikes down the backbone.

tellar /ste-lar/ *adj* having to do with the stars.

tellular /stel-yu-lar/ *adj* shaped like a star, covered with small stars or starlike spots.

tem¹ /stem/ *n* **1** the trunk of a tree, the stalk of a flower, leaf, etc. **2** the front part of a ship. **3** the main unchanging part of a word, prefixes and suffixes left out. ● *adj* **stemmed** /stemd/ referring objects that have a stem or stemlike object, such as a goblet.

tem² /stem/ *vb* (**stemmed** /stemd/, **stemming** /ste-ming/) to check, to delay, to stop (something) flowing (*stem the flow of blood*).

tench /stench/ *n* a foul smell (*the stench from the sewer*).

tencil /sten-sil/ *n* **1** a thin plate or card with a design cut through it so that patterned markings can be painted or printed on a surface beneath. **2** a waxed paper from which copies of typewritten material can be printed. ● *vb* (**stenciled** /sten-sild/, **stenciling** /sten-si-ling/) to make a design or copy by using a stencil.

tep /step/ *n* **1** a pace taken by one foot. **2** the distance covered by such a pace. **3** a footprint. **4** the sound of a footfall (*hear steps on the stair*). **5** a complete series of steps in a dance. **6** one of a series of rungs or small graded platforms that allow a person to climb or walk from one level to another (*the steps of a ladder*). **7** *pl* a flight of stairs. **8** *pl* a stepladder. ● *vb* (**stepped** /stept/,

stepping /ste-ping/) to walk. ● **out of step 1** out of time with others in performing a regular movement. **2** behaving or thinking differently from others (*older workers are out of step with the ideas of the young people*). ● **step out** to move boldly or quickly forward. ● **step up** to increase (*step up the interest payments on the loan*). ● **take steps** to take action.

stepchild /step-childe/ *n* the child of a husband or wife by a previous marriage. ● *also* **stepdaughter** / step-daw-ter/, **stepfather** /step-fa-ther/, **stepmother** /step-mu-ther/, **stepson** /step-sun/, **stepfamily** / step-fam-lee/.

stepladder /step-la-der/ *n* a portable self-supporting ladder.

steppe /step/ *n* in Russia or Asia, a vast treeless uncultivated plain.

stereo /ste-ree-o/ *n* a device used to play music in stereoscopic sound. ● *also adj*.

stereoscopic sound /ste-ree-o-scop-ic-sound/ *n* sound relayed from two transmitters so that it seems to come from an area and not one point.

stereotype /ste-ree-o-tipe/ *n* **1** a metal plate on which type is reproduced so that it may be reprinted over and over again. **2** an idea, image, etc., that has become fixed and unchanging.

stereotyped /ste-ree-o-tiept/ *adj* fixed and unchanging (*actors worried about becoming stereotyped by playing the same kind of role too often*).

sterile /ste-rul/ *adj* **1** bearing no fruit or children, barren. **2** germ-free (*sterile operating theaters*). ● *n* **sterility** /ste-ri-li-tee/.

sterilize /ste-ri-lize/ *vb*, *also* **sterilise** (*Br*) **1** to make sterile. **2** to get rid of germs (by boiling, etc.).

sterling /ster-ling/ *adj* genuine, of worth.

stern¹ /stern/ *adj* severe, strict, harsh.

stern² /stern/ *n* the back part of a ship.

sternum /ster-num/ *n* a thin, flat bone to which most of the ribs are attached in the front of the chest.

stethoscope /ste-thu-scoap/ *n* an instrument by means of which a person can listen to the sound of another's breathing or heartbeats.

stew /stoo/ *vb* to boil slowly in little liquid in a closed vessel. ● *n* **1** stewed meat and vegetables. **2** (*inf*) a state of anxiety (*in a stew about the exams*). ● *adj* **stewed** cooked by stewing.

steward /stoo-wurd/ *n* **1** a person paid to manage another's land or property. **2** a manservant on a ship or airplane. **3** an official at a concert, race, meeting, show, etc. ● *f* **stewardess** /stoo-wur-dess/.

stick[1] /stick/ *vb* (*pt, pp* **stuck** /stuck/) **1** to pierce or stab (*stick a marshmallow on the skewer*). **2** to fasten or be fastened to, as with glue (*stick pictures on a piece of cardboard*). **3** to be unable to move (*cars stuck in the mud*).

stick[2] /stick/ *n* **1** a rod, a long, thin piece of wood, especially one carried when walking. **2** something shaped like a stick (*a stick of butter*).

stickball /stick-bawl/ *n* a game like baseball played by children in city streets with a stick, such as a broom handle, and a soft rubber ball.

sticker /sti-ker/ *n* a person or thing that sticks.

stickle /sti-kul/ *vb* to raise objections or make difficulties, especially in a stubborn manner and usually about small things.

stickler /sti-kler/ *n* a person who is fussy about details or unimportant matters (*a stickler for the school rules*).

sticky /sti-kee/ *adj* **1** smeared with glue, etc., for fixing to other things (*sticky paper*). **2** tending to fasten on by sticking. **3** (*inf*) difficult (*a sticky situation*).

stiff /stiff/ *adj* **1** hard to bend. **2** firm. **3** unable to move easily (*feel stiff after the exercise*). **4** cold and severe in manner.

stiffen /sti-fen/ *vb* to make or become stiff.

stifle /stie-ful/ *vb* **1** to smother, to choke, to cut off the supply of air. **2** to prevent from expressing (*stifle the child's natural talent*). **3** to keep down by force (*stifle a laugh*). ● *also adj*.

stigma /stig-ma/ *n* (*pl* **stigmas** /stig-maz/) **1** a mark of shame or disgrace (*the stigma of having been in prison*). **2** the part of a flower that receives the pollen. **3** (*pl* **stigmata** /stig-ma-ta/) marks like those of the wounds on Jesus's body.

stigmatic /stig-ma-tic/ *adj* of, like, or having a stigma.

stigmatize /stig-ma-tize/ *vb, also* **stigmatise** (*Br*) to blame as being shameful or disgraceful (*stigmatized as cowardly*).

stile /stile/ *n* a set of steps over a fence or wall.

stiletto /sti-le-toe/ *n* **1** a small dagger. **2** a small, sharp tools used for making small holes in cloth.

still[1] /still/ *adj* **1** at rest, motionless (*still water*). **2** calm, silent. ● *n* a single photograph out of a series taken by a moving camera. ● *vb* to make still. ● *adj* **1** even so (*he is old—still he wants to go on working*). **2** up to this moment (*they are still fighting*).

still[2] /still/ *n* a device for distilling spirits, or making alcoholic drinks (*a whiskey still*).

stillbirth /still-burth/ *n* the birth of a stillborn baby.

stillborn /still-bawrn/ *adj* born dead (*stillborn babies*).

still life /still-life/ *n* (*pl* **still lifes** /still-laeevz/) nonliving objects (e.g. fruit, ornaments, etc.) as subjects for painting, paintings of such objects.

stilt /stilt/ *n* one of a pair of poles with footrests so that a person can walk some height above the ground (*the clown walked on stilts*).

stilted /stil-tid/ *adj* **1** unnatural or pompous in manner. **2** awkwardly expressed (*stilted English*).

stimulant /sti-myu-lant/ *n* something that increases energy for a time (*coffee is a stimulant*). ● *also adj*

stimulate /sti-myu-late/ *vb* **1** to rouse or make more alert, active, etc. (*stimulating her into learning to paint*). **2** to stir up, cause (*the teacher stimulated discussion on the arts*). ● *adj* **stimulating** /sti-myu-lay-ting/.

stimulus /sti-myu-lus/ *n* (*pl* **stimuli** /sti-myu-lie/) something that arouses a person's feelings or excites a person to action (*the competition acted as a stimulus to get him to practice running*).

sting /sting/ *n* **1** a sharp-pointed defensive organ of certain animals or insects by means of which they can inject poison into an attacker. **2** in plants, a hair containing poison. **3** the pain caused by a sting (*a wasp sting*). **4** any sharp pain. ● *vb* (*pt, pp* **stung** /stung/). **1** to pierce or wound with a sting. **2** to pierce painfully with a sharp point. **3** to drive or provoke (a person) to act (*stung into making an angry reply*).

stinger /sting-er/ *n* a person or thing that stings.

stingray /sting-ray/ *n* a kind of flat fish that has a long, whiplike tale that can sting its enemies.

stingy /stin-jee/ *adj* mean, unwilling to spend or give money.

stink /stingk/ *vb* (*pt* **stank** /stangk/ *or* **stunk** /stungk/ *pp* **stunk**) to give an unpleasant smell. ● *n* an unpleasant smell (*the stink of rotten meat*).

stint /stint/ *vb* to give or allow only a small amount of (*stinted on materials*). ● *n* limit, a set amount of work

stipple /sti-pul/ *vb* to paint or draw in very small dots instead of lines.

stipulate /sti-pyu-late/ *vb* to lay down conditions in advance (*stipulating the terms of her employment in writing*).

stipulation /sti-pyu-lay-shun/ *n* conditions demanded as part of an agreement.

stir /stir/ *vb* (**stirred** /stird/, **stirring** /sti-ring/) **1** to move or set in motion (*stir the sauce*). **2** to arouse (*stir up hatred*). ● *n* excitement, noisy movement, sensation (*their divorce caused quite a stir*).

stir-fry /stir-frie/ *vb* to fry very quickly in a wok with a little oil while stirring constantly. ● *n* a dish prepared this way.

stirring /sti-ring/ *adj* rousing, exciting (*a stirring song*).

stirrup /sti-rup/ *n* a metal foot support hung from the saddle for a horse-rider.

stitch /stitch/ *n* 1 a single complete movement of the needle in knitting, sewing, etc. 2 the thread, wool, etc., used in such a movement. 3 a sharp pain in the side as a result of running, etc. ● *vb* to join by stitches (*a wound requiring stitching*).

stock /stock/ *n* 1 the main stem of a plant, the trunk of a tree. 2 the wooden handle of a gun. 3 a band of cloth worn around the neck, sometimes also covering the shirt front. 4 the families from which a person is descended. 5 goods kept for selling (*have a varied stock of candies*). 6 shares in a business. 7 the animals of a farm. 8 liquid in which marrow bones, vegetables, etc., have been boiled. 9 a sweet-smelling garden flower. 10 *pl* (*old*) a frame with holes for the hands and feet into which lawbreakers could be fastened for punishment. 11 *pl* the wooden frame on which a ship rests while being built. ● *adj* always in use or ready for use. ● *vb* to provide with necessary goods, to keep a store of (*stock greetings cards*). ● **take stock** 1 to list and check goods. 2 to consider all the aspects of a situation (*take stock of his future prospects*).

stockade /stock-ade/ *n* a fence of strong posts built for defense.

stockbroker /stock-bro-ker/ *n* a person who buys and sells shares in business companies on behalf of others.

stock car /stock car/ *n* a normal automobile adapted for racing with.

stock exchange /stock-eks-change/, **stock market** / stock-mar-kit/ *ns* a place where shares are bought and sold.

stockholder /stock-hole-der/ *n* a person owning stock in a given company.

stocking /stock-ing/ *n* a close-fitting covering for the foot and leg.

stockpile /stock-pile/ *n* a supply of goods for use in case of a shortage.

stocktaking /stock-tay-king/ *n* the checking of all the goods held in a store (*undertake a stocktaking of their winter stock*).

stocky /stock-ee/ *adj* short and broad (*a stocky young man*).

stodgy /stodge-ee/ *adj* 1 dull (*a stodgy piece of writing*). 2 (*of food*) heavy or hard to digest.

stoic /stoe-ic/ *n* a person who accepts good and bad, pleasure and pain without excitement or complaint. ● *adj* **stoical** /stoe-ic-al/. ● *n* **stoicism** /stoe-i-si-zum/.

stoke /stoke/ *vb* to put fuel on a fire.

stole[1] /stole/ *n* 1 a band of cloth worn around the neck by a clergyman during services. 2 a long scarf worn around the shoulders by women (*wearing a fur stole over her evening dress*).

stole[2] /stole/ *pt of* **steal.**

stolen /sto-len/ *pp of* **steal.** ● *also adj.*

stomach /stu-mac/ *n* 1 the baglike bodily organ that receives and digests food. 2 courage (*not have the stomach for battle*). ● *vb* to bear with, to put up with (*could not stomach his treatment of animals*).

stomp /stomp/ *vb* a jazz tune with a lively rhythm and a strong beat, dancing to this music.

stone /stone/ *n* 1 a hard mass of rock. 2 a piece of rock, a pebble. 3 the hard center of some fruits (*cherry stones*). 4 a piece of hard matter that forms in the body in certain diseases (*kidney stones*). 5 a precious stone or gem. ● *adj* made of stone. ● *vb* 1 to throw stones at. 2 to remove the stones from (fruit) (*stoning the cherries*). ● **leave no stone unturned** to do everything possible (*the police left no stone unturned in the search for the murderer*).

Stone Age /stoe-nayj/ *n* an early period in history during which humans made tools, weapons, etc., of stone.

stonemason /stone-may-sun/ *n* a person who cuts stone to shape and uses it to make walls, buildings, etc.

stoneware /stone-ware/ *n* a coarse pottery with a glazed finish.

stonewashed /stone-wawsht/ *adj* usually of material, washed with rough stones to cause fading and make softer.

stonework /stone-wurk/ *n* the art or process of working in stone, as in masonry or jewelry.

stony /stoe-nee/ *adj* 1 like stone. 2 covered with stones (*a stony beach*). 3 hard, unsympathetic (*listen in stony silence*).

stood /stood/ *pt of* **stand.**

stooge /stoodge/ *n* 1 a person made a fool of (*a comedian's stooge*). 2 a person who does unpleasant work for another, a person who takes the blame due to others.

stool /stool/ *n* a low, backless seat.

stoop /stoop/ *vb* 1 to bend forward and downward. 2 to agree to do something unworthy, to give in (*refuse to stoop to lying*). ● *n* a downward bending of the head and shoulders.

stop /stop/ vb (**stopped** /stopt/, **stopping** /stop-ing/) **1** to cease or prevent from moving or doing something. **2** to come or bring to a standstill. **3** to block or close up (*stop the hole in the pipe*). ● n **1** a pause. **2** a place where a bus, etc., halts to pick up passengers. **3** time spent standing still or doing nothing (*a stop for lunch*). **4** one of the knobs controlling the flow of air in the pipes of an organ, thereby regulating the sounds produced.

stopper /stop-er/ n something closing a small hole (e.g. in the neck of a bottle).

stopwatch /stop-wach/ n a watch, used for timing events, that can be started or stopped at will (*use a stopwatch to time the race*).

storage /sto-ridge/ n **1** the putting of goods in warehouses, etc., until they are required (*the storage of their furniture while they were away*). **2** the charge for storing goods.

store /store/ n **1** a large quantity. **2** a supply of goods that can be drawn on when necessary. **3** a room or building where such goods are kept. **4** a shop selling many different kinds of articles (*a department store*). ● vb **1** to keep for future use (*storing her summer clothes in the attic*). **2** to put in warehouses, etc. ● **set store by** to regard as valuable.

stork /stawrk/ n a white wading bird of the heron family, with long legs and bill.

storm /stawrm/ n **1** a spell of very bad weather (e.g. rain, wind, snow, etc.). **2** a display of violent emotion, public anger. ● vb **1** to make a sudden violent attack on a defended place (*the enemy storming the castle*). **2** to rage (*storming about the damage to his car*). ● **take by storm** to capture by sudden violent attack.

stormy /stawr-mee/ adj **1** of, like, or troubled by storms. **2** violent, marked by angry feelings (*a stormy reaction to his defeat*).

story[1] /sto-ree/ n **1** an account of events, real or imagined. **2** (*inf*) a lie (*feel that his account of the event was just a story*).

story[2] /sto-ree/ n a level of a building (*five-story building*).

storyboard /sto-ree-board/ n a large board on which a series of sketches of shots or scenes are arranged for outlining the action of a film, video, etc.

storybook /sto-ree-book/ n a book of stories, especially those for children.

storyteller /sto-ree-te-ler/ n a person who tells stories.

stout /stout/ adj **1** strong or thick (*a stout stick*). **2** fat (*so stout that he was breathless walking along the road*). **3** brave (*a stout attempt*). ● n a strong dark beer.

stove /stove/ n a closed-in fireplace or metal device for warming a room, cooking, etc.

stow /stoe/ vb to put away, to pack tightly (*stow the luggage in the trunk of the car*).

stowaway /stoe-a-way/ n a person who hides on a ship, etc., so as to travel without paying the fare.

straddle /stra-dul/ vb **1** to spread the legs wide apart. **2** to sit or stand with a leg on either side of.

straggle /stra-gul/ vb **1** to move in widely scattered formation. **2** to fall behind the main body.

straggler /stra-gler/ n a person who wanders from the main body.

straggly /stra-glee/ adj spread out in an irregular way.

straight /strate/ adj **1** not curving or crooked. **2** honest. ● adv directly, at once. ● vb **straighten** /straten/ to make straight (*straighten the bedclothes*).

straightaway /stray-ta-way/ adv at once.

straightforward /strate-fawr-ward/ adj **1** simple, easy to understand. **2** honest (*a straightforward person*).

strain[1] /strain/ vb **1** to stretch tightly (*a dress straining at the seams*). **2** to make the utmost effort. **3** to harm by trying to do too much with (*strain themselves by pushing the cart*). **4** to put in a sieve to draw liquid off (*strain the sauce*). ● n **1** violent effort. **2** harm caused to muscles, etc., by straining them. **3** manner or style of speaking or writing. **4** a tune.

strain[2] /strain/ n **1** breed, stock (*a strain of plant*). **2** an element of character (*a family with an artistic strain*). **3** a tune.

strained /straind/ adj **1** stretched too far. **2** not natural (*a strained relationship*).

strainer /stray-ner/ n a small sieve or filter (*a metal strainer*).

strait /strait/ adj narrow, strict. ● n **1** a narrow strip of water between two land masses. **2** pl distressing difficulties.

strait-jacket /strait-ja-ket/ n a strong, tightly fitting garment that can be laced onto violent persons to make them helpless or to people with a back injury for support.

strait-laced /strait-layst/ adj having strict rules of behavior for oneself and others.

strand[1] /strand/ n (*fml*) the shore. ● vb **1** to run aground. **2** to be left helpless without money, friends, etc. (*find herself stranded with nowhere to stay*).

strand[2] /strand/ n one of the threads of a rope or string.

strange /straynj/ *adj* **1** unusual, odd (*strange animals*). **2** unfamiliar (*strange to the job*). **3** (*lit*) foreign (*strange lands*). **4** peculiar, uncomfortable, unwell (*feel strange*).

strangeness /straynj-ness/ *n* the state or quality of being strange.

stranger /strane-jer/ *n* **1** a person previously unknown. **2** a new arrival to a place, town, etc. **3** a person who is unfamilar with or ignorant of something (*a stranger to the truth*).

strangle /strang-gul/ *vb* to kill by pressing the throat tightly, to choke.

strap /strap/ *n* **1** a narrow band of leather or other material (*a strap around the suitcase*). **2** a leather belt. ● *vb* (**strapped** /strapt/, **strapping** /stra-ping/) **1** to fasten with a strap (*strap the load to the donkey*). **2** to beat with a strap.

strapless /strap-less/ *adj* having no strap (*strapless dress*).

strapping /stra-ping/ *adj* tall and strong (*strapping athletes*).

strata *see* **stratum**.

stratagem /stra-ta-jum/ *n* a trick intended to deceive (*a stratagem to get into the house unnoticed*).

strategic(al) /stra-**tee**-jic(-al)/ *adj* having to do with strategy.

strategist /stra-te-jist/ *n* a person skilled in strategy.

strategize /stra-te-jize/ *vb*, *also* **strategise** (*Br*) to plan a strategy.

strategy /stra-te-jee/ *n* **1** the art of dealing with a situation in such a way as to gain from it the greatest advantage possible (*the strategy required to get the council to agree to the building of the new road*). **2** in war, the planning of a campaign.

stratify /stra-ti-fie/ *vb* to form into or set out in layers. ● *n* **stratification** /stra-ti-fi-cay-shun/.

stratosphere /stra-tu-sfeer/ *n* a layer of Earth's atmosphere (5–10 miles up) in which temperature does not become lower as a person goes higher.

stratum /stra-tum/ *n* (*pl* **strata** /stra-ta/) **1** a layer of rock, earth, etc., forming part of Earth's surface. **2** a level (*a stratum of society*).

straw /straw/ *n* **1** the dried stalks of corn, etc. (*lay straw for the cattle to lie on*). **2** one such stalk or something resembling it (*suck lemonade through a straw*). **3** something of no worth (*not worth a straw*).

strawberry /straw-ber-ee/ *n* **1** a wild or garden plant. **2** the juicy red fruit it bears.

stray /stray/ *vb* to wander, to lose the way (*find the animal that had strayed*). ● *adj* **1** lost, off the right path (*stray animals*). **2** occasional (*stray flowers in the wood*). ● *n* a lost or wandering person, animal, or thing.

streak /streek/ *n* **1** a long, narrow mark or stain, a stripe, a narrow band (*streaks of red in the sky*). **2** part of a person's character (*a streak of nastiness*). ● *vb* to mark with streaks.

streaky /stree-kee/ *adj* consisting of or marked with streaks (*streaky hair*).

stream /streem/ *n* **1** a current of any liquid or gas. **2** a small river. **3** a succession of people moving in one direction (*a stream of people leaving the office*). ● *vb* **1** to move in a stream. **2** to flow freely.

streamer /stree-mer/ *n* **1** a long, narrow flag. **2** a narrow strip of ribbon or colored paper for flying in the wind (*streamers flying from the bus window*).

streamline /streem-line/ *vb* **1** to build so as to offer minimum resistance to air or water. **2** to make more efficient.

street /street/ *n* a public road lined with buildings in a city or town.

streetcar /street-car/ *n* a large coach or car on rails for the public to use.

streetlight /street-lite/ *n* a light mounted on a tall pole used to light up a street.

streetwise /street-lite/ *adj* knowing how to keep out of trouble.

strength /strength/ *n* **1** bodily power (*not have the strength to lift the load*). **2** might, force. **3** the number of persons of a class, army, etc., present or on the roll (*when the staff is at full strength*).

strengthen /streng-then/ *vb* to make or become stronger (*strengthen the wall/strengthen our case*).

strenuous /stren-yu-wus/ *adj* requiring much energy (*a strenuous task*).

stress /stress/ *vb* **1** to point out the importance of. **2** to emphasize with the voice (*stress the second syllable of the word*). ● *n* **1** importance (*put some stress on the cost of the project*). **2** strain, pressure (*not coping with the stress of the job*). **3** the special emphasis given to particular syllables, words, etc., when speaking.

stressed /strest/, **stressed-out** /strest-out/ *adj* tired, nervous, or depressed as a result of overwork, pressure, etc.

stretch /stretch/ *vb* **1** to make or become longer or broader by pulling. **2** to draw out to the fullest extent (*stretch muscles after exercise*). **3** to reach out (*stretch out for the salt*). **4** to exaggerate, to make seem more important, bigger, etc., than in actuality. ● *n* a full length of time or space.

stretcher /**stret**-cher/ *n* a light frame for carrying a sick or wounded person.

stretchy /**stret**-chee/ *adj* that can be stretched (*stretchy shirt*).

strew /**stroo**/ *vb* (*pp* strewn /stroon/) to scatter about, to spread at intervals over (*strewed flowers in the bride's path*).

stricken /**stri**-ken/ *adj* affected by (*stricken with a fatal illness*).

strict /**strict**/ *adj* 1 severe. 2 demanding others to obey the rules (*a strict teacher*).

stricture /**stric**-chur/ *n* 1 blame, unfavorable criticism of a person. 2 limit (*strictures on their freedom*).

stride /**stride**/ *vb* (*pt* strode /strode/) to walk with long steps. ● *n* a long step.

strident /**strie**-dent/ *adj* loud and harsh in sound (*strident voices*).

strife /**strife**/ *n* open disagreement, arguing, fighting.

strike /**strike**/ *vb* (*pt, pp* struck /struck/) 1 to hit (*he struck his opponent*). 2 (*of a clock*) to sound the hours or quarters. 3 to stop work to try to make employers grant better pay or conditions. 4 to come suddenly to mind (*it struck me that they were late*). 5 to make and stamp (a coin or medal). 6 to take down (a flag or tent). 7 to light (a match) by rubbing. 8 to come upon by chance (*strike a bad patch*). ● *n* a stopping of work.

striking /**strie**-king/ *adj* attracting attention because of being fine or unusual (*a striking dress*).

string /**string**/ *n* 1 a cord or strong thread. 2 the cord or wire of a musical instrument. 3 a number of persons or things, one following the other (*a string of applicants for the job*). ● *vb* 1 to put on a string. 2 to put a string into (a musical instrument).

string bean /**string** been/ *n* a long, thin, green, edible bean pod.

stringent /**strin**-jent/ *adj* 1 severe, strict, laying down exact rules to be obeyed (*stringent measures*). 2 marked by severe lack of money or firm control (*stringent financial conditions*). ● *n* stringency / strin-jen-see/.

stringy /**string**-ee/ *adj* 1 like string (*stringy beans*). 2 thin and muscular (*stringy arms*).

strip /**strip**/ *vb* (stripped /stript/, stripping /stri-ping/) 1 to pull off the outer covering. 2 to undress (*they stripped to swim*). 3 to take everything from (*strip the room of everything valuable*). ● *n* a long, narrow piece.

stripe /**stripe**/ *n* 1 a band or streak of different color from those on either side of it (*a pattern of blue and white stripes*). 2 a stroke from a whip, rod, etc ● *adj* **stripy** /strie-pee/, **striped** /striept/ marked with stripes.

strive /**strive**/ *vb* (*pt* strove /strove/ *or* strived /strievd/ *pp* striven /stri-ven/) to try as hard as possible, to struggle (*strive to reach the top*).

strobe light /**strobe**-lite/ *n* a light that gives off very bright, rapid flashes.

stroganoff /**strog**-an-of/ *adj* cooked with sour cream onions, mushrooms, etc. (*beef stroganoff*).

stroke[1] /**stroke**/ *n* 1 a blow. 2 a sudden turn of luck good or bad. 3 a sudden attack of illness, especially one affecting the brain. 4 a line made by a pen, pencil, etc. 5 one sound from a bell (*at the stroke of 10*). 6 in a boat, the oarsman with whom the others keep time when rowing.

stroke[2] /**stroke**/ *vb* to rub gently with the hand in one direction (*stroking the cat's fur*).

stroll /**strole**/ *vb* to walk in a leisurely way (*stroll along the path*). ● *n* a short leisurely walk.

stroller /**stroa**-ler/ *n* 1 a person who strolls. 2 a baby carriage.

strong /**strong**/ *adj* 1 powerful (*a strong influence*) 2 healthy (*children getting strong after their illness*) 3 possessing bodily power.

stronghold /**strong**-hoald/ *n* 1 a fort. 2 a place difficult to capture by attack.

structure /**struc**-chur/ *n* 1 a building. 2 anything consisting of parts put together according to a plan. 3 the way in which a thing is put together (*the structure of the organization*). ● *adj* **structural** /struc-chural/.

strudel /**stroo**-dul/ *n* a kind of pastry made of a very thin sheet of double covered with fillings and then rolled and baked.

struggle /**stru**-gul/ *vb* 1 to try hard. 2 to fight. ● *n* 1 a hard effort (*put up a struggle*). 2 a fight.

strum /**strum**/ *vb* (strummed /strumd/, strumming /stru-ming/) 1 to play a tune carelessly. 2 to play on a stringed instrument by plucking the strings (*strum on a guitar*).

strut[1] /**strut**/ *vb* (strutted /stru-tid/, strutting /strutting/) to walk stiffly, as if trying to look important (*the bully was strutting around the playground*). ● *also n*.

strut[2] /**strut**/ *n* a supporting bar, a prop or support.

strychnine /**stric**-neen/ *n* a highly poisonous drug.

stub /**stub**/ *n* 1 a short piece left when the rest is cut off or used up. 2 the retained section of a ticket etc. ● *vb* (stubbed /stubd/, stubbing /stu-bing/) to strike (the toes) against something by accident.

stubbed /stubd/ *adj* like a stub, short.

stubble /stu-bul/ *n* **1** the stumps of the corn stalks left in the ground after reaping. **2** the short bristly hairs that grow after a person has shaved.

stubborn /stu-burn/ *adj* unwilling to change point of view, not ready to give in.

stubby /stu-bee/ *adj* short and broad, short and thick (*stubby fingers*).

stud[1] /stud/ *n* **1** a nail with a large head or knob. **2** a fastener with a head at each end for linking two buttonholes (*collar studs*). **3** one of the supporting wooden beams in a wall. ● *vb* (**studded** /stu-did/, **studding** /stu-ding/) **1** to decorate with many small ornaments. **2** to cover with (*a dress studded with sequins*). ● *adj* covered with studs (*studded belt*).

stud[2] /stud/ *n* a number of horses kept for breeding.

student /stoo-dent/ *n* a person who studies, a person who goes to school (*university students*).

studied /stu-deed/ *adj* done with care, deliberate (*with studied politeness*).

studio /stoo-dee-o/ *n* **1** the room in which a painter, sculptor, photographer, etc., works. **2** a building in which films are made. **3** a workshop in which records are made or from which programs are broadcast. **4** a one-room apartment.

studious /stoo-dee-us/ *adj* of, given to, or engaged in study (*studious pupils*).

study /stu-dee/ *vb* **1** to read about or look at to obtain knowledge (*studied local history*). **2** to examine closely, to think deeply about (*studying the evidence*). ● *n* **1** the obtaining of information, especially by reading. **2** a subject studied. **3** an office, a room set aside for reading and learning (*the professor's study*). **4** a work of art done to improve a person's skill.

stuff /stuff/ *n* **1** the material or substance of which something is made. **2** anything said, done, written, composed, etc. **3** cloth (*clothes of hard-wearing stuff*). ● *vb* **1** to fill full or tightly. **2** to fill something hollow with another material.

stuffing /stu-fing/ *n* **1** material used to stuff something hollow (*stuffing for cushions*). **2** a mixture of breadcrumbs, seasoning, etc., put inside chickens, etc., when cooking (*turkey stuffing*).

stuffy /stu-fee/ *adj* hot and airless (*a stuffy room*).

stumble /stum-bul/ *vb* **1** to trip and nearly fall (*stumbling over an uneven piece of road*). **2** to make an error, to do wrong. **3** to come upon by chance (*stumble upon the solution*). ● *n* a trip, a false step when walking, nearly causing a person to fall.

stump /stump/ *n* **1** the part of a tree left above ground when the rest is cut down. **2** the part of a limb left after the rest has been amputated. ● *vb* **1** to walk heavily (*she stumped out of the room angrily*). **2** to ask someone a question that he or she is unable to answer.

stumpy /stum-pee/ *adj* short and thick, short and broad (*stumpy fingers*).

stun /stun/ *vb* (**stunned** /stund/, **stunning** /stu-ning/) **1** to knock senseless. **2** to amaze (*stunned by the changes in the city center*). ● *n* **stunner** /stu-ner/ a person or thing that stuns. ● *adj* **stunning** /stu-ning/ extremely attractive.

stunt[1] /stunt/ *vb* to prevent the full growth of (*plants stunted because of frost*).

stunt[2] /stunt/ *n* **1** a trick to display special skill or daring. **2** anything done to attract attention or gain publicity (*a publicity stunt for their new product*).

stunted /stun-tid/ *adj* undersized.

stupefaction /stoo-pi-fac-shun/ *n* (*fml*) amazement.

stupefy /stoo-pi-fie/ *vb* **1** to make stupid, to make the senses less acute (*stupefied by the drug*). **2** to amaze.

stupendous /stoo-pen-dus/ *adj* extraordinary, so large or powerful that it amazes.

stupid /stoo-pid/ *adj* foolish, not intelligent, slow to understand. ● *n* **stupidity** /stoo-pi-di-tee/.

stupor /stoo-pur/ *n* temporary inability to think clearly, confusion of mind (*in a stupor because he just woke up*).

sturdy /stur-dee/ *adj* strong, well-built (*sturdy country children*).

sturgeon /stur-jin/ *n* a large fish from whose eggs caviar is made.

stutter /stu-ter/ *vb* to speak with difficulty, to repeat the first sound of a word several times before saying the whole word. ● *n* a stammer.

sty[1] /stie/ *n* an enclosure or a pen in which pigs are kept.

sty[2], **stye** /stie/ *n* a swelling on the edge of the eyelid.

style /stile/ *n* **1** manner of doing anything (*her style of teaching*). **2** a way of writing, painting, etc., by which works of art can be recognized as the work of a particular artist, school, or period (*discuss the style of the writer in the essay*). **3** a fashion (*the style of the 1920s*). **4** elegance (*dress with style*).

stylish /stie-lish/ *adj* well-dressed, smart, fashionable.

stylist /stie-list/ *n* a person who designs, creates, or advises on current styles of clothing, hair, etc.

stylistic /stie-li-stick/ *adj* having to do with style.

stylistics /stie-li-sticks/ *n* the study of style as a way of figuring out meaning.

stylize /stie-lize/ *vb*, *also* **stylise** (*Br*) to make part of one particular style.

suave /swav/ *adj* agreeable in manner, especially in an insincere way. ● *n* **suavity** /swa-vi-tee/.

sub- /sub/ *prefix* under, below.

subconscious /sub-con-shus/ *adj* not fully aware of what one is doing (*a subconscious hatred of his father*). ● *n* mental processes that go on without a person being fully aware of them.

subdivide /sub-di-vide/ *vb* to divide into smaller parts or groups. ● *n* **subdivision** /sub-di-vi-zhun/.

subdue /sub-doo/ *vb* to conquer, to force to be tame or obedient.

subdued /sub-dood/ *adj* not bright, not loud (*subdued lighting*).

subject /sub-jict/ *adj* 1 ruled by another. 2 liable to (*subject to colds*). ● *n* 1 a person who owes loyalty to a ruler or government. 2 that about which something is said or written (*he was the subject of the newspaper article*). 3 something studied (*French and other school subjects*). 4 in a clause or sentence, the word with which the verb agrees grammatically. ● *vb* **subject** /sub-ject/ 1 to bring under the power of (*a country subjected to tyranny*). 2 to expose to (*subject them to ridicule*).

subjection /sub-jec-shun/ *n* control, the state of being under another's rule or power.

subjective /sub-jec-tiv/ *adj* having to do with a person's own ideas and feelings rather than with objects outside (*a subjective judgment*).

sublet /sub-let/ *vb* to rent to another what that person is already paying rent for. ● *also n.*

sublime /su-blime/ *adj* noble, awe-inspiring, grand and lofty.

subliminal /su-bli-mi-nal/ *adj* not quite at a conscious level, pertaining repeating things over and over again so that they stick in the mind without the person realizing it (*TV commercials with subliminal messages*).

sublimity /su-bli-mi-tee/ *n* greatness of feeling or expression.

submarine /sub-ma-reen/ *adj* under the surface of the sea. ● *n* a ship that can travel under the surface of the sea.

submerge /su-merj/ *vb* to put or sink under water. ● *n* **submergence** /sub-mer-jense/.

submersion /sum-mer-shun/ *n* the act of putting or sinking under water.

submission /sum-mi-shun/ *n* 1 surrender, obedi-

ence, the act of giving in or yielding. 2 a proposa or opinion (*their submission was rejected*).

submissive /sub-mi-siv/ *adj* willing to accept orders ready to give in without fighting back.

submit /sub-mit/ *vb* (**submitted** /sub-mi-tid/, **sub mitting** /sub-mi-ting/) 1 to give in (*submit to the enemy*). 2 to put forward for consideration (*sub mit a claim for expenses*).

subordinate /su-bawr-di-nate/ *adj* 1 less importan (*subordinate issues*). 2 of lower rank. ● *n* a per son who is lower in rank, a person who is work ing under the orders of another. ● *vb* 1 to plac in a lower rank, to put under the command of. ² to regard as less important. ● *n* **subordination** su-bawr-di-nay-shun/.

subpoena /su-pee-na/ *n* an order to appear as a wit ness in a court of law.

subscribe /sub-scribe/ *vb* 1 to sign the name unde 2 to agree with (*unable to subscribe to his views*) 3 to give or promise to give money to a fund o collection (*subscribing to a children's charity*) 4 to give money to receive a weekly, monthly, etc. magazine, newspaper, etc. (*subscribe to* Tim *magazine*). ● *n* **subscriber** /sub-scrie-ber/.

subscription /sub-scrip-shun/ *n* 1 a signature. 2 sum of money given to a fund, collection, maga zine, newspaper, etc.

subsequent /sub-si-kwent/ *adj* following, later (*o subsequent occasions*).

subservient /sub-ser-vee-ant/ *adj* ready to do all person is told to gain favor (*subservient member of staff*).

subside /sub-side/ *vb* 1 to sink gradually dow (*buildings subsiding*). 2 to become less, to disap pear gradually (*the wind subsided*).

subsidence /sub-sie-dense/ *n* a gradual sinkin down, especially of land.

subsidiary /sub-si-dee-a-ree/ *adj* of less importanc (*subsidiary issues*).

subsidize /sub-si-dize/ *vb*, *also* **subsidise** (*Br, Cdn* to pay a subsidy to (*subsidizing the children' theater*).

subsidy /sub-si-dee/ *n* money paid by the governmen to certain groups, trades, etc., to enable them to pro vide the public with necessary services without los ing money (*subsidies for renovating old houses*).

subsist /sub-sist/ *vb* to live or exist, to have the mean of living (*subsisting on very little money*).

subsistence /sub-si-stense/ *n* existence, being, tha which is necessary to support life (food, clothing shelter).

ubstance /sub-stanse/ n 1 the material of which a thing is made (a waterproof substance). 2 that which really exists (not what is imagined). 3 the chief ideas in a speech or written work. 4 (fml) wealth (a man of substance).

ubstantial /sub-**stan**-shal/ adj 1 really existing. 2 solid. 3 fairly large or important (a substantial improvement).

ubstantiate /sub-**stan**-shee-ate/ vb to prove the truth of (substantiating his claim to the truth).

ubstitute /sub-sti-toot/ vb to put in place of (substituting tofu for meat). ● n a person or thing put in the place of another (the teacher had a substitute yesterday). ● also adj (substitute teacher). ● n substitution /sub-sti-**too**-shun/.

ubterranean /sub-tu-**ray**-nee-an/ adj underground (subterranean caves).

ubtitle /sub-tie-tul/ n 1 a second, less important, title of a book. 2 explanatory comments, etc., printed on silent or foreign-language films.

ubtle /su-tul/ adj 1 cunning, clever, not obvious (he succeeded in persuading her by subtle means). 2 difficult to understand completely (a subtle difference). 3 faint or delicate (subtle colors).

ubtlety /su-tul-tee/ n 1 skill, cleverness. 2 refinement.

ubtract /sub-tract/ vb to take (one number) from another. ● n subtraction /sub-**trac**-shun/.

uburb /su-**burb**/ n an outlying part of a city. ● adj suburban /su-**bur**-ban/.

ubversive /sub-**ver**-siv/ adj intended or likely to overthrow or destroy, directed against the government, management, organization, etc. (a subversive section of the club).

ubvert /sub-**vert**/ vb (fml) to overthrow, to try to destroy (try to subvert the government). ● n subversion /sub-**ver**-shun/.

ubway /sub-way/ n 1 an underground passage (use the subway to get across the busy road). 2 an underground railway.

ucceed /suc-**seed**/ vb 1 to do what a person has attempted or desired to do (succeeded in climbing the mountain). 2 to come after, to follow in order and take the place of (the president who succeeded George Washington/he succeeded his father as chairman).

uccess /suc-**sess**/ n 1 the doing of what a person has attempted or desired to do. 2 a favorable result or outcome. 3 a person or thing that does as well as was hoped or expected. ● adj successful /suc-**sess**-ful/.

succession /suc-se-shun/ n 1 a number of persons or things following one another in order (a succession of people for the post). 2 the order in which people may inherit a title when it becomes available.

successive /suc-se-siv/ adj coming in order, following one after another (on successive occasions).

successor /suc-se-sur/ n a person who comes after or takes the place of another (the president's successor).

succinct /suc-**sinct**/ adj short and to the point, concise (a succinct account of the meeting).

succor /su-cur/ vb, also succour (Br, Cdn) (fml) to help when in difficulty. ● n aid, help (give succor to the injured).

succotash /su-cu-tash/ n a dish of lima beans and kernels of corn cooked together.

succulent /su-cyu-lent/ adj juicy (succulent peaches).

succumb /su-cum/ vb 1 to give way to, to be overcome. 2 to die.

such /such/ adj 1 of a like kind or degree, similar. 2 so extreme, so much, so great, etc. (happy with such praise). ● adv to so great a degree (such good news).

suck /suck/ vb 1 to draw into or in with the mouth (suck juice from a straw). 2 to draw the liquid from the mouth or something in it with the tongue (suck sweets). ● also n.

sucker /su-cler/ n 1 a person or thing that sucks. 2 (inf) a foolish or gullible person.

suckle /su-cul/ vb to allow to suck milk from the breast (sows suckling their piglets).

suckling /su-cling/ n a baby or animal still feeding from its mother's breast.

suction /suc-shun/ n the act of sucking, the drawing up of a fluid into a tube, etc., by expelling the air so that the fluid fills where the air once was.

sudden /su-den/ adj happening without warning, unexpected, hurried (a sudden change in the weather).

suds /sudz/ npl the froth on soapy water. ● adj sudsy /sud-zee/.

sue /soo/ vb 1 to bring a case against in a court of law (sue him for slander). 2 (fml) to beg for (suing for mercy).

suede /swade/ n a soft kind of leather that is brushed and buffed so that it has a soft, sort of furry feal to it. ● also adj.

suet /soo-it/ n a hard fat from cattle and sheep, used in cooking.

suffer /su-fer/ vb 1 to undergo pain or great anxiety

(*families suffering during the strike*). **2** to experience or undergo (*suffer defeat*). **3** to put up with (*unable to suffer the noise*). ● *n* **suffering** /su-fring/ the bearing of pain, distress, etc.

suffice /su-**fise**/ *vb* (*fml*) to be enough (*a little will suffice*).

sufficiency /su-fi-shen-see/ *n* a big enough supply.

sufficient /su-fi-shent/ *adj* enough (*not sufficient money to buy food*).

suffix /su-fiks/ *n* a syllable added to the end of a word (e.g., -ness, -ly) to change its use or meaning.

suffocate /su-fu-cate/ *vb* **1** to choke for lack of air (*people suffocating in the heat*). **2** to kill by preventing from breathing. ● *n* **suffocation** /su-fu-**cay**-shun/.

suffrage /su-fridge/ *n* (*fml*) the right to vote in elections. ● *n* **suffragist** /su-fri-jist/ a person who believes in giving people the right to vote.

suffragette /su-fri-**jet**/ *n* in the 19th century, a woman who claimed and obtained the right for women to vote (*Susan B Anthony was a suffragette*).

suffuse /su-**fyooz**/ *vb* (*fml*) to spread over (*a blush suffusing her cheeks*). ● *n* **suffusion** /su-**fyoo**-zhun/.

sugar /**shoo**-gar/ *n* a sweet substance manufactured from sugar cane, beets, etc. ● *vb* **1** to sweeten with sugar (*sugared the strawberries*) **2** to try to make more acceptable (*try to sugar the insult*). ● *adj* **sugary** /**shoo**-gree/.

sugar beet /**shoo**-gar-beet/ *n* a plant with a root from which sugar is obtained.

sugar cane /**shoo**-gar-cane/ *n* a tall, stiff reed from which sugar is obtained.

sugarcoat /**shoo**-gar-coat/ *vb* **1** to cover or coat with sugar. **2** to make something unpleasant not seem so bad (*sugarcoat an idea so everyone will agree*).

suggest /su-**jest**/ *vb* **1** to put forward (*suggest some improvements*). **2** to hint (*she thought that he was suggesting that she was a liar*). **3** to cause an idea to come into the mind (*a perfume suggesting roses*).

suggestion /su-**jes**-chun/ *n* **1** a proposal. **2** a hint.

suggestive /su-**jes**-tiv/ *adj* **1** putting ideas into the mind (*suggestive of Victorian times*). **2** rather indecent (*suggestive remarks about her appearance*).

suicide /**soo**-i-side/ *n* **1** the killing of oneself on purpose. **2** a person who kills himself or herself on purpose (*the police found the suicide*). ● *adj* **suicidal** /soo-i-**sie**-dal/.

suit /soot/ *vb* **1** to please or satisfy (*it suits him to go*). **2** to go well with. **3** to look nice on (*a dress that suits her*). ● *n* **1** a set of clothes of the same mate-

rial (*a business suit*). **2** attentions paid to a lad with the intention of marrying her. **3** one of the four sets (hearts, clubs, etc.) in a pack of playin cards. **4** the taking of a case to a court of law. ● **follow suit 1** to play a card from the same suit. **2** t do the same as or follow the example of anothe (*he left, and she followed suit*).

suitable /**soo**-ta-bul/ *adj* what is wanted for the pur pose, fitting the occasion (*suitable clothes for th job*).

suitcase /**soot**-case/ *n* a traveling bag for clothes.

suite /sweet/ *n* **1** a set of rooms or furniture (*th bedroom suite*). **2** all the attendants who wait upo a certain person. **3** a series of connected pieces o music. **4** a group of connected rooms (*the brida suite in the hotel*).

suitor /**soo**-tur/ *n* **1** a person making a request o asking for a favor. **2** a man paying attention to lady with the intention of marrying her.

sulfate /**sul**-fate/ *n*, *also* **sulphate** (*Br, Cdn*) a salt o sulfuric acid.

sulfur /**sul**-fur/ *n*, *also* **sulphur** (*Br, Cdn*) a yellow non metallic element.

sulfuric *adj*, *also* **sulphuric** (*Br, Cdn*) /**sul**-few-ric having to do with or containing sulfur.

sulfurous *adj*, *also* **sulphurous** (*Br, Cdn*) /**sul**-fur-uss having to do with or like sulfur.

sulk /sulk/ *vb* to behave in an ill-humored, unfriendl way, to refuse to speak to others because of ill-tem per (*she sulked when she didn't get her own way*)

sulky /**sul**-kee/ *adj* ill-natured, not mixing with oth ers because of ill-humor (*sulky because he didn get his own way*).

sullen /**su**-len/ *adj* ill-natured, silently bad-tempered gloomy, sad.

sultan /**sul**-tan/ *n* the ruler of a Muslim country.

sultana /sul-**ta**-na/ *n* **1** the wife of a sultan. **2** a white seedless grape used for raisins and wine making

sultry /**sul**-tree/ *adj* very hot and close (*sultr weather*).

sum /sum/ *n* **1** the answer obtained by adding sev eral numbers together. **2** the total or entire amoun especially of money (*the sum gathered for the cha ity*). **3** a problem in arithmetic. ● *vb* (**summed** sumd/, **summing** /**su**-ming/) to add up. ● **sum up t** summarize.

summarize /**su**-ma-rize/ *vb*, *also* **summarise** (*Br*) t give a brief account of the main points (*summa rizing the discussion of the committee*).

summary /**su**-ma-ree/ *n* a brief account of the mai points (*summaries of their speeches*). ● *adj* **1** shor

2 done quickly or by a short method (*their summary dismissal of him*).

summation /su-**may**-shun/ *n* the act or process of summing up or of finding a total.

summer /su-mer/ *n* the warmest season of the year, in the Northern Hemisphere, generally June, July, and August. ● *adj* **summery** /su-mer-ee/ of or like summer.

summit /su-mit/ *n* **1** the highest point, the top. **2** a meeting of heads of government, or other high-ranking officials, of several countries to discuss matters of great importance (*a summit on environment pollution*).

summon /su-mun/ *vb* **1** to call upon to appear before an official (*summoned by the court*). **2** to call upon to do something (*summon all his strength*).

summons /su-munz/ *n* an order to appear for trial by a court of law. ● *vb* to present with such on order.

sumo wrestling /**soo**-mo-ress-ling/ *n* a Japanese form of wrestling, performed by very large men. ● *n* **sumo wrestler.**

sump /sump/ *n* a hole or hollow in which liquid collects (e.g., an oil sump in an engine).

sumptuous /sum-shu-wus/ *adj* splendid, very expensive, luxurious (*a sumptuous palace*).

sun /sun/ *n* **1** (*often cap*) the heavenly body that gives light and heat to the Earth and other planets in the same solar system. **2** the warmth or light given by the sun.

sunbathe /sun-bathe/ *vb* to lay out in the sun.

sunblock /sun-block/ *n* sunscreen.

sunburn /sun-burn/ *n* a reddening of the skin's color caused by exposure to the sun. ● *also vb.*

sundae /sun-day/ *n* ice cream served with fruit, nuts, syrup, etc.

Sunday /sun-day/ *n* the first day of the week.

sundial /sun-dile/ *n* an instrument that tells the time by casting the shadow of an indicator on a face marked with the hours.

sun-dried /sun-dried/ *adj* dried by the sun (*sun-dried tomatoes*).

sunflower /sun-flour/ *n* a tall plant with a large yellow flower.

sunglasses /sun-gla-siz/ *n* tinted glasses to shade the eyes from the brightness of the sun.

sunlight /sun-lite/ *n* the light of the sun. ● *adj* **sunlit** /sun-lit/.

sunny /su-nee/ *adj* **1** brightly lit by the sun. **2** cheerful, happy (*a sunny nature*).

sunrise /sun-rize/ *n* the first appearance of the sun in the morning.

sunscreen /sun-screen/ *n* a cream or oily substance worn on the skin to protect it from the sun's rays.

sunset /sun-set/ *n* the disappearance of the sun below the horizon in the evening.

sunshine /sun-shine/ *n* **1** the light or warmth of the sun. **2** cheerfulness (*the sunshine of her nature*).

sunstroke /sun-stroke/ *n* a severe illness caused by the effect of the sun's heat on the body.

suntan /sun-tan/ *n* a darkening of the skin caused by the sun.

sunward /sun-ward/ *adj* facing the sun.

sup /sup/ *vb* (**supped** /supt/, **supping** /su-ping/) **1** (*old*) to take supper. **2** to eat or drink in small mouthfuls. ● *n* a small mouthful.

super /**soo**-per/ *adj* outstanding, great, wonderful.

super- /**soo**-per/ *prefix* above, over.

superb /soo-**perb**/ *adj* magnificent, excellent (*a superb performance*).

supercilious /soo-per-**si**-lee-us/ *adj* **1** overproud, having a scornful manner, looking down on others (*a supercilious young woman*). **2** disdainful, scornful (*a supercilious look*).

superficial /soo-per-**fi**-shal/ *adj* **1** on the surface (*superficial wounds*). **2** not deeply felt or thought about (*a superficial knowledge*). **3** shallow, incapable of deep thought or feeling (*a superficial person*). ● *n* **superficiality** /soo-per-fi-shee-a-li-tee/.

superfluous /soo-**per**-floo-us/ *adj* more than enough, unnecessary (*his advice was superfluous*). ● *n* **superfluity** /soo-per-**floo**-i-tee/.

superhero /**soo**-per-hee-rous/ *n* an all-powerful hero of a kind found in comic books.

superhuman /soo-per-**hyoo**-man/ *adj* more than human, extraordinary, divine (*make a superhuman effort*).

superimpose /soo-per-im-**poaz**/ *vb* to lay on top of something else (*superimposing one photograph on another*).

superintendent /soo-per-in-**ten**-dent/ *n* **1** one who superintends. **2** a person in charge of a department, group, school, etc.

superior /soo-**pir**-ee-ur/ *adj* **1** higher in rank (*his superior officer*). **2** better (*a superior player*). ● *n* **1** a person higher in rank. **2** a person better than others (*he is his brother's superior on the football field*). **3** the head of a monastery or convent. ● *n* **superiority** /soo-pir-ee-**aw**-ri-tee/.

superlative /soo-**per**-la-tiv/ *adj* **1** excellent, above all others in quality (*a superlative musical performance*). **2** expressing the highest degree (*best is the superlative degree of good*).

superman /**soo**-per-man/ *n* a man of extraordinary powers, the imagined perfect human being of the future.

supermarket /**soo**-per-mar-kit/ *n* a large store selling (usually by self-service) food and household goods.

supernatural /soo-per-**nach**-ral/ *adj* **1** not to be explained by natural causes (*supernatural forces*). **2** caused by direct divine intervention in human affairs. ● *n* immortal beings existing outside the known universe and having the power to intervene in human affairs.

supernova /**soo**-per noe-vah/ *n* an exploding star giving off millions of times more light than the sun.

supersede /soo-per-**seed**/ *vb* to take the place of, to put another in the place of (*some hobbies have been superseded by television viewing*).

supersonic /soo-per-**son**-ic/ *adj* faster than sound (*the Concorde was a supersonic passenger aircraft*).

superstition /soo-per-**sti**-shun/ *n* **1** a tendency to believe that certain human beings or objects have more than natural powers. **2** belief in magic, luck, etc. (*the superstition that black cats are unlucky*). ● *adj* **superstitious** /soo-per-**sti**-shus/.

supervise /**soo**-per-vize/ *vb* **1** to watch others to see that they do their work properly (*supervising the students doing homework*). **2** to be in charge of (*supervised the dress department*). ● *n* **supervision** / soo-per-**vi**-zhun/. ● *n* **supervisor** /**soo**-per-vie-zur/.

supper /**su**-per/ *n* a light evening meal.

supple /**su**-pul/ *adj* **1** (*fml*) easily bent. **2** bending or moving easily and gracefully (*supple gymnasts*).

supplement /**su**-pli-mint/ *n* **1** something added to make up what is lacking (*vitamin supplements*). **2** an addition. ● *vb* **supplement** /**su**-pli-ment/ to make additions to.

supplementary /su-pli-**men**-tree/ *adj* given in addition, given to make up what is lacking (*supplementary income*).

suppliant /**su**-**plie**-ant/ *adj* (*fml*) begging for as a favor. ● *n* (*fml*) a person humbly asking for a favour.

supply /su-**plie**/ *vb* to provide what is needed (*supplied food for the party*). ● *n* **1** a store of what is needed. **2** *pl* stores.

support /su-**poart**/ *vb* **1** to help to hold up (*struts supporting the bridge*). **2** to give help or encouragement to (*support the cause*). **3** to provide the necessities of life for (*support a family*). **4** to put up with (*unable to support the noise of the machinery*). ● *n* **1** a prop. **2** assistance, encouragement. **3** a person or thing that supports. ● *adj* **supportive** su-**poar**-tiv/.

supporter /su-**poar**-ter/ *n* a person who helps or encourages (*supporters of the president's cause*).

suppose /su-**poaz**/ *vb* **1** to believe to be true without sure evidence (*we suppose that he is honest*). **2** to imagine. **3** to think probable (*I suppose she has gone home*). ● *adv* **supposedly** /su-**poa**-zid-lee/ according to what is, was, or may be supposed.

supposition /su-pu-**zi**-shun/ *n* **1** a guess. **2** something taken as true or imagined.

suppress /su-**press**/ *vb* **1** to put down, to crush (*suppress the rebellion*). **2** to prevent from being known (*suppress information*). ● *n* **suppression** /su-**presh**-un/.

suppressant /su-**press**-ant/ *n* something, especially a drug, that suppresses an action, condition, etc (*cough suppressant*).

supremacist /soo-**prem**-a-sist/ *n* a person who believes that one group is superior to others.

supremacy /soo-**prem**-a-see/ *n* the highest power or authority.

supreme /soo-**preem**/ *adj* **1** highest in power or authority. **2** greatest (*supreme happiness*).

sura /**soo**-ra/ *n* any of the main chapters in the Koran.

surcharge /**sur**-charge/ *n* an extra charge (*a surcharge for taxis ordered after midnight*).

sure /**shoor**/ *adj* **1** certain (*I'm sure he'll come*). **2** convinced of (*sure of her own ability*). **3** unfailing (*a sure remedy*).

surely /**shoor**-lee/ *adv* without doubt.

surf /**surf**/ *n* the foamy water caused by waves breaking on a sloping shore.

surfboard *see* **surfing**.

surface /**sur**-fiss/ *n* **1** the outside or top part of anything. **2** outside appearance (*she seems happy on the surface*). ● *vb* to rise to the surface (*divers surfacing*).

surfeit /**sur**-fut/ *n* too much of anything (*a surfeit of rich food*). ● *vb* to overfeed.

surfing /**sur**-fing/ *n* **1** the sport of riding on the crest of large waves while standing on a long, narrow board with a rounded or pointed front end, called a **surfboard** /**surf**-board/. **2** the act of moving from site to site on the Internet looking for something interesting. ● *vb* **surf** /**surf**/.

surge /**surge**/ *n* the rising of a wave, the up-and-down movement of the surface of the sea. ● *vb* to rise, to well up, as a wave.

surgeon /**sur**-jin/ *n* a doctor skilled in surgery.

surgery /**sur**-je-ree/ *n* **1** the art or science of curing disease by cutting the body open to fix whatever is wrong. **2** the room in which surgery takes place.

surgical /sur-ji-cal/ *adj* having to do with surgery (*surgical treatment*).

surly /sur-lee/ *adj* gloomy and ill-humored. ● *n* **surliness** /sur-lee-ness/.

surname /sur-name/ *n* a person's family name.

surpass /sur-**pass**/ *vb* to do better than (*his performance surpassed that of the others*).

surpassing /sur-**pa**-sing/ *adj* excellent.

surplus /sur-plus/ *n* the amount by which anything is more than is required (*a surplus of apples that autumn*).

surprise /sur-**prize**/ *n* **1** the feeling caused by what is sudden or unexpected. **2** a sudden or unexpected event, gift, piece of news, etc. (*it was a surprise when she arrived*). ● *vb* **1** to come upon when not expected. **2** to take unawares, to startle, to astonish (*surprising the enemy*). ● *adj* **surprising** /sur-**prie**-zing/.

surreal /su-**reel**/ *adj* bizarre, strange, of or related to surrealism.

surrealism /su-**ree**-ul-iz-um/ *n* an artistic style that focuses on the unconscious mind, dreams, and fantastic, irrational subject material. ● *adj* **surrealistic** /su-**ree**-u-li-stic/.

surrender /su-**ren**-der/ *vb* **1** to stop fighting and accept the enemy's terms, to give up. **2** to hand over (*have to surrender his passport at the border*). ● *also n*.

surrey /su-ree/ *n* a light, four-wheeled carriage of the late 19th and early-20th centuries.

surrogate /su-ru-gate/ *n* **1** a substitute. **2** a woman who, by agreement, has the baby of another woman who cannot for some reason bear the child. ● *adj* (*surrogate mother*). ● *n* **surrogacy** /su-ru-ga-see/ the fact or condition of being a surrogate.

surround /su-**round**/ *vb* to go, put, or be on all sides of (*trees surrounding the house/an army surrounding the city*).

surroundings /su-**round**-dingz/ *npl* the objects or country around a person or place (*live in beautiful surroundings*).

surveillance /sur-**vay**-lanse/ *n* a careful watch (*he was under police surveillance*).

survey /sur-**vay**/ *vb* **1** to look over. **2** to look at carefully. **3** to measure an area of land and make a plan of it. ● *n* **survey** /sur-vay/ **1** a general view. **2** the measuring of a piece of land. **3** a plan made of a piece of land.

surveyor /sur-**vay**-ur/ *n* a person who surveys land.

survival /sur-**vie**-val/ *n* **1** act of surviving. **2** a person or thing that has lived on from a past age. ● **survival of the fittest** the belief that only those kinds of plants, animals, etc., live on that have been able to adapt themselves to their surroundings.

survivalist /sur-**vie**-va-list/ *n* a person who is determined to survive.

survive /sur-**vive**/ *vb* **1** to live on after (*she survived her husband*). **2** to continue to live or exist (*several were killed, but she survived*).

survivor /sur-**vie**-vur/ *n* a person who has lived on, especially after a disaster (*survivors of the plane crash*).

susceptible /su-**sep**-ti-bul/ *adj* easily influenced or affected by (*susceptible to colds/susceptible children*). ● *n* **susceptibility** /su-sep-ti-**bi**-li-tee/.

sushi /**soo**-shee/ *n* a Japanese dish of small cakes of cold rice served with raw or cooked fish, vegetables, etc.

suspect /su-**spect**/ *vb* **1** to think something is the case but have no proof (*I suspect that he is leaving*). **2** to mistrust, to doubt the truth of. **3** to believe to be guilty (*suspect him of murder*). ● *n* **suspect** /**su**-spect/ a person who is suspected. ● *adj* **suspect** /**su**-spect/ doubtful, not worthy of trust.

suspend /su-**spend**/ *vb* **1** to hang from (*hooks suspended from the roof*). **2** to cause to stop for a time (*sales of the product have been suspended*).

suspenders /su-**spen**-derz/ *n* **suspenders** *n pl* elastic straps for holding up pants.

suspense /su-**spense**/ *n* uncertainty or anxiety about what may happen in the future (*the suspense of waiting for exam results*).

suspension /su-**spen**-shun/ *n* the state of being suspended.

suspension bridge /su-**spen**-shun-bridge/ *n* a bridge suspended by chains or steel ropes from towers or arches.

suspicion /su-**spi**-shun/ *n* a feeling of doubt or mistrust.

suspicious /su-**spi**-shus/ *adj* doubtful, mistrustful (*suspicious about his neighbor's activities*).

sustain /su-**stane**/ *vb* **1** to keep up, to support (*sustain the weight of the statue*). **2** to give strength to (*sustained by a good meal*). **3** to keep in existence over a long period (*sustain his interest*). **4** to undergo (*sustain damage*). ● *adj* **sustainable** /su-**stay**-na-bul/ able to be sustained.

sustenance /su-sti-nanse/ *n* food, nourishment.

suture /soo-chur/ *n* the act of joining together as by sewing. ● *vb* to join together by sewing.

SUV /ess-yoo-vee/ *abbr* = **Sport Utility Vehicle**: a vehicle the size of a truck that can be driven off-road.

svelte /svelt/ *adj* slender and graceful, polished, sophisticated.

swab /swob/ *n* **1** a pad of cotton (sometimes wrapped around a stick) used for cleansing wounds, applying medicines, etc. **2** a mop for cleaning decks, etc. ● *vb* (**swabbed** /swobd/, **swabbing** /swob-ing/) to clean with a swab.

swagger /swa-ger/ *vb* to walk proudly, to behave boastfully (*swagger down the road after winning the fight*). ● *also n.*

swallow[1] /swaw-loe/ *vb* **1** to draw down the throat and into the stomach (*swallow pills*). **2** to enclose in the middle of something bigger (*villages swallowed up by the growing city*). **3** to believe without question (*did not swallow the story*). ● *n* the act of swallowing.

swallow[2] /swaw-loe/ *n* a bird with long wings and a forked tail.

swami /swa-mee/ *n* a Hindu title of respect, especially for a religious leader.

swamp /swawmp/ *n* wet, marshy ground. ● *vb* **1** to flood. **2** to overwhelm by greater numbers or strength (*swamped by letters of application*).

swampy /swawm-pee/ *adj* soft and wet, marshy.

swan /swon/ *n* a long-necked bird of the duck family.

swank /swangk/ *n* a stylish display of dress, behavior, etc. ● *adj* swanky /swang-kee/.

swap /swop/ *vb* (**swapped** /swopt/, **swapping** /swop-ing/) to exchange (one thing for another) (*the children are swapping model cars*).

swarm /swawrm/ *n* **1** a large number of insects (e.g., bees) moving as a group. **2** a large, closely packed crowd (*swarms of people going to the sales*). ● *vb* **1** to come together in large numbers. **2** (*of bees, etc.*) to leave the hive in a body.

swarthy /swawr-thee/ *adj* dark-skinned.

swash /swosh/ *n* a body of swift, dashing water, the splashing of water or the sound of this.

swastika /swos-ti-ca/ *n* an ancient symbol of a cross with four equal arms each bent at right angles. Found throughout history, but during the 20th century it was used to symbolize Nazi Germany and Nazi beliefs.

swat /swot/ *vb* (**swatted** /swot-ider/, **swatting** /swot-ing/) to hit sharply, to crush (*swat the flies*).

swatch /swotch/ *n* a sample piece of cloth.

swathe /swathe/ *vb* to wrap up in bandages o clothing. ● *n* swathe *or* swath.

sway /sway/ *vb* **1** to move with a rocking motion from side to side or backward and forward (*tree. swaying in the wind*). **2** to rule, to have influence over (*he's easily swayed*). ● *n* **1** a rocking movement. **2** control, rule.

swear /sware/ *vb* (*pt* **swore** /swore/, *pp* **sworn** swoarn/) **1** to promise to tell the truth. **2** to declare something is true. **3** to use bad words o bad language, to use words that are considered offensive and socially unacceptable.

sweat /swet/ *n* the moisture that oozes from the body when it is overheated, perspiration. ● *vb* to perspire. **2** to work very hard (*sweat to pass the exams*). **3** to employ for low wages.

sweater /swe-ter/ *n* a heavy close-fitting knitted woolen outer garment for the upper body; a close fitting garment put on over the head (*he wears a warm sweater over his shirt*).

sweaty /swe-tee/ *adj* (*inf*) damp with perspiration (*sweaty feet*).

sweep /sweep/ *vb* (*pt, pp* **swept** /swept/) **1** to clean with a brush or broom (*sweep the floor*). **2** to move over swiftly and smoothly (*the waves swept toward the shore/panic swept through the crowd*) **3** to remove with an extensive or curving move ment (*sweep the papers into the drawer*). ● *n* an extensive or curving movement. **2** a quick look over. **3** a person who cleans chimneys. ● **sweep the board** to win everything offered or at stake.

sweeping /swee-ping/ *adj* **1** wide, extensive (*sweeping changes*). **2** not taking sufficient account o exceptions (*a sweeping generalization*).

sweet /sweet/ *adj* **1** tasting like honey or sugar (*sweet fruit*). **2** having a pleasing smell (*the swee smell of roses*). **3** pleasing to the senses (*swee music*). **4** gentle and likable (*she's a sweet old lady*). **5** pretty (*a sweet dress*). ● *n* **1** a candy. **2** dessert. ● *adv* sweetly /sweet-lee/. ● **have sweet tooth** to like eating sweet-tasting things

sweeten /swee-ten/ *vb* to make or become swee (*sweeten the pudding with honey*). ● *n* sweetene a thing that makes something sweet. ● *n* **sweet ening** /sweet-ning/ the process of making some thing sweet.

sweetheart /sweet-hart/ *n* a person dearly loved, lover.

sweet pea /sweet-pee/ *n* a garden plant with sweet smelling flowers.

sweet potato /sweet-pu-**tay**-toe/ *n* a plant whose orange-colored root is used as a vegetable.

swell /swell/ *vb* (*pp* **swollen** /**swo**-len/) **1** to grow larger (*the lump is swelling*). **2** to make or become louder (*the music swelled*). **3** to bulge out (*with stomach swelling*). **4** (*of the sea*) to rise and fall in large waves that do not break. ● *n* **1** movement of the sea in large waves that do not break. **2** (*inf*) a very well-dressed person.

swelling /**swe**-ling/ *n* a lump raised for a time on the body by a bruise, infected cut, etc. (*a swelling on her neck*).

swelter /**swel**-ter/ *vb* to be very hot, to be uncomfortable because of great heat (*tourists sweltering in high temperatures*). ● *adj* **sweltering** /**swel**-tring/.

swerve /swerv/ *vb* to turn or move suddenly to one side (*the driver swerved to avoid the dog*). ● *also n.*

swift /swift/ *adj* quick-moving, speedy.

swig /swig/ *vb* (**swigged** /swigd/, **swigging** /**swi**-ging/) (*inf*) to drink in large mouthfuls. ● *n* (*inf*) a large mouthful (*a swig of water*).

swim /swim/ *vb* (**swam** /swam/, **swimming** /**swi**-ming/, *pp* **swum** /swum/) **1** to move through the water by moving the arms and legs. **2** to float in or on the top of (*a stew swimming with fat*). **3** to be dizzy (*with head swimming*). ● *n* act of swimming. ● *n* **swimmer** /**swi**-mer/. ● **in the swim** knowing what is going on, knowing important people.

swimmingly /**swi**-ming-lee/ *adv* smoothly, with great success (*everything went swimmingly*).

swimsuit /**swim**-soot/ *n* a bathing suit; a garment worn for swimming.

swimwear /**swim**-ware/ *n* garments worn for swimming.

swindle /**swin**-dul/ *vb* to cheat. ● *n* a deception intended to cheat people, a fraud (*the cheap holiday offer was a swindle*).

swindler /**swin**-dler/ *n* a cheat, a person who tricks people out of money.

swine /swine/ *n* (*pl* **swine**) **1** a pig. **2** (*inf*) a very nasty person.

swing /swing/ *vb* (*pt, pp* **swung** /swung/) **1** to move to and fro, especially when suspended from above (*children swinging from a branch*). **2** to whirl around (*dancers swinging*). **3** to turn around when at anchor. **4** to walk quickly with a swaying movement (*swing along the promenade*). ● *n* **1** a seat suspended by ropes, etc., on which a person can swing to and fro (*the swings in the park*). **2** a swinging movement. **3** a type of jazz music. **4** a long-range blow given with a curved arm. ● **in full swing** in progress (*the party was in full swing*).

swinging /**swing**-ing/ *adj* **1** moving to and fro. **2** done with a swing; lively, fashionable.

swipe /swipe/ *vb* **1** to hit hard with a swinging movement (*swipe the mosquito*). **2** (*inf*) to steal. ● *n* a hard, sweeping blow.

swirl /swirl/ *vb* to flow or move with a circular motion (*water swirling/her skirt swirled*). ● *n* a circular motion of water.

swish /swish/ *n* the sound made by a light or thin object moving through the air (*the swish of her skirt*). ● *vb* to move through the air with a swish.

switch /switch/ *n* **1** an easily bent stick. **2** a small lever for turning on and off electric current (*the light switch*). ● *vb* **1** to hit with a switch. **2** to turn electric current (on or off). **3** to change suddenly (*switch courses*).

switchboard /**switch**-board/ *n* a board at which connection can be made between one telephone line and another.

swivel /**swi**-vul/ *n* a ring that turns freely around a stable pin. ● *vb* [**swiveled** /**swi**-vuld/, **swiveling** /**swiv**-ling/; *also* **swivelled**, **swivelling** (*Br, Cdn*)] to turn around, as on a swivel.

swoon /swoon/ *vb* to faint. ● *n* a fainting turn.

swoop /swoop/ *vb* **1** to fly down upon with a sudden swift movement (*hawks swooping*). **2** to come upon swiftly and suddenly (*the police swooped down on the smugglers in a dawn raid*). ● *n* **1** a sudden downward rush. **2** a sudden attack.

sword /sawrd/ *n* a weapon with a long blade and sharp point for cutting or thrusting.

swordfish /**sawrd**-fish/ *n* a large fish whose upper jaw sticks out and comes to a point like a sword.

sycamore /**si**-ca-more/ *n* a large tree, of the same family as the maple and fig tree.

sycophant /**si**-cu-fant/ *n* a person who flatters another to gain his or her favor. ● *adj* **sycophantic** /si-cu-**fan**-tic/.

syllable /**si**-la-bul/ *n* a part of a word or a word containing one vowel sound. ● *adj* **syllabic** /si-**la**-bic/.

syllabus /**si**-la-bus/ *n* a plan for a course of study, giving subjects to be studied, times of classes, etc.

symbol /**sim**-bul/ *n* **1** an emblem or sign made to stand for or represent something else (*Ag is the symbol for silver*). **2** a sign that all recognize as bearing a certain meaning (*the symbol of peace is an olive branch*).

symbolic /sim-**bol**-ic/ *adj* standing for or representing something else. ● *adv* **symbolically** /sim-**bol**-ic-lee/.

symbolism /**sim**-bu-li-zum/ *n* the use of symbols.

symbolize /**sim**-bu-lize/ *vb, also* **symbolise** (*Br*) to stand as a sign for (*an olive branch symbolizing peace*).

symmetrical /si-**met**-ri-cal/ *adj* **1** having a balanced or regular design (*symmetrical patterns*). **2** graceful because the parts are in pleasing proportion to one another and to the whole.

symmetry /**si**-mi-tree/ *n* **1** sameness between the two halves of a design. **2** a pleasing similarity or contrast between parts, beauty resulting from graceful proportions.

sympathetic /sim-pa-**thet**-ic/ *adj* showing or feeling understanding or pity.

sympathize /**sim**-pa-thize/ *vb, also* **sympathise** (*Br*) **1** to feel with and for another. **2** to be in agreement with.

sympathy /**sim**-pa-thee/ *n* **1** understanding of the sorrow or distress of another, pity. **2** agreement with the opinion of another (*in sympathy with his views on the environment*).

symphony /**sim**-fu-nee/ *n* **1** a piece of music written for a full orchestra. **2** (*lit*) a pleasant unison of sounds, colors, etc. ● *adj* **symphonic** /sim-**fon**-ic/.

symptom /**sim**(p)-tum/ *n* **1** a sign or mark by which something can be recognized. **2** one of the signs by which a doctor is able to recognize the disease affecting a patient. ● *adj* **symptomatic** /sim(p)-tu-**ma**-tic/.

synagogue /**si**-nu-gog/ *n* a place where Jewish people go to worship.

synchronize /**sing**-cru-nize/ *vb also* **synchronise** (*Br*) **1** to happen or cause to happen at the same time (*synchronize our plans*). **2** to set to exactly the same time (*synchronizing watches*).

syncopate /**sing**-cu-pate/ *vb* to change the rhythm of music by beginning or ending notes slightly sooner or later than is strictly correct. ● *n* **syncopation** /sing-cu-**pay**-shun/.

syndicate /**sin**-di-cit/ *n* **1** a group of persons or companies who are working together for busines reasons or financial gain. ● *vb* **1** to join together i a syndicate. **2** to sell for publication in more tha one journal, newspaper, etc. (*syndicating his co umn across the United States*).

syndrome /**sin**-drome/ *n* a number of symptoms oc curring together and being from a specific diseas or condition.

synonym /**si**-nu-nim/ *n* a word having the same c nearly the same meaning as another word.

synonymous /si-**non**-im-us/ *adj* having the sam meaning.

synopsis /si-**nop**-sis/ *n* a summary, a short accou of the main happenings or ideas in a book.

syntax /**sin**-taks/ *n* the putting of words in a sen tence in order and in the correct relation to eac other. ● *adjs* **syntactic**(**al**) /sin-**tac**-tic-(al)/.

synthesis /**sin**-thi-sis/ *n* the putting together of part to make a whole.

synthetic /sini-**thet**-ic/ *adj* made or put together b artificial means, not natural (*synthetic materials*)

syphon /**sie**-fun/ *n same as* **siphon**.

syringe /si-**rinj**/ *n* a tube filled with a piston by mean of which fluid can be drawn up or squirted out. ● *vb* to squirt or spray with a syringe.

syrup /**si**-rup/ *n* **1** any thick, sweet-tasting liqui (*maple syrup*). **2** the thick liquid obtained whe refining cane sugar.

system /**si**-stum/ *n* **1** a method by which a numbe of parts of different kinds are made to work to gether as a unified whole (*the nervous system/ transport system/the solar system*). **2** a regula method of doing things (*he has no system in work ing*). **3** a plan (*a system for winning the lottery*).

systematic /si-stu-**mat**-ic/ *adj* methodical, arrange in an orderly or reasonable manner, following a pre arranged plan.

systematize /**si**-stu-ma-tize/ *vb, also* **systematis** (*Br*) to reduce to a system.

T

T, t /**tee**/ the twentieth letter of the alphabet.

tab /**tab**/ *n* a small piece of paper, fabric, etc., sticking out from something larger, a small flap (*the tab on the box of detergent*).

tabby /**ta**-bee/ *n* a female cat.

tabernacle /**ta**-ber-na-cul/ *n* a place of worship.

table /**tay**-bul/ *n* **1** an article of furniture with legs and a flat top, used for placing or resting things on (*the dining table*). **2** a list of figures, names, facts, etc., arranged in columns (*a table showing the times of the buses*). ● *vb* to put forward for discussion (*tabling a motion*). ● **turn the tables on** to begin doing to another what he or she has been doing to you.

tableau /**ta**-blo/ *n* (*pl* **tableaux** /**ta**-bloaz/) a scene in which people stand motionless as if figures in a picture (*the pageant consisted of a series of historical tableaux*).

tablecloth /**tay**-bul cloth/ *n* a piece of material that is spread over a dining table.

table manners /**tay**-bul **man**-ers/ *npl* good behavior while at the dinner table.

tablespoon /**tay**-bul-spoon/ *n* a large spoon used for serving at the table or as a measure in cooking.

tablet /**ta**-blet/ *n* **1** a piece of cardboard or flat piece of metal or stone with some writing or signs on it (*a tablet on the wall in memory of a local hero*). **2** a small flat slab (*a tablet of paper*). **3** a pill (*sleeping tablets*).

table tennis /**tay**-bul-te-nis/ *n* a game like tennis, played with paddles and a light plastic ball on a table with a net across the middle.

tabloid /**ta**-bloid/ *n* a small-format newspaper, usually with emphasis on photographs and news in condensed form.

taboo, tabu /**ta**-boo/ *adj* set apart so as not to be touched or used, forbidden for religious reasons or because it is against social custom (*alcohol is taboo in Muslim countries*). ● *n* an order not to touch or use something.

tabular /**ta**-byu-lar/ *adj* set out in columns or tables (*information in tabular form*).

tabulate /**ta**-byu-late/ *vb* to arrange in columns or tables in a systematic way (*tabulate the results of the experiment*). ● *ns* **tabulation** /**ta**-byu-**lay**-shun/, **tabulator** /**ta**-byu-lay-tor/.

tacit /**ta**-sit/ *adj* thought or intended, but not spoken (*tacit agreement*).

taciturn /**ta**-si-turn/ *adj* speaking little, silent by nature (*he was so taciturn that it was difficult to get to know him*). ● *n* **taciturnity** /**ta**-si-**tur**-ni-tee/.

tack /**tack**/ *n* **1** a small sharp nail with a broad head. **2** a long, loose stitch. **3** the zigzag course of a sailing ship when sailing against the wind. ● *vb* **1** to nail with tacks (*tack the notice to the wall*). **2** to sew with long, loose stitches. **3** (*of a sailing ship*) to change course to catch the wind. **4** to add on (*they had tacked on an extra question to the test paper*). ● **on the wrong tack** on the wrong trail (*the police were on the wrong tack in the murder investigation*).

tackle /**ta**-cul/ *n* **1** all the equipment needed for some sport or game (*fishing tackle*). **2** all the things necessary for a task. **3** a series of ropes, pulleys, etc., for raising weights, sails, etc. ● *vb* **1** to struggle with, to seize and pull down (*tackle the bank robber*). **2** (*in football*) to prevent from advancing with the ball. **3** to try to do (*tackle the job*). **4** to speak to or put questions to (*he tackled him about the unemployment issue*).

tacky[1] /**ta**-kee/ *adj* sticky (*the paint is still tacky*). ● *n* **tackiness** /**ta**-kee-ness/.

tacky[2] /**ta**-kee/ *adj* (*inf*) cheap, in bad taste (*tacky décor*). ● *n* **tackiness** /**ta**-kee-ness/.

taco /**ta**-co/ *n* a tortilla that is fried until crisp and folded, with a filling, used in Mexican cooking.

tact /**tact**/ *n* the ability to speak or behave without hurting the feelings of others, consideration (*husband and wife are not speaking to each other and so act with tact*). ● *adjs* **tactful** /**tact**-ful/, **tactless** /**tact**-less/. ● *advs* **tactfully** /**tact**-fu-lee/, **tactlessly** /**tact**-less-lee/.

tactical /**tac**-ti-cul/ *adj* having to do with tactics (*tactical military maneuvers*). ● *adv* **tactically** /**ta**-ti-cu-lee/.

tactician /**tac**-**ti**-shun/ *n* **1** a person who is skilled in tactics. **2** a person who is quick to see a possible advantage.

tactics /**tac**-tics/ *npl* **1** the art of moving armies or other warlike forces during battle. **2** any actions intended to gain an immediate advantage (*tactics required to win the match*).

tactile /**tac**-tile/ *adj* having to do with the sense of touch (*the tactile qualities*).

tadpole /**tad**-pole/ *n* the young of a frog, toad, etc., just after it has come out of the egg.

taffeta /**ta**-fi-ta/ *n* a shiny silk material.

tag[1] /**tag**/ *n* **1** the metal point at the end of a shoe-lace. **2** an address label. **3** a common quotation or saying. ● *vb* (**tagged** /**tagd**/, **tagging** /**ta**-ging/) to fasten on.

tag[2] /**tag**/ *n* a children's game in which one person chases the others, tapping on the shoulder the first one caught, who then becomes the chaser.

tail /**tail**/ *n* **1** a long hanging part of an animal's body, situated at the end of the spine. **2** the back part of anything (*the tail of the line*).

tailcoat /**tail**-coat/ *n* a man's coat, short in front, long and divided down the middle at the back.

tail end /**tail**-end/ *n* the last or back part (*he was at the tail end of his speech*).

tailgate /**tail**-gate/ *n* a board for closing the back of a cart or truck. ● *vb* to drive too closely to another vehicle.

tail light /**tail** lite/ *n* the light at the back of a vehicle.

tailor /**tay**-lor/ *n* a person who makes clothing, especially for men. ● *vb* to make clothing.

tails /**tailz**/ *npl* **1** the reverse side of a coin. **2** a tailcoat.

taint /**taint**/ *vb* to spoil or make bad (*tainted meat/taint his reputation*). ● *n* **1** a stain, an evil element that spoils the rest. **2** a mark of shame or disgrace.

take /**take**/ *vb* (*pt* **took** /**took**/, *pp* **taken** /**tay**-ken/) **1** to seize or grasp. **2** to receive or accept. **3** to capture (*the army took the city*). **4** to carry. **5** to travel by (bus, etc.). **6** to eat (*take fruit*). **7** to require (numbers, time, material, etc.). ● **take after** to be like. ● **take down** to write (notes, etc.). ● **take for** to think to be (*they took him for a fool*). ● **take heart** to become braver. ● **take in 1** to deceive (*they pretended to be workingmen and took in the old lady*). **2** to understand (*scarcely able to take in the news*). **3** to make (a garment) smaller. ● **take off 1** to remove. **2** to leave the ground when beginning to fly. **3** to imitate mockingly (*to take off their boss*). ● **take on** to agree to play or fight against. ● **take over** to get control of (*take over the running of the store*). ● **take place** to happen. ● **take to** to begin to like (*he did not take to her*). ● **take up** to begin to do or study. ● **take up with** to begin to go about with.

take-out /**tay**-kout/ *n* ready-cooked food bought from a restaurant or store to be eaten elsewhere.

takeover /**take**-oa-ver/ *n* an instance of getting control if something, especially a business.

talc /**talc**/ *n* **1** a glasslike mineral. **2** a fine powder for the skin made from this.

talcum powder /**tal**-cum-pow-der/ *n* a fine, perfumed powder made from talc (*powder the baby with talcum*).

tale /**tale**/ *n* a story.

talent /**ta**-lent/ *n* special ability or skill (*a talent for dealing with people*).

talented /**ta**-len-tid/ *adj* very clever.

talisman /**ta**-liz-man/ *n* (*pl* **talismans** /**ta**-liz-manz/) an object, word or words supposed to possess magic powers.

talk /**tawk**/ *vb* to speak. ● *n* **1** a conversation. **2** a lecture (*a talk on local history*). **3** gossip (*there is a lot of talk about their affair*). ● **talk over** to discuss. ● **talk (someone) around** to convince. ● **talk to** to scold.

talkative /**taw**-ka-tiv/ *adj* fond of talking.

tall /**tawl**/ *adj* **1** high (*he was over six feet tall*). **2** above the usual height.

tallow /**ta**-lo/ *n* the melted fat of animals.

tally /**ta**-lee/ *n* **1** an account. **2** a score or count (*keep a tally of money spent*). ● *vb* to agree with, to fit (*his account of events does not tally with hers*).

Talmud /**tal**-mood/ *n* the Jewish system of law.

talon /**ta**-lon/ *n* the claw of a bird of prey (*the eagle's talons*).

tamale /tuh-**ma**-lee/ *n* a Mexican dish of spicy chopped meat rolled in cornmeal dough that is cooked by steaming.

tambourine /tam-bu-**reen**/ *n* a small one-sided drum with rattling metal disks around its sides, played by hand.

tame /**tame**/ *adj* **1** not wild. **2** trained to be obedient. **3** not exciting, dull (*life in the little village was considered tame*). ● *vb* to make tame.

tamper /**tam**-per/ *vb* to meddle with, to interfere with dishonestly or unlawfully (*tamper with the evidence*).

tan /**tan**/ *n* **1** bark of trees crushed for use in preparing leather. **2** a light brown color. **3** suntan (*hope to get a tan on vacation*). ● *vb* (**tanned** /**tand**/, **tanning** /**ta**-ning/) **1** to treat animal skins so as to turn them into leather. **2** to make or become brown from sunburn. ● *adj* light brown in color (*tan shoes*).

tandem /**tan**-dem/ *adj* one behind the other. ● *n* a bicycle for two persons, one sitting behind the other.

tandoori /tan-**doo**-ree/ *n* an Indian way of cooking meat in a clay pot.

tang /**tang**/ *n* **1** a sharp taste (*the tang of the sea air*). **2** a characteristic flavor.

tangent /**tan**-jent/ *n* a straight line touching a circle but not cutting it. ● **go off at a tangent** to begin talking about something quite different (*his speech was difficult to follow because he would often go off at a tangent*).

tangible /**tan**-ji-bul/ *adj* **1** able to be touched. **2** real, actual (*no tangible evidence*). ● *adv* **tangibly** /**tan**-ji-blee/.

tangle /**tang**-gul/ *vb* **1** to interweave in a confused way that is difficult to undo. **2** to muddle. ● *n* **1** a mass of confusedly interwoven thread, string, etc. **2** a muddle, a complication.

tango /**tang**-go/ *n* a South American dance.

tank /**tangk**/ *n* **1** a large container for storing water, oil, etc. **2** a fighting vehicle protected by thick metal plates and moving on caterpillar tracks (*the advance of enemy tanks*).

tankard /**tang**-kard/ *n* a large metal drinking mug (*a tankard of beer*).

tanker /**tang**-ker/ *n* a cargo ship with tanks for carrying oil.

tanned /**tand**/ *adj* **1** made brown by the sun (*they were tanned after their vacation*). **2** made into leather.

tannery /**ta**-ne-ree/ *n* a place where leather is made.

tannic /**ta**-nic/ *adj* having to do with tannin (*tannic acid*).

tannin /**ta**-nin/ *n* a substance found in the bark of the oak and certain other trees, used in tanning leather.

tantalize /**tan**-ta-lize/ *vb, also* **tantalise** (*Br*) to torment by raising false hopes (*hungry people tantalized by the cooking smells*).

tantrum /**tan**-trum/ *n* a fit of bad temper or ill-humor (*the angry child had a tantrum*).

tap[1] /**tap**/ *n* **1** a stopper. **2** (*Br*) see **faucet**. ● *vb* (**tapped** /**tapt**/, **tapping** /**ta**-ping/) **1** to fit with a tap. **2** to draw liquid out of. **3** to obtain information from.

tap[2] /**tap**/ *vb* (**tapped** /**tapt**/, **tapping** /**ta**-ping/) **1** to strike lightly (*tap him on the shoulder*). **2** to knock gently (*tap the door*). ● *also n*.

tap-dance /**tap**-danse/ *vb* to dance with shoes with metal plates on the soles, making elaborate tapping sounds on the floor. ● *ns* **tap-dancer** /**tap**-dan-ser/, **tap-dancing** /**tap**-dan-sing/.

tape /**tape**/ *n* **1** a long, narrow strip of cloth, paper, or sticky material (*he used tape to seal the parcel*). **2** a sensitized strip for recording and transmitting sound or pictures (*audiotape*). ● *also vb*.

tape measure /**tape**-me-zhur/ *n* a strong tape of cloth, metal, etc., used for measuring (*measure her waist with a tape measure*).

taper /**tay**-per/ *n* a long wick coated with wax, like a thin candle. ● *vb* to become narrow or thinner at one end.

tape recorder /**tape**-ri-**cawr**-der/ *n* a machine for recording and transmitting sounds on magnetic tape. ● *n* **tape-recording** /**tape**-ri-**cawr**-ding/.

tapestry /**ta**-pe-stree/ *n* a large piece of cloth in which different colored threads are worked together to make a picture, sometimes hung on walls as a decoration.

tapeworm /**tape**-wurm/ *n* a long tapelike worm sometimes found in the intestines.

tapioca /**ta**-pee-yo-ca/ *n* **1** an edible grain obtained from a West Indian plant. **2** a pudding made from it.

tapir /**tay**-pir/ *n* a piglike animal of South America.

tar /**tar**/ *n* **1** a thick, black, sticky substance obtained from wood or coal (*get tar on his shoes from the road*). **2** (*old*) a sailor. ● *vb* (**tarred** /**tard**/, **tarring** /**ta**-ring/) to coat with tar.

tarantula /**ta**-ran-chu-la/ *n* a large poisonous spider.

tardy /**tar**-dee/ *adj* (*old*) slow, late (*tardy in making a decision*). ● *n* **tardiness** /**tar**-dee-ness/.

target /**tar**-git/ *n* **1** something set up for aiming or shooting at (*the archers set up a target*). **2** a goal or result that you hope to achieve (*the charity's target was $20,000*). ● *vb* to make someone the object or focus of something (*target single parents with their advertising campaign*).

tariff /**ta**-rif/ *n* **1** the tax to be paid on an imported commodity. **2** a list of the taxes to be paid on imported goods. **3** a list of charges.

tarnish /**tar**-nish/ *vb* **1** to make less bright, to discolor (*it tarnished with age*). **2** to spoil (*tarnish their reputation*).

tarpaulin /**tar**-paw-lin/ *n* strong cloth or canvas covered with tar to make it waterproof (*cover the load in the trailer with a tarpaulin*).

tarragon /**ta**-ra-gon/ *n* a plant with leaves that are used to add flavor in cooking.

tarry[1] /**ta**-ree/ *adj* coated with tar.

tarry[2] /**ta**-ree/ *vb* (*old or lit*) to stay, to delay, to wait behind.

tart[1] /**tart**/ *n* a pastry containing jam or fruit.

tart[2] /**tart**/ *adj* **1** sharp-tasting (*a tart sauce*). **2** sour, biting, sarcastic (*tart remarks*).

tartan /**tar**-tan/ *n* a plaid cloth with stripes and squares of different colors, especially when worn as part of Scottish Highland dress.

tartar /**tar**-tar/ *n* **1** a crust of lime left by wine in a barrel. **2** a hard substance that forms on the teeth.

3 a hot-tempered person, a person who is hard to manage (*everyone is afraid of her, she is a real tartar*).

task /task/ *n* a piece of work to be done (*given the task of washing the dishes*). ● *vb* to lay upon as a burden.

task force /task-foarss/ *n* a group of people brought together to deal with a particular problem (*a police task force appointed to reduce youth crime*).

taskmaster /task-ma-ster/ *n* (*old*) a person who sets work to be done and sees that it is done properly.

tassel /ta-sel/ *n* an ornamental knot with loose threads hanging down from it (*a beret with a tassel on it*).

taste /tayst/ *n* **1** the sense by which you judge whether food is pleasant or unpleasant (*had a cold and lost her sense of taste*). **2** the ability to distinguish what is fine, beautiful, or correct from what is not so (*have good taste in décor*). **3** the flavor of food when eaten (*soup lacking in taste*). **4** a small portion of food for testing. ● *vb* **1** to eat to see whether pleasant or unpleasant. **2** to have a flavor (of) (*taste of lemon*).

tasteful /tayst-ful/ *adj* showing good taste or judgment (*tasteful wallpaper*). ● *adv* **tastefully** /tayst-fu-lee/.

tasteless /tayst-less/ *adj* **1** having no flavor (*tasteless food*). **2** showing bad taste or judgment (*a tasteless remark*).

tasty /tay-stee/ *adj* having a pleasing flavor (*tasty food*).

tattered /ta-terd/ *adj* ragged (*tattered clothing*).

tatters /ta-terz/ *npl* ragged clothing.

tattle /ta-tul/ *vb* to tell someone in authority about another's mistake or wrongdoing to get them into trouble.

tattletale /ta-tul tale/ *n* a person who tells others, in a gossipy way, about someone's mistakes, wrong-doings or secrets to get them into trouble.

tattoo[1] /ta-too/ *vb* to make a colored design on the skin by pricking holes in it and filling them with colored matter (*got her arm tattooed with a red butterfly*). ● *also n*.

tattoo[2] /ta-too/ *n* **1** beating of a drum, blowing of a bugle, etc., to recall soldiers to camp at night. **2** a night display of military drill, exercises, etc., to music.

tatty /ta-tee/ *adj* shabby, worn (*a tatty old coat*).

taught /tawt/ *pt of* teach.

taunt /tawnt/ *vb* to make fun of in order to hurt, to mock, to sneer at (*taunt the boy because he is poor*). ● *n* a mocking or hurtful remark.

taut /tawt/ *adj* stretched tight (*pull the rope taut*).

tautology /taw-tol-o-jee/ *n* saying the same thing again in different words. ● *adj* **tautological** /taw-tu-lodge-i-cal/.

tavern /ta-vern/ *n* an inn, a bar.

tawdry /taw-dree/ *adj* showy but cheap or of bad quality (*a store selling tawdry souvenirs*). ● *n* **tawdriness** /taw-dree-ness/.

tawny /taw-nee/ *adj* yellowish brown.

tax /taks/ *n* money paid to the government to help pay for public services. ● *vb* **1** to raise a tax. **2** to charge a tax on. **3** to accuse (*tax him with cruelty*). **4** to be a hard test for (*tax his strength*). ● *adj* **taxable** /tak-sa-bul/.

taxation /tak-say-shun/ *n* **1** all the taxes paid. **2** the charging of taxes.

taxi /tak-see/ *n* a motor car for hire, especially one fitted with a machine (**taximeter**) showing the amount to be paid as a fare. ● *also* **taxicab** /tak-see-cab/. ● *vb* (*of an airplane*) to run along the ground (*planes taxied down the runway*).

taxidermist /tak-si-der-mist/ *n* a person who is skilled in taxidermy.

taxidermy /tak-si-der-mee/ *n* the art of stuffing the skins of dead animals to make them look like living animals.

tea /tee/ *n* **1** a shrub found in India and China. **2** its leaves, dried. **3** a drink made by pouring boiling water on dried tea leaves (*a cup of tea*). **4** a light afternoon or evening meal (*invite them to tea*).

teach /teech/ *vb* (*pt, pp* **taught** /tawt/) **1** to give information about (*teach English*). **2** to show how to do something (*teach him how to drive*). **3** to give lessons to (*teach elementary students*). ● *n* **teaching** /tee-ching/.

teacher /tee-cher/ *n* **1** a person who teaches (*a piano teacher*). **2** a schoolmaster or schoolmistress.

teak /teek/ *n* an Indian tree producing very hard wood (*a table made of teak*).

teal /teel/ *n* a small freshwater wild duck.

team /teem/ *n* **1** a number of persons working together for the same purpose (*a team of workers*). **2** a set of players on one side in a game (*a baseball team*). **3** a number of horses, oxen, etc., harnessed together.

teamwork /teem-wurk/ *n* united effort for the common good.

tear[1] /tear/ *n* a drop of water appearing in or falling from the eyes (*the tragedy brought tears to his eyes*)

tear[2] /tare/ *vb* (*pt* **tore** /tore/, *pp* **torn** /toarn/) **1** to pull apart or into pieces (*tear paper*). **2** to pull with violence (*tear her hair*). **3** (*inf*) to rush (*tear upstairs*). ● *n* a hole or division made by tearing.

tearful /teer-ful/ *adj* weeping (*in a tearful mood*). ● *adv* **tearfully** /teer-fu-lee/.

tear gas /teer-gas/ *n* a gas that makes your eyes water, sometimes used to disperse a crowd

tease /teez/ *vb* **1** to annoy by making fun of. **2** to pull apart wool, etc., into separate strands. **3** to comb wool to give it a hairy surface. ● *n* a person who annoys another by teasing.

teaser /tee-zer/ *n* a difficult problem.

teaspoon /tee-spoon/ *n* a small spoon for use with tea or as a measure in cooking.

teat /teet/ *n* **1** the part of the breast from which milk may be sucked or drawn. **2** (*Br*) a rubber attachment through which a baby sucks milk from a bottle, a nipple.

technical /tec-ni-cal/ *adj* having to do with a particular art, science, or craft (*the manual was full of technical language*).

technicality /tec-ni-**ca**-li-tee/ *n* **1** a technical word or phrase. **2** a small detail or rule (*disqualified on a technicality*)

technically /tek-ni-cal-lee/ *adv* strictly speaking (*the tomato is, technically, a fruit*).

technician /tek-ni-shan/ *n* a person who is skilled in a particular art or craft.

technique /tek-**neek**/ *n* the method of doing something that requires skill (*his technique as a portrait painter*).

technology /tek-**nol**-o-jee/ *n* the study of methods of manufacturing. ● *adj* **technological** /tek-nu-**lodge**-ic-al/. ● *n* **technologist** /tek-**nol**-o-jist/.

teddy /te-dee/, **teddy bear** /te-dee-bare/ *n* a child's toy bear.

tedious /tee-dee-us/ *adj* long and boring, tiresome (*it was a tedious job*).

tedium /tee-dee-um/ *n* boredom; long, drawn-out dullness (*the tedium of factory work*).

tee /tee/ *n* **1** the starting place for each "hole" in golf. **2** a peg or small mound on which the ball may be placed for the first shot at each hole in golf.

teem /teem/ *vb* to be full of (*rivers teeming with fish*).

teenager /tee-nay-jer/ *n* a person who is between the ages of 13 and 19. ● *adj* **teenage** /tee-nayj/.

teens /teenz/ *npl* the ages from 13 to 19.

teeth *see* **tooth**.

teethe /teethe/ *vb* to grow your first teeth (*babies teethe during their first year*).

teetotal /tee-**toe**-tal/ *adj* taking no alcoholic drinks. ● *n* **teetotaler** /tee-**toe**-tu-ler/.

tele- /**te**-lee/ *prefix* far, at, or to a distance.

telecommunications /te-li-cu-myoo-ni-**cay**-shunz/ *n* the technology or industry involved in transmitting information electronically over long distances by means of wires, radio signals, satellite, etc.

telegram /**te**-li-gram/ *n* a message sent by telegraph.

telegraph /**te**-li-graf/ *n* an apparatus for sending messages to a distance, especially by means of electricity. ● *vb* to send by telegraph. ● *adj* **telegraphic** /te-li-**gra**-fic/. ● *n* **telegraphy** /ti-**leg**-ra-fee/.

telepathy /ti-**le**-pa-thee/ *n* the power to pass thoughts to or receive them from another, even if far away, without the use of words or signs (*he knew by telepathy that his sister was sick*).

telephone /**te**-li-foan/ *n* (*abbr* = **phone** /foan/) an apparatus by means of which you may speak with a person at a distance by means of electric currents carried along wires. ● *vb* to speak with or communicate by telephone (*he telephoned his doctor*).

telephonist /te-**le**-fu-nist/ *n* (*Br*) a person who operates a telephone switchboard; **operator**.

telephoto lens /tel-uh-**foe**-toe-lens/ *n* a lens on a camera enabling it to take pictures from a great distance.

telescope /**te**-le-scope/ *n* an instrument consisting of lenses set in a tube or tubes that, when looked through, makes distant objects appear larger. ● *vb* **1** to slide together, one section fitting into another, as with a telescope. **2** to become shorter by one part sliding over the other.

telescopic /te-le-**scop**-ic/ *adj* **1** having to do with a telescope. **2** able to be seen only by means of a telescope (*a telescopic image*). **3** something that telescopes (*a telescopic umbrella*).

televise /**te**-le-vize/ *vb* to transmit by television.

television /te-le-**vi**-zhun/ *n* the transmitting of pictures by sound waves so as to reproduce them on a screen.

tell /tell/ *vb* (*pt, pp* **told** /toald/) **1** to give an account of (*tell about the accident*). **2** to let another know of by speaking. **3** to count. **4** to have an effect (*his illness is telling on him*).

teller /**te**-ler/ *n* **1** a bank clerk who receives and pays out cash. **2** a person who is appointed to count votes.

telling /**te**-ler/ *adj* very effective (*a telling remark*).

telltale /**tel**-tale/ *adj* **1** giving information (*telltale signs*). **2** revealing what was meant to be secret.

● *n* a **tattletale**; a person who tells what another has done to get him or her into trouble.

temerity /te-**mer**-i-tee/ *n* boldness, rashness (*have the temerity to question the judge*).

temper /**tem**-per/ *n* **1** anger (*in a real temper*). **2** mood, state of mind (*in a good temper*). **3** the correct hardness of metal. ● *vb* **1** to make less severe. **2** to harden (metal). **3** to mix in proper proportions.

temperament /**tem**-pra-ment/ *n* **1** your character. **2** the usual state of your mind or feelings.

temperamental /tem-pra-**men**-tal/ *adj* easily excited, changing mood quickly. ● *adv* **temperamentally** /tem-pra-**men**-ta-lee/.

temperate /**tem**-prit/ *adj* **1** taking neither too much nor too little. **2** neither too hot nor too cold (*a temperate climate*).

temperature /**tem**-pri-chur/ *n* degree of heat or cold. ● **take your temperature** to find the degree of heat of your body (*take the baby's temperature*).

tempest /**tem**-pest/ *n* a violent storm.

tempestuous /tem-**pes**-chu-wus/ *adj* **1** very stormy. **2** violent (*a tempestuous relationship*).

template /**tem**-plit/ *n* a pattern or mold used as a guide for shaping things.

temple[1] /**tem**-pul/ *n* **1** a place of worship. **2** a church.

temple[2] /**tem**-pul/ *n* the side of the head above the end of the cheekbone and between the ear and the forehead.

tempo /**tem**-po/ *n* (*pl* **tempos** /**tem**-poaz/ *or* **tempi** /**tem**-pie/) the speed at which a piece of music is played.

temporal /**tem**-pral/ *adj* **1** (*fml*) having to do with time. **2** worldly. **3** having to do with life on earth.

temporary /**tem**-pra-ree/ *adj* lasting for a time only, not permanent (*a temporary job*). ● *adv* **temporarily** /tem-po-**ra**-ri-lee/.

tempt /**tem**(p)t/ *vb* **1** to try to get someone to do what he feels he ought not to do (*he tried to tempt her with another drink*). **2** to arouse desire in. ● *ns* **tempter** /**tem**(p)-ter/, **temptress** /**tem**(p)-tress/.

temptation /tem(p)-**tay**-shun/ *n* attraction to what is wrong or forbidden.

tempting /**tem**(p)-ting/ *adj* **1** attractive. **2** arousing desire.

ten /ten/ *n* and *adj* the number 10. ● **tenth** *adj and n*.

tenacious /ti-**nay**-shus/ *adj* **1** holding on firmly (*a tenacious hold on the branch*). **2** not giving in easily, stubborn (*a tenacious fighter*). ● *adv* **tenaciously** /ti-**nay**-shus-lee/. ● *n* **tenacity** /ti-**na**-si-tee/.

tenancy /**te**-nan-see/ *n* **1** the renting of property.

2 property for which a rent is paid. **3** the time during which you rent property.

tenant /**te**-nant/ *n* a person who occupies rented property.

tend[1] /**tend**/ *vb* **1** to incline to (*tend to get angry easily*). **2** to have a leaning toward.

tend[2] /**tend**/ *vb* to care for, to look after (*tend sheep*).

tendency /**ten**-den-see/ *n* a leaning toward, an inclination, liability to do certain things more than others (*a tendency to drink too much*).

tender[1] /**ten**-der/ *adj* **1** soft, gentle, and loving. **2** easily hurt. ● *adv* **tenderly** /**ten**-der-lee/. ● *n* **tenderness** /**ten**-der-ness/.

tender[2] /**ten**-der/ *vb* (*fml*) to offer or present (*to tender his resignation*). ● *n* an offer, especially one to do work at a certain price.

tender[3] /**ten**-der/ *n* **1** a small boat carrying stores, etc., to a larger one. **2** a wagon or truck attached to a locomotive to carry coal, water, etc., for it.

tendon /**ten**-don/ *n* a strong cord-like band joining a muscle to a bone.

tendril /**ten**-dril/ *n* **1** a slender curling shoot by which some plants cling to supports when climbing. **2** a wispy curl of hair.

tenement /**te**-ni-ment/ *n* an apartment building, especially a rundown and crowded one in the city.

tennis /**te**-nis/ *n* a game played across a net by striking a ball to and fro with rackets.

tenor /**te**-nor/ *n* **1** the higher of two kinds of men's singing voices. **2** the general meaning (*the tenor of his speech*).

tense[1] /**tense**/ *n* a set of forms of the verb that indicate time.

tense[2] /**tense**/ *adj* **1** stretched tight (*keep the rope tense*). **2** strained (*his job makes him feel tense*). **3** excited from expectation (*tense with excitement*). ● *adv* **tensely**.

tension /**ten**-shun/ *n* **1** act of stretching. **2** tightness, strain. **3** excitement due to expectation.

tent /**tent**/ *n* a portable shelter of canvas, supported by a pole or poles and stretched and held in position by cords.

tentacle /**ten**-ta-cul/ *n* a slender boneless limb of various creatures, used for feeling, gripping, or moving (*the tentacles of an octopus*).

tentative /**ten**-ta-tiv/ *adj* done as an experiment or trial (*a tentative approach*). ● *adv* **tentatively** /**ten**-ta-tiv-lee/.

tenterhooks /**ten**-ter-hooks/ *npl*. ● **on tenterhooks** anxious or excited because of doubt or suspense (*on tenterhooks waiting for the test results*).

tenth see **ten.**

tenuous /ten-yu-wus/ adj thin, slender (a tenuous connection between the events).

tenure /ten-yur/ n the holding or conditions of holding land, office, etc.

tepee /tee-pee/ n a cone-shaped Native American tent made of skins.

tepid /te-pid/ adj lukewarm (a tepid bath).

term /term/ n 1 a limited period of time (during the term of the contract). 2 a word or phrase used in a particular study (a technical term he did not understand). 3 a time when law courts are dealing with cases. 4 (Br) a division of the school year. ● vb to name, to call (he is not what you would term a friendly person). ● npl **terms** /termz/ conditions, charge, price (the terms of the loan agreement). ● **come to terms** to make an agreement. ● **on good terms** friendly.

terminal /ter-mi-nal/ adj having to do with the end or last part (a terminal illness). ● n 1 the station at the end of a railroad line or route. 2 an airport building where passengers arrive and depart from. 3 one of the screws to which an electric wire is attached to make a connection. 4 a computer monitor and keyboard for entering data. ● adv **terminally** /ter-mi-na-lee/.

terminate /ter-mi-nate/ vb to bring or come to an end (terminate the agreement).

termination /ter-mi-nay-shun/ n end, ending.

terminology /ter-mi-nol-o-jee/ n the words, phrases, etc., special to a particular branch of study (the terminology of computing).

termite /ter-mite/ n a white ant.

tern /tern/ n a sea bird like a gull, but smaller.

terrace /te-riss/ n 1 a raised bank of earth with a flat area on top. 2 a row of houses.

terraced /te-rist/ adj having terraces (terraced houses).

terracotta /te-ra-cot-a/ n 1 a reddish brown pottery. 2 its color. ● also adj.

terrain /te-rain/ n a stretch of country (rocky terrain).

terrapin /te-ra-pin/ n a type of tortoise.

terrestrial /te-re-stree-al/ adj having to do with the Earth.

terrible /te-ri-bul/ adj 1 frightening, causing dread (a terrible scream). 2 very bad (a terrible experience). ● adv **terribly** /te-ri-blee/.

terrier /te-ree-er/ n a small dog that is good at hunting.

terrific /te-ri-fic/ adj 1 exceptionally good (a terrific concert). 2 frightening, causing dread. ● adv **terrifically** /te-ri-fi-ca-lee/.

terrify /te-ri-fie/ vb to make very frightened (she was terrified of the dog).

territorial /te-ri-toe-ree-al/ adj having to do with a certain district or piece of land.

territory /te-ri-toe-ree/ n a district or piece of land, especially one that belongs to a person, a nation, etc.

terror /te-ror/ n 1 great fear, dread. 2 terrorism (the war against terror).

terrorism /te-ror-i-zum/ n the use of, or the threat of, extreme violence for political purposes (the bombing was an act of terrorism).

terrorist /te-ror-ist/ n a person who uses, or threatens to use, extreme violence for political purposes.

terrorize /te-ror-ize/ vb, also **terrorise** (Br) 1 to make very frightened. 2 to make do what is desired by causing fear.

terror-stricken /te-ror-stri-ken/ adj full of fear or dread.

terse /terss/ adj short and to the point (a terse statement of resignation). ● adv **tersely.** ● n **terseness** / terss-ness/.

test /test/ n an examination or trial intended to reveal quality, ability, progress, etc. ● vb 1 to try the quality of (test the new car). 2 to examine (test his French).

testament /tes-ta-ment/ n 1 in law, a person's will. 2 one of the two main divisions of the Bible (Old Testament, New Testament).

testator /tes-tay-tor/ n a person who leaves a will at death. ● f **testatrix** /tes-tay-triks/.

testify /te-sti-fie/ vb 1 to give evidence. 2 to say publicly what you believe to be true (he testified to her honesty).

testimonial /te-sti-moe-nee-al/ n 1 a letter stating a person's good qualities and abilities. 2 a gift presented as a sign of respect.

testimony /te-sti-mo-nee/ n evidence, a public statement of belief (give his testimony in court).

test pilot /test-pie-lot/ n a person who tests an aircraft by making it perform difficult maneuvers.

test tube /test-toob/ n a glass tube open at one end, used for scientific experiments.

testy /te-stee/ adj irritable, easily angered (a testy old man).

tetanus /tet-nus/ n a disease causing cramp in the muscles and making the jaw so stiff that it cannot move.

tête-à-tête /te-ta-**tet**/ *n* a private talk between two people.

tether /**te**-ther/ *vb* to tie an animal by a rope to a stake or peg. ● *n* a stake, etc. ● **at the end of your tether** at the end of your strength or endurance (*she left the job because she was at the end of her tether*).

tetra- /**te**-tra/ *prefix* four.

tetragon /**te**-tra-gon/ *n* a four-sided figure.

tetrahedron /te-tra-**hee**-dron/ *n* a solid figure with four sides shaped like a pyramid.

text /**tekst**/ *n* **1** the words actually written by the author (not including notes, drawings, etc.). **2** a short passage from the Bible. **3** subject, topic (*the text of his speech*). **4** a text message. ● *vb* to send a text message to.

textbook /**tekst**-book/ *n* a book about a subject written for those studying it (*a math textbook*).

textile /**tek**-stile/ *n* a fabric made by weaving. ● *adj* having to do with or made by weaving.

text message /**tekst**-meh-sidge/ *n* a message typed into a cell phone using its keys, and sent to another cell phone.

texture /**teks**-chur/ *n* **1** the way in which a fabric or cloth, etc., is woven. **2** the quality of woven cloth.

than /**than**/ *conj* compared with (*Jack is older than Kristina*).

thank /**thangk**/ *vb* to express pleasure to another for something done, etc., to express gratitude.

thankful /**thangk**-ful/ *adj* grateful, full of gratitude (*thankful that the children were safe*). ● *adv* **thankfully** /**thangk**-fu-lee/.

thankless /**thangk**-less/ *adj* ungrateful, for which you will receive no thanks (*a thankless task*).

thanks /**thangks**/ *npl* an expression of gratitude.

thanksgiving /**thangks**-gi-ving/ *n* the act of giving thanks, especially to God at harvest time (*a service in the church for thanksgiving*).

Thanksgiving Day /**thangks**-gi-ving day/ *n* **1** the fourth Thursday in November, observed as a holiday in the United States for giving thanks to God for health and harvest. **2** in Canada, the second Monday in October when thanks are given to God for health and harvest.

that /**that**/ *adj* and *pron* being the person or thing there (*that man with the black hair; that is my house over there*). ● *pron* who or which (*this is the dress that I bought in New York*). ● *conj* introduces a statement, a wish, etc. (*he said that he was hungry*).

thatch /**thatch**/ *n* straw used as a cover for the roof

of a house. ● *vb* to put thatch on (*thatch the cottage roof*). ● *n* **thatcher** /**thatch**-er/.

thaw /**thaw**/ *vb* **1** to melt (*the snow began to thaw in the sun*). **2** to become more friendly. ● *n* a state or time of thawing.

the /**thi**/ *adj* referring to a particular person or thing (*the woman in black*).

theater /**thee**-a-tor/ *n* **1** a building or hall in which plays are acted. **2** a lecture hall. **3** a scene of action (*the theater of war*). **4** (*Br*) *see* **operating room**.

theatrical /**thee**-a-tri-cal/ *adj* **1** having to do with plays or the theater. **2** behaving as if acting in a play (*her theatrical reaction to the news*). ● *adv* **theatrically** /**thee**-a-tri-**ca**-lee/.

theatricals /**thee**-a-tri-calz/ *npl* dramatic performances.

thee /**thee**/ *pron* you (*sing*).

theft /**theft**/ *n* act of stealing (*the theft of her car*).

their /**thayr**/, **theirs** /**thayrz**/ *poss adj* and *pron* belonging to them.

theism /**thee**-iz-um/ *n* belief in the existence of God. ● *n* **theist**.

them /**them**/ *n* the form of "they" used when the object of a sentence (*I saw them at the ball game*).

theme /**theem**/ *n* **1** subject, topic (*the theme of his talk*). **2** a set of notes played several times in a piece of music.

theme park /**theem**-park/ *n* an amusement park based around a particular theme.

themselves /them-**selvz**/ *pron* the reflexive form of "they" (*the girls are old enough to take care of themselves*).

then /**then**/ *adv* **1** at that time. **2** after that. **3** therefore.

thence /**thenss**/ *adv* **1** from that time or place. **2** for that reason.

theologian /thee-ol-**odge**-ee-an/ *n* an expert in or a student of theology.

theological /thee-ol-**odge**-ic-al/ *adj* having to do with theology.

theology /thee-**ol**-odge-ee/ *n* the study of the existence of God and people's beliefs about God.

theorem /**thee**-ur-em/ *n* an idea that can be proved true by reasoning (*geometrical theorem*).

theoretical /thee-ur-**et**-i-cal/ *adj* based on ideas, not on practice (*a theoretical solution to the problem*). ● *adv* **theoretically** /thee-ur-**et**-i-ca-lee/.

theorize /**thee**-ur-ize/ *vb*, *also* **theorise** (*Br*) **1** to suggest explanations. **2** to put forward theories (*he was theorizing on the problem*).

theory /**thee**-ur-ee/ *n* **1** an explanation that seems satisfactory but has not been proved true. **2** a set of ideas or rules on how something should be done.

therapeutic /ther-a-**pyoo**-tic/ *adj* having to do with therapy.

therapy /**ther**-a-pee/ *n* the treatment and cure of disease (*cancer therapy*). ● *n* **therapist** /**ther**-a-pist/.

there /thare/ *adv* in that place.

thereafter /thay-**raf**-ter/ *adv* after that.

thereby /thare-**bie**/ *adv* by that means.

therefore /**thare**-fore/ *adv* for this or that reason.

thermal /**ther**-mal/ *adj* having to do with heat, hot (*thermal currents*).

thermodynamics /ther-mo-die-**na**-mics/ *n* the study of heat as a source of power.

thermometer /ther-**mom**-e-ter/ *n* an instrument for measuring degree of heat (*an oven thermometer*).

thermos bottle /**ther**-mus bot-l/ *n* (*trademark*) a flask for keeping hot liquid hot or cold liquid cold.

thermostat /**ther**-mu-stat/ *n* an instrument that mechanically controls temperature and keeps it steady (*a central heating thermostat*).

thesaurus /thi-**sawr**-us/ *n* a reference book containing synonyms and antonyms.

these /theez/ *pl of* **this** /this/.

thesis /**thee**-sis/ *n* **1** an opinion to be defended in writing or discussion. **2** an essay on a subject submitted for a higher university degree.

they /thay/ *pron* the people or things already mentioned (*the boys lost their ball*).

they'd /thayd/ *contraction* they had.

they'll /thayl/ *contraction* they will.

they're /thayr/ *contraction* they are.

they've /thayv/ *contraction* they have.

thick /thick/ *adj* **1** broad (*thick slices of meat*). **2** fat. **3** not easily seen through (*thick fog*). **4** slow to understand (*her boyfriend is really thick*). ● *n* the most crowded part (*the thick of the crowd*). ● *adv* **thickly** /**thick**-lee/. ● *n* **thickness** /**thick**-ness/.

thicken /**thi**-ken/ *vb* to make or become thicker (*the sauce would not thicken*).

thicket /**thi**-ket/ *n* a group of trees, shrubs, etc., growing close together.

thick-skinned /**thick**-skind/ *adj* slow to feel or resent insults.

thief /theef/ *n* (*pl* **thieves** /theevz/) a person who steals (*the thief took her purse*).

thievish /**thee**-vish/ *adj* given to stealing.

thigh /thie/ *n* the part of the leg above the knee.

thimble /**thim**-bul/ *n* a metal or plastic cap to protect the finger in sewing.

thin /thin/ *adj* **1** not thick. **2** not fat, lean, skinny, slim. **3** not crowded (*the audience was a little thin*). **4** not convincing (*a thin excuse*). ● *vb* to make or become thin. ● *adv* **thinly** /**thin**-lee/. ● *n* **thinness** /**thin**-ness/.

thing /thing/ *n* **1** any single existing object. **2** whatever may be thought of or spoken about. **3** a happening. ● *npl* **things** /thingz/ your belongings.

think /thingk/ *vb* (**thought** /thot/, **thinking** /**thing**-king/) **1** to form ideas in the mind, to consider (*no time to think*). **2** to believe, to hold as an opinion (*he thinks it is wrong*).

thinker /**thi**-ker/ *n* **1** a person who thinks. **2** a person who tries to work out an explanation of life, etc., for himself or herself.

thinking /**thing**-king/ *adj* able to think or reason.

thin-skinned /**thin**-skind/ *adj* quick to feel or resent insults, easily upset.

third /thurd/ *adj* coming after second. ● *n* one of three equal parts.

thirst /thurst/ *n* **1** the need or desire to drink. **2** a strong desire for anything (*a thirst for learning*). ● *vb* **1** to feel thirst. **2** to desire strongly.

thirsty /**thur**-stee/ *adj* **1** wanting or needing a drink. **2** dry. **3** causing thirst (*thirsty work*). ● *adv* **thirstily** /**thur**-sti-lee/.

thirteen /**thur**-teen/ *n and adj* the number 13. ● *adj and n* **thirteenth** /**thur**-teenth/.

thirty /**thur**-tee/ *n and adj* the number 30. ● *adj and n* **thirteeth** /**thur**-tee-eth/.

this /this/ *adj and pron* being the person or thing here (*this painting here; this is my sister*).

thistle /**thi**-sul/ *n* a prickly plant with a purple head, the national emblem of Scotland.

thong /thong/ *n* **1** a strap of hide or leather. **2** a sandal consisting of a sole and straps from either side that pass between the first and second toe. **3** a woman's very skimpy undergarment for the lower body that leaves the buttocks uncovered.

thorn /thawrn/ *n* **1** a prickle on the stern of a plant. **2** a bush or plant with prickles. ● **thorn in the flesh** a cause of trouble or difficulty (*he thinks his sister is a thorn in his flesh*).

thorny /**thawr**-nee/ *adj* **1** prickly. **2** difficult, troublesome (*a thorny situation*).

thorough /**thu**-ro/ *adj* **1** complete (*a thorough job*). **2** doing work with great care (*a thorough person*). ● *adv* **thoroughly** /**thu**-ro-lee/. ● *n* **thoroughness** /**thu**-ro-ness/.

thoroughfare /**thu**-ro-fare/ *n* a road open to the public and to traffic.

those /thoaz/ *pl of* **that**.

though /thoa/ *prep* despite the fact that.

thought /thawt/ *pt of* **think.** ● *n* **1** the power or act of thinking. **2** what you think, an idea (*a sad thought*).

thoughtful /thawt-ful/ *adj* **1** given to thinking (*a thoughtful mood*). **2** considerate, thinking of others (*the gift was typical of such a thoughtful person*). ● *adv* **thoughtfully** /thawt-fu-lee/. ● *n* **thoughtfullness** /thawt-ful-ness/.

thoughtless /thawt-less/ *adj* **1** not thinking before acting. **2** inconsiderate, not thinking of others (*a thoughtless remark that hurt her mother*). ● *adv* **thoughtlessly.** ● *n* **thoughtlessness** /thawt-less-ness/.

thousand /thou-zand/ *adj and n* 10 hundred.

thrash /thrash/ *vb* to beat hard, to flog.

thrashing /thra-shing/ *n* a good beating, a flogging.

thread /thred/ *n* **1** a fine strand of any substance (e.g., cotton, wool, etc.) drawn out and twisted to make a cord. **2** the spiral ridge running around and around a screw, etc. **3** the main connected points running through an argument (*lose the thread of the speech*). ● *vb* **1** to pass thread or fine cord through. **2** to make your way through.

threadbare /thred-bare/ *adj* (*of clothing*) having the fluffy surface worn off, shabby, frequently used, and so no longer fresh or new.

threat /thret/ *n* **1** a promise to hurt or punish another in future. **2** a warning of harm to come (*the threat of unemployment*).

threaten /thre-ten/ *vb* **1** to make threats to. **2** to be a sign of coming harm, evil, etc. (*it was threatening to snow*). ● *adj* **threatening** /thre-te-ning/. ● *adv* **threateningly** /thre-te-ning-lee/.

three /three/ *adj and n* the number 3.

thresh /thresh/ *vb* to separate seed from straw by beating it or putting it through a machine.

threshing machine /thre-shing-ma-sheen/ *n* a machine that separates seed from straw.

threshold /thresh-hoald/ *n* **1** the plank or stone you cross when passing through a door. **2** the beginning (*on the threshold of a new career*).

threw /throo/ *pt of* **throw.**

thrice /thrice/ *adv* three times.

thrift /thrift/ *n* care in spending or using up, the habit of saving and not wasting.

thrifty /thrif-tee/ *adj* careful in spending, saving (*a thrifty attitude to money*). ● *adv* **thriftily** /thrif-ti-lee/.

thrill /thrill/ *n* a sudden feeling of excitement or emotion. ● *vb* to excite, to cause a thrill in.

thriller /thri-ler/ *n* a story written to excite or horrify.

thrilling /thri-ling/ *adj* very exciting (*a thrilling experience*).

thrive /thrive/ *vb* **1** to do well (*the baby continues to thrive*). **2** to be or become strong or successful (*a business that was thriving*).

throat /throat/ *n* **1** the front of the neck. **2** the opening downward at the back of the mouth and the pipe leading down from it.

throb /throb/ *vb* **1** to beat, as the heart. **2** (*of pain*) to increase and decrease at short regular intervals. ● *also n.*

throne /throan/ *n* the chair occupied by a monarch or bishop.

throng /throng/ *n* a crowd. ● *vb* to go in crowds, to crowd together (*people thronged to the hall*).

throttle /throt-ul/ *n* **1** the throat or windpipe. **2** a lever working a valve that controls the supply of steam, gasoline, etc., to an engine. ● *vb* **1** to choke or strangle. **2** to cut down the supply of steam, etc., by using a throttle.

through /throo/ *prep* **1** from end to end. **2** from beginning to end. **3** by means of (*get to the top through hard work*). **4** because of. ● *adv* from end to end. ● *adj* going all the way without requiring changes.

throughout /throo-out/ *adv* in every way or part (*a house painted throughout*). ● *prep* right through (*throughout the day*).

throw /thro/ *vb* (*pt* **threw** /throo/, *pp* **thrown** /throan/) **1** to fling or cast (*throw a stone in the river*). **2** to make to fall on the ground (e.g., in wrestling). ● *n* **1** act of throwing. **2** the distance to which something can move or be flung through the air.

thrum /thrum/ *vb* (**thrummed** /thrumd/, **thrumming** /thru-ming/) **1** to play (a musical instrument) carelessly. **2** to play by pulling the strings of.

thrush[1] /thrush/ *n* a songbird.

thrush[2] /thrush/ *n* a disease of the mouth and throat.

thrust /thrust/ *vb* **1** to push with force (*thrust the door open*). **2** to stab at or into. **3** to push forward (*thrust himself to the front of the line*). ● *n* **1** a sudden or violent push. **2** a stab.

thud /thud/ *n* a low dull sound, as of a muffled blow (*the thud of the heavy packet hitting the floor*). ● *also vb* (**thudded** /thu-did/, **thudding** /thu-ding/).

thug /thug/ *n* a ruffian.

thumb /thum/ *n* the shortest and thickest of the fingers. ● *vb* to dirty with marks of the thumb or fingers. ● **rule of thumb** a rough rule based on practice. ● **under someone's thumb** under the control or influence of someone (*he is said to under his girlfriend's thumb*).

thump /thump/ *n* a dull heavy blow. ● *vb* to beat heavily.

thunder /thun-der/ *n* **1** the sound that follows lightning. **2** any loud rumbling noise (*the thunder of passing trucks*). ● *vb* **1** to make thunder. **2** to make a loud noise. ● *adj* **thundery** /thun-de-ree/ (*of weather*) hot and close, as before a thunderstorm.

thunderbolt /thun-der-boalt/ *n* a flash of lightning.

thunderclap /thun-der-clap/ *n* a peal of thunder.

thunderous /thun-der-us/ *adj* like thunder, very loud (*thunderous applause*).

thunderstorm /thun-der-stawrm/ *n* a spell of thunder, lightning, and heavy rain.

thunderstruck /thun-der-struck/ *adj* amazed, astonished (*thunderstruck at the news*).

Thursday /thurz-day/ *n* the fifth day of the week.

thus /thus/ *adv* in this way.

thwack /thwack/ *vb* to beat hard. ● *n* a heavy blow.

thwart /thwawrt/ *vb* to prevent from succeeding (*thwart him in his attempts to gain promotion*).

thyme /time/ *n* a herb with sweet-smelling leaves, used in cooking.

tiara /tee-ya-ra/ *n* a jeweled band, like a small crown, worn on the head by ladies.

tibia /ti-bee-ya/ *n* the shin bone (*a fracture of the tibia*).

tic /tic/ *n* an involuntary movement of a muscle, especially in the face.

tick[1] /tick/ *n* **1** the sound made by a watch or clock (*he heard the tick of the clock*). **2** a mark made when checking or correcting. ● *also vb*.

tick[2] /tick/ *n* a small blood-sucking insect.

ticket /ti-ket/ *n* **1** a marked card giving its possessor the right to do something (e.g., travel by train, enter a theater, etc.) (*his weekly rail ticket*). **2** a label.

tickle /ti-cul/ *vb* **1** to cause discomfort or make laugh by touching or prodding lightly a sensitive part of the body. **2** (*inf*) to please, to amuse.

ticklish /ti-clish/ *adj* **1** easily tickled. **2** difficult, requiring careful management (*a ticklish problem*).

tidal /tie-dal/ *adj* having to do with tides.

tidal wave /tie-dal-wave/ *n* a tsunami.

tidbit /tie-bit/ *n* a tasty piece of food (*tidbits for the dog*).

tide /tide/ *n* **1** the regular rise and fall, or ebb and flow, of the sea. **2** time, season.

tidings /tie-dingz/ *npl* (*old or fml*) news (*bring tidings of his death*).

tidy /tie-dee/ *adj* neatly arranged, orderly. ● *vb* to arrange neatly (*tidy the room*). ● *adv* **tidily** /tie-di-lee/. ● *n* **tidiness** /tie-dee-ness/.

tie /tie/ *vb* **1** to fasten with cord, rope, etc. (*tie the dog up*). **2** to make a knot in. **3** (*in a game or contest*) to be equal (with). ● *n* **1** a connection, bond (*family ties*). **2** a draw (i.e., an equal score). **3** a match in a knockout competition (*the third-round tie*). **4** (*Br*) see **necktie** /neck-tie/.

tie breaker /tie-brake-ur/ *n* an extra game played to decide between participants in a game that has resulted in a **tie**, sense **3**.

tier /teer/ *n* one of a series of rows of seats arranged on the slope, so that each row is slightly higher than the one below it.

tiff /tiff/ *n* a slight quarrel (*a lover's tiff*).

tiger /tie-ger/ *n* a large fierce striped animal of the cat family. ● *f* **tigress**.

tiger lily /tie-ger-li-lee/ *n* a lily with spotted orange flowers.

tight /tite/ *adj* **1** close-fitting (*a tight dress*). **2** closely packed (*a tight fit*). **3** (*inf*) difficult, especially because of shortage of money. **4** (*inf*) drunk (*get tight at the office party*).

tighten /tie-ten/ *vb* to make or become tight (*tighten the rope*). ● *adv* **tightly** /tite-lee/. ● *n* **tightness** /tite-ness/.

tightrope /tite-rope/ *n* a tightly stretched rope on which an acrobat walks and performs tricks.

tights /tites/ *npl* **1** a light, close-fitting garment covering the lower trunk and legs, worn by dancers. **2** (*Br*) see **pantyhose**.

tigress see **tiger**.

tile /tile/ *n* a thin slab of baked clay or other suitable material for covering roofs, floors, etc. ● *vb* to cover with tiles (*tile the wall*).

till[1] /till/ *prep* up to the time of. ● *conj* up to the time when.

till[2] /till/ *n* in a store, a drawer for money.

till[3] /till/ *vb* to plow and prepare for seed (*farmer tilling the land*).

tiller /ti-ler/ *n* the handle of a rudder, a blade at the back of a boat by means of which it is steered.

tilt /tilt/ *vb* to make to slope to one side, to lean (*a floor that tilts*). ● *n* a slant, a sloping position.

timber /tim-ber/ *n* **1** wood for building, carpentry, etc. **2** trees from which such wood can be obtained. **3** a wooden beam used in the framework of a house or ship.

time /time/ *n* **1** the measure of the passage of past, present, and future. **2** the moment of the hour, day, year, etc. **3** a season. **4** an occasion (*a happy time*). **5** the rhythm of a piece of music. ● *vb* **1** to see how long something lasts (*time the race*).

2 to see that something happens at the right moment (*time his arrival well*). ● **for the time being** meanwhile.

timekeeper /**time**-kee-per/ *n* a person who notes the times at which something begins and ends.

timely /**time**-lee/ *adj* (*inf*) happening at the right time (*his timely arrival*).

timepiece /**time**-peess/ *n* a watch or clock.

timer /**tie**-mer/ *n* a device used for timing something.

times /**tiemz**/ *prep* multiplied by (*two times three equals six*).

timetable /**time**-tay-bul/ *n* **1** a list of classes, giving times when they begin and end. **2** a list giving the times of arrival and departure of trains, buses, etc.

timid /**ti**-mid/ *adj* easily made afraid, shy (*too timid to complain*). ● *adv* **timidly** /**ti**-mid-lee/. ● *n* **timidity** /**ti**-mi-di-tee/.

timorous /**ti**-mu-russ/ *same as* **timid**.

timpani /**tim**-pa-nee/ *npl* kettledrums.

tin /**tin**/ *n* **1** a soft, light white metal. **2** (*Br*) *see* **can**. ● *vb* (**tinned** /**tind**/, **tinning** /**ti**-ning/) (*Br*) *see* **can**.

tincture /**ting**-chur/ *n* **1** a shade of color. **2** a slight taste or flavor of something. **3** a drug dissolved in alcohol.

tinder /**tin**-der/ *n* an easily lit substance that catches light from a spark (used before the invention of matches).

tinge /**tinge**/ *vb* **1** to color slightly. **2** to have a slight effect on. ● *n* **1** a shade, a slight color (*a reddish tinge*). **2** a small amount.

tingle /**ting**-gul/ *vb* to feel a prickly or thrilling sensation (*her fingers tingled with cold*).

tinker /**ting**-ker/ *n* **1** a person who goes from door to door, mending pots, kettles, etc. **2** a vagabond. ● *vb* **1** to mend roughly. **2** to work at unskillfully (*tinker with the car*).

tinkle /**ting**-kul/ *vb* to make soft, bell-like sounds (*the doorbell tinkled*). ● *also n*.

tinned /**tind**/ (*Br*) *see* **canned**.

tinny /**ti**-nee/ *adj* sharp and harsh in sound.

tin-opener /**tin**-o-pe-ner/ (*Br*) *see* **can-opener**.

tinsel /**tin**-sel/ *n* **1** thin strips, threads, disks, etc., of shiny metal. **2** anything showy but of little value.

tint /**tint**/ *n* **1** a shade of color (*a bluish tint*). **2** a faint color. ● *vb* to color slightly.

tiny /**tie**-nee/ *adj* very small (*tiny insects*).

tip /**tip**/ *n* **1** a narrow end or point. **2** a light blow. **3** money given as a present or for special help (*a tip for the waiters*). **4** a helpful hint (*tips on removing stains*). ● *vb* (**tipped** /**tipt**/, **tipping** /**ti**-ping/) **1** to put a tip on. **2** to make to tilt. **3** to give a money tip

to (*tip the waiter*). **4** to give a useful hint to. **5** to throw out (of) (*tip the peas out of the can*).

tipple /**ti**-pul/ *vb* to make a habit of taking strong liquor, to drink often.

tipsy /**tip**-see/ *adj* drunk, confused by strong liquor (*tipsy after the office party*).

tiptoe /**tip**-toe/ *n* the point of the toe. ● *vb* **1** to walk on the points of the toes. **2** to walk very quietly (*tiptoe out of the room*).

tiptop /**tip**-**top**/ *adj* splendid, excellent (*in tiptop condition*).

tirade /**tie**-rade/ *n* a long,0 angry speech, a violently critical speech (*a tirade on the subject of punctuality*).

tire[1] /**tire**/ *vb* to make or become weary (*the long journey tired her*). ● *adj* **tiring** /**tir**-ring/.

tire[2] /**tire**/ *n* a ring of iron or rubber around the outside rim of a wheel.

tired /**tierd**/ *adj* weary.

tireless /**tire**-less/ *adj* not easily wearied, having much energy. ● *adv* **tirelessly** /**tire**-less-lee/.

tiresome /**tire**-sum/ *adj* boring, annoying (*a tiresome day*).

tiring /**tie**-ring/ *see* **tire**[1].

tissue /**ti**-shoo/ *n* **1** any fine woven material. **2** substance (fat, muscle, etc.) of which the parts of animals and plants are made. **3** a complete connected set.

tissue paper /**ti**-shoo-pay-per/ *n* thin soft paper for wrapping (*wrap the china in tissue paper*).

tit[1] /**tit**/ *n* a small bird (*blue tit*).

tit[2] /**tit**/ *n*. ● **tit for tat** getting your own back.

titanic /**tie**-ta-nic/ *adj* huge, gigantic.

titanium /**tie**-tay-nee-yum/ *n* a silver-gray metal that is used to make alloys.

titbit /**tit**-bit/ (*Br*) *see* **tidbit**.

titillate /**ti**-ti-late/ *vb* **1** to tickle. **2** to give pleasure to (*titillate the audience*). ● *n* **titillation** /**ti**-ti-lay-shun/.

titivate /**ti**-ti-late/ *vb* to make neat or smart (*titivating herself for the party*).

title /**tie**-tul/ *n* **1** the name of a book, piece of writing or music, picture, etc. **2** a name or word used in addressing someone, to indicate rank, office, etc. **3** a claim to ownership, a right.

titled /**tie**-tuld/ *adj* being a member of the nobility.

title role /**tie**-tul-role/ *n* the part of a character in a play whose name is the same as that of the play, e.g., Macbeth in *Macbeth*.

titter /**ti**-ter/ *vb* to giggle (*they tittered behind his back*). ● *also n*.

tittle-tattle /ti-tul-ta-tul/ n gossip, foolish talk.

titular /ti-chu-lar/ adj having the rank or title but no powers (*the titular head of the country*).

Tlingit /tling-kut or kling-kut/ n native Americans of the islands and coast of southern Alaska.

to /too/ prep used to show movement toward (*driving to school*).

toad /toad/ n a froglike animal that lives both on land and in water.

toadstool /toad-stool/ n a poisonous fungus, like a mushroom in shape.

toady /toa-dee/ n (*inf*) a person who flatters another in order to gain his or her favor. ● vb to flatter or try to please in order to gain favor (*toadied to the boss*).

toast /toast/ vb 1 to dry and brown by heat. 2 to warm at the fire (*toast themselves by the fire*). 3 to drink the health of (*toast his friends*). ● n 1 sliced bread browned by heat. 2 a person whose health is drunk. 3 a sentiment or thing to which you drink.

toaster /toa-ster/ n an electrical implement for toasting bread.

tobacco /tu-ba-co/ n the dried leaves of the tobacco plant, used for smoking or taken as snuff.

tobacconist /tu-ba-cu-nist/ n a person who sells tobacco, cigarettes, etc.

toboggan /tu-bog-an/ n a narrow sled for sliding down snow-covered slopes. ● vb (**tobogganed** /tu-bog-and/, **tobogganing** /tu-bog-a-ning/) to go on a toboggan.

today /to-day/ adv on this day.

toddle /tod-ul/ vb to walk with short unsteady steps, as a small child.

toddler /tod-ler/ n a small child just beginning to walk.

toddy /tod-ee/ n a mixture of liquor, sugar, and hot water.

toe /toe/ n one of the five fingerlike members at the end of the foot. ● **toe the line** to behave as you are told.

toffee /taw-fee/ n a kind of candy made of sugar and butter.

toga /toe-ga/ n in ancient times, the cloak of a Roman citizen.

together /to-ge-ther/ adv with another or others, in company.

toil /toil/ vb to work hard. ● n hard work. ● n **toiler** /toi-ler/.

toilet /toi-let/ n 1 (*old*) the act of making yourself clean and tidy. 2 (*Br*) a bathroom or lavatory. **toilet soap** /toi-let-soap/ n soap for washing the body.

token /toe-ken/ n 1 a mark or sign (*a token of his friendship*). 2 an object often used to help to remember. 3 something used instead of money (*bus token*).

told /toald/ pt of **tell**.

tolerable /tol-ra-bul/ adj able to be put up with. ● adv **tolerably** /tol-ra-blee/.

tolerance /tol-er-anse/, **toleration** /tol-er-ay-shun/ ns 1 patience. 2 readiness to allow what is displeasing, strange, or different to continue to exist.

tolerant /tol-er-ant/ adj ready to tolerate, broadminded (*tolerant of their beliefs*).

tolerate /tol-er-ate/ vb 1 to put up with (*he could not tolerate the noise*). 2 to allow (*she will not tolerate shoddy work*).

toll[1] /tole/ n a tax charged for the use of a bridge, road, etc.

toll[2] /tole/ vb to ring slowly, as a bell at a funeral (*church bells tolling*). ● n a single stroke of a large bell.

tomahawk /tom-a-hawk/ n a battle-ax once used as a tool or a weapon by Native American peoples.

tomato /tom-ay-toe/ n (*pl* **tomatoes** /tom-ay-toaz/) 1 a plant with a soft edible fruit. 2 the fruit of the tomato.

tomb /toom/ n 1 a grave. 2 a cellar in which dead bodies are placed.

tomboy /tom-boy/ n an energetic girl who is fond of boyish games and sports.

tombstone /toom-stone/ n a stone placed over a grave giving the name, etc., of the person buried underneath.

tome /tome/ n a large, heavy book (*a tome on philosophy*).

tommy gun /tom-ee-gun/ n a small machine gun.

tomorrow /to-mor-ow/ adv the day after today.

ton /tun/ n a measure of weight (= 20 hundredweight, 2000 lbs).

tone /tone/ n 1 a sound. 2 the quality or pitch of a voice or sound. 3 the prevailing spirit or atmosphere (*the tone of the meeting*). 4 a shade of color (*in tones of blue*). ● vb to fit in with. ● **tone down** to soften, to make less harsh. ● adj **tonal** /toe-nal/.

tongs /tongz/ npl an instrument with two arms between which things can be gripped for moving (*lift the coal with tongs*).

tongue /tung/ n 1 an organ in the mouth with the help of which you speak or taste. 2 anything shaped like a tongue (e.g., a leather flap in a shoe). 3 a language (*a foreign tongue*). 4 the clapper of a bell. ● **hold your tongue** to remain silent.

tongue-tied /**tung**-tied/ *adj* unable to speak because of excitement or nervousness.

tongue-twister /**tung**-twi-ster/ *n* a group of words that it is difficult to pronounce quickly.

tonic /**ton**-ic/ *adj* **1** strengthening, giving vigor or health. **2** having to do with musical tones. ● *n* a strengthening medicine (*the sick boy was given a tonic*).

tonight /to-**nite**/ *adv* on this night.

tonnage /**tu**-nidge/ *n* the weight of goods a ship can carry.

tonne /tun/ *n* a metric ton (=2204.6lbs, 1000kg).

tonsil /**ton**-sil/ *n* one of the two glands at the back of the mouth.

tonsillitis /ton-si-**lie**-tis/ *n* a disease causing the tonsils to become swollen and sore.

too /too/ *adv* **1** also (*Steve is hungry, and I am too*). **2** excessively (*too young to get married*).

took /took/ *pt of* **take**.

tool /tool/ *n* **1** an instrument for working with. **2** a person who does exactly what another wants him or her to do (*a tool of the company's management*).

toot /toot/ *n* the sound of a horn. ● *also vb* (*drivers tooting their horns in impatience*).

tooth /tooth/ *n* (*pl* **teeth** /teeth/) **1** one of the bony projections rooted in the jaw, used for biting or chewing. **2** any tooth-shaped projection, as on a saw, comb, etc. ● **have a sweet tooth** to like eating sweet things. ● **long in the tooth** (*inf*) old (*he is a bit long in the tooth to be at a disco*). ● **tooth and nail** with great violence or fury (*fight tooth and nail*).

toothache /**tooth**-ake/ *n* a pain in a tooth (*go to the dentist with a toothache*).

toothbrush /**tooth**-brush/ *n* a brush for cleaning the teeth.

toothpaste /**tooth**-paste/ *n* a paste for cleaning the teeth.

toothpick /**tooth**-pick/ *n* a small stick used for removing anything stuck in or between the teeth.

toothy /**too**-thee/ *adj* having or showing large or sticking-out teeth (*a toothy grin*).

top /top/ *n* **1** the highest part or place (*the top of the tree*). **2** the summit (*the top of the mountain*). **3** a toy for spinning. **4** a garment worn on the upper body, e.g., a sweater or a T-shirt. ● *adj* **1** highest. **2** most important. ● *vb* (**topped**, **topping**) **1** to be at the top of. **2** to hit the top of. **3** to do better than.

topaz /**to**-paz/ *n* a precious stone.

top hat /**top**-hat/ *n* a tall cylindrical hat covered with silk (*the wedding guests wore top hats*).

top-heavy /**top**-he-vee/ *adj* so heavy at the top that it may fall over (*the load was top-heavy*).

topic /**top**-ic/ *n* a subject of discussion.

topical /**top**-ic-al/ *adj* having to do with events of the present day (*topical stories*).

topmost /**top**-moast/ *adj* highest.

topping /**top**-ing/ *n* a sauce or garnish that is put on the top of a hamburger, ice cream, etc.

topple /**top**-ul/ *vb* **1** to fall over, to overbalance (*much of the load toppled off*). **2** to cause to fall.

topsy-turvy /top-see-**tur**-vee/ *adj* confused, upside-down.

torch /tawrch/ *n* **1** (*old*) a piece of blazing wood carried or stuck up to give light. **2** (*Br*) *see* flashlight.

tore /tore/ *pt of* **tear**.

toreador /**taw**-ree-ya-dore/ *n* a Spanish bullfighter.

torment /**tawr**-ment/ *n* **1** great suffering or agony. **2** great anxiety (*the torment of waiting for the results of the test*). ● *vb* **torment** /tawr-**ment**/ **1** to cause distress or suffering to, to torture. **2** to tease (*students tormenting the new boy*). ● *n* **tormentor** /tawr-**men**-tor/.

torn /toarn/ *pp of* **tear**.

tornado /tor-**nay**-doe/ *n* (*pl* **tornadoes** /tor-**nay**-doaz/) a violent swirling wind or hurricane.

torpedo /tor-**pee**-doe/ *n* (*pl* **torpedoes** /tor-**pee**-doaz/) a long fish-shaped shell that can be fired along the surface of the water to hit another ship and explode on touching it. ● *vb* to hit or damage with a torpedo.

torpid /**tawr**-pid/ *adj* lacking energy, numb, inactive, dull (*feeling torpid in the extreme heat*).

torrent /**taw**-rent/ *n* **1** a rushing stream. **2** a heavy downpour (*rain came down in a torrent*).

torrential /taw-**ren**-shal/ *adj* flowing with great violence, falling heavily and steadily (*torrential rain*).

torrid /**taw**-rid/ *adj* **1** extremely hot. **2** dried up by heat.

torso /**tawr**-so/ *n* the body without the head or limbs (*a statue of a torso*).

tortilla /tawr-**tee**-ya/ *n* a thin pancake made with cornmeal or wheat flour and wrapped around a filling, used in Mexican cooking.

tortoise /**tawr**-toyz/ (*Br*) *see* **turtle**.

tortoiseshell /**tawr**-tus-shell/ *n* the shell of a type of sea turtle used to make combs, rims of spectacles, etc., colored brown and yellow.

tortuous /**tawr**-chu-wus/ *adj* crooked, twisting (*tortuous mountain roads*).

torture /**tawr**-chur/ *vb* **1** to cause great suffering or anxiety to. **2** to cause pain to as a punishment or in order to obtain information from (*he was tortured* *by the enemy*). ● *n* extreme pain or anxiety. ● *adj* **torturous** /**tawr**-chu-rus/.

toss /tawss/ *vb* **1** to throw upward, to jerk upward, as the head (*toss a coin in the air*). **2** (*of a ship*) to roll about in rough seas. **3** to drink (off) quickly (*toss off his soda*). ● *n* a throw. ● **toss up** to throw up a coin to decide something by chance.

tot /tot/ *n* a small child.

total /**toe**-tal/ *adj* **1** whole (*the total cost*). **2** complete (*the car was a total wreck*). ● *n* **1** the whole amount. **2** the result when everything has been added up. ● *vb* **1** to add up (*total the items on the check*). **2** to add up to. ● *adv* **totally** /**toe**-ta-lee/.

totalitarian /toe-ta-li-**tay**-ree-n/ *adj* allowing only one political party.

totality /toe-**ta**-lity/ *n* the complete amount.

totem /**toe**-tem/ *n* an animal or plant taken by a tribe as an emblem and regarded as mysteriously connected with the tribe.

totem pole /**toe**-tem-pole/ *n* a pole on which the totem or symbols of it are carried.

totter /**tot**-er/ *vb* to stand or walk unsteadily, to stagger (*tottering down the street in high-heeled shoes*).

toucan /**too**-can/ *n* a South American bird with a huge bill.

touch /tuch/ *vb* **1** to come to rest against with any part of the body, especially the hand. **2** to be in contact. **3** to cause to feel emotion (*touched by the poem*). **4** to make a difference to, to concern (*the changes in management did not touch her*). ● *n* **1** act of coming against or being in contact with. **2** the ability to do really well something requiring skill. **3** the sense of feeling. **4** (*in soccer*) the ground at the side of the marked field of play. ● **touch on** to mention briefly. ● **touch up** to improve by making small changes.

touching /**tu**-ching/ *adj* moving the feelings, causing pity.

touchline /**tuch**-line/ *n* (*in soccer*) the side lines of the marked field of play.

touchstone /**tuch**-stone/ *n* something by comparison with which you judge other things, ideas, etc. (*a touchstone for the other students' work*).

touchy /**tu**-chee/ *adj* easily angered or hurt (*in a touchy mood*). ● *n* **touchiness** /**tu**-chee-ness/.

tough /tuff/ *adj* **1** hard to cut, tear, or chew (*tough meat*). **2** hardy and strong (*people living there have to be tough*). **3** rough-mannered (*a tough neighborhood*). **4** difficult to deal with (*a tough problem*). ● *n* a street ruffian.

toughen /**tu**-fen/ *vb* **1** to make tough. **2** to make better able to resist (*toughen the plastic*).

tour /toor/ *n* a journey, made for pleasure, to various places, usually ending up at the starting point. ● *vb* to go for a tour, to travel here and there (*tour Canada*).

tourism /**too**-ri-zum/ *n* the providing of hotels, routes, etc., for tourists.

tourist /**too**-rist/ *n* a person who travels for pleasure, a sightseer.

tournament /**toor**-na-ment/ *n* **1** a series of games between different competitors to see which is the best player or team (*a tennis tournament*). **2** in olden times, a display of fighting on horseback in which the warriors carried blunted arms.

tourniquet /**toor**-ni-ket/ *n* a bandage twisted tightly around a limb to prevent the flow of blood from a cut artery.

tousle /**tou**-zel/ *vb* **1** to disarrange, especially the hair (*the wind had tousled her hair*). **2** to make untidy.

tout /tout/ *vb* to go about looking for customers or buyers (*tout for business*). ● *n* a person who touts (*a ticket tout*).

tow[1] /toe/ *vb* to pull along with a rope, chain, etc. ● *n* the act of towing.

tow[2] /toe/ *n* fibers of flax or hemp.

toward /**too**-ord/ *prep* in the direction of.

towel /**taoo**-el/ *n* a cloth for drying the body. ● *vb* to rub with a towel (*towel the child after bathing him*).

tower /**taoo**-wer/ *n* **1** a building much higher than it is broad. **2** a high part of another building, projecting above it. **3** a fortress. ● *vb* to rise high into the air (*the mountains tower above the village*).

towering /**taoo**-wer-ing/ *adj* **1** very high or tall (*a towering mountain*). **2** very great (*a towering rage*).

town /taoon/ *n* a group of houses, stores, etc., larger than a village but smaller than a city.

toxic /**tok**-sic/ *adj* poisonous (*the toxic substance in some plants*). ● *n* **toxicity** /tok-**si**-si-tee/.

toxicology /tok-si-**col**-o-jee/ *n* the study of poisons. ● *n* **toxicologist** /tok-si-**col**-o-jist/.

toxin /**tok**-sin/ *n* a poison (*the toxins in some plants*).

toy /toy/ *n* a plaything. ● *vb* to play with (*the dog was toying with the kitten*).

trace /trace/ *n* **1** a mark left behind (*a trace of blood on the knife*). **2** a footstep. **3** a sign of something that has happened or existed (*there were traces of a struggle*). ● *vb* **1** to copy a drawing on to transparent paper laid on top of it. **2** to follow the tracks of (*the police traced him to his hideout*). ● *adj* **traceable** /**tray**-sa-bul/.

tracery /**tray**-se-ree/ *n* stone carved to form an open design, as in the windows of old churches.

tracing /**tray**-sing/ *n* a drawing made by copying another drawing on to transparent paper laid on top of it.

track /**track**/ *n* **1** a footprint. **2** the mark or rut left by a wheel. **3** a path made by coming and going (*a track up the mountain*). **4** a railroad line. **5** a course for races. ● *vb* **1** to follow the marks left by (*track the wolf to its lair*). **2** to pursue or search for someone or something until found (*track down the source of the gas leak*).

track-and-field /**trac**-and-**feeld**/ *n* competitive athletic events that involve running, jumping, or throwing (*the track-and-field events*).

tract /**tract**/ *n* **1** a wide area of land. **2** a short booklet, especially one about religion.

traction /**trac**-shun/ *n* **1** the drawing of vehicles. **2** treatment of an injured limb by pulling on it gently with a device using weights and pulleys.

traction engine /**trac**-shun-en-jin/ *n* a steam engine for dragging loads on roads.

tractor /**trac**-tor/ *n* a heavy motor vehicle used for drawing other vehicles or farm implements.

trade /**trade**/ *n* **1** the buying and selling of goods. **2** the exchanging of goods in large quantities. ● *vb* **1** to buy and sell. **2** to exchange in large quantities.

trademark /**trade**-mark/ *n* an officially registered mark (such as ™) or name put on goods to show who manufactured them and that they are not to be used by any other party.

trader /**tray**-der/ *n* a person who buys and sells goods, a merchant.

tradesman /**traydz**-man/, **tradesperson** /**traydz**-persun/ *n* **1** a skilled manual worker (*the carpenter and other men in the building trade*). **2** a storekeeper. ● *See also* **journeyman**.

tradition /tra-**di**-shun/ *n* **1** the handing down of knowledge, customs, etc., from age to age by word of mouth (*according to tradition*). **2** any story, custom, etc., so handed down (*village traditions*).

traditional /tra-**di**-shnal/ *adj* according to or handed down by tradition (*traditional Thanksgiving customs*). ● *adv* **traditionally** /tra-**di**-shna-lee/.

traffic /**tra**-fic/ *n* **1** the coming and going of persons, vehicles, etc., between places. **2** trade. **3** the carrying of goods or persons in vehicles, etc. **4** all the vehicles on the roads (*freeway traffic*). ● *vb* (**trafficked** /**tra**-fict/, **trafficking** /**tra**-fi-cing/) to trade.

tragedy /**tra**-je-dee/ *n* **1** a sad event, a disaster (*his death was a tragedy*). **2** a play showing the suffering caused by man's inability to overcome evil (*Shakespeare's tragedies*).

tragic /**tra**-jic/ *adj* **1** having to do with tragedy (*a tragic actor*). **2** very sad (*a tragic story*). ● *adv* **tragically** /**tra**-jic-lee/.

trail /**trail**/ *n* **1** the track or scent left by a moving creature (*the stag's trail*). **2** a path or track made by coming and going (*the mountain trail*). ● *vb* **1** to drag along the ground (*the child trailing her teddy bear*). **2** to draw along behind. **3** to walk wearily (*children trailing home from school*). **4** to follow the tracks of (*trail the fox to its lair*).

trailer /**tray**-ler/ *n* **1** a vehicle without an engine towed by another. **2** a mobile home. **3** a short part of a movie shown in advance by way of advertisement. **4** a climbing plant.

train /**train**/ *vb* **1** to prepare or make to prepare by constant practice or teaching (*train the basketball team*). **2** to aim (*train his gun on them*). **3** to make to grow in a particular direction (*train the vine along the wall*). ● *n* **1** railroad cars or trucks drawn by an engine. **2** part of a dress that trails behind the wearer (*the bride's train*). **3** a series (*train of thought*). ● *n* **trainee** /tray-**nee**/.

trainer /**tray**-ner/ *n* a person who teaches animals or people to do something, often a sport, well (*a trainer of racehorses*).

training /**tray**-ning/ *n* education, practice (*football training*).

trait /**trate**/ *n* a special characteristic by which you may know a person (*his humor was his most endearing trait*).

traitor /**tray**-tor/ *n* a person who helps an enemy against his or her own country friends. ● *adj* **traitorous** /**tray**-tor-us/.

trajectory /tra-**jec**-tree/ *n* the path of a moving body (e.g., a bullet, a comet, etc.).

tram /**tram**/, **tramcar** /**tram**-car/ (*Br*) *see* **streetcar**.

tramp /**tramp**/ *vb* **1** to walk heavily. **2** to travel on foot (*it was a day's tramp for the army*). ● *n* **1** a journey on foot. **2** a person who has no home and walks about the countryside begging (*the tramp begged for spare change*). **3** the sound of heavy steps or many steps together (*the tramp of soldiers*).

trample /**tram**-pul/ *vb* to walk heavily on top of (*the animals trampled the crops*).

trampoline /**tram**-pu-lee/ *n* a large piece of canvas or strong nylon joined to a metal frame by springs, used for jumping on.

trance /**transs**/ *n* a state in which you are unconscious of your surroundings (*the hypnotist put her into a trance*).

tranquil /**tran**-kwil/ *adj* **1** calm, peaceful. **2** still. ● *n*

tranquility /tran-**kwi**-li-tee/, *also* **tranquillity** (*Br,* *Cdn*).

ranquilize /tran-kwi-lize/ *vb, also* **tranquilise** (*Br*) to calm (someone) down (*tranquilize the patient before surgery*).

ranquilizer /**tran**-kwi-lie-zer/ *n, also* **tranquiliser** (*Br*) anything (e.g., a pill) that calms a person down.

ransact /tran-**zact**/ *vb* to carry on or put through (*transact business with his firm*).

ransaction /tran-**zac**-shun/ *n* a piece of business (*a property transaction*). ● *npl* **transactions** /tran-**zac**-shunz/ a written record of the doings of a society.

ransatlantic /tran-zat-**lan**-tic/ *adj* across or crossing the Atlantic (*a transatlantic flight*).

ranscend /**tran**-send/ *vb* **1** to rise above (*his desire for power transcends everything else*). **2** to be superior to (*his new symphony transcends his other musical works*).

ranscendent /tran-**sen**-dent/ *adj* marvelous (*her transcendent beauty*).

ranscendental /tran-sen-**den**-tal/ *adj* beyond human understanding, supernatural.

ranscribe /tran-**scribe**/ *vb* to copy in writing.

ranscript /**tran**-script/ *n* a written copy (*a transcript of the broadcast*).

ransept /**tran**-sept/ *n* one of the two parts representing the arms in a cross-shaped church.

ransfer /tran-**sfer**/ *vb* (**transferred** /tran-**sferd**/, **transferring** /tran-**sfe**-ring/) to send or remove from one place or owner to another. ● *n* **transfer** /**tran**-sfer/ **1** the act of transferring (*seek a transfer from one firm to another*). **2** a design that can be pressed from one surface onto another.

ransferable /tran-**sfe**-ra-bul/ *adj* that can be transferred (*his property is transferable to his wife*).

ransference /tran-**sfe**-rense/ *n* act of transferring.

ransfigure /tran-**sfi**-gyur/ *vb* **1** to change in form, shape, or appearance. **2** to make more beautiful or splendid (*a face transfigured with happiness*). ● *n* **transfiguration** /tran-sfi-gyu-**ray**-shun/.

ransfix /tran-**sfiks**/ *vb* **1** to pierce through (*transfixed by a spear*). **2** to cause to be unable to move (*transfixed with terror*).

ransform /trans-**fawrm**/ *vb* **1** to change the form of. **2** to change completely (*computers transformed the office system*). ● *n* **transformation** /trans-fawr-**may**-shun/.

ransformer /trans-**fawr**-mer/ *n* a machine for changing the voltage of an electric current.

transfuse /trans-**fyooz**/ *vb* to transfer from one thing to another (e.g., by pouring).

transfusion /trans-**fyoo**-zhun/ *n* **1** the act of transfusing. **2** the passing of the blood of one person into another.

transient /**tran**-shent/ *adj* **1** not lasting for long, passing quickly (*transient pleasures*). **2** not staying for long (*a transient population*). ● *n* **transience** /**tran**-shense/.

transistor /tran-**sis**-tor/ *n* a simple radio receiving set in which the current is produced by sensitive wires in contact with a crystal. ● *adj* **transistorized** /tran-**sis**-tor-ized/, *also* **transistorised** (*Br, Cdn*).

transit /**tran**-sit/ *n* **1** going or being moved from one place to another (*passengers in transit at the airport*). **2** the passing of a planet between the sun and the earth.

transition /tran-**si**-shun/ *n* changing from one state or condition to another (*in transition between high school and college*). ● *adj* **transitional** /tran-**si**-shnal/.

transitive /**tran**-si-tiv/ *adj*. ● **transitive verb** a verb taking a direct object.

transitory /**tran**-si-toe-ree/ *adj* passing quickly, not lasting for long (*transitory pleasures*).

translate /tran-**slate**/ *vb* to give the meaning of what is said or written in one language in another language. ● *n* **translator** /tran-**slate**-or/.

translation /tran-**slay**-shun/ *n* a turning from one language into another.

translucent /tran-**sloo**-sent/ *adj* allowing light to pass through (*translucent glass*).

transmission /tran-**smi**-shun/ *n* **1** the act of sending messages, etc. **2** a radio or television broadcast.

transmit /tran-**smit**/ *vb* (**transmitted** /tran-**smi**-tid/, **transmitting** /tran-**smi**-ting/) **1** to send (a message, news, etc.). **2** to send by radio or television. **3** to send or pass from one person to another (*a disease transmitted by mosquitoes*).

transmitter /tran-**smi**-ter/ *n* a radio apparatus able to send messages or make broadcasts.

transmute /tran-**smyoot**/ *vb* (*fml*) to change from one form into another. ● *n* **transmutation** /tran-smyoo-**tay**-shun/.

transom /**tran**-sum/ *n* a window over a door.

transparent /tran-**spa**-rent/ *adj* **1** that can be clearly seen through. **2** obvious (*her misery was transparent to all*). ● *ns* **transparence** /tran-**spa**-rense/, **transparency** /tran-**spa**-ren-see/.

transpire /tran-**spire**/ *vb* **1** to become known (*it later transpired that he was not there*). **2** to happen (*wait and see what transpires*). **3** to exhale.

transplant /tran-**splant**/ *vb* 1 to uproot and plant in another place. 2 to replace an organ of the body by one belonging to someone else (*transplant a kidney*). ● *ns* **transplant** /tran-splant/, **transplantation** /tran-splan-**tay**-shun/.

transport /tran-**spoart**/ *vb* 1 to carry from one place to another (*transport children to school*). 2 (*old*) to convey to another country as a punishment. 3 (*fml*) to fill with emotions, anger, etc. ● *n* **transport** /tran-spoart/ 1 any means of carrying persons or goods from one place to another. 2 a ship for carrying troops. 3 (*fml*) great delight, ecstasy (*in transports after their victory*).

transportation /tran-spoar-**tay**-shun/ *n* the conveying of convicts to another country as a punishment.

transpose /tran-**spoaz**/ *vb* 1 to interchange the places of. 2 to change the order of (*transpose the words in the sentence*). ● *n* **transposition** /tran-spu-**zi**-shun/.

transverse /tran-**sverse**/ *adj* lying across.

trap /**trap**/ *n* 1 an instrument or device for catching wild animals and holding them alive or dead. 2 any device that, by its appearance, deceives you into advancing or progressing into unseen difficulties (*he walked into the trap*). 3 an S-shaped bend in drainpipes to prevent foul air rising. 4 a light two-wheeled horse carriage. ● *vb* (**trapped** /trapt/, **trapping** /tra-ping/) 1 to catch in a trap or snare. 2 to deceive (*they trapped her into admitting her guilt*).

trapdoor /**trap**-dore/ *n* a door in a floor, ceiling, or roof.

trapeze /tra-**peez**/ *n* a bar suspended from two swinging ropes, some distance above the ground, and used in gymnastic or acrobatic exercises.

trapezium /tra-**pee**-zee-um/ *n* a four-sided figure of which two sides are parallel and unequal in length.

trapper /**tra**-per/ *n* a person who traps animals, especially for their furs.

trappings /**tra**-pingz/ *npl* 1 finery, decoration. 2 an ornamental harness for a horse.

trash /**trash**/ *n* 1 that which is thrown away as useless, useless material (*put the trash in the trashcan*). 2 nonsense (*talk trash*). ● *adj* **trashy** /**tra**-shee/.

trashcan /**trash**-can/ *n* a container for household trash.

trauma /**traw**-ma/ *n* a shock that has a long-lasting effect. ● *adj* **traumatic** /traw-**ma**-tic/. ● *adv* **traumatically** /traw-**ma**-ti-ca-lee/.

travel /**tra**-vel/ *vb* 1 to make a journey (*travel by train to the city*). 2 to move on your way (*the speed at which light travels*). ● *n* **travel**. ● *vb, adj* **traveled** /

tra-veld/, **traveling** /**trav**-ling/; *also* **travelled**, **travelling** (*Br, Cdn*).

travel agent /**tra**-vel-ay-jent/ *n* a person who makes travel arrangements for customers. ● *n* **travel agency** /**tra**-vel-ay-jen-see/.

traveler /**trav**-ler/ *n, also* **traveller** (*Br, Cdn*) 1 a person who journeys. 2 a person who goes from place to place trying to obtain orders for a business firm (*also* **traveling salesman**).

traverse /tra-**verse**/ *vb* to go across (*traversing the desert*).

travesty /**tra**-ve-stee/ *vb* to imitate in such a way as to make appear ridiculous. ● *n* a silly imitation.

trawl /**trawl**/ *n* a large wide-mouthed net for deep sea fishing. ● *vb* to fish by drawing a trawl through the water.

trawler /**traw**-ler/ *n* a fishing boat using a trawl.

tray /**tray**/ *n* a flat piece of wood, metal, etc., with rim, used for carrying dishes, etc.

treacherous /**tre**-che-rus/ *adj* 1 faithless, disloyal, deceitful (*treacherous followers*). 2 dangerous, but seeming safe (*a treacherous beach full of mines*).

treachery /**tre**-che-ree/ *n* unfaithfulness to those who have placed trust in you, disloyalty.

treacle /**tree**-cul/ (*Br*) *see* **molasses**.

tread /**tred**/ *vb* (*pt* **trod** /trod/, *pp* **trodden** /**trod**-en or **trod**) 1 to step or walk (*tread softly*). 2 to walk heavily on (*tread grapes to crush them*). ● *n* 1 step (*hear her tread on the stairs*). 2 your way of walking. 3 the sound of walking. 4 the flat part of the step of a stair. 5 the part of a tire that touches the ground.

treadle /**tre**-dul/ *n* a pedal used for operating a machine.

treadmill /**tred**-mill/ *n* 1 a millwheel turned by persons treading on steps sticking out from it. 2 an exercise machine with an endless belt on which you walk or run.

treason /**tree**-zun/ *n* disloyalty to your country or ruler.

treasonable /**tree**-zu-na-bul/ *adj* having to do with treason (*treasonable actions*).

treasure /**tre**-zhur/ *n* 1 something greatly valued (*family treasures such as photographs*). 2 a store of great wealth. ● *vb* to value greatly.

treasurer /**tre**-zhu-rer/ *n* a person who is in charge of the money of a society, business firm, etc.

treasure trove /**tre**-zhur-trove/ *n* treasure found hidden and ownerless (*the children dug up some treasure trove on the beach*).

treasury /**trezh**-ree/ *n* 1 (*with cap*) the government department in charge of a nation's finances. **2** a store where public money is kept. **3** (*old*) a book containing a collection of facts, poems, etc.

treat /treet/ *vb* **1** to deal with. **2** to act toward. **3** to talk or write about. **4** to try to cure by certain remedies. **5** to pay for another's entertainment. **6** to discuss conditions for an agreement. ● *n* **1** an entertainment. **2** something that gives great pleasure.

treatise /tree-tize/ *n* a piece of writing giving information on a certain subject (*a treatise on diseases*).

treatment /treet-ment/ *n* the way of treating anything.

treaty /tree-tee/ *n* an agreement between two nations (*a treaty that ended the war*).

treble /tre-bul/ *adj* threefold, three times. ● *vb* to multiply by three. ● *n* the highest part in singing, soprano.

tree /tree/ *n* a plant with a trunk and branches of wood.

trek /trek/ *vb* (**trekked** /trekt/, **trekking** /tre-king/) to journey on foot, often wearily (*trek around the stores buying presents*). ● *also n*.

trellis /tre-liss/ *n* a light framework of crisscrossing bars of wood or metal for supporting climbing plants.

tremble /trem-bul/ *vb* **1** to shake with fear, cold, fever, etc. **2** to feel great fear.

tremendous /tre-men-dus/ *adj* **1** huge. **2** very great, impressive (*a tremendous achievement*). ● *adv* **tremendously** /tre-men-dus-lee/.

tremor /tre-mur/ *n* a slight shaking or shivering (*earth tremors*).

trench /trench/ *n* a long, narrow hole or ditch dug in the ground, especially one to shelter soldiers from enemy gunfire.

trenchant /tren-chant/ *adj* (*of remarks*) sharp and forceful (*trenchant criticism*).

trend /trend/ *n* **1** a tendency. **2** a general inclination toward (*a trend toward smaller families*).

trendy /tren-dee/ *adj* (*inf*) very fashionable (*a trendy nightclub*).

trepidation /tre-pi-day-shun/ *n* fear.

trespass /tress-pass/ *vb* **1** to go unlawfully on another's land (*walkers trespassing on the farmer's land*). **2** (*old*) to sin. ● *also n*. ● *n* **trespasser** /tress-passer/.

tress /tress/ *n* a lock of hair. ● *npl* **tresses** long hair worn loose.

trestle /tre-sul/ *n* a frame that supports a bridge or railroad track.

tri- /trie/ *prefix* three.

trial /trie-al/ *n* **1** the examining of a prisoner in a court of law. **2** a test (*give the young woman a trial as a secretary*). **3** hardship or distress undergone (*the trials of being homeless*).

triangle /trie-ang-gul/ *n* **1** a figure with three sides and three angles. **2** a musical instrument consisting of a triangle-shaped steel rod, played by striking it with a small rod.

triangular /trie-ang-gyu-lar/ *adj* having three sides and three angles.

triathlon /trie-ath-lon/ *n* an athletic contest consisting of three events, usually swimming, cycling, and long-distance running.

tribe /tribe/ *n* a group of people or families living together under the rule of a chief. ● *adj* **tribal** / trie-bal/. ● *n* **tribesman** /triebz-man/.

tribulation /tri-byoo-lay-shun/ *n* great suffering or trouble (*the trials and tribulations of the refugees*).

tribunal /trie-byoo-nal/ *n* **1** a court of justice. **2** a body appointed to look into and report on a matter of public interest.

tribune /tri-byoon/ *n* a Roman magistrate chosen by the people.

tributary /tri-byu-ta-ree/ *n* a stream that flows into a larger stream or river

tribute /tri-byoot/ *n* **1** deserved praise (*pay tribute to her bravery*). **2** money paid by a defeated nation to its conquerors.

trice /trice/ *n*. ● **in a trice** in a moment.

trick /trick/ *n* **1** something said or done in order to deceive (*gain entry to the house by a trick*). **2** something done quickly and skillfully in order to amuse (*a conjurer's trick*). **3** a special way of doing something (*the trick of getting the car to start*). **4** cards played and won in a round. ● *vb* to deceive, to cheat.

trickery /trik-ree/ *n* cheating, deceitful conduct (*use trickery to get the old woman's money*).

trickle /tri-cul/ *vb* to flow very slowly (*blood trickling from the wound*). ● *n* a thin stream of liquid.

tricky /tri-kee/ *adj* **1** cunning (*a tricky customer*). **2** requiring skill (*a tricky piece of engineering*). **3** difficult (*a tricky situation*).

tricycle /trie-si-cul/ *n* a three-wheeled cycle.

trident /trie-dent/ *n* a spear with three prongs.

tried /tried/ *pt of* **try**. ● *adj* reliable, proved good.

trifle /trie-ful/ *n* **1** a thing of little value or importance (*worry about trifles*). **2** a small amount (*she was a trifle annoyed*). **3** a pudding consisting of sponge cake, fruit, and cream. ● *vb* **1** to treat without seriousness. **2** to idle.

trifling /trie-fling/ *adj* **1** of no value or importance. **2** very small (*a trifling animal*).

trigger /tri-ger/ *n* a small lever that when pulled fires a gun. ● *vb* **1** to cause something to happen (*trigger an allergic reaction*), **2** to cause something to start functioning (*trigger the alarm*).

trigonometry /tri-gu-**nom**-et-ree/ *n* the science dealing with the measurement of triangles, and the relation between their sides and angles.

trillion /**trill**-yun/ *n* **1** a million million (10^{12}; 1,000,000,000,000) **2** (*inf*) a very large number.

trilogy /tri-lo-jee/ *n* a series of three connected plays, novels, etc.

trim /trim/ *vb* (**trimmed** /trimd/, **trimming** /tri-ming/) **1** to make neat, especially by cutting (*have her hair trimmed*). **2** to decorate (*trim the coat with fake fur*). **3** to rearrange cargo so that a ship is properly balanced. **4** to make ready for sailing. ● *adj* neat, tidy. ● **in good trim 1** in good condition. **2** well-prepared.

trimester /trie-**mes**-ter/ *n* **1** an academic term. **2** three months. **3** one third of the length of a human pregnancy.

trimming /tri-ming/ *n* something added as an ornament (*gold trimming on the evening dress*).

trinity /tri-ni-tee/ *n* a union of three in one. ● **the Trinity** the Christian belief that in one God there are three persons—the Father, Son, and Holy Spirit.

trinket /tring-ket/ *n* an ornament of little value, a piece of cheap jewelry.

trio /tree-yo/ *n* **1** a set of three, especially three musicians who play together (*the trio of rascals who broke the windows*). **2** a piece of music for three performers.

trip /trip/ *vb* (**tripped** /tript/, **tripping** /tri-ping/) **1** to stumble or fall over (*she tripped getting off the bus*). **2** to cause to stumble or fall (*they deliberately tripped her up*).**3** (*fml*) to move with quick light steps (*trip upstairs*). ● *n* **1** a stumble. **2** a short journey or outing.

tripe /tripe/ *n* **1** part of the stomach of a sheep, cow, etc., prepared as food. **2** (*inf*) nonsense, rubbish (*the movie was just tripe*).

triple /tri-pul/ *adj* made up of three parts, threefold. ● *vb* to make or become three times as large or many (*tripled his income in a year*).

triplet /tri-plit/ *n* one of three children born at one birth.

triplicate /tri-pli-kit/ *adj* threefold. ● *n*: **in triplicate** with three copies.

tripod /trie-pod/ *n* a three-legged stand or suppor‹ (e.g., for a camera).

tripper /tri-per/ *n* (*inf*) a person who is on vacatio‹ or on an outing for pleasure (*the trippers set out fo‹ the shore*).

trite /trite/ *adj* often used, commonplace (*her word‹ of comfort were rather trite*).

triumph /trie-yumf/ *n* **1** joy at success or victory. **2** great success or victory (*the crowd cheered her tr‹ umph*). ● *vb* to gain a great success or victory (*tr‹ umphed over the opposition*).

triumphal /trie-**yum**-fal/ *adj* having to do with a vic‹ tory (*a triumphal procession*).

triumphant /trie-**yum**-fant/ *adj* **1** successful, victo‹ rious (*the triumphant team*). **2** joyous at succes‹ or victory (*triumphant at the team's win*). ● *ad‹* **triumphantly** /trie-**yum**-fant-lee/.

triumvirate /trie-**yum**-vi-rit/ *n* a group of three peo‹ ple sharing the power of government.

trivet /tri-vet/ *n* a three-legged stand for a pot, ket‹ tle, etc.

trivia /tri-vee-ya/ *npl* (*now often regarded as a sin‹ gular noun*) facts of small importance (*a head fu‹ of trivia*).

trivial /tri-vee-yal/ *adj* of small importance, triflin‹ (*waste time on trivial matters*). ● *n* **triviality** /tri‹ vee-ya-li-tee/.

troglodyte /trog-lo-dite/ *n* a cave-dweller.

troll /trole/ *n* a dwarfish elf or goblin.

trolley /trol-ee/ *n* (*pl* **trolleys** /trol-eez/) **1** a pole tha‹ conveys electric current from an overhead wire t‹ a streetcar. **2** a streetcar. **3** (*Br*) a cart for trans‹ porting goods in a supermarket or baggage at a‹ airport.

trombone /trom-**bone**/ *n* a deep-toned type of trum‹ pet with a sliding tube moved in and out when it i‹ being played.

troop /troop/ *n* **1** a collection or group of people o‹ animals (*a troop of monkeys in the circus*). **2** a‹ organized group of soldiers, scouts, etc. ● *vb* t‹ move or gather in large numbers. ● *npl* **troop‹** /troops/ soldiers.

trooper /troo-per/ *n* a cavalryman, *see* **cavalry**.

trophy /troe-fee/ *n* something given or kept as a re‹ ward for or reminder of success or victory (*a tro‹ phy for winning the tournament*).

tropic /trop-ic/ *n* one of two imaginary lines aroun‹ the earth marking the farthest distance north an‹ south of the equator at which the sun rises an‹ sets during the year. ● *npl* **tropics** /trop-ics/ the h‹ regions north and south of the equator.

tropical /**trop**-ic-al/ *adj* **1** having to do with the tropics (*a tropical fruit*). **2** very hot.

trot /trot/ *vb* (**trotted** /**trot**-id/, **trotting** /**trot**-ing/) **1** (*of a horse*) to go at a pace between a walk and a gallop. **2** to run with short steps (*a child trotting behind his mother*). ● *n* a medium pace.

troth /troth/ *n* —**plight your troth** (*old*) to promise to marry.

trotter /**trot**-er/ *n* the foot of a pig or sheep.

trouble /**tru**-bl/ *vb* **1** to cause anxiety, difficulty, or distress to (*he was troubled by his daughter's absence*). **2** to disturb (*please don't trouble to get up*). ● *n* **1** worry, anxiety, distress (*her son causes her a lot of trouble*). **2** difficulty (*having trouble closing the door*).

troublesome /**tru**-bl-sum/ *adj* causing trouble (*a troublesome task*).

trough /troff/ *n* **1** a long, narrow vessel to hold water or food for animals. **2** a hollow (e.g., between two waves).

trounce /trounss/ *vb* to beat severely (*they trounced the opposing team*).

troupe /troop/ *n* a company of actors or other performers.

trousers /**trou**-zers/ (*Br*) *see* **pants**.

trousseau /**troo**-so/ *n* (*pl* **trousseaux** *or* **trousseaus** / **troo**-soaz/) a bride's outfit.

trout /trout/ *n* an edible freshwater fish.

trowel /**trow**-el/ *n* **1** a tool with a flat blade used for spreading mortar, plaster, etc. **2** a tool with a curved blade used in gardening.

troy /troy/, **troy weight** *n* a system of measures used in weighing precious metals or gems.

truant /**troo**-ant/ *n* a child who stays off school without leave (*the teacher saw the truants at the supermarket*). ● **play truant** to stay off school without leave. ● *n* **truancy**.

truce /trooss/ *n* an agreement to stop fighting for a time (*both armies agreed on a truce at Christmas*).

truck[1] /truck/ *n* a large motor vehicle for carrying goods.

truck[2] /truck/ *n* dealings (*have no truck with the people next door*).

trucker /**tru**-ker/ *n* a truck driver.

truck farm /**truck**-farm/ *n* a garden in which vegetables are grown for sale (*they get organically grown vegetables from a truck farm*). ● *n* **truck farmer** / **truck** far-mer/.

truculent /**tru**-cyu-lent/ *adj* quarrelsome, trying to find a cause for quarreling or fighting (*children in a truculent mood*). ● *n* **truculence** /**tru**-cyu-lenss/.

trudge /trudge/ *vb* to walk, especially with heavy steps, to walk in a tired manner (*trudge home after a hard day's work*). ● *also n*.

true /troo/ *adj* **1** in agreement with fact, not false (*the true facts*). **2** genuine (*the true heir*). **3** honest. **4** faithful, loyal (*true friends*). **5** exact, close (*a true copy*). ● *adv* **truly** /**troo**-lee/.

truffle /**tru**-ful/ *n* an edible fungus that grows underground (*truffles are an expensive delicacy*).

truism /**troo**-i-zum/ *n* a remark that is obviously true and therefore unnecessary (*"look before you leap" is a truism*).

trump /trump/ *n* one of a suit of cards that, in a particular hand, beats a card of any other suit. ● *vb* to play a trump on a card of another suit. ● **trump up** to make up, to invent.

trump card /**trump**-card/ *n* a means of ensuring success.

trumpet /**trum**-pet/ *n* a metal wind instrument. ● *vb* **1** to make known far and wide. **2** to make a noise, like an elephant (*trumpet as he blew his nose*).

trumpeter /**trum**-pe-ter/ *n* a person who plays the trumpet.

truncate /trung-**cate**/ *vb* to cut off, to cut short (*a truncated meeting*).

truncheon /**trun**-shun/ *n* **1** a club carried by a police officer. **2** a short staff carried as a sign of authority.

trundle /**trun**-dul/ *vb* to roll, push, or bowl along (*the bus trundled along the country road*).

trunk /trungk/ *n* **1** the main stem of a tree. **2** the body without the head or limbs (*the rash was confined to his trunk*). **3** the long tubelike nose of an elephant. **4** a box or chest for clothing, etc. (*store the clothing in the trunk*). **5** the storage place for luggage at the back of an automobile.

trunks /trungks/ *npl* men's shorts worn for swimming or other sports.

truss /truss/ *n* **1** a bundle of hay or straw. **2** a supporting bandage (*a truss for a hernia*). ● *vb* **1** to tie (*the burglars trussed up the guard*). **2** to tie up (a fowl) for cooking.

trust /trust/ *n* **1** a firm belief that another person or a thing is what it claims or is claimed to be, confidence (*put your trust in him*). **2** a union of several firms to advance their business interests. **3** the holding and controlling of money or property for the advantage of someone (*money held in trust until she is 21*). **4** care or responsibility (*a child placed in her trust*). ● *vb* **1** to rely upon, to have faith in. **2** to hope. ● **take on trust** to accept without examination or inquiry.

trustee /tru-**stee**/ *n* a person who is appointed to hold and look after property on behalf of another. ● *n* **trusteeship** /tru-**stee**-ship/.

trustful /**trust**-ful/, **trusting** /**trust**-ing/ *adjs* ready to trust.

trustworthy /**trust**-wur-thee/ *adj* deserving trust or confidence, reliable.

trusty /**tru**-stee/ *adj* (*fml*) that can be trusted, reliable (*his trusty followers*).

truth /**trooth**/ *n* that which is true (*always tell the truth*). ● *adj* **truthful** /**trooth**-ful/. ● *adv* **truthfully** /**trooth**-ful-ee/.

try /**trie**/ *vb* (**tried** /**tried**/, **trying** /**trie**-ing/) **1** to attempt (*try to climb the tree*). **2** to test (*try the new flavor*). **3** to examine and judge in a court of law.

trying /**trie**-ing/ *adj* difficult, worrying, annoying (*a trying time for all*).

tsar, tzar, czar /**zar**/ *n* the title of the emperor of Russia. ● *f* **tsarina**.

tsetse /(t)**set**-see/ *n* an African fly whose bite is fatal to horses, cattle, etc., and which carries the disease of sleeping sickness.

T-shirt /**tee**-shirt/ *n* a short-sleeved collarless shirt or undershirt.

tsunami /(t)soo-**na**-mee/ *n* a huge sea wave produced by an underwater earthquake.

tub /**tub**/ *n* **1** a large open container used for bathing, washing clothing, growing things, etc. (*an old wooden washing tub*). **2** a bath tub.

tuba /**too**-ba/ *n* a low-pitched brass wind instrument.

tubby /**tu**-bee/ *adj* (*inf*) round and fat (*a tubby child*).

tube /**toob**/ *n* **1** a pipe. **2** a hollow cylinder.

tuber /**too**-ber/ *n* a swelling on the root of a plant (e.g. a potato).

tuberculosis /too-ber-cyu-**lo**-sis/ *n* a wasting disease caused by the growth of tubercles on the lungs or other organs, consumption. ● *adj* **tubercular** /too-ber-cyu-lar/.

tubing /**too**-bing/ *n* **1** a length of tube. **2** a series of tubes.

tubular /**too**-byu-lar/ *adj* **1** like a tube. **2** consisting of tubes (*tubular construction/tubular bells*).

tuck /**tuck**/ *vb* **1** to push, to stuff (*tucks his shirt into his pants*). **2** to put in a secure or private place (*tucked his book under his arm*). ● *n* a fold in a garment. ● **tuck in 1** to cover up comfortably (*tuck the baby in*). **2** (*inf*) to eat hungrily (*tuck into milk and cookies*).

Tuesday /**tooz**-day/ *n* the third day of the week.

tuft /**tuft**/ *n* **1** a bunch or clump of grass, hair, etc., growing together. **2** a bunch of threads, etc., held together.

tufty /**tuf**-tee/ *adj* growing in tufts (*tufty hair*).

tug /**tug**/ *vb* (**tugged** /**tugd**/, **tugging** /**tu**-ging/) **1** to pull with effort (*tug the gate open*). **2** to pull sharply (*tugged his sister's hair*). ● *n* **1** a strong sharp pull. **2** a small boat used to pull larger ones.

tug-of-war /tu-gu-**wawr**/ *n* a contest in which two teams pull opposite ways on a rope until one is pulled across a mark.

tuition /too-**wi**-shun/ *n* teaching (*private tuition in French*).

tulip /**too**-lip/ *n* a plant growing from a bulb and having a single brightly colored flower.

tumble /**tum**-bul/ *vb* **1** to fall (*the child tumbled down the hill*). **2** to do acrobatic and jumping tricks. ● *n* a fall.

tumbler /**tum**-bler/ *n* **1** a drinking glass (*a tumbler of cold water*). **2** an acrobat (*tumblers in the circus*).

tumbleweed /**tum**-bul-weed/ *n* a plant broken away from its roots in the fall and rolled about by the wind.

tummy /**tu**-mee/ *n* (*inf*) a stomach (*a pain in my tummy*).

tumor /**too**-mur/ *n, also* **tumour** (*Br, Cdn*) a mass of diseased cells in the body causing swelling (*a brain tumor/a malignant tumor*).

tumult /too-**mult**/ *n* **1** noisy confusion, uproar (*his statement went unheard in the tumult*). **2** disorderly behavior by a crowd.

tumultuous /too-**mul**-chu-wus/ *adj* noisy and disorderly (*a tumultuous welcome*).

tuna /**too**-na/ *n* a large edible fish of the mackerel family.

tundra /**tun**-dra/ *n* a wide plain of frozen marshy land in northern Siberia or North America.

tune /**toon**/ *n* **1** the melody or air of a piece of music. **2** a short pleasing piece of music. **3** the correct relation of one musical note to others. ● *vb* **1** to see that the strings of an instrument are adjusted to play the correct notes. **2** to adjust a radio, etc, until it is receiving as clearly as possible.

tuneful /**toon**-ful/ *adj* having a pleasing air or melody (*a tuneful air*). ● *adv* **tunefully** /**toon**-fu-lee/.

tungsten /**tung**-sten/ *n* a rare metallic element, used for filaments in electric light bulbs.

tunic /**too**-nic/ *n* **1** a loose upper garment covering the body, sometimes to below the waist. **2** a soldier's uniform jacket.

tuning fork /**too**-ning-fawrk/ *n* a two-pronged fork that, when struck, gives a musical note to which instruments can be adjusted.

tunnel /tu-nel/ *n* an underground passage, especially one that enables a road or railroad to pass under or through an obstacle (*the train went through a tunnel*).

turban /tur-ban/ *n* a headdress, common in the East, made by winding a band of fabric around and around the head.

turbine /tur-bin/ *n* a type of wheel that, when moved by steam or water power, drives an engine.

turbot /tur-but/ *n* a large edible flatfish.

turbulent /tur-byu-lent/ *adj* 1 moving violently and irregularly. 2 disorderly, hard to control or rule, rebellious (*a turbulent crowd of protestors*). ● *n* **turbulence** /tur-byu-lense/.

tureen /tu-reen/ *n* a large deep dish for soup.

turf /turf/ *n* earth covered thickly with short grass (*the turf of the golf course*). ● *vb* to cover with turf.

turkey /tur-kee/ *n* a large farmyard fowl (*roast turkey for Thanksgiving*).

Turkey Day /tur-kee day/ *n* an informal name for **Thanksgiving Day**.

Turkish bath /tur-kish-bath/ *n* 1 a treatment in which you sit in a room of steam to induce a sweat and then follow it with a shower and massage. 2 the place where you would go for a Turkish bath.

turmoil /tur-moil/ *n* noisy confusion, disorder (*the office was in turmoil after she left*).

turn /turn/ *vb* 1 to move or cause to move around (*she turned to face him*). 2 to shape wood by cutting it as it revolves. 3 to change (*turn into a beautiful young woman*). 4 (*of milk*) to become sour. ● *n* 1 a change of direction. 2 (*of a wheel*) a revolution. 3 a bend (*the accident happened at the turn in the road*). 4 an act (*she did him a good turn*). 5 a short walk (*take a turn along the promenade*). 6 a sudden feeling of sickness. ● **turn down** to refuse (*turn down the invitation*). ● **turn in** (*inf*) to go to bed. ● **turn out 1** to have (good or bad) results (*it turned out for the best*). 2 to attend a meeting, etc. (*very few turned out because of the weather*). ● **turn over a new leaf** to change yourself for the better. ● **turn turtle** to turn completely over, to capsize. ● **turn up** to appear unexpectedly (*she did not turn up at the meeting*). ● **turn upon** to attack suddenly (*the dog turned upon its master*). ● **in turn** one after the other, in the proper order (*they drove the car in turns*).

turning /tur-ning/ *n* 1 a bend in the road. 2 a corner leading off to another road.

turnip /tur-nip/ *n* 1 a plant of the mustard family with a thick edible root. 2 (*Br*) see **rutabaga**.

turnout /tur-nout/ *n* the number of people in an assembly (*a large turnout at the concert*).

turnover /tur-no-ver/ *n* in business, the amount of money paid in and out in a certain period (*the store's turnover is down this year*).

turnpike /turn-pike/ *n* a gate or bar across a road at which travelers must pay a tax for the use of the road.

turnstile /turn-stile/ *n* a revolving gate through which only one person can pass at a time (*pay at the turnstile*).

turntable /turn-tay-bul/ *n* 1 a revolving platform for turning round railroad engines, etc. 2 a round spinning surface on a phonograph on which the record is placed.

turpentine /tur-pen-tine/ *n* 1 a resin obtained from certain trees. 2 an oil made from this.

turquoise /tur-kwoiz/ *n* a greenish-blue precious stone or its color (*dressed all in turquoise*). ● *also adj*.

turret /tu-ret/ *n* 1 a small tower forming part of a building (*a castle with many turrets*). 2 a revolving tower to protect guns and gunners on a warship or in a fort.

turtle /tur-tul/ *n* a four-footed reptile almost entirely covered by a hard shell.

turtle dove /tur-tul-duv/ *n* a dove with a soft, cooing note.

turtle neck /tur-tul nek/ *n* 1 a high collar that turns down and fits closely around the neck. 2 a sweater or shirt with such a collar.

tusk /tusk/ *n* a long, pointed tooth sticking out from the mouth, as in an elephant, walrus, etc.

tussle /tu-sul/ *n* a short struggle, a disorderly fight (*the children had a tussle over the toys*). ● *vb* to struggle.

tut /tut/ *interj* an exclamation expressing disappointment or disapproval.

tutor /too-tur/ *n* a private teacher (*she has a tutor to help with the subjects with which she is having difficulty*). ● *vb* to teach, to act as tutor.

tutorial /too-toe-ree-al/ *adj* having to do with a tutor or teaching. ● *n* 1 a group of students who study with a tutor. 2 study time spent with a tutor.

tutu /too-too/ *n* a very short stiff skirt worn by a female ballet dancer.

TV /tee-vee/ *n* television.

twaddle /twod-ul/ *n* nonsense, foolish talk (*he was talking twaddle*).

twang /twang/ *n* 1 the sound made by plucking a tightly stretched string or wire. 2 a tone that sounds as if you were speaking through your nose. ● *vb* to pluck a tightly stretched string or wire.

tweak /tweek/ *vb* to twist sharply, to pinch (*she tweaked his ear in fun*). ● *also n*.

tweed /tweed/ *n* a rough woolen cloth, suitable for outer garments.

tweezers /twee-zerz/ *npl* small pincers for pulling out hairs, lifting tiny things, etc. (*plucked her eyebrows with tweezers*).

twelve /twelv/ *n* and *adj* the number 12. ● *adj* and *n* **twelfth** /twelfth/.

twenty /twen-tee/ *n* and *adj* the number 20. ● *adj* and *n* **twentieth** /twen-tee-yeth/.

twice /twice/ *adv* two times (*he has been beaten only twice*).

twiddle /twi-dul/ *vb* to play with (*sit twiddling your fingers with nothing to do*).

twig /twig/ *n* a small shoot or branch of a tree or shrub.

twilight /twie-lite/ *n* the faint light just after sundown.

twill /twill/ *n* a strong cloth with ribbed lines or ridges running from end to end (*pants made of twill*).

twin /twin/ *n* **1** one of two children born at one birth. **2** a person or thing that looks exactly the same as another (*the twin of her china vase*). ● *adj* **1** born at one birth (*twin babies*). **2** double. **3** consisting of two like parts or things (*twin engines*). ● *vb* (**twinned** /twinnd/, **twinning** /twin-ing/) to pair together.

twine /twine/ *n* strong string (*garden twine*). ● *vb* **1** to twist or wind around. **2** to twist together (*garden plants twining around each other*).

twinge /twinge/ *n* a sudden sharp pain (*a twinge in his back when he bent down*).

twinkle /twing-kul/ *vb* **1** to sparkle. **2** to shine with a light that very quickly increases and decreases (*stars twinkling in the sky*). ● *n* **1** a gleam of light. **2** a quick look of amusement in the eyes.

twinkling /twing-kling/ *n* a moment.

twirl /twirl/ *vb* to spin or turn around rapidly (*she twirled the baton*). ● *also n*.

twist /twist/ *vb* **1** to turn quickly out of shape or position. **2** to wind strands around each other (to make a cord). **3** to put a wrong meaning on (*she deliberately twisted his words*). ● *n* **1** something made by twisting. **2** a sudden turning out of shape or position.

twister /twi-ster/ *n* a tornado.

twitch /twich/ *n* **1** a jerk. **2** a sudden quick move-

ment. ● *vb* **1** to pull sharply (*twitch her dress into position*). **2** to make a quick movement unintentionally (*her eye twitches*).

twitter /twi-ter/ *vb* to chirp, as a bird. ● *n* **1** a chirp. **2** a state of nervous excitement (*in a twitter about the party*).

two /too/ *adj* and *n* one more than one.

two-faced /too-fayst/ *adj* deceitful, not sincere (*supposed loyal supporter who turned out to be two-faced*).

tycoon /tie-coon/ *n* a very successful and influential businessman, a business magnate.

type /tipe/ *n* **1** a class or kind (*a kind of vegetable*). a person or thing possessing most of the qualities of a certain group, class, nationality, etc. **3** a letter or symbol cut in metal, etc., and used for printing. **4** the kind and size of a set of letters used in printing. ● *vb* to use a typewriter (*he is learning to type*).

typescript /tipe-script/ *n* typewritten material (*sent the typescript to her publisher*).

typeset /tipe-set/ *vb* to set a written piece of work in a typed form. ● *n* **typesetter**. ● *adj* **typeset**.

typewriter /tipe-rie-ter/ *n* a machine operated by keys that, when struck, cause letters or symbols to be printed through an inked ribbon on to paper.

typhoid /tie-foid/ *n* an infectious disease causing acute pain in the intestines (*get typhoid from infected food*).

typhoon /tie-foon/ *n* a violent storm of wind and rain especially in the China seas.

typical /ti-pi-cal/ *adj* **1** characteristic (*it was typical of him not to apologize*). **2** serving as an example of a class or group (*a typical village store*). ● *adv* **typically** /ti-pi-clee/.

typify /ti-pi-fie/ *vb* to serve as an example of.

typist /tie-pist/ *n* a person who uses a typewriter.

typography /tie-pog-ra-fee/ *n* the art of printing. ● *n* **typographer** /tie-pog-ra-fer/.

tyrannical /ti-ran-ic-al/, **tyrannous** /ti-ran-us/ *adj* cruel, ruling unjustly (*a tyrannical emperor*).

tyrannize /ti-ra-nize/ *vb, also* **tyrannise** (*Br*) to use power cruelly or unjustly (*the dictator was known to tyrannize the people*).

tyrannosaurus /ti-ran-o-saw-rus/ *n* a very large meat-eating dinosaur that walked on its hind legs and had two small front legs.

tyranny /ti-ra-nee/ *n* cruel or unjust use of power.

tyrant /tie-rant/ *n* **1** a person who uses power cruelly. **2** an unjust ruler.

tyre /tire/ (*Br*) *see* tire².

tzar /zar/ *see* **tsar**. ● *f* **tsarina** /za-ree-na/.

U

u, u /yoo/ the twenty-first letter of the alphabet.

ubiquitous /yoo-**bi**-kwi-tus/ *adj* being or seeming to be in more than one place at the same time, seemingly occurring everywhere (*broccoli seems to be ubiquitous in restaurants these days*). ● *n* **ubiquity** /yoo-**bi**-kwi-tee/.

U-boat /**yoo**-boat/ *n* a German submarine.

udder /**u**-der/ *n* the organ containing the milk-producing gland of a cow, sheep, etc.

UFO /yoo-ef-**oa**/ *abbr* = **unidentified flying object**: a strange, unidentified object seen in the sky, believed by some people to be an alien spacecraft.

ugly /**ug**-lee/ *adj* **1** unpleasant to see or hear. **2** unpleasant, dangerous (*an ugly occurrence in the bar*). ● *n* **ugliness** /**ug**-lee-ness/.

ukulele /yoo-ca-**lay**-lee/ *n* a stringed musical instrument similar to a guitar played by plucking the strings.

ulcer /**ul**-sur/ *n* an open, painful sore on the skin, or inside the mouth or stomach (*mouth ulcers*).

ulcerated /**ul**-su-ray-tid/, **ulcerous** /**ul**-su-russ/ *adjs* having an ulcer or ulcers.

ulema /yoo-lu-**ma**/ *n* a group of Muslim men who have authority in religion and law.

ulna /**ul**-na/ *n* the larger of the two bones of the forearm in humans, on the opposite side of the thumb.

ulterior /ul-**ti**-ree-ur/ *adj* further, secret, hidden.

ulterior motive /ul-ti-ree-ur-**mo**-tiv/ *n* a reason for action that one does not make known to others.

ultimate /**ul**-ti-mit/ *adj* **1** last, final (*his ultimate destination*). **2** greatest or highest possible.

ultimately /**ul**-ti-mit-lee/ *adv* in the end.

ultimatum /ul-ti-**may**-tum/ *n* (*pl* **ultimatums** /ul-ti-**may**-tumz/ *or* **ultimata** /ul-ti-**may**-ta/) a last offer of conditions, to be followed, if refused, by action without more discussion (*she gave an ultimatum that if he did not stop bothering her, she would call the police*).

ultra- /**ul**-tra/ *prefix* **1** very, extremely (*ultraviolet light*). **2** beyond (*ultramicroscopic*).

ultramarine /ul-tra-ma-**reen**/ *n* a deep blue color. ● *also adj.*

ultrasound /**ul**-tra-sound/ *n* the use of ultrasonic waves to form images of inside the body (*she saw her unborn baby while having an ultrasound*).

ultraviolet /ul-tra-**vie**-lit/ *adj* having to do with a kind of radiation present in sunlight that is harmful to the eyes and skin, the wavelengths of which are shorter than violet light.

ultravirus /**ul**-tra-vie-rus/ *n* a virus so small that it can pass through even the finest filters.

ulu /**oo**-loo/ *n* a knife with a broad, almost semicircular blade, used traditionally by Eskimo women.

umber /**um**-ber/ *n* a reddish brown color.

umbilicus /um-**bi**-li-cus/ *n* (*pl* **umbilici** /um-**bi**-li-kie/) the navel. ● *adj* **umbilical** /um-**bi**-li-cul/.

umbrage /**um**-bridge/ *n*: **take umbrage** to be offended or made angry by.

umbrella /um-**bre**-la/ *n* a folding frame covered with waterproof material that can be opened out and held over the head at the end of a stick as protection against rain.

umiak /**oo**-mee-ak/ *n* a large, open boat made of skins stretched on a wooden frame, used by Eskimos for moving goods.

umpire /**um**-pire/ *n* a person who acts as judge in a dispute or contest, a referee (*a baseball umpire*).

umpteen /**um**-teen/ *adj* a great number of, a great many. ● *adj* **umpteenth** (*for the umpteenth time, clean your room!*).

un- /**un**/ *prefix* not.

unabashed /u-na-**basht**/ *adj* not ashamed, not put off, confident (*she was unabashed by the complaints*).

unable /u-**nay**-bul/ *adj* not able, lacking the ability, means or power to do something.

unabridged /u-na-**bridgd**/ *adj* not shortened, complete (*unabridged edition of the book*).

unacceptable *adj* unwelcome, not good enough to be acceptable.

unaccommodating *adj* not ready to oblige.

unaccountable /u-na-**coun**-ta-bul/ *adj* that cannot be explained (*for some unaccountable reason*).

unaccustomed /u-na-**cu**-stumd/ *adj* not usual (*the unaccustomed warmth of a day in March*).

unacknowledged /u-nak-**nol**-idgd/ *adj* not recognized, ignored (*his unacknowledged skill*).

unaffected /u-na-**fec**-tid/ *adj* **1** simple, sincere (*his unaffected manner*). **2** unmoved (*unaffected by the child's tears*).

unanimous /yoo-**na**-ni-mus/ *adj* **1** being all of the same opinion (*they were unanimous in their decision*). **2** agreed to by all present (*a unanimous vote*).

unapproachable /u-na-**pro**-cha-bul/ *adj* unfriendly in manner.

unarmed /u-**narmd**/ *adj* having no weapons, especially firearms or armor.

unassuming /u-na-**soo**-ming/ *adj* modest, not boastful.

unauthorized /un-**aw**-thu-riezd/ *adj*, *also* **unauthorised** (*Br, Cdn*) done without permission.

unaware /u-na-**ware**/ *adj* not knowing, ignorant (of).

unawares u-na-**wayrz**/ *adv* unexpectedly (*catch the thief unawares*).

unbearable /un-**bay**-ra-bul/ *adj* that cannot be accepted or allowed.

unbecoming /un-bi-**cu**-ming/ *adj* not suitable, not proper, unattractive (*her behavior was unbecoming*).

unbelief /un-bi-**leef**/ *n* lack of faith, doubt.

unbeliever /un-bi-**lee**-ver/ *n* a person who does not believe in the accepted religion.

unbend /un-**bend**/ *vb* **1** to make straight. **2** to behave in a more friendly way (*she was unfriendly at first but she unbent later*).

unbiased /un-**bi**-ast/ *adj* fair to all parties, just (*the judge made an unbiased decision*).

unblock /un-**block**/ *vb* to remove a block from (*unblock the sink so it drains properly*).

unbounded /un-**boun**-did/ *adj* great, without limits (*unbounded enthusiasm*).

unbridled /un-**brie**-duld/ *adj* uncontrolled (*unbridled rage*).

unburden /un-**bur**-din/ *vb* **1** (*fml*) to take a load off. **2** to tell about something that has caused worry or anxiety (*unburden himself of his worries*).

unbutton /un-**bu**-tin/ *vb* to unfasten the button or buttons of something.

uncalled-for /un-**cawld**-fawr/ *adj* not required, unnecessary and rude (*uncalled-for comments about her perfomance*).

uncanny /un-**ca**-nee/ *adj* strange, mysterious.

uncap /un-**cap**/ *vb* to remove the cap from.

uncertain /un-**ser**-tin/ *adj* **1** not sure (*uncertain about how to proceed*). **2** doubtful (*uncertain plans*). ● *n* **uncertainty** /un-**ser**-tin-tee/.

uncharitable /un-**cha**-ri-ta-bul/ *adj* harsh, severe, unkind, ungenerous (*uncharitable thoughts*).

unclasp /un-**clasp**/ *vb* to unfasten the clasp of.

uncle /un-**cul**/ *n* **1** the brother of a person's father or mother. **2** the husband of a person's aunt.

Uncle Sam /un-cul **sam**/ *n* a made-up person, who represents the United States, who is a tall, thin man with white hair and a beard, dressed in a red, white, and blue costume of a coat jacket with tails, striped pants, and a tall hat with a band of stars.

uncoil /un-**coil**/ *vb* to unwind (*the rope wa uncoiled*).

uncomfortable /un-**cumf**-ta-bul/ *adj* **1** uneasy (*fee uncomfortable about going to the party alone*). giving no comfort (*an uncomfortable chair*).

uncommunicative /un-cu-**myoo**-ni-cay-tiv/ *adj* no speaking much to others.

uncomplimentary /un-com-pli-**men**-tree/ *adj* critical, insulting.

uncompromising /un-**com**-pru-mise-ing/ *adj* firm not ready to give in (*both sides had uncompro mising attitudes*).

unconcerned /un-cun-**sernd**/ *adj* **1** unmoved. uninterested.

unconditional /un-cun-**dish**-nal/ *adj* without con ditions (*unconditional surrender*).

unconformity /un-cun-**fawr**-mi-tee/ *n* not bein the same as others.

unconscious /un-**con**-shus/ *adj* **1** not knowing, una ware (*unconscious of what was going on*). stunned, as by a blow to the head, and so una ware of what is going on (*knocked unconsciou by the blow*).

unconstitutional /un-con-sti-**too**-shnal/ *adj* agains the principles of a constitution, especially said o the US Constitution; unlawful.

unconventional /un-cun-**ven**-shnal/ *adj* not boun by custom, natural, free and easy (*unconventiona dress and manners*).

uncouth /un-**cooth**/ *adj* rough in manner, awkward clumsy (*uncouth manners*).

uncover /un-**cu**-ver/ *vb* to make known, to reveal.

uncultivated /un-**cul**-ti-vay-tid/ *adj* **1** not prepare for crops (*uncultivated land*). **2** uncivilized, crud (*an uncultivated people*).

undaunted /un-**dawn**-tid/ *adj* bold, fearless (*un daunted, they went through the jungle*).

undecided /un-di-**sie**-did/ *adj* not having made u the mind, doubtful (*undecided about how to vote*)

undemonstrative /un-di-**mon**-stra-tiv/ *adj* no showing feelings, calm by nature (*the judge wa an undemonstrative man*).

undeniable /un-di-**nie**-a-bul/ *adj* that cannot b argued against, certain (*his undeniable guilt*).

under /un-der/ *prep* **1** below. **2** beneath. **3** subjec to. **4** less good than. ● *adv* in a lower condition degree, or place. ● *pref* **under-** /un-der/ in, on, t or from a lower place or side, beneath or below

underachieve /un-der-a-**chee**-va-bul/ *vb* to fail to do as well as expected, as in school classes.

underage /un-der-**ayj**/ *adj* below the age required by law.

underarm /un-der-**arm**/ *adj* of, for, in, or used on the area under the arm or the armpit.

underbelly /un-der-be-lee/ *n* 1 the lower part of an animal's belly. 2 any unprotected area.

underbrush /un-der-brush/ *n* small trees, shrubs, etc. that grow underneath large trees in woods or forests.

undercarriage /un-der-ca-ridge/ *n* the wheels or other parts on the underside of an aircraft needed for landing.

underclothes /un-der-cloathz/, **underclothing**, /un-der-cloathe-ing/ *n* clothes worn under others or next to the skin, underwear.

undercoat /un-der-coat/ *n* 1 a layer of short hair or fur under the longer hair or fur on an animal's coat. 2 *also* **undercoating** a coating, like a primer, which prepares a surface for another layer of paint, varnish etc.

undercover /un-der-**cu**-ver/ *adj* acting or carried out in secret.

undercurrent /un-der-**cu**-rint/ *n* 1 a current, as of air or water, flowing beneath the surface. 2 an influence or popular feeling that cannot easily be noticed (*undercurrent of discontent in the office*).

undercut /un-der-**cut**/ *vb* to offer to sell at a lower price (than). ● *n* undercut /un-der-cut/ 1 the underside of a loin of beef. 2 in a fight, a blow from below.

underdog /un-der-**dawg**/ *n* a person or group that is expected to lose.

underdone /un-der-**dun**/ *adj* not sufficiently cooked, lightly cooked (*the underdone chicken was still pink*).

underestimate /un-der-e-sti-mate/ *vb* to have too low an opinion of (*underestimate his ability*).

underfur /un-der-fur/ *n* the soft, shorter layer of fur under the longer layer of fur on an animal's coat.

undergo /un-der-**go**/ *vb* to bear, to suffer (*undergo much pain*).

undergraduate /un-der-**gra**-ju-wit/ *n* a university student who has not yet earned a degree.

underground /un-der-**ground**/ *adj and adv* 1 beneath the ground. 2 secret (*an underground political organization*). ● *n* underground /un-der-ground/ 1 a place below the surface of the earth. 2 a railway running through underground tunnels.

Underground Railroad /un-der-ground-**rail**-road/ *n*
in the United States before the Civil War, a network of people and a system of secret hiding places that slaves could use when running away to Canada and the free states in the North.

undergrowth /un-der-**groath**/ *n* shrubs and low bushes growing among trees.

underhand /un-der-**hand**/ *adj* sly, secret, dishonest (*an underhand action*).

underline /un-der-**line**/ *vb* 1 to draw a line under. 2 to emphasize (*underline the need*).

undermine /un-der-**mine**/ *vb* 1 to make holes underground. 2 to destroy gradually, to seek to harm by underhand methods (*undermine his confidence*).

underneath /un-der-**neeth**/ *adv* under, below, beneath, on the underside.

underpants /un-der-**pants**/ *n* underwear for the lower part of the body, long or short, with two openings for the legs.

underpass /un-der-**pass**/ *n* part of a road or footpath that goes underneath a road or railway.

underrate /un-der-**rate**/ *vb* to have too low an opinion of (*underrate their ability*).

undersell /un-der-**sell**/ *vb* to sell at a lower price (than) (*he tried to undersell his competitors*).

undershirt /un-der-**shurt**/ *n* a collarless shirt with or without sleeves worn under an outer shirt.

undersized /un-der-**siezd**/ *adj* less than the normal size, very small.

understand /un-der-**stand**/ *vb* 1 to see the meaning of (*understand the poem*). 2 to know thoroughly (*understand the filing system*). 3 to work out the truth from what has been said (*understand his motives*).

understanding /un-der-**stan**-ding/ *n* 1 intelligence, powers of judgment. 2 an agreement, especially an unwritten one (*an understanding that the money would be paid every month*).

understate /un-der-**state**/ *vb* to talk of something as smaller or less important than it really is (*understate his role in the events*).

understudy /un-der-**stu**-dee/ *n* an actor or actress who learns the same part as another to be able to take his or her place if necessary (*the understudy took the place of the sick actor*).

undertake /un-der-**take**/ *vb* to take upon oneself to do, to attempt.

undertaker /un-der-**tay**-ker/ *n* a funeral director.

undertaking /un-der-**tay**-king/ *n* 1 a task (*an undertaking requiring great skill*). 2 a promise (*he gave an undertaking that he would be present*).

undertow /**un**-der-toe/ *n* the backward flow of water after a wave breaks on the shore, an undercurrent.

underwear /**un**-der-ware/ *n* underclothes.

underwire /un-der-**wire**/ *n* a curved wire inserted into the bottom cups of certain brassieres for added support.

underworld /**un**-der-wurld/ *n* **1** the mythical place to which the spirits of people go after death. **2** those members of society who live by violence and crime.

undies /**un**-deez/ *n* an informal term for underwear.

undisguised /un-dis-**giezd**/ *adj* open, not hidden (*her undisguised jealousy*).

undisturbed /un-di-**sturbd**/ *adj* calm, tranquil (*an undisturbed night*).

undo /un-**doo**/ *vb* to reverse what has been done, to untie or unfasten, to ruin (*undo the damage*).

undoing /un-**doo**-ing/ *n* ruin (*lying was her undoing*).

undone /un-**dun**/ *pp* of **undo.** ● *adj* **1** not done. **2** ruined.

undoubted /un-**dou**-tid/ *adj* certain, undeniable (*her undoubted honesty*).

undress /un-**dress**/ *vb* **1** to take your clothes off (*she undressed in private*). **2** to take off the clothes of (*undress the doll*).

undue /un-**doo**/ *adj* greater than is necessary (*an undue panic*).

undulate /**un**-ju-late/ *vb* **1** to rise and fall like waves. **2** to have a wavy appearance.

unduly /un-**doo**-lee/ *adv* more than is necessary, excessively (*not unduly worried*).

unearth /un-**erth**/ *vb* **1** to discover by searching (*unearth the truth*). **2** to dig up (*police unearthed the evidence*).

unearthly /un-**erth**-lee/ *adj* weird, supernatural, ghostly (*there was an unearthly scream*).

uneasy /un-**ee**-zee/ *adj* uncomfortable, worried, anxious (*an uneasy feeling that all was not well*).

unemployed /un-im-**ployd**/ *adj* having no paid job, out of work.

unemployment /un-im-**ploy**-mint/ *n* the state of not having a job.

unequivocal /un-i-**kwi**-vu-cal/ *adj* clear, that cannot be misunderstood (*an unequivocal reply*).

unerring /un-**er**-ing/ *adj* true, going straight to the target (*with unerring accuracy*).

uneven /un-**ee**-vin/ *adj* **1** not flat, not smooth (*uneven ground*). **2** sometimes not as good as at other times (*his work is uneven*).

unfailing /un-**fay**-ling/ *adj* sure, reliable (*an unfailing remedy*).

unfamiliar /un-fa-**mil**-yar / *adj* strange (*unfamiliar territory*).

unfasten /un-fa-sin/ *vb* to undo, to unfix, to set loose (*unfasten the belt*).

unfathomable /un-fa-thu-ma-bul/ *adj* **1** very deep. **2** mysterious.

unfetter /un-**fet**-ur/ *vb* to free from restraint of any kind. ● *adj* **unfettered.**

unforeseen /un-fur-**seen**/ *adj* unexpected (*unforeseen circumstances*).

unfortunate /un-**fawrch**-nit/ *adj* unlucky (*it was unfortunate that she missed the bus*).

unfounded /un-**foun**-did/ *adj* not based on fact (*unfounded accusations*).

unfurl /un-**furl**/ *vb* to spread out (*unfurl the flag*).

ungainly /un-**gane**-lee/ *adj* clumsy, awkward (*her ungainly way of walking*).

ungodly /un-**god**-lee/ *adj* not religious, sinful, wicked.

ungrateful /un-**grate**-ful/ *adj* not showing due thanks (*an ungrateful remark*).

unhappiness /un-**ha**-pee-nis/ *n* misfortune, misery.

unhappy /un-**ha**-pee/ *adj* **1** miserable, sad (*unhappy that she had failed*). **2** unlucky (*an unhappy set of circumstances*).

unhealthy /un-**helth**-ee/ *adj* **1** not having good health. **2** bad for health (*unhealthy diet*). **3** having a bad influence.

uni- /**yoo**-nee/ *pref* having or consisting only of one.

unicorn /**yoo**-ni-cawrn/ *n* in fables, an animal like a horse with a single straight horn on its head.

unicycle /**yoo**-ni-sie-cul/ *n* a one-wheeled cycle straddled by the rider who pushes its peddles.

uniform /**yoo**-ni-fawrm/ *adj* **1** unchanging. **2** of the one kind, shape, size, etc. ● *n* distinctive clothing worn by all members of the same organization, institution, etc. (*school uniform/police uniform*).

unify /**yoo**-ni-fie/ *vb* to unite, to form into one (*unify the political factions into a single party*). ● *n* **unification** /yoo-ni-fi-cay-shun/.

unilateral /yoo-ni-la-tu-rul/ *adj* affecting one side or party only (*a unilateral attitude to nuclear weapons*).

unintentional /un-in-**ten**-shnal/ *adj* not done on purpose.

union /**yoon**-yun/ *n* **1** a putting together to make one. **2** act of joining together. **3** a trade union (*the print unions*).

unique /yoo-**neek**/ *adj* being the only one of its kind, unequalled (*she has a unique beauty*).

unisex /**yoo**-ni-seks/ *adj* designed for use by both men and women, not for one particular sex (*a unisex hair salon*).

unison /**yoo**-ni-sun/ *n* agreement. ● **in unison** all at the same time together.

unit /**yoo**-nit/ *n* 1 the number one. 2 a single person, thing, or group. 3 a fixed amount, etc., taken as a standard in measuring.

unite /yoo-**nite**/ *vb* 1 to make or become one (*unite the two organizations*). 2 to join, to act or work together (*the people united to defeat the tyrant*).

unity /**yoo**-ni-tee/ *n* 1 oneness. 2 agreement.

universal /yoo-ni-**ver**-sal/ *adj* 1 total, whole. 2 affecting all, done by everyone (*a universal effort*). ● *adv* **universally** /yoo-ni-**ver**-sa-lee/.

universality /yoo-ni-ver-**sa**-li-tee/ *n* the state of being universal.

universe /**yoo**-ni-verse/ *n* 1 the whole of creation. 2 the world.

university /yoo-ni-**ver**-si-tee/ *n* a place of higher education in which advanced study in all branches of knowledge is carried on, and by which degrees are awarded to those showing proper ability in their subjects.

unjust /un-**just**/ *adj* unfair, dishonest, not just.

unkempt /un-**kempt**/ *adj* (of hair) uncombed.

unlawful /un-**law**-ful/ *adj* against the law, illegal.

unleaded /un-**led**-id/ *adj* not containing lead compounds, said of gasoline.

unleavened /un-**le**-vend/ *adj* not mixed with yeast (*unleavened bread*).

unless /un-**less**/ *conj* if not, except that.

unlimited /un-**li**-mi-tid/ *adj* 1 as much as is wanted, that cannot be used up (*unlimited supply of money*).

unload /un-**load**/ *vb* to remove the load or burden from (*unload the truck*).

unlucky /un-**lu**-kee/ *adj* unfortunate.

unmask /un-**mask**/ *vb* to remove a mask or disguise from.

unmentionable /un-**men**-shna-bul/ *adj* unfit to be mentioned, especially in polite conversation.

unmitigated /un-**mi**-ti-gay-tid/ *adj* complete, with no good qualities, thorough (*an unmitigated disaster*).

unmoved /un-**moovd**/ *adj* firm, calm, not affected (by) (*unmoved by the child's plea*).

unnerve /un-**nerv**/ *vb* to take away the strength or courage of (*unnerved by the confidence of the opposition*).

unobtrusive /un-nub-**troo**-siv/ *adj* not attracting attention, modest.

unoccupied /un-**oc**-yu-pied/ *adj* empty (*unoccupied houses*).

unorthodox /un-**or**-thu-doks/ *adj* holding unusual views, differing from the accepted view.

unpack /un-**pack**/ *vb* to open and removed the packed contents of.

unpalatable /un-**pa**-la-ta-bul/ *adj* 1 unpleasant to taste (*unpalatable food*). 2 unpleasant (*an unpalatable set of events*).

unpopular /un-**pop**-yu-lar/ *adj* widely disliked.

unparalleled /un-**par**-a-leld/ *adj* that has no equal, unmatched.

unprecedented /un-**pre**-su-den-tid/ *adj* without a previous example of the same kind (*an unprecedented set of ideas*).

unprejudiced /un-**pre**-ju-dist/ *adj* fair, showing favor to no one.

unpremeditated /un-pree-**med**-i-tay-tid/ *adj* done without forethought (*an unpremeditated crime*).

unprepossessing /un-pre-pu-**ze**-sing/ *adj* unattractive at first sight (*an unprepossessing sight*).

unpretentious /un-pri-**ten**-shus/ *adj* modest, not attracting attention.

unprincipled /un-**prin**-si-puld/ *adj* immoral, wicked, recognizing no standards of right or wrong.

unproductive /un-pru-**duc**-tiv/ *adj* 1 yielding no crops, etc. 2 giving no profit (*an unproductive scheme*).

unprofessional /un-pru-**fesh**-nal/ *adj* against the rules or customs of a profession (*unprofessional conduct*).

unqualified /un-**kwawl**-i-fied/ *adj* 1 not having the necessary training or skill. 2 complete (*an unqualified success*).

unquestionable /un-**kwes**-chu-na-bul/ *adj* undoubted, certain (*unquestionable proof*).

unravel /un-**ra**-vel/ *vb* 1 to untangle. 2 to solve (*unraveled the problem*).

unrelenting /un-ri-**len**-ting/ *adj* refusing to yield.

unrelieved /un-ri-**leevd**/ *adj* 1 without relief (from pain, etc.). 2 lacking variety (*unrelieved boredom*).

unremitting /un-ri-**mi**-ting/ *adj* without pause, ceaseless (*his unremitting effort*).

unrequited /un-ri-**kwie**-tid/ *adj* not rewarded, not returned (*unrequited love*).

unresolved /un-ri-**zolvd**/ *adj* not settled, undecided (*the matter remains unresolved*).

unrest /un-**rest**/ *n* discontent, rebellion.

unruly /un-**roo**-lee/ *adj* disorderly, badly behaved (*the unruly behavior of the schoolchildren*).

unsavory /un-**save**-ree/ *adj*, *also* **unsavoury** (*Br, Cdn*) unpleasant, without taste or smell (*an unsavory dinner*).

unscathed /un-**scaythd**/ *adj* unhurt (*he climbed from the wreck unscathed*).

unscrupulous /un-**scroo**-pyu-lus/ *adj* having no standards of good and evil, wicked (*an unscrupulous criminal*).

unseemly /un-**seem**-lee/ *adj* not fitting, improper (*unseemly behavior*).

unsettle /un-**se**-tul/ *vb* to upset, to disturb (*the incident unsettled them*).

unsheathe /un-**sheethe**/ *vb* to draw from a sheath or holder (*unsheathe the sword*).

unsightly /un-**site**-lee/ *adj* ugly, unpleasant to look at (*an unsightly scar*).

unskilled /un-**skild**/ *adj* having no special skill or training.

unsociable /un-**so**-sha-bul/ *adj* avoiding others, not sociable, unfriendly.

unsolicited /un-su-**li**-si-tid/ *adj* not asked for (*unsolicited advice*).

unsophisticated /un-su-**fi**-sti-cay-tid/ *adj* simple, natural, innocent.

unsound /un-**sound**/ *adj* **1** not healthy. **2** faulty (*equipment that is unsound*).

unspeakable /un-**spee**-ca-bul/ *adj* better or worse than can easily be expressed in words (*his unspeakable rudeness*).

unstudied /un-**stu**-deed/ *adj* natural, without having tried, not got by study (*with unstudied grace*).

unsuspecting /un-su-**spec**-ting/ *adj* free from fear of danger or evil, trusting (*too unsuspecting to think he was lying*).

untangle /un-**tang**-gul/ *vb* to free from a snarl, to free from confusion.

unthinkable /un-**thing**-ka-bul/ *adj* beyond the ability to understand or imagine (*the unthinkable crime*).

unthinking /un-**thing**-king/ *adj* showing lack of thought, attention, or consideration.

untie /un-**tie**/ *vb* to loosen, undo, or unfasten something tied or knotted.

until /un-**til**/ *prep* up to the time of. ● *conj* up to the time when.

untimely /un-**time**-lee/ *adj* happening at a wrong or an inconvenient time (*an untimely visit*).

untold /un-**toald**/ *adj* **1** not related, not told (*untold stories*). **2** vast (*untold wealth*).

untouchable /un-**tu**-cha-bul/ *n* **1** a person or thing that cannot be touched. **2** a member of the lowest Hindu caste, whom a higher-caste Hindu may not touch.

untoward /un-tu-**wawrd**/ *adj* awkward, unsuitable, undesirable (*a journey in which nothing untoward happened*).

untrue /un-**troo**/ *adj* **1** not true. **2** not loyal, faithless (*untrue followers*).

untruth /un-**trooth**/ *n* (*fml*) a lie, a falsehood (*tell an untruth*).

untruthful /un-**trooth**-ful/ *adj* given to lying.

unusual /un-**yoozh**-wal/ *adj* rare, peculiar, strange (*unusual patterns*).

unutterable /un-**u**-tu-ra-bul/ *adj* that cannot be described in words (*his unutterable rudeness*).

unveil /un-**vale**/ *vb* to uncover, to reveal, to disclose to view (*unveil the portrait*).

unwelcome /un-**wel**-cum/ *adj* not gladly received

unwell /un-**wel**/ *n* ill; sick.

unwieldy /un-**weel**-dee/ *adj* **1** huge. **2** hard to move. **3** clumsy.

unwilling /un-**wi**-ling/ *adj* not willing, reluctant (*unwilling to get involved*).

unwind /un-**winde**/ *vb* to undo, to straighten out, to make relaxed or less tense.

unwitting /un-**wi**-ting/ *adj* not knowing (*the unwitting cause of her injury*).

unworldly /un-**wurld**-lee/ *adj* **1** not interested in things in this life. **2** lacking experience of public life.

unworthy /un-**wur**-thee/ *adj* **1** not deserving (*a remark unworthy of comment*). **2** dishonorable (*unworthy thoughts*).

unwrap /un-**rap**/ *vb* to open, to take off the wrapping.

unzip /un-**zip**/ *vb* to open a zipper, to separate the edges by opening a zipper.

up /up/ *adv* **1** in or to a higher place, amount, etc. **2** above. ● *prep* to, toward, or at a higher place or in.

up- /up/ *pref* combining form to suggest an upward movement.

up-and-coming /up-and-**cu**-ming/ *adj* gaining in importance or status, promising.

upbeat /up-**beet**/ *n* **1** an upward trend. **2** in music, an unaccented beat, especially on the last note of a bar. ● *adj* lively, cheerful.

upbringing /up-**bring**-ing/ *n* a person's early training at home and school.

upcoming /up-**cum**-ing/ *adj* coming soon.

upcountry /up-**cun**-tree/ *adj* of or located in the central part of a country, inland.

update /up-**date**/ *vb* to bring up to date, to make aware of the most recent facts.

updraft /up-**draft**/ *n* an upward air current.

upend /up-**end**/ *vb* to set or turn on end.

upfield /up-**feeld**/ *adv, adj* into, toward, or in the opposite end of the field.

upfront /up-**frunt**/ *adj* very honest and open.

upgrade /up-**grade**/ *n* **1** an upward slope, especially in a road. **2** an improvement of the position or status of something.

upheaval /up-**hee**-val/ *n* **1** the pushing up of part of the earth's surface by forces below it. **2** a great change (*the upheaval of moving houses*).

uphill /up-**hill**/ *adv* in an upward direction. ● *adj* **1** sloping upward. **2** very difficult (*an uphill task*).

uphold /up-**hoald**/ *vb* **1** to support (*upholding the right of free speech*). **2** to defend as correct (*the appeal judge upheld the original sentence*).

upholster /up-**hole**-ster/ *vb* to provide (chairs, sofas, etc.) with springs, stuffing, covering, etc. ● *n* **upholstery** /up-**hole**-stree/. ● *n* **upholsterer** /up-**hole**-stur-er/.

upkeep /up-**keep**/ *n* **1** the money needed to keep anything in good condition. **2** the act of keeping in good health or condition (*the upkeep of the large house*).

upland /up-**land**/ *n* land above other land, as along a river.

uplift /up-**lift**/ *vb* **1** to raise. **2** to make to think of higher things. ● *n* **uplift** /up-**lift**/ the act or process of lifting up.

upload /up-**load**/ *vb* to load or transfer a file or program from a personal computer to a central computer.

upon /up-**on**/ *adv* on, used only for completing a verb.

upper /up-**er**/ *adj* higher in place or rank. ● *n* the upper part of a shoe.

uppercase /up-er-**case**/ *n* capital-letter type used in printing, rather than lower case or small letters.

uppercut /up-**er**-cut/ *n* in boxing, a short, swinging blow directed upward toward the chin.

uppermost /up-**er**-moast/ *adj* highest in place or rank (*the thought was uppermost in his mind*).

upright /up-**rite**/ *adj* **1** standing straight up. **2** honest (*an upright member of the community*). ● *n* a vertical post.

uprising /up-**rie**-zing/ *n* the action of rising up, as in a rebelling against the government.

upriver /up-**ri**-ver/ *adj, adv* toward the source of a river.

uproar /up-**roar**/ *n* loud, confused noise (*there was an uproar when the concert was cancelled*). ● *adj* **uproarious** /up-ro-**ree**-us/.

uproarious /up-ro-**ree**-us/ *adj* noisy (*an uproarious party*).

uproot /up-**root**/ *vb* to tear up by the roots (*the trees were uprooted in the storm*).

upset /up-**set**/ *vb* **1** to overturn, to knock over (*tables upset during the fight*). **2** to spoil completely (*plans upset because of a change in the weather*). **3** to cause to be sad, worried, etc. (*his remarks upset her*). ● *adj* **1** worried. **2** ill. ● *n* **upset** /up-set/ **1** disturbance. **2** trouble. **3** a sudden misfortune.

upset price /up-set-**price**/ *n* the minimum price something can be sold for at an auction.

upshot /up-shot/ *n* result, outcome (*the upshot of the meetings was a raise for the workers*).

upside /up-**side**/ *n* the upper side or part.

upside-down /up-side-**down**/ *adv* with the top down and the bottom upward.

upstage /up-**stage**/ *adv* toward or at the rear of a stage. ● *adj*. ● *vb* to draw the attention of the audience away from a fellow actor/actress and put the focus on oneself.

upstairs /up-**stares**/ *adv* on an upper floor of a house with stairs.

upstanding /up-**stan**-ding/ *adj* **1** standing straight. **2** upright in character and behavior.

upstart /up-**start**/ *n* a person who has risen quickly to a position of wealth or importance (*older members regard him as an upstart*).

upstate /up-**state**/ *n* that part of a state farther to the north or away from a large city.

upstream /up-**streem**/ *adv, adj* in the direction against the current of a stream.

uptight /up-**tite**/ *adj* tense and worried (*uptight about the test results*).

up-to-date /up-tu-**date**/ *adj* containing the most recent information.

uptown /up-**town**/ *adj, adv* of, in, like, to, or toward the upper part of a city or town, usually the part away from the main business section.

upward /up-**ward**/ *adj, adv* toward a higher place, position, degree, amount, etc.

uranium /yoo-**ray**-nee-um/ *n* a heavy, white, radioactive metal.

Uranus /yoo-ra-nus/ *n* the seventh planet from the sun, and the third-largest planet in the solar system.

urban /ur-ban/ *adj* having to do with a city or city life (*urban areas of the country*).

urbane /ur-**bane**/ *adj* polite, refined, smooth (*his urbane manner charmed everyone*). ● *n* **urbanity** /ur-**ba**-ni-tee/.

urchin /ur-chin/ *n* **1** (*old*) a ragged, poor street boy. **2** a sea creature with a prickly shell.

urethra /yoo-**ree**-thra/ *n* the duct through which urine is passed through the body in most mammals.

urge /urge/ *vb* **1** to press to do (*urge her to take the job*). **2** to suggest strongly (*urge caution*).

urgent /ur-jent/ *adj* requiring to be done quickly or at once, needing immediate attention (*it is an urgent matter*). ● *n* **urgency** /ur-jen-see/.

urinal /yoo-ra-nul/, **urinal** /yoo-**rie**-nul/ *n* a place for passing urine.

urine /yoo-rin/ *n* fluid passed from the kidneys and bladder. ● *adj* **urinary** /yoo-ri-ne-ree/ having to do with urine.

urn /urn/ *n* **1** a vase for the ashes of the dead. **2** a large container with a tap for making and serving tea or coffee.

usable /yoo-za-bul/ *adj* that can be used.

usage /yoo-sidge/ *n* treatment (*furniture subjected to rough usage*).

use /yooz/ *vb* **1** to do something with for a purpose (*use a knife to cut the butter*). **2** to employ (*use a great many long words*). **3** consume (*use all the butter*). ● *n* **1** the act of using, the state of being used (*for use in emergencies*). **2** advantage, benefit, value (*a book that is of no use to us*). **3** the power of using (*lose the use of her legs*). **4** permission to use, the right to use (*give them the use of the car*). ● **use up** to consume or exhaust, leaving nothing.

useful /yoos-ful/ *adj* **1** of help (*useful advice*). **2** able to be used (*tools no longer useful*).

useless /yoos-less/ *adj* **1** of no help. **2** not any use.

user /yoo-zer/ *n* a person or thing that uses something.

user-friendly /yoo-zer-**frend**-lee/ *adj* designed to be used easily by a wide range of people who are not experts (*a user-friendly computer program*).

usher /u-sher/ *n* a person who meets people at the door (of a church, hall, etc.) and shows them to their seats (*usher the guests to their seats*). ● *vb* to show in. ● *f* **usherette** /u-sher-**ret**/.

usual /yoo-zh-wal/ *adj* common, normal (*the usua price*).

usurer /yoo-zhu-rer/ *n* a person whose busines consists of lending money at high interest.

usurp /yoo-**surp**/ *vb* to seize power or property t which that person has no right (*attempt to usur the king's authority*). ● *n* **usurpation** /yoo-sur-**pay** shun/. ● *n* **usurper** /yoo-**sur**-per/.

usury /yoo-zhu-ree/ *n* (*fml*) the lending of mone at high interest.

Ute /yoot/ *n* a member of the Native American peopl formerly ranging throughout the south-wester plains regions, now living mainly in western Colo rado and eastern Utah, the language of this people

utensil /yoo-**ten**-sil/ *n* a vessel or object in com mon household use, such as a fork or knif (*kitchen utensils*).

uterine /yoo-te-rine/ *adj* **1** of the uterus. **2** havin; the same mother but different fathers.

uterus /yoo-te-rus/ *n* a female organ in mammal in which babies are developed, womb.

utilitarian /yoo-ti-li-**tay**-ree-an/ *n* a person wh considers that a thing or action is good only if i is useful. ● *also adj*.

utilitarianism /yoo-ti-li-**tay**-ree-a-ni-zum/ *n* th belief that only what is useful is good.

utility /yoo-**ti**-li-tee/ *n* **1** usefulness. **2** benefit. **3** public service (*gas and other utilities*).

utilize /yoo-**ti**-li-tize/ *vb* (*fml*), *also* **utilise** (*Br*) t make use of (*utilize her powers of observation*).

utmost /ut-moast/ *adj* **1** the farthest (*the utmos parts of the earth*). **2** the greatest (*utmost tact*).

utopia /yoo-**toe**-pee-ya/ *n* an imaginary state i which everything is perfect.

utopian /yoo-**toe**-pee-yan/ *adj* perfect but impos sible to achieve.

utter[1] /u-ter/ *adj* complete, total (*he is an utter fool*

utter[2] /u-ter/ *vb* to speak, to pronounce (*utter h first words*).

utterance /u-ter-anse/ *n* **1** something said. **2** a wa of speaking.

uttermost /u-ter-moast/ *adj* **1** farthest (*the utter most parts of the Earth*). **3** greatest (*the uttermos care*).

U-turn /yoo-turn/ *n* a turn made so as to head i the opposite direction.

uvula /yoo-vyu-la/ *n* a small piece of flesh hangin inside the back of the mouth.

V

V, v /**vee**/ the twenty-second letter of the alphabet.

vacancy /**vay**-can-see/ *n* **1** an empty space. **2** a job to be filled (*advertise vacancies in the paper*).

vacant /**vay**-cant/ *adj* **1** empty, not occupied (*vacant flats*). **2** unthinking (*in a vacant mood*). ● *adv* **vacantly** /**vay**-cant-lee/.

vacate /**vay**-can-see/ *vb* **1** (*fml*) to leave empty (*vacate the flat*). **2** to give up (*vacate his position in the firm*).

vacation /**vay**-**cay**-shun/ *n* a period away from home for rest or relaxation.

vaccinate /**vac**-si-nate/ *vb* to inject with vaccine or with fluids giving protection against diseases. ● *n* **vaccination** /vac-si-**nay**-shun/.

vaccine /**vac**-seen/ *n* **1** fluid taken from a cow infected with cowpox and injected into a person's bloodstream to cause a mild attack of smallpox and so protect against worse attacks later. **2** a substance made from the germs that cause a particular disease and given to someone to prevent the disease.

vacillate /**va**-si-late/ *vb* (*fml*) to keep on changing your mind, to hesitate to come to a decision (*vacillate about moving house*). ● *n* **vacillation** /va-si-**lay**-shun/.

vacuous /**va**-cyu-wus/ *adj* **1** (*fml*) empty, meaningless (*a vacuous life*). **2** without expression (*look vacuous*).

vacuum /**va**-cyoom/ *n* a space from which all the air has been taken.

vacuum cleaner /**va**-cyoom clee-ner/ *n* a machine that cleans carpets, etc., by sucking dust into a bag.

vacuum flask /**va**-cyoom flask/ (*Br*) *see* **thermos**.

vagabond /**va**-ga-bond/ *n* a person who wanders aimlessly from place to place. ● *adj* wandering.

vagary /**vay**-ga-ree/ *n* a piece of odd or unexpected behavior (*the vagaries of human life/the vagaries of the weather*).

vagrant /**vay**-grant/ *adj* wandering. ● *n* a wanderer or hobo. ● *n* **vagrancy** /**vay**-gran-see/.

vague /**vage**/ *adj* not clear, not definite (*a vague idea of where he might be*). ● *adv* **vaguely** /**vage**-lee/. ● *n* **vagueness** /**vage**-ness/.

vain /**vain**/ *adj* **1** having no meaning or value (*vain words*). **2** too proud of yourself (*so vain that he is always looking in the mirror*). **3** useless (*a vain attempt to swim the river*). ● *adv* **vainly** /**vain**-lee/.

● **in vain** without result or effect.

valance /**va**-lanse/ *n* a short drapery hanging from a couch, bedstead, etc.

vale /**vale**/ *n* (*fml*) a valley.

valediction /va-li-**dic**-chun/ *n* (*fml*) a farewell. ● *adj* **valedictory** /va-li-**dic**-tree/.

valency /**vay**-lin-see/ *n* the power of chemical elements to combine.

valentine /**va**-lin-tine/ *n* **1** a person who is chosen as a lover or beloved on St Valentine's Day, February 14. **2** a card expressing love sent on this day.

valet /**va**-lay/ *n* a man's personal servant.

valiant /**va**-lee-ent/ *adj* brave (*a valiant attempt to save the drowning man*). ● *adv* **valiantly** /**va**-lee-ent-lee/.

valid /**va**-lid/ *adj* **1** correct according to law (*a regulation no longer valid*). **2** good, sound (*asked to validate her husband's alibi*). ● *n* **validity** /va-li-di-tee/.

validate /**va**-li-date/ *vb* (*fml*) to make valid.

valley /**va**-lee/ *n* the low ground between neighboring hills or mountains, often watered by a river.

valor /**va**-lur/ *n, also* **valour** (*Br, Cdn*) bravery, courage (*pay tribute to the valor of the soldiers*). ● *adj* **valorous** /**va**-lu-rus/.

valuable /**val**-yu-bul/ *adj* **1** of great worth or importance (*valuable advice*). **2** costly (*valuable jewels*).

valuables /**val**-yu-bulz/ *npl* precious things (*have her valuables insured*).

valuation /val-yu-**way**-shun/ *n* the estimated worth, price, or importance of a thing (*ask for a valuation of the property*).

value /**val**-yoo/ *n* **1** worth, importance (*information that was of value to the police*). **2** price, cost (*the marked value of the vase*). ● *npl* **values** /**val**-yooz/ the standards by which you judge the worth of things (*moral values*). ● *adj* **valueless** /**val**-yoo-less/.

valuer /**val**-yoo-er/ *n* a person who estimates the value of things.

valve /**valv**/ *n* **1** a device that, when opened, allows gas, air, fluid, etc., to pass through in one direction only. **2** in radio sets, a device by which you can control the power of waves transmitted or received.

469

vamp /vamp/ *n* the upper part of a boot or shoe. ● *vb* to play music made up as you play.

vampire /vam-pire/ *n* **1** in old stories, a ghost supposed to suck the blood of the living. **2** a bloodsucking bat.

van[1] /van/ *n* a covered wagon for goods or animals.

van[2] /van/ short for **vanguard**.

vandal /van-dal/ *n* a person who purposefully and pointlessly destroys or damages public buildings or other property. ● *n* **vandalism** /van-da-li-zum/. ● *vb* **vandalize** /van-da-lize/, *also* **vandalise** (*Br*).

vane /vane/ *n* **1** a weathercock. **2** the blade of a windmill, propeller, etc.

vanguard /van-gard/ *n* (*abbr* = **van**) **1** the front part of an army or fleet. **2** those leading the way.

vanilla /va-ni-lla/ *n* a flavoring prepared from a tropical plant (*a dessert flavored with vanilla essence*).

vanish /va-nish/ *vb* **1** to disappear (*the chill seems to have vanished*). **2** to pass out of sight (*the car vanished around the corner*).

vanity /va-ni-tee/ *n* **1** lack of meaning or value (*the vanity of human ambition*). **2** too great pride in yourself, conceit (*she was disliked for her vanity*).

vanquish /vang-kwish/ *vb* to defeat completely (*vanquish the enemy*).

vantage /van-tidge/ *n* **1** (*old*) advantage. **2** a point in lawn tennis (after deuce).

vantage point /van-tidge-point/ *n* a good position (*the hill was a good vantage point from which to see the procession*).

vapid /va-pid/ *adj* lacking in spirit, dull (*so vapid as to bore everyone*).

vapor /vay-pur/ *n*, *also* **vapour** (*Br, Cdn*) **1** the gas given off by a body when sufficiently heated. **2** mist.

vaporize /vay-pu-rize *vb*, *also* **vaporise** (*Br*) to turn into vapor.

variable /vay-ree-a-bul/ *adj* **1** quick to change (*variable in her opinions*). **2** changing often or easily (*variable temperature*).

variance /vay-ree-anse/ *n*. ● **at variance with** in disagreement with.

variant /vay-ree-ant/ *n* a different or alternative form. ● *adj* different (*variant spellings of the word*).

variation /vay-ree-ay-shun/ *n* change, difference (*variations in temperature*).

varicose /vay-ri-coas/ *adj*. ● **varicose veins** /vay-ri-coas-vaynz/ swollen veins.

varied /vay-reed/ *adj* including many differen things.

variegate /vay-ree-u-gate/ *vb* to mark with differ ent colors (*the leaves were variegated*). ● *ad* **variegated**.

variety /va-rie-i-tee/ *n* **1** the state of being differ ent. **2** a collection of different or slightly differ ent things. **3** a class or species. **4** a theater shov with performers of different kinds.

various /vay-ree-us/ *adj* of several different type (*various pets, such as cats, dogs, and rabbits*).

varmint /var-mint/ *n* (*inf*) **1** an animal regarded a a pest. **2** a despicable person.

varnish /var-nish/ *n* a clear, sticky liquid used t give a shiny surface to wood, metal, paper, etc. ● *vb* to coat with varnish (*varnish the floorboards*)

vary /vay-ree/ *vb* to make or become different, t change (*his rate of work never varies*).

vase /vayss/ *n* a vessel used for holding flowers o as an ornament.

Vaseline /va-su-leen/ *n* (*trademark*) a jelly mad from petroleum, used on the skin as an ointmen

vassal /va-sal/ *n* in the feudal system, a person wh held land from a lord on condition that he per formed certain services for the lord.

vast /vast/ *adj* **1** of great extent (*vast plans*). **2** hug (*a vast improvement*). ● *adv* **vastly** /vast-lee/. ● *r* **vastness** /vast-ness/.

vat /vat/ *n* a large tub or tank.

Vatican /va-ti-can/ *n* the Pope's palace in Rome.

vaudeville /vaw-vil/ *n* an entertainment includin songs and dances, usually comic, a light variet entertainment.

vault[1] /vawlt/ *n*. **1** an arched roof. **2** a room, usual underground, with an arched roof (e.g., a cella a tomb, etc.).

vault[2] /vawlt/ *vb* to jump over while resting th hand on something for support (*vault over th fences*). ● *n* a leap (over something).

v-chip /vee-chip/ *n* a device that can be attached t a television to block unsuitable shows from be ing viewed.

VCR /vee-see-ar/ *n* video cassette recorder.

VDU /vee-dee-yoo/ *n* visual display unit.

veal /veel/ *n* the flesh of a calf.

veejay /vee-jay/ *n* a person on a television musi show who presents music videos.

veer /veer/ *vb* to change direction (*the wind ha veered to the north*).

vegan /vee-gan/ *n* a person who eats no food mad from animal products.

vegetable /**vedge**-ta-bul/ *n* a plant grown for food (*soup made with fresh vegetables*).

vegetarian /ve-ji-**tay**-ree-an/ *n* a person who eats only vegetable food, taking no meat. ● *n* **vegetarianism** /ve-ji-**tay**-ree-a-ni-zum/.

vegetate /**ve**-ji-tate/ *vb* **1** to live a plant's life. **2** to lead a dull, inactive life (*she is vegetating staying in her house all day*).

vegetation /ve-ji-**tay**-shun/ *n* **1** plants in general. **2** the plants of a particular region (*jungle vegetation*).

vehement /**vee**-i-ment/ *adj* **1** full of strong feeling, passionate (*a vehement protest*). **2** having a forceful way of speaking. ● *n* **vehemence** /**vee**-i-mense/. ● *adv* **vehemently** /**vee**-i-ment-lee/.

vehicle /**vee**-i-cul/ *n* **1** any type of carriage, cart, etc., used on land for carrying people or things. **2** (*fml*) a means of doing something (*the newspaper is a vehicle of communication*). ● *adj* **vehicular** /vee-**hi**-cyu-lar/.

veil /**vale**/ *n* **1** a cloth worn over the face to hide or protect it (*a bridal veil*). **2** something that hides or conceals (*a veil of mist*). ● *vb* **1** to conceal (*try to conceal her dislike of him*). **2** to cover (*mist veiling the hill*).

vein /**vane**/ *n* **1** one of the blood vessels through which blood flows back to the heart. **2** a sap tube or small rib of a leaf. **3** a layer of mineral in a rock. **4** a mood (*in a light-hearted vein*).

Velcro /**vel**-cro/ (*trademark*) *n* a type of fastening for clothing, etc., consisting of two strips of fabric that stick to each other when pressed together.

veld, veldt /**velt**/ *n* in South Africa, a wide expanse of grassy country with few trees.

velocity /vu-**los**-i-tee/ *n* speed.

velour /vu-**loor**/, **velours** /vu-**loorz**/ *n* a material like velvet.

velvet /**vel**-vet/ *n* a thick silk fabric or substitute, with a soft pile on one side.

velvety /**vel**-vi-tee/ *adj* soft and smooth, like velvet (*the velvety skin of a peach*).

venal /**vee**-nal/ *adj* ready to take bribes, corrupt. ● *n* **venality** /vee-na-li-tee/.

vendetta /ven-**de**-ta/ *n* a feud between two families in which each is bound to revenge the death of any of its members killed by the other.

vending machine /**ven**-ding-ma-sheen/ *n* a machine from which certain items can be bought by putting coins in it (*candy from a vending machine*).

vendor /**ven**-dur/ *n* a person who sells (*a street vendor selling newspapers*).

veneer /vu-**neer**/ *n* **1** a thin layer (of fine wood, plastic, etc.) glued on the surface of another inferior one. **2** something that appears fine but is not deep or lasting (*a veneer of sincerity*). ● *vb* to cover with veneer.

Venetian /vu-**nee**-shin/ *adj* from or of Venice.

venetian blind /vu-nee-shin-**blinde**/ *n* a window blind made from horizontal strips of thin wood, plastic, etc.

vengeance /**ven**-jinse/ *n* harm done in return for harm or injury received, revenge (*seek vengeance for his brother's death*).

vengeful /**venj**-ful/ *adj* desiring revenge.

venison /**ve**-ni-sun/ *n* the flesh of deer.

venom /**ve**-num/ *n* **1** (*fml*) poison (*the venom of the cobra*). **2** spite (*a look full of venom*).

venomous /**ve**-nu-mus/ *adj* **1** poisonous (*venomous reptile*). **2** spiteful (*venomous remarks*).

vent /**vent**/ *n* **1** a hole or opening through which air, smoke, etc., can pass. **2** an outlet. **3** expression (*give vent to his rage*). ● *vb* to give free expression to (*vented his rage on the children*).

ventilate /**ven**-ti-late/ *vb* **1** to allow fresh air to pass into or through (*ventilate the room by opening the windows*). **2** to discuss freely (*ventilate topics of interest to all*). ● *n* **ventilation** /ven-ti-**lay**-shun/.

ventilator /**ven**-ti-lay-tur/ *n* any device to let in fresh air.

ventriloquist /ven-**tri**-lu-kwist/ *n* a person who is able to speak without moving his or her lips, in such a way that the voice seems to come from another person. ● *n* **ventriloquism** /ven-**tri**-lu-kwi-zum/.

venture /**ven**-chur/ *n* an undertaking that may lead you into loss or danger (*a business venture*). ● *vb* **1** to dare (*venture to go into the jungle alone*). **2** to risk (*venture his savings on the scheme*).

venturesome /**ven**-chur-sum/ *adj* (*fml*) ready to take risks, daring.

venue /**ven**-yoo/ *n* the place appointed for a public event (*the venue of the concert*).

Venus /**vee**-nus/ *n* **1** the Roman goddess of love. **2** one of the planets in the solar system.

veranda, verandah /vu-**ran**-da/ *n* a covered platform or open balcony along the wall of a house.

verb /**verb**/ *n* a word that tells of the action or state of the subject of a sentence.

verbal /**ver**-bal/ *adj* **1** of or in words. **2** by word of mouth. **3** word for word. ● *adv* **verbally** /**ver**-ba-lee/.

verbatim /ver-**bay**-tim/ *adv* word for word (*she wrote down the statement verbatim*).

verbose /ver-**boass**/ adj (fml) using too many words, using more words than are necessary (a verbose style). ● n **verbosity** /ver-**bos**-i-tee/.

verdict /**ver**-dict/ n **1** the decision of a jury. **2** a considered opinion or judgment (their verdict on the food at the new restaurant).

verdigris /**ver**-di-grees/ n the green rust on metals of various kinds.

verge /verj/ n **1** the edging of a road, etc. (the grass verges of the highway). **2** edge, brink (on the verge of losing his temper). ● also vb.

verger /**ver**-jer/ n a church attendant or usher.

verify /**ve**-ri-fie/ vb **1** confirm (verify the statement). **2** to prove to be true. ● n **verification** /ve-ri-fi-cay-shun/.

veritable /**ve**-ri-ta-bul/ adj (fml or hum) true, real, actual (a veritable feast).

verity /**ve**-ri-tee/ n (fml) truth.

vermicelli /ver-mi-**chel**-ee/ n long, thin threads of pasta made from wheaten flour.

vermilion /ver-**mil**-yun/ n a bright red color.

vermin /**ver**-min/ npl **1** small animals that do harm (e.g., to crops), as rats, mice, etc. **2** insects connected with discomfort to human beings or dirt.

vernacular /ver-**na**-cyu-lar/ n the language spoken from infancy by the people of a certain country or district.

verruca /vu-**roo**-ca/ n a plantar wart on the sole of the foot.

versatile /**ver**-sa-tile/ adj able to do many different kinds of things (a versatile tool). ● n **versatility** /ver-sa-**ti**-li-tee/.

verse /verss/ n **1** poetry. **2** writing set down in the form of poetry. **3** a stanza. **4** a short division of a chapter of the Bible.

versed /verst/ adj skilled, having knowledge (a student versed in Latin).

version /**ver**-shun/ n **1** an account or description peculiar to a particular person (his version of the events before the accident). **2** a translation.

versus /**ver**-sus/ prep against.

vertebra /**ver**-ti-bra/ n (pl **vertebrae** /**ver**-ti-brae/) one of the bones of the spine.

vertebrate /**ver**-ti-brit/ adj having a backbone.

vertex /**ver**-teks/ n (pl **vertices** /**ver**-ti-seez/) the highest point, the top (the vertex of the pyramid).

vertical /**ver**-ti-cal/ adj upright, at right angles to the bottom or ground level, running straight from top to bottom.

vertigo /**ver**-ti-go/ n dizziness, giddiness (suffer from vertigo at the top of the ladder).

verve /verv/ n enthusiasm, liveliness (set about the task with verve).

very /**ve**-ree/ adv extremely. ● adj true, real (the very person we were looking for).

vespers /**ve**-spers/ npl evening service in church.

vessel /**ve**-sul/ n **1** a container for holding things. **2** a ship or boat.

vest /vest/ n **1** a sleeveless garment worn by men below a suit coat. **2** (Br) see **undershirt**.

vested interests /ve-**stid**-**in**-trest/ npl rights that have been long held and will not readily be given up.

vestibule /**ve**-sti-byool/ n a porch or small compartment between the outer and inner front doors of a house, a small entrance hall.

vestige /**ve**-stidge/ n **1** a mark or trace (vestiges of old customs). **2** a very small amount (not a vestige of the truth).

vestment /**vest**-ment/ n a garment or robe, especially that worn by a priest or official.

vestry /**ve**-stree/ n a room in a church where the robes of priests, etc., are kept.

vet[1] /vet/ short for **veteran** or **veterinarian**.

vet[2] /vet/ vb (**vetted** /**ve**-tid/, **vetting** /**ve**-ting/) to approve, to pass as sound (has to have his application vetted by the committee).

veteran /**ve**-te-ran/ n **1** an old person having long experience. **2** a soldier who has served in a war (a Vietnam veteran). ● also adj.

veterinarian /ve-tu-ri-**nay**-ree-an/ n (abbr = **vet**) an animal doctor.

veterinary /**ve**-tu-ri-nay-ree/ adj having to do with the diseases of domestic animals.

veterinary surgeon (Br) see **veterinarian**.

veto /**vee**-toe/ n (pl **vetoes** /**vee**-toaz/) the right to refuse or forbid. ● vb to forbid, to refuse to allow discussion of (vetoing the suggestion).

vex /veks/ vb to make angry, to annoy (their mother was vexed by the children's behavior). ● n **vexation** /vek-**say**-shun/.

vexatious /vek-**say**-shus/ adj annoying, troublesome.

via /**vee**-a/ prep by way of.

viable /**vie**-a-bul/ adj **1** able to exist or survive (a viable fetus). **2** workable (a viable proposition). ● n **viability** /vie-a-**bi**-li-tee/.

viaduct /**vie**-a-duct/ n a long arched bridge carrying a road or railroad over a valley, etc.

vibrant /**vie**-brant/ adj **1** quivering (singing in a vibrant voice). **2** full of energy (a vibrant personality). **3** bright, shining (vibrant colors). ● n

vibrancy /vie-bran-see/. ● *adv* **vibrantly** /vie-brant-lee/.

vibrate /vie-**brate**/ *vb* **1** to move quickly backward and forward. **2** to shake, to quiver. ● *n* **vibration** /vie-**bray**-shun/.

vicar /vi-car/ *n* the priest or minister in charge of a parish.

vicarage /vic-ridge/ *n* the house of a vicar.

vicarious /vie-**cay**-ree-us/ *adj* **1** suffered or undergone in place of another. **2** enjoyed or experienced through the medium of other people (*vicarious pleasures*).

vice[1] /vice/ *n* a fault, a bad habit (*smoking was his only vice*).

vice[2] /vice/ *n* an instrument for holding something (a piece of wood, metal, etc.) steady while you are working on it.

vice[3] /vice/ *prep* in place of.

vice- /vice/ *prefix* in the place of, next in order to (*vice-admiral, vice-president, etc.*).

viceroy /**vice**-roy/ *n* a person who rules in behalf of a king or queen.

vice versa /vie-si-**ver**-sa/ *adv* the other way around (*dogs dislike cats and vice versa*).

vicinity /vi-**si**-ni-tee/ *n* neighborhood (*look for a restaurant in the vicinity of the hotel*).

vicious /**vi**-shus/ *adj* wicked, evil, ill-tempered (*a vicious temper/a vicious dog*). ● *adv* **viciously** /vi-shus-lee/. ● *n* **viciousness** /vi-shus-ness/.

vicious circle /vi-shus-**sir**-cul/ *n* a series in which each bad event or action or argument leads on to a worse one.

victim /**vic**-tim/ *n* **1** a person who suffers either from his or her own faults or from outside circumstances (*the police have not named the victims killed in the explosion*). **2** a person or animal killed and offered in sacrifice.

victimize /**vic**-ti-mize/ *vb, also* **victimise** (*Br*) to make to suffer, to treat unfairly (*people victimized for their beliefs*). ● *n* **victimization** /vic-ti-mi-zay-shun/, *also* **victimisation** (*Br*).

victor /**vic**-tur/ *n* a person who wins or conquers.

victorious /vic-**toe**-ree-us/ *adj* successful in a war, battle, contest, or match (*the victorious team*).

victory /**vic**-tree/ *n* the winning of a battle, contest, or game (*victory in the tennis tournament*).

victuals /**vi**-tulz/ *npl* food.

video /**vi**-dee-oe/ *n* the transmission or recording of television shows or movies using a television set and a **video cassette recorder** and **videotape**. ● *also vb.*

video game /vi-dee-oe-game/ *n* an electronic game with images that you can manipulate on a video screen.

vie /vie/ *vb* to try hard to do better than, to compete with (*the two boys spent the evening vying for her attention*).

view /vyoo/ *n* **1** all that can be seen at one look or from one point, a scene (*the view from the hill*). **2** opinion (*in his view she is not suitable for the job*). **3** intention (*buy the house with the intention of building an extension*). ● *vb* **1** to look at (*view the property*). **2** to examine, to consider (*view all possible solutions to the problem*).

viewer /**vyoo**-wer/ *n* a person who watches television.

viewpoint /**vyoo**-point/ *n* **1** a place from which you can see the surroundings well. **2** the way in which you consider or think of something (*try to see the problem from the viewpoint of the teacher*).

vigil /**vi**-jil/ *n* an act of staying awake all night or of remaining watchful (*keep a vigil at his injured son's bedside*).

vigilance /**vi**-ji-lanse/ *n* watchfulness, care.

vigilant /**vi**-ji-lant/ *adj* watchful, careful (*the police asked the public to remain vigilant*). ● *adv* **vigilantly** /**vi**-ji-lant-lee/.

vigilante /vi-ji-**lan**-tee/ *n* a member of an unauthorized group who try to prevent, or who punish, crime in their neighborhood.

vigor /**vi**-gur/ *n, also* **vigour** (*Br, Cdn*) strength and energy, power of mind.

vigorous /**vi**-grus/ *adj* full of strength or energy, active (*vigorous young athletes/a vigorous attack on her writing*). ● *adj* **vigorously** /vi-grus-lee/.

Viking /**vie**-king/ *n* a Norse pirate or sea rover of the 8th to 10th centuries.

vile /vile/ *adj* **1** wicked, evil (*a vile crime/a vile old man*). **2** disgusting, horrible (*a vile meal at the new restaurant*).

vilify /**vi**-li-fie/ *vb* to speak ill of (*he was vilified by the press for his part in the affair*). ● *n* **vilification** /vi-li-fi-**cay**-shun/.

villa /**vi**-la/ *n* **1** a country house. **2** in a town, a house with a garden and a space between it and the houses on either side.

village /**vi**-lidge/ *n* a group of houses, stores, etc., smaller than a town.

villager /**vi**-li-jer/ *n* a person who lives in a village.

villain /**vi**-lin/ *n* a bad or wicked person, a scoundrel (*police are looking for the dangerous villain*).

villainous /**vi**-li-nus/ *adj* wicked.

villainy /vi-li-nee/ *n* wickedness.

vim /vim/ *n* energy, strength, force (*a gymnastic performance that was full of vim*).

vindicate /vin-di-cate/ *vb* 1 to show that charges made are untrue, to free from blame (*the testimony of the witness completely vindicated him*). 2 to prove that something is true or right, to justify (*her success vindicates his faith in her*). ● *n* **vindication** /vin-di-**cay**-shun/.

vindictive /vin-**dic**-tiv/ *adj* eager to obtain revenge, spiteful (*have a vindictive streak*).

vine /vine/ *n* a climbing plant that bears grapes.

vinegar /vi-ni-gar/ *n* a sour liquid, dilute acetic acid, made from wine or malt and used in cooking or for seasoning.

vinegary /vi-ni-gree/ *adj* sour.

vineyard /vin-yard/ *n* a field or area in which vines are cultivated.

vintage /vin-tidge/ *n* 1 the number of grapes or amount of wine obtained from one vineyard in a year. 2 all the wine made from the grapes grown in a certain year. ● *adj* 1 of a good vintage (*vintage champagne*) 2 classic, the best of its kind (*that album is vintage Rolling Stones*) 3 of a time gone by (*vintage clothing*)

vinyl /vie-nil/ *n* a kind of strong plastic that can bend easily, used to make wall and floor coverings, etc., and, especially formerly, records.

viola[1] /vie-oe-la/ *n* a large type of violin.

viola[2] /vie-oe-la/ *n* a family of plants, including the violet, pansy, etc.

violate /vie-u-late/ *vb* to break (*violate the peace treaty*). ● *n* **violation** /vie-u-**lay**-shun/. ● *n* **violator** /vie-u-lay-tur/.

violence /vie-lense/ *n* 1 great force (*the violence of the wind*). 2 harm, injury (*he was so angry that he resorted to violence*).

violent /vie-lent/ *adj* 1 strong (*a violent quarrel*). 2 using force (*the man grew more violent*). ● *adv* **violently** /vie-lent-lee/.

violet /vie-let/ *n* 1 a small bluish-purple flower. 2 a bluish-purple color. ● *adj* bluish-purple (*violet eyes*).

violin /vie-u-lin/ *n* a four-stringed musical instrument played with a bow. ● *n* **violinist**.

violoncello /vie-u-li-che-lo/ *n* (*abbr = cello* /che-lo/) a large violin giving deep notes. ● *n* **violoncellist** /vie-u-li-che-list/.

viper /vie-per/ *n* 1 a poisonous snake. 2 (*lit*) a treacherous or spiteful person.

virago /vi-ra-go/ *n* (*pl* **viragoes** *or* **viragos** /vi-ra-goaz/) a bad-tempered scolding woman.

virgin /vir-jin/ *adj* 1 pure. 2 untouched; still in its original condition (*virgin territory*). ● *n* **virginity** /vir-ji-ni-tee/. ● *adj* **virginal** /vir-ji-nal/.

virile /vi-rile/ *adj* manly, strong (*virile athletes*). ● *n* **virility** /vi-ri-li-tee/.

virtual /vir-chal/ *adj* being so in fact but not in name or title (*her husband is so weak that she is virtual head of the company*). ● *adv* **virtually** /vir-cha-lee/.

virtual reality /vir-chal ree-a-li-tee/ *n* the simulation by a computer of three-dimensional images that creates the impression of surrounding the person looking at them and that allows him or her to interact with the images, using special electronic equipment.

virtue /vir-choo/ *n* 1 goodness of life or character. 2 a good quality, power, strength (*generosity is her greatest virtue*).

virtuoso /vir-choo-wo-so/ *n* (*pl* **virtuosi** /vir-choo-wo-sie/ *or* **virtuosos** /vir-choo-wo-soaz/) an exceptionally highly skilled musician or other artist. ● *n* **virtuosity** /vir-choo-**woss**-i-tee/.

virtuous /vir-choo-wus/ *adj* morally good, of good character, leading a good life. ● *adv* **virtuously** /vir-choo-wus-lee/.

virulent /vir-yu-lent/ *adj* 1 powerful, dangerous (*virulent passions*). 2 full of hatred, spiteful (*virulent criticisms*). ● *n* **virulence** /vir-yu-lense/.

virus /vie-rus/ *n* any of various types of germ that are smaller than bacteria and cause infectious diseases in the body.

visa /vee-za/ *n* a permit stamped on a passport giving the owner the right to enter or leave a particular country.

visage /vi-**zazh**/ *n* (*fml*) the face.

vis-à-vis /vee-za-vee/ *prep* (*fml*) with regard to (*the committee's position vis-à-vis the proposed changes*).

viscose /vis-coass/ *n* a kind of rayon made from viscous cellulose.

viscount /vie-count/ *n* a nobleman of the rank below an earl.

viscous /vis-cuss/ *adj* sticky (*viscous substances*). ● *n* **viscosity** /vi-**scoss**-i-tee/.

visibility /vi-zi-**bi**-li-tee/ *n* 1 clearness to sight. 2 the state of weather, atmosphere, etc., as they affect your ability to see clearly (*visibility was poor on the highway*).

visible *adj* able to be seen. ● *adv* **visibly** /vi-zi-blee/.

vision /vi-zhun/ *n* 1 the ability to see, sight (*have poor vision in one eye*). 2 something imagined as in a dream (*God came to him in a vision*). **3** something seen that has no bodily existence (*see a ghostly vision*). **4** the power to foresee consequences (*he had a vision of the result*).

visionary /**vi**-zhin-ree/ *adj* **1** existing only in the imagination (*visionary scheme*). **2** full of fancies or hopes of perfection (*a visionary writer*). ● *n* a person who believes in ideals that cannot be achieved in his or her lifetime.

visit /**vi**-zit/ *vb* **1** to go to see or stay with (*visiting his parents*). **2** to call upon (*we visited with the bride's family*). ● *n* **1** a call upon. **2** a short stay.

visitation /vi-zi-**tay**-shun/ *n* **1** an official visit. **2** suffering believed to be sent by God as punishment.

visitor /**vi**-zi-tur/ *n* a person who visits.

visor /**vie**-zur/ *n* **1** (*old*) a movable part of a helmet, protecting the face when closed. **2** the peak of a cap.

vista /**vi**-sta/ *n* a narrow view, as seen between rows of houses, trees, etc.

visual /**vi**-zhu-wal/ *adj* of the sense of sight. ● *adv* **visually** /**vi**-zhu-wa-lee/.

vital /**vie**-tal/ *adj* **1** very important (*a meeting vital to the peace treaty*). **2** unable to be done without, necessary to life (*vital organs*). ● *adv* **vitally** /**vie**-ta-lee/.

vitality /vie-**ta**-li-tee/ *n* energy, vigor, liveliness.

vitals /**vie**-talz/ *npl* the organs of the body necessary to life.

vitamin /**vi**-ta-min, **vie**-ta-min/ *n* one of several substances found in food, necessary to the health of the body.

vitreous /**vi**-tree-us/ *adj* of or like glass.

vitriol /**vi**-tree-ole/ *n* **1** sulfuric acid. **2** hostile language.

vitriolic /vi-tree-**ol**-ic/ *adj* using violent language, full of hatred (*a vitriolic attack on the government policy*).

vivacious /vi-**vay**-shus/ *adj* lively, bright, and talkative (*a vivacious personality*). ● *adv* **vivaciously** /vi-**vay**-shus-lee/.

vivacity /vi-**va**-si-tee/ *n* liveliness (*the girl's vivacity*).

vivid /**vi**-vid/ *adj* **1** bright, striking, **2** appearing true to life (*a vivid dream/a vivid description*). ● *adv* **vividly** /**vi**-vid-lee/.

vivisection /vi-vi-**sec**-shun/ *n* the cutting up of a living animal to assist scientific experiment.

vixen /**vik**-sun/ *n* a female fox.

vizier /vi-**zeer**/ *n* a high political official in Moslem countries.

vocabulary /vu-**ca**-byu-la-ree/ *n* **1** all the words used by a certain person or a certain work (*a child with a large vocabulary*). **2** a list of words with their meaning (*a vocabulary at the back of the book*).

vocal /**vo**-cal/ *adj* **1** having to do with the voice, spoken or sung (*the vocal organs*). **2** intended to be heard (*vocal opposition to the plan*). ● *adv* **vocally**.

vocal cords /**vo**-cal-cawrds/ *npl* two membranes in the throat that produce vocal sounds.

vocalist /**vo**-ca-list/ *n* a singer.

vocation /vo-**cay**-shun/ *n* **1** your employment, profession, or trade. **2** the particular work you feel you are specially fitted for (*being a minister of the church is a vocation*).

vocational /vo-**cay**-shnal/ *adj* concerned with your profession or trade.

vociferous /vu-**si**-frous/ *adj* **1** noisy. **2** expressing opinions loudly or openly (*a vociferous protest from the crowd*).

vodka /**vod**-ka/ *n* a kind of strong liquor, made from grain or potatoes, originating in Russia.

vogue /**voag**/ *n* a popular or passing fashion (*the length of skirt currently in vogue*).

voice /**voiss**/ *n* **1** the sound produced through the mouth when speaking or singing (*the choir boy has a lovely voice*). **2** a vote, an opinion (*the voice of the people*). **3** the right to speak or express an opinion (*the workers had no voice*). **4** (*gram*) a grouping of forms of the verb according to whether they are active or passive. ● *vb* **1** to say. **2** to express (*voice their disapproval*).

voicemail /**voiss**-male/ *n* an electronic system for storing telephone messages so that they can be listened to later.

void /**void**/ *adj* **1** (*fml*) empty (*a statement void of meaning*). **2** having no effect, having no force (*regulations that are now void*). ● *n* empty space.

volatile /**vol**-a-tile/ *adj* **1** easily changing into gas. **2** able to evaporate readily. **3** changing moods or ideas often (*a volatile personality*). ● *n* **volatility** /vol-a-**ti**-li-tee/.

volcano /vol-**cay**-no/ *n* (*pl* **volcanoes** /vol-**cay**-noaz/) a mountain with an opening at its summit through which molten rock, metals, etc., are occasionally forced up in a red-hot stream from beneath the surface of the earth. ● *adj* **volcanic** /vol-**ca**-nic/.

vole /**vole**/ *n* the water-rat.

volition /vu-**li**-shun/ *n* willpower (*leave of his own volition*).

volley /**vol**-ee/ *n* **1** the firing of several guns or throwing of many things at the same time. **2** the speaking of a number of words in quick succession (*a volley of questions addressed to the speaker*). **3** in tennis, the hitting of a ball before it touches the ground. ● *vb* **1** to send a volley. **2** to hit (a ball) before it touches the ground.

volleyball /**vol**-ee-bawl/ *n* a game in which two teams volley a ball back and forth over a net.

volt /voalt/ *n* the unit used in measuring electrical power or force.

voltage /**voal**-tidge/ *n* electrical power measured in volts.

voluble /**vol**-yu-bul/ *adj* speaking much (*she is voluble on the subject of her son's education*). ● *n* **volubility** /vol-yu-**bi**-li-tee/.

volume /**vol**-yum/ *n* **1** a book. **2** one of a series in a set of books (*volume three of the encyclopedia*). **3** the amount of space taken up by anything (*the volume of water in the tank*). **4** a large mass or amount (*the volume of trade*). **5** level of sound (*turn up the volume on the radio*).

voluminous /vu-**loo**-mi-nus/ *adj* **1** taking up much space (*a voluminous skirt*). **2** very big, holding a lot (*a voluminous suitcase*).

voluntary /**vol**-un-tree/ *adj* done of your own free will, not forced (*face voluntary early retirement*). ● *n* an organ solo before or after a church service.

volunteer /vol-un-**teer**/ *n* a person who offers to do something without being asked or ordered (*volunteers required to visit the elderly*). ● *vb* **1** to offer your services. **2** to give (information) unasked (*she volunteered that she had no experience of doing the job*).

voluptuous /vu-**lup**-chu-wus/ *adj* **1** having a full, rounded figure (*voluptuous women*). **2** tempting to bodily pleasures (*the voluptuous movements of the dancers*). **3** giving pleasure to the senses (*the voluptuous feel of velvet*).

vomit /**vom**-it/ *vb* **1** to throw up from the stomach through the mouth, to be sick. **2** to put out in large clouds, e.g., of smoke (*factory chimneys vomiting black smoke*).

voodoo /**voo**-doo/ *n* a primitive and degraded form of worship, witchcraft.

voracious /vu-**ray**-shus/ *adj* very greedy. ● *adv* **voraciously** /vu-**ray**-shus-lee/. ● *n* **voracity** /vu-ra-si-tee/.

vortex /**vawr**-teks/ *n* **1** a whirlpool. **2** a whirlwind.

vote /vote/ *n* **1** an expression of opinion for or against a proposal (*60 votes for the proposal and 10 against*). **2** the support given by an individual to a person contesting an election. ● *vb* **1** to give a vote. **2** to decide by vote. ● *n* **voter**.

vouch /vouch/ *vb* to speak (on behalf of) with confidence, to confirm, to guarantee (*able to vouch for his friend's statement*).

voucher /**vou**-cher/ *n* **1** a paper handed over in exchange for goods instead of cash (*the company provided staff with luncheon vouchers*). **2** a receipt.

vouchsafe /**vouch**-safe/ *vb* (*fml*) to be good enough to give or grant (*reluctant to vouchsafe a reply*).

vow /vow/ *n* a solemn promise, a promise made to God. ● *vb* to promise solemnly.

vowel /**vow**-el/ *n* **1** a simple sound (*a, e, i, o, u*) made by the voice without obstruction to the air passage. **2** the letter representing it.

voyage /**voy**-idge/ *n* a long journey, especially by sea (*a voyage to Australia*).

vulcanize /**vul**-ca-nize/ *vb, also* **vulcanise** (*Br*) to treat rubber with sulfur.

vulgar /**vul**-gar/ *adj* **1** coarse in manners or behavior, rude (*a vulgar comment/it is vulgar to eat with your mouth open*). **2** (*old*) having to do with ordinary people, low. ● *adv* **vulgarly** /**vul**-gar-lee/.

vulgar fraction /vul-gar-**frac**-shun/ *n* a fraction other than a decimal fraction (e.g., $5/8$).

vulgarity /vul-ga-**ri**-tee/ *n* rudeness, coarseness.

vulnerable /**vuln**-ra-bul/ *adj* **1** able to be wounded or hurt (*he liked to pick on vulnerable people*). **2** weakly defended against attack (*the vulnerable position of the army*). ● *n* **vulnerability** /vuln-ra-bi-li-tee/.

vulture /**vul**-chur/ *n* a large bird that feeds on the flesh of dead animals.

W

W, w /**du**-bul-yoo/ the twenty-third letter of the alphabet.

wacky /**wa**-kee/ *adj* mad or eccentric.

wad /**wod**/ *n* **1** a lump of soft fibrous material for padding garments, stopping holes, etc. **2** a bundle (*a wad of paper money*).

wadding /**wod**-ing/ *n* soft material used for padding, etc.

waddle /**wod**-ul/ *vb* to walk, rolling from side to side, as a duck (*she was so fat she waddled*). ● *also n.*

wade /**wade**/ *vb* **1** to walk through water. **2** to walk slowly and with difficulty. **3** to read through with difficulty.

wader /**way**-der/ *n* any long-legged bird that wades in water in search of food.

waders /**way**-derz/ *npl* high waterproof boots worn by fishermen, etc.

wafer /**way**-fer/ *n* a very thin cake or cracker.

waffle[1] /**waf**-ul/ *n* a batter cake with a grid pattern, baked in a waffle iron

waffle[2] /**waf**-ul/ *vb* (*inf*) to talk in a rambling way (*the teacher waffled*).

waffle iron /**wof**-ul-eye-urn/ *n* a device with a grid pattern for baking waffles.

waft /**waft**/ *vb* to bear along gently through the air.

wag /**wag**/ *vb* (**wagged** /**wagd**/, **wagging** /**wag**-ing/) to shake up and down or to and fro (*he wagged his finger while giving the children a warning*). ● *n* **1** a wagging movement. **2** a person who is fond of telling jokes or making amusing comments.

wage /**wayj**/ *n* money paid regularly for work done (*often pl*). ● *vb* to carry on (*wage war*).

wager /**way**-jer/ *n* a bet. ● *vb* to bet.

waggle /**wa**-gul/ *vb* to wag.

wagon /**wa**-gun/ *n* **1** a four-wheeled vehicle used to carry loads. **2** a four-wheeled toy vehicle or cart, pulled by a long handle.

wagtail /**wag**-tail/ *n* a small bird with a long tail that it wags constantly.

waif /**waif**/ *n* a homeless child or animal.

wail /**wail**/ *vb* to cry aloud in grief, distress (*the children wailed when their parents went away*). ● *n* a loud cry of grief, a moaning cry.

waist /**waist**/ *n* the narrowest part of the human trunk, just below the ribs.

waistcoat /**waist**-coat/ (*Br*) *see* **vest**.

wait /**wait**/ *vb* **1** to stay in a place in the hope or expectation of something happening (*wait for the lights to change*). **2** to serve at table. ● *n* time spent waiting (*a wait of five hours*).

waiter /**way**-ter/ *n* a person employed to serve food at table. ● *f* **waitress** /**way**-triss/.

waiting list /**way**-ting-list/ *n* a list of people who are waiting for something.

waiting room /**way**-ting-room/ *n* a room where people may wait (*the doctor's waiting room*).

waitperson /**wait**-per-sun/ *n* a waiter or waitress.

waitress *see* **waiter**.

waive /**waiv**/ *vb* to give up, not to insist on (*waive his usual fee*).

wake[1] /**wake**/ *vb* (*pt* **woke** /**woke**/, *pp* **woken** /**wo**-kin/) **1** to arouse from sleep (*wake the baby with the loud music*). **2** to return to full consciousness after sleep (*she woke early*). ● *n* a watch kept over a dead body until the time of burial, sometimes with feasting.

wake[2] /**wake**/ *n* the track left on water by a moving ship. ● **in the wake of** behind, following.

wakeful /**wake**-ful/ *adj* not sleeping (*a wakeful child*).

waken /**way**-kin/ *vb* to wake.

walk /**wawk**/ *vb* **1** to advance step by step. **2** to go on foot. ● *n* **1** an outing on foot. **2** your manner of walking. **3** a road or path. ● **walk of life** your rank or work in life (*people in a humble walk of life*).

walking stick /**waw**-king-stick/ *n* a stick carried when walking.

walkover /**waw**-koa-ver/ *n* **1** an easy victory (*they were so bad that our team had a walkover*). **2** a victory granted because there has been no opposition (*she had a walkover in the match because her opponent did not turn up*).

wall /**wawl**/ *n* **1** a barrier of stone, brick, etc. **2** one of the sides of a building, room, etc. ● *vb* to provide with a wall (*the garden was walled in*).

wallaby /**waw**-la-bee/ *n* a small marsupial of the kangaroo family.

wallet /**waw**-let/ *n* (*mostly Br*) a man's flat case for holding money and credit cards *see* **pocketbook**, **billfold**.

wallflower /**wawl**-flour/ *n* **1** a sweet-smelling garden flower. **2** a person who is not dancing because he or she has no partner.

wallop /**waw**-lup/ *vb* to thrash soundly, to strike heavily. ● *also n.*

wallow /**waw**-lo/ *vb* **1** to roll about in mud, dirt, etc.

2 to enjoy what is dirty or unpleasant (*wallow in his rival's misfortune*).

wallpaper /wawl-pay-per/ *n* colored or decorative paper covering the walls of rooms.

walnut /wawl-nut/ *n* **1** a tree whose wood is much used for making furniture. **2** its edible nut.

walrus /wawl-rus/ *n* a large tusked sea mammal that can live on both land and sea.

waltz /wawltz/ *n* **1** a dance for two people. **2** music for such a dance. ● *vb* to dance a waltz (*dancers waltzing around the room*).

wan /wan/ *adj* pale, sickly-looking (*wan after her long illness*). ● *adv* **wanly** /wan-lee/. ● *n* **wanness** /wawn-ness/.

wand /wawnd/ *n* **1** a long, thin stick. **2** the rod of a magician or conjurer (*waved his magic wand*).

wander /wawn-der/ *vb* **1** to go purposelessly from place to place. **2** to lose your way (*wander off the path*). **3** to talk in a disconnected manner (*the professor began to wander*). **4** to go off the point. ● *n* **wanderer** /wawn-der-er/.

wane /wane/ *vb* **1** to grow less or smaller. **2** to lose strength or power. ● **on the wane** growing less.

wangle /wang-gul/ *vb* to arrange cleverly or by trickery (*try to wangle a ticket for the ballgame*).

want /wawnt/ *n* **1** need. **2** longing. **3** shortage. **4** poverty. ● *vb* **1** to lack. **2** to need. **3** to desire.

wanting /wawn-ting/ *adj* **1** not as good as required (*he found his work wanting*). **2** lacking (*a car wanting a tire*). **3** foolish-minded.

wanton /wawn-tun/ *adj* **1** immoral. **2** malicious. ● *n* an immoral person.

war /wawr/ *n* **1** a state of fighting and enmity between nations or within a nation. **2** an active campaign against something (*the war against racism*). ● *vb* (**warred** /wawrd/, **warring** /waw-ring/) to make war.

warble /wawr-bul/ *vb* to sing, as a bird.

warbler /wawr-blur/ *n* a songbird.

ward /wawrd/ *vb* (*with* **off**) **1** to defend oneself against (*warded off the blow with his arm*). **2** to defeat (an attack) for the time being. ● *n* **1** in a hospital, a large room containing several beds. **2** a division of a town for the purposes of local government. **3** a person under the legal care of another until he or she is old enough to manage his or her own affairs (*he is the ward of his uncle*).

-ward /wurd/ *suffix* in the direction of (*homeward*).

warden /wawr-din/ *n* **1** a person who guards or helps to protect. **2** the head of a college or hostel.

warder /wawr-der/ *n* a guard in a prison. ● *f* **wardress** /wawr-dress/.

wardrobe /wawr-droab/ *n* **1** a closet for hanging clothing. **2** all of a person's clothing (*get a new spring wardrobe*).

ware /ware/ *n* articles manufactured out of some material (*hardware*). ● *npl* **wares** goods for sale (*a flower girl selling her wares*).

warehouse /ware-houss/ *n* a building for storing goods.

warfare /wawr-fare/ *n* the carrying-on of fighting in war.

warlock /wawr-lock/ *n* a person who has magical powers (*witches and warlocks*).

warm /wawrm/ *adj* **1** quite hot (*warm water*). **2** affectionate (*a warm greeting*). **3** sincere (*with warm regards*). ● *vb* to make or become warm. ● *adv* **warmly** /wawrm-lee/.

warm-hearted /wawrm-har-tid/ *adj* kindly, generous.

warmth /wawrmth/ *n* **1** gentle heat. **2** excitement. **3** sincerity.

warn /wawrn/ *vb* **1** to advise against possible danger or error (*warned against walking home alone*). **2** to tell to be careful (*warn the children not to cross the road*).

warning /wawr-ning/ *n* **1** advice to be careful. **2** advice that danger or trouble lies ahead.

warp /wawrp/ *vb* **1** to twist or bend out of shape (*warp the metal rod*). **2** to become twisted or bent. **3** to spoil the nature or character of (*the unhappy childhood warped her*). ● *n* **1** the lengthwise threads in a loom (a weaving machine).

warrant /wawr-rant/ *n* a written document giving the right to do certain things (*a warrant for his arrest*). ● *vb* **1** to give the right or permission to. **2** to be good reason for, to justify (*that does not warrant his rudeness*) **3** (*fml*) to be sure (that) (*I warrant that he has run away*).

warren /wawr-rin/ *n* many rabbit burrows in one piece of land.

warrior /wawr-yur/ *n* **1** a person who is good at fighting. **2** a soldier.

wart /wawrt/ *n* a hard dry growth on the skin.

wary /way-ree/ *adj* careful, cautious, not rushing into danger (*wary of trusting strangers*).

wash /wawsh/ *vb* **1** to clean with water (*wash her hair*). **2** to flow against or over (*waves washing against the rocks*). **3** to carry away (on a rush of liquid) (*wash the mud away*). **4** to color lightly. ● *n* **1** the act of cleaning with water. **2** a washing, the flow or dash of water. **3** a healing liquid. **4** a thin coat of color. ● **wash your hands of** to refuse to have anything more to do with. ● *adj* **washable** /waw-sha-bul/.

washbowl /**wawsh**-boal/ *n* a large bowl for washing your hands and face.

washer /**wawsh**-er/ *n* a ring of metal, rubber, etc., to keep a bolt, etc., firmly in position (*top washer*).

washing /**wawsh**-ing/ *n* **1** dirty clothing or linen to be washed. **2** clothing newly washed.

washing machine /**wawsh**-ing-ma-sheen/ *n* a machine for washing clothing and linen.

washstand /**wawsh**-stand/ *n* a table for a basin of water.

wasp /**wawsp**/ *n* a stinging winged insect, with black and yellow stripes on its body.

waspish /**waw**-spish/ *adj* sharp-tempered, spiteful (*a waspish remark*).

wastage /**way**-stidge/ *n* that which is lost by waste (*the wallpaper wastage when decorating*).

waste /**waste**/ *vb* **1** to fail to put to a useful purpose (*waste talent*). **2** to spend or use foolishly (*waste money*). **3** to destroy, to damage. **4** to make or become weaker (*muscles wasting without exercise*). ● *adj* **1** left over (*waste product*). **2** uncultivated, undeveloped (*waste land*). ● *n* **1** what is left over as useless (*industrial waste*). **2** useless spending.

wasteful /**waste**-ful/ *adj* spending foolishly or uselessly.

waste paper /**waste**-pay-per/ *n* paper thrown away as useless.

waste pipe /**waste**-pipe/ *n* a pipe to carry away dirty water.

waster /**way**-ster/, **wastrel** /**way**-stril/ *ns* (*inf*) a lazy useless person.

watch /**wawch**/ *vb* **1** to look at or observe with care (*watch how he changes the tire*). **2** to look at (*watch television*). **3** to guard (*watch the princess*). **4** to look after (*watch the children*). ● *n* **1** a guard. **2** a careful look-out. **3** a four-hour spell of duty for half the crew on board a ship. **4** a clock carried in the pocket or on the wrist.

watchdog /**wawch**-dawg/ *n* **1** a dog used to guard a house or other building. **2** a person who watches out for wrongdoing, especially by a business firm.

watchful /**wawch**-ful/ *adj* keeping a look-out, observant, alert (*under her watchful eyes*).

watchmaker /**wawch**-may-kur/ *n* a person who makes or repairs watches.

watchman /**wawch**-man/ *n* a man employed to look after a building or site when it is unoccupied (*a night watchman*).

watchword /**wawch**-wurd/ *n* **1** a word known only to members of a group so that by using it they may be recognized as members (*only let them in if they know the watchword*). **2** a motto.

water /**waw**-ter/ *n* **1** the clear liquid that falls as rain and flows in streams and rivers. **2** a large area of water, as a lake, sea, etc. ● *vb* **1** to supply with water. **2** to pour or sprinkle water on (*water the garden*).

watercolor /**waw**-ter-cu-lur/ *n*, *also* **watercolour** (*Br, Cdn*) **1** coloring matter to be mixed with water, not oil. **2** a painting in watercolors (*a watercolor of the old mill*).

watercress /**waw**-ter-cress/ *n* an edible water plant.

waterfall /**waw**-ter-fawl/ *n* a stream falling over steep rocks or stones to a lower level.

water-lily /**waw**-ter-li-lee/ *n* a plant with floating flowers and leaves, found in ponds, etc.

waterlogged /**waw**-ter-logd/ *adj* soaked or filled with water (*a waterlogged field*).

watermark /**waw**-ter-mark/ *n* the faint trademark on a piece of paper.

watermelon /**waw**-ter-mel-on/ *n* a large juicy type of melon with red flesh.

water polo /**waw**-ter-po-lo/ *n* a ball game for swimmers.

water power /**waw**-ter-pow-ur/ *n* mechanical power got from running water.

waterproof /**waw**-ter-proof/ *adj* able to keep out water, that water cannot pass through (*waterproof tents/a waterproof coat*). ● *n* **1** waterproof cloth. **2** (*Br*) *see* **raincoat**.

watershed /**waw**-ter-shed/ *n* **1** a ridge or hill separating two river valleys. **2** a point at which events take a different turn (*a watershed in the war*).

water-ski /**waw**-ter-skee/ *n* a board on which a person can stand and be towed over water by a speedboat. ● *also vb*. ● *n* **water-skier** /**waw**-ter-skee-ur/. ● *n* **water-skiing** /**waw**-ter-skee-ing/.

waterspout /**waw**-ter-spout/ *n* a column of water sucked by a whirlwind.

watertight /**waw**-ter-tite/ *adj* so tight that water can pass neither in nor out (*a watertight container*).

waterworks /**waw**-ter-wurks/ *n* an apparatus for supplying water through pipes to a town, etc.

watery /**waw**-ter-ee/ *adj* **1** full of water (*watery eyes*). **2** tasteless, weak, thin (*watery soup*).

watt /**wat**/ *n* a unit of measurement of electric power. ● *n* **wattage** /**wat**-idge/.

wattle /**wat**-ul/ *n* **1** a twig. **2** a fence made of twigs woven together. **3** an Australian tree that is the country's emblem.

wave /**wave**/ *n* **1** a moving ridge of water rising above the surface of the sea and then sinking down again. **2** any movement resembling this (*light waves/sound waves*). **3** one of several ridges in the hair. **4** a moving of the hand as a signal (*a friendly wave*). ● *vb* **1** to move or make to move up and down or to and fro. **2** to shake in the air as a sign. **3** to put waves in hair. **4** to signal with your hand (*the police officer waved me on*).

waveband /**wave**-band/ *n* a band of radio waves between specific limits.

wavelength /**wave**-length/ *n* the distance (on the sea or in the air) between the crest of one wave and that of the next.

waver /**way**-ver/ *vb* **1** to be uncertain, to hesitate (*wavering about whether to be good or not*). **2** to move unsteadily. **3** to flicker (*a candle flame wavering*).

wavy /**way**-vee/ *adj* **1** rising and falling in waves (*wavy hair*). **2** covered with waves.

wax[1] /**waks**/ *n* **1** a sticky yellow substance made by bees. **2** any material resembling this. **3** a substance used to seal letters, packets, etc.

wax[2] /**waks**/ *vb* (*old*) **1** to grow larger (*the moon waxing*). **2** to become (*wax eloquent*).

waxen /**wak**-sin/ *adj* like wax (*a waxen skin*).

wax museum /waks-myoo-**zee**-um/ *n* a museum where waxworks are exhibited.

waxwork /**waks**-wurk/ *n* the image of a famous person made in wax for showing to the public. ● *n* **waxworks** *same as* **wax museum**.

way /**way**/ *n* **1** a track, path, or road (*the way of passage*). **2** a method of doing something (*a new way of teaching*). **3** distance traveled (*it is a long way to the next village*). **4** the route to a place (*the way to the station*). **5** a custom or habit (*have an unpleasant way*). ● **have a way with you** to be attractive in character (*he has a way with women*). ● **under way** in movement (*the expansion of the firm is under way*). ● **ways and means** methods.

wayfarer /**way**-fay-rer/ *n* a traveler, especially on foot.

waylay /**way**-lay/ *vb* to hide and wait for in order to surprise or attack (*they waylaid the enemy*).

wayside /**way**-side/ *n.* ● **fall by the wayside** not to continue.

wayward /**way**-ward/ *adj* fond of having your own way, not heeding the advice or orders of others (*wayward children*).

WC /du-bul-yoo-**see**/ *n* a water closet.

weak /**week**/ *adj* **1** not strong, feeble. **2** giving in too easily to others. **3** not good at (*weak at foreign languages*). ● *adv* **weakly** /**weel**-lee/.

weaken /**wee**-kin/ *vb* to make or become weak (*she was determined not to go but finally weakened*).

weakling /**week**-ling/ *n* a person who is weak in body or character.

weakly /**week**-lee/ *adj* not strong, not having good health (*weakly children*).

weakness /**week**-ness/ *n* **1** lack of strength or determination. **2** a bad point in your character (*telling white lies is her major weakness*). **3** a foolish liking for (*a weakness for ice cream*).

weal /**weel**/ *n* a raised mark on the skin caused by a blow from a whip, thin stick, etc.

wealth /**welth**/ *n* **1** riches (*the miser's great riches*). **2** plenty (*a wealth of talent*).

wealthy /**wel**-thee/ *adj* very rich (*wealthy enough not to have to work*).

wean /**ween**/ *vb* **1** to change from feeding (an infant) only on milk to more solid food. **2** to get someone to change his or her habits or desires (*wean him from his criminal ways*).

weapon /**wep**-un/ *n* any instrument that can be used in fighting or attack (*weapons such as guns and knives*).

wear /**ware**/ *vb* (*pt* **wore** /**wore**/, *pp* **worn** /**woarn**/) **1** to have on the body as clothing. **2** to put or stick on your clothing for show (*wear a badge*). **3** to damage or waste by rubbing or use (*the waves wear away at the rocks*). ● *n* **1** clothing (*evening wear*). **2** damage caused by rubbing or use. ● *n* **wearer** /**way**-rer/. ● **wear away** to become gradually less, to rub or be rubbed away. ● **wear on** to pass slowly (*time is wearing on*). ● **wear off** to become gradually less (*the effects of the painkillers wore off*). ● **wear out 1** to exhaust (*worn out by his continual complaining*). **2** to make useless by using too often.

wearisome /**wee**-ree-sum/ *adj* tiring, boring (*a wearisome journey*).

weary /**wee**-ree/ *adj* **1** tired by continued effort, exhausted (*weary from the long journey*). **2** fed up, bored (*weary of listening to complaints*). ● *adv* **wearily** /**wee**-ri-lee/.

weasel /**wee**-zul/ *n* a small bloodthirsty reddish-brown animal that eats frogs, mice, birds, etc.

weather /**weth**-er/ *n* the general conditions of the atmosphere (e.g., sunshine, rain, wind, etc.) at any particular time. ● *vb* **1** to come safely through (*succeeded in weathering the selection process*). **2** to be damaged or discolored by the effects of weather (*stone weathered with age*). ● **make heavy weather of** to find difficulty in doing (*he made* *heavy weather of the work).* ● **under the weather** feeling unwell.

weather-beaten /weth-er-bee-tin/ *adj* marred or colored by the effects of the weather.

weather vane /weth-er vane/ *n* a pointer that turns around to show the direction from which the wind is blowing.

weave /weev/ *vb* (*pt* **wove** /woav/, *pp* **woven** /woa-vin/) **1** to form cloth by intertwining threads. **2** to put together sticks, twigs, etc., by interlacing them. **3** to make up (*weave a story about his childhood*). ● *n* **weaver** /wee-ver/.

web /web/ *n* **1** cloth made by weaving. **2** the net of fine threads made by a spider. **3** the skin between the toes of water birds. **3** (*with cap*) short for the World Wide Web, the Internet. ● *adj* **webbed** / webd/.

webbing /web-ing/ *n* a narrow band of strong material used for belts, etc.

web-footed /web-foo-tid/ *adj* having skin between the toes.

Web page /web-payj/ *n* a computer file accessed on the Internet or World Wide Web.

Web site /web-site/ *n* an Internet location that consists of a number of related documents or files (*a Web site about allergies*).

wed /wed/ *vb* (**wed** *or* **wedded** /wed-id/, **wedding** / wed-ing/) to marry (*he wed his childhood sweetheart*).

wedding /wed-ing/ *n* a marriage.

wedge /wedge/ *n* a piece of wood, metal, etc., thick at one end and narrowing to a sharp edge at the other. ● *vb* to split open, fix, or fasten with a wedge (*wedge the door open*).

wedlock /wed-lock/ *n* the married state.

Wednesday /wed-anz-day/ *n* the fourth or middle day of the week.

weed /weed/ *n* a useless plant growing in a garden or field. ● *vb* **1** to clear of weeds (*weed the garden*). **2** to pull up weeds (*pay him to weed*).

weeds /weedz/ *npl* the black clothing worn by a widow in mourning.

weedy /wee-dee/ *adj* thin and weak-looking (*a weedy youth*).

week /week/ *n* a period of seven days.

weekday /week-day/ *n* any day of the week except Sunday and often Saturday.

weekend /week-end/ *n* the period from the time your work ceases on Friday or Saturday until you begin it again on Monday.

weekly /week-lee/ *adj* happening once a week (*a weekly meeting*). ● *n* a newspaper or magazine published once a week.

weep /weep/ *vb* (*pt, pp* **wept** /wept/) **1** to shed tears, to cry. **2** to mourn (*weep for a lost cause*). ● *adj* **weepy** /wee-pee/.

weeping /wee-ping/ *adj* **1** crying. **2** (*of a tree*) having drooping branches (*a weeping willow*).

weevil /wee-vil/ *n* a type of beetle that destroys stored grain.

weft /weft/ *n* the cross-threads of a piece of cloth.

weigh /way/ *vb* **1** to measure the heaviness of (*weigh the baggage*). to raise (anchor). **3** to be of a certain heaviness (*she weighs 140 pounds*). ● **weigh down** to trouble. ● **weigh up** to consider carefully. ● **weigh with** to seem important to.

weight /wate/ *n* **1** heaviness (*measure the weight of the load*). **2** a piece of metal, etc., of known heaviness, used in finding how heavy another object is or in fitness training. **3** importance, influence (*her opinion does not carry much weight*). **4** a heavy load. ● *adj* **weightless** /wate-less/. ● *n* **weightlessness** / wate-less-ness/.

weightlifting /wate-lif-ting/ *n* the sport of lifting heavy weights.

weight training /wate-tray-ning/ *n* a kind of fitness training involving the use of light weights.

weighty /way-tee/ *adj* **1** heavy (*a weighty load*). **2** important, deserving careful consideration (*weighty matters*).

weir /weer/ *n* a barrier built across a stream to make the water approaching it deeper.

weird /weerd/ *adj* **1** odd, very strange (*she looks weird in that outfit*). **2** strange, eerie, unearthly (*a weird scream*). ● *adv* **weirdly** /weerd-lee/. ● *n* **weirdness** /weerd-ness/.

welcome /wel-cum/ *adj* **1** pleasing. **2** allowed to use or take at any time. ● *n* a kindly greeting or reception. ● *vb* **1** to greet kindly (*welcome the guests*). **2** to receive or hear with pleasure (*welcome the news*). ● **make welcome** to make (a guest) feel at home.

weld /weld/ *vb* to join two pieces of metal by heating them and hammering them together. ● *n* **welder** /wel-der/.

welfare /wel-fare/ *n* **1** happiness, success. **2** health, good living conditions (*the department concerned with the welfare of the community*). **3** payments provided by the government for those in need.

well[1] /well/ *adv* **1** in a good way or style (*she does her job well*). **2** thoroughly (*examine the house well before buying*). **3** rightly (*you may well apologize*).

4 with approval (*speak well of him*). ● *adj* **1** in good health. **2** all right. ● **as well as** in addition to.

well² /well/ *n* **1** a spring of water. **2** a hole in the ground from which water can be drawn. **3** a pit made in the ground to reach oil. **4** a fountain. ● *vb* **1** to come up as from a spring. **2** to gush out (*tears welling from her eyes*).

we'll /weel/ *contraction* we will.

well-being /well-bee-ing/ *n* success, happiness (*only interested in his wife's well-being*).

well-informed /well-in-**fawrmd**/ *adj* having much knowledge.

well-known /well-**noan**/ *adj* famous (*well-known actors*).

well-nigh /well-nie/ *adv* (*old or fml*) almost (*it was well-nigh impossible to take him seriously*).

well-off /well-**awf**/ *adj* rich.

well-read /well-**red**/ *adj* having read much.

well-spoken /well-**spo**-kin/ *adj* always pronouncing clearly with a pleasing, educated accent.

well-wisher /well-wi-sher/ *n* a friendly supporter (*well-wishers giving donations to charity*).

well-worn /well-**woarn**/ *adj* much worn, much used (*well-worn phrases*).

welter /well-ter/ *n* a confused mass, disorder (*a welter of useless information*).

welterweight /well-ter-wate/ *n* a boxer between middleweight and heavyweight.

wench /wench/ *n* (*old*) a young woman.

wend /wend/ *vb* (*old*) to go, to make (your way).

were /wer/ a form of be, in the past tense, used with we, you or they or with plural nouns

we're /weer/ *contraction* we are.

west /west/ *n* one of the four principal points of the compass, the direction in which the sun sets.

westerly /west-er-lee/ *adj* from or toward the west (*a westerly wind*).

western /west-ern/ *adj* in or from the west. ● *n* a movie, usually about cowboys and American Indians, set in the west of North America during the 19th or early 20th century.

westward /west-ward/ *adv* toward the west.

wet /wet/ *adj* **1** covered or soaked with water or other liquid (*get wet standing in the rain at the bus stop*). **2** not dry, moist. **3** rainy (*a wet day*). ● *n* rainy weather. ● *vb* (**wet** *or* **wetted** /wet-id/, **wetting** /wet-ing/) to make wet. ● *n* **wetness** /wet-ness/.

we've /weev/ *contraction* we have.

whack /whack/ *vb* (*inf*) to strike sharply, to beat severely (*he whacked the carpet with the beater*). ● *n* **1** a blow (*a whack on the head*). **2** a share (*I want my fair whack*). **3** an attempt (*have a whack at this quiz*)

whale /whale/ *n* a large sea mammal. ● *vb* to hunt whales. ● *n* **whaling** /whay-ling/.

whalebone /whale-bone/ *n* an elastic horny substance got from the jaw of a whale.

whaler /whay-ler/ *n* a ship engaged in whale hunting.

wharf /whawrf/ *n* (*pl* **wharfs** /whawrfs/ *or* **wharves** /whawrvz/) a platform or quay at which ships are loaded and unloaded.

what /whawt/ *adj and pron* used to ask for information about someone or something (*what dress should I wear?/what is your favorite movie?*)

whatever /whaw-te-ver/ *pron* no matter what, any thing concerned.

whatnot /whawt-nawt/ *n* an object not easily described or defined (*buy a few whatnots for her vacation*).

wheat /wheet/ *n* the grain from which bread flour is obtained.

wheat bread /wheet-bred/ *n* bread made with white and wholewheat flour.

wheaten /whee-tin/ *adj* made from wheat (*wheaten bread*).

wheedle /whee-dul/ *vb* to try to please a person in order to get him or her to do something, to coax (*he tried to wheedle more money out of his father*).

wheel /wheel/ *n* a round frame, often strengthened by spokes, turning on an axis. ● *vb* **1** to move on wheels. **2** to turn like a wheel. **3** to change direction by a wheeling movement when marching in line.

wheelbarrow /wheel-ba-ro/ *n* a handcart, usually with one wheel, two legs, and handles.

wheelchair /wheel-chair/ *n* a chair with wheels for people who are unable to walk.

wheelwright /wheel-rite/ *n* a maker of wheels and carts.

wheeze /wheez/ *vb* to breathe with a hoarse or hissing sound (*she is asthmatic and wheezes badly*). ● *also n.* ● *adj* **wheezy** /whee-zee/.

when /when/ *adv and conj* at what or which time.

whence /whenss/ *adv and conj* from what place.

whenever /whe-ne-ver/, **whensoever** /when-so-ever/ *advs and conjs* at no matter what time.

where /whare/ *adv and conj* at, to, or in what place.

whereabouts /whay-ra-bouts/ *n* the place you are in (*the police want to know the accused's whereabouts*).

whereas /whay-**raz**/ *conj* since, although.

whereby /whare-**bie**/ *adv* and *conj* by which.

wherefore /whare-**fore**/ *adv* and *conj* for which or what reason.

whereupon /whare-up-**awn**/ *adv* after which.

wherever /whare-**ev**-er/ *adv* and *conj* at, to, or in whatever place.

whet /whet/ *vb* **1** to sharpen. **2** to make (a desire) more strongly felt (*whet their appetites*).

whether /**whe**-ther/ *conj* if. ● *pron* which of two.

whey /whay/ *n* the watery part of the milk, separated from the curd.

which /which/ *adj* and *pron* what particular (person or thing) (*which picture do you prefer?*).

whiff /whiff/ *n* **1** a puff of air or smoke. **2** a quick or slight smell (*think she smelled a whiff of gas*). ● *vb* **1** to puff. **2** to smell.

while /while/ *n* a space of time. ● *conj* during the time that. ● *vb* to pass (time) in pleasure or leisure (*while away the afternoon reading*).

whilst /whilste/ *conj* (*Br*) *see* **while**.

whim /whim/ *n* a sudden strange desire or idea, a passing fancy.

whimper /**whim**-per/ *vb* to cry brokenly, to whine (*the child was whimpering in his cot*). ● *also n.*

whimsical /**whim**-zi-cal/ *adj* full of whims, odd, unusual, fantastic.

whimsy /**whim**-zee/ *n* whim (*she went to the shore for the day on a sudden whimsy*). ● *n* **whimsicality** /whim-zi-ca-li-tee/. ● *adv* **whimsically** /**whim**-zi-clee/.

whine /whine/ *n* a long cry of complaint, a wail. ● *vb* **1** to utter a sad or complaining cry (*dogs whining*). **2** to speak in a complaining voice (*whine about her misfortune*).

whinny /**whi**-nee/ *n* the high-pitched cry of a horse. ● *also vb*

whip /whip/ *n* a cord attached to a stick for beating or driving animals. ● *vb* (**whipped** /whipt/, **whipping** /**whi**-ping/) **1** to strike with a whip (*whip the wrong-doers*). **2** to beat eggs, cream, etc., into a froth (*whip the mixture*). **3** to take or move (something) quickly (*she whipped her apron off*).

whippet /**whi**-pit/ *n* a dog like a greyhound used for racing.

whippoorwill /**whip**-pur-will/ *n* a nightjar with spotted brown feathers and a loud call.

whir(r) /whir/ *vb* (**whirred** /whird/, **whirring** /**whi**-ring/) to move through the air or spin with a buzzing or clicking sound (*the propellers whirred*). ● *also n.*

whirl /whirl/ *vb* to move quickly around and around, to spin quickly (*the dancers whirl around the dance floor*). ● *n* a quick round-and-round movement, confusion.

whirlpool /**whirl**-pool/ *n* a current of water turning around and around with a circular motion.

whirlwind /**whirl**-wind/ *n* a violent wind blowing around and around in a circle.

whisk /whisk/ *vb* **1** to knock or brush with a quick light movement. **2** to beat lightly into a froth (*whisk the eggs*). **3** to take with a quick movement (*whisked her apron off*). ● *n* **1** a quick or jerky movement. **2** an implement for beating eggs, etc. (*an electric whisk*). **3** a bunch of hair, etc., for brushing away flies, dust, etc.

whisker /**whi**-sker/ *n* **1** the hair growing on the cheeks, the stiff hairs growing on the cheeks of men. **2** the stiff hairs growing above the mouth of certain animals (*the cat's whiskers*).

whiskey /**whi**-skee/ *n* **1** a strong alcoholic drink made from barley, rye, etc. **2** (*Br*) a strong alcoholic drink made in Ireland or North America from barley, rye, etc.

whisky /**whi**-skee/ *n* (*Br*) a strong alcoholic drink made in Scotland from barley.

whisper /**whi**-sper/ *vb* **1** to speak very softly, using the breath instead of the voice. **2** to rustle (*silk skirts whispering as she walked*). ● *n* **1** a very soft voice. **2** what is whispered (*he heard her whispers*). **3** a rumor (*there is a whisper that he embezzled money*).

whist /whist/ *n* a game of cards for four persons.

whistle /**whi**-sul/ *vb* **1** to make a high, shrill sound with the lips or a special instrument. **2** to play a tune by whistling. ● *n* **1** a shrill sound made with the lips or a special instrument. **2** an instrument that makes a whistling sound when blown (*the referee blew his whistle*).

whit /whit/ *n* a tiny piece (*not a whit of truth in his statement*).

white /white/ *adj* **1** of the color of clean snow or milk. **2** pale (*her illness has made her look rather white*). **3** having a pale skin (as opposed to yellow, brown, or black). ● *also n.*

White House /white howss/ *n* the official residence, and office of power, of the president of the United States of America. Located on Pennsylvania Avenue, Washington, DC.

white lie /white-lie/ *n* a lie told for what is believed to be a good purpose.

whiten /**white**-en/ *vb* to make or become white (*buy something to whiten the sheets*).

whitewash /**white**-wawsh/ *n* a mixture of lime or chalk and water used for painting walls, etc., white. ● *vb* **1**

to paint with whitewash (*whitewash the walls of the house*). **2** to try to make what is wrong appear blameless, to try to make a guilty person seem innocent (*they tried to whitewash the crime*).

whither /whi-ther/ *adv* and *conj* to which or what place.

whiting /whie-ting/ *n* a small edible sea fish.

whittle /whi-tul/ *vb* **1** to pare off short strips with a knife. **2** to make smaller or thinner (*whittle the budget*). **3** to cut down or reduce a little at a time (*the bills are whittling away at our budget*).

whiz(z) /whizz/ *vb* (**whizzed** /whizd/, **whizzing** /whizing/) to make a hissing or swishing sound when moving through the air (*children whizzing down our road on roller skates*). ● *also n.*

whizkid or **whizzkid** /whiz-kid/ *n* (*inf*) a young person who is exceptionally successful at something, often in business (*the financial world is full of whizkids*).

who /hoo/ *pron* which person (*the man who died*).

whoever /hoo-ev-er/ *pron* no matter who, any person concerned.

whole /hole/ *adj* **1** complete, entire (*tired of the whole affair*). **2** unharmed (*escape whole from the accident*). ● *n* the total, all.

wholefood /hole-food/ *n* food which has not been refined or processed very much and which does not contain artificial substances.

wholehearted /hole-har-tid/ *adj* enthusiastic, keen (*give the cause his wholehearted support*). ● *adv* **wholeheartedly** /hole-har-tid-lee/.

wholemeal /hole-meel/ (*Br*) *see* **wholewheat** /hole-wheet/.

wholesale /hole-sale/ *n* the selling of goods in large quantities to those who will resell them to others. ● *adj* on a large scale (*wholesale slaughter*). ● *n* **wholesaler** /hole-say-ler/.

wholesome /hole-sum/ *adj* **1** having a good effect on health (*wholesome food*). **2** healthy, morally healthy (*a wholesome young girl*).

wholewheat /hole-wheet/ *adj* of flour or bread, made from the complete grain of wheat, including the husk.

wholly /hole-lee/ *adv* completely (*not wholly committed*).

whom /hoom/ *pron* the form of "who" used when the object of a sentence or following a preposition (*to whom are you referring?*).

whoop /whoop/ *n* a loud shout. ● *vb* to make a whoop (*whooping with joy*).

whooping cough /whoo-ping-coff/ *n* a disease, chiefly

of children, with long fits of coughing, during which the breath is taken in again with a gasping sound.

whorl /whawrl/ *n* **1** a ring of leaves around a stem. **2** one turn of a spiral shell.

whose /hooz/ *pron* belonging to whom (*whose is this sweater?*).

why /whie/ *adv* and *conj* for what reason.

wick /wick/ *n* the thread in a candle, in an 0lamp or oil heater, the band of cloth that draws up the oil and is burned to give light.

wicked /wi-kid/ *adj* bad, sinful, evil (*wicked people*). ● *adv* **wickedly** /wi-kid-lee/. ● *n* **wickedness** /wi-kid-ness/.

wicker /wi-ker/ *n* a willow twig. ● *adj* made of willow twigs woven together.

wickerwork /wi-ker-wurk/ *n* basket work.

wicket /wi-kit/ *n* a small gate, a small door in or near a larger one.

wide /wide/ *adj* broad, extending far in all directions. ● *adv* **1** missing the target by passing beside it (*shoot wide*). **2** fully (*wide awake*). ● *adv* **widely** /wide-lee/.

widen /wie-den/ *vb* to make or become wide (*widen the garden*).

widespread /wide-spred/ *adj* occurring or found far and wide (*a widespread belief*).

widow /wi-doe/ *n* a woman whose husband is dead.

widower /wi-doe-wer/ *n* a man whose wife is dead.

width /width/ *n* breadth (*measure the width of the room*).

wield /weeld/ *vb* **1** to use with the hands (*wield a knife in self-defense*). **2** to use or put into practice (*wield power*).

wiener /wee-ner/ *n* a frankfurter.

wife /wife/ *n* (*pl* **wives** /waeevz/) a married woman.

wifely /wife-lee/ *adj* like a wife (*wifely affection*).

wig /wig/ *n* an artificial covering of hair for the head (*he wore a wig to cover his baldness*).

wiggle /wi-gul/ *vb* to wag, to shake from side to side (*wiggling her hips as she walked*).

wigwam /wig-wam/ *n* the hut or tent of an American Indian.

wild /wilde/ *adj* **1** not tamed or civilized. **2** not cultivated (*a wild stretch of countryside*). **3** savage. **4** uncontrolled (*wild passions*). **5** very excited (*crowds growing wild at the arrival of the pop star*). ● *n* a desert area, an area unaltered by man. ● *adv* **wildly**.

wildcat /wilde-cat/ *n* **1** a fierce wild animal of the cat family. **2** a fierce person. ● *adj* foolish, reckless, risky (*a wildcat strike*).

wildebeest /wil-di-beest/ *n* a gnu.

wilderness /wil-der-ness/ *n* a desert, an uncultivated or uninhabited area (*the place was a wilderness after the bombing*).

wildfire /wilde-fire/ *n.* ● **spread like wildfire** to spread very quickly.

wild-goose chase /wilde-**goos**-chase/ *n* an undertaking that cannot possibly succeed.

wildlife /wilde-life/ *n* animals, birds, and insects, and sometimes plants, which live in their natural environment (*damaging the forest wildlife*).

wile /wile/ *n* a trick (*use her wiles to get her own way*).

will /will/ *n* **1** your power to make decisions or choices, self-control (*believe in freedom of the will*). **2** desire (*done against her will*). **3** a written document made by a person to say what is to be done with his or her property after death. ● *vb* **1** to desire (*we are willing her to win*). **2** to leave property to others by a signed will.

willful /will-ful/ *adj* always wanting your own way, done deliberately. ● *adv* **willfully** /will-fu-lee/.

willing /wi-ling/ *adj* ready, eager (*willing helpers*). ● *adv* **willingly** /wi-ling-lee/.

willow /wi-loe/ *n* a tree with slender, easily bent branches.

willowy /wi-lo-wee/ *adj* **1** easily bent. **2** slender, graceful (*a willowy figure*).

willpower /will-pow-er/ *n* determination to control what you do.

wilt /wilt/ *vb* **1** to droop (*plants wilting*). **2** to lose freshness or vigor (*people wilting in the heat*).

wily /wie-lee/ *adj* cunning (*a wily plan to get into the building*).

wimple /wim-pul/ *n* (*old*) a headdress, fitting closely around the face, worn by nuns.

win /win/ *vb* (**won** /wun/, **winning** /wi-ning/) **1** to be successful in a match or contest, to be victorious (*he is bound to win against the younger player*). **2** to obtain in a competition (*win a prize*). ● *n* **1** a success. **2** a victory. ● *n* **winner** /wi-ner/.

wince /winss/ *vb* **1** to make a quick movement back because of pain or fear. **2** to twist the face from pain (*she winced as the dentist touched her sore tooth*).

winch /winch/ *n* **1** a handle for turning a wheel. **2** a device for moving a heavy object by winding a rope attached to it around a drum or wheel, so drawing the object up or along.

wind[1] /wind/ *n* **1** air moving. **2** a current of air, a breeze or gale. **3** breath. ● *vb* (*pt, pp* **winded** /win-did/) to put out of breath by a blow in the stomach

(*the boxer was winded and fell*).

wind[2] /waeend/ *vb* (*pt, pp* **wound** /wound/) **1** to twist. **2** to coil. **3** to gather up by turning. **4** to follow a twisting course (*the path winding up the mountain*). ● **wind up 1** to turn a handle to tighten a spring in a machine. **2** to bring to an end (*wind up the firm*).

windbag /wind-bag/ *n* (*inf*) a person who talks too much (*bored listening to the old windbag*).

windfall /wind-fawl/ *n* **1** fruit blown down (*gather windfalls in the orchard*). **2** a piece of unexpected luck, an unexpected gift of money.

wind instrument /wind-in-stru-mint/ *n* a musical instrument, such as the trombone, played by blowing into it.

windmill /wind-mill/ *n* a mill with sails driven by wind.

window /win-doe/ *n* an opening in the wall of a house, etc., to let in light (usually filled with a sheet of glass) (*bay windows*).

windpipe /wind-pipe/ *n* the air passage from the mouth to the lungs.

windshield /wind-sheeld/ *n* the glass panel at the front of a motor car that acts like a shield (*a windshield shattered by a pebble*).

windsurfing /wind-sur-fing/ *n* a sport involving moving along the surface of the sea or a stretch of water while standing on a board with a sail attached to it. ● *n* **windsurfer** /wind-sur-fer/.

windward /wind-ward/ *n* the direction from which the wind is blowing. ● *also adj*.

windy /win-dee/ *adj* open to the winds, breezy, gusty (*a windy day/a windy stretch of countryside*).

wine /wine/ *n* a strong drink made from the fermented juice of grapes.

wing /wing/ *n* **1** the limb with the help of which birds, insects, etc., fly. **2** a side part or extension of a building, stage, etc. (*one wing of the building had burned down*). **3** the supporting parts of an airplane. **4** the side part of an army when drawn up for battle. ● *vb* **1** to fly (*swallows winging their way south*). **2** to wound in the wing or arm. ● *adj* **winged** /wingd/. ● *adj* **wingless** /wing-less/. ● **on the wing** in flight.

wink /wingk/ *vb* **1** to shut and open one eyelid with a quick movement. **2** to flicker, to twinkle (*lights winking*). **3** (*fml*) (*usually with* **at**) to pretend not to see (*wink at her son's misdeeds*). ● *n* **1** the act of winking. **2** a hint given by winking. ● **forty winks** a nap, a short sleep.

winner *see* **win**.

winning /wi-ning/ adj 1 successful (a winning formation). 2 charming (winning manners). ● npl **winnings** /wi-ningz/ money that you have won.

winnow /win-noe/ vb to separate the grain from the chaff by a draft of air.

winsome /win-sum/ adj (fml) attractive, pleasant.

winter /win-ter/ n the coldest season of the year. ● vb to spend the winter (wintering in Florida).

wintry /win-tree/ adj like winter, cold, stormy, or snowy (wintry weather).

wipe /wipe/ vb to clean or dry by gentle rubbing (wipe the table). ● n a rub intended to clean or dry. ● **wipe out** to destroy, to cause to cease to exist (an entire city wiped out by the war).

wiper /wie-per/ n a device for wiping rain from a car windshield (a windshield wiper).

wire /wire/ n a thread or cord of metal. ● vb to provide with wire or wires. ● n **wiring**.

wiry /wie-ree/ adj thin but muscular (the boxer did not look strong but he had a wiry build).

wisdom /wiz-dum/ n 1 the ability to make good use of your knowledge and experience. 2 good sense.

wisdom tooth /wiz-dum-tooth/ n a back tooth that grows when you are a young adult.

wise /wize/ adj 1 having or showing wisdom (a wise man). 2 sensible (a wise decision).

-wise /wize/ suffix (fml) with regard to (healthwise I am doing just fine).

wish /wish/ vb to have a desire, to want (to do), to long. ● n 1 a desire. 2 the thing wanted.

wishful thinking /wish-ful-thing-king/ n something believed in spite of the facts because you want it to be true (she said she was going to the Caribbean, but it was only wishful thinking).

wishy-washy /wi-shee-waw-shee/ adj weak and pale, feeble (too wishy-washy to defend herself).

wisp /wisp/ n a small bundle of straw, hay, etc. (wisps of hair). ● adj **wispy** /wi-spee/.

wistful /wist-ful/ adj thoughtful, longing (she looked wistful as the other children left on vacation). ● adv **wistfully** /wist-fu-lee/.

wit /wit/ n 1 the ability to say things shortly, neatly, and cleverly, often in a way that makes them amusing. 2 a person who has this ability. 3 intelligence, understanding. ● **at your wits end** so worried that you do not know what to do next. ● **to wit** namely, that is to say.

witch /witch/ n 1 a woman believed to have magical powers granted by the devil. 2 an ugly old woman.

witchcraft /witch-craft/ n magic performed with the aid of the devil.

witch-doctor /witch-doc-tor/ n among certain African tribes, a man believed to be able to control evil spirits and cure illness by magic.

with /with/ prep 1 in the company of (come with me). 2 having (the girl with red hair).

withdraw /with-draw/ vb 1 to draw or pull back, to retreat. 2 to take back (something said) as not meant (withdraw his apology). 3 to take money, etc., from your bank or stock (withdrew money from his bank account). ● n **withdrawal** /with-drawl/.

withdrawn /with-drawn/ adj shy or unfriendly.

wither /wi-ther/ vb to make or become dry and faded, to shrivel, to rot away (flowers withering without water).

withering /wi-ther-ing/ adj 1 drying, fading. 2 hurtful, sarcastic (a withering reply).

withers /wi-therz/ npl the ridge between the shoulder blades of a horse.

withhold /with-hoald/ vb to refuse to grant or give, to keep back (withhold information).

within /wi-thin/ prep inside. ● adv 1 indoors. 2 inwardly.

without /wi-thout/ prep not having.

withstand /with-stand/ vb to resist, to oppose.

witless /wit-less/ adj (fml) foolish, stupid.

witness /wit-ness/ n 1 a person who sees an event taking place. 2 a person who tells in a court of law what took place on an occasion at which he or she was present. 3 (fml) evidence pointing to the truth. ● vb 1 to see happening (witnessed the accident). 2 to sign a document to confirm that another has signed it in your presence (witness the signature on the agreement). ● **bear witness** to give evidence.

witticism /wi-ti-si-zum/ n a clever or humorous saying, shortly and neatly expressed.

wittingly /wi-ting-lee/ adv with knowledge or understanding of what you are doing (he did not wittingly hurt her).

witty /wi-tee/ adj able to say clever things briefly and often amusingly (a witty after-dinner speech). ● adv **wittily** /wi-ti-lee/.

wives see **wife**.

wizard /wi-zard/ n 1 a man who claims magical powers. 2 a conjurer.

wizardry /wi-zard-ree/ n 1 magic. 2 great skill.

wizened /wi-zend/ adj dried up and wrinkled (a wizened old lady).

wobble /wob-ul/ vb to sway from side to side, move unsteadily (cyclists wobbling along the street). ● also n.

wobbly /**wob**-lee/ adj unsteady (a wobbly table).

woe /woe/ n (fml) grief, sorrow, misery (tell a tale of woe).

woebegone /**wo**-bi-gawn/ adj (fml) full of sorrow or grief (she felt woebegone when they left).

woeful /**wo**-ful/ adj 1 sad. 2 deplorably bad (a woeful lack of understanding). • adv **woefully** /**wo**-fu-lee/.

wok /wak/ n a large bowl-shaped cooking pan used for stir-frying.

woke /woke/ pt of **wake**.

wolf /woolf/ n (pl wolves /woolvz/) a fierce wild animal of the dog family. • vb to eat greedily.

woman /**woo**-man/ n (pl women /**wi**-min/) a grown-up female human being.

womanhood /**woo**-man-hood/ n the state or qualities of a woman (the age at which girls reach womanhood).

womanish /**woo**-ma-nish/ adj 1 having the qualities of a woman. 2 unmanly.

womankind /**woo**-man-kiend/, **womanfolk** /**woo**-man-foke/ ns women in general.

womanly /**woo**-man-lee/ adj having the good qualities of a woman, gentle.

womb /woom/ n the female organ in which the young are kept and fed until birth.

wombat /**wom**-bat/ n a pouched Australian animal, like a small bear.

women see **woman**.

women's movement /**wi**-minz-moov-mint/ n a movement whose aim is to improve the position of women in society and obtain equality with men.

won /wun/ pt of **win**.

wonder /**wun**-der/ n 1 great surprise or astonishment (look at the sight with wonder). 2 anything giving rise to such feelings, a marvel or miracle (the wonders of the world). • vb 1 to think about the reasons for something (wonder why he behaved like that). 2 to feel surprise or astonishment.

wonderful /**wun**-der-ful/ adj very surprising, extraordinary (a wonderful gift/a wonderful surprise). • adv **wonderfully** /**wun**-der-fu-lee/.

wonderment /**wun**-der-ment/ n surprise, astonishment.

wondrous /**wun**-druss/ adj (old) wonderful.

wont /wawnt/ n custom, habit. • adj accustomed.

won't /woant/ contraction will not.

woo /woo/ vb to make love to, to seek to marry. • n **wooer** /**woo**-er/.

wood /wood/ n 1 a large collection of growing trees (the pine wood below the hill). 2 the hard substance of which the trunks and branches of trees are made.

woodchuck /**wood**-chuck/ n a North American animal with brown fur that lives underground and hibernates in winter. • Also called **groundhog**.

woodcut /**wood**-cut/ n a print made from a picture carved on wood.

wooded /**woo**-did/ adj covered with trees or woods (wooded areas).

wooden /**woo**-din/ adj 1 made of wood. 2 dull, lacking feeling (wooden acting).

woodland /**wood**-land/ n country covered with trees or woods.

woodpecker /**wood**-pe-ker/ n a bird that taps holes in trees with its long pointed beak and takes out insects from them with its tongue.

woodwind instrument /**wood**-wind **in**-stru-mint/ n a wind instrument usually made of wood, such as the clarinet.

woodwork /**wood**-wurk/ n 1 the art of making objects out of wood (take classes in woodwork). 2 objects so made.

woodworm /**wood**-wurm/ n a grub that eats its way into wood and destroys it.

woody /**woo**-dee/ adj 1 made of wood. 2 covered with woods (a woody area).

woof /woof/ n the sound that a dog makes when it barks.

wool /wool/ n 1 the soft, wavy hair covering the body of certain animals (e.g., sheep, goats, etc.). 2 thread or cloth made from wool (knit a sweater with wool).

woolen /**woo**-len/ adj made of wool (woolen sweaters). • also n.

wooly /**woo**-lee/ adj 1 covered with wool. 2 like wool.

word /wurd/ n 1 a sound or group of sounds expressing an idea. 2 a message, information (send him word about his wife's health). 3 a promise (he gave his word that he would be there). • vb to express in words. • **have words with** to quarrel with. • **word for word** in exactly the same words as those used before.

wording /**wur**-ding/ n the way that something is expressed in words.

word-perfect /**wurd**-per-fect/ adj able to say without an error the words of something learned (actors who were not word-perfect).

word processor /**wurd**-**pro**-se-sur/ n a computer system used for editing and printing documents.

wordy /**wur**-dee/ adj using more words than are necessary (a wordy letter).

wore /wore/ pt of **wear**.

work /wurk/ n **1** effort (*put a lot of work into the project*). **2** a task, tasks (*bring work home from the office*). **3** that which you do for a living (*she is at work seven hours a day*). **4** a book, picture, piece of music, etc. ● vb **1** to labor, to toil (*they really worked at getting the house ready*). **2** to be in a job. **3** to make to do work (*to work the servants hard*). **4** to have the desired effect or result (*the painkillers did not work*). **5** to cause, to bring about. **6** to give shape to (*work the clay into a pot*). ● npl **works 1** a factory. **2** the parts of a machine that make it go. ● **work up** to excite.

workable /wur-ka-bul/ adj that can be done or used (*a workable plan*).

worker /wur-ker/ n **1** a person who works (*the factory workers*). **2** an insect (e.g., a bee) that does all the work.

workforce /wurk-foarss/ n the number of people who work in a particular firm, place, industry, etc.

workman /wurk-man skill of a worker. **2** the quality of a piece of work.

work-out /wurk-out/ n a session of physical exercise or training (*regular work-outs at the gym keep her fit*). ● vb **work out** /wurk-out/.

workshop /wurk-shap/ n a building or room in which work is carried on (*mending the radio in the workshop*).

world /wurld/ n **1** the Earth on which we live. **2** any planet or star. **3** the universe and all created things. **4** all human beings. **5** any sphere of activity, study, etc. (*the world of science*). **6** a great amount (*a world of difference*).

worldly /wurld-lee/ adj **1** having to do with this world or life (*worldly pleasures*). **2** interested only in the things of this life (*worldly people*).

worldwide /wurld-wide/ adj spread throughout or found everywhere in the world (*a worldwide organization*).

World Wide Web /world wide web/ n (abbr = WWW) the Internet network that stretches across the world. Each Internet page is indexed (by a function called hypertext) and can be linked to a related document and searched for using search engines.

worm /wurm/ n **1** a small creeping animal without a backbone or legs. **2** the thread of a screw. **3** (*inf*) a despicable person (*he is an absolute worm*). ● vb **1** to wriggle or crawl along. **2** to do something slowly and secretly (*worm his way into her favor*). **3** to persuade to tell by persistent questioning (*worm the truth out of her*).

worn /woarn/ pp of **wear**. ● adj showing signs of wear (*worn furniture*).

worn-out /woarn-out/ adj **1** exhausted. **2** overused or worn.

worry /wu-ree/ vb **1** to feel anxiety (*she worries when the children are late*). **2** to trouble, to vex (*the child's behavior worries her*). **3** to tear with the teeth (*the dog worrying a bone*). ● n **1** anxiety, trouble. **2** a cause of anxiety.

worse /wurss/ adj more bad, less good, more sick. ● adv more badly.

worsen /wur-sin/ vb to make or become worse (*interference would only worsen the situation*).

worship /wur-ship/ n **1** prayers and praise offered to God. **2** a religious service. **3** great love or reverence for. ● vb (**worshiped** /wur-shipt/, **worshiping** /wur-shi-ping/) **1** to pray to. **2** to honor greatly. **3** to join in a religious service (*the congregation worships every Sunday*). ● n **worshiper** /wur-shi-per/.

worst /wurst/ adj most bad or sick. ● adv most badly. ● n the greatest evil or ill possible. ● vb to defeat (*he was worsted by his opponent*).

worth /wurth/ adj **1** equal in value to (*a vase worth $200*). **2** deserving of (*a movie worth seeing*). **3** having such-and-such an amount of money or property (*he's worth millions*). ● n **1** value (*the painting's worth is incalculable*). **2** price (*$20 worth of gas*). **3** merit, excellence (*he proved his worth by going*).

worthless /wurth-less/ adj of no use or value. ● n **worthlessness** /wurth-less-ness/.

worthwhile /wurth-while/ adj profitable, repaying the money, work, etc., expended (*a worthwhile job*).

worthy /wur-thee/ adj deserving, deserving respect (*worthy of respect/a worthy cause*).

would /wood/ pt of **will**.

would-be /wood-be/ adj wishing to be, intending (*a would-be doctor*).

wound /woond/ n a hurt, cut, or bruise, an injury. ● vb **1** to injure, to cause a wound to (*wounded in battle*). **2** to hurt the feelings of (*wounded by his nasty remarks*).

wound /wound/ pt of **wind**. ● **wound-up** over-excited (*she was wound-up before the job interview*).

wove /wove/ pt of **weave**. ● pp **woven**.

wraith /raith/ n (*fml*) a ghost.

wrangle /rang-gul/ vb to quarrel, to argue angrily (*wrangle over their father's will*). ● n a quarrel, dispute. ● n **wrangler** /rang-gler/.

wrap /rap/ vb (**wrapped** /rapt/, **wrapping** /ra-ping/) to fold paper, cloth etc. around so as to cove (*wrap presents*). ● *n* **1** a shawl, a loose cloak. **2** a sandwich consisting of a tortilla with a filling inside. ● *n* **wrapping** /rah-ping/.

wrapper /ra-per/ *n* a cover for books, etc.

wrath /rath/ *n* great anger, rage (*show her wrath by walking out*).

wrathful /rath-ful/ *adj* very angry.

wreak /reek/ vb to carry out, to put into effect (*wreak revenge*).

wreath /reeth/ *n* **1** flowers, leaves, etc, woven together to form a ring or crown (*put a wreath on her grave*). **2** a curling or spiral cloud (*wreaths of smoke*).

wreathe /reethe/ *vb* to put a wreath on or around.

wreck /reck/ *n* **1** destruction, especially of a ship at sea. **2** a ruin (*a wreck of a car*). **3** the remains of a ship destroyed by the sea. **4** a person weakened by ill health or evil living. ● *vb* to ruin, to destroy (*wrecked their plans*).

wreckage /re-kidge/ *n* the broken parts of a wrecked ship.

wren /ren/ *n* a very small songbird.

wrench /rench/ *n* **1** a violent twist (*open the bottle with a wrench*). **2** the sorrow caused by parting from or giving away (*leaving her children was a wrench*). **3** a tool for gripping and turning nuts, bolts, etc. ● *vb* **1** to give a sudden twist or pull to. **2** to sprain.

wrest /rest/ *vb* to twist, to pull violently from (wrest the property from his hands).

wrestle /re-sul/ *vb* **1** to struggle with another by gripping and trying to throw down. **2** to try hard to solve (*wrestle with the problem*).

wrestler /re-sler/ *n* a person who wrestles for sport.

wrestling /re-sling/ *n* the sport of wrestling.

wretch /rech/ *n* **1** a very unfortunate or miserable person (*the poor wretch has lost everything*). **2** a wicked or worthless person (*that wretch stole my money*).

wretched /rech-ed/ *adj* **1** miserable. **2** worthless.

wriggle /ri-gul/ *vb* **1** to twist from side to side (*children wriggling with impatience*). **2** to move with a wriggling movement. ● also *n*. ● *adj* **wriggly** /ri-glee/.

wright /rite/ *suffix* worker at, maker of (*shipwright/ playwright*).

wring /ring/ *vb* (*pt, pp* **wrung** /rung/) **1** to squeeze hard, to twist tightly. **2** to get by pressure or persuasion (*wring a confession from him*).

wringer /ring-er/ *n* a machine for squeezing the water out of clothing.

wrinkle /ring-cul/ *n* a fold or furrow in the skin, or in cloth, etc. (*have wrinkles in her skirt after sitting for so long*). ● *vb* to make wrinkles in.

wrist /rist/ *n* the joint between the hand and the arm.

wristwatch /rist-wawch/ *n* a watch attached to a band worn around the wrist.

writ /rit/ *n* a written order from a law court to do or not to do certain acts (*issue a writ for his arrest*).

write /rite/ *vb* (*pt* **wrote** /rote/, *pp* **written** /ri-ten/) **1** to make marks standing for sounds, letters, or words on paper, etc, with a pen or pencil (*learn to read and write*). **2** to make up stories, poems, etc, for publication (*writing fairy stories*). **3** to write a letter to (*I wrote him yesterday*).

writer /rie-ter/ *n* **1** an author. **2** a person who writes.

writhe /rithe/ *vb* to twist and turn the body about (*writhe in agony*).

writing paper /rie-ting pay-per/ *n* paper for writing letters on.

writings /rie-tingz/ *npl* the written works of an author.

wrong /rong/ *adj* **1** not correct, false (*the wrong set of figures*). **2** incorrect in your opinion, etc. (*she was proved wrong*). **3** not good, not morally right, evil (*wrong deeds*). ● *vb* **1** to treat unjustly (*wronged his wife*). **2** to do harm to. ● *n* **1** an injustice. **2** harm. ● *adv* **wrongly** /rong-lee/.

wrongdoer /rong-doo-er/ *n* a criminal, a sinner. ● *n* **wrongdoing** /rong-doo-ing/.

wrongful /rong-ful/ *adj* **1** unjust (wrongful arrest). **2** criminal, wrong (*wrongful actions*). ● *adv* **wrongfully** /rong-fu-lee/.

wrote /rote/ *pt* of write.

wrought /rawt/ *old pt* of work. ● *adj* beaten or rolled into shape (*wrought iron*).

wrought iron /rawt-eye-urn/ *n* hammered iron.

wry /rie/ *adj* **1** twisted, turned to one side (*a wry neck*). **2** slightly mocking (*a wry smile*). ● *adv* wryly /rie-lee/. ● *n* **wryness** /rie-ness/.

WWW *see* **World Wide Web.**

X

X, x /eks/ **1** the twenty-fourth letter of the alphabet. **2** (*algebra*) the first unknown quantity. **3** (*math*) the first coordinate.

xenophobia /ze-nu-**fo**-bee-ya/ *n* hatred of foreigners and their ways.

xerox /**zee**-roks/ *vb* to make photograph copies by machine (*xeroxing the documents for each of the committee*).

Xmas /**eks**-mas/ short for **Christmas**.

X-rays /**eks**-raze/ *npl* electric rays that are able to pass through solid substances and so can be used in photographing broken bones, or other objects hidden behind a solid surface. ● *n* **X-ray** /**eks**-ray/ an X-ray photograph. ● *vb* **X-ray** to make an X-ray photograph of.

xylophone /**zie**-lu-fone/ *n* a musical instrument of hanging wooden bars that give notes when struck with a wooden hammer.

Y

Y, y /why/ **1** the twenty-fifth letter of the alphabet. **2** (*algebra*) the second unknown quantity. **3** (*math*) the second coordinate.

yacht /yot/ *n* a ship, especially a sailing ship, used for pleasure or racing. ● *n* **yachting**.

yachtsman /**yots**-man/, **yachtswoman** /**yots**-woo-man/ *n* a person who sails a yacht.

yak /yak/ *n* a type of ox with long silky hair, found in Tibet.

yam /yam/ *n* a tropical plant with an edible root, a sweet potato.

yank /yangk/ *vb* to move suddenly or with a jerk (*yank the door open*).

Yankee /**yang**-kee/ *n* a citizen of the North of the United States.

yap /yap/ *vb* (**yapped** /yapt/, **yapping** /**ya**-ping/) to yelp, to bark shrilly (*little dogs yapping*).

yard /yard/ *n* **1** a measure of length (= 3 feet or 0.9144 meters). **2** a pole fixed across a mast for supporting a sail. **3** an enclosed piece of ground near or behind a building. **4** the grounds surrounding a house, a garden. **5** a piece of ground enclosed for a particular purpose (*a building yard*).

yardstick /**yard**-stick/ *n* a standard by which you measure or judge other things (*used her mother's behavior as a yardstick for her own*).

yarn /yarn/ *n* **1** any type of spun thread. **2** (*inf*) a made-up or improbable story (*the old man was spinning a yarn about his days as a sailor*).

yashmak /**yash**-mak/ *n* a veil worn by Muslim women in public.

yawn /yawn/ *vb* **1** to open the mouth wide because of tiredness or boredom. **2** to be wide open (*the cave yawned below them*). ● *n* the act of yawning.

ye /yee/ *pron* old form of you (*pl*).

yea /yay/ *adv* yes.

yeah /yeh/ *adv* (*inf*) yes.

year /yeer/ *n* the time taken by the Earth to travel once around the sun, 365 days, especially from 1 January to December 31, 12 months.

yearling /**yeer**-ling/ *n* a one-year-old animal.

yearly /**yeer**-lee/ *adj* **1** happening once a year. **2** happening every year. ● *also adv*.

yearn /yurn/ *vb* to desire greatly, to long (for) (*yearn for a better way of life*).

yearning /**yur**-ning/ *n* a strong desire, a longing.

yeast /yeest/ *n* a frothy substance used for making bread rise and in making beer, etc.

yell /yell/ *vb* to scream, to shout loudly and suddenly (*yell for help*). ● *also n*.

yellow /**ye**-lo/ *n* a bright golden color, as of daffodils. ● *adj* **1** of golden color. **2** (*inf*) cowardly (*too yellow to stand up for himself*).

yellow-fever /ye-lo-**fee**-ver/ *n* a dangerous tropical disease spread by mosquitoes.

yelp /yelpg/ *vb* to utter a sharp cry, as a dog in pain (*she yelped as the boulder fell on her foot*). ● *also n*.

yen[1] /yen/ *n* (*pl yen*) a Japanese coin.

yen[2] /yen/ *n* (*inf*) desire (*have a yen for sunshine*).

yeoman /**yoe**-man/ *n* a farmer, one who owns a small farm of his own.

yesterday /ye-ster-dee/ *n* the day before today. ● *also adv.*

yet /yet/ *adv* 1 still. 2 in addition. 3 up to the present. 4 however. 5 all the same.

yeti /ye-tee/ *n* a legendary very large creature said to live in the Himalayas.

yew /yoo/ *n* a large evergreen tree often grown in churchyards.

Yiddish /yid-ish/ *n* a language, partly German and Hebrew, spoken by modern Jews.

yield /yeeld/ *vb* 1 to produce (fruit, crops, profit, etc.) (*the milk yielded by the cattle*). 2 to give in, to surrender (*the soldiers yield to the enemy*). 3 to give way (*the door finally yielded to pressure*). ● *n* 1 the amount produced or made in profit. 2 a crop.

yielding /yeel-ding/ *adj* giving in easily, easily influenced or managed.

yodel /yo-dul/ *vb* (**yodeled** /yo-duld/, **yodeling** /yo-dling/) to sing with frequent changes from one's ordinary voice to a higher-pitched one. ● *n* **yodeler**.

yoga /yo-ga/ *n* a Hindu belief that by prayer and complete control over the body and its desires, you may become one with God.

yogi /yo-gee/ *n* a person who practices yoga.

yogurt /yo-gurt/ *n* a food made from fermented milk (*have yogurt and fruit for breakfast*).

yoke /yoke/ *n* 1 the part of a garment that fits over the shoulders and round the neck (*a black dress with a white yolk*). 2 a frame of wood that fits over the necks of two oxen, making them work together when pulling a plow, cart, etc. 3 something that forces people to do something (*the yoke of slavery*). ● *vb* 1 to put together under a yoke. 2 to link together.

yokel /yo-kul/ *n* (*derog*) a country fellow.

yolk /yoke/ *n* the yellow part of an egg.

Yom Kippur /yom-ki-**poor**/ *n* the Day of Atonement, a Jewish festival involving fasting and repenting.

Yon /yon/, **yonder** /yon-dur/ *adjs* (*old*) that (one) over there. ● *adv* **yonder** over there.

yore /yore/ *n* (*old*) olden times. ● **of yore** in olden times.

you /yoo/ *pron* the person or people being addressed (*you look well*).

young /yung/ *adj* not old, not grown up, childish, youthful. ● *n* 1 all the children or offspring (of) (*the lioness and her young*). 2 young people in general (*entertainments for the young*).

youngster /yung-ster/ *n* a young person.

your /yoor/ *adj* belonging to you (*I like your perfume*).

yours /yoorz/ *pron* something belonging to you (*is this book yours?*).

yourself /yoor-self/ *pron* (*pl* **yourselves** /yoor-selvz/) the reflexive form of "they" (*take care of yourself*).

youth /yooth/ *n* 1 the early part of one's life (*she lived overseas in her youth*). 2 a young man (*youths who have just left school*). 3 young people (*clothes designed for youth*).

youthful /yooth-ful/ *adj* young, young-looking (*youthful old people*). ● *adv* **youthfully** /yooth-ful-ee/.

yowl /yowl/ *vb* to cry or howl like a dog. ● *also n.*

yo-yo /yo-yo/ *n* a toy consisting of a double disk that you move up and down on a string.

Yule /yool/ *n* Christmas.

Yuletide /yool-tide/ *n* the Christmas season.

Z

Z, z /zee, zed/ **1** the twenty-sixth letter of the alphabet. **2** (*algebra*) the third unknown quantity. **3** (*math*) the third coordinate.

zany /**zay**-nee/ *adj* crazy (*a zany comedy*).

zap /zap/ *vb* **1** to destroy or kill, especially in computer games. **2** to change television channel using a remote control.

zeal /zeel/ *n* keenness, eagerness, enthusiasm (*show a great deal of zeal for keeping fit*).

zealot /**zel**-ut/ *n* a person who is so keen on a cause or idea that he or she can talk of nothing else.

zealous /**zel**-uss/ *adj* very keen, eager (*zealous supporters of the cause*). ● *adv* **zealously** /**zel**-u-slee/.

zebra /**zee**-bra/ *n* a striped horselike animal found in Africa.

zenith /**ze**-nith/ *n* **1** the point of the heavens directly overhead. **2** the highest point (*the zenith of his career*).

zephyr /**ze**-fur/ *n* (*lit*) a gentle breeze.

zero /**zee**-ro/ *n* **1** the figure 0. **2** the 0-mark on a measuring scale.

zero hour /**zee**-ro-our/ *n* the time fixed for the beginning of something, such as a military attack.

zest /zest/ *n* keen enjoyment, enthusiasm (*the old lady's zest for life*). ● *adj* **zestful**.

zigzag /**zig**-zag/ *adj* turning sharply to the left, following a straight line, then turning sharply to the right, and so on. ● *n* a zigzag line or course. ● *vb* (**zigzagged** /**zig**-zagd/, **zigzagging** /**zig**-za-ging/) to follow a zigzag course (*the path zigzags up the hill*).

zinc /zingk/ *n* a bluish white metal

Zionism /**zie**-u-ni-zum/ *n* the movement to found and develop Israel. ● *adj and n* **Zionist** /**zie**-u-nist/.

zip /zip/ *vb* (**zipped** /zipt/, **zipping** /**zi**-ping/) **1** (*inf*) to whiz (*zipping to the drugstore*). **2** to fasten with a zipper (*zip up her dress*).

zip code /**zip**-code/ *n* a number identifying a postal area of the United States.

zipper /**zi**-per/ *n* a sliding fastener that causes two strips of metal teeth to engage in or disengage from each other as it moves.

zither /**zi**-ther/ *n* a flat stringed musical instrument played with the fingers.

zodiac /**zo**-dee-ac/ *n* the band of the heavens within which the sun, moon, and planets seem to move and containing the 12 groups of stars known as the signs of the zodiac.

zone /zone/ *n* **1** a belt or stripe. **2** any region with distinctive characteristics of its own. **3** one of the five great belts running around the earth (e.g. *Arctic zone*).

zoo /zoo/ *n* a park in which animals are kept in cages, enclosures, ponds, etc., for show.

zoological /zoo-u-**lodge**-ic-al/ *adj* having to do with the study of animals.

zoological gardens /zoo-u-**lodge**-ic-al-gar-denz/ *n* a zoo.

zoologist /zoo-**ol**-u-jist/ *n* a person who studies animals.

zoology /zoo-**ol**-u-jee/ *n* the study of animals.

zoom /zoom/ *vb* **1** to climb rapidly at a steep angle. **2** (*inf*) to increase rapidly (*prices have zoomed*). **3** (*inf*) to move very quickly (*cars zooming along the road*).

zoom lens /zoom-**lenz**/ *n* a camera lens that is adjusted for focusing on close or distant objects.

zucchini /zoo-**kee**-nee/ *n* a cylindrical summer squash with dark green skin.

Zulu /**zoo**-loo/ *n* **1** a member of an African tribe. its language.

THESAURUS AND PHRASEFINDER

A

abandon *vb* **1** (*abandon the nest*) desert, leave, forsake, depart from. **2** (*abandon the attempt*) give up, drop, discard, (*inf*) quit.

abate *vb* (*the storm abated*) die down, lessen, ease, decrease, diminish, moderate, wane.

abbreviate *vb* (*abbreviate a word or phrase*) shorten, reduce, cut, cut short, cut down, contract. ⟳

abbreviations include **CIA** = Central Intelligence Agency, **FBI** = Federal Bureau of Investigation, **IRS** = Internal Revenue Service, **IT** = information technology, **NASA** = National Aeronautics and Space Administration, **PR** = public relations, **SF** = science fiction.

abdicate *vb* **1** (*the king abdicated in 1936*) give up, resign, stand down, retire, quit. **2** (*abdicate responsibilities*) give up, renounce, relinquish.

abdomen *n* (*a pain in the abdomen*) stomach, belly, (*inf*) tummy, (*inf*) insides, intestines.

abduct *vb* (*abduct someone else's child*) kidnap, carry off, seize, hold as hostage, (*inf*) snatch.

abhor *vb* dislike, hate, loathe, despise (*she abhors garlic*).

ability *n* (*a performer of great ability*) talent, skill, expertise, cleverness, competence.

able *adj* (*an able student*) clever, talented, capable, competent.

abnormal *adj* (*an abnormal thing to do*) unusual, strange, odd, peculiar, queer, extraordinary.

abolish *vb* (*abolish slavery*) do away with, put an end to, end, stop, eliminate.

about *adv* (*there were about five people there*) in the neighborhood of, near, around. • *prep* regarding, in relation to.

above *adv* (*clouds up above*) high, overhead. • *prep* **1** (*clouds above us*) over. **2** (*he was above the limit*) in excess of. **3** (*you think you're above me*) superior.

abridge *vb* (*abridge the book for children*) shorten, cut down, condense, compress.

abroad *adv* (*go abroad on vacation*) overseas, to a foreign country, to a foreign land, out of the country.

abrupt *adj* **1** (*come to an abrupt end*) sudden, quick, hurried, hasty, swift, rapid, unexpected, unforeseen. **2** (*an abrupt reply*) curt, blunt,

brusque, short, rude. **3** (*an abrupt slope*) steep, sheer, sudden.

absence *n* (*the teacher reported the absence of her students*) leave, non-attendance, disappearance, truancy, (*inf*) hooky. ⟳

absence makes the heart grow fonder being separated from someone makes your feelings for them grow stronger.

absent *adj* (*absent from school*) not present, away, off, missing, truanting. ⟳

absent without leave being away without having permission to do so <The term and its abbreviation AWOL, are army terms>.

absent-minded *adj* (*so absent-minded that she didn't hear what people were saying to her*) distracted, preoccupied, absorbed, vague, inattentive.

absolute *adj* (*absolute trust*) complete, total, utter, out-and-out, outright, perfect, unqualified, sheer.

abstain *vb* (*abstain from voting/abstain from drinking soda*) refrain, desist, hold back, keep from.

absurd *adj* (*absurd plan*) ridiculous, foolish, silly, idiotic, stupid, nonsensical, senseless, crazy, ludicrous, hare-brained.

abundance *n* (*there was food in abundance*) plenty, plentifulness, (*inf*) heaps, (*inf*) oodles.

abundant *adj* (*an abundant supply of fresh food*) plentiful, ample, large, great, copious, lavish.

abuse *vb* **1** (*abuse children*) mistreat, maltreat, ill-treat, injure, hurt, harm. **2** (*abuse power*) misuse, misapply, mishandle. **3** (*abuse the person who ran into his car*) swear at, curse, insult, rebuke.

abuse *n* **1** (*child abuse*) mistreatment, maltreatment, ill-treatment, ill-use, injury, hurting, harming. **2** (*the abuse of power/the abuse of alcohol*) misuse, misapplication, misapplying, mishandling.

abysmal *adj* **1** (*abysmal ignorance*) utter, extreme, complete, thorough, profound. **2** (*an abysmal performance*) dreadful, appalling, very bad, worthless.

accelerate *vb* **1** (*the car accelerated*) speed up, go faster, go quicker, pick up speed. **2**

(*accelerate the process of change*) speed up, hasten, hurry along, spur on.

accent *n* **1** (*a French accent*) way of speaking, pronunciation, inflection. **2** (*the accent is on the first syllable*) stress, emphasis, force, accentuation. **3** (*the accent must be on efficiency*) emphasis, stress, importance.

accept *vb* **1** (*accept the gift*) receive, take, take receipt of. **2** (*accept their decision*) agree to, consent to, comply with, acquiesce in, concur with, endorse.

acceptable *adj* **1** (*a very acceptable gift*) welcome, agreeable, delightful, pleasing, pleasant, desirable, (*inf*) cool. **2** (*work that is not acceptable*) satisfactory, good enough, adequate, passable, tolerable.

access *n* (*no direct access to the building from the main road*) entry, entrance, way in, admittance, approach.

accessible *adj* (*accessible sources of information*) attainable, available, reachable, obtainable.

accessory *n* **1** (*accessories for an electric drill*) attachment, fitment, extra, addition. **2** (*accessories to the crime*) accomplice, associate, confederate, abettor.

accident *n* **1** (*people injured in the mining accident*) casualty, disaster, catastrophe, calamity, mishap. **2** (*old friends who met by accident*) chance, fate, good fortune, luck, (*inf*) fluke.

accidental *adj* (*accidental death/an accidental meeting*) chance, unintentional, unintended, unexpected, unforeseen, unplanned, unpremeditated.

accommodations *npl* (*find accommodations for the visitors*) housing, lodging, shelter, board, quarters.

accompany *vb* (*accompany her to the dance*) partner, escort, go with, go along with.

accomplice *n* (*an accomplice in crime*) confederate, accessory, collaborator, abettor, ally, helper, henchman, (*inf*) sidekick.

accomplish *vb* (*accomplish a task*) finish, complete, do, perform, execute.

accomplished *adj* (*an accomplished pianist*) skilled, skillful, expert, gifted, talented, masterly.

accomplishment *n* (*person of many accomplishments*) talent, gift, ability, skill, attainment, achievement.

account *n* **1** (*give a full account of the accident*) statement, report, description, record, story,

tale. **2** (*send in the account for the work done*) bill, check, invoice, charges.

accumulate *vb* **1** (*garbage accumulating in the streets*) gather, collect, pile up, build up. **2** (*accumulate many books over the years*) gather, collect, amass, stockpile, hoard.

accredited *adj* (*an accredited representative of the firm*) official, authorized, legal, approved, certified.

accurate *adj* **1** (*accurate measurements*) correct, precise, exact, right. **2** (*an accurate description*) correct, exact, close, true, faithful, strict.

accusation *n* (*deny the accusations*) charge, allegation, incrimination.

accuse *vb* **1** (*accuse her of murder*) charge, indict. **2** (*accuse the boys of breaking windows*) blame, put the blame on, lay the blame on, hold responsible for, hold accountable for, lay at the door of.

accustom *vb* (*accustom herself to her new surroundings*) adapt, adjust, acclimatize, get used to.

accustomed *adj* **1** (*our accustomed route home*) usual, normal, customary, regular, habitual, routine. **2** (*accustomed to public speaking*) used to, in the habit of, familiar with, acquainted with.

ache *vb* (*my head aches*) hurt, be sore, be painful, throb.

ache *n* (*an ache in his back*) pain, soreness, throbbing, twinge, pang.

achieve *vb* (*achieve one's aim*) accomplish, reach, attain, gain, obtain, acquire.

achievement *n* (*proud of his achievements in track and field*) accomplishment, attainment, deed, act, effort, feat.

acid *adj* **1** (*an acid taste*) sour, tart, sharp, bitter vinegary. **2** (*acid remarks*) sharp, sarcastic, caustic, acerbic.

acknowledge *vb* **1** (*acknowledge a letter*) answer, reply to, respond to. **2** (*acknowledge defeat*) admit, accept, recognize, grant, concede.

acquire *vb* (*acquire enough money*) obtain, get, come by, gain, procure.

acquit *vb* (*the judge will acquit the accused*) clear, set free, release, discharge, pardon, absolve.

act *vb* **1** (*act like a fool*) behave, do, operate. **2** (*act quickly to put out the fire*) take action, move, be active, perform. **3** (*act the part of Peter Pan*) play, perform, enact. **4** (*act in a new play*) be an actor, play a part, perform.

act n **1** (*a brave act*) action, deed, undertaking, feat, exploit. **2** (*enjoy the magician's act*) performance, show, turn, routine. **3** (*an act to forbid smoking*) law, ruling, rule, regulation, order, bill, decree, statute. ✧

act out to perform (*Act out the role of Macbeth*).

act up to misbehave (*If you don't stop acting up we are not going to the funfair*).

act your age to stop behaving in an immature way (*Act your age, and stop crying over nothing*).

catch someone in the act to find someone actually doing something wrong or bad (*The thief was breaking into the car and was caught in the act by the police*).

clean up your act to behave in a better way (*The teacher told the boy to clean up his act*).

acting adj (*the acting principal*) temporary, substitute.

action n **1** (*his action saved their lives*) act, deed, move, behavior, undertaking, feat, exploit. **2** (*a movie full of action*) activity, movement, liveliness, energy, vitality. ✧

actions speak louder than words what a person does is more important than what he or she says (*Karen says she loves Gary, but actions speak louder than words*).

active adj **1** (*active children tiring their mothers/lead active lives*) energetic, full of energy, lively, busy, nimble, (*inf*) on the go. **2** (*athletic clubs that are still active*) in action, working, operating, in operation, functioning.

activity n **1** (*city streets full of activity*) movement, bustle, hustle and bustle, liveliness. **2** (*activities enjoyed after school*) pastime, interest, hobby, pursuit, project.

actual adj **1** (*the actual cost was far less than the newspapers reported*) real, true, genuine, authentic. **2** (*no actual evidence of burglary*) existing, definite, certain, positive, concrete.

actually adv (*the boy seems unhealthy, but he is actually quite well*) really, in fact, in reality, in truth, truly.

adapt vb **1** (*adapt the scheme to suit younger children*) adjust, alter, change, convert, modify, vary, reshape, remodel. **2** (*find it difficult to adapt to a new way of life*) adjust, fit in, accustom yourself, become accustomed to, acclimatize.

add vb **1** (*add some more details to the report*) put in, include. **2** (*add the rows of figures*) add up, count, count up, (*inf*) tot up, total. **3** (*money problems added to his worry*) increase, intensify, aggravate.

addicted adj (*be addicted to alcohol*) dependent on, (*inf*) hooked on.

addiction n (*try to cure his drug addiction*) dependence, dependency, craving, habit.

additional adj (*require additional supplies*) more, extra, further, supplementary.

additive n (*additives listed on food labels*) supplement, preservative.

address n **1** (*find out his address*) where you live, home, house, residence. **2** (*the address of the company's head office*) location, place, whereabouts. **3** (*unable to read the address on the parcel*) label, directions, inscription. **4** (*the principal's end-of-year address*) speech, talk, lecture.

address vb **1** (*address a parcel*) write the address on, label, write the directions on, direct, inscribe. **2** (*how do you address a bishop?*) name, call, speak to, write to, describe. **3** (*address your remarks to the manager*) direct, communicate, convey, send.

adequate adj **1** (*adequate supplies for the week*) enough, sufficient, ample. **2** (*workers who are not adequate*) fit, able, competent, qualified, (*inf*) up to scratch.

adhesive n (*an adhesive to stick the tiles to the wall*) glue, cement, gum, fixative.

adjacent adj (*living in the adjacent house*) adjoining, next, next door, neighboring, bordering.

adjourn vb (*adjourn the meeting till the next day*) break off, discontinue, defer, postpone, put off, shelve.

adjudicate vb (*adjudicate at the singing contest*) judge, arbitrate, referee, umpire.

adjust vb **1** (*unable to adjust to the new situation*) adapt, become accustomed to, accustom yourself to, get used to, acclimatize. **2** (*adjust the saddle of the bike*) alter, change, modify, rearrange.

administration n (*in hospital administration*) management, direction, government.

administrator n (*business administrators*) manager, director, executive, controller.

admire vb **1** (*admire her hat/admire the view*) express admiration of, approve of, like, compliment, praise. **2** (*admire their courage*) approve of, respect, think highly of, appreciate, applaud, praise, esteem.

admit vb **1** (*admit his guilt/admit that she could be wrong*) acknowledge, confess, own up, reveal, make known, declare, disclose, divulge, (*inf*) fess up. **2** (*a ticket that admits only one person*) let in, allow in, allow entry, permit entry.

admittance n (*no admittance to the private building*) entry, right of entry, entrance, access.

adolescence n (*a young person just reaching adolescence*) teenage years, (*inf*) teens, growing up.

adopt vb **1** (*adopt a child*) take as your own, take in, take care of, be adoptive parents to. **2** (*adopt a candidate*) select, choose, pick, vote for. **3** (*adopt modern customs/adopt a foreign style of dress*) assume, take on, take over, affect, embrace.

adorable adj (*an adorable little baby*) lovable, sweet, dear, darling, delightful, appealing, charming, enchanting, cute.

adore vb **1** (*they adore their children*) love dearly, be devoted to, dote on, cherish, idolize. **2** (*adore ice cream*) like very much, love, be fond of, enjoy, relish. **3** (*adore God*) worship, praise, glorify, revere.

adorn vb (*flowers adorning the room/adorn the tree with lights*) decorate, embellish, ornament, beautify.

adroit adj (*her adroit handling of the situation*) skillful, skilled, deft, expert, clever, able, adept.

adult adj **1** (*adult people*) grown-up, (*fml*) of age. **2** (*adult trees*) mature, fully grown, developed.

advance[1] vb (*the armies advance*) move forward, go forward, proceed, press on, forge ahead, make progress.

advance[2] adj **1** (*the advance party*) leading, first, in front. **2** (*advance warning*) early, previous, prior, beforehand.

advanced adj **1** (*advanced technology*) progressive, modern, up-to-date, ultra-modern, sophisticated, avant-garde. **2** (*advanced studies/schoolwork that is more advanced*) higher-level, complicated, difficult.

advantage n **1** (*one of the advantages of being tall*) benefit, asset, good point, blessing, boon. **2** (*have an advantage over his rivals*) superiority, ascendancy, supremacy, upper hand. **3** (*there is little advantage in going into business with her*) benefit, profit, gain, good. ✧

take advantage of someone or something to make use of someone or something in such a way as to be of benefit to yourself (*People*

take advantage of her generosity and are always borrowing money from her/her neighbors take advantage of the kind old lady and use her as an unpaid babysitter*).

advantageous adj **1** (*an advantageous position*) favorable, helpful, beneficial, useful. **2** (*advantageous to his hopes of promotion*) of benefit, beneficial, of assistance, useful, valuable.

adventure n **1** (*tell her grandchildren of her adventures at sea*) exploit, escapade, deed, feat, experience. **2** (*a journey full of adventure*) risk, precariousness, danger, hazard, peril, uncertainty.

adventurous adj (*an adventurous life*) risky, precarious, dangerous, hazardous, perilous.

adversary n (*their adversaries in the battle/her adversary in the tournament*) opponent, enemy, foe, antagonist, rival.

adversity n **1** (*a homeless person leading a life of adversity*) misfortune, ill-luck, bad luck, trouble, hardship, distress, misery. **2** (*many adversities in his life*) misfortune, mishap, setback, trial, disaster, catastrophe, calamity.

advertise vb (*advertise a new product*) promote, give publicity to, publicize, (*inf*) push, (*inf*) plug.

advice n (*give careers advice/get advice on a personal problem*) guidance, counseling, counsel, help, suggestions, hints, tips.

advisable adj (*such action is not advisable*) desirable, wise, sensible, prudent, suitable, appropriate, recommended.

advise vb **1** (*advise them on future careers*) give advice to, give guidance on, guide, counsel, give recommendations, offer suggestions, give hints. **2** (*advise carefulness*) recommend, suggest, urge, commend, advocate.

advocate vb (*advocate spending less money*) advise, recommend, suggest, urge, press for, favor, support.

affable adj (*an affable neighbor/in an affable mood*) friendly, amiable, genial, cordial, pleasant, agreeable, good-natured, sociable, courteous.

affair n **1** (*it's my affair*) concern, business, matter, responsibility. **2** (*the sacking of the boss was an unfortunate affair*) event, happening, occurrence, incident, episode, state of affairs.

affect vb **1** (*a tragedy that affected all of us*) hav an effect on, influence, have an influence on, act on, work on, change, alter. **2** (*a disease affecting his stomach*) attack, infect. **3** (*deeply affected by the orphan's sad story*) move, touch, upset, disturb, trouble, stir.

affected *adj* (*an affected way of speaking*) pretentious, artificial, false, pretended, unnatural, assumed.

affection *n* (*feel affection for his children*) love, fondness, caring, devotion, liking, warmth.

affectionate *adj* (*an affectionate farewell*) loving, fond, devoted, tender, warm.

afflict *vb* (*people afflicted by a terrible disease*) trouble, distress, torment, plague.

affliction *n* (*the afflictions associated with old age*) trouble, disorder, disease, ailment, pain, suffering, hardship.

affluent *adj* (*affluent people living in expensive houses*) wealthy, rich, well-off, prosperous, well-to-do, (*inf*) well-heeled.

afford *vb* (*unable to afford a new car*) buy, purchase, pay for, pay the price of, meet the expense of.

affront *n* (*sexist remarks that are an affront to women*) insult, offense, slight, snub, indignity.

afraid *adj* **1** (*afraid of the wild animal/afraid to enter the haunted house*) frightened, scared, nervous, terrified, apprehensive, fearful. **2** (*I'm afraid that I cannot help you*) sorry, regretful, apologetic, unhappy.

against *prep* **1** (*sit against the wall*) near to, close to, next to, opposite to, up against, touching. **2** (*the team played against their biggest rivals*) in competition with, up against. **3** (*I'm against animal cruelty*) in disagreement with, opposed to, resisting, anti. ✧

against all odds in spite of great difficulties (*Against all odds they built the house in two months*).
against the clock/against time with very little time (*They worked against the clock to get the newspaper to press*).
against the grain to go against your own better judgment (*Not recycling that paper really goes against the grain*).

age *n* **1** (*the wisdom that comes with age*) old age, maturity, seniority, advancing years. **2** (*in the Bronze Age*) era, period, epoch, time.

agency *n* (*an advertising agency*) organization, business, firm, company, office, bureau.

agenda *n* (*on the agenda for tonight's meeting*) program, schedule, timetable, list. ✧

hidden agenda intentions or a motive that is deliberately hidden by another activity: (*Debbie seemed to act like Ashley's new best friend, but she had a hidden agenda—she was after Ashley's boyfriend*).

agent *n* **1** (*an insurance agent/a travel agent*) representative, negotiator, operator, (*inf*) rep. **2** (*an enemy agent*) spy, (*inf*) mole, (*inf*) spook.

aggravate *vb* **1** (*aggravate the situation/aggravate the illness*) make worse, worsen, intensify, increase. **2** (*inf*) (*children aggravating their mother with their noise*) annoy, irritate, anger, exasperate, provoke, get on someone's nerves. ✧

aggravate should be used in the meaning of "annoy" only in informal situations, such as in speech or personal letters between friends. Many people regard this as a wrong use of the word, and it should be avoided in formal writing, such as compositions.

aggressive *adj* **1** (*people getting aggressive when they are stressed*) quarrelsome, argumentative, belligerent, pugnacious. **2** (*aggressive salesmen/aggressive young workers seeking rapid promotion*) assertive, forceful, dynamic, thrusting, (*inf*) pushy.

aghast *adj* (*aghast at the decision to close the local steelworks*) horrified, appalled, astounded, amazed, shocked, flabbergasted.

agile *adj* (*old people still agile/agile young gymnasts*) active, nimble, lithe, supple, sprightly.

agitate *vb* **1** (*the news agitated her*) upset, work up, fluster, perturb, ruffle, disconcert, flurry, excite. **2** (*demonstrators agitating for more nursery schools*) campaign, argue.

agonizing *adj* (*an agonizing pain*) excruciating, painful, unbearable, insufferable, piercing.

agony *n* (*accident victims in agony*) suffering, pain, torture, torment, distress, anguish. ✧

agree *vb* **1** (*agree with the suggestions*) concur, comply, accord. **2** (*agree to the demands*) consent to, accept, assent to, acquiesce in. **3** (*the accounts of the accident do not agree with one another*) match, accord, correspond, coincide, tally, (*inf*) square.

agreeable *adj* **1** (*we are agreeable to your coming with us*) willing, amenable, compliant, consenting, assenting, accommodating. **2** (*an agreeable occasion*) pleasant, delightful, enjoyable, pleasurable. **3** (*an agreeable young man*) pleasant, likable, amiable, friendly, nice, affable.

agreement *n* **1** (*all in complete agreement*) accord, assent, concurrence, harmony, unity. **2** (*sign an agreement to purchase*) contract, compact, covenant, pact, pledge, deal.

aid *vb* **1** (*aid the rescue workers*) assist, help, support, lend a hand. **2** (*medicine to aid his recovery*) assist, help, speed up, hasten, facilitate. ⋄

aid and abet *vb* to provide help and encouragement in some bad or illegal activity (*She was arrested for aiding and abetting the bank robber by hiding him from the police*).

aid *n* **1** (*stop to give aid to a motorist who had broken down*) assistance, help, support, a helping hand. **2** (*give aid to poor countries*) assistance, help, contributions, subsidy, gift, donation. **3** (*a hospital aid*) helper, assistant, girl/man Friday.

ailment *n* illness, complaint, disease, disorder.

aim *vb* **1** (*aim a gun at*) point, direct, train, level. **2** (*aim to get there before dark*) plan, intend, propose, try.

aim *n* (*their aims in life/their aim is to make a lot of money*) goal, ambition, objective, object, target, purpose, intention, plan, aspiration, design, desire.

aimless *adj* **1** (*lead an aimless life*) pointless, purposeless, futile, undirected. **2** (*aimless young people wandering the streets*) unambitious, drifting, wandering.

air *n* **1** (*fly through the air*) atmosphere, sky. **2** (*an air of loneliness about her*) impression, appearance, atmosphere, mood, quality, look, feeling. **3** (*playing a sad air on the piano*) tune, melody, song, theme. ⋄

be up in the air to be undecided, yet to be decided (*We were going on vacation tomorrow, but our plans are up in the air now because our daughter has chickenpox*).

air *vb* **1** (*air clothes/air a room*) ventilate, freshen. **2** (*air your views*) make known, make public, publicize, voice, express, vent, communicate, reveal.

aisle *n* (*the aisles in planes/trains*) gangway, passageway, passage, corridor.

alarm *vb* (*alarmed by a loud bang in the night*) frighten, scare, startle, terrify, unnerve, disturb, upset.

alarm *n* **1** (*a burglar alarm/a fire alarm*) alarm signal, alarm bell, danger signal, siren, warning. **2** (*a burglar causing alarm in the neighborhood*) fear, fright, apprehension, terror, panic, disturbance, anxiety, upset, disquiet.

alert *adj* (*stay alert when on sentry duty*) awake, wide awake, aware, attentive, watchful, wary, observant, vigilant.

alien *adj* **1** (*alien lands*) foreign, overseas. **2** (*find themselves in an alien environment*) strange, unfamiliar, unknown.

alien *n* **1** (*aliens deported from the country at the start of the war*) foreigner, non-native, immigrant. **2** (*aliens from another planet*) extraterrestrial, (*inf*) little green man.

alight *vb* **1** (*alight from the bus*) get off, dismount, descend. **2** (*butterflies alighting on leaves*) land, come down, come to rest, settle, touch down.

alike *adj* (*sisters who are very much alike*) like, similar, the same, identical, indistinguishable.

alive *adj* **1** (*soldiers wounded, but still alive*) living, live, breathing, (*inf*) in the land of the living. **2** (*streets alive with shoppers*) crowded, packed, teeming, swarming, overflowing, thronged, (*inf*) crawling.

allegation *n* (*deny their allegations that he was a thief*) claim, charge, accusation, declaration, assertion, statement.

allergic *adj* (*allergic to cows' milk*) hypersensitive, sensitive.

alley *n* (*attacked in a dark alley leading off the high street*) alleyway, lane, passage, passageway, backstreet. ⋄

blind alley an action or situation that cannot be of advantage to you (*His present job is just a blind alley—he has no hope of promotion*) <Literally, a "blind alley" is a lane that is blocked off at one end so that no exit is possible>.

alliance *n* (*foreign countries forming an alliance against the enemy*) union, association, league, coalition, federation, partnership, affiliation.

allot *vb* (*allot work to each of the students/allot grants of money to those in need*) allocate, distribute, give out, share out, dispense, apportion.

allow *vb* **1** (*allow them to use her swimming pool*) let, permit, give permission to, authorize, (*inf* give the go-ahead to. **2** (*allow half a roll of wastepaper for wastage*) plan for, make provision for, provide for, take into account, take into consideration.

allowance *n* (*a dress allowance*) money, payment, contribution, grant, subsidy. ⋄

make allowances for someone *or* **something** to expect a less high standard from someone because of special circumstances (*You must make allowances for his wife—she is not usually so short-tempered, but she is still upset about her mother's death*).

allude *vb* (*allude to the history of the town in the speech*) refer to, mention, mention in passing, touch upon, make an allusion to.

alluring *adj* (*a woman of alluring beauty*) attractive, fascinating, charming, enchanting, captivating, bewitching, beguiling, tempting.

ally *n* (*their allies in the war*) confederate, associate, collaborator, partner, friend.

almost *adv* (*almost four o'clock/almost two miles long*) nearly, close to, just about, around, not quite, practically, approximately.

alone *adj* **1** (*go to the party alone*) by yourself, unaccompanied, unescorted, companionless. **2** (*left all alone by her father's death*) solitary, lonely, isolated, desolate, deserted, forlorn. • *adv* (*he alone can answer the questions*) only, solely, just.

aloof *adj* (*people who are aloof do not have many friends*) distant, remote, unresponsive, unapproachable, standoffish, unsociable, unfriendly, cold.

aloud *adv* (*cry aloud*) out loud, audibly, clearly, distinctly.

also *adv* **1** (*buy a bed and a dressing table also*) too, as well, besides, in addition, into the bargain. **2** (*he's poor; also he's ill*) furthermore, besides, moreover, in addition. ⋄

also-ran *n* an unsuccessful person (*She was not one of the leading competitors—she was just an also-ran./He will never gain promotion—he is an also-ran*) <A horse-racing term for a horse that is not one of the first three horses in a race>.

alter *vb* **1** (*alter the dress*) change, adjust, modify, convert, reshape, remodel, vary, transform. **2** (*thehe village has scarcely altered*) change, become different, vary.

alteration *n* **1** (*make alterations to the dress/make alterations to the letter*) change, adjustment, modification, amendment, revision, variation. **2** (*the alteration of his appearance after his illness*) change, difference, variation, transformation, metamorphosis.

alternative *n* (*offer an alternative on the menu for vegetarians*) choice, option, possibility, preference.

altitude *n* (*the altitude of the ski-resort*) height, elevation.

altogether *adv* **1** (*six of us altogether*) in all, all told, in total. **2** (*not altogether sure*) completely, quite, entirely, totally, thoroughly, absolutely, fully, perfectly. ⋄

in the altogether is a humorous informal way of saying naked or nude (*You don't expect me to answer the door in the altogether, do you?*).

always *adv* **1** (*we always shop there*) regularly, invariably, consistently, unfailingly, repeatedly, without exception. **2** (*she's always cheerful*) continually, continuously, constantly, incessantly, perpetually. **3** (*promise to love her always*) forever, forever and ever, evermore, eternally, endlessly, everlastingly.

amaze *vb* (*his sheer stupidity amazed us*) astonish, astound, surprise, dumbfound, flabbergast, daze, shock, stun, (*inf*) stagger, nonplus.

amazing *adj* (*to have an amazing memory*) exceptional, extraordinary, remarkable, phenomenal.

ambiguous *adj* (*her message was ambiguous*) unclear, uncertain, doubtful, dubious, vague, obscure, puzzling, perplexing, enigmatic.

ambition *n* **1** (*young members of the firm full of ambition*) aspiration, drive, striving, force, enterprise, enthusiasm. **2** (*her ambition is to go on the stage*) aim, goal, objective, purpose, intent, dream, hope.

ambitious *adj* (*ambitious people seeking promotion*) aspiring, forceful, purposeful, enterprising, go-ahead, assertive.

ambush *n* **1** (*terrorists waiting in ambush for the soldiers*) hiding, concealment, cover. **2** (*lay an ambush for the enemy soldiers*) trap, snare, pitfall.

amiable *adj* (*in the company of amiable people*) friendly, pleasant, agreeable, charming, good-natured, sociable, genial.

amnesty *n* (*declare an amnesty for all political prisoners*) general pardon, pardon, reprieve, forgiveness, absolution.

among *prep* **1** (*a house among the trees/live among enemies*) in the midst of, amid, amidst, surrounded by, in the thick of. **2** (*divide it among you*) between, to each of.

amount *n* (*a small amount of wood/a large amount of attention*) quantity, mass, measure, volume, extent.

amount *vb* (*the bill amounts to hundreds of dollars*) add up to, total, come to, run to.

ample *adj* **1** (*ample food for everyone*) enough, sufficient, plenty, adequate, more than enough. **2** (*an ample supply of money*) plentiful, abundant, copious, liberal, generous, lavish. **3** (*her ample bosom*) large, big, substantial.

amplify *vb* **1** (*amplify the sound level*) make louder, increase, boost, augment. **2** (*amplify your suggestion*) expand, enlarge on, elaborate on, develop.

amputate *vb* (*amputate the injured leg*) cut off, remove, sever, excise.

amuse *vb* **1** (*try to amuse the children on a cold, rainy day*) entertain, occupy, interest, divert. **2** (*the comedian's jokes amused everyone*) make laugh, entertain, cheer up, delight.

amusement *n* **1** (*various forms of amusement in the resort*) entertainment, diversion, fun, interest, pastime, hobby, recreation. **2** (*smile with amusement at the comedian's jokes*) laughter, mirth, hilarity, pleasure, enjoyment.

amusing *adj* (*an amusing story*) funny, humorous, comical, entertaining, hilarious.

analyze *vb* (*analyze the election results*) examine, study, investigate, enquire into, dissect.

anarchy *n* **1** (*the fall of the government was followed by a period of anarchy*) absence of government, lawlessness, revolution. **2** (*anarchy on the streets when the police went on strike*) lawlessness, disorder, chaos, confusion, mayhem.

ancestor *n* (*trace his ancestors back to the time of Abraham Lincoln*) forebear, forefather, progenitor, forerunner, predecessor.

ancestry *n* (*she is of royal ancestry*) descent, extraction, origin, derivation, parentage, blood, family tree.

ancient *adj* **1** (*ancient customs*) very old, age-old, time-worn. **2** (*in ancient times*) earliest, early, primeval, prehistoric. **3** (*his ideas on fashion are ancient*) antiquated, old-fashioned, out-of-date, outdated, outmoded, obsolete.

and *conj* (*my family and I*) along with, with, together with, as well as, in addition to, plus.

angel *n* **1** (*angels in heaven*) seraph, cherub, archangel, guardian angel. **2** (*my kind neighbor is an absolute angel*) saint, gem, dear, darling.
↪

on the side of the angels supporting or agreeing with what is regarded by most people as being the good or the right side (*The teacher has to pretend to be on the side of the angels and support his colleagues, although he has a lot of sympathy for the students' complaints*).

anger *n* (*feelings of anger at cruelty to animals*) annoyance, rage, fury, indignation, wrath, irritation, ire.

anger *vb* (*they were angered by his rudeness*) annoy, infuriate, enrage, irritate, incense, madden, provoke, rile.

angry *adj* (*angry parents scolding their children*) annoyed, cross, furious, infuriated, indignant, irate, livid, enraged, wrathful, incensed, (*inf*) mad.

anguish *n* (*the children were in anguish when their pet died*) agony, suffering, pain, torment, torture, distress, misery.

animated *adj* (*an animated discussion*) lively, spirited, excited, enthusiastic, passionate, fiery, dynamic, energetic.

annex *n* (*add an annex to the house*) extension, wing.

annihilate *vb* (*annihilate the enemy army*) destroy, wipe out, exterminate, eliminate, obliterate.

announce *vb* (*announce that the president was dead*) make known, make public, proclaim, publish, broadcast, report, state, declare, reveal, disclose.

announcement *n* (*an announcement of the president's death*) report, statement, notice, proclamation, declaration, bulletin.

announcer *n* (*a TV announcer*) commentator, presenter, newscaster, broadcaster, reporter.

annoy *vb* **1** (*her attitude annoyed her parents*) anger, infuriate, enrage, irritate, incense, madden, provoke, rile. **2** (*don't annoy your mother while she is working/children annoying the dog*) bother, disturb, pester, worry, torment, tease.

annul *vb* (*annul the marriage/annul the agreement*) declare null and void, nullify, invalidate, cancel.

anomaly n (*anomalies in the tax system*) abnormality, irregularity, deviation, aberration, oddity, peculiarity, inconsistency.

anonymous adj (*the money for the charity was from an anonymous donor*) unnamed, nameless, unknown, unidentified, incognito.

another adj 1 (*another cup of tea*) additional, second, further. 2 (*go another time/get another car*) different, some other.

answer vb 1 (*answer the question*) reply to, give a response to, respond to, retort. 2 (*answer our requirements*) meet, satisfy, fulfill, fill, serve. 3 (*a man answering the description issued by the police*) fit, match, correspond to, be like.

answer n 1 (*receive no answer to his question/ waiting for an answer to his letter*) reply, response, acknowledge, retort. 2 (*the answer to the puzzle*) solution, explanation. ✧

know all the answers to have all the information that is required to deal successfully with a situation, especially when you are conceited about this (*She never listens to any advice from other people—she always acts as if she knows all the answers*).

antagonism n (*a great deal of antagonism between the two sides*) hostility, opposition, animosity, antipathy, conflict, friction.

anthology n (*an anthology of poetry*) collection, selection, miscellany, compendium.

anticipate vb 1 (*the organizers are anticipating a large audience for the concert*) expect, foresee, predict, forecast, look for, await. 2 (*anticipate his opponent's move*) forestall, intercept, prevent, (*inf*) beat someone to it.

anticipation n 1 (*buy champagne in anticipation of victory*) expectation, prediction. 2 (*girls full of anticipation before the dance*) expectancy, hopefulness, hope.

anticlimax n (*after all the fun of planning the actual vacation was rather an anticlimax*) disappointment, letdown, disillusionment.

antiquated adj (*children thinking that their parents have antiquated ideas/an antiquated TV set*) out-of-date, old-fashioned, outmoded, outworn, obsolete, archaic.

antique adj (*antique furniture*) old, antiquarian, vintage, early.

antisocial adj 1 (*antisocial people dislike parties*) unsociable, reserved, aloof, withdrawn, retiring, uncommunicative, unfriendly. 2 (*playing loud music late at night is an example of unsocial behavior*) disruptive, disorderly, lawless, unruly, obstreperous.

antithesis n (*the antithesis of "good" is "bad"*) opposite, reverse, converse, inverse, other extreme.

anxiety n (*full of anxiety about the lateness of her husband*) worry, concern, uneasiness, disquiet, nervousness, apprehension, tenseness.

anxious adj 1 (*anxious parents out looking for their children*) worried, concerned, uneasy, nervous, apprehensive, fearful, tense. 2 (*anxious to learn*) eager, keen, longing, avid.

apart adv 1 (*blow the place apart*) to pieces, in pieces, to bits, asunder. 2 (*a couple living apart*) separated, separately, divorced. 3 (*a man standing apart at the party*) to one side, aside, separately, by yourself. ✧

be poles or **worlds apart** to be completely different (*The two girls are sisters, but their attitudes to work and money are poles apart*).

apathy n (*because of apathy many people did not vote*) lack of interest, indifference, unresponsiveness, unconcern, lethargy.

apex n 1 (*the apex of the triangle*) top, tip, pinnacle, vertex, peak. 2 (*the apex of his career*) peak, summit, top, zenith, acme.

apologetic adj (*feel apologetic for the trouble they caused*) sorry, regretful, contrite, remorseful, repentant, penitent, rueful.

apologize vb (*apologize for his error*) say you are sorry, express regret, ask forgiveness, (*inf*) eat humble pie.

apology n (*accept his apology for his wrongdoing*) regret, regrets. ✧

an apology for (*inf*) a very poor example of (*The café served us up an apology for a meal/The tradesman we employed was an apology for a carpenter*).

appalling adj 1 (*an appalling accident*) shocking, frightful, horrifying, terrible, dreadful, awful, ghastly. 2 (*a piece of work that is quite appalling/appalling behavior*) very bad, unacceptable, unsatisfactory, intolerable.

apparent adj 1 (*it was apparent that she was sick/ problems that were apparent from the start*) obvious, clear, plain, evident, discernible, perceptible, manifest. 2 (*he eventually saw* *through her apparent sincerity*) seeming, ostensible, outward, superficial.

apparition *n* (*they thought they saw an apparition in the graveyard*) ghost, specter, phantom, spirit, wraith, (*inf*) spook.

appeal *n* 1 (*make an appeal for help*) request, call, plea, entreaty. 2 (*a possibility that holds little appeal for her*) attraction, attractiveness, charm, allure, interest. 3 (*he has been convicted of the crime, but the case is going to appeal*) review, reconsideration, reexamination.

appear *vb* 1 (*a figure appeared out of the mist*) come into view, come into sight, emerge, materialize, surface. 2 (*the visitors were very late, but they finally appeared*) come, arrive, make an appearance, turn up, (*inf*) show up. 3 (*she appeared rather thoughtful*) seem, look, have the appearance of, have the air of, give the impression of. 4 (*he once appeared in a production of "Hamlet"*) act, perform, play, take part.

appearance *n* 1 (*the sudden appearance of the police*) arrival, advent, materialization, surfacing. 2 (*having an appearance of sadness*) look, air, expression, impression, manner. 3 (*his statement had the appearance of truth, but it was a lie*) semblance, outward appearance, guise, show, pretense. ▵

keep up appearances to behave in public in such a way as to hide what is going on in private (*He has lost his job, but he tries to keep up appearances by leaving the house at his usual time each morning*).

appease *vb* (*try to appease his angry wife by giving her flowers*) calm down, placate, make peace with, pacify, soothe, mollify.

appetizer *n* (*serve smoked salmon as an appetizer*) starter, hors d'oeuvre, antipasto.

appetizing *adj* 1 (*an appetizing dish*) tasty, mouth-watering, flavorsome, delicious. 2 (*appetizing smells coming from the kitchen*) tempting, inviting, enticing, alluring.

applaud *vb* 1 (*the audience applauded*) clap, give a standing ovation to, (*inf*) give a big hand to. 2 (*everyone applauded his courage*) praise, admire, compliment on, commend, acclaim, extol, laud.

appliance *n* (*electrical appliances in the kitchen*) gadget, tool, implement, apparatus, device, machine.

applicant *n* (*applicants for the job*) candidate, entrant, competitor, interviewee.

apply *vb* 1 (*apply for a job*) put in an application for, ask, put in for, try for. 2 (*apply ointment to the sore*) put on, rub in, cover with, spread, smear. 3 (*have to apply force to open the box*) use, employ, administer, utilize, exercise, bring to bear. 4 (*these regulations do not apply*) be applicable, be relevant, be pertinent, be apposite, be appropriate.

appoint *vb* (*appoint a new manager*) name, select, choose, pick, elect, designate, nominate.

appointment *n* 1 (*have a business appointment this afternoon/a dinner appointment*) meeting, engagement, date, rendezvous, assignation. 2 (*take up his new appointment as manager*) job, post, position, situation, place.

appreciate *vb* 1 (*appreciate offers of help*) be grateful for, be thankful for, be appreciative of, give thanks for. 2 (*appreciate the urgency of the situation*) recognize, acknowledge, realize, know, be aware of, be conscious of, understand. 3 (*appreciate good wine*) value, prize, treasure, respect, hold in high regard, think highly of, enjoy, take pleasure in. 4 (*a house that has appreciated in value over the years*) increase, gain, grow, rise.

apprehensive *adj* (*apprehensive at the thought of going into hospital*) frightened, fearful, scared, nervous, anxious, worried, uneasy, concerned.

apprentice *n* (*find work as an apprentice in the garage*) trainee, learner, beginner, probationer, novice.

approach *vb* 1 (*visitors approaching the house*) come/go near, draw near, move toward, advance toward. 2 (*beggars approaching strangers to ask for money*) go up to, speak to, talk to, engage in conversation, address, hail. 3 (*approach the task with energy*) set about, tackle, begin, start, commence, embark on, make a start on. 4 (*temperatures approaching freezing point*) come close to, come near to, approximate.

approach *n* 1 (*the approach to the house*) driveway, drive, access, entrance, entry, way in. 2 (*a new approach to education*) method, system, technique, procedure, style, mode, way. 3 (*make approaches to the government for money*) application, appeal, advances, overtures.

appropriate *adj* (*an appropriate time/an appropriate reply*) suitable, fitting, proper, right, apt, apposite, opportune.

approval n 1 (*the audience showed its approval by applauding*) favor, liking, admiration, appreciation, approbation, regard. 2 (*the committee gave its approval to their plans*) acceptance, agreement, consent, assent, sanction, authorization, (*inf*) the go-ahead, the green light, (*inf*) the OK. ▽

on approval an expression used of goods that a customer takes home to try on or try out and that can be returned to the store if the goods are not suitable or if the customer is not satisfied (*The young lady took several ball gowns home on approval*).

seal of approval evidence of the quality of something (*The critic gave the restaurant the seal of approval*).

approve vb 1 (*unable to approve of their actions*) think well of, think highly of, think favorably of, look upon with favor, like, admire, hold in high regard. 2 (*the committee approved her plans*) accept, pass, agree to, consent to, assent to, sanction, authorize, (*inf*) give the go-ahead to, give the green light to.

approximately adv (*a distance of approximately five miles*) about, just about, around, roughly, nearly, close to, almost, more or less, in the neighborhood of, in the region of, circa.

apron n pinafore. ▽

tied to someone's apron strings completely dependent on a woman, especially your mother or wife (*He is so tied to his wife's apron strings that he never goes out with his friends*).

apt adj 1 (*apt to lose his temper*) inclined, given, likely, liable, ready, disposed, prone. 2 (*an apt comment*) appropriate, suitable, fitting, applicable, relevant, apposite. 3 (*an apt student*) clever, bright, intelligent, quick, able.

aptitude n (*have an aptitude for word games*) talent, gift, flair, skill, ability, capability, bent, knack.

arbitrary adj 1 (*a purely arbitrary decision/The choice of players seemed arbitrary*) personal, subjective, discretionary, unreasoned, unsupported, random, chance, whimsical, capricious, erratic. 2 (*an arbitrary ruler*) despotic, tyrannical, absolute, dictatorial, domineering.

arbitrate vb (*asked to arbitrate in the dispute between union and management*) adjudicate, judge, umpire, referee.

arc n (*the arc of a rainbow*) curve, bow, arch, bend, crescent, semicircle.

arch vb (*a cat arching its back*) curve, bend, bow.

archaic adj (*archaic language/archaic attitudes*) old, out-of-date, old-fashioned, outmoded, antiquated, obsolete, (*inf*) old hat.

architect n (*the architect of the new church*) designer, planner, building consultant.

archives npl (*study the archives of the firm*) records, annals, chronicles, register, documents.

arctic adj (*arctic temperatures*) freezing, frozen, icy, glacial, frosty, chilly, cold.

ardent adj (*an ardent supporter of the local football team*) passionate, avid, fervent, zealous, eager, enthusiastic, keen.

arduous adj (*an arduous task*) difficult, hard, taxing, laborious, strenuous, tough, onerous, burdensome, tiring, exhausting, grueling, Herculean.

area n 1 (*live in a pleasant area of the city*) district, part, region, quarter, neighborhood, locality, sector, zone, territory. 2 (*a specialist in the area of computing*) field, sphere, department, discipline, realm, sector. 3 (*measure the area of the room*) dimensions, extent, size, expanse. 4 (*the changing area of the swimming pool*) section, part, portion, space.

arena n (*the sport arena*) ground, field, stadium, ring. ▽

arena is Latin in origin and meant "sand." The central area of Roman amphitheaters, where the gladiators fought, was covered in sand to soak up the blood from the wounded or dead contestants. In time, the word was used for the central area itself and then for any enclosed area used for contests.

argue vb 1 (*her brother and sister are always arguing*) quarrel, disagree, bicker, squabble, wrangle, fight, dispute, (*inf*) fall out. 2 (*he argued that his method was the best*) assert, declare, maintain, hold, claim, contend.

argument n 1 (*children having an argument over toys*) quarrel, disagreement, squabble, wrangle, fight, dispute, (*inf*) spat. 2 (*the argument against the new scheme*) reasoning, line of reasoning, reasons, grounds, case, defense, evidence, proof.

argumentative adj (*argumentative people/an argumentative mood*) quarrelsome, belligerent, contentious.

arid *adj* **1** (*arid areas of the world*) dry, dried up, desert, waterless, parched, barren. **2** (*an arid discussion*) uninspiring, uninteresting, dull, dreary, dry, colorless, lifeless, boring, monotonous, tedious.

arise *vb* **1** (*deal with any problems that arise*) appear, make an appearance, come to light, crop up, turn up, emerge, occur. **2** (*matters arising from our discussion*) result, proceed, follow, stem, originate, emanate, ensue. ⋄

> **arise** in its original meaning of "get up" or "stand up," as in "They arose at dawn," "He arose slowly from his chair," is not used in modern English and is now considered an old or literary use.

aristocracy *n* (*a member of the British aristocracy*) nobility, peerage, gentry, upper class, high society, (*inf*) upper crust.

arm *n* **1** (*have an arm amputated*) upper limb. **2** (*an arm of the civil service*) branch, offshoot, section, department, division, sector. ⋄

> **the long arm of the law** the power or authority of the police (*The crook thought that he had got away with the bank robbery, but the long arm of the law caught up with him as he tried to leave the country*).

arm *vb* (*arm yourself with a gun/arm yourself with a stick to protect yourself against attack*) provide, supply, equip, furnish.

armaments *npl* (*a military armaments store*) arms, weapons, firearms, munitions.

armistice *n* (*the armistice that ended the war*) truce, ceasefire, peace.

armor, armour (*Br, Cdn*) *n* (*knights wearing armor*) armor plate, chain mail, coat of mail, mail, protective covering. ⋄

> **a chink in someone's armor** a weak or vulnerable spot in someone who is otherwise very strong and difficult to get through to attack (*The old man is very stern, but his little granddaughter has found a chink in his armor/The opposition is always trying to find a chink in the government's armor*).
> **knight in shining armor** a hero (*Dave was my knight in shining armor when my car broke down*).

arms *npl* **1** (*soldiers laying down their arms*)

weapons, firearms, guns, armaments. **2** (*the family arms*) coat of arms, emblem, crest, insignia, heraldic device.

army *n* **1** (*the invading army*) military force, troops, soldiers. **2** (*armies of tourists on the island in the summer*) horde, crowd, host, multitude, swarm, throng, mob.

aroma *n* (*the aroma of freshly baked bread*) smell, scent, fragrance, perfume, odor, bouquet.

aromatic *adj* (*aromatic spices*) fragrant, sweet-smelling, scented, perfumed, piquant, spicy, pungent.

around *adv* **1** (*turn around*) in the opposite direction, in reverse. **2** (*around nine o'clock/around five miles away*) approximately, roughly, close to, near to, nearly. **3** (*flowers planted around the tree*) about, on all sides of, on every side of, surrounding, circling, encircling. **4** (*newspapers scattered around the room*) about, here and there in, all over, everywhere in, in all parts of. ⋄

> **to have been around 1** (*inf*) to have had a lot of experience of life (*She is unlikely to be deceived by him—she's been around a bit*). **2** to have been alive (*The old man said that he had been around so long that he could remember President Roosevelt*).

arouse *vb* **1** (*the noise aroused the neighbors*) rouse, awaken, waken, wake, wake up. **2** (*behavior arousing suspicion/actions arousing panic*) cause, induce, stir up, provoke, call forth, whip up.

arrange *vb* **1** (*arrange the books*) put in order, set out, order, sort, organize, group, classify, categorize. **2** (*arrange a meeting*) fix, fix up, organize, settle on, plan, schedule.

arrangement *n* (*make an arrangement to meet tomorrow*) preparations, plans, provisions, agreement, deal, contract.

arrest *vb* **1** (*police arrested the thieves*) take into custody, take prisoner, detain, seize, capture, catch, (*inf*) run in. **2** (*try to arrest the spread of the disease*) stop, halt, bring to a halt, end, check, nip in the bud.

arresting *adj* (*her arresting appearance*) striking, noticeable, conspicuous, impressive, remarkable, extraordinary, unusual.

arrival *n* **1** (*the arrival of winter*) coming, advent, appearance, occurrence. **2** (*several new arrivals in the village*) newcomer, immigrant, alien.

arrive *vb* **1** (*arrive at their destination*) reach, come to, attain. **2** (*when mother arrives*) come, get here, appear, put in an appearance, turn up, come on the scene, (*inf*) show up.

arrogant *adj* (*a very arrogant young woman/have a very arrogant manner*) haughty, proud, conceited, vain, self-important, egotistic, overbearing, condescending, disdainful, snobbish, supercilious, presumptuous, boastful, (*inf*) cocky, (*inf*) stuck-up.

art *n* **1** (*studying art at college*) painting, drawing, visual arts. **2** (*the art of conversation*) skill, craft, aptitude, knack, technique, facility, talent, flair, gift.

artful *adj* (*get his own way by artful means*) cunning, crafty, wily, sly, deceitful, scheming, shrewd, ingenious, clever.

article *n* **1** (*a range of articles going on sale*) thing, object, item, commodity. **2** (*an article in the newspaper on violence*) item, piece, story, feature, report, account, write-up.

artificial *adj* (*artificial flowers/an artificial leg*) manmade, synthetic, imitation, simulated, ersatz, mock, sham, fake, bogus, counterfeit, (*inf*) phony.

ashamed *adj* (*she was obviously ashamed of what she had done*) sorry, shame-faced, abashed, repentant, remorseful, sheepish.

ask *vb* **1** (*we asked where they were going*) inquire. **2** (*they asked a favor from her/You should ask for more money*) request, demand, apply for, beg for, plead for. **3** (*the police asked him about his movements on the night of the murder*) question, interrogate, cross-examine, give the third degree to, pump, (*inf*) grill.

assault *vb* (*they assaulted the old man to get his pocketbook*) attack, set upon, strike, hit, (*inf*) mug.

assemble *vb* **1** (*the children assembled in the school hall to hear the news*) gather, come together, congregate, convene. **2** (*he is assembling the evidence for the prosecution*) get together, gather together, collect, accumulate, amass. **3** (*you have to assemble the furniture yourself*) put together, fit together, construct, build, erect.

assist *vb* (*he assisted the doctor to care for the accident victims*) help, aid, give assistance to, lend a hand to, support.

associate *vb* **1** (*she associates home with security*) connect, link, relate. **2** (*the clubs are associated in some way*) connect, link, join, attach, affiliate. **3** (*he associates with crooks*) mix, keep company with, socialize, fraternize.

astonish *vb* (*their boldness astonished us*) amaze, astound, dumbfound, stun, surprise.

attach *vb* **1** (*they should attach baggage labels to their suitcases*) fasten, tie, secure, stick, affix. **2** (*we attach no importance to that*) place, lay, put, apply, ascribe.

attend *vb* **1** (*he is unable to attend the meeting*) be at, be present at, put in an appearance at, be there/here. **2** (*she promised to attend to the matter immediately*) deal with, see to, cope with, handle. **3** (*you should attend to what your teacher says*) pay attention to, pay heed to, heed, listen to, take note of.

attitude *n* **1** (*I don't like her attitude toward people from other countries*) view, point of view, opinion, outlook, thoughts, ideas. **2** (*she stood in an attitude of thought*) stance, pose, position.

attractive *adj* **1** (*she is a very attractive girl*) good-looking, pretty, beautiful, handsome. **2** (*that is an attractive idea*) appealing, pleasing, tempting.

authentic *adj* (*he is the authentic heir to the estate*) real, genuine, rightful, lawful, legal, valid.

authority *n* **1** (*he does not have the authority to stop us going*) power, right, control, force, influence. **2** (*we have the authority of the king to be present*) permission, sanction, authorization, (*inf*) say-so. **3** (*he is an authority on local history*) expert, specialist, pundit.

available *adj* **1** (*have to make do with the material that is available*) obtainable, handy, to hand, accessible, ready. **2** (*there are still tickets available*) free.

average *adj* **1** (*she was of average height for her age*) normal, typical, ordinary, common. **2** (*her work was just average*) run-of-the mill, mediocre, unexceptional.

awful *adj* **1** (*she has an awful cold*) dreadful, nasty, unpleasant, troublesome, bad. **2** (*in the awful presence of God*) awesome, awe-inspiring.

awkward *adj* **1** (*they arrived at an awkward time*) inconvenient, difficult, problematic. **2** (*she is a very awkward child and keeps bumping into things*) clumsy, ungainly, inelegant. **3** (*it is an awkward piece of furniture*) clumsy, unwieldy.

B

baby *n* (*babies in their strollers*) infant, child, toddler. ⋄

throw out the baby with the bath water to accidentally to get rid of something valuable or wanted in the process of getting rid of something worthless or unwanted (*They threw out the baby with the bathwater when they modernised that lovely old house*).

babyish *adj* (*older children acting in a babyish way*) childish, immature, infantile, juvenile.

back *n* **1** (*the back of the building*) rear, far end. **2** (*the back of the envelope*) reverse, other side. **3** (*break his back in the accident*) spine, backbone.

back *adv* (*without looking back*) backward, behind, to the rear.

back *vb* **1** (*back the plan*) support, give support to, help, assist, encourage, favor. **2** (*look for someone to back the theatrical production*) finance, subsidize, sponsor. **3** (*back the horse*) bet on, place a bet on, gamble on. **4** (*back the car out of the garage*) reverse, drive backward.

backer *n* (*the backers of the theatrical production*) sponsor, promoter, financier, benefactor.

background *n* **1** (*people from a wealthy background*) upbringing, family circumstances, environment, experience. **2** (*photographed against a white background*) setting, backdrop, scene. **3** (*in the background of the photograph*) rear, distance.

backlog *n* (*a backlog of work*) accumulation, stockpile, arrears, (*inf*) mountain.

backward *adj* **1** (*a backward look*) to the rear, rearward. **2** (*a backward area of the world*) underdeveloped, slow, unprogressive. ⋄

know something backward and forward to know a great deal about something (*She knows Shakespeare's plays backward and forward*).

bacteria *npl* (*bacteria from rotting food*) germs, micro-organisms, (*inf*) bugs.

bad *adj* **1** (*bad people*) wicked, evil, immoral, wrong, sinful, dishonest, dishonorable, criminal, (*inf*) crooked, naughty, mischievous. **2** (*a bad accident*) serious, severe, terrible, shocking, appalling. **3** (*a bad performance*) poor, unsatisfactory, inadequate, inferior, substandard, defective, shoddy, (*inf*) lousy. **4** (*smoking is a bad*

habit) harmful, damaging, dangerous, unhealthy. **5** (*bad food/food gone bad*) rotten, decayed, moldy, tainted, putrid, (*inf*) off. **6** (*bad weather*) unpleasant, nasty, dreadful, terrible, disagreeable. **7** (*feel bad about hurting her*) sorry, regretful, apologetic, guilty, sad. **8** (*an invalid feeling bad today*) sick, ill, unwell, under the weather, (*inf*) below par. ⋄

a bad egg a wicked or dishonest person (*He's a bad egg—he's been in trouble with the police.*

hit a bad patch to experience difficulties or a difficult or unsuccessful period (*The team was playing well, but the players have now hit a bad patch*).

badge *n* (*wear the club badge on their blazers*) crest, emblem, symbol.

badly *adv* **1** (*do the work badly*) poorly, unsatisfactorily, inadequately, shoddily. **2** (*things worked out badly*) unsuccessfully, unfortunately, unfavorably, unluckily, unhappily. **3** (*want something badly*) greatly, very much, enormously, to a great degree. **4** (*behave badly*) wrongly, naughtily, improperly, wickedly, immorally, sinfully, criminally.

baffle *vb* (*police baffled by the crime/students baffled by the exam question*) puzzle, perplex, mystify, nonplus, stump, flummox, bamboozle, bewilder.

baggage *n* (*collect your baggage at the airport*) luggage, bags, suitcases, things, belongings, gear, paraphernalia. ⋄

bag and baggage absolutely all your belongings (*We had to move out of the apartment bag and baggage when the new tenants arrived*).

baggy *adj* (*wear baggy clothing*) loose, slack, roomy, floppy, ballooning.

bake *vb* **1** (*bake cakes*) cook. **2** (*earth baked by the sun*) scorch, burn, parch, dry, harden.

balance *n* **1** (*weigh the substance on a balance*) scales, weighing machine. **2** (*trip and lose your balance*) steadiness, stability, equilibrium. **3** (*pay the balance of the account*) remainder, rest, difference, surplus, excess.

bald *adj* **1** (*men going bald*) bald-headed, hairless, (*inf*) thin on top. **2** (*a bald statement*) direct, forthright, blunt, plain, unadorned.

ball *n* **1** (*a glass ball*) sphere, globe, orb. **2** (*be invited to a ball*) dance, formal dance. ✧

> **a whole new ball game** a completely different situation (*I enjoy swimming, but deep-sea diving is a whole new ball game*).
>
> **drop the ball** to make a mistake or fail to do something (*The export manager said that the French firm would definitely place an order with us, but he dropped the ball during the negotiations and the deal is off*).
>
> **have the ball at your feet** to be in a position to be successful (*When he left college he thought that he had the ball at his feet but he could not find the job he wanted*) <From soccer>.

ballot *n* (*choose the new leader by ballot*) vote, poll, election.

ban *vb* (*ban smoking in the hall*) prohibit, forbid, debar, bar, veto, make illegal.

ban *n* (*impose a ban on smoking*) prohibition, veto.

band *n* **1** (*the jazz band playing at the wedding celebrations*) group, ensemble, orchestra. **2** (*a band of thieves*) group, troop, company, gang, pack, bunch, mob, team. **3** (*a metal band/a rubber band*) binding, cord, tie, link, ring, hoop. **4** (*a band of blue on the white sweater*) strip, stripe, streak, line, bar. **5** (*a band around her hair*) ribbon, braid.

bang *n* **1** (*a loud bang when the bomb went off*) boom, crash, blast, explosion, report. **2** (*get a bang on the head*) blow, knock, bump, hit, smack.

bang *vb* **1** (*the door banged shut*) slam, crash. **2** (*bang the table with his fist*) strike, hit, beat, thump, rap, whack, (*inf*) bash. ✧

> **bang your head against a brick wall** to do something, usually to keep doing something, in vain (*You'll be banging your head against a brick wall if you try to persuade him to change his mind*).

bang *adv* (*bang in the middle of his speech*) right, exactly, precisely, absolutely, directly, (*inf*) smack.

banish *vb* **1** (*banish them from their native land*) exile, deport, cast out, send away, expel. **2** (*banish the child's fears*) drive away, dispel, dismiss, get rid of, cast out.

bank *n* **1** (*borrow money from the bank*) financial institution, high-street bank. **2** (*a child's bank*) piggy bank, savings bank, cash box. **3** (*a bank of information*) store, stock, reserve. **4** (*children sliding down grassy banks*) slope, rise, incline, hillock. **5** (*the river bank*) edge, side, shore. ✧

> **bank on** to rely on, count on, depend on, pin your hopes on (*I'm banking on your help in this project*).

bankrupt *adj* (*bankrupt after the failure of his business*) ruined, insolvent, penniless, (*inf*) in the red, (*inf*) on the rocks, (*inf*) broke.

banner *n* (*banners flying for the Fourth of July*) flag, standard, pennant, streamer.

banquet *n* feast, dinner, dinner party, (*inf*) spread.

baptize *vb* (*baptize a baby*) christen, name.

bar *n* **1** (*an iron bar*) rod, pole, rail, girder. **2** (*a bar of soap*) block, cake, lump, wedge. **3** (*getting drunk in bars*) pub, public house, tavern, saloon.

bar *vb* **1** (*bar the door*) bolt, lock, padlock, fasten, secure. **2** (*bar them from joining the club*) debar, prohibit, forbid, preclude, ban. **3** (*fallen trees barring their way*) block, hinder, impede, obstruct.

bare *adj* **1** (*sunbathing bare*) nude, naked, stark-naked, undressed, unclothed, without clothing, unclad. **2** (*a bare room*) empty, vacant, unfurnished, unadorned. **3** (*a bare landscape*) barren, bleak, desolate.

barely *adv* (*barely enough food*) hardly, scarcely, only just, just.

bargain *n* **1** (*make a bargain not to quarrel*) agreement, pact, contract, deal. **2** (*get a bargain at the sales*) good buy, (*inf*) snip. ✧

> **drive a hard bargain** to haggle, argue, negotiate (*She drove a hard bargain for those carpets in the market*).

barge *vb* **1** (*people barging into each other in the crowded stores*) bump, collide, cannon, crash. **2** (*barge into a private meeting*) interrupt, intrude on, burst in on, (*inf*) butt in on.

barn *n* outbuilding, outhouse, shed, byre.

barrel *n* (*a barrel of beer*) cask, keg, vat. ✧

> **have someone over a barrel** to get someone into such a position that you can get him or her to do anything that you want (*They owe him a lot of money, and so he has them over a barrel*).

barren *adj* **1** (*barren fields*) infertile, unproductive, arid, desert, waste. **2** (*barren women*) infertile, sterile, childless. **3** (*barren discussions*) fruitless, worthless, useless, valueless, purposeless.

barricade *n* (*barricades keeping back the crowds*) barrier, blockade, obstacle, bar.

barrier *n* (*a barrier to keep the spectators off the playing field*) barricade, bar, fence, railing, blockade.

base *n* **1** (*the base of the statue*) foundation, support, prop, foot. **2** (*paints with an oil base*) basis, essence, source. **3** (*climbers setting up a base*) headquarters, depot, center, camp, starting point.

base *vb* **1** (*base his statement on the facts available*) found, build, establish, ground. **2** (*base the novel on his childhood memories*) locate, situate, station.

bashful *adj* shy, reserved, retiring, modest, self-conscious.

basic *adj* (*the basic facts/the basic principles*) fundamental, elementary, rudimentary, primary, essential, chief.

basis *n* **1** (*the basis for his conclusions*) grounds, foundation, base. **2** (*issues that form the basis of the discussion*) starting point, foundation, base.

batch *n* (*a batch of new students/a batch of old magazines*) group, quantity, collection, set.

bathe *vb* **1** (*bathe the wound*) clean, cleanse, wash. **2** (*bathe in the sea*) swim, go swimming, (*inf*) take a dip.

batter *vb* (*batter the door*) bang, beat, strike, knock, pound, thump.

battle *n* (*a battle to prevent the enemy army invading*) conflict, fight, clash, skirmish, engagement, encounter, struggle, contest.

bawl *vb* (*bawl in order to attract attention*) shout, cry out, yell, roar, bellow, scream.

bay *n* (*ships anchored in the bay*) inlet, cove, gulf, basin, bight.

bay *vb* howl, bark, yell, cry, growl.

bazaar *n* (*tourists at an eastern bazaar*) market, marketplace.

beach *n* (*pull the boat on to the beach*) seaside, coast, shore, sands.

beam *n* **1** (*roof beams*) board, timber, plank, joist, rafter, support. **2** (*a beam of light*) ray, shaft, stream, streak, flash, gleam, glint.

bear *vb* **1** (*bearing gifts*) carry, bring, take, convey.

2 (*bear the weight*) carry, support, hold up, sustain. **3** (*unable to bear the pain*) put up with, stand, suffer, endure, tolerate. **4** (*bear a son*) give birth to, produce. **5** (*bear a grudge*) have, hold, harbor. ✧

bear up to keep cheerful or strong under strain or stress (*She is in a great deal of pain, but she somehow succeeds in bearing up*).

bearded *adj* (*a bearded man*) unshaven, whiskered, stubbly, hirsute.

bearings *npl* (*lose our bearings on the mountain*) location, position, whereabouts, way, course, direction.

beast *n* **1** (*the beasts of the jungle*) animal, creature, mammal. **2** (*he was an absolute beast*) brute, monster, savage, pig, ogre.

beat *vb* **1** (*beat the drum*) bang, hit, strike, pound. **2** (*with hearts beating*) throb, pound, thump, pulsate, pulse, palpitate. **3** (*they beat their animals*) hit, strike, batter, thump, wallop, thrash, slap. **4** (*birds with their wings beating*) flap, flutter, vibrate, **5** (*beat the butter and sugar*) mix, blend, whisk, stir. **6** (*beat the opposition*) defeat, conquer, vanquish, rout, trounce, crush, overwhelm, (*inf*) lick. **7** (*beat the record*) outdo, surpass, exceed, excel, transcend. ✧

beat around the bush to approach something in a very indirect way (*He was beating around the bush instead of telling her frankly that her work was not good enough*) <In game-bird hunting bushes are beaten to make the birds appear>.

beat it! go away! (*Beat it, you're not wanted here!*).

beat *n* **1** (*the beat of the music*) rhythm, time, measure, pulse, throb. **2** (*the policeman's beat*) round, circuit, course, route.

beautiful *adj* **1** (*a beautiful woman*) lovely, pretty, attractive, handsome, glamorous, gorgeous. **2** (*a beautiful view*) lovely, attractive, picturesque, charming, delightful, magnificent, splendid.

beauty *n* **1** (*a woman of great beauty*) loveliness, prettiness, attractiveness, handsomeness, glamor. **2** (*the beauty of the scheme*) advantage, benefit, asset. ✧

beauty is only skin-deep people have more important qualities than how they look

(She is not pretty but she is very interesting and amusing. After all, beauty is only skin-deep).

becoming *adj* **1** (*a becoming dress*) flattering, attractive, elegant. **2** (*behavior that was hardly becoming*) fitting, suitable, appropriate, apt, proper, seemly

before *adv* (*we had met before*) previously, earlier, formerly, in the past.

beg *vb* **1** (*homeless people begging in the streets*) ask for money, (*inf*) cadge, (*inf*) scrounge. **2** (*beg for mercy*) ask for, require, plead for, entreat, beseech, implore. ✧

beg the question in an argument or debate, to take for granted the very point that requires to be proven (*It begs the question to say that I can trust the president because he's honest*). Often used, erroneously, with the meaning to inspire or elicit a line of questioning (*Her behavior begs the question: 'Can she be trusted?' ''*). This usage is now becoming more common than the original one <From philosophy>.

beggar *n* vagrant, down-and-out, hobo, bum.

begin *vb* **1** (*begin work*) start, commence, set about, embark on. **2** (*when the trouble begins*) start, commence, get going, arise.

beginning *n* **1** (*the beginning of the relationship*) start, starting-point, commencement, outset, onset. **2** (*the beginning of the book*) start, commencement, first part, introduction, opening, preface.

begrudge *vb* (*begrudge him his success*) grudge, envy, be envious of, resent, be jealous of.

behave *vb* (*behave in a responsible way*) act, conduct yourself.

behavior, behaviour (*Br, Cdn*) *n* (*criticize the behavior of the football crowd*) actions, conduct, manners.

being *n* **1** (*the reason for our being*) existence, life, living. **2** (*beings from another planet*) creature, living thing, individual.

belief *n* **1** (*it is her belief that he is still alive*) opinion, feeling, impression, view, viewpoint, way of thinking, theory. **2** (*religious beliefs*) faith, creed, doctrine. **3** (*have no belief in their ability*) faith, trust, reliance.

belligerent *adj* (*a belligerent fellow who started a fight*) aggressive, quarrelsome, argumentative, pugnacious.

belong *vb* **1** (*the car belongs to me*) be owned by, be the property of. **2** (*she belongs to the tennis club*) be a member of, be associated with.

belongings *npl* (*lose all her belongings*) possessions, things, property, personal effects.

beloved *adj* (*her beloved husband*) dearest, darling, loved, adored.

beloved *n* (*wish to marry her beloved*) sweetheart, boyfriend/girlfriend, fiancé/fiancée.

belt *n* **1** (*wear a plastic belt around her waist*) girdle, sash, strap, cummerbund. **2** (*a belt of green fields between the towns*) area, region, tract, zone. **3** (*a belt of blue across the white walls*) strip, stripe, streak, line, band. ✧

tighten your belt to reduce the amount of money which you spend (*Since their father now earns less money the family will have to tighten their belts*) <Belts have to be tightened if you lose weight—in this case because less money will be spent on food>.

bench *n* **1** (*students sitting on a bench*) form, seat. **2** (*a carpenter's bench*) workbench, worktable, table, counter.

bend *vb* **1** (*try to bend the iron band*) curve, flex, loop, arch, twist, contort, warp. **2** (*the road bends to the left*) curve, turn, twist, swerve, veer, incline. **3** (*she bent down to pick up the letter*) stoop, crouch down, lean down, bow down. ✧

get bent out of shape to become angry (*No need to get all bent out of shape – I'm just leaving*).
on bended knees very humbly or earnestly (*She asked him to forgive her on bended knees*).

bend *n* (*a bend in the road*) curve, turn, twist, corner, angle.

beneficial *adj* (*a climate beneficial to her health*) of benefit, advantageous, favorable, helpful.

benefit *n* **1** (*one of the benefits of living near the sea*) advantage, gain, good point, asset, boon. **2** (*things that are of benefit to all*) advantage, good, profit, use, value, help, service.

benevolent *adj* **1** (*a benevolent old man*) kind, kindly, kind-hearted, generous, helpful. **2** (*benevolent institutions*) charitable, nonprofit-making.

bent *adj* **1** (*a bent iron rod*) curved, crooked, angled, twisted, contorted, warped. **2** (*with bent backs*) bowed, arched, stooped, hunched.

bent *n* (*of a musical bent*) inclination, leaning, tendency, predisposition, talent, aptitude, flair.

bequest *n* (*receive a bequest in her employer's will*) legacy, inheritance.

bereavement *n* (*their grandfather has died—we must sympathize with them on their bereavement*) loss, death, decease.

bereft *adj* (*bereft of speech*) deprived of, robbed of, devoid of, lacking.

berserk *adj* (*he went berserk when he saw the damage to his car*) mad, insane, frenzied, out of your mind, wild, enraged, raging, amok.

besides *adv* (*I do not want to go—besides, it is too late*) also, in addition, additionally, moreover, furthermore.

besides *prep* (*four people besides us*) as well as, apart from, in addition to, not counting.

besiege *vb* (*a city besieged by the enemy*) lay siege to, blockade, surround, encircle.

best *adj* 1 (*the best player*) top, foremost, leading, finest. 2 (*the best thing to do*) right, correct, most suitable, most fitting.

bet *vb* (*bet $100 on a horse*) gamble, wager, stake, risk, venture.

bet *n* 1 (*place a bet on a horse*) wager, stake. 2 (*your best bet*) choice, option, alternative, course of action. ✧

hedge your bets to try to protect yourself from possible loss, failure, disappointment, etc. (*We decided to hedge our bets and book seats for both performances*) <From betting the same amount on each side to make sure of not losing>.

betray *vb* 1 (*betray his friend to the police*) be disloyal to, break faith with, inform on, double-cross, (*inf*) blow the whistle on, sell down the river. 2 (*betray her secret*) reveal, disclose, divulge, let slip, give away.

beware *vb* (*advised to beware of thieves*) be careful, be wary, be on your guard, guard against, watch out.

bewilder *vb* (*bewildered by all the traffic signs*) confuse, muddle, puzzle, perplex, baffle, nonplus, bamboozle, bemuse.

bewitch *vb* 1 (*bewitched by the pianist's performance*) captivate, enchant, entrance, beguile, charm. 2 (*the wizard bewitched the prince*) put a spell on, cast a spell over, enchant.

biased *adj* (*accuse the referee of being biased/a biased attitude*) prejudiced, one-sided, influenced, partial, bigoted, unfair, unjust.

bid *vb* 1 (*bid $100 for the vase at the auction*) offer, tender, proffer, put forward. 2 (*bid them farewell*) wish, greet, tell, say.

big *adj* 1 (*a big house/a big car*) large, sizable, great, substantial, huge, enormous, vast, colossal, gigantic. 2 (*a big man*) large, tall, heavy, burly, thickset. 3 (*a big decision*) important, significant, major, serious, grave, weighty. ✧

a big fish in a small pond a person who seems better, more important, etc., than they are because they work or live in a small, limited area (*He did well in the village school, where he was a big fish in a small pond, but when he went to a large city school, he was just average*).
a big shot an important person (*Her father is a big shot in the publishing world*).

bigotry *n* (*religious bigotry*) prejudice, intolerance, bias, partiality, narrow-mindedness, fanaticism.

bilious *adj* 1 sick, nauseated, queasy. 2 (*walls of a bilious color*) garish, violent, nauseating.

bill *n* 1 (*send them the bill for the work!*) account, invoice, check, (*inf*) tab. 2 (*post bills to advertise the show*) poster, advertisement, notice, circular.

bin *n* (*a bin for corn*) container, receptacle, box, can.

bind *vb* 1 (*bind the sheaves of corn together*) tie, tie up, fasten, secure, attach, truss. 2 (*bind the wound*) bandage, dress, cover. 3 (*bind the seams*) edge trim, hem, finish.

birth *n* 1 (*present at the birth*) delivery, childbirth, confinement. 2 (*of humble birth*) origin, descent, family, parentage, extraction, ancestry. 3 (*the birth of civilization*) origin, beginning, start, creation.

bit *n* (*a bit of chocolate/a bit of cheese*) piece, section, segment, lump, chunk, scrap, sliver, morsel, grain, speck, particle.

bite *vb* 1 (*bite into the apple/biting her nails*) chew, munch, crunch, nibble at, gnaw at, eat. 2 (*the dog bit the postman*) sink your teeth into, snap at, nip. 3 (*bitten by mosquitoes*) sting, puncture.

bite *n* 1 (*a bite of the apple/a bite of food*) mouthful, piece, morsel, bit. 2 (*the dog gave her a bite*) snap, nip. 3 (*insect bites*) sting, prick, puncture. 4 (*food with a bite*) sharpness, spiciness, piquancy, pungency.

bitter *adj* 1 (*a bitter taste*) acid, tart, sour, acrid, harsh, pungent, vinegary. 2 (*a bitter old man*) embittered, resentful, sour, spiteful, vindictive. 3 (*a bitter wind*) biting, sharp, raw, penetrating, stinging, freezing. 4 (*from bitter experience*) painful, distressing, unhappy, sad, tragic.

black *adj* 1 (*black clothing/black horses*) jet-black, pitch-black, inky, sable, dusky. **2** (*black nights*) dark, pitch-black, inky, murky, unlit, starless. **3** (*in a black mood*) depressed, gloomy, pessimistic, melancholy, sad. ▽

in black and white in writing or in print (*We had a conversation and agreed to work together but our lawyer says we should put the details in black and white*) <From black print on white paper>.

blame *vb* **1** (*blame her for the crime*) hold responsible, hold accountable, accuse, charge, find guilty, condemn. **2** (*blame the crime on her*) attribute, ascribe, lay at the door of, (*inf*) pin on.

blame *n* (*put the blame for the crime on her*) responsibility, accountability, liability, fault, accusation, guilt, condemnation, (*inf*) rap.

bland *adj* **1** (*bland food*) tasteless, flavorless, insipid, mild. **2** (*a bland manner*) smooth, suave, urbane, gracious.

blank *adj* **1** (*a blank piece of paper*) empty, unfilled, unwritten-on, unmarked, bare. **2** (*a blank tape*) clean, empty, unfilled, unused. **3** (*a blank face*) expressionless, vacant, empty, deadpan, impassive.

blast *n* **1** (*hear the blast several streets away*) explosion, bang, report, eruption. **2** (*a blast of cold air*) gust, rush, draft, wind, gale. **3** (*a blast of loud music*) blare, boom, roar.

blatant *adj* (*a blatant crime*) glaring, flagrant, obvious, conspicuous, unmistakable, brazen.

blaze *n* **1** (*old people killed in the blaze*) fire, flames, inferno. **2** (*a sudden blaze of light*) flash, flare, beam, streak.

blaze *vb* **1** (*logs blazing in the fire*) burn, be ablaze, flame. **2** (*lights blazing*) shine, beam, flash, flare.

bleak *adj* **1** (*a bleak countryside*) bare, barren, desolate, dismal, exposed. **2** (*a bleak future*) gloomy, depressing, miserable, dismal, grim, dark.

blemish *n* **1** (*blemishes on the fruit*) mark, spot, blotch, bruise, imperfection. **2** (*a blemish in his character*) flaw, fault, defect. **3** (*a blemish on her reputation*) stain, blot.

blend *vb* (*blend the ingredients for the pudding*) mix, combine, mingle.

blessing *n* **1** (*the minister said a blessing*) benediction, grace, prayer, dedication. **2** (*the rain is a blessing for the dried-out gardens*) boon, advantage, benefit, asset, help. **3** (*give the*

scheme his blessing) approval, support, sanction, endorsement. ▽

a blessing in disguise something that turns out to be an advantage after at first seeming unfortunate (*Being laid off was a blessing in disguise. She got a much more interesting job*).

blind *adj* **1** (*a blind person with a guide dog*) unsighted, sightless, unseeing, visually impaired, visually challenged. **2** (*blind to the problems*) unmindful of, heedless of, oblivious to, indifferent to, unaware of, unconscious of, ignorant of.

blind *n* **1** (*the blind kept out the sunlight*) screen, shade, shutters, drape. **2** (*his store was a blind for drug-pushing*) front, screen, smoke screen, camouflage, cloak, disguise.

blink *vb* **1** (*people blinking in the bright light*) screw up your eyes, wink, squint. **2** (*with eyelids blinking*) flicker, wink, bat. **3** (*Christmas trees blinking*) flicker, twinkle, wink, glimmer, glitter.

bliss *n* (*the bliss of being in love*) ecstasy, elation, euphoria, joy, rapture, happiness, delight.

block *n* **1** (*a block of chocolate*) bar, cake, brick, slab, chunk, lump, hunk, wedge. **2** (*a block in the waste pipe*) blockage, obstruction, stoppage. **3** (*the science block of the university*) building, complex.

block *vb* **1** (*leaves blocking the drains*) clog, choke, stop up, obstruct, (*inf*) bung up. **2** (*fallen trees blocking the flow of traffic*) bar, halt, obstruct, hinder, impede, hold back.

bloodshed *n* (*a battle that resulted in great bloodshed*) killing, murder, slaughter, massacre, carnage.

bloom *vb* **1** (*flowers that bloom in the summer*) flower, be in flower, come into flower, blossom. **2** (*children blooming in their new environment*) flourish, thrive, blossom, get on well, prosper, succeed.

blot *n* **1** (*ink blots/blots of grease*) blotch, spot, smudge, splotch, smear. **2** (*a blot on her character*) stain, blemish, flaw, fault, defect, taint.

blot *vb* **1** (*paper blotted with ink spots*) spot, smudge, blotch, smear, mark. **2** (*blot their reputation*) sully, blacken, stain, tarnish, besmirch. **3** (*blot out memories of the past*) wipe out, rub out, erase, obliterate, destroy.

blow *n* **1** (*a blow on the head*) hit, knock, bang,

thump, smack, slap, rap, (*inf*) clout. **2** (*it was a blow when her friend went away*) shock, upset, jolt, setback, disappointment, misfortune, disaster, catastrophe.

blue *adj* **1** (*blue skies*) azure, indigo, sapphire, ultramarine, navy, navy blue, sky blue, powder-blue, royal blue. **2** (*feeling blue*) depressed, gloomy, miserable, downcast, glum, sad, unhappy, melancholy. **3** (*blue jokes*) obscene, indecent, improper, dirty, smutty. ⇨

out of the blue without any warning (*The news of his death came out of the blue*).

bluff *vb* (*she believed him but he was only bluffing*) pretend, sham, fake, feign, put it on, lie, deceive, fool, hoax, hoodwink.

bluff *n* (*he said that he would report her but it was only a bluff*) pretense, sham, fake, deception, subterfuge, hoax.

bluff *adj* (*a bluff manner*) outspoken, plain-spoken, blunt, direct, frank, candid.

blunder *n* (*make a blunder in the calculations*) mistake, error, slip, inaccuracy, (*inf*) slip-up, (*inf*) boob.

blunder *vb* **1** (*discover that someone had blundered and had forgotten to book the hall*) make a mistake, err, (*inf*) slip up. **2** (*blundering about in the dark without a torch*) stumble, lurch, stagger, flounder.

blunt *adj* **1** (*a blunt knife*) dull, dulled, unsharpened. **2** (*a blunt statement*) abrupt, curt, brusque, outspoken, plain-spoken, direct, frank, straightforward, candid.

blur *vb* **1** (*tears blurred her vision*) obscure, dim, make hazy, make misty, make fuzzy, cloud. **2** (*grease blurred the windshield*) smear, smudge. **3** (*time had blurred her memory*) dim, make hazy, make vague, dull, confuse.

blur *n* (*when she did not have her eyeglasses on, everything was just a blur*) haze, mist.

blurred *adj* (*blurred vision*) hazy, misty, fuzzy, indistinct, unclear.

blush *vb* (*she blushed with embarrassment*) redden, go red, turn red, go scarlet, go crimson, flush, color.

board *n* **1** (*a bridge made of wooden boards*) plank, slat, beam. **2** (*charge her for her board*) food, meals.

board *vb* **1** (*board the plane*) get on, enter, go on board, mount, embark. **2** (*board up the windows*) cover up, shut up, seal. **3** (*he boards with*

a friend of his mother) lodge, live, have rooms. ⇨

go by the boards to be abandoned (*His dreams of going to university have gone by the boards since he failed his exams*) <The board here is a ship's board or side—"to go by the board" literally was to vanish overboard>.

boast *vb* (*she was always boasting about how well she could sing*) brag, crow, blow your own horn, show off, swagger, (*inf*) swank.

boastful *adj* (*a boastful person always telling people about her fine house*) bragging, swaggering, conceited, vain, (*inf*) big-headed, (*inf*) swanking.

boat *n* vessel, craft, dinghy, yacht, ship, rowboat. ⇨

miss the boat to fail to take advantage of an opportunity (*She meant to apply for the job but she missed the boat. She posted the application letter too late*).

rock the boat to do something to spoil or put at risk a happy or comfortable situation (*It was a happy neighborhood until you came along and rocked the boat by complaining about everything*).

body *n* **1** (*healthy bodies*) physique. **2** (*pains in his body and in his limbs*) trunk, torso. **3** (*bodies in the mortuary*) dead body, corpse, carcass, cadaver. **4** (*the ruling body in the organization*) group, party, band, company, bloc. **5** (*a large body of water*) mass, expanse, extent.

bodyguard *n* (*the president's bodyguard*) guard, protector, defender.

bog *n* (*the walkers got stuck in the bog*) marsh, marshland, swamp, mire, quagmire.

bogus *adj* **1** (*the man in the hospital turned out to be a bogus doctor*) fraudulent, fake, sham, (*inf*) phony. **2** (*pay for the goods with bogus $10 bills*) counterfeit, forged, fake, fraudulent, sham, (*inf*) phony.

boil *vb* (*soup boiling on the stove*) bubble, cook, simmer.

boisterous *adj* **1** (*boisterous children*) lively, active, spirited, noisy, loud, rowdy, unruly. **2** (*a boisterous wind*) blustery, gusting, stormy, wild.

bold *adj* **1** (*a bold adventurer*) brave, courageous, valiant, gallant, daring, adventurous, intrepid, fearless, heroic. **2** (*a bold young woman/so bold* *as to invite themselves to the party*) brazen, impudent, forward, audacious. **3** (*bold colors*) striking, bright, vivid, eye-catching, showy.

bolt *n* **1** (*bolts on the door*) bar, catch, latch, fastener, lock. **2** (*nuts and bolts*) rivet, pin, peg. **3** (*make a bolt for it*) dash, run, sprint, dart, rush. ✧

> **a bolt from the blue** something very sudden and unexpected (*His decision to leave was a bolt from the blue*).

bolt *vb* **1** (*they bolted the door*) bar, lock, fasten, secure. **2** (*bolt from the room in fear*) dash, run, sprint, dart, rush, hurtle, flee. **3** (*the children bolted their food*) gulp, gobble, wolf, guzzle.

bomb *n* (*a building blown up by a bomb*) incendiary device, incendiary, explosive, shell.

bombard *vb* **1** (*the enemy bombarded the military stores*) bomb, shell, torpedo, blitz, attack. **2** (*bombard them with questions*) assail, attack, besiege, subject to.

bond *n* **1** (*the bond between mother and child*) tie, link, connection, attachment. **2** (*prisoners escaping from their bonds*) chains, fetters, shackles, rope.

bonus *n* **1** (*the good food on vacation was a welcome bonus*) extra, addition, (*inf*) plus, benefit, gain, boon. **2** (*staff getting an annual bonus*) gift, tip, gratuity, (*inf*) perk, reward.

bony *adj* angular, scraggy, gaunt, skinny, skeletal.

book *vb* (*book theater seats/book hotel rooms*) reserve, make reservations for.

book *n* (*borrow a book from the library*) volume, tome, publication. ✧

> **read someone like a book** to understand someone completely, not to be deceived by someone (*I knew that he was lying—I can read him like a book*).

bookish *adj* (*she is rather a bookish child*) studious, scholarly, academic, intellectual, learned, highbrow.

boom *n* **1** (*hear the boom of guns*) bang, blast, roar, rumble. **2** (*a boom in the number of tourists*) increase, growth, upsurge, upswing, upturn, boost.

boor *n* (*boors with bad manners*) lout, oaf, redneck.

boost *vb* (*boost the morale of the troops*) raise, increase, heighten, improve, encourage, help, assist.

booth *n* **1** (*a market booth*) stall, stand, counter. **2** (*a telephone booth*) cubicle, compartment.

booty *n* (*the booty hidden by the burglars*) loot, spoils, plunder, haul, (*inf*) swag.

border *n* **1** (*sew a colorful border on the skirt*) edging, edge, fringe, trim. **2** (*a flower border*) bed. **3** (*the borders of the lake*) edge, verge, perimeter, margin. **4** (*show your passport at the border*) frontier, boundary.

bore *vb* **1** (*bore into the wood/bore a hole in the wood*) drill, pierce, perforate, penetrate, puncture. **2** (*an audience bored by the comedian*) weary, tire, fatigue, be tedious to, bore to tears, bore to death.

boring *adj* (*a boring speech*) dull, tedious, monotonous, unexciting, uninteresting, wearisome, tiring.

borrow *vb* (*borrow money from someone/borrow someone's pen*) ask for the loan of, take as a loan, use temporarily, (*inf*) scrounge, (*inf*) cadge.

boss *n* (*the workers asked the boss for a wage rise*) employer, manager, director, owner, (*inf*) honcho.

bossy *adj* domineering, bullying, overbearing, dominating, dictatorial.

bother *vb* **1** (*the children were told not to bother their mother when she was resting*) disturb, trouble, worry, pester, annoy, harass, (*inf*) hassle. **2** (*please don't bother to wait for me*) take the trouble, trouble yourself, inconvenience yourself, make the effort. **3** (*it bothers me that she is not here yet*) concern, worry, trouble, upset.

bother *n* **1** (*please don't go to any bother over dinner*) trouble, inconvenience, effort, fuss. **2** (*there was a bit of bother at the rally*) trouble, disturbance, commotion, disorder, fighting.

bottle *n* (*a bottle of milk/a bottle of wine*) container, flask, carafe. ✧

> **crack a bottle** to open a bottle (*Let us celebrate by cracking a bottle of champagne*).

bottom *n* **1** (*at the bottom of the hill*) foot, base. **2** (*the bottom of the sea*) floor, bed, depths. **3** (*the bottom of the garden*) the far end, the farthest point.

bound *vb* (*bound into the room/bound over the fence*) leap, jump, spring, vault.

bound *adj* (*she thought that she was bound to win*) certain, sure, very likely, destined.

boundary *n* **1** (*the boundary between the countries*) border, frontier, dividing line. **2** (*the boundary of the estate*) bounds, border, perimeter, periphery, confines, limits, margin.

bouquet n (*the bride's bouquet/a bouquet of roses*) bunch of flowers, bunch, spray, posy.

bout n **1** (*a boxing bout*) combat, contest, match, round, fight. **2** (*a bout of coughing*) fit, attack, turn, spell.

bow vb (*bow his head*) incline, bend, nod, stoop.

bowl n (*a bowl of cereal*) dish, basin, container.

bowl vb (*bowl a ball*) pitch, throw, fling, hurl, toss.

box n container, receptacle, carton, case, pack, chest, bin, crate.

box vb **1** (*he used to box for the United States*) fight. **2** (*box the child on the ears*) strike, hit, cuff, slap, smack, wallop, (*inf*) belt.

boy n (*when he was a boy*) youth, lad.

boycott vb **1** (*boycott goods from that country*) bar, ban, black, blacklist, embargo, place an embargo on, prohibit. **2** (*boycott their company*) shun, avoid, spurn.

boyfriend n (*she has a new boyfriend*) sweetheart, young man, lover, partner.

bracing adj (*a bracing climate*) invigorating, refreshing, stimulating, exhilarating, reviving, health-giving.

brag vb (*he brags about having a lot of money*) boast, crow, blow your own horn, show off, (*inf*) talk big.

brain n (*have a good brain*) intellect, mind, intelligence, powers of reasoning, head. ▭

pick someone's brains to find out someone's ideas and knowledge about a subject so that you can put them to your own use.

branch n **1** (*the branch of a tree*) bough, limb. **2** (*the local branch of the business*) division, subdivision, section, department, part.

brand n **1** (*a brand of breakfast cereal*) make, kind, variety, type, sort, line, label, trade name, trademark. **2** (*her brand of wit*) kind, variety, type, sort, style.

brandish vb (*a criminal brandishing a knife*) wave, flourish, swing, wield, shake.

brash adj (*a brash young man*) bold, cocky, self-confident, self-assertive, insolent, impudent, fresh, brazen.

brave adj (*a brave soldier*) courageous, valiant, intrepid, fearless, plucky, gallant, heroic, bold, daring.

brawl n (*a brawl in a tavern*) fight, wrangle, rumpus, row, quarrel, argument, squabble, free-for-all, scrap.

brawny adj (*brawny hammer-throwers*) burly, muscular, hefty, powerful, strong, strapping.

bray vb (*donkeys braying*) whinny, neigh, hee-haw.

brazen adj (*it was brazen of her to kiss a complete stranger on the lips*) bold, audacious, forward, brash, impudent, insolent, impertinent, immodest, shameless.

breach n **1** (*a breach in the sea wall*) break, split, crack, gap, hole, opening. **2** (*a breach of the legal agreement*) breaking, violation, infringement.

breadth n **1** (*measure the breadth of the room*) width, wideness, broadness, span. **2** (*discover the breadth of her knowledge of the subject*) extent, range, scope, scale, degree.

break vb **1** (*break a cup*) smash, shatter, crack. **2** (*break the handle of the bag*) snap, split, tear. **3** (*the machine broke*) break down, become damaged, stop working, cease to operate, (*inf*) go kaput. **4** (*break the law*) violate, contravene, breach, infringe, disobey, disregard, defy. **5** (*break his arm*) fracture, crack. **6** (*break the news*) tell, impart, announce, communicate, reveal, disclose. ▭

break even to have your losses balanced by your gains, to make neither a loss nor a profit (*We did not make any money on our investment, but at least we broke even*).

break n **1** (*a break in the water pipe*) crack, hole, gash, split, fracture, chink, tear. **2** (*a break in her career to look after her children*) interruption, discontinuation, pause. **3** (*have a cup of tea during her break*) rest period, interval, intermission, breathing space. **4** (*take a weekend break*) vacation, time off.

breakthrough n (*a breakthrough in cancer research*) advance, step forward, development.

breathe vb **1** (*breathe in/breathe out*) inhale/exhale, inspire/expire, puff, pant. **2** (*as long as he breathes*) be alive, live, have life. ▭

breathe down someone's neck 1 to be very close behind someone (*He was in the lead in the race but there were several other runners breathing down his neck*). **2** to be waiting impatiently for something from someone (*The boss is breathing down her neck for those letters that she is typing*).

breathless adj (*breathless after running for the bus*) out of breath, gasping, panting, puffing.

breed n (*a breed of cattle*) variety, kind, strain.

breed vb 1 (*rabbits breed very rapidly*) reproduce, multiply, give birth. 2 (*he breeds horses*) raise, rear. 3 (*poverty that can breed crime and violence*) cause, bring about, give rise to, create, produce, stir up.

breeze n (*a cool breeze on a hot day*) puff of wind, gust of wind, current of air, draft.

bribe vb (*try to bribe a member of the jury*) buy off, corrupt, give an inducement to, (*inf*) grease the palm of, (*inf*) give a backhander to, (*inf*) give a sweetener to.

bridge n (*a bridge over the freeway*) overpass, flyover, viaduct, suspension bridge. ▽

cross a bridge when you come to it to worry about something or attempt to deal with something only when it actually happens instead of worrying about it beforehand (*She is worrying about losing her job, although she might not. She should learn to cross a bridge when she comes to it*).

brief adj 1 (*a brief statement*) short, concise, succinct, to the point, compact, terse. 2 (*a brief friendship*) short, short-lived, fleeting, passing.

brief vb (*brief a lawyer*) instruct, give instructions to, direct, give directions to, inform, give information to, prime.

bright adj 1 (*a bright light*) shining, brilliant, dazzling, blazing, gleaming, radiant. 2 (*bright colors*) vivid, brilliant, intense, glowing, bold, rich. 3 (*bright children*) clever, intelligent, sharp, quick, quick-witted, (*inf*) smart, brilliant, (*inf*) brainy, gifted, talented. 4 (*a bright future*) promising, favorable, hopeful, optimistic, encouraging, fortunate, good. ▽

bright-eyed and bushy-tailed very lively and cheerful (*She is always bright-eyed and bushy-tailed early in the morning but her sister is sleepy and bad-tempered*) <From squirrels who have bright eyes and bushy tails>.

brilliant adj 1 (*a brilliant light*) bright, shining, dazzling, gleaming, radiant. 2 (*brilliant children*) bright, clever, intelligent, sharp, quick, quick-witted, (*inf*) smart, (*inf*) brainy, gifted, talented.

brim n (*glasses full to the brim*) rim, lip, top, edge.

brim vb (*glasses brimming with wine/eyes brimming with tears*) be full, be filled with, overflow, run over.

bring vb 1 (*bring food home*) carry, take, convey, transport, fetch. 2 (*famine which brought disease*) cause, produce, create, result in, give rise to.

brink n 1 (*on the brink of the lake*) edge, verge, boundary, border, margin. 2 (*on the brink of the disaster*) edge, verge, threshold, point.

brisk adj 1 (*walk at a brisk speed*) quick, fast, rapid, swift, speedy, energetic, lively. 2 (*business was brisk*) busy, active, hectic.

brittle adj (*toffee is a brittle substance*) hard, crisp, breakable, splintery.

broad adj 1 (*a broad street*) wide. 2 (*a broad range of subjects*) wide, wide-ranging, broad-ranging, general, comprehensive. 3 (*a broad statement of their plans*) general, non-detailed, imprecise, vague. ▽

have broad shoulders to be able to accept a great deal of responsibility, criticism, etc. (*He never minds being blamed when things go wrong. He says that he has broad shoulders*).

brochure n (*an advertising brochure*) booklet, leaflet, pamphlet, circular, notice, bill.

brooch n (*she wears a silver brooch on her lapel*) pin, clip.

brow n 1 (*wipe the sweat from his brow*) forehead, temple. 2 (*the brow of the hill*) top, summit, crown, peak.

brown adj (*go brown in the summer*) tanned, suntanned, bronze, bronzed. ▽

in a brown study deep in thought (*She did not hear anything he said. She was in a brown study*).

brush vb 1 (*brush the back yard*) sweep, clean. 2 (*brush her hair*) groom, tidy. 3 (*brush her cheek with his lips*) touch, flick, glance. ▽

brush up on something to refresh your knowledge of something (*Brushing up on their French before going on vacation*).

brusque adj (*a brusque reply*) abrupt, blunt, curt, sharp, gruff, rude.

brutal adj (*a brutal attack*) savage, cruel, vicious, callous, ruthless.

bubble vb 1 (*champagne bubbling*) fizz, effervesce, sparkle, foam, froth. 2 (*a sauce bubbling on the stove*) boil, simmer.

bucket n (*need a bucket of water to wash the floor*) pail, container. ⌖

kick the bucket (*inf*) to die (*He hoped to be left a lot of money when the old man kicked the bucket*) <'bucket" here is perhaps a beam from which pigs were hung after being killed>.

buckle n (*the buckle of the belt*) clasp, catch, fastener, fastening, clip.

bug n 1 (*bitten by bugs when sitting on the grass*) insect, mite, (*inf*) creepy-crawly. 2 (*he caught a bug and is off work*) infection, virus, germ, bacterium, micro-organism.

build vb 1 (*build a new school*) construct, put up, erect. 2 (*build model planes*) make, construct, assemble, put together. 3 (*build his own business*) found, set up, establish, start, begin, develop, institute. ⌖

build castles in Spain to have dreams or hopes that are very unlikely to be realized.

building n (*old buildings that are tourist attractions*) edifice, structure.

bulge n (*the pack of candy made a bulge in her pocket*) swelling, bump, lump.

bulk n 1 (*the armoire was difficult to move because of its sheer bulk*) size, mass, extent, largeness, hugeness. 2 (*the bulk of the people voted against the proposal*) majority, most, preponderance, mass.

bulky adj (*bulky furniture*) large, big, massive, substantial, heavy, unwieldy, cumbersome, awkward.

bully vb (*older boys bullying the younger ones*) browbeat, domineer, intimidate, threaten, persecute, torment, tyrannize, (*inf*) push around.

bump vb (*the car that bumped into ours*) knock, hit, strike, crash into, bang, collide with, ram.

bump n 1 (*the child fell out of the tree with a bump*) thud, thump, bang, jolt, crash. 2 (*he has a bump on the head from the accident*) lump, swelling, bulge.

bumpy adj (*bumpy roads*) uneven, rough, rutted, pitted, potholed.

bunch n 1 (*a bunch of flowers*) bouquet, spray, posy, sheaf. 2 (*a bunch of grapes*) cluster, clump. 3 (*a friendly bunch of people*) group, band, crowd, gang.

bundle n (*a bundle of old clothes*) pile, heap, stack, bale.

burden n 1 (*the pony's burden*) load, pack. 2 (*the burden of being head of the family*) responsibility, obligation, onus, worry, weight, strain. ⌖

the burden of proof the responsibility for proving something (*The burden of proof lies with the accusers*) <A legal term>.

burglar n (*catch a burglar breaking into the house*) housebreaker, cat burglar, thief, robber.

burglary n (*he was sent to prison on a charge of burglary*) house-breaking, breaking and entering, forced entry, theft, robbery, larceny.

burly adj (*a burly figure*) muscular, powerful, thickset, strapping, hefty, beefy, stout.

burn vb 1 (*the house was burning*) be on fire, be ablaze, blaze. 2 (*burn the leaves*) set on fire, set alight, ignite. 3 (*burn the shirt with the iron*) scorch, singe, sear. ⌖

the burning question a question that is of great interest to many people (*The burning question is which of the men will she marry*).

burst vb 1 (*the water pipes have burst*) crack, split, fracture, rupture. 2 (*they burst into the room*) push your way, barge. 3 (*burst into tears*) break out, explode, erupt, begin suddenly.

bury vb 1 (*bury the corpse*) inter, lay to rest. 2 (*bury her head in her hands*) hide, conceal, cover, put, submerge.

business n 1 (*she owns her own business*) company, firm, concern, organization, establishment. 2 (*we don't know what business he is in*) occupation, line, work, profession, job, career. 3 (*people employed in business*) commerce, industry, private enterprise, e-commerce. 4 (*it was none of their business*) concern, affair, problem, responsibility. 5 (*an odd business*) affair, situation, matter, circumstance, thing. ⌖

mean business to be determined to do something, to be serious about something (*He'll pass the exam —he means business*).
mind your own business to occupy yourself with the things that concern yourself and not to interfere in those that concern others.

busy adj 1 (*don't disturb your mother—she's busy*) occupied, engaged, working, at work. 2 (*have a busy day*) active, energetic, full, hectic.

buy vb (*buy a new house*) purchase, make a purchase of, pay for, invest in.

C

café *n* (*they stopped for a snack at a café*) coffee bar, coffee shop, cafeteria, snack bar, tearoom, tea shop, restaurant, wine bar, bistro.

cajole *vb* (*try to cajole him into coming with us*) wheedle, coax, inveigle, persuade.

cagey *adj* (*they seemed rather cagey about where they were going*) secretive, guarded, noncommittal.

cake *n* **1** (*have some cake and coffee*) gateau. **2** (*a cake of soap*) bar, block, slab, lump. ♦

a piece of cake something that is very easy to do (*Winning the race was a piece of cake*).
a slice of the cake a share of something that is desirable, profitable or valuable (*You should invest some money in your brother's firm and get a slice of the cake*).
have one's cake and eat it, eat one's cake and have it to have the advantage of two things or two situations when doing, possessing, etc., one of them would normally make doing, possessing, etc. the other one impossible (*He's engaged to one of the sisters, but he would like to eat his cake and have it and go out with the other one too*).

calculate *vb* (*calculate the cost*) work out, count, estimate, gauge, figure out, reckon.

call *vb* **1** (*she called out in fear*) cry, shout, yell, scream. **2** (*they called their son Peter*) name, christen. **3** (*the vegetables are called courgettes/ That is called wind-surfing*) name, style, designate, term, describe, dub, label. **4** (*she called you from a public telephone box*) telephone, phone, ring. **5** (*he will call tomorrow to do his aunt's shopping*) pay a call, pay a visit, stop by, drop in. **6** (*if the child is ill you had better call a doctor*) send for, ask for, summon. **7** (*they called a meeting of the committee*) call together, convene, summon. **8** (*I call it shocking that he got away with the crime*) think, consider, regard, judge. ♦

call off to cancel (*They were to be married next week, but she suddenly called off the wedding*).
call a spade a spade to speak bluntly and in a forthright manner (*I don't think you should try to break the bad news to her gently. She would much rather that you called a spade a spade*).

calm *adj* **1** (*she remains calm even in an emergency*) cool, composed, self-possessed, unruffled, tranquil, quiet, relayed, (*inf*) laid-back. **2** (*the sea was calm when the boat set out*) still, smooth. **3** (*it was a calm day for their trip to the seaside*) still, windless, mild.

camouflage *n* (*the polar bear's coat is a camouflage in the snow*) protective coloring, disguise, cover, screen, concealment.

camp *n* **1** (*the soldier's camp*) encampment, campsite, camping ground. **2** (*he is in the left-wing camp of the party*) group, set, faction, clique. ♦

have a foot in both camps to have associations with two groups that have opposing and conflicting views and attitudes (*He is one of the workers but he has shares in the company so he has a foot in both camps*).

can *n* (*a can of soup*) tin, container. ♦

carry the can take all the blame (*Jake broke the vase but I'll carry the can since I was meant to be looking after him*).
get the can to fire someone from their job or to reject them somehow (*I'm sorry, he's a nice guy but he's going to get the can because of his incompetence*).
in the can (*inf*) certain, agreed or decided upon (*He had a good interview and he thinks the job's in the can*) <A reference to a completed cinema film that is stored in large metal containers or cans>.

cancel *vb* **1** (*they had to cancel the meeting because of bad weather*) put off, call off. **2** (*they canceled the order because it was late*) call off, retract, declare void, declare null and void, revoke.

candid *adj* (*he was quite candid with them about his reasons for leaving*) frank, open, honest, direct, forthright, blunt, plainspoken.

cap *n* **1** (*he wore a cap to hide his baldness*) hat, bonnet. **2** (*I can't get the cap off the bottle*) top, lid, stopper, cork. ♦

put on one's thinking cap to begin to think very carefully about something (*If you put on your thinking cap I am sure that you will* come up with a solution to the problem).

to cap it all on top of everything else, usually everything else that has already gone wrong (*I was late, and to cap it all, the car would not start*).

cap in hand very humbly, usually when asking for something (*Although he had quarrelled with his father he had to go cap in hand to ask for a loan to pay the rent*).

capable *adj* **1** (*she is a very capable person*) able, competent, efficient, effective. **2** (*he is quite capable of cheating*) likely to, liable to.

capital *n* **1** (*Edinburgh is the capital of Scotland*) first city, chief city, seat of administration. **2** (*he does not have enough capital to buy the company*) money, finance, funds, cash, means, resources, wherewithal, assets. **3** (*write the title in capitals*) capital letter, upper case letter, (*inf*) cap. ▷

make capital out of (something) to make use of (something), usually something that is in some way disadvantageous to someone else, for one's own advantage (*In the court case the counsel for the defence made capital out of the fact that the witness for the prosecution was very nervous*).

capsize *vb* **1** (*the boat capsized in heavy seas*) overturn, turn over, upend, keel over, turn turtle. **2** (*the child capsized the bucket of water*) upset, overturn, upend.

captivity *n* (*enjoy freedom after months in captivity*) imprisonment, custody, confinement, incarceration.

capture *vb* (*the police have captured the escaped prisoners*) catch, take prisoner, take captive, take into custody, arrest, apprehend, seize.

card *n* **1** (*she sent a card to her mother on her birthday*) greetings card, postcard. **2** (*the salesman handed them his card*) business card, identification, ID. **3** (*he was asked to deal the cards*) playing card. ▷

have a card up one's sleeve to have an idea, plan of action, etc., in reserve to be used if necessary to get what one wants (*The person who wants to build the new flats thinks that he has won but I have a feeling that the protesters have a card up their sleeve*) <A reference to cheating at cards>.

in the cards very likely (*The company is losing money and so the closure of the factory is in the cards*). <A reference to reading the cards in fortune-telling>.

play one's cards close to one's chest to be secretive or non-communicative about one's plans or intentions (*I think that they are moving overseas but they are playing their cards close to their chest*) <From holding one's cards close to one in card-playing so that one's opponents will not see them>.

care *n* **1** (*the children were told to cross the road with care*) carefulness, caution, heed, heedfulness, wariness, attention, vigilance, prudence. **2** (*she iced the cake with care*) carefulness, conscientiousness, accuracy, meticulousness, punctiliousness. **3** (*the child is in the care of the local authorities*) protection, charge, keeping, custody, supervision. **4** (*they show no care for other people*) concern, regard, interest, solicitude, sympathy. **5** (*she looked older than she was after a life full of care*) worry, anxiety, trouble, distress, hardship, stress.

careful *adj* **1** (*the children were told to be careful crossing the road*) cautious, heedful, wary, attentive, vigilant, prudent. **2** (*you must be careful of your belongings at the airport*) mindful, heedful, protective. **3** (*you must be careful what you say to the lawyer*) mindful, attentive, heedful, thoughtful. **4** (*they are all careful workers*) conscientious, painstaking, accurate, meticulous, punctilious. **5** (*they do not earn much and so they have to be very careful with money*) thrifty, economic, frugal, cautious, canny.

careless *adj* **1** (*a careless pedestrian who walked out in front of the moving car*) unthinking, inattentive, thoughtless, forgetful, remiss, negligent. **2** (*the pupil's exercise is very careless*) inaccurate, slapdash, disorganized, (*inf*) sloppy.

carpet *n* **1** (*they laid a new carpet in the hall*) rug, floor covering, mat. **2** (*a carpet of autumn leaves on the grass*) covering, layer. ▷

be on the carpet to be scolded or punished by someone in authority (*She will be on the carpet when the boss finds out she's late*) <A reference to the piece of carpet in front of a desk where someone might stand to be scolded by a head teacher, etc>..

sweep (something) under the carpet to try to hide or forget about (something unpleasant)

(They try to sweep under the carpet the fact that their son steals money from them).

arry *vb* **1** (*she was asked to carry the shopping home*) bring, take, transport, convey, lug. **2** (*will the bridge carry the weight of the car?*) take, support, bear, sustain. **3** (*the store carries a wide range of goods*) sell, stock, offer. ✧

carry coals to Newcastle to do something that is completely unnecessary, especially to take something to a place where there is already a great deal of it (*Taking a cake to her was like carrying coals to Newcastle. She spends most of her time baking*) <Newcastle, in England, used to be a large coal-mining center>.

ase *n* **1** (*put the cases in the boot of the car*) suitcase, briefcase, piece of luggage. **2** (*a silver cigarette case*) container, box, receptacle. **3** (*a display case for ornaments*) cabinet, cupboard. **4** (*it was the case that she had been ill*) situation, position, circumstance. **5** (*they decided that it had been a case of misunderstanding*) instance, occurrence, occasion, example. **6** (*he has been accused of murder and the case comes up next week*) lawsuit, trial, legal proceedings. **7** (*the heart cases in the ward*) patient, sufferer, victim, invalid.

ash *n* **1** (*he earns quite a lot, but he never seems to have any cash, when we go out*) money, wherewithal, funds, (*inf*) dough, (*inf*) the ready. **2** (*they want us to pay in cash, but we have only credit cards*) money, ready money.

ast *vb* **1** (*snakes casting their coats*) shed, slough, discard, throw off. **2** (*the street lamps cast a yellow light*) give off, send out, shed, emit, radiate. **3** (*the children were casting stones in the river*) throw, fling, pitch, toss, hurl, heave. **4** (*she cast him a glance of contempt*) send, throw, bestow. ✧

cast pearls before swine to offer something valuable, desirable, enjoyable, to someone who does not appreciate it (*Taking her to the opera would be a case of casting pearls before swine*) <A biblical reference to Matthew 7:6>.

asual *adj* **1** (*she wears casual clothes at the weekend*) informal, leisure. **2** (*he is a casual acquaintance not a close friend*) slight, superficial. **3** (*casual hotel work in the summer*) irregular, temporary, part-time. **4** (*he just made a casual remark about the state of the business*) spontaneous, offhand, impromptu. **5** (*they have a very casual attitude to the dangers of the journey*) unconcerned, nonchalant, blasé, indifferent. **6** (*I did not arrange to meet her— it was just a casual meeting*) chance, accidental, unintentional, unforeseen, unexpected.

catch *vb* **1** (*he failed to catch the ball*) get hold of, grasp, grab, seize, snatch, grip. **2** (*the police are determined to catch the escaped prisoner*) capture, take captive, seize, apprehend, arrest. **3** (*did you catch what he said?*) get, understand, follow, grasp, make out, comprehend, fathom. **4** (*something bright caught his attention*) attract, draw, capture. **5** (*the child has caught a cold*) contract, develop, get, become infected with, come down with. ✧

catch it to be scolded or punished (*He will catch it when his father sees what he has done to the car*).

catch (someone) with his *or* **her pants** *or* **trousers down** to surprise (someone) when he or she is unprepared or is doing something wrong (*When the boss came into his office he was sitting snoozing with his feet on the desk. He was certainly caught with his pants down*).

catch *n* **1** (*the catch of the bag is broken*) lock, fastener, fastening, clasp. **2** (*there is no catch on the door*) lock, snib, latch, bolt. ✧

catch-22 a situation in which one can never win or from which one can never escape, being constantly hindered by a rule or restriction that itself changes to block any changes in one's plans; a difficulty that prevents one from an unpleasant or dangerous situation (*You can get money from Social Security if you have somewhere to live but you cannot get anywhere to live without money. It's a catch-22 situation*) <From the title of a novel by Joseph Heller>.

cause *n* **1** (*what was the cause of the accident?*) origin, source, root, agent. **2** (*the patient's condition gives cause for concern*) reason, justification, grounds, call. **3** (*the cause of animals' rights*) ideal, principle, belief.

cautious adj (be cautious about trusting strangers) careful, wary, watchful, guarded, chary, heedful, attentive, alert, vigilant.

cease vb (the firm has ceased to operate/It ceased operating) stop, halt, finish, leave off, suspend, quit, desist from.

celebrated adj (the celebrated painter) famous, renowned, well-known, notable, noted, distinguished, eminent, illustrious.

center n 1 (the store is in the center of the town) middle, heart. 2 (at the center of the quarrel) middle, hub, core, focus, focal point, hub, kernel.

central adj 1 (occupying a central position in the town) middle. 2 (central London) middle, inner. 3 (that is the central issue of the discussion) main, chief, principal, key, core, focal.

certain adj 1 (they are certain that he will arrive) sure, positive, confident, assured. 2 (failure is certain) sure, assured, inevitable, inescapable, (inf) in the bag. 3 (it is certain that they have already left) sure, definite, unquestionable, beyond question, indubitable, undeniable, incontrovertible. 4 (there is no certain remedy for the disease) sure, definite, definite, unfailing, dependable, reliable, foolproof, (inf) sure-fire. 5 (there were certain people who did not believe him) particular, specific.

chain n (a chain of events) series, succession, string, sequence, train, progression.

chance n 1 (they took a chance when they crossed the bridge—it is very rickety) risk, gamble, hazard. 2 (there is a good chance that we will get there on time) prospect, possibility, probability, likelihood. 3 (youou will not get another chance like that again) opportunity, opening. 4 (we haven't been in touch for years—we met again quite by chance) accident, coincidence, luck, fortuity. ◇

chance it to take a risk (I don't think I'll take an umbrella—I'll chance it).
have a sporting chance to have a reasonable chance of success (A great many people have applied for the job, but with his qualifications he must have a sporting chance).

change vb 1 (we have had to change the arrangements for the meeting) alter, modify, vary, reorganize, transform. 2 (she has changed com-pletely since I last saw her) alter, be trans-formed, metamorphose. 3 (she has changed jobs) switch. ◇

change one's tune to change one's attitude or intention (He disagreed with me completely on the issue but he changed his tune when he heard the facts).
change horses in midstream to change one's opinion, plans, sides, etc., in the middle of something (At the beginning of the campaign he was in favor of the new road but he changed horses in midstream and joined the protesters).

character n 1 (he seems to have changed in character since I first knew him/The character of the seaside village has altered) nature disposition, temperament, temper personality, make-up, ethos. 2 (we need a person of character in the job) strength backbone, integrity, uprightness, honesty. (his former teacher gave him a letter saying he was of good character/The incident damaged his character) reputation, name standing. 4 (one of the characters in Shakespeare's Hamlet) role, part, persona. (one of the village's characters) eccentric individual, (inf) card.

characteristic adj (he treated the occasion with characteristic arrogance) typical distinguishing, individual, particular.

charge vb 1 (the accused has been charged with murder) accuse, indict. 2 (the French force charged the enemy army) attack, rush, assault storm. 3 (the soldier charged the cannon) load fill. 4 (what did they charge for the car?) ask levy. 5 (tell them to charge it to my account) debit put down to, bill.

charge n 1 (the charge was one of murder accusation, indictment, arraignment. 2 (he ha charge of the accounts) responsibility, care protection, custody. 3 (what is the charge fo hiring the boat?) cost, price, fee, rate, amoun payment.

charm n 1 (she had a great deal of charm/The were taken with the charm of the village attractiveness, attraction, appeal, allure fascination. 2 (she has a tiny horseshoe as lucky charm) amulet, talisman. 3 (she has bracelet with charms on it) trinket, ornamen 4 (the sorcerer's charm) spell, magic. ◇

lead a charmed life regularly to have good fortune and to avoid misfortune, harm or danger (*The racing driver seems to lead a charmed life. He has been in many serious accidents but has never been badly injured*) <It is as though someone has cast a spell on him or her to ensure protection>.

work like a charm to be very effective, to work very well (*His efforts to get the old woman to like him worked like a charm*) <It is as though a sorcerer has cast a spell>.

hart *n* (*record the information in the form of charts*) table, graph, diagram.

hase *vb* **1** (*the hounds were chasing the fox*) run after, pursue, follow. **2** (*they chased away the burglar*) put to flight, drive away. ⋄

chase (after) rainbows to spend time and effort in thinking about, or in trying to obtain, things that it is quite impossible for one to achieve (*He is always applying for jobs that are away beyond his qualifications. He should concentrate on finding a job which he can do and stop chasing rainbows*).

heap *adj* **1** (*fruit is very cheap in the summer there*) inexpensive, low-cost, low-priced, reasonable, economical. **2** (*she wears cheap and gaudy jewelry*) inferior, shoddy, tawdry, trashy, tatty, cheap-jack, (*inf*) tacky.

heat *vb* **1** (*he cheated the old lady into giving him her savings*) deceive, trick, swindle, dupe, hoodwink. **2** (*his brother cheated him out of his inheritance*) deprive of, deny, thwart, prevent from.

heck *vb* **1** (*the police checked the car's tires*) examine, inspect, look at, scrutinize, test. **2** (*you must check that the door is locked*) confirm, make sure, verify. **3** (*they had to find some way to check the vehicle's progress*) stop, halt, slow down, delay, obstruct, impede.

heeky *adj* (*he was scolded for being cheeky to the teacher*) impertinent, impudent, insolent, disrespectful, forward .

heer *vb* **1** (*the crowds began to cheer*) applaud, shout hurrah, hurrah. **2** (*the arrival of her friends cheered her*) brighten up, buoy up, perk up, enliven, hearten, exhilarate, gladden, elate.

heerful *adj* **1** (*they were in a cheerful mood when the sun shone*) happy, merry, bright, glad, light-hearted, carefree, joyful. **2** (*she was wearing a dress in cheerful colors*) bright.

cherish *vb* **1** (*she cherishes memories of her father*) treasure, prize, hold dear, revere. **2** (*the children cherish their pets*) look after, care for, tend, protect. **3** (*they cherish hopes of success*) have, entertain, cling to, harbor.

chest *n* **1** (*he was wounded in the chest*) breast, sternum. **2** (*the miser kept his treasure in a chest*) box, trunk, casket, coffer, container, receptacle. ⋄

get (something) off one's chest to tell (someone) about (something) that is upsetting, worrying, or annoying one (*If you know something about the accident you must get it off your chest and tell the police*).

chew *vb* (*children told to chew their food thoroughly*) munch, crunch, champ, masticate. ⋄

chew the cud to think deeply about something (*You will have to chew the cud before coming to a decision on such an important issue*) <A reference to cows literally chewing the cud>.

chief *adj* **1** (*the chief man of the tribe*) head, leading, foremost, principal. **2** (*we must discuss the chief points in the report*) main, principal, most important, essential, prime, key, central.

child *n* **1** (*when he was a child*) young one, little one, youngster, young person, (*inf*) kid. **2** (*parents and their child*) offspring, progeny, son/daughter. ⋄

child's play something that is very easy to do (*With your experience you will find the work child's play*).

choice *n* **1** (*you have some choice in the matter—the meeting is not compulsory*) option, selection, preference. **2** (*there is a wide choice of fruit and vegetables in the supermarket*) selection, range, variety. **3** (*we have little choice but to go*) option, alternative, possibility. ⋄

Hobson's choice no choice at all; a choice between accepting what is offered or having nothing at all (*The hotel has only one room available for tonight. It's Hobson's choice, I'm afraid*).

choke *vb* **1** (*the murderer choked her to death*) strangle, throttle. **2** (*he choked to death on the smoke from the fire*) suffocate, smother, stifle, asphyxiate. **3** (*the drains are choked and had to be cleared*) block, clog, obstruct.

choose *vb* **1** (*the children were told to choose some candy from the store's selection*) pick, select, settle on, opt for, decide on. **2** (*he always does just as he chooses*) like, wish, want, prefer, fancy, desire.

chop *vb* **1** (*they began to chop the old trees down*) cut down, fell, hew, hack down. **2** (*they chopped up the vegetables for the soup*) cut up, dice, cube. ✧

chop and change to keep altering (something), to keep changing (something) (*I am supposed to be going on vacation with them but they keep chopping and changing the arrangements*).

get the chop (*inf*) **1** to be dismissed or discontinued (*Both he and his research project got the chop when the budget was cut*). **2** to be killed (*The gang made sure that their enemy got the chop*).

chronic *adj* **1** (*she suffers from a chronic illness*) long-standing, long-term, persistent, lingering. **2** (*they are chronic liars*) habitual, hardened, inveterate.

circle *n* **1** (*the children were asked to draw a circle*) ring, round, ball, globe, sphere, orb, loop, disc. **2** (*she has a large circle of friends*) group, set, crowd, ring, clique.

circuit *n* (*they had to run three circuits of the track*) round, lap, turn, loop, ambit.

circulate *vb* **1** (*they circulated information to the club members*) spread, distribute, issue, give out, disseminate, advertise. **2** (*blood constantly circulating*) flow, move around, go round, revolve, rotate.

circumstances *npl* (*the family lives in poverty-stricken circumstances*) state, situation, conditions.

civil *adj* **1** (*there had been a civil war in the country*) internal, domestic, home. **2** (*the army were in control but there is now a civil government*) civilian, nonmilitary. **3** (*she might have asked in a more civil way/They are very civil people*) polite, courteous, mannerly, well-mannered, refined, civilized, cultured.

civilized *adj* **1** (*peoples of the world who were not then civilized*) enlightened, educated, socialized. **2** (*she is a very civilized person*) cultivated, cultured, educated, sophisticated, refined, polished.

claim *vb* **1** (*he wrote in to claim his prize*) lay claim to, request, ask for, demand. **2** (*they claim that they had nothing to do with the crime*) assert, declare, maintain, profess, allege.

clash *vb* **1** (*the child clashed the cymbals*) strike, bang, clang, clatter, clank. **2** (*I have another appointment which clashes with my proposed meeting with you*) coincide, conflict. **3** (*one group of the committee clashed with the other*) be in conflict, have a disagreement, argue, quarrel, fight. **4** (*the curtains clashed horribly with the carpet*) jar, be incompatible, be discordant, (*inf*) scream.

class *n* **1** (*what appeals to the middle classes*) social division. **2** (*the awards are divided into four classes*) grade, rank, level, classification, category, set, group. **3** (*a lot consisting of one class of objects*) category, group, set, order, sort, type, variety, order, species, genre, genus. **4** (*the two pupils are in the same class*) study group. ✧

in a class by oneself, itself, *etc.*, **in a class of its,** *etc.*, **own** far better than other people or things of the same type, without equal (*No one ever beats her at the tennis club. She is in a class by herself*).

clean *adj* **1** (*the children had no clean clothes*) unsoiled, spotless, laundered. **2** (*the village is in need of a clean water supply*) pure, clear, unpolluted, untainted, uncontaminated. **3** (*the pupil asked for a clean piece of paper*) unused, blank. **4** (*people who live clean lives*) good, virtuous, upright, honorable, righteous ✧

a clean slate a record free of any discredit, an opportunity to make a fresh start (*He has paid the penalty for his crime and now that he is out of prison he hopes to start again with a clean slate*).

come clean to tell the truth about something, especially after lying about it (*He finally decided to come clean and tell the police about his part in the crime*).

clear *adj* **1** (*it was clear that she was ill*) obvious, evident, plain, apparent, unmistakable. **2** (*you must try to give a clear account of what happened*) plain, explicit, lucid, coherent, intelligible. **3** (*we had a clear day for our flight*) bright, fair, fine, cloudless. **4** (*a door made of clear glass*) transparent. **5** (*you have to stay five clear days*) whole, complete, entire. ✧

as clear as crystal extremely easy to gasp or understand (*It was as clear as crystal that she was lying*).

be in the clear to be free from suspicion (*The police suspected him of the crime but they have now discovered that he is in the clear*).

the coast is clear the danger or difficulty is now over (*She has quarreled with her father and does not want to go into the house while he is still there. Could you tell her when he has gone out and the coast is clear?*).

lever *adj* 1 (*he is a very clever pupil*) intelligent, bright, smart, gifted. 2 (*it was clever of them to open a new restaurant at that time*) smart, shrewd, astute, ingenious. 3 (*they are not very academic, but they are clever with their hands*) skillful, deft, handy, dexterous.

limate *n* 1 (*a cold climate*) weather, weather pattern. 2 (*an unstable political climate*) atmosphere, feeling, mood, spirit.

limb *vb* (*the boy climbed the ladder*) go up, ascend, mount, scale, clamber up.

ling *vb* 1 (*she began to cling to her mother's hand*) hold on to, grip, clutch, grasp, clasp. 2 (*they tried to change her mind, but she clings to her old beliefs*) stick to, hold to, stand by, adhere to.

lip *vb* (*she clipped her son's hair*) cut, trim, snip, crop, shear, prune. ✂

clip (someone's) wings to limit the freedom, power, or influence of (someone) (*She used to go out every night but her wings have been clipped since she has had a baby*) <A reference to the practice of clipping the wings of a bird to prevent it from flying>.

loak *n* 1 (*she wore a black evening cloak*) cape, mantle, shawl, wrap. 2 (*there was a cloak of secrecy surrounding the whole affair*) cover, screen, mask, mantle, veil, shield. ✂

cloak-and-dagger involving or relating to a great deal of plotting and scheming (*There was lot of cloak-and-dagger stuff surrounding the sacking of the chairman*) <The combination of a cloak and dagger suggests conspiracy>.

log *vb* 1 (*they thought that it was leaves that were clogging up the drains*) block, obstruct, stop up.

2 (*the sheer volume of correspondence has clogged up the system*) obstruct, impede, hinder, hamper.

close *vb* 1 (*they were asked to close the gate*) shut, fasten, secure, lock, bolt. 2 (*they closed the meeting with the chairman's speech*) end, bring to an end, conclude, finish, wind up. 3 (*the gap between the two runners closed*) narrow, lessen, grow less, dwindle. 4 (*they finally closed the bargain*) conclude, complete, settle, seal, clinch.

close *adj* 1 (*the cottages were very close to one another*) near. 2 (*they have been close friends for years*) intimate, devoted, close-knit, bosom. 3 (*you must pay close attention to what she says*) careful, attentive, intense, assiduous. 4 (*she was able to give a close description of the man who attacked her*) exact, precise, accurate. 5 (*the weather was very close*) humid, muggy, stuffy, airless, oppressive. 6 (*the whole family is extremely close with money*) mean, miserly, parsimonious, stingy. ✂

too close for comfort so near that one feels uncomfortable, worried, etc. (*That car behind us is a bit close for comfort*).
a close shave something that was only just avoided, especially an escape from danger, failure, etc. (*He had a close shave when his car skidded and hit a wall*).

clothing *n* (*they washed all their clothing*) clothes, garments, attire, apparel.

cloudy *adj* 1 (*under cloudy skies*) overcast, hazy, grey, leaden, heavy. 2 (*the liquid in the glass was cloudy*) opaque, milky, murky, muddy. 3 (*her vision is rather cloudy*) unclear, blurred, hazy.

clumsy *adj* 1 (*the antique wardrobe is a clumsy piece of furniture*) awkward, unwieldy, hulking, heavy, solid. 2 (*the child is clumsy and is always bumping into things*) awkward, ungainly, uncoordinated, blundering, maladroit, like a bull in a china shop.

coarse *adj* 1 (*the coat was made of a very coarse fabric*) rough, bristly, hairy, shaggy. 2 (*she prefers to bake with a coarse flour*) unrefined, unprocessed, crude. 3 (*they all have rather coarse features*) heavy, rugged. 4 (*he tells coarse jokes*) crude, vulgar, smutty, blue, dirty, bawdy, earthy, obscene, pornographic.

cold *adj* 1 (*it was a cold winter's day*) chilly, cool, freezing, icy, raw, frosty, glacial. **2** (*the children were feeling cold*) chilly, freezing, frozen, frozen to the marrow, shivery. **3** (*she seems rather a cold woman/She received them with rather a cold manner*) frigid, unresponsive, unemotional, indifferent, apathetic, distant, remote, reserved, detached. ▱

come in from the cold to be allowed to take part in some activity from which one was excluded before (*After months of not being selected for the team he has come in from the cold and has been offered a game this week*).

leave (someone) cold to fail to impress or excite (someone) (*The comedian was meant to be very funny but he left the audience cold*).

cold *vb* **1** (*the children were collecting firewood for a bonfire*) gather, accumulate, amass, pile up, stockpile, store, hoard. **2** (*they are collecting money for a children's charity*) gather, raise. **3** (*she collected the shoes from the repair store*) fetch, call for, go and get. **4** (*a crowd collected round the speaker*) gather, assemble, converge, congregate.

collide *vb* (*the cars collided*) crash, smash, bump.

color *n* **1** (*she has sweaters in several colors*) shade, hue, tint, tone. **2** (*people of different color*) skin-coloring, skin-tone, complexion, coloring. **3** (*the children were told to add a bit of color to their stories*) vividness, life, animation. ▱

change color to become either very pale or very flushed through fear, distress, embarrassment, anger, etc. (*She changed color when she realized that her crime had been discovered*).

show your true colors to reveal what you are really like after pretending to be otherwise (*She pretended to be his friend but she showed her true colors by reporting him to the boss*) <A reference to a ship raising its colors or flag to indicate which country or side it was supporting>.

combine *vb* **1** (*they combined the ingredients*) mix, blend, amalgamate, bind. **2** (*they have combined their resources to open a restaurant*) join, put together, unite, pool, merge. **3** (*they have combined to form one team*) get together, join

forces, team up, club together, cooperate associate, amalgamate, merge.

comfort *n* **1** (*they were poor but they now live ii comfort*) ease, cosiness, snugness, well-being affluence. **2** (*they tried to bring some comfort t the widow*) solace, consolation, condolence sympathy, support. **3** (*the children were a comfort to their mother*) solace, help, support ▱

cold comfort no consolation at all (*When one suffers misfortune it is cold comfort to be told that there are many people who are worse off than oneself*).

comic *adj* (*it was a comic situation*) funny, amusing, entertaining, diverting, droll, hilarious, farcical.

command *vb* **1** (*the king commanded them to go`* order, direct, instruct, bid. **2** (*he commands th force*) be in command of, be in charge of, control, rule, govern, direct, preside over, head lead, manage.

comment *n* (*the man passed comment on how il she looked*) remark, observation, statement view.

commercial *adj* **1** (*he has undertaken a commercial training*) business, trade, marketing. **2** (*the seaside village is becoming too commercial money-orientated, profit-orientated, merce nary, materialistic. **3** (*his business idea was no a commercial one*) profit-making, profitable.

commitment *n* **1** (*she has a great deal of commitment to her job*) dedication, devotion, involve ment. **2** (*he had many financial commitments responsibility, obligation, undertaking, duty, li ability.

common *adj* **1** (*fighting in the street is commor there*) usual, ordinary, everyday, regular, fre quent, customary, habitual, standard, routine commonplace, run-of-the-mill, traditional. : (*there is a common belief that the place i haunted*) widespread, universal, general, preva lent, popular. **3** (*things that appeal to the com mon people*) ordinary, normal, average, typica. run-of-the-mill. **4** (*it was a very common typ of watch*) ordinary, commonplace, common-or garden, unexceptional, undistinguished. **5** (*th politicians said that they were working for th common good*) communal, collective, public. (*they regard her as a very common girl*) vulga: coarse, uncouth, low. ▱

the common touch the ability to get on well with ordinary people (*He is a wealthy prince but most of his friends are ordinary students. He has the common touch*).

communicate *vb* **1** (*they were unable to communicate the information back to headquarters*) pass on, convey, make known, impart, report, relay. **2** (*we do not communicate with them anymore*) be in touch, be in contact, have dealings with. **3** (*in order to get a job in some industries, it is important to be able to communicate*) be articulate, be fluent, be coherent, be eloquent.

compatible *adj* **1** (*the couple are just not compatible*) suited, well-suited, like-minded, in tune, having rapport. **2** (*the two accounts of the incident are not at all compatible*) in agreement, consistent, in keeping.

compel *vb* (*they plan to compel him to go*) force, make, coerce, oblige, dragoon, pressurize, pressure.

compete *vb* **1** (*will they all compete in the race?*) take part, participate, go in for, be a competitor, be a contestant. **2** (*the two brothers are competing against each other in the final*) vie, contend.

competent *adj* (*they are very competent workers*) capable, able, proficient, efficient, skilful.

complaint *n* **1** (*they made a complaint about the standard of the food*) protest, criticism, grievance. **2** (*nothing ever pleases them—they are full of complaints*) grumble, (*inf*) grouse, (*inf*) gripe. **3** (*he has a stomach complaint*) illness, disease, disorder, ailment.

complete *vb* (*they failed to complete the job on time*) bring to completion, finish, conclude, accomplish, fulfil, achieve, execute, perform.

complete *adj* **1** (*he has the complete set of books*) whole, entire, full, total, intact, unbroken. **2** (*they think that she is a complete fool*) absolute, utter, thorough, total, out-and-out.

complicated *adj* (*it is a very complicated problem*) difficult, involved, complex, puzzling, perplexing.

compose *vb* **1** (*the children were asked to compose a poem*) make up, think up, create, concoct, invent, produce. **2** (*she was upset but tried to compose herself*) calm, calm down, quieten, control.

comprehend *vb* **1** (*unable to comprehend the scientific information*) understand, grasp, fathom, take in. **2** (*we cannot comprehend how*

they could behave like that) understand, imagine, conceive, fathom, perceive, get to the bottom of.

comprehensive *adj* (*his knowledge of the subject is quite comprehensive*) inclusive, thorough, extensive, exhaustive, full, broad, widespread.

compulsory *adj* (*attendance at school assembly is compulsory*) obligatory, mandatory, forced, essential, de rigueur.

conceal *vb* **1** (*she concealed the papers under her mattress*) hide, keep hidden, cover up, secrete, tuck away. **2** (*they tried to conceal their fears*) hide, cover up, disguise, mask.

conceited *adj* (*she is so conceited that she spends ages looking in the mirror*) vain, proud, arrogant, haughty, immodest, egotistical, (*inf*) big-headed.

concern *n* **1** (*we were full of concern for the safety of the missing children*) worry, anxiety, distress, apprehension. **2** (*the news was of concern to all parents*) interest, importance, relevance. **3** (*they were told that it was none of their concern*) business, affair, interest, responsibility, job, duty. **4** (*they are partners in a manufacturing concern*) business, firm, company, establishment.

concise *adj* (*a concise report that gave all the main points*) brief, short, succinct, terse, crisp, to the point.

conclude *vb* **1** (*we concluded the talks at midnight*) finish, end, close. **2** (*we were unable to conclude an agreement with the other side*) negotiate, bring about, pull off, clinch. **3** (*we were forced to conclude that he was lying*) come to the conclusion, deduce, gather, assume, suppose.

condemn *vb* **1** (*we condemned them for injuring children*) blame, censure, criticize, disapprove of, upbraid. **2** (*the murderer was condemned to death*) sentence.

condition *n* **1** (*housing conditions*) state, situation, circumstances, position. **2** (*the horses were in good condition*) form, shape, order, fitness, health. **3** (*they were allowed to rent the land but with certain conditions*) restriction, proviso, provision, stipulation, prerequisite, stipulation. **4** (*the old lady has a heart condition*) complaint, disorder, disease, illness, ailment, problem.

conduct *n* **1** (*the teacher reported the child's conduct to his parents*) behavior, actions. **2** (*their conduct of the economy was criticized*) direction, organization, management, control.

confess *vb* **1** (*she confessed when she heard that her friend was being blamed for the crime*) own up, admit guilt, plead guilty, accept blame, make a clean breast of it. **2** (*I must confess that I know nothing about it*) admit, acknowledge, concede, allow, grant.

confidence *n* **1** (*the people have no confidence in the government*) trust, faith, reliance. **2** (*competitors full of confidence*) self-confidence, self-assurance, poise, aplomb. **3** (*the girls exchanged confidences*) secret, private affair. ⇨

confidence trick the act of a swindler who gains the trust of someone and then persuades him or her to hand over money or something valuable (*She thought she was giving money to charity, but the collector was playing a confidence trick on her and kept the money for himself*).

conflict *n* **1** (*there has been conflict between the neighbors for years*) disagreement, discord, dissension, friction, strife, hostility, ill will. **2** (*the conflict between love and duty*) clash, friction. **3** (*there were many killed in the military conflict*) battle, fight, war, clash.

confuse *vb* **1** (*all the questions confused the child*) bewilder, puzzle, perplex, muddle. **2** (*his remarks just confused the situation*) muddle, mix up, jumble, obscure, make unclear. **3** (*the old man became confused in old age*) muddle, disorientate, befuddle. **4** (*she confused the two books, which looked alike*) mix up, mistake.

congratulate *vb* (*we congratulated them on the birth of their son*) wish joy to, offer good wishes to, compliment, felicitate.

connect *vb* **1** (*the gardener connected the garden hose to the tap*) attach, fasten, join, secure, clamp, couple. **2** (*only a path connects the two mountain villages*) link, join, unite. **3** (*the child connects his mother with security*) associate, link, equate, identify.

connection *n* **1** (*there is no connection between the crimes*) relationship, link, association, correspondence. **2** (*they had a meeting in connection with staff redundancies*) reference, relation. **3** (*one of her husband's connections*) relative, relation, kindred.

conscientious *adj* (*conscientious workers*) careful, diligent, painstaking, hardworking, assiduous, meticulous, punctilious.

consequence *n* **1** (*unable to foresee the consequences of their actions*) result, effect, upshot, outcome, repercussion. **2** (*it was a matter of no consequence*) importance, significance, note.

considerate *adj* (*she has very considerate children*) thoughtful, attentive, concerned, solicitous, obliging, kind, sympathetic.

consistent *adj* (*keep the room at a consistent temperature*) uniform, steady, constant, unchanging.

conspicuous *adj* **1** (*there had been conspicuous alterations to the city*) obvious, clear, noticeable, evident, apparent, discernible, visible. **2** (*her clothes were conspicuous by their bright colors*) obvious, striking, obtrusive, blatant, showy.

constant *adj* **1** (*keep it at a constant temperature*) uniform, even, regular, steady, stable, unchanging, invariable. **2** (*we have had a constant stream of enquiries*) continuous, uninterrupted, unbroken. **3** (*tired of her constant complaints*) never-ending, nonstop, endless, unending, incessant, continual, perpetual, interminable. **4** (*he was constant in his love for her*) faithful, devoted, staunch, loyal, true.

contact *vb* (*they tried to contact her parents*) get in touch with, communicate with, be in communication with.

container *n* (*containers to transport the food*) receptacle, vessel.

content *adj* (*he is quite content with his life*) contented, satisfied, pleased, happy, comfortable.

contest *n* (*the competitors in the contest*) competition, tournament, match, game.

continual *adj* **1** (*tired of their continual questions*) frequent, regular, repeated, recurrent, persistent, habitual. **2** (*there was continual noise from their flat*) continuous, endless, nonstop, incessant, constant, interminable.

continue *vb* **1** (*the road continues beyond the village*) go on, extend, keep on, carry on. **2** (*he may continue as chairman*) go on, carry on, stay, remain, persist. **3** (*we continued the search all night*) maintain, sustain, prolong, protract. **4** (*they continued looking for the ring*) go on, carry on, keep on, persist in, persevere in. **5** (*they stopped the search overnight but continued it at dawn*) resume, renew, recommence, carry on with.

continuous *adj* (*they have a continuous supply of fuel/upset by the continuous traffic noise*) constant, uninterrupted, unbroken, nonstop, endless, perpetual, incessant, unceasing, interminable, unremitting.

contract *n* (*a business contract*) agreement, arrangement, deal, settlement, pact, bargain, transaction.

ontrast *n* **1** (*the contrast between the two styles of government*) difference, dissimilarity, distinction, disparity. **2** (*he is a complete contrast to his father*) opposite, antithesis.

ontribute *vb* **1** (*they were all asked to contribute to the charity*) give, give a contribution, donate, give a donation to, subscribe to, help, give assistance to, assist, aid, support. **2** (*his leadership contributed to the success of the company*) add to, help, assist, have a hand in, be conducive to, be instrumental in.

ontrol *vb* **1** (*it is she who controls the budget of the company*) be in control of, be in charge of, manage, administrate, direct, govern, head. **2** (*the fire fighters could not control the fire*) contain, keep in check, curb, limit.

onvenient *adj* **1** (*select a time convenient for both of us*) suitable, appropriate, fitting, favourable, advantageous. **2** (*houses convenient for schools*) handy, within reach, within easy reach, accessible.

onvert *vb* **1** (*we converted the attic into another bedroom*) alter, adapt, make into, turn into, change into, transform. **2** (*convert pounds into dollars*) change, exchange. **3** (*the missionary converted the tribesmen to Christianity*) cause to change beliefs, reform, convince of. ▵

preach to the converted to speak enthusiastically in favor of something to people who are already convinced of its good points and are in favor of it (*You are preaching to the converted by singing the praises of that make of car to us. We have had one for years*) <A reference to someone trying to convert someone else to a religion that the person already believes in>.

onvict *n* (*the convict escaped*) prisoner, jailbird, criminal, felon, (*inf*) crook.

onvincing *adj* **1** (*her argument seemed very convincing*) persuasive, plausible, credible, cogent, powerful. **2** (*our team had a convincing victory*) decisive, conclusive.

ool *adj* **1** (*the weather was rather cool*) cold, coldish, chilly, fresh. **2** (*they wanted a cool drink*) cold, refreshing. **3** (*people who can remain cool in an emergency*) calm, composed, self-possessed, unexcited, unruffled, unperturbed, **4** (*she was rather cool when we went to see her*) aloof, distant, remote, offhand, unfriendly, chilly, unwelcoming, unresponsive, apathetic. **5** (*they were amazed at the cool way*

she stole the goods from the store) bold, audacious, brazen, impudent. ▵

as cool as a cucumber extremely calm and unexcited (*Everyone else was agitated when the fire started but she remained as cool as a cucumber*).

cool, calm and collected completely calm, in full control of one's emotions (*Even when her car broke down on the highway she remained cool, calm, and collected*).

cool one's heels to be kept waiting (*They were late for the meeting and I was left cooling my heels in the hall*).

cope *vb* **1** (*he found it difficult to cope when his wife died*) manage, carry on, get by, get along. **2** (*he had to cope with the money problems*) deal with, handle, contend with, manage.

copy *n* **1** (*give out copies of the report at the meeting*) duplicate, facsimile, photocopy, Xerox (trademark), Photostat (trademark). **2** (*it was not the original vase but a clever copy*) reproduction, replica, fake, sham, counterfeit. **3** (*buy several copies of the newspaper*) issue, example. ▵

carbon copy a person or thing that is extremely like another (*Her new boyfriend seems like a carbon copy of her previous one*) <A reference to carbon paper used in copying documents>.

correct *adj* **1** (*that is not the correct answer*) right, accurate, true, precise, exact, (*inf*) spot on. **2** (*what is the correct behavior on such an occasion?*) proper, suitable, fitting, seemly, appropriate, apt, accepted, usual.

cost *vb* **1** (*how much does a car like that cost?*) be priced at, sell for, come to, fetch. **2** (*you should get the mechanic to cost the repairs for you*) price, put a price on, estimate, evaluate. ▵

cost the earth to cost a great deal of money (*The meal at that restaurant costs the earth*).

at all costs no matter what must be done, given, suffered, etc., whatever happens (*You must stop her finding out at all costs*).

cosy *adj* (*a cosy room*) snug, comfortable, homely, homelike, secure.

count *vb* **1** (*pupils asked to count the row of numbers*) count up, add up, total, calculate, compute. **2** (*could you count the people as they enter the hall?*) keep a count of, keep a tally of, enumerate. **3** (*what he thinks does not count*) matter, be important, be of account, mean anything. **4** (*they counted themselves fortunate to have somewhere to live*) consider, regard, think, judge. ⋄

out for the count unconscious or deeply asleep (*The children were so tired after their long walk that they are still out for the count*) <A reference to boxing when a boxer who has been knocked down by his opponent has to get up again before the referee counts to 10 in order to stay in the match>.

count one's chickens before they are hatched to make plans which depend on something that is still uncertain (*You should not give up this job before you get the offer for the other one in writing. Don't count your chickens before they are hatched*).

count the cost to consider the risks, difficulties and possible losses involved in doing something (*He did not stop to count the cost before he drove without a licence. Now that he has been charged by the police he is counting the cost*).

counterfeit *adj* (*counterfeit banknotes*) fake, forged, fraudulent, sham, bogus, (*inf*) phoney.

country *n* **1** (*all the countries of the world*) nation, state, realm. **2** (*he would do anything for his country*) native land, homeland, fatherland, mother country. **3** (*they left the city to live in the country*) countryside, rural area. **4** (*the government should listen to what the country thinks*) public, general public, people, nation, population. **5** (*the country around there is very flat*) land, terrain, territory. ⋄

country cousin a person from the country, considered unsophisticated by a town or city dweller (*They regard her as a country cousin because she has never been to a pop concert*).

go to the country to hold a general election (*When the government was defeated on the bill the prime minister decided to go to the country*).

courage *n* (*the courage of the soldiers in battle*) bravery, valour, gallantry, heroism, boldness, daring. ⋄

Dutch courage courage that is not real courage but brought on by drinking alcohol (*He went out for a drink at lunchtime. He needed some Dutch courage before he asked the boss for an increase in salary*).

course *n* **1** (*in the course of a varied career*) progress, progression, development. **2** (*the ship was a bit off course*) route, way, track, direction, path, tack, orbit. **3** (*you should try a different course of action*) method, procedure, process, system, technique. **4** (*the car disappeared in the course of a few minutes*) duration, passage, lapse, period, interval, span. **5** (*the race was cancelled as the course was flooded*) track, circuit. ⋄

run its course to continue to its natural end, to develop naturally (*Your child will recover soon. The infection just has to run its course*).

stay the course to continue to the end or completion of (something) (*She has started on a new diet but we don't think that she will stay the course*).

courtesy *n* (*she showed a lack of courtesy towards elderly people*) politeness, civility, good manners, respect, deference.

cover *n* **1** (*there was a cover of snow over the ground*) covering, layer, coat, blanket, carpet, mantle, film. **2** (*they sought cover from the storm*) shelter, protection, refuge, sanctuary. **3** (*his business is just a cover for his drug-dealing*) cover-up, concealment, disguise, pretext, front, camouflage, screen, mask, cloak, veil. **4** (*the insurance policy provides cover against fire and theft*) insurance, protection, compensation. **5** (*the design on the cover of the book*) jacket, dust jacket, wrapper. **6** (*pull up the covers over the sleeping child*) bedcover, bedclothes, blankets, duvet.

cowardly *adj* (*he is too cowardly to complain*) timid, timorous, fearful, faint-hearted, lily livered, (*inf*) yellow, (*inf*) chicken.

crack *n* **1** (*there is a crack in this cup*) chip, chink. **2** (*there are several cracks in the wall*) fracture, split, crevice, slit. **3** (*the crack on the head made him pass out*) blow, knock, bump, smack, whack, thump, wallop. **3** (*they heard the crack of a pistol*) report, bang.

crash *vb* **1** (*the cymbals crashed*) clash, clang, clank, clatter, bang. **2** (*the car crashed into the wall*) bang into, bump into, hit, collide with. (*his son crashed his car*) smash, wreck, write off. **4** (*the chimney crashed on to the pavement*) topple, fall, plunge, tumble. **5** (*they listened to the sea crashing against the ship*) dash, batter, smash, break. **6** (*their business crashed*) fail, collapse, fold, go under, go to the wall.

credit *n* **1** (*he received little credit for a fine per* *formance*) praise, commendation, acclaim, tribute, applause, recognition. **2** (*the famous artist was regarded as being a credit to the town*) honor, asset, glory. **3** (*his credit is not good*) financial standing, solvency.

reep *vb* **1** (*creatures that creep along the ground*) crawl, slither, wriggle. **2** (*they began creeping up on the burglar*) steal, sneak, slink, tiptoe. ✧

give (someone) the creeps to arouse dislike, disgust or fear in (someone) (*This house is so dark and damp. It gives me the creeps*).

rime *n* **1** (*he was convicted of the crime of theft*) offence, misdeed, wrong, misdemeanor, felony. **2** (*crime is on the increase*) law-breaking, wrongdoing, felony, evil, vice.

riticize *vb* (*she is always criticizing him*) find fault with, blame, censure, pick holes in, (*inf*) slam, (*inf*) nit-pick.

rooked *adj* **1** (*a crooked stick*) bent, curved, twisted. **2** (*the old man had a crooked back*) deformed, misshapen. **3** (*that picture is crooked*) tilted, at an angle, askew, slanted, sloping. **4** (*a crooked salesman*) dishonest, dishonorable, unscrupulous, fraudulent.

ross *adj* **1** (*cross at the children's naughtiness*) angry, annoyed, irritated, vexed. **2** (*a cross old woman*) irritable, short-tempered, bad-tempered, ill-humoured, disagreeable, surly, crotchety, cantankerous.

rush *vb* **1** (*crush the grapes*) squash, squeeze, compress. **2** (*crush the stones*) break up, smash, pulverize, ground, pound. **3** (*a crushed dress*) crease, crumple, rumple, wrinkle, crinkle. **3** (*crush the rebellion*) quell, quash, suppress, subdue, put down, stamp out, overpower.

ry *vb* **1** (*to cry for your mother*) weep, shed tears, sob, wail. **2** (*cry out in pain*) call out, shout out, yell, scream. ✧

a far cry from (something) a long way from (something), very different from (something) (*His present wealthy lifestyle is a far cry from his poverty-stricken childhood*).

be crying out for (something) to be badly in need of (something) or to be badly in need of (something) being done (*The house is crying out for a coat of paint*).

cure *n* (*trying to find a cure for cancer*) remedy, treatment, panacea.

curious *adj* **1** (*we are curious to hear what happens at the meeting*) interested. **2** (*she is always curious about the affairs of her neighbors*) inquisitive, prying, meddlesome, snooping, (*inf*) nosy. **3** (*it was a curious sight*) odd, strange, unusual, peculiar, queer, weird, bizarre, mysterious.

current *adj* **1** (*the current fashion for pale-colored clothes*) present, present-day, contemporary, existing, modern. **2** (*those traditions are no longer current*) around, prevalent, common, general, popular.

curved *adj* (*a curved stick/a curved back*) bent, arched, bowed, crooked, rounded, humped.

custom *n* **1** (*the local customs are dying out*) tradition, practice, convention, ritual. **2** (*it was his custom to go for a walk before breakfast*) habit, practice, routine, wont, way. **3** (*he is grateful for their custom*) trade, business, patronage.

customer *n* (*shops trying to attract new customers*) client, patron, buyer, shopper, consumer.

cut *vb* **1** (*cut the meat into cubes*) cut up, chop, divide, carve, slice. **2** (*he cut his finger with a razor blade*) wound, gash, slash, pierce. **3** (*she cut her son's hair*) trim, clip, crop, snip, prune, shear. **4** (*the firm must cut its expenditure*) cut back on, reduce, decrease, curtail, slash. **5** (*the essay is too long—you must cut it*) shorten, abridge, condense, abbreviate. **6** (*she cut some paragraphs from the article*) cut out, delete, excise. **7** (*the driver cut the engine*) switch off, turn off. ✧

a cut above (someone *or* **something)** superior to (someone or something) (*The office workers think that they are a cut above the factory workers*).

cut it out to stop doing (something) (*The children were teasing the cat and I had to tell them to cut it out*).

cut up upset (*She was very cut up about the death of her dog*).

not cut out for (something) not naturally suited to (something) (*He was not cut out for the army*).

cynical *adj* (*she is cynical about our chances of success/They are very cynical people*) pessimistic, sceptical, doubting, distrustful, suspicious.

D

dagger *n* (*he killed his enemy with his dagger*) stiletto, knife. ⟿

look daggers at (someone) to look with great dislike or hostility at (someone) (*When she won the prize, her fellow contestants looked daggers at her*).

dainty *adj* **1** (*a dainty little girl*) petite, neat, graceful. **2** (*dainty china cups*) delicate, fine, exquisite.

damage *n* **1** (*there was a great deal of damage to his car*) harm, destruction, accident, ruin. **2** (*the incident caused damage to his reputation*) harm, injury, hurt, detriment, loss, suffering. ⟿

what's the damage? (*inf*) how much is it?, what does it cost? ("*What's the damage?*" *the diner asked the waiter*).

damp *adj* **1** (*they hung up their damp clothing to dry*) wet, soaking, sopping. **2** (*the ground was damp*) wet, soggy. **3** (*it was a damp day*) wet, rainy, drizzly, humid, muggy. ⟿

danger *n* **1** (*there was an element of danger in the job*) peril, jeopardy, risk, hazard. **2** (*pollution is a danger to lives*) risk, menace, threat, peril.

dangerous *adj* **1** (*they were in a dangerous situation*) risky, perilous, hazardous, precarious, insecure. **2** (*the police say that he is dangerous*) threatening, menacing, alarming, nasty.

dare *vb* **1** (*he did not dare climb the high tree*) have the courage, pluck up courage, have the nerve, risk, venture. **2** (*his friends dared him to jump from the high wall*) challenge, throw down the gauntlet.

daring *adj* (*a daring deed*) bold, adventurous, brave, courageous, plucky, reckless, rash.

dark *adj* **1** (*it was a very dark night*) black, pitch-dark, pitch-black, inky, dim, murky, unlit. **2** (*she has dark hair*) dark brown, brunette, black, jet-black. **3** (*they lived in the dark ages*) unenlightened, ignorant, uneducated, uncultivated, uncultured. **4** (*dark, dingy rooms*) gloomy, dismal, drab, dim, dingy, bleak, dreary, cheerless. **5** (*she was in a dark mood*) gloomy, depressed, morose. ⟿

a shot in the dark an attempt or guess based on very little information (*We don't know his address but it's worth taking a shot in the dark and trying the telephone book*).

keep (someone) in the dark to keep (someone) unaware or ignorant of (something) (*They kept their parents in the dark about their marriage*).

dawdle *vb* (*they dawdled on their way to school*) dally, loiter, linger, delay, tarry.

day *n* **1** (*she doesn't mind driving during the day*) daylight, daytime. **2** (*in this modern day*) time, age, era, epoch. ⟿

have had your *or* **its day** to be past the most successful part of your or its life (*I thought the movies had had their day when television came in but they are flourishing now*).

make (someone's) day to make (someone) very pleased or happy (*He really made his mother's day by sending her flowers*).

dead *adj* **1** (*her father is dead/the dead man*) deceased, departed, lifeless, gone. **2** (*dead village traditions*) extinct, gone, perished. (*dead matter*) without life, lifeless, inanimate. **4** (*her fingers were dead with cold*) numb, benumbed, without feeling. **5** (*the small town is dead at night*) boring, dull, uneventful, unexciting. ⟿

a dead duck a person or thing that is very unlikely to survive or continue (*The proposed new traffic scheme is a dead duck. The department does not have the money for it*).

as dead as a dodo completely dead or extinct, no longer popular or fashionable (*They are trying to revive village traditions that have been as dead as a dodo for years*) <A reference to a flightless bird that has been extinct since 1700>.

over my dead body in the face of fierce opposition from me (*The authorities will pull my house down over my dead body*).

deadly *adj* **1** (*he drank a deadly poison*) fatal, lethal, toxic, poisonous. **2** (*he was struck* *deadly blow*) fatal, mortal, lethal, dangerous, life-threatening, terminal. **3** (*they were deadly enemies*) fierce, hostile, grim, hated.

deaf *adj* **1** (*the accident left him deaf*) with impaired hearing, stone-deaf, as deaf as a post. **2** (*they were deaf to her pleas*) indifferent to, unmoved by, oblivious to, heedless of. ✧

fall on deaf ears to go unnoticed or unheeded, not to be listened to (*There is no point in offering her any advice. It will only fall on deaf ears*).
turn a deaf ear to (something) to refuse to listen to (something), to take no notice of (something) (*He turned a deaf ear to her pleas for help*).

deal *vb* **1** (*she was unable to deal with the problem*) cope with, handle, attend to, sort out, tackle, manage. **2** (*they need a book that deals with the early history of the town*) be about, have to do with, concern, discuss. **3** (*he does not know how to deal with children*) act toward, behave toward, cope with, manage. **4** (*he was asked to deal the cards*) distribute, give out, share out, divide out, dole out. **5** (*they dealt him a fatal blow*) give, deliver, administer.

deal *n* **1** (*a business deal*) arrangement, agreement, transaction, contract, pact. **2** (*he did not get a fair deal*) treatment, usage. ✧

a done deal something that has already been decided (*I was going to apply for the manager's position, but it seems it's going to the assistant manager—it's a done deal, apparently*).
a good deal *or* **a great deal of (something)** a great amount of (something) (*He is in a great deal of danger*).
a raw deal unfair treatment (*The younger son got a raw deal when his father's estate was divided*).

dear *adj* **1** (*he lost his dear wife*) beloved, loved, darling, cherished. **2** (*she was a dear child*) sweet, adorable, lovable, darling, attractive, winning, enchanting. **3** (*it was a dear car*) expensive, costly, high-priced, valuable, exorbitant.

death *n* **1** (*death was caused by strangling*) dying, demise, decease, loss of life, passing away,

killing, murder, slaughter. **2** (*there were many deaths in the flu epidemic*) fatality, dead people. **3** (*the close of the firm marked the death of his hopes*) end, finish, destruction, ruin. ✧

at death's door extremely ill, dying (*She seemed to be at death's door but she has made a complete recovery*).
be in at the death to be present at the end or final stages of something (*The factory closed today. It was sad to be in at the death*) <Refers originally to being present at the death of the prey in a hunt>.

decay *vb* **1** (*the food had begun to decay*) go bad, rot, decompose, putrefy, spoil. **2** (*the Roman Empire decayed*) decline, degenerate, deteriorate, wane, ebb.

deceitful *adj* **1** (*she is a very deceitful child*) lying, untruthful, dishonest, false, insincere, untrustworthy, underhand. **2** (*he got into the house by deceitful means*) underhand, fraudulent, crooked, dishonest, cheating, crafty, sneaky.

deceive *vb* (*his friends did not realize that he was deceiving them*) delude, mislead, take in, hoodwink, pull the wool over (someone's) eyes, swindle, dupe.

decent *adj* **1** (*he seemed a decent enough fellow*) honest, honorable, trustworthy, worthy, civil. **2** (*her behavior was not considered decent*) seemly, proper, appropriate, decorous, pure. **3** (*he earns a decent salary*) reasonable, ample, good, adequate, sufficient.

decide *vb* **1** (*they decided to stay*) come to a decision, reach a decision, make up your mind, resolve, commit yourself. **2** (*that decided the matter*) settle, resolve, determine. **3** (*the judge will decide the case*) judge, make a judgment on, make a ruling on, give a verdict.

decision *n* **1** (*they finally reached a decision*) resolution, conclusion, determination, settlement. **2** (*the judge will announce his decision*) judgment, verdict, ruling. **3** (*he is a man of decision*) decisiveness, determination, resolution, resolve, firmness.

decisive *adj* **1** (*her personality was the decisive factor in her getting the job*) deciding, determining, conclusive, critical, crucial. **2** (*they need someone decisive in charge of the firm*) determined, resolute, firm, forceful.

decline *vb* **1** (*they declined the invitation*) turn down, refuse, say no to. **2** (*the influence of the leader has declined*) get less, lessen, decrease, diminish, dwindle, fade. **3** (*the Roman Empire was declining then*) deteriorate, degenerate.

decorate *vb* **1** (*they decorated the Christmas tree*) adorn, ornament, embellish, trim. **2** (*they have begun to decorate the house*) paint, paper, renovate, (*inf*) do up. **3** (*the soldier was decorated for bravery*) honor, give a medal to, cite.

decrease *vb* **1** (*the number of the pupils at the school is decreasing*) grow less, lessen, diminish, dwindle, drop, fall off, decline. **2** (*they have decreased the number of places available at the school*) reduce, lower, lessen, cut back, curtail. **3** (*the storm finally decreased*) die down, abate, subside.

deed *n* **1** (*a dishonest deed*) act, action, feat, exploit, undertaking, enterprise. **2** (*the deeds to the house*) document, contract, title deed.

deep *adj* **1** (*they dug a deep hole in the garden*) yawning, cavernous. **2** (*they have a deep affection for each other*) intense, fervent, ardent, heart-felt. **3** (*he has a deep distrust of doctors*) profound, extreme, intense, great. **4** (*he has a very deep voice*) low, low-pitched, bass, booming, resonant. **5** (*she always wears clothing in deep colors*) rich, strong, vivid, intense, dark. ✧

be thrown in at the deep end to be put suddenly into a difficult situation of which you have no experience (*The trainee journalist was thrown in at the deep end and set out on a story on his first morning on the newspaper*) <A reference to the deep end of a swimming pool>.

go off the deep end to become mentally unstable (*His father went off at the deep end and spent some time in a psychiatric hospital*) <A reference to the deep end of a swimming pool>.

defeat *vb* **1** (*the army finally defeated the enemy*) beat, conquer, vanquish, win a victory over, get the better of, overcome. **2** (*the parliamentary motion was defeated*) reject, overthrow, throw out, outvote.

defect *n* **1** (*a defect in the material*) fault, flaw, imperfection, blemish. **2** (*they tried to find the defects in the system*) deficiency, weakness, shortcoming, failing, inadequacy, snag.

defense, defence (*Br, Cdn*) *n* **1** (*walls built as a defense for the house*) protection, safeguard, guard, security, cover, fortification, barricade. **2** (*a report in defense of the system*) justification, vindication, argument, apology, exoneration.

defer *vb* (*they had to defer the date of the meeting*) put off, postpone, delay, hold over, adjourn.

deficiency *n* **1** (*she suffers from vitamin deficiency*) lack, want, shortage, dearth, insufficiency, scarcity, deficit. **2** (*it was the only deficiency in the system*) defect, flaw, fault, imperfection, failing, shortcoming, drawback, snag.

definite *adj* **1** (*they have no definite plans*) clear-cut, fixed, established, precise, specific, particular. **2** (*it is not definite that he is leaving*) certain, sure, settled, decided, fixed.

defy *vb* **1** (*they decided to defy their parents and go to the movies*) disobey, disregard, ignore. **2** (*the army defied the enemy*) withstand, resist, stand up to, brave, confront.

degree *n* **1** (*there was a marked degree of improvement in her work*) extent, amount, level, measure. **2** (*the dancers reached a high degree of expertise*) level, stage, grade, point. ✧

be one degree under to feel slightly unwell (*She is not at work—she is feeling one degree under*).

give (someone) the third degree to subject (someone) to intense questioning, especially by using severe or harsh methods (*The enemy officers gave the captured soldiers the third degree*).

dejected *adj* (*she was feeling dejected after her friends left*) miserable, wretched, downcast, depressed, sad, despondent.

delay *vb* **1** (*we have had to delay our vacation*) postpone, put off, put back, defer, adjourn, put on ice. **2** (*they were delayed by heavy traffic*) hold up, hold back, detain, hinder, impede, hamper, obstruct.

deliberate *adj* (*his murder was quite deliberate*) intentional, on purpose, planned, calculated, prearranged, premeditated.

delicate *adj* **1** (*she was very delicate as a child*) weak, frail, sickly, unwell, infirm. **2** (*cups made of delicate china*) fine, exquisite, fragile, thin. **3** (*it was a very delicate matter*) difficult, sensitive, tricky. **4** (*the situation required delicate handling*) careful, tactful, discreet, diplomatic.

delicious *adj* (*they serve delicious food at the restaurant*) tasty, flavorsome, appetizing, luscious, (*inf*) scrumptious, (*inf*) yummy.

delight *n* (*she was filled with delight at seeing her friend again*) joy, pleasure, gladness, happiness.

delightful *adj* **1** (*we had a delightful evening at the theater*) pleasant, enjoyable, entertaining, amusing, diverting. **2** (*she is a delightful person*) charming, engaging, attractive, nice.

deliver *vb* **1** (*he delivers morning newspapers*) distribute, bring, take round. **2** (*they delivered the little girl to her mother*) hand over, convey, present. **3** (*she delivered a moving speech/deliver a sigh of relief*) give, give voice to, utter, speak, express, pronounce. **4** (*they were able to deliver the prisoners*) free, set free, liberate, release.

demand *vb* **1** (*the workers demanded a wage rise*) call for, ask for, request, press for, insist on, clamor for. **2** (*the work demanded patience*) call for, require, need, take, involve.

demanding *adj* (*they have very demanding jobs*) difficult, taxing, exacting, hard, tough.

demolish *vb* (*they began to demolish the old buildings*) knock down, tear down, pull down, level, flatten, raze, dismantle.

demonstrate *vb* **1** (*she demonstrated how to change an electric plug*) show, illustrate, teach, explain. **2** (*her expression demonstrated how she was feeling*) show, indicate, display, exhibit, manifest. **3** (*the documents demonstrated that she was telling the truth*) show, establish, prove, confirm, verify. **4** (*they planned to demonstrate against the new road*) protest, stage a protest.

dense *adj* **1** (*they were lost in a dense forest*) thick, close-packed, impenetrable. **2** (*he was too dense to follow the instructions*) stupid, thick, dim, slow.

deny *vb* **1** (*he began to deny that he had said it*) contradict, refute, retract, negate, disagree with. **2** (*the committee might deny their request*) refuse, reject, turn down, decline, dismiss.

depart *vb* **1** (*we have to depart at dawn*) leave, go, take your leave, take yourself off, set out, start out, (*inf*) make tracks. **2** (*results that depart from the norm*) deviate, diverge, differ, vary.

depend *vb* **1** (*the firm depends on him to look after the place*) rely on, count on, bank on, lean on, put your faith in. **2** (*the success of the business will depend on the order*) be dependent on, hinge on, turn on, hang on, rest on, revolve around.

deport *vb* (*they decided to deport the refugees*) banish, expel, exile, evict, transport.

depreciate *vb* (*the houses have depreciated in value*) decrease, lessen, lower.

depressed *adj* (*he was feeling depressed having lost his job*) miserable, downcast, low in spirits, melancholy, gloomy, glum, dejected, sad, unhappy.

depth *n* **1** (*measure the depth of the water*) deepness. **2** (*it was a book of great depth*) profoundness, profundity, wisdom, insight, understanding, weight, importance. ▽

be out of your depth to be in a situation that you cannot cope with (*The child is out of depth in that class. The work is too hard for him*) <Refers literally to being in water deeper than you can stand up in or swim easily in>.
in depth thoroughly (*The committee must study the problem in depth before coming to a decision*).
plumb the depths of (something) to reach the lowest level of unhappiness, misfortune, etc. (*He plumbed the depths of misery when his wife died*).

deprived *adj* (*deprived children brought up in poverty*) poor, needy, in want, disadvantaged.

derelict *adj* (*derelict farmhouses*) dilapidated, tumbledown, rundown, ramshackle, broken-down, abandoned, forsaken.

descend *vb* **1** (*she descended the stairs gracefully*) come down, go down, climb down. **2** (*the hot air balloon descended*) go down, come down, drop, fall, sink, plummet. **3** (*they descended from the train with their baggage*) get off, get down, alight, dismount.

describe *vb* **1** (*he was asked to describe the incident*) give a description of, give an account of, give details of, recount, relate, report, explain, tell about, narrate. **2** (*they have described her as beautiful*) call, label, designate.

desert *vb* **1** (*a man who had deserted his family*) abandon, forsake, leave, turn your back on, leave in the lurch, throw over. **2** (*the army are looking for the soldiers who deserted*) abscond, run away, quit, defect.

deserve *vb* (*he deserves reward*) merit, be worthy of, warrant, rate, be entitled to, have a claim on.

design *n* **1** (*the architect showed the committee the designs for the new building*) plan, blueprint, sketch, drawing, outline. **2** (*the fabric designs are very modern*) pattern, motif, style. **3** (*it was a cunning design to break into the building*) plan, scheme, plot, stratagem, aim. **4** (*they did it with the design of stealing money*) aim, intention, goal, objective, purpose. ⇨

have designs on (someone *or* something) to wish to possess (someone or something, usually belonging to someone else) (*I think he has designs on my job*).

desire *vb* **1** (*she desires some comfort in her old age*) wish, want, long for, yearn for, crave, covet, hanker after, (*inf*) have a yen for. **2** (*they desire to leave at once*) wish, want, feel like.

desolate *adj* **1** (*on the edge of a desolate moor*) bare, barren, bleak, wild. **2** (*an area full of desolate farms*) deserted, forsaken, solitary, lonely, isolated. **3** (*she was desolate when he went away*) miserable, wretched, sad, unhappy, dejected, forlorn, lonely.

despair *vb* (*he has despaired of ever getting a job*) lose hope, give up hope, lose heart, be discouraged, give up, throw in the towel.

desperate *adj* **1** (*it was a desperate attempt to save the town*) daring, risky, hazardous, wild, reckless, rash, imprudent. **2** (*some desperate criminals have escaped*) wild, violent, lawless, reckless. **3** (*they are in desperate need of more food*) urgent, pressing, critical, crucial, serious, dire, great. **4** (*they are desperate for money*) in great need of, in want of. **5** (*the family is in a desperate state*) dreadful, shocking, appalling, deplorable, intolerable. **6** (*help required for desperate people*) despairing, hopeless, despairing, distressed, wretched.

despise *vb* (*she despises people who tell lies*) scorn, look down on, shun, disdain, sneer at, mock, hate, loathe.

despondent *adj* (*the pupil was despondent when she heard that she had failed the exam*) downcast, cast down, low in spirits, disheartened, discouraged, disappointed, gloomy, melancholy, wretched, miserable.

destroy *vb* (*the bridge was destroyed in the war*) demolish, knock down, pull down, tear down, wreck, smash, shatter, blow up, wipe out.

detach *vb* **1** (*she detached the hood from her coat*) unfasten, remove, separate, uncouple, free. **2** (*she detached herself from her group to join us*) move away from, separate, dissociate.

detail *n* **1** (*the police try to notice every detail at the scene of the crime*) particular, point, circumstance, feature, aspect. **2** (*draw up a general plan and not bother with the details*) particular, fine point, minutia.

detect *vb* **1** (*they thought that they detected a smell of gas*) notice, note, make out, spot, identify, distinguish, sense, observe. **2** (*the police were detecting the crime*) investigate, probe.

deter *vb* (*they hope the stiff sentence will deter others from committing such a crime*) put off, prevent, stop, discourage, restrain, scare off.

determined *adj* **1** (*he is a very determined person and will probably win*) firm, resolute, tenacious, single-minded, strong-willed, dogged, persistent, stubborn, inflexible. **2** (*they are determined to leave*) set on, intent on, bent on.

detest *vb* (*the rivals detest each other*) hate, loathe, abhor, feel aversion to, feel hostility to.

detrimental *adj* (*the incident was detrimental to his reputation*) harmful, damaging, hurtful, disadvantageous, destructive.

develop *vb* **1** (*children quickly developing into adults*) grow, turn, mature. **2** (*modern cities developing rapidly*) grow, expand, enlarge, spread, progress, evolve. **3** (*they are trying to develop a scheme for expansion*) originate, set in motion, establish, form, institute. **4** (*they have the beginnings of a plan but they have to develop it*) elaborate, work out, enlarge on, flesh out. **5** (*the child has developed a cough*) acquire, get, contract. **6** (*a quarrel developed between the two women*) begin, start, commence, happen, come about, break out.

device *n* **1** (*a handy device for use in the kitchen*) gadget, appliance, utensil, implement, tool, apparatus, contrivance, contraption. **2** (*they thought of a cunning device to get into the building*) ploy, ruse, trick, stratagem, scheme, dodge, plan.

devil *n* **1** (*a story about the devil and hell*) Satan, Beelzebub. **2** (*she dreamt that she was being pursued by devils*) demon, evil spirit, fiend. **3** (*the slave's master was a devil*) brute, savage, monster, beast, fiend, scoundrel, villain. **4** (*the child is a little devil*) scamp, rascal, rogue. ⇨

be between the devil and the deep blue sea to be faced with two possible courses of action each of which is as unacceptable, difficult, dangerous, etc., as the other (*He is between*

the devil and the deep blue sea. If he stays in his present job he will have to take a big cut in salary. If he leaves he will have to move to the other side of the country to get a job).
speak of the devil here is the very person that we have just been speaking about or referred to (*Speak of the devil! Here is Jim and we were just talking about him playing in the game tomorrow*).
there will be the devil to pay there will be serious trouble (*There will be the devil to pay when your father sees the broken window*) <From legends in which bargains are struck with the devil by which you could have immediate worldly success, happiness, and riches, if you gave him your soul at a later date when he asked for it>. ⟳

devious *adj* (*they are very devious people/They will get what they want only by devious means*) underhand, cunning, sly, crafty, wily, deceitful.
devoted *adj* **1** (*the king's devoted followers*) loyal, faithful, true, staunch, dedicated, committed, constant. **2** (*time devoted to hobbies*) set aside, allocated, assigned, allotted.
devout *adj* **1** (*devout churchgoers*) pious, religious, godly, holy, churchgoing. **2** (*it was their devout hope that he would be present*) sincere, deep, profound, earnest, heart-felt, fervent, genuine.
diagnose *vb* (*the doctor diagnosed mumps*) identify, recognize, distinguish, detect, pronounce.
dialog, dialogue (*Br, Cdn*) *n* (*a dialog between the presidents*) conversation, talk, exchange of views, discussion, conference, tête-à-tête.
die *vb* **1** (*the doctors think that he is going to die*) pass away, breathe your last, lose your life, meet your end, (*inf*) give up the ghost, (*inf*) kick the bucket, expire. **2** (*all hope died when they heard the news*) end, come to an end, vanish, disappear, pass, fade. **3** (*the car's engine died*) stop, fail, break down, peter out. ⟳

die hard to take a long time to disappear or become extinct (*He is trying to give up smoking but old habits die hard*).
die with your boots on to die while you are still working (*He did not want to retire. He would have wanted to die with his boots on*).
never say die never give up hope (*It is going

to be difficult to pass the exam but never say die—just work as hard as you can*).

differ *vb* **1** (*their tastes differ completely*) be different, be dissimilar, be unlike, vary, diverge. **2** (*the two sides still differ on the best course of action*) disagree, dissent, be at variance, be in dispute, be in conflict, clash, argue, quarrel. **3** (*the scientist's results differ from the norm*) vary, diverge, deviate, depart from, contradict. ⟳

agree to differ to agree not to argue about something any more since neither party is likely to change his or her opinion (*Having spent many hours arguing about what is the right course of action, they finally decided that it was a waste of time and agreed to differ*).

difference *n* **1** (*there was marked difference between the two sisters*) dissimilarity, distinction, variation, contrast. **2** (*they had several differences over the years*) difference of opinion, disagreement, dispute, clash, argument, quarrel, row.

bury your differences to forget about past disagreements (*The two members of the board hold different views but in the interests of the company they decided to bury their differences*).
split the difference to agree on an amount of money halfway between two amounts, especially between the amount that one person wants to charge for something and the amount of money that someone else is willing to pay for it (*If he is asking $200 for the table and you only want to pay $100 why don't you split the difference and offer him $150?*).

different *adj* **1** (*their tastes in clotheing are very different*) dissimilar, unlike, at variance, contrasting. **2** (*with her new hairstyle she looks completely different*) changed, altered, transformed. **3** (*she wears a different sweater every day*) another, fresh. **4** (*the dress is available in different colors*) various, several, varied, assorted. **5** (*she was looking for something a bit different to wear to the wedding*) unusual, out of the ordinary, uncommon, distinctive, special, singular, extraordinary, rare. ⟳

a different kettle of fish a completely different set of circumstances (*I know that we turned down his first suggestion, but this one is a completely different kettle of fish*).
different strokes for different folks different people have different tastes or views (*My sister likes to go travel whereas I like to stay at home – different strokes for different folks*).

difficult *adj* **1** (*working on the building site was very difficult work*) hard, strenuous, arduous, demanding, taxing, laborious, tiring. **2** (*it is a difficult problem to solve*) hard, complicated, complex, involved, intricate, problematic, tough. **3** (*I felt that we had arrived at a difficult time*) inconvenient, ill-timed, unfavorable. **4** (*the family has gone through a difficult period*) hard, tough, distressing, grim. **5** (*she has always been a difficult child*) troublesome, unmanageable, willful.

dig *vb* **1** (*dig the earth before planting potatoes*) break up, work, turn over, loosen. **2** (*the prisoners dug a tunnel to try to escape*) dig out, excavate, hollow out, gouge out, scoop out, burrow, mine. **3** (*she dug her friend in the ribs at the lecture to wake him up*) prod, jab, poke, push, elbow. **4** (*the newspaper reporter is trying to dig up facts about the politician's private life*) search, probe, investigate, research, delve. ✧

dig your heels in to show great determination, especially in order to get your own wishes carried out (*There's no point in trying to persuade him to attend the meeting. He's digging his heels in and refusing to go*).
dig your own grave to be the cause of your own misfortune or ruin (*It is a pity that he lost his job but in fact he dug his own grave. He kept taking days off and was hardly ever there*).

dignity *n* **1** (*she was anxious not to lose her dignity in front of people*) pride, self-esteem, self-respect. **2** (*the dignity of the royal procession*) stateliness, formality, decorum, majesty, grandeur, nobility.
dilapidated *adj* (*an area full of dilapidated houses*) rundown, tumbledown, brokendown, ramshackle, crumbling, in disrepair, decaying, neglected.
diligent *adj* (*diligent pupils studying hard*) conscientious, industrious, hardworking, assiduous, painstaking, studious, zealous.

dim *adj* **1** (*the light from the street lamps was dim*) faint, feeble, weak. **2** (*people frightened to walk along the dim corridors*) dark, gloomy, badly lit, dingy. **3** (*they saw a dim shape in the mist*) vague, indefinite, ill-defined, blurred, shadowy, fuzzy. **4** (*they have only a dim recollection of the incident*) vague, indistinct, hazy, blurred, confused. **5** (*he failed to understand because he is a bit dim*) stupid, dense, (*inf*) dumb, dull, slow-witted. **6** (*his prospects of getting a job are rather dim*) gloomy, unpromising, depressing, discouraging. ✧

take a dim view of (something) to look with disapproval on (something) (*The boss takes a dim view of people making private telephone calls from the firm's phones*).

dingy *adj* (*they live in run-down dingy houses*) dim, dark, gloomy, dull, drab, murky, dirty, discolored, shabby.
direct *adj* **1** (*the direct route to the city*) straight, shortest. **2** (*a very direct manner/a direct statement*) frank, straightforward, blunt, forthright, clear, plain, candid, open.
direction *n* **1** (*they complained about his direction of the project*) administration, management, government, leadership, supervision, conduct, handling, control, guidance. **2** (*you must obey the teacher's directions*) order, command, instruction, bidding. **3** (*the climbers have gone in the wrong direction*) route, way, course, path.
dirt *n* **1** (*they cleaned the dirt from their boots*) grime, mud, muck, filth, dust. **2** (*piles of dirt in the garden*) soil, earth. **3** (*she is given to spreading dirt about her neighbors*) scandal, slander, gossip. ✧

do (someone) dirt to treat (someone) in an unfair, dishonest, or disloyal way (*My friend did me dirt by going out with my girlfriend*).
treat (someone) like dirt to treat (someone) with contempt, to treat (someone) very badly (*The head of production treats his staff like dirt*).

dirty *adj* **1** (*their boots were dirty*) unclean, soiled, grubby, grimy, muddy, mucky, filthy, dusty, messy, stained, polluted. **2** (*that was a dirty trick*) nasty, unfair, dishonest, dishonorable, deceitful, underhand, fraudulent. ✧

do (someone's) dirty work to do something wrong or unpleasant in behalf of someone else (*The manager has asked his deputy to do his dirty work and sack some of the workers*).

disability n (*help for people with some form of disability*) incapacity, learning difficulty, learning disability, infirmity, handicap.

disadvantage n **1** (*discover the disadvantages of the system*) drawback, snag, weak spot, weakness, flaw, defect, fault, handicap, obstacle, minus. **2** (*children who suffer from financial disadvantage*) deprivation, hardship. **3** (*the incident turned out to be to their disadvantage*) detriment, disservice, harm, damage, injury, hurt, loss.

disadvantageous adj (*the circumstances were disadvantageous to them*) unfavorable, adverse, unfortunate, detrimental, damaging.

disagree vb **1** (*the two sides had talks but they still disagreed*) differ, diverge, be at variance, be at odds. **2** (*the police said that the stories of the witnesses disagreed*) differ, be dissimilar, be unlike, be different, vary, clash, conflict, diverge. **3** (*the children were always disagreeing*) argue, quarrel, bicker, wrangle.

disagreeable adj **1** (*it was a very disagreeable experience*) unpleasant, nasty, horrible, foul, dreadful, revolting. **2** (*he is a disagreeable old man*) bad-tempered, cross, irritable, surly, churlish, rude, nasty, unpleasant.

disappear vb **1** (*the sun disappeared behind the cloud*) vanish, recede, fade, retire, retreat. **2** (*traditions that have now disappeared*) die out, be no more, end, pass, fade, perish, become extinct.

disappoint vb **1** (*we hated to disappoint the children by canceling the picnic*) let down, dishearten, upset, sadden. **2** (*we had to disappoint their hopes*) thwart, frustrate, baulk, foil, baffle, hinder, obstruct, hamper, impede.

disapprove vb (*she disapproves of the young people's behavior*) find unacceptable, dislike, be against, be displeased by, frown on, blame.

disaster n **1** (*earthquakes and other natural disasters*) catastrophe, calamity, tragedy, mishap, setback, reversal. **2** (*the play was a disaster*) failure, flop, (*inf*) bomb.

discard vb (*discard old newspapers*) throw away, throw out, dispose of, jettison, scrap, dump.

discharge vb **1** (*the pipe was discharging a foul-smelling liquid*) give off, send out, emit, exude, excrete, ooze, leak. **2** (*several workers were discharged*) dismiss, sack, get rid of, lay off, (*inf*) fire, (*inf*) ax. **3** (*she did not discharge her duties*) carry out, do, perform, execute. **4** (*he discharged a firearm*) let off, fire, shoot. **5** (*the prisoner has been discharged*) set free, free, release, let go, acquit, clear, reprieve.

disclose vb (*she finally disclosed her reasons for leaving*) make known, reveal, divulge, tell, communicate, impart.

discomfort n **1** (*she experiences some discomfort in her eye*) ache, pain, soreness, twinge, irritation, throbbing. **2** (*the discomfort of traveling long journeys in a very small car*) inconvenience, difficulty, trouble, bother, drawback.

discordant adj (*she has a discordant voice/discordant sounds*) harsh, strident, shrill, grating, jarring.

discourage vb **1** (*the young man was discouraged by failing his driving test*) dishearten, dispirit, deject, depress, disappoint, demoralize. **2** (*they tried to discourage the woman from applying for the job*) deter, dissuade, talk out of, advise against, restrain.

discover vb **1** (*the police discovered a new clue*) uncover, find, come across, bring to light, turn up, unearth. **2** (*the scientists have discovered a new cancer drug*) invent, devise, originate. **3** (*we discovered that he was very sick!*) learn, find out, come to realize.

discreet adj (*behavior that was far from discreet/a few discreet remarks*) careful, cautious, prudent, tactful, diplomatic, wise.

discriminate vb **1** (*children should be taught to discriminate between right and wrong*) distinguish, differentiate, separate. **2** (*she said that her employers discriminated against women*) show prejudice toward, show bias toward, be biased toward.

discuss vb (*the committee discussed the problem*) talk about, confer about, debate, consider, deliberate.

disease n (*the old man is suffering from a brain disease*) illness, disorder, complaint, condition, malady, ailment.

disgrace n **1** (*he found it difficult to endure the disgrace of being in prison*) shame, humiliation, dishonor. **2** (*the pupil is in disgrace for playing truant*) disfavor, discredit, disrepute.

disgraceful adj **1** (*their behavior was disgraceful*) shameful, shameless, dishonorable, shocking, outrageous, unseemly, improper. **2** (*the pupil's work is disgraceful*) very bad, appalling, dreadful, terrible, shocking.

disguise vb **1** (*they disguised themselves as police* officers) dress up, camouflage. **2** (*he tried to disguise the scar on his face*) conceal, hide, cover up, mask, screen.

disgust *vb* **1** (*the thought of eating snails disgusts them*) revolt, repel, put off, sicken, nauseate, (*inf*) turn off. **2** (*they were disgusted by the behavior of the teenagers*) scandalize, shock, appall, outrage, offend.

disheveled, dishevelled (*Br, Cdn*) *adj* (*they were disheveled after their long journey*) untidy, unkempt, bedraggled, messy, tousled.

disinterested *adj* **1** (*the judges of the competition must be disinterested*) unbiased, unprejudiced, impartial, detached, objective, neutral, fair. **2** (*they were completely disinterested in the subject*) uninterested, bored, indifferent, apathetic.

dismal *adj* **1** (*feeling dismal because he was ill and had to stay in bed*) miserable, wretched, despondent, gloomy, sad, unhappy. **2** (*they plan to redecorate the dismal room*) dark, dim, dull, dingy, drab, dreary, bleak, cheerless.

dismiss *vb* (*he was dismissed from his job*) sack, give notice to, discharge, lay off, lay off, (*inf*) fire.

disobey *vb* (*they disobeyed the rules*) defy, disregard, flout, contravene, infringe, violate.

disorderly *adj* **1** (*they tried to tidy the disorderly office*) untidy, messy, cluttered, disorganized, out of order, chaotic. **2** (*the police tried to control the disorderly crowds*) unruly, rowdy, boisterous, rough, wild, lawless, rebellious.

display *vb* **1** (*they displayed the goods in the store window*) exhibit, put on show, show, present, set out. **2** (*the young gymnasts displayed their expertise*) demonstrate, exhibit, show, show off, flaunt. **3** (*the accused displayed no emotion as he was sentenced by the judge*) show, exhibit, indicate, manifest, show evidence of, demonstrate.

dispose:— dispose of *vb* (*they disposed of the garbage by burying it*) get rid of, throw away, throw out, discard, jettison, scrap, dump.

dispute *n* (*the two friends had a dispute over money*) argument, quarrel, row, wrangle, clash, altercation, feud.

disrupt *n* (*the protesters disrupted the meaning*) disturb, interrupt, interfere with, obstruct, impede, hamper.

dissolve *vb* **1** (*salt dissolves in water*) liquefy, melt. **2** (*they both dissolved in tears*) break into, be overcome by. **3** (*they have decided to dissolve their partnership*) end, terminate, break up, discontinue, wind up. **4** (*the crowds dissolved when the police arrived*) break up, split up, disband, separate, go their separate ways.

distance *n* **1** (*measure the distance between the two trees*) space, gap, interval, span, stretch. **2** (*they were concerned about the distance of the house from the town*) remoteness. ⟳

go the distance to complete something successfully, to last until the end of something (*It was such a long university course that we thought that he would not go the distance, but he got his degree last week*) <A reference to a racehorse finishing the course>.

keep your distance from (someone *or* something) not to come too close to (someone or something), not to be too friendly with (someone) (*It is advisable for teachers to keep their distance from pupils*).

within striking distance of (something) reasonably close to, or very close to (something) (*He was within striking distance of the town when he collapsed*).

distant *adj* **1** (*the children like to hear stories of distant places*) far-off, remote, out-of-the-way, outlying, far-flung. **2** (*in distant times*) long ago, far-off. **3** (*the two villages are 10 miles distant from each other*) away, apart, separate. **3** (*I have only a distant recollection of what happened*) dim, vague, faint, hazy, indistinct. **4** (*she is rather a distant person*) aloof, detached, remote, reserved, unfriendly, unsociable, uncommunicative, standoffish, unapproachable.

distinct *adj* **1** (*there was a distinct resemblance between the two crimes*) clear, clear-cut, plain, obvious, marked, definite, unmistakable, manifest. **2** (*there are two distinct issues to be discussed*) separate, individual, different.

distinguish *vb* **1** (*he found it difficult to distinguish some colors from others*) tell apart, tell the difference between, differentiate, discriminate. **2** (*they thought that they could distinguish a dim shape in the mist*) make out, detect, discern, notice, see, observe. **3** (*the soldier distinguished himself in the battle*) make famous, bring fame to, bestow honor on.

distress *n* **1** (*the child's distress on being separated from her parents*) suffering, pain, agony, misery, wretchedness, heartache, sorrow, sadness. **2** (*homeless people in distress*) hardship, adversity, misfortune, need, want, poverty, deprivation.

distribute *vb* **1** (*they distributed advertising leaflets on the street*) issue, pass out, pass round, circulate. **2** (*the teacher distributed books to the children*) give out, hand out, allocate, issue, allot, dispense.

district *n* (*they live in a district at the edge of the city*) area, region, place, locality, neighborhood, sector.

disturb *vb* **1** (*they don't like being disturbed when they are at work*) interrupt, distract, bother, trouble, pester, intrude on, interfere with, harass, (*inf*) hassle. **2** (*the cleaner was asked not to disturb the documents on the desk*) disarrange, disorganize, muddle, confuse. **3** (*the news of the closure of the school disturbed them*) concern, worry, upset, fluster, perturb.

dive *vb* (*he dived into the water to save the drowning child*) jump, leap, drop, nose-dive, plunge.

diverge *vb* (*the roads diverge at the end of the village*) separate, divide, split, part, fork, branch off.

divide *vb* **1** (*you should divide the rope in two*) sever, cut, split, separate. **2** (*the road divides suddenly*) diverge, separate, divide, split, part, fork, branch off. **3** (*they divided the cake out among the children*) distribute, deal out, share out, allocate, allot, apportion.

divine *adj* **1** (*divine beings*) godly, heavenly, celestial, holy. **2** (*taking part in divine worship*) religious, holy, spiritual. **3** (*the bride looked divine*) lovely, beautiful, charming, wonderful, marvelous.

doctor *n* (*they called a doctor when the child was sick*) medical practitioner, hospital doctor, consultant, specialist, intern. ⌖

just what the doctor ordered exactly what is required at the time (*When they arrived back hot and thirsty, a cold drink was just what the doctor ordered*).

document *n* (*the documents relating to the business deal*) paper, official paper, certificate, record, deed.

dogged *adj* (*they admired her dogged determination*) determined, resolute, stubborn, obstinate.

dominant *adj* **1** (*he is the dominant member of the group*) supreme, controlling, influential, authoritative, domineering. **2** (*It was the dominant issue on the agenda*) chief, main, principal, leading, predominant.

domineering *adj* (*he is so domineering that everyone is afraid of him*) overbearing, arrogant, masterful, tyrannical, bullying, (*inf*) bossy.

doom *n* (*people who are always predicting doom*) catastrophe, disaster, destruction, ruin, downfall.

door *n* (*stand at the door of the block of apartment building*) doorway, entrance, entry. ⌖

darken (someone's) door to go into (someone's) house (*He told his son never to darken his door again*).

on (someone's) doorstep very close to where (someone) lives (*Naturally, they do not wish a freeway built on their doorstep*).

show (someone) the door to make (someone) leave your house or premises (*Some of the guests at the party were causing such a disturbance that he was forced to show them the door*).

doting *adj* (*doting parents*) indulgent, adoring, devoted, fond.

double *adj* **1** (*a double yellow line*) duplicate, two-fold, in pairs. **2** (*a double thickness of cloth*) twofold, folded, two-ply. **3** (*his words had a double meaning*) dual, ambiguous, ambivalent, two-edged. ⌖

on the double extremely quickly (*We are very late—we had better get there on the double*) <A military term, literally at twice the normal marching speed>.

doubt *n* **1** (*they are having doubts about his efficiency as a leader*) misgiving, mistrust, distrust, reservations. **2** (*they are full of doubts about what they ought to do*) uncertainty, indecision, hesitation, irresolution.

doubtful *adj* **1** (*it is doubtful that he will be present*) uncertain, in doubt, unsure. **2** (*the genuineness of the signature is doubtful*) open to question, questionable, uncertain, dubious, debatable, inconclusive. **3** (*the meaning of the word is doubtful*) dubious, unclear, ambiguous, obscure. **4** (*his parents thought that he was associating with doubtful people*) dubious, questionable, suspicious, suspect.

down *adj* **1** (*they were feeling down at the end of the vacation*) downcast, dejected, depressed, gloomy, miserable, sad, unhappy. **2** (*the computer system is down*) malfunctioning, inoperative, not working. ⌖

down the drain completely wasted (*Something went wrong with the computer and I lost all my*

material. *It was a day's work down the drain*).
down under Australia or New Zealand (*He has many relatives down under*).
get down to (something) to begin to work at (something) in earnest (*The exams are coming up and we'll have to get down to some studying*).
be down on (someone or something) to be very hostile or opposed to (someone or something) (*The teacher seems to be down on the new student*).

downright *adv* (*she was downright rude*) utterly, completely, totally, absolutely, thoroughly, positively.
drab *adj* (*they live in very drab surroundings*) dingy, dull, dismal, dreary, gloomy, cheerless, dim, dark.
drag *vb* 1 (*they dragged the fallen trees from the forest*) haul, pull, draw, tug, yank, tow. 2 (*time dragged*) move slowly, crawl.
drastic *adj* (*a drastic remedy*) extreme, severe, rigorous, harsh, radical, dire.
draw *vb* 1 (*draw a house*) sketch, make a picture of, make a diagram of, portray, depict, design. 2 (*draw a chair up to the table*) pull, drag, haul, tow, tug, yank. 3 (*he drew a sword from its sheath*) take out, bring out, withdraw, extract, produce. 4 (*her hat drew a lot of attention*) attract, catch, captivate. 5 (*draw the curtains*) pull, close, shut. 6 (*they drew level with the other car*) move, go, proceed.
dreadful *adj* 1 (*it was a dreadful accident*) terrible, frightful, horrible, grim, awful, shocking, appalling, ghastly, gruesome. 2 (*what a dreadful man!*) nasty, unpleasant, disagreeable, horrible, frightful, odious.
dream *vb* 1 (*the child seems to dream every night*) have dreams, have nightmares. 2 (*he said that he saw a ghost, but he must have been dreaming*) see things, hallucinate, imagine things. 3 (*she was dreaming instead of concentrating on her work*) daydream, be in a reverie, be lost in thought, be in a brown study. 4 (*he would not dream of upsetting her*) think, consider.
dreary *adj* (*they live in dreary surroundings*) dismal, drab, dingy, dull, gloomy, cheerless, gloomy, dark.
dress *vb* 1 (*they were all dressed in black*) clothe, attire, array, garb. 2 (*she was late and had to dress quickly*) get dressed, put on clothes. 3 (*the nurse

dressed the wound) cover, bandage, bind up. 4 (*the children dressed the Christmas tree*) decorate, adorn, ornament, trim, deck. ✧

be dressed to kill, be dressed to the nines to be dressed in your smartest and most eye-catching clothing to attract attention (*She was dressed to kill when she went to the party*).

drink *vb* (*she drank the water quickly*) swallow, gulp down, partake of, quaff, (*inf*) swig, slug.
drip *vb* (*water began to drip from the faucet*) trickle, dribble, plop, leak, splash, ooze, exude.
drive *vb* 1 (*young people learning to drive a car*) operate, steer, handle, direct, manage. 2 (*they came by train but we drove here*) go by car, come by car, travel by car, motor. 3 (*they drove the cattle to the milking parlor*) press, urge, push, prod, goad, spur. 4 (*poverty drove them to steal*) force, compel, oblige, make, pressure, coerce. 5 (*they began to drive posts into the ground to make a fence*) hammer, ram, bang, plunge, sink. ✧

be driving at (something) to be suggesting or trying to say (something) (*We weren't sure what he was driving at, but we thought that he might be suggesting that we were lying*).
drive a coach and horses through (something) to destroy (an argument, etc.) completely by detecting and making use of the weak points in it (*The defense lawyer was able to drive a coach and horses through the prosecution's case against his client*) <A reference to the fact that the defects or holes in the argument are so large that you could drive a coach and horses through them>.

drop *vb* 1 (*the hot-air balloon dropped out of the sky*) drop down, descend, fall, plummet, plunge. 2 (*water dropped from the branches*) fall, drip, trickle, dribble, plop. 3 (*she dropped her baggage and fell into a chair*) let fall, let go. 4 (*he has decided to drop piano lessons*) give up, stop, abandon, discontinue, cease, end, finish. 5 (*she has dropped her latest boyfriend*) leave, forsake, abandon, jilt, (*inf*) dump. 6 (*house prices have dropped*) fall, lessen, decrease, decline, dwindle, plummet, plunge. ✧

drop off to fall asleep (*Grandfather usually drops off in his chair after dinner*).

drop out to withdraw from school, university, etc., or from society (*After his first year at college he decided to drop out/He reacted against his wealthy parents' lifestyle and decided to drop out and live rough*).
let (something) drop, let it drop to let (something) be known by accident, or supposedly by accident (*Her father found out that her boyfriend was married, but felt that he shouldn't let it drop to his daughter*).

drowsy *adj* (*people often feel drowsy after a heavy meal*) sleepy, tired, weary, lethargic, sluggish.

drug *n* 1 (*medical scientists have discovered a new cancer drug*) medical drug, medicine, medication, cure, remedy. 2 (*concern over young people who are addicted to drugs*) addictive drug, narcotic, opiate, barbiturate, (*inf*) dope.

drunk *adj* (*drunk people staggering down the road*) intoxicated, under the influence, tipsy.

dry *adj* 1 (*the dry regions of the world*) arid, parched, scorched, dehydrated. 2 (*dry autumn leaves*) withered, shriveled, wilted. 3 (*the cheese has become very dry*) dried out, hard, stale. 4 (*the lecture was very dry and the audience was bored*) boring, dull, uninteresting, tedious, monotonous, tiresome. ♥

a dry run a practice attempt, a rehearsal (*The principal wanted to have a dry run of the next day's school concert*).
as dry as dust extremely dull and boring (*The students thought that the play which they had to read was as dry as dust*).
dry up to forget what you were going to say (*The bride's father started to give a speech at the wedding and then dried up*).

dual *adj* (*he plays a dual role in the firm*) double, duplicate.

dubious *adj* 1 (*he is dubious about going to the meeting*) doubtful, unsure, uncertain, hesitant, irresolute, wavering. 2 (*the result is still dubious*) doubtful, uncertain, unsure, unsettled, up in the air. 3 (*he seems rather a dubious character*) suspicious, suspect, questionable, untrustworthy.

dull *adj* 1 (*it was a dull day*) overcast, cloudy, dark, gloomy, dismal, bleak. 2 (*she always wore dull colors*) drab, dreary, dark, somber. 3 (*we heard the dull thud of something falling*) muffled, muted, indistinct. 4 (*the professor gave a very dull talk*) boring, uninteresting, dry, tedious, monotonous.

dumb *adj* 1 (*he has been dumb since birth*) without speech, mute. 2 (*they were struck dumb at the beauty of the view*) speechless, silent, wordless, mute, inarticulate, at a loss for words. 3 (*he is so dumb that he did not get the job*) stupid, unintelligent, dense, slow-witted.

duplicate *vb* 1 (*she was asked to duplicate the documents*) copy, photocopy, reproduce. fax. 2 (*there does not seem to be work around and workers are duplicating tasks*) repeat, do over again.

duplicity *n* (*his duplicity in swindling the old lady*) deceit, deceitfulness, double-dealing, trickery, guile, dishonesty.

durable *adj* 1 (*the durable effects of the drug*) long-lasting, lasting, persisting, permanent, 2 (*the boots must be durable*) long-lasting, lasting, hard-wearing, sturdy, strong, tough.

dust *vb* 1 (*dust the furniture*) wipe, brush, clean, mop. 2 (*she dusted the cake with sugar*) sprinkle, dredge, scatter. ♥

bite the dust to suffer a defeat (*The senator I supported bit the dust at the last election*).
throw dust in (someone's) eyes to attempt to confuse or deceive (someone) (*They threw dust in the police officer's eyes by saying that they had seen an intruder in the garden, but this was just to give the real burglar time to get away*) <Dust temporarily blinds people if it gets into their eyes>.

duty *n* 1 (*he has a sense of duty toward his parents*) responsibility, obligation. 2 (*he failed to carry out his duties and was sacked*) job, task, chore, assignment. 3 (*they had to pay duty on the goods which they brought into the country*) tax, levy, tariff, excise.

dwindle *vb* (*their hopes are dwindling as time goes on*) grow less, lessen, decrease, diminish, fade.

E

eager *adj* **1** (*eager students*) keen, enthusiastic, avid, earnest, zealous, fervent. **2** (*people eager to learn/eager for information*) avid for, anxious for, longing for, yearning for, desirous of. ⟳

eager beaver a very enthusiastic and hardworking person (*The new student is a real eager beaver who works late into the night*) <Beavers are small animals that build dams with great speed and skill and are traditionally thought of as being very hardworking>.

early *adv* **1** (*get up early*) at dawn, at daybreak, with the lark, at cockcrow. **2** (*visitors who arrived early*) too soon, ahead of time, prematurely. **3** (*it is very important that you arrive early for your interview*) in good time, ahead of schedule, punctually.
early *adj* **1** (*an early reply*) prompt, speedy, quick, rapid, fast, without delay. **2** (*an early crop*) advanced, forward, premature, precocious. **3** (*early man*) primitive, prehistoric, primeval. ⟳

the early bird catches the worm a person who arrives early or acts promptly is in a position to gain an advantage over others who are later or slower to act.

earn *vb* **1** (*earn an extremely high salary*) make, get, receive, obtain, draw, clear, take home. **2** (*earn the respect of his colleagues*) gain, win, attain, secure, merit, deserve.
earnest *adj* **1** (*an earnest young man who studies hard*) serious, solemn, grave, intense, staid, studious, diligent. **2** (*make an earnest plea for mercy*) fervent, ardent, passionate, intense, heartfelt, sincere, urgent.
earnest:—in earnest 1 (*they were in earnest about walking all the way home*) serious, sincere, not joking. **2** (*they set to work in earnest*) zealously, wholeheartedly, with a will, with commitment, determinedly.
earnings *npl* (*she tries to save part of her earnings*) income, salary, wages, pay.
earth *n* **1** (*earth, moon, and stars*) globe, world, planet. **2** (*the earth and the sky*) land, ground. **3** (*children getting covered in earth from playing in the garden*) soil, dirt. ⟳

bring (someone) back down to earth to make (someone) aware of the practical nature of life or a situation and so stop dreaming or imagining (*She was daydreaming about a vacation in the sun when the sight of the pouring rain brought her back down to earth*).

earthenware *n* (*a store selling local earthenware to the tourists*) pottery, crockery, stoneware, ceramics.
earthly *adj* **1** (*a book about creatures that were not earthly*) terrestrial. **2** (*earthly pleasures*) worldly, non-spiritual, material. **3** (*they have no earthly chance of success*) feasible, possible, conceivable, likely, realistic.
earthy *adj* **1** (*the earthy smell of a newly dug garden*) soillike, dirtlike. **2** (*tell jokes that were rather earthy*) bawdy, crude, coarse, indecent.
ease *n* **1** (*wealthy people leading a life of ease*) comfort, contentment, wealth, prosperity, luxury. **2** (*do the job with ease*) effortlessness, facility, no difficulty, deftness, adroitness. **3** (*ease of manner is important in his job*) naturalness, relaxedness, composure.
ease *vb* **1** (*receive some pills to ease the pain*) lessen, reduce, diminish, relieve, soothe. **2** (*the storm finally eased*) lessen, grow less, abate, moderate, slacken off. **3** (*a letter would ease his mother's mind*) comfort, give comfort to, calm, soothe. **4** (*try to ease the part of the machine into the right position*) guide, maneuver, inch, edge, steer, slide.
easy *adj* **1** (*an easy task*) simple, effortless, uncomplicated, straightforward, undemanding. **2** (*she had an easy mind when she knew her family was safe*) at ease, untroubled, unworried, at peace, calm, tranquil, composed. **3** (*an easy manner*) natural, relaxed, easygoing, composed, unreserved, (*inf*) laid-back. ⟳

as easy as falling off a log extremely easy (*She was worried about having to use the computer, but she discovered that it was as easy as falling off a log*).

easygoing *adj* (*he is too easygoing to get upset about anything*) even-tempered, relaxed, placid, happy-go-lucky, tolerant, understanding, undemanding, patient, (*inf*) laid-back.

eat *vb* **1** (*eat sweets*) consume, devour, chew, swallow, gulp down, bolt, wolf, (*inf*) tuck into, scoff. **2** (*what time do you eat?*) have a meal, take food. **3** (*acid had eaten away the material*) erode, corrode, wear away, rot. ✧

have (someone) eating out of your hand to have (someone) doing everything that you wish, because they like or admire you or are trying to flatter you (*That class is meant to be very wild, but the teacher has them eating out of her hand*) <From an animal that is so tame that it will take food from your hand>.

eavesdrop *vb* (*the child tried to eavesdrop on her parents' conversation*) listen in on, overhear.

ebb *vb* **1** (*when the tide ebbed*) go out, flow back, retreat, draw back, recede. **2** (*the popularity of the president ebbed*) decline, lessen, decrease, dwindle, fade away, peter out.

eccentric *adj* (*the villagers think he is eccentric/ She has an eccentric way of dressing*) strange, peculiar, odd, queer, weird, outlandish, bizarre, zany, freakish, unconventional, (*inf*) off-beat, (*inf*) way-out.

echo *vb* **1** (*the sound echoed around the hall*) resound, reverberate, ring. **2** (*she simply echoed what her father said*) repeat, reproduce, copy, imitate, parrot.

economical *adj* **1** (*have to be economical with fuel so that it will last the winter*) sparing, thrifty, careful, frugal. **2** (*an economical form of transport*) inexpensive, reasonable, low-cost, low-price, cheap. ✧

be economical with the truth not to tell the whole truth, or to lie (*We did not believe the figures which the politician quoted—we thought that he was being economical with the truth*).

economize *vb* (*since prices have gone up we will have to economize*) cut back, spend less, cut expenditure, tighten your belt, draw in your horns.

ecstasy *n* (*her idea of ecstasy was to lie on a beach all day*) bliss, rapture, joy, elation, delight, happiness, pleasure.

ecstatic *adj* (*they were ecstatic when their team won the championship*) elated, in raptures, overjoyed, joyful, jumping for joy, on cloud seven, in seventh heaven.

edge *n* **1** (*the edge of the road*) side, verge. **2** (*the edge of the town*) border, boundary, perimeter. ✧

have the edge on (someone or **something)** to have an advantage over (someone or something), to be superior to (someone or something) (*He has the edge over the other basketball players because he is so tall/This washing machine definitely has the edge over the other one*).

take the edge off (something) to make (something) less sharp, to reduce (something) (*An apple took the edge off our appetite/Her smile took the edge off her criticism*).

edgy *adj* (*she felt edgy when her children came home late*) on edge, anxious, nervous, tense, uneasy, worried, stressed out, (*inf*) nervy, (*inf*) uptight.

edible *adj* (*food that is scarcely edible*) eatable, consumable, digestible, palatable.

edict *n* (*by edict of the emperor/obey the official edicts*) order, decree, command, law, rule, act, statute.

edit *vb* **1** (*they edited the manuscript that he had written*) revise, correct, alter, adapt, emend. **2** (*he edits the daily newspaper*) be the editor of, be in charge of, direct.

edition *n* (*last week's edition of the magazine*) issue, number, publication.

educate *vb* (*children who were educated at the little local school*) teach, instruct, school, train.

educated *adj* (*the kind of books that educated people might read*) well-read, knowledgeable, literate, cultivated, cultured.

education *n* (*receive a good education*) schooling, teaching, instruction, training, tuition.

eerie *adj* (*hear an eerie noise in the middle of the night*) strange, unnatural, uncanny, ghostly, frightening, (*inf*) scary.

effect *n* **1** (*it is difficult to say what the effect of the changes will be*) result, consequences, outcome, influence, impact. **2** (*I like the general effect of the color scheme*) impression, impact.

effect:—take effect *vb* **1** (*new regulations taking effect from next week*) come into force, come into operation, begin, become law, become valid. **2** (*when the sleeping pills take effect*) work, be effective.

effective *adj* **1** (*an effective government*) successful, competent, capable, efficient, productive. **2** (*an effective color scheme*) striking, impressive, attractive. **3** (*rules that will be effective from next year*) valid, in force, in operation, operative.

effects *npl* (*her personal effects*) belongings, possessions, goods, things, baggage.

effervescent *adj* (*effervescent soft drinks*) sparkling, fizzy, bubbly, carbonated.

efficient *adj* **1** (*a very efficient worker*) capable, competent, able, effective, productive, skillful, organized. **2** (*an efficient system*) effective, well-organized, well-run, streamlined.

effigy *n* (*effigies of ancient kings*) likeness, image, statue, bust.

effort *n* **1** (*work requiring a great deal of effort*) exertion, power, energy, work, force, application, struggle, strain, (*inf*) elbow grease. **2** (*she passed the driving test at her second effort*) attempt, try, endeavor, (*inf*) shot, (*inf*) go.

effortless *adj* (*he made lifting the heavy weights seem effortless*) easy, simple, uncomplicated, trouble-free, unexacting, undemanding.

effrontery *n* (*she had the effrontery to go straight to the front of the line*) impudence, impertinence, (*inf*) nerve.

egg, egg on *vb* (*his friends egged him on to steal the apples*) encourage, urge, spur, goad, prod, prompt. ⟳

be left with egg on your face to be left looking foolish (*She boasted that she would win easily, but she lost and was left with egg on her face*) <From having forgotten to wipe your face after having got your breakfast egg smeared on it>.
lay an egg to be particularly unsuccessful (*Her first novel was a bestseller, but her second really laid an egg*).

eject *vb* **1** (*he was ejected from the club for trying to start a fight*) throw out, remove, banish, evict, (*inf*) kick out, (*inf*) chuck out. **2** (*she was ejected from the plane*) thrust out, throw out, propel.

eke:—eke out *vb* **1** (*eke out the lamb stew by adding a lot of vegetables*) stretch out, increase, supplement. **2** (*we must try to eke out our fuel supplies*) be economical with, be sparing with,

economize on. **3** (*the poor peasants eke out a living from the soil*) scrape, scratch.

elaborate *adj* **1** (*elaborate carvings/elaborate patterns*) detailed, intricate, complex, ornate, fancy, showy, fussy, (*inf*) flashy. **2** (*draw up an elaborate plan*) complicated, detailed, complex, involved, intricate.

elaborate *vb* (*asked to elaborate on his suggestion*) expand, enlarge, flesh out.

elapse *vb* (*a long time elapsed before they met again*) pass, go by, roll by, slip by.

elastic *adj* **1** (*elastic materials*) stretchy, springy, pliant, flexible, rubbery. **2** (*our vacation plans are elastic*) flexible, fluid, adaptable, adjustable.

elated *adj* (*they were elated at their victory*) overjoyed, jumping for joy, joyful, delighted, gleeful, ecstatic, on cloud seven, in seventh heaven.

elation *n* (*their elation at their victory*) joy, joyfulness, delight, glee, ecstasy.

elbow *vb* (*elbow him out of the way to get to the front of the crowd*) push, jostle, shoulder, knock, bump. ⟳

elbow grease hard physical work (*New polishes are all very well, but it will take elbow grease to get a good shine on that furniture*).
give (someone) the elbow (*inf*) to get rid of (someone), to dismiss (someone) from a job or to end a relationship with (someone) (*He has given his girlfriend the elbow and is going out with someone else*).

elderly *adj* (*the elderly couple next door*) oldish, old, advanced in years.

elderly:—the elderly *npl* elderly people, older people, senior citizens, retired people (*be kind to the elderly*).

elect *vb* **1** (*elect a team captain*) choose, select, pick, opt for, appoint, decide on. **2** (*elect an senator*) vote for, choose.

election *n* (*vote in an election for a new leader*) ballot, poll.

electrify *vb* (*he electrified the audience with his performance*) excite, thrill, rouse, stir, move, fire.

elegance *n* (*admire the elegance of the model*) stylishness, style, grace, gracefulness, fashion, fashionableness.

elegant *adj* (*the elegant women at the wedding*

party) stylish, graceful, fashionable, tasteful, artistic.

element *n* **1** (*the main elements of the project*) component, ingredient, constituent, factor, feature, detail. **2** (*the natural element of the lion*) environment, habitat, sphere. ▽

in your element in a situation in which you are very happy or at your best (*She is in her element when she is organizing something*) <A reference to the four elements of medieval science—fire, earth, air, and water>.

elementary *adj* **1** (*he said that the problem was elementary*) easy, simple, uncomplicated, straightforward. **2** (*students taking a course in elementary mathematics*) basic, fundamental, rudimentary, primary.

elements *npl* (*climbers braving the elements*) weather, climate, atmospheric conditions.

elicit *vb* (*try to elicit the information from them*) draw out, extract, obtain, get.

eligible *adj* (*not eligible for the post/not eligible to take part in the race*) qualified, suitable, acceptable, authorized.

eliminate *vb* **1** (*she was eliminated from the team*) drop, leave out, exclude, omit, reject. **2** (*a gunman hired to eliminate the members of the other gang*) get rid of, dispose of, destroy, put an end to, kill.

elocution *n* (*take lessons in elocution*) speech, voice production, delivery.

eloquent *adj* (*an eloquent speech*) articulate, expressive, fluent, persuasive, forceful.

elude *vb* (*try to elude the police*) avoid, dodge, evade, escape from, get away from.

embark *vb* **1** (*passengers were asked to embark early*) board ship, board a plane, go on board. **2** (*someone embarking on a new career*) set out on, begin, start, commence, enter on, set about.

embarrassed *adj* (*feel embarrassed when she forgot the words of her speech*) awkward, uncomfortable, self-conscious, upset, disconcerted, flustered, confused, abashed, ashamed, mortified.

embarrassment *n* (*overcome with embarrassment when she forgot the words of her speech*) awkwardness, discomfort, self-consciousness, confusion, shame.

embezzle *vb* (*embezzle money from his company*) steal, rob, thieve, pilfer.

emblem *n* (*the emblem of the society*) crest, badge, symbol, sign, device.

embrace *vb* (*he embraced his daughter as she got on the train*) hug, cuddle, clasp, cling to, squeeze.

emerge *vb* **1** (*they stood around the pool as the swimmers emerged*) come out, come into view, appear, surface, become visible. **2** (*waiting for the facts to emerge*) come out, become known, come to the fore.

emergency *n* (*emergencies such as fires*) crisis, danger, accident.

emigrate *vb* (*people emigrating to find work*) move overseas, move abroad, migrate, relocate.

eminent *adj* (*an eminent writer*) famous, well-known, distinguished, renowned, notable, noteworthy, great, important, prominent.

emit *vb* **1** (*chimneys emitting smoke*) give out, pour out, issue, send forth, discharge, issue. **2** (*emit a scream for help*) utter, express, voice.

emotion *n* (*in a voice in which there was no emotion*) feeling, sentiment, passion.

emotional *adj* **1** (*an emotional person*) passionate, ardent, demonstrative, excitable. **2** (*an emotional moment*) moving, touching, affecting.

emphasis *n* **1** (*as far as the interviews were concerned the emphasis was on qualifications*) stress, priority, importance, weight, urgency. **2** (*put the emphasis on the first syllable*) stress, accent.

emphasize *vb* **1** (*emphasize the importance of working hard*) stress, underline, highlight, spotlight, point up. **2** (*emphasize the first syllable*) stress, put the stress on.

emphatic *adj* (*he issued an emphatic denial*) definite, decided, firm, positive, absolute.

employ *vb* **1** (*he wishes to employ three more people in his office*) engage, hire, take on, sign on. **2** (*his work employs all his time*) take up, occupy, fill, use up. **3** (*employ modern methods in their factory*) use, make use of, apply.

employment *n* (*he is looking for employment in the computing industry*) work, occupation, job.

empty *adj* **1** (*an empty house*) vacant, unoccupied, uninhabited, unfilled. **2** (*an empty page*) blank, unused, clean. **3** (*empty threats*) meaningless, futile, ineffective, idle, insubstantial. ▽

empty vessels make most noise the most foolish or least informed people are most likely to voice their opinions (*They know* *nothing whatsoever about the new scheme, but they are protesting about them—empty vessels make most noise).*

enchant *vb* (*the children were enchanted by the ballet*) captivate, fascinate, entrance, bewitch, charm, delight.

enclosure *n* (*the enclosure for the animals at the dog show*) compound, ring, arena, paddock, fold.

encounter *vb* **1** (*she encountered an old friend in the mall*) meet, run into, run across, come upon, (*inf*) bump into. **2** (*encounter problems*) meet, be faced with, face, confront.

encourage *vb* **1** (*encourage those who had given up hope*) inspire, hearten, stimulate, motivate, incite, prompt. **2** (*a plan to encourage exports*) boost, promote, help, assist, aid.

end *n* **1** (*the far end of the lake*) edge, border, boundary, extremity, tip. **2** (*the end of the movie*) ending, conclusion, close, finish. **3** (*the end of the train*) rear, back. **4** (*their end in mind*) aim, objective, intention, purpose. **5** (*meet a peaceful end*) death, demise.

end *vb* **1** (*when his membership of the club ends*) come to an end, finish, come to a stop, stop, cease, conclude. **2** (*the incident ended their friendship*) bring to an end, bring to a close, finish, stop, discontinue, wind up. ✧

make ends meet to live within the limits of your means (*They have a large family and find it difficult to make ends meet*) <The ends referred to are the start and finish of your annual financial accounts>.

endanger *vb* (*things which endanger the species*) put in danger, expose to danger, put at risk, risk, jeopardize.

endearing *adj* (*one of her endearing features*) charming, attractive, lovable, adorable, engaging, sweet.

endeavor, endeavour (*Br, Cdn*) *vb* (*endeavor to do better*) attempt, try, exert yourself, make an effort, strive.

ending *n* (*a happy ending to the novel*) end, finish, close, conclusion.

endless *adj* **1** (*endless patience*) unending, without end, unlimited, infinite, everlasting, boundless. **2** (*an endless chain*) continuous, unbroken, uninterrupted, unbroken.

endorse *vb* (*endorse their course of action*) approve, support, back, champion, uphold, subscribe to.

endow *vb* (*she was endowed with good looks*) give, provide, supply, gift.

endure *vb* **1** (*unable to endure the traffic noise any longer*) put up with, stand, bear, tolerate, abide. **2** (*hope that their love would endure*) last, continue, remain, live on, persist.

enemy *n* (*the army of the enemy/regard his former friend as an enemy*) foe, opponent, adversary, rival.

energetic *adj* (*not feeling energetic enough to go for a walk*) active, lively, sprightly, vigorous, animated, enthusiastic.

energy *n* (*lacking in energy after her illness*) strength, stamina, vigor, power, force, liveliness, vitality, animation, (*inf*) get-up-and-go.

enforce *vb* **1** (*enforce the law*) apply, carry out, administer, implement, impose. **2** (*enforce silence on the group*) force, compel, insist on.

engage *vb* **1** (*engage a new nanny*) employ, hire, appoint, take on. **2** (*engage in a game of chess/be engaged in a bitter argument*) take part in, join in, participate in, enter into. **3** (*an attempt to engage their attention*) attract, catch, draw, gain, capture.

engaged *adj* **1** (*the manager is engaged*) busy, occupied, unavailable, (*inf*) tied up. **2** (*the toilet is engaged*) occupied, in use. **3** (*engaged couples*) going to be married, betrothed.

engaging *adj* (*an engaging smile*) charming, attractive, appealing, winning, pleasing, sweet.

engineer *vb* (*engineer a secret meeting between them*) bring about, cause, contrive, devise, (*inf*) wangle.

engrave *vb* **1** (*engrave their initials on the tree*) carve, etch, inscribe, cut. **2** (*her words are engraved on his heart*) fix, set, imprint, stamp.

engross *vb* (*the book engrossed me*) occupy, absorb, preoccupy, engage, rivet.

engulf *vb* (*a town engulfed by a tidal wave*) flood, swamp, swallow, submerge.

enjoy *vb* (*enjoy a trip to the shore*) like, love, be entertained by, take pleasure in, delight in.

enjoy:—enjoy yourself *vb* have a good time, have fun, (*inf*) have a ball (*the children are enjoying themselves at the funfair*).

enjoyable *adj* (*an enjoyable occasion*) entertaining, amusing, delightful, pleasant, nice.

enlarge *vb* (*enlarge the garden*) expand, extend, add to.

enormous *adj* (*an enormous creature/an enormous load*) huge, immense, massive, vast, colossal, gigantic, mammoth.

enough *adj* (*we have enough food*) sufficient, adequate, ample, abundant. ⋄

enough is as good as a feast if you have enough of something for your needs that is all that matters and large quantities are not necessary (*We had only a little bread and cheese for a snack on our walk, but it stopped us from being hungry—enough is as good as a feast*).

have had enough of (someone or **something)** to be unable to put up with (someone or something) any longer (*I have had enough of listening to her complaining*).

enroll *vb* **1** (*enroll for a French course*) register, sign up, enter, volunteer. **2** (*we enrolled several new recruits in the society*) register, sign up, take on, admit, accept.

ensue *vb* (*the argument and the fight that ensued*) follow, come after, result, arise.

ensure *vb* (*you must try to ensure that he will be present*) make sure, make certain, guarantee, certify.

enter *vb* **1** (*enter the hall*) come into, go into, pass into, move into. **2** (*a bullet entered his chest*) go into, pierce, penetrate. **3** (*enter a competition*) go in for, take part in, participate in. **4** (*enter your name on the form*) put down, register, record, mark down, note.

enterprise *n* **1** (*the festival is an annual enterprise*) project, undertaking, operation, venture. **2** (*the wool firm is a private enterprise*) business, industry, firm, establishment. **3** (*young people showing some enterprise*) resourcefulness, initiative, drive, imagination, spirit, enthusiasm, boldness, (*inf*) get-up-and-go.

enterprising *adj* (*an enterprising member of staff*) resourceful, go-ahead, imaginative, spirited, enthusiastic.

entertain *vb* (*he entertained the children with conjuring tricks*) amuse, divert, please, delight, interest.

entertainment *n* **1** (*several forms of entertainment for nonworking hours*) amusement, fun, recreation, diversion, distraction. **2** (*sing for the entertainment of the children*) amusement, enjoyment, diversion, pleasure, delight, interest. **3** (*the entertainment at the club that evening*) show, performance.

enthralling *adj* (*the acrobats gave an enthralling performance*) fascinating, gripping, riveting, spellbinding, enchanting, captivating, entrancing.

enthusiastic *adj* (*enthusiastic members of the flying club*) eager, keen, ardent, zealous, passionate, wholehearted, devoted, earnest, fanatical.

entice *vb* (*try to entice customers into his store*) lure, tempt, attract, coax.

entire *adj* **1** (*his entire collection of CDs*) whole, total, complete, full. **2** (*not an entire success*) total, absolute, unqualified, thorough, outright.

entirely *adv* (*not entirely true*) absolutely, completely, totally, wholly, altogether.

entitle *vb* **1** (*your pass entitles you to go to three matches*) allow, permit, enable, qualify, give the right to. **2** (*his novel is entitled* Lost Dreams) call, name.

entrance *n* **1** (*the entrance to the apartment building*) way in, entry, doorway, gateway, lobby, porch, foyer. **2** (*gain entrance to the building*) entry, access, admission, admittance. **3** (*the entrance of the school principal*) entry, arrival, appearance.

entrance *vb* (*we were entranced by their graceful dancing*) hold spellbound, fascinate, captivate, enchant, enthrall.

entrant *n* (*count the number of entrants for the competition*) competitor, contestant, participant, candidate, applicant.

entreat *vb* (*she entreated us to go with her*) beg, implore, beseech, plead with, appeal to.

entry *n* **1** (*the entry to the high-rise*) entrance, doorway, gateway, lobby, porch, foyer. **2** (*gain entry to the apartment building*) entrance, access, admission, admittance. **3** (*the entry of the ballet dancers*) entrance, arrival, appearance. **4** (*an entry in her diary*) statement, item, record, note, listing.

envelop *vb* (*mountaintops enveloped in mist*) cover, blanket, surround, engulf, swathe.

enviable *adj* (*he has an enviable collection of CDs*) desirable, tempting, impressive, excellent.

envious *adj* (*she was envious when she saw her friend's new car*) jealous, green, begrudging, resentful.

environment *n* (*children need a loving environment/the ideal environment for tigers*) surroundings, habitat, background, situation, conditions, circumstances, atmosphere.

envy *n* (*her envy of her neighbor's garden*) enviousness, jealousy, resentment.

envy *vb* (*she envies her friend her new car*) be envious of, be jealous of, begrudge, grudge, resent.

episode *n* **1** (*the second episode of the TV serial*) part, installment, section. **2** (*an unhappy episode in their lives*) incident, event, occurrence, happening, experience.

equal *adj* **1** (*children of equal ability*) the same, identical, like, comparable. **2** (*an equal contest*) even, evenly matched, level. **3** (*not feeling equal to the task*) up to, fit for, ready for, capable of. ⟡

all things being equal if all other facts when taken into consideration make no difference (*She is much younger than her husband and should, all things being equal, live longer than he will*).

equal *vb* **1** (*six plus six equals twelve*) be equal to, come to, amount to, add up to, make, total. **2** (*the runner equaled the record for the race*) match, be level with, reach.

equate *vb* (*they equate money with happiness*) associate, bracket, link, connect.

equip *vb* **1** (*equip the children for their skiing trip*) fit out, kit out, rig out, dress. **2** (*equip the hall with gymnastic apparatus*) fit out, furnish, supply, stock.

equipment *n* (*the equipment needed to do the job*) tools, gear, apparatus, materials, things, paraphernalia.

equivalent *adj* (*ask the store to exchange the item for something of equivalent value*) equal, the same, identical, similar, like, comparable, corresponding, matching.

equivalent *n* (*the equivalent of our attorney general in their country*) counterpart, opposite number, equal.

era *n* (*furniture from the Colonial era*) age, period, time, days, eon, epoch.

eradicate *vb* (*try to eradicate the weed from his garden/A government tries to eradicate tax avoidance*) get rid of, do away with, root out, wipe out, eliminate.

erase *vb* (*erase the incorrect passage from the report*) remove, rub out, wipe out, delete, cancel.

erect *adj* (*human beings stand erect*) upright, vertical, straight.

erect *vb* **1** (*erect a tent*) put up, set up, set upright, pitch, assemble. **2** (*erect an apartment building*) build, construct, put up, raise.

erode *vb* (*cliffs eroded by the sea*) wear away, wear down, eat away, corrode.

err *vb* **1** (*they erred when they accused him of theft*) be in error, be wrong, be incorrect, make a mistake, be mistaken, get it wrong, miscalculate, (*inf*) slip up. **2** (*ministers who urge the members of their congregation not to err*) do wrong, sin, behave badly, misbehave. ⟡

err on the side of (something) to be guilty of what might be seen as a fault in order to avoid an opposite and even greater fault (*He tended to err on the side of leniency when punishing children*).

to err is human it is part of human nature to do wrong or sin at some point.

errand *n* task, job, chore, assignment, mission. ⟡

a fool's errand a journey or task that turns out to have been a waste of time, a pointless or useless journey or task (*They sent us on a fool's errand to the bank—it was closed on Saturdays*).

erratic *adj* **1** (*worried about her erratic behavior*) inconsistent, irregular, variable, unstable, unpredictable, unreliable, capricious. **2** (*a driver steering an erratic course*) wandering, meandering, wavering.

error *n* **1** (*an error in their calculation of the building costs*) mistake, inaccuracy, miscalculation, blunder, fault, oversight, (*inf*) slip-up. **2** (*see the error of his ways*) wrongdoing, sin, evil, misbehavior, misconduct. ⟡

trial and error the trying-out of various methods or approaches of doing something until you find the right one (*They found a cure for her allergy by trial and error*).

erupt *vb* **1** (*a flow of lava erupted from the volcano*) be discharged, gush, pour out, issue, belch. **2** (*violence erupted between the two gangs*) break out, flare up, blow up, burst forth.

eruption *n* (*an eruption of violence*) outburst, outbreak, flare-up.

escalate vb 1 (*the violence has escalated/The war escalated*) increase, intensify, heighten, accelerate, be stepped up, mushroom. 2 (*prices have escalated*) go up, mount, climb, soar.

escapade n (*the children were punished for their escapades*) adventure, prank, stunt, trick, (*inf*) lark.

escape vb 1 (*the prisoners escaped from prison*) get away, run away, abscond, bolt, break free, make your getaway, (*inf*) do a runner, (*inf*) do a bunk. 2 (*succeed in escaping punishment*) avoid, evade, dodge, elude, steer clear of, side-step. 3 (*gas escaping*) leak, seep out, discharge, spurt, gush.

escort n (*require an escort for the dance*) partner, companion, attendant, (*inf*) date.

especially adv 1 (*the products sell well, especially in the summer*) particularly, above all, chiefly, mainly, principally. 2 (*designed especially for her*) specially, specifically, expressly, particularly, exclusively.

essay n (*asked to write an essay on a favorite author*) composition, paper, article.

essence n 1 (*the essence of good speech*) essential part, main ingredient, nature. 2 (*vanilla essence*) extract, concentrate. ✧

of the essence of the greatest importance (*Speed is of the essence if we are to reach the hospital in time*).

essential adj 1 (*essential equipment/It is essential to arrive early*) necessary, vital, indispensable, crucial, important. 2 (*the essential theme of the novel*) basic, fundamental, principal.

establish vb 1 (*establish a computing firm*) set up, form, found, institute, create, inaugurate. 2 (*try to establish his innocence*) prove, show, demonstrate, verify, certify.

estate n 1 (*he owns a town house and a country estate*) real estate, property, land, land-holding. 2 (*his estate at his death amounted to nearly a million dollars*) assets, resources, effects, possessions, belongings, wealth.

esteem n (*hold the writer in great esteem*) regard, respect, admiration, honor, reverence, appreciation.

estimate vb (*estimate the cost of repairs*) work out, calculate, assess, gauge, reckon, guess, (*inf*) guesstimate.

estimation n 1 (*in our estimation he is the best player*) opinion, view, judgment, consideration,

way of thinking, feeling. 2 (*when she lied she went down in our estimation*) good opinion, regard, respect, admiration, approval, favor.

estuary n (*boats in the estuary*) river mouth, inlet, cove, bay.

eternal adj 1 (*life eternal*) everlasting, endless, without end, never-ending, perpetual, immortal, infinite. 2 (*we are tired of their eternal quarreling*) endless, never-ending, incessant, ceaseless, nonstop, constant, continuous, continual, interminable. ✧

eternal rest death (*The old man has gone to his eternal rest after enduring much pain*).
The Eternal City Rome.
the eternal triangle a relationship involving one man and two women or one woman and two men (*He sometimes lives with his wife and sometimes with his girlfriend—a definite case of the eternal triangle*).

ethical adj (*not an ethical thing to do*) moral, honorable, virtuous, good, decent, honest.

ethnic adj (*ethnic restaurants/ethnic customs*) racial, cultural, national.

etiquette n (*wedding etiquette*) rules of conduct, accepted behavior, custom, convention.

evacuate vb 1 (*people asked to evacuate areas likely to be bombed by the enemy*) leave, vacate, quit, abandon, retreat from, (*inf*) pull out. 2 (*the police evacuated everyone from the area*) move out, clear.

evade vb 1 (*try to evade her responsibilities*) avoid, escape from, dodge, shirk, side-step, (*inf*) duck. 2 (*succeed in evading the enemy*) avoid, escape from, elude, shake off, give the slip to, keep out of the way of, steer clear of.

even adj 1 (*even ground*) level, flat, smooth, uniform. 2 (*the temperature of the room must remain even*) constant, uniform, steady, stable, unchanging. 3 (*we gave the children even amounts of money*) equal, the same, identical, like, similar, comparable. 4 (*the score was even at the end of the second quarter*) level, equal, all square, tied, drawn. 5 (*people of an even disposition*) even-tempered, calm, placid, serene, composed, unexcitable, imperturbable. ✧

break even to have your losses balanced by your gains or profit (*We did not make much*

money from the restaurant in its first year,
but at least we broke even).

get even with (someone) to be revenged on
(someone), do something bad to (someone
who has done something bad to you) (*When
they deliberately damaged his car he vowed
to get even with them*).

get on an even keel to get into a steady or
stable situation with no sudden changes
(*We would be all right if we could just get our
finances on an even keel*).

event *n* **1** (*the sad and happy events in their lives*)
happening, occurrence, occasion, episode, inci-
dent, experience. **2** (*the track events in the
Olympic Games*) contest, competition, match. ⟡

in the event as it happened, as it turned out
(*We thought our team would lose, but in the
event they won easily*).
in the event of (something) if something
should happen (*You will get your money
back in the event of the goods being faulty*).

eventually *adv* (*she took her driving test several
times and eventually passed*) in the end, finally,
at last, ultimately.

everlasting *adj* **1** (*everlasting life*) eternal,
endless, without end, never-ending, perpetual,
abiding, immortal, infinite. **2** (*their everlasting
complaints*) endless, never-ending, nonstop,
incessant, ceaseless, continuous, continual.

evict *adj* (*get evicted from their apartment for not
paying the rent/get evicted from the club for being
under age*) throw out, put out, turn out, eject,
remove, oust, (*inf*) kick out.

evidence *n* **1** (*they will have to produce evidence
of his guilt*) proof, confirmation, verification. **2**
(*there was evidence of a struggle at the scene of
the murder*) sign, indication, mark. ⟡

in evidence easily seen (*The police were very
much in evidence at the protest match*).

evident *adj* (*it was evident that he was unwell/
an evident improvement*) obvious, clear, apparent, plain, noticeable, conspicuous, visible.

evil *adj* (*appalled at his evil deeds*) wicked, bad,
wrong, sinful, immoral, villainous. ⟡

exact *adj* **1** (*an exact description*) precise, accurate, close, faithful, true. **2** (*the exact time*) precise, accurate, right.

exacting *adj* (*an exacting task*) demanding, difficult, hard, tough, laborious, taxing.

exactly *adv* **1** (*his estimate was exactly right*) precisely, absolutely, just, quite, (*inf*) on the nail,
(*inf*) bang on, (*inf*) spot on. **2** (*repeat the information exactly*) word for word, literally, to the
letter, closely, faithfully.

exaggerate *vb* **1** (*exaggerate the length of time the
journey took*) overstate, overemphasize,
overstress, overestimate. **2** (*it's not that
expensive—you're exaggerating*) overstate,
embroider, embellish, overdraw, over-elaborate,
make a mountain out of a molehill, (*inf*) lay it
on with a trowel, (*inf*) lay it on thick.

examine *vb* **1** (*it is necessary to examine the facts*)
look at, study, inspect, survey, analyze, review,
observe, check out, weigh up. **2** (*examine a
patient*) look at, check over, give a check-up,
assess.

example *n* **1** (*buy an example of the artist's early
work*) sample, specimen, instance, illustration.
2 (*follow his brother's example*) model, pattern,
standard. **3** (*punish some pupils as an example
to the others*) warning, caution, lesson.

exasperate *vb* (*she was exasperated by their objections*) annoy, irritate, anger, infuriate, enrage.

excavate *vb* **1** (*excavate a trench*) dig, dig out,
hollow out, scoop out. **2** (*excavate an ancient
Roman settlement*) unearth, dig up, uncover.

exceed *vb* **1** (*his talent as a musician exceeds that
of his brother*) be greater than, be more than,
be superior to, surpass, outstrip, outshine, overshadow, top, cap. **2** (*exceed the speed limit*) go
beyond, go over, do more than, overstep. **3** (*at a
price not exceeding £5000*) be greater than, be
more than, go beyond, top.

exceedingly *adv* (*she was exceedingly beautiful*)
extremely, exceptionally, extraordinarily, tremendously, enormously, vastly, greatly, highly, hugely.

excellent *adj* (*an excellent player*) very good,
first-rate, first-class, great, fine, distinguished,
superb, outstanding, marvelous, brilliant, (*inf*)
A1, (*inf*) top-notch.

exception *n* **1** (*the whole school will go with the
exception of the first class*) exclusion, omission.
2 (*their case is an exception*) special case, deviation, irregularity, oddity, freak. ⟡

the exception that proves the rule the fact
that an exception has to be made for a
particular example of something proves that

the general rule is valid (*All the family have black hair. The youngest member is the exception that proves the rule*).
take exception to (something) to take offense at (something) (*She took exception to his remarks about her outfit*).

exceptional *adj* **1** (*exceptional weather for the time of year*) unusual, uncommon, abnormal, out of the ordinary, extraordinary, atypical, rare. **2** (*people of exceptional talent*) excellent, extraordinary, remarkable, outstanding, phenomenal.

excerpt *n* (*read an excerpt from one of Shakespeare's plays*) extract, passage, quotation, quote, piece, section, clip.

excessive *n* **1** (*an excessive amount of water*) too much, extravagant, immoderate, undue, (*inf*) over-the-top. **2** (*the prices seem excessive*) exorbitant, outrageous, unreasonable.

exchange *vb* (*the children agreed to exchange toys*) swap, trade, barter.

excite *vb* **1** (*the thought of the party excited the children*) thrill, stimulate, rouse, animate, (*inf*) turn on. **2** (*excite feelings of anger in the crowd*) cause, bring about, rouse, arouse, incite, provoke, stir up.

exclamation *n* (*he gave an exclamation of surprise*) cry, call, shout, yell, shriek.

exclude *vb* **1** (*she was excluded from their talks*) leave out, keep out, debar, bar, ban. **2** (*they cannot exclude the possibility of murder*) rule out, set aside, eliminate.

exclusive *adj* **1** (*an exclusive club*) select, private, fashionable, chic. **2** (*gave them her exclusive attention*) complete, undivided, full, absolute, entire, total. **3** (*the price exclusive of drinks*) excluding, not including, omitting, not counting, excepting.

excruciating *adj* (*an excruciating pain in her stomach*) agonizing, acute, severe, intense, extreme.

excursion *n* (*go on an excursion to the shore*) trip, expedition, jaunt, outing, journey.

excuse *vb* **1** (*impossible to excuse their crime*) forgive, pardon, condone, justify, defend. **2** (*ask to be excused from the gymnastics class*) let off, exempt, release.

excuse *n* **1** (*their excuse for not arriving on time*) defense, justification, reason, grounds, vindication. **2** (*his supposed illness was just an*

excuse for staying out of school) pretext, cover-up, front, pretense.

execute *vb* **1** (*murderers used to be executed*) put to death, kill, hang. **2** (*execute a plan*), carry out, perform, accomplish, fulfill, put into effect, implement.

exercise *vb* **1** (*the women were exercising in order to keep fit*) do exercises, work out, train. **2** (*try to exercise a little patience*) use, employ, apply, exert.

exercise *n* **1** (*do exercises every morning to keep fit*) physical training, workout, drill. **2** (*some exercise is necessary to keep healthy*) activity, physical exertion, physical effort. **3** (*pupils given an English exercise*) assignment, task, piece of work, problem.

exert *vb* **1** (*they could finish the job in time if they exerted themselves*) make an effort, spare no effort, put yourself out, try hard, do your best, strive, struggle, strain, labor. **2** (*it was necessary to exercise some pressure*) employ, use, apply, wield.

exhaust *vb* **1** (*the long walk exhausted her*) tire, tire out, wear out, fatigue, weary, (*inf*) poop. **2** (*we have exhausted our supplies of food*) use up, consume, finish, deplete, expend.

exhaustive *adj* (*the police made an exhaustive search*) intensive, all-out, comprehensive, extensive, thorough.

exhibit *vb* **1** (*the firm exhibited their latest works*) put on show, show, put on display, display, put on view, demonstrate, present. **2** (*exhibit patience/exhibit signs of improvement*) show, indicate, reveal, demonstrate, express.

exhibition *n* **1** (*a book exhibition*) show, display, demonstration, presentation, fair. **2** (*an exhibition of bad temper*) display, show, expression, indication, demonstration. ▽

make an exhibition of yourself to behave embarrassinmgly in public.

exile *vb* (*exiled from their native land*) banish, deport, expel, outlaw.

exile *n* **1** (*sent into exile*) banishment, deportation. **2** (*exiles from their native land*) deportee, outlaw, refugee, displaced person, asylum seeker.

exist *vb* **1** (*children believing that fairies exist*) be, have being, have existence, live, be living. **2** (*difficult to exist on such a low income*) live, stay alive, survive.

exit *n* (*the exit from the movie theater*) way out, door.

expand *vb* **1** (*substances that expand when heated*) grow larger, get larger, increase in size, swell. **2** (*expand the business*) make larger, make bigger, increase, amplify, add to, extend, grow.

expanse *n* (*an expanse of blue water*) stretch, area, extent, tract, sweep.

expect *vb* **1** (*I expect that they will arrive soon*) believe, think, assume, suppose, imagine, presume, surmise. **2** (*I am expecting a parcel from them*) await, wait for, look for, anticipate, hope for.

expedition *n* **1** (*an expedition to the center of the jungle*) journey, exploration, safari, undertaking, quest. **2** (*a shopping expedition*) trip, outing, excursion, jaunt. **3** (*the members of the expedition to climb Mount Everest*) group, team, party, company.

expel *vb* **1** (*expel him from school/expel him from the club*) throw out, oust, drum out, bar, ban, blackball. **2** (*expel them from their native land*) banish, exile, drive out, cast out, deport.

expense *n* **1** (*victory in the war at the expense of many lives*) cost, sacrifice. **2** (*go to a great deal of expense to buy her a present*) outlay, cost, spending. ⟡

at the expense of (someone or **something)** causing harm, loss, embarrassment, etc. (*He got to the top of the mountain, but at the expense of his health*).

expensive *adj* (*expensive clothing*) costly, high-priced, dear, overpriced, exorbitant, extortionate, (*inf*) steep.

experience *n* **1** (*a terrifying experience*) event, incident, occurrence, happening, affair, episode. **2** (*a job requiring experience as well as a university degree*) practical knowledge, skill, practice, training, (*inf*) know-how, (*inf*) hands-on experience.

experiment *n* (*medical experiments to find new drugs*) test, trial, investigation, research, pilot study.

expert *n* (*an expert on local history*) authority, specialist, professional, pundit, (*inf*) buff.

expert *adj* (*an expert chess player*) knowledgeable, specialist, experienced, professional, skillful, proficient, adept, (*inf*) crack, ace.

expire *vb* **1** (*her club membership has expired*) run out, be no longer valid, end, come to an end, finish, stop, cease, lapse. **2** (*people expiring from lack of food*) die, pass away, breathe your last, decease.

explain *vb* **1** (*explain how to operate the machine*) give an explanation of, describe, define, make clear, spell out, throw light on. **2** (*called upon to explain their actions*) give an explanation of, account for, give a reason for, justify, defend, vindicate.

explanation *n* **1** (*a clear explanation as to how the machine works*) description, definition, clarification, interpretation. **2** (*unable to accept their explanation for their absence*) account, reason, grounds, excuse, justification, defense, vindication

explode *vb* **1** (*the bomb exploded*) blow up, go off, detonate, burst. **2** (*the gas boiler exploded*) blow up, burst open, fly into pieces, erupt.

exploit *n* (*a book about the exploits of the knights of old*) deed, feat, adventure, stunt.

exploit *vb* **1** (*exploit the resources which they have*) make use of, use, utilize, put to good use, turn to your advantage, profit by, make capital out of. **2** (*a mill owner exploited the workers/a man who exploited his friends*) make use of, take advantage of, abuse, impose upon.

explore *vb* **1** (*explore areas of jungle*) travel in, survey. **2** (*explore every possibility*) examine, look into, investigate, inquire into, consider, research.

explosion *n* **1** (*there was a loud explosion and we discovered the boiler had blown up*) bang, blast, boom, rumble, crash, crack, report. **2** (*an explosion in the population figures*) increase, escalation, mushrooming, rocketing. boom, upsurge.

expose *vb* **1** (*expose her skin to the sun*) bare, lay bare, uncover. **2** (*newspapers exposing the details of the scandal*) reveal, disclose, divulge, make known, uncover, unveil. **3** (*expose the baby to harsh weather*) lay open to, leave unprotected by, put at risk from.

express *vb* **1** (*express their gratitude in a short speech*) voice, state, put into words, articulate, utter, make known, communicate. **2** (*express their appreciation with a gift of money*) show, demonstrate, indicate, convey. **3** (*express juice from the oranges*) press, squeeze, force out, extract.

expression *n* **1** (*we could tell from her expression that she was angry*) face, countenance, look, appearance, air. **2** (*find the right expression to say what she means*) word, words, phrase, term, wording, language, turn of phrase. **3** (*play the violin piece with expression*) feeling, emotion, passion, intensity, vividness.

extant *adj* (*a species of bird that is still extant*) still existing, in existence, living, alive, existent, surviving, remaining.

extend *vb* **1** (*extend the territory which he rules over*) expand, increase, enlarge, lengthen. **2** (*extend the ladder to its full length*) stretch out, draw out, lengthen, elongate. **3** (*extend the period of his employment*) increase, prolong, lengthen, stretch out, protract. **4** (*the lake extends for many miles*) continue, stretch, stretch out, carry on, run on. **5** (*extend a warm welcome to the guests*) offer, give, proffer, hold out.

extensive *adj* **1** (*a house with extensive grounds*) large, large-scale, sizable, substantial, vast, immense. **2** (*have extensive knowledge of the Bible*) comprehensive, thorough, wide-ranging, wide, broad. **3** (*the storm caused extensive damage to the crops*) great, widespread, wholesale, universal.

extent *n* **1** (*the extent of her knowledge/the extent of the damage*) scope, range, coverage, degree. **2** (*the extent of the land around the house*) area, expanse, length, stretch.

exterior *adj* (*the exterior surface*) outside, outer, outermost, outward, external, surface.

extinct *adj* **1** (*a species of bird now extinct*) died out, wiped out, gone, defunct. **2** (*an extinct volcano*) inactive, extinguished, burned out.

extinguish *vb* (*extinguish the candles*) put out, blow out, quench, snuff out.

extra *adj* **1** (*they need extra help to finish the job*) more, additional, added, further, supplementary, auxiliary. **2** (*we have extra food in our picnic—would you like some?*) surplus, spare, left-over, superfluous, excess, reserve.

extract *vb* (*extract a tooth*) pull out, draw out, take out, remove.

extract *n* (*read extracts from her novel on the radio*) excerpt, passage, selection, quotation, citation.

extraordinary *adj* **1** (*have an extraordinary memory*) exceptional, unusual, uncommon, rare, striking, remarkable. phenomenal. **2** (*it was extraordinary that she survived*) amazing, astonishing, remarkable, astounding, surprising, strange.

extravagant *adj* **1** (*an extravagant way of life/It was extravagant to buy such an expensive dress*) spendthrift, wasteful. **2** (*he tried to flatter her by paying her extravagant compliments*) exaggerated, excessive, outrageous, absurd, (*inf*) over-the-top.

extreme *adj* **1** (*in the extreme north of the country*) farthest, furthest, outermost, most remote. **2** (*in extreme danger*) very great, greatest, maximum, utmost, severe. **3** (*people who hold extreme political views*) immoderate, fanatical, exaggerated.

extremely *adv* (*she is extremely beautiful*) very, exceedingly, exceptionally, extraordinarily, markedly, uncommonly.

eye *n* **1** (*have sharp eyes*) eyesight, sight, vision. **2** (*the police are keeping an eye on her/She is under the eagle eye of the head teacher*) watch, observation, notice, surveillance. ⟳

have an eye for (something) to be a good judge of (something), to be able to spot (something) as a good example (*She has an eye for a bargain in the housing market*).

not bat an eye not to react to something that you might be expected to be shocked by (*I thought my mother would be uspet when I said I would not be home for Thanksgiving, but she didn't bat an eye*).

F

fabric *n* **1** (*drapes made of a brightly colored fabric*) cloth, material, textile, stuff. **2** (*the fabric of the building/the fabric of society*) framework, frame, structure, constitution.

fabulous *adj* **1** (*stories about fabulous creatures such as dragons*) mythical, imaginary, fictitious, fictional, legendary. **2** (*an emperor of fabulous wealth*) incredible, unbelievable, unimaginable, inconceivable, astonishing. **3** (*they had a fabulous time on vacation*) marvelous, wonderful, superb, great, (*inf*) super.

face *n* **1** (*she had a beautiful face*) countenance, features. **2** (*she came rushing out with an angry face*) expression, look, air. **3** (*the faces of a cube*) front, side, surface. **4** (*she was afraid of losing face in the firm*) prestige, status, standing, dignity. ○

on the face of it judging from what you can see or find out from first impressions, especially when this turns out to be wrong (*On the face of it, he seemed ideal for the job, but he turned out to be hopeless*).
take (someone or **something) at face value** to judge (someone or something) on outward appearance only without bothering to get any more information (*He seemed genuine and she took him at face value, but he turned out to be a crook*).

face *vb* **1** (*an apartment building facing the sea*) look onto, overlook, be opposite to, front onto. **2** (*they are facing many difficulties*) meet, encounter, confront.

facetious *adj* (*please don't make facetious remarks—it is a serious situation*) flippant, frivolous, light-hearted, joking, jocular, funny, amusing.

fact *n* **1** (*difficult to separate fact from fiction*) reality, actuality, truth. **2** (*wish to have all the facts of the case*) detail, particular, factor, piece of information, piece of data, circumstance.

factor *n* (*consider all the factors connected with the situation*) element, point, detail, feature, item, circumstance.

fade *vb* **1** (*the drapes had faded in the sunlight*) lose color, become bleached, become pale, become washed out, dull, dim. **2** (*fresh flowers that had faded*) wilt, wither, droop, die. **3** (*hope had faded/*

Memories of the occasion had faded) dim, grow less, die away, dwindle, grow faint, vanish, die.

fail *vb* **1** (*their attempt to climb the mountain failed*) be unsuccessful, fall through, be in vain, come to nothing, come to grief, (*inf*) flop. **2** (*they failed the exam*) not pass, (*inf*) flunk. **3** (*the engine failed*) break down, stop working, cut out, (*inf*) conk out. **4** (*he failed to keep us informed*) omit, neglect, forget. **5** (*her health is failing*) decline, deteriorate, diminish, dwindle, wane. **6** (*his business has failed*) collapse, crash, go under, go bankrupt, go to the wall, fold, (*inf*) go bust, (*inf*) flop.

failing *n* (*untidiness is his main failing*) fault, shortcoming, weakness, flaw, imperfection, defect, foible.

failure *n* (*our attempt was a complete failure*) nonsuccess, disaster, fiasco, (*inf*) flop.

faint *adj* **1** (*faint traces of paint on the table*) indistinct, unclear, dim, faded, obscure. **2** (*hear a faint sound of laughter*) indistinct, soft, low, muted, feeble. **3** (*a faint smell of violets*) slight, indistinct, delicate. **4** (*have a faint chance of winning the match*) slight, small, remote, vague. **5** (*feel faint*) dizzy, giddy, light-headed, (*inf*) muzzy. ○

faint heart never won fair lady if you want to achieve what you desire you must be bold and determined.

faint *vb* (*she fainted in the heat*) pass out, collapse, black out, lose consciousness, swoon, (*inf*) conk out.

fair *adj* **1** (*she had fair hair*) blond, yellow, flaxen, pale, light brown. **2** (*the accused was given a fair trial*) just, impartial, unprejudiced, unbiased, objective. **3** (*a fair judge*) fair-minded, just, impartial, unprejudiced, unbiased, open-minded, honest. **4** (*the weather was fair for the picnic*) fine, dry, bright. **5** (*the standard of his work is just fair*) satisfactory, all right, middling, so-so, average, adequate. ○

by fair means or foul in any way possible, whether just or unjust (*He intends to get that by fair means or foul*).
fair-haired boy a male who is someone's favorite (*He certainly will not lose his job. He is the manager's fair-haired boy*).

fairly *adv* (*she was fairly good at playing the piano*) quite, rather, somewhat, reasonably, passably, moderately, tolerably, (*inf*) pretty.

faith *n* **1** (*they have faith in their doctor*) trust, confidence, belief, reliance. **2** (*they are of the Jewish faith*) religion, creed, belief, persuasion. ⋄

keep faith with (someone) to be loyal to (someone) (*They tried to get her to betray her leader, but she kept faith with him*).

faithful *adj* **1** (*the leader's faithful followers*) loyal, constant, true, devoted, dependable, reliable, trustworthy, staunch. **2** (*a faithful account of the event/a faithful copy of the picture*) accurate, true, exact, precise, close.

fake *adj* **1** (*fake ten-dollar bills*) counterfeit, forged, fraudulent, false, imitation, (*inf*) phony. **2** (*wearing a string of fake pearls*) imitation, artificial, synthetic, simulated, mock, sham.

fall *vb* **1** (*the leaves fall in autumn*) drop, descend. **2** (*the child fell as she left the bus*) fall down, trip over, stumble, topple over, go head over heels, (*inf*) take a spill. **3** (*the level of the water in the river was falling in the drought*) sink, subside, abate. **4** (*the price of houses has fallen*) decrease, decline, go down, grow less, plummet, slump. **5** (*a memorial to the soldiers who fell in battle*) die, be killed, be slain, perish, be a fatality, be a casualty. **6** (*her birthday falls on a Monday this year*) be, take place, occur, happen. ⋄

fall flat to have no effect, to fail to have the expected or desired effect, to fail (*The comedian was supposed to be very funny, but his jokes fell flat*).

fall over yourself to (do something) to set about (doing something) with great willingness and eagerness (*They were all falling over themselves to be charming to the wealthy man*).

false *adj* **1** (*they gave a false account of their movements to the police*) untrue, wrong, incorrect, inaccurate. **2** (*he gave a false name*) assumed, made-up, invented, fictitious, (*inf*) phony. **3** (*false friends*) disloyal, unfaithful, faithless, treacherous, untrustworthy. ⋄

under false pretenses by being deceitful (*The burglars got into the house under false pretenses by pretending to be workmen*).

falsehood *n* (*accuse him of telling falsehoods*) lie, untruth, fib, story.

falter *vb* **1** (*the young boxer faltered when he saw the size of his opponent*) hesitate, waver, flinch, stumble. **2** (*the speaker was nervous and faltered over his speech*) stumble, stutter, stammer.

fame *n* (*his fame as an artist has spread/seek fame in Hollywood*) renown, distinction, notability, greatness, glory, honor.

familiar *adj* **1** (*the old man was a familiar sight in the village store*) well-known, common, customary, accustomed, regular, commonplace, everyday. **2** (*workers who were familiar with the computing system*) acquainted with, conversant with, versed in, experienced in, with knowledge of. ⋄

familiarity breeds contempt people do not appreciate people or things that they know very well or see frequently.

family *n* **1** (*people of noble family*) ancestry, parentage, descent, extraction, bloodline. **2** (*the poor old woman has no family*) relatives, relations, people, your own flesh and blood, kin. **3** (*the couple have no family*) children, offspring, (*inf*) kids. ⋄

run in the family to be a characteristic found in many members of the same family (*Red hair runs in the family*).

fan *n* (*a football fan/a fan of the pop star*) admirer, follower, enthusiast, devotee, fanatic, addict, (*inf*) buff, (*inf*) freak.

fancy *n* **1** (*the fancy of the poet*) imagination, creativity. **2** (*the person from Mars was just a fancy on the child's part*) figment of the imagination, hallucination, illusion, delusion, fantasy. **3** (*have a fancy for some chocolate*) desire, urge, notion, wish, want, hankering, longing, yearning, (*inf*) yen. ⋄

footloose and fancy-free to be not married, engaged or in love with someone (*He said that he was engaged once, but he is now footloose and fancy-free*).

fancy *vb* **1** (*he fancied he saw a ghostly figure*) imagine, think, believe. **2** (*he said that he fancied a drink*) would like, wish, want, desire, hanker after, long for, yearn for, (*inf*) have a yen for.

fancy *adj* (*fancy patterns/fancy decorations*) ornate, elaborate, ornamental, decorated, adorned, embellished, showy, (*inf*) jazzy.

fantastic *adj* **1** (*he had fantastic notions about seeing aliens from Mars*) fanciful, imaginary, wild, strange. **2** (*fantastic figures and shapes in his painting*) strange, weird, bizarre, outlandish, fanciful, whimsical. **3** (*he earns a fantastic amount of money*) huge, enormous, tremendous. **4** (*he thought the concert was fantastic*) marvelous, wonderful, sensational, superb, excellent, (*inf*) cool.

fantasy *n* **1** (*a children's book that is full of fantasy*) fancy, imagination, creativity, originality, vision. **2** (*she is always having fantasies about winning a lot of money*) flight of fancy, dream, daydream, illusion.

far *adv* **1** (*it is not far to the next village*) a long way, a great distance. **2** (*it is far too soon to know*) by a long way, to a great extent, very much. ⟳

go far to be very successful, especially in your career (*The teacher said that the boy would go far*).
go too far to do or say something that is beyond the limits of what is acceptable (*He has always had a hot temper, but he went too far when he hit a police officer*).

far *adj* (*the far places of the world*) faraway, far-off, distant, remote.

fare *n* (*train fares have gone up*) ticket, charge, cost, price.

far-fetched *adj* (*they found his story rather far-fetched*) unlikely, improbable, incredible, unbelievable, unconvincing .

farm *vb* (*farmland in the north*) cultivate, work.

fascinate *vb* (*the children were fascinated by the mime artist*) captivate, enchant, enthrall, entrance, hold spellbound, charm, absorb, engross.

fashion *n* **1** (*the fashions of the 19th century*) style, trend, taste, craze, vogue. **2** (*she has a job in fashion*) clothing, the clothing industry. **3** (*she arranged things in an organized fashion*) way, manner, method, style, system.

fashionable *adj* (*fashionable clothing/furniture that is no longer fashionable*) in fashion, stylish, up-to-date, in vogue, modern, contemporary, (*inf*) trendy.

fast *adj* **1** (*at a fast pace*) quick, rapid, swift, brisk, speedy, hurried. **2** (*fast colors*) fixed, indelible, permanent. ⟳

pull a fast one on (someone) to succeed in tricking or deceiving (someone) (*She pulled a fast one on her friend by selling him her old car, which she knew was in bad condition*) <From bowling a fast ball in cricket>.

fast *adv* **1** (*walk fast*) quickly, rapidly, swiftly, briskly, speedily, hurriedly, like the wind. **2** (*a truck stuck fast in the mud*) firmly, tightly, securely, immovably. **3** (*children who were fast asleep*) sound, deeply.

fast *vb* (*people who fast during certain religious holidays/fasting in aid of a famine charity*) go without food, eat nothing, go hungry, starve yourself, deny yourself food.

fasten *vb* **1** (*she fastened a pin to her dress*) attach, fix, clip, pin. **2** (*fasten the dog to the gatepost*) attach, tie, bind. **3** (*the links of the chain are fastened to one another*) join, connect, couple, unite, link.

fat *adj* **1** (*fat people trying to lose weight*) plump, obese, stout, overweight, chubby, tubby, pudgy, flabby. **2** (*fat reference books*) thick, big, substantial. **3** (*people told to avoid fat substances for the sake of their health*) fatty, greasy, oily.

fat *n* **1** (*require some form of fat to make a cake*) animal fat, vegetable fat, lard,, butter, margarine. **2** (*she was embarrassed by her fat*) fatness, plumpness, obesity, stoutness, chubbiness, tubbiness, flab. ⟳

the fat is in the fire trouble has been started and nothing can be done to stop it (*The fat was in the fire when his boss discovered that he was at the ball game instead of being at work*).

fatal *adj* (*a fatal blow/a fatal illness*) mortal, deadly, lethal, killing, terminal.

fatality *n* (*there were several fatalities in the freeway crash*) death, dead, casualty, mortality.

fate *n* (*she wondered what fate had in store for him*) destiny, providence, chance, luck, fortune, the stars. ⟳

seal (someone's) fate to ensure that something, usually something unpleasant, happens to someone (*Her fate was sealed when the teachers discovered that she had been cheating in the exam*).

fateful adj (a fateful meeting) critical, crucial, decisive, momentous, important.

father n 1 (her father left her a lot of money) male parent, (inf) dad, (inf) daddy, (inf) pop. 2 (the father of modern medicine) founder, originator, initiator, creator.

fatigue n (he was suffering from fatigue after climbing the mountain) tiredness, overtiredness, weariness, exhaustion.

fatty adj (fatty foods) fat, greasy, oily.

fault n 1 (discover a fault in the material) flaw, defect, imperfection. 2 (one of the main faults in her character) flaw, defect, failing, shortcoming, weakness, weak point, deficiency. 3 (the accident was her fault) blame, responsibility.

faulty adj 1 (a faulty lock) broken, damaged, unsound. 2 (take the faulty goods back to the store) flawed, imperfect.

favor, favour (Br, Cdn) n 1 (he did her a favor by giving her a ride to the station) good turn, good deed, service, kindness. 2 (he looked on the new scheme with favor) approval, goodwill, friendliness. ⊃

curry favor with (someone) to try to win the approval or friendship of (someone) by the use of insincere flattery or by being extremely agreeable to (Them) (She is currying favor with the teacher to try to get into the school play).

favorable, favourable (Br, Cdn) adj 1 (in less favorable circumstances/favorable winds) advantageous, beneficial, helpful, promising. 2 (she hoped to make a favorable impression on her friend's parents) good, pleasing, agreeable. 3 (he received a favorable report from his teacher) good, approving, praising, enthusiastic.

favorite, favourite (Br, Cdn) adj (the child's favorite toy) best-loved, dearest, favored, chosen, preferred.

favorite, favourite (Br, Cdn) n (the youngest child is her grandfather's favorite) pet, darling, idol, (inf) fair-haired boy/girl.

fear n (filled with fear at the sight of the strange man) fright, terror, alarm, panic, apprehensiveness, dread, horror, nervousness. ⊃

there is no fear of (something) it is not at all likely that (something) will happen (There is no fear of our getting any extra money).

fear vb 1 (they fear their grandfather) be afraid of, be scared of, be apprehensive of, dread. 2 (we fear for their safety) worry, be anxious, feel concerned. 3 (we fear that they could be right) be afraid, suspect, have a suspicion.

fearful adj 1 (they were fearful of disturbing the guard dogs) afraid, frightened, terrified, alarmed, apprehensive. 2 (the smashed cars were a fearful sight) terrible, frightful, appalling, ghastly, horrific, horrible, shocking. 3 (the house was in a fearful mess) terrible, frightful, appalling, very great.

fearless adj (fearless soldiers fighting the enemy/ fearless explorers) brave, courageous, gallant, bold, heroic.

feasible adj (it was not feasible to leave earlier) possible, practicable, workable, reasonable, realistic, within reason.

feat n (read about the daring feats of the knights of old) deed, act, action, exploit, achievement.

feather n (the bird's feathers) plumage, down. ⊃

a feather in your cap something of which you can be justly proud (Winning the tournament was a real feather in his cap because he was the youngest person taking part) <Perhaps from the custom of American Indians who wore feathers on their head as a sign of their bravery in war>.
feather your own nest to make a profit for yourself, often at the expense of someone else, such as your employer (All the time he was a storekeeper with the firm, he was feathering his own nest).

feature n (the feature of the burglary that confused the police) aspect, characteristic, side, detail, quality.

features npl (she had very regular features) face, countenance.

fee n (the fee for membership of the club) charge, price, cost, payment.

feeble adj 1 (people who have grown feeble with age) weak, weakly, frail, infirm, delicate, failing, helpless. 2 (they made a feeble attempt to get there on time) ineffective, ineffectual, weak, futile, inadequate.

feed vb (not make enough money to feed the family) give food to, nourish, provide for, cater for.

feel vb 1 (feel faint at her father's words) experience, undergo, know, be conscious of, be aware of, notice. 2 (feel the silky cloth) touch, stroke, caress, finger, handle, fondle. **3** (*he tried to feel his way to the house in the dark*) grope, fumble. **4** (*the weather feels warmer today*) seem, appear. **5** (*feel the temperature of the water before bathing the baby*) test, try out. **6** (*we feel that we ought to go*) believe, think, consider, be of the opinion, judge. ▷

feeling *n* **1** (*blind people are able to identify objects by feeling*) feel, touch, sense of touch. **2** (*he could not describe his feelings when he lost his job*) emotion, sentiment, sensation. **3** (*there was a feeling of unhappiness about the place*) feel, atmosphere, mood, impression, air, aura. **4** (*my feeling is that we should go*) thoughts, opinion, view, way of thinking, instinct. **5** (*I had a feeling that he would win*) idea, suspicion, funny feeling, hunch.

feign *vb* **1** (*feign illness*) pretend, fake, simulate, sham, affect, give the appearance of. **2** (*we thought that he was sleeping, but he was only feigning*) pretend, put on an act, put it on, fake, sham, act, play-act.

fellow *n* (*a suspicious-looking fellow over there*) man, boy, individual, (*inf*) chap, (*inf*) bloke, (*inf*) guy, (*inf*) character.

female *n* (*a club just for females*) woman, lady, girl.

feminine *adj* **1** (*a very feminine young woman/feminine clothing*) womanly, ladylike, soft, delicate. **2** (*a rather feminine man*) effeminate, womanish, unmanly .

fence *n* (*build a fence around the garden*) barrier, barricade, rail, paling, hedge, wall. ▷

mend fences to put things right after a quarrel or disagreement (*I quarreled with my sister years ago, and I would like to try and mend fences now*).

sit on the fence to decline or refuse to take sides in a dispute or to commit yourself to a point of view (*Her two best friends are having a terrible argument, but she is sitting on the fence because she does not want to offend either of them*).

fence *vb* **1** (*fence the garden*) enclose, surround, encircle. **2** (*fence in the cows*) shut in, confine, pen.

fend *vb* (*he tried to fend off his attacker's blows with his arm/a speaker trying to fend off questions*) ward off, turn aside, deflect, avert, keep off.

ferment *vb* (*beer fermenting in vats*) foam, froth, bubble.

ferocious *adj* **1** (*ferocious animals*) fierce, savage, wild. **2** (*he was injured in a ferocious attack*) fierce, savage, brutal, vicious, violent, murderous, barbaric.

fertile *adj* **1** (*fertile soil*) fruitful, productive, rich. **2** (*a fertile imagination*) inventive, creative, resourceful, ingenious.

fertilizer *n* (*put fertilizer on the garden*) plant food, manure, compost.

fervent *adj* (*his fervent enthusiasm for football/a fervent supporter of animal rights*) passionate, ardent, zealous, devout, vehement, eager, earnest.

festival *n* (*the village's annual festival*) fête, carnival, gala day.

fetch *vb* **1** (*fetch the milk from the store*) get, go for, bring, carry, collect, transport. **2** (*an antique table that fetched thousands of dollars at the auction*) sell for, go for, realize. ▷

fetch and carry for (someone) to run about doing a series of small jobs for (someone) as though you were a servant (*He expects his wife to fetch and carry for him*).

feud *n* (*there had been a bitter feud between the families for generations*) quarrel, dispute, conflict.

fiasco *n* (*the picnic was a fiasco because of the weather*) disaster, catastrophe, failure, (*inf*) flop.

fickle *adj* (*so fickle that she is always changing boyfriends/fickle weather*) changeable, variable, unpredictable, unstable, unreliable.

fictitious *adj* **1** (*not a real person, but a fictitious character*) fictional, made up, invented, imaginary, unreal, mythical. **2** (*he gave a fictitious address to the police*) false, invented, bogus, fake, sham.

fiddle *vb* **1** (*fiddling with his pencil instead of writing his essay*) play, fidget, toy, twiddle. **2** (*fiddle his accounts*) falsify, forge, (*inf*) cook. ▷

fiddle while Rome burns to do absolutely nothing while something important is being ruined, destroyed, or damaged (*The government is being accused of fiddling while Rome burns as the rate of unemployment rises*) <The Roman emperor Nero was said to have played on a lyre, a musical instrument similar to a fiddle, while the city of Rome was burning>.

fidelity *n* (*a leader who looked for fidelity in his followers*) faithfulness, loyalty, devotion, allegiance, constancy, trustworthiness.

fidget *vb* **1** (*children fidgeting in boredom*) be restless, wriggle, squirm. **2** (*students fidgeting with their pencils*) fiddle, play, toy, twiddle.

field *n* **1** (*look at the cows in the field*) pasture, meadow, paddock. **2** (*working in the field of computing*) area, sphere, line, specialty. ⋄

fresh fields and pastures new new places, new activities (*She is tired of her current job and is seriously thinking about moving overseas to explore fresh fields and pastures new*).
have a field day to have a very busy, successful, or enjoyable day (*The reporters had a field day when the scandal about the movie star was announced*) <A field day is a day on which soldiers practice for battle in front of high-ranking officers and so is a special occasion>.

fierce *adj* **1** (*a fierce animal*) ferocious, savage, wild. **2** (*a fierce attack*) ferocious, savage, brutal, vicious, violent, murderous. **3** (*her fierce love of liberty*) passionate, ardent, intense, fervent. **4** (*a fierce wind*) strong, violent, stormy, blustery. **5** (*face fierce competition in the race*) keen, intense, strong, competitive.

fight *vb* **1** (*enemy armies fighting*) do battle, wage war, take up arms, meet in combat. **2** (*armies fighting a battle*) wage, carry on, be engaged in. **3** (*two men fighting in the street*) exchange blows, hit each other, punch each other, brawl. **4** (*the two sisters are always fighting with each other*) quarrel, argue, bicker, squabble, disagree, (*inf*) fall out, feud. **5** (*decide to fight the plans for a new road*) contest, take a stand against, oppose, object to, protest against. ⋄

fight *n* **1** (*our army lost the fight*) battle, encounter, engagement. **2** (*the champion lost the fight*) boxing match. **3** (*two men in a fight outside the tavern*) brawl, (*inf*) scrap, (*inf*) punch-up. **4** (*she has had a fight with her sister*) quarrel, argument, disagreement, difference of opinion, squabble, dispute, feud.

figure *n* **1** (*write down the figures from 1 to 10*) number, numeral, digit. **2** (*what figure did you have in mind as a salary?*) amount, sum. **3** (*fail to recognize the figures disappearing into the mist*) shape, form, outline, silhouette. **4** (*have rather a plump figure*) body, shape, build,

physique. **5** (*a bronze figure of the saint*) likeness, image, statue, carving. **6** (*the figures in the text*) diagram, illustration, drawing, chart.

figure *vb* **1** (*figure out the cost of the vacation*) calculate, count, work out, reckon, add up. **2** (*try to figure out why he did it*) work out, make out, understand, fathom. **3** (*his mother figures in his novel*) appear, feature, play a part, be mentioned.

fill *vb* **1** (*fill the supermarket shelves*) load, stock, supply. **2** (*food that will fill the children*) make full, satisfy, stuff. **3** (*the perfume of roses filled the air*) spread through. **4** (*they filled the hole with sand*) stop up, block up, plug. **5** (*fill in the form*) fill out, answer. ⋄

fill the bill to be exactly what is required (*She was looking for a new hat for the wedding and finally found one that filled the bill*) <Originally referred to a handbill or public notice>.

film *n* **1** (*a film of oil on the road*) layer, coat, coating, covering, sheet. **2** (*see it through a film of tears*) haze, mist, blur.

film *vb* (*film the wedding ceremony*) photograph, take photographs of, take pictures of, shoot, video, make a film of, televise.

filter *vb* (*filter the coffee*) strain, sieve, sift.

filth *n* (*an old basement covered in filth*) dirt, grime, muck, mud, squalor.

filthy *adj* (*filthy houses/filthy hands*) dirty, grimy, grubby, mucky, muddy, squalid, unwashed, unclean.

final *adj* **1** (*the final minutes of the ballgame*) last, closing, concluding, finishing, terminal. **2** (*the decision of the judges is final*) conclusive, decisive, unalterable, indisputable, definitive, absolute.

finalize *vb* (*finalize our arrangements*) complete, conclude, settle, put the finishing touches to.

finance *n* **1** (*look for a job relating to finance*) money matters, money management, economics. **2** (*our finances are low at this time of year*) money, cash, capital, funds, assets, resources.

finance *vb* (*look for someone to finance*) pay for, fund, provide capital for, provide backing for.

find *vb* **1** (*we found a pocketbook in the street*) come across, stumble on, discover. **2** (*she lost her purse and never found it*) get back, recover, retrieve. **3** (*doctors trying to find a cure for* cancer) discover, come upon, bring to light, uncover, unearth, hit upon. **4** (*he is trying to find a new job*) get, obtain, acquire, procure. **5** (*she found that the food did not agree with her*) discover, realize, become aware, learn. ⋄

find out the hard way to find out something by your own experience (*We told her that she would not enjoy the job, but she had to find out the hard way*).
find your feet to be in the process of becoming used to a situation (*He is not very experienced in the job yet—he's just feeling his feet*).

fine *adj* **1** (*hope for a fine day for their picnic*) dry, fair, clear, sunny. **2** (*ornaments made of fine porcelain*) delicate, fragile, dainty. **3** (*summer dresses made of fine material*) light, lightweight, thin, delicate, filmy, flimsy. **4** (*a beach with fine sand*) powdery, fine-grained. **5** (*there is only a fine distinction between the two schemes*) tiny, minute, subtle. **6** (*the musician gave a fine performance*) splendid, excellent, first-class, first-rate, outstanding. **7** (*a wedding party wearing fine clothing*) elegant, stylish, expensive. **8** (*he was sick, but he is fine now*) all right, well. **9** (*if you want to leave early that is fine with us*) all right, acceptable, suitable, (*inf*) OK. ⋄

have (something) down to a fine art to have learned to do something extremely skillfully and usually rapidly (*She has dealing with unwelcome visitors down to a fine art*).

fine *n* (*a fine for speeding*) penalty.
finger *vb* (*children told not to finger the fruit before buying it*) touch, handle, feel, fiddle with. ⋄

be all fingers and thumbs to be clumsy or awkward when using your hands (*She was so nervous about holding a dinner party that she was all fingers and thumbs and kept dropping things*).
let (something) slip through your fingers to lose (an opportunity or advantage) by your own neglect or inactivity.

finish *vb* **1** (*workmen who did not finish the job in time*) complete, accomplish, carry out, get done, fulfill. **2** (*when the concert finished/when the work finished*) end, come to an end, conclude, cease, stop, terminate. **3** (*we finished the bread*

at breakfast) use, use up, consume, exhaust. **4** (*they finish work at five o'clock*) stop, cease, end, discontinue, halt. ⋄

the finishing touches the final details which complete something or make it very good or perfect (*She put the finishing touches to the dinner table by putting an arrangement of flowers on it*).

fire *n* **1** (*modern homes that do not have a fire*) fireplace, hearth, grate. **2** (*fortunately no one was hurt in the fire*) blaze, flames. **3** (*make a fire to burn the garbage*) bonfire. **4** (*her playing of the piece was without fire*) passion, ardor, inspiration. ⋄

like a house afire in a very speedy manner (*The tickets sold like a house afire*).
play with fire to take risks, to do something dangerous (*The child is playing with fire by teasing that dog. It will bite her*).

fire *vb* **1** (*he fired the gun*) shoot, let off, discharge. **2** (*his performance fired them up with enthusiasm*) inspire, rouse, arouse, stir up, stimulate. **3** (*he was fired for always being late*) sack, dismiss, lay off, (*inf*) ax.
firm *adj* **1** (*the ice was not firm enough to skate on*) hard, hardened, solid, set, rigid. **2** (*the poles for the fence must be firm in the ground*) fixed, secure, fast, stable, set, tight. **3** (*we have no firm plans/make a firm arrangement*) fixed, settled, agreed, definite, decided, established. **4** (*they were quite firm about refusing the invitation*) determined, resolute, resolved, decided, adamant, unwavering, obstinate, stubborn. **5** (*they have become firm friends*) devoted, faithful, loyal, dependable.
firm *n* (*he started his own publishing firm*) business, company, organization, establishment, concern.
first *adj* **1** (*the first stages of the manufacturing process*) early, earliest, opening, introductory. **2** (*the first airplane*) earliest, original. **3** (*the first people to arrive*) earliest, soonest. ⋄

first thing early in the morning or early in the working day (*The student was told to go to see the principal first thing*).
get to first base to achieve the first stage toward reaching your goal (*He had big plans, but he never even got to first base with them*).

not to know the first thing about (it/ something) to know nothing whatsoever about (something), to have no knowledge or experience of (something) (*He has opened a music store, although he does not know the first thing about music*).

first *n* (*we knew from the first that he was not suitable*) beginning, start, outset, commencement, (*inf*) the word go.

fit *adj* **1** (*is the water fit to drink?*) suitable, good enough, satisfactory, appropriate. **2** (*she was not fit for the job*) suitable, good enough, satisfactory, able, capable, competent, adequate, trained, qualified. **3** (*the football player was injured, but he is fit now*) well, healthy, in good health, strong, in good condition, in good shape, toned. ⌕

fit to be tied very angry or annoyed (*Jared was fit to be tied when the other boys insulted his mother*).

fit *vb* **1** (*the shoes do not fit*) be the right size, be the correct size. **2** (*fit the parts of the doll's house together*) assemble, put together, join, connect. **3** (*fit the tiles to the floor*) lay, fix, put in place, put in position, position. **4** (*clothing that does not fit the occasion*) suit, be suitable for, be appropriate for, be apt for. **5** (*his account of the accident does not fit with hers*) agree, be in agreement, match, accord, tally. ⌕

fit like a glove to fit very well and comfortably (*She did not have to have the wedding dress altered. It fit her like a glove*).
if the shoe fits, wear it if you think that what has been said might apply to you then you should take particular notice of it.

fit *n* **1** (*she had a coughing fit*) bout, attack, spell. **2** (*an epileptic fit*) convulsion, seizure, spasm.

fitting *adj* **1** (*the criminal should receive a fitting punishment*) suitable, appropriate, due, apt. **2** (*it was not fitting for her to wear that clothing to a funeral*) proper, right, seemly, decent, suitable, appropriate.

fix *vb* **1** (*fix the bookshelves to the study wall*) attach, fasten, secure, stick, screw, nail. **2** (*fix a date for the party*) set, decide on, settle, arrange, agree on, name. **3** (*he is trying to fix the car*) repair, mend, sort, put right, put to rights.

fizzy *adj* (*fizzy drinks*) sparkling, bubbly.

flabbergasted *adj* (*he was flabbergasted at how much the new car was going to cost*) astounded, amazed, dumbfounded, stunned, staggered, nonplussed.

flag *n* (*decorate the streets with flags for the coronation*) banner, streamer, standard. ⌕

fly the flag to attend an event only so that you can say that you have been present, or in order to make sure that your firm, organization, etc. is represented (*I don't really want to go to the advertising firm's party, but no one else from our firm is going and someone really ought to go and fly the flag*).

flag *vb* **1** (*their interest in the subject matter is flagging*) fade, fail, decrease, decline, diminish. **2** (*the speeding motorist was flagged down by the police*) wave down, signal to stop.

flair *n* (*have a flair for languages*) talent, gift, ability, aptitude, bent, genius.

flake *n* (*flakes of paint*) chip, shaving, sliver, fragment, bit.

flame *n* (*burn with a bright flame*) fire, glow, gleam, brightness. ⌕

an old flame a former boyfriend or girlfriend (*His wife objected to the fact that he had lunch with an old flame*) <The suggestion is that the flame of love has died down>.

flame *vb* (*the dry wood flamed up*) burn, blaze, burst into flames, catch fire.

flap *vb* **1** (*the flags were flapping in the wind*) flutter, wave, swing. **2** (*birds with wings flapping*) beat, flail, vibrate, thrash. **3** (*the hostess started to flap when the oven broke down*) panic, go into a panic, become flustered, become agitated, (*inf*) be in a state.

flare *vb* **1** (*the fire suddenly flared up*) blaze, flame. **2** (*trouble flared up when the army left*) break out, burst out, recur. **3** (*she flares up whenever anyone disagrees with her*) lose your temper, go into a rage, get angry, fly off the handle.

flash *n* **1** (*a flash of light*) blaze, burst, flare, gleam, beam, streak. **2** (*she was there in a flash*) instant, moment, second, trice, twinkling of an eye. ⌕

a flash in the pan a sudden and short-lived success (*Our team did unexpectedly well in* *the first round of the tournament, but it turned out to be just a flash in the pan. We were knocked out in the next round*) <A reference to a flintlock gun in which the spark from the flint ignited the gunpowder in the priming pan, the flash then traveling to the main barrel. If this failed to go off there was only a flash in the pan instead of the gun firing>.

flashy *adj* (*wear flashy clothing*) showy, gaudy, ostentatious, flamboyant, loud, garish, tawdry, (*inf*) jazzy, (*inf*) tacky, (*inf*) glitzy.

flat *adj* **1** (*flat surfaces*) level, horizontal, even, smooth. **2** (*lying in a flat position*) spread out, stretched out, prone. **3** (*a flat tire*) deflated, collapsed, burst, punctured. **4** (*the party was rather flat after she had left*) boring, dull, tedious, unexciting, lifeless, uninspired. ✧

in a flat spin in a state of confused excitement, in a state of panic or agitation (*They were in a flat spin when they heard that their guests were going to arrive a day early*).

flatten *vb* **1** (*flatten the surface to make the new road*) make flat, level, even out, smooth out, plane. **2** (*flatten the old buildings to make way for a new housing development*) pull down, knock down, tear down, demolish, raze to the ground. **3** (*gales which flattened the crops*) crush, squash, compress.

flatter *vb* **1** (*he flatters her whenever he wants to borrow her car*) pay compliments to, compliment, praise, sing the praises of, humor, (*inf*) sweet-talk. **2** (*the dress flatters her*) suit, become, show to advantage.

flavor, flavour (*Br; Cdn*) *n* **1** (*people who dislike the flavor of garlic*) taste, savor. **2** (*a sauce in need of flavor*) flavoring, seasoning, spiciness. **3** (*a book that captured the flavor of the times*) spirit, character, feel, feeling, tone, nature, essence. ✧

flavor of the month a person or thing that is very popular only for a short time (*The new secretary is flavor of the month with the boss/Words that are flavor of the month with the media*) <From the practice of some ice-cream firms of trying to persuade customers to try out new flavors>.

flaw *n* **1** (*a flaw in the dress material*) defect, imperfection, fault. **2** (*a flaw in the porcelain*) defect, imperfection, fault, crack, chip.

flee *vb* (*the villagers fled as the enemy army approached*) run away, run off, escape, take flight, make off, (*inf*) do a bunk, retreat.

fleeting *adj* (*a fleeting feeling of regret*) brief, short-lived, momentary.

flesh *n* **1** (*the flesh and bones of the animals*) meat, brawn, muscle. **2** (*prefer the pleasures of the flesh to those of the spirit*) body, human body, physical nature. ✧

get your pound of flesh to obtain everything that you are entitled to, especially if this causes difficulties or suffering to those who have to give it (*He is well paid, but he works such long hours that the company certainly get their pound of flesh*) <A reference to Shakespeare's *Merchant of Venice*, in which Shylock, the moneylender, tries to enforce an agreement by which he is allowed to cut a pound of flesh from Antonio>.

press the flesh to go around shaking hands with members of the public (*The presidential candidate went around the crowd pressing the flesh*).

flexible *adj* **1** (*flexible materials*) pliable, pliant, elastic, springy, bendable. **2** (*our vacation plans are flexible at the moment*) adaptable, adjustable, variable, changeable, open to change.

flight *n* **1** (*the flight of the refugees from the war zone*) fleeing, running away, escape, retreat. **2** (*write a book on the history of flight*) flying, aviation. **3** (*the flight to Australia from New York is very long*) plane journey, plane trip.

flimsy *adj* **1** (*a summer dress made of a flimsy material*) thin, lightweight, light, delicate, sheer. **2** (*a flimsy hut to shelter the refugees*) insubstantial, frail, rickety, ramshackle, makeshift. **3** (*a flimsy excuse for being absent*) feeble, weak, poor, thin, inadequate, unconvincing.

flinch *vb* **1** (*the boy flinched as his father raised his fist*) draw back, recoil, shrink, quail, wince. **2** (*soldiers who do not flinch from their duty*) shrink from, shy away from, shirk, dodge, duck.

fling *vb* (*fling the garbage into the dump*) throw, toss, hurl, cast, pitch, lob, heave, (*inf*) chuck.

flippant *adj* (*she gave a flippant reply to his serious question*) frivolous, shallow, glib, offhand, carefree.

float *vb* 1 (*things that can float on water*) stay afloat, be buoyant. 2 (*marker buoys floating along*) bob, drift. 3 (*balloons floating in the air*) drift, hover, hang.

flog *vb* (*people who think that wrongdoers should be flogged*) whip, lash, beat, thrash. ✧

flog a dead horse to continue to try to arouse interest, enthusiasm, etc., in something which is obviously not, or no longer, of interest (*He's canvassing for votes, but he's flogging a dead horse. His opponent is bound to win*).

flood *n* 1 (*property damaged in the flood*) deluge, torrent, spate. 2 (*after the article in the newspaper there was a flood of correspondence*) abundance, overabundance.

flood *vb* 1 (*houses damaged by rivers flooding*) overflow, break its banks. 2 (*water that flooded the town*) pour over, submerge, immerse.

floor *n* (*a house on three floors*) story, level. ✧

flop *vb* 1 (*his head flopped to one side and he fell asleep*) droop, sag, dangle. 2 (*she flopped into a chair after a hard day's work*) slump, drop, collapse, fall. 3 (*his first play flopped*) fail, be unsuccessful, be a disaster, (*inf*) bomb.

flourish *vb* 1 (*plants that flourish in a dry climate*) thrive, bloom, grow, do well, develop. 2 (*the company is flourishing now*) be in good condition, thrive, be successful, succeed, make progress, grow. 3 (*he flourished the trophy that he had won*) brandish, wave, wield, swing, shake, twirl, hold aloft.

flow *vb* 1 (*rivers flowing*) run, glide, course, stream, ripple, surge. 2 (*a serious wound with blood flowing from it*) gush, well, spurt, spill, ooze.

flower *n* (*put the flowers in a vase*) bloom, blossom. ✧

the flower of (something) the best and finest of (something) (*The young men who were killed in the battle were the flower of the nation*).

flowery *adj* 1 (*drapes with a flowery pattern*) floral, flower-covered. 2 (*dislike the flowery language of his writing*) high-flown, ornate, elaborate.

fluent *adj* 1 (*a fluent speaker*) eloquent, articulate, smooth-spoken. 2 (*we admired his fluent French*) smooth, flowing, effortless, unhesitating.

flurry *n* 1 (*a sudden flurry of snow*) shower, gust, squall. 2 (*in a flurry of excitement waiting for the visitors to arrive*) fluster, bustle, whirl, fuss, flap.

flush *vb* 1 (*flush the toilet*) rinse out, wash out, cleanse. 2 (*she flushed with embarrassment*) blush, redden, go red, turn red, crimson, color. ✧

in the first flush of (something) in the early and strongest stages of (something) (*They raised a lot of money for the project in the first flush of their enthusiasm*).

fluster *vb* (*the guests flustered her by arriving early*) agitate, unsettle, upset, ruffle, panic, confuse, disconcert, (*inf*) rattle.

flutter *vb* 1 (*birds fluttering their wings*) flap, beat, quiver, vibrate. 2 (*streamers fluttering in the wind*) flap, wave, fly, ripple.

fly *vb* 1 (*we decided to fly to Paris rather than go by train*) go by air, go by plane. 2 (*he was flying the plane*) pilot, control, operate. 3 (*watch the birds flying overhead*) hover, flutter, soar. 4 (*flags flying to celebrate the victory*) wave, flap, flutter. 5 (*she flew to the window when she heard the car*) rush, race, run, dash, dart. 6 (*they decided to fly when the enemy army approached*) flee, run away, take flight, make your escape, escape, retreat. ✧

be flying high to be extremely successful, to be in a position of power or influence (*He was flying high a few years ago, but he was laid off and is now unemployed*).
pigs might fly an expression used to show that you think that something is extremely unlikely to happen (*You seriously think that he will lend us his car. Pigs might fly!*)

foam *n* 1 (*the foam on the beer*) froth, head. 2 (*the foam on the soapy water*) froth, bubbles, lather, suds.

foe *n* (*they easily defeated their foes*) enemy, opponent, rival.

fog *n* (*the fog was making it difficult for motorists to see*) mist, haze, smog.

foil *vb* (*the police foiled the thief's attempt to rob the bank*) thwart, frustrate, stop.

foist *vb* (*he tried to foist some of his work on to the junior employees*) force, unload, thrust, impose.

fold *vb* 1 (*fold the sheets*) double over, overlap, crease. 2 (*the firm lost money and folded*) fail, collapse, shut down, go bankrupt, (*inf*) go bust.

folder *n* (*the documents for the meeting were in a folder*) file, binder, cover.

follow vb 1 (she followed her brother into the house) walk behind, go behind, go after. 2 (we asked the taxi to follow the car with the thieves in it) go after, pursue, chase, (inf) tail. 3 (he followed his father as king) come after, succeed, replace, take the place of. 4 (they were told to follow the instructions) obey, observe, keep to, comply with, heed, take notice of. 5 (the students could not follow what the professor was saying) understand, grasp, fathom. 6 (he follows the local football team) be a follower of, be a fan of, be an admirer of, be a supporter of. ⇨

follow suit to do just as someone else has done (She got up from the dinner table and everyone else followed suit) <A reference to card-playing when a player plays a card of the same suit as the previous player>.

fond adj (he is very fond of his grandchildren/She is fond of spicy food) having love for, having a liking for, keen on, attached to, having a soft spot for.

food n 1 (children with not enough food to survive on) nourishment, provisions. 2 (the hostess served delicious food) refreshment, fare, diet, (inf) grub, (inf) nosh. ⇨

food for thought something that makes you think very carefully (The manager's letter about the financial state of the firm gave all the workers food for thought).

foolish adj 1 (it was a foolish idea/They thought it was a foolish thing to do) silly, absurd, senseless, unintelligent, unwise. 2 (he is a foolish fellow) stupid, silly, unintelligent, brainless, dense, ignorant, (inf) dumb.

foot n 1 (the foot of the pillar) base, bottom. 2 (we met at the foot of the road) bottom, end. ⇨

put your foot down to be firm about something, to forbid someone to do something (She wanted to go hitchhiking, but her mother put her foot down and now she's going by bus).

put your foot in your mouth to do or say something tactless or something that will upset or embarrass someone or cause trouble (You put your foot in your mouth when you mentioned her husband. He has just left her).

shoot yourself in the foot to make a mistake or do something stupid which causes problems for yourself or harms your chances of success (Dave shot himself in the foot when he stole money from his grandmother; she was going to leave him all her money, but she changed her will before she died).

forbid vb (they were forbidden to go on the farmer's land) prohibit, ban, bar, debar.

force n 1 (it required a great deal of force to open the door) strength, power, might, energy, effort, exertion, pressure, vigor. 2 (they were accused of using force to get him to confess) pressure, compulsion, violence. 3 (recognize the force of his arguments) persuasiveness, effectiveness, strength, power.

force vb 1 (you cannot force them to go with you) use force on, make, compel, bring pressure to bear on, pressurize. 2 (we lost the key and had to force the drawer) break open, burst open.

forecast vb (we could have forecast that they would win) predict, foretell, prophesy, foresee, speculate.

foreign adj (customs that were foreign to them) alien, unfamiliar, strange, unknown, unfamiliar, exotic.

foresee vb (we could not have foreseen those problems) anticipate, predict, foretell, forecast, prophesy.

forfeit vb (she had to forfeit her pocket money to pay for the damage) give up, hand over, relinquish, surrender.

forge vb (he forged his father's signature on the check) falsify, fake, counterfeit, imitate, copy.

forget vb 1 (I forget their address) be unable to remember, be unable to recall. 2 (he tried to forget the terrible event) put out of your mind, ignore, disregard. 3 (she forgot her husband's birthday) overlook, neglect, disregard. 4 (she forgot her gloves) leave behind, omit to take.

forgive vb (their mother forgave them for being late) excuse, pardon, let off.

form n 1 (describe the form of the crystals) shape, formation, structure. 2 (the human form) body, figure, shape, build, frame, physique, anatomy 3 (a form of entertainment) kind, type, sort, variety. 4 (fill out a form to apply for the job) document, paper, application.

form vb 1 (form clay into animal shapes) shape, mold, fashion, model, make. 2 (they formed a committee to raise money for charity) set up, establish, found, institute. 3 (begin to form plans to solve the problem) put together, draw up, think up, devise, frame. **4** (*icicles began to form in the cold weather*) take shape, develop, appear, materialize. ◇

be bad form not to be in keeping with social customs or accepted manners (*It is bad form to smoke before the end of a meal*).
true to form in keeping with someone's usual pattern of behavior (*True to form, they arrived very late*).

orthcoming *adj* **1** (*forthcoming events in the town*) future, coming, approaching, imminent. **2** (*the children were not very forthcoming about where they had been*) communicative, talkative, informative, open.

orthright *adj* (*a very forthright person who told them the truth*) direct, frank, candid, blunt, plainspeaking.

ortunate *adj* **1** (*he was fortunate to survive the accident*) in luck. **2** (*they are in a fortunate position to have been offered jobs*) favorable, lucky, advantageous.

ortune *n* **1** (*it was only by good fortune that he found the book*) chance, luck, accident. **2** (*he amassed a great fortune*) wealth, riches, assets, possessions.

orward *adj* **1** (*the forward part of the army*) front, foremost, leading **2** (*they were annoyed at her forward behavior*) bold, brash, brazen, impudent, impertinent, (*inf*) pushy.

oul *adj* **1** (*the rotting meat was a foul sight*) disgusting, revolting, repulsive, nauseating, nasty, dirty. **2** (*the air was foul/foul water*) polluted, contaminated, impure, dirty. **3** (*foul weather*) rainy, stormy, wild, rainy, wet, nasty, disagreeable. **4** (*foul language*) blasphemous, vulgar, crude, coarse, rude, filthy. **5** (*what a foul thing to do*) horrible, nasty, hateful, disgraceful, low, wicked, evil. ◇

foul play a criminal act, especially one involving murder (*The police have found a body and they suspect foul play*).

ound *vb* (*found a new company*) set up, establish, institute, start, create.

racture *n* (*fractures in the outer wall*) break, crack, split.

ragile *adj* (*porcelain that is very fragile*) delicate, fine, breakable, brittle, frail.

ragment *n* (*fragments of glass*) piece, bit, chip, sliver, splinter, particle.

frail *adj* **1** (*frail old ladies*) delicate, infirm, weak, slight. **2** (*frail model airplanes*) fragile, breakable, flimsy, insubstantial.

frame *n* **1** (*ships built on a frame of steel*) framework, foundation, shell, skeleton. **2** (*a photograph frame*) mounting, mount. **3** (*wrestlers with huge frames*) body, physique, figure,

frank *adj* (*he answered in a frank manner*) direct, candid, forthright, plain, open, outspoken, blunt.

fraud *n* **1** (*he was accused of fraud*) swindling, sharp practice, dishonesty, crookedness, deceit, deception. **2** (*the magician's act was a fraud*) swindle, hoax, deception, (*inf*) con, (*inf*) rip-off. **3** (*the bank-note was a fraud*) fake, counterfeit, sham, (*inf*) phony.

frayed *adj* (*frayed shirt cuffs*) ragged, tattered, worn.

freak *adj* (*a freak storm*) abnormal, unusual, atypical, exceptional, odd, strange, bizarre.

free *adj* **1** (*we got free tickets for the concert*) free of charge, for nothing, without charge, at no cost, complimentary. **2** (*they were free of any worries*) without, devoid of, unaffected by, clear of. **3** (*we were free to go anywhere we wanted*) allowed, permitted, able. **4** (*they asked us to the party, but we were not free*) available, unoccupied, not busy, at leisure. **5** (*we looked for a free table in the café*) unoccupied, empty, vacant, spare. **6** (*nations that wanted to be free*) independent. ◇

free and easy informal, casual, at ease (*He is the boss, but he is always very free and easy with the employees*).
give (someone) a free hand give (someone) permission to do as they wish (*They gave their gardener a free hand to choose the plants*).

freedom *n* **1** (*prisoners longing for their freedom*) liberty, release. **2** (*nations seeking freedom*) independence.

freezing *adj* **1** (*freezing weather*) icy, frosty, chilly, arctic, wintry. **2** (*we were freezing while waiting for the bus*) chilled through, chilled to the marrow, numb with cold.

frequent *adj* **1** (*they have frequent storms in that area*) many, numerous, repeated, recurrent, persistent. **2** (*a frequent visitor*) regular, habitual, common, usual, constant.

fresh *adj* **1** (*serve fresh fruit for dessert*) raw, unpreserved, unprocessed. **2** (*a supply of fresh water*) pure, unpolluted, uncontaminated, clean.

3 (*they are hoping for some fresh ideas*) new, modern, original. **4** (*we felt fresh after our vacation*) energetic, invigorated, lively, refreshed, revived.

friend *n* (*the children invited their friends to a party*) companion, (*inf*) pal, (*inf*) chum, (*inf*) mate. ✧

a friend in need is a friend indeed a friend who provides help when you are in trouble is truly a friend.
fair-weather friends people who are friendly toward you only when you are not in trouble of any kind (*All his fair-weather friends deserted him when he lost his job*).

friendly *adj* (*friendly neighbors*) sociable, hospitable, approachable, good-natured, kindly.

frighten *vb* (*the children were frightened when they heard the noise*) scare, alarm, startle, terrify.

front *n* **1** (*the front of the line*) head, top, beginning. **2** (*they painted the front of the building red*) frontage, façade, face. **3** (*his business is just a front for drug-dealing*) cover, cover-up, disguise, blind, mask.

froth *n* **1** (*froth on the soapy water*) bubbles, lather, suds. **2** (*froth on the beer*) bubbles, head.

frown *vb* **1** (*she frowned in anger*) scowl, glower, glare. **2** (*they frowned upon casual clothes at the club*) disapprove of, take a dim view of, dislike.

fulfill *vb* **1** (*he failed to fulfill the tasks given to him*) carry out, perform, discharge, accomplish, complete. **2** (*he was the only person who fulfilled the job requirements*) satisfy, meet, answer, obey.

full *adj* **1** (*their glasses were full*) filled, brimming, brimful. **2** (*all the hotel rooms are full*) occupied, taken, in use. **3** (*the supermarket was full on Saturdays*) crowded, packed, crammed, chock-full. **4** (*she gave us a full list of the names of people present*) complete, whole, entire, comprehensive, detailed, thorough.

fumble *vb* **1** (*fumbled for his keys in the dark*) grope, feel for. **2** (*fumble a catch at baseball*) miss, mishandle.

fumes *npl* (*the fumes from the car's exhaust pipe*) gases, smoke, vapor, smell.

fun *n* (*the children had fun at the party*) entertainment, amusement, enjoyment, pleasure, a good time. ✧

make fun of (someone or **something)** to laugh at or make mocking remarks about (someone or something) (*Her classmates made fun of her for wearing old-fashioned clothing*).

function *n* **1** (*his function in the firm*) role, job, duty, task, responsibility. **2** (*the function of the machine*) use, purpose. **3** (*invited to the firm's annual function*) party, reception, gathering, social occasion, social event.

fundamental *adj* (*learn fundamental cooking skills*) basic, rudimentary, elementary, essential, primary.

funny *adj* **1** (*they laughed at his funny stories*) amusing, comic, comical, humorous, hilarious, laughable, riotous. **2** (*there was something funny about the way he was behaving*) odd, peculiar, strange, queer, weird, bizarre, suspicious.

furious *adj* (*they were furious at being treated rudely*) enraged, infuriated, indignant, angry.

furnish *vb* **1** (*furnish the room with modern furniture*) equip, fit out. **2** (*furnish the committee with the required information*) provide, supply, equip, present.

furniture *n* (*buy antique furniture for the house*) furnishings, appointments, effects.

further *adj* (*require further supplies*) additional, more, extra.

furtive *adj* (*the police were suspicious of his furtive behavior*) secretive, stealthy, sneaky, surreptitious, sly.

fury *n* (*her parent's fury at the damage caused during the party*) anger, rage.

future *n* **1** (*hope for better things in the future*) time to come, time ahead, time hereafter. **2** (*there is little future for that industry*) prospects, expectations, outlook, likely success.

future *adj* (*an advertisement for future events*) coming, approaching, to come.

G

gadget *n* (*a kitchen with a lot of labor-saving gadgets*) appliance, device, piece of apparatus, implement.

gag *n* (*the comedian told a series of old gags*) joke, jest, quip, witticism, wisecrack.

gain *vb* (*they tried to gain an advantage over the opposition*) get, obtain, acquire, procure, secure, achieve.

gain *n* (*their gains from the sale of the company*) profit, return, yield, proceeds, earnings, reward, benefit, (*inf*) pickings. ✧

gain ground to make progress, to become more generally acceptable or popular (*The campaign in favor of animal rights is gaining ground*).

nothing ventured, nothing gained you cannot achieve anything worthwhile in life if you are not prepared to take any risks (*It's risky starting a new business without much capital,, but there again nothing ventured, nothing gained*).

gale *n* (*ships damaged at sea in a gale*) storm, hurricane, tempest, tornado, cyclone.

gallant *adj* (*gallant soldiers who died in battle*) brave, courageous, heroic, plucky, fearless, intrepid.

gallop *vb* **1** (*horses galloping around the field*) canter, prance, frisk. **2** (*the children always gallop home for tea*) rush, run, dash, race, sprint, hurry.

gamble *vb* **1** (*he loves to gamble and loses a lot of money*) bet, place a bet, wager, lay a wager, (*inf*) punt. **2** (*he gambled when he invested in the company*) take a risk, take a chance, speculate, venture.

game *n* **1** (*the children's games*) amusement, entertainment, diversion, sport, pastime, hobby. **2** (*we are all going to the game tomorrow*) match, competition, contest, tournament, athletics event, sports meeting. ✧

beat (someone) at their own game to be more successful than (someone) at the kind of activity they usually take part in, especially a cunning or dishonest one (*In previous years he won the cross-country race by taking a short cut, but this year another competitor did the same and beat him at his own game*).

give the game away to reveal a secret plan, trick, etc., usually accidentally.

play the game to behave in a fair and honorable way (*He didn't play the game. He got his friend's job when she was out sick*).

gang *n* **1** (*a gang of people had gathered to listen to the speaker*) group, band, crowd, mob, horde. **2** (*the boys formed a gang*) club, clique, circle, set. **3** (*a gang of workmen*) squad, team, troop.

gap *n* **1** (*crawl through a gap in the wall*) opening, hole, space, chink. **2** (*the police are trying to fill in a few gaps in the account of the accident*) omission, blank, void.

gape *vb* **1** (*they gaped at the sheer size of the huge man*) stare, goggle, gaze. **2** (*the caves gaped before them*) open wide, yawn.

garden *n* (*he grows vegetables in his garden*) yard, plot. ✧

garden variety completely ordinary (*I'm not going to wear anything special to the ceremony. I'll just put on a garden-variety skirt and top*).

lead (someone) down the garden path to mislead or deceive (someone) (*She thought that he was going to marry her, but he was just leading her down the garden path*).

garish *adj* (*the vacationers were wearing garish clothing*) flashy, loud, gaudy, bold, flamboyant.

garland *n* (*wearing garlands of flowers around their necks*) wreath, festoon.

garment *n* (*wearing a strange black garment*) piece of clothing, item of clothing, article of clothing.

garments *npl* (*wearing mourning garments*) clothes, clothing, dress, attire, apparel, outfit.

gash *vb* (*he gashed his hand when carving the meat*) cut, slash, wound, nick.

gasp *vb* (*he was gasping as he reached the top of the mountain*) pant, puff, puff and pant, blow, choke, wheeze. ✧

at your last gasp just about to collapse, to be ruined, to die, etc. (*She was at her last gasp when the ambulance arrived*).

gate *n* (*the gate at the end of the driveway to the house*) gateway, barrier, entrance.

gather *vb* **1** (*a crowd gathered to hear the speaker*) collect, come together, assemble, congregate, meet. **2** (*gather food for the fire*) collect, get together, accumulate, heap up, store, stockpile, hoard. **3** (*gather blackberries*) pick, pluck, harvest, collect. **4** (*we gather that she is ill*) understand, believe, be led to believe, hear, learn.

gathering *n* (*be invited to the firm's annual gathering*) party, function, get-together, social.

gaudy *adj* garish, bold, overbright, loud, glaring, flashy, showy.

gauge *vb* **1** (*he was asked to gauge the length of the yard*) measure, calculate, determine, estimate. **2** (*it is difficult to gauge the extent of his interest in the project*) assess, estimate, judge, guess.

gaunt *adj* (*he looked gaunt after his long illness*) haggard, drawn, skinny, bony, scrawny.

gay *adj* **1** (*people feeling gay on vacation*) merry, jolly, light-hearted, glad, happy, cheerful, in good spirits. **2** (*girls wearing summer dresses in gay colors*) bright, brightly colored, vivid, brilliant, flamboyant.

gaze *vb* (*tourists gazing at the beauty of the sunset*) stare, eye, contemplate, look fixedly.

gear *n* **1** (*the mountaineers and all their gear*) equipment, apparatus, kit, implements, tackle, things, possessions, belongings, (*inf*) stuff. **2** (*young people who like to be dressed in the latest gear*) clothes, clothing, dress, garments, attire, apparel.

gem *n* (*an engagement ring with sparkling gems*) jewel, precious stone, stone.

general *adj* **1** (*the general feeling is that he is guilty*) common, widespread, broad, wide, accepted, universal. **2** (*the general rule is that people have to have three years' experience before getting a job there*) usual, customary, common, normal, standard, ordinary, typical. **3** (*he gave them a general idea of his plans for the business*) broad, nondetailed, vague, indefinite, inexact, rough.

generous *adj* **1** (*he was a generous contributor to the charity*) kind, liberal, lavish, open-handed. **2** (*there was a generous supply of food and drinks at the party*) abundant, plentiful, ample, rich.

genius *n* **1** (*he is a genius at mathematics*) mastermind, intellectual, expert, (*inf*) Einstein. **2** (*people of genius*) brilliance, brains, intellect, intelligence. **3** (*have a genius for making delicious low-cost meals*) gift, talent, flair, bent, knack, aptitude, ability.

gentle *adj* **1** (*she remembered with love her gentle mother*) kind, kindly, lenient, tender-hearted, sweet-tempered, mild, soft, peaceful. **2** (*her gentle touch*) soft, light, smooth, soothing. **3** (*a gentle breeze*) mild, light, soft, moderate, temperate. **4** (*children learning to ski on gentle slopes*) gradual, slight. **5** (*the dog was a very gentle animal*) tame, placid, docile. **6** (*she tried to give him a gentle hint about his bad manners*) indirect, subtle.

genuine *adj* **1** (*his excuse for being absent turned out to be genuine*) real, true, authentic, sound, legitimate, valid. **2** (*they doubted that his feelings were genuine*) real, sincere, honest, truthful, true.

gesture *n* (*he made a gesture to indicate that he agreed*) signal, sign, motion.

get *vb* **1** (*she wondered where she could get a book on antiques*) obtain, acquire, get hold of, come by, procure, buy, purchase. **2** (*he went upstairs to get a book for his mother*) fetch, bring, carry, go for, retrieve. **3** (*they get a high salary*) earn, be paid, bring in, make, clear, take home. **4** (*she got flu last winter*) catch, become infected by, contract. **5** (*the children were getting tired*) become, grow. **6** (*when do you expect to get there?*) arrive at, reach. **7** (*I didn't get what he was talking about*) understand, comprehend, follow, grasp. **8** (*we eventually got her to agree*) persuade, coax, induce, talk (someone) into. ↻

get nowhere to make absolutely no progress (*The two sides have been having talks to try to find a solution, but they are getting nowhere*).

tell (someone) where to get off to tell (someone) that you will not tolerate their behavior or actions anymore.

ghastly *adj* (*she looked ghastly when she went to hospital*) white, white as a sheet, pale, pallid, wan, colorless, drawn.

ghost *n* (*she imagined that she saw a ghost in the graveyard*) apparition, specter, phantom, spirit, (*inf*) spook. ↻

give up the ghost to die, to stop working, to stop trying, etc. (*Our old car has finally given up the ghost*) <Ghost refers to a person's spirit—a biblical reference to Job 14:10>.

not to have a ghost of a chance not to have

the slightest possibility of success (*He has decided to enter the race, but he doesn't have a ghost of a chance*).

gibberish *n* (*they accused him of talking gibberish*) nonsense, garbage, drivel.

gibe *n* (*she was upset at the gibes of her fellow-students*) sneer, jeer, taunt, mocking, scorn.

giddy *adj* **1** (*feel giddy at the top of the ladder*) dizzy, light-headed, faint, (*inf*) woozy. **2** (*giddy girls who had no interest in having a career*) silly, flighty, frivolous, irresponsible, thoughtless, unstable.

gift *n* **1** (*birthday gifts*) present. **2** (*he was thanked for his gift to the charity*) present, donation, contribution, offering. **3** (*the student has a gift for foreign languages*) talent, flair, aptitude, knack, ability, expertise, genius. ✧

look a gift horse in the mouth to criticize something that has been given to you (*She was complaining about flaws in the antique table which he gave her. She really shouldn't look a gift horse in the mouth*) <Looking at a horse's teeth is a way of telling its age and of estimating its value>.

gigantic *adj* (*they caught sight of a gigantic mountain through the mist*) huge, enormous, colossal, immense, vast.

giggle *vb* (*students giggling at the back of the class*) titter, snicker, laugh, (*inf*) tee-hee.

girl *n* **1** (*she lived in the village as a girl*) young woman, (*inf*) lass. **2** (*the couple have a boy and a girl*) daughter. **3** (*he went to the pictures with his girl*) girlfriend, sweetheart, fiancée.

gist *n* (*some of his lecture was a bit difficult for the audience, but most of them got the gist of it*) drift, substance, essence, sense.

give *vb* **1** (*she lifted the book and gave it to him*) hand, hand over, pass. **2** (*the old lady gave a very large sum of money to the local hospital*) donate, contribute, present, bestow, make over. **3** (*the charity worker was giving out soup and bread to homeless people*) hand out, distribute, allot, allocate, dole out. **4** (*they were given some bad advice*) provide, supply, furnish, offer. **5** (*she gives the impression of being very efficient*) show, display, demonstrate, indicate. **6** (*the chair gave and the child fell to the floor*) give way, collapse, break, come apart, fall apart. ✧

give and take willingness to compromise (*There has to be some give and take in a friendship, but she wanted to get her own way all the time*).

give as good as you get to be as successful as your opponent in an argument, quarrel, contest, etc. (*He tries to bully his wife, but she gives as good as she gets*).

giver *n* (*the giver of the money to the hospital*) donor, contributor.

glad *adj* **1** (*we were very glad to see our visitors*) happy, pleased, delighted. **2** (*hear the glad news*) happy, delightful, joyful, welcome, cheerful. ✧

glad rags (*inf*) your best clothes worn on special occasions (*They put on their glad rags and went to the most expensive restaurant in town*).

glamorous *adj* **1** (*glamorous movie stars*) beautiful, lovely, attractive, elegant, smart, dazzling, alluring. **2** (*she has a glamorous career in advertising*) exciting, fascinating, dazzling, high-profile, (*inf*) glitzy.

glance *vb* **1** (*he only glanced at the stranger*) take a quick look at, look briefly at, glimpse, peep. **2** (*glance through the newspapers at breakfast*) skim through, leaf through, flick through, flip through, thumb through, scan. **3** (*the bullet glanced off the tree*) bounce, rebound, ricochet. **4** (*the car glanced the wall as he drove it into the garage*) graze, brush, touch, skim.

glare *n* **1** (*he was unaware of her angry glares*) scowl, frown, black look, (*inf*) dirty look. **2** (*the glare from the headlights of oncoming cars*) flare, blaze, dazzle.

glass *n* (*a glass of cold water*) tumbler, beaker, goblet. ✧

people who live in glass houses shouldn't throw stones people who have certain faults or disadvantages themselves should not criticize similar faults or disadvantages in others (*He complains about his neighbors playing music loudly, but he does the same. Somebody should tell him that people in glass houses shouldn't throw stones*).

gleam *n* **1** (*a gleam of light*) beam, glow, ray, shimmer, sparkle. **2** (*the gleam of the polished tables*) glow, shine, gloss, sheen, luster. **3** (*there* *is still a gleam of hope*) glimmer, ray, trace, suggestion, hint, flicker.

glib *adj* (*she was persuaded into buying the goods by a glib sales clerk*) smooth, plausible, smooth-talking, fluent, suave.

glide *vb* (*they watched the yachts gliding by*) sail, slide, slip, skim, float, drift.

glimpse *vb* (*she thought that she glimpsed a stranger through the trees*) catch sight of, spot, make out, notice.

glitter *vb* (*the diamonds glittered in the candlelight*) sparkle, flash, twinkle, flicker, blink, wink, shimmer, gleam, glint.

gloat *vb* (*she was gloating over her rival's misfortunes*) relish, delight in, take pleasure in, revel in, rejoice in, glory in, crow about.

global *adj* **1** (*the possibility of global war*) world, worldwide, universal, international. **2** (*a global pay settlement on all public service employees*) general, universal, across-the-board, comprehensive.

gloomy *adj* **1** (*a gloomy November day*) dark, overcast, cloudy, dull, dismal, dreary. **2** (*an old house full of gloomy rooms*) dark, somber, dingy, dismal, dreary, depressing. **3** (*he is in a gloomy mood today*) in low spirits, depressed, sad, unhappy, miserable, dejected, downcast, downhearted, glum, melancholy.

glorious *adj* **1** (*it was a glorious day*) bright, beautiful, lovely, sunny. **2** (*the procession was a glorious sight*) splendid, magnificent, wonderful, marvelous. **3** (*celebrate a glorious victory*) famous, celebrated, renowned, noble, distinguished.

glossy *adj* (*the glossy surfaces of the polished tables*) gleaming, shining, shiny, bright, sparkling, shimmering, polished.

glow *vb* (*the lights glowed*) gleam, shine, glimmer.

glow *n* **1** (*the glow from the table lamps*) gleam, brightness, glimmer. **2** (*the glow from the fire*) warmth, heat, redness. **3** (*she felt a warm glow when she thought of her friends*) warmth, happiness, contentment, satisfaction.

glue *vb* (*glue the broken pieces together*) stick, gum, paste, cement.

glum *adj* (*in a glum mood*) gloomy, depressed, sad, unhappy, miserable, dejected, downcast, downhearted, melancholy.

glut *n* (*a glut of soft fruit on the market*) surplus, excess, surfeit, overabundance, oversupply.

gnaw *vb* **1** (*the dog was gnawing on a bone*) chew, munch, crunch, bite, nibble, worry. **2** (*the metal had been gnawed away by rust*) erode, corrode, wear away, eat away.

go *vb* **1** (*go carefully on the icy roads*) move, proceed, walk, travel. **2** (*it is time to go*) go away, leave, depart, withdraw, set off, set out. **3** (*the pain has gone*) stop, cease, vanish, disappear, fade, be no more. **4** (*the machine has stopped going*) work, be in working order, function, operate, run. **5** (*his beard has gone white*) become, grow, turn, get, come to be. **6** (*this road goes to the next town*) extend, stretch, reach, lead to. **7** (*time went slowly while they were waiting for the train*) pass, elapse, slip by. **8** (*how did the party go?*) turn out, work out, progress, fare. **9** (*drapes and carpets that don't go*) go together, match, blend, harmonize. ▷

from the get go (*inf*) right from the very start (*We knew from the get go that he was not the right person for the job*).
make a go of (something) to make a success of (something) (*They tried very hard to make a go of the restaurant*).
on the go always very active or busy (*She has three small children and is on the go all day*).

goal *n* (*making a lot of money was his one goal in life/He read out a statement of the goals of the organization*) aim, objective, end, purpose, object, target, ambition.

gobble *vb* (*the children were told not to gobble their food*) wolf, bolt, gulp, (*inf*) scoff.

god *n* (*the gods of ancient Greece*) deity, divinity, divine being, idol. ▷

in the lap of the gods uncertain, left to chance or fate (*There's nothing else we can do. Whether we get the job or not is in the lap of the gods*).

God *n* (*the biblical story about God and Moses*) God Almighty, the Almighty, God the Father, Our Maker. ▷

there, but for the grace of God go I if I had not been fortunate then that piece of misfortune could easily have happened to me (*There were a lot of layoffs in the company and as I said goodbye to some of my colleagues I thought "There but for the grace of God go I"*).

think that you are God's gift to (someone) to have a very high opinion of yourself (*He thinks that he is God's gift to women*).

golden *adj* **1** (*girls with golden hair*) gold-colored, blond, yellow, fair, flaxen. **2** (*a golden opportunity*) splendid, superb, excellent, favorable, fortunate, advantageous, profitable. ⋄

a golden handshake a large amount of money given to someone who is leaving a job, usually because he or she is retiring (*Bill will be quite comfortable in his retirement, having received a golden handshake from the firm*).

the golden rule a rule or practice that it is vital to remember if things are to run smoothly (*The golden rule when baking a sponge cake is never to open the oven door when it is cooking*) <Originally the golden rule was that you should do to others as you would wish them to do to yourself>.

good *adj* **1** (*the children were told to be good*) well-behaved, well-mannered, obedient, manageable. **2** (*she is such a good person, who never treats anyone badly*) honorable, virtuous, righteous, upright, honest, decent, moral, ethical. **3** (*she is noted for her good deeds*) helpful, kind, thoughtful, virtuous, admirable. **4** (*he is not a very good driver*) competent, capable, able, skillful, adept, proficient, expert, first-class, (*inf*) A1. **5** (*the car does not have very good brakes*) efficient, reliable, dependable, trustworthy. **6** (*athletes in good condition*) fine, healthy, sound, strong, robust, vigorous. **7** (*the party was very good*) enjoyable, agreeable, entertaining, pleasant, lovely, nice. **8** (*we had good weather on vacation*) fine, sunny, pleasant. ⋄

be up to no good to be planning to do something wrong or illegal (*The police officer thought that the boys standing by the cars were up to no good*).

make good to be successful in your career or business (*He comes from a very poor background, but he made good at an early age in the advertising business*).

as good as gold very well behaved (*The children were as good as gold at the party*).

gossip *n* **1** (*I heard that he had been in prison, but it turned out to be just gossip*) rumor, tittle-tattle, scandal, hearsay, (*inf*) mud-slinging. **2** (*she was having a good gossip with her neighbor*) chat.

govern *vb* (*the party that is governing the country*) rule, manage, lead, be in power over, be in charge of, preside over, control.

government *n* (*he is a member of the government*) administration, parliament, congress, ministry, council, (*inf*) the powers that be.

grab *vb* **1** (*he was told to grab the end of the rope*) catch hold of, take hold of, grasp, clutch, grip. **2** (*he grabbed the money and ran*) seize, snatch. ⋄

up for grabs ready to be taken, bought, etc. (*There are several jobs up for grabs in the firm*).

grace *n* **1** (*admire the grace of the dancers*) gracefulness, elegance. **2** (*he did not to have the grace to apologize*) manners, courtesy, decency. **3** (*he was at one time the king's favorite courtier, but he fell from grace*) favor, goodwill. **4** (*pray for God's grace*) forgiveness, mercy, pardon. **5** (*say grace before dinner*) blessing, thanksgiving. ⋄

saving grace a good quality that prevents someone or something from being completely bad, unpleasant, useless, etc. (*She is not very bright, but her saving grace is that she is a very hard worker*).

with a bad *or* **good grace** in an unwilling or willing way (*She had the good grace not to run for office*).

graceful *adj* **1** (*they admired the gymnasts' graceful movements*) smooth, flowing, supple, agile, easy, elegant. **2** (*he gave a graceful speech of thanks*) elegant, polished, suave, refined.

gracious *adj* **1** (*the old duchess was a very gracious lady*) kind, kindly, benevolent, friendly, amiable, pleasant, cordial, courteous, polite, civil. **2** (*their gracious lifestyle*) elegant, tasteful, comfortable, luxurious. **3** (*believe in a gracious God*) merciful, compassionate, lenient, gentle.

grade *n* **1** (*what grade has he reached in the firm?*) level, stage, position, rank, standard. **2** (*grades of eggs*) category, class, classification.

gradual *adj* (*there has been a gradual improvement*) slow, steady, gentle, moderate, step-by-step, systematic.

grain *n* 1 (*have grains of sand in her shoes*) particle, granule, bit, piece, fragment, speck. 2 (*the farmer grows grain*) cereal crop, corn. 3 (*we found that there was not a grain of truth in his statement*) particle, scrap, trace, hint, suggestion. 4 (*the grain of the wood*) texture, surface. ✧

go against the grain to be against someone's inclinations, feelings, or wishes (*It goes against the grain for him to lie, but he did not want to tell the truth and hurt her feelings*) <Refers to the direction of the grain in wood, it being easier to cut or smooth wood with the grain rather than across or against it>.

grand *adj* 1 (*the grand houses of the rich*) great, impressive, magnificent, splendid, imposing, majestic, stately. 2 (*a grand occasion*) important, great, splendid, magnificent.

grant *vb* 1 (*the president granted the journalist an interview*) agree to, consent to, allow, permit. 2 (*I grant that you may be right*) acknowledge, admit, concede, allow.

grapple *vb* 1 (*the police officer grappled with the burglar*) struggle, wrestle, fight, tussle, clash. 2 (*he is still grappling with the problem of how to get there*) struggle, tackle, handle, deal with, cope with, attend to. ✧

grasp *vb* 1 (*He grasped the handrail to prevent himself from falling*) grip, clutch, grab, take hold of, hold on to, clench. 2 (*He seemed unable to grasp the situation*) understand, follow, comprehend, take in, get the drift of.

grateful *adj* 1 (*they were grateful to him for his help*) thankful, filled with gratitude, indebted, obliged, appreciative. 2 (*we received a grateful letter for our contribution*) appreciative, thankful.

grave *n* (*the grave of the unknown soldier*) burial place, tomb .

grave *adj* 1 (*he was in a grave mood when he came back from the hospital*) solemn, serious, earnest, sober, somber, grim, severe, unsmiling. 2 (*there were grave matters to discuss at the meeting*) serious, important, significant, weighty, pressing, urgent, vital, crucial.

graveyard *n* (*the funeral procession arrived at the graveyard*) cemetery, burial ground, churchyard.

graze *vb* 1 (*he grazed his knee*) scrape, skin, scratch, wound, bruise. 2 (*the car grazed the garage wall*) brush, touch, glance off, shave, skim.

greasy *adj* 1 (*dislike greasy foods*) fatty, fat, oily. 2 (*the car skidded on the greasy roads*) slippery, slimy.

great *adj* 1 (*a great stretch of water*) large, big, extensive, vast, immense, huge. 2 (*the invalid was in great pain*) extreme, severe, intense, acute. 3 (*they have traveled to all the great cities of the world*) major, main, chief, principal, leading. 4 (*the great people of the country*) important, prominent, leading, top, distinguished, notable, famous. 5 (*he was a great tennis player*) expert, skillful, adept, masterly, (*inf*) ace, (*inf*) crack. 6 (*they had a great time at the party*) enjoyable, splendid, wonderful, marvelous, (*inf*) fabulous. ✧

go great guns to be performing very well (*The runner got off to a slow start, but he is going great guns now*).

great minds think alike an expression used humorously when someone else shares your opinion or has had the same idea as yourself (*John came up with the same solution to the problem as I did—great minds think alike*).

greedy *adj* 1 (*greedy children ate all the cakes before some people arrived*) gluttonous. 2 (*people greedy for information*) avid, eager, hungry, desirous of, craving. 3 (*a greedy miser hoarding gold*) grasping, miserly, tight-fisted.

greet *vb* 1 (*he greeted his neighbor as he walked down the street*) say "hello" to, address, hail. 2 (*the hostess greeted her guests*) receive, welcome, meet.

grief *n* (*her grief at the death of her husband*) sorrow, sadness, misery, distress, heartbreak, dejection, mourning. ✧

come to grief to suffer misfortune, to be unsuccessful (*All their schemes for making money came to grief*).

grievance *n* (*management refused to listen to the workers' grievances*) complaint, protest, charge, grumble.

grieve *vb* 1 (*the widow is still grieving*) mourn, be in mourning, lament, be sorrowful, sorrow, be sad, be distressed, fret. 2 (*she was grieved by her son's behavior*) hurt, upset, distress, sadden, wound.

grim *adj* **1** (*she held on with grim determination*) determined, resolute, obstinate, unwavering, relentless. **2** (*the teacher was wearing a grim expression*) stern, severe, fierce, forbidding, somber. **3** (*the murdered corpse was a grim sight*) horrible, dreadful, terrible, frightful, shocking, ghastly, gruesome.

grime *n* (*trying to clean the grime from the old house*) dirt, filth, dust, (*inf*) muck, (*inf*) grunge.

grin *vb* smile, smile broadly, smile from ear to ear. ⋄

grin like a Cheshire cat to smile very broadly, often with self-satisfaction (*She was grinning like a Cheshire cat as she was handed the prize*) <Refers to *Alice's Adventures in Wonderland* by Lewis Carroll, in which the Cheshire cat gradually disappears, leaving his smile behind>.

grind *vb* **1** (*grind coffee beans*) crush, pound, pulverize, powder, mill. **2** (*grind knives*) sharpen, whet, file, polish. **3** (*she had a habit of grinding her teeth*) gnash, grate, rasp.

grip *vb* **1** (*she gripped the handrail of the ship*) grasp, clutch, clasp, clench, grab, take hold of, seize. **2** (*the audience was gripped by the exciting play*) absorb, rivet, engross, fascinate, enthrall, hold spellbound.

grit *n* **1** (*put grit on icy roads*) gravel, pebbles, dirt, sand, dust. **2** (*he did not have the grit to tell her himself that he was breaking off the engagement*) courage, bravery, pluck, nerve, backbone. ⋄

grit your teeth to make every effort not to show your feelings of pain, distress, disappointment, anger, etc. (*He had to grit his teeth when his boss read out a list of his faults*).

groan *vb* **1** (*the accident victim groaned in pain*) moan, whimper, wail, cry. **2** (*the workers were groaning about their low wages*) grumble, complain, moan.

grope *vb* **1** (*they had to grope their way in the pitch dark*) fumble, feel. **2** (*she groped for her keys in her purse*) fumble, feel for, fish for, scrabble for.

ground *n* **1** (*the ground is very wet after all the rain*) earth, soil, dirt, land. **2** (*she became sick and fell to the ground*) earth, floor. **3** (*they would like a new sport ground*) stadium, pitch, field, arena. ⋄

get (something) off the ground to get (a project) started and under way (*It sounds like a good idea, but I think the scheme is too expensive ever to get off the ground*).

hit the ground running to start a new activity immediately with a great deal of energy and enthusiasm (*We expected the new manager to hit the ground running and introduce new ideas immediately, but she said that she would rather wait and see how things were done*) <From soldiers leaving a helicopter or getting up from being dropped by parachute and immediately running into battle>.

shift your ground to change your opinions, attitudes, ideas, etc. (*We thought that we were going to lose the vote, but several members of the opposition have shifted their ground*).

grounds *npl* **1** (*they have grounds for concern about their missing son*) reason, cause, basis, foundation, justification. **2** (*the house was set in beautiful grounds*) land, surroundings, property, estate, lawns, gardens, park.

group *n* **1** (*we divided the books into groups*) category, class, set, lot, batch. **2** (*she has joined a cookery group*) society, association, club, circle. **3** (*a group of people gathered to watch the fight*) band, gathering, cluster, crowd, flock, bunch.

grow *vb* **1** (*the farmers grow wheat*) cultivate, produce, raise, farm. **2** (*the plants will not grow in this very dry soil*) shoot up, spring up, sprout, thrive, flourish. **3** (*the boy is growing rapidly*) become taller, get bigger, grow larger, stretch, lengthen, expand, fill out. **4** (*the situation is growing serious*) become, come to be, get, get to be, turn, turn out to be.

grudge *vb* (*she grudges them their success*) begrudge, resent, be jealous of, envy, mind.

grumble *vb* (*the passengers were grumbling about the train being late*) complain, protest, object, moan, (*inf*) beef.

guarantee *vb* **1** (*he guaranteed that he would attend the meeting*) promise, pledge, give your word, give an assurance, vow, swear. **2** (*this ticket guarantees you a seat at the match*) ensure, secure. **3** (*he guaranteed his daughter's car loan*) act as guarantor, provide security for, vouch for.

guard *n* **1** (*prison guards*) warder, jailer, keeper.

2 (*the castle guards*) sentry, sentinel, custodian, watchman, lookout. **3** (*put a new guard on the machine*) safety guard, safety device, shield. ⋄

be on your guard to be unprepared for a difficult or dangerous situation (*He was told to beware of thieves so he was on his guard*) <Refers to fencing>.

guard *vb* **1** (*the people who were guarding the jewels*) stand guard over, watch over, protect, safeguard, defend, shield, look after, preserve. **2** (*the people guarding the prisoners*) keep under guard, keep watch over, mind, supervise. **3** (*tourists are asked to guard against thieves*) beware of, be on the alert for, be on the look-out for, keep an eye out for.

guess *vb* **1** (*we were asked to guess the weight of the cake*) estimate, predict, (*inf*) guesstimate. **2** (*we guessed that they would take the shortest route*) surmise, conjecture, suppose, assume, reckon.

guest *n* (*the hostess welcomed her guests*) visitor, company, caller.

guide *vb* **1** (*he guided them down the mountain*) lead, conduct, show, usher, direct, show the way to, escort. **2** (*they asked for someone to guide them in their choice of career*) advise, give advice to, counsel, direct.

guide *n* **1** (*they hired a guide to show them around the city sights*) escort, leader, advisor. **2** (*buy a guide to Rome*) guidebook, handbook, directory, manual. **3** (*the lights acted as a guide to shipping*) landmark, marker, signal, beacon. **4** (*the students were given an essay as a guide*) model, pattern, standard, example, yardstick.

guilt *n* **1** (*it was impossible to prove his guilt*) guiltiness, blame, blameworthiness, fault, responsibility. **2** (*feelings of guilt at their treatment of her*) guiltiness, guilty conscience, remorse, penitence, shame.

guilty *adj* **1** (*he was tried and found guilty*) to blame, blameworthy, at fault, responsible. **2** (*they felt guilty about not inviting her*) conscience-stricken, remorseful, repentant, penitent, ashamed, shamefaced, sheepish.

gulf *n* **1** (*they were asked to find the Gulf of Mexico on the map*) bay, cove, inlet. **2** (*they had a quarrel and there is now a gulf between the two families*) rift, split, division, divide.

gullible *adj* (*the old lady was not gullible enough to be taken in by his story*) naive, foolish, credulous.

gulp *vb* **1** (*the children were told not to gulp their food*) bolt, wolf, gobble, devour. **2** (*she tried to gulp back her tears*) fight back, choke back, suppress, stifle, smother.

gush *vb* **1** (*water gushed from the burst pipe*) pour, stream, rush, spout, spurt, flood, cascade. **2** (*she embarrassed the little girls by gushing about their prettiness*) enthuse, babble, fuss.

gust *n* (*a gust of wind*) puff, rush, flurry, blast.

gutter *n* (*floodwater running down the gutter*) drain, sewer, sluice, ditch.

H

habit n **1** (*it was their habit to eat late in the evening*) custom, practice, routine, convention. **2** (*smoking and other harmful habits*) addiction, dependence, compulsion, obsession.

habitat n (*the animal's usual habitat*) environment, background, home.

habitual adj (*they went home by their habitual route*) usual, customary, accustomed, regular, routine.

hack vb (*they hacked down the trees*) chop down, cut down, fell, hew.

hackneyed adj (*the writer is too apt to use hackneyed phrases*) overused, stale, stereotyped, unoriginal, run-of-the-mill, stock.

haggard adj (*she looked haggard with tiredness*) drawn, gaunt, hollow-cheeked.

haggle vb (*haggle over the price of a shawl in the market*) bargain.

hail vb (*she hailed her friend in the street*) greet, salute, wave to, say "hello" to.

hair n **1** (*she has beautiful hair*) locks, tresses. **2** (*the animal's hair*) fur, coat. ↻

let your hair down to behave in an informal, relaxed manner (*She always seemed reserved, but she let her hair down at the party and danced on the table*).

split hairs to argue about small, unimportant details, to quibble (*She is leaving the job. There is no point in splitting hairs as to whether she was bored with it or tired*).

half-hearted adj (*they made a half-hearted attempt at saving the business*) lukewarm, unenthusiastic, apathetic, indifferent.

hall n **1** (*the guests left their coats in the hall*) entrance hall, hallway, lobby. **2** (*the crowds surged into the hall*) concert hall, theater.

hallucination n (*she thought that she had seen a ghost, but it was only a hallucination*) illusion, figment of the imagination, vision, fantasy, apparition.

halt vb **1** (*the traffic has to halt at the end of the road*) come to a halt, stop, come to a stop, pull up, draw up. **2** (*work halted when the heating system broke down*) stop, finish, end, break off, discontinue. **3** (*the strike halted progress on the export order*) stop, put a stop to, put an end to, arrest, interrupt, obstruct, impede.

halve vb (*halve the orange for the two children*) cut in half, divide in two. ↻

go halves with (someone) to share costs with (someone) (*When they go to the movies, they go halves on the tickets*).

hamper vb (*the bad weather hampered progress on the building*) hinder, impede, obstruct, hold up.

hand n **1** (*the hand of a clock*) pointer, indicator, needle. **2** (*they had to fire some of the hands*) worker, employee, helper. ·♀'

be hand and glove with (someone) to be closely associated with (someone) for a bad or illegal purpose (*The police discovered that one of the assistants in the jewelry store had been hand and glove with the jewel thieves*). **have a hand in (something)** to be involved in (something), to have contributed to the cause of (something) (*She had a hand in the surprise birthday party for her friend*). **keep your hand in** to retain your skill at (something) by doing it occasionally (*The ex-champion does not play tennis very often, but he keeps his hand in by playing with his son occasionally*).

hand vb (*hand the prize to the winner*) hand over, give, pass, transfer, transmit.

handbook n (*read the instructions in the handbook*) manual, directions, instructions, guide, guidebook.

handicap n (*her lack of qualifications was a handicap to her in her career*) disadvantage, impediment, obstruction, hindrance, block.

handle n (*the handle of the tool/the handle of the pan*) shaft, grip, hilt. ↻

fly off the handle to lose your temper (*She flies off the handle whenever anyone disagrees with her*) <A reference to an ax head that flies off the handle when it is being used>.

handle vb **1** (*they were asked not to handle the goods before they bought them*) touch, finger, feel, pick up, lift. **2** (*he cannot handle the more difficult students*) cope with, deal with, manage, control.

handsome *n* **1** (*her husband is a very handsome man*) attractive, good-looking. **2** (*the antique table was a handsome piece of furniture*) attractive, fine, elegant, tasteful. **3** (*her parents gave them a handsome gift as a wedding present*) generous, lavish, sizeable.

handy *adj* **1** (*do you have the book handy?*) to hand, available, within reach, accessible, nearby. **2** (*that is a handy kitchen utensil*) useful, helpful, convenient, practical. **3** (*it is useful to have someone handy to do repairs around the house*) good with your hands, practical, capable.

hang *vb* **1** (*there were mobiles hanging from the ceiling in the nursery*) hang down, be suspended, dangle, swing. **2** (*she hung the picture from the picture rail*) suspend, put up. **3** (*she employed him to hang wallpaper*) put up, stick on. **4** (*they used to hang murderers in Britain*) send to the gallows, put a noose on, execute, (*inf*) string up. ⟡

a hanging matter a very serious deed, often one which receives a harsh punishment (*I was surprised that he was expelled from school. I would not have thought that his action was a hanging matter*) <A reference to a crime that was punishable by execution or hanging>.
get the hang of (something) to learn how to do (something) or to begin to understand (something) (*I think the learner driver finally has the hang of changing gears*).
hang a left *or* **right** to turn left *or* right when driving (*Hang a left at the drugstore*).

hanker *vb* (*she hankers after a cottage in the country*) desire, long for, yearn for, crave, covet, fancy, (*inf*) have a yen for.

haphazard *adj* (*the books were arranged in a haphazard way*) random, unsystematic, unmethodical, disorganized, slapdash, careless.

happen *vb* **1** (*the accident happened on an icy road*) occur, take place, come about. **2** (*we happened to meet her in the supermarket*) chance. **3** (*whatever happened to them?*) become of, befall. **4** (*they happened upon some valuable old books*) find, come upon, chance upon, stumble upon.

happening *n* (*there has been a series of sad happenings in her life*) event, incident, occurrence, experience.

happy *adj* **1** (*the children were happy playing in the sunshine*) cheerful, merry, light-hearted, joyful, carefree. **2** (*they were happy to see their grandparents*) pleased, glad, delighted. **3** (*by a happy chance we found the lost necklace*) fortunate, lucky. ⟡

a happy event the birth of a baby (*The young couple is expecting a happy event*).
a happy hunting ground a place where someone finds what he or she desires or where he or she is successful (*That store is a happy hunting ground for her. She has bought all her nicest clothing there*).

harass *vb* (*the children were bored and were harassing their mother*) pester, disturb, bother, annoy, badger, torment, (*inf*) hassle.

harbor, harbour (*Br, Cdn*) *n* (*the ships were tied up in the harbor*) quay, jetty, pier, wharf, dock.

harbor, harbour (*Br, Cdn*) *vb* **1** (*she was accused of harboring an escaped prisoner*) shelter, give protection to, give asylum to. **2** (*they still harbor resentment against their mother for abandoning them*) nurse, retain, maintain, cling to.

hard *adj* **1** (*the ground was hard*) solid, solidified, stony, rocky. **2** (*a hard substance*) solid, rigid, stiff, inflexible, tough. **3** (*the work was very hard*) strenuous, heavy, tiring, demanding, taxing. **4** (*the problem was a hard one*) difficult, complicated, complex, involved, intricate. **5** (*they are hard workers*) industrious, diligent, energetic, keen. **6** (*their father was a hard man*) harsh, stern, severe, ruthless. **7** (*he was wounded by a hard blow to the head*) strong, forceful, powerful, violent. **8** (*she had a hard life*) difficult, uncomfortable, harsh, grim, unpleasant, distressing. ⟡

be hard put to have great difficulty (*You would be hard put to find a more comfortable hotel than the one in the village*).

hardship *n* (*the refugees are suffering hardship*) deprivation, want, need, distress.

harm *vb* **1** (*the kidnappers did not harm the child*) hurt, injure, wound, abuse, maltreat. **2** (*the incident harmed his reputation*) damage, mar, spoil.

harm *n* **1** (*no harm came to the child*) injury, hurt, pain, suffering, abuse. **2** (*some harm was done to his reputation*) damage, loss.

harmful *adj* (*the drug is not thought to have any*

harmful effects) hurtful, injurious, disadvantageous, detrimental.

harmless adj **1** (a weed-killer that is thought to be harmless to pets) safe, non-toxic. **2** (he was just a harmless old man) inoffensive, blameless, innocent.

harmony n (the different nationalities lived in harmony in the country) peace, peacefulness, agreement, friendship.

harsh adj **1** (the harsh noise grated on their ears) grating, jarring, rasping, discordant. **2** (the colors of the walls were a bit harsh) gaudy, garish, loud, bold. **3** (it had been a harsh winter) hard, severe, cold. **4** (she was brought up under harsh conditions) severe, grim, rough, austere. **5** (he was a harsh ruler) cruel, brutal, merciless, ruthless. **6** (the school rules used to be very harsh) severe, stern, inflexible.

haste n (haste is required to get the order delivered on time) speed, swiftness, rapidity, fastness.

hasty adj **1** (you should avoid making hasty decisions) hurried, rushed, impetuous, impulsive. **2** (she had a hasty look at her notes before she spoke) quick, rapid, swift, brief, fleeting, cursory, superficial. **3** (she has a hasty temper) hot, fiery, quick, irritable.

hat n (he wore a hat to protect his head from the sun) cap, bonnet. ✧

hats off to (someone) (someone) should be praised and congratulated (Hats off to the new boy for standing up to the school bully).
pass the hat around to ask for contributions of money (We passed the hat around the office for a wedding gift for her).

hate vb (he hates his rival/She hates football) loathe, detest, dislike, have an aversion to.

hateful adj (she thinks that he is a hateful person) loathsome, detestable, revolting, offensive, horrible, nasty.

hatred n (he is full of hatred toward his rivals) hate, loathing, dislike, aversion, ill will.

haughty adj (she looks at everyone in a very haughty way) arrogant, proud, disdainful, condescending, snobbish.

haul vb (they hauled the dead body from the river) pull, tug, drag, draw, heave. ✧

haul (someone) over the coals to scold severely (The sales clerk was hauled over

the coals for being rude to the customer) <A reference to an old practice of burning people alive because of their religious beliefs>.

have vb **1** (they have two cats) own, possess, keep. **2** (the house has five rooms) contain, comprise, include. **3** (she had a lot of trouble with her eldest son) experience, undergo, go through, endure. **4** (she will not have such behavior in her house) permit, allow, tolerate, stand for. ✧

have had it to have no hope of survival, success, etc. (The owners of the local deli will have had it when the new supermarket opens).
let (someone) have it suddenly to attack (someone) either physically or verbally (The boy was tired of being beaten and turned around and let the bully have it).

hay n (they gave hay to the horses) fodder, straw. ✧

make hay while the sun shines to take advantage of an opportunity while you have the chance (He has been offered some overtime, and he needs the money. He might as well make hay while the sun shines).

hazard n (one of the hazards of being a soldier) danger, risk, peril, menace.

hazy adj **1** (it was rather a hazy day) misty, foggy. **2** (her memory of the event is a bit hazy) unclear, vague, blurred, fuzzy, muddled.

head n **1** (he has a good head for business) mind, brain, intellect. **2** (he was the head of the whole organization) chief, leader, director, manager, principal, boss. **3** (she is at the head of the company) top, control, command, charge, leadership. **4** (at the head of the hill) top, summit, crest, brow, apex. **5** (she was at the head of the line) top, front. ✧

bring (something) to a head to bring (something) to a state where something must be done about it (There has been hostility between them for some time, but his public criticism of her brought matters to a head) <A reference to a boil, etc. coming to a head>.

go to (someone's) head to make (someone) conceited or arrogant (*Winning first prize went to his head and he goes around boasting all the time*).

the head honcho the person in charge of an organization (*Her father is the head honcho of an international corporation*).

head *vb* **1** (*he was heading the expedition*) be in charge of, lead, be in control of, direct. **2** (*they headed for town*) make for, set out for, go to.

heal *vb* **1** (*the ointment will heal the wound*) cure, make better, remedy, treat. **2** (*the wound began to heal*) get better, mend, improve.

health *n* (*the children are full of health*) healthiness, fitness, strength, vigor.

healthy *adj* **1** (*healthy young men playing football*) well, fit, robust, strong, vigorous. **2** (*they live in a healthy climate*) health-giving, invigorating, bracing. **3** (*they eat a healthy diet*) health-giving, healthful, nutritious, nourishing, wholesome.

heap *n* (*heaps of leaves in the garden*) pile, mound, stack, mass, stockpile.

heap *vb* (*the children heaped up the leaves in the garden*) pile, stack, stockpile, accumulate.

hear *vb* **1** (*I could not hear what she said*) catch, take in. **2** (*we heard that they had gone overseas*) find out, discover, gather, learn.

heart *n* **1** (*he loves her with all his heart*) love, passion, affection, emotion. **2** (*she thinks he has no heart*) tenderness, compassion, sympathy, humanity, kindness. **3** (*the discussion did not get to the heart of the matter*) center, core, hub, crux. ✧

his, her, etc., **heart is in the right place** he, she, etc., is basically kind, sympathetic, etc., although sometimes not appearing to be so (*Our neighbor seems very stern toward the children, but her heart is in the right place*).

take (something) to heart 1 to be upset by (something) (*He was only teasing, but she took his remarks to heart*). **2** to be influenced by and take notice of (something) (*She took the doctor's advice to heart and tried to get more rest*).

hearten *vb* (*the team were heartened by their success*) cheer, cheer up, uplift, encourage, elate, buoy up.

hearty *adj* **1** (*they were given a hearty welcome*) enthusiastic, eager, warm, friendly. **2** (*he has a hearty dislike of deceit*) wholehearted, great, complete, thorough. **3** (*they ate a hearty breakfast*) substantial, solid, filling, ample.

heat *n* **1** (*the heat melted the ice*) hotness, warmth. **2** (*there was heat between them*) passion, emotion **3** (*qualify for the third heat*) contest, game, round, semi-final, qualifying round. ✧

in the heat of the moment while influenced by the excitement or emotion of the occasion (*They were having a quarrel and in the heat of the moment she threatened to kill him*).

turn up the heat to make a situation seem more important, urgent, etc. (*The boss, sick of his employees' time wasting, really turned up the heat to get them to meet the deadline*).

heave *vb* **1** (*he hurt his back heaving heavy weights*) lift, raise, haul, pull, tug. **2** (*they heaved a sigh of relief*) utter, give, let out.

heaven *n* **1** (*Bible stories about heaven*) paradise. **2** (*she thought that lying on a beach in the sun was heaven*) bliss, ecstasy, rapture, supreme happiness. ✧

be in seventh heaven to be extremely happy (*She was in seventh heaven when her twins were born*) <In Jewish literature the seventh heaven is the highest of all heavens where God lives>.

heavy *adj* **1** (*he had to carry heavy weights in his job*) weighty, hefty, substantial, burdensome. **2** (*it proved a heavy task*) hard, difficult, laborious, demanding, exacting. **3** (*he received a heavy blow to the head*) hard, strong, powerful, forceful, violent. **4** (*he was a heavy man*) large, bulky, hefty, stout, overweight, fat, obese. **5** (*a heavy mist*) dense, thick, solid. **6** (*with heavy heart*) depressed, gloomy, downcast, despondent.

hectic *adj* (*they had a hectic day at the office*) busy, frantic, bustling, frenzied.

hedge *vb* **1** (*the trees hedged in the garden*) surround, enclose, encircle, fence in. **2** (*she simply hedged when they asked her a direct question*) hem and haw, beat around the bush.

hedge one's bets lessen your chance of loss by spreading or balancing your investments or bets (*I'm hedging my bets by putting some of my money into shares and some into savings*).

heed n (*they pay no heed to what anyone says*) attention, notice, note, consideration.

hefty adj (*he is a hefty young man*) heavy, bulky, stout, brawny, muscular, powerfully built.

height n 1 (*measure the height*) tallness, altitude. 2 (*he died at the height of his career*) culmination, peak.

heir/heiress ns (*he was heir to his father's estate*) inheritor, beneficiary, legate.

help vb 1 (*she did it to help her parents*) assist, aid, support, lend a hand to. 2 (*they gave her something to help the pain*) ease, soothe, relieve, cure.

help n 1 (*the old lady is in need of some help*) assistance, aid, support. 2 (*there was no help for the condition*) ease, relief, cure.

helpful adj 1 (*he made some helpful suggestions*) useful, of use, beneficial, advantageous, valuable. 2 (*their neighbors are very helpful people*) supportive, obliging, cooperative, caring, charitable, friendly.

hereditary adj (*the disease is hereditary*) inherited, genetic.

hero n 1 (*he was the hero of the battle*) victor, champion, celebrity. 2 (*the pop singer is the girl's hero*) idol, ideal. 3 (*the hero in the play*) male lead.

heroic adj (*it was a heroic act to try and save his friend's life*) brave, courageous, gallant, fearless, bold.

hesitate vb 1 (*she hesitated before making such an important decision*) pause, delay, hang back, wait, waver, shilly-shally. 2 (*they hesitate to interfere in their daughter's life*) be reluctant, be unwilling, be disinclined, shrink from. 3 (*he hesitates a bit when he gets nervous*) stammer, stutter, stumble, falter.

hide vb 1 (*the thieves hid the jewels in the garden*) conceal, secrete. 2 (*the escaped prisoners were hiding in the cellar*) take cover, lie low, conceal yourself, go to ground. 3 (*clouds hiding the sun*) obscure, block, eclipse, obstruct. 4 (*she tried to hide her motives*) conceal, keep secret, suppress, hush up.

hide n (*the animal's hide*) skin, pelt, coat, fur. ✧

neither hide nor hair of (someone or something) no trace at all of (someone or something) (*The police are searching for the missing prisoner, but so far they have found neither hide nor hair of him*) <"Hide" here means skin>.

tan (someone's) hide to beat or thrash (someone) (*the boy's father threatened to tan his hide if he got into trouble at school again*) <A reference to leather-making>.

hideous adj 1 (*the new drapes are hideous*) ugly, unsightly, gruesome, grim, repulsive, revolting. 2 (*it was a hideous crime*) horrible, horrific, shocking, outrageous, dreadful, appalling.

high adj 1 (*a street with high buildings*) tall, lofty, towering. 2 (*he has a high rank in the organization*) top, leading, prominent, important, powerful. 3 (*they have a high opinion of his work*) favorable, good, approving, admiring. 4 (*she has a very high voice*) high-pitched, shrill, sharp, piercing. 5 (*the ship was in difficulties in the high winds*) strong, intense, forceful, violent. ✧

a high flier a person who is bound to be very successful or who has achieved great success (*She was one of the high fliers in our year at university*).

high and mighty arrogant (*Since he has become so rich, he is so high and mighty that he won't speak to his former neighbors*).

leave (someone) high and dry to leave (someone) in a difficult or helpless state (*His secretary walked out and left him high and dry in the middle of the busiest time of the year*) <A reference to a ship left stranded>.

live high on the hog to have a very comfortable lifestyle, with more than enough to eat and drink (*Since they won the lottery, they have been living high on the hog, eating in the finest restaurants*).

highbrow adj (*her taste in books is rather highbrow*) intellectual, scholarly, educated, bookish.

highlight n (*the trip to the theater was one of the highlights of our trip*) high spot, feature, peak, climax.

hijack vb (*the thieves hijacked the truck*) seize, take over, commandeer.

hike vb (*they hiked over the hills*) tramp, march, walk, ramble, trek, trudge.

hilarious adj (*the comedian's jokes were hilarious*) uproarious, hysterical, side-splitting, funny, amusing, humorous, comic, entertaining.

hill *n* **1** (*the hills behind the town*) heights, highland, rising ground, mountain, peak. **2** (*the cars went slowly up the steep hill*) slope, rise, incline, gradient. ▷

> **as old as the hills** extremely old (*Some of the village traditions are as old as the hills*).
> **not be worth a hill of beans** not to be very important (*All your promises to help are not worth a hill of beans if you don't actually do something constructive*).
> **over the hill** past your best or past your prime (*In that firm you are considered over the hill at 30*).

hinder *vb* (*the bad weather hindered their efforts to get the bridge built*) hamper, impede, hold up, obstruct, delay, curb, block.

hindrance *n* (*their long tight skirts were a hindrance to them when they tried to hurry*) impediment, obstacle, obstruction, handicap, drawback.

hint *n* **1** (*she gave no hint that she was planning to leave*) inkling, clue, suggestion, indication, mention. **2** (*he writes a column in the newspaper giving gardening hints*) tip, suggestion, pointer. **3** (*there was just a hint of ginger in the sauce*) trace, touch, dash, suggestion.

hire *vb* **1** (*they hired a boat*) rent, lease, charter. **2** (*the firm is hiring more staff*) engage, take on, sign on, appoint, employ.

hiss *vb* **1** (*the kettle was hissing*) whistle, wheeze. **2** (*the audience hissed at the comic's bad jokes*) boo, jeer.

historic *adj* (*it was a historic battle/It was a historic event when the country gained its independence*) famous, notable, celebrated, memorable, important, significant, outstanding.

hit *vb* **1** (*the bully hit the little boy*) strike, slap, smack, punch, bang, thump. **2** (*the car was out of control and hit the truck*) bang into, crash into, knock into, smash into. ▷

> **hit it off** to get on well, to become friendly immediately (*I knew those two would hit it off. They have so much in common*).
> **hit the hay** (*inf*) to go to bed (*He was so tired that he decided to hit the hay immediately after dinner*) <Beds were formerly filled with hay>.

hitch *n* (*our travel arrangements were going well, but then there was a sudden hitch*) snag, hindrance, holdup, obstacle, difficulty, stumbling-block, (*inf*) glitch.

hoard *vb* (*they hoarded food in the summer in case of bad weather in the winter/misers hoarding gold*) store, stock up, save, accumulate, pile up, gather, collect.

hoarse *adj* (*she had a cold and her voice was hoarse*) harsh, gruff, husky, croaking, grating, rasping, raucous.

hoax *n* (*the bomb threat was a hoax*) practical joke, joke, prank, trick, (*inf*) spoof.

hobble *vb* (*her feet were sore and she had to hobble down to the store*) limp, shuffle, totter.

hobby *n* (*they work so hard that they have little time for hobbies*) pastime, amusement, sport.

hold *vb* **1** (*they held their baggage tightly*) hold on to, clutch, grip, grasp, cling to. **2** (*they held each other close*) embrace, cuddle, hug, clasp. **3** (*the bank holds all their private documents*) have, keep, retain, own, possess. **4** (*he holds a position of responsibility*) hold down, have, be in, occupy, fill. **5** (*one suitcase will not hold all these clothes*) contain, take, carry, include. **6** (*the bridge will not hold his weight*) bear, carry, support, sustain. **7** (*police are holding him for questioning*) detain, hold in custody, confine, keep, imprison. **8** (*it is difficult to hold the interest of the children*) keep, retain, occupy, engage. **9** (*I wonder if the warm weather will hold*) last, continue, go on, remain, stay. **10** (*the old rule does not hold anymore*) be valid, be in force, apply. **11** (*they hold him responsible for the accident*) consider, think, regard, view. **12** (*the club holds meetings every month*) have, conduct, run. ▷

> **have a hold over (someone)** to have power or influence over (someone), often because you know something bad about him or her (*We thought that he had a hold over her and then we discovered that he had found out that she had been in prison*).
> **hold forth** to talk for a long time forcefully or pompously about (something) (*He bored everyone by holding forth about his opinion of the government*).
> **hold true** to be valid, to still apply (*The rule about no smoking still holds true*).

hole *n* **1** (*there was a hole in the hedge/The material was full of holes*) opening, gap, breach, break, crack, rent, slit, perforation. **2** (*there was a huge hole in the ground after the explosion*) crater, cavity, chasm, hollow, depression, dip. **3** (*the animal's hole*) lair, burrow, earth. ✧

pick holes in (something) to find faults in (something) (*They spent their time picking holes in her theory*).

hollow *adj* **1** (*a hollow space*) hollowed out, empty, vacant. **2** (*she has hollow cheeks*) sunken, concave. **3** (*we heard a hollow sound*) dull, low, muffled, deep.

hollow *vb* (*they hollowed out a tree trunk to make a canoe*) scoop out, gouge out, excavate.

holy *adj* **1** (*the saint's grave was a holy place*) blessed, consecrated, sacred, hallowed. **2** (*they are holy people*) God-fearing, religious, pious, devout. ✧

the holy of holies a private or special place inside a building (*That's her father's study. It's the holy of holies in the house*) <A literal translation of the Hebrew name of the inner sanctuary in the Jewish temple where the Ark of the Covenant was kept>.

home *n* **1** (*I know where he works, but not where his home is*) house, residence, abode, dwelling place. **2** (*the home of the chimpanzee*) habitat, environment, abode. **3** (*the old lady is in a home*) residential home, institution. ✧

a home away from home a place where you feel comfortable and relaxed (*Her friend's house is a home away from home for her*).

honest *adj* **1** (*honest people who do not steal other people's goods*) honorable, upright, good, decent, righteous, moral, virtuous, trustworthy, law-abiding. **2** (*she gave honest replies to the questions*) true, truthful, sincere, genuine, direct, frank, candid. **3** (*he gave an honest judgment*) fair, just, impartial, objective, unbiased.

honor, honour (*Br, Cdn*) *n* **1** (*he was a man of honor and handed in the money which he had found*) honesty, integrity, uprightness, decency, principle, righteousness, morals, virtue. **2** (*his honor was at stake*) reputation, good name. **3** (*he did not care about the honor of winning*) glory, prestige, fame, renown, distinction.

honorable, honourable (*Br, Cdn*) *adj* **1** (*honorable people who tell the truth*) honest, upright, good, decent, righteous, moral, virtuous, trustworthy, admirable. **2** (*it was an honorable victory for*

the army) famous, renowned, prestigious, notable, distinguished.

hook *n* **1** (*a hook used for cutting corn*) scythe, sickle. **2** (*hooks for the children's coats*) peg. **3** (*the hook of the dress*) fastener, catch.

hook *vb* **1** (*they hooked a fish*) catch, take. **2** (*hook the trailer on to the car*) fasten, secure. ✧

get (someone) off the hook to free (someone) from some difficulty, problem, etc., or from something that he or she does not want to do (*I did not want to go to the party and my friends got me off the hook by asking me to baby-sit*) <A reference to angling>.

hooked *adj* (*she has a hooked nose*) hook-shaped, curved, bent.

hooligan *n* (*the police are looking for the hooligans who damaged the cars*) ruffian, thug, vandal.

hoop *n* (*hoops of steel*) ring, band, circle, circlet. ✧

put (someone) through the hoop to cause (someone) to experience something unpleasant or difficult (*The interviewers certainly put the candidates for the job through the hoop*) <A reference to circus performers who jump through hoops set on fire or to circus animals that are made to jump through hoops>.

hop *vb* (*the frogs were hopping everywhere*) jump, leap, bound, spring, skip.

hope *n* **1** (*we were full of hope for a victory*) hopefulness, optimism, confidence, expectation, faith. **2** (*is there any hope of success?*) likelihood, prospect.

hope *vb* (*we are hoping for victory*) have hopes of, be hopeful of, expect, anticipate, look forward to, have confidence in.

hopeful *adj* **1** (*we are hopeful of winning*) expectant, optimistic, confident. **2** (*the news is hopeful*) optimistic, promising, encouraging, favorable. ✧

hope against hope to continue to hope although there is very little reason to be hopeful (*She is seriously sick, but they are hoping against hope that she will recover*).

horde *n* (*hordes of shoppers*) crowd, swarm, mob, throng, multitude, host.

horizontal *adj* (*both the horizontal and vertical*

supports of the frame/an invalid lying horizontal) flat, level, prone.

horrible *adj* **1** (*it was a horrible sight*) dreadful, awful, horrid, terrible, frightful, shocking, appalling, grim, hideous, ghastly, gruesome, disgusting, revolting. **2** (*she was a horrible old woman*) disagreeable, nasty, unpleasant, mean, obnoxious.

horrify *vb* (*we were horrified at her behavior*) shock, appall, outrage, scandalize, disgust.

horror *n* (*they looked at the dead body with horror*) terror, fear, alarm, shock.

horse *n* (*she rode a brown horse*) mount, hack, pony, steed, stallion, mare, racehorse. ✧

a horse of a different color a different matter entirely (*If you can't afford to go on the trip with us, that's one thing, but if you just don't want to go, that's a horse of a different color*).
horse sense common sense (*She has no specialist business knowledge, but she has horse sense*).

hospitable *adj* (*the people we stayed with were most hospitable*) generous, kind, cordial, sociable, friendly.

hostage *n* (*they kept the child hostage*) captive, prisoner, pawn.

hostile *adj* **1** (*the crowd grew hostile*) belligerent, aggressive, antagonistic, angry, unfriendly. **2** (*they were quite hostile to the idea*) opposed, averse, antagonistic.

hot *adj* **1** (*there was no hot food left in the restaurant/hot food straight from the oven*) warm, piping hot, boiling, sizzling, scalding. **2** (*it was a very hot day*) boiling, sweltering, scorching, baking, blistering, sultry, torrid. **3** (*the sauce was too hot for their taste*) spicy, peppery, pungent, sharp. **4** (*she had a hot temper*) fiery, fierce, furious, violent. ✧

a hot potato something which it is difficult or dangerous to deal with (*The complaint about bad food is a hot potato. You had better pass it on to the restaurant manager*).
be hot under the collar to be very angry or agitated (*He got hot under the collar when she refused to believe him*).
make things hot for (someone) to make a situation unpleasant or impossible for (someone) (*She might as well leave if the boss does not like her. He'll just make things hot for her if she stays*).

hotel *n* (*book in at the local hotel*) inn, tavern, guest house, boardinghouse.

house *n* **1** (*the house they live in is very old*) abode, residence, dwelling, home. **2** (*they own a publishing house*) firm, company, business, establishment, concern. ✧

bring the house down cause great amusement or applause (*The comedian's jokes brought the house down*).
on the house paid by the owner of the store, restaurant, or bar rather than by the customer (*The owner's wife has just had a baby, so the drinks are on the house*).

house *vb* (*the apartments house about 30 people*) accommodate, lodge, have room for.

hover *vb* **1** (*children's kites hovering in the air*) hang, flutter, fly, drift, float. **2** (*she was hovering behind them, hoping to hear what they were talking about*) linger, hang about, wait.

howl *vb* **1** (*hear the dogs howling*) bay, yowl, yelp. **2** (*children howling for their mothers*) cry, weep, scream, bawl, wail.

huddle *vb* **1** (*the children huddled together to keep warm*) cuddle up, snuggle, nestle, curl up. **2** (*the sheep huddled in the corner of the field*) crowd, cluster, squeeze, pack.

hue *n* (*ribbons of many hues*) color, shade, tone, tint. ✧

a hue and cry a loud protest, an outcry (*There was a real hue and cry when they threatened to close the local school*) <An old legal term meaning a summons for people to join in a hunt for a wanted criminal>.

hug *vb* (*the children hugged their mother*) embrace, cuddle, hold close.

huge *adj* (*a story about huge monsters*) enormous, massive, vast, immense, colossal, gigantic.

hum *vb* **1** (*machines humming in the factory*) drone, vibrate, throb, whirr, buzz. **2** (*she was humming a happy tune*) croon, murmur, mumble, sing.

human *n* (*animals and humans/fairies and humans*) human being, mortal.

humane *adj* (*it is humane to put animals down when they are in pain*) kind, compassionate, sympathetic, merciful, charitable.

humble *adj* **1** (*he has achieved much fame but is very humble*) modest, unassuming, unpretentious. **2** (*the humble people of the village*) common, ordinary, low-born, lowly, poor, unimportant. ⟜

> **eat humble pie** to be forced to admit that you were wrong (*He said that his wife would never pass her driving test and had to eat humble pie when she passed it first time*).

humid *adj* (*a humid atmosphere*) damp, moist, muggy, sticky, steamy, clammy.

humiliate *vb* (*she humiliated her husband by criticizing him in public*) mortify, make ashamed, humble, disgrace, embarrass.

humility *n* (*he showed humility even when he won*) humbleness, modesty, self-effacement.

humor *n* **1** (*he could not see the humor in the situation*) funny side, comedy, farce, absurdity. **2** (*his own particular brand of humor*) comedy, jokes, jests, wit. **3** (*he is not in a very good humor*) mood, temper, temperament, frame of mind, disposition.

humorous *adj* (*he told a very humorous story*) funny, amusing, comic, hilarious, facetious, entertaining.

hunch *n* **1** (*he has a hunch on his back*) hump, swelling, bump, bulge. **2** (*the police have a hunch that he is guilty*) feeling, intuition, sixth sense, inkling, suspicion.

hunger *n* **1** (*the children died of hunger*) starvation, famine. **2** (*he has a hunger for knowledge*) desire, longing, yearning, craving, thirst.

hungry *adj* **1** (*hungry children with nothing to eat*) starving, famished, ravenous. **2** (*they are hungry for knowledge*) eager, anxious, avid, craving, longing for.

hunk *n* (*a hunk of cheese*) lump, block, chunk, wedge, mass.

hunt *vb* **1** (*they are hunting stags*) chase, pursue, stalk, track. **2** (*she was hunting for her glasses*) look for, search for, seek, rummage for, scrabble for.

hurdle *n* **1** (*the runner failed to clear the first hurdle*) fence, rail, railing, barrier. **2** (*there were several hurdles in the way of progress*) obstacle, obstruction, barrier, stumbling block.

hurl *vb* (*the crowd hurled stones at the police*) throw, fling, cast, pitch, toss.

hurricane *n* (*lives lost in the hurricane*) tornado, cyclone, typhoon, storm, tempest.

hurry *vb* (*you must hurry if you want to catch the train*) hurry up, hasten, make haste, speed up, run, dash, (*inf*) get a move on.

hurt *vb* **1** (*his leg was hurt in the accident*) injure, wound, bruise, maim. **2** (*her leg hurts*) be sore, be painful, ache, throb. **3** (*she was hurt by his unkind remarks*) upset, wound, grieve, sadden, offend.

hurtle *vb* (*the runner hurtled toward the finishing post*) race, dash, sprint, rush.

hush *vb* **1** (*try to hush the children*) quiet, silence, (*inf*) shut up. **2** (*the crowd suddenly hushed*) fall silent, quiet down, (*inf*) shut up. **3** (*they tried to hush up the scandal but the press found out*) conceal, suppress, cover up.

hut *n* (*a garden hut*) shed, lean-to, shack, cabin.

hygienic *adj* (*hospitals must be hygienic*) sanitary, clean, sterile, germ-free.

hymn *n* (*sing hymns in church*) psalm, religious song.

hypnotic *adj* (*hypnotic effects*) mesmerizing, mesmeric.

hypocritical *adj* (*it is hypocritical of him to go to church because he is a very evil person*) insincere, false, deceitful, dishonest.

hypothetical *adj* (*let us take a hypothetical case*) supposed, assumed, theoretical, imagined.

hysterical *adj* **1** (*she became hysterical at the news of his death*) frantic, frenzied, in a frenzy, out of control, berserk, beside yourself, distracted, overwrought, demented, crazed. **2** (*she told us a hysterical story about her travels*) hilarious, uproarious, side-splitting, comical, funny, amusing.

I

idea *n* **1** (*the idea of death terrifies him*) concept, notion. **2** (*we asked for their ideas on the subject*) thought, view, opinion, feeling. **3** (*I had an idea that he was dead*) thought, impression, belief, suspicion. **4** (*their idea is to sail around the world*) plan, aim, intention, objective. **5** (*we need some idea of the cost*) estimation, approximation, guess.

ideal *adj* (*the conditions were ideal*) perfect, faultless, excellent.

identify *vb* **1** (*she was able to identify her attacker*) recognize, name, distinguish, pinpoint. **2** (*they were able to identify the cause of the problem*) establish, find out, diagnose. **3** (*she identifies her mother with security*) associate, connect. **4** (*she identifies with homeless people*) relate.

identical *adj* **1** (*the twins wear identical clothing*) like, similar, matching. **2** (*that is the identical dress that her sister wore last week*) same.

idiot *n* (*he was an idiot to behave in that way*) fool, dolt, ass, dunce.

idiotic *adj* (*it was an idiotic thing to do*) stupid, foolish, senseless.

idle *adj* **1** (*he was an idle fellow who did not want to work*) lazy, slothful. **2** (*the workers are idle through no fault of their own*) unemployed, jobless, laid off.

idol *n* **1** (*the heathens were worshiping idols*) god, icon, image. **2** (*he is a pop idol to the teenagers*) hero/heroine, favorite, darling.

idolize *vb* (*the children idolize their grandfather*) adore, love, worship.

ignite *vb* **1** (*ignite the fire*) set alight, set fire to, kindle. **2** (*the dry material ignited easily*) catch fire, burn, burst into flames.

ignorant *adj* **1** (*they had never gone to school and were quite ignorant*) uneducated, illiterate. **2** (*they were ignorant of the legal facts*) unaware, unconscious, uninformed.

ignore *vb* **1** (*the child was told to ignore their insulting remarks*) disregard, take no notice of. **2** (*the students were told to ignore the last question in the test paper*) disregard, omit, (*inf*) skip.

ill *adj* **1** (*she has been ill and out of work for some time*) unwell, sick, poorly, indisposed, unhealthy, (*inf*) under the weather. **2** (*the medicine has no ill effects*) harmful, detrimental. **3** (*there is ill feeling between the two families*) hostile, antagonistic, unfriendly.

illegal *adj* (*they were imprisoned for their illegal deeds*) unlawful, criminal.

illegible *adj* (*her handwriting was illegible*) unreadable, indecipherable, unintelligible.

illiterate *adj* (*people who never went to school and so are illiterate*) uneducated, unschooled, ignorant.

illness *n* (*she is suffering from a mysterious illness*) complaint, ailment, disease, disorder, affliction, (*inf*) bug.

illogical *adj* (*his behavior was illogical*) irrational, unreasonable, unsound.

illusion *n* **1** (*the magician did not really do that—it was just an illusion*) deception. **2** (*the supposed ghost was just an illusion*) hallucination, dream, fantasy **3** (*she was under the illusion the he was unmarried*) delusion, misapprehension, misconception.

illustrate *vb* **1** (*she illustrated the children's book*) decorate, ornament. **2** (*he illustrated his theory with examples*) demonstrate, exemplify.

illustration *n* **1** (*the colored illustrations in the book*) picture, drawing, sketch, diagram. **2** (*the illustrations which he used to prove his point*) example, case, instance.

image *adj* **1** (*there were images of famous saints in the churchyard*) likeness, statue, figure, representation. **2** (*you can see your image in the mirror*) reflection, likeness. ⟳

> **be the spitting image of (someone** *or* **something)** to be extremely like (someone or something) (*The child is the spitting image of his father*).

imaginary *adj* (*the child has an imaginary friend*) fictitious, invented, made up, legendary, mythical, unreal, fanciful.

imagination *n* **1** (*the poem shows imagination*) creativity, vision, inspiration, fancifulness. **2** (*she thought she saw her father but it was only her imagination*) illusion, fancy, hallucination, dream, figment of the imagination.

imagine *vb* **1** (*can you imagine what life will be like in 50 years?*) picture, visualize, conceive. **2** (*he imagined that the meeting would last an hour*) presume, assume, suppose, think, believe.

imitate *vb* **1** (*she imitated the style used by the* writer) copy, follow. **2** (*the cruel children imitated the boy with the limp*) mimic, impersonate, mock, parody.

imitation *n* (*the portrait is not genuine but an imitation*) copy, reproduction, counterfeit, forgery, fake.

immature *adj* **1** (*it was immature of the young man to behave like that*) childish, juvenile, infantile. **2** (*the fruit was picked when it was immature*) unripe, green.

immediate *adj* **1** (*there was an immediate reaction to his speech*) instant, instantaneous, prompt, swift, sudden. **2** (*he turned to his immediate neighbor in the hall*) next, near, nearest, adjacent. **3** (*we have no immediate plans to go*) existing, current.

immediately *adv* **1** (*he plans to leave immediately*) right away, straight away, at once, without delay. **2** (*they were sitting immediately behind us*) directly, right.

immense *adj* **1** (*an immense figure of a man*) huge, enormous, vast, colossal, gigantic, giant. **2** (*there has been an immense improvement*) huge, immense, vast.

immerse *vb* **1** (*she immersed the dress in the soapy water*) submerge, plunge, dip, lower. **2** (*they immersed themselves in their work before the test*) absorb, engross, occupy, preoccupy.

immoral *adj* (*everyone disapproved of his immoral acts*) bad, wrong, evil, wicked, sinful, unethical.

immortal *adj* (*human beings are not immortal*) everlasting, endless, eternal, undying.

impact *n* **1** (*both cars were damaged in the impact*) collision, crash, bump, smash, clash. **2** (*his speech had a powerful impact on the crowd*) effect, influence, impression. **3** (*his nose took the full impact of the blow*) force, shock, impetus, brunt.

impartial *adj* (*we had to make sure that the judge was impartial*) unbiased, unprejudiced, disinterested, objective, detached.

impatient *adj* **1** (*the children were impatient to get out to play*) eager, anxious, keen, avid. **2** (*the show was late in starting, and the audience was growing impatient*) restless, agitated, edgy, fidgety.

impeccable *adj* (*his performance was impeccable*) faultless, flawless, perfect, exemplary.

impede *vb* (*the weather impeded their progress*) hinder, obstruct, hamper, block, check, delay, deter.

impediment *n* **1** (*the weather was an impediment to their plans*) hindrance, obstruction, obstacle, handicap, block, check, bar, barrier. **2** (*she has a speech impediment and has to speak slowly*) stammer, stutter.

imperative *adj* (*it is imperative that we leave now*) essential, necessary, urgent, vital, important, crucial.

imperceptible *adj* (*the difference between the two vases was imperceptible*) undetectable, unnoticeable, slight, small, minute.

impersonal *adj* (*the nurse had a very impersonal manner*) cold, cool, aloof, distant, stiff, formal, detached.

impersonate *vb* (*the pupil began to impersonate the teacher*) imitate, copy, mimic, mock, ape.

impertinent *adj* (*it was impertinent to speak to the old lady like that*) insolent, impudent, cheeky, rude, impolite, ill-mannered.

imperturbable *adj* (*she is imperturbable even in an emergency*) calm, cool, composed, unruffled.

impetuous *adj* (*he is given to impetuous actions*) hasty, impulsive, spontaneous, rash, foolhardy.

implement *n* (*the garden implements have been stolen/buy new kitchen implements*) tool, utensil, appliance, instrument, device, gadget.

implore *vb* (*she implored him to help*) beg, plead with, appeal to, entreat, beseech.

imply *vb* (*he implied that she was not telling the truth*) insinuate, hint, suggest, indicate.

important *adj* **1** (*it is important to arrive on time*) necessary, essential, vital, crucial, urgent. **2** (*the two countries are having important talks*) significant, critical, crucial, serious, momentous, of great import. **3** (*she noted the important points in the lecture*) chief, main, principal, significant. **4** (*all the important people in the town were invited to the reception*) prominent, notable, leading, distinguished, eminent.

impose *vb* **1** (*the judge imposed a heavy fine on him*) exact, charge, inflict, enforce. **2** (*she tries to impose her views on all her colleagues*) force, foist, inflict, thrust. **3** (*they felt she was imposing on their mother's generosity*) take advantage, exploit, abuse.

impossible *adj* **1** (*it was obviously an impossible task*) unimaginable, inconceivable, impracticable, impractical, hopeless. **2** (*life became impossible for them in the damp conditions*) unbearable, intolerable.

impostor, imposter *ns* (*they thought that he was a*

doctor, but he was an impostor) fake, fraud, swindler, cheat, (*inf*) con man.

impotent *adj* (*the small army was impotent in the face of the enemy*) powerless, helpless, weak, feeble.

impoverished *adj* (*impoverished people with no homes*) poor, poverty-stricken, penniless, destitute.

impracticable *adj* (*the task was totally impracticable*) impossible, out of the question.

impractical *adj* **1** (*the proposed solution was totally impractical*) impossible, nonviable, hopeless, ineffective, useless. **2** (*they are impractical people*) unrealistic, idealistic.

impress *vb* **1** (*the crowd was impressed by his speech*) make an impression on, affect, influence, sway, move, stir. **2** (*you must impress on them the need for silence*) stress, emphasize.

impression *n* **1** (*his speech made a powerful impression on his audience*) effect, influence, impact. **2** (*we had the impression that he disliked us*) feeling, idea, notion, sensation, suspicion, hunch. **3** (*he does impressions of the prime minister*) impersonation, imitation, mimicry, parody.

impressive *adj* **1** (*it was an impressive building*) imposing, grand, splendid, magnificent. **2** (*he made an impressive speech*) moving, stirring, powerful.

imprison *vb* (*the criminals were imprisoned*) put in prison, jail, lock up, take into custody, confine, detain.

impromptu *adj* (*he made an impromptu speech at the wedding reception*) unrehearsed, unprepared, spontaneous, improvised, off-the-cuff, ad-lib.

improve *vb* **1** (*they tried to improve conditions for the poor*) better, make better. **2** (*the standard of her work has improved*) get better, advance, progress, move on.

improvise *vb* **1** (*they had to improvise a shelter when they lost their tent*) put together, devise, rig up, concoct. **2** (*he has not prepared a speech and so he will have to improvise*) make do, ad-lib.

impudent *adj* (*the girl was impudent enough to swear at the teacher*) impertinent, insolent, cheeky, bold, forward, brazen, presumptuous.

impulsive *adj* (*he was given to impulsive decisions*) impetuous, impromptu, spontaneous, hasty, rash, thoughtless.

in *adj* **1** (*short skirts are in*) fashionable, stylish, (*inf*) trendy. **2** (*she is in with the boss*) in favor, favored. ○

be in for (something) likely to experience (something, often something unpleasant) (*The sky is so dark that I think we are in for a storm*).

be in on (something) to be involved in (something), to know about (something) (*Not many people were in on the scheme*).

have it in for (someone) to try to cause trouble for (someone) (*They have had it in for the boy since he reported them to the teacher*).

the ins and outs of (something) the details of (something) (*I don't know the ins and outs of their business arrangement*).

inadequate *adj* **1** (*their supplies of fuel are inadequate*) insufficient, deficient, scanty, meager. **2** (*she feels that she is an inadequate mother*) incompetent, inefficient, inept.

inadvertent *adj* (*there were a few inadvertent omissions from the list of guests*) accidental, unintentional.

inane *adj* (*it was an inane thing to do*) foolish, stupid, idiotic, absurd, ridiculous.

inanimate *adj* (*inanimate objects*) lifeless, without life.

inapt *adj* (*her inapt remarks*) inappropriate, unsuitable.

inaugurate *vb* (*they are inaugurating a new club*) launch, initiate, begin, commence, found, establish.

inborn *adj* (*his inborn pessimism*) inherent, innate, inbred, inherited.

incense *vb* (*he was incensed at the children's behavior*) enrage, annoy, anger, infuriate, exasperate.

incentive *n* (*they gave the workers more money as an incentive*) inducement, incitement, encouragement, motivation, spur.

incessant *adj* (*they were tired of their neighbor's incessant noise*) never-ending, unending, endless, unceasing, continuous, continual, unremitting.

incident *n* (*various sad incidents in her life*) event, happening, occurrence, episode, occasion.

incite *vb* **1** (*the speaker tried to incite the crowd to rebellion*) egg on, urge, goad, spur on, excite, rouse, stimulate. **2** (*they incited a rebellion*) provoke, instigate, stir up.

inclination *n* **1** (*he has an inclination to put on weight*) tendency, predisposition, habit. **2** (*flat ground with a slight inclination*) slope, gradient, rise. **3** (*with a slight inclination of his head*) bow, bending, nod.

incline *vb* **1** (*the land inclines toward the shore*) slope, slant, tilt, bend. **2** (*he inclines toward the left in politics*) tend, lean, veer.

incline, be inclined to *vbs* (*they are inclined to tell lies*) be apt to, have a tendency to, have a habit of, be liable to, be likely to.

include *vb* **1** (*the menu includes all their favorite dishes*) contain, take in, incorporate, comprise. **2** (*remember to include their names on the list*) put in, add, insert, enter.

inclusive *adj* **1** (*the hotel quoted an inclusive price*) all-in. **2** (*the total bill inclusive of service charge*) including.

incognito *adj/adv* (*he traveled incognito*) in disguise, disguised.

incoherent *adj* (*she was badly shaken and gave a very incoherent account of the accident*) confused, muddled, jumbled, disjointed, garbled.

income *n* (*his income after tax*) salary, wages, pay, earnings, profits.

incompatible *adj* **1** (*their two statements are incompatible*) conflicting, contradictory, inconsistent. **2** (*it was obvious before they married that they were incompatible*) unsuited, mismatched, ill-assorted.

incongruous *adj* (*the modern steel furniture looked incongruous with the old style of decoration*) out of keeping, unsuitable, unsuited, inappropriate, discordant, strange, odd.

increase *vb* **1** (*demand for the product has increased*) grow, go up, rise, multiply, mushroom, escalate. **2** (*they have increased the number of college places*) add to, augment, enlarge, extend, expand, raise, (*inf*) step up.

incredible *adj* **1** (*his story seemed quite incredible*) unbelievable, far-fetched, unconvincing, unlikely. **2** (*the gymnast's performance was quite incredible*) extraordinary, marvelous, amazing.

incriminate *vb* (*he was found guilty of the crime and tried to incriminate his friend*) accuse, charge, blame, implicate, involve.

indecent *adj* (*the comic told indecent jokes*) vulgar, crude, coarse, rude.

indefinite *adj* **1** (*he gave us rather an indefinite answer*) vague, unclear, confused, ambiguous. **2** (*she was rather indefinite about whether to go or not*) undecided, indecisive, uncertain, irresolute. **3** (*the date for the meeting is indefinite as yet*) undecided, unsettled, uncertain. **4** (*an indefinite shape in the mist*) indistinct, blurred, vague, dim.

independent *adj* **1** (*it is an independent state*) self-governing, free. **2** (*the children are grown up and independent*) self-supporting, self-sufficient. **3** (*the firms are independent of each other*) unattached, unconnected, unrelated, separate.

indicate *vb* **1** (*his ragged clothes indicated his poverty*) show, demonstrate, point to, be a sign of, suggest, mean. **2** (*he indicated which direction he was turning*) show, point out, make known.

indication *n* **1** (*her paleness is an indication of her illness*) sign, symptom, mark, signal. **2** (*he frowned as an indication of his anger*) demonstration, display, show.

indifferent *adj* **1** (*he seemed indifferent about the result of his trial*) apathetic, unconcerned, detached, unemotional. **2** (*he gave an indifferent performance*) mediocre, run-of-the-mill, commonplace, uninspired, undistinguished.

indignant *adj* (*they were indignant at being ignored*) angry, annoyed, irate, furious.

indispensable *adj* (*employees who were considered indispensable*) essential, necessary, crucial, imperative.

indisposed *adj* sick, ill, unwell, (*inf*) under the weather.

indistinct *adj* **1** (*indistinct noises*) muffled, low. **2** (*the picture was rather indistinct*) blurred, fuzzy, hazy, misty.

individual *adj* **1** (*the individual petals of the flower*) single, separate, particular, specific. **2** (*the writer has a very individual style*) characteristic, distinctive, peculiar, original.

induce *vb* **1** (*the sales clerk tried to induce them to buy a new car*) persuade, prevail upon, get, press. **2** (*the drug induced a skin reaction*) produce, cause, give rise to, bring about.

indulgent *adj* (*the children's grandparents are too indulgent*) permissive, easygoing, doting.

industrial *adj* (*an industrial area of the country*) manufacturing.

industrious *adj* (*industrious students*) hardworking, conscientious.

inert *adj* (*people lying inert after the previous night's party*) inactive, motionless, still.

inevitable *adj* (*a guilty verdict seemed inevitable*) unavoidable, unpreventable, inescapable, irrevocable.

infallible *adj* (*she claims that it is an infallible cure*) unfailing, foolproof, reliable, sure, certain.

infamous *adj* **1** (*he is an infamous criminal*) notorious, villainous, wicked. **2** (*it was an infamous crime*) notorious, scandalous, disgraceful, shocking, outrageous.

infant *n* (*she was very ill as an infant*) baby, young child.

infatuation *n* (*his infatuation with one of his female colleagues*) love, fancy, obsession, fixation, (*inf*) crush.

infect *vb* **1** (*waste material that infected the town's water supply*) contaminate, pollute, taint. **2** (*the wound was infected*) poison, make septic. **3** (*he infected others with his enthusiasm*) influence, affect.

infectious *adj* (*an infectious disease*) communicable, transmittable, catching.

infer *vb* (*from the evidence, the jury inferred that he was guilty*) deduce, reason, conclude, gather.

inferior *adj* **1** (*she occupies an inferior position in the firm)* subordinate, lower, lesser, junior, minor, low, humble. **2** (*the firm produces inferior goods*) imperfect, faulty, defective, substandard, shoddy. **3** (*they do not employ inferior workers*) incompetent, second-rate.

infest *vb* (*houses infested with rats*) overrun, invade, plague.

infidelity *n* **1** (*accused of infidelity to their king*) disloyalty, unfaithfulness, treachery. **2** (*his wife's infidelity*) unfaithfulness, adultery.

infinite *adj* **1** (*space is infinite*) boundless, unbounded, limitless, unlimited, endless. **2** (*she has infinite patience*) unlimited, endless, unending, inexhaustible.

infirm *adj* (*the old people are becoming infirm*) frail, failing, feeble, weak.

inflamed *adj* **1** (*a badly inflamed arm*) red, reddened, sore, infected, festering, septic. **2** (*inflamed passions*) aroused, roused, excited.

inflammable *adj* (*nightdresses made of inflammable material*) flammable, combustible.

inflammation *n* (*he was given some ointment to cure the inflammation*) redness, sore, swelling.

inflate *vb* **1** (*he had to stop and inflate his bicycle tires*) blow up, pump up. **2** (*a decision that might inflate prices*) increase, raise, boost, escalate.

inflexible *adj* **1** (*inflexible substances*) rigid, stiff, hard. **2** (*an inflexible work schedule*) fixed, rigid, unalterable. **3** (*their inflexible attitudes*) stubborn, obstinate, adamant, firm, unaccommodating, unbending.

inflict *vb* (*inflict distress on his parents*) administer, deal out, mete out, impose, give.

influence *vb* **1** (*her state of health influenced her decision*) affect, have an effect on, have an impact on, sway, control, determine. **2** (*they would like to influence the jury*) sway, bias, prejudice, bribe.

influence *n* (*she had a great deal of influence on her colleagues*) effect, impact, sway, control, power.

influential *adj* (*he is an influential figure in the government*) powerful, important, leading.

inform *vb* **1** (*we had to inform her that he was dead*) tell, advise, notify, communicate to. **2** (*he informed on his friends to the police*) betray, (*inf*) grass on, (*inf*) blow the whistle on.

informal *adj* **1** (*wear informal clothing at weekends*) casual, comfortable. **2** (*an informal party*) casual, unceremonious, unofficial, simple, relaxed.

information *n* **1** (*collect information on all of the countries of the world*) data, facts, statistics. **2** (*when will we receive information about the next meeting?*) news, word, communication, advice, instruction.

infuriate *vb* (*they were infuriated at being overcharged in the restaurant*) enrage, incense, annoy, anger, exasperate.

ingenious *adj* (*they thought up an ingenious plan*) clever, shrewd, cunning, inventive, resourceful.

inhabit *vb* (*they inhabit a remote area of the country*) live in, dwell in, reside in, occupy.

inherent *adj* **1** (*there is an inherent tendency to heart disease in the family*) inborn, inbred, hereditary, congenital. **2** (*it was an inherent part of the design of the building*) intrinsic, innate, essential, basic, fundamental.

inherit *vb* **1** (*she inherited a great deal of money from her grandmother*) be left, be bequeathed. **2** (*he inherited the title on his father's death*) succeed to, accede to, assume.

inheritance *n* (*he has already spent his inheritance from his father*) legacy, estate.

inhibited *adj* (*she feels inhibited in the presence of her parents*) shy, reticent, reserved, self-conscious, subdued.

initial *adj* (*he was involved right from the initial stages of the company*) first, beginning, commencing, opening, early, introductory.

initiate *vb* **1** (*they asked him to initiate the proceedings*) begin, start off, commence, open, institute, launch. **2** (*the boys initiated a new member into their gang*) admit, introduce, induct, install, enroll.

initiative *n* **1** (*he took the initiative and made the opening speech*) first move, first step, lead, start, beginning. **2** (*there will be promotion prospects for workers with initiative*) enterprise, resourcefulness, inventiveness, drive.

injection *n* (*he was given an injection against tetanus*) inoculation, vaccination, shot, (*inf*) jab.

injure *vb* **1** (*he injured his leg in the accident*) hurt, damage, wound. **2** (*his behavior has injured his reputation*) damage, ruin, spoil, mar.

inkling *n* (*the workers had no inkling that the firm was going to shut down*) hint, clue, indication, suspicion.

inlet *n* (*they tied the boat up in a sandy inlet*) cove, bay.

inn *n* (*they had a meal at the local inn*) pub, tavern.

inner *adj* (*the inner layer*) inside, interior.

innocent *adj* **1** (*the accused was found innocent*) not guilty, guiltless, blameless. **2** (*innocent young girls*) simple, naive, artless, trusting, inexperienced, gullible, virtuous, pure. **3** (*it was just innocent fun*) harmless, safe, inoffensive.

innocuous *adj* (*the substance was found to be innocuous*) harmless, safe, nontoxic.

innovation *n* (*the new owner introduced some innovations*) new measure, change, alteration.

innuendo *n* (*she made an innuendo about his lack of honesty*) insinuation, suggestion, hint.

inordinate *adj* (*they caused an inordinate amount of trouble*) excessive, undue, unreasonable, uncalled for.

inquire *vb* **1** (*the police are inquiring into the cause of the fire*) make inquiries, investigate, look into, probe, query. **2** (*we inquired about her mother's health*) ask, make inquiries.

inquiry *n* **1** (*the police are conducting a murder inquiry*) investigation, inquest, interrogation, examination. **2** (*she is employed to answer customers' inquiries*) query, question.

inquisitive *adj* (*she is inquisitive about other people's business*) curious, prying, snooping, (*inf*) nosy.

insane *adj* **1** (*the murderer has been declared insane*) mad, deranged, demented, unhinged, out of your mind. **2** (*it was insane to take such risks*) mad, crazy, idiotic, foolish, stupid, absurd.

inscription *n* **1** (*the inscription on the gravestone*) writing, engraving, epitaph. **2** (*the inscription in the front of the book*) dedication, message.

insert *vb* **1** (*she inserted the letter in the envelope*) put in, push in, thrust in, slip in. **2** (*he decided to insert a few more lines into his report*) put in, introduce, enter.

inside *adv* (*she decided to stay inside in the cold weather*) indoors.

insignificant *adj* (*concentrate on the main points in the report and ignore the insignificant details*) unimportant, minor, trivial, trifling, negligible.

insinuate *vb* **1** (*she insinuated that she did not trust him*) hint, suggest, imply, indicate. **2** (*she succeeded in insinuating herself into the old lady's affections*) worm your way, work your way, ingratiate youself.

insipid *adj* (*she is a very insipid person*) colorless, dull, drab, uninteresting.

insist *vb* **1** (*at first they refused to go, but their parents insisted*) stand firm, be firm, stand your ground, be determined, not take no for an answer. **2** (*she insisted that they go immediately*) demand, command, urge. **3** (*he insists that he is innocent*) maintain, assert, declare, swear.

insolent *adj* (*the student was accused of being insolent*) impertinent, impudent, cheeky, rude.

inspect *vb* (*the police inspected the stolen car*) examine, check, scrutinize, study.

inspiration *n* **1** (*his wife acts as an inspiration to the artist*) stimulus, stimulation, encouragement, motivation, spur. **2** (*his poetry lacks inspiration*) creativity, originality, inventiveness, imagination. **3** (*they were completely puzzled, but then he had a sudden inspiration*) bright idea.

install *vb* **1** (*they have installed a new bathroom*) put in, insert, fix, establish. **2** (*they installed themselves in comfortable chairs*) settle.

installment *n* **1** (*they are paying for the goods by installment*) part payment. **2** (*they published the novel in installments*) part, portion, section.

instance *n* (*that was just one instance of his impertinence*) case, example, illustration.

instant *adj* (*she demanded an instant reply*) instantaneous, immediate, on-the-spot, rapid, prompt.

instant *n* (*he was gone in an instant*) moment, minute, second, trice, (*inf*) jiffy.

instinct *n* **1** (*some birds migrate by instinct*) intuition, sixth sense. **2** (*she has an instinct for* *doing the right thing*) ability, knack, aptitude, gift, talent.

institution *n* **1** (*he has been living in an institution since he was very young*) home, hospital. **2** (*it was one of the village's institutions*) custom, tradition, practice.

instruct *vb* **1** (*he instructs the students in gymnastics*) teach, train, coach, educate. **2** (*she instructed the bank to close her account*) tell, order, command, direct, bid.

instructor *n* (*a sports instructor*) teacher, coach, trainer, tutor.

instrument *n* **1** (*instruments used by dentists*) implement, tool, appliance, apparatus, utensil, gadget. **2** (*she plays several instruments*) musical instrument.

insult *n* (*his insults were quite unjustified*) slur, abuse, affront, slight, gibe. ▷

add insult to injury to make matters worse (*Having given his first play a bad review the critic added insult to injury by ignoring the writer's second one*).

insult *vb* (*she was deeply insulted by his accusations*) affront, give offense to, abuse, slight, hurt.

intact *adj* (*they were pleased to find all their furniture intact after they moved house*) whole, in one piece, sound, unbroken, complete, undamaged.

integrate *vb* (*they integrated the various parts into a whole*) combine, unite, join, amalgamate, merge, fuse.

integrity *n* (*no person of integrity would have got involved in the scheme*) honor, honesty, uprightness, righteousness, decency.

intellect *n* (*people of limited intellect*) brain, mind, intelligence.

intellectual *adj* (*they are an intellectual family*) academic. well-educated, well-read, scholarly, bookish, clever.

intelligent *adj* (*the more intelligent pupils*) clever, bright, sharp, quick, smart, (*inf*) brainy.

intend *vb* (*she intends to leave soon*) aim, mean, plan.

intense *adj* **1** (*she could not stand the intense heat*) severe, acute, fierce, extreme, strong, powerful. **2** (*she has an intense desire to travel*) deep, profound, passionate, fervent, burning, eager, ardent.

intent *adj* **1** (*they were intent on getting there on time*) set on, bent on, determined to. **2** (*the child wore an intent expression as he worked*) absorbed, engrossed, attentive, concentrating.

intention *n* (*it is his intention to go to university*) aim, purpose, intent, goal, objective, design.

intentional *adj* (*it was not an accident that he hurt her—it was intentional*) deliberate, meant, purposeful, planned, calculated.

interest *n* **1** (*he showed no interest in the project*) concern, heed, regard, notice, attention, curiosity. **2** (*stamp collecting is one of his interests*) hobby, pastime, diversion. **3** (*this is a matter of interest to us all*) concern, importance, import, consequence.

interested *adj* **1** (*the children were not interested*) attentive, absorbed, curious. **2** (*the interested parties*) concerned, involved.

interesting *adj* (*it was an interesting book*) absorbing, engrossing, fascinating, riveting, gripping, amusing, entertaining.

interfere *vb* **1** (*he is always interfering in other people's business*) meddle with, pry into, intrude into, (*inf*) poke your nose into, (*inf*) stick your oar into. **2** (*he lets his sports training interfere with his schoolwork*) hinder, impede, hamper, obstruct, get in the way of.

interior *n* **1** (*they are painting the interior of the building*) inside. **2** (*they traveled to the interior of the country*) center, middle, heart.

interlude *n* (*during the interlude at the theater*) interval, intermission, break, lull, pause.

intermediate *adj* (*the team is in an intermediate position in the league*) middle, midway, halfway.

interminable *adj* **1** (*the journey seemed interminable*) endless, never-ending, everlasting **2** (*she was tired of his interminable questions*) endless, everlasting, ceaseless, incessant, continuous, continual, constant, persistent.

intermittent *adj* (*their telephone has an intermittent fault*) occasional, irregular, sporadic, fitful, recurrent.

internal *adj* **1** (*they knocked down an internal wall*) interior, inside, inner, inward. **2** (*the country's internal affairs*) home, domestic,.

international *adj* (*international issues*) global, universal, worldwide.

interpret *vb* **1** (*the students need someone to interpret the difficult text*) explain, clarify. **2** (*they interpreted her silence as agreement*) take, construe, read, understand. **3** (*she is employed to interpret for foreign businesspeople*) translate.

interrogate vb (*the police are interrogating the accused*) question, ask questions, examine, cross-examine, quiz, give the third degree to, (*inf*) grill.

interrupt vb 1 (*people in the audience kept interrupting his speech*) cut in on, break in on, butt in on, intrude on, disturb. 2 (*they interrupted the meeting to make an important announcement*) discontinue, break off, suspend, leave off, delay.

intersection n (*there was a bad road accident at the intersection*) junction, interchange, crossroad.

interval n 1 (*there was quite an interval between the two meetings*) gap, wait, space, period. 2 (*during the interval in the theater*) intermission, interlude, break, pause, lull.

intervene vb 1 (*the quarrel between the children was so bad that their parents had to intervene*) intercede, mediate, step in, interfere. 2 (*a period of several years intervened before they met again*) occur, pass, happen, take place, ensue.

interview n 1 (*the candidates for the job had to attend an interview*) meeting, discussion, dialog, evaluation. 2 (*the president was giving an interview to the press*) audience, press conference, dialog, question-and-answer session.

intimate adj 1 (*they were intimate friends*) close, dear, near, loving, friendly, amicable. 2 (*the intimate details of her life, as noted in her diary*) personal, private, confidential, secret.

intimidate vb (*they felt intimidated by the three huge men*) frighten, scare, alarm, terrify, terrorize, threaten.

intolerable adj (*an intolerable level of pain*) unbearable, unendurable, insufferable.

intolerant adj (*intolerant members of the community who objected to the activities of young people*) bigoted, illiberal, narrow-minded, biased, prejudiced, provincial.

intrepid adj (*intrepid explorers who went into the heart of the jungle*) fearless, bold, daring, brave, courageous.

intricate adj 1 (*an intricate pattern*) elaborate, fancy, ornate. 2 (*intricate problems*) complex, complicated, involved, difficult.

intriguing adj (*an intriguing story*) fascinating, riveting, absorbing, interesting, captivating.

introduce vb 1 (*she introduced the speaker*) present, announce. 2 (*she introduced her friends to each other*) present, make known. 3 (*they introduced new business methods*) bring in, initiate, launch, establish, start.

introduction n (*the introduction to the book*) preface, foreword, front matter, prolog.

introverted adj (*her sister is very outgoing but she is introverted*) inward-looking, withdrawn.

intrude vb (*although they had been invited to the party they felt as though they were intruding*) interrupt, barge in, interfere, butt in.

intruder n (*the police arrested the intruder*) burglar, housebreaker, thief.

intuition n (*she seemed to know by intuition where her child was*) instinct, sixth sense.

inundate vb (*they were inundated with complaints*) overwhelm, swamp, bog down.

invade vb (*the enemy army invaded the city*) overrun, storm, take over, attack, raid.

invalid adj (*the doctor visited their invalid mother*) ill, sick, ailing, unwell, infirm.

invalid n (*the invalid was confined to bed*) sick person, sufferer, patient, case.

invaluable adj (*we thanked them for their invaluable help*) useful, helpful, precious.

invariable adj (*an invariable temperature/Her style of dress was quite invariable*) unchanging, constant, unvarying, fixed, regular, uniform.

invasion n (*the enemy's invasion of the city*) attack, assault, raid.

invent vb 1 (*the person who invented television*) originate, create, discover, design, devise, think up. 2 (*he invented an excuse for not being present*) make up, concoct, fabricate, hatch, (*inf*) cook up.

investigate vb (*investigate a murder case*) research, examine, explore, inquire into, study.

invincible adj 1 (*their army seemed invincible*) unbeatable, unconquerable. 2 (*the obstacles to progress seem invincible*) insurmountable, overwhelming.

invisible adj 1 (*the high hedge made the cottage invisible to passers-by*) unseen, unnoticed, out of sight, hidden, concealed. 2 (*an invisible repair*) inconspicuous, unnoticeable.

invite vb 1 (*we invited them to dinner*) ask, send an invitation to. 2 (*the company is inviting applications for sales clerks*) ask, request, seek, call for.

involuntary adj (*blinking is usually an involuntary reaction*) reflex, automatic, instinctive, unthinking, mechanical.

involve vb 1 (*his new job involves working with*

computers) entail, include, necessitate, require. **2** (*they hoped to involve all the children in the scheme*) include, take in, incorporate, concern, interest. **3** (*he tried to involve his friends in his plans for the robbery*) implicate, associate, mix up. **4** (*find a hobby that involves them*) interest, absorb, occupy, grip, engross.

involved *adj* (*her excuse seemed very involved*) complicated, complex, intricate, elaborate, confused, muddled.

irate *adj* (*they tried to calm the irate old man*) angry, furious, indignant, infuriated.

iron *vb* (*they had to iron their creased shirts*) press, smooth.

iron, iron out *vbs* (*they had talks to try to iron out their problems*) sort out, clear up, straighten out, settle, solve. ᴏ

have several irons in the fire to be involved in several projects, schemes, etc., at the same time (*One of his businesses has gone bankrupt, but he still has several irons in the fire*) <A reference to a blacksmith who heats pieces of iron before shaping them>.
strike while the iron is hot to act at a point at which things are favorable to you (*Your father seems to be in a good mood. Why don't you strike while the iron is hot and ask him for an increase your allowance?*)

ironic *adj* (*he has a tendency to make ironic remarks*) satirical, mocking, scoffing, scornful, sneering, sarcastic.

irritable *adj* (*he gets irritable when he is tired*) bad-tempered, ill-tempered, cross, touchy, grumpy.

irritate *vb* **1** (*his constant stream of jokes irritates her*) annoy, get on your nerves, try your patience, exasperate, infuriate. **2** (*the material irritated her skin*) inflame, redden, chafe, cause discomfort to.

isolated *adj* **1** (*they live in an isolated place*) remote, out-of-the-way, secluded, desolate, inaccessible. **2** (*she felt isolated living far away from her family and friends*) lonely, solitary, alone, forsaken **3** (*the doctors do not think it is an epidemic, but just an isolated example of the disease*) single, solitary, abnormal, unusual, atypical.

issue *vb* **1** (*smoke issued from the factory chimney*) pour forth, discharge. **2** (*a steady stream of people issued from the building*) come out, emerge, leave, appear from. **3** (*new stamps have been issued to mark the occasion/They issued a press release*) put out, distribute, circulate, release.

issue *n* **1** (*they argue over political issues*) matter, subject, topic, affair, problem. **2** (*they plan to buy the next issue of the magazine*) edition, number, installment. **3** (*they have been having talks about peace, but the issue is still in doubt*) result, outcome, decision, conclusion.

itch *n* **1** (*she has an itch in her head*) tingling, prickling, irritation. **2** (*she has an itch to travel*) desire, longing, yearning, craving, hankering, (*inf*) yen.

item *n* **1** (*make a list of items for sale*) object, article, thing. **2** (*there are several items to be discussed at the meeting*) point, matter, issue, thing. ᴏ

be an item to be regarded as having a romantic relationship (*I didn't realize that Ralph and Carol are an item; I thought they were just good friends*).

itinerant *adj* (*an itinerant salesperson*) traveling.
itinerary *n* (*our itinerary takes us through Belgium*) route, journey, travels.

J

jab *vb* (*she jabbed him in the ribs to wake him*) prod, poke, nudge, dig.

jagged *adj* (*the jagged edge of the bread knife*) rough, uneven, pointed, notched, serrated.

jail *n* (*the prisoners have escaped from jail*) prison, lock-up, slammer, (*inf*) cooler, (*inf*) jug.

jail *vb* (*the judge jailed him for life*) imprison, send to prison, lock up, put away, confine.

jam *vb* **1** (*they tried to jam too many people into the hall*) crowd, pack, cram, squeeze, crush. **2** (*roads jammed by the sheer volume of traffic*) block, obstruct, congest, clog. **3** (*they jammed a piece of paper under the door to keep it open*) wedge, stick, force, push, stuff.

jar *vb* **1** (*the knife jarred against the metal surface of the box*) grate, rasp, scratch, squeak. **2** (*he jarred his shoulder in the car crash*) jolt, jerk, shake.

jealous *adj* **1** (*she was jealous because her sister won the race*) envious, grudging, resentful, covetous, green with envy. **2** (*he had a jealous wife*) suspicious, distrustful, mistrustful, possessive.

jeer *vb* (*when the politician tried to speak the crowd jeered*) mock, scoff, ridicule, taunt, sneer.

jerk *vb* **1** (*his leg was jerking uncontrollably*) twitch, shake, tremble. **2** (*she jerked the child out of his seat*) pull, yank, tug, wrench. **3** (*the old bus jerked along the country roads*) jolt, bump, lurch, jar.

jewel *n* (*she kept her jewels in a safe*) gem, precious stone. ✧

the jewel in the crown the best or most valued part of something (*The cathedral is the jewel in the city's crown*).

jewelry, jewellery (*Br, Cdn*) *n* (*she wore silver jewelry on her black dress*) jewels, gems, trinkets, ornament.

jittery *adj* (*he was jittery before the exam*) nervous, nervy, jumpy, uneasy, anxious.

job *n* **1** (*he took days to finish a simple job*) task, piece of work, assignment, undertaking. **2** (*what is her job?*) occupation, profession, employment, career, trade. **3** (*it was his job to take out the garbage*) task, responsibility, concern, function, role.

jog *vb* **1** (*they jogged around the park*) go jogging, run, trot, lope. **2** (*we tried to jog her memory*) prompt, stir, stimulate, refresh.

join *vb* **1** (*we had to join the two pieces of string*) fasten, attach, put together, link, connect, tie. **2** (*we joined in the search party to look for the dog*) take part in, participate in, contribute to. **3** (*we were asked to join the tennis club*) become a member of, take up membership of, enroll in, sign up for. **4** (*the two clubs have joined together*) join forces, amalgamate, merge, combine, ally. **5** (*their garden joins ours*) adjoin, border, border on, meet. ✧

if you can't beat 'em, join 'em if you cannot persuade other people to think and act as you do, then often the easiest thing to do is to begin to think and act like them (*We tried to keep the apartment tidy, but they always left a mess. Finally we decided that if you can't beat 'em, join 'em*).

joint *n* (*the joints in the water pipes*) join, junction, coupling, seam.

joint *adj* (*the organization of the party was a joint effort*) common, shared, mutual, combined, collective, cooperative, united.

joke *n* **1** (*her uncle tells very funny jokes*) jest, gag, witticism, (*inf*) funny. **2** (*we took his bike for a joke*) practical joke, prank, hoax, piece of fun, trick, (*inf*) lark. ✧

be beyond a joke to be no longer amusing, to be rather serious or annoying (*We were a bit amused by the child's smart remarks at first but they are now beyond a joke*).

joke *vb* **1** (*she was hurt by his remark but he was only joking*) tease, fool, pull (someone's) leg. **2** (*he can be rather annoying as he jokes all the time*) tell jokes, crack jokes, jest.

jolly *adj* (*he was a very jolly old man*) merry, happy, gay, joyful, cheerful, light-hearted.

jolt *vb* **1** (*the old car jolted along the bumpy roads*) jerk, lurch, bump, bounce. **2** (*the little boy kept getting jolted by the crowd*) bump, jostle, push, shove, nudge. **3** (*he was jolted by the news of her death*) upset, disturb, perturb, shake, disconcert, stun.

jostle *vb* (*people in the crowd jostling each other*

to the front) push, shove, elbow, nudge, bump, knock, jolt.

jot *vb* (*jot down the names of the students*) note, make a note of, take down, write down, mark down, list.

journalist *n* (*the local artist was interviewed by a journalist*) reporter, newsman/newswoman, member of the press.

journey *n* (*they were tired after their long train journey*) trip, excursion, expedition, travels.

joy *n* (*their joy at the birth of their daughter*) delight, pleasure, happiness, gladness, rapture. ⇆

joyful *adj* (*it was a joyful occasion*) happy, cheerful, merry, gay, jolly, light-hearted.

judge *vb* **1** (*a senior member of the legal profession judged the case*) try, pronounce a verdict. **2** (*the local mayor judged the pets' competition*) adjudicate, arbitrate, evaluate, assess. **3** (*he is too ready to judge others*) pass judgment on, criticize, find fault with. **4** (*we judge that the meat would take an hour to cook*) estimate, guess, surmise, reckon, suppose, consider, think, believe.

judgment *n* **1** (*the magistrate will give his judgment tomorrow*) verdict, ruling, decision, finding, conclusion. **2** (*he is not a good businessman as he is lacking in judgment*) good sense, sense, shrewdness, wisdom.

juicy *adj* (*juicy fruit*) moist, ripe.

jump *vb* **1** (*the dog escaped by jumping over the fence*) leap over, vault, clear, hurdle. **2** (*the game involved the children jumping*) leap, spring, bound, bounce. **3** (*the sudden noise made everyone jump*) start, flinch, jerk.

junction *n* (*the cars collided at the junction*) intersection, interchange, crossroad.

jungle *n* (*wild animals in the jungle*) forest, tropical forest, undergrowth. ⇆

the law of the jungle the unofficial rules for survival or success in a dangerous or difficult situation where the usual civilized laws do not apply or are not effective (*Forget the normal rules, it's the law of the jungle out on those streets*).

junior *adj* **1** (*the junior members of the family*) younger. **2** (*the junior posts in the company*) subordinate, lower, lesser, minor.

just *adj* (*we felt it was a just decision*) fair, honest, impartial, unprejudiced, unbiased, objective.

just *adv* **1** (*he's just a boy*) only, merely. **2** (*I just met them*) now, a moment ago, recently. **3** (*we just caught the bus*) only just, barely, scarcely, (*inf*) by the skin of your teeth. **4** (*the house was just right for them*) exactly, absolutely, precisely, entirely.

justice *n* (*he expects justice from the US courts*) justness, fairness, fair-mindedness, impartiality, lack of bias, objectivity.

justify *vb* **1** (*he was asked to justify his absence*) account for, give reasons for, give grounds for, explain, defend, excuse. **2** (*his behavior justified our concern for his health*) support, warrant, bear out, confirm.

jut *vb* (*the cliff juts out over the road*) stick out, project, protrude, overhang.

juvenile *adj* **1** (*the juvenile section of the musical competition*) junior, young, youthful. **2** (*we were amazed at their juvenile attitude to losing the game*) childish, immature, infantile, purile.

K

keen *adj* **1** (*a keen sense of smell*) sharp, acute, sensitive. **2** (*admire her keen mind*) sharp, astute, shrewd, quick, clever, bright, intelligent. **3** (*the keen students asked for extra practice*) enthusiastic, eager, willing, avid, zealous, conscientious. **4** (*people who are keen on football*) fond of, devoted to, having a liking for, being a fan of. **5** (*people who are keen to get more education*) eager, anxious, avid. **6** (*a keen edge on the sword*) sharp, sharp-edged. **7** (*a keen frost*) intense, extreme, severe.

keep *vb* **1** (*she kept the ring that he had given her*) hold on to, retain, (*inf*) hang on to. **2** (*the child keeps all his old magazines*) save up, store, accumulate, hoard, collect. **3** (*the firm tried to keep going*) continue, carry on, persist, persevere. **4** (*the local deli keeps a wide range of goods*) stock, sell, stock, carry. **5** (*he does not earn enough to keep a wife and children*) provide, support, maintain, feed. **6** (*everyone should keep to the rules*) obey, comply with, observe, abide by, carry out. **7** (*try to keep the news of his accident from his mother*) keep back, keep secret, hide, conceal, withhold, suppress. **8** (*he is late—something must have kept him*) keep back, delay, hold back, detain, hinder. ↻

keep to yourself not to seek the company of others, to tell others very little about yourself (*We do not know our new neighbors— they keep very much to themselves*).
keep up with the Joneses to make an effort to remain on the same social level as your neighbors or friends by buying everything that they buy, etc. (*She insists that they change their car every time one of her friends gets a new one. She spends all her time keeping up with the Joneses*).

keep *n* (*she pays for her own keep*) board, food, maintenance, support.
keepsake *n* (*be given a keepsake of her vacation*) memento, souvenir, reminder, remembrance.
keg *n* (*kegs of beer*) barrel, cask, vat, butt.
kernel *n* **1** (*hazelnut kernels*) nut, stone, seed. **2** (*try to get to the kernel of the problem*) nub, core, center, heart, (*inf*) nitty-gritty.
key *n* **1** (*musical keys*) tone, pitch, timbre. **2** (*find the key to the problem*) clue, guide, pointer, answer, solution, explanation.

kick *vb* **1** (*kick the ball*) boot, punt. **2** (*kick the man lying on the ground*) boot, take your boot to, take your feet to. **3** (*try to kick the smoking habit*) give up, stop, abandon, quit. ↻

kick yourself to be annoyed with yourself (*He could have kicked himself when he realized that he had been tactless*).

kidnap *vb* (*the president's son has been kidnapped*) abduct, snatch, seize, hold to ransom, take hostage.
kill *vb* **1** (*he was killed by a member of a rival gang*) take (someone's) life, slay, murder, do to death, put to death, execute, assassinate, (*inf*) bump off. **2** (*the news of his death killed all our hopes*) destroy, put an end to, ruin, extinguish. ↻

kill (someone) with kindness to spoil (someone) to the extent that it is a disadvantage to him or her (*The old lady is killing her dog with kindness by giving him too much food*).
kill two birds with one stone to succeed in fulfilling two purposes with one act (*He was able to kill two birds with one stone when he went to a conference in New York. He gave a lecture and visited old friends*).

kind *adj* (*kind people helped him/They appreciated his kind action*) kind-hearted, kindly, generous, charitable, benevolent, helpful, considerate, obliging, thoughtful, friendly, amiable.
kind *n* (*a kind of dog/a kind of car*) type, sort, variety, class, category, brand, make, species.

two of a kind two people of a very similar type or character (*Don't worry about him treating her badly, because she treats him just as badly. They're two of a kind*).

king *n* (*he was crowned king of Denmark*) monarch, ruler, sovereign.
kingdom *n* (*the ruler's kingdom extended to the sea*) realm, domain, land, country, territory. ↻

till kingdom come for an extremely long time (*They will talk about the problem till kingdom come but they will not take any action*)

<Refers to the Lord's Prayer from the bible>.

to kingdom come to death (*The bomb is powerful enough to blow us all to kingdom come*).

kink *n* **1** (*there were some kinks in the rope*) twist, bend, coil, loop, tangle. **2** (*the kinks in her character*) quirk, eccentricity.

kit *n* (*he forgot his football kit*) equipment, gear, tackle, stuff, things, paraphernalia.

knack *n* (*he has the knack of getting people to tell him things*) talent, gift, aptitude, flair, ability, skill, expertise.

kneel *vb* (*he knelt to pick out some weeds*) get down on your knees, bend, stoop, crouch.

knife *vb* (*he was knifed to death*) stab, pierce, run through, impale. ⌦

knob *n* **1** (*turn the knob of the door*) handle. **2** (*turn the knob of the radio*) switch. **3** (*trees with knobs on the bark*) bump, bulge, lump, swelling, knot, nodule. **4** (*a knob of butter*) lump, piece, bit.

knock *vb* **1** (*they knocked at the door*) tap, rap, bang. **2** (*the child knocked into the table and hurt his head*) bang, bump, collide with, crash into. **3** (*he knocked his son on the head for being naughty*) strike, hit, slap, smack, box, thump, (*inf*) wallop.

know *vb* **1** (*we don't really know the other people in the street*) be acquainted with, have dealings with, socialize with. **2** (*we knew what they were saying about us*) realize, be aware of, be conscious of, notice, recognize. **3** (*he does not know any Spanish*) have knowledge of, understand, comprehend. **4** (*she has known great misfortune*) experience, go through, be familiar with. **5** (*he does not know one of the twins from the other*) distinguish, differentiate, tell.

knowledgeable *adj* (*she is very knowledgeable about local history*) informed, well-informed, educated, learned.

knowledge *n* **1** (*he showed his knowledge by doing well in the test*) learning, education, scholarship. **2** (*admire the taxi driver's knowledge of the area*) familiarity, acquaintanceship. **3** (*he has little knowledge of the subject*) understanding, grasp, comprehension, expertise, skill, know-how.

L

label *n* (*put a label on the baggage/the label on the article*) tag, tab, sticker, ticket.

labor, labour (*Br, Cdn*) *n* **1** (*they did not receive much money for their labor*) work, toil, effort, exertion, drudgery. **2** (*employ local labor in the new factory*) workers, employees, work force. ⟶

a labor of love a long or very difficult job done for your own satisfaction or from affection for someone rather than for any form of payment or reward (*He didn't get paid a cent for writing that piece about the history of the school—it was a real labor of love*).

labored, laboured (*Br, Cdn*) *adj* **1** (*the labored breathing of the invalid*) heavy, strained, forced, difficult. **2** (*he has a labored style of writing*) stilted, strained, stiff, unnatural.

laborer, labourer (*Br, Cdn*) *n* (*laborers on the construction site*) workman, worker.

laborious *adj* (*undertake a laborious task*) hard, difficult, strenuous, tiring.

labyrinth *n* **1** (*a labyrinth in the grounds of the stately home*) maze. **2** (*a labyrinth of cellars under the house/try to make their way through the labyrinth of rules and regulations*) maze, network, tangle, jungle.

lace *n* (*lose a lace from her shoe*) shoelace, cord, string.

lacerate *vb* (*he lacerated his hand on the cut glass*) cut, tear, gash, slash, rip.

lack *n* (*there is a lack of fresh water in the area*) shortage, dearth, insufficiency, scarcity, want.

lack *vb* (*she lacks training for the job*) be lacking, be without, have need of, be short of, be deficient in.

laconic *adj* (*she gave a laconic reply*) brief, concise, terse, succinct.

lad *n* (*they hired a lad to deliver the newspapers*) boy, youth, young man.

ladder *n* (*stand on a ladder to paint the ceiling*) stepladder, steps.

laden *adj* (*people laden with shopping*) loaded, burdened, weighed down.

lag *vb* **1** (*he lagged behind the rest of the runners in the race*) fall behind, ail, linger, dawdle, dally. **2** (*they lagged their hot-water tank*) wrap up, insulate.

lair *n* (*the fox's lair*) den.

lake *n* (*the children waded in the lake*) reservoir.

lame *adj* **1** (*he has been lame since the accident*) limping, crippled. **2** (*she has a lame leg*) crippled, game. **3** (*he gave a lame excuse for being late*) weak, feeble, flimsy, inadequate. ⟶

a lame duck a weak or inefficient person or organization (*The manager is a lame duck less than two years into the job*).

lamp *n* (*the lamps were still burning*) light.

land *n* **1** (*he went to live in a foreign land*) country, nation, state. **2** (*the land there will not grow much*) soil, earth, ground. **3** (*a large house with a great deal of land around it*) ground, estate, property, real estate. **4** (*prefer traveling on land to traveling by sea*) dry land, terra firma. ⟶

a land of milk and honey a place where life is pleasant, with plenty of good things and possibilities of success (*The refugees saw the country to which they were sent as a land of milk and honey*) <A biblical reference to the Promised Land of the Israelites described in Exodus 3:8>.

see how the land lies to look carefully at a situation before taking any action or decision (*She does not know how long she is going to stay with her friends. She is going to see how the land lies*).

land *vb* **1** (*the plane landed*) touch down, come down, alight. **2** (*they met us as we landed at the dock*) dock, disembark.

landscape *n* (*a country with a flat landscape*) countryside.

lane *n* **1** (*take a walk down a country lane*) path, track. **2** (*freeway lanes*) track, course.

language *n* **1** (*the Spanish language*) tongue, speech, mother tongue. **2** (*children acquire language at different rates*) speech, speaking, talking, words, vocabulary, communication.

lap *n* **1** (*the cat was sitting in its owner's lap*) knee, knees. **2** (*we are on our last lap of the journey*) round, section, stage. **3** (*the runners ran several laps of the track*) circuit, course. ⟶

drop into (someone's) lap to happen to (someone) without any effort on his or her part (*The job just dropped into his lap. He didn't even apply for it—the employers contacted him*).

in the lap of luxury in extremely comfortable or luxurious conditions (*She was a wealthy movie star living in the lap of luxury*).

lap *vb* **1** (*the cats lapped up the milk*) drink, lick up. **2** (*the water lapped against the rocks*) wash, beat.

lapse *n* (*we saw him again after a lapse of time*) interval, break, gap, pause, passage.

large *adj* **1** (*they have a large garden/They are putting up large buildings*) big, sizable, substantial, tall, high, huge, immense, enormous. **2** (*he is a very large man*) big, burly, heavy, strapping, hulking, hefty, fat. **3** (*we have large supplies of fuel*) big, ample, abundant, copious, liberal, plentiful. ✧

large as life in person, actually present (*We thought he had drowned but he suddenly came into the room large as life*).

lash *vb* **1** (*the guard lashed the prisoner with a whip*) whip, flog, flail, trash, beat. **2** (*they lashed the boat to the side of the ship*) tie, bind, fasten, tether, strap.

last *adj* **1** (*the last words of the speaker*) final, closing, concluding. **2** (*the last runners arrived exhausted*) hindmost, rearmost, final. ✧

as a last resort when all other methods have proved unsuccessful (*As a last resort we could walk to the next village although it is a long way*).

the last straw an event which, when added to everything that has already taken place, makes a situation impossible (*Everything had gone wrong that day, and when she missed the last bus, it was the last straw. She burst into tears*) <A shortened version of the saying "it is the last straw that breaks the camel's back," indicating that, if a camel is carrying the absolute maximum load for its strength, even an extra straw might be too much for it and might break its back>.

last *vb* **1** (*how long is the meeting likely to last?*) continue, go on, carry on, remain, persist. **2** (*the climbers cannot last on the mountains in these blizzard conditions*) survive, live, endure. **3** (*people said that their marriage would not last*)

survive, be permanent, hold out, last long. **4** (*buy shoes that will last*) wear well, last long, be durable.

late *adj* **1** (*don't wait for her. She is always late*) unpunctual, overdue, behind schedule, slow. **2** (*she still misses her late husband*) dead, deceased. **3** (*some late news has just arrived*) recent, new, fresh, up-to-the-minute. ✧

better late than never better for something to arrive, happen, etc., late than for it never to happen at all (*The letter offering him the job was a few days overdue but it was a case of better late than never*).

lather *n* (*the soap made a lot of lather*) suds, soapsuds, bubbles.

latter *adj* (*the latter brand is the more expensive*) last-named, second, the second of two.

laugh *vb* **1** (*the children laughed heartily at the antics of the clown*) chuckle, chortle, (*inf*) split your sides, (*inf*) fall about, (*inf*) be rolling in the aisles. **2** (*the children laughed at the old-fashioned clothing that the little girl was wearing*) jeer, mock, ridicule, sneer, make fun of, poke fun at. ✧

have the last laugh be victorious or proved right in the end, especially after being scorned, criticized, etc. (*His neighbors teased him for entering the best-kept garden competition but he had the last laugh when he won*) <A reference to the saying "He who laughs last laughs longest">.

laugh out of the other side of your mouth to suffer disappointment or misfortune after seeming to be successful or happy (*They were in good spirits because they thought their team had won the game but they laughed out of the other side of their mouths when the opposing team scored a late goal*).

launch *vb* **1** (*they launched the ship*) float, se afloat. **2** (*they launched a missile*) fire, discharge, send forth. **3** (*we launch our new business tomorrow*) begin, start, embark upon, se up, establish.

laundry *n* (*she does the laundry on Mondays*) washing, wash.

lavish *adj* (*a lavish supply of food*) generous, lib eral, abundant, copious, plentiful.

law *n* **1** (*it was a new law issued by Parliament*) rule, regulation, act, decree. **2** (*all players mus* *obey the laws of the game*) rule, regulation, instruction, guideline. ⟿

be a law unto yourself to behave as you wish rather than obeying the usual rules and conventions (*He was the only person at the formal party who was not wearing evening dress but then he's always been a law unto himself*).

take the law into your own hands to take action against a crime or injustice without involving the police or law courts (*When a child was murdered the villagers took the law into their own hands and nearly killed the person who they thought had committed the murder*).

lawful *adj* **1** (*they are looking for the lawful owner of the car*) legal, legitimate, rightful. **2** (*it is not lawful to play baseball on the grass in the park*) legal, permitted, permissible, allowed, authorized.

lawyer *n* (*he hired a lawyer to sue his neighbor for damage to his property*) solicitor, legal practitioner, legal adviser.

lay *vb* **1** (*we were asked to lay our books on the table*) put down, set down, place, deposit. **2** (*laid the blame on his friend*) place, put, attribute, assign.

layer *n* (*a layer of ice on the road*) coat, sheet, skin, film.

lazy *adj* (*he is very lazy and does not want to work*) idle, slothful, inactive, work-shy.

lead *n* **1** (*they need a strong person to lead the country*) be in charge of, direct, govern, be in command of, manage, head. **2** (*the horse was leading but fell just before the finish*) be in the lead, be in front, be first, be winning. **3** (*he was asked to lead the visitors to their seats*) conduct, guide, direct, escort, usher. **4** (*we hope that they will lead a happy life*) have, live, pass, experience. ⟿

lead (someone) by the nose to get (someone) to do whatever you want (*There is one student in the class who is very naughty and he seems to be able to lead all the other children by the nose*) <A reference to the ring on a bull's nose by which he can be led if necessary>.

lead *n* **1** (*the runners in the lead*) first place, leading position, forefront, vanguard. **2** (*she has the*

lead in the new play) leading part, leading role, starring role, principal part. **3** (*we lost the dog's lead*) leash, chain, tether.

leader *n* **1** (*the leader of the team of climbers*) head, captain. **2** (*the leader of the country*) head, ruler, commander, chief. **3** (*a leader in the field of fashion/a leader in medical research*) front runner, trend-setter, pioneer, trailblazer.

leading *adj* **1** (*they played a leading role in the peace talks*) chief, principal, foremost, important. **2** (*he was one of the leading artists of his day*) foremost, chief, most important, celebrated, eminent, outstanding.

leaf *vb* (*he leafed through the book to see if it was what he was looking for*) flick, skim, browse, glance. ⟿

take a leaf out of (someone's) book to use (someone) as an example (*You should take a leaf out of your sister's book and start doing some studying for your test*).

turn over a new leaf to change your behavior, etc., for the better (*He was wild as a teenager but has turned over a new leaf now that he is older*).

leaflet *n* (*an advertising leaflet*) pamphlet, booklet, brochure, circular, handbill.

league *n* (*clubs forming a soccer league*) alliance, federation, association, union, group, society. ⟿

be in league with (someone) to have joined together with (someone) usually for a bad purpose (*The police were sure that he was in league with the men who broke into the bank*).

leak *vb* **1** (*water was leaking from the hole in the pipe*) escape, ooze, drip, seep, discharge, issue. **2** (*a member of the department leaked information to the press*) reveal, divulge, disclose, make known, pass on.

lean *vb* **1** (*lean the ladder against the wall*) rest, prop, support. **2** (*the ship leaned to one side*) incline, bend, slant, tilt, slope.

lean *adj* **1** (*he was tall and lean*) thin, slender, slim, spare, skinny **2** (*lean meat*) nonfat, low-fat.

leaning *n* (*he has a leaning toward scientific subjects*) tendency, inclination, bent.

leap *vb* **1** (*the dog leaped over the fence*) jump, spring, bound, vault. **2** (*the children were* *leaping around excitedly before the party*) jump, bound, bounce, skip, hop, dance. **3** (*house prices have leaped*) soar, rocket, mount, shoot up.

learn *vb* **1** (*they had to learn a new method*) grasp, master, take in, pick up. **2** (*we go to school to learn*) be educated. **3** (*how did you learn that they had gone?*) find out, discover, gather, hear.

learned *adj* (*the learned men of the community*) educated, well-educated, well-read, scholarly, clever, intellectual.

learner *n* (*drivers who were learners*) trainee, student, apprentice.

lease *vb* (*they leased a car from an agency*) hire, rent, charter.

leash *n* (*a dog's leash*) lead, chain, cord. ⟳

be straining at the leash to be very impatient or eager to do something (*It was a lovely afternoon, and the children were straining at the leash to get out to play*) <A reference to a dog straining to get free from its leash>.

leather *n* (*coats made of leather*) skin, hide.

leave *vb* **1** (*the guests left hurriedly*) depart, go away, take your leave, set off. **2** (*he left his job and emigrated*) give up, quit, move from. **3** (*he left his wife and children*) abandon, desert, forsake, turn your back on. **4** (*he left his gloves in the bus*) leave behind, forget, mislay. **5** (*they were asked to leave their boots by the front door*) place, put, deposit. **6** (*she plans to leave all her money to her nephew*) bequeath, will. ⟳

leave (someone) in the lurch leave (someone) in a difficult or dangerous situation without any help (*She walked out and left her husband in the lurch with three young children*) <A lurch refers to a position at the end of certain games, such as cribbage, in which the loser has either lost by a huge margin or scored no points at all>.

leave *n* **1** (*the soldiers are taking some leave*) vacation, time off. **2** (*they were given leave to take some time off*) permission, consent, authorization. **3** (*they took their leave at midnight*) departure, leave-taking, farewell, goodbye.

lecture *n* (*the students attended a lecture on local history*) talk, speech, address.

leg *n* **1** (*she broke her leg*) lower limb. **2** (*the legs of the tripod for the telescope*) support, upright. **3** (*on the second leg of their journey*) stage, round, stretch, lap, part, portion. ⟳

not have a leg to stand on not to have any defense or justification for your actions (*He was definitely speeding when the police stopped him. He does not have leg to stand on*).

pull (someone's) leg to try as a joke to get (someone) to believe something that is not true (*There is not really a lion walking down the street. He was pulling your leg*).

legacy *n* (*he received a legacy in his aunt's will*) bequest, inheritance.

legal *adj* (*his action was not quite legal*) lawful, legitimate, law-abiding, permissible.

legend *n* (*legends about giants*) myth, saga, epic, folktale.

legendary *adj* **1** (*giants and other legendary figures*) mythical, fictitious, fictional, fabled. **2** (*legendary Hollywood actors*) famous, renowned, celebrated.

legible *adj* (*writing that was scarcely legible*) readable, decipherable, clear.

leisure *n* (*hobbies he pursued in periods of leisure*) free time, spare time.

lend *vb* **1** (*she lent him a book on gardening*) loan, give (someone) a loan of, let (someone) have the use of. **2** (*the flowers lend a freshness to the room*) add, give, supply.

length *n* **1** (*what length is the room?*) distance. **2** (*the audience were bored by the sheer length of the speech*) lengthiness, extensiveness, longwindedness.

lengthen *vb* **1** (*they lengthened the skirts*) make longer, elongate, let down **2** (*it will lengthen the time the job takes*) make longer, draw out, prolong, extend, protract. **3** (*it is early spring and the days are lengthening*) become longer, draw out.

lengthy *adj* (*he gave a lengthy speech/The meeting was a lengthy affair*) long, long-lasting, prolonged, protracted, too long.

lenient *adj* **1** (*a lenient judge*) merciful, forgiving, compassionate, tolerant, gentle. **2** (*the accused was given a lenient sentence*) mild, moderate.

lessen *vb* **1** (*they hoped that the storm would lessen*) grow less, get less, abate, subside, ease off, let up, dwindle, decrease. **2** (*he was given pills to lessen the pain*) reduce, decrease, ease, relieve, soothe.

lesson *n* **1** (*the children are having a French*

lesson) class. **2** (*the Bible story is meant to teach a lesson*) moral, message, example, warning.

let *vb* **1** (*they let the children play in the garden*) allow, permit, give permission to, authorize. **2** (*he lets his apartment to students*) let out, rent, rent out, lease, hire.

lethal *adj* (*the blow to his head proved lethal*) fatal, deadly, mortal, terminal, destructive.

lethargic *adj* (*they felt lethargic after a heavy lunch*) sluggish, inactive, listless, sleepy, lazy, languid.

letter *n* **1** (*the letters of the alphabet*) character, symbol. **2** (*we sent a letter of thanks*) message, note, epistle. ✧

the letter of the law the exact wording of a law, rule, agreement, etc. (*According to the letter of the law he is responsible for repairs to the house but he refuses to carry them out*).

level *adj* **1** (*we need a level surface to build it on*) even, flat, smooth, flush, horizontal. **2** (*the scores were level at half-time*) equal, even, neck and neck. **3** (*we need to keep the room at a level temperature*) even, uniform, regular, consistent, stable, constant.

level *n* **1** (*at eye-level*) height, altitude. **2** (*the lift will take you to the second level*) floor, story. **3** (*the two gymnasts are at about the same level of competence*) stage, standard, grade.

liable *adj* **1** (*the hotel is not liable for customers' lost goods*) responsible, accountable, answerable, at fault. **2** (*people who climb high buildings are liable to injury*) exposed, open to, in danger of, at risk of, subject to, vulnerable. **3** (*she is liable to burst into tears if you criticize her*) likely, apt, inclined, prone.

liberal *adj* **1** (*a liberal supply of food*) abundant, copious, ample, plentiful, generous, lavish. **2** (*her parents have very liberal ideas*) tolerant, broad-minded, unprejudiced, enlightened.

liberty *n* **1** (*a country that values its liberty*) freedom, independence. **2** (*the prisoners were suddenly given their liberty*) freedom, release, discharge.

license *n* (*he showed his driver's license as proof of identity*) permit, certificate, document, documentation.

license *vb* (*the store is licensed to sell liquor*) authorize, permit, allow.

lid *n* (*he removed the lid from the jar*) cover, top, cork, stopper. ✧

blow the lid off (something), take the lid off (something) (*inf*) to reveal the truth about (something) about which there has formerly been some secrecy (*When the worker was fired he blew the lid off the firm's illegal methods of accounting*).

lie *n* (*it was obvious that he was telling a lie*) untruth, falsehood, fib, white lie.

lie *vb* **1** (*the jury felt that the witness was lying*) tell a lie, tell a falsehood, fib. **2** (*the doctor asked him to lie on the sofa*) recline, stretch out, be horizontal. **3** (*the village lies at the foot of a hill*) be situated, be located, be. **4** (*the volcano lies dormant*) be, continue, remain. ✧

lie through your teeth to tell lies in an obvious and unashamed way (*He was lying through his teeth when he told her that he had been working late at the office*).
take (something) lying down to accept an unpleasant situation without protesting or taking action against it.

life *n* **1** (*when life began on earth*) existence, being. **2** (*they worked hard all their lives*) lifetime, life span, existence. **3** (*the children were full of life*) liveliness, animation, vitality, vivacity. **4** (*he was the life of the party*) spirit, vital spark, moving force. **5** (*they published a life of Winston Churchill*) biography, autobiography. ✧

come to life to become active or lively (*The restaurants there don't come to life until late in the evening*).
see life to have wide experience of varying conditions and situations (*As a social worker she certainly sees life*).
take your life in your hands to take the risk of being killed, injured, or harmed (*So many cars speed along that road that you take your life in your hands when you cross it*).

lifeless *adj* **1** (*a lifeless figure lay on the shore*) dead, deceased. **2** (*he seems to prefer lifeless objects to people*) inanimate, without life. **3** (*lifeless stretches of the world*) infertile, barren, sterile, bare, desolate. **4** (*the actor gave rather a lifeless performance*) spiritless, colorless, uninspired, flat, lackluster.

lift *vb* **1** (*they lifted the sacks onto the truck*) hoist, pick up, raise, carry. **2** (*they lifted the ban*) raise, remove, withdraw, revoke, relax, end. **3** (*the mist soon lifted*) rise, disperse, disappear.

light *n* **1** (*by the light of the candles*) illumination, brightness, brilliance, shining. **2** (*they carried a light to the window*) lamp, torch, flashlight. **3** (*they struck a light*) flame, spark. **4** (*we would prefer to arrive in the light*) daylight, daytime, day. **5** (*he began to see things in a different light*) aspect, angle, slant, approach, viewpoint, point of view. ✧

hide your light under a bushel to be modest or silent about your abilities or talents (*We discovered quite accidentally that she has a marvelous singing voice. She certainly had been hiding her light under a bushel*) <A biblical reference to Matthew 5:15>.
light at the end of the tunnel the possibility of success, happiness, etc., after a long period of suffering, depression, misery, etc. (*He has been depressed about being out of work, but now that there is a possibility of some work coming up there may be light at the end of the tunnel for him*).

light *adj* **1** (*a light, airy room*) bright, well-lit **2** (*wearing light clothing*) light-colored, pale, pastel. **3** (*she had very light hair*) light-colored, fair, blond, pale. **4** (*the suitcases are quite light*) easy to carry, portable. **5** (*a suit of a light material*) lightweight, thin, flimsy, delicate. **6** (*the child is very light for her age*) slight, small, thin. **7** (*he is able to do only light tasks*) easy, simple, effortless, undemanding. **8** (*she woke up with a light heart*) happy, merry, carefree, cheerful. **9** (*they were told that it was not a light matter*) frivolous, unimportant, insignificant, trivial, trifling. **10** (*there was a light wind blowing*) gentle, soft, slight.

light *vb* **1** (*they light the fire in the evenings*) ignite, kindle, set fire to, set alight. **2** (*the fireworks lit up the sky*) illuminate, brighten, lighten.

lighten *vb* **1** (*the sky lightened*) grow light, grow bright, grow brighter, brighten. **2** (*we had to lighten the donkey's load*) make lighter, lessen, reduce.

lightweight *adj* **1** (*wearing a lightweight suit in the heat*) light, thin, flimsy. **2** (*he is rather a lightweight writer*) insignificant, unimportant, trivial.

like *prep* **1** (*it was like her to lose her temper*) typical, characteristic, in keeping with. **2** (*she writes rather like Jane Austen*) in the manner of, in the same way as, resembling.

like *adj* (*they have like tastes*) similar, identical, corresponding, compatible.

like *vb* **1** (*they seemed to like each other right away*) have a liking for, be fond of, be attracted to, be keen on, love, admire, appreciate, approve of. **2** (*she does not like pop music*) enjoy, delight in, relish, be partial to, have a preference for. **3** (*we would like to go to the party but we have another engagement*) wish, want, desire, prefer.

likelihood *n* (*there is no likelihood of our arriving on time*) possibility, probability, chance, prospect.

likely *adj* **1** (*it is likely that she will fail*) probable, to be expected, possible. **2** (*it is likely to be wet there at that time of year*) liable, apt, inclined. **3** (*they gave a likely enough reason for being absent*) plausible, feasible, reasonable, credible. **4** (*she found a likely place to build a house*) suitable, appropriate, fitting, acceptable, reasonable.

likeness *n* (*there is a distinct likeness between the two faces*) similarity, resemblance, sameness.

limb *n* **1** (*he injured his limbs in the accident*) arm, leg, extremity. **2** (*they cut a limb from the tree because it was keeping out the light from the house*) branch, bough. ✧

out on a limb to be in a risky and often solitary position, having ideas, opinions, etc., that are different from those of other people (*Most of the members of the research department said that the new drug was absolutely safe, but the young scientist went out on a limb and said that it could have serious side effects*).

limelight *n* (*she was a movie actress who enjoyed the limelight*) public eye, public notice.

limit *n* **1** (*they were fishing outside the agreed limits*) boundary, border, extremity, cut-off point. **2** (*they tried to impose some kind of limit on their expenditure*) limitation, ceiling, maximum, restriction, restraint. **3** (*the climb up the mountain pushed their powers of endurance to the limit*) utmost, maximum, extremity, end.

limit *vb* **1** (*they tried to limit their expenditure*) restrict, restrain, curb, hold in check, **2** (*she felt* *that having children would limit her freedom)* restrict, restrain, curb, impede, hinder, hamper.

limp *vb (he still limps after the accident to his leg)* be lame, hobble.

limp *adj* **1** *(a salad consisting of tomatoes and a few limp lettuce leaves)* drooping, floppy, wilting, sagging. **2** *(they felt limp in the heat)* drooping, wilting, lethargic, exhausted.

line *n* **1** *(the students were asked to draw a line)* stroke. **2** *(there was a dirty line around the edge of the tub)* band, strip, stripe, seam. **3** *(the old woman had a face full of lines)* wrinkle, furrow, crease, groove. **4** *(a line of police kept back the crowd)* row, column, chain, cordon, procession, file. **5** *(she is hanging the washing on a line in the backyard)* rope, string, cable, wire. **6** *(the police are taking a tough line against the wrongdoers)* course of action, policy, approach, position, procedure. **7** *(what line is he in?)* line of work, work, business, employment, job, occupation, profession, trade. ⬦

lay it on the line to make the situation absolutely clear to someone *(His boss really laid it on the line to the workers. They had to arrive punctually or be sacked)*.

step out of line to behave differently from what is considered acceptable or expected *(Any student who steps out of line and does not wear school uniform will be punished)* <A reference to a line of soldiers on parade>.

toe the line to obey rules or orders or act in a way that is considered to be acceptable *(The children have been used to being disobedient but the new principal will soon get them to toe the line)* <A reference to competitors having to stand with their toes to a line when starting a race, etc.>.

line *vb* **1** *(age had lined her face)* wrinkle, furrow, crease. **2** *(beech trees lined the avenue)* border, edge. **3** *(the children were asked to line up outside their classroom)* form a line.

linger *vb* **1** *(the smell of fried fish lingered in the hall)* stay, remain, persist, hang around. **2** *(some of the students lingered to ask the professor questions)* stay behind, wait behind, hang around, loiter, delay, stay, remain.

link *n* **1** *(a link has been established between smoking and certain illnesses)* connection, association, relationship, tie-up. **2** *(they have*

strong family links) bond, attachment, tie. **3** *(the links of the chain)* loop, ring, coupling.

link *vb* **1** *(she has lost the piece that links the two parts together)* join, connect, fasten together, attach, couple. **2** *(the police are linking the murder with a previous one)* connect, associate, relate, bracket together.

lip *n* *(the lip of the cup)* edge, rim, brim, border, brink. ⬦

lick your lips to look forward to something with great pleasure *(He was positively licking his lips at the thought of a vacation in the sun)*.

liquid *adj (a liquid substance)* fluid, flowing, runny, watery.

liquor *n (he drinks only fruit juice, not liquor)* spirits, alcohol, alcoholic drink, strong drink, *(inf)* the hard stuff.

list *n (make a list of the titles of the books)* record, catalogue, register, inventory, table.

list *vb* **1** *(please list the articles that you bought)* make a list of, note down, write down, itemize, enter, record, register. **2** *(the ship listed in the storm)* lean, tilt, tip, heel over.

listen *vb (they listened carefully to what the teacher was saying)* pay attention to, take heed, heed, take notice of, hear.

listless *adj (feeling listless in the heat)* lethargic, sluggish, weak, exhausted, inactive.

litter *n* **1** *(with litter lying all over the park)* debris, refuse, waste, junk, trash, garbage. **2** *(a litter of pups)* family.

little *adj* **1** *(a little man/a little object)* small, slight, short, tiny, minute, diminutive, mini, infinitesimal, microscopic. **2** *(a little book)* small, concise, compact. **3** *(you will gain little advantage from doing that)* hardly any, slight, negligible. **4** *(they had a little argument about which of them should pay the check)* small, minor, petty, trivial, trifling, unimportant, insignificant. **5** *(they have nasty little minds)* mean, narrow, small, shallow.

little *n* **1** *(he will take a little of the milk)* touch, trace, bit, dash, spot. **2** *(you will see him in a little)* short time, little while, minute, moment.

live *adj (live animals/live bodies)* alive, living, breathing, existing, animate. ⬦

a live wire an energetic, enthusiastic person *(She's a real live wire who always makes parties very enjoyable)*.

live *vb* **1** *(in the days when dinosaurs lived)* be alive, exist, have life, be. **2** (*the casualty was not expected to live*) survive, last, endure. **3** (*old customs that live on*) survive, stay, remain, continue, abide. **4** (*they live on fruit and vegetables*) eat, feed on. **5** (*they live by begging*) make a living, support yourself, maintain yourself. **6** (*they live in an apartment downtown*) dwell, inhabit, reside, lodge, occupy. ✧

live and let live to get on with your own life and let other people get on with theirs without you interfering (*Everyone else complains about the noise made by the neighbors in the apartment upstairs but we believe we should live and let live*).

live it up to have an enjoyable and expensive time (*They really lived it up when they were on vacation and now they are faced with lots of debts*).

lively *adj* **1** (*they are very lively children*) active, energetic, spirited, sprightly, perky. **2** (*they had a lively discussion on local politics*) animated, spirited, stimulating, enthusiastic.

livid *adj* **1** (*their father was livid when he saw the damage which they had done to the car*) furious, enraged, infuriated, fuming. **2** (*he had a livid mark on his forehead*) bruised, discolored, black-and-white, purplish, bluish. **3** (*the livid faces of the dead*) ashen, pale, pallid, ghastly.

load *n* **1** (*the donkey had a heavy load*) burden, weight. **2** (*the truck's load*) cargo, freight, contents.

load *vb* **1** (*they helped to load the truck*) fill, fill up, pack, stack. **2** (*he loaded the gun*) prime, charge, fill. ✧

a loaded question a question intended to lead someone into admitting or agreeing with something when he or she does not wish to do so (*The accused was tricked into admitting his presence at the crime by a loaded question from the prosecuting lawyer*).

loaf *vb* (*loafing around the house instead of working*) laze, idle, lounge.

loan *vb* (*they loaned him money*) lend, give on loan.

loathe *vb* (*they used to be friends, but now they loathe each other*) hate, detest, have an aversion to.

local *adj* (*they attend the local school*) nearby, near, neighborhood.

locality *n* (*there are several hotels in the locality*) area, district, region, neighborhood, vicinity.

locate *vb* **1** (*they plan to locate the hotel on the outside of the village*) place, position, situate, site, build, establish. **2** (*we finally located the cause of the trouble with the engine*) find, discover, detect, identify, pinpoint.

lock *vb* **1** (*they locked the door*) bolt, bar, fasten, secure. **2** (*the guards locked the prisoners up*) shut up, confine, imprison.

logical *adj* **1** (*his argument was not at all logical*) reasoned, rational, sound, coherent. **2** (*it seemed the logical thing to do*) rational, reasonable, sensible, intelligent.

loiter *vb* **1** (*there were gangs of youths loitering around the street corners*) hang around, wait, skulk, lounge, loaf, idle. **2** (*they loitered along the road to school*) dawdle, dally, saunter, dilly-dally.

lone *adj* (*the sailors saw a lone yachtsman*) solitary, single, sole, unaccompanied, by yourself.

lonesome *adj* (*she lived by herself and sometime felt lonesome*) friendless, lonely, forlorn, neglected, desolate, isolated, unhappy, sad.

long *adj* **1** (*a piece of wood three meters long*) in length, lengthways, lengthwise. **2** (*it was a long journey*) lengthy, extended, slow, prolonged. **3** (*he gave a long speech*) lengthy, prolonged, protracted, long-drawn-out, wordy, long-winded.

long *vb* (*they longed for a cool drink*) yearn for, wish for, desire, crave, pine for, hanker after.

longing *n* (*they had a longing for some sunshine*) yearning, wish, desire, craving.

long-winded *adj* (*a long-winded speech*) wordy, rambling, lengthy, long-drawn-out, prolonged, protracted.

look *vb* **1** (*we looked and saw a beautiful painting*) take a look, observe, view, contemplate, gaze, stare, examine, study. **2** (*she looks sick*) appear, seem. **3** (*the dining room looks south*) face, overlook.

loom *vb* **1** (*a dark figure loomed out of the shadows*) appear, emerge, materialize. **2** (*the tests are looming*) be imminent, be close, be ominously close.

loop *n* (*loops of ribbon*) coil, hoop, circle, curl.

loose *adj* **1** (*they wore loose clothing*) loose-fitting, slack, wide, baggy. **2** (*the table leg is loose*) not secure, insecure, movable, wobbly, unsteady, shaky. **3** (*the rope was loose*) slack, untied, unfastened. **4** (*the pigs were loose in the village* *street*) at large, at liberty, free, unconfined.

loose *vb* (*she loosed the dogs when she saw the strange man in the yard*) let loose, set free, release, unleash, untie.

loosen *vb* 1 (*he loosened his belt*) slacken, let out, undo, unfasten, unhook. 2 (*he loosened his grip on the rail*) relax, slacken, weaken.

loot *n* (*the police found the burglar's loot*) booty, haul, plunder, spoils.

loot *vb* (*gangs looted the stores after the fire in the mall*) plunder, pillage, ransack, rob, burgle.

lose *vb* 1 (*we lost our keys*) mislay, misplace, forget. 2 (*they lost their way in the dark*) stray from, wander from. 3 (*she lost a lot of blood*) be deprived of. 4 (*they lost several opportunities*) miss, pass, neglect, waste. 5 (*our team lost*) be defeated, suffer defeat, be conquered.

loss *n* (*the firm made a loss that year*) deficit, non-profit.

lost *adj* 1 (*they eventually found the lost gloves*) missing, misplaced, mislaid, forgotten. 2 (*lost opportunities*) missed, passed, neglected, wasted.

lot *n* 1 (*a lot of people were present*) a great many, many, a good deal, a great deal, numerous, an abundance, plenty, masses. 2 (*she weeps a lot*) a good deal, much, many times. 3 (*the furniture was sold at auction as one lot*) collection, set, batch, quantity.

lotion *n* (*a lotion to soothe his sunburned skin*) cream, salve, ointment.

lottery *n* (*he hoped to gain a lot of money in the lottery*) draw, sweepstake, drawing of lots.

loud *adj* 1 (*the children were frightened by the loud noise*) noisy, blaring, booming, deafening, ear-splitting. 2 (*she disliked the loud colors in the restaurant*) garish, gaudy, flamboyant, flashy, vulgar. 3 (*she disapproved of their loud behavior*) noisy, rowdy, boisterous, rough.

loutish *adj* (*because of their loutish behavior, he was asked to leave the bar*) boorish, oafish, doltish, churlish.

love *n* 1 (*he showed his love by sending her red roses*) affection, fondness, care, concern, attachment, devotion, adoration, passion. 2 (*the child has a great love of chocolates*) liking, weakness, partiality, relish.

love *vb* 1 (*it was obvious that she loved him*) be in love with, care for, be fond of, adore, (*inf*) have a crush on. 2 (*she loves fresh peaches*) like, have a weakness for, be partial to, enjoy.

lovely *adj* 1 (*she is a lovely girl*) beautiful, pretty, attractive, good-looking, gorgeous, charming, enchanting. 2 (*we had a lovely time at the party*) delightful, pleasant, nice, marvelous, wonderful.

low *adj* 1 (*a low table*) short. 2 (*a low position in the firm*) inferior, humble, subordinate, junior. 3 (*she spoke in a low voice*) soft, quiet, whispered, hushed. 4 (*she was feeling low after her defeat*) in low spirits, down, down-hearted, dejected, depressed, despondent. 5 (*they have a low opinion of him*) unfavorable, poor, bad, adverse, negative, hostile. 6 (*our supplies of food are low*) sparse, meager, scarce, scanty, paltry, inadequate. 7 (*it was a low thing to do*) nasty, mean, foul, vile, base, dishonorable, despicable, wicked, evil.

lower *vb* 1 (*they lowered the flag*) let down, take down, haul down. 2 (*they have lowered the prices*) reduce, decrease, bring down, cut, slash. 3 (*she was asked to lower her voice/They lowered the volume of the radio*) quieten, soften, hush, turn down.

loyal *adj* (*they were loyal subjects of the king*) faithful, true, trusted, trustworthy, trusty, reliable, dependable, devoted, constant.

loyalty *n* (*they showed their loyalty to the king*) faith, faithfulness, fidelity, allegiance, trustworthiness, reliability, dependability, devotion, constancy.

lucid *adj* 1 (*her explanation was extremely lucid*) clear, crystal-clear, plain, graphic. 2 (*an old man who was scarcely lucid*) sane, in your right mind, rational, (*inf*) all there.

luck *n* 1 (*she found the perfect apartment just by luck*) chance, fortune, destiny, fate, accident. 2 (*we wished them luck*) good luck, good fortune, success, prosperity.

lucky *adj* 1 (*she seemed a very lucky person who always got what she wanted*) fortunate, favored, advantaged. 2 (*she didn't know the answer—it was just a lucky guess*) fortunate, opportune, timely.

lucrative *adj* (*his firm is very lucrative*) profitable, profit-making, money-making.

ludicrous *adj* (*it was a really ludicrous suggestion*) absurd, ridiculous, laughable, foolish, silly, crazy, preposterous.

lull *vb* 1 (*they lulled the child to sleep*) soothe, hush, quieten. 2 (*their fears were lulled*) soothe, quieten, silence, calm, ease.

lull *n* (*they left while there was a lull in the storm*) pause, respite, interval, break, let-up.

lumbering *adj* (*he was a great lumbering creature*) awkward, clumsy, bumbling, blundering, hulking, ungainly.

luminous *adj* (*a clock with a luminous dial*) lighted, lit, shining.

lump *n* (*he got a lump on the head when he fell*) bump, swelling, bulge, knob, bruise. **1** (*a lump in the middle of the nice flat lawn*) chunk, hunk, wedge, piece, mass.

lunatic *adj* (*it was a lunatic thing to do*) mad, insane, foolish, stupid, idiotic, senseless, absurd, ludicrous.

lunge *vb* **1** (*she lunged at her attacker with a knife*) stab, jab, thrust, poke. **2** (*he lunged toward the door when he saw his attacker*) charge, dive, spring, leap, bound.

lurch *vb* (*drunk men lurching home*) stagger, sway, reel, roll, weave, stumble, totter.

lure *vb* (*the evil men lured the children into their car*) entice, attract, induce, inveigle, decoy, tempt.

lurid *adj* **1** (*she hated the lurid colors on the walls of the restaurant*) overbright, gaudy, garish, flamboyant, loud. **2** (*the newspaper published the lurid details of the murder*) gory, gruesome, sensational, melodramatic, explicit.

lurk *vb* (*she saw a figure lurking in the shadows*) skulk, lie in wait, crouch, slink, prowl.

luscious *adj* (*luscious peaches*) juicy, delicious, succulent, mouth-watering.

lust *n* (*they needed to satisfy their lust for power*) greed, craving, desire, yearning, hunger.

luxurious *adj* (*they live in luxurious surroundings*) sumptuous, splendid, magnificent, wealthy, expensive, rich, costly, lavish, de luxe.

luxury *n* (*after they won the lottery they lived in luxury*) splendor, magnificence, wealth, ease.

lynch *vb* (*the townspeople lynched the man who had murdered the child*) put to death, execute, hang, kill, murder.

lyrics *npl* (*he wrote the lyrics of the pop songs*) words, libretto, book, text.

M

machine *n* apparatus, appliance, instrument, device, mechanism.

machinery *n* **1** (*the machinery in the factory*) apparatus, equipment, gear, plant. **2** (*the machinery of government*) workings, organization, system, agency.

mad *adj* **1** (*she went mad with grief*) insane, demented, deranged, of unsound mind, crazed, crazy, unbalanced. **2** (*mothers who were mad with their children*) annoyed, angry, furious, enraged. **3** (*he is always engaging in mad schemes*) insane, crazy, idiotic, foolish, absurd, foolhardy, rash. **4** (*they are mad about jazz*) passionate, enthusiastic, , fervent, fanatical.

magazine *n* (*she was looking for a gardening magazine*) periodical, journal, paper, (*inf*) glossy.

magic *n* **1** (*people who believe in magic*) witchcraft, sorcery, wizardry, enchantment, the occult, voodoo. **2** (*the magic performed by the entertainer*) conjuring tricks, illusion, sleight of hand.

magician *n* **1** (*rather a frightening story about a magician*) sorcerer, witch, wizard, warlock, enchanter. **2** (*they hired a magician for the children's party*) conjuror, illusionist.

magnificent *adj* **1** (*a magnificent royal procession/ a magnificent feast*) splendid, grand, impressive, superb, glorious. **2** (*it was a magnificent game of tennis*) excellent, skillful, fine, impressive, outstanding.

magnitude *vb* **1** (*try to estimate the magnitude of the explosion*) extent, size, dimensions, volume, bulk. **2** (*we were surprised at the magnitude of the flu epidemic*) size, extent, vastness, extensiveness. **3** (*fail to appreciate the magnitude of the problem*) scale, importance, significance.

maid *n* (*the hotel maids*) domestic worker, domestic, servant. ⟁

maiden voyage the first voyage undertaken by a ship (*The ship ran aground on its maiden voyage*).

mail *n* **1** (*the mailman delivered the morning mail*) letters, junk mail, e-mail, snail mail. **2** (*she sent the package by mail*) postal service. **3** (*the knights of old wore mail*) chain, coat of mail, armor.

main *adj* (*the main points in the discussion/the main cities in the world*) chief, principal, leading, foremost, major, important.

mainly *adv* (*they mainly lived on fruit and vegetables*) for the most part, mostly, on the whole, largely.

maintain *vb* **1** (*he has always maintained that he is innocent*) declare, insist, assert, state, proclaim, claim. **2** (*he has a family to maintain*) keep, support, provide for, take care of, look after. **3** (*he maintained a steady speed throughout the journey*) keep, keep up, continue, sustain.

major *adj* **1** (*play a major part in the victory*) important, leading, principal, great, crucial. **2** (*the major part of his fortune*) larger, greater, bigger, main. **3** (*one of our major artists*) leading, chief, foremost, greatest, main, outstanding, notable, eminent.

majority *n* (*the majority of the people*) most, bulk, mass, main body.

make *vb* **1** (*make furniture at his woodwork class*) build, construct, assemble, fabricate, form, fashion. **2** (*try not to make a noise*) create, produce, bring about. **3** (*he made a bow to the audience*) perform, execute, carry out, effect. **4** (*they made him apologize*) force, compel. **5** (*the bride's father made a speech*) give, deliver, utter. **6** (*he made a fortune before he was 35*) earn, gain, acquire, obtain, get. **7** (*she will make a wonderful mother*) become, grow into, turn into. **8** (*we made an appointment to see him*) arrange, fix, agree on, settle on, decide on. **9** (*6 and 2 make 8*) add up to, amount to, come to, total. **10** (*he made the "v" into a "y" by mistake*) alter, change, turn, transform. **11** (*he hoped to make his destination by nightfall*) reach, arrive at, get to, achieve. **12** (*we could not make out what he was saying*) understand, follow, work out, hear. **13** (*he made up an excuse for not being present*) invent, think up, concoct, fabricate. ⟁

make it 1 to be successful, especially financially (*He said that if you don't make it by 35, you never do*). **2** to arrive somewhere e, to succeed in reaching somewhere (*When the car broke down on the way to the*

wedding we thought we would not make it).
make it up to become friendly again after a quarrel (*The two families have not spoken to each other for years but they have now agreed to make it up*).

make *n* (*various makes of car*) brand, kind, variety, sort, type. ✧

on the make (*inf*) with the intention of making a profit for yourself (*She thought he was trying to help her by giving her financial advice but he was really on the make*).

make-believe *n* (*she said that she saw a fairy but it was only make-believe*) fantasy, pretense, imagination.
make-believe *adj* (*the child's make-believe friend*) fantasy, made-up, pretended, feigned, imaginary, fictitious, unreal.
makeup *n* (*she put on her makeup in the powder room*) cosmetics: lipstick, powder, blusher, eyeshadow, eyeliner, mascara.
male *adj* (*male creatures*) masculine, manly, virile, macho.
male *n* (*two males and a female*) man, boy, gentleman.
malicious *adj* (*she received an anonymous malicious letter*) spiteful, vindictive, vicious, venomous, nasty, bitter, evil.
malignant *adj* **1** (*the doctor discovered that she had a malignant growth*) cancerous. **2** (*a malignant disease/a malignant influence*) dangerous, destructive, fatal, deadly, harmful.
mammoth *adj* (*they faced a mammoth task/a mammoth serving of ice cream*) huge, enormous, gigantic, vast, colossal, massive.
man *n* **1** (*three men and a woman*) male, gentleman, (*inf*) guy, (*inf*) dude. **2** (*man and animals*) mankind, humankind, the human race, humans. ✧

be your own man to be independent with regard to your opinions, attitudes, actions, etc. (*He's not his own man. He just agrees with whatever his friends say*).
the man in the street the ordinary, average person (*Politicians should pay more attention to the man in the street*).
to a man everyone without exception (*The workers voted to a man to go on strike*).

manage *vb* **1** (*he manages the whole firm*) run, be in charge of, be head of, control, preside over,

administer. **2** (*we don't know how they managed to survive/manage the work*) succeed in, contrive, achieve, accomplish, effect. **3** (*it is going to be a large dinner party. Will you manage?*) cope, get by. **4** (*she really cannot manage such a lively horse*) handle, cope with, deal with, control.
manager *vb* (*the workers and the departmental manager*) head, superintendent, supervisor, boss, chief, administrator.
mandatory *adj* (*taking part in the conference was not mandatory*) compulsory, obligatory, imperative, essential
maneuver, manoeuvre (*Br, Cdn*) *vb* (*he maneuvered the piece of metal into position*) guide, steer, ease, move, negotiate, manipulate.
maneuver, manoeuvre (*Br, Cdn*) *n* **1** (*army maneuvers*) movement, operation, exercise. **2** (*it was a clever maneuver to try to obtain a promotion*) move, tactic, trick, stratagem, scheme, ploy, ruse.
manful *adj* (*make a manful attempt to get to the summit of the mountain*) brave, courageous, gallant, heroic, bold, determined.
manhandle *vb* **1** (*the removal men had to manhandle the piano upstairs*) maneuver, haul, heave, push. **2** (*the police were accused of manhandling the protesters*) knock about, maul, mistreat, ill-treat, abuse, (*inf*) beat up.
mania *n* **1** (*sometimes he suffers from depression and sometimes from mania*) frenzy, hysteria, wildness, derangement, madness, insanity. **2** (*they have a mania for attending auctions*) fixation, obsession, compulsion, fascination, passion, enthusiasm, fad.
manipulate *vb* **1** (*manipulate the controls of the aircraft*) handle, operate, use, manage, maneuver. **2** (*a clever lawyer can manipulate a jury*) influence, control, guide, exploit.
mankind *n* (*the history of mankind*) man, humankind, the human race, Homo sapiens.
manly *adj* **1** (*a manly figure*) masculine, virile. **2** (*showing manly characteristics*) manful, brave, courageous, gallant.
manner *n* **1** (*she does the work in an efficient manner*) way, means, fashion, style, method, system. **2** (*they dislike his bossy manner*) attitude, behavior, conduct, bearing, look. ✧

in a manner of speaking in a way, in a sense (*I suppose you could call him her guardian in a manner of speaking*).

manners *npl* (*the children should be taught manners*) polite behavior, politeness, courtesy, social graces, etiquette.

mannish *adj* (*rather a mannish voice*) masculine, unfeminine, unwomanly, (*inf*) butch.

mansion *n* (*the rich family live in a huge mansion*) manor house, stately home.

manual *adj* **1** (*a manual gear change*) by hand, hand-operated. **2** (*manual workers rather than desk workers*) physical, laboring.

manual *n* (*an instruction manual with the washing machine*) handbook, instructions, guide, guidebook.

manufacture *vb* (*a factory manufacturing computer parts*) make, produce, build, construct, turn out.

manure *n* (*farmers spreading manure on the ground*) dung, fertilizer.

many *adj* (*many people did not turn up*) numerous, a large number, innumerable, countless, (*inf*) a lot of, (*inf*) lots of, (*inf*) oodles of. ✧

many hands make light work a job is easier to do if there are several people involved in doing it (*It looks as though the weeding of the garden will take a long time. Still there are a lot of us and many hands make light work*).

map *n* (*a map of the city*) chart, plan, diagram, guide. ✧

put (somewhere) on the map to become well-known or important (*Building a theme park there really put the town on the map*).

march *vb* **1** (*the soldiers marched along*) walk, stride, tramp, parade, file. **2** (*time marches on*) progress, advance, go on, continue.

margin *n* **1** (*they won by a narrow margin*) amount, difference. **2** (*we have so little money that there is little margin for error*) scope, room, allowance, latitude, leeway. **3** (*the margin of the lake*) edge, side, border, verge, boundary.

marginal *adj* (*there has been only a marginal improvement*) slight, minimal, small, tiny, minor, insignificant.

mark *n* **1** (*the dirty marks on the tablecloth*) stain, spot, speck, smear, streak, blotch, smudge. **2** (*a mark of respect*) sign, symbol, indication, token. **3** (*his war experiences had left their mark on him*) impression, effect, impact, influence, imprint. ✧

be up to the mark to reach the required or normal standard (*They fired him on the grounds that his work was just not up to the mark*).

make your mark to make yourself well-known or famous, to make a lasting impression (*When he was a student his teachers were sure that he would make his mark on the art world*).

mark *vb* **1** (*the hot coffee cups marked the table*) stain, smear, streak, blotch, smudge. **2** (*mark the battle sites on the map*) indicate, label, flag, tag. **3** (*they marked his birthday with a huge party*) celebrate, commemorate, observe. **4** (*you should mark what the principal says*) pay attention to, take heed of, heed, note, take notice of, mind.

market *n* **1** (*tourists buying souvenirs in the market*) marketplace, bazaar. **2** (*there is no market for such expensive goods in this part of the city*) demand, call, need.

maroon *vb* (*he was marooned on a desert island*) abandon, forsake, desert, strand.

marriage *n* **1** (*the marriage of their daughter to the son of their best friends*) wedding. **2** (*their marriage lasted 20 years*) matrimony, union.

marry *vb* **1** (*the couple will marry later in the year*) be married, wed, be wed, become man and wife, (*inf*) tie the knot. **2** (*they decided to marry their skills and set up business together*) join, unite, combine, merge.

marsh *n* (*plants that grow in marshes*) marshland, bog, swamp, mire, quagmire.

martial *adj* **1** (*the martial arts*) warlike, militant, combative, belligerent. **2** (*martial law*) military, army.

martyr *n* (*early martyrs killed because of their Christian faith*) victim, sufferer.

marvel *n* (*the pyramids are one of the marvels of the world*) wonder, sensation, phenomenon, miracle.

marvel *vb* (*we marveled at the exploits of the acrobats*) be amazed, be astonished, stare, gape, wonder at.

marvelous, marvellous (*Br, Cdn*) *adj* **1** (*admire the marvelous exploits of the acrobats*) amazing, astonishing, astounding, sensational, breathtaking, spectacular, remarkable, extraordinary. **2** (*we had a marvelous evening at the theater*) splendid, wonderful, glorious, excellent, enjoyable.

masculine *adj* **1** (*that tends to be a masculine*

habit) male, manlike. **2** (*she says she likes really masculine men*) manly, virile, (*inf*) macho.

mash *vb* (*mash the potatoes*) pulp, purée, crush, pound.

mask *vb* (*we planted trees to mask the view of the factory*) screen, camouflage, hide, conceal, cover up, blot out.

mass *n* **1** (*a mass of wood*) block, lump, hunk, chunk, piece. **2** (*measure the mass of the body*) size, dimension, bulk, capacity. **3** (*a mass of people attended the meeting*) many, crowd, throng, mob, crowd, host.

massacre *n* (*the world was shocked at the massacre of civilians*) slaughter, carnage, mass murder, butchery.

massage *vb* (*she massaged their stiff limbs*) knead, rub, pommel.

masses *npl* (*the leader did not care what the masses thought*) the people, the common people, the public, the populace, the mob.

massive *adj* (*they built a massive wall around their estate*) huge, enormous, immense, vast, colossal, gigantic, mammoth.

master *n* **1** (*in earlier time a master would have many servants*) lord, owner, employer. **2** (*he likes to think that he is master in the household*) chief, head, boss. **3** (*he is master of the ship*) captain, skipper. **4** (*several golf masters took part in the tournament*) expert, professional, virtuoso, genius, (*inf*) ace. ☞

past master someone extremely talented or **old master** any great painter, or a work painted by any of them, who painted before the 19th century, especially a painter of the 15th and 16th centuries.

master *vb* **1** (*unable to master his horse/He must try to master his emotions*) control, subdue, check, curb, quell. **2** (*she seems unable to master the techniques of driving*) learn, grasp, understand, (*inf*) get the hang of.

match *n* **1** (*take bets on who will win the soccer match*) contest, competition, game, tournament, trial, bout. **2** (*she was no match for the stronger player*) equal, equivalent, counterpart, rival. **3** (*their parents tried to arrange a match*) marriage, union. ☞

meet your match to find yourself opposing someone who has the ability to defeat you in a contest, argument, or activity (*She has*

been winning the annual tennis match for years but she has met her match in this new young player*).

mate *n* **1** (*a plumber's mate*) apprentice, assistant. **2** (*her friends think she is looking for a mate*) spouse, partner, husband/wife.

material *n* **1** (*dresses made of a silky material*) cloth, fabric, stuff, textile. **2** (*organic material*) matter, substance, stuff. **3** (*research material for his novel*) information, facts, details, data, (*inf*) gen.

materialize *vb* **1** (*we had very elaborate plans, but they did not materialize*) happen, come into being, come about, occur. **2** (*suddenly figures materialized out of the fog*) appear, come into view, become visible, emerge.

maternal *adj* (*maternal feelings*) motherly.

matrimony *n* (*she feels she is not ready for matrimony*) marriage, wedlock.

matted *adj* (*the child's hair was dirty and matted*) tangled, knotted, tousled, unkempt.

matter *n* **1** (*there are important matters to discuss*) topic, issue, subject. **2** (*it was no laughing matter*) affair, business, situation, circumstance. **3** (*waste matter*) material, substance, stuff. **4** (*what is the matter with the car?*) problem, trouble, difficulty. **5** (*matter oozing from the wound*) pus, discharge. ☞

a matter of life and death something of great urgency that may involve loss of life or some kind of other disaster (*Send for an ambulance and tell the driver that it is a matter of life and death/Please give me a ride downtown. It's a matter of life and death— I'm late for work*).

matter *vb* (*will it matter if we arrive a bit late?*) be of importance, be important, make any difference, count, be relevant.

mature *adj* **1** (*mature human beings*) adult, grown-up, grown, fully grown. **2** (*mature fruit/ mature cheese*) ripe, ripened, ready, mellow.

maul *vb* **1** (*the zookeeper was mauled by a lion*) tear to pieces, mutilate, mangle. **2** (*he was accused of mauling the female employees*) paw, molest.

maximum *adj* (*the maximum number*) highest, greatest, utmost.

maybe *adv* perhaps, possibly.

maze *n* (*get lost in the maze of corridors in the hospital*) labyrinth, network, mesh, confusion.

meadow n (*cows grazing in the meadow*) field, grassland, pasture.

meager, meagre (*Br, Cdn*) adj (*unable to feed themselves on their meager supply of money*) sparse, scarce, scanty, paltry, inadequate, insufficient, (*inf*) measly.

mean vb **1** (*what did his words mean?*) signify, indicate, convey, denote, stand for, suggest, imply. **2** (*we did not mean to hurt her*) intend, plan, set out, aim, propose. **3** (*I am afraid that this will mean war*) lead to, involve, result in, give rise to.

mean adj **1** (*he's too mean to buy anyone a present*) miserly, penny-pinching, grasping, greedy. **2** (*it was a mean thing to take the child's candy*) nasty, disagreeable, foul, vile, contemptible, hateful, cruel.

meaning n **1** (*he does not know the meaning of the word*) sense, significance, drift, gist, implication. **2** (*his life seems to have no meaning anymore*) point, value, worth. **3** (*she gave him a look full of meaning*) significance, eloquence.

means n **1** (*we have no means of getting there*) way, method, manner, course. **2** (*his father is a man of means*) wealth, riches, money, property, substance. **3** (*they have not the means to buy the car*) money, capital, finance, funds, resources.

measure n **1** (*use a linear measure*) standard, scale, system. **2** (*they had to take drastic measures to stop the truancy in the school*) action, act, course of action, step, means. ✧

for good measure something in addition to what is necessary (*She locked the door and for good measure put a table in front of it*).

measure vb (*measure the length of the room*) calculate, estimate, compute.

measurement n (*take the measurements of the room*) size, dimensions, proportions, extent, capacity.

mechanism n (*the mechanism that drives the machine*) machinery, workings, apparatus, device.

meddle vb (*his neighbors tried to meddle in his affairs*) interfere, intrude, pry, butt in.

media npl (*the politician blamed his unpopularity on the media*) the press, journalists, radio and television.

medicine n (*the doctor gave the patient some medicine*) medication, drug. ✧

a dose of your own medicine something unpleasant done to a person who is in the habit of doing similar things to other people (*He is always bullying the younger boys but he got a dose of his own medicine when their brothers beat him up*).

mediocre adj (*she used to be at the top of the class but her work this semester has been mediocre*) average, ordinary, indifferent, middling, passable, adequate, uninspired.

meditate vb (*take time to meditate on the gravity of the matter*) think about, contemplate, reflect on, consider, deliberate on.

medium adj (*of medium height*) average, middling.

meek adj (*meek people being bullied by the others*) docile, gentle, humble, patient, long-suffering.

meet vb **1** (*I met an old friend by chance in the mall*) encounter, come across, run into, bump into. **2** (*the committee meets on Thursday afternoons*) gather, assemble, congregate. **3** (*they met the demands of the job*) satisfy, fulfill, comply with. **4** (*meet your responsibilities*) carry out, perform, execute. **5** (*he met death bravely*) face, encounter, confront. **6** (*where the two roads meet*) join, connect, unite, adjoin. ✧

meet your Waterloo to be finally defeated, ruined, etc., often after a period of success (*He had been tennis champion at the club for years but met his Waterloo when the new member beat him*) <Napoleon Bonaparte was finally defeated at the battle of Waterloo>.

meeting n **1** (*a politician addressed the meeting*) gathering, assembly, conference. **2** (*a happy meeting between the two old friends*) encounter.

melancholy adj (*in a melancholy mood*) depressed, dejected, gloomy.

melancholy n depression, gloom, blues, low spirits.

mellow adj **1** (*mellow fruit*) ripe, mature, juicy, luscious. **2** (*she spoke in mellow tones*) sweet, tuneful, melodious, dulcet. **3** (*in a mellow mood after a good dinner*) cheerful, happy, genial, jovial.

melodious adj (*melodious sounds*) tuneful, musical, harmonious, dulcet.

melodramatic *adj* (*her reaction to the news was rather melodramatic*) theatrical, overdone, extravagant.

melt *vb* 1 (*the sun had melted the snow*) thaw, soften. 2 (*solids melting rapidly*) dissolve, thaw, defrost, soften.

memento *n* (*he gave her a memento of their holiday*) souvenir, keepsake, token, remembrance.

memorable *adj* (*a memorable occasion*) unforgettable, momentous, significant, notable,.

memory *n* 1 (*her memory of the event is rather hazy*) recollection, recall. 2 (*they built a statue in memory of the soldiers killed in the war*) remembrance, commemoration, honor.

menacing *adj* (*he gave them a menacing look*) threatening, ominous, frightening, sinister.

mend *vb* 1 (*he mended the broken table*) repair, fix, renovate, restore. 2 (*she mended the children's socks*) darn, sew, patch.

mention *vb* 1 (*she mentioned your name as someone who might be interested in the job*) refer to, allude to, touch on. 2 (*she did mention that she was thinking of leaving*) remark, comment, observe.

mercenary *adj* (*she is very mercenary and wants to marry a rich man*) grasping, greedy, avaricious, (*inf*) gold-digging.

merciful *adj* (*a merciful judge*) lenient, compassionate, forgiving, sympathetic, humane.

mercy *n* (*the judge showed mercy to the man who had stolen money to feed his children*) leniency, clemency, pity, compassion, forgiveness. ⇨

at the mercy of (someone) wholly in the power or control of (someone) (*The villagers are at the mercy of the cruel tyrant who owns the land which they rent*).

merge *vb* 1 (*the two firms have merged and staff have been made redundant*) amalgamate, combine, unite, join forces. 2 (*the colors in the picture seemed to merge*) blend, fuse, mingle.

merit *n* 1 (*he put forward the merits of the scheme*) advantage, asset, plus, good point. 2 (*she received a certificate of merit*) distinction, credit. 3 (*the artist's work is thought to have little merit*) worth, value.

merry *adj* (*merry children*) cheerful, gay, happy, light-hearted, joyful.

mess *n* 1 (*their mother asked them to clear up the mess in the kitchen*) clutter, litter, shambles, disorder, untidiness.

message *n* (*they were out and so we left a message for them*) note, memo, word, information, news, communication. ⇨

get the message (*inf*) to understand something, especially something that is not directly referred to (*He began yawning, hoping that his guests would get the message*).

method *n* (*teaching methods*) system, technique, procedure, routine. ⇨

there is method in his or **her madness** someone has a good, logical reason for acting as he or she does, although his or her actions seem strange or unreasonable (*We thought that he was a fool to resign but he got his severance package. The firm went bankrupt a few months later—there was method in his madness*).

microscopic *adj* (*microscopic insects*) tiny, minute, minuscule.

middle *n* (*the children formed a circle and the little girl was in the middle/right in the middle of the city*) center, heart.

might *n* (*unable to overcome the might of the enemy*) power, force, strength.

mighty *adj* 1 (*a mighty blow*) powerful, strong, forceful, hefty. 2 (*mighty mountains*) huge, massive, vast, enormous, colossal.

migrate *vb* (*swallow migrating to the south in the summer/people migrating to find work*) move, relocate.

mild *adj* 1 (*mild climate/mild weather*) moderate, warm, soft, balmy. 2 (*she is usually of a mild disposition but she really lost her temper at the children*) gentle, tender, soft-hearted, warm-hearted, compassionate, lenient, calm. 3 (*a mild sauce*) subtle, bland, non-spicy.

militant *adj* (*in a militant mood*) belligerent, aggressive, warlike.

mimic *vb* (*the student was caught mimicking the teacher*) impersonate, give an impersonation of, imitate, copy, parody, (*inf*) take off.

mind *vb* 1 (*I am sure that they won't mind if you use the phone*) object, care, bother, be upset, complain, disapprove. 2 (*you should mind your own business*) attend to, pay attention to, concentrate on. 3 (*tell him to mind the low ceiling—he might bump his head*) be careful of, watch out for, look out for, beware of.

mind *n* 1 (*she failed her test, although she has a*

good *mind*) brain, intellect, powers of reasoning. **2** (*it brought thoughts of her father to mind*) memory, recollection, remembrance. ▽

have a mind of your own to be in the habit of forming your own opinions, to be independent (*Her parents try to get her to do what they want, but she has a mind of her own*).
put (someone) in mind of (someone or **something)** to remind (someone) of (someone or something) because of some kind of similarity (*He puts me in mind of his father at that age*).

mingle *vb* **1** (*the colors mingled*) mix, blend. **2** (*she was too shy to mingle with the other guests at the party*) mix, socialize, circulate.

miniature *adj* (*a miniature railroad*) small-scale, mini, diminutive, minute, tiny.

minimum *adj* (*the minimum price*) lowest, smallest, least, bottom.

minute *adj* **1** (*insects which are minute creatures*) tiny, diminutive, microscopic, minuscule. **2** (*there is just a minute difference between the two*) tiny, insignificant, infinitesimal, negligible.

miracle *n* (*miracles described in the Bible*) wonder, marvel.

miraculous *adj* (*she made a miraculous recovery from the accident*) amazing, remarkable, extraordinary, incredible.

mirage *n* (*the travelers thought they saw an oasis in the desert, but it was a mirage*) hallucination, illusion, vision.

mirror *n* (*she looked in the mirror to apply her makeup*) looking glass, glass.

mirth *n* (*there was a lot of mirth at the party*) laughter, merriment, hilarity, revelry.

misbehave *vb* (*the children misbehaved when their mother was away*) behave badly, be naughty, be disobedient, (*inf*) act out.

miscellaneous *adj* (*a miscellaneous collection of old clothing for the sale*) assorted, mixed, varied, motley.

mischief *n* (*children who are bored may get into mischief*) mischievousness, naughtiness, bad behavior, misbehavior, misconduct, wrongdoing, trouble.

mischievous *adj* **1** (*mischievous children*) naughty, badly behaved, disobedient, rascally, roguish. **2** (*they were upset by the mischievous rumors that*

their *neighbors spread about them*) malicious, spiteful.

miser *n* (*the old miser would not give any money to charity*) Scrooge, skinflint, (*inf*) cheapskate.

miserly *adj* (*they were too miserly to give any money to charity*) mean, niggardly, parsimonious, tight-fisted, Scroogelike, (*inf*) tight.

misery *n* (*the misery of being homeless and hungry*) wretchedness, hardship, suffering, unhappiness, distress, sorrow. ▽

put (someone) out of his or **her misery** to end a time of anxiety or suspense (for someone) (*Finally the teachers put the students out of their misery by giving them their test results*).

misfortune *n* **1** (*he endured many misfortunes before becoming a successful businessman*) trouble, setback, adversity, calamity, disaster. **2** (*by misfortune, we missed the last bus*) bad luck, ill luck, accident.

misgiving *n* (*we had misgivings about lending them the car*) qualm, doubt, reservation, suspicion.

mislay *vb* (*Grandfather has mislaid his eyeglasses again*) lose, misplace.

mislead *vb* (*she deliberately tried to mislead her parents*) misinform, deceive, hoodwink.

miss *vb* **1** (*he missed a great opportunity*) pass up, let go, **2** (*the children are missing their mother*) long for, pine for. **3** (*he missed the shot*) bungle, botch, muff. **4** (*we tried to miss heavy traffic by leaving early*) avoid, evade, escape, dodge. **5** (*try not to miss anything out when you give an account of the accident*) leave out, omit, forget, overlook.

missile *n* (*guided missiles*) projectile, rocket.

mist *n* (*there was a morning mist but it soon lifted*) haze, fog.

mistake *n* (*his homework was full of mistakes*) error, inaccuracy, fault, blunder, (*inf*) slip-up.

mistreat *vb* (*her parents were accused of mistreating her*) abuse, ill-treat, harm, injure, molest.

misty *adj* **1** (*a misty morning*) hazy, foggy. **2** (*only a misty idea of what we are supposed to be doing*) vague, hazy. **3** (*my eyesight is a bit misty just now*) blurred, fuzzy.

mix *vb* **1** (*mix the ingredients for the cake*) blend, combine, put together. **2** (*she never mixes with the rest of the people in the street*) socialize, associate with, have dealings with. **3** (*the* demands of her job and looking after children just don't mix) be compatible. **4** (*she mixed up the two packages and sent us the wrong one*) muddle, jumble, confuse. **5** (*I think that he is mixed up in the crime*) involve, implicate.

mixed *adj* (*a mixed lot of old clothing for the rummage sale*) miscellaneous, assorted, varied, motley. ➪

a mixed bag a very varied mixture (*The new class of students were a mixed bag*).
a mixed blessing something that has disadvantages as well as advantages (*Having a tenant was a mixed blessing. The extra income was useful, but she interfered with their privacy*).

mixture *n* **1** (*pour the cake mixture into a bowl*) mix, blend, compound, concoction. **2** (*there was quite a mixture of people on the jury*) miscellany, assortment, variety, mix, collection.

moan *vb* **1** (*the injured woman moaned in pain*) groan. **2** (*she was always moaning about how poor she was, although she spent a lot of money on clothes*) complain, grumble, (*inf*) grouse, (*inf*) gripe.

mob *n* **1** (*an angry mob of protesters*) crowd, horde, throng, multitude. **2** (*she thinks she is too aristocratic to mix with the mob*) the common people, the masses, the populace, the rabble.

mobile *adj* **1** (*a mobile caravan*) movable, transportable, traveling. **2** (*the patients are mobile*) moving, walking.

mock *vb* (*the children mocked the new girl because she was wearing very thick eyeglasses*) ridicule, jeer at, sneer at, laugh at, tease, mimic.

model *n* **1** (*a model of an old airplane*) replica, copy, imitation. **2** (*what model of car would you like?*) design, style, variety, type. **3** (*the architects showed us the model of the new housing project*) prototype, design, pattern. **4** (*she wants to be a model*) fashion model, mannequin. **5** (*the art teacher used one of the students as a model*) artist's model, subject, sitter.

moderate *adj* **1** (*moderate winds*) mild, gentle, light. **2** (*we had moderate success*) reasonable, acceptable, tolerable, adequate, middling, average. **3** (*the prisoners' demands seemed moderate*) reasonable, within reason, fair. **4** (*a moderate lifestyle*) restrained, controlled, sober, steady.

modern *adj* **1** (*politicians in modern times*) present-day, present, contemporary, current. **2** (*her ideas on education are very modern/ modern styles of clothing*) up to date, new, advanced, progressive, state-of-the-art, fashionable, (*inf*) trendy.

modest *adj* **1** (*he had accomplished a great deal in life but was very modest*) unassuming, self-effacing, humble. **2** (*she was asked to wear modest clothing for the occasion*) demure, seemly, decent, decorous. **3** (*they are rich but live in a modest house*) humble, plain, simple, inexpensive. **4** (*their demands seemed very modest*) small, slight, limited, reasonable, moderate.

modify *vb* (*they may have to modify the design of the new plane slightly*) alter, change, adjust, vary.

moist *adj* **1** (*moist weather*) wet, damp, dank, rainy, humid, clammy. **2** (*soil moist after the rain*) wet, damp. **3** (*a moist fruitcake*) juicy, soft.

moisture *n* (*moisture running down the walls of the damp house*) water, liquid, wetness, wet, dampness.

mold, mould (*Br, Cdn*) *n* **1** (*cheese covered in mold/old wood with a layer of mold*) fungus, mildew, must. **2** (*put the Jell-O in a mold to set/ hot metal left to set in a mold*) shape, cast. ➪

cast in the same mold as (someone) very similar to (someone) (*She's cast in the same mold as her mother. They both have very hot tempers*).

moldy, mouldy (*Br, Cdn*) *adj* (*food having gone moldy in the closet*) mildewed, musty.

mole *n* (*a small mole on her back*) blemish, blotch, discoloration.

moment *n* **1** (*the peculiar noise lasted only a moment*) short time, instant, second, flash, (*inf*) jiffy. **2** (*it was a moment of great importance when the leaders first met*) time, occasion, point in time. **3** (*discuss matters of great moment*) importance, significance, note, seriousness. ➪

have had your moments to have experienced times of success, happiness, excitement (*The old lady seems to lead a very boring life now, but she has certainly had her moments*).
on the spur of the moment suddenly, without previous planning (*On the spur of the moment they decided to go away for the weekend*).

momentous *adj* (*a momentous event in history*) crucial, important, significant, serious.

monarch *n* (*French monarchs*) ruler, sovereign, king/queen.

money *n* (*they have enough money to buy a new car*) cash, capital, finance, (*inf*) wherewithal. ✧

have money to burn to have so much money that you can afford to spend it in ways considered overly extravagant or foolish (*That child has more toys than she knows what to do with. Her parents have money to burn*).

right on the money exactly right (*Your guess was right on the money*).

throw good money after bad to spend money in an unsuccessful attempt to get back money which you already lost (*He is trying to borrow thousands of dollars from the bank to invest in a firm that is losing money rapidly. He is simply trying to throw good money after bad*).

monitor *vb* (*doctors monitoring the patient's condition*) watch, observe, check, keep an eye on.

monotonous *adj* **1** (*people who have to do monotonous jobs*) without variety, repetitious, routine, humdrum, boring, dull, tedious. **2** (*he has a very monotonous voice*) flat, droning.

monstrous *adj* **1** (*they serve monstrous helpings of food/monstrous trucks speeding down the freeways*) huge, immense, vast, colossal. **2** (*firing them for asking for more money was a monstrous thing to do*) shocking, outrageous, disgraceful, scandalous, terrible, dreadful, foul, vile, despicable.

monument *n* (*a monument to soldiers who died in the war*) memorial, statue, shrine.

mood *n* **1** (*they were in a happy mood*) humor, temper, state of mind, disposition. **2** (*she is in a mood*) bad mood, bad temper, sulks.

moody *adj* (*teenagers are often accused of being moody*) temperamental, unpredictable, irritable, short-tempered, bad-tempered, touchy, sulky.

moon *vb* (*mooning around complaining of boredom*) mope, idle, languish. ✧

ask for the moon *or* **cry for the moon** to ask for something that is impossible, or virtually impossible, to obtain (*She keeps asking to go to Disneyland but she is crying for the moon. Her parents have scarcely enough to live on*).

moor *vb* (*moor the boat in the harbor*) secure, tie up, fasten, anchor.

mope *vb* (*since her boyfriend went away she has been moping around the house*) be miserable, be unhappy, brood, fret, sulk, idle, languish.

moral *adj* (*they are far too moral to break the law*) upright, honorable, virtuous, righteous, law-abiding, pure. ✧

moral support encouragement without actual physical, financial, etc., help (*Her parents could not afford to help her out financially when she was in college but they gave her moral support*).

morale *n* (*the team's morale was low after their third defeat in a row*) spirit, confidence, self-confidence, heart.

morsel *n* (*a morsel of cheese*) mouthful, bite, piece, bit, crumb, little.

mortal *adj* **1** (*a mortal blow*) deadly, fatal, lethal, destructive. **2** (*all of us are mortal*) human, earthly.

mostly *adv* (*the people in the group were mostly quite young*) for the most part, mainly, in the main, on the whole, largely, chiefly.

mother *n* (*her mother and father*) female parent, (*inf*) mom, mum, (*inf*) mommy, mummy.

motherly *adj* (*the school nurse is a very motherly person*) maternal, kind, loving, warm.

motion *n* (*sickness caused by the motion of the boat*) movement, moving. ✧

go through the motions to make a show of doing something, to pretend to do something (*He was bored stiff at the concert to which she took him but, to be polite, he had to go through the motions of enjoying himself*).

motivate *vb* (*trying to motivate the children into reading novels*) stimulate, inspire, stir, persuade.

motive *n* (*she seems to have had no motive for the murder*) reason, cause, grounds, basis.

mottled *adj* (*skin with rather a mottled appearance*) blotchy, speckled, flecked, spotted, marbled.

motto *n* ("*Service with a smile*" *is the store's motto*) slogan, saying, watchword.

mound n (*mounds of leaves in the garden*) heap, pile, stack, bank.

mount vb 1 (*mount the stairs to go to bed*) climb, ascend, go up. 2 (*mount the bus*) get on, board. 3 (*he mounted the picture*) frame. 4 (*mount a book exhibition*) put on, set up, stage, organize, arrange. 5 (*if you save a little each week your savings will soon mount up*) grow, increase, accumulate, pile up. 6 (*house prices are mounting*) rise, go up, increase, soar, escalate.

mountain n 1 (*a climber was injured on the mountain*) peak, hill. 2 (*they received mountains of mail complaining about the show*) pile, mound, heap, stack. ✧

make a mountain out of a molehill greatly to exaggerate the extent of a problem, etc. (*She is talking of going to the emergency room with a small cut on her finger. She is really making a mountain out of a molehill*).

mourn vb (*she is still mourning after the death of her husband last year*) grieve, sorrow, be sad.

mournful adj (*wearing a mournful expression*) sad, sorrowful, dejected, gloomy.

mouth n 1 (*the mouth of the river*) outlet, estuary. 2 (*the mouth of the cave*) opening, entry, entrance. ✧

foam at the mouth to be very angry (*He was foaming at the mouth at getting a parking ticket*) <Mad dogs foam at the mouth>.

move vb 1 (*they moved slowly around the room*) walk, go, proceed, progress. 2 (*we moved the furniture from one room to another*) carry, transport, transfer, convey, shift. 3 (*he is moving because he has a new job*) move house, relocate, leave, go away. 4 (*she was moved by the sight of the orphan children*) affect, touch, upset, disturb. 5 (*the sight moved her to tears/They finally felt moved to act*) rouse, stir, influence, induce, prompt. 6 (*at the meeting she moved that the chairman resign*) propose, put forward, suggest.

move n (*it is difficult to predict what our opponent's next move will be*) act, action, step, deed. ✧

make the first move to be the person who acts first, especially in a situation where two people are romantically or sexually attracted to each other (*Sam and Laura have been sitting looking longingly at each other all night, but both of them are too shy to make the first move*).

moving adj 1 (*the moving parts of the machinery*) movable, mobile. 2 (*the moving force behind the scheme*) driving, stimulating, dynamic. 3 (*a moving story about two orphans*) touching, affecting, emotional, emotive.

mow vb (*mow the grass*) cut, clip, trim.

mud n dirt, slime, sludge, (*inf*) muck.

muddle vb 1 (*she accidentally muddled the books in the library*) confuse, mix up, jumble up, disorganize, mess up. 2 (*new faces tend to muddle the old woman*) confuse, bewilder, perplex, puzzle.

muffle vb 1 (*try to muffle the loud noise*) stifle, suppress, deaden, quiet. 2 (*you must muffle yourself up against the cold*) wrap up, cover up.

mug n (*a mug of cocoa*) beaker, cup.

mug vb (*they mugged an old man to get his wallet*) attack, assault, rob, (*inf*) beat up.

muggy adj (*muggy weather*) close, stuffy, sultry, oppressive, humid, clammy.

multiple adj (*she received multiple fractures in the accident*) many, several, numerous, various.

multiply vb 1 (*mice multiplying rapidly*) reproduce, breed. 2 (*their troubles seem to be multiplying*) increase, grow, spread, accumulate.

multitude n (*they were surprised at the multitude of people who turned up for the meeting*) crowd, horde, mob.

mumble vb (*mumbling a few words*) mutter, whisper, murmur.

munch vb (*munching an apple*) chew, bite, gnaw.

mundane adj (*a meeting supposedly designed to discuss important church issues but ending up discussing mundane matters*) commonplace, common, ordinary, everyday, routine, normal, typical.

murder n (*he was charged with murder*) killing, slaying, homicide, slaughter.

murder vb (*convicted of murdering his father*) kill, slay, put to death.

murky adj 1 (*murky water*) muddy, dirty, cloudy, opaque. 2 (*a murky time of day*) dark, dim, gloomy.

murmur vb (*she murmured that she wanted to leave*) whisper, mutter, mumble.

muscle n (*he strained the muscle while high-jumping*) tendon, sinew, ligament.

muscular *adj* (*muscular young men involved in bodybuilding*) brawny, strapping, hefty, burly.

muse *vb* (*he mused over the situation*) think about, consider, contemplate, meditate on, reflect on.

mushroom *vb* (*housing estates mushrooming everywhere*) spring up, shoot up, sprout, boom, thrive.

music *n* (*people enjoying the music*) melody, tune, air, rhythm.

musical *adj* (*a musical sound*) tuneful, melodic, melodious, sweet-sounding.

muss *vb* (*climbing through the bushes had mussed her hair*) disarrange, tousle, dishevel, make untidy.

muster *vb* (*the general mustered the troops/He had to muster all his energy to climb the stairs*) gather, summon, rally.

musty *adj* (*a musty smell in the old house*) moldy, stale, fusty, stuffy, airless, damp.

mute *adj* (*animals making a mute appeal for help*) silent, speechless, unspoken, dumb, wordless.

muted *adj* (*muted colors*) soft, subtle, subdued, discreet, understated.

mutilate *vb* (*soldiers horribly mutilated in the war*) cripple, maim, mangle, disfigure, dismember.

mutinous *adj* (*a mutinous crew on board ship*) rebellious, revolutionary, insubordinate, disobedient, unruly.

mutiny *n* (*mutiny on board ship*) rebellion, revolt, revolution, riot.

mutter *vb* (*she muttered that she did not want to go*) mumble, murmur, whisper, complain.

mutual *adj* (*they have mutual friends*) common, shared, joint.

mysterious *adj* **1** (*there were mysterious noises coming from the room where they were getting ready for the party*) peculiar, strange, odd, weird, curious, puzzling. **2** (*they were being very mysterious about where they were going*) secretive, reticent, evasive.

mythical *adj* **1** (*the dragon is a mythical creature*) legendary, mythological, fabulous, imaginary, fictitious. **2** (*she is always talking about her rich uncle but we think that he is a mythical figure*) imaginary, fantasy, make-believe, invented, made-up, (*inf*) pretend.

N

nag *vb* **1** (*she is always nagging her husband*) scold, carp at, find fault with, bully. **2** (*children nagging their mother to buy them sweets*) pester, badger, harass, (*inf*) hassle.

nail *n* (*the carpenter's wood and nails*) pin, tack. ⬦

> **hit the nail on the head** to be extremely accurate in one's description, judgment, etc. (*You certainly hit the nail on the head when you said that he was lazy*).

naive *adj* (*she was so naive that she believed every word he said*) gullible, trusting, innocent.

naked *adj* **1** (*she could not answer the door because she was naked after her shower*) nude, in the nude, undressed, unclothed, bare, stark naked. **2** (*a naked flame*) unprotected, uncovered, exposed. **3** (*the naked truth*) undisguised, unadorned, stark, plain, simple.

name *n* **1** (*we don't know the name of the book*) title. **2** (*he made his name in the theater*) reputation, fame, renown, distinction. ⬦

> **call (someone) names** to use insulting or rude names to (someone) (*The other children called the poor boy names because he wore ragged clothes*).
> **name names** *vb* to give the names of people, especially people who have been involved in some form of crime or wrongdoing (*The children are being bullied at school, but they are afraid of naming names in case they are attacked*).

nap *n* catnap, sleep, doze, (*inf*) snooze, (*inf*) 40 winks.

narrate *vb* (*the old man narrated the story of his life*) tell, relate, recount, describe.

narrow *adj* **1** (*they have very narrow wrists*) slender, slim, thin. **2** (*they stock only a narrow range of goods*) limited, restricted, small.

narrow-minded *adj* (*she was too narrow-minded to listen to other people's points of view*) intolerant, prejudiced, bigoted, biased.

nasty *n* **1** (*the rotting meat was a nasty sight*) unpleasant, disagreeable, horrible, foul. **2** (*a nasty old woman*) disagreeable, bad-tempered, spiteful, mean.

nation *n* (*the nation of Spain*) country, land, state.

nationalistic *adj* (*he is nationalistic and does not like foreigners*) patriotic, chauvinistic.

native *adj* **1** (*the native plants of the region*) indigenous, original, local. **2** (*their native instincts*) natural, inborn.

natural *adj* **1** (*a store selling natural produce*) organic, pure. **2** (*natural behavior*) unaffected, simple, genuine, spontaneous. **3** (*their natural instincts*) inborn, native, instinctive. **4** (*the disease took its natural course*) usual, normal, regular, ordinary, common.

nature *n* **1** (*the children are interested in nature*) environment, Mother Nature, creation. **2** (*he has a warm nature*) temperament, disposition, character, personality. ⬦

> **second nature** a firmly established habit (*It was second nature to him to work as hard as he could*).

naughty *adj* (*the children were being naughty*) badly behaved, bad, mischievous, misbehaving, disobedient.

nauseate *vb* (*the sight of the rotting meat nauseated her*) sicken, make sick, turn one's stomach, disgust, revolt.

navigate *vb* (*he navigated the ship through the narrow straits*) steer, pilot, direct, guide.

near *adj* (*the station is very near*) nearby, close, at hand, handy. ⬦

> **a near miss** something unpleasant that very nearly happened, often the near collision of two planes in the sky (*The chimney fell to the ground just in front of me. It was certainly a near miss*).
> **one's nearest and dearest** one's close family (*Even her nearest and dearest think that she is bad-tempered in the morning*).

nearly *adv* **1** (*we nearly drowned*) almost, all but, as good as, practically. **2** (*they collected nearly $500*) almost, roughly, approximately.

neat *adj* **1** (*the children looked neat going to school*) tidy, smart, spruce. **2** (*they made a mess of the neat room*) tidy, orderly.

necessary *adj* (*they took the necessary action in time*) essential, needful, indispensable, required, vital.

need *n* **1** (*there is no need to shout*) necessity,

requirement, obligation, call. **2** (*their needs are very few*) want, wish, demand, requirement. **3** (*the charity helps people in need*) want, poverty, deprivation.

neglect *vb* (*she went to the movies and neglected her work*) pay no attention to, disregard, ignore, overlook, skip, shirk.

negligent *adj* (*he was found negligent for falling asleep on duty*) neglectful, careless, inattentive, sloppy.

negotiate *vb* **1** (*the two sides succeeded in negotiating a settlement*) work out, arrange, agree on. **2** (*the two sides are negotiating a financial settlement*) bargain, hold talks, discuss.

neighborhood *n* (*they are moving to a new neighborhood*) district, area, region, locality. ◇

in the neighborhood of (something) around, about, approximately, roughly.

nerve *n* **1** (*climbing the outside of the tower requires nerve*) courage, bravery, daring, pluck, (*inf*) guts. **2** (*they had the nerve to ask us to pay more*) impertinence, impudence, cheek, brazenness, effrontery, temerity. ◇

a bag of nerves a very nervous, anxious person (*She was a bag of nerves, waiting to hear the results of her exams*).

nervous *adj* **1** (*he was feeling nervous about his visit to the doctor*) edgy, on edge, tense, anxious, agitated. **2** (*they are very nervous people*) timid, anxious, edgy, tense, apprehensive.

network *n* **1** (*the pattern consisted of a network of lines*) latticework, mesh. **2** (*when looking for work she contacted her network of old friends*) system, organization.

neutral *n* **1** (*it is essential for referees to be neutral*) impartial, unbiased, unprejudiced, open-minded, detached, disinterested. **2** (*she was looking for curtains in neutral colors*) indefinite, colorless, beige, stone.

never *adv* (*she never lies*) not ever, not at all, under no circumstances. ◇

never-never land an imaginary land where conditions are absolutely ideal (*They are hoping for a never-never land in which they will have no money worries*) <A corruption of never-land in JM Barrie's play *Peter Pan*>.

new *adj* **1** (*they are buying a new car*) brand new, unused. **2** (*we need some new ideas*) fresh, original, imaginative. **3** (*they have introduced a new system of cataloging books*) different, modern, up-to-date. ◇

a new broom sweeps clean a new person will bring good changes to an organisation because (*Our new manager is just what we need—a new broom sweeps clean*).

turn over a new leaf to make changes in one's behavior, etc. which are for the better (*The student always used to arrive at school late, but he has turned over a new leaf*).

news *npl* (*there has been no news of the missing climbers*) information, facts, communication, word, data. ◇

no news is good news if one has not received any information about someone or something then one can probably assume that all is well, since, if something bad, such as an accident, had happened, one would have heard.

next *adj* **1** (*the next bus/the next president*) following, subsequent, succeeding. **2** (*the next house*) neighboring, adjacent, adjoining, closest, nearest.

nibble *vb* (*mice nibbling on a piece of cheese*) bite, gnaw, munch.

nice *adj* **1** (*his father is a nice person*) pleasant, friendly, kind, agreeable, charming. **2** (*we had a nice time at the theater*) pleasant, enjoyable, delightful. **3** (*it was a nice day for the wedding*) fine, sunny, dry. **4** (*there is a nice distinction in meaning between the two words*) fine, subtle, minute, precise.

night *n* (*when night fell*) night-time, darkness, dark. ◇

a night owl someone who is in the habit of staying up very late at night (*She is a real night owl and rarely goes to bed before 2:00 a.m.*).

nimble *adj* **1** (*the old lady was still very nimble*) agile, lithe, quick-moving, spry. **2** (*the knitters had very nimble fingers*) supple, deft.

nip *vb* **1** (*the dog nipped her ankle*) bite, snap at. **2** (*the little boy cried out when his friend nipped him*) compress, pinch, tweak, squeeze. ◇

nip and tuck very close (*It was nip and tuck until the final round of the match*). In modern times it is also used to describe having plastic surgery (*Hannah's had a little nip and tuck—she looks fabulous*).

nip (something) in the bud to put a stop or end to (something) at an early stage in the development of (something) (*Her father tried to nip her new romance in the bud by finding her a job overseas*).

noble *adj* **1** (*the king and the noble people of the land*) aristocratic, high-born, titled, blue-blooded. **2** (*a knight noted for his noble deeds*) brave, courageous, gallant, heroic, honorable, chivalrous. **3** (*the tourists admired the city's noble buildings*) impressive, imposing, magnificent, stately, grand.

nod *vb* **1** (*he nodded his head in agreement*) bow, incline, bob. **2** (*the audience began to nod*) nod off, drop off, fall asleep, doze. ⟳

the land of Nod sleep (*It is time that you children were in the land of Nod*).

noise *n* (*they were kept awake by the noise of traffic*) sound, loud sound, din, racket, clamor, row, commotion, hubbub, bedlam, pandemonium.

noisy *adj* **1** (*the teacher tried to quieten the noisy children*) rowdy, boisterous, loud. **2** (*noisy music*) loud, blaring, deafening, ear-splitting.

nondescript *adj* (*she was wearing nondescript clothes*) unremarkable, undistinguished, commonplace, ordinary.

nonsense *n* (*they told her that she was talking absolute nonsense*) rubbish, drivel, gibberish, balderdash.

normal *adj* **1** (*temperatures that were normal for the time of year*) average, usual, common, standard, ordinary, typical. **2** (*he is of more than normal size*) average, standard.

nosey, nosy *adjs* (*they have nosey neighbors*) inquisitive, prying, curious, interfering, (*inf*) snooping.

notable *adj* **1** (*the notable achievements of the politician*) noteworthy, outstanding, remarkable, memorable, important, significant. **2** (*all the notable people in the town were present at the reception*) noted, of note, distinguished, well-known, eminent, prominent.

notch *n* (*make notches in the stick*) nick, dent, cut, indentation.

note *n* **1** (*it is wise to keep a note of how much you spend*) record, account. **2** (*I wrote her a note thanking her*) letter, line, message. **3** (*his advice is worthy of note*) notice, attention, heed,

observation, **4** (*people of note in the community*) distinction, eminence, prestige, fame. **5** (*there was a note of sadness in her voice*) tone, sound. **6** (*he changed his notes into coins*) banknote, paper money. ⟳

strike the right note to say or do something suitable for the occasion (*Her dark clothes struck just the right note at the funeral*).

note *vb* **1** (*she noted the details in her diary*) write down, jot down, put down, enter. **2** (*the police noted that he seemed frightened*) notice, observe, perceive, detect.

notice *n* **1** (*very little escapes the principal's notice*) attention, observation, heed. **2** (*we have received notice of a meeting to be held next week*) notification, information, news, announcement. **3** (*a notice on the board giving details of the meeting*) poster, handbill, information sheet, bulletin, circular. **4** (*several workers have received their notice*) notice to quit, notice, (*inf*) marching orders.

notice *vb* (*we could not help noticing the bruise on her face*) see, observe, note, detect, spot, perceive, discern.

noticeable *adj* **1** (*the scar on her cheek was quite noticeable*) visible, obvious, plain, plain to see. **2** (*there had been a noticeable improvement in the pupil's work*) marked, obvious, evident, conspicuous, distinct.

notify *vb* (*they notified the police about the stranger in the backyard*) inform, tell, advise, acquaint.

notion *n* (*they have some peculiar notions*) idea, belief, opinion, conviction, theory, thought.

notorious *adj* (*he is a notorious criminal*) infamous, well-known, scandalous.

nourishing *adj* (*give the children nourishing food*) nutritious, healthy, wholesome, beneficial.

novel *adj* (*he had a novel approach to the teaching of history*) new, fresh, different, original, unusual.

novelty *n* (*a stand on the boardwalk selling novelties*) knick-knack, trinket, bauble, souvenir, memento, gimmick.

novice *n* (*they are complete novices at the game*) beginner, learner, trainee, apprentice, newcomer, recruit.

nude *adj* (*they were sunbathing nude*) in the nude, naked, stark naked, bare, undressed, unclothed.

nudge *vb* (*she nudged him in the ribs to tell him to keep quiet*) prod, jab, poke, dig, elbow, push.

nuisance *n* (*she regards the cat next door as a nuisance*) pest, bother, irritant, problem, trial, bore.

numb *adj* (*her fingers were numb with cold*) without feeling, immobilized, frozen, paralyzed.

number *n* **1** (*write down all the numbers*) figure, numeral, digit. **2** (*a large number of people attended the event*) quantity, amount, collection. **3** (*this is last week's number of the magazine*) issue, edition, copy. ♢

(someone's) number is up (*inf*) someone is about to suffer something unpleasant, such as dying, failing, being punished, etc. (*He has been stealing from the company for years but his number is up now. The manager has just begun to conduct an investigation*).

numerous *adj* (*he has numerous reasons for leaving*) many, very many, innumerable, several.

nurse *vb* **1** (*she nursed the sick child*) take care of, look after, tend, treat. **2** (*they still nurse feelings of resentment against their parents*) have, hold, harbor, entertain.

nutritious *adj* (*get the children to eat nutritious food instead of junk food*) nourishing, healthy, health-giving, wholesome, beneficial.

O

oath *n* **1** (*take the oath of office*) vow, promise, pledge, word. **2** (*she was offended by the oaths used by the drunk man*) swear word, curse, obscenity.

obedient *adj* (*obedient children/obedient dogs*) biddable, well-behaved, well-trained, docile.

obey *vb* **1** (*obey the school rules*) observe, abide by, comply with, keep to. **2** (*soldiers obeying orders*) carry out, perform, fulfill, execute. **3** (*children taught to obey their parents*) be dutiful to, follow the orders of.

object *n* **1** (*pick up a wooden object lying on the pavement*) thing, article, item. **2** (*the object of the exercise was to collect money for charity*) aim, goal, purpose, point, objective. **3** (*the object of their abuse*) target, focus, recipient. ◇

money, distance, etc.**, is no object** it does not matter how much money, distance etc. is involved (*Money was obviously no object at the lavish wedding reception/The delivery service advertised the fact that distance was no object*).

object *vb* (*we objected to the way they handled the situation*) raise objections to, protest against, complain, take exception to, grumble.

objection *n* (*there were several objections to the scheme*) protest, complaint, grumble.

objectionable *adj* (*he is a most objectionable young man/We found her manner objectionable*) offensive, obnoxious, unpleasant, disagreeable, nasty.

objective *adj* (*referees have to be objective*) impartial, unbiased, unprejudiced, neutral, disinterested, detached.

objective *n* (*our objective was to get there before dark*) object, aim, goal, target, intention.

obliged *adj* (*you are not obliged to say anything at this stage*) bound, compelled, forced, required.

obliging *adj* (*we have very obliging neighbors*) helpful, accommodating, willing, generous, cooperative.

oblivious *adj* (*they were oblivious to the danger they were in*) unaware, heedless, unheeding, unmindful, unconscious, ignorant.

obnoxious *adj* (*a most obnoxious sales person*) offensive, objectionable, unpleasant, disagreeable, nasty, horrible, odious.

obscene *adj* (*obscene videos*) pornographic, indecent, blue, bawdy, smutty, dirty.

obscure *adj* **1** (*for some obscure reason they suddenly decided to leave*) unclear, hidden, concealed, puzzling, mysterious. **2** (*a book by some obscure poet*) unheard of, unknown, little known, insignificant.

obscure *vb* **1** (*the new apartment building obscures our view of the lake*) hide, conceal, screen, block out. **2** (*his remarks simply obscured the issue*) confuse, muddle, complicate, cloud, obfuscate.

observant *adj* (*the observant lad was able to get the car's registration number*) sharp-eyed, eagle-eyed, attentive, heedful, vigilant.

observe *vb* **1** (*he observed a man watching his neighbor's house*) see, catch sight of, notice, perceive, witness. **2** (*all players must observe the rules of the game*) obey, keep, abide by, adhere to, comply with, follow, heed. **3** (*she observed that it was going to rain*) remark, comment, state, announce.

obsession *n* (*she has an obsession about having a spotlessly clean house*) fixation, preoccupation, compulsion, mania.

obsolete *adj* (*the factory uses obsolete machinery/The book has a great many obsolete words*) outworn, outmoded, antiquated, out of date, old-fashioned, archaic.

obstacle *n* (*the obstacles in the way of progress*) hindrance, impediment, obstruction, barrier, bar, hurdle.

obstinate *adj* (*the two sisters had a quarrel and were too obstinate to apologize*) stubborn, pigheaded, mulish, headstrong, unyielding.

obstreperous *adj* (*the police tried to control the obstreperous football crowd*) unruly, disorderly, rowdy, boisterous, rough, wild, turbulent, riotous.

obstruct *vb* **1** (*fallen trees obstructing the flow of traffic*) block, bar, check, halt. **2** (*the protesters tried to obstruct progress on the building of the new highway*) hinder, delay, impede, hamper, block, interrupt, hold up.

obstruction *n* (*obstructions to progress*) obstacle, impediment, hindrance, hurdle, barrier, bar.

obtain *vb* (*we tried to obtain a copy of the book*) get, get hold of, acquire, come by, procure, gain.

obvious *adj* (*it was obvious that she was crying/ The bruise on his face was very obvious*) clear, clear-cut, plain, noticeable, evident, apparent.

occasion *n* **1** (*they met on several occasions*) time, point. **2** (*the retirement party was a sad occasion*) event, incident, occurrence, happening. **3** (*she will go abroad if the occasion arises*) opportunity, chance, opening. **4** (*they met at a festive occasion*) function, gathering, party, (*inf*) do. ⌁

rise to the occasion to be able to carry out whatever action is required in an important or urgent situation (*Her father was very nervous about speaking in public, but he rose to the occasion at her wedding reception*).

occasional *adj* (*it will be a fine day with occasional showers*) infrequent, irregular, sporadic, rare, odd.

occupation *n* (*write down your occupation on the application form*) job, employment, profession, business, trade, career.

occupied *adj* **1** (*all the hotel rooms are occupied*) full, in use, engaged, taken. **2** (*the houses in the new development are all occupied already*) inhabited. **3** (*the manager is occupied just now and cannot speak to you*) busy, engaged, (*inf*) tied up.

occupy *vb* **1** (*how many people occupy this apartment?*) inhabit, live in, reside in, dwell in. **2** (*the enemy army occupied the city*) take possession of, seize, invade, capture. **3** (*how does she occupy her leisure hours?*) fill, use, utilize, take up. **4** (*they occupy less senior jobs*) hold, have, fill.

occur *vb* **1** (*the police think the murder occurred last night*) take place, happen, come about. **2** (*the same mistakes occur throughout the piece of work*) arise, be found, appear, be present. **3** (*it occurred to me that I had seen her before*) come to, enter one's head, strike.

occurrence *n* (*car theft is a common occurrence these days*) event, incident, happening.

odd *adj* **1** (*we thought her behavior was odd*) strange, peculiar, queer, weird, bizarre, outlandish, abnormal, curious. **2** (*she thinks of him at odd moments*) occasional, random, irregular. **3** (*he found an odd sock*) spare, left over, single, unmatched.

odious *adj* (*our new neighbors are odious people*) horrible, nasty, loathsome, detestable, hateful, objectionable, offensive.

odor *n* (*the odor of frying onions*) smell, aroma, scent, fragrance, stink, stench.

offense *n* **1** (*they were punished for the offense which they committed*) crime, misdeed, wrong. **2** (*his ungrateful behavior caused offense*) upset, displeasure, annoyance, disapproval.

offend *vb* (*he offended her parents by not thanking them for the meal*) hurt, upset, displease, annoy.

offensive *adj* **1** (*he was forced to apologize for his offensive remarks*) hurtful, upsetting, distressful, abusive. **2** (*he is an offensive person/We noticed an offensive smell*) unpleasant, nasty, horrible, foul, vile, objectionable, odious.

offer *vb* **1** (*he offered several suggestions*) put forward, propose, submit, suggest. **2** (*we offered to babysit for them*) volunteer. **3** (*the job offers good career prospects*) give, present, afford, supply, furnish.

office *n* **1** (*his office is on the top floor*) place of business, workplace, room. **2** (*he has the office of president*) post, position, appointment, job.

official *adj* **1** (*receive official permission/the official documents*) authorized, formal, licensed, certified, legal. **2** (*we had to wear evening attire to the official function*) formal, ceremonial.

officious *adj* (*the officious man at the counter in the unemployment office*) interfering, meddlesome, bumptious, self-important.

offspring *n* (*a couple with no offspring*) children, family, young.

oil *n* **1** (*fry the food in oil, not lard*) cooking oil. **2** (*oil to lubricate the hinges of the gate*) grease, lubrication. ⌁

strike oil to obtain exactly what one wants, to be successful (*We have been looking for our ideal house for ages and now we've struck oil*).

oil *vb* (*oil the door's rusty hinges*) grease, lubricate.

oily *adj* (*she dislikes oily food*) greasy, fat, fatty.

ointment *n* (*put ointment on his wound*) medication, cream, lotion. ⌁

a fly in the ointment something that spoils something otherwise perfect, enjoyable, etc. (*She really enjoyed her job. The only fly in the ointment is that she has to work on Saturdays*).

old *adj* **1** (*a ward in the hospital full of old people*) elderly, aged, (*inf*) long in the tooth. **2** (*she was wearing old clothes to work in*) worn, shabby. **3** (*tired of his old ideas*) old-fashioned, outdated, out-of-date, outmoded, antiquated. **4** (*the old fountain in the center of town*) dilapidated, run-down, ramshackle, crumbling. **5** (*he collects old cars*) antique, veteran, vintage. **6** (*in the old days*) past, bygone, earlier. **7** (*an old girlfriend*) former, ex-, previous. ✧

an old hand someone who is very experienced at doing something (*She's an old hand at looking after children*).
old hat old-fashioned, no longer popular (*He used to be thought very modern but his ideas are considered old hat these days*).

old-fashioned *adj* (*old-fashioned clothes/old-fashioned ideas*) outdated, out-of-date, unfashionable, outmoded, (*inf*) past the sell-by date.
omen *n* (*they were superstitious and thought that walking under a ladder was a bad omen*) sign, portent, forewarning, prophesy.
ominous *adj* (*we heard the ominous sound of gunfire*) threatening, menacing.
omit *vb* (*we omitted his name from the invitation list in error*) leave out, exclude, miss out, delete, eliminate.
onlooker *n* (*the police asked the onlookers at the accident scene to move*) observer, witness, eyewitness, spectator, bystander.
ooze *vb* (*pus was oozing from the wound*) flow, discharge, seep, exude, leak, drip.
opaque *adj* **1** (*opaque glass*) nontransparent, cloudy. **2** (*the waters were opaque with mud*) cloudy, dark, murky, hazy.
open *adj* **1** (*the door was open*) ajar, unlocked, unbolted, unfastened. **2** (*open boxes*) uncovered, unsealed. **3** (*find some open spaces for the children to run around in*) unfenced, unenclosed, extensive, broad, spacious. **4** (*maps lying open on the table*) spread out, unfolded. **5** (*she was quite open about her hatred of them*) frank, candid, forthright, honest, blunt, plain-spoken. **6** (*there was open hostility between them*) obvious, evident, visible, unconcealed. ✧

an open-and-shut case something that is free from uncertainty, having an obvious outcome (*I do not think that the trial of the accused murderer will take long. It seems like an open-and-shut case*).
lay oneself wide open to (something) to put oneself in a position in which one is liable to

be in receipt of (blame, criticism, accusations, attack, etc.) (*If the personnel officer goes out to dinner with one of the applicants for the job he will be laying himself wide open to charges of prejudice*).

opening *n* **1** (*an opening in the wall*) gap, space, aperture, hole, breach. **2** (*at the opening of the meeting*) beginning, start, commencement, outset. **3** (*there is an opening in the firm for a receptionist*) vacancy, position, post, place.
operate *vb* **1** (*the machine suddenly ceased to operate*) work, function, go, run. **2** (*can you operate this machine?*) work, use, handle. **3** (*the surgeon had to operate on her leg*) perform surgery on.
operation *n* **1** (*she had to have an operation on her leg*) surgery. **2** (*the troops took part in a military operation*) maneuver, campaign, action.
opinion *n* (*we were asked to give our opinions on the state of the company*) view, point of view, viewpoint, thought, belief, idea.
opponent *n* (*his opponent in the chess game*) rival, adversary, opposition, enemy, foe.
opportunity *n* **1** (*you should go abroad if the opportunity arises*) chance, occasion. **2** (*it was a good opportunity to spend some time with her family*) chance, occasion, time, moment.
oppose *vb* (*some of the board members opposed the company's plans for expansion*) contest, take a stand against, argue against.
opposite *adj* **1** (*rows of houses opposite one another*) facing, face-to-face. **2** (*the two brothers were on opposite sides in the dispute*) opposing, rival, competitive, warring. **3** (*they hold opposite views*) differing, different, contrary, conflicting, contradictory, incompatible.
oppress *vb* (*the tyrant oppressed the poor people*) crush, abuse, maltreat, persecute.
oppressive *adj* **1** (*the oppressive regimes in the world*) tyrannical, despotic, repressive, undemocratic, harsh, severe, brutal. **2** (*they were unable to sleep in that oppressive weather*) close, stifling, stuffy, suffocating, sultry.
opt *vb* (*he opted for a red car*) choose, select, pick, settle on, decide on.
optimistic *adj* **1** (*we were optimistic about our chances of success*) hopeful, confident. **2** (*he was in an optimistic mood*) hopeful, confident, cheerful, positive.
option *adj* (*we had only two options—to accept his offer or resign*) choice, alternative. ✧

keep one's options open delay making a definite decision so that all possible choices remain available for as long as possible (*Avoid replying to the job offer until you hear from the other companies. It is best to keep your options open*).

optional *adj* (*attendance at the meeting is optional*) voluntary, non-compulsory, discretionary.

oral *adj* (*he was asked to give an oral report of the events*) spoken, verbal, by word of mouth.

orator *n* (*the crowds gathered to hear the orator*) speaker, public speaker.

orbit *n* (*the spacecraft made an orbit of the Earth*) revolution, circle.

ordeal *n* (*the climb up the mountain in blizzard conditions was a real ordeal*) test, trial, tribulation, suffering, torment, torture, nightmare.

order *n* 1 (*soldiers must obey orders*) command, direction, instruction, decree. 2 (*the teacher restored order in the rowdy class*) calm, peace, control, discipline, good behavior. 3 (*they restored the room to order after the party*) orderliness, neatness, tidiness. 4 (*is the machine in working order?*) condition, state, shape. 5 (*arrange the words in alphabetical order*) arrangement, grouping, sequence, series, system, categorization. 6 (*place an order for his new book*) request, booking, reservation. ▷

a tall order a very difficult or problematic task (*She said that she must receive the book by the next day but that was a tall order*).
in apple-pie order with everything tidy and correctly arranged (*She always leaves the office files in apple-pie order*).

order *vb* 1 (*the general ordered the soldiers to shoot*) command, direct, instruct, bid. 2 (*the store did not have the book, so we ordered it*) place an order for, book, reserve.

orderly *adj* 1 (*an orderly piece of work*) organized, methodical, systematic. 2 (*an orderly crowd*) well-behaved, disciplined, quiet, peaceful, restrained.

ordinary *adj* 1 (*we followed our ordinary procedure*) usual, normal, standard, common, customary, regular, routine, typical. 2 (*lead ordinary lives/ordinary people*) unremarkable, unexceptional, average, run-of-the-mill, commonplace, humdrum.

organization *n* (*he is head of the organization*) company, firm, corporation, association, society, club, group.

organize *vb* 1 (*organize the books in alphabetical order by the name of the author*) arrange, group, sort, classify, categorize. 2 (*we organized a Christmas party for the children*) arrange, co-ordinate, set up, put together, run, see to.

origin *n* 1 (*discuss the origin of life*) source, basis, creation, start, commencement. 2 (*the origin of the word*) derivation, etymology, root.

original *adj* 1 (*the original owners of the house*) first, earliest, initial. 2 (*the judges are looking for original work*) innovative, inventive, creative, new, fresh, novel, unusual.

ornament *n* 1 (*there was an assortment of ornaments on the mantelpiece*) knick-knack, trinket, bauble, whatnot. 2 (*an outfit entirely without ornament*) decoration, adornment.

ornate *adj* 1 (*an ornate style of architecture*) decorated, elaborate, fancy, fussy, showy. 2 (*her ornate writing style*) elaborate, flowery, high-flown, pompous, pretentious.

orthodox *adj* (*people who question orthodox ideas*) conventional, accepted, established, traditional, standard.

ostentatious *adj* (*she was wearing a very ostentatious dress*) showy, conspicuous, obtrusive, loud, pretentious, over-elaborate.

other *adj* 1 (*we shall have to use other methods*) different, alternative. 2 (*give some other examples*) more, additional, further. ▷

look the other way deliberately to ignore or disregard something wrong, illegal, etc. (*The local policeman would look the other way when the village pub was open after hours*).

outbreak *n* (*an outbreak of measles*) epidemic, flare-up.

outcast *n* (*he was an outcast from his native land*) exile, refugee, outlaw.

outcome *n* (*the outcome of the talks was that the workers went on strike*) result, consequence, upshot, conclusion, effect.

outcry *n* (*the outcry when the village post office was threatened with closure*) protest, commotion, outburst, uproar, clamour, hullabaloo.

outer *adj* (*the outer layer*) outside, exterior, external.

outfit *n* 1 (*her wedding outfit*) clothes, ensemble, costume, clothes, (*inf*) gear, (*inf*) rig-out. 2 (*a bicycle repair outfit*) kit, equipment, gear, apparatus.

outing n (*the children went on an outing to the seaside*) trip, excursion, jaunt, expedition.

outlaw n (*a book about outlaws who escaped from prison*) criminal, fugitive, outcast, bandit.

outlet n 1 (*water pouring through the outlet*) way out, exit, vent, opening. 2 (*an outlet for their farm produce*) market.

outline n 1 (*they saw the outline of someone against the wall*) silhouette, shadow, profile, shape. 2 (*they gave an outline of their plans*) summary, synopsis, rough idea.

outline vb (*we outlined our plans to the planning committee*) sketch out, rough out, summarize.

outlook n 1 (*the attic bedroom has a wonderful outlook*) view, prospect, aspect. 2 (*she is quite ill, but the outlook is good*) future, prediction, forecast. 3 (*he has a depressed outlook on life*) view, opinion, attitude.

outlying adj (*outlying areas of the country*) remote, distant, far-flung.

outrageous adj 1 (*they objected to the drunk's outrageous behavior*) disgraceful, shocking, scandalous, offensive, intolerable. 2 (*the invading army committed outrageous acts*) terrible, dreadful, abominable, foul, vile. 3 (*the prices in that restaurant are outrageous*) exorbitant, excessive, preposterous.

outside n 1 (*they painted the outside of the building white*) exterior, surface. 2 (*the fruit is dark green on the outside*) exterior, surface, skin, shell. ⟳

at the outside at the most, at the absolute maximum (*The drive to the city will take two hours at the outside*).

outskirts npl (*a shopping complex on the outskirts of the town*) suburbs, outlying area.

outstanding adj 1 (*he is an outstanding artist*) excellent, exceptional, remarkable, eminent, noted, well-known. 2 (*his bill is still outstanding*) unpaid, owing, due.

outward adj 1 (*the outward layers*) outer, outside, external, exterior. 2 (*his outward cheerfulness hid his grief*) external, superficial, visible, discernible.

outwit vb (*he tried to cheat in order to win, but the other player outwitted him*) outsmart, trick, fool, dupe.

oval adj (*an oval face*) egg-shaped, ovoid.

overcome vb 1 (*our army succeeded in overcoming the enemy*) defeat, conquer, beat, vanquish, overthrow, crush. 2 (*he tried to overcome his disability*) conquer, master, triumph over.

overdue adj (*the train is overdue*) late, behindhand, delayed, unpunctual.

overheads npl (*try to reduce the firm's overheads*) expenses, expenditure, outlay, running costs.

overjoyed adj (*they were overjoyed when their baby was born*) elated, thrilled, delighted, ecstatic.

overlook vb 1 (*her bedroom window overlooks the lake*) face, have a view of, look out on. 2 (*he said he would overlook the error just this once*) disregard, ignore, pay no attention to, let pass, turn a blind eye to, condone. 3 (*he overlooked a note at the foot of the contract*) miss, fail to notice.

oversight n (*omitting your name from the list was an oversight*) mistake, error, blunder, slip-up.

overtake vb (*the car overtook us on the highway*) pass, overhaul, outdistance, catch up with.

overthrow vb (*overthrow the invading army*) overcome, defeat, conquer, vanquish, beat, overwhelm.

overwhelm vb 1 (*a tidal wave overwhelmed the village*) flood, swamp, inundate, deluge, engulf. 2 (*they overwhelmed the invading army*) overcome, defeat, conquer, vanquish, crush.

owe v (*pay what you owe*) indebted, obliged, financially committed.

owing adj (*we had to pay the money owing right away*) outstanding, unpaid, due.

own adj (*each of the girls had her own car*) individual, personal, particular, private. ⟳

come into one's own to have the opportunity to show one's good qualities, talent, skill, etc. (*She is a marvelous artist and really comes into her own with her painting*).
hold one's own 1 to perform as well as one's opponents in a contest, argument, etc. (*The younger player succeeded in holding his own against the champion*). 2 to be surviving, to be holding on to life (*He was badly injured in the accident but he is holding his own*).

own vb 1 (*they own two cars*) have, possess, keep. 2 (*you have to own that he may be right*) admit, acknowledge, allow, concede. 3 (*the boy finally owned up to his crime*) confess, admit, acknowledge, (*inf*) come clean.

owner n 1 (*the owner of the car*) possessor, keeper, holder. 2 (*the owner of the business*) proprietor, boss.

P

pack *vb* **1** (*they packed their bags*) fill, load, stuff, cram. **2** (*they packed their old clothing in a trunk*) place, put, store, stow. **3** (*protesters packed the hall*) fill, crowd, throng, mob, cram, jam, press into, squeeze into. ⟳

send (someone) packing to send (someone) away firmly and frankly (*She never buys anything from door-to-door salesmen—she sends them packing immediately*).

packet *n* **1** (*a packet of soap powder*) carton, pack, package, container. **2** (*the mailman tried to deliver a packet*) package, parcel.

painful *adj* (*the leg that she injured is very painful*) sore, hurting, aching, throbbing, smarting, agonizing, excruciating.

paint *vb* **1** (*they are painting the walls*) apply paint to, decorate. **2** (*he painted the view from his bedroom window*) portray, depict, draw, sketch. ⟳

paint the town red to go out and celebrate in a lively, noisy manner (*As soon as they finished their exams, the students went out to paint the town red*).

painting *n* (*the paintings hanging in the gallery*) picture, portrait, sketch, drawing.

pale *adj* **1** (*she looks pale after her illness*) white, whitish, white-faced, colorless, wan, drained, pallid, pasty, peaky, ashen, as white as a sheet, as white as a ghost. **2** (*she always wears pale colors*) light, light-colored, muted, subdued, pastel.

pan *n* (*the pans on the stove*) saucepan, pot, frying pan.

panic *n* (*they were filled with panic at the sight of the flames*) alarm, agitation, hysteria, fear, fright, terror, trepidation.

paper *n* **1** (*the paper is delivered on a Sunday*) newspaper. **2** (*chose a paper for the den*) wallpaper, wall-covering. **3** (*the students have to write a paper on Shakespeare's* Hamlet) essay, report, dissertation, article, treatise, thesis. **4** (*get a photocopy of all the papers for today's meeting*) document, legal paper. ⟳

paper tiger someone or something that has the outward appearance of being powerful and threatening but is in fact ineffective

(*The president used to be feared by everyone but since the rebellion he is regarded as a paper tiger*).

paralyze *vb* **1** (*his legs were paralyzed in the accident*) immobilize, make powerless, numb, deaden, disable. **2** (*the traffic system was paralyzed in the snow storm*) immobilize, bring to a halt, bring to a stop, bring to a standstill.

parcel *n* (*the mailman tried to deliver a parcel*) package, packet.

parcel *vb* (*parcel the Christmas presents*) parcel up, wrap, wrap up, pack, tie up. ⟳

parcel out to divide into parts; to distribute in portions (*Parcel out the party gifts to the children*).

pardon *vb* **1** (*the prisoner was pardoned by the king*) reprieve, let off, release, absolve, acquit, exonerate. **2** (*he asked her to pardon him for being so ill-tempered*) excuse, forgive, let off, condone.

part *n* **1** (*the last part of the book*) section, portion, segment, bit. **2** (*the parts of the machine*) component, bit, constituent. **3** (*she went to the northern part of the island*) section, area, district, quarter, sector. **4** (*originally the book was issued in several parts*) section, bit, episode, volume. **5** (*he apologized for the part that he played in the hoax*) role, function, responsibility, job. **6** (*she plays the part of Joan of Arc in the play*) role, character. ⟳

look the part to have the appearance appropriate to a particular kind of person (*If she wants to be a top executive, she will have to look the part—at the moment she is too casually dressed*).

part *vb* **1** (*they had to part when he went back to his own country*) separate, say "goodbye". **2** (*after three years of marriage they have decided to part*) separate, leave each other, split up, break up, divorce, go their separate ways. **3** (*the police parted the crowd to reach the troublemakers at the front*) divide, separate, break up.

partial *adj* **1** (*there was only a partial improvement in his work*) part, in part, incomplete, limited, imperfect. **2** (*the referee was accused of* being *partial*) biased, prejudiced, partisan, discriminatory, unfair, unjust.

partial *adj*:—**be partial to** (*she is partial to seafood*) like, have a liking for, love, be fond of, have a weakness for.

particular *adj* **1** (*you must pay particular attention to what he says*) special, exceptional, unusual. **2** (*in this particular case I think we should be generous*) specific, individual, single. **3** (*she is particular about who cuts her hair*) fussy, fastidious, selective, discriminating, (*inf*) persnickety, (*inf*) choosy.

partner *n* **1** (*they are business partners*) associate, colleague, co-owner. **2** (*the burglar and his partner in crime*) ally, confederate, accomplice. **3** (*all her friends and their partners were invited to the wedding*) husband/wife, spouse, boyfriend/girlfriend.

party *n* **1** (*it was he who was host at the party*) social gathering, social function, function, reception, (*inf*) get-together **2** (*they were part of the bridal party*) group, band, company, contingent. **3** (*a certain party who shall remain nameless*) person, individual. ✧

the party's over a pleasant or happy time has come to an end (*This used to be a very free-and-easy department, but I think the party's over. The new manager is said to be very strict*).

pass *vb* **1** (*the car passed us on a dangerous stretch of road*) overtake. **2** (*trucks passed along the road all night*) go, proceed, drive, run, travel. **3** (*time passed quickly*) go past, advance, roll by, flow by, slip by. **4** (*how does he pass the time now he has retired?*) spend, fill, occupy, take up, use, while away. **5** (*he passed her the papers for the meeting*) hand over, give, reach. **6** (*the estate passes to his eldest son on his death*) be passed on, be transferred, be signed over to. **7** (*all the students have passed the test*) be successful, get through, gain a pass. **8** (*Congress passed the new bill*) vote for, accept, prove, adopt, sanction. **9** (*the judge passed sentence*) pronounce, utter, deliver, declare. **10** (*eventually the hurricane passed*) run its course, die out, fade, finish. ✧

make a pass at (someone) to try to start a romantic relationship with (someone) (*At the dinner he made a pass at the girl who was sitting next to him*).

pass for (someone *or* **something)** to be mistaken for (someone or something) (*Her mother could easily pass for her sister*).

past *adj* **1** (*they were congratulated on their past successes*) former, previous, prior, foregoing. **2** (*he has become very ill in the past few days*) recent, preceding, last. **3** (*the history of past ages*) gone by, bygone, former. ✧

not put it past (someone) to think that (someone) is quite capable of doing something bad (*I would not put it past him to tell a lie to get a job*).

past it less good, effective, etc., than you used to be when you were young (*He used to be a good football player, but he is past it now*).

pastime *n* (*he is going to have to take up a pastime in his retirement*) hobby, recreation, distraction, leisure activity, amusement, entertainment.

path *n* **1** (*a winding path up the mountain*) pathway, trail, track, way. **2** (*they are studying the moon's path*) course, route, circuit, orbit. ✧

beat a path to (someone's) door to visit with (someone) very frequently or in large numbers (*The world's press beat a path to her door when she said that she had witnessed a miracle*).

pathetic *adj* **1** (*the starving children were a pathetic sight*) pitiful, pitiable, moving, touching, affecting, poignant, distressing, heart-breaking. **2** (*he could not play baseball and made only a few pathetic attempts to hit the ball*) feeble, inadequate, unsatisfactory, poor.

patient *adj* (*there is nothing to be done about the delayed flight—we'll have to be patient*) calm, composed, even-tempered, restrained, tolerant, resigned, stoical, uncomplaining.

pause *n* (*there was a pause in the music while he changed the CD*) interval, lull, break, halt, gap.

pay *vb* **1** (*they had to pay a huge amount for that house*) pay out, spend, lay out, part with, (*inf*) shell out, (*inf*) fork out. **2** (*he will get paid at the end of the job*) give payment to. **3** (*he enjoys the work but it doesn't really pay*) be profitable, make money. **4** (*he pays his bills right away*) settle. **5** (*he likes to pay compliments to women*) bestow, offer, extend. ✧

pay the piper to provide the money for something and therefore be entitled to have a say in the organization of it (*Their parents feel that they should choose where the family goes on vacation, since they are paying the piper*).

peaceful *adj* **1** (*they were at war but conditions between the countries are now peaceful*) peaceable, at peace, friendly, amicable. **2** (*the old man looked peaceful lying asleep in his chair*) at peace, tranquil, serene, calm, composed, placid, undisturbed. **3** (*they longed for a house in a peaceful country setting*) quiet, restful, tranquil, calm, still.

peculiar *adj* **1** (*she wears such peculiar hats*) strange, odd, queer, funny, weird, bizarre, eccentric, outlandish, unconventional, offbeat. **2** (*there was a peculiar smell in the hall*) odd, unusual, strange, curious, abnormal. **3** (*a manner of walking that is peculiar to her*) characteristic, typical, individualistic, special, unique.

peel *vb* **1** (*peel the skin from the fruit*) pare, remove. **2** (*peel the fruit*) pare, skin. **3** (*her skin was peeling after sunbathing*) flake off, scale off.

peg *n* (*they fastened the pieces of wood with a peg*) pin, nail, screw, bolt, spike, skewer.

penetrate *vb* **1** (*the knife of the attacker did not penetrate the skin*) pierce, bore, perforate, stab. **2** (*unable to penetrate the dense jungle*) go through, get through, enter.

people *npl* **1** (*an issue that should be decided by the people*) the public, the general public, the common people, the electorate. **2** (*an area inhabited by a nomadic people*) population, tribe, race, nation. **3** (*a lot of people were expected to attend*) individuals, persons. **4** (*her people should be looking after her*) relatives, relations, family, folks, kin, kinfolk.

perfect *adj* **1** (*her performance on the piano is perfect*) flawless, faultless, impeccable, consummate, ideal, supreme, excellent, marvelous. **2** (*a perfect set of the encyclopedia*) complete, full, whole, entire. **3** (*the boy is a perfect fool*) absolute, utter, complete, out-and-out, thoroughgoing.

perform *vb* (*they performed all the tasks that they were given*) carry out, do, execute, discharge, fulfill.

perfume *n* (*a garden full of the perfume of roses*) scent, fragrance, aroma, smell, bouquet.

peril *n* (*animals in peril*) danger, risk, jeopardy, menace, threat.

period *n* **1** (*during the Colonial period of American history*) time, age, era, epoch. **2** (*her condition worsened over a period of years*) time, space, interval, spell, stretch, span. ▽

period piece someone or something that is exceptionally typical of the time when he or she was born or when it was made (*She has a household full of Victorian furniture—real period pieces*).

perish *vb* **1** (*the food perished in the heat*) go bad, go off, decay, rot, decompose. **2** (*villagers who perished in the earthquake*) die, be killed, lose your life.

permanent *adj* (*the accident left him with a permanent limp*) lasting, perpetual, persistent, enduring, abiding, eternal, endless, never-ending, unending.

permission *n* (*he took his father's car without permission*) authorization, leave, sanction, consent, assent, agreement, approval.

permit *vb* (*her parents would not permit her to stay out late*) give permission to, allow, let, give leave, authorize, action, consent to, assent to, agree to,.

persecute *vb* (*people who were persecuted for their religious beliefs*) oppress, abuse, maltreat, torment, torture, victimize.

persevere *vb* (*you must persevere in your attempts to get a job*) persist, keep at, keep on, continue, carry on, be resolute, be determined, be insistent.

persistent *adj* **1** (*their persistent attempts to get planning permission*) determined, relentless, unrelenting, constant, continual, incessant, endless. **2** (*persistent people who will not give up trying*) persevering, determined, resolute, insistent, obstinate, tenacious.

personal *adj* **1** (*his reason for not being at work is purely personal*) private, confidential, individual, secret. **2** (*her personal interpretation of the piece of music*) individual, individualistic, idiosyncratic, peculiar.

personality *n* **1** (*she has a very pleasant personality*) nature, disposition, temperament, character. **2** (*it is a job for someone with personality*) character, charisma, magnetism, charm. **3** (*there were many sporting personalities at the dinner*) celebrity, dignitary, famous name, VIP.

personnel n (*the person in the firm in charge of personnel*) staff, employees, workers, work force, human resources.

persuade vb (*could you try to persuade her to go?*) influence, induce, talk into, win over, cajole, wheedle.

pessimistic adj (*he has a pessimistic outlook on life*) gloomy, cynical, defeatist, fatalistic, resigned, distrustful.

pest n (*he thought the child was a pest*) nuisance, bother, irritant, trouble, worry, problem, inconvenience, trial.

pet n (*the boy is teased about being the teacher's pet*) favorite, darling, apple of your eye.

petty adj (*have no time to discuss the petty details of the case*) trivial, trifling, minor, unimportant, inconsequential, slight.

phobia n (*she has a phobia about spiders*) aversion, fear, dread, horror, loathing, revulsion, (*inf*) thing, (*inf*) hang-up.

pick vb 1 (*they are picking fruit*) gather, collect, harvest, pull. 2 (*the little girl was asked to pick a toy*) choose, select, single out, opt for, decide upon, settle on. 3 (*the burglar picked the lock*) break open, force, prize open. ✧

pick and choose to choose very carefully from a range of things (*There is such a huge selection of dresses here that you can pick and choose*).

picture n 1 (*a picture painted by a famous artist*) painting, drawing, sketch, likeness, portrait, illustration. 2 (*he was paid to take pictures at the wedding*) photograph, photo, snapshot, snap, shot. 3 (*the novel painted a distressing picture of Victorian England*) scene, view, vision, impression, description, portrayal, account, report. 4 (*a horror picture*) movie, motion picture.

pie n (*a piece of apple pie*) tart, quiche, pastry, flan. ✧

pie in the sky something expected or promised in the future which is unlikely to come about (*He is planning a trip around the world but it's all pie in the sky. He'll never save that much money*) <A reference to a quotation from a poem by the poet Joe Hills>.

piece n 1 (*put the pieces of the jigsaw together*) bit, part, section, segment, component, unit. 2 (*a quilt made of pieces of cloth*) length, bit, remnant, scrap. 3 (*a piece of pie*) bit, chunk, wedge, hunk, lump, (*inf*) wodge. 4 (*each of his children will get a piece of his estate*) bit, share, slice, portion, percentage. 5 (*the valuable vase was smashed to pieces*) bit, fragment, smithereens, shard. 6 (*an impressive piece of antique furniture*) example, sample, specimen, instance, illustration. 7 (*a musical piece*) work, creation, composition. 8 (*the journalist wrote a piece on the war*) article, item, story, report. ✧

go to pieces to be unable to continue coping with a situation, life, etc. (*She goes to pieces in an emergency*).

pierce vb 1 (*did the knife pierce the skin?*) penetrate, puncture, prick, perforate, stab, pass through, enter. 2 (*pierce the piece of leather to make a leash for the dog*) perforate, bore, drill. 3 (*the cries of the bird pierced the air*) fill, penetrate.

pile n 1 (*dead leaves in piles around the yard*) heap, mound, stack, collection, stockpile, mountain. 2 (*we have a pile of homework*) great deal, abundance, (*inf*) lots. 3 (*he made his pile forging money*) fortune, wealth, money.

pill n (*medicine in the form of pills*) tablet, capsule. ✧

sugar-coat the pill to make something unpleasant more palatable.

pillar n (*the pillars at the front of the temple*) column, post, upright, support.

pin vb 1 (*can you pin the badge to my coat?*) fasten, fix, secure, attach. 2 (*the man was pinned under the overturned tractor*) hold, press, pinion, restrain, immobilize.

on pins and needles anxious about the outcome of something (*Michael was on pins and needles waiting for the results of the test*).

pinch vb 1 (*she pinched her friend's arm to wake her up*) nip, tweak, squeeze. 2 (*her new shoes are pinching her toes*) hurt, crush, squeeze.✧

feel the pinch (*inf*) to have financial problems (*They are feeling the pinch now that they have retired*).
in a pinch if it is absolutely necessary (*We do not have much space, but in a pinch we could accommodate three of you*).

pious adj (pious members of the parish) religious, godly, devout, God-fearing, righteous.

pitch vb 1 (they pitched their tent in a field) put up, set up, erect, raise. 2 (the children began to pitch stones into the lake) throw, cast, fling, hurl, toss, heave, lob, (inf) chuck. 3 (the ships were pitching in the high winds) roll, rock, lurch, sway.

pity n 1 (they felt pity for the poor orphans) compassion, sympathy, commiseration, distress, sadness. 2 (the tyrant showed the prisoners no pity) mercy, leniency, kindness. 3 (it was a pity that their bus was late) shame, crying shame, misfortune.

placard n (placards advertising the show) poster, notice, bill, sticker.

place n 1 (this is the place where she lost the ring/ the place where he built the houses) spot, location, site, setting, position, situation, area, region. 2 (she won third place in the competition) position, grade, level, rank. 3 (it was not his place to sort out the dispute) responsibility, job, task, function, role. 4 (the student returned to her place) seat, position.

plain adj 1 (it was plain to all of us that she was in pain) clear, crystal-clear, obvious, evident, apparent, manifest, unmistakable, noticeable, conspicuous. 2 (we need a plain statement of what happened) clear, straightforward, simple, lucid. 3 (the style of decoration is very plain) simple, restrained, bare, austere, stark, basic, unadorned, spartan. 4 (she was rather plain as a child) unattractive, ugly.

plan n 1 (they have plans to expand the firm/The prisoners have an escape plan) scheme, strategy, tactics, system, method, project. 2 (their vacation plans have been ruined) arrangements, schedule, program, procedure, method, system. 3 (their plan was to travel overnight) aim, intention, objective, scheme, proposal. 4 (the architect's plans for the new building are on show) drawing, blueprint, representation, model.

play vb 1 (children need time to play) amuse yourself, enjoy yourself, entertain yourself, have fun. 2 (the children were playing in the garden with the dog) play games, frolic, romp, frisk, gambol, cavort. 3 (he likes to play football) take part in, engage in, be involved in, participate in. 4 (our team is playing against strong opposition) compete against, take on, oppose, challenge, vie with, contend with. 5 (she plays the piano) perform on. 6 (the children played tricks on their

grandfather) perform, carry out, do, execute, discharge. 6 (he played Hamlet in school) play the part of, act the part of, perform, portray. ⟡

make a play for (someone or **something)** to try to obtain (someone or something) (He is not really qualified for the job but he is making a play for it).
play possum to pretend to be asleep, unconscious or dead (Their father played possum when the children went into his room early in the morning) <The possum is an animal that pretends to be dead when it is under threat of attack from another animal>.

plead vb (they pleaded for mercy) beg, entreat, implore.

pleasant adj 1 (it was a very pleasant occasion) agreeable, enjoyable, pleasing, delightful, nice, good, lovely, entertaining, amusing 2 (our neighbors are very pleasant) agreeable, friendly, amiable, affable, likable, charming.

please vb 1 (we were going to go to the theater, but it is difficult to find a show that will please everyone) give pleasure to, satisfy, suit, delight, amuse, entertain. 2 (whatever advice you give her she will do as she pleases) wish, want, like, choose, prefer, see fit.

pleasure n 1 (a gift that will bring their mother a great deal of pleasure) happiness, joy, delight, enjoyment, amusement, entertainment, satisfaction. 2 (one of the old man's few pleasures) joy, delight, enjoyment, recreation.

plentiful adj (plentiful supplies of fuel) abundant, copious, ample, profuse, generous, liberal, large.

plot n 1 (they uncovered a plot to murder the president) conspiracy, intrigue. 2 (the novel has a complicated plot) theme, action, story line, subject. 3 (he grows potatoes in his vegetable plot) allotment, patch. ⟡

the plot thickens the situation is getting more complicated and more interesting (He is trying to get her job but he doesn't know that she is trying to get him fired. The plot thickens).

plump adj (she was plump as a little girl) chubby, tubby, fat.

plunder vb (they crossed the border and plundered the enemy villages) rob, raid, loot, pillage, lay waste.

pocketbook n (her pocketbook was stolen and she now has no money) note case, purse.

poetry *n* (*he writes poetry as a hobby*) poems, verse, verses.

point *n* **1** (*the spear had a very sharp point*) tip, end, top. **2** (*she reached a point where she could not go on*) stage, position, situation, circumstances, time. **3** (*at some point during the meeting*) time, juncture, stage. **4** (*they discussed the various points in the report*) detail, item, particular, issue, subject, topic. **5** (*the speaker spoke at length but few people got the point of his talk*) meaning, significance, substance, gist, drift. **6** (*he took ages to get to the point when he told them they were fired*) main point, crux of the matter, crux, heart of the matter, (*inf*) nitty-gritty. **7** (*what is the point of this discussion?*) aim, purpose, intention, object, objective, goal. **8** (*that is one of the weak points of the argument/He has many good points*) aspect, feature, attribute, quality, characteristic, trait. **9** (*the team that has the most points*) mark. ✧

make a point of (doing something) to be exceptionally careful about (doing something) (*He makes a point of visiting his elderly parents once a week*).
up to a point to some extent but not completely (*I agree with him up to a point but there are weaknesses in his argument*).

point:— point out *vb* (*we pointed out the benefits*) draw attention to, call attention to, identify, indicate, show, mention, specify.

pointless *adj* **1** (*it was pointless to continue the search after dark*) in vain, useless, futile, to no purpose, senseless, stupid **2** (*they made a few pointless comments*) worthless, meaningless, insignificant, irrelevant.

poisonous *adj* **1** (*an area with poisonous snakes*) venomous. **2** (*poisonous chemical substances*) toxic, deadly, lethal, fatal.

poke *vb* **1** (*the child tried to poke a pencil in the electric socket*) jab, push, thrust, shove, stick. **2** (*he poked his friend in the ribs to get him to stop laughing*) jab, prod, dig, nudge, elbow.

polish *vb* **1** (*she has to polish the furniture*) wax, shine, buff up, burnish. **2** (*she wants to polish up her French before she goes on vacation*) improve, revise, perfect, brush up.

polite *adj* **1** (*children should be taught to be polite*) well-mannered, mannerly, courteous, civil, well-bred, well-behaved. **2** (*the way things are done*

in polite society) well-bred, civilized, cultured, refined, genteel.

pollute *vb* (*chemicals that pollute the water*) contaminate, taint, infect, poison, dirty.

pompous *adj* (*they were kept out of the building by a pompous official*) self-important, presumptuous, overbearing, egotistic.

poor *adj* **1** (*poor people with not enough money to live on*) poverty-stricken, penniless, needy, in need, impoverished, deprived, destitute, hard up, badly off. **2** (*it was a poor attempt*) inadequate, unsatisfactory, inferior.

popular *adj* **1** (*the place is popular with young people*) liked, favored, approved, in demand, in fashion. **2** (*ideas that were popular at the time*) current, accepted, widespread, common, general.

population *n* (*the population of the area is mainly elderly*) people, inhabitants, residents, community.

portion *n* **1** (*each of his children got an equal portion of his fortune*) part, share, division, piece, bit, quota, percentage. **2** (*the restaurant serves children's portions on request*) serving, helping, quantity. **3** (*they bought four portions of the cake*) piece, bit, slice, section, segment, lump, chunk.

position *n* **1** (*he had been sitting in an uncomfortable position*) posture, attitude, pose. **2** (*try to find the position of the wrecked ship*) location, whereabouts. **3** (*these trees grow well in a shady position*) situation, location, place, spot, area, setting. **4** (*he is in a very fortunate position*) situation, state, circumstances, condition. **5** (*the position of the team in the league tables*) place, level, grade, status, rank, ranking. **6** (*the position of manager is vacant*) situation, post, job, role. **7** (*people of position in society*) rank, status, influence, standing, prestige.

positive *adj* **1** (*she is positive that she saw him*) sure, certain, confident, convinced. **2** (*try to give some positive criticism of the essays*) constructive, helpful, useful. **3** (*he should try to have a more positive attitude to life*) optimistic, hopeful, confident, determined. **4** (*the results of the medical tests were positive*) affirmative. **5** (*he is a positive fool*) absolute, utter, complete, total, out-and-out.

possess *vb* **1** (*they do not possess a car*) own, be the owner of, have. **2** (*he thought that he was possessed by devils*) control, dominate, influence, bewitch.

possessions *npl* (*our apartment is full of her possessions*) belongings, property, goods, things, personal effects.

possible *adj* **1** (*it is not possible to get there on time*) feasible, practicable, achievable. **2** (*one possible solution*) likely, potential, conceivable, imaginable.

post *n* **1** (*hammer in posts to make a fence*) stake, pole, upright. **2** (*the post has been filled*) job, position, appointment, situation.

postpone *vb* (*they have had to postpone the wedding*) put off, put back, delay, put on ice.

pounce *vb* (*the cat pounced on the mouse*) swoop, spring, leap, jump.

pound *vb* **1** (*she pounded the seeds to a powder*) crush, smash, beat, pulverize, grind. **2** (*she pounded her father's chest with her fists*) beat, pommel, strike, hit, hammer. **3** (*her heart was pounding*) beat heavily, throb, pulse, pulsate, palpitate. **4** (*they pounded the sidewalks looking for somewhere to live*) tramp, tread, trudge.

pour *vb* **1** (*water began to pour from the burst pipe*) rush, gush, stream, spout, spurt, flow. **2** (*pour custard over the tart*) let flow, splash, spill. **3** (*it was pouring*) come down in torrents, rain cats and dogs, come down in sheets, (*inf*) be bucketing. ⟡

it never rains but it pours when something goes wrong it goes wrong very badly or other things go wrong too (*I forgot where I had parked the car and then I got a parking ticket. It never rains but it pours*).

poverty *n* need, want, deprivation, hardship.

power *n* **1** (*the power of speech*) ability, capability, capacity, faculty. **2** (*the tyrant had her in his power*) control, command, rule, domination, mastery, authority. **3** (*people of power gaining victory over the weak*) powerfulness, strength, force, forcefulness, might, vigor, effectiveness. **4** (*electricity and other kinds of power*) energy. ⟡

the power behind the throne the person who is really in control or makes all the decisions while giving the impression that someone else is (*He is the president of the company but his wife is the power behind the throne*).
the powers that be the people who are in charge, the authorities. (*The powers that be have decided that all sales staff should wear uniform*).

powerful *adj* **1** (*weight lifters of powerful build*) strong, sturdy, strapping, tough, mighty. **2** (*the most powerful members of the community*) dominant, controlling, influential, authoritative, strong, forceful, vigorous. **3** (*she drew up a powerful argument against the scheme*) strong, forceful, effective, convincing, persuasive, compelling.

practical *adj* **1** (*they want people with practical experience of the job*) applied, experienced, skilled, hands-on. **2** (*she is very bright academically but not at all practical*) sensible, down-to-earth, realistic, businesslike. **3** (*wear practical footwear for walking*) sensible, functional, useful, utilitarian.

practice *vb* **1** (*she has to practice her piano performances*) rehearse, go over, run through, work at, prepare, train for, study for, polish up. **2** (*she seems quite unable to practice self-control*) carry out, perform, execute, do. **3** (*they practice medicine*) work in, be engaged in. ⟡

practice what you preach to act in a way that you recommend to others (*The manager always reminds all the workers that they must get there on time but he is often very late himself. He really should practice what he preaches*).

praise *vb* **1** (*they praised her performance*) applaud, express admiration for, admire, compliment, pay tribute to, sing the praises of. **2** (*praise God*) worship, glorify, honor, exalt. ⟡

sing (someone's *or* **something's) praises** to praise (someone or something) with great enthusiasm (*She keeps singing the praises of her new car*).

precarious *adj* **1** (*it was rather a precarious journey through the jungle*) risky, dangerous, hazardous, perilous. **2** (*a precarious way to earn your living*) risky, unreliable, uncertain, unsure, chancy, unpredictable.

precious *adj* **1** (*a necklace full of precious stones*) valuable, costly, expensive. **2** (*family photographs that are very precious to her/her precious memories*) valued, treasured, cherished, prized, beloved, dear.

precise *adj* **1** (*we need to know her precise words*) exact, actual, literal. **2** (*at that precise moment*) very, exact, actual, particular. **3** (*he is a very precise person*) exact, careful, accurate, meticulous.

predict vb (she claimed to be able to predict the future) foretell, forecast, foresee, prophesy.

predominant adj (red is the predominant color in the pattern) chief, main, principal, dominant.

prefer vb 1 (she prefers the blue pattern to the yellow) like better, favor, choose, select, pick, opt for, plump for. 2 (they could drive but they prefer to go by train) like better, would rather, would sooner, favor, choose.

prejudiced adj (they have a prejudiced attitude toward people of a different race/prejudiced employers) biased, discriminatory, partial, partisan, bigoted, intolerant, unfair, unjust.

premature adj (the premature birth of the baby) too soon, too early.

premonition n (she had a premonition that something tragic was going to happen) feeling, foreboding, intuition, hunch.

prepare vb 1 (they must prepare their proposal to present it to the committee) get ready, arrange, assemble, draw up, put together. 2 (prepare a meal) make, cook, put together.

presence n 1 (the presence of chemical waste in the drinking water) existence. 2 (they are asking for our presence at the meeting) attendance. 3 (they felt inadequate in the presence of the great man) company. ◇

presence of mind the ability to keep calm and think and act sensibly whatever the situation (She had the presence of mind to throw a wet cloth over the pan when it caught fire).

present adj 1 (pollutants were present in the water supply) existing, existent. 2 (there should be a nurse present) in attendance, here, there, on hand. 3 (in the present situation) current, existing, present-day, contemporary.

present n 1 (thinking about the present rather than the future) now, today, the present moment. 2 (a present on her birthday/a present for all their hard work) gift, reward. ◇

there's no time like the present if you have decided on a course of action you should get started on it right away (If you are going to sell the house, phone the Realtor. There's no time like the present).

presentable adj (make yourself presentable before you see the principal) tidy, well-groomed, smart, spruce.

preserve vb 1 (try to preserve the old village

traditions) keep, keep up, continue, maintain, uphold, conserve. 2 (a substance to preserve wood) protect, conserve. 3 (they had to preserve the city from enemy attack) protect, save, safeguard, keep, defend. 4 (preserve some money for your old age) keep, put aside, save, retain.

press vb 1 (you should press the doorbell again) push. 2 (villagers pressing grapes to make wine) crush, squeeze, compress. 3 (need an iron to press her skirt) iron, smooth. 3 (the mother pressed the tired child against her) clasp, hold, pull, squeeze, crush, hug. 4 (they are pressing the planning committee for a decision) urge, pressure, put pressure on, pressurize. ◇

be pressed for (something) to be short of (something) such as time or money (I can't stay and talk. I'm really pressed for time).

pressure n 1 (they had to exert a great deal of pressure to get the door open) force, strength, weight. 2 (she tried to withstand the pressure of her parents to get her to stay at home) force, compulsion. 3 (the pressures of modern living) strain, stress, tension. ◇

pressure group a group of people formed to bring the attention of the authorities, etc., to certain issues, with a view to influencing them into making some changes (They formed a pressure group to persuade the authorities to save the local school).

prestige n (he does not want to lose his prestige in the community) status, kudos, standing, importance, reputation, esteem, influence.

pretend vb (he was not sleeping at all—he was just pretending) put on an act, put it on, play-act, sham, fake.

pretense n 1 (she did not really faint—it was just pretense) dissembling, shamming, faking, make-believe. 2 (they left on the pretense that they were going to a meeting) pretext, excuse.

pretty adj (she is a very pretty girl) attractive, good-looking, lovely, nice-looking. ◇

be sitting pretty to be in a very comfortable or advantageous position (She's the boss's daughter. While the rest of us are worrying about our jobs she is sitting pretty).

pretty adv (she was feeling pretty annoyed) rather, quite, very.

prevent vb 1 (her parents tried to prevent her from

marrying him) stop, halt, restrain, prohibit, bar, hinder, obstruct, impede, hamper. **2** (*try to prevent the spread of the infection*) stop, halt, arrest, check, block, check, hinder, obstruct, impede.

previous *adj* **1** (*the previous chairman*) former, preceding, ex-, foregoing. **2** (*we met on a previous occasion*) earlier, prior, former.

price *n* (*ask the price of the bookcase*) cost, charge. ⋄

a price on (someone's) head a reward offered for the capture or killing (of someone), such as an outlaw (*The escaped prisoner was never caught although there was a price on his head*).

prick *vb* **1** (*the child pricked the balloon with a pin*) pierce, puncture, stab, gash. **2** (*she pricked her finger on the needle*) jab, stab, wound.

pride *n* **1** (*they take pride in their work*) satisfaction, gratification, pleasure. **2** (*her pride was hurt when he left her for another woman*) self-esteem, self-respect, ego. **3** (*he is guilty of the sin of pride*) conceit, vanity, arrogance, egotism, self-importance, (*inf*) big-headedness. ⋄

pride goes before a fall being too conceited often leads to misfortune (*The player who was boasting about how good she was got beaten. It just shows you that pride goes before a fall*).

pride of place the most important or privileged position (*His children's photograph took pride of place on his desk*).

swallow your pride to behave in a more humble way than you usually do or than you would wish to do (*When she could not pay the rent she swallowed her pride and asked her father for a loan*).

prim *adj* (*he is much too prim to join in the fun*) proper, demure, strait-laced, stuffy, prudish, (*inf*) goody-goody.

prime *adj* **1** (*meat of prime quality*) top, best, first-class, superior, choice, select. **2** (*his prime ambition was to make money*) chief, main, principal. **3** (*the prime cause of the infection was the water*) basic, fundamental.

prime *n* (*in the prime of life*) peak, height. ⋄

be cut off in your prime to die or be killed in your youth or at the most successful part of your life (*The people in the town mourned*

the soldiers cut off in their prime).

prime mover someone or something that gets something started (*She was the prime mover in the campaign against the new highway*).

principal *adj* **1** (*the principal members of the organization*) chief, leading, foremost, dominant. **2** (*the principal issues to be discussed*) main, major, key, essential.

principle *n* **1** (*the principles of socialism*) idea, theory, philosophy, basis, code. **2** (*he is a man of principle*) morals, ethics, integrity, uprightness, honor.

prison *n* (*he was sent to prison for theft*) jail, lock-up.

private *adj* **1** (*a private discussion between senators*) confidential, secret, privileged, (*inf*) hush-hush. **2** (*she wished to be private to think about things*) undisturbed, uninterrupted, alone, solitary. **3** (*she would not disclose her private thoughts*) personal, intimate, secret. **4** (*a private place in the large garden*) secluded, quiet, out-of-the-way.

privileged *adj* (*she comes from a privileged background*) advantaged, favored, elite.

probable *adj* (*the probable outcome/It is probable that he will lose*) likely, expected.

problem *n* **1** (*an arithmetical problem*) question, puzzle, poser, brain-teaser. **2** (*they have had a few financial problems*) difficulty, trouble, complication, predicament. **3** (*their teenage son is a real problem*) trouble, bother, nuisance, pest.

proceed *vb* **1** (*we were unsure as to how to proceed*) act, take action, move, progress. **2** (*we proceeded up the mountain as fast as we could*) make your way, carry on, go on, advance, go forward, progress.

process *n* **1** (*the manufacturing process*) operation, activity, stages. **2** (*a new process for cleaning carpets*) system, method, technique, procedure.

process *n*:—**in the process of (something)** (*they are in the process of moving house*) in the midst of, in the course of.

procession *n* (*a procession to celebrate the town's centenary*) parade, march, cavalcade.

produce *vb* **1** (*an agricultural area that produces a wide variety of crops*) yield, bear, give. **2** (*a cat that has just produced kittens*) give birth to, bear. **3** (*his article produced an angry response*) cause, give rise to, evoke, generate, start, spark off. **4** (*the country produces a great many goods for export*) make, manufacture, turn out. **5** (*the police have produced proof that he is guilty*) bring forward, present, advance.

product *n* (*a firm specializing in electronic products*) goods, wares, merchandise.

profit *n* (*they made little profit from the sale*) gain, return, yield, proceeds, income.

profitable *adj* (*the business is no longer profitable*) profit-making, money-making, commercial, lucrative.

program *n* (*the program of events for the fete*) schedule, plan, scheme, list, calendar.

progress *n* **1** (*they have been discussing the matter for ages but they have made little progress*) headway, advancement. **2** (*her work shows no sign of progress*) headway, advancement, improvement.

project *n* (*take part in a project to build a new swimming pool*) scheme, plan, undertaking, enterprise, venture, operation.

prominent *adj* **1** (*prominent members of the government*) leading, chief, foremost, eminent, top. **2** (*the palm trees are a prominent feature of the area*) striking, conspicuous, noticeable, obvious, eye-catching. **3** (*she has prominent cheekbones*) protruding, obvious.

promise *n* **1** (*she made a promise that she would be there*) pledge, vow, bond, assurance, commitment. **2** (*a young skater of promise*) potential, talent, flair. **3** (*there was a promise of good times to come*) indication, sign, suggestion, hint.

promote *vb* **1** (*they plan to promote him to manager*) upgrade, elevate. **2** (*the company is promoting a new line in perfume*) advertise, publicize, push, (*inf*) plug. **3** (*they need volunteers to promote the cause of animal rights*) support, champion, further, advance, help, assist, boost.

prompt *adj* (*they will expect a prompt reply*) rapid, swift, quick, fast, speedy, immediate, instant.

proof *n* **1** (*the police had little proof of his guilt*) evidence, confirmation. **2** (*the workmen had no proof of their identity*) evidence, verification, authentication, certification.

proper *adj* **1** (*the proper behavior on such an occasion*) right, correct, suitable, fitting, appropriate, acceptable, conventional. **2** (*put the plates in their proper place in the kitchen*) right, correct, usual, own.

property *n* (*items that were his property*) belongings, possessions, things, goods.

proportion *n* **1** (*an area with a high proportion of agricultural workers*) ratio, distribution. **2** (*he gives a large proportion of his earnings to the church*) part, share, percentage, measure.

a sense of proportion the ability to decide what is important, etc., and what is not (*She went into hysterics just because she got a small stain on her dress. She has no sense of proportion*).

propose *vb* **1** (*we are proposing to go by train*) plan, intend, aim, suggest. **2** (*they proposed some alterations to the system*) put forward, submit, recommend. **3** (*they proposed him as chairman*) put forward, nominate, suggest.

prosper *vb* (*the family began to prosper*) thrive, do well, succeed, flourish, make good.

prosperous *adj* (*prosperous people with a great deal of money to spend*) well-off, wealthy, rich, successful.

protect *vb* (*they wished to protect the child from danger*) safeguard, guard, keep, preserve, shield, defend.

protest *n* (*they lodged a protest against the closure of the school*) objection, opposition, complaint, disagreement, outcry.

proud *adj* **1** (*he is rich and now too proud to talk to his former neighbors*) conceited, vain, arrogant, egotistical, haughty, boastful, (*inf*) snooty. **2** (*he was proud of his son's achievement*) gratified, appreciative, pleased, happy.

prove *vb* (*evidence that proved his innocence*) establish, determine, confirm.

provide *vb* **1** (*they provided the money for the trip*) give, supply, donate, contribute. **2** (*a job that provides the opportunity for travel*) give, grant, offer, afford, present.

prowl *vb* (*burglars prowling around the house*) roam, skulk, slink, sneak.

pry *vb* (*she likes to pry into her neighbors' affairs*) interfere, meddle, snoop.

public *adj* **1** (*public feeling is against the new road*) popular, general, common. **2** (*make their views public*) known, plain. **3** (*public figures*) well-known, prominent, eminent, influential.

publicity *n* **1** (*she only did it to get publicity in the press*) public attention, public interest. **2** (*the reception was part of the publicity for her book*) promotion, advertisement, advertising, (*inf*) hype.

pull *vb* **1** (*he pulled the nail out of the wall*) pull out, draw out, take out, extract, remove. **2** (*they began to pull the rope*) haul, tug, (*inf*) yank. **3** (*the child was pulling a toy train behind him*) haul, drag, trail, tow, tug. **4** (*the athlete has pulled a muscle*) strain, sprain, wrench. ⋄

pull (something) off to be successful in (something) (*We were all surprised when he pulled off a victory against the golf champion*).
pull through to survive, to get better (*We thought that he was going to die after the operation but he pulled through*).

punch *vb* (*the boy punched him on the nose*) strike, hit, box. ⋄

as pleased as Punch extremely pleased or happy (*The little girl was as pleased as Punch with her new bike*)
pull your punches to be less forceful or harsh in your attack or criticism than you are capable of (*The manager rarely pulls his punches when he is criticizing the employees' work*) <A reference to striking blows in boxing without using your full strength>.

punctual *adj* (*it is important to be punctual at meetings*) on time, prompt, in good time.
punish *vb* **1** (*she punished the children for being naughty*) discipline, chastise, smack, slap. **2** (*punished for doing wrong*) discipline, penalize.
puny *adj* (*too puny to fight against such a strong opponent*) weak, weakly, frail, feeble, undersized, stunted, slight, small.
pure *adj* **1** (*breathing in the pure mountain air*) clean, clear, fresh, unpolluted, uncontaminated, untainted, wholesome. **2** (*dishes of pure gold*) unalloyed, unmixed, unadulterated, true, real. **3** (*people who are expected to be of pure character*) virtuous, honorable, moral, ethical, righteous, blameless, uncorrupted, impeccable, flawless, spotless. **4** (*it was pure folly to do that*) sheer, utter, absolute, downright, total, complete, out-and-out. **5** (*the students are studying pure science*) theoretical, abstract. ⋄

as pure as the driven snow extremely virtuous or moral (*He will expect his bride to be as pure as the driven snow*).

purpose *n* **1** (*what was the purpose of their inquiries?*) reason, point, motivation, cause, grounds, justification. **2** (*the young man should try to get a purpose in life*) aim, goal, objective, object, target, aspiration, ambition. **3** (*the search for the missing goods lacked purpose*) determination, resoluteness, resolve, firmness, perseverance. **4** (*the talks went on all night but to little purpose*) worth, use, usefulness, value, advantage, benefit, avail. ⋄

be at cross purposes of two people or groups, to be involved in a misunderstanding because of talking or thinking about different things without the people involved realizing it (*No wonder I couldn't understand what she was talking about. We were talking at cross purposes*).
serve the purpose to be useful in a particular situation, to fulfill a need (*I really need a screwdriver for this job but a knife will serve the purpose*).

pursue *vb* **1** (*the police officer pursued the bank robber*) go after, run after, follow, chase, give chase to, trail, stalk, shadow, (*inf*) tail. **2** (*the police are pursuing a line of inquiry in the murder case*) follow, proceed with, go on with, continue with. **3** (*she wishes to pursue a career in medicine*) follow, be engaged in, work in. **4** (*they are pursuing their goal of making a fortune*) strive toward, be intent on.
push *vb* **1** (*the little boy pushed his friend into the pool*) shove, thrust, propel, ram, drive. **2** (*she pushed her way to the front of the crowd*) force, shove, thrust, press, elbow, shoulder, jostle. **3** (*push the button to start the machine*) press. **4** (*he said that his parents pushed him into going to university*) force, coerce, press, dragoon, browbeat, prod, goad, urge. **5** (*the company held a reception to push their new product*) promote, advertise, publicize, boost, (*inf*) plug. ⋄

a pencil pusher someone who works in an office (*She works for the police department as a pencil pusher*).
push your luck to risk failure by trying to gain too much (*He is pushing his luck by asking for yet more time off*).

put *vb* **1** (*they were asked to put the books on the desk*) place, lay, set down, deposit. **2** (*they tried to put the blame on their friend*) place, lay, attach, attribute, assign. **3** (*she put the value of the antique vase at $4000*) assess, evaluate, calculate, reckon, guess, (*inf*) guesstimate. **4** (*you should put the idea to your parents*) put forward, propose, present, submit. **5** (*he put a large sum of money on the horse*) place, bet, wager, gamble. ⬠

a put-up job (*inf*) something done to deceive or trick (someone) (*The police pretended to believe him but it was a put-up job. They were just trying to get him to confess*).
be put upon to be made use of for someone else's benefit, to be taken advantage of (*She is really put upon by her daughter. She is expected to baby-sit every night*).
put it on to pretend, to feign (*She said that she had sprained her ankle but she was just putting it on because she didn't want to walk any farther*).

puzzle *vb* (*her parents were puzzled by the change in her behavior*) perplex, mystify, baffle, bewilder, nonplus, stump.

Q

qualified *adj* **1** (*a qualified doctor/She is qualified to teach*) trained, certificated, equipped. **2** (*they gave the plan qualified approval*) limited, conditional, modified, restricted.

quarrel *n* (*the sisters have had a quarrel*) disagreement, argument, row, fight, difference of opinion, dispute, wrangle, misunderstanding.

queer *adj* (*their behavior seemed very queer*) strange, odd, peculiar, funny, weird, bizarre.

question *n* **1** (*she was unable to answer his questions*) inquiry, query, interrogation. **2** (*we must consider the question of safety*) issue, matter, point, subject, topic. ↪

be out of the question not to be possible (*It is out of the question for you to take a vacation now—we are too busy*).

pop the question to ask someone to marry you (*He popped the question on her birthday*).

rhetorical question a question which does not require or expect an answer (*"What happened to the happy times of our youth?" is a rhetorical question*).

quick *adj* **1** (*you will have to be quick to catch the bus*) fast, swift, rapid, speedy. **2** (*she wants a quick reply to her letter*) prompt, without delay, immediate. **3** (*she took a quick look at the instructions*) hasty, brief, fleeting, cursory.

quiet *adj* (*it was very quiet in the church*) hushed, silent, soundless, noiseless. **2** (*he spoke in quiet tones*) soft, low, hushed, whispered, inaudible. **3** (*lead a quiet life in the country*) peaceful, tranquil, calm, serene, placid, untroubled, undisturbed. **4** (*they are both rather quiet people*) reserved, uncommunicative, reticent, placid, unexcitable. **5** (*she dresses in quiet colors*) restrained, unobtrusive, muted, subdued, subtle, conservative, sober, dull. **6** (*they kept the news of their engagement quiet*) secret, confidential, private, (*inf*) hush-hush.

quite *adj* **1** (*has he quite recovered after his accident?*) completely, totally, entirely, fully, wholly. **2** (*she is quite good at tennis but she will not win the match*) fairly, relatively, moderately, somewhat, rather. ↪

quite something something special or remarkable (*The house that he designed is quite something*).

R

race *vb* (*runners racing toward the finishing post*) run, sprint, dash, speed, bolt, dart. ⋄

the rat race the fierce competitive struggle for success in business, etc. (*He has given up the rat race of the advertising world and has gone off to live on a remote island*).

race *n* (*humankind is divided into races*) ethnic group, racial division.

racial *adj* (*racial discrimination*) ethnic, race-related.

racism *n* racial discrimination, racial prejudice.

rack *n* (*a plate rack*) frame, framework, stand, support, holder. ⋄

go to rack and ruin to fall into a state of disrepair or into a worthless condition (*The estate has gone to rack and ruin because the owner has no money*) <"Rack" here means destruction>.

racket *n* **1** (*we couldn't sleep because of the racket from the party next door*) din, noise, commotion, row, hubbub, disturbance. **2** (*they think he was involved in a drugs racket*) fraud, criminal scheme.

radiant *adj* **1** (*they could not see properly in the radiant light*) brilliant, shining, bright, gleaming **2** (*the winners looked radiant*) joyful, elated, ecstatic, delighted.

radiate *vb* **1** (*the fire radiated a fierce heat*) send out, emit, disperse. **2** (*roads radiating out from the Center City*) branch out, spread out, diverge.

radical *adj* **1** (*there have been radical changes in their business methods*) thorough, complete, total, sweeping, exhaustive, drastic, violent. **2** (*she holds radical political views*) extremist, fundamental.

rage *n* **1** (*she went into a rage when they criticized her*) temper, tantrum. **2** (*she was filled with rage at the sight of her rival*) fury, anger, annoyance, exasperation. ⋄

be all the rage to be extremely fashionable or popular (*Shoulder pads were all the rage then*).

rags *npl* (*the homeless woman was dressed in rags*) tatters.

raid *n* **1** (*enemy raids on the town*) attack, assault,

onslaught, invasion. **2** (*a bank raid*) robbery, break-in.

railing *n* (*the rail around the balcony*) rail, barrier, fence.

rain *vb* (*it was raining during the ballgame*) pour, drizzle, (*inf*) rain cats and dogs. ⋄

as right as rain perfectly all right, completely well (*She was injured in the accident but she is as right as rain now*).

rainy *adj* (*we got a rainy day for the picnic*) wet, damp, showery, drizzly. ⋄

keep (something) for a rainy day to keep (something, especially a sum of money) until you really have need of it (*The old lady does not have enough food to eat but she insists on keeping a large sum of money for a rainy day*) <Formerly many jobs, such as farm jobs, could not be carried out in wet weather and so no money was earned then>.

raise *vb* **1** (*they need a crane to raise the wrecked car*) lift, hoist, heave up, elevate. **2** (*they are going to raise an apartment building there*) put up, build, construct, erect. **3** (*the news raised our hopes*) increase, boost, build up, stimulate. **4** (*they had to raise the temperature in the glasshouse*) put up, increase, intensify. **5** (*the local hotels raise their prices in the summer*) put up, increase, inflate, (*inf*) hike up. **6** (*they raise turkeys*) breed, rear. **7** (*he raises cereal crops*) grow, cultivate, produce, farm. **8** (*they have raised several children*) rear, bring up, nurture.

rake *vb* **1** (*rake up the dead leaves*) scrape up, collect, gather. **2** (*they raked the soil before planting the seeds*) smooth, level, flatten, even out. **3** (*the burglars raked through her things*) search, hunt, ransack, rummage, rifle.

rally *n* **1** (*they held a rally to demonstrate against the war*) meeting, mass meeting, gathering, assembly, convention, demonstration, (*inf*) demo. **2** (*stock market prices fell but then there was a sudden rally*) recovery, revival, improvement, comeback.

rally *vb* **1** (*the troops rallied to support the king*) assemble, gather, convene, unite. **2** (*the invalid was seriously ill but she has rallied*) recover, recuperate, revive, get better, improve, pull through, take a turn for the better.

ram *vb* **1** (*ram the clothing into the bag in a hurry*) force, cram, stuff, thrust. **2** (*his car rammed ours*) hit, strike, run into, collide with, bump. ✧

> **ram (something) down (someone's) throat** to try forcefully to make (someone) accept ideas, opinions, a course of action, etc.

ramble *vb* **1** (*they rambled over the hills for the afternoon*) walk, hike, wander, roam. **2** (*the professor rambled on without the students understanding a word*) babble, rattle on.

rampage *vb* (*children rampaging around their neighbor's garden*) rush, charge, tear, run riot.

ramshackle *adj* (*they bought a ramshackle cottage and are going to rebuild it*) tumbledown, broken-down, run-down, dilapidated, derelict, crumbling.

random *adj* (*ask a random selection of the population how they were going to vote*) haphazard, chance, arbitrary, indiscriminate, unsystematic, unmethodical, unplanned, accidental.

range *n* **1** (*a range of mountains*) row, line, chain. **2** (*it was not within their range of vision*) scope, field, area, limit, reach. **3** (*the store stocks a wide range of goods*) selection, assortment, variety.

range *vb* **1** (*prices range from $10 to $200*) extend, stretch, go, vary. **2** (*the books are ranged according to subject*) classify, categorize, group, class. **3** (*sheep ranging over the hills*) roam, rove, ramble, wander, stray.

rank *n* **1** (*what is the soldier's rank?*) grade, position. **2** (*salary in the organization is according to rank*) grade, level, position, status. ✧

> **close ranks** to act together and support each other as a defensive measure (*The dead patient's husband tried to inquire into the cause of her death but the doctors closed ranks and would tell him nothing*).
> **the rank and file** the ordinary people or the ordinary members of an organization, etc. (*It was suggested that the union leaders should listen more to the opinions of the rank and file*) <Literally ranks and files were the horizontal and vertical lines in which ordinary soldiers were drawn up on parade>.

ransack *vb* **1** (*raiders ransacked the shops after the explosion*) loot, plunder, rob, rifle, pillage. **2** (*we ransacked the house to try to find the lost passport*) search, rummage, scour, turn upside down.

rap *vb* **1** (*she rapped on the door*) knock, tap, bang. **2** (*she rapped him over the knuckles with a ruler*) hit, strike, tap, bang, whack.

rapid *adj* (*they set off at a rapid pace*) swift, fast, quick, speedy, hurried, hasty, brisk, lively.

rapture *n* (*their rapture at the birth of their child*) joy, ecstasy, bliss, delight.

rare *adj* **1** (*the wild flower was a rare specimen*) unusual, uncommon, out of the ordinary, atypical, remarkable. **2** (*he made one of his rare appearances*) infrequent, few and far between, sparse.

rascal *n* (*the child was a real little rascal*) imp, scamp, scalawag.

rash *adj* (*leaving her job to go around the world proved to be a rash decision*) impetuous, reckless, hasty, impulsive, unthinking, foolhardy.

rash *n* **1** (*she woke up with a rash on her face*) spots, redness, eruption, hives. **2** (*there has been a rash of car thefts in the area*) spate, outbreak, wave, flood, series, run, plague, epidemic.

rasping *adj* (*she has a rasping voice/the rasping noise of a knife on metal*) grating, jarring, harsh, rough, gruff, croaky.

rate *n* **1** (*they walked at a very fast rate*) pace, speed, tempo. **2** (*the bank's rate of interest*) ratio, proportion, scale, degree. **3** (*the hotel is charging its winter rates*) price, charge, cost, tariff, fee, payment.

rate *vb* **1** (*how would you rate the team's performance?*) judge, assess, evaluate, measure, weigh up, rank, class. **2** (*she rates more respect from them*) deserve, merit, be entitled to.

rather *adv* **1** (*she would rather go than stay*) for preference, sooner, from choice. **2** (*she is pretty rather than beautiful*) more. **3** (*she tends to be rather blunt*) quite, fairly, somewhat, slightly.

ratify *vb* (*the two sides still have to ratify the agreement*) confirm, endorse, sign, approve.

ratio *n* (*the ratio of staff to students in the school*) proportion, percentage, fraction.

rational *adj* **1** (*it seemed a rational decision*) sensible, reasonable, logical, sound, intelligent, wise, judicious. **2** (*his mind has been affected but he has a few rational moments*) sane, balanced, lucid.

rattle *vb* **1** (*the windows rattled in the wind*) bang, clatter, clank, jangle. **2** (*she rattled the door knocker*) bang, knock, rap. **3** (*he was rattling on about his hobbies and boring everyone*) chatter, babble, prattle, jabber. **4** (*the speaker was obviously rattled by some of the questions from the audience*) agitate, disturb, fluster, upset, shake.

raucous *adj* (*the raucous singing of the students*) shrill, grating, jarring, piercing.

ravenous *adj* (*they were ravenous after walking all day*) famished, starving, hungry.

raw *adj* **1** (*she prefers to eat raw vegetables*) uncooked, fresh. **2** (*raw sugar*) unrefined, unprocessed, crude, natural. **3** (*it was a raw winter's day*) cold, chilly, bitter. **4** (*she has a raw place on her elbow from when she fell over*) red, sore, inflamed, tender, grazed. **5** (*raw recruits to the job*) inexperienced, untrained, unskilled, green.

ray *n* **1** (*the rays of light showed up the dust on the furniture*) beam, shaft, streak, gleam, flash. **2** (*there did not seem to be a ray of hope left*) glimmer, flicker, trace, indication, suggestion.

reach *vb* **1** (*he reached his hand out for the book*) stretch, extend. **2** (*the child could not reach the door handle*) get hold of, grasp, touch. **3** (*we finally reached our destination*) get to, arrive at. **4** (*he has not reached the required standard*) get to, achieve, attain.

react *vb* **1** (*how did he react when he discovered that she had gone?*) behave, act, respond. **2** (*the teenagers are reacting against their parents' beliefs*) rebel against.

read *vb* **1** (*she read a book while she waited*) study, pore over, browse through. **2** (*can you read his handwriting?*) decipher, make out. **3** (*they read his silence as consent*) interpret, take to mean.

ready *adj* **1** (*the meal is ready*) prepared, completed. **2** (*they are ready for battle*) prepared, equipped, organized, all set. **3** (*her neighbors are always ready to help*) willing, eager, keen, inclined, disposed. **4** (*she was ready to collapse when she got to the bottom of the mountain*) about to, on the point of, in danger of. **5** (*she always has a ready answer*) prompt, quick, rapid, swift, speedy. **6** (*have you got your ticket ready for collection?*) available, to hand, accessible.

real *adj* **1** (*things connected with the real world*) actual, factual. **2** (*the coat was made of real leather*) genuine, authentic. **3** (*she showed signs of real emotion*) genuine, authentic, sincere, honest, truthful. **4** (*he has been a real friend*) true, sincere. ▭

the real McCoy something that is genuine and very good as opposed to something that is not (*This lasagne is the real McCoy, not something from the supermarket freezer*).

realistic *adj* **1** (*the model of the bear was very realistic*) lifelike, true-to-life, naturalistic, authentic. **2** (*he has to try to be realistic about his job prospects*) practical, down-to-earth, matter-of-fact, sensible, level-headed, unromantic, no-nonsense.

realize *vb* **1** (*we began to realize that she was sick*) understand, grasp, take in, become aware, appreciate, recognize. **2** (*I hope that she realizes her dreams*) fulfill, achieve, attain, accomplish.

really *adv* **1** (*it was a really beautiful day*) truly, genuinely, undoubtedly, unquestionably, indeed. **2** (*the performer is dressed as a woman but is really a man*) in fact, in actual fact, in truth.

rear *n* **1** (*they sat at the rear of the train*) back. **2** (*they were at the rear of the line for the theater*) back, tail, end.

rear *vb* **1** (*she reared three children on her own*) bring up, raise, care for. **2** (*the farmer rears turkeys*) breed, raise, keep.

reason *n* **1** (*there was no reason for his behavior*) grounds, cause, basis, motive, justification. **2** (*the old man has lost his reason*) sanity, mind. ▭

it stands to reason that it is logical or obvious that (*It stands to reason that she would be in pain. She has broken her leg in two places*).
see reason to be persuaded by someone's advice, etc., to act or think sensibly (*At first he refused to go to the doctor with his sore leg but he finally saw reason*).
within reason within sensible limits (*She was told that she could have anything she wanted for her birthday—within reason*).

reasonable *adj* **1** (*it seemed a reasonable thing to do*) logical, rational, practical, sensible, intelligent, wise, sound. **2** (*I thought that he was quite a reasonable person*) fair, just, decent, unbiased. **3** (*the prices in the new restaurant were quite* *reasonable*) inexpensive, moderate, modest, cheap.

rebel *vb* **1** (*the crew are rebelling*) mutiny, riot, revolt, rise up. **2** (*teenagers rebelling against their parents' authority*) defy, disobey.

rebellion *n* (*they joined in a rebellion against the king*) revolt, revolution, insurrection, uprising, rising, riot.

rebellious *adj* (*the rebellious troops/the rebellious schoolgirls*) defiant, disobedient, unruly, unmanageable, mutinous.

rebuke *vb* (*her teacher rebuked her for being late*) scold, admonish, (*inf*) tell off.

recall *vb* **1** (*she was unable to recall his name*) call to mind, remember, recollect, think of. **2** (*the manufacturers have recalled a batch of cars with faulty brakes*) call back, withdraw.

recede *vb* **1** (*the flood water began to recede*) go back, retreat, subside, ebb. **2** (*the danger seems to have receded*) grow less, lessen, fade, diminish.

receive *vb* **1** (*she said that she posted the goods but we never received them*) get, be in receipt of. **2** (*she received many benefits from the scheme*) get, obtain, gain, acquire. **3** (*she received the best of treatment in the hospital*) get, experience, undergo, meet with. **4** (*she got ready to receive her dinner guests*) welcome, greet, entertain.

recent *adj* (*the doctor tries to keep up with recent medical developments*) new, fresh, latest, modern.

recite *vb* (*the little girl was asked to recite a poem*) say, repeat, speak, deliver.

reckless *adj* (*he later regretted his reckless action*) rash, careless, thoughtless, inattentive, incautious, irresponsible, negligent.

reclaim *vb* **1** (*they went to the police station to reclaim their property*) get back, recover, retrieve. **2** (*they reclaimed some land from the sea to build a bird sanctuary*) get back, recover, retrieve, regain, store, save, salvage, rescue.

recline *vb* (*the invalid reclined on a sofa*) lie down, lie, stretch out, lean back, rest, lounge.

recognize *vb* **1** (*I failed to recognize my cousin after all these years*) know, know again, identify, recall, call to mind, recollect, remember. **2** (*the authorities are refusing to recognize his claim to the title*) acknowledge, accept, allow, grant, validate. **3** (*he recognized that he had been at fault*) realize, be aware, appreciate, admit,

acknowledge. **4** (*his genius as a composer was not recognized in his lifetime*) appreciate, honor, pay homage to, reward.

recoil *vb* (*he recoiled when he realized that his fellow thief had a gun*) flinch, shrink, draw back, wince.

recollect *vb* (*I cannot recollect his name*) remember, recall, call to mind, think of.

recommend *vb* **1** (*he recommended a treatment for a cold*) commend, advocate, speak favorably of, approve, vouch for. **2** (*they recommend caution in that case*) advise, urge.

reconcile *vb* **1** (*the couple separated for a time but have now been reconciled*) bring together, reunite. **2** (*they quarreled but have now reconciled their differences*) settle, resolve, put to rights. **3** (*we have now reconciled ourselves to our misfortune*) resign yourself, accept, make the best of it.

record *n* **1** (*he is using parish records to write a history of the area*) register, documents, information, data, chronicles, annals. **2** (*she kept a diary of her vacation experiences*) account, note, description, report, diary, register. **3** (*she played a dance record*) recording, disc, CD, album, vinyl.

record *vb* **1** (*all births, marriage, and deaths must be recorded*) register, enter, note, document, minute, catalogue. **2** (*the group have recorded some folk songs*) make, cut, tape, videotape, video. ↺

break the record to do something better, faster, etc., than has been done before (*The sprinter has broken the world record*).
off the record not to be made public (*Although the politician said that he had made the remark off the record the newspaper published it*).
set the record straight to put right a mistake or misunderstanding (*People thought that he had been fired but he was able to set the record straight*).

recount *vb* (*they recounted the tale of their vacation adventures*) tell, relate, narrate, unfold, repeat.

recover *vb* **1** (*she has been very sick but she is now recovering*) get well, get better, recuperate, improve, rally, pull through. **2** (*they recovered some of their stolen property*) get back, regain, recoup, retrieve, reclaim, repossess, redeem. **3** (*they recovered land from the sea*) reclaim, restore, salvage, save.

recreation *n* **1** (*his recreations include wind-surfing*) hobby, pastime, amusement, distraction. **2** (*what does he do for recreation?*) leisure, relaxation, amusement, entertainment, fun, pleasure, distraction.

recruit *vb* (*the club is hoping to recruit new members*) enroll, enlist, sign up, take on.

recur *vb* (*his illness has recurred*) come back, return, reappear.

recurrent *adj* (*a recurrent fault*) recurring, repeated, repetitive, periodic, frequent.

recycle *vb* (*recycle paper products*) re-use, use again, reprocess, salvage.

red *adj* **1** (*she was red with embarrassment*) flushed, blushing. **2** (*her face goes red in the cold*) ruddy, florid. ✧

like a red flag before a bull certain to make someone extremely angry (*Any criticism of the government is like a red flag before a bull to the old man*) <From the widespread belief that bulls are angered by the sight of the color red although they are in fact color-blind>.

red tape the rules and regulations, official papers, etc. that are thought to be typical of government departments (*With all the red tape it took a long time for us to get a work permit*) <From the reddish tape used by government offices to tie bundles of official papers>.

see red to get extremely angry (*She is usually very calm but she saw red when she witnessed him whipping the dog*).

reduce *vb* **1** (*reduce the amount of food they eat*) cut, curtail, decrease, lessen, diminish. **2** (*drivers should reduce speed*) decrease, moderate, lessen, lower. **3** (*prices have been reduced*) cut, lower, mark down, take down, slash, cheapen.

refer *vb* **1** (*he referred to the difficulty of the task in his speech*) mention, allude to, touch on, speak of. **2** (*she referred the complaint to the manager*) pass, hand on, direct, transfer. **3** (*if you do not know the meaning of the word you should refer to a dictionary*) consult, look up, turn to.

referee *n* (*select a referee for the match*) umpire, judge.

reference *n* **1** (*she made no reference to the previ-*ous day's quarrel) mention, allusion. **2** (*his comments have no reference to the case being discussed*) relation, relevance, connection, bearing, application. **3** (*she asked her former teacher for a reference when she applied for a job*) character reference, testimonial, commendation.

refined *adj* **1** (*refined sugar*) processed, purified, treated. **2** (*she felt she was too refined to mix with them*) polished, cultivated, cultured, civilized, well-bred.

reflect *vb* **1** (*glass reflects light*) send back, throw back, diffuse. **2** (*his expression reflected his mood*) show, indicate, reveal, communicate. **3** (*she needed time to reflect on her problems*) think about, consider, contemplate, mull over, ponder.

reflection *n* (*his reflection in the mirror*) image, likeness.

reform *vb* (*make efforts to reform the educational system*) improve, make better, better, amend, rectify, reorganize, revolutionize.

refreshing *adj* **1** (*a refreshing cool drink/ a refreshing cool breeze*) invigorating, reviving, bracing, exhilarating. **2** (*some of his ideas seemed very refreshing*) fresh, new, novel, original, different.

refuge *n* **1** (*they sought refuge from their enemies/ seek refuge from the storm*) asylum, sanctuary, protection, safety, shelter, cover. **2** (*the building was a refuge for the homeless*) safe house, sanctuary, shelter, retreat, haven.

refugee *n* (*refugees from the famine area*) fugitive, exile, displaced person, stateless person, asylum seeker, alien.

refuse *vb* (*she refused their invitation*) turn down, reject, decline.

refuse *n* (*dispose of household refuse*) waste, debris, litter, garbage.

regard *vb* **1** (*the police officer was regarding them closely as they tried to get into the car*) look at, watch, observe, study, eye. **2** (*he regards his job prospects with optimism*) look on, view, consider. **3** (*they regard him as rather a fool*) consider, judge, rate, assess.

regard *n* **1** (*they paid no regard to his advice*) heed, notice, attention. **2** (*he is looked upon with regard in the firm*) respect, esteem, admiration.

region *n* (*the cold regions of the world*) area, territory, section, tract, zone, part, place. ✧

in the region of (something) approximately, roughly (*The price will be in the region of $50,000*).

register *vb* **1** (*the hotel guests were asked to sign the register*) list, record, directory. **2** (*he used the parish registers for his research*) record, chronicle. **3** (*the register of her voice*) range, scale, reach.

register *vb* **1** (*they registered the birth of their son/ They had to register their arrival on the list*) record, put on record, enter, write down. **2** (*the thermostat registered 20 degrees*) read, indicate, show, display. **3** (*her face registered her surprise*) show, express, display, reveal.

regret *vb* (*she regrets that she did it*) feel sorry, feel repentant, feel remorse, repent, to be ashamed of.

regretful *adj* (*she gave a regretful smile*) apologetic, repentant, contrite, remorseful, penitent.

regular *adj* **1** (*the mailman did not follow his regular route*) usual, customary, accustomed, habitual, normal. **2** (*the breathing of the patient is regular*) even, steady, rhythmic. **3** (*they planted the trees at regular intervals*) even, fixed, uniform. **4** (*you will have to apply through the regular channels*) usual, standard, official, conventional, orthodox.

regulation *n* (*traffic regulations*) rule, order, law, decree.

rehearse *vb* (*the actors were rehearsing the play*) practise, try out, go over, run through.

reject *vb* **1** (*she has rejected their invitation*) refuse, turn down, decline. **2** (*she rejected the baby at birth*) abandon, forsake, renounce, cast aside.

rejoice *vb* (*they rejoiced on hearing that they had won*) be joyful, be happy, be glad, be delighted, be overjoyed, celebrate.

relapse *n* (*the patient was improving but then suffered a relapse*) setback, turn for the worse.

relate *vb* **1** (*he related the story of his misfortune*) tell, recount, describe, narrate, report. **2** (*information not relating to the matter*) apply, be relevant, concern, have a bearing on.

relations *npl* **1** (*she has no relations in the area*) family, kin. **2** (*they have business relations*) dealings, associations.

relationship *n* **1** (*I don't think there is any relationship between the two events*) connection, association, link. **2** (*their relationship is over*) friendship, partnership, love affair.

relax *vb* **1** (*he relaxes by swimming*) rest, unwind, take it easy, be at leisure, amuse yourself. **2** (*he relaxed his grip on the dog's leash*) loosen, loose, slacken, weaken **3** (*the police will not relax their efforts to find the criminal*) reduce, lessen, decrease, diminish.

release *vb* **1** (*the police have released the accused*) free, set free, let out, set loose, liberate. **2** (*they were tied up by the burglars and could not release themselves*) set free, free, untie, undo. **3** (*they have released the news of the royal engagement*) make public, make known, issue, announce, disclose, put out, circulate, publish.

relentless *adj* **1** (*the judge was completely relentless*) ruthless, unmerciful, merciless, pitiless, unforgiving, harsh, cruel. **2** (*their relentless efforts to persuade him*) persistent, persevering, nonstop, unceasing.

relevant *adj* (*the information was not relevant to the discussion*) applicable, pertinent, apposite, appropriate.

reliable *adj* **1** (*her most reliable friends*) dependable, trustworthy, true, loyal, devoted. **2** (*the evidence was not considered reliable*) dependable, trustworthy, well-founded, sound.

relieve *vb* **1** (*a drug to relieve the pain*) alleviate, soothe, ease, reduce. **2** (*collect money to relieve the distress of the famine victims*) help, assist, aid, bring aid to. **3** (*she was to relieve the nurse on duty*) take over from, take the place of, stand in for, substitute for. **4** (*look for something to relieve the monotony of her life*) break up, interrupt, vary, lighten.

religious *adj* **1** (*take part in a religious ceremony/ a religious discussion*) church, holy, divine, theological. **2** (*she comes from a religious family*) church-going, pious, devout, God-fearing.

relinquish *vb* (*he relinquished his right to the title*) give up, renounce, surrender.

reluctant *adj* **1** (*a reluctant witness*) unwilling, unenthusiastic, grudging **2** (*she was reluctant to go*) unwilling, disinclined, loath, averse.

rely *vb* (*she was relying on her parents for help*) depend on, count on, bank on, trust, put your faith in.

remain *vb* **1** (*she remained calm in the emergency*) stay, keep, continue. **2** (*only a few of the original inhabitants remained*) be left, survive, last, endure. **3** (*he has to remain in hospital*) stay, wait.

remark *n* (*she made some critical remarks*) comment, statement, observation.

remarkable *adj* (*it was a remarkable achievement for one so young*) extraordinary, unusual, exceptional, outstanding, impressive.

remedy n (*a remedy for the common cold*) cure, treatment.

remember vb **1** (*I cannot remember his name*) recall, call to mind, recollect, think of. **2** (*try to remember to post the letter*) keep in mind, bear in mind.

reminisce vb (*old people reminiscing about their youth*) call to mind, recall, remember, recollect, think back on.

remorse n (*she showed remorse for her wrongdoing*) regret, penitence.

remote adj **1** (*they live in a remote mountain village*) distant, far-off, out-of-the way, isolated. **2** (*she is rather a remote person*) distant, aloof, reserved, unfriendly. **3** (*there is a remote possibility that he will win*) outside, unlikely, slender, slight.

remove vb **1** (*they removed their shoes*) take off. **2** (*she was asked to remove her books from the table*) move, shift, take away, carry away. **3** (*they tried to remove him from his post*) get rid of, throw out, dismiss, sack, expel, evict, oust. **4** (*she has had a tooth removed*) take out, pull out, extract.

renounce vb **1** (*he renounced his claim to the title*) give up, relinquish, surrender, waive. **2** (*he renounced the smoking habit*) give up, swear off, abstain from, desist from. **3** (*they renounced their religion*) give up, abandon, turn your back on, forsake.

renovate vb (*they are renovating an old country cottage*) modernize, restore, recondition, overhaul.

renown n (*her renown as a singer spread*) fame, acclaim, reputation, eminence, prestige.

rent vb (*they rented a boat*) hire, lease, charter.

repair vb **1** (*the mechanic repaired the car*) mend, fix, put right. **2** (*they repaired the torn clothing*) mend, sew, darn, patch.

repeat vb **1** (*he was asked to repeat his statement to the committee*) say again, restate, recapitulate. **2** (*the boy repeated his father's words*) say again, echo, quote. **3** (*they have to repeat the task*) re-do, do again, duplicate.

repel vb **1** (*they succeed in repelling their attackers*) drive back, push back, repulse, fend off, ward off. **2** (*the sight of the rotting meat repelled them*) revolt, disgust, nauseate, sicken.

repent vb (*she committed a sin but she has repented*) feel regret, feel remorse, be sorry, be repentant, be penitent, be contrite.

repercussion n (*he could not have foretold the repercussions of his actions*) consequence, effect, result, reverberation.

repetitive adj (*his work consists of repetitive tasks*) repeated, unchanging, monotonous.

replica n (*the original of the necklace is in the bank—this is a replica*) copy, duplicate, reproduction, imitation, model.

reply n **1** (*she gave no reply to his question*) answer, response, retort, rejoinder. **2** (*he received a reply to his letter*) answer, response, acknowledgment.

report n **1** (*the firm's annual financial report*) statement, record, register. **2** (*a newspaper report of the accident*) account, article, piece, story, write-up. **3** (*they heard the report of a gun*) bang, explosion, blast, boom, crack.

report vb **1** (*they reported that they had been successful*) announce, communicate, tell, relate. **2** (*the soldiers were to report to the sergeant at noon*) present yourself, announce yourself, appear, arrive. **3** (*they reported him to the police*) inform on, accuse, tell on, complain about, (*inf*) rat on, (*inf*) grass on.

repose n (*enjoy some repose after his hard work*) rest, relaxation, respite, time off, sleep.

represent vb **1** (*a closed fist represents violence*) symbolize, stand for, personify. **2** (*the queen was represented in the picture as a warrior*) depict, portray, picture, show. **3** (*his lawyer represented him*) appear for, act for, speak for, be the representative of.

repressive adj (*a repressive regime*) tyrannical, oppressive, harsh, stern.

reprieve vb (*the woman was reprieved because she had killed in self-defense*) pardon, let off, spare.

reprimand vb (*the pupils were reprimanded for being late*) scold, chide, reprove, admonish, reproach, (*inf*) tell off, (*inf*) tick off.

reprisal n (*when their village was attacked they took reprisals on the attackers*) retaliation, vengeance, revenge, retribution, redress, requital.

reproach n (*she was upset by his words of reproach*) criticism, censure, condemnation, reprimand, reproof.

reproduce vb **1** (*can the photocopier reproduce colored documents?*) copy, photocopy, duplicate. **2** (*we were unable to reproduce the lighting effect we produced last week*) repeat, recreate.

emulate. **3** (*rabbits reproduce quickly*) breed, bear young, multiply.

repulsive *adj* (*it was a repulsive sight*) revolting, repellent, disgusting, nauseating, offensive, objectionable, loathsome, nasty, horrible, foul.

reputable *adj* (*get a reputable firm to do the work*) respected, respectable, well-thought-of, esteemed, reliable, dependable.

reputation *n* **1** (*the firm has a bad reputation for shoddy work*) name, character. **2** (*the incident damaged their reputation*) good name, respectability, esteem. ✧

live up to your reputation to behave in the way that you are reputed or expected to behave (*He lived up to his reputation for meanness by refusing to give a contribution to the charity*).

request *vb* (*they requested more help*) ask for, seek, apply for, demand, beg for, plead for.

require *vb* **1** (*they require more money*) need, have need of, be short of, lack, want. **2** (*the job requires concentration*) need, involve, take, call for. **3** (*the police required him to go to the police station*) order, instruct, command.

rescue *vb* (*they rescued the drowning man from the river/They rescued the men from prison*) save, get out, free, liberate.

research *n* (*they were carrying out medical research into new drugs*) investigation, exploration, inquiry, study, analysis.

resemble *vb* (*she resembles her mother*) look like, be like, bear a semblance to, be similar to, take after, put you in mind of, remind you of.

resent *vb* (*she resents the fact that her sister earns more money than she does*) begrudge, grudge, be bitter, feel aggrieved, envy, be jealous.

reserve *vb* **1** (*we reserved seats for the play*) book, order. **2** (*you should reserve some fuel for the winter*) keep, put aside, conserve, save, store. **3** (*they should reserve judgment until they have heard all the facts*) postpone, delay, defer.

reserved *adj* (*she is very reserved and does not speak to many people*) shy, retiring, reticent, aloof, distant, uncommunicative.

reside *vb* (*he resides in a large house in New Orleans now*) live in, stay in, occupy, inhabit, dwell in.

residence *n* **1** (*they have an impressive Georgian residence*) house, dwelling place. **2** (*they take up residence next week*) occupation, occupancy, tenancy.

resident *n* **1** (*the residents of the new apartment building*) occupant, occupier, inhabitant. **2** (*the hotel residents*) guest, visitor.

resign *vb* **1** (*he resigned yesterday*) give notice, hand in your notice, leave. **2** (*he resigned from his job yesterday*) leave, quit, give up.

resist *vb* (*the troops resisted the invading army*) fight against, stand up to, withstand, hold out against, defy, oppose, repel.

resolve *vb* **1** (*she resolved to try harder*) decide, make up your mind, determine, settle. **2** (*they seemed unable to resolve the problem*) solve, sort out, work out, clear up, answer.

resourceful *adj* (*resourceful people who made do with what they had*) ingenious, inventive, creative, imaginative, clever, capable.

respect *n* **1** (*they had great respect for him as a painter*) esteem, high regard, admiration, reverence, deference. **2** (*with respect to the matter under discussion*) reference, relevance, regard, relation. **3** (*the plan was not perfect in all respects*) aspect, facet, feature, way, sense, particular, point, detail.

respectable *adj* (*her neighbors do not think that she is very respectable*) of good reputation, upright, honorable, honest, decent, worthy.

response *n* (*they asked several questions but received no response*) answer, reply, acknowledgment, reaction.

responsible *adj* **1** (*they said that he was responsible for the damage*) blameworthy, to blame, guilty, at fault, accountable, answerable. **2** (*they need a responsible person to look after the children*) mature, sensible, level-headed, stable, reliable, dependable, trustworthy.

rest *n* **1** (*a period of rest after work*) repose, relaxation, leisure, ease, inactivity, sleep. **2** (*she is going away for a rest*) break, vacation.

restless *adj* **1** (*the children got restless in the afternoon*) fidgety, restive, agitated. **2** (*they passed a restless night*) wakeful, fitful.

restrain *vb* **1** (*they tried to restrain him from jumping off the bus*) prevent, hold back, impede. **2** (*she tried to restrain her laughter*) suppress, curb, check, stifle, contain. **3** (*it was her job to restrain the dogs*) control, keep under control, subdue, curb.

restrict *vb* **1** (*the long tight skirt restricted her freedom of movement*) hinder, hamper, impede, obstruct. **2** (*he was told by the doctor to restrict his consumption of salt*) limit, regulate, control, moderate.

restricted *adj* **1** (*a restricted space*) cramped, confined. **2** (*there is a restricted area around the military camp*) out of bounds, off limits, private.

result *n* (*his illness was a result of overwork*) effect, consequence, upshot, outcome, repercussion.

retain *vb* **1** (*they were asked to retain their train tickets*) keep, hold on to, hang on to. **2** (*the village still retains some of the old traditions*) keep, maintain, continue, preserve.

retaliate *vb* (*they hit the new boy and he retaliated*) take revenge, seek retribution, take reprisals, get even, give tit for tat.

reticent *adj* (*he was very outgoing but his wife was very reticent*) reserved, diffident, uncommunicative, unforthcoming, silent.

retiring *adj* (*very few people know her because she is very retiring*) shy, bashful, unassertive.

retreat *vb* **1** (*the army retreated before the enemy*) withdraw, go back, fall back, take flight, flee, beat a retreat. **2** (*the tide retreated*) go back, recede, ebb.

retrieve *vb* (*he tried to retrieve his stolen property*) get back, recover, regain, recoup, reclaim.

return *vb* **1** (*their parents will return tomorrow*) come back, go back, reappear. **2** (*she asked him to return the book that she had lent him*) give back, send back.

reveal *vb* **1** (*she took off her coat and revealed a white dress*) show, display, exhibit, expose, uncover. **2** (*the press revealed the truth about the affair*) disclose, divulge, tell, let out, make known.

revenge *n* (*he wanted revenge for his brother's murder*) vengeance, retribution, retaliation, reprisal.

reverse *vb* **1** (*they reversed their roles for the day*) change, exchange, swap, trade. **2** (*they have reversed their previous decision*) alter, change, overturn, repeal, revoke. **3** (*he reversed the car*) back. **4** (*reverse the coat*) turn around, put back to front.

revise *vb* **1** (*the students are revising the term's work*) go over, reread. **2** (*she had to revise the text of the manuscript*) amend, emend, correct, alter, edit. **3** (*we have had to revise our vacation plans*) reconsider, review, alter, change.

revolt *vb* **1** (*the sight of the dried blood revolted her*) disgust, repel, nauseate, sicken, (*inf*) turn you off. **2** (*the citizens are revolting against the tyrant*) rebel, rise up, take up arms, mutiny.

revolution *n* **1** (*there was a revolution against the king*) rebellion, revolt, uprising, mutiny, riot. **2** (*there has been a revolution in the computer industry*) complete change, transformation, reformation, innovation. **3** (*one revolution of the wheel*) rotation, round, whirl, spin. **4** (*the satellite made a revolution of the sun*) orbit, circuit, turn.

revolve *vb* **1** (*the wheel revolved slowly*) go round, turn, rotate, spin, whirl. **2** (*the planet revolves around the sun*) orbit, circle. **3** (*his world revolves around his family*) center on, focus on, concentrate on.

reward *n* (*he received a reward for bravery*) award, prize, recompense, gift, decoration, medal.

rhythm *n* (*the tune had a fast rhythm*) beat, pulse, throb, tempo, cadence.

rich *adj* **1** (*rich people who owned several houses*) wealthy, affluent, well off, prosperous, well-to-do, moneyed. **2** (*a house with rich furnishings*) costly, expensive, opulent, luxurious, sumptuous, splendid, magnificent. **3** (*the area has a very rich soil*) fertile, fruitful, productive. **4** (*drapes of a very rich color*) strong, deep, vivid, intense, brilliant. **5** (*the country has rich supplies of oil*) abundant, copious, ample, plentiful.

rid:—get rid of *vb* (*she should get rid of those old clothes*) dispose of, throw away, throw out, dump.

riddle *n* (*unable to solve the riddle*) puzzle, conundrum, poser, brain-teaser.

ridiculous *adj* **1** (*it was a ridiculous thing to do*) absurd, pointless, senseless, foolish, inane. **2** (*he told us a ridiculous story about his vacation/She always wears ridiculous hats*) absurd, comical, funny, laughable, humorous, ludicrous. **3** (*it is ridiculous that he got away with the crime*) shocking, outrageous, monstrous, preposterous, incredible.

right *adj* **1** (*they all gave the right answer*) correct, accurate. **2** (*he was not the right person for the job*) suitable, appropriate, fitting, desirable. **3** (*he is not in his right mind*) sane, sound, rational, sensible. **4** (*they thought the judge did not make the right decision*) just, fair, impartial, good, honest, virtuous. ✧

serve (someone) right to be something unpleasant that (someone) deserves (*It serves her right* *that she has lost her job as manager—she was responsible for getting rid of so many other workers).*

igid *adj* **1** (*it was made of a rigid substance*) stiff, hard, taut, inflexible, unbending. **2** (*the principal was a rigid disciplinarian*) strict, severe, stern, stringent, harsh, inflexible.

ing *n* **1** (*she wore a gold ring*) band, hoop. **2** (*they saw a ring around the moon*) circle, loop. **3** (*he jumped into the boxing ring*) arena, area, enclosure. **4** (*the police have discovered a spy ring*) gang, organization, league, combine, syndicate.

ing *vb* **1** (*church bells ringing*) toll, sound, peal, chime. **2** (*the hall rang with music*) resound, reverberate, echo, resonate. **3** (*he said that he would ring back*) call, phone, telephone. ✧

have a ringside seat to be in a position to observe clearly what is happening (*We all had a ringside seat during the couple's constant quarrels*) <A reference to a boxing ring>.
ring down the curtain on (something) to cause (something) to come to an end (*The government is ringing down the curtain on the new roads scheme because it is too expensive*) <A reference to curtains in a theater being lowered at the end of a performance>.

iot *n* (*there was a riot in the crowd when their leader was arrested*) rebellion, revolt, uprising, mutiny, uproar. ✧

read the riot act to (someone) to scold (someone) severely and warn him or her to behave better (*Their mother read the riot act to the children about the untidy state of their rooms*) <The Riot Act of 1715 was read to gatherings of people who were considered unlawful in order to break up the gatherings. If the people refused to disperse, action could be taken against them>.

pe *adj* (*ripe fruit*) mature, ready to eat, ready, mellow.

se *vb* **1** (*the balloon will rise into the air*) go up, climb, ascend. **2** (*the mountains rising behind the village*) rear up, tower, soar, loom. **3** (*she always rises early*) get up. **4** (*prices are set to rise*) go up, increase, mount, escalate, rocket. **5** (*the stream rises in the mountains*) originate, begin, start, flow from.

sk *n* **1** (*there is a risk of flooding*) danger, chance,

possibility, likelihood. **2** (*their actions put lives at risk*) danger, peril, jeopardy.

rival *n* (*her rival in the competition*) opponent, opposition, adversary.

roar *vb* **1** (*the lion roared*) bellow. **2** (*he roared in rage*) bellow, yell, bawl, shout.

robbery *n* (*the criminals committed robbery*) burglary, theft, stealing, larceny. ✧

highway robbery the charging of prices that are far too high (*Taxi fares in that city are highway robbery*).

robust *adj* (*in robust health*) strong, vigorous, tough, rugged, sturdy, stalwart.

rock *vb* **1** (*the boat began to rock in the storm*) roll, lurch, pitch, swing, sway, wobble. **2** (*rock the cradle*) sway, swing.

rogue *n* (*he was a rogue who ended up in prison*) villain, scoundrel, rascal.

role *n* **1** (*her role in the play*) part, character. **2** (*he attended in his role as chairman*) capacity, position, function, post.

roll *vb* **1** (*the wheels began to roll*) turn, go around, rotate, revolve, spin. **2** (*roll up a newspaper to swat a fly*) furl, coil, fold. **3** (*roll the lawn*) flatten level, smooth, even out. **4** (*as time rolls on*) pass, go by. **5** (*as the ship rolled*) rock, lurch, pitch, toss, swing, sway. ✧

a rolling stone gathers no moss a person who does not stay very long in one place does not acquire much in the way of possessions, responsibilities, etc. (*He has been a rolling stone all his life and has no furniture to put in the house he has been left*).
be rolling in the aisles to laugh extremely heartily (*The comedian had the audience rolling in the aisles*).

romantic *adj* **1** (*she has a very romantic idea of what it is like to live in a remote village*) unrealistic, impractical, idealistic, starry-eyed. **2** (*romantic words on a greetings card*) loving, amorous, sentimental. **3** (*she seemed to them a romantic figure*) fascinating, glamorous, mysterious, exotic, exciting.

rope *n* (*tie the logs up with a rope*) string, cord, cable, line. ✧

at the end of your rope at the end of your patience, tolerance, etc. (*She is at the end of her rope looking after two small children*).

give (someone) enough rope and he *or* **she will hang himself** *or* **herself** let (someone foolish) act as he or she pleases and he or she will bring about his or her own downfall, ruin, etc. (*I know that he is running the department badly but don't say anything just now. Give him enough rope and he will hang himself*).
know the ropes to know the details and methods associated with a business, procedure, activity, etc. (*We need someone for the job who knows the ropes*).

rotate *vb* **1** (*the wheels rotate*) turn, go around, revolve, spin. **2** (*the two doctors rotate between the two wards*) alternate, take turns.
rotten *adj* **1** (*rotten food*) bad, moldy, decaying, decomposed, putrid, rancid, stinking. **2** (*rotten wood*) decaying, crumbling, disintegrating, corroding. **3** (*what a rotten thing to do!*) nasty, mean, foul, despicable, contemptible.
rough *adj* **1** (*sand down the rough surface of the table*) uneven, bumpy, jagged, rugged, irregular. **2** (*they have a dog with a rough coat*) shaggy, bushy, hairy, coarse, bristly. **3** (*people with rough voices*) gruff, hoarse, harsh, husky. **4** (*rough weather at sea*) stormy, squally, wild. **5** (*he goes around with a rough crowd*) rowdy, disorderly, wild, uncouth, coarse, loutish, boorish. **6** (*at a rough estimate*) approximate, inexact, imprecise. **7** (*he made a rough sketch of the house*) rough-and ready, hasty, quick, sketchy.
round *adj* (*a round shape*) circular, ring-shaped, spherical. ◇

a round trip the journey to somewhere and the journey back (*The round trip to my parents' house takes about four hours*).
get around to (something) to find the time and opportunity to (do something) (*I never seem to get around to writing letters*).

route *n* (*they went home by a different route*) way, road, course.
routine *n* (*he hates to have his routine upset*) custom, habit, practice, procedure.
row *n* **1** (*children standing in rows*) line, column, series. **2** (*empty rows of seats in the theater*) line, tier, rank.
row *n* **1** (*the two brothers had a row over money*) argument, disagreement, dispute, squabble,

fight. **2** (*the row coming from the party*) noise, din, rumpus, uproar, commotion.
rowdy *adj* (*the rowdy drunks in the tavern*) unruly, disorderly, noisy, boisterous, loud, wild.
rub *vb* **1** (*she rubbed his sore neck*) massage, knead. **2** (*the child began to rub the cat's back*) pat, caress, fondle. **3** (*rub off the dirty mark*) wipe off, remove, erase. **4** (*rub the ointment into the skin*) apply, work in, spread. ◇

rub (something) in to keep reminding someone about (something) (*I know that I made a fool of myself but there is no need to rub it in*).
rub (someone) the wrong way to irritate (someone) (*He tries to be friendly but he has a habit of rubbing people the wrong way*).

rude *adj* **1** (*the children were very rude*) ill-mannered, bad-mannered, impolite, impertinent, impudent, cheeky. **2** (*they told rude jokes*) vulgar, coarse, dirty, bawdy, blue. **3** (*the peasants had only a few rude tools*) crude, primitive, rough, rudimentary, simple.
ruffian *n* (*the old man was attacked by a gang of ruffians*) rogue, thug, villain, hooligan, scoundrel.
rugged *adj* **1** (*a rugged landscape*) rough, uneven, irregular, bumpy, rocky, jagged. **2** (*rugged men who do hard physical work*) tough, strong, stalwart, robust, sturdy, muscular, brawny.
ruin *vb* **1** (*the storm ruined the crops*) spoil, damage, wreck, wreak havoc on, destroy, lay waste. **2** (*the recession ruined many small businesses*) bring to ruin, bankrupt, make insolvent, impoverish.
rule *vb* **1** (*the emperor ruled over several countries*) govern, preside over, have control over, have authority over, be in command of. **2** (*the judge ruled that the accused be released*) order, command, direct, decide. ◇

rule the roost to be the person in charge whose orders or wishes are obeyed (*When his father is away his elder brother tries to rule the roost*) <A reference to a cockerel in the farmyard>.
rule of thumb a rough or inexact guide used for calculations of some kind (*I did not have a tape measure but I estimated the length of the drapes by rule of thumb*).

rumor, rumour (*Br, Cdn*) *n* (*rumor has it that h*

has gone) gossip, hearsay, the grapevine.

run *vb* **1** (*they had to run to catch the bus*) race, sprint, dash, rush, bolt, charge. **2** (*do the trains run on Sundays?*) operate, go, travel. **3** (*water running down the walls*) flow, stream, pour, gush. **4** (*the dye from the black pants ran on to the white shirt*) spread, mix with. **5** (*he runs a successful business*) operate, conduct, carry on, manage, administer, control, be in charge of, rule. **6** (*they left the engine running*) go, operate, function. ✍

run the gauntlet to be exposed or subjected to extreme criticism, blame, or risk (*Before he married her he had to run the gauntlet of her family's disapproval*) <"Gauntlet" is a mistaken form of Swedish *gatlopp*. "Running the gatlopp" was a Swedish military punishment in which the culprit had to run between two lines of men with whips who struck him as he passed>.

run the show to be in charge of an organization, etc.: *I don't know what will happen to our jobs* (*There's a new man running the show now*). <Refers literally to the theater>.

rural *adj* (*a house in a rural setting*) country, rustic, pastoral.

ruse *n* (*he gained entrance to the house by a ruse*) trick, stratagem, dodge, ploy, deception, hoax.

rush *vb* (*they rushed to switch off the water*) hurry, hasten, make haste, run, race, dash. ✍

the rush hour a period when there is a lot of traffic on the roads, usually when people are going to, or coming from, work.

ruthless *adj* (*he was a ruthless tyrant*) merciless, pitiless, relentless, unforgiving, harsh, severe, heartless, cruel.

S

sacred *adj* **1** (*playing sacred music*) religious, church, spiritual, devotional. **2** (*the temple was a sacred place*) holy, blessed, hallowed, consecrated, godly, divine. **3** (*In Hinduism the cow is a sacred animal*) sacrosanct, protected. ✧

a sacred cow something that is regarded with too much respect for people to be allowed to criticize it freely (*Don't let anyone hear you saying that City Hall is ugly. It is one of the community's sacred cows*).

sad *adj* **1** (*she felt sad when her friend went away*) unhappy, miserable, wretched, dejected, downcast, in low spirits, depressed, gloomy, melancholy. **2** (*she tried to forget the sad events of her childhood*) unhappy, unfortunate, distressing, tragic. **3** (*he thought that the country was in a sad state*) sorry, wretched, unfortunate, regrettable, deplorable, disgraceful.

safe *adj* **1** (*the children are safe indoors*) safe and sound, secure, protected, uninjured, unscathed, free from harm, free from danger, out of harm's way. **2** (*is the building a safe place for the children to play?*) secure, sound, risk-free. **3** (*she is a safe person to look after the children*) reliable, dependable, trustworthy. **4** (*a safe driver*) careful, cautious, prudent. ✧

there's safety in numbers it is safer to undertake a risky venture if there are several people involved (*He would not go on strike on his own in case he got fired but his colleagues are joining him and there's safety in numbers*).
to be on the safe side not to take any risks (*I don't think it will rain but to be on the safe side I'll take my umbrella*).

sail *vb* (*we sail at dawn*) set sail, embark, put to sea, put off.
salary *n* (*he earns a good salary*) wage, pay, earnings.
same *adj* **1** (*that is the same dress which she wore yesterday*) identical, selfsame, the very. **2** (*the restaurant sells the same old food, week after week*) identical, similar, unchanging, unvarying. ✧

be all the same to (someone) to be a matter of no importance to (someone) (*It's all the same to us whether he goes or stays*).
not be in the same league as (someone) not to be as able, talented, etc., as (someone) (*The new teacher is just not in the same league as the previous one*).
the same old story a situation, etc., that recurs frequently (*It was the same old story. They said that he couldn't have the job because he had no experience but he couldn't find a job to gain the experience*).

sample *n* **1** (*the artist showed the advertising agency a sample of her work*) specimen, example, illustration, instance. **2** (*they gave the questionnaire to a sample of the population*) cross-section, sampling, random sample.
sane *adj* (*he said that he had not been sane when he committed the murder*) of sound mind, in your right mind, rational, rational, lucid, (*inf*) all there.
sarcastic *adj* (*they were hurt by her sarcastic remarks*) caustic, sneering, mocking, scoffing, derisive.
satisfactory *adj* (*they did not find her work satisfactory*) adequate, good enough, all right, acceptable, passable, up to scratch, up to standard.
satisfied *adj* **1** (*they were satisfied with the results, satisfied customers*) pleased, happy, content. (*the police were satisfied that he was innocent*) convinced, sure, certain, positive. **3** (*they felt satisfied after one course of the meal*) full.
satisfy *vb* **1** (*students who satisfy the university entrance requirements*) fulfill, meet, be sufficient for. **2** (*products that satisfy the demands of the customers*) fulfill, gratify. **3** (*find some cool water to satisfy their thirst*) quench, satiate. **4** (*he was able to satisfy her parents that she was telling the truth*) convince, persuade, assure.
savage *adj* **1** (*attacked by a savage animal*) ferocious, fierce, wild. **2** (*during the attack she received a savage blow to the head*) vicious, brutal. **3** (*he was really savage to his family*) brutal, cruel, vicious, harsh, grim, barbarous, merciless. **4** (*the explorers were attacked by*

savage tribe) primitive, uncivilized, wild. ⌖

noble savage a primitive person brought up in primitive surroundings who is thought of as being less corrupt, worthier, etc., than people brought up in ordinary modern circumstances (*The child whom they found living alone in the jungle was hailed as a noble savage*).

save *vb* 1 (*try to save some money for a vacation*) put aside, set aside, put by, keep, reserve, conserve, stockpile, hoard. 2 (*it will save a lot of inconvenience*) prevent, obviate, rule out. 3 (*he saved his friend from death*) rescue, deliver, snatch, free. ⌖

saved by the bell rescued from an unpleasant situation by something suddenly bringing that situation to an end (*The teacher asked him for his homework which he had not done. He was saved by the bell when a parent arrived to see the teacher*) <A reference to a bell that marks the end of a round in boxing>.

say *vb* 1 (*say a few words*) speak, utter, voice, pronounce. 2 (*you should say what you are thinking*) express, tell, put into words, state, communicate, make known, articulate. 3 ("*It's snowing heavily,*" *she said*) state, remark, announce. ⌖

say the word say what you want and your wishes will be carried out (*If you want some food just say the word*).
you can say that again you are absolutely right (*I told her that I thought that the restaurant was very expensive. "You can say that again!" she said*).

scandalous *adj* 1 (*a politician who had to resign because of his scandalous behavior*) disgraceful, dishonorable, shocking, outrageous, disreputable, improper. 2 (*scandalous rumors circulating about the family*) slanderous, libelous.
scant *adj* (*took scant notice of what her mother said*) little, slight, minimal, inadequate, insufficient.
scar *n* (*the accident left him with a scar on his face*) blemish, mark, blotch, disfigurement.
scarce *adj* (*copies of the book are scarce now*) rare, few, few and far between, in short supply, scant, uncommon, unusual.
scare *vb* (*the sight of the man scared the children*)

frighten, make afraid, alarm, startle, terrify, terrorize.
scatter *vb* 1 (*scatter the breadcrumbs for the birds*) spread, sow, sprinkle. 2 (*the crowd scattered when the police arrived*) disperse, break up, separate, disband.
scene *n* 1 (*they visited the scene of the battle*) site, location, position, spot. 2 (*the photographs were taken against a winter scene*) background, setting, landscape, view, vista, outlook. 3 (*it was a moving scene when child and mother were reunited*) event, incident, happening, situation. 4 (*the child made a scene when she did not get her own way*) fuss, outburst, commotion, exhibition, to-do, upset, row. ⌖

behind the scenes out of sight of the public etc. (*Our hostess took all the credit for the successful dinner party but she had a team of caterers behind the scenes*) <A reference to people in a theatrical production who work behind the scenery offstage>.
come on the scene to arrive or appear (*They were happily married until that young woman came on the scene*).
not (someone's) scene not the kind of thing that (someone) likes (*Opera is not his scene*).

scenery *n* (*tourists admiring the scenery*) view, outlook, prospect, vista, landscape.
scent *n* 1 (*he bought her an expensive scent for her* birthday) perfume, fragrance. 2 (*the scent of roses in the room*) perfume, fragrance, smell. 3 (*the scent of newly baked bread*) aroma, smell, bouquet, odor. 4 (*dogs following the scent of the fox*) trail, track, spoor. ⌖

throw (someone) off the scent to distract (someone) from a search for someone or something, eg by giving him or her wrong information (*The police were put off the scent of the real killer when someone made a false confession*) <Refers literally to distracting dogs from the scent of someone or something that they are following>.

scheme *n* 1 (*they have developed a new training scheme for young people*) plan, program, project, system, procedure, strategy, design, tactics. 2 (*a modern color scheme*) arrangement, system.
scoff *vb* (*they began to scoff at his efforts to bake a cake*) jeer at, mock at, laugh at, ridicule.

scold *vb* (*her parents scolded her for being late*) rebuke, reprimand, chide, upbraid.

score *n* **1** (*what was the final score?*) result, outcome. **2** (*she noticed a deep score on the table*) scrape, scratch, groove, cut, mark. ✧

know the score (*inf*) to know exactly what is involved, to know all the facts of a situation (*She knew the score when she married him. He has been in and out of jail all his life*).
settle old scores to get revenge for wrongs committed in the past (*He has just met the man who killed his brother in a fight years ago and wants to settle old scores*).

scorn *n* (*he treated everyone else's ideas with scorn*) contempt, disdain, mockery, derision.

scowl *vb* (*he scowled when they disagreed with him*) frown, glower, glare, look daggers.

scrap *n* **1** (*use scraps of material to make a patchwork quilt*) remnant, fragment, bit, piece, snippet. **2** (*feed the dog scraps of food*) piece, bit, morsel, particle. **3** (*he is a scrap merchant*) waste, junk. **4** (*there was not a scrap of sincerity in what she said*) bit, grain, iota, trace, whit.

scrape *vb* **1** (*scrape the surface of the table*) scratch. **2** (*the child fell and scraped her knee*) graze, scratch, cut.

scratch *vb* **1** (*try to scratch an itchy spot on her back*) rub, tear at. **2** (*she scratched her hand on a rusty nail*) graze, cut, skin, wound. ✧

start from scratch to start from the very beginning without any advantages (*She had absolutely no educational qualifications. She had to start from scratch with her studying*).

scream *vb* (*he screamed when the heavy weight fell on him*) shriek, shout, yell, howl, squeal, yelp, wail.

screen *n* **1** (*a screen at the window to stop people looking in*) drape, blind. **2** (*trees to act as a screen from the wind*) shelter, shield, protection, guard. **3** (*the business was a screen for his drug-dealing*) front, façade, blind, disguise, camouflage, cover, cloak.

scruffy *adj* (*he was told to tidy up, that he was too scruffy to go to school*) untidy, unkempt, disheveled, messy, slovenly.

scurry *vb* (*the children were late and scurried home*) hurry, hasten, rush, run, race, dash, scamper.

seal *vb* **1** (*they sealed the parcel before posting it*) fasten, secure, close up, shut. **2** (*they filled the jars with fruit and sealed them*) make airtight, close, shut, cork. **3** (*the police sealed off the area*) cordon off, shut off, close off. **4** (*they have sealed a bargain*) settle, secure, clinch. ✧

set your seal of approval on (something) to give your agreement or approval to (something) (*The council has set its seal of approval on the new leisure center*).

search *vb* **1** (*the police are searching for clues to the crime*) look for, seek, hunt for, ferret out. **2** (*they searched the building for the missing jewels*) look through, hunt through, rifle through, scour. ✧

search high and low for (someone *or* something) to search absolutely everywhere for (someone or something) (*We searched high and low for the missing ring but did not find it*).

secluded *adj* (*a secluded part of the large garden*) sheltered, private, remote, out-of-the way.

secret *adj* **1** (*they were told to keep the matter secret*) confidential, private, under wraps, (*inf*) hush-hush. **2** (*a desk with a secret drawer*) hidden, concealed.

secretive *adj* (*she is very secretive about where she is going*) reticent, uncommunicative, unforthcoming, silent.

section *n* **1** (*he bought the wood in sections*) part, segment, piece, portion, bit. **2** (*a book divided into sections*) part, division, chapter. **3** (*the children's section of the bookstore*) part, department.

secure *adj* **1** (*the children feel secure at their grandparents' house*) safe, protected, free from danger, out of harm's way. **2** (*they can no longer look forward to a secure future*) safe, settled, solid, dependable, reliable. **3** (*the stepladder is not very secure*) steady, stable, sturdy, solid.

see *vb* **1** (*they could not see the cottage through the mists*) make out, catch sight of, spot, glimpse, look at, discern, perceive, notice, observe, view. **2** (*I see what he means*) understand, grasp, get, comprehend, follow, take in. **3** (*I will go and see where he is*) find out, discover, learn **4** (*we asked her to see that the children went to bed early*) make sure, be sure, ensure, mind, see to it, take care. **5** (*when she asked if she could go on vacation her parents said that they would have to see*) think, have a think, give it some thought, consider, reflect. **6** (*the two friends see each other once a week*) meet, arrange to meet. **7** (*he saw his mother to her door*) escort, accompany, usher, guide, lead. **8** (*did you see the documentary on TV last night?*) watch, look at, view. ▭

see daylight to be coming to the end of a long task (*I have been working for months on this research project but I'm beginning to see daylight*).

see stars to see flashes of light as a result of a bang on the head (*When he bumped his head on the wooden beam he saw stars*).

eek *vb* **1** (*the police are seeking more information*) search for, look for, hunt for. **2** (*after the accident she was advised that she should seek help from a counselor*) request, ask for, solicit.

eem *vb* (*they seem rather pleasant people*) appear to be, look to be, give the impression of being.

eemly *adj* (*they thought that her behavior was far from seemly*) decent, proper, decorous, fitting, suitable, appropriate, becoming.

eize *vb* **1** (*he seized a hanging branch to pull himself out of the water*) grab, grab hold of, take hold of, grasp, grip, clutch at. **2** (*kidnappers seized the children*) snatch, kidnap, abduct.

eldom *adv* (*we seldom see them*) rarely, hardly ever, infrequently.

elect *vb* (*the little boy was asked to select a toy as a present*) choose, pick, opt for, decide on, settle on, plump for.

elfish *adj* (*the child is selfish and will not share anything with his friends*) self-centered, self-seeking, egotistic, egocentric.

ell *vb* **1** (*they plan to sell their house soon*) put on sale, put up for sale. **2** (*stores selling foodstuffs*) offer for sale, stock, carry, deal in, market. ▭

sell (someone) down the river to betray or be disloyal to (someone) (*He sold his friend down the river by telling the police that she had been present at the crime*) <Refers historically to selling slaves in America from the upper Mississippi states to buyers in Louisiana where working and living conditions were much harsher>.

end *vb* **1** (*send a parcel by airmail*) dispatch, convey, transport, mail. **2** (*she sent her parents a message that she was well*) communicate, convey, transmit.

sensational *adj* (*tabloid newspapers with a sensational story about a politician*) spectacular, exciting, dramatic, startling, shocking, scandalous.

sense *n* **1** (*a sense of smell*) sensation, faculty, feeling. **2** (*they have no sense of honor*) awareness, understanding, appreciation. **3** (*he now has a sense of shame*) feeling. **4** (*the child had the sense to wait for her mother*) common sense, intelligence, cleverness, wisdom, practicality. **5** (*a word with more than one sense*) meaning, definition. ▭

come to your senses to begin to behave or think sensibly (*He was going to leave his job and go around the world but he came to his senses when he counted up the cost*).

sixth sense intuition, an ability to feel or realize something not perceived by the five senses of sight, hearing, smell, taste, and touch (*He could not see anyone but a sixth sense told him that he was not alone*).

take leave of your senses to become deranged or very foolish (*I think that she's taken leave of her senses. She has left her husband and children to go off with an absolutely horrible man*).

sensitive *adj* **1** (*she has very sensitive skin*) delicate, fine, soft. **2** (*she is very sensitive to noise*) easily affected by, susceptible to. **3** (*she is a very sensitive person*) responsive, perceptive, sympathetic, understanding. **4** (*she is too sensitive to work in such a competitive firm*) over-sensitive, thin-skinned, touchy. **5** (*the two sides were discussing a very sensitive issue*) delicate, difficult, problematic, thorny.

sentence *n* **1** (*the judge delivered his sentence*) judgment, verdict, ruling, decision. **2** (*her attacker is serving a 10-year sentence*) prison sentence, prison term.

sentimental *adj* **1** (*the vase is not valuable but she has a sentimental attachment to it*) emotional, nostalgic. **2** (*the group was singing sentimental love songs*) emotional, overemotional, romantic, mawkish, maudlin, (*inf*) soppy, (*inf*) schmaltzy.

separate *adj* **1** (*the two issues are quite separate*) unconnected, unrelated, divorced, distinct, different. **2** (*they have separate apartments*) individual, independent, different. ▭

separate the men from the boys to distinguish the good, useful, strong, etc., people from the bad, useless, weak, etc., ones (*The coach said that this game would separate the men from the boys*).

series *n* (*a series of sporting events/a series of misfortunes*) succession, progression, sequence, chain, train, run, cycle, order.

serious *adj* **1** (*the principal was looking very serious*) solemn, grave, earnest, unsmiling, somber, sober. **2** (*the accident victim has serious injuries*) bad, grave, critical, acute, dangerous. **3** (*they have several serious matters to discuss*) grave, important, weighty, of consequence, urgent, pressing, crucial, vital. **4** (*make a serious attempt at the championship*) earnest, determined, resolute, honest, sincere.

serve *vb* **1** (*he has served his master loyally for many years*) be in the service of, work for, be employed by. **2** (*people who have served the community*) be of service to, be of use to, help, assist, benefit, support. **3** (*he served three years as a plumber's apprentice*) spend, carry out, fulfill, complete. **4** (*a couch that will also serve as a bed*) function, act as, do duty as. **5** (*the hostess is just about to serve the first course*) dish up, give out, deal out. **6** (*she is trying to find a sales clerk to serve her*) attend to, assist.

service *n* **1** (*she retired after 40 years' service with the firm*) work, employment. **2** (*we did him a service by telling him the truth about his friends*) good turn, benefit, advantage, help, assistance. **3** (*his car is due for a service*) overhaul, checkup, repair, maintenance. **4** (*guests at the wedding service*) ceremony, rite, ritual. ✧

at (someone's) service ready to be of assistance to (someone) (*He said that his chauffeur was at our service for the day*).

session *n* (*old friends having a good gossip session*) time, period, spell.

set *vb* **1** (*set their bags down on the sidewalk*) put, put down, lay down, place, deposit. **2** (*set the jewel in a gold ring*) fix, embed, arrange, mount. **3** (*set the thermostat*) regulate, adjust. **4** (*set the house on fire*) put, cause to be, start. **5** (*the Jell-o will not set*) solidify, thicken, harden, gel. **6** (*at what time does the sun set?*) go down, sink, subside. **7** (*the runner set a new record for the course*) set up, establish, create, institute. **8**

(*we must set a date for the annual dinner*) fix establish, settle, agree on, decide on, select. (*his behavior set them talking*) start, cause **10** (*the teacher set the children a test*) assign allot. ✧

set about (someone *or* **something) 1** to begin (something or doing something) (*How will you set about finding your father after all these years?*). **2** to attack (someone or something) (*The thug set about the old man with an iron bar*).

settle *vb* **1** (*we must settle on a date for the annual dance*) set, decide on, agree on, fix, arrange choose, select. **2** (*I hope they settle the dispute soon*) clear up, resolve, bring to an end conclude. **3** (*he wants to settle his financial affairs before he dies*) set to rights, put in order arrange, clear out, straighten up. **4** (*enough money to settle their bills*) pay, meet. **5** (*the coffee dregs had settled at the foot of the cup*) sink subside, fall. **6** (*she was so upset that the doctor had to give her something to settle her*) calm calm down, quiet, sedate, compose, tranquilize **7** (*the family emigrated from Ireland to settle in America*) make your home, take up residence go to live, move to. **8** (*a part of America settled by Scots*) establish, colonize, occupy, inhabit populate.

sever *vb* **1** (*in the accident he severed his leg at the knee*) cut off, chop off, lop off. **2** (*he had to sever the logs in two*) divide, split. **3** (*the two families quarreled and severed relations with each other*) break off, suspend, end, terminate

several *adj* **1** (*she has invited several people to dinner*) some, a number of, a few. **2** (*eventually we all went our several ways*) separate, different, respective, individual, particular.

severe *adj* **1** (*he wore a very severe expression*) stern, grim, forbidding, disapproving, somber serious. **2** (*the tyrant ruled over a severe regime*) harsh, hard, strict, cruel, brutal, savage merciless. **3** (*she always wore severe clothing*) plain, simple, unadorned, austere. **4** (*we have had a severe winter*) harsh, hard, extreme. (*she suffers from severe pain in her legs*) extreme, intense, fierce, strong, violent, very bad

shabby *adj* **1** (*she wore shabby clothing*) worn threadbare, scruffy. **2** (*the house is looking rather shabby*) dilapidated, run-down, broken-down tumbledown, ramshackle, dingy, seedy, squalid slumlike. **3** (*the way he treated her was shabby*) despicable, dishonorable, mean, shoddy.

shade *n* **1** (*they sat in the shade of a tree*) shadow, cover. **2** (*a shade of blue*) color, tint, tone, hue. **3** (*a shade against the light*) screen, shield, cover, blind. ✧

shades of (someone *or* something) that reminds me of (someone or something) (*The food at the conference reminded me of school dinners. Shades of childhood!*) <It is as though the shade or ghost of someone or something was present>.

hadow *n* **1** (*we sat in the shadow of the tree*) shade, cover. **2** (*the shadow of the children on the wall*) silhouette, outline, shape. ✧

cast a shadow over (something) to lessen the happiness or joy of (something) (*Knowing that he was going away cast a shadow over her last meeting with him*).

hady *adj* **1** (*sit in a shady part of the garden on a hot day*) shaded, shadowy, sheltered, screened, dark, dim. **2** (*the store is run by rather a shady character*) suspicious, suspect, questionable, devious, underhand, dishonest, dishonorable.

hake *vb* **1** (*the child shook her bank to hear the coins jingling*) rattle, jolt, jerk. **2** (*the car shook as we drove over the stony roads*) bump, jolt, bounce, rock, roll. **3** (*the child was feverish and was shaking*) shiver, quiver, tremble, quake, shudder. **4** (*her failure had shaken her confidence for future tournaments*) undermine, lessen, weaken. **5** (*she was obviously shaken by the news of the accident*) disturb, upset, shock, agitate, perturb, disquiet, disconcert. ✧

in two shakes of a lamb's tail in an extremely short time (*Your mother will be back in two shakes of a lamb's tail*).
no great shakes not very good or important (*I think our team is bound to win. The opposition is no great shakes*).

hame *n* **1** (*he seemed to feel no shame at his crime*) guilt, remorse, humiliation. **2** (*it was a shame that it rained on the picnic*) pity, misfortune, bad luck. **3** (*she felt that he had brought shame to the school by his action*) disgrace, dishonor, scandal, discredit, disrepute, ignominy.

hape *n* **1** (*children playing with pieces of card-board of different shapes*) form, formation, outline. **2** (*help came in the shape of a passing motorist*) form, guise, appearance. **3** (*put the Jello in shapes*) mold. **4** (*the players must be in good shape for tomorrow's game*) condition, state, fettle, trim. ✧

knock (someone *or* something) into shape to get (someone or something) into the desired or good condition (*The present office system is chaotic but we will soon knock it into shape*).
shape up to be developing into the desired state or form (*The new player was not very good to start with but he is shaping up now*).

share *n* (*each of them will receive a share of the profits*) portion, part, quota, percentage, division, allocation.

sharp *adj* **1** (*need a sharp knife to carve the meat*) keen, razor-edged. **2** (*the child was injured by a sharp length of metal*) pointed, spiky. **3** (*she felt a sharp pain in her side*) acute, intense, keen, piercing, stabbing, severe. **4** (*the sauce had rather a sharp taste*) pungent, sour, tart, bitter, biting. **5** (*there is a sharp drop to the sea just there*) steep, sheer, abrupt. **6** (*he was sharp enough to realize that they were trying to swindle him*) clever, shrewd, bright, smart, intelligent. **7** (*she sounded rather sharp on the phone*) abrupt, brusque, curt, short.

sheer *adj* **1** (*it was sheer stupidity to behave like that*) utter, downright, total, complete, out-and-out. **2** (*it was a sheer drop to the sea*) steep, abrupt, sharp.

sheet *n* **1** (*a sheet of glass*) piece, length, panel. **2** (*a sheet of ice on the roadway*) layer, coat, coating, cover, covering, film, blanket, carpet. **3** (*sheets of water left after the flood*) expanse, stretch.

shelf *n* (*build a shelf for the books*) ledge.

shield *vb* (*try to shield her eyes from the sun/shield the children from danger*) protect, screen, guard, safeguard.

shine *vb* (*the street lights were shining*) gleam, glow, glint, sparkle, flash, glitter, shimmer.

shiver *vb* (*they began to shiver with cold*) shake, quiver, tremble, shudder, quake.

shock *vb* (*she was shocked by the state of the slum housing*) appall, horrify, outrage, disturb, amaze, astound, traumatize.

short *adj* **1** (*he is too short to reach the branch*) small, tiny, diminutive. **2** (*a short vacation/a short relationship*) brief, short-lived, short-term, fleeting. **3** (*she was asked to write a short account of the incident*) brief, concise, succinct, terse. **4** (*she was rather short on the phone*) sharp, brusque, abrupt, curt. **5** (*their supply of money is getting a bit short*) deficient, insufficient, scarce, scanty, sparse, meager, tight. ✧

give (someone *or* something) short shrift to spend very little time or thought on (someone or something) (*She resigned and then asked for her job back but she was given short shrift*).
short and sweet to the point, short and to the point (*When he left the firm his farewell speech was short and sweet*).

shot *n* **1** (*hear a shot*) gunfire, report of a gun, bang, blast, explosion. **2** (*have a shot at winning*) try, attempt, effort, (*inf*) go, (*inf*) stab. **3** (*take shots at trying to hit the target*) turn, opportunity. **4** (*tourists taking shots of the beauty spot*) photograph, photo, snapshot, snap, film. **5** (*have to have several shots before going on a trip to the tropics*) vaccination, inoculation, injection, (*inf*) jab. ✧

like a shot very quickly (*They were out of the office like a shot at five o'clock*).

shout *vb* (*they shouted to attract his attention/He shouted out in pain*) cry, call, yell, howl, roar, scream, bellow.
show *vb* **1** (*show the new products to the customers*) display, exhibit, present, demonstrate, set forth. **2** (*show them how to use the machine*) demonstrate, point out, explain, teach, instruct. **3** (*he showed his displeasure by leaving the meeting early*) indicate, demonstrate, express, manifest, make known, reveal. **4** (*the effects of his illness are beginning to show*) be visible, be seen, be obvious, appear. **5** (*ushers to show them to their seats at the wedding service*) escort, accompany, guide, usher, conduct. ✧

for show for appearance, in order to impress people (*The country's annual military procession is just for show*).
show off to behave in such a way as to try to impress others with your possessions, abilities, etc. (*The child has just learned to dance and is showing off*).

shrewd *adj* (*a shrewd businessman*) astute, clever, smart, sharp.
shrill *adj* (*a shrill voice*) high-pitched, high, sharp, piercing, penetrating, screeching, shrieking.
shrink *vb* **1** (*that blouse might shrink in the wash*) get smaller. **2** (*the market for goods like that will shrink*) grow less, become smaller, contract, diminish, fall off, drop off. **3** (*they shrank from him in fear*) draw back, coil, flinch, cringe.
shut *vb* (*please shut the door when everyone is here*) close, fasten, secure, lock.
shy *adj* (*she is too shy to say much in public*) bashful, reserved, reticent, retiring, withdrawn, self-effacing, self-conscious, timid.
sick *adj* **1** (*she has been sick and is staying home from work*) ill, unwell, indisposed, poorly, ailing, below par, (*inf*) under the weather. **2** (*she felt sick on the sea voyage*) nauseated, queasy, bilious. **3** (*he is sick of his present job*) tired, weary, bored, jaded, (*inf*) fed up. **4** (*that was rather a sick joke*) morbid, macabre, ghoulish, gruesome.
side *n* **1** (*flowers growing by the side of the river*) edge, border, verge. **2** (*the upper side of the desk*) surface, part. **3** (*they live on the north side of the town*) part, area, region, district, quarter, section, neighborhood. **4** (*discuss all sides of the problem*) aspect, angle, facet, point of view, viewpoint, standpoint. **5** (*on his side in the dispute*) camp, faction, party, group, wing. **6** (*the side that is playing against them tomorrow*) team, squad. ✧

on the side in a way other than by means of your ordinary occupation (*He has a full-time job as a teacher but he earns a bit on the side as a bartender*).
side by side beside one another (*They climbed the hill side by side*).
take sides to support a particular person, group, etc., against another (*Two of the workers quarreled and the whole office took sides*).

sight *n* **1** (*it was her first sight of the old family house*) view, glimpse. **2** (*the child was told to stay within sight of her parents*) view, range of vision, field of vision. **3** (*her sight is now poor*) eyesight, vision, eyes, power of sight. **4** (*visitor going on a tour of the town's sights*) spectacle. **5** (*what a sight she was in that hat!*) spectacle, eyesore, mess, (*inf*) fright. ✧

set your sights on (something) to try to obtain (something) (*She has set her sights on that big house at the edge of the village*) <A reference to the sight of a gun>.

sign *n* **1** (*her thinness was a sign of her illness*) indication, symptom, evidence, clue. **2** (*a sign indicating the way to the museum*) signpost, notice, placard. **3** (*he gave them a sign to stay still*) signal, gesture, motion, movement, gesticulation. **4** (*mathematical signs*) symbol. **5** (*they believed that they would be given a sign of forthcoming tragedy*) omen, portent, warning.

silent *adj* **1** (*it was very silent on the hills at night*) quiet, hushed, peaceful, tranquil. **2** (*they were completely silent as he told them the news*) speechless, wordless, unspeaking, without speaking, mute, taciturn, mum, uncommunicative. **3** (*she was upset by their silent reproach*) unspoken, wordless, unsaid, unexpressed, tacit, implicit. ⇨

the silent majority the people who make up most of the population but who rarely make their views known although these are thought to be moderate and reasonable (*The politicians stated that it was time that the silent majority had an influence on the running of the country*).

silly *adj* **1** (*she is a very silly person*) foolish, stupid, irresponsible, giddy, frivolous, immature. **2** (*it was a very silly thing to do*) foolish, stupid, senseless, idiotic, unwise, foolhardy, irresponsible, ridiculous, absurd.

simple *adj* **1** (*it was a very simple task*) easy, uncomplicated, elementary, straightforward, effortless. **2** (*you will have to explain it to them in simple language*) plain, uncomplicated, clear, straightforward, direct, intelligible. **3** (*they are wealthy but lead a very simple life*) ordinary, modest, unpretentious, humble. **4** (*she was a simple peasant girl*) unsophisticated, innocent, naive, inexperienced. **5** (*the boy is a bit simple*) simple-minded, feeble-minded, backward.

sin *n* (*they will be punished for their sin*) wrong, wrongdoing, evil, evildoing, badness, crime, offense, immorality.

sincere *adj* (*her apology was obviously sincere*) genuine, real, true, honest, wholehearted, heartfelt.

single *adj* **1** (*only a single flower was left bloom-*

ing) sole, solitary, one, lone, isolated, by itself. **2** (*he is still single*) unmarried, unwed, unattached, free.

sink *vb* **1** (*the ship began to sink*) go under, submerge, founder, capsize. **2** (*he sank to his knees to ask forgiveness*) fall, drop, slump. **3** (*the invalid is thought to be sinking rapidly*) decline, deteriorate, fail, fade.

sit *vb* **1** (*the audience was asked to sit*) sit down, take a seat, be seated. **2** (*their bags were sitting on the sidewalk*) be placed, be situated. **3** (*the assembly was sitting all night*) be in session, meet, assemble. **4** (*we require a table that sits 12 people*) seat, accommodate, hold, have room for.

situation *n* **1** (*a cottage in a picturesque situation*) place, position, location, setting, site. **2** (*the firm is in an unstable financial situation*) circumstances, state, state of affairs, condition, predicament. **3** (*there is a vacant situation in the accounts department*) post, position, job, place.

size *n* (*measure the size of the room*) dimensions, measurements, proportions, area, extent. ⇨

size (someone *or* **something) up** to consider carefully and form an opinion of the worth, nature, etc., of (someone or something) (*You should size up the employment position before you leave your job*).

skeptical, sceptical (*Br, Cdn*) *adj* (*she was skeptical about her chances of success*) doubtful, dubious, distrustful, mistrustful, unconvinced.

skillful *adj* (*he is a very skillful carpenter*) skilled, able, good, competent, adept, accomplished, expert, deft, masterly.

slack *adj* **1** (*she has lost a lot of weight and her clothing is now slack*) loose, baggy. **2** (*since he stopped exercising his muscles have got slack*) limp, flabby, flaccid. **3** (*business is slack just now*) slow, quiet, inactive, sluggish. **4** (*the students have got rather slack about their work*) negligent, neglectful, remiss, careless, slapdash, slipshod.

slap *vb* (*she slapped his face*) strike, hit, whack, cuff (*inf*) wallop. ⇨

a slap on the wrist a reprimand (*She will get a slap on the wrist for forgetting to give the boss the message*).

sleep n (*have a short sleep after lunch*) nap, doze, rest, (*inf*) snooze, (*inf*) forty winks. ✧

put (something) to sleep to kill (an animal) painlessly because it is incurably ill, etc. (*The vet put the dog to sleep when it lost the use of its legs*).
sleep like a log to sleep extremely soundly (*I didn't hear a noise in the night. I slept like a log*).

sleepy adj 1 (*she had not had much rest and was feeling sleepy*) tired, drowsy, lethargic, sluggish. 2 (*a sleepy little village*) quiet, peaceful, inactive.

slight adj 1 (*there had been a slight improvement*) small, little, minute, subtle, modest. 2 (*slight matters*) unimportant, minor, insignificant, trifling, trivial. 3 (*she was very slight*) slightly built, slender, slim, small, delicate.

slip vb 1 (*the old lady slipped on the ice and broke her leg*) slide, skid, slither, lose your footing. 2 (*the cup slipped from her grasp*) fall, slide, drop. 3 (*she became upset and slipped from the room*) steal, creep, sneak. 4 (*she just had time to slip on some clothing*) put on, pull on. 5 (*some people think that educational standards have slipped*) drop, fall, decline, deteriorate. ✧

let (something) slip to say or reveal (something) accidentally (*I'm sorry that I let slip that you're leaving*). ✧

slope n 1 (*the floors of the building are on a slight slope*) slant, angle, inclination, tilt, dip. 2 (*they had a picnic on a grassy slope*) hill, hillock, bank, rise.

slow adj 1 (*they moved along at a very slow pace*) slow-moving, leisurely, unhurried, dawdling, snail-like. 2 (*getting planning permission can be a slow process*) slow-moving, drawn-out, long-drawn-out, prolonged, protracted, time-consuming. 3 (*pupils who are rather slow*) slow-witted, backward, stupid, unintelligent. 4 (*business is rather slow*) slack, quiet, sluggish.

sly adj (*it is difficult to know what he is doing—he is very sly*) cunning, crafty, wily, artful, sneaky, devious, underhand, scheming, shifty, furtive.

small adj 1 (*the child is very small for her age*) little, tiny, slight, short, diminutive, undersized, (*inf*) pint-sized. 2 (*it was just a small mistake*) slight, minor, unimportant, insignificant, trifling, trivial. 3 (*he is rich and powerful but came from small beginnings*) humble, low, lowly, modest, poor, inferior. ✧

make (someone) look small to make (someone) seem foolish or insignificant (*He made her look small by criticizing her in front of the whole school*).
small talk light conversation about unimportant or light-hearted matters (*He always talks about his work. He has absolutely no small talk*).

smart adj 1 (*you must try to look smart for your job interview*) well-dressed, elegant, neat, spruce, (*inf*) natty. 2 (*the child is smart for her age*) clever, bright, intelligent, sharp. ✧

a smart aleck someone who thinks that he or she is very clever and acts as though this were the case (*He is such a smart aleck that he tried to teach us our jobs when we have been doing them for years*).

smash vb 1 (*she smashed several plates when doing the dishes*) break, shatter. 2 (*he smashed his father's car*) crash, wreck, collide. 3 (*our hopes of success were smashed*) shatter, ruin, wreck.

smell n 1 (*the smell of roses*) scent, perfume, fragrance. 2 (*the smell of freshly baked bread*) aroma, odor. 3 (*the smell of rotting meat*) stink, stench. ✧

smell a rat to have a suspicion that something is wrong or that you are being deceived (*I smelled a rat when she did not ask me into the house*) <A reference to a terrier hunting rats>.

smooth adj 1 (*smooth surfaces*) even, level, flat, plane. 2 (*the sea was very smooth*) calm, still, flat, tranquil. 3 (*he is responsible for the smooth running of the firm*) trouble-free, steady, regular, effortless. 4 (*young men with smooth faces*) clean-shaven, hairless. 5 (*she was approached in the store by a smooth sales clerk*) smooth-tongued, suave, glib, urbane, courteous, gracious.

smother vb 1 (*she was accused of trying to smother the old lady with a pillow*) suffocate, stifle. 2 (*she tried to smother a giggle*) suppress, stifle, muffle.

snag n (*he did not see the possible snags in his plans*) drawback, hitch, catch, obstacle, stumbling-block.

snap vb 1 (*the branch suddenly snapped*) break

splinter, fracture, crack. **2** (*she snapped her fingers*) click, crack. **3** (*the dog snapped at our ankles*) bite, snarl, growl. **4** (*she was tired and began to snap at the children*) speak irritably, shout, growl, snarl. **5** (*she was behaving very calmly and then she suddenly snapped*) collapse, break down.

snatch *vb* **1** (*she was late and had to snatch a piece of toast from the table and run for the bus*) grab, seize, take hold of. **2** (*the thief snatched my purse at the airport*) rob, steal, make off with. **3** (*they snatched the millionaire's child and demanded a ransom*) kidnap, abduct, seize, grab.

sneer *vb* (*sneering at her attempts*) smirk, snicker, scoff, scorn, mock, jeer.

snobbish *adj* (*she has a very snobbish attitude toward people who are badly off*) arrogant, haughty, proud, disdainful, condescending, (*inf*) snooty, (*inf*) uppity.

soak *vb* **1** (*they got soaked in the storm*) drench, wet through, saturate. **2** (*soak the dress in cold water to remove the stain*) steep, immerse. **3** (*blood soaking through the bandage*) penetrate, permeate.

sob *vb* (*she began to sob as her mother left*) weep, cry, wail.

sociable *adj* (*our neighbors are very sociable people*) friendly, affable, social, communicative, outgoing.

soft *adj* **1** (*the car got stuck in soft mud*) spongy, mushy. **2** (*the ground by the river was very soft*) swampy, spongy, boggy. **3** (*soft substances such as modeling clay*) pliable, pliant, flexible. **4** (*a dress of a soft material*) smooth, silky, velvety. **5** (*dresses in soft colors*) pale, light, pastel, muted, subdued, restrained. **6** (*the lighting in the room was very soft*) low, dim, faint, muted, subdued. **7** (*she spoke in a soft voice so that the others would not hear*) quiet, hushed, low, faint, whispered. **8** (*parents accused of being too soft with their children*) lenient, indulgent, easygoing, permissive, liberal. ▷

a soft touch (*inf*) someone who is easily taken advantage of, deceived, etc. (*He would lend money to anyone who asked him. He's a really soft touch*).

soil *n* **1** (*the soil is very poor in that area*) earth, ground, dirt. **2** (*troops killed on foreign soil*) land, country.

solemn *adj* **1** (*she wore a solemn expression*) grave, serious, unsmiling, somber. **2** (*it was a*

solemn occasion) serious, grave, important, formal, grand, stately, dignified, ceremonious. **3** (*a solemn promise*) earnest, sincere, genuine, honest.

solid *adj* **1** (*a solid rather than a liquid substance*) firm, hard, dense, thick. **2** (*jewelry made of solid gold*) pure, unalloyed, complete. **3** (*solid houses made of stone and built to last*) substantial, strong, sturdy.

solitary *adj* **1** (*he leads a solitary life with no family or friends*) lonesome, friendless, unsociable. **2** (*a solitary tree in the barren landscape*) single, lone, sole, by yourself/itself.

solution *n* **1** (*unable to find the solution to the mathematical problem*) answer, result, resolution. **2** (*a solution of salt and water*) suspension, mixture.

soothe *vb* **1** (*an ointment to soothe the painful sunburn*) ease, alleviate, lessen, reduce. **2** (*he tried to soothe the crying baby*) quiet, calm, pacify.

sophisticated *adj* **1** (*she regards herself as being a sophisticated city-dweller*) worldly, experienced, cultivated, cultured, urbane, suave, cosmopolitan. **2** (*an office equipped with sophisticated electronic equipment*) advanced, complex, complicated, elaborate.

sore *adj* **1** (*she has a sore patch on her arm*) painful, in pain, aching, tender, raw, smarting, inflamed, bruised. **2** (*people in sore need of somewhere to live*) urgent, pressing, desperate, critical, dire.

sorry *adj* **1** (*he is not at all sorry for his misdeeds*) apologetic, regretful, ashamed, repentant, penitent, remorseful. **2** (*we were sorry to hear that she was sick*) sad, unhappy, distressed, regretful. **3** (*they felt sorry for the homeless people*) sympathetic, compassionate, full of pity, moved.

sort *n* (*several different sorts of vegetable/a new sort of computer*) kind, variety, type, class, category, make, brand. ▷

it takes all sorts a saying indicating that you should be tolerant of all people, whatever they are like (*The new neighbors seem a bit odd to us but I suppose it takes all sorts*).
out of sorts not feeling very well, not in a very good mood (*He has been out of sorts since he had the flu*).

sound *n* **1** (*there was not a sound from the children's room*) noise. **2** (*the sound of someone playing the recorder*) noise, music. **3** (*we did*

not like the sound of their plans for improvement)
impression, idea.

sour *adj* **1** (*a sauce that was rather sour*) tart, acid,
bitter, sharp. **2** (*milk that had turned sour*)
curdled, bad, rancid, off. **3** (*he is a sour old man*)
ill-tempered, disagreeable, irritable, cross.

space *n* **1** (*travel in space*) outer space, infinity. **2**
(*large pieces of furniture that take up a great
deal of space*) room, expanse, area, scope. **3**
(*there was only a narrow space between each
house*) gap, interval, opening, break. **4** (*there is
a space on the form to explain why you want the
job*) blank space, blank, empty space, gap. **5**
(*they both died within the space of two years*)
time, period, span, interval, duration. **6** (*there
are no spaces left on the course*) place, room.

spare *adj* **1** (*take a spare pair of socks*) extra, additional, reserve, supplementary, surplus. **2** (*she
works long hours and has little spare time*) free,
unoccupied, leisure.

sparse *adj* (*a sparse covering of grass*) scanty,
meager, slight.

spasm *n* **1** (*he is in agony with stomach spasms*)
contraction, cramp. **2** (*limb spasms*) twitching,
convulsion. **3** (*a sudden spasm of coughing*) fit,
convulsion, bout, attack.

speak *vb* **1** (*did he speak the truth?*) say, tell, state,
utter, voice, express, pronounce. **2** (*the two sisters quarreled and have not spoken to each other
for years*) talk to, converse with, communicate
with, chat. **3** (*the lecturer is to speak for an hour*)
talk, lecture, deliver a speech.

special *adj* **1** (*we were asked to take special care of
the book*) especial, particular, exceptional,
extraspecial. **2** (*it was a special occasion for the
old people*) unusual, exceptional, remarkable,
out-of-the ordinary, notable, outstanding,
memorable, significant, important, momentous.

spectacular *adj* (*a spectacular firework display*)
striking, remarkable, impressive, magnificent,
splendid, sensational, breathtaking, dramatic.

speech *n* **1** (*the power of speech*) talk, communication. **2** (*he was drunk and his speech was
slurred*) diction, pronunciation. **3** (*he gave a
speech thanking everyone*) talk, lecture, address.

speed *n* **1** (*the speed at which they were going*) rate.
2 (*they moved with amazing speed*) rapidity,
swiftness, fastness, quickness, haste, hurry.

spend *vb* **1** (*they will have to spend a great deal
of money on that house*) pay out, lay out, expend,
(*inf*) fork out, (*inf*) shell out. **2** (*they spend hours

on the beach) pass, while away, fill, occupy. **3** (*a
great deal of effort was spent on the task*) use,
employ, apply, devote.

spill *vb* (*water was spilling from the bucket as she
walked*) flow, pour, overflow, brim over, run
over, slop over.

spirit *n* **1** (*his spirit was troubled*) soul, psyche,
inner self. **2** (*they were people of determined
spirit*) character, temperament, disposition,
quality. **2** (*he required spirit to undertake the
journey*) courage, bravery, mettle, pluck, determination. **4** (*the children performed the play
with spirit*) liveliness, animation, enthusiasm,
energy, vivacity, verve.

spite *n* (*she damaged her friend's bike out of spite*)
malice, maliciousness, ill-will, hostility, resentment, vindictiveness.

splendid *adj* **1** (*we had a splendid vacation*) excellent, fine, first-class, superb, marvelous,
wonderful, great. **2** (*a splendid royal palace*)
magnificent, sumptuous, imposing, impressive,
glorious, luxurious.

split *vb* **1** (*split the logs for the fire*) break, chop,
cut. **2** (*the plate seemed just to split in two*) break,
snap, splinter. **3** (*the robbers split the profits from
the burglary amongst themselves*) divide, share,
apportion, distribute. **4** (*the argument over the
local school split the village into two groups*)
divide, separate. **5** (*the couple have split up*)
separate, part, divorce, break up.

spoil *vb* **1** (*a substance that spoiled the surface of
the table*) damage, mar, impair, blemish, deface,
ruin, destroy. **2** (*she spoils her daughter*)
overindulge, indulge, pamper, cosset,
mollycoddle.

spot *n* **1** (*spots of soot on the washing on the line*)
mark, speck, fleck, dot, smudge, stain, blotch.
2 (*get ointment for the spots on her chin*) pimple,
pustule, boil, blemish. **3** (*a pleasant spot for a
country cottage*) place, area, location, site,
situation, setting.

spread *vb* **1** (*they spread rumors*) circulate,
transmit, publicize. **2** (*feeling against the new
road is spreading*) extend, increase, escalate,
mushroom. **3** (*the farmer spread fertilizer on
the fields*) lay, put, apply, cover. **4** (*the bird spread
its wings and flew off*) stretch, extend, open out,
unfurl.

squeeze *vb* **1** (*squeeze limes to make a cool drink*)
squash, crush, compress. **2** (*she squeezed his
arm to attract his attention*) pinch, press, grip.

3 (*she squeezed the water from the dress and hung it up*) wring, twist, press. **4** (*they squeezed the water from the wet sweaters*) extract, press, force, express. **5** (*the speaker was so popular that the audience was squeezed into the hall*) crush, squash, pack, crowd, cram, jam, wedge.

stage *n* **1** (*the stages in the production process*) point, step, period, level, phase. **2** (*the first stage of the journey*) lap, leg, phase. **3** (*she was too nervous to go on the stage*) platform, dais, rostrum, podium.

stand *vb* **1** (*the audience was asked to stand*) rise, get to your feet, get up, be upright, be erect, be vertical. **2** (*the apartment building that used to stand here*) be, be situated, be located. **3** (*stand the bookcase against the wall near the fireplace*) place, put, position, erect, set up. **4** (*they appealed against the judge's ruling but the sentence stood*) remain, stay, hold, hold good, prevail. **5** (*she cannot stand loud noise*) put up with, tolerate, bear, endure, abide.

start *vb* **1** (*before the war started*) begin, commence, get underway, come into being. **2** (*start the machine*) turn on, put on, set in motion, activate. **3** (*she started a new society*) begin, commence, set up, establish, found, launch.

state *n* **1** (*a system in a state of chaos*) condition, situation, circumstances, position, state of affairs, predicament. **2** (*she was in a tearful state*) condition, mood, humor, frame of mind. **3** (*his mother got into a state when he did not come home*) panic, fluster, (*inf*) flap. **4** (*occasions of state attended by the queen*) pomp, ceremony, majesty, grandeur. **5** (*the various states in the world*) country, nation, land.

state *vb* (*state their reasons for going*) express, voice, utter, say, declare, tell, announce.

stay *vb* **1** (*they left but we decided to stay*) remain, wait, linger. **2** (*she stayed angry a long time*) remain, continue. **3** (*they stayed at a small hotel*) put up, reside.

steady *adj* **1** (*drive at a steady pace*) uniform, even, regular, consistent. **2** (*try to keep the table steady on the moving ship*) stable, immovable, unmoving, motionless. **3** (*her steady love for him*) constant, unchanging, unfaltering, continuous, endless. **4** (*require a steady young person for the job*) sensible, level-headed, calm, reliable.

step *n* **1** (*take one step nearer the sea*) stride. **2** (*she listened for her father's steps on the stairs*) footstep, footfall, tread. **3** (*she took a rash step*)

act, course of action, move, deed. **4** (*looking for the next step in his promotion*) stage, level, grade, rank, degree. **5** (*a rotten step on the ladder*) rung, tread.

stick *vb* **1** (*the child began to stick the pictures in a book*) glue, paste, gum, attach, fix, pin, tack. **2** (*she stuck a knife in the meat to see if it was cooked*) thrust, push, jab, poke, insert. **3** (*the machine has stuck*) jam, stop, halt, come to a halt.

stiff *adj* **1** (*a piece of stiff card*) rigid, hard, unyielding, inflexible. **2** (*her muscles are stiff after the long climb*) tight, tense, taut. **3** (*the robbers received a stiff sentence*) severe, harsh, hard, heavy, drastic, stringent. **4** (*she was rather stiff when we arrived*) formal, cold, aloof.

still *adj* **1** (*it was a still day*) calm, windless. **2** (*they were asked to stay completely still*) motionless, immobile, stationary. **3** (*the house was still*) quiet, peaceful, silent, hushed.

stop *vb* **1** (*they tried to stop the fight*) bring to a halt, halt, end, finish, terminate, bring to a standstill, wind up. **2** (*she could not stop shivering*) refrain from, desist, cease, leave, hinder, impede, obstruct.

story *n* **1** (*a story about dragons*) tale, fairy story, myth, legend, fable. **2** (*the story of how he got home*) account, report.

straight *adj* **1** (*the picture is not straight*) level, in line. **2** (*a straight line*) uncurving, unbent. **3** (*they would not give a straight answer*) direct, forthright, frank, candid, honest, sincere.

strange *adj* **1** (*it was a strange sight*) peculiar, odd, queer, bizarre, weird. **2** (*a market stocking strange fruits*) exotic, foreign, alien, unfamiliar.

strong *adj* **1** (*require someone strong to lift the heavy furniture*) powerful, muscular, well-built, burly, sturdy, strapping, robust. **2** (*strong doors at the castle entrance*) solid, heavy, sturdy. **3** (*they have a very strong argument against closing the station*) sound, powerful, compelling. **4** (*there is a strong similarity between the two styles*) marked, noticeable, pronounced, distinct, definite, striking. **5** (*they have strong feelings on the subject of education*) intense, fervent, passionate. **6** (*wearing strong colors*) bright, vivid, deep, intense. **7** (*strong coffee*) concentrated. **8** (*take strong measures*) active, firm, severe, drastic, extreme.

stupid *adj* **1** (*he is too stupid to follow the instructions*) unintelligent, thick, dense, dim, dull-witted, foolish. **2** (*it was a stupid thing to do*) foolish, absurd, silly, idiotic, unwise, unintelligent.

suggest *vb* **1** (*suggest a plan of action*) propose, put forward, recommend, advocate. **2** (*what are you suggesting?*) hint at, insinuate, imply.

suit *vb* **1** (*find a time for the meeting that suits both of them*) be suitable for, be convenient for. **2** (*a style of dress that does not suit her*) become. **3** (*you must try to suit your speech to the occasion*) fit, tailor, adapt, adjust. ⟁

suit yourself to do as you wish (*We have all decided to go to the meeting but you can suit yourself*).

suitable *adj* **1** (*the books are not suitable for the course*) suited, right, appropriate, apt, in keeping with. **2** (*come at a suitable time*) convenient, acceptable.

supply *n* (*have a supply of fuel for the winter*) store, stock, reserve, pile, mass, heap, hoard, stockpile.

supply *vb* (*they supply us with fuel*) give, provide, furnish, equip.

support *vb* **1** (*the uprights that support the bridge*) bear, prop up, hold up, shore up, underpin. **2** (*he supported the local candidate in the election*) back, champion, assist, aid, help, be on the side of, vote for. **3** (*support the cause of animal rights*) back, champion, promote, further, favor, defend. **4** (*evidence to support his point of view*) back, bear out, substantiate, corroborate, confirm. **5** (*she works long hours to support the family*) maintain, provide for, look after, sustain.

suppose *vb* (*I suppose he will get there as soon as he can*) assume, presume, think, believe, expect, imagine.

sure *adj* **1** (*the police have to be sure that he is guilty*) certain, definite, positive, convinced, confident. **2** (*he felt that the project was a sure winner*) certain, definite, guaranteed, inevitable, (*inf*) in the bag. **3** (*a sure remedy for warts*) certain, unfailing, infallible, reliable, dependable.

suspicious *adj* **1** (*we are a bit suspicious of his story*) doubtful, distrustful, mistrustful, skeptical, disbelieving. **2** (*the circumstances of the case are rather suspicious*) odd, strange, queer, questionable, (*inf*) fishy. **3** (*a house now occupied by a suspicious character*) shady, shifty.

sweet *adj* **1** (*children who love sweet foods*) sugary, syrupy. **2** (*the sweet smell of roses*) fragrant, perfumed, scented. **3** (*the sweet sound of the flute*) musical, tuneful, melodious. **4** (*what a sweet little girl*) delightful, charming, appealing, attractive. **5** (*she was always very sweet to us*) charming, pleasant, friendly, generous, kind, kindly, amiable.

sympathy *n* **1** (*they expressed their sympathy to the widow*) compassion, commiseration, pity, condolence, support, concern, consideration. **2** (*they have some sympathy for the cause of the protesters*) good will, approval, favor, support.

synthetic *adj* (*objects made of synthetic material*) man-made, manufactured, artificial, fake, mock.

system *n* **1** (*the public transport system*) structure, organization, arrangement, setup. **2** (*a new system for filing information*) method, process, means, technique.

T

table *n* **1** (*students doing their assignments at a table*) counter, bench, desk. **2** (*a book containing many tables*) diagram, chart, figure. **3** (*a table of contents at the front of the book*) list, catalog, index. ⬦

tablet *n* **1** (*take tablets for a headache*) pill, capsule. **2** (*the hotel provided tablets of soap*) bar, cake.

tackle *vb* (*he is going to tackle the job alone*) deal with, undertake, attempt, take on, apply yourself to.

tactful *adj* (*you will have to be tactful as she is very sensitive*) diplomatic, discreet, delicate, subtle, sensitive.

tactics *npl* (*they used dishonest tactics to win*) strategy, maneuvers, scheme, plan, policy.

tail *n* **1** (*a fox's tail*) brush, scut. **2** (*we were at the tail of the line*) end, rear, back. **3** (*the police were on his tail*) trail, scent.

tail *vb* **1** (*police tailing the crook*) follow, shadow, stalk. **2** (*business tails off at the end of the fall*) dwindle, decrease, drop off, fall away, peter out, die away. ⬦

take *vb* **1** (*the child took his mother's hand*) take hold of, grasp, seize, grip, grab, clutch, **2** (*the soldiers took several prisoners*) seize, catch, capture, arrest. **3** (*someone has taken the teacher's pen*) remove, go off with, pick up, move, steal. **4** (*she took her sister to the movies*) escort, accompany, conduct, guide. **5** (*the journey takes two hours*) take up, use, need, require, call for. **6** (*the bus will take you right there*) transport, carry, convey. **7** (*he took the books to school with him*) carry, bear, fetch, convey. **8** (*she decided to take the red dress*) choose, pick, select, buy, purchase. **9** (*she took the bad news well*) receive, accept, deal with, cope with. **10** (*she takes Spanish at school*) study, learn, be taught. **11** (*I take it that you do not agree*) understand, gather, assume, believe. ⬦

tale *n* **1** (*a fairy tale*) story, anecdote, legend, fable, narrative. **2** (*we hear tales of his bad behavior*) talk, rumor, gossip. ⬦

talented *adj* (*they are very talented musicians*) gifted, accomplished, able, capable, expert.

talk *vb* **1** (*the children were scolded for talking in class*) speak, express yourself, communicate, chatter, chat, gossip. **2** (*he was talking nonsense*) speak, say, utter, voice. **3** (*people are talking about her wild behavior*) gossip, comment, spread rumors.

talk *n* **1** (*the lecturer gave an interesting talk*) lecture, speech, address. **2** (*she wanted to have a talk with him about her career*) chat, discussion, conversation, tête à tête. ⬦

tall *adj* **1** (*many good basketball players are tall*) big. **2** (*a town with many tall buildings*) high, lofty, towering. ⬦

a tall story a story which is extremely unlikely to be true (*His latest tall story is that he saw a man from Mars*).

tame *adj* (*the animal is quite tame*) domesticated, gentle.

tamper *vb* (*someone had tampered with the papers on her desk*) interfere with, meddle with, fiddle with.

tangled *adj* 1 (*tangled hair/tangled wool*) entangled, twisted, knotted, matted. 2 (*tangled financial affairs*) confused, muddled, jumbled, complicated, involved.

tap *vb* 1 (*tap on the door*) knock, rap, bang. 2 (*someone tapped me on the shoulder*) touch, pat.

target *n* 1 (*the archer failed to hit the target*) mark, bull's eye. 2 (*the target for the appeal is $50,000*) goal, aim, objective. 3 (*the new girl is the target of all their teasing*) butt, victim, scapegoat.

task *n* (*tasks to be done around the house*) job, chore, duty, assignment. ⋄

take (someone) to task to reprimand or criticize (someone) (*The teacher took the student to task for his untidy work*).

taste *n* 1 (*the dessert had an odd taste*) flavor, tang. 2 (*her taste in literature*) like, liking, preference, inclination, predilection. 3 (*a house furnished with great taste*) stylishness, elegance, refinement, discrimination.

tasteless *adj* 1 (*the soup was tasteless*) flavorless, bland, insipid, watery. 2 (*tasteless decorations*) vulgar, tawdry, flashy, garish. 3 (*she made a few tasteless remarks*) unseemly, indelicate, vulgar.

teach *vb* 1 (*she teaches the younger children*) educate, give lessons to, instruct, coach, train. 2 (*he teaches history*) give lessons in, give instruction in. 3 (*his father taught him how to ride a bike*) instruct, train, show.

tease *vb* 1 (*the cat will scratch you if you tease it*) torment, annoy, bother, provoke. 2 (*she was upset by his remark but he was only teasing*) joke, fool.

technique *n* 1 (*the tennis player is trying out a new technique*) method, system, approach, way, strategy. 2 (*we admired the technique of the sculptor*) skill, expertise, artistry, proficiency, knack.

tedious *adj* (*the work is tedious*) boring, monotonous, dull, wearisome.

tell *vb* 1 (*we told them the news*) inform, make known, impart, communicate, announce, disclose, declare. 2 (*he told the children a story*) recount, relate, narrate. 3 (*the children were told to go home*) instruct, order, command, direct. 4 (*they know her secret but promised not to tell*) tell tales, give the game away, let the cat out of the bag, (*inf*) spill the beans, (*inf*) grass. 5 (*we could not tell which twin was which*) distinguish, differentiate. ⋄

tell tales to report someone's wrongdoing to someone in authority (*Don't mention to her that I've torn my jacket. She'll tell tales to my mother*).

you're telling me! that is definitely the case (*You're telling me it's a difficult job!*).

temper *n* 1 (*she is in a temper*) bad mood, ill humor, rage, fury, tantrum. 2 (*he is of uncertain temper*) temperament, disposition, nature, character, mood. 3 (*she lost her temper*) composure, self-control, coolness, calm, good humor.

temperamental *adj* (*she is a good worker but she is very temperamental*) excitable, emotional, volatile, moody.

temporary *adj* 1 (*they have temporary jobs*) short-term, provisional, impermanent. 2 (*his interest in golf was only temporary*) short-lived, brief, fleeting.

tempt *vb* (*she was on a diet but was tempted by the sight of the chocolates*) entice, lure, attract, seduce.

tendency *n* 1 (*they have a tendency to tell lies*) inclination, leaning. 2 (*the upward tendency of the temperature graph*) movement, direction, trend, bias.

tender *adj* 1 (*the meat was tender*) not tough, juicy, succulent, soft. 2 (*she has a tender area on her head*) sore, painful, aching, irritated, inflamed. 3 (*the old man seems fierce but has a tender heart*) compassionate, soft-hearted, kind, sympathetic, caring, gentle.

tense *adj* 1 (*they are feeling tense as they wait for the results of the test*) strained, under a strain, under pressure, overwrought, distraught, worked up, anxious, uneasy. 2 (*you have to keep the rope tense*) tight, taut, rigid, stretched, strained.

tentative *adj* 1 (*the young child took a few tentative steps*) hesitant, hesitating, faltering, uncertain, cautious. **2** (*she asked if she could make a tentative suggestion*) speculative, exploratory, experimental, trial, untried.

term *n* **1** (*a document full of technical terms*) word, expression, phrase, name, title. **2** (*the mayor's term of office*) period, time, spell, interval, duration. ⬦

come to terms with (something) to accept (something) as inevitable and try to cope with it as well as you can.

terrible *adj* **1** (*refugees who endured terrible hardship*) dreadful, appalling, shocking, horrible, horrific, grim. **2** (*the terrible heat from the fire*) extreme, severe, intolerable. **3** (*there was a terrible smell from the drains*) nasty, foul, vile, offensive, obnoxious. **4** (*he is a terrible dancer*) very bad, poor, incompetent, useless, dreadful.

terrify *vb* (*walking through the cemetery at night would terrify her*) frighten, scare, alarm, petrify, terrorize.

terror *n* **1** (*she was gripped with terror when she heard noise*) fear, dread, alarm, panic. **2** (*that boy's a little terror*) rogue, imp, hooligan.

test *n* **1** (*the children are having an English test*) exam, examination. **2** (*a hearing test*) examination, exam, check, assessment, appraisal, investigation, exploration. **3** (*the test of a successful movie*) criterion, touchstone, yardstick, standard, measure.

test *vb* **1** (*test the child's hearing*) examine, check, assess, appraise, investigate, explore, analyze. **2** (*the children's behavior really tested his patience*) try, tax, strain. **3** (*test the car*) try out, try.

text *n* **1** (*the text of his speech was world poverty*) topic, subject, subject matter, theme. **2** (*in the introduction, not in the text of the book*) body, main part. **3** (*he is responsible for the text but not the illustrations of the book*) words.

thankful *adj* (*her parents were thankful that she was safe*) grateful, full of gratitude, appreciative, relieved.

thaw *vb* (*the ice began to thaw*) melt, defrost, liquefy.

theft *n* (*there has been a series of thefts from stores*) stealing, robbery, thieving, burglary.

theoretical *adj* (*he was describing a theoretical situation rather than an actual one*) hypothetical, speculative, assumed.

thick *adj* **1** (*thick snow lay on the roads*) deep. **2** (*she was reading a very thick book*) fat, substantial. **3** (*she thinks that she has thick legs*) broad, wide, fat, large, solid. **4** (*a thick rope to tie up the logs*) strong, stout, sturdy. **5** (*a thick mist descended*) dense, heavy, sold. **6** (*a voice thick with emotion*) husky, gruff, hoarse, rough, guttural, throaty. ⬦

through thick and thin no matter what difficulties or dangers arise (*He has vowed to support his leader through thick and thin*).

thief *n* (*the thief got away with his watch*) robber, pickpocket, burglar, housebreaker.

thin *adj* **1** (*she is thin and ill-looking*) underweight, skinny, scrawny, gaunt, anorexic. **2** (*she is on a diet to try to get thin*) slim, slender, svelte, light. **3** (*a design formed of thin lines*) fine, narrow, delicate. **4** (*a dress made of a very thin material*) light, lightweight, delicate, flimsy, sheer, filmy. **5** (*she is worried about having thin hair*) sparse, scanty, wispy. **6** (*the custard was too thin*) dilute, watery, runny. **7** (*they had hoped for a large crowd but the audience was rather thin*) sparse, scarce, scanty, meager. **8** (*rather a thin voice*) weak, low, feeble, faint. **9** (*it was rather a thin excuse*) flimsy, weak, feeble, poor, unconvincing, inadequate. ⬦

be as thin as a rake to be extremely thin (*She keeps dieting but she is already as thin as a rake*).
be thin on top to be going bald (*He often wears a hat to hide the fact that he is thin on top*).

thing *n* **1** (*there was a huge pile of things on the table*) article, item, object. **2** (*it was a sensible thing to do*) action, act, deed, undertaking. **3** (*it was a dreadful thing to happen*) incident, event, occurrence, happening. **4** (*calmness is a useful thing to have in a crisis*) quality, characteristic, attribute, trait. **5** (*there are a few things which we should discuss*) fact, point, detail, particular. **6** (*the poor thing had nowhere to go*) wretch, creature. **7** (*she has a thing about spiders*) phobia, fear, aversion, dislike, horror. ⬦

just one of those things something that just has to be accepted (*Our flight has been delayed but that is just one of those things*).
see things to imagine that you see something

or someone that is not there (*She must be seeing things. She says there was a woman dressed in black in her bedroom*).

the thing is the most important point or question is (*It would be good to expand the business but the thing is where will we get the money?*).

think *vb* **1** (*you must think before you act*) reflect, deliberate, concentrate, contemplate, ponder. **2** (*the old lady was thinking about the past*) remember, recall, call to mind, reminisce. **3** (*we think that they will arrive tomorrow*) believe, expect, suppose, imagine, assume. **4** (*he is thought to be brilliant*) consider, regard, hold, deem. ⟳

not think much of (someone *or* something) to have a low opinion of (someone or something) (*We didn't think much of the play*).

thirst *n* **1** (*they nearly died of thirst in the desert*) thirstiness, dehydration. **2** (*they had a great thirst for knowledge*) desire, craving, longing, yearning, eagerness, keenness.

thorough *adj* **1** (*the police conducted a thorough investigation*) exhaustive, in depth, comprehensive, intensive, extensive. **2** (*he is a slow worker but he is thorough*) meticulous, painstaking, careful. **3** (*he is a thorough villain*) utter, out-and-out, absolute, sheer, complete.

thought *n* **1** (*he is now incapable of rational thought*) thinking, powers of reasoning. **2** (*she was deep in thought*) thinking, reflection, contemplation, musing. **3** (*I had a sudden thought as to what we should do*) idea, line of thought, notion. **4** (*we shall give the matter some thought*) consideration, attention, heed, regard. **5** (*we asked her for her thoughts on the subject*) idea, opinion, view, feeling. **6** (*in giving gifts it is the thought that counts*) thoughtfulness, consideration, care, kindness, compassion.

thoughtful *adj* **1** (*he seemed in a thoughtful mood*) introspective, absorbed. **2** (*she is a thoughtful daughter*) considerate, attentive, caring, helpful, kind, kindly.

threaten *vb* **1** (*the bully threatened the younger children*) make threats, menace, intimidate, browbeat, bully, pressurize. **2** (*pollution threatens the environment*) be a threat to, menace, be a danger to, endanger, put at risk,

jeopardize, put in jeopardy, imperil. **3** (*rain was threatening*) be imminent, loom, be impending.

thrifty *adj* (*they have to be thrifty because they do not have much money*) economical, careful, frugal, sparing.

thrill *vb* (*the children were thrilled by the display of acrobatics*) excite, stimulate, arouse, stir, electrify, give joy to, (*inf*) get a kick out of.

thrive *vb* **1** (*the house plants thrive in that room*) flourish, do well. **2** (*the firm is now thriving*) flourish, proper, do well, boom.

throb *vb* (*his pulse throbbed normally/Her heart throbbed*) beat, pulse, palpitate, pound, vibrate, thump.

throw *vb* **1** (*he threw a brick through the window*) hurl, fling, toss, cast, lob, sling, (*inf*) chuck. **2** (*she threw him a warning glance*) cast, send, give, bestow on. **3** (*she threw away all her old clothing*) throw out, discard, dispose of, get rid of, dispense with, (*inf*) dump. **4** (*the question completely threw him*) baffle, bamboozle, dumbfound, disconcert, astonish. ⟳

throw in the towel to give up, to admit defeat (*He started a college course but he threw in the towel in his second year*) <From a method of conceding defeat in boxing>.

thrust *vb* **1** (*he thrust the present into her hands*) push, shove, ram. **2** (*they thrust the door open*) push, shove, drive, press, propel. **3** (*they thrust their way to the front of the line*) push, shove, press, force, shoulder, elbow, jostle.

thud *n* (*the box fell with a loud thud*) thump, bang, crash, wham.

thug *n* (*the thug attacked the old man*) ruffian, villain, hoodlum, rogue, rough, tough.

thump *vb* **1** (*he turned around and thumped his attacker*) strike, hit, punch, smack, slap, batter. **2** (*her heart was thumping in terror*) thud, pulse, pulsate, throb, palpitate. **3** (*he thumped on the table*) bang, batter, beat, crash, knock.

thwart *vb* (*their plans for expansion were thwarted*) frustrate, foil, baulk, check, block, obstruct, impede, hamper, stop.

tidy *adj* **1** (*the room was very tidy*) neat, orderly, in order, in good order, clean, shipshape, spick and span, spruce. **2** (*everyone had to be tidy for the school photograph*) neat, well-groomed, spruce. **3** (*he is not a tidy person*) neat, orderly, organized, methodical, systematic.

tie *vb* **1** (*he tied the string*) knot, make a bow in. **2** (*they tied the packet with string*) bind. **3** (*they had to tie the dog to the gate*) tie up, tether, fasten, secure, attach, fix. **4** (*the two teams tied for first place*) draw, be equal, be even, be neck and neck.

tight *adj* **1** (*she wore a tight skirt instead of a full one*) tight-fitting, close-fitting, figure-hugging, narrow. **2** (*you must keep the rope tight*) taut, rigid, stiff, tense, stretched, strained. **3** (*she kept a tight grip on her mother's hand*) fast, secure. **4** (*we need a jar with a tight lid*) airtight, watertight, sealed, hermetically sealed. **5** (*make sure that the screws are tight*) secure, fast, fixed. **6** (*a tight mass of fibers*) compact, compressed. **7** (*space was tight in the small house*) cramped, restricted, limited. **8** (*security was tight at the meeting of the presidents*) strict, rigorous, stringent. **9** (*money was tight*) scarce, scant, in short supply, limited, inadequate, insufficient. ✧

in a tight corner in a difficult or dangerous situation (*The troops were in a tight corner completely surrounded by the enemy*).
run a tight ship to run an efficient, well-organized firm, etc. (*During a recession it is exceptionally important to run a tight ship*).

time *n* **1** (*in the time of the cavemen*) period, age, era, epoch. **2** (*he seemed fine the last time I saw him*) occasion, point, juncture. **3** (*he felt that it was time to leave*) moment, point, stage. **4** (*I worked in Spain for a time*) while, period, spell. **5** (*it was a tune in waltz time*) rhythm, measure, tempo, beat. ✧

have no time for (someone *or* something) to have a very low opinion of (someone or something) and to wish not to associate with him/her/it (*I have no time for people who tell lies*).
have the time of your life to have a very enjoyable time (*The child had the time of her life at the theme park*).
have time on your hands to have more free time than you can usefully fill with work, hobbies, etc. (*If you have time on your hands you should do some volunteer work*).

timetable *n* (*give out copies of the conference timetable*) schedule, program, list, agenda.
timid *adj* **1** (*the students were too timid to stand up to the bullies*) timorous, fearful, afraid, ap-

prehensive, frightened, scared, cowardly. **2** (*she was too timid to ask the pop star for his autograph*) timorous, shy, bashful, diffident, reticent, retiring.

tingle *vb* (*her fingers were tingling*) prickle, tickle, itch, sting, quiver, tremble.

tint *n* **1** (*the artist had several tints to chose from*) color, shade, tone. **2** (*an auburn hair tint*) dye, colorant, coloring.

tiny *adj* **1** (*a tiny insect*) minute, diminutive, miniature, microscopic, infinitesimal, minuscule. **2** (*a tiny amount of water*) small, trifling, negligible, minor, insignificant.

tip *vb* **1** (*the dog tipped over the trash can*) upset, overturn, topple, capsize. **2** (*she tipped the water into the bucket*) pour, empty. **3** (*the dresser tends to tip*) tilt, lean, list, cant. **4** (*he tipped the horse to win*) back, put your money on, recommend. **5** (*tip the waiter*) give a tip to, reward.
tip *n* **1** (*the tip of the iceberg*) point, peak, top, apex. **2** (*the tips of his fingers*) end, extremity. **3** (*give the waiter a tip*) gratuity, reward, remuneration. **4** (*she gave him a few tips on cooking*) hint, suggestion, advice. **5** (*a racing tip*) recommendation. ✧

be on the tip of your tongue to be about to be said (*It was on the tip of my tongue to tell her that he was married but I decided not to mention it*).
tip (someone) off to give (someone) some private or secret information.

tired *adj* **1** (*they were tired after their long walk*) weary, fatigued, worn out, exhausted. **2** (*the comic told a series of tired jokes*) stale, hackneyed, outworn, trite, banal. **3** (*they were tired of her endless complaints*) bored, weary.
tiresome *adj* (*she finds the work tiresome*) wearisome, tedious, boring, dull, monotonous, unexciting, uninteresting.
title *n* **1** (*the title of the book*) name. **2** (*what title does the king's nephew have?*) form of address, name, designation.
toilet *n* (*public toilets*) bathroom, restroom, lavatory, WC.
tolerate *vb* **1** (*we could not tolerate the noise from next door*) put up with, stand, bear, endure. **2** (*people should be able to tolerate views that are different from theirs*) permit, allow, recognize, sanction, brook.
tone *n* **1** (*he enjoys the sweet tone of the flute*)

sound, pitch, timbre. **2** (*he spoke in a whispered tone*) voice, intonation, inflection. **3** (*the tone of his letter was threatening*) mood, spirit, manner, vein, gist. **4** (*she was dressed in tones of blue*) tint, shade, tinge.

tool *n* (*the workman forgot one of his tools*) implement, instrument, utensil, gadget, appliance.

top *n* **1** (*they reached the top of the mountain*) peak, summit, crest, apex. **2** (*they are at the top of their careers*) height, peak, pinnacle, zenith, acme, culmination, climax. **3** (*replace the top on the bottle*) lid, cap, stopper, cork. **4** (*they were at the top of the line*) head, front. **5** (*the child wore a white summer top*) sweater, blouse, shirt, T-shirt. ✧

be over the top to be excessive, to be extreme (*She went completely over the top with the catering for the party*).

topical *adj* (*the students were asked to write about something topical*) newsworthy, in the news, current, contemporary, up to date.

toss *vb* **1** (*toss the book on the couch*) throw, fling, hurl. **2** (*Ships tossing on the waves*) rock, roll, sway, lurch, pitch, heave. **3** (*The horse tossed its head*) throw back, jerk. **4** (*They tossed and turned unable to sleep*) thrash, writhe, tumble.

total *adj* **1** (*the total amount of money*) complete, entire, whole, full. **2** (*he's a total fool*) complete, thorough, utter, absolute, downright.

touch *vb* **1** (*the two wires should touch*) be in contact, come together, meet. **2** (*she touched his arm*) put her hand on, tap, pat. **3** (*you shouldn't touch his private things*) handle, pick up, hold, fiddle with, interfere with. **4** (*they were touched by the orphan's sad story*) affect, move, upset, disturb. **5** (*some firms were not touched by the recession*) affect, have an effect on, concern, have a bearing on. ✧

be in touch with (someone) to be in communication with (someone) (*She tried to get in touch with an old friend*).
it's touch and go it is a very uncertain or precarious situation (*It's touch and go whether he lives or dies*) <Perhaps a reference to a ship that touches rocks or the ground but goes on past the hazard without being damaged>.

tough *adj* **1** (*objects made of a tough substance*)

strong, durable, solid, sturdy, rigid, stiff. **2** (*the meat was tough*) chewy, leathery, gristly, sinewy. **3** (*they had to be tough to survive the weather conditions*) hardy, rugged, robust, sturdy, strong. **4** (*the job was very tough*) difficult, hard, strenuous, laborious. **5** (*they had a tough life*) hard, harsh, rugged, rough, grim, difficult. **6** (*the tough kids of the district*) rough, rowdy, unruly, disorderly, wild, violent, lawbreaking

tourist *n* (*foreign tourists visiting the city*) visitor, traveler, sightseer, vacationer.

tower *n* (*a church tower*) spire, steeple, belfry, turret. ✧

a tower of strength someone who is very helpful and supportive (*He was a tower of strength when her husband died*).
live in an ivory tower to have a way of life that is protected from difficulty or unpleasantness (*The writer lives in an ivory tower. He doesn't realize the struggle that his wife has to keep the family together*).

trace *n* **1** (*we could find no trace of where they had camped*) mark, sign, remains, vestige, indication, evidence. **2** (*there was not a trace of shame in his facial expression*) bit, hint, suggestion, suspicion, shadow, jot, iota. **3** (*follow the animal's traces*) track, trail, spoor, scent.

trace *vb* (*they were unable to trace their lost son/ we tried to trace the missing letter*) find, discover, detect, track down, unearth, ferret out.

track *n* **1** (*the hunters were following the tracks of the bear*) marks, traces, prints, trail, spoor, scent. **2** (*they followed the track up the mountain*) path, road, trail. **3** (*the train suddenly left the track*) rail, line. **4** (*the runners had to run 10 times around the track*) course, running track, racetrack. ✧

cover your tracks to conceal your activities or movements (*The bank raiders tried to cover their tracks by changing cars*).
make tracks (*inf*) to leave or set out (*If we are to get there before night we had better be making tracks*).

trade *n* (*he is in the export trade*) commerce, business.

tradition *n* (*keep up the old village traditions*)

custom, habit, belief, practice, convention, institution.

traffic n (*the noise of traffic kept him awake*) vehicles, cars.

tragedy n (*she was sad because of some tragedy in her life*) disaster, calamity, misfortune, adversity.

tragic adj 1 (*appalled at her tragic story about her childhood*) sad, unhappy, pathetic, moving, distressing, pitiful. 2 (*she was killed in a tragic accident*) disastrous, calamitous, catastrophic, terrible, dreadful, appalling, dire.

trail vb 1 (*they trailed the fallen trees behind them*) tow, pull, drag, haul, draw. 2 (*they trailed the fox to its earth*) follow, pursue, track, trace, tail, shadow.

train vb 1 (*she is training the students in cooking techniques*) teach, coach, instruct, educate, give lessons to. 2 (*she is training to be a vet*) study, learn. 3 (*the football players have to train every evening*) work out, do exercises, practice.

tramp n (*go for a tramp over the moors*) hike, trek, march, ramble, wander, roam, walk.

tranquil adj 1 (*a tranquil country scene*) peaceful, restful, quiet, still, serene. 2 (*a very tranquil person*) calm, serene, placid, composed.

transfer vb (*he transferred the furniture from one house to another*) move, shift, take, carry, convey, transport.

transform vb (*the new furnishings transformed the room*) change, alter, revolutionize.

transmit vb (*transmit the information electronically*) pass on, transfer, communicate, spread, send, carry.

transparent adj 1 (*things made of a transparent material*) clear, see-through. 2 (*they were impressed by his transparent honesty*) obvious, clear, unmistakable, evident, noticeable, apparent.

travel vb 1 (*they travel a lot in the course of their work*) journey, move around, take a trip. 2 (*the speed at which sound travels*) be transmitted, proceed, progress. 3 (*they travel the country begging*) journey, cross, traverse, roam, wander.

treacherous adj (*he was betrayed by a treacherous friend*) traitorous, disloyal, faithless, double-dealing, untrustworthy.

treasure n (*they looked for buried treasure*) riches, valuables, wealth, fortune.

treat vb 1 (*he treated his children badly*) act to-ward, behave toward, deal with, cope with, use. 2 (*they treated his remarks as a joke*) regard, consider, view. 3 (*the doctor treated the patient*) attend to, cure, heal, give treatment to, give medication to. 4 (*treat the wood with something to preserve it*) apply to, put on. 5 (*they treated us to dinner*) pay for, stand, entertain, take out. 6 (*she treats the subject in an original way*) deal with, discuss, consider, write about, speak about.

tremble vb (*they were trembling with fear*) shake, quiver, quake, shudder.

tremendous adj 1 (*it made a tremendous difference to their lives*) huge, enormous, great, immense, vast, colossal. 2 (*she is a tremendous cook*) excellent, exceptional, remarkable, wonderful, fabulous.

trend n 1 (*witness an upward trend in prices*) tendency, drift, swing, course. 2 (*she always follows fashion trends*) fashion, style, fad.

trial n 1 (*she was a witness at a murder trial*) court case, case, hearing. 2 (*he is giving the young man a trial as a trainee mechanic*) trial period, probation. 3 (*cars having passed safety trials*) test, tryout, check. 4 (*facing the trials of life*) trouble, worry, burden, hardship, suffering.

✧

trial and error the trying-out of various approaches or methods of doing something until you find out the right one (*The doctor found a cure for my son's skin rash by trial and error*).

trials and tribulations difficulties and hardships (*She was complaining about the trials and tribulations of being a single parent*).

trick n 1 (*he gained entry to her house by a trick*) deception, hoax, ruse, stratagem, subterfuge. 2 (*the children played tricks on each other*) practical joke, joke, hoax, prank.

trick vb (*he was tricked into giving her his life's savings*) cheat, deceive, delude, mislead, hoodwink, dupe, swindle, defraud.

trip vb (*she tripped over her shoe laces*) stumble, lose your footing, lose your balance, slip, fall, tumble.

trip n (*they went on a trip to the shore*) excursion, outing, jaunt, expedition.

triumphant adj 1 (*he gave a triumphant shout when he won*) exultant, joyful, jubilant. 2 (*the* *triumphant team*) winning, victorious, successful.

trivial *adj* (*they quarreled over something trivial*) unimportant, insignificant, inconsequential, petty, minor, negligible.

trouble *n* **1** (*their teenage children are causing them some trouble*) worry, bother, anxiety, disquiet, unease, inconvenience, difficulty, problems. **2** (*there has been a great deal of trouble in her life*) misfortune, difficulty, hardship, distress, suffering, unhappiness, sadness. **3** (*our hosts went to a great deal of trouble*) bother, inconvenience, disturbance, fuss, effort. **4** (*there was a bit of trouble in the restaurant last night*) disturbance, disorder, strife, fighting, commotion. **5** (*he has chest trouble*) disorder, disease, illness.

truck *n* (*they loaded the truck*) van, juggernaut.

trust *vb* **1** (*we do not trust his judgment*) place your trust in, have confidence in, have faith in, believe in, be convinced by. **2** (*you can trust them to help if they offer*) rely on, bank on, depend on, count on, be sure of. **3** (*we trust that you will be there*) hope, assume, presume, expect, suppose.

true *adj* **1** (*what she said is true*) truthful, accurate, right, correct, genuine, reliable. **2** (*they are true friends*) real, genuine, loyal, faithful, trustworthy, reliable, dependable. **3** (*the book gives a true account of the war*) accurate, correct, exact, precise, faithful, close.

trustworthy *adj* (*he thinks that all his employees are trustworthy*) reliable, dependable, loyal, staunch, faithful, trusty, honest, honorable.

truth *n* **1** (*there seemed little truth in what he said*) truthfulness, accuracy, correctness, rightness, validity, veracity. **2** (*truth is often stranger than fiction*) reality, actuality.

try *vb* **1** (*you must try to do well*) attempt, aim, endeavor, make an effort, exert yourself, strive, struggle. **2** (*we tried a new kind of cereal*) try out, test, evaluate. **3** (*the children are trying her patience*) tax, strain, exhaust. **4** (*he was the judge who tried the case*) hear, judge, adjudicate.

trying *adj* **1** (*they had had a trying day*) taxing, demanding, difficult, stressful, hard, tough. **2** (*the children were particularly trying that day*) troublesome, tiresome, annoying, irritating, exasperating.

tuck *vb* **1** (*she tucked her blouse into her skirt*) push, ease, insert, stuff. **2** (*tuck the child up in bed*) cover up, wrap up. **3** (*they tucked into a hearty meal*) eat, devour, wolf down, gobble up.

tug *vb* **1** (*she tugged at the rope*) pull, jerk, yank. **2** (*the child tugged a toy cart behind him*) drag, draw, tow, lug. ✧

tug of love a struggle involving the custody of a child <A variation on a tug-of-war, which involves two teams pulling on a rope>.

tumble *vb* **1** (*watch that the child does not tumble*) fall over, fall headlong, topple, stumble, trip. **2** (*prices have tumbled*) fall, drop, plummet, plunge, slump. **3** (*acrobats tumbling*) turn somersaults, go head over heels.

tune *n* (*a group playing a folk tune*) melody, air, song. ✧

in tune with (something) in agreement with (something), compatible with (something) (*Their ideas on the new scheme are very much in tune*).

turn *vb* **1** (*the wheel began to turn*) go around, rotate, revolve, spin, whirl, twirl. **2** (*he turned the car in the driveway*) turn around, reverse, make a U-turn. **3** (*he turned the steaks over on the grill*) turn over, flip over, invert, reverse. **4** (*the weather turned stormy*) become, grow, get. **5** (*tadpoles turn into frogs*) become, change into. **6** (*the car turned the corner*) go around, round. **7** (*he turned the dusty attic into a bedroom*) convert, change, transform, alter, modify. ✧

tussle *n* (*the two boys had a tussle to gain possession of the bag*) struggle, fight, scuffle, skirmish.

tweak *vb* (*the boy tweaked his friend's ear*) twist, pinch, nip, pull, jerk.

twilight *n* (*they walked home at twilight*) dusk, half-light.

twinkle *vb* (*the stars twinkled*) sparkle, glitter, glint, flicker, shimmer.

twist *vb* **1** (*the extreme heat had twisted the metal*) bend, warp, distort, buckle. **2** (*he twisted the string around his finger*) wind, coil, curl, twine, twirl, loop. **3** (*the road twists up the mountain*) curve, wind, zigzag, snake, meander. **4** (*the ropes became twisted*) entangle,

tangle, entwine. **5** (*they twisted his words*) distort, garble, misrepresent, falsify. **6** (*she twisted her head around to look at him*) turn, swivel, screw.

type *n* **1** (*a type of plant/a type of person*) kind, variety, sort, form, class. **2** (*in italic type*) print, face, fount.

twitch *n* **1** (*her arm gave a twitch*) spasm, jerk, jump, quiver, tremor. **2** (*he has a twitch in his eye*) blink, flutter, tic.

U

ugly *adj* **1** (*an ugly monster/ugly buildings*) hideous, unattractive, unprepossessing, horrible, frightful. **2** (*the war situation grew more ugly*) dangerous, threatening, menacing, ominous, hostile, nasty. ▽

ugly duckling an unattractive or uninteresting person or thing that develops in time into something or someone very attractive, interesting, successful, etc. (*She is now a beautiful movie star but as a child she was a real ugly duckling*) <A reference to a story by Hans Christian Andersen about a baby swan that is brought up by two ducks who consider it ugly by their standards until it grows into a beautiful swan>.

umpire *n* (*the umpire in the tournament*) referee, judge, adjudicator, arbitrator.

unanimous *adj* (*the committee was unanimous in its decision to close down the club*) agreed, united, like-minded, at one, in harmony, with one voice.

unaware *adj* (*they were unaware of what people were saying about them*) unconscious, ignorant, oblivious, heedless, (*inf*) in the dark.

uncanny *adj* **1** (*there were uncanny happenings in the cemetery at night*) strange, odd, queer, mysterious, eerie, weird, unnatural, supernatural. **2** (*she bore an uncanny resemblance to her grandmother*) remarkable, striking, extraordinary, astonishing, incredible.

uncertain *adj* **1** (*the result of the talks is still uncertain*) unknown, undetermined, unsettled, up in the air. **2** (*we are uncertain about whether to go or stay*) unsure, doubtful, undecided, dubious, unresolved, indecisive, wavering, in two minds. **3** (*the future is uncertain*) unpredictable, risky, chancy.

uncouth *adj* (*uncouth table manners*) rough, coarse, uncivilized, unrefined, unpolished, boorish, ill-bred.

under *prep* **1** (*she sat under the tree*) below, underneath, beneath. **2** (*prices under $10*) below, less than, lower than. **3** (*army ranks under major*) low, lower than, inferior to, subordinate to, junior to. ▽

under your very nose 1 right in front of you and so very easily seen (*She could not find her book although it was under her very nose*). **2** while one is actually present (*The thief stole my baggage from the train under my very nose*).

under your own steam entirely through your own efforts (*There is no transportation to the picnic site, so we will have to get there under our own steam*) <A reference to steam engines>.

under the influence under the influence of alcohol, drunk (*It is an offense to drive while you are under the influence*).

underclothing *n* (*wear warm underclothing in the winter*) underwear, underclothes, undergarments, lingerie.

undergo *vb* (*undergo a terrible experience*) go through, experience, be subjected to, endure.

underground *adj* **1** (*an underground shelter*) subterranean, sunken. **2** (*an underground organization*) secret, clandestine, undercover, surreptitious.

undergrowth *n* (*the animals emerged from the undergrowth*) thicket, brushwood.

underhand *adj* (*she got the job by underhand methods*) deceitful, devious, crafty, cunning, sneaky, furtive, dishonest.

underline *vb* (*the burglary underlined the need for security staff*) emphasize, stress, highlight.

undermine *vb* (*they tried to undermine the authority of the manager*) weaken, impair, damage, destroy.

understand *vb* **1** (*we did not understand his instructions*) comprehend, grasp, take in, follow, fathom, interpret. **2** (*she failed to understand how the homeless people felt*) appreciate, sympathize with. **3** (*we understand that he has left*) gather, hear, be informed, learn, believe.

understanding *n* **1** (*have a poor understanding of the facts*) comprehension, grasp, knowledge, awareness. **2** (*his powers of understanding are poor*) reasoning, brain power, (*inf*) gray matter. **3** (*the two businessmen did not sign a contract but they had an unofficial understanding*) agreement, gentleman's agreement, arrangement, deal, pact. **4** (*she treated the difficult situation with great understanding*) sensitivity, consideration, insight, compassion, sympathy. **5** (*it was our understanding that he was leaving*) belief, opinion, feeling.

undertake vb (*they agreed to undertake the difficult task*) take on, assume, tackle, set about, enter upon.

underwear n (*wear warm underwear in winter*) underclothes, underclothing, undergarments, lingerie.

undo vb 1 (*she undid the hook on her dress*) unfasten, unhook, unbutton, untie, loosen, open. 2 (*they undid all his good work*) destroy, ruin, wreck, upset. 3 (*she rang to undo the arrangements for the meeting*) cancel, annul, revoke, set aside.

unearth vb 1 (*the police have unearthed new information about the murder*) uncover, discover, find, come across, bring to light, expose, turn up. 2 (*the dog unearthed an old bone*) dig up, excavate, exhume.

unearthly adj (*they heard an unearthly shriek*) eerie, uncanny, supernatural, ghostly, weird.

uneasy adj (*they felt uneasy when their son did not arrive home*) anxious, worried, concerned, troubled, nervous.

unemployed adj (*he has been unemployed for a year*) jobless, out of work.

unfasten vb (*unfasten the gate/unfasten the knot*) undo, open, loose, untie, unlock.

unfortunate adj 1 (*in unfortunate circumstances*) adverse, disadvantageous, unfavorable. 2 (*the unfortunate girl lost all her money*) unlucky, out of luck, luckless, wretched, unhappy. 3 (*it was a most unfortunate remark*) regrettable, inappropriate, tactless.

unhappy adj (*she was unhappy when her dog died*) sad, miserable, sorrowful, dejected, gloomy.

uniform adj 1 (*pieces of cloth of uniform length*) same, alike, like, equal, identical. 2 (*keep the room at a uniform temperature*) constant, unvarying, unchanging, regular, even.

union n (*a union of youth clubs*) association, alliance, league, federation.

unique adj 1 (*a unique specimen*) one and only, single, sole, solitary, exclusive. 2 (*the salesclerk pointed out the unique features of the dishwasher*) distinctive, unequaled, unparalleled.

unit n 1 (*the English course is divided into units*) component, part, section, portion, element. 2 (*the meter is a unit of length*) measurement, measure, quantity.

unite vb 1 (*the two sides united to fight their common enemy*) join, join together, get together, join forces, amalgamate, combine, merge. 2 (*they decided to unite the two teams*) join, combine, amalgamate, merge, link, fuse.

universal adj (*poverty is a universal problem*) general, widespread, common, global, international, worldwide.

universe n (*the wonders of the universe*) world, cosmos.

unlikely adj (*it is unlikely that they will arrive on time*) improbable, doubtful.

unlucky adj 1 (*he was unlucky not to win/a most unlucky young man*) out of luck, luckless, down on your luck, unfortunate, hapless. 2 (*by an unlucky set of circumstances they failed to arrive on time*) unfortunate, adverse, disadvantageous, unfavorable.

unmarried adj (*she is unmarried and lives with her parents*) single, unwed, unattached.

unpleasant adj (*an unpleasant experience/an unpleasant person*) disagreeable, nasty, horrible.

unreal adj (*a story about an unreal world*) imaginary, fictitious, make-believe, mythical.

unruly adj (*the teacher could not control the unruly children*) rowdy, wild, disorderly, noisy, uncontrollable, unmanageable.

unsightly adj (*unsightly modern apartment buildings in a historical area*) ugly, unattractive, hideous, horrible.

unsuccessful adj (*their attempt to save the firm was unsuccessful*) without success, in vain, failed, futile, useless, ineffective.

untangle vb (*untangle the knots*) disentangle, unravel, straighten out.

untidy adj 1 (*the room where the children were playing was very untidy*) in disorder, disordered, disarranged, chaotic, disorganized. 2 (*the children were scolded for being untidy*) disheveled, unkempt, rumpled, messy.

untie vb (*untie the gate/untie the string*) undo, unfasten, loosen.

untrue adj (*we felt that his account of the accident was untrue*) false, wrong, inaccurate.

unusual adj (*his behavior was unusual*) uncommon, out of the ordinary, abnormal, odd, different, irregular.

unwell adj (*she is unwell and is staying home*) sick, ill, ailing, unhealthy, (*inf*) under the weather.

unwilling adj (*they were unwilling to set off so late*) reluctant, disinclined, loath, averse.

up:— ✧

be on the **up-and-up** to be above board or legal

(We questioned how he made his money, but it all seems to be on the up-and-up).
be up to (something) 1 to be involved in something mischievous or dishonest *(Their mother could tell by the children's faces that they were up to something)*. **2** to be good enough, competent enough, strong enough, etc., to do something *(She was under a lot of stress at work because she was not really up to the job)*.
up-and-coming likely to be successful, rising in importance or popularity *(She is an up-and-coming young musician)*.

upbringing *n* *(they had a very strict upbringing)* rearing, training.
upheaval *n* *(moving to a new house caused a terrible upheaval and stress)* disturbance, disruption, disorder, turmoil, chaos, confusion.
upkeep *n* *(pay for the upkeep of the house)* maintenance, running, support.
upper *adj* **1** *(the upper shelf)* higher. **2** *(the upper ranks in the army)* higher, superior, senior. ⊳

have the upper hand to be in control or have the advantage *(The two roommates are quarreling but she has the upper hand because the apartment belongs to her mother)*.
upper-crust *(inf)* belonging to the upper class or aristocracy *(She has an upper-crust accent)* <Refers literally to the upper part of the pastry of a pie above the filling>.

upright *adj* **1** *(the upright posts in the fence)* erect, vertical, perpendicular. **2** *(he is an upright member of the community)* honest, honorable, decent, respectable, law-abiding, upstanding.
uproar *n* *(there was uproar when the soccer player kicked the ball into his own goal)* disturbance, turmoil, tumult, commotion, riot, rumpus
upset *vb* **1** *(his remarks upset her)* hurt, distress, worry, bother. **2** *(the animals were upset by the thunderstorm)* agitate, alarm, frighten. **3** *(he got a new job and upset our vacation plans)* disorganize, disarrange, *(inf)* mess up. **4** *(the child upset the pail of water)* overturn, knock over, upend, capsize, tip over.
upshot *n* *(the upshot of the quarrel was that he left)* result, outcome, end, conclusion.
up-to-date *adj* *(his ideas are very up-to-date)* modern, current, contemporary, fashionable.
urban *n* *(urban areas)* city, town, metropolitan, inner city.
urbane *adj* *(an urbane man whom women found*

charming) suave, smooth, sophisticated, elegant, cultivated, polished, refined, gracious, courteous.
urge *vb* **1** *(urge the cattle to the milking shed)* drive, propel, force, push, hurry. **2** *(we urged her to accept the invitation)* advise, encourage, prompt, entreat, exhort. **3** *(the applause of the crowd urged the players on to greater effort)* spur, incite, stimulate, prod, goad, encourage, egg on.
urge *n* *(she had a sudden urge to laugh)* desire, compulsion, need, wish, impulse, longing.
urgent *adj* **1** *(it is urgent that we get him to hospital)* imperative, a matter of life or death, vital, crucial, critical, essential. **2** *(we have urgent matters to discuss)* important, crucial, vital, serious, grave, pressing.
use *n* **1** *(the lotion we bought at the drugstore is for external use only)* application, utilization, employment. **2** *(what use is this old chair?)* usefulness, good, benefit, service. **3** *(we have no use for this old bike)* need, purpose. ⊳

use *vb* **1** *(do you know how to use this machine?)* make use of, utilize, work, operate, employ, wield. **2** *(you will have to use tact)* exercise, employ, apply. **3** *(have you used all the flour?)* consume, get through.

used *adj* *(a store selling used clothing)* secondhand, nearly new, cast-off.
useful *adj* *(this is a useful kitchen gadget)* of use, practical, of service, handy, convenient. ⊳

come in useful to be useful at some time in the future *(She keeps a lot of old boxes in her garage in case they come in useful, but they never do)*.

usual *adj* **1** *(the mailman's usual route)* regular, accustomed, customary, habitual, normal, routine, set, established. **2** *(the weather was usual for the time of year)* common, typical, standard, normal, average, run-of-the-mill.
usually *adv* *(we usually go out to lunch on Saturday)* generally, as a rule, normally, mostly, for the most part.
utter *vb* *(we heard him utter threats)* say, speak, voice, pronounce, express.
utter *adj* *(they are utter fools)* complete, absolute, total, thorough, out-and-out, perfect.
utterly *adv* *(we were utterly delighted at the news)* absolutely, completely, totally, thoroughly, perfectly.

V

vacant *adj* **1** (*the house is vacant*) empty, unoc-cupied, uninhabited, to let, deserted. **2** (*several vacant posts in the firm*) free, available, unfilled, unoccupied, empty. **3** (*look for a vacant seat*) empty, free, unoccupied, unused. **4** (*he wore a vacant look*) expressionless, blank, inexpressive, deadpan.

vagrant *n* (*vagrants begging for money for food*) homeless person, hobo, person of no fixed abode.

vague *adj* **1** (*she has only a vague idea about her duties in her new job*) hazy, imprecise, ill-de-fined, uncertain. **2** (*our vacation plans are still rather vague*) hazy, uncertain, undecided, in-definite, (*inf*) up in the air, doubtful. **3** (*he gave rather a vague description of the person who at-tacked him*) imprecise, inexact, loose, hazy, wooly. **4** (*a vague shape loomed out of the mist*) indistinct, shadowy, unclear, hazy, dim, fuzzy. **5** (*she is rather a vague person*) absent-minded, dreamy, with your head in the clouds.

vain *adj* **1** (*they made a vain attempt to save the drowning man*) unsuccessful, futile, useless, ineffective, abortive, unprofitable. **2** (*he is a very vain young man*) conceited, proud, arrogant, cocky, (*inf*) big-headed. ⌕

valiant *adj* (*make a valiant attempt to save his friend's life*) brave, courageous, gallant, heroic, bold.

valid *adj* **1** (*the school regulation is still valid*) in force, effective, in effect, legal, lawful. **2** (*he has valid reasons for lodging an objection*) sound, well-founded, reasonable, justifiable, authen-tic.

valuable *adj* **1** (*the burglars took some valuable jewelry*) expensive, costly, high-priced, pre-cious, priceless. **2** (*the old man gave them some valuable advice*) useful, helpful, beneficial, worthwhile.

value *n* **1** (*it is difficult to place a value on the antique table*) price, market price, cost. **2** (*she tried to convince the children of the value of a balanced diet*) worth, benefit, merit, advantage, gain, importance.

value *vb* **1** (*they asked him to value their house*) set a price on, price, place a value on. **2** (*she values the contribution that parents make to sports events*) appreciate, think highly of, rate highly, set store by.

vanish *vb* **1** (*the figure seemed to vanish into the mist*) disappear, fade, melt. **2** (*they were talk-ing about a way of life that has now vanished*) go, die out, disappear, end, come to an end.

vanquish *vb* (*they vanquished the enemy army*) conquer, defeat, triumph over, overcome, crush, trounce.

varied *adj* (*a varied selection of magazines*) as-sorted, mixed, miscellaneous.

variety *n* **1** (*they tried to introduce some variety into the diet*) variation, diversity, change. **2** (*a huge variety of flowers*) assortment, miscellany, mixture, range, collection. ⌕

various *adj* **1** (*the dress comes in various colors*) varying, diverse, different, many, assorted. **2** (*for various reasons we are unable to attend the meeting*) numerous, several, many, varied.

vary *vb* **1** (*they tend to vary slightly in size*) dif-fer, be different, be unlike, be dissimilar. **2** (*the temperature varies throughout the day*) change, alter. **3** (*try to vary your speed on a long jour-ney*) change, alter, modify.

vast *adj* **1** (*the vast plains covered in ripe corn*) extensive, immense, expansive, wide, sweep-ing. **2** (*a vast shape suddenly loomed out of the fog*) huge, enormous, massive, colossal, gigan-tic.

vegetation *n* (*an area of the world with little veg-etation*) plant life, plants, greenery, flora.

vehement *adj* (*a vehement denial*) emphatic, vig-orous, forceful, strong, fervent, passionate.

vehicle *n* **1** (*no parking for unauthorized vehicles*) conveyance, car, bus, truck, means of transport. **2** (*they use the magazine simply as a vehicle for* *spreading their political views*) medium, means of expression, agency, instrument.

veil *n* (*the mountain peaks were hidden under a veil of mist/They moved the body under a veil of secrecy*) cover, covering, screen, blanket, cloak, mantle, mask, shroud, cloud.

vein *n* 1 (*blood gushed from the vein*) blood vessel. 2 (*a vein of ore in the rocks*) seam, lode, stratum. 3 (*the marble fireplace had a pink vein in it*) streak, stripe, strip, line, thread. 4 (*there was a vein of humor in her criticism*) streak, strain, dash, hint. 5 (*the poem was in a serious vein*) mood, tone.

vengeance *n* (*they sought vengeance for the murder of their brother*) revenge, retaliation, reprisal, retribution, tit for tat. ⋄

with a vengeance very strongly, very much, etc. (*It began to snow with a vengeance*).

venom *n* 1 (*find an antidote for the snake's venom*) poison, toxin. 2 (*she spoke with venom about her fellow competitor*) spite, malice, ill will, animosity.

venture *n* (*a business venture*) enterprise, undertaking, project.

verbal *adj* (*asked to give a verbal account of the accident*) oral, spoken, in speech.

verdict *n* (*the jury delivered its verdict*) decision, findings, conclusion, judgment, ruling, opinion.

verge *n* (*the grass verge by the road*) edge, border, boundary. ⋄

be on the verge of (something) to be about to experience something (*The research scientist thought that she was on the verge of a major medical discovery*).

verify *vb* (*he was asked to verify that he had been present*) confirm, corroborate, endorse, ratify.

versatile *adj* 1 (*a versatile kitchen gadget*) adaptable, multipurpose. 2 (*she is a very versatile musician*) adaptable, adjustable, flexible, resourceful.

version *n* 1 (*she gave us her version of what happened*) account, story, report, side, interpretation. 2 (*there are several versions of that song around*) variant, variation, form.

vertical *adj* (*hammer vertical posts into the ground to make a fence*) upright, erect, perpendicular.

very *adj* 1 (*those were her very words*) actual, exact, precise. 2 (*the beauty of the dress lay in its very simplicity*) sheer, utter, pure. 3 (*he has*

been a member from the very beginning) absolute. ⋄

the very thing exactly what is required (*That scarf is the very thing to complete her outfit*).

vessel *n* 1 (*there was a foreign flag flying from the vessel*) ship, boat, craft. 2 (*we need some kind of vessel to give the dog a drink*) container, receptacle.

veto *vb* (*some members vetoed his membership of the club*) ban, bar, place an embargo on, forbid, disallow, reject, turn down, give the thumbs down to.

vex *vb* (*her mother was vexed by her refusal to come home for Thanksgiving*) annoy, irritate, upset, put out, distress.

vibrate *vb* 1 (*the music vibrated throughout the hall*) throb, pulsate, resonate, reverberate, ring, echo. 2 (*the whole bus vibrated as the driver tried to start the engine*) shudder, tremble, shake, quiver, shiver.

vice *n* 1 (*vice seems to be on the increase in the modern world*) sin, sinfulness, evil, wickedness, badness, wrongdoing. 2 (*one of his many vices*) sin, offense, misdeed, failing, flaw, defect.

vicious *adj* 1 (*the mailman was attacked by a vicious dog*) fierce, ferocious, savage, dangerous. 2 (*the attack on the old man was a particularly vicious one*) violent, savage, brutal, fierce, ferocious, inhuman. ⋄

a vicious circle an unfortunate or bad situation, the result of which produces the original cause of the situation or something similar (*It is a vicious circle. They are so much in debt that they have to borrow money to pay their debts and end up even deeper in debt*).

victim *n* 1 (*they were victims of a vicious attack*) casualty, sufferer. 2 (*tracking down their victims*) prey, quarry.

victorious *adj* (*the victorious army/the victorious team*) conquering, winning, triumphant, champion.

victory *n* (*we celebrated our victory*) win, success, conquest, triumph, achievement. ⋄

landslide victory a victory in an election by a very large number of votes (*Early on in the counting of the votes it was obvious that the government was heading for a landslide victory*).

Pyrrhic victory a success of some kind in which what you achieve is not worth the effort or sacrifice that you have had to make in the process of attaining it (*She won her case against her employers for unfair dismissal but it was a Pyrrhic victory. All her compensation money went toward the cost of the legal fees*) <From the costly victory of Pyrrhus, King of Epirus, over the Romans at Heracles in 280 BC>.

view *n* **1** (*the view from our balcony was beautiful*) outlook, prospect, panorama, vista. **2** (*a strange figure came into view*) sight, range of vision, eyeshot. **3** (*our view is that he is dishonest*) opinion, point of view, viewpoint, belief, feeling, idea. ⊙

a bird's-eye view of (something) 1 a view of (something) seen from high above (*We got a marvelous bird's-eye view of the town from the top of the tower*). **2** a brief description or account of (something) (*The book gives a bird's-eye view of the use of herbs in cooking*).

vigorous *adj* (*a vigorous attempt at winning the game*) strong, powerful, forceful, determined, enthusiastic, lively, energetic, strenuous.

vile *adj* (*what a vile thing to do!*) nasty, foul, unpleasant, disagreeable, horrible, dreadful, disgusting, hateful, shocking.

villain *n* (*the police have caught the villains*) rogue, scoundrel, wrongdoer, ruffian, (*inf*) crook.

violent *adj* **1** (*a violent attack*) brutal, ferocious, cruel, savage, vicious. **2** (*he has a violent temper*) uncontrollable, unrestrained, wild, passionate, forceful. **3** (*he took a violent dislike to her at first sight*) strong, great, intense, extreme, vehement.

virtually *adv* (*traffic was virtually at a standstill*) more or less, nearly, practically, as good as, effectively, in effect, in essence, for all practical purposes.

virtue *n* (*the church admires virtue and discourages vice*) goodness, righteousness, morality, integrity, uprightness, honesty, decency.

visible *adj* **1** (*the hilltops were scarcely visible in the mist*) in view, discernible, perceptible. **2** (*his unhappiness was visible to us all*) obvious, evident, apparent, noticeable, plain, clear, unmistakable.

vision *n* **1** (*certain jobs call for good vision*) eyesight, sight. **2** (*he claims to have seen a vision in the cemetery*) apparition, ghost, specter. **3** (*he saw his dead brother in a vision*) dream, hallucination. **4** (*men of vision*) insight, perception, discernment, intuition.

visit *vb* (*he visits his aunt once a year*) pay a visit to, go to see, pay a call on, call on, (*inf*) drop in on.

vital *adj* **1** (*it is vital that you attend the meeting*) imperative, essential, necessary, crucial. **2** (*hold vital discussions*) indispensable, urgent, essential, necessary, key. **3** (*she was a very vital person*) lively, energetic, vivacious. ⊙

vital statistics your chest, waist, and hip measurements (*The announcer in the beauty contest gave the vital statistics of all the contestants*).

vitality *n* (*well-nourished children full of vitality*) energy, liveliness, vigor, zest, vivacity.

vivacious *adj* (*she is so vivacious that everyone else seems dull beside her*) lively, animated, sparkling, scintillating, dynamic, vibrant.

vivid *adj* **1** (*vivid colors*) bright, brilliant, strong, intense. **2** (*a vivid description*) clear, graphic, powerful, dramatic.

vocabulary *n* (*the difficult vocabulary in the piece*) language, words.

voice *n* **1** (*she lost her voice when she had a cold*) speech. **2** (*they finally gave voice to their feelings*) expression, utterance. **3** (*governments refusing to listen to the voice of the people*) opinion, view, comment. ⊙

a voice crying in the wilderness someone expressing an opinion or warning to which no one pays any attention (*She told them that the suggested new range of goods would not sell but she was a voice crying in the wilderness*).

the still small voice of reason the expression of a calm, sensible point of view of the kind often given by your conscience. <A biblical reference to John the Baptist in Matthew 3:3>.

volume *n* **1** (*an encyclopedia in several volumes*) book. **2** (*measure the volume*) capacity, bulk. **3** (*the sheer volume of water pouring out*) amount, quantity, mass. **4** (*we asked them to turn down the volume of their radio*) loudness, sound.

voluntary *adj* **1** (*attendance at the meeting is entirely voluntary*) of your own free will, optional, non-compulsory. **2** (*she is unemployed but does voluntary work*) unpaid, without payment, volunteer.

vote *vb* **1** (*they are voting to elect a new president*) cast your vote, go to the polls. **2** (*she voted for the woman candidate*) elect, opt for, select. ✧

vote with your feet to show your disapproval, dissatisfaction, etc., by leaving (*The workers have no confidence in the firm's management and are voting with their feet*).

vote *n* (*have a vote on who should lead the team*) ballot, poll, election. ✧

a vote of no confidence a vote taken to find out whether the government, a person, group of people, etc., is still trusted and supported.

voucher *n* (*lunch vouchers*) token, ticket, slip.

vow *n* (*marriage vows*) oath, promise, pledge.

vow *vb* (*he vowed to be true*) swear, promise, pledge, give your word.

vulgar *adj* **1** (*they objected to his vulgar language*) rude, indecent, obscene, bawdy, smutty. **2** (*vulgar table manners*) rude, impolite, unmannerly, ill-mannered. **3** (*they thought her clothing was vulgar*) tasteless, flashy, gaudy, tawdry.

vulnerable *adj* (*they felt vulnerable camping out in that area*) exposed, unprotected, defenseless.

W

wad *n* **1** (*use a wad of cotton to clean the wound*) lump, chunk, plug. **2** (*wads of dollar bills*) bundle, roll.

wadding *n* (*use cotton wadding to pack the jewelry*) filling, packing, padding, lining, stuffing.

waddle *vb* (*the very fat lady waddled down the street*) wiggle, sway, totter.

wade *vb* **1** (*the children were wading in the pool in the park*) paddle, splash. **2** (*there was no bridge and they had to wade across the stream*) ford, cross.

waffle *vb* (*she did not have much to say about the subject but she waffled on*) ramble, babble, prattle.

wag *vb* **1** (*the dog's tail was wagging*) swing, sway, shake, twitch, quiver. **2** (*the teacher wagged her finger angrily at the children*) waggle, wiggle.

wage *vb* (*wage war*) carry on, conduct, engage in, undertake.

wager *n* (*he laid a wager that she would not win*) bet, gamble, stake, (*inf*) flutter.

wager *vb* (*she wagered that the horse would come first in the race*) bet, place a bet, lay a bet, lay odds, put money on, gamble.

wages *npl* (*she has asked for a raise in her wages*) pay, salary, earnings, income.

wail *vb* (*the children were wailing because their mother would not give them candy*) cry, weep, sob, lament, howl, whine.

wait *vb* **1** (*the children were told to wait at the side of the road*) stay, remain, stop, halt. **2** (*she does not know if she has got the job—she will just have to wait and see*) be patient, stand by, hang fire, mark time, (*inf*) sit tight. **3** (*they asked us to wait for them*) await, watch out for, expect. **4** (*they are employed to wait at table*) serve, be a waiter/waitress. ✧

be waiting in the wings to be in a state of readiness to do something, especially to take over someone else's job (*She is afraid to be away from the office for long because she feels that her assistant is just waiting in the wings*).

lie in wait (for someone) to be on the watch (for someone), to ambush (someone) (*The soldier was attacked by terrorists who were lying in wait for him/The reporters were lying in wait for the movie star as she left the studio*).

wake *vb* **1** (*he asked us to wake him early*) wake up, waken, rouse. **2** (*we woke at dawn*) awake, waken, wake up, get up, arise.

walk *vb* **1** (*we were able to walk to the mall*) go by foot, go on foot. **2** (*the children were told to walk and not to run*) stroll, saunter, amble, march.

walk *n* **1** (*they went for a walk after lunch*) stroll, saunter, amble, ramble, hike. **2** (*I recognized him by his walk*) gait, step, stride. ✧

walk of life occupation or profession, your way of earning a living (*people from all walks of life attended the funeral of the governor*).

walker *n* (*we passed a few walkers as we drove to the village*) pedestrian, hiker, rambler.

wall *n* **1** (*the garden had a wall around it*) enclosure, barrier. **2** (*we tore down a wall of the house to knock two rooms into one*) partition. **3** (*tourists went to visit the old city walls*) fortifications, ramparts, barricade. ✧

walls have ears someone unnoticed or unseen may be listening (*I asked him not to discuss our private business in the restaurant. It was not busy, but walls have ears*).

wallow *vb* **1** (*the animals were wallowing in mud*) roll, splash, tumble. **2** (*she was wallowing in self-pity*) bask, revel, delight.

wan *adj* (*she looked wan after having had flu*) pale, white, pallid, (*inf*) peaky.

wand *n* (*the fairy godmother waved her wand*) stick, baton, rod.

wander *vb* **1** (*the child wandered off while his mother was shopping*) go off, get lost, stray, lose your way. **2** (*they loved to wander over the hills when they were on vacation*) roam, ramble, rove, range. **3** (*the old man does not recognize his family and has started to wander*) ramble, rave, babble.

wane *vb* **1** (*the moon is waning*) decrease, diminish, dwindle. **2** (*the power of ancient Greece waned*) decrease, decline, diminish, dwindle, fade, subside, dim, vanish, die out.

want *vb* **1** (*the children wanted some candy*) wish for, desire, demand, long for, crave, yearn for, hanker after. **2** (*poor people wanting food*) lack, be lacking in, be without, be devoid of, be short of.

war *n* **1** (*the war between the neighboring countries lasted many years*) warfare, fighting, conflict, struggle, hostilities, battles. **2** (*there was a state of war between the two nations*) conflict, strife, hostility, enmity, ill-will. **3** (*she took part in the war against poverty in the area*) battle, fight, crusade, campaign. ✧

be on the warpath to be extremely angry and out for revenge (*Their father has discovered the broken window and is now on the warpath*) <A Native American expression>.

ward *n* (*her parents are dead and she is a ward of her uncle*) charge, dependant.

ward *vb* **1** (*she succeeded in warding off his attack*) fend off, stave off, deflect, avert, rebuff. **2** (*they warded off the intruders*) drive back, repel, beat back.

warden *n* **1** (*he is a game warden in Africa*) keeper, custodian, guardian, guard. **2** (*the prisoners attacked a warden*) prison officer, guard, jailer, (*inf*) screw.

wardrobe *n* **1** (*she hung her clothes up in the wardrobe*) closet. **2** (*she is buying a new wardrobe for her vacation*) clothing.

warehouse *n* (*they collected the books from the warehouse*) store, depot, stockroom.

wares *npl* (*there were many people selling their wares in the market*) goods, products, merchandise, stock.

warlike *adj* (*they encountered warlike tribes in the jungle*) belligerent, aggressive, hostile.

warlock *n* (*a story about a warlock*) wizard, sorcerer, magician, witch.

warm *adj* **1** (*she bathed the wound in warm water*) heated, tepid, lukewarm. **2** (*go for a swim on a warm day*) sunny, hot, close, sultry. **3** (*she has a warm heart*) kind, kindly, sympathetic, tender, loving, affectionate. **4** (*we received a warm welcome*) hearty, cordial, friendly, enthusiastic.

warm *vb* **1** (*the mother warmed the food for the baby*) heat, heat up. **2** (*the competitors warmed up for the race*) loosen up, limber up, exercise. ✧

warm the cockles of the heart to make you feel happy and contented (*It warmed the cockles of her heart to watch her children looking after the old woman*).

warn *vb* (*they were warned that they were entering a dangerous area*) advise, caution, make aware, notify, inform, (*inf*) tip off.

warning *n* **1** (*they had no warning of the terrible storm*) forewarning, notification, notice, information, indication, hint. **2** (*he was superstitious and regarded his experience as a warning of things to come*) omen, signal, threat.

warrior *n* (*a book about the deeds of ancient warriors*) fighter, combatant, champion, soldier, knight.

wary *adj* (*the children were taught to be wary of strangers*) cautious, careful, on your guard, watchful, chary, suspicious, distrustful.

wash *vb* **1** (*they washed their hands before dinner*) clean, cleanse, scrub. **2** (*the children washed before going to bed*) have a wash, wash yourself, clean yourself, sponge yourself down. **3** (*they washed their clothes and hung them out to dry*) launder, clean. **4** (*waves washing against the boats*) splash, dash, beat. ✧

wash your hands of (someone or something) to refuse to be held responsible for (someone or something) or to be involved any longer in (something) (*He has tried to help the student to get through her test but since she refuses to work he has washed his hands of her*).

waste *vb* **1** (*They waste a lot of money/Try not to waste time*) squander, fritter, misuse, misspend. **2** (*Because of his illness his limbs are wasting away*) grow weak, grow thin, wither.

waste *n* **1** (*find a way of getting rid of the waste*) garbage, trash, refuse, debris. **2** (*doing research in the wastes of the Antarctic*) wasteland, wilderness, desert, vastness.

wasteful *adj* (*a wasteful use of money*) thriftless, extravagant, spendthrift.

watch *vb* **1** (*we watched the sun going down*) look at, observe, view, contemplate, survey, stare at, gaze at. **2** (*if you watch what the teacher does you will be able to do the experiment yourself*) pay attention to, take notice of, to heed, concentrate on. **3** (*the police are watching him*) keep watch on, keep an eye on, keep under surveillance, follow, spy on. **4** (*watch and don't get attacked in that area of the town*) take care, look out, take heed, beware, be alert. **5** (*she asked her mother *to watch the children*) mind, take care of, look after, keep an eye on, tend. ▽

a watched pot never boils when you are waiting for something to happen the time taken seems much longer if you are constantly thinking about it.

watch (someone) like a hawk to watch (someone) very carefully (*The teacher has to watch the boy like a hawk as he always tries to bully the other children*) <Birds of prey are thought to have particularly sharp eyesight>.

watchman *n* security guard, guard, caretaker, custodian, sentry.

water *n* **1** (*have a glass of water with the meal*) tap water, bottled water, mineral water. **2** (*children playing by the water*) pond, pool, lake, river, sea. ▽

water off a duck's back to be totally ineffective or unsuccessful (*We tried to warn him that his journey would be dangerous but our warnings washed off him like water off a duck's back*) <Refers to the fact that water runs straight off the oily feathers on a duck's back>.

hold water to be able to be proved to be true, to be accurate (*The scientist's theory seemed interesting but when we put it to the test it did not hold water*) <A reference to a container of some kind that is not broken and so can hold liquids>.

watery *adj* **1** (*the gravy was watery/The soup was watery*) thin, weak, dilute, runny, tasteless, flavorless. **2** (*watery eyes*) wet, moist, damp, tearful, weepy.

wave *vb* **1** (*flags waving in the breeze*) flutter, flap, ripple, shake. **2** (*he waved his sword angrily*) shake, swing, brandish. **3** (*he waved his hand to his friends*) flutter, waggle. **4** (*he waved to the driver*) gesture. **5** (*her hair waves*) curl, kink.

wave *n* **1** (*the children were splashing in the waves*) breaker, swell, surf, billow. **2** (*the waves in her hair*) curl, kink. **3** (*a town hit by a crime wave*) upsurge, surge, rash, outbreak.

waver *vb* **1** (*his courage did not waver*) falter, vary, change. **2** (*we had been determined to go but then we began to waver*) hesitate, think twice, shilly-shally. **3** (*lights wavering*) flicker, tremble, quiver.

wax *vb* (*the moon was waxing*) increase, enlarge.

way *n* **1** (*they asked which was the way to Philadelphia*) road, route, direction. **2** (*she said that it was a long way to Philadelphia from there*) distance, journey. **3** (*they were taught the correct way to change the wheel of a car*) method, procedure, technique, system, manner, means. **4** (*the children laughed at the way the old lady dressed*) manner, fashion, style, mode. **5** (*they have old-fashioned ways*) habit, custom, practice, conduct, behavior. **6** (*his business affairs are in a bad way*) state, condition, situation. **7** (*in some ways I will miss them although mostly I am glad that they've gone*) respect, aspect, feature, detail, point. ▽

go out of your way to make a special effort, to do more than is really necessary (*our hosts went out of their way to make us feel welcome*).

have a way with (someone *or* **something)** to have a special knack when dealing with (someone or something), to be good at dealing with (someone or something) (*she wants to become a nanny and she certainly has a way with children*).

weak *adj* **1** (*she felt very weak after her long illness*) weakly, frail, delicate, feeble, shaky, tired. **2** (*their leader was too weak to stand up to the enemy*) cowardly, timid, soft, spineless, powerless. **3** (*she made a weak excuse for being late*) feeble, lame, pathetic, unconvincing, unsatisfactory. **4** (*the tea was too weak*) watery, tasteless, wishy-washy. ▽

in a weak moment at a time when you are feeling unusually generous, sympathetic, etc. (*In a weak moment I offered to lend them my car and then regretted it*).

weaken *vb* **1** (*the illness had obviously weakened her*) make weak, tire, wear out. **2** (*our chances of winning were weakened*) lessen, decrease, reduce, diminish, undermine. **3** (*our parents refused to let us go but then they weakened*) relent, come round, give in.

weakness *n* **1** (*a tendency to lie is her major weakness*) fault, failing, flaw, defect, shortcoming, imperfection, foible. **2** (*she has a weakness for chocolate*) fondness, liking, love, soft spot, preference, penchant.

wealth *n* (*he shared his great wealth among his family*) riches, fortune, money, capital, assets.

wealthy *adj* (*an area of the town where wealthy people live*) affluent, rich, well-off, well-to-do, moneyed, (*inf*) well-heeled.

wear *vb* **1** (*the children were wearing warm coats*) be dressed in, be clothed in, have on. **2** (*she wore a gloomy expression*) have, show, display. **3** (*rocks worn away by water*) erode, eat away, rub away. **4** (*she was worn out by the long walk*) tire, fatigue, exhaust. ▷

wear your heart on your sleeve to let your feelings be very obvious (*She is not one to wear her heart on her sleeve and so people did not realize that she was in love with him*).

weary *adj* **1** (*the children were weary at the end of the long school day*) tired, fatigued, exhausted, worn out, (*inf*) dead beat. **2** (*she is weary of her present job*) bored, discontented, jaded, (*inf*) fed up.

weather *n* (*what is the weather like there in August?*) climate. ▷

be under the weather to be slightly unwell (*She left work early because she was under the weather*).

web *n* (*a spider's web*) mesh, net, network, lattice.

wedding *n* wedding ceremony, marriage, marriage ceremony.

wedge *vb* **1** (*since it was very hot they wedged the door open*) jam, secure. **2** (*four of them were wedged in the back seat*) squeeze, jam, cram, pack.

wedge *n* (*a wedge of cheese*) chunk, hunk, lump.

weep *vb* (*the child wept when her mother went away*) cry, sob, shed tears.

weight *n* **1** (*estimate the weight of the cake*) heaviness. **2** (*a weight fell on his toe*) heavy object. **3** (*when their daughter returned it was a weight off their minds*) burden, load, onus, worry, trouble. **4** (*they attach a great deal of weight to his opinion*) importance, significance, value, substance. ▷

pull your weight to do your fair share of work, etc. (*They were all supposed to help with the housework but she did not pull her weight*).

throw your weight around to use your power or influence in a domineering, bullying way (*When her father is away her elder brother says that he is head of the house and throws his weight around*).

weird *adj* **1** (*we heard weird noises in the cellar*) eerie, strange, queer, uncanny, creepy, ghostly, unearthly, (*inf*) spooky. **2** (*she always wears weird clothing*) strange, queer, odd, bizarre, eccentric, outlandish, off-beat.

welcome *vb* **1** (*they welcomed their guests at the door*) greet, receive, meet. **2** (*we welcomed the news*) be pleased with, be glad at.

welfare *n* (*she was worried about her children's welfare*) well-being, health, happiness.

well *adj* **1** (*she has been sick but is now quite well*) in good health, healthy, fit, strong. **2** (*they found that all was well*) all right, satisfactory, fine, (*inf*) OK.

well *adv* **1** (*he plays the piano well*) competently, skillfully, expertly. **2** (*the children behaved well*) properly, correctly, suitably, satisfactorily. **3** (*they speak well of him*) highly, admiringly, approvingly, favorably. **4** (*they may well be right*) probably, likely, possibly.

wet *adj* **1** (*the ground was wet after the rain/Her clothes were wet*) damp, moist, soaked, drenched, saturated, sopping. **2** (*we had wet weather on vacation*) rainy, damp, showery.

wet *vb* **1** (*she wet the shirts before ironing them*) dampen, moisten, sprinkle, spray. **2** (*the rain really wet them*) soak, drench, saturate. ▷

a wet blanket a dull, uninteresting person who make s other people feel depressed (*We were enjoying the party until he arrived but he is such a wet blanket*).

be wet behind the ears to be young and inexperienced (*Don't let the young sales clerk deal with that difficult customer. He's still wet behind the ears*).

wharf *n* (*ships being unloaded at the wharf*) dock, quay, pier, jetty, landing stage.

wheeze *vb* (*she had a bad cold and was wheezing*) pant, puff, gasp.

whimper *vb* (*the dog was sitting whimpering on the doorstep*) whine, cry.

whine *vb* (*the children were bored and began to whine*) wail, cry, whimper, complain, (*inf*) grizzle.

whip *n* (*the jockey used his whip on the horse*) switch, crop, horsewhip, cat o' nine tails.

whip *vb* **1** (*they used to whip people who had done* *wrong*) lash, flog, scourge, birch, beat, thrash. **2** (*she whipped the cream*) beat, whisk, mix, blend. **3** (*he whipped his handkerchief from his pocket*) pull, yank, jerk, snatch, whisk. ↻

have the whip hand to have control or an advantage (*He has the whip hand in that partnership. He makes all the decisions*) <A reference to driving a coach>.

whipping boy someone who is blamed and punished for someone else's mistakes (*The young clerk is the whipping boy for the whole department*) <Refers historically to a boy who was punished by a tutor for any misdeeds a royal prince made, since the tutor was not allowed to strike a member of the royal family>.

whirl *vb* (*they watched the dancers whirling around the floor*) turn, spin, rotate, revolve, wheel, circle, twirl.

whisper *vb* (*she whispered to her friend at the back of the classroom*) murmur, mutter, breathe.

white *adj* **1** (*she was white with fear*) pale, wan, pallid, ashen, peaky. **2** (*her hair is white with age*) gray, silver, snowy white. ↻

white elephant something which is useless and often troublesome to look after (*The vase that my aunt gave me is a real white elephant. It's large and ugly and difficult to dust*) <White elephants were formerly given by the Kings of Siam to followers who had displeased them since the cost of keeping such an elephant was so great that it might well ruin the followers>.

white lie a not very serious lie (*I told a white lie when she asked me if I liked her dress. I didn't want to upset her*).

whole *adj* **1** (*we asked her to tell us the whole story*) full, entire, complete. **2** (*not a single wineglass was left whole*) intact, in one piece, undamaged, unbroken. ↻

go whole hog to do something completely and thoroughly (*We decorated one room and then decided to go whole hog and paint the entire house*) <Perhaps refers to buying a whole pig at market instead of just parts of it for meat>.

wholesome *adj* (*wholesome food*) health-giving, healthy, nutritious, nourishing.

wholly *adv* **1** (*we are not wholly against the scheme*) entirely, completely, fully, thoroughly, utterly. **2** (*the responsibility lies wholly with him*) only, solely, purely, exclusively.

wicked *adj* (*the wicked people who attacked and robbed the old man*) evil, bad, sinful, vicious, immoral, unethical, villainous, criminal.

wide *adj* **1** (*a city with wide streets*) broad, spacious. **2** (*a wide range of subjects is available at the school*) broad, large, extensive, comprehensive, wide-ranging. **3** (*he always wears very wide pants*) loose, baggy, roomy.

widespread *adj* (*there were widespread rumors of war*) general, common, universal, extensive, prevalent, rife.

width *n* **1** (*measure the width of the material*) wideness, breadth, broadness, span. **2** (*we admired the width of his knowledge*) wideness, breadth, scope, range, comprehensiveness.

wield *vb* **1** (*a knight wielding a sword*) brandish, flourish, wave, swing. **2** (*it is the deputy president who wields the power*) have, hold, exercise, exert.

wife *n* spouse, partner, (*inf*) better half.

wild *adj* **1** (*an area where wild animals roamed*) untamed, undomesticated, fierce, savage, ferocious. **2** (*the wildflowers of the area*) uncultivated, native. **3** (*the ship sank in wild weather*) stormy, rough, blustery, turbulent, windy. **4** (*they had to travel across wild country*) rough, rugged, desolate, waste. **5** (*the wild behavior of the crowd*) rowdy, disorderly, unruly, violent, turbulent, uncontrolled. ↻

a wild goose chase a search or hunt that is unlikely to end in success (*I knew it was a wild goose chase to look for a restaurant that was open at that time in the morning*).

spread like wildfire to spread extremely rapidly (*The disease spread like wildfire in the overcrowded community*) <Wildfire was probably a kind of fire started by lightning>.

wild horses would not drag (someone) to something *or* **somewhere** nothing would persuade (someone) to attend something or go somewhere (*Wild horses would not drag me to the mall on a Saturday afternoon. I hate crowds*).

will *n* **1** (*he seems to have lost the will to live*) desire, wish, inclination, determination. **2** (*he died without making a will*) last will and testament, testament.

willful, wilful (*Br, Cdn*) *adj* **1** (*a nanny finding it difficult to cope with such willful children*) headstrong, strong-willed, obstinate, stubborn, determined, disobedient, contrary. **2** (*the jury decided that it was a case of willful homicide*) deliberate, intentional, planned, premeditated, calculated.

willing *adj* **1** (*they had a lot of willing helpers at the church bazaar*) eager, keen, enthusiastic, avid. **2** (*there was no one willing to take responsibility for the organization of the event*) ready, prepared, disposed, agreeable.

wilt *vb* (*the flowers in the vase were wilting*) droop, wither, shrivel, dry up.

wily *adj* (*he was wily enough to convince the old lady that he was a representative of the church*) cunning, crafty, artful, scheming, sly, sharp.

win *vb* **1** (*we were not surprised when their team won*) be victorious, be the victor, come first, triumph, carry the day. **2** (*she won first prize*) gain, get, achieve, attain, acquire.

wince *vb* (*she winced when they reminded her of her tactless remark*) grimace, flinch, cringe, recoil.

wind *n* (*the wind blew the papers all around the room*) breeze, gale, gust, blast, draft. ✧

get wind of (something) to receive information about (something) usually indirectly or secretly (*They were planning to steal our bicycles but fortunately we got wind of their plans*) <A reference to the scent of an animal carried by the wind>.

take the wind out of (someone's) sail to reduce (someone's) pride in his or her cleverness, abilities, achievements, etc. (*She was boasting about how many tests she had passed when we took the wind out of her sail by telling her that everyone else had passed more*) <A reference to the fact that a ship takes the wind out of another ship's sails if it passes too close to it on the windward side>.

wind *vb* **1** (*her grandmother asked her to wind her wool*) twist, twine, coil, roll. **2** (*the road winds up the mountain*) twist, twist and turn, curve, loop, zigzag, spiral, snake, meander.

wing *n* **1** (*the family occupies just the west wing of the castle*) side, annex. **2** (*they are on the right wing of the party*) section, side, group, segment. ✧

take (someone) under your wing to take (someone) under your protection and guidance (*The girl has been neglected. She needs an older woman to take her under her wing*).

wink *vb* **1** (*he winked an eye*) blink, flutter, bat. **2** (*lights winking on the water*) twinkle, flash, sparkle, glitter, gleam.

winner *n* (*they were the winners in the battle/the winner in the tennis tournament*) victor, champion, conqueror.

wipe *vb* (*wipe the kitchen surfaces*) clean, sponge, mop, rub, brush. ✧

wipe the floor with (someone) to defeat (someone), to scold (someone) very severely (*The visiting team wiped the floor with us/ Mum wiped the floor with us when we arrived home late*).

wisdom *n* **1** (*admire their wisdom in getting out of the industry at the right time*) sense, common sense, prudence, good judgment, shrewdness, smartness. **2** (*the young people benefited from the wisdom of their grandparents*) knowledge.

wise *adj* **1** (*we thought it wise to leave early when it began to snow*) sensible, well-advised, prudent, shrewd, smart. **2** (*they asked the wise old men of the village for advice*) knowledgable, learned, well-informed, enlightened, sage.

wish *vb* (*they could not have wished for friendlier neighbors*) want, desire, long for, yearn for, covet, (*inf*) have a yen for.

wish *n* **1** (*they were supposed to obey the king's every wish*) want, desire, demand, request. **2** (*at last she was able to satisfy her wish to travel*) desire, longing, yearning, fancy, inclination, craving, (*inf*) yen. ✧

wishful thinking believing that, or hoping that, something unlikely is true or will happen just because you wish that it would (*We hoped our team would win but it was just wishful thinking. They were not very good*).

wistful *adj* (*she had a wistful expression as she watched them leave on vacation*) yearning, longing, forlorn, sad, pathetic.

wit *n* **1** (*he did not have the wit to realize that she was teasing him*) intelligence, brains, sense, common sense, shrewdness. **2** (*we had to admire his wit as he kept us all amused*) wittiness, humor. ✧

at your wits' end extremely worried and desperate (*We were at our wits' end when all our money was stolen*).
live by your wits to make a living from cunning schemes rather than from working.

witch *n* (*a story about a witch and her broomstick*) enchantress, sorceress. ⟳

witch-hunt a search for people who are thought to have done something wrong, hold opinions which are considered dangerous, etc., in order to persecute them (*There was a witch-hunt to remove people from the club who held different political opinions from the majority*) <Formerly there were organized searches for people thought to be witches in order that they might be punished>.

withdraw *vb* **1** (*she withdrew from the tennis match because of ill health*) pull out, come out, retire. **2** (*they withdrew their son from the school*) remove, take away, pull out. **3** (*the troops withdrew when they were defeated*) pull back, fall back, move back, retreat, retire, depart.

wither *vb* (*the flowers in the vase had withered*) fade, dry up, dry out, shrivel, die.

witness *vb* (*they witnessed a terrible accident*) see, observe, look on at, watch, view, be present at.

witness *n* (*the police asked for witnesses at the scene of the accident*) eye-witness, onlooker, observer, spectator, bystander.

witty *adj* (*witty stories/witty people*) amusing, funny, humorous, comic, clever.

wizard *n* (*a fairy story about wizards*) warlock, sorcerer, magician, enchanter.

wobble *vb* **1** (*this table wobbles*) rock, teeter, shake. **2** (*wobble down the street on stiletto heels*) totter, teeter, sway, stagger, waddle. **3** (*her voice wobbled and she began to cry*) shake, tremble, quiver.

woe *n* (*we listened to her tale of woe*) misfortune, distress, suffering, trouble, misery, unhappiness.

wonder *n* **1** (*watched with wonder as the acrobats performed*) amazement, astonishment, awe, bewilderment, curiosity. **2** (*the acrobats are a wonder*) marvel, miracle, prodigy, surprise. ⟳

a nine days' wonder something that has aroused interest or talk for a short time only (*It was in all the papers when he was sent to prison but it was a nine days' wonder*).

wonder *vb* **1** (*wondering at the immensity of the sky*) admire, gape, marvel. **2** (*I wonder if they will marry*) conjecture, ponder, query, question, speculate.

wonderful *adj* **1** (*the church ceiling was a wonderful sight*) marvelous, remarkable, extraordinary, amazing, astonishing, fantastic. **2** (*she was a wonderful pianist*) superb, marvelous, brilliant, excellent, first-rate, outstanding.

wood *n* **1** (*houses made of wood*) timber. **2** (*go for a walk in the wood*) woods, forest, copse, thicket. ⟳

be out of the woods to be free from danger or difficulty (*She was very sick and nearly died but she is out of the woods now*).
knock on wood to touch something made of wood supposedly in an effort to keep away bad luck or misfortune <A reference to a well-known superstition>.

wooly, woolly (*Br, Cdn*) *adj* **1** (*buy the child a wooly toy*) fluffy, fleecy, furry. **2** (*woolly thoughts*) hazy, vague, muddled, confused, indefinite, uncertain.

word *n* **1** (*she was trying to think of another word for "work"*) term, expression. **2** (*she gave him her word that she would be there*) promise, pledge, assurance, guarantee, undertaking. **3** (*they have had no word about their missing son*) news, information, communication. ⟳

have words to quarrel or argue (*From the expressions on their faces I would say that they have had words*).
take (someone) at his *or* **her word** to believe (someone) without question and act accordingly (*He said we could borrow the car any time and we took him at his word*).

work *n* **1** (*making a dollhouse for his daughter involved a lot of work*) effort, exertion, labor, toil, trouble. **2** (*her work involves meeting a great many people*) job, employment, occupation, profession, trade. ⟳

have your work cut out to face a very difficult task (*You will have your work cut out to persuade him to stay*) <Literally to have a lot of work ready for you to do>.

work *vb* **1** (*he works in banking*) be employed,

have a job. **2** (*the students will have to work at their studies to pass the exams*) exert yourself, apply yourself, make an effort, labor, toil. **3** (*can you work this machine?*) operate, use, control, handle. **4** (*this machine does not work*) go, operate, function, run. **5** (*that idea will not work*) succeed, be successful, go well, be effective.

world *n* **1** (*the peoples of the world*) earth, globe, planet. **2** (*the world was shocked by the terrorist attack*) people, everyone, the public. **3** (*the medical world*) society, sector, section, group. ✧

out of this world remarkably good (*The food in the new restaurant is out of this world*).
think the world of (someone or something) to be extremely fond of (someone or something) (*She thinks the world of her dog*).

worry *n* **1** (*his behavior caused her a lot of worry*) anxiety, trouble, bother, distress, disturbance, upset, uneasiness. **2** (*she was a real worry to her parents*) trouble, nuisance, pest, problem, trial, thorn in the flesh.

worsen *vb* **1** (*the situation between workers and management has worsened*) get worse, take a turn for the worse, deteriorate. **2** (*his efforts to help simply worsened the situation*) make worse, aggravate, exacerbate, increase.

worship *vb* **1** (*go to church to worship God*) pray to, praise, glorify, pay homage to. **2** (*he simply worships his wife*) idolize, adore, be devoted to, cherish, dote on.

worth *n* **1** (*the jewelry is of little financial worth but is of sentimental worth*) value. **2** (*we regarded his advice as being of little worth*) value, use, advantage, benefit, gain. ✧

for all you are worth using maximum effort (*We tried for all we were worth to finish the job in time*).
make (something) worth (someone's) while to make (something) worth (someone's) time and effort, to give (someone) sufficient reward or recompense (*If you want a workman to do repairs on a Sunday you will have to make it worth his while*).

worthy *adj* **1** (*they were not worthy of respect*) deserving, meriting. **2** (*the worthy people in the community*) good, decent, honorable, upright,

virtuous, admirable, commendable, deserving.
wound *n* **1** (*he got his wound dressed in hospital*) injury, sore, cut. **2** (*her remark was a wound to his pride*) blow, injury, hurt, damage, slight.

wrap *vb* **1** (*wrap the child in a blanket and take him to a hospital*) cover, bundle up. **2** (*she wrapped the Christmas presents*) wrap up, parcel up, package, tie up, gift-wrap. ✧

be wrapped up in (someone or something) to give (someone or something) all your attention (*She complains about the fact that her husband is completely wrapped up in his work*).
keep (something) under wraps to keep (something) secret or confidential (*We are keeping our plans for the firm under wraps at the moment so that our rivals don't find out about them*).

wrath *n* (*they had to face the wrath of the teacher when they played truant*) anger, rage, fury, indignation, annoyance.

wreck *vb* **1** (*he wrecked his father's car*) crash, smash, demolish, ruin, damage. **2** (*his illness wrecked their vacation plans*) ruin, destroy, spoil, shatter.

wrench *vb* (*he wrenched the lid from the container*) twist, pull, tug, jerk, force. ✧

throw a wrench into the works to hinder or spoil (a plan, project, etc.) (*We were going away for the weekend but my boss threw a wrench into the works by asking me to work on Saturday*).

wretched *adj* **1** (*she was feeling wretched about being away from home*) miserable, depressed, unhappy, sad. **2** (*he felt wretched when he had flu*) sick, ill, unwell, (*inf*) under the weather. **3** (*he has a wretched cold*) nasty, unpleasant, disagreeable.

wriggle *vb* **1** (*children wriggling with impatience in their seats*) twist, squirm, writhe. **2** (*she tried to wriggle out of helping with the housework*) dodge, evade, avoid, duck out of.

wring *vb* **1** (*wring the clothes out*) squeeze, twist. **2** (*his enemies wrung the information from him*) extract, force, wrench.

wrinkle *n* (*she ironed her blouse to remove the wrinkles*) crease, pucker, fold, furrow.

write *vb* **1** (*write an essay*) compose, pen. **2** (*she wrote down the names of the people present*) put down, take down, note, list, record. ✧

be nothing to write home about to be unremarkable, to be nothing special (*The meal in the new restaurant was all right but it was nothing to write home about*).

writer *n* (*he is a professional writer*) author, novelist, journalist.

writing *n* **1** (*she teaches children writing*) handwriting, penmanship, script. **2** (*a list of his writings*) work, book, publication. ✧

the writing on the wall something which indicates that something unpleasant, such as failure, unhappiness, disaster, etc., will happen (*She should have seen the writing on the wall when her boss kept complaining about her work*) <A Biblical reference to Daniel 5:5-31, in which the coming destruction of the Babylonian empire is made known to Belshazzar at a feast through mysterious writing on a wall>.

wrong *adj* **1** (*it is wrong to steal*) bad, wicked, sinful, illegal, unlawful, criminal, crooked. **2** (*there is something wrong with the computer*) broken, faulty, defective, out of order. **3** (*it was the wrong way to deal with the problem*) incorrect, improper, inappropriate, unsuitable. **4** (*she gave the wrong answer to the mathematical question*) incorrect, inaccurate, erroneous, mistaken. ✧

get on the wrong side of (someone) to cause (someone) to dislike or be hostile to you (*She seemed to get on the wrong side of the boss from her first day in the firm*).

not to put a foot wrong not to make a mistake of any kind (*It was not surprising that he won the tennis match. He did not put a foot wrong throughout the game*).

wrong *n* **1** (*be taught right from wrong*) badness, evil, sin, sinfulness, unlawfulness. **2** (*he committed several wrongs*) misdeed, offense, crime. ✧

be in the wrong to be to blame, to be guilty of some kind of error (*The accident was his fault but he refused to admit that he had been in the wrong*).

Y Z

yearn *vb* (*they yearned for some sunshine*) long, pine, crave, desire, covet, fancy, hanker after, (*inf*) have a yen for.

yield *vb* **1** (*they refuse to yield to the invading army*) submit, give in, surrender, concede defeat. **2** (*they finally yielded to his demands*) give in, comply with, consent to, grant. **3** (*investments which yield a good return*) bring in, earn, return, produce. **4** (*an area which yields heavy crops*) produce, give, bear, grow, supply.

young *adj* (*young people*) youthful, juvenile, adolescent.

zealous *adj* (*zealous followers of the sport/zealous in their efforts to gain support*) eager, keen, enthusiastic, passionate, fervent, earnest, fanatical.

zenith *n* (*when the Roman empire was at the zenith of its power*) peak, height, top, pinnacle, acme, apex.

zero *n* **1** (*how many zeroes are there when you write a million in figures?*) nought, nothing. **2** (*we won absolutely zero*) nothing, naught, nil, (*inf*) zilch.

zest *n* (*the old lady's zest for life*) enthusiasm, eagerness, relish, energy.

zone *n* (*a traffic-free zone*) area, sector, region.

Atlas of World History

Timelines

EUROPE	AMERICAS	ASIA	AFRICA
BC	BC	BC	BC
c. 20,000 Paintings showing hunting scenes in caves in southern France and Spain			
		c. 8000 First farming in the Middle East	
c. 6500 Agriculture in Greece			*c.* 5000 Agricultural settlements in Egypt
		c. 4000 Beginning of Bronze Age in the Near East	
		c. 3100 First writing on clay tablets	
	c. 3000 First ceramics in Mexico	*c.* 3000 First cities in Sumer	*c.* 3200 King Menes unites Egypt
		c. 2750 Growth of civilizations in Indus valley	*c.* 2658 Beginning of 'Old Kingdom' in Egypt
c. 2200 Beginnings of Bronze Age Minoan civilization in Crete	*c.* 2000 First metal-working in Peru		*c.* 2650 First pyramid built for King Zoser of Egypt
		c. 1750 Collapse of Indus Valley civilization	
c. 1600 Mycenaean civilization in Greece		*c.* 1600 Rise of Shang Dynasty in China	*c.* 1552 Beginning of 'New Kingdom' in Egypt
c. 1000 Destruction of Minoan Crete			1361–52 Rule of Tutankhamun in Egypt
c. 1200 Collapse of Mycenaean Empire	1200 Rise of the Oltec civilization	*c.* 1100 Chou Dynasty supplants Shang in China	
c. 1100 Phoenicians develop first phonic alphabet			
c. 800 Rise of city states in Greece		*c.* 720 Height of Assyrian power	*c.* 800 Carthage founded by Phoenicians
753 Foundation of Rome		*c.* 650 First iron used in China	
		586 Babylonian captivity of Jews	
510 Foundation of Roman Republic		*c.* 486 Death of Siddhartha Gautama, founder of Buddhism	
431–404 Peloponnesian War between Athens and Sparta		476–221 'Warring States' period in China	
334–327 Alexander the Great of Macedonia conquers Persia		*c.* 320 Mauryan Empire in India	
290 Roman conquest of central Italy			
264–146 Three Punic Wars between Rome and Carthage		221 Ch'in Dynasty	
146 Greece becomes part of Roman Empire		202 China under control of Han Dynasty	
31 Roman victory at the Battle of Actium			

EUROPE		AMERICAS		ASIA		AFRICA	
AD		AD		AD		AD	
43	Roman invasion of Britain			c. 0	Buddhism spreads from India to South East Asia and China		
116	Roman Empire at greatest extent			25	Han Dynasty restored in China	30	Egypt becomes Roman province
238	First raids on Roman Empire by Goths			131–36	Jewish revolt against Rome		
285	Roman Empire divided into Eastern Empire and Western Empire	c. 300	Mayan civilization rises to prominence in Central America	220	End of Han Dynasty: China splits into three states		
				214	Great Wall of China built		
370	Huns from Asia begin to invade Europe			330	Constantinople becomes capital of Roman Empire		
410	Visigoths sack Rome	c. 400	Pre-Inca civilizations in western South America	350	Huns invade western Central Asia	429–535	Vandal kingdom in northern Africa
449	Angles, Saxons and Jutes invade Britain			407–553	Early Mongol Empire	533–552	Justinian restores Roman power in North Africa
486	Frankish Empire founded by Clovis			552	Buddhism introduced to Japan		
497	Franks converted to Christianity			c. 570 –632	Muhammad: founder of Islamic religion		
597	St Augustine's Christian mission to England	c. 600	Height of Mayan civilization			641	Conquest of Egypt by Arabs
711	Second Muslim conquest of Spain			618	China reunited under T'ang Dynasty	c. 700	Rise of Empire of Ghana
793	Viking raids begin			622	First year of Islamic calendar		
800	Charlemagne crowned Holy Roman Emperor			635–74	Muslim conquests of Syria and Persia		
843	Treaty of Verdun divides Carolingian or Frankish Empire into three parts			730	First printing in China		
874	First Viking settlers in Iceland			821	Conquest of Tibet by Chinese		
886	Danelaw established in England					920 –1050	Height of Ghana Empire
911	Vikings granted Duchy of Normandy by Frankish king			907	Last T'ang Emperor deposed in China	969	Fatimids conquer Egypt and found Cairo
				939	Civil wars in Japan		
c. 1000	Vikings discover North America			960 –1127	Northern Sung Dynasty	c. 1000	First Iron Age settlement at Zimbabwe
1016	King Cnut rules England, Denmark and Norway			1127 –1279	Southern Sung Dynasty		
1054	Great Schism finally divides Church into Western Church and Eastern Church						

EUROPE	AMERICAS	ASIA	AFRICA
1066 Defeat of Anglo-Saxons by William the Conqueror			
1071 Normans conquer Byzantine Italy		**1071** Asia Minor conquered by Seljuk Turks	
1095–99 First Crusade	**1100** Toltecs build capital city at Tula in Mexico	**c. 1100** Polynesian Islands colonized	**c. 1150** Beginnings of Yoruba city states (Nigeria)
1147–49 Second Crusade		**1156–59** Civil wars in Japan	**1174** Ottoman Turks under Saladin conquer Egypt
1189–92 Third Crusade		**1174–87** Ottoman Turks under Saladin conquer Syria and Levant	
1202–04 Fourth Crusade and capture of Constantinople	Cuzco founded by the Incas		**c. 1200** Rise of Empire of Mali in West Africa
1217–21 Fifth Crusade		**1206** Mongol Empire founded under Genghis Khan	
1228–29 Sixth Crusade	**c. 1250** End of Toltec Empire in Mexico	**1234** Mongols invade and destroy Northern China	Emergence of Hausa city states (Nigeria)
1237 Mongols invade Russia			**1240** Collapse of Empire of Ghana
1241 Mongols invade Poland, Hungary, Bohemia then withdraw			
1248–54 Seventh Crusade			
1250 Collapse of Imperial power in Germany and Italy on death of Holy Roman Emperor, Frederick II		**1261** Beginning of Greek Palaeologian dynasties: ruled the Byzantine Empire until 1453	
1270–71 Eighth Crusade			**c. 1300** Emergence of Ife kingdom, city state of the Yoruba (West Africa)
1271–72 Ninth Crusade			
1305 Papacy moves from Rome to Avignon	**1325** Rise of Aztecs in Mexico	**c. 1334** Black Death in China	
1337 –1453 Hundred Years' War between France and England	Founding of city of Tenochtitlán	**1336** Revolution in Japan	
		c. 1370 Tamerlane begins conquest of Asia	
1378 –1417 Second Great Schism: break between Rome and Avignon, rival Popes elected	**1370** Expansion of Chimu kingdom in South America	**1368** Ming Dynasty founded in China	
	c. 1375 Beginning of Aztec expansion	**1380** Tartars (the Golden Horde) defeated by the Grand Duke of Moscow	
1381 Peasants' Revolt in England			
1385 Portugal's independence from Spain assured	**1438** Inca Empire established in Peru	**1398– 1402** Tamerlane conquers kingdom of Delhi and Ottoman Empire	**1415** Portuguese begin to establish colonies in Africa
1415 Henry V of England defeats French at battle of Agincourt	**1440–69** Montezuma I rules Aztecs		**1450** Height of Songhai Empire in northwest Africa
1453 England loses all her French possessions except for Calais	**1450** Incas conquer Chimu kingdom	**1453** Ottoman Turks capture Constantinople	
	1493 First New World settlement by Spanish		**1482** Portuguese settle Gold Coast (now Ghana)
1455–85 Wars of the Roses in England		**1498** Explorer Vasco da Gama reaches India around Cape of Good Hope	**1492** Spain begins conquest of North African coast
1492 Last Muslims in Spain conquered by Christians			

EUROPE	AMERICAS	ASIA	AFRICA
	1502–20 Aztec conquests under Montezuma II		1505 Portuguese begin establishing trading posts in East Africa
1517 Martin Luther nails '95 theses' to church door at Wittenberg	c. 1510 First African slaves taken to America	1517 Ottoman Turks conquer Syria, Egypt and Arabia	
1520 Zwingli leads Protestant Reformation in Switzerland			
1522 First circumnavigation of world by Portuguese navigator, Magellan	1521 Cortes conquers Aztec capital, Tenochtitlán	1526 Foundation of Mughal Empire (till 1857)	
1529–36 Reformation Parliament begins in England	1533 Pizarro conquers Peru: end of Inca Empire	1533 Ivan the Terrible succeeds to Russian throne	
1532–36 Calvin starts Protestant movement in France	1535 Spaniards explore Chile		
1540 Potato introduced to Europe from New World			1546 Destruction of Mali Empire in northwest Africa by the Songhai
1545 Council of Trent marks start of the Counter-Reformation (till 1563)			
1558 England loses Calais to French			
1562–98 Wars of Religion in France			1570 Kanem-Bornu Empire in the Sudan flourishes
1568 –1648 Eighty Years' War or Dutch Revolt			1571 Portuguese establish colony in Angola (Southern Africa)
1571 Battle of Lepanto: end of Turkish sea power			
1588 Spanish Armada defeated by English	1607 First successful English settlement in America at Jamestown, in Virginia		1591 Moroccans destroy Songhai Empire
1600 Foundation of English East India Company	1608 French colonists found Quebec		
1618–48 Thirty Years' War in Europe	1620 Puritans (Pilgrim Fathers) land in New England		
	1624 Dutch settle New Amsterdam	1630s Japan isolates itself from the rest of the world	
1649 Execution of Charles I in London	1654 Portuguese take Brazil from Dutch	1644 Ch'ing Dynasty founded in China by Manchus	1652 Foundation of Cape Colony by Dutch
	1664 New Amsterdam seized by British: later renamed New York		1686 French annex Madagascar
1688 England's 'Glorious Revolution'	1693 Gold discovered in Brazil	1690 Foundation of Calcutta by British	

EUROPE	AMERICAS	ASIA	AFRICA
1700–14 War of Spanish Succession		1707 Break-up of Mughal Empire	1700 Rise of Ashanti power in the Gold Coast)
1704 Battle of Blenheim		1724 Hyderabad in India gains freedom from Mughals	
1707 Union of England and Scotland			
1740–48 War of Austrian Succession	1759 British capture Quebec from French	1757 British rule in India established by battle of Plassey	
1756–63 Seven Years' War	1775–83 American War of Independence	1768 Captain James Cook begins exploration of the Pacific	
1765 Invention of James Watts' steam engine	1776 Declaration of American Independence	1773–75 Peasant revolts in Russia	
Beginning of Industrial Revolution in Britain	1789 Washington becomes first US president	1784 India Act gives Britain control of India	1787 British acquire Sierra Leone
1789 French Revolution	1791 Slave revolt in Haiti	1788 British penal colony at Botany Bay, Australia	1798 Napoleon attacks Egypt
1804 Napoleon proclaimed Emperor	1803 Louisiana Purchase doubles size of USA	1799 Napoleon invades Syria	1811 Muhammad Ali massacres Mameluke leaders and takes control in Egypt
1812 Napoleon's Russian campaign	1808–26 Independence movements in South America	1804–15 Serbs revolt against Ottoman Turks	
1815 Napoleon defeated at Waterloo		1819 British establish a trading post at Singapore	1814 British acquire the Cape Colony in South Africa from the Dutch
1821–29 Greek War of Independence	1821 Spain grants Mexico independence		1818 Zulu Empire founded in southern Africa
1825 First commercial steam railway	1840 Union of Upper and Lower Canada		1822 Liberia founded on the west coast of Africa for freed American slaves
1830 Revolutions in France, Germany, Poland and Italy	1845 Texas annexed by US	1840 Britain establishes sovereignty over New Zealand	
	1846–48 War between US and Mexico	1840–42 First Opium War between Britain and China	1830 French begin conquest of Algeria
1845–46 Irish potato famine	1848 Gold is found in California	1842 Hong Kong ceded to Britain by China	1835–37 Great Trek of Boers in South Africa
1848 Year of Revolutions		1854 Trade treaties between Japan and the US	1860 French expansion in West Africa begins
	1861–65 American Civil War	and 1858	
1854–56 Crimean War	1865 Assassination of US president, Abraham Lincoln	1856–60 Second Opium War	1869 Opening of Suez Canal
1861 Kingdom of Italy proclaimed		1857 Indian troops mutiny against British Army	1879 Anglo-Zulu War
	1867 Dominion of Canada formed	1877 Queen Victoria proclaimed Empress of India	1880–81 First Anglo-Boer War
1870–71 Franco-Prussian War	Alaska is purchased by the US from Russia	1885 Indian National Congress formed	1882 British occupy Egypt
1871 German Empire created		1886 Upper and Lower Burma united under British India	1884 Germany acquires African colonies
			1885 Belgium acquires Congo
1882– Triple Alliance 1914 between Germany, Austria and Italy	1898 Spanish-American War	1894–95 First Sino-Japanese War	1886 Germany and Britain divide East Africa
			1899 Second Anglo-Boer –1902 War

EUROPE		AMERICAS		ASIA		AFRICA	
1904	Anglo-French Entente			1901	Unification of Australia		
1905	First Revolution in Russia			1904–05	Russo-Japanese War		
1912–13	Balkan Wars	1911	Revolution in Mexico	1906	Revolt in Persia	1910	Union of South Africa formed
		1914	Panama Canal opens	1910	Japan annexes Korea	1911	Italy takes Libya from the Ottoman
1914–18	First World War	1917	US enters First World War	1911–49	Chinese revolution		Empire
1917	Russian Revolution			1922	Republic proclaimed in Turkey	1914	Egypt a British Protectorate
1919	Treaty of Versailles			1928	Chiang Kai-shek unites China	1919	Nationalist revolt in Egypt against British occupation
		1929	Wall Street crash heralds the	1931	Japanese occupy Manchuria		
1920	League of Nations established		Depression	1934–35	Mao Tse-tung's Long March	1922	Egypt achieves independence
1922	Irish Free State created by Anglo-Irish Treaty of 1921	1933	Roosevelt introduces New Deal in the US	1937–45	Second Sino-Japanese War	1935	Mussolini invades Abyssinia (Ethiopia)
				1940	Japan allies with Germany		
	Mussolini takes power in Italy			1941	Japanese attack US fleet at Pearl Harbor		
1926	General Strike in Britain	1941	US enters Second World War	1942	Japanese fleet defeated by US at battle of Midway		
1933	Hitler becomes German Chancellor			1945	Nuclear bombs dropped on Japan	1949	Apartheid is established in South
1936–39	Civil war in Spain			1946–49	Civil war in China		Africa
1939–45	Second World War			1947	India, Pakistan and Burma gain independence		
1945	United Nations established						
				1948	Jewish state of Israel founded		
1948	Communists seize power in Czechoslovakia			1948–49	First Arab-Israeli War		
				1950–53	Korean War		
				1954–75	Vietnam War		
1956	Hungarian revolt crushed by Russians	1959	Cuban revolution	1956	Second Arab-Israeli War	1956	Suez crisis
1958	European Economic Community (EEC) comes into being	1962	Cuban missile crisis	1957	Federation of Malaya independent	1957	Ghana becomes independent, followed by other African states
		1963	President Kennedy assassinated	1962	Sino-Indian War		
				1967	Third Arab-Israeli War	1960	Civil war follows independence in the Congo
1961	Berlin Wall built: beginning of Cold War in Europe	1963–73	US involvement in Vietnam War	1971	East Pakistan becomes Bangladesh	1962	Algeria gains independence from France
		1969	Neil Armstrong becomes first man on the moon	1973	Fourth Arab-Israeli War		
1968	USSR invades Czechoslovakia	1973	Political unrest in Chile culminates in a military coup	1974	Portuguese African colonies independent	1967–70	Civil war in Nigeria
1973	Britain, Eire and Denmark join EC (9 member states)			1978	Fifth Arab-Israeli War		
		1974	Resignation of US President Nixon: Gerald Ford becomes US president	1979	Soviet invasion of Afghanistan	1979	General Amin flees from Uganda
1975	Restoration of monarchy in Spain				Shah of Iran deposed: Islamic republic declared		

EUROPE	AMERICAS	ASIA	AFRICA
1980 Polish Solidarity Trade Union, led by Lech Walesa, confronts the Polish Communist government	1981 US hostages in Iran freed	1980–88 Iran-Iraq War	1980 Rhodesia, last British colony in Africa, becomes independent as Zimbabwe
1981 Greece becomes tenth member of the EC	1982 Falklands War between Argentina and Britain: Britain retains Falklands	1984 Indian prime minister, Indira Gandhi, is assassinated	1981 President Sadat of Egypt is assassinated
1985 Mikhail Gorbachev elected new Soviet leader	1983 US troops invade Grenada		
1986 Prime Minister Palme of Sweden assassinated. Spain and Portugal join the EC (12 member states)	1986 US raid on Libya	1986 Overthrow of Marcos regime in Philippines	1985 Renewed unrest in South Africa
	Nuclear arms talks resume between USA and USSR	1987 Ongoing civil war in Lebanon	1986 Ethiopia has worst famine in more than ten years
1989 Berlin Wall dismantled	1987 Falling dollar and Wall Street crash	1990 Gulf War begins: Iran invades Kuwait	
1991 Break up of the Soviet Union. West and East Germany are united	1989 US troops invade Panama	US and Allies send troops to Gulf region	1990 Nelson Mandela, African National Congress (ANC) political prisoner, is freed in South Africa: process of dismantling apartheid begins
1992 Bloody civil war in Yugoslavia: European Commission recognizes independence of Croatia and Slovenia	1992 Bill Clinton is elected US president	1994 Israel and PLO sign pact ending Israeli occupation of Gaza Strip and Jericho	
1993 Czechoslovakia is split into Slovakia and the Czech Republic		1995 Israeli Prime Minister Yitzakh Rabin is assassinated	1994 In South Africa ANC wins first multiracial election in Africa
1994–96 First Russian-Chechen War	1994 US troops invade Haiti to oust military government	1997 Hong Kong returned to Chinese rule	Massacre of Tutsis by Hutus in Rwanda leaves estimated 500,000 dead and 1.5 million homeless
1995 Dayton Peace Accords signed to end civil war in Bosnia and Herzegovina		1999 King Hussein of Jordan dies: Prince Abdullah is king	1997 End of civil war in Zaire and country is renamed as the Democratic Republic of Congo
Austria, Finland and Sweden join the EC now the EU (15 member states)		Allied jets attack missile sites in Iraq	
1997 Labour Party wins British general election: Tony Blair is prime minister	1999 Self-governing region of Nunavut in northwest Canada comes into being	Inhabitants of East Timor vote for independence from Indonesia: UN sends in an Australian peacekeeping force when Indonesian militia go on the rampage	1999 UN troops pull out of Angola
1998 Good Friday Agreement in Northern Ireland			President Nelson Mandela of South Africa stands down from politics: Thabo Mbeki is new president
1999 Entire European Commission resigns following a report on corruption	Lost Mayan city found at border of Mexico and Guatemala	Military coup ends civilian government in Pakistan	

EUROPE	AMERICAS	ASIA	AFRICA
1999 –2002 Major combat in Second Russian-Chechen War	**2000** President Fuyimori of Peru decamps to Japan	**2000** Fijian government overthrown by armed coup	**2000** Devastating floods in Mozambique
2000 Spain and Britain agree on administrative arrangements for Gibraltar	**2001** George W. Bush becomes US president	Israel withdraws from South Lebanon	**2001** More devastating floods in Mozambique
2001 Former Yugoslav president, Slobodan Milosevic, extradited to the Hague to stand trial for war crimes	IMF lends $8 billion to Argentina to stave off the country's financial collapse	**2001** Ongoing violence in Israeli-Palestinian conflict	Zimbabwe approves legislation for white-owned farms to be confiscated without compensation
2001–02 Outbreak of foot and mouth disease rocks British agricultural industry	US is target of coordinated terrorist attacks on World Trade Center and the Pentagon: US Senate enacts anti-terrorism legislation	United Islamic Front for the Salvation of Afghanistan, with US and British air support, defeats the Taliban government	**2002** Mt Nyiragongo erupts in DR Congo
2002 The euro, a single currency shared by 12 members of the EU, successfully launched	**2002** US slaps a heavy tariff on steel imports	**2002** East Timor recognised internationally as an independent state	Robert Mugabe re-elected as President of Zimbabwe
2003 London's biggest ever political demonstration against impending war in Iraq but British troops are part of Coalition forces that invade Iraq	**2003** NASA spacecraft breaks up on re-entry: 7 astronauts killed	**2003** US-led Coalition forces invade Iraq: US-led transitional authority is set up to oversee transference of rule to a civilian government	**2003** Nigerian peacekeeping force enters Liberia to stop civil war
Heatwave in Europe causes around 10,000 deaths among the elderly in France	US lifts much-criticized tariff on steel imports	North Korea withdraws from Nuclear Non-Proliferation Treaty	**2004** African National Congress wins South African general election with 70% of the vote
2004 10 more countries join the EU (25 member states)	Invasion of Iraq by US-led Coalition Forces	**2004** Insurgency in Iraq reaches new heights of violence in a sustained suicide bombing campaign	In Sudan, the government and the People's Liberation Army agree to end the civil war: ongoing violence in the Darfur region
Swedish foreign minister, Anna Lindh, is stabbed to death in Stockholm	**2004** Haitian President Aristide resigns and goes into exile	Asian Tsunami devastates shoreline communities in Indonesia, Sri Lanka and India	A UN report states that life expectancy in 7 African countries has fallen below 40
2005 Suicide bombers in London underground trains and a bus kill 52 people and wound over 700: British born al-Qaeda activists are identified as responsible	NASA lands a mobile robot on Mars

Venezuela votes to keep President Hugo Chavez in office by 52% to 48%

George Bush re-elected as US president | **2005** Parliamentary elections held in Iraq: Shiites largest party but do not have majority vote | **2005** A forced 'slum clearance' by the government of Zimbabwe drives fringe town dwellers back into the countryside |
| | **2005** US continues its presence in Iraq

Hurricane Katrina devastates US Gulf coast | Israel withdraws settlers from Gaza Strip

North Korea admits possession of nuclear weapons | Ellen Johnson is elected President of Liberia: first woman president in Africa |

The First Humans

Our closest relations in the animal world are chimpanzees and gorillas. By about 4 million years ago, the earliest human ancestors had evolved in Africa. They were called *Australopithecus* (which means "southern ape"), but unlike apes they had the ability to walk upright. The first *Homo* (man) fossils which have been found date to 2 million years ago, but it was not until about 100,000 years ago that the first fully modern humans evolved in Africa. Over these millions of years of human evolution, the most noticeable development was in the size of the skull and the brain. As our ancestors' brains became larger, they developed other skills: the ability to make tools, to use language, to work together as a group, to create the first art.

During the cold phases of the last Ice Age, which lasted from about 2 million to 10,000 years ago, temperatures were, on average, 10–15°C lower than the present day. Humans were therefore forced to adapt to a hostile world. In cold climates, they learned to use fire, find or build shelters and make warm clothes. They became skilled at making tools and weapons, and were lethal hunters. By about 10,000 years ago modern humans had spread from Africa to the most remote corners of the globe. During cold periods, a great deal of water was locked up in the large ice sheets (glaciers) that covered much of the northern hemisphere. This caused sea levels to fall, revealing land "bridges" that linked the continents, enabling our ancestors to cross from Asia into North America and from South East Asia into Australia.

When the ice finally retreated, large game, such as woolly mammoths, was increasingly scarce. Humans had to find new sources of food and began to experiment with the domestication of certain plants and animals – the agricultural revolution had begun.

Homo Habilis
Homo habilis (handy man) was so called because of his ability to make tools. Feet and hand fossils show some similarities to modern humans' feet and hands. They indicate that he would have had a strong grip and would have been able to manipulate tools effectively. He was probably a meat-eater – tools were needed to separate the flesh from the carcass.

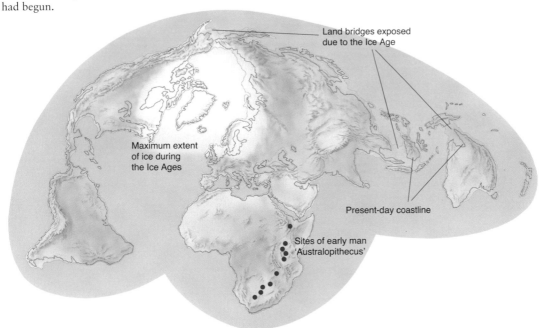

Land bridges exposed due to the Ice Age

Maximum extent of ice during the Ice Ages

Present-day coastline

Sites of early man 'Australopithecus'

703

The First Civilizations 3500–1000 BC

The cultivation of plants, such as wheat and barley, and the domestication of animals, such as sheep, goats and cattle, began in the Near East in about 8500 BC. As people turned to farming, they began to live in fixed settlements, which became small towns. In about 5000 BC, farmers moved down into the fertile river valleys of Mesopotamia, and built dykes and ditches to irrigate the arid land. Their labors bore fruit; surplus food freed some of the population from farming. These people became merchants, craftsmen and priests. As the settlements grew into cities, they became more organized; laws were made, writing evolved, and religious and public buildings were built.

Between 3500 and 1800 years ago, three great civilizations evolved in Mesopotamia, Egypt and the Indus valley of northern India. All three civilizations were located in the fertile valleys of great rivers. Each civilization was based on substantial cities, inhabited by several thousand people and containing imposing public buildings, such as temples and palaces. Each civilization had evolved a form of writing. All three civilizations show evidence of a strong, centralized administration or all-powerful rulers – in Mesopotamia, for example, rulers were buried with their sacrificed servants as well as a vast array of their worldly possessions.

Egypt

The cities, tombs and temples of Ancient Egypt lined the banks of the River Nile. Every year the river flooded, depositing fertile mud along its banks – when the waters receded, these lands could be cultivated. During the Nile flood (August to October), the vast majority of the Egyptian population, who lived by farming, could work for the pharaoh, building temples, tombs and pyramids. During the Old Kingdom (c. 2685–2185 BC), when all of Egypt was under the rule of one pharaoh, the important centers were in the north, around Giza and Memphis. In the New Kingdom (c. 1552–1071), the main royal city was Thebes, in Middle Egypt.

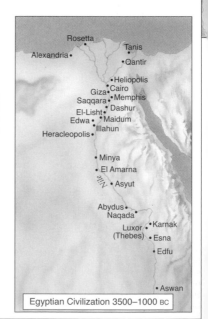

Egyptian Civilization 3500–1000 BC

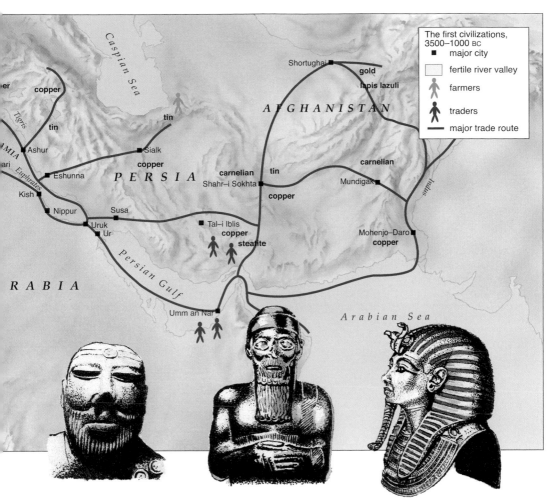

This head from the Indus valley city of Mohenjo-Daro, c. 2100 BC, may represent a priest-king.

Ishtup-Ilum, c. 2100 BC, was the ruler of Mari, a city-state in northern Mesopotamia.

The solid gold funeral mask of the Egyptian pharaoh, Tutankhamun, c. 1340 BC.

The Temple of Ur

The temple at the Mesopotamian city of Ur was a ziggurat, comprising an ascending series of terraces, made from mud bricks, and decorated with mosaics. Each terrace would have been planted with a "hanging garden" of trees. The temple was dedicated to the worship of the city's patron deity, the moon-god, Nanna. Surrounding the temple stood the houses of the lower town, which contained 20,000 people at its peak.

The Bronze Age 2000–1000 BC

Metal-working first occurred in Turkey and Iran in about 6000 BC, when people began to smelt copper and lead. By 3000 BC, it was a flourishing craft in the city-states of Mesopotamia and it became increasingly specialized as craftsmen began to experiment with mixing together different metals to produce alloys. By adding a small quantity of tin to copper they produced bronze, a harder metal that could be used for making stronger weapons, with sharper cutting edges. By about 2500 BC, copper was in use over a region that stretched from the Iberian peninsula to Scandinavia and, within a thousand years, bronze was being used by craftsmen in Europe. At this time, much of Europe was still thickly forested, and people lived in widely scattered agricultural villages. Tin, a vital component of bronze, was a rare resource, found mainly along the Atlantic coast of Europe. It was transported along long-distance trade routes and exchanged for other highly valued goods, such as Baltic amber and salt. Control of these precious resources led to the rise of a wealthy social elite, who turned to metalsmiths to produce bronze regalia, symbolic of their rank. Costly daggers, bronze sheaths and helmets, and metal breastplates were buried with chieftains in "barrow burials" – graves that were crowned with large mounds of earth or stone. As the European population grew, there was increasing pressure on limited resources. Conflict began to break out between communities, and people began to build fortified villages or fortresses, which could be defended against groups of marauders. In Crete and the Greek mainland, two sophisticated Bronze Age societies began to emerge between 2000 BC and 1500 BC, centered on palaces which ruled over an agricultural hinterland. The Minoans of Crete built substantial palaces, whose magnificent wall paintings depict young acrobats leaping over a bull's horns. The Cretans

Scandinavia flourished during the second millennium BC, growing rich on its trade in precious Baltic amber. Bronze-working was greatly valued. The sun was probably worshiped and sun symbolism was widespread. This bronze, wheeled model of a horse pulling a disk (the sun), was probably a revered religious object.

When the royal tombs of Mycenae in mainland Greece were excavated in the nineteenth century, gold death-masks, tiaras, bowls, daggers and wine cups were found. One of the gold masks was associated with Agamemnon, the Mycenaean warlord celebrated by the poet Homer in his epic works, the Iliad and the Odyssey.

were skilled craftsmen and traders, and examples of Minoan jewelry and pottery have been found in Egypt, Greece and Italy. It is thought that a massive volcanic eruption on the island of Santorini *c.* 1450 BC shattered Minoan civilization. On the Greek mainland, Mycenaean civilization was more warlike. Great Mycenaean cities, such as Mycenae and Pylos, were fortresses that ruled over the surrounding countryside, and Mycenaean traders dominated the eastern Mediterranean. But by 1000 BC internal conflict, or possibly foreign invasion, had brought about their downfall.

Meanwhile, in East Asia, the Shang state developed *c.* 1800 BC from earlier agricultural communities that had evolved on the Yellow River. It was a feudal society, ruled by the Shang Dynasty of kings who lived in elaborate, luxurious palaces. The Shang were fierce soldiers, who used ancestor worship and human sacrifice to assert their power. Ancestors were consulted through oracle bones – animal bones heated to produce cracks which were then interpreted. Elaborate bronze vessels were used by the king and his aristocrats to offer wine and food to the spirits of their ancestors. But Shang rule was not to last, and in about 1100 BC the dynasty collapsed and the era of Chou China began.

Shang Bronze
Bronze halberds, with decorated hilts, were the main weapons of war in Shang China. Metalworking in China dates back to about 1800 BC, and bronze was widely used for everyday objects and weapons. More elaborate ritual vessels, cast from ceramic molds, were decorated with vigorous animal motifs.

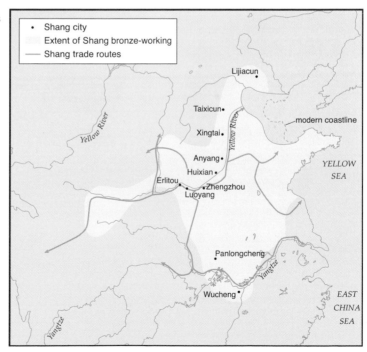

- • Shang city
- Extent of Shang bronze-working
- — Shang trade routes

Lijiacun
Taixicun
Xingtai
Anyang
Huixian
Erlitou
Zhengzhou
Luoyang
Panlongcheng
Wucheng
Yellow River
modern coastline
YELLOW SEA
Yangtze
Yangtze
EAST CHINA SEA

Greece 750–150 BC

Europe's earliest advanced civilization flourished on the island of Crete from 2200 to 1400 BC. Minoan civilization, centered on palace-cities, prospered by trading goods such as olive oil and pottery within the Mediterranean. Meanwhile, on the Peloponnese peninsula, another Bronze Age civilization was emerging, based on fortified palace-cities such as Mycenae. This more warlike civilization collapsed in about 1200 BC. A period known as the "dark ages" followed but, in about 800 BC, populations began to expand, and small city-states, consisting of a city surrounded by towns, villages and agricultural land, began to evolve. By about 500 BC, Athens had become the richest and most important city-state in Classical Greece, as well as the cultural and intellectual center of the Greek world. Democracy was born in Athens: Athenian citizens (free men) had the right to vote on all matters of government, and any citizen could serve for a year as a city magistrate, paid by the state. But, in 404 BC, Athens was crushed by Sparta, a rival city-state, where a small elite ruled over their subject peoples with the help of a well-trained army. In the fourth century BC the Greeks were united under the Macedonian leader, Alexander, who conquered the mighty empire of Persia. Wherever he went, he founded cities, spreading Greek culture and language throughout the Middle East.

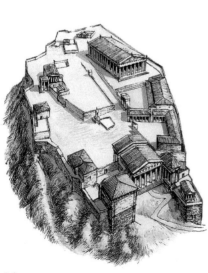

Alexander the Great
Alexander the Great, son of King Philip of Macedonia, conquered a vast area, stretching from Greece to the borders of India from 334–323 BC. He died when he was just 33.

Athens
Most Greek cities clustered around a rocky outcrop, or acropolis, which could be defended in times of crisis. The Athenian acropolis is crowned by the famous Parthenon, dedicated to Athena, the city's patron deity. Below the acropolis, lay the market place, or agora, and the law courts and government offices. The Greeks were dedicated to the health of both mind and body, so large public gymnasia and amphitheaters were found in most Greek cities.

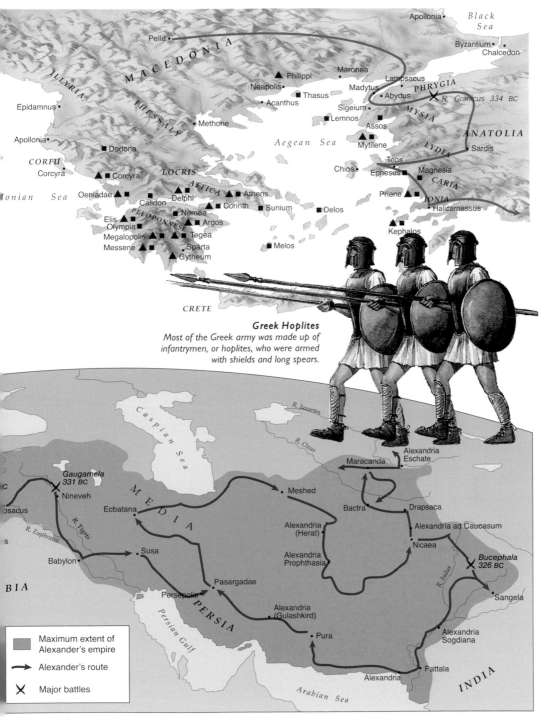

Greek Hoplites
Most of the Greek army was made up of infantrymen, or hoplites, who were armed with shields and long spears.

Black Sea

Apollonia•

Byzantium•
Chalcedon•

MACEDONIA

Pella•

Maronea•

Philippi▲

Lampsacus•

Neapolis•
Thasus▪

Madytus•

Abydus•

PHRYGIA

✕ *R. Granicus 334 BC*

THESSALY

Acanthus•

Sigeium•

MYSIA

Epidamnus•

Methone•

Lemnos▪

ANATOLIA

Assos▪

Apollonia•

CORFU

▪Dodona

Aegean Sea

Mytilene▲

LYDIA

Sardis•

Corcyra•

LOCRIS

Teos•

Chios•

Ephesus▲

Magnesia▪

onian Sea

Oeniadae▲▲

ATTICA

▲Athens

Priene▲▲

CARIA

Calidon•

Delphi▲

Corinth•

Sunium▪

▪Delos

IONIA

Halicarnassus•

Elis▲

Nemea▪

Argos▪

Kephalos•

PELOPONNESE

Olympia▲

Megalopolis▲▲

Tegea▪

Messene▲▪

Sparta•

Melos▪

Gytheum▲

CRETE

R. Jaxartes

Caspian Sea

R. Oxus

Alexandria
Eschate

Maracanda•

*Gaugamela
331 BC*
✕
•Nineveh

Meshed•

•osacus

Bactra•

Drapsaca•

MEDIA

Ecbatana•

Alexandria ad Caucasum

R. Euphrates

R. Tigris

Alexandria
(Herat)•

Nicaea•

s•

Susa•

Alexandria
Prophthasia•

*Bucephala
326 BC*
✕

Babylon•

R. Indus

Pasargadae•

BIA

Sangela•

Persepolis•

PERSIA

Alexandria
(Gulashkird)•

Alexandria
Sogdiana•

Persian Gulf

•Pura

Pattala•

INDIA

Alexandria•

Arabian Sea

	Maximum extent of Alexander's empire
→	Alexander's route
✕	Major battles

Rome 500 BC–AD 500

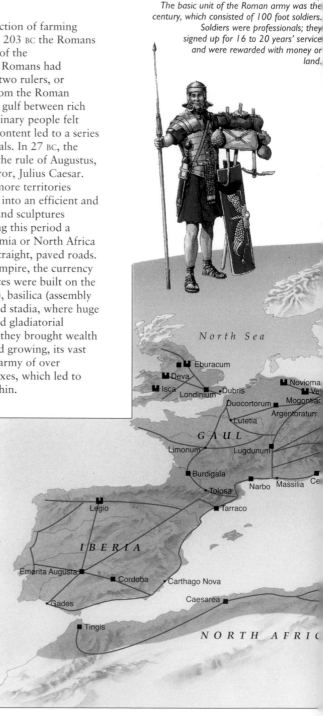

In 1000 BC Rome was no more than a collection of farming villages clustered around seven hills. Yet by 203 BC the Romans controlled the Italian peninsula, the whole of the Mediterranean Sea, Spain and Greece. The Romans had evolved a form of republican government: two rulers, or consuls, presided over the senate, drawn from the Roman aristocracy and rich landowners. But as the gulf between rich and poor within Rome grew wider, the ordinary people felt that they held none of the power. This discontent led to a series of bitter civil wars between powerful generals. In 27 BC, the Roman Republic became an empire under the rule of Augustus, the adopted son of the general and conqueror, Julius Caesar.

Under the rule of the Emperor Augustus more territories were conquered, the army was reorganized into an efficient and loyal fighting force, magnificent buildings and sculptures adorned all the empire's major cities. During this period a Roman citizen could travel from Mesopotamia or North Africa to the northern borders of England along straight, paved roads. Latin was spoken throughout the Roman Empire, the currency was universal. Even cities in distant provinces were built on the Roman model, with a forum (market place), basilica (assembly hall), temples, theaters, palaces, libraries and stadia, where huge crowds gathered to watch chariot racing and gladiatorial combat. As new provinces were conquered they brought wealth to the empire. But when the empire stopped growing, its vast size became a problem; the expenses of an army of over 300,000 men had to be met by increased taxes, which led to discontent, weakening the empire from within.

The Roman Empire

As new provinces were added to the Roman empire, the conquerors set about "Romanizing" them. Towns and capital cities were built to follow the layout and design of Rome. Straight, paved roads and aqueducts linked these new settlements. In the countryside, land was cleared and irrigated so that it was ready for cultivation. A provincial governor was appointed to run the province and ensure that there were no revolts against Roman rule. Legions of the Roman army were sent to the provinces to help keep the peace and were often stationed in fortresses along the borders of the empire.

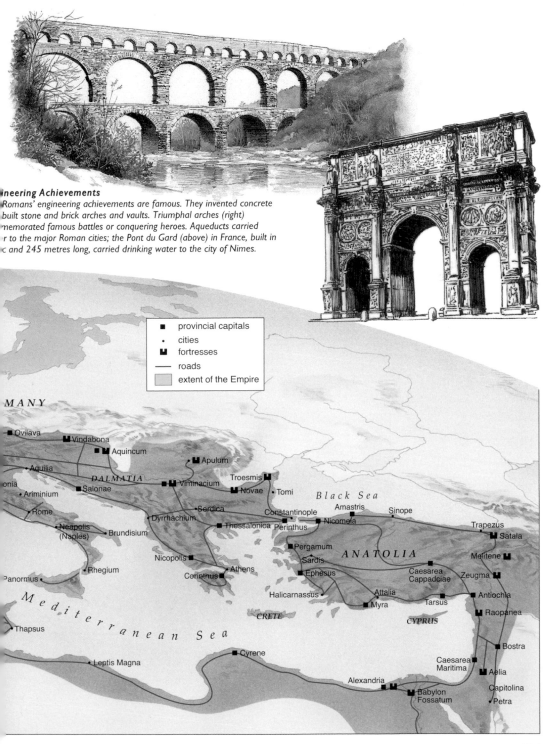

...ineering Achievements

...Romans' engineering achievements are famous. They invented concrete
...built stone and brick arches and vaults. Triumphal arches (right)
...memorated famous battles or conquering heroes. Aqueducts carried
...r to the major Roman cities; the Pont du Gard (above) in France, built in
...c and 245 metres long, carried drinking water to the city of Nimes.

- ■ provincial capitals
- · cities
- ⛫ fortresses
- — roads
- ▨ extent of the Empire

MANY

- ■ Ovilava
- ⛫ Vindabona
- ■ Aquincum
- · Apulum
- · Aquilia
- DALMATIA
- Troesmis ⛫
- ...onia
- ■ Salonae
- ⛫ Viminacium
- ⛫ Novae
- · Tomi
- · Ariminium
- · Serdica
- Black Sea
- · Rome
- Dyrrhachium
- Constantinople
- Amastris
- · Sinope
- · Neapolis (Naples)
- · Brundisium
- ■ Thessalonica
- Perinthus
- Nicomeia
- Trapezus
- ⛫ Satala
- Nicopolis ■
- ■ Pergamum
- ANATOLIA
- Melitene ⛫
- · Rhegium
- · Athens
- Sardis
- Caesarea Cappadciae
- Zeugma ⛫
- ...anormus ·
- Corinthus ·
- · Ephesus
- Antiochia
- Halicarnassus ·
- Attalia
- Tarsus
- CRETE
- · Myra
- CYPRUS
- ⛫ Raopanea
- M e d i t e r r a n e a n   S e a
- · Thapsus
- · Bostra
- · Cyrene
- Caesarea Maritima
- ⛫ Aelia
- · Leptis Magna
- Alexandria
- Babylon Fossatum
- Capitolina
- · Petra

Europe Attacked AD 600–1100

The success of the Roman Empire led to its downfall, its sheer size making administration increasingly difficult. In the third century the empire split into the Byzantine Empire and the Western Empire. Throughout the 3rd century AD, nomadic tribes from central Asia, such as the Visigoths and Franks, had been pressing on Rome's northern frontiers. With the weakening of the empire, they broke through, sweeping south in search of new lands. These tribes were pastoralists; accompanied by their animal herds they traveled long distances, living in tented camps. With the collapse of the Western Roman Empire in the fifth century AD, one of the nomadic tribes, the Franks, became Europe's most powerful rulers. Under their great king, Charlemagne, the Frankish Carolingian Empire became known as the "Holy Roman Empire" and extended from France to Italy.

Charlemagne
A gold bust of Charlemagne (742–814), King of the Franks.

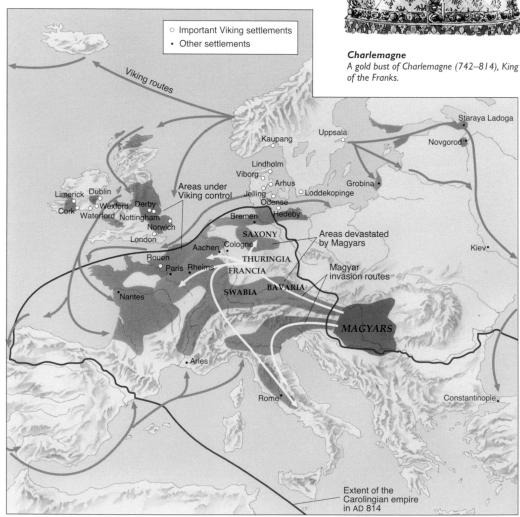

- ○ Important Viking settlements
- • Other settlements

Viking routes

Staraya Ladoga
Novgorod
Kaupang
Uppsala
Lindholm
Viborg
Arhus
Grobina
Jelling
Loddekopinge
Odense
Limerick
Dublin
Wexford
Derby
Cork
Waterford
Nottingham
Bremen
Hedeby
Areas under Viking control
Norwich
London
SAXONY
Areas devastated by Magyars
Kiev
Aachen
Cologne
Rouen
THURINGIA
Paris
Rheims
FRANCIA
Magyar invasion routes
Nantes
SWABIA
BAVARIA
MAGYARS
Arles
Rome
Constantinople

Extent of the Carolingian empire in AD 814

The Vikings

In the eighth century, a seafaring people called the Vikings sailed in their longboats from Norway, Denmark and Sweden to find new lands to colonize. They raided coastal settlements, murdering and terrorizing the native populations and plundering their monasteries, returning to their homelands laden with treasure. In the mid-ninth century, instead of returning home, Viking raiders began to make permanent settlements. They were good farmers, adapting themselves to the culture of the peoples they conquered. Accomplished traders, they established trade routes throughout northwestern Europe. Some reached America. By crossing the Baltic Sea, Vikings entered the great river systems of European Russia, and *c.* 862 formed the first Russian state in Novgorod. Using the south-flowing rivers, they penetrated the forests and frozen wastes of Russia, establishing trading stations as far as the Black Sea and the Mediterranean. Though fearless warriors, the Vikings were also good craftsmen, producing fine swords and beautiful woodcarvings.

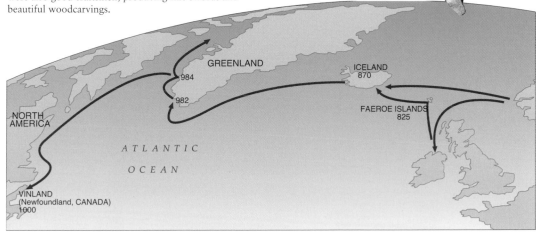

A Viking Settlement

The Vikings established a trading center at Hedeby in Denmark where several major trade routes intersected. Over the years, Hedeby became a major trading center. To protect the town from hostile German tribes, an earth embankment topped with a timber palisade was built around it. The houses were constructed of wood and earth. The entire family slept, ate, worked and played together in one small room. The house of a more prosperous Viking might have two or three rooms. Their food came from fishing, hunting and from local farms.

Asian Empires 100 BC–AD 1300

China was first united under the short-lived Ch'in Dynasty in 221 BC. The succeeding Han Dynasty (202 BC–AD 220) ruled a united China for over four centuries. During this period, China grew prosperous, with an efficient administration, extensive road and canal network, and a growing number of large towns. Paper was invented. Chang'an (or Xi'an), the Han capital, stood at the beginning of the Silk Road, the great trade route across central Asia. Merchants traveled the road, their camels laden with silk. After a long period of decline, the Han Empire collapsed and for 400 years China was fragmented. Its unification, begun during the Sui Dynasty, was consolidated by the T'ang (618–907), one of the greatest periods in Chinese history. Ch'ang-an became one of the world's largest cities. The T'ang were famed for their arts, literature and poetry. With the decline of the T'ang, a new dynasty, the Sung or Song (AD 960–1279), began. The Sung built a centrally controlled bureaucracy and army. Ocean-going junks laden with tea, silk and porcelain sailed for India and Africa. Urban centers grew and flourished. Printing was invented, developing later into movable type, 400 years before it reached the West. Among the Sung's finest products were its superb pottery and porcelain. The refinement of the Sung period lasted for 300 years until it was shattered by the Mongol invasion. In Japan, Imperial rule was established in about the fifth century AD. In the ninth century, Japan was dominated by military overlords, called shoguns.

Samarkand

Area und
Chinese
control

Model Army
In 221 BC Shi Huang Ti founded the Ch'in Dynasty. On his death he was buried with thousands of life-size pottery figures and horses.

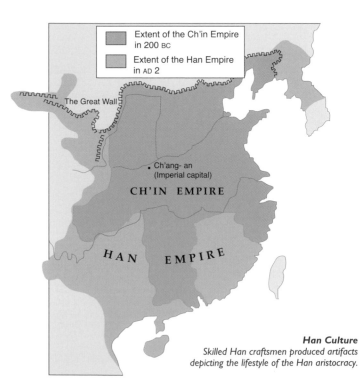

Extent of the Ch'in Empire in 200 BC

Extent of the Han Empire in AD 2

The Great Wall

Ch'ang- an
(Imperial capital)

CH'IN EMPIRE

HAN EMPIRE

Han Culture
Skilled Han craftsmen produced artifacts depicting the lifestyle of the Han aristocracy.

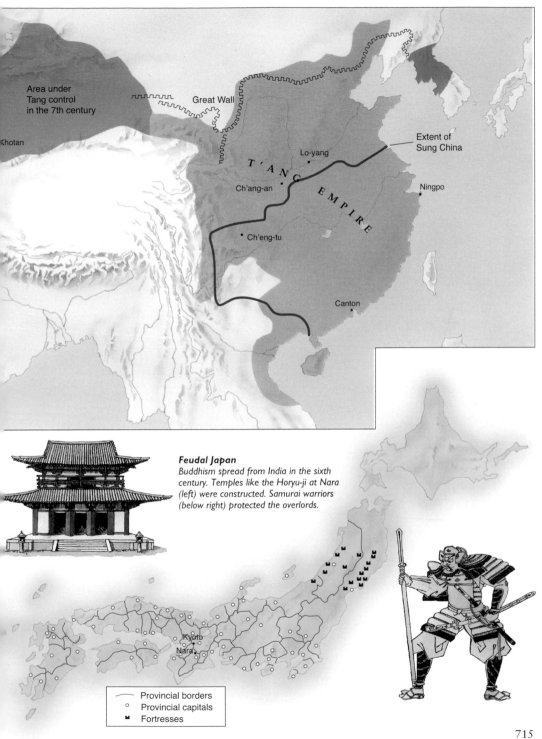

Area under
Tang control
in the 7th century

Great Wall

Khotan

Extent of
Sung China

T'ANG

Lo-yang

Ch'ang-an

EMPIRE

Ningpo

Ch'eng-tu

Canton

Feudal Japan
Buddhism spread from India in the sixth
century. Temples like the Horyu-ji at Nara
(left) were constructed. Samurai warriors
(below right) protected the overlords.

Kyoto
Nara

‒‒‒‒ Provincial borders
○ Provincial capitals
ᴎ Fortresses

The Rise of Islam AD 632

In the seventh century, the Prophet Muhammad founded the Islamic
religion. Based on the simple message that there is no God but the one
God, Allah, the religion united the warring nomadic tribes of the
Arabian peninsula. Arab armies advanced east and west, engulfing the
ancient world. By the time of the Prophet Muhammad's death in AD 632
the tide of conquest had spread from West Africa to the Far East. Today
there are some 1.6 billion Muslims in the world.

While Western Europe struggled through the "dark ages" (fifth–tenth
century), the Arab world pushed forward the frontiers of learning in
science, medicine, astronomy and mathematics. Arab merchants
traveled the trade routes, carrying with them not only goods but a new
and sophisticated culture. A prosperous Arab bathed in a "Turkish"
bath, strolled among the geometrically laid-out paths and water courses
of his garden, or went shopping in the great covered markets – or souks
– where everything was for sale under one roof. He could even send his
son to university, whereas it was to be three hundred years before such
centers of learning existed in Europe. Islamic architects designed
exquisite buildings that contained intricate mosaics, brilliantly colored
glazed tiles and splashing fountains.

The Minaret
The tall slender minaret of the Ahmad ibn
Tulun Mosque towers above the rooftops
of Cairo, capital of Egypt.

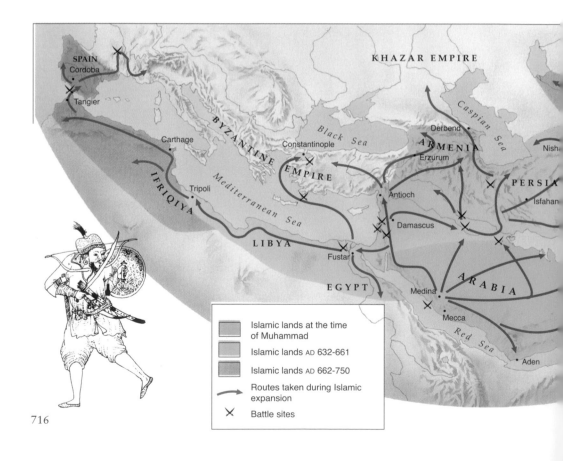

Islamic lands at the time
of Muhammad

Islamic lands AD 632-661

Islamic lands AD 662-750

Routes taken during Islamic
expansion

✕ Battle sites

Islamic Religion

The Islamic religion is based on a series of revelations that Muslims (followers of Islam) believe were received directly from God by the Prophet Muhammad (*c.* 570–632). These revelations are contained in the Koran, the Holy Book of Islam. Islam means submission to the will of God, known as Allah to Muslims. The Koran lays down strict rules for every aspect of a Muslim's life. A devout Muslim should pray to Allah five times a day, either in a mosque or wherever he happens to be so long as he kneels facing towards Mecca, the birthplace of Muhammad and the holiest city of Islam. The Koran also decrees that once in a lifetime every Muslim should make a pilgrimage to Mecca to worship at the Ka'aba, the holy shrine of Islam. It is also a Muslim's duty to fast during the daylight hours of the holy month of Ramadan.

Dome of the Rock
The magnificent Dome of the Rock in Jerusalem is one of the holiest places of Islam.

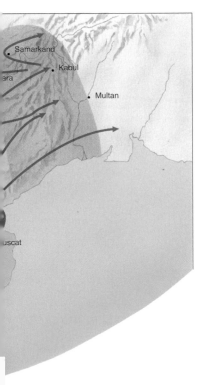

Samarkand

Kabul

ara

Multan

uscat

Arab Trade

With the coming of Islam to North Africa in the eleventh century, Arab merchants opened up trade routes across the Sahara Desert. Their camel caravans carried salt, ivory, African slaves and gold from West Africa to the Mediterranean lands. Dates and grain were stored in pottery jars, like the one below from Syria. From the Arab markets, traveling merchants traded spices along the trade routes of Asia, returning with silk from China.

Europe in the Middle Ages 1100–1300

By the mid-tenth century, the invasions of the northern tribes, like the Vikings, had been halted. Western Europe was divided into kingdoms, ruled by kings or lords. Society was organized under a system called the feudal system whereby the king or lord gave land to nobles who in return swore an oath of loyalty and provided soldiers, or knights, for his protection. Throughout Europe these rulers built castles in strategic positions as defenses against their potential enemies. Peasants were owned by the lord; they farmed his land for nothing but in return were given strips of land of their own and protected by his soldiers. Trade expanded during the Middle Ages, and towns developed into cities. As Christianity spread, the church played an increasingly important part in people's lives. Religious communities called monasteries were founded, where monks devoted their lives to prayer. As centers of pilgrimage, learning and medical care, they became an integral part of medieval life. The most powerful ruler in Western Europe was the pope, head of the Roman Catholic Church. The church owned vast amounts of land and grew rich on the payment of taxes.

Christianity
The Christian religion is based on the teachings of Jesus Christ whom Christians believe was the son of God. It began in Palestine, and after its adoption by the Romans in the fourth century, spread throughout Europe. Churches and cathedrals, like Santiago de Compostela in Spain, shown below, were built for worship and to glorify God.

Pagan religions
Muslim religions
Scandinavian-influenced religions

Craftsmen
Craftsmen, such as the carpenter below, tended to live in towns. They were independent of the feudal system and were paid for their work.

Daily Life
Most people lived as farmers, cultivating crops, such as wheat, barley and beans, and grazing livestock. The wool trade flourished in the Middle Ages, especially in England.

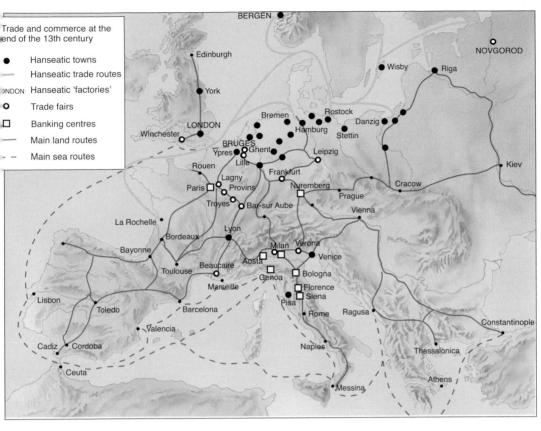

Trade and commerce at the end of the 13th century

- ● Hanseatic towns
- — Hanseatic trade routes
- ︶NDON Hanseatic 'factories'
- ○ Trade fairs
- □ Banking centres
- — Main land routes
- - - Main sea routes

BERGEN

NOVGOROD

Edinburgh

Wisby

Riga

York

Bremen · Rostock

LONDON · Danzig

Winchester · Hamburg · Stettin

Bruges · Ghent · Leipzig

Ypres · Lille

Rouen · Frankfurt

Lagny · Nuremberg · Cracow

Paris □ ○ Provins · Prague

Troyes ○ Bar-sur Aube · Vienna

La Rochelle

Lyon

Bordeaux · Milan · Verona

Bayonne · Aosta · Venice

Toulouse · Beaucaire · Bologna

Marseille · Genoa · Florence · Siena

Lisbon · Pisa

Toledo · Barcelona · Rome · Ragusa

Valencia · Constantinople

Cadiz · Cordoba · Naples · Thessalonica

Ceuta · Athens

Messina

Kiev

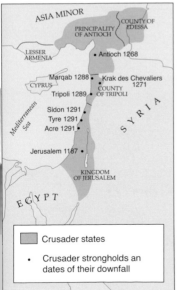

ASIA MINOR

PRINCIPALITY OF ANTIOCH

COUNTY OF EDESSA

LESSER ARMENIA

· Antioch 1268

CYPRUS

Marqab 1288 · Krak des Chevaliers 1271

Tripoli 1289 · COUNTY OF TRIPOLI

Sidon 1291 ·

Tyre 1291 ·

Acre 1291 ·

SYRIA

Jerusalem 1187 ·

KINGDOM OF JERUSALEM

EGYPT

Mediterranean Sea

▨ Crusader states

· Crusader strongholds an dates of their downfall

The Hansa
In northern Europe an association of trading towns, the Hansa, regulated commerce. Banking originated in the city states of medieval Italy. See above.

The Crusades

With the spread of Christianity, pilgrims journeyed to Palestine (or the Holy Land) to worship at the Christian holy places. When Seljuk Turks conquered Palestine in 1071, these pilgrimages were forbidden. This sparked off the Crusades, a series of military campaigns fought by Christians against Muslims for control of the holy places. The Crusaders built magnificent castles, like Krak des Chevaliers in Syria (below), to protect the pilgrim routes.

The Mongol Empire 1200–1405

Covering a vast area of northern Asia are the steppes – windswept grasslands inhabited by tribes of pastoral nomads grazing their sheep and horses. In the early thirteenth century the Mongol tribes were united under Genghis Khan (*c.* 1162–1227) who welded them into a formidable fighting force. The Mongol's first target was China. Despite the Great Wall, built by the Chinese in the third century BC to repel northern barbarians, the Mongol hordes invaded China, occupying it until driven out by the Ming Dynasty in 1368. In 1219 Genghis Khan's armies swept westwards, overrunning central Asia, Russia, entering Hungary and Poland and continuing their conquests until they reached the Black Sea. The Mongols then withdrew into central Asia, but within a few years a fresh onslaught began. Total domination of Europe and Muslim Asia was probably prevented only by the defeat of a Mongol army near Baghdad and by disputes between Genghis Khan's successors. Attempts to invade Java and Japan were also unsuccessful. In the late fourteenth century one of Genghis Khan's greatest successors, Tamerlane, led campaigns south of the Caspian Sea and as far as northern India. At its height, the Mongol Empire was the largest the world had ever seen. Though the hordes left a trail of death and destruction in their wake, once the empire was established it was followed by a period of peace and consolidation.

Liegnitz

EUROPE

1242

Ragusa

Constantino

AFRICA

Ain J

Mongol Horsemen
Superb horsemen, the Mongols rode ponies that could travel immense distances without tiring. The Mongols could fire their arrows from the saddle at full gallop. Their maneuverability was aided by stirrups, such as those above, which were reputedly made for Genghis Khan himself. It was their speed, mobility and firepower that gave the Mongols their military superiority.

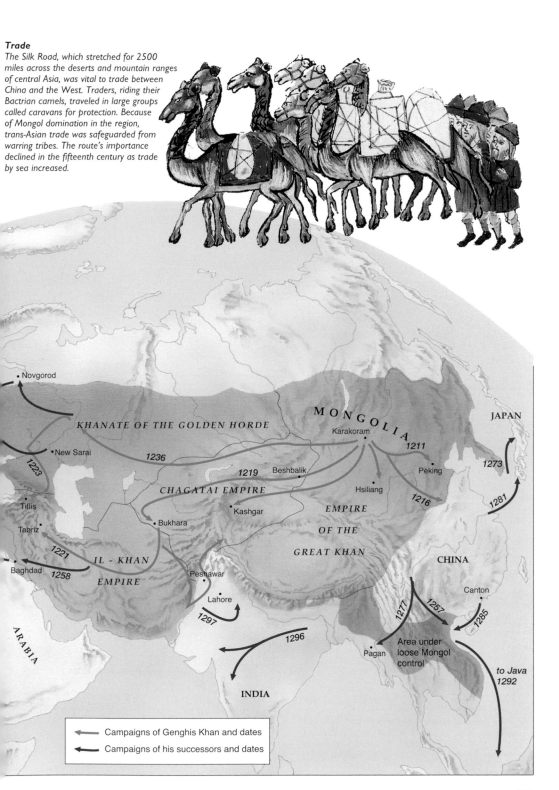

Trade

The Silk Road, which stretched for 2500 miles across the deserts and mountain ranges of central Asia, was vital to trade between China and the West. Traders, riding their Bactrian camels, traveled in large groups called caravans for protection. Because of Mongol domination in the region, trans-Asian trade was safeguarded from warring tribes. The route's importance declined in the fifteenth century as trade by sea increased.

• Novgorod

JAPAN

KHANATE OF THE GOLDEN HORDE

M O N G O L I A

Karakoram

1211

1273

1236

• New Sarai

1223

1219   Beshbalik

Peking

1281

CHAGATAI EMPIRE

Hsiliang

1216

• Tiflis

• Kashgar

EMPIRE

• Bukhara

Tabriz

OF THE

CHINA

1221

GREAT KHAN

IL - KHAN

Baghdad   1258

Peshawar

Canton

EMPIRE

•

1257

1277

1285

Lahore

•

1297

1296

to Java
1292

Pagan   Area under
•   loose Mongol
control

ARABIA

INDIA

| Campaigns of Genghis Khan and dates |
| Campaigns of his successors and dates |

Europe in Crisis 1300–1400

In the early fourteenth century Europe suffered from a number of disasters. A change in the climate caused harvests to fail, resulting in widespread famine. This was followed by a pandemic plague (called "the Black Death"), and the beginning of the Hundred Years' War between England and France. This war was not one continuous conflict but a series of attempts by English kings to dominate France, which began with Edward III's claim to the French throne. The English armies won battles at Sluys, Crécy, Calais and Poitiers, but these were countered by later French victories, and by 1377 France had recovered most of its lost territories. War was renewed by Henry V of England who won a crushing victory over the French at Agincourt in 1415 and then went on to conquer much of Normandy. France's recovery was begun by Joan of Arc who led an army against the English at Orleans in 1429. By the mid-fifteenth century Calais was the only English possession left in France. The misery caused by war, famine, plague and high taxes led to popular uprisings, like the Peasants' Revolt in England in 1381.

Knights
Medieval knights went into battle wearing plate armor over a layer of chain mail.

- ◻ English domains in 1339
- ◻ English domains after Peace of Bretigny (1360)
- ○ English bases in 1380

✗ Sluys
○ Calais   • Brussels
✗ ✗ Agincourt
Cherbourg
Crécy
• Paris
○ Brest
BRITTANY
✗ Orléans
FRANCE
✗ Poitiers
Lyon
Bordeaux
Bayonne
Carcassonne

Archers
English archers at the battle of Crécy. A skilled archer could fire as many as twelve arrows per minute.

Lisbon
PORTUGAL

Changes in Warfare
The various conflicts during the Hundred Years' War were dominated by sieges of fortified castles and towns. An assault began with the mining of the outer walls and bombardment by cannon, as seen here in the siege of Rouen by the English in 1419.

722

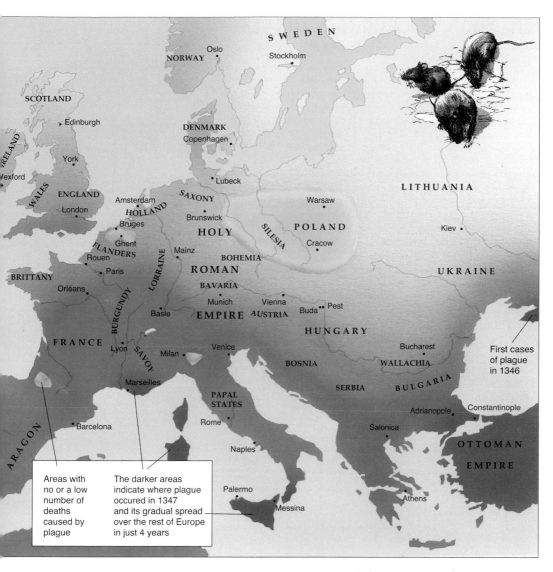

SWEDEN

NORWAY
Oslo
Stockholm

DENMARK
Copenhagen

SCOTLAND
Edinburgh

York

IRELAND

Wexford

WALES

ENGLAND
London

Lubeck

SAXONY
Brunswick

Warsaw

LITHUANIA

Amsterdam
HOLLAND
Bruges

POLAND
Cracow

Kiev

HOLY

Ghent
Rouen
FLANDERS
Mainz
BOHEMIA

SILESIA

BRITTANY
Orléans
Paris
LORRAINE
ROMAN
BAVARIA

UKRAINE

FRANCE

BURGUNDY
Basle
EMPIRE
AUSTRIA
Munich
Vienna
Buda Pest

HUNGARY

Lyon
SAVOY
Milan
Venice
Bucharest

Marseilles
BOSNIA
WALLACHIA

First cases
of plague
in 1346

ARAGON
Barcelona
PAPAL
STATES
Rome

SERBIA
BULGARIA

Salonica

Adrianople
Constantinople

OTTOMAN

EMPIRE

Areas with no or a low number of deaths caused by plague	The darker areas indicate where plague occured in 1347 and its gradual spread over the rest of Europe in just 4 years

Palermo
Messina

Athens

Naples

Black Death

In the fourteenth century, Western Europe was ravaged by a terrible scourge called the Black Death. Carried by infected fleas on rats, it made its first appearance in the Crimea in 1346, probably brought by ships from Asia. Victims were covered by black swellings that oozed blood and were incredibly painful. Few people who contracted the plague survived. Its effect on the populations of Europe was devastating: some towns and villages were left virtually uninhabited. The dead had to be buried in mass graves. It is estimated that some 20 million Europeans died.

The Ottoman Empire 1300–1500

Until the late thirteenth century, the Ottoman Turks were nomadic tribesmen who patrolled the eastern borders of the Byzantine Empire. United by a strong leader – Othman or Osman I – in the early fourteenth century, they began their conquest of Eastern Europe, extending as far west as Hungary and the Balkans. In 1453, after a prolonged siege, the Ottomans captured Constantinople (now Istanbul), thus bringing to an end the Christian Byzantine Empire which had lasted some six hundred years.

Constantinople became the empire's cultural and administrative centre, and the residence of the sultan. In the Topkapi Palace overlooking the city, the sultan ruled his empire, surrounded by his family and protected by his personal bodyguard, the janissaries – Christians who had been captured by the Turks, converted to Islam and given a rigorous military training. No sultan could rise to power or maintain it without their support.

Under Suleiman I, further expansion into Europe began, but with the failure of the siege of Vienna in 1529, westward expansion by land halted. In their shipyards in Constantinople the Ottomans built a magnificent fleet of galleys with which they ravaged the coasts of Spain, Italy and Greece. But in 1571 they were defeated in a great sea battle at Lepanto, off the coast of Greece. This defeat meant further expansion was only possible to the east. Expansion continued until 1680 when the empire's slow decline began.

Turkish Janissaries
Turkish janissaries served the sultan, both as soldiers and administrators, with unquestioning obedience.

Hagia Sophia
Influenced by both Muslim and Byzantine architecture, the Ottomans developed a style of their own. Magnificent mosques, surmounted by several domes and often with as many as six minarets, pierced the city skylines. St Sophia in Constantinople began life as a Christian church but was converted into an Islamic mosque when the city fell to the Turks in 1453.

Algiers

Tunis

Tripoli

Maximum extent
of the Ottoman
Empire in 1680

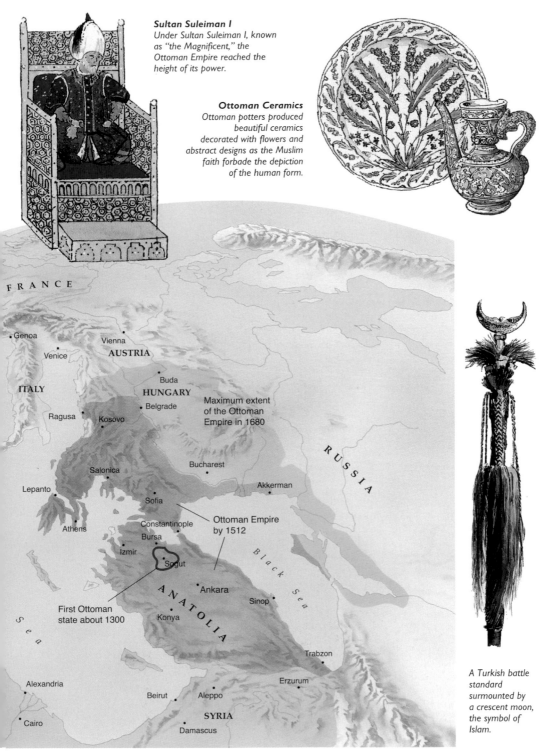

Sultan Suleiman I
Under Sultan Suleiman I, known as "the Magnificent," the Ottoman Empire reached the height of its power.

Ottoman Ceramics
Ottoman potters produced beautiful ceramics decorated with flowers and abstract designs as the Muslim faith forbade the depiction of the human form.

FRANCE

Genoa

Vienna

Venice

AUSTRIA

ITALY

Buda

HUNGARY

Belgrade

Maximum extent of the Ottoman Empire in 1680

Ragusa

Kosovo

RUSSIA

Salonica

Bucharest

Lepanto

Akkerman

Sofia

Athens

Constantinople

Ottoman Empire by 1512

Bursa

Izmir

Black Sea

Söğüt

First Ottoman state about 1300

Ankara

Sinop

ANATOLIA

Konya

Sea

Trabzon

Alexandria

Erzurum

Beirut

Aleppo

Cairo

SYRIA

Damascus

A Turkish battle standard surmounted by a crescent moon, the symbol of Islam.

725

The Americas from the Eve of Conquest to 1519

Sometime between 40,000 and 25,000 years ago, hunters from Asia migrated to North America by crossing the Bering Strait. Living as hunter-gatherers, they gradually spread throughout the continent. Their descendants moved southwards, reaching Mexico in *c.* 20,000 BC. There they settled and became farmers, cultivating crops of maize and beans. Two warrior societies rose to power, first the Olmecs and then the Toltecs. The Olmecs are known for their huge helmeted stone heads and small jade axes, while the Toltecs erected temples and monumental stone warriors in their city at Tula. In the thirteenth century, the Toltecs were succeeded by the warlike Aztecs, who established a powerful empire centerd on their capital, Tenochtitlán, built on an island in Lake Texcoco – the site of Mexico City today. Believing that their gods required to be fed on human blood, the Aztecs waged continuous war on their neighbors, sacrificing their prisoners to the gods.

Further south, in the tropical rain forests of Guatemala and Belize, a sophisticated civilization called the Maya had been in existence since AD 300. Great builders, their huge temple complexes and spectacular pyramids can still be seen in the jungles of Yucatán. In Peru another great civilization, the Inca, had established its empire in the Cuzco valley in the twelfth century. The Inca and the Aztec were conquered by the Spanish conquistadors in the early sixteenth century.

Murder of Atahualpa
At its height, the Inca Empire stretched for 2000 miles along the Andes. In 1532 Spaniards, led by the conquistador Pizarro, invaded Peru, murdered the Inca leader, Atahualpa, (see left) and brought the empire to an end.

Totem Pole
Tribes who settled along the Pacific coast of North America erected painted wooden totem poles on which were carved symbolic animals and spirits.

Machu Picchu
In 1911, some four centuries after it was built, archeologists discovered a remarkable Inca town high in the Andes. Extensive buildings and great terraces clung to the bare hillsides, evidence of a thriving community. Although only 70 kilometers from the Inca capital at Cuzco, Machu Picchu was never discovered by the Spanish conquistadors.

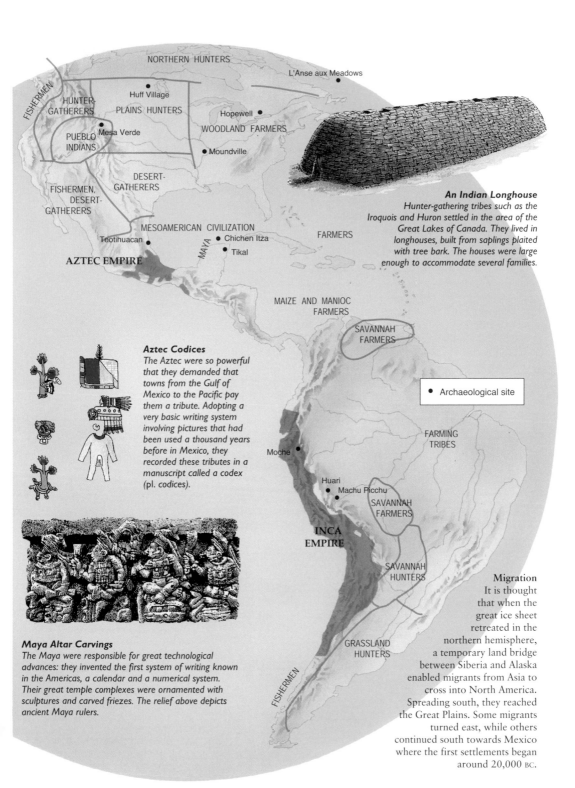

NORTHERN HUNTERS

L'Anse aux Meadows

FISHERMEN

HUNTER-
GATHERERS

Huff Village
PLAINS HUNTERS

Hopewell

WOODLAND FARMERS

PUEBLO
INDIANS

Mesa Verde

Moundville

FISHERMEN,
DESERT-
GATHERERS

DESERT-
GATHERERS

MESOAMERICAN CIVILIZATION

Teotihuacan

MAYA

Chichen Itza

Tikal

FARMERS

AZTEC EMPIRE

MAIZE AND MANIOC
FARMERS

SAVANNAH
FARMERS

● Archaeological site

FARMING
TRIBES

Moche

Huari
Machu Picchu

SAVANNAH
FARMERS

**INCA
EMPIRE**

SAVANNAH
HUNTERS

GRASSLAND
HUNTERS

FISHERMEN

An Indian Longhouse
*Hunter-gathering tribes such as the
Iroquois and Huron settled in the area of the
Great Lakes of Canada. They lived in
longhouses, built from saplings plaited
with tree bark. The houses were large
enough to accommodate several families.*

Aztec Codices
*The Aztec were so powerful
that they demanded that
towns from the Gulf of
Mexico to the Pacific pay
them a tribute. Adopting a
very basic writing system
involving pictures that had
been used a thousand years
before in Mexico, they
recorded these tributes in a
manuscript called a codex
(pl. codices).*

Maya Altar Carvings
*The Maya were responsible for great technological
advances: they invented the first system of writing known
in the Americas, a calendar and a numerical system.
Their great temple complexes were ornamented with
sculptures and carved friezes. The relief above depicts
ancient Maya rulers.*

Migration
It is thought
that when the
great ice sheet
retreated in the
northern hemisphere,
a temporary land bridge
between Siberia and Alaska
enabled migrants from Asia to
cross into North America.
Spreading south, they reached
the Great Plains. Some migrants
turned east, while others
continued south towards Mexico
where the first settlements began
around 20,000 BC.

Europe: the Expansion of Knowledge 1400–1600

In the fifteenth century the great age of discovery began. Europeans sailed the seven seas in search of knowledge, goods to trade and new lands to conquer. Vasco da Gama's ships buffeted their way around the Cape of Good Hope, continuing east until they reached India. Christopher Columbus stumbled upon the Americas. Amerigo Vespucci gave his name to the American continent after his journeys along the coasts of what are now Brazil and Guiana. Ferdinand Magellan achieved the first circumnavigation of the world; the Spanish invaded Mexico and Peru; and the Portuguese explored Africa's west coast. The world began to take shape and maps began to look as they do today. These great voyagers returned with knowledge of other cultures and with their ships loaded with cargoes of gold, silver and tobacco from the Americas, ivory and slaves from Africa and spices from Indonesia. Trade routes formed a network across the oceans. The Dutch, Spanish, English, French and Portuguese founded colonies in foreign lands that grew into vast territorial possessions. In Italy a great flowering of the arts – known as the Renaissance, or rebirth – began. New forms of architecture, painting, music and literature evolved. Powerful families and wealthy members of the Church became patrons of the arts, commissioning work from artists like Raphael and Michelangelo and financing the construction of great cathedrals and palaces. The opening up of the world stimulated an interest in geography and cartography. Advances were made in navigation, astronomy and medicine, while the development of printing accelerated the spread of knowledge and new ideas throughout Europe and beyond.

PACIFIC OCEAN

NO
AME

Magellan

European Christianity

From its early beginnings, European Christianity had been dominated by the Roman Catholic Church – so-called because it was ruled by the Pope in Rome. In the sixteenth century a German priest called Martin Luther led a movement of protest – later called the Reformation – against the corruption of the Catholic Church, which resulted in the establishment of the Protestant Church.

The Printing Press

Until the mid-fifteenth century, information was communicated by word of mouth or written by hand. In the 1450s, communication was revolutionized by the printing press, invented by Johannes Gutenberg. The first book to be printed was the Bible. Individual letters were made which could be moved and reused – movable type. The interior of a printing shop on the left shows two men choosing the letters required to compose the manuscript page in front of them; paper is fed into the printing press and as each printed sheet comes off the press, a boy arranges it in order.

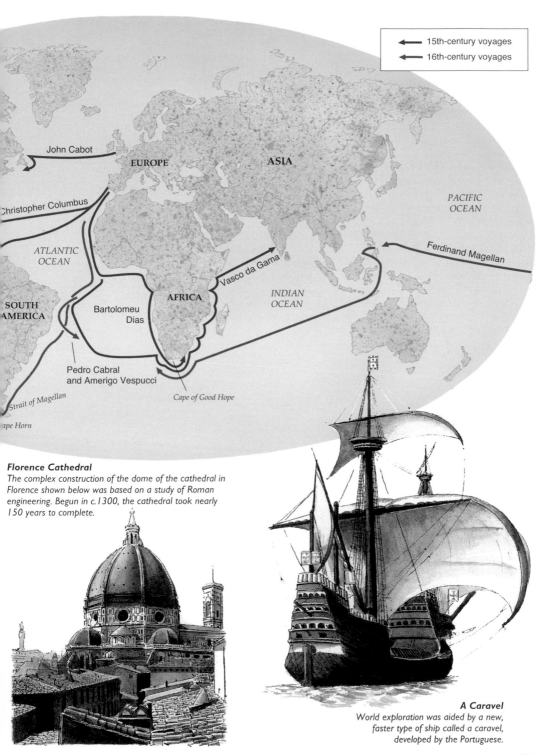

15th-century voyages
16th-century voyages

EUROPE

ASIA

John Cabot

Christopher Columbus

PACIFIC OCEAN

ATLANTIC OCEAN

Ferdinand Magellan

Vasco da Gama

SOUTH AMERICA

AFRICA

INDIAN OCEAN

Bartolomeu Dias

Pedro Cabral and Amerigo Vespucci

Strait of Magellan

Cape Horn

Cape of Good Hope

Florence Cathedral
The complex construction of the dome of the cathedral in Florence shown below was based on a study of Roman engineering. Begun in c.1300, the cathedral took nearly 150 years to complete.

A Caravel
World exploration was aided by a new, faster type of ship called a caravel, developed by the Portuguese.

729

Colonial Expansion 1500–1700

The great voyages of discovery had defined the areas of interest for the seafaring and trading nations of Western Europe. In the sixteenth and seventeenth centuries they began to expand their settlements into colonies and their colonies into empires. In the Americas the Spanish consolidated their empire in Mexico, extending it throughout Central America, to the Caribbean and southwards from Peru to Chile and beyond. The Portuguese settled in Brazil. The success of these overseas empires was dependent on forced labor by the native populations – as in Mexico – or by Africans who were shipped from Africa to be sold as slaves. In North America, French fur traders penetrated along the St Lawrence River deep into Canada; the Dutch settled along the Hudson Valley; in 1607 the English established a colony at Jamestown, Virginia. Trade was not the only motive for conquest and colonization; religion too played its part, some colonizers fleeing from religious persecution. In 1620 a group, later known as the "Pilgrim Fathers", left England for America and founded a settlement at Plymouth. On the other side of the globe, the Portuguese founded a colony at Goa and set up slave-trading stations along the East African coast, while the Dutch established control of the spice trade in Indonesia. By the end of the seventeenth century, only Oceania remained undiscovered by the Europeans.

The Slave Trade
Between the mid-fifteenth century and the end of the seventeenth century, some 10 million Africans were crammed into the holds of slave ships and transported across the Atlantic to work the sugar, cotton and tobacco plantations of the European colonies. In the picture below sugar cane is crushed in a Spanish sugar mill.

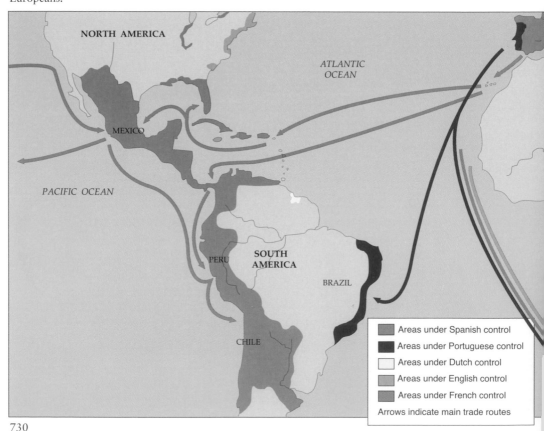

NORTH AMERICA

ATLANTIC OCEAN

MEXICO

PACIFIC OCEAN

PERU   SOUTH AMERICA

BRAZIL

CHILE

Areas under Spanish control
Areas under Portuguese control
Areas under Dutch control
Areas under English control
Areas under French control
Arrows indicate main trade routes

New York

New York began as a Dutch trading post on Manhattan Island at the mouth of the Hudson River. Its fine natural harbor attracted a flourishing trade, especially in furs. Here ships enter the Great Dock. In 1664 New York was captured by the English.

A Benin brass statue of a Portuguese soldier.

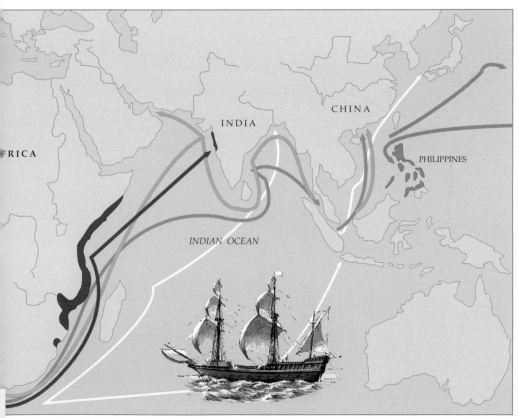

731

Asian Empires 1300–1700

Although Europeans had established trading ports in South East Asia, the continent remained largely unaffected by the European quest for colonization. Only the Indian subcontinent, invaded in the early sixteenth century by the Mughals, was radically altered by an alien culture. Of mixed Mongol and Turkish descent, the Mughals brought the Islamic religion to India. A series of remarkable rulers extended the empire and introduced the distinctive Islamic style of architecture which changed the face of Indian cities forever.

China was ruled by an equally successful dynasty, the Ming, which brought peace and stability to a population twice the size of all Europe. The arts flourished, especially the production of silk and pottery. But, threatened from without by Japan and a tribe from Manchuria called the Manchus, the Ming dynasty was ended in 1644 when the Manchus seized power and founded a new Imperial dynasty – the Ch'ing. During Ch'ing rule, the Chinese Empire reached its greatest extent, developed a successful economy and improved cultivation, especially of rice, the staple diet. Trade with Western nations, except Russia, was not permitted.

Throughout the 1400s and 1500s Japan had been torn by civil strife, but in the late sixteenth century a series of powerful warriors broke the power of the feudal overlords and restored peace and prosperity. In 1639 all foreigners were expelled from Japan and for the next 200 years it existed in virtual isolation from the rest of the world.

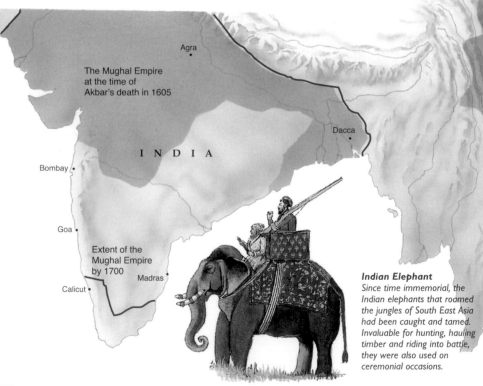

Great

Ch

Agra

The Mughal Empire
at the time of
Akbar's death in 1605

Dacca

Yun-na

I N D I A

Bombay

Goa

Extent of the
Mughal Empire
by 1700

Madras

Calicut

Indian Elephant
Since time immemorial, the Indian elephants that roamed the jungles of South East Asia had been caught and tamed. Invaluable for hunting, hauling timber and riding into battle, they were also used on ceremonial occasions.

732

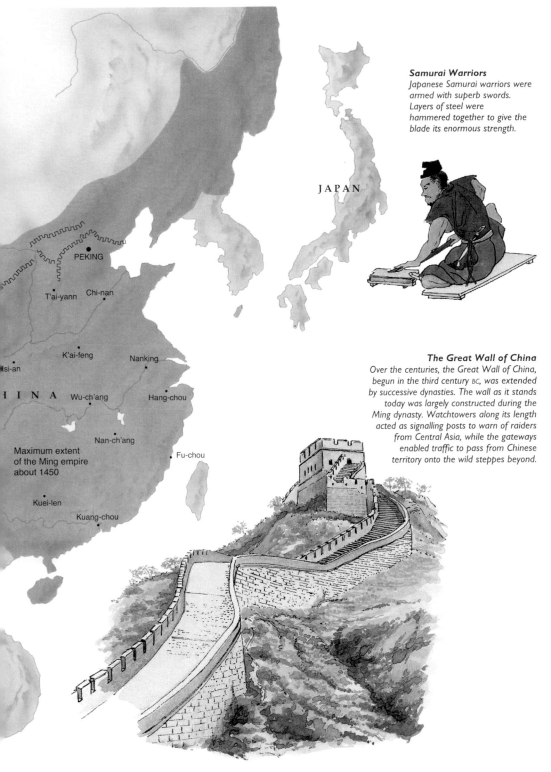

Samurai Warriors
Japanese Samurai warriors were armed with superb swords. Layers of steel were hammered together to give the blade its enormous strength.

JAPAN

PEKING

T'ai-yann   Chi-nan

K'ai-feng   Nanking

si-an

H I N A   Wu-ch'ang   Hang-chou

Nan-ch'ang
· Fu-chou

Maximum extent
of the Ming empire
about 1450

Kuei-len

Kuang-chou

The Great Wall of China
Over the centuries, the Great Wall of China, begun in the third century BC, was extended by successive dynasties. The wall as it stands today was largely constructed during the Ming dynasty. Watchtowers along its length acted as signalling posts to warn of raiders from Central Asia, while the gateways enabled traffic to pass from Chinese territory onto the wild steppes beyond.

Europe: Nations and Conflict 1600–1715

In the fifteenth and sixteenth centuries Europe was divided into a number of small states, but in the seventeenth century these states were absorbed into strong nations, larger and fewer in number, and ruled by powerful kings and emperors. The nations began to compete with one another for political supremacy in Europe. A nation's strength depended on its wealth, administration, military and naval forces and on its agriculture – 90 per cent of Europe's population still derived its living from the land. Conflicts which had previously been largely religious now became territorial. To maintain a balance of power in Europe, nations formed alliances with each other.

An illustrated drill manual of 1607 shows how soldiers in the Dutch army used their muskets.

The Thirty Years' War (1618–48)

This began as a religious war between the Catholic Habsburg emperors and their Protestant subjects in the Holy Roman Empire, but evolved into a major conflict involving the majority of the European states of the time. The war devastated central Europe, especially large areas of Germany, which was left with its economy in ruins and its population greatly reduced. The war was ended by the Peace of Westphalia in 1648.

A musketeer of the English Civil War period with his flintlock musket. Over his shoulder he carries his bandolier in which he kept his cartridge pouches.

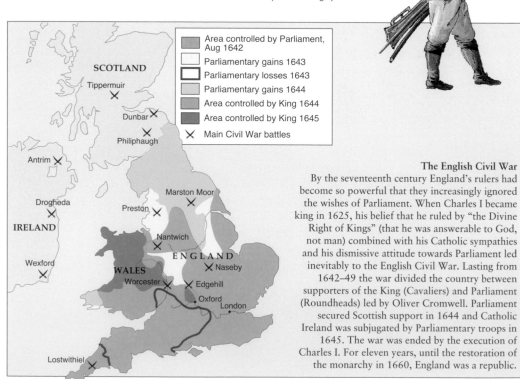

Area controlled by Parliament, Aug 1642
Parliamentary gains 1643
Parliamentary losses 1643
Parliamentary gains 1644
Area controlled by King 1644
Area controlled by King 1645
✕ Main Civil War battles

SCOTLAND
Tippermuir ✕
Dunbar ✕
✕ Philiphaugh
Antrim ✕
Drogheda ✕
IRELAND
Wexford ✕
Marston Moor ✕
Preston ✕
Nantwich
ENGLAND
WALES
Worcester ✕
✕ Naseby
✕ Edgehill
Oxford
London
Lostwithiel ✕

The English Civil War

By the seventeenth century England's rulers had become so powerful that they increasingly ignored the wishes of Parliament. When Charles I became king in 1625, his belief that he ruled by "the Divine Right of Kings" (that he was answerable to God, not man) combined with his Catholic sympathies and his dismissive attitude towards Parliament led inevitably to the English Civil War. Lasting from 1642–49 the war divided the country between supporters of the King (Cavaliers) and Parliament (Roundheads) led by Oliver Cromwell. Parliament secured Scottish support in 1644 and Catholic Ireland was subjugated by Parliamentary troops in 1645. The war was ended by the execution of Charles I. For eleven years, until the restoration of the monarchy in 1660, England was a republic.

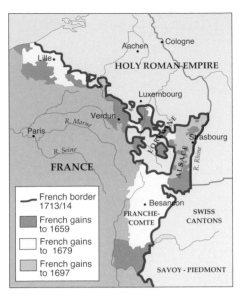

Louis XIV's France

King of France from 1643 to 1715, Louis XIV was a prime example of an absolute monarch. Aided by a few brilliant ministers, he ruled France almost single-handedly, dispensing with the French version of parliament, the Estates General. During his reign France's frontiers were extended and French culture became the envy of all Europe. But France's ascendancy was bought at a price: the country was crippled by the taxes required to finance the wars that Louis waged throughout his reign.

On the map (image 1):

Cologne
Aachen
Lille
HOLY ROMAN EMPIRE
Luxembourg
Verdun
R. Marne
Paris
R. Seine
Strasbourg
LORRAINE
ALSACE
R. Rhine
FRANCE
Besançon
FRANCHE-COMTE
SWISS CANTONS
SAVOY - PIEDMONT

French border 1713/14
French gains to 1659
French gains to 1679
French gains to 1697

Louis XIV
Louis XIV's reign was the golden age of French art and literature. In his splendid palace at Versailles the "Sun King" surrounded himself with the aristocracy.

The Rise of Russia

From the thirteenth to fourteenth centuries much of European Russia was controlled by the Mongols. But in the fifteenth century the Princes of Muscovy drove out the Mongols and created a centralized Russian state. Ivan IV (known as Ivan the Terrible), the first tsar of Russia, extended Russia's territories. During the reign of Peter the Great (1682–1725) Russia became a vast empire stretching from the Baltic to the Pacific. After traveling widely in Europe, Peter the Great began the modernization of Russia by introducing Western ideas and technology. He founded St Petersburg as the new Russian capital, modeling its architecture on European examples.

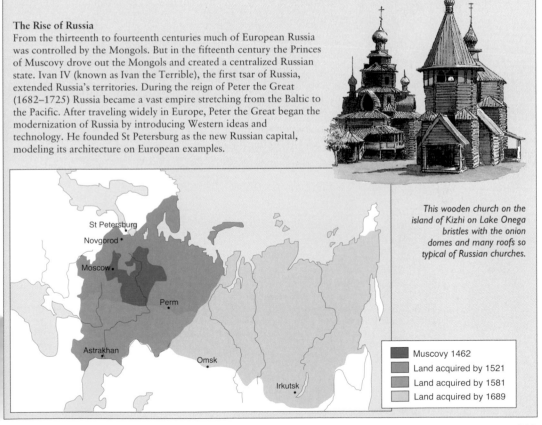

This wooden church on the island of Kizhi on Lake Onega bristles with the onion domes and many roofs so typical of Russian churches.

On the map (image 3):

St Petersburg
Novgorod
Moscow
Perm
Astrakhan
Omsk
Irkutsk

Muscovy 1462
Land acquired by 1521
Land acquired by 1581
Land acquired by 1689

The Age of Revolution 1770–1815

The eighteenth century was an age of prosperity, elegance and new ways of thinking. It witnessed the beginning of the Industrial Revolution, the rise of the press, the novel and the publication of the first encylopedias. The population of Europe doubled, and people moved increasingly from the country to the town. It was also the age of absolute monarchy. Western Europe was ruled by monarchs who presided over their subjects from magnificent palaces which became centres of art and fashion. In the latter part of the century, minor upheavals erupted in many parts of the Western hemisphere, but these were overshadowed by major revolutions in France and America. The French Revolution sent shock waves throughout Europe, changing for ever the relationship between the rulers and the ruled, and precipitating over twenty years of conflict which devastated Europe.

George Washington
George Washington commanded the colonial forces which expelled the British from America.

The Stamp Act
A British tax collector is tarred and feathered by an angry mob of American colonists protesting against the Stamp Act imposed on them by the British parliament. The colonists argued that they could not be legally taxed since they were not represented in parliament.

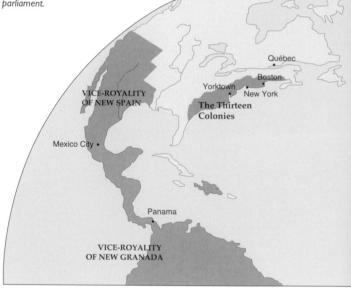

VICE-ROYALITY OF NEW SPAIN

Québec

Boston

Yorktown • • New York

The Thirteen Colonies

Mexico City •

Panama

VICE-ROYALITY OF NEW GRANADA

The American War of Independence

Having defeated the French at Québec in 1759, Britain became the dominant power in North America. The original settlements – known as the Thirteen Colonies – now extended along the Atlantic coast. Increased resentment among the colonials against British rule led to war. In 1776 the Thirteen Colonies proclaimed the Declaration of Independence. With the defeat of British forces at Yorktown in 1781, America became independent.

Soldiers of the American War of Independence
The British "redcoats" (left) were well-trained professional soldiers. The American volunteers (far left) were largely untrained and often ill-equipped.

Maximilien Robespierre
Robespierre was one of the most influential members of the French National Assembly, formed by the Third Estate to challenge the power of the aristocracy and the church.

Marie Antoinette
Louis XVI's Austrian queen, Marie Antoinette, went to her death on the scaffold nine months after her husband.

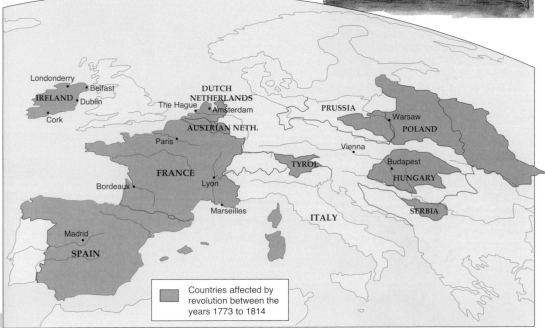

Countries affected by revolution between the years 1773 to 1814

The French Revolution

While the French aristocracy lived in luxury, the peasants, who made up over 90 per cent of the population, existed in a state of abject poverty. Opposition to the old order grew, erupting into full-scale revolution when a Paris mob stormed the Bastille prison. The monarchy was overthrown, the king executed and a republic established.

These cataclysmic events were followed by the Terror, in which some 40,000 people were guillotined. For the first time in history, the middle and lower classes had taken power into their own hands. In the picture on the right, French citizens of the Revolution march through Paris with a banner proclaiming "Liberty or Death".

The Napoleonic Years 1799–1815

Alarmed by the Revolution in France and the execution of Louis XVI, neighboring states, including Britain, formed a coalition against France. The French then mobilized an army of some 750,000 men and went on the offensive. Led by Napoleon, the French forces defeated one European state after another but failed to drive the British out of Egypt. The first coalition broke up, leaving Britain as Napoleon's only opponent. A second coalition was formed, this time including Russia. In 1799, Napoleon seized control of the French government and appointed himself First Consul. After a brief period of peace, war was renewed in 1803. A year later Napoleon crowned himself Emperor of France. The French armies continued their inexorable progress, and by 1810 Napoleon was at the peak of his power. Only Britain continued to withstand his ambitions to dominate the whole of Europe. In 1805 the British navy confirmed its superiority at sea by defeating the French at Trafalgar, thus frustrating Napoleon's plans for invasion. When French forces invaded Spain, Britain sent an army commanded by Wellington to confront them. After six years of conflict, the Peninsular Wars ended in a French withdrawal. In 1812 Napoleon made the fatal decision to invade Russia. The French army's subsequent retreat from Moscow, and its crushing defeat by the allies at Leipzig, forced Napoleon's abdication and exile to Elba. But he escaped, gathered up an army and confronted the British and Prussians, commanded by his old enemy, Wellington, at Waterloo. The French were defeated. Napoleon again abdicated and was exiled to St Helena where he died in 1821. The French monarchy was restored, and Louis XVI's brother was crowned Louis XVIII. After nearly 23 years of war, the victorious powers met at the Congress of Vienna and began the task of reorganizing Europe.

Napoleon Bonaparte
Napoleon Bonaparte (1769–1821), a man of magnetic personality and vaunting ambition, was a military genius. A brilliant general and a skillful administrator, he introduced reforms that shaped modern France. The Code Napoléon reorganized the French legal system and is still used by a large part of the world today.

Napoleon's invasion of Russia, 1812
Napoleon's invasion of Russia in 1812 was the turning point in his fortunes. Prophesying a quick victorious campaign, he marched his armies over the frontier. After one of the bloodiest battles of the Napoleonic Wars, at Borodino, the Russians withdrew towards Moscow, luring the French deeper into Russian territory. When Napoleon reached Moscow, he found it almost deserted. A day later, the Russian holy city was virtually destroyed by fire. Napoleon, with his goal in ruins, his supply lines threatened and the terrible Russian winter approaching, retreated.

The retreat became a disaster: short of food, transport and adequate clothing, and hounded by the Russians, the exhausted troops struggled through deep snow and icy winds towards the frontier. Of the 400,000 French soldiers who entered Russia, only 25,000 survived. For Napoleon, it was the beginning of the end of his empire.

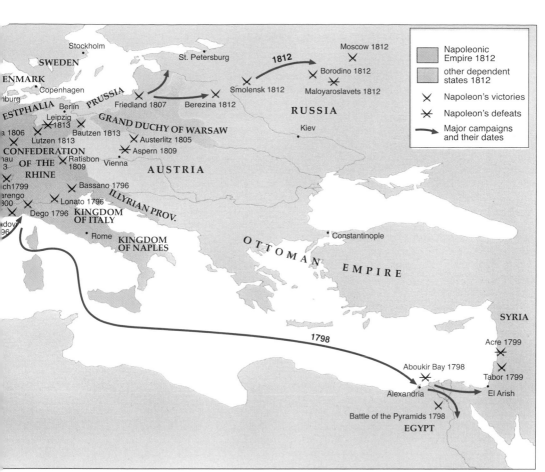

Stockholm

SWEDEN

ENMARK
DENMARK
Copenhagen
nburg

ESTPHALIA Berlin PRUSSIA
Leipzig
a 1806 ×1813
Lutzen 1813 Bautzen 1813
CONFEDERATION × Austerlitz 1805
nau OF THE ×Ratisbon Vienna
3 **RHINE** 1809
ch1799
arengo
300 × ×Lonato 1796 **ILLYRIAN PROV.**
Dego 1796 **KINGDOM**
dovi **OF ITALY**
96

Friedland 1807 Berezina 1812

St. Petersburg

1812

Moscow 1812

× Borodino 1812
Smolensk 1812 × Maloyaroslavets 1812

RUSSIA

Kiev

GRAND DUCHY OF WARSAW
×Aspern 1809

× Bassano 1796

• Rome **KINGDOM**
OF NAPLES

AUSTRIA

• Constantinople

O T T O M A N   E M P I R E

	Napoleonic Empire 1812
	other dependent states 1812
×	Napoleon's victories
✕	Napoleon's defeats
→	Major campaigns and their dates

SYRIA

Acre 1799
×

1798
× Tabor 1799
Aboukir Bay 1798
× El Arish
Alexandria
×
Battle of the Pyramids 1798
EGYPT

The Making of America 1800–1900

During the nineteenth century, the United States grew from the thirteen colonies strung out along the North Atlantic coast to become the world's most powerful and prosperous nation, stretching "from sea to shining sea." The push westwards began with the sale of Louisiana by the French to America. It cost the US government $15 million and immediately doubled the country in size. The opening up of the far west was a more gradual process: hunters in search of game, and settlers seeking land to farm, drifted ever deeper into the interior of the country. This relentless progression was disastrous for the American Indians, whose ancestral lands were overrun by settlers, miners and cattlemen, and whose game – particularly the buffalo – were slaughtered. Some Indian tribes fiercely resisted these incursions, but by 1890 they had been confined to reservations. The construction of the railway did much to open up the west, the gleaming rails penetrating the wilderness until by 1869 the east coast was joined to the west by 85,000 kilometers of track. The midwest was largely populated by immigrants from Europe in search of a new life and freedom from political or religious persecution; many also found work in the industrial cities of the north. Further west, from Texas to Montana, the plains became home to the cowboy and the cattle barons, who sent countless head of cattle by train to feed the growing populations of cities like Chicago. In the Deep South slaves worked the cotton and tobacco plantations. Despite the horrors of the American Civil War (1861–65), by the end of the nineteenth century the 48 separate states in North America had become the United States of today, with a population of 76 million.

American Civil War

The disparity between the rich industrial states in the north and the poverty of much of the population in the south was one of the main causes of the American Civil War. So too was the north's hatred of slavery, and its fear that it would be extended into the western states of America. When Abraham Lincoln became president in 1860, his declared opposition to slavery led to the withdrawal of eleven southern states (the Confederacy) from the Union. The war, which began in 1861, raged from Pennsylvania to Mississippi. It ended with the Confederacy's defeat in 1865; slavery was abolished. More Americans died in the American Civil War than in all the country's other wars combined.

The Union soldier, shown here in regulation dress, was better equipped than his Confederate opponent . . .

. . . but the Confederate soldier shown here in battle dress, w better led.

Map legend:
- Confederate states
- Union states
- Border slave states
- ✗ Confederate victory
- ✱ Confederate defeat

OHIO, PENN., Gettysburg, DEL., Antietam, MD., Bull Run, WEST VIRGINIA, The Wilderness, VIRGINIA, Seven Days, Norfolk, MISSOURI, KENTUCKY, Fort Donelson, Chattanooga, NORTH CAROLINA, Raleigh, TENNESSEE, ARKANSAS, Shiloh, Atlanta, Columbia, SOUTH CAROLINA, MISSISSIPPI, ALABAMA, GEORGIA, Savannah, Vicksburg, Jacksonville, LOUISIANA, FLORIDA, New Orleans

740

Settlers

Pioneers returned from the far west with tales of limitless fertile land to be had for the taking. Families loaded their possessions into covered wagons and set off on the long hazardous journey. As the trails became established, forts (see map below) were built as staging posts and to provide refuge from hostile Indians.

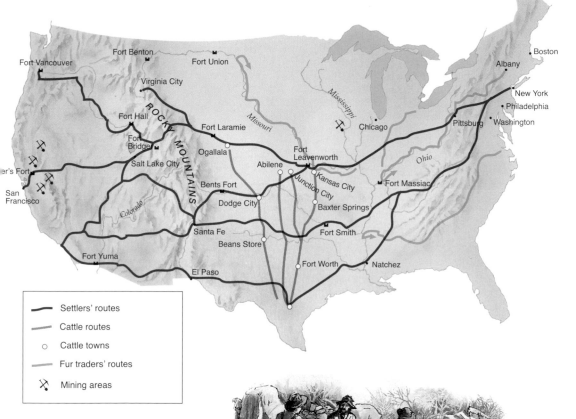

Settlers' routes

Cattle routes

○ Cattle towns

Fur traders' routes

⚔ Mining areas

Gold Rush

In 1848 a settler found a lump of gold in a stream in California. As news spread, gold-hungry adventurers from all over America and the world converged on California. In five years, half a billion dollars of gold were dug from the Californian mud. In 1850 the state became part of the Union.

Canada: The Creation of a Nation 1600–1880

Humans have inhabited the land now known as Canada for perhaps 20,000 years. A theory says that animals and humans may have traveled from Asia to North America over a land bridge that joined the North American and Asian land masses where the Bering Straits now are. These humans might be the ancestors of the people we now know as Canada's First Nations peoples. They adapted to the varied climates of a vast country.

Fishing brought contact between Canada's Native peoples and Europeans. The first Europeans to come to Canada were the Vikings in the eleventh century, meeting with Native peoples in Newfoundland. Later fishermen, ventured from Portugal, Spain, France, and England to North America. However, it was men searching for a westward sea route to China who "found" Canada. The first colonists were Portuguese. France sent the first large group of settlers in the seventeenth century, but Canada came to be dominated by the British until its independence.

The country's name given to it by Jacques Cartier, who, on hearing the Native peoples in the St Lawrence River area refer to their villages as "kanata," took it to be the name of their country.

Demand in Europe for fur drove explorers further into Canada. The Native peoples were astute traders. At first peaceful trade with European immigrants strengthened Native societies. However, European diseases were introduced into Native societies that did not have any immunity against them, devastating these populations. The Europeans introduced guns and alcohol, which also had a destructive influence on Native societies.

First Nations peoples

Inuit and Aleut peoples in the north perfected a way of life that suited the icy hostile environment there – hunting, whaling and fishing, and using their prey for food, tools and clothes (like the furs pictured opposite). In the forested regions, Woodland Indian groups made canoes to travel along the many lakes and rivers. In the north and west, nomadic hunter-gatherers traveled the land. To the southeast, First Nations peoples made permanent settlements and farmed. The inhabitants of the Plains hunted bison for food, tools and clothes. The wooded Pacific Coast region provided plentiful fish, land, wildlife and timber for its Native peoples.

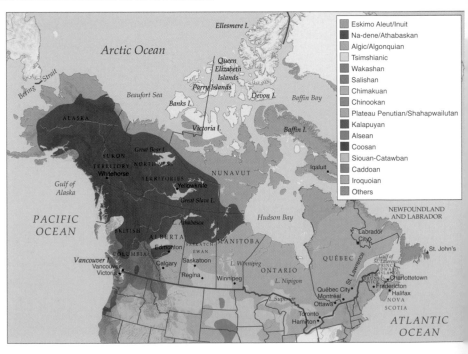

Distribution of native peoples, shown by language, c. 1823

Legend:
- Eskimo Aleut/Inuit
- Na-dene/Athabaskan
- Algic/Algonquian
- Tsimshianic
- Wakashan
- Salishan
- Chimakuan
- Chinookan
- Plateau Penutian/Shahapwailutan
- Kalapuyan
- Alsean
- Coosan
- Siouan-Catawban
- Caddoan
- Iroquoian
- Others

In 1604, French colonists began to establish settlements in the east, first in Acadia (the name given to a territory in northeastern North America that includes parts of eastern Quebec), then in Quebec City in 1608, to exploit the fishing and fur trade. Over the next 150 years, the region of Acadia expanded to reach the St Lawrence River, the Great Lakes and the Mississippi Valley. The British waged a series of wars defeating France. By 1763, France had lost all its North American colonies except for the islands of Saint-Pierre and Miquelon. Following the American Revolution of 1775, British North America (Newfoundland, Nova Scotia, Prince Edward Island and Quebec) still remained part of the British Empire.

Following the Treaty of Paris of 1783, which ended the American Revolutionary War, the international border between the colonies, that would divide the United States and British North America, was established. In 1791, the British divided Quebec into two provinces: Lower Canada and Upper Canada.

In the late eighteenth century, the western coast began to be populated by immigrants, as Europeans, mostly Scots who worked for the North West Company, crossed the Rocky Mountains and reached the coast.

In 1812 the United States invaded British North America. While this war ended in stalemate, a greater sense of nationhood had emerged that would lead towards the emergence of Canada as a nation. From 1837–1838, rebellions led by William Lyon Mackenzie and Louis Joseph Papineau against British control took place. These rebellions were defeated, however, they prompted the British government to allow elected local assemblies in 1841. This was a step towards Canadian self-government. However, this electorate did not include Native peoples.

After the rebellions, the colonies of Lower and Upper Canada were united under one government, the Province of Canada, with the 1840 Act of Union. This act failed to assimilate the French Canadians. The Charlottetown Conference and Quebec Conference, in 1864, were held to work out the details of a federal union.

On July 1, 1867, with the passing of the *British North America Act*, three colonies of British North America (the Province of Canada, New Brunswick and Nova Scotia) became a confederation called the Dominion of Canada, composed of four provinces: Ontario, Quebec, New Brunswick and Nova Scotia.

By 1880, Canada included all the areas it has now, including Arctic lands, except for Newfoundland and Labrador, which joined in 1949. In 1982, Canada broke the last legal link of subordination with the United Kingdom. However, Canada has continued to be an independent constitutional monarchy and a member of the British Commonwealth.

Canadian bison
Almost 200,000 once roamed the north but by the early 1900s there were fewer than 300 left. A recovery program brought their numbers up to approximately 4500

Canada before Confederation

743

Age of Empire 1800–1914

Until the early nineteenth century, European imperialism had been motivated by trade. But the Industrial Revolution, which began in Britain in the mid-nineteenth century and spread throughout Europe, required cheap raw materials to feed its hungry machines. Countries like China and Japan, which had been closed to outsiders, now opened their doors to European trade.

Britain, which had retained trading posts at strategic points around the world, such as the Cape of Good Hope and Ceylon, now added others in the Far East, such as Hong Kong and Singapore, which became thriving British colonies. The opening of the French-built Suez Canal in 1869 gave Britain the justification for adding Egypt to its empire. Britain also laid claim to Australia and New Zealand. Since the establishment of the East India Company in the seventeenth century, British power in India had grown until it dominated the subcontinent.

Mexican Independence
The people of Mexico, resentful of Spanish rule and inspired by the ideals of the French Revolution, demanded their independence. Their struggle went on till 1821 when Spain granted Mexico its independence.

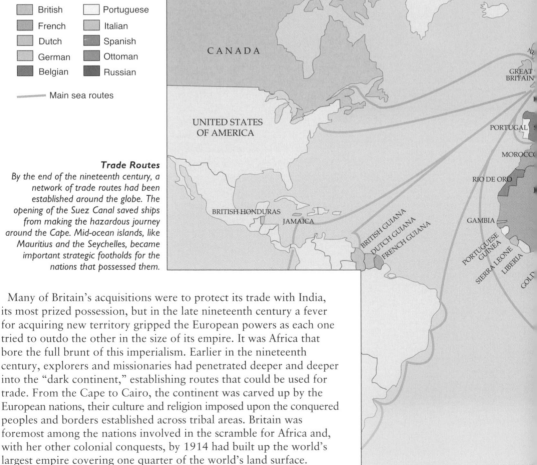

COLONIAL EMPIRES IN 1914
- British
- French
- Dutch
- German
- Belgian
- Portuguese
- Italian
- Spanish
- Ottoman
- Russian

—— Main sea routes

CANADA

UNITED STATES OF AMERICA

BRITISH HONDURAS
JAMAICA
BRITISH GUIANA
DUTCH GUIANA
FRENCH GUIANA

GREAT BRITAIN
PORTUGAL
MOROCCO
RIO DE ORO
GAMBIA
PORTUGUESE GUINEA
SIERRA LEONE
LIBERIA
GOLD

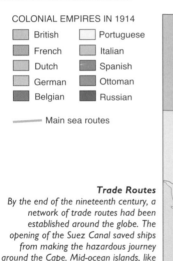

Trade Routes
By the end of the nineteenth century, a network of trade routes had been established around the globe. The opening of the Suez Canal saved ships from making the hazardous journey around the Cape. Mid-ocean islands, like Mauritius and the Seychelles, became important strategic footholds for the nations that possessed them.

Many of Britain's acquisitions were to protect its trade with India, its most prized possession, but in the late nineteenth century a fever for acquiring new territory gripped the European powers as each one tried to outdo the other in the size of its empire. It was Africa that bore the full brunt of this imperialism. Earlier in the nineteenth century, explorers and missionaries had penetrated deeper and deeper into the "dark continent," establishing routes that could be used for trade. From the Cape to Cairo, the continent was carved up by the European nations, their culture and religion imposed upon the conquered peoples and borders established across tribal areas. Britain was foremost among the nations involved in the scramble for Africa and, with her other colonial conquests, by 1914 had built up the world's largest empire covering one quarter of the world's land surface.

Anglo-Boer War

In 1814 the British took control of South Africa from the original Dutch settlers – known as "Boers" (farmers). Determined to maintain their independence from Britain, the Boers trekked into the interior and founded two republics, the Orange Free State and the Transvaal. When gold and diamonds were discovered in Boer territory, the massive influx of prospectors, and Britain's refusal to withdraw its troops from the Transvaal, led to war. Although British forces were superior in numbers, they were steadily out-fought by the brilliant guerilla tactics of the Boers. But the arrival of British reinforcements forced a Boer surrender in 1902.

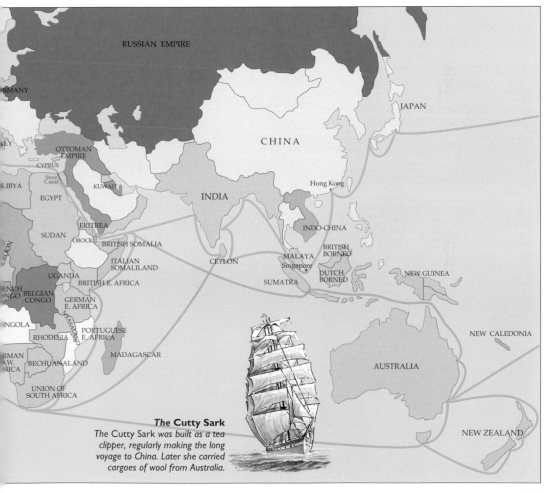

The Cutty Sark

The Cutty Sark was built as a tea clipper, regularly making the long voyage to China. Later she carried cargoes of wool from Australia.

The First World War 1914–1918

By 1900, Germany had become the most powerful industrial power in Europe. Fearing Germany's ambitions to increase its colonial empire, and alarmed by its formidable army and navy, France, Britain and Russia formed an alliance (Allied forces), while Germany allied itself with Austria (Central forces). In an atmosphere of mutual suspicion, an arms race developed. But it was increased tension in the Balkans – which had long been a center of conflict – that precipitated matters. Serbia's emergence as the strongest state threatened the collapse of Austria's shaky empire in the region, which would isolate Germany in Europe. When the heir to the Austrian throne was assassinated in June 1914 at Sarajevo, Austria blamed Serbia and declared war. By August, all the European powers had mobilized and war was inevitable. Most of the fighting took place in Europe, but campaigns were fought as far afield as Mesopotamia (today's Iraq), the Middle East and in Germany's colonies in Africa and the Pacific.

During the course of the war, other countries, such as Greece and Italy, joined the war against Germany. At sea, the British navy was faced by German warships and submarines, which caused havoc to ships carrying supplies to the embattled French and British armies in France. In January 1917 American ships were sunk by German submarines. The United States entered the war, bringing massive reinforcements of men and arms to the aid of Britain and its allies. Germany surrendered in 1918: 10 million had died and over 20 million were wounded. For future generations the First World War became a symbol of the futility and senseless destruction of war.

North Sea

GREAT BRITAIN

NETHERL
Amsterdam

London

Trench line
in the West, 1914

BELGIUM
• Bruss

Amiens •

Farthest German
advance in the West, 1914

Paris •

Armistice line
in the West,
November 1918

FRANCE

SPAIN

Trench Warfare
In Western Europe the war took the form of two lines of opposing trenches stretching from the English Channel to the Swiss border. The British and French faced the Germans across an area of neutral territory, known as "no-man's land." Both sides fought in conditions of unbearable squalor. Living in the trenches, up to their knees in mud, their quarters infested by rats, they were shelled and gassed.

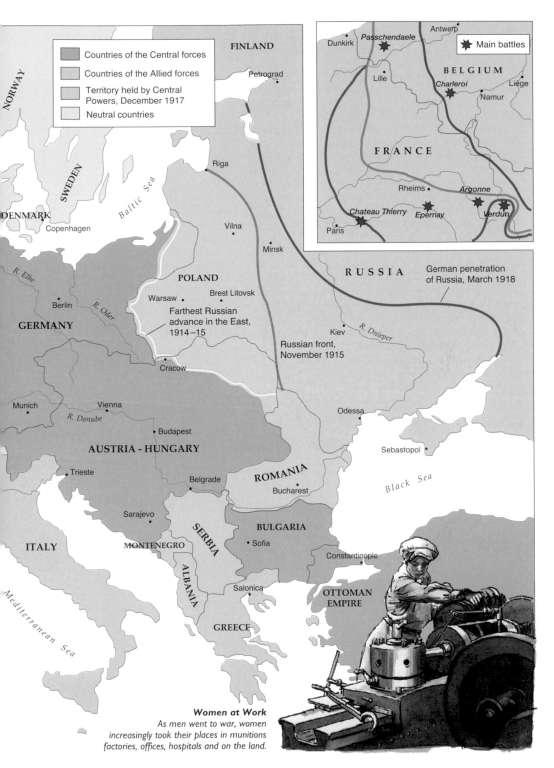

FINLAND

NORWAY

SWEDEN

DENMARK

Copenhagen

Petrograd

Baltic Sea

Riga

Vilna

Minsk

Countries of the Central forces
Countries of the Allied forces
Territory held by Central Powers, December 1917
Neutral countries

R. Elbe

Berlin

R. Oder

GERMANY

POLAND

Warsaw

Brest Litovsk

Farthest Russian
advance in the East,
1914–15

Russian front,
November 1915

RUSSIA

German penetration
of Russia, March 1918

Kiev

R. Dnieper

Cracow

Munich

R. Danube

Vienna

Budapest

AUSTRIA - HUNGARY

Odessa

Sebastopol

Trieste

Belgrade

ROMANIA

Bucharest

Black Sea

ITALY

Sarajevo

MONTENEGRO

SERBIA

BULGARIA

Sofia

Constantinople

ALBANIA

Salonica

OTTOMAN
EMPIRE

Mediterranean Sea

GREECE

Dunkirk

Passchendaele

Antwerp

BELGIUM

Lille

Charleroi

Liège

Namur

Main battles

FRANCE

Rheims

Argonne

Chateau Thierry

Epernay

Verdun

Paris

Women at Work
*As men went to war, women
increasingly took their places in munitions
factories, offices, hospitals and on the land.*

Between the Wars 1919–1939

In 1919, a shattered Europe, crippled by the cost of the First World War, began the struggle toward recovery. The thirty victorious states met at Versailles (1919) to work out peace conditions. Germany was blamed for the war and made to pay huge reparations, which led to inflation, high unemployment and resentment against the European powers. In America a loss of confidence in the economy caused the collapse of the New York Stock Exchange in 1929: banks closed and thousands were thrown out of work. The American Depression sent shock waves round the world. Unemployment in America rose to 6 million by the end of 1930, while world unemployment doubled. The Great Depression had political repercussions: with promises of a "New Deal" which would get people back to work, FD Roosevelt became US president. In Germany, mounting unemployment and fear of social chaos created support for the National Socialist (or Nazi) Party, led by Adolf Hitler. The Nazis created jobs in the armed forces and munitions factories. Nationalism swept through Europe. In Italy, the Fascist dictator, Mussolini, rose to power, pledging to increase Italy's prestige in Europe. In Spain, a conflict erupted between Republicans and Nationalists – who were supported by Italy and Germany – which developed into three years of civil war. The failure of Britain and France to aid the Republicans in Spain encouraged Italian and German expansion in Europe. In the Far East, Japanese economic growth threatened the region's stability. The stage was set for the Second World War.

Wall Street Crash 1929
Thousands of panic-stricken investors thronged Wall Street after the collapse of the New York Stock Exchange in 1929. In the next three years 5000 American banks closed and thousands lost their savings.

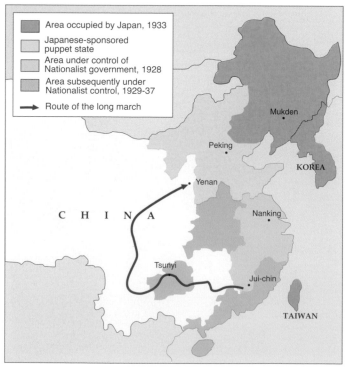

- ■ Area occupied by Japan, 1933
- □ Japanese-sponsored puppet state
- □ Area under control of Nationalist government, 1928
- ■ Area subsequently under Nationalist control, 1929-37
- → Route of the long march

Mukden

Peking

KOREA

Yenan

C H I N A

Nanking

Tsunyi

Jui-chin

TAIWAN

The Chinese Revolution (1911–1949)
With the end of Imperial rule, provincial warlords controlled China. The misery they caused precipitated an upsurge of nationalism.

Chiang Kai-shek united much of China, ruling from Nanking with his Nationalist Party. But his Republic of China collapsed in the face of the Japanese invasion of Manchuria and civil war with Chinese Communists.

Led by Mao Tse-tung, the remnants of the Communist forces set off on "the Long March," gathering widespread support as they journeyed north. After a brief truce, civil war resumed. The Nationalists were defeated and the People's Republic of China was proclaimed in 1949.

Adolf Hitler

To the German people, suffering the aftermath of the First World War, Hitler's promises of a return to prosperity ensured his rise to power. Hitler believed that the Germans were a "master race" and that people who were not members of the master race, such as the Jews, must be eliminated.

The Russian Revolution (1917–21)

The First World War brought great hardship to the Russian people, and a loss of confidence in the government. In 1917, there was an uprising in St Petersburg and Tsar Nicholas II was forced to abdicate. A provisional government was formed, but the Bolsheviks (communists), led by Lenin, seized power, declared Russia a Soviet republic and made peace with Germany. The Revolution was followed by a conflict between anti-communist forces (the Whites), supported by certain Western powers, and the communists (the Reds). The conflict became widespread. The Whites were defeated. In 1921 the new Soviet Union was established.

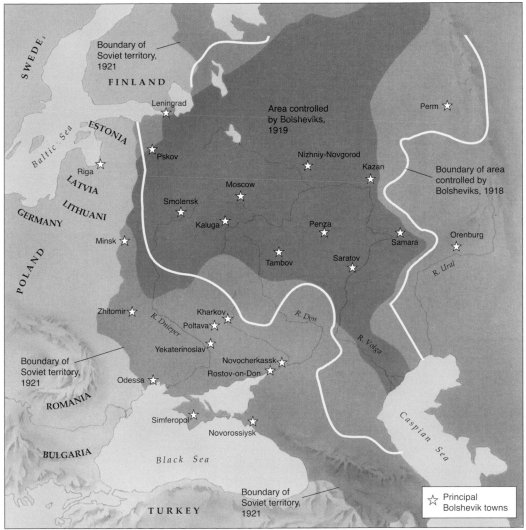

The Second World War 1939–1945

The Second World War was primarily fought between two large
alliances: the Axis Powers – a group of countries led by Germany and
Japan and including Italy – and the Allies – Britain, France, the Soviet
Union and the USA. Adolf Hitler's ambitions for a Greater Germany
had been demonstrated by his annexation of Austria in March 1938,
followed by the seizure of Czechoslovakia. British and French attempts
to curb German aggression by negotiation (the Munich agreement) had
failed. Fearful that Germany would overrun central Europe, Britain and
France guaranteed to protect Greece, Poland and Romania. When
Germany invaded Poland, Britain and France declared war. Surprised
but undeterred, Hitler invaded Denmark, Norway and the Low
Countries. The French, British and Belgian forces were forced to retreat
into northern France and to evacuate their armies from Dunkirk. The
Germans pressed inexorably into France. Italy joined Germany in the
war and France surrendered. By June 1940, with little cost in either
men or equipment, Germany dominated Western Europe. Only Britain
remained at war with Germany. Hitler's attempt to bomb Britain into a
surrender in August–September 1940 failed. The war now spread
farther east; Yugoslavia fell and Italy attacked Greece. In June 1941,
confident of victory, Hitler invaded Russia. Instead of yielding
to German aggression, the Russians resisted fiercely and
in December 1941 began a counter-offensive.

Tank Warfare
*The Germans were masters of tank warfare:
fast-moving tanks and mobile infantry,
supported by dive bombers, were used to
great effect in Poland, France and Greece.
But by 1942 the Allies were better equipped,
winning decisive tank battles in the deserts
of North Africa. In 1943, the Russians
successfully stemmed the tide of German
invasion in a massive tank battle at Kursk.*

Axis territory Sept. 1939

Axis satellites

Axis-occupied

Soviet occupied 1939–40

British Empire

Neutral countries

German advances

At the end of 1941 an event took place that altered the course of the war: Japan bombed the US naval base at Pearl Harbor in the Pacific. The US had been reluctant to become involved but Japan's unprovoked attack was a decisive factor and the US entered the war. A series of crucial battles in late 1942 and 1943 gave the initiative to the Allies on land and at sea. In June 1944, the Allies invaded France and liberated Western Europe, while Russia advanced on the eastern front. War in Europe ended on 8 May 1945.

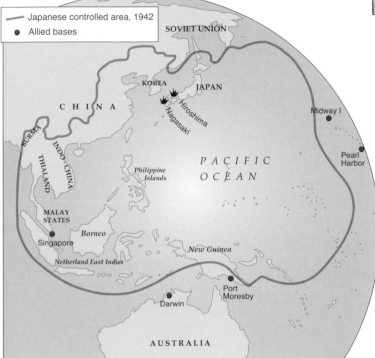

Legend:
- Japanese controlled area, 1942
- Allied bases

SOVIET UNION

KOREA JAPAN

CHINA

Hiroshima

Nagasaki

Midway I

BURMA

INDO-CHINA

THAILAND

Philippine
Islands

PACIFIC
OCEAN

Pearl
Harbor

MALAY
STATES

Borneo

Singapore

Netherland East Indies

New Guinea

Port
Moresby

Darwin

AUSTRALIA

War in the Pacific
With the collapse of European empires in the Far East, Japan saw its chance for expansion. In 1941, it bombed Pearl Harbor and overran much of South East Asia. War in the Pacific now became inevitable. At Midway in 1942, Japanese naval power was shattered by the US fleet. Japanese land forces, however, fought on. In 1945, fearing Japanese resistance would continue indefinitely, the Allies dropped atomic bombs (above) on Hiroshima and Nagasaki, causing the death of 155,000 people in Hiroshima alone. Japan surrendered in August 1945.

Civilian Populations in the Second World War
In no previous conflict had civilian populations become so deeply involved. The bombing of Europe's cities took the war into people's homes. In the first four months of the German air raids on London – the Blitz – over 30,000 people were killed or injured. Hitler's persecution of the Jews and other civilians caused the death of more than 6 million people in German concentration camps.

The Postwar World 1946–1997

At the end of the Second World War much of Europe lay in ruins. Germany was divided into four zones, controlled by the victorious nations. Berlin, the pre-war German capital, was also divided into four zones. Under the dictator Stalin, the Soviet Union (USSR) took control of the eastern part of Germany and regained much of the territory it had lost at the end of the First World War. Repressive one-party (communist) regimes replaced the previous democracies. Fears that the Soviet Union would extend its control into the West accelerated the division of the continent into two armed camps, divided by the so-called "Iron Curtain." Mutual suspicion was aggravated by the formation in the West of the North Atlantic Treaty Organization (NATO) – which included the US – and the Warsaw Pact in the East. What became known as the Cold War developed between the two opposing blocs. The Western economies, stimulated by American aid, began to recover. In 1957 a number of them became founding members of the European Economic Community. But recovery in Eastern Europe was painfully slow. Harsh conditions led to widespread strikes and unrest. Uprisings in Hungary (1956) and Czechoslovakia (1968) were brutally suppressed by Soviet troops.

Nuclear Weapons
After the Second World War, the Soviet Union rapidly increased its hold on Eastern Europe and extended its control into the Baltic states. In the arms race between the US and the Soviet Union, each side stockpiled nuclear weapons like the Atlas missile above.

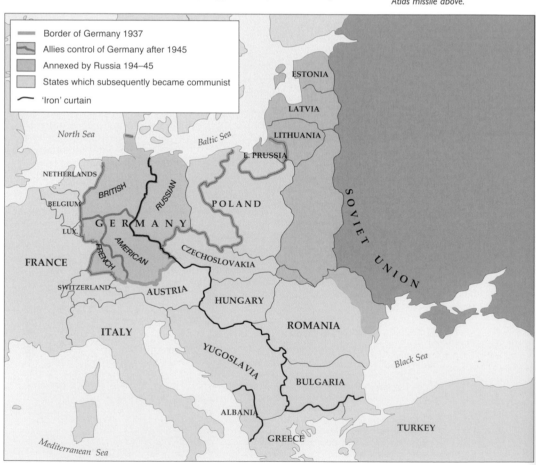

Border of Germany 1937

Allies control of Germany after 1945

Annexed by Russia 194–45

States which subsequently became communist

'Iron' curtain

The West's fear of the spread of communism caused a series of confrontations around the world. In the civil war between communist North Vietnam and non-communist South Vietnam, America became involved on the side of the South, while China and the USSR supported the North. After enormous losses, America withdrew in 1975. When Gorbachev became leader of the USSR in 1985, a new era in East–West relations began. With the USSR on the verge of economic collapse, it could no longer afford to maintain its place in the arms race, and agreements were reached between the USSR and the US to reduce nuclear weapons. Discontented with communist rule, the republics within the USSR began to demand independence, and in 1991 the USSR officially ceased to exist. In the Far East, China had experienced two major upheavals: Mao Tse-tung's reforms, embodied in the Great Leap Forward (1958–59), met with opposition that Mao sought to suppress with the Cultural Revolution. A decade of chaos and political unrest followed, during which millions of Chinese died.

War in Vietnam
The retreat from empire caused conflict in both the Middle East and South East Asia. In Asia, the withdrawal of French colonists led to a communist takeover in North Vietnam. The US's involvement in the conflict, despite a huge injection of men and arms, ultimately led to their withdrawal and humiliation.

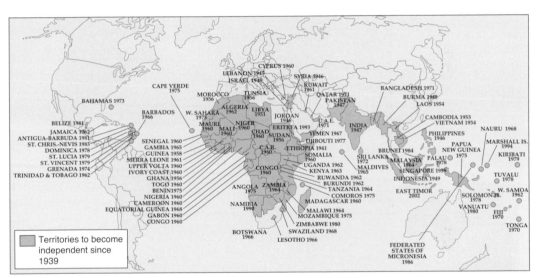

CYPRUS 1960
LEBANON 1943
ISRAEL 1948
SYRIA 1946
CAPE VERDE 1975
KUWAIT 1961
QATAR 1971
BANGLADESH 1971
BAHAMAS 1973
MOROCCO 1956
TUNISIA 1956
BURMA 1948
LAOS 1954
BARBADOS 1966
W. SAHARA 1975
ALGERIA 1962
LIBYA 1951
JORDAN 1946
PAKISTAN 1947
BELIZE 1981
MAURI 1960
MALI 1960
NIGER 1960
CHAD 1960
SUDAN 1956
U.A.E. 1971
INDIA 1947
CAMBODIA 1953
VIETNAM 1954
JAMAICA 1962
ANTIGUA-BARBUDA 1981
ST. CHRIS.-NEVIS 1983
ERITREA 1993
YEMEN 1967
PHILIPPINES 1946
NAURU 1968
SENEGAL 1960
DJIBOUTI 1977
MARSHALL IS. 1994
DOMINICA 1978
ST. LUCIA 1979
GAMBIA 1965
GUINEA 1958
C.A.R. 1960
ETHIOPIA 1941
SOMALIA 1960
BRUNEI 1984
PAPUA NEW GUINEA 1975
PALAU 1978
KIRIBATI 1979
ST. VINCENT 1979
SIERRA LEONE 1961
SRI LANKA 1972
MALAYSIA 1964
SINGAPORE 1956
GRENADA 1974
UPPER VOLTA 1960
UGANDA 1962
KENYA 1963
MALDIVES 1965
TRINIDAD & TOBAGO 1962
IVORY COAST 1960
GHANA 1956
CONGO 1960
RUWANDA 1962
INDONESIA 1949
TUVALU 1978
TOGO 1960
BURUNDI 1962
ANGOLA 1975
ZAMBIA 1964
TANZANIA 1964
COMOROS 1975
EAST TIMOR 2002
W. SAMOA 1962
BENIN 1975
NIGERIA 1960
MADAGASCAR 1960
SOLOMON IS. 1978
CAMEROON 1960
NAMIBIA 1990
MALAWI 1964
VANUATU 1980
EQUATORIAL GUINEA 1968
GABON 1960
MOZAMBIQUE 1975
FIJI 1970
CONGO 1960
ZIMBABWE 1980
TONGA 1970
BOTSWANA 1966
SWAZILAND 1968
LESOTHO 1966
FEDERATED STATES OF MICRONESIA 1986

Territories to become independent since 1939

Independence for Many
Within a few years of the end of the Second World War, virtually all of Europe's empires had collapsed. France lost Indo-China and Algeria; Indonesia regained the territories previously under Dutch control. India's long struggle for independence from Britain came to a successful conclusion in 1947. Independence for Burma, Sri Lanka (Ceylon) and Singapore followed. In Africa, all of the European colonies won independence mainly during the 1950s and 60s. In 1947, when Palestine was partitioned into a Jewish and an Arab state, the plan was disputed by the Palestinians and war broke out in 1948. Since then further wars have erupted between Israel and her Arab neighbours.

Civil War and Famine
For some African nations, independence brought new and terrible problems. Old tribal enmities, suppressed by colonial rule, resurfaced and boiled over into civil wars. In Ethiopia, civil war caused an appalling famine in 1984–1985 which shocked the world.

The World in Conflict 1985–2006

With the fall of the Berlin Wall in 1989, the Cold War era came to an end, and a new world order began to emerge. The USSR was broken into separate republics and former communist states in Europe gained their independence. In some regions, this fragmentation led to civil war, especially when it was fuelled by ethnic nationalism as in Yugoslavia. In the Middle East, disputes between Israel and her Arab neighbours remained unresolved, and Palestinians continued their violent struggle to eject Israeli settlers from the Autonomous Palestinian Territories. Islamic fundamentalism in Iran fuelled the tension, while Saddam Hussein, the dictator of Iraq, turned his attention to oil-rich Kuwait, igniting the Gulf War of 1991, when a US-led coalition of 29 states launched air and ground attacks against the Iraqis. In South Africa, political protest led to the breakdown of apartheid, with the first democratic elections held in 1994. The rest of the continent did not fare so well, however; ethnic warfare in east and central Africa led to the displacement of millions, and brutal genocide in Rwanda; in northeast Africa, Islamic fundamentalism continues to cause severe tension. On September 11 2001, terrorists belonging to an Islamic group called al-Qaeda hijacked passenger airliners and used them as bombs to attack the World Trade Center in New York City and the Pentagon in Washington, DC. This attack unleashed a "war against terror" by the US. In 2001, US troops invaded Afghanistan, ruled by

the aggressively Islamic Taliban, and installed a democratic government. In 2003 they turned their attention to Iraq, and led a coalition of international forces into the country. They captured Saddam Hussein and eventually sponsored democratic elections, but Islamic insurgency against coalition forces continues to cause severe problems.

Terrorism
Terrorists are people who are prepared to risk their own lives to make a political point, whether it is to attack a hated target or an individual, or to destroy whole communities. Terrorist outrages are happening all over the world, and the US government has identified seven countries as state sponsors of terrorism.

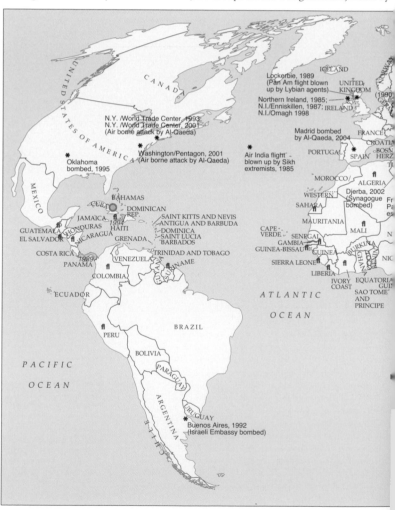

754

US-led Intervention

Since September 2001, the US has been a leader in the war against terror. It has led international coalitions into Afghanistan and Iraq, using a wide variety of economic and other sanctions to pressure states into abandoning their support of terrorism. The price is high, however, and many coalition troops have lost their lives overseas.

Osama bin Laden

Considered the world's foremost terrorist, Osama bin Laden has been implicated in a string of deadly attacks against the United States and its allies. He is the chief suspect behind the World Trade Center attacks of 2001.

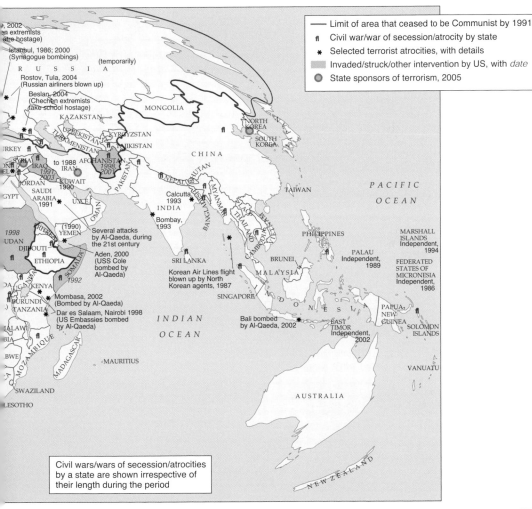

- —— Limit of area that ceased to be Communist by 1991
- ⚑ Civil war/war of secession/atrocity by state
- ✳ Selected terrorist atrocities, with details
- ▨ Invaded/struck/other intervention by US, with *date*
- ◉ State sponsors of terrorism, 2005

, 2002
an extremists
atre hostage)

Istanbul, 1986; 2000
(Synagogue bombings)
(temporarily)

R U S S I A

Rostov, Tula, 2004
(Russian airliners blown up)

Beslan, 2004
(Chechen extremists
take school hostage)

KAZAKSTAN

MONGOLIA

NORTH KOREA

SOUTH KOREA

UZBEKISTAN
KYRGYZSTAN
TURKMENISTAN
TAJIKISTAN

URKEY

IRAQ   to 1988   AFGHANISTAN
1991   IRAN   1998,
2003   2001

CHINA

BHUTAN

JORDAN   KUWAIT
GYPT   1990
SAUDI   NEPAL
ARABIA   1991   UAE   OMAN

Calcutta,
1993
INDIA

MYANMAR

TAIWAN

PACIFIC
OCEAN

Bombay,
1993

1998
UDAN
YEMEN   (1990)

DJIBOUTI   Several attacks
by Al-Qaeda, during
the 21st century

ETHIOPIA   Aden, 2000
(USS Cole
bombed by
Al-Qaeda)

SOMALIA
1992

KENYA

Korean Air Lines flight
blown up by North
Korean agents, 1987

SRI LANKA

BRUNEI

MALAYSIA

PHILIPPINES

SINGAPORE

MARSHALL
ISLANDS
Independent,
1994

PALAU
Independent,
1989

FEDERATED
STATES OF
MICRONESIA
Independent,
1986

BURUNDI   Mombasa, 2002
TANZANIA   (Bombed by Al-Qaeda)

Dar es Salaam, Nairobi 1998
(US Embassies bombed
by Al-Qaeda)

MALAWI

MADAGASCAR

BIA

BWE

MAURITIUS

SWAZILAND

LESOTHO

INDIAN

OCEAN

Bali bombed
by Al-Qaeda, 2002

EAST
TIMOR
Independent,
2002

PAPUA
NEW
GUINEA

SOLOMON
ISLANDS

VANUATU

AUSTRALIA

NEW ZEALAND

Civil wars/wars of secession/atrocities
by a state are shown irrespective of
their length during the period

The World Tomorrow?

Despite huge strides in technology in the twentieth century, with an estimated global population of more than 6.5 billion in the year 2006, many basic problems remain in the twenty-first century. Hunger and famine, war and disease stalk our world today just as they have done in the past. Will the citizens of tomorrow's world be any better off?

Urban populations have exploded in recent years: many Asian and African cities, such as Lagos and Bombay, are experiencing very rapid growth that is projected to continue at this pace. In 1950 there were just eight "megacities" with populations of 5 million or more but by 2000 the number had grown to forty-one.

We are beginning to face the consequences of climate change and global warming: the United Nations Framework Convention on Climate Change has set an overall framework for intergovernmental efforts to tackle the challenge posed by climate change. For example, under the Convention governments now work together to gather and share information on greenhouse gas emissions, national policies and best practices.

There is a also a growing awareness – highlighted by the Earth Summits held in Stockholm (1972), Rio (1992), and Johannesburg (2002) – of the need to conserve the planet's natural resources, such as its wildlife and rainforests, and to develop alternative sources of energy – the present rate of oil consumption is now so great that oil supplies will have run out by 2050.

In 1997, pictures were received from a space probe on Mars and in 2004 another probe reached Saturn and sent back the closest photographs yet of the planet's rings. Manned space stations have circled the earth.

Will our exploration of space provide a pathway to future worlds? What will globalization bring? Can we save our world and its habitat? Can there be world peace and prosperity for all our peoples? The world tomorrow will certainly demand much from its citizens in the years to come.

MAPS OF THE WORLD

Contents

Symbols for maps on pages:
8-22, 27-38, 40-54, 60-62

Inhabitants

More than 5 million

New York

1 000 000 - 5 000 000

Seattle

250 000 - 1 000 000

Mexicali

100 000 - 250 000

Tijuana

25 000 - 100 000

Sparks

Less than 25 000

Monterey

National capital (UPPERCASE)

OTTAWA

State capital

Boise

International boundary

Disputed international boundary

State boundary

Disputed state boundary

Major road

Other road

Road under construction

Seasonal road

Railway

Canal

Highest peak in continent

▲
McKinley

Highest peak in country

△
Logan

Height in feet

17000ft

Depth in feet

▽
185ft

Coral reef

Dam

| Kainji
Dam

Waterfall

| Niagara
Falls

Pass

)(

International airport

National airport

Historical site

Scientific site

Scale 1:20 000 000

| 0 | 200 | 400 | 600 km |
| 0 | 100 | 200 | 300 miles |

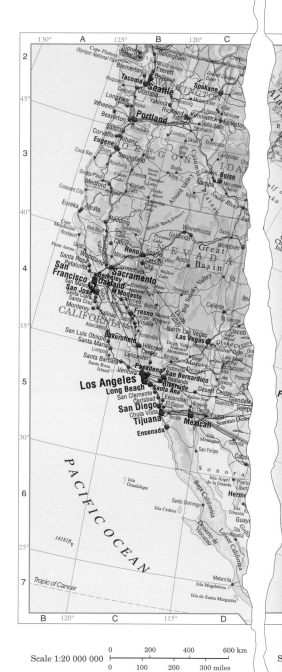

Symbols for maps on pages:
7, 24-25, 56-59

Inhabitants

Chicago	More than 5 million
Columbus	1 000 000 - 5 000 000
Quebec	250 000 - 1 000 000
Halifax	100 000 - 250 000
Anderson	Less than 100 000
NASSAU	National capital (UPPERCASE)
Sacramento	State capital
	International boundary
	Disputed international boundary
	Major road
	Road under construction
	Major railway
	Canal
McKinley	Highest peak in continent
Logan	Highest peak in country
17000ft	Heights in feet
185ft	Depths in feet
	Coral reef
	Scientific station
	Territorial claims in Antarctica
	Disputed territorial claims in Antarctica
Grand Coulee Dam	Dam
Virginia Falls	Waterfall

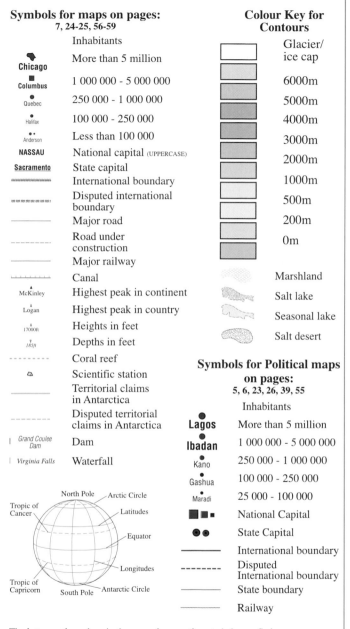

North Pole — Arctic Circle
Tropic of Cancer
Latitudes
Equator
Longitudes
Tropic of Capricorn
South Pole — Antarctic Circle

Colour Key for Contours

	Glacier/ ice cap
	6000m
	5000m
	4000m
	3000m
	2000m
	1000m
	500m
	200m
	0m
	Marshland
	Salt lake
	Seasonal lake
	Salt desert

Symbols for Political maps on pages:
5, 6, 23, 26, 39, 55

Inhabitants

Lagos	More than 5 million
Ibadan	1 000 000 - 5 000 000
Kano	250 000 - 1 000 000
Gashua	100 000 - 250 000
Maradi	25 000 - 100 000
	National Capital
	State Capital
	International boundary
	Disputed International boundary
	State boundary
	Railway

The letters and numbers in the map edges are there to help you find names. Look for London in the index **29** D4. Turn to page 29 and look top or bottom for number 4 and left or right for letter D. In this blue grid square you will find the city of London.

Scale 1:50 000 000 means that a distance on the map is 50 000 000 times longer on the Earth's surface e.g. 1 cm on the map represents 500 km on the surface and 1 inch on the map represents 800 miles.

0   500   1000   1500 km

0   250   500   750 miles

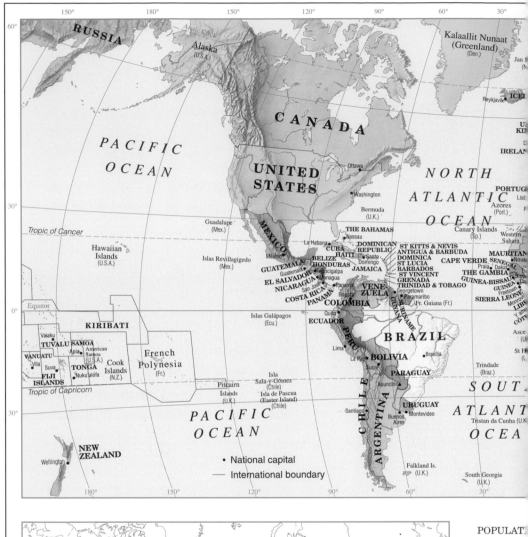

POPULAT...

- 10 million inhab...
- 1 million inhab...

The density of po...
varies over the Ea...
surface. Some p...
sparsely populated...
of geographical co...
high mountains, ho...
or cold tundra. Con...
maps on pages 8...
Some parts are...
populated due to g...
conditions, econor...
physically convenie...
big cities, as well...
reasons such as r...
ethnic grouping. P...
growth is mainly c...
the already densely...
populated areas.

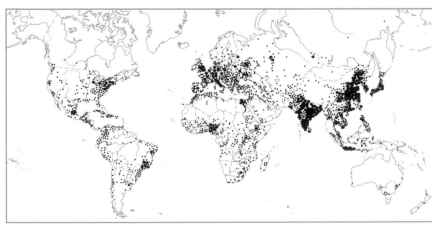

- National capital
- — International boundary

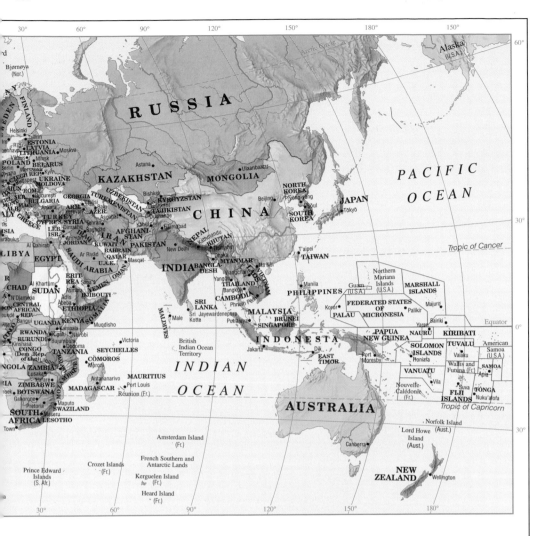

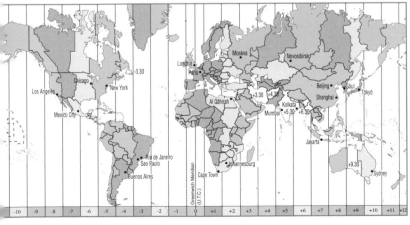

TIME ZONES

The Earth spins around its axis anticlockwise and completes one turn every 24 hours. As the world rotates it is day on the part facing the Sun and night on the side in shadow. As shown on this map, we have divided the Earth into 24 standard time zones. They are based upon lines of longitude at 15 degree intervals but mainly follow country or state boundaries. You can compare times around the world by using the map. For example; when it is 12 noon in London it is 5 hours earlier in New York or 7 am.

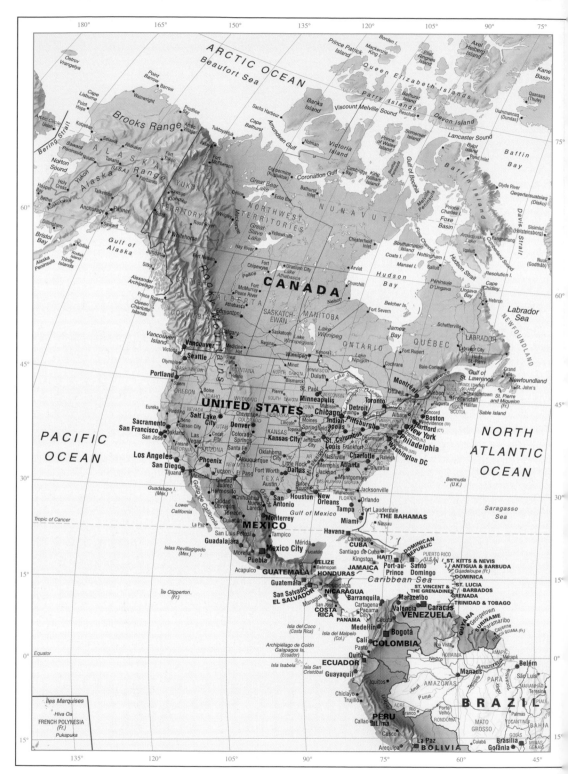

Scale 1: 31 250 000

| 0 | 500 | 1000km |

| 0 | 300 | 600miles |

© Geddes & Grosset

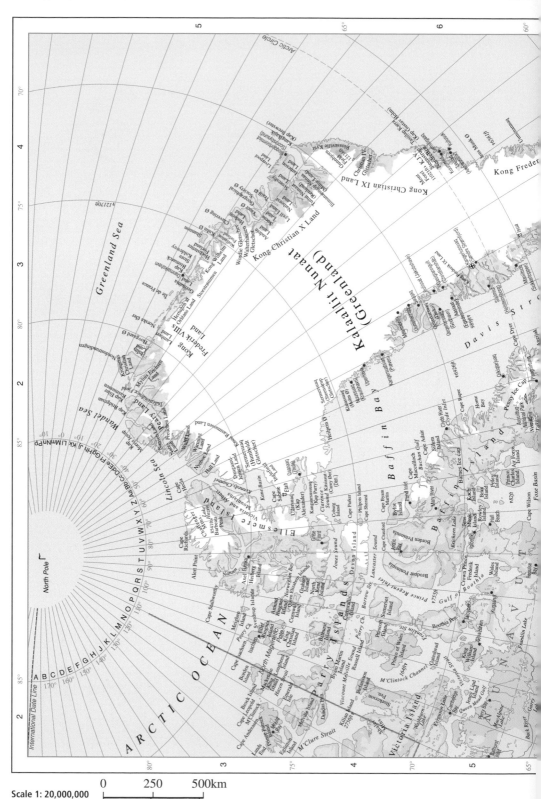

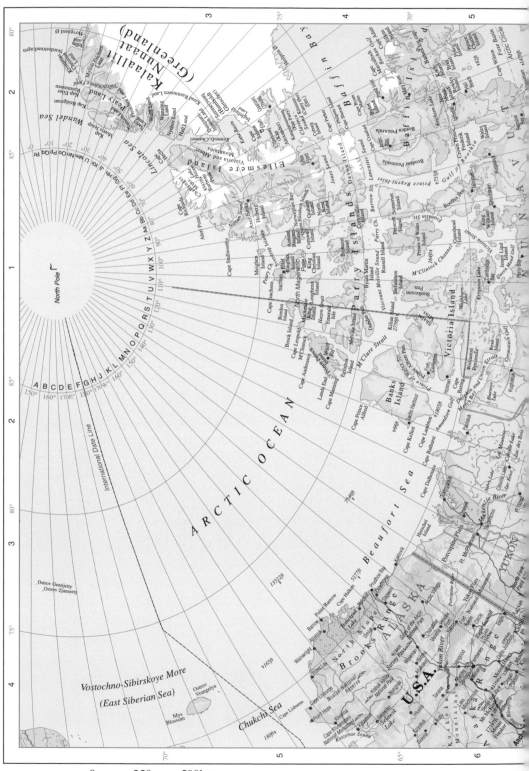

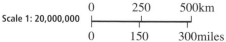

Scale 1: 20,000,000

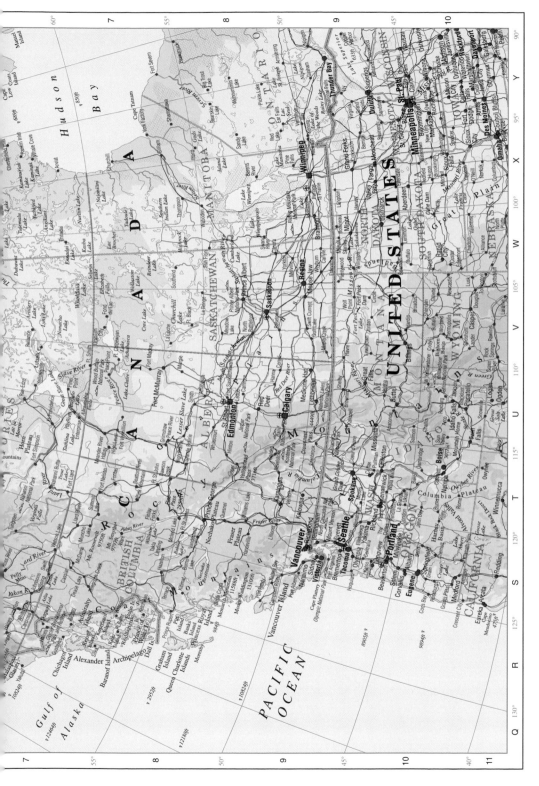

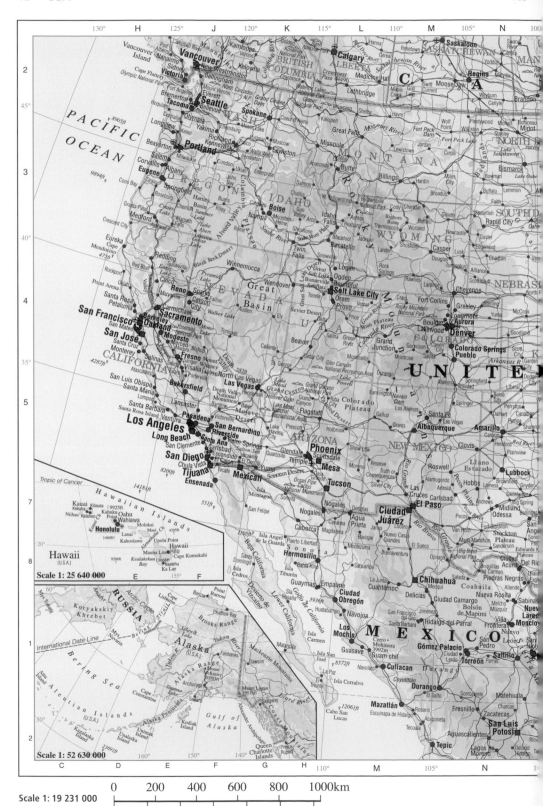

| 0 | 200 | 400 | 600 | 800 | 1000km |

| 0 | 100 | 200 | 300 | 400 | 500 | 600miles |

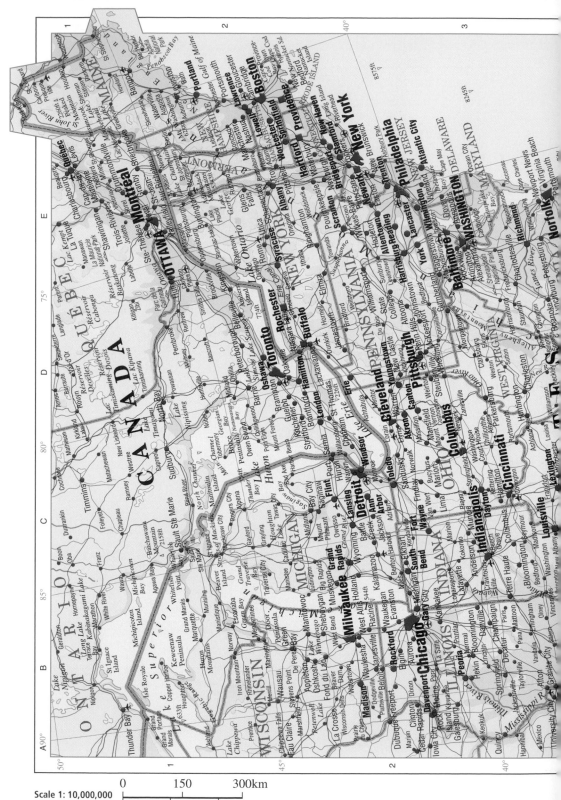

Scale 1 : 10,000,000

| 0 | 150 | 300km |

| 0 | 75 | 150miles |

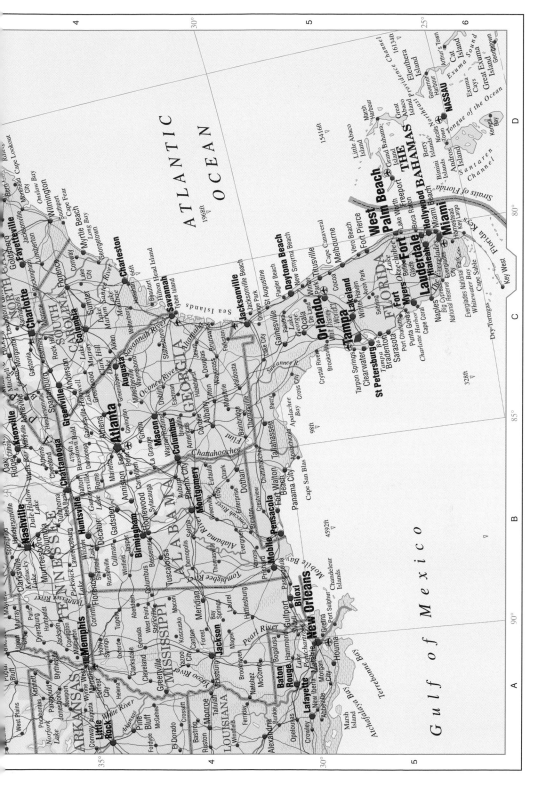

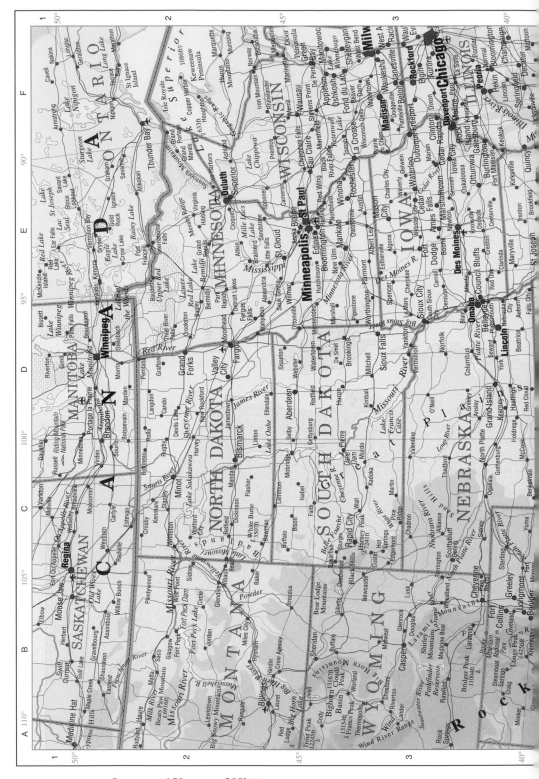

Scale 1: 10 000 000

0   150   300km

0   75   150miles

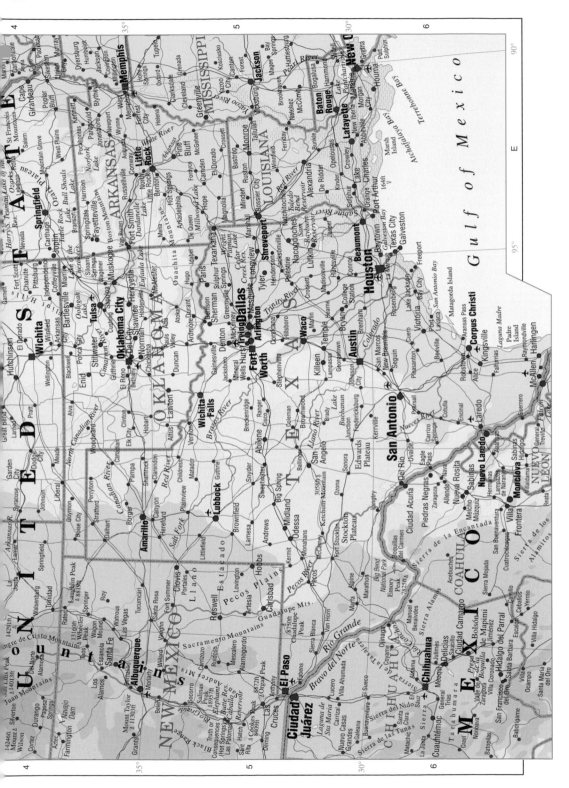

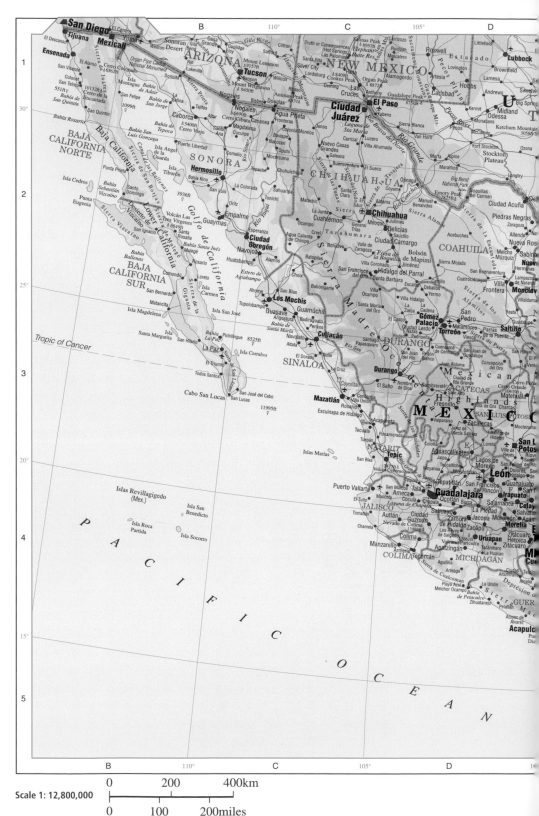

Scale 1: 12,800,000

0	200	400km

0	100	200miles

Gulf of Mexico

CUBA

LA HABANA (HAVANA)

MEXICO

YUCATÁN

Yucatan Peninsula

CAMPECHE

QUINTANA ROO

TABASCO

CHIAPAS

OAXACA

VERACRUZ

BELIZE

GUATEMALA

HONDURAS

EL SALVADOR

NICARAGUA

TEGUCIGALPA

SAN SALVADOR

GUATEMALA

Bahía de Campeche

Golfo de Tehuantepec

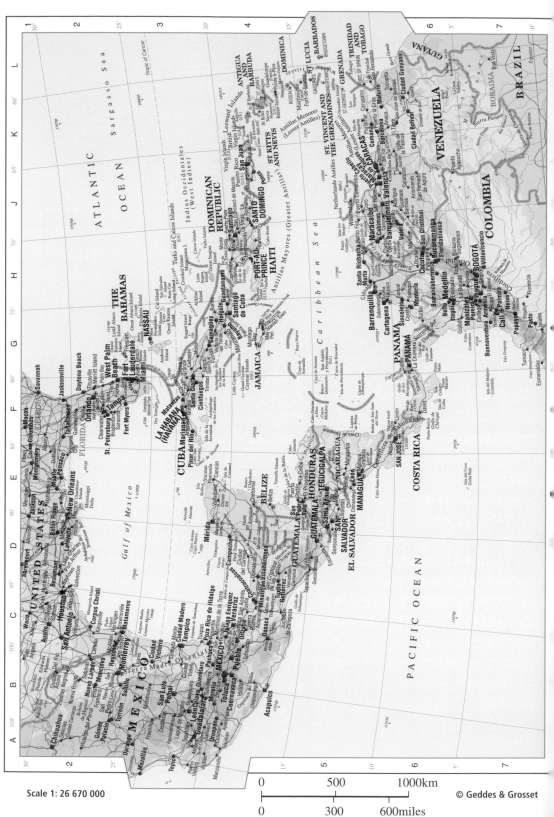

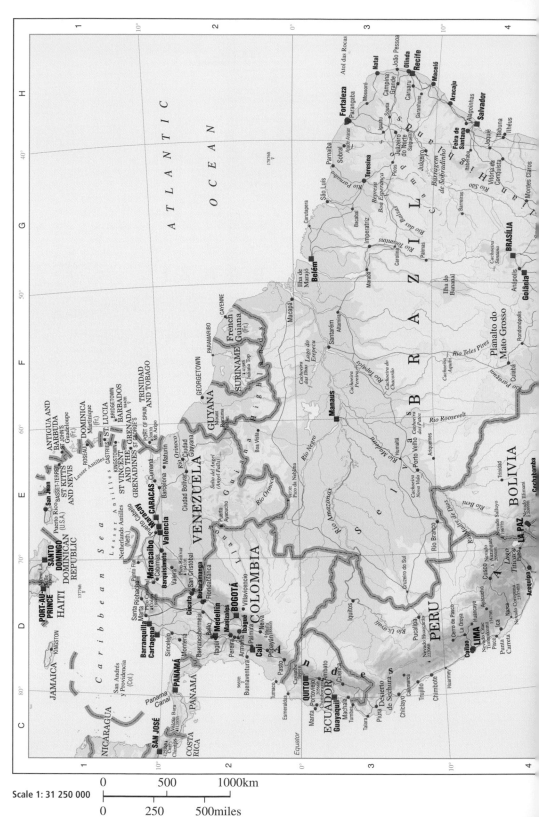

Scale 1: 31 250 000

| 0 | 500 | 1000km |

| 0 | 250 | 500miles |

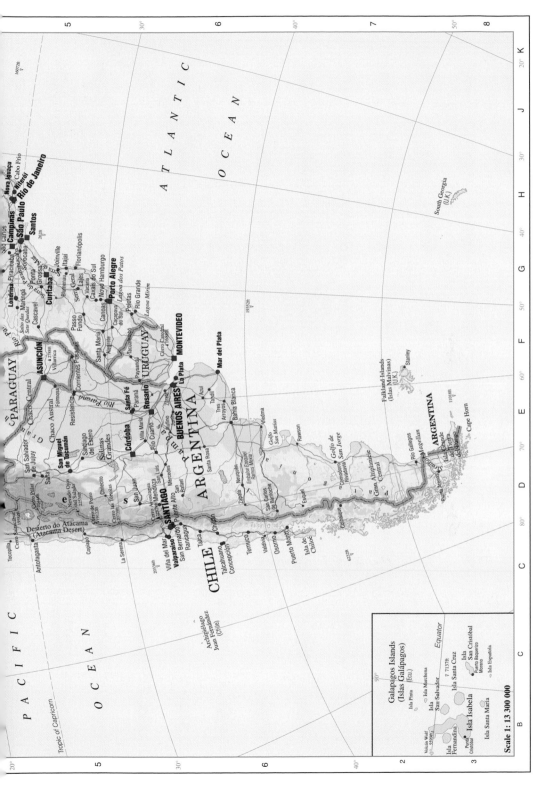

Scale 1: 13 300 000

Galapagos Islands
(Islas Galápagos)

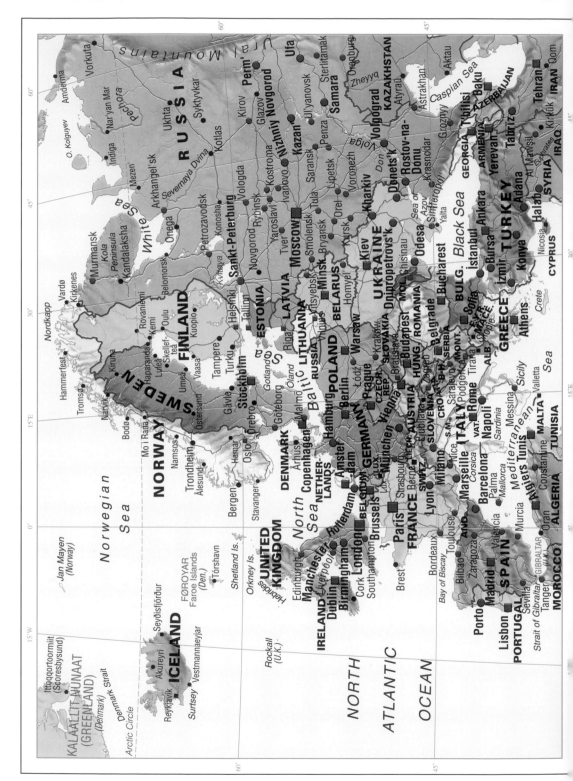

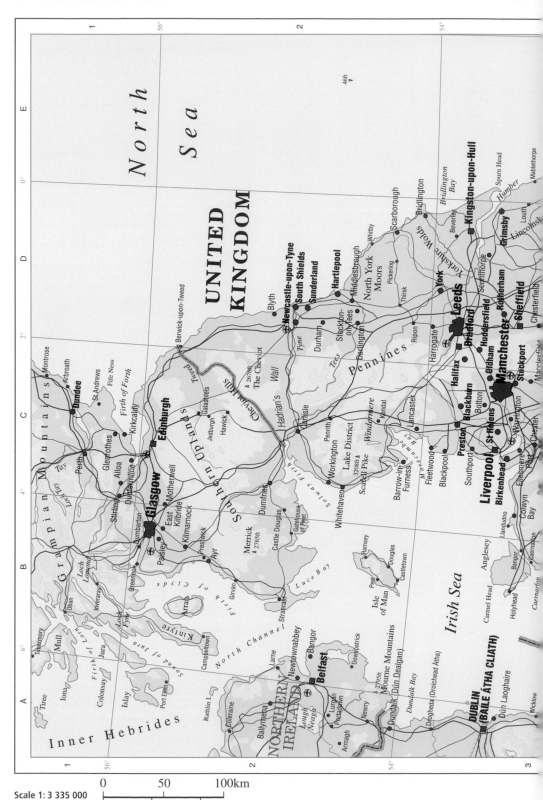

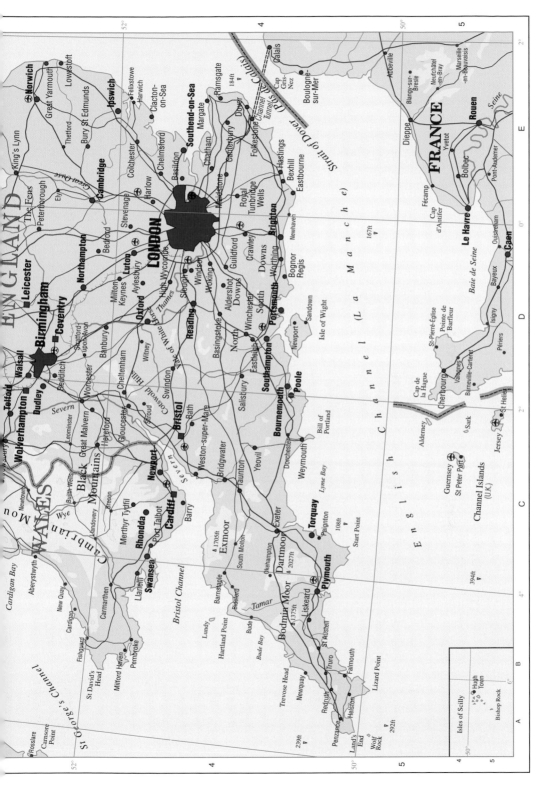

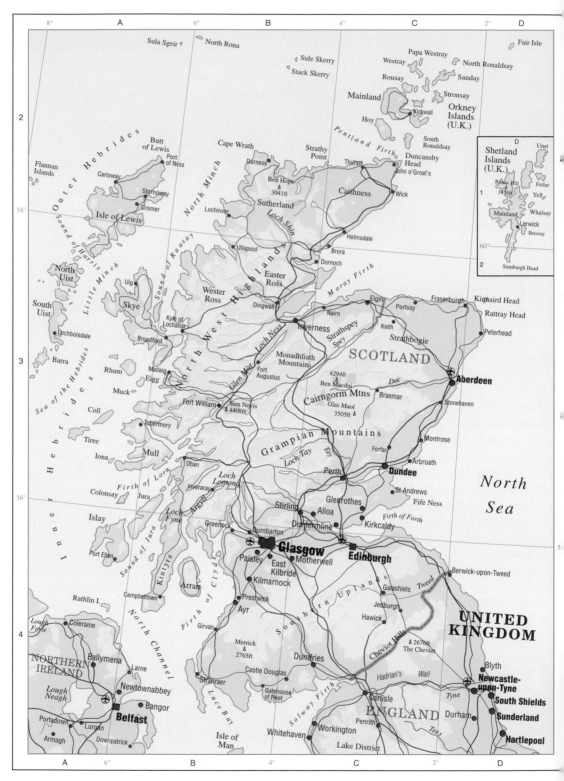

Sula Sgeir
North Rona
Fair Isle
Sule Skerry
Stack Skerry
Papa Westray
Westray
North Ronaldsay
Rousay
Sanday
Mainland
Stronsay
Kirkwall
Orkney
Islands
(U.K.)
Hoy
South
Ronaldsay
Pentland Firth
Duncansby
Head
John o'Groat's
Thurso
Wick
Caithness

Butt
of Lewis
Port
of Ness
Cape Wrath
Strathy
Point
Durness
Ben Hope
3041ft
Strathy
Point

Outer Hebrides
Carloway
Stornoway
Cromer
Isle of Lewis
North Minch
Lochinver
Sutherland
Loch Shin
Helmsdale
Brora
Dornoch

Shetland
Islands
(U.K.)
Unst
Ronas Hill
1476ft
Fetlar
Yell
Mainland
Whalsay
Lerwick
Bressay
Sumburgh Head

Flannan
Islands
Sound of Harris
North
Uist
South
Uist
Lochboisdale
Barra
Sea of the Hebrides
Rhum
Eigg
Muck
Coll
Tiree
Iona
Mull
Colonsay
Jura
Islay
Port Ellen

Uig
Skye
Kyle of
Lochalsh
Broadford
Mallaig
Tobermory
Oban
Inveraray
Loch
Fyne
Greenock
Dumbarton

Little Minch
Sound of Raasay
North West Highlands
Wester
Ross
Dingwall
Loch Ness
Glen Mor
Fort
Augustus
Fort William
Ben Nevis
4408ft
Glen More

Easter
Ross
Moray Firth
Elgin
Portsoy
Fraserburgh
Kinnaird Head
Rattray Head
Peterhead
Inverness
Nairn
Strathspey
Spey
Keith
Strathbogie
Monadhliath
Mountains
4294ft
Ben Macdui
Cairngorm Mtns
Dee
Braemar
Glas Maol
3505ft
Stonehaven
Aberdeen

SCOTLAND

Grampian Mountains
Loch Tay
Tay
Forfar
Arbroath
Montrose
Perth
Dundee
St Andrews
Fife Ness

Loch
Lomond
Stirling
Alloa
Glenrothes
Dunfermline
Firth of Forth
Kirkcaldy
Edinburgh
North
Sea

Firth of Lorn
Sound of Jura
Kintyre
Arran
Campbeltown
Firth of Clyde
Prestwick
Ayr
Girvan
Rathlin I.
Coleraine
North Channel
Lough
Foyle
Ballymena
Larne
Newtownabbey
Bangor
Belfast
Portadown
Lurgan
Armagh
Downpatrick
NORTHERN
IRELAND
Lough
Neagh

Paisley
Glasgow
East
Kilbride
Motherwell
Kilmarnock
Galashiels
Tweed
Berwick-upon-Tweed
Jedburgh
Hawick
Southern Uplands
Cheviot Hills
2676ft
The Cheviot
UNITED
KINGDOM
Merrick
2765ft
Dumfries
Castle Douglas
Stranraer
Luce Bay
Gatehouse
of Fleet
Solway Firth
Hadrian's Wall
Carlisle
Tyne
Penrith
ENGLAND
Blyth
Newcastle-
upon-Tyne
South Shields
Sunderland
Durham
Tees
Hartlepool

Portrush
Whitehaven
Workington
Lake District
Isle of
Man

58°
56°
60°
8°
6°
4°
2°
A
B
C
D

Scale 1: 3 117 000

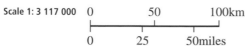

© Geddes & Grosset

Scale 1: 3 335 000

0   50   100km

0   25   50miles

© Geddes & Grosset

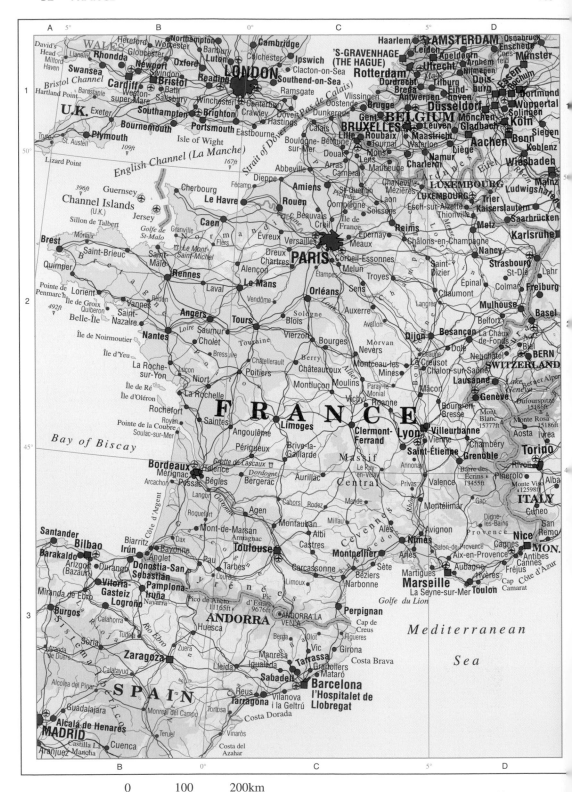

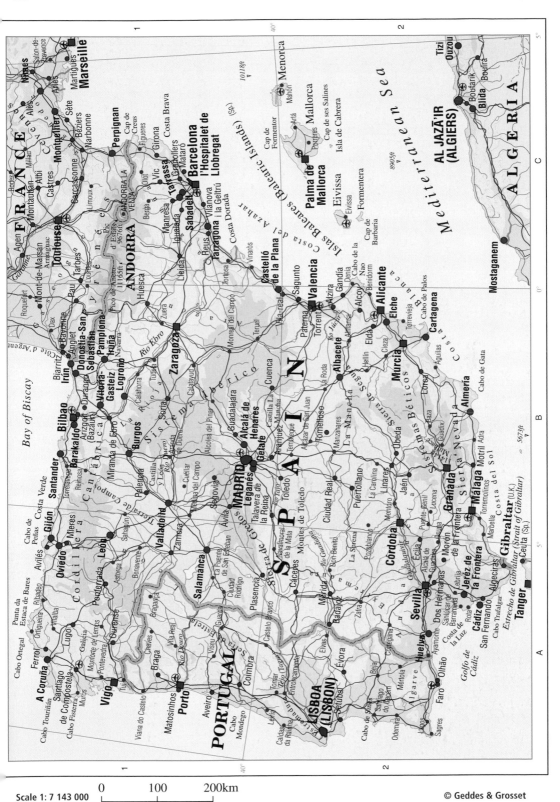

Scale 1: 10 893 000

0   200   400km

0   100   200miles

© Geddes & Grosset

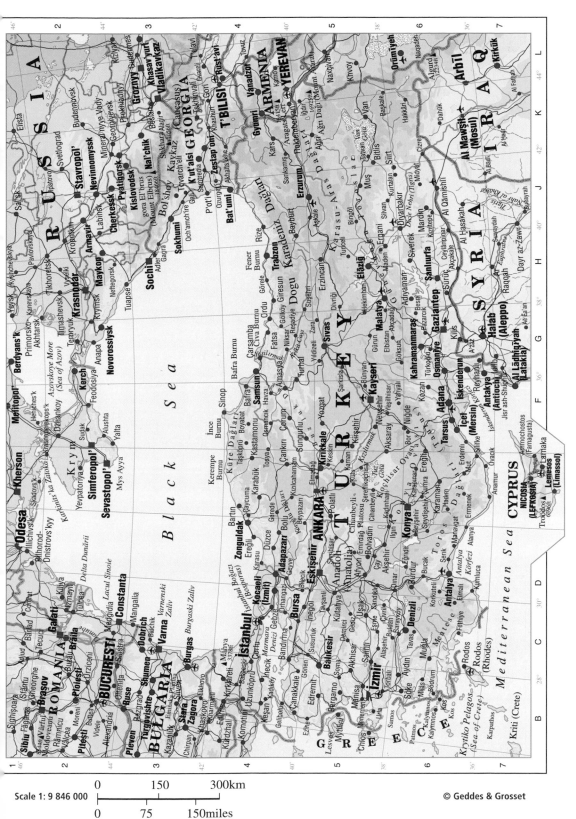

Scale 1: 9 846 000

0   150   300km

0   75   150miles

© Geddes & Grosset

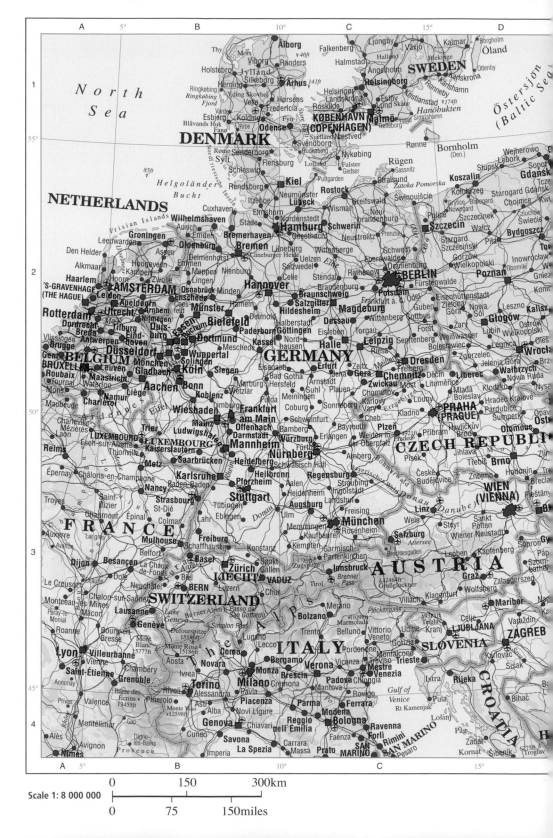

Scale 1: 8 000 000

| 0 | 150 | 300km |

| 0 | 75 | 150miles |

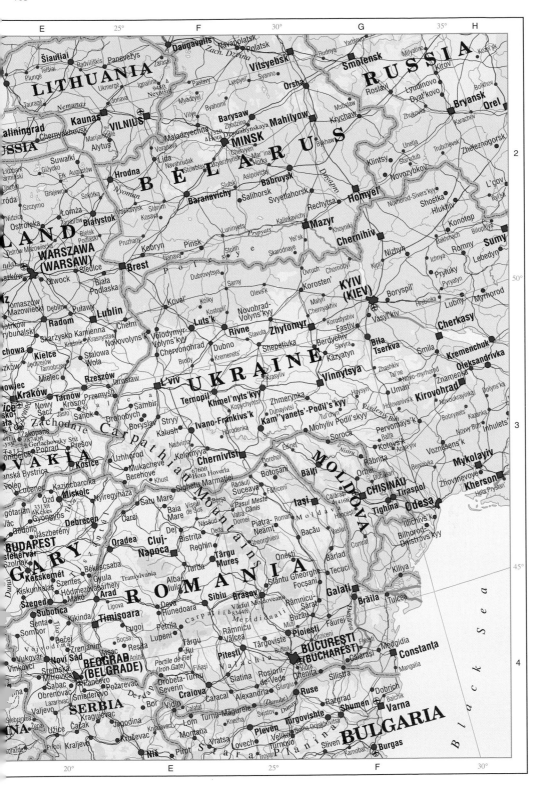

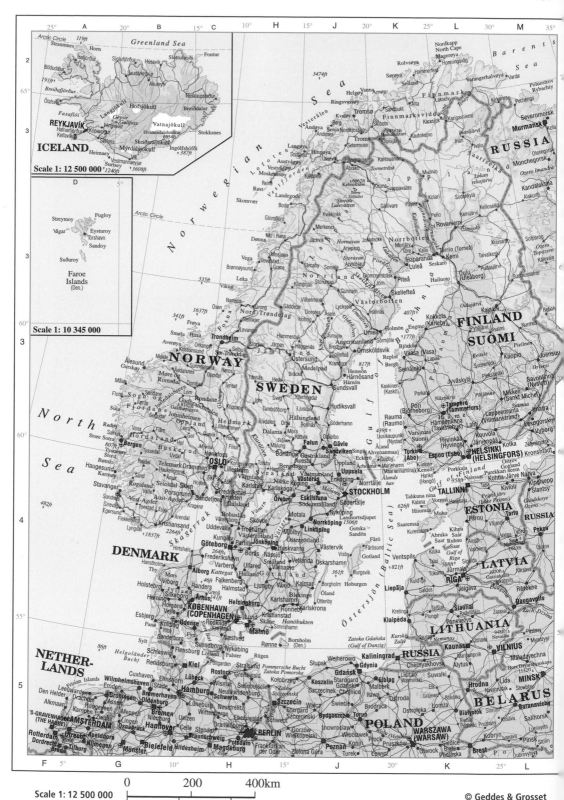

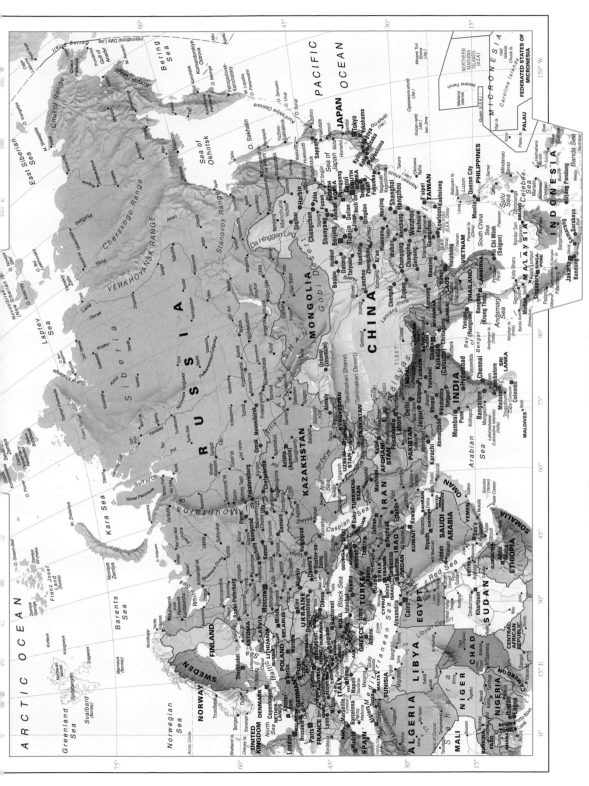

Spitsbergen Nordaustlandet K. Płoten
Longyearbyen Barentsøya Bolshiy Lyakhov
Storfjorden Edgeøya Kong Karls Land
Svalbard (Nor.)
Nordkappet Franz Josef Land
Bjørnøya (Bear Island) (Nor.)

Norwegian Sea

Ostrov Kil'din

NORWAY
SWEDEN
FINLAND (SUOMI)

Barentsevo More (Barents Sea)

Novaya Zemlya

Ostrov
Belush'ya Guba

Murmansk Severomorsk
Kola
Ozero Imandra Olenegorsk
Monchegorsk
Apatity Kirovsk Kandalaksha Kol'skiy Poluostrov
Mys Svyatoy Nos
Kanin Nos
Mezenskaya Guba
Cheshskaya Guba

Pechorskoye More
Ostrov Kolguyev
Ostrov Dolgiy
Yugorskiy Poluostrov
Ust'-Kara
Kara

Arctic Circle

Beloye More (White Sea)

Nar'yan Mar
Vorkuta
Chum
Inta
Labytnangi
Salekhard

Severodvinsk Arkhangel'sk
Novodvinsk
Onega

Pechora
Ukhta
Sosnogorsk

Polyarnyy Ural

Zapadno

Syktyvkar

Khanty-Mansiysk

Kotlas
Velikiy Ustyug
Koryazhma

Vologda
Sokol
Yaroslavl'
Rybinsk
Kostroma
Ivanovo
Tver' (Kalinin)

Kirov
Berezniki
Solikamsk Karpinsk
Kudymkar Kizel
Serov
Krasnotur'insk

MOSKVA
Vladimir
Yoshkar-Ola
Izhevsk
Perm'
Nizhniy Tagil
Yekaterinburg
Chelyabinsk

Nizhniy Novgorod
Kazan'
Naberezhnyye Chelny
Ufa
Magnitogorsk

Saransk
Penza
Tol'yatti
Samara
Saratov
Orenburg

KAZAKHSTAN
Qostanay
Kokshetau
Petropavlovsk
Kurgan

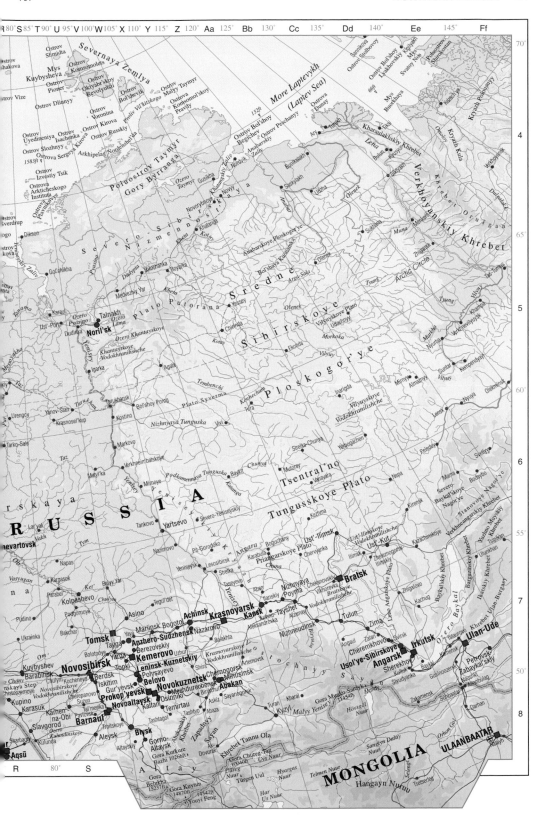

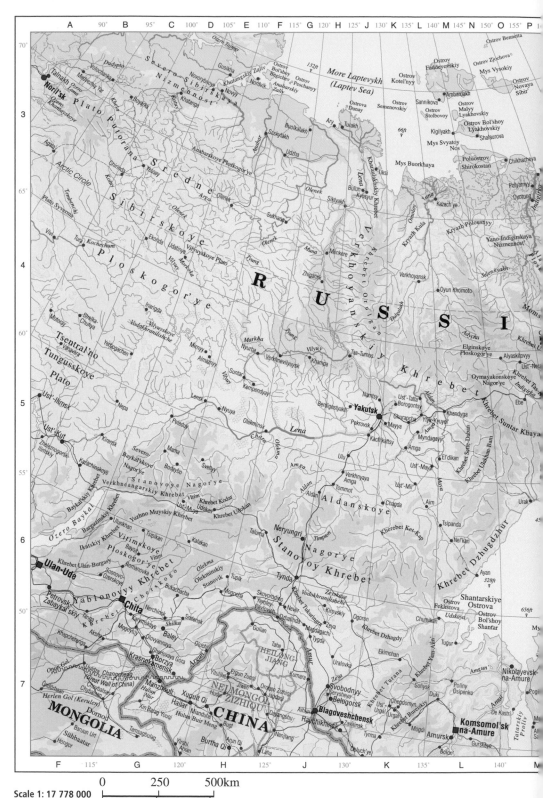

Scale 1: 17 778 000

```
0        250      500km
├───────┼────────┤
0      150      300miles
```

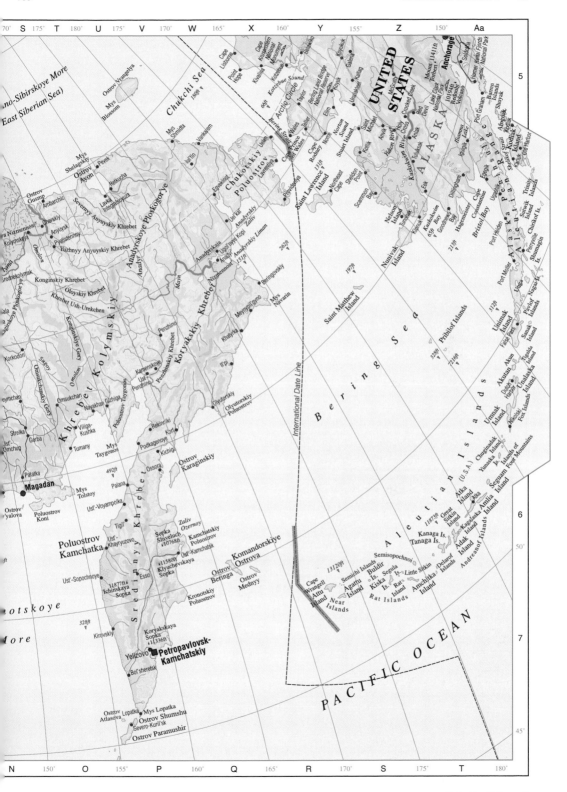

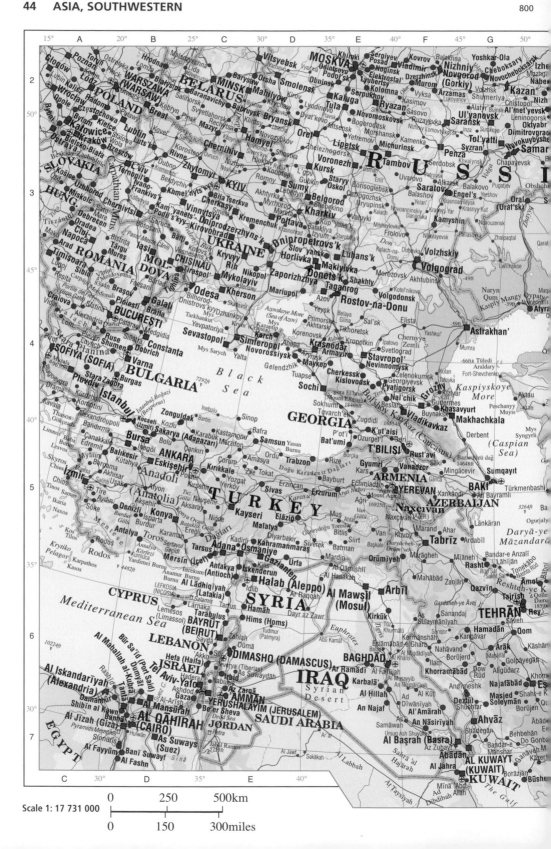

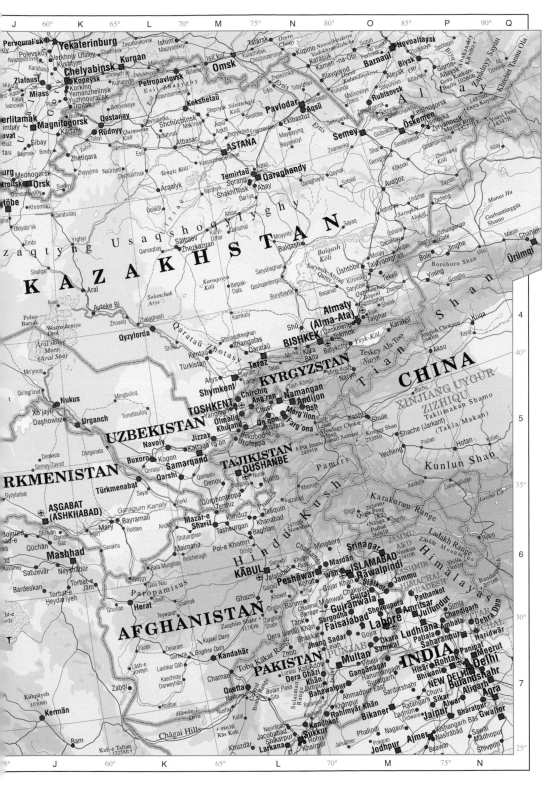

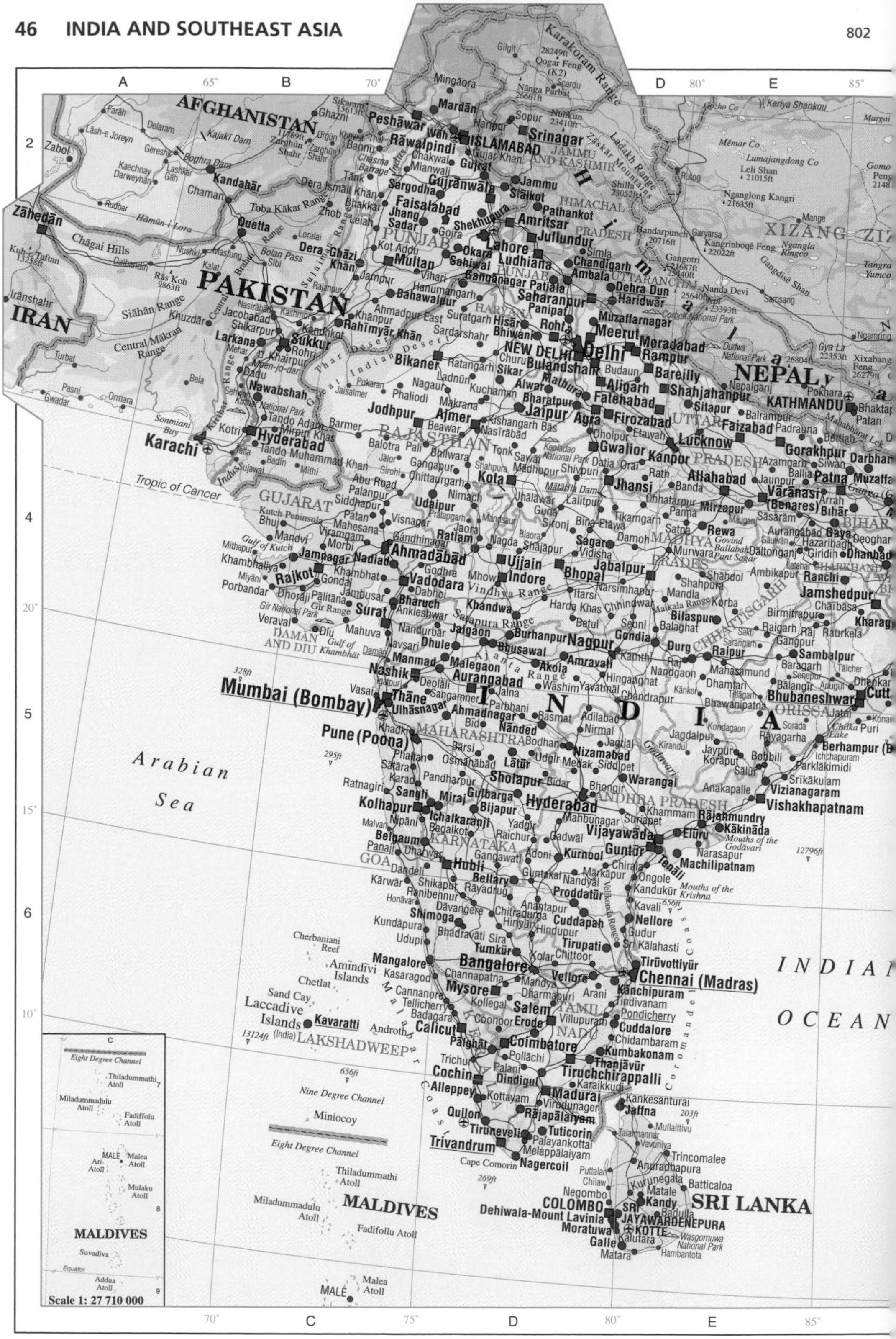

AFGHANISTAN

PAKISTAN

IRAN

JAMMU AND KASHMIR

XIZANG

NEPAL

KATHMANDU

NEW DELHI

PUNJAB

RAJASTHAN

GUJARAT

Karachi

UTTAR PRADESH

MADHYA PRADESH

BIHAR

CHHATTISGARH

ORISSA

JHARKHAND

Mumbai (Bombay)

MAHARASHTRA

Pune (Poona)

GOA

KARNATAKA

Hyderabad

ANDHRA PRADESH

Arabian Sea

Bangalore

TAMIL NADU

Chennai (Madras)

Mysore

Calicut

LAKSHADWEEP

Laccadive Islands (India)

Amindivi Islands

Cochin

Trivandrum

Cape Comorin

MALDIVES

MALÉ

COLOMBO

SRI JAYAWARDENEPURA KOTTE

SRI LANKA

INDIAN OCEAN

Tropic of Cancer

Equator

Eight Degree Channel

Nine Degree Channel

Eight Degree Channel

Scale 1: 27 710 000

Scale 1: 19 245 000

0   250   500km

0   150   300miles

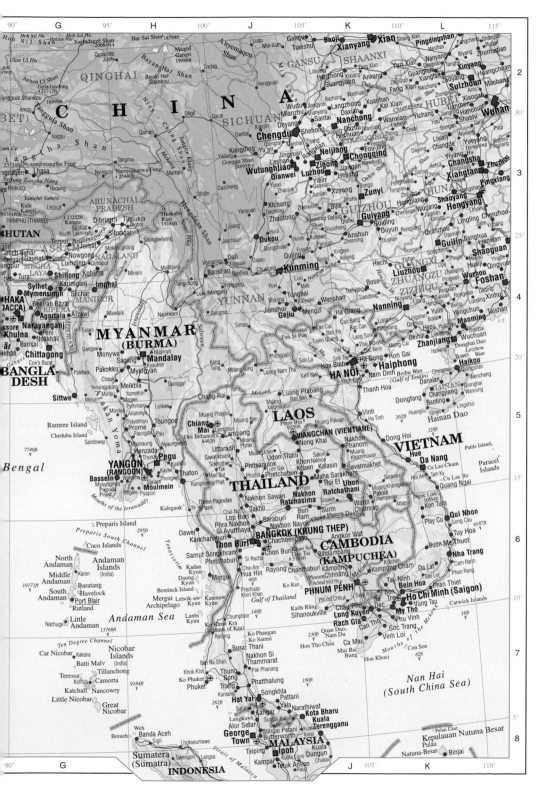

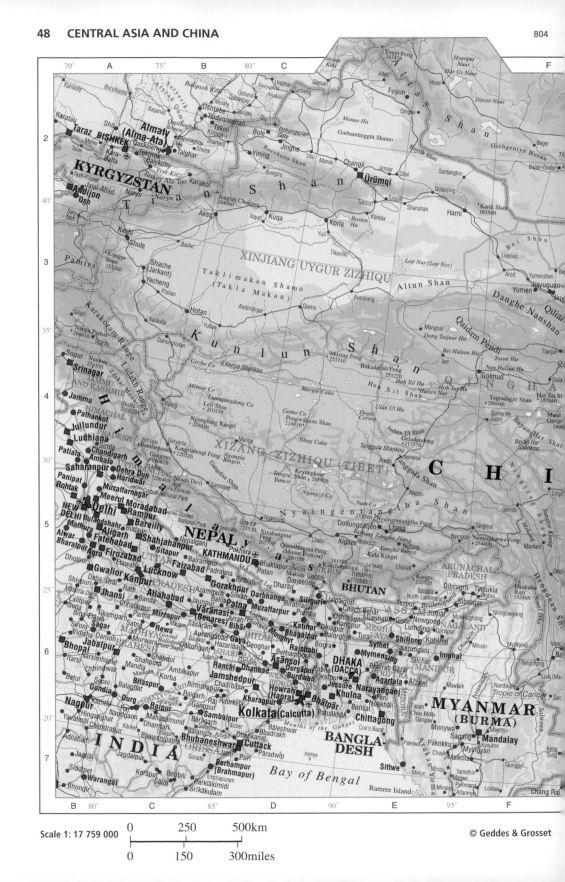

Scale 1: 17 759 000

| 0 | 250 | 500km |

| 0 | 150 | 300miles |

© Geddes & Grosset

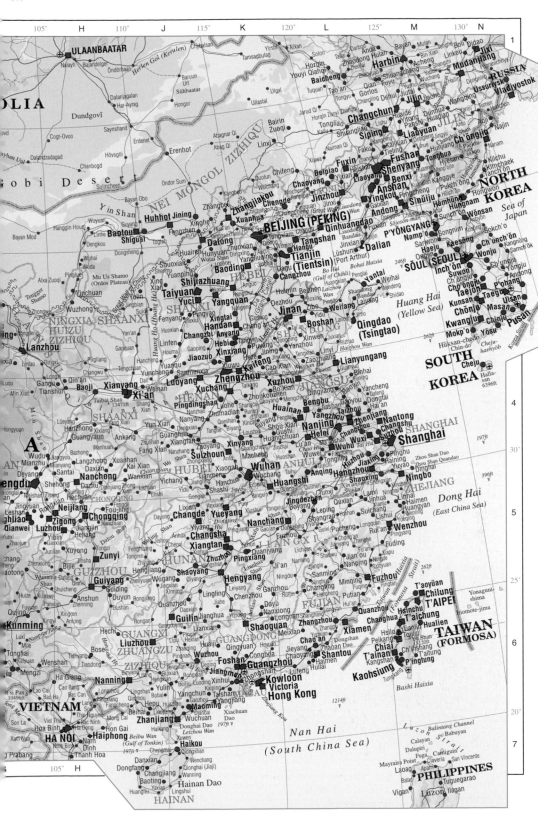

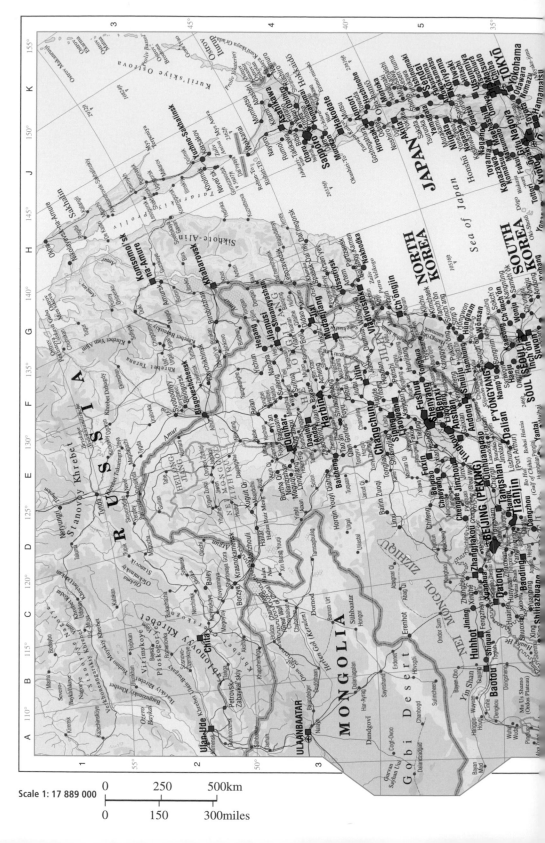

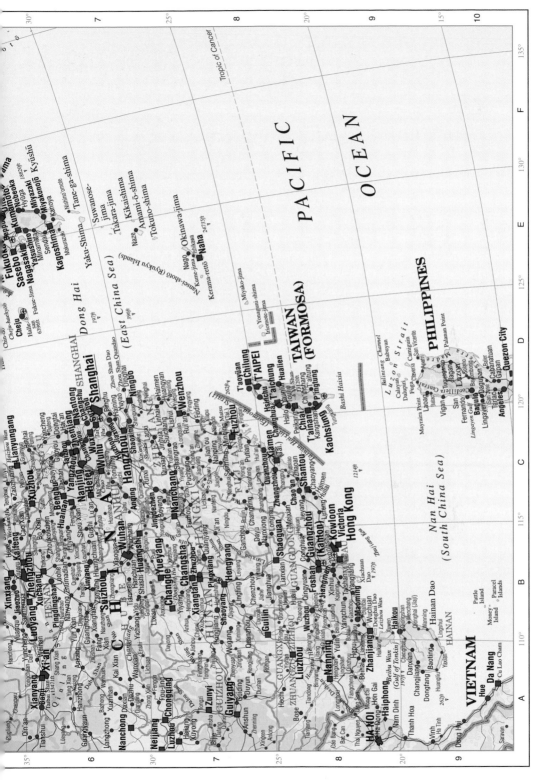

0   250   500km

0   150   300miles

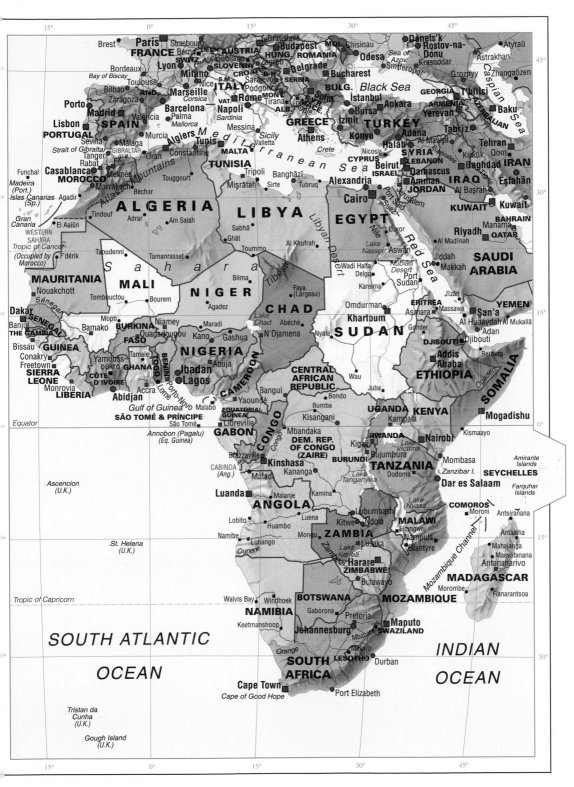

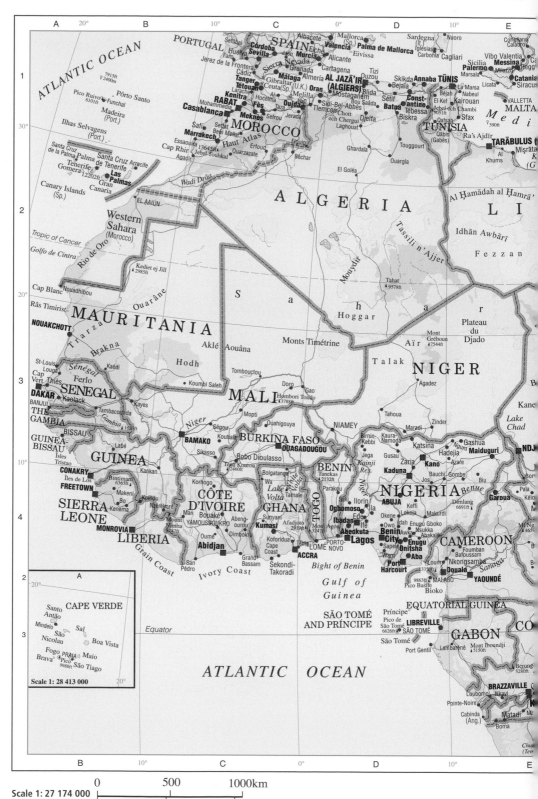

ATLANTIC OCEAN

PORTUGAL

SPAIN

Albacete
Mallorca
Valencia
Palma de Mallorca
Sardegna
Nuoro
Cagliari
Carbonia
Iglesias
Oristano
Conigliano
Calabro

Setúbal
Córdoba
Sevilla
Elche
Murcia
Eivissa
Alicante

Huelva
Jerez de la Frontera
Cádiz
Sierra Nevada
Granada
Almería
Cartagena
Tizi Ouzou
Skikda
Annaba
TÚNIS
Palermo
Marsala
Licata
Messina
Milazzo
Catania
Siracusa

7915ft
2400m
Pôrto Santo
Funchal
Madeira
(Port.)

Tanger
Tétouan
Gibraltar (U.K.)
Ceuta(Sp)
Melilla
Oran
Mostaganem
AL JAZĀ'IR
(ALGIERS)
Bejaia
Sétif
Constantine
El Kef
Béjah
Nabeul
La Marsa
Kairouan
VALLETTA
MALTA
Medi

Pico Ruivo
6101ft
Larache
Al Hoceima
Sidi-Bel-Abbès
Blida
Bou Saâda
Batna
Jebel ech Chambi
5051ft
Qafsah
Sfax
TARĀBULUS

Santa Cruz
de la Palma
Santa Cruz
Arrecife
RABAT
Casablanca
Kentra
Fes
Meknes
Sefrou
Oujda
Jerada
Tlemcen
Djelfa
Biskra
Qābis
(Gābes)
Ra's Ajdīr

Ilhas Selvagens
(Port.)
Mohammedia
Settat
Beni Mellal
El Goléa
Ghardaïa
Touggourt
Al Khums
Mişrātah
(G

Tenerife
La Palma
de Tenerife
Gomera
12202ft
Gran
Canaria
Las Palmas
Safi
Marrakech
Essaouira
Haut Atlas
13645ft
Jebel Toubkal
Erfoud
Béchar
Ouargla

MOROCCO

TUNISIA

Canary Islands
(Sp.)
Cap Rhir
Agadir
Quarzazate

EL AAIÚN

Western
Sahara
(Morocco)

ALGERIA

LI

Al Hamādah al Hamrā'

Idhān Awbārī

Fezzan

Tropic of Cancer

Golfo de Cintra

Rio de Oro

Kediet ej Jill
2985ft

Tassili n' Ajjer

Cap Blanc
Nouadhibou

Ouarâne

S   a
h   a   r
Hoggar
Mouydir
Tahat
9578ft

Plateau
du
Djado

Rås Timirist

MAURITANIA

Trarza

Brakna

Aklé Aouâna
Hodh

Monts Timétrine

Aïr
Mont
Gréboun
7544ft

Talak

NOUAKCHOTT

Tombouctou

Doro
Koumbi Saleh
Gao
Hombori Tondo
4378ft

Agadez

NIGER

St-Louis
Louga
Cap Vert
Thiès
DAKAR
Kaédi

Mopti

Tahoua

Kano

Lake
Chad

20°

Sénégal
Ferlo

Kayes
Ségou

Ouahigouya

Maradi
Zinder

NDJ

Senegal
Tambacounda
Gambia
1633ft

Niger
Koutiala
NIAMEY
Birnin-Kebbi
Kaura-Namoda
Katsina
Gusau
Nguru
Hadejia
Gashua
Maiduguri

BANJUL
THE
GAMBIA

Kaolack
BAMAKO

Sikasso

Bobo Dioulasso

Jega
Zaria
Bauchi
Gombe
Biu

GUINEA-BISSAU
BISSAU

Labé
Kankan
Korhogo
Bolgatanga

OUAGADOUGOU
Tenkas
2132ft
BENIN
Parakou
Kaduna
ABUJA
Keffi
Makurdi
Garoua

CONAKRY
FREETOWN

Bintimani
6363ft
Îles de Los
Makeni

Kindia
Nzérékoré
Bouaké
YAMOUSSOUKRO
Dimbokro
Sunyani
Tamale
Saki
Ogbomoso
Ibadan
Ilorin
Ife
Ila
Okene
Idah
Lokoja
Owo
Enugu
Nsukka
Gboko
Dimlang
6691ft
MENG
465

SIERRA
LEONE
MONROVIA
LIBERIA

Bo
Kenema

CÔTE
D'IVOIRE
GHANA
TOGO
Abeokuta
Benin
City
Enugu
Aba
CAMEROON

NIGERIA
Fouban
Bafoussam
Nkongsamba

Mount
Nimba
5747ft
Man
Abengourou
Oumé

Koforidua
LOMÉ
PORTO-NOVO
Lagos
Onitsha
Port
Harcourt
Douala

Grain Coast
Abidjan
Grand-Bassam
Sekondi-Takoradi
ACCRA
Bight of Benin
Warri
Sapele
MALABO
YAOUNDÉ

San Pédro
Koforidua
Cape
Coast

Gulf of
Guinea

Pico Basile
Bioko

Ivory Coast

EQUATORIAL GUINEA

Príncipe
Pico de
São Tomé
6626ft
LIBREVILLE
GABON
CO

SÃO TOMÉ
AND PRÍNCIPE

São Tomé
Port Gentil
Lambaréné
Mont Iboundji
5150ft

Equator

ATLANTIC OCEAN

BRAZZAVILLE

Pointe-Noire
Cabinda
(Ang.)
Boma
Matadi

CAPE VERDE

Santo
Antão
Mindelo
São
Nicolau
Sal
Boa Vista

Fogo
Brava
Pico
9988ft
PRAIA
São Tiago
Maio

Scale 1: 28 413 000

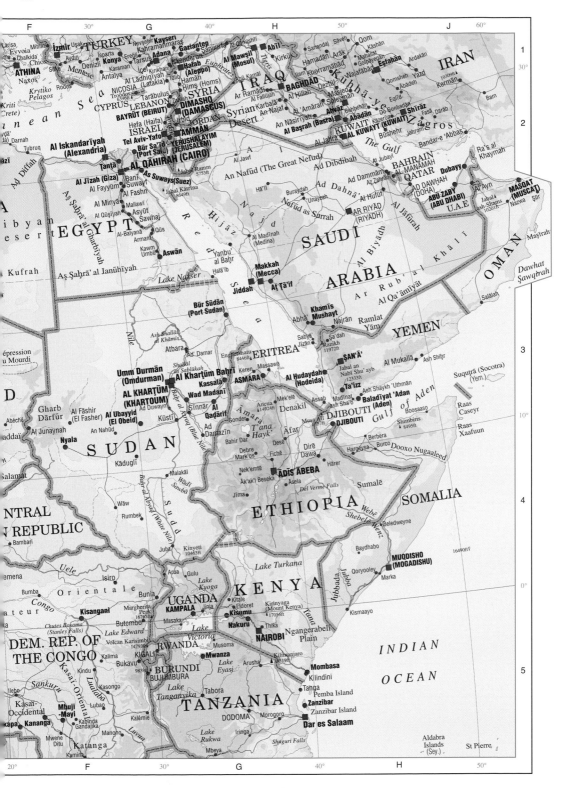

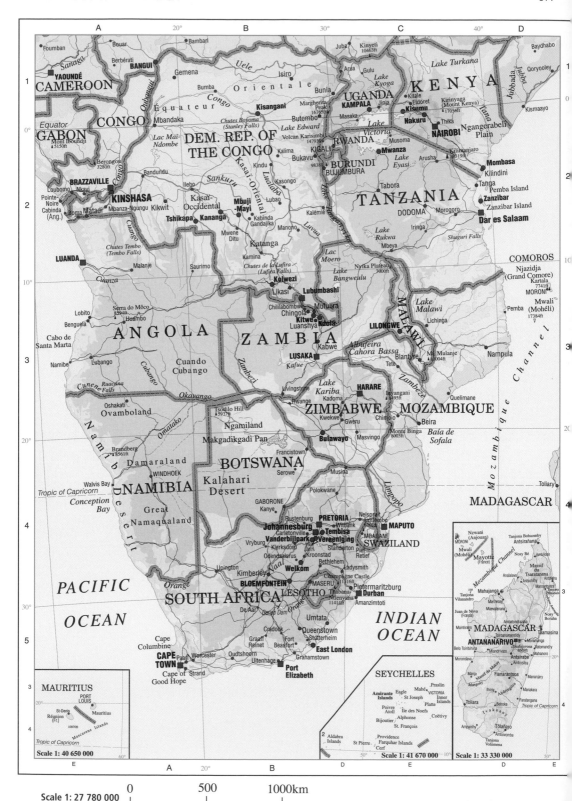

Foumban
Bouar
Bambari
Juba
Kinyeti 10463ft
Gulu
Arua
Lake Turkana
Baydhabo
Qoryooley
Berbérati
BANGUI
Gemena
Uele
Isiro
Bunia
Lake Kyoga
K E N Y A
Jubbada
YAOUNDÉ
CAMEROON
Sanaga
Bumba
Oubangui
Orientale
Margherita Peak 16760ft
Kitale
Kirinyaga (Mount Kenya) 17058ft
Kisangani
UGANDA
Eldoret
KAMPALA Jinja
Kismaayo
CONGO
Mbandaka
Équateur
Chutes Boyoma (Stanley Falls)
Butembo
Lake Edward
Masaka
Kisumu
Thika
Congo
Volcan Karisimbi 1479ft
Ngangerabeli Plain
Equator
GABON
Lac Mai-Ndombe
DEM. REP. OF THE CONGO
RWANDA
Nakuru
NAIROBI
Mont Iboundji 5150ft
Kalima
Kindu
KIGALI
Bukavu 9384ft
BURUNDI
Mwanza
Kilimanjaro 19319ft
Mombasa
Berongou 3280ft
Bandundu
Kasai-Oriental
BUJUMBURA
Lake Eyasi
Arusha
Kilindini
BRAZZAVILLE
Congo
Sankuru
Kasongo
Tabora
Lake Victoria
Tanga
Pemba Island
Loubomo Nkavi
KINSHASA
Ilebo
Lualaba
TANZANIA
Zanzibar
Pointe-Noire
Boma Matadi
Mbanza-Ngungu Kikwit
Kasai-Occidental
Mbuji-Mayi
Lubao
Kalémié
DODOMA
Zanzibar Island
Cabinda (Ang.)
Tshikapa
Kananga
Kabinda Gandajika
Manono
Iringa
Morogoro
Dar es Salaam
Mwene-Ditu
Katanga
Lavua
Lake Rukwa
Mbeya
Shuguri Falls
Kamina
LUANDA
Chutes Tembo (Tembo Falls)
Chutes de la Lufira (Lufira Falls)
Lac Moero
Nyika Plateau 7600ft
COMOROS
Njazidja (Grand Comore) 7741ft
Malanje
Lake Bangweulu
Kolwezi
Lake Malawi
Lichinga
Pemba
MORONI
Cuanza
Saurimo
Likasi
Lubumbashi
Mwali (Mohéli) 17384ft
Lobito
Serra do Môco 8594ft
Huambo
Chililabombwe
Mufulira
MALAWI
Benguela
ANGOLA
Chingola
Kitwe
Ndola
ZAMBIA
Cabo de Santa Marta
Luanshya
Kabwe
LILONGWE
Namibe
Lubango
Cuando Cubango
Zambezi
LUSAKA
Kafue
Albufeira Cahora Bassa
Blantyre
Mt Mulanje 10004ft
Nampula
Cunene
Ruacana Falls
Cubango
Okavango
Livingstone
Lake Kariba
Tete
Zambeze
Oshakati
Tsodilo Hill 4593ft
Kadoma
HARARE
Inyangani 8495ft
Quelimane
Ovamboland
Ngamiland
Hwange
Gweru
ZIMBABWE
Kwekwe
Chimoio
Beira
Omatako
Makgadikgadi Pan
Bulawayo
Masvingo
Monte Binga 8003ft
Baía de Sofala
Brandberg 8556ft
Francistown
MOZAMBIQUE
Damaraland
Serowe
Musina
NAMIBIA
Kalahari Desert
BOTSWANA
Polokwane
Limpopo
Toliary
MADAGASCAR
Walvis Bay
WINDHOEK
Tropic of Capricorn
GABORONE
Kanye
Nelspruit
Conception Bay
Great Namaqualand
Rustenburg
PRETORIA
Witbank
Komombo
MBABANE
MAPUTO
Johannesburg
Tembisa
Carletonville
Vanderbijlpark
Vereeniging
SWAZILAND
Vryburg
Klerksdorp
Standerton
Piet Retief
Upington
Oldendaalsrus
Kroonstad
Bethlehem
Ladysmith
Kimberley
Welkom
MASERU
Thabana 11166ft
Pietermaritzburg
Orange
BLOEMFONTEIN
LESOTHO
Mlenyisa 11414ft
Durban
PACIFIC OCEAN
SOUTH AFRICA
De Aar
Gariep Dam
Orange
Umtata
Amanzimtoti
Cradock
Queenstown
INDIAN OCEAN
Cape Columbine
Graaff Reinet
Fort Beaufort
Stutterheim
East London
CAPE TOWN
Paarl
Worcester
Oudtshoorn
Grahamstown
Cape of Good Hope
Strand
Uitenhage
Port Elizabeth

MAURITIUS
PORT LOUIS
St-Denis
Réunion (Fr.)
Mauritius
10070ft
Mascarene Islands
Tropic of Capricorn
Scale 1: 40 650 000

SEYCHELLES
Amirante Islands
Eagle
St Joseph
Mahé
Praslin
VICTORIA
Inner Islands
Poivre Atoll
Île des Noefs
Bijoutier
Alphonse
Coëtivy
St François
Aldabra Islands
St Pierre
Providence
Farquhar Islands
Cerf
Scale 1: 41 670 000

Nzwani (Anjouan)
MORONI
Mwali (Mohéli)
Mayotte (France)
Mozambique Channel
Tanjona Bobaomby
Antsiranana
Nosy Bé
Massif du Tsaratanana
Antsohihy
Mahajanga
Tanjona Vilanandro
Maintirano
MADAGASCAR
ANTANANARIVO
Toamasina
Fianarantsoa
Toliara
Tropic of Capricorn
Tôlañaro
Tanjona Vohimena
Scale 1: 33 330 000

Scale 1: 27 780 000
0   500   1000km
0   300   600miles

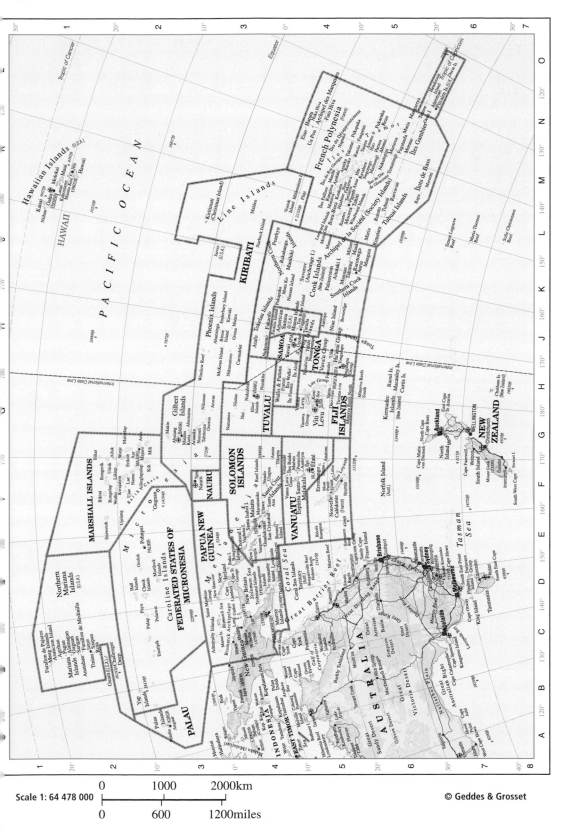

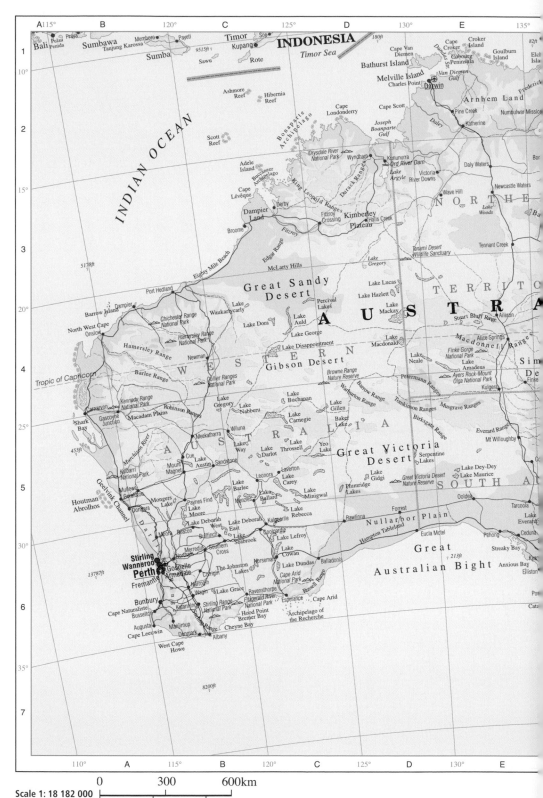

Scale 1: 18 182 000

0   300   600km
|————————|————————|

0   150   300miles
|————————|————————|

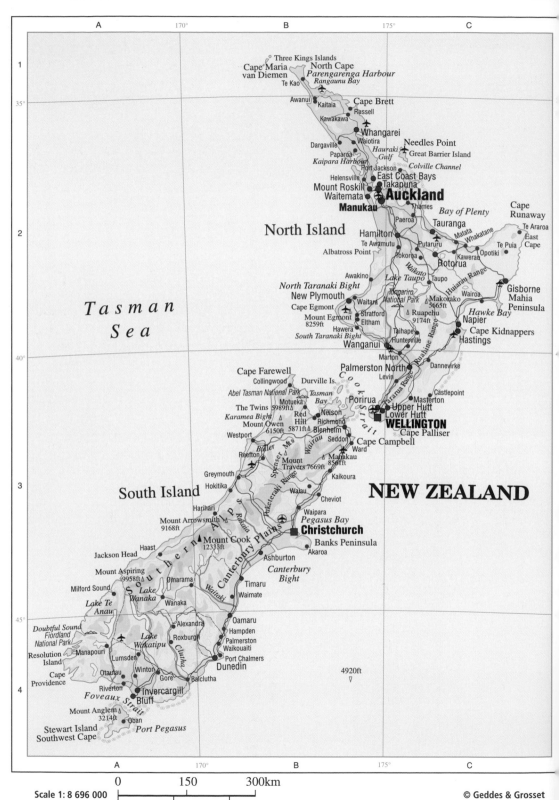

Scale 1: 8 696 000

0   150   300km

0   75   150miles

© Geddes & Grosset

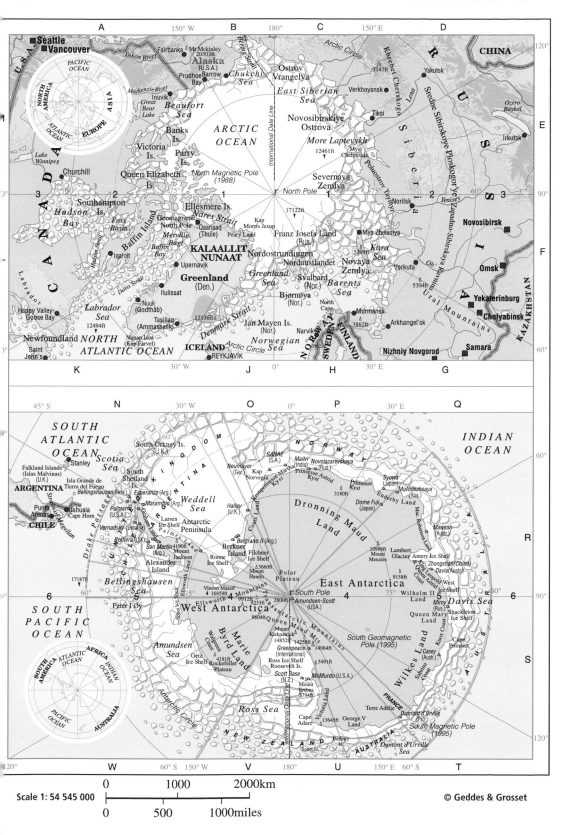

Seabed treasures

In the deeper sea regions mineral exploitation has concentrated on manganese nodules. These lumps grow at rates of between 3–8 mm, 25 in each million years, and they are valuable for the copper, nickel and cobalt they contain. Granules vary in size and may be up to 150 mm, 6 ins in diameter.

On the continental shelves and near coastal regions placer deposits are often commercially viable. They consist of heavy mineral particles which have been weathered from locally occuring ore bodies and deposited on beaches and in estuaries. Gold is extracted from placer deposits off Alaska.

- ☐ Moderate coverage of manganese nodules
- ☐ Extensive coverage of manganese nodules
- ● Nodules with >1.8% nickel and copper
- ● Nodules with >1% cobalt
- ● Nodules with >35% manganese
- • Placer deposits

s Metalliferous muds

Underwater landscapes

Topography of the ocean floor can be divided into two distinct features: the continental margins and the deep sea basins.

The character of the ocean basin depends on the extent to which sediments mask the crust and also the degree of volcanic activity. The sediments may be either pelagic or terrigenous. The latter are brought down by turbidity currents which are avalanches of salt and sand from the continental shelf. These powerful currents can cut channels in the continental shelf such as the Hatteras Canyon off North America and transport material thousands of kilometres.

On the continental shelf, sediments are affected by waves, tidal currents and changes in sea level.

a. Shallow areas are most accessible, they may overlie oil and gas bearing rock.
b. The continental slope defines the edge of the continental block.
c. Deep sea floors can be very flat with gradients less than 1:1000.
d. A Guyot is a submarine volcanic mountain with a completely smooth top.
e. Volcanic islands can be higher above the seabed than Everest is above sea level.
f. Mid ocean ridges. New oceanic crust is formed along these.
g. Atolls are extinct volcanoes which have been colonized by coral.
h. Deep sea trenches. Oceanic crust is destroyed under neighbouring plates.

Map Index

Flags of the World

Afghanistan
Area: 251,773 sq mi
(652,225 sq km)
Population: 20,833,000
Capital: Kabul
Other cities: Herat, Kandahar,
Mazar-e-Sharif
Government: Republic
Religions: Sunni Islam, Shia Islam
Currency: Afghani

Angola
Area: 481,354 sq mi
(1,246,700 sq km)
Population: 11,185,000
Capital: Luanda
Other cities: Huambo, Lobito
Government: People's Republic
Religions: Roman Catholicism,
African traditional religions
Currency: Kwanza

Albania
Area: 11,009 sq mi (28,748
sq km)
Population: 3,670,000
Capital: Tirana (Tiranè)
Other cities: Durrès, Shkodèr,
Vlorë
Government: Socialist Republic
Religion: Constitutionally
atheist but mainly Sunni
Islam
Currency: Lek

Anguilla
Area: 37 sq mi (96 sq km)
Population: 12,400
Capital: The Valley
Government: British Overseas
Territory
Religion: Christianity
Currency: East Caribbean
dollar

African Union
53 Members: Algeria, Angola, Benin,
Botswana, Burkina Faso, Burundi,
Cameroon, Cape Verde, Central African
Republic, Chad, Comoros, Democratic
Republic of the Congo, Republic of the
Congo, Côte d'Ivoire, Djibouti, Egypt,
Equatorial Guinea, Eritrea, Ethiopia,
Gabon, Gambia, Ghana, Guinea,
Guinea-Bissau, Kenya, Lesotho, Liberia,
Libya, Madagascar, Malawi, Mali,
Mauritius, Mozambique, Namibia, Niger,
Nigeria, Rwanda, Western Sahara, São
Tomé and Príncipe, Senegal, Seychelles,
Sierra Leone, Somalia, South Africa,
Sudan, Swaziland, Tanzania, Togo,
Tunisia, Uganda, Zambia, Zimbabwe

Antigua and Barbuda
Area: 171 sq mi (442 sq km)
Population: 66,000
Capital: St John's
Government: Constitutional
monarchy
Religion: Christianity (mainly
Anglican)
Currency: East Caribbean
dollar

Algeria
Area: 919,595 sq mi
(2,381,741 sq km)
Population: 29,168,000
Capital: Algiers (Alger)
Other cities: Oran,
Constantine, Annaba
Government: Republic
Religion: Sunni Islam
Currency: Algerian dinar

Argentina
Area: 1,073,518 sq mi
(2,780,400 sq km)
Population: 35,220,000
Capital: Buenos Aires
Other cities: Cordoba,
Rosario, Mar del Plata,
Mendoza, La Plata, Salta
Government: Federal republic
Religion: Roman Catholicism
Currency: Peso

Andorra
Area: 175 sq mi (453 sq km)
Population: 65,900
Capital: Andorra la Vella
Government: Republic
Religion: Roman Catholicism
Currency: Euro

Arab League
Members: Egypt, Iraq ,
Jordan, Lebanon, Saudi
Arabia, Syria, Yemen, Libya,
Sudan, Morocco, Tunisia,
Kuwait, Algeria, United Arab
Emirates, Bahrain, Qatar,
Oman, Mauritania, Somalia,
Palestine, Djibouti, Comoros

Armenia
Area: 11,506 sq mi (29,800 sq km)
Population: 3,893,000
Capital: Yerevan
Other major city: Kunmayr (Gyumri)
Government: Republic
Religion: Armenian Orthodox
Currency: Dram

Bahamas, The
Area: 5,358 sq mi (13,878 sq km)
Population: 284,000
Capital: Nassau
Other important city: Freeport
Government: Constitutional Monarchy
Religion: Christianity
Currency: Bahamian Dollar

Aruba
Area: 75 sq mi (193 sq km)
Population: 87,000
Capital: Oranjestad
Government: Self-governing Dutch territory
Religion: Christianity
Currency: Aruban florin

Bahrain
Area: 268 sq mi (694 sq km)
Population: 599,000
Capital: Manama (Al Manamah)
Government: Hereditary Monarchy
Religions: Shia Islam, Sunni Islam
Currency: Bahrain Dinar

Australia
Area: 2,988,902 sq mi (7,741,220 sq km)
Population: 18,871,800
Capital: Canberra
Other cities: Melbourne, Sydney
Government: Federal parliamentary state
Religion: Christianity
Currency: Australian dollar

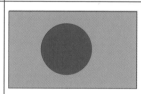

Bangladesh
Area: 55,598 sq mi (143,998 sq km)
Population: 120,073,000
Capital: Dhaka
Other cities: Chittagong, Khulna, Narayanganj, Saidpur
Government: Republic
Religion: Sunni Islam
Currency: Taka

Austria
Area: 32,378 sq mi (83,859 sq km)
Population: 8,106,000
Capital: Vienna (Wien)
Other cities: Graz, Linz, Salzburg
Government: Federal republic
Religion: Roman Catholicism
Currency: Euro

Barbados
Area: 166 sq mi (430 sq km)
Population: 265,000
Capital: Bridgetown
Government: Constitutional Monarchy
Religions: Anglicanism, Methodism
Currency: Barbados Dollar

Azerbaijan
Area: 33,436 sq mi (86,600 sq km)
Population: 7,625,000
Capital: Baku
Other major city: Sumqayit
Government: Republic
Religions: Shia Islam, Sunni Islam, Russian Orthodox
Currency: Manat (= 100 gopik)

Belarus (Belorussia, Byelorussia)
Area: 80,155 sq mi (207,600 sq km)
Population: 10,203,000
Capital: Minsk
Other cities: Homyel, Mahilyov
Government: Republic
Religions: Russian Orthodox, Roman Catholicism
Currency: Rouble

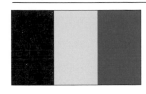

Belgium
Area: 11,783 sq mi (30,519 sq km)
Population: 10,159,000
Capital: Brussels
Other cities: Antwerp, Charleroi, Liège
Government: Constitutional monarchy
Religion: Roman Catholicism
Currency: Euro

Bolivia
Area: 424,165 sq mi (1,098,581 sq km)
Population: 8,140,000
Capital: La Paz (admin.), Sucre (legal)
Other cities: Cochabamba, Santa Cruz
Government: Republic
Religion: Roman Catholicism
Currency: Boliviano

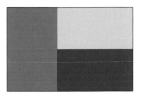

Belize
Area: 8,763 sq mi (22,696 sq km)
Population: 222,000
Capital: Belmopan
Other major city: Belize City
Government: Constitutional monarchy
Religions: Roman Catholicism, Protestantism
Currency: Belize Dollar

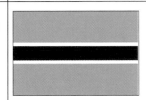

Bosnia-Herzegovina
Area: 19,735 sq mi (51,129 sq km)
Population: 4,510,000
Capital: Sarajevo
Other cities: Banja Luka, Mostar, Tuzla
Government: Republic
Religions: Eastern Orthodox, Sunni Islam, Roman Catholicism
Currency: Dinar (unofficially the Euro)

Benin
Area: 43,484 sq mi (112,622 sq km)
Population: 5,563,000
Capital: Porto-Novo
Government: Republic
Religions: African traditional religions, Sunni Islam, Christianity
Currency: CFA Franc

Botswana
Area: 224,607 sq mi (581,730 sq km)
Population: 1,490,000
Capital: Gaborone
Other cities: Francistown, Molepolole
Government: Republic
Religions: African traditional religions, Christianity
Currency: Pula

Bermuda
Area: 20 sq mi (53 sq km)
Population: 64,000
Capital: Hamilton
Government: British Overseas Territory
Religions: Protestantism, Roman Catholicism
Currency: Bermuda dollar

Brazil
Area: 3,300,171 sq mi (8,547,403 sq km)
Population: 157,872,000
Capital: Brasília
Other cities: Rio de Janeiro, São Paulo
Government: Federal Republic
Religion: Roman Catholicism
Currency: Cruzeiro

Bhutan
Area: 18,147 sq mi (47,000 sq km)
Population: 1,812,000
Capital: Thimphu
Government: Constitutional Monarchy
Religions: Buddhism, Hinduism
Currency: Ngultrum

British Indian Ocean Territory
The Chagos Archipelago, a group of five coral atolls in the middle of the Indian Ocean.
A British colony.
Area: 20 square miles/52 square kilometres.)

Brunei
Area: 2,226 sq mi (5,765 sq km)
Population: 300,000
Capital: Bandar Seri Begawan
Other cities: Kuala Belait, Seria
Government: Monarchy (sultanate)
Religion: Sunni Islam
Currency: Brunei dollar

Cameroon
Area: 183,569 sq mi (475,442 sq km)
Population: 13,560,000
Capital: Yaoundé
Other major city: Douala
Government: Republic
Religions: African traditional religions, Roman Catholicism, Sunni Islam
Currency: CFA franc

Bulgaria
Area: 42,823 sq mi (110,912 sq km)
Population: 8,356,000
Capital: Sofiya
Other cities: Burgas, Ruse, Varna
Government: Republic
Religion: Eastern Orthodox
Currency: Lev

Canada
Area: 3,849,674 sq mi (9,970,610 sq km)
Population: 29,964,000
Capital: Ottawa
Cities: Calgary, Toronto, Montréal, Vancouver, Québec City
Government: Federal Parliamentary State
Religions: Roman Catholicism, United Church of Canada, Anglicanism
Currency: Canadian dollar

Burkina Faso (Burkina)
Area: 105,792 sq mi (274,000 sq km)
Population: 10,780,000
Capital: Ouagadougou
Other cities: Bobo-Dioulasso, Koudougou
Government: Republic
Religions: African traditional religions, Sunni Islam
Currency: CFA franc

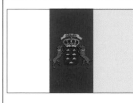

Canary Islands
Area: 2,808 sq mi (7,273 sq km)
Population: 1,493,000
Islands: Gran Canaria, Tenerife, Lanzarote, La Palma, La Gomera, El Hierro, Fuerteventura.
Capitals: Las Palmas de Gran Canaria, Santa Cruz de Tenerife
Government: Autonomous community of Spain
Currency: Euro

Burundi
Area: 10,747 sq mi (27,834 sq km)
Population: 6,088,000
Capital: Bujumbura
Government: Republic
Religion: Roman Catholicism
Currency: Burundi franc

Cape Verde
Area: 1,557 sq mi (4,033 sq km)
Population: 396,000
Capital: Praia
Government: Republic
Religion: Roman Catholicism
Currency: Cape Verde Escudo

Cambodia
Area: 69,898 sq mi (181,035 sq km)
Population: 10,273,000
Capital: Phnom-Penh
Other cities: Battambang, Kampong Cham
Government: People's Republic
Religion: Buddhism
Currency: Riel

Cayman Islands
Area: 102 sq mi (264 sq km)
Population: 38,000
Capital: George Town, on Grand Cayman
Government: British overseas territory
Religion: Christianity
Currency: Cayman Islands dollar

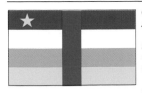

Central African Republic
Area: 240,535 sq mi (622,984 sq km)
Population: 3,344,000
Capital: Bangui
Other cities: Bambari, Bangassou
Government: Republic
Religions: African traditional religions, Roman Catholicism
Currency: CFA Franc

Christmas Island
Area: 108 sq mi (135 sq km)
Population: 1600
Towns: Settlement, Silver City, Kampong, Poon Saan, and Drumsite
Government: self-governing Territory of Australia
Religion: Buddhism, Islam, Christianity, Taoism
Currency: Australian dollar

Chad
Area: 495,755 sq mi (1,284,000 sq km)
Population: 6,515,000
Capital: N'Djamena
Other cities: Sarh, Moundou, Abéché
Government: Republic
Religions: Sunni Islam, African traditional religions
Currency: CFA Franc

Colombia
Area: 439,737 sq mi (1,138,914 sq km)
Population: 35,626,000
Capital: Bogotá
Other cities: Barranquilla, Cali, Cartagena, Medellin
Government: Republic
Religion: Roman Catholicism
Currency: Colombian peso

Channel Islands
Area: 75 square miles/194 square km
Population: 143,000
Main islands: Jersey (top flag), Guernsey (bottom), also Alderney, Sark, Herm and Brechou.
Government: British Crown dependencies.
Religion: Christianity
Currency: Pound sterling

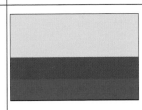

Commonweath of Independent States (CIS)
A confederation of 11 former Soviet Republics: Armenia, Azerbaijan, Belarus, Georgia, Kazakhstan, Kyrgyzstan, Moldova, Russia, Tajikistan, Ukraine, and Uzbekistan. Turkmenistan discontinued permanent membership as of August 2005 and is now an associate member.

Chile
Area: 292,135 sq mi (756,626 sq km)
Population: 14,419,000
Capital: Santiago
Other cities: Arica, Concepcion, Valparaiso, Viña del Mar
Government: Republic
Religion: Roman Catholicism
Currency: Chilean Peso

Comoros, The
Area: 720 sq mi (1,865 sq km) excluding Mayotte
Population: 538,000
Capital: Moroni
Other cities: Dornoni, Fomboni
Government: Federal Islamic Republic
Religion: Sunni Islam
Currency: Comorian franc

China
Area: 3,705,408 sq mi (9,596,961 sq km)
Population: 1,246,872,000
Capital: Beijing (Peking)
Other cities: Guangzhou, Shanghai
Government: People's Republic
Religions: Buddhism, Confucianism, Taoism
Currency: Yuan

Congo
Area: 132,047 sq mi (342,000 sq km)
Population: 2,668,000
Capital: Brazzaville
Other major city: Pointe-Noire
Government: Republic
Religions: Christianity, African traditional religions
Currency: CFA franc

Congo, Democratic Republic of
Area: 905,355 sq mi
(2,344,858 sq km)
Population: 46,812,000
Capital: Kinshasa
Other cities: Lubumbashi,
Mbuji-Mayi, Kananga,
Kisangani
Government: Republic
Religions: Christianity, Islam
Currency: Congolese Franc

Cuba
Area: 42,804 sq mi (110,861
sq km)
Population: 11,019,000
Capital: Havana (La Habana)
Other cities: Camaguey,
Holguin, Santa Clara,
Santiago de Cuba
Government: Socialist
Republic
Religion: Roman Catholicism
Currency: Cuban peso

Cook Islands
Area: 93 sq mi (240 sq km)
Population: 18,500
Capital: Avarua, on
Rarotonga
Government: Self-governing
in association with New
Zealand
Religion: Christianity
Currency: Cook Islands
Dollar/New Zealand dollar.

Cyprus
Area: 3,572 sq mi (9,251 sq
km)
Population: 756,000
Capital: Nicosia
Other cities: Famagusta,
Larnaca
Government: Republic
Religions: Greek Orthodox,
Sunni Islam
Currency: Cyprus pound

Costa Rica
Area: 19,730 sq mi (51,100
sq km)
Population: 3,398,000
Capital: San José
Other cities: Alajuela, Límon,
Puntarenas
Government: Republic
Religion: Roman Catholicism
Currency: Colon

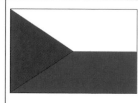

Czech Republic, The
Area: 30,450 sq mi (78,864
sq km)
Population: 10,315,000
Capital: Prague (Praha)
Other cities: Brno, Olomouc,
Plzen
Government: Republic
Religions: Roman Catholi-
cism, Protestantism
Currency: Koruna

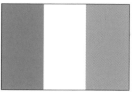

Côte d'Ivoire
Area: 124,504 sq mi (322,463
sq km)
Population: 14,781,000
Capital: Yamoussoukro
Other cities: Abidjan, Bouaké,
Daloa
Government: Republic
Religions: African traditional
religions, Sunni Islam,
Roman Catholicism
Currency: CFA franc

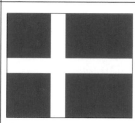

Denmark
Area: 16,639 sq mi (43,094 sq km)
Population: 5,262,000
(excluding the Faeroe Islands)
Capital: Copenhagen
(København)
Other cities: Ålborg, Århus,
Odense
Government: Constitutional
Monarchy
Religion: Lutheranism
Currency: Danish krone

Croatia (Hrvatska)
Area: 21,824 sq mi (56,538
sq km)
Population: 4,501,000
Capital: Zagreb
Other cities: Osijek, Rijeka,
Split
Government: Republic
Religions: Roman Catholi-
cism, Eastern Orthodox
Currency: Kuna (unofficially
the euro)

Djibouti
Area: 8,958 sq mi (23,200 sq
km)
Population: 617,000
Capital: Djibouti
Government: Republic
Religion: Sunni Islam
Currency: Djibouti franc

Dominica
Area: 290 sq mi (751 sq km)
Population: 74,000
Capital: Roseau
Government: Republic
Religion: Roman Catholicism
Currency: East Caribbean
dollar

El Salvador
Area: 8,124 sq mi (21,041 sq
km)
Population: 5,796,000
Capital: San Salvador
Other cities: Santa Ana, San
Miguel
Government: Republic
Religion: Roman Catholicism
Currency: Colón

Dominican Republic
Area: 18,816 sq mi (48,734
sq km)
Population: 8,052,000
Capital: Santo Domingo
Other cities: Barahona,
Santiago, San Pedro de
Macoris
Government: Republic
Religion: Roman Catholicism
Currency: Dominican
Republic peso

Equatorial Guinea
Area: 10,830 sq mi (28,051
sq km)
Population: 410,000
Capital: Malabo
Other major city: Bata
Government: Republic
Religion: Roman Catholicism
Currency: CFA franc

East Timor
Area: 5,743 sq mi (14,874 sq
km)
Population: 857,000
Capital: Dili
Government: Republic
Religions: Roman Catholism
Currency: US dollar

Eritrea
Area: 45,406 sq mi (117,600
sq km)
Population: 3,280,000
Capital: Asmara
Other cities: Mitsiwa, Keren,
Nak'fa, Ak'ordat
Government: Republic
Religions: Sunni Islam,
Christianity
Currency: Ethiopian birr

Ecuador
Area: 109,484 sq mi (283,561
sq km)
Population: 11,698,000
Capital: Quito
Other cities: Ambato,
Guayaquil, Cuenca,
Machala
Government: Republic
Religion: Roman Catholicism
Currency: Sucre

Estonia
Area: 17,413 sq mi (45,227
sq km)
Population: 1,453,800
Capital: Tallinn
Other cities: Tartu, Narva,
Pärnu
Government: Republic
Religions: Eastern Orthodox,
Lutheranism
Currency: Kroon

Egypt
Area: 386,662 sq mi
(1,001,449 sq km)
Population: 60,603,000
Capital: Cairo (El Qâhira)
Other cities: Alexandria, Giza,
Port Said, Suez
Government: republic
Religions: Sunni Islam,
Christianity
Currency: Egyptian pound

Ethiopia
Area: 426,373 sq mi
(1,104,300 sq km)
Population: 58,506,000
Capital: Addis Ababa (Adis
Abeba)
Other cities: Dire Dawa, Gonder,
Jima
Government: Federation
Religions: Ethiopian Orthodox,
Sunni Islam
Currency: Ethiopian Birr

European Union (EU)
A union of 25 European counries. *Members*: Belgium, France, West Germany, Italy, Luxembourg, Netherlands, Denmark, Ireland, United Kingdom, Greece, Portugal, Spain, Austria, Finland, Sweden, Cyprus, Czech Republic, Estonia, Hungary, Latvia, Lithuania, Malta, Poland, Slovakia, Slovenia. In 2007 Bulgaria and Romania will become members.

France
Area: 212,935 sq mi (551,500 sq km)
Population: 58,375,000
Capital: Paris
Other cities: Bordeaux, Lyon, Marseille, Nantes, Nice
Government: Republic
Religion: Roman Catholicism
Currency: Euro

Faeroe (Faroe) Islands (Føroyar)
Area: 540 sq mi (1,399 sq km)
Population: 47,000
Capital: Tørshavn
Government: Self-governing Region of Denmark
Religion: Lutheranism
Currency: Danish Krone

French Polynesia
Area: 1,544 sq mi (4,000 sq km)
Population: 223,000
Capital: Papeete
Government: French Overseas Territory
Religions: Protestantism, Roman Catholicism
Currency: CFP franc

Falkland Islands
Area: 4,700 sq mi (12,173 sq km)
Population: 2,200
Capital: Stanley
Government: British Crown Colony
Religion: Christianity
Currency: Falkland Islands Pound

French Southern and Antarctic Territories
Territories in Antarctica and the Antarctic Ocean administered by FRANCE. They include the Crozet Islands and Kerguelen.

Fiji
Area: 7,056 sq mi (18,274 sq km)
Population: 797,000
Capital: Suva
Government: Republic
Religions: Christianity, Hinduism
Currency: Fijian dollar

Gabon
Area: 103,347 sq mi (267,668 sq km)
Population: 1,106,000
Capital: Libreville
Other major city: Port Gentile
Government: Republic
Religions: Roman Catholicism, African traditional religions
Currency: CFA Franc

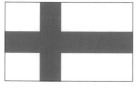

Finland
Area: 130,559 sq mi (338,145 sq km)
Population: 5,125,000
Capital: Helsinki (Helsingfors)
Other cities: Turku, Tampere
Government: Republic
Religion: Lutheranism
Currency: Euro

Gambia
Area: 4,361 sq mi (11,295 sq km)
Population: 1,141,000
Capital: Banjul
Government: Republic
Religions: Sunni Islam, Christianity
Currency: Dalasi

Georgia
Area: 26,911 sq mi (69,700 sq km)
Population: 5,411,000
Capital: T'bilisi
Other cities: Kutaisi, Rustavi, Batumi
Government: Republic
Religions: Georgian and Russian Orthodox, Islam
Currency: Lari

Greenland (Kalaallit Nunaat)
Area: 840,000 sq mi (2,175,600 sq km)
Population: 58,200
Capital: Gothåb (Nuuk)
Government: Self-governing region of Denmark
Religion: Lutheranism
Currency: Danish krone

Germany
Area: 137,735 sq mi (356,733 sq km)
Population: 81,912,000
Capital: Berlin
Other cities: Bonn, Cologne, Munich
Government: Republic
Religions: Lutheranism, Roman Catholicism
Currency: Euro

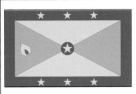

Grenada
Area: 133 sq mi (344 sq km)
Population: 92,000
Capital: St George's
Government: Independent state within the Common-wealth
Religions: Roman Catholi-cism, Anglicanism, Methodism
Currency: East Caribbean dollar

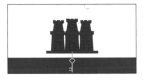

Ghana
Area: 92,100 sq mi (238,537 sq km)
Population: 17,459,350
Capital: Accra
Other cities: Sekondi-Takoradi, Tamale
Government: Republic
Religions: Christianity, African traditional religions
Currency: Cedi

Guadeloupe
Area: 658 sq mi (1,705 sq km)
Population: 431,000
Capital: Basse Terre
Other main town: Pointe-à-Pitre
Government: French overseas department
Religion: Roman Catholicism
Currency: Euro
NB.The pictured flag is local but unofficial. the French flag is official.

Gibraltar
Area: 2.5 sq mi (6.5 sq km)
Population: 27,100
Capital: Gibraltar
Government: Self-governing British colony
Religion: Christianity
Currency: Gibraltar pound

Guam
Area: 212 sq mi (549 sq km)
Population: 153,000
Capital: Agana
Government: Unincorporated territory of the USA
Religion: Roman Catholicism
Currency: US dollar

Greece
Area: 50,949 sq mi (131,957 sq km)
Population: 10,475,000
Capital: Athens (Athínai)
Other cities: Iráklian, Thessaloníki
Government: Republic
Religion: Greek Orthodox
Currency: Euro

Guatemala
Area: 42,042 sq mi (108,889 sq km)
Population: 10,928,000
Capital: Guatemala City
Other cities: Cobán, Puerto Barrios
Government: Republic
Religion: Roman Catholicism
Currency: Quetza

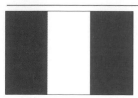

Guiana (French) *or* **Guyane**
Area: 34,749 sq mi (90,000
    sq km)
Population: 153,000
Capital: Cayenne
Government: French
    Overseas Department
Religion: Roman Catholicism
Currency: Euro

Honduras
Area: 43,277 sq mi (112,088
    sq km)
Population: 6,140,000
Capital: Tegucigalpa
Other cities: San Pedro Sula,
    La Ceiba, Puerto Cortès
Government: Republic
Religion: Roman Catholicism
Currency: Lempira

Guinea
Area: 94,926 sq mi (245,857
    sq km)
Population: 7,518,000
Capital: Conakry
Other cities: Kankan, Kindia,
    Labé
Government: Republic
Religion: Sunni Islam
Currency: Guinea franc

Hong Kong
Area: 415 sq mi (1,075 sq
    km)
Population: 6,687,200
Government: Special
    Autonomous Province of
    China
Religions: Buddhism, Taoism,
    Christianity
Currency: Hong Kong dollar

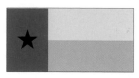

Guinea-Bissau
Area: 13,948 sq mi (36,125
    sq km)
Population: 1,091,000
Capital: Bissau
Government: Republic
Religions: African traditional
    religions, Sunni Islam
Currency: Peso

Hungary
Area: 35,920 sq mi (93,032
    sq km)
Population: 10,193,000
Capital: Budapest
Other cities: Debrecen, Pécs,
    Szeged
Government: Republic
Religions: Roman Catholi-
    cism, Calvinism, Lutheran-
    ism
Currency: Forint

Guyana
Area: 83,000 sq mi (214,969
    sq km)
Population: 838,000
Capital: Georgetown
Other cities: Linden, New
    Amsterdam
Government: Cooperative
    republic
Religions: Hinduism,
    Christianity
Currency: Guyana dollar

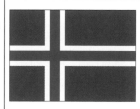

Iceland
Area: 39,769 sq mi (103,000
    sq km)
Population: 275,300
Capital: Reykjavík
Other cities: Akureyri,
    Kópavogur
Government: Republic
Religion: Lutheranism
Currency: Icelandic króna

Haiti
Area: 10,714 sq mi (27,750
    sq km)
Population: 7,336,000
Capital: Port-au-Prince
Other towns: Cap-Haïtien,
    Gonaïves
Government: Republic
Religions: Roman Catholi-
    cism, Voodooism
Currency: Gourde

India
Area: 1,269,346 sq mi
    (3,287,590 sq km)
Population: 970,930,000
Capital: New Delhi
Other cities: Mumbai,
    Calcutta, Delhi
Government: Federal Republic
Religions: Hinduism, Islam,
    Sikkism, Christianity,
    Jainism, Buddhism
Currency: Rupee

Indonesia
Area: 735,358 sq mi
  (1,904,569 sq km)
Population: 196,813,000
Capital: Jakarta
Other cities: Palembang,
  Surabaya
Government: Republic
Religions: Sunni Islam,
  Christianity, Hinduism
Currency: Rupiah

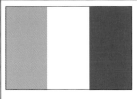

Italy
Area: 116,320 sq mi (301,268
  sq km)
Population: 57,339,000
Capital: Rome (Roma)
Other cities: Milan, Naples, Turin,
  Florence
Government: Republic
Religion: Roman Catholicism
Currency: Euro

Iran, Islamic Republic of
Area: 634,293 sq mi
  (1,648,195 sq km)
Population: 61,128,000
Capital: Tehran
Other cities: Esfahan,
  Mashhad, Tabriz
Government: Islamic Republic
Religion: Shia Islam
Currency: Rial

Jamaica
Area: 4,243 sq mi (10,990 sq
  km)
Population: 2,491,000
Capital: Kingston
Other town: Montego Bay
Government: Constitutional
  monarchy
Religions: Anglicanism,
  Roman Catholicism,
  Protestantism
Currency: Jamaican dollar

Iraq
Area: 169,235 sq mi (438,317
  sq km)
Population: 20,607,000
Capital: Baghdad
Other cities: Al-Basrah, Al
  Mawsil
Government: Republic
Religions: Shia Islam, Sunni
  Islam
Currency: Iraqi dinar

Japan
Area: 145,870 sq mi (377,801
  sq km)
Population: 125,761,000
Capital: Tokyo
Other cities: Nagoya, Kyoto,
  Yokohama
Government: Constitutional
  Monarchy
Religions: Shintoism,
  Buddhism, Christianity
Currency: Yen

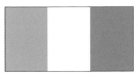

Ireland, Republic of
Area: 27,137 sq mi (70,284
  sq km)
Population: 3,626,000
Capital: Dublin (Baile Atha
  Cliath)
Other cities: Cork, Galway,
  Limerick, Waterford
Government: Republic
Religion: Roman Catholicism
Currency: Euro

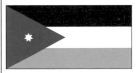

Jordan
Area: 37,738 sq mi (97,740
  sq km)
Population: 5,581,000
Capital: Amman
Other cities: Aqaba, Irbid,
  Zarqa
Government: Constitutional
  monarchy
Religion: Sunni Islam
Currency: Jordanian dinar

Israel
Area: 8,130 sq mi (21,056 sq
  km)
Population: 6,100,000
Capital: Tel Aviv (Tel Aviv-
  Yafo)
Other cities: Jerusalem, Haifa
Government: Republic
Religions: Judaism, Sunni
  Islam, Christianity
Currency: New Israeli shekel

Kazakhstan
Population: 15,671,000
Capital: Astana
Other major city: Almaty
Government: Republic
Religion: Sunni Islam
Currency: Tenge

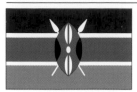

Kenya
Area: 224,081 sq mi (580,367 sq km)
Population: 31,806,000
Capital: Nairobi
Other towns: Mombasa, Nakuru
Government: Republic
Religions: Christianity, African traditional religions
Currency: Kenya shilling

Kiribati
Area: 280 sq mi (726 sq km)
Population: 80,000
Capital: Tarawa
Government: Republic
Religions: Roman Catholicism, Protestantism
Currency: Australian dollar

Korea, Democratic People's Republic of (North)
Area: 46,540 sq mi (120,538 sq km)
Population: 22,466,000
Capital: Pyongyang
Other cities: Wonsan, Hamhung
Government: Socialist Republic
Religions: Buddhism, Confucianism, Chondogyo
Currency: Won

Korea, Republic of (South)
Area: 38,368 sq mi (99,373 sq km)
Population: 46,430,000
Capital: Seoul (Soul)
Other cities: Pusan, Taegu
Government: Republic
Religion: Buddhism, Christianity, Chondogyo, Confucianism, Unification Church
Currency: Won

Kuwait
Area: 6,880 sq mi (17,818 sq km)
Population: 1,866,100
Capital: Kuwait City (Al Kuwayt)
Government: Constitutional Monarchy
Religions: Sunni Islam, Shia Islam
Currency: Kuwaiti dinar

Kyrgyzstan
Area: 76,641 sq mi (198,500 sq km)
Population: 4,575,000
Capital: Bishkek
Other major city: Osh
Government: Republic
Religion: Sunni Islam
Currency: Som

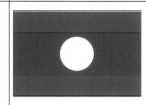

Laos
Area: 91,429 sq mi (236,800 sq km)
Population: 5,035,000
Capital: Vientiane
Other cities: Luang Prabang, Savannakhét, Paksé
Government: People's Republic
Religion: Buddhism
Currency: New Kip

Latvia
Area: 24,942 sq mi (64,600 sq km)
Population: 2,491,000
Capital: Riga
Other cities: Liepaja, Daugavpils
Government: Republic
Religion: Lutheranism
Currency: Lat

Lebanon
Area: 4,015 sq mi (10,400 sq km)
Population: 3,084,900
Capital: Beirut (Beyrouth)
Other important cities: Tripoli, Sidon
Government: Republic
Religions: Shia Islam, Sunni Islam, Christianity
Currency: Lebanese pound

Lesotho
Area: 11,720 sq mi (30,355 sq km)
Population: 2,078,000
Capital: Maseru
Government: Constitutional monarchy
Religions: Roman Catholicism, other Christianity
Currency: Loti

Liberia
Area: 43,000 sq mi (111,369
sq km)
Population: 2,820,000
Capital: Monrovia
Other major city: Buchanan
Government: Republic
Religions: African traditional
religions, Sunni Islam,
Christianity
Currency: Liberian dollar

Macao *or* **Macau**
Area: 7 sq mi (18 sq km)
Population: 440,000
Capital: Macao
Government: Special
Administrative Region
under Chinese Sovereignty
Religions: Buddhism, Roman
Catholicism
Currency: Pataca

Libya
Area: 679,362 sq mi
(1,759,540 sq km)
Population: 4,389,739
Capital: Tripoli (Tarabulus)
Other cities: Benghazi,
Misrāta
Government: Socialist People's
Republic
Religion: Sunni Islam
Currency: Libyan dinar

**Macedonia, The Former
Yugoslav Republic of
(FYROM)**
Area: 9,928 sq mi (25,713 sq
km)
Population: 2,174,000
Capital: Skopje
Other cities: Kumanovo, Ohrid
Government: Republic
Religions: Eastern Orthodox,
Islam
Currency: Dinar

Liechtenstein
Area: 62 sq mi (160 sq km)
Population: 31,320
Capital: Vaduz
Government: Constitutional
monarchy (principality)
Religion: Roman Catholicism
Currency: Swiss franc

Madagascar
Area: 226,658 sq mi (587,041
sq km)
Population: 15,353,000
Capital: Antananarivo
Other cities: Mahajanga,
Toamasina
Government: Republic
Religions: African traditional
religions, Christianity
Currency: Franc Malgache

Lithuania
Population: 3,701,300
Capital: Vilnius
Other cities: Kaunas,
Klaipeda, Siauliai
Government: Republic
Religion: Roman Catholicism
Currency: Litas

Malawi
Area: 45,747 sq mi (118,484
sq km)
Population: 10,114,000
Capital: Lilongwe
Other cities: Blantyre, Zomba
Government: Republic
Religions: African traditional
religions, Christianity
Currency: Kwacha

**Luxembourg, Grand Duchy
of**
Population: 412,000
Capital: Luxembourg City
Other cities: Differdange,
Dudelange
Government: Constitutional
Monarchy (Duchy)
Religion: Roman Catholicism
Currency: Euro

**Malaysia, The Federation
of**
Area: 127,320 sq mi (329,758
sq km)
Population: 20,581,000
Capital: Kuala Lumpur
Other cities: Ipoh, Johor Baharu
Government: Federal
Constitutional Monarchy
Religion: Islam
Currency: Ringgit or
Malaysian dollar

Maldives, Republic of
Area: 115 sq mi (298 sq km)
Population: 263,000
Capital: Malé
Government: Republic
Religion: Sunni Islam
Currency: Rufiyaa

Mauritania or the **Islamic Republic of Mauritania**
Area: 395,956 sq mi
(1,025,520 sq km)
Population: 2,351,000
Capital: Nouakchott
Other cities: Kaédi,
Nouadhibou
Government: Republic
Religion: Sunni Islam
Currency: Ouguiya

Mali
Area: 478,841 sq mi
(1,240,192 sq km)
Population: 11,134,000
Capital: Bamako
Other towns: Gao, Kayes,
Sikasso
Government: Republic
Religions: Sunni Islam,
African traditional religions
Currency: CFA franc

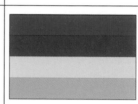

Mauritius
Area: 788 sq mi (2,040 sq
km)
Population: 1,160,000
Capital: Port Louis
Government: Republic
Religions: Hinduism, Roman
Catholicism, Sunni Islam
Currency: Mauritian rupee

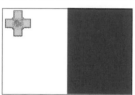

Malta
Area: 122 sq mi (316 sq km)
Population: 376,500
Capital: Valletta
Government: Republic
Religion: Roman Catholicism
Currency: Maltese pound

Mexico
Area: 756,066 sq mi
(1,958,201 sq km)
Population: 96,578,000
Capital: México City
Other cities: Guadalajara,
León, Monterrey, Puebla,
Tijuana
Government: Federal
Republic
Religion: Roman Catholicism
Currency: Mexican peso

Marshall Islands
Area: 70 sq mi (181 sq km)
Population: 58,000
Capital: Dalag-Uliga-Darrit
(on Majuro atoll)
Government: Republic in free
association with the USA
Religion: Protestantism
Currency: US dollar

Micronesia, Federated States of
Area: 271 sq mi (702 sq km)
Population: 109,000
Capital: Palikir
Government: Republic
Religion: Christianity
Currency: US dollar

Martinique
Area: 425 sq mi (1,102 sq
km)
Population: 384,000
Capital: Fort-de-France
Government:Overseas
Department of France
Religion: Roman Catholicism
Currency: Euro

Moldova (Moldavia)
Area: 13,012 sq mi (33,700
sq km)
Population: 4,327,000
Capital: Chisinau
Other cities: Tiraspol, Tighina,
Bel'tsy
Government: Republic
Religion: Russian Orthodox
Currency: Leu

Monaco
Area: 0.4 sq mile (1 sq kilometre)
Population: 32,000
Capital: Monaco
Government: Constitutional Monarchy
Religion: Roman Catholicism
Currency: Euro

Myanmar, Union of
Area: 261,228 sq mi (676,578 sq km)
Population: 45,922,000
Capital: Rangoon (Yangon)
Other cities: Mandalay, Moulmein, Pegu
Government: Republic
Religion: Buddhism
Currency: Kyat

Mongolia
Area: 604,829 sq mi (1,566,500 sq km)
Population: 2,354,000
Capital: Ulaanbaatar
Other cities: Altay, Saynshand, Hovd, Choybalsan, Tsetserleg
Government: Republic
Religions: Buddhism, Shamanism, Islam
Currency: Tughrik

Namibia
Area: 318,261 sq mi (824,292 sq km)
Population: 1,575,000
Capital: Windhoek
Government: Republic
Religions: Lutheranism, Roman Catholicism, other Christianity
Currency: Namibian dollar

Montserrat
Area: 91 sq km
Population: 8,400
Capital:Plymouth (abandoned; destroyed by volcanic eruption
Government: British overseas territory
Religions: Christian denominations
Currency: East Carribean Dollar

Nauru
Area: 8 sq mi (21 sq km)
Population: 11,000
Capital: Nauru
Government: Republic
Religions: Protestantism, Roman Catholicism
Currency: Australian dollar

Morocco
Area: 172,414 sq mi (446,550 sq km)
Population: 27,623,000
Capital: Rabat
Other cities: Casablanca, Fès, Marrakech, Tangier
Government: Constitutional Monarchy
Religion: Sunni Islam
Currency: Dirham

Nepal, Kingdom of
Area: 56,827 sq mi (147,181 sq km)
Population: 21,127,000
Capital: Kathmandu
Other city: Biratnagar
Government: Constitutional monarchy
Religion: Hinduism, Buddhism
Currency: Nepalese rupee

Mozambique
Area: 309,496 sq mi (799,380 sq km)
Population: 16,916,000
Capital: Maputo
Other towns: Beira, Nampula
Government: Republic
Religions: African traditional religions, Roman Catholicism, Sunni Islam
Currency: Metical

Netherlands, The
Area: 15,770 sq mi (40,844 sq km)
Population: 15,517,000
Capital: Amsterdam
Other cities: Rotterdam, Eindhoven
Government: Constitutional Monarchy
Religions: Roman Catholicism, Dutch Reformed, Calvinism
Currency: Euro

Netherlands Antilles
Area: 309 sq mi (800 sq km)
Population: 207,300
Capital: Willemstad
Government: Self-governing
  Dutch Territory
Religion: Roman Catholicism
Currency: Netherlands
  Antilles guilder

Nigeria
Area: 356,669 sq mi (923,768
  sq km)
Population: 115,120,000
Capital: Abuja
Other cities: Lagos, Onitsha,
  Kano
Government: Federal
  Republic
Religions: Sunni Islam,
  Christianity, African
  traditional religions
Currency: Naira

New Caledonia or **Nouvelle
Calédonie**
Area: 7,172 sq mi (18,575 sq
  km)
Population: 189,000
Capital: Noumea
Government: French Overseas
  Territory
Religion: Roman Catholicism
Currency: CFP franc

Niue
Area: 260 km
Population: 2,145
Capital: Alofi
Government: Self-governing
  in free association with
  New Zealand
Religions: Ekalesia Niue, Latter-
  Day Saints, Roman Catholic,
  Jehovah's Witnesses,
  Seventh-Day Adventist
Currency: New Zealand Dollar

New Zealand
Area: 104,454 sq mi (270,534
  sq km)
Population: 3,681,546
Capital: Wellington
Other cities: Auckland,
  Dunedin,
Government: Constitutional
  monarchy
Religions: Anglicanism, Roman
  Catholicism, Presbyterianism
Currency: New Zealand dollar

Norfolk Island
Area: 34.6 sq km
Population: 1853
Capital: Kingston
Government: Constitutional
  monarchy. Non-self-
  governing territory of
  Australia. (Some claim it was
  actually granted independ-
  ence by Queen Victoria.)
Religion: Christianity
Currency: Australian dollar

Nicaragua
Area: 50,193 sq mi (130,668
  sq km)
Population: 4,663,000
Capital: Managua
Government: Republic
Religion: Roman Catholicism
Currency: Córdoba oro

Northern Mariana Islands
Area: 179 sq mi (464 sq km)
Population: 49,000
Capital: Saipan
Government: Common-
  wealth in union with the
  USA
Religion: Roman Catholicism
Currency: US dollar

Niger
Area: 489,191 sq mi (1,267,000
  sq km)
Population: 9,465,000
Capital: Niamey
Other cities: Agadez, Maradi,
  Tahoua
Government: Republic
Religion: Sunni Islam
Currency: CFA franc

Norway
Area: 125,050 sq mi (323,877
  sq km)
Population: 4,445,500
Capital: Oslo
Other cities: Bergen,
  Trondheim, Stavanger,
  Kristiansand, Tromsö
Government: Constitutional
  monarchy
Religion: Lutheranism
Currency: Norwegian krone

Organization of Islamic Conference (OIC)
57 members, including: Afghanistan, Algeria, Chad, Egypt,Guinea, Indonesia, Iran, Jordan,Kuwait, Lebanon, Libya, Malaysia, Mali, Morocco, Niger, Pakistan, Palestine, Yemen, Saudi Arabia, Senegal, Sudan, Somalia, Tunisia,Turkey, Bahrain, Oman,Qatar, Syria, UAE, Sierra Leone, Bangladesh, Gambia, Uganda, Cameroon, Iraq, Maldives, Benin, Brunei, Nigeria, Azerbaijan, Albania, Kyrgyzstan, Tajikistan, Turkmenistan, Mozambique, Kazakhstan, Uzbekistan, Suriname, Guyana, Côte d'Ivoire.

Panama
Area: 29,157 sq mi (75,517 sq km)
Population: 2,674,000
Capital: Panama City
Other cities: Colón, Puerto Armuelles, David
Government: Republic
Religion: Roman Catholicism
Currency: Balboa

Oman (Sultanate of Oman)
Area: 119,498 sq mi (309,500 sq km)
Population: 2,302,000
Capital: Mascat (Musqat)
Other towns: Salalah, Al Khaburah, Matrah
Government: Monarchy
Religions: Ibadi Islam, Sunni Islam
Currency: Rial Omani

Papua New Guinea
Area: 178,704 sq mi (462,840 sq km)
Population: 4,400,000
Capital: Port Moresby
Government: Republic
Religions: Protestantism, Roman Catholicism
Currency: Kina

Pakistan or the Islamic Republic of Pakistan
Area: 307,374 sq mi (796,095 sq km)
Population: 134,146,000
Capital: Islamabad
Other cities: Hyderabad, Karachi
Government: Federal Islamic Republic
Religions: Sunni Islam, Shia Islam
Currency: Pakistan rupee

Paraguay
Area: 157,048 sq mi (406,752 sq km)
Population: 4,955,000
Capital: Asunción
Other cities: Concepción, Ciudad del Este, Encarnación
Government: Republic
Religion: Roman Catholicism
Currency: Guaraní

Palau
Area: 177 sq mi (459 sq km)
Population: 17,000
Capital: Koror
Government: Free Associated Republic (USA)
Religions: Roman Catholicism and Modekngei
Currency: US dollar

Peru
Area: 496,225 sq mi (1,285,216 sq km)
Population: 25,015,000
Capital: Lima
Other cities: Arequipa, Callao, Chiclayo, Cuzco, Trujillo
Government: Republic
Religion: Roman Catholicism
Currency: Nuevo sol

Palestine (Palestinian Territories)
Area: Gaza Strip 146 sq mi (360 sq km); West Bank 2,269 sq mi (5,860 sq km)
Population: Gaza 1,376,289; West Bank 2,385,615
Government: Palestinian National Authority; future status yet to be determined
Religions: Sunni Islam, Shia Islam
Currency: Israeli and Jordanian currency

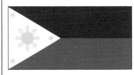

Philippines
Area: 115,813 sq mi (300,000 sq km)
Population: 71,899,000
Capital: Manila
Other cities: Cebu, Davao, Quezon City, Zamboanga
Government: Republic
Religions: Sunni Islam, Roman Catholicism, Protestantism
Currency: Philippine peso

Pitcairn Islands
Area: 2 sq mi (5 sq km)
Population: 50
Government: British Overseas
  Territory
Religion: Seventh Day
  Adventism
Currency: New Zealand dollar

Réunion
Area: 969 sq mi (2,510 sq
  km)
Population: 664,000
Capital: St Denis
Government: French overseas
  department
Religion: Roman Catholicism
Currency: Euro

Poland
Area: 124,808 sq mi
  (323,250 sq km)
Population: 38,628,000
Capital: Warsaw (Warszawa)
Other cities: Gdansk, Kraków,
  Lódz, Poznan, Wroclaw
Government: Republic
Religion: Roman Catholicism
Currency: Zloty

Romania
Area: 92,043 sq mi (238,391
  sq km)
Population 22,520,000
Capital: Bucharest (Bucuresti)
Other cities: Brasov, Constanta,
  Galati, Iasi, Timisoara,
  Craiova, Brâila, Arad, Ploiesti
Government: Republic
Religions: Romanian Orthodox,
  Roman Catholicism
Currency: Leu

Portugal
Area: 35,514 sq mi (91,982
  sq km)
Population: 9,920,800
Capital: Lisbon (Lisboa)
Other cities: Braga, Faro,
  Oporto, Setúbal
Government: Republic
Religion: Roman Catholicism
Currency: Euro

Russia or the **Russian
  Federation**
Area: 6,592,850 sq mi
  (17,075,400 sq km)
Population: 146,100,000
Capital: Moscow (Moskva)
Other cities: St Petersburg,
  Nizhniy Novgorod
Government: Republic
Religions: Russian Orthodox,
  Sunni Islam, Shia Islam,
  Roman Catholicism
Currency: Rouble

Puerto Rico
Area: 3,427 sq mi (8,875 sq
  km)
Population: 3,736,000
Capital: San Juan
Government: Self-governing
  commonwealth (in
  association with the USA)
Religions: Roman Catholi-
  cism, Protestantism
Currency: US dollar

Rwanda
Area: 10,169 sq mi (26,338
  sq km)
Population: 5,397,000
Capital: Kigali
Other major city: Butare
Government: Republic
Religions: Roman Catholi-
  cism, African traditional
  religions
Currency: Rwandan franc

Qatar
Area: 4,247 sq mi (11,000 sq
  km)
Population: 558,000
Capital: Doha (Ad Dawhah)
Government: Absolute
  Monarchy
Religion: Wahhabi Sunni
  Islam
Currency: Qatar riyal

**St Christopher (St Kitts)
  and Nevis**
Area: 101 sq mi (261 sq km)
Population: 41,000
Capital: Basseterre
Other major city:
  Charlestown
Government: Constitutional
  monarchy
Religions: Anglicanism,
  Methodism
Currency: East Caribbean
  Dollar

St Helena
Area: 47 sq mi (122 sq km)
Population: 5,200
Capital: Jamestown
Government: British Overseas
　Territory
Currency: St Helena pound

Samoa, American
Area: 77 sq mi (199 sq km)
Population: 56,000
Capital: Pago Pago
Government: Unincorporated
　Territory of the USA
Religion: Christianity
Currency: US dollar

St Lucia
Area: 240 sq mi (622 sq km)
Population: 144,000
Capital: Castries
Government: Constitutional
　Monarchy
Religion: Roman Catholicism
Currency: East Caribbean
　Dollar

San Marino
Area: 24 sq mi (61 sq km)
Population: 25,000
Capital: San Marino
Other cities: Borgo Maggiore,
　Serravalle
Government: Republic
Religion: Roman Catholicism
Currency: Euro

St Pierre and Miquelon
Area: 93 sq mi (240 sq km)
Population: 6,300
Capital: Saint Pierre
Government: French overseas
　territory
Religion: Roman Catholicism
Currency: Euro

São Tomé and Príncipe
Area: 372 sq mi (964 sq km)
Population: 135,000
Capital: São Tomé
Government: Republic
Religion: Roman Catholicism
Currency: Dobra

**St Vincent and the
　Grenadines**
Area: 150 sq mi (388 sq km)
Population: 113,000
Capital: Kingstown
Government: Constitutional
　monarchy
Religions: Anglicanism,
　Methodism, Roman
　Catholicism
Currency: East Caribbean
　dollar

Saudi Arabia
Area: 830,000 sq mi
　(2,149,690 sq km)
Population: 18,836,000
Capital: Riyadh (Ar Riyād)
Other cities: Ad Dammam,
　Mecca, Jeddah, Medina
Government: Monarchy
Religions: Sunni Islam, Shia
　Islam
Currency: Riyal

Samoa (Western)
Area: 1,093 sq mi (2,831 sq
　km)
Population: 166,000
Capital: Apia
Government: Constitutional
　Monarchy
Religion: Protestantism
Currency: Tala

Senegal
Area: 75,955 sq mi (196,722
　sq km)
Population: 8,572,000
Capital: Dakar
Other cities: Kaolack, Thiès,
　St Louis
Government: Republic
Religions: Sunni Islam, Roman
　Catholicism
Currency: CFA franc

Serbia and Montenegro
Area: 39,449 sq mi (102,173 sq km)
Population: 10,829,175
Capital: Belgrade
Other cities: Nis, Novi Sad, Pristina
Government: Republic
Religions: Eastern Orthodox, Islam
Currency: New dinar (Kosovo and Montenegro have adopted the euro).

Slovenia
Area: 7,821 sq mi (20,256 sq km)
Population: 1,991,000
Capital: Ljubljana
Other cities: Maribor, Kranj
Government: Republic
Religion: Roman Catholicism
Currency: Tolar

Seychelles
Area: 175 sq mi (455 sq km)
Population: 76,000
Capital: Victoria
Government: Republic
Religion: Roman Catholicism
Currency: Seychelles rupee

Solomon Islands
Area: 11,157 sq mi (28,896 sq km)
Population: 391,000
Capital: Honiara
Government: Parliamentary Democracy within the Commonwealth
Religion: Christianity
Currency: Solomon Islands dollar

Sierra Leone
Area: 27,699 sq mi (71,740 sq km)
Population: 4,297,000
Capital: Freetown
Other city: Bo
Government: Republic
Religions: African traditional religions, Sunni Islam, Christianity
Currency: Leone

Somalia
Area: 246,201 sq mi (637,657 sq km)
Population: 9,822,000
Capital: Mogadishu (Muqdisho)
Other major towns: Hargeysa, Burco
Government: Republic
Religion: Sunni Islam
Currency: Somali shilling

Singapore
Area: 239 sq mi (618 sq km)
Population: 3,044,000
Capital: Singapore
Government: Parliamentary Democracy
Religions: Buddhism, Sunni Islam, Christianity, Hinduism
Currency: Singapore dollar

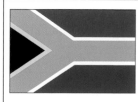

South Africa
Area: 471,445 sq mi (1,221,037 sq km)
Population: 42,393,000
Capital: Pretoria (administrative), Cape Town (legislative)
Other cities: Johannesburg, Durban, Port Elizabeth, Soweto
Government: Republic
Religions: Christianity, Hinduism, Islam
Currency: Rand

Slovakia (Slovak Republic)
Area: 18,928 sq mi (49,035 sq km)
Population: 5,374,000
Capital: Bratislava
Other cities: Kosice, Zilina, Nitra
Government: Republic
Religion: Roman Catholicism
Currency: Slovak koruna

Spain
Area: 195,365 sq mi (505,992 sq km)
Population: 39,270,400
Capital: Madrid
Other cities: Barcelona, Valencia, Seville, Zaragoza, Malaga, Bilbao
Government: Constitutional Monarchy
Religion: Roman Catholicism
Currency: Euro

Sri Lanka
Area: 25,332 sq mi (65,610 sq km)
Population: 18,354,000
Capital: Colombo
Other cities: Trincomalee, Jaffna, Kandy, Moratuwa
Government: Republic
Religions: Buddhism, Hinduism, Christianity, Sunni Islam
Currency: Sri Lankan rupee

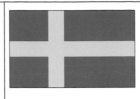

Sweden
Area: 173,732 sq mi (449,964 sq km)
Population: 8,843,000
Capital: Stockholm
Other cities: Göteborg, Malmö, Uppsala, Örebro, Linköping
Government: Constitutional Monarchy
Religion: Lutheranism
Currency: Krona

Sudan
Area: 967,500 sq mi (2,505,813 sq km)
Population: 27,291,000
Capital: Khartoum (El Khartum)
Other cities: Omdurman, Khartoum North, Port Sudan
Government: Republic
Religions: Sunni Islam, African traditional religions, Christianity
Currency: Sudanese dinar (of 10 pounds)

Switzerland
Area: 15,940 sq mi (41,284 sq km)
Population: 7,076,000
Capital: Bern
Other cities: Zürich, Basle, Geneva, Lausanne
Government: Federal Republic
Religions: Roman Catholicism, Protestantism
Currency: Swiss franc

Suriname
Area: 63,037 sq mi (163,265 sq km)
Population: 423,000
Capital: Paramaribo
Government: Republic
Religions: Hinduism, Roman Catholicism, Sunni Islam
Currency: Suriname guilder

Syria or the **Syrian Arab Republic**
Area: 71,498 sq mi (185,180 sq km)
Population: 14,619,000
Capital: Damascus (Dimashq)
Other cities: Halab, Hims, Dar'a
Government: Republic
Religion: Sunni Islam
Currency: Syrian pound

Svalbard
Area: 62,049 sq km
Population: 2,756
Capital: Longyearbyen
Islands: Spitsbergen, Nordaustlandet,Edgeøya, Barentsøya
Government: Norwegian sovereignty
Currency: Norwegian krone

Taiwan
Area: 13,800 sq mi (35,742 sq km)
Population: 21,854,270
Capital: T'ai-pei
Other cities: Kao-hsiung, T'ai-nan, Chang-hua, Chi-lung
Government: Republic
Religions: Taoism, Buddhism, Christianity
Currency: New Taiwan dollar

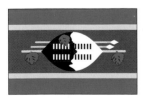

Swaziland
Area: 6,704 sq mi (17,364 sq km)
Population: 938,700
Capital: Mbabane
Other towns: Big Bend, Manzini, Mankayane, Lobamba
Government: Monarchy
Religions: Christianity, African traditional religions
Currency: Lilangeni

Tajikistan
Area: 55,250 sq mi (143,100 sq km)
Population: 5,919,000
Capital: Dushanbe
Other major city: Khujand
Government: Republic
Religion: Shia Islam
Currency: Tajik rouble

Tanzania
Area: 362,162 sq mi
   (938,000 sq km)
Population: 30,799,100
Capital: Dodoma
Other towns: Dar es Salaam,
   Zanzibar, Mwanza, Tanga
Government: Republic
Religions: Sunni Islam, Roman
   Catholicism, Anglicanism,
   Hinduism
Currency: Tanzanian shilling

Tunisia
Area: 62,592 sq mi (162,155
   sq km)
Population: 9,092,000
Capital: Tunis
Other cities: Sfax, Bizerte,
   Sousse
Government: Republic
Religion: Sunni Islam
Currency: Dinar

Thailand
Area: 198,115 sq mi
   (513,115 sq km)
Population: 60,206,000
Capital: Bangkok (Krung Thep)
Other cities: Chiang Mai,
   Nakhon Ratchasima, Ubon
   Ratchathani
Government: Constitutional
   monarchy
Religions: Buddhism, Sunni Islam
Currency: Baht

Turkey
Area: 299,158 sq mi
   (774,815 sq km)
Population: 62,697,000
Capital: Ankara
Other cities: Istanbul, Izmir,
   Adana, Bursa
Government: Republic
Religion: Sunni Islam
Currency: Turkish lira

Togo
Area: 21,925 sq mi (56,785
   sq km)
Population: 4,201,000
Capital: Lomé
Other major city: Sokodé
Government: Republic
Religions: African traditional
   religions, Roman Catholi-
   cism, Sunni Islam
Currency: CFA franc

Turkmenistan
Area: 188,456 sq mi
   (488,100 sq km)
Population: 4,569,000
Capital: Ashkhabad
   (Ashgabat)
Other cities: Chardzhou,
   Mary, Turkmenbashi
Government: Republic
Religion: Sunni Islam
Currency: Manat

Tonga
Area: 288 sq mi (747 sq km)
Population: 99,000
Capital: Nuku'alofa
Government: Constitutional
   monarchy
Religions: Methodism, Roman
   Catholicism
Currency: Pa'anga

Turks and Caicos Islands
Area: 166 sq mi (430 sq km)
Population: 23,000
Capital: Grand Turk
Government: British Crown
   Colony
Religion: Christianity
Currency: US dollar

Trinidad and Tobago
Area: 1,981 sq mi (5,130 sq km)
Population: 1,297,000
Capital: Port of Spain
Other towns: San Fernando,
   Arima
Government: Republic
Religions: Roman Catholi-
   cism, Hinduism,
   Anglicanism, Sunni Islam
Currency: Trinidad and
   Tobago dollar

Tuvalu
Area: 10 sq mi (24 sq km)
Population: 10,000
Capital: Funafuti
Government: Constitutional
   Monarchy
Religion: Protestantism
Currency: Tuvalu dollar/
   Australian dollar

Uganda
Area: 93,065 sq mi (241,038 sq km)
Population: 19,848,000
Capital: Kampala
Other cities: Entebbe, Jinja, Soroti, Mbale
Government: Republic
Religions: Roman Catholicism, Protestantism, African traditional religions, Sunni Islam
Currency: Uganda shilling

United States of America
Area: 3,536,278 sq mi (9,158,960 sq km)
Population: 270,299,000
Capital: Washington DC
Other cities: New York, Boston, Chicago, Houston, Los Angeles, Philadelphia, San Francisco
Government: Federal republic
Religions: Christianity, Judaism, Eastern Orthodox, Islam
Currency: US dollar

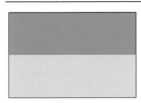

Ukraine
Area: 233,090 sq mi (603,700 sq km)
Population: 51,094,000
Capital: Kiev (Kiyev)
Other cities: Dnepropetrovsk, Donetsk, Khar'kov, Odessa, Lugansk, Sevastopol
Government: Republic
Religions: Russian Orthodox, Roman Catholicism
Currency: Rouble

Uruguay
Area: 68,500 sq mi (177,414 sq km)
Population: 3,203,000
Capital: Montevideo
Government: Republic
Religions: Roman Catholicism, Protestantism
Currency: Peso Uruguayos

United Arab Emirates (UAE)
Area: 32,278 sq mi (83,600 sq km)
Population: 2,260,000
Capital: Abu Zabi (Abu Dhabi)
Other cities: Dubai, Sharjh, Ras al Khaymah
Government: Monarchy
Religion: Sunni Islam
Currency: Dirham

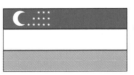

Uzbekistan
Area: 172,742 sq mi (447,400 sq km)
Population: 24,000,000
Capital: Tashkent
Other cities: Urgench, Nukus, Bukhara, Samarkand
Government: Republic
Religion: Sunni Islam
Currency: Soum

United Kingdom of Great Britain and Northern Ireland
Area: 94,248 sq mi (244,101 sq km)
Population: 58,784,000
Capital: London
Other cities: Glasgow, Edinburgh, Cardiff, Belfast
Government: Constitutional Monarchy
Religions: Christianity, Islam
Currency: Pound sterling
The top flag depicts the union of England, Northern Ireland, Scotland and Wales; flags are shown respectively below. There is no de facto flag for Northern Ireland but the flag pictured is used in many official and sporting occasions.

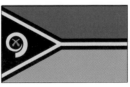

Vanuatu
Area: 4,706 sq mi (12,189 sq km)
Population: 169,000
Capital: Vila
Government: Republic
Religion: Roman Catholicism
Currency: Vatu

Vatican City State
Area: 0.2 sq mile (0.44 sq kilometre)
Population: 1,000
Capital: Vatican City
Government: Papal commission
Religion: Roman Catholicism
Currency: Euro

Venezuela
Area: 352,145 sq mi
   (912,050 sq km)
Population: 21,710,000
Capital: Caracas
Other cities: Maracaibo,
   Valencia, Barquisimeto
Government: Federal republic
Religion: Roman Catholicism
Currency: Bolívar

Western Sahara
Area: 102,703 sq mi
   (266,000 sq km)
Population: 266,000
Capital: Laâyoune (El Aaiún)
Government: Republic. It is
   disputed whether this
   territory is part of Morocco,
   or governed by the Sahrawi
   Arab Democratic Republic
   (SADR).
Religion: Sunni Islam
Currency: Moroccan dirham

Vietnam
Area: 128,066 sq mi
   (331,689 sq km)
Population: 75,181,000
Capital: Hanoi
Other cities: Ho Chi Minh City,
   Haiphong, Hué, Dà Nang
Government: Socialist
   Republic
Religions: Buddhism, Taoism,
   Roman Catholicism
Currency: New dong

Yemen
Area: 203,850 sq mi
   (527,978 sq km)
Population: 15,919,000
Capital: San'a
Commercial Capital: Aden
   (Adan)
Other cities: Al Hudaydah, Ta'izz
Government: Republic
Religions: Zaidism, Shia Islam,
   Sunni Islam
Currency: Riyal

Virgin Islands, British
Area: 58 sq mi (151 sq km)
Population: 19,000
Capital: Road Town
Government: British overseas
   territory
Religion: Protestantism
Currency: US dollar

Zambia
Area: 290,587 sq mi
   (752,618 sq km)
Population: 8,275,000
Capital: Lusaka
Other cities: Kitwe, Ndola,
   Mufulira
Government: Republic
Religions: Christianity, African
   traditional religions
Currency: Kwacha

Virgin Islands, US
Area: 134 sq mi (347 sq km)
Population: 106,000
Capital: Charlotte Amalie
Government: Self-governing
   US Territory
Religion: Protestantism
Currency: US dollar

Zimbabwe
Area: 150,872 sq mi
   (390,757 sq km)
Population: 11,908,000
Capital: Harare
Other cities: Bulawayo,
   Mutare, Gweru
Government: Republic
Religions: African traditional
   religions, Anglicanism,
   Roman Catholicism
Currency: Zimbabwe dollar

Wallis and Futuna Islands
Area: 77 sq mi (200 sq km)
Population: 15,000
Capital: Mata-Uru
Government: French overseas
   territory
Religion: Roman Catholicism
Currency: CFP franc

US States

Alabama (AL)

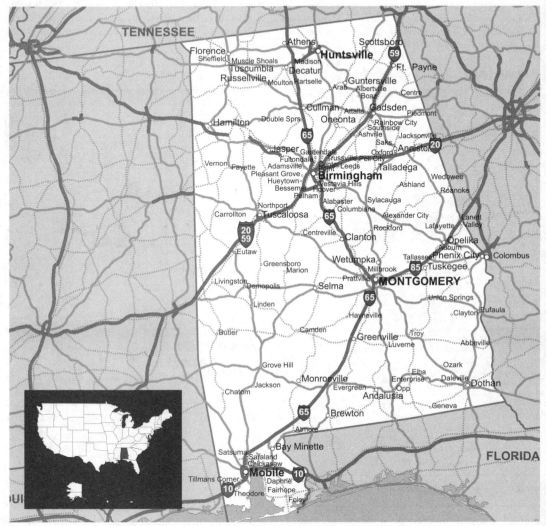

Name: the name may come from the native American Choctaw language meaning "thicket-clearers" or "vegetation-gatherers."

Nickname: Heart of Dixie; Camellia State; The Cotton State.

State flower: Camellia.

State bird: Yellowhammer.

Motto: Crossroads of America.

Population: 4,557,808 (2005).

Capital: Montgomery.

Physical description: Alabama is the 30th-largest state in the United States. It borders Tennessee to the north, Florida to the south, and Georgia to the east. Around three fifths of the land is made up of plains, while the region is mostly mountainous to the north. Its highest point is Mount Cheaha reaching 2408 feet (734m). Its lowest point is the Gulf of Mexico. Notable sights of interest include Horseshoe bend National Military park and Little River Canyon National Preserve.

Area: 52,423 sq mi (135,775 sq km).

Climate: mild weather all year round with average temperatures of 27°C in summer and above 7°C in winter. There is occasional winter snowfall in the north.

Agriculture: agricultural output includes poultry and eggs, cattle, peanuts, cotton, grains, vegetables, milk, soybeans, and peaches.

Minerals: steel and coal.

Industry: iron and steel products; paper, lumber, and wood products; coal mining; plastic products; cars and trucks; aerospace and electronic products.

History: The Native American people once living in Alabama were Alabama (Alibamu), Cherokee, Chickasaw, Choctaw, Creek, Koasati, and Mobile. The French established the first European settlement in the state in 1702, and southern Alabama was French till 1763. The British gained control of the area from 1763 till 1780, and from 1780 till 1814 it was part of Spanish west Florida. Afterwards it became part of the American Mississippi territory. Alabama became the 22nd state in 1819. Alabama became a Confederate state in 1861, known as the Alabama Republic. For a time Montgomery was the Confederate capital. After the war the state was re-admitted to the union in 1868. In the 1950s is was the center of black civil rights action.

Alaska (AK)

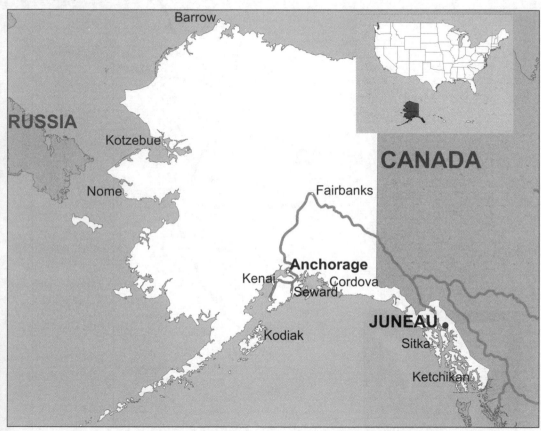

Name: from the word Aleut word Alyeska, meaning "greater land" or "that which the sea breaks against."

Nickname: The Last Frontier; Land of the Midnight Sun.

State flower: Forget-me-not.

State bird: Willow ptarmigan.

Motto: North to the future.

Population: 626,932.

Capital: Juneau.

Physical description: Alaska is the USA's largest state. It is an exclave, (a territory that belongs to a country but is not connected to it by land and is surrounded by other countries) of the USA, bordered by Yukon Territory and British Colombia, Canada to the east, and the Gulf Of Alaska to the south. It has the longest coastline of all of the American states. It has four regions: South central Alaska (Palmer, Wasilia), The Alaska panhandle (Juneau), the Alaska Interior (Fairbanks, Arctic tundra) and the Alaskan Bush (Nome, Bethel, Kotzebue, Barrow). There are 3.5 million lakes. Marshlands and wetland permafrost cover 188,320 sq mi (487,747 sq km). Glacier ice, covers 16,000 sq mi (41,440 sq km) of land and 1200 square miles (3,108 sq km) of coast. The Bering Glacier complex near the southeastern border with Yukon, Canada, covers 2,250 square miles (5,827 sq km). It's highest point is Mt McKinley at 20,320 ft (6,194 m).

Area: 663,267 sq mi (1,717,854 sq km)

Climate: Unpredictable weather with long, dark, cold winters, but potentially warm beautiful summers. Alaska's enormous size means the weather varies greatly. Summer: some areas can reach the 80ºF and 90ºF, others barely reach

30°F. Winter: along the southern coast, temperatures may be as high as 20°F, while in the north they can reach -50 and even lower. Southern areas have well-defined four seasons while northern areas have winter and summer. Daylight hours are also given to dramatic changes, for example in Barrow, the sun sets at 12:50pm on November 18 and rises at 11:50am on January 24; but by 1:00am on May 10 there is 24-hour daylight.

Agriculture: nursery stock, dairy products, vegetables, and livestock.

Minerals: crude petroleum, natural gas, coal, gold, precious metals and zinc.

Industry: natural resource extraction, shipping, and transportation

History: Alaska's first inhabitants came across the Bering

Land Bridge, and area of around 1000 miles (1600 km) in length, which joined present-day Alaska and eastern Siberia during the ice ages. Alaska became populated by the Inupiaq, Inuit and Yupik Eskimos, Aleuts, and other American Indian groups. The first Europeans to discover Alaska were Vitus Bering, a Dane working for Russia, and Alexei Chirikov in 1741. In 1867 US Secretary of State William Seward purchased the unexplored territory from Russia for $7,200,000. It was at this time, known as the Department of Alaska. From 1884 it was known as the District of Alaska, and in 1912 it was a territory. On January 3, 1959 President Eisenhower granted it statehood, making it the 49th US state.

Arizona (AZ)

Name: There are many theories about the name, including that it is from the Spanish arida zona, meaning arid zone, or the Aztec word alizuma, meaning silver-bearing.
Nickname: Grand Canyon State.
State flower: Saguaro flower.
State bird: Cactus wren.
Motto: Diat Deus ("God enriches").
Population: 4,668,000.
Capital: Phoenix.
Physical description: Arizona is famed for its desert landscape, as exemplified by its most spectacular tourist attractions, the Grand Canyon, a vast gorge carved out by the movement of the Colorado River over millions of years, and the Painted Desert, so called because of its layers of red and yellow sand, and bentonite clay. But this great state, the sixth largest in the union, also has its highlands of lush pine forests, mountains and plateaus, including the 600 meter Mogollon Rim, at the Southwestern edge of the Colorado Plateau.
Arizona's modern topography owes much to the volcanic activity of prehistoric times, which accounts for its deep ravines and vertiginous slopes. Its past can also be seen at the Petrified Forest National Park, part of the Painted Desert; this is the largest prehistoric forest in the world, dating back to the Triassic period.
Area: 114,000 sq mi (295,259 sq km).
Climate: Arizona has a very varied climate to match its varied landscape. The desert regions have a typical desert climate of hot, dry summers with chilly nights, and mild winters which only occasionally dip to below freezing. Spring comes as early as February and temperatures can climb, by midsummer, to as high as 40ºC, sometimes even 50ºC.
In the highlands, the climate is considerably cooler, with cold fronts sometimes coming in from as far north as Canada, driving winter temperatures down to as low as -18ºC.
Rainfall averages at 322mm per year, thanks to two rainy seasons, one comprising fronts drifting in from the Pacific Ocean during winter, and a summer monsoon.
Agriculture: Lettuce, cotton, hay, fruit, vegetables, cattle and dairy produce
Minerals: Copper, silver and lead
Industry: Cotton, cattle, dairy products, manufacturing (electrical) and IT.
History: The modern state of Arizona was once part of Mexico, but was partially annexed to the USA in 1848, following the Battle of Mexico. The remainder was acquired in 1853 is the Gadsden Purchase. It became a separate state from New Mexico in 1863, and the 48th state of the USA on Valentine's Day, 1912.
One of the great "Wild West" states, Arizona was the backdrop to the battles fought between white settlers and the great Apache chiefs, Cochise and Geronimo. So fiercely did the Apaches resist the white man's encroachment that, in 1861, the US forces were driven from Arizona almost entirely. But a generation later, under Geronimo, they were heavily outnumbered and defeated, thus ending the warfare between the "Cowboys and Indians" forever.
Not that Arizona quietened down any. On 26 October 1881 came the most famous shoot-out in American history, when Wyatt Earp and Doc Holliday took on the Clantons and McLaurys at the OK Corral in Tombstone.
During the twentieth century, the state's staple industries, copper mining and cattle-ranching, were knocked for six by the Great Depression of the 1920s. The state's economy recovered thanks largely to tourism, both in the form of Wild West-style holiday ranches and upmarket hotels from the late 1920s onwards.
The advent of air-conditioning made the sweltering state's population soar, from just under 300,000 in 1910 to nearly 2 million by the 1970s.
Its warm climate makes it a magnet for wealthy retirees, coming to live in purpose-built communities such as Sun City, built in 1960, and Green Valley, near Tucson.
The state is also home to America's largest Native American population, with members of 14 tribes living across 20 reservations.

Arkansas (AR)

Name: French pronunciation of the Quapaws or Arkansas, native Americans who lived in the north of the state.
Nickname: Land of Opportunity.
State flower: Apple blossom.
State bird: Mockingbird.
Motto: Regnat Populus ("The people rule")
Population: 2,538,000.
Capital: Little Rock.
Physical description: Bordering Texas, Louisiana, Mississippi, Tennessee, Missouri and Oklahoma, Arkansas is at the very heart of America, both physically and in terms of concentration of population.
Its eastern border is formed by the great Mississippi River, and the landscape there is characterized by alluvial valleys, a fertile land that yields rich crops of cotton, rice and soy beans. The Arkansas River also runs through here.

The north is quite different, a mountainous landscape dominated by the Quachita and Ozark ranges, with peaks rising to a top height of 2,753 feet.
The state is also known for its vast forests.
Area: 53,187 sq miles (137,754 sq km).
Climate: Summers are hot and humid, with temperatures soaring to 100ºF in the south, though the north and west, particularly in the mountains, experience much milder conditions.
Winters in the mountains can be bitterly cold with average annual snowfall of 10.4 inches. The south is warmer, with less than 3 inches of snow per year and temperatures rarely dipping below freezing.
Rainfall is less in the mountains, at around 45 inches a year, rising to 55 inches in the lowlands.

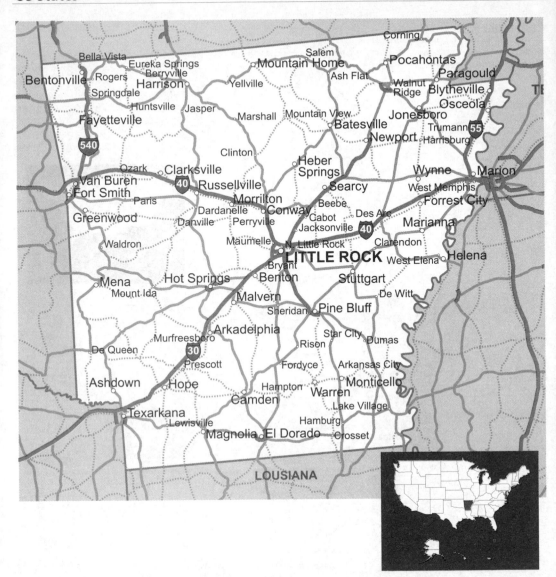

Agriculture: rice, soybeans, dairy produce, cotton and grapes

Minerals: Bauxite, quartz crystal, silica stone.

Industry: food processing, electric equipment, fabricated metal products, machinery, paper products.

History: Long before the Spanish explorer Hernando de Soto arrived here in 1541, Arkansas was home to a range of First Nation tribes, including Cherokee, Choctaw, Osage and Quapaws, and there remains much evidence of their ancient life here, in mounds and bluffs, stone artifacts and pottery.

European settlement was steady and by 1819, Arkansas was recognized as a territory. It achieved statehood in 1836, becoming the 25th state of the union.

Like those around it, Arkansas was a slave state. In 1860, its 435,000-strong population was comprised one quarter slaves. They mostly worked the rich farmlands to the south and east, this being a predominantly agricultural region.

Like other slave states, Arkansas fought against the north during the Civil War, and two major battles – Pea Ridge and Prairie Grove – were fought here. The subsequent period of Reconstruction saw a major political and social upheaval in Arkansas, as across the south generally, as the rights and freedoms of blacks were established. Changes were felt agriculturally too, as the vast plantations and farms built on slave labour were broken up into smaller concerns.

Modern Arkansas is a prosperous region with a strong showing in the agricultural, manufacturing and tourism sectors.

California (CA)

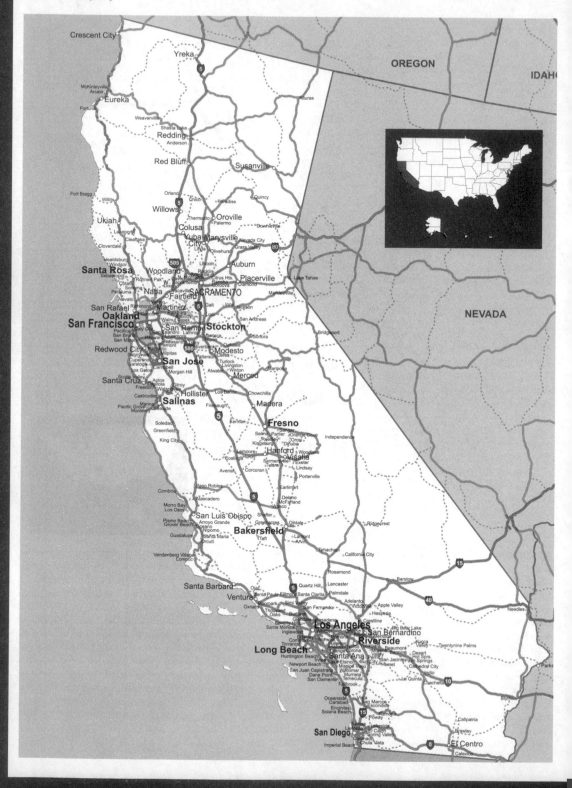

Name: derives from a fictional island in a 16th century Spanish novel, popular at the time of European settlement.
Nickname: Golden State.
State flower: Golden poppy.
State bird: California valley quail.
Motto: Eureka ("I have found it").
Population: 32,670,000.
Capital: Sacramento.
Physical description: California has everything, from the plunging depths of Death Valley, 282 feet below sea level, to the soaring heights of Mount Whitney, at 14,495 feet, great rivers and endless beaches, desert and farmland.

The state extends 825 miles from its northwest corner which touches the Pacific Ocean to its southeast corner at the junction of the Gila and Colorado Rivers.

Its coastline stretches 1264 miles, taking in inlets and beaches and even mountains, the Coast Ranges, which border the Pacific Ocean from Oregon to Marin County.

But California's greatest mountains are the Sierra Nevadas to the south, which cover a vast 400 miles and are bordered on the south by the Mojave Desert and on the east by the Great Basin mountains.

The Salton Trough, which also borders the Mojave, is an area of immense geological interest, it being the spot where the land that is now Mexico broke off from the American mainland.

To the north are the Klamath and Cascade Mountains and the Modoc Plateau, with the Great Valley of the Sacramento and San Joaquin Rivers running from it to the south.
Area: 158,706 sq mi (411,047 sq km).
Climate: Like its topography, California's climate has a little of everything. In the mountains, expect heavy snow and cold winters, and dry hot days and chilly nights in the desert regions. The coast and much of the interior, by contrast, is warm yet temperate, its hottest days fanned by Pacific breezes.
The ocean, specifically, the California Current, creates summer fog near the coast, particularly in the coastal valleys, even in summer.

Temperatures vary wildly, from an astonishing 120°F in Death Valley, the hottest spot in the western hemisphere, to -20°F in the mountains. In general, however, the climate is continental in character, with cool, rainy winters and warm, dry summers.

Rainfall can vary extremely, from 80 inches annually in the Coast Redwoods, to 1.5 inches annually in Death Valley. In general, around 15-50 inches of rain falls in a year.
Agriculture: fruit, vegetables, dairy produce, wine.
Minerals: sand and gravel.
Industry: entertainment, light manufacturing, tourism, IT, wine
History: Spanish settlers arrived during the late 1700s, displacing the native populations that had lived there for centuries.

Following the Mexican War of Independence, 1810-21, California was annexed to Mexico, only freeing itself through a popular rebellion to become the California Republic on the eve of the Mexican-American war of 1846-48. After which, it became part of the US.

California sustained a huge population boost during its famous Gold Rush of 1849, which brought prospectors in droves from across the states. It became the 31st state in 1850.

The arrival of the railroad facilitated a second population boom, as people discovered that, as well as gold, California had a fine, fertile soil, ideal for fruit cultivation, especially citrus fruit.

It quickly became the agricultural heart of the Pacific west, its fortunes later boosted by the establishment of what it became world famous for, its film industry, based in Hollywood.

It later also became a major center for information technology and is today one of the wealthiest, most culturally diverse states in the union.

Colorado (CO)

Name: From the Spanish, meaning "ruddy" or "red."
Nickname: Centennial State
State flower: Blue (Rocky Mountain) Colombine
State bird: Lark Bunting
Motto: Nil sine numine ("Nothing without providence")
Population: 3,971,000
Capital: Denver
Physical description: Colorado is characterized by its mountains, of which it has more over 14,000 feet than any other state and the highest peaks in the Rocky Mountain chain which stretches from Alaska to Mexico. Thus it has the highest mean altitude of any state, at 2073 meters above sea-level.

It has four distinct regions:

The Great Plains region, which runs through the American interior, from Canada to Mexico, is largely flat and dry.

The Rocky Mountains region, which includes the Rocky Mountain National Park, a treasure of wildlife, including bears and cougars, great rivers and peaks, and a famous leaf show during the autumn, caused by the Aspen forests reacting to the unique climate, creating vivid hues of yellow, red, orange, even blue.

The Continental Divide runs through the mountains. On one side, the rivers run to the Atlantic, on the other, to the Pacific.

The Colorado Plateau region, which runs along the Utah border, is characterized by hills, valleys and flat-topped mountains, and the Intermontane Basin region, by rolling hills covered in lush woodlands and dry, flat plateau.

Finally, Colorada is the source of some of the great American rivers, including the Rio Grande, the 20th longest river in the world, and the Colorado.

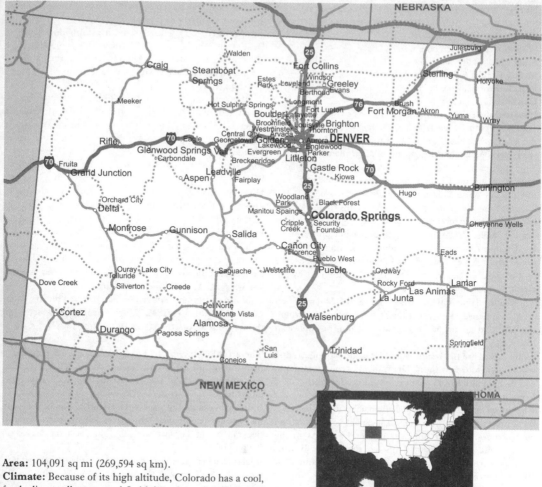

Area: 104,091 sq mi (269,594 sq km).

Climate: Because of its high altitude, Colorado has a cool, fresh climate all year round. In high summer, hot spells and humidity are short-lived while in winter, though nights are chilly and sub-Arctic in the Rockies, the days are bright. However, there are pronounced regional variations. The south east, for example, is around 35°C warmer than in the mountains, where snow falls to the tune of 300 inches a year compared to just 25 inches in the San Luis Valley.

Colorado is a dry, landlocked state, with most rain falling in the spring and early summer. Winters can be dry with snow, sometimes becoming blizzards in the mountains. Winter also brings the "chinooks," a sudden rise in temperature caused by westerly winds moving down rapidly from the mountains causing the air pressure to compress and warm the air.

Agriculture: cattle, corn, wheat

Minerals: aquamarine, rhodochrosite, quartz

Industry: service industries and manufacturing (foodstuffs, printing, machinery, electrical instruments)

History: Colorado was first inhabited over 1000 years ago by the mysterious and fascinating Anasazi Indians, the ancestors of the modern Pueblo Indians. Their name is Navajo, meaning "Ancient Ones" and they left behind many artifacts, including their spectacular, multi-storey cliff dwellings. By the 13th century, however, they had gone, leaving it to the nomadic tribes of the Kiowa, Comanche, Arapaho and Cheyenne, and the Utes, the only indigenous Native American tribe.

The Spanish arrived in the 16th century, in search of mythical, gold-paved cities. They didn't find any and, in 1800, ceded the territory to the French who, three years later, sold it to America in the "Louisiana Purchase."

The 1849 California gold rush sparked interest in Colorado and over 50,000 settlers arrived between 1858-9, creating the cities of Denver and San Luis, which, dating from 1851, is Colorado's oldest white settlement.

Colorado achieved statehood in 1876, becoming the 38th in the union and was called the "Centennial State" because it was the 100th anniversary of the Declaration of Independence.

Today, this beautiful state is a magnet for tourists who come to enjoy its spectacular scenery, national parkland, ski resorts and great rivers.

Connecticut (CT)

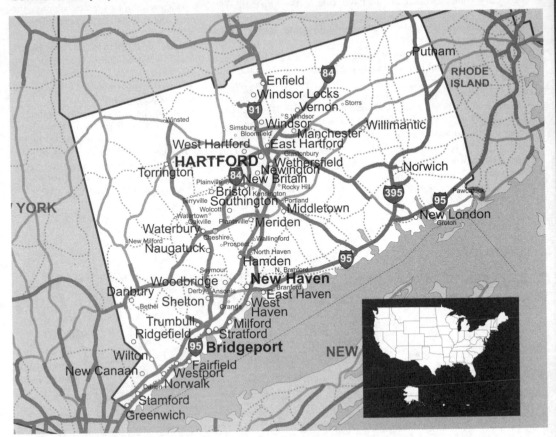

Name: from the Mohican word Quinnehtukqut, meaning "beside the tidal river."

Nicknames: Constitution State; Nutmeg State.

State flower: Mountain laurel.

State bird: American robin.

Population: 3,275,000.

Motto: Qui transtulit sustinet ("He who transplanted still sustains").

Capital: Hartford.

Physical description: The most southerly of the New England states, Connecticut borders New York to the west and Massachusetts and Rhode Island to the east, and is divided topographically into five regions.

The Western New England Upland is a rugged, hilly upland, rising to an altitude of 1200 feet. Its landscape, like that of the Eastern New England Upland, is covered in boulders, the calling card of continental glaciation.

The Eastern uplands are lower, rising to only 700 feet, with narrow river valleys and plentiful forestry.

The Western and Eastern uplands are divided by the Connecticut Valley Lowland, which is around 30 miles wide on average, a stretch of small rivers and ridges running in to Massachusetts.

The Taconic Mountains, and Litchfield Hills, are characterized by steep slopes and narrow valleys and have quite barren terrain.

Finally, the Coastal Lowlands, which runs along the south shore at Long Island Sound, is a narrow region, 6-16 miles wide, with many small bays and inlets.

Area: 5,018 sq mi (12,997 sq km).

Climate: Blessed with a temperate climate, Connecticut experiences mild winters and warm summers with only very occasional extreme weather events, such as the drought of 1963-66, which saw crops fail and water rationed, and the 1982 floods, sustaining $266 million-worth of damage.

In general, the state enjoys quite diverse weather in quite short periods of time.

In summer, temperatures average 21°C, in winter -3°C. Rainfall is distributed relatively evenly across the seasons, with snow in January and February and, rarely, in December.

Located on a middle latitude, the state is subject to the prevailing westerly – eastward winds that circle the earth and help maintain a steady climate.

The only truly hazardous weather occurs in winter in the

form of northeasterlies, storms from the sea which generate very strong winds and rain and, in severe cold, snowstorms.

Agriculture: dairy produce, eggs, tobacco, mushrooms and apples.

Minerals: garnet, tourmaline, copper, tungsten

Industry: manufacturing (jet engines, helicopters), electronics, insurance.

History: The home of the Pequot tribe, in 1614, Dutch ships began exploring the Connecticut coastline, finally establishing a fort at Hartford in 1633. In the same year, members of the Plymouth Colony set up a trading post at Windsor and, in 1635, came the English Puritans from Massachusetts Bay, who also set up a trading post, this time at Wethersfield.

The Pequot fought back but were defeated in the Pequot War of 1637.

In 1638, representatives from the three white settlements met and established Connecticut as a colony, adopting the Fundamental Orders, the original state constitution, in 1639.

By 1643, Connecticut had expanded to include New Haven, Massachusetts Bay and the Plymouth Colony. It went on to become one of the first states to approve the US Constitution, and a staunch supporter of the Union during the Civil War, providing 60,000 troops.

Its industries were built on the backs of waves of immigration and, during World Wars I and II, prospered through the manufacture of munitions, though it was hit hard by the 1920s Depression. In 1954, it built the first nuclear-powered submarine and became an important manufacturer of weaponry during the Cold War. Today it is a wealthy state, with many of its residents working in New York.

Delaware (DE)

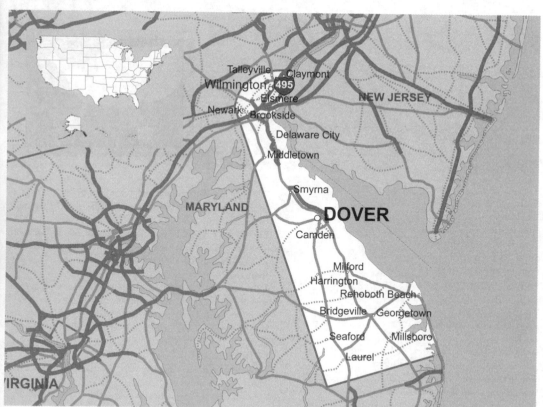

Name: After Lord de la Warr, the first governor of Virginia.
Nickname: First State; Diamond State Delaware (DE).
State flower: Peach blossom.
State bird: Blue hen chicken.
Motto: Liberty and independence.
Population: 745,000.

Capital: Dover.
Physical description: Due to its small size, there is little variety topographically. The state is part of two major land regions.

The Piedmont, which runs from New Jersey to Alabama, straddles the northernmost tip of Delaware, is ten miles wide at its widest point, and is gently hilly.

However, 95% of Delaware comprises the Delmarva Peninsula, part of the Atlantic Coastal Plain – a low, flat region, including 30,000 acres of swampland on the southern border.

Generally flat, Delaware rises from sea level at the coast to 442 feet at its highest altitude.

Area: 2,044 sq miles (5,294 sq km).

Climate: a temperate climate that varies little across the state. In summer, temperatures average 24°C, and in winter, -1 degree C. August is the wettest month, with average rainfall of 5.5 inches (140mm), while February is the driest, with only 3 inches. Average yearly rainfall is 45 inches (1140 mm).

Extreme weather is rare.

Agriculture: soy beans, corn, chickens, dairy produce

Minerals: sand, gravel, sillimanite

Industry: chemicals, plastics, synthetic rubber, food and paper products.

History: The Lenape, meaning "original people," were indigenous to Delaware and the first Native Americans to come into contact with Europeans, causing their population to plummet from as many as 20,000 in 1600 to just a few thousand by 1700 through warfare with white settlers and exposure to European diseases to which they had no immunity. This ancient "grandfather" tribe gradually migrated westward as their lands were appropriated, first by the Swedish, who established a colony in 1638, and then the Dutch, who forcibly took over in 1655.

In 1776, the year of the Declaration of Independence, Delaware announced its independence from Britain and supplied 4000 troops to the Revolutionary war – quite a force for such a small state.

Of the 13 original states, it was the first to approve the US Constitution, hence its nickname of "First State."

Delaware was an avowed slave state and though it mostly fought on the Union side during the Civil War, on 18 February 1865, it voted unsuccessfully to reject the 13th Amendment and retain slavery, which was not abolished in Delaware until the amendment came into effect.

Modern Delaware is a highly industrialized state, specializing in chemical research and manufacture.

District of Columbia (DC)

Name: Columbia is an old, romantic name for the US, derived possibly from Christopher Columbus

Nickname: Capital city

State flower: American beauty rose

State bird: Wood thrush

Population: 606,900

Motto: Justitia omnibus ("Justice for all")

Capital: Washington

Physical description: Columbia's most notable geographic features are its rivers, notably the Potomac, the 21st largest river in the US, which flows to Chesapeake Bay on the Atlantic Coast, and the Anacostia, bordering reclaimed flatlands to the south. Rock Creek, the third Columbia River, flows from the northwest to join the Potomac.

The landscape is predominantly flat, rising to a maximum elevation of 410 feet at Tenleytown.

Area: 68 sq mi (108.8 sq km).

Climate: Columbia's summers are hot and humid, rising to temperatures in excess of 30°C. Thunderstorms are a regular occurrence during these months. Winters are very cold, with temperatures plunging to 20°F. Snowstorms are not unusual. Columbia also experiences hurricanes occasionally.

Agriculture: there is no commercial farming in the District of Columbia

Minerals: n/a

Industry: government

History: Columbia was created out of land from neighboring states Maryland and Virginia, and was declared a federal district on 16 July 1790. The site was chosen by General Washington himself and it quickly became established as the seat of government, housing the Capitol, White House, Supreme Court and other important governmental buildings.

On 24 August 1814, much of it was razed to the ground by British forces but it was rebuilt and became a major center after the Civil War, its population peaking in 1950 though declining thereafter.

Today, it remains a focal point for America, the site of government decree and a locus for political protest. It now also houses offices of international organizations including the International Monetary Fund and the World Bank.

Florida (FL)

Name: From the Spanish Pascua florida, the Easter celebration, meaning "feast of the flowers."

Nickname: Sunshine State.

State flower: Orange blossom.

State bird: Mockingbird.

Motto: in God we trust.

Population: 14,916,000.

Capital: Tallahassee.

Physical description: Florida is a very flat, low-lying state, with the lowest high point of any state in the US, at only 345 feet. The northwest, the Florida Panhandle, is characterized by a series of rolling, red clay hills that, as they descend to the Gulf coast, give way to swampland.

The east coast, part of the Atlantic Coastal Plain, extends into the sea as coral reefs and sandbars, which offer shelter to the bays and lagoons. To the south is a drenched land-

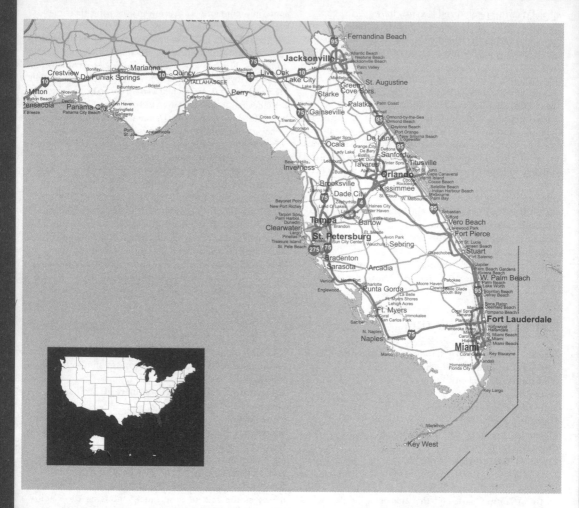

scape, including the Big Cyprus Swamp and the Everglades.

Finally, the southwest, extending to the Gulf of Mexico, includes the Florida Keys and many tiny islands.

The Straits of Florida divide the mainland from Cuba.

Area: 58,664 sq mi (151,939 sq km).

Climate: A warm, sunny climate thanks to tropical and subtropical waters cooled by trade winds. Winters are mild and summers are hot, with temperatures soaring beyond the 80s. The heat and humidity is tempered, however, by thunderstorms which lower the temperature by 10-20°F.

Florida has more thunderstorms than anywhere else in the union, and more violent ones. The "Lightning Belt," which runs from Orlando to Tampa, is particularly hazardous and contributes to the state's appalling record of deaths by lightning.

April, May and June constitute tornado season, though these dramatic weather events tend to be more benign than they look.

Rainfall varies considerably, from 100 inches a year in one area, to less than 50 in another. There are two rainy seasons, one in early spring, the other in summer, with the northwest and southeast the wettest, and the interior the driest.

Agriculture: citrus, cattle and dairy produce.

Minerals: limestone, phosphate, quartz and aragonite

Industry: electronics, plastics, construction, real estate, tourism.

History: The Seminoles occupied Florida long before Juan Ponce de Leon arrived from Spain in 1513 and named the state, which he thought was an island, after the Easter celebrations. The area was very desirable for settlement but the first colony failed following fierce resistance from the native Americans.

The Spanish controlled Florida till 1763, when they exchanged it with the British for Cuba, which the latter had seized during the Seven Years' War (1756-63), though Spain got it back after the American Revolution. They finally ceded it to the US in 1821, in the Adams-Onis Treaty. For mass settlement to occur, the native population had to be displaced and the US government spent $20 million and countless army and civilian lives in doing just that. The Seminoles were unpopular not only for living on covetable land but also for sheltering runaway slaves. Many left in the end, others retreating to the Everglades to live apart from the settlers.

The slave state became the 27th of the union on 3 March 1845 but joined the Confederate States for the Civil War which, following defeat and military rule by Congress, ef-

fectively ended Florida's cotton plantation industry.

In the late 19th century, manufacturing and large-scale farming boomed, as did tourism. The Great Depression blighted the economy, as did devastating hurricanes and the Mediterranean fruit fly, which threatened to wipe out the citrus industry.

However, the post-war boom established Florida as a wealthy state, rich in industry and natural resources and one of the most popular tourist destinations in the world.

Georgia (GA)

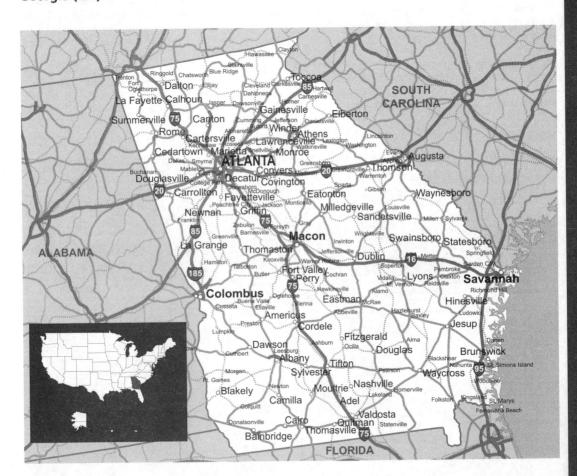

Name: After King George II of England, who granted the colony its royal charter in 1752.

Nickname: Peace State; Empire State of the South.

State flower: Cherokee rose.

State bird: Brown thrasher.

Motto: Wisdom, justice and moderation.

Population: 7,643,000.

Capital: Atlanta.

Physical description: Georgia is a huge, mostly flat state, rising to the Blue Ridge Mountains at its northernmost

edge. The East Gulf and Atlantic Coastal Plains comprise the south, a flat swampland giving way to rivers, sandy plains and the Atlantic shoreline.

The central region, the Piedmont, sweeps up towards the Appalachians in the north, to a top elevation of 1500 feet. The Fall Line occurs where Piedmont meets the Coastal Plains and is characterized by river rapids and waterfalls due to the sudden drop in ground level.

To the north are the Appalachian Ridge and Plateau, a region of lush wide valleys and sandstone ridges. The

Plateau is 2000 feet above sea level.

Area: 58,910 sq mi (152,576 sq km).

Climate: Georgia is a warm, sunny state with snow only appearing on the peaks of the Blue Ridge Mountains. Summers are hot and humid, with temperatures in the mid-80s (F), while winters are mild and cool, though temperatures never fall below 15°F thanks to a combination of polar air warmed by subtropical air masses.

Cyclonic activity in early spring makes February and March a rainy season, the other wet months being June and July thanks to thunderstorms. Rainfall ranges from 45 inches a year in the interior, to up to 75 inches in the northeast.

Agriculture: chickens, cotton, timber, peanuts

Minerals: Kaolin, Barite, Ochre, Marble

Industry: textiles, paper products, food processing, manufacture (cars and aircraft), tourism.

History: The earliest inhabitants were the "Moundbuilders," a prehistoric race who established a complex society linked by waterways. By the time the first white settlers arrived, the Creek and Cherokee nations were dominant, but were later ruthlessly driven out.

The Spanish established a base here first, but after much wrangling, the British took control and, on 12 February 1733, HMS Anne brought 113 settlers from England to what is now Savannah.

The Creek nation was forced out by 1827, the Cherokee remaining until 1838 when the Treaty of New Echota decreed their removal to Oklahoma. Men, women and children were dragged from their homes and forced to march 1000 miles under brutal military escort; a shameful event subsequently known as the "Trail of Tears."

Georgia became the 4th United State on 2 January 1788 but joined the Confederate States for the Civil War, when it was well and truly routed by General William Tecumseh's March to the Sea, which destroyed everything in its path, from Atlanta to Savannah. This provided the inspiration for Margaret Mitchell's Civil War epic, Gone With The Wind, published in 1936.

Georgia is now a prosperous state, famous in the 20th century as the birthplace of Coca-cola, Jimmy Carter and Martin Luther King.

Hawaii (HI)

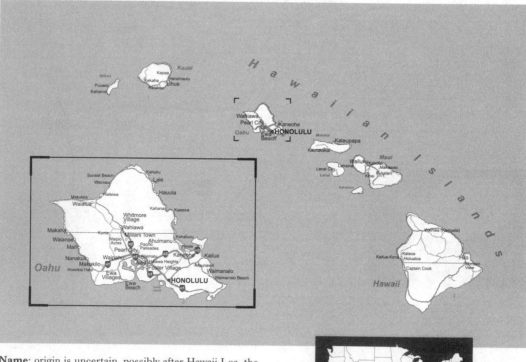

Name: origin is uncertain, possibly after Hawaii Loa, the original discoverer, or after the Polynesian traditional home, of Hawaii or Hawaiki.

Nickname: Aloha State.

State flower: Hibiscus.

State bird: Nene Goose/Hawaiian Goose.

Motto: The life of the land is perpetuated in righteousness.

Population: 1,194,000.
Capital: Honolulu.
Physical description: Hawaii is the world's longest island chain, at 1523 miles comprising 132 islands, only 7 of which are inhabited. All were formed by volcanic eruptions and as such, are characterized by sheer cliffs rising from the sea and some black sand beaches. Hawaii, the biggest island, has two active volcanoes, including Mauna Loa, the biggest volcano in the world, which rises 17 km from the seabed and has erupted 33 times since 1843, the last time in 1984. Maui was created from two volcanoes which form a fertile, central valley, ideal for sugar cane cultivation. Moloka'i is mountainous on one side and a plateau on the other, with a fertile central region. Lana'i is the pineapple island, of which 98% is owned by Dole, the fruit company. O'ahu is rich in sugar and pineapple plantations and the striking feature of a 700 feet wide extinct volcano crater, known as the Diamond Head. Kaua'i, the "Garden Island" is lush and green. It also boasts the rainiest place on earth, at the summit of Mount Waialeale, 5080 feet above sea level, which records 460 inches of rain a year. Niihau is dry, arid, and privately owned and Kaho'olawe is also arid, and uninhabited.
Area: 6,471 sq miles (16,760 sq km).
Climate: Hawaii has only two seasons, summer and winter, with generally mild temperatures all year round. Winter temperatures are only about 20°F lower than summer temperatures.
The surrounding Pacific Ocean acts as a natural thermostat and keeps temperatures stable though extreme weather events, such as tornadoes and hurricanes, are not unheard of.
The mountains affect local weather conditions. Land to the windward side receive northeast trade winds, which bring rain, while those to the leeward side are drier and hotter. Most resorts are on the leeward side.
Agriculture: sugar cane, pineapples, macadamia nuts, livestock.

Minerals: sand, gravel, black and precious coral.
Industry: tourism, food processing, apparel, stone, clay and glass products
History: The islands of Hawaii were settled by Polynesians from the South Pacific many centuries before Captain James Cook set foot on Oahu and Kauai in 1778, but written history begins with the arrival of Europeans.
The Hawaiians thought Cook was a reincarnation of one of their gods, Lonu, but he proved to be a harbinger of disease and death. Because they had no natural immunity to them, the white settlers' diseases decimated the native population, which shrank from nearly one million to less than 50,000 within a century.
Kamehameha I, who became ruler in 1782, unified the islands of Hawaii, having conquered all but Kauai, with whom he negotiated a peace settlement. He was keen to promote trade with Europe, a modernising theme taken up by Kamehameha II, who abolished idol worship and traditional Hawaiian religion.
In 1842, the US recognized the Kingdom of Hawaii which, in 1893, became a republic. By now, the US was seriously interested in Hawaii thanks to its sugar industry and annexed the kingdom in 1898, granting it the status of a territory in 1900, which is how it remained for nearly 60 years.
Meantime, the plantations were thriving on the backs of immigrant labour; in all, 400,000 came to work Hawaii's sugar industry. The plantation owners were happy that Hawaii remained a territory rather than a state because, if they were not American, they need not abide by American law and could continue to import cheap labour and pay it very little.
But the labour won and, in 1959, Hawaii became the 50th state of the union, a richly diverse, multicultural region with a strong, proud spirit. In 1978, for example, the Hawaii State Constitutional Convention heralded something of a Hawaiian renaissance, granting the indigenous language official status and native diacritical marks fit for official usage.

Idaho (ID)

Name: coined by mining lobbyist George M Willing, it is not a Shoshone word as legend suggests.
Nickname: Gem State.
State flower: Syringa.
State bird: Mountain bluebird.
Motto: Esto perpetua ("It is perpetual").
Population: 1,229,000.
Capital: Boise.
Physical description: Idaho is blessed with some stunning scenery, from the vast Rocky Mountain peaks – Borah Peak in the Lost River Mountains is the highest at 12,622 feet – to deep, dark waters, such as Hell's Canyon, which is deeper even than Arizona's Grand Canyon.
Mostly, Idaho is known for its mountains – it has 80 mountain ranges – and the world's most celebrated national park, Yellowstone.
The Rocky Mountain region includes the Bitterroot

Mountains, through which run the Continental Divide, and the Sawtooth Mountains, so-called because of their jagged, granite peaks, 33 of which rise above 10,000 feet.
Central Idaho is made up of flat plains that follow the path of the Snake River. This land is ideal for the cultivation of potatoes and sugar beets, two of Idaho's mainstay crops.
To the south is the Basin and Range Region, comprising mountains and deep valleys, and rolling grassy plains.
Area: 83,564 sq miles (216,430 sq km).
Climate: Idaho has a very varied climate, though its proximity to the Pacific Ocean keeps extreme temperatures in check. Nor is Idaho particularly subject to extreme weather events, like tornadoes and hurricanes.
Generally speaking, the north is cooler and wetter, with winter temperatures plunging to -15°F and annual rainfall averaging 25 inches, while the south and east are drier and hotter, summer temperatures soaring to 90°F and annual

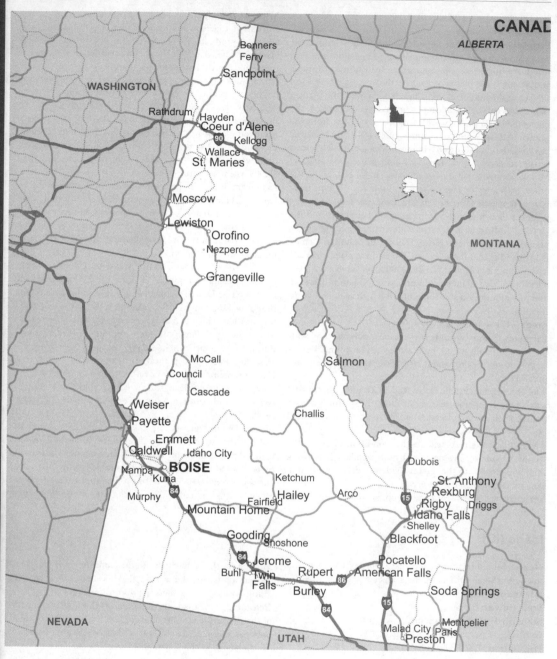

rainfall averaging only 10.5 inches.

Snow is heavy in the mountains, up to 52 inches in a year, and scarce on low ground to the south, around 10 inches per year.

Winter temperatures throughout the state stay within the range of 10-20ºF while summer temperatures are around 80-90ºF.

Agriculture: cattle, potatoes, dairy produce, wheat, sugar beets.

Minerals: silver, gold, lead, copper, tungsten, cobalt.

Industry: chemical products, food processing, silver and other mining.

History: The Shoshone were the first inhabitants of Idaho, and followed a highly efficient, ecologically sustainable way of life. But the beginning of the end for them was spelled by the arrival, in 1805, of Captains Meriwether Lewis and William Clark. Idaho was the last American state to be reached by the Europeans though, for a long time, it served as little more than a through road to Oregon, where gold rush succeeded gold rush.

Then, in 1860, Idaho had a little gold rush of its own, and its first city, Franklyn, was established. The state bloomed suddenly, as lead and silver, as well as gold mines sprang up and trade was lubricated by the arrival of the railroad. Today, these once prosperous hamlets with optimistic names like Silver City and Bonanza are ghost towns, decaying matchstick main streets crumbling alongside caved-in mine shafts and overgrown roads.

Idaho has other ghosts – those of the victims of the Bear River Massacre where, in a bid to drive out the Shoshone, Colonel Patrick Edward Connor and 200 volunteers at-

tacked their winter camp and murdered 250, including 90 women and children. The subsequent Treaty of Box Elder, signed 30 July 1863, saw the once proud natives herded into the Fort Hall Reservation.

Statehood came on 3 July 1890.

Idaho became a very important mining and farming state, and currently produces one quarter of America's potato crop. In the 1990s, its IT industry took off though latterly this has been eclipsed by the tourism industry, particularly winter tourism, which has burgeoned thanks to the development of winter sports infrastructure.

Illinois (IL)

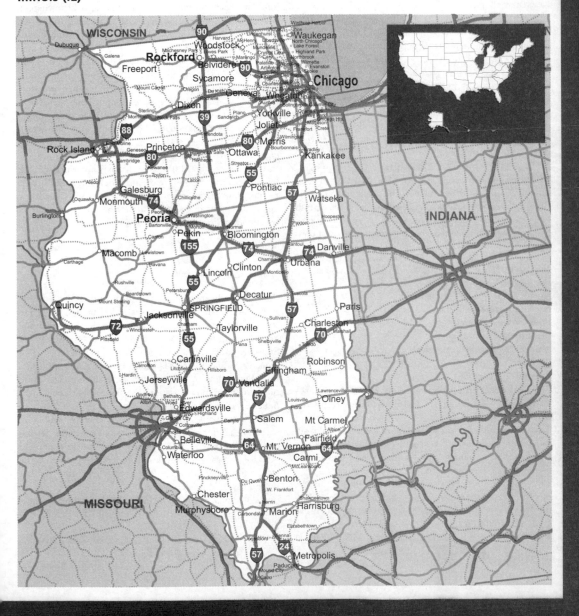

Name: named by French explorers after the indigenous Illiniwek people
Nickname: Prairie State
State flower: Native violet
State bird: Cardinal
Motto: State sovereignty – national union
Population: 12,046,000
Capital: Springfield
Physical description: Illinois, which lies within the Interior Plains, is divided into three major regions, Chicagoland, central Illinois and the south.

Chicagoland, as the name suggests, centers around Chicago and is very urban and thus densely populated and highly industrialized.

Everywhere that is not Chicagoland is referred to as Downstate Illinois.

The central region is almost all rolling prairie-land. To the west of the Illinois River is the so-called Land of Lincoln, or Heart of Illinois, a richly agricultural area with many small towns and even some major cities, including Springfield and Bloomington-Normal.

Lastly, the south is hotter and busier than elsewhere in Downstate Illinois, and includes Little Egypt, near the junction of the Mississippi and Ohio Rivers, and the great city of St Louis. More mountainous and with greater mineral deposits, this area has a mining industry and even a small-scale oil industry.

Area: 57,871 sq miles (149, 885 sq km).
Climate: Illinois covers a huge area, and thus has the widely variable climate to match. The north, in and around Chicagoland, sees heavy snowfall, influenced by lake conditions, of up to 33 inches. In the south, an annual fall of 15 inches is something to talk about. Rainfall is heaviest down south, at just over 48 inches per year, and lightest up north, at 35 inches. Temperatures also dip in the north, with lows of 10°F in the winter, while in the south, summer extremes can peak at over 100°F.

Agriculture: corn, soybeans, cattle, dairy produce, wheat.
Minerals: cement, clays, sand, gravel, stone, petroleum, coal.
Industry: machinery, food processing, electrical equipment, chemical products, publishing, fabricated metal products
History: White settlers arrived in 1673, though the first town, Cahokia, was not established for over twenty years, in 1899. The French initially claimed the region, incorporating it into French Louisiana in 1717, but the British took possession of it following the French-Indian War in 1763.

The American Revolution put paid to colonialism when, in 1778, Colonel George Rogers Clark, an Irish American, launched a surprise attack at Kaskaskia, ultimately claiming the region for the US.

Illinois finally achieved territory status in 1809, and full statehood in 1818, making it the 21st state in the union.

Though not a slave state – Illinois fought for the union during the Civil War – it did allow the importation of slaves to work the salt mines of Saline County because, quite simply, no free person would do it. This loophole led to the dreadful practice of freed slaves being captured and sold, illegally, to other states as slaves once again.

In the 19th century, Illinois' industrialization began, with the construction of the Illinois and Michigan, and Chicago Sanitary and Ship Canals.

Today, it is a bustling state, with both a strong rban character and a thriving agriculture.

Indiana (IN)

Name: means "Land of the Indians."
Nickname: Hoosier State.
State flower: Peony.
State bird: Cardinal.
Motto: Crossroads of America.
Population: 5,900,000.
Capital: Indianapolis.
Physical description: Indiana is one of the Great Lakes states, with Lake Michigan to the north, and the Ohio River to the south.

The northern part of the state is mostly agricultural land, though the northwest is urban, being part of greater Chicago whose suburbs sprawl across the Illinois state boundary as far as the shores of Lake Michigan.

The southern part of the state is also agricultural, though much of the land is also given over to forestry, including the Hoosier National Forest, a nature reserve which extends across 200,000 acres.

The south is also hillier than the north, which tends to flatness.

One of Indiana's most notable topographical features is the Wabash River, which is 475 miles long and crosses the state from northeast to southwest. Its tributary, the White River, also traverses the state and is the river on which the great cities of Indianapolis and Muncie are built.

Southern Indiana is a mixture of farmland and forest. The Hoosier National Forest is a 200,000 acre nature preserve near Bedford. Southern Indiana generally contains more hills and geographic variation than the northern portion.

Area: 36,413 sq miles (94,309 sq km).
Climate: Indiana has an invigorating climate, with cold, sometimes bitter winters and hot, humid summers. Spring can be a turbulent time, marked by thunderstorms and even tornadoes while autumn is generally regarded as the state's finest period, with glorious weather, sunny but not humid days and fresh breezes.

Average annual rainfall is 40 inches, with summer temperatures ranging between 70-80°F, and winter temperatures ranging between 25-35°F.

Agriculture: corn, soybeans, diary produce, melons, tomatoes, grapes, mint, tobacco.
Minerals: coal, clay, Portland cement, gypsum, limestone.

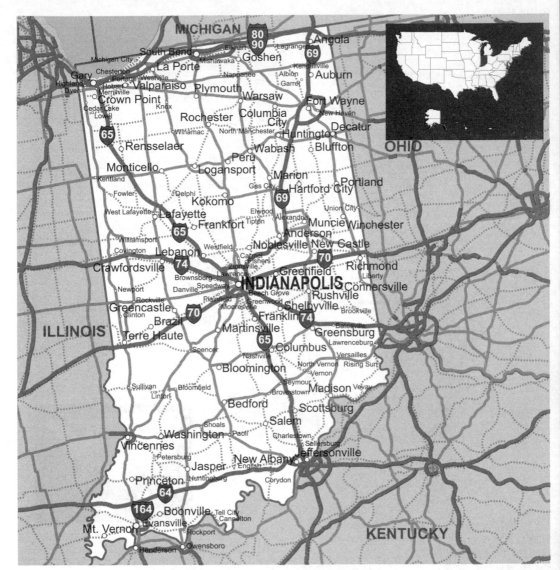

Industry: Manufacture (cars, electrical equipment, transportation equipment), chemical products, rubber, petroleum and coal products, and factory machinery.

History: The First Nation tribes which inhabited Indiana were the Miami and the Shawnee.

White settlement began when France claimed the territory during the 17th century, finally ceding it to the British at the culmination of the French and India War.

The American Revolution saw it become part of the US, specifically part of the Northwest Territory and, in 1816, Indiana became a state in its own right, the 19th in the union.

Immigration was rapid thereafter, with the population doubling between 1820 and 1830 to 343,031, as people came to work the land. But a breadbasket needs its transport links and the development of canals and railroads during the 19th century brought a degree of wealth to the region, and more and more settlers. Due to its history of religious tolerance, it also attracted Amish and Mennonite communities.

During the Civil War, Indiana provided 196,000 troops for the union army – and made a vital contribution in terms of food.

Nowadays, Indiana is probably most famous for its steel industry, though with 1.1 million acres devoted to outdoor recreation, it is also renowned for its outdoor facilities, from parks to forests, wildlife reserves to mountains, rivers to, of course, great lakes.

Mostly, however, it is a rural state, as famous for its round barns and ploughed fields as anything else.

Iowa (IA)

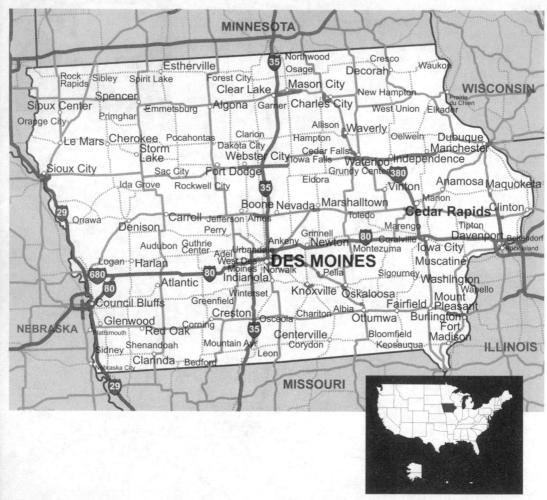

Name: believed to derive from a Native American word, meaning The Beautiful Place.

Nickname: Hawkeye State.

State flower: Wild rose.

State bird: Goldfinch.

Motto: Our liberties we prize and our rights we will maintain.

Population: 2,863,000.

Capital: Des Moines.

Physical description: Iowa is characterized by its rolling plains and generally low-lying terrain. With a mean elevation of 335 meters, don't expect sharp peaks and deep valleys.

Perhaps its most interesting topographical features are its lakes, which include Spirit Lake, at 5684 acres, Iowa's biggest natural lake, and the West and East Okoboji Lakes, all rich in wildlife and a magnet for outdoors enthusiasts.

In the northeast, along the border where it meets the Mississippi River, is to be found part of the Driftless Zone, a region of gentle, pine-forested hills. This almost Alpine terrain lends it its nickname, the "Switzerland of America." To the west, the Missouri River forms a boundary to the south of Sioux City, with the Big Sioux River, which rises in South Dakota and flows 420 miles to join the Missouri, forming the state boundary to the north.

And at the center are the Young Drift Plains, an extremely fertile region which ensures Iowa's status as America's biggest corn producer.

Area: 56,275 sq mi (145,752 sq km).

Climate: Iowa's climate ranges from extreme cold, particularly in the spring, to hot humidity, with summer temperatures rising beyond 100ºF.

Snowfall averages 36.3 inches per year, with annual rainfall ranging from 28 inches in the northwest, to 38 inches in the southeast and 32-34 inches in the central plains.

Agriculture: cattle, corn, soy beans, dairy produce

Minerals: coal, lead-zinc, gypsum, sand, gravel, stone

Industry: food processing, chemical products, publishing, primary metals, ethanol, insurance

History: Iowa was once home to at least 15 Native American tribes but today, only the Meskwaki remain. They were driven out by white settlers, who began to arrive following the "discovery: by French explorers Louis Joliet and Jacques Marquette of the state's rich, fertile lands.

Settlement officially began late, in 1833, when American families moved in from Illinois, Indiana and Missouri. Shortly afterwards, on 28 December 1846, Iowa became the 29th state of the union.

Iowa's agricultural export market began in earnest with the advent of the railroad, which linked Iowa up to the great Union Pacific Railroad, so that by the 20th century, its reputation as a beef, corn and pork state was well established. Iowa provided 75,000 troops to the Civil War, which equates to nearly 60% of all eligible males. Quite something for an agricultural state dependent on its male workforce.

The Great Depression was a time of real hardship here, and many family farms went to the wall when subsidies, established during the First World War, were withdrawn.

A farm crisis during the 1980s brought agriculture to its knees again and many small farmers sold their assets and left the state for good.

Kansas (KS)

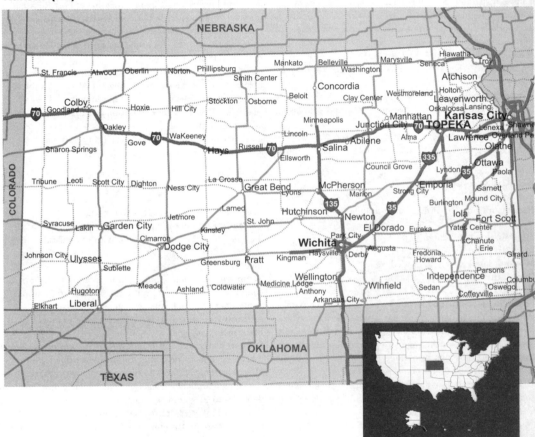

Name: after Konza or Kaw, Native Americans who lived here.

Nickname: Sunflower State.

State flower: Sunflower.

State bird: Western meadowlark.

Population: 2,629,000.

Motto: Ad astra per aspera ("To the stars through difficulties").

Capital: Topeka.

Physical description: The Wheat State is famous for its rolling, golden plains and can be divided into three regions. The Great Plains rise to an elevation of 4000 feet to the west, to form the High Plains, an area of stunning contrasts, such as the Castle and Monument Rocks rising dramatically from the plains, to the outstanding beauty of the Cimarron National Grasslands. And at the Colorado border stands Sunflower Mountain, the state's highest point, at 4039 feet.

The Southeastern Plains are a gently undulating landscape, with a wonderfully fertile soil.

And finally, a section of the Dissected Till Plain, north of the Kansas River and east of the Big Blue River, with its rich soil, sharp bluffs and deep streams and rivers.

Climate: Kansas' climate is highly variable, not just from area to area, but from hour to hour, with sunshine one minute and electrical storms the next.

The mean temperature of the state is 55°F, rising to over 100 in some areas in high summer, and plunging to -20 or even -30 in some areas in the depths of winter.

Annual rainfall ranges from 40 inches in the southeast, to 16 inches in the west, most rain falling during the hot months of summer.

Annual snowfall can be as much as 36 inches in the north, dropping to just 11 inches in the southeast.

Kansas tornadoes don't just happen in the Wizard of Oz, they are a regular occurrence with Dodge City reputedly the windiest city in the union with an average windspeed of 14 mph.

Area: 82,277 sq miles (213,096 sq km).

Agriculture: wheat, feed grains, live animals and meat, corn, soy beans

Minerals: sulfur, gypsum, barite, garnet.

Industry: car and aircraft manufacture, food processing (meat-packing), mining, machinery

History: The Spanish explorer Francisco Vasquez de Coronado came here in 1541, but in 1682, La Salle claimed the region for France.

All this notwithstanding, life went on as it had for centuries, the land settled by Native Americans with much of it roamed by great herds of buffalo.

The US bought the region as part of the Louisiana Purchase in 1803, though it was more a through-route to Utah and Oregon than a destination in itself. However, by the mid-19th century, settlers were streaming in, drawn by reports of the land's fertility.

On 29 January 1861, Kansas became the 34th state of the union.

Gas and oil fields were developed in the late 19th century, though agriculture remained a primary force in the economy. It was around this time that

Wild Bill Hickok was a deputy marshal at Fort Riley and a marshal at Hays and Abilene, and Bat Masterson and Wyatt Earp were lawmen in Dodge City, the "cowboy capital" so-called because of the thousands of head of cattle that rode through it every year.

In the 1930s, Kansas was doubly hit by the Great Depression and the cataclysmic winds that lifted the topsoil and turned it into vast blinding dust clouds. A whole season's crops were gone in hours, and the farmers stared starvation in the face.

The state later built its fortunes on its aircraft manufacture and meatpacking plants.

Kentucky (KY)

Name: an Iroquois word, meaning Land of Tomorrow

Nickname: Bluegrass State

State flower: Goldenrod

State bird: Kentucky cardinal

Motto: United we stand, divided we fall

Population: 3,937,000

Capital: Frankfort

Physical description: Kentucky is a small state with a wildly varying topography. Most famous perhaps is the Bluegrass Region, an area of flat plains and sandstone hills known collectively as the Knobs Region. These Knobs are cone-shaped hills that were once part of the Mississippi Plateau before stream erosion separated them.

To the east are mountains, including the state's highest peak, Black Mountain, at 4145 feet, and the Pine and Cumberland mountain ranges.

To the northwest is the Western Coal Field, where the state's mining industry is based, and to the south is Pennyroyal, an area of hills and plains, named after a wild-flower that grows there.

Central Pennyroyal is called The Barrens because of its arid, treeless terrain while to the north is a rocky region famous for its extensive cave systems, including the Mammoth Cave system, believed to be the most extensive in the world.

Finally, to the west are flood plains, an area that crosses the Madrid Fault zone, though the most spectacular earthquakes occurred more than 200 years ago.

Area: 40,409 sq miles (104,659 sq km).

Climate: Kentucky is a warm state, with a high rainfall.

The north is the driest region, with annual rainfall of 40 inches, while the south records an average of at least 50 inches.

Temperatures range from a summer average of 85°F to a winter average of 23°F, with the season from March to September notable for its storminess.

Agriculture: horses, cattle, tobacco, dairy produce

Minerals: coal, agate, gold, silver

Industry: transportation equipment, chemical products, machinery, food processing, tobacco products

History: Many Native American tribes roamed these plains, including Cherokee, Chickasaw and Shawnee, but none settled here to any significant degree.

Then, in 1750, the Cumberland Gap was discovered, allowing easy overland travel between Virginia and Kentucky, and settlers began to arrive from 1770 onwards, encouraged by a liberal Virginia land law (1779) allowing Kentucky lands to be bought, often at knock-down prices.

Settlers petitioned for Kentucky to be recognized as a state and, on 1 June 1792, it became the 15th state of the union.

The agricultural economy boomed, largely due to the slave labor that worked the great tobacco plantations. Wheat, livestock, hemp and horses were other agricultural mainstays.

In the 19th century, business boomed, in the form of banks, sawmills and gristmills.

These days, Kentucky is as well-known for its rural poverty as its urban fiscal health.

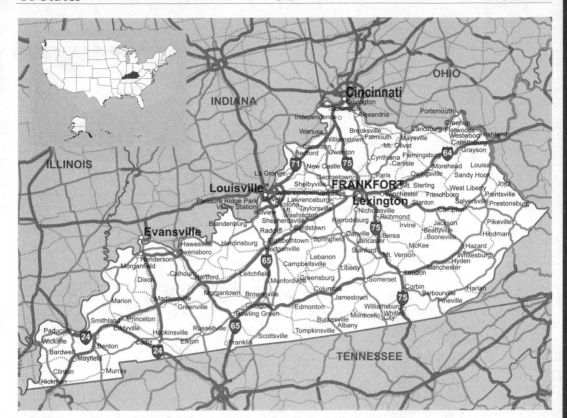

Louisiana (LA)

Name: after Louis XIV of France
Nickname: Pelican State
State flower: Magnolia
State bird: Eastern brown pelican
Motto: Union, justice, and confidence
Population: 4,369,000
Capital: Baton Rouge
Physical description: This low-lying coastal state has as its highest point Driskill Mountain, almost at the Arkansas border, which rises to 535 feet.

The Louisiana coastline is comprised of marshlands which account for one quarter of America's total wetlands and is one of the world's largest, most biologically diverse estuaries, supporting major populations of sea fish, oysters, crabs and waterfowl.

One of the world's greatest rivers, the 3705 km-long Mississippi, which rises in the Minnesota North Woods, ends here in the 13,000 square mile Mississippi Delta, an incredibly fertile region and the key to Louisiana's agricultural success.

Inland are the Louisiana Prairies which rise gradually to the west towards Arkansas.

Area: 47,752 sq miles 123,677sq km.

Climate: a semitropical state, the rule of thumb is that, the nearer you are to the Gulf of Mexico, the hotter and more humid it is. In summer, temperatures average 80ºF, and in

winter they center around the 50ºF mark.

Rainfall averages 64 inches per year across the state.

The summer and autumn are turbulent periods in terms of weather, the seasons of hurricanes and wild, tropical storms.

Louisiana's most famous, and devastating hurricanes include Betsy, in 1965, which led to 58 deaths, and Katrina, in 2005, which virtually destroyed New Orleans and killed over 1000 people.

Agriculture: sweet potatoes, rice, sugar cane, pecans, corn, cotton

Minerals: coal, oil, sulfur

Industry: natural gas, oil refining, petrochemicals, salt, coal, lumber

History: Louisiana was claimed for Spain in 1541 by Hernando de Soto and claimed again, this time for France, by La Salle a few years later, then for Britain, then Florida. White settlement began in 1715 in the Mississippi valley, a richly fertile area, and New Orleans was founded in 1718.

America was desperate to own Louisiana because it controlled the mouth of the Mississippi, a key trading point, and finally acquired it from Napoleon in the 1803 Louisiana Purchase.

On 30 April 1812, Louisiana became the 18th state of the union and became rich through world trade in indigo, sugar and cotton. Its plantations were particularly prof-

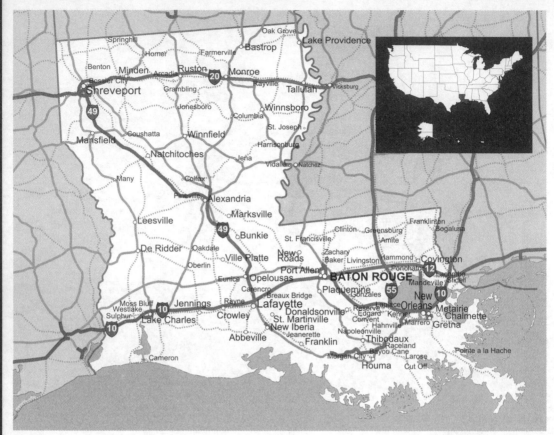

itable and made their owners incredibly rich, but this system, built on the back of slavery, was destroyed by the Civil War.

During the period of Reconstruction, Louisiana's agricultural output slumped. In time, however, it became a major exporter of farmed produce once again.

The discovery of natural gas, oil and sulfur in the late 19th century boosted the economy even further and today, it is a center for oil refining and petrochemical manufacture.

However, as the aftermath of Hurricane Katrina made clear, this rich state still has a wretchedly poor underbelly and, over a century on from emancipation, it is a predominantly black one.

Maine (ME)

Name: origin unknown, though some speculate that it refers to the mainland.

Nickname: Pine Tree State.

State flower: White Pine cone and tassel.

State bird: Chickadee.

Motto: Dirigo ("I direct").

Population: 1,245,000.

Capital: Augusta.

Physical description: Maine is the largest New England state, is mostly forested (90%) and forms part of the American Atlantic coastline.

This coastal region is comprised of flat, sandy beaches become smaller beaches to the north, divided by sheer cliffs and narrow inlets.

There are around 400 islands off the coast, the best known being Mount Desert, which forms the base of Cadillac Mountain, rising 1530 feet above sea level.

Inland are salt marshes and tidal rivers while the central region includes part of the New England Uplands, which run from Canada down to Connecticut, taking in the Aroostook Plateau and the Longfellow Mountains.

In the northwest are found the White Mountains, including Mount Katahdin, the state's highest point at 5267 feet, situated at the end of the Appalachian Trail.

Area: 33,265 sq miles (86,156 sq km).

Climate: Maine's climate is very changeable, though in general summers are cool, even chilly at night, with average temperatures of 70°F, while winters are long and snowy, with temperatures dipping as low as 5°F and an average annual snowfall of 78 inches across the state.

Coastal regions are generally warmer and wetter while the north is cooler and drier.

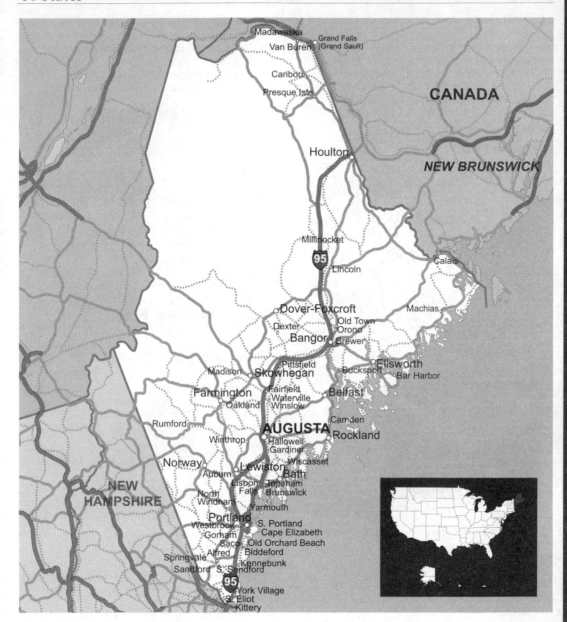

Agriculture: seafood, dairy produce, potatoes, blueberries, apples.

Minerals: tourmaline, gold, rose quartz, uranium

Industry: paper, lumber and wood products, food processing, tourism, hydro electricity.

History: Many Native American tribes lived here, notably the bellicose Micmacs in the east, and the more peaceful and populous Abnakis. Today only the Passamaquoddies, with a population of 1500, and the Penobscots, with a population of 1200, remain in any significant numbers.

The first white settlement was in 1607 at Popham, established by the Plymouth Company, though it did not last long, allegedly beaten back by the harsh Maine winter.

The 18th century was marked by strife over ownership of the region, as the Spanish, French and British tussled over it, and the Native Americans resisted the rising tide of land-grabbing incomers.

Maine fought the British during the American Revolution and this fight exerted a dreadful toll; 1000 dead and the seaport and civil infrastructure all but razed to the ground. The state was left in terrible debt.

On 15 March 1820, Maine became the 23rd state of the union as part of the Missouri Compromise, which decreed that one state (Missouri) would be a slave state while

Maine was a free state, thus maintaining the balance of the union.

Interestingly, Maine was the birthplace of Harriet Beecher Stowe, author of Uncle Tom's Cabin, one of the definitive and, in its time, controversial anti-slavery novels.

Industry took off after the Civil War in areas such as ship-building, mining and ice harvesting.

In time, small-scale farming gave way to mass production of potatoes and dairy produce, and industries such as textiles and leather to hydroelectricity, pulp and paper production and tourism.

Today, Maine strives to create a balance between its often polluting industries and environmental responsibility.

Maryland (MD)

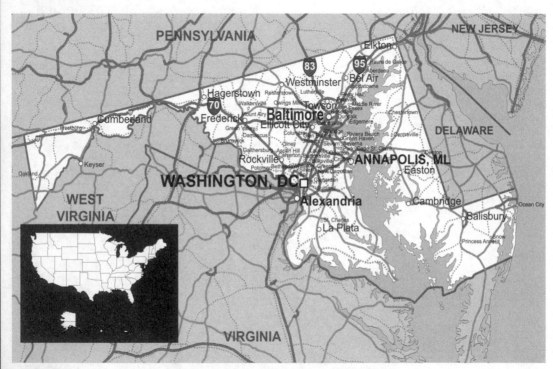

Name: **Name**d after King Charles I of England's wife, Henrietta Maria

Nickname: Old line state; Free State

State flower: Black-eyed Susan

State bird: Baltimore oriole

Motto: Fatti maschii, parole femine ("Manly deeds, womanly words")

Population: 5,135,000

Capital: Annapolis

Physical description: Maryland is a richly fertile, beautiful region of mountains, grassy plains and lush valleys, and is divided in two by the mighty Chesapeake Bay.

To the warm country of the east is the Delmarva (Delaware, Maryland, Virginia) Peninsula, a marshy land including the Great Pocomoke, or Cypress, Swamp. This freshwater marsh, comprising 50 square miles, was once a major source of cypress wood but over-logging has stripped it of much of its natural resources and a devastating fire in the 1930s depleted it still further.

The Monocacy River flows here, the largest tributary into the Potomac River, which broadens to 11 miles as it enters Chesapeake Bay.

Early Maryland settlers enjoyed the Potomac's bountiful supply of crabs, oysters and fish and, while environmental pollution is starting to reduce stocks, it remains a rich source of wildlife to this day.

On the cooler West Shore are found a section of the Blue Ridge Mountains, which run from south Pennsylvania to northern Georgia and include South Mountain, a spectacular quartzite peak. Here too are 41 miles of the interstate footpath that is the Appalachian Trail.

Also to the west is the densely forested Appalachian Plateau, including Backbone Mountain, the highest point in Maryland at 3360 feet.

Area: 10,460 sq miles (27,091sq km).

Climate: For such a small state, the climate is very variable. Temperatures vary quite widely from the cool mountains, with their almost Canadian climate, and the subtropical shoreline to the east.

The weather in the east is influenced by the proximity of

the Atlantic, giving it long, hot summers and short winters. Temperatures climb as high as 90ºF and beyond.

In the western mountains, winters are truly cold, with temperatures below freezing and up to 100 inches of snow annually. Quite a contrast to the 8-10 inches seen in the south east.

Summer is the hottest and also the wettest month, and towards August become intensely humid, with frequent thunderstorms. January is the coldest time of year, with average temperatures of 20ºF.

Agriculture: chickens, dairy produce, soy beans

Minerals: stone, coal, sand, gravel, cement clay

Industry: foodstuffs, IT, primary metals, chemicals.

History: Maryland Day marks the anniversary of the arrival, on 25 March 1634, of the state's first white settlers, led by Leonard Calvert, from the Isle of Wight.

Initially, it served as a refuge for English Roman Catholics who were persecuted at home, though it did not always prove to be the most peaceful of sanctuaries when Puritan rebels briefly overturned the government and imposed their religion.

However, in 1649, the Maryland Toleration Act was passed, permitting freedom of worship, Christian worship that is. This act is believed to be the inspiration for the First Amendment.

The Mason and Dixie Line was drawn up in the 1760s, following a dispute between the Calvert family, who ran Maryland, and the Penn family, who ran Pennsylvania. The Mason and Dixie established the boundary between the two states and came to be seen as the divide between the North and the South.

In 1788, Maryland became one of the 13 original states that formed the union.

The British attack on Baltimore in 1814 was one of the most dramatic events of the American Revolution, the assault on Fort McHenry inspiring Francis Scott Key to pen The Star Spangled Banner.

But it was the Civil War that tore Maryland apart. A slave state, it had 87,000 slaves in 1860, mostly working the vast tobacco plantations. But it also had industrialists and businessmen who felt a strong allegiance to the North and refused to vote for secession. In the end, Maryland was occupied by union forces, and Maryland families were split, some fighting for the Confederates, some for the union.

Industrialization, which had begun with the construction of the National Road and the Chesapeake and Delaware Canal, accelerated as railroads arrived. The state became a north/south crossing point, and during the two World Wars, an important center for shipbuilding and aircraft construction.

Massachusetts (MA)

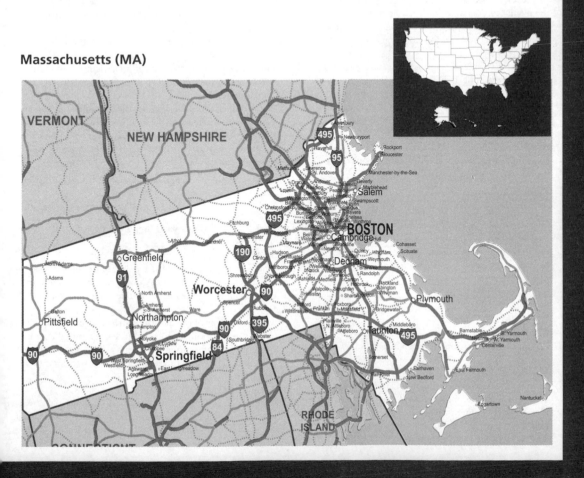

Name: from the Native American tribe the Massachusett, meaning "at or about the great hill."

Nickname: Bay State; Colony State.

State flower: Mayflower.

State bird: Chickadee.

Motto: Ense petit placidam sub libertate ("By the sword we seek peace, but peace only").

Population: 6,148,000.

Capital: Boston.

Physical description: A small state with a jagged coastline that hooks around Cape Cod, Massachusetts' landscape varies in slices as you work your way inland.

The coastal regions include Martha's Vineyard and Nantucket, both very much summer holiday islands for the wealthy, with their white sands, surf and private beaches.

Inland are the Eastern New England Uplands, which rise to 1000 feet to meet the narrow strip that is the Connecticut Valley Lowland. Only 20 miles wide, this Lowland is ideal farming country.

Next are the Western New England Uplands, which rise to 2000 feet and are part of the Green Mountains of Vermont and include Mount Greylock, at 3487 feet, the highest point in Massachusetts.

The Berkshire Hills and Valley are next, rising up to the Taconic Mountains. **Name**d by the then state geologist Ebenezer Emmons in 1844 to describe their formation – the result of underwater rocks being thrust together by the collision of the North American continent with a volcanic island arc – the Taconics form the boundary with New York.

Area: 8,284 sq mi (21,455 sq km).

Climate: As a rule of thumb, the further west you go, the colder it gets. The Berkshires are the coldest, with cool summers and truly bitter winters. The interior is significantly warmer, with temperatures up a few degrees, while the coast is warmest of all, with a subtropical climate tempered by Atlantic winds.

Summer temperatures rise above the mid-70s°F at the coast, but rarely breach 70°F in the far west.

Rainfall averages at 39-45 inches across the state, with a similar annual snowfall of 42 inches on average.

The greatest season to see Massachusetts is undoubtedly the autumn when the bright, almost Canadian cool weather turns the hardwood leaves vivid shades of red through gold and yellow.

Agriculture: seafood, dairy produce, cranberries, vegetables

Minerals: clay, lime, marble, silica, sand and gravel, quartz

Industry: machinery, electrical equipment, paper and publishing, tourism.

History: The first white colonists were Puritans from England seeking a place to worship unmolested. Settlers arrived in small groups and then, in 1630, John Winthrop arrived in Salem, at the head of a large group, brandishing the charter allowing Massachusetts the status of a colony.

By 1640, an incredible 16,000 people had settled here from Europe.

Puritan political organization, a highly democratic affair of allowing every tax -payer to vote in town elections and have equal say in decision-making, set the template for American democracy.

Massachusetts developed as an international trading point, Boston being known as the "Mart(market) of the West Indies". And it was this enviable position that sparked the first bloodshed of the American Revolution, when Bostonians rebelled against British rule in what became known as the Boston Tea Party of 1733.

In 1788, Massachusetts became one of the original 13 colonies to ratify the Constitution.

The 19th century saw a move from agriculture to industry as the Erie Canal, opened in 1825, brought cheaper produce from the breadbasket of the west.

Massachusetts excelled in textiles, woolen goods and leather tanning. Industrialization brought waves of immigrants to Massachusetts and, by 1930, over 65% of its population was foreign-born, making it the fascinating, multicultural state it is today.

Michigan (MI)

Name: from Chippewa word Michigana, meaning "great lake."

Nicknames: Great Lake State; Wolverine State.

Motto: Si quaeris peninsulam amoenam ("If you seek a pleasant peninsula, look about you").

State flower: Apple Blossom.

State bird: Robin.

Population: 9,818,000.

Capital: Lansing

Physical description: Michigan has 11,000 lakes, and touches on four of the five Great Lakes: Superior, Michigan, Huron and Erie. Thus it has 3288 miles of shoreline, the longest in the union after Alaska.

Michigan is divided into two land masses, the Great Lake Plains and the Superior Upland, connected only by the five mile stretch of the Mackinac Bridge.

The Great Lake Plain's lower peninsula is a low-lying flat land bordered the Lakes, though it rises to hills in the north and south.

The upper peninsula is partly swamp area.

The Superior Upland to the north is more rugged, leading ultimately to the Porcupine Mountains in the far northwest. Mount Arvon is here, the state's highest peak at 1979 feet.

Michigan is one of the most industrialized states and some of its most striking natural features, notably the Lakes, have been compromised by chemical and manufacturing pollution, though there are many agencies seeking to address this problem.

Area: 97,102 sq mi (251,493 sq km).

Climate: Michigan has well-defined seasons – cold winters, with temperatures plunging below freezing and lots of snow, and hot, muggy summers, temperatures soaring above 70°F.

Rainfall is an annual average of 32.9 inches while snow is heaviest in the regions of the Great Lakes, where cold air blows across the warmer waters, creating annual snowfall up to 183 inches in some places.

The lakes also cause heavy cloud cover. Detroit has only 49% days of sunshine, and overall humidity is an annual average of 81%.

Early summer is a time of frequent tornadoes.

Agriculture: corn, soy beans, wheat

Minerals: sand, gravel, limestone, iron ore, marble

Industry: car manufacture, timber, fishing

History: The French were exploring the Great Lakes region since the early 17th century, where they established a fur trade and tried to convert the Native American tribes to Christianity, with mixed results.

Settlements began to pop up in the late 17th/early 18th century. In 1701, Antoine de la Mothe Cadillac, a French Army officer, established the settlement of Fort Pontchartrain, on the site of modern-day Detroit. His wife, Marie-Therese, was the first white woman to live in this wild territory.

The British seized control in 1760 and a period of intense resistance by the native Ottawa nation, led by Pontiac, ensued. At one stage, Detroit was the only British stronghold that had not fallen, west of Niagara.

Michigan was such a lucrative place that the British held fast to it and the 1812 war brought a lot of bloodshed to the region.

However, by the 1820s, the economy was in recovery and in 1837, Michigan became the 26th state of the union.

Very much an anti-slavery society, Michigan fostered underground networks that assisted escaping slaves from the south. In 1854, such was the opposition to slavery, that the Republican Party was formed, largely to promote personal freedom laws.

Michigan fought fiercely for the union during the Civil War, prompting Lincoln to say: "Thank God for Michigan."

During the 19th century, the logging and furniture industries took off, but were eclipsed in the 20th by the car industry, for which Detroit will always be world-famous.

Minnesota (MN)

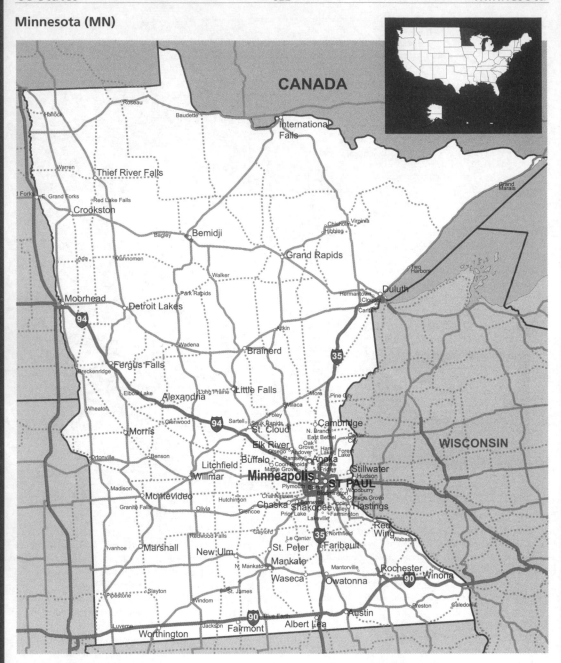

Name: from Dakota word, meaning "cloudy water"
Nicknames: North Star State; Gopher State
State flower: Pink and white lady's slipper
State bird: Common loon
Motto: L'Étoile du nord ("Star of the North")
Population: 4,726,000
Capital: St Paul
Physical description: Bordering Canada to the north, Minnesota's northern reaches have a similar topography – high rocky mountains and deep lakes, formed by thousands

of years of glacier activity, surrounded by wilderness and great forests.

Eagle Mountain, a stunning peak set amidst a vast swathe of unspoilt terrain, fast flowing rivers and deep, dark forests, with a rich wildlife, including wolves, bears and moose, is Minnesota's highest point, at 2301 feet.

To the south is a gentler, more rolling landscape, with excellent farmland, said to be the most fertile region in the US.

Flatter lands are to be found in the southeast, where it

touches on the Mississippi River, a tributary of which is the 320 mile long Minnesota River.

Area: 86,614 sq miles (224,329 sq km).

Climate: Located in the geographical center of America, Minnesota is as given to droughts and floods, tornadoes and snow blizzards, as it is to temperate weather.

Rainfall averages 18 inches in the north, 32 inches in the south. The proximity of the Gulf of Mexico makes the latter wetter, particularly during summer.

Snowfalls are heavy around Lake Superior, up to 70 inches a year, due to cold winds crossing the warmer lake waters. Expect winter blizzards roughly twice a year. To the south, snowfall is less than 40 inches annually.

Temperatures range from below freezing to well below freezing in January to 70-100ºF in summer, depending on how far south/north you are.

An average of 18 tornadoes occur every year in the south.

Agriculture: corn, soy beans, sugar beets, wheat, dairy produce

Minerals: copper, iron ore, calcite, agate

Industry: paper and pulp, mining ore, lumber

History: Originally the homeland of Dakota and Ojibwe (including Chippewa) nations, Minnesota was settled by Europeans drawn by the promise of a slice of the fur trade. As such, Minnesota is a striking example of how greed kills the goose that lays the golden eggs. Settlers, initially French, later displaced by the British, then by the Americans, trapped, poisoned, snared and speared their way through entire populations of beaver, muskrat, otter and mink. They even drained ponds and dismantled lodges, such was their hunger for fur, which was then shipped dangerously down the Lawrence and Ottawa Rivers and across Lakes Superior and Huron, in canoes to Hudson Bay and Montreal, to be shipped to Europe.

By the 1820s, the fur supply was exhausted and the American Fur Company bankrupt. Only strict laws and careful management allowed the animal population to recover, and over many decades.

Similarly, the rich land, which bore wheat like gold, was crudely carved up into saleable lots by incomers with no respect for the ancient ways of life that preceded them. Woods were cut down to clear the way for farms, and mass immigration ratcheted up the need for yet more land, and more cutting down.

It is incredible that so much wilderness survives, though this may be solely down to its rugged inaccessibility.

Agriculture is still important here, as is the state's greatest asset – its ravishing beauty.

On 11 May 1858, Minnesota became the 32nd state of the US.

Mississippi (MS)

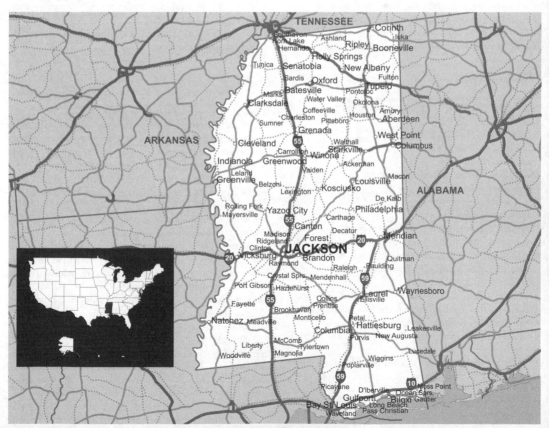

Name: Chippiwa word, meaning "father of waters."
Nickname: Magnolia State.
State flower: Magnolia.
State bird: Mockingbird.
Population: 2,752,000.
Motto: Virtute et armis ("By valor and arms").
Capital: Jackson.
Physical description: This low-lying region has, as its highest point, Woodall Mountain which, at 806 feet, hardly deserves to be called a mountain at all.

The focal point of this state is the Mississippi Delta, an alluvial plain nestling between the Yazoo and Mississippi Rivers, with a dense and diverse population of marine and bird life.

To the northeast, Mississippi is a hilly landscape leading to prairie and flatlands.

The south is predominantly covered in piney forests, comprising longleaf yellow pine.

Area: 47,689 sq mi (123,514 sq km).
Climate: Mississippi's is a subtropical climate, given to long, hot summers, cool, but rarely cold, winters and rainfall throughout the year. Which is not to say that the climate is not given to quite violent extremes. Floods are as common as droughts, while violent thunderstorms occur some 60 days a year, and tornadoes are frequent, and highly dangerous, in the spring.

The summers are very hot due to prevailing southwesterly winds, with temperatures frequently peaking above 100°F. By contrast, winter temperatures only dip below freezing about once every five years on average.

Rainfall averages 50 inches a year across the state.

Missouri (MO)

Name: Missouri word meaning, "town or river of the large canoes."
Nickname: Show-Me-State.
State flower: Hawthorn.
State bird: Bluebird.
Motto: Salus popull suprema lex esto ("The welfare of the people shall be the supreme law").
Population: 5,439,000.
Capital: Jefferson City.
Physical description: Rich farmland abounds in Missouri, a state of the American midwest, from the high tableland in the southwest where delicious strawberries are cultivated, to the irrigated plains of the north, ideal for corn growing.

The Mississippi alluvial plain covers much of southern Missouri, where drained swampland has been turned over to the farming of cotton, soy beans and rice.

Grains are grown in the Osage Plains, the rolling prairies to the west.

The state's highest point is Taum Sauk Mountain, in the igneous St Francois Mountains in the southeast, at 1772 feet.

Finally, the Ozark Plateau in the south is a heavily forested region of mountains, sinkholes, caves and clear lakes.

Agriculture: cotton, rice, soy beans, aquaculture
Minerals: petroleum, natural gas
Industry: chemicals, plastics, foodstuffs, fish and seafood processing, wood products
History: Chickasaw lived here in the northeast, Chocktaw in the central region and Natchez in the southwest, long before the Spanish explorer Hernando de Soto "discovered" the Mississippi River in 1540.

The French settled first, establishing themselves at a site near modern day Ocean Springs in 1699, before the British took over in 1763, following the French and Indian war.

The US did not annex the region until 1810, as part of West Florida.

Mississippi was one of the slave states, and is most famous for its vast plantations and the opulent lifestyles of the plantation owners. And, of course, the wretched lives of the slaves who made them rich.

The Civil War ended that era and brought Mississippi's economy to its knees. By 1865, it was facing ruin and its white minority was struggling with the concept of emancipation. In the end, they refused to accept it and the segregation laws were the result. This was not remedied till the 1960s when the Civil Rights movement forced the Mississippi legislature to modernize.

Economically, Mississippi remained dependent on agriculture until relatively recently, moving into lumber only in the 20th century.

In the 1980s, it developed industries in furniture-making, catfish culture, and casinos.

Once a rich state, modern Mississippi has the lowest per capita income in the US.

Area: 69,697 sq mi (180,415 sq km).
Climate: Missouri has a continental climate with many local variations, including a 10 degree F differential between north and south. In summer, temperatures rise to the high 70°F, and in winter dip well below freezing.

Rain is heaviest in the southeast, where it averages at 48 inches a year, and lightest in the northwest, where it averages 35 inches a year.

Snowfall again is variable, up to 20 inches in the north, 10 inches in the south.

Extremes of heat are not unknown. In 1980, during a heatwave, 311 people died in Missouri, more than anywhere else in the US. In 1983, another heatwave claimed 51 lives. In spring, tornadoes can occur.

Agriculture: beef, soy beans, pork, dairy, hay, corn
Minerals: lead, coal, limestone, Portland cement
Industry: aerospace, transportation equipment, food processing, chemicals, wine
History: Native nations to Missouri include, of course, the Missouri but also Osages, Sacs, Foxes, Otos, Iowas, Miamis, Delawares and Shawnees. None of these tribes exist in any significant numbers in modern Missouri.

French settlers came in 1682, followed by the Spanish in 1762, though the region was finally ceded to the US in

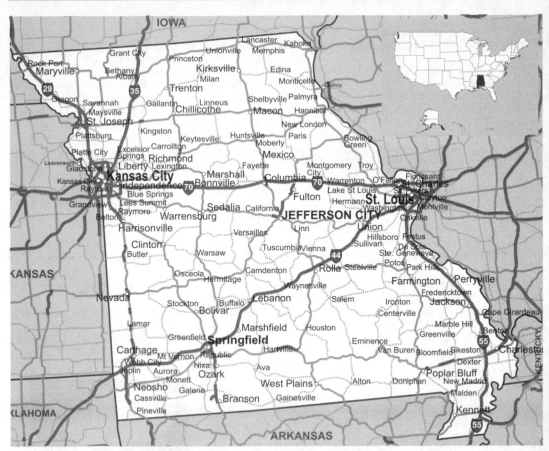

Lead ore, Galena, was discovered as early as 1701 and aided Missouri's development. A mining industry was on its feet within 20 years, encouraging settlement and infrastructure. Fur was another major draw, upon which the city of St Louis was founded, economically speaking. The Missouri and Mississippi rivers facilitated the trade. Missouri became the 24th state of the union on August 10 1821, following the Missouri Compromise, which allowed Missouri to remain a slave state and Maine to remain a free state, thus maintaining the slave/free balance of the united states.

Despite being a slave state, Missouri fought on the side of the union during the Civil War, providing 109,000 troops. However, the state legislature did try to make it otherwise and pledged support for the south – without the support of its citizens. They were forced to flee.

One of the most famous battles of the Civil War, the Battle of Wilson's Creek, was fought in Missouri.

Today, Missouri is a highly modernized economy with a fledgling wine industry and strong tourism.

Montana (MT)

Name: From the Spanish, meaning mountain.
Nickname: Treasure State.
State flower: Bitterroot.
State bird: Western meadowlark.
Motto: Oro y plata ("Gold and silver").
Population: 881,000.
Capital: Helena.
Physical description: Montana is America's fourth largest state, and half of it has an elevation in excess of 4000 feet.

And it certainly deserves its name, being home to 50 rocky mountain ranges, including the Bitterroot, Cabinet, Flathead, Beartooth and Beaverhead mountains. These rocky mountains, similar in geological formation to their Canadian counterparts across the border to the north, reside on an earthquake zone and are dissected by the Continental Divide, to the east of which, all rivers flow towards the Atlantic and to the west of which, all waters flow to the Pacific.

The highest point is Granite Peak, at 12,799 feet.

To the south are plains, part of the Interior Plain of North America, which extends from Canada to Mexico. These plains are cut through by rivers and valleys and punctuated by isolated groups of hills, such as the Bear Paws and the

Little Rockies.

Area: 147,046 sq miles (380,847sq km).

Climate: Winter is characterized by cold waves and chi-nooks.

Cold waves combine freezing temperatures with strong winds bearing snow and can be treacherous. Chinooks provide welcome relief, being warm winds caused by cold air descending rapidly from the mountains and thus generating heat.

Lakes freeze over during a Montana winter, and snowfall can reach an annual total of as much as 300 inches in some places, though snowfall in the more temperate east is more akin to 20 inches.

Summers are hot, particularly in the east, and can have temperatures exceeding 100°F, but they are never oppressive as the nights are always cool.

Rain is heavier in the mountains, with annual averages of 34.7 inches, the wettest season being early summer. Rainfall in drier areas, by contrast, may be as little as 6.5 inches.

Another feature of Montana weather are hail storms which can be very violent and destructive, causing annual damages of around $5 million.

Agriculture: cattle, wheat, barley, sugar beets, hay

Industry: mining, metal refining, oil and timber

History: The Cheyenne and Blackfoot lived here before white settlers began arriving in the 18th and 19th centuries.

Explorers Lewis and Clark ventured into Montana in 1804, followed by the fur trappers from Canada and the US, including the so-called Mountain Men, who came to trap beaver in the often hazardous mountain streams. The American Fur Company came to dominate the industry here, until it collapsed as fashions in Europe changed and animal populations were hunted into near-extinction.

Cattle and sheep ranching expanded as land was appropriated from the Native Americans, who put up a fierce resistance, culminating in the most famous victory of them all, at the Battle of Little Bighorn. Here, in 1876, Lieutenant Colonel Custer and 255 soldiers were killed by the Sioux and Cheyenne, led by Crazy Horse and Sitting Bull.

In the end, however, through sheer weight of numbers, the Native Americans were defeated.

Mining began in earnest in the late 19th century, following the discovery of first silver (1875), then copper (1880) at Butte, the "richest hill on earth."

By the 1980s, however, the copper and silver mining industry had all but gone.

Today, Montana has a thriving coal industry and boasts some magnificent national parkland, including parts of Waterton, which extends into Canada, and Yellowstone, America's first national park.

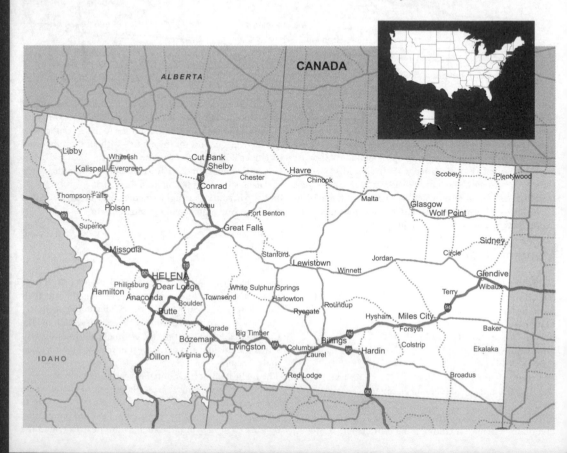

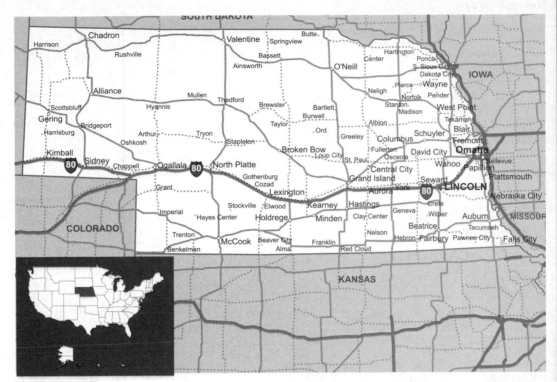

Nebraska (NE)

Name: Oto word meaning "flat water" in reference to Platte River.

Nickname: Cornhusker State.

State flower: Goldenrod.

State bird: Western Meadowlark.

Motto: Equality before the law.

Population: 1,663,000.

Capital: Lincoln.

Physical description: Nebraska has two regions, the Dissected Till Plains to the east and the Great Plains to the west. The Dissected Till Plains, the result of glacier activity over several millennia, is a gently undulating country, mostly turned over to farming. The Great Plains include prairie, high tableland and semi-arid plain, the forested hills of the Pine Ridge and the 7000 square mile farmland region of the Loess Plains, also known as the Rainwater Basin. Central Nebraska has the largest area – 20,000 sq mi – of sand dunes in America. The area is known as the Sand Hills. And tucked away in the northwest corner are the Badlands with their eerie yet beautiful sandstone and clay wind sculptures. These vertiginous rocks and toadstool-shaped pedestals are natural formations, created by wind and water, and are quite breathtaking to behold.

Area: 77,355 sq mi (200,349 sq km).

Climate: An arid-looking country, it has an arid climate – at least in the west. The east, however, though given to hot summers, has a generous annual rainfall of 31 inches. Winters can be harsh here, though the chinook winds, caused by rapidly descending air from the mountains, softens the blow.

Snowfall is an average of 25-35 inches a year. Tornadoes occur often in the spring and powerful thunderstorms characterize the hotter, more humid portion of summer.

Agriculture: cattle, corn, wheat, sorghum

Minerals: petroleum, sand, gravel, clay, natural gas

Industry: food processing, machinery, electrical equipment, printing and publishing

History: The first Europeans to visit Nebraska called it the Great Desert, owing to its flat, arid-looking terrain. But Native American nations had been cultivating the land for years, growing sunflowers and corn, and hunting roaming herds of buffalo.

Omaha, Ponca, Pawnee and Oto were amongst the tribes that lived in settlements, while the Sioux, Cheyenne and Arapaho were more nomadic, following the buffalo. Before white settlement, Nebraska had a population of over 40,000. Fur trappers were the first non-native settlers, establishing trading posts as they went, though the Platte Valley led to Nebraska becoming a through-route to Oregon and California.

In 1854, Nebraska became a territory, and the Homestead Act of 1862 finally brought mass settlement with the promise of 160 acres of free land in the east.

The unpromising looking land proved to be hugely rewarding, and the region's fortunes progressed steadily, only curbed by farming slumps in the 1890s, 1920s and 1930s. Nebraska became the 37th state of the union on 1 March 1867, the same year the Union Pacific railroad came.

Nevada (NV)

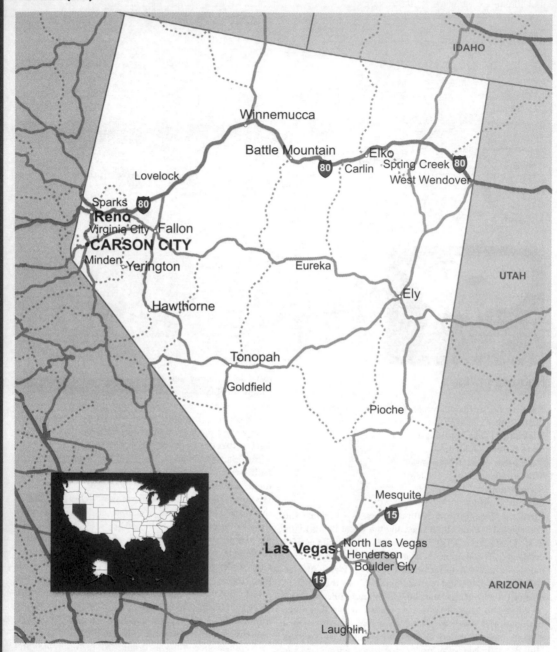

Name: from the Spanish, meaning "snow-capped"
Nickname: Sagebrush State; Battle-Born State
State flower: Sagebrush
State bird: Mountain Bluebird
Motto: All for our country
Population: 1,745,000
Capital: Carson City
Physical description: This once volcanic region lies

within the Great Basin of the Basin and Range region of America.

It is the driest state of all, its landscape typified by arid terrain with sparse vegetation – such as sagebrush and creosote – and rugged mountain ranges.

These ranges include the mighty Sierra Nevada to the north, with Boundary Peak the state's highest point at 13,140 feet. In the center of Nevada are found the Toiyabe and Toquima mountains, with the Snake and Toana ranges to the east. Also seen are small, lone hills and mesas, distinctive, flat-topped mountains.

The Columbia Plateau forms the border region to the south, and is a landscape of deep canyons finally giving way to open prairie.

The Mojave Desert is to the south.

None of Nevada's rivers reach the sea, disappearing instead into shallow drainage basins known as alkali sinks, unless artificially diverted for irrigation purposes. Hot springs and geysers pay testament to a volcanic past.

Area: 110,561 sq miles (286,352 sq km).

Climate: This semi-arid state experiences extremely cold winters, with temperatures below freezing, and oppressively hot summers, where temperatures climb to 100°F and beyond. The highest temperature ever recorded was at Laughlin on 29 June 1994, when it rose to 125°F.

Rainfall is sparse, with annual averages of 7.5 inches.

Snow is more abundant, though only in the mountains, with yearly averages of 60 inches in some places.

Nevada has very little humidity, and enjoys over 300 days of sunshine a year.

Agriculture: cattle, hay, potatoes, onions

Minerals: gold, silver, mercury, petroleum, diatomite

Industry: IT, gaming machines, aerospace equipment, seismic monitoring equipment, warehousing, trucking, tourism

History: Native American tribes in this region included the Paiute, Shoshone and Washoe and they had the place to themselves right up into the 19th century, when the first European settlers, fur traders, began moving in.

The US acquired Nevada after the 1846-48 Mexican War, and it served initially as little more than a wagon-trail to California's gold fields, in 1849.

Las Vegas, on the Old Spanish Trail, became a significant stopping-off point at this time.

In 1859, gold was struck in Nevada, followed by silver at Comstock Lode, the richest silver seam in the US, sparking a frenzy of activity as speculators rushed in and a local economy sprang up around them. Mad riches ensued but the bubble had burst by 1898, the mines exhausted and silver's value plummeted through demonetization.

Nevada became a territory in 1861, and a state in 1864, when President Lincoln needed the extra vote to push through the Thirteenth Amendment.

In the 20th century, Nevada has been at the cutting edge of technology, with one of the world's largest dams, the Hoover Dam, constructed in 1936, and the Nevada desert the scene of controversial nuclear testing in the 1950s.

Today, it has a thriving IT and tourism industry and its population has soared a spectacular 1200% between 1950 and 2000, making it the fastest-growing state in America.

New Hampshire (NH)

Name: named after English county of Hampshire.
Nickname: Granite State.
State flower: Purple lilac.
State bird: Purple finch.
Motto: Live free or die.
Population: 1,185,000.
Capital: Concord.
Physical description: This small, mountainous state has long been beloved of artists and writers for its stunning beauty. The White Mountain ranges, part of the Appalachian chain, dominate much of the north and central region, their progress interrupted by passes, called notches, which have been worn through by thousands of years of glacier activity. The state is also known for its incredible water features, including the clear blue waters of Profile Lake, overlooked by the Old Man of the Mountain, an almost human-like edifice of red granite layers, and the Flume, which pours down an 800 foot chasm. The state's highest point is Mount Washington, at 6288 feet, which is part of the Presidential Range of White Mountains. While the northern landscape is characterized by rocky peaks, forests, lakes and streams, this gives way, moving westward, to the pastoral, fertile lands of the Connecticut River Valley, known as Coos Country. The shoreline on the Atlantic, at 13 miles, is the shortest state shoreline in the union, with sandy beaches and, extending inland, wetlands.

Area: 9,279 sq mi (24,032 sq km).

Climate: Temperatures vary throughout New Hampshire, and from day to day, throughout the seasons.

Summers tend to be short and quite brisk, with temperatures rarely rising beyond 70°F, while winters are long and cold, with temperatures in the 20°F range. High winds are common in the mountains, particularly through the passes. Indeed, the highest wind ever recorded – not including tornadoes – was at Mount Washington on 12 April 1934, when wind speeds topped 231 mph.

Rainfall is an annual average of 40 inches, while snowfall can top 8 feet in some mountainous regions.

Agriculture: dairy, apples, cattle

Minerals: gravel, sand, mica

Industry: IT, electrical machinery, metals and plastics, paper

History: First explored by Europeans in the early 1600s, the region between Piscataqua and Merrimack became New Hampshire in 1629 when Captain John Mason, of the Council for New England, took possession of the land rights.

There ensued over the next century a deal of wrangling over state boundaries with neighboring New York and Massachusetts, and modern boundaries were not established until after the American Revolution.

New Hampshire was the first state to declare its independence from the British, in January 1776, and was one of the union's 13 original states, fighting on the union side during the Civil War.

Early industry centered around textiles and lumber, and vast swathes of forestry were destroyed in the process. But

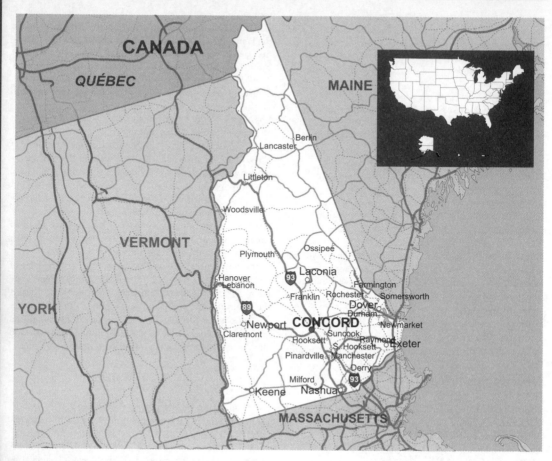

New Hampshire proved to have remarkable foresight and, before too much damage was done, began preserving its beautiful landscape under a series of conservation laws from the early 20th century onwards.

Its fortunes were battered by the Great Depression of the 1930s, though it recovered to the extent that, by the 1980s, it was the fastest-growing economy in the US.

New Jersey (NJ)

Name: After Channel Island of Jersey
Nickname: Garden State
State flower: Purple violet
State bird: Eastern goldfinch
Motto: Liberty and prosperity
Population: 8,116,000
Capital: Trenton
Physical description: The fourth smallest state in the union, over half of New Jersey's land mass forms part of the Atlantic Coastal Plain. This gently rolling landscape becomes the Pine Barrens to the east, a densely forested region, and rich farmland to the west.

The actual coast is a highly developed resort area.

Northeast of this is the Piedmont, a lowland region with many rivers, including the Raritan and Passaic, and home to the industrial heartland of this state, location of the great cities of Newark and Jersey City.

To the west are the highlands, a country of flat-topped ridges and glacial lakes, north of which are found the Kittatinny Mountains, including the state's highest point, High Point, at 1803 feet. The Delaware River cuts through this range at the so-called Delaware Water Gap.
Area: 7,787 sq mi (20,168 sq km).
Climate: New Jersey experiences hot summers, with average July temperatures of 75°F and above, and cold winters, with January temperature of 31°F. It is cooler all year round in the mountains and intensely humid in the summer elsewhere, up to 87%.

Coastal storms, hurricanes and droughts are not unknown, but weather is generally predictable and moderate.
Agriculture: cranberries, blueberries, potatoes, corn, hay, peaches, poultry
Minerals: granite, marble, limestone, slate, sand and gravel, clay, zinc, iron ore

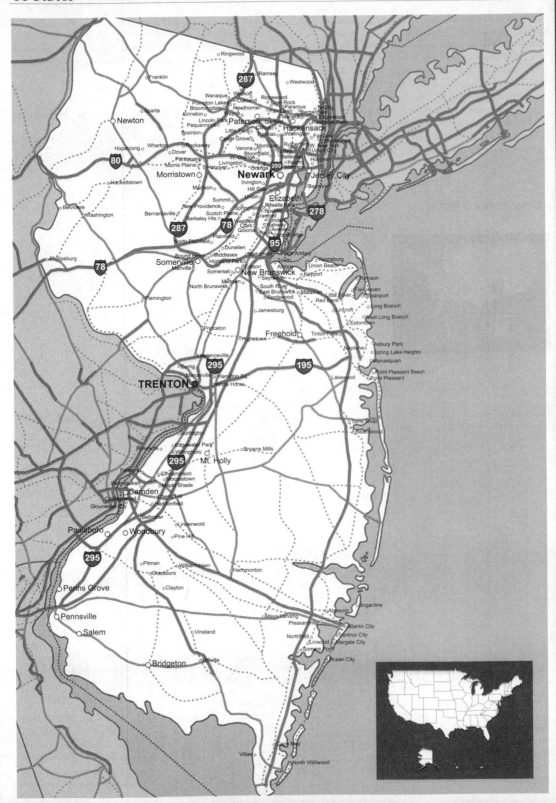

Industry: chemicals, pharmaceuticals, biotechnology, finance, warehousing, food processing, machinery

History: The Lenape, or Delaware, were here first, with the first Europeans to settle being the Scandinavians in the early 1600s, to form New Sweden, and the Dutch, in the 1630s, settling in a site near modern-day Jersey City.

In 1664, the British took over and, in 1676, the Quintipartite Deed carved the region into two blocks, East and West Jersey, the former settled by Quakers and others, the latter by Calvinists from New England and Scotland.

New Jersey finally came together as a single entity in 1702. Endless, complicated disputes over land ownership led to riots in the 1740s, and New Jersey was one of the first states to declare its independence from the British. It became a major theatre of war during the American Revolution, the site of over 90 battles, including that at Monmouth, in June 1778.

In 1787, it became the 3rd of the original 13 states to ratify the Constitution.

Industry took off from the mid-18th century, facilitated by rivers, canals and the railroad.

During the Civil War, it even turned a profit, attracting waves of immigrants, thus becoming the populous, industrious region it is today.

New Mexico (NM)

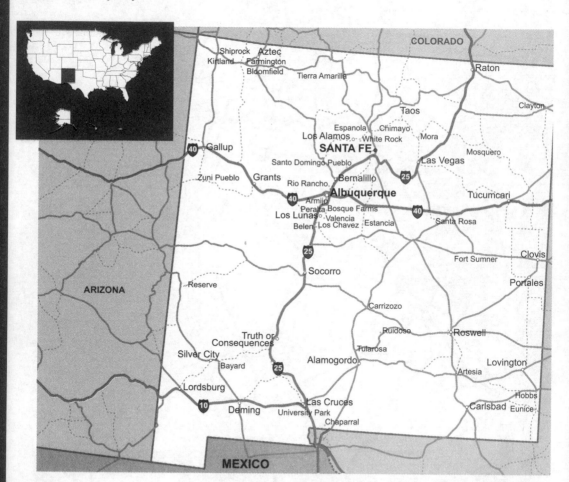

Name: after Mexico, a Spanish word, meaning "place of Mexitli," an Aztec god.

Nickname: Land of Enchantment.

State flower: Yucca.

State bird: Roadrunner.

Motto: Crescit eundo ("It grows as it goes").

Population: 1,737,000.

Capital: Santa Fe.

Physical description: This high, dry land, with a mean elevation of 5700 feet, is typified by broad deserts with scant vegetation, and high, bare peaks. It divides into three regions, the Great Plains, Rocky Mountains and Basin and Range region. The Great Plains form a high plateau cut through by rivers in the north, with low-lying, dry land to the south. The Rockies, extending in from Colorado, are divided by the Rio Grande River, running due south. Wheeler Peak, the highest point in New Mexico at 13,161 feet, is here, part of the Sangre de Christo range. In the south, the Basin and Range region, are mountains and desert, including the Gila Wilderness. Vegetation is sparse, typically comprising cactus, yucca, sagebrush and creosote, with very little rain or groundwater.

Area: 121,593 sq mi (314,924 sq km).

Climate: An arid to semi-arid climate, characterized by sparse rain and dry, hot summers. The light precipitation is accounted for by the state being 500 miles from both the Pacific Ocean and the Gulf of Mexico. Less than 10 inches fall annually in the south, 20 inches in the mountains. Summer temperatures often exceed 100°F in the south, 70°F in the mountains, with July and August given to thunderstorms which account for most of the summer rain, delivered in brief downpours leading to localized flooding. Winters rarely reach subzero temperatures, ranging between 30°F in the extreme north to 50°F in the south. There is very little humidity.

Agriculture: cattle, dairy produce, hay, chilies

Minerals: jasper, turquoise, petroleum

Industry: electrical equipment, petroleum and coal products, food processing, stone, glass and clay products, printing and publishing

History: The Pueblo nation was well established here before the Spanish arrived in the mid-16th century in search of the legendary seven cities of Cibola.

From the outset, the incomers treated the Native Americans badly, leading to violent uprising and suppression, notably the Apache uprising of 1676 and the Pueblo uprising of 1680, which drove the Spanish briefly from New Mexico altogether. Even today, the native nations are strong, with a combined population in excess of 130,000.

Sante Fe was founded in 1610 by New Mexico's first governor, Pedro de Peralta, though it was not until 1821 that it declared its independence from Spain, becoming British territory in 1846, following the Mexican War. The British ceded the lands to the US in 1848, under the Treaty of Guadalupe Hidalgo.

Cattle ranching became a real staple from the 17th century and the advent of the railroad facilitated the 1880s cattle boom, a time of huge wealth and high criminality. Billy the Kid, one of the West's most famous outlaws, was shot by Sheriff Pat Garrett in Fort Suma, in 1881.

The 1850 compromise denied New Mexico statehood, forcing it to wait until 1912, when it became the 47th of the union.

During the Civil War, it was occupied by Confederate troops until 1862, when Union forces took over.

During the 20th century, New Mexico perhaps became best known as the site of Los Alamos, the US nuclear testing laboratory, and Trinity Site, where the first Atomic bomb was detonated in the 1950s.

This is also home to Roswell where, in 1947, the story goes that a UFO crash-landed and its contents kept secret by the US government ever since.

New York (NY)

Name: named after the Duke of York.
Nickname: Empire State.
State flower: Rose (any color).
State bird: Bluebird.
Motto: Excelsior ("ever upward").
Population: 18,176,000.
Capital: Albany.
Physical description: New York state borders Lakes Erie and Ontario to the north, and Pennsylvania, New Jersey and the Atlantic to the south.

Between Lakes Ontario and Champlain are the Adirondacks, high, rugged peaks – including Mount Marcy, the state's highest peak, at 5344 – interspersed with cool, mountain lakes.

The clear, fresh climate and spectacular scenery has made this a playground for the rich. The Vanderbilts and Rockerfellers both had summer homes here.

Due south are the Hudson-Mohawk lowlands, bordered by the Appalachian highlands, home Bear Mountain National Park, created in the 1900s to save the environment from the ravages of rapid industrialization, and now welcoming more visitors annually even than Yellowstone.

Further south is a section of the Atlantic Coastal Plain, on which is found the Catskill Mountains, a region famous for its forests, mountains, waterfalls and fast-flowing rivers, and recognized as America's first wilderness, because of the pioneering work done here by early conservationists.

Mention should also be made of Niagara Falls, on the boundary between the US and Canada, and one of the great wonders of the world, attracting some 12 million tourists a year.

The Horseshoe Falls are the most spectacular, at 167 feet high, disgorging 600,000 gallons of water per second.

Area: 52,735 sq mi (136,583 sq km).

Climate: For such a small state, New York is given to extremes.

Winter is a time of subzero temperatures and freezing rainstorms, sometimes called ice storms, which occur one or two times a year. Temperatures are as low as -10°F in the south, -25°F in the mountainous north.

These prolonged, icy winters are the result of arctic air masses moving down from Canada and Hudson Bay.

Oppressively hot summers, with temperatures soaring above 90°F, are the result of high pressure systems moving in from the Atlantic.

By contrast, the mountainous regions of the Catskills and Adirondacks are wonderfully cool.

Rainfall is fairly uniform throughout the year, with precipitation averaging 30-50 inches annually.

Snow is heavy, up to 40 inches in places, and can create hazardous conditions.

Hurricanes are rare.

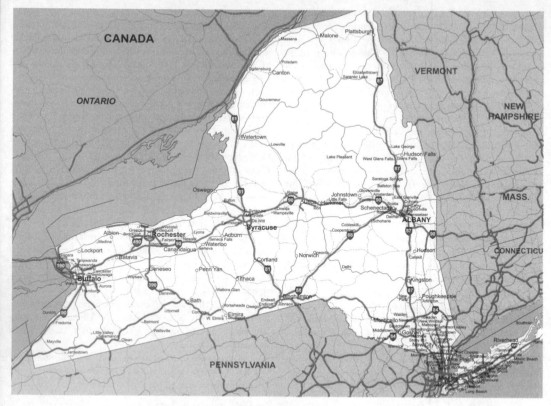

Agriculture: dairy produce, cattle, apples, cherries, potatoes, onions

Minerals: sand, gravel, limestone, gypsum, garnet, talc, zinc

Industry: electrical equipment, printing and publishing, scientific instruments, machinery, tourism

History: The Iroquois nations dominated this region for hundreds of years, but were beaten back by the settlers and, after making the disastrous decision to side with the British during the American Revolution, were all but ruined.

Europeans arrived in 1524, when Giovanni de Verrazano sailed into Hudson Bay. Henry Hudson, who gave the bay its name, arrived in 1609, claiming the region for France.

The Dutch founded a settlement at Fort Orange, now Albany, in 1624.

New York was central to the Revolutionary war and, despite being occupied by the British, provided many troops and goods to the American side.

On 26 July 1788, New York City became one of the original 13 states to form the union and became the first American capital. George Washington was inaugurated here, on 30 April 1789.

Philadelphia became the new capital in 1790, though New York City overtook it in size by 1835.

During the Civil War, conscription provoked the Draft Riots of 1863, when for four days in July, 50,000 people took to the streets and hundreds lost their lives.

New York City, home to Wall Street and the New York Stock Exchange as well as the headquarters of many multinational corporations, became the engine-house of the state economy but industry, notably mining, which developed rapidly in the 19th century, played a huge part.

The construction of the Erie (1825) and Welland (1833) Canals opened up the interior to commerce, allowing towns like Buffalo and Niagara Falls to expand. The state was also an important center for immigration, attracting people from across the globe in search of a better life in the New World.

North Carolina (NC)

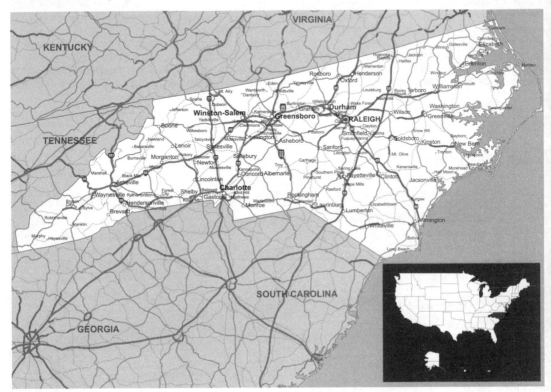

Name: after Charles I of England. Carolus is the Latin name for Charles.

Nickname: Tar Heel State; Old North State.

State flower: Dogwood.

State bird: Cardinal.

Motto: Esse quam videri ("To be rather than to seem").

Population: 7,547,000.

Capital: Raleigh.

Physical description: At 560 miles, North Carolina is the widest state in the Mississippi regions. Bordering Tennessee to the west and Virginia to the north, it divides into three recognizable regions.

The Coastal Plain is a low, flat farmland with coastal regions sheltered by the Outer Banks, a string of barrier islands with three capes, Cape Hatteras, Cape Lookout and Cape Fear.

Further inland is the 200-mile wide Piedmont, or 'Foothills' a- a high, flat area rising to meet the Appalachian Mountains region, which includes the Blue Ridge and the Great Smokey Mountains. North Carolina's highest peak, indeed the highest peak in the whole of the Mississippi, is

Mount Mitchell, at 6684 feet.

The Continental Divide runs along the top of the Blue Ridge range, so that rivers on the eastern side flow to the Atlantic, while those on the west, flow towards the Pacific.

Area: 52,669 sq mi (136,412 sq km).

Climate: North Carolina has a subtropical climate, with short, cool winters and long, hot, humid summers. Spring and autumn are refreshing periods by comparison.

January temperatures range between 29°F and 51°F, while July temperature run to an average of 87°F.

The Bermuda High ushers in high pressure fronts which contribute to summer's intense humidity. Heat can often be stagnant, making polluted areas extremely unpleasant, and requiring strong breezes from Canada to shift them.

Rain is most plentiful in the northwest, where the Blue Ridge mountains experience up to 80 inches of precipitation a year. Further east and south, rain fall is much less.

Snow can fall up to 50 inches in the mountains, but is rarely seen in the southeast.

This is also hurricane country. Hurricane Diane, in 1984, caused $36 million of damage. Hurricanes Hugo (1989)

and Fran (1994) also caused immense destruction.

Agriculture: poultry, eggs, tobacco, diary produce, soy beans

Minerals: emerald, feldspar, mica, pyrophyllite

Industry: tobacco products, textiles, chemicals, electrical equipment

History: Native American nations included the Cherokee, who lived in the Appalachians predominantly, the Catawba and the Croatian.

White settlement was unsuccessful to begin with, colonies established in 1585 and 1587 all but vanishing from the face of the earth.

In 1650, however, a permanent settlement was established at Albemarle by the 'overflow' settlers from Virginia, and in 1663, King Charles I of England granted it the royal charter.

Until 1712, North and South Carolinas were governed as a single entity.

By 1776, North Carolina had been independent for a long time and took this one stage further, calling for independence from the British through the Halifax Resolves.

It seceded from the Union in 1861 to fight with the Confederates during the Civil War, finally surrendering to Union forces in 1865, and being readmitted to the Union in 1868.

North Carolina was known as the Rip Van Winkle state in the early 1800s because it made so little progress it appeared to be asleep. The 20th century saw a quite different North Carolina emerge.

Here, in 1903, the Wright brothers made the first successful powered flight, an ambitious roads building program of the 1920s saw it christened the "Good Roads State" and, in 1994, the Raleigh-Durham area was designated the best place to live in the US.

North Dakota (ND)

Name: From the Dakota, the other name for the Sioux, who lived here.
Nickname: Peace Garden State.
State flower: Wild prairie rose.
State bird: Western Meadowlark.
Motto: Liberty and union, now and forever, one and inseparable.
Population: 639,000.
Capital: Bismarck.
Physical description: North Dakota divides into four regions.
The Red River Valley, drained by the Red River of the North, is a flat, fertile region where wheat and sugar beet grow in abundance.
The Drift Plains, which rise to an elevation of 2000 feet, are bordered on the north by the Turtle Mountains, and form a landscape of undulating hills, valleys and lakes, to which thousands of ducks migrate every spring to nest.
The Great Plains, to the west, constitute hilly, mining country. The lower region along the Missouri River is known as the Missouri Break.
Finally, the state's best known geological feature is the Badlands valley, where wind and rain have carved weird statues, pedestals and domes, in the stone and clay.
There are also rocks containing lignite coal which has been burning for years, rendering the baked clay vivid shades of pink, orange and red. These baked rocks are known locally as 'clinker'.
Area: 70,702 sq mi (183,117 sq km).
Climate: Expect long, hard winters, where temperatures dip to -15°F.
Summers are intense and brief, with temperatures soaring to 80°F or more and rainfall quite frequent, the months June to August being generally the wettest.
Annual precipitation is around 22 inches on average in the east, dropping to only 14 inches in the west.

Snowfall amounts to an annual average of 32 inches.
Agriculture: wheat, barley, oats, flaxseed, sugar beets
Minerals: lignite, soft coal
Industry: mining, electricity production
History: The Sioux (Dakota) were one of the region's established tribes, pursuing a roaming existence, following the buffalo trails. The Mandan and Arikara were settled, agricultural nations, living in their distinctive earth lodges. The first white contact was with Pierre Gaultier de Varennes, who arrived at the site of present-day Bismarck in 1738, a harbinger of the fur traders to come, who shipped over the border from Canada to establish a series of trading posts to furnish the fashion houses of Europe. This lucrative trade was highly competitive and native Americans became a part of it, a development that, though it promoted harmony between the whites and natives, also brought trouble. In 1837, for example, smallpox – a disease to which they had no immunity – virtually wiped out the Mandan at Fort Clark.
In 1803, North Dakota became part of the US through the Louisiana Purchase, and in 1818, the disputes over the border were settled with Canada.
The 1870s saw a surge in settlement, facilitated by the railroad. An estimated 100,000 people flooded into North Dakota to partake of the farming boom that mostly comprised small farms, though there were also some pioneering large-scale, "bonanza" enterprises.
The Great Depression devastated the region, as crop prices collapsed. Dust storms and crop failures sabotaged the farming industry still further and at one time, some 70% of the population relied on public assistance.
The 1940s saw a recovery, but rural decline continued thereafter as the state became increasingly urbanized. Nowadays, more people live in cities than in the countryside – quite a reversal for a state once characterized by its farming culture and scattered population.

Ohio (OH)

Name: from Iroquois word, meaning "great river."
Nickname: Buckeye State.
State flower: Scarlet carnation.
State bird: Cardinal.
Motto: With God all things are possible.
Population: 11,210,000.
Capital: Columbus.
Physical description: Ohio is a state of rolling plains bordering Lakes Erie and Michigan to the north and Kentucky and West Virginia to the south.
Once covered in virgin forest, much of it was cleared to build cities and for farmland. The Lake Erie Plains in the north are low-lying lands, virtually treeless, with broad, sweeping horizons.
To the south is a section of the Corn Belt, called the Till Plains. This exceptionally fertile region is characterized by lowlands and hills, including Campbell Hill, 1550 feet, the highest peak in the state.
The rugged terrain of the Appalachians can be found to the

southeast. A scenic region, with rich mineral deposits, it is barely cultivated due to its poor soil.
The hilly region of Bluegrass also extends into Ohio, from Kentucky in the south.
Area: 44,787 sq mi (115,998 sq km).
Climate: Ohio experiences cold, snowy winters, with temperatures dipping to 15°F and below, and an average maximum snowfall of 56.3 inches in the region of Lake Erie.
Lake Erie also creates the conditions which make Cleveland the windiest city in the state, with average wind speeds of 11 mph.
Summers are warm, to 85°F, and rainy, providing a long growing season.
Annual average precipitation is 38-42 inches, and falls mostly between May and October.
Agriculture: soy beans, corn, wheat, hay, strawberries, peaches, apples, grapes, sheep and dairy
Minerals: limestone, sand, gravel
Industry: car assembly, rubber, jet engines, machinery

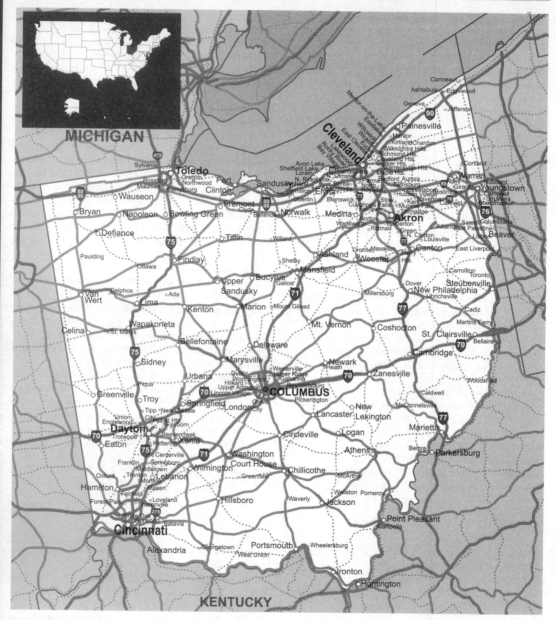

History: French explorer La Salle was the first white arrival, in 1669, and claimed it for France. Following the France and Indian Wars, Britain took it over, finally ceding it to the US after the Revolution, in 1783.

White settlement provoked horrendous clashes with native populations culminating in the battle of Fallen Timbers of 1794, when the native Americans were heavily defeated and resistance was all but quelled.

Moving forward to the 19th and 20th centuries, Ohio became a major industrial center, its city names synonymous with the goods they produce – Cleveland with car assembly, Akron with rubber, Cincinnati with machine tools and jet engines, Dayton with office, refrigeration and heating equipment.

Oklahoma (OK)

Name: from two Choctaw words, meaning "red people."
Nickname: Sooner State.

State flower: Mistletoe.
State bird: Scissor-tailed flycatcher.

Motto: Labor omnia vincit ("Labor conquers all things").

Population: 3,347,000.

Capital: Oklahoma City.

Physical description: The state of Oklahoma could be characterized as one great rolling plain, with mountain ranges to the south and north, and extensive forestry along the Missouri and Arkansas border.

Oklahoma has four mountain ranges, the Ouachita to the southeast, a heavily forested, rugged terrain interspersed with lakes, streams and springs, the Ozarks to the northeast, not mountains so much as igneous rocks worn down to form rounded hills or "knobs", the Arbuckles in the south central area, and the Wichita to the southwest.

The Black Mesa, Oklahoma's highest peak at 4973 feet, and named for its formation from black lava rock, is found in the Panhandle region, an area of sandstone outcrops and stark ravines.

The Red River (not to be confused with the Red River of the North) runs along the border with Texas.

Area: 69,956 sq mi (181,185 sq km).

Climate: A dry, warm climate, cooler and drier in the northwest, with annual rainfall averages of 15 inches, warmer and wetter in the southeast, with annual rainfall averages of 50 inches.

Snow is scarce in the south, to the tune of 2 inches a year on average, while in the northern Panhandle, you can expect a yearly total of 25 inches.

Average temperatures are 37°F statewide in January, 82°F in July.

Oklahoma is afflicted by tornadoes, the worst on record occurring on 9 April 1947, when a twister ripped through Ellis, Woods and Woodward counties, killing 101 people and injuring 782.

Agriculture: wheat, cattle

Minerals: zinc, lead, iodine, natural gas, oil

Industry: mining, machinery, aircraft and aerospace equipment, food processing

History: The native tribes living here were the Osage and Quapaw predominantly. As with other native experiences across America, they were brutally forced off the land and herded into reservations, but more of that later.

The first white explorers were Spanish, stumbling into Oklahoma in search of legendary gold cities. But the territory was finally bought by the US as part of the 1803 Louisiana Purchase.

As settlers continued to arrive in Oklahoma, the federal government agreed to "open up" the Native American heartland in six land runs between 1889 and 1895, prompting a further surge of immigrants including Europeans and freed slaves from across the southern states. Many farms were established in Oklahoma by black pioneers.

On 16 November 1907, Oklahoma became the 47th state of the union, just as it struck oil. As the oil boom took hold, towns like Oklahoma City and Tulsa flourished.

As a footnote, the Osage were forced into a reservation they called Osage City. It was here that oil was struck, making them overnight the richest, per capita, people in the US!

The Quapaw struck gold, of a sort, too. They were cheated out of their ancestral lands by the government and could only afford to buy a miserable strip of land in the northeast. But it was rich in zinc and lead which, during the 1920s, brought them an income of over $1 million a year.

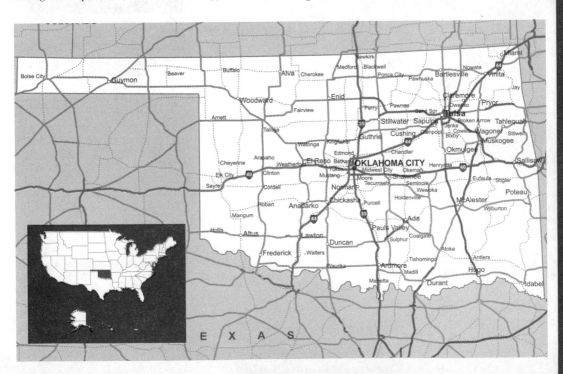

Oregon (OR)

Name: unknown, though may related to the French word "ouragan," meaning "hurricane."

Nickname: Beaver State.

State flower: Oregon grape.

State bird: Western meadowlark.

Motto: The union.

Population: 3,282,000.

Capital: Salem.

Physical description: Oregon is a heavily forested state, particularly along the coast, where the low mountains are densely covered with spruce and fir trees.

Spectacular cliffs, rising sheer over 1000 feet above the Pacific Ocean characterize the immediate coast.

To the east are the Cascade Mountains, which include the chain of volcanoes called the High Cascades, which form part of the Pacific Rim of Fire, the circle of volcanoes around the Pacific Ocean.

Some of Oregon's highest peaks and deepest lakes are here, including Mount Hood, at 11,239 feet, the highest in the state, and the Three Sisters, each over 10,000 feet, not to mention America's deepest lake, Crater Lake, which plunges to a depth of 1932 feet.

Oregon's famous wheat fields are found on the Columbia Plateau, to the east, with mountains rising to the north.

Finally, one of Oregon's most striking physical features is Hell's Canyon at the Idaho border, which is more than a mile deep and has no roads across it.

Area: 97,073 sq mi (251,418 sq km).

Climate: The Pacific Ocean moderates temperatures in this state, ensuring very little extreme weather. Thus summers are hot, but not unbearable and winters cold, but dry. The Cascade Mountains have a major influence on the climate, creating two climate zones. The west is warm with heavy rainfall, around 37 inches annually, while the east is dry, with average annual rainfall of only 8 inches in places, with lower temperatures. The difference is caused by the fact that air masses from the Pacific must ascend the Cascades to reach the east, losing much of their moisture on the way.

The west is around 5-10°F warmer than the east, with July

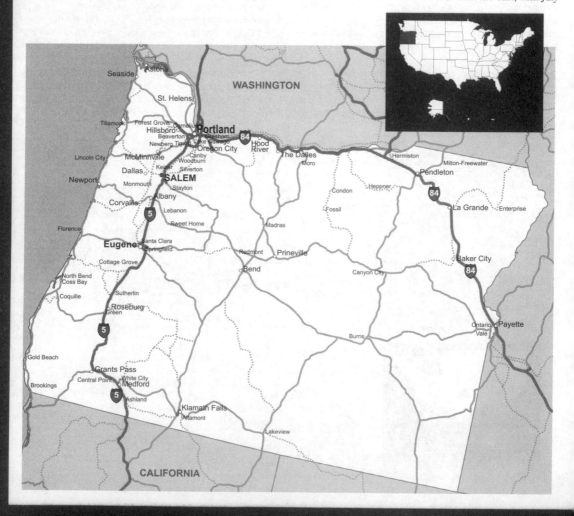

temperatures averaging 75°F and January temperatures averaging 45°F.

Agriculture: wheat, cattle

Minerals: gold, silver, copper, iron, asbestos, nickel, platinum, coal

Industry: timber, paper products, electronics, coal mining

History: The Cayuse, a hunter-gatherer tribe, lived here, as did Cherokee, Klamath and Bannock, long before the Europeans arrived, drawn by the lure of fur trapping.

New Yorker John Jacob Aster was one of the earliest, establishing Fort Astoria at the mouth of the Columbia River as a means of linking up the fur trading posts further inland. The British took over the region in 1812 and the British Hudson Bay Company took over the fur trade.

But the US needed Oregon too, to provide land for the Midwest overspill, and settlements began taking root in the Willamette Valley from the 1830s, with tens of thousands traversing the 2000-mile long Oregon Trail during the 1850s to get to this land of plenty, now that the government, via the Donation Land Act, was giving 350 acres to every male over 23, twice that if he had a wife.

All of which was devastating for peoples like the Cayuse, who resisted the white tide but were beaten back ruthlessly. In 1847, in retaliation for an epidemic of measles they believed had been deliberately unleashed on them, Cayuse attacked a mission in Waiilaptu, killing 14. Five men were hanged for the massacre and the land appropriation went on.

On 14 February 1859, Oregon became a state, the 33rd in the union.

The railroad opened the area up to trade and Oregon became an important supplier of timber to the American continent.

In the 20th century, it also became important for its electricity production.

Pennsylvania (PA)

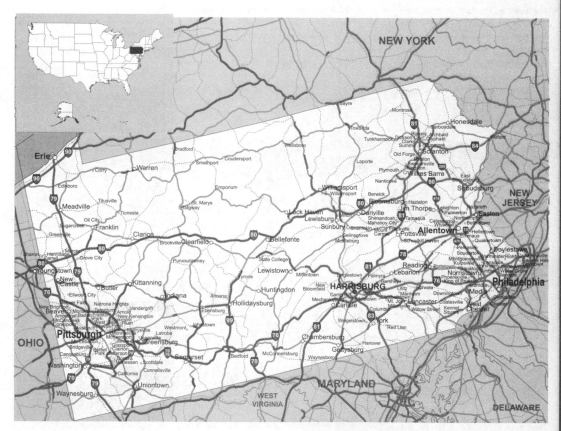

Name: after the father of William Penn, the colony's founder.

Nickname: Keystone State.

State flower: Mountain laurel.

State bird: Ruffed grouse.

Motto: Virtue, liberty and independence.

Population: 12,002,000.

Capital: Harrisburg.

Physical description: Though technically a landlocked state, as its shoreline gives onto an estuary of the Delaware River rather than open sea, Pennsylvania has one of the largest seaports in the US, the Port of Philadelphia.

This is not Pennsylvania's only physical anomaly.

The western third of the state, part of the US manufacturing belt, is almost a separate state in itself, cut off as it is by both the Appalachian mountains and the Appalachian Plateau, a high, flat elevation so scored by erosion it looks more like a range of unending hills.

This latter is rich in fossils, and fossil fuels, notably natural gas and petroleum.

Not only is Western Pennsylvania cut off, its rivers drain west, into the Mississippi, and its climate is drier and cooler.

Area: 46,063 sq mi (119,251 sq km).

Climate: As aforementioned, temperatures vary across the state, from an annual mean of 54°F in Philadelphia to an annual mean of 50°F in Pittsburgh, 42 inches of rain in Philadelphia, 37.5 in Pittsburgh, 21 inches of snow in Philadelphia, 44 inches in Pittsburgh, 56% sunshine in Philadelphia, 44% in Pittsburgh.

Flooding is a problem in Pennsylvania. In May 1889, the South Fork dam burst after a bout of heavy rain, flooding the town of Johnstone in minutes and killing 2200 people. Floods in Johnstone in 1977 killed 68.

Violent hurricanes and tornadoes also cause immense damage and death.

Agriculture: dairy produce, eggs, poultry, pears, apples, grapes, sweetcorn, Christmas trees

Minerals: limestone, slate, coal, petroleum

Industry: cement, chemicals, food processing, electrical machinery, clay products such as bricks and tiles.

History: The Delaware, Susquehannocks, Shawnee and Iroquois were the first inhabitants of what became Pennsylvania, but they were driven out in time, as white settlement increased from its tiny base as a refuge for English Quakers seeking freedom of worship.

William Penn, the leader of this colony, obtained a royal charter from King Charles II, arriving in 1681.

Immigration developed the colony, which became a prosperous farming and home manufacturing region. Weaving and textile industries, saw and grist mills, tanning factories and printing presses sprang up, just as stagecoach lines opened the area up to trade.

The arts and education also flourished, the University of Pennsylvania being the only non-denominational college in the colonial period.

During the American Revolution, Philadelphia served as the US capital and was crucial in shaping the Constitution and the anti-slavery movement. During the Civil War, Pennsylvania citizens aided slaves escaping the south over the border to Canada.

Pennsylvania later became a major center of the steel and mining industry, and of organized labor in trade unions.

These industries declined in the 20th century, replaced by retail and service sectors.

Pennsylvania is a magnet for tourists, thanks to its centrality to so much American history.

Rhode Island (RI)

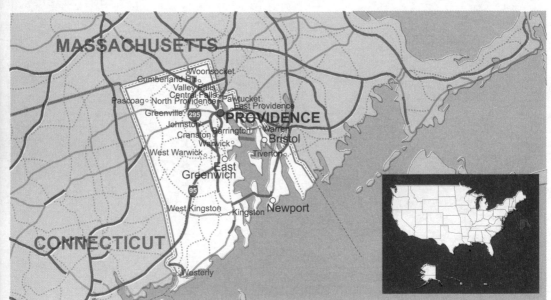

Name: After Rhodes, the Greek island.
Nickname: Little Rhody; Ocean State.
State flower: Violet.
State bird: Rhode Island hen.
Motto: Hope.
Population: 989,000.

Capital: Providence.
Physical description: Rhode Island is the smallest state, and is mostly wooded. Its coastal region has sandy beaches to the east, becoming more rugged to the west.

The Western Rocky Upland is, as its name suggests, higher and rockier, interspersed with cool, clear lakes. Jerimoth

Hill, at 812 feet, is the state's highest point.

Area: 1,212 sq mi (3,139sq km).

Climate: Four distinct seasons, with a cold winter, temperatures dropping to 30°F, and hot summers, with temperatures peaking at 80°F. Temperatures are generally higher the further inland you travel.

There is an average of 45 inches of rain annually.

Agriculture: greenhouse produce, dairy produce, sweetcorn, cattle and calves, potatoes

Minerals: granite, stone

Industry: textiles, jewellery, rubber products, machinery

History: On land purchased from the Narragansett nation, clergyman Roger Williams founded Providence, the state capital, following his exile by the Puritans of Massachusetts Bay.

His colony became a brisk trading point, where ships pulled in to exchange slaves for goods. Angry at the levies imposed by the British on all this business, Rhode Islanders rebelled, burning two British revenue cutters, the Liberty and Gaspee, and declaring their independence from Britain in 1776.

It became the 13th of the original 13 states to form the union on 13 May 1790.

In 1842, unrest broke out again, this time in the cause of universal suffrage. Dorr's Rebellion became an armed struggle against the property qualification and led to the arrest of many Dorrites, including Dorr himself, for treason. Rhode Island became very industrialized, proving central to the American textiles industry and, later, manufacturing. Today it is still busy, still prosperous, and a huge tourist attraction.

South Carolina (SC)

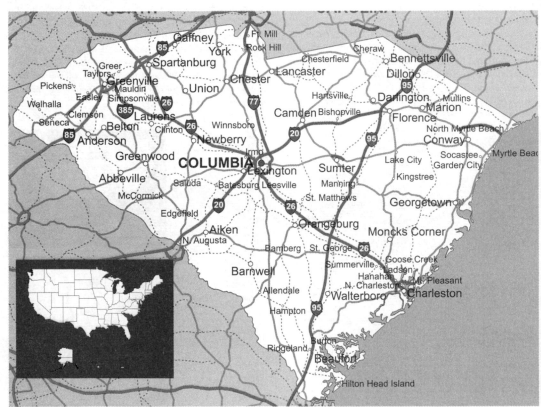

Name: named after Charles I of England, Carolus being the Latin translation of Charles.

Nickname: Palmetto State.

State flower: Carolina Jessamine.

State bird: Carolina wren.

Motto: Dum spiro spero ("While I breathe, hope").

Population: 3,836,000.

Capital: Columbia.

Physical description: South Carolina's long coastline forms part of the Atlantic Coast Plain and is celebrated for its beautiful, sandy beaches, including the Grand Strand near Georgetown.

Due south, the coastline is broken up by inlets, marshier areas which extend inland, and the Pine Barrens, a heavily forested region.

The Piedmont is higher land, rising from 400 to 1400 feet, and is a hilly country with a discernible Fall Line, where the rivers coursing across the Piedmont towards the Atlantic 'fall' to the lower ground of the Coastal Plain.

The progress of these rivers, including the Savannah,

Edisto, Santee and Pee Dee, creates a landscape of rushing whitewater and waterfalls.

In the extreme northwest are the Blue Mountains, including Sassafras, the highest peak, at 3560 feet.

Area: 31,113 sq mi (80,852 sq km).

Climate: A subtropical climate exists at the coast, becoming a little more moderate inland.

Summers are hot, humid and long, with temperatures soaring as high as 90°F, though higher ground is considerably cooler.

Winters are short and cool rather than cold, with Columbia recording a mean temperature for January of 44°F.

Rainfall is abundant throughout the state, with a Columbia annual average of 48.3 inches, dropping to 38 inches in the interior, and rising to 52 inches in higher elevations.

Snow and sleet occur two to three times a year, more frequently in the mountains.

Agriculture: cotton, tobacco, soy beans, cattle, peanuts, pecans

Minerals: cement, stone, sand, gravel

Industry: chemicals, machinery, cars, timber, paper

History: The first white settlers were Spanish, expanding their missions from Florida. Undaunted, Charles I claimed it for England in 1629, issuing a royal charter for a colony that was never established. Charles II tried again, granting a charter to eight of his supporters, including Lord Ashley, first Lord of Shaftesbury.

The first colony at Albemarle was set up under the Fundamental Constitution of Carolina. Hardly a progressive document, it simply enshrined feudal privileges and led to enormous dissent.

The area grew rich through cotton and tobacco plantations, worked by vast numbers of slaves. So many, indeed, that white immigrants were actively encouraged, simply to restore a white majority.

In 1712, North and South Carolina were separated, the southern state going on to lead the movement for independence from Britain, despite having once been so tied to it.

It was later the first state to secede and is regarded as the cradle of the Civil War. Thus, when routed, Union troops wreaked a terrible revenge, and all but razed Columbia to the ground.

The agricultural economy was ruined by the end of slavery, and hard times fell on the state's farmers. Recovery was succeeded by another slump in the 1920s when the boll weevil destroyed the cotton, then in the 1930s, when the Great Depression bit deep.

Black migration from the state was also pronounced at this time as white supremacists, including the Ku Klux Klan, began to mobilize. Desegregation was achieved by 1970, but there are many underlying racial tensions in this most southern of southern states.

South Dakota (SD)

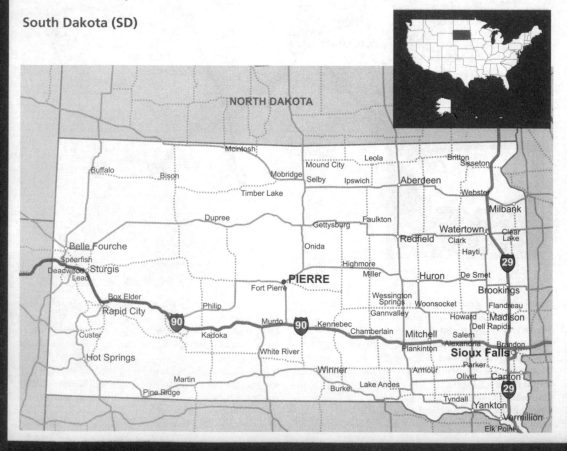

Name: after the Dakota nation, which lived here.
Nickname: Coyote State; Sunshine State.
State flower: Pasque flower.
State bird: Ring-knecked pheasant.
Population: 739,000.
Motto: Under God, the people rule.
Capital: Pierre.
Physical description: This prairie state rises some 6000 feet from east to west, the lower lands comprising the Drift Plains, a gently hilly region, and the Dissected Till Plains, again hilly and criss-crossed with rivers.
The land begins to rise as you reach the Great Plains, an area of hills, flatlands, canyons and flat-topped hills called "buttes."
The land rises again towards the Black Hills which, including the Badlands, are believed to be the oldest rock formations on the North American continent.
The area is rich in fossils and mineral deposits, including gold, silver and lead, and extends into Wyoming to form an area of 6000 square miles.
The highest peak in South Dakota, Harney Peak, stands here at 7242 feet.
Area: 77,116 sq mi (199,730 sq km).
Climate: South Dakota is unprotected compared to other coastal southern states, and thus feels the full impact of arctic winds moving south in winter, and the influence of the Gulf of Mexico in summer.
Winter temperatures fall to average lows of 12°F, while summer temperatures soar to the mid-70s.
Rainfall reaches an annual average of 24.7 inches in the southeast, 13 inches in the southwest. The southeast also clocks up about 41 inches of snow every year.
South Dakota is subject to high winds and occasional but nonetheless devastating droughts.
Agriculture: cattle, sheep, corn, soy beans, oats, wheat
Minerals: gold, silver, lead, copper
Industry: electronics, meatpacking, food processing, service and finance industries.
History: The Arikara and Dakota nations lived here together until the Dakota, a more warlike and nomadic tribe, achieved dominance in the 1830s.
Early white settlers came for the fur trade and co-existed reasonably well with the Dakota, but when settlers came looking for land, the troubles began.
Undaunted by droughts, locusts and native resistance, the immigrants came, more speedily once the railroad arrived in 1872.
Serious conflict ensued when gold was discovered in the Black Hills, an area the Dakota held sacred and refused to sell. The 1876 defeat of General Custer at the Battle of Little Bighorn notwithstanding, Dakota resistance began to falter as the buffalo they had hunted for generations began to die out, their leader Sitting Bull died and the massacre at Wounded Knee, in which 200 men, women and children were slaughtered, broke their spirit.
The white settlers got their Black Hills in the end, though it was not gold that made South Dakota prosper, but cattle ranching, which became big business as the 19th century progressed.
Today, little farms have been superseded by big businesses and manufacturing displaced by the service and finance industries.

Tennessee (TN)

Name: from "Tanasi," the name of a group of Cherokee villages.
Nickname: Volunteer State.
State flower: Iris.
State bird: Mockingbird.
Motto: Agriculture and commerce.
Population: 5,431,000.
Capital: Nashville.
Physical description: Tennessee's biggest area is its Coastal Plain, which includes the bottom lands, a wide, gently hilling region rolling all the way to Memphis.
To the west, the Plain dips down towards the Mississippi Delta.
Working inland comes first the Nashville Basin, a great farming country, surrounded by the Highland Rim, or Pennyroyal, named after a wildflower of the region.
The land then rises to the Appalachian Plateau, an area of flat-topped mountains and sudden valleys, which effectively forms a dividing line between east and west Tennessee.
Beyond the Appalachian Valley and Ridge are the Blue Mountains, comprising the Great Smokies, which include Clingman's Dome, at 6643, Tennessee's highest point, and the Chilhowee and Snowbird mountains.
Area: 42,144 sq mi (109,152 sq km).
Climate: Tennessee has four distinct seasons, with cool winters, warm summers and temperate springs and autumns, and is not plagued by either extreme temperatures or weather events.
It is warmest at the coast, getting cooler as you move due easterly.
Memphis in the west has an annual mean temperature for January of 40°F, compared to 36°F in Nashville, and 83°F for July, compared to 79°F.
The extreme west also has a longer growing season, by as much as 100 days, compared to the extreme east.
Rainfall is heaviest in winter, with 54.7 inches falling annually in Memphis, and snowfall is heaviest in the east, Nashville having a yearly average of 10 inches compared to Memphis's 5 inches.
Agriculture: soy beans, tobacco, hay, cotton, wheat
Minerals: stone, bitumous coal, zinc
Industry: chemicals (acids, pharmaceuticals, plastics), textiles and apparel, machinery, transportation equipment
History: Chickasaw, Cherokee and Creek were amongst the nations that dwelt here prior to the establishment of the first settlement by the French, in 1682, at the mouth of the Hatchie River.
Fur trappers came first, then settlers seeking land to culti-

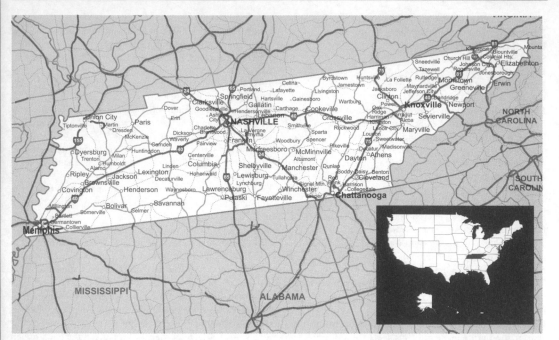

vate. In 1779-80, an expedition of pioneers pushed west along the Columbia River to the site of modern Nashville. After the American Revolution, native Americans were pushed out and slaves were shipped in, to work the plantations. Tennessee sided with the Confederates during the Civil War and many battles, including Shiloh and Chattanooga, were fought here.

In its wake came difficult times economically, but a rapid industrialization, centered primarily on timber, coal, iron and copper, restored some degree of prosperity to the state. Industrialization continued into the 20th century, bringing with it a new problem – environmental degradation. This latter is Tennessee's new challenge.

Texas (TX)

Name: From the Caddo word meaning "hello friends" or "friends."
Nickname: Lone Star State.
State flower: Bluebonnet.
State bird: Mockingbird.
Population: 19,760,000.
Motto: Friendship.
Capital: Austin.
Physical description: Texas is a vast state with a varied terrain.
To the east, between the Sabine and Trinity Rivers, is an area of pine forests, hills and swamps, a typically southern landscape.
The Gulf Coast too, with its lush vegetation and sultry climate, is redolent of the Deep South.
But move inland and the semi-arid landscape more typical of Mexico becomes apparent.
The Rio Grande valley and Blackland Prairies give way to the High Plains, a hot, dry land with punishing cold winters.
In the Trans-Pecos region, the plains rise to the rugged mountains of the Guadalupe, Davis and Chicos ranges, creating some of the most unexpectedly stunning scenery

in Texas, right in the heart of a wilderness.
Area: 266,807 sq mi (691,027 sq km).
Climate: Texas has two seasons, summer and winter, and two climates, the semitropical one at the coast, and the drier one of the interior.
Gulf winds keep the coastal regions humid throughout summer, and warm in winter. In Galveston, on the Gulf, mean temperatures for January are 48°F, while El Paso's are 29°F. In July, Galveston has 88°F, El Paso, 96°F.
But perhaps the most striking contrast is in humidity levels, where Galveston records 72% on a given day at noon, El Paso records 34%.
Rain is heavier near the Gulf, up to 56 inches per year, and scant in the interior, less than 8 inches in some places.
In winter, Northers can cause radical temperature drops as cold fronts pass through, as much as 30-40°F.
Though summer thunderstorms provide relief from humidity, they can cause flash flooding too. More extreme weather comes through rarely but causes monumental destruction when it does. Texas has learnt some hard lessons and hurricane defenses are now in place.
Agriculture: cattle, sheep, lambs, cotton, rice
Minerals: oil, natural gas, helium, salt, sulfur

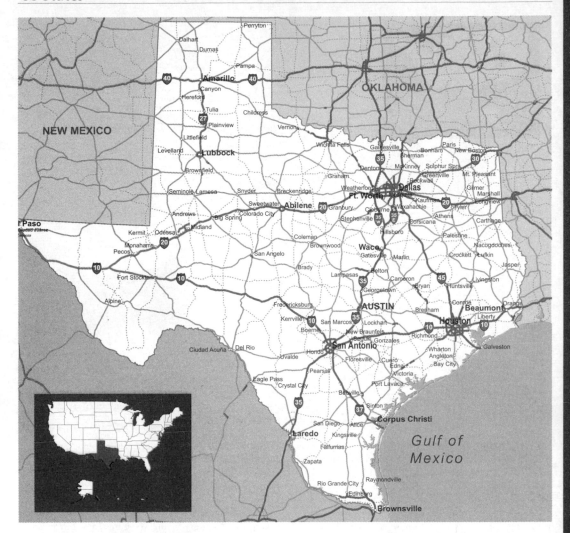

Industry: oil, lumber, chemicals, food processing, machinery

History: The first Spanish settlements of the 1680s and 90s were flushed out by the native Americans, including the Comanche and Apache.

But in the 19th century, Stephen F Austin, after whom the state capital is named, acquired colonization rights from the authorities in Mexico and led 300 families into Texas. Thousands followed and, by 1830, Americans outnumbered Spanish – something the Spanish did not like. The Texas Revolution of 1835 was won by the Americans, and eventually Texas became an independent republic, only annexed to the US in 1845.

The 19th century saw cattle ranching become a dominant agricultural force and, in 1901, oil was struck, becoming a booming industry by the 1920s. So booming, in fact, it all but cushioned the blow of the 1930s Depression.

Military bases were established in Texas during World War II, expanding the state's fortunes and it is now also a center for major corporations and high tech companies.

Utah (UT)

Name: from Ute word, meaning "people of the mountains."

Nickname: Beehive State.

State flower: Sego lily.

State bird: Seagull.

Motto: Industry.

Population: 2,010,000.

Capital: Salt Lake City.

Physical description: Utah is a very high state, dominated by Rocky Mountains, and with a mean elevation of 6100 feet.

The Rocky Mountain region includes the Wasatch and Uinta ranges. This latter includes King's Peak, at 13,528 feet, the highest point in Utah. The Basin and Ridge region

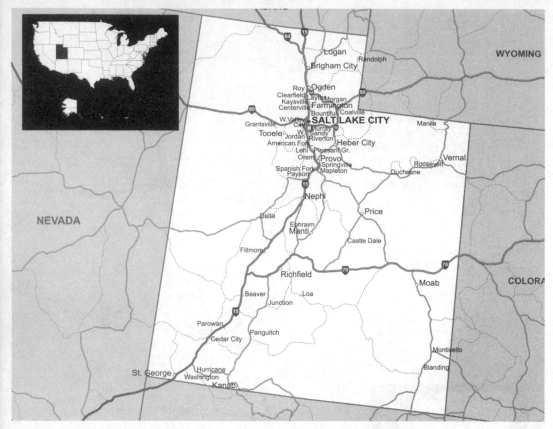

is a very dry area, extending into the heart of Utah and including the Great Salt Lake, believed to have once been part of the much greater Lake Bonneville, but now landlocked and thus one of the biggest saltwater lakes in the world. The Great Salt Lake Desert includes the Bonneville Salt Flats, 4000 acres of hard salt beds. To the east are the high plateaus, including Aquarius, Fish Lake and Markagunt.

Area: 84,899 sq mi (219,887 sq km).

Climate: Utah is semi-arid, and as such, less than 5 inches of rain fall annually over the Great Salt Lake, though more than 40 inches do in the Wasatch Mountains.

Rain water from mountain regions is diverted to farmland, where annual rainfall comes in at 10-15 inches.

Snowfall achieves an annual average of 59 inches, thanks to the mountains, which are usually snow-capped all year round.

Temperatures range from 28ºF in winter, to 78ºF in summer.

Agriculture: cattle, sheep, dairy products

Minerals: coal, copper, iron ore, silver, gold

Industry: oil, mining, steel-making, tourism

History: The Ute, Navajo and Shoshone lived here before Juan Maria Antonia led two Spanish expeditions here in 1765.

At first, Utah was seen as a through-route to California, following the discovery of the Wyoming Pass, but in 1847, Mormons came to settle on the shores of the Great Salt Lake. Despite the harsh conditions, their spirit of industry and cooperation enabled them to survive.

Conflicts with the native tribes, who resented their presence, led to the Walker War of 1850 in which many Mormons and native Americans were killed.

As the 19th century progressed, Pony Express, overland telegraph wires and the railroad opened Utah up to the American continent, and non-Mormons began to arrive.

Mining became a major industry and in 1896, Utah achieved statehood.

Today it is a booming region, with a burgeoning tourist and film industry.

Vermont (VT)

Name: from the French "les verts mont," meaning "green mountains."

Nickname: Green Mountain State

State flower: Red clover

State bird: Thrush

Motto: Freedom and unity

Population: 591,000

Capital: Montpelier

Physical description: Vermont is best known for its mountains and its ranges include the Green Mountains, from which it takes its name, in the center of the state. These mountains include Mount Mansfield, at 4393 feet, the highest in the state. They are not only beautiful to look at but rich in mineral deposits. The Taconic Mountains in the southwest extend out of Massachusetts and include the famous Bear Mountain, Dorset Peak, Equinox and Little Equinox Mountains. The granite peaks of the northeast create a wonderfully rocky landscape cut through by sparkling, fast-flowing streams. These highlands include Gore Peak and Burke Mountain. Finally, the Piedmont is a region of fertile plains running through the Connecticut River Valley.

Area: 9,614 sq mi (24,900 sq km).

Climate: Vermont has four seasons, and a continental moist climate.

Winter sees 60 inches of snowfall in lower regions and up to 150 inches in the Green Mountains. Temperatures average at 22°F.

Spring is known as the "mud season" as snow thaws, causing localized flooding.

Summer temperatures can rise to 90°F, and is a time of violent thunderstorms, hail showers and powerful winds.

Autumn is widely regarded as the best season of all, bright but cool, with a spectacular show of color as the leaves turn.

Agriculture: dairy

Minerals: granite, marble, slate

Industry: maple syrup, tourism, electronics, paper and timber

History: Iroquois were dominant here by the time Samuel de Champlain arrived in 1609 and gave the state its name. He claimed Vermont for New France, but the Dutch settled here too, then the British, who finally took control after the France and India War, in 1763.

But surrounding colonies continued to bicker over ownership, until Vermont declared itself a republic and even drew up its own constitution, in 1777, which advocated the abolition of slavery and property rights to vote, and the establishment of public schools.

During the Civil War, Vermont provided 30,000 troops, many of whom never came back.

The state is now most famous for its liberal policies, fabulous scenery, and maple syrup.

Virginia (VA)

Name: after Queen Elizabeth I of England, the so-called "Virgin Queen."

Nickname: Old Dominion.

State flower: Flowering dogwood.

State bird: Cardinal.

Motto: Sic semper tyannis ("Thus always to tyrants").

Population: 6,792,000.

Capital: Richmond.

Physical description: Virginia borders the Atlantic and has five recognizably different regions.

The coastal plain features salt marshes and swamps that extend 100 miles inland in places.

The Piedmont, immediately inland, sees the land rise up from 200-900 feet. The 'Fall Line' where this region falls down to the lower coastal plain is clearly visible and where rivers turn into waterfalls.

The Blue Ridge mountains effectively bisect the state, with the highest peak being Mount Rogers, at 5729 feet.

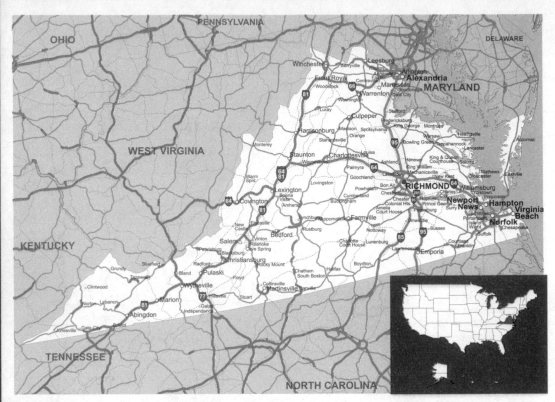

The Appalachian Ridge and Valley, also known as the Valley of Virginia, is actually a series of valleys, including the Shanandoah.

Finally, the plateau, which rises to an elevation of 2000 feet and is a landscape of rivers and forests.

Area: 40,767 sq mi (105,586 sq km).

Climate: Virginia has a "Goldilocks climate," neither too hot, nor too cold.

The coastal plain can be hot and humid in summer, but temperatures drop as you move inland and the elevation increases. The mountains are around 10°F cooler all year round.

Rainfall is heaviest near the coast too, with an annual precipitation of 45.7 inches, compared to 33 inches in the Shenandoah.

Most snow falls in the mountains, between 16 and 24 inches, where polar air masses cause winters to be as bitterly cold as in Chicago. Coastal winters are much milder.

Agriculture: cattle, peanuts, tobacco

Minerals: kaolin clay, gold

Industry: defense contracts, communications, manufacturing, IT

History: The first European settlement was a corporate affair; the English pioneers who came here in 1607 were sponsored by the London Company. Many came for easy riches in the New World and found instead a difficult land with hostile natives. Many tried desperately to get home.

Pocahontas, the daughter of the Powhatan chief, came to make peace and negotiate with these early settlers but was kidnapped by them in the hope she could be used as a bargaining chip with the natives.

She married a white settler, John Rolfe, returning with him to England. She died there, on the eve of her return to Virginia.

The first slaves brought to America arrived in Virginia, on a Dutch ship in 1619. Ultimately, so many slaves were shipped to Virginia to work the tobacco, cotton and hemp plantations that they comprised half the population by the mid-18th century. Following the Civil War and emancipation, many moved away to the urban north. Such was the exodus that today, only one fifth of the population of Virginia is African American.

Though Virginia was hurt economically by the Civil War, it recovered faster than any of the other southern states and remains the richest region, with thriving industries in communications, manufacturing and IT.

Washington (WA)

Name: after George Washington.
Nickname: Evergreen State.
State flower: Rhododendron.
State bird: Willow Goldfinch.

Motto: Alki ("By and by").
Population: 5,690,000.
Capital: Olympia.
Physical description: The state is characterized by its

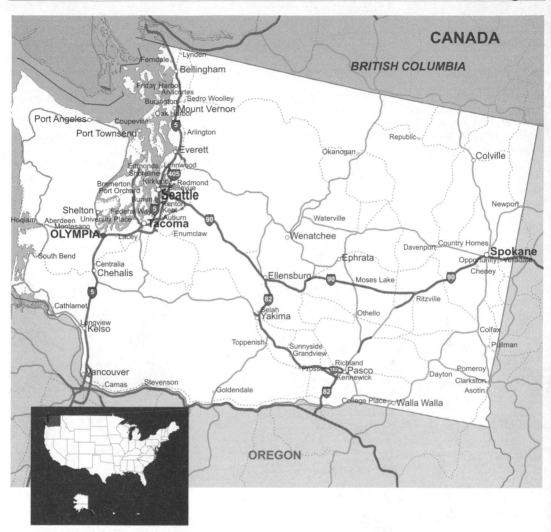

mountains, formed through volcanic activity. The most prominent ranges are the almost totally inaccessible Olympic Mountains, on the north Pacific coast, the Coastal mountains, including the geologically fascinating Willapa Hills, the stunning, permanently snow-capped Cascades, including the state's high point, Mount Rainier, at 14,411 feet, and the active volcano, Mount St Helen's, which last erupted in 1980, and the Columbia Mountains, part of the Rocky Mountain chain, which are rich in mineral deposits. The Columbia Plateau, called here the Columbia Basin, accounts for much of Washington's lower ground. The largest lava plateau in the world, the Basin features "coulees," waterless canyons cut into the rock over millennia, and "scablands," lave deposits on the plateau surface. Here too are rolling wheat fields and pasture.

The most populous region is the Puget Sound Lowland, which is sheltered from the Pacific Ocean by the Olympic Mountains and Willapa Hills.

Area: 68,139 sq mi (176,479 sq km).

Climate: The Cascade Mountains create two climates within the one state.

The west is exposed to the ocean, and experiences the full brunt of storms, rain and high winds. This is the wettest region in the US, with 70-100 inches of rain annually. Snowfall ranges from 10-30 inches a year, to 250-500 inches in the mountains.

Summer temperatures hit the mid-70s°F, with winter temperatures ranging between 32-42°F.

The Puget Sound area is more sheltered, with a fresh breezy climate due to prevailing south/southwesterly winds in summer, and lighter rainfall, typically 32-35 inches a year.

January temperatures hit 41-45°F, July temperatures 73-75°F on average.

In the east are hot, dry summers tending to desert-like conditions in the extreme southeast, and cold winters, moderated occasionally by chinook winds that temporarily but quite dramatically raise the temperature.

Thunderstorms are common, though rainfall is not, annual averages reaching only 7-15 inches across the region.

Agriculture: wheat, raspberries, apples, cherries, potatoes, lentils

Minerals: copper, gold, lead, limestone, magnesite, silver, zinc

Industry: jet aircraft, computer software development, biotechnology, aluminum production, lumber, mining

History: First nations who dwelt here included the Spokane, Chinook, Cayuse and Nez Perce, who together created a rich, diverse culture.

They were first disturbed by Bruno Heceta in 1775, who claimed the region for Spain. Britain wanted a slice of the action too, as the local wildlife, including sea otter and beaver, was highly prized for its pelts. In 1790, the Noolka Sound Agreement opened the area up to settlement by both British and Spanish.

Following the famous Lewis and Clark expedition of 1804-6, the US wanted in too, and in 1811, New Yorker John Jacob Astor established the first trading post at the mouth of the Columbia River.

Britain ceded the land to the US in 1846, when it became part of Oregon. In 1852, it became a territory in its own right, with Puget Sound the main locus of settlement.

The railroad's arrival in 1889 boosted the already abundant agriculture and fledgling industries.

In the 20th century, Washington became a major manufacturer of jet aircraft, thanks to the presence of Boeing, and electricity, following construction of the Grand Coulee Dam in 1941, the biggest dam in the US.

West Virginia (WV)

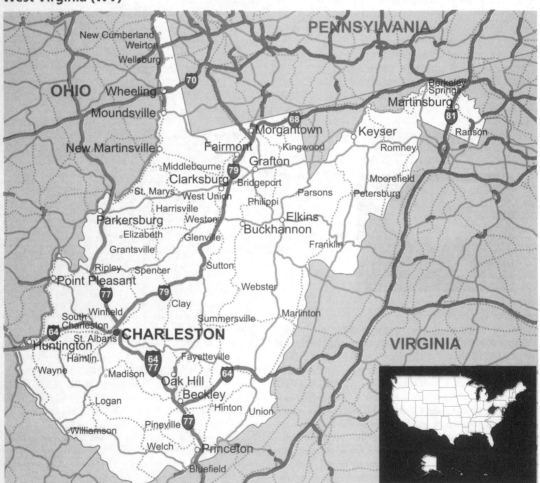

Name: as for Virginia. The West was added when the state refused to secede, instead breaking away and forming its own government.

Nickname: Mountain State.

State flower: Rhododendron.

State bird: Cardinal.

Population: 1,812,000.

Motto: Montani semper liberi ("Mountaineers are always free").

Capital: Charlestown.

Physical description: This small state is characterized by rivers, high mountains and lush forests. There is very little low-lying ground.

West Virginia has an odd, pincer-like outline, due to the two panhandles which stick out, due east and north, following the contour of rivers.

The Eastern Panhandle, bordered by the Potomac and Shenandoah Rivers, drives a wedge between Maryland and Virginia and contains West Virginia's highest peak, Spruce Knob, at 4863 feet, and its only natural lake, Trout Pond.

The Northern Panhandle, defined by the Ohio River and Texan border, is a heavily industrial region.

The Blue Ridge and Allegheny Mountains comprise West Virginia's section of the Appalachian Ridge, and also form a natural physical barrier with Virginia.

This region is famous not only for its spectacular peaks, but also its hot mineral springs, the best known being the White Sulfur Springs.

Area: 24,231 sq mi (62,758 sq km).

Climate: This state enjoys four seasons. In low-lying areas, these seasons are warm and mild, while at higher elevations, though the summers are warm, the winters are harsh and very snowy.

Statewide, summer temperatures average in the high 79°F, while winter sees them drop to the mid-30°F.

Rainfall is heavier the higher you go, with a 55 inch average in the mountains compared to a statewide average of 40 inches.

Snowfall, again, is considerable in the mountains, up to 64 inches annually, but less so in the lowlands, at 16 inches annually.

Thunderstorms and flash floods are reasonably common in high summer, but wilder weather, such as tornadoes and hurricanes, are extremely rare.

Agriculture: cattle, hay, broiler chickens, dairy produce

Minerals: coal, natural gas, petroleum, stone, sand, gravel

Industry: coal mining, glass-making, tourism

History: The Adena, or Mound Builders, settled here in ancient times and evidence of their civilization can still be seen today.

As for the state's colonial history, it is the same as Virginia's up until 1861, when it refused to secede and instead, delegates from 40 counties came together to form an independent government.

Opposition to slavery was pronounced here, as evidenced by abolitionist John Brown's raid on the arsenal at Harper's Ferry in 1859. He sought to drum up and equip an army to free the slaves of the south. His mission failed, but it lit the spark for the Civil War.

Coal had been discovered in 1742 and in fact, coal lies underneath two thirds of the state. But the industry did not take off significantly until after the Civil War, when the railroad opened up the region to trade.

But with heavy industrialization came labor and social unrest. Miners agitated, mainly over safety issues and working conditions, and mine-owners did all they could to suppress them.

This 'other civil war' raged between 1912-54.

Coal mining also had huge environmental implications, as valleys, stripped bare by mineworks, became vulnerable to flooding, and protests arose over open-cast mining.

Today, it is one of the poorest states with a very fragile economy.

Wisconsin (WI)

Name: unknown. Possibly derived from a Chippewa word "Ouisconsin," meaning "gathering of waters."

Nickname: Badger State.

State flower: Wood violet.

State bird: Robin.

Motto: Forward.

Population: 5,224,000.

Capital: Madison.

Physical description: Whatever the origin of its name, Wisconsin truly is a gathering of the waters; it has 15,000 lakes to its name, formed by the activity of glaciers, which also accounts for the mountain scenery and rich, fertile valleys. The highest elevations are in the Northern Highlands, a heavily forested region including Timms Peak, at 1951 feet, the highest point in Wisconsin, and hundreds of glacial lakes. The v-shaped central region is a surprising terrain, more like Texas than a state nearly touching the Canadian border. The long, flat plain is broken up only by abrupt, flat-topped mesas and weirdly-shaped sandstone crags, formed through the erosion of near-horizontal sedimentary rocks. The glaciers that formed the mountains did not reach here. More typical land for this part of America is found in the east, an area of gently rolling hills and cool, clear lakes, including Lake Winnebago, which has the largest volume of any lake in Wisconsin, at 137,708 acres.

Area: 66,215 sq mi (171,496 sq km).

Climate: Wisconsin has a typically continental climate, with warm summers and cold, snowy winters. The mountain regions are noticeably cooler, with temperatures reaching -30°F in winter, while lower-lying, more southerly regions clock temperatures upwards of 80°F during summer. Rainfall is heavier in the higher areas, some 30-34 inches annually compared to 28 inches elsewhere. The same goes for snow, which reaches an average of 100 inches in the mountains, compared to 30 inches at lower elevations. Ice covers most streams and lakes from November to late March, when the thaw, combined with spring rains, can cause flooding.

Agriculture: dairy produce, corn, small grains, hay

Minerals: sand and gravel, limestone, lead, zinc, clay

Industry: machinery, paper, beer

History: The Winnebago and Menominee were the original inhabitants of this region, later joined by migrating Fox, Sauk and Potawatomi. However, by the 19th century, these ancient civilizations were almost wiped out, their last major stand occurring in 1832 in the Black Hawk War.

French explorers were the first Europeans to reach here, in the 17th century, and fur traders moved in thereafter, the trade dominated by the French almost uninterrupted until

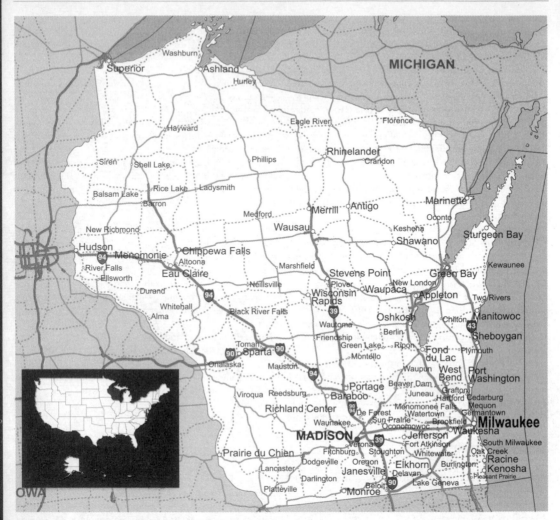

the 19th century, when the US took over. Statehood came in 1783 and in the 1820s, miners from Kentucky and Missouri began to arrive to work the rich lead seams of the south west, establishing the first permanent white settlements other than fur trading posts. A second wave of immigration came ten years later, this time bringing people who came mostly to work the land or build on it. In the late 19th and early 20th centuries, an influx of Poles, Germans and Scandinavians brought a new skill set to the region and in-

dustries such as brewing, leather tanning and ironworking were established. Thus a strong rural economy was buttressed by a thriving industrial one. Politically, Wisconsin has always been very diverse, producing progressive figures such as Emil Seidel, the first socialist mayor of Milwaukee in 1910, and less progressive figures such as Senator Joe McCarthy, who led the anti-Communist witch hunts in the 1950s.

Wyoming (WY)

Name: A Delaware word, meaning "mountains and valleys alternating."
Nickname: Equality State.
State flower: Indian paintbrush.
State bird: Meadowlark.
Population: 481,000.
Motto: Equal rights.
Capital: Cheyenne.
Physical description: Wyoming has two distinct terrains

– flat plains and rocky mountains. The plains are a flat, dry region, part of the Great Plains that extend from Mexico to Canada. An amazing feature of this region in Wyoming is the Devil's Tower, a vertiginous remnant of volcanic neck, which is 40 million years old and rises straight up from the flat plain to a height of 5112 feet. The Rocky Mountains traverse Wyoming and include the "shining" Big Horn mountains, named by the native Americans for the big horn sheep that roam the area and described as "shining" by

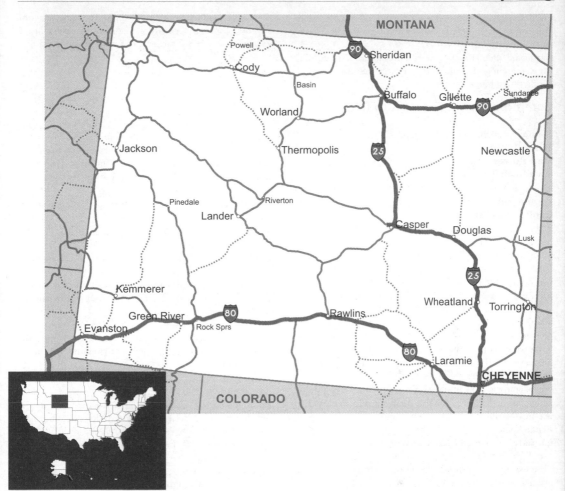

early travelers on account of their snow-capped peaks. The Wind River range are also Rocky Mountains, and include Gannett Peak, the state's highest point, at 13,804 feet. The Continental Divide cuts through the Rockies, causing rivers to the east, including the Yellowstone and Big Horn, to drain to the Atlantic, and those to the west, including the Snake and Green Rivers, to drain towards the Pacific. Between the mountains are found flat, bare areas called Intermontane Basins, which are very dry and support only minimal life. One such is the Red Desert Basin, where the Continental Divide splits to surround it. This stunning, cold desert region of 6 million acres has features such as fossil beds, volcanic necks, shifting sand dunes and prehistoric rock art to recommend it.

Area: 97,809 sq mi (253,324 sq km).

Climate: Because of its generally high elevation, Wyoming has a cool climate, only the Basins really building up any heat.

Due to low humidity, summers are very pleasant, warm and breezy, with temperatures averaging 85-95°F on lower elevations, dropping to 70°F in the mountains.

Winters are cold, with snow falling between November and May, often followed by wind, causing drifts. The Big Horn Basin has an annual snowfall of just 15-20 inches, compared to 200 inches in some of the higher mountain reaches.

Winds are high, reaching speeds of up to 30-40mph in winter. Such is the tenacity of the prevailing winds from the west that some trees actually grow bent towards the east. Hail is the most destructive force, sudden storms sometimes ruining entire crops and damaging property. Tornadoes are sometimes seen but tend to only touch the ground for a few minutes before vanishing back up into the clouds.

Agriculture: cattle, sheep, hay, sugar beets, wheat

Minerals: petroleum, uranium, coal

Industry: mining, electricity production, tourism

History: Shoshone, Crow and Arapaho lived here long before John Colter, the first white man, set foot in Wyoming in 1807. A fur trapper, he triggered the advance of the fur trade into the region.

As part of the Oregon Trail, Wyoming saw many settlers pass through on their way to Oregon, California and Utah. But the Homestead Laws of the 1860s encouraged some of them to stop off, and the arrival of the Union Pacific Railroad made trade and immigration an altogether easier and more attractive prospect.

Cattle and sheep ranching were a major part of the agricultural economy, though ranchers often came into bloody conflict with homesteaders.

Commonwealth: Puerto Rico (PR)

Name: Spanish, meaning "rich port".
Name: Equality State.
State flower: Maga.
State bird: Reinita.
Motto: Joannes est nomen eius ("John is his name").
Population: 3,829,000.
Capital: San Juan.
Physical description: Puerto Rica is a small, rectangular island in the Greater Antilles, in the Caribbean Sea, 1000 miles off the southeast coast of Florida.

It has a very variable landscape, with a mountainous interior dominated by the Cordillera Central range, which run from east to west across the island and has, as its highest peak, Cerro La Punta, standing at 4389 feet.

The Karst region to the north is an area with a fascinating geology, of limestone hills and sinkholes, the Rio Camuy River which runs partially underground, making it the third longest subterranean river in the world, and the Cuevo del Infierno, which has some 2000 caves.

The island also has a rainforest, the 28,000 acre El Yunque, which has an incredibly diverse plant and animal life and on which 100 billion gallons of rainwater fall every year.

Area: 3,349 sq mi (8,647 sq km).
Climate: The island has a tropical marine climate, with very little variation in temperature throughout the seasons. To most visitors, it feels like summer year-round with an average temperature of 82°F.

But there are variations.

November to May is the dry season, with June to November the rainy season. El Yunque, in the north, receives 180 inches of rain every year while the south, where it always a

Following statehood in 1890, Wyoming became a boom state, first through agriculture, then the discovery of oil and then, in the mid-20th century, uranium and trona.

few degrees warmer, receives only 40 inches.

This is also hurricane season, and the island has been devastated by these 200 mph winds in the past. Hurricane Georges, in 1998, caused floods and landslips and left a terrible trail of destruction.

Agriculture: sugarcane, coffee, pineapples, plantains, bananas.

Minerals: copper, nickel, oil

Industry: pharmaceuticals, electronics, apparel

History: The Taino Indians from South America settled here and lived peaceably for centuries.

This did not stop Christopher Columbus, in 1493, claiming the island for Spain, though European settlement did not actually begin until 1508, when Ponce de Leon founded a town near the site of present day San Juan.

The Spanish ruled for four centuries, in which time the Tainos were enslaved, brutalized and then either driven out or murdered.

Following the Spanish-American War, the US took the island over in 1898.

Despite a gold rush and a roaring trade in horses, the island's fortunes had slumped and Puerto Rica was the poorest island in the Caribbean.

The US launched Operation Bootstrap to remedy this, pouring billions of dollars into the economy.

Puerto Ricans are US citizens, but have no US tax liability and no voting rights in American elections.

Migration to the US by Puerto Ricans has made New York the place where more Puerto Ricans are to be found than anywhere else on earth, with a population of one million people.

Canadian Provinces and Territories

Alberta

Name: the name is in honour of Queen Victoria's daughter, Princess Louise Alberta, wife of the Marquis of Lorne, Governor General. Alberta, along with Manitoba and Saskatchewan is one of the so-called Prairie Provinces.

Emblems: the wild rose, the lodgepole pine, the great horned owl.

Motto: Fortis et Liber, 'Strong and free'.

Population (2002): 3,113,600.

Capital: Edmonton, Canada's fifth largest city. The 36 municipalities forming Greater Edmonton are home to over 900,000 people. Focally placed on transcontinental routes running east, west, north, south, and northwest, the city is a major communications hub.

Physical description: with a land area of 661,848 square kilometres (243,560 square miles), it is the sixth largest of the provinces and territories. Southwestern Alberta is a mountainous region that includes the Monashee and Cariboo ranges of the Western Cordillera, rising to high peaks and with glaciers in the upper valleys. Alberta's highest point is Mt. Columbia (3,747 metres, 12,293 feet). Towards the central south, the foothills gradually give way to flat prairie country. The central area of the province is rich farming land, with woods, hills, and lakes. South of the 55th parallel the rivers flow east into Saskatchewan. To the north of the 55th parallel is a vast region of woods and grassland, still thinly populated, and with large extents of marsh known as muskeg. In it two great river systems flow northwards: the Peace River flows to the Great Slave Lake; the Athabasca to the lake of the same name.

Climate: Alberta has a continental-type climate, with long, cold winters, a brief, brilliant spring, and hot summers. On the west, the rain shadow of the mountains can produce long periods of drought.

Agriculture: in the eastern prairie area, wheat and other cereal crops are grown. To the west, stock rearing is more common. In the country between Calgary and Edmonton, mixed farming is practiced, with dairy herds and market gardens.

Minerals: southwest and central-south Alberta have large deposits of coal and natural gas, and the latter is a prime source of energy, along with hydroelectricity generated in the mountain valleys. Oil is extracted from a major field centred on the city of Drumheller. In the north of the province there are further oil and gas deposits, and rock salt is mined.

Industry: much of Alberta's mineral wealth is transported elsewhere by train and pipeline, but manufacturing industry related to mining, transport, and farming is important in the cities.

History: long a wilderness inhabited by nomadic tribes, the region was part of the Hudson's Bay grant of 1670. For another 200 years, little changed, though trading stations were established here and there, and pioneer families and communities began to establish farms. The completion of the Canadian Pacific Railway in 1885 opened up the area, and towns like Calgary and Edmonton began to grow. In the early twentieth century there was a rush of settlement, as not only the farmlands but also the mineral resources of the south began to be exploited. Alberta was constituted a province in 1905.

British Columbia

Name: the name of Canada's westernmost province ultimately honours Christopher Columbus and also recalls its original status as part of the British Empire.

Emblem: the dogwood.

Motto: *Splendor sine occasu*, 'Splendour undiminished'.

Population (2002): 4,141,300.

Capital: Victoria, on Vancouver Island, a pleasant city on a fine natural harbour, with tourism, service industries, and administration its main occupations.

Physical description: with a land area of 944,735 square kilometres (364,668 square miles), it is the fifth in size among the territories and provinces. Mountains, deep valleys, and a heavily indented and islanded coastline largely define the landscape of British Columbia: geologically it is a continuation of the Western Cordillera, which covers most of the province, dividing between the Rocky Mountains on the border with Alberta, and the Coast Range, with a wide central area of mountains and plateaus separating the two main ranges. The highest peaks extend far above the tree line into regions of perpetual snow and ice with large glaciers. The highest point is Mt. Fairweather (4,663 metres, 15,298 feet). Rivers drain to east and west from the watersheds, with the Fraser system dominating in the south of the province and leading to the Pacific; and the Peace River flowing from the vast man-made Williston Lake to the east and north. The lower slopes, valleys, and islands are heavily forested, with cedar, spruce, and Douglas fir among the most common trees.

Climate: on the coastal side, the sea promotes a mild, moist climate, without great extremes. In the south of the province, there is an almost Mediterranean-type climate. Inland of the coastal range, it can be very dry, and temperatures vary from summer maxima of around 37° to winter lows of -32° or lower. On the eastern slopes of the mountains, the warm Chinook wind has an alleviating effect, though it also promotes a dry climate and dry soil. In the north, the climate becomes subarctic both on the coast and inland.

Agriculture: forestry is by far the most important form of cultivation. Forest parks now preserve the remaining specimens of the giant firs and cedars which once grew in vast numbers. Softwood trees are grown in huge plantations and the logs are usually floated down to the sea. In valleys and on grassy plateau areas, cattle and sheep are raised, and wheat and other cereals are grown in the Peace River valley. On the coastal side, fruit trees are also cultivated. Fisheries are important in the sea and the rivers, especially salmon.

Minerals: falling water is an important resource in British Columbia and virtually all its electricity is hydrogenerated. The province also has deposits of lead, zinc, gold, copper, asbestos, and silver. Coal is mined around Fernie, in the Rocky Mountains, and there are also coal deposits on Vancouver Island.

Industry: cheap power has encouraged the growth of power-intensive industry such as aluminium smelting. Lumber-related industry is widespread, with sawmills and pulp mills. In the Vancouver–Victoria area there is a diversity of industry including chemicals and electronics. Tourism is also a major contributor to the province's economy.

History: occupied by coastal Indian tribes from prehistoric times, British Columbia's first European visitors came by sea up the Pacific coast. The Spanish explorer, Juan Pérez, came in 1774, and the British Captain Cook in 1778. The coast was surveyed between 1792–94 by Captain George Vancouver of the Royal Navy, and was at that time claimed for Great Britain. In 1793, Alexander Mackenzie, a Scottish fur trader, crossed the Rockies to Cascade Inlet. The North West Company was established to trade in furs and other natural products of the region; in 1821 it merged with the Hudson's Bay Company. In 1843, Fort Victoria, site of the present provincial capital, was established by Sir James

Douglas on behalf of the Hudson's Bay Company. Vancouver Island later became a Crown colony, with Douglas as its governor. In 1858, shortly after gold was found in the Fraser River valley, the mainland was also designated as a colony and named British Columbia. Vancouver Island was incorporated with it as a single colony in 1866. Five years later, British Columbia agreed to join as one of the provinces of the newly formed Dominion of Canada, so long as a railway connection was provided to link it to the eastern provinces. The first transcontinental line was completed in 1885. Despite this, the western province naturally has many north–south links with the U.S. states

on either side, as well as a 'Pacific rim' presence.

Vancouver: though not the provincial capital, Vancouver is by far the largest city of British Columbia, and third largest in Canada, with a population of 545,674 in 2001, and with almost 2,000,000 people living in the metropolitan area. It is the chief port, and manufacturing and business centre of the province. A city of many ethnic groups, it has one of the largest and oldest 'Chinatowns' in North America. Vancouver's location, its parks, botanical gardens, and museums, make it a popular tourist venue, and it is the country's main film production centre.

Manitoba

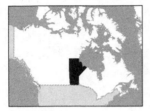

Name: the name is said to come from an Indian phrase, meaning 'God that speaks'. It is the easternmost of the Prairie Provinces.

Emblems: the great grey owl, the crocus, the white spruce.

Motto: Gloriosus et liber, 'Glorious and free'.

Population (2002): 1,150,800.

Capital: the city of Winnipeg, whose name comes from the Cree Indian phrase *win nipee* ('muddy water'), referring to the great lake of the same name. It is a spacious city of 640,000 people, spread over 462.1 square kilometres (178.4 square miles), and it is home to almost half the province's population.

Physical description: with an area of 647,797 square kilometres (250,050 square miles), it is eighth in size among the provinces and territories, and only very slightly smaller than Saskatchewan. Much of the area was once submerged under a huge lake, and it remains a lowland region still dominated by water features. Lake Winnipeg is the largest of many thousands of lakes, and north of it lies an extraordinary complex of inland waters, reaching to and beyond the province's northern boundary at the 60th parallel. On the northeast, Manitoba is bounded by Hudson Bay. On the west side, reaching into Saskatchewan, is a more hilly re-

gion, rising to summits mostly of around 750 metres (2,250 feet). The highest point is Mt. Baldy (832 metres, 2,729 feet). In the south there are great extents of almost level prairie.

Climate: the Manitoban climate is similar to that of Alberta, with long, cold winters and short but hot summers.

Agriculture: on the prairie, wheat is the prime crop, though oats, barley, potatoes, rye, and sugar beet are also grown. There are also large areas of pasture land and, apart from stock rearing, much of Canada's honey production is located here. In the northern part of the province there is little farming, and the prime form of cultivation is forestry. Commercial fishing is based chiefly on Lake Winnipeg.

Minerals: Flin Flon, in the northwest of the province, is the main centre for a mining industry that extracts copper, zinc, gold, silver, cadmium, and tellurium. Other gold-producing areas are at Bissett, Herb Lake, and Snow Lake, and nickel is extracted at Mystery Lake and Moak Lake, near Thompson. In the southwest, near Virden, there are oil deposits. Sands and gravels are also extracted in large quantities.

Industry: most manufacturing industry is concentrated in and around Winnipeg and the industrial base is quite diverse. Parts are made for the automotive and aircraft industries. There is textile weaving and a clothing industry based on this plus locally available furs and leather. Mineral smelting and processing is carried out at Flin Flon, and nickel is refined at Thompson.

Transport: Winnipeg's international airport is the central hub of internal Canadian air services. The port of Churchill on Hudson Bay is a major grain exporter in the ice-free mid-July to mid-November period, as it stands at the end of the shortest sea route from the prairies to Europe. A branch of the transcontinental railroad links it to the main system.

History: the first recorded European explorer was Pierre de la Vérendrye in 1739, but the first serious attempt at settling was made from Scotland in 1812, when a pioneering community established the township of Selkirk. The population remained very small through most of the nineteenth century. Up until 1867, Manitoba was the property of the Hudson's Bay Company, but in that year the new Dominion government purchased a large part of the territory lying on both sides of the Red River. At that time there was a rebellion among the Métis who lived and hunted in the region. This ended peacefully in 1870, but its leader Louis Riel had incurred deep hostility in Ontario. He was unable to take up his parliamentary seat and lived in exile in the U.S.A. In 1870 Manitoba was established as a province (albeit a much smaller province than today's Manitoba). By 1878 the railway had come, and this led to a substantial increase in population from the 12,000 or so of 1870. Land speculation led to further unrest among the Métis in 1885, and Riel returned to lead a second rebellion. This was put down by force, and Riel was captured, tried, and hanged at Regina. Manitoba joined the Confederation in 1905.

New Brunswick

Name: named after the German state of Braunschweig, a possession of the royal British Hanoverians, New Brunswick, along with Newfoundland, Nova Scotia, and Prince Edward Island, is one of the Maritime Provinces.

Emblems: the purple violet, the black-capped chickadee.

Motto: *Spem reduxit*, 'Hope was restored'.

Population (2002): 756,700. Most people live around the coast and in the main river valleys (the St. John and Matapedia), which also form important lines of road and rail communication. The interior of the province is very sparsely populated.

Capital: Fredericton, population 46,500, an attractive town with many nineteenth-century buildings. The cultural centre of the province, it has two universities and the famous Beaverbrook Art Gallery.

Physical description: with a land area of 72,908 square kilometres (28,142 square miles), it is eleventh in size among the provinces and territories. The province occupies the end of the 'peninsula' formed between the St. Lawrence Estuary, the Gulf of St. Lawrence, and the Bay of

Fundy. The interior, forming the end of the long Appalachian range, consists of hilly and often wild countryside penetrated by long river valleys. The highest point is Mt. Carleton (817 metres, 2,610 feet).

Climate: away from the coast, the climate takes on more continental characteristics. Winters can be very cold, especially in the uplands, and are accompanied by heavy snowfalls. On the coast and in sheltered valleys, the weather is generally milder.

Agriculture: the relatively dry and cool climate has encouraged vegetable growing, notably of seed potatoes. Mixed farming prevails, with much pasture land. Much of the province remains covered in forest, with extensive hardwood forests as well as quick-growing softwood to feed the wood pulp and paper industries. Shellfish are an important resource along the coast.

Minerals: zinc, potash, silver, lead, copper, and coal are all found. There are also extensive peat deposits, cut for horticultural use.

Trade and industry: New Brunswick employment is divided 72% to services, 22% to industry, and 6% to agriculture.

History: until the seventeenth century, the region was the hunting ground of nomadic Indian tribes. The first European settlers were French, but as in the rest of eastern Canada, the French and the British were soon in a contest for ownership. British possession was confirmed in 1713, and there was a steady increase in settlement during the eighteenth century. At this time the region was included in Nova Scotia. In 1784, New Brunswick was formally recognized as a separate province and it became one of the provinces of Canada in 1867.

Newfoundland and Labrador

Name: its name bestowed by the explorer, John Cabot, in 1497, Canada's easternmost and most recent province is formed by this large island and the adjacent coastal region of Labrador. It is one of the four Maritime Provinces.

Emblems: the caribou, the pitcher plant. Other provincial emblems are the Newfoundland dog and pony, the black spruce, and the gemstone, labradorite.

Motto: *Quaerite prime regnum dei*, 'Seek first the kingdom of God'.

Population (2002): 531,600.

Capital: St. John's with a population of 102,000. With an average annual precipitation of 1,482 millimetres (58 inches), and 217 wet days a year, St. John's is Canada's wettest provincial capital.

Physical description: with a land area of 405,212 square kilometres (156,412 square miles), it is tenth in size among the provinces and territories. Lying across the entry to the Gulf of St. Lawrence, Newfoundland is shaped rather like an irregular triangle, with many peninsulas, and sides slightly less than 500 kilometres (310 miles) long. It is formed of the same rocks as the continent. These are at their highest on the western side, where the Long Range Mountains reach to around 800 metres (2,400 feet), with the highest point being Mt. Caubvik (1,652 metres, 5,420 feet); the height gradually reduces towards the eastern coast. Like the landscape of the Canadian Shield, the landscape is rugged and rocky, dotted with many lakes. Rivers, mostly short, drain from the interior to all coasts.

Climate: oceanic influences dominate, with a prevailing moistness and coolness and no great extremes, except on the northern Long Range coast where winter conditions can be severe. The Strait of Belle Isle is normally icebound between December and June. The Atlantic coasts are often enveloped in thick fog that comes in from the sea, a product of cold northern air meeting the relatively warm waters of the Gulf Stream.

Agriculture: the landscape is on the whole poorly suited to farming and farms exist mostly to supply local communities, but some two-fifths of the land surface is covered in forest, and lumber is an important industry. Newfoundland also has a large fishing industry, though over-exploitation by many nations of the once cod-rich Newfoundland Banks has brought about a reduction in catches and a shift of emphasis to crab and shrimp. It is the world's largest producer of cold-water cooked and peeled shrimp. In 2001, fisheries employed 14,600 people in the province, compared to 20,800 in 1991. Aquaculture (fish farming) now produces around 8,000 tonnes of fish a year and is still growing rapidly.

Minerals: there are many mineral deposits. Newfoundland is Canada's main source of fluorspar, while zinc, copper, lead, and gold are among the metals found. Substantial oil reserves are known to exist in the offshore Ben Nevis-Hebron Field, but in 2002 Chevron Canada Resources abandoned a plan to go ahead with exploitation.

Industry: the main industries are wood and fish-related: pulp and newsprint mills, and fish processing.

Transport: the highway between Port aux Basques and St. John's is a continuation of the trans-Canada highway, but the topography is such that it more than doubles the direct distance between these cities. Land travel is often compelled to take devious routes around the mountains. In the days of sea travel, and early transatlantic air travel, the island was strategically placed in global terms, on the routes between New York, the St. Lawrence, and the ports of northwest Europe, with Gander an important refuelling point.

History: in 1583 the Elizabethan adventurer, Sir Humphrey Gilbert, claimed Newfoundland on behalf of the English Queen Elizabeth I. The first colonial settlement was made in 1610, but English possession was challenged by the French, who established a colony at Placentia. It was not until 1713 that, under the Treaty of Utrecht, Newfoundland was formally accepted as a British colony. Unusually, the founding of settlements was resisted by the British government. This had much to do with the control of fishing rights. The wealthy few who controlled the Newfoundland fishing did not want to see colonists taking a share of their lucrative business. Settlers were refused permission to build houses or cut wood within six miles of the shore. These laws, very hard to enforce, were gradually relaxed. By 1832 the island had its own Parliament and in 1855 it became a self-governing British colony. The inhabitants voted against joining in the formation of Canada in 1867, and Newfoundland remained a self-governing colony. But in the slump year of 1933, with the island's economy in a state of collapse, elective government was suspended and a 'commission of government' controlled affairs through the 1930s, and the years of World War II. During 1939–45, the strategic position of Newfoundland again worked in its favour, and a strong war economy brought renewed prosperity. In a referendum in 1948, the islanders voted in favour of union with Canada, and Newfoundland, together with Labrador, became the country's tenth province on 1 April 1949.

Labrador: the name comes from the Portuguese explorer of 1530, João Fernandes, who was a *lavrador*, or landholder, in the Azores. The easternmost territory of Canada, administratively part of Newfoundland province, Labrador is very thinly populated. Stretching from the Hudson Bay coast to the Strait of Belle Isle, it has never been settled and was little explored before the twentieth century. The cold arctic current that sweeps past its coast means that the prevailing climate is chilly, and the landscape is usually snowbound except for the summer months. The south of the territory is thickly forested, mostly with black spruce; the ground cover of the north consists mostly of mosses and lichens. A varied wildlife is supported, including bear, beaver, muskrat, lynx, wolverine, red squirrel, and caribou among the animals, and ptarmigan, geese, grouse, and partridge among the birds. Fur trapping is Labrador's oldest human pursuit, but by far the most important nowadays is iron mining from the ore beds found between the headwaters of the Hamilton and Kaniapiskau Rivers, with Labrador City as the centre. Another centre of activity is Schefferville, just over the border in Québec province. A railway runs south through Labrador linking it to the St. Lawrence at Sept Îles. Copper and nickel are also mined, and prospecting for other minerals continues. Labrador's main settlements are Battle Harbour, the capital, Labrador City, Nain, and Goose Bay.

Northwest Territories

A vast semi-autonomous region lying north of the 60th parallel, east of the Yukon and bordering the Prairie Provinces to the south.

Emblem: the mountain avens.

Population (2002): 41,400. The population is very small and scattered in a number of mining communities.

Capital: Yellowknife. With a population of just under 18,000, it is said to be Canada's fastest-growing city. It provides administration, medical, and college facilities as well as being the region's main market centre.

Physical description: with a land area of 1,346,106 square kilometres (519,597 square miles), it is third in size among the territories and provinces. Lakes cover more than 10% of the surface. The western area is mountainous, with the Mackenzie Mountains rising to meet the Selwyn and Cassiar ranges. The highest point is Unnamed Peak (2,773 metres, 9,098 feet). The land falls away eastwards towards the long valley of the Mackenzie River, Canada's longest, which flows from the Great Slave Lake to the Arctic Ocean. East of the Mackenzie, a bare and rocky landscape reaches to the shore of Hudson Bay. To the north there is subarctic tundra. Beyond the north coast is the Arctic Archipelago, composed of many islands, some of them of great size, merging into the frozen sea towards the North Pole.

Climate: its far northern situation and proximity to the polar icecap ensure long, dark winters with deep snow and very low temperatures. During its brief summer, temperatures

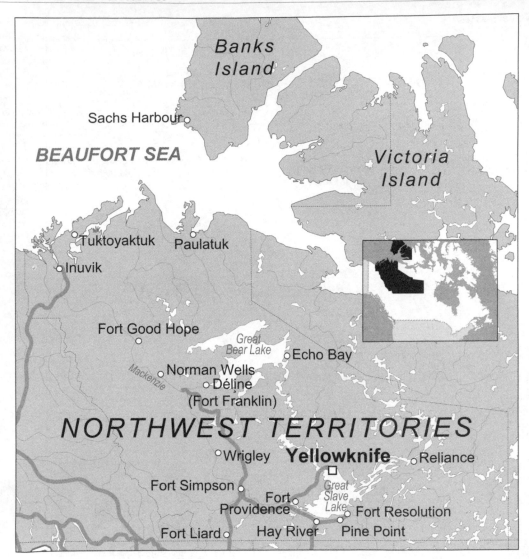

can rise as high as 27°C (80°F) around the Great Slave Lake.

Agriculture: virtually all of the foodstuffs consumed by the population are imported from elsewhere, as the soil and climate are not conducive to farming. There are extensive stands of forest in the Mackenzie Plains. Fur trapping remains an important activity.

Minerals: the region is rich in minerals. Gold, silver, uranium, copper, and nickel have all been identified in significant quantities. In addition there are oil and natural gas deposits. Canada's first diamond deposits have also been found here.

Industry: the only industries are those associated with the extraction and primary processing of metals and other mineral reserves.

Transport: the territory is very much dependent on air transport and every community has its airstrip. Hay River, on the south shore of the Great Slave Lake, is the terminus of a rail link to the national system, and there are road connections to other towns in the same region. Lack of suitable transport is a serious problem for the mining industries.

Wildlife: muskrats, foxes, beavers, lynxes, wolves, and martens live in the woods and marshes. Migratory birds, including vast numbers of wild geese and duck, flock to the Arctic coast springtime nesting sites

History: from 1670 the southern part of the region was part of what was known as Rupert's Land, and was administered by the Hudson's Bay Company. The northern part was under nominal British suzerainty. In 1870 both parts were integrated into the Dominion of Canada. The formation of the Prairie Provinces and northern extensions of Ontario and Québec reduced the size of Northwest Territories somewhat. The greatest reduction came with the formation of the separate territory of Nunavut in 1999, though even in its reduced form Northwest Territories is far bigger than many nation states.

Nova Scotia

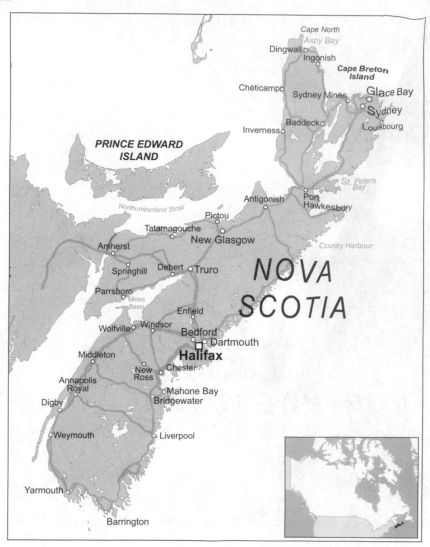

Name: the name means 'New Scotland'. Nova Scotia is one of the smallest but longest-established provinces. Nova Scotians have a keen sense of their own identity. Cape Breton Island, in particular, maintains the tradition of Gaelic speech and has many links with Celtic Scotland and Ireland. It is one of Canada's so-called Maritime Provinces.

Emblems: the red spruce, the mayflower, the osprey.

Motto: *Munit haec et altera vincit*, 'This defends, the other conquers'.

Population (2002): 944,800.

Capital: Halifax, with some 340,000 people in its metropolitan area, is the largest town and main port as well as the provincial capital. Its large and ice-free harbour is a major container port as well as Canada's prime Atlantic naval base. Founded in 1749, it is also one of Canada's oldest cities.

Physical description: with a land area of 55,284 square kilometres (21,340 square miles), Nova Scotia is twelfth in size among the provinces and territories. The province consists of the peninsula of Nova Scotia, joined to the continent by a narrow neck of land, and Cape Breton Island to the north, which is linked to Nova Scotia by a causeway across the Strait of Canso. Many small islands, mostly uninhabited, surround the coasts. The terrain is similar to that of New Brunswick, across the Bay of Fundy: hilly, wooded country with many valleys, the highest point being 532 metres (1,745 feet) above sea level. The watershed runs along the spinal ridge, with short, swift rivers reaching the sea on both sides. Cape Breton Island has a lower-lying area round the large Bras d'Or saltwater lake, but rises in the north to the Cape Breton Highlands. The Bay of Fundy has the world's largest tides, with a difference of 15 metres (45 feet) between high and low water at the head of the bay.

Climate: summers are pleasant, but winters are severe with heavy snowfalls, though without the extreme temperature lows found in the Prairie Provinces. Generally the influence of the sea makes for a milder, if wetter and windier, climatic regime.

Agriculture: the main agricultural area lies in and around the Annapolis Valley on the Fundy coast, where there is good soil and the mountain ridge provides shelter from northeasterly cold winds. There are many apple orchards. Mixed farming is the staple of the province and there is extensive breeding of stock and poultry. Although remote from the main centres of Canadian population, Nova Scotia has access to the New England region of the U.S.A. As elsewhere in Canada, forestry is of great importance, and the slopes of the province's low mountain ranges are clothed in spruce, fir, birch, maple, and pine. Fishing was an important industry for many coastal communities but, with dwindled stocks, its significance has receded in recent years. Fish farming has to a degree replaced sea fishing.

Minerals: coal is the main mineral resource, with mining districts around Sydney in Cape Breton Island and Pictou in northern Nova Scotia. Nova Scotia is an important source of gypsum, and rock salt is also produced.

Industry: steelworks at Sydney and New Glasgow use local coal and Newfoundland iron ore. Some lumber is exported but the province also has lumber mills.

History: originally populated by Indian tribes, the region's first European settlers were from France in 1604. They called the land Acadia. Possession was contested by the British. King James I granted the territory to the Scottish entrepreneur, Sir William Alexander, in 1621, under the name Nova Scotia. A large French element remained and the colony remained in dispute until 1713, when the Treaty of Utrecht confirmed British possession. In 1755 many French residents were expelled. After the American War of Independence, many American colonists who remained loyal to Britain sailed or travelled to set up new lives in Nova Scotia. The 'Highland Clearances' in Scotland during the late eighteenth and early nineteenth centuries resulted in the arrival of many Gaelic-speaking colonists who settled around Pictou and in Cape Breton Island – areas that still retain a Gaelic tradition. The province was the first to be established as self-governing from 1848. It also had Canada's first university, printing-press and newspaper. In 1867 it was one of the founding provinces of the new Dominion of Canada.

Nunavut

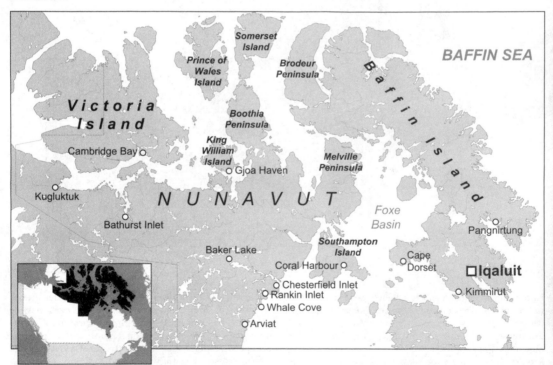

Name: the name means 'our land' in the Inuktitut language
Emblems: the purple saxifrage, the rock ptarmigan.
Motto: *Nunavut Sanginivut*, 'Nunavut our strength'.
Population (2002): 28,700. About 85% of the people are Inuit, and 56% of the population is under 25.
Capital: Iqaluit. Formerly Frobisher Bay, on Baffin Island, Iqaluit has a population of 3,600. It is also a trading and educational centre, and home to the Arctic

College, whose courses focus on Nunavut's cultures and environment.

Physical description: with a land area of 2,093,190 square kilometres (807,971 square miles), Nunavut is by far the largest of the territories and provinces, occupying almost a quarter of the entire country. The highest point is Barbeau Peak on Ellesmere Island (2,626 metres, 8,615 feet). Most of the landscape is bare and bleak, and covered in snow all or most of the year, but its austere beauty attracts more visitors each year.

Climate: the brief summers can be warm, but the territory lies mostly north of the Arctic Circle, and long, dark, very cold winters are the dominant aspect of the climate.

Minerals: the bleak landscape contains a variety of mineral deposits, with more still being prospected. The Polaris lead-zinc mine on Little Cornwallis Island is the most northerly mine in the world, producing 1,000,000 tonnes of refinable ores annually.

Economy and industry: though extreme climatic conditions mean that mining is expensive, and only high grade and valuable ores are exploited, minerals are one of the three main bases of the economy. The others are fur trading and tourism. Government salaries and subsidies are a further support.

History: human occupancy of the subarctic region goes back for many thousands of years. Under British rule it became part of the Northwest Territories. Its modern development began in 1965 when the Canadian government first unveiled plans to reorganize the administration of the arctic territories. Years of discussion and campaigning by the Inuit people followed. A plebiscite held in the Northwest Territories in 1982 resulted in a 90% majority vote among the Inuit for a separate eastern division. Another decade of wrangling ensued over the border between the Northwest Territories and Nunavut until a new plebiscite in 1992 brought agreement. In June 1993 the Canadian government passed the Nunavut Act, and in 1999 the territory and government of Nunavut finally came into being.

Ontario

Name: the province's name has been traced to the Iroquois for 'beautiful lake', and also to Seneca's *entohonorous*, 'the people'.

Emblems: the white trillium flower, the eastern white pine, the common loon.

Motto: *Ut incepit fidelis, sic permanet*, 'Loyal it began, loyal it remains'.

Population (2002): 12,068,300. More than a third of the country's population live in Ontario, making it Canada's most populous province.

Capital: Toronto, Canada's largest city, has 2.8 million inhabitants, and around 4 million in the metropolitan region. Toronto is the fifth largest municipal government region in North America. It is the main industrial and economic centre of Ontario and of all Canada. Ethnically it is highly diverse, with over 100 different ethnic and language groups represented. Over 50% of its citizens were born outside Canada. The name comes from an Indian word for 'meeting place', and it was an Indian centre before the first European settlement was made by the French in 1750. Under British control it was named York until its present name was given in 1834, when it became a city. Today, metropolitan Toronto covers 632 square kilometres (244 square miles). It was the first Canadian city to construct a subway, and its CN tower, at 533 metres (1,750 feet), is among the world's tallest buildings. Among other 'firsts', it claims the world's largest underground pedestrian area. Some 90% of foreign banks in Canada are established here, and electronics and telecommunications are important aspects of a very diverse industrial base. Toronto is also a major publishing and media centre, and is the largest centre of English-language theatre after London and New York.

Physical description: with a land area of 1,076,395 square kilometres (415,488 square miles), it is fourth largest among the provinces and territories. To the south, Ontario's shape is defined by the line of the Upper St. Lawrence River and the north coasts of Lakes Superior, Huron, and Ontario. The part of the province south of the Ottawa River, once a vast forested zone, is now a region of fertile rolling farmlands. To the north, the landscape is an enormous plateau region, scraped by ice sheets, and often lacking soil and vegetation. On glacial soils there are forests, but much of the ground is heath or bare rock, interspersed with a multitude of lakes. The highest point of land is Ishpatina Ridge (693 metres, 2,273 feet). In the north the rivers drain into Hudson Bay, in the west to Lake Winnipeg, in the south to the Great Lakes and the St. Lawrence.

Climate: the climate is essentially a continental one, of cold winters and hot summers, but in the south it is modified by the presence of the Great Lakes, making winters and summers a little moister and milder. Nevertheless it can become cold enough to freeze up Niagara Falls. In the scantily populated north, there is again a marine influence on the climate.

Agriculture: climate, fertile soil, and a densely packed population have influenced the development of mixed farming in the southern part of the province. In the Lake Peninsula between Toronto and Niagara, vines, tobacco and peaches can be grown. In the north, farming is much more localized, depending on the soil and the proximity of a market. Lumbering is much more important, with spruce and poplar grown for packaging and newsprint.

Minerals: north of Georgian Bay there is a region of rich mineral deposits, including uranium, nickel, and copper. The Creighton nickel-copper mine near Sudbury is the deepest in Canada at 2,200 metres (7,218 feet). Other minerals mined in Ontario include iron, platinum, gold, and zinc.

Trade and industry: Ontario is the most highly industrialized of the provinces. Employment is divided 64% to services, 34% to industry, and 2% to agriculture. Oil from the Alberta field comes across Canada by pipeline to be refined at Sarnia. A variety of manufacturing industry is located in the cities of Toronto, Hamilton, London, and smaller centres. Mineral processing is a major industry at Sudbury. Transport, trading, banking, and media are all important.

History: the region had been Indian territory since prehistoric times when the first European exploring party, under Samuel de Champlain, reached Lake Huron in 1615. French trading posts and mission stations were established along the shores of the Great Lakes, but the inland regions remained Indian territory. The British took possession in 1763. At that time it was all part of Québec, or New France. Between 1783 and 1791 many British Loyalists removed from the U.S.A. to set up home in British North America; and in 1791 the eastern and western areas of Québec were separated politically and known as Lower and Upper Canada respectively. Upper Canada's first capital, at Niagara, was uncomfortably close to the U.S.A., and York (later renamed Toronto) replaced it. In 1812 invading American forces destroyed the town. The Act of Union of 1840 once again brought Upper and Lower Canada together in a single province. However, with the establishment of the Confederation in 1870, Upper Canada became the province of Ontario. By this time it was already well populated in the southern part and, with the development of railways and the discovery of mineral reserves, it quickly became Canada's most industrialized province.

Prince Edward Island (P.E.I.)

Name: the name was given in 1798, in honour of the Duke of Kent, father of Queen Victoria. This is Canada's smallest province, both in size and population, and is one of the four Maritime Provinces.

Emblems: lady's slipper flower, northern red oak, the blue jay.

Motto: Parva sub ingenti, 'The small protected by the great'.

Population (2002): 139,900. P.E.I. is the most densely populated province of the Confederation, with almost 25 persons to the square kilometre, compared to a national average of 3.

Capital: Charlottetown. With a population of 33,000, Charlottetown is the island's only urban centre. It has the highest average snowfall of the provincial capitals, with 338.7 centimetres (133 inches) a year.

Physical description: with a land area of 5,660 square kilometres (2,185 square miles), P.E.I. is the smallest of the provinces and territories, occupying 0.1% of Canada's total area. Lying in the south of the Gulf of St. Lawrence, it is separated from New Brunswick by the Northumberland Strait, some 30 kilometres (18 miles) wide. Much indented by the sea, it is almost divided in two at Hillsborough Bay. The island terrain is relatively low, nowhere rising over 150 metres (450 feet) and is intensively farmed, with most of the original forest cover long vanished.

Climate: the climate is much the same as Nova Scotia, with pleasant summers but heavy snowfalls in winter. The influence of the sea makes for a milder, if wetter and windier, climate.

Agriculture: a well-developed pattern of farmland covers most of the island. The red soil is fertile and produces crops of potatoes, wheat, and barley. Stock rearing is important, both for beef and dairy farming, and there are many pasture fields. Pigs and poultry are also farmed. On the coast, shellfish rearing is important, notably lobsters.

Industry: industry revolves around the needs and products of the farms. Food processing, freezing, and canning are important. There is also a substantial tourist industry, with coastal fishing and first-rate golf links among the attractions.

Transport: the Confederation Bridge, 12.9 kilometres (8 miles) long, joins the island to the mainland, between Borden and Carleton. Opened in 1997, this is the world's longest bridge over seasonally icebound waters. There is a good road network, and a railway links Charlottetown with Tignish in the north. Train ferries between Tormentine and Borden provide a connection with the mainland network. Car ferries also operate on this route and from Pictou in Nova Scotia. Icebreakers make it a year-round service.

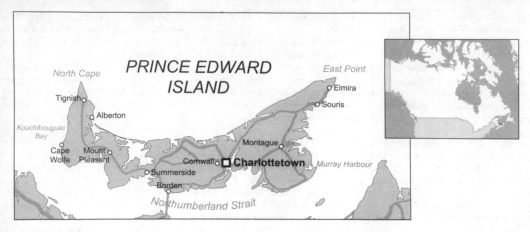

The main airport is at Charlottetown.

History: originally occupied by Indians of the Micmac and other tribes (who still occupy a reservation on the island) and called by them *Abegweit*, 'Home cradled in the waves', the island was identified by Jacques Cartier in 1534. Samuel de Champlain gave it the name Île de St. Jean. During the French-British war over possession of eastern Canada, the British landed in 1758 and drove out some of the French residents. It was confirmed as a British possession in 1763, and given colony status in 1769. Charlottetown was the venue of the inter-provincial conference of 1864 which led to the formation of the Dominion of Canada in 1867, but Prince Edward Island was not one of the founding provinces. It joined the federation soon after, in 1873.

Tradition: the island was the home of L. M. Montgomery, author of the *Anne of Green Gables* stories enjoyed by generations of children. Her house is now a museum.

Québec

Name: Québec is Canada's second largest province, three times the size of France. The name is from *kebek*, the Iroquois for 'narrowing of the waters', describing the St. Lawrence at Québec City.

Emblems: the Madonna lily, the snowy owl.

Motto: *Je me souviens*, 'I remember'.

Population (2002): 7,455,200.

Capital: Québec City. Canada's oldest city, Québec City has a population of 180,000. Winding, narrow streets link its Upper and Lower Towns. There are many historic sites, including the Ursuline Convent (1639) and the Basilica Notre Dame (1647) as well as the fortress. Its industries include shipbuilding and repair, wood pulp, textiles, food, and drinks.

Physical description: with a land area of 1,542,056 square kilometres (595,233 square miles), it is exceeded in size only by the vast area of Nunavut. Bounded on the east by Labrador, on the south by New Brunswick and the U.S. state of New York, and on the west by Ontario and Hudson Bay, the vast spread of Québec province reaches from the St. Lawrence to the Arctic. North of the St. Lawrence lie the rocky uplands of forest and wilderness known as the Canadian Shield, an ancient landscape formed by ice sheets and pocked with innumerable lakes. Its southern boundary is the Laurentian Mountains, a range stretching 1,600 kilometres (1,000 miles) and rising to heights of around 900 metres (2,700 feet) north of Québec City. The highest point in the province is Mt. D'Iberville (1,652 metres, 5,124 feet). The St. Lawrence valley forms a wide lowland region between Montréal and Québec, and to the south the land rises into forested hills bordering on the U.S. states of Vermont and Maine. Rivers flow to all points of the compass, but the main systems are those of the Ottawa River in the west, the Saguenay in the east and the Caniapiscau in the north.

Climate: the southern part of the province has warm summers and cold, snowy winters. Autumn, though brief, is brilliant with the red and gold foliage of the maple and other deciduous trees. To the north the climate is increasingly subarctic.

Agriculture: the St. Lawrence lowlands are intensively farmed. Meat and dairy products, eggs and poultry, and market gardening reflect the needs of a substantial urban population. South of the St. Lawrence, farmland and deciduous forest share the valleys and hill slopes. In the north there are huge forest areas, chiefly of softwood trees. Québec supplies almost half the softwood used in Canada's vast lumber industry.

Minerals: iron ore is extracted at Schefferville, close to the Labrador border, and to the west of Ungava Bay in the far north of the province. In the south there are large deposits of the minerals that produce asbestos and have given the town of Asbestos its name. Gold, silver, and copper deposits are also worked. Québec has Canada's only titanium mine. There are mining centres at Abitibi, Temiscamingue, North Shore, Eastern Townships, and on the Gaspé peninsula.

Trade and industry: unlimited water power provides the province with cheap electricity and this is utilized in many forms of industry, including aluminium smelting, using imported bauxite, and other forms of metal processing. Automobiles, chemicals, textiles, and electronics also form part of a diverse industrial base. Apart from wood pulp and

paper, many other timber products and by-products are manufactured and packaged. Employment in Québec is divided 68% to services, 29% to industry, and 3% to agriculture.

Political life: politics in Québec are quite different to those of any other province and impact heavily on federal politics. The reason for this lies in the fact that the great majority of the Québecois, over 6 million people, are of French descent and remain French-speaking, and in many ways form part of the French cultural universe. Although Canada is a secular state, with an increasingly secular outlook, the fact that the Québec population adheres overwhelmingly to the Roman Catholic Church serves to increase the sense of cultural difference. A separatist movement has become increasingly vocal and influential during the latter part of the twentieth century. Two provincial referendums on the issue have been held, in 1980 and 1995, and though both resulted in a vote in favour of continued union with the other provinces, the latter produced a majority of only 1%, and the issue of separatism remains very much an open one.

History: on his second voyage, in 1535, the French explorer Jacques Cartier sailed up the St. Lawrence and claimed the land he found on behalf of King François I of France. It was inhabited by numerous large Indian tribes,

including Iroquois and Huron. The first French settlement was established by Samuel de Champlain in 1608 at Québec, head of navigation for seagoing ships, where he built a fort. The colony was known as La Nouvelle France, and run from 1627 by a monopoly business, the 'Company of One Hundred' (also known as the 'Company of New France'). But it attracted few settlers and there was little activity. From 1663 it was established as a royal province ruled by a Governor General, with an intendant as his head of administration.

Steady population growth now began, with towns forming round the forts at Québec, Montréal and Trois Rivières. As explorers pushed out further west, the area of the colony enlarged, but the bulk of the population was in the St. Lawrence Lowlands; by the middle of the eighteenth century it numbered around 65,000 people. Farming was the main occupation, though furs remained the chief source of wealth. Land was apportioned to a seigneur, who allocated it to tenants (the habitants) in long rectangular lots. From the earliest stage, however, the French domain was challenged by the English, who had settled in New England, and whose search for the Northwest Passage had introduced them to the northern wilderness. They used the voyages of John Cabot, Martin Frobisher, Henry Hudson, and others to claim possession of the regions north and west of

New France. In 1629 they captured Québec City and held it for three years.

The original inhabitants, well organized in the Iroquois League, were alternately courted and attacked by the contending colonial powers. Caught in the middle, the Iroquois attempted to play off both sets of Europeans but their power was ultimately broken by the French. As a Catholic state, France included a missionary element in its colonial activity, and New France's first bishop arrived in 1659. By then, monks and nuns had already established convents and hospitals. Among the French governors were some very able men, but a fatal error was made in 1668 when two French explorers, Radisson and Des Groseilliers, failing to get backing from France, but receiving it in England, opened up the Hudson Bay fur trade for the new English Hudson's Bay Company.

From 1672, under one of its most energetic governors, the Comte de Frontenac, the colony's area and activities expanded, but from the late seventeenth and into the eighteenth centuries, as a result of warfare in Europe, decline began. Following the loss of Nova Scotia and Newfoundland in 1713, a great fort was begun in 1717 at Louisbourg, to guard access to the St. Lawrence. A fort-building race characterized the next thirty years, but, neglected by the French government, and with access to France made difficult by naval warfare, the colony was increasingly open to attack. Though at this time French explorers and settlers, such as the La Vérendrye family, were still establishing themselves in the west, the western forts, in the plains and on the Great Lakes, fell one by one to the British. The culmination came in the warfare that took place between 1754 and 1760; in 1759 the British captured the Québec fortress and in the following year the Governor General, the Marquis de Vaudreuil, was forced to surrender. In the Treaty of Paris, 1763, British possession of the French colony was confirmed.

Although large numbers of English-speaking settlers came to the province after 1760, Québec (characterized in 1791 as Lower Canada) has retained its French-speaking population, its language, religion, and traditions, at first under British rule and later as part of federal Canada. In the American invasions of 1775 and 1812, the Québecois fought with the other Canadian provincials for the defence of the British colony (though they had no cause to love the New Englanders). In 1841 the province was granted a degree of self-government and in 1849 the French language was given legal recognition. In 1867 Lower Canada was one of the founding provinces of the Confederation, and received the name of Québec province.

In the twentieth century the province shared in the eco-nomic growth of Canada, and the gradual shedding of colonial British links was welcomed. But Québec continued to be different, as shown by the resistance to conscription at the start of both world wars. Socially a conservative province, it was the last in Canada to give women the vote. In the 1960s the issue of separation became a dominant one and has remained so. Although the 'Quiet Revolution' initiated by the Liberal government of 1960 brought about progressive changes in federal attitudes to the province's unique status, it also saw the rise of political violence from the *Front pour la Libération de Québec* (FLQ), with bombs in Montréal in 1960, and the kidnap and murder of British diplomat James Cross and Québec government minister Pierre Laporte in 1970. In that year martial law was imposed for a time, and over 500 persons were arrested. In 1973 the *Parti Québecois* (PQ) emerged as a separatist party pledged to peaceful methods, and in 1976, under René Levesque, it won control of the provincial government. On a state visit that year, the French President, Charles de Gaulle, infuriated the Canadian government by expressing support for 'free Québec'. Many English speakers left the province in the wake of Bill 101, designed to preserve the supremacy of the French language in the province. A referendum in 1980 rejected independence for the province. Both federal and provincial governments have been preoccupied with the question of how to reconcile the Québecois desire for independence with the province's remaining part of Canada. The 'Meech Lake Accord' promoted by federal Premier Mulroney in 1987 fell in 1990 against opposition from other provinces, resulting in the formation of the *Bloc Québécois* by Québec politicians. A referendum on independence in 1995 rejected it by a majority of only 1%, resulting in controversy as some politicians accused immigrant voters of sabotaging the aspirations of the French-speaking Québecois. Discussions on the constitutional issue continue.

Montréal: though not the capital, this is by far Québec's largest city, the second largest in Canada, and the world's largest French-speaking city after Paris. The population is 2,800,000. Montréal is a major industrial, commercial and media centre, and an important port. Although it has always been an important city, its population doubled between 1941 and 1971. In 1976 it was the site of the Olympic Games. There are many modern buildings, and an underground pedestrian zone of 29 kilometres (18 miles). The city's four-line *Métro* runs on rubber tires. Montréal is ethnically diverse, with an Italian population of some 200,000 as the largest language group after French and English.

Saskatchewan

Name: the name comes from an Indian word, *kisikatchewin*, 'swift river'. It is one of the three Prairie Provinces.
Emblem: the prairie lily.
Motto: *Multis e gentibus vires*, 'Strength from many peoples'.
Population (2002): 1,011,800.
Capital: Regina, with a population of 187,500. The name was given in honour of Queen Victoria. Given city status in 1903, Regina is Canada's sunniest and driest capital city, with an average annual precipitation of 364 millimetres (14 inches), and 109 wet days a year. With potash mines and sodium sulphate extraction close by, the city has an industrial base as well as being an administrative and market centre. Steel, chemicals, and telecommunications are other important industries.
Physical description: with a land area of 651,036 square kilometres (251,300 square miles), it is seventh in size among the provinces and territories. The south of the province is prairie country, with wide level plains and gently rolling uplands. The

Saskatchewan River, with its north and south branches, flows westward in deeply incised valleys. Farther north is 'parkland' country with groves of aspen and poplar trees. The north of the province is more rugged, with rocky and marshy terrain, and many lakes and rivers. The highest point is at Cypress Hills (1,468 metres, 4,816 feet). The largest lake is Lake Athabasca (7,935 square kilometres, 3,063 square miles).

Climate: remote from the sea, the province has a continental climate, with hot summers and cold winters. Snow may lie on the ground for up to four months of the year.

Agriculture: more than 16,000,000 hectares (40 million acres) of arable land are under cultivation, and Saskatchewan produces about two thirds of Canada's wheat crop. Wheat is sown in spring, and grows and ripens rapidly during the hot summer months. Other crops include oats, barley, rye, rape, and flax. Mixed farming is practiced in the parkland regions, with beef and dairy cattle. Pigs and poultry are also farmed in large numbers.

Minerals: the southern part of the province has reserves of lignite (brown coal), oil, and natural gas. In the north there is extensive exploitation of metallic ores, notably around Uranium City, northeast of Lake Athabasca. Copper, zinc, gold, silver, and cadmium are also mined in addition to uranium. Canada is the world's main potash producer, and the province produces about 90% of the country's supply.

Industry: Saskatchewan is a primary producer region rather than a manufacturing one. Most industry is concerned with the preparation and packing of agricultural products, lumber, and metal processing.

History: once Plains Indian territory and very thinly populated (as much of it still is), this area formed part of the Hudson's Bay grant of 1670. The first white man to explore it was Henry Kelsey, a Hudson's Bay employee, during 1691 and 1692. French and British traders set up trading stations. During the nineteenth century it was thought unlikely that the vast plains could be used for anything other than grazing, with organized ranching replacing the huge herds of buffaloes. The arrival of the railroad, linking Regina with the east by 1882, increased the rate of settlement and also provided a means of bulk transport for farm produce. The development of new cereal strains such as quick-ripening wheat, and the mechanization of agriculture, followed. The old way of life made a last stand with the rising in 1885 of Indian and Métis nomadic peoples against the new order of things. Troops quelled the rising and its leader, Riel, was captured and hanged at Regina. From 1896 the pace of settlement increased further, with the population quadrupling in the first decade of the twentieth century, from around 100,000 to over 400,000. Many of the immigrants were from central and eastern Europe. In 1905 Saskatchewan province was formed and became part of the Confederation.

Yukon Territory

Name: consisting of the semi-autonomous far northwest of Canada, the Yukon Territory's name is taken from an Indian word, *yukoo*, 'clear water'.

Emblems: fireweed, the sub-alpine fir, the raven, and the gemstone, lazulite.

Population (2002): 29,900.

Capital: the capital, Whitehorse, is situated on the west bank of the Yukon River, and is the only city in the territory.

It has a population of 23,000, and its main activities are administration, social and medical services, tourism, and mining support industries.

Physical description: with a land area of 482,443 square kilometres (186,223 square miles), it is ninth in size among the provinces and territories. The Yukon is a mountainous region, where the Western Cordillera spreads into the Selwyn and Ogilvie ranges. Here can be found Canada's highest

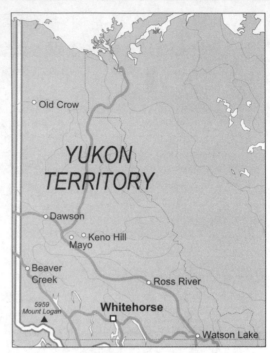

point, Mt. Logan (5,959 metres, 19,550 feet). The main rivers drain eastwards into the Mackenzie system, apart from the Yukon River itself, which rises in the south of the territory and flows westwards through Alaska.

Climate: most of the territory is south of the Arctic Circle, but winters are long, dark, cold, and severe. Spring and summer are short seasons.

Minerals: gold, zinc, lead, and silver ores are mined, with a value to the territory of $97,000,000 in 2001. Of this, 92% was contributed by gold. There are also petroleum wells, while sands and gravels are excavated in vast quantities. In 1997, emeralds were discovered.

Transport: a railroad links Whitehorse with Skagway in Alaska, and the Fairbanks–Edmonton highway also passes through Whitehorse. The only other permanent routes are by river. Dirt roads extend into the country from various mining sites. Air transport is the main lifeline of the remote communities.

History: unexplored and uninhabited except by migratory Indians and wandering fur trappers until the nineteenth century, the name of the Yukon became synonymous with panning for gold in the mid-1890s. Fortune hunters flocked there and a new town, Dawson City, grew almost overnight to a population of 30,000. By 1899, when the surface gold was exhausted, the population had diminished with equal rapidity, though gold-mining by industrial methods continued at Dawson City until 1966. Dawson was superseded by Whitehorse as the capital in 1953.

The United States Constitution

Followed by the Bill of Rights and Other Amendments

Preamble

We the people of the United States, in order to form a more perfect union, establish justice, insure domestic tranquility, provide for the common defense, promote the general welfare, and secure the blessings of liberty to ourselves and our posterity, do ordain and establish this Constitution for the United States of America.

Article I
Section 1

All legislative Powers herein granted shall be vested in a Congress of the United States, which shall consist of a Senate and House of Representatives.

Section 2

The House of Representatives shall be composed of Members chosen every second Year by the People of the several States, and the Electors in each State shall have the Qualifications requisite for Electors of the most numerous Branch of the State Legislature.

No Person shall be a Representative who shall not have attained to the Age of twenty five Years, and been seven Years a Citizen of the United States, and who shall not, when elected, be an Inhabitant of that State in which he shall be chosen.

Representatives and direct Taxes shall be apportioned among the several States which may be included within this Union, according to their respective Numbers, which shall be determined by adding to the whole Number of free Persons, including those bound to Service for a Term of Years, and excluding Indians not taxed, three fifths of all other Persons. The actual Enumeration shall be made within three Years after the first Meeting of the Congress of the United States, and within every subsequent Term of ten Years, in such Manner as they shall by Law direct. The Number of Representatives shall not exceed one for every thirty Thousand, but each State shall have at Least one Representative; and until such enumeration shall be made, the State of New Hampshire shall be entitled to chuse three, Massachusetts eight, Rhode-Island and Providence Plantations one, Connecticut five, New-York six, New Jersey four, Pennsylvania eight, Delaware one, Maryland six, Virginia ten, North Carolina five, South Carolina five, and Georgia three.

When vacancies happen in the Representation from any State, the Executive Authority thereof shall issue Writs of Election to fill such Vacancies.

The House of Representatives shall chuse their Speaker and other Officers; and shall have the sole Power of Impeachment.

Section 3

The Senate of the United States shall be composed of two Senators from each State, chosen by the Legislature thereof for six Years; and each Senator shall have one Vote.

Immediately after they shall be assembled in Consequence of the first Election, they shall be divided as equally as may be into three Classes. The Seats of the Senators of the first Class shall be vacated at the Expiration of the second Year, of the second Class at the Expiration of the fourth Year, and of the third Class at the Expiration of the sixth Year, so that one third may be chosen every second Year; and if Vacancies happen by Resignation, or otherwise, during the Recess of the Legislature of any State, the Executive thereof may make temporary Appointments until the next Meeting of the Legislature, which shall then fill such Vacancies.

No Person shall be a Senator who shall not have attained to the Age of thirty Years, and been nine Years a Citizen of the United States, and who shall not, when elected, be an Inhabitant of that State for which he shall be chosen.

The Vice President of the United States shall be President of the Senate, but shall have no Vote, unless they be equally divided.

The Senate shall chuse their other Officers, and also a President pro tempore, in the Absence of the Vice President, or when he shall exercise the Office of President of the United States.

The Senate shall have the sole Power to try all Impeachments. When sitting for that Purpose, they shall be on Oath or Affirmation. When the President of the United States is tried, the Chief Justice shall preside: And no Person shall be convicted without the Concurrence of two thirds of the Members present.

Judgment in Cases of Impeachment shall not extend further than to removal from Office, and disqualification to hold and enjoy any Office of honor, Trust or Profit under the United States: but the Party convicted shall nevertheless be liable and subject to Indictment, Trial, Judgment and Punishment, according to Law.

Section 4

The Times, Places and Manner of holding Elections for Senators and Representatives, shall be prescribed in each State by the Legislature thereof; but the Congress may at any time by Law make or alter such Regulations, except as to the Places of chusing Senators.

The Congress shall assemble at least once in every Year, and such Meeting shall be on the first Monday in December, unless they shall by Law appoint a different Day.

Section 5

Each House shall be the Judge of the Elections, Returns and Qualifications of its own Members, and a Majority of each shall constitute a Quorum to do Business; but a smaller Number may adjourn from day to day, and may be authorized to compel the Attendance of absent Members, in such Manner, and under such Penalties as each House may provide.

Each House may determine the Rules of its Proceedings, punish its Members for disorderly Behaviour, and, with the Concurrence of two thirds, expel a Member.

Each House shall keep a Journal of its Proceedings, and from time to time publish the same, excepting such Parts as may in their Judgment require Secrecy; and the Yeas and Nays of the Members of either House on any question shall, at the Desire of one fifth of those Present, be entered on the Journal.

Neither House, during the Session of Congress, shall, without the Consent of the other, adjourn for more than three days, nor to any other Place than that in which the two Houses shall be sitting.

Section 6

The Senators and Representatives shall receive a Compensation for their Services, to be ascertained by Law, and paid out of the Treasury of the United States. They shall in all Cases, except Treason, Felony and Breach of the Peace, be privileged from Arrest during their Attendance at the Session of their respective Houses, and in going to and returning from the same; and for any Speech or Debate in either House, they shall not be questioned in any other Place.

No Senator or Representative shall, during the Time for which he was elected, be appointed to any civil Office under the Authority of the United States, which shall have been created, or the Emoluments whereof shall have been encreased during such time; and no Person holding any Office under the United States, shall be a Member of either House during his Continuance in Office.

Section 7

All Bills for raising Revenue shall originate in the House of Representatives; but the Senate may propose or concur with Amendments as on other Bills.

Every Bill which shall have passed the House of Representatives and the Senate, shall, before it become a Law, be presented to the President of the United States: If he approve he shall sign it, but if not he shall return it, with his Objections to that House in which it shall have originated, who shall enter the Objections at large on their Journal, and proceed to reconsider it.If after such Reconsideration two thirds of that House shall agree to pass the Bill, it shall be sent, together with the Objections, to the other House, by which it shall likewise be reconsidered, and if approved by two thirds of that House, it shall become a Law. But in all such Cases the Votes of both Houses shall be determined by yeas and Nays, and the Names of the Persons voting for and against the Bill shall be entered on the Journal of each House respectively. If any Bill shall not be returned by the President within ten Days (Sundays excepted) after it shall have been presented to him, the Same shall be a Law, in like Manner as if he had signed it, unless the Congress by their Adjournment prevent its Return, in which Case it shall not be a Law.

Every Order, Resolution, or Vote to which the Concurrence of the Senate and House of Representatives may be necessary (except on a question of Adjournment) shall be presented to the President of the United States; and before the Same shall take Effect, shall be approved by him, or being disapproved by him, shall be repassed by two thirds of the Senate and House of Representatives, according to the Rules and Limitations prescribed in the Case of a Bill.

Section 8

The Congress shall have Power To lay and collect Taxes, Duties, Imposts and Excises, to pay the Debts and provide for the common Defence and general Welfare of the United States; but all Duties, Imposts and Excises shall be uniform throughout the United States;

To borrow Money on the credit of the United States;

To regulate Commerce with foreign Nations, and among the several States, and with the Indian Tribes;

To establish an uniform Rule of Naturalization, and uniform Laws on the subject of Bankruptcies throughout the United States;

To coin Money, regulate the Value thereof, and of foreign Coin, and fix the Standard of Weights and Measures;

To provide for the Punishment of counterfeiting the Securities and current Coin of the United States;

To establish Post Offices and post Roads;

To promote the Progress of Science and useful Arts, by securing for limited Times to Authors and Inventors the exclusive Right to their respective Writings and Discoveries;

To constitute Tribunals inferior to the supreme Court;

To define and punish Piracies and Felonies committed on the high Seas, and Offences against the Law of Nations;

To declare War, grant Letters of Marque and Reprisal, and make Rules concerning Captures on Land and Water;

To raise and support Armies, but no Appropriation of Money to that Use shall be for a longer Term than two Years;

To provide and maintain a Navy;

To make Rules for the Government and Regulation of the land and naval Forces;

To provide for calling forth the Militia to execute the Laws of the Union, suppress Insurrections and repel Invasions;

To provide for organizing, arming, and disciplining, the Militia, and for governing such Part of them as may be employed in the Service of the United States, reserving to the States respectively, the Appointment of the Officers, and the Authority of training the Militia according to the discipline prescribed by Congress;

To exercise exclusive Legislation in all Cases whatsoever, over such District (not exceeding ten Miles square) as may, by Cession of particular States, and the Acceptance of Congress, become the Seat of the Government of the United States, and to exercise like Authority over all Places purchased by the Consent of the Legislature of the State in which the Same shall be, for the Erection of Forts, Magazines, Arsenals, dock-Yards, and other needful Buildings;—And

To make all Laws which shall be necessary and proper for carrying into Execution the foregoing Powers, and all other Powers vested by this Constitution in the Government of the United States, or in any Department or Officer thereof.

Section 9

The Migration or Importation of such Persons as any of the States now existing shall think proper to admit, shall not be prohibited by the Congress prior to the Year one thousand eight hundred and eight, but a Tax or duty may be imposed on such Importation, not exceeding ten dollars for each Person.

The Privilege of the Writ of Habeas Corpus shall not be suspended, unless when in Cases of Rebellion or Invasion the public Safety may require it.

No Bill of Attainder or ex post facto Law shall be passed.

No Capitation, or other direct, Tax shall be laid, unless in Proportion to the Census or enumeration herein before directed to be taken.

No Tax or Duty shall be laid on Articles exported from any State.

No Preference shall be given by any Regulation of Commerce or Revenue to the Ports of one State over those of another; nor shall Vessels bound to, or from, one State, be obliged to enter, clear, or pay Duties in another.

No Money shall be drawn from the Treasury, but in Consequence of Appropriations made by Law; and a regular Statement and Account of the Receipts and Expenditures of all public Money shall be published from time to time.

No Title of Nobility shall be granted by the United States: And no Person holding any Office of Profit or Trust under them, shall, without the Consent of the Congress, accept of any present, Emolument, Office, or Title, of any kind whatever, from any King, Prince, or foreign State.

Section 10

No State shall enter into any Treaty, Alliance, or Confederation; grant Letters of Marque and Reprisal; coin Money; emit Bills of Credit; make any Thing but gold and silver Coin a Tender in Payment of Debts; pass any Bill of Attainder, ex post facto Law, or Law impairing the Obligation of Contracts, or grant any Title of Nobility.

No State shall, without the Consent of the Congress, lay any Imposts or Duties on Imports or Exports, except what may be absolutely necessary for executing it's inspection Laws: and the net Produce of all Duties and Imposts, laid by any State on Imports or Exports, shall be for the Use of the Treasury of the United States; and all such Laws shall be subject to the Revision and Control of the Congress.

No State shall, without the Consent of Congress, lay any Duty of Tonnage, keep Troops, or Ships of War in time of Peace, enter into any Agreement or Compact with another State, or with a foreign Power, or engage in War, unless actually invaded, or in such imminent Danger as will not admit of delay.

Article II
Section. 1

The executive Power shall be vested in a President of the United States of America. He shall hold his Office during the Term of four Years, and, together with the Vice President, chosen for the same Term, be elected, as follows:

Each State shall appoint, in such Manner as the Legislature thereof may direct, a Number of Electors, equal to the whole Number of Senators and Representatives to which the State may be entitled in the Congress: but no Senator or Representative, or Person holding an Office of Trust or Profit under the United States, shall be appointed an Elector.

The Electors shall meet in their respective States, and vote by Ballot for two Persons, of whom one at least shall not be an Inhabitant of the same State with themselves. And they shall make a List of all the Persons voted for, and of the Number of Votes for each; which List they shall sign and certify, and transmit sealed to the Seat of the Government of the United States, directed to the President of the Senate. The President of the Senate shall, in the Presence of the Senate and House of Representatives, open all the Certificates, and the Votes shall then be counted. The Person having the greatest Number of Votes shall be the President, if such Number be a Majority of the whole Number of Electors appointed; and if there be more than one who have such Majority, and have an equal Number of Votes, then the House of Representatives shall immediately chuse by Ballot one of them for President; and if no Person have a Majority, then from the five highest on the List the said House shall in like Manner chuse the President. But in chusing the President, the Votes shall be taken by States, the Representation from each State having one Vote; A quorum for this purpose shall consist of a Member or Members from two thirds of the States, and a Majority of all the States shall be necessary to a Choice. In every Case, after the Choice of the President, the Person having the greatest Number of Votes of the Electors shall be the Vice President. But if there should remain two or more who have equal Votes, the Senate shall chuse from them by Ballot the Vice President.

The Congress may determine the Time of chusing the Electors, and the Day on which they shall give their Votes; which Day shall be the same throughout the United States.

No Person except a natural born Citizen, or a Citizen of the United States, at the time of the Adoption of this Constitution, shall be eligible to the Office of President; neither shall any Person be eligible to that Office who shall not have attained to the Age of thirty five Years, and been fourteen Years a Resident within the United States.

In Case of the Removal of the President from Office, or of his Death, Resignation, or Inability to discharge the Powers and Duties of the said Office, the Same shall devolve on the Vice President, and the Congress may by Law provide for the Case of Removal, Death, Resignation or Inability, both of the President and Vice President, declaring what Officer shall then act as President, and such Officer shall act accordingly, until the Disability be removed, or a President shall be elected.

The President shall, at stated Times, receive for his Services, a Compensation, which shall neither be increased nor diminished during the Period for which he shall have been elected, and he shall not receive within that Period any other Emolument from the United States, or any of them.

Before he enter on the Execution of his Office, he shall take the following Oath or Affirmation:—"I do solemnly swear (or affirm) that I will faithfully execute the Office of President of the United States, and will to the best of my Ability, preserve, protect and defend the Constitution of the United States."

Section 2

The President shall be Commander in Chief of the Army and Navy of the United States, and of the Militia of the several States, when called into the actual Service of the United States; he may require the Opinion, in writing, of the principal Officer in each of the executive Departments, upon any Subject relating to the Duties of their respective Offices, and he shall have Power to grant Reprieves and Pardons for Offences against the United States, except in Cases of Impeachment.

He shall have Power, by and with the Advice and Consent of the Senate, to make Treaties, provided two thirds of the Senators present concur; and he shall nominate, and by and with the Advice and Consent of the Senate, shall appoint Ambassadors, other public Ministers and Consuls, Judges of the supreme Court, and all other Officers of the United States, whose Appointments are not herein otherwise provided for, and which shall be established by Law: but the Congress may by Law vest the Appointment of such inferior Officers, as they think proper, in the President alone, in the Courts of Law, or in the Heads of Departments.

The President shall have Power to fill up all Vacancies that may happen during the Recess of the Senate, by granting Commissions which shall expire at the End of their next Session.

Section 3

He shall from time to time give to the Congress Information of the State of the Union, and recommend to their Consideration such Measures as he shall judge necessary and expedient; he may, on extraordinary Occasions, convene both Houses, or either of them, and in Case of Disagreement between them, with Respect to the Time of Adjournment, he may adjourn them to such Time as he shall think proper; he shall receive Ambassadors and other public Ministers; he shall take Care that the Laws be faithfully executed, and shall Commission all the Officers of the United States.

Section 4

The President, Vice President and all civil Officers of the United States, shall be removed from Office on Impeachment for, and Conviction of, Treason, Bribery, or other high Crimes and Misdemeanors.

Article III
Section 1

The judicial Power of the United States shall be vested in one supreme Court, and in such inferior Courts as the Congress may from time to time ordain and establish. The Judges, both of the supreme and inferior Courts, shall hold their Offices during good Behaviour, and shall, at stated Times, receive for their Services a Compensation, which shall not be diminished during their Continuance in Office.

Section 2

The judicial Power shall extend to all Cases, in Law and Equity, arising under this Constitution, the Laws of the United States, and Treaties made, or which shall be made, under their Authority;—to all Cases affecting Ambassadors, other public Ministers and Consuls;—to all Cases of admiralty and maritime Jurisdiction;—to Controversies to which the United States shall be a Party;— to Controversies between two or more States;— between a State and Citizens of another State;—between Citizens of different States;—between Citizens of the same State claiming Lands under Grants of different States, and between a State, or the Citizens thereof, and foreign States, Citizens or Subjects.

In all Cases affecting Ambassadors, other public Ministers and Consuls, and those in which a State shall be Party, the supreme Court shall have original Jurisdiction. In all the other Cases before mentioned, the supreme Court shall have appellate Jurisdiction, both as to Law and Fact, with such Exceptions, and under such Regulations as the Congress shall make.

The Trial of all Crimes, except in Cases of Impeachment, shall be by Jury; and such Trial shall be held in the State where the said Crimes shall have been committed; but when not committed within any State, the Trial shall be at such Place or Places as the Congress may by Law have directed.

Section 3

Treason against the United States, shall consist only in levying War against them, or in adhering to their Enemies, giving them Aid and Comfort. No Person shall be convicted of Treason unless on the Testimony of two Witnesses to the same overt Act, or on Confession in open Court.

The Congress shall have Power to declare the Punishment of Treason, but no Attainder of Treason shall work Corruption of Blood, or Forfeiture except during the Life of the Person attainted.

Article IV
Section 1

Full Faith and Credit shall be given in each State to the public Acts, Records, and judicial Proceedings of every other State. And the Congress may by general Laws prescribe the Manner in which such Acts, Records and Proceedings shall be proved, and the Effect thereof.

Section 2

The Citizens of each State shall be entitled to all Privileges and Immunities of Citizens in the several States.

A Person charged in any State with Treason, Felony, or other Crime, who shall flee from Justice, and be found in another State, shall on Demand of the executive Authority of the State from which he fled, be delivered up, to be removed to the State having Jurisdiction of the Crime.

No Person held to Service or Labour in one State, under the Laws thereof, escaping into another, shall, in Consequence of any Law or Regulation therein, be discharged from such Service or Labour, but shall be delivered up on Claim of the Party to whom such Service or Labour may be due.

Section 3

New States may be admitted by the Congress into this Union; but no new State shall be formed or erected within the Jurisdiction of any other State; nor any State be formed by the Junction of two or more States, or Parts of States, without the Consent of the Legislatures of the States concerned as well as of the Congress.

The Congress shall have Power to dispose of and make all needful Rules and Regulations respecting the Territory or other Property belonging to the United States; and nothing in this Constitution shall be so construed as to Prejudice any Claims of the United States, or of any particular State.

Section 4

The United States shall guarantee to every State in this Union a Republican Form of Government, and shall protect each of them against Invasion; and on Application of the Legislature, or of the Executive (when the Legislature cannot be convened), against domestic Violence.

Article V

The Congress, whenever two thirds of both Houses shall deem it necessary, shall propose Amendments to this Constitution, or, on the Application of the Legislatures of two thirds of the several States, shall call a Convention for proposing Amendments, which, in either Case, shall be valid to all Intents and Purposes, as Part of this Constitution, when ratified by the Legislatures of three fourths of the several States, or by Conventions in three fourths thereof, as the one or the other Mode of Ratification may be proposed by the Congress; Provided that no Amendment which may be made prior to the Year One thousand eight hundred and eight shall in any Manner affect the first and fourth Clauses in the Ninth Section of the first Article; and that no State, without its Consent, shall be deprived of its equal Suffrage in the Senate.

Article VI

All Debts contracted and Engagements entered into, before the Adoption of this Constitution, shall be as valid against the United States under this Constitution, as under the Confederation.

This Constitution, and the Laws of the United States which shall be made in Pursuance thereof; and all Treaties made, or which shall be made, under the Authority of the United States, shall be the supreme Law of the Land; and the Judges in every State shall be bound thereby, any Thing in the Constitution or Laws of any State to the Contrary notwithstanding.

The Senators and Representatives before mentioned, and the Members of the several State Legislatures, and all executive and judicial Officers, both of the United States and of the several States, shall be bound by Oath or Affirmation, to support this Constitution; but no religious Test shall ever be required as a Qualification to any Office or public Trust under the United States.

Article VII

The Ratification of the Conventions of nine States, shall be sufficient for the Establishment of this Constitution between the States so ratifying the Same.

Amendments 1 through 10
The Bill of Rights

Amendment I

Congress shall make no law respecting an establishment of religion, or prohibiting the free exercise thereof; or abridging the freedom of speech, or of the press; or the right of the people peaceably to assemble, and to petition the Government for a redress of grievances.

Amendment II

A well regulated Militia, being necessary to the security of a free State, the right of the people to keep and bear Arms, shall not be infringed.

Amendment III

No Soldier shall, in time of peace be quartered in any house, without the consent of the Owner, nor in time of war, but in a manner to be prescribed by law.

Amendment IV

The right of the people to be secure in their persons, houses, papers, and effects, against unreasonable searches and seizures, shall not be violated, and no Warrants shall issue, but upon probable cause, supported by Oath or affirmation, and particularly describing the place to be searched, and the persons or things to be seized.

Amendment V

No person shall be held to answer for a capital, or otherwise infamous crime, unless on a presentment or indictment of a Grand Jury, except in cases arising in the land or naval forces, or in the Militia, when in actual service in time of War or public danger; nor shall any person be subject for the same offence to be twice put in jeopardy of life or limb; nor shall be compelled in any criminal case to be a witness against himself, nor be deprived of life, liberty, or property, without due process of law; nor shall private property be taken for public use, without just compensation.

Amendment VI

In all criminal prosecutions, the accused shall enjoy the right to a speedy and public trial, by an impartial jury of the State and district wherein the crime shall have been committed, which district shall have been previously ascertained by law, and to be informed of the nature and cause of the accusation; to be confronted with the witnesses against him; to have compulsory process for obtaining witnesses in his favor, and to have the Assistance of Counsel for his defence.

Amendment VII

In Suits at common law, where the value in controversy shall exceed twenty dollars, the right of trial by jury shall be preserved, and no fact tried by a jury, shall be otherwise re-examined in any Court of the United States, than according to the rules of the common law.

Amendment VIII

Excessive bail shall not be required, nor excessive fines imposed, nor cruel and unusual punishments inflicted.

Amendment IX

The enumeration in the Constitution, of certain rights, shall not be construed to deny or disparage others retained by the people.

Amendment X

The powers not delegated to the United States by the Constitution, nor prohibited by it to the States, are reserved to the States respectively, or to the people.

Amendments 11 through 27

AMENDMENT XI

Passed by Congress March 4, 1794. Ratified February 7, 1795.

Note: Article III, section 2, of the Constitution was modified by amendment 11.

The Judicial power of the United States shall not be construed to extend to any suit in law or equity, commenced or prosecuted against one of the United States by Citizens of another State, or by Citizens or Subjects of any Foreign State.

AMENDMENT XII

Passed by Congress December 9, 1803. Ratified June 15, 1804.

Note: A portion of Article II, section 1 of the Constitution was superseded by the 12th amendment.

The Electors shall meet in their respective states and vote by ballot for President and Vice-President, one of whom, at least, shall not be an inhabitant of the same state with themselves; they shall name in their ballots the person voted for as President, and in distinct ballots the person voted for as Vice-President, and they shall make distinct lists of all persons voted for as

President, and of all persons voted for as Vice-President, and of the number of votes for each, which lists they shall sign and certify, and transmit sealed to the seat of the government of the United States, directed to the President of the Senate; — the President of the Senate shall, in the presence of the Senate and House of Representatives, open all the certificates and the votes shall then be counted; — The person having the greatest number of votes for President, shall be the President, if such number be a majority of the whole number of Electors appointed; and if no person have such majority, then from the persons having the highest numbers not exceeding three on the list of those voted for as President, the House of Representatives shall choose immediately, by ballot, the President. But in choosing the President, the votes shall be taken by states, the representation from each state having one vote; a quorum for this purpose shall consist of a member or members from two-thirds of the states, and a majority of all the states shall be necessary to a choice. [And if the House of Representatives shall not choose a President whenever the right of choice shall devolve upon them, before the fourth day of March next following, then the Vice-President shall act as President, as in case of the death or other constitutional disability of the President. —]* The person having the greatest number of votes as Vice-President, shall be the Vice-President, if such number be a majority of the whole number of Electors appointed, and if no person have a majority, then from the two highest numbers on the list, the Senate shall choose the Vice-President; a quorum for the purpose shall consist of two-thirds of the whole number of Senators, and a majority of the whole number shall be necessary to a choice. But no person constitutionally ineligible to the office of President shall be eligible to that of Vice-President of the United States.

*Superseded by section 3 of the 20th amendment.

AMENDMENT XIII

Passed by Congress January 31, 1865. Ratified December 6, 1865.

   Note: A portion of Article IV, section 2, of the Constitution was superseded by the 13th amendment.

Section 1

Neither slavery nor involuntary servitude, except as a punishment for crime whereof the party shall have been duly convicted, shall exist within the United States, or any place subject to their jurisdiction.

Section 2

Congress shall have power to enforce this article by appropriate legislation.

AMENDMENT XIV

Passed by Congress June 13, 1866. Ratified July 9, 1868.

   Note: Article I, section 2, of the Constitution was modified by section 2 of the 14th amendment.

Section 1

All persons born or naturalized in the United States, and subject to the jurisdiction thereof, are citizens of the United States and of the State wherein they reside. No State shall make or enforce any law which shall abridge the privileges or immunities of citizens of the United States; nor shall any State deprive any person of life, liberty, or property, without due process of law; nor deny to any person within its jurisdiction the equal protection of the laws.

Section 2

Representatives shall be apportioned among the several States according to their respective numbers, counting the whole number of persons in each State, excluding Indians not taxed. But when the right to vote at any election for the choice of electors for President and Vice-President of the United States, Representatives in Congress, the Executive and Judicial officers of a State, or the members of the Legislature thereof, is denied to any of the male inhabitants of such State, being twenty-one years of age,* and citizens of the United States, or in any way abridged, except for participation in rebellion, or other crime, the basis of representation therein shall be reduced in the proportion which the number of such male citizens shall bear to the whole number of male citizens twenty-one years of age in such State.

Section 3

No person shall be a Senator or Representative in Congress, or elector of President and Vice-President, or hold any office, civil or military, under the United States, or under any State, who, having previously taken an oath, as a member of Congress, or as an officer of the United States, or as a member of any State legislature, or as an executive or judicial officer of any State, to support the Constitution of the United States, shall have engaged in insurrection or rebellion against the same, or given aid or comfort to the enemies thereof. But Congress may by a vote of two-thirds of each House, remove such disability.

Section 4

The validity of the public debt of the United States, authorized by law, including debts incurred for payment of pensions and bounties for services in suppressing insurrection or rebellion, shall not be questioned. But neither the United States nor any State shall assume or pay any debt or obligation incurred in aid of insurrection or rebellion against the United States, or any claim for the loss or emancipation of any slave; but all such debts, obligations and claims shall be held illegal and void.

Section 5

The Congress shall have the power to enforce, by appropriate legislation, the provisions of this article.

*Changed by section 1 of the 26th amendment.

AMENDMENT XV

Section 1

Passed by Congress February 26, 1869. Ratified February 3, 1870.

The right of citizens of the United States to vote shall not be denied or abridged by the United States or by any State on account of race, color, or previous condition of servitude—

Section 2

The Congress shall have the power to enforce this article by appropriate legislation.

AMENDMENT XVI

Passed by Congress July 2, 1909. Ratified February 3, 1913.
Note: Article I, section 9, of the Constitution was modified by amendment 16.

The Congress shall have power to lay and collect taxes on incomes, from whatever source derived, without apportionment among the several States, and without regard to any census or enumeration.

AMENDMENT XVII

Passed by Congress May 13, 1912. Ratified April 8, 1913.
Note: Article I, section 3, of the Constitution was modified by the 17th amendment.

The Senate of the United States shall be composed of two Senators from each State, elected by the people thereof, for six years; and each Senator shall have one vote. The electors in each State shall have the qualifications requisite for electors of the most numerous branch of the State legislatures.

When vacancies happen in the representation of any State in the Senate, the executive authority of such State shall issue writs of election to fill such vacancies: Provided, That the legislature of any State may empower the executive thereof to make temporary appointments until the people fill the vacancies by election as the legislature may direct.

This amendment shall not be so construed as to affect the election or term of any Senator chosen before it becomes valid as part of the Constitution.

AMENDMENT XVIII

Passed by Congress December 18, 1917. Ratified January 16, 1919. Repealed by amendment 21.

Section 1

After one year from the ratification of this article the manufacture, sale, or transportation of intoxicating liquors within, the importation thereof into, or the exportation thereof from the United States and all territory subject to the jurisdiction thereof for beverage purposes is hereby prohibited.

Section 2

The Congress and the several States shall have concurrent power to enforce this article by appropriate legislation.

Section 3

This article shall be inoperative unless it shall have been ratified as an amendment to the Constitution by the legislatures of the several States, as provided in the Constitution, within seven years from the date of the submission hereof to the States by the Congress.

AMENDMENT XIX

Passed by Congress June 4, 1919. Ratified August 18, 1920.

The right of citizens of the United States to vote shall not be denied or abridged by the United States or by any State on account of sex.

Congress shall have power to enforce this article by appropriate legislation.

AMENDMENT XX

Passed by Congress March 2, 1932. Ratified January 23, 1933.

Note: Article I, section 4, of the Constitution was modified by section 2 of this amendment. In addition, a portion of the 12th amendment was superseded by section 3.

Section 1

The terms of the President and the Vice President shall end at noon on the 20th day of January, and the terms of Senators and Representatives at noon on the 3d day of January, of the years in which such terms would have ended if this article had not been ratified; and the terms of their successors shall then begin.

Section 2

The Congress shall assemble at least once in every year, and such meeting shall begin at noon on the 3d day of January, unless they shall by law appoint a different day.

Section 3

If, at the time fixed for the beginning of the term of the President, the President elect shall have died, the Vice President elect shall become President. If a President shall not have been chosen before the time fixed for the beginning of his term, or if the President elect shall have failed to qualify, then the Vice President elect shall act as President until a President shall have qualified; and the Congress may by law provide for the case wherein neither a President elect nor a Vice President shall have qualified, declaring who shall then act as President, or the manner in which one who is to act shall be selected, and such person shall act accordingly until a President or Vice President shall have qualified.

Section 4

The Congress may by law provide for the case of the death of any of the persons from whom the House of Representatives may choose a President whenever the right of choice shall have devolved upon them, and for the case of the death of any of the persons from whom the Senate may choose a Vice President whenever the right of choice shall have devolved upon them.

Section 5

Sections 1 and 2 shall take effect on the 15th day of October following the ratification of this article.

Section 6

This article shall be inoperative unless it shall have been ratified as an amendment to the Constitution by the legislatures of three-fourths of the several States within seven years from the date of its submission.

AMENDMENT XXI

Passed by Congress February 20, 1933. Ratified December 5, 1933.

Section 1

The eighteenth article of amendment to the Constitution of the United States is hereby repealed.

Section 2

The transportation or importation into any State, Territory, or Possession of the United States for delivery or use therein of intoxicating liquors, in violation of the laws thereof, is hereby prohibited.

Section 3

This article shall be inoperative unless it shall have been ratified as an amendment to the Constitution by conventions in the several States, as provided in the Constitution, within seven years from the date of the submission hereof to the States by the Congress.

AMENDMENT XXII

Passed by Congress March 21, 1947. Ratified February 27, 1951.

Section 1

No person shall be elected to the office of the President more than twice, and no person who has held the office of President, or acted as President, for more than two years of a term to which some other person was elected President shall be elected to the office of President more than once. But this Article shall not apply to any person holding the office of President when this Article was proposed by Congress, and shall not prevent any person who may be holding the office of President, or acting as President, during the term within which this Article becomes operative from holding the office of President or acting as President during the remainder of such term.

Section 2

This article shall be inoperative unless it shall have been ratified as an amendment to the Constitution by the legislatures of three-fourths of the several States within seven years from the date of its submission to the States by the Congress.

AMENDMENT XXIII

Passed by Congress June 16, 1960. Ratified March 29, 1961.

Section 1

The District constituting the seat of Government of the United States shall appoint in such manner as Congress may direct:

A number of electors of President and Vice President equal to the whole number of Senators and Representatives in Congress to which the District would be entitled if it were a State, but in no event more than the least populous State; they shall be in addition to those appointed by the States, but they shall be considered, for the purposes of the election of President and Vice President, to be electors appointed by a State; and they shall meet in the District and perform such duties as provided by the twelfth article of amendment.

Section 2

The Congress shall have power to enforce this article by appropriate legislation.

AMENDMENT XXIV

Passed by Congress August 27, 1962. Ratified January 23, 1964.

Section 1

The right of citizens of the United States to vote in any primary or other election for President or Vice President, for electors for President or Vice President, or for Senator or Representative in Congress, shall not be denied or abridged by the United States or any State by reason of failure to pay poll tax or other tax.

Section 2

The Congress shall have power to enforce this article by appropriate legislation.

AMENDMENT XXV

Passed by Congress July 6, 1965. Ratified February 10, 1967.
Note: Article II, section 1, of the Constitution was affected by the 25th amendment.

Section 1

In case of the removal of the President from office or of his death or resignation, the Vice President shall become President.

Section 2

Whenever there is a vacancy in the office of the Vice President, the President shall nominate a Vice President who shall take office upon confirmation by a majority vote of both Houses of Congress.

Section 3

Whenever the President transmits to the President pro tempore of the Senate and the Speaker of the House of Representatives his written declaration that he is unable to discharge the powers and duties of his office, and until he transmits to them a written declaration to the contrary, such powers and duties shall be discharged by the Vice President as Acting President.

Section 4

Whenever the Vice President and a majority of either the principal officers of the executive departments or of such other body as Congress may by law provide, transmit to the President pro tempore of the Senate and the Speaker of the House of Representatives their written declaration that the President is unable to discharge the powers and duties of his office, the Vice President shall immediately assume the powers and duties of the office as Acting President.

Thereafter, when the President transmits to the President pro tempore of the Senate and the Speaker of the House of Representatives his written declaration that no inability exists, he shall resume the powers and duties of his office unless the Vice President and a majority of either the principal officers of the executive department or of such other body as Congress may by law provide, transmit within four days to the President pro tempore of the Senate and the Speaker of the House of Representatives their written declaration that the President is unable to discharge the powers and duties of his office. Thereupon Congress shall decide the issue, assembling within forty-eight hours for that purpose if not in session. If the Congress, within twenty-one days after receipt of the latter written declaration, or, if Congress is not in session, within twenty-one days after Congress is required to assemble, determines by two-thirds vote of both Houses that the President is unable to discharge the powers and duties of his office, the Vice President shall continue to discharge the same as Acting President; otherwise, the President shall resume the powers and duties of his office.

AMENDMENT XXVI

Passed by Congress March 23, 1971. Ratified July 1, 1971.
Note: Amendment 14, section 2, of the Constitution was modified by section 1 of the 26th amendment.

Section 1

The right of citizens of the United States, who are eighteen years of age or older, to vote shall not be denied or abridged by the United States or by any State on account of age.

Section 2

The Congress shall have power to enforce this article by appropriate legislation.

AMENDMENT XXVII

Originally proposed Sept. 25, 1789. Ratified May 7, 1992.

No law, varying the compensation for the services of the Senators and Representatives, shall take effect, until an election of representatives shall have intervened.

The US Declaration of Independence

IN CONGRESS, JULY 4, 1776

The unanimous Declaration of the thirteen united States of America

When in the Course of human events it becomes necessary for one people to dissolve the political bands which have connected them with another and to assume among the powers of the earth, the separate and equal station to which the Laws of Nature and of Nature's God entitle them, a decent respect to the opinions of mankind requires that they should declare the causes which impel them to the separation.

We hold these truths to be self-evident, that all men are created equal, that they are endowed by their Creator with certain unalienable Rights, that among these are Life, Liberty and the pursuit of Happiness. --That to secure these rights, Governments are instituted among Men, deriving their just powers from the consent of the governed, --That whenever any Form of Government becomes destructive of these ends, it is the Right of the People to alter or to abolish it, and to institute new Government, laying its foundation on such principles and organizing its powers in such form, as to them shall seem most likely to effect their Safety and Happiness. Prudence, indeed, will dictate that Governments long established should not be changed for light and transient causes; and accordingly all experience hath shewn that mankind are more disposed to suffer, while evils are sufferable than to right themselves by abolishing the forms to which they are accustomed. But when a long train of abuses and usurpations, pursuing invariably the same Object evinces a design to reduce them under absolute Despotism, it is their right, it is their duty, to throw off such Government, and to provide new Guards for their future security. --Such has been the patient sufferance of these Colonies; and such is now the necessity which constrains them to alter their former Systems of Government. The history of the present King of Great Britain is a history of repeated injuries and usurpations, all having in direct object the establishment of an absolute Tyranny over these States. To prove this, let Facts be submitted to a candid world.

He has refuted his Assent to Laws, the most wholesome and necessary for the public good.

He has forbidden his Governors to pass Laws of immediate and pressing importance, unless suspended in their operation till his Assent should be obtained; and when so suspended, he has utterly neglected to attend to them.

He has refused to pass other Laws for the accommodation of large districts of people, unless those people would relinquish the right of Representation in the Legislature, a right inestimable to them and formidable to tyrants only.

He has called together legislative bodies at places unusual, uncomfortable, and distant from the depository of their Public Records, for the sole purpose of fatiguing them into compliance with his measures.

He has dissolved Representative Houses repeatedly, for opposing with manly firmness his invasions on the rights of the people.

He has refused for a long time, after such dissolutions, to cause others to be elected, whereby the Legislative Powers, incapable of Annihilation, have returned to the People at large for their exercise; the State remaining in the mean time exposed to all the dangers of invasion from without, and convulsions within.

He has endeavoured to prevent the population of these States; for that purpose obstructing the Laws for Naturalization of Foreigners; refusing to pass others to encourage their migrations hither, and raising the conditions of new Appropriations of Lands.

He has obstructed the Administration of Justice by refusing his Assent to Laws for establishing Judiciary Powers.

He has made Judges dependent on his Will alone for the tenure of their offices, and the amount and payment of their salaries.

He has erected a multitude of New Offices, and sent hither swarms of Officers to harass our people and eat out their substance.

He has kept among us, in times of peace, Standing Armies without the Consent of our legislatures.

He has affected to render the Military independent of and superior to the Civil Power.

He has combined with others to subject us to a jurisdiction foreign to our constitution, and unacknowledged by our laws; giving his Assent to their Acts of pretended Legislation:

For quartering large bodies of armed troops among us:

For protecting them, by a mock Trial from punishment for any Murders which they should commit on the Inhabitants of these States:

For cutting off our Trade with all parts of the world:

For imposing Taxes on us without our Consent:

For depriving us in many cases, of the benefit of Trial by Jury:

For transporting us beyond Seas to be tried for pretended offences:

For abolishing the free System of English Laws in a neighbouring Province, establishing therein an Arbitrary government, and enlarging its Boundaries so as to render it at once an example and fit instrument for introducing the same absolute rule into these Colonies

For taking away our Charters, abolishing our most valuable Laws and altering fundamentally the Forms of our Governments:

For suspending our own Legislatures, and declaring themselves invested with power to legislate for us in all cases whatsoever.

He has abdicated Government here, by declaring us out of his Protection and waging War against us.

He has plundered our seas, ravaged our Coasts burnt our towns, and destroyed the lives of our people.

He is at this time transporting large Armies of foreign Mercenaries to compleat the works of death, desolation, and tyranny, already begun with circumstances of Cruelty & Perfidy scarcely paralleled in the most barbarous ages, and totally unworthy the Head of a civilized nation.

He has constrained our fellow Citizens taken Captive on the high Seas to bear Arms against their Country, to become the executioners of their friends and Brethren, or to fall themselves by their Hands.

He has excited domestic insurrections amongst us, and has endeavoured to bring on the inhabitants of our frontiers, the merciless Indian Savages whose known rule of warfare, is an undistinguished destruction of all ages, sexes and conditions.

In every stage of these Oppressions We have Petitioned for Redress in the most humble terms: Our repeated Petitions have been answered only by repeated injury. A Prince, whose character is thus marked by every act which may define a Tyrant, is unfit to be the ruler of a free people.

Nor have We been wanting in attentions to our British brethren. We have warned them from time to time of attempts by their legislature to extend an unwarrantable jurisdiction over us. We have reminded them of the circumstances of our emigration and settlement here. We have appealed to their native justice and magnanimity, and we have conjured them by the ties of our common kindred. to disavow these usurpations, which would inevitably interrupt our connections and correspondence. They too have been deaf to the voice of justice and of consanguinity. We must, therefore, acquiesce in the necessity, which denounces our Separation, and hold them, as we hold the rest of mankind, Enemies in War, in Peace Friends.

We, therefore, the Representatives of the United States of America, in General Congress, Assembled, appealing to the Supreme Judge of the world for the rectitude of our intentions, do, in the Name, and by Authority of the good People of these Colonies, solemnly publish and declare, That these United Colonies are, and of Right ought to be Free and Independent States, that they are Absolved from all Allegiance to the British Crown, and that all political connection between them and the State of Great Britain, is and ought to be totally dissolved; and that as Free and Independent States, they have full Power to levy War, conclude Peace contract Alliances, establish Commerce, and to do all other Acts and Things which Independent States may of right do. And for the support of this Declaration, with a firm reliance on the protection of Divine Providence, we mutually pledge to each other our Lives, our Fortunes and our sacred Honor.

New Hampshire:
Josiah Bartlett, William Whipple, Matthew Thornton

Massachusetts:
John Hancock, Samuel Adams, John Adams, Robert Treat Paine, Elbridge Gerry

Rhode Island:
Stephen Hopkins, William Ellery

Connecticut:
Roger Sherman, Samuel Huntington, William Williams, Oliver Wolcott

New York:
William Floyd, Philip Livingston, Francis Lewis, Lewis Morris

New Jersey:
Richard Stockton, John Witherspoon, Francis Hopkinson, John Hart, Abraham Clark

Pennsylvania:
Robert Morris, Benjamin Rush, Benjamin Franklin, John Morton, George Clymer, James Smith, George Taylor, James Wilson, George Ross

Delaware:
Caesar Rodney, George Read, Thomas McKean

Maryland:
Samuel Chase, William Paca, Thomas Stone, Charles Carroll of Carrollton

Virginia:
George Wythe, Richard Henry Lee, Thomas Jefferson, Benjamin Harrison, Thomas Nelson, Jr., Francis Lightfoot Lee, Carter Braxton

North Carolina:
William Hooper, Joseph Hewes, John Penn

South Carolina:
Edward Rutledge, Thomas Heyward, Jr., Thomas Lynch, Jr., Arthur Middleton

Georgia:
Button Gwinnett, Lyman Hall, George Walton

Presidents of the
United States of America

F: Federalist   D–R: Democratic Republican   D: Democratic   W: Whig   R: Republican

Year of President	Term	Birth–Death	Party
1. George Washington	4/30/1789–3/3/1797	1732–1799	F
2. John Adams	3/4/1797–3/3/1801	1735–1826	F
3. Thomas Jefferson	3/4/1801–3/3/1805	1743–1826	D–R
	3/4/1805–3/3/1809		
4. James Madison	3/4/1809–3/3/1813	1751–1836	D–R
	3/4/1813–3/3/1817		
5. James Monroe	3/4/1817–3/3/1825	1758–1835	D–R
6. John Quincy Adams	3/4/1825–3/3/1829	1767–1848	D–R
7. Andrew Jackson	3/4/1829–3/3/1833	1767–1845	D
	3/4/1833–3/3/1837		
8. Martin Van Buren	3/4/1837–3/3/1841	1782–1862	D
9. William Henry Harrison	3/4/1841–4/4/1841	1773–1841	W
10. John Tyler	4/6/1841–3/3/1845	1790–1862	W
11. James K. Polk	3/4/1845–3/3/1849	1795–1849	D
12. Zachary Taylor	3/4/1849–7/9/1850	1784–1850	W
13. Millard Fillmore	7/10/1850–3/3/1853	1800–1874	W
14. Franklin Pierce	3/4/1853–3/3/1857	1804–1869	D
15. James Buchanan	3/4/1857–3/3/1861	1791–1868	D
16. Abraham Lincoln	3/4/1861–3/3/1865	1809–1865	R
	3/4/1865–4/15/1865		
17. Andrew Johnson	4/15/1865–3/3/1869	1808–1875	D
18. Ulysses S. Grant	3/4/1869–3/3/1873	1822–1885	R
	3/4/1873–3/3/1877		
19. Rutherford B. Hayes	3/4/1877–3/3/1881	1822–1893	R
20. James Garfield	3/4/1881–9/19/1881	1831–1881	R
21. Chester A. Arthur	9/20/1881–3/3/1885	1829–1886	R
22. Grover Cleveland	3/4/1885–3/3/1889	1837–1908	D
23. Benjamin Harrison	3/4/1889–3/3/1893	1833–1901	R
24. Grover Cleveland	3/4/1893–3/3/1897	1837–1908	D
25. William McKinley	3/4/1897–3/3/1901	1843–1901	R
	3/4/1901–9/14/1901		
26. Theodore Roosevelt	9/14/1901–3/3/1905	1858–1919	R
	3/4/1905–3/3/1909		
27. William H. Taft	3/4/1909–3/3/1913	1857–1930	R
28. Woodrow Wilson	3/4/1913–3/3/1921	1856–1924	D
29. Warren G. Harding	3/4/1921–8/2/1923	1865–1923	R

30. Calvin Coolidge	8/3/1923–3/3/1925	1872–1933	R
	3/4/1925–3/3/1929		
31. Herbert C. Hoover	3/4/1929–3/3/1933	1874–1964	R
32. Franklin D. Roosevelt	3/4/1933–1/20/1941	1882–1945	D
	1/20/1941–1/20/1945		
	1/20/1945–4/12/1945		
33. Harry S. Truman	4/12/1945–1/20/1949	1884–1972	D
	1/20/1949–1/20/1953		
34. Dwight D. Eisenhower	1/20/1953–1/20/1961	1890–1969	R
35. John F. Kennedy	1/20/1961–11/22/1963	1917–1963	D
36. Lyndon B. Johnson	11/22/1963–1/20/1965	1908–1965	D
	1/20/1965–1/20/1969		
37. Richard M. Nixon	1/20/1969–1/20/1973	1913–1994	R
	1/20/1973–8/9/1974		
38. Gerald R. Ford	8/9/1974–1/20/1977	1913–	R
39. James (Jimmy) Carter	1/20/1977–1/20/1981	1924–	D
40. Ronald Reagan	1/20/1981–1/20/1989	1911–	R
41. George H. W. Bush	1/20/1989–1/20/1993	1924–	R
42. William Clinton	1/20/1993–1/20/2001	1946–	D
43. George W. Bush	1/20/2001–	1946–	R

Prime Ministers of Canada
Since Confederation (1867)

Parties: Con – Conservative; Lib – Liberal; PC – Progressive Conservative

Prime Minister	Term of Office	Party
J. A. Macdonald	1867–73	Con/Lib
Alexander Mackenzie	1873–78	Lib
J. A. Macdonald	1878–91	Con
John Joseph Caldwell Abbott	1891–1892	Lib/Con
John Sparrow David Thompson	1892–94	Con
Mackenzie Bowell	1894–96	Con
Charles Tupper	1896	Con
Wilfrid Laurier	1896–1911	Lib
Robert L. Borden	1911–17, 1917–20	Con/Unionist
Arthur Meighen	1920-21	Con/Unionist
William Lyon Mackenzie King	1921–26	Lib
Arthur Meighen	1926	Con
William Lyon Mackenzie King	1926–30	Lib
Richard Bedford Bennett	1930–35	Con
William Lyon Mackenzie King	1935–48	Lib
Louis St. Laurent	1948–57	Lib
John G. Diefenbaker	1957–63	PC
Lester Pearson (	1963–68	Lib
Pierre Elliott Trudeau	1968–79	Lib
Charles Joseph Clark	1979–80	PC
Pierre Elliott Trudeau	1980–84(	Lib
John Napier Turner	1984	Lib
M. Brian Mulroney	1984–93	PC
A. Kim Campbell	1993	PC
Jean Chrétien	1993–2003	Lib
Paul Martin	2003–2006	Lib
Stephen Harper	2006–	Con

Accredited political parties in Canada (2005)
(* indicates seats in House of Commons)

*Bloc Québecois**
Canadian Action Party
Christian Heritage Party of Canada
Communist Party of Canada
Green Party of Canada
Liberal Party of Canada*

Marijuana Party
Marxist-Leninist Party of Canada
New Democratic Party*
Conservative Party of Canada*
Progressive Canadian Party
Libertarian Party of Canada

Weights and Measures:
Conversions and Equivalents

Measurement of mass or weight

avoirdupois		metric equivalent
	1 grain (gr)	= 64.8 mg
	1 dram (dr)	= 1.772 g
16 drams	= 1 ounce (oz.)	= 28.3495 g
16 oz (= 7000gr)	= 1 pound (lb)	= 0.4536 kg
100 lb	= 1 short hundredweight	= 45.3592 kg
112 lb	= 1 long hundredweight	= 50.8024 kg
2000 lb	= 1 short ton	= 0.9072 kg
2240 lb	= 1 long ton	= 1.01605 tonnes

metric		avoirdupois equivalent
	1 milligram (mg)	= 0.015 gr
10 mg	= 1 centigram	= 0.154 gr
10 cg	= 1 decigram (dg)	= 1.543 gr
10 dg	= 1 gram (g)	= 15.43 gr = 0.035 oz
10 g	= 1 decagram (dag)	= 0.353 oz
10 dag	= 1 hectogram (hg)	= 3.527 oz
10 hg	= 1 kilogram (kg)	= 2.205 lb
1000 kg	= 1 tonne (metric ton)	= 0.984 (long) ton
		= 2204.62 lb

Troy weight

		metric equivalent
	1 grain	= 0.065 g
4 grains	= 1 carat of gold or silver	= 0.2592 g
6 carats	= 1 pennyweight (dwt)	= 1.5552 g
20 dwt	= 1 ounce (oz)	= 31.1035 g
12 oz	= 1 pound (lb)	= 373.242 g
25 lb	= 1 quarter (qr)	= 9.331 kg
100 lb	= 1 hundredweight (cwt)	= 37.324 kg
20 cwt	= 1 ton of gold or silver	= 746.68 kg

Note: The grain troy is the same as the grain avoirdupois, but the pound troy contains 5760 grains, the pound avoirdupois 7000 grains. Jewels are not weighed by this measure.

Linear measure

		metric equivalent
	1 inch (in)	= 25.4 mm
12 in	= 1 foot (ft)	= 0.305 m
3 ft	= 1 yard (yd)	= 0.914 m
2 yds	= 6 ft = 1 fathom (fm)	= 1.829 m
5.5 yds	= 16.5 ft = 1 rod	= 5.029 m
4 rod	= 22 yds = 66 ft = 1 chain	= 20.12 m
10 chain	= 220 yds = 660 ft = 1 furlong (fur.)	= 0.201 km
8 fur.	= 1760 yds = 5280 ft = 1 (statute) mile (mi)	= 1.609 km
3 mi	= 1 league	= 4.827 km

metric		US equivalent
	1 millimeter (mm)	= 0.0394 in
10 mm	= 1 centimeter (cm)	= 0.3937 in
10 cm	= 1 decimeter (dm)	= 3.937 in
10 dm	= 1 meter (m)	= 39.37 in
10 m	= 1 decameter (dam)	= 10.94 yds
10 dam	= 1 hectometer (hm)	= 109.4 yds
10 hm	= 1 kilometer (km)	= 0.621 mi

Surveyor's measure

Surveyor's linear units		metric equivalent
1 link	= 7.92 in	= 20.117 cm
25 links = 1 rod	= 5.50 yds	= 5.029 m
100 links = 1 chain	= 22 yds	= 20.12 m
10 chains = 1 fur.	= 220 yds	= 0.201 m
80 chains = 8 fur.	= 1 mile	= 1.609 km

Surveyor's square units	metric equivalent
100 x 100 links or 10,000 sq. links	= 1 sq. chain = 484 sq. yds = 404.7 m^2
4 x 4 poles or 16 sq. poles	= 1 sq. chain
22 x 22 yds or 484 sq. yds	= 1 sq. chain
100,000 sq. links or 10 sq. chains	= 1 acre = 4840 sq. yds = 0.4047 ha

Square measure

		metric equivalent
	1 square inch (sq. in)	= 6.4516 cm^2
144 sq. in	= 1 square foot (sq. ft)	= 0.0929 m^2
9 sq. ft	= 1 square yard (sq. yd)	= 0.8361 m^2
30$^1/4$ sq. yds	= 1 square perch	= 25.29 m^2
40 sq. perch	= 1 rod	= 0.1012 ha
4 sq. rods or 4840 sq. yds	= 1 acre	= 0.4047 ha
640 acres	= 1 square mile (sq. mi)	= 2.5900 km^2

metric units		**U.S. equivalent**
	1 square millimeter (mm^2)	= 0.0016 sq. in
100 mm^2	= 1 square centimeter (cm^2)	= 0.1550 sq. in
100 cm^2	= 1 square decimeter (dm^2)	= 15.500 sq. in
100 dm^2	= 1 square meter (m^2)	= 10.7639 sq. ft
		(= 1.1959 sq. yds)
100 m^2	= 1 square decameter (dam^2)	= 1076.3910 sq. ft
100 dam^2	= 1 square hectometer (hm^2)	= 0.0039 sq. mi
100 hm^2	= 1 square kilometer (km^2)	= 0.3861sq. mi

*Note: The square hectometer is also known as a hectare (ha.).

The hectare can be sub-divided into ares:

metric units		
100 m^2	= 1 are	= 119.59 sq. yds
1000 m^2	= 10 ares = 1 dekare	= 1195.9 sq. yds
10,000 m^2	= 100 ares = 1 hectare	= 2.471 acres

Cubic measure

		metric equivalent
	1 cubic inch (cu. in)	= 16.39 cm^3
1728 cu. in	= 1 cubic foot (cu. ft)	= 0.0283 m^3
27 cu. ft	= 1 cubic yard (cu. yd)	= 0.7646 m^3

metric units		
1000 cubic millimeters (mm^3)	= 1 cubic centimeter (cm^3)	= 0.0610 cu. in
1000 cubic centimeters (cm^3)	= 1 cubic decimeter (dm^3)	= 610 cu. in
1000 cubic decimeters (dm^3)	= 1 cubic meter (m^3)	= 35.3147 cu. ft

The stere is also used, in particular as a unit of measurement for timber:

1 cubic meter	= 1 stere	= 35.3147 cu. ft
10 decisteres	= 1 stere	= 35.3147 cu. ft
10 steres	= 1 decastere	= 353.1467 cu. ft
		(= 13.0795 cu. yds)

Liquid measure

		metric equivalent
	1 fluid ounce (fl. oz)	= 29.573 ml
4 fl. oz	= 1 gill	= 118.291 ml
4 gills	= 1 pint (pt)	= 473.163 ml
2 pt	= 1 quart (qt)	= 0.9463 l
4 qt	= 1 gallon (gal)	= 3.7854 l

U.S. and British equivalents

U.S.	British
1 fluid ounce	1.0408 fl oz
1 pint	0.8327 pt
1 gallon	0.8327 gal

metric units

10 milliliters (ml)	= 1 centiliter (cl)	= 0.0211 pt
10 cl	= 1 decileter (dl)	= 0.211 pt
10 dl	= 1 liter (l)	= 2.11 pt
		(= 0.264 gal)
10l	= 1 decaliter (dal)	= 2.64 gal
10 dal	= 1 hectoliter (hl)	= 26.4 gal
10 hl	= 1 kiloliter (kl)	= 264.0 gal

Temperature

Equations for conversion

°Fahrenheit = (9/5 x x°C) + 32 °Centigrade = 5/9 x (x°F - 32)
°Kelvin = x°C + 273.15

Some equivalents

	Centigrade	Fahrenheit
Normal temperature of the human body	36.9°C	98.4°F
Freezing point	0°C	32°F
Boiling point	100°C	212°F

Table of equivalents

Fahrenheit	Centigrade	Centigrade	Fahrenheit
100°C	212°C	30°C	86°F
90°C	194°F	20°C	68°F
80°C	176°F	10°C	50°F
70°C	58°F	0°C	32°F
60°C	140°F	-10°C	14°F
50°C	122°F	-20°C	4°F
40°C	104°F	-30°C	-22°F

The International System of Units (SI units)

Quantity	Symbol	Unit	Symbols
acceleration	a	meters per second squared	ms^{-2} or m/s^2
area	A	square meter	m^2
capacitance	C	farad	F ($1F = 1 AsV^{-1}$)
charge	Q	coulomb	C ($1C = 1 As$)
current	I	ampere	A
density	ρ	kilograms per cubic meter	kgm^{-3} or kg/m^3
force	F	newton	N ($1N = 1kg\ ms^{-2}$)
frequency	f	hertz	Hz ($1Hz = 1s^{-1}$)
length	l	meter	m
mass	m	kilogram	kg
potential difference	V	volt	V ($1V = 1JC^{-1}$ or WA^{-1})
power	P	watt	W ($1W = 1Js^{-1}$)

Quantity	Symbol	Unit	Symbols
resistance	R	ohm	Ω $(1\ \Omega = 1V/A = 1m^{-2}\ kg\ s^{-3}\ A^2)$
specific heat capacity	c	joules per kilogram	$Jkg^{-1}\ K^{-1}$
temperature	T	kelvin	K
time	t	second	s
volume	V	cubic meter	m^3
velocity	v	meters per second	m^{s-1} or m/s
wavelength	λ	meter	m
work, energy	W, E	joule	J $(1J = 1Nm)$

Useful prefixes adopted with SI units

Prefix	Symbol	Factor	Name	Decimal Equivalent
exa	E	10^{18}	quintillion	1 000 000 000 000 000 000
peta	P	10^{15}	quadrillion	1 000 000 000 000 000
tera	T	10^{12}	trillion	1 000 000 000 000
giga	G	10^{9}	billion	1 000 000 000
mega	M	10^{6}	million	1 000 000
kilo	k	10^{3}	thousand	1 000
hecto	h	10^{2}	hundred	100
deca	da	10^{1}	ten	10
deci	d	10^{-1}	tenth	0.1
centi	c	10^{-2}	hundredth	0.01
milli	m	10^{-3}	thousandth	0.001
micro	μ	10^{-6}	millionth	0.000 001
nano	n	10^{-9}	billionth	0.000 000 001
pico	p	10^{-12}	trillionth	0.000 000 000 001
femto	f	10^{-15}	quadrillionth	0.000 000 000 000 001
atto	a	10^{-18}	quintillionth	0.000 000 000 000 000 001

Chemical elements listed by symbol

Symbol	Element	Symbol	Element
Ac	Actinium	Br	Bromine
Al	Aluminum	C	Carbon
Am	Americium	Ca	Calcium
Ar	Argon	Cd	Cadmium
As	Arsenic	Ce	Cerium
At	Astatine	Cf	Californium
Au	Gold	Cl	Chlorine
B	Boron	Cm	Curium
Ba	Barium	Co	Cobalt
Be	Beryllium	Cr	Chromium
Bi	Bismuth	Cs	Caesium
Bk	Berkelium	Cu	Copper

Symbol	Element	Symbol	Element
Dy	Dysprosium	Pa	Protactinium
Er	Erbium	Pb	Lead
Es	Einsteinium	Pd	Palladium
Eu	Europium	Pm	Promethium
F	Fluorine	Po	Polonium
Fe	Iron	Pr	Praseodymium
Fm	Fermium	Pt	Platinum
Fr	Francium	Pu	Plutionium
Ga	Gallium	Ra	Radium
Gd	Gadolinium	Rb	Rubidium
Ge	Germanium	Rh	Rhodium
H	Hydrogen	Rn	Radon
He	Helium	Ru	Ruthenium
Hf	Hafnium	S	Sulphur
Ho	Holmium	Sb	Antimony
I	Iodine	Sc	Scandium
In	Indium	Se	Selenium
Ir	Iridium	Si	Silicon
Kr	Krypton	Sm	Samarium
La	Lanthanum	Sn	Tin
Li	Lithium	Sr	Strontium
Lu	Lutetium	Ta	Tantalum
Md	Mendelevium	Tn	Terbium
Mg	Magnesium	Tc	Technetium
Mn	Manganese	Te	Tellerium
Mo	Molybdenum	Th	Thorium
N	Nitrogen	Ti	Titanium
Na	Sodium	Tl	Thallium
Nb	Niobium	Tm	Thulium
Nd	Neodymium	U	Uranium
Ne	Neon	V	Vanadium
Ni	Nickel	W	Tungsten
No	Nobelium	Xe	Xenon
Np	Neptunium	Y	Yttrium
O	Oxygen	Yb	Ytterbium
Os	Osmium	Zn	Zinc
P	Phosphorous	Zr	Zirconium